Paul and Tracey
AAA members,
bargain hunters

Northern California & Nevada

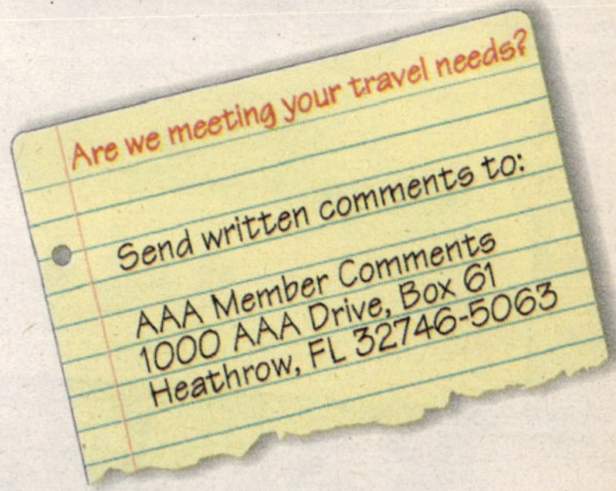
Are we meeting your travel needs?
Send written comments to:
AAA Member Comments
1000 AAA Drive, Box 61
Heathrow, FL 32746-5063

Published by:
AAA Publishing
1000 AAA Drive
Heathrow, FL 32746-5063

Advertising Rate and Circulation Information
Call: (407) 444-8280

Printed in the USA by Quebecor World, Buffalo, NY

***Photo Credit:* (Cover & Title Page)**
Lake Tahoe, CA/NV border
© Royalty-Free / Corbis

Printed on recyclable paper.
Please recycle whenever possible.

Stock #9975

TourBook Navigator

Comprehensive City Index

Northern California

Nevada

Featured Information

aaa.com
Travel Planning Made Easy!

Trust the AAA TourBook® guide for objective travel information. Follow the pages of the TourBook Navigator to thoroughly understand this unique member benefit.

Making Your Way Through the AAA Listings

Attractions, lodgings and restaurants are listed on the basis of merit alone after careful evaluation, approval and rating by one of our full-time, professionally trained Tourism Editors. Annual evaluations are unannounced to ensure that our Tourism Editors see an establishment just as our members would see it.

Those lodgings and restaurants listed with an [fyi] icon have not gone through the same evaluation process as other rated properties. Individual listings will typically denote the reason why this icon appears. Bulleted recreational activity listings are not inspected but are included for member information.

An establishment's decision to advertise in the TourBook guide has no bearing on its evaluation or rating. Advertising for services or products does not imply AAA endorsement.

How the TourBook is Organized

Geographic listing is used for accuracy and consistency. This means attractions, lodgings and restaurants are listed under the city in which they physically are located—or in some cases under the nearest recognized city. The Comprehensive City Index located in the back of the book contains an A-to-Z list of cities. Most listings are alphabetically organized by state, province, region or island; city; and establishment name. A color is assigned to each state or province so that you can match the color bars at the top of the page to switch from ❶ **Points of Interest** to ❷ **Lodgings and Restaurants.**

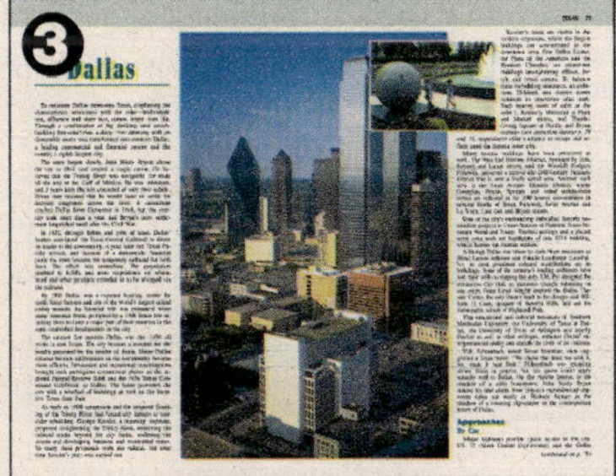

Dallas

Destination Cities and Destination Areas

The TourBook guide also groups information by destination city and destination area. If a city is grouped in a destination vicinity section, the city name will appear at its alphabetical location in the book, and a handy cross reference will give the exact page on which listings for that city begin. Maps are placed at the beginning of these sections to orient you to the destinations.

❸ **Destination cities,** established based on government models and local expertise, are comprised of metropolitan areas plus nearby vicinity cities.

Destination areas are regions with broad tourist appeal. Several cities will comprise the area.

All information in this TourBook guide was reviewed for accuracy before publication. However, since changes inevitably occur between annual editions, we suggest you contact establishments directly to confirm prices and schedules.

Points of Interest Section

Orientation maps

near the start of each Attractions section show only those places we call points of interest. Coordinates included with the city listings depict the locations of those cities on the map. A GEM symbol (⛉) accents towns with "must see" points of interest which offer a *Great Experience for Members*®. And the black ovals with white numerals (**22** for example) locate items listed in the nearby Recreation Areas chart.

Destination area maps

illustrate key travel areas defined by local travel experts. Communities shown have listings for AAA approved attractions.

National park maps

represent the area in and around the park. Some campground sites and lodges spotted on the maps do not meet AAA/CAA criteria, but are shown for members who nevertheless wish to stay close to the park area.

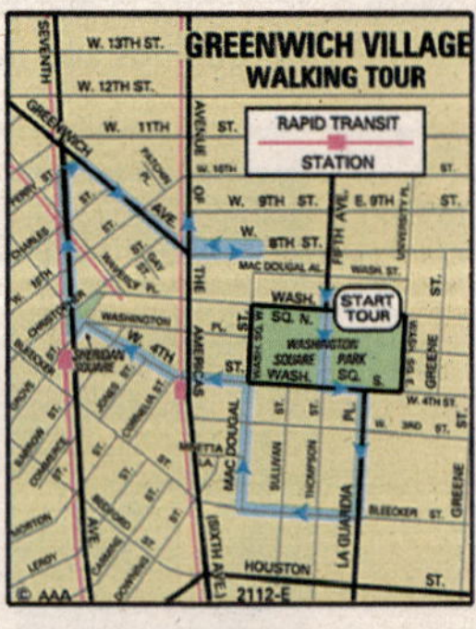

Walking or self-guiding tour maps

correspond to specific routes described in TourBook guide text.

City maps

show areas where numerous points of interest are concentrated and indicate their location in relation to major roads, parks, airports and other landmarks.

Lodgings & Restaurants Section

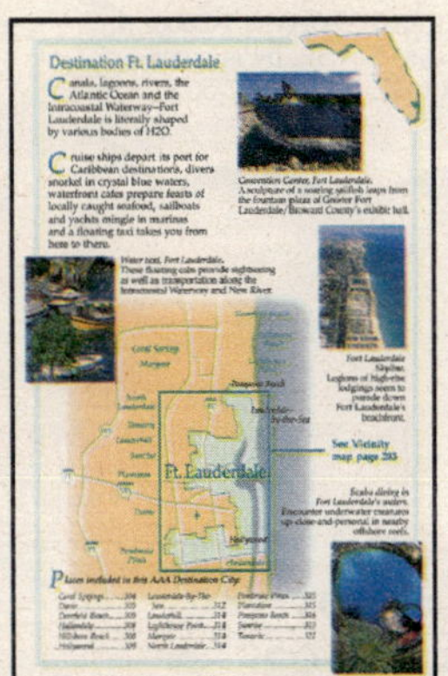

Destination area maps
illustrate key travel areas defined by local travel experts. Communities shown have listings for AAA-RATED® lodgings and/or restaurants.

Spotting maps
show the location of lodgings and restaurants. Lodgings are spotted with a black background (22 for example); restaurants are spotted with a white background (23 for example). Spotting map indexes have been placed immediately after each map to provide the user with a convenient method to identify what an area has to offer at a glance. The index references the map page number where the property is spotted, indicates if a property is an Official Appointment and contains an advertising reference if applicable. It also lists the property's diamond rating, high season rate range and listing page number.

Downtown/city spotting maps
are provided when spotted facilities are very concentrated. GEM points of interest also appear on these maps.

Vicinity spotting maps
spot those properties that are outside the downtown or city area. Major roads, landmarks, airports and GEM points of interest are shown on vicinity spotting maps as well. The names of suburban communities that have AAA-RATED® accommodations are shown in magenta type.

Featured Information Section

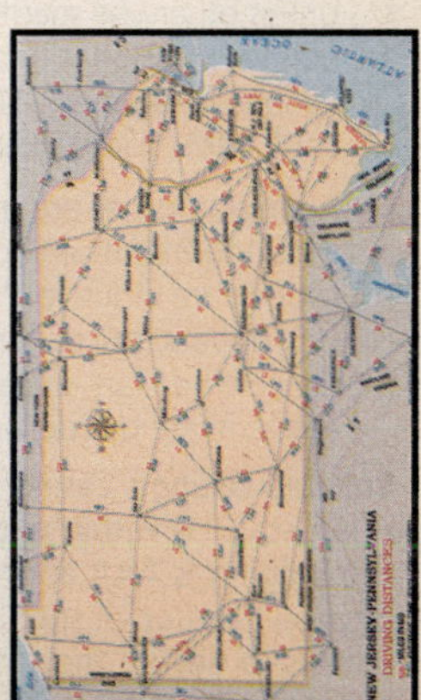

Driving distance maps
are intended to be used only for trip-distance and driving-time planning.

Sample Attraction Listing

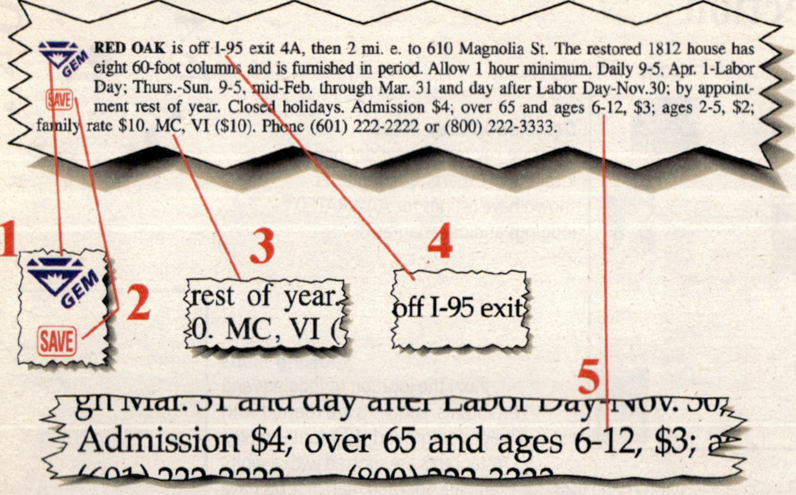

RED OAK is off I-95 exit 4A, then 2 mi. e. to 610 Magnolia St. The restored 1812 house has eight 60-foot columns and is furnished in period. Allow 1 hour minimum. Daily 9-5, Apr. 1-Labor Day; Thurs.-Sun. 9-5, mid-Feb. through Mar. 31 and day after Labor Day-Nov.30; by appointment rest of year. Closed holidays. Admission $4; over 65 and ages 6-12, $3; ages 2-5, $2; family rate $10. MC, VI ($10). Phone (601) 222-2222 or (800) 222-3333.
1
GEM
SAVE
2
3
rest of year.
0. MC, VI (
4
off I-95 exit
5
Admission $4; over 65 and ages 6-12, $3;

1 This attraction is of exceptional interest and quality and therefore has been designated a AAA GEM—offering a *Great Experience for Members*®.

2 SAVE Participating attractions offer AAA/CAA, AAA MasterCard or AAA Visa cardholders a discount off the attraction's standard admission; members should inquire in advance concerning the validity of the discount for special rates. Present your card at the admission desk. A list of participating points of interest appears in the Indexes section of the book. The SAVE discount may not be used in conjunction with other discounts. Attractions that already provide a reduced senior or child rate may not honor the SAVE discount for those age groups. All offers are subject to change and may not apply during special events, particular days or seasons or for the entire validity period of the TourBook. Shopping establishments preceded by a SAVE icon also provide discounts and/or gift with purchase to AAA/CAA members; present your card at the mall's customer service center to receive your benefit.

3 AX=American Express
CB=Carte Blanche
DC=Diners Club
DS=Discover
JC=Japan Credit Bureau
MC=MasterCard
VI=VISA

Minimum amounts that may be charged appear in parentheses when applicable.

4 Unless otherwise specified, directions are given from the center of town, using the following highway designations: I (interstate highway), US (federal highway), Hwy. (Canadian or Caribbean highway), SR (state route), CR (county road), FM (farm to market road), FR (forest road), MM (mile marker), Mex. (Mexican highway).

5 Admission prices are quoted without sales tax. Children under the lowest age specified are admitted free when accompanied by an adult. Days, months and age groups written with a hyphen are inclusive. Prices pertaining to points of interest in the United States are quoted in U.S. dollars; prices for Canadian province and territory points of interest are quoted in Canadian dollars; prices for points of interest in Mexico and the Caribbean are quoted as an approximate U.S. dollar equivalent.

Bulleted Listings: Casino gambling establishments are visited by AAA personnel to ensure safety; casinos within hotels are presented for member information regardless of whether the lodging is AAA approved. Recreational activities of a participatory nature (requiring physical exertion or special skills) are not inspected. Wineries are inspected by AAA Tourism Editors to ensure they meet listing requirements and offer tours. All are presented in a bulleted format for informational purposes.

These Show Your Card & Save® partners provide the listed member benefits. Admission tickets that offer greater discounts may be available for purchase at the local AAA/CAA club. A maximum of six tickets is available at the discount price.

Attraction Partners

SeaWorld/Busch Gardens

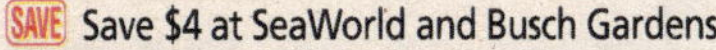

- SAVE Save $4 at SeaWorld and Busch Gardens

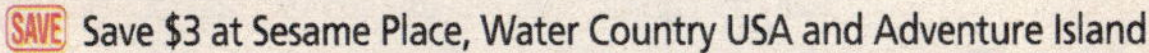

- SAVE Save $3 at Sesame Place, Water Country USA and Adventure Island
- SAVE Save 10% on select up-close dining. Reservations are required; visit Guest Relations for details

Six Flags Theme Parks

- SAVE Save $4 on general admission at the gate
- SAVE Save $12 on general admission at the gate each Wednesday
- SAVE Save 10% on selected souvenirs and dining (check at main gate for details)

Universal Orlando (www.aaa.com/Universal)

- SAVE Save $4 on a 2-day/2-park pass or $5 on a 3-day/2-park pass at Universal Orlando's theme parks (savings apply to tickets purchased at the gate)

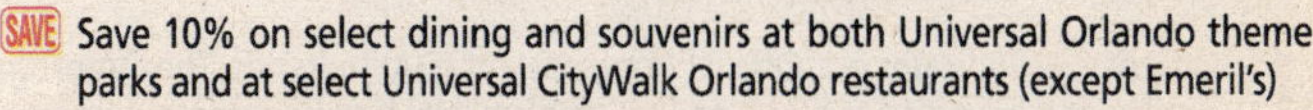

- SAVE Save 10% on select dining and souvenirs at both Universal Orlando theme parks and at select Universal CityWalk Orlando restaurants (except Emeril's)

Universal Studios Hollywood

- SAVE Save $3 on a 1-day Universal Hollywood pass (savings applies to tickets purchased at the gate)

- SAVE Save 10% on select dining and souvenirs at Universal Studios Hollywood and Universal CityWalk

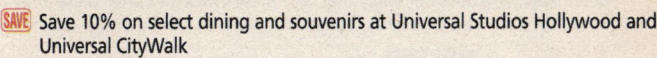

Gray Line

- SAVE Save 10% on sightseeing tours of 1 day or less

Restaurant Partners

Landry's Seafood House, The Crab House, Chart House, Muer Seafood Restaurants, Joe's Crab Shack

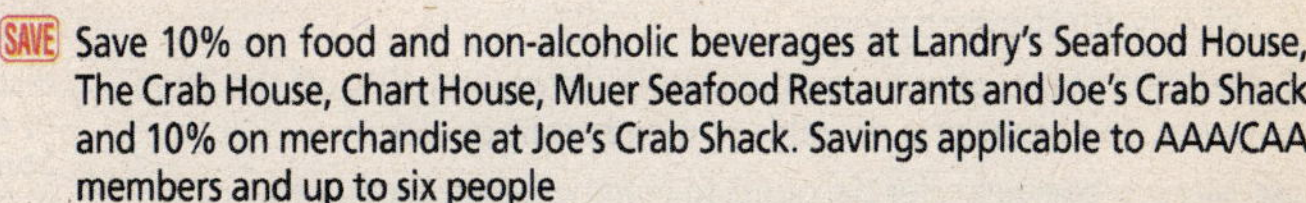

- SAVE Save 10% on food and non-alcoholic beverages at Landry's Seafood House, The Crab House, Chart House, Muer Seafood Restaurants and Joe's Crab Shack and 10% on merchandise at Joe's Crab Shack. Savings applicable to AAA/CAA members and up to six people

Hard Rock Cafe

- SAVE Save 10% on food, beverage, and merchandise at all U.S., Canada, and select international locations. Members also save 10% at The Hard Rock Vault.

Mexican Partners

- SAVE An alliance between AAA/CAA and AMA (Mexican Automobile Association) provides members visting Mexico savings from Mexicana Airlines, Tony Roma restaurants and Six Flags of Mexico

Visit aaa.com to discover all the great Show Your Card & Save® discounts in your area.

Sample Lodging Listing

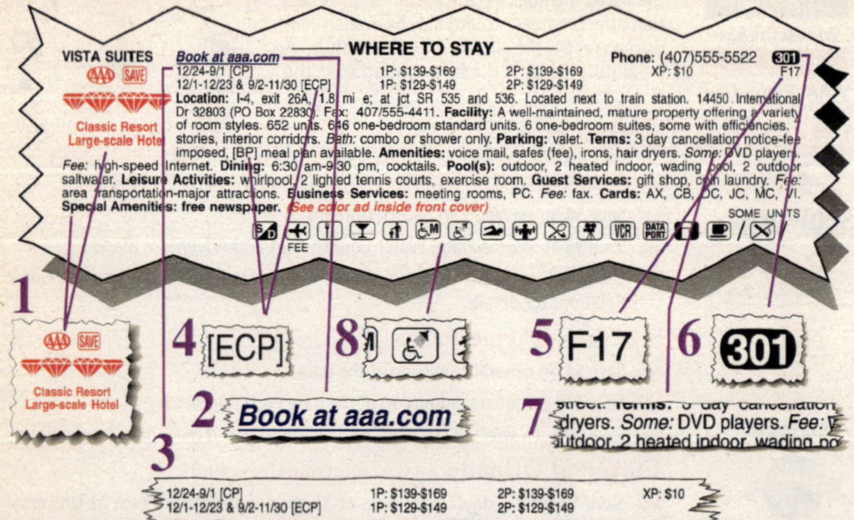

1 (AAA) or (CAA) indicates our Official Appointment (OA) lodgings. The OA program permits properties to display and advertise the (AAA) or (CAA) emblem. We highlight these properties with red diamonds and classification. Some OA listings include special amenities such as free continental breakfast; expanded continental breakfast or full breakfast; early check-in/late check-out; free room upgrade or preferred room, such as ocean view or poolside (subject to availability); free local phone calls; and free daily newspaper. This does not imply that only these properties offer these amenities. The (AAA) or (CAA) sign helps traveling members find accommodations that want member business.

(red diamonds) or (black diamonds) The number of diamonds—not the color—informs you of the overall level of quality in a lodging's amenities and service. More diamond details appear on page 16.

Classic Resort Large-scale Hotel or Classic Resort Large-scale Hotel: All diamond rated lodgings are classified using three key elements: style of operation, overall concept and service level. See pages 22-23 for details about our Lodging Classifications and Subclassifications.

Member Values

SAVE Official Appointment properties guarantee members a minimum 10% discount off the standard room rates published in TourBook guides or the lowest public rate available at the time of booking for the dates of stay, for standard rooms.

S/D Establishments offer a minimum senior discount of 10% off the listed rates. This discount is available to members 60 or older.

A$K Many properties offer discounts to members even though the lodgings do not participate in a formal discount program. The A$K is another reminder to inquire about available discounts when making your reservations or at check-in.

Discounts normally offered at some lodgings may not apply during special events or holiday periods. Special rates and discounts may not apply to all room types. Some Member Values may not apply in Mexico or the Caribbean.

To obtain published rates or discounts, you must identify yourself as a AAA or CAA member, request AAA rates when making reservations and have written confirmation sent to you. The SAVE or senior discount may not be used in conjunction with other discounts. At registration, show your membership card and verify the room rate.

Discounts normally offered at some lodgings may not apply during special events or holiday periods. Special rates and discounts may not apply to all room types. Some Member Values may not apply in Mexico or the Caribbean.

The rates listed for approved properties are provided to AAA by each lodging and represent the regular (rack) rate for a standard room. Printed rates, based on rack rates and last room availability, are rounded to the nearest dollar. Rates do not include taxes and discounts. U.S., Mexican and Caribbean rates are in U.S. dollars; rates for Canadian lodgings are in Canadian dollars.

NAVIGATOR N W E S • Lodgings •

2 **Book at aaa.com - Internet Reservations**

Indicates AAA/CAA members can conveniently check room availability and make reservations in a secure online environment at aaa.com.

3 **Rate Lines**

Shown from left to right: dates the rates are effective; meal plan provided with rates (see Meal Plan Indicators-if no plan noted, rate includes room only); rates for 1 person or 2 persons; extra person charge (XP); and any applicable family plan indicator.

Rates Guaranteed

AAA/CAA members are guaranteed that they will not be charged more than the maximum regular rate printed in each rate range for a standard room. Rates may vary within the range depending on season and room type. Listed rates are based on last standard room availability. Rates for properties operating as concessionaires for the U.S. National Park Service are not guaranteed due to governing regulations. Rates in the Mexico TourBook are not guaranteed and may fluctuate based on the exchange rate of the peso.

Exceptions

Lodgings may temporarily increase room rates, not recognize discounts or modify pricing policies during special events. Examples of special events range from Mardi Gras and Kentucky Derby (including pre-Derby events) to college football games, holidays, holiday periods and state fairs. Although some special events are listed in AAA/CAA TourBook guides, it is always wise to check, in advance, with AAA travel professionals for specific dates.

Discounts

Member discounts will apply to rates quoted, within the rate range, applicable at the time of booking. Special rates used in advertising, and special short-term, promotional rates lower than the lowest listed rate in the range, are not subject to additional member discounts.

4 **Meal Plan Indicators**

The following types of meal plans may be available in the listed room rate:

AP = American Plan of three meals daily
BP = Breakfast Plan of full hot breakfast
CP = Continental Plan of pastry, juice and another beverage
ECP = Expanded Continental Plan, which offers a wider variety of breakfast items
MAP = Modified American Plan of two meals daily

See individual listing "Terms" section for additional meal plans that are not included in the room rate.

Check-in times are shown in the listing only if they are after 3 p.m.; check-out times are shown only if they are before 10 a.m.

5 **Family Plan Indicators**

F = Children stay free
D = Discounts for children
F17 = Children 17 and under stay free (age displayed will reflect property's policy)
D17 = Discount for children 17 and under

6 **Lodging Locators**

Black ovals with white numbers are used to locate, or "spot," lodgings on maps we provide for larger cities.

7 **Unit Types**

Unit types, amenities and room features preceded by the word "Some" indicate the item is available on a limited basis, potentially within only one unit.

8 **Lodging Icons**

A row of icons is included with each lodging listing. These icons represent the member values, member services, and facilities offered by that lodging. See page 19 for an explanation of each icon.

The Lodging Diamond Ratings

AAA Tourism Editors evaluate and rate each lodging based on the overall quality, the range of facilities and the level of services offered by a property. The size, age and overall appeal of an establishment are considered as well as regional architectural style and design.

While guest services are an important part of all diamond ratings, they are particularly critical at the four and five diamond levels. A property must provide a high level of service, on a consistent basis, to obtain and support the four and five diamond rating.

These establishments typically appeal to the budget-minded traveler. They provide essential, no-frills accommodations. They meet the basic requirements pertaining to comfort, cleanliness, and hospitality.

These establishments appeal to the traveler seeking more than the basic accommodations. There are modest enhancements to the overall physical attributes, design elements, and amenities of the facility typically at a modest price.

These establishments appeal to the traveler with comprehensive needs. Properties are multifaceted with a distinguished style, including marked upgrades in the quality of physical attributes, amenities and level of comfort provided.

These establishments are upscale in all areas. Accommodations are progressively more refined and stylish. The physical attributes reflect an obvious enhanced level of quality throughout. The fundamental hallmarks at this level include an extensive array of amenities combined with a high degree of hospitality, service, and attention to detail.

These establishments reflect the characteristics of the ultimate in luxury and sophistication. Accommodations are first-class. The physical attributes are extraordinary in every manner. The fundamental hallmarks at this level are to meticulously serve and exceed all guest expectations while maintaining an impeccable standard of excellence. Many personalized services and amenities enhance an unmatched level of comfort.

The lodging listings with fyi in place of diamonds are included as an "information only" service for members. The icon indicates that a property has not been rated for one or more of the following reasons: too new to rate; under construction; under major renovation; not evaluated; or may not meet all AAA requirements. Those properties not meeting all AAA requirements are included for either their member value or because it may be the only accommodation available in the area. Listing prose will give insight as to why the fyi designation was assigned.

Guest Safety

Room Security

In order to be approved for listing in AAA/CAA TourBook guides for the United States and Canada, all lodgings must comply with AAA's guest room security requirements.

In response to AAA/CAA members' concern about their safety at properties, AAA-RATED® accommodations must have dead-bolt locks on all guest room entry doors and connecting room doors.

If the area outside the guest room door is not visible from inside the room through a window or door panel, viewports must be installed on all guest room entry doors. Bed and breakfast properties and country inns are not required to have viewports. Ground floor and easily accessible sliding doors must be equipped with some other type of secondary security locks.

Tourism Editors view a percentage of rooms at each property since it is not feasible to evaluate every room in every lodging establishment. Therefore, AAA cannot guarantee that there are working locks on all doors and windows in all guest rooms.

Fire Safety

Because of the highly specialized skills needed to conduct professional fire safety inspections, AAA/CAA Tourism Editors cannot assess fire safety.

Properties must meet all federal, state and local fire codes. Each guest unit in all U.S. and Canadian lodging properties must be equipped with an operational, single-station smoke detector. A AAA/CAA Tourism Editor has evaluated a sampling of the rooms to verify this equipment is in place.

For additional fire safety information, read the page posted on the back of your guest room door, or write:

National Fire Protection Association
1 Batterymarch Park
P.O. Box 9101
Quincy, MA 02269-9101

Requirements for some features, such as door locks and smoke detectors/sprinkler systems, differ in Mexico and the Caribbean. If a property met AAA's security requirements at the time of the evaluation, the phrase "Meets AAA guest room security requirements" appears in the listing.

Access for Mature Travelers and Travelers with Disabilities

Qualified properties listed in this guide are shown with symbols indicating they meet the needs of the hearing-impaired or offer some accessible features for mature travelers or travelers with disabilities.

Hearing Impaired

Indicates a property has the following equipment available for hearing-impaired travelers: TDD at front desk or switchboard; visual notification of fire alarm, incoming telephone calls, door knock or bell; closed caption decoder; text telephone or TDD for guest room use; telephone amplification device, with shelf or electric outlet next to guest room telephone.

Accessible Features

Indicates a property has some accessible features meeting the needs of mature travelers and travelers with disabilities. Lodging establishments will provide at least one guest room meeting the designated criteria as well as accessible restrooms and parking facilities. Restaurants provide accessible parking, dining rooms and restrooms.

AAA/CAA strongly urges members to call the property directly to fully understand the property's exact accessibility features. Some properties do not fully comply with AAA/CAA's exacting accessibility standards but may offer some design standards that meet the needs of some guests with disabilities.

AAA/CAA does not evaluate recreational facilities, banquet rooms, or convention or meeting facilities for accessibility.

Service Animals

No fees or deposits, even those normally charged for pets, may be charged for service animals. Service animals fulfill a critical need for their owners—they are *not* pets.

The Americans With Disabilities Act (ADA) prohibits U.S. businesses that serve the public from discriminating against persons with disabilities. Some businesses have mistakenly denied access to persons who use service animals. ADA, a federal mandate, has priority over all state and local laws, as well as a business owner's standard of business, which might bar animals from the premises. Businesses must permit entry to guests and their service animals, as well as allow service animals to accompany guests to all public areas of a property. A property is permitted to ask whether the animal is a service animal or a pet, and whether the guest has a disability. The property may not, however, ask questions about the nature of the disability, the service provided by the animal or require proof of a disability or certification that the animal is a service animal.

Note: These regulations may not apply in Canada, Mexico or the Caribbean.

What The Lodging Icons Mean

NAVIGATOR Lodgings

Member Values

(see p. 14)

AAA or CAA Official Appointment

SAVE Offers minimum 10% discount or lowest public rate *(see p. 14)*

ASK May offer discount

S/D Offers senior discount

fyi Informational listing only

Member Services

Airport transportation

Pets allowed

Restaurant on premises

Restaurant off premises (walking distance)

24 24-hour room service

Cocktail lounge

Child care

Accessibility Feature

(see p. 18)

Accessible features

Roll-in showers

Hearing impaired

Safety Features

(Mexico and Caribbean only)

S Sprinklers

D Smoke detectors

Leisure Activities

Full service casino

Pool

Health club on premises

Health club off premises

Recreational activities

In-Room Amenities

Designated non-smoking rooms

AC No air conditioning

TV No TV

CTV No cable TV

VCR VCR

Movies

DATA PORT Data port/modem line

No telephones

Refrigerator

Microwave

Coffee maker

Availability and Additional Fees

If an in-room amenity is available only on a limited basis (in one or more rooms), the term "SOME UNITS" will appear above those icons. Fees may be charged for some of the services represented by the icons listed here. The word "FEE" will appear below each icon when an extra charge applies.

SOME UNITS

VCR / DATA PORT /

FEE FEE FEE

Preferred Lodging Partners

SAVINGS. SELECTION. SATISFACTION. — When contacting one of the partners listed, you will be given AAA's best rates for your dates of stay. Your valid membership card must be presented at check-in.

SATISFACTION GUARANTEE — If you are not satisfied with any part of your stay, you must provide the property the opportunity to correct the situation during your stay. If the matter cannot be resolved, you will be entitled to recompense for a portion of, or your entire, stay. Satisfaction guarantee varies by chain.

Select the chain you want and have your membership card available when making a reservation and checking in.

Visit	Over 1,100 AAA Offices	Click	aaa.com	Call	866-AAA-SAVE

Comfort Inn · Comfort Suites · Quality · Sleep Inn · Clarion · MainStay Suites · Econo Lodge · Rodeway Inn

CHOICE HOTELS INTERNATIONAL®

Best Western · Days Inn · Hyatt Hotels & Resorts

Hilton · Hilton Garden Inn · Hampton Inn · Hampton Inn & Suites

Embassy Suites Hotels · DoubleTree Hotels·Suites·Resorts·Clubs · Homewood Suites Hilton · La Quinta Inn

La Quinta Inn & Suites · Marriott Hotels & Resorts · Renaissance. Hotels & Resorts · Courtyard Marriott

Fairfield Inn Marriott · Residence Inn Marriott · SpringHill Suites Marriott · Marriott TownePlace Suites

Westin Hotels & Resorts · Sheraton Hotels & Resorts · Four Points Sheraton

St. Regis · Luxury Collection · W Hotels

Special rates and discounts may not apply to all room types. All discounts are off full rates and vary by location and time of year. Special rates and discounts are not available to groups and cannot be combined with other discounts. Restrictions apply to satisfaction guarantees. Valid AAA/CAA membership card must be presented at check-in. Offers good at time of publication; chains and offers may change without notice. Lodging partners offering discounts to AAA/CAA members may vary in Mexico and the Caribbean.

Making Reservations

When making reservations, you must identify yourself as a AAA or CAA member. Give all pertinent information about your planned stay. Ask about the lodging's pet policy, or the availability of any other special feature that is important to your stay. Request written confirmation to guarantee: type of room, rate, dates of stay, and cancellation and refund policies. At registration, show your membership card. Note: Age restrictions may apply.

Confirm Deposit, Refund and Cancellation Policies

Most establishments give full deposit refunds if they have been notified at least 48 hours before the normal check-in time. Listing prose will note if more than 48 hours notice is required for cancellation. However, when making reservations, confirm the property's deposit, cancellation and refund policies. Some properties may charge a cancellation or handling fee.

When this applies, "cancellation fee imposed" will appear in the listing. If you cancel too late, you have little recourse if a refund is denied.

When an establishment requires a full or partial payment in advance, and your trip is cut short, a refund may not be given.

When canceling reservations, phone the lodging immediately. Make a note of the date and time you called, the cancellation number if there is one, and the name of the person who handled the cancellation. If your AAA/CAA club made your reservation, allow them to make the cancellation for you as well so you will have proof of cancellation.

Review Charges for Appropriate Rates

When you are charged more than the maximum rate listed in the TourBook guide for a standard room, question the additional charge. If management refuses to adhere to the published rate, pay for the room and submit your receipt and membership number to AAA/CAA within 30 days. Include all pertinent information: dates of stay, rate paid, itemized paid receipts, number of persons in your party, the room number you occupied, and list any extra room equipment used. A refund of the amount paid in excess of the stated maximum will be made if our investigation indicates that unjustified charging has occurred.

Get the Room You Reserved

When you find your room is not as specified, and you have written confirmation of reservations for a certain type of accommodation, you should be given the option of choosing a different room or finding one elsewhere. Should you choose to go elsewhere and a refund is refused or resisted, submit the matter to AAA/CAA within 30 days along with complete documentation, including your reasons for refusing the room and copies of your written confirmation and any receipts or canceled checks associated with this problem.

How to Get the Best Room Rates

You'll find the best room rate if you book your reservation in advance with the help of a travel professional or agent at your local AAA/CAA office.

If you're not yet ready to make firm vacation plans or if you prefer a more spontaneous trip, take advantage of the partnerships that preferred hotel chains have arranged with AAA. Phone the toll-free number 866-AAA-SAVE that has been set up exclusively for members for the purpose of reserving with these Show Your Card & Save® chain partners.

Even if you were unable to make a reservation, be sure to show your membership card at the desk and ask if you're being offered the lowest rate available for that time. Many lodgings offer reduced rates to members.

Lodging Classifications

To ensure that your lodging needs/preferences are met, we recommend that you consider an establishment's classification when making your travel choices.

While the quality and comfort at properties with the same diamond rating should be consistent (regardless of the classification), there are differences in typical décor/theme elements, range of facilities and service levels. Please see the descriptions below.

Hotel Royal Plaza, Lake Buena Vista, FL

Large-scale Hotel

A multistory establishment with interior room entrances. A variety of guest unit styles is offered. Public areas are spacious and include a variety of facilities such as a restaurant, shops, fitness center, spa, business center, or meeting rooms.

Baymont Inn, Dallas/Ft. Worth-Airport North, TX

Small-scale Hotel

A multistory establishment typically with interior room entrances. A variety of guest unit styles is offered. Public areas are limited in size and/or the variety of facilities available.

Best Western Deltona Inn, Deltona, FL

Motel

A one- to three-story establishment typically with exterior room entrances facilitating convenient access to parking. The standard guest units have one bedroom with a bathroom and are typically similar in décor and design throughout. Public areas are limited in size and/or the variety of facilities available.

Greenville Inn, Greenville, ME

Country Inn

Similar in definition to a bed and breakfast, but usually larger in scale with spacious public areas and offers a dining facility that serves at least breakfast and dinner.

Harbour Town Inn, Boothbay Harbor, ME

Bed & Breakfast

Small-scale properties emphasizing a high degree of personal touches that provide guests an "at home" feeling. Guest units tend to be individually decorated. Rooms may not include some modern amenities such as televisions and telephones, and may have a shared bathroom. Usually owner-operated with a common room or parlor separate from the innkeeper's living quarters, where guests and operators can interact during evening and breakfast hours. Evening office closures are normal. A continental or full, hot breakfast is served and is included in the room rate.

Sands of Kahana, Kahana, Maui, HI

Condominium

Vacation-oriented or extended-stay, apartment-style accommodations that are routinely available for rent through a management company. Units vary in design and décor and often contain one or more bedrooms, living room, full kitchen, and an eating area. Studio-type models combine the sleeping and living areas into one room. Typically, basic cleaning supplies, kitchen utensils and complete bed and bath linens are supplied. The guest registration area may be located off-site.

NAVIGATOR Lodgings

Desert Rose Inn, Bluff, UT

Cabin/Cottage

Vacation-oriented, small-scale, freestanding houses or cabins. Units vary in design and décor and often contain one or more bedrooms, living room, kitchen, dining area, and bathroom. Studio-type models combine the sleeping and living areas into one room. Typically, basic cleaning supplies, kitchen utensils, and complete bed and bath linens are supplied. The guest registration area may be located off-site.

C Lazy U Ranch, Granby, CO

Ranch

Typically a working ranch with an obvious rustic, Western theme. In general, equestrian-related activities are featured, but ranches may include other animals and activities as well. A variety of guest unit styles is offered in a family-oriented atmosphere.

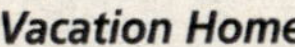

Vacation Home

Vacation-oriented or extended-stay, large-scale, freestanding houses that are routinely available for rent through a management company. Houses vary in design and décor and often contain two or more bedrooms, living room, full kitchen, dining room, and multiple bathrooms. Typically, basic cleaning supplies, kitchen utensils, and complete bed and bath linens are supplied. The guest registration area may be located off-site.

ResortQuest, Hilton Head Island, SC

Lodging Subclassifications

The following are subclassifications that may appear along with the classifications listed above to provide a more specific description of the lodging.

Casino

Extensive gambling facilities are available such as blackjack, craps, keno, and slot machines. **Note:** This subclassification will not appear beneath its diamond rating in the listing. It will be indicated by a dice icon and will be included in the row of icons immediately below the lodging listing.

Classic

Renowned and landmark properties, older than 50 years, well-known for their unique style and ambience.

Historic

These properties are typically over 75 years of age and exhibit many features of a historic nature with respect to architecture, design, furnishings, public record, or acclaim. Properties must meet one of the following criteria:

- Maintained the integrity of the historical nature
- Listed on the U.S. National Register of Historic Places
- Designated a U.S. National Historic Landmark
- Located in a U.S. National Register Historic District

Separate criteria designate historic properties in Canada, Mexico and the Caribbean.

Resort

Recreation-oriented, geared to vacation travelers seeking a specific destination experience. Travel packages, meal plans, theme entertainment, and social and recreational programs are typically available. Recreational facilities are extensive and may include spa treatments, golf, tennis, skiing, fishing, or water sports, etc. Larger resorts may offer a variety of guest accommodations.

Sample Restaurant Listing

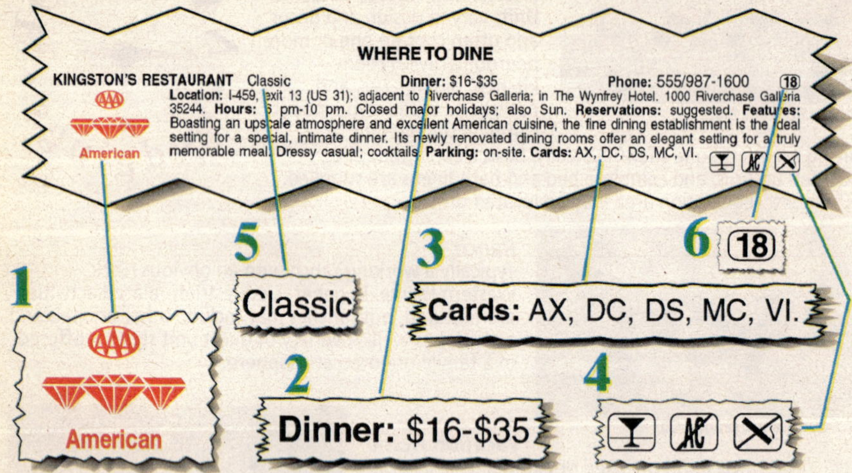

1 AAA or CAA indicates our Official Appointment (OA) restaurants. The OA program permits properties to display and advertise the AAA or CAA emblem. We highlight these properties with red diamonds and cuisine type. The AAA or CAA sign helps traveling members find restaurants that want member business.

or The number of diamonds—not the color—informs you of the overall level of quality for food and presentation, service and ambience. Menus for red Diamond restaurants can be viewed on aaa.com.

A cuisine type is assigned for each restaurant listing. AAA currently recognizes more than 90 different cuisine types.

2 Prices represent the minimum and maximum entree cost per person. Exceptions may include one-of-a-kind or special market priced items.

3 AX=American Express
CB=Carte Blanche DS=Discover MC=MasterCard
DC=Diners Club JC=Japan Credit Bureau VI=VISA

4 These three icons are used in restaurant listings. When present, they indicate: the presence of a cocktail lounge, the lack of air conditioning, and/or that the restaurant has a designated non-smoking section or is entirely smoke-free.

5 If applicable, restaurants may be further defined as:

Classic—renowned and landmark restaurant operations in business longer than 25 years, known for unique style and ambience.

Historic—properties must meet one of the following criteria:

- Listed on the U.S. National Register of Historic Places
- Designated a U.S. National Historic Landmark
- Located in a U.S. National Register Historic District

Separate criteria designate historic properties in Canada, Mexico and the Caribbean.

6 These white ovals with black numbers serve as restaurant locators and are used to locate, or "spot," restaurants on maps we provide for larger cities.

The Restaurant Diamond Ratings

AAA Tourism Editors are responsible for determining a restaurant's diamond rating based on established criteria.

These criteria were established with input from AAA trained professionals, members, and restaurant industry experts. They are purposely broad to capture what is typically seen throughout the restaurant industry at each diamond rating level.

These establishments appeal to a diner seeking good, wholesome, no-nonsense eating at an affordable price. They typically provide simple, familiar, and unadorned foods served in a sensible, casual or self-service style. Often quick service and family oriented.

Examples include coffee shops, diners, cafeterias, short order, and modest full service eateries.

These establishments provide for dining needs that are increasingly complex, but still reasonably priced. They typically exhibit noticeable efforts in rising above the ordinary in many aspects of food, service and decor. Service is typically functional yet ambitious, periodically combining informal style with limited self-service elements. Often well-suited to traditional, special occasion, and family dining.

Examples include a varied range of specific concept (theme) and multi-purpose establishments.

These establishments impart an increasingly refined and upscale, adult-oriented experience. This is the entry level into fine dining. Creative and complex menus offer a blend of traditional and trendy foods. The service level is typically semi-formal with knowledgeable and proficient staff. Routinely these restaurants appeal to the diner in search of an experience rather than just a meal.

Examples include high-caliber, chic, boutique, and conventional restaurants.

These establishments impart a luxurious and socially refined experience. This is consistent fine dining. Menus typically reflect a high degree of creativity and complexity, featuring elaborate presentations of market-driven or traditional dishes. A cultured, professional, and highly proficient staff consistently demonstrates a profound desire to meet or exceed guest expectations. Restaurants of this caliber are geared to individuals with an appetite for an elite, fine-dining experience.

Examples include dining rooms associated with luxury lodgings, or exclusive independent restaurants often found in metropolitan areas.

Often renowned, these establishments impart a world-class and opulent, adult-oriented experience. This is "haute cuisine" at its best. Menus are often cutting edge, with an obvious dedication to use of only the finest ingredients available. Even the classic dishes become extraordinary under the masterful direction of highly acclaimed chefs. Presentations are spectacular, reflecting impeccable artistry and awareness. An expert, formalized staff continuously anticipates and exceeds guest expectations. Staff members' unfailing attention to detail appears effortless, well-rehearsed and unobtrusive. Undoubtedly, these restaurants appeal to those in search of the ultimate dining experience.

Examples include renowned dining rooms associated with luxury lodgings, or exclusive independent restaurants often found in metropolitan areas.

The restaurants with fyi in place of diamonds are included as an "information only" service for members. These listings provide additional dining choices but have not yet been evaluated.

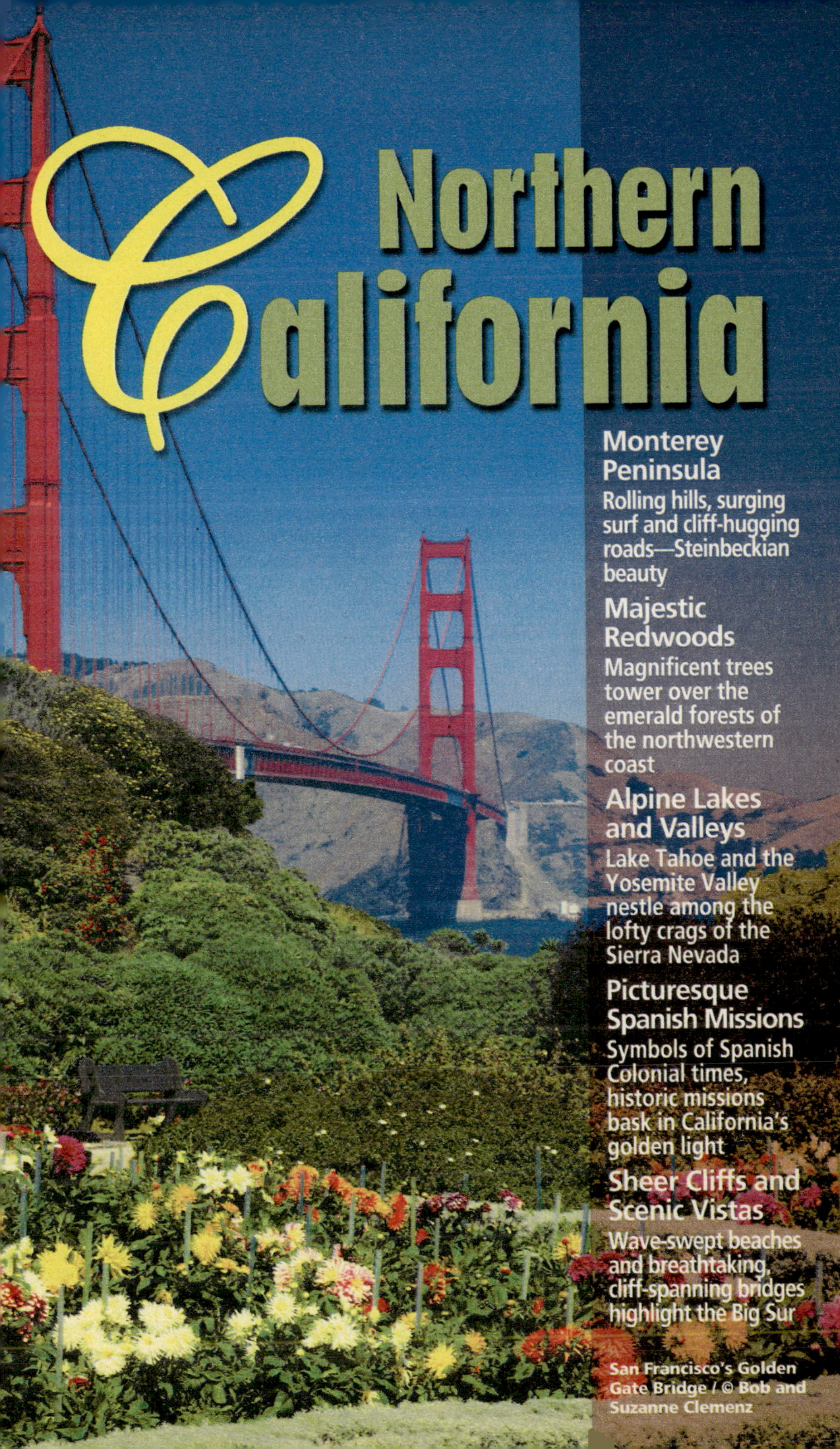

Northern California
Monterey Peninsula
Rolling hills, surging surf and cliff-hugging roads—Steinbeckian beauty
Majestic Redwoods
Magnificent trees tower over the emerald forests of the northwestern coast
Alpine Lakes and Valleys
Lake Tahoe and the Yosemite Valley nestle among the lofty crags of the Sierra Nevada
Picturesque Spanish Missions
Symbols of Spanish Colonial times, historic missions bask in California's golden light
Sheer Cliffs and Scenic Vistas
Wave-swept beaches and breathtaking, cliff-spanning bridges highlight the Big Sur

San Francisco's Golden Gate Bridge / © Bob and Suzanne Clemenz

Pfeiffer Big Sur State Park / © Christopher Talbot Frank / Ambient Images Inc.

The allure of the Golden State must be powerful: Nearly 34 million people can't be wrong. Abundant resources, some of the nation's most agreeable weather and a stunningly varied landscape go a long way toward explaining the attraction.

Most Americans who have never set foot west of the Rockies have heard of the Yosemite Valley, Lake Tahoe, Big Sur, Death Valley, the Golden Gate Bridge, the San Diego Zoo and L.A.'s Getty Center. Thanks to Hollywood movies and TV shows, California and all its associations—surfing, sun, starlets lounging by pools, environmentalists chaining themselves to condemned trees, urban sprawl, pollution, earthquakes—have all entered the popular imagination.

the promised land

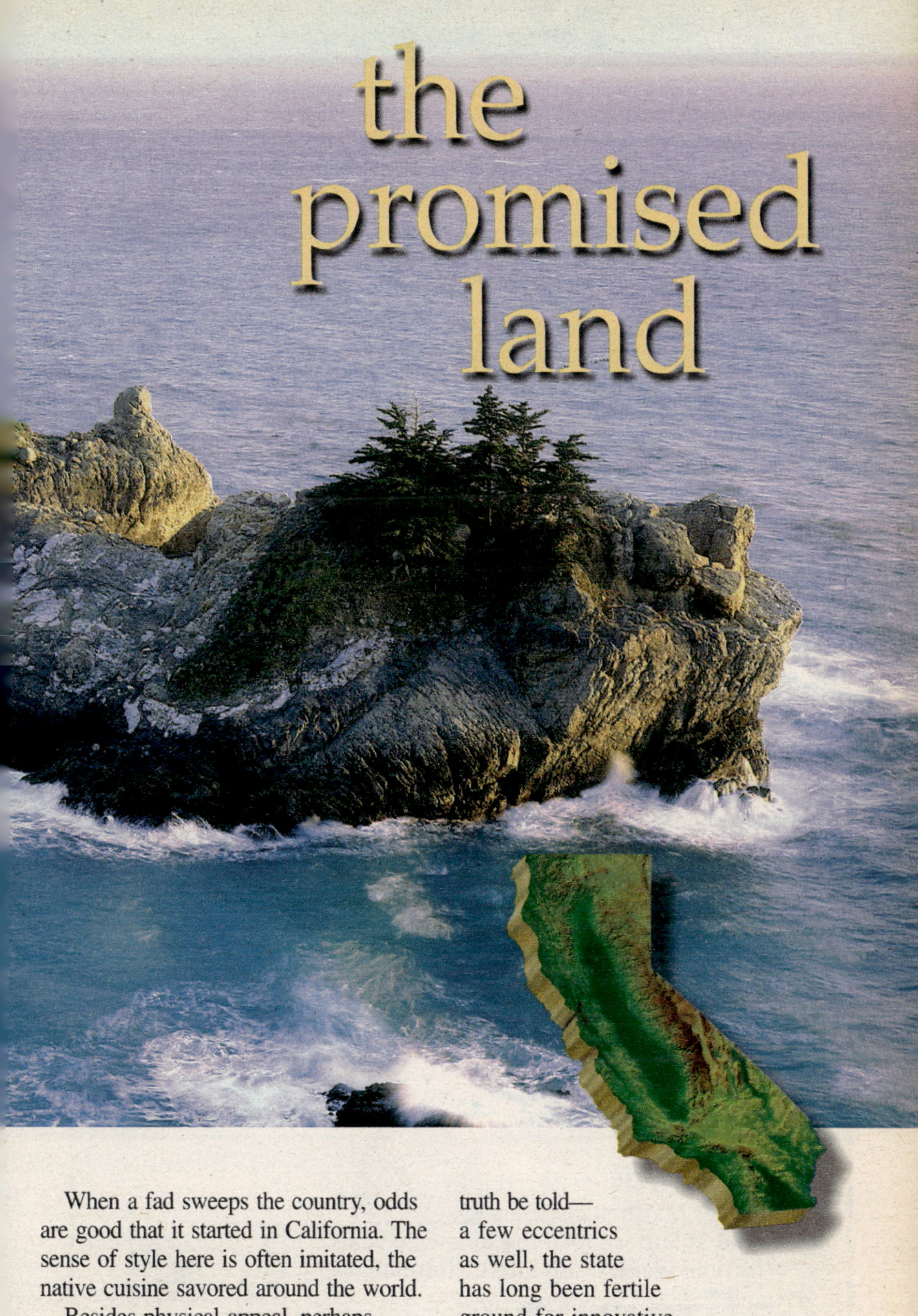

When a fad sweeps the country, odds are good that it started in California. The sense of style here is often imitated, the native cuisine savored around the world.

Besides physical appeal, perhaps nothing epitomizes the "Left Coast" more than the people and their almost mythical lifestyle. Populated by entrepreneurs, visionaries, counterculture radicals, trendsetters, go-getters and—truth be told—a few eccentrics as well, the state has long been fertile ground for innovative ideas, technological breakthroughs and entirely new ways of living. No wonder Americans looking toward the future often face west.

Fade in: A snow-clad mountainside. A man and woman dressed in ski gear swoosh down an alpine slope. Cut to: A sun-washed beach hours later. The same couple strolls along the shore, waves rolling in, water lapping at their feet. Next scene: A swank urban bistro an hour later. The twosome sit across from each other savoring a sumptuous dinner as they discuss which of the many local nightclubs they should visit. Fade out.

Although unusually energetic, the happy duo described above is realistic enough. It's the setting that seems unreal, dreamed up. Skiing in the mountains within hours of a walk on a picture-postcard beach? Both within reach of a major city? A place that could only exist in movies, right?

Well, no. Though the beautiful scenery is nearly unbelievable, the place is real, and it is where movies are *made*. As you've probably guessed, this far-fetched locale could only be California.

Appropriately named after a fictional island rich with gold from a Spanish romance novel, the state attracted early movie-making pioneers with its plentiful sunshine, mild climate and tremendously varied terrain. What better background for drama?

And drama has long been a hallmark of the state. From that first emotion-filled cry of "Eureka!" at Sutter's Mill to the chaotic human tidal wave of the ensuing gold rush and the tragedy of the San Francisco earthquake decades later, drama has been one of the state's most notable characteristics.

Better Than Fiction

Those first filmmakers arriving in the early 1900s must have realized they couldn't dream up a better setting for their celluloid fantasies; the California landscape itself is dramatic. Breathtaking only begins to describe the rocky, sea-splashed cliffs of Big Sur, the snow-capped cone of volcanic Mount Shasta or the jagged, glacier-sculpted peaks of the Sierra Nevada.

And vistas that are impossible to truly capture on film abound in the Yosemite Valley and the surrounding national park. Even frequent visitors find it difficult to comprehend the size of the park's colossal escarpments and the height of its waterfalls. And what camera could do justice to the super-saturated blues of frigid Lake Tahoe or the emerald greens of Muir Woods?

California Historical Timeline

1769-1823

Fathers Junípero Serra and Fermín Lasuén build 21 missions extending from San Diego to Sonoma.

©Gibson Stock Photography

1848

James Marshall discovers gold at Sutter's Mill; the following year fortune seekers rush into California.

©SuperStock

1850

California becomes the 31st state.

1890

Yosemite National Park is established.

©Jack Novak/SuperStock

©Underwood Photo Archives/SuperStock

1906

An earthquake and resulting fire destroy most of San Francisco.

There's also drama in the diversity of landscapes: the nation's second tallest mountain, Mount Whitney, stands within 90 miles of Death Valley, the Western Hemisphere's lowest point. Even the lighting varies enough to please the fussiest cinematographer, ranging from the soft, mist-dimmed glow of the northwest coast to the harsh, unfiltered glare of the southeast deserts. And speaking of lighting, who can count the number of movies that have ended with a lingering view of heroes and heroines riding off into the trademark, Technicolor California sunset?

And like a movie star from Hollywood's golden age, the state's ready for its close-up. Zoom in on the mountains, valleys, deserts and shore areas and you'll find a fascinating array of plants and animals. Off the coast, migrating gray and humpback whales are the stars while sea lions, elephant seals and playful sea otters make their appearances closer to shore. California's signature flora includes chaparral scrub, desert-loving Joshua trees, giant sequoias and ancient bristlecone pines.

Following the Sun

But what motion picture would be complete without actors? Even before the flood of fortune hunters following the sun from the East arrived, the lands west of the Sierra Nevada were home to a cast of characters that included Franciscan missionaries, Spanish ranchers, and the American Indians who had lived in the region for thousands of years. Then the gold rush created cities and towns almost overnight, and people have never stopped being drawn to the spectacle of the place. Since the '60s more people have called the Golden State home than any other in the union.

The results of their labors take myriad forms: centuries-old Spanish missions that dot the coast; the futuristic glass-and-steel skyscrapers of Los Angeles and San Francisco; the lovely beach resorts of Carmel and Santa Cruz; the unlikely desert oasis of Palm Springs; and the quaint gold rush towns sprinkled along the western slopes of the Sierra Nevada. And what more fitting testament to surreal beauty than the magnificent Hearst Castle or the celebration of imagination that is Disneyland?

Of course, no better symbol of California's blend of the fantastic and the real exists than Hollywood: the capital of an industry which has for nearly a century drawn inspiration from a location that seems like make-believe but somehow isn't.

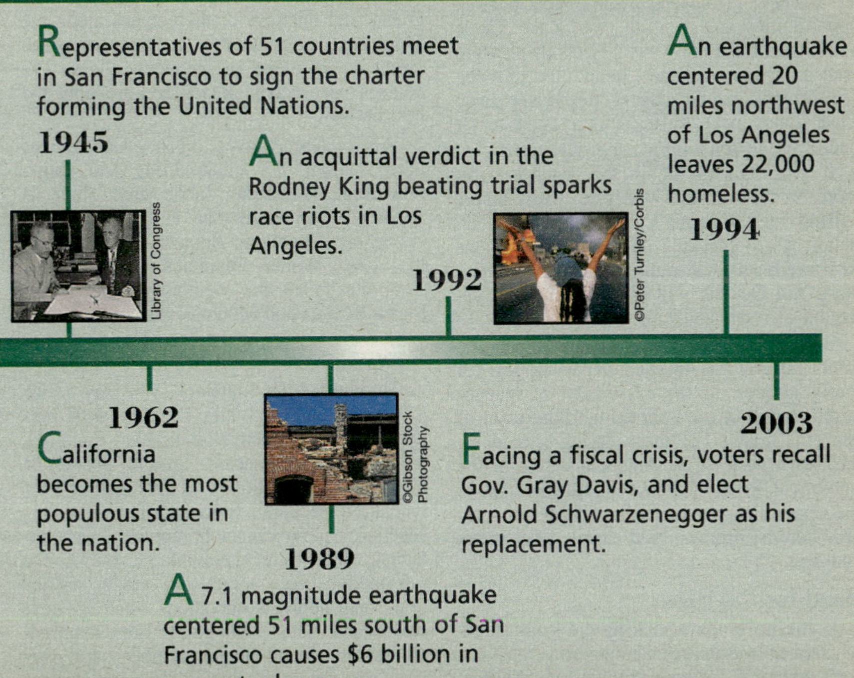

Representatives of 51 countries meet in San Francisco to sign the charter forming the United Nations.
1945
Library of Congress
1962
California becomes the most populous state in the nation.
©Gibson Stock Photography
1989
A 7.1 magnitude earthquake centered 51 miles south of San Francisco causes $6 billion in property damage.
An acquittal verdict in the Rodney King beating trial sparks race riots in Los Angeles.
1992
©Peter Turnley/Corbis
An earthquake centered 20 miles northwest of Los Angeles leaves 22,000 homeless.
1994
2003
Facing a fiscal crisis, voters recall Gov. Gray Davis, and elect Arnold Schwarzenegger as his replacement.

Recreation

Enjoying life outside in California is easy; choosing from the many options is where things get difficult. The great outdoors truly is great here, and the amazing variety of landscapes and activities attracts nature lovers from far and wide.

Splish Splash

California's scenic 1,264-mile-long coastline isn't just for taking snapshots. With that much H_20 readily available, water sports enthusiasts have it made in the Golden State. Wet-suited surfers flock to the chilly waters of Monterey Bay, especially around Santa Cruz's renowned Steamer Lane. And if you want to make a splash with something bigger than a surfboard, the coastline's countless inlets and coves are perfect for **boating.**

Consistent winds March through October also make Santa Cruz a great locale for **wind surfing,** although rough surf and riptides rule it out for beginners. San Francisco Bay offers a variety of wind surfing conditions, with Crissy Field in the Presidio offering spectacular urban views and the chance to sail under the Golden Gate Bridge.

Anglers can easily rent all the gear necessary for saltwater **fishing** in many coastal towns. Salmon is among the most sought after catches. Freshwater fishing and boating opportunities are plentiful, too. Lake Tahoe and Shasta Lake draw small fleets of pleasure craft on balmy weekends. In addition to being California's second largest freshwater lake, Clear Lake, near Kelseyville, is said to be one of the nation's finest bass repositories.

If your idea of fun in the water is a bit more on the wet and wild side, **white-water rafting** on California's rushing rivers is an option worth checking out. Due to variations in water levels, scheduling your trip between April and October will give you the best selection of rivers and trips.

Rafting on the Lower Klamath or the South Fork of the American River is ideal for family groups, as the excitement of maneuvering rapids is interspersed with the calm of peaceful floats. The more daring should try the North Fork of the American River or the Tuolumne River. A bonus of rafting trips is the opportunity to see such wildlife as great blue herons, ospreys, bald eagles, river otters and deer.

Head for the Hills

If **hiking** or **backpacking** are your sports of choice, lace up your boots, strap on your pack and head for the 600-mile-long California Coastal Trail or the Pacific Crest Trail, which stretches from Mexico to Canada. And you won't have to travel far from California's big cities to enjoy tromping through the outdoors. Check out Mount Tamalpais State Park, Mount Diablo State Park and the Golden Gate National Recreation Area near San Francisco. By the way, Marin County, on the north end of the Golden Gate Bridge, offers several great trails for **mountain biking** if you opt to pedal instead of walk.

No self-respecting hiker visiting Lake Tahoe should miss the incredible views from the Tahoe Rim Trail. And then there's Yosemite, which fully deserves its reputation for amazing scenery. But don't limit yourself to the valley floor; the park's high country, accessible during the summer months, offers spectacular panoramas.

If the strange, otherworldly landscapes of the desert interest you, try backpacking or off-road biking through Death Valley National Park. Just remember to bring water and plenty of sunscreen. Want to just sit still a bit? Many parks and recreation areas are great for **camping,** too. In fact, Tahoe National Forest alone claims to have 1,400 camping sites.

If you've brought your driver and putter with you, you're in luck, as California boasts some of the nation's finest **golfing.** The greens and fairways of the courses along the Monterey Peninsula offer a choice of windswept ocean views or forested valleys. The courses near Pebble Beach are probably the best known.

When temperatures drop, Californians head outdoors for great **skiing** and **snowboarding.** The Lake Tahoe area alone is sprinkled with more than a dozen different ski resorts, including Squaw Valley, site of the 1960 Winter Olympics. Add to this Yosemite Valley and Mammoth Lakes in the Sierra Nevada and Mount Shasta in the north.

Recreational Activities

Throughout the TourBook, you may notice a Recreational Activities heading with bulleted listings of recreation-oriented establishments listed underneath. Similar operations also may be mentioned in Destination City recreation sections. Since normal AAA inspection criteria cannot be applied, these establishments are presented only for information. Age, height and weight restrictions may apply. Reservations often are recommended and sometimes are required. Addresses and/or phone numbers are provided so visitors can contact the attraction for additional information.

California Fast Facts

POPULATION: 33,871,648.

AREA: 158,693 square miles; ranks 3rd.

CAPITAL: Sacramento.

HIGHEST POINT: 14,494 ft., Mount Whitney.

LOWEST POINT: -282 ft., Death Valley.

TIME ZONE(S): Pacific. DST.

MINIMUM AGE FOR DRIVERS: 16 with drivers' training, 18 without.

SEAT BELT/CHILD RESTRAINT LAWS: Safety belts required for driver and all passengers; child restraints required for children under age 6 or under 60 pounds.

HELMETS FOR MOTORCYCLISTS: Required.

RADAR DETECTORS: Permitted.

FIREARMS LAWS: Vary by state and/or county. Contact Department of Justice, Firearms Program, P.O. Box 820200, Sacramento, CA 94203-0200; phone (916) 227-3703.

HOLIDAYS: Jan. 1; Martin Luther King Jr. Day, Jan. (3rd Mon.); Lincoln's Birthday, Feb. 12; Washington's Birthday, Feb. (3rd Mon.); Easter; Memorial Day, May (last Mon.); July 4; Labor Day, Sept. (1st Mon.); Admission Day, Sept. 9; Columbus Day, Oct. (2nd Mon.); Veterans Day, Nov. 11; Thanksgiving; Dec. 25.

TAXES: California's statewide sales tax is 7.25 percent; an additional district tax of .25 to 1.25 percent may be imposed in various counties. A transient occupancy tax may be imposed in various counties and cities.

STATE INFORMATION CENTERS: California Welcome Centers are in Arcata at jct. US 101 and SR 299, in Rohnert Park off US 101 Golf Course Rd. exit, in San Francisco at Pier 39, in Los Angeles at Beverly and La Cienega blvds., in Oceanside off I-5 Coast Highway exit, in Barstow off I-15 Lenwood Rd. exit, in Anderson off I-5 Deschutes Rd. exit, in Merced on W. 16th St., in Yucca Valley on SR 62, in Santa Ana on N. Main St. and in Auburn on Lincoln Way.

SPECIAL REGULATIONS: The State Department of Food and Agriculture inspects all produce, plant materials and wild animals at the borders to see if they are admissible under current quarantine regulations. For California regulations concerning plants phone (916) 654-0312; for regulations concerning animals phone (916) 654-1447. Dogs older than 4 months must be accompanied by a current rabies vaccination certificate.

ROAD CONDITIONS: CalTrans provides current information about road conditions; phone (800) 427-7623 in Calif.

FURTHER INFORMATION FOR VISITORS:

California Division of Tourism
P.O. Box 1499
Sacramento, CA 95812-1499
(800) 862-2543

RECREATION INFORMATION:

State Parks:

California State Park System
Department of Parks and Recreation
P.O. Box 942896
Sacramento, CA 94296-0001
(916) 653-6995
(800) 444-7275 (reservations)
TTY (800) 274-7275 (reservations)

National Forests:

Pacific-Southwest Region
U.S. Forest Service
1323 Club Dr.
Vallejo, CA 94592
(707) 562-8737
(877) 444-6777 (reservations)
TTY (888) 433-0287 (reservations)

National Parks:

National Park Service
Fort Mason, Bldg. 201
Bay and Franklin sts.
San Francisco, CA 94123
(415) 561-4700
(800) 365-2267 (reservations)
TTY (888) 530-9796 (reservations)

FISHING AND HUNTING REGULATIONS:

California Department of Fish and Game
1416 9th St.
12th Floor, Room 1240
Sacramento, CA 95814
(916) 653-7664

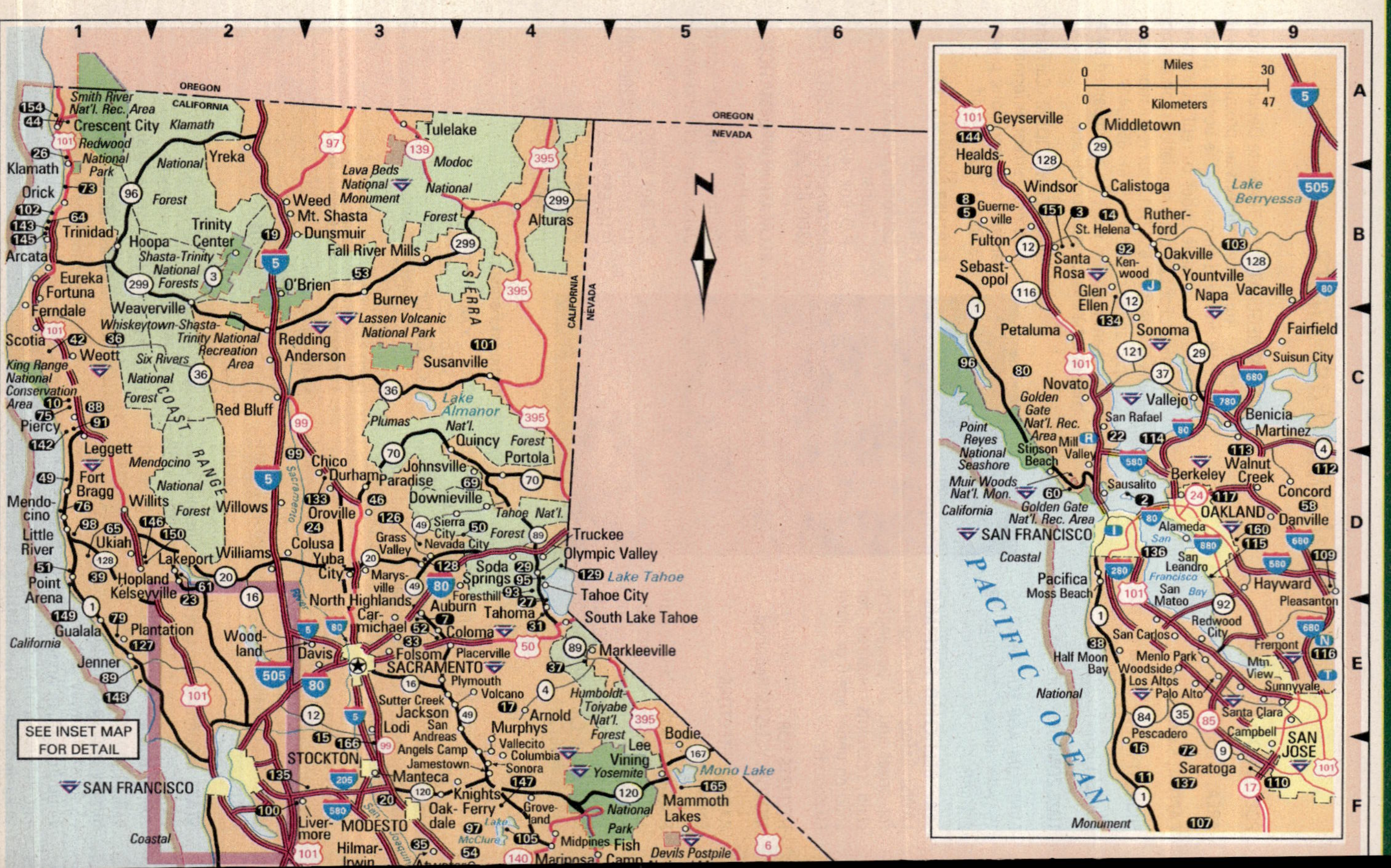

OREGON
CALIFORNIA
NEVADA
Crescent City
Klamath
Yreka
Eureka
Arcata
Weaverville
Redding
Red Bluff
Chico
Susanville
Tulelake
Alturas
Lake Almanor
Truckee
Lake Tahoe
South Lake Tahoe
Mono Lake
Mammoth Lakes
Yosemite
SACRAMENTO
STOCKTON
MODESTO
SAN FRANCISCO
SEE INSET MAP FOR DETAIL
Miles
Kilometers
OAKLAND
SAN JOSE
PACIFIC OCEAN
Lake Berryessa
Santa Rosa
Napa
Vallejo
Berkeley
Hayward
Palo Alto
Santa Clara

Only places listed in Attractions section appear on this map.
See AAA GEM Attractions
See chart of Recreation Areas
PACIFIC OCEAN
Northern California
ORIENTATION
Miles
Kilometers
0
77
124
MISSIONS OF NORTHERN CALIFORNIA
C NUESTRA SEÑORA DE LA SOLEDAD
D SAN ANTONIO DE PADUA
G SAN CARLOS BORROMEO DEL RIO CARMELO
I SAN FRANCISCO DE ASIS
J SAN FRANCISCO SOLANO
L SAN JUAN BAUTISTA
N SAN JOSE
O SAN LUIS OBISPO DE TOLOSA
Q SAN MIGUEL ARCANGEL
R SAN RAFAEL ARCANGEL
T SANTA CLARA DE ASIS
U SANTA CRUZ
SEE SOUTHERN CALIFORNIA TOURBOOK
Los Gatos
Morgan Hill
New Almaden
Big Basin
Felton
Soquel
Santa Cruz
Capitola
Gilroy
Moss Landing
Watsonville
Pacific Grove
Monterey
Carmel
San Juan Bautista
SALINAS
Soledad
Pinnacles National Monument
Big Sur
King City
National Monument
San Simeon
Cambria
Morro Bay
Pismo Beach
Oceano
Santa Maria
Nipomo
Arroyo Grande
San Luis Obispo
Atascadero
Paso Robles
San Miguel
Coalinga
COAST RANGE
Santa Nella
Los Baños
Merced
Oakhurst
North Fork
FRESNO
Clovis
Kingsburg
Hanford
Dunlap
VISALIA
Tulare
Three Rivers
Earlimart
Porterville
Giant Sequoia National Monument
Kernville
BAKERSFIELD
Tupman
Taft
Tehachapi
Boron
Ridgecrest
Barstow
Bishop
Big Pine
Kings Canyon National Park
Sequoia National Park
NEVADA
Independence
Lone Pine
Death Valley National Park
Death Valley Junction
NEVADA
CALIFORNIA
ARIZONA
SANTA BARBARA
LOS ANGELES
SAN BERNARDINO
SAN DIEGO
Colorado River
BAJA CALIFORNIA
USA
MEXICO
G
H
I
J
K
L
© AAA
4000-L

GEM Points of Interest Offering A *Great Experience for Members®*

Berkeley (D-8)

UNIVERSITY OF CALIFORNIA—This college campus encompasses more than a thousand scenic acres that include archives, art and science museums, a botanical garden and a 307-foot-tall bell tower. See p. 63.

Big Basin (G-2)

BIG BASIN REDWOODS STATE PARK—California's first state park features the giant redwoods for which California is famous. See p. 64.

Carmel (G-2)

MISSION SAN CARLOS BORROMEO DEL RIO CARMELO—Called Carmel Mission, this church was founded in 1770. Relics of the mission's early days as well as books and documents are displayed. A Moorish bell tower and courtyard gardens are of interest. See p. 99.

POINT LOBOS STATE RESERVE—Rocky bluffs along the sea are home to rare plants, archeological sites and unusual geological formations. See p. 99.

Coloma (E-4)

MARSHALL GOLD DISCOVERY STATE HISTORIC PARK—This is where the great California gold rush of 1849 began; James Marshall discovered gold here near Capt. John Sutter's mill, and the rest is history. See p. 67.

Columbia (F-4)

COLUMBIA STATE HISTORIC PARK—Once a Mother Lode mining town, Columbia boasts a restored business district that evokes the town's heady gold rush days. See p. 68.

Death Valley National Park (H-7)

DEATH VALLEY NATIONAL PARK—The Western Hemisphere's lowest point, Death Valley is blazingly hot and prone to flash floods, yet is home to rare foliage and geological phenomena. See p. 69.

SCOTTY'S CASTLE—Walter E. Scott had been a prospector, a mule team driver and a member of Buffalo Bill's Wild West Show before he began this nine-building, Moorish-Mexican-Spanish-style home for Chicago businessman Albert Johnson. See p. 70.

Devils Postpile National Monument (F-5)

DEVILS POSTPILE NATIONAL MONUMENT—A sheer wall of 60-foot-high basaltic columns distinguishes this monument in the eastern Sierra Nevada range. See p. 70.

Fort Bragg (D-1)

MENDOCINO COAST BOTANICAL GARDENS—Overlooking the Pacific Ocean, formal gardens, flower-covered bluffs, a pine forest, meadows and trails await exploration by nature lovers. See p. 192.

Fremont (E-9)

DON EDWARDS SAN FRANCISCO BAY NATIONAL WILDLIFE REFUGE—A 20,000-acre habitat for migratory birds and local endangered species, this refuge also features an interpretive center. See p. 76.

MISSION SAN JOSE CHAPEL AND MUSEUM—An unusually elegant interior features crystal chandeliers, murals, religious paintings and an ornate altar. A museum displays photographs, paintings and artifacts. See p. 76.

Lassen Volcanic National Park (C-3)

LASSEN VOLCANIC NATIONAL PARK—Four types of volcanoes as well as lava flows, boiling springs and lakes, fumaroles and mudpots are among the uncommon sights in this national park. See p. 90.

Lava Beds National Monument (B-3)

LAVA BEDS NATIONAL MONUMENT—Exploring the national monument's rugged terrain will lead to lava tube caves and volcanic formations used as fortifications by the Modoc Indians. See p. 91.

Monterey (G-2)

MONTEREY BAY AQUARIUM—More than 700 species of marine life are exhibited. Touch pools, life-size models, a shorebird aviary, a theater and historical displays also are featured. See p. 102.

MONTEREY STATE HISTORIC PARK—A 7-acre site preserves the historical and architectural heritage of old Monterey. Guided walking tours are available. See p. 102.

Muir Woods National Monument (D-7)

MUIR WOODS NATIONAL MONUMENT—Named for noted conservationist John Muir, Muir Woods is one of the most beautiful and accessible of the noted redwood groves. Some coast redwoods reach a height of 250 feet with diameters of more than 12 feet. Trails for hiking and exploring are available. See p. 158.

Napa (B-8)

COPIA: THE AMERICAN CENTER FOR WINE, FOOD & THE ARTS—Named for the Roman goddess of abundance, Copia celebrates the integral part food and wine play in American culture. See p. 195.

Oakland (D-9)

OAKLAND MUSEUM OF CALIFORNIA—The state's natural and cultural history can be traced through artwork and exhibits. See p. 110.

Palo Alto (E-8)

IRIS & B. GERALD CANTOR CENTER FOR VISUAL ARTS—Bronze sculptures by Auguste Rodin are the focal point of this world-class museum on the Stanford University campus. See p. 112.

Pinnacles National Monument (G-3)

PINNACLES NATIONAL MONUMENT—Jagged crags and stark spires that serve as remnants of an ancient volcano rise above a countryside rich with flora and fauna. See p. 113.

Redding (C-2)

SHASTA STATE HISTORIC PARK—In 1849 Shasta—the "Queen City"—was the supply point for the gold mines in the northern Klamath Range. See p. 116.

Sacramento (E-3)

CALIFORNIA STATE RAILROAD MUSEUM—Several restored locomotives along with exhibits describing railroad history are housed in this museum's striking brick and glass building. See p. 121.

STATE CAPITOL—The 40 acres of gardens surrounding the restored 1869 capitol include the Vietnam Veterans' Memorial. See p. 122.

SUTTER'S FORT STATE HISTORIC PARK—The site, once part of a 48,000-acre ranch named New Helvetia (New Switzerland), has been restored to the way it was 2 years before gold was discovered here in 1849. See p. 122.

San Francisco (D-7)

CALIFORNIA ACADEMY OF SCIENCES—This San Francisco institution features a natural history museum and an aquarium. See p. 135.

CALIFORNIA PALACE OF THE LEGION OF HONOR—The museum, on a hill overlooking the Pacific Ocean and the Golden Gate Bridge, has a magnificent art collection spanning 4,000 years. See p. 135.

CHINATOWN—Enjoy a taste of the Far East in this bustling "city within a city" where Chinese shops and restaurants abound. See p. 140.

exploratorium

EXPLORATORIUM—With more than 650 interactive exhibits, this science museum inside the Palace of Fine Arts teaches visitors about a wide variety of topics. See p. 140.

GOLDEN GATE PARK—This magnificent city park has it all: museums, gardens, recreation facilities, ponds, streams, lakes—even a buffalo enclosure and a Dutch-style windmill. See p. 141.

MISSION SAN FRANCISCO DE ASIS—One of the oldest buildings in San Francisco, the mission's redwood roof timbers still are lashed together with rawhide. A small museum displays relics and old manuscripts. See p. 142.

San Jose (F-9)

LICK OBSERVATORY—Dedicated in 1888, this facility on the summit of 4,209-foot Mount Hamilton now serves as an observation station overlooking the Santa Clara Valley. See p. 163.

ROSICRUCIAN EGYPTIAN MUSEUM—In the beautiful gardens of Rosicrucian Park, this museum showcases one of the country's largest collections of Egyptian, Babylonian and Assyrian antiquities. See p. 163.

WINCHESTER MYSTERY HOUSE—Told by a psychic she was being tormented by vengeful spirits, rifle heiress Sarah Winchester fled her home in Connecticut and built this elaborate and unusual West Coast mansion in which to hide. See p. 163.

San Juan Bautista (G-3)

MISSION SAN JUAN BAUTISTA—Still an active Roman Catholic Church, the 1797 mission features a three-aisle entrance to the altar. Displays include relics and period furnishings. See p. 164.

SAN JUAN BAUTISTA STATE HISTORIC PARK—In the early 1800s the town that sprang up around the mission was the largest in central California. See p. 164.

San Luis Obispo (I-4)

MISSION SAN LUIS OBISPO DE TOLOSA—In order to repel flaming arrow attacks by unfriendly natives, the mission was built with a tile roof rather than the usual ignitable thatch roof. A museum contains Chumash Indian artifacts and memorabilia from early settlers. See p. 164.

San Miguel (H-4)

MISSION SAN MIGUEL ARCANGEL—Many original decorations, frescoes and paintings adorn the 1797 mission. The vaulted corridor is known for its arches. See p. 165.

San Simeon (H-3)

HEARST CASTLE—Overlooking the Pacific Ocean, this palatial Mediterranean Revival-style mansion pays homage to the wealth and vision of its late owner, newspaper tycoon William Randolph Hearst. See p. 165.

Santa Clara (E-9)

MISSION SANTA CLARA DE ASIS—Relics displayed include three bells given to the mission by the king of Spain. Gardens and artifacts also are noteworthy. See p. 166.

PARAMOUNT'S GREAT AMERICA—Five themed areas offer thrilling rides, dazzling shows and magical children's attractions. See p. 166.

Santa Cruz (G-2)

SANTA CRUZ BEACH BOARDWALK—Roller coasters, a 1911 carousel and the Pacific Ocean as a backdrop are all part of this beachfront amusement park. See p. 167

Santa Rosa (B-8)

SAFARI WEST—Exotic animals and birds can be spotted from open-air safari vehicles during tours of this wildlife preserve. See p. 200.

Sequoia and Kings Canyon National Parks (H-5, G-5)

SEQUOIA AND KINGS CANYON NATIONAL PARKS—For variety you can't beat this second-oldest national park: rivers, waterfalls, meadows, caves, played-out gold mines, trees 200 feet high and marmots that eat radiator hoses. See p. 169.

Sonoma (C-8)

SONOMA STATE HISTORIC PARK—Sonoma, completed in 1823, is the last of California's 21 missions; the surrounding buildings were constructed 1823-55. See p. 201.

Vallejo (C-8)

SIX FLAGS MARINE WORLD—Denizens of the deep are not the only attractions at this wildlife park; elephants, Bengal tigers, exotic birds, shows and interactive exhibits also are part of the entertainment. See p. 178.

Weott (C-1)

AVENUE OF THE GIANTS—Some of California's most beautiful redwood groves line this 33-mile section of highway in Humboldt Redwoods State Park. See p. 181.

Yosemite National Park (F-5)

YOSEMITE NATIONAL PARK—One of the jewels of the national park system, Yosemite includes the spectacular valley for which it was named, along with more than 1,100 square miles of nearly pristine land in the Sierra Nevada. See p. 204.

RECREATION AREAS

RECREATION AREAS	MAP LOCATION	CAMPING	PICNICKING	HIKING TRAILS	BOATING	BOAT RAMP	BOAT RENTAL	FISHING	SWIMMING	PETS ON LEASH	BICYCLE TRAILS	NATURE PROGS.	VISITOR CENTER	LODGE/CABINS	FOOD SERVICE
NATIONAL PARKS *(See place listings)*															
Death Valley (H-7) 3,367,628 acres. Wildflower viewing.		•	•	•					•	•		•	•	•	•
Lassen Volcanic (C-3) 106,000 acres.		•	•	•	•			•	•	•		•	•	•	•
Redwood (A-1) 110, 232 acres. Kayaking; horse rental.		•	•	•				•	•	•	•	•	•		•
Sequoia and Kings Canyon (H-5 & G-5) 1,351 square miles. Horse rental.		•	•	•				•		•		•	•	•	•
Yosemite (F-5) 1,189 square miles. Horse rental. Motorized vessels prohibited.		•	•	•	•			•	•	•	•	•	•	•	•
NATIONAL FORESTS *(See place listings)*															
Eldorado 676,780 acres. Central California. Bird-watching, rock climbing; motorcycle trails.		•	•	•	•	•		•	•	•	•	•	•		•
Inyo 1,944,040 acres. Central California. Horse rental.		•	•	•	•	•	•	•	•	•	•	•	•	•	•
Klamath 1,726,000 acres. Northern California. Bird-watching, cross-country skiing, horseback riding.		•	•	•	•	•		•	•	•	•		•		
Lassen 1,375,000 acres. Northern California.		•	•	•	•	•	•	•	•	•	•	•	•	•	•
Mendocino 886,048 acres. Northwestern California.		•	•	•	•	•	•	•	•	•	•	•	•	•	•
Modoc 1,654,392 acres. Northeastern California.		•	•	•	•	•		•	•	•	•		•	•	
Plumas 1,162,863 acres. Northern California. Horse rental, motorcycle trails.		•	•	•	•	•	•	•	•	•	•	•	•	•	•
Sequoia 1,139,519 acres. South-central California. Horse rental.		•	•	•	•	•		•	•	•	•	•	•		•
Shasta-Trinity 2,129,524 acres. Northern California. Horse rental.		•	•	•	•	•	•	•	•	•		•	•	•	•
Sierra 1,304,476 acres. Central California. Horse rental.		•	•	•	•	•	•	•	•	•	•	•	•	•	•
Six Rivers 990,000 acres. Northwestern California. Kayaking.		•	•	•	•	•		•	•	•	•	•	•	•	•
Stanislaus 898,602 acres. Central California. Horse rental.		•	•	•	•	•	•	•	•	•	•	•		•	•
Tahoe 797,205 acres. North-central California. Horse rental.		•	•	•	•	•	•	•	•	•		•	•	•	•
NATIONAL CONSERVATION AREAS *(See place listings)*															
King Range (C-1) 60,000 acres w. of Garberville. Horseback riding, wildlife viewing.		•	•	•	•	•		•	•	•	•		•	•	•
NATIONAL RECREATION AREAS *(See place listings)*															
Golden Gate (C-7) 74,000 acres. Bird-watching, golfing, sailing; horse rental.		•	•	•	•		•	•	•	•	•	•	•	•	•
Smith River (A-1) 305,337 acres. Historic. Gold panning, scuba diving; horse trails, scenic byway. *(See Six Rivers National Forest p. 173)*		•	•	•	•	•		•	•	•	•	•		•	
Whiskeytown-Shasta-Trinity (C-2) 42,500 acres. Horse rental.		•	•	•	•	•	•	•	•	•	•	•	•		•
NATIONAL SEASHORES *(See place listings)*															
Point Reyes (C-7) 65,300 acres. Wildlife viewing; horse rental.		•	•	•				•		•	•	•	•		•
ARMY CORPS OF ENGINEERS															
Lake Mendocino (D-2) 5,000 acres 5 mi. n.w. of Ukiah on SR 20. Nature trails.	150	•	•	•	•	•	•	•	•	•	•	•	•		•
Lake Sonoma (A-7) 17,600 acres 26 mi. n.w. of Santa Rosa on Dry Creek Rd. Horseback riding; fish hatchery, interpretive trails.	144	•	•	•	•	•	•	•	•	•	•	•	•		•
STATE															
Anderson Marsh (D-2) 1,065 acres .75 mi. n. of Lower Lake on SR 53. Bird-watching; nature trail.	61		•	•	•			•		•		•	•		
Andrew Molera (H-2) 4,800 acres 21 mi. s. of Carmel on SR 1. Bird-watching, beachcombing; horse rental.	1	•	•	•				•	•	•	•				
Angel Island (D-8) 758 acres in San Francisco Bay; ferry from San Francisco or Tiburon. Historic. Beachcombing, kayaking; bicycle rentals, interpretive services, museum, nature trails, tours.	2	•	•	•	•	•		•			•	•	•		•
Annadel (B-8) 4,913 acres s.e. of Santa Rosa on Channel Dr. Horse rental.	3		•	•				•		•	•		•		

RECREATION AREAS

	MAP LOCATION	CAMPING	PICNICKING	HIKING TRAILS	BOATING	BOAT RAMP	BOAT RENTAL	FISHING	SWIMMING	PETS ON LEASH	BICYCLE TRAILS	NATURE PROGS.	VISITOR CENTER	LODGE/CABINS	FOOD SERVICE
Armstrong Redwoods (B-7) 752 acres 2 mi. n. of Guerneville on Armstrong Woods Rd. Horse rental, nature trails.	5		•	•						•		•	•		
Auburn (E-3) 30,000 acres 1 mi. s. of Auburn on SR 49. Historic. Gold panning, hunting, rafting, water skiing; farm, marina, pond.	7	•	•	•	•	•		•	•	•					
Austin Creek (B-7) 4,236 acres 2 mi. n. of Guerneville on Armstrong Woods Rd. Horse rental.	8	•	•	•						•					
Benbow Lake (C-1) 1,200 acres 3 mi. s. of Garberville on US 101. Motorboats not permitted. Golfing.	10	•	•	•	•		•	•	•	•		•			
Bethany Reservoir (F-2) 600 acres 7 mi. n. of I-580 via Altamont Pass, Mountain House and Christensen rds. Windsurfing.	135		•		•	•		•		•	•				
Bidwell/Sacramento River (D-3) 180 acres 5 mi. w. of Chico on River Rd. Canoeing, kayaking, rafting, tubing.	133		•	•	•	•		•	•						
Big Basin Redwoods (F-8) 18,000 acres. Horse rental, nature trails. *(See Big Basin p. 64)*	11	•	•	•						•	•	•	•	•	•
Bothe-Napa Valley (B-8) 1,916 acres 4 mi. n. of St. Helena on SR 29. Bird-watching, wildlife viewing; horse rental.	14	•	•	•					•	•		•	•		
Brannan Island (F-3) 336 acres 3.25 mi. s. of Rio Vista. Water skiing, windsurfing; nature trails, wildlife habitat.	15	•	•	•	•	•	•	•	•	•		•	•		•
Butano (F-8) 2,200 acres 7 mi. s. of Pescadero on Cloverdale Rd. Wildlife viewing.	16	•	•	•				•		•	•	•	•		
Calaveras Big Trees (E-4) 6,073 acres. Cross-country skiing; nature trails; wildlife site. *(See Arnold p. 60)*	17	•	•	•				•	•	•	•	•	•		
Candlestick Point (D-8) 37 acres in San Francisco e. of US 101 via Candlestick exit. Windsurfing; cultural programs, guided nature walks.	136		•	•				•			•	•	•		
Castle Crags (B-2) 4,350 acres. Nature trails. *(See Dunsmuir p. 72)*	19	•	•	•	•			•	•	•			•		
Castle Rock (F-8) 4,350 acres 2 mi. w. of Los Gatos via SRs 9 and 35. Wildlife viewing; horse trails, nature trails.	137	•		•							•	•			
Caswell Memorial (F-3) 258 acres 6 mi. s.w. of Ripon on Austin Rd. Wildlife habitat.	20	•	•	•	•			•	•	•	•	•			
China Camp (C-8) 1,640 acres n. of San Rafael via US 101 and N. San Pedro Rd. Windsurfing; wildlife site.	22	•	•	•	•			•	•			•	•		•
Clear Lake (D-2) 565 acres 3.5 mi. n. of Kelseyville on Soda Bay Rd. Water skiing, wildflower viewing; nature trails. *(See Kelseyville p. 194)*	23	•	•	•	•	•	•	•	•	•		•	•		
Colusa-Sacramento River (D-3) 67 acres near downtown Colusa on SR 20. Nature trails.	24	•	•		•	•		•	•	•					
Del Norte Coast Redwoods (A-1) 6,400 acres 7 mi. s. of Crescent City on US 101. Nature trails. *(See Crescent City p. 69)*	26	•	•	•				•		•	•	•	•		
D.L. Bliss (E-4) 1,830 acres on the w. shore of Lake Tahoe on SR 89. Nature trails. *(See South Lake Tahoe p. 87)*	27	•	•	•				•	•	•		•	•		
Donner Memorial (D-4) 353 acres. Cross-country skiing; nature trails. *(See Truckee p. 88)*	29	•	•	•	•		•	•	•	•		•	•		
Emerald Bay (E-4) 593 acres on the s.w. shore of Lake Tahoe.	31	•	•	•	•			•	•	•		•			
Empire Mine (D-3) 788 acres. Horse rental. *(See Grass Valley p. 78)*	128		•	•						•	•	•	•		
Folsom Lake (E-3) 17,718 acres 2 mi. n.w. of Folsom off US 50. Water skiing, windsurfing; horse rental, nature trails.	33	•	•	•	•	•	•	•	•	•	•	•	•		•
Forest of Nisene Marks (G-2) 9,960 acres 4 mi. n. of Aptos on Aptos Creek Rd.	138	•	•	•						•	•				
Fort Ross (E-1) 3,386 acres. *(See Jenner p. 194)*	127	•	•	•				•		•		•	•		
Fremont Peak (G-3) 244 acres 11 mi. s. of San Juan Bautista on San Juan Canyon Rd. Nature trails.	139	•	•	•						•		•	•		
George J. Hatfield (F-3) 47 acres 28 mi. w. of Merced on Kelly Rd.	35	•	•				•	•		•					
Grizzly Creek Redwoods (C-1) 390 acres 15 mi. e. of Fortuna on SR 36. Nature trails.	36	•	•	•				•	•	•		•	•		

RECREATION AREAS

	MAP LOCATION	CAMPING	PICNICKING	HIKING TRAILS	BOATING	BOAT RAMP	BOAT RENTAL	FISHING	SWIMMING	PETS ON LEASH	BICYCLE TRAILS	NATURE PROGS.	VISITOR CENTER	LODGE/CABINS	FOOD SERVICE
Grover Hot Springs (E-4) 700 acres 4 mi. w. of Markleeville on Hot Springs Rd. Nature trails. *(See Markleeville p. 94)*	37	•	•	•				•	•	•	•	•			
Half Moon Bay Beach (E-8) 170 acres .5 mi. w. of US 1 on Kelly Ave. Horse rental.	38	•	•	•				•		•	•				
Hendy Woods (D-1) 690 acres 3 mi. w. of Philo off SR 128. Nature trails.	39	•	•	•				•	•	•	•	•			
Henry Cowell Redwoods (G-2) 4,082 acres 3 mi. e. of Felton on Graham Hill Rd. Nature trails.	40	•	•	•				•		•	•	•	•		•
Henry W. Coe (G-3) 80,000 acres 14 mi. e. of Morgan Hill on E. Dunne Ave. Nature trails.	41	•	•	•				•		•	•	•	•		
Hollister Hills (G-3) 6,627 acres 8 mi. s. of Hollister via Cienega Rd. Nature trails, motorcycle trails, trails for four-wheel-drive vehicles.	140	•	•	•						•	•	•			•
Humboldt Lagoons (B-1) 1,886 acres 4 mi. s. of Orick on US 101. *(See Orick p. 110)*	102	•	•	•	•	•		•	•	•		•	•		
Humboldt Redwoods (C-1) 52,000 acres. Horse rental, nature trails. *(See Weott p. 181)*	42	•	•	•	•			•	•	•	•	•	•		
Jack London (C-8) 800 acres. Horse rental. *(See Glen Ellen p. 193)*	134		•	•						•	•	•	•		
Jedediah Smith Redwoods (A-1) 10,000 acres 9 mi. n.e. of Crescent City on US 199. Horse rentals, nature trails.	44	•	•	•	•			•	•	•		•	•		
Julia Pfeiffer Burns (H-2) 3,583 acres 37 mi. s. of Carmel on SR 1.	157	•	•	•						•					
Kings Beach (D-4) 8 acres 12 mi. n.e. of Tahoe City on SR 28.	129		•		•	•	•	•	•						
Lake Oroville (D-3) 28,450 acres 6 mi. n.e. of Oroville off SR 70. Water skiing, windsurfing; horse rental, nature trails.	46	•	•	•	•	•	•	•	•	•	•	•	•		•
Lakes Earl and Talawa (A-1) 5,000 acres n. of Crescent City off US 101. Horse rental.	154	•	•	•	•	•		•			•	•			
Los Baños Creek Reservoir (G-3) 10 mi. s.w. of Los Baños via SR 165, Pioneer and Canyon rds. Horseback riding trails.	161	•	•	•	•			•	•	•					
MacKerricher (D-1) 2,030 acres 3 mi. n. of Fort Bragg on SR 1. Horse rental.	49	•	•	•	•	•		•		•	•	•			
Malakoff Diggins (D-3) 3,000 acres n.e. of Nevada City on N. Bloomfield Rd. Historic. Nature trails. *(See Nevada City p. 106)*	50	•	•	•				•	•	•	•	•	•	•	
Manchester Beach (D-1) 760 acres 7 mi. n. of Point Arena on SR 1.	51	•	•	•				•		•	•				
Manresa Beach (G-2) 83 acres 5 mi. w. of Watsonville off SR 1.	162	•	•					•	•	•					
Marshall Gold Discovery (E-3) 274 acres in Coloma on SR 49. Historic. Nature trails. *(See Coloma p. 67)*	52		•	•	•			•		•		•	•		•
McArthur-Burney Falls Memorial (B-3) 910 acres. Scenic. Water skiing, nature trails. *(See Burney p. 65)*	53	•	•	•	•	•	•	•	•	•	•	•	•		•
McConnell (F-4) 74 acres 5 mi. e. of Delhi on the Merced River.	54	•	•		•			•	•	•		•			
Millerton Lake (G-4) 6,553 acres 21 mi. n.e. of Fresno via SR 41. Historic. Water skiing, windsurfing.	55	•	•	•	•	•	•	•	•	•	•	•	•		
Mono Lake Tufa (F-5) 10 mi. s.e. of Lee Vining off US 395. *(See Lee Vining p. 92)*	165		•	•	•	•			•			•	•		
Montaña de Oro (I-3) 8,066 acres 7 mi. s. of Los Osos on Pecho Rd. Horse rental, nature trails.	56	•	•	•				•			•	•	•		
Morro Bay (I-3) 2,435 acres 3 mi. s. of Morro Bay. Bird-watching, golf.	57	•	•	•	•		•	•	•			•	•		•
Morro Strand Beach (I-3) 117 acres 1 mi. n. of Morro Bay on SR 1. Surfing.	120	•	•					•	•	•	•	•			
Mount Diablo (D-9) 18,000 acres. Horse rental. *(See Danville p. 69)*	58	•	•	•						•	•	•	•		
Mount Tamalpais (D-7) 6,300 acres. Horse rental, nature trails. *(See Mill Valley p. 158)*	60	•	•	•				•			•	•	•	•	•

RECREATION AREAS

	MAP LOCATION	CAMPING	PICNICKING	HIKING TRAILS	BOATING	BOAT RAMP	BOAT RENTAL	FISHING	SWIMMING	PETS ON LEASH	BICYCLE TRAILS	NATURE PROGS.	VISITOR CENTER	LODGE/CABINS	FOOD SERVICE
Navarro River Redwoods (D-1) 12 acres 6 mi. w. of Navarro on SR 128.	65	•	•		•			•	•	•					
New Brighton Beach (G-2) 94 acres off SR 1 New Brighton/Park Ave. exit in Capitola.	62	•	•	•				•	•			•			
Oceano Dunes (I-3) 1,500 acres 3 mi. s. of city of Pismo Beach on SR 1. Off-road vehicles permitted. Surfing; horse rental.	118	•	•	•				•	•	•		•			
Patrick's Point (B-1) 632 acres. Nature trails. *(See Trinidad p. 177)*	64	•	•	•				•		•	•	•	•	•	
Pfeiffer Big Sur (H-2) 821 acres. Nature trails. *(See Big Sur p. 64)*	66	•	•	•					•	•	•	•	•	•	•
Pismo Beach (I-3) 1,051 acres 3 mi. s. of city of Pismo Beach on SR 1. Surfing; nature trails.	68	•	•	•				•	•	•	•	•			•
Plumas-Eureka (D-4) 6,749 acres 4 mi. w. of Johnsville on CR A14. Horse rental, nature trails. *(See Johnsville p. 80)*	69	•	•	•				•		•	•	•	•		
Portola (F-8) 2,010 acres 20 mi. s.w. of Palo Alto off SR 35. Nature trails.	72	•	•	•						•	•	•	•		
Prairie Creek Redwoods (B-1) 14,000 acres. *(See Orick p. 110)*	73	•	•	•				•			•	•	•		
Red Rock Canyon (I-6) 4,000 acres. Scenic. Nature trails. *(See place listing p. 117)*	122	•	•	•						•		•			
Richardson Grove (C-1) 1,000 acres 8 mi. s. of Garberville on US 101. Nature trails.	75	•	•	•	•			•	•	•		•	•	•	•
Russian Gulch (D-1) 1,300 acres 2 mi. n. of Mendocino on US 101. Skin diving.	76	•	•	•				•		•	•	•			
Salt Point (E-1) 5,676 acres 24 mi. n. of Jenner on SR 1. Skin diving.	79	•	•	•	•	•		•		•	•		•		
Samuel P. Taylor (C-7) 2,708 acres 15 mi. w. of San Rafael on Sir Francis Drake Blvd. Nature trails.	80	•	•	•			•		•	•	•	•			
San Luis Reservoir (G-3) 26,026 acres 12 mi. w. of Los Baños on SR 152. Water skiing, windsurfing; motorbike area.	84	•	•		•	•		•	•	•	•	•	•		
San Simeon Beach (H-3) 541 acres 5 mi. s. of San Simeon on SR 1.	111	•	•		•			•	•	•		•			
Seacliff Beach (G-2) 85 acres 5.5 mi. s. of Santa Cruz on SR 1.	86	•	•					•	•	•		•	•	•	•
Sinkyone Wilderness (C-1) 7,302 acres 30 mi. w. of Redway on CR 435 (Briceland Rd.).	142	•	•	•				•		•					
Smithe Redwoods (C-1) 665 acres 4 mi. n. of Leggett on US 101.	88		•					•	•	•		•			
Sonoma Coast Beach (E-1) 5,333 acres n. of Bodega Bay on SR 1. Horse rental.	89	•	•	•	•	•		•	•	•	•		•		
South Yuba River (D-3) 2,000 acres 8 mi. n.w. of Nevada City on SR 49. Nature trail. *(See Nevada City p. 106)*	126		•	•				•	•	•		•	•		
Standish-Hickey (C-1) 1,012 acres 2 mi. n. of Leggett on US 101. Nature trail.	91	•	•	•				•	•	•		•			
Sugarloaf Ridge (B-8) 2,700 acres 7 mi. e. of Santa Rosa on SR 12. Horse rental, nature trails.	92	•	•	•				•	•	•	•	•			
Sugar Pine Point (D-4) 1,975 acres 10 mi. s. of Tahoe City on SR 89. Historic. Nature trails, cross-country ski trails.	93	•	•	•	•			•	•	•	•	•	•		
Sunset Beach (G-3) 324 acres 4 mi. w. of Watsonville via SR 1 and San Andreas Rd.	94	•	•					•	•	•		•			
Tahoe (E-4) 57 acres on Lake Tahoe .25 mi. s. of Tahoe City.	95	•	•		•			•	•	•	•				
Tomales Bay (C-7) 2,000 acres 4 mi. n. of Inverness on Pierce Point Rd. Nature trails.	96	•	•	•				•	•	•		•	•		
Trinidad Beach (B-1) 159 acres 19 mi. n. of Eureka on US 101.	143		•	•	•	•	•	•	•		•	•			
Turlock Lake (F-4) 408 acres 23 mi. e. of Modesto off SR 132. Water skiing.	97	•	•	•	•	•		•	•	•		•			
Van Damme (D-1) 1,831 acres 3 mi. s. of Mendocino on SR 1. Nature trails.	98	•	•	•				•		•	•	•	•		
William Randolph Hearst Memorial Beach (H-3) 8 acres in San Simeon on SR 1.	132		•		•			•	•			•			•

RECREATION AREAS

	MAP LOCATION	CAMPING	PICNICKING	HIKING TRAILS	BOATING	BOAT RAMP	BOAT RENTAL	FISHING	SWIMMING	PETS ON LEASH	BICYCLE TRAILS	NATURE PROGS.	VISITOR CENTER	LODGE/CABINS	FOOD SERVICE
Woodson Bridge (D-2) 428 acres 6 mi. e. of Corning and I-5. Nature trails.	99	•	•	•	•	•		•		•		•			
OTHER															
Anthony Chabot Regional Park and Lake Chabot Marina (D-9) 5,242 acres e. of Oakland on Redwood Rd. Horse rental, horse trails.	160	•	•	•	•		•	•		•	•	•			•
Avila Beach (I-3) 10 acres in Avila. Surfing.	9		•		•	•		•	•						•
Big Lagoon (B-1) 50 acres 7 mi. n. of Trinidad on US 101.	145	•	•	•	•	•		•	•	•					
Cayucos Beach (I-3) 16 acres s.w. of Cayucos on SR 1. Surfing.	21		•	•				•	•	•					
Contra Loma (D-9) 776 acres 1 mi. s. of Antioch. Windsurfing, sailboarding.	112		•	•	•	•	•	•	•	•	•				•
Cow Mountain (D-2) 50,000 acres e. of Ukiah on Talmage Rd.	146	•	•	•					•	•			•		
Del Valle (F-2) 4,500 acres 10 mi. s. of Livermore via Arroyo Rd.	100	•	•	•	•	•	•	•	•	•	•	•	•		•
Don Pedro Lake (F-4) 12,960 acres n.e. of La Grange on Bond's Flat Rd.	147	•	•	•	•	•	•	•	•		•		•	•	•
Doran (E-1) 120 acres on Doran Park Rd. s. of Bodega Bay.	148	•	•	•	•	•		•	•	•					
Eagle Lake (C-4) 22,000 acres 20 mi. n.w. of Susanville. *(See Susanville p. 175)*	101	•	•	•	•	•	•	•	•	•		•		•	•
Gualala Point (E-1) 300 acres off SR 1 s. of Gualala.	149	•	•	•	•			•		•	•		•		
Lake Berryessa (B-9) 13,000 acres 20 mi. n.w. of Napa on SR 121.	103	•	•	•	•	•	•	•	•	•			•	•	•
Lake McClure (F-4) 7,100 acres 4 mi. w. of Coulterville on SR 132.	105	•	•		•	•	•	•	•						•
Lake Nacimiento (H-3) 5,370 acres 17 mi. w. of Paso Robles off US 101.	106	•	•		•	•	•	•	•	•	•	•	•	•	•
Lake San Antonio (H-3) 5,000 acres 40 mi. s. of King City off US 101. Bird-watching; horse rental.	156	•	•	•	•	•	•	•	•		•		•	•	•
Loch Lomond (F-8) 2,100 acres n. of Ben Lomond.	107		•	•	•	•	•	•		•		•	•		•
Lopez Lake (I-4) 4,376 acres 11 mi. n.e. of Arroyo Grande on Lopez Dr.	158	•	•	•	•	•	•	•	•						
Martinez Shoreline (C-9) 343 acres in Martinez. Bird-watching; nature trails.	113		•	•	•	•		•	•	•	•	•			
Martin Luther King Jr. Shoreline (D-9) 1,220 acres in Oakland. Bird-watching; fishing pier.	115		•	•	•	•		•		•	•				•
Oak Grove Regional Park (F-3) 180 acres off I-5 at Eight Mile Rd. in Stockton. Outdoor amphitheater, nature center.	166		•	•				•		•		•	•		
Oceano Memorial (I-3) 11.8 acres on Dewey Rd. in Oceano.	159	•	•					•	•						
Point Pinole Shoreline (C-8) 2,147 acres n.w. of San Pablo. Fishing pier.	114		•	•				•	•	•	•				
Shadow Cliffs East Bay Regional Recreation Area (D-9) 249 acres at Pleasanton. Waterslide. *(See Pleasanton p. 114)*	109		•	•	•	•	•	•	•	•	•				•
Spring Lake (B-7) 320 acres e. of Santa Rosa at Newanga Ave.	151	•	•	•	•	•	•	•	•	•	•				•
Sunol Wilderness (E-9) 6,858 acres 6 mi. s. of Sunol. Bird-watching; nature trails.	116	•	•	•						•	•	•	•		
Temescal (D-9) 48 acres in Oakland.	117		•	•				•	•	•	•	•			•
Vasona Park and Reservoir (F-9) 151 acres near Los Gatos. Motorboats not permitted.	110		•	•	•	•	•	•		•	•	•	•		

Northern California Temperature Averages
Maximum/Minimum
From the records of the National Weather Service

	JAN	FEB	MAR	APR	MAY	JUNE	JULY	AUG	SEPT	OCT	NOV	DEC
Bakersfield	57/37	63/41	69/45	76/50	85/56	92/62	100/68	98/66	92/61	81/53	69/43	59/39
Barstow	59/31	63/34	70/40	77/45	84/51	96/60	101/67	100/65	92/57	80/47	70/37	60/30
Bishop	53/21	56/25	64/30	73/38	81/44	90/50	97/55	95/52	89/47	77/37	64/28	55/23
Bridgeport	38/9	41/12	48/19	59/27	66/33	74/38	84/45	83/44	77/37	65/29	53/21	44/15
Chico	54/36	60/39	67/41	73/44	82/49	91/55	98/59	96/58	88/53	79/47	66/40	55/36
Eureka	54/41	54/42	55/43	56/45	58/48	60/51	61/52	61/53	62/51	60/49	58/45	55/43
Fresno	55/36	61/39	67/42	75/47	83/52	90/57	99/63	97/60	91/56	80/48	67/39	56/37
Merced	55/36	62/39	66/41	73/45	81/50	91/56	97/61	95/59	88/54	79/47	67/39	56/35
Mount Shasta	41/25	47/28	52/30	60/35	68/40	75/46	85/51	85/49	78/45	66/38	53/31	45/27
Redding	54/37	59/40	64/43	71/48	80/54	88/61	97/67	95/65	87/59	77/52	64/44	56/38
Sacramento	53/39	59/42	65/44	72/47	80/52	89/56	95/59	94/58	90/57	79/51	65/44	55/40
San Francisco	55/42	58/43	62/45	64/47	67/50	70/52	72/54	72/54	74/54	71/51	64/46	57/43
Truckee	38/16	38/16	46/21	53/29	60/36	73/41	81/43	81/41	73/37	63/30	52/24	40/15
Willits	49/31	53/34	56/35	64/39	70/43	77/47	86/52	86/50	83/49	71/44	57/38	50/34

Exploring Northern California

For descriptions of places in bold type, see individual listings.

California's Outback

Not just sand and occasional palm oases, California's desert country is a land of diversity and drama. Mountain peaks thousands of feet high look down on valleys that lie below sea level. A seemingly arid wilderness supports a variety of fascinating flora and fauna, and the harsh terrain contains remnants of prosperous mines and boom towns.

To explore this back country, begin on I-10 in **Los Angeles** and head east. Seven miles past the Upland turnoff, go north on I-15 headed for **Victorville** and **Barstow.** In Barstow visit the California Desert Information Center for information about geology, desert plants and animals, recreation, and road and weather conditions.

Interstate 40 begins at Barstow; take it and go east. The highway stretches through an arid expanse where cactus and brush conceal small wildlife, dry lakes signify prehistoric seas, and mountains shelter old mining sites.

Approximately 80 miles from Barstow, Kelbaker Road—a narrow, paved road—runs north of I-40 through desert vistas that include mountains, ancient lava beds and the dramatic Kelso Dunes, a sand formation rising 600 feet from the desert floor. The only town is Kelso, once an important stop for the Union Pacific Railroad.

For a different perspective of the desert, stay on I-40 past Kelbaker Road and turn north on Essex Road to Providence Mountains State Recreation Area. Red volcanic peaks punctuate this high desert area, and within its Mitchell Caverns are intricate limestone formations. Guided tours are available.

Because of the poor condition of the east-west roads between Essex and Kelbaker roads, it is advisable to return to I-40, then Kelbaker Road. Thirty-five miles north of Kelso, Kelbaker meets I-15 in the tiny town of Baker.

Death Valley National Park / © Bill Ross / Corbis

California Cruisin'

North out of Baker, take SR 127 about 59 miles to SR 178.

Turn west and drive over the Greenwater mountain range and through Greenwater Valley into **Death Valley National Park.** Here is a vast region of remarkable scenery: sand dunes and rocks sculpted by wind, and sub-sea-level valleys bordered by mountain walls of every hue. The lowest point in the United States (282 feet below sea level) lies within the national park, and not far away Telescope Peak rises to 11,049 feet.

As SR 178 curves north it becomes Badwater Road and, having offered some spectacular views along the way, reaches the visitor center at Furnace Creek. Another 55 miles north from Furnace Creek brings you to extravagant Scotty's Castle.

Leave Death Valley by driving south and west on SR 190, then south on Panamint Valley Road. Within 14 miles the highway becomes Trona-Wildrose Road as it goes through Panamint Valley, a smaller version of Death Valley. Mountains rise on either side of the highway, and side roads lead to dry lakes or old mines.

At Trona pick up SR 178 leading southwest to **Ridgecrest.** From there China Lake Boulevard goes south to US 395. Continue down to the Randsburg turnoff. Randsburg, along with the camps at Johannesburg and Red Mountain, was the site of frenzied gold and silver mining in the late 1800s.

Twenty-one miles west of Randsburg, Red Rock-Randsburg Road intersects SR 14. You can choose to make a side trip to **Red Rock Canyon State Park** by turning north on SR 14 and traveling 4 miles. The sight of the park's fantastically shaped cliffs and columns makes this a worthwhile detour.

Back on SR 14 head south through Mojave and **Rosamond.** Within about 1.5 hours after leaving Red Rock Canyon you will be in the Antelope Valley, with the San Gabriel Mountains just ahead. SR 14 takes you through the western portion of the **Angeles National Forest,** then ends at I-5, the highway leading south to Los Angeles.

Gold Country

For this tour along former stagecoach routes to the jewel of the Sierras—Lake Tahoe, haven for summer and winter sports and home of varied casinos and accommodations—it is strongly suggested you allow several days to enjoy the many scenic and historic attractions. During the tour you will ascend from an altitude of 30 feet in Sacramento to 7,382 feet at Echo Summit and then to 6,229 feet in Lake Tahoe.

Your vehicle should be in good condition with good brakes. Remember that down-shifting can sometimes be used to slow your vehicle instead of or in addition to using your brakes. Tire chains should be carried in all mountain areas from mid-October through April. For up-to-date travel advisory information, phone CalTrans at (800) 427-7623 in California.

Perhaps one of the most exciting and scenic drives in northern California is that from the flat farmland of Sacramento to the resort area of Lake Tahoe. The area changes from rich, black soil with deciduous trees to red clay with its distinctive aroma and pines in the lower Sierras to craggy mountain peaks cloaked in snow.

Begin your trip in **Sacramento,** the state capital. The restored Old Sacramento area has restaurants, shops and museums, including the impressive California State Railroad Museum. Take US 50 east to **Placerville;** a *placer* is a deposit of sand or gravel containing valuable minerals. This once-raucous mining town—infamous for its prosperity and consequent lawlessness—has reminders of its past in its museums, municipally owned gold mine and many buildings constructed 1850-70, including fine Victorian-style residences.

Continue east on US 50 through Camino, originally a station on the Placerville-Lake Tahoe stagecoach route. About 2 miles farther is a road to Apple Hill where some of the more than 40 apple farms are open to the public during the fall harvest from mid-September through December.

Taste locally made wines and purchase fruits, nuts, vegetables, apple products, arts and crafts or a Christmas tree from one of the nearly 20 Christmas tree farms. October offers the widest variety of events, but the Apple Blossom Festival from mid-April through May has many highlights, including hayrides and a trout derby.

About 10 miles from Camino you come to Pacific House, an 1859 inn which can boast of such guests as Horace Greeley and Mark Twain. On the 30 miles from Camino to Echo Summit you will pass several entrances to Desolation Wilderness, a hiking and backpacking area open only by permit. After passing through Strawberry, another stagecoach stop, you reach Echo Summit at an altitude of 7,382 feet and begin a 22-mile descent to **Lake Tahoe.**

Lake Tahoe is in a high valley between the Sierra Nevada and the Carson ranges and is one of the premier U.S. winter sports areas. Tahoe's forests were nearly destroyed 1860-90. Lumber was needed for fuel and to support the web of mines constructed beneath Virginia City. The decline of the Comstock Lode was likely the saving grace for Tahoe's forests.

The headquarters of the U.S. Forest Service-Lake Tahoe Basin Management Unit provides year-round information about forest activities, including camping, fishing and hiking in summer and cross-country skiing in winter. Phone (530) 543-2600, or TTY (530) 541-4036.

Several companies operate cruises around the lake. These trips offer scenic views of the lakeshore as well as surrounding resorts and estates.

Hotels and gambling establishments have proliferated on the south shore on the Nevada side of the state line. The larger casinos each have several restaurants and coffee shops in which the meals may be both above average in quality and below average in price—the casinos derive most of their income from gambling.

Follow US 50 north and east, a particularly scenic drive along the shore of the lake and through **Humboldt-Toiyabe National Forest.** When US 50 merges with US 395 turn north and 3 miles later you are in **Carson City,** the capital of Nevada. The city's convention and visitors bureau distributes a map of historic sites and attractions.

In downtown Carson City, 2 blocks north of the State Museum and 1 block north of Washington Street at E. William Street, US 50 diverges from US

395 and resumes its eastward course. Take US 50 east forabout 7 miles to its intersection with scenic SR 341.

On SR 341 travel north for about 10 miles to **Virginia City.** This former haunt of such notables as Mark Twain and Bret Harte has been restored to its 1870 boomtown appearance. The town's restored buildings, its many large and small museums, its mine and its railroad can easily keep you busy for an entire day.

Continue northwest on SR 341 until it intersects US 395; take US 395 north into **Reno,** "The Biggest Little City in the World." While nationally known for quick and easy marriages and divorces as well as for gambling, it also has fine schools and museums. Not to be missed is the collection of more than 200 antique, classic and special-interest automobiles at the National Automobile Museum.

Now it is time to leave the gambling fever of today and return to yesterday's gold fever. Leave Reno via I-80 heading west, and after 32 miles you are in the small California town of **Truckee,** where restored 19th-century false-front buildings now house shops and restaurants. As with most of the lakes and rivers in the Sierras, the Truckee River is popular with trout fishermen.

Continuing west along I-80 you will find an exit to the 353-acre Donner Memorial State Park. Only 9 miles farther along I-80 you reach 7,239-foot Donner Pass.

Continuing west you pass exits to **Soda Springs,** which has a ski museum, and Cisco Grove. Near Emigrant Gap take SR 20 west; this road is lined with tall pines and offers views of old mining camps and sweeping views of the foothills, sometimes as far as 40 miles.

Nevada City was built on seven steep hills, and the streets follow miners' trails. The chamber of commerce offers a brochure outlining a walking tour. Some of its many Victorian-era buildings are a hodgepodge of styles. The town has several museums, many restaurants and arts and crafts stores.

Continuing west on SR 49 for 5 miles you come to **Grass Valley,** once California's richest gold-mining town. The chamber of commerce can provide you with walking-tour information.

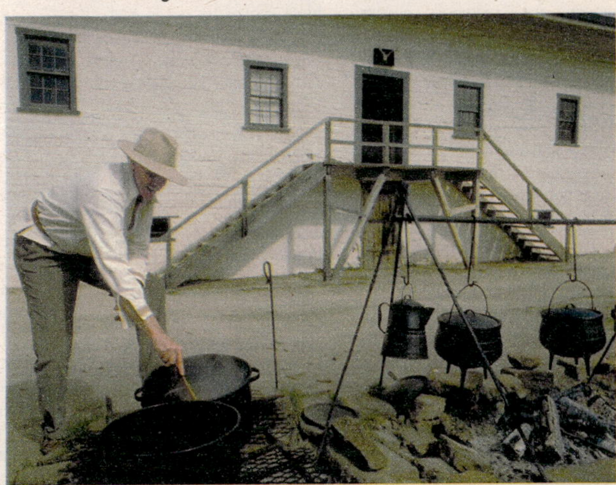

Sutter's Fort State Historic Park, Sacramento / Robert Holmes / CalTour

The 784-acre Empire Mine State Historic Park, with California's largest and richest gold mine, and North Star Mining Museum are worthwhile stops.

Head southwest on SR 49 to **Auburn** and its well-preserved 19th-century buildings. The visitor center at 13464 Lincoln Way has walking tour brochures of Old Town. In addition to the museums, do not miss the 1891 firehouse and the 1849 post office.

Continuing southwest on SR 49 for about 25 miles you come to **Coloma,** the birthplace of the California gold rush. Most of the town is within the 300 acres of the Marshall Gold Discovery State Historic Park. The best way to see the park, with its many 1800s buildings and replica of Sutter's Mill, is to first visit the Gold Discovery Museum for a detailed brochure. The more adventurous may enjoy a whitewater rafting trip down the American River; several outfitters operate locally.

SR 49 intersects US 50 near Placerville; take US 50 southwest toward Sacramento. About 25 miles from Placerville is the exit for **Folsom.** Reminders of the past of this 1850s gold rush town remain in a restored four-block section of Sutter Street. Folsom State Prison is 2 miles north of town. The nearly 18,000 acres of Folsom Lake State Recreation Area offer such a variety of recreational opportunities that it is one of the state's most popular multiuse parks.

Return to US 50 and drive west about 22 miles to return to Sacramento.

The Northern California Coast and the Redwood Empire

Leave downtown **San Francisco** on US 101, north across the Golden Gate Bridge, to enjoy panoramic views of the city. A brief side trip to the suburban community of Larkspur will take you back to a turn-of-the-20th-century small California town that has been preserved and is listed on the National Register of Historic Places. Continue north on US 101 to enjoy views of the coastal mountains, passing suburban communities, San Pablo Bay and agricultural lands for about 50 miles to exit SR 116 west.

Your target is **Sebastopol,** a well-known Gravenstein apple orchard, berry and winery center. Small farms and antique and woodcarving shops are at the roadside; a weekend flea market is a popular mecca. In April the countryside blooms during the Apple Blossom Festival with music, food and fun for all as the downtown shops feature local wares.

The countryside is a carpet of orchards and pastures as you approach the redwood covered mountains where winding SR 116 enters the deep shade and passes occasional small rustic cabins. Crossing the Russian River on a narrow bridge you enter **Guerneville** where fine food, lodging and shops are an invitation to stop. Here you may swim, canoe, hike or tour a winery.

Anglers driving along the Russian River to the coast through the tiny town of Monte Rio will bite at the sign "Monte Rio Angling Access," developed by the California Department of Fish and Game. Here too is a 7-mile byway drive to Occidental, a popular weekend dining spot.

Your ride will open out of the trees along riverbottom pasture lands to the junction with old SR 1. Turn right and another mile brings you to **Jenner** and an ocean view. Check your gas tank here, as few refueling facilities lie en route to **Fort Bragg.**

The 100-mile drive to Fort Bragg and on to Rockport—one of the most scenic on the Pacific Coast—hugs the shoreline as it winds sharply around headlands high above the ocean and offering views of narrow coves and inlets. Occasionally it turns in for straight stretches, passing farms and cattle.

Visit Fort Ross, a trading post established by Russian fur traders in 1812. Most of the redwood buildings are faithfully reconstructed.

A few miles further is Salt Point State Park, extending 4 miles along the rugged coastline. This is an excellent place for camping, picnicking, fishing and skin diving and has marked trails for hiking and horseback riding. The scenery varies dramatically from protected, sandy coves to sharp bluffs and sheer sandstone caves. The park has tidal pools rich in marine organisms.

Just down the road in **Plantation** is Kruse Rhododendron State Reserve, a springtime mecca for flower lovers.

The well-spaced little towns of Mendocino County—**Gualala, Point Arena** and Elk—offer a palette of ever-changing scenery. Whale-watching from the light station at Point Arena, which offers daily tours, is spectacular December through April. California gray whales stop briefly in the cove near the lighthouse before voyaging down the coast to Baja California. The cove has a concrete and steel 330-foot pier, 15 feet above high-water level. Fishing from the pier requires no state license.

Fort Ross State Historic Park, Jenner / Robert Holmes CalTour

Little River, formerly a lumber port, is now a hostelry hub. Less than 3 miles north is Van Damme State Park, with an underwater skin diving park, a bike trail, fishing and excellent camping. Fern Canyon, via Ukiah Airport Road south of the park entrance on SR 1, or Pygmy Forest Self-Guiding Trail via Little River Road from SR 1, provide a view of freak dwarfed pines and cypress trees growing on the coastal shelf.

Continue your drive to **Mendocino,** a former lumber port that is now an artists' and vacation colony with quiet shops and an unhurried atmosphere. The Mendocino coastline, the setting for many movies, is a spectacle of nature.

Five miles north at Jughandle State Reserve is a remarkable "ecological staircase," a series of terraces formed beneath the ocean by the action of the waves. Five terraces support a distinctive association of plants, animals and soil that many scientists believe to be the finest record anywhere of the glacial movement during the great Pleistocene Ice Age.

Just 2 miles south of Fort Bragg is Mendocino Coast Botanical Gardens, a seaside garden of native and ornamental plants in a woodland setting.

If you have not stayed overnight along the way, Fort Bragg offers traditional and bed and breakfast lodgings, restaurants, shops and entertainment. Stop for a map from the chamber of commerce and take the historic walking tour. Noyo Harbor offers sandy beaches, tidepools, ocean fishing, year-round seal watching and seasonal whale watching. Train buffs will enjoy riding the "Old 45" steam locomotive (The

Skunk) through the redwoods from Fort Bragg to **Willits.**

State campsite reservations are available by phoning ReserveAmerica, (800) 444-7275, for MacKerricher State Park just 3 miles north of Fort Bragg.

Continuing north on SR 1, you pass through the community of Westport, a picturesque remnant of a New England-like coastal mill town. Abalone and surf fishing are popular sports. Your route goes onward past Rockport for 28 miles to the junction of US 101 at **Leggett,** marking the official start of your journey north through vast preserves of towering coastal redwoods.

Trinidad / © Gibson Stock Photography

Richardson Grove State Park is the northbound traveler's first look at giant redwoods in the 1,000-acre park along US 101. Camping, swimming and fishing are permitted, and there are trails for hiking, bicycling and scenic walks, including Lookout Trail and Toumey Trail.

After driving 5 miles north to Richardson Grove you will find Benbow Lake and State Recreation Area, with 786 forested acres and the lake. The historic Benbow Inn holds a Shakespeare Festival in mid-summer.

There is a visitor center at the south exit of US 101 at Garberville. This also is a take-off point for Shelter Cove, King Range National Conservation Area, Sinkyone Wilderness and a section of Humboldt Redwoods State Park.

Ahead 6 miles on US 101 is the turn-off to scenic SR 254, a two-lane, 31-mile road parallel to US 101 that traverses the area known as the "Avenue of the Giants." The 52,222-acre Humboldt Redwood State Park winds along this beautiful section of highway sprinkled with memorial groves and picnic groves, an interpretive center, lodgings, restaurants, grocery, souvenir and art shops, and other services.

Continuing through **Scotia,** Rio Dell and **Fortuna,** you travel on to **Eureka** and **Arcata.** This has been a major lumber center, along with fishing and shipping, since the 1850s. The Carson Mansion, not open for tours, is a splendid example of classical Victorian architecture. An aviary delight is the National Wildlife Refuge at the south end of Humboldt Bay. As you continue on north, **Trinidad** and Patrick's Point State Park are fine beach and picnicking areas.

At **Orick,** a southern gateway to **Redwood National Park,** there is an information center at Freshwater Lagoon. You may purchase tickets there for the Tall Trees Shuttle. Visits to Lady Bird Johnson Grove and Elk Prairie are a must; however, watch out for the Roosevelt elk that roam the beaches and meadows.

Upon entering Del Norte County you will cross the Klamath Bridge into **Klamath.** This is part of the Yurok Indian Reservation and a magnet for steelhead and salmon fishermen. The Klamath Salmon Festival in early August is a popular event. North of Klamath is the Trees of Mystery park where Paul Bunyan stands guard over unusual redwoods. Indian artifacts fill a museum.

Within Del Norte Coast State Park, in Redwood National Park, are more than 6,000 acres of redwoods, rhododendrons, azaleas and other spring and summer flowers.

Further north is **Crescent City,** with its beautiful crescent-shaped beach and harbor. At low tide a walk to the Battery Point Lighthouse is a seasonal delight—just don't stay too long! There are many fine restaurants, museums, galleries and shops. Just half a mile north are Earl and Talawa lakes, where dunes, marshes and ponds make for excellent bird-watching.

For a flower lover's treat, travel 1.5 miles north to Smith River, the "Easter Lily Capital of the World." The Easter in July Lily Festival celebrates the harvest of the blooming plants.

To start the trip back to San Francisco, drive south on US 101 to Eureka. You may take a side trip and visit the beautiful Victorian village of **Ferndale,** now a State Historic Landmark; exit US 101 at Loleta and drive over the Fernbridge. A walking tour map is available at most shops. The wonderful gingerbread buildings are well-preserved. The services here are varied.

Half Moon Bay / © Robert Holmes / Corbis

Soon you pass the rocky promontory Devil's Slide and proceed to gentle, fertile agricultural land where Brussels sprouts, artichokes and flowers grow in abundance and splendor.

Moss Beach has the James V. Fitzgerald Marine Reserve, just off SR 1 via California Avenue, one of the state's most diverse intertidal regions. Courageous surfers challenge the breaking waves along the beach at Pillar Point Harbor, adjacent to **Half Moon Bay** Airport in Princeton. Beaches in this area also are popular for fishing and whale-watching cruises.

You have a choice now of either returning to US 101 or, as an alternate route, experiencing the beautiful "Lost Coast of California" by continuing on the Mattole Road for 45 miles past Cape Mendocino and inland to Honeydew. If you wish to continue on to the King Range National Conservation Area and Shelter Cove via Wilder Range, be advised that this is an unpaved road.

Continue on Mattole Road from Honeydew through the Humboldt Redwoods State Park to US 101 and drive south to Redway. From Redway the 25-mile winding road to Shelter Cove and Sinkyone Wilderness State Park gives you breathtaking views of beaches and ocean. There are 4.5 miles of tidal beach for avid beachcombers. South of Shelter Cove, Usal Road is an unpaved county road and very remote. Returning to Redway and US 101, continue back to Leggett.

The most direct route back to the Bay Area is south on US 101 and across the Golden Gate Bridge, but to continue on a scenic tour exit US 101 at Leggett to SR 1. Traveling south approximately 65 miles, leave SR 1, go inland on SR 128 and follow the Navarro River into Anderson Valley.

Northwest of Boonville 8 miles is Hendy Woods State Park with its virgin redwoods, making a great camping spot. On through Philo, with vineyards close by to sample, then to Boonville. It helps to speak the native dialect, "Boontling," to get along with the locals. Continue to Yorkville and the junction with US 101 just above Cloverdale. The drive from Cloverdale to San Francisco is approximately 90 miles.

San Francisco to Monterey

Leave downtown **San Francisco** for a picturesque 1-day or weekend tour by driving south on US 101 to an immediate junction with I-280 to the junction of SR 1 in Daly City. Stay on SR 1 as the freeway turns toward the scenic community of **Pacifica,** nestled against the rolling Peninsula hills on the edge of the Pacific Ocean.

Another 10 miles south is San Gregorio State Beach, one of many tempting beaches along this tour. Año Nuevo State Reserve, 13 miles south of **Pescadero,** is known for its large colony of northern elephant seals. Their population peaks during the December-through-March breeding season.

Davenport, about 10 miles north of **Santa Cruz,** was a whaling station in the 1850s. A nearby cement company is an oddity; it has churned concrete since 1915.

Still viewing the waving ocean shores you enter Santa Cruz, the site of one of Father Junípero Serra's historic California missions.

Santa Cruz and the other Monterey Bay communities of **Capitola, Soquel,** Aptos and Rio Del Mar are on your path. The 26 miles of Santa Cruz County's coast are scalloped into a succession of state beaches that are the warmest and gentlest ocean waters in northern California.

In addition to Lighthouse Field and Natural Bridges State

Beach—where winter migrating monarch butterflies stop, there is Twin Lakes, across from Schwan Lagoon, where you can watch myriad waterfowl. New Brighton, Seacliff and Sunset offer camping among the evergreens. For camping reservations on all state beaches phone ReserveAmerica at (800) 444-7275.

Best known for its Begonia Festival in September, Capitola is an arts and crafts lover's haven. There are many fine galleries and eateries along the esplanade to explore.

Aptos, an Indian word for "meeting of the streams," adjoins SR 1 just past Capitola. The Forest of Nisene Marks State Park is the location of the epicenter of the 1989 earthquake. Except for a placard, there is no evidence above ground of the powerful quake.

As you continue on SR 1 toward Monterey, the redwoods level to cultivated farmlands. Apples, strawberries and flowers are the basis of the **Watsonville** economy.

Maps for walking and driving tours of Watsonville and the Pajaro Valley are available from the chamber of commerce. The county's farm trail headquarters, Country Crossroads, 141 Monte Vista Ave. in Watsonville, has information and a map of farms you can visit and pick produce.

Crossing Elkhorn Slough at **Moss Landing** there is an 8-mile side drive inland to Elkhorn Slough National Estuarine Research Reserve. The slough is on a migratory flyway and is an important feeding and resting ground for many kinds of waterfowl and shorebirds.

Back on SR 1 it is a few miles to Castroville, "The Artichoke Capital of the World," and only 15 miles to your destination, **Monterey.**

The colorful blue Monterey Bay terminates in the vision of historic Monterey, rich with natural beauty and many attractions from Fisherman's Wharf to Cannery Row, the Monterey adobes to city parks and the Monterey Bay Aquarium.

Add the Seventeen-Mile Drive to your tour of the peninsula and end at the charming village of **Carmel** for delightful shopping, a stroll on the white sand beach and a visit to Mission San Carlos Borromeo del Rio Carmelo.

To enjoy some of the points you may have missed, return to San Francisco via SR 1 through Santa Cruz, where the boardwalk amusements include an arcade, rides, saltwater taffy and an entertainment center.

The University of California at Santa Cruz (UCSC) offers many noteworthy attractions, including a Shakespeare Festival in July and August. You can visit the school's two art galleries, a world-class arboretum, a birds of prey project with wild falcons and a 25-acre farm and garden. Campus tours cover the fascinating architecture.

Leave Santa Cruz and SR 1 via a different scenic route immediately past the junction of SR 17. Exit SR 9 right, going north on the redwood-shaded highway.

In **Felton,** Henry Cowell Redwoods State Park has picnic areas and campgrounds. Consider taking the Roaring Camp & Big Trees Narrow Gauge Railroad from Felton to the Santa Cruz Beach Boardwalk and return.

© Gunter Marx Photography Corbis

The oldest state park in California is Big Basin Redwoods State Park, established in 1902 in **Big Basin.** Access is via a 9-mile drive on SR 236 at Boulder Creek, a town with the nearest automotive and other service facilities.

The magnificent 18,000-acre park has about 100 miles of hiking trails, a museum/nature center, a large picnic area, family campsites, several group camping areas and backpacker trail camps. Reservations can be made through ReserveAmerica, (800) 444-7275.

Leaving the park, SR 236 narrowly winds through the redwoods and rejoins SR 9 at Waterman Gap; therefore, campers and trailers must return on SR 236 to the Boulder Creek junction of SR 9. Whichever your exit route, proceed north on SR 9 for a gradual downhill ride to **Saratoga** and the junction of SR 58. Take SR 85 north to Cupertino and then continue north on the Junípero Serra Freeway, I-280.

To make a side tour to Stanford University in **Palo Alto,** exit at Page Mill Expressway to El Camino Real. Turn left to the campus entrance. Resuming your tour on I-280, a last stop can be enjoyed on a clear, sunny day from the top of 1,000-acre Sweeney Ridge, site of the Spanish explorer Gaspar de Portolá's discovery of San Francisco Bay in 1769. This part of the **Golden Gate National Recreation Area** has sweeping views of the Pacific coastline, San Francisco Bay and open space to the south.

To get there, exit I-280 on SR 35 (Skyline Boulevard) to Sneath Lane. Turn left. Major access is from the west end of Sneath Lane. It is a 1.5-mile walk to the Discovery Site. In springtime the hills turn gold with California poppies and dozens of other wildflowers. The Ridge has a great diversity of wildlife.

Return on Sneath Lane to I-280 and enter, driving north to San Francisco and the junction of US 101 to downtown.

San Francisco to Yosemite

A description of two routes follows for the tour from San Francisco to Yosemite. Both leave **San Francisco** via I-80. Once across the Bay Bridge take I-580 through Alameda County and east into the Livermore Valley. Upon entering the Central Valley it is easy to understand why this is called the agricultural heartland of California. Nestled between the coastal foothills and the western slopes of the Sierra Nevada range, the valley is laced with waterways, orchards, fields and vineyards.

For the more direct route, which is 39 miles shorter, continue on I-580 to I-205, heading east across the middle of California's breadbasket. When I-205 meets I-5, follow I-5 north for 2 miles to the SR 120 exit. Take SR 120 east for approximately 28 miles to **Oakdale.** The city celebrates its cowboy heritage in early April at the Oakdale Rodeo, held outdoors—rain or shine—every year since 1954. Continue east on SR 120, the Northern Yosemite Highway, which has now merged with SR 108. This combination route takes you into Tuolumne County to Yosemite Junction, where SR 120 continues its easterly trek, merging, after about 3 miles, with SR 49.

Steadily gaining in elevation, SR 120 eventually enters the southwestern portion of **Stanislaus National Forest** before reaching the Big Oak Flat Entrance Station to **Yosemite National Park.**

For the alternate route, continue on I-580 to SR 132 and turn east to **Modesto** where SR 99 intersects. Turning south on SR 99 and crossing the Tuolumne River, you travel approximately 35 miles to Merced, then take SR 140 northeast to **Mariposa.**

Renamed from Logtown, Mariposa is Spanish for "butterfly." It is one of the major towns along the Golden Chain. The mines around Mariposa yielded some of the richest finds in the Mother Lode. The California State Mining and Mineral Museum, 2 miles south at the county fairgrounds, has one of the world's largest gem and mineral collections. Climbing in altitude on SR 140, past Briceburg, the Merced River guides you through the Stanislaus National Forest to El Portal and the Arch Rock Entrance Station to Yosemite National Park.

Yosemite Valley / © Galen Rowell / Corbis

When Abraham Lincoln signed the Yosemite Grant in 1864, he gave the state of California the deed to Yosemite Valley and the Mariposa Grove of Giant Sequoias. In 1890 Congress declared Yosemite a national park, thanks to the tireless efforts of naturalist John Muir.

The center of activity in Yosemite is the Valley, which comprises only 7 of the almost 2,000 square miles of the park. One of the best ways to see Yosemite Valley is to leave your car at your hotel, campground or the Curry Village day-use lot (shuttle bus stop #1) and take a 2-hour Valley Floor Tour. An informed tour guide will take you to some of the most scenic sites in the park.

You will not want to miss beautiful Bridalveil Falls, named "Pohono, Spirit of the Puffing Wind" by the Ahwahneechee, the Yosemite Indians.

The highest waterfall in North America is Ribbon Falls, which drops 2,425 feet. Other equally beautiful falls are Vernal Fall, Nevada Fall and Horsetail Fall at El Capitan.

About midway through the valley on the north side is El Capitan, the largest single granite monolith on earth. Rock climbers come from all over the world to challenge the summit which rises 3,593 feet above the valley floor.

The symbol of Yosemite National Park is Half Dome. At a height of 5,000 feet, the split rock is full of mystery. The Yosemite Indians tell a story of an Indian princess and her face stained on the side of the rock.

Most people find they cannot limit their visit to the park to just a day. There are several types of accommodations in Yosemite. You may camp in the high country along Tioga Pass, or there are housekeeping cabins in the valley. These facilities require reservations well in advance. You also may stay at lodges throughout the park or, if you prefer an elegant hotel in a wooded setting, The Ahwahnee is open all year; its dining room has long been known for fine cuisine.

If you prefer accommodations away from the bustle of the valley, then the Wawona Hotel, south on SR 41, is the perfect choice. This National Historic Landmark with its Victorian architecture and beautiful, spacious grounds gives the weary traveler an excellent rest.

Leaving the valley floor from the northwest side, take the New Big Oak Flat Road entrance station past the Tuolumne and Merced groves of giant sequoias to the Big Oak Flat entrance station. Continue on SR 120 approximately 45 miles west down Priest Grade to Moccasin, where SR 49 junctions with SR 120. Heading north on SR 49 through the southern end of the Gold Country is **Jamestown,** one of the more commercially developed mining towns.

Railtown 1897 State Historic Park operates a 19th-century steam locomotive in summer.

Continuing north to **Sonora,** the Tuolumne County Museum will have on display many gold rush-era artifacts.

The next stop is 2.5 miles north in **Columbia,** the best preserved of all mining towns. The old business district is a state historic park which allows for leisurely walks through history.

From Columbia return on SR 49 to the junction with SR 108. Take SR 108 approximately 6 miles to the junction with SR 120 and proceed to **Knights Ferry.** This gold town boasts a covered bridge—a rare sight in California.

Starting back to San Francisco, stay on SR 120 through the Central Valley to I-205 for 12 miles, then take I-580. For the next 11 miles the windmill farms stand high on the hills. Continue to the Oakland Bay Bridge and back to "The City by the Bay."

The Sierras

A journey from the hectic pace of a big city to the quiet solitude of a mountain forest can be accomplished in less than a day. Begin by taking I-5 north from downtown **Los Angeles.** Make your first stop at **Lebec,** site of the long-ago U.S. Camel Corps, about 70 miles north of Los Angeles. Continue to Wheeler Ridge, where I-5 splits off to the west and SR 99 begins; travel north on SR 99 to **Bakersfield.**

The next 70 miles lead through farm and cattle country. Along the way you will come to **Earlimart** and beyond that, **Tulare,** both with interesting histories to share.

Nine miles north of Tulare at Goshen, take SR 198 east. The highway goes through the attractive town of **Visalia,** then climbs through the foothills of the Sierra Nevada mountain range. Approximately 7 miles beyond Three Rivers, SR 198 becomes Generals Highway as it enters Sequoia National Park at Ash Mountain.

The highway connects **Sequoia and Kings Canyon National Parks** and provides an especially scenic 2-hour drive from the entrance station to Grant Grove. (Normally open year-round, the road may be closed for brief periods during heavy winter snowfalls.) On the mountainsides and in the meadows are giant sequoia trees, descendants of those that covered Earth millions of years ago. Throughout the parks are wonderful places to picnic, hike or camp.

Just south of Grant Grove, SR 180 heads back down the mountains, across the Kings River and into **Fresno.** Then for a sampling of California's Mother Lode, take SR 41 north from Fresno to **Oakhurst** and turn northwest on SR 49 to **Mariposa.** Continue on the trail of the gold seekers as you drive to Coulterville.

Eleven miles north of Coulterville go east on SR 120 through Big Oak Flat and **Groveland.** Soon you are back in the mountains as you travel through **Stanislaus National Forest** and enter **Yosemite National Park** at the Big Oak Flat station. Here SR 120 becomes Tioga Road (closed in winter) and enables you to enjoy the grandeur of one of the world's most scenic spectacles. If unaccustomed to mountain driving on a road carved out of a nearly vertical cliff, motorists may find the driving challenging, but will be rewarded with magnificent views. In addition to its magnificent cliffs and waterfalls, Yosemite offers a full range of recreational activities.

Exiting via the eastern side of the park on SR 120 takes you over breathtaking Tioga Pass and down through **Inyo National Forest.** At the highway's junction with US 395 is **Lee Vining,** gateway to Mono Lake. The lake and its surrounding landscape are worth exploring, for they contain unusual and dramatic geological formations.

Before starting back to Los Angeles, you might enjoy an interesting side trip of approximately 30 miles to **Bodie** for a visit at Bodie State Historic Park, the preserved site of a rip-roaring gold-rush town. Take US 395 north to Bodie Road (SR 270) and turn east to the park. **Note:** During winter months US 375 may be closed due to bad weather conditions.

From Lee Vining, a trip south on US 395 leads along the eastern base of the Sierra Nevada, an area abounding in beautiful and varied landscapes. Among possible side trips, **Mammoth Lakes** and **Devils Postpile National Monument,** (there is a shuttle from the Mammoth Mountain Ski Area parking lot) west on SR 203, are well worth the day you will want to spend there.

Thirty-eight miles south of Mammoth Lakes, US 395 reaches **Bishop** and from there goes through the Owens Valley to **Lone Pine.** The town is best known for its views of spectacular 14,494-foot Mount Whitney, the highest mountain in the contiguous United States. You can reach the 8,371-foot level of the mountain via Whitney Portal Road out of Lone Pine.

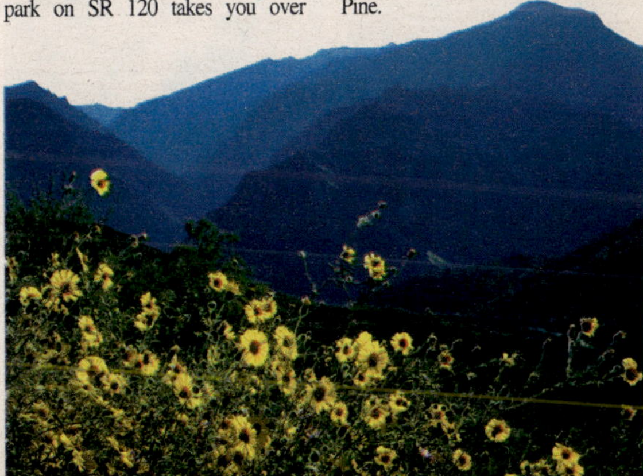

Kings Canyon National Park / © Phil Schermeister / Corbis

As you continue south on US 395, mountain scenery gives way to desert landscape. Sixty-three miles south of Lone Pine, pick up SR 14 where it intersects US 395 and turns southwest to Mojave. **Red Rock Canyon State Park** is just off SR 14 about 25 miles below that junction. Within the park ancient sedimentary rock has eroded into fantastically shaped cliffs and columns.

Continue on SR 14 and approximately 25 miles south of the park you will reach the high-desert town of Mojave. **Rosamond** is 5 miles farther south, and now you are in the Antelope Valley, with the San Gabriel Mountains on the southern horizon. Within the area is the 1,700-acre California Poppy Reserve, a state park offering wildflower lovers the chance to see millions of orange poppy blossoms blanket the hills from late March to early April (depending upon weather conditions).

From there SR 14 cuts through the **Angeles National Forest** on its way to I-5, the highway you will take south to return to Los Angeles.

The Southern and Central Coast

Seasoned by salt air and sunshine, the southern and central California coast offers a variety of Pacific settings, from grassy bluffs above rocky shores to sandy beaches or busy harbors. California history is reflected along the way in such places as bustling Santa Monica with its famous pier, picturesque Santa Barbara that grew from a Hispanic settlement, and beautiful Monterey, the town that was once the capital of Spanish California. Inland detours lead to such pastoral scenes as small towns, missions and farmland.

Interstate 10 west from downtown Los Angeles leads to **Santa Monica,** where the coastal highway turns north and northwest and, as SR 1, continues to **Malibu.** On your right are steep, eroded bluffs with plateaus on which houses seemingly perch precariously; here and there buildings cluster at the foot of the bluffs. On your left, wide beaches, beach parking, and oceanfront houses separate the highway from the ocean.

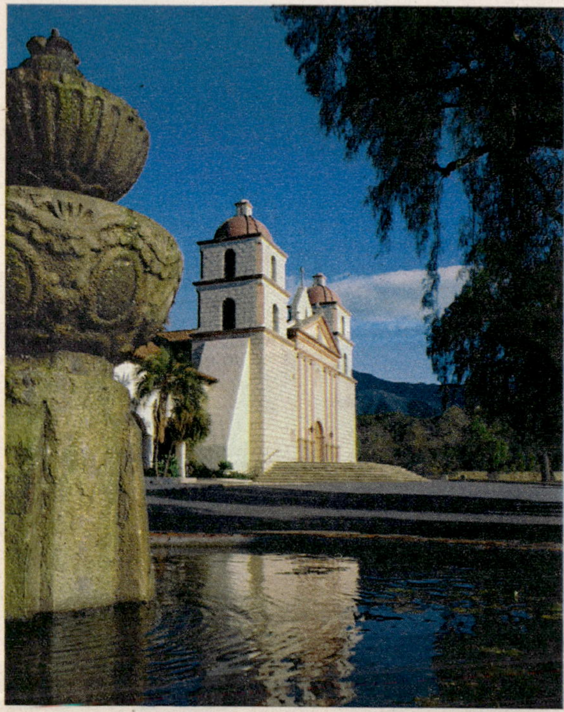

Santa Barbara Mission / © Ralph A. Clevenger / Corbis

North of Malibu SR 1 begins to climb through foothills covered with wild grasses. The coastline faces the Pacific on the south; to the north lie portions of the **Santa Monica Mountains National Recreation Area.** At the line separating Los Angeles and Ventura counties is Leo Carrillo State Beach, and farther west the highway cuts through Point Mugu State Park.

Now swinging northwest, SR 1 goes into **Oxnard.** Turn north on Oxnard Boulevard to pick up US 101 heading for **Ventura.** In Ventura watch for the Seaward Avenue turn-off and follow signs to the **Channel Islands National Park** visitor center. Here you will receive a good introduction to the five islands that make up a most unusual park.

At **Santa Barbara** either continue on US 101 along the coast or take an inland detour. US 101 goes west from Santa Barbara through **Goleta,** then along the coast past El Capitan and Refugio state beaches to Gaviota Pass. The pass cuts through the inland portion of Gaviota State Park and the western section of the Santa Ynez Mountains before meeting SR 154 about 5 miles past **Buellton.**

An alternate route begins at the western edge of Santa Barbara where San Marcos Pass Road (SR 154) goes north from US 101. This highway leads through the Santa Ynez Mountains past Lake Cachuma and through Santa Ynez Valley to rejoin US 101. On a clear day some of the Channel Islands are visible from the mountain road. Lake Cachuma is a pleasant place for a shoreline picnic. Within the valley are wineries to tour. And a side trip to **Solvang** provides a make-believe trip to Denmark.

Just beyond **Los Olivos** SR 154 rejoins US 101. As it heads toward San Luis Obispo County, the highway goes through oak-dotted ranchland backed by gently rolling hills.

About 12.5 miles north of **Santa Maria** US 101 bisects the charming little town of **Arroyo Grande,** then heads out to the coast and through **Pismo Beach.** At Pismo State Beach it is possible to drive right onto the hard-packed sand.

Just out of Pismo Beach US 101 leads north to the university and mission city of **San Luis Obispo,** then meets SR 1. Turn north to **Morro Bay,** a small town with a big rock presiding over a bay where sea otters swim, seagulls soar and pelicans perch. The highway then makes its way along the coast to the pine groves and tempting shops of **Cambria.** Another 8 miles brings you to **San Simeon,** with Hearst Castle high on a hill beyond the town.

North of San Simeon SR 1 becomes a winding, cliff-top road that affords spectacular coastal views. A word of caution: Slides caused by storms may close the road periodically during the winter, and fog can sometimes make driving hazardous, particularly in the summer. **Big Sur,** 64 miles north of San Simeon, is the site of artists' secluded residences as well as scenic Pfeiffer Big Sur State Park.

North of Big Sur the Pacific is in sight almost continuously, and one of the best views is at Point Lobos State Preserve, with its Monterey cypress, tidepools, marine mammals and ocean birds. The lovely town of **Carmel** is less than 5 miles north, and **Monterey** is approximately 2 miles farther. Monterey, prominent in California history and the setting for John Steinbeck's "Cannery Row," is the terminus of this drive along California's coast.

For variety, the return trip to Los Angeles can be taken inland as far as San Luis Obispo. Southeast of Monterey, SR 68 leads to **Salinas,** self-proclaimed "Lettuce Capital of the World." Turning south on US 101 leads into an agricultural valley where, seasonally, fields of lettuce, beans, grains, beets, berries and other crops cover the landscape. Orchards and pastureland complete the bucolic scene. This is John Steinbeck country, with farms, small towns and distant hills seemingly from the pages of "The Red Pony," "Of Mice and Men" and "East of Eden."

Robert Holmes / CalTour

Just south of **Soledad** there is an interesting side trip east on SR 146 to **Pinnacles National Monument,** with its volcanic spires and caves. The monument is a popular spot for hiking and rock climbing.

Return to US 101 and continue south along the Salinas River, over creek beds and through farming communities. To the east lies the Diablo mountain range; to the west, the Santa Lucias.

Sixty-three miles south of Soledad, tiny **San Miguel** and its well-preserved mission are just off US 101. About 12 miles farther south is **Paso Robles** where you will find rest and refreshment and a chance to visit nearby wineries. Not far south of Paso Robles are the small, quiet, attractive towns of Templeton and **Atascadero.** On US 101 San Luis Obispo lies 16.5 miles south of Atascadero.

Wine Country

If Southern California is synonymous with motion pictures, then northern California is synonymous with wine. Just 40 miles north of San Francisco are Sonoma and Napa counties and their more than 150 wineries.

Begin this tour by taking US 101 across the Golden Gate Bridge from **San Francisco** to **Sausalito.** Tourists flock to this small town to walk streets familiar to them from motion pictures and television shows and to frequent many quaint arts and crafts shops, eateries and bars.

Resume your northward journey on US 101 and continue until you reach the exit for SR 116 east at **Petaluma.** Do not be surprised if you experience *déjà vu:* Many scenes from the movies "American Graffiti" and "Peggy Sue Got Married" were filmed here. Petaluma Adobe State Historic Park is an unusual and popular attraction.

After sightseeing continue east on Stage Gulch Road (SR 116) to **Sonoma,** with its reminders of California's multicultural heritage. Around Sonoma Plaza are many of the buildings of Sonoma State Historic Park. In the Plaza the Vasquez House offers a walking tour brochure for $2.75. Sonoma Wineries Association provides visitors with an overview of the county's wine production through a videotape, demonstrations and tour packages.

Sebastiani Vineyards, a few blocks east of the Plaza, offers not only tours and tastings but also a fine collection of Indian artifacts. Within a 5-mile radius are more than 10 wineries. North of town near **Glen Ellen** is the 800-acre Jack London State Historic Park.

Continue east on SR 12/121 to find several wineries open primarily by appointment. At the junction with SR 29 turn north onto SR 29 heading to **Napa.**

Napa is an Indian word meaning "plenty" and is most appropriate for this fertile valley. The Napa Valley Conference and Visitors Bureau has local maps and information. The nearly 30-mile stretch of SR 29 between Napa and **Calistoga** runs past lush vineyards, farmhouses, wineries and small towns.

To the east and roughly parallel to SR 29 runs the Silverado Trail, never more than 3 miles from SR 29. Just off and between these roads lie more than 60 wineries, from small concerns to large, such as Beringer.

As you travel north on SR 29 the concentration of wineries really begins at **Yountville.** Here you can take a hot air balloon ride over the Napa Valley or eat and shop in the restaurants, boutiques and art galleries which now occupy Vintage 1870, a former winery.

Traveling north you come to **Oakville** and **Rutherford,** an area which produces some of the world's best cabernet sauvignons. The area around **St. Helena,** with more than 100 wineries, is considered by many to be the capital of this wine region.

St. Helena is a sophisticated town of stone buildings, parks, shops, restaurants and a resort. Silverado Museum contains manuscripts and first editions of works by Robert Louis Stevenson. While learning about wine production and sampling its fruits, do not ignore the architecture, such as the Gothic style of the Rhine House at Beringer Vineyards.

Three miles north on SR 29 you come to Bale Grist Mill State Historic Park, with its 36-foot waterwheel. Continuing north toward Calistoga the number but not the quality of the wineries decreases. One interesting variation is 3 miles south of town at Sterling Vineyards. An aerial tram takes visitors the 300 feet from the parking lot to the winery.

Calistoga, besides being a well-known spa and winery area, also offers visitors glimpses of Russian churches as well as hot air balloon and glider flights. Three miles north of town is one of the world's three regularly erupting geysers. Five miles west of town is a petrified forest of giant redwoods.

Take SR 128 from Calistoga northwest to **Geyserville** to rejoin US 101 and head south to **Santa Rosa,** a large city with many lodgings and restaurants and several attractions, including the former home of horticulturist Luther Burbank. Either continue on US 101 to return to San Francisco or choose a more scenic route.

For a scenic return to San Francisco, head west on the Luther Burbank Memorial Highway/SR 12. **Sebastopol** is an apple-growing town with an ornate Buddhist temple on Gravenstein Highway. In Sebastopol, Luther Burbank Memorial Highway/SR 12 becomes Bodega Highway and meanders west to intersect SR 1, the scenic Coast Highway.

Turn south onto SR 1, which travels between **Point Reyes National Seashore** on the west and **Golden Gate National Recreation Area** on the east. South of Marshall, SR 1 intersects Sir Francis Drake Boulevard, which travels west to Point Reyes Light Station. Farther south on SR 1 near Olema, Bear Valley Road goes west to the park headquarters.

At Point Reyes National Seashore, blunt headlands jut into the sea and grass-tufted dunes lie along miles of secluded beaches. Inland are rolling hills, freshwater lakes and Inverness Ridge, where the Douglas fir, typical of the northern California coastal ranges, and the Bishop pine of the southern forest areas merge.

Continue south on SR 1 to pass through **Stinson Beach** and then **Muir Woods National Monument,** one of the most beautiful and accessible of the redwood groves. Some of these coastal redwoods reach a height of 250 feet, with diameters of more than 12 feet.

Still continuing south on SR 1 you come to Mount Tamalpais State Park—6,233 acres of picturesque coastal hill country dominated by triple-peaked Mount Tamalpais. Hiking trails and a winding road lead to the summit, where spectacular vistas encompass much of Marin County, the San Francisco Bay area and beyond.

Just past Muir Beach, SR 1 turns inland and merges with US 101 at Marin City. From here it is a short southward trip across the Golden Gate Bridge and back into "The City," San Francisco.

© Dave Bartruff / Corbis

Points of Interest

Phone Ahead.

Because of budget considerations, the schedules and fees of all state-owned facilities are subject to change. Travelers are advised to phone ahead.

ALAMEDA (D-8) pop. 72,259, elev. 30'

See map page 109.

Fall and winter in Alameda are the best times to observe such sea birds as loons, grebes and ducks at Robert W. Crown Memorial Beach. Crab Cove, at the north end of the beach, has been designated a marine reserve. Crab Cove Visitor Center, on McKay near Central, features exhibits about shoreline and undersea life and a saltwater aquarium with live bay creatures; phone (510) 521-6887.

Daily ferry service through Alameda Harbor Bay Maritime is available between the Ferry Building, at the foot of Market Street across from the Embarcadero in San Francisco, and Bay Farm Island in Alameda at 2990 Main St. Phone (510) 769-5500 for information, departure times and rates.

The Alameda/Oakland Ferry also departs from 2990 Main St. in Alameda, proceeds to Jack London Square in Oakland and then on to the Ferry Building and Fisherman's Wharf in San Francisco; seasonal service is available to Pacific Bell Park and to Angel Island State Park. Phone (510) 522-3300 for schedule information.

Alameda Chamber of Commerce: 1416 Park Ave., Alameda, CA 94501; phone (510) 522-0414.

ALAMEDA HISTORICAL MUSEUM AND CULTURAL CENTER, 2324 Alameda Ave., contains city memorabilia. Displayed are vintage clothing, photographs, art, toys, household furnishings and a bicycle built for six. A gallery features changing exhibits of contemporary arts and crafts created by local artists. Allow 30 minutes minimum. Wed.-Fri. and Sun. 1:30-4, Sat. 11-4, Jan.-Nov.; closed holidays. Free. Phone (510) 521-1233.

USS *HORNET* MUSEUM is docked at Pier 3 at the former Alameda Naval Air Station on Alameda Point. This World War II aircraft carrier performed a wide variety of tasks, from shooting down enemy planes to recovering astronauts Neil Armstrong and Buzz Aldrin following their splash-down re-entry after walking on the moon. Visitors get a feel for life aboard a carrier, without having to enlist.

Wed.-Mon. 10-5; closed Thanksgiving and Dec. 25. Last admission 1 hour before closing. Admission $12; over 64 and military with ID $10; ages 5-18, $5. AX, DS, MC, VI. Phone (510) 521-8448.

ALTURAS (B-4) pop. 2,892, elev. 4,366'

Until 1874 Alturas was called Dorris Bridge after the Dorris family, the town's first European settlers. The Dorrises built a simple wooden bridge across the Pit River at the south end of town and later erected a house that served as a stopover for travelers. The county seat, Alturas is a marketing center for ranchers who raise livestock, potatoes and alfalfa.

Alturas Chamber of Commerce: 522 S. Main St., Alturas, CA 96101; phone (530) 233-4434.

MODOC COUNTY HISTORICAL MUSEUM, 600 S. Main St., documents area development via displays of American Indian artifacts and firearms, including pieces dating from the 15th century to World War II. A steam engine once used locally is outside. Tues.-Sat. 10-4, May-Oct. Donations. Phone (530) 233-6328 or (530) 233-2944.

ANDERSON (C-3) pop. 9,022, elev. 430'

The railroad arrived in the area near Anderson in 1872. The town was named for Elias Anderson, the owner of the largest land grant in the area at that time. Today part of that grant is Anderson River Park which offers free summer concerts.

Anderson Chamber of Commerce: P.O. Box 1144, Anderson, CA 96007; phone (530) 365-8095.

COLEMAN NATIONAL FISH HATCHERY is 11 mi. s.e. via Balls Ferry Rd. to Ashcreek and Gover rds., then onto Coleman Fish Hatchery Rd. The largest salmon hatchery in the continental United States, Coleman raises fingerlings in rearing ponds year-round. Salmon and steelhead migrate up the ladders to the hatchery early October to early February during spawning season. Self-guiding tours are available. Picnicking is permitted. Daily 8-4. Free. Phone (530) 365-8622.

ANGELS CAMP (F-3) pop. 2,400, elev. 1,379'

Named after shopkeeper Henry Angel who started a trading post at this site in 1848, Angels Camp was a popular spot for gold miners. Early diggers uncovered riches, and within 1 year approximately 4,000 miners populated the town to try their luck. Angels Camp sits atop numerous tunnels, which proved to be successful mines.

Angels Camp inspired Mark Twain to write his famous short story "The Celebrated Jumping Frog of Calaveras County"—his first published success.

Calaveras County Visitor Center: 1192 S. Main St., P.O. Box 637, Angels Camp, CA 95222; phone (209) 736-0049 or (800) 225-3764.

Self-guiding tours: A packet that includes walking-tour maps and information about the town's historic district, as well as other areas in Calaveras County, is available from the visitor center. A Calaveras County Visitors Guide also is available.

ANGELS CAMP MUSEUM, 753 S. Main St., features early mining equipment, wagons, a blacksmith shop, minerals and artifacts from the gold rush era and a carriage house with horse-drawn vehicles from the gold-rush days. Allow 1 hour minimum. Daily 10-3, Mar.-Dec.; Sat.-Sun. 10-3, rest of year. Closed Jan. 1, Easter, Thanksgiving and Dec. 25. Admission $2; ages 6-12, 50c. Phone (209) 736-2963.

RECREATIONAL ACTIVITIES

White-water Rafting

- **O.A.R.S. River Trips**, 1.7 mi. s. on SR 49, P.O. Box 67, Angels Camp, CA 95222. Daily Apr.-Oct. Phone (209) 736-4677 or (800) 346-6277.

ARCATA (B-1) pop. 16,651, elev. 33'

Founded in 1858 as a mining supply center, Arcata also was where author Bret Harte once worked as a journalist and miner; he used Arcata as the setting for some of his stories of mining camp life. The 7,500-student Humboldt State University is in Arcata.

Southwest on Humboldt Bay is the 175-acre Arcata Marsh and Wildlife Sanctuary, a recently transformed industrial area and county landfill that now is host to more than 200 species of birds. About 4.5 miles of foot trails wind past seven wetland habitats.

Arcata Chamber of Commerce: 1635 Heindon Rd., Arcata, CA 95521-5816; phone (707) 822-3619.

Self-guiding tours: Maps detailing a walking tour of Greek Revival structures and Victorian houses, as well as maps of the city-owned Redwood Park within Arcata Community Forest can be obtained at the chamber of commerce.

AZALEA STATE RESERVE is 5 mi. n. off US 101 McKinleyville exit, then 2 mi. e. on N. Bank Rd. The 30-acre reserve features western azaleas as well as other plantings common to the area. The reserve is loveliest when the azaleas are in bloom April through May. Parking is limited; the reserve is not recommended for trailers. Picnicking is permitted. Allow 30 minutes minimum. Daily dawn-dusk. Free. Phone (707) 488-2041.

HUMBOLDT STATE UNIVERSITY NATURAL HISTORY MUSEUM, 1315 G St., exhibits almost 2,000 animal and plant specimens from around the world, local natural history displays and fossils dating from 500 million years ago.

Exhibits, which change periodically, include a 60-gallon tidepool tank; local salamanders, toads, turtles and snakes; a dire wolf jaw fossil; a 50 million-year-old fish skeleton; birds of the Redwoods; Western minerals and ores; butterflies; and Pacific seashells. Tues.-Sat. 10-5; closed Jan. 1, Thanksgiving and Dec. 25. Donations. Phone (707) 826-4479.

ARNOLD (E-4) pop. 4,218, elev. 4,000'

The logging industry sustained Arnold until Blagen Mill closed in 1962. Because of the area's proximity to recreational opportunities, a full slate of winter recreation, from snowmobiling to skiing, as well as summer activities in parks, lakes and rivers is available.

Calaveras County Visitors Bureau: P.O. Box 637, Angels Camp, CA 95222; phone (209) 736-0049 or (800) 225-3764.

CALAVERAS BIG TREES STATE PARK, 4 mi. e. on SR 4, consists of 6,073 acres and contains some of the finest specimens of Sierra redwoods. Hiking trails of various lengths lead through the groves of trees. Interpretive programs are available in summer; snowshoeing and cross-country skiing are available in winter. Daily dawn-dusk. Day use fee $4 per private vehicle. Phone (209) 795-2334. *See Recreation Chart and the AAA California & Nevada CampBook.*

RECREATIONAL ACTIVITIES

White-water Rafting

- **Beyond Limits Adventures** departs from Calaveras Big Tree State Park, 4 mi. e. on SR 4. Write P.O. Box 215, Riverbank, CA 95367. Daily Apr.-Sept. (depending upon water flow). Phone (209) 869-6060 or (800) 234-7238.

ARROYO GRANDE (I-3) pop. 15,851, elev. 114'

Although Spanish explorers discovered the creek flowing from the Santa Lucia Mountain Range to the ocean, Arroyo Grande was not founded until 1862; it was another 5 years before the first two structures—a smithy and a schoolhouse—were built.

To bridge the gap between the town's two sections, which grew on opposite banks of the river, a rope bridge was constructed during the 1880s. A local landmark, the Swinging Bridge still is used by pedestrians. Arroyo Grande Village, a quarter-mile east of US 101 along E. Branch Street, reflects an 1890s atmosphere, including a farmers market Saturdays noon-3.

Arroyo Grande Chamber of Commerce: 800 W. Branch St., Arroyo Grande, CA 93420-1901; phone (805) 489-1488.

Self-guiding tours: A walking-tour brochure outlining historic structures is available from the chamber.

ATASCADERO (I-4) pop. 26,411, elev. 834′

Atascadero City Administration Building, Palma Avenue at West Mall, was built in the Italian Renaissance style. Completed in 1918, it houses the city hall and Atascadero Historical Society Museum, which has photographs and household items pertaining to Atascadero's early days. About 2 miles west off SR 41, Atascadero Lake Park offers fishing, picnicking, a wading pool for children under age 6 and the Charles Paddock Zoo.

Atascadero Chamber of Commerce: 6550 El Camino Real, Atascadero, CA 93422-4202; phone (805) 466-2044.

ATWATER (F-3) pop. 23,113, elev. 151′

The 1991 announcement that Castle Air Force Base would close—as well as its closure 4 years later—thrust Atwater into a temporary economic crisis that waned as local markets flourished and interest rates remained steady.

Atwater Chamber of Commerce: 1181 Third St., Atwater, CA 95301; phone (209) 358-4251.

CASTLE AIR MUSEUM is .5 mi. e. of SR 99 on Buhach Rd., then n. on Santa Fe Dr. In a remodeled barracks, the museum is named for Brig. Gen. Frederick W. Castle, who earned a posthumous Medal of Honor for his role in a World War II bombing mission over Europe. Historical photographs, weapons, uniforms and 44 vintage aircraft, including an SR-71 Blackbird and a B-36 bomber, depict the U.S. Air Force's development during the World War II, Korea and Vietnam eras.

Guided tours and food are available. Allow 1 hour minimum. Daily 10-5, Memorial Day weekend-Sept. 30; 10-4, rest of year. Closed Jan. 1, Easter, Thanksgiving and Dec. 25. Admission $7; over 59 and ages 8-17, $5. MC, VI. Phone (209) 723-2178.

AUBURN (E-3) pop. 12,462, elev. 1,255′

Historic Old Auburn, the central section of the city, has many restored mid-1800s buildings, including a firehouse and the oldest continuously used post office in California.

Placer County Visitor Counsel: 13411 Lincoln Way, Auburn, CA 95603; phone (530) 887-2111 or (866) 752-2371.

GOLD COUNTRY MUSEUM, 1273 High St. on the fairgrounds, depicts Placer County's early days through old mining equipment, exhibits about early transportation and mining methods, a stamp mill and a period saloon. Visitors may try gold-panning at a small stream; salted goldbags are available. The Bernhard Museum, at 291 Auburn-Folsom Rd., has a restored Victorian house and outbuildings with coopering, blacksmithing and winemaking displays.

Guided tours are available. Allow 1 hour minimum. Gold Country Museum open Tues.-Fri. 10-3:30, Sat.-Sun. 11-4. Bernhard Museum open Tues.-Fri. 10:30-3, Sat.-Sun. noon-4. Both closed holidays. Both museums free. Salted goldbags $1.50. Phone (530) 889-6500.

PLACER COUNTY MUSEUM & COURTHOUSE, 101 Maple St., features an American Indian habitat with a recorded narration and a 10-minute videotape presentation about the history of the transcontinental highway that runs through the county. Also inside the 1898 courthouse is a restored sheriff's office circa 1915 and the Pate Native American Collection, which contains more than 400 American Indian artifacts from around the country. Allow 1 hour minimum. Tues.-Sun. 10-4. Free. Phone (530) 889-6500.

BAKERSFIELD (I-5) pop. 247,057, elev. 408′

Bakersfield, near the southern end of the San Joaquin Valley, is an important shipping and marketing center for oil, natural gas and farm products. It also is known as California's Country and Western music capital. Mesa Marin Raceway is host to NASCAR stock car races in March and mid-October. Each October, the NHRA Hot Rod Reunion, presented by the Automobile Club of Southern California, takes place at Famoso Raceway near Bakersfield; phone (909) 622-8562.

Greater Bakersfield Chamber of Commerce: 1725 Eye St., P.O. Box 1947, Bakersfield, CA 93303; phone (661) 327-4421.

Shopping areas: East Hills Mall, at Mall View Road and Oswell Street off SR 178, offers Harris'-Gottschalks and Mervyn's. Valley Plaza, SR 99 at Ming Avenue, has a Harris'-Gottschalks, JCPenney, Macy's, Robinsons-May and Sears.

SAVE **CALIFORNIA LIVING MUSEUM,** 3.5 mi. n.w. off SR 178 at 10500 Alfred Harrell Hwy., presents more than 70 species of native California mammals, birds, amphibians, and reptiles, some of which are rare or endangered. Species include the desert tortoise, rattlesnakes, kit fox, black bear, raccoon, black-crowned night heron and bald eagle. Gardens feature plants in representative plant communities, as well as specimen gardens to attract butterflies and hummingbirds.

Picnic facilities are available. Tues.-Sun. 9-5; closed Jan. 1, Thanksgiving and Dec. 25. Admission $4.50; over 59, $3.25; students with ID and ages 3-12, $2.75. Phone (661) 872-2256.

SAVE **KERN COUNTY MUSEUM,** 3801 Chester Ave., contains exhibits that represent the human science and natural history of the area. This 16-acre, 56-building museum depicts life in the late 19th and early 20th centuries. Black Gold: The Oil Experience is an interactive exhibit explaining how oil is formed, found, and extracted from the ground. Lori Brock Children's Discovery Center features hands-on exhibits.

Mon.-Sat. and some holidays 10-5, Sun. noon-5; closed Jan. 1, Easter, July 4, Thanksgiving and Dec. 24-25 and 31. Last admission 2 hours before closing. Admission $7; over 60 and ages 13-17, $6; ages 6-12, $5; ages 3-5, $4. MC, VI. Phone (661) 852-5000.

BARSTOW (I-7) pop. 21,119, elev. 2,106′

A thriving mining center in the late 19th century, Barstow is at the junction of three major highways—I-15, I-40 and SR 58—that provide access to the Mojave Desert. Several local military installations anchor the city's economy. Near Yermo, east of town along Route 66, one of the visual kicks is Peggy Sue's Nifty 50's Diner, where patrons enter through a replica of a jukebox.

Barstow Area Chamber of Commerce: 409 E. Fredericks St., P.O. Box 698, Barstow, CA 92312-0698; phone (760) 256-8617.

Shopping areas: Approximately 120 outlet stores draw bargain hunters to Factory Merchants Barstow, 4 miles south near the I-15 Lenwood Road exit, and SAVE Tanger Outlet Center, across the street.

CALICO EARLY MAN ARCHAEOLOGICAL SITE, 15 mi. n.e. via I-15 and Minneola Rd., is an excavation begun by Dr. Louis Leakey in 1964. More than 12,000 stone tools dating back possibly 200,000 years have been unearthed. The site has active digs Oct.-May and the first full weekend of the month. Examples of early tools can be seen in the walls and floors of the excavated pits, in the visitor center and in the county museum.

Guided tours are available. Unescorted visitors must stay on designated trails. Allow 1 hour minimum. Thurs.-Sun. 8-4:30, closed holidays. Admission $5 per private vehicle. MC, VI. Phone (909) 307-2669, ext. 265.

SAVE **CALICO GHOST TOWN REGIONAL PARK** is 10 mi. n. via I-15. Named for the varicolored surrounding mountains, Calico was a booming silver-mining town 1881-96. Its mines produced more than $13 million in ore. In 1895 the price of silver dropped, the mines quit producing and the town became a ghost town. Attractions include a mine tour, mystery shack and train ride. Mock gunfights, panning for gold and historic tours are offered.

Camping is permitted. Food is available. Daily 9-5; closed Dec. 25. Town admission $6; ages 6-15, $3. Train ride $2. Mystery shack each $1. Mine tour $1. DS, MC, VI. Phone (760) 254-2122 or (800) 862-2542.

RAINBOW BASIN NATIONAL NATURAL LANDMARK is 8 mi. n. via old Hwy. 58, 6 mi. n. on Irwin Rd., then 2 mi. w. on Fossil Bed Rd. (last 3 mi. are unpaved). This desert basin was formed by millions of years of the shifting and upheaval of the Earth's crust. Rock walls, in shades of red, brown, green and white, hold fossils and an abundance of minerals. The 8-mile loop road offers good views of colorful rock formations.

Note: Collecting of rocks, plants or wildlife is prohibited. Only vehicles less than 25 feet in length are permitted on the loop; motor homes, buses and towed vehicles are prohibited. Hiking and camping are permitted at Owl Canyon Campground. Daily 24 hours. Admission free. Camping $6. Phone the Bureau of Land Management field office at (760) 252-6000.

BENICIA (C-9) pop. 26,865, elev. 33′

Named after the wife of Mariano Guadalupe Vallejo, one of its founders, Benicia boasts California's oldest standing capitol building. The city supported an Army arsenal and barracks as well as the Pacific Mail Steamship Co. before becoming the state's third capital in 1853. Several well-preserved houses date back to those early years of statehood.

Benicia also boasts the oldest Masonic temple in the state and Saint Paul's Episcopal Church, the first Episcopal cathedral in northern California. Scandinavian shipwrights who worked on the church created a ceiling that resembles an inverted ship's hull, a design similar to those of Norwegian stave churches.

Other historic structures include the four sandstone buildings of the Benicia Camel Barn Museum, built 1853-57. The museum contains exhibits recounting the history of Benicia and the U.S. Army Arsenal. It was at the arsenal that the last of the animals from the Army's camel corps were auctioned off in 1864; the camel corps was a brief attempt at using camels as draft animals in the deserts of the Southwest.

Benicia Chamber of Commerce and Visitor Center: 601 First St., Benicia, CA 94510; phone (707) 745-2120, or (800) 559-7377 in Calif.

Self-guiding tours: The chamber distributes a visitors guide that includes information about driving and walking tours of historic Benicia.

BENICIA CAPITOL STATE HISTORIC PARK, First and West G sts., preserves the Greek Revival building that served as the third state capitol Feb. 4, 1853-Feb. 25, 1854. The structure is restored and furnished in period. Fischer-Hanlon House, at 135 West G St. next to the park, is a renovated gold rush hotel furnished in period.

Allow 30 minutes minimum. Park open Wed.-Sun. 10-5; closed Jan. 1, Thanksgiving and Dec. 25. Tours of the Fischer-Hanlon House are by appointment; check at the capitol for availability. Admission (includes Fischer-Hanlon House) $2, under 17 free. Phone (707) 745-3385.

BERKELEY (D-8) pop. 102,743, elev. 152′

Lively, inquiring and experimental, Berkeley exudes an atmosphere befitting its position as one of the country's leading educational centers. The University of California, with its 39,000 students, is often the vanguard of any campus movement, be it political, artistic or philosophic.

At the foot of University Avenue lies the center for one of the city's favorite activities—sport fishing. Berkeley Marina, base for a large charter boat fleet, also has a free fishing pier; phone (510) 644-6376. No license is required. Water sports and model yacht racing are popular on the mile-long saltwater lake in Aquatic Park at the foot of Bancroft Avenue. Golden Gate Fields in nearby Albany offers seasonal horse racing; phone (510) 559-7300.

Note: Policies concerning admittance of children to pari-mutuel betting facilities vary. Phone for information.

Berkeley Convention & Visitors Bureau: 2015 Center St., Berkeley, CA 94704; phone (510) 549-7040 or (800) 847-4823.

Self-guiding tours: A brochure about a walking tour that outlines downtown's architectural flavor is available from the convention and visitors bureau.

BERKELEY MUNICIPAL ROSE GARDEN, Euclid Ave. at Bayview Pl., contains more than 3,000 rose bushes representing 250 varieties of the flower. The garden is best viewed in late spring and early summer. A terraced amphitheater and arbor overlook the bay and Golden Gate Bridge. Daily dawn-dusk. The garden may be closed during special occasions; phone ahead. Free. Phone (510) 981-5150.

GRIZZLY PEAK BOULEVARD, which can be reached from the head of Spruce St. or from other points along the city's n.e. edge, winds along the crest of the hills behind the city at elevations up to 1,600 feet. The scenic drive provides access to attractions within Tilden Regional Park as well as a view of San Francisco Bay.

JUDAH L. MAGNES MUSEUM is at 2911 Russell St. The museum features changing exhibits of Jewish art and artifacts from ancient to contemporary, the Western Jewish History Center and a Judaica library. Allow 1 hour minimum. Sun.-Thurs. 10-4; closed Jewish and federal holidays. Hours may vary; phone ahead. Donations. Phone (510) 549-6950.

PACIFIC SCHOOL OF RELIGION, LeConte and Scenic aves., is an interdenominational seminary. A museum displays Palestinian artifacts dating from 3200 B.C. Allow 30 minutes minimum. Mon.-Fri. 8:30-5; closed major holidays. Free. Phone (510) 848-0528.

SCHARFFEN BERGER CHOCOLATE MAKER is at 914 Heinz Ave. at 7th St. The company specializes in making dark chocolate, using restored vintage machinery from Europe. One-hour guided tours begin with an overview of the history of chocolate and how it is made. Chocolate samples are provided and the differences between them are explained. A factory tour details the manufacturing process, including bean selection and cleaning, blending, roasting and conching.

Open-toed sandals or shoes are not permitted on the factory portion of the tour. Allow 1 hour minimum. Guided tours are given daily at 10:30, 2:30 and 3:30; closed Jan. 1, Thanksgiving and Dec. 25. Free. Under 10 are not permitted. Reservations are suggested. Phone (510) 981-4050.

TAKARA SAKE USA INC., 708 Addison St., has an exhibit that explains how sake is made as well as a collection of sake artifacts. A video pertaining to the production of Japanese rice and plum wines is presented on request. A tasting room also is available. Daily noon-6; closed Jan. 1, Easter, July 4, Thanksgiving and Dec. 25. Free. Phone (510) 540-8250, ext. 20.

TILDEN REGIONAL PARK, off Grizzly Peak Blvd. adjoining the city on the n.e. edge, has a botanic garden, golf course, a Herschell Spillman merry-go-round, picnicking, camping, a nature area and hiking, biking and horse trails as part of its 2,077 acres. The Environmental Education Center near Jewel Lake has a miniature farm with livestock, farm implements and an exhibit hall. Swimming and fishing in Lake Anza and pony rides are offered as are miniature steam train rides.

Park open daily 8 a.m.-10 p.m. Environmental center open Tues.-Sun. 10-5; closed Jan. 1, Thanksgiving and Dec. 25. Merry-go-round daily 11-5, Memorial Day-Labor Day; Sat.-Sun. 11-5, rest of year. Pony rides Tues.-Fri. 11-4, Sat.-Sun. 11-5, mid-June through Labor Day; Sat.-Sun. 11-5, rest of year. Train rides Mon.-Fri. noon-5, Sat.-Sun. 11-6, mid-June through Labor Day; Sat.-Sun. 11-6, rest of year. Closed Thanksgiving and Dec. 25. Phone ahead to confirm schedules.

Park admission free. Swimming fee $3.50; over 65 and ages 1-15, $2.50. Merry-go-round $1. Pony rides $3. Train rides $1.75, under 2 free, family ticket $7 for 5 rides. Phone (510) 562-7275 or (510) 635-0135 for the park, (510) 528-6619 for the environmental center, (510) 524-6773 for the merry-go-round, (510) 548-6100 for the train, or (510) 527-0421 for pony rides.

GEM **UNIVERSITY OF CALIFORNIA,** e. of Oxford St. between Hearst St. and Bancroft Way, occupies a beautiful 1,232-acre campus. Guided 90-minute walking tours of the campus depart from the visitor center in the lobby of University Hall at 2200 University Ave. at Oxford Street Mon.-Fri. at 10, and from the clock tower Sat. at 10 and Sun. at 1.

The Ernest Orlando Lawrence Berkeley National Laboratory, above the campus on Cyclotron Road, is a Department of Energy laboratory that performs scientific research and operates national scientific user facilities in the energy, life and physical sciences. Two- to 2.5-hour guided tours of different research areas are offered on Fridays; reservations are required 2 weeks in advance. Phone (510)

642-5215 for the visitor center or (510) 486-7292 for the laboratory.

Botanical Garden, in Strawberry Canyon off Centennial Dr., contains 9,800 species of plants arranged according to their native regions. The 34-acre complex includes a Chinese herb garden and a large collection of cactuses and other succulents. Greenhouse exhibits and a visitor center also are available.

Allow 1 hour minimum. Daily 9-5 (also Wed.-Sun. 5-8, Memorial Day weekend-Labor Day); closed Jan. 1, Martin Luther King Jr. Day, Thanksgiving, Dec. 24-25 and 31 and first Tues. of each month. One-hour tours are given Thurs. and Sat.-Sun. at 1:30. Admission $3; over 64, $2; ages 3-18, $1; free to all Thurs. Parking 50c per hour. Phone (510) 643-2755.

Campanile, at the center of the campus, is 307 feet tall and contains a 61-bell carillon which chimes on the hour and plays music. Also known as Sather Tower, the campus landmark was built in 1914. An elevator takes visitors to a viewing platform. Music is played Sun.-Fri. at 7:50 a.m., noon and 6 p.m., Sat. at noon and 6 p.m., during the school year; schedule varies rest of year. Recitals lasting 45 minutes are performed Sun. at 2. Elevator operates Mon.-Fri. 10-4, Sat.-Sun. 10-5; closed university holidays. Elevator fee $2. Phone (510) 642-5215.

Lawrence Hall of Science, Centennial Dr. on the e. side of the campus, is a public science center that incorporates the Holt Planetarium as well as hands-on exhibits involving computers, telescopes, laboratory equipment and animals.

Allow 2 hours minimum. Science hall open daily 10-5; closed Thanksgiving and Dec. 25. Planetarium shows daily at 1, 2:15 and 3:30, mid-June to late Aug.; Sat.-Sun. and holidays at 1, 2:15 and 3:30, rest of year. Science hall admission $8; over 61 and ages 5-18, $6; ages 3-4, $4. Planetarium shows an additional $3; under 19, $2.50. CB, DC, DS, JC, MC, VI. Phone (510) 642-5132.

Pacific Film Archive, at the UC Berkeley Art Museum, 2575 Bancroft Way near Bowditch St., houses a large collection of films and videotapes from around the world. Showings are held nightly, except some Mon. Admission $8; over 64, non-UC Berkeley students, physically impaired and under 18, $5. Second feature $2 extra. AX, DS, MC, VI. Phone (510) 642-1124, or (510) 642-5249 to order tickets in advance.

Phoebe A. Hearst Museum of Anthropology, in Kroeber Hall on Bancroft Way, has exhibits about ethnology, archeology and anthropology. The 3.8 million items in the museum's collections include artifacts from California as well as other countries throughout the world. Wed.-Sat. 10-4:30, Sun. noon-4; closed major holidays. Admission $4; over 54, $3; non-UC Berkeley students with ID $1; under 13 free; free to all Thurs. Phone (510) 643-7648.

UC Berkeley Art Museum, 2626 Bancroft Way between College and Telegraph aves., features contemporary and Asian art as well as 18th- and 19th-century works and touring exhibits. Allow 1 hour, 30 minutes minimum. Wed.-Sun. 11-7. Admission $8; over 64, non-UC Berkeley students and ages 12-17, $5; free to all first Thurs. of each month. DS, MC, VI. Phone (510) 642-0808.

BIG BASIN (G-2) elev. 1,000'

GEM **BIG BASIN REDWOODS STATE PARK** is on SR 236; the headquarters is 9 mi. n.w. of Boulder Creek. Covering more than 18,000 acres surrounding Big Basin, the park was established in 1902 as California's first state park. Some trees have attained a diameter of 18 feet and a height of 330 feet. Trails for hikers and equestrians, waterfalls and a chance to spot wildlife draw nature lovers. A natural history museum is on the grounds. Camping supplies and naturalist services are available June through October.

Allow 2 hours minimum. Park and museum open daily 8-dusk. Day use fee $5 per private vehicle. Phone (831) 338-8860. *See Recreation Chart and Boulder Creek in the AAA California & Nevada CampBook.*

BIG PINE (G-6) pop. 1,350, elev. 3,985'

ANCIENT BRISTLECONE PINE FOREST, reached from Big Pine by the Westgard Pass Rd. (SR 168) and White Mountain Rd. to Schulman Grove (elev. 10,000 ft.), is 28,000 acres in Inyo National Forest *(see place listing p. 79)*. This forest preserves these gnarled trees, some more than 4,000 years old—a millennium older than the oldest redwoods. Three self-guiding trails are available. During the summer, naturalist services are provided daily at Schulman Visitor Center in the White Mountain District.

Dress warmly, bring adequate water and have a full tank of gas; there are no telephones, gas or water in the area. Forest daily early June-late Oct. (weather permitting). The visitor center is open daily Memorial Day-Oct. 31. Admission $2 ($5 maximum per private vehicle), under 18 free. Phone (760) 873-2500.

BIG SUR (H-2) elev. 155'

Point Sur State Historic Park, facing SR 1, encompasses Point Sur Lighthouse and its seven light-station buildings as well as an interpretive center. Because access is through private land, the park is open only by guided tour. Phone (831) 625-4419 for 24-hour information. Camping facilities are found at Limekiln State Park, south on SR 1 near Lucia.

PFEIFFER BIG SUR STATE PARK, s. on SR 1, covers 821 acres of coastal redwood and chaparral on the Big Sur River. Visitors can see groves of redwood trees while traversing the hiking trails within the park. Rangers conduct naturalist and campfire programs Memorial Day weekend through

Labor Day. Year-round overnight camping is permitted. Park open daily 9-dusk. Day use fee per private vehicle $5; over 64, $4 per private vehicle. Phone (831) 667-2315. *See Recreation Chart and the AAA California & Nevada CampBook.*

BISHOP (G-6) pop. 3,575, elev. 4,147′

Near the northern end of the Owens River Valley, between the state's two highest mountain ranges, Bishop is the center of a vast recreation and resort area and is an outfitting point for pack trips. Bishop Creek Canyon is west on Bishop Creek Highway (SR 168) within Inyo National Forest *(see place listing p. 79).*

Bishop Area Chamber of Commerce and Visitors Bureau: 690 N. Main St., Bishop, CA 93514; phone (760) 873-8405.

LAWS RAILROAD MUSEUM AND HISTORICAL SITE, 5 mi. n.e. on US 6 to Silver Canyon Rd., features the original narrow-gauge railroad depot that served the once-active railroad community of Laws. On site are exhibit buildings such as an old time doctor's office, an agent's house and a carriage house. Also shown is Locomotive No. 9, with its string of cars. Daily 10-4 (weather permitting); closed Jan. 1, Thanksgiving and Dec. 25. Donations. Phone (760) 873-5950.

OWENS VALLEY PAIUTE-SHOSHONE INDIAN CULTURAL CENTER, 2300 W. Line St. on Bishop Paiute Reservation, features exhibits of historic Native American food sources, clothing, shelter, tools and basketry. Daily 9-4; closed Jan. 1, Easter, Thanksgiving and Dec. 25. Admission $4; over 59, $2; students with ID $1; under 12 free. MC, VI. Phone (760) 873-4478.

BODIE (E-5) elev. 8,375′

Once a bustling mining town with an estimated population of 10,000, Bodie was notorious for its saloons, brothels, gambling halls and opium dens. Devastated in the early 1900s by fire, the town now is said to house only an assortment of colorful spirits.

BODIE STATE HISTORIC PARK, reached via SR 270 (last 3 mi. unpaved), is more than 1,000 acres embracing the ghost town of Bodie, one of the most lawless gold-mining camps in the West. The 170 buildings that remain are preserved in a state of arrested decay; they will not be restored, but are prevented from decaying further. The park often is inaccessible by automobile in winter. **Note:** Smoking is restricted to the parking lot.

Pets on leashes are permitted. Park open daily 8-7, Memorial Day weekend-early Sept.; 8-6, May 1-day before Memorial Day weekend and mid-Sept. through Oct. 31; 8-4, Nov.-Feb.; 8-5, rest of year. Museum open daily 9-6, Memorial Day weekend-Labor day. Admission $2, under 17 free. Phone (760) 647-6445.

BORON (I-6) pop. 2,025, elev. 2,460′

The chamber of commerce has exhibits about area history and minerals, and a video presentation about borax mining; phone (760) 762-5810. Among the displays at the Colonel Vernon P. Saxon Jr. Aerospace Museum is an F-4 fighter jet; phone (760) 762-6600

Boron Chamber of Commerce and Visitor Information Center: 26962-20 Mule Team Rd., Boron, CA 93516; phone (760) 762-5810.

BORAX VISITOR CENTER, 14486 Borax Rd., allows guests to view mammoth mining equipment operating in California's largest open pit mine. The center is divided into six areas: Mining, Processing, Distribution, Use, Responsibility and Heritage. Daily 9-5; closed major holidays. Admission $2 per private vehicle, $1 per motorcycle. Phone (760) 762-7588.

BURNEY (B-3) pop. 3,217, elev. 3,173′

Named for an early English settler killed in an American Indian raid in 1857, Burney is a marketing center for lumber, produce and livestock. Its location between Lassen National Forest and Mount Shasta makes it popular with campers and anglers *(see place listings p. 90 and p. 106).*

Burney Chamber of Commerce: 37028 N. Main St., P.O. Box 36, Burney, CA 96013; phone (530) 335-2111.

McARTHUR-BURNEY FALLS MEMORIAL STATE PARK, 6 mi. n. on SR 89, features a 129-foot waterfall that flows down several levels over moss-covered lava rock in a lush forest setting. Daily dawn-dusk. Admission $4 per private vehicle; over 62, $3 per private vehicle. Phone (530) 335-2777. *See Recreation Chart and the AAA California & Nevada CampBook.*

CALICO GHOST TOWN REGIONAL PARK—*see Barstow p. 62.*

CALIFORNIA COASTAL NATIONAL MONUMENT

Consisting of thousands of islands, rocks, exposed reefs and pinnacles extending up to 12 miles out from the shore off California's entire 840-mile coastline, California Coastal National Monument was established to preserve these uninhabited outcroppings.

The diverse geological formations found within the national monument's fragile coastal ecosystem provide feeding and nesting grounds for many sea birds, including gulls; brown pelicans, a threatened species; snowy plovers; bald eagles; peregrine falcons; and the California least tern, an endangered species. Two threatened species, southern sea otters and Steller sea lions, as well as California sea lions and Guadalupe fur seals are examples of marine mammals that find shelter and breeding habitats within the monument's boundaries.

Visitor centers for the offshore sanctuaries will be established along the California coast in the near future. For additional information contact the California Coastal National Monument, 299 Foam St., Monterey, CA 93940; phone (831) 372-6115.

CALISTOGA—*see Wine Country p. 191.*

CAMBRIA (H-3) pop. 6,232, elev. 60'

Cambria, with its stately pines and panoramic ocean views, is about 33 miles northwest of San Luis Obispo off SR 1. Originally developed in 1866, the town became a center for shipping, lumbering, whaling and mining. Today specialty shops, art galleries and restaurants line Main Street. Overlooking the town on Hillcrest Drive is Nitt Witt Ridge, a 2.5-acre folk art landmark. Terraced gardens and a multi-level house were hand-built by a local eccentric, using salvaged materials including driftwood, abalone shells, auto parts and beer cans; phone (805) 927-2690 for guided tour information.

Two coastal parks, Shamel County Park and Leffingwell Landing, a state day-use park, offer picnic areas, beachcombing, tide pools and vantage points for viewing sea otters, sea lions and the winter migration of California gray whales. Cambria lies on a scenic stretch of SR 1 that extends from San Francisco to San Luis Obispo.

Cambria Chamber of Commerce: 767 Main St., Cambria, CA 93428; phone (805) 927-3624.

CAMPBELL (F-9) pop. 38,138, elev. 196'

SAVE **CAMPBELL HISTORICAL MUSEUM & THE AINSLEY HOUSE** are at the corner of N. Central Ave. and Civic Center Dr. at 51 N. Central Ave. Campbell's rich agricultural history is depicted in the museum. Hands-on exhibits focus on the canneries that were the city's lifeblood, home life, and recreation enjoyed during free time.

The 1925 Tudor-style Ainsley House, just across the green, is lavishly furnished appropriate to the status of its English-born canning pioneer owner and his wife. Many furnishings are original to the house.

Allow 30 minutes minimum each for house and museum. Museum Thurs.-Sun. noon-4. House Thurs.-Sun. noon-4, Mar.-Dec. Closed major holidays. Last house tour begins 30 minutes before closing. Museum admission $2. House $6; over 54, $4; ages 7-17, $2.50. Combination admission $7; over 54, $5; ages 7-17, $4. Phone (408) 866-2119 for the museum or (408) 866-2118 for the house.

CAPITOLA (G-2) pop. 10,033, elev. 50'

Capitola is a resort community on the north shore of Monterey Bay facing New Brighton Beach State Park *(see Recreation Chart and the AAA California & Nevada CampBook)*. Capitola's begonia gardens bloom July through September. The city lies on a scenic stretch of SR 1 that extends from San Francisco to San Luis Obispo.

Capitola Chamber of Commerce: 716-G Capitola Ave., Capitola, CA 95010; phone (831) 475-6522 or (800) 474-6522.

CARMEL—*see Monterey Peninsula p. 98.*

CARMICHAEL (E-3) pop. 49,742, elev. 123'

EFFIE YEAW NATURE CENTER is along the American River in Ancil Hoffman Park at 6700 Tarshes Dr. In addition to rotating hands-on exhibits, the nature center is home to rescued animals—including birds, snakes and turtles—unable to be reintroduced into the wild. Three nature trails through the center's 77 acres provide opportunities for spotting wildlife such as deer, hawks, woodpeckers, jackrabbits and wild turkeys. Trailheads are at the rear of the center.

Picnicking is permitted. Allow 1 hour minimum. Daily 9-5, Mar.-Oct.; 9:30-4, rest of year. Closed Jan. 1, Thanksgiving and Dec. 25. Free. Park admission $4 per private vehicle. Phone (916) 489-4918.

CHICO (D-3) pop. 59,954, elev. 200'

Bidwell Park, a 2,250-acre city park spanning an area from downtown to the foothills of the Sierra Nevada, offers hiking and bicycling trails, a playground and various sports facilities as well as Chico Creek Nature Center *(see attraction listing)*.

Chico Chamber of Commerce & Visitor Bureau: 300 Salem St., Chico, CA 95928; phone (530) 891-5556 or (800) 852-8570.

BIDWELL MANSION STATE HISTORIC PARK, 525 The Esplanade, preserves a three-story, 26-room Victorian residence built 1865-68 for city founder Gen. John Bidwell and his wife Annie. Guests entertained at the mansion included such well-known figures as Susan B. Anthony, President Rutherford B. Hayes, John Muir and Gen. William Tecumseh Sherman.

Allow 1 hour minimum. Guided tours are given on the hour Wed.-Fri. noon-4, Sat.-Sun. 10-4; closed Jan. 1, Thanksgiving and Dec. 25. Last tour begins 1 hour before closing. Admission $2, under 16 free. Phone (530) 895-6144.

CHICO CREEK NATURE CENTER is just s. off SR 32 at 1968 E. 8th St. in Bidwell Park. The center features nature exhibits, gardens, hiking trails and a collection of non-releasable wild animals, including squirrels, tortoises and snakes. Picnicking is permitted. Tues.-Sun. 11-4; closed major holidays. Donations. (530) 891-4671.

CHICO MUSEUM, 2nd and Salem sts., offers permanent and changing exhibits of regional history and art as well as a late-1800s Chinese Taoist temple that was used in Chico 1860-1939. Wed.-Sun. noon-4. Donations. Phone (530) 891-4336.

SIERRA NEVADA BREWING CO. is e. of SR 99 at 1075 E. 20th St. Thirty- to 40-minute guided tours of the microbrewery explain how the ales and lagers are produced, from their beginnings in the brewhouse, through the fermentation process to the keg or bottle. Food is available (except on Mon.). Daily 10-5. Guided tours are offered Sun.-Fri. at 2:30, Sat. noon-3. Free. Phone (530) 893-3520.

CLOVIS (G-4) pop. 68,468, elev. 361′

The town of Clovis was named after Clovis Cole, the area's largest grain grower, who donated land for a rail station in the late 19th century. The city was incorporated in 1912. Lumbering was the initial economic mainstay, though fruit farming also became important. Many buildings date to the early 1900s, and today the Old Town section of Clovis is a reflection of the city as it was at the turn of the 20th century.

Clovis Tourist Information & Visitors Center: 399 Clovis Ave., Clovis, CA 93612; phone (559) 324-2084 or (877) 725-6847.

Self-guiding tours: Brochures describing walking tours of the historic district are available at the visitors center.

CLOVIS BIG DRY CREEK MUSEUM is at jct. 4th St. and Pollasky Ave. in the Old Town area. The museum displays photographs, documents and memorabilia pertaining to area history. Allow 1 hour minimum. Tues.-Thurs. and Sat.-Sun. 11-2, Fri. 5-9, May-Sept.; Tues.-Sun. 11-2, rest of year. Closed major holidays. Donations. Phone (559) 297-8033.

WILD WATER ADVENTURE PARK, 11413 E. Shaw Ave., offers more than 20 water rides and amusements, including water slides and flumes; Gold Rush Mountain, a water tube ride; Vortex, an enclosed inner tube with special effects; a large wave pool; a large swimming pool; a small fishing lake; Adventure Bay, a children's play area; baseball fields; and volleyball courts.

Glass items and containers are not permitted. Picnic facilities and food are available. Daily 11-6, mid-June to late Aug.; Sat.-Sun. 10-6, Memorial Day weekend to mid-June and late Aug.-early Sept. Hours may vary; phone ahead. Admission $21.99; age 3 to under 48 inches tall $15.99; over age 61, $9.99. Admission after 4 p.m. $15.99, over age 61 and age 3 to under 48 inches tall $9.99. DS, MC, VI. Phone (559) 299-9453 or (800) 564-9453.

COALINGA (H-3) pop. 11,668, elev. 671′

Coalinga began as a loading point for the Southern Pacific Railroad Co., which transported coal from area mines. Eventually "Coaling Station A" grew into a permanent oil-boomer settlement and its name was abbreviated. Nine miles north is a group of oil pumps decorated as animals, clowns and imaginary creatures.

Coalinga Area Chamber of Commerce: 380 Coalinga Plaza, Coalinga, CA 93210; phone (559) 935-2948 or (800) 854-3885.

R.C. BAKER MEMORIAL MUSEUM, 297 W. Elm St., displays fossils, American Indian artifacts, Western ranch hand equipment, early 20th-century household items, a 1924 American La France fire engine and a large collection of oilfield equipment. Allow 1 hour minimum. Mon.-Fri. 10-noon and 1-5, Sat. 11-5, Sun. and holidays 1-5; closed Jan. 1, Easter, Thanksgiving and Dec. 24-25. Donations. Phone (559) 935-1914.

COLOMA (E-4) elev. 750′

In January 1848, near Capt. John Sutter's sawmill on the American River, James Marshall discovered the first yellow flecks of metal that launched the great California gold rush. By the summer more than 2,000 miners were sifting for gold along the river near Sutter's mill, and Coloma, the first of the gold rush towns, was born. Finds grew scarce within a few years, and the once thriving city of 10,000 dwindled to the quiet village it is today.

GEM **MARSHALL GOLD DISCOVERY STATE HISTORIC PARK** is on SR 49. The 274-acre park preserves the site where James Marshall's discovery of gold began the California gold rush. Hired by John Sutter to construct a sawmill to provide lumber for Sutter's many enterprises, Marshall chose a site convenient to the American River and a stand of pine trees. It was there, in January 1848, that Marshall noticed the glint of gold in the water.

A statue of Marshall, marking his gravesite, points toward the site of his discovery, a half-mile away. The gold-rush era and its historical impact are depicted through exhibits, mining memorabilia and video presentations at a museum, while a working replica of Sutter's mill stands near the river not far from the site of the original mill. Also part of the park is the 1860 cabin in which Marshall lived.

Panning for gold is allowed, and fishing is permitted in season. Picnicking is permitted. Allow 1 hour minimum. Park open daily 8-5. Museum open daily 10-4:30. Closed Jan. 1, Thanksgiving and Dec. 25. Day use fee $4 per private vehicle. Phone (530) 622-3470. *See Recreation Chart.*

RECREATIONAL ACTIVITIES

White-water Rafting

- SAVE **All-Outdoors Whitewater Rafting** departs from several locations near Coloma. Write 1250 Pine St., Suite 103, Walnut Creek, CA 94596. Daily Apr.-Oct. Phone (925) 932-8993 or (800) 247-2387.
- **Beyond Limits Adventures** departs from River Park Resort, off SR 49 at the end of River Park Dr. Write P.O. Box 215, Riverbank, CA 95367. Daily Apr.-Sept. (depending upon water flow). Phone (209) 869-6060 or (800) 234-7238. *See color ad p. 88.*
- **Whitewater Connection** departs from Point Pleasant Beach campground, .2 mi. n. of Sutter's

Mill on SR 49. Write P.O. Box 270, Coloma, CA 95613-0270. Trips depart Tues.-Sun., Apr.-Sept. (depending upon water flow). Phone (530) 622-6446 or (800) 336-7238.

- **Whitewater Voyages** meets at varying departure points. Write 5225 San Pablo Dam Rd., El Sobrante, CA 94803. Daily Apr.-Sept. (depending upon water flow). Reservations office open all year. Phone (510) 222-5994 or (800) 400-7238.

COLUMBIA (F-4) pop. 2,405, elev. 2,143′

In the foothills of the Sierra Nevada, Columbia was one of the largest and most important mining towns along the Mother Lode. Local placer mines yielded $87 million in gold 1850-70.

Columbia Chamber of Commerce: P.O. Box 1824, Columbia, CA 95310; phone (209) 536-1672.

GEM **COLUMBIA STATE HISTORIC PARK,** covering 12 square blocks in the old business district, depicts a typical boomtown of the 1850s. Never completely deserted, the settlement has been partially restored to its appearance in gold-rush days. Among the town's buildings are a schoolhouse, bank, newspaper building, barbershop, saloons, the Wells Fargo Express Co. building, Fallon Hotel and the City Hotel, which still houses guests. The Masonic Temple has been reconstructed on its original site.

A museum presents a slide show about Columbia history. The Firemen's Muster is held the first weekend in May. Plays are presented in the restored Fallon House Theater. Stagecoach rides, horseback tours, gold panning and 90-minute gold-mine tours also are available.

Park open daily 24 hours. The museum and most stores are open 10-5. Plays are presented Thurs.-Sat. at 8 p.m., Sun. at 2 (also Sat. at 2 if the production is a musical), except during breaks between one closing and another opening. Stagecoach rides Tues.-Sun. 10-4:30, Apr.-Sept.; Wed.-Sun. 10-4, rest of year (weather permitting). Horseback riding Wed.-Sun. 10-4 (weather permitting), Memorial Day-Labor Day.

Park admission free. Play admission $12-$18. Stagecoach fare (inside) $5; over 54 and under 13, $4.50. Fare $1 additional to ride on top. Reserved seat $10. Guided .5-hour horseback tour $18; .75-hour tour $24; 1-hour tour $30. Gold mine tour $12; ages 5-12, $10. Gold panning $3-$10. Phone (209) 532-0150 for park office, (209) 532-3120 for play information, (209) 588-0808 for stagecoach or horseback rides, or (209) 532-9693 for gold panning and mine tour schedules.

COURTNEY AVIATION, departing from Columbia Airport at 10723 Airport Rd., offers scenic tours. Passengers can choose from various trips that fly over such scenic areas as the Yosemite Valley, Mt. Lyell Glacier, Mammoth Lakes, John Muir Wilderness, Kings Canyon and Sequoia National Parks, Mt. Whitney and Mono Lake. Flights depart daily. Fares range from $99-$349. Yosemite tour $149. Reservations are required. AX, DS, MC, VI. Phone (209) 532-2345.

Note: The mention of the preceding airplane tour is for information only and does **not** imply endorsement by AAA.

COLUSA (D-3) pop. 5,402, elev. 61′

More than 4,000 acres of seasonal marsh, permanent ponds, watergrass and uplands west of Colusa shelter large flocks of ducks and geese during fall and winter; the best viewing is during November and mid-January. The Colusa National Wildlife Refuge's 3-mile self-guiding auto tour route and 1-mile walking trail lead through part of the area; phone (530) 934-2801.

CONCORD (D-9) pop. 121,780, elev. 80′

SAVE **WATERWORLD USA** is .3 mi. e. off I-680 Willow Pass Rd. exit, then n. on Waterworld Pkwy. More than 25 rides and slides include the massive wave produced by Honolulu Halfpipe, Cliff Hanger's dual racing slides, the tranquil Kannapali Kooler river ride and the family-oriented Wild Water Kingdom and Treasure Island. Daily 10:30-6, mid-June through Labor Day; hours vary Sat.-Sun., mid-May to mid-June and day after Labor Day-late Sept. Admission $25.99; under 49 inches tall $17.99; over age 54, $12.99; under age 3 free. Parking $8. AX, MC, VI. Phone (925) 609-1364.

CRESCENT CITY (A-1) pop. 4,006, elev. 44′

Founded in 1853 as a gold mining supply center, Crescent City edges a harbor defined by a crescent-shaped beach. Point St. George, just above the harbor, protects the city from strong north winds; it was on Point St. George Reef that the side-wheeler *Brother Jonathan* wrecked on July 30, 1865. Brother Jonathan Cemetery, 9th Street and Pebble Beach Drive, contains the graves of many victims.

Lake Earl Wildlife Area, 5 miles north at the junction of Northcrest Drive and Old Mill Road, is 5,000 acres of wildlife habitat open for nature study, boating, hiking, waterfowl hunting and fishing.

Crescent City is the southern terminus of a scenic 42-mile stretch of US 199 that heads northeast to the Oregon border through Smith River National Recreation Area.

Crescent City-Del Norte County Chamber of Commerce: 1001 Front St., Crescent City, CA 95531; phone (707) 464-3174 or (800) 343-8300.

BATTERY POINT LIGHTHOUSE, on Battery Point Island at the end of H St., is a working 1856 lighthouse that houses a museum, nautical artifacts, antique clocks, and photographs of shipwrecks and American and foreign lighthouses. Guided tours are available, tide permitting. Allow 30 minutes minimum. Wed.-Sun. 10-4, Apr.-Sept. Admission $2; ages 6-12, 50c. To confirm hours phone (707) 464-3089.

DEL NORTE COAST REDWOODS STATE PARK, 7 mi. s. on US 101, contains 15 memorial redwood groves within its 6,400 acres. The growths extend down steep slopes almost to the ocean shore at Damnation Creek. Wildlife can be seen. Daily 24 hours. Day use fee $4 per private vehicle; over 64, $3 per private vehicle. Phone (707) 464-6101, ext. 5101, or ReserveAmerica at (800) 444-7275 for camping information. *See Recreation Chart and the AAA California & Nevada CampBook.*

OCEAN WORLD, 304 US 101S, features a half-million-gallon aquarium with a sandy bottom and reef exhibit. Guided tour highlights include a touch tidepool, shark petting tank and performances by trained sea lions. Daily 8 a.m.-9 p.m., June-Sept.; 9-5, rest of year. Closed Thanksgiving and Dec. 25. Guided 40-minute aquarium tours are available every 20 minutes. Admission $7.95; ages 4-11, $4.95. AX, DS, MC, VI. Phone (707) 464-3522.

DANVILLE (D-9) pop. 41,715, elev. 368′

Historic buildings and tree-lined streets connect Danville to its Old West past. The symbol of the town, a massive 300-year-old oak tree, stands on Diablo Road. Behind the restored Southern Pacific Railroad Depot is the Iron Horse Trail, a rails-to-trails conversion that is now a popular jogging, biking and walking route. The paved pathway extends 12 miles, meandering through Danville and the San Ramon Valley.

Scenic views of Mount Diablo, visible throughout Danville, are what brought playwright Eugene O'Neill to the area. His home in the Las Trampas foothills, where he lived 1937-44 and wrote many of his most well-known plays, is now the Eugene O'Neill National Historic Site. The house can be toured by reservation; phone (925) 838-0249. Mount Diablo State Park *(see attraction listing)*, popular with hikers and for the views from its summit, is east on Diablo Road.

Danville Area Chamber of Commerce: 117-E Town and Country Dr., Danville, CA 94526; phone (925) 837-4400.

BLACKHAWK MUSEUM, 3700 Blackhawk Plaza Cir., at the intersection of Crow Canyon Rd., Camino Tassajara and Blackhawk Rd., features traveling exhibits from the Smithsonian Institution. The museum's permanent exhibit consists of distinctive automobiles built 1894-1971. The Automotive Art Gallery is in the museum.

Wed.-Sun. and Mon. holidays 10-5; closed Jan. 1, Thanksgiving and Dec. 25. One-hour guided tours are given Sat.-Sun. at 2. Admission $8, over 65 and students with ID $5, under 6 free with an adult. AX, DS, MC, VI. Phone (925) 736-2277 or (925) 736-2280.

MOUNT DIABLO STATE PARK is off I-680 Diablo Rd. exit, then 3 mi. e. to Mount Diablo Scenic Blvd. A paved road leads to the 3,849-foot summit of Mount Diablo, from which as much as 600 miles of the Sierra Nevada Range and portions of 35 counties are visible on clear days. An interpretive center is on the summit. Dogs are permitted except on trails. Park open daily 8-dusk. Interpretive center open Wed.-Sun. 11-5, Mar.-Oct.; 10-4, rest of year. Day use fee $4 per private vehicle. Phone (925) 837-2525. *See Recreation Chart.*

DAVIS (E-3) pop. 60,308, elev. 50′

As a result of its foresight and commitment to conservation, Davis has received several energy conservation awards. The University of California, Davis, with 27,000 students, offers free guided 90-minute walking tours of the campus; reservations are required and should be made at least 1 week in advance. Tours, given weekdays at 10 and 2 and Sat.-Sun. at 11:30, depart from the Walter A. Buehler Alumni and Visitors Center; phone (530) 752-8111.

Students and residents alike shop at the Farmers Market Saturday mornings year-round, and Wednesday evenings in the summer when a festival atmosphere prevails with music, a carousel, a portable fountain and play areas for children.

Davis Chamber of Commerce: 130 G St., Suite B, Davis, CA 95616; phone (530) 756-5160.

DEATH VALLEY JUNCTION (H-8) elev. 2,042′

SAVE **MARTA BECKET'S AMARGOSA OPERA HOUSE,** near jct. SRs 127 and 190, is the backdrop for dance-mime performances created and presented by Marta Becket. Murals painted by Becket adorn the walls and ceiling of the opera house. Performances Mon. and Sat. at 8:15 p.m., Feb.-Apr. and in Nov.; Sat. at 8:15 in Jan., the first 2 Sats. in May, and in Oct. and Dec. Admission $15; ages 2-12, $10. AX, MC, VI. Phone (760) 852-4441.

GEM DEATH VALLEY NATIONAL PARK (H-7)

Elevations in the park range from -282 ft. near Badwater to 11,049 ft. at Telescope Peak. Refer to AAA maps for additional elevation information.

Death Valley National Park straddles the Nevada border in the east central part of California. Death Valley's formation began about 3 million years ago when forces within the Earth broke the crust into blocks. Some of these blocks tilted and rotated, creating the alternating mountain and valley pattern. During the ice ages large lakes intermittently occupied the basin; their evaporation left alternating layers of mud and large salt deposits that still are visible.

American Indian peoples have occupied the area during the past 9,000 years, but the valley gained its forbidding name and reputation relatively recently. In the late autumn of 1849 a group of pioneers and gold seekers left Salt Lake City for

California following the Old Spanish trail. After two weeks of slow-going, a splinter group decided to take a route across the desert which would cut 500 miles from their journey.

Early on, the man with the map of the route abandoned the travelers, who were left to just head west. After a month of traveling the shortcut, the band again split into groups taking different routes. Each faction escaped the area on its own and met at Ash Meadows, east of Death Valley. More than 3 months after starting on the Old Spanish Trail, their journey ended, and with only one human death occurring in the valley.

Although miners later found precious metals in the area, the discovery of another mineral—borax—initiated the exploitation of the valley. The borax company built the roads over which the famous 20-mule teams drew wagon loads weighing as much as 40 tons.

A place of unexpected contrasts, Death Valley National Park encompasses 3,336,000 acres. The valley itself ranges from less than 10 miles to about 61 miles in width and is about 146 miles long. Elevations range from 282 feet below sea level near Badwater (the lowest point in the Western Hemisphere) to 11,049 feet above sea level at Telescope Peak. One of the hottest regions in the world, the valley experienced a record temperature of 134 F, through summer temperatures in the 110s and 120s are the norm. Although summer thunderstorms sometimes send flash floods tearing down narrow canyons, the average yearly rainfall on the valley floor is less than 2 inches.

Of the more than 900 species of plants found, 19 are unique to the area, including the Desert Bird's Beak, Napkinring Buckwheat, and Golden Carpet.

The area also contains a wealth of geological phenomena: large sand dune formations, sculpted rocks, isolated valleys and volcanic craters. The canyon and mountain walls change color with the shifting sunlight.

Mankind's marks on the desert are limited. The park boundaries encompass the route of the Jayhawkers Trail taken from Utah's Great Salt Lake in 1849; the route taken by the Darwin-French party in 1860; the first mine worked in the region; several beehive charcoal kilns; and the ghost town site of Skidoo.

General Information and Activities

Death Valley attracts many visitors between mid-October and late April. Presidents' Day, Easter Week, Thanksgiving, Christmas and Death Valley Encampment in early November are particularly busy times.

Artists Drive is a scenic 9-mile route among the foothills of the Black Mountains. Golden Canyon, about 5 miles north of the entrance to Artists Drive, is cut by an easy 1-mile trail that winds through carved rock formations; parking and trail guides are available at the trail entrance. East of Furnace Creek, SR 190 leads to Zabriskie Point and views of an area of eroded, contoured hills.

Furnace Creek Visitor Center, on SR 190, has exhibits, literature and a 12-minute slide show about the park. It is open daily 8-5; phone (760) 786-3200. Evening programs and naturalist walks are conducted Nov. 1 through mid-Apr. Horses can be rented at Furnace Creek Ranch Oct.-Apr. phone (760) 786-2345.

Note: Travelers are cautioned that the valley is subject to intense heat during the summer. Those affected by extreme temperatures should plan to travel in the cooler evening or night hours. Carry extra water. If your car breaks down, stay with it until help arrives.

ADMISSION fee $10 per private vehicle, $5 per person arriving by other means, free to holders of National Park passes, Golden Age and Golden Access passports. AX, DS, MC, VI. *See Recreation Chart and the AAA California & Nevada CampBook.*

PETS on leash are allowed in the valley on all roads, but not in public facilities, on the trails or in the backcountry.

ADDRESS inquiries to the Superintendent, Death Valley National Park, P.O. Box 579, Death Valley, CA 92328. Phone (760) 786-3200.

Points of Interest

GEM **SCOTTY'S CASTLE,** at the valley's n. boundary, is an amazing sight in this isolated region. Built in the 1920s as a vacation retreat by a wealthy Chicagoan, it contains beautiful furnishings and art. The decoration of the house is as it would have appeared in 1939.

Picnicking is permitted. Allow 1 hour minimum. Rangers in period garb conduct 50-minute living history tours on the hour daily 9-5. Last tour begins at 5. Grounds open daily 7-6. Grounds free. Guided castle tour $9; over 62, $7; ages 6-15, $5. Phone AX, DC, DS, MC, VI. (760) 786-2392.

GEM DEVILS POSTPILE NATIONAL MONUMENT (F-5)

Near Mammoth Lakes and surrounded by Inyo National Forest, Devils Postpile National Monument lies at an elevation of 7,600 feet in the eastern Sierra Nevada. The highlight of this 800-acre monument is a sheer wall of symmetrical basaltic columns more than 60 feet high. The formation is a remnant of a basalt flow worn smooth on top by glacial action. A trail leads to the top where the surface resembles a tile inlay.

The Middle Fork of the San Joaquin River drops more than 100 feet at Rainbow Falls, 2 miles by trail from the Postpile. Fishing is permitted; anyone over 16 must have a California license. Hunting is prohibited.

The monument is reached via SR 203, which leads west from US 395 and Mammoth Visitor Center to the Mammoth Mountain Ski Area parking lot, then by shuttle bus to the Postpile ranger station *(see Inyo National Forest p. 79 for shuttle bus nformation)*. The shuttle, which runs 7 a.m.-7 p.m., lso departs from Minaret Vista. A half-mile trail eads to the Postpile. Except for vehicles with amping permits, private vehicles with 11 or more passengers, resort guests or the physically impaired, private vehicles are not allowed beyond Minaret ummit (just beyond the ski area parking lot) durng the day, mid-June through Labor Day.

Rangers conduct interpretive walks and campfire programs early July through Labor Day (weather permitting). Leashed pets are permitted. Monument open mid-June through Oct. 31. Ranger station open daily 9-4, July 1-Labor Day. Daily access fee $7; ages 3-12, $4. Shuttle bus free with access fee. Golden passports and the National Parks Pass are not valid at this site. Phone (760) 934-2289.

DOWNIEVILLE (D-4) elev. 2,899'

Once the center of enormously rich gold diggings, Downieville retains much of its earlier atmosphere. Old brick and stone buildings with picturesque iron doors and shutters flank narrow, tree-lined Main Street. Some sections of sidewalk still are made of planks. Gold panning is available downtown in the Yuba River.

DOWNIEVILLE MUSEUM, Main St., was built in 1852 and features eclectic exhibitions including collections of antique bottles and horse snowshoes. The stone structure once was a Chinese store and gambling house and contains period artifacts. Daily 11-4, Memorial Day weekend-second weekend in Oct.; Sat.-Sun. 11-4 (weather permitting), rest of year. Donations. Phone (530) 289-3423.

RECREATIONAL ACTIVITIES

White-water Rafting

- **Beyond Limits Adventures** departs from Convict Flat Picnic Area, 8 mi. w. on SR 49. Write P.O. Box 215, Riverbank, CA 95367. Daily Apr.-Sept. (depending upon water flow). Phone (209) 869-6060 or (800) 234-7238.
- **Whitewater Voyages** meets at varying departure points. Write 5225 San Pablo Dam Rd., El Sobrante, CA 94803. Daily Apr.-Sept. (depending upon water flow). Reservations office open all year. Phone (510) 222-5994 or (800) 488-7238.

DUNLAP (G-4) elev. 1,914'

SIERRA ENDANGERED CAT HAVEN is on SR 180 at 38257 E. Kings Canyon Rd. A .25-mile guided tour of this wild animal park devoted to cats provides an up-close look at tigers, lions and several types of leopards in natural settings. Picnicking is permitted. Allow 1 hour, 30 minutes minimum. Wed.-Mon. 10-4; closed Jan. 1, Easter, Thanksgiving and Dec. 25. Last tour departs 1 hour before closing. Admission $7.50; over 61, $6.25; ages 5-12, $4.50. AX, DS, JC, MC, VI. Phone (559) 338-1336.

DUNSMUIR (B-3) pop. 1,923, elev. 2,289'

Dunsmuir is an old railroad town just south of Mount Shasta. The Sacramento River, which runs

The Sea Otter

That pointy-nosed, long-whiskered creature floating on its back in central and northern California's waters isn't one of California's typical sunbathers—it's the sea otter.

The sea otter is a thickset, sturdy, fur-bearing marine mammal with small ears and short limbs. Its large hind feet are webbed and flipper-like; its front feet are comparatively small but agile enough to use rocks as tools to break open shellfish. The average adult weighs up to 80 pounds and can be 5 feet long including its tail, making it the largest otter.

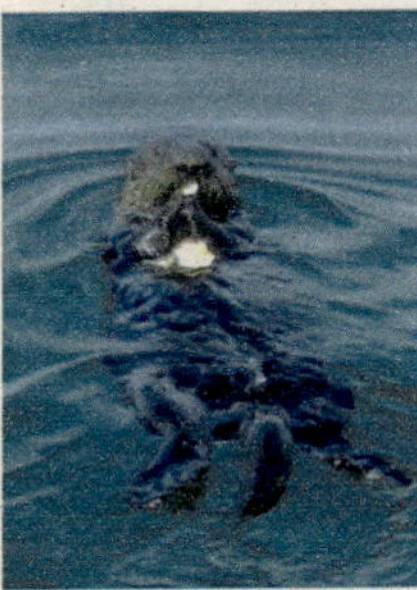
Digital Archive

The sea otter differs from most marine animals in that it doesn't have a layer of blubber under its skin to keep it warm. Instead, air trapped in its fur serves as a waterproof blanket, insulating the animal and helping it stay afloat.

Weaving through the water at speeds up to 10 miles per hour and diving as deep as 100 feet, sea otters swim with the ease of fish, but they're not fast enough to escape their natural enemies, killer whales and sharks. Vast populations of sea otters once lived in kelp beds along the northern Pacific coast until man proved to be their worst enemy.

Hunters virtually exterminated the species for its lustrous, brown-black fur. In 1911 Russia, Japan, Great Britain and the United States signed a treaty protecting them.

The sea otter has reoccupied about one-fifth of its original range, reestablishing colonies in California, western Alaska and near the Commander and Kurile islands. Slowly, but in steadily increasing numbers, the bewhiskered sea otter is reclaiming its place in the Pacific ecosystem.

through town, offers fishing. Other recreational opportunities in the area include camping, hiking and skiing.

Dunsmuir Chamber of Commerce: 4118 Pine St., Dunsmuir, CA 96025; phone (530) 235-2177.

CASTLE CRAGS STATE PARK lies 6 mi. s. off I-5. The granite crags tower more than 4,000 feet over the nearby Sacramento River. In addition to its own 28 miles of hiking trails, the Pacific Crest Trail also passes through the park. Camping is available. Pets must be leashed. Park open daily 7:30 a.m.-10 p.m. Day use fee $4 per private vehicle; over 62, $3 per private vehicle. Phone (530) 235-2684, or ReserveAmerica at (800) 444-7275 for camping reservations. *See Recreation Chart and the AAA California & Nevada CampBook.*

DURHAM (D-3) pop. 5,220, elev. 158′

BARRY R. KIRSHNER WILDLIFE FOUNDATION is on Laura Ln. behind Durham Park. Dedicated to educating the public about the importance of wildlife and their habitats, the foundation is home to a variety of endangered, non-releasable and exotic animals, including many species of cats, such as lions, tigers, leopards and bobcats. Hands-on interaction with the animals is encouraged. Guided tours are available by appointment. Daily 9-5. Donations. Reservations are required. Phone (530) 345-1700.

EARLIMART (H-4) pop. 6,583, elev. 283′

COLONEL ALLENSWORTH STATE HISTORIC PARK, 7 mi. w. on CR J22, was the only California town founded, financed and governed by African-Americans. Founded in 1908 as an agricultural community, it flourished until a declining and unpredictable water supply, the Great Depression and the manpower drain of World War II lead to its gradual demise. Allensworth offers a visitor center, a picnic area and a campground.

Allow 2 hours minimum. Park daily dawn-dusk. Visitor center open when staffing is available; closed major holidays. Guided tours are available by advance arrangements. Admission $3 per private vehicle, senior citizens $2 per private vehicle. Phone (661) 849-3433.

ELDORADO NATIONAL FOREST

Elevations in the forest range from 3,382 ft. in the foothills to 9,983 ft. at Pyramid Peak. Refer to AAA maps for additional elevation information.

Bounded on the west by the Mother Lode Country and on the east by Lake Tahoe, Eldorado National Forest encompasses 676,780 acres in the rugged, lake-strewn Sierra Nevada. US 50 and SR 88 provide access to most of the forest's recreational facilities. Carson Pass Highway (SR 88) is a 58-mile scenic route through the forest.

Although the forest is most popular in spring and summer, three downhill ski areas and trails for cross-country skiing and snowmobiling attract winter visitors as well. Segments of the Pacific Crest National Scenic Trail pass through the forest; snow renders some sections impassable until mid-June or July. Hikers wishing to camp on the trail should obtain campfire permits. Permits also are required for day use and overnight stays in the Desolation Wilderness and Mokelumne Wilderness.

Designated routes for off-road vehicles are outlined on a Vehicle Travel Plan Map. For information contact Eldorado National Forest Visitor Center, 3070 Camino Heights Dr., Camino, CA 95709; phone (530) 644-6048. *See Recreation Chart and the AAA California & Nevada CampBook.*

EUREKA (B-1) pop. 26,128, elev. 44′

The chief port between San Francisco Bay and the Columbia River, Eureka is a lumbering, industrial and commercial city on Humboldt Bay. Such ornate Victorian dwellings as Carson Mansion at 2nd and M streets reflect the days of the lumber barons. Fort Humboldt, where Ulysses S. Grant was stationed 1853-54, is now a state historic park housing exhibits about local Native American cultures and past methods of logging.

The renovated 19th-century Old Town consists of specialty shops, restaurants, art galleries and studios.

Humboldt Bay also is an important fishing port, boasting catches of crab, salmon, shrimp, albacore and bottom fish. Fishing fleets dock just across the Samoa Bridge at Woodley Island Marina, where a copper-clad redwood statue of a fisherman commemorates fishermen lost at sea. Humboldt Bay Maritime Museum, 423 First St., displays marine artifacts and early photographs of the area; phone (707) 444-9440.

Eureka/Humboldt County Convention and Visitors Bureau: 1034 Second St., Eureka, CA 95501; phone (707) 443-5097 or (800) 346-3482.

Self-guiding tours: A map of a driving tour that passes 100 vintage residences is available from the Greater Eureka Chamber of Commerce, 2112 Broadway, Eureka, CA 95501-2189; phone (707) 442-3738 or (800) 356-6381.

BLUE OX MILLWORKS SCHOOL AND HISTORIC PARK is at 1 X St., 4 blks. n. of US 101. In this Victorian millwork shop visitors can learn about boatbuilding and the craftsmanship of late 19th-century woodworking in general. Among the vintage tools are those of a blacksmith; a ceramics kiln and an old printing press also can be seen. A re-creation of a logging skid camp is on the grounds.

Visitors may watch the artisans at work via a self-guiding tour. Casual dress and low-heeled shoes are advised. Mon.-Sat. 9-5. Admission $7.50; over 64, $6.50; ages 6-12, $3.50. Phone (707) 444-3437 or (800) 248-4259.

CLARKE HISTORICAL MUSEUM, 240 E St., displays Native American artifacts, antique weapons and exhibits about regional and natural history. The museum also has a significant collection of northwestern California Native American basketry, ceremonial regalia and stone artifacts from the Yurok, Karuk, Hupa and Wiyot tribes. Allow 1 hour minimum. Tues.-Sat. 11-4; closed Jan. 1, Thanksgiving and Dec. 25. Donations. Phone (707) 443-1947.

HUMBOLDT BAY HARBOUR CRUISE leaves from the foot of C St. The MV *Madaket*, an original 1910 ferry, takes visitors on a 75-minute narrated history cruise around Humboldt Bay. Bring a sweater or jacket. Holiday brunch cruises and cocktail cruises also are available. Harbor cruise departs Wed.-Sat. at 1, 2:30 and 4, Sun. and Tues. at 1 and 2:30, May-Oct. Harbor cruise $12.50; over 54 and ages 13-17, $10.50; ages 5-12, $6.50. Phone (707) 445-1910.

THE MORRIS GRAVES MUSEUM OF ART is at 636 F St. Named for noted 20th-century Northwest artist and Humboldt County resident Morris Graves, the museum features many of Graves' works in its seven galleries. Also included are a sculpture garden and changing exhibits. Thurs.-Sun. noon-5; closed major holidays. Free. Phone (707) 442-0278.

SAMOA COOKHOUSE MUSEUM off US 101 across the Samoa Bridge at 79 Cookhouse Ln., was established in the late 1800s as a large lumber camp chowhouse. The museum and dining rooms contain equipment, utensils and memorabilia from the lumber and logging industry. Food is available. Mon.-Sat. 7-3:30 and 5-10, Sun. 7 a.m.-10 p.m., Memorial Day weekend-Labor Day; Mon.-Sat. 7-3:30 and 5-9, Sun. 7 a.m.-9 p.m. (Thanksgiving noon-8 and Dec. 24 7 a.m.-3 p.m.), rest of year. Closed Dec. 25. Free. Phone (707) 442-1659.

SEQUOIA PARK AND ZOO, Glatt and W sts., contains a 52-acre grove of redwoods more than a century old, a formal flower garden, duck pond, zoo, bear grotto, playground and deer and African nyala and llama paddocks. Picnic facilities are available. Park open daily 10-7, May-Sept.; 10-dusk, rest of year. Zoo open Tues.-Sun. 10-7, May-Sept; 10-5, rest of year. Petting zoo open Fri.-Sun. 11-3:30, mid-June through Labor Day. Donations. Phone (707) 442-6552.

FAIRFIELD (C-9) pop. 96,178, elev. 15′

Founded in 1903, Fairfield sits southeast of the Vaca Mountains. Major industries sustaining Fairfield include agriculture, manufacturing and the military.

Travis Air Museum, on Travis Air Force Base, has planes, photographs, uniforms and memorabilia detailing base history. Access to the base is limited; phone (707) 424-5605 in advance to determine whether security restrictions allow visitors.

Fairfield-Suisun Chamber of Commerce: 1111 Webster St., Fairfield, CA 94533; phone (707) 425-4625.

Shopping areas: Westfield Shoppingtown Solano, off I-80 at junction Travis Boulevard and Pennsylvania Avenue, houses JCPenney, Macy's, Mervyn's and Sears.

ANHEUSER-BUSCH FAIRFIELD BREWERY TOUR, 3101 Busch Dr., details the brewing process via a 1-hour guided tour of the brewery. A videodisc also is shown. Tours are given on the hour Mon.-Sat. 10-4, June-Aug.; Tues.-Sat. 10-4, rest of year. Free. Under 5 are not allowed on the production floor (the last 5 minutes of the tour). Phone (707) 429-7595.

JELLY BELLY FACTORY TOUR is offered at the Herman Goelitz Candy Co. at 2400 N. Watney Way. The company offers 40-minute guided tours of its jelly bean-making facilities. Visitors can see the entire process which includes pouring and curing the jelly centers, coating the centers with a candy shell and polishing and seasoning the jelly beans before they are packaged.

Allow 30 minutes minimum. Tour are given daily 9-5; closed Jan. 1, Easter, Thanksgiving and Dec. 25. Last tour departs 30 minutes before closing. Schedule may vary; phone ahead. Since production takes place Mon.-Fri., tours Sat.-Sun. are by video presentation. Free. Phone (707) 428-2838 or (800) 522-3267.

SCANDIA FAMILY CENTER—
see Suisun City p. 175.

FALL RIVER MILLS (B-3)
pop. 648, elev. 3,291′

FORT CROOK MUSEUM, Fort Crook Museum Rd., features American Indian artifacts, photographs and items from the late 1800s to the early 1900s, a dugout canoe and a 360-degree view. Adjacent are a turn-of-the-20th-century schoolhouse, a barn housing a 1911 Wichita Flat-Bed Motorstage, an 1860 log cabin, a jailhouse, a working blacksmith shop and the James Showcase building. Genealogical records are available. Allow 30 minutes minimum. Tues.-Sun. noon-4, May-Oct. Donations. Phone (530) 336-5110.

FELTON (G-2) pop. 1,051, elev. 286′

One of the tallest covered bridges in the United States—and the only one made of redwood—can be found in Felton. The city lies on a scenic stretch of SR 9 that extends from Los Gatos to Santa Cruz.

San Lorenzo Valley Chamber of Commerce: P.O. Box 67, Felton, CA 95018-0067; phone (831) 335-2764.

ROARING CAMP & BIG TREES NARROW GAUGE RAILROAD, 1 mi. s.e. on Graham Hill Rd., runs south from Roaring Camp Station through the redwoods of the Santa Cruz Mountains. Late 19th- and early 20th-century steam locomotives pull open-air and covered passenger cars along a 6-mile,

75-minute round-trip route as the conductor recounts area history. A barbecue lunch is offered on summer weekends.

Departures daily at 11, 12:15, 1:30 and 3, mid-June to late Aug.; Mon.-Fri. at 11, Sat.-Sun. at 11, 12:15, 1:30 and 3, late Aug.-Sept. 30; Mon.-Fri. at 11, Sat.-Sun. at 11, 12:15 and 2, Apr. 1 to mid-June and Oct. 1-late Nov.; Sat.-Sun. at 11, 12:15 and 2 (also Jan. 1 and Dec. 26-31), rest of year. Closed Dec. 25. Schedule may vary; phone ahead. Fare $17; ages 3-12, $12. Parking $5 per private vehicle. AX, DS, MC, VI. Phone (831) 335-4400.

Santa Cruz, Big Trees & Pacific Railway departs Roaring Camp Station for a 3-hour round-trip excursion to the Santa Cruz Beach Boardwalk *(see attraction listing in Santa Cruz p. 167)*. Mid-20th-century passenger coaches and open-air excursion cars travel through Henry Cowell Redwoods State Park and along the San Lorenzo River gorge. Conductors point out scenic highlights and provide information about the line's history—the railway was established in 1875.

Departures daily at 10:30 and 2:30, mid-June to late Aug.; Sat.-Sun. at 10:30 and 2:30, early May to mid-June and late Aug.-Oct. 31. Schedule may vary; phone ahead. Fare $19; ages 3-12, $15. Parking $5 per private vehicle. AX, DS, MC, VI. Phone (831) 335-4400.

FERNDALE (C-1) pop. 1,382, elev. 30'

Ferndale was settled in 1852 by Vermonters Seth and Stephen Shaw, but it was Danish pioneers who established the town's dairying industry in the 1850s, producing the butter that Ferndale has been identified with ever since. The houses that the Danish and Portuguese dairymen built, known as "butterfat palaces," reflect the town's past and present. Fern Cottage, 3 miles west on Ocean Avenue, features 19th-century items. The village is a state historical landmark; it plays host to a December Christmas gala.

Ferndale Repertory Theatre offers eight productions each year, including contemporary American, musical and classic plays; phone (707) 786-5483 for schedule and ticket information.

Ferndale Chamber of Commerce: P.O. Box 325, Ferndale, CA 95536-0325; phone (707) 786-4477.

Self-guiding tours: A souvenir newspaper detailing walking and driving tours can be obtained at various shops on Main Street.

FERNDALE MUSEUM, Third and Shaw sts., features period rooms, a smithy, a seismograph, farm and logging equipment, microfilmed newspapers dating from 1878 and cemetery records. Tues.-Sat. 11-4, Sun. 1-4, June-Sept.; Wed.-Sat. 11-4, Sun. 1-4, Feb.-May and Oct.-Dec. Admission $1; ages 6-16, 50c. Phone (707) 786-4466.

FISH CAMP (F-5) elev. 4,990′

SAVE **YOSEMITE MOUNTAIN-SUGAR PINE RAILROAD** is 2 mi. s. on SR 41. The scenic narrow-gauge railroad offers 4-mile excursions through Sierra National Forest aboard authentic steam-powered trains or gas-powered railcars. A Moonlight Special journey with barbecue dinner and entertainment also is available.

The narrow-gauge train runs daily mid-Mar. through Oct. 31 and some fall and winter holidays. Departure times for the Logger steam train vary, Apr.-Oct.; phone for schedule. Jenny Railcars operate daily every half-hour 9-3, mid-Mar. through Oct. 31, except when the steam train is running; phone for limited winter schedule. Moonlight Special runs Wed. and Sat. evenings during the summer; reservations are recommended. Steam train $14; ages 3-12, $7. Rail cars $10; ages 3-12, $5. Moonlite Special $37.50; ages 3-12, $21. MC, VI. Phone (559) 683-7273. *See ad p. 204 & p. 821.*

FOLSOM (E-3) pop. 51,884, elev. 218′

A gold-mining town dating from the 1860s, Folsom retains much of its historic character. Many restored houses and buildings of that era line Sutter Street; they include the Wells Fargo Office—the terminus of the Pony Express.

The old Southern Pacific Depot, 200 Wool St., now houses the chamber of commerce. A Southern Pacific railcar, boxcar and caboose are displayed. Alongside the cars is the 1868 Ashland Freight Depot, said to be the oldest standing station west of the Mississippi River.

A self-guiding tour at Gekkeikan Sake provides visitors with an understanding of the steps taken in the sake brewing process. The facility, at 1136 Sibley St., also has a koi pond and a small Japanese garden in addition to tastings of its products; phone (916) 985-3111 for information.

Folsom City Park and Zoo, behind the city hall complex on Natoma Street, has picnic facilities, a children's play area, a railway and a small zoo. Two miles north of town is the massive granite Folsom State Prison. A museum contains displays of photographs and other items that describe the prison's history. An arts and gift shop at the main gate has items crafted by inmates; sales contribute to trust funds for the creators upon their release.

Folsom Chamber of Commerce: 200 Wool St., Folsom, CA 95630; phone (916) 985-2698 or (800) 377-1414.

Shopping areas: Folsom Premium Outlets, 13000 Folsom Blvd., has more than 80 factory-direct and specialty stores.

FOLSOM POWERHOUSE STATE HISTORIC PARK, on the American River at the foot of Riley St., performed the first long-distance transmission of hydroelectric power to Sacramento in 1895. Now a national landmark as well as a state park, it is part of Folsom Lake State Recreation Area *(see Recreation Chart and the AAA California & Nevada CampBook).*

Wed.-Sun. noon-4; closed major holidays. Tours of powerhouse and dam free. Parking $2. Phone (916) 985-4843 or (916) 988-0205 to arrange powerhouse tours, (916) 989-7275 for dam tours or (916) 988-1707 for additional information.

FORESTHILL (D-3) pop. 1,791, elev. 3,225′

RECREATIONAL ACTIVITIES

White-water Rafting

- SAVE **All-Outdoors Whitewater Rafting** departs from the Rafters parking lot e. of the Starlite Cafe on Foresthill Rd. Write 1250 Pine St., Suite 103, Walnut Creek, CA 94596. Daily Apr.-Oct. Phone (925) 932-8993 or (800) 247-2387.

FORT BRAGG—*see Wine Country p. 192.*

FORTUNA (B-1) pop. 10,497, elev. 51′

Established in 1875 as Springville, after the numerous springs in the surrounding hills, Fortuna was renamed Slide and finally, Fortuna by its "fortunate" citizens. The Redwood Empire surrounds the town.

Fortuna Chamber of Commerce: 735 14th St., P.O. Box 797, Fortuna, CA 95540; phone (707) 725-3959.

CHAPMAN'S GEM AND MINERAL SHOP AND MUSEUM, 4 mi. s. off US 101, has displays of fossils, gems, minerals, petrified wood and American Indian artifacts. Allow 30 minutes minimum. Mon.-Sat. 10-5, Sun. 11-5; closed Easter and Dec. 25. Donations. Phone (707) 725-4732.

THE FORTUNA DEPOT MUSEUM, e. of US 101 in Rohner Park, presents local history exhibits in a restored 1893 Northwestern-Pacific depot. Included are displays about fishing, logging, railroading and barbed wire. Allow 30 minutes minimum. Daily noon-4:30, June-Aug.; Thurs.-Sun. noon-4:30, rest of year. Free. Phone (707) 725-7645.

FREMONT (E-9) pop. 203,413, elev. 53′

Fremont was created in 1956 by the incorporation of five southeastern San Francisco Bay communities and their adjacent agricultural lands.

Spanish priests and native Ohlones founded a mission in this area in 1797. Reputedly, pioneer John Fremont, for whom the city is named, was so taken with the mission that he offered to buy the adjacent property for his house. The gold rush transformed the mission-based trade and agricultural center into a boisterous supply stop for miners. The use of salt in extracting silver from the Comstock Lode stimulated salt production along San Francisco Bay.

By the 1800s artesian springs had turned Fremont into a resort area. It was a motion picture location as well; Essanay Studio began a 4-year production stint in 1912, and Charlie Chaplin filmed "The Tramp" in 1915. Traces of the past provide a backdrop for the futuristic city hall that overlooks Lake Elizabeth and Central Park.

Fremont Chamber of Commerce: 39488 Stevenson Pl., Suite 100, Fremont, CA 94539; phone (510) 795-2244.

ARDENWOOD HISTORIC FARM, on Ardenwood/Newark Blvd., .2 mi. n. of SR 84, is a living-history project depicting farm life from the 1870s to the 1920s. The complex contains the Patterson house, a farmyard, gardens, period shops, a picnic area and farm animals. Haywagon and horse-drawn rail car rides as well as 40-minute guided house tours are available. The farm is open for Christmas tours in early December.

Tues.-Sun. 10-4; closed Thanksgiving and Dec. 25. Last admission 1 hour before closing. Admission Thurs.-Fri. and Sun. $5; over 61 and ages 4-17, $3.50 (includes house tour, grounds and rides). Admission Tues.-Wed. and Sat. $1; ages 4-17, 50c (rides not open Tues.-Wed. and Sat.). House tour on Sat. $3; ages 4-12, $2. Additional admission is charged during events. AX, DC, DS, MC, VI. Phone (510) 796-0663, or (510) 791-4196 for information about house tours, or (510) 797-5621 for picnic reservations.

CENTRAL PARK AT LAKE ELIZABETH, 40000 Paseo Padre Pkwy., includes a waterfowl refuge; lake; bicycling and jogging trails; a skate park; basketball court; and sailboat, kayak, canoe and paddleboat rentals. A golf driving range and tennis courts are available. Picnicking is permitted. Park open daily dawn-10 p.m. Visitor center daily 8-5. Free. Nonmotorized boat launch fee $5. Phone (510) 790-5540 or (510) 790-5541.

COYOTE HILLS REGIONAL PARK is at 8000 Patterson Ranch Rd. The park is a 966-acre wildlife sanctuary containing 2,400-year-old American Indian shell mounds and a reconstructed Indian village. The park also has more than 40 miles of hiking, bicycling and jogging trails; a museum; a visitor center; a boardwalk through a freshwater marsh; picnic facilities; a butterfly garden; and weekend nature programs.

Park open daily 8-dusk. Visitor center and museum open Tues.-Sun. 9:30-5; closed Thanksgiving and Dec. 25. Day-use fee $4 per private vehicle. Leashed dogs are permitted; fee $1. Phone (510) 795-9385.

GEM **DON EDWARDS SAN FRANCISCO BAY NATIONAL WILDLIFE REFUGE,** on Marshlands Rd., protects 20,000 acres for migratory birds using the Pacific flyway and for the endangered species of San Francisco Bay. A visitor center overlooking Dumbarton Bridge has an observation deck and dioramas depicting area wildlife; weekend interpretive walks are offered. Several self-guiding trails are accessible from the visitor center.

To protect nesting birds, the road to a fishin pier, 2.5 miles from the center, is closed to automo bile traffic April through August; a weekend shutt service is available during this time. Wildlife view ing is best October through April. Trails daily 8-8 Apr.-Oct.; 7-6, rest of year. Center open Tues.-Su 10-5. Free. Phone (510) 792-0222.

GEM **MISSION SAN JOSE CHAPEL AND MU SEUM,** 43300 Mission Blvd., was founde in 1797 by Father Fermin Francisco de La suen. The original adobe structure was destroyed b an 1868 earthquake. The interior of the recon structed church, based on church inventories fro the 1830s, is unusually elegant, containing cryst chandeliers, murals, religious paintings and a gol leaf altar. Several statues, the baptismal font an the mission bells remain from the original structure

The mission contains a small museum, whic displays old paintings, photographs, mission perio artifacts and exhibits about the Ohlone Indians an the mission restoration. Daily 10-5; closed Jan. 1 Easter, Thanksgiving and Dec. 25. Donations Phone (510) 657-1797.

FRESNO (G-4) pop. 427,652, elev. 294′

More than a million acres in the San Joaquin Valley are irrigated; on this land grow the grapes oranges and cotton that make Fresno County one o the nation's agricultural leaders. More turkeys are raised in this area than anywhere else in the country.

Guided tours of SAVE Kearney Mansion Museum, 7160 W. Kearney Blvd. in Kearney Park, are offered Saturday and Sunday and feature many original furnishings and wallcoverings; phone (559) 441-0862. Also of historical interest is the 1889 Meux Home Museum, 1007 R St. at Tulare. Guided tours are offered weekends; phone (559) 233-8007.

Fresno Convention & Visitors Bureau: 848 M St., 3rd floor, Fresno, CA 93721; phone (559) 233-0836 or (800) 788-0836.

Self-guiding tours: Blossom Trail is a scenic 63-mile self-guiding tour encompassing vineyards, orchards and historical points of interest. The trail is a profusion of almond, apricot, peach, plum and nectarine blossoms from late February through March. A map of the trail is available from the convention and visitors bureau.

FORESTIERE UNDERGROUND GARDENS is .3 mi. e. off SR 99 Shaw Ave. exit at 5021 W. Shaw Ave. It took Sicilian immigrant Baldasare Forestiere 40 years to create this underground retreat by hand, beginning in the early 1900s. Subterranean rooms, passageways, gardens, patios and courtyards with fruit trees and exotic plants are connected by tunnels and lit by skylights. The arches and stonework resemble the catacombs in Rome, Italy. The underground complex also contains a home and a chapel.

Allow 1 hour, 30 minutes minimum. Guided tours are given Wed.-Sun. at 10, noon and 2, Memorial Day weekend-Labor Day weekend; Sat.-Sun.

t noon and 2, Jan. 1-day before Memorial Day weekend and day after Labor Day weekend-Nov. 30. Schedule may vary; phone ahead. Fee $9; senior citizens $8; ages 13-19, $7; ages 4-12, $6. Under 4 are not permitted. Phone (559) 271-0734.

SAVE **FRESNO ART MUSEUM,** 2233 N. First St. in Radio Park, offers changing exhibits of national and international artists in eight galleries. Bonner Auditorium features the Fresno Public Theater and a series of lectures by artists. Allow 1 hour minimum. Tues.-Fri. 10-5, Sat.-Sun. noon-5, mid-Sept. through July 31; closed Jan. 1, Thanksgiving and Dec. 25. Admission $4, over 61 and students with ID $2, under 5 free; free to all Tues. Phone (559) 441-4221.

FRESNO METROPOLITAN MUSEUM OF ART, HISTORY AND SCIENCE, 1555 Van Ness Ave., features an Asian art collection and the Salzer collection of European and American still-life paintings. Also displayed is memorabilia from author William Saroyan, a native of Fresno. A science gallery has more than 40 interactive stations with exhibits geared to youngsters.

Allow 1 hour minimum. Tues.-Sun. 11-5 (also Thurs. 5-8); closed Jan. 1, Easter, July 4, Thanksgiving and Dec. 25. Last admission 30 minutes before closing. Admission $7; over 61 and students with ID $4; ages 3-12, $3; free to all first Thurs. of each month 5-8 (admission $1 other Thurs. nights). AX, MC, VI. Phone (559) 441-1444.

LEGION OF VALOR MUSEUM, near downtown at 2425 Fresno St. at "O" St., honors those who have received the nation's highest military honors—the Medal of Honor, the Distinguished Service Cross, the Navy Cross, and the Air Force Cross. Uniforms, weapons, war memorabilia dating as far back as the Civil War and military equipment also are exhibited. Allow 30 minutes minimum. Mon.-Sat. 10-3. Free. Phone (559) 498-0510.

ROEDING PARK, e. of US 99 via Olive Ave. or Belmont Ave. exits, features recreational facilities; Rotary Playland, which has a carousel, rides and a miniature railway; and the Japanese-American War Memorial. Allow 1 hour, 30 minutes minimum. Daily 7 a.m.-10 p.m. Park fee $1 per private vehicle. Phone (559) 621-2905.

SAVE **Chaffee Zoological Gardens,** on Olive Ave. in Roeding Park, houses mammals, birds and reptiles amid dense vegetation and winding pathways. The computerized Reptile House modifies temperature, humidity and light cycles to mimic the environment from which each species comes. South American plants and animals share the rain forest habitat.

Food is available. Daily 9-4, Feb.-Oct.; 10-3, rest of year. Admission $7; over 61 and ages 2-11, $3.50. Half-price to all Wed., Nov.-Feb. Park admission $1 per private vehicle. Under 14 must be with an adult. AX, DS, MC, VI. Phone (559) 498-2671.

Rotary Storyland, 890 W. Belmont Ave., is a children's attraction with a fairy-tale theme featuring a castle. Mon.-Fri. 10-4:30, Sat.-Sun. 10-5:30, June 1-Labor Day; Sat.-Sun. 10-5, day after Labor Day-Oct. 31; Sat.-Sun. 10-4, Feb.-May. Admission $4; over 62, $3.50; ages 3-12, $3. Phone (559) 264-2235.

FULTON—*see Wine Country p. 192.*

GEYSERVILLE—*see Wine Country p. 192.*

GILROY (G-3) pop. 41,464, elev. 194′

Renowned as the Garlic Capital of the World, garlic was first commercially grown by immigrant Japanese farmers following World War I. For Gilroy, this darling of cooks and bane of vampires has become a $100-million-a-year industry. During the annual Garlic Festival in July, this unignorable vegetable is found in every imaginable edible form throughout this southern Silicon Valley town.

A local wine industry fostered by Italian immigrant families has been productive on a small scale since the time of the ranchos. Ideal climatic and soil conditions also enabled the seed industry to blossom in Gilroy; Goldsmith Seeds, (408) 847-7333, offers guided tours.

Among the nearly 50 historic buildings along Monterey Street are the 1897 I.O.O.F. Children's Home for California, the 1906 old City Hall, and the 1910 Carnegie Library building which now houses the Gilroy Historical Museum. The museum, on the corner of Fifth and Church streets, displays historical photographs and artifacts of the area, and offers a pamphlet detailing a walking tour of the historic district; phone (408) 848-0470.

Gilroy Visitors Bureau: 7780 Monterey St., Gilroy, CA 95020; phone (408) 842-6436.

Self-guiding tours: The visitors bureau and the Gilroy Historical Museum offer a walking tour booklet for 50c.

Shopping areas: Gilroy Premium Outlets, 681 Leavesley Rd., has more than 145 shops, including those representing Ann Taylor, Eddie Bauer, Esprit, Farberware, Gap, London Fog, Polo Ralph Lauren and Royal Doulton. Gilroy's downtown historic district, a five-block area along Monterey Street, tempts bargain hunters with antique shops.

BONFANTE GARDENS FAMILY THEME PARK is w. on SR 152 (Hecker Pass Hwy. W.), just past Burchell Rd., following signs. This 28-acre theme park centered around trees and horticulture has 19 rides and 21 attractions, including a roller coaster, a rock maze, a 1927 carousel, antique car rides, pitch and win games, educational areas and extensive theme gardens. Also featured is a group of 19 unusual trees known as circus trees; these are trees that have been grafted together to form interesting shapes.

Food is available. Sun.-Fri. 10-7, Sat. 10-8, late June-late Aug. and Labor Day weekend; Mon.-Thurs. 11-5, Fri.-Sun. 10-7, early June-late June; Sat.-Sun. 11-5, day after Labor Day-Oct. 31; schedule varies mid-Apr. to early June. Admission $29.95; over 64 and ages 3-6, $21.95. Parking $7. AX, MC, VI. Phone (408) 840-7100. *See color ad p. 139.*

GLEN ELLEN—*see Wine Country p. 193.*

GOLDEN GATE NATIONAL RECREATION AREA—

see San Francisco p. 157.

GRASS VALLEY (D-3)

pop. 10,922, elev. 2,420′

In 1850 George Knight stubbed his toe on a piece of quartz laced with gold and put Grass Valley on the map. Aided by advanced mining techniques that first were developed and used in this region, Grass Valley ultimately became the richest gold-mining town in California. Unlike most gold-rush towns, Grass Valley achieved prosperity that outlasted its mining industry. Agriculture, high-tech manufacturing and tourism now anchor the economy.

Grass Valley-Nevada County Chamber of Commerce: 248 Mill St., Grass Valley, CA 95945-6783; phone (530) 273-4667, or (800) 655-4667 in Calif.

EMPIRE MINE STATE HISTORIC PARK, 1 mi. e. of SR 49 at 10791 E. Empire St., produced nearly 6 million ounces of gold during its operation. The park has 10 miles of hiking trails and a mine with 367 miles of passageways. Restored buildings include the owner's cottage, clubhouse, a smithy, a hoist house and a machine shop.

Free guided tours of the cottage and the mine yard are offered. Living-history tours, with guides in period garb, are conducted weekends in summer.

Picnic facilities are in the parking area; food is not permitted inside the park. Allow 2 hours minimum. Park open daily 9-6, May-Aug.; 10-5, rest of year. Closed Jan. 1, Thanksgiving and Dec. 25. Cottage and mine yard tours are given daily Mar.-Dec.; Sat.-Sun., rest of year. Hours vary; phone ahead. Admission $2, under 17 free. Phone (530) 273-8522 to verify summer opening time. *See Recreation Chart.*

NORTH STAR MINING MUSEUM, on Allison Ranch Rd. at the s. end of Mill St., houses the three-story Pelton wheel, a type of water wheel used for hydropneumatic power; an assay room; a smithy; a stamp mill; and a dynamite-packing machine. The museum features one of the few operating Cornish pumps in the country. A collection of gold samples also is shown. Picnicking is permitted. Daily 10-5, May 1-Oct. 15. Donations. Phone (530) 273-4255.

GROVELAND (F-4) elev. 2,846′

In its formative years, the gold-boom town went through a pair of unpleasant names—Savage's Diggings and Garrotte—before its citizens agreed on a more placid one, Groveland.

GROVELAND YOSEMITE GATEWAY MUSEUM is at 18990 Main St., next to Wayside Park in the same building as the county library. Changing exhibits in the museum depict area life since the beginning of the gold mining era in 1849. A theater features programs about local history and pioneer families. Allow 1 hour minimum. Daily 1-4:30, Mar.-Oct.; Wed.-Mon. 1-4, rest of year. Closed Jan. 1, Thanksgiving and Dec. 25. Free. Phone (209) 962-0300.

RECREATIONAL ACTIVITIES

White-water Rafting

- SAVE **All-Outdoors Whitewater Rafting** departs from 8 mi. e. on SR 120. Write 1250 Pine St., Suite 103, Walnut Creek, CA 94596. Daily Apr.-Oct. Phone (925) 932-8993 or (800) 247-2387.
- **ARTA River Trips** has departure points on several rivers. Write 24000 Casa Loma Rd., Groveland, CA 95321. Daily Apr.-Oct. Phone (209) 962-7873 or (800) 323-2782.
- **Whitewater Voyages** meets at varying departure points. Write 5225 San Pablo Dam Rd., El Sobrante, CA 94803 Daily Apr.-Sept. (depending upon water flow). Reservations office open all year. Phone (510) 222-5994 or (800) 488-7238.

GUALALA—*see Wine Country p. 193.*

GUERNEVILLE—*see Wine Country p. 193.*

HALF MOON BAY—*see San Francisco p. 158.*

HANFORD (H-4) pop. 41,686, elev. 248′

Founded in 1882 in the San Joaquin Valley, Hanford was named for a Southern Pacific Railroad paymaster who became a power in the community. He paid millions of dollars of workers' wages in gold. Hanford once claimed one of the largest Chinese communities in California. In China Alley, a remnant of that community, are a Taoist Temple and a landmark restaurant operated by the descendants of the family who started the business in 1883.

Courthouse Square, the center of historic Hanford, includes a renovated carousel and many specialty shops.

Hanford Visitor Agency: 200 Santa Fe Ave., Suite D, Hanford, CA 93230; phone (559) 582-5024.

Self-guiding tours: Maps for tours of historic Hanford are available from the visitor agency.

HANFORD CARNEGIE MUSEUM, 109 E. Eighth St., is in a Romanesque-style library built in 1905.

Among items depicting Hanford and Kings County history are clothes, including a dress that belonged to Amelia Earhart, furniture and photographs. Guided tours are available by appointment. Allow 30 minutes minimum. Tues.-Fri. noon-3, Sat. noon-4. Admission $2, students $1. Phone (559) 584-1367.

HAYWARD (D-9) pop. 140,030, elev. 111′

HAYWARD AREA HISTORICAL SOCIETY MUSEUM, 22701 Main St., is a former post office that houses memorabilia of early Hayward and southern Alameda County. Photographs, maps and tools are displayed. Changing exhibits also are presented. Allow 1 hour minimum. Tues.-Sat. 11-4; closed holidays. Admission $1; ages 6-12, 50c. Phone (510) 581-0223.

JAPANESE GARDENS, 22325 N. Third St. off Crescent Ave., encompasses 3.3 acres of Japanese and native California trees, rocks and plants arranged in the traditional Japanese style. The area includes a small pond containing koi and goldfish, and a gazebo. Daily 8:30-4. Free. Phone (510) 881-6700.

HEALDSBURG—*see Wine Country p. 193.*

HEARST CASTLE—*see San Simeon p. 165.*

HILMAR-IRWIN (F-3)

HILMAR CHEESE CO. is at 9001 N. Lander Ave. (SR 165). The company's visitor center has viewing windows through which guests can watch the cheese-making and packaging process. More than a million pounds of cheddar and Monterey Jack cheese are produced here each day. Hands-on exhibits allow young visitors to dress like a cheese-maker; see a model of a cow; learn about nutrition; and view a choice of five videotapes.

Picnicking is permitted. Food is available. Allow 30 minutes minimum. Daily 8-6; closed major holidays. Guided tours are given Sat.-Sun. at 11 and 1. Free. Phone (209) 656-1196 or (800) 577-5772.

HOOPA (B-1) elev. 300′

HOOPA TRIBAL MUSEUM, on SR 96 in Hoopa Shopping Center, displays baskets, jewelry, tools, a redwood canoe, hats and ceremonial clothing still used in Hoopa tribal events. Tours to the ceremonial grounds and villages may be arranged by appointment. Displayed are collections of new and restored baskets. Allow 1 hour minimum. Tues.-Fri. 8-5, Sat. 10-4. Donations. Phone (530) 625-4110.

HOPLAND—*see Wine Country p. 193.*

HUMBOLDT-TOIYABE NATIONAL FOREST—*see Nevada p. 226.*

INDEPENDENCE (G-6) pop. 574, elev. 3,925′

EASTERN CALIFORNIA MUSEUM, 3 blks. w. of the courthouse at 155 Grant St., illustrates area history, anthropology, botany and geology. Highlights include an extensive Native American basketry exhibit and antique farm and mining equipment. Of interest is the exhibit dealing with the Manzanar World War II Relocation Camp for Japanese-Americans. The camp, now Manzanar National Historic Site, is 5 miles south of Independence off US-395.

Museum open Wed.-Mon. 10-4; closed Jan. 1, Easter, Thanksgiving and Dec. 25. Donations. Phone (760) 878-0364 or (760) 878-0258.

INYO NATIONAL FOREST

Elevations in the forest range from 3,700 ft. in Owens Valley to 14,494 ft. at the summit of Mount Whitney. Refer to AAA maps for additional elevation information.

Inyo National Forest parallels US 6 and US 395 for 165 miles between the eastern California towns of Inyokern and Lee Vining. The forest contains Mount Whitney—at 14,494 feet, the highest point in the contiguous United States—as well as portions of the Pacific Crest Trail and the John Muir Trail. The eastern escarpment of the Sierra Nevada and the Ancient Bristlecone Pine Forest *(see attraction listing p. 64)* in the White Mountains rise to 14,246 feet between US 6 and the Nevada border; the forest has a visitor center open to the public in the summer. Almost all of the Sierra's highest peaks are visible from US 395.

Vehicle travel is restricted to Devils Postpile National Monument *(see place listing p. 70)* and the Reds Meadow area of the forest: Only vehicles with camping permits are allowed beyond the Minaret Vista turnoff between 7:30 a.m. and 5:30 p.m., June 1-Labor Day.

All others are required to use a shuttle bus that operates during the restricted times. The 2-hour round trip makes 10 stops, including the Devils Postpile ranger station, where trails lead to recreation areas. Tickets, schedule and fare information are available at Mammoth Mountain Inn. Parking is free.

Mammoth and June mountains have ski areas that are popular in winter, while mountain biking, hiking, camping, fishing and backpacking are the main summertime diversions. Chairlift rides to the top of Mammoth Mountain provide outstanding views and access to hiking trails. Chairlift rides are available daily 9-5, mid-June to mid-Nov. (weather and wind permitting). Fare $16; senior citizens $12; ages 7-12, $8. Phone (760) 934-2571 or (800) 626-6684.

Minaret Vista, at 9,175 feet, offers a sweeping view of Ritter Range. A store and cafe, as well as saddle and pack horses, are available at Reds Meadow. Permits are required for all overnight trips in wilderness areas. Contact the Inyo National Forest.

Roads throughout the remainder of the forest provide scenic drives. An interagency visitor center is south of Lone Pine at the junction of US 395 and SR 136. Center open daily 8-5:50 in summer; 8-4:50 rest of year. Closed Jan. 1, Thanksgiving and Dec. 24-25. Phone (760) 876-6222. For additional information the Forest Supervisor's office is at 351 Pacu Lane, Suite 200, Bishop, CA 93514; phone (760) 873-2400. For camping permits phone (760) 873-2483. *See Recreation Chart and the AAA California & Nevada CampBook.*

BISHOP CREEK CANYON is 9 mi. w. of Bishop on SR 168. Lined by 1,000-foot granite cliffs, the canyon is a popular fishing area late April through October. Developed campgrounds, hiking trails and food are available. Phone (760) 873-8405

JUNE LAKE LOOP RECREATION AREA off SR 158, covers approximately 60,000 acres and contains portions of the Pacific Crest and John Muir trails, Mono Basin National Forest Scenic Area *(see place listing p. 96)* and June Mountain Winter Sports Area. Mono Craters, Lee Vining Canyon and Tioga Pass are nearby. A visitor center is on US 395 one-half mile north of Lee Vining. Visitor center open daily 9-4:30, otherwise varies. Free. Phone (760) 873-2408.

JACKSON (E-3) pop. 3,989, elev. 1,200′

Many buildings along Jackson's narrow streets were destroyed by fire in 1862 and subsequently were rebuilt. North of town are several mine headframes; one shaft is approximately 6,000 feet deep. Kennedy Gold Mine Tours allows visitors to see the buildings and other structures that make up a mining site closed in 1942. The tours are offered weekends, March through October; phone (209) 223-9542.

Amador County Chamber of Commerce: 125 Peek St., Suite B, P.O. Box 596, Jackson, CA 95642; phone (209) 223-0350 or (800) 649-4988.

AMADOR COUNTY MUSEUM, 225 Church St., is in the 1859 home built by one of Jackson's first settlers. Its 15 rooms contain artifacts depicting the county's history from its earliest period through the present. The museum grounds feature flower and herb gardens. Also displayed is a working scale model of Kennedy Mine. Allow 30 minutes minimum. Wed.-Sun. 10-4. Mine model tours are offered Sat.-Sun. on the hour 11-3. Donations. Mine model tours $2. Phone (209) 223-6386.

JAMESTOWN (F-3) pop. 3,017, elev. 1,405′

The first gold discovery in Tuolumne County was made near Jamestown in 1848. "Jimtown," as it once was called, has served as a backdrop for such movies as "High Noon" and "Butch Cassidy and the Sundance Kid." Several buildings in town date to the 1870s.

JIMTOWN 1849 GOLD MINING CAMP, 18170 Main St., is a living-history re-creation. Among the camp's buildings is a cabin said to be once inhabited by Mark Twain. Gold panning is available. Allow 1 hour minimum. Daily 10-5. Admission free. Gold panning $15-$140. MC, VI. Phone (209) 984-4653 or (800) 596-0009.

RAILTOWN 1897 STATE HISTORIC PARK, on 5th Ave., comprises 26 acres which include an interpretive center, a roundhouse, station, trains and yard facilities. Sierra Railway Co. began operating from Jamestown in 1897, carrying passengers and freight throughout the gold-mining area. Visitors can observe the maintenance and restoration of the railroad equipment. A videotape presentation and seasonal train excursions are available.

Picnicking is permitted. Tours of the roundhouse and shop are given daily 9:30-4:30; closed Jan. 1, Thanksgiving and Dec. 25. Train rides are given Sat.-Sun. and holidays on the hour 11-3, early Apr.-Oct. 31. Park admission free. Tours $2; ages 6-12, $1. Train $6; ages 6-12, $3. AX, DC, DS, MC, VI. Phone (209) 984-3953.

JENNER—*see Wine Country p. 194.*

JOHNSVILLE (D-3) pop. 21

Johnsville was established in 1872 on the flat at the base of Eureka Peak. Two fires destroyed many of the town's original structures. Ski racing, which originated nearby, is among the popular recreational pursuits.

PLUMAS-EUREKA STATE PARK AND MUSEUM is 4 mi. w. on CR A14 at 310 Johnsville Rd. The museum, originally a miners' bunkhouse, has a collection of photographs, tools and memorabilia of mining days. A partially restored stamp mill is featured. Recreational activities available include hiking, fishing and skiing.

Allow 30 minutes minimum. Park open daily 24 hours, early May to mid-Oct. Museum open daily 8-4:30, early June to mid-Oct.; schedule may vary according to staff availability, rest of year. Closed Jan. 1, Thanksgiving and Dec. 25. Park admission free. Museum $2, under 17 free. Phone (530) 836-2380. *See Recreation Chart.*

KELSEYVILLE—*see Wine Country p. 194.*

KENWOOD—*see Wine Country p. 194.*

KERNVILLE (H-5) pop. 1,736, elev. 2,251′

Kernville is a high desert lake resort community that began as a gold town in 1860. The Onyx Store, believed to be the oldest continuously operating store in the state, has been selling its wares since 1861. Today visitors enjoy the biodiversity that Kernville and Kern Valley offer and its concomitant variety of recreational opportunities such as fishing, golfing, snowmobiling, skiing, rock climbing, panning for gold and camping.

Kernville Chamber of Commerce: 11447 Kernville Rd., P.O. Box 397, Kernville, CA 93238-0397; phone (760) 376-2629.

KERN RIVER FISH HATCHERY, 14400 Sierra Way (SR 99), produces trout for release into the wild. In addition to the usual aquariums and interpretive displays, visitors can view and feed llamas which are used as pack animals. Picnicking is permitted. Open Thurs.-Sun. 10-4; closed major holidays. Free. Phone (760) 376-2846 or (760) 376-8719.

KERN VALLEY MUSEUM, 49 Big Blue Rd., exhibits American Indian, gold mining, ranching, farming and lumber industry artifacts, as well as providing information about the many 1930s-50s Western motion pictures filmed in the Kern River Valley. Thurs.-Sun. 10-4; closed holidays. Free. Phone (760) 376-6683.

RECREATIONAL ACTIVITIES

White-water Rafting

- SAVE **Chuck Richards' Whitewater Inc.**, departs from various points. Write Box W.W. Whitewater, Lake Isabella, CA 93240. Daily May-Sept. Phone (760) 379-4444 or (800) 624-5950.
- **Kern River Tours** departs from various points. Write P.O. Box 3444, Lake Isabella, CA 93240. Daily Mar. 15-Sept. 15. Phone (760) 379-4616 or (800) 844-7238.
- **Kern River's Eagle Rafting** departs Kernville. Write 610 N. Brady, Ridgecrest, CA 93555. Daily Apr.-July or Aug. (depending upon water level); phone to verify schedule. Phone (760) 376-3648 or (800) 375-7395.
- **Whitewater Voyages Kern Outdoor Center**, 11252 Kernville Rd., Kernville, CA 93238. Daily Apr.-Aug. (depending upon water flow). Reservations office open all year. Phone (510) 222-5994 or (800) 488-7238.

KING CITY (H-3) pop. 11,094, elev. 330'

King City takes its name from pioneer Charles H. King who bought 13,000 acres of land in 1884 and founded King Ranch. The town was incorporated in 1911. Agriculture sustains King City; products range from broccoli, lettuce and wine grapes to barley and beans.

King City Chamber of Commerce & Agriculture: 200 Broadway, Suite 40, King City, CA 93930; phone (831) 385-3814.

MISSION SAN ANTONIO DE PADUA is 29 mi. s.w. in Fort Hunter Liggett via Jolon Rd. Founded by Father Junípero Serra on July 14, 1771, it is one of the largest restored and rebuilt missions. Original remains include the well, gristmill, tannery and parts of the aqueduct system. A museum exhibits American Indian artifacts. The mission's annual fiesta is held the second Sunday in June. Daily 8-6, June-Sept.; 8-5, rest of year. Closed Dec. 25. Donations. Phone (831) 385-4478.

MONTEREY COUNTY AGRICULTURAL AND RURAL LIFE MUSEUM, in San Lorenzo County Park at 1160 Broadway, features a barn with more than 20 exhibits tracing the evolution of agriculture in Monterey County. Other buildings include the restored 1898 Spreckels farmhouse, a smithy, an 1887 schoolhouse, and the original 1903 King City train depot.

Guided tours are available by appointment. Picnicking is permitted. Allow 30 minutes minimum. Main exhibit barn open daily 10-4; closed Jan. 1, Thanksgiving, day after Thanksgiving and Dec. 25. Historic buildings open Sat.-Sun. (and July 4) 12:30-3:30, Apr.-Oct. or by appointment. Donations. Parking Mon.-Fri. $3, Sat.-Sun. and holidays $5; parking Mon.-Fri. free for senior citizens. Phone (831) 385-8020.

KINGSBURG (G-5) pop. 9,199, elev. 297′

Kingsburg was established in 1875 by the Southern Pacific Railroad. Swedish emigrants influenced the town's customs and architecture. Today Kingsburg is known as a Swedish village, with many restored buildings dating back to the early 1900s and featuring steep wood-shingled roofs, dormer windows and half-timbers.

Kingsburg District Chamber of Commerce: 1475 Draper St., Kingsburg, CA 93631; phone (559) 897-1111.

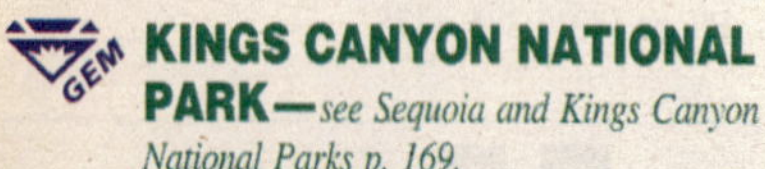

KINGS CANYON NATIONAL PARK—*see Sequoia and Kings Canyon National Parks p. 169.*

KLAMATH (B-1) pop. 651, elev. 29′

Above the Klamath River on aptly named Bear Bridge, two golden bears welcome visitors to the city. Originally gray, the bears were painted in the late 1950s or early 1960s by a group of residents who set out to give the town a face-lift. State government officials repeatedly painted the bears gray to expunge what they had believed was the work of vandals. Upon realizing that the citizens were behind the golden bears, the government relented.

TREES OF MYSTERY, 4 mi. n. on US 101, is a forest of redwoods containing a number of oddly formed trees, some nearly 2,000 years old and 300 feet tall. The Trail of Tall Tales has chainsaw-carved redwood sculptures depicting the legend of Paul Bunyan and other loggers' stories. A museum has artifacts and crafts from American Indian tribes. The SkyTrail, a six-passenger gondola, transports guests through the forest canopy.

Complex open daily 8-8, June 1 to mid-Sept.; 9-5, mid-Sept. through Easter; 9-6, rest of year. Closed Thanksgiving and Dec. 25. Gondola and trail open daily 8-6:30, June 1 to mid-Sept.; 9-3:30, mid-Sept. through Easter; 9-4:30, rest of year. Museum open daily 8-7:30, June 1 to mid-Sept.; 9-4:30, mid-Sept. through Easter; 9-5:30, rest of year. Hours may vary; phone ahead. Admission $12; over 59, $10; ages 4-10, $5; family rates available for more than four people. AX, DC, DS, MC, VI. Phone (707) 482-2251 or (800) 638-3389. *See ad p. 117.*

KLAMATH NATIONAL FOREST

Elevations in the forest range from 523 ft. at Somes Bar to 8,563 ft. at Caribou Mountain. Refer to AAA maps for additional elevation information.

Covering about 1,726,000 acres in northern California with a small segment also extending into Oregon, Klamath National Forest is characterized by rugged forested ridges, rushing rivers and high mountain lakes and streams. Much of this scenic area is included in the Marble Mountain Wilderness and Trinity Alps Wilderness, which are accessible only by trail. Vehicular traffic is prohibited in wilderness areas. Hunting, fishing and white-water rafting opportunities are available.

Good fishing spots abound, and the forest is a prime location for anglers in search of steelhead and salmon. Trout fishing is popular in creeks and high mountain lakes. Outdoor enthusiasts also can camp, hike, horseback ride, ski and snowmobile.

Klamath River Highway and forest roads and trails provide access to the region. For information contact the Forest Supervisor, Klamath National Forest, 1312 Fairlane Rd., Yreka, CA 96097; phone (530) 842-6131. *See Recreation Chart and the AAA California & Nevada CampBook.*

KLAMATH NATIONAL FOREST INTERPRETIVE MUSEUM, 1312 Fairlane Rd. in Yreka, has exhibits about national forests and how they are managed. Displays include dioramas about timber and wildlife preservation, geology, soils, mining and fire prevention. Another exhibit honors Hallie Daggett, the first female forest-fire lookout in the country. Mon.-Fri. 8-4:30; closed holidays. Free. Phone (530) 841-4484 or (530) 842-6131.

RECREATIONAL ACTIVITIES

White-water Rafting

- **Marble Mountain Ranch/Access to Adventure Whitewater Rafting** departs from various points. Write 92520 Hwy. 96, Somes Bar, CA 95568. Other activities are available. Daily Apr.-Oct. Phone (530) 469-3322 or (800) 552-6284.

KNIGHTS FERRY (F-3) elev. 200′

Dating from the town's Gold Rush days, a 330-foot-long covered bridge crosses the Stanislaus River to the north of Knights Ferry. Said to be the longest covered bridge west of the Mississippi River, the structure was completed in 1863, replacing an earlier bridge destroyed by a flood. The covered bridge is open to foot traffic only.

RECREATIONAL ACTIVITIES

White-water Rafting

- **Beyond Limits Adventures** departs from Stanislaus River Park, 14842 Orange Blossom Rd. Write P.O. Box 215, Riverbank, CA 95367. Daily Apr.-Sept. Phone (209) 869-6060 or (800) 234-7238.

LAKEPORT—*see Wine Country p. 194.*

Lake Tahoe Area

Lake Tahoe, which holds enough water to cover the entire state of California to a depth of 14 inches, was named "big water" by the Washoe Indians. Their legend says Lake Tahoe was created when an Evil Spirit was in pursuit of an innocent American Indian. Attempting to aid the Indian, the Great Spirit gave him a branch of leaves; each leaf dropped would produce a body of water that the Evil Spirit would have to circumvent. But during the chase, the Indian dropped the whole branch in fright—creating Lake Tahoe.

It is said that the water in Lake Tahoe is 97 percent pure, nearly the same as distilled water. Remarkably clear and deep blue, the lake is 22 miles long and 12 miles wide; about one-third lies in Nevada. Its average depth is 989 feet; the deepest point is 1,645 feet, making Tahoe the third deepest lake in North America. The first 12 feet below the surface can warm to 68 F in summer, while depths below 700 feet remain a constant 39 F.

The "lake in the sky," at an elevation of 6,229 feet, lies in a valley between the main Sierra Nevada and an eastern offshoot, the Carson Range. The mountains rise more than 4,000 feet above the resort-lined shore. Most of the surrounding area is within the Eldorado *(see place listing p. 72)*, Humboldt-Toiyabe *(see place listing p. 226)* and Tahoe *(see place listing p. 176)* national forests.

Immigrants and miners were lured to the rugged Sierras by tales of fortunes made during the California gold rush. The discovery of the Comstock Lode increased traffic and depleted the Tahoe Basin's natural resources to a dangerously low level. Between 1860 and 1890 lumber was needed for fuel and to support the web of mines constructed beneath Virginia City. The decline of the Comstock Lode was likely the saving grace for Tahoe's forests.

By the early 1900s the lake had become a retreat for the rich. Elaborate hotels began dotting the shores. Roads were paved during the 1920s and '30s, and Lake Tahoe no longer was available only to the wealthy. As development continued in the 1950s, roads were plowed during the winter, enabling year-round residence. In 1968 the Tahoe Regional Planning Agency was established, ensuring environmentally responsible development for years to come.

Snow skiing enthusiasts flock to Lake Tahoe each year to enjoy their favorite winter sport. Well-known Tahoe ski areas include Heavenly, Alpine Meadows, Sierra Tahoe and Squaw Valley.

The Tahoe Rim Trail, a 165-mile loop running along the ridges and peaks surrounding Lake Tahoe, offers both

Squaw Valley ski lodge / © Gibson Stock Photography

© Vic Bider / Index Stock

a splendid panorama of the lake, California's High Sierra and Nevada's Great Basin as well as providing a scenic path for hiking, horseback riding and snowshoeing. Mountain biking is allowed in certain areas. Phone the Tahoe Rim Trail Association, (775) 298-0012, for additional information.

The headquarters of the U.S. Forest Service-Lake Tahoe Basin Management Unit provides year-round information about forest activities, including camping and hiking in summer and cross-country skiing in winter. The headquarters is open Mon.-Fri. 8-4:30 (weather permitting). For information contact Lake Tahoe Basin Management Unit, 35 College Dr., South Lake Tahoe, CA 96150; phone (530) 543-2600, or TTY (530) 541-4036.

The U.S. Forest Visitor Center on SR 89 between Camp Richardson and Emerald Bay offers free orientation programs; a Stream Profile Chamber, an underground viewing chamber allowing an underwater cross-section view of Taylor Creek; and a 10-minute, quarter-mile walking trail. Open daily 8-4:30, mid-June through Sept. 30; Sat.-Sun. 8-4:30, Memorial Day weekend to mid-June (weather permitting); phone (530) 543-2674. Wilderness permits for hiking are available adjacent to the visitor center; phone (530) 543-2736.

The lake has two distinct approaches: the North Shore via I-80 and the South Shore via US 50. The North Shore has a more rural atmosphere with small lakeside towns, while South Shore places such as South Lake Tahoe and Stateline, Nev., are more metropolitan and have casinos, more shopping areas and restaurants.

Both roads that surround the lake are two-lane highways providing excellent views and interesting drives. SR 89 on the west side around Emerald Bay occasionally is closed in times of heavy snow. Road information is available from CalTrans; phone (800) 427-7623 in California. Rotary phone users and those outside California should phone CalTrans at (916) 445-1534.

OLYMPIC VALLEY (D-4)

SQUAW VALLEY CABLE CAR, 1960 Squaw Valley Rd., provides a full aerial view of Lake Tahoe and Squaw Valley, site of the 1960 Winter Olympics and a year-round recreation area. Passengers are taken to the trailhead of the Pacific Crest Trail, where activities such as ice skating and swimming are offered. Activities packages are available.

Daily 9:40 a.m.-10 p.m., late June to mid-Oct.; 9-9, mid-Nov. to mid-May (weather permitting). Fare $17; over 64, $14; ages 4-12, $5. Fee charged for activities. AX, DS, MC, VI. Phone (530) 583-6985 to verify schedule and prices.

(continued on p. 87)

Destination Lake Tahoe Area

Lake Tahoe, in a high valley between the Sierra Nevada and the Carson mountain ranges, is a premier winter sports area.

The scenery is spectacular. In the summer, pockets of shade-sheltered snow look down on wildflower strewn meadows, and conifers extend to the sapphire lake's shores.

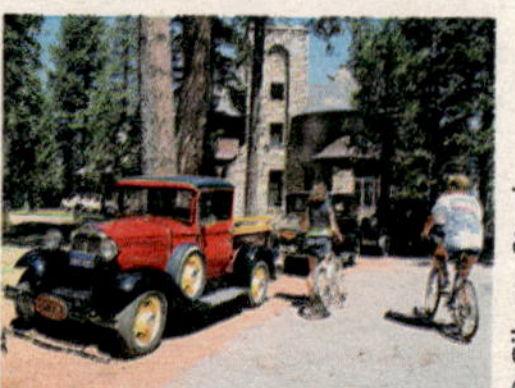

© Gibson Stock Photography

Hellman-Ehrman Mansion, Tahoma. At one time similar cars undoubtedly graced the driveway of this grand Lake Tahoe summer retreat, built in 1902 for a wealthy San Francisco family. (See listing page 88)

Gatekeeper's Museum & Marion Steinbach Indian Basket Museum, Tahoe City. Formerly the residence of Lake Tahoe's dam attendant, the reconstructed log cabin now contains historical artifacts and a basket collection representing more than 85 tribes. (See listing page 88)

© Gibson Stock Photography

© Gibson Stock Photography

Vikingsholm, South Lake Tahoe. This Scandinavian-style summer "castle" on Emerald Bay is accessible by boat or a steep hiking trail. (See listing page 87)

Donner Memorial State Park, Truckee. A monument to the westward-bound pioneers marks the spot of one of the fateful Donner Party's cabins. (See listing page 88)

© Robert Holmes / Corbis

Places included in this AAA Destination Area:

SOUTH LAKE TAHOE (E-4)
pop. 23,609, elev. 6,254'

As its name implies, the city of South Lake Tahoe sits at the southern tip of the lake. Myriad summer and winter recreational activities abound, courtesy of the lake and nearby mountains.

South Lake Tahoe Chamber of Commerce: 3066 Lake Tahoe Blvd., South Lake Tahoe, CA 96150; phone (530) 541-5255.[11]

D.L. BLISS STATE PARK, on the w. shore of Lake Tahoe between Meeks and Emerald bays, occupies 1,830 acres of forested mountain terrain. A sandy beach is at Rubicon Point, 2 miles north of Emerald Bay. Naturalist programs are available in the summer (staff permitting). Allow 3 hours minimum. Daily 8 a.m.-dusk, mid-June to mid-Sept. Day use fee $4 per private vehicle. Phone (530) 525-7277. *See Recreation Chart.*

THE GONDOLA AT HEAVENLY is at US 50 and Stateline. Eight-passenger gondola cabins transport riders 2.4 miles up the mountain, providing scenic views of Lake Tahoe and the Sierra Nevada range. A mid-station viewing deck is placed around a granite outcropping, while hiking trails can be accessed from the top of the mountain at an elevation of 9,123 feet.

Allow 1 hour minimum. Mon.-Fri. 10-dusk, Sat.-Sun. 9-dusk, Memorial Day weekend-Labor Day weekend; daily 10-7, day after Labor Day weekend-late Oct.; Mon.-Fri. 9-4, Sat.-Sun. 8:30-4, early May-day before Memorial Day weekend. Fare $20; over 65 and ages 13-17, $18; ages 6-12, $12. AX, DS, MC, VI. Phone (775) 586-7000.

LAKE TAHOE ADVENTURES departs from the w. shore of Lake Tahoe at Meeks Bay on SR 89. Guided tours of the Rubicon Trail, 9,150-foot Genoa Peak, the High Sierra and the high desert of Nevada are available by ATVs, Jeeps and Hummers. Guides drive and show you the sights in Jeeps and Hummers, or guests, led by guides, drive themselves in ATVs. Snowmobile tours also are available.

Daily 9-4. Fee for 2-hour Jeep tour begins at $49 (two person minimum); under 12, $25. Two-hour Hummer tour $75 (three adult minimum); under 12, $35. One-hour ATV tour $49, 2-hour tour $95; longer tours are available. Reservations are required. AX, DS, MC, VI. Phone (530) 577-2940 or (800) 865-4679.

TALLAC HISTORIC SITE is on SR 89 n. of Camp Richardson. Elaborate summer estates were built at this site by California's newly rich during the late 19th and early 20th centuries. Three estates on the shore of Lake Tahoe are open to visitors. Some buildings are being restored. Highlights include a visitor center and an art gallery with artists at work. Concerts, plays and classic films are presented daily during the summer.

Guided tours are available. Picnicking is permitted. Site open daily dawn-dusk, Memorial Day weekend-third weekend in Sept. Artists in Action program and art exhibits daily 11-3, May-Oct. Visitor center open daily 8-5, mid-June through Labor Day; Sat.-Sun. 8-5, Memorial Day weekend to mid-June. Free. Phone the historic site at (530) 541-5227, (530) 543-2600 year-round to verify schedule, (530) 543-2674 for the visitor center, or (530) 542-4166 for Artists in Action.

VIKINGSHOLM, at the s.w. end of Emerald Bay, is a 38-room reproduction of a ninth-century Norse fortress, built as a summer home in 1929 in a setting of pines and cedars. It is accessible by boat or by a steep 1-mile hiking trail; park in the Harvey West parking lot by SR 89 at Emerald Bay. Allow 1 hour minimum. Guided tours every half-hour daily 10-4, mid-June through Labor Day; Sat.-Sun. 10-4, Memorial Day weekend to mid-June. Admission $3, under 17 free. Phone (530) 525-7277.

TAHOE CITY (D-4) elev. 6,302′

GATEKEEPER'S MUSEUM & MARION STEINBACH INDIAN BASKET MUSEUM is 1 blk. s. on SR 89. The museum is a reconstruction of the original gatekeeper's cabin, which served as the residence for the dam attendant. Included are historic photographs and displays about Lake Tahoe, natural history and pioneers. The handiwork of more than 85 tribes is represented in the 800 baskets featured in the basket museum.

Picnicking is permitted. Allow 30 minutes minimum. Daily 11-5, June 15-Labor Day; Wed.-Sun. 11-5, May 1-June 14 and day after Labor Day-Oct. 1. Admission $2, under 13 free. Phone (530) 583-1762.

TAHOMA (E-4)

HELLMAN-EHRMAN MANSION is 1 mi. s. on SR 89 in Sugar Pine Point State Park. The two-story Queen Anne-style house was built in 1902 and is a fine example of a Tahoe summer house. Exhibits pertaining to the Hellman-Ehrman family can be seen on the second floor. On the grounds are an 1870 cabin, a nature center and nature trails.

Park interpretive specialists conduct guided 45-minute tours of the mansion daily on the hour 11-4, July 1-Labor Day. Park entrance fee $4 per private vehicle. Tour $3, under 17 free. Phone (530) 525-7982.

TRUCKEE (D-4) pop. 13,864, elev. 5,820′

Truckee, named for Washoe Indian Chief Trokay, was once a lawless lumber and railroad town, and much of its Old West charm remains; 19th-century false-front buildings and a train that runs through the middle of town can be seen.

Truckee-Donner Chamber of Commerce: 10065 Donner Pass Rd., Truckee, CA 96161; phone (530) 587-2757.

Self-guiding tours: Maps outlining a self-guiding walking tour of the historic downtown district are available from the chamber of commerce.

DONNER MEMORIAL STATE PARK, 2 mi. w. on Donner Pass Rd., is near the site where the Donner party was stranded trying to cross the Sierra Nevada Mountains during the severe winter of 1846-47. As members of the 89-person party died, some of those remaining resorted to cannibalism; only 47

were rescued. The Emigrant Trail Museum has exhibits about railroad and natural history, logging and immigrants. The Pioneer Monument is near the museum.

Park open daily 8-dusk, Memorial Day weekend to mid-Oct. Museum open daily 9-4. Video presented daily at 9:15 and then on the hour 10 until closing. Closed Jan. 1, Thanksgiving and Dec. 25. Day use fee $4 per private vehicle. Museum admission $2, under 16 free. Phone (530) 582-7892. *See Recreation Chart and the AAA California & Nevada CampBook.*

Nearby Nevada

INCLINE VILLAGE pop. 9,952, elev. 6,420′

PONDEROSA RANCH, 100 Ponderosa Ranch Rd. off SR 28, is a Western-style theme park featuring the original Cartwright ranch house from the television show "Bonanza." Park highlights include a saloon, museum, kiddyland, playground, petting farm and mystery mine. A pancake breakfast is the culmination of a morning haywagon ride. Two-hour guided ATV tours of the ranch are available.

Allow 2 hours minimum. Daily 9:30-6, mid-Apr. through Oct. 31. Breakfast hay rides 8-9:30, Memorial Day weekend-Labor Day. Last admission 1 hour before closing. Admission $11.50; ages 5-11, $6.50. Breakfast (includes ranch admission) $13.50; ages 6-11, $8.50; ages 4-5, $3. AX, DS, MC, VI. Phone (775) 831-0691.

ZEPHYR COVE pop. 1,649

THE MS *DIXIE II*, departing from the Zephyr Cove Resort, is a paddlewheeler offering 2-hour narrated sightseeing cruises of Emerald Bay and Lake Tahoe. Breakfast, brunch and dinner dance cruises also are available. Sightseeing cruises depart daily at 11 and 2, mid-June to mid-Oct.; at 1, rest of year. Sightseeing cruise fare $25; ages 3-11, $8. Reservations are recommended. AX, DS, MC, VI. Phone (775) 589-4906 or (800) 238-2463. *See color ad.*

WOODWIND SAILING CRUISES departs from the Zephyr Cove Resort on US 50. Sightseeing cruises aboard the 55-foot, glass-bottom catamaran *Woodwind II* take visitors along the Nevada shoreline of Lake Tahoe where the geological formation Cave Rock and views of the Sierra Nevada mountains can be seen. The boat offers both indoor and outdoor seating on the 1.75-hour trips. Other cruises also are available.

Allow 2 hours minimum. Cruises depart daily at 11:30, 1:30, 3:30 and 5:30 (weather permitting), mid-Apr. to mid-Oct. Fare $26; over 59, $23; ages 3-12, $12. Reservations are recommended. AX, DC, DS, MC, VI. Phone (775) 588-3000 or (888) 867-6394.

The previous listings were for the Lake Tahoe Area.
This page resumes the alphabetical listings of cities in Northern California.

LASSEN NATIONAL FOREST

Elevations in the forest range from 800 ft. near Butte Meadows to 8,172 ft. at West Prospect Peak. Refer to AAA maps for additional elevation information.

Covering approximately 1,375,000 acres surrounding Lassen Volcanic National Park, Lassen National Forest includes numerous lakes formed by ancient volcanic action.

Several highways, forest roads and trails afford access to the region. The Caribou, Thousand Lakes and Ishi wilderness areas allow backpacking. Campfire permits are required, except in campgrounds with developed facilities. Obtain permits in person at any Forest Service, Bureau of Land Management or California Department of Forestry Office. Hunting, fishing, cross-country skiing and snowmobiling are permitted.

Lake Almanor, one of the largest man-made bodies of water in California, and Eagle Lake, the second largest natural lake in California, offer fishing, sailing, water skiing and swimming. Eagle Lake and Hat Creek offer trout fishing. Recreation sites usually are open mid-May to mid-October (weather permitting); the season is shorter at higher elevations. For more information contact the Supervisor's Office, Lassen National Forest, 2550 Riverside Dr., Susanville, CA 96130; phone (530) 257-2151. *See Recreation Chart and the AAA California & Nevada CampBook.*

SUBWAY CAVE is off SR 89 about .1 mi. n. of SR 44. This lava tube winds 1,300 feet through a lava flow that covered the Hat Creek Valley nearly 20,000 years ago. Carry a jacket and a reliable lantern or flashlight while exploring the self-guiding interpretive trail through this cave. Free. Phone (530) 336-5521.

GEM LASSEN VOLCANIC NATIONAL PARK (C-3)

Elevations in the park range from 6,000 ft. at Warner Valley to 10,457 ft. at Lassen Peak. Refer to AAA maps for additional elevation information.

Accessible via SR 36, 9 miles east of Mineral, Lassen Volcanic National Park covers 106,000 acres in northeastern California where the Cascades join the Sierra Nevada. In addition to Lassen Peak (10,457 ft.) and Cinder Cone (6,907 ft.), the park boasts Prospect Peak (8,338 ft.) and Mount Harkness (8,045 ft.), two shield volcanoes topped by cinder cones with trails leading to their summits. Other features include smaller volcanoes and lava flows, fumaroles, boiling springs, boiling lakes and mudpots.

For a period of several thousand years Lassen Peak was quiescent; then in the spring of 1914 a series of relatively small eruptions began. After reaching its peak in 1915, the activity continued until about 1921.

A plug dome volcano, Lassen Peak once protruded from the north flank of ancestral Mount Tehama. This great stratovolcano was destroyed by glaciers, hydrothermal activity and erosion by Mill Creek and other water. Lassen Park Road winds around Lassen Peak, affording views of the volcano and evidence of its destructive might.

In the southern half of the park gurgling mudpots and roaring fumaroles contribute to the bizarre atmosphere. The eastern sector encompasses a splendid chain of lakes, extending from Juniper Lake at the northern base of Mount Harkness to Butte Lake near the eastern base of Prospect Peak.

General Information and Activities

Although the park is open all year, heavy snows render most sections inaccessible from late October to early June. Winter roads are maintained from the northern gate to the district ranger's office (about 1 mile) and from the southern gate to the winter sports area at Lassen Chalet, the hub of winter sports activity. Cross-country skiing is usually possible from early December to late spring. Mountain bikes are not permitted on trails in the park.

Some of the park's many lakes and streams contain trout. A state fishing license is required, and catch limits are posted. Wilderness permits issued by the park are required for back-country camping. Permits are available by mail; phone the park headquarters 2 weeks in advance. Gates are open 24 hours daily, but the hours they are attended vary. Motorists entering the park in summer when the station is unattended must obtain a permit before leaving.

Park headquarters is 1 mile west of Mineral on SR 36. Maps, information and bulletins can be obtained at the headquarters, Loomis Museum and the Southwest Information Station. Interpretive and evening programs, guided nature walks and self-guiding trails are available. The visitor center at the park headquarters in Mineral is open Mon.-Fri. 8-4:30; closed holidays. *See Recreation Chart and the AAA California & Nevada CampBook.*

Note: Stay on established trails at all times in boiling springs or steaming areas; small children should be kept under strict control. Ground crusts that appear safe can be dangerously thin.

ADMISSION to the park is $10 per private vehicle, or $5 per person by other means. Entrance fees are good for 7 days, with a receipt.

PETS are permitted in the park only if they are on a leash, crated or otherwise physically restrained at all times. Pets are not allowed on trails or in buildings.

ADDRESS inquiries to the Superintendent, Lassen Volcanic National Park, Box 100, Mineral, CA 96063-0100. Phone (530) 595-4444.

Points of Interest

BUMPASS HELL TRAIL, about .5 mi. beyond Emerald Lake, leads 1.5 mi. off the Lassen Park Road to Bumpass Hell, a large area of spectacular boiling springs, mudpots, boiling pools and other types of hydrothermal activity.

BUTTE LAKE is 6 mi. off SR 44 in the n.e. corner of the park. A marked nature trail with wayside exhibits leads to the Cinder Cone summit; interpretive leaflets are available at the trailhead.

CINDER CONE, accessible from a trail beginning at Butte Lake, is known for Fantastic Lava Beds and multicolored volcanic ash and cinders. It is possible that some lava flows occurred as recently as 1650.

LASSEN PARK ROAD, between the s. entrance and Manzanita Lake in the n.w. region, is a 30-mile drive. A road guide to points of interest along the route is available for a fee at the park's contact stations. Most of the road is impassable late Oct.-early June due to heavy snowfall.

Chaos Crags and Chaos Jumbles are 2 mi. s. from the n.w. boundary. The Chaos Crags are lava plugs believed to have been pushed up more than 1,000 years ago; subsequent rockfalls formed the Chaos Jumbles. The small coniferous trees in the Chaos Jumbles—some more than 300 years old—constitute the Dwarf Forest.

Devastated Area begins about 2.5 mi. n. of Summit Lake. It was stripped of all vegetation by hot blasts, avalanches and mudflows from the May 1915 eruptions of Lassen Peak. Natural reforestation is taking place. Another eruption remnant is Hot Rock, a large black lava rock near the north end of the area.

Diamond Peak is reached by Lassen Park Rd., which, from 2 mi. n. of the Sulphur Works, winds up the remains of old Mount Tehama. The road, which encompasses Diamond Peak, offers a glimpse of steam vents across the canyon in Little Hot Springs Valley.

Kings Creek Meadows (7,400 ft.) are 4.5 mi. n. from the summit. A trail leads 1.3 miles to beautiful Kings Creek Falls. Both the cascades and falls are visible from the left side of the creek downstream.

Loomis Museum, .5 mi. beyond the n.w. entrance station, has a visitor contact station where park information, exhibits, books, wilderness maps and assistance are available.

Sulphur Works Thermal Area, about 1 mi. n. of the s.w. entrance station, has steam vents and mudpots. Stay on the trails in these areas at all times. Ground that appears safe might be dangerously thin.

Summit Lake, 5 mi. n.e. of Kings Creek Meadows, has two lakeside campgrounds with trailer spaces. They are convenient to hiking, fishing and points of interest. Campfire programs several nights a week are available in summer.

LASSEN PEAK TRAIL leaves Lassen Park Rd. less than 1 mi. beyond Lake Helen and travels 2.5 miles to the top of the volcano. The round trip requires 4 to 5 hours.

WARNER VALLEY, in the s. part of the park, is reached by road from Chester or by trail from Summit Lake to Drakesbad. Marked trails lead to Boiling Springs Lake and Devils Kitchen, a large area of boiling pools and other volcanic features.

GEM LAVA BEDS NATIONAL MONUMENT (B-3)

In northeastern California, reachable from SR 139 south of Tulelake, Lava Beds National Monument was created from molten lava spewed centuries ago from Medicine Lake volcano. When the lava cooled, the monument's rugged terrain was formed. The 46,500-acre area is characterized by cinder cones, deep chasms and more than 450 lava tube caves of various sizes.

Some of the caves contain permanent ice. The Modoc Indians used the volcanic formations as fortifications 1872-73 during the only major Indian war fought in California. Visitors can explore a lava tube cave on their own or on a ranger-guided tour. Mushpot, a lighted cave, is accessible from the visitor center parking lot. Free-use flashlights for cave exploration are available at the visitor center.

Hiking trails, some as short as .75 mile in length, lead to other caves, pictographs and petroglyphs, the fire lookout, crater rims, overlooks and battlefield sites. The visitor center has trail brochures.

DID YOU KNOW

Because of budget considerations, the schedules and fees of all state-owned facilities are subject to change. Travelers are advised to phone ahead.

Camping is allowed, but no lodgings, supplies, gas or oil are available. Pets on leash are permitted in certain areas of the park, but not on the trails. The monument is open all year, and although there are no specified visiting hours, those planning to camp should arrive before 5 p.m. The geology and history of the area are interpreted at a visitor center.

Daily 8-6, June 15-Labor Day; 8-5, rest of year. Closed Thanksgiving and Dec. 25. Admission $10 per private vehicle; $5 per person arriving by other means. For more information contact the Supervisor's Office, Lava Beds National Monument, 1 Indian Well Headquarters, P.O. Box 867, Tulelake, CA 96134; phone (530) 667-2282, ext. 230. *See the AAA California & Nevada CampBook.*

LEE VINING (F-5) elev. 6,781′

Lee Vining is a center for recreational and scenic attractions around Mono Lake. Mono Lake County Park, 5 miles north off US 395, has a shady streamside picnic area and a boardwalk trail that winds through meadows to the lakeshore. Contact the information center for details about naturalist tours and canoe trips.

Mono Lake Committee Information Center and Bookstore: US 395, P.O. Box 29, Lee Vining, CA 93541; phone (760) 647-6595.

MONO LAKE TUFA STATE RESERVE is at South Tufa Area off SR 120, 5 mi. e. of US 395 in the Mono Basin National Forest Scenic Area *(see place listing p. 96)*. The combined state reserve and scenic area is a 48,000-acre tract that preserves tufa, a calcium-carbonate rock created by the interaction of freshwater springs under the lake with the alkaline lake waters. The lowering of the lake level due to stream diversion has exposed unusual tower formations. The Mono Basin Scenic Area Visitor Center features a free 20-minute movie.

Reserve open daily 24 hours. Visitor center open daily 9-4, May-Oct.; Fri.-Sun. 9-4, rest of the year. Free guided 90-minute tours of the reserve are given daily at 10, 1 and 6, July 1-Labor Day; at 1, day after Labor Day-Sept. 30; Sat.-Sun. at 1, rest of year. Bird walks are offered Fri. and Sun. mornings at 8, mid-June through Labor Day in Mono Lake County Park. Admission $3, under 19 free. Phone (760) 647-6331 for reserve information, or (760) 647-3044 for the visitor center. *See Recreation Chart.*

LEGGETT—*see Wine Country p. 194.*

LITTLE RIVER—*see Wine Country p. 194.*

LIVERMORE (F-3) pop. 73,345, elev. 486′

Livermore is the principal community in Livermore Valley, a scenic area with vineyards and cattle lands. Sycamore trees—some more than 2 centuries old—grow along the banks of the Arroyo del Valle.

Livermore Chamber of Commerce: 2157 First St., Livermore, CA 94550-4543; phone (925) 447-1606.

LAWRENCE LIVERMORE NATIONAL LABORATORY'S DISCOVERY CENTER, off Greenville Rd. about 2.2 mi. s. of I-580 at East Gate entrance, presents a broad-based display of the scientific technology developed at the laboratory and highlights the lab's research in defense, homeland security, biotechnology and new energy sources.

Allow 30 minutes minimum. Mon.-Fri. 1-4; closed holidays. Two-hour guided tours are given Tues. and Thurs. Tour reservations must be made at least 2 weeks in advance. Free. Under 18 are not permitted. Phone (925) 424-6575 for tour reservations.

WINERIES

- **Livermore Valley Cellars**, 1 mi. s. off SR 84 at 1508 Wetmore Rd. Daily 11:30-5. Phone (925) 447-1751.

- **Wente Vineyards**, 3 mi. s. off I-580 Vasco Rd. exit, then w. to 5565 Tesla Rd. Daily 11-4:30. Tours are given at 11, 1, 2 and 3. Phone (925) 456-2305.

LODI (E-3) pop. 56,999, elev. 52′

With more than 40 wineries nearby, Lodi is growing as an important wine-producing center. Nearby Lodi Lake Park offers water skiing, boating, swimming and hiking. Hill House Museum, 826 S. Church St., is one of the few Victorian houses in Lodi. The museum is open Sunday and by appointment; phone (209) 369-6073.

Lodi Conference & Visitor's Bureau: 2545 W. Turner Rd., Lodi, CA 95242; phone (209) 365-1195 or (800) 798-1810.

MICKE GROVE REGIONAL PARK, 11793 N. Micke Grove Rd., has picnic facilities, amusement rides, a Japanese garden, historical museum and zoo. Park open daily 8-dusk. Zoo open daily 10-5. Park admission per private vehicle Mon.-Fri. $2, Sat.-Sun. $4, holidays $5. Zoo admission $2; ages 6-17, $1. Phone (209) 331-7400.

San Joaquin County Historical Museum has permanent and changing exhibits about local history, agriculture, transportation and American Indian culture. Of interest is the Sunshine Trail, which recreates a trip across California from west to east. An enclosed garden contains native California plants and a waterfall.

Allow 2 hours minimum. Wed.-Sun. 10-3. Museum admission (in addition to park admission fee) $2; over 59 and ages 6-12, $1. Phone (209) 331-2055.

LONE PINE (G-6) pop. 1,655, elev. 3,733′

Many Western movies have been filmed among the Alabama Hills, a mass of weather-beaten rock bordering US 395 on the west side of Lone Pine.

Eastern Sierra Interagency Visitor Center, at US 395 and SR 136, has information and exhibits about

Inyo National Forest, Sequoia and Kings Canyon National Parks, Yosemite National Park, Death Valley National Park and Inyo and Mono counties recreation areas; phone (760) 876-6222. The center is open daily 8-4:50; closed Jan. 1, Thanksgiving, Dec. 24-25.

Vestiges of Manzanar are about 7 miles north off SR 395. This internment camp, the first of several established to hold Japanese-Americans during World War II, had more than 10,000 inhabitants at its peak population. While today little remains but stone entrance gates, some concrete foundations, a cemetery and roads in varying stages of disrepair, a restoration project is underway and will an interpretive center.

Lone Pine Chamber of Commerce: 128 S. Main St., P.O. Box 749, Lone Pine, CA 93545; phone (760) 876-4444.

MOUNT WHITNEY, 13 mi. w. on W. Whitney Portal Rd., rises to 14,496 feet, making it the highest mountain in the lower 48 states The summit is 11 miles by a strenuous trail from the end of Whitney Portal Road, which reaches the height of 8,360 ft. Wilderness permits are required year-round.

Day- and overnight-use quotas are in effect May through October; November-April wilderness permits are available at the Eastern Sierra Interagency Visitor Center. For details or permit reservations write Inyo National Forest Wilderness Reservation Service, 351 Pacu Ln., Suite 200, Bishop, CA 93514.

Mount Whitney Ranger Station in Lone Pine is open daily 8-5, late May to mid-Oct.; Mon.-Fri. 8-4:30, rest of year. Phone (760) 876-6200 for general information, or (760) 873-2483 for permits.

LOS ALTOS (E-8) pop. 27,693, elev. 165′

LOS ALTOS HISTORY MUSEUM is in the Civic Center complex behind the library at 51 S. San Antonio Rd. The museum's permanent exhibit follows area development from the days when the Ohlone Indians occupied the land to the present. Recorded sounds add realism to each display, which include information about the early ranchos, the apricot orchards prevalent in the early 20th century and an animated model train display depicting the city during the 1930s. Changing exhibits also are featured.

Picnicking is permitted. Allow 30 minutes minimum. Thurs.-Sun. noon-4; closed Jan. 1, July 4, Thanksgiving and Dec. 25. Free. Phone (650) 948-9427.

LOS BAÑOS (G-3) pop. 25,869, elev. 120′

The town is named for Los Baños Creek, once a popular bathing spot for missionaries. Cotton, rice and alfalfa crops were introduced to the town's hardy soil in the mid- to late 1800s. Agriculture remains the key industry.

Los Baños Chamber of Commerce: 503 J St., Los Baños, CA 93635; phone (209) 826-2495, or (800) 336-6354 in most states.

SAN LUIS DAM RESERVOIR, 12 mi. w. on SR 152, is an important link in the Central Valley Project and the California Water Project. Swimming, windsurfing, boating, camping and picnicking are permitted at San Luis Reservoir, San Luis Creek, Los Baños Detention Dam and O'Neill Forebay state recreation areas. Romero Visitors Center has a videotape program, telescopes and information about the projects.

Park open daily dawn-dusk (weather permitting). Visitor center open daily 9-5; closed Jan. 1, Thanksgiving and Dec. 25. Day use pass $4. Boating fee $4. Phone (209) 826-1196 for dam complex information or (209) 827-5353 for the visitor center.

LOS GATOS (G-2) pop. 28,592, elev. 385′

Los Gatos is guarded by two mountain ridges, El Sombroso (the shadowing one) and El Sereno (the night watchman). The town was founded about 1868 on a portion of an 1840 Spanish land grant. The original grant was known as *La Rinconada de los Gatos* (corner of the cats), a name derived from the many mountain lions and wildcats that inhabited the nearby hills.

By the early 1900s Los Gatos was a rural community supporting mostly orchards. The town was thrust into urbanization with the onset of World War II. Forbes Mill Museum at 75 Church St. has exhibits about local and regional history. Los Gatos is the northern terminus of a scenic 38-mile stretch of SR 17 to Santa Cruz.

Los Gatos Chamber of Commerce: 349 N. Santa Cruz Ave., Los Gatos, CA 95031; phone (408) 354-9300.

Shopping areas: Oldtown, on University Avenue, with its many restored buildings of Spanish and Victorian architecture, topiary trees and gardens, encompasses shops, restaurants and an outdoor amphitheater.

ART MUSEUM OF LOS GATOS, at W. Main St. and Tait Ave., has two stories of changing exhibits by area artists. Wed.-Sun. noon-4; closed holidays. Donations. Phone (408) 354-2646.

OAK MEADOW PARK/VASONA PARK are at University Ave. and Blossom Hill Rd. Vasona Lake County Park has a playground and fishing, picnicking and boating facilities; boat rentals are available *(see Recreation Chart)*. Oak Meadow Park has a playground, sports field, a 1910 English carousel and a lake stocked for fishing.

Daily 8 a.m.-dusk. Free. Parking $4 mid-June to mid-Sept. and Sat.-Sun., Mar. 1 to mid-June; free other days. Carousel fare $1 per ride, under 2 free. Phone (408) 399-5770 for Oak Meadow Park or (408) 356-2729 for Vasona Park.

Billy Jones Wildcat Railroad, in Oak Meadow Park, is a restored 1905 steam train, although a diesel train occasionally is featured. The scenic 1-mile trip passes over Los Gatos Creek and proceeds through Vasona Park. Train departs daily 10:30-4:30, mid-June through Labor Day; Sat.-Sun.

10:30-4:30, Nov. 1 to mid-Mar. (weather permitting). Fare $1.50 per ride, physically impaired and under 2 with paying adult free. Phone (408) 395-7433.

MAMMOTH LAKES (F-5)

pop. 7,093, elev. 7,860′

One of California's more popular four-season resorts, Mammoth Lakes provides access to the recreational facilities and points of interest in Inyo National Forest *(see place listing p. 79).*

Mammoth Lakes Visitors Bureau: on SR 203 in the center of town, P.O. Box 48, Mammoth Lakes, CA 93546; phone (760) 934-2712 or (888) 466-2666. *See ad p. 416.*

MAMMOTH LAKES AREA, 12 miles n. of Crowley Lake off US 395, encompasses 200,000 acres in east central California, and contains portions of Pacific Crest Trail, Ansel Adams Wilderness Area, John Muir Wilderness Area, Devils Postpile National Monument *(see place listing p. 70),* Mammoth Mountain Ski Area, Rainbow Falls, Mammoth City Historical Site, Mammoth Lakes Basin and geothermal springs. The area has facilities for fishing, boating, rock climbing, snowmobiling, cross-country and downhill skiing and hiking.

The Mammoth Lakes Visitor Center and Ranger Station on SR 203 at the entrance to town, is open daily 8-5; closed Jan. 1, Thanksgiving and Dec. 25 Visitor center free. Phone (760) 924-5500 for visitor center, or (800) 427-7623 for weather and road information.

MANTECA (F-3) pop. 49,258, elev. 38′

OAKWOOD LAKE RV CAMPGROUND/MANTECA WATERSLIDES is between I-5 and SR 99 at 874 E. Woodward. The water park features more than 30 water rides and a wading pool. A 75-acre lake adjoins a campground and picnic sites. Daily 10:30-6, mid-June through Labor Day; Sat.-Sun. 10:30-5, May 1 to mid-June and day after Labor Day-Sept. 30. Phone to verify schedule. All-inclusive pass $25, under 42 inches free. Admission only $15. Parking $6. DS, MC, VI. Phone (209) 239-9566 or (209) 239-2500.

MARIPOSA (F-4) pop. 1,373, elev. 1,953′

Originally called Logtown, Mariposa was renamed after the Spanish word for butterfly. Gold mining has been supplanted by the scenic riches of nearby Yosemite Valley, which draw thousands of visitors each year.

Mariposa County Visitors Bureau: 5158 Hwy. 140, P.O. Box 967, Mariposa, CA 95338; phone (866) 425-3366. *See color ad p. 206.*

CALIFORNIA STATE MINING AND MINERAL MUSEUM, 1.8 mi. s. on SR 49 at the county fairgrounds, contains a collection of minerals, gold, diamonds and other gems that reflect the wealth found in Mariposa mines. Benitoite, the California state gemstone, is displayed. Other exhibits include models of an assay office and stamp mill and a full-scale replica of a mine. The museum also features temporary exhibits of gem and mineral specimens from other institutions and private collections.

Allow 1 hour minimum. Daily 10-6, May-Sept.; Wed.-Mon. 10-4, rest of year. Hours may vary; phone ahead. Closed Thanksgiving and Dec. 25. Admission $2, under 17 free. Phone (209) 742-7625.

COURTHOUSE, 5088 Bullion St., was built in 1854 and is the oldest courthouse in the state still in use. Wooden pegs were used in the construction of the two-story white pine building; the second floor contains original furnishings. The old clock in the square clock tower was brought by way of Cape Horn, at the southern tip of South America. Guided tours are available by appointment. Daily 8-5, Memorial Day weekend-Labor Day; Mon.-Fri. 8-5, rest of year. Free. Phone (866) 425-3366, or (209) 966-3685 for guided tours.

MARIPOSA MUSEUM AND HISTORY CENTER INC., SR 140 at 12th and Jessie sts., contains a re-created 1850s street, including a five-stamp mill, horse-drawn vehicles and mining and printing equipment. Featured are replicas of a schoolroom, an American Indian village, a miner's cabin, a print shop, a sheriff's office, a saloon and an apothecary as well as the restored house of the 1860s county treasurer. Allow 1 hour minimum. Daily 10-4, Feb.-Dec. Donations. Phone (209) 966-2924.

MARKLEEVILLE (E-5) pop. 197, elev. 5,525′

ALPINE COUNTY HISTORICAL COMPLEX, .2 mi. w. of SR 89 at School and Montgomery sts., includes an 1882 schoolhouse and a jail that have been restored and furnished in period. A museum contains exhibits about mining, the history and culture of the Washoe Indians and the history of the Vaquero Camp (a vaquero is a cowboy or herder). Thurs.-Mon. 11-4, Memorial Day weekend-Oct. 31. Donations. Phone (530) 694-2317.

GROVER HOT SPRINGS STATE PARK is 4 mi. w. at the end of Hot Springs Rd. Known for its two pools filled with natural hot springs water, the 700-acre park also offers hiking and mountain biking trails and camping as well as cross-country skiing and snowshoeing in winter. One pool is kept at 102-104 F, the other at 75-85 F (depending on the season).

Picnicking is permitted. Park hours daily dawn-dusk; closed Jan. 1, Thanksgiving, Dec. 25 and for maintenance 2 weeks in late Sept. Pool operation varies; phone ahead for schedule. Park admission $4 per private vehicle. Fee for pool usage $3; under 17, $1. Phone (530) 694-2248. *See Recreation Chart and the AAA California & Nevada CampBook.*

MARTINEZ (C-9) pop. 35,866, elev. 23′

JOHN MUIR NATIONAL HISTORIC SITE, 4202 Alhambra Ave., was the residence of the conservationist and founder of the Sierra Club. His crusade for wilderness preservation aided in the establishment of national parks and forests. The 1882 house contains original furnishings. Visitors may tour the 17-room mansion and the surrounding orchards. A 30-minute videotape about Muir's life is shown. The two-story Martinez Adobe, built in 1848, also is on site.

Guided tours are available. Picnicking is permitted. Allow 1 hour, 30 minutes minimum. Wed.-Sun. 10-5; closed Jan. 1, Thanksgiving and Dec. 25. Schedule may vary; phone ahead. Videotape shown at 10, 11, noon, 1:30, 2:30 and 3:30. Admission $3, under 17 free when accompanied by an adult. Phone (925) 228-8860.

MARYSVILLE (D-3) pop. 12,268, elev. 63'

Central to Marysville is Ellis Lake, named for W.T. Ellis, a prosperous town merchant in the early 1900s. The boulevard along the shore testifies to the merchant's efforts to beautify the lake; a jogging/exercise course also circles the lake. Paddleboats are available seasonally.

Riverfront Park is beneath the 5th and 10th street bridges, which link Marysville and Yuba City. Recreational facilities include a boat-launching dock, picnic area, playgrounds, soccer fields, baseball fields and motorbike trails. The park also has a concert bowl with grassy slopes for seating.

Yuba-Sutter Chamber of Commerce: 429 10th St., P.O. Box 1429, Marysville, CA 95901; phone (530) 743-6501.

MENDOCINO—*see Wine Country p. 194.*

MENDOCINO NATIONAL FOREST

Elevations in the forest range from 1,000 ft. at Elk Creek to 8,110 ft. at the summit of Mount Linn. Refer to AAA maps for additional elevation information.

In the North Coast Mountain Range north of San Francisco, Mendocino National Forest encompasses nearly 886,048 acres. Hang gliding and motorcycling areas are available. Roads and trails afford access to scenic points. Many roads within the forest are unsurfaced; driving can be hazardous, especially in the dusty, dry months.

Yolla Bolly-Middle Eel Wilderness at the north end of the forest and Snow Mountain Wilderness in the south provide peaceful settings for horseback riding and hiking. Wilderness entry permits are not required, but users should sign the registry at trailheads.

Campfire permits are required in some areas; check with the Forest Supervisor, 420 E. Laurel St., Willows, CA 95988, or a district ranger. For recorded information phone (530) 934-2350, (530) 934-3316, or TTY (530) 934-7724. *See Recreation Chart and the AAA California & Nevada CampBook.*

MENLO PARK (E-8) pop. 30,785, elev. 70'

ALLIED ARTS GUILD, off SR 82 at the end of Cambridge Ave. on Arbor Rd., stands on 3.5 acres of land granted by the King of Spain to the Commandant of the Presidio de San Francisco in the early 19th century. Spanish-style buildings, courtyards, gardens, fountains, murals and frescoes create an Old World atmosphere where artisans practice their crafts. **Note:** The complex is closed for renovations; reopening is scheduled for late 2004. Food is available. Mon.-Sat. 10-5 (also Sun. noon-5, Nov.-Dec.). Free. Phone (650) 322-2405.

SUNSET PUBLISHING CORP., 80 Willow Rd. at Middlefield Rd., the publisher of *Sunset* magazine, offers self-guiding walking tours of the company's gardens. Divided into zones that represent the West, the gardens contain more than 300 varieties of trees, shrubs, vines, ground cover, annuals and perennials. Allow 1 hour minimum. Mon.-Fri. 9-4:30; closed holidays. Free. Phone (650) 321-3600.

MERCED (G-4) pop. 63,893, elev. 167'

Merced, in the agricultural San Joaquin Valley, is the principal western gateway to Yosemite National Park for travelers from the north.

The 1875 Old County Courthouse at 21st and N streets in Courthouse Park is built in the Italianate Renaissance style and resembles the state Capitol building. Merced County Museum in the courthouse contains exhibits about local history. Merced National Wildlife Refuge is 16 miles southwest. Water sports are offered 7 miles northeast at Lake Yosemite. Applegate Park and Zoo at 25th and R streets features wild animals, birds and children's rides.

Merced Conference and Visitors Bureau: 690 W. 16th St., Merced, CA 95340; phone (209) 384-7092 or (800) 446-5353. *See color ad p. 208.*

Self-guiding tours: The conference and visitors bureau distributes a guide to historic Merced as well as a blossom guide.

MIDDLETOWN—*see Wine Country p. 195.*

MIDPINES (F-4) elev. 2,575'

RECREATIONAL ACTIVITIES

White-water Rafting

- SAVE **All-Outdoors Whitewater Rafting** departs from the Midpines Country Store on SR 140. Write 1250 Pine St., Suite 103, Walnut Creek, CA 94596. Daily Apr. 1 to mid-July. Phone (925) 932-8993 or (800) 247-2387.

MILL VALLEY—*see San Francisco p. 158.*

MODESTO (F-3) pop. 188,856, elev. 88'

In the northern San Joaquin Valley on the Tuolumne River, Modesto is near the geographic center of the state. When the Central Pacific Railroad brought about the city's founding in 1870, its proponents wanted to name it after a San Francisco banker. When the banker rejected the idea, his modesty was commemorated in the chosen name.

Modesto provides access to Sonora Pass in Stanislaus National Forest, the Mother Lode Country and the Big Oak Flat route to Yosemite.

Great Valley Museum of Natural History, 1100 Stoddard Ave., features exhibits about Central Valley ecosystems; phone (209) 575-6196.

Native son and filmmaker George Lucas is remembered at a plaza named in his honor at Downey, McHenry Avenue and 17th and J streets. His movie "American Graffiti" recalls the times he spent cruising the streets of his hometown in the early 1960s. A statue in George Lucas Plaza depicts two teenagers leaning against a '57 Chevrolet.

Modesto Convention and Visitors Bureau: 1150 9th St., Suite C, Modesto, CA 95354; phone (209) 526-5588.

Shopping areas: Off SR 99 Standiford/Beckwith exit between Sisk and Dale roads, Vintage Faire Mall offers Gottschalk's, JCPenney, Macy's, Sears and 125 other stores to tempt shoppers.

BLUE DIAMOND ALMOND, 4800 Sisk Rd., offers a videotape presentation about the growing and harvesting of almonds. A tasting room is available. Mon.-Fri. 9-5, Sat. 10-4; closed holidays. Last videotape presentation is 1 hour before closing. Free. Phone (209) 545-3222.

McHENRY MUSEUM, 1402 I St., includes a schoolroom, smithy, dentist's and doctor's offices, kitchen, country store, historical photographs and documents, and changing exhibits. Tues.-Sun. noon-4; closed holidays. Donations. Phone (209) 577-5366.

MODOC NATIONAL FOREST

Elevations in the forest range from 4,500 ft. at Devils Gardens to 9,892 ft. at Eagle Peak. Refer to AAA maps for additional elevation information.

Encompassing much of the state's remote northeastern corner, Modoc National Forest's 1,654,392 acres were covered millions of years ago by an immense lava flow. Although geologically the area is known as the Modoc Plateau, it doesn't look like a plateau. The region is distinguished by basins, mountains, lakes and meadows. And despite the relatively dry climate, the plateau supports some of the country's most significant wetlands.

The forest is home to more than 300 species of wildlife, including Rocky Mountain mule deer, pronghorn antelopes, bald and golden eagles and wild horses. The Pacific Flyway for migratory birds crosses directly over the forest.

Volcanism has left many marks on the forest's terrain, and some of the most dramatic examples are in the Medicine Lake highlands. There are such unusual features as Glass Mountain, a huge flow of obsidian, and the Burnt Lava Flow, which is a jumble of black lava interspersed with islands of timber. Medicine Lake itself fills an old volcanic crater and is popular for boating and swimming.

On the forest's eastern boundary, the Warner Mountains are a rolling upland that drops steeply on its eastern edge. Most of the range is above 5,000 feet, and some of the peaks reach an altitude over 9,000 feet in the 70,385-acre South Warner Wilderness, which includes Modoc's highest mountain, Eagle Peak. The forest has 118 miles of trails, accessible by eight trailheads, suited for hikers and horseback riders. Carrying a topography map is advised. Fishing is prime in many reservoirs. Cross-country skiing is a popular wintertime diversion.

Maps, brochures and information about recreational opportunities are available at the district ranger stations and the forest headquarters in Alturas. For more information write the Forest Supervisor, Modoc National Forest, 800 W. 12th St., Alturas, CA 96101; phone (530) 233-5811. *See the Recreation Chart and AAA California & Nevada CampBook.*

MONO BASIN NATIONAL FOREST SCENIC AREA

Accessible via SRs 120 and 167 and I-395, the scenic area is near Lee Vining, within Inyo National Forest *(see place listing p. 79)*. The area covers 116,000 acres surrounding Mono Lake and includes volcanic hills on its borders. The Bodie Hills to the north and the Anchorite Hills to the east are about 11 million years old, while the Mono Craters to the south are the youngest mountain range in North America, starting to form about 3.6 million years ago. One of the craters erupted about 600 years ago. The islands in Mono Lake also are volcanic, as evidenced by hot springs and steam vents. The islands cannot be visited April through July due to the nesting season of the California Seagull.

The lake itself is more than 750,000 years old. Over time the salts and minerals in the water have become too concentrated for most species to survive. However, the indigenous brine shrimp and flies attract millions of migratory birds and waterfowl. The word "mono" is an American Indian word for "flies." Most tourists come to see the tufa, spires and knobs formed of calcium carbonate that were exposed as the lake's water level dropped, but in recent years the water level has been rising. **Note:** Tufa, pumice and obsidian are protected by state and federal laws and may not be collected or damaged.

Many basin roads are unsuitable for conventional vehicles; off-road driving is not permitted. Self-guiding nature trails and interpretive signs are at the South Tufa and Panum Crater day-use areas. Guided tours are available; phone for schedule.

The scenic area is open daily 24 hours. A visitor center a half-mile north of Lee Vining is open daily May-Oct.; phone for schedule. Free. South Tufa and Panum Crater areas $3; under 18 free. For more information contact Mono Basin Scenic Area Visitor Center, P.O. Box 429, Lee Vining, CA 93541; phone (760) 873-2408.

Monterey Peninsula

Although Spanish explorer Juan Rodriguez Cabrillo, the first European to reach Monterey Bay, came within visual contact of the bay's beaches and pine forests in 1542, he was unable to land due to high seas. It would be 60 years before Sebastián Vizcaíno explored the bay and named it for the Count of Monte Rey, viceroy of Mexico. Vizcaíno also was responsible for naming a nearby valley after his patron saint, Our Lady of Carmel.

Although officially claimed for Spain, the area was not settled until Franciscan priest Junípero Serra and Spanish governor Gaspar de Portolá arrived in 1770 to build a mission and establish a seat of government, respectively.

The fishing industry was the original anchor of the area's economy, with whaling the mainstay. By the 1880s tourism took economic precedence over whaling. But it was only natural that the ocean should beckon once again, and sardine harvesting led to the birth of Monterey's Cannery Row during the 1920s.

The peninsula's natural beauty restored tourism to the economic forefront after the collapse of the sardine industry. In addition to the obvious attractions offered by the dramatic coastline, beaches and the surf, the Monterey Peninsula also consists of gently rolling hills, streams and forests, and the area has become a mecca for golf aficionados. The AT&T Pebble Beach National Pro-Am, held in late January, is one of the highlights of professional golf.

For those seeking more active pursuits, the Monterey Peninsula Recreational Trail is a walking, jogging and biking path that parallels the coastline from Seaside, through Monterey to Pacific Grove.

CARMEL (G-2) pop. 4,081, elev. 20′

Carmel, also known as Carmel-by-the-Sea, was established in 1904 by a group of artists and writers as a bucolic retreat. As the settlement grew, its founders fought the encroachment of paved streets, gas, electricity and other modern amenities, and stringent zoning ordinances have preserved Carmel's village flavor and individuality. Even today there are no street addresses; locations are indicated by intersections.

The best way to see Carmel is by walking—perhaps a stroll along the beach, or exploring the city's numerous art galleries or courtyards. Carmel is an architectural conglomerate of international styles, reflecting the whims of the residents.

Each summer the Outdoor Forest Theatre delivers live performances and the audience is encouraged to picnic.

Point Lobos State Reserve, Carmel / © Gibson Stock Photography

© Lee Foster / Lonely Planet Images

Carmel lies on a scenic stretch of SR 1 that extends from San Francisco to San Luis Obispo. North of Carmel's white sand beach is an entrance to Seventeen-Mile Drive, a scenic route from Pacific Grove to Carmel *(see Monterey p. 104)*.

Downtown parking time limits are strictly enforced. A city lot on Third at Torres offers free, unlimited parking; enter from Third.

Carmel Visitor Center: San Carlos between 5th and 6th streets, P.O. Box 4444, Carmel, CA 93921; phone (831) 624-2522.

Shopping areas: The compact business center contains unusual shops and galleries that display the work of local artists. The Barnyard, SR 1 and Carmel Valley Road with access from Carmel Rancho Boulevard, is as popular for its garden setting and country atmosphere as for its galleries and specialty shops. The Crossroads, east of SR 1 and Father Serra's Carmel Mission on Rio Road, offers nearly 100 boutiques and specialty shops.

CARMEL WALKS tours meet in the outdoor courtyard of the Pine Inn, Lincoln St. at Ocean Ave. The 2-hour guided walking tours show visitors Carmel's hidden treasures—the town's secluded courtyards, gardens and cottages. A narrative gives the town's history as well as information about the artists, writers and movie stars who call Carmel home. Allow 2 hours minimum. Tours depart Tues.-Fri. at 10, Sat. at 10 and 2. Fee $20. Reservations are recommended. Phone (831) 642-2700.

GEM **MISSION SAN CARLOS BORROMEO DEL RIO CARMELO,** at 3080 Rio Rd., is called Carmel Mission. Established by Father Junípero Serra at Monterey in 1770 and moved to its present site the following year, the mission was Father Serra's residence and headquarters until his death in 1784. He is buried beneath the church floor in front of the altar.

Relics of the mission's early days and some of Father Serra's books and documents are displayed. The courtyard gardens and Moorish bell tower are of interest, and a museum contains exhibits about the mission. A fiesta usually is held the last Sunday in September.

Allow 1 hour minimum. Mon.-Sat. 9:30-5, Sun. 10:30-5, June-Aug.; Mon.-Sat. 9:30-4, Sun. 10:30-4, rest of year. Closed Easter, Easter Monday, Thanksgiving and Dec. 25. Admission $4; ages 5-17, $1. Phone (831) 624-3600.

GEM **POINT LOBOS STATE RESERVE,** 3 mi. s. on SR 1, covers 1,225 acres of land and water along the rugged seacoast. Maps of the 10 miles of well-marked trails along the cliffs are available at the entrance station. Plants specially adapted to the coastal climate abound in and among

(continued on p. 101)

Destination Monterey Peninsula

The city of Monterey has rich natural beauty and a variety of man-made attractions–from Fisherman's Wharf to Cannery Row, from Monterey Adobes to the Monterey Bay Aquarium.

Add the stunning Seventeen-Mile Drive to your tour of the peninsula and you'll arrive at the charming village of Carmel, where you can indulge in delightful shopping, stroll on the beach and visit one of Fr. Junípero Serra's missions.

© W. Talarowski / Robertstock

Mission San Carlos Borromeo del Rio Carmelo, Carmel. The bells in the Carmel Mission's Moorish tower have called the faithful since 1797. (See listing page 99)

© Jonathan Blair / Corbis

Monterey Bay Aquarium, Monterey. Many stranded and orphaned sea otters rescued by the aquarium are rehabilitated and returned to the wild. (See listing page 102)

© Robert Holmes / Corbis

Fishing tours, Monterey. Explore the peninsula on land, but don't forget about the bounty waiting in its offshore waters.

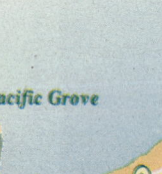

Pacific Grove

Carmel-by-the-Sea

Monterey

Monterey Peninsula

Colton Hall, Monterey. California's first constitution was written in this historic hall in 1849. (See listing page 103)

© Gibson Stock Photography

Places included in this AAA Destination Area:

the rocks, particularly the Monterey cypress, Monterey pine, seaside daisy and bluff lettuce. Wildlife includes deer, squirrels and rabbits.

About half the reserve is designated as an underwater reserve. Harbor seals, gray whales, California sea lions and California sea otters can be seen. Sea birds, such as cormorants and pelicans, nest along the coast. A museum at Whalers Cove documents the late 19th-century whaling industry at Point Lobos. Diving is allowed only by permit. Nature walks are offered; phone for schedule.

Pets are not permitted. Allow 2 hours minimum. Daily 9-7, Memorial Day-Oct. 31; 9-5, rest of year. Admission $6 per private vehicle; over 61, $4 per private vehicle. Phone (831) 624-4909, or (831) 624-8413 for diving reservations.

MONTEREY (G-2) pop. 29,674, elev. 60′

The capital of Alta California under the Spanish, Mexican and American flags, Monterey lies on the Monterey Peninsula and ranges in altitude from sea level to 360 feet. The peninsula is a popular year-round playground boasting several golf courses. South of Monterey SR 1 winds through redwood forests and along the cliffs of the spectacular Big Sur coast.

On Cannery Row, the colorful locale of John Steinbeck's novels "Cannery Row" and "Sweet Thursday," galleries, shops and restaurants have replaced the sardine canneries. Along Fisherman's Wharf an art gallery, handicraft shops and the Wharf Theater have superseded the commercial fishing activities of the early 20th century.

Every Tuesday afternoon bargain hunters flock to Monterey Farmers Market to meander among the produce, food, and arts and crafts booths.

The Monterey Presidio, 1 block from the theater on Pacific Street, was founded in 1770 by Capt. Gaspar de Portolá, assisted by fathers Junípero Serra and Juan Crespi. It is now the Defense Language Institute Presidio of Monterey. The Lower Presidio Historic Park is open to the public below the Sloat Monument.

Monterey County Convention and Visitors Bureau: 150 Olivier St., Monterey, CA 93940; phone (831) 657-6400 or (888) 221-1010. *See color ad.*

Self-guiding tours: Maps for the 2-mile Monterey Path of History walking tour, detailing gardens, adobes and historic sites, are available from the convention and visitors bureau, the visitor center at Camino el Estero between Del Monte Avenue and Fremont Street, and at Monterey State Historic Park *(see attraction listing p. 102).*

DENNIS THE MENACE PLAYGROUND is in the park on Lake El Estero. Hank Ketcham, creator of the cartoon strip "Dennis the Menace," aided in its development. The playground contains climbing structures, slides, a balancing bridge, a maze, a railroad switch engine and a lion-shaped drinking fountain. Daily 10-dusk, June-Aug.; Tues.-Sun. and Mon. holidays 10-dusk, rest of year. Free. Phone (831) 646-3866.

SAVE **MARITIME MUSEUM,** 5 Custom House Plaza, contains the collections of Allen Knight, a seaman who built a stone ship next to his home to store his collected artifacts. The nearly 10,000-pound Fresnel lens of Point Sur Lighthouse illuminates the museum's exhibits, including navigational instruments, ship models, chronicles, photos and charts. A 14-minute videotape about regional history is presented every 20 minutes.

Allow 1 hour minimum. Tues.-Sun. 11-5; closed Jan. 1, Thanksgiving and Dec. 25. Last videotape showing is 30 minutes before closing. Admission

$5; over 64, military and ages 13-18, $2.50. AX, MC, VI. Phone (831) 373-2469.

GEM **MONTEREY BAY AQUARIUM,** 886 Cannery Row, houses more than 700 species of marine life in more than 200 galleries and exhibits. The Outer Bay Galleries present the mysteries of the open ocean; sunfish, barracudas, tuna, sharks and sea turtles are visible through an acrylic panel in a million-gallon tank. Other exhibits include an elliptical, overhead anchovy tank and a remarkable display of jellyfish.

A living kelp forest can be seen in Nearshore Galleries. Other exhibits feature octopuses, rockfish, sand dollars, an aviary with shorebirds, a touch pool, sea otters, wharf pilings and an indoor/outdoor coastal stream.

Splash Zone depicts the reef and rocky shore habitats of almost 60 species of marine life. The aquarium also has life-size models of whales and other marine animals and historical displays.

Food is available. Allow 3 hours minimum. Daily 9:30-6, Memorial Day weekend-Labor Day and holidays; 10-6, rest of year. Closed Dec. 25. Admission $19.95; over 64, full-time college students with ID and ages 13-17, $15.95; ages 3-12, $8.95. AX, DS, MC, VI. Phone (831) 648-4800, (831) 648-4888 for recorded information, or (800) 756-3737 in Calif. for advance tickets. *See color ad.*

MONTEREY MUSEUM OF ART AT CIVIC CENTER, 559 Pacific St., presents permanent and changing displays of regional, Oriental and folk art as well as photography. Allow 1 hour minimum. Wed.-Sat. 11-5 (also third Thurs. of the month 5-7), Sun. 1-4; closed Jan. 1, Thanksgiving and Dec. 25. Admission $5, military and students with ID $2.50, under 12 free (includes admission to Monterey Museum of Art at La Mirada). AX, DS, MC, VI. Phone (831) 372-7591.

MONTEREY MUSEUM OF ART AT LA MIRADA, 720 Via Mirada off Fremont St., presents permanent collections and changing exhibits in an exquisitely furnished, two-story house in which regional and international celebrities were once entertained. On the grounds are rose and rhododendron gardens. Wed.-Sat. 11-5, Sun. 1-4; closed major holidays. Admission $5, military and students with ID $2.50, under 12 free (includes admission to Monterey Museum of Art at Civic Center). AX, DS, MC, VI. Phone (831) 372-3689.

GEM **MONTEREY STATE HISTORIC PARK,** 20 Custom House Plaza, is a 7-acre site that preserves the historical and architectural heritage of old Monterey. Nearby is the original 1602 landing site of Sebastián Vizcaíno and—more than 150 years later—Father Junípero Serra.

Guided 45-minute walking tours allow visitors to see buildings and residences from early California history. Morning tours depart from the Pacific House Museum on Custom House Plaza; weekend afternoon tours depart from the Cooper-Molera Adobe at Polk, Alvarado and Munras streets.

House tours also are available; phone to confirm times. Gardens, some with fountains or arbors, can be seen on self-guiding or 75-minute guided tours; guided tours begin at the Cooper-Molera Adobe. The visitor center has brochures and showings of a videotape about Monterey history.

Daily 10-5; closed Jan. 1, Thanksgiving and Dec. 25. Guided walking tours of the park are given Mon.-Fri. at 10:30, Sat.-Sun. at 10:30 and 2. Guided garden tours are given Tues. and Sat. at noon, June-Aug. Admission, including guided tours, free. Phone (831) 649-7118 to verify schedules.

Casa Soberanes and Garden, 336 Pacific St., was built in 1842 and occupied by members of the Soberanes family until 1922. Known for its blue entrance gate, the well-preserved adobe house contains period antiques and terraced garden walkways. Guided half-hour tours are available Mon., Wed. and Fri. at 11:30, Sun. at 1. Phone ahead to confirm schedule. Phone (831) 649-7118.

Colton Hall, in the civic center on Pacific St. facing Friendly Plaza, is where the first Constitution of California was written in 1849; it now contains a museum dedicated to city history. Adjoining Colton Hall, completed in 1849, is the old jail, built in 1854. Allow 30 minutes minimum. Daily 10-4; closed Jan. 1, Thanksgiving and Dec. 25. Donations. Phone (831) 646-5640.

Cooper-Molera Adobe and Garden, 525 Polk St. at jct. Alvarado and Munras sts., is the restored Victorian home of the Yankee sea captain, rancher and adventurer who married the sister of Gen. Mariano Vallejo. The 3-acre grounds also have four other structures and a period garden that are open to the public. Grounds open daily 10-4. Guided 45-minute tours are available Mon., Wed. and Fri.-Sat. at 1. Phone ahead to confirm schedule. Phone (831) 649-7118.

Custom House, on Custom House Plaza at Fisherman's Wharf, is the oldest government building in California, its north section having been constructed about 1827. When Commodore John Drake Sloat raised the American flag over the building in 1846, approximately 600,000 square miles became part of the United States. The house displays trade goods from the 1840s. A cactus garden provides views of Monterey's harbor. Thurs.-Tues. 10-4. Phone (831) 649-7118

First Brick House is adjacent to the Old Whaling Station. The structure marks one of the first uses in California of fired clay bricks for building purposes. The new material was stronger and more durable and water-repellent than the traditional sun dried mud bricks. Displays about Monterey history are presented. Daily 10-4.

First Theatre and Garden, Pacific and Scott sts., once was a lodging house for sailors as well as the first building in Monterey to charge admission for a theatrical performance. The 1846 building contains relics of early California. Dramatic productions still are staged. Succulents and cypress trees grace the garden. **Note:** The theater is currently closed for renovation. Phone (831) 649-7118 for information.

Larkin House and Garden is at Calle Principal and Jefferson St. Its combination of Mexican Colonial and New England architectural features reflects the New England origins of the builder, merchant Thomas Oliver Larkin. The 1835 two-story adobe house served as the American consulate 1843-46. Its rooms hold antiques from many parts of the world. The garden was planted by Larkin's granddaughter. Guided 45-minute tours are available Mon., Wed. and Fri. at 2, Sat.-Sun. at 3.

Pacific House Museum is on Custom House Plaza. The 1847 adobe building, built as a U.S. army storage facility, is now a museum with interactive displays depicting the history of Monterey during its days as the capital of Spanish and Mexican California. A second floor museum features American Indian baskets and pottery. Tues.-Sun. 10-4.

Stevenson House and Garden is at 530 Houston St. Robert Louis Stevenson spent the fall of 1879 in this former rooming house, then known as the French Hotel, writing "Vendetta of the West," an essay about Henry David Thoreau and blocking out "Amateur Emigrant" and "Prince Otto." The two-story adobe building is restored and furnished in period. An early Mexican garden can be seen. **Note:** The house and garden are temporarily closed; reopening is scheduled for late 2003.

MY MUSEUM is at 601 Wave St., Suite 100. This hands-on children's museum offers interactive exhibits where youngsters can pretend to be a fisherman on Cannery Row, be a puppeteer, create a masterpiece on a loom to take home and participate in building a house. Allow 1 hour minimum. Thurs.-Tues. 10-5, Sun. noon-5. Admission $5.50, under 2 free. AX, MC, VI. Phone (831) 649-6444.

NATIONAL STEINBECK CENTER—
see attraction listing in Salinas p. 123.

THE PRESIDIO OF MONTEREY MUSEUM is in Lower Presidio Historic Park, Corporal Ewing Rd., Bldg. 113, just n.w. of Monterey State Historic Park at the e. end of the Defense Language Institute Foreign Language Center. The museum traces the history of this site from its inhabitation by American Indians through its rich military history, beginning with the mission and presidio established in 1770 by Spanish missionary Junípero Serra and Capt. Gaspar de Portolá.

Exhibits include the Spanish and Mexican periods and the presidio's development as a U.S. Army training base, with an emphasis on its cavalry post period.

Allow 30 minutes minimum. Thurs.-Sat. 10-4, Sun. 1-4, Mon. 10-1; closed Jan. 1, Thanksgiving and Dec. 25. Donations. Phone (831) 646-3456.

SAN CARLOS CATHEDRAL, at 500 Church St., also is known as Royal Presidio Chapel. Founded in 1770 to be the mission church of the port, San Carlos Cathedral became the church for the Spanish colonists and soldiers instead, as the mission was moved to Carmel the following year. The present church has been in continuous use since 1795. Mon.-Fri. 7:30-4:30. Donations. Phone (831) 373-2628.

SEVENTEEN-MILE DRIVE can be entered through several gates off SRs 1 and 68 between Pacific Grove and Carmel. This scenic route along the Monterey Peninsula is a highlight of a visit to this coastal region. A private toll-road, the drive meanders through Pebble Beach, offering stopping points for grand views of the craggy Pacific Ocean shoreline, Seal Rock, Cypress Point, The Lone Cypress and six golf courses. The toll includes a map listing 21 points of interest along the road.

Bicycles are permitted during daylight when no major sporting event is scheduled; no motorcycles or motorbikes are allowed. Bicyclists must enter through the Pacific Grove gate on weekends, holidays and during events. Allow at least 1 hour to complete the drive. Route open daily dawn-30 minutes before dusk. The toll for cars is $8.25. For additional information and toll confirmation phone (831) 625-8426. *See color ad.*

STEINBECK'S SPIRIT OF MONTEREY WAX MUSEUM, 700 Cannery Row in the Monterey Cannery Building, displays wax figures from Monterey's turbulent history. Allow 30 minutes minimum. Daily 10:30-8, May-Oct.; 10:30-7, rest of year. Admission $5.95; senior citizens, military and students with ID $4.95; ages 6-18, $3.95. Phone (831) 375-3770.

RECREATIONAL ACTIVITIES

Kayaking

- SAVE **Monterey Bay Kayaks**, 693 Del Monte Ave., Monterey, CA 93940. Daily 9-6; closed Jan. 1, Thanksgiving and Dec. 25. Phone (831) 373-5357 or (800) 649-5357.

PACIFIC GROVE (G-2) pop. 15,522, elev. 55'

Adjoining Monterey, Pacific Grove is one of the starting points for the popular Seventeen-Mile Drive *(see Monterey p. 104)*. Another way of experiencing the scenic waterfront is by hiking or biking the Monterey Peninsula Recreational Trail, which runs from Pacific Grove to Seaside. The trail passes such area landmarks as Point Piños Lighthouse and Del Monte Beach.

Point Piños Lighthouse, in operation since 1855, is on Asilomar Boulevard, off Lighthouse Avenue. The lighthouse's levels, connected by a spiral staircase, depict a typical lightkeeper's quarters in the 1800s and early 1900s; phone (831) 648-3116. Downtown residential neighborhoods contain numbers of well-preserved Victorian houses.

For years thousands of monarch butterflies visited an area of pine trees on Ridge Road off Lighthouse Avenue from early October through March; sadly, their number is greatly diminished.

Pacific Grove Chamber of Commerce: Central and Forest aves., P.O. Box 167, Pacific Grove, CA 93950; phone (831) 373-3304. *See color ad p. 489.*

Shopping areas: American Tin Cannery Premium Outlets, 125 Ocean View Blvd., includes factory-direct and specialty stores.

PACIFIC GROVE MUSEUM OF NATURAL HISTORY, 165 Forest Ave., emphasizes the natural history of Monterey County through an extensive collection of rocks and minerals, 400 mounted birds and a monarch butterfly display. Changing exhibits focus on American Indians. Allow 1 hour minimum. Tues.-Sun. and holidays 10-5; closed Jan. 1, Thanksgiving and Dec. 24-25. Free. Phone (831) 648-5716.

The previous listings were for the Monterey Peninsula.
This page resumes the alphabetical listings of cities in Northern California.

MORGAN HILL (G-3) pop. 33,556, elev. 345′

Before the arrival of Spanish soldiers and priests in 1776, the area was home to the peaceful Costanoan Indians. The first English-speaking community sprang up around a prosperous estate known as Morgan Hill's Ranch in 1845 and was incorporated in 1906. Morgan Hill is at the southern end of the agriculturally rich Santa Clara Valley, where the French prune was developed.

Morgan Hill Chamber of Commerce: 17450 Monterey Rd., P.O. Box 786, Morgan Hill, CA 95038-0786; phone (408) 779-9444.

MORRO BAY (I-3) pop. 10,350, elev. 80′

Both the town of Morro Bay and the bay that fronts it are named for Morro Rock, the great conical rock that juts 578 feet out of the Pacific Ocean. In the 1870s Morro Bay was a port for the region's cattle ranching and dairy industries, which were later replaced by commercial fishing and oyster farming enterprises. Morro Bay still maintains a large commercial fishing fleet.

Boat tours and boat rentals are available at Marina Square on the Embarcadero. A few miles south of SR 1 is Morro Bay State Park *(see Recreation Chart and the AAA California & Nevada CampBook).*

Morro Bay Chamber of Commerce: 880 Main St., Morro Bay, CA 93442; phone (805) 772-4467 or (800) 231-0592.

MORRO BAY STATE PARK MUSEUM OF NATURAL HISTORY, in Morro Bay State Park off South Bay Blvd., includes 26 state-of-the-art interactive exhibits explaining how natural forces, including man, shape the world as we know it. Audiovisual presentations, nature walks and lectures are featured. Trails from the museum lead to scenic viewpoints. Daily 10-5; closed Jan. 1, Thanksgiving and Dec. 25. Admission $2, under 17 free. Phone (805) 772-2694.

SUB-SEA TOURS, which depart from Marina Sq. at the Embarcadero at Pacific St., lets visitors view sea life—including fish and diving birds—from both above and below the water. Tours last 45 minutes and generally begin on the hour, depending upon the tide and demand. Kayak rentals are available.

Allow 1 hour minimum. Daily 9-5, May-Oct. and holidays; 11-3, rest of year. Fare $14; senior citizens $11; under 13, $7. Phone for schedule. MC, VI. Phone (805) 772-9463 for the office, or (805) 772-3349 for the marina.

***TIGER'S FOLLY II* HARBOR CRUISES** depart from 1205 Embarcadero. One-hour narrated trips on the paddlewheeler cruise past Morro Rock, the harbor entrance and the Embarcadero. Sunday brunch and weekend dinner cruises are available. One-hour trips offered daily, June-Sept.; Sat.-Sun. and holidays, rest of year. Fare $10; under 12, $5. AX, DS, MC, VI. Phone (805) 772-2257 or (800) 958-4437.

MOSS BEACH—*see San Francisco p. 158.*

MOSS LANDING (G-2) pop. 300, elev. 10′

ELKHORN SLOUGH SAFARI NATURE BOAT TOURS departs from the Moss Landing Marina, w. off SR 1 onto Moss Landing Rd., n. onto Sandholt Rd., then e. into the marina parking lot. Two-hour cruises on a 27-foot pontoon boat explore the Elkhorn Slough habitat. Led by a naturalist, the tours provide opportunities for sighting sea otters, harbor seals, terns, grebes and other species of waterfowl and shorebirds. The captain and naturalist provide information about slough ecology and natural history; photographs circulated during the trip help identify wildlife.

Allow 2 hours, 30 minutes minimum. Departures daily. Times vary depending on the tide and the migration of species; phone ahead. Closed Thanksgiving and Dec. 25. Fare $26; senior citizens $24; ages 3-14, $19. Parking $2. Reservations are recommended at least 1 week in advance. Phone (831) 633-5555.

MOUNTAIN VIEW (E-9) pop. 70,708, elev. 97′

Mountain View is a commercially diversified city in the Santa Clara Valley. To the east is Moffett Field, a combined-services military field.

In addition to being a sanctuary for wildlife and 154 species of birds, Shoreline at Mountain View is a regional recreation area off US 101 Shoreline Boulevard exit near San Francisco Bay. Migratory birds frequent Shoreline from October through February on their way to Mexico, sharing the park with year-round visitors who utilize 7 miles of jogging, hiking and bicycling trails; a saltwater lake for windsurfing and sailing; expanses for kite flying; an 18-hole golf course; an outdoor amphitheater that draws major entertainers; and mountain views.

Mountain View Chamber of Commerce: 580 Castro St., Mountain View, CA 94041; phone (650) 968-8378.

NASA AMES RESEARCH CENTER, off US 101 Moffett Field exit, is a NASA field center that conducts research on information technology, astrobiology and aeronautics. The visitor center features a moon rock, Mercury spacecraft, research aircraft, the largest space shuttle wind tunnel model, space suits and interactive displays highlighting past and current projects. Visitor center open Mon.-Fri. 8-4:30; closed federal holidays. Free. Phone (650) 604-6274.

THE RENGSTORFF HOUSE is off US 101 Shoreline Blvd. exit in Shoreline at Mountain View park at 3070 N. Shoreline Blvd. German immigrant Henry Rengstorff came to California in 1850 to seek his fortune. Too late for the gold rush, he accumulated acreage in the Santa Clara Valley and built this 12-room, two-story Victorian Italianate home in 1867.

Featured are four fireplaces, a large dining room, a staircase with handcrafted newel post, and parlors with period wallpaper. Docents in period attire conduct guided tours. Allow 30 minutes minimum. Tues.-Wed. and Sun. 11-5. Free. Phone (650) 903-6088.

MOUNT SHASTA (B-3)
pop. 3,621, elev. 3,554′

A small city named for a tall mountain, Mount Shasta is the northern gateway via scenic SR 89 to Whiskeytown-Shasta-Trinity National Recreation Area *(see place listing p. 181)*, Shasta-Trinity National Forests *(see place listing p. 172)*, and nearby Lake Siskiyou.

Mount Shasta Visitors Bureau: 300 Pine St., Mount Shasta, CA 96067; phone (530) 926-4865 or (800) 926-4865.

MOUNT SHASTA STATE FISH HATCHERY AND SISSON HATCHERY MUSEUM, .5 mi. w. of I-5 via central Mount Shasta exit at Three, Old Stage Rd., produces 3 to 5 million trout annually to stock the streams and lakes of northern California. The museum has exhibits pertaining to the geological and human history of the region.

Allow 1 hour minimum. Museum open Mon.-Sat. 10-4, Sun. 1-4, June-Sept.; daily 1-4, Apr.-May and Oct.-Dec. Hatchery open daily 7 a.m.-dusk. Free. Phone (530) 926-2215 for the hatchery or (530) 926-5508 for the museum.

GEM MUIR WOODS NATIONAL MONUMENT—*see San Francisco p. 158.*

MURPHYS (E-4) pop. 2,061, elev. 2,171′

MERCER CAVERNS, 1.5 mi. n. via Sheep Ranch Rd., has been open since 1885. Guided tours lasting 45 to 50 minutes visit 10 rooms with various crystalline formations. Tours are given Sun.-Thurs. 9-5, Fri.-Sat. 9-6, Memorial Day weekend-Labor Day; daily 10-4:30, rest of year. Closed Dec. 25. Last tour begins at closing. Admission $10; ages 5-12, $6. Phone (209) 728-2101.

WINERIES

- **Stevenot Winery**, 2 mi. n. on Sheep Ranch Rd., then w. .2 mi. on San Domingo Rd. Daily 10-5; closed Dec. 25. Phone (209) 728-3436.

NAPA—*see Wine Country p. 195.*

NEVADA CITY (D-3) pop. 3,001, elev. 2,525′

In the foothills of the High Sierras, Nevada City has been a gold-mining center for more than a century. It also is the seat of Nevada County, whose lode and placer mines have yielded more than one-half of California's total production of gold. Among the buildings dating from gold rush days is Old Nevada Theater, said to be the oldest theater in California. It opened in July 1865.

Just 8 miles northwest on SR 49 is South Yuba River State Park, a 2,000-acre scenic corridor noted for its spring wildflowers, kayaking possibilities and, at 251 feet, what is believed to be the longest single-span covered bridge in the United States. *See Recreation Chart and the AAA California & Nevada CampBook.*

Nevada City Chamber of Commerce: 132 Main St., Nevada City, CA 95959; phone (530) 265-2692 or (800) 655-6569.

FIREHOUSE NO. 1 MUSEUM, at 214 Main St., displays pioneer relics and American Indian and Donner party artifacts. A highlight is a Chinese collection that includes an altar from an 1870s Chinese joss house as well as a Quan Yin altar (Quan Yin is the goddess of compassion and mercy). Tours are available by appointment. Allow 30 minutes minimum. Thurs.-Mon. 11-4, May-Dec.; Thurs.-Sun. 11:30-4, rest of year (weather permitting). Closed most holidays. Donations. Phone (530) 265-5468.

MALAKOFF DIGGINS STATE HISTORIC PARK, 27 mi. n.e. of SR 49 off Tyler Foote Crossing Rd., was the world's largest hydraulic gold mine before it ceased operation in 1884. The park museum has exhibits and a 20-minute videotape explaining hydraulic mining methods and describing the miners' way of life. Highlights include a restored church, 1860s general store, drugstore, barber shop, livery stable and house. The homecoming celebration is held in mid-June.

Camping and picnicking facilities are available. Dogs are not permitted in buildings or on trails. Allow 1 hour minimum. Daily 10-5, June 1-Labor Day; Sat.-Sun. 10-4, rest of year. Admission $4 per vehicle. Reservations for camping are required. Phone (530) 265-2740 for information and cabin reservations or ReserveAmerica at (800) 444-7275 for camping reservations. *See Recreation Chart and the AAA California & Nevada CampBook.*

MINERS FOUNDRY CULTURAL CENTER, 325 Spring St., was built in 1856 for industrial metal working and metal casting. The complex is now a cultural center with performing arts facilities. A hall built of stones native to the area also is featured. Special programs are scheduled throughout the year. Guided tours are available by appointment. Mon.-Fri. 9-4. Free. Phone (530) 265-5040 for information about programs.

NEW ALMADEN (F-2) elev. 440′

NEW ALMADEN QUICKSILVER MINING MUSEUM is 2.5 mi. w. off Almaden Expwy. (CR G8) at 21350 Almaden Rd. in Almaden Quicksilver County Park. The museum, in the 1854 La Casa

Grande, the brick residence that was home to the New Almaden Quicksilver Mine manager and his family, depicts the mercury mining operations that began in New Almaden in 1845. Exhibits explain the process of extracting mercury from the cinnabar ore found in the area. Artifacts from mining families are shown, and a diorama replicates the interior of a mine shaft.

Allow 30 minutes minimum. Fri.-Sun. 10-4, July-Aug.; Fri. noon-4, Sat.-Sun. 10-4, rest of year. Closed major holidays. Free. Phone (408) 323-1107.

NIPOMO (I-4) pop. 12,626, elev. 330′

Originally a private 38,000-acre ranch, Nipomo grew into a stopover on El Camino Real (The King's Highway) between missions San Luis Obispo and Santa Barbara. Citrus orchards, vegetable farms and commercial nurseries thrive in the rich soil that washes down from the Nipomo Foothills. Thousands of blue gum eucalyptus trees, unsuccessfully planted to yield hardwood, populate the mesa area of Nipomo. The Dana Adobe, built in 1839 with the help of mission American Indians, still stands. Nipomo is on a scenic stretch of US 101.

Nipomo Chamber of Commerce: 267 W. Tefft, P.O. Box 386, Nipomo, CA 93444; (805) 929-1583.

NORTH FORK (G-5) elev. 2,629′

SIERRA MONO INDIAN MUSEUM, jct. CRs 225, 228 and 274, displays artifacts and items unique to the Mono Indians. Central to the museum's exhibits, as well as to the Mono culture, is an extensive collection of baskets. Other highlights include wildlife exhibits and tools, jewelry and baskets from other North American Indian tribes. Tues.-Sat. 9-3:30; closed Jan. 1, July 4, Thanksgiving and Dec. 25. Admission $5, over 59 and physically impaired $3, students $2. Phone (559) 877-2115.

NORTH HIGHLANDS (E-3) pop. 44,187, elev. 100′

McCLELLAN AVIATION MUSEUM is at 3204 Palm St. at McClellan Air Park; enter through the Palm Gate off Watt Ave. Military aircraft and aviation memorabilia featured at this site of the former McClellan Air Force Base include restored aircraft engines dating from World War I, flight simulators and pilot ejector seats. Outdoors are 30 planes including a Korean War F-86, a C-53 from World War II that towed gliders into Normandy on D-Day, a Russian MiG 21 and an F-105D Thunderchief.

Allow 1 hour, 30 minutes minimum. Mon.-Sat. 9-4, Sun. noon-4; closed Jan. 1, Easter, Thanksgiving and Dec. 25. Admission $4; senior citizens and ages 12-18, $2. Phone (916) 643-3192.

NOVATO (C-8) pop. 47,630, elev. 18′

North of San Francisco on US 101, Novato was named for a chief of the Coast Miwok Indians. Although a national leader in the production of CD-ROMs, the area still retains an outlying dairy region. Novato History Museum, 815 DeLong Ave., is in the circa 1856 house of the town's first postmaster. Exhibits include photographs and relics depicting life in Novato from its earliest days.

Novato Chamber of Commerce: 807 DeLong Ave., Novato, CA 94945; phone (415) 897-1164 or (800) 897-1164.

MARIN MUSEUM OF THE AMERICAN INDIAN, 2200 Novato Blvd. in Miwok Park, displays American Indian art and culture as well as exhibits of the prehistoric period in Marin County. The museum also has a native plant garden. Changing exhibits highlight various other American Indian cultures. Allow 30 minutes minimum. Tues.-Fri. 10-3, Sat.-Sun. noon-4. Admission $5, senior citizens $3, under 12 free. Phone (415) 897-4064.

OLOMPALI STATE HISTORIC PARK, 2.5 mi. n. on US 101 (southbound only), is a 700-acre park featuring several historic buildings including the ruins of the 1913 Burdell Mansion, which consists of three older structures built 1830-66. A traditional Victorian garden surrounds the ruins and an 1870s frame house stands nearby. A reconstruction of a Coast Miwok village from which the state park takes its name also is featured. Allow 30 minutes minimum. Daily 10-6. Admission $1 per private vehicle. Phone (415) 892-3383.

OAKDALE (F-3) pop. 15,503, elev. 155′

In an area with many cattle farms and ranches, Oakdale bills itself as "The Cowboy Capital of the World." Just east of town, Woodward Reservoir offers both local wranglers and visitors a chance to unwind; swimming, fishing, sailing, water skiing, camping and picnicking can be enjoyed.

At Oakdale Cheese & Specialties, 10040 SR 120, visitors can watch Gouda cheese being made several days a week; at other times the process can be seen courtesy of a videotape presentation. Phone (209) 848-3139.

Oakdale District Chamber of Commerce & Visitors Bureau: 590 N. Yosemite Ave., Oakdale, CA 95361; phone (209) 847-2244 or (209) 848-9484.

OAKDALE COWBOY MUSEUM is at 355 E. F St., just off SR 120. In the town's former Southern Pacific train depot, the museum celebrates Oakdale's ranching heritage through displays of rodeo memorabilia, items belonging to local cowboys enshrined in halls of fame, saddles, photographs, awards, branding irons and different types of barbed wire. Allow 30 minutes minimum. Mon.-Sat. 10-2. Admission $1. Phone (209) 847-5163.

OAKHURST (G-4) pop. 2,868, elev. 2,289′

FRESNO FLATS HISTORICAL PARK, n.e. via SR 41 and CR 426 on School Rd., has a museum and a collection of historic buildings typical of those found in a local late 19th-century community. Highlights include Taylor Log House; Laramore House with its collection of antiques; a smithy; a logging exhibit; a late 1800s agricultural barn; a schoolhouse; a riverwalk; and a collection of wagons and stagecoaches. A research library is available.

Picnicking is permitted. Park open daily dawn-dusk; closed Jan. 1, Thanksgiving and Dec. 25. Museum and research library open Mon.-Fri. 10-3, Sat.-Sun. noon-4. Guided tours are offered Sat.-Sun. Free. Guided tour $3. Phone (559) 683-6570.

YOSEMITE SIGHTSEEING TOURS picks up passengers at area hotels for full-day narrated tours of Yosemite National Park. Visitors can see Yosemite Valley, the Mariposa Grove of giant sequoias and Glacier Point. Daily 8-8. Times vary depending on location of hotel and the season. Fare $66-$70; under 12, $35. Rates may vary; phone ahead. Reservations are required. AX, DS, MC, VI. Phone (559) 877-8687.

OAKLAND (D-9) pop. 399,484, elev. 42'

Oakland is a major West Coast port and manufacturing center that stretches along the mainland side of San Francisco Bay and varies in elevation from sea level to 1,500 feet. The San Francisco-Oakland Bay Bridge links the city with San Francisco; a westbound toll of $2 is charged.

The city's rich cultural heritage is demonstrated through ethnic festivals and varied events. Rolling hills and forested areas offer hiking and riding trails, and lakes and parks dot the countryside.

Nine regional parks adjoin Oakland: Anthony Chabot *(see Recreation Chart and the AAA California & Nevada CampBook)*, Claremont Canyon Regional Preserve, Huckleberry Botanic Regional Preserve, Martin Luther King Jr. Shoreline *(see Recreation Chart)*, Miller/Knox, Redwood, Temescal *(see Recreation Chart)*, Robert Sibley Volcanic Regional Preserve, and Tilden *(see Berkeley p. 63)*. Opportunities for hiking, picnicking, fishing and swimming are available. Facilities vary from park to park.

Woodminster Amphitheater, on Joaquin Miller Road in Joaquin Miller Park, is an open-air theater built by the federal WPA program during the mid-20th century. Presentations, mostly Broadway musicals, are scheduled early July to early September; phone (510) 531-9597.

Bret Harte Boardwalk on 5th Street between Jefferson and Clay streets adjoins the site of the author's boyhood home. A block of renovated Victorian houses and barns has been converted to shops and restaurants. Visitor centers are at 14th Street and Broadway and at Jack London Square, Broadway and Embarcadero.

Network Associates Coliseum, off Nimitz Freeway (I-880) at the 66th Avenue exit, includes a stadium, indoor arena and exhibit hall. The complex is the home of two of Oakland's professional sports teams—the A's (baseball) and the Raiders (football). The Golden State Warriors (basketball) play at The Arena, off I-880 at the 66th Avenue or Hegenberger Road exit; the venue also is utilized for concerts, wrestling and the circus. Phone (510) 569-2121 for either arena.

Oakland Convention & Visitors Bureau: 475 14th St., Suite 120, Oakland, CA 94612; phone (510) 839-9000.

CHABOT SPACE & SCIENCE CENTER, 10000 Skyline Blvd. in Joaquin Miller Park, is a hands-on learning center with an emphasis on astronomy and space exploration. The center has a planetarium that presents both live and recorded shows, large format films in a domed theater, interactive exhibits, and the Discovery Room for children ages 3-7. Telescopes are available for free public viewing.

Food is available. Exhibits, planetarium and theater Tues.-Thurs. and Mon. holidays 10-5, Fri.-Sat. 10-7:30 (planetarium and theater also Fri.-Sat. 7:30-9 p.m.), Sun. noon-5, mid-June through Labor Day; Tues.-Sat. and Mon. holidays 10-3 (exhibits also Fri.-Sat. 3-7:30, planetarium and theater also Fri.-Sat. 3-9), Sun. noon-5, rest of year. Closed Thanksgiving and Dec. 25. Observatory open Fri.-Sat. dusk-11 p.m., Apr.-Oct.; 7-10 p.m., rest of year (weather permitting).

Admission (includes exhibits and planetarium show) $11; over 64, students with ID and ages 4-12, $8. Planetarium or theater admission $6; over 64, students with ID and ages 4-12, $5. MC, VI. Phone (510) 336-7300.

GREEK ORTHODOX CATHEDRAL OF THE ASCENSION, 4700 Lincoln Ave., overlooks Oakland and the bay. Designed in the Byzantine style, the copper-domed church houses colorful mosaics and icons of Christ and the disciples. It is crowned with a 12-foot cross set with light-catching Baccarat crystals. A 3-day Greek festival is held in mid-May. Allow 1 hour minimum. Mon.-Fri. 9-4; closed holidays. Free. Phone (510) 531-3400.

JACK LONDON SQUARE, bounded by Clay St., Alice St., the Embarcadero and the Oakland estuary, is a colorful waterfront area. Heinolds' First and Last Chance Saloon, a favorite haunt of the author, is at the foot of Webster Street. The area also contains an Amtrak station and several museums. Jack London Village is an early 19th-century-style shopping and restaurant complex. Phone (866) 295-9853 for information and special events and activities at the square.

LAKESIDE PARK embraces the n. shore of Lake Merritt, a saltwater tidal lake in the center of the city. Boat rentals, windsurfing and sailing lessons and bowling greens are available. A tour boat also plies the lake. Picnicking is permitted. Park admission free. Parking $2 Sat.-Sun. and holidays. Phone (510) 238-2196 for tour boat information and reservations.

Children's Fairyland, corner of Grand and Bellevue aves., is a child-size attraction depicting fairy tales and nursery rhymes. Children's rides are available. Allow 2 hours minimum. Mon.-Fri. 10-4, Sat.-Sun. 10-5, mid-June through Labor Day; Wed.-Sun.

10-4, Apr. 1 to mid-June and day after Labor Day-Oct. 31; Sat.-Sun. 10-4, rest of year. Closed Jan. 1 and Dec. 25. Puppet shows are presented at 11, 2 and 4. Admission $6. Parking $2 Sat.-Sun. and holidays. MC, VI. Phone (510) 238-6876 or (510) 452-2259.

Gondola Servizio, Lake Merritt Boating Center, offers 55-minute cruises in authentic, handmade Venetian gondolas. Daily 10-10. Fare $45-$225 per couple. While frequently it is possible to accommodate walk-ups, reservations are suggested. AX, MC, VI. Phone (510) 663-6603 or (866) 737-8494.

Lake Merritt Wildlife Refuge and Rotary Nature Center, Bellevue Ave. and Perkins St., has seasonal displays of birds, mammals and reptiles. In winter hundreds of wild geese, herons, egrets and ducks take sanctuary at the wildlife refuge outside the museum; founded in 1870, this is said to be the oldest refuge in North America. The nature center also contains a native plant garden. Allow 30 minutes minimum. Daily 10-5. Free. Phone (510) 238-3739.

Lakeside Park Garden Center, 666 Bellevue Ave., is surrounded by Japanese, Polynesian, cactus, dahlia, palm, fuchsia, firescape and chrysanthemum gardens, and also has an herb and fragrance garden. The center presents flower shows in season. Allow 2 hours minimum. Mon.-Fri. 10-6, Sat.-Sun. and holidays 10-5, May-Nov.; Mon.-Fri. 10-3, Sat.-Sun. 10-4, rest of year. Parking $2 Sat.-Sun. and holidays. Phone (510) 238-3208.

MILLS COLLEGE ART MUSEUM, on campus at 5000 McArthur Blvd., offers changing exhibits by contemporary artists and senior art students at this 1,000-student noted liberal arts college. Allow 1 hour, 30 minutes minimum. Tues.-Sat. 11-4 (also Wed. 4-7:30), Sun. noon-4; closed holidays. Free. Phone (510) 430-2164.

MORCOM AMPHITHEATER OF ROSES is 1 blk. w. of Grand Ave. at 700 Jean St.; additional street parking is available on Olive Ave. The site features 8 acres of gardens, reflecting pools and trees, with various species in bloom May through November; the peak season is May through September. Garden information is available. Daily dawn-dusk. Free. Phone (510) 238-3187.

MORMON TEMPLE, 4770 Lincoln Ave., is a magnificent example of religious architecture and offers

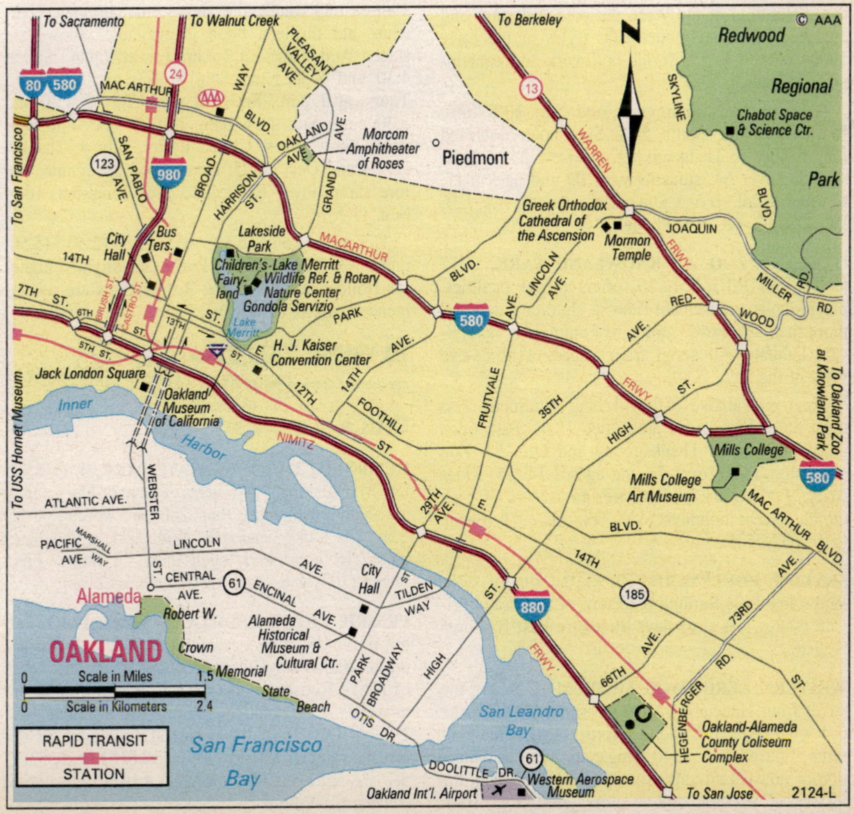

a scenic vista of Oakland and San Francisco. Guided 25-minute tours of the gardens and visitor center include a 12-minute videotape presentation about the temple, and begin as needed. A family history center is located below the visitor center. The interior of the temple is closed to non-Mormons.

Allow 1 hour minimum. Grounds open 8 a.m.-10 p.m. Visitor center open 9-9. Last tour departs 30 minutes before closing. Free. Phone (510) 531-3200, or (510) 531-1475 for the visitor center.

GEM **OAKLAND MUSEUM OF CALIFORNIA,** 10th and Oak sts., is a complex of terraced gardens and three main galleries reflecting the state's ecology, history and art.

The Natural Sciences Gallery depicts California's ecology through a walk across the state from ocean to mountains and desert with native plants and animals shown in realistic settings, while the Cowell Hall of California History preserves the state's past from its pre-Spanish period to current times, with an emphasis on events such as earthquakes, countercultures, the computer chip and the diverse groups of people that influenced the state's development.

The Gallery of California Art presents pieces dating from the early 19th century; works of art depict the exploration of the West, the gold rush days and the decorative and modernistic styles of the early 1900s as well as California craftwork and contemporary pieces.

Allow 1 hour minimum. Wed.-Sat. 10-5 (also first Fri. of the month 5-9), Sun. noon-5; closed Jan. 1, July 4, Thanksgiving and Dec. 25. Admission $8; over 64, students with ID and ages 6-17, $5; free to all second Sun. of the month. AX, CB, DC, DS, JC, MC, VI. Phone (510) 238-2200.

OAKLAND ZOO AT KNOWLAND PARK, 9777 Golf Links Rd. off I-580, offers picnic facilities, playgrounds, amusement rides, a children's zoo and more than 400 exotic and native animals in naturalistic habitats. An aerial tram affords a bird's-eye view of the area.

Food is available. Allow 1 hour minimum. Zoo open daily 10-4 (rides area open 11-4). Park open daily 9-5. Closed Thanksgiving and Dec. 25. Zoo admission $8.50; over 54 and ages 2-14, $5. Rides $1-$2. Parking $4; parking free first Mon. of each month except holidays. AX, DS, MC, VI. Phone (510) 632-9525.

SKYLINE BOULEVARD follows the rim of Oakland's low hills through a section of parks and private estates. On clear days the entire East Bay area is visible.

WESTERN AEROSPACE MUSEUM is across the street from Hangar 6 (Alaska Airlines) in Building 621 on Oakland Airport's North Field. This museum, housed in a 1940 hangar, presents a collection of unusual aircraft as well as exhibits about the history of aviation and aviators. Wed.-Sun. 10-4; closed Jan. 1, Thanksgiving and Dec. 25. Admission $7; over 60, $6; ages 6-12, $3. MC, VI. Phone (510) 638-7100.

OAKVILLE—*see Wine Country p. 198.*

O'BRIEN (B-3)

LAKE SHASTA CAVERNS is reached from Shasta Caverns Rd., 1.5 mi. e. of I-5. Columns, stalactites, stalagmites and flowstone deposits can be seen on 2-hour tours; more than 600 steps are included. The caverns remain a constant temperature of 58 F. Round-trip boat and bus transportation are provided.

Food is available. Allow 3 hours minimum. Tours depart every half-hour daily 9-4, Memorial Day weekend-Labor Day; every hour 9-3, Apr. 1-day before Memorial Day weekend and day after Labor Day-Sept. 30; at 10, noon and 2, rest of year (weather permitting). Closed Thanksgiving and Dec. 25. Admission $19; ages 4-12, $9. AX, DS, MC, VI. Phone (530) 238-2341 or (800) 795-2283.

OCEANO (I-3) pop. 7,260, elev. 25'

THE GREAT AMERICAN MELODRAMA AND VAUDEVILLE, 1863 Pacific Blvd. (SR 1), presents 19th-century vaudeville shows, melodramas, comedies and thrillers. Food is available. Shows are staged Wed.-Thurs. at 7 p.m., Fri. at 8 p.m., Sat. at 4:30 and 8:30 p.m., Sun. at 6 p.m., Mar.-Dec.; Thurs. at 7 p.m., Fri. at 8 p.m., Sat. at 4:30 and 8:30 p.m., Sun. at 6 p.m., rest of year. Phone to verify show times. Closed Easter, July 4, Thanksgiving and Dec. 24-25. Doors open 30 minutes before show times. Box office open Mon.-Sat. 10-6, Sun. 11-5.

Tickets $13.50-$16.50; over 62, $12.50-$15.50; under 13, $10.50-13.50. Prices are slightly higher for Holiday Extravaganza. Reservations are recommended. AX, DS, MC, VI. Phone (805) 489-2499.

OLYMPIC VALLEY—

see Lake Tahoe Area p. 85.

ORICK (B-1) elev. 34'

HUMBOLDT LAGOONS STATE PARK, 4 mi. s. on US 101, contains 1,886 acres. The park has a sandy marshland with more than 200 bird species, a lagoon and rocky headlands. Wild azaleas and lilacs bloom in June. Park open daily 24 hours. Free. Phone (707) 488-2041. *See Recreation Chart.*

PRAIRIE CREEK REDWOODS STATE PARK is 6 mi. n. on US 101. A coastal redwood park consisting of 40,000 acres, it protects one of the last herds of native Roosevelt elks. Beach access, guided nature hikes and campfire programs are available June 1-Labor Day. Daily dawn-dusk. Day use fee $2 per private vehicle. Phone (707) 464-6101, ext. 5301. *See Recreation Chart and the AAA California & Nevada CampBook.*

OROVILLE (D-3) pop. 13,004, elev. 174'

Cherokee Indians migrated to Oroville from Georgia in the 1850s to work in gold mines north of town. In 1870 alone, hydraulic mining operations at the site yielded $5 million in gold. Later diamonds were discovered; Cherokee Diamond Mine opened in 1873 and produced some 300 diamonds of industrial quality.

The reserves soon were depleted however, and the nearby town of Cherokee, like so many other mining towns in California, was forgotten. Ruins of brick stores and foundations identified by markers are all that remain in this ghost town on Cherokee Road, 10 miles north via SR 70, the Feather River Scenic Byway.

Recreational opportunities are abundant, considering the city's access to Lake Oroville *(see Recreation Chart)* and the Feather River. The lake's 167 miles of shoreline are utilized for water skiing, sailing, jet skiing, camping and houseboating, while the river is popular with anglers in search of salmon, sturgeon, bass and steelhead.

Oroville Area Chamber of Commerce: 1789 Montgomery St., Oroville, CA 95965; phone (530) 538-2542 or (800) 655-4653.

BUTTE COUNTY PIONEER MUSEUM, 2332 Montgomery St., has a room resembling an 1849 cabin, a replica of a Victorian parlor and varied collections ranging from American Indian artifacts to early home furnishings. Fri.-Sun. noon-4. Admission $2, under 12 free. Phone (530) 538-2529, or (530) 538-2497 for tour information.

CHINESE TEMPLE is at 1500 Broderick St. The 1863 temple contains furnishings donated by the Emperor of China. A self-guiding tour includes three chapels—Confucianism, Taoism and Buddhism, a courtyard garden and collections of puppets, costumes and tapestries. Allow 1 hour minimum. Thurs.-Mon. noon-4, Tues.-Wed. 1-4, Feb. 1-Dec. 14. Admission $2, under 12 free. Phone (530) 538-2496.

FEATHER RIVER HATCHERY, 5 Table Mountain Blvd., releases more than 10 million salmon and steelhead yearlings into the Feather River each year. The best time to visit the hatchery is during the spawning season, October 1 to mid-November. Guided tours are available by appointment. Allow 30 minutes minimum. Daily 7:30-dusk. Free. Phone (530) 538-2222, or (530) 534-2306 for guided tours.

LAKE OROVILLE VISITOR CENTER is 7 mi. n.e. of SR 162 to Kelly Ridge, then 1.5 mi. n. The center, overlooking Lake Oroville and Oroville Dam, displays exhibits depicting the gold-rush era; state water projects; wildlife; the Beckwourth Trail, a safer route across the Sierra Nevada; and the Maidu Indians. Videotapes about the area are shown upon request. Allow 1 hour minimum. Daily 9-5; closed Jan. 1, Thanksgiving and Dec. 25. Free. Phone (530) 538-2219.

LOTT HOME MUSEUM is between 3rd and 4th aves. at 1067 Montgomery St. in Sank Park. The 1856 house, built by a prominent lawyer for his bride, is furnished in period. A Victorian garden is in the park. Picnic facilities are available. House open Sun.-Mon. and Fri. 11:30-3:30 and by appointment, Feb. 1-Dec. 14. Park open daily 9-8. House $2, under 12 free. Park free. Phone (530) 538-2497.

PACIFICA—*see San Francisco p. 159.*

PACIFIC GROVE—

see Monterey Peninsula p. 104.

PALO ALTO (E-8) pop. 58,598, elev. 23'

Palo Alto (Spanish for tall tree) was named for a double-trunked redwood tree, a landmark used by travelers and explorers as early as 1769. A likeness of the tree appears on the seal of Stanford University. The opening of the university in 1891 provided the impetus for Palo Alto's growth, and the livelihoods of the two remain closely intertwined. Palo Alto is the southeastern terminus of a scenic 31-mile stretch of I-280 that heads northwest to San Francisco.

Palo Alto Chamber of Commerce: 122 Hamilton Ave., Palo Alto, CA 94301; phone (650) 324-3121.

MUSEUM OF AMERICAN HERITAGE, downtown at 351 Homer Ave. in the Williams House and Gardens, offers a glimpse at the evolution of American technology during the 19th and 20th centuries. Housed in the 1907 English Country-style home of a prominent local physician, the museum displays a kitchen typical of the 1920s and '30s, a doctor's examining room, a general store, and radio repair and print shops. Fri.-Sun. 11-4. Donations. Phone (650) 321-1004.

STANFORD UNIVERSITY, about 1 mi. w., stands on what is known as the Stanford Farm, an estate of 8,200 acres. Frederick Law Olmstead created the general concept for the grounds and the unifying architectural theme: Romanesque sandstone buildings with arched arcades and red-tiled roofs. One-hour tours of the 14,000-student campus depart Memorial Hall, across from Hoover Tower on Serra Street. Tours are given daily at 11 and 3:15, except holidays and the last 2 weeks in Dec. Phone (650) 723-2560.

Hoover Tower, on Serra Mall, houses the Hoover Institution on War, Revolution and Peace, a public policy research center devoted to the study of world conflict. The institution was founded in 1919 by Herbert Hoover, who would later become the nation's 31st president. The 285-foot-tall tower is topped by a 48-bell carillon. The building and an observation platform can be visited. Allow 30 minutes minimum. Open daily 10-4:30; closed holidays, examination weeks and during school breaks.

Admission $2; over 64 and under 14, $1. Phone (650) 723-2053.

GEM **Iris & B. Gerald Cantor Center for Visual Arts**, just off Campus Dr. E. at Lomita Dr. and Museum Way, contains 27 galleries displaying sculpture, decorative arts, photographs, paintings and sketchings. Works from ancient days to the early 20th century represent African, American, Asian, European, ancient Mediterranean and American Indian artists and craftspeople.

Two galleries are dedicated to Auguste Rodin sculpture; his famous "Age of Bronze" and "The Kiss" are crowd-pleasers. Outside, the Rodin Sculpture Garden displays more life-size bronze figures. "Adam and Eve at the Gates of Hell" has large figures of Adam and Eve flanking the elaborate gates, which contain many smaller figures within.

Georgia O'Keeffe paintings, Andy Warhol pop art sculpture, Ansel Adams photography and Edgar Degas sculpture and paintings also are highlights.

Food is available. Allow 2 hours minimum. Wed.-Sun. 11-5 (also Thurs. 5-8); closed Jan. 1, Thanksgiving and Dec. 25. Guided tours are given Wed. at noon, Sat.-Sun. at 1. Free. Phone (650) 723-4177 or TTY (650) 723-1216.

Stanford Linear Accelerator Center is on Sand Hill Rd. Also known as SLAC, the center is a research facility with a 2-mile-long linear accelerator that generates high-energy electron beams. Stanford University operates the 426-acre basic research laboratory for the U.S. Department of Energy. An orientation precedes the guided bus tour. Allow 2 hours minimum for the orientation and tour. Visitor center open Mon.-Fri. 8-5. Tour schedule varies; phone ahead. Free. Phone (650) 926-2204 for schedule and reservations.

PARADISE (D-3) pop. 26,408, elev. 1,708'

It was gold that brought prospectors in search of their fortunes to this area in the foothills of the Sierra Nevada during California's gold rush. Although a 54-pound nugget was found nearby, the frenzy for gold eventually died down. Many of the miners stayed, however, establishing the farms, orchards, sawmills and shops that became the community of Paradise.

Visitors to Paradise today enjoy a variety of outdoor activities such as hiking, nature trails, boating, bicycling, fishing, gold panning and backroad adventures to old mining sites.

Paradise Ridge Chamber of Commerce and Visitors Bureau: 5550-A Skyway, Paradise, CA 95969; phone (530) 877-9356 or (888) 845-2769.

GOLD NUGGET MUSEUM, 502 Pearson Rd., exhibits a miner's cabin, smithy, general store and a replica of a gold mine. Also displayed are exhibits depicting the history of Paradise and Magalia Ridge. A research library is available. Living-history weekends take place June 1 through Labor Day, when skills such as gold panning and blacksmithing are demonstrated. Events also are scheduled the rest of the year. Allow 1 hour minimum. Wed.-Sun. noon-4; closed major holidays. Donations. Phone (530) 872-8722.

PASO ROBLES (H-4) pop. 18,600, elev. 721'

Twenty-five miles east on SR 46 is Cholame, the small town where motion-picture legend James Dean died in an automobile accident; a stainless steel monument is beside the road.

Paso Robles Chamber of Commerce and Visitors and Conference Bureau: 1225 Park St., Paso Robles, CA 93446-2234; phone (805) 238-0506.

EL PASO DE ROBLES AREA PIONEER MUSEUM, 2010 Riverside Ave., preserves the history of the Paso Robles area. Objects displayed include American Indian artifacts; vintage farm and ranching equipment, including a barbed wire collection; early 20th-century vehicles; household items, including furniture and clothing; and business machinery. Open Thurs.-Sun. 1-4. Free. Phone (805) 239-4556.

WINERIES

- **Eberle Winery**, 4 mi. e. on SR 46 to 3810 Hwy. 46E. Daily 10-6, Apr.-Sept.; 10-5, rest of year. Closed Thanksgiving and Dec. 25. Phone (805) 238-9607.
- **EOS Estate Winery at Arciero Vineyards**, 6 mi. e. on SR 46. Daily 10-5; closed Jan. 1, Thanksgiving and Dec. 25. Phone (805) 239-2562 or (800) 249-9463.

PESCADERO (E-8) elev. 30'

AÑO NUEVO STATE RESERVE, 13 mi. s on SR 1, is known for its colony of northern elephant seals, which come ashore to give birth, breed and molt. Guided 3-mile, 2.5-hour walks are scheduled December through March, the best viewing months; tickets must be bought in advance by phone through ReserveAmerica. Obtain hiking permits for the wildlife protection area, required April through November, at the entrance station or visitor center.

Layered clothing and sturdy shoes are recommended. Pets are not allowed. Park open daily 8-dusk, year-round; the wildlife protection area has some seasonal restrictions. Guided walks every quarter-hour daily 8:30-3:30, mid-Dec. through Mar. 31; closed Jan. 24 and Dec. 25. Walks operate regardless of weather; no refunds are issued. Hiking permits available on a first-come, first-served basis daily 8:30-3:30.

Guided walk tickets $4 per person. Parking $2 per private vehicle. Phone (650) 879-0227 or (650) 879-2025, or (800) 444-4445 for ReserveAmerica.

PETALUMA—*see Wine Country p. 198.*

PIERCY—*see Wine Country p. 198.*

GEM PINNACLES NATIONAL MONUMENT (G-3)

Entered from the east via SR 146, 35 miles south of Hollister via SR 25, or 35 miles north of King City via CR G13, the monument also can be approached from the west via SR 146, off US 101 in Soledad. Pinnacles National Monument embraces about 24,000 acres of precipitous bluffs, spires and crags of colorful volcanic rock and a series of caves underneath the formations. The forces of heat, cold, water and wind have worn the contours of the rocky terrain.

Bear Gulch Visitor Center is accessible by car from the east entrance. The west entrance has a ranger station; the entrance road is winding and narrow. Trailers and motorhomes are advised to use the east entrance. No roads connect the east and west districts. The visitor center is open daily 9-5.

Pinnacles is strictly a hiking park, although some major formations can be seen from the roadway into the monument. The best viewing by car is from the west side. Hiking trails range from easy 1-mile treks to strenuous hikes of more than 10 miles.

The monument is bisected from north to south by a 1,000-foot-high ridge. Most of the spirelike formations, some more than 600 feet high, are found on or alongside the ridge. This central backbone has been cut in two places by streams; huge fragments of rock have fallen into the resulting deep clefts, creating caves. Bear Gulch Caves and Balconies Caves require visitors to carry flashlights. Bear Gulch Caves are closed temporarily.

Note: Neither pets nor bicycles are permitted on the trails; in parking lots, roads and picnic areas, pets must be kept leashed and under physical control. Beware of poison oak.

In addition to geological and scenic interest, the monument has an abundant bird population as well as deer and wildflowers. The plants and animals within the national monument are examples of a coast range chaparral ecosystem. Picnic facilities are available. Admission is $5 per private vehicle; parking areas fill up early on weekends and during spring, the monument's busiest season. Phone (831) 389-4485. *See the AAA California & Nevada CampBook.*

PISMO BEACH (I-3) pop. 8,551, elev. 70′

Pismo Beach lies on a scenic stretch of US 101 that extends from San Luis Obispo to Los Angeles. Pismo Beach is perhaps best known for its namesake mollusk, the Pismo clam. At one time the clams were so plentiful that 45,000 could be harvested commercially in a day. Decades of unrestricted clamming and the appetites of sea otters have depleted the supply, resulting in strict limits. Digging for no more than 10 legal-size clams is permitted with a California state license.

These days butterflies outrank clams as a local attraction. From late October through February thousands of migrating monarchs alight on Pismo Beach's Butterfly Trees, a grove of Monterey pines and eucalyptus. Some come from as far as Canada to pass the winter in this mild climate.

Popular beach activities include horseback riding and kite boarding. Pismo State Beach *(see Recreation Chart)* has camping and a dune area where off-highway vehicles are allowed. Vehicles are prohibited in Pismo Dunes Preserve, which contains extensive coastal dunes.

Pismo Beach Visitor Information Center: 581 Dolliver St., Pismo Beach, CA 93449; phone (805) 443-7778.

PLACERVILLE (E-4) pop. 9,610, elev. 1,860′

Placerville, originally known as Dry Diggin's, became so prosperous and lawless that lawbreakers were hanged first singly, then in pairs. As a result, the settlement was named Hangtown. By working as a wheelwright in a smithy during the 1850s, John Studebaker accumulated enough capital to move east and establish the factory where the first Studebaker automobile was produced.

Less than 10 miles from the original California gold discovery site, Placerville's past is reflected in the 19th-century architecture prevalent in its historic downtown. As the county seat, the city is the center of area commerce.

El Dorado County Chamber of Commerce: 542 Main St., Placerville, CA 95667; phone (530) 621-5885 or (800) 457-6279.

EL DORADO COUNTY HISTORICAL MUSEUM is 1 mi. n. of US 50 at 104 Placerville Dr. in the El Dorado County Fairgrounds. Exhibits—which include ranching, logging, mining equipment, farming, housing, a country store, a stagecoach, a Shay locomotive and other railroad rolling stock—reflect local history and the gold-rush days. Changing exhibits and a research library also are offered.

Allow 1 hour minimum. Wed.-Sat. 10-4, Sun. noon-4, or by appointment; closed Jan. 1, Thanksgiving and Dec. 25. Research library open Tues. 9-3. Donations. Phone (530) 621-5865.

GOLD BUG MINE is 1 mi. n. off US 50 Bedford Ave. exit within Gold Bug Park. The nation's only municipally owned mine, Gold Bug Mine lies on the eastern side of the Mother Lode vein. The wood-floored mine has a 352-foot horizontal drift. Also in the park are the Priest Mine and the Hendy Stamp Mill and Museum. Self-guiding tours utilizing hand-held cassettes are available in several languages. Hiking trails and panning for gold are available.

Picnicking is permitted. Allow 30 minutes minimum. Mines, museum and stamp mill open daily 10-4, mid-Apr. through last Sun. in Oct.; mine only Sat.-Sun. noon-4, rest of year. Park grounds open daily 8:30-5 (weather permitting), year-round. Admission $3; ages 5-16, $1. Under 16 must be with an adult. Cassette rental $1. Phone (530) 642-5207.

PLANTATION—*see Wine Country p. 199.*

PLEASANTON (E-9) pop. 63,634, elev. 352′

Many well-maintained old buildings and houses lend Pleasanton an early 19th-century atmosphere. The Amador-Livermore Valley Historical Society operates a museum at 603 Main St. that depicts regional history; phone (925) 462-2766.

The Alameda County Fairgrounds has one of the oldest racetracks in America; it was built in 1858 by the sons of a Spanish don, Augustin Bernal. The presence of limestone in the soil is credited with making this an exceptionally fine track.

Shadow Cliffs East Bay Regional Recreation Area on the outskirts of town was developed from an abandoned gravel quarry. A lake in the park offers swimming, boating and fishing. *See Recreation Chart.*

Pleasanton Chamber of Commerce: 777 Peters Ave., Pleasanton, CA 94566; phone (925) 846-5858.

RAPIDS WATERSLIDE AT SHADOW CLIFFS EAST BAY REGIONAL PARK, 2 mi. e. at 2500 Stanley Blvd., has four flumes in a rustic corner of the site. Daily 10:30-5:30, June 1-Labor Day; Sat.-Sun. 10:30-5:30, in May and day after Labor Day-Sept. 30 (weather permitting). All-day pass $15; half-day pass (Mon.-Fri. 10:30-2 or 2-5:30) $10; regular admission $7 per hour. Parking $5. Under 42 inches tall are not permitted on the slides. AX, MC, VI. Phone (925) 846-4900, or (925) 829-6230 for reservations.

PLUMAS NATIONAL FOREST

Elevations in the forest range from 1,000 ft. at Feather River Canyon to 8,372 ft. at the summit of Mount Ingalls. Refer to AAA maps for additional elevation information.

In northern California, the 1,162,863 acres of Plumas National Forest straddle the transition zone between two of the West's great mountain ranges, the Sierra Nevada and the Cascades. Although the Sierra block disappears under the younger volcanic rock of the Cascades on the forest's northern boundary near Lake Almanor, it is difficult to tell where one range ends and the other begins.

The mountains of the northern Sierra Nevada, which make up most of the forest lands, are neither as high nor as spectacular as those south of Lake Tahoe. Yet within these mountains are a history of hidden treasure and a wealth of scenery.

The forest's principal gem is the Feather River watershed. The Feather River has carved numerous canyons and ravines full of cascades and white water. Portions of the Middle Fork of the river and three of its tributaries have been designated Feather Falls Scenic Area. The centerpiece of this 15,000-acre scenic area is 640-foot Feather Falls, which is just above Lake Oroville and is the highest of the numerous waterfalls on the 93-mile-long Middle Fork of the Feather River—a designated wild and scenic river. Water from this forest creates the headwaters for the California state water system.

Because of the rugged terrain and dangerous rapids, canoeing and tubing are recommended only in the recreation zone. Hiking trails and campgrounds are available along the river. Near the headwaters of the South Fork is Little Grass Valley Lake Recreation Area, which offers swimming, fishing and camping.

An extensive network of roads crisscrosses the national forest. Many routes, such as the Feather River National Scenic Byway, which crosses the lowest pass in the Sierra Nevada, are a legacy of the gold era when such towns as Rich Bar, Pulga and La Porte were flourishing mining camps. Anglers and hikers have replaced the miners and frequent such popular areas as Bucks Lake, Lake Davis, Frenchman Lake and Antelope Lake. Seventy-one miles of the Pacific Crest Trail run through the national forest.

Information about campgrounds and recreational opportunities is available at the District Ranger stations and the Forest Headquarters in Quincy. Maps and guides to the Pacific Crest Trail and the Feather Falls Scenic Area also are available at the headquarters. For more information contact Plumas National Forest, 159 Lawrence St., P.O. Box 11500, Quincy, CA 95971; phone (530) 283-2050. *See the Recreation Chart and AAA California & Nevada CampBook.*

PLYMOUTH (E-4) pop. 980, elev. 1,086′

AMADOR FLOWER FARM is at 22001 Shenandoah School Rd. More than 800 varieties of daylilies are featured among the farm's 12 acres of gardens. Included are 4 acres of landscaped demonstration gardens. Picnicking is permitted. Daily 9-4; closed Jan. 1, Thanksgiving and Dec. 25. Free. Phone (209) 245-6660.

WINERIES

- **Sobon Estate**, 7.5 mi. n.e. of SR 49 at 14430 Shenandoah Rd. Daily 9:30-5; closed Jan. 1, Easter, Thanksgiving and Dec. 25. Phone (209) 245-6554.

POINT ARENA—*see Wine Country p. 199.*

POINT REYES NATIONAL SEASHORE—*see San Francisco p. 159.*

PORTERVILLE (H-5) pop. 39,615, elev. 455′

Porterville Chamber of Commerce: 93 North Main St., Suite A, Porterville, CA 93257; phone (559) 784-7502.

PORTERVILLE HISTORICAL MUSEUM, 257 N. D St., is housed in a 1913 Southern Pacific passenger station. The museum's exhibits include vignettes of a dentist's office, drug store and attorney's office. China, glassware, furniture and American Indian artifacts, including baskets created by Yokuts, are displayed.

Thurs.-Sat. 9-3, June-Sept.; 10-4, rest of year. Closed Jan. 1, during Porterville Fair Week in May, Thanksgiving and Dec. 25. Admission $2, students with ID 50c, under 6 free. Phone (559) 784-2053.

ZALUD HOUSE, 393 N. Hockett St. at Morton Ave., was built about 1891. The rococo-style house with a mansard roof contains most of its original furnishings. The flower garden, initially planted in the 1930s, retains its original design. Guided 20-minute tours are given as needed Wed.-Sat. 10-4, Sun. 2-4, Feb.-Dec.; closed holidays. Admission $2; under 18, 50c. Phone (559) 782-7548.

PORTOLA (D-4) pop. 2,227, elev. 4,850′

Portola is intersected by the Union Pacific Railroad and the Middle Fork of the Feather River. Nearby Lake Davis is a favorite of trout fishermen.

Plumas County Visitors Bureau: P.O. Box 4120, Quincy, CA 95971; phone (530) 283-6345 or (800) 326-2247.

PORTOLA RAILROAD MUSEUM, 1 mi. s. of SR 70 on CR A15 (Gulling St.), contains more than 100 historical Western railroad locomotives and railcars, including a 1950 streamline diesel and a Union Pacific Centennial, billed as the world's largest diesel locomotive. Housed in a former diesel shop, the museum also displays railroad relics. Train rides are available.

Picnic facilities are available. Allow 1 hour minimum. Daily 10-5. Caboose train rides every half-hour, Sat.-Sun. 11-4, Memorial Day weekend-Labor Day. Museum admission by donations. All-day train ride pass $5, family pass $12. Phone (530) 832-4131.

QUINCY (C-4) pop. 1,879, elev. 3,432′

Quincy is nestled against the western slope of the Sierra Nevada range, at the top of the scenic Feather River Canyon. A walking tour of its preserved and restored downtown begins at the Plumas County Museum *(see attraction listing).*

Plumas County Visitors Bureau: P.O. Box 4120, Quincy, CA 95971; phone (530) 283-6345 or (800) 326-2247.

PLUMAS COUNTY MUSEUM, 500 Jackson St., displays historical documents and photographs; permanent and rotating exhibits; cultural and natural history displays that illustrate area history since the 1850s; mining, logging and railroad exhibits; and woven baskets and artifacts from the native Maidu Indians. The restored 1878 Victorian house next to the museum is furnished with museum pieces; phone for house schedule.

Allow 30 minutes minimum. Mon.-Sat. 8-5 (also Sun. and holidays 10-4, May-Sept.). Admission $2; ages 12-17, $1. Phone (530) 283-6320.

RED BLUFF (C-2) pop. 13,147, elev. 304′

Named for the colored sand and gravel cliffs characteristic of the surrounding area, Red Bluff is a gateway to Lassen Volcanic National Park *(see place listing p. 90)*.

Red Bluff-Tehama County Chamber of Commerce: 100 Main St., P.O. Box 850, Red Bluff, CA 96080; phone (530) 527-6220 or (800) 655-6225.

GAUMER'S is off I-5 SR 36W exit at 78 Belle Mill Rd. This jewelry shop houses a mining and mineral museum with displays of rocks, gems, minerals and crystals. Fossils, American Indian artifacts and a reproduction of a mine entrance—with an ore car used by the owner's grandfather as well as tracks and mining equipment—also are shown. Mon.-Fri. 9-5; closed major holidays. Free. Phone (530) 527-6166.

SALMON VIEWING PLAZA, .1 mi. e. of I-5 on SR 36, then 2 mi. s. on Sale Ln., is at Diversion Dam on the Sacramento River. Underwater television cameras monitor the fish ladders. There is no viewing mid-September through mid-May. The plaza has exhibits about salmon as well as camping, picnicking and boat-launching facilities. Nearby is the Sacramento River Discovery Center.

DID YOU KNOW

Because of budget considerations, the schedules and fees of all state-owned facilities are subject to change. Travelers are advised to phone ahead.

Viewing plaza open daily 6 a.m.-8 p.m. River ramp closed in Aug. Free. Phone (530) 527-3043, (530) 527-2813 for camping information, or (530) 527-1196 for the discovery center.

WILLIAM B. IDE ADOBE STATE HISTORIC PARK, 1 mi. n. on Adobe Rd., has an 1850 adobe that is a memorial to the founder and president of the short-lived California Republic.

In 1846 rumors that Mexican authorities were about to expel American settlers compelled Ide to join a band of settlers in the Bear Flag Revolt. Subsequently, California became an independent country with Ide as its president for 24 days until the Mexican-American War began and the area was occupied by U.S. troops. Picnicking is permitted. Daily 8-dusk. Free. Parking $4. Phone (530) 529-8599.

REDDING (C-2) pop. 80,865, elev. 560′

Redding, in the center of a year-round recreation area, provides scenic access via I-5 to the surrounding Shasta-Trinity National Forests *(see place listing p. 172)* and Whiskeytown-Shasta-Trinity National Recreation Area *(see place listing p. 181)*.

The Sacramento River National Recreation Trail, a 10-mile hiking and bicycling path, runs along both sides of the Sacramento River; the Pedestrian Bridge connects the two sides. Benches along the trail afford a respite from which to enjoy scenic views of the river.

Redding Convention & Visitors Bureau: 777 Auditorium Dr., Redding, CA 96001; phone (530) 225-4100 or (800) 874-7562.

SHASTA DAM is 10 mi. n.w. off I-5 Shasta Dam Blvd. exit, following signs. Shasta Dam is reputedly the world's highest center-overflow spillway. A 30-minute videotape depicting water usage in California is shown at the visitor center upon request. Guided walking tours provide information about visitor center displays and the dam. A 1-hour tour of the dam departs daily at 9, 11, 1 and 3. Visitor center open Mon.-Fri. 8-4:30, Sat.-Sun. 8:30-5; closed winter federal holidays. Free. Phone (530) 275-4463.

GEM **SHASTA STATE HISTORIC PARK** is 6 mi. w. on SR 299. Formerly a robust mining town with a population of 2,500, Shasta was the gateway to a large area of riches and a rendezvous for gamblers; it is now an interesting gold-rush relic. The old courthouse has been converted to a museum that contains historical exhibits as well as the Boggs Collection—100 Years of California Art.

A restored barn and stagecoach can be seen. Also in the park are unrestored buildings that stand as reminders of Shasta's mining heyday. Picnic facilities are available. Wed.-Sun. 10-5; closed Jan. 1,

Thanksgiving and Dec. 25. Admission $2, under 17 free. Phone (530) 243-8194 or (530) 225-2065.

TURTLE BAY EXPLORATION PARK is off SR 299W Auditorium Dr. exit. The 300-acre interpretive park explores the people, cultures and natural resources of the Northern Valley region. The complex contains the Turtle Bay Museum featuring regional history, art and natural science; Paul Bunyan's Forest Camp, with logging and ecology exhibits; and the Butterfly House, a summer favorite.

Food is available. Complex open daily 9-5, early June-Sept. 30; Tues.-Sun. 9-5, rest of year. Closed Jan. 1, Thanksgiving and Dec. 25. Admission $11; over 64, $9; ages 4-15, $6. Rates may vary; phone ahead. AX, DC, DS, MC, VI. Phone (530) 243-8850 or (800) 887-8532.

WATERWORKS PARK, 151 N. Boulder Dr., has three flumes, the Flash Flood, the Avalanche, the Raging River inner tube ride, an activity pool, a children's pool with slides and a fountain, and facilities for basketball and video games.

Lockers, dressing rooms, picnic tables and food are available. Daily 10-7 (also Tues. and Thurs. 7-8 p.m.), Memorial Day weekend-Labor Day. Hours may be reduced in early June and late Aug.; phone ahead. Admission $17; ages 3-11, $14; over 63 free. Reduced admission 3 hours before closing. DS, MC, VI. Phone (530) 246-9550.

RED ROCK CANYON STATE PARK (I-6)

Red Rock Canyon State Park is 25 miles northeast of Mojave via SR 14. Red, brown and gray sandstone cliffs have eroded into spectacular shapes. The colorful formations served as landmarks for freight wagons that stopped at the canyon's springs. Included in this desert community are Joshua trees, cholla cactus, golden eagles, desert tortoises and coyotes. A visitor center provides information about geology and history, and a pamphlet for a self-guiding half-mile nature trail is available.

The park is open daily 24 hours. The visitor center is open Sat.-Sun. 9-3, mid-Sept. through Memorial Day; otherwise varies. Day use fee, $3. Primitive camping fee $9; over 61, $7. Phone (661) 942-0662. *See Recreation Chart and AAA California & Nevada CampBook.*

REDWOOD CITY (E-9) pop. 75,402, elev. 15′

LATHROP HOUSE is in the county government center at 627 Hamilton St. The restored 1863 house, built by Benjamin Lathrop, is an example of early Gothic Revival architecture and is furnished in period. Its two floors feature period clothing and changing exhibits. The house was moved to its present site in 1905 and survived the earthquakes of 1906 and 1989. Tues.-Thurs. 11-3, Sept.-July; closed holidays and the last 2 weeks in Dec. Hours may vary; phone ahead. Donations. Phone (650) 365-5564.

SAN MATEO COUNTY HISTORY MUSEUM is at 777 Hamilton St. Changing exhibits in the 1908 county courthouse depict peninsula history from the days of the Ohlone Indians to the present. Nature's Bounty explains how the area's natural resources have been utilized. A second floor courtroom, in use 1910-98, retains its witness stand, judge's bench and jury box. Other permanent exhibits include a collection of 20 model ships and a look at the peninsula commute 1853 to the present.

Allow 1 hour, 30 minutes minimum. Tues.-Sun. 10-4; closed Jan. 1, Easter, Thanksgiving and Dec. 25. Admission $2; over 64 and ages 6-12, $1. AX, MC, VI. Phone (650) 299-0104.

REDWOOD NATIONAL PARK (A-1)

Elevations in the park range from sea level at Crescent City to 3,262 ft. at an unnamed peak. Refer to AAA maps for additional elevation information.

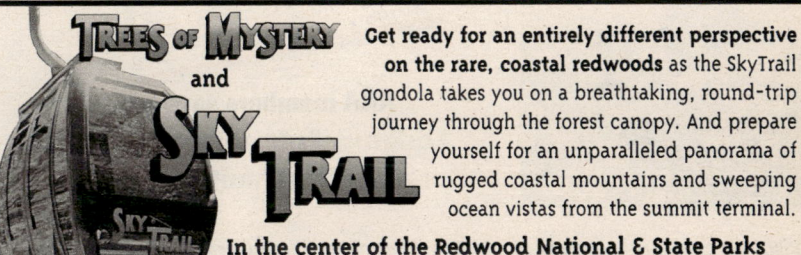

Along the northern California coast between Crescent City and Orick, 302 miles north of San Francisco on US 101, Redwood National Park encompasses 110,232 acres. Within its boundaries are the 34,780 combined acres of Del Norte Coast *(see Crescent City p. 69)*, Jedediah Smith and Prairie Creek Redwoods *(see Orick p. 110)* state parks *(see Recreation Chart and Crescent City and Orick in the AAA California & Nevada CampBook)*. In addition to dense forests of coast redwoods, the park embraces marshland, beaches, rugged coastline, rivers, streams, prairies and oak woodlands.

General Information and Activities

The beaches are open all year, but visitors should use caution when swimming or surfing. The coastline in northern California is a dangerous combination of steeply descending beaches, heavy undertows, very cold water and jagged rocky shoals. Visitors to the beach should be aware of the tides.

Coastal Drive, reached from the US 101 Klamath Beach Road exit, affords 8 miles of spectacular coastal scenery. Gold Bluffs Beach, off US 101 on Davison Road about 2 miles north of Orick, was the site of gold-mining operations in the 1850s. Howland Hill Road east of Crescent City is a 6-mile drive through old-growth redwoods along an unimproved stage route. Coastal Drive, Gold Bluffs and Howland Road are not suitable for RV or trailer travel.

Some public roads also serve adjoining private forest lands; logging truck traffic and other private activities take place along some of the routes.

Trails traverse the 37 miles of wild and untouched coastline along rock promontories that protrude into the sea, affording vistas of sea lion colonies and migrating whales. Birds inhabit bluffs, lagoons and offshore rocks; bird-watching is particularly rewarding during waterfowl migrations. More than 170 miles of trails provide access to the magnificent redwood groves. The park also contains 41 miles of horse trails and 54 miles of bicycle trails.

The park staff provides free guided walks, evening programs and other activities from mid-June through Labor Day. Information stations are in Crescent City, Hiouchi and Orick as well as at Prairie Creek Redwoods and Jedediah Smith state parks. Hiouchi and Jedediah Smith are open only during the summer.

Developed campgrounds are within the state parks and along US 101 nearby. Reservations are recommended in summer; phone (800) 444-7275. There also are five primitive walk-in campsites in the national park although space is limited. Freshwater and surf fishing are permitted; a California fishing license is required. *See Recreation Chart.*

ADMISSION to the national park is free. The state parks charge day use and overnight fees for developed picnicking and camping areas.

PETS must be kept under physical restraint while in the park and are prohibited on most trails. Campers are required to have proof of rabies shots for pets.

ADDRESS inquiries to the Superintendents, Redwood National and State Parks, 1111 2nd St., Crescent City, CA 95531. Phone (707) 464-6101, ext. 5064 or 5265.

RIDGECREST (I-6) pop. 24,927, elev. 2,289′

MATURANGO MUSEUM, 100 E. Las Flores Ave., has exhibits pertaining to the natural and cultural history of the upper Mojave Desert, a children's discovery area with hands-on displays and an art gallery. In spring and fall, the museum offers guided tours with the emphasis on rock art, geology, local history, wildflowers, mining and natural history. Also in the museum is the Death Valley Tourist Center and Northern Mojave Visitors Center.

Daily 10-5; closed major holidays. Admission $2; over 54, military with ID and ages 6-18, $1. Phone (760) 375-6900.

RUTHERFORD—*see Wine Country p. 199.*

SACRAMENTO (E-3) pop. 407,018, elev. 30′

See map page 120.

Capt. John Sutter, a Swiss emigrant, settled at the confluence of the American and Sacramento rivers in 1839 on a 50,000-acre land grant from the Mexican government. The town of Sacramento was laid out on Sutter's property in 1848—the same year that James Marshall discovered gold near the South Fork of the American River to start the great California gold rush.

Sacramento quickly grew into a major supply center for the northern Mother Lode country. It was devastated 1849-53 by two floods and two fires that leveled two-thirds of the town. Nonetheless, it was chosen as the state capital in 1854 and fought off subsequent challenges by Berkeley, San Jose and Monterey.

In 1856 the first railroad in California connected Sacramento with Folsom, and in 1860 the town became the western terminus of the Pony Express line from St. Joseph, Mo. The transcontinental railroad was completed in 1869. Agriculture took hold in the fertile Sacramento Valley, and the city's continued prosperity was assured.

Today Sacramento is an important highway, rail and river hub; the state capital; and the marketing center for a rich agricultural region. Nearby military installations and the space and aviation industries also contribute to Sacramento's economy. A deepwater channel to San Francisco Bay was completed in 1963, making the city a major inland port.

A landmark in the heart of downtown Sacramento, the Cathedral of the Blessed Sacrament at 1017 11th St. at K Street is part of a complex of Victorian buildings. Built in the Italian Renaissance style in 1886, it was the largest Roman Catholic church west of the Mississippi River until 1966. The cathedral's 218-foot bell tower and stained glass windows are noteworthy.

The Wells Fargo History Museum, in the Wells Fargo Center at 400 Capitol Mall, has exhibits illustrating the commercial development of Wells Fargo Bank and its role during the gold rush, including such historical subjects as stagecoach travel, the Pony Express and gold rush banking. Items exhibited include a fully restored Wells Fargo stagecoach, photographs and a postal collection; phone (916) 440-4161.

ARCO Arena, at 1 Sports Pkwy. near the intersection of I-5 and I-80, is the home of the Sacramento Kings professional basketball team. The arena also is the scene of many other events and performances; phone (916) 928-8499 for ticket information.

Sacramento is the northern terminus of a scenic 33-mile stretch of SR 160 that heads south to Isleton along the Sacramento River.

Sacramento Convention and Visitors Bureau: 1303 J St., Suite 600, Sacramento, CA 95814; phone (916) 264-7777 or (800) 292-2334.

Self-guiding tours: Maps and brochures for walking tours of Old Sacramento are available at the Old Sacramento Visitor Center at 1101 2nd St.; phone (916) 442-7644. Another self-guiding tour takes participants past nine kiosks where tokens activate a descriptive narrative by Mark Twain; the tokens and a map, obtainable for a fee, are available at the visitor center.

Shopping areas: Among the malls in the Sacramento area are Arden Fair, I-80 and Arden Way, and Westfield Galleria at Roseville, off I-80 SR 65 exit, both with JCPenney, Macy's, Nordstrom and Sears. Sunrise Mall, Sunrise Boulevard and Greenback Lane, features JCPenney, Macy's and Sears.

BLUE DIAMOND GROWERS, 1701 C St., presents a 20-minute videotape about almond growing and processing and offers tastings. Allow 1 hour minimum. Mon.-Fri. 10-5, Sat. 10-4. Free. Phone (916) 446-8439.

CALIFORNIA VIETNAM VETERANS MEMORIAL is at 15th and L sts., at the e. end of State Capitol Park. The 22 shiny black granite panels, built entirely with donations, are engraved with the 5,822 names of California's dead and missing. Full-relief bronze figures depict daily military life during the war.

CROCKER ART MUSEUM, 216 O St., exhibits paintings, drawings, sculpture and decorative arts, featuring both European and northern California artists. Traveling exhibits are displayed in the main room. Guided tours are available upon request. Tues.-Sun. 10-5 (also Thurs. 5-9); closed Jan. 1, Thanksgiving and Dec. 25. Admission $6; over 65, $4; ages 7-17, $3; free to all Sun. 10-1. AX, MC, VI. Phone (916) 264-5423.

SAVE **DISCOVERY MUSEUM SCIENCE & SPACE CENTER** is at 3615 Auburn Blvd. A separate facility of the Discovery Museum History Center in Old Sacramento *(see attraction listing p. 121)*, this branch has exhibits about animals, reptiles and insects, hands-on science displays and a planetarium. A wildlife pond is part of the center's 14 acres.

Picnicking is permitted. Allow 30 minutes minimum. Daily 10-5, July-Aug.; Tues.-Fri. noon-5, Sat.-Sun. 10-5, rest of year. Closed Jan. 1, Easter, July 4, Thanksgiving and Dec. 25. Planetarium shows Sat.-Sun. at 1 and 3, July-Aug. Admission (includes Discovery Museum History Center in Old Sacramento) $5; over 59 and ages 13-17, $4; ages 4-12, $3. AX, DS, MC, VI. Phone (916) 575-3941.

SAVE **GOLDEN STATE MUSEUM** is at 1020 O St. at the California State Archives, 1 blk. s. of the State Capitol. Four galleries tell the story of California: the People Gallery, through stories of its immigrants; the Place Gallery, with features about its landscape and ecology; the Promise Gallery, with a videotape presentation about Hollywood and the California dream; and the Politics Gallery, spotlighting people who made a difference in the state.

Allow 1 hour, 30 minutes minimum. Tues.-Sat. 10-5, Sun. noon-5; closed major holidays. Admission $5; over 54, $4; ages 6-13, $3.50. AX, MC, VI. Phone (916) 653-7524.

GOVERNOR'S MANSION STATE HISTORIC PARK, 1526 H St., features the 19th-century governor's mansion. Furnishings and personal items of former governors are displayed. Included are a 1902 Steinway piano, Persian carpets acquired by Mrs. Earl Warren in 1943 and many reminders of the Victorian era. The last governor to reside in the mansion was Ronald Reagan. The mansion grounds contain flowers, shrubs and trees, some dating to 1877.

Guided 45-minute tours are given daily on the hour 10-4; closed Jan. 1, Thanksgiving and Dec. 25. Fee $2, under 17 free. Phone (916) 323-3047.

THE HISTORIC PADDLEWHEELER *SPIRIT OF SACRAMENTO*, departing from the L St. Landing in Old Sacramento, is a 110-foot paddlewheel riverboat that conducts 1-hour sightseeing cruises on the Sacramento River. Dinner, brunch, happy hour and murder mystery excursions also are available. Sunday sunset cruises are offered April through October.

Sightseeing cruises depart Wed.-Sun. at 1:30 and 3, June-Aug.; otherwise varies. Sightseeing fare $10; under 12, $5. Reservations are recommended. MC, VI. Phone (916) 552-2933 or (800) 433-0263.

McCLELLAN AVIATION MUSEUM—
see North Highlands p. 107.

OLD SACRAMENTO, a four-block section delineated by Capitol Mall, I and Second sts., and the Sacramento River, was the commercial district during the gold rush. The area has been redeveloped with museums, restaurants and shops that preserve its historical character.

The California Military Museum, 1119 Second St., honors Californians who served and protected their state and country in times of war, peace and disaster. Exhibits include weapons, uniforms, battle flags, photographs, medals and documents dating from the Spanish explorers through the Civil War, World Wars I and II, Korea, Vietnam, Desert Storm, Bosnia and California earthquakes. A research center covers all branches of the military.

Allow 1 hour minimum. Tues.-Sun. 10-5; closed Jan. 1, Thanksgiving and Dec. 25. Admission $3; over 54, $1.50; ages 6-17 and military with ID $1. Phone (916) 442-2883.

GEM **California State Railroad Museum**, Second and I sts., is a three-story steel, brick and glass structure housing 21 restored locomotives and train cars. More than 40 interpretive exhibits, dioramas, pictures, murals and a 20-minute film presentation document the history of American railroading 1860-1960. A film is presented in the museum's theaters. The building's striking thematic design and gleaming exhibits are impressive.

Steam trains of the Sacramento Southern Railroad transport visitors on a 6-mile journey weekends April through September. The trains depart from the Public Market in Old Sacramento at Front and K streets.

Allow 2 hours minimum. Museum open daily 10-5; closed Jan. 1, Thanksgiving and Dec. 25. Last admission 30 minutes before closing. Trains operate Sat.-Sun. and holidays on the hour 11-5, Apr.-Sept. Museum admission $4, under 17 free. Tickets are good for a same-day visit to the Central Pacific Passenger Station. Train fare $6; ages 6-12, $3. Phone (916) 445-6645.

Central Pacific Passenger Station, Front and J sts. across from the railroad museum, was the first California terminal for the transcontinental railroad. The self-guiding tour of the reconstructed building recalls the 1870s. Allow 30 minutes minimum. Daily 10-5. Admission included in fee for California State Railroad Museum.

SAVE **Discovery Museum History Center,** 101 I St., comprises five themed areas offering exhibits about history, science and technology. Original artifacts and hands-on exhibits are featured. Displays include a million-dollar Mother Lode gold collection, ethnic photographs and a historic print shop. Programs and a planetarium are featured at a separate facility, the Discovery Museum Science & Space Center *(see attraction listing p. 119).*

Allow 1 hour minimum. Museum open daily 10-5, Memorial Day-Labor Day; Tues.-Sun. 10-5, rest of year. Closed Jan. 1, Thanksgiving and Dec. 24-25 and 31. Admission (includes Discovery Museum Science & Space Center) $5; over 59 and ages 13-17, $4; ages 4-12, $3. AX, DS, JC, MC, VI. Phone (916) 264-7057.

Eagle Theatre, 925 Front St., opened in October 1849 for a 3-month run and then was closed by the 1850 flood. The structure was rebuilt in 1974. A 13-minute slide presentation about the history of Sacramento is shown March through June and September 1 through November 15. Museum open Tues.-Fri. 10-4:30. Hours may vary; phone ahead. Theater performances occasionally. Museum admission free. Admission to performances varies. Phone (916) 445-6645 for general information or (916) 323-6343 for show schedule.

PORT OF SACRAMENTO, s. of West Sacramento off I-80 along Harbor Blvd., is the terminus of the Sacramento River Deepwater Ship Channel. Self-guiding tours of the port begin at the main entrance. Daily dawn-dusk. Free. Phone (916) 371-8000.

SACRAMENTO-SAN JOAQUIN RIVER DELTA, bounded by the cities of Sacramento, Stockton, Tracy and Pittsburg, was reclaimed in the 19th-century with labor by Chinese workers. Renowned for its relaxed lifestyle, the delta is northern California's water sports destination. Throughout this rich farmland winds a series of waterways punctuated by hundreds of islands, historical towns, marinas and resorts. Houseboating is a favorite means of exploring the delta. Fishing, camping and picnicking also are popular. Phone (209) 367-9840.

GEM **STATE CAPITOL,** bounded by 10th, 15th, L and N sts., was built 1860-74 in a style similar to that of the U.S. Capitol. The main building contains art exhibits, murals and statuary. Marble floors and the rotunda dome are highlights; murals depicting important events in California's history are at the base of the rotunda. One-hour guided tours cover the restored main building, legislative chambers and several offices of state officials.

The surrounding 40-acre Capitol Park has trees, shrubs and other plants from around the world as well as memorials and statues commemorating significant events in California's history. Tours of Capitol Park also are offered.

Allow 1 hour minimum. Daily 9-5; closed Jan. 1, Thanksgiving and Dec. 25. Capitol Tour offered daily on the hour 9-4. Capitol Park Tour departs daily at 10:30, mid-June through Labor Day; by reservation rest of year. Tour sign-in is available 30 minutes before the beginning of both tours; phone for schedule and location. Free. Children must be with an adult. Phone (916) 324-0333.

STATE LIBRARY, 914 Capitol Mall, is a handsome granite structure with a 100-foot mural by Maynard Dixon. A second building at 900 N St. houses the state history section, including an interesting collection of early state newspapers. Mon.-Fri. 9:30-4. Free. Phone (916) 654-0261.

GEM **SUTTER'S FORT STATE HISTORIC PARK,** 27th and L sts., was the first European outpost in the California interior. Established by Swiss immigrant John Sutter after the receipt of a 48,000-acre land grant from the Mexican government, the fort's walls were 2.5-feet thick and 15- to 18-feet tall. The settlement was initially known as New Helvetia (New Switzerland).

After the discovery of gold, Sutter's lands were virtually taken over by prospectors and he eventually left California for the East. The restored 1839 adobe fort has relics of pioneer and gold rush days. Allow 1 hour minimum. Self-guiding tours daily 10-5; 10-4 during events. Closed Jan. 1, Thanksgiving and Dec. 25. Admission $4; ages 6-16, $1. Admission may increase during special events. Phone (916) 445-4422.

State Indian Museum, 2618 K St., on the grounds of Sutter's Fort, depicts aspects of California's American Indian cultures with displays of feather baskets, jewelry, clothing and art. Daily 10-5; closed Jan. 1, Thanksgiving and Dec. 25. Admission $2, under 17 free. Phone (916) 324-0971.

SAVE **TOWE AUTO MUSEUM,** 2200 Front St. at V St., displays more than 150 vintage automobiles. The development of the automobile is depicted via representations of varied models and makes, including Buicks, Fords, Packards and Studebakers. The vehicles are displayed in a series of exhibits built around "Dream Themes."

Guided tours are available. Allow 30 minutes minimum. Daily 10-6; closed Jan. 1, Thanksgiving and Dec. 25. Last tour begins 1 hour before closing. Admission $7; ages 14-18, $3; ages 5-13, $2. MC, VI. Phone (916) 442-6802.

SAVE **WATERWORLD USA,** 1600 Exposition Blvd., has a wading pool, wave pool, waterslides, a river tube ride, an in-line water luge and a children's play area featuring a five-story interactive playhouse.

Daily 10:30-6, Memorial Day weekend-Labor Day. Admission, including all rides, $21.99; under 49 inches tall $16.99; over age 59, $9.99; under age 3 free. Admission to the California State Fair Aug. 20-Sept. 6 required for entrance to Waterworld USA. Parking $6. Additional charges for lockers, inner tubes and observers. AX, MC, VI. Phone (916) 924-0556 or (916) 924-3747.

WILLIAM LAND PARK, bounded by Freeport and Riverside blvds., 13th Ave. and Sutterville Rd., encompasses 600 acres, including picnic facilities, a public golf course and a grove of cherry trees. Phone (916) 277-1207 for golf information.

Fairytale Town, 3901 Land Park Dr. across from Sacramento Zoo, is a 2.5-acre park with sets based on themes from popular children's nursery rhymes and fairy tales. Arts and crafts take place daily. Special events are scheduled throughout the year.

Daily 9-5, Mar.-Aug.; 10-5, Sept.-Dec. Closed Thanksgiving and Dec. 25. Last admission 1 hour before closing. Admission Mon.-Fri. $3.50; ages 3-12, $3.25. Admission Sat.-Sun. and holidays $3.75; ages 3-12, $3.50. Phone (916) 264-7462, or (916) 264-5233 for schedule and price information.

Sacramento Zoo, at the corner of Sutterville Rd. and Land Park Dr., exhibits more than 400 animals, including lions, Sumatran tigers, Grevy's zebras, African cheetahs, chimpanzees and red pandas. A reptile house maintains 53 species in 60 exhibits. Daily 9-4, Memorial Day-Labor Day; 10-4, rest of year. Closed Thanksgiving and Dec. 25. Admission Mon.-Fri. $6.75; ages 3-12, $4.50. Admission Sat.-Sun. $7.25; ages 3-12, $5. MC, VI. Phone (916) 264-5885.

ST. HELENA—*see Wine Country p. 199.*

SALINAS (G-3) pop. 151,060, elev. 55′

Salinas is best known as the birthplace of John Steinbeck and the setting for many of his novels. Winner of the Nobel and Pulitzer prizes, Steinbeck continues to be a source of pride in Salinas. First editions, letters, photographs and memorabilia are displayed in a room of John Steinbeck Public Library, 350 Lincoln Ave.; phone (831) 758-7311. A statue of the author stands on the library's lawn.

The vast quantities and varieties of vegetables and fruits grown in the area have earned the Salinas Valley the nickname "Salad Bowl of the Nation."

Salinas Valley Chamber of Commerce: 119 E. Alisal St., P.O. Box 1170, Salinas, CA 93901; phone (831) 424-7611.

Shopping areas: Northridge Mall, US 101 at Boronda Road and N. Main Street, offers shoppers JCPenney, Macy's, Mervyn's and Sears.

JOSE EUSEBIO BORONDA ADOBE, 333 Boronda Rd., was built 1844-46 and is the town's oldest structure. The wood shingles used on the adobe are a departure from the traditional red-clay tiles. The 1897 Old Lagunita School House also is at the site. Allow 30 minutes minimum. Guided 30- to 60-minute tours are given Mon.-Fri. 10-2. Donations. Phone (831) 757-8085.

NATIONAL STEINBECK CENTER, One Main St., features interactive, multisensory exhibits about John Steinbeck's life and works that are of interest to all ages; film clips; and educational programs celebrating this Nobel prize-winning author's life, work and values. There are seven themed theaters and changing art exhibits as well.

Food is available. Allow 2 hours minimum. Daily 10-5; closed Jan. 1, Easter, Thanksgiving and Dec. 25. Admission $10.95; over 61 and students with ID $8.95; ages 13-17, $7.95; ages 6-12, $5.95. AX, DS, MC, VI. Phone (831) 796-3833.

SALINAS COMMUNITY CENTER, 940 N. Main St., displays varied artwork and stages musical and theatrical performances throughout the year. Allow 30 minutes minimum. Mon.-Fri. 8-5. Admission free. A fee may be charged for some displays or performances. Phone (831) 758-7351.

"Hat In Three Stages of Landing", on the lawn of Salinas Community Center, is a giant sculpture by Claes Oldenberg. The three hats, at various elevations, are painted a vivid yellow and weigh 3,500 pounds each. The sculpture is a tribute to farmers and ranchers and represents a Western hat tossed in the air from the nearby rodeo stands.

WILD THINGS is 4 mi. e. off SR 68 River Rd./Reservation Rd. exit, following signs to Vision Quest Ranch at 400 River Rd. The organization provides professionally trained wild, exotic and domestic animals for use in movies, television, music videos, print and education. Guided tours introduce some of the more than 100 residents, including lions, tigers, cheetahs, servals, elephants, porcupines, bears, kangaroos and baboons. Visitors learn about the animal's personality, in which media they have appeared and how they are trained.

Allow 1 hour minimum. Guided tours are given daily at 1 and 3, June-Aug.; at 1, rest of year. Closed Thanksgiving and Dec. 25. Admission $10; under 15, $8. AX, DS, MC, VI. Phone (831) 455-1901 or (800) 228-7382.

SAN ANDREAS (E-3) pop. 2,615, elev. 1,008′

Just 16 miles west of San Andreas via SR 12, Paloma Road, Watertown Road and Campo Seco-Chile Camp Road are the remains of Campo Seco, a once thriving gold and copper town. Dubbed Campo Seco (dry camp) by prospectors, the site produced some gold, but the real treasure was copper. In the early 1860s Penn Copper Co. supplied the Union Army with the metal during the Civil War. Though considered a ghost town, Campo Seco has a post office and claims the largest cork oak tree in California.

Calaveras County Visitor Center: 1192 S. Main St., P.O. Box 637, Angels Camp, CA 95222-0637; phone (209) 736-0049 or (800) 225-3764.

CALAVERAS COUNTY MUSEUM, 30 N. Main St., served as the county jail and the county courthouse 1867-1962. Featured are a garden of native California plants and trees, Miwok Indian artifacts, mining relics, 1850-1900 period exhibits and an Italian stone oven. Allow 30 minutes minimum. Daily 10-4; closed holidays. Admission $2, over 59 and students with ID $1, under 6 free. Phone (209) 754-1058.

CALIFORNIA CAVERN AT CAVE CITY is 8 mi. e. on Mountain Ranch Rd., then about 2.5 mi. s.e. on Michel and Cave City Rd. Chambers and passageways contain glittering formations ranging from fragile soda straws on the ceiling to colossal stalagmites rising from the floor. Discovered in 1849, the cavern offers gemstone mining and a nature trail in addition to a variety of cave trips. A 60- to 80-minute guided walking tour provides information about area history as well as the history and geology of the cave.

Picnicking is permitted. Walking tour departs (weather permitting) daily on the hour 10-5, May-Oct.; 10-4 in Apr. and Nov.-Dec. Since the cave's water level determines when tours can operate, seasons may vary; phone ahead to verify schedule. Last tour begins at closing. Walking tour fee $11; over 59, $10; ages 3-13, $5.50. MC, VI. Phone (209) 736-2708 or (866) 762-2837.

SAN CARLOS—*see San Francisco p. 160.*

San Francisco

City Population: 776,733 **Elevation:** 63 ft.

Popular Spots

Just blocks from a looming 853-foot-tall skyscraper, an elderly vendor hawks exotic-looking vegetables piled under signs hand-lettered in Chinese characters. A woman sporting a pierced nose and blue fingernails gulps down a cappuccino before dashing off to work at a boutique selling vintage hippie clothing. In an antique shop, two young men search for a table to furnish a renovated Victorian. An early morning jogger weaves through a serene park where ghostly fog frames eucalyptus trees. And under an evening sky, the Golden Gate Bridge arches over San Francisco Bay as the green- and brown-flecked hills of the Marin Headlands blur into the distance.

It seems that everywhere one turns in San Francisco an intriguing juxtaposition or a picture-postcard view appears. The city's popular image is that of a worldly seaport whose sophisticated citizens are blessed with the finer things—good food, culture, magnificent settings. Obviously, such an ideal is in part misrepresentative. San Franciscans have had to cope with a litany of typical urban ills, from air and water pollution to inner-city decay to political violence.

Still, San Francisco is seductive. Its disparate geography, architecture, people and ideas defy an orderly blueprint yet somehow manage to coexist in harmony. Certainly the city's location is one of the loveliest anywhere. Varying in elevation from sea level to 933 feet, it rests on some 40 hills at the northern end of a narrow peninsula, bounded on one side by the Pacific Ocean and on the other by San Francisco Bay. The nearly landlocked bay is connected to the ocean by a narrow strait.

A pair of notable bridges arch over the bay's waters. While more than 280,000 vehicles a day cross

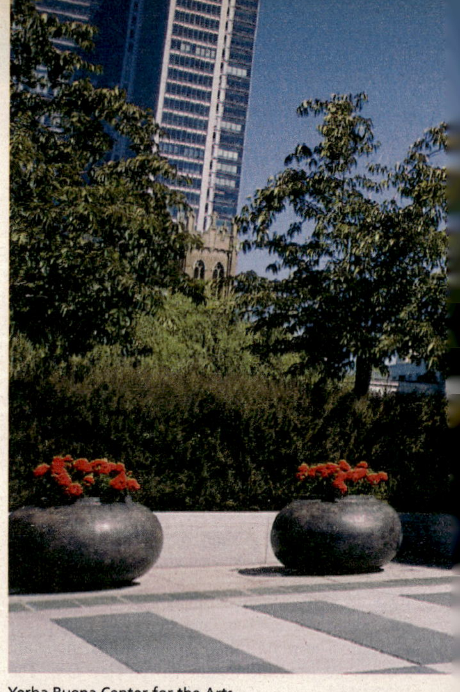

Yerba Buena Center for the Arts

the San Francisco-Oakland Bay Bridge, the Golden Gate Bridge has become a symbol of San Francisco—even more so than cable cars or Victorian houses. Completed in 4 years, its single-suspension span is anchored by 746-foot-high twin towers—the world's tallest. The structure was built to withstand 100-mile-per-hour winds, and its 220-foot clearance allows even the tallest vessels to pass underneath. For a great panorama, throw on a jacket, brave the gusty conditions and hike across its 1.7-mile walkway; pedestrians are allowed on the bridge during daylight hours.

The Greater San Francisco Bay Area is home to more than 7 million people. It wasn't always so, although the city's bayside location attracted its first colonizers. Spaniards established the Presidio, a military post, at the northern end of the San Francisco peninsula in 1776; that same year Franciscan priest Junípero Serra founded the Mission San Francisco de Asis.

Meanwhile, the town that was to become San Francisco was coalescing around what is now Portsmouth Square in present-day Chinatown. The settlement of Yerba Buena—under Mexican rule—was christened in 1835. It was renamed San Francisco in 1847 after fighting broke out between the United States and

Getting There — starting on p. 130
Getting Around — starting on p. 131
What To See — starting on p. 134
What To Do — starting on p. 145
Where To Stay — starting on p. 605
Where To Dine — starting on p. 649

Mexico and the latter was forced to relinquish territory that soon became California. The city was incorporated in 1850.

In 1848 nuggets of gold were discovered in the American River near Coloma, northeast of San Francisco. By 1849 adventurers, dubbed "Forty-niners," were arriving by the thousands; riches were accumulated and lost, and the drowsy village exploded into a frontier boomtown. While many Forty-niners became farmers or shopkeepers rather than millionaires, their impact was such that the city's football team was named for them.

Along with wealth came vice, and San Francisco became notorious for its murders. From the gold rush era to the end of the 19th century, the waterfront district was known as the Barbary Coast. The term was a reference to the same-named coastal region of northern Africa that once was dominated by pirates; the city's saloons, gambling dens and brothels had a similar lawless reputation. When the gold dried up in the late 1850s, the Comstock Silver Lode, discovered in the territory of Nevada, kept coffers full. San Francisco became a financial metropolis; its bankers and investors patronized grand hotels and dined in sumptuous restaurants.

Perhaps the city's most epochal event was the 1906 earthquake. Strong tremors had been felt before, notably in 1868, but this temblor proved disastrous. And more destructive than the quake itself was the subsequent fire. Ignited by gas leaking from ruptured mains and fanned by high winds, it destroyed much of the city, including its central business district. Rebuilding was quick; in 1915 the Panama-Pacific International Exposition celebrated both San Francisco's renaissance and the opening of the Panama Canal.

San Francisco's reputation for tolerance and unconventionality continued to grow. The Beat movement of the 1950s flourished in San Francisco's North Beach, where beatniks frequently dressed in black and affected a vocabulary of hip terms borrowed primarily from jazz musicians. The flower children of the 1960s, a generation of long-haired, tie-dyed clad youth, also migrated to San Francisco. By 1967 the city was the undisputed capital of peace, love and psychedelic music, with the Haight-Ashbury neighborhood serving as the hippie movement's spiritual center. And during the 1970s the Castro neighborhood in particular fostered an open expression of identity and lifestyle for gay men and women.

This human melting pot was shaken by the 1989 Loma Prieta earthquake. Centered near Santa Cruz, it struck Oct. 17 just before the third World Series game between the San Francisco Giants and the Oakland A's, stunning the television-watching world. City damage was relatively minor, although portions of freeways in Oakland buckled or collapsed in rubble. The quake was a sobering reminder of the geologic volatility of the region, where earthquake safety drills are a grade school routine.

San Francisco was at one time home base for the Pacific whaling industry and an embarkation point for imports and exports between the United States and the Orient. Piers still line the Embarcadero, the waterfront area facing the bay's eastern shoreline. They radiate like fingers both north and south of the Ferry Building at the foot of Market Street—headquarters for port activities. The waterfront has since transformed into somewhat of a tourist attraction, with Pier 39 as its centerpiece.

The city is a financial center and the administrative heart of the West, one of the country's biggest tourist destinations and a major convention, commerce and manufacturing center. San Francisco is the seat of the Pacific Stock Exchange and has been a financial power since gold rush days. Bank of California, Union Bank and Wells Fargo & Co. all are headquartered here.

Architecturally, San Francisco is characterized by two sharply contrasting styles: sleek skyscrapers and late 19th-century wooden houses collectively known as Victorians. In an area where space is at a premium, both types of structures stress the vertical. San Francisco's skyline is notably compact. The skyscrapers—many more than 500 feet tall—seem even more impressive due to the many elevated vantage points from which they can be seen. Their area of concentration, the blocks around Montgomery Street, is known as Wall Street West.

While the majority of downtown's steel-and-glass towers date only from the late 1960s, most of the finest Victorians were built 1870-1906. Standing close together, as there is precious little room for extensive gardens or grounds, these "painted ladies" are another San Francisco symbol. Many along Van Ness Avenue and on Nob Hill sadly were destroyed by the 1906 earthquake and fire. But thousands of Victorians remain, and their loving (and expensive) renovation is a full-time industry.

The original houses were constructed primarily of redwood and were called "stick" houses because of the vertical orientation; most were attached and crowned by gables. Italianate Victorians borrowed architectural details from the Romanesque decorative tradition. Queen Anne Victorians, appearing in the 1890s, were embellished with intricately ornamented towers, turrets and cupolas, all painted in vibrant colors.

Rows of the dwellings are scattered throughout San Francisco's residential neighborhoods. Haight-Ashbury, Noe Valley, Potrero Hill and the Mission District are all rich with Victorians. From the corner of Hayes and Steiner streets in Alamo Square, a row of quaint Victorians huddles against a backdrop of towering modern skyscrapers. And picturesque Italianate Victorians line the 1800 block of Laguna Street (between California and Pine streets) in Pacific Heights. Such delightful views contribute in no small measure to the charms of this captivating city by the bay.

The crests of many city hills, particularly Twin Peaks, afford matchless views of downtown and the East Bay. At night when the bridges are lighted, the view is even more impressive. Standing on a hilltop, watching the fog swirl in through the Golden Gate and looking at the city's skyline, it is easy to understand Rudyard Kipling's lament: "San Francisco has only one drawback—'tis hard to leave."

The Informed Traveler

Whom To Call

Emergency: 911

Police (non-emergency): (415) 553-0123

Time: (415) 767-1111

Hospitals: California Pacific Medical Center, (415) 563-4321; St. Francis Memorial, (415) 353-6000; St. Mary's Medical Center, (415) 668-1000; University of California San Francisco, (415) 476-1000.

Where To Look

Newspapers

The major daily newspapers are the morning *Chronicle* and the evening *Examiner.* They produce a joint Sunday paper.

Radio

San Francisco radio station KCBS (740 AM) is an all-news/weather station; KQED (88.5 FM) is a member of National Public Radio.

Visitor Information

The San Francisco Visitor Information Center, (415) 391-2000, or TTY (415) 392-0328, is on the lower level of Hallidie Plaza at 900 Market St., San Francisco, CA 94102. The center is open Mon.-Fri. 9-5, Sat.-Sun. and holidays 9-3; closed Jan. 1, Easter, Thanksgiving and Dec. 25.

What To Pack

San Francisco's weather is noted not for its extremes but for its consistency. Temperatures usually do not rise above 80 or fall below 40 degrees. September is the warmest month; in January (the coolest month), highs average in the mid-50s, lows in the mid-40s.

Precipitation totals about 21 inches annually, more than 80 percent of it falling November through March. Winter storms can bring occasional heavy rains, yet thunderstorms can be expected only 2 days a year—from May through September it hardly ever rains. In summer expect morning fog from the Pacific; it usually dissipates by noon but frequently re-forms again in the late afternoon, accompanied by strong sea breezes. *For additional information see temperature chart p. 46.*

The Golden Gate Bridge / © Neil Rabinowitz / Corbis

A sweater, light jacket or all-weather coat come in handy just about anytime in San Francisco. Bring at least one suit or dressy outfit for dinner or an evening at the symphony or theater.

Sales Tax: State and county sales taxes total 8.5 percent in San Francisco. In addition a hotel room tax of 14 percent is levied.

Destination San Francisco

Millions of visitors have left their hearts in *The City*–San Francisco.

When the sun rises *The City* is gilded from stem to stern and daytime diversions are plentiful and varied. The setting sun spectacularly vanishes into the Pacific and fog creeps in on soft paws to embrace theater- and concert-goers, and other pleasure seekers.

© Gibson Stock Photography

Yerba Buena Gardens, San Francisco.
Museums, galleries, shopping, dining and outdoor esplanades are all part of this developing arts district.

© Gibson Stock Photography

Alcatraz Island, Golden Gate National Recreation Area.
A ferry provides transportation from San Francisco to this isolated, former federal prison known as "The Rock." (See listing page 157)

Places included in this AAA Destination City:

Robert Holmes / CalTour

Japanese Tea Garden, San Francisco.
One of the treasures in Golden Gate Park, the garden's pagodas, statuary and ponds are treasures in their own right. (See listing page 141)

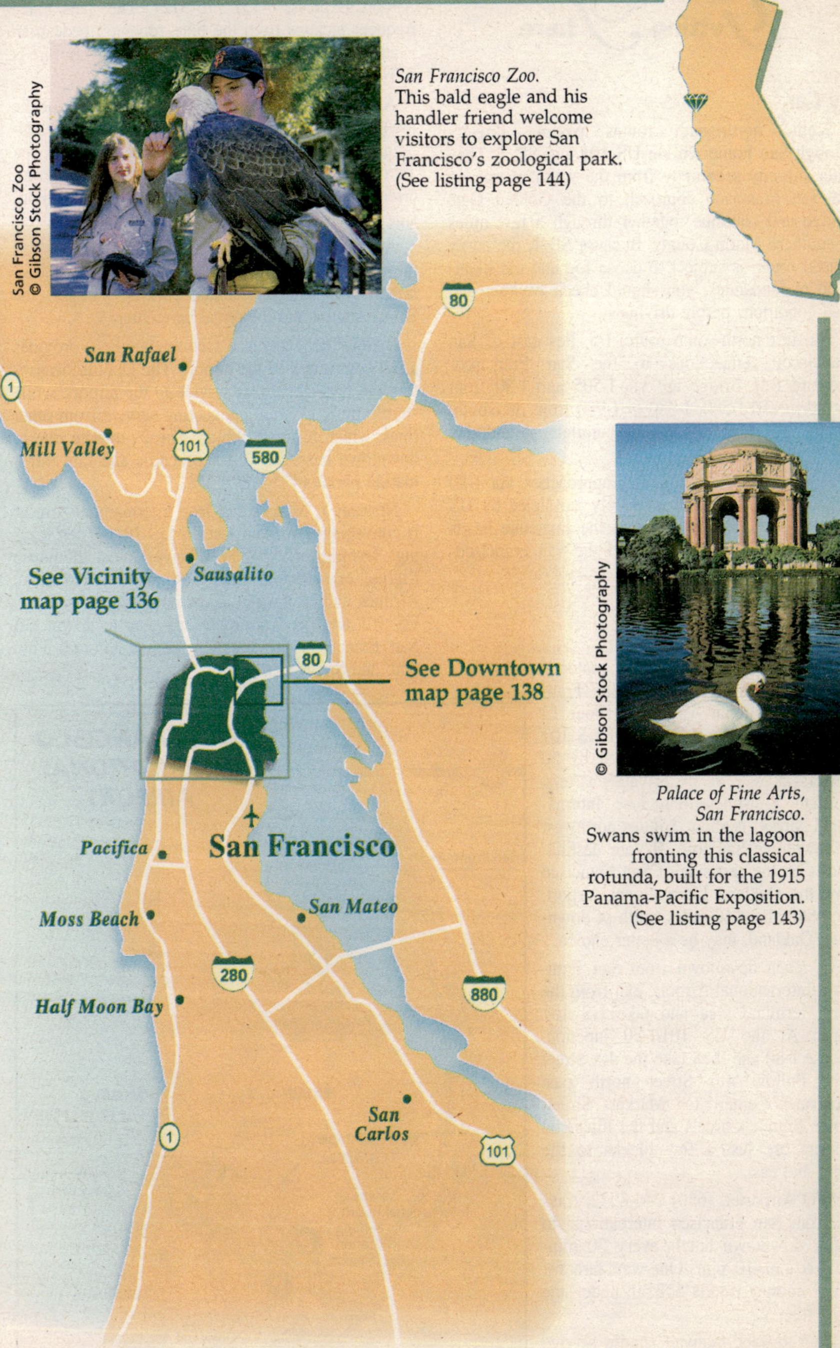

San Francisco Zoo.
This bald eagle and his handler friend welcome visitors to explore San Francisco's zoological park. (See listing page 144)

Palace of Fine Arts, San Francisco.
Swans swim in the lagoon fronting this classical rotunda, built for the 1915 Panama-Pacific Exposition. (See listing page 143)

By Car

Scenic north-south routes passing directly through San Francisco are US 101 and SR 1. They enter the city separately from the south, merge on the San Francisco approach to the Golden Gate Bridge and continue together through a few miles of southern Marin County. Because SR 1, the curvy coastal route, is subject to dense fog and the likelihood of landslides, you should check weather and road conditions before driving it.

The fast north-south route, I-5, lies east of San Francisco; connections to the San Francisco-Oakland Bay Bridge are via I-505 and I-80 from the north and I-580, I-880 or I-980 from the south. Another route, SR 99, closely parallels I-5 and also has connections into the city.

Most traffic from the east approaches via I-80 across the Sierras. I-80 is closely paralleled by US 50 to Sacramento, from where the Interstate heads west, leading into the city over the San Francisco-Oakland Bay Bridge.

Air Travel

The area is served by three major airports. One of the nation's five busiest, San Francisco International Airport is about 12 miles south near San Bruno off US 101 (Bayshore Freeway); it's served by 50 carriers as well as by private charters. Norman Y. Mineta San Jose International Airport is about 3 miles northwest of downtown San Jose. If your destination is on the east side of San Francisco Bay, the Oakland International Airport, off I-880 about 10 miles south of downtown Oakland, may be a better choice.

To reach downtown from San Francisco International Airport, exit from the north terminal area and take US 101 north. At the US 101/I-80 junction, choose I-80 and then take the 4th Street exit. Follow 4th Street north past Moscone Center to Market Street; Union Square's hotels and the Financial District are just a few blocks to the north and east.

SFO Airporter, (650) 246-8942, travels from San Francisco International to major downtown hotels every 30 minutes, 6 a.m.-10 p.m. One-way fare for the 30-minute ride is $12.50; under age 13 is free.

Door-to-door minivan shuttle service between the airport and hotels, businesses and residences is offered by several companies, including Supershuttle San Francisco, (800) 258-3826, and Door-to-Door Airport Express, (415) 775-5121. The vans make frequent pickups from the blue zones on pedestrian islands on the airport's upper level. One-way fare is $13-$17 per person.

Airport shuttle buses pick up passengers on the lower level pedestrian islands near the blue columns. Or take a taxi or limousine to downtown. Taxi fares between the Civic Center and San Francisco International Airport average $35-$50; limousine service costs $50-$60.

An automated light rail system, with nine stops throughout the airport, links the International Terminal with other terminals, parking garages, the BART station and the rental car center.

BART, San Francisco's commuter line, provides a rail connection to the airport. The Dublin/Pleasanton line provides direct service to the airport, while shuttle trains provide connecting service from other lines, which run to Millbrae. The 29-minute ride to downtown costs $4.70; for schedule and fare information phone (415) 989-2278.

Norman Y. Mineta San Jose International Airport is conveniently located just off US 101. When leaving Terminal C (which receives most domestic flights) or Terminal A (which receives American Airlines and two regional carriers), follow signs to US 101 and head north. On its way to downtown San Francisco, the highway passes through Palo Alto and San Mateo.

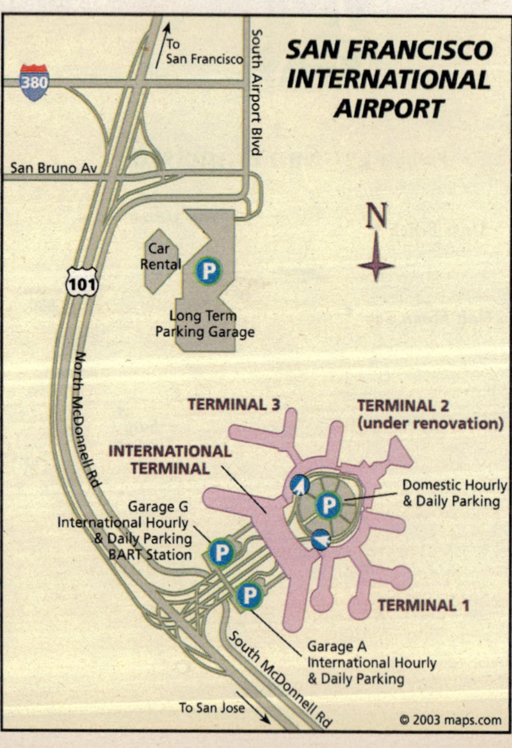

To reach downtown San Francisco from Oakland International Airport, exit the terminal building and take Airport Drive east toward downtown Oakland. Exit north onto I-880 (Nimitz Freeway). Take I-880 north to the I-980 detour, which connects with I-80. Take I-80 west over the San Francisco-Oakland Bay Bridge ($2 toll). Once across, take the 5th Street exit north to Market Street and the Union Square/Financial District area.

Hertz, at San Francisco International, offers discounts to AAA members; phone (415) 771-2200 or (800) 654-3080. For listings of other agencies check the telephone directory.

Rail Service

Most rail service terminates in Oakland at Jack London Square, Alice Street and the Embarcadero, or at Emeryville. From there, passengers are transported via shuttle bus to the following stops: San Francisco's Ferry Building at the foot of Market Street; Fisherman's Wharf at the plaza bus stop at Pier 39; Westfield San Francisco Shopping Centre (SFS), 4th and Market streets; in front of Macy's at 835 Market St.; outside the Hyatt Regency Hotel at California and Drumm streets; and at the CalTrain depot, 4th and King streets. For schedule, fare and additional information phone Amtrak at (800) 872-7245.

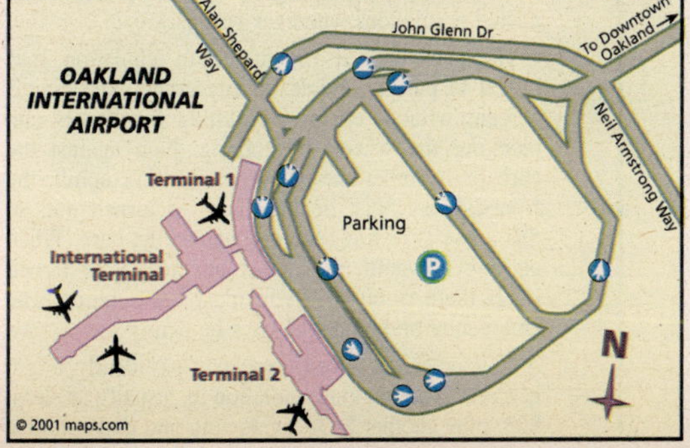

Buses

Greyhound Lines Inc., (800) 231-2222, departs from the Transbay Terminal at 1st and Mission streets.

Street System

Market Street, the main thoroughfare, runs diagonally through the city. Major east-west arteries are Bush and Pine, each one-way streets with synchronized traffic signals. Bush goes into the city, while Pine goes out. Numbered avenues run north-south in the western section of the city, and for the most part streets form a grid pattern.

Skyscrapers and office buildings are concentrated in the Financial District, centered around Montgomery Street. Major stores and hotels surround Union Square, bordered north-south by Post and Geary streets and east-west by Stockton and Powell streets. Government buildings cluster around the Civic Center, between Van Ness Avenue and Market Street. All three districts are north of Market Street; numbered streets are south of Market.

Van Ness Avenue is a principal north-south downtown artery and San Francisco's widest street. Many major thoroughfares are one way; a good street map comes in handy. Although the street layout looks straightforward on a map, keep the city's extremely variable topography in mind when traveling: The steep hills are difficult to negotiate. Depending upon your agenda, it may be more advantageous to use public transportation or walk rather than drive. If driving your own car, it is strongly recommended that you have your brakes checked before you visit.

San Francisco intersections are subject to strict enforcement of the Anti-Gridlock Act, which prohibits entering an intersection when traffic makes it questionable that you will get through before the light turns red. Motorists convicted of violating the act are subject to a fine of $103.

"The Boot" (also known as "The Denver Boot") is a metal clamp that immobilizes a car when attached to its wheel. This device is applied when five or more parking tickets have accumulated or if registration is not current; it is removed only when all outstanding fines and/or registration fees and a $50 de-booting fee have been paid. If the fines are not paid, the car may be towed within 72 hours.

CityPass

CityPass offers savings to those who plan visits to many San Francisco attractions. The pass covers a week of unlimited use of all Muni transportation (including the city's cable cars) as well as the price of admission to the San Francisco Museum of Modern Art, California Palace of the Legion of Honor, Exploratorium, California Academy of Sciences and Steinhart Aquarium, and a San Francisco bay cruise aboard the Blue & Gold Fleet. (A tour of Alcatraz may be substituted for the bay cruise, but only if the tickets are purchased through the Blue & Gold Fleet by phoning (415) 705-5555.)

A pass, valid for 9 days once the first attraction is visited, is $39; ages 5-17, $30. CityPass is available from participating attractions and in advance from any participating U.S. travel agent. For additional information phone (707) 256-0490. *See color ad p. 144.*

Digital Archives

The downtown speed limit, unless otherwise posted, is 25 mph—15 mph at blind intersections. Right turns on red are legal unless otherwise posted. Pedestrians using designated crosswalks **always** have the right-of-way. Avoid driving around the city in general and across the San Francisco-Oakland Bay Bridge in particular during rush hours, generally 7-9 a.m. and 4-6 p.m.

Parking

San Francisco is not a parking-friendly city. There is a shortage of on-street spaces and a plethora of parking regulations, which are strictly enforced. On-street meter parking is permitted in some areas, but much neighborhood parking is reserved for local residents and is by permit only.

Downtown does have some large garages and many convenient smaller garages and lots. There are garages at Fisherman's Wharf, 655 Beach St. at Hyde Street, (415) 673-5197; downtown at 833 Mission St. (at 5th Street), (415) 982-8522; at the Moscone Center, 255 3rd St., (415) 777-2782; and in Chinatown at 733 Kearny St., (415) 982-6353. Fees range about $2-$6 per hour and $13-$29 per day. The only public parking available for recreational vehicles is at San Francisco Stadium at Candlestick Point (formerly known as 3Com Park and Candlestick Park), south of the city off US 101; phone (415) 822-2299.

On-street parking in hilly San Francisco is strictly regulated. In addition to posted tow-away zones, pay particular attention to curb colors, which determine parking availability. Red means no stopping, standing or parking whatsoever; yellow curbs indicate commercial loading and unloading (7 a.m.-6 p.m.). Passenger cars left unattended in downtown loading zones are subject to heavy fines and towing.

White curbs allow a 5-minute limit to pick up or discharge passengers during the hours the adjacent public building is open. White curbs marked with a taxi sign are within a taxi zone. Green curbs indicate 10-minute parking 9 a.m.-6 p.m. Blue marks spaces for use by the disabled; the fine for illegal parking in designated spaces for the disabled is $275, while the fine for parking in bus zone spaces is $250. In several areas of the city local residents have priority parking rights; be sure to check all posted regulations wherever you park.

How you park also is subject to regulation. It is illegal to park a vehicle on any grade exceeding 3 percent without effectively setting the brakes and blocking the wheels by turning them against the curb or by other means. When parking uphill, the front wheels must be "heeled," or turned out, so that a tire is resting securely against the curb. When parking downhill, they must be "toed," or turned in. If there is no curb you must use a block. The emergency brake must always be firmly set.

If your car is towed, expect to pay dearly to get it back. The parking violation is usually at least $23, plus another $138 for towing and daily storage fees. Fines for illegally parking in disabled-designated spaces, in bus zones or in an area blocking access to a wheelchair ramp are $250-$275. To settle your fees and release your car, go to City Tow offices at 850 Bryant St., Room 145, at the Hall of Justice. For additional information phone the City of San Francisco Parking and Traffic Department, (415) 553-1200.

Taxis & Limousines

Taxis in San Francisco are metered, with fares averaging about $2.50 for the first mile and $2 for each additional mile. Either phone for a cab or wait at a hotel taxi stand (hailing one on the street is rarely successful). Limousine service ranges from $55-$70 per hour.

Public Transportation

San Francisco Municipal Railway (Muni) provides public transportation consisting of buses, streetcars, trolley buses and cable cars. The fare for buses, streetcars and trolley buses is $1; over 64, the physically impaired and ages 5-17, 35c. Exact change is required. Fare includes a free transfer good for use on any two other vehicles within a 2-hour period; ask for a transfer when you board. Transfers are not valid on cable cars.

Muni buses are numbered and destinations are marked on the front of the vehicle. Major routes have 24-hour service. Muni streetcars operate underground in the downtown area and above ground in outlying neighborhoods. There are seven lines: F (Market), J (Church), K (Ingleside), L (Taraval), M (Ocean View), N (Judah) and S (Castro-Embarcadero shuttle).

The Muni's F Line (also called the Market Street Railway) escorts passengers on colorful vintage streetcars. Although some of the cars are original to San Francisco, others ran their routes in such diverse locales as Milan, Italy; Melbourne, Australia; and Osaka, Japan. The route, beginning at Market and Castro streets, follows Market Street through downtown to Fisherman's Wharf; the route ends at Jones and Beach streets.

The Muni Passport, valid on all Muni buses and cable cars, offers unlimited usage each day and is $6 for a daily pass, $10 for a 3-day pass, and $15 for a 7-day pass. The $35 fast pass is valid for 1 month; over 64 and ages 5-17, $8. Passports can be obtained at the San Francisco Visitor Information Center, Hallidie Plaza (lower level) at Market and Powell streets, or at TIX Bay Area, inside the Union Square Garage at the Geary Street entrance. **Note:** You must possess proof of payment (Muni pass, ticket or transfer) for the duration of your travels. A citation for up to $76 may be issued to passengers without proof of payment. For schedules, routing and other information phone (415) 673-6864.

AC Transit is a bus service that runs from the Transbay Terminal to various destinations in the East Bay Area and Alameda and Contra Costa counties.

BART (Bay Area Rapid Transit), (650) 992-2278, connects San Francisco with East Bay cities, terminating at Richmond (north), Pittsburg/Bay Point (east), Pleasanton (southeast) and Fremont (south). On the Peninsula (West Bay side) the terminus is Millbrae, approximately 30 minutes south of the Civic Center area. BART operates Mon.-Fri. 4 a.m.-midnight, Sat. 6 a.m.-midnight and Sun. 8 a.m.-midnight. Color-keyed wall maps at the stations list destinations and fares; tickets are dispensed from machines at each station. The maximum fare between San Francisco stations is $1.10; a maximum of $4.70 will transport you to East Bay locations. Information is posted near the machines.

Tiburon Ferry / © Richard Cummins / Photophile

In addition, passenger ferries link San Francisco with the north Bay Area. The Blue and Gold Fleet, (415) 773-1188, operates daily commuter service to Tiburon and Sausalito.

Golden Gate Transit, (415) 923-2000, operates daily ferries to Larkspur and Sausalito; no service is available Jan. 1, Thanksgiving or Dec. 25. Larkspur ferry one-way rates Mon.-Fri. are $3.25; ages 6-12, $2.45; over 64 and the physically impaired $1.60. Weekend and holiday rates are $5.60; ages 6-12, $4.20; over 64 and the physically impaired $2.50. Sausalito ferry one-way daily rates are $5.60; ages 6-12, $4.20; over 64 and the physically impaired $2.80. The family rate for both routes allows two children under 12 free with a paid adult on weekends.

Bus service linking San Francisco to Marin County and the cities of Sausalito, Mill Valley, Tiburon and Santa Rosa in Sonoma County via the Golden Gate Bridge is available; phone (415) 923-2000.

Passenger ferries cross San Francisco Bay, providing both commuter service and sightseeing

The Lincoln Highway

The horseless carriage rolled onto the American landscape in the 1890s. By 1910 there were more than 450,000 registered automobiles, yet the country still lacked a public road system.

Organized movements for better roads brought issues to the attention of the federal government, which had not participated in major road construction since it funded the National Road project in 1806.

But one particular initiative captured the public's support with a unique idea. In 1913 Carl Fisher—the man who built the Indianapolis Motor Speedway in 1909—and automobile industry leaders chartered the Lincoln Highway Association for the purpose of defining a direct coast-to-coast automobile route.

The LHA's first official act was to delineate a 3,389-mile, 12-state continuous route from New York to California—one that would be passable before the opening of the 1915 Panama-Pacific International Exposition in San Francisco. Although not perfect, the throughway was ready as promised, and a motion picture of America's transcontinental highway was shown at the exposition. Over time, the association improved surfaces by using better materials, shortened the driving distance with realignments and published guidebooks about the Lincoln Highway. Automobile touring had never been so good.

Through example, the LHA educated the public as well as state and federal governments about the value of good roads for almost 15 years. The 1919 moving of a military convoy over the "Lincolnway" foretold the utility of an integrated highway system for national defense and interstate commerce.

With the 1921 Federal Highway Act came the funds for states to construct and maintain connecting arteries. Four years later the United States adopted a highway numbering system, and most of the Lincoln

pleasure. Harbor Bay Maritime, (510) 769-5500, operates ferries from Alameda to the San Francisco Ferry Building. Fares are $5; over 62, military and the physically impaired $3; ages 2-12, $2.25.

The Alameda/Oakland Ferry, (510) 522-3300, provides service to Alameda, Angel Island, Oakland and San Francisco. The Alameda/Oakland/San Francisco one-way fare is $5; active military with ID $3.75; over 64 and the physically impaired $3; ages 5-12, $2.25. Round-trip fare to Angel Island is $12; over 61, physically impaired and ages 13-18, $9; ages 5-12, $6.

Golden Gate and Harbor Bay Maritime ferries depart from the Ferry Building at the foot of Market Street and north of the San Francisco-Oakland Bay Bridge. Red and White ferries depart Pier 43½ at Fisherman's Wharf. For schedules phone the respective companies at the above numbers.

Preserved as national historic landmarks and purportedly the only such on wheels, San Francisco's famous cable cars are painted in their original 1873 colors—maroon with cream and blue trim. The cable cars run 6 a.m.-1 a.m. and travel three routes. The Powell-Hyde line begins at Powell and Market streets and runs to Victorian Park at Beach and Hyde streets; the Powell-Mason line also begins at Powell and Market streets but ends at Bay and Taylor streets near Fisherman's Wharf; and the California Street line runs between Market Street and Van Ness Avenue.

Although there are frequent stops and the trip is slow (travel speed is 9.5 mph), taking a cable car ride is an essential part of any San Francisco visit. One-way fare is $2 (over 64 and the physically impaired $1, 9 p.m.-7 a.m.); an all-day pass costs $6. No transfers are issued or accepted. If you're just riding for fun, the California Street line is likely to be the least crowded.

ALCATRAZ ISLAND—
see Golden Gate National Recreation Area p. 157.

SAVE **THE AQUARIUM OF THE BAY,** Pier 39 at the Embarcadero and Beach St., is a "diver's eye" view aquarium. Clear acrylic tunnels give visitors a subsea perspective on such San Francisco Bay area marine life as sharks, rays, jellyfish and eels. Naturalists are available to answer questions. Self-guided tours through the tanks last an hour.

Daily 9-8, Memorial Day-Labor Day; 10-6, rest of year. Closed Dec. 25. Admission $12.95; over 64 and ages 3-11, $6.50. Public transit riders receive $2 discount. MC, VI. Phone (415) 623-5300 or (888) 732-3483.

ASIAN ART MUSEUM OF SAN FRANCISCO, 200 Larkin St. on Civic Center Plaza, is in the former 1917 Beaux Arts-style main library. The museum, one of the Western world's largest dedicated to Asian art, houses a collection of 15,000 pieces spanning 6,000 years. A large portion of the museum's collection was donated by industrialist Avery Brundage. Paintings, jades, sculptures, ceramics and other treasures introduce the major cultures of Asia.

Guided tours are available. Food is available. Tues.-Sun. 10-5 (also Thurs. 5-9); closed Jan. 1, Thanksgiving and Dec. 25. Admission $10; over 64, $7; college students with ID and ages 13-17, $6; free to all first Tues. of each month. AX, DS, MC, VI. Phone (415) 379-8800.

CABLE CAR MUSEUM AND POWERHOUSE VIEWING GALLERY, 1201 Mason St. at Washington St., contains models, photographs and relics of San Francisco's early transit system, including the first cable car, built in 1873. A videotape presentation about cable cars describes how they work, and an underground viewing room enables visitors to observe the huge sheaves that guide the vehicles from under the street.

Allow 1 hour minimum. Daily 10-6, Apr.-Sept.; 10-5, rest of year. Closed Jan. 1, Thanksgiving and Dec. 25. Donations. Phone (415) 474-1887.

GEM SAVE **CALIFORNIA ACADEMY OF SCIENCES,** 875 Howard St., includes the Natural History Museum and Steinhart Aquarium. **Note:** The attraction will relocate to this temporary facility spring 2004 pending completion of a new building in Golden Gate Park. The Morrison Planetarium will be closed during this time. Reopening at the new facility is planned for summer 2008. Daily 10-5. Admission $6; ages 12-17, $4; ages 4-11, $2. Admission includes the museum and aquarium. AX, DS, MC, VI. Phone (415) 750-7145. *See color ad p. 144.*

Natural History Museum encompasses Wild California Hall, African Hall, Hall of Gems and Minerals, The Far Side of Science Gallery and Earth and Space Hall, where a shake table lets visitors safely experience a simulated California earthquake. Another exhibit hall, Life Through Time—The Age of the Dinosaurs, demonstrates evolution based on scientific evidence.

Steinhart Aquarium houses some 14,000 aquatic animals, including octopuses, alligators, turtles, reptiles, sharks, anemones and sea horses, presented in 189 displays. Highlights include the Fish Roundabout and Sharks of the Tropics, featuring several species of sharks in a re-created tropical reef habitat. Penguins are fed at daily at 11:30 and 4; Roundabout feedings take place daily at 1:30. *See color ad p. 144.*

GEM **CALIFORNIA PALACE OF THE LEGION OF HONOR** is in Lincoln Park near 34th Ave. and Clement St. overlooking the Golden Gate Bridge. Founded to honor Californians who died in France during World War I, the Beaux Arts building is a three-quarter-scale replica of the 18th-century Palais de la Légion d'Honneur in Paris. The museum's collections include decorative arts, sculpture, tapestries and more than 87,000 paintings spanning 4,000 years. Ancient and medieval

The Lincoln Highway (continued)

route became US 30, 40 and 50. The association disbanded in 1928, but not before it engaged Boy Scout troops across the country to place some 3,000 concrete Lincoln Highway markers along the route in all 12 states: New York, New Jersey, Pennsylvania, Ohio, Indiana, Illinois, Iowa, Nebraska, Wyoming, Utah, Nevada and California. Many of these markers still exist.

San Francisco's Lincoln Park marked the western terminus of the Lincoln Highway. To get there from the Nevada border, motorists entered California through **Truckee** and negotiated the Sierra Nevada via historic Donner Pass; an optional route from Carson City took motorists along the southern shore of **Lake Tahoe,** followed the American River toward **Placerville,** then went through **Folsom.** The roads converged at **Sacramento** and the highway continued south through **Lodi** to **Stockton,** west through **Livermore** to **Hayward,** then north into **Oakland,** where a ferry served as the only connector to San Francisco until a bridge was completed in 1936. Another route from Sacramento approached Oakland from the north through **Davis** and **Vacaville. Look for these California Lincoln Highway landmark towns in this TourBook guide.**

For more information about the old Lincoln Highway contact the new Lincoln Highway Association, P.O. Box 308, Franklin Grove, IL 61031; phone (815) 456-3030.

Digital Archives

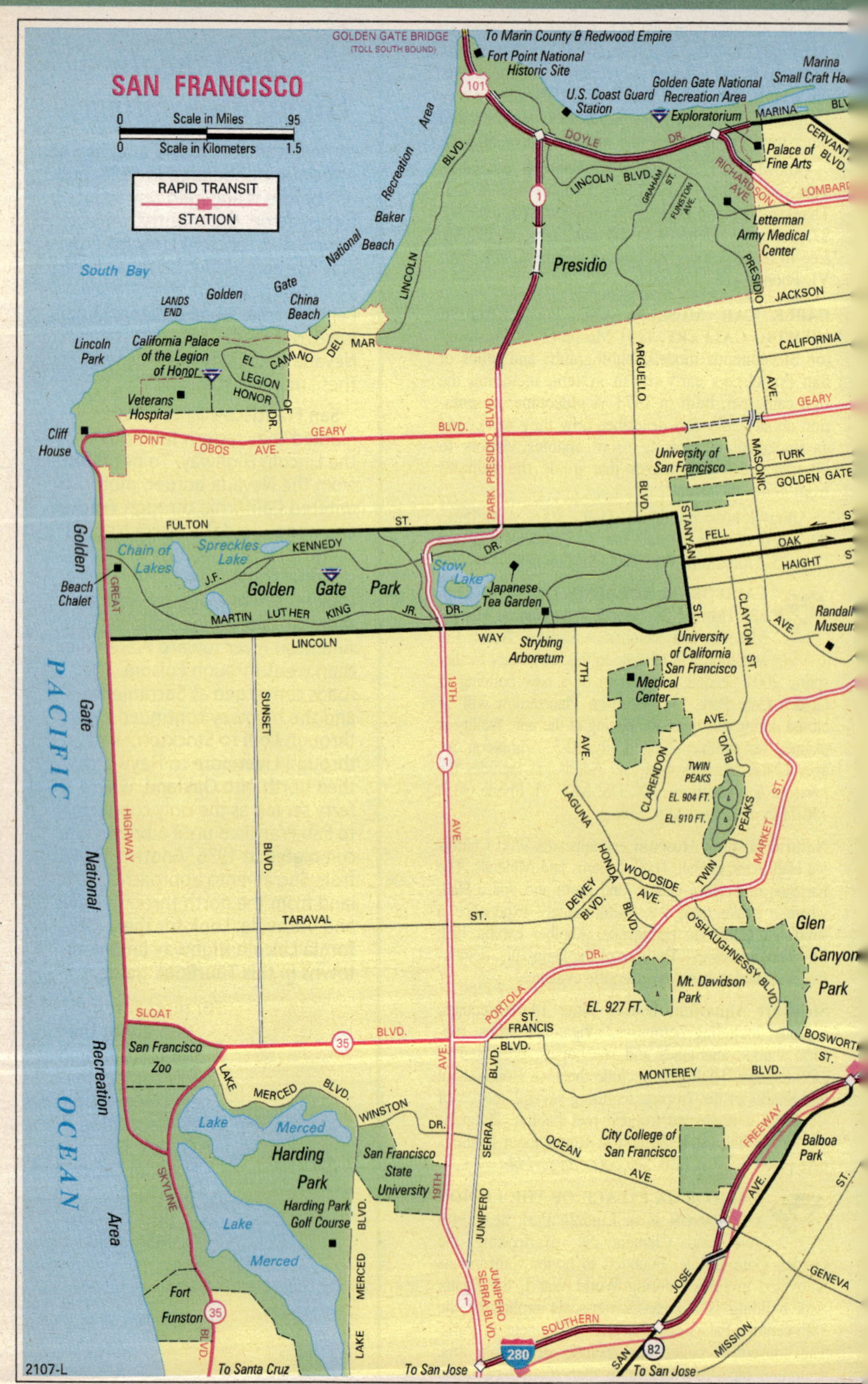
SAN FRANCISCO
Scale in Miles 0 .95
Scale in Kilometers 0 1.5
RAPID TRANSIT
STATION
GOLDEN GATE BRIDGE
(TOLL SOUTH BOUND)
To Marin County & Redwood Empire
Fort Point National Historic Site
U.S. Coast Guard Station
Golden Gate National Recreation Area
Exploratorium
Marina Small Craft Harbor
Palace of Fine Arts
Letterman Army Medical Center
Presidio
Baker Beach
China Beach
National Recreation Area
South Bay
Lands End
Golden Gate
Lincoln Park
California Palace of the Legion of Honor
Veterans Hospital
Cliff House
University of San Francisco
Golden Gate National Recreation Area
Beach Chalet
Chain of Lakes
Spreckles Lake
Golden Gate Park
Stow Lake
Japanese Tea Garden
Strybing Arboretum
University of California San Francisco Medical Center
Randall Museum
TWIN PEAKS
EL. 904 FT.
EL. 910 FT.
Mt. Davidson Park
EL. 927 FT.
Glen Canyon Park
PACIFIC OCEAN
San Francisco Zoo
Lake Merced
Harding Park
Harding Park Golf Course
San Francisco State University
City College of San Francisco
Balboa Park
Fort Funston
To Santa Cruz
To San Jose
2107-L

Pier 45
USS Pampanito
Ferry to Alcatraz Island
Fisherman's Wharf
Pier 39
Pier 35
Maritime Museum
The Jeremiah O'Brien
The Cannery
Fort Mason
Ghirardelli Square
Coit Tower
Ferry to Marin County & Vallejo
To Treasure Island
YERBA BUENA ISLAND
To Oakland & East Bay Cities
80
U.S. Coast Guard Reservation
FERRY
Ferry Plaza East World Trade Center
SAN FRANCISCO-OAKLAND BAY BRIDGE
(TOLL WEST BOUND)
To Alameda/Oakland
THE EMBARCADERO
BROADWAY
COLUMBUS AVE.
WASHINGTON
CLAY
Cable Car Mus. & Powerhouse Viewing Gallery
Transit-Bay Transit Term. Greyhound Bus Terminal
Japan Center
GEARY
EXPWY.
Visitor Information Ctr. Hallidie Plaza
Pacific Bell Mus. & Archives
California Academy of Sciences
The Seymour Pioneer Mus.
Pacific Bell Park
China Basin
Mary's Cathedral
Civic Center and Asian Art Museum of San Francisco
MARKET ST.
MISSION
HOWARD
FOLSOM
HARRISON
BRYANT
BRANNAN
TOWNSEND
KING
CALTRAIN Depot
San
Francisco
Bay
16TH ST.
Mission San Francisco de Asis
MISSION ST.
S. VAN NESS AVE.
FOLSOM ST.
HARRISON ST.
DOLORES ST.
FREE WAY
280
Central Basin
San Francisco General Hospital
POTRERO AVE.
LICK
CESAR CHAVEZ ST.
JAMES
101
3RD ST.
Indian Basin
BAYSHORE
San Francisco Bay Naval Shipyard
South Basin
Mc Laren Park
GILMAN AVE.
JAMESTOWN AVE.
San Francisco Stadium at Candlestick Point
HUNTERS POINT EXPWY.
Bay View Park
BAYSHORE BLVD.
FREEWAY
Cow Palace AVE.
To San Francisco International Airport & San Jose
© AAA

DOWNTOWN
SAN FRANCISCO
Scale in Miles
Scale in Kilometers
San Francisco Bay
Fort Mason
San Francisco Maritime National Historical Park
Balclutha
Municipal Pier
Hyde St. Pier Hist. Ships
Eureka
Thayer
Ferry to Tiburon
Pier 45
USS Pampanito
Ferry to Angel Island
Ferry to Alcatraz Island
Fisherman's Wharf
Pier 43½
The Jeremiah O'Brien
Bay Cruise & Sausalito
Pier 39
Bay Cruise
The Aquarium of the Bay
Pier 35
Restaurants
Maritime Museum
Ghirardelli Square
The Cannery
Ripley's Believe It or Not! Museum
Wax Museum at Fisherman's Wharf
Statue of St. Francis
Russian Hill Park
San Francisco Art Institute
Telegraph Hill
Coit Memorial Tower
Washington Square
RUSSIAN HILL
JACK KEROVAC ALLEY
U.S. Customs
JACKSON SQ. HISTORICAL DISTRICT
Cable Car Museum and Powerhouse Viewing Gallery
CHINESE HISTORICAL SOCIETY OF AMERICA MUS. AND LEARNING CENTER
CHINATOWN
Grace Cathedral
NOB HILL
PACIFIC HERITAGE MUSEUM
Wells Fargo History Museum
Old St. Mary's Church
Financial District
"Wall Street" West
Victorian Home Walk
START TOUR
Union Square
CARTOON ART MUS.
PACIFIC BELL MUSEUM AND ARCHIVES
SAN FRANCISCO MUSEUM OF MODERN ART
YERBA BUENA CENTER FOR THE ARTS
Moscone Convention Center
Visitor Information Center
Hallidie Plaza
Federal Bldg.
State Bldg.
Asian Art Mus.
United Nations Plaza
Veterans War Mem.
San Francisco Ballet
Opera House
City Hall
Civic Center
Brooks Hall
Library
Symphony Hall
Bill Graham Civic Auditorium
California State Automobile Association
P.O.
JEFFERSON
BEACH
NORTH POINT
BAY
FRANCISCO
CHESTNUT
LOMBARD
GREENWICH
FILBERT
UNION
GREEN
VALLEJO
BROADWAY
PACIFIC AVE.
JACKSON
WASHINGTON
CLAY
SACRAMENTO
CALIFORNIA
PINE
BUSH
SUTTER
POST
MAIDEN LA.
GEARY
O'FARRELL
ELLIS
EDDY
TURK
GOLDEN GATE AVE.
MC ALLISTER
GROVE
HAYES
FRANKLIN
VAN NESS AVE.
POLK
LARKIN
HYDE
LEAVENWORTH
JONES
TAYLOR
CUSHMAN
MASON
POWELL
CYRIL MAGNIN
STOCKTON
WAVERLY PL.
BRENHAM PL.
GRANT AVE.
KEARNY
MONTGOMERY
SANSOME
NEW MONTGOMERY
COLUMBUS AVE.
THE EMBARCADERO
MARKET ST.
PETER YORKE WAY
STAR KING WAY
FULTON
MINT ST.
2ND
3RD
4TH
5TH
6TH
7TH
8TH ST.
9TH ST.
HOWARD
FOLSOM
MISSION ST.
101
© AAA
2109-L
RAPID TRANSIT
STATION
SELF-GUIDING TOUR
WALKING
BUS
CABLE CAR
PUBLIC PARKING

art is featured as are works by El Greco, Claude Monet, Pablo Picasso, Rembrandt, Pierre Auguste Renoir and Auguste Rodin.

The "Thinker," one of more than 70 Rodin sculptures in the museum's collections, is a highlight of the outdoor Court of Honor. European paintings span the 14th through 20th centuries and include works by Fra Angelico, Henri Matisse and Peter Paul Rubens. A collection of antiquities features objects from the Mediterranean and Near East.

Food is available. Allow 2 hours minimum. Tues.-Sun. 9:30-5; closed major holidays. Admission $8; over 64, $6; ages 12-17, $5; free to all Tues. An additional fee is charged for special exhibitions. AX, MC, VI. Phone (415) 863-3330, TTY (415) 750-3509, or (415) 750-7645 for sign language tour requests. *See color ad p. 144.*

THE CANNERY—*see Shopping p. 154.*

SAVE **CARTOON ART MUSEUM** is at 655 Mission St. Focusing on original cartoon and animation art, the museum presents rotating exhibits in addition to its permanent collection. Categories of cartoon art displayed include Underground, which emerged in the late 1960s San Francisco hippie scene; Editorial, typically found in newspapers; Magazine; and Animation, art used to produce animated films. Also shown are comic strip and comic book art.

Allow 1 hour minimum. Tues.-Sun. 11-5; closed Jan. 1, Easter, July 4, Thanksgiving and Dec. 25. Admission $6; senior citizens and students with ID $4; ages 6-12, $2. MC, VI. Phone (415) 227-8666.

GEM **CHINATOWN** covers about 16 square blks. and is bounded by Broadway, Bush, Kearny and Stockton sts. More Chinese live in this "city within a city" than in any other place in the world outside China. Grant Avenue, the main thoroughfare, is lined with tearooms, shops, temples, Christian missions, Chinese schools, theaters and grocery stores. The Bank of Canton, 743 Washington St., has an unusual exterior.

© Richard Cummins / Corbis

SAVE All About Chinatown! Walking Tours features the area's history, culture and traditions with 2- and 3-hour tours; the 3-hour tour includes a dim sum lunch. The Wok Wiz Chinatown Tours offers a historical walking tour of Chinatown and lunch. Chinese Culture Center, 3rd floor of the Holiday Inn at 750 Kearny St., has information about Chinatown and displays Chinese art. The center offers a 2-hour culinary walking tour ending with a dim sum lunch as well as 90-minute heritage walking tours.

All About Chinatown! tours daily at 10 and 1 (tours require six or more participants). Wok Wiz tours daily at 1. Chinese Culture Center open Tues.-Sat. 10-4; closed holidays.

Two-hour All About Chinatown! tour $25; 3-hour lunch tour $40. Wok Wiz tours $40. Chinese Culture Center free; culinary walking tour $30; heritage walking tour $15. Reservations are required for all tours. Phone All About Chinatown! Walking Tours at (415) 982-8839, Wok Wiz Chinatown Tours at (415) 981-8989, or Chinese Culture Center at (415) 986-1822.

CHINESE HISTORICAL SOCIETY OF AMERICA MUSEUM AND LEARNING CENTER, 965 Clay St., is in the historic Julia Morgan Chinese YWCA building, dating to 1930. The museum recalls the important role of the Chinese in the settlement of the city and the West through a variety of exhibits. Allow 30 minutes minimum. Tues.-Fri. 11-4, Sat.-Sun. noon-4. Admission $3; senior citizens and students with ID $2; ages 6-17, $1; free to all first Thurs. of each month. Phone (415) 391-1188.

CIVIC CENTER, covering 8 blks. and bordered by Market, Hayes and Franklin sts. and Golden Gate Ave., groups federal, state and city structures and parklands. With a dome taller than the U.S. Capitol, City Hall commands a view of the plaza, which is surrounded by the State and Federal buildings, Main Public Library, Auditorium and the Health Center, all of French and Neo-Renaissance style.

Performing Arts Center is across Van Ness Ave. opposite City Hall; guided tours of the Herbst Theatre, the War Memorial Opera House and Davies Symphony Hall leave from the Grove St. entrance of the symphony hall. The center is comprised of the San Francisco Performing Arts Library, Herbst Theatre in the Veterans Memorial Building, War Memorial Opera House, Davies Symphony Hall and the San Francisco Ballet Association. The San Francisco Symphony's electro-pneumatic Ruffatti organ has more than 10,000 pipes, five manuals and 163 ranks.

Tours are given on the hour Mon. 10-2, except on holidays. Tours $5, over 64 and students with ID $3. Phone (415) 552-8338 for reservations or (415) 255-4800 for library information.

CLIFF HOUSE—
see Golden Gate National Recreation Area p. 158.

GEM SAVE **EXPLORATORIUM,** 3601 Lyon St. inside the Palace of Fine Arts, contains more than 650 interactive exhibits that invite visitors to see, touch, hear, feel and explore the fields of science, mathematics, technology, animal behavior and human perception. Subjects covered include color, electricity, language, motion, touch and weather. The Tactile Dome is a totally dark geodesic dome with 13 chambers and no right angles. Visitors make their way through the chambers by crawling and sliding, using only their sense of touch.

Food is available. Allow 2 hours minimum. Tues.-Sun. and Mon. holidays 10-5; closed Thanksgiving and Dec. 25. Admission $12; over 64, students with ID, the physically impaired and ages 13-17, $9.50; ages 4-12, $8; free to all first Wed. of the month. Tactile Dome $15 (includes Exploratorium admission); reservations are recommended. AX, MC, VI. Phone (415) 561-0360, or (415) 561-0362 for Tactile Dome reservations. *See color ad p. 144.*

FISHERMAN'S WHARF—*see Shopping p. 154.*

FORT MASON CENTER, Buchanan St. and Marina Blvd., is a World War II embarkation point that has been transformed into a regional cultural center. Among the art galleries converted from former warehouses are SAVE Museo ItaloAmericano; San Francisco African American Historical and Cultural Society; and Museum of Craft & Folk Art, which specializes in exhibitions of contemporary craft, contemporary American folk art and worldwide tribal-ethnic art.

The center also contains six theaters. Events are presented weekly. Daily 8 a.m.-midnight. Free. A fee may be charged for some events and galleries. Phone (415) 441-3400.

FORT POINT NATIONAL HISTORIC SITE—*see Golden Gate National Recreation Area p. 158.*

GHIRARDELLI SQUARE—*see Shopping p. 154.*

GOLDEN GATE BRIDGE, over the bay, connects San Francisco with Marin County and the Redwood Hwy. (US 101). With a length of 8,981 feet and main span length of 4,200 feet, it is one of the longest single-span suspension bridges ever built. Its two massive towers are the world's highest bridge towers, at 746 feet above the water. A clearance of 220 feet allows passage of the largest oceangoing vessels. A crew of painters constantly maintains the bridge's distinctive coat of international orange. A toll of $5 is charged southbound; northbound free.

GOLDEN GATE NATIONAL RECREATION AREA—*see place listing p. 157.*

GEM **GOLDEN GATE PARK** is bordered by the Great Hwy. on the w., Lincoln Way on the s., Stanyan St. on the e. and Fulton St. on the n., extending 3 miles from Fell and Stanyan sts. to the ocean. John McLaren, a Scottish landscape gardener and park superintendent 1887-1943, transformed a barren wasteland lapped by shifting dunes into this lush oasis with a dozen artificial lakes and a collection of trees and plants of worldwide scope. Miles of roads, bridle paths and foot trails weave through the 1,017-acre park.

Among the park's attractions are the Conservatory of Flowers, a bison paddock, a restored Dutch-style windmill, an equestrian center, trotting track, tennis courts, archery field, golf course, polo field stadium, playground, boat rentals, a restored carousel, the National AIDS Memorial Grove and an outdoor music concourse, which offers concerts all year.

The visitor center, in the Beach Chalet on Great Highway, features murals with scenes of the city during the Great Depression, mosaics and wood carvings.

Picnic facilities are available. Park open daily 24 hours. Visitor center open daily 9-6. Guided tours of various parts of the park are offered Sat. at 11, Sun. at 11 and 2, May-Oct.; most tours last 1-2 hours, but duration varies greatly and tours are not restricted to the hours listed. Certain roads are closed to automobile traffic Sun. Phone (415) 831-2700, or (415) 263-0991 for tour information.

California Academy of Sciences—*see attraction listing p. 135.*

Japanese Tea Garden, 8th Ave. and Kennedy Dr., is a 3.8-acre site landscaped with bridges, walks, ponds, miniature waterfalls, statuary and pagodas. The garden is spectacular in spring when the cherry trees bloom. Daily 8:30-6, Mar.-Oct.; 8:30-5, rest of year. Admission $3.50; over 64 and ages 6-12, $1.25. Admission first and last hours of each day free. Phone (415) 752-1171.

Natural History Museum—*see California Academy of Sciences p. 135.*

Steinhart Aquarium—*see California Academy of Sciences p. 135.*

Strybing Arboretum, 9th Ave. and Lincoln Way, has more than 7,000 varieties of plants from around the world. Within its 55 acres are a cloud forest, a fragrance garden, a redwood grove, a primitive plant garden and a Japanese moonviewing garden. Mon.-Fri. 8-4:30, Sat.-Sun. and holidays 10-5. Free guided 45-minute tours are given daily at 1:30 (also Sat.-Sun. at 10:30). Donations. Phone (415) 661-1316.

JAPAN CENTER (Nihonmachi), is bounded by Post, Geary, Laguna and Fillmore sts.; underground parking is available. The 5-acre complex has diverse cultural and commercial points of interest. The Miyako Hotel adjoins the Japanese consulate. The Peace Pagoda, a gift of the Japanese people, stands in the central plaza. Music, dance, tea ceremonies and martial arts presentations are given many weekends in summer.

Golden Gate Park / © Jan Butchofsky-Houser / Corbis

California Missions

To secure its northern territorial claims in the New World, Spain ordered the creation of a series of Franciscan missions in California. Begun under the leadership of Father Junípero Serra, who died in 1784, 21 missions and one asistencia were established 1769-1823, spaced about a day's journey apart along the northern extension of El Camino Real, the Royal Road.

Each mission had its own herd of cattle, fields and vegetable gardens, which were tended by native converts. For furniture, clothing, tools and other implements, the missions traded their surplus of meal, wine, oil, hemp, hides and tallow. Their attempts to "civilize" the indigenous population yielded mixed results: For the thousands of Indians brought under the wing of the church, thousands of others died at the hands of the Spanish or from their diseases. But the missions succeeded in other regards: Around them and their accompanying presidios, or military posts, grew the first permanent settlements in California.

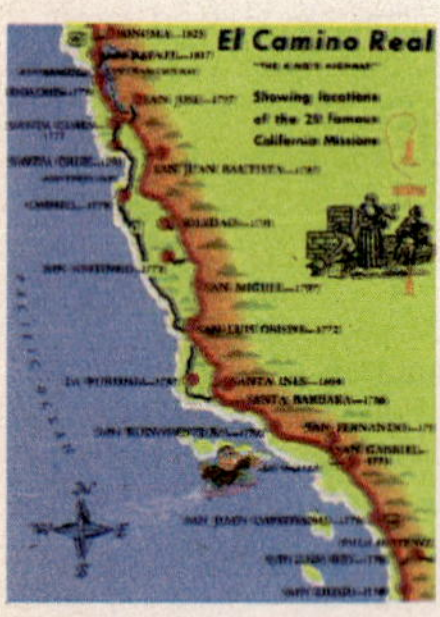

Digital Archives

After winning its independence from Spain and during the secularization, Mexico removed control of the missions from the Franciscans and subdivided much of their land among the Mexican soldiers and settlers. During the ensuing years, neglect and earthquakes took their toll; many of the missions were severely damaged or destroyed. Subsequent restoration and reconstruction have revitalized these historic structures, and today US 101 roughly traces the route of the old El Camino Real.

The area has restaurants, art galleries, movie theaters, gardens, Japanese baths and shops *(see Specialty Districts in the Shopping section p. 153)*. Phone (415) 922-6776.

JAPANESE TEA GARDEN—
see Golden Gate Park p. 141.

THE *JEREMIAH O'BRIEN*, berthed at Pier 45, is a restored World War II liberty ship in operating condition. During "steaming" weekends, usually the third weekend of the month, the ship's engine is in operation and the ship's store is set up. Daily 9-4; closed Jan. 1, Thanksgiving and Dec. 25. Cruises are offered in May and Oct. Admission $7; over 64, $5; ages 6-14, $4. MC, VI. Phone (415) 544-0100.

LANDS END, overlooking the Pacific Ocean and the Golden Gate Bridge, is part of Golden Gate National Recreation Area *(see place listing p. 157)*. It has a memorial to the men who died on the USS *San Francisco* during the Battle of Guadalcanal, Nov. 12-13, 1942. The memorial is a piece of the ship's bridge.

LINCOLN PARK, at 34th Ave. and Clement St., consists of 193 acres and contains American artist George Segal's memorial to the victims of the World War II Holocaust. The park is noted for its encompassing views of the Golden Gate area and includes the California Palace of the Legion of Honor *(see attraction listing p. 135)*.

LOMBARD STREET, between Hyde and Leavenworth sts., is often referred to as "the crookedest street in the world." In a series of S-curves, this one-block portion descends a 40-degree slope. Stairs are available. Campers and trailers are prohibited on this block of Lombard Street.

GEM **MISSION SAN FRANCISCO DE ASIS** (Mission Dolores) is at 3321 16th St. at Dolores St. One of the oldest buildings in San Francisco, it was founded June 29 and opened Oct. 9, 1776, by Father Junípero Serra. The rough-hewn redwood roof timbers still are lashed together with rawhide. The altar was one of the most ornate among the missions; the original books and decorations were brought from Spain and Mexico. California's first book—Palou's "Life of Junípero Serra"—was written here. A small museum displays old manuscripts and mission relics.

The basilica next door, with its combination of Moorish, Mission and Corinthian styles, is a striking contrast to the mission's appearance. Limited street parking is available. Daily 9-4:30; closed Thanksgiving and Dec. 25. Donations. Phone (415) 621-8203.

NATURAL HISTORY MUSEUM—
see California Academy of Sciences p. 135.

NOB HILL, in the vicinity of California, Sacramento, Jones and Taylor sts., was the center of luxurious living in the last half of the 19th century, when men who had made fortunes in railroading and gold mining built their houses in this territory. Elegant apartment buildings and hotels now occupy the hilltop.

Grace Cathedral (Episcopal), one of the nation's oldest cathedrals, contains replicas of the bronze doors of the Baptistry in Florence, Italy, by Lorenzo Ghiberti. Cathedral tours Mon.-Fri. 1-3, Sat. 11:30-1:30, Sun. 12:30-2. Donations. Phone (415) 749-6300 for cathedral information.

NORTH BEACH, spread around Telegraph Hill and down to the waterfront, is noted for its art galleries, bookshops, international restaurants and informal approach to life. The area once was on the water, but landfill efforts have placed it farther inland.

OLD ST. MARY'S CHURCH is in Chinatown at Grant Ave. and California St. The 1854 church's interior was patterned after the Spanish church of California's first bishop, Joseph Sadoc Alemany. Mon.-Fri. 7-4:30, Sat. 10-6, Sun. 8-3:30. Donations. Phone (415) 986-4388.

PACIFIC BELL MUSEUM AND ARCHIVES, 140 New Montgomery St., Suite 111, offers a small collection of antique telephones, switchboards and related objects, photographs and memorabilia tracing the history of the telephone and PacBell. Allow 30 minutes minimum. Tues.-Thurs. 10-2; closed holidays. Free. Phone (415) 542-0182.

SAVE **PACIFIC BELL PARK TOURS** is at 24 Willie Mays Plaza, at Third and King sts. Guided walking tours of the San Francisco Giants' baseball stadium allow fans to visit the press box, dugout, visitors' clubhouse and luxury suites. Tours are given daily 10-2 (no tours are given on dates when day games are scheduled, and tours are limited on days when night games will be played); closed Jan. 1, Easter and Dec. 25. Fee $10; over 54, $8; under 13, $5. DS, JC, MC, VI. Phone (415) 972-2400.

PACIFIC HERITAGE MUSEUM, 608 Commercial St., displays changing exhibits chronicling the history and culture of peoples from both sides of the Pacific Basin. Housed in the restored U.S. Subtreasury Building, the museum features an exhibit depicting the building's history. Allow 30 minutes minimum. Tues.-Sat. 10-4; closed holidays. Free. Phone (415) 399-1124 or (415) 362-4100.

PIER 39—*see Shopping p. 154.*

PALACE OF FINE ARTS, s.e. approach to the Golden Gate Bridge at Bay and Lyon Sts., is the last remaining structure of the 1915 Panama-Pacific Exposition. The temporary structure survived until 1962 when the Beaux Arts rotunda and colonnade were re-created in concrete from castings of the original ornamentation. The palace is now in a park with a lagoon where swans and ducks swim. Also in the park is a 1,000-seat theater. Daily dawn-dusk. Free. Phone (415) 567-6642 for theater information.

PRESIDIO—
see Golden Gate National Recreation Area p. 158.

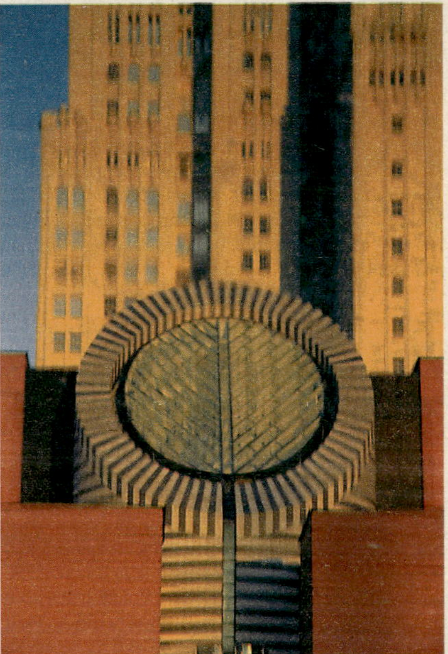

San Francisco Museum of Modern Art
© Richard Cummins / Photophile

RANDALL MUSEUM, off Roosevelt Way at 199 Museum Way, has animals, arts and crafts and exhibits about sciences and model trains. Tues.-Sat. 10-5. Donations. Phone (415) 554-9600.

SAVE **RIPLEY'S BELIEVE IT OR NOT! MUSEUM,** 175 Jefferson St. at Fisherman's Wharf, displays the bizarre and unusual. Sun.-Thurs. 9 a.m.-11 p.m., Fri.-Sat. 9 a.m.-midnight, mid-June through Labor Day; Sun.-Thurs. 10-10, Fri.-Sat. 10 a.m.-midnight, rest of year. Admission $11.95; over 59, $8.95; ages 5-12, $7.95. AX, DC, MC, VI. Phone (415) 771-6188.

ST. MARY'S CATHEDRAL, 1111 Gough St. on Cathedral Hill, is a modern structure of Italian marble. A baldachino, or canopy, of aluminum and gold; a large mosaic; and a Ruffati organ highlight the interior of the cathedral. Mon.-Fri. 6:30-4:30, Sat. 6:30 a.m.-7 p.m., Sun. 7:30-4:30, except during masses. Docents lead tours Mon.-Sat. 9-noon and Sun. after 11 mass, Mar.-Oct. Donations. Phone (415) 567-2020.

SAN FRANCISCO ART INSTITUTE, 800 Chestnut St. at Jones and Leavenworth sts., presents artworks in two galleries, one of which contains a mural by Diego Rivera. The architecture effectively combines the traditional Spanish style of the original structure with the contemporary look of the addition. Daily 9-8. Free. Phone (415) 771-7020.

SAN FRANCISCO MARITIME NATIONAL HISTORICAL PARK is at the w. end of Fisherman's Wharf. In addition to a fleet of historic ships, a museum and a library, the site also includes Aquatic

Park, a bayside park and recreation area with a quarter-mile stretch of beach and a lagoon.

Hyde Street Pier Historic Ships, at the foot of Hyde St., displays ships dating from the late 19th century. Visitors can board three ships: *Balclutha,* a three-masted square-rigged sailing vessel containing ship relics, marine paintings and photographs; *C.A. Thayer,* a coastal lumber schooner; and *Eureka,* the largest ferry operating on San Francisco Bay in her time. The tugboats *Eppleton Hall* and *Hercules* are anchored nearby. Programs and demonstrations are offered.

Daily 9:30-5:30; closed Jan. 1, Thanksgiving and Dec. 25. Admission $5; over 61, $4; under 17 free. Phone (415) 561-7100.

Maritime Museum displays the history of water transportation from the 1800s to the present. Model ships, maritime artifacts, fine arts and photographs are displayed. Daily 10-5; closed Jan. 1, Thanksgiving and Dec. 25. Free. Phone (415) 556-3002.

San Francisco Maritime Library is at Fort Mason, Building E, and houses more than 250,000 historic photographs, documents and maritime literature. Wed.-Fri. 1-5, Sat. 10-5, Tues. 5-8. Free. Phone (415) 561-7080 or (415) 561-7030.

SAVE **SAN FRANCISCO MUSEUM OF MODERN ART,** 151 Third St., is in a modernistic, five-story building designed by Swiss architect Mario Botta in 1994. A brick, granite and glass exterior contains spacious galleries illuminated by a skylight. The museum houses a comprehensive collection of modern and contemporary art, including traditional paintings and sculpture, multimedia installations and photography. Rotating exhibits are featured.

Food is available. Thurs.-Tues. 10-6 (also Thurs. 6-9 p.m.), Memorial Day-Labor Day; Thurs.-Tues. 11-6 (also Thurs. 6-9 p.m.), rest of year. Closed Jan. 1, July 4, Thanksgiving and Dec. 25. Guided 45-minute tours are offered. Admission $10; over 61, $7; students with ID $6; under 12 free; free to all first Tues. of the month. Guided tours free. Admission half-price to all Thurs. 6-9 p.m. Under 12 must be with an adult. MC, VI. Phone (415) 357-4000, (415) 357-4096 for guided tours, or TTY (415) 357-4154. *See color ad.*

SAN FRANCISCO-OAKLAND BAY BRIDGE spans San Francisco Bay and links San Francisco with the East Bay cities. Including approaches, it is 8.4 miles long, 4.5 miles of it over navigable water. The east and west spans are connected by a double-deck tunnel through Yerba Buena Island. A $2 toll is charged westbound only. Phone (510) 286-1148.

SAN FRANCISCO ZOO, on Sloat Blvd. with an entrance near 45th Ave., has approximately 1,000 mammals and birds. Of interest are the Primate Discovery Center, Gorilla World, Koala Crossing which features an Australian Walk-About, a feline conservation center, a warthog exhibit, broad-snouted caymans and an antique carousel. Daily 10-5. Big cats are fed Tues.-Sun. at 2. Admission $10; over 64 and ages 12-17, $7; ages 3-11, $4; free to all first Wed. of the month. Carousel ride $2. AX, MC, VI. Phone (415) 753-7080.

Children's Zoo includes nature trails, a barnyard, an insect zoo and animals that may be petted and fed. Daily 10:30-4:30 in summer; Mon.-Fri. 11-4, Sat.-Sun. 10:30-4, rest of year. Admission included with fee for San Francisco Zoo.

THE SEYMOUR PIONEER MUSEUM is at 300 Fourth St. Changing annual exhibits highlight the early years of California's heritage and history. The museum's collections were gathered by pioneer families and their descendants and include 19th- and early 20th-century paintings, artifacts, photographs and manuscripts. Allow 1 hour minimum. Wed.-Fri. and first and third Sat. of the month 10-4; closed holidays. Admission $3, over 61 and students with ID $1. Phone (415) 957-1849.

STEINHART AQUARIUM—
see California Academy of Sciences p. 135.

STRYBING ARBORETUM—
see Golden Gate Park p. 141.

TELEGRAPH HILL rises near the e. end of Lombard St. Topped by a park, the hill provides a panorama. Coit Memorial Tower, built roughly in the shape of a fire hose nozzle, memorializes volunteer firefighters. The observation deck is 542 feet above the bay. Tower open daily 10-6. Tower admission $3.75; over 64, $2.50; ages 6-12, $1.50. Phone (415) 362-0808.

SAVE **USS *PAMPANITO*,** at the end of Taylor St. at Pier 45, is a World War II submarine that saw action in the Pacific theater. Self-guiding audiotape tours require climbing stairs and stooping through low bulkheads. Thurs.-Tues. 9-8, Wed. 9-6, mid-May to mid-Oct.; Fri.-Sat. 9-8, Sun.-Thurs. 9-6, rest of year. Admission $7; over 61, $5; ages 6-12, $3; family rate (two adults and up to four family members) $20. AX, MC, VI. Phone (415) 775-1943.

SAVE **WAX MUSEUM AT FISHERMAN'S WHARF** is at 145 Jefferson St. between Taylor and Mason. Lifelike wax creations are displayed in such settings as the Chamber of Horrors, Hall of Religion, Library of U.S. Presidents, King Tut's Tomb and Palace of Living Art. Among the figures displayed are Leonardo DiCaprio, Marilyn Monroe, Donny and Marie Osmond, Sylvester Stallone and John Wayne.

Allow 1 hour minimum. Daily 9 a.m.-midnight, Memorial Day-Labor Day; Sun.-Thurs. 10-9, Fri.-Sat. 9 a.m.-11 p.m., rest of year. Admission $12.95; over 55, $10.55; ages 4-11, $6.95. DC, DS, MC, VI. Phone (415) 202-0400 or (800) 439-4305.

WELLS FARGO HISTORY MUSEUM is in Wells Fargo Bank Building at 420 Montgomery St. The museum contains a stagecoach, relics of the gold rush, nuggets, Western franks and stamps and other articles from 1848 to the present. Mon.-Fri. 9-5; closed bank holidays. Free. Phone (415) 396-2619.

YERBA BUENA CENTER FOR THE ARTS, bordered by Mission, Howard and Third sts., comprises three galleries, a screening room, an esplanade, an outdoor stage, a theater, a waterfall, a sculpture court and a garden. The complex emphasizes a range of art forms, from painting and electronic music to ballet and videotape. Lectures and workshops are offered.

Food is available. Galleries open Tues.-Sun. 11-5. Admission to galleries $6; over 64, students with ID and under 16, $3; free to all first Tues. of the month. AX, DC, MC, VI. Phone (415) 978-2787.

What To Do

Sightseeing

Sightseeing tours are available by land, sea and air; if your time is limited, the bus tours that touch briefly on city highlights are recommended. A list of events and sightseeing tips is recorded daily by the San Francisco Convention & Visitors Bureau; phone (415) 391-2000.

Boat Tours

Tours of the harbor operate from Fisherman's Wharf. The Red and White Fleet, (415) 447-0597 or (800) 229-2784, schedules 1-hour daytime cruises that depart from Pier 43½. Tours to Sonoma and the Napa wine country as well as tours of the city and Yosemite National Park depart from Pier 43½ or from area hotels with advance notice.

If you're interested in seeing what life on Alcatraz Island *(see attraction listing p. 157)* was like, be sure and buy your tickets ahead of time, as the tours frequently sell out. Ferries operated by the Blue & Gold Fleet *(see color ad p. 144)* depart from Pier 41 at Fisherman's Wharf. Reservations a week or more in advance are recommended during the summer and holiday periods; phone (415) 705-5555.

Cruises to Six Flags Marine World *(see attraction listing p. 178)* in Vallejo and to Angel Island are scheduled by Vallejo Ferry and depart from the Ferry Building; phone (707) 643-3779.

The Angel Island-Tiburon Ferry, (415) 435-2131, runs daily; times vary with the season. Angel Island State Park offers picnic facilities, beaches and hiking trails. The park includes the Angel Island Immigration Station, which received thousands of Chinese emigrants 1910-40 *(see Recreation Chart).*

Blue and Gold Fleet Bay Cruises and Motor Coach Tours, (415) 705-5555, has 60-minute bay cruises leaving Pier 39 at frequent intervals daily. The company also offers daily San Francisco, Napa and Sonoma wine country, Muir Woods, Monterey, Carmel and Yosemite trips; phone (415) 773-1188.

Hornblower Dining Yachts, (415) 788-8866, Pier 33 on the Embarcadero, offers daily dinner and lunch cruises and weekend brunch cruises aboard the motor yacht *California Hornblower.* Live music is provided with dinner and brunch, and there are dance floors on two decks. Reservations are required.

Bus and Limousine Tours

Many companies offer limousine tours of San Francisco, the Bay Area and Wine Country. See the telephone directory for information.

SAVE **GRAY LINE** tours depart from Pier 43½ at the Embarcadero; pick-up service also is available at most hotels. Various full- and half-day excursions of San Francisco and the Bay Area are offered. The 3.5-hour Deluxe City Highlights tour departs daily at 9:15, 11:15 and 2:15. Deluxe City Highlights fare $37; ages 5-11, $19. Reservations are required. AX, DC, DS, MC, VI. Phone (415) 434-8687.

GREAT PACIFIC TOUR CO. offers pick-up service at local hotels. The half-day City Tour gives passengers a comprehensive overview of San Francisco, including Fisherman's Wharf, Haight-Ashbury, Nob Hill and the city's famous Victorian homes. Stops are made at Twin Peaks and at the Marin Headlands across the Golden Gate Bridge (weather permitting). Tours are conducted in 14-passenger minivans. Other tours are available.

Allow 3 hours, 30 minutes minimum. City Tour departs daily at 9, 11 and 2. Fare $40; over 61, $38; ages 5-11, $28. Reservations are required. AX, MC, VI. Phone (415) 626-4499.

Driving Tours

Skyline Boulevard (SR 35) follows the scenic peninsula divide south of the city into the Santa Cruz Mountains, affording simultaneous views of the bay and ocean.

DID YOU KNOW

Because of budget considerations, the schedules and fees of all state-owned facilities are subject to change. Travelers are advised to phone ahead.

Upon presentation of your AAA membership card, the California State Automobile Association can furnish a map with a suggested tour covering much of San Francisco. This 49-Mile Scenic Drive map also is available from the San Francisco Convention & Visitors Bureau Visitor Information Center on the lower level of Hallidie Plaza at Market and Powell streets, where the cable cars turn around.

An audio cassette and map guide produced by OmniNav also provide a self-guiding tour of the 49-Mile Scenic Drive. The $10.95 tour package is available at the San Francisco Visitor Information Center at Powell and Market streets. For additional information phone (650) 219-8029.

Walking Tours

AAA Walking Tour: Downtown San Francisco

Refer to the Downtown San Francisco map. The tour takes 4-6 hours, depending on your pace and the number of listed sites you visit along the way. Those that appear in bold type have detailed listings in the What to See or Shopping sections. Even if you decide not to visit a listed site, reading the listing when you reach that point should make the tour more interesting.

Let's face it, San Francisco is known for its treacherous hills. Even so, areas like Union Square, the Financial District, Chinatown, North Beach, Telegraph Hill, Fisherman's Wharf and Russian Hill are best explored on foot. While the route makes the most of the city's flat streets, we still recommended wearing comfortable shoes for any unavoidable climbs. We'll warn you about approaching hills, and should you choose not to hoof it, you can hop on a bus or cable car at certain points along the tour.

Union Square, bordered by Geary, Powell, Post and Stockton streets, is a good place to start. To get there, take the Powell-Hyde cable car, which stops on the south side of the square. Parking is pricey, but if you must drive, underground spots are available at the Union Square Garage, accessed from Geary Street (one-way, westbound). Cheaper rates can be found at 330 Sutter St. (one-way, westbound) near Stockton Street.

Built in 1850, the square was named for demonstrations held here to support Union troops at the start of the Civil War. Standing in the palm-tree-framed park, you'll notice its focal point: the 97-foot-tall Dewey Monument, erected in 1903 to honor Commodore George Dewey's 1898 Manila Bay victory over the Spanish. A patina Goddess of Victory tops the column.

The square—heart of the downtown scene—teems with life. Vendors sell flowers, streetcar bells clang and people crowd the luxury hotels and department stores extending from the square. One such hotel is the historic Westin St. Francis, 335 Powell St., which survived the 1906 earthquake, purportedly serving breakfast to the masses on the morning of the disaster. Its spectacular lobby protects an antique grandfather clock: The ornate timepiece has served as a local meeting spot for years, coining the well-known phrase "Meet me at the St. Francis." The city's cable cars sport the expression.

Shopaholics may mistake Union Square and its environs for heaven. Some of the world's fanciest retailers and department stores can be found here: A gigantic Macy's dominates the Geary block, and Saks Fifth Avenue rubs elbows with Tiffany. Neiman-Marcus, at Geary and Stockton streets, boasts a six-story rotunda topped with an elaborate stained-glass dome. Original to the City of Paris department store (1909), the arched ceiling features a mural of a sailing ship and crowns the store's restaurant—a perfect spot for afternoon tea.

After window-shopping along the square, head east on Maiden Lane. Part of the raucous Barbary Coast in the early 1900s, this small side street, then called Morton Street, was once lined with bordellos. Now the tract serves clients of a different sort at its chic bistros and boutiques. Look to the left: The brick gallery at 140 Maiden Ln. was designed by Frank Lloyd Wright; it served as a prototype for the Guggenheim Museum in New York.

At Grant Avenue, turn left. A few blocks ahead is the entrance to Chinatown, marked by the famous green-tiled gate, bedecked with golden dragons. The gate was a gift to the city from the Republic of China in 1969. It is traditional for Chinese villages to have ceremonial gates similar to this one; the carved concrete guard dogs are said to ward off evil.

At Post, turn right. Admire the treasures in the windows of more swanky shops along this block. Note the Crocker Galleria, 50 Post St. at Kearny, designed to mimic the Galleria Vittorio Emanuele II in Milan, Italy. Beneath its dome you'll find large English ivy topiaries among elite shops and cafes.

Make a sharp left onto Montgomery Street. You have entered the concrete canyons of "Wall Street West" San Francisco's financial district. Here, between Market and Sacramento streets and east toward the Embarcadero, is where deals have been made since the 1850s, when prospectors returned from the gold mines with treasure and created a demand for banks. The district remains one of the country's top four financial centers. From 9 a.m.-5 p.m., the wide sidewalks are choked with hurried, well-dressed businesspeople, yet the street is nearly deserted when bankers' hours are over.

As befits a financial district, Montgomery is lined with skyscrapers that tickle the clouds. Lean and seemingly striped, the Wells Fargo Building, just north of Post Street at 44 Montgomery St., was built to house the bank's world headquarters. The concrete and steel structure stands 561 feet tall. At Bush Street, look right to locate the Mills Building at 220 Montgomery St. Built in 1892 (the tower was added in 1907), the steel building nearly occupies the entire block; its large lobby displays varied artwork. The 1928 Russ Building, 235 Montgomery St. just north of Bush, was the city's tallest building until the 1960s when the Transamerica Pyramid was constructed. Citizens referred to the 435-foot-tall building simply as "the skyscraper." Its Gothic design was modeled after the Chicago Tribune tower.

Union Square / © Richard Cummins / Photophile

Speaking of "the pyramid" San Francisco's most famous (and tallest) skyscraper, look north to spot this 48-story structure. Situated at 600 Montgomery St. where Columbus Avenue meets Washington Street, it sports nearly 6,000 windows, is topped with a 212-foot-tall spire and can be seen from almost anywhere in the city.

In its shadow is the **Jackson Square Historical District,** dating from gold rush heydays. Brick buildings with iron shutters lining Gold and Balance streets now contain antiques shops. Restaurants are decorated in Victorian style, and lampposts and hitching posts give the area an old-time feel.

Make a left onto California, a street shaded by more imposing buildings. Carved concrete faces, marble, brown stone and red brick decorate the facades of more banks and title companies; inside, magnificent chandeliers dangle in extravagant lobbies. Most notable is the 52-story Bank of America headquarters, 555 California St. (the accordionlike building on your left). The modern structure features carnelian marble; its top-floor restaurant, aptly named the Carnelian Room, provides stunning panoramas of the city. Bring your camera and some cash—you'll pay for the view with the price of one cocktail.

Continue up a relatively short but steep hill to Grant Avenue. **Old St. Mary's Church** is on the right, sandwiched between sleek high-rises and Chinese architecture. Built in 1854, the Catholic church is said to be the first cathedral in California. It survived the 1906 earthquake and subsequent fires; following renovation, it was rededicated in 1909. Across the street in St. Mary's Square is a 12-foot-tall metal and granite statue of Dr. Sun Yat-sen, founder of the Republic of China.

As you turn right onto Grant Avenue, **Chinatown's** main drag, be prepared for sensory overload. Originally called Calle de Fundacion, the street is the city's oldest. Now, beneath Chinese calligraphy street signs, lampposts dressed like pagodas (entwined with golden dragons' tails) and colorful filigreed balconies draped with laundry, there is an explosion of smells, sounds and activity. The narrow, crowded avenue is crammed with restaurants advertising dim sum; herb shops tempting passersby with ancient potions; delicatessens parading roasted ducks (with the heads still attached) hanging upside-down in the windows; newsstands selling Chinese reading materials; stores displaying fine antiques and jade sculpture; and souvenir shop bins filled with Chinese Barbie dolls, plastic Buddha statues, tea sets, embroidered slippers, postcards, ear-piercing cricket toys, bamboo flutes, Chinese iron balls, three-for-ten-dollar T-shirts and mah-jongg games—all identified with colorful Chinese signs.

Chinatown / © Richard Cummins / Photophile

To get a true feel for the neighborhood, visit on a Saturday morning, when residents pack the sidewalks, running errands and socializing. Women crowd the vegetable markets, picking over fresh water chestnuts and giant jackfruit. Scents of barbecued pork, simmering soup and incense mingle in the air, and you may be the only one speaking English; Chinatown is home to nearly 10,000 Chinese.

Browse the selections at the Canton Bazaar, 616 Grant Ave., a popular import shop; the Chinatown Kite Shop, 717 Grant Ave., a great spot for fish kites or hand-painted paper kites; and the Wok Shop, 718 Grant Ave., which peddles all sorts of Chinese kitchenware.

Check out the Bank of America branch at the northwest corner of Grant Avenue and Sacramento Street (701 Grant Ave.). In true pagoda style, dragons adorn the columns and guard the front doors.

Chinatown is known for its maze of tucked-away back alleys. Waverly Place, called "the street of the painted balconies," is just west of Grant between Sacramento and Washington streets. Turn left on Clay, then right on Waverly Place. The smell of incense pervades the crowded little alley, which is reminiscent of streets found in New Orleans' French Quarter—with a Chinese flair, of course. Red and green, considered symbols of happiness and longevity, respectively, embellish three temples: Jeng Sen at 146, Tin How at 125 and Norras at 109.

At Washington Street, turn right and continue just past Grant to the three-tiered Bank of Canton at 743 Washington St. Awash in blue, gold and vibrant red, it was built in 1909 to house the Chinatown Telephone Exchange (known as "China-5")—which it did until 1945. Sandwiched between two brick buildings, it's the area's oldest pagoda-style edifice.

Backtrack to Grant Avenue and turn right. Leaving Chinatown, you're now approaching the old stomping grounds of the Beat poets of the 1950s. Proceed about two blocks to Jack Kerouac Alley (just past Pacific) and turn right. A quasi-nucleus of the Beat movement, the Vesuvio saloon, 255 Columbus Ave. at Jack Kerouac Alley, is one of few remaining Beat landmarks. A faded sign over the front door proclaims, "We are itching to get away from Portland, Oregon!" Established in 1948, the bar was a favorite hangout for Bohemian types; its signature drink is appropriately named the Jack Kerouac.

Across the alley and just north of the saloon, at the corner of Columbus and Broadway, is City Lights, the first all-paperback bookstore in the country. Established in 1953 by poet Lawrence Ferlinghetti, the three-story, poetry-packed den also attracted Beat writers; a large section is devoted to their works.

Continue northwest along busy Columbus Avenue. Any idea where you are now? There are plenty of clues. First, notice the street signs, which say "Cristóforo Colombo Avenue." Second, the light posts are emblazoned with Italian flags. Third, what's with all the cafes, bakeries, delis, coffeehouses and gelato parlors? And that House of Gnocci? Why, it's obvious—you're in **North Beach,** San Francisco's Little Italy. Italians settled here first, and later the writers followed. The name dates to early days when the neighborhood overlooked the water; the bay was filled in the mid-1800s.

If it's time for lunch, this is the place. Settle into a chair at one of the many outdoor cafes and savor homemade Italian delicacies, or sample as you go. Visit a deli for a hard roll with salami and a bakery for a cannoli or cream puff, then stop by Caffe Trieste for the best coffee in town. To get there, turn right off of Columbus onto Vallejo Street, then follow Vallejo to Grant. The coffeehouse, painted turquoise and red, is on the corner. Said to be the first espresso coffeehouse on the West Coast, it has been operated by the singing Giotta family since 1956.

Backtracking to Columbus, you'll pass the imposing National Shrine of St. Francis of Assisi, 610 Vallejo St. at Columbus. The 1860 Norman Gothic church is dedicated to St. Francis, the city's namesake.

Make a right on Columbus (continuing north), passing restaurants and the occasional cigar shop and pottery store until you reach Washington Square, at Union and Columbus.

In the same manner that North Beach is not a real beach, Washington Square is not a true square, but a pentagon. If the weather is good, you'll likely find people sunbathing and picnicking. Local artists sell their works, and residents practice tai chi in the grassy piazza, which features a statue of Benjamin Franklin (not George Washington, as its name would suggest), donated to the city in 1879.

Wander through the square. The terra-cotta towers of the 1884 Romanesque Church of Saints Peter and Paul overlook the north side. Known as the "fisherman's church," it offers mass in English, Italian and Cantonese and holds the Blessing of the Fleet each October.

Follow Filbert east to Stockton. At the corner of Filbert and Stockton, look directly east. Coit Tower, which some say resembles a fire hose nozzle, is visible above the neat row houses. That's your next stop. To get there, you have two options. You can walk (it's a scenic yet demanding uphill hike), or catch the number 39 (Coit) Muni bus ($1 fare) to the top of **Telegraph Hill.** Meet the bus at the corner of Columbus and Union, in front of Fior d'Italia, the city's oldest Italian restaurant (in operation since 1886).

Walkers should make a left onto Stockton, continue north for two blocks (following signs to Coit Tower), then turn right on Lombard Street. It's approximately two blocks to the base of Telegraph Hill, but keep in mind that in San Francisco, distance is misleading—these two blocks are nearly vertical.

If you get tired, stop to admire the pretty row houses and gardens. Look left at Grant Avenue for a great view of the bay (in good weather it will be dotted with sailboats), the Golden Gate Bridge and, behind it, the rolling hills of Marin County. Also look west (behind you) for a great view of the zigzag block of Lombard, known as "the crookedest street in the world."

Once at the base of Telegraph Hill, catch your breath (or exit the bus) and take a peek at the Oakland Bay Bridge (to the east), with piers in the foreground. Follow shaded Telegraph Hill Boulevard as it circles to the top of the hill. A regal bronze statue of Christopher Columbus—donated by the Italian community and the focus of annual Columbus Day festivities—overlooks a panorama of the city. Behind the statue is the 210-foot-tall Coit Memorial Tower, built in 1933 with a donation from Lillie Hitchcock Coit, a local eccentric.

At the summit, the entire city and bay spread out before you. Notice crooked Lombard Street among the hilly lanes crammed with row houses (directly west); the Golden Gate Bridge and Presidio (northwest); **Alcatraz** (directly north); and the towers of the financial district (south). An elevator leading to the top of the tower offers more spectacular views.

No visit to Telegraph Hill is complete without exploring the Greenwich and Filbert steps—staircases hugging the east side of the slope. Locate the "Greenwich" sign behind the statue and follow the brick stairs down through a tropical oasis—flowering hillside gardens are hidden among quaint cottages, where social cats and wild parrots dwell.

Fisherman's Wharf / © Tom Tracy / Photophile

You might choose to climb all the way down (the stairs end at Sansome Street), but to minimize the return hike, we recommend turning right onto Montgomery (about halfway down) and heading back up the wooden Filbert Steps. (Follow the lower—or eastern—side of Montgomery.) Where Montgomery meets the Filbert Steps, note the Malloch Apartment Building at 1360 Montgomery St. This 1937 Art Deco dwelling was featured in the movie "Dark Passage," which starred Lauren Bacall and Humphrey Bogart. Return up the Filbert Steps to the base of Telegraph Hill.

From there, retrace your steps (or bus route), heading downhill along Telegraph Hill Boulevard and continuing down Lombard for about five blocks. At Lombard and Powell, look straight up Lombard (directly west) to catch another glimpse of cars winding their way down the city's crookedest street. Glances to the right as you pass Stockton and Powell streets afford splendid views of Victorian row houses with the bay as a backdrop. At Columbus, make a quick right, then another right onto Taylor Street, heading north. Follow Taylor three blocks to Bay Street, where you can see the cable cars being turned around (with a great deal of physical effort) at the end of the Powell-Mason line. Continue along Taylor; here, postcard stands hint of the kitschy souvenirs to come.

At Taylor and Jefferson streets is **Fisherman's Wharf,** marked by a nifty sign that makes its way into many a vacation photo. The wharf, built during the gold rush, is home to the city's fishing fleet, which docks along the Jefferson Street promenade. In the fog of the early morning, fishermen can be spotted unloading the catch of the day on Pier 45.

If you'd like, head east along the waterfront to Pier 39 and stroll past tourist shops selling everything from fog in a can to T-shirts proclaiming "I escaped from Alcatraz." Street performers pack Jefferson, Hyde, Beach, Leavenworth and Taylor streets—here you'll see folks painted from head to toe in silver or gold; mimes; stilt-walkers; palm readers; those dressed in goofy outfits posing for pictures; and others twirling hoops or juggling. Look out for the "Bushman"; he hides behind a tree branch and startles unsuspecting pedestrians.

More performers take the stage at **Pier 39.** Arguably the best entertainers are the barking sea lions that sunbathe on the dock just west of the pier; unlike much in this area, they were not transplanted to attract tourists. After exploring the shops and perhaps taking a whirl on the carousel, head west along Jefferson; you'll pass more souvenir shops as well as the **Wax Museum at Fisherman's Wharf** and **Ripley's Believe It or Not! Museum.**

At Jefferson and Taylor, the smell of fresh fish wafts in the air. Seagulls hover and squawk, looking for treats. You've entered "Fish Alley," where smart visitors will nibble on some "take-away" shrimp or Dungeness crab cocktails—cooked on site at one of the sidewalk vendors. Or indulge in some clam chowder: Boudin's is excellent, served in a sourdough bowl.

Continue along Jefferson for two blocks. At the corner of Leavenworth and Jefferson is the three-story brick **Cannery,** packed with shops and restaurants. The building, constructed in 1907, was originally owned by Del Monte and used to can peaches until it closed during the Great Depression. Its courtyard, shaded by 100-year-old olive trees, is a great place to kick back and listen to jazz bands that frequent the stage.

At Hyde Street, turn right and stroll along Hyde Street Pier, part of the **San Francisco Maritime National Historical Park.** Here, four antique vessels comprise the nation's only floating national park, where you can tour the ships or participate in a boat building class. From the end of the pier, spot the giant Ghirardelli sign. That's your next stop. Leave the pier by heading south on Hyde to Beach Street, then turn right on Beach and proceed for two blocks to **Ghirardelli Square.** This collection of 19th-century brick factory buildings is where the chocolatier whipped up sweet concoctions until the 1960s. Visit the soda fountain to indulge in a sinfully delicious Ghirardelli hot fudge sundae.

Backtrack along Beach to Hyde, the end of the Powell & Hyde cable car line. While walking back (uphill) to Union Square may be an attractive option to some, it's much more fun to hop on a streetcar—the fare is $2. Across from the cable car turnaround is the Buena Vista Cafe, where Irish coffee was introduced to America based on a recipe brought from Dublin in the 1950s.

Hold on tight while the car is pulled up Russian Hill (named for Russian sailors buried here), one of the city's steepest, and marvel at the mansions along the route. If you like, disembark at **Lombard Street** to peer (or climb) down the stairs—the view is best from the bottom, although the climb back up is a bit grueling. Neatly manicured hedges, hydrangea bushes and Art Deco-style houses frame the curvy brick road. (If you depart the cable car, you will need to pay $2 upon reboarding.)

Once en route again, look east at Greenwich Street for a great view of Coit Tower and one of San Francisco's extreme hills. The cable car will make a swift turn at Washington, passing the **Cable Car Museum** at Washington and Mason streets. Depart at Geary (Union Square), which is where the tour began.

Guided Walking Tours

City Guides Walking Tours, a part of the San Francisco Friends of the Library, provides free 1.5- to 2-hour tours of historic Market Street, the Civic Center, North Beach, Chinatown, Golden Gate Bridge, the mission murals, the Palace of Fine Arts, Victorian San Francisco, Pacific Heights mansions and other parts of the city; phone (415) 557-4266 for schedules and information.

San Francisco Architectural Heritage offers 1-hour guided tours of San Francisco's only Queen Anne Victorian open to the public, the Haas-Lilienthal House. The tours are available Wednesday, Saturday and Sunday. A 2-hour Pacific Heights walking tour is conducted on Sunday. The tours cost $5; over 64 and under 12, $3. Phone (415) 441-3004.

The murals along Balmy Alley in the Mission District can be viewed via walking tours. Tours offered by the Precita Eyes Mural Arts Center depart Sat.-Sun. at 11 and 1:30. Fee $10-$12; college students with ID $8; over 64, $5; under 18, $2. Monthly bicycle and Mexican bus tours also are available. Phone (415) 285-2287.

SAVE **VICTORIAN HOME WALK** departs from the lobby of the Westin St. Francis Hotel on Union Square at 335 Powell St. After a brief trolley bus ride, participants explore the interior of a Queen Anne bed-and-breakfast, then embark on an easy (no hills) walk among the "painted ladies" of the Victorian neighborhoods of Pacific Heights and Cow Hollow.

The guide explains differences between Italianate, Queen Anne and Stick Style architecture while relating the history of the era and pointing out homes used in films. Allow 2 hours, 30 minutes minimum. Tours depart daily at 11; closed Jan. 1 and Dec. 25. Fee $20; under 13, $10. Phone (415) 252-9485.

Self-guiding Walking Tours

Alamo Square, at Hayes and Steiner streets, is a historic area of Victorian row houses backdropped by downtown skyscrapers. The grassy square itself is a good spot for a mid-day break. The area contains several bed and breakfast inns.

Spectator Sports

Bay Area fans vigorously support both professional and college sports teams. San Francisco's and nearby Oakland's professional and college teams—the Giants, Oakland A's, 49ers, Golden State Warriors, Raiders and Sharks—offer plenty to cheer for.

In addition to the venues listed below, the **Cow Palace**, 2600 Geneva Ave. at Santos Street (in Daly City), plays host to rodeos, ice shows and other events; phone (415) 404-4111.

Baseball

The **San Francisco Giants** play at **Pacific Bell Park**. The stadium, at 24 Willie Mays Plaza, is in southeastern San Francisco; phone (415) 972-2000 for ticket information. The rival **Oakland A's** play at **Network Associates Coliseum**, I-880 at the 66th Avenue exit in Oakland; phone (510) 638-4900.

Basketball

The Bay Area's **Golden State Warriors** play at **The Arena** in Oakland, off I-880 at either the 66th Avenue or Hegenberger exit; phone (510) 986-2222 for ticket information. Area universities whet hoop appetites as well. The **San Jose State University Spartans** play at the **San Jose Event Center** at 7th and E. San Carlos streets; phone (408) 924-7589. The **University of California Golden Bears** compete at **Haas Pavillion** in Berkeley; phone (510) 642-3277 or (800) 462-3277. And the **University of San Francisco Dons** draw fans to **War Memorial Gymnasium**, 2335 Golden Gate Ave.; phone (415) 422-2873.

Football

Two NFL teams serve the Bay Area. The **San Francisco 49ers,** dubbed the "team of the '80s" for its four Super Bowl wins following the 1981, 1984, 1988 and 1989 seasons, not to mention its clinching of the title following the 1994 season, play at **San Francisco Stadium at Candlestick Point** (formerly known as 3Com Park), south of the city off US 101. For ticket information phone (415) 468-2249. The **Oakland Raiders** play at the Network Associates Coliseum; phone (800) 949-2626 for Raiders ticket information.

Hockey

Farther south, members of the **San Jose Sharks** circle their prey. The Bay Area's NHL representatives take to the ice at the **Compaq Center at San Jose Arena**, 525 W. Santa Clara St. at Autumn Street; phone (408) 287-9200.

Recreation

San Francisco, frequently considered a metropolitan mecca, has an alter ego. The 76,500-acre **Golden Gate National Recreation Area** *(see place listing p. 157)* represents the city's pastoral side. Encompassing the northern and western city shoreline, it offers bracing scenery, miles of trails and several camping sites. The area attracts birdwatchers, beachcombers, hikers, bicyclists, surfers, surf fishers, picnickers and naturalists.

Bicycling

The recreational center of San Francisco is wooded **Golden Gate Park**, a refuge plunked in the middle of this compact city. Facilities are available for all sorts of activities, including bicycling, hiking, boating, horseback riding, golf and tennis.

Two marked bicycle routes meander through San Francisco. One winds its way through Golden Gate Park, ending up at Lake Merced in the southwestern city limits; the second proceeds from the south end of the city north across the Golden Gate Bridge into Marin County. The straightaway near the Ferry Building at the foot of Market Street, created by the demolition of the Embarcadero Freeway following the 1989 earthquake, offers a mercifully hill-free stretch.

Bicycle rental outfits congregate along Stanyan Street and Geary Boulevard near Golden Gate Park. Several area touring companies organize jaunts to the Sonoma wine country and other scenic spots around the Bay Area. **Golden Gate Park Skate and Bike**, 3038 Fulton St. at 6th Avenue, is a convenient outlet from which to rent a bike for a ride through Golden Gate Park, the **Presidio** or across the Golden Gate Bridge. You also can rent roller blades and roller skates; phone (415) 668-1117.

Fishing

Lake Merced, south of the San Francisco Zoo, sports largemouth bass, trout and catfish. Fly-casting pools are south of the bison paddock in Golden Gate Park next to the Angler's Lodge; bring your own equipment. Municipal fishing piers are scattered along the northern waterfront and at Aquatic Park, and fishing boats ply the waters of San Francisco Bay for striped bass and giant sturgeon.

Golden Gate Promenade / © Morton Beebe / Corbis

Golf

Rain may dampen fairways during winter, but otherwise the mild weather is nearly ideal for a game. With space at such a premium, there are only a few public golf courses within city limits.

Municipal golf courses include Harding Park Golf Course on Lake Merced, Harding Road off Skyline Boulevard, (415) 664-4690; Lincoln Park Municipal Golf Course, 34th Avenue and Clement Street, overlooking the Golden Gate Bridge, (415) 221-9911; and the Presidio Golf Course on Finley at Arguello, (415) 561-4664. There also is a nine-hole course in Golden Gate Park, at 47th Avenue and John F. Kennedy Drive; phone (415) 751-8987.

Hiking

Hikers have numerous choices in both the city and its environs. **Ocean Beach**, the 4-mile stretch of sandy shoreline running along San Francisco's Pacific back door, offers few frills but maximum atmosphere for a brisk hike. The Golden Gate National Recreational Area's **Mount Tamalpais State Park** and the **Marin Headlands,** just across the Golden Gate Bridge, contain terrain ranging from gentle to strenuous. Miles of hiking trails run through the Presidio as well.

Jogging & Walking

Stroll the foot trails from Golden Gate Park's eastern boundary to the ocean, admiring the manicured gardens and lush parklands along the way. For those who don't mind windy conditions, the **Golden Gate Bridge** has a walkway that offers breathtaking views.

One of the city's most popular jogging areas is the paved **Golden Gate Promenade**, which traverses Crissy Field. Run at the water's edge with a wonderful view of the Golden Gate Bridge.

If it's plain old exercise you're looking for, simply step outside your hotel room door. The city's steep hills provide challenging climbs and great views, and many of the steeper sidewalks have stairs. Try walking up the block of Lombard Street dubbed "the crookedest street in the world."

Tennis

Twenty-one well-maintained courts are located in Golden Gate Park off John F. Kennedy Drive opposite the Conservatory of Flowers. A fee is charged and reservations are required on weekends; phone (415) 753-7001. The **San Francisco Recreation and Parks Department** maintains some 150 public courts available on a first-come, first-served basis as well as eight indoor swimming pools and an outdoor pool; phone (415) 831-2700.

Water Sports

Sailing the blue waters of the bay offers year-round enjoyment and a close-up look at Alcatraz and Angel islands, the Golden Gate Bridge, the San rancisco-Oakland Bay Bridge and Marin County's icturesque waterfront towns. Currents are tricky, owever, so it's best to leave the sailing to others.

Boat rentals and charters are available throughout ne greater Bay Area. **Cass' Charters and Sailing chool,** 1702 Bridgeway in Sausalito, rents sail-oats for cruising about the bay. Skippered charters nd gourmet catering also are available. Rental oats must depart from Sausalito; phone (415) 32-6789.

Row, paddle and electric boats can be rented at **tow Lake** in Golden Gate Park—just the thing for lazy sojourn around Strawberry Hill, which rises p out of the lake's middle. Phone (415) 752-0347 or rates and information.

Shopping

Shopping is a passionate pastime in San Fran-cisco. The city is a world marketplace where every-hing from souvenirs to fine art is readily available. Neighborhood enclaves, specialty districts and so-phisticated retail/restaurant complexes abound. In act, many San Francisco shopping areas—with in-novative architectural forms and sleek glass and steel facades—are attractions on their own without he shops they offer. In general, hours for down-town department stores are Mon.-Sat. 9:30-5:30; some stores are open evenings and Sun. noon-5.

No visitor would want to miss **The Cannery, Fisherman's Wharf, Ghirardelli Square** or **Pier 39.** *See attraction listings following this section.*

Antiques

Jackson Square, a six-block historic district north of Washington Street and east of Columbus Avenue, once was a part of the rough Barbary Coast; Victorian architecture remains along the area's narrow streets. Today some 20 shops along Jackson and Sansome streets constitute the center of San Francisco's antiques trade. Knowledgeable dealers can offer valuable advice to both novices and seasoned collectors.

Malls

Bounded by Sacramento, California, Clay, Battery and Drumm streets, the four-tower **Embarcadero Center** complex, with 125 shops and restaurants, encompasses eight blocks and is dominated by the Hyatt Regency San Francisco. Offices, chic restaurants and pricey boutiques sit on three levels of open-air, tree-lined plazas. The center's modern design is typified by Louise Nevelson's soaring steel sculpture, Sky Tree.

Three blocks from Union Square at 5th and Market streets is **Westfield San Francisco Shopping Centre**, a nine-story vertical mall featuring a 150-foot-high atrium covered by a retractable skylight. Competing with the polished green granite and gleaming glass are more than 70 establishments selling mostly upscale merchandise; the center's crown is a five-story Nordstrom, complete with six spiral escalators.

Near Union Square and bordered by Post, Kearney, Sutter and Montgomery streets, **Crocker Galleria** offers more than 50 specialty shops, restaurants and services under a glass dome modeled after Galleria Vittorio Emanuele II in Milan, Italy. The three-level pavilion features a rooftop garden and one-of-a-kind collectibles by American and European designers. The quality of the merchandise is outstanding, and prices are equally dear.

Specialty Districts

Union Square, bordered by flower stands, is the heart of the city's downtown shopping district; it is bounded by Powell, Geary, Post and Stockton streets. Stores line the square and extend a few blocks down each street. Shopaholics can wander through Macy's department store, and Borders Books, The Disney Store, Nike and Virgin Megastore also entice shoppers and browsers.

Those with champagne taste can peruse the elegant offerings at the likes of Alfred Dunhill of London Inc., Brooks Brothers, Bullock and Jones, Neiman-Marcus, Saks Fifth Avenue and such international names as Cartier, Chanel, Giorgio Armani, Gucci, Hermes, Louis Vuitton, Ralph Lauren and Gump's, which is famous for its selection of fine gifts, china, glass and jade.

The Anchorage, near Fisherman's Wharf, is decorated with flags and banners and has an appropriately nautical look—outdoor promenades and decks provide great spots from which to view the bay. Inside are galleries specializing in crafts, jewelry and leather goods. Musicians, magicians and street entertainers perform in the courtyard.

San Francisco's multifaceted neighborhoods also are great places to browse. The **Japan Center**, bordered by Post, Geary, Laguna and Fillmore streets, is a complex of shops, sushi bars and restaurants sheltered under one roof and crowned by a five-tiered pagoda. Three buildings (Kintetsu, East and Kinokuniya) contain stores selling antiques, silk-embroidered kimonos, exquisite porcelains and rainbow-colored fish kites.

Chinatown, bounded by Broadway, Bush, Kearny and Stockton streets, is a veritable zoo of activity and sells practically anything, from plastic Buddha trinkets to produce to fine ivory and jade imports.

The section of **Union Street** between Van Ness Avenue and Steiner Street is the "main street" of Cow Hollow, named as such when it was dairy land. Restored Victorians on the blocks between Scott and Webster streets now are home to boutiques, antique stores and gift shops proffering furniture, contemporary fashions, jewelry, books and music. In between are cozy pubs and coffeehouses.

Or head for the Haight. In addition to the incense, used books and records, shops along **Haight Street** also offer interesting art, offbeat jewelry and good-quality vintage clothing.

The most recent addition to the city's entertainment and shopping scene is the **Metreon**. This 350,000-square-foot, four-story Sony Entertainment

Center is at 4th and Mission streets in Yerba Buena Center for the Arts. Stores include the Discovery Channel Store, PlayStation and microsoftSF.

THE CANNERY is on the e. side of the block bordered by Jefferson, Leavenworth, Beach and Hyde sts. Formerly a Del Monte fruit cannery, it houses two levels of specialty shops, art galleries and restaurants, all linked by arcades, bridges and balconies. Street performers also frequent this spot. Phone (415) 771-3112.

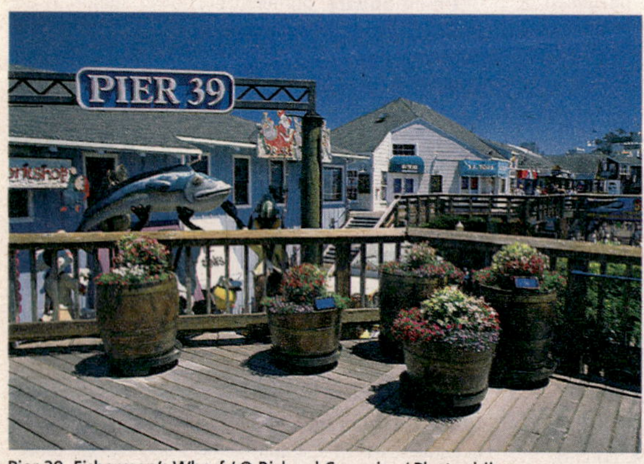

Pier 39, Fisherman's Wharf / © Richard Cummins / Photophile

FISHERMAN'S WHARF is part of the n. waterfront; parking is available in public lots along Beach, North Point, Bay and Francisco sts. The wharf has picturesque sights and pungent smells that attract millions of visitors annually. The area contains many restaurants, markets, import houses and souvenir shops. Fresh seafood and sourdough bread are favorite buys.

GHIRARDELLI SQUARE, between Beach, Polk, North Point and Larkin sts., is within walking distance of Fisherman's Wharf and the Cannery. The 2.5-acre site comprises a complex of crenellated, white-trimmed brick buildings of the old Ghirardelli chocolate company, a woolen mill, apartments and other buildings that have been refurbished to house specialty shops, bakeries and international restaurants. Many "human statues" and mimes perform next to the square. Phone (415) 775-5500.

PIER 39, at the foot of Stockton St. on the Embarcadero, is a two-story waterfront shopping and dining complex. Three stage areas present live entertainment, and the Palace of Fun Arts provides an amusement section for children, while The Turbo Ride combines moving seats with images displayed on a big screen. Sea lions live on the pier's docks, and three stage areas serve as venues for street performers. An information center is at the pier's entrance. Phone (415) 705-5500.

Performing Arts

San Francisco's tempestuous 19th-century adolescence was more attuned to drinking and gambling than to the refined pleasures of the performing arts. Even so, 15 legitimate theaters operated amid the saloons of the Barbary Coast. Today residents and visitors alike can take advantage of a world-class symphony, opera and ballet companies, and theatrical fare—from touring Broadway blockbusters to a full house of offbeat experimental productions.

The city's two major performing arts facilities are just west of the Civic Center. A bronze Henry Moore sculpture squats in front of **Louise M. Davies Symphony Hall**. The building's wraparound design places seating around and even behind the orchestra. The **War Memorial Opera House**, opposite the Davies, plays host to opera, dance and performing arts troupes. The venerable structure appears as it did in 1931.

The *San Francisco Chronicle's* pink-page Datebook section, published in the newspaper's Sunday edition, carries complete listings of area theaters and nightspots as well as information about upcoming events. TIXBay Area offers cash-only, half-price tickets for selected theater, dance and music events on the day of the performance, and also serves as a TicketMaster ticket outlet (for credit card purchases). It is located inside the Union Square Garage, accessible through the Geary Street entrance; phone (415) 433-7827.

Dance

Innovative new productions as well as classics are performed by the **San Francisco Ballet** at the War Memorial Opera House. The company's repertory season lasts from February into early May, although the Nutcracker Suite is performed in December. For information phone (415) 865-2000.

Across the bay, the **Oakland Ballet** has been presenting its own revivals and contemporary productions since 1965. The season begins in September; performances take place at the **Paramount Theater of the Arts**, 2025 Broadway near the 19th Street BART station. Phone (510) 452-9288 for information, or (510) 625-8497 or (510) 286-8914 for tickets.

Film

The Bay Area is a mecca for film lovers. Independent film-making tradition thrives here: Documentaries and experimental features are produced on cut-rate budgets throughout the city. Movie theaters in San Francisco are likely to show exclusively art-house or foreign films, and several colleges and universities also ensure a wide variety of fare.

The following show a mix of foreign and independent films in addition to repertory programs and revivals of old classics: the **Castro Theatre**, 429

Castro St., (415) 621-6120; **Embarcadero Cinema**, promenade level 1 at Embarcadero Center, (415) 352-0810; the **Red Vic Movie House**, 1727 Haight St., (415) 668-3994; the **Roxie Cinema**, 3117 16th St., (415) 863-1087; and **Yerba Buena Center for the Arts**, 701 Mission St. in the Yerba Buena Gardens complex, (415) 978-2787.

Music

Under the direction of Michael Tilson Thomas, the **San Francisco Symphony** performs in Louise M. Davies Symphony Hall from September through June and also at the **Flint Center for the Performing Arts**, 21250 Stevens Creek Blvd. in Cupertino. Guest conductors and soloists of international stature round out the repertoire of standards. For ticket information phone (415) 864-6000.

As a free alternative to the often sold-out symphony productions, orchestral and band concerts take place summer Sundays in the natural amphitheater of **Sigmund Stern Memorial Park**, at Sloat Boulevard and 19th Avenue; phone (415) 252-6252 for concert information. **Golden Gate Park** also plays host to concerts throughout the year; phone (415) 831-2700.

During the academic year both students and faculty perform at the San Francisco Conservatory of Music's **Hellman Hall**, 1201 Ortega St. in the Sunset District. Phone (415) 759-3477 for 24-hour schedule and price information; for tickets phone (415) 759-3475 Mon.-Fri. 10-3. Occasional classical music concerts take place at the **Nob Hill Masonic Center**, 1111 California St.; phone (510) 762-2277.

Opera

The **San Francisco Opera**, founded in 1923, is the resident company at the War Memorial Opera House. International names frequently appear during the season, which begins in early September and lasts into December. Many performances are sold out long in advance, but standing-room tickets are always made available the day of performance; they go on sale (cash only and one per person) at the box office, 199 Grove St., beginning at 10. Phone (415) 864-3330 for performance and additional ticket information.

Theater

Major touring plays and productions of Broadway shows are presented at the **Curran Theater**, 445 Geary St., and the **Orpheum Theater**, 1192 Market St. Musicals run at the **Golden Gate Theater**, at the intersection of Market and Taylor streets and Golden Gate Avenue, and at the Curran Theatre.

The **American Conservatory Theater** (ACT) is San Francisco's major repertory group and presents plays at the 1910 Edwardian-style **Geary Theatre**, 415 Geary St.; phone (415) 749-2228. Another repertory company, **Lamplighters Music Theatre**, specializes in operettas and musical spoofs, with an emphasis on Gilbert & Sullivan musicals. Performances are given Wednesday through Sunday at the Yerba Buena Center for the Arts, 700 Howard St. at Third Street; the **Ira and Leonore S. Gershwin Theatre**, 2350 Turk Blvd.; and at the **Dean Lesher Regional Center for the Arts**, 1601 Civic Dr. at Locust Street in Walnut Creek; phone (415) 227-4797.

A uniquely San Francisco theater experience is "Beach Blanket Babylon" at **Club Fugazi**, 678 Green St. Running since 1974, the show features cabaret-style entertainment paired with outlandish costumes; phone (415) 421-4222 for reservations.

The **Lorraine Hansberry Theatre**, 620 Sutter St., showcases the works of African-American writers; phone (415) 474-8800. The **Magic Theatre** in Building D of Fort Mason, Marina Boulevard and Buchanan Street, presents West Coast premieres and occasional solo shows; phone (415) 441-8822. And the **Cowell Theater**, at Fort Mason, Marina Boulevard at Buchanan, features one-man shows and smaller performances; phone (415) 345-7575.

Special Events

San Francisco's calendar is packed with events ranging from gigantic exhibits of boats, cars, vacation equipment, furniture and antiques to small one-man sidewalk art shows.

The year begins with the **Sports and Boat Show**, a huge exhibition held in January at the Cow Palace. Also in early January college all-stars compete in the **East West Shrine Game** at Pacific Bell Park. Following is one of the most colorful of all celebrations—**Chinese New Year**. Featuring the Golden Dragon Parade, it is held in January or February in Chinatown.

March's main event, the **St. Patrick's Day Parade**, is held the Sunday nearest the 17th; it starts at Second and Market streets and proceeds to City Hall. Festivities also include religious services at St. Patrick's Church.

Mid-April brings the **Northern California Cherry Blossom Festival**, an elaborate display of Japanese culture and customs. The **San Francisco International Film Festival**, which spotlights adventurous filmmakers, is presented in various locations. The festival has been held nearly every spring since 1956.

In May **Armed Forces Day** is observed; the festivities include a parade, entertainment, arts and crafts and an open house at several nearby military installations. Also in May is the **Bay to Breakers Footrace**, which has included up to 100,000 runners—many who sport creative, crazy costumes. The race covers some 7.5 miles from bay to ocean via Golden Gate Park.

In late May or early June, **Carnaval**, a Mardi Gras-inspired street festival, takes place in the Mission District; a parade is followed by a masquerade ball. On a different note, the San Francisco Symphony presents a series of **Beethoven concerts** in June and a series of pops concerts in July.

In early June the **Union Street Spring Festival Arts & Crafts Fair** takes place. The mood is that of an elegant garden party, with gourmet food, California wines, musical entertainment and art and craft exhibits.

A parade from the Civic Center to the Embarcadero is the highlight of the **San Francisco Lesbian, Gay, Bisexual, Transgender Pride Celebration and Parade** in late June. The 2-day festival rivals Chinese New Year as the city's biggest event.

The **California Shakespeare Festival** is held in Orinda from late May to early October. Golden Gate Park provides a sylvan setting for the Bard's works. Also celebrated in September is **The Chinatown Autumn Moon Festival**.

North Beach's Italian community holds a week-long **Columbus Day Celebration** in early October. The event, which continues the centuries-old Sicilian custom of blessing the fishing fleet, features the Italian Heritage Parade beginning at Fisherman's Wharf and ending at Washington Square in front of the Church of Saints Peter and Paul.

In late October the Cow Palace is the scene of the **Grand National Rodeo, Horse and Stock Show**, which includes rodeo events along with prize-winning horse and livestock exhibits. The **San Francisco International Auto Show** revs up in late November at Moscone Center.

Nightlife

With glorious views the rule rather than the exception, it's only natural that evening entertainment frequently revolves around elegant cocktail lounges sitting atop San Francisco's classier hotels. If your style is more down to earth, however, there are plenty of options. Nightclubs are plentiful, and bars run the gamut from oh-so-chic singles spots to friendly neighborhood pubs.

Chinese New Year / © Phil Schermeister / Corbis

The Datebook, published in the Sunday edition of the *San Francisco Chronicle,* has listings of area nightspots, as does the *San Francisco Bay Guardian,* a free weekly found at curbside vending machines.

San Francisco's upwardly mobile professional congregate at watering holes all over the city, but few are particularly popular. **Harry Denton's Starlight Room,** 450 Powell St., at the top of the Si Francis Drake Hotel, has a stunning 300-degre view of the city; phone (415) 395-8595. **Perry's** 1944 Union St. between Buchanan and Lagun streets, draws a similar dress-to-be-seen crowd an offers a full-range menu as well; phone (415 922-9022.

Finally, for an elegant nightcap stop by the **Redwood Room** in the Clift Hotel, downtown at Taylo and Geary streets. This modern lounge exude class, from its redwood paneling to the changin display of digital artwork; phone (415) 775-4700.

Comedy Clubs

While comedy clubs are usually not thought o as elegant, the **Punch Line,** 444 Battery St. (between Washington and Clay streets) could almost fi that description. Whoopi Goldberg paid her due here. Weekend shows often sell out; phone (415) 397-7573.

At **Cobb's Comedy Club,** 2801 Leavenworth St in the Cannery, established comics like Margaret Cho and Janeane Garofalo alternate with up-and-coming stand-up acts. There's also an adjoining restaurant; phone (415) 928-4320.

Dance Clubs

Join the herd of locals and tourists at **Holy Cow,** 1535 Folsom St., for a mix of disco music, funk from the '70s, '80s and '90s, and the latest releases; phone (415) 621-6087. For an elegant evening out, the **Tonga Room and Hurricane Bar** at the Fairmont Hotel, 950 Mason St., offers a live band and dancing nightly beginning at 8; phone (415) 772-5278.

Entertainment Complexes

The **Great American Music Hall,** 859 O'Farrell St. (between Polk and Larkin streets), has been around since the early 20th century. The building was renovated and reopened in the early 1970s. Marble pillars, opulent balconies and elaborately frescoed ceilings provide a stylish setting for a wide-ranging roster of live performances—big-name blues, rock and folk musicians, plus a sprinkling of jazz, world music, bluegrass, punk and alternative. Dance parties also take place; phone (415) 885-0750.

Jazz & Blues

Jazz at Pearl's, in North Beach at 256 Columbus Ave. near Broadway, is a sophisticated venue with nightly live music; phone (415) 291-8255.

Lou's Pier 47, 300 Jefferson St. at Fisherman's Wharf, boasts 65 blues bands each month. You can eat dinner here, too; phone (415) 771-5687.

Yoshi's, 510 Embarcadero W. in Oakland, is worth the trek for aficionados of Japanese cuisine as well as live music. Outstanding acoustics attract big-name jazz acts; phone (510) 238-9200.

Rock

Gone are the days when Bill Graham's old Fillmore ballroom brought the best rock acts of the day to San Francisco audiences. Now, **The Fillmore,** 1805 Geary St. at Fillmore Street, spotlights mainstream and classic rock acts as well as blues groups and the latest sensations; phone (415) 346-6000. The **Warfield,** 982 Market St., is a former movie palace retooled as a rock 'n' roll showcase. Eclectic is the keyword here; phone (415) 775-7722.

The San Francisco Vicinity

GOLDEN GATE NATIONAL RECREATION AREA (C-7)

Encompassing both the rolling coastal hill country north of the Golden Gate Bridge and the diverse urban parklands strung around San Francisco's northern and western edges, Golden Gate National Recreation Area contains approximately 74,000 acres of land and water.

The Marin Headlands across the Golden Gate Bridge contrast dramatically with the cityscape to the south. Smooth grassy ridges slope down through valleys to a craggy shoreline scalloped with sandy coves. Abandoned gun emplacements stud the hillsides above the Golden Gate and provide good vantage points for viewing the bridge and the city.

Northward from the Marin Headlands are Mount Tamalpais State Park *(see Mill Valley p. 158)* and Muir Woods National Monument *(see place listing p. 158)*. Beyond the state park, the Olema Valley section of the recreation area abuts Point Reyes National Seashore *(see place listing p. 159)*.

About 100 miles of hiking and riding trails traverse the pastoral countryside between Point Reyes and the Golden Gate. Hikers should stay on the trails, as the hillsides are often laced with poison oak. Because of the cool ocean winds and frequent fog, visitors should be prepared for changeable weather by dressing in layers. Swimming is permitted at Stinson Beach, China Beach, Muir Beach and Aquatic Park. Back-country campsites are available and require reservations. Fishing spots and picnic facilities are scattered throughout the parklands.

The Marine Mammal Center, 4 miles west of US 101 in the Marin Headlands, is an animal hospital that rescues and rehabilitates sick, injured or distressed marine animals from the California coast. Self-guiding tours are available; phone (415) 289-7325.

The southern extreme of the recreation area is Fort Funston, where hang gliders commonly fly along the cliffs. The long windswept strand of Ocean Beach links Fort Funston with Cliff House, the Victorian gardens of Sutro Heights and Lands End at the northwestern shoulder of the city. The Coastal Trail threads through Lands End to China and Baker beaches and the abandoned coastal batteries just south of the Golden Gate Bridge.

The Golden Gate Promenade extends 3.5 miles along San Francisco Bay and connects Fort Point below the Golden Gate Bridge with Crissy Field and Fort Mason. Alcatraz Island in the bay also is part of the recreation area. An information center is open Mon.-Fri. 9:30-4:30.

For further information write the Information Center, Golden Gate National Recreation Area, Building 201, Fort Mason, San Francisco, CA 94123; phone (415) 561-4700. *See Recreation Chart.*

ALCATRAZ ISLAND, in San Francisco Bay, can be reached via the Blue & Gold Fleet's ferries that leave Pier 41 at Fisherman's Wharf. Known as "The Rock," Alcatraz was a maximum security federal penitentiary that once held such notorious criminals as Al Capone, Machine Gun Kelly and Robert Stroud, the "Birdman of Alcatraz."

A self-guiding trail, guided cellblock tour, slide shows, exhibits and ranger programs are available. Special 2.5-hour evening cruises feature guided tours and scenic skyline views of San Francisco after dark.

Ferries depart daily at 9:30 and 10:15, then every half-hour 10:45-4:15, mid-May through first Sun. in Oct.; at 9:30 and 10:15, then every half-hour 10:45-2:15, rest of year. Guided 90-minute tours begin every half-hour. Evening cruises depart Thurs.-Sun.; phone for schedule.

Round-trip fare with admission (includes audiotape tour) $16; over 61, $14.25; ages 5-11, $10.75. Evening cruise $23.50; over 61, $20.75; ages 5-11, $14.25. Wear comfortable shoes and warm clothing. Visitors are strongly advised to buy tickets 2 to 4 weeks in advance, May-Sept.; 2 days in advance, rest of year. AX, DS, MC, VI. Phone (415) 705-5555. *See color ad p. 144.*

SAVE **BAY AREA DISCOVERY MUSEUM** is off US 101 at 557 McReynolds Rd. in Golden Gate National Recreation Area at the n. end of Golden Gate Bridge. The hands-on children's museum features both indoor exhibitions and outdoor activities. Crawling through an underwater sea tunnel, decorating a doll house and fishing off a boat or pier are some of the activities offered. Tot Spot is a storybook environment for ages 1-3.

Food is available Tues.-Fri. 9-4, Sat.-Sun. 10-5; closed Jan. 1, Easter, July 4, Thanksgiving and Dec. 25. Admission $7, under 1 free. All children must be with an adult. AX, DS, MC, VI. Phone (415) 339-3900.

CLIFF HOUSE, Great Hwy. and Point Lobos Ave., overlooks the ocean and nearby Seal Rocks, habitat of sea lions September through June. A visitor center under the aegis of Golden Gate National Recreation Area is at the viewing platform. Mechanical Museum (Musée Mécanique) displays coin-operated, automatic musical instruments.

Note: Cliff House is closed for renovations; reopening is expected summer 2004. The museum's collections can be seen at Fisherman's Wharf, Pier 45 at the end of Taylor Street. Museum daily 10-8. Free. Phone (415) 386-1170.

FORT POINT NATIONAL HISTORIC SITE, reached by turning off Lincoln Blvd. at Long Ave. to the fort, is part of Golden Gate National Recreation Area. Built by the U.S. Army 1853-61, Fort Point is similar in design to Fort Sumter, S.C. Although it once was the principal defense bastion on the West Coast, no battle ever occurred at Fort Point.

Videotape presentations about the history of the fort and the building of the Golden Gate Bridge are provided. Free guided 30-minute tours and cannon-loading demonstrations are offered. **Note:** During security alerts the fort may be closed.

Open Fri.-Sun. 10-5; closed Jan. 1 and Dec. 25. Tours are given at 11 and 3. Cannon-loading demonstrations are given at noon. Donations. Phone (415) 556-1693.

PRESIDIO, in the n.w. corner of the city, served as an active military garrison almost continuously for 218 years; it closed as an Army post in 1994. The higher hills of the Presidio and its 1,480 acres offer spectacular bay and ocean vistas. Maps for 11 miles of hiking trails and 14 miles for cyclists are available at the visitor center, Building 102 on Montgomery Street at Lincoln Boulevard, which also has displays and brochures.

Guided tours are available. Visitor center open daily 9-5. Park admission and guided tours free. Phone (415) 561-4323, or TTY (415) 561-4314.

HALF MOON BAY (E-8)

pop. 11,842, elev. 69′

Half Moon Bay has a rugged coastline with many sandy beaches for walking and exploring. The bay is a popular launching spot for sightseeing, fishing and whale-watching cruises; contact Huck Finn Sport Fishing at (650) 726-7133. The town also is known for its Flower Market, held every third Saturday of the month at Kelly and Main streets. Half Moon Bay lies on a scenic stretch of SR 1 that extends from San Francisco to San Luis Obispo.

Half Moon Bay Coastside Chamber of Commerce and Visitors Bureau: 520 Kelly Ave., Half Moon Bay, CA 94019; phone (650) 726-8380.

MILL VALLEY (D-8) pop. 13,600, elev. 70′

Mill Valley is a residential community at the base of Mount Tamalpais. The heavy redwood frame of the sawmill for which the town was named still stands in Old Mill Park on Throckmorton Avenue. Hikers can follow a nearby trail up the mountain.

Mill Valley Chamber of Commerce: 85 Throckmorton Ave., P.O. Box 5123, Mill Valley, CA 94941; phone (415) 388-9700.

MOUNT TAMALPAIS STATE PARK, 6 mi. w., covers 6,300 acres of picturesque coastal hill country dominated by triple-peaked Mount Tamalpais whose profile from the south is said to resemble a sleeping American Indian girl.

Hiking and bicycling trails and a winding road lead to spectacular vistas at the summit, where a visitor center can be found. Theatrical productions known as the Mountain Play are presented in Cushing Memorial Amphitheatre.

Park open daily dawn-dusk. Visitor center open Sat.-Sun and holidays 10-5. Ranger station open daily 8:30-dusk. Plays are presented mid-May to mid-June. Parking $2 per private vehicle. Phone (415) 388-2070, or (415) 383-1100 for the amphitheater. *See Recreation Chart and the AAA California & Nevada CampBook.*

MOSS BEACH (D-8) pop. 1,953, elev. 80′

JAMES V. FITZGERALD MARINE RESERVE, w. off SR 1 via California Ave., preserves marine life in one of the state's most diverse intertidal regions. Marine life typically visible includes crabs, abalone, mussels, starfish, sea slugs and isopods. Low tide is the best time to explore; consult a local tide chart or phone the reserve for information. Collecting shells, rocks and plants is strictly prohibited. Daily dawn-dusk. Free. Phone (650) 728-3584.

GEM MUIR WOODS NATIONAL MONUMENT (D-7)

Seventeen miles northwest of San Francisco on the southwestern slope of Mount Tamalpais, Muir Woods National Monument is reached via the Golden Gate Bridge and SR 1. Named for noted conservationist John Muir, the 560-acre Muir Woods National Monument is one of the most beautiful and accessible of the famous redwood groves which 140 million years ago blanketed much of the Northern Hemisphere. The Sequoia sempervirens, tallest of all tree life—though not as large in girth as the Sequoia gigantea—is well represented. Some coast redwoods reach a height of 250 feet with diameters of more than 12 feet.

Although coast redwood trees are most common in the forest, Douglas fir, maple, oak and bay laurel also thrive. Due to a lack of food caused by the shady forest conditions, animal life is sparse. Trails for hiking and exploring range from a half-mile to 2 miles long. Some trails combine with others in

Mount Tamalpais State Park near Mill Valley *(see attraction listing)*.

Neither picnicking nor camping is permitted at the monument, and pets are not allowed. Since roads leading to the park are steep and winding, vehicles longer than 35 feet are not permitted. Food is available. Monument open daily 8-dusk. A visitor center is open daily 9-6, Apr.-Oct.; 9-5, rest of year. For a less crowded summer visit, plan to arrive before 10 or after 3. Admission $3, under 17 free. For additional information contact the Site Supervisor, Muir Woods National Monument, Mill Valley, CA 94941; phone (415) 388-2595, or TTY (916) 556-2766.

PACIFICA (D-8) pop. 38,390, elev. 60′

One of California's newest towns, Pacifica was formed in 1957. Its history, however, goes back to 1769, when Gaspar de Portolá first sighted San Francisco Bay from Discovery Point in the mountains behind present-day Pacifica. Francisco Sanchez, an alcalde of San Francisco under the Spanish government, later was awarded the land in return for his service to Mexico. His adobe was built 1842-46. The two-story house, a half-mile east of SR 1 at 1000 Linda Mar Blvd., is preserved as Sanchez Adobe Historic Site and is decorated with period furniture, objects, implements and clothing.

Pacifica Chamber of Commerce and Visitors Center: 225 Rockaway Beach Ave., Suite 1, Pacifica, CA 94044; phone (650) 355-4122.

POINT REYES NATIONAL SEASHORE (D-7)

Twenty-two miles north of San Francisco along SR 1, the blunt headlands of Point Reyes National Seashore jut into the sea, and grass-tufted dunes lie along miles of secluded beaches. Inland are rolling hills, freshwater lakes and Inverness Ridge, where the Douglas fir, typical of the northern California coastal ranges, and the Bishop pine of the southern forest areas merge. More than 350 species of birds and 72 species of mammals inhabit Point Reyes National Seashore's 65,300 acres. In addition fragile tidepool life can be observed at several locations.

Park headquarters is at Bear Valley, .2 miles west of Olema on Bear Valley Road. The headquarters is adjacent to Bear Valley Visitor Center, which provides information about facilities, nature trails and exhibits; it is open daily. Point Reyes Lighthouse and Visitor Center is open Thurs.-Mon. 10-4:30 (weather permitting). Visitors must descend 300 narrow steps from an observation deck to reach the oceanfront lighthouse. Kenneth C. Patrick Visitor Center at Drakes Beach is open Sat.-Sun. and holidays 10-5 (weather permitting). Admission, backpack camping and use of facilities are free; reservations are suggested for camping.

Point Reyes Morgan Horse Ranch; Kule Loklo, a replica of a Miwok Indian village; the Pierce Ranch, a former dairy ranch with self-guiding trail exhibits; and the Earthquake Trail are near park headquarters. At the end of Mesa Road is Point Reyes Bird Observatory. Bird-banding demonstrations are held Saturday and Sunday mornings.

Popular activities within the seashore include hiking, bird-watching, beachcombing, picnicking and swimming. Panoramic views are available at many observation spots and overlooks; from some locations it is possible to spot harbor seals, sea lions and migrating gray whales.

The park has four hike-in campgrounds. The required free permits can be obtained at Bear Valley Visitor Center; phone (415) 663-8054 daily 9-2 for camping reservations. More than 140 miles of foot and horse trails fan out from the Bear Valley trailhead. Some 35 miles of trails are open to bicyclists; trail maps are available at the visitor centers. Hikers and campers should carry a canteen, since the stream water is not potable. Pets are barred from all trails and campgrounds, but may be taken to North and South beaches and a portion of Limantour Beach if leashed.

Point Reyes National Seashore lies on a scenic stretch of SR 1 that extends from Leggett to Sausalito. Varied programs are conducted.

For additional information contact the Superintendent, Point Reyes National Seashore, Point Reyes, CA 94956; phone (415) 464-5100. *See Recreation Chart and the AAA California & Nevada CampBook.*

SAN CARLOS (E-8) pop. 27,718, elev. 76′

SAVE **HILLER AVIATION MUSEUM** is at 601 Skyway Rd. at the San Carlos Airport. The museum exhibits, through both hanging and ground displays, Northern California's contributions to aviation history. Restored aircraft, full-size replicas and models range from an unmanned 1869 aeroplane to a 21st-century robotic flying wing. Young guests can climb into the cockpit of a Navy jet.

Interactive displays, multimedia presentations, and a glass-fronted restoration workshop can be seen. Daily 10-5; closed Jan. 1, Easter, Thanksgiving and Dec. 25. Admission $8; over 64 and ages 8-17, $5. AX, MC, VI. Phone (650) 654-0200.

SAN MATEO (E-8) pop. 92,482, elev. 29′

San Mateo is a residential suburb of San Francisco. Central Park contains a lovely Japanese garden. San Mateo-Hayward Bridge, constructed with five steel spans, is one of the longest highway bridges in the country. Bay Meadows Race Track features horse racing; phone (650) 574-7223.

Note: Policies concerning admittance of children to pari-mutuel betting facilities vary. Phone for information.

San Mateo Area Chamber of Commerce: 1021 S. El Camino Real, 2nd floor, San Mateo, CA 94402; phone (650) 341-5679.

COYOTE POINT MUSEUM FOR ENVIRONMENTAL EDUCATION is on Coyote Point Dr. in Coyote Point Park. Environmental Hall exhibits are on four descending levels of ramps to symbolize the eastward flow of water from the Santa Cruz Mountains to San Francisco Bay and its westward flow to the Pacific. Displays include dioramas, a working beehive and other insect colonies. Interactive demonstration stations stress man's impact on nature. The wildlife habitats feature reptiles, birds and mammals.

Picnicking is permitted. Tues.-Sat. 10-5, Sun. noon-5; closed Jan. 1, Thanksgiving and Dec. 25 and 31. Admission (includes museum and wildlife habitats) $6; over 61 and ages 13-17, $4; ages 3-12, $2; free to all first Wed. of the month. Park admission $5 per private vehicle. Phone (650) 342-7755.

JAPANESE TEA GARDEN, El Camino at 5th Ave., was designed by Nagao Sakurai, the chief landscape architect at the Imperial Palace in Tokyo. The garden has labeled plants, evergreens, waterfalls and koi ponds. Parking lots are under the tennis courts. Mon.-Fri. 10-4, Sat.-Sun. 11-4. Free. Phone (650) 522-7440.

SAN RAFAEL (C-8) pop. 56,063, elev. 34′

San Rafael began as a village that developed in the early 19th century around Mission San Rafael. It is now a residential area. Marin Shakespeare Company presents plays by the bard at Forest Meadows Amphitheatre, on the campus of Dominican College, from July through September. Performances are scheduled Friday, Saturday and Sunday evenings, with a matinee on Sunday; phone (415) 499-1108, or (415) 499-4488 for the box office.

Thursday evenings from 6 to 9, early May to late October, Fourth Street between Lincoln Avenue and B Street is the setting for a five-block-long farmers market. In addition to fresh produce and flowers, expect to find a festival-like atmosphere with music, arts and crafts, merchants, children's activities, baked goods and food vendors.

San Rafael Chamber of Commerce: 817 Mission Ave., San Rafael, CA 94901; phone (415) 454-4163 or (800) 454-4163.

MARIN COUNTY CIVIC CENTER, just n. off US 101, was the last major project of Frank Lloyd Wright. The 140 landscaped acres include fairgrounds, theaters, a lake and a water conservation garden with drought-resistant plants. The building itself is divided into administrative offices and the Hall of Justice; both parts of the building are included on a 1.5- to 2-hour tour. Allow 1 hour minimum. Mon.-Fri. 9-5; closed holidays. Tour offered Wed. at 10:30. Building free. Tour by donations. Phone (415) 499-6646.

MISSION SAN RAFAEL ARCANGEL, 1104 5th Ave. at A St., is a replica built in 1949 on the approximate site of the original mission. Relics and old pictures are displayed. Allow 30 minutes minimum. Mon.-Sat. 11-4, Sun. 10-4. Free. Phone (415) 454-8141.

WILDCARE—TERWILLIGER NATURE EDUCATION AND WILDLIFE REHABILITATION is at 76 Albert Park Ln. off B St. The hospital treats and shelters injured, orphaned and sick animals until they are able to return to their natural habitats. An exhibit hall offers photographic and California wildlife displays in addition to hands-on exhibits for children. Allow 30 minutes minimum. Daily 9-5. Donations. Phone (415) 456-7283.

SAUSALITO (D-8) pop. 7,330, elev. 14′

A focal point for artists, Sausalito (originally *Saucelito,* meaning "little willow") is a pleasant blending of bohemian and marine influences. Its setting of hilly terrain plunging into the bay contributes to its popularity.

Ferry service links Sausalito with San Francisco; the entire Bay Area is visible from Sausalito and from Vista Point at the north end of the Golden Gate Bridge. Sausalito is the southern terminus of a scenic 212-mile stretch of SR 1 that heads north along the ocean to Leggett.

Sausalito Chamber of Commerce: 10 Liberty Ship Way, Suite 250, Sausalito, CA 94965; phone (415) 331-7262.

BAY MODEL VISITOR CENTER is at 2100 Bridgeway at the foot of Spring St.; use Marinship Way access rd. An environmental education facility operated by the U.S. Army Corps of Engineers, the model simulates the tidal action and current, as well as the mixing of saltwater and freshwater, in a 1.5-acre scale model of the San Francisco Bay and the Sacramento-San Joaquin Delta region. While not always filled with water, the model still provides an interesting view of the estuary.

Tues.-Fri. 9-4, Sat.-Sun. and holidays 10-5, Memorial Day weekend-Labor Day; Tues.-Sat. 9-4, rest of year. Phone to verify schedule. Free. Phone (415) 332-3870 or (415) 332-3871.

VALLEJO—*see place listing p. 178.*

Maritime Museum / © Richard Cummins / Photophile

This ends listings for the San Francisco Vicinity. The following page resumes the alphabetical listings of cities in Northern California.

SAN JOSE (F-9) pop. 894,943, elev. 94'

San Jose lies in the Santa Clara Valley between the Mount Hamilton and Santa Cruz ranges. Founded as Pueblo de San José de Guadalupe in November 1777, the settlement was established to raise crops and cattle for the nearby presidios of San Francisco and Monterey. In 1849 San Jose became the state's first capital—until 1851. San Jose now is known as the "Capital of Silicon Valley" for the technological innovations that have been forthcoming.

At the junction of I-280, I-680 and US 101, just off King Road—in the middle of bustling, high-tech San Jose—is Emma Prusch Farm Park, a reminder of the city's agricultural past. This former dairy farm retains its barn, vintage farm equipment and fruit orchards as well as pens of sheep, pigs, cows, geese and rabbits, so that visitors can see what life was formerly like in the Santa Clara Valley.

The San Jose area has more than 50 wineries ranging from family-run establishments to large corporations. Throughout the year there are festivals, concerts and other events celebrating viticulture. Santa Clara Valley Transit Authority offers transportation to the various wineries.

The Peralta Adobe & Fallon House Historic Site is at 175 W. St. John St. The two-room 1797 adobe, the last remaining adobe structure from El Pueblo de San José de Guadalupe, illustrates daily life in San Jose during its Spanish and Mexican periods. Fallon House, built by the mayor of San Jose 1859-60, is a Victorian house furnished in period. The two dwellings are open on weekends.

San Jose is host to community events as well; Mexican, Japanese, Italian, Spanish, German, Portuguese and Vietnamese festivals take place throughout the year. San Jose's events line is answered daily 24 hours at (408) 295-2265, with a touch-tone phone. San José State University has an enrollment of 26,000.

Compaq Center at San Jose Arena at W. Santa Clara and Autumn streets is home to the San Jose Sharks hockey team. College and professional sporting events, in addition to musical and entertainment events, are held at the arena.

San Jose Convention & Visitors Bureau: 125 S. Market St., Suite 300, San Jose, CA 95113-2257; phone (408) 295-9600 or (888) 726-5673.

Self-guiding tours: Driving-tour maps are available from the convention/visitors bureau. The San Jose Visitor Information and Business Center is in the lobby of the San Jose McEnery Convention Center, 150 W. San Carlos St.

Shopping areas: The anchor sites of Eastridge Mall, east of US 101 on Tully Road, are occupied by JCPenney, Macy's and Sears. Westfield Shoppingtown Oakridge, Blossom Hill Road and Santa Teresa Boulevard, features Macy's and Sears.

Great Mall of the Bay Area, off I-880 in nearby Milpitas, features more than 180 outlet stores, including Donna Karan, Off 5th—Saks Fifth Avenue Outlet and The Sharper Image. The San Jose Flea Market, 12000 Berryessa Rd., which features thousands of booths and 25 restaurants, draws an average of 80,000 people on a sunny weekend.

ALUM ROCK PARK is e. of US 101 on Alum Rock Ave.; use Penitencia Creek Rd. for vehicle access to the park. A 730-acre site in the foothills, the park contains views of the Santa Clara Valley, picnic facilities, mineral springs, marked trails and the Youth Science Institute. The institute's nature center features animal exhibits such as a group of birds of prey that have been injured and cannot be released back into the wild.

Dogs are not permitted. Allow 30 minutes minimum. Park open daily 8 a.m.-30 minutes after dusk. Institute open Tues.-Sun. noon-4:30. Landslides sometimes close the road through the park. Because of brush-fire danger, the park may be closed at times June-Oct.; phone ahead. Park free. Institute admission 50c. Parking $6 per private vehicle, Memorial Day weekend-Labor Day and Sat.-Sun. and holidays, rest of year; free other times. Phone (408) 259-5477, or (408) 258-4322 for the institute.

CHILDREN'S DISCOVERY MUSEUM OF SAN JOSE, intersection of Woz Way and Auzerais St., offers changing interactive exhibits and programs that lead children to discoveries about themselves and the world around them. Guadalupe Park surrounds the museum.

Mon.-Sat. and holidays 10-5, Sun. noon-5, mid-June through Labor Day; Tues.-Sat. and holidays 10-5, Sun. noon-5, rest of year. Closed Jan. 1, Easter, Thanksgiving and Dec. 24-25. Admission $7; over 59, $6; under 1 free. Under 13 must be with an adult. DS, MC, VI. Phone (408) 298-5437.

KELLEY PARK, at Senter and Story rds., contains two parks—one geared to children's activities, the other to area history and culture—as well as a Japanese-themed garden. Park open daily 8 a.m.-30 minutes after dusk. Parking fee $5 per private vehicle. Phone (408) 277-5562.

Happy Hollow Park and Zoo, 1300 Senter Rd., is a family park with a playground, riverboat replica, tree house, rides and a zoo. Allow 1 hour minimum. Mon.-Fri. 10-5, Sat.-Sun. 10-6, July 1-Labor Day weekend (weather permitting); daily 10-5, rest of year. Closed Dec. 25. Combination ticket for playground, rides and zoo $5.50, ages 65-74 and the physically impaired $5, under 2 free. DS, MC, VI. Phone (408) 277-3000.

History Park, 1650 Senter Rd. at Phelan Ave., comprises 28 structures that highlight the history and culture of San Jose and the Santa Clara Valley, depicting area life at the turn of the 20th century. Visitors can experience a Chinese temple and a Portuguese *império* (church), observe letterpress printing and hop aboard a historic trolley.

Allow 2 hours minimum. Tues.-Sun. noon-5; closed Jan. 1, Thanksgiving and Dec. 25. Admission $6; over 64, $5; ages 6-17, $4. Rates vary for events. MC, VI. Phone (408) 287-2290.

Japanese Friendship Garden, 1500 Senter Rd., features landscaping and lanterns representing Japanese culture. The garden is patterned after a park in Okayama, Japan—San Jose's sister city. Daily 10-dusk. Free. Phone (408) 277-4192.

GEM **LICK OBSERVATORY** is e. via Alum Rock Rd. and 19-mi.-long, narrow, winding Mount Hamilton Rd. Mount Hamilton Rd. is closed when there is snow at the observatory. The observatory, on the 4,209-foot summit of Mount Hamilton, is now an observation station overlooking the Santa Clara Valley. It was dedicated in 1888 and is a division of the University of California, Santa Cruz.

A visitor center in the Main Building contains exhibits, photographic displays and a 36-inch telescope. Guided tours, given in the dome of the 36-inch refractor, relate the history of the observatory and discuss the research currently taking place. A short walk leads to the Shane Dome, where the 120-inch reflector can be seen from a visitors gallery. An audiovisual presentation and interpretive displays are available. **Note:** Food and automotive services are not available nearby.

Allow 2 hours minimum. Tours of the visitor center are given every half-hour Mon.-Fri. 12:30-5, Sat.-Sun. 10-5. The Main Building is open 30 minutes before and 30 minutes after the tours begin. The visitor gallery at the 120-inch telescope is open daily 10-5; closed Thanksgiving and Dec. 24-25. Phone to verify schedule. Free. Phone (408) 274-5061 for information and detailed directions.

MUNICIPAL ROSE GARDENS is on Naglee Ave. between Dana Ave. and Garden Dr. The gardens contain more than 5,000 plants and 186 varieties of roses. The peak of color is in May and June, but blooms continue throughout the summer. Allow 30 minutes minimum. Daily dawn-30 minutes after dusk. Free. Phone (408) 277-5422.

OVERFELT GARDENS, Educational Park Dr. and McKee Rd., has a self-guiding arboreal trail, wildflower path, fragrance garden and three small lakes. The 5-acre Chinese Cultural Garden contains statues, memorials and displays devoted to ancient Chinese architecture and culture. Allow 1 hour, 30 minutes minimum. Daily 10-dusk; closed Jan. 1, Thanksgiving and Dec. 25. Free. Phone (408) 251-3323.

RAGING WATERS, off Capitol Expwy. at Tully Rd. in Lake Cunningham Regional Park, is a 16-acre water park with more than 10 waterslides and a wave pool set in a tropical atmosphere.

Allow 4 hours minimum. Open daily at 10:30 (closing time varies), mid-June to mid-Sept. (weather permitting); schedule varies mid-May to mid-June and mid-Sept. to late Sept. Admission $25.99; over age 54, $15.99; under 48 inches tall $19.99; under age 2 free. After 3 p.m. $18.99. Parking $5. AX, MC, VI. Phone (408) 238-9900.

GEM SAVE **ROSICRUCIAN EGYPTIAN MUSEUM,** on Park Ave. between Naglee and Randol, is in a gardenlike setting in a building resembling the Temple of Amon at Karnak. The museum has a collection of Egyptian artifacts, including human and animal mummies, funerary boats, textiles, sculptures, jewelry and objects from daily life; a replica of an Egyptian rock tomb; and Babylonian, Sumerian and Assyrian artifacts, including seals and tablets with examples of early writing.

Allow 2 hours minimum. Tues.-Fri. 10-5, Sat.-Sun. 11-6; closed Jan. 1, Easter, Thanksgiving and Dec. 24-25 and 31. Last admission 30 minutes before closing. Admission $9; over 64 and students with ID $7; ages 5-10, $5. AX, DS, MC, VI. Phone (408) 947-3635.

SAN JOSE MUSEUM OF ART, 110 S. Market St., was built in 1892 by local architect Willoughby Edbrooke. The museum contains changing exhibits of contemporary art. Text panels are available in several languages. Food is available. Allow 2 hours minimum. Tues.-Sun. 11-5 (also Fri. 5-10); closed Jan. 1, Thanksgiving and Dec. 25. Guided 45-minute tours are given Tues.-Sun. at 12:30 and 2:30. Free. Phone (408) 294-2787.

THE TECH MUSEUM OF INNOVATION, jct. Park Ave. and Market St., contains nearly 250 permanent exhibits and interactive displays that show how high technology affects everyday life. The museum has four themed galleries focusing on innovation, communication, the human body and exploration. Visitors can design virtual roller coasters, learn about computer chips and experiment with special effects. Films are shown in the Hackworth IMAX Dome Theater.

Daily 10-5; closed Dec. 25. Exhibits *or* IMAX film $9; over 64, $8; ages 3-12, $7. Exhibits *and* IMAX film $16; over 64, $15; ages 3-12, $13. AX, DS, MC, VI. Phone (408) 294-8324.

GEM **WINCHESTER MYSTERY HOUSE,** 525 S. Winchester Blvd. between I-280 and Stevens Creek Blvd., is a Victorian mansion designed to baffle the evil spirits that haunted Sarah Winchester, eccentric heiress to the Winchester Arms fortune, and mistress of the house. With 160 rooms, 2,000 doors, 13 bathrooms, 10,000 windows, 47 fireplaces, blind closets, secret passageways and 40 staircases, the house is so complex that even the owner and servants needed maps to find their way.

The Mansion Tour includes a 65-minute guided interior tour, a self-guiding tour of the Victorian gardens and entrance to two museums containing collections of Winchester rifles and other products made by the arms manufacturing company. The 50-minute Behind-the-Scenes Tour shows how the estate operated when Winchester lived in it. The

Estate Tour combines the Mansion and Behind-the-Scenes tours.

Allow 2 hours minimum. Daily 9-7, mid-June through Labor Day; Sun.-Thurs. 9-5, Fri.-Sat. 9-7, mid-Apr. to mid-June; daily 9-5, rest of year. Closed Dec. 25. Mansion Tour $17.95; over 64, $14.95; ages 6-12, $11.95. Behind-the-Scenes Tour $14.95; over 64, $13.95. Estate Tour $24.95; over 64, $21.95. Under 13 not permitted on Behind-the-Scenes or Estate tours. AX, MC, VI. Phone (408) 247-2101.

WINERIES

- **Mirassou Vineyards**, 3000 Aborn Rd. Mon.-Sat. noon-5, Sun. noon-4; closed holidays. Phone (408) 274-4000.

SAN JUAN BAUTISTA (G-3)

pop. 1,549, elev. 200′

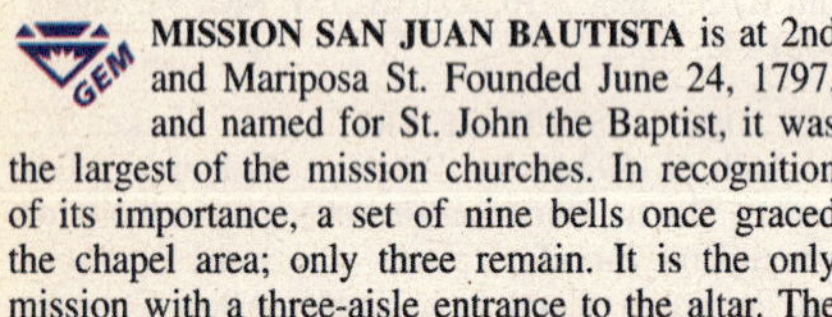

MISSION SAN JUAN BAUTISTA is at 2nd and Mariposa St. Founded June 24, 1797, and named for St. John the Baptist, it was the largest of the mission churches. In recognition of its importance, a set of nine bells once graced the chapel area; only three remain. It is the only mission with a three-aisle entrance to the altar. The mission has period furnishings, and the convent wing contains relics.

Original artifacts include altar statues, wall decorations and a baptismal font as well as an 1816 altar screen. It is still an active Catholic church. Daily 9:30-4:45; closed Jan. 1, Good Friday, Thanksgiving eve, Thanksgiving and Dec. 24-25. Donations. Phone (831) 623-4528, or (831) 623-2127 for the office.

SAN JUAN BAUTISTA STATE HISTORIC PARK, on the plaza, includes the old Plaza Hotel, built in 1858 on the site of the old Spanish soldiers' barracks, and the 1840 Castro House, headquarters of the Mexican government and later home of the Patrick Breen family, survivors of the ill-fated Donner party.

Other attractions are the 1868 Zanetta House, gardens, a Spanish orchard, a livery stable with old carriages and a slide show about the history of San Juan Bautista. Allow 30 minutes minimum. Daily 10-4:30; closed Jan. 1, Thanksgiving and Dec. 25. Admission $2, under 17 free. Phone (831) 623-4881.

SAN LEANDRO (D-8) pop. 79,452, elev. 59′

CASA PERALTA is at 384 W. Estudillo. This 1901 casa has been restored to its 1920s appearance. Spanish tiles inside the fence relate the story of Don Quixote. Allow 30 minutes minimum. Fri.-Sun. noon-4; closed holidays. Hours may vary; phone ahead. Donations. Phone (510) 577-3971 or (510) 577-3474.

SAN LUIS OBISPO (I-4)

pop. 44,174, elev. 230′

Founded as a mission in 1772, San Luis Obispo grew into a full-fledged town only after completion of the Southern Pacific Railroad in 1894. Today the city is accessible via US 101 and is known as the home of California Polytechnic State University; for information about free guided tours phone (805) 756-5734. The university's Christopher Cohan Center for Performing Arts hosts cultural events; phone (805) 756-2787 for ticket information.

A Farmers Market takes place on the 600-900 blocks of Higuera Street each Thursday evening from 6 to 9. There are stalls of fresh produce as well as barbecue stands. Many retail stores remain open, and free street entertainment includes bands and puppet shows.

Mission Plaza, a developed wooded creek and urban oasis, offers events throughout year. Five miles north of town off SR 1, the California Conservation Corps State Museum traces the history of the federal organization begun during the Great Depression; phone (805) 788-0517.

San Luis Obispo is part of a scenic 252-mile stretch of SR 1 to San Francisco. Continuing southward, San Luis Obispo provides access to an interesting 204-mile drive on US 101 to Los Angeles.

San Luis Obispo Chamber of Commerce: 1039 Chorro St., San Luis Obispo, CA 93401; phone (805) 781-2777.

APPLE FARM, 2015 Monterey St., features a working reproduction of a 19th-century millhouse on San Luis Creek. Visitors can watch a 14-foot waterwheel that, through a series of pulleys and gears, powers a gristmill, ice cream maker and cider press. Food is available. Tours are available. Daily 9-6. Free. Phone (805) 544-2040.

MISSION SAN LUIS OBISPO DE TOLOSA, Chorro and Monterey sts., is often called "The Prince of Missions." Named for a 13th-century French saint, the Bishop of Toulouse, the 1772 mission is now a parish church. In order to repel flaming arrow attacks by unfriendly natives, the mission was built with a tile roof instead of the usual ignitable thatch roof. A museum contains Chumash Indian artifacts and memorabilia from early settlers. There also are gardens.

Daily 9-5, during DST; 9-4, rest of year. Closed Jan. 1, Good Friday, Easter, Thanksgiving and Dec. 25. Donations. Phone (805) 543-6850.

SAVE **SAN LUIS OBISPO CHILDREN'S MUSEUM,** 1010 Nipomo St. at Monterey St., lets visitors learn through play and exploration in more than 25 interactive exhibits. Budding thespians can perform at the Kids' Theater; future firefighters can learn to extinguish fires. Tues.-Sat. 11-5, Sun. noon-4; closed July 4, Easter, Thanksgiving and Dec. 24-26. Phone to verify schedule. Admission $5, under 2 free. Under 16 must be with an adult. MC, VI. Phone (805) 544-6212.

SAN LUIS OBISPO COUNTY HISTORY CENTER AND MUSEUM, 696 Monterey St. in the historic Carnegie Library building, contains rotating exhibits covering local history from the Chumash and

Salinan Indian periods to the present. Wed.-Sun. 10-4; closed holidays. Free. Phone (805) 543-0638 to verify schedule and prices.

WINERIES

- **Edna Valley Ranch**, 2585 Biddle Ranch Rd. Daily 10-5; closed major holidays. Guided tours Sat.-Sun. on the hour 11-3. Phone (805) 544-5855.

SAN MATEO—*see San Francisco p. 160.*

SAN MIGUEL (H-4) pop. 1,427, elev. 620′

GEM **MISSION SAN MIGUEL ARCÁNGEL**, 775 Mission St. on the s. edge of US 101, is still a parish church. The 1797 mission has many original decorations, frescoes and paintings. The vaulted corridor is noted for its arches. The mission holds a fiesta the third Sunday in September. Mission and museum open daily 9:30-4:15; closed Jan. 1, Easter, Thanksgiving and Dec. 25. Donations. Phone (805) 467-3256.

RIOS-CALEDONIA ADOBE is at 700 S. Mission St. This Adobe was built about 1846 by American Indians from the mission, and served as an inn and stage stop 1868-86; it is restored and furnished in period. Wed.-Sun. 10-4; closed Thanksgiving and Dec. 25. Donations. Phone (805) 467-3357.

SAN RAFAEL—*see San Francisco p. 160.*

SAN SIMEON (H-3) elev. 20′

San Simeon lies on a scenic stretch of SR 1 that extends from San Francisco to San Luis Obispo.

San Simeon Chamber of Commerce: 250 San Simeon Ave., San Simeon, CA 93452; phone (805) 927-3500.

GEM **HEARST CASTLE** has visitor parking in a lot off SR 1; buses provide transportation to the castle. The Castle consists of 165 rooms that include the main house of 115 rooms and three guesthouses, as well as and 127 acres of what was once the estate of newspaper publisher William Randolph Hearst.

The estate is open only by tour. Four distinct 1.75-hour daytime tours and one 2-hour evening tour are available. Tour 1 is suggested for first-time visitors. *Tour 1* conducts visitors through the gardens, one guesthouse, both pools and the ground floor of the main building. *Tour 2* visits the upper floors of the main building, including Hearst's private quarters.

Tour 3 includes the north wing of the main building, gardens, both pools and a videotape about the castle's construction. *Tour 4* covers mostly the gardens and includes the wine cellar. Evening tours cover highlights of the estate.

Comfortable shoes are recommended; there are many stairways. A sweater or jacket is advised; part of each tour is outdoors. Photography without the use of supports or flash attachments is permitted.

Mission Architecture

The architecture of the 21 Spanish missions built along El Camino Real 1769-1823 reflects both the simple tastes of their Franciscan founders and the limited resources of material and skilled labor available. The missions were constructed of stone and adobe, finished inside and out with whitewashed mud plaster and topped with pitched roofs of hewn timber covered with red tile. They were modestly adorned, compared to much of the Spanish architecture in the New World at that time.

The mission usually centered on a courtyard enclosed by the church and other buildings. These minor structures included quarters for friars, native workers, servants and soldiers; guest rooms; workshops; a convent; a kitchen; and a dining hall. Cloisters—arched covered passageways—fronted the courtyard and often the surrounding outer plaza.

Digital Archives

The mission church followed one of three general designs. The first, typified by Mission San Miguel Arcangel in San Miguel, consisted of a simple nave, or central hall. A more elaborate design, such as San Buenaventura Mission in Ventura, included a single bell tower. Two belfry towers adorned churches of the third design, exemplified by the graceful Mission Santa Barbara.

After the secularization of the missions in 1833, earthquakes and neglect took their toll; many of the missions were severely damaged or destroyed. Restoration and reconstruction have revitalized these historic structures.

Estate tours daily 8:20-3:20. Hours vary depending upon the season. Tour 4 offered Apr.-Oct. Evening tours available most Fri.-Sat., Mar.-May and Sept.-Dec. Closed Jan. 1, Thanksgiving and Dec. 25.

Tour 1 is $18; ages 6-17, $9. Tours 2, 3 and 4 are $12; ages 6-17, $7. Evening tours $24; ages 6-17, $12. Reservations are recommended and can be made by phone up to 8 weeks in advance. Tours for the physically challenged are available with at least 10 days advance notice. AX, DS, MC, VI. Phone (805) 927-2020. To charge by telephone, phone Reserve America at (800) 444-4445 or TTY (800) 274-7275.

SANTA CLARA (E-9) pop. 102,361, elev. 88′

Once an agricultural community renowned for its orchards, Santa Clara is now world-famous as the core of the Silicon Valley. Santa Clara University has an enrollment of 4,000 undergraduates and 3,800 graduate and law students.

Santa Clara Convention and Visitors Bureau: 1850 Warburton Ave., Santa Clara, CA 95050; phone (408) 244-9660.

Shopping areas: Westfield Shoppingtown Valley Fair, off I-880 at Stevens Creek Boulevard, features Macy's, Nordstrom and 165 upscale specialty stores.

DE SAISSET MUSEUM, on the Santa Clara University campus, displays paintings, decorative arts, an early California history collection relating to Mission Santa Clara and changing exhibits. Allow 1 hour minimum. Tues.-Sun. 11-4; closed holidays. Donations. Phone (408) 554-4528.

INTEL MUSEUM is .5 mi. n. off US 101 Montague Expwy. exit, then .4 mi. w. to 2200 Mission College Blvd., in the Intel Corp.'s Robert Noyce Building. Exhibits focus on the manufacture and use of computer chips. Visitors can communicate in binary code and learn how a computer performs simple calculations using a giant talking microprocessor. A section about clean rooms ("fabs") details 47 steps workers perform before entering a chip-making factory. A "bunny suit" also is on display.

A timeline details the progress of computers and Intel history. Allow 1 hour minimum. Mon.-Fri. 9-6, Sat. 10-5; closed holidays. Free. Phone (408) 765-0503.

GEM **MISSION SANTA CLARA DE ASIS,** on the Santa Clara University campus, off US 101 De La Cruz exit to 500 El Camino Real, was founded in 1777, the eighth of 21 missions built in California in the 1700s. It has the distinction of being the first mission named for a woman, Saint Clare of Assisi, the founder of the Poor Clares order. Established as protection for the San Francisco Bay area, it is the only mission associated with a university.

The present building is a replica of the third mission, which was built in 1825. Relics include three bells given to the mission by the king of Spain. The original garden still can be seen; it is in full bloom April through May. Allow 30 minutes minimum. Mission church open daily 8-6; office open Mon.-Fri. 1-5. Free. Phone (408) 554-4023.

GEM SAVE **PARAMOUNT'S GREAT AMERICA,** on Great America Pkwy. between US 101 and SR 237, is a 100-acre family theme park combining movie magic with theme park thrills and excitement. Among more than 50 rides and attractions are a double-decker carousel; Drop Zone Stunt Tower, a 22-story free-fall ride; Delirium, a spinning pendulum-like ride; and 10 roller coasters.

Other highlights include Rip Roaring Rapids, a white-water raft ride; Kidsville; an aerial gondola; Loggers Run, a water flume ride; an antique auto turnpike ride; and roaming Nickelodeon characters.

Nickelodeon Splat City features Slime Time: The Live Show, an outdoor participatory game show, and Green Slime Zone Definery, an interactive maze of pipework. Theaters present stage shows, and concerts are held in an outdoor amphitheater. Laser tag, games galleries and video game arcades also are featured.

Open daily at 10 during spring break and late May-Labor Day; Sat.-Sun., late Mar. to mid-May (except during spring break) and day after Labor Day to mid-Oct. Closing time varies. Hours and dates may vary; phone ahead. Closed Easter. Admission $45.99; over 59, $39.99; ages 3-6, $33.99. Parking $10. AX, DS, MC, VI. Phone (408) 988-1776. *See color ad p. 139.*

TRITON MUSEUM OF ART, across from the Santa Clara Civic Center at jct. Lincoln St. and Warburton Ave., features rotating exhibits relating to local history and culture. Exhibits are changed every 4 months. Allow 30 minutes minimum. Thurs.-Tues. 11-5 (also Thurs. 5-9); closed holidays. Donations. Phone (408) 247-3754.

SANTA CRUZ (G-2) pop. 54,593, elev. 20′

Santa Cruz, on the coast off scenic SR 1, is the site of one of Father Junípero Serra's 21 missions. A half-scale replica of the mission is on the grounds of Holy Cross Church facing the plaza. All that remains of the original mission, built in 1791 and destroyed by the 1857 earthquake, are the ruins of the soldiers' barracks and part of the stone foundation. The chapel is open to visitors.

Also of interest are McPherson Center for Art and History at Santa Cruz County Art Museum, 705 Front St., which has family programs featuring exhibitions, films and lectures; and Santa Cruz County Historical Trust Museum at McPherson Center, with exhibits and programs relating to local history. The Surfing Museum, on the ground level of Mark Abbott Memorial Lighthouse on West Cliff Drive, displays a collection of surfboards and surfing photographs from the 1930s to the present; phone (831) 420-6289.

Santa Cruz County Conference and Visitors Council: 1211 Ocean St., Santa Cruz, CA 95060; phone (831) 425-1234 or (800) 833-3494.

SAVE **CHARDONNAY SAILING CHARTERS** departs from Santa Cruz Yacht Harbor. Two-hour cruises through Monterey Bay National Marine Sanctuary aboard a 70-foot sailing yacht feature winemakers, brewmasters, sunsets and brunch. Three-hour cruises offer whale-watching.

Two-hour cruises depart Wed.-Sun., Apr.-Oct. Whale-watch cruises Sat.-Sun., Jan.-Mar.; Sat., July-Aug. Hours vary; phone ahead. Each cruise $39.50, children $29.50. Reservations are required. AX, MC, VI. Phone (831) 423-1213 for schedules and reservations.

MYSTERY SPOT, 2.5 mi. n. on Market St., which becomes Branciforte Dr., is a section of redwood forest where the law of gravity seemingly does not apply. Allow 30 minutes minimum. Guided 35-minute tours are given daily every half-hour 9-7, Memorial Day-Labor Day; 9-5, rest of year. Last tour begins at closing. Admission $5; ages 2-5, $2. Phone (831) 423-8897.

NATURAL BRIDGES STATE BEACH, 65 acres on West Cliff Dr., has many tide pools for exploring. The migration of monarch butterflies can be observed from about mid-October through February; a boardwalk leads to the grove. A visitor center offers exhibits about area ecology and wildlife. Allow 2 hours minimum. Beach open daily 8-dusk. Visitor center open Sat.-Sun. 10-4; schedule varies rest of week. Day use fee $5 per private vehicle. Phone (831) 423-4609.

SANTA CRUZ ART LEAGUE GALLERIES, 526 Broadway, presents changing art exhibits in all forms of media as well as performance space for theater, dance and music. Allow 30 minutes minimum. Wed.-Sat. noon-5 (also Thurs. 5-7), Sun. noon-4; closed Jan. 1, Thanksgiving and Dec. 25. Donations. Phone (831) 426-5787.

GEM SAVE **SANTA CRUZ BEACH BOARDWALK** is off SR 1 following signs to the beach area. Established in 1904, the half-mile-long boardwalk is reminiscent of turn-of-the-20th-century amusement parks. A Looff carousel, with a rare brass ring machine and an original 342-pipe organ, dates from 1911, and the Giant Dipper wooden roller coaster, built in 1924, ranks among the nation's most thrilling.

More than 34 rides and attractions are complemented by arcades, games, shops and eateries; a dozen rides tempt the youngsters in the family. The boardwalk features the Casino Arcade and Neptune's Kingdom, which includes miniature golf, games and historical displays. The Pacific Ocean beach provides a scenic backdrop to the amusement park. A beach bandstand is the site of Friday night concerts late June through late August.

Food is available. Allow 1 hour minimum. Open daily at 11, closing times vary, Memorial Day-Labor Day; open Sat.-Sun. and holidays at 11, closing times vary, Jan. 1-day before Memorial Day and day after Labor Day-Nov. 30. Boardwalk free. Individual rides $1.80-$3.60; unlimited rides $24.95. Parking $8. DS, MC, VI. Phone (831) 426-7433 or (831) 423-5590. *See color ad p. 139 & p. 710.*

SANTA CRUZ MUSEUM OF NATURAL HISTORY, 1305 E. Cliff Dr., contains displays of American Indian artifacts, rocks, fossils, a touch tide pool exhibit and specimens of local fauna. The museum sponsors programs, field trips and special events. Allow 1 hour minimum. Tues.-Sun. 10-5; closed holidays. Donations. Phone (831) 420-6115.

SEYMOUR MARINE DISCOVERY CENTER AT LONG MARINE LABORATORY is w. off SR 1 (Mission St.) on Swift St., then n. on Delaware Ave. to end of rd. The center is a marine research and educational facility of the University of California, Santa Cruz. The facility features an 87-foot blue whale skeleton, an exhibit hall with interactive displays, demonstrations, discovery labs, teaching aquariums and touch pools. Guided 45-minute tours of the research lab areas are available.

Open Tues.-Sat. 10-5, Sun. noon-5; closed July 4. Lab tours Tues.-Sun. 1-3. Admission $5, over 59, students with ID and ages 6-16 $3; free to all first Tues. of each month. Phone (831) 459-3800.

UNIVERSITY OF CALIFORNIA AT SANTA CRUZ (UCSC), corner of Bay and High sts., was founded in 1965 on a 2,000-acre portion of the Cowell Ranch overlooking Monterey Bay and Santa Cruz. Roads and walkways situated amid redwoods and meadows connect nine residential colleges. Barn Theater, just inside the main entrance, is a converted horse barn now functioning as a 158-seat theater. Self-guiding tour maps are available at the main entrance information booth.

Student-led tours lasting 1.75 hours are given Mon.-Fri. and some Sat. Times for tours vary; phone ahead. Reservations are required at least 2 to 3 weeks in advance. Tours free. Parking permits $5; limited metered spaces. Phone (831) 459-4008.

Arboretum, 1500 High St., .5 mi. w. of the main entrance, maintains rare plant collections. Many specimens are not otherwise available for study in American botanical gardens. Hummingbirds and butterflies frequently can be seen. Open daily 9-5. Donations. Phone (831) 427-2998.

Center for Agroecology & Sustainable Food System, reached by footpath from Coolidge Dr., is a 25-acre teaching and research facility. The organic farm supports vegetable crops, flowers, herbs and fruit trees. Daily dawn-dusk. Free. Phone (831) 459-3248.

Cook House, 1156 High St., is now the college's admissions office. Built in 1860, the building is the former Cowell Ranch cookhouse. The well-preserved structure also has served as the chancellor's office and headquarters for the campus police. Phone (831) 459-4008.

Theater Arts Center, 1156 High St., is a complex that contains a 530-seat indoor theater as well as dance, drama and sound recording studios; a 231-seat second stage; a 390-seat music and recital hall; and specialized visual arts facilities. The Shakespeare Santa Cruz Festival takes place outdoors in a glen of redwoods; seating capacity is 700. Phone (831) 459-2121.

SANTA MARIA (I-4) pop. 77,423, elev. 217′

Santa Maria's scenic location can best be viewed by a drive along the Foxen Canyon Wine Trail, a 21-mile rural road with 13 wineries along it. West of town, the Guadalupe Nipomo Dunes Preserve offers a nature trail, birding and the highest coastal dunes on the West Coast.

Residents assert that no visit to Santa Maria is complete without sampling the city's renowned Santa Maria Style Barbecue, which consists of beef tri-tip, fresh salsa, pinquito beans and toasted French bread. After dinner take in a production staged by the acclaimed Pacific Conservatory of the Performing Arts (PCPA) of Allan Hancock College. Year-round performances range from Shakespeare through Broadway standards; for tickets phone the box office Tuesday through Sunday at (805) 922-8313.

Santa Maria Valley Chamber of Commerce and Visitors and Convention Bureau: 614 S. Broadway, Santa Maria, CA 93454; phone (805) 925-2403 or (800) 331-3779. *See color ad.*

Self-guiding tours: The free Santa Barbara County Wineries Touring Map and a $1 Santa Maria historic walking-tour map/booklet are available at the chamber of commerce office.

Shopping areas: Santa Maria Town Center, at Broadway and Main Street, has Gottschalks, Robinsons-May and Sears among its more than 70 establishments.

SANTA MARIA HISTORICAL MUSEUM, 616 S. Broadway, depicts early area history. Changing displays include artifacts from the Chumash Indian, Spanish rancho and American pioneer eras. The museum also has a replica of a portion of a turn-of-the-20th-century schoolroom. Tues.-Sat. noon-5; closed holidays. Free. Phone (805) 922-3130.

SANTA MARIA MUSEUM OF FLIGHT, 3015 Airpark Dr., displays within two hangars such airplanes as the Fleet Model 2, F-4 Phantom, F-86 Saber, a full-scale Wright 1902 Glider and the Stinson V77-Reliant. An extensive collection of model planes depicts aviation history from the Wright brothers' pioneering effort to the "flying wing" Stealth bomber. Also on view is the once-secret Norden bombsight and its accessories.

Picnicking is permitted. Fri.-Sun. 10-4 and by appointment; closed Jan. 1 and Dec. 25. Donations. Phone (805) 922-8758.

WINERIES

- **Cottonwood Canyon Vineyard & Winery**, 8 mi. s.e. at 3940 Dominion Rd. Daily 10:30-5:30; closed holidays. Phone (805) 937-8463.

SANTA NELLA (G-3) elev. 78′

REMEMBRANCE MEMORIAL FOR CALIFORNIA KOREAN WAR VETERANS is in the San Joaquin Valley National Cemetery on McCabe Rd. Dedicated to the 2,496 Californians missing or killed in action during the Korean War, the memorial consists of 16 5-foot-high white granite panels engraved with the soldiers' names. Services are conducted on Memorial Day and Veterans Day. Allow 1 hour minimum. Daily dawn-dusk. Free. Phone (209) 854-1040.

SANTA ROSA—*see Wine Country p. 200.*

SARATOGA (F-8) pop. 29,843, elev. 480′

Saratoga is the northern terminus of a scenic 38-mile stretch of SR 9.

Saratoga Chamber of Commerce: 20460 Saratoga-Los Gatos Rd., Saratoga, CA 95070; phone (408) 867-0753.

HAKONE GARDENS, 21000 Big Basin Way, is a 15-acre park containing four gardens—Hill and Pond Garden; Tea Garden; Zen Garden; and Kizuna En, a bamboo garden. A tea ceremony is performed the first Thursday of the month. Allow 1 hour minimum. Mon.-Fri. 10-5, Sat.-Sun. and holidays 11-5;

closed Jan. 1 and Dec. 25. Donations. Parking $7 per private vehicle. Phone (408) 741-4994.

MONTALVO CENTER FOR THE ARTS AND PARK is .5 mi. s.e. on SR 9, then 1 mi. s.w. on Montalvo Rd. Formerly the summer home of U.S. senator and San Francisco mayor James D. Phelan, the estate now serves as a center for fine arts. The 1912 Mediterranean-style structure has a formal garden and trails to lookout points on the surrounding hills. The villa regularly sponsors art exhibits, theater events and concerts.

Allow 1 hour minimum. Park open Mon.-Fri. 8-5, Sat.-Sun. and holidays 9-5, Oct.-Apr.; otherwise varies, rest of year. Gallery open Wed.-Sun. 1-4. The garden occasionally closes for events. Hours may vary; phone ahead. Free. Phone (408) 961-5800 for recorded information.

SAUSALITO—*see San Francisco p. 160.*

SCOTIA (C-1) elev. 164'

PACIFIC LUMBER CO., Main St., offers self-guiding, 45-minute tours of their redwood-processing plant. A logging museum features samples of former and current products, logging equipment, Scotia coins (produced for and used by employees), and photographs. Allow 1 hour minimum. Plant tours Mon.-Fri. 8-10:30 and 11:30-2. Museum open Mon.-Fri. 8-4:30, day after Memorial Day-Labor Day; closed holidays. Free. Phone (707) 764-2222.

SEBASTOPOL—*see Wine Country p. 201.*

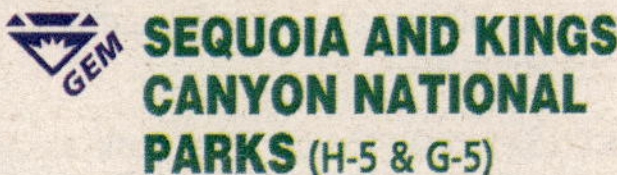

SEQUOIA AND KINGS CANYON NATIONAL PARKS (H-5 & G-5)

Elevations in the parks range from 1,500 ft. near the headquarters at Ash Mountain to 14,494 ft. at the summit of Mount Whitney. Refer to AAA maps for additional elevation information.

Stretching northward from 35 miles east of Visalia to 55 miles east of Fresno, and from the foothills of the San Joaquin Valley to the crest of the High Sierras, the two parks abut and are managed together. Sequoia is the second-oldest national park, behind Yellowstone National Park.

One way to turn back the clock 3,000 years is to take a trip through Sequoia and Kings Canyon National Parks. The landscape is studded with the largest of trees, the giant sequoia trees (Sequoiadendron giganteum). Many of the trees are more than 200 feet high and some have trunks more than 30 feet in diameter. Mount Whitney, at 14,494 feet the highest point in the contiguous United States, is on the eastern edge of Sequoia National Park.

Although the sequoias sparked the formation of these parks, magnificent forests of sugar and ponderosa pine, white and red fir and incense-cedar also exist here. Sugar pines have been known to grow to a base diameter of 11 feet.

Its variable climate has endowed this region with a significant variety of plants. About 1,400 species trees, shrubs, plants and flowers have been identified.

Mule deer, marmots, chipmunks and squirrels are common. Because American black bears frequently are seen in campgrounds, proper food storage is strictly enforced. Raccoons, gray foxes and bobcats can be seen occasionally at night. Rarely seen, however, are Sierra bighorns, mountain lions, pine martens and fishers. About 200 species of birds, including the golden eagle, have been spotted, and the streams along with some high-country lakes support rainbow, brook, brown and golden trout.

Only trails penetrate the alpine wilderness of both parks; therefore, the beauties of the High Sierra or backcountry are available only to hikers and horseback riders. Park trails are off-limits to bicyclists. *See Recreation Chart and the AAA California & Nevada CampBook.*

General Information and Activities

Sequoia and Kings Canyon National Parks are open all year, although the more remote areas are inaccessible in winter. High mountain passes are seldom open to travel before July 1. The roads to Giant Forest, Lodgepole and the Big Stump entrance are open all year; however, the Generals Highway between Lodgepole in Sequoia National Park and Grant Grove in Kings Canyon is closed by heavy snow for periods during winter. Tire chains may be necessary at any time.

Vehicles longer than 22 feet are not recommended on the Generals Highway in Sequoia National Park between Potwisha Campground and Giant Forest. An alternate route for longer vehicles to access the area is SR 180 from Fresno, a straighter, less steep and wider road.

Accommodations generally are open all year. While most campgrounds usually operate from late May through October, some campgrounds are open all year.

Lodgepole and Grant Grove visitor centers, in Sequoia and Kings Canyon National Parks, respectively, are headquarters for activities. Naturalists give illustrated talks or campfire programs several nights a week in summer at Cedar Grove, Dorst, Grant Grove, Lodgepole, and Mineral King amphitheaters. Schedules of programs and daily guided walks are posted on bulletin boards and in prominent public places. The parks' free newspaper contains information. It is available at park entrance stations and visitor centers.

A state fishing license is required for all persons 16 years and over; fee for residents $30.70 (annual), non-residents $30.70 (good for 10 days). A 2-day resident or non-resident license costs $11.05. A second-pole license is $9. Hunting is prohibited.

Horseback trips over the hundreds of miles of backpacking trails are popular. Current information is available at the park visitor centers. Guided trail rides and pack trips or rental saddle stock are available from Grant Grove, Cedar Grove, Horse Corral and Mineral King at the southern section of Sequoia. Pack trips also can be arranged from the Owens Valley area on the east side of the Sierra. Cross-country ski rentals and lessons are available at Grant Grove and Waksachi Lodge.

Headquarters for both parks, which are administered jointly, is at Ash Mountain, on the Generals Hwy. 7 mi. above Three Rivers via SR 198. The Foothills Visitor Center includes a photographic exhibit depicting life in the foothills.

ADMISSION to the parks is $10 per private vehicle, good for 7 days, or $5 per person by other means.

PETS are permitted only if they are on a leash, crated or otherwise restricted at all times. They are prohibited on all trails and in buildings.

ADDRESS inquiries to the Superintendent, 47050 General's Hwy., Sequoia and Kings Canyon National Parks, Three Rivers, CA 93271-9651; phone (559) 565-3341.

Points of Interest

Connecting the two national parks is the Generals Highway, a 46-mile-long scenic road that extends from SR 198 at Ash Mountain through Giant Forest to SR 180 at Grant Grove in Kings Canyon National Park. The highway reaches 7,643 feet at Big Baldy Saddle. **Note:** From Ash Mountain to Giant Forest, the road is particularly difficult for motor homes and large trailers. The road is not recommended for vehicles longer than 22 feet. Vehicle combinations over 50 feet are prohibited between Hospital Rock and Giant Forest.

ALTA PEAK (Sequoia), about 7 mi. from the Wolverton parking area, is 11,204 feet high; it can be reached on foot by a strenuous hike.

CEDAR GROVE (Kings Canyon) is within the canyon of the South Fork of the Kings River. Peaks rise nearly a mile above the stream, and spectacular views are available from road and trail. The level valley floor is especially well suited to leisurely bicycling. Cedar Grove also is a popular base point for trail trips into the high country. The area is inaccessible during winter.

CRYSTAL CAVE (Sequoia) is 14 mi. from Lodgepole Visitor Center and is reached by a narrow, winding road that descends 2,000 feet to Marble Fork Kaweah River Bridge, and then from the parking area down a steep half-mile trail to the cave entrance. **Note:** Vehicles longer than 22 feet are prohibited on the road.

This the only one of the more than 200 caves within these national parks that is open to the public. Three tours are offered: The Regular Tour, lasting 45 minutes; the 2-hour Discovery Tour for ages 13 and older; the crawling and climbing off-trail Wild Cave Tour for those 16 and older.

The temperature inside the cave is approximately 48 F, so visitors should bring warm clothing. Strollers, baby backpacks and tripods are prohibited. Tickets must be bought at least 90 minutes in advance at Lodgepole Visitor Center or at Foothills Visitor Center.

The Regular Tour leaves daily every 30 minutes 11-4, mid-June through Labor Day; Sat.-Sun. on the hour 11-4, Mon.-Fri. 11, noon, 3, 4, mid-May to mid-June; and Sat.-Sun. on the hour 11-4, Mon.-Fri. at 10, 2, 3, day after Labor Day-last Sun. in Sept.; Thurs.-Mon. at 11, 2 and 3, in Oct. and (weather permitting) Nov. 1-11. Phone for the Discovery and the Wild Cave tour schedules and availability.

Regular Tour fee $9; over 61, $7; ages 6-12, $5. Phone for the Discovery and the Wild Cave tour fees. DS, MC, VI. Phone (559) 565-3759.

GENERAL GRANT AND REDWOOD MOUNTAIN GROVES are in Kings Canyon. In Grant Grove is General Grant Tree, third largest of known sequoias. It is 267 feet high with a circumference of 107.6 feet. Robert E. Lee is the second largest sequoia in Grant Grove. Big Stump Basin, the result of early lumbering pursuits, is nearby. Hart Tree, another large sequoia, is in Redwood Mountain Grove. Phone (559) 565-4307.

Grant Grove Visitor Center (Kings Canyon) is 3 mi. e. of Big Stump entrance station on SR 180. The center contains exhibits about the logging history of the sequoias and the wildlife and early native inhabitants of the area. Daily 8-6, June-Sept.; hours may vary rest of the year due to staffing. Free. Phone (559) 565-4307.

GIANT FOREST (Sequoia), 16 mi. from park entrance station via the steep and winding Generals Hwy., was named in 1875 by conservationist John Muir. General Sherman Tree is about 275 feet high and 103 feet in circumference, with a maximum diameter of 36.5 feet at the base. The volume of its trunk is 52,500 cubic feet; it is the largest known sequoia.

Giant Forest Museum offers exhibits focused on giant sequoia ecology and the trees' relationship with mankind.

HEATHER LAKE (Sequoia), 4 mi. by trail from Wolverton, is the most easily accessible of the parks' alpine lakes. Two miles beyond is Pear Lake, in a barren granite basin.

THE HIGH COUNTRY extends from Coyote Peaks at the s. border of Sequoia to the n. boundary of Kings Canyon at Pavilion Dome. Trail trips are the only way to become acquainted with this rugged country. Mount Whitney is 72 miles from Giant Forest along the High Sierra Trail.

HOSPITAL ROCK (Sequoia) is 5 mi. beyond Ash Mountain entrance station on the road to Giant Forest. American Indian pictographs on the boulder mark an old village site once occupied by the Potwisha tribe of the Western Mono Indians. Also at the site are 71 mortar-and-pestle holes used by the women to grind acorns into flour. Exhibits are on the site of an ancient village.

LODGEPOLE VISITOR CENTER (Sequoia) is 4 mi. n.e. of Giant Forest on the Generals Hwy. The center has displays about the sequoias, geologic history and plant life. Daily 8-6, June-Sept.; daily 9-4:30, rest of year. Phone to confirm schedule. Free. Phone the visitor center at (559) 565-4436. Phone Spherix at (800) 365-2267 for camping reservations for Lodgepole and Dorst (in summer only).

MINERAL KING (Sequoia) 25 mi. e. of Three Rivers via Mineral King Rd. and a steep, narrow, winding and partially paved road. Once a silver-mining area, it is now a peaceful valley retreat lying at an altitude of 7,500 feet in the shadow of the towering peaks of the Great Western Divide. Rangers lead walks and campfire programs in summer. The area is unsuitable for RVs (trailers are not permitted) and is inaccessible in winter. Road open late May-Oct. 31.

MORO ROCK (Sequoia), 2 mi. by narrow road or trail from Giant Forest, is 6,725 feet above sea level and more than 6,000 feet above the San Joaquin Valley floor. Scenic views of the Great Western Divide, especially at sunset, are the rewards of reaching the top. A steep stairway, inaccessible in winter, leads to the summit.

PANORAMIC POINT (Kings Canyon) at the e. boundary of General Grant Grove is accessible via a 2.3 mi. road and then a 0.25 mi. walk from the parking lot. **Note:** The road is narrow and winding and not recommended for trailers or motor homes.

The point offers views of the High Sierra to the east and the San Joaquin Valley and Coast Range to the west. Within walking distance is another observation point at Park Ridge. Road closed to vehicular traffic in the winter, when it becomes a cross-country ski trail.

THARP'S LOG (Sequoia) is at the end of Log Meadow, 1 mi. by trail from Crescent Meadow; or by Circle Meadow and Congress trails. This is an old pioneer cabin built within a fire-hollowed sequoia log.

SEQUOIA NATIONAL FOREST

Elevations in the forest range from 1,000 ft. at the Kings and Kern rivers along the forest's western edge to 12,432 ft. at Florence Peak in the Golden Trout Wilderness. Refer to AAA maps for additional elevation information.

Sequoia National Forest, in central California at the southern end of the Sierra Nevadas, extends from Kings River southward to the Kern River and

The Mother Lode

Mexican miners called it "La Veta Madre"—the Mother Lode—a rich vein of gold lacing the western slopes of the Sierra Nevada for 120 miles. The name eventually came to denote the entire band of territory extending roughly from Mariposa to Sierra City, where the gleaming metal was mined during the frenetic years of the California gold rush.

The discovery of gold near Coloma in 1848 lured thousands of prospectors to the Mother Lode. Tales of nuggets littering the hillsides were not entirely unfounded during the early years of the gold rush, and the possibility of unearthing a mammoth find, like the 195-pound nugget found near Carson Hill, stoked the get-rich-quick dreams of many a '49er.

Digital Archives

Nearly 550 mining towns proliferated in the Mother Lode; fewer than half remain today. Like the fortunes of many of the miners, the towns rose and fell precipitately and often were simply abandoned when the miners moved on to more profitable stakes. A few, such as Sonora, Placerville, Auburn and Grass Valley, weathered the diminishing reserves to become prosperous small cities. Others survive as little more than intriguing names on a map.

Aptly numbered SR 49 traverses the length of the Mother Lode country. The facades of the surviving buildings, the historical parks along the route and the ghost towns and empty mines scattered throughout the hills still retain a sense of the atmosphere from this colorful period.

Piute Mountains, and westward from the Sierra Nevada summit to the brush-covered foothills of the San Joaquin Valley.

Thirty-eight groves of giant sequoias, the Kern Plateau and the Golden Trout, Monarch, Jennie Lakes, South Sierra, Dome Land and Kiavah wildernesses are among the more popular attractions of this approximately 1,139,500-acre forest. South Fork Kings Wild and Scenic River, Kings River Special Management Area, North Fork Kern Wild and Scenic River, and South Fork Kern Wild and Scenic River also are among the attractions.

To permanently protect most of the nation's remaining giant sequoia trees, the Giant Sequoia National Monument was created in 2000. The monument's 327,000 acres, all within Sequoia National Forest, include 38 groves of the soaring trees. These largest trees on Earth can grow to become more than 300 feet tall and can live more than 3,000 years. The monument is in two sections divided by Sequoia National Park; the northern portion is in Fresno and Tulare counties, the southern entirely within Tulare County. Hiking and horseback riding are permitted, and motorcycles, all-terrain vehicles and snowmobiles may be used, though with restrictions. For additional information phone the national forest office.

Within the national forest more than 50 campgrounds and picnic areas provide bases for fishing, swimming, boating, hiking, horseback riding, rock climbing and hunting. White-water rafting is popular on the Kern and Kings rivers. Swimming along the shoreline is permitted on 87-acre Hume Lake. Fall color is particularly spectacular at Quaking Aspen, Indian Basin and the Kern Plateau. Winter activities include cross-country and downhill skiing and snowmobiling.

For information contact the Information Receptionist, Sequoia National Forest, 900 W. Grand Ave., Porterville, CA 93257-2035; phone (559) 784-1500. *See Recreation Chart and the AAA California & Nevada CampBook.*

DID YOU KNOW

Because of budget considerations, the schedules and fees of all state-owned facilities are subject to change. Travelers are advised to phone ahead.

BALCH PARK is within Mountain Home State Forest and the general boundary of the Sequoia National Forest, 32 mi. n.e. of Porterville. At an elevation of 6,325 feet stands a beautiful sequoia grove. Two small stocked ponds are in the park. Day use fee $1 per person. Phone (559) 539-3896.

BOYDEN CAVERN is 22 mi. n.e. of Grant Grove on SR 180 at 74101 E. Kings Canyon Rd. within Sequoia National Forest. Guided 45-minute tours wind through underground chambers filled with a variety of interesting formations. The temperature inside is a cool 55 F; a sweater or light jacket is advised. Picnicking is permitted. Allow 1 hour minimum.

Tours depart on the hour daily 10-5, June-Sept.; 11-4 last week in Apr.-May 30 and Oct. 1-first week in Nov. Tour $10; senior citizens, $9; ages 3-13, $5. MC, VI. Phone (209) 736-2708 or (866) 762-2837.

LAKE ISABELLA, off SR 178, is one of Southern California's largest reservoirs, with more than 11,000 surface acres. With fishing, boating, kayaking, wind surfing, water skiing, camping and picnicking, the lake offers freshwater recreation well within a few hours drive of Los Angeles. Rentals are available at three marinas. **Note:** Sudden gusts of 60 mph winds may arise, making crossing open water unsafe. Phone (760) 379-5646.

SHASTA-TRINITY NATIONAL FORESTS

Elevations in the forests range from 620 ft. at Lake Shasta to 14,162 ft. at Mount Shasta. Refer to AAA maps for additional elevation information.

In northern California, Shasta-Trinity National Forests covers more than 2,100,000 acres, including portions of Yolla Bolly-Middle Eel Wilderness Area and Trinity Alps Wilderness. Mount Shasta, a dormant volcano with five living glaciers, towers to 14,162 feet.

Three impounded lakes—Whiskeytown, Shasta and Clair Engle—are within Whiskeytown-Shasta-Trinity National Recreation Area *(see place listing p. 181)*. Some 1,269 miles of trails lace the area, including 154 miles of the Pacific Crest Trail. The forest offers opportunities for lake and stream fishing as well as hunting for waterfowl, upland birds, deer, bears and small game. For forest reservations phone the National Recreation Reservation Service at (877) 444-6777, or TTY (877) 833-6777.

For more information contact the Forest Supervisor, Shasta-Trinity National Forests, 2400 Washington Ave., Redding, CA 96001; phone (530) 244-2978. *See Recreation Chart and the AAA California & Nevada CampBook.*

SIERRA CITY (D-4) elev. 4,187'

KENTUCKY MINE PARK AND MUSEUM, .5 mi. e. via SR 49 in Sierra County Historical Park, is on the site of a hard-rock gold mine. Guided 1-hour walking tours go from the mine portal through an operable ten stamp mill. Tools, photographs, documents and mineral samples displayed in the museum depict mining-camp life during California's gold rush era. Other exhibits include American Indian and Chinese artifacts.

Picnic facilities are available. Open Thurs.-Mon. 10-4, Memorial Day weekend-Sept. 30. Guided stamp mill and mine tours at 11 and 2. Admission, including museum and tours, $5; ages 7-17, $2.50. Museum $1. Phone (530) 862-1310.

SIERRA NATIONAL FOREST

Elevations in the forest range from 990 ft. at the Merced River to 13,157 ft. at the summit of Mount Ritter. Refer to AAA maps for additional elevation information.

Set between two of California's crown jewels, Kings Canyon and Yosemite national parks *(see place listings p. 169 and 204)*, Sierra National Forest is a gem in its own right. The forest's 1,300,000 acres embrace almost all the land between these national parks—from the gently rolling foothills bordering the San Joaquin Valley to the jagged Sierra crest. Within the forest's boundaries is much of John Muir's famed "Range of Light." More commonly called the High Sierra, this is a landscape of craggy peaks, giant glacial stairways, and mountainside amphitheaters filled with lakes and open meadows.

How this rugged landscape came to be was a major issue among many 19th-century scientists. Yet it was Muir's remark that "tender snow-flowers noiselessly falling through unnumbered centuries" came closest to the truth. Glacial ice gave these peaks their distinctive shape, a profile further refined by the swift streams and rivers fed by the yearly snowpack. Such major rivers as the San Joaquin, the Merced, the Kings and their tributaries carved deep canyons and gorges within the forest.

Hidden deep within these watersheds are clusters of sequoias. One stand of these majestic trees is the Nelder Grove south of Yosemite National Park near Bass Lake; another is farther south near Dinkey Creek in the McKinley Grove.

Two major highways that penetrate the forest are SRs 41 and 168; the most accessible recreation areas lie along or just off these routes. Shaver and Bass lakes are two popular destinations, offering camping and water sports. Other recreation areas, such as Florence Lake, Edison Lake, Redinger Lake and Pine Flat Reservoir, are accessible from forest roads branching off SR 168.

The John Muir and Ansel Adams wilderness areas straddle the forest's eastern border and the Sierra crest. The former, with its snowcapped peaks, dense forests and numerous lakes, is one of California's largest wilderness areas. Highlights of this wild area include John Muir Trail—a segment of Pacific Crest Trail—and Humphreys Basin, with its countless lakes and views of Mount Humphreys, a favorite for world-class climbers.

Within Ansel Adams Wilderness Area are the jagged peaks of Ritter Range, one of the most dramatic mountain ranges in the national forest. Smaller areas include the Monarch, Dinkey Lakes and Kaiser wilderness areas. The John Muir, Kaiser and portions of the Ansel Adams wilderness areas are so popular that a quota system for visitors is in effect; reservations at least 3 weeks in advance are recommended. Other recreation highlights include 1,100 miles of hiking trails, 411 lakes and five wilderness areas.

Wildlife native to the forest include deer, bears, quails, bobcats, foxes, beavers and coyotes. Anglers can expect to find an abundance of rainbow, golden, brown and eastern brook trout as well as large and small mouth bass, crappie and bluegill.

Although the forest has no visitor center, information about campgrounds and recreational opportunities is available at the district ranger stations and the forest headquarters in Clovis. Campground reservations, usually required for June, July and August at Shaver Lake, Huntington Lake, Dinkey Creek and Bass Lake, can be made through the National Recreation Reservation Service, (877) 444-6777. Downhill skiing is available nearby.

For more information contact the Forest Headquarters, Sierra National Forest, 1600 Tollhouse Rd., Clovis, CA 93611; phone (559) 297-0706. *See Recreation Chart and the AAA California & Nevada CampBook.*

SIX RIVERS NATIONAL FOREST

Elevations in the forest range from 350 ft. at Adams Station to 6,957 ft. at the summit of Salmon Mountain. Refer to AAA maps for additional elevation information.

Extending 135 miles south from the Oregon border along the west slope of the Coast Range, Six Rivers National Forest covers almost 990,000 acres; it is named for the Smith, Klamath, Trinity, Mad, Van Duzen and Eel rivers.

Many routes, including SR 96 along the Trinity and Klamath rivers northward from Willow Creek through the Hoopa Valley Indian Reservation, penetrate the forest. Much of the region is accessible only on foot or by horseback.

As the forest's name implies, many recreational opportunities center around the rivers. Rafting and kayaking are especially popular on the Klamath, Trinity and Smith rivers. Trout, steelhead and salmon fishing and deer hunting also are popular pastimes.

Within the national forest is Smith River National Recreation Area, which offers numerous leisure activities. More than 65 miles of trails accommodate horseback riders, mountain bikers or hikers, and animals lovers will find rare and endangered species such as the bald eagle and peregrine falcon. For information contact the Forest Supervisor, Six Rivers National Forest, 1330 Bayshore Way, Eureka, CA 95501; phone (707) 442-1721. *See Recreation Chart and the AAA California & Nevada CampBook.*

SODA SPRINGS (D-4) elev. 6,768′

WESTERN SKISPORT MUSEUM, s. of I-80 at the Boreal Ski Area, has displays depicting the development of snow skiing as a sport. Exhibits date from 1850 to the present. Videotapes are shown by request. Allow 30 minutes minimum. Wed.-Sun. 10-4, Nov.-Apr.; Sat.-Sun. 10-4, July-Aug. Free. Phone (530) 426-3313.

SOLEDAD (G-3) pop. 11,263, elev. 190′

MISSION NUESTRA SEÑORA DE LA SOLEDAD, 1.3 mi. w. off US 101 at 36641 Fort Romie Rd., was founded in 1791. It consists of adobe ruins, a museum and a restored chapel. Allow 30 minutes minimum. Daily 10-4; closed Jan. 1, Easter, Thanksgiving and Dec. 25. Donations. Phone (831) 678-2586.

SONOMA—*see Wine Country p. 201.*

SONORA (F-4) pop. 4,423, elev. 1,796′

Sonora was first settled by miners from Sonora, Mexico, and became one of the largest and wealthiest towns in the Mother Lode country. Still a bustling community, Sonora now relies on tourism, lumbering and agriculture. It also is the seat of Tuolumne County and a market center for the surrounding region. Sonora's past is proudly reflected in its fine collection of Victorian houses.

Tuolumne County Visitors Bureau: 542 Stockton St., Sonora, CA 95370; phone (209) 533-4420 or (800) 446-1333.

BRADFORD STREET PARK, Bradford St. at SR 49, has exhibits about mining equipment used in Sonora during the gold rush era. A drag-stone mill used for pulverizing ores (an arrastra), stamp mill and pelton wheel are included. Picnic areas are available. Daily 24 hours. Free.

TUOLUMNE COUNTY MUSEUM AND HISTORY CENTER, 158 W. Bradford Ave., is housed in the 1857 county jail. Displays depicting the gold-rush era include photographs, guns, antiques, artifacts and gold exhibits. A Pioneer Trails exhibit is available. Picnicking is permitted. Sun.-Fri. 10-4, Sat. 10-3:30; closed Jan. 1, Mother's Day and Dec. 24-25 and 31. Donations. Phone (209) 532-1317.

SOQUEL (G-2) pop. 5,081, elev. 40′

WINERIES

- **Bargetto's Santa Cruz Winery**, 3535 N. Main St. Mon.-Sat. 11-6, Sun. noon-6; closed Jan. 1, Easter, Thanksgiving and Dec. 25. Tours are offered; phone for reservations. Phone (831) 475-2258.

SOUTH LAKE TAHOE—

see Lake Tahoe Area p. 87.

STANISLAUS NATIONAL FOREST

Elevations in the forest range from 1,200 ft. in the Lumsden area to 11,462 ft. at Sonora Peak. Refer to AAA maps for additional elevation information.

On the western slope of the Sierra Nevada Range, Stanislaus National Forest covers nearly 900,000 acres and outlines the northwestern boundary of Yosemite National Park *(see place listing p. 204).* The Merced, Mokelumne, Clavey, Stanislaus and Tuolumne rivers cut deep canyons through this region.

Popular summer activities include swimming, camping, picnicking, boating, rafting, canoeing and hunting. More than 800 miles of rivers and streams offer myriad opportunities for fishing. The forest offers an abundance of trails suitable for hiking, horseback riding, backpacking, off-roading and mountain biking. Snow skiing is available at Dodge Ridge off SR 108 and at Mount Reba off SR 4. Snowmobiling and cross-country skiing also are popular during the winter.

Reservations for Pinecrest campground can be made through the U.S. National Forest Service Reservation Center, (877) 444-6775 in summer.

Visitor tours and programs are offered June through August in Pinecrest. The Emigrant and Carson-Iceberg wildernesses are on the eastern side of the forest. Permits may be obtained at any Stanislaus National Forest office. For general forest information contact the Supervisor's Office, Stanislaus National Forest, 19777 Greenley Rd., Sonora, CA 95370; phone (209) 532-3671. *See Recreation Chart and the AAA California & Nevada CampBook.*

STINSON BEACH (D-7) pop. 751, elev. 18′

AUDUBON CANYON RANCH, 3.5 mi. n. on SR 1, is a wildlife preserve and educational center. The ranch contains a major heronry frequented by great blue herons and great egrets. Allow 2 hours minimum. Sat.-Sun. and holidays 10-4, during the mid-Mar. to mid-July nesting period. Donations. Phone (415) 868-9244.

STOCKTON (F-3) pop. 243,771, elev. 14′

The first of California's two inland seaports, Stockton is connected with San Francisco Bay by a channel 60 miles long and 37 feet deep. The San Joaquin waterways, 1,000 miles of navigable inland waters, offer boating and fishing. The city also is the home of the University of the Pacific, which in 1852 became the first chartered university in California; current enrollment is approximately 4,000.

Greater Stockton Chamber of Commerce: 445 W. Weber Ave., Suite 220, Stockton, CA 95203; phone (209) 547-2770.

THE CHILDREN'S MUSEUM OF STOCKTON is downtown across from the deep water channel at 402 W. Weber Ave. This hands-on museum has a fire truck, police car and an ambulance for youngsters to explore as well as a child-sized grocery store, emergency room and TV studio where pretending is the order of the day. Allow 30 minutes minimum. Tues.-Fri. 9-4, Sat. 10-5, Sun. noon-5. Admission $4, under 2 free. Phone (209) 465-4386.

THE HAGGIN MUSEUM, .3 mi. n. of I-5 Pershing Ave. exit (northbound) or off I-5 Oak-Fremont exit (southbound) to 1201 N. Pershing Ave. at Rose St., following signs, houses 19th-century American and European paintings as well as local historical artifacts. Works by Albert Bierstadt, Paul Gauguin, George Inness and Pierre Auguste Renoir are exhibited. American Indian baskets; a tractor and harvester, both developed locally; an Egyptian mummy; and reconstructed interiors of several turn-of-the-20th-century businesses are highlights.

Tours are available by appointment. Allow 1 hour, 30 minutes minimum. Tues.-Sun. 1:30-5; closed major holidays. Admission $5; over 64, students with ID and ages 10-17, $2.50; free to all first Tues. of the month. Phone (209) 940-6300.

PIXIE WOODS WONDERLAND, jct. Occidental Ave. and Monte Diablo Blvd. in Louis Park, is a children's playland featuring sets from popular children's stories and legends. Theater programs are held during the afternoon. The park also offers amusement rides. Wed.-Fri. and holidays 11-5, Sat.-Sun. 11-6, early June-early Sept.; Sat.-Sun. and holidays noon-5, late Feb.-early June and early Sept.-late Oct. Admission $2.25; under 13, $1.75. Rides $1.25 each. Phone (209) 937-8220 or (209) 937-7366.

SUISUN CITY (C-9) pop. 26,118

SCANDIA FAMILY CENTER, I-80 and Suisun Valley Rd., includes two 18-hole miniature golf courses, a large arcade, waterbug bumper boats and a 10-minute train ride on the Copenhagen Express. A children's clubhouse also is part of the center.

Food is available. Allow 2 hours minimum. Indoor activities daily 10-10. Outdoor activities Sun.-Thurs. 10-8:30, Fri.-Sat. 10-10. Admission, including 10 game tokens, golf, junior track, boats and train, $18; individual prices for other rides $2-$6. Miniature golf $7.50; over 55 and ages 6-10, $5. DS, MC, VI. Phone (707) 864-8558.

WESTERN RAILWAY MUSEUM, e. on SR 12 to 5848 SR 12, operates vintage streetcars, including Key System trains, California's last 5-cent street car and other equipment on 9.5-mile trips. Other trips are offered in April and October. Picnicking is permitted. Wed.-Sun. 10:30-5, early June-Labor Day; Sat.-Sun. 10:30-5, rest of year. Closed Jan. 1 and Dec. 25. Last train departs 1 hour before closing. Admission $8; over 65, $7; ages 2-12, $5. AX, DS, MC, VI. Phone (707) 374-2978.

SUNNYVALE (E-9) pop. 131,760, elev. 105'

Although Silicon Valley doesn't appear on any map, people the world over know that the nickname refers to the area around Sunnyvale. The city is the headquarters of more than 650 computer-related manufacturers whose products, whether software or hardware, are based on silicon chip technology.

Local manufacturers make good use of The Sunnyvale Center for Innovation, Invention and Ideas (SCI^3) at 465 S. Mathilda Ave., Suite 300. The center, which has facilities for patent and trademark research, also has on-line access to the full patent database used by the Patent and Trademark Office in Washington, D.C. A research library features patents from 1790 to the present as well as trademark/logo information. Phone (408) 730-7290.

Sunnyvale Chamber of Commerce: 101 W. Olive Ave., Sunnyvale, CA 94086; phone (408) 736-4971.

SUSANVILLE (C-4) pop. 13,541, elev. 4,258'

Founded by pioneer Isaac Roop in 1854 and named for his daughter, the town of Susanville lies at the head of the Honey Lake Valley and is flanked by the cliffs of the Susan River Canyon. In the 19th century Susanville served as a stopping point on the Nobles Emigrant Trail, a popular alternate route to the Donner Pass Overland Trail.

The Bizz Johnson Trail follows an old branch line of the Southern Pacific Railroad for approximately 26 miles between Susanville and Westwood. Administered by the Bureau of Land Management and Lassen National Forest, the trail is popular with hikers, railroad history buffs and cross-country skiers. The Susanville Depot & Museum at the beginning of the trail houses historic photographs and railroad memorabilia in a restored 1920s train station.

Of particular interest in downtown are the Susanville murals, eight on outdoor walls, one indoor. All are within a five-block area. To drive or walk by all nine, begin your tour at the corner of Main and Union streets. Continue west on Main to Roop Street and turn south; when you reach Cottage Street turn east—the last mural is at the corner of Gay Street. The indoor mural is at the corner of Main and S. Lassen streets.

Lassen County Chamber of Commerce: 84 N. Lassen St., P.O. Box 338, Susanville, CA 96130; phone (530) 257-4323.

EAGLE LAKE, 16 mi. n.w. on Eagle Lake Rd., is the second largest natural lake in California. In summer campfire programs and slide presentations are held; phone ahead for schedule. Mon.-Fri. 8-4:30. Free. Phone (530) 257-4188 or (530) 825-3212. *See Recreation Chart and the AAA California & Nevada CampBook.*

SUTTER CREEK (E-3)

pop. 2,303, elev. 1,198′

In the Sierra foothills, Sutter Creek is popular with outdoor enthusiasts due to its mild climate. On SR 49 wayfarers are often waylaid by the 1850s charm of this small town's antiques shops and bed and breakfasts.

Sutter Creek Visitor Center: 11A Randolf St., P.O. Box 1234, Sutter Creek, CA 95685; phone (209) 267-1344, or (800) 400-0305 in Calif.

Self-guiding tours: A brochure describing a walking tour past Sutter Creek's historic buildings is available from the visitor center.

SUTTER GOLD MINE is at 13660 SR 49. A 1-hour family tour takes visitors, wearing hard hats, on a shuttle ride underground to see mining equipment, learn about area geology and mining technology and discover the differences between real gold versus "fools gold." The temperature in the mine is a constant 64 F. Gold panning, gemstone mining and a 3.5-hour Deep Mine Experience tour also are available.

Picnicking is permitted. Allow 1 hour minimum. Tours are given daily on the hour 9-5, May-Oct.; 10-4, rest of year. Tours may leave on the half-hour on busy days. Admission $14.50; over 55, $12.50; ages 3-13, $10. Under 3 are not permitted. An additional fee is charged for gold panning and gemstone mining. MC, VI. Phone (209) 736-2708 or (866) 762-2837.

TAFT (I-4) pop. 6,400, elev. 984′

WEST KERN OIL MUSEUM, w. of SR 33 and SR 119 at 1168 Wood St., celebrates the story of oil from the American Indian's uses of asphaltum 8,000 years ago to the present. It preserves artifacts, photographs and equipment from the early oil fields on an 8-acre property that is being turned into a replica of an old time oil company camp. Exhibits include a 1912 oilfield office, tent house, motor transport building and a wooden derrick drilled in 1917.

Tues.-Sat. 10-4, Sun. 1-4; closed Jan. 1, Easter, July 4, Thanksgiving and Dec. 25. Donations. Phone (661) 765-6664.

TAHOE CITY—*see Lake Tahoe Area p. 88.*

TAHOE NATIONAL FOREST

Elevations in the forest range from 1,300 ft. on the Middle Fork of the American River to 9,143 ft. at the summit of Mount Lola. Refer to AAA maps for additional elevation information.

North and west of Lake Tahoe, Tahoe National Forest—despite its name—has little to do with the lake. Much of the national forest's 797,205 acres lie in the Yuba River drainage. Here miners used the placer pan, pick and hydraulic cannon, which used tons of pressurized water to tear away the hillsides, in their frantic pursuit of gold. The lake and its immediate environs are part of the Lake Tahoe Basin Management Unit.

Today, where pack trains and stagecoaches once traveled, automobiles now follow SR 49 past the remnants of mining camps since reclaimed by forest. Along the twisting course of the North Yuba River are steep-walled canyons and the dramatic Sierra Buttes, which are riddled with old quartz mines.

Miners weren't the only ones to leave their mark on the landscape. Touring the region as an entertainer in 1853, famed *femme-fatale* Lola Montez christened Independence Lake during a Fourth of July picnic. Just north of the site of her picnic, Mount Lola honors the adventuress.

Independence Lake is but one of many lakes within the forest boundaries. Some of the most popular areas are the French Meadows Reservoir, cradled in the upper reaches of the American River watershed; a cluster of glacial lakes north of Sierra City; and Bullards Bar Reservoir, on the edge of the Sacramento Valley.

Recreational opportunities abound in the forest. Alpine and Nordic skiing and snowmobiling are popular winter diversions, while hiking, camping, boating, horseback riding and fishing are available the rest of the year. Hikers enjoy the 400 miles of trails, and those who prefer water sports are attracted to the sailing, water skiing, swimming, rafting, kayaking and canoeing available within the forest. Reservations for Logger Campground can be made through the U.S. National Forest Service Reservation Center; phone (877) 444-6777.

Publications about recreational opportunities and maps are available at most forest service stations and the forest headquarters in Nevada City. For more information contact the Forest Supervisor, Tahoe National Forest, 631 Coyote St., Nevada City, CA 95959; phone (530) 265-4531. *See Recreation Chart and the AAA California & Nevada CampBook.*

TAHOMA—*see Lake Tahoe Area p. 88.*

TEHACHAPI (I-5) pop. 10,957, elev. 3,973′

This old railroad town in the Tehachapi Mountains is in an area known as the Tehachapi-Mojave Wind Resource Area, site of more than 4,500 wind turbines. These turbines collectively generate 2.4 billion kilowatt-hours of electricity per year, enough to meet the annual residential needs of almost 650,000 people. The best time to see the turbines spinning is late afternoon when hot winds blow from the nearby Mojave Desert. For guided tours contact the Kern Wind Energy Association at (661) 831-1038; brochures outlining a self-guiding tour are available from the chamber of commerce.

In spring Tehachapi's apple orchards burst into bloom, and between mid-August and mid-November visitors can pick and purchase or just purchase samples of more than 20 varieties. Mourning Cloak Ranch and Botanical Gardens has more than 2,200 species of plants on 20 acres of hillside. Open by appointment only, the ranch and gardens also feature a horse-drawn carriage collection; phone (661) 822-1661.

Greater Tehachapi Chamber of Commerce: 209 E. Tehachapi Blvd., P.O. Box 401, Tehachapi, CA 93581; phone (661) 822-4180.

Self-guiding tours: Brochures outlining walking tours of the downtown historic district and the surrounding area are available from the chamber of commerce.

TEHACHAPI LOOP, 8.5 mi. n.w. on the railroad track, was conceived by a railroad engineer in 1876 to overcome a steep grade. The loop enables the last car of an 85-car train to pass above the engine in the tunnel below. For more information phone the chamber of commerce at (661) 822-4180.

TEHACHAPI MUSEUM, 310 S. Green St., displays items of local historical significance including ranching, farming and mining equipment, along with exhibits describing the importance of Native Americans, lumber, cement, the railroads and agriculture to the area. Tues.-Sun. noon-4, Memorial Day-Labor Day; otherwise varies. Free. Phone (661) 822-8152 or (661) 822-3937.

THREE RIVERS (H-5) pop. 2,248, elev. 826'

RECREATIONAL ACTIVITIES

White-water Rafting

- **Beyond Limits Adventures** departs from 40501 Sierra Dr., .2 mi. e. of Kaweah Park Resort on SR 198. Write P.O. Box 215, Riverbank, CA 95367. Daily Apr.-Sept. (depending upon water flow). Phone (209) 869-6060 or (800) 234-7238.

TOIYABE NATIONAL FOREST—

see Humboldt-Toiyabe National Forest in Nevada p. 226.

TRINIDAD (B-1) pop. 311, elev. 175'

Sighted by a Portuguese sea captain around 1595, the area now known as Trinidad was first settled by the Tsurai Indians around 1620. Spanish explorers came ashore on Trinity Sunday in 1775 and named the port *La Santisima Trinidad,* "the most holy Trinity." The Spanish were followed by Capt. George Vancouver in 1793 and, in the early 19th century, by a succession of fur traders.

Trinidad became a boomtown during the gold-rush days as prospectors in search of instant wealth along nearby rivers loaded up with supplies before heading on to the mines. One of California's oldest incorporated cities, Trinidad achieved that distinction in 1870.

Known later as a mill town and then as a whaling port, the coastal village now welcomes those in search of secluded beaches, hiking, fishing and whale watching. A working lighthouse is near the edge of the promontory.

Greater Trinidad Chamber of Commerce: P.O. Box 356, Trinidad, CA 95570; phone (707) 677-1610.

PATRICK'S POINT STATE PARK, 632 acres 5 mi. n. via US 101, is noted for its agate beach, numerous tide pools, American Indian village and spring wildflowers. A naturalist service is available in summer. Dogs are restricted from the beach and trails. Camping is permitted. Daily dawn-dusk. Day use fee $4 per private vehicle. Phone (707) 677-3570, or ReserveAmerica at (800) 444-7275 for camping. *See Recreation Chart and the AAA California & Nevada CampBook.*

TRINITY CENTER (B-2) elev. 2,311'

SCOTT MUSEUM OF TRINITY CENTER is 1 mi. e. off SR 3 on Airport Rd. Among the exhibits are horse-drawn vehicles, a barbed-wire collection, American Indian artifacts and old utensils. Free guide service is available. Tues.-Sat. 1-5, June 1-Labor Day. Donations. Phone (530) 266-3378.

TRINITY NATIONAL FOREST—

see Shasta-Trinity National Forests p. 172.

TRUCKEE—*see Lake Tahoe Area p. 88.*

TULARE (H-4) pop. 43,994, elev. 288'

Tulare, in the heart of one of the country's largest milk and dairy producing areas, has become known as a dairy processing center. Other agriculture also plays an important part in the area's economy.

Tulare Chamber of Commerce: 220 E. Tulare Ave., P.O. Box 1435, Tulare, CA 93275-1435; phone (559) 686-1547.

Shopping areas: Dozens of factory outlet stores, including IZOD, Mikasa and Polo Ralph Lauren, are in the Horizon Outlet Center adjacent to the Prosperity Avenue exit from SR 99. In the center is the chamber of commerce welcome center; phone (559) 684-9681.

TULARE HISTORICAL MUSEUM, 444 W. Tulare Ave., displays dioramas, artifacts, photographs and replicas of rooms and small businesses which reveal the colorful history of the town, from Yokuts Indian villages to the present. The museum also houses art glass, the Manuel Toledo Military Collection and memorabilia of Adm. Elmo R. Zumwalt Jr. who graduated from high school here, and of Olympians Bob Mathias, a native son, and Sim Iness.

Thurs.-Sat. 10-4, Sun. 12:30-4; closed holidays. Admission $5; over 54, $3; students with ID $2; under 5 free. Phone (559) 686-2074.

TULELAKE (A-3) pop. 1,020, elev. 4,035'

KLAMATH BASIN NATIONAL WILDLIFE REFUGES, near Tulelake, include the Lower Klamath and Tule Lake refuges. They offer some 30 miles of auto tour routes for observing wildlife. An estimated 60 to 70 percent of Pacific flyway waterfowl stop here in the fall, with peak migration from late October to mid-November.

As many as 500 bald eagles can be seen during January and February, many from the auto tour routes.

Visitor center open Mon.-Fri. 8-4:30, Sat.-Sun. and holidays 10-4; closed Jan. 1 and Dec. 25. Day-use fee $5 per private vehicle for the automobile tour. Phone (530) 667-2231.

TUPMAN (I-4) pop. 227, elev. 320′

TULE ELK STATE RESERVE, 3 mi. w. of I-5 on Stockdale Hwy., protects 956 acres and a herd of Tule elk. The elk can be observed best in the viewing area near park headquarters. A visitor center offers natural history displays and information about the Tule elk. Picnicking is permitted. Reserve open daily 8-dusk. Visitor center open when staffing is available; phone ahead. Day use fee $3 per private vehicle. Phone (661) 764-6881.

UKIAH—*see Wine Country p. 202.*

VACAVILLE (B-9) pop. 88,625, elev. 179′

VACAVILLE MUSEUM—A CENTER FOR SOLANO COUNTY HISTORY, 213 Buck Ave., displays photographs, documents and memorabilia pertaining to the history of Solano County. The museum also contains changing exhibits and an interpretive garden of native plants. Guided walking tours of old downtown are offered periodically; phone for schedule. Allow 30 minutes minimum. Wed.-Sun. 1-4:30. Donations. Phone (707) 447-4513.

VALLECITO (F-4) pop. 427, elev. 1,745′

MOANING CAVERN, 2 mi. s.w. on Parrots Ferry Rd., was explored in 1851 by miners, who discovered not the precious metal they sought but prehistoric human remains. Guided 45-minute walking tours descend 165 feet, 100 feet of which are by a steel spiral staircase into a room big enough to hold the Statue of Liberty.

Daily 9-6, Memorial Day-Labor Day; Mon.-Fri. 10-5, Sat.-Sun. 9-5, rest of year. Last tour begins 30 minutes before closing. Walking tour fee $12; over 61, $11; ages 3-13, $6. MC, VI. Phone (209) 736-2708 or (866) 762-2837.

VALLEJO (C-8) pop. 116,760, elev. 40′

In 1851 Gen. Mariano Guadalupe Vallejo (val-LEH-hoh) founded the town that bears his name at the junction of the Carquinez Straits and the Napa River. The general was a citizen of California under both Mexican and U.S. rule. The town served as state capital on two occasions 1851-53. Today Vallejo is the home of the 1,000-student California Maritime Academy and the Sperry Division of General Mills.

From 1854 until 1996 the Mare Island Naval Shipyard was a vital defense installation—during World War I the destroyer USS *Ward* was built here in 17.5 days. Since the installation was closed in the 1990s, the Mare Island Historic Park Foundation has formed to purchase and preserve some of its facilities. Of particular interest is the 1900 St. Peter's Chapel, believed to be the oldest naval chapel in the country. The chapel has 29 Tiffany windows. Arrangements to view the chapel sometimes can be made at the ferry building in Vallejo.

Service by Vallejo Ferry is offered from Pier 39 and the Ferry Building in San Francisco to Vallejo, where shuttle buses can transport visitors to the Six Flags Marine World theme park as well as to Napa Valley.

Vallejo Convention and Visitors Bureau: Vallejo Ferry Terminal, 495 Mare Island Way, Vallejo, CA 94590; phone (707) 642-3653 or (800) 482-5535.

GEM SAVE **SIX FLAGS MARINE WORLD** is at Marine World Pkwy. (SR 37) exit off I-80. This 160-acre wildlife park, oceanarium and theme park combines rides, shows, play areas and educational encounters with wildlife. Dolphins, sea lions, birds, tigers and elephants perform in daily shows.

Highlights include the tropical Butterfly Habitat; Elephant Encounter, where pachyderms are featured in shows, demonstrations and rides; Lorikeet Aviary, where visitors can feed the colorful birds; Giraffe Feeding Dock; Shark Experience, where the predators can be seen through an underwater tunnel; Tiger Island Splash Attack; and Looney Tunes Seaport, with kid-sized rides, play zones and a chance to meet Bugs Bunny and his friends.

Walrus Experience showcases the massive marine mammals in their rocky habitat. Other features include a 3-D motion simulator ride, an animal nursery and veterinary clinic, and a games area. Roller coasters include Zonga, a twisting coaster whose name is Swahili for "loop"; Vertical Velocity, a spiraling coaster that propels riders up and down two 150-foot towers; Medusa, a floorless, seven-loop mega coaster; ROAR, a classic wooden coaster; Kong; and Boomerang.

Food is available. Allow a full day. Park open daily at 10, Memorial Day weekend-Labor Day and during spring break in Apr.; Sat.-Sun. at 10, mid-Mar. through day before Memorial Day weekend (except spring break) and day after Labor Day-Oct. 31. Closing times vary. Phone ahead to confirm hours.

Admission $43.99, over 59 or physically impaired $32.99, under 49 inches tall $26.99, under 3 free. Parking $10. AAA members save 10 percent on select in-park dining and merchandise. Check at the park's Guest Relations window for details. AX, DC, MC, VI. Phone (707) 643-6722 to verify schedule and prices.

SAVE **VALLEJO NAVAL AND HISTORICAL MUSEUM,** in the old Vallejo City Hall building at 734 Marin St., offers exhibits about naval history, including relics and papers from Mare Island Naval Shipyard. Ships models, murals and an operating periscope are displayed. The museum also offers changing exhibits and exhibits about local and regional history.

Tues.-Sat. 10-4:30; closed holidays. Guided 40-minute tours are available by reservation. Admission $2; over 59 and ages 12-17, $1. There is an additional fee for guided tours. Phone (707) 643-0077.

VISALIA (G-5) pop. 91,565, elev. 331′

Founded in 1852, Visalia, known as the gateway to the Sierras, is the oldest city between Stockton and Los Angeles. By the early 20th century its countryside was rich with ranches and farms, and the city's prosperity was reflected in its many lavish houses.

Visalia Chamber of Commerce and Visitors Bureau: 720 W. Mineral King St., Visalia, CA 93291; phone (559) 734-5876 or (877) 847-2542.

MOONEY GROVE PARK, 5 mi. s. at jct. Mooney Blvd. and Ave 272, embraces 155 grassy acres covered with valley oaks and date palms, picnic areas, a lake and recreational facilities. Paddleboats, bicycles and concessions are available weekends. Daily 8 a.m.-9 p.m., Memorial Day-Labor Day; Mon. 8-6, Thurs.-Sun. 8-7, Mar. 1-day before Memorial Day and day after Labor Day-Sept. 30; Thurs.-Mon. 8-5, rest of year. Closed Jan. 1, Dec. 24-31 and county holidays. Admission $5 per private vehicle, over 61 free. Phone (559) 733-6291.

Tulare County Museum, in Mooney Grove Park at 27000 S. Mooney Blvd., displays American Indian artifacts and Tulare County pioneer memorabilia of the late 1800s. Guided tours are available by appointment. Allow 30 minutes minimum. Thurs.-Mon. 10-4; closed President's Day, Martin Luther King, Jr. Day, July 4, Thanksgiving and third Mon. in Dec.-Jan. 2. Free with Mooney Grove Park admission. Under 12 must be with an adult. Phone (559) 733-6616.

VOLCANO (E-4) elev. 2,053′

Volcano, in a deep depression resembling a crater, was aptly named. During the gold rush the city was famous for its dance halls and saloons. Daffodil Hill, 3 miles north, is covered with daffodils originally planted during the 1850s. Blooming season is late March to mid-April.

BLACK CHASM is at 15701 Pioneer-Volcano Rd. The cavern has foot-long crystal formations, large rooms and deep lakes. Visitors descend 60 feet (152 steps) on a 50-minute tour to view stalactites, stalagmites, helictites, draperies, flowstones, columns and keystone bridges, while learning about area history and geology. The cave maintains a constant temperature of 57 F. Gemstone mining also is available.

Allow 1 hour minimum. Daily 9-5, May-Oct.; 10-4, rest of year. Admission $11; ages 3-13, $5.50. An additional fee is charged for gemstone mining. MC, VI. Phone (209) 736-2708 or (866) 762-2837.

INDIAN GRINDING ROCK STATE HISTORIC PARK, 2 mi. off SR 88 at 14881 Pine Grove-Volcano Rd., is a 135-acre park where Miwok Indians chiseled in the main bedrock more than a thousand mortar cups in which they pulverized acorns and other seeds for food. A ceremonial roundhouse and re-created village are featured. Chaw Se' Regional Indian Museum includes artifacts, presentations, exhibits and videotaped programs representing 10 Sierra Nevada Indian tribes.

Camping and picnicking are permitted. Park open daily dawn-dusk. Museum open Mon.-Fri. 11-3, Sat.-Sun. 10-4; closed Jan. 1, Thanksgiving and Dec. 25. Admission $3 per private vehicle; over 61, $2 per private vehicle. Phone (209) 296-7488.

WALNUT CREEK (D-9) pop. 64,296, elev. 135'

THE GARDENS AT HEATHER FARM is at 1540 Marchbanks Dr. Walkways wind among the center's 6 acres, which feature 20 landscaped gardens and learning sites. Included are rose, English meadow, water conservation, sensory, butterfly, native plant, waterfall and rock gardens. A gazebo overlooks a lagoon where ducks and birds gather. Daily dawn-dusk. Gardens free. Guided tours $4; reservations are required. Phone (925) 947-1678, or (925) 947-6712.

SAVE **LINDSAY WILDLIFE MUSEUM,** 1931 First Ave., houses native animals that are unfit for release into the wild. The museum's Wildlife Rehabilitation Hospital, closed to the public, tends to these animals. An exhibit hall features more than 50 species of animals rescued and returned to health. Other displays include natural history items, aquariums, insects and a children's room with hands-on exhibits.

Tues.-Sun. 10-5, mid-June through Labor Day; Tues.-Fri. noon-5, Sat.-Sun. 10-5, rest of year. Holiday hours vary. Admission $6; over 64, $5; ages 3-17, $4. MC, VI. Phone (925) 935-1978.

MOUNT DIABLO STATE PARK—
see Danville p. 69.

WATSONVILLE (G-2) pop. 44,265, elev. 23'

Watsonville's economy relies heavily on the growing of apples, strawberries and flowers. The main harvest time is celebrated in late September and early October.

Pajaro Valley Chamber of Commerce: 444 Main St., P.O. Box 1748, Watsonville, CA 95077-1748; phone (831) 724-3900.

Self-guiding tours: Maps for walking and driving tours of Watsonville and the Pajaro Valley are available from the chamber of commerce.

ELKHORN SLOUGH NATIONAL ESTUARINE RESEARCH RESERVE is e. of SR 1 off Dolan Rd. exit at 1700 Elkhorn Rd. The 1,400-acre coastal area protects the habitat of hundreds of species of birds, fish and invertebrates. It also is an important feeding and resting ground for many waterfowl and migratory shorebirds. Walking trails wind through live oak and eucalyptus groves and along fingers of salt marsh.

Picnicking is permitted near the visitor center; smoking is prohibited on the trails. Dogs are not permitted. Wed.-Sun. 9-5. Guided nature walks originate at the visitor center near the Elkhorn Road entrance and are offered Sat.-Sun. at 10 and 1. Admission $2.50, under 16 free. Phone (831) 728-2822.

WEAVERVILLE (B-2) pop. 3,554, elev. 2,045'

A mining town in the days of '49, Weaverville retains the flavor and colorful atmosphere depicted by author Bret Harte. The town is a starting point for trips into Shasta-Trinity National Forests *(see place listing p. 172)* and Whiskeytown-Shasta-Trinity National Recreation Area *(see place listing p. 181).*

Trinity County Chamber of Commerce: 211 Trinity Lakes Blvd., P.O. Box 517, Weaverville, CA 96093; phone (530) 623-6101 or (800) 487-4648.

J.J. "JAKE" JACKSON MEMORIAL MUSEUM, 508 Main St., displays American Indian relics, Chinese weapons, fossils, a bottle collection and old jail cells with an emphasis on the early pioneer era. Picnic facilities are available. Daily 10-5, May-Oct.; daily noon-4, in Apr. and Nov.; Tues. and Sat. noon-4, rest of year. Donations. Phone (530) 623-5211.

WEAVERVILLE DRUG STORE is at 219 Main St. Said to be California's oldest pharmacy, the drug store has been at the same location since 1852. Apothecary jars, medicine bottles, pill-making machines, tonics, patent medicines and mortars and pestles line the store's top shelves. Mon.-Fri. 10-6, Sat. 11-3; closed Jan. 1, Thanksgiving and Dec. 25. Free. Phone (530) 623-4343.

WEAVERVILLE JOSS HOUSE STATE HISTORIC PARK, at the corner of Main and Oregon sts., contains the oldest wooden Chinese temple still in use in California. Exhibits depict Chinese life, early history and contributions to the state's development. Wed.-Sun. 10-5; closed Jan. 1, Thanksgiving and Dec. 25. Guided 30-minute tours are given every hour 10-4. Admission $2, under 17 free. Phone (530) 623-5284.

WEED (B-3) pop. 2,978, elev. 3,466'

LIVING MEMORIAL SCULPTURE GARDEN is 13 mi. n.e. on US 97 near jct. CR A12. This 132-acre memorial features metal sculptures grouped into 11 themed areas. In addition to American veterans in general, those specifically memorialized include refugees, army nurses, prisoners of war, World War II and Korean War veterans, and helicopter pilots from the Vietnam War. Daily dawn-dusk. Free. Phone (530) 938-2218 or (530) 842-2477.

WEOTT (C-1) elev. 338′

HUMBOLDT REDWOODS STATE PARK, along the Redwood Hwy. between Miranda and Redcrest, covers more than 52,000 acres. The park is famous for the 362-foot Dyerville Giant Tree, considered the world's tallest until it was felled by another tree in 1991; the Rockefeller Forest; and more than 100 memorial redwood groves. Naturalist service is offered in the summer. A visitor center contains redwood and wildlife exhibits.

Park open daily 8 a.m.-11:30 p.m. Visitor center open daily 9-5, Apr.-Oct.; 10-4, rest of year. Closed Dec. 25. Day use fee $4 per private vehicle; over 61, $3 per private vehicle. Visitor center free. Phone (707) 946-2409 for the park or (707) 946-2263 for the visitor center. *See Recreation Chart and the AAA California & Nevada CampBook.*

GEM **Avenue of the Giants**, a 33-mi. section of highway paralleling US 101 between Phillipsville and Pepperwood, winds along the course of Eel River. While the surrounding hills support oak, maple, madrone and pepperwood trees, the magnificent redwoods along this route overshadow all. The two-lane road has numerous parking areas, picnic sites and nature trails that afford a closer look at some of California's most beautiful redwood groves.

WHISKEYTOWN-SHASTA-TRINITY NATIONAL RECREATION AREA (C-2)

At the head of the Sacramento Valley and Upper Trinity River country, north and west of Redding, the 42,500-acre Whiskeytown-Shasta-Trinity National Recreation Area's three components embrace four major dam-created lakes: Whiskeytown, about 8 miles west of Redding via SR 299; Trinity and Lewiston, northeast of Weaverville; and Shasta, north of Redding.

Recreational gold panning using a metal or plastic gold pan is permitted in the Whiskeytown unit only; annual permits are required and are available at the park for $1. Other recreational activities include hiking, swimming, personal watercraft riding, boating and sailing.

Area open daily dawn-dusk. Visitor center open daily 9-5 in summer; otherwise varies. Day-use fee $5 per private vehicle; a fee is charged for camping. Phone (530) 242-3400 for park information, or Biospherics Inc. at (800) 365-2267 for camping reservations. *See Recreation Chart and the AAA California & Nevada CampBook.*

WILLIAMS (D-2) pop. 3,670, elev. 80′

SAVE **SACRAMENTO VALLEY MUSEUM,** 1 mi. w. of I-5 at 1491 E St. in the two-story Williams High School building, includes 27 rooms that depict life in the Sacramento Valley area from the mid-1800s to the 1930s. Among them are an apothecary, a kitchen, a children's room with dolls in 1500-1920s apparel, a millinery and dress shop, an old-fashioned general store and a documents room with deeds signed by United States presidents.

Thurs.-Sat. 10-4, Mar.-Nov.; closed major holidays. Tours are available by appointment Mon.-Fri. 10-4. Admission $2; under 17, $1. Additional charge for events. Phone (530) 473-2978.

WILLITS—*see Wine Country p. 202.*

WILLOWS (D-2) pop. 6,220, elev. 135′

SACRAMENTO NATIONAL WILDLIFE REFUGE, 7 mi. s. on SR 99W, affords a 10,783-acre wintering area for migratory birds, especially ducks and geese. The best season to view waterfowl is November through January. Among the more than 265 bird species frequenting the area are hawks, egrets and herons. A 6-mile auto route and 2-mile self-guiding walking trail meander through part of the refuge.

Refuge open daily dawn-dusk. Visitor center open daily 7:30-4, Oct.-Mar.; Mon.-Fri. 7:30-4, rest of year. Admission $3 per private vehicle. Phone (530) 934-2801, or (530) 934-7774 for recorded information.

WINDSOR—*see Wine Country p. 202.*

Wine Country

You're in a basket beneath a hot air balloon, soaring over a two-lane country road cradled in a lush valley. Acre upon acre of the landscape is planted with neat rows of leafy grapevines, forming pale green pinstripes against the fertile soil. Red rosebushes mark the beginnings of some rows, which extend from the road and seem to disappear into forested hills. Beyond the rolling hills are rocky ocean bluffs and dark stands of redwoods, their feathery branches sheltering a damp, fern-carpeted ground. The ride is quiet and seemingly still, following the whim of the wind with only the roar of the burners to break the silence.

"Heaven?" you ask. Close. You're in Wine Country. And while the views in Napa, Sonoma, Lake and Mendocino counties are enough to make you dizzy with delight, this pinstriped countryside isn't for shutterbugs alone.

There's a business growing here, and a fruitful one at that. Every year some 300 wineries produce nearly 2 billion bottles of wine thanks to an ideal, varied climate—balmy days with cool mornings and evenings interspersed with floating blankets of Pacific fog. Add relatively cheap labor and mineral-rich soil, and the bottled result has caught the eyes, noses and palates of connoisseurs around the globe.

With all its options for fun—hot air ballooning, shopping in elite boutiques, hiking, touring historical sites, kayaking, gorging on sinfully delicious gourmet food, horseback riding, relaxing with a massage, sinking into a mud or mineral bath or bicycling—it still comes as no surprise that most visitors are here for one thing: fermented grape juice. Yes, the sweet nectar of the gods.

It's All About the Wine

Napa Valley's main drag, SR 29—as well as its parallel counterpart, the Silverado Trail—is a north-south valley bisector with stunning mountain views to the east and west. The rural route leads from the town of Napa north through St. Helena's picturesque Main Street to the hot springs and mud bath mecca of Calistoga. Farmers in pickup trucks along with locals in Land Rovers pack the lanes, making way for bicyclists. Small wooden signs facing the road denote grapes grown here: Cabernet Sauvignon, Chardonnay, Chenin Blanc, Merlot, Pinot Noir, Riesling, Sauvignon Blanc or the precious, California-grown Zinfandel.

Large signs proclaim grape owners, names no doubt you've seen adorning labels on wine bottles in your local grocery store—Beringer, Robert Mondavi, Sutter Home

Sonoma / © Lee Foster / Lonely Planet Images

Napa / © Roland & Karen Muschenetz / Alamy Images

and hundreds of others sharing soil in this world famous viticultural region.

Peppering the valley floor are magnificent winery estates: orange-hued, postmodern Clos Pegase; Sterling Vineyard's white, Greek island-style stucco building; Oscar-winning Francis Ford Coppola's giant, gray stone chateau; the gabled, Victorian Rhine House (complete with Art Nouveau-style stained-glass windows) at Beringer; and the simple, California mission-style Robert Mondavi Winery.

Choose a winery—perhaps St. Supéry, Domaine Chandon, Niebaum-Coppola or Beaulieu—and follow the drive to its majestic mansion. You'll pass workers tending to the expansive rows of vines. Take a tour to learn about the delicate art of winemaking, from the plucking of sweet, plump grapes to the long-awaited popping of the cork.

You may be surprised to find how scientific the process is; gone are the days when ladies tied up their skirts, removed their shoes and stomped on juicy grapes until their toes turned purple. Winemaking is a complicated, subjective blend of technology, nature and experience. Biologists, chemists and winemakers each have a hand in the steps from grape to glass.

After you've walked through a vineyard, felt the cold steel of a giant, shiny fermentation tank, smelled the scent of grapes fermenting, watched bottles clattering along an assembly line and glimpsed the winery's high-tech presses, filters and computers, you might be convinced that paying $75 for a bottle of Cabernet Sauvignon is reasonable. But how does it *taste?*

First-time tasters might be intimidated by the overwhelming and confusing terminology used to evaluate wines. Don't fret! When sampling, just remember four little words: Look. Swirl. Smell. Taste.

Wine Tasting 101

First, take a good look at the wine. Hold the glass (by the stem, please) up to the light, or place a white napkin behind it. Note the *color* of the wine, a clue to its age. White wines, ranging from pale yellow (straw) to amber, darken with age. Red wines, which appear light purple to deep ruby, lighten with age. Also notice the *clarity* of the wine. Is it clear or cloudy? Next look at the *brightness*—brilliant or opaque?

Second, swirl the wine. Not only is this quite fun, but it oxygenates the wine, releasing its aromas. Observe its *legs,* little drops running down inside the glass after it's swirled.

Now hold the glass under your nose and sniff sharply. (Don't worry, everyone's doing it.) Remark about its *nose*—the scent determined by smelling

(continued on p. 190)

Destination Wine Country

Hills are covered in vines. Wineries line the roadsides. Festivals celebrate the grape "crush." Gift shops sell bottle tags, assorted varieties of corkscrews, decanters and other wine-related sundries. Phrases like "full-bodied, good nose, assertive and complex" are most likely compliments about a Pinot Noir. And a feeling of luxury hangs heavy as morning fog.

Did you bring cheese and crackers? The wine is waiting.

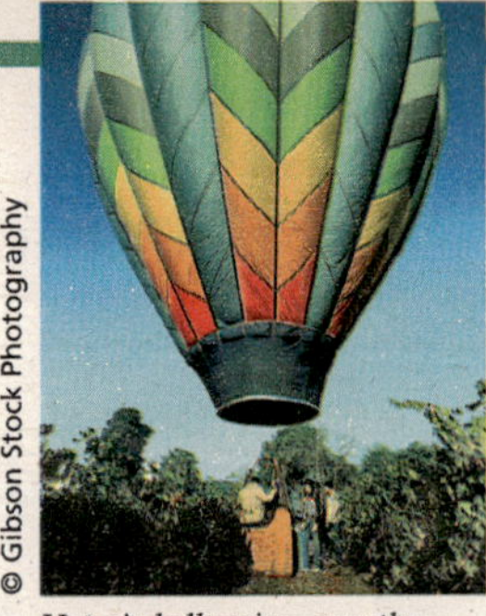

© Gibson Stock Photography

Hot air ballooning over the Napa Valley.
Colorful hot air balloons provide spectacular views of green valleys, forested hills and lazy rivers as well as grape-laden vineyards.

© Gibson Stock Photography

Beringer Winery, St. Helena.
Tastings are given in this mansion, which was modeled after a family home in Germany. (See listing page 199)

© Gibson Stock Photography

Culinary Institute of America, St. Helena.
The prestigious culinary school's Napa Valley campus offers cooking demonstrations and top-notch dining featuring local ingredients. (See mention page 199)

Places included in this AAA Destination Area:

© Gibson Stock Photography

Napa Valley Wine Train, Napa.
The elegance of a 1917 Pullman dining car and a gourmet meal make for a memorable 36-mile journey through the heart of Wine Country. (See listing page 196)

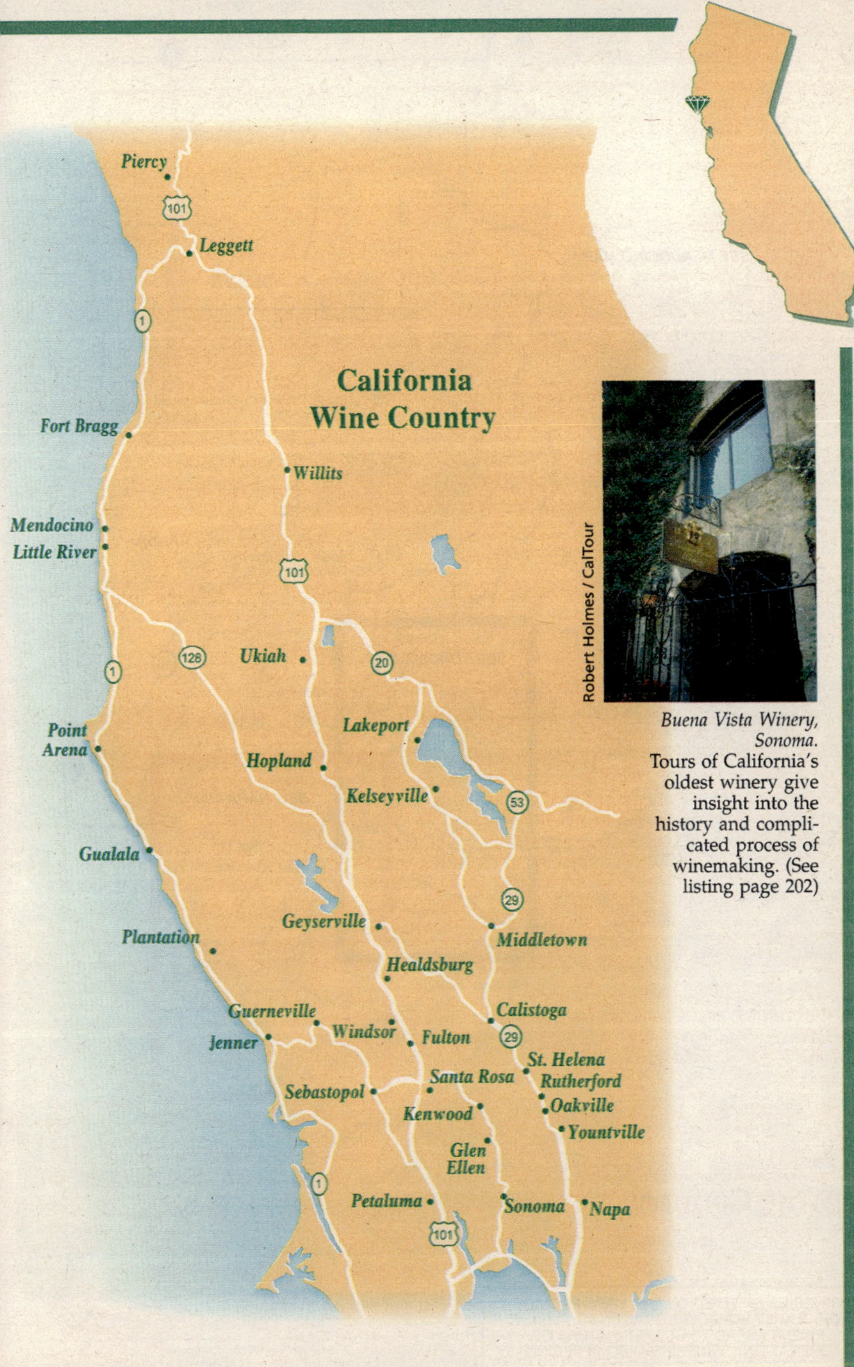

Buena Vista Winery, Sonoma. Tours of California's oldest winery give insight into the history and complicated process of winemaking. (See listing page 202)

WINERIES SPOTTED ON THE MAPS PROVIDE REGULARLY SCHEDULED TASTINGS; PLEASE PHONE AHEAD TO CONFIRM HOURS OF OPERATION. WINERIES ALSO OFFERING GUIDED OR SELF-GUIDED TOURS ARE BULLETED IN THE WINE COUNTRY DESCRIPTIVE SECTION UNDER THE APPROPRIATE TOWN.

Sonoma County Wineries
Miles 0 5.2
MENDOCINO
SONOMA
LAKE
MARIN
Cloverdale
Cloverdale Municipal Airport
Fritz Winery
Lake Sonoma Winery
Lake Sonoma Visitor Center
Ferrari-Carano Vineyards & Winery
Preston Vineyards & Winery
Quivira Vineyards
F Teldeschi Winery
Pezzi King Vineyards
Dry Creek Vineyard
Lambert Bridge Winery
Healdsburg Municipal Airport
Geyserville
De Lorimier Winery
Chateau Souverain Winery
Canyon Road Winery
Clos Du Bois Winery
Trentadue Winery
Murphy-Goode Winery
Ridge-Lytton Springs Winery
Mazzocco Vineyards
Sausal Winery
Alexander Valley Vineyards
Johnson's Alexander Valley Wines
Hanna Winery
Field Stone Winery
Simi Winery
The Healdsburg Museum
Windsor Vineyards
Healdsburg
Seghesio Winery
Bellerose Vineyard
Everett Ridge Winery
Alderbrook Winery
Rabbit Ridge Vineyards
Foppiano Vineyards
Christopher Creek Winery
Limerick Lane
Mill Creek Vineyards
Armida
Rodney Strong Vineyards
Belvedere Winery
J Vineyards & Winery
Hop Kiln Winery
Rochioli Vineyards & Winery
Korbel Champagne Cellars
Davis Bynum Winery
Mark West Vineyard
Windsor
Windsor Waterworks and Slides
Fulton
Sonoma County Airport
Kendall-Jackson
Martinelli Winery
Z Moore Winery
Paradise Ridge Winery
Hartford Family Winery
Joseph Swan Vineyards
Martini and Prati Winery
De Loach Vineyards
Topolos Winery
Iron Horse Vineyards
Fountain Grove Vineyard
Sebastopol Vineyards
Sonoma County Museum
Charles M Schulz Museum
Luther Burbank Home & Gardens
Santa Rosa
Annadel State Park
Matanzas Creek Winery
Taft Street Winery
Guerneville
Monte Rio
Occidental
Sebastopol
Rohnert Park
Cobb
Middletown
Robert Louis Stevenson State Park
Chateau Montelena Winery
Old Faithful Geyser of California
Safari West
Petrified Forest
Russian River
©2003 NAVIGATION TECHNOLOGIES
1203-A

Napa & Sonoma Valleys
Miles
0
3.9
N
Lake Berryessa
BERRYESSA KN OXVILLE RD
POPE CANYON RD
CHILES & POPE VALLEY RD
LOWER CHILES VALLEY RD
HOWELL MOUNTAIN RD
CAPELL VALLEY RD
MONTICELLO RD
ATLAS PEAK RD
SAGE CANYON RD
SILVERADO TRL
ST HELENA HWY
SPRING MOUNTAIN RD
ST HELENA RD
CALISTOGA RD
PETRIFIED FOREST RD
FOOTHILL BLVD
TUBBS LN
LARKMEAD LN
OAKVILLE CROSS RD
OAKVILLE GRADE RD
YOUNTVILLE CROSS RD
DRY
TRINITY RD
SONOMA HWY
WARM SPRINGS RD
BENNETT VALLEY RD
GRANGE RD
SEE INSET MAP FOR DETAIL
Chateau Montelena
Old Faithful Geyser of California
Zahtila Vineyards
Sharpsteen Museum
Calistoga
Clos Pegase
Dutch Henry Winery
Cuvaison Winery
Sterling Vineyards
Stonegate Winery
Villa Amorosa
Larkmead Vineyards
Rombauer Vineyards
Chateau Boswell
Petrified Forest
Safari West
Bothe-Napa Valley State Park
Bale Grist Mill State Historic Park
St. Helena
Nichelini Winery
Plump Jack Winery
Miner Family Winery
Rudd Vineyards and Winery
Rutherford
Peju Province Winery
St Supery Vineyards
Oakville
Cakebread Cellars
Robert Mondavi Winery
Sequoia Grove Vineyards
Silver Oak Cellars
Cardinal Winery
Napa Cellars
Cosentino Winery
S Anderson/ Cliff Lede Vineyards
Robert Sinskey Vineyards
Silverado Vineyards
Steltzner Vineyards
Pine Ridge Winery
Stag's Leap Wine Cellars
Chimney Rock Winery
Clos Du Val Wine Co
White Rock Vineyards
Signorello Vineyards
Monticello Vineyards
Van Der Heyden Vineyards & Winery
Trefethen Vineyards
Yountville
Domaine Chandon Winery
Bernard Pradel Cellars
Koves-Newland Vineyards & Winery
Laird Family Estate
Chateau Potelle
Hood Mountain Regional Park
Sugarloaf Ridge State Park
Landmark Vineyards
Kaz Vineyard & Winery
Chateau St Jean
Kenwood Vineyard
Kenwood
Kunde Estate Winery
St Francis Winery
Annadel State Park
Matanzas Creek Winery
Spring Lake Park
Wellington Vineyards
Glen Ellen
Sonoma Valley Regional Park
Arrowood Vineyards & Winery
B R Cohn Winery
Benziger Family Winery
128
29
12
121
1204-A

Jack London State Historic Park
SONOMA
Goodtime Touring Company
Petaluma Adobe State Historic Park
Petaluma Municipal Airport
Mrs. Grossman's Tours
Petaluma History Museum
Petaluma
PETALUMA HILL
ADOBE RD
WASHINGTON ST
PETALUMA BLVD
SPRING HILL RD
FRATES RD
LAKEVILLE HWY
STAGE GULCH RD
MADRONE RD
ARNOLD DR
BOYES BLVD
VERANO AVE
PETALUMA AVE
SONOMA HWY
Ravenswood Winery
Sonoma State Historic Park
Sonoma
E NAPA ST
Train Town
BROADWAY
LEVARONI RD
WATMAUGH RD
Schug Carneros Estate Winery
GEH RICKE RD
Collection Winery
Bartholomew Park Winery
Buena Vista Carneros Winery
Sebastiani Vineyards
Codorniu Napa
Gundlach-Bundschu Winery
Carneros Creek Winery
HENRY RD
NAPA RD
Homewood Winery
Gloria Ferrer Champagne Caves
Viansa Winery
Cline Cellars
Roche Winery
BUHMAN RD
DEALY LN
DUHIG RD
LAS AMIGAS RD
Domaine Carneros
Madonna Estate
Bouchaine Vineyards
NAPA
BROWNS VALLEY RD
CREEK RD
TRANCAS ST
Napa
Vineyards
HAGEN RD
Round Hill Cellars
Copia The American Center For Wine, Food & The Arts
COOMBSVILLE RD
IMOLA AVE
Skyline Park
NAPA VALLEJO HWY
Hakusan Sake Gardens
Napa County Airport
JAMESON CANYON RD
SONOMA BLVD
AMERICAN CANYON RD
FLOSDEN RD
Six Flags Marine World
SOLANO
LAKE HERMAN RD
TENNESSEE ST
MARINE WORLD PKY
SEARS POINT RD
San Pablo Bay
Vallejo Naval and Historical Museum
Vallejo
Benicia State Park
©2003 NAVIGATION TECHNOLOGIES
0 Miles 1
Ehlers Grove Cartlidge/Brown Winery
Folie a Deux Winery
DEER PARK RD
Freemark Abbey Winery
Markham Vineyards
St Clement Vineyards
Charles Krug Winery
William Harrison Vineyards
Robert Louis Stevenson Silverado Museum
SPRING MOUNTAIN RD
Beringer Vineyards
St. Helena
Napa Valley Museum
Sutter Home Winery
Prager Winery
Edgewood Estate Winery
Milat Vineyards
POPE ST
Merryvale Vineyards
Louis M Martini Winery
V Sattui Winery
SILVERADO TRL
HELENA HWY
Rutherford Grove
Grgich Hills Cellar
Niebaum-Coppola Estate Winery
Beaulieu Vineyards
ZINFANDEL LN
Raymond Vineyard & Cellar
Franciscan Oakville Estate
Opus One
Mumm Napa Valley Winery
Conn Creek Winery
Heitz Wine Cellars
Rutherford Hill Winery
CONN VALLEY RD
Anderson's Conn Valley Vineyards
Villa Mt Eden Winery
CONN CREEK RD
RUTHERFORD RD
Rutherford
Zd Wines

alone. A good nose reveals a strong *bouquet*—the fragrance acquired as a result of the wine's aging process. Usually, the bigger the bouquet, the older the wine. But here's the best part: determining the wine's *aroma*. Scents recall the grape used to make the wine, and there are numerous aromas associated with each varietal. They range from grapefruit to cream to butterscotch for a Chardonnay; mint to grass to apricot for a Sauvignon Blanc; or blackberry to cloves to olives for a Zinfandel.

Take a big drink of the wine. Let it flow over your tongue and chew it like pasta, allowing it to reach all the taste buds. Identify its *taste*—a Chenin Blanc may suggest red apple, while a Cabernet Sauvignon might hint of cedar. Determine the *balance* (how the flavors combine): A good wine evenly blends its sugar, tannins (astringents found in red wines) and fruit. Observe the *body*, the way the liquid feels on your tongue. This may range from thin and light to full and heavy. Finally, swallow and note the *length* or *finish*, the aftertaste: How long does it last, and how does the taste differ from the initial flavor?

Sound confusing? It just takes time, similar to how the region attained notoriety for its wine. Missionary Padre José Altimira brought vine cuttings to Sonoma Valley in 1823 to make wine for Catholic mass, but it was Hungarian nobleman "Count" Agoston Haraszthy who created the California wine industry as we know it. In 1857 he planted European varieties and established Buena Vista, the state's oldest winery. You'll find the original, ivy-clad stone buildings tucked away near the town of Sonoma, where the winery shares a quiet, rustic road alongside homes, farms and vineyards.

A peaceful bike ride along Sonoma's streets may afford a glimpse of a resident peacock, often seen trotting along Lovall Valley Road. Pedal to Sebastiani Winery for a sample. Then tour Sonoma State Historic Park, comprised of numerous sites near Sonoma Plaza. Together they tell the story of early "Alta" California and the establishment of a brief, 26-day California Republic.

Drive along SR 12, Sonoma Valley's thoroughfare, for more tastings at Benziger, Glen Ellen,

Chateau St. John or Kunde. Vintners here are especially friendly and easygoing. West of SR 12, the Russian River Wine Road traverses through the Russian River Valley, where vineyards are neighbors to Gravenstein apple orchards, redwood forests and a lazy river.

If you've reached your tolerance for wine, visit Petaluma for enough brightly-colored Victorians to make your jaw drop; Santa Rosa for gorgeous gardens; and Healdsburg for scads of antique shops and art galleries. Or pack your fishing pole and head to giant Clear Lake.

But by all means, don't pass up a trip to the spectacular Pacific coast. Mendocino, a sleepy hamlet with adorable New England-style architecture, rests on bluffs overlooking a lively blue ocean. Rainbow-colored wildflowers dot the grassy headlands in spring, and eruptive white water spills over jagged ocean rocks. Day-trippers have the option of hiking, kayaking or horseback riding, and a coastal drive along winding SR 1 is sure to elicit gasps and silly grins on the faces of photographers, artists and nature buffs.

To end the day, stop by a deli, bakery or roadside produce stand and fill a picnic basket with homegrown and homemade delicacies. Find a quiet spot to relax on the coast and watch the sunset. Pull the cork on a bottle of the area's claim to fame, make a toast and drink it all up.

CALISTOGA (B-8) pop. 5,190, elev. 362′

At the head of Napa Valley, Calistoga is known for its natural hot-water geysers, mineral springs and mineralized mud baths. Numerous day spas reside downtown, which has an Old West feel. Some of California's finest vineyards cover the surrounding region, and an extinct volcano lies north of town.

Calistoga is the southern terminus of a scenic 94-mile stretch of SR 128 that heads northwest to the coastal city of Albion. Scenic SR 29 runs 28 miles south to Napa through the valley.

Calistoga Chamber of Commerce and Visitor's Center: 1458 Lincoln Ave. #9, Calistoga, CA 94515; phone (707) 942-6333.

SAVE **OLD FAITHFUL GEYSER OF CALIFORNIA,** 1 mi. n. on Tubbs Ln. between SRs 29 and 128, is one of the few regularly erupting geysers in the world. Fed by an underground river, the water heats to 350 degrees Fahrenheit and erupts about every 30 minutes for 1 to 2 minutes on average, spewing 60 feet into the air. Earthquake activity might disrupt normal eruption patterns. Self-guiding geothermal tours are available.

Picnicking is permitted. Daily 9-6, May-Sept.; 9-5, rest of year. Admission $8; over 60, $7; ages 6-12, $3. MC, VI. Phone (707) 942-6463.

PETRIFIED FOREST, 5 mi. w. on Petrified Forest Rd., preserves the texture and fiber of giant petrified redwoods. The grounds also contain a museum and picnic facilities. Allow 30 minutes minimum.

Wine Country

The Automobile Club of Southern California publishes *Southern and Central California Wineries* and *Northern California Wineries* which feature maps and information about California wineries and the process of winemaking and its history in the state. The publications are available at offices of the Automobile Club of Southern California and the California State Automobile Association and are free to AAA/CAA members. They are not available by mail.

Spotlight's Wine Country Guide, a 100-page brochure providing maps and detailed information about towns, events, wineries, attractions, accommodations and retail establishments in Lake, Lower Mendocino, Napa and Sonoma counties is available free at the concierge desk of most Bay Area hotels, at most retail establishments in Wine Country and at northern California AAA offices. The brochure's 4-month calendar of events is updated monthly.

Digital Archives

The brochure is available from the publisher for $3.50 to cover postage and handling. Write *Spotlight's Wine Country Guide,* 5 Kenilworth Ct., Novato, CA 94945; phone (415) 898-7908, or fax (415) 898-7751.

Daily 9-7, Memorial Day-Labor Day; 9-6, day after Labor Day-Oct. 31; 9-5, rest of year. Closed Dec. 25. Admission $5; over 59 and ages 12-17, $4; ages 6-11, $3. AX, DS, MC, VI. Phone (707) 942-6667.

SHARPSTEEN MUSEUM, 1311 Washington St., displays artifacts, photographs and dioramas depicting 19th-century Calistoga; a scale model of Calistoga Hot Springs Resort is included. Next to the museum is one of the resort's 1860s cottages. In addition to the permanent exhibits, which include an interactive geothermal display, is a rotating exhibit that changes every 3 months. Docents conduct tours on request. Daily 11-4; closed Thanksgiving and Dec. 25. Donations. Phone (707) 942-5911.

RECREATIONAL ACTIVITIES

Hot Air Ballooning

- **Calistoga Ballooning** departs from various locations. Write P.O. Box 985, Calistoga, CA 94515. Trips depart daily at dawn (weather permitting). Phone (707) 944-2822 or (800) 359-6272.

WINERIES

- **Clos Pegase** is e. off SR 29 at 1060 Dunaweal Ln. Daily 10:30-5; closed some holidays. Guided tours are given daily at 11 and 2. Phone (707) 942-4981.
- **Cuvaison Winery** is e. off SR 29 on Dunaweal Ln., then s. to 4550 Silverado Tr. Daily 10-5, early Apr.-late Oct.; Sun.-Thurs. 11-4, Fri.-Sat. 10-5, rest of year. Phone (707) 942-6266.
- **Sterling Vineyards** is between SR 29 and Silverado Tr. at 1111 Dunaweal Ln. Daily 10:30-4:30; closed Jan. 1, Thanksgiving and Dec. 25. Phone (707) 942-3344 or (800) 726-6136.

FORT BRAGG (D-1) pop. 7,026, elev. 80'

Fort Bragg, on a scenic stretch of SR 1 that extends from Leggett to Sausalito, was established in 1857 to oversee the Mendocino Indian Reservation. When the reservation was moved, the fort was abandoned and subsequently became a lumber and port town. Noyo Harbor, at the south end of town, is a small commercial fishing port; fishing and whale-watching cruises are available.

More than 60,000 fuchsia plants are on display at Fuchsiarama, a nursery and garden at 23201 N. SR 1; phone (707) 964-0429. Just north of town is MacKerricher State Park *(see Recreation Chart)*, home to tidal flats, headlands and a lagoon. The park offers horseback riding and camping opportunities.

Fort Bragg-Mendocino Coast Chamber of Commerce: 332 N. Main St., P.O. Box 1141, Fort Bragg, CA 95437; phone (707) 961-6300 or (800) 726-2780.

GEM SAVE **MENDOCINO COAST BOTANICAL GARDENS,** 1 mi. s. on SR 1, encompasses 47 acres of gardens featuring numerous varieties of camellias, dahlias, fuchsias, heathers, Pacifica irises, rhododendrons and roses. Two creeks wind through a lush native forest filled with ferns and pines, and perennials and succulents are planted in beds along grass trails.

Paths lead from a nursery to scenic ocean bluffs adorned with wildflowers and ice plants. Three miles of trails meander through the gardens, leading to the ocean. A vegetable garden, a meadow and picnic areas flank the trails. Free electric carts are available.

Allow 1 hour minimum. Daily 9-5, Mar.-Oct.; 9-4, rest of year. Closed Sat. after Labor Day, Thanksgiving and Dec. 25. Admission $7.50; over 60, $6; ages 13-17, $3; ages 6-12, $1. DS, MC, VI. Phone (707) 964-4352.

SKUNK TRAIN, departing from the Skunk Depot on Laurel St. w. off SR 1, travels from Fort Bragg to Willits through Northspur. The 40-mile trip passes through redwood groves and two tunnels and across 30 bridges. The unusual name is from the gas engines that power the 1925 passenger rail cars. The Skunk Line operates different trains, including vintage 1925 and 1935 motorcars as well as engines powered by diesel and steam. Half- and full-day trips are available.

Note: At press time the status of the train for the 2004 season was uncertain; phone ahead to confirm schedule. Half-day trips depart daily Mar.-Nov. Full-day trips depart daily mid-May to late Oct. Closed Thanksgiving. Half-day fare $29-$39; ages 3-14, $18. Full-day round-trip fare $45; ages 3-14, $25. Family rates are available. Reservations are recommended. MC, VI. Phone (707) 964-6371 or (800) 777-5865.

RECREATIONAL ACTIVITIES

Horseback Riding

- **Ricochet Ridge Ranch**, 2 mi. n. of Pudding Creek Bridge at 24201 SR 1, Fort Bragg, CA 95437. Rides are offered daily at 10, noon, 2, 4 and by appointment. Phone (707) 964-7669 or (888) 873-5777.

FULTON (B-7) elev. 132'

WINERIES

- **Kendall-Jackson Wine Center** is w. off US 101 at 5007 Fulton Rd. Daily 10-5. Tours are given at 11, 1 and 3 (weather permitting). Phone (707) 571-7500.

GEYSERVILLE (A-7) elev. 209'

LAKE SONOMA VISITOR CENTER, 3333 Skaggs Springs Rd., displays Pomo Indian baskets and arrowheads and local flora and fauna. The center provides information about recreational activities in the Lake Sonoma/Warm Springs Dam area. King salmon, silver salmon and steelhead are raised at Don Clausen Fish Hatchery. A swim area is available at Yorty Creek. Allow 2 hours minimum. Visitor center open Wed.-Sun. 8-8. Fish hatchery Wed.-Sun. 9-3:45. Free. Phone (707) 433-9483.

GLEN ELLEN (B-8) pop. 992, elev. 230′

JACK LONDON STATE HISTORIC PARK, 1 mi. w. on London Ranch Rd., contains 800 acres and encompasses the author's ranch, house and grave. The two-story museum house contains his papers, personal belongings and mementos of his travels, including South Pacific art objects. The burnt ruins of Wolf House, the 26-room mansion he built but never lived in, are nearby. The original cottage which London purchased is open weekends.

Off-road vehicles are not permitted. Leashed dogs are permitted in historic area only. Allow 1 hour, 30 minutes minimum. Park open daily 9:30-7, mid-May to mid-Oct.; 9:30-5, rest of year. Museum open daily 10-5; closed Jan. 1, Thanksgiving and Dec. 25. Fee $5 per private vehicle; over 61, $4 per private vehicle. Phone (707) 938-5216. *See Recreation Chart.*

WINERIES

- **Benziger Family Winery** is at 1883 London Ranch Rd. Daily 10-5; closed Jan. 1, Thanksgiving and Dec. 25. Tours are given daily on the half-hour 11-3. Phone (888) 490-2739.
- **B.R. Cohn Winery** is at 15000 Sonoma Hwy. Tastings and self-guiding tours daily 10-5. Phone (707) 938-4064 or (800) 330-4064, ext. 24.

GUALALA (E-1) elev. 67′

Originally settled by Pomo Indians, Gualala (wa-LA-la) means "where the water meets," due to its location above the mouth of the Gualala River and the Pacific Ocean. Formerly sustained by redwood logging and milling, the town is now a popular weekend retreat known for its steelhead fishing, abalone diving and kayaking.

Redwood Coast Chamber of Commerce: P.O. Box 199, Gualala, CA 95445; phone (707) 884-1080 or (800) 778-5252.

RECREATIONAL ACTIVITIES

Kayaking

- **Adventure Rents** is downtown on SR 1 in the Cantamare Center. Write P.O. Box 489, Gualala, CA 95445. Daily 9:30-5:30, May-Oct.; by reservation (weather permitting), rest of year Phone (707) 884-4386 or (888) 881-4386.

GUERNEVILLE (B-7) pop. 2,441, elev. 56′

Lumber mills flourished during Guerneville's early years. Railroads were built to ship wood from the town, and agricultural endeavors were undertaken on the cleared land.

The Russian River Chamber of Commerce and Visitor Information Center: 16201 First St., P.O. Box 331, Guerneville, CA 95446; phone (707) 869-9000.

WINERIES

- **Korbel Champagne Cellars**, 13250 River Rd. Daily 9-5, May-Sept.; 9-4:30, rest of year. Phone (707) 824-7000.

HEALDSBURG (A-7) pop. 10,722, elev. 106′

Healdsburg, founded in 1867, was once a part of the 48,800-acre Sotoyome Rancho owned by widow Josefa Fitch and her 11 children. While the family sought refuge at Sutter's Fort during American Indian uprisings and the Mexican War, Harmon Heald and many other failed gold miners illegally squatted on her land. Fitch won ownership of the original title to the rancho, but Heald donated some of the rancho he had bought for a park, school, cemetery and church and then named this new town after himself.

Healdsburg Chamber of Commerce and Visitors Bureau: 217 Healdsburg Ave., Healdsburg, CA 95448; phone (707) 433-6935, or (800) 648-9922 in Calif.

Self-guiding tours: Maps for tours of historic buildings as well as a winery map are available at the chamber of commerce and visitors bureau for $2.

THE HEALDSBURG MUSEUM is 2 blks. e. of the downtown plaza at 221 Matheson St. Housed in the refurbished 1910 Healdsburg Carnegie Library, the museum preserves and exhibits a range of relics and documents pertaining to northern Sonoma County history. Items displayed include 19th-century weapons, tools, textiles and crafts along with Pomo Indian basketry and other artifacts. Allow 30 minutes minimum. Tues.-Sun. 11-4; closed major holidays. Free. Phone (707) 431-3325.

WINERIES

- **Foppiano Vineyards** is just s. at 12707 Old Redwood Hwy. Tastings and self-guiding tours daily 10-4:30. Phone (707) 433-7272.
- **Johnson's Alexander Valley Wines** is 7 mi. n.e. at 8333 SR 128. Daily 11-4; closed Jan. 1, Thanksgiving and Dec. 25. Phone (707) 433-2319.
- **Rodney Strong Vineyards** is 3 mi. s. off US 101 at 11455 Old Redwood Hwy. Daily 10-5; closed Thanksgiving and Dec. 25. Tours are given daily at 11 and 3. Phone (707) 431-1533.
- **Simi Winery**, US 101 to Dry Creek Rd., e. to Healdsburg Ave., then 1 mi. n. Daily 10-5; closed holidays. Guided tours are given at 11, 1 and 3. Phone (707) 433-6981.

HOPLAND (D-1) elev. 488′

REAL GOODS' SOLAR LIVING CENTER, 13771 US 101S, encompasses 12 acres of outdoor displays about energy conservation, recycling and solar power. Highlights include permaculture gardens, unusual living structures, solar timepieces and a building constructed of rice straw bales. Mon.-Sat. 10-7, Sun. 10-6, Memorial Day-Labor Day; Mon.-Sat. 10-6, Sun. 10-5, rest of year. Closed Thanksgiving and Dec. 25. Guided tours available Fri.-Sun. at 11 and 3. Free. Phone (707) 744-2100.

JENNER (E-1) elev. 12′

FORT ROSS STATE HISTORIC PARK, 12 mi. n. on SR 1, was the site of a trading post and fort established by Russians in 1812 to protect their claim against the Spanish. Restored or reconstructed buildings within the stockade include the chapel, officers' barracks, commandant's house and blockhouses. The visitor center includes a museum. Cultural Heritage Day is held the last Saturday in July. Russian Orthodox services are held Memorial Day and July 4.

Allow 1 hour minimum. Grounds daily dawn-dusk. Visitor center daily 10-4:30. Closed Jan. 1, Thanksgiving and Dec. 25. Fee $4 per private vehicle; over 61, $3 per private vehicle. Cultural Heritage Day admission $15. Phone (707) 847-3286. *See Recreation Chart and the AAA California & Nevada CampBook.*

KELSEYVILLE (D-1) pop. 2,928, elev. 1,386′

Called the "Bartlett Pear Capital of the World," Kelseyville is the agricultural center of Lake County. Pear and walnut orchards share the surrounding valley with vineyards.

CLEAR LAKE STATE PARK VISITORS CENTER, 3 mi. n.e. at 5300 Soda Bay Rd., has wildlife dioramas and exhibits depicting the lake environment both on land and in water. A theater presents videos, films and demonstrations. Allow 1 hour minimum. Tues.-Fri. 1-4, Sat.-Sun. 10-4, July-Aug. Park admission $4 per private vehicle; over 62, $3 per private vehicle. Phone (707) 279-4293. *See Recreation Chart and the AAA California & Nevada CampBook.*

KENWOOD (B-8) elev. 415′

WINERIES

- **Kunde Estate Winery & Vineyards** is at 10155 Sonoma Hwy. (SR 12). Daily 10:30-4:30. Guided tours are given Mon.-Thurs. at 11, Fri.-Sun. on the hour 11-3. Phone (707) 833-5501.

LAKEPORT (D-1) pop. 4,820, elev. 1,343′

On the western shore of Clear Lake *(see Recreation Chart and the AAA California & Nevada CampBook)*, one of California's largest, Lakeport is known for its excellent fishing (especially bass) and water recreation.

Lake County Visitor Information Center: 6110 E. Hwy. 20, P.O. Box 1025, Lucerne, CA 95458; phone (707) 274-5652 or (800) 525-3743.

LAKE COUNTY HISTORIC COURTHOUSE MUSEUM, 255 N. Main St., contains displays of items depicting Pomo Indian culture, period rooms of the late 1800s and early 1900s, and a gem and mineral collection. Changing exhibits also are featured. Allow 1 hour minimum. Wed.-Sat. 10-4, Sun. noon-4. Donations. Phone (707) 263-4555.

LEGGETT (C-1)

Leggett is at the crossroads of the Redwood Highway (US 101) and scenic SR 1. The town is near the ocean, wine country and redwood forests.

CHANDELIER TREE, in Drive-Thru Tree Park on US 101, towers 315 feet into the air and is 21 feet in diameter. Visitors can drive a full-size automobile through the hand-hewn opening at the base of the tree. Picnicking is permitted. Daily 8:30-8:30, Memorial Day weekend to mid-Oct.; 9-dusk, rest of year. Admission $3 per private vehicle. Phone (707) 925-6464.

LITTLE RIVER (D-1) elev. 90′

Founded as a lumber and shipbuilding town in the mid-19th century, Little River boasts architecture to reflect its settlers' New England heritage. The town is a popular spot for divers. Little River lies on a scenic stretch of SR 1 on the north coast that runs from Leggett southward to Sausalito and the San Francisco Bay.

PYGMY FOREST, s. edge on SR 1 and 3 mi. e. on Little River Airport Rd., is thought to be the result of acidic soil. Even though they are decades old, some of the rare pygmy pine and pygmy cypress trees are only 2 feet high.

MENDOCINO (D-1) pop. 824, elev. 90′

A picturesque community off scenic SR 1 on the rugged northern California coast, Mendocino has many well-preserved 19th-century buildings and houses. The architecture reflects the New England roots of early settlers, who were drawn by the rich timber resources of the surrounding countryside. Nearby Anderson Valley (southeast of town near Boonville) is peppered with wineries.

The stark beauty of the region attracted many artists in the 1950s, and the town remains a haven for creative folks. Mendocino Art Center, 45200 Little Lake Rd., offers exhibits and festivals.

Visitors to Mendocino may find it familiar; the town was featured as the fictional Cabot Cove, Maine, in the television show "Murder She Wrote."

Self-guiding tour: A 60-mile tour up the Mendocino coastline on the Pacific Coast Highway, SR 1, is one of the most rewarding to be taken anywhere. You can begin in the south at the small town of **Gualala** *(see place listing p. 193)*; born a lumber town, it now offers travelers art galleries, restaurants, boutiques and accommodations in a mix of 19th-century and contemporary properties. **Point Arena** *(see place listing p. 199)* is one of the better spots from which to watch the migration of the grey whale November through March.

Elk is a cliff-top cluster of country inns, restaurants and shops featuring the works of local artisans. Albion is thought by some to have been the site of Sir Francis Drake's 1579 fort; it definitely is the site of the last wooden bridge, built in 1944, on the Pacific Coast Highway. The architecture of

Little River *(see place listing p. 194)* reflects the tastes of its mid-19th century New England settlers. The entire town of **Mendocino** is on the National Register of Historic Places.

Fort Bragg *(see place listing p. 192)*, with a population of more than 7,000, is far larger than its neighbors but still is a small town—a happy combination of the 19th-century and the present. The northernmost town on the Mendocino coast is Westport, where the highway swings eastward in deference to a coastline so rugged it is best explored by foot or four-wheel-drive vehicles. Continue on SR 1 until it joins the Redwood Highway (US 101) in **Leggett** *(see place listing p. 194)*, fortuitously near the ocean, the redwoods and wine country. If you head south you will come to **Willits** *(see place listing p. 202)* and to **Ukiah** *(see place listing p. 202)*, center of a flourishing wine region.

KELLEY HOUSE MUSEUM, 45007 Albion St., contains photographs and brief histories of many historic buildings and houses in the area. The 1861 house has been restored. Genealogy records also are on site. Thurs.-Tues. 1-4, June-Aug.; Fri.-Mon. 1-4, rest of year. Admission $2. Phone (707) 937-5791.

RECREATIONAL ACTIVITIES

Canoeing

- **Catch a Canoe & Bicycles, Too!**, SR 1 and Comptche-Ukiah Rd. Write P.O. Box 487, Mendocino, CA 95460. Daily 9-5. Phone (707) 937-0273.

MIDDLETOWN (A-8) pop. 1,020, elev. 1,105′

WINERIES

- **Guenoc and Langtry Estate Vineyards and Winery** is at 21000 Butts Canyon Rd. Tastings and self-guiding tours daily 11:30-5. Phone (707) 987-2385.

NAPA (B-8) pop. 72,585, elev. 17′

Napa is nestled in one of California's most famous wine producing regions, the Napa Valley. The area was a gold-rush center in the 1850s. Original grapevine cuttings were supplied by priests from the missions at Sonoma and San Rafael, and today Napa Valley is a leader in the American table wine industry.

Napa is the southern terminus of a scenic 28-mile stretch of SR 29, which heads northwest through the valley to Calistoga. The two-lane road passes acres of vineyards and more than 40 wineries. The Silverado Trail, running parallel to SR 29 to the east, provides stunning views of the valley and Napa River. Additional wineries can be found along this less-traveled route.

Downtown Napa has many turn-of-the-20th-century houses and buildings, representing Art Deco, Classic Revival, Italianate, Spanish Colonial and Victorian Gothic architectural styles. About 2,500 buildings are on the National Historical Registry.

TravelBrains Napa Valley Expedition Guide, available at visitor centers in San Francisco and Napa and by mail, features a self-guiding driving tour of 11 wineries and five historic locations that explain Napa Valley's wine heritage and history. An audio driving tour (CD or tape), an 88-page guidebook and a CD-ROM are included; phone (888) 458-6475.

Napa Valley Conference and Visitors Bureau: 1310 Napa Town Center, Napa, CA 94559; phone (707) 226-7459.

Self-guiding tours: Maps of wineries and historic downtown are available from the conference and visitors bureau.

GEM **COPIA: THE AMERICAN CENTER FOR WINE, FOOD & THE ARTS** is at 500 First St. In a perfect setting for such an institution, a 12-acre site on the Napa River, Copia explores the relationship of wine, food and the arts through exhibitions, programs, classes and demonstrations. The cultural center, whose name is derived from the Roman goddess of abundance, shows how food and wine are an integral part of American culture.

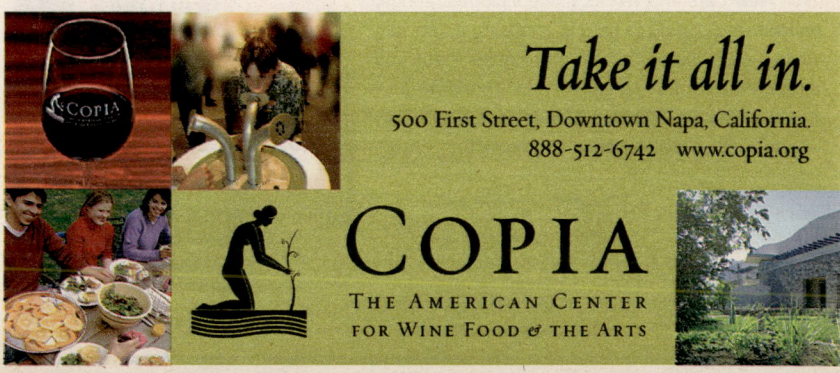

The permanent exhibit—Forks in the Road: Food, Wine and the American Table—has displays showcasing ingenious food products, early cooking utensils, kitchen gadgets, frozen food packaging and American wines as well as several interactive exhibits. Changing exhibits focusing on food and wine also are featured. Organic gardens have seasonal plantings of vegetables, herbs, fruits and flowers. Orientation, garden and exhibition tours are conducted daily.

Food is available. Allow 2 hours minimum. Wed.-Mon. 10-5; closed Jan. 1, Thanksgiving and Dec. 25. Admission (includes daily tours and most programs) $12.50; over 61 and ages 13-17, $10; ages 6-12, $7.50. AX, DS, MC, VI. Phone (707) 259-1600 or (888) 512-6742. *See color ad p. 195.*

NAPA VALLEY WINE TRAIN, 1275 McKinstry St., is a 36-mile journey that winds through the heart of Napa Valley wine country. Pullman dining cars offer brunch, lunch and dinner, while hors d'oeuvres and wine tasting are offered in lounge cars. Allow 3 hours minimum. Departures daily, times vary. Lunch train fare $37, meal $35; brunch train fare $30, meal $29.50; dinner train fare $36, meal $44. Reservations and pre-payment are required. AX, CB, DC, DS, JC, MC, VI. Phone (707) 253-2111 or (800) 427-4124. *See color ad.*

RECREATIONAL ACTIVITIES

Hot Air Ballooning

- **Balloons Above the Valley** trips depart from the Vineyard Gardens at 5091 Solano Ave. (mid-Mar. to mid-Nov.) and from the Napa Valley Marriott at 3425 Solano Ave. (rest of year). Write 5091 Solano Ave., Napa, CA 94558. Trips depart daily at sunrise (weather permitting). Phone (707) 253-2222 or (800) 464-6824.

WINERIES

- **Artesa Vineyards & Winery** is at 1345 Henry Rd. Daily 10-5. Guided tours are given daily at 11 and 2. Phone (707) 224-1668.

- **Domaine Carneros**, 4 mi. s.w. just off SR 121/12 at 1240 Duhig Rd. Daily 10-6; closed

Jan. 1, Thanksgiving and Dec. 25. Phone (707) 257-0101.

- **Hakusan Sake Gardens**, s. on SR 29 then e. on SR 12 to N. Kelly Rd. exit. Daily 10-5. Phone (707) 258-6160.

- **Monticello Vineyards** is 2 mi. s. between SR 29 and Silverado Tr. at 4242 Big Ranch Rd. Tasting room daily 10-4:30; closed major holidays. Tours are given daily at 10:30 and 2:30, May-Aug. Phone ahead to confirm tour schedule. Phone (707) 253-2802.

OAKVILLE (B-8) elev. 155′

WINERIES

- **Robert Mondavi Winery**, .5 mi. n. on SR 29. Daily 9-5; closed Jan. 1, Easter, Thanksgiving and Dec. 25. Phone (707) 259-9463 or (888) 766-6328.

PETALUMA (C-7) pop. 54,548, elev. 12′

Petaluma has one of California's older and better preserved downtowns: 19th-century Victorian homes, theaters, taverns and iron-front commercial buildings have been painstakingly restored. An interesting way to experience this distinctive area is by free, 1-hour guided walking tours led by docents dressed in Victorian garb. The tours are conducted on weekends, May through October; phone (707) 778-4398.

The town and the surrounding area have appeared in such movies as "American Graffiti," "Peggy Sue Got Married" and "The Horse Whisperer." In Sonoma County's wine country but still just 32 miles from the Golden Gate Bridge, the city is a good location from which to explore the county's wineries, its dramatic coastline, Point Reyes National Seashore and the state's towering redwoods.

A stroll along the Petaluma River Walk at Shollenberger Park on S. McDowell Boulevard provides glimpses of many varieties of birds as well as other animals, fish and plants that reside in this wetlands preserve. A brochure and a list of birds that can be seen are available from the Petaluma Visitors Program.

Petaluma Visitors Center: 800 Baywood Dr., Suite A, Petaluma, CA 94954; phone (707) 769-0429 or (877) 273-8258. *See color ad p. 796.*

Self-guiding tours: Brochures detailing a self-guiding walking tour past 19th-century iron-front buildings and Victorian houses, survivors of the 1906 earthquake; film sites; and heritage trees can be obtained from the visitors center.

GARDEN VALLEY RANCH is at 498 Pepper Rd. Self-guiding tours of this 9-acre rose ranch, which specializes in garden roses, include such areas of interest as the Fragrance Garden and the All-America Rose Selection Test Garden—one of only 22 official test gardens in the country. Rose arbors and a duck pond accent the property. Allow 1 hour minimum. Wed.-Sun. 10-4; closed major holidays and during special events. Admission $4; under 13, $2. AX, MC, VI. Phone (707) 792-0377.

MARIN FRENCH CHEESE FACTORY, 9 mi. s.w. at 7500 Red Hill Rd. (Petaluma-Point Reyes Rd.), offers tours of its cheesemaking operation. Picnicking is permitted. Allow 30 minutes minimum. Tours are given daily at 10, 11, noon and 3 (visitors can see cheese being made Wed.-Thurs.). Free. Phone (707) 762-6001 or (800) 292-6001.

MRS. GROSSMAN'S TOURS is at 3810 Cypress Dr. at jct. S. McDowell Blvd. Angus the dog narrates a 20-minute video presentation explaining how decorative stickers are made—the printing, assembling and finishing process. During a walking tour of this sticker manufacturing plant, visitors can see the presses at work and how laser-cut stickers are produced. A sticker art class where guests create their own masterpiece follows the tour. Sticker samples are provided.

Allow 1 hour minimum. Guided tours are given Mon.-Fri. at 9:30, 11, 1 and 2:30. Free. Reservations are required. Phone (800) 429-4549.

PETALUMA ADOBE STATE HISTORIC PARK, .7 mi. e. on Adobe Rd., preserves the large adobe ranch headquarters built by General Mariano Vallejo about 1836. Exhibits include furnished rooms, weaving tools, outdoor ovens, live animals and interpretive displays. Allow 1 hour minimum. Daily 10-5; closed Jan. 1, Thanksgiving and Dec. 25. Admission (including house) $2, under 17 free. Phone (707) 762-4871.

PETALUMA HISTORICAL MUSEUM/LIBRARY, 20 4th St., houses permanent and rotating exhibits reflecting life in early 19th-century Petaluma. Philanthropist Andrew Carnegie awarded the town $12,500 toward the building's construction in 1903; a highlight of the building is its stained glass free-standing dome. Exhibits include historic photographs and materials indicative of the poultry industry.

Allow 30 minutes minimum. Wed.-Sat. 10-4, Sun. noon-3. Costumed docents offer 1-hour guided tours Sat. and the first and third Sun. of the month at 10:30, May-Oct. Donations. Phone (707) 778-4398.

PIERCY (C-1) elev. 622′

CAMPBELL BROS. CONFUSION HILL, on US 101, is an experience in contradictory optical and physical sensations in an apparently confused gravitational or magnetic field. In addition to the gravity house, an optional 1.25-mile, 30-minute miniature mountain train ride meanders (weather permitting) through a redwood forest to a hilltop and back, with the engineer pointing out historical logging artifacts along the way.

Allow 1 hour minimum. Gravity house open daily 8-7, late May-Labor Day; 9-5, rest of year. Train operates daily 10-5, early June-Labor Day; Sat.-Sun. 10-5, in May. Admission to gravity house $3.50; ages 4-12, $2.50. Train ride $4.50; ages 4-12, $3.50. Phone (707) 925-6456.

WORLD FAMOUS TREE HOUSE, 5 mi. s. on US 101, is in a 4,000-year-old living tree—250 feet high, 33 feet in diameter and 101.5 feet in circumference. The room is built in a 50-foot-high cavity in the tree. Allow 30 minutes minimum. Daily 9-8; closed Thanksgiving and Dec. 25. Schedule may vary; phone ahead. Free. Phone (707) 925-6406.

PLANTATION (E-2) elev. 741′

KRUSE RHODODENDRON STATE RESERVE is .5 mi. e. off SR 1 on Kruse Ranch Rd. The rhododendrons, some growing to 14 feet tall, usually reach full bloom late April to early June. A variety of mosses, ferns, sorrel and other forest undergrowth bloom even earlier. Four miles of hiking trails wind through the reserve's 317 acres. The reserve is not suitable for vehicles larger than a van or pickup truck; trailers are not permitted. Allow 1 hour minimum. Daily dawn-dusk. Free. Phone (707) 847-3221.

POINT ARENA (D-1) pop. 474, elev. 220′

POINT ARENA LIGHTHOUSE AND MUSEUM are 1 mi. n.w. of SR 1 on Lighthouse Rd. The 115-foot-tall, steel-reinforced concrete lighthouse opened in 1908 to replace the 1870 structure that was destroyed by the 1906 earthquake; guided tours are available. The point is a popular spot from which to watch migrating whales. Historical items are displayed in the adjacent maritime museum.

Daily 10-4:30, May-Sept.; 10-3:30, rest of year. Closed Thanksgiving and Dec. 25. Admission $5; under 12, $1. Phone (707) 882-2777.

RUTHERFORD (B-8) elev. 170′

WINERIES

- **Beaulieu Vineyard**, off SR 29 at 1960 St. Helena Hwy. Daily 10-5; closed Jan. 1, Easter, Thanksgiving and Dec. 25. Phone (707) 963-2411 or (707) 967-5233.
- **Mumm Napa Valley Winery**, 8445 Silverado Tr. Daily 10-5. Guided tours are offered on the hour 10-3. Phone (707) 942-3434 or (800) 686-6272.
- **Niebaum-Coppola Winery**, off SR 29 at 1991 St. Helena Hwy. Daily 10-5; closed holidays. Phone (707) 968-1177.
- **Peju Province Winery** is at 8466 St. Helena Hwy. (SR 29). Tastings and self-guiding tours daily 10-6. Phone (707) 963-3600 or (800) 446-7358.
- **Rutherford Hill Winery**, e. off Silverado Tr. at the end of Rutherford Hill Rd. Daily 10-5; closed Jan. 1, Easter, Thanksgiving and Dec. 25. Phone (707) 963-7194 or (707) 963-1871.
- **St. Supéry Vineyards and Winery**, off SR 29 at 8440 St. Helena Hwy. Daily 10-5:30. Hours may vary; phone ahead. Guided tours are offered at 1 and 3. Phone (707) 963-4507.
- **Sequoia Grove Vineyards** is at 8338 St. Helena Hwy. (SR 29). Tastings daily 10:30-5. Tours are given Fri.-Sun. at 11:30 and 2. Phone (707) 944-2945 or (800) 851-7841.

ST. HELENA (B-8) pop. 5,950, elev. 255′

In addition to its many wineries, St. Helena in Napa Valley has other industries, such as the production of handcrafted candles by Hurd Beeswax Candle Factory, 2.5 miles north on SR 29 in the Freemark Abbey complex. St. Helena lies on a scenic stretch of SR 29 from Calistoga to Napa.

The Culinary Institute of America has a campus in St. Helena, housed in the imposing Greystone Cellars building on a 30-acre campus accessible from SR 29.

St. Helena Chamber of Commerce: 1010 Main St., Suite A, St. Helena, CA 94574; phone (707) 963-4456 or (800) 799-6456.

BALE GRIST MILL STATE HISTORIC PARK is 3 mi. n.w. on SR 29. The 1847 mill has a 36-foot-diameter wheel that was once used to grind flour for local farmers. It has been restored and once again grinds flour and cornmeal. Hiking trails lead from the access road to the mill pond as well as to Bothe-Napa Valley State Park *(see Recreation Chart)*. Daily 10-5; closed Jan. 1, Thanksgiving and Dec. 25. Admission $2, under 17 free. Phone (707) 942-4575.

ROBERT LOUIS STEVENSON SILVERADO MUSEUM, 1490 Library Ln., off E. Adams St., contains more than 8,000 items related to Scottish author Robert Louis Stevenson, who spent 2 months during 1880 in Northern California. Tues.-Sun. noon-4; closed holidays. Donations. Phone (707) 963-3757.

RECREATIONAL ACTIVITIES

Hot Air Ballooning

- SAVE **Bonaventura Balloons of Napa Valley** departs from various locations. Write P.O. Box 150, Oakville, CA 94562. Trips depart daily at dawn (weather permitting). Phone (707) 944-2822 or (800) 359-6272.

WINERIES

- **Beringer Winery**, 2000 Main St. Daily 10-5; closed Jan. 1, Thanksgiving and Dec. 25. Phone (707) 963-7115.
- **Louis M. Martini Winery**, 254 S. St. Helena Hwy. Daily 10-4:30; closed holidays. Phone (707) 963-2736 or (800) 321-9463.
- **V. Sattui Winery**, 1.5 mi. s. at jct. White Ln. and US 29 at 1111 White Ln. Daily 9-6, Mar.-Oct.; 9-5, rest of year. Closed Dec. 25. Phone (707) 963-7774.

SANTA ROSA (B-8) pop. 147,595, elev. 164′

CHARLES M. SCHULZ MUSEUM is at 2301 Hardies Ln. at jct. W. Steele Ln. The museum relates the life of the creator of the "Peanuts" comic strip and the development of the "Peanuts" gang—the lovable Charlie Brown, Snoopy, Lucy and their friends. A replica of Schulz's studio, a collection of his pencil sketches and doodles, a Snoopy labyrinth in an outdoor garden and a morphing Snoopy sculpture are highlights. Original "Peanuts" comic strips and other art by Schulz can be viewed.

Allow 1 hour, 30 minutes minimum. Mon. and Wed.-Fri. noon-5:30, Sat.-Sun. 10-5:30; closed Jan. 1, July 4, Thanksgiving and Dec. 24-25. Admission $8; over 61, college students with ID and ages 4-18, $5. AX, DS, MC, VI. Phone (707) 579-4452.

LUTHER BURBANK HOME & GARDENS is at the corner of Santa Rosa and Sonoma aves. Half-hour guided tours describe the life and work of the horticulturist who introduced 800 varieties of fruits, vegetables, nuts, grains and ornamental flowers, including the Santa Rosa plum and the Shasta daisy. Examples of roses, fruit trees and other plants developed by Burbank are featured on the grounds. The house, greenhouse and carriage house museum contain original furnishings and changing exhibits.

Gardens open daily 8-7, Apr.-Oct.; 8-5, rest of year. Guided house tours available every half-hour Tues.-Sun. 10-3:30, Apr.-Oct. only. Gardens free. House tours $4, under 13 free with adult. Phone (707) 524-5445.

GEM SAVE **SAFARI WEST** is at 3115 Porter Creek Rd. Tours of the 400-acre wildlife preserve, home of 350 exotic animals and birds, are conducted by a naturalist in open-air safari vehicles. Information about each animal is provided as they are spotted. Sightings might include zebras, ostriches, antelopes, cape buffalo, gazelles and elands. Passengers also visit an open-air aviary and walk through an animal compound for up-close meetings with giraffes and primates.

Allow 3 hours minimum. Tours are given daily (weather permitting) at 9, 1 and 3, early Apr.-late Oct.; at 10 and 2, rest of year. Closed Jan. 1, Thanksgiving and Dec. 25. Fare $58; over 61, $52; ages 3-12, $28. Reservations are required. AX, MC, VI. Phone (707) 579-2551 or (800) 616-2695.

SAVE **SONOMA COUNTY MUSEUM,** in the restored post office building at 425 Seventh St., exhibits photographs, paintings and other items pertaining to regional history and culture. Programs and lectures are offered periodically. Allow 30 minutes minimum. Wed.-Sun. 11-4. Admission $5; over 64 and ages 12-18, $2. Phone (707) 579-1500.

RECREATIONAL ACTIVITIES

Hot Air Ballooning

- **Above the Wine Country Ballooning** departs from Kal's Kaffe Mocha, 3 mi. n. off US 101

Airport Blvd. exit, then e. to 397 Aviation Blvd. Write 2508 Burnside Rd., Sebastopol, CA 95472. Trips depart daily at dawn; closed Dec. 25. Phone (707) 829-9850 or (888) 238-6359.

WINERIES

- **De Loach Vineyards** is 5 mi. w. off US 101 River Road exit, then w. to 1791 Olivet Rd. Daily 10-4:30. Guided tours are given daily at 11 and 2 by appointment. Phone (707) 526-9111.

SEBASTOPOL (B-7) pop. 7,774, elev. 78'

Named after Sevastopol, the Russian seaport on the Crimean peninsula, Sebastopol became a center of canned applesauce production in the late 19th century. The industry is still important to the town today, as are the Gravenstein apple orchards and vineyards that cover the region.

Sebastopol Chamber of Commerce and Visitors Center: 265 S. Main St., Sebastopol, CA 95472; phone (707) 823-3032.

SONOMA (C-8) pop. 9,128, elev. 84'

After overthrowing the Spanish government in 1823, the Mexican government issued a decree that all church properties be secularized. This included Mission San Francisco Solano, recently established by Spanish priest Jose Altimira. Gen. Mariano Guadelupe Vallejo was sent from Monterey to confiscate the property, which he did; during his post he also created the town of Sonoma, with a plaza serving as its centerpiece.

Settlers, lured to the area by the promise of free land, later were denied the opportunity to own property. Faced with the threat of deportation, their dissatisfaction came to a climax on June 14, 1846, when the group, calling themselves Osos (bears), arrested Vallejo at his home. They proclaimed California a republic and Sonoma its capital. The Bear Flag—fashioned from unbleached muslin, a red petticoat and a crude berry-stained picture of a bear—was raised in Sonoma Plaza.

The revolt was short-lived, however; on July 9 the flag was replaced by the Stars and Stripes. In 1911 the State Legislature adopted the Bear Flag as the state flag.

Depot Park Museum, in the original town depot, preserves the history of the California Republic through displays of 19th-century clothing, railroad artifacts and furniture; phone (707) 938-1762.

Sonoma Valley Visitors Bureau: 453 1st St. E., Sonoma, CA 95476; phone (707) 996-1090.

SONOMA STATE HISTORIC PARK, 20 E. Spain St. on Sonoma Plaza, consists of 49 acres that include more than a dozen buildings important to early California history. The Toscano Hotel and Sonoma Barracks are on the Plaza. The hotel, built during the 1850s, resembles its appearance around the turn of the 20th century. The two-story, partially restored adobe barracks were built to house Gen. Mariano Vallejo's Mexican troops. Following the raising of the Bear Flag in 1846, the building was used by U.S. troops.

The 1823 Mission San Francisco Solano was the last of the California missions, located a day's journey apart along the coast. Destroyed and rebuilt several times, the mission houses the Jorgensen watercolors of Missions of California. Gen. Vallejo's home has gardens and family furnishings. Self-guiding tours of the mission are available.

Several guided tours are available; phone ahead for schedules. Allow 1 hour minimum. Daily 10-5; closed Jan. 1, Thanksgiving and Dec. 25. Park free. Mission, barracks and house $2, under 17 free. Phone (707) 938-1519.

TRAIN TOWN, 1 mi. s. on SR 12, offers a 20-minute miniature steam train ride through a forested railroad park past scaled-down reproductions of buildings and waterfalls. A diesel engine is featured Monday through Friday, while a steam engine is used Saturday, Sunday and holidays. A petting zoo, Ferris wheel, merry-go-round and other rides are on the grounds.

Allow 30 minutes minimum. Trips daily 10-5, June-Sept.; Fri.-Sun. and some holidays 10-5, rest of year. Closed Thanksgiving and Dec. 25. Admission $3.75; over 54 and ages 16 months-16 years, $3.25. Merry-go-round $1.75. Phone (707) 938-3912.

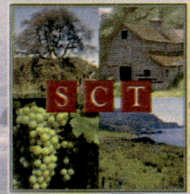

RECREATIONAL ACTIVITIES

Bicycling

- **Goodtime Touring Company** delivers bicycles to local hotels. Daily 9-6. Phone (707) 938-0453 or (888) 525-0453.

WINERIES

- **Bartholomew Park Winery** is e. off SR 12 onto Napa St., n. onto 7th St. E., then w. on Castle Rd. Tastings and self-guiding tours daily 11-4:30; closed Jan. 1, Easter, Thanksgiving and Dec. 25. Phone (707) 935-9511, ext. 206.
- **Buena Vista Winery** is 2 mi. n.e. at 18000 Old Winery Rd. Daily 10-5; closed Jan. 1, Thanksgiving and Dec. 25. Phone (707) 938-1266 or (800) 926-1266.
- **Cline Cellars** is at 24737 SR 121. Daily 10-6; closed Dec. 25. Guided tours are given daily at 11, 1 and 3. Phone (707) 940-4030 or (800) 546-2070.
- **Gloria Ferrer Champagne Caves** is at 23555 Carneros Hwy. (SR 121). Daily 10:30-5:30. Guided tours are given daily at noon, 2 and 4; phone ahead to confirm tour schedule. Phone (707) 996-7256, or (707) 933-1917 to confirm the day's tour schedule.
- **Gundlach Bundschu Winery** is e. off SR 12 onto E. Napa St., s. onto 8th St. E., then e. to 2000 Denmark St. Daily 11-4:30; closed Jan. 1, Easter, Thanksgiving and Dec. 25. Guided tours are given Mon.-Fri. at 11 and 2, Sat.-Sun. on the hour noon-3. Phone (707) 938-5277.
- **Sebastiani Vineyards**, 389 4th St. E. Tasting room open daily 10-5. Vineyards open Mon.-Fri. 8-5. Closed holidays. Phone (707) 938-5532 or (800) 888-5532.
- **Viansa Winery** is at 25200 Arnold Dr. (SR 121). Daily 10-5. Guided tours are given at 11 and 2. Phone (707) 935-4700 or (800) 995-4740.

UKIAH (D-1) pop. 15,497, elev. 635′

Ukiah, center of a flourishing wine region, gets its name from a Pomo Indian word meaning "deep valley." It is home to the Redwood Empire Fairgrounds.

Greater Ukiah Chamber of Commerce: 200 S. School St., Ukiah, CA 95482; phone (707) 462-4705.

GRACE HUDSON MUSEUM AND SUN HOUSE, 431 S. Main St., is a complex that includes a historic house, a park and a museum of art, history and anthropology. The museum displays works by noted painter Grace Carpenter Hudson, who chose Pomo Indians as her subjects; a small collection of Pomo Indian basketry; family artifacts; and historical photographs. Sun House was the home of the artist, who lived there for 25 years before her death in 1937.

Allow 1 hour minimum. Museum open Wed.-Sat. 10-4:30, Sun. noon-4:30; closed major holidays. Free guided 15-minute tours of Sun House are available on the hour Wed.-Sun. noon-3. Donations. Phone (707) 467-2836.

LAKE MENDOCINO VISITOR CENTER is .2 mi. s. of SR 20 at Marina Dr. The center offers information that features the lake, Pomo Indian culture and the Coyote Valley. Highlights include the Interpretive Cultural Center, featuring exhibits of Pomo Indian crafts and decorative arts. Guided tours are available by appointment. Picnicking is permitted. Wed.-Sun. 9-5, mid-Apr. through Sept. 30; Sat.-Sun. 1-5, Oct. 1 to mid-Nov. Donations. Phone (707) 485-8685 or (707) 462-7581.

WILLITS (D-1) pop. 5,000, elev. 1,364′

Willits is the terminus for the California Western Railroad trip aboard "The Skunk" from Fort Bragg *(see place listing p. 192)*.

Willits Chamber of Commerce: 239 S. Main St., Willits, CA 95490-3591; phone (707) 459-7910.

MENDOCINO COUNTY MUSEUM, 400 E. Commercial St., displays collections of Pomo and Yuki Indian baskets, artifacts of Mendocino County, steam-powered equipment and locomotives, and contemporary and traditional art. Allow 30 minutes minimum. Wed.-Sun. 10-4:30; closed holidays except July 4. Donations. Phone (707) 459-2736.

WINDSOR (B-7) pop. 22,744, elev. 118′

WINDSOR WATERWORKS AND SLIDES, 8225 Conde Ln., has a children's slide, a speed slide, an inner-tube ride, an aqua tube, a splash fountain and a heated pool. Height requirements are imposed on certain rides and all slides.

Picnic facilities and food are available. Allow 4 hours minimum. Daily 11-7, mid-June to early Sept.; Sat.-Sun. 11-7, May 1 to mid-June. Afternoon splash daily 4-7, mid-June to early July. All-day pass $16.95. After 4 p.m. (mid-June to early July) $11.95. AX, MC, VI. Phone (707) 838-7760.

YOUNTVILLE (B-8) pop. 2,916, elev. 100′

Yountville, on a scenic stretch of SR 29 extending from Calistoga to Napa, was founded by George Yount in 1835. Yount is said to have planted the first grapevines in Napa Valley.

Yountville Chamber of Commerce: 6516 Yount St., P.O. Box 2064, Yountville, CA 94599; phone (707) 944-0904.

Shopping areas: Vintage 1870 offers shopping and dining in a restored 19th-century winery.

SAVE **NAPA VALLEY MUSEUM** is at 55 Presidents Cir., on the grounds of the Veterans Home. The culture of the Napa Valley is depicted in the museum's two permanent exhibits. The process of winemaking from the growing of the grapes to the bottling of the final product is interactively examined, while the environment and history of the region also are explored. Changing art exhibits are featured.

Allow 1 hour minimum. Wed.-Mon. 10-5; closed Jan. 1, Thanksgiving and Dec. 25. Admission $4.50; over 65 and students with ID $3.50; ages 7-17, $2.50. AX, MC, VI. Phone (707) 944-0500.

RECREATIONAL ACTIVITIES

Hot Air Ballooning

- **Above the West Ballooning** departs from Cucina à la Carte in the courtyard of the Vintage 1870 shopping complex, 6525 Washington St., Yountville, CA 94599. Trips depart daily at dawn (weather permitting); closed Dec. 25. Phone (707) 944-8638 or (800) 627-2759.
- **Adventures Aloft** departs from Cucina à la Carte in the courtyard of the Vintage 1870 shopping complex, 6525 Washington St., Yountville, CA 94599. Trips depart daily at dawn (weather permitting); closed Dec. 25. Phone (707) 944-4408 or (800) 944-4408.
- **Balloon Aviation** departs from Cucina à la Carte in the courtyard of the Vintage 1870 shopping complex, 6525 Washington St., Yountville, CA 94599. Trips depart daily at dawn (weather permitting); closed Dec. 25. Phone (707) 944-4400 or (800) 367-6272.
- **Napa Valley Balloons** departs from Napa Valley Grille in Washington Square, 6795 Washington St. Write P.O. Box 2860, Yountville, CA 94599. Trips depart daily at dawn (weather permitting). Phone (707) 944-0228 or (800) 253-2224.

WINERIES

- **Domaine Chandon**, 1 California Dr. Daily 10-6; closed Jan. 1, Thanksgiving and Dec. 25. Tours are given Mon.-Fri. at 11, 2 and 5, Sat.-Sun. on the hour 11-5. Phone ahead to confirm schedule. Phone (707) 944-2280.
- **S. Anderson/Cliff Lede Vineyards**, n. on SR 29, e. on Madison St., n. onto Yount St., then 1.5 mi. e. to 1473 Yountville Cross Rd. Daily 10-5; closed Jan. 1, Thanksgiving and Dec. 25. Guided tours are given daily at 10:30 and 2:30. Phone (707) 944-8642.

This ends listings for the Wine Country.
The following page resumes the alphabetical listings of cities in Northern California.

WOODLAND (E-3) pop. 49,151, elev. 65′

First known as Yolo City, Woodland was a gold rush town established in 1861. Agriculture and industrial plants feed the economy.

Woodland Chamber of Commerce: 307 First St., Woodland, CA 95695; phone (530) 662-7327.

HEIDRICK AG HISTORY CENTER, 1962 Hays Ln., houses collections of antique agricultural equipment, trucks and tractors. The center chronicles the history of agricultural machinery and commercial trucking through displays and interactive exhibits. Trucks dating from 1901 through the '50s represent many manufacturers. Also shown are vehicles from an 1890 horse-drawn Deering Reaper to gasoline and diesel equipment from the early 1900s.

Guided tours are available. Open Mon.-Fri. 10-5, Sat. 10-6, Sun. 10-4; closed Jan. 1, Easter, Mother's Day, Thanksgiving and Dec. 24-25 and 31. Admission $6; over 62, $5; ages 6-14, $4. MC, VI. Phone (530) 666-9700. *See ad p. 121.*

YOLO COUNTY HISTORICAL MUSEUM is at 512 Gibson Rd. Furnishings of various styles and eras are displayed in an 1857-77 Classical Revival-style mansion in a parklike setting. Three outbuildings on the grounds have historical exhibits, and a barn features a display about Yolo County's agriculture and horticulture. There also is an herb garden. Picnicking is permitted. Allow 30 minutes minimum. Mon.-Tues. 10-4, Sat.-Sun. noon-4; closed Jan. 1, Easter, Thanksgiving and Dec. 25. Admission $2, under 13 free. Phone (530) 666-1045.

WINERIES

- **Satiety Winery**, at SR 113 and CR 25-A. Mon.-Fri. 7-7, Sat.-Sun. and holidays 11-7. Phone (530) 661-0680.

WOODSIDE (E-8) pop. 5,352, elev. 382′

Woodside came into being in 1849 when the gold rush drastically increased the size and population of San Francisco. The wood needed for wharves, houses and commercial buildings was harvested from virgin redwood forests in this section of San Mateo County. At one time there were 14 lumber mills here.

FILOLI, off I-280 via Edgewood Rd. to Cañada Rd., is a 654-acre estate built 1916-19 for Mr. and Mrs. William B. Bourn II, wealthy San Franciscans. The estate includes a 43-room mansion and 16 acres of themed formal gardens. The focal points of the garden are the Italian Renaissance tea house and the nearby carriage house, which is dominated by a bell tower.

Estate may be seen via a 2-hour guided tour Tues.-Sat. at 10, 11:30 and 1, Apr.-June; Tues.-Sat. at 10 and 1, mid-Feb. through Mar. 31 and July 1-late Oct. Estate is open for self-guiding tours Tues.-Sat. 10-3:30, mid-Feb. to late Oct. Last admission for self-guiding tour is 1 hour before closing. Admission $10; students with ID $5; ages 7-12, $1. Reservations are required for guided tours. MC, VI. Phone (650) 364-8300, ext. 507.

THE WOODSIDE STORE, 3300 Tripp Rd. at King's Mountain Rd., was built in 1854 and operated as a country store and post office until 1909. Restored to its 1880's appearance, this living museum contains many examples of clothing, hardware and fixtures of that period. Tues. and Thurs. 10-4, Sat.-Sun. noon-4. Free. Phone (650) 851-7615.

GEM YOSEMITE NATIONAL PARK (F-5)

See map page 207.

Elevations in the park range from 2,000 ft. at the park boundary at El Portal on SR 140 to 13,014 ft. at the summit of Mount Lyell. Refer to AAA maps for additional elevation information.

Reached by SR 140 (El Portal Road) from Merced, SR 41 (Wawona Road) from Fresno, and SR 120 (Big Oak Flat Road) from Stockton, Yosemite National Park lies in central California on the western slope of the Sierra Nevada in a region of unusual beauty.

Glaciers transformed the rolling hills and meandering streams of pre-Pleistocene Yosemite into the colossal landscape of the present. To preserve it for posterity, Abraham Lincoln set aside the Mariposa grove of giant sequoias in the Yosemite Valley as the nation's first state park on June 30, 1864. Twenty-six years later Yosemite became a national park.

The park is much greater both in area and beauty than most people generally realize; Yosemite Valley actually comprises only 7 of the 1,189 square miles of park land. The territory above the rim of the valley is less celebrated principally because it is less well-known. However, 196 miles of primary roads and more than 800 miles of trails now make much of this mountain region easily accessible to both motorist and hiker.

The crest of the Sierra Nevada is the park's eastern boundary, and the two rivers that flow through the park—the Merced and Tuolumne—originate among the snowy peaks. The Merced River flows through Yosemite Valley, and the Tuolumne River carves a magnificent gorge through the northern half of the park. Though spectacular through most of the year, many of the park's famous waterfalls are often dry during the late summer months.

With the exception of the Tioga Pass Road portion of SR 120, the Glacier Point Road and the Mariposa Grove Road, all of which are closed late fall through early summer, all roads are open year round; chains may be needed in winter.

The road to Mirror Lake and Happy Isles, at the eastern end of Yosemite Valley, is closed to most cars but is served by a free shuttle bus. Southside Drive is one-way eastbound from Bridalveil Fall to Curry Village; Northside Drive is one-way westbound from Yosemite Lodge; and the road between Curry Village and Yosemite Village also is one-way westbound.

General Information and Activities

Yosemite National Park is open daily all year. Maps and information are available at the Yosemite Valley Visitor Center, and schedules of events are provided at park entrances and posted throughout the valley. A free shuttle bus operates in the east end of the valley daily 7 a.m.-10 p.m., mid-May to mid-Sept.; 9 a.m.-10 p.m., rest of year. In the winter a shuttle runs from Yosemite Lodge to the Badger Pass Ski Area.

Wilderness permits, required of all overnight backpackers, are free at the Yosemite Valley Wilderness Center or $5 if obtained by phone or mail; phone (209) 372-0740. To make reservations by mail write Wilderness Reservations, P.O. Box 545, Yosemite, CA 95389. For information about wilderness permits phone (209) 372-0200.

A California fishing license is required for all park waters; an annual permit costs $30.45 for residents. A 10-day non-resident pass also is $30.45. A 2-day resident or non-resident license costs $11.05. Information about bicycle rentals is available at Curry Village and Yosemite Lodge; tour bus information also is given at these spots and at Yosemite Village and The Ahwahnee Hotel.

High-Altitude Health

Temples throbbing, gasping for breath and nauseated, you barely notice the scudding clouds or the spectacular view.

You might be suffering from Acute Mountain Sickness (AMS). Usually striking at around 8,000 feet (2,450 m) in altitude, AMS is your body's way of coping with the reduced oxygen and humidity of high altitudes. Among the symptoms are headaches, shortness of breath, loss of appetite, insomnia and lethargy. Some people complain of temporary weight gain or swelling in the face, hands and feet.

Digital Archive

If your AMS is severe, you should stop ascending; you will recover in a few days. If the AMS is mild, a quick descent will end the suffering immediately.

You can reduce the effect of high altitude by being in top condition. If you smoke or suffer from heart or lung ailments, consult your physician. Alcohol and certain drugs will intensify the symptoms.

A gradual ascent with a couple days of acclimatization is best if you have time. On the way up, eat light, nutritious meals and drink plenty of water. A spicy, high-carbohydrate diet may mitigate the effects of low oxygen and encourage you to drink more.

Other high-altitude health problems include sunburn and hypothermia. Dress in layers to protect yourself from the intense sun and wide fluctuations in temperature.

Finally, after you lounge in the sauna or whirlpool bath at your lodgings, remember to stand up carefully, for the heat has relaxed your blood vessels and lowered your blood pressure.

Ranger-naturalists conduct year-round nature walks that last from a half-hour to 2 hours; snowshoe walks are available in the winter. Evening programs are presented all year at the Yosemite Lodge, and in summer at Curry Village, Lower Pines, Glacier Point, Tuolumne Meadows, Crane Flat, Wawona and White Wolf campgrounds.

An open-air tram offers frequent 2-hour tours of the valley during summer and occasional trips after Labor Day; reservations can be made at The Ahwahnee Hotel, Curry Village and Yosemite Lodge. Other tours depart daily in summer to Glacier Point and Mariposa Grove. Guided horseback tours of Wawona, Tuolumne Meadows and the valley also are available. A hiker shuttle goes to Glacier Point and Tuolumne Meadows.

Four- and 6-day saddle trips and a 7-day guided hiking trip are available; contact Yosemite Concession Services Corp., Yosemite National Park, CA 95389; phone (559) 252-4848.

Skiing and skating can be enjoyed in winter. Curry Village has an outdoor skating rink; Badger Pass Ski Area has downhill and cross-country skiing. Cross-country ski trails lead from the Badger Pass and Crane Flat areas. Snowshoe tours are offered.

Child care is available in winter for a fee at Ski Tots Playhouse at Badger Pass. During the summer the Junior Ranger Program of nature walks and classes welcomes students in grades 3 through 6; phone (209) 372-0200.

For recorded information about camping, roads, weather conditions and recreation, phone (209) 372-0200. Campground reservations are available through the National Park Reservation System, (800) 436-7275, 9450 Carroll Park Dr., San Diego, CA 92121. *See Recreation Chart and the AAA California & Nevada CampBook.*

The visitor center in Yosemite Valley has exhibits and audiovisual programs and is open all year. The adjacent Indian Cultural Museum depicts the history of the Miwok and Paiute. The visitor centers at Big Oak Flat and Tuolumne Meadows usually are open June through September.

The Wilderness Center, in Yosemite Valley, provides detailed information about the park's back country and wilderness areas. The center, open daily 8-5 with extended hours during the summer, contains a variety of displays for hikers and climbers as well as trip planning information, including guide books and maps; phone (209) 372-0200 for additional information or (209) 372-0740 for back country reservations.

ADMISSION to the park is by $20 private vehicle fee, good for 7 days. **Note:** Chains might be required at any time during winter months.

PETS are not allowed on the trails or in public buildings and accommodations and must be leashed at all times. Pets are permitted in Upper Pines in Yosemite Valley, the west end of the campground at Tuolumne Meadows, and at White Wolf (Section

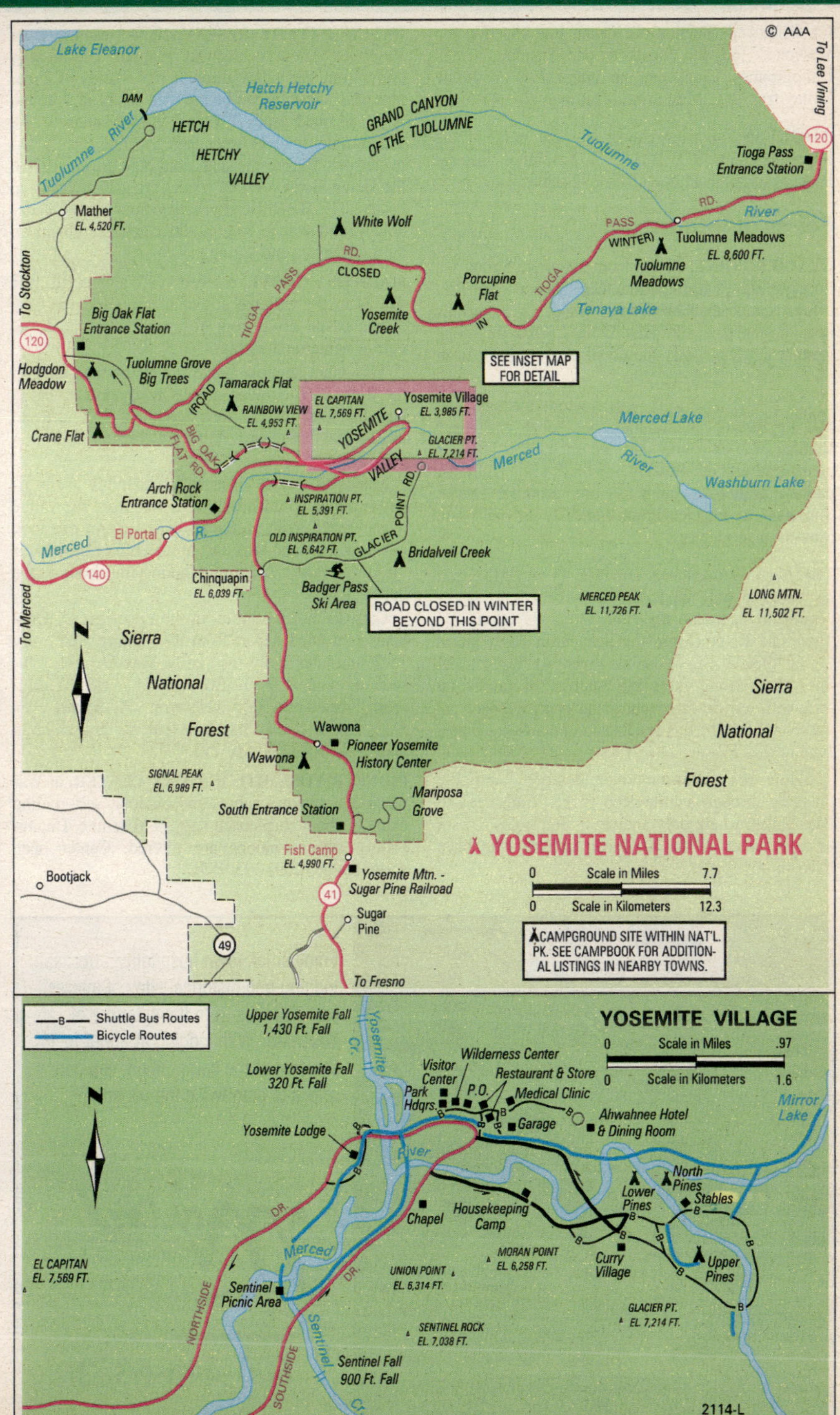
© AAA
YOSEMITE NATIONAL PARK
Lake Eleanor
Hetch Hetchy Reservoir
DAM
HETCH HETCHY VALLEY
GRAND CANYON OF THE TUOLUMNE
Tuolumne River
To Lee Vining
Tioga Pass Entrance Station
Mather EL. 4,520 FT.
White Wolf
Tuolumne Meadows EL. 8,600 FT.
Tuolumne Meadows
TIOGA PASS RD. CLOSED IN WINTER
Porcupine Flat
Yosemite Creek
Tenaya Lake
To Stockton
Big Oak Flat Entrance Station
Tuolumne Grove Big Trees
Hodgdon Meadow
Tamarack Flat
SEE INSET MAP FOR DETAIL
RAINBOW VIEW EL. 4,953 FT.
EL CAPITAN EL. 7,569 FT.
Yosemite Village EL. 3,985 FT.
GLACIER PT. EL. 7,214 FT.
Merced Lake
Merced River
Washburn Lake
Crane Flat
(BIG OAK FLAT RD.)
YOSEMITE VALLEY
Arch Rock Entrance Station
INSPIRATION PT. EL. 5,391 FT.
OLD INSPIRATION PT. EL. 6,642 FT.
GLACIER POINT RD.
Bridalveil Creek
El Portal
Merced R.
To Merced
Chinquapin EL. 6,039 FT.
Badger Pass Ski Area
ROAD CLOSED IN WINTER BEYOND THIS POINT
MERCED PEAK EL. 11,726 FT.
LONG MTN. EL. 11,502 FT.
Sierra National Forest
Wawona
Pioneer Yosemite History Center
SIGNAL PEAK EL. 6,989 FT.
Mariposa Grove
South Entrance Station
Fish Camp EL. 4,990 FT.
Yosemite Mtn. - Sugar Pine Railroad
Bootjack
Sugar Pine
To Fresno
Scale in Miles 0 7.7
Scale in Kilometers 0 12.3
CAMPGROUND SITE WITHIN NAT'L. PK. SEE CAMPBOOK FOR ADDITIONAL LISTINGS IN NEARBY TOWNS.
120
140
41
49
N
YOSEMITE VILLAGE
Shuttle Bus Routes
Bicycle Routes
Scale in Miles 0 .97
Scale in Kilometers 0 1.6
Upper Yosemite Fall 1,430 Ft. Fall
Lower Yosemite Fall 320 Ft. Fall
Yosemite Cr.
Wilderness Center
Visitor Center
Park Hdqrs.
P.O.
Restaurant & Store
Medical Clinic
Garage
Ahwahnee Hotel & Dining Room
Mirror Lake
Yosemite Lodge
Merced River
North Pines
Lower Pines
Stables
Chapel
Housekeeping Camp
Curry Village
Upper Pines
MORAN POINT EL. 6,258 FT.
UNION POINT EL. 6,314 FT.
EL CAPITAN EL. 7,569 FT.
Sentinel Picnic Area
NORTHSIDE DR.
SOUTHSIDE DR.
SENTINEL ROCK EL. 7,038 FT.
GLACIER PT. EL. 7,214 FT.
Sentinel Cr.
Sentinel Fall 900 Ft. Fall
2114-L

C), Bridalveil (Section A), Crane Flat (Section A), Wawona, Hodgdon Meadows and Yosemite Creek campgrounds. Dogs can be boarded in Yosemite Valley from late May to mid-October.

ADDRESS inquiries concerning the park to the Superintendent, P.O. Box 577, Yosemite National Park, CA 95389. Phone (209) 372-0200.

Points of Interest

GLACIER POINT, 30 mi. from Yosemite Valley via Wawona Rd. to Chinquapin, then Glacier Point Rd., offers a panorama of domes, pinnacles, waterfalls and—dominating all—Half Dome. From the stone lookout you can study the detail of the distant High Sierra and its flanking ranges.

The paved road to the point winds through pine and fir forests. In summer, bus tours and hiker shuttles to the point are available and ranger-naturalists are on duty. A 1.5-mile walk from the parking area leads to 8,122-foot Sentinel Dome. The road to Glacier Point normally is open late May through October.

THE GRAND CANYON OF THE TUOLUMNE can be traversed only on foot; Waterwheel Falls is accessible by a trail 6 mi. from Tioga Rd. along the Tuolumne River Gorge to Glen Aulin High Sierra Camp, then 3 mi. down the river. At Waterwheel Falls the rushing river hits shelves of projecting rock with terrific force, throwing enormous arcs of water into the air; this spectacle is best viewed mid-June to mid-July.

Below the falls the river descends abruptly, plunging through a mile-deep gorge. Trails lead to Pate Valley, where only ancient mortar holes remain as a reminder of the American Indians who once lived in this region.

HETCH HETCHY RESERVOIR is reached from Yosemite Valley via Big Oak Flat Rd. The 38-mile drive from the valley through fine stands of sugar pine and white fir can be covered easily in 2 hours. A paved road leads 7 miles from Mather to the 312-foot dam, which impounds San Francisco's water supply. Before the dam was built in the 1920s, the Hetch Hetchy Valley rivaled Yosemite Valley in beauty. The Hetch Hetchy Valley floor is now under 300 feet of water. You should carry tire chains in the fall, winter and spring.

MARIPOSA GROVE, reached via Wawona Rd. (SR 41), is in the extreme s. end of the park; the easy 36-mi. paved drive from Yosemite Valley is closed during winter and spring.

This giant sequoia grove is one of the finest in the Sierras. The oldest tree, Grizzly Giant, has a base diameter of 30.7 feet, a girth of 96.5 feet and is 210 feet high; the 232-foot California Tree is a tunnel tree.

Mariposa Grove Museum has exhibits about giant sequoias. Guided bus tours run from the valley to the grove, with a stop in Wawona. An overlook at the 4,233-foot Wawona tunnel offers a view of the entire valley. A 2.5-mile hiking trail leads to the upper grove.

Cars are not permitted in the upper grove. One-hour tram tours depart from the parking area every 15-20 minutes daily 9-5, early May-Oct. 31. Museum open daily 9:30-4:30, early May-Oct. 31. Museum free. Tram fare $11; over 61, $8.50; ages 5-12, $5.50; family rate $30 (parents and children under 17). AX, DS, MC, VI.

PIONEER YOSEMITE HISTORY CENTER, at Wawona, has historic cabins and outdoor, self-guiding exhibits about stagecoach days in Yosemite. Living-history demonstrations are offered. Center open daily. Phone (209) 375-9531.

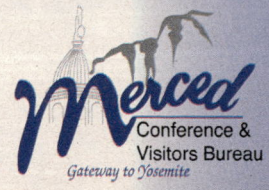

TIOGA PASS ROAD begins at jct. SR 120 and US 395 just s. of Lee Vining; also known as SR 120, the road traverses the park and provides the only entrance from the e.

The first 12 miles of the two-lane paved road ascend nearly a mile and overlook a vast canyon. The road traverses Tuolumne Meadows, descends to Tenaya Lake and continues west to Big Oak Flat Road, offering a scenic trip with frequent overlooks.

Although portions of the drive are more demanding than relaxing, the magnificent scenery attracts many motorists. Motorists should carry tire chains, since weather and road conditions can change quickly. The road is usually open late May-Oct. 31 (weather permitting). For road conditions phone (209) 372-0200.

TUOLUMNE GROVE, on old Big Oak Flat Rd., 17 mi. from Yosemite Valley, contains 20 giant sequoia trees, including the Dead Giant stump. Automobiles are no longer permitted on the section of Big Oak Flat Road adjacent to the grove. Visitors may park their cars near the Crane Flat Junction at a lot off of Tioga Road and walk to Tuolumne Grove; however, the mile-long route descends approximately 700 feet and the return ascent to the parking lot is a moderately strenuous climb.

TUOLUMNE MEADOWS is in the High Sierra, about 56 mi. from Yosemite Valley over Big Oak Flat and Tioga rds. At 8,600 feet in elevation and surrounded by lofty peaks, the area is ideal for camping and fishing, hiking and mountain-climbing.

Trips can be taken on foot or horseback to Waterwheel Falls, Mount Lyell, Lyell Glacier, Lembert Dome, Glen Aulin, Muir Gorge, Soda Springs and Tenaya Lake. Nature walks, hikes and evening campfire programs are conducted seasonally. The meadows is accessible by car from about early June-Oct. 31. Daily bus service from Yosemite Valley is available early June-Labor Day (weather permitting), as are walks, hikes and campfire programs.

WASHBURN AND MERCED LAKES, accessible by trail only from Yosemite Valley, are typical of the many lakes bordering the western slopes of the Sierras. One of six High Sierra camps is at the head of Merced Lake and can be reached by trail from Yosemite Valley, Tenaya Lake or Tuolumne Meadows.

WAWONA BASIN is on Wawona Rd., 27 mi. s. of the Yosemite Valley near Mariposa Grove. In a beautiful meadow, Wawona provides a recreation area of several square miles that includes camping, riding, golf, swimming and tennis facilities. Saddle and pack animals are available in summer.

YOSEMITE VALLEY, 27 mi. n. on SR 41 or also accessible from SRs 120 and 140, is 7 miles long and averages .7 mile wide; its walls rise to 3,200 feet. Immense precipices and lofty waterfalls are impressive natural features.

Upper Yosemite Fall drops 1,430 feet in one fall, a height equal to nine Niagaras. Lower Yosemite Fall drops 320 feet. The falls are at their fullest in May and June while winter snows melt.

The valley's domes and pinnacles—Three Brothers, El Capitan, Cathedral Spires, North Dome and Half Dome—are as celebrated as the falls. The valley is open all year.

YOUNTVILLE—*see Wine Country p. 202.*

YREKA (A-2) pop. 7,290, elev. 2,625′

Yreka was incorporated in 1857, 6 years after Abraham Thompson's mules pulled gold flecks up on the roots of the grass they were eating. Miners soon swarmed into this lush valley, which had long been a home to the Karuk and Shasta Indians. I-5 provides a scenic route.

Yreka Chamber of Commerce: 117 W. Miner St., Yreka, CA 96097; phone (530) 842-1649.

BLUE-GOOSE STEAM TRAIN departs the depot at the Center exit. The 3.5-hour tour provides views of Mount Shasta, Shasta Valley and cattle ranch country as well as a visit to the old railroad town of Montague. Steam train departs Wed.-Sun. at 11, mid-June through Labor Day; Sat.-Sun. at 11, late May to mid-June and day after Labor Day-late Oct. Fare $14; over 59, $11; ages 3-12, $7. An additional fee is charged to ride in the locomotive or caboose. DS, MC, VI. Phone (530) 842-4146.

GREENHORN PARK, s. off Greenhorn Rd. at Greenhorn Reservoir, features a restored miner's cabin and mining equipment. A nature trail, playground and picnic facilities are available. Fishing is permitted. Daily 7 a.m.-10 p.m., May-Sept.; 7-6, rest of year. Free. Phone (530) 841-2386.

DID YOU KNOW

Because of budget considerations, the schedules and fees of all state-owned facilities are subject to change. Travelers are advised to phone ahead.

SISKIYOU COUNTY COURTHOUSE, 311 Fourth St., exhibits various forms of gold. Mon.-Fri. 8-5; closed holidays. Free. Phone (530) 842-8084 or (888) 854-2000.

SISKIYOU COUNTY MUSEUM, 910 S. Main St., contains exhibits of the region dating from prehistoric times to the 20th century. Featured are displays about American Indians, fur trappers and the military. The outdoor museum displays equipment and restored buildings in an 1800s mining and pioneer settlement. Allow 2 hours minimum. Tues.-Fri. 9-5, Sat. 9-4; closed holidays. Admission $2; ages 7-12, 75c. Phone (530) 842-3836.

RECREATIONAL ACTIVITIES

White-water Rafting

- SAVE **Orange Torpedo Trips** travels the Klamath River. Write P.O. Box 1111, Grants Pass, OR 97528-0294. Daily Apr.-Oct. Phone (541) 479-5061.

YUBA CITY (D-3) pop. 36,758, elev. 60′

Yuba City was founded in 1849 as a gold rush development; it is now a marketing center for the surrounding agricultural area.

COMMUNITY MEMORIAL MUSEUM, 1333 Butte House Rd., contains American Indian and pioneer artifacts, furniture, clothing, agricultural equipment, photographs and historical documents from Sutter County. Tues.-Fri. 9-5, Sat.-Sun. noon-4. Donations. Phone (530) 822-7141.

GRAY LODGE WILDLIFE AREA, 15 mi. n.w. off SR 99, comprises 9,100 acres. The refuge is an important Pacific flyway stopover for waterfowl, in addition to being a nesting ground for doves, pheasants, coots and hawks. More than 200 bird species use the refuge. Bird-watching and walking trails are available. An auto route traverses the area; fishing and hunting are permitted in season.

Daily dawn-dusk, except during waterfowl season, when hours coincide with the operational hunting regulations. Admission $2.50; free to holders of current California fishing and hunting licenses or California Wildlife Pass. Phone (530) 846-7500, or (530) 846-7505 for information about interpretive programs.

SUTTER BUTTES are 10 mi. w. on Butte House Rd. Sometimes referred to as the world's smallest mountain range, this brooding cluster of dark rocks rises some 2,000 feet and covers about 75 square miles. The buttes are a volcanic upthrust formation, something of a geologic anomaly for this area, and are popular with nature lovers, who enjoy the abundant bird life and wildflowers.

Although much of the region is private property, visitors can join nature study groups and guided hikes. For more information phone (530) 741-6825.

Nevada
"The City that Never Sleeps"
Nonstop gambling, neon signs, flashy shows—this is Las Vegas
The Extraterrestrial Highway
Bring your binoculars and watch for UFOs along this lonely stretch of road
Sandy Lows and Icy Highs
Nevada's terrain ranges from parched deserts to snowcapped peaks
Pioneer Routes
Many Nevada highways retrace the routes blazed by intrepid pioneers
Ghost Towns Still Live
Old mining towns such as Virginia City, Rhyolite and Eureka are open for business

Black Rock Desert
© Scott T. Smith

Great Basin National Park / © Scott T. Smith

You could drive completely across Nevada and see nothing but lonely, deserted highway, or you could drive across Nevada and see everything. It's all in your expectations and attitude.

You can see it as it is now, some of the most arid territory in the entire country. Or you could imagine what this land must have been like millions of years ago when it was a vast inland sea.

You might glance at your surroundings and think: hot, sandy, dry. Or you could look a little further and see snowcapped peaks and green valleys with fertile farms.

You might think that nothing could live in such a desolate place. But closer inspection might reveal wild horses, tortoises and any number of raptors.

take a closer look

You could look toward the horizon and see only sage, juniper and yucca palms. Or you could venture off the beaten path and find pines, firs, roses and wild strawberries.

You might conclude that all the people you see are tourists or visiting weekend gamblers. Yet a little investigation will show that the state is one of the fastest growing in the country and that Clark County has more than tripled its citizenry over the past 25 years.

So take a second look at Nevada. Don't be fooled by what you think you see.

OK, you were lured to Nevada by the temptation of turning a quarter into a million dollars. Hitting the jackpot. Early retirement. A life of ease. Then reality sets in. As it turns out, you don't have the Midas touch after all. But here you are in Nevada, the Silver State, with no silver to show for your troubles. What should you do?

Your dreams of monetary riches may have faded, but there are other riches to be had here: wide open spaces, endless blue skies, deserts, mountains and the culture of the American Indians who lived here long before neon invaded the Las Vegas Valley.

Las Vegas is man's excuse for excess. In the beginning there were slot machines, which begat all-you-can-eat buffets, which begat elaborate star-studded shows, which begat themed megaresorts. But leave the glitz and glamour of Vegas and you will find the Nevada of the ancient Anasazi, of the early pioneers who braved the harsh extremes of barren deserts and inhospitable mountains, of the dashing pony express riders and the ghost towns left behind by grizzled miners.

For there's another side to this state, one where Mother Nature, history and geography are intertwined. Take a gamble on what you will find here. You might discover that you struck it rich after all.

Of Deserts and Mountains

Some of Nevada's earliest inhabitants left their calling cards at Grimes Point near Fallon. Follow a trail past 150 boulders inscribed with rock art etched by these ancient peoples. But don't become too engrossed in deciphering their symbolism. You might be rudely returned to the present by the roar of jet aircraft engines—the Navy Fighter Weapons School, commonly known as "Top Gun," is nearby.

When you consider Nevada's setting in the Great Basin—an area characterized by dry deserts, mountain ranges, and valleys often interrupted by mesas and buttes—it's easy to understand why permanent settlement did not occur until the 1850s. It was greed and the potential of hitting pay dirt in the burgeoning mining districts that finally brought rudimentary civilization to this part of the nation.

It takes hardy species such as yucca, cacti and sagebrush to survive the arid climate, where annual rainfall in some areas is no more than 4 inches. While geckos and rattlesnakes handle the desert heat, bighorn sheep and pronghorn antelopes have adapted to the

Nevada Historical Timeline

1826
A year after Hudson's Bay Co. trapper Peter Skene Ogden crosses the Humboldt River, explorer Jedediah Smith leads a party into the Las Vegas Valley.

©Bettmann/Corbis

1855
A Mormon mission in the Las Vegas Valley is begun; the mission eventually fails, but is the predecessor of today's glittery Las Vegas.

1859
The discovery of gold at the Comstock Mines in Virginia City prompts a surge in population and turns the region into a major mining center.

1861
The territory of Nevada is carved from the existing Utah Territory.

Nevada Commission on Tourism

1864
Nevada is proclaimed the 36th state.

higher elevations, where some peaks are snow-covered most of the year.

E.T. Meets the Old West

If this reminds you of the Old West, you have an accurate picture of much of Nevada. The occupation of cowboy still thrives in this part of the country, where old Pony Express stations line US 50, now known as "The Loneliest Road in America." But more futuristic means of travel are sought out along SR 375, designated the Extraterrestrial Highway for its many UFO sightings and proximity to the Air Force's top-secret Area 51.

Head away from the population hubs of Las Vegas and Reno and you will find highways leading to historic outposts—vestiges of the frontier era. Old mining towns such as Virginia City retain their 19th-century boomtown appearance from the days when the Comstock Lode's vast deposits generated prosperity and a surge in population as well as saloons and brothels. The assay office is open again in the ghost town of Berlin, east of Gabbs on SR 844, but this time strictly for the edification of visitors to the state park encompassing the site.

Present-day reminders of Nevada's Western heritage include rodeos, powwows and cultural exhibits about the American Indians who lived here long before Capt. John C. Frémont explored this land. For a look at one tribe's legacy, pay a visit to the Lost City Museum in Overton, which is actually on the site of a prehistoric Anasazi village. On the cowboy side of the ledger, get a ticket for June's Helldorado Days rodeo in Las Vegas for bull riding and bucking bronco action.

Wealth from Different Sources

As spectacular as the man-made scenery is in Las Vegas and Reno, it pales in comparison with that created by Mother Nature. Seemingly crafted with a heavy hand, Nevada's landscape is studded with jagged peaks, vividly hued rock formations and alkali flats—sometimes surreal, always majestic. The high desert setting of Red Rock Canyon, a short drive west of Las Vegas; the eroded sandstone formations at Valley of Fire, near Overton; and the spires and pillars of Cathedral Gorge, outside Caliente, attest to nature's prowess.

Nevada appeals to the gambler in each of us, from pioneers seeking fortune and wealth to today's casino cowboys, who pursue instant riches—not from the sweat of their brows, but with poker chips or a lucky roll of the dice.

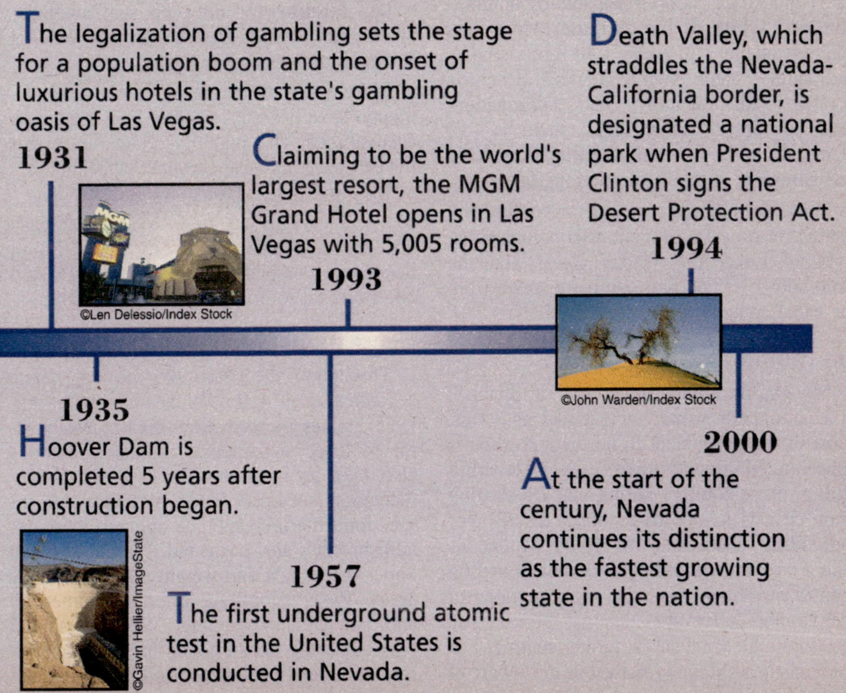

The legalization of gambling sets the stage for a population boom and the onset of luxurious hotels in the state's gambling oasis of Las Vegas.
1931
©Len Delessio/Index Stock
Claiming to be the world's largest resort, the MGM Grand Hotel opens in Las Vegas with 5,005 rooms.
1993
Death Valley, which straddles the Nevada-California border, is designated a national park when President Clinton signs the Desert Protection Act.
1994
©John Warden/Index Stock
1935
Hoover Dam is completed 5 years after construction began.
©Gavin Hellier/ImageState
1957
The first underground atomic test in the United States is conducted in Nevada.
2000
At the start of the century, Nevada continues its distinction as the fastest growing state in the nation.

Recreation

Conventional wisdom holds that recreational opportunities would be clustered near a state's largest cities. And you *can* enjoy **swimming, golf, tennis** and **racquetball** at any number of places in Las Vegas and Reno. However, the rest of the state holds its own as far as outdoor pursuits are concerned.

In or On the Water

If **fishing** is on the agenda, Nevada is the right place to be. Grab your pole and head to lakes Mead or Mohave in Lake Mead National Recreation Area for some of the nation's premier sport fishing spots. Lake Mead, created when Hoover Dam was completed in 1935, is known for striped bass, while rainbow trout prefer the waters of Lake Mohave. Other prime fishing holes can be found at Cave Lake State Park near Ely, where German brown trout are prevalent, and at Wild Horse State Recreation Area, off SR 225 between Mountain City and North Fork, where several varieties of trout populate the reservoir. State fishing licenses and/or special use stamps may be required.

Lake Mead is where to go for just about any water-based activity. **Boating** enthusiasts enjoy hidden coves not reachable by automobile, and **scuba diving** and **snorkeling** fans take advantage of the lake's 30-foot visibility and calm waters. While Boulder Beach is popular with swimmers and **sailboarders** seek out breezy shore areas, there is still plenty of room for **water skiing, kayaking** and **canoeing** at this 110-mile-long lake.

Tribal permits are required for boating and fishing on American Indian reservations along Pyramid Lake, the Walker River and the Colorado River; permits can be obtained from the tribal council at the reservation site.

On (Somewhat) Dry Land

Nevada, meaning "snow clad" in Spanish, is a natural for winter recreational activities. Most of the excitement in northern Nevada is concentrated around Lake Tahoe. **Downhill skiing, cross-country skiing** and **ice skating** draw crowds to the area's many resorts. For **heli-skiing** check out the Ruby Mountains near Elko; **snowmobiling** and **snowboarding** enthusiasts should visit the many sections of the Humboldt-Toiyabe National Forest. You can enjoy the same sports farther south at Lee Canyon, near Mount Charleston northwest of Las Vegas.

Lace up your **hiking** boots and explore Nevada. Miles of trails within most state parks await the adventurous. Just west of Las Vegas, Red Rock Canyon has more than 30 miles of hiking trails, including Pine Creek Canyon Trail, where eagle eyes might spot wild burros. Trekking cross-country through Lake Mead National Recreation Area can lead you to colorful sandstone formations, centuries-old petroglyphs and panoramic views. Brochures describing various trails as well as safety hints are available from the Nevada Commission on Tourism, 401 N. Carson St., Carson City, NV 89701; phone (775) 687-4322.

Among the miles of **backpacking** and hiking trails in Humboldt-Toiyabe National Forest are those in the Ruby Mountains outside Elko where mountain goats and bighorn sheep can be seen among the high mountain lakes. But don't forget your long johns, as evening temperatures can drop below freezing even during the summer. There also are many miles of trails suitable for **horseback riding.**

Duck hunters should head to the national wildlife refuges of Pahranagat, south of Alamo; Ruby Lake, in the Ruby Valley; and Stillwater, in the Fallon area. Other game includes rabbits, quails and pheasants. Controlled **hunting** for deer, elk and antelopes takes place at the Desert National Wildlife Range northwest of Las Vegas.

Most state parks are open all year, although severe winter weather may limit their accessibility. The majority charge user fees for **camping**, day use and boat launching.

And for those more attuned to spectator sports, Las Vegas has more to offer than casinos and nightclubs. The Las Vegas Motor Speedway complex, northeast off I-15 exit 54, offers all forms of **automobile racing.**

Recreational Activities

Throughout the TourBook, you may notice a Recreational Activities heading with bulleted listings of recreation-oriented establishments listed underneath. Similar operations also may be mentioned in Destination City recreation sections. Since normal AAA inspection criteria cannot be applied, these establishments are presented for information only. Age, height and weight restrictions may apply. Reservations are often recommended and sometimes required. Visitors should phone or write the attraction for additional information, and the address and phone number are provided for this purpose.

Fast Facts

POPULATION: 1,998,257.

AREA: 110,540 square miles; ranks 7th.

CAPITAL: Carson City.

HIGHEST POINT: 13,143 ft., Boundary Peak, White Mountains.

LOWEST POINT: 470 ft., on the Colorado River.

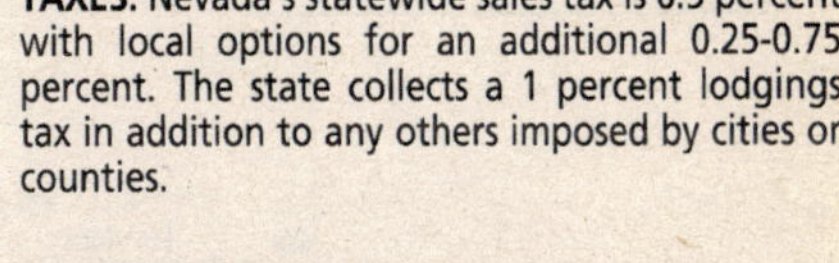

TIME ZONE(S): Pacific. DST.

MINIMUM AGE FOR DRIVERS: 16.

MINIMUM AGE FOR GAMBLING: 21.

SEAT BELT/CHILD RESTRAINT LAWS: Seat belts required for driver and all passengers; restraints required for children under 5 and under 40 pounds.

HELMETS FOR MOTORCYCLISTS: Required.

RADAR DETECTORS: Permitted.

FIREARMS LAWS: Vary by state and/or county. Contact the Legislative Council Bureau, Capitol Complex, Carson City, NV 89710; phone (775) 684-6800.

HOLIDAYS: Jan. 1; Washington's Birthday, Feb. (3rd Mon.); Memorial Day, May (last Mon.); July 4; Labor Day; Nevada Day, Oct. 31; Veterans Day, Nov. 11; Thanksgiving; Dec. 25.

TAXES: Nevada's statewide sales tax is 6.5 percent with local options for an additional 0.25-0.75 percent. The state collects a 1 percent lodgings tax in addition to any others imposed by cities or counties.

STATE INFORMATION CENTERS: Centers are maintained on US 93 at Boulder City; on I-15 at Jean; at 195 US 50 at Lake Tahoe; in Las Vegas at 3150 Paradise Rd.; in Laughlin at 1555 S. Casino Dr.; on I-15 at Mesquite; and on I-80 at West Wendover.

FURTHER INFORMATION FOR VISITORS:

Nevada Commission on Tourism
401 N. Carson St.
Carson City, NV 89701
(775) 687-4322
(800) 237-0774

RECREATION INFORMATION:

Nevada Division of State Parks
1300 S. Curry St.
Carson City, NV 89703
(775) 687-4384

FISHING AND HUNTING REGULATIONS:

Nevada Division of Wildlife
State Headquarters
1100 Valley Rd.
Reno, NV 89512
(775) 688-1500

NATIONAL FOREST INFORMATION:

Intermountain Region
2501 Wall Ave.
Ogden, UT 84401
(801) 625-5306
(877) 444-6777 (reservations)

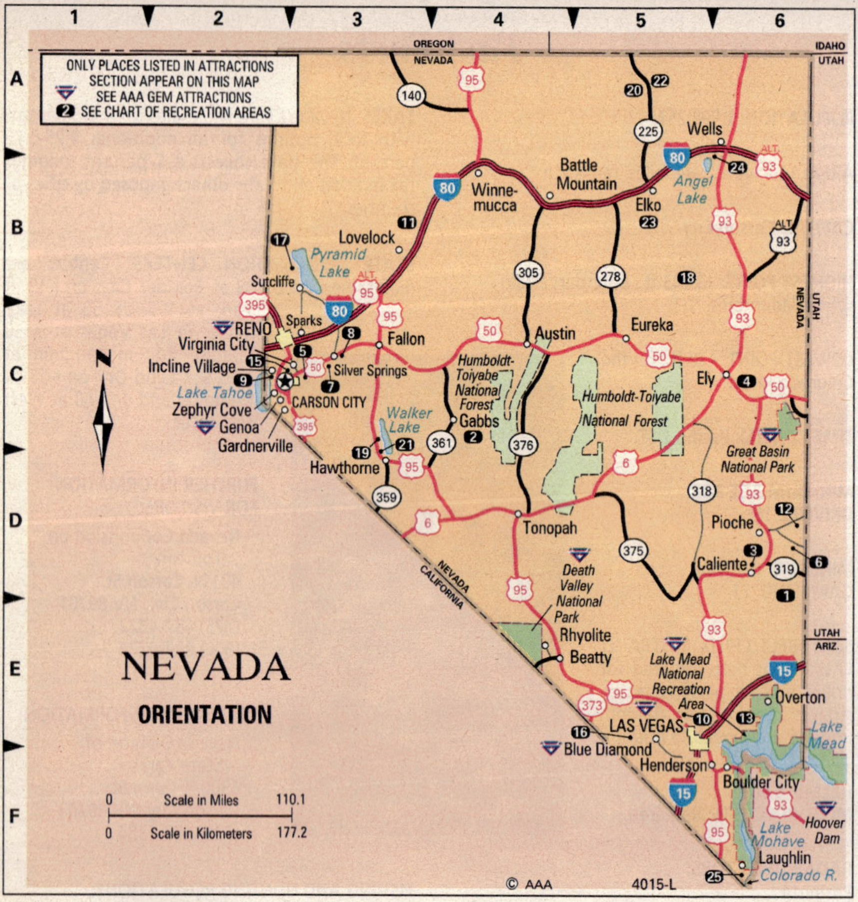

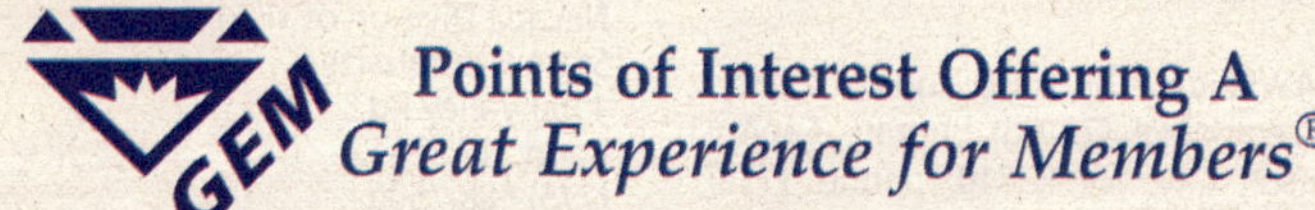

Points of Interest Offering A *Great Experience for Members®*

Blue Diamond (E-5)

SPRING MOUNTAIN RANCH STATE PARK—A spring-fed creek and a variety of wildlife and vegetation occupy this 528-acre park. See p. 251

Death Valley National Park (E-4)

DEATH VALLEY NATIONAL PARK—The Western Hemisphere's lowest point, Death Valley is blazingly hot and prone to flash floods, yet is home to rare foliage and geological phenomena. See p. 69 in California.

Genoa (C-2)

MORMON STATION STATE HISTORIC PARK—The log trading post at Mormon Station has been rebuilt to portray its place in history as a way station on the grueling overland trek to California. See p. 225.

Great Basin National Park (D-6)

GREAT BASIN NATIONAL PARK—Flora and fauna in this mountainous park range from that typically found in arid climates to examples that survive in frigid tundra conditions. See p. 225.

LEHMAN CAVES—Marble and limestone passageways are the focus of this cave at the base of Wheeler Peak. See p. 226.

Lake Mead National Recreation Area (E-5)

HOOVER DAM—Explore the history and operation of this engineering marvel built in the desert during the Great Depression. See p. 252.

LAKE MEAD NATIONAL RECREATION AREA—A year-round recreation mecca, Lake Mead beckons boaters, fishermen, hikers and water skiers as well as those simply in search of scenic drives. See p. 252.

Las Vegas (E-5)

GUGGENHEIM HERMITAGE MUSEUM—Masterworks and traveling exhibitions cover more than 7,600 square feet in the showroom of this museum designed by Pritzker Prize-winning architect Rem Koolhaas. See p. 237

THE LIBERACE MUSEUM—The glittering costumes and jewelry and the elaborate pianos and automobiles collected by the legendary pianist and entertainer are the highlights of this museum. See p. 237.

Reno (C-2)

FLEISCHMANN PLANETARIUM—Realistic images projected on the planetarium's domed screen transport visitors to the stars and beyond. See p. 254.

NATIONAL AUTOMOBILE MUSEUM—Drive on over and check out more than 200 classic automobiles displayed in period street scenes and galleries. See p. 255.

Nevada Temperature Averages Maximum / Minimum

From the records of the National Weather Service

	JAN	FEB	MAR	APR	MAY	JUNE	JULY	AUG	SEPT	OCT	NOV	DEC
Beatty	55/25	59/30	66/33	73/39	81/46	92/55	99/61	97/59	89/52	76/43	65/33	55/26
Elko	35/10	40/16	49/22	60/29	69/35	79/41	91/48	89/45	80/36	66/28	49/19	39/14
Ely	37/9	40/13	47/20	58/28	67/34	77/40	87/48	85/47	77/38	63/29	49/18	41/13
Hawthorne	45/23	49/26	57/31	64/36	72/44	82/52	90/59	89/59	79/51	67/40	57/31	46/24
Las Vegas	55/32	60/36	69/42	79/51	88/60	98/69	105/76	102/73	95/66	81/53	66/40	57/33
Reno	47/17	51/21	57/25	65/30	73/34	81/39	91/45	90/43	83/37	71/29	58/21	49/17

RECREATION AREAS

	MAP LOCATION	CAMPING	PICNICKING	HIKING TRAILS	BOATING	BOAT RAMP	BOAT RENTAL	FISHING	SWIMMING	PETS ON LEASH	BICYCLE TRAILS	WINTER SPORTS	VISITOR CENTER	LODGE/CABINS	FOOD SERVICE
NATIONAL PARKS *(See place listings)*															
Great Basin 77,100 acres 5 mi. w. of Baker near the Nevada-Utah border.		•	•	•				•		•		•	•		•
NATIONAL FORESTS *(See place listings)*															
Humboldt-Toiyabe 6,343,735 acres. Central, western, southern and northern Nevada and eastern California. Horse rental, interpretive trails.		•	•	•	•		•	•		•	•	•		•	
NATIONAL RECREATION AREAS *(See place listings)*															
Lake Mead (E-5) Southeastern Nevada. Scuba diving.		•	•	•	•	•	•	•	•	•	•	•	•	•	•
STATE															
Beaver Dam (D-6) 2,393 acres 3.5 mi. n.e. of Caliente on US 93, then 28 mi. e. on a gravel road. Interpretive trails.	1	•	•	•	•	•		•	•	•					
Berlin-Ichthyosaur (C-4) 1,127 acres 23 mi. e. of Gabbs via SR 844. Historic. Horse trails, interpretive trails. *(See Gabbs p. 224)*	2	•	•	•						•		•	•		
Big Bend of the Colorado (F-6) 2,500 acres 5 mi. s. of Laughlin on the Needles Hwy. Scenic.	25		•		•	•		•	•	•					
Cathedral Gorge (D-6) 1,633 acres 2 mi. n. of Panaca off US 93. Scenic. Horse trails, interpretive trails.	3	•	•	•						•			•		
Cave Lake (C-6) 1,240 acres 8 mi. s. of Ely off US 93, then 7 mi. e. on Success Summit Rd. Cross-country skiing, snowmobiling.	4	•	•	•	•	•		•		•		•			
Dayton (C-3) 152 acres in Dayton on US 50. Historic. Nature trail.	5	•	•	•				•		•					
Echo Canyon (D-6) 1,080 acres 12 mi. e. of Pioche via SRs 322 and 323. Interpretive trail.	6	•	•	•	•	•		•		•					
Floyd Lamb (E-5) 2,040 acres 15 mi. n.w. of Las Vegas on US 95.	10		•	•				•		•	•				
Fort Churchill (C-3) 4,461 acres 7 mi. s. on US 9A, then 1 mi. w. on Old Fort Churchill Rd. Historic. Interpretive trail. *(See Silver Springs p. 255)*	7	•	•	•						•			•		
Lahontan (C-3) 30,522 acres 18 mi. w. of Fallon off US 50. Water sports. Scenic drives.	8	•	•		•	•	•	•	•	•					
Lake Tahoe Nevada (C-2) 14,242 acres 4 mi. s. of Incline Village on SR 28. Water skiing, cross-country skiing.	9		•	•	•	•		•	•	•	•	•			
Rye Patch (B-3) 20,241 acres 22 mi. n.e. of Lovelock off I-80.	11	•	•		•	•		•	•	•					
South Fork (B-5) 3,924 acres 16 mi. s.w. of Elko via SR 228 to Lower South Fork Rd. Water skiing.	23	•	•	•	•	•		•	•	•		•			
Spring Valley (D-6) 1,281 acres 20 mi. e. of Pioche via SR 322.	12	•	•	•	•	•		•		•		•			
Valley of Fire (E-6) 34,830 acres 14 mi. s.w. of Overton via SR 169. Historic sites. Bird-watching, horse trails. *(See Overton p. 253)*	13	•	•	•						•			•		
Walker Lake (C-3) 280 acres 11 mi. n.w. of Hawthorne on US 95. Water skiing.	21	•	•		•	•	•	•	•	•					
Washoe Lake (C-2) 8,038 acres between Reno and Carson City e. of US 395.	15	•	•	•	•	•		•	•	•					
Wild Horse (A-5) 120 acres 65 mi. n. of Elko via SR 225. Bird-watching, cross-country skiing, snowmobiling.	20	•	•		•	•		•		•		•			
OTHER															
Angel Lake (B-5) 13 mi. s.w. of Wells via SR 582.	24	•	•	•	•			•	•	•		•			
Mount Charleston (E-5) 30 mi. n.w. of Las Vegas via US 95 and SR 157.	16	•	•	•						•	•	•	•	•	•
Pyramid Lake (B-2) off SR 445. *(See Sutcliffe p. 256)*	17	•	•		•	•	•	•	•	•			•	•	•
Ruby Lake (B-5) 60 mi. s.e. of Elko.	18	•	•		•	•		•		•			•		•
Walker Lake/Sportsman's Beach (D-3) 4 mi. n. of Hawthorne. Water skiing.	19	•	•		•	•		•	•	•	•				
Wild Horse Reservoir (A-5) 65 mi. n. of Elko on SR 225.	22	•	•	•	•	•		•	•	•		•		•	•

Points of Interest

AUSTIN (C-4) pop. 400, elev. 6,527′

Popular legend says that Austin sprang up in 1862 just west of the present townsite after a Pony Express horse kicked over a rock that capped the mouth of a silver-laden cavern. Within 2 years Austin boasted a population of 10,000, as bullion poured from 11 ore-reduction mills. By 1867 some 6,000 mining claims had been filed.

A reminder of Austin's former affluence is Stoke's Castle, built in 1897 for Anson Phelps Stokes, an eastern financier who had considerable mining interests in the area. Built of hand-hewn granite slabs, the deserted three-story replica of a Roman tower can be seen for miles in the desert. Also of interest is Lander County Courthouse, the second-story balcony of which was used by vigilantes as a gallows.

Near Austin are a number of historical sites. Hickson Petroglyph Recreation Site, 24 miles east on US 50 near the old Pony Express Trail, and the Toquima Caves, 6 miles farther east, feature stones etched with American Indian drawings dating from 1000 B.C. to A.D. 1500. About 65 miles west of Austin off SR 50 are the remains of the Cold Springs Pony Express Station. A sign near the highway explains the history of the site and marks the beginning of an interpretive 1.5-mile trail to the Pony Express station site.

Mountain biking and hiking as well as trout fishing and waterfowl hunting are available in the Humboldt-Toiyabe National Forest *(see place listing p. 226).*

Greater Austin Chamber of Commerce: Austin Courthouse, P.O. Box 212, Austin, NV 89310; phone (775) 964-2200 or (775) 964-2447.

BATTLE MOUNTAIN (B-5) pop. 2,871, elev. 4,507′

Battle Mountain is named for a nearby mountain range that commemorates an American Indian raid against pioneers in 1857. The discovery of minerals in Copper Canyon in 1870 brought permanent settlers, and Battle Mountain became the point of transfer for mining supplies between stage lines and railroads.

Ranching and transportation have largely replaced mining. There are two barite mines near Battle Mountain and a gold and silver mine at Copper Canyon. Battle Mountain straddles I-80, which follows the old Bidwell, Donner and Fremont pioneer trails. To the south along SR 305 is the scenic Reese River Valley, part of the Arc Dome Wilderness in the Humboldt-Toiyabe National Forest.

Battle Mountain Chamber of Commerce: 625 S. Broad, P.O. Box 333, Battle Mountain, NV 89820; phone (775) 635-8245.

BEATTY (E-5) pop. 1,154, elev. 3,308′

A picturesque desert town in the Amargosa River Valley, Beatty is the Nevada approach to Death Valley National Park *(see place listing in California p. 69).* Chloride Cliff, reached via a rough 5-mile dirt road off SR 374, offers an excellent view of Death Valley. Also en route to the national park are the ghost towns of Rhyolite *(see place listing p. 255)* and Bullfrog. Six miles north of Beatty on US 95 is Bailey's Hot Springs. With a water temperature of about 104 degrees Fahrenheit, the springs are open year-round.

Beatty Chamber of Commerce: 119 E. Main, P.O. Box 956, Beatty, NV 89003; phone (775) 553-2424.

BLUE DIAMOND—*see Las Vegas p. 251.*

BOULDER CITY—*see Las Vegas p. 251.*

CALIENTE (D-6) pop. 1,123, elev. 4,403′

Caliente, named for the hot springs originally found in the area, is near several state parks, including Beaver Dam, Cathedral Gorge, Echo Canyon and Spring Valley *(see Recreation Chart and the AAA California & Nevada CampBook).* Also nearby is the ghost town Delamar, marked by a few stone buildings, mill ruins and a cemetery; check locally for road conditions.

A mural displaying points of interest in Lincoln and Clark counties is in the lobby of the Amtrak station, a Spanish-style railroad depot built in 1923. Guided tours of the Lincoln County Art Room, also in the lobby of the station, and other area attractions can be arranged through the chamber of commerce.

Caliente Chamber of Commerce: 101 Depot St., P.O. Box 553, Caliente, NV 89008; phone (775) 726-3129.

CARSON CITY (C-3) pop. 52,457, elev. 4,660′

Carson City, founded in 1858 and named for Kit Carson, was designated as the state capital in 1864. The 19th-century silver-domed Capitol, with additions and restorations, still is in use. The old Assembly and Senate chambers, including a museum display about the Capitol, can be visited. Self-guiding tour brochures are available at the Capitol; at the Nevada State Library and Archives at 100 N. Stewart St., (775) 684-3360; or from the State Historic Preservation Office, (775) 684-3448. The Legislative Building, south of the Capitol, also is open to the public; phone (775) 684-6800.

As the social center for nearby mining settlements in the mid-1800s, Carson City prospered.

The federal government established a mint for coining the copious silver output of the Comstock Lode, 15 miles northeast near Virginia City *(see place listing p. 257)*. Gold found its way here also, as evidenced by the rare gold display at the Carson City Nugget, across from the Capitol.

Antique firefighting equipment, old photographs and a series of Currier & Ives prints dealing with firefighters are displayed at Warren Engine Company No. 1 Fire Museum, 777 S. Stewart St.; phone (775) 887-2210.

The Sierra Seminary, one of the first coeducational schools in the West, was established in Carson City in 1860 by Hannah Clapp. An outspoken advocate of women's rights, Clapp operated the school for about 25 years before moving to Reno. There she and the university president temporarily served as the entire staff of the infant University of Nevada.

Carson City lies along US 50, which has been called "The Loneliest Road in America." Once part of the Pony Express Trail across central Nevada, the route has long stretches without roadside services and passes through such historic mining towns as Austin *(see place listing p. 221)*, Ely *(see place listing p. 223)* and Eureka *(see place listing p. 223)*.

The portion of US 50 heading west to Lake Tahoe and the California border is especially scenic. From its junction with US 395 downtown, US 50 cuts through the Humboldt-Toiyabe National Forest *(see place listing p. 226)* and then follows the lake's southeastern shoreline. Beginning at its junction with US 50 at Spooner Summit, SR 28, another scenic route, follows the lake's northeastern shoreline into California.

Carson City Convention and Visitors Bureau: 1900 S. Carson St:, Suite 100, Carson City, NV 89701; phone (775) 687-7410 or (800) 638-2321. *See color ad p. 88.*

Self-guiding tours: A walking tour map containing illustrations and descriptions of the town's historic sites is available from the convention and visitors bureau.

BOWERS MANSION PARK, 10 mi. n. on old US 395, overlooks Washoe Lake. The restored mansion, built by a Comstock Lode millionaire at a cost of $200,000 in 1864, contains some of the original furnishings. The surrounding park has picnic facilities, a playground and a swimming pool.

Park open daily 8 a.m.-9 p.m., Memorial Day-Labor Day; 8-7, first weekend in Apr.-day before Memorial Day and day after Labor Day-late Oct.; 8-5, rest of year. Closed Thanksgiving and Dec. 25. Guided mansion tours are given daily every 30 minutes 11-4:30. Park free. Mansion tours $4; over 63 and under 16, $3. Pool $3; under 16, $2. Phone the mansion at (775) 849-0201 or the ranger station at (775) 849-1825.

BREWERY ARTS CENTER is at 449 W. King St. near the Capitol. Situated in the city's historic district, the gallery presents the work of Nevada artists. Changing exhibits include paintings, sculpture, photography, jewelry and fine arts and crafts. Allow 1 hour minimum. Mon.-Sat. 10-4; closed Jan. 1, Thanksgiving and Dec. 25. Free. Phone (775) 882-6411.

SAVE **THE CHILDREN'S MUSEUM OF NORTHERN NEVADA,** 813 N. Carson St., presents hands-on exhibits allowing children to discover what it is like to work in a grocery store, conduct an orchestra and make a movie. Star Labs, a planetarium presentation, is offered on weekends. Traveling art and science exhibits are featured throughout the year. Allow 1 hour minimum. Tues.-Sun. 10-4:30. Admission $5; ages 3-14, $3. MC, VI. Phone (775) 884-2226.

NEVADA STATE MUSEUM, 600 N. Carson St., is in the former United States Branch Mint Building, where Carson City silver dollars were stamped 1870-93. Exhibits include historical relics, a ghost town replica, a gun collection, one of the largest mammoths ever found in North America, a mintmark coin collection, minerals and ores. In addition, an American Indian room displays willow baskets woven by Dot-So-La-Lee of the Washoe tribe.

Allow 1 hour, 30 minutes minimum. Daily 8:30-4:30; closed Jan. 1, Thanksgiving and Dec. 25. Admission $3, senior citizens $2.50, under 17 free. Phone (775) 687-4810.

NEVADA STATE RAILROAD MUSEUM, 2180 S. Carson St. (US 395), contains more than 60 pieces of rolling stock, most from the Virginia and Truckee Railroad line, including seven restored steam engines. Established in 1869, the line carried ore from the Comstock Lode to the Carson River for 69 of its 81 years. It was later discovered by Hollywood, which used V & T passenger cars, freight cars and vintage engines from the late 1930s through the 1950s.

Rides on the historic trains are available. Allow 30 minutes minimum for museum, 1 hour for museum and train ride. Museum daily 8:30-4:30; closed Jan. 1, Thanksgiving and Dec. 25. Train schedules vary; phone ahead. Museum admission $2, under 18 free. Steam train ride $2.50; ages 6-11, $1. Motorcar ride $1; ages 6-11, 50c. Phone (775) 687-6953.

GEM DEATH VALLEY NATIONAL PARK—

see place listing in California p. 69.

ELKO (B-5) pop. 16,708, elev. 5,060′

The center of Nevada's cattle country, Elko served as a way station for wagon trains during the western migration. Tourism accounts for a large portion of the town's revenue. The Cowboy Poetry Gathering, the nation's first such festival, is held from late January to early February. The event helps preserve the culture of the cowboy through music, stories, tall tales, dance, poetry and exhibits of cowboy gear.

South of Elko lie the Ruby Mountains, where miles of trails lead to back-country lakes and marshes offering hunting, fishing and boating. Lamoille Canyon *(see Humboldt-Toiyabe National Forest p. 226)* in the Ruby Mountains is known for its steep glacial walls, free-flowing streams and scenic vistas.

Elko Chamber of Commerce: 1405 Idaho St., Elko, NV 89801; phone (775) 738-7135 or (800) 428-7143.

NORTHEASTERN NEVADA MUSEUM, 1515 Idaho St., chronicles natural history with exhibits pertaining to the area's American Indian heritage, mining, ranching and railroad traditions. Frontier displays include a pioneer kitchen, a schoolroom and a printing plant. Also included are wildlife displays, a photograph library, an antique gun collection, an 1860 Pony Express cabin, two "mudwagon" stagecoaches and a 1918 Dodge touring car. Allow 1 hour minimum. Mon.-Sat. 9-5, Sun. 1-5; closed Jan. 1, Thanksgiving and Dec. 25. Admission $5; over 65 and ages 13-18, $3; ages 3-12, $1. Phone (775) 738-3418.

WESTERN FOLKLIFE CENTER, off I-80 exit 301, downtown at 501 Railroad St., preserves and presents folk art of the American West with a variety of exhibits, performances and activities. Its gallery features changing exhibits about cowboy and American Indian art. An original 44-foot mahogany Brunswick bar is displayed in homage to the Western saloon. The center also hosts the National Cowboy Poetry Gathering as well as a nationally broadcast radio show, "The Open Road." Allow 1 hour minimum. Mon.-Sat. 10-5:30; closed Jan. 1, Thanksgiving and Dec. 25. Free. Phone (775) 738-7508 or (888) 880-5885.

ELY (C-5) pop. 4,041, elev. 6,421'

Founded in 1868 as a silver-mining camp, Ely bloomed with the arrival of the Nevada Northern Railway, which chugged into town in 1906 bedecked with flags, bunting and sagebrush wreaths. When Ely converted to large-scale copper mining, the town grew from 500 to 3,000 residents in a year.

Kennecott Copper Corp.'s renowned Liberty Pit produced more than $550 million in copper, gold and silver deposits. Kennecott also operated the giant Ruth pit, which produced from about 1905 to the late 1970s. Ely continues to be a center for mining as well as ranching and recreation.

The surrounding mountain ranges provide fine hunting and trout fishing. High-country hikers are fond of nearby Wheeler Peak Scenic Area, which includes 13,063-foot Wheeler Peak, Baker and Snake creeks, Big Wash Canyon and the upper parts of Lehman Creek. The garnet-studded rhyolite outcropping at the peak of Garnet Hill, 5 miles west off US 50, is popular with rockhounds. Swimming and fishing are available at Cave Lake State Recreation Area *(see Recreation Chart and the AAA California & Nevada CampBook).*

Several old mining camps and ghost towns still can be found in the Ely vicinity; these include Cherry Creek, Fort Schellbourne, Hamilton, Lane City, Osceola, Taylor and Ward. Ely also is the western terminus of a scenic route consisting of US 93, US 50/6 and SR 487. Crossing the Schell Creek and Snake ranges, the route leads to the Utah border and Great Basin National Park *(see place listing p. 225).*

White Pines County Tourism: 150 6th St., Ely, NV 89301; phone (775) 289-3720 or (800) 496-9350.

NEVADA NORTHERN RAILWAY MUSEUM, e. of town at 1100 Ave. A, includes a restored depot, a dispatcher's office, a roundhouse and a machine shop in addition to cars and locomotives from various eras. Ninety-minute train rides to Lane City or Lavon and 2.25-hour trips to Keystone or Adverse are offered. Sunset and holiday excursions are available. Museum Wed.-Mon. 8-5, Memorial Day-Sept. 30. Guided tours are given at 11 and 2. Trains depart Mon. and Wed.-Sun., June-Sept. Departure times vary; phone ahead. Museum admission $3, under 5 free. Train fare $18; ages 4-12, $12. Phone (775) 289-2085.

WARD CHARCOAL OVENS STATE HISTORIC PARK is 5 mi. s.e. on US 6/50/93, then 11 mi. s. on Cave Valley Rd. The six 30-foot-high stone "beehive" kilns, constructed during the 1870s mining boom, burned wood to produce charcoal for use in area smelters. The park affords outstanding views of the Steptoe Valley. Picnicking is permitted. Daily dawn-dusk (weather permitting). Admission $3 per private vehicle. Camping $9. Phone (775) 728-4460.

WHITE PINE PUBLIC MUSEUM, 2000 Aultman St., displays gems and minerals, mining equipment, Pony Express memorabilia, American Indian relics, furniture, clothes and guns. In addition the museum has a collection of 1,000 dolls, with more than 400 displayed on a rotating basis. An outdoor train exhibit also is offered. Mon.-Sat. 9-5, Sun. 1-5; closed major holidays. Donations. Phone (775) 289-4710.

EUREKA (C-5) elev. 6,837'

Eureka lies along US 50 at the southern end of scenic SR 278. During the town's heyday in the 1870s, its lead-based economy and the attendant smelters led the town to be called the "Pittsburgh of the West." The population, which at one point reached nearly 11,000, supported 100 saloons, several newspapers, hotels, an opera house, five fire companies and a brass band.

The renovated Eureka Opera House, 31 S. Main St., which dates from 1880, presents a variety of cultural shows and serves as a convention, visitor and cultural arts center. A videotape describing Eureka's history also is featured.

Eureka Sentinel Museum, at Bateman and Monroe streets, houses the original printing equipment of the newspaper, which began operations in 1870, and displays reprints, posters and placards printed by the *Sentinel* in the 1870s and '80s; phone (775) 237-5010.

The Eureka County Courthouse, at Ruby Hill Avenue and Main Street, typifies late 19th-century architecture. Completed in 1880, it features a large upstairs courtroom with a bench made of imported Spanish cedar. Two outdoor bells once served as alarms for the town's volunteer fire companies. The courthouse is still in use today; phone (775) 237-6006.

Eureka Economic Development Program: 31 S. Main St., Eureka, NV 89316; phone (775) 237-5484.

Self-guiding tours: A walking tour map containing descriptions of the town's historic sites is available from the economic development program.

FALLON (C-3) pop. 7,536, elev. 3,963′

Completion of Lahontan Dam in 1914 and subsequent reclamation and irrigation changed the area from barren desert to one of the state's largest farming districts. Major farm products include livestock, alfalfa and "Hearts o' Gold" cantaloupes. Besides supplying water for irrigation, the impounded lake is popular for recreation as part of the 30,522-acre Lahontan State Recreation Area *(see Recreation Chart and the AAA California & Nevada CampBook).*

East of Fallon US 50 parallels the old Pony Express route for a number of miles. About 20 miles east of town is a 1-mile-long road leading to Sand Mountain and Sand Springs Pony Express Station. One of the few "singing mountains" in the country, Sand Mountain is composed of grains of sand that sometimes create a low moan as they shift. A more contemporary means of getting across the desert now exists, however, as Fallon is the headquarters for the U.S. Navy Fighter Weapons School; the flight school is more commonly known as "Top Gun."

The Bureau of Land Management offers free expeditions on the second and fourth Saturday of each month to Hidden Cave, an archeological zone 11 miles east of Fallon on US 50; phone (775) 885-6000. Tours depart from the Churchill County Museum and Archives *(see attraction listing).*

Fallon Convention & Tourism Authority: 100 Campus Way, Fallon, NV 89406; phone (775) 423-4556 or (800) 874-0903.

CHURCHILL COUNTY MUSEUM AND ARCHIVES, 1050 S. Maine St., features an extensive collection of Western Americana focusing on the history of Churchill County and the Lahontan Valley. Displays of memorabilia pertain to the Emigrant Trail and transcontinental telegraph, while notable collections include rocks, minerals and gemstones, artifacts of Nevada Indian tribes and an early 1900s novelty store. An exhibit about the Carson Desert includes a diorama.

Allow 1 hour minimum. Mon.-Sat. 10-5, Sun. noon-5, Apr.-Dec.; Mon.-Sat. 10-4, Sun. noon-4, rest of year. Donations. Phone (775) 423-3677.

GABBS (C-4) pop. 318, elev. 4,597′

BERLIN-ICHTHYOSAUR STATE PARK is 23 mi. e. via SR 844. This 1,153-acre park has fossils of gigantic marine reptiles known as ichthyosaurs, which once swam in an ocean that covered Nevada 225 million years ago. The park contains the late 19th-century ghost town of Berlin, where fortunes rose and fell with the silver boom. Interpretive signs outline self-guiding tours among the town's 13 preserved buildings.

Park daily 24 hours (weather permitting). Guided 90-minute tours of the townsite are given Sat.-Sun. at 3, Memorial Day-Labor Day. Guided tours of the Ichthyosaur Fossil Shelter are given daily at 10, 2 and 4, Memorial Day-Labor Day; Sat.-Sun. at 10 and 2, mid-Mar. through day before Memorial Day and day after Labor Day to mid-Nov. The 1-hour Diana Mine tour is offered Fri.-Sun. at 11, mid-Apr. to mid-Oct. Mine tour is limited to 8 people; reservations are recommended.

Park $3. Guided tours $2; ages 6-12, $1. Camping fee additional $8. Phone (775) 964-2440. *See Recreation Chart and the AAA California & Nevada CampBook.*

GARDNERVILLE (C-2)
pop. 3,357, elev. 4,746′

The Lahontan National Fish Hatchery, 4 miles south on US 395, raises the threatened Lahontan cutthroat trout for stocking in western Nevada waters. The hatchery is open daily; phone (775) 265-2425.

Carson Valley Chamber of Commerce and Visitors Authority: 1513 US 395, Gardnerville, NV 89410; phone (775) 782-8144 or (800) 727-7677.

CARSON VALLEY MUSEUM & CULTURAL CENTER is at 1477 US 395N. The museum is housed in the former Douglas County High School, constructed in 1915. Exhibits depict the history of the Carson Valley community and its settlers. Allow 1 hour minimum. Tues.-Sat. 10-4; closed major holidays. Admission $3; ages 6-18, $2; free to all first Sat. of the month. Phone (775) 782-2555.

GENOA (C-2) elev. 4,800′

Founded by one of the traders sent out by Brigham Young in 1849, Genoa became the first permanent settlement in Nevada. In 1859 Nevada's first territorial legislature met in Genoa for a 9-day session that drafted a declaration of cause for separation from Utah Territory. Recognizing the value of the famed Comstock Lode in financing the Union's efforts in the Civil War, Congress established the Territory of Nevada in 1861.

Norwegian immigrant John Torsteinson-Rue, better known as Snowshoe Thompson, is buried in

Genoa. From 1856 to 1876 Thompson made 90-mile treks over the rugged, snow-covered Sierra Nevada range to deliver mail between Genoa and Sacramento, Calif.

GENOA COURTHOUSE MUSEUM is at 2304 Main St. The restored 1865 courthouse contains exhibits about Snowshoe Thompson and the Pony Express, replicas of an old schoolroom, a courtroom, a jail and a kitchen as well as American Indian basketry, needlework and artifacts. Changing exhibits also are offered. Allow 1 hour minimum. Daily 10-4:30, early May 1 to mid-Oct. Admission $3; ages 6-18, $2; free to all first Sat. of the month. Phone (775) 782-4325.

GEM **MORMON STATION STATE HISTORIC PARK,** off US 395, then w. on Genoa Ln. to jct. SR 206 (Foothill Rd.), is a restored log stockade and trading post built in 1851 in the Carson Valley, where pioneers often rested before continuing over the Sierra Nevada to California. A museum with state history exhibits also is on the grounds. Picnicking is permitted. Daily 9-4:30, May 1 to mid-Oct. Donations. Phone (775) 782-2590 or (775) 687-4379.

GEM GREAT BASIN NATIONAL PARK (D-6)

Elevations in the park range from 6,200 ft. at Snake Creek to 13,063 ft. at Wheeler Peak. Refer to AAA maps for additional elevation information.

Approximately 5 miles west of Baker on SR 488 near the Nevada-Utah border, the 77,100-acre Great Basin National Park, established in 1986, contains many of the features common to the Great Basin, including impressive mountain peaks, lush meadows, sparkling streams, alpine lakes and a small glacier.

Rising abruptly 7,700 feet from the desert floor, the park exhibits a wide variety of plant and animal habitats that range from the Upper Sonoran life zone with its jackrabbits, sagebrush and cacti to the frigid Arctic-Alpine Tundra life zone at the highest elevations.

In spring and summer many kinds of wildflowers bloom on the mountain slopes. Pine, spruce, fir and mountain mahogany make up the forests, and wildlife includes mule deer, mountain lions, coyotes, porcupines and golden eagles. Rocky Mountain bighorn sheep, once locally extinct, were reintroduced to this area in 1971.

General Information and Activities

A highlight of the park is Lehman Caves, a limestone-solution cave. Cave walks, exhibits, films, maps and park information are offered *(see attraction listing)*. The park's visitor center is open daily 8:30-4:30; phone (775) 234-7331. Food is available April through October.

Wheeler Peak Scenic Drive extends 12 miles to the 10,000-foot elevation on the flank of Wheeler Peak. Hiking trails pass several alpine lakes to the 13,063-foot summit or to a rare ancient bristlecone pine forest. Park interpreters conduct various campfire programs in the summer. It is recommended that motor homes and trailers longer than 24 feet not attempt Wheeler Peak Scenic Drive.

Camping is permitted at three campgrounds along Wheeler Peak Scenic Drive and at Baker Creek Campground on Baker Creek Road. Fishing for rainbow trout is popular in the park's many clear creeks. Anglers over age 11 need a Nevada fishing license and a trout stamp; both are available in Ely and Baker. There are no developed cross-country ski trails, but winter brings ample opportunity for back-country skiing.

Note: A few warnings should be kept in mind when visiting the park. The area is dry, so carry plenty of drinking water when hiking and treat any surface water before use. Rattlesnakes are found at all elevations during warm weather, and extreme weather conditions are likely throughout the year. *See Recreation Chart.*

ADMISSION to the park is free. Fees for cave walks range $2-$8. Camping $10.

PETS must be on a leash at all times. They are not allowed in buildings, in the cave or on trails.

ADDRESS inquiries to the Superintendent, Great Basin National Park, 100 Great Basin National Park, Baker, NV 89311; phone (775) 234-7331.

Points of Interest

BRISTLECONE PINE FOREST consists of 150 acres of trees considered to be among the oldest living things on Earth. One stand includes pines approaching 4,000 years old. An interpretive trail branches off the scenic area's main loop trail. Another spur off the main loop climbs to the summit

---

DID YOU KNOW

Lake Mead, formed by Hoover Dam, is one of the world's largest artificially created lakes.

---

of Wheeler Peak, the second highest peak in Nevada. Park interpreters lead walks daily in summer (weather permitting).

LEHMAN CAVES, 5 mi. w. of Baker at the foot of Wheeler Peak, consists of illuminated marble and limestone passages that have many colorful formations and curious shield or palette shapes.

Although the first written mention of the cave was found in an 1885 newspaper, it is possible the cave was discovered earlier by homesteaders or miners. Absalom S. Lehman probably was the first to realize the significance of the underground galleries. After conducting his own exploration, he guided parties through the cave until his death in 1891.

The tour covers about a half-mile and includes six stairways. Flash cameras are allowed, but tripods and backpacks are not. The cave temperature is 50 degrees Fahrenheit, so a sweater or light jacket is recommended.

Guided 30-, 60- and 90-minute cave tours are given daily year-round. Tour times vary; phone ahead. Closed Jan. 1, Thanksgiving and Dec. 25. Tickets may be purchased up to 30 days in advance. Fee for 30-minute tour $2, bearers of Golden Age Passports $1, under 12 free. Fee for 60-minute tour $6; bearers of Golden Age Passports and under 12, $3. Fee for 90-minute tour $8, bearers of Golden Age Passports and under 12, $4. Under 5 are not permitted on 90-minute tour. AX, DC, DS, MC, VI. Phone (775) 234-7331, ext. 242, Mon.-Fri. 7:30-4:30.

HAWTHORNE (D-3) pop. 3,311, elev. 4,375′

MINERAL COUNTY MUSEUM, 10th and D sts., features mining, firefighting and railroad equipment, clothing, housewares and archeological specimens from the area's early days. A collection of mission bells recovered from the desert also is displayed. Tues.-Sat. noon-4. Donations. Phone (775) 945-5142.

HENDERSON—*see Las Vegas p. 251.*

HUMBOLDT-TOIYABE NATIONAL FOREST (C-5)

Elevations in the forest range from 100 ft. below sea level at Death Valley in Calif. to 12,374 ft. at Castle Peak. Refer to AAA maps for additional elevation information.

Scattered across divisions in central, northern, western and southern Nevada and in eastern California, Humboldt-Toiyabe National Forest is the second largest national forest in the country, totaling 6,343,735 acres. Ranges in north-central Nevada include the Independence, Santa Rosa, Ruby, White Pine, Jarbidge, Schell Creek and Quinn Canyon. Part of the forest lies along the rugged Monitor, Toquima, Toiyabe, Shoshone and Paradise ranges of central Nevada and along the eastern slopes of the Sierra Nevada and the Spring Mountains near Las Vegas.

Jarbidge Wilderness is north of Elko; no motorized vehicles are allowed, but six trails suitable for hiking and horseback riding traverse the area. The Ruby Mountains Wilderness, southeast of Elko, offers backpacking and other recreational opportunities within 90,000 acres of alpine lakes, glaciated canyons and rugged mountains. Other wilderness areas include Currant Mountain, East Humboldt, Grant Range, Mount Moriah, Quinn Canyon and Santa Rosa-Paradise Peak.

Three national hiking trails are within the forest. The Pacific Crest National Scenic Trail traverses 74 miles of forest land; the Toiyabe Crest National Recreation Trail runs 67 miles along the Toiyabe Range; and the Mount Charleston National Recreation Trail ascends the 11,918-foot summit of Charleston Peak. Due to unpredictable weather conditions, hiking on these trails should be limited to June through October; high elevations can receive snow during any month of the year.

Recreational activities within the forest include backpacking and hiking on nearly 900 miles of trails, fishing, hunting, camping and picnicking. Several mountain biking trails have been developed near Austin in central Nevada. Winter sports areas are at Heavenly Valley, Lee Canyon and Mount Rose. Winter sports such as heli-skiing, snowmobiling and cross-country skiing are popular. Other areas noted for visual and recreational appeal are Lake Tahoe, the Sierra Nevada near Bridgeport, Calif., and Mount Rose.

For further information contact the Forest Supervisor, Humboldt-Toiyabe National Forest, 1200 Franklin Way, Sparks, NV 89431; phone (775) 331-6444. *See Recreation Chart and the AAA California & Nevada CampBook.*

LAMOILLE CANYON SCENIC AREA is in Humboldt-Toiyabe National Forest, 20 mi. s.e. of Elko via SR 227. A paved, two-lane scenic drive, overshadowed by towering cliffs, winds 12 miles along the canyon. Several overlooks with posted information enable visitors to observe the effects of glacial activity. Picnicking, rest areas and limited campgrounds are available.

INCLINE VILLAGE—

see Lake Tahoe Area in California p. 89.

LAKE MEAD NATIONAL RECREATION AREA—

see Las Vegas p. 252.

LAKE TAHOE—

see Lake Tahoe Area in California p. 84.

Las Vegas

City Population: 478,434 **Elevation:** 2,174 ft.

Popular Spots

Lago di Bellagio at Bellagio...... *(see p. 240)*

Céline Dion at Caesars Palace..... *(see p. 248)*

The "Battle of Buccaneer Bay" at Treasure Island .... *(see p. 242)*

Sin City. Gambleville. The Entertainment Capital of the World. Open 24 hours. City of Lost Wages. The City Without Clocks. The Garden of Neon. Las Vegas is known as all of these. A city of approximately 478,434 people—1.4 million in the metro area—it did not even exist at the turn of the 20th century. Its explosive growth, particularly over the last 20 years or so, is largely a testament to the eternal conflict between fate and free will that lies at the heart of a dice roll, a dealt card or a pull on a slot. Gambling, in other words, is big business. According to the Las Vegas Convention and Visitors Authority, more than 35 million fun seekers arrived in 2001 and spent more than $31.5 billion (casino profits made up about $6 billion of that total).

Las Vegas has traditionally been considered the refuge of adults, but the shift toward family values was in full swing by the early 1990s, when the opening of theme hotels such as Excalibur, Treasure Island and the Luxor signaled a new effort to lure affluent baby boomers and their children.

It is true that you can have a great time in Las Vegas without gambling. Dining and shopping opportunities are plentiful and varied. The city arguably boasts more entertainment superstars and out-of-this-world production spectaculars per square mile than any other in the world. And spectacular natural attractions—from Red Rock Canyon National Conservation Area to Valley of Fire State Park *(see attraction listings p. 238 and p. 253)* to Arizona's Grand Canyon—are all within a day's drive.

The bottom line, however, is that "casinos are king," as one city advertising slogan puts it. So although children and nongamblers will find plenty of ways to have fun, it is the over-21 visitor, preferably with money to burn at the blackjack table or the slot machine, that the city seeks to attract.

Paris Las Vegas Eiffel Tower / © M. Gibson / Robertstock

Although the Strip and downtown's "Glitter Gulch" are the two major tourist areas, there are whole other sides to this city that the average visitor never sees while shuttling between the airport and his or her hotel. A large percentage of locals work in the service industry, and their shifts often do not reflect a conventional routine—there aren't many other places where you will see a cocktail waitress in full regalia circulating through a crowd and serving drinks at 7 in the morning.

Las Vegas is one of the most isolated major cities in the United States. It is 270 miles from Los Angeles, 293 miles from Phoenix, 570 miles from San Francisco and 447 miles from Reno, the only other city of any size in Nevada. Visitors arriving by air in the daytime see two small clusters of buildings (the hotels downtown and along the Strip) and odd incongruities like the Luxor pyramid and sphinx.

In fact, it is hard to imagine a man-made paradise sprouting from a more unlikely natural setting. Las Vegas—just over 2,000 feet in elevation—lies in the Las Vegas Valley, a long, flat expanse of terrain formed over time by the advance-and-retreat movements of glaciers. The valley is enclosed by mountain ranges, notably the Spring Mountains to

Getting There — *starting on p. 234*

Getting Around — *starting on p. 234*

What To See — *starting on p. 235*

What To Do — *starting on p. 240*

Where To Stay — *starting on p. 846*

Where To Dine — *starting on p. 860*

the west, a popular hiking and skiing area dominated by 11,918-foot Mount Charleston. Prehistoric southern Nevada was a virtual marsh; the valley assumed its present arid characteristics roughly 12,000 years ago when it was overtaken by the Mojave Desert. But beneath the parched valley floor a system of aquifers, fed by rainwater and snowmelt coming off the surrounding mountains, periodically surfaced to create a life-giving oasis.

American Indians, from primitive hunters and foragers to the later Anasazi and Paiute tribes, had inhabited the Las Vegas Valley as far back as 11,000 B.C. It was not until 1829 that the valley oasis was stumbled upon by Rafael Rivera, a scout for Mexican trader Antonio Armijo, who was leading a 60-man expedition to Los Angeles via the Old Spanish Trail. Searching for water, Rivera discovered the artesian springs that he named Las Vegas ("the meadows").

The discovery shortened the route to Los Angeles but sadly hastened the dissolution of the Paiute, not only through the depredations of invading white settlers but the raids of the warlike Ute tribe. In 1844, surveyor and explorer John C. Frémont, leading an overland expedition west to California, camped at the Las Vegas Springs; today a downtown street and casino both bear his name. By the early 1850s, Mormon wagon trains traveling from central Utah to Los Angeles had tamed the Old Spanish Trail, which by then was known as the Mormon Trail.

The Mormon Trail became the preferred route for settlers, immigrants and California gold seekers. Mormon missionaries established a settlement in the Las Vegas Valley in 1855. But although they dug irrigation ditches, managed to cultivate fruit trees and vegetables, and mined lead for bullets from nearby Potosi Mountain, the harsh environment caused the outpost to be abandoned by 1858. During the next few decades hardscrabble prospectors coexisted uneasily with the Paiute, and the only development of any note was the ranch built by Octavius Decatur Gass on the site of the fort erected by the Mormons.

Stratosphere Tower coaster ride
© Gibson Stock Photography

The coming of the railroads brought about the birth of Las Vegas. Due to the area's strategic location and plentiful water supply, the San Pedro, Los Angeles and Salt Lake Railroad (later absorbed by Union Pacific) in 1902 designated it a service stop on the route from Los Angeles to Salt Lake City. A dusty tent settlement sprang up as track was laid across the valley. The train's inaugural run was in January 1905; the railroad yards were located at Main and Fremont streets, where the Plaza Hotel now stands. Four months later the city of Las Vegas was founded through a land auction of individual lots. Clark County, named for railroad magnate William Clark, was created in 1909 from neighboring Lincoln County; Las Vegas was incorporated 2 years later.

The desert town languished in its early years, but the announcement of plans to construct the Hoover Dam less than 30 miles away spurred growth. By the end of the 1920s a federal highway connected Las Vegas with Los Angeles and Salt Lake City, the population had increased to about 5,000, and long-distance telephone service finally became a reality. It was largely insulated from the Great Depression years due to the jobs created by dam construction, Union Pacific Railroad growth and the reinstatement of legitimate gambling.

Casino-style gaming would eventually prove to be the city's savior, but not before several legal ups and downs. Nevada passed a strict anti-gambling law in 1910—even the local custom of flipping a coin for the price of a drink was outlawed. But wagering simply went underground until 1931, when the Nevada Legislature passed into law a bill proposed by rancher Phil Tobin, who designed it to generate tax revenue in support of public schools. (Ironically, Tobin never visited Las Vegas.) With the additional incentives of bootlegging, legal prostitution and a residency requirement for divorce of just 6 weeks, Las Vegas suddenly became a bright magnet in the otherwise gloomy national mood that followed the Roaring Twenties.

The 1940s saw the beginning of resort growth, although World War II initially delayed its onset. The Strip—then US 91, also known as the Los Angeles Highway, and now Las Vegas Boulevard—was inaugurated with the opening of El Rancho Vegas in April 1941.

After World War II came the big resort hotels, and with them big entertainment. The purpose was simply to lure people in to sample the thrill of slot machines and blackjack. As more hotels moved onto the Strip, each vied with the others for the most opulent casino and the showroom with the most glamorous stars.

The siren song was simple: Visit Las Vegas and see the world's largest and best collection of singers, comedians, dancers and musicians, and visitors heeded the call in increasing numbers. Hotels and casinos, enriched by the increased revenue, offered more and more—shows grew bigger, the Strip flashier, the casinos slicker. Las Vegas became a city that thrived on illusion and fantasy.

The city's incredible success can be measured by the number of hotel rooms it boasts: 123,000 and counting. And in addition to new construction and the ongoing expansion and modernization of existing properties, older hotels are being razed and replaced by newer, glitzier megaresorts. And judging from visitor statistics, odds are good the boom will last well into the 21st century.

Harrah's-Las Vegas / © R. Kord / Robertstock

The Informed Traveler

Whom To Call

Emergency: 911

Police (non-emergency): (702) 795-3111 or TTY (702) 795-3111

Fire: (702) 383-2888

Weather: (702) 736-3854

Time: (775) 782-3456

Hospitals: Desert Springs Hospital, (702) 733-8800; Mountainview Hospital, (702) 255-5000; Summerlin Hospital Med Center, (702) 233-7000; Sunrise Hospital and Medical Center,(702) 731-8000; University Medical Center, (702) 383-2000; Valley Hospital Medical Center, (702) 388-4000.

Where To Look

Newspapers

Las Vegas has two daily newspapers, the morning *Review-Journal* and the evening *Sun*. Check the daily events section for current entertainment offerings.

Radio

Las Vegas radio station KNUU (970 AM) is an all-news/weather station; KNPR (89.5 FM) is a member of National Public Radio.

Visitor Information

The Las Vegas Convention and Visitors Authority, 3150 S. Paradise Rd., Las Vegas, NV 89109, and the Las Vegas Chamber of Commerce, 3720 Howard Hughes Pkwy., Las Vegas, NV 89104, provide entertainment, transportation, recreation, city tour and visitor information. The authority's reservation department is open daily 6 a.m.-10 p.m., office hours are daily 8-5; phone (702) 892-7575. The chamber is open Mon.-Fri. 8-5; phone (702) 735-1616. phone (702) 735-1616.

What To Pack

Las Vegas has four distinct seasons defined by the thermometer rather than by precipitation. Winter days are mild and usually sunny, and evenings are cool to chilly, with a fair number of nights below freezing. Summers are characterized by furnace-like heat, which is uncomfortable despite the very low humidity. Even on the hottest days, evenings are cooler in comparison. Universally air-conditioned interiors also offer relief. The danger of flash flooding is possible during severe thunderstorms.

Spring and fall offer the most pleasant weather for outdoor activity—dry, warm and sunny. April, May and October are the nicest months. But whenever you visit, leave the umbrella at home. Las Vegas receives an average of just 4 inches of rain a year. *For additional information see temperature chart p. 219.*

Las Vegas Convention Center / © Richard Cummins / Corbis

Informal business attire is the rule, particularly in the summer. Most vacationers wear casual clothing around the clock, and the casinos do not enforce any sort of dress code. Some women—and a few men—do dress up for dinner or to take in a show. A sweater or jacket will come in handy during the winter; sunglasses are a must regardless of the time of year.

Sales Tax: Clark County's sales is 7.25 percent. It also imposes a 9 percent tax on lodgings, a 6 percent tax on automobile rentals and a 10 percent entertainment tax on hotel shows.

Destination Las Vegas

Las Vegas is glitter and glamour, gawking and gaming. This is the place of non-stop neon, sparkling sequins and get-rich dreams.

True to its reputation for standout entertainment and celebrated excess, the town entices tourists with promises of fantastic surroundings and 24-hour fun. And like a slot machine showing nothing but cherries, it delivers.

© Lester Lefkowitz / Corbis

Hoover Dam.
This 1930s engineering marvel tamed the flood-prone Colorado River, transformed desert into irrigated farmland, introduced electricity to rural areas and created Lake Mead, one of the nation's largest man-made bodies of water. (See listing page 252)

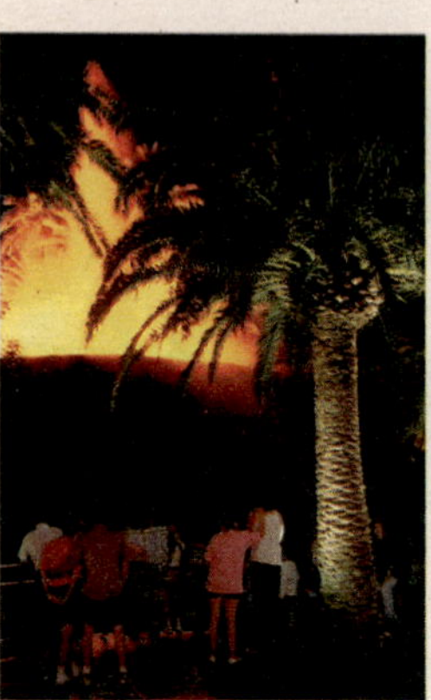

© Richard Cummins / Corbis

The Mirage.
A volcano, the resort's signature attraction, erupts on schedule each night spewing smoke and flames 100 feet into the desert sky. (See mention page 242)

© Gibson Stock Photography

Fremont Street Experience.
More than 2 million lights illuminate this high-wattage spectacle spanning four blocks. Nearby hotels and casinos dim outdoor lights during the nightly shows on the pedestrian promenade. (See mention page 250)

Places included in this AAA Destination City:

The Main Event. Set against the backdrop of glitz and ringside glamour, many of boxing's biggest matches take place in Las Vegas. (See mention page 244)

Cirque du Soleil. This international troupe of acrobats, jugglers, clowns, musicians and trapeze artists presents two of the most mesmerizing shows on the Strip. (See mention page 249)

Getting There

By Car

The major route into Las Vegas is I-15, which passes through the city from southern California to Arizona and Utah. Other routes are US 95 from the northwest, which becomes the Las Vegas Expressway in the downtown area, and US 93/95 from the southeast.

Travelers from California should be prepared for desert driving, regardless of their departure point. Basic precautions include making certain that the car's engine and cooling system are working well, that tires are inflated properly, and that the gas tank is filled adequately. It always is prudent to carry extra coolant or water in case of overheating.

Air Travel

McCarran International Airport is about 5 miles south of downtown Las Vegas via Las Vegas Boulevard and 3.5 miles south of the Las Vegas Convention Center via Paradise Road, just a few minutes' drive from the Strip's southern end. One of the nation's busier airports, it serves most major airlines.

From the airport rental car lots, take Kitty Hawk Way to Swenson Street, then Swenson north to Tropicana Avenue. Turning west on Tropicana will take you to the Strip and I-15. Taxi and limousine services also are available from the airport to the Strip and points downtown. Cab fare to the Strip hotels varies depending on traffic and routes taken, but in general, plan on $9-$10 to Tropicana Avenue (Luxor Las Vegas, MGM Grand, Excalibur, Tropicana and New York-New York); $10-$11 to Flamingo Road (Bally's Las Vegas, Caesars Palace, Flamingo Las Vegas); $11-$12 to the Treasure Island and Stardust hotels; $13 to the Stratosphere; and $16-$20 to the downtown area.

Private transportation to and from the airport is provided 4:30 a.m.-2 a.m. by Bell Trans; phone (702) 739-7990.

Hertz offers discounts to AAA members; phone (702) 736-4900 for the airport, (702) 866-2330 for the Strip or (800) 654-3131.

Buses

Greyhound Lines Inc., 1 Main St., is the major bus company serving Las Vegas; phone (702) 384-8009 or (800) 231-2222.

Street System

Las Vegas is compact, and even first-time visitors will have no trouble finding their way around. The two areas of interest to tourists are the Strip and downtown (also known as Glitter Gulch and Casino Center).

Las Vegas Boulevard parallels I-15 and is the main north-south thoroughfare. Fremont Street downtown is the dividing line for Las Vegas Boulevard North and Las Vegas Boulevard South addresses. The part of the boulevard constituting the Strip extends from Sahara Avenue south to Hacienda Avenue. All of the big resort hotels are along this 3.5-mile stretch.

Downtown, anchored by Fremont Street, is the original hotel/casino area. Almost everything of interest to visitors is located along Fremont between Main Street and Las Vegas Boulevard, or a few blocks to the north or south.

Paradise Road and Maryland Parkway are major north-south arteries east of the Strip. The area around the Las Vegas Convention Center, at Paradise and Desert Inn roads, is the location of the Las Vegas Country Club and several big hotels, notably the Las Vegas Hilton. The University of Nevada Las Vegas campus sits between Paradise Road and Maryland Parkway, a short distance north of the airport.

The main east-west thoroughfares south of Fremont Street (in geographic order from north to south) are Charleston Avenue, Sahara Avenue, Desert Inn Road, Spring Mountain Road/Sands Avenue, Flamingo Road and Tropicana Avenue. Residential subdivisions spread east, west and north of Las Vegas' core commercial area, bounded roughly east and west by Maryland Parkway and the Strip and north and south by SR 93/95/I-515 and the airport.

Note: Although distances are fairly short between any two points in greater Las Vegas, traffic is often heavy on I-15, Flamingo Road, Tropicana Avenue and Las Vegas Boulevard. The Strip is frequently bumper to bumper—especially at night—and crawling with pedestrians. Avoid driving on the Strip if possible, or use Paradise Road as an alternative.

Parking

Parking is rarely a problem in Las Vegas, as most of the hotels provide guest, valet and customer parking. Valet parking is a boon in a city where temperatures routinely top 100 F in the summer and the walk from an outer parking lot to the hotel's front door can take 10 minutes. The $1 or $2 tip is well worth it. If you have restaurant or show reservations, keep in mind that valet parking lots sometimes fill up.

Several downtown hotel and commercial garages are open 24 hours; rates average from $1-$2 per hour. Check hours of operation, as some lots close at 6 p.m. If you're staying on the Strip and want to visit the downtown area, it's much easier to use public transportation to get there.

Taxis and Limousines

Major cab companies include ABC Union, (702) 736-8444; Ace, (702) 736-8383; Checker/Yellow Cab/Star, (702) 873-2227; and Whittlesea Blue Cab, (702) 384-6111. Base fare is $2.70 for the first mile and $1.80 for each additional mile; trips to the airport incur a $1.20 surcharge.

Limousine service averages $40-$55 per hour; a super stretch limo averages $65-$80 per hour. Licensed limousine services include Ambassador Limo, (702) 362-6200; Bell Trans, (702) 385-5466; and Presidential Limo, (702) 731-5577.

Public Transportation

Citizens Area Transit (CAT) provides bus service to most parts of the city. Buses serving the Strip, or Las Vegas Boulevard, run every 7-10 minutes. Some routes provide 24-hour-a-day service. The fare is $2 on the Strip, $1.25 all other routes. Exact change is required; transfers are free. Buses serve other Las Vegas routes from 5:30 a.m.-1:30 a.m. The fare is $1.25. For schedule and route information phone (702) 228-7433.

Enclosed, air-conditioned trolleys run along the Strip every 15 minutes from the Stratosphere Hotel to Mandalay Bay for a fare of $1.65. Exact change is required; phone (702) 382-1404 for information.

New York-New York Casino
© Gibson Stock Photography

The Las Vegas Monorail serves a 4-mile stretch of the Strip from the MGM Grand to the Sahara Hotel including the convention center. Daily 6 a.m.-2 a.m.; phone (702) 699-8200.

What To See

ADVENTUREDOME is in Circus Circus at 2880 Las Vegas Blvd. Encased in a pink glass dome, the 5-acre indoor theme park showcases the Canyon Blaster, a double-loop, double-corkscrew roller coaster that whips past life-size animated dinosaurs and cascading waterfalls. A white-water raft ride, IMAX theaters, simulator rides, miniature golf, rock climbing, trampolines, virtual-reality games and an arcade also are included.

Food is available. Allow 2 hours minimum. Daily 10 a.m.-midnight, June-Aug.; Mon.-Thurs. 10-6, Fri.-Sat. 10 a.m.-midnight, Sun. 10-8, rest of year. Fees for rides and games vary. All-day ride pass $18.95, under 48 inches tall $13.95. AX, CB, DS, MC, VI. Phone (702) 794-3745 or (702) 794-3939.

SAVE **ADVENTURE PHOTO TOURS** meets passengers at prearranged locations. Half- and full-day narrated tours are offered to the Grand Canyon, Mojave Desert, Hoover Dam, Red Rock Canyon,

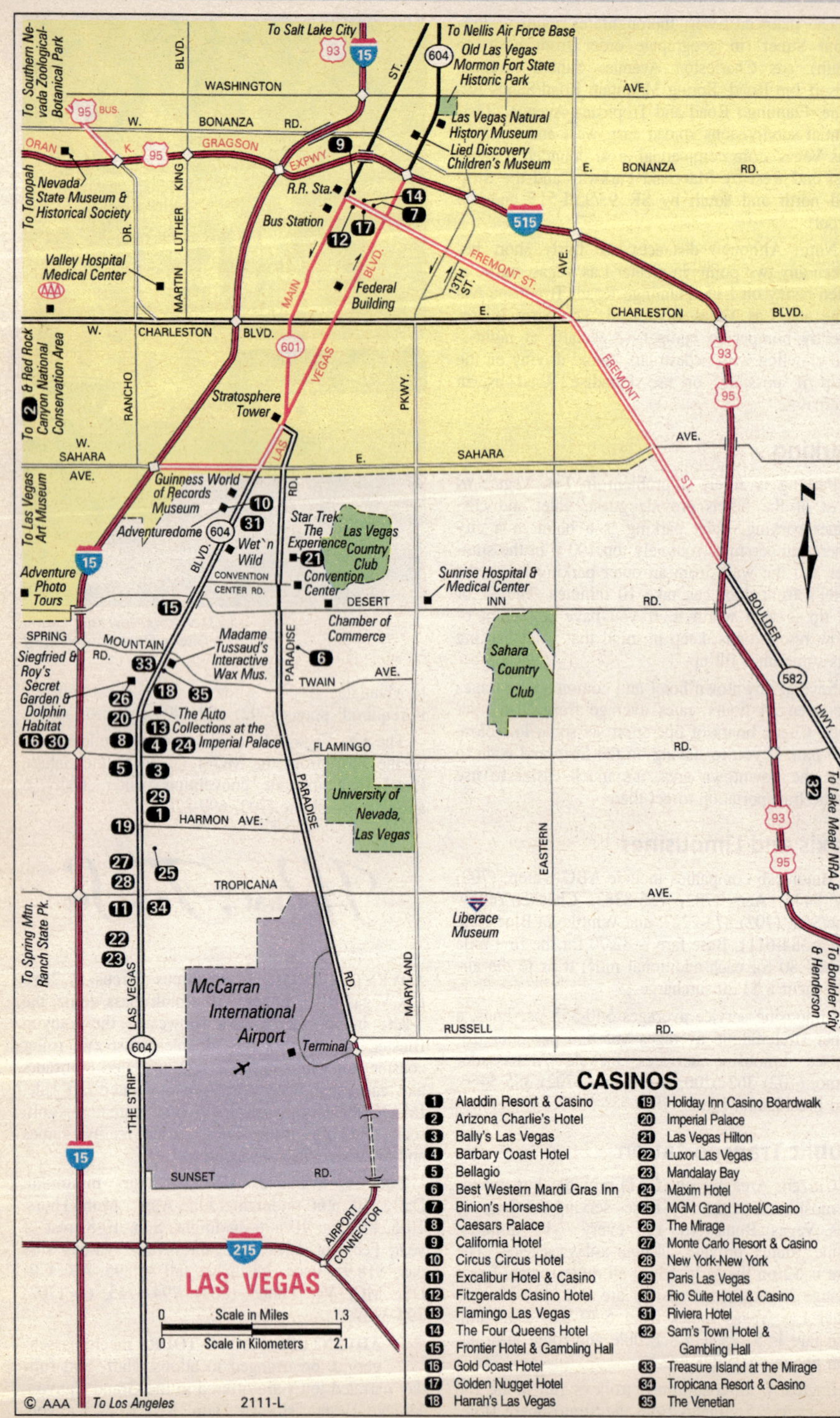
LAS VEGAS
To Salt Lake City
To Nellis Air Force Base
Old Las Vegas Mormon Fort State Historic Park
Las Vegas Natural History Museum
Lied Discovery Children's Museum
To Southern Nevada Zoological-Botanical Park
To Tonopah
Nevada State Museum & Historical Society
Valley Hospital Medical Center
R.R. Sta.
Bus Station
Federal Building
Stratosphere Tower
To 2 & Red Rock Canyon National Conservation Area
To Las Vegas Art Museum
Guinness World of Records Museum
Adventuredome
Wet 'n Wild
Adventure Photo Tours
Star Trek: The Experience
Las Vegas Country Club
Convention Center
Chamber of Commerce
Sunrise Hospital & Medical Center
Sahara Country Club
Madame Tussaud's Interactive Wax Mus.
Siegfried & Roy's Secret Garden & Dolphin Habitat
The Auto Collections at the Imperial Palace
University of Nevada, Las Vegas
Liberace Museum
McCarran International Airport
Terminal
To Spring Mtn. Ranch State Pk.
To Lake Mead NRA & 32
To Boulder City & Henderson
To Los Angeles
WASHINGTON AVE.
W. BONANZA RD.
E. BONANZA RD.
ORAN K. GRAGSON EXPWY.
W. CHARLESTON BLVD.
E. CHARLESTON BLVD.
W. SAHARA AVE.
E. SAHARA AVE.
CONVENTION CENTER RD.
DESERT INN RD.
SPRING MOUNTAIN RD.
TWAIN AVE.
FLAMINGO RD.
HARMON AVE.
TROPICANA AVE.
RUSSELL RD.
SUNSET RD.
AIRPORT CONNECTOR
MARTIN LUTHER KING BLVD.
RANCHO DR.
MAIN ST.
LAS VEGAS BLVD.
"THE STRIP"
PARADISE RD.
MARYLAND PKWY.
EASTERN AVE.
FREMONT ST.
13TH ST.
BOULDER HWY.
Scale in Miles 0 1.3
Scale in Kilometers 0 2.1
© AAA
2111-L
CASINOS
1 Aladdin Resort & Casino
2 Arizona Charlie's Hotel
3 Bally's Las Vegas
4 Barbary Coast Hotel
5 Bellagio
6 Best Western Mardi Gras Inn
7 Binion's Horseshoe
8 Caesars Palace
9 California Hotel
10 Circus Circus Hotel
11 Excalibur Hotel & Casino
12 Fitzgeralds Casino Hotel
13 Flamingo Las Vegas
14 The Four Queens Hotel
15 Frontier Hotel & Gambling Hall
16 Gold Coast Hotel
17 Golden Nugget Hotel
18 Harrah's Las Vegas
19 Holiday Inn Casino Boardwalk
20 Imperial Palace
21 Las Vegas Hilton
22 Luxor Las Vegas
23 Mandalay Bay
24 Maxim Hotel
25 MGM Grand Hotel/Casino
26 The Mirage
27 Monte Carlo Resort & Casino
28 New York-New York
29 Paris Las Vegas
30 Rio Suite Hotel & Casino
31 Riviera Hotel
32 Sam's Town Hotel & Gambling Hall
33 Treasure Island at the Mirage
34 Tropicana Resort & Casino
35 The Venetian

'alley of Fire, Area 51 and Goodsprings Valley nining ghost towns. Some tours include short ikes, helicopter rides, river rafting and boat excurions. Each tour stops at several scenic locations for icture-taking. Photographic assistance is offered nd 35 mm cameras may be rented for a fee. Priate and custom tours are available. Allow 3 hours, 0 minutes minimum. Daily 6 a.m.-10 p.m. Tour imes vary; phone ahead. Fares $89-$279; over 65, 76-$238; under 12, $67-$210. Camera rental $25. AX, DC, DS, JC, MC, VI. Phone (702) 889-8687 r (888) 363-8687.

THE AUTO COLLECTIONS AT THE IMPERIAL PALACE, in the Imperial Palace hotel at 3535 Las Vegas Blvd., includes more than 350 antique, classic and special-interest automobiles displayed in a gallery setting. Since each car is for sale, the collection is constantly changing.

Vehicles have included an 1897 Haynes-Apperson, the King of Siam's 1928 Delage limousine, President Dwight D. Eisenhower's parade car, President Kennedy's 1962 Lincoln Continental "bubble top" and Elvis Presley's 1976 Cadillac El Dorado.

Allow 1 hour minimum. Daily 9:30-9:30. Admission $6.95; over 65, military with ID and ages 4-12, $3. AX, DS, JC, MC, VI. Phone (702) 794-3174.

GEM **GUGGENHEIM HERMITAGE MUSEUM** is at 3355 Las Vegas Blvd. S. (inside the Venetian Hotel). The 7,600 foot museum was designed by Pritzker Prize-winning architect Rem Koolhaas. Permanent collections include masterworks from the Guggenheim in New York, the Hermitage in St. Petersburg, Russia, and the Kunsthistorisches in Vienna. Guided tours are available. Allow 1 hour, 30 minutes minimum. Daily 9:30-8:30. Admission $15; over 60, $12; students with ID $11; ages 6-12, $7. AX, DS, MC, VI. Phone (702) 414-2440.

SAVE **GUINNESS WORLD OF RECORDS MUSEUM,** 2780 Las Vegas Blvd. S., features exhibits, videotape presentations, computerized data banks and interactive computers containing world records, feats and facts from the "Guinness Book of Records." A display highlights the history of Las Vegas. Daily 9-5:30. Admission $6.50; over 55, military with ID and ages 13-18, $5.50; ages 5-12, $4.50. AX, DS, MC, VI. Phone (702) 792-3766.

LAS VEGAS ART MUSEUM, 9600 W. Sahara Ave., houses permanent or rotating collections. In between special exhibits, which have included the works of Marc Chagall and Salvador Dali, visitors can view more than 170 works representing all mediums, including bronze and ceramics. Allow 30 minutes minimum. Tues.-Sat. 10-5, Sun. 1-5. Admission $5, over 54, $3; students with ID $2; under 13 free. Rates may increase during special exhibits. Phone (702) 360-8000.

SAVE **LAS VEGAS NATURAL HISTORY MUSEUM,** 900 Las Vegas Blvd. N., features walk-through dioramas representing animals in their natural habitats. The museum displays marine life and species from around the world. Animated dinosaurs are presented as well as exhibits about the African savanna and rain forest. Additional highlights include mounted sharks, a 3,000-gallon shark tank, videotape presentations, plants and animals indigenous to Nevada and hands-on exhibits.

Madame Tussaud's Interactive Wax Museum

Allow 30 minutes minimum. Daily 9-4; closed Thanksgiving and Dec. 25. Admission $6; over 55, military and students with ID $5; ages 3-11, $3. AX, DS, MC, VI. Phone (702) 384-3466.

GEM **THE LIBERACE MUSEUM,** 1775 E. Tropicana Ave., houses a rare piano collection, antiques, jewelry, customized automobiles and elaborate costumes from the entertainer's million-dollar wardrobe. Of particular interest are a Louis XV desk owned by Czar Nicholas II of Russia, a black mink coat lined with more than 40,000 rhinestones, a rare 1788 piano and a Rolls Royce covered with mirrored tiles etched with galloping horses. The performer's stage jewelry, including a piano-shaped ring set with 260 diamonds, also is displayed.

Food is available. Allow 1 hour, 30 minutes minimum. Mon.-Sat. 10-5, Sun. noon-4; closed Jan. 1, Thanksgiving and Dec. 25. Free guided tours are given daily at 11 and 2. Last admission 45 minutes before closing. Admission $12, over 65 and students with ID $8, under 6 free. AX, MC, VI. Phone (702) 798-5595.

SAVE **LIED DISCOVERY CHILDREN'S MUSEUM,** 833 Las Vegas Blvd. N., contains more than 200 hands-on exhibits about science, arts and humanities that teach as well as entertain. An everyday-living section, where children pretend to choose a job, earn a paycheck, deposit savings in a bank and buy groceries, offers an opportunity to sample adult life. Another section lets children feel what it is like to be physically impaired. A science tower with fiber optics and a weather station also are featured.

Allow 2 hours minimum. Tues.-Sun. and Mon. school holidays 10-5. Admission $6; senior citizens, college students and military with ID and ages 1-17, $5. AX, DS, MC, VI. Phone (702) 382-3445.

SAVE **MADAME TUSSAUD'S INTERACTIVE WAX MUSEUM** is near the Venetian Hotel at 3377 Las Vegas Blvd. S., Suite 2001. Visitors enter the museum to find themselves "mingling" at a cocktail party with such lifelike wax celebrities as Nicholas Cage, Princess Diana, Frank Sinatra and Oprah Winfrey. Sports legends, rock stars and Las Vegas entertainers of past and present also are represented. A behind the scenes exhibit illustrates how the wax figures are painstakingly created to resemble their real-life counterparts. Allow 1 hour minimum. Daily 10-10. Hours may vary; phone ahead. Admission $19.95; over 64, students with ID and Nevada residents $14; ages 6-12, $9.95. AX, CB, DS, MC, VI. Phone (702) 862-7800.

NEVADA STATE MUSEUM AND HISTORICAL SOCIETY, 700 Twin Lakes Dr. in Lorenzi Park, portrays the history, cultures, geography and wildlife of southern Nevada from the Ice Age to the present. Exhibits include an ichthyosaur fossil from the Triassic Period and a 48-foot carved relief depicting the full size of the prehistoric marine reptile. The rambling Spanish Colonial-style museum also houses the Nevada Historical Society's research library. Daily 9-5; closed Jan. 1, Thanksgiving and Dec. 25. Admission $2, under 18 free. Phone (702) 486-5205.

Stratosphere Tower / © Richard Cummins / Photophile

OLD LAS VEGAS MORMON FORT STATE HISTORIC PARK, at Washington Ave. and Las Vegas Blvd., is the site where an adobe fort was built by Mormons in 1855 to give refuge to travelers bound for California. After the departure of the Mormons in 1858, the site was developed as a ranch that provided blacksmith services and supplies to westward bound pioneers; it later became a railroad stop, prompting land speculation that transformed the town into what would become Las Vegas.

Guided tours are available. Allow 30 minutes minimum. Daily 8:30-4:30; closed Thanksgiving, day after Thanksgiving and Dec. 25-Jan. 1. Admission $2; ages 6-12, $1. Phone (702) 486-3511.

RED ROCK CANYON NATIONAL CONSERVATION AREA, 20 mi. w. off Charleston Blvd. (SR 159), is a 196,000-acre preserve containing such outstanding geological formations as the Keystone Thrust Fault, which reveals the contrast between layers of gray limestone and red sandstone.

Self-guiding hiking trails lead to a spring, a waterfall, water containment areas, small canyons and the ruins of an old homestead. Picnicking at Willow Spring on the scenic loop road and camping at 13-Mile Campground, 2 miles east of the visitor center on SR 159, are permitted. Scenic loop road open daily 6 a.m.-8 p.m., DST. Winter hours may vary; phone ahead. Visitor center daily 8-5:30; closed Thanksgiving and Dec. 25. Admission $5 per private vehicle. Phone (702) 363-1921.

SHOWTIME TOURS meets passengers at prearranged locations. Luxury coach tours of Las Vegas and to Gold Mine/Ghost Town, Grand Canyon, Hoover Dam and Laughlin are offered. Lake Mead cruises, Colorado River raft tours and air tours of Grand Canyon and Hoover Dam also are available. Allow 1 hour minimum. Daily 6 a.m.-10 p.m. Fare $26-$239. AX, DS, MC, VI. Phone (702) 895-9976 or (800) 704-7011.

SIEGFRIED & ROY'S SECRET GARDEN AND DOLPHIN HABITAT is at 3400 Las Vegas Blvd. S. at the Mirage Hotel. Visitors can view the white lions of Timbavati, rescued from the brink of extinction by a conservation program established by entertainers Siegfried & Roy. Heterozygous golden tigers also can be seen lounging, swimming or roaming in naturalistic settings. A dolphin habitat contains an area from which the creatures can be observed frolicking underwater.

Allow 1 hour minimum. Secret Garden Mon.-Tues. and Thurs.-Fri. 11-5, Sat.-Sun. 10-5, Memorial Day-day before Labor Day; Mon.-Tues. and Thurs.-Fri. 11-3:30, Sat.-Sun. 10-3:30, rest of year. Dolphin habitat Mon.-Fri. 11-7, Sat.-Sun. 10-7, Memorial Day-day before Labor Day; Mon.-Fri. 11-5:30, Sat.-Sun. 10-5:30, rest of year. Admission $10 (includes dolphin habitat), under 11 free with adult. Admission Wed. (Secret Garden only) $5, under 11 free with adult. AX, CB, DS, MC, VI. Phone (702) 791-7111.

SOUTHERN NEVADA ZOOLOGICAL-BOTANICAL PARK, 1.5 mi. n. of US 95N at 1775 N. Rancho Dr., is a 3-acre zoo featuring African, Asian and western American animals along with more than 150 varieties of plants. Of interest is the children's petting zoo. Allow 30 minutes minimum. Daily 9-5; closed Jan. 1, Thanksgiving and Dec. 25. Admission $6.50; over 62 and ages 2-12, $4.50. AX, MC, VI. Phone (702) 648-5955.

STAR TREK: THE EXPERIENCE, in the Las Vegas Hilton Hotel at 3000 Paradise Rd., features an interactive 24th-century space adventure aboard the USS *Enterprise.* A highlight is the simulated voyage on a shuttlecraft that emulates warp speed and battles Klingons. Costumes, props and memorabilia from "Star Trek" films are displayed in the museum. Food is available. Daily 11-11. Hours may vary; phone ahead. Admission $24.99; under 13, $21.99. Under 42 inches tall are not allowed on motion simulator voyage. AX, CB, DC, DS, JC, MC, VI. Phone (702) 697-8700.

STRATOSPHERE TOWER, 2000 Las Vegas Blvd. S. at the Stratosphere Hotel, affords a spectacular panorama of Las Vegas. Said to be America's tallest freestanding tower, the 1,149-foot-high structure contains indoor and outdoor observation decks. Rides include the High Roller, a roller coaster that meanders around the tower's base, and the Big Shot, where the brave at heart are launched 150 feet up into the air to be rewarded with a free fall.

Allow 1 hour minimum. Sun.-Thurs. 10 a.m.-1 a.m., Fri.-Sat. 10 a.m.-2 a.m. Tower $8; senior citizens and ages 4-12, $4. Big Shot $8. High Roller $5. Combination ticket for the tower and the Big Shot $13; combination ticket for the tower and High Roller $11; all three rides $17. AX, CB, DC, DS, JC, MC, VI. Phone (702) 380-7777.

UNIVERSITY OF NEVADA, LAS VEGAS is 1.5 mi. e. of the Strip at 4505 Maryland Pkwy. UNLV, one of the nation's fastest-growing universities, offers free 45-minute to 1-hour tours of its 335-acre campus Mon., Wed. and Fri. at 10:30 and 2, Tues. and Thurs. at 10 and 2, Sat. at 9:30, early Sept. to mid-May; Mon.-Fri. at 9, Sat. at 9:30, rest of year. Phone (702) 895-3443. *Also see What To Do, Theater.*

Donna Beam Fine Art Gallery, in the Alta Ham Fine Arts Building on campus, displays works of modern art by professional touring artists, faculty and students. Guided tours are available by reservation. Allow 30 minutes minimum. Mon.-Fri. 9-5, Sat. 10-2; closed holidays. Free. Phone (702) 895-3893.

Flashlight is in the small plaza next to the Judy Bayley Theatre on Maryland Ave. on campus. The university commissioned Swedish pop sculptor Claes Oldenburg to create a work symbolizing the school. The resulting sculpture is a 38-foot black steel flashlight that is mounted lens down.

Marjorie Barrick Museum of Natural History, at the corner of Swenson and Harmon sts. on campus, focuses on the natural history of southern Nevada and the Mojave Desert. Traveling exhibits also are featured. An outdoor garden features drought-resistant plants from deserts around the world. Allow 1 hour minimum. Mon.-Fri. 8-4:45, Sat. 10-2; closed holidays and Oct. 31. Free. Phone (702) 895-3381.

Mandalay Bay Resort and Casino / © Richard Cummins / Photophile

VALLEY OF FIRE STATE PARK— *see Overton p. 253.*

WETLANDS PARK NATURE PRESERVE is at 7050 Wetlands Park Ln., 1 mi. e. of Boulder Hwy. Five miles of walking trails wind through the 130-acre preserve that provides a wetland habitat for native species. A visitor center and amphitheater are highlights. Bicycles, dogs, fishing and swimming are prohibited. Allow 1 hour minimum. Daily dawn-dusk. Visitor center 10-4. Free. Phone (702) 455-7522.

SAVE **WET 'N WILD,** 2601 Las Vegas Blvd., is a 26-acre water park. Attractions include a wave pool, water flumes and a water roller coaster. Also featured are a hydra-hurricane ride that transports riders on inner tubes around a pool at 15 mph and a capsule that drops riders feet-first into the water. Allow 3 hours minimum. Park open daily at 10, last weekend in Apr.-last weekend in Sept. Closing times vary; phone ahead. Admission $26.99; under 48 inches tall $20.99; over 55, $15.99; under 3 free. AX, DS, MC, VI. Phone (702) 737-3819.

What To Do

Casino Megaresorts

Aladdin Resort & Casino

Tales of Arabia set the scene for the reborn Aladdin Resort and Casino. Built on the site where the original Aladdin Hotel was imploded in 1998, the new resort conjures up the Arabian Nights legend at every turn. The hotel is smaller than its megaresort neighbors along the Strip, but it rivals all with its elaborately themed design.

Recalling the tale of Aladdin, a 35-foot golden lamp emits mystical smoke; flying carpets abound and an enchanted light garden creates a constantly blooming wall of flowers. Central to the theme of wealth and riches is the adjoining Desert Passage mall, which features some 130 shops and more than 20 restaurants. Though designed to evoke the feeling of an ancient journey along arid trade routes, the mall is decidedly chic and upscale. The resort also features a 7,000-seat theater for concerts and theatrical productions as well as a separate, exclusive European-style casino for high rollers.

Aladdin is at 3667 Las Vegas Blvd. S. (just south of Flamingo Road); phone (702) 785-5555.

Bellagio

Inspired by the village of Bellagio on the shores of northern Italy's Lake Como, this $1.6 billion resort may have been the most anticipated hotel in Las Vegas history. Nearly a million people visited the new resort in the first 20 days after its grand opening on Oct. 15, 1998. With ornate fountains, sculptures, stained glass and a botanical conservatory, Bellagio's elegant atmosphere appeals to adults, a major shift in Las Vegas' recent family-friendly philosophy.

Perhaps the resort's most dramatic feature is the 11-acre Lago di Bellagio. A series of fountains spans the quarter-mile length of the lake, using 1,000 water launchers capable of blasting water up to 240 feet in the air. Musically choreographed water shows run every half-hour Mon.-Fri. 3-7, Sat.-Sun. noon-7, every 15 minutes daily 7 p.m.-midnight.

Bellagio is at 3600 Las Vegas Blvd. S. (at Flamingo Road); phone (702) 693-7111 or (888) 987-6667.

Caesars Palace

Opened in 1966 and arguably Las Vegas' first themed hotel/casino, Caesars Palace exemplifies opulence. A 20-foot statue of Julius Caesar himself—hailing a cab, of all things—stands at the driveway leading to the main entrance. A Roman theme pervades this resort hotel, from the 18 fountains to the statuary gracing the public areas.

A circular pool surrounded by fluted columns is the centerpiece of the resort's elaborate Garden of the Gods. The grounds also feature two elongated swimming pools and two outdoor whirlpool spas set among almost 700 trees and other meticulously groomed greenery.

The gods themselves come alive at the elegantly upscale Forum Shops at Caesars Palace *(see Shopping p. 246)*, with an animatronic show staged every hour at the Festival Fountain. Also found at the Forum Shops, the Race for Atlantis IMAX simulator ride creates the multisensory sensation of being a rider in a visually dazzling chariot race through the streets of the legendary city.

The Caesars Palace Omnimax Theatre presents 70 mm films on a six-story, dome-shaped screen enhanced by reclining seats and a state-of-the-art sound system. At night the geodesic dome's exterior glows with computerized light patterns visible to passersby on the Strip.

Caesars Palace is at 3570 Las Vegas Blvd. S. (just north of Flamingo Road); phone (702) 731-7110 or (800) 634-6001.

Excalibur Hotel & Casino

As the name implies, the theme here is medieval (carried out in a thoroughly Vegas style). Two 2,000-room towers rise behind a white turreted castle (complete with moat and drawbridge) capped by red and blue spires. The Excalibur's attractions are spread out on three levels within the castle. Singers, jugglers, magicians and puppeteers provide free entertainment throughout the day from the Court Jester's Stage.

The lower level has Fantasy Faire, a video-game arcade resembling a carnival midway. Visitors also can witness a fearsome dragon battling within the Excalibur's moat. The dragon appears daily on the hour from dusk until midnight, and the show is free. Excalibur's Tournament of Kings *(see Nightlife p. 250)* is a dinner show featuring jousting, dragons, fire-wizards and invading armies.

Excalibur is at 3850 Las Vegas Blvd. S. (just south of Tropicana Avenue); phone (702) 597-7777 or (800) 937-7777. *See color ad p 851.*

Luxor Las Vegas

Rising 30 stories into the Nevada skyline, this sleek, black, pyramid-shaped hotel is instantly recognizable. Its base measures nearly 562 feet wide on each side, and its exterior is covered by more than 26,750 glass plates—the equivalent of 13 acres. At night, a beam of light projected from the pyramid's apex pierces the sky above and is said to be visible from space. From the Strip, the main entrance to the hotel passes through a huge sphinx sporting a blue-and-gold-striped headdress. In front of the sphinx is a 190-foot-tall obelisk emblazoned with the hotel's name.

Inside is reputedly the world's largest atrium, encompassing 29 million cubic feet. Within this open space, the Luxor's casino, shops, restaurants and showroom are located on the casino level; on the level above are the attractions. Guest rooms are located along the pyramid's sides. The four elevators (called "inclinators") that ascend from the base of each corner to the open hallways do so at a 39-degree incline.

Throughout the property an Egyptian motif prevails. A life-size replica of the temple of Ramses II—flanked by 35-foot-tall ram sphinx statues—is the gateway to Luxor's 120,000-square-foot casino, decorated with gold statues, friezes, wall hieroglyphics and reproductions of Egyptian artifacts. Ramses figures are incorporated into the carpet design; a Nile barge complete with a pharaoh statue sits atop a bar.

The attractions level, an open-air mezzanine, has more sphinxes and statues. Here visitors will find a motion simulator ride and a video arcade. Nearby, large-format films are shown on a seven-story screen at the Luxor IMAX Theatre.

Also on the attractions level is The Tomb and Museum of King Tut, a painstaking re-creation of the ruler Tutankhamen's antechamber, burial chamber and treasury. All of the replicas, which were handcrafted in Egypt, are based on artifacts discovered by archeologists in 1922 inside the pharaoh's tomb in the Valley of Kings at Luxor, Egypt. The 15-minute audiotape tour is preceded by a brief introductory film.

Luxor Las Vegas is at 3900 Las Vegas Blvd. S. (south of Tropicana Avenue); phone (702) 262-4000 or (800) 288-1000.

Mandalay Bay

This 43-story resort contains more than 3,300 rooms as well as 11 specialty restaurants and numerous shops. Features of this lush tropical oasis are an 11-acre lagoon complete with a sand-and-surf beach, waterfalls, three exotic pools, a lazy river ride and a swim-up shark tank. The Mandalay Bay Events Center is a 12,000-seat arena hosting top entertainment.

The Treasures of Mandalay Bay Museum, on the casino level, displays rare coins and currency and contains an exhibit of Wells Fargo memorabilia. A monorail links Mandalay Bay to the Excalibur Hotel with stops at the Luxor Las Vegas on the return trip.

Mandalay Bay is at 3950 Las Vegas Blvd. S. (just south of the Luxor Las Vegas); phone (702) 632-7777.

MGM Grand Hotel/Casino

This gargantuan complex bills itself as "The City of Entertainment" and while gaming figures prominently, there are numerous other facilities and recreational opportunities for those who are not interested in trying their luck.

Everything about the MGM Grand is big. It cost a billion dollars to build. It sprawls over 114 acres. Some 5,000 guest rooms are divided among the four emerald-green towers that soar 280 feet into the air. Just beyond the registration area is the 170,000-square-foot casino that is equivalent in size to four football fields.

Entertainment Tips

Las Vegas entertainment falls into two categories: big room and lounge. The big rooms, seating 600 to 1,500, offer different types of shows, the best known of which is the star performer backed by an orchestra and supported by a lesser-known singer or comic. Extravagant production shows are another popular option; most feature some combination of elaborately costumed dancers, comics, illusionists, impressionists, celebrity hosts, female impersonators and special effects.

Big room shows generally run about 90 minutes. Guests for cocktail shows should arrive about 1 hour early; 2 hours early for dinner shows. Children are not admitted to shows with nude performers.

© Ian Vaughn/Lance Burton

There is no cover charge for shows in the big rooms, but depending on the entertainer being featured, admission can range from $25 to $100 per person. Production show admissions vary from $10 to $25 per person. Big rooms usually require reservations well in advance for the more popular performances. Give the name of your hotel—chances of getting in are always better when staying at a hotel where a popular entertainer is performing. If your seat is not pre-assigned on the ticket, tip the maitre d' $5 to $20 for a couple and double that for a larger party to get a good seat. As in restaurants, servers at a dinner show also expect a tip.

Lounges seat 200 to 400 in more intimate surroundings. Here, too, a folding favor will spur the captain to seat you quickly and at a good table on crowded nights. Some big room and lounge shows include two drinks per person.

The massive MGM lion posing at the hotel entrance weighs some 100,000 pounds, making it one of the largest bronze statues in the country. MGM's signature lion also is part of the carpet pattern throughout, and the decor includes ornate ceilings of gilded red and gold, or gold stars embedded on a white background. At the Lion Habitat, next to the MGM Grand box office on the casino level, cubs frolic behind glass.

The MGM Grand is at 3799 Las Vegas Blvd. S. (just north of Tropicana Avenue); phone (702) 891-1111 or (800) 929-1111.

The Mirage

This resort's tropical theme creates the lushest hotel environment on the Strip. A variety of palm trees (not just the usual desert-acclimated date palms), manicured shrubbery and clipped lawns are kept green with constant watering from a sprinkler system. Pools, waterfalls and dolphin sculptures also are sprinkled about the grounds. Inside is an atrium with a 100-foot-tall glass dome that shelters a living rain forest of palms, banana plants and other vegetation. This may be the only Vegas hotel where visitors will feel like lingering at the registration area, courtesy of a 20,000-gallon tropical reef aquarium built into the wall behind the check-in desks.

The Mirage is home to Siegfried & Roy's Secret Garden and Dolphin Habitat. Heterozygous golden tigers reside at an outdoor area near the landscaped pool. Also within the habitat is a 2.5-million-gallon saltwater pool where Atlantic bottlenose dolphin frolic.

The hotel also is known for its erupting volcano, a man-made mountain rising some 50 feet out of a lagoon surrounded by palms. Water normally cascades peacefully down the volcano's sides, but after dark, approximately every 15-minutes the spotlights go down, smoke issues forth, the crater glows an angry red, and flames leap into the air.

The Mirage is at 3400 Las Vegas Blvd. S. (between Flamingo and Spring Mountain roads); phone (702) 791-7444 or (800) 627-6667.

Monte Carlo Resort & Casino

The theme here is turn-of-the-20th-century French Riviera, replete with French Victorian architectural accents. The entrance area in front of the lofty, two-wing guest room tower is alabaster white trimmed with gold—all Romanesque archways, recessed niches, fountains and classically inspired statuary. Set off from the casino, its dome ceiling, marble floors and stately crystal chandeliers evoke the grandness of a European hotel. Hallways at one side of the lobby, decorated to look like European streets, lead to a collection of gift, clothing and other shops.

Monte Carlo Resort & Casino is at 3770 Las Vegas Boulevard S. (north of Tropicana Avenue next to New York-New York); phone (702) 730-7777 or (800) 311-8999.

New York-New York

One of Las Vegas' most popular themed megaresorts since it opened in January 1997, New York-New York is impossible to miss. The re-creation of the Big Apple's skyline, which rises incongruously above the intersection of Las Vegas Boulevard and Tropicana Avenue, is one of the Strip's most distinctive landmarks.

A 150-foot-tall version of the Statue of Liberty, copied down to the last detail, stands atop a stone pedestal rising from a pool of water with a tugboat and gushing fountains. A row of building fronts along the Strip are reminiscent of turn-of-the-20th-century New York architecture. There is even a 300-foot replica of the Brooklyn Bridge, cleverly positioned to be part of the main entryway into the hotel.

Looming behind are 12 connected guest room towers that are look-guggenheimalikes of such signature New York skyscrapers as the Empire State Building, the Seagrams Building and the Chrysler Building. Looping in and around the entire complex at speeds up to 65 mph is a red-tracked, Coney Island-style roller coaster dubbed the *Manhattan Express*.

The casino is decked out like Central Park; trees (nonliving, but still impressive) sprout up from the floor, providing a canopy over the slot machines. A rabbit warren of shops and eateries along winding walkways recall Greenwich Village, Wall Street, Soho and other familiar New York neighborhoods—down to the street signs and false storefronts.

New York-New York is at 3790 Las Vegas Blvd. S. (just north of Tropicana Avenue across from the MGM Grand); phone (702) 740-6969 or (800) 693-6763.

Paris Las Vegas

The City of Light comes to the desert in this 34-story luxury resort. Impressive re-creations of scaled-down versions of the Eiffel Tower and the Arc de Triomphe as well as the Champs Elysées, the Paris Opera House, the Louvre, Parc Monceau and the River Seine make visitors feel as if they are a continent away. Cobblestone streets and winding alleys lead past the European-inspired shops and restaurants of "Le Boulevard." The signature landmark is the 50-story Eiffel Tower, where guests can travel on a glass elevator to an observation deck for a panoramic view of the Strip.

Paris Las Vegas is at 3655 Las Vegas Blvd. S. (just south of Bally's Las Vegas); phone (702) 946-7000.

Treasure Island

Treasure Island is next door to the Mirage, its sister property. The Mirage's South Seas ambience carries over to Treasure Island, but it more closely resembles something out of a Robert Louis Stevenson adventure. Just off the Strip is Buccaneer Bay, a palm-edged lagoon. The portion of Strip sidewalk fronting the lagoon becomes an elevated wooden gangplank; another gangplank walkway leads over the lagoon into the hotel's shops, restaurants and casino. Along the shore spreads a re-created pirate village with building facades situated among rocky cliffs.

Buccaneer Bay is the backdrop for a free entertainment spectacular. The "Battle of Buccaneer Bay" is re-enacted daily in the lagoon. The staged battle between the HMS *Britannia* and the *Hispaniola,* a pirate ship, begins with some verbal sallies before escalating into full-fledged pyrotechnics—cannon and musket fire, big explosions, and a large, enthusiastic cast of dueling pirates and sailors.

Shows take place daily every 90 minutes from 5:30 to 11:30, mid-June through Labor Day. Schedule varies rest of year; phone ahead. No performances are given during high winds. The spectacle has more impact at night. It is necessary to arrive at least 30 minutes before show time for the best views, as the sidewalks on both sides of the Strip usually become very congested.

Treasure Island is at 3300 Las Vegas Blvd. S. (at Spring Mountain Road); phone (702) 894-7111 or (800) 288-7206.

The Venetian

Situated where the old Sands Hotel Casino once stood, The Venetian transports guests to the Italian city of Venice. The all-suite Venezia Tower offers 1,013 additional rooms. From the Campanile Tower entrance to the lavish re-creations of the Doge's Palace and the Ca' d'Oro (Palace of Gold), this megaresort presents a remarkable facsimile of the Italian city's architectural glory. Gondola rides past cobblestone walkways and a replica of St. Marks Square are available on the hotel's Grand Canal.

The Venetian is at 3355 Las Vegas Blvd. S. (just north of Harrah's Las Vegas); phone (702) 733-5000 or (888) 283-6423.

Gambling

The rattle of the "bones," then a sigh of disappointment or a cry of exultation—such are the sounds of Las Vegas, where gambling is by no means limited to the craps table. Slot machines, "21" or blackjack, keno, bingo, poker, baccarat and roulette all await the hopeful.

Gambling is easier than buying toothpaste, since casinos never close and most drugstores do. Many hotels strategically place their casinos near the registration desk; visitors are immediately greeted with the lure of fortune. Rows of slot machines stand like sentries in most establishments—restaurants, drugstores, supermarkets, even laundromats.

Visitors who resist the temptation to gamble are rare. If you decide to take a chance, obtain a book about gambling and bone up. Generally speaking, beginners never should approach any gaming table without some knowledge about the game to be played. Many casinos provide literature and some even give classes for novice patrons. Although the state regulates casinos and gambling, the odds ultimately favor the house.

In terms of betting and playing strategies, poker in all its varieties can be termed the most complex. Baccarat requires a high stake to be successful, though "mini-baccarat," in which the dealer keeps the bank, provides cheaper play.

The Venetian Resort Hotel Casino / © Gibson Stock Photography

The many ways of playing number combinations, the difficulty in understanding the payoffs and general unfamiliarity with the game have made craps the most challenging game of all. It also is a difficult game for dealers to learn. While not a game for the novice, craps is mesmerizing to watch.

Casinos and separate betting parlors also have sports books that allow patrons to wager on almost any horse race, boxing match or professional or collegiate game.

Remember that if you are a first-time visitor to Las Vegas, credit at the gaming tables will be tight or nonexistent. With further visits, once credit has been established, gamblers will be able to obtain $1,000 as easily as $1.

Sightseeing

There are other ways to spend time and money in Las Vegas than inside a casino. A daylong sightseeing tour of the city and nearby attractions can be a relaxing intermission from the hectic agenda of casino hopping and shows.

Boat Tours

A combination tour of Hoover Dam and a cruise on Lake Mead is offered by SAVE Lake Mead Cruises; phone (702) 595-4927.

Bus Tours

Guided bus tours of downtown and surrounding points of interest, including the Grand Canyon,

Hoover Dam, Red Rock Canyon, Bryce Canyon, Death Valley, Lake Mead and Valley of Fire State Park, are offered by SAVE Gray Line; phone (702) 384-1234 or (800) 634-6579.

Plane or Helicopter Tours

Air tours of the Grand Canyon or Lake Mead area are available from Las Vegas or Boulder City. The following list represents a sampling of companies available and is provided for information only. Air Vegas Airlines, (702) 736-3599; Biplane Rides of Las Vegas, (702) 375-0048; A Grand Canyon Tour, (702) 361-7628; Lake Mead Air, (702) 293-1848; Maverick Helicopters, (702) 261-0007; SAVE Papillon Grand Canyon Helicopter Tours, (702) 736-7243 or (800) 528-2418; SAVE Scenic Airlines, (702) 638-3300 or (800) 634-6801; and Sundance Helicopters, (702) 597-5525 or (800) 653-1881.

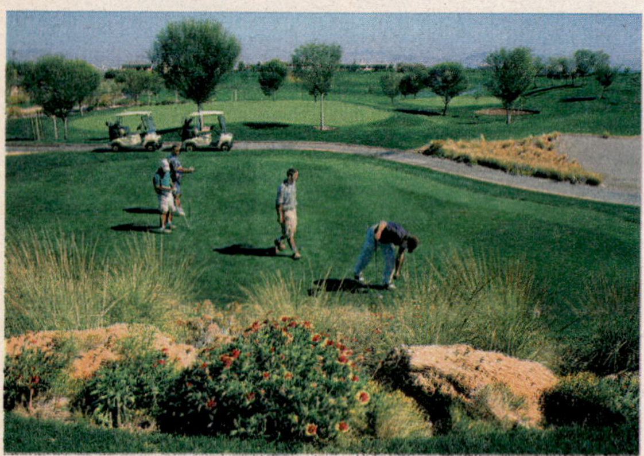

© Gibson Stock Photography

Spectator Sports

The biggest games in this town are played at green felt tables, not sports arenas. Yet despite more money being *bet* on sports in Las Vegas than is ever taken in at the turnstiles, the city nevertheless presents a fine selection of spectator sports. College basketball, especially, has a rich tradition in Las Vegas.

Auto Racing

Fans of automobile racing will find plenty of company at the **Las Vegas Motor Speedway**, 7000 Las Vegas Blvd. N., 17 miles northeast of Las Vegas off the I-15 Speedway Boulevard exit. The facility, set on 1,500 acres, has 24 race tracks, seating for 140,000, plus 75,000 square feet of meeting and exhibit space. The complex hosts NASCAR and Winston Cup events; phone (702) 644-4444 for information.

Nearby, the **Carroll Shelby Museum** at 6755 Speedway Blvd. displays 35 years of performance cars, including Shelby Cobras. Tours of the manufacturing facility are available; phone (702) 643-3000.

Baseball

The **Las Vegas 51s** appear for professional baseball at **Cashman Field**, 850 Las Vegas Blvd. N., just after 7 in the evening April through the first week in September. These Class AAA, Pacific Coast League affiliates of the Los Angeles Dodgers adopted an unusual team logo: a bald-headed space alien. Their name refers to Area 51, the top secret U.S. Air Force base north of the city where some speculate that extraterrestrials visit. Phone (702) 386-7200 for ticket and schedule information.

The **Hustlin' Rebels** of UNLV play at the on-campus **Earl E. Wilson Baseball Stadium** during the college season.

Basketball

The Rebels of UNLV hope to one day live down an outlaw image that's swirled like an Old West legend around the team for years—often overshadowing enormous success with a truly exciting style of basketball.

The basketball program came to national prominence under former coach Jerry "Tark the Shark" Tarkanian, who first took the Rebels to the NCAA Final Four in 1977. Tarkanian built the program into a perennial powerhouse and an object of local idolatry. The Rebels play on the UNLV campus at the **Thomas & Mack Center** between November and February; phone (702) 739-3267.

Boxing

Vegas and professional boxing have had a close relationship for nearly 40 years. Despite a rocky history—government scrutiny, a confusing mishmash of championship titles (IBF, WBA and WBC) and the scurrilous out-of-ring antics of a few of the sport's biggest names—heavyweight title fights have always captured the public interest. The absurdly high purses, flamboyant promoters, glamorous ringside spectators and attendant media hoopla all seem appropriate against a Las Vegas backdrop.

Some of the sport's most memorable bouts have taken place here: Muhammad Ali vs. Floyd Patterson, Ali vs. Leon Spinks, Sugar Ray Leonard vs. Marvin Hagler. In November 1997 Evander Holyfield—none the worse for wear after being bitten by Mike Tyson 4 months earlier—defeated Michael Moorer for the IBF crown at the Thomas & Mack Center. Most big fights now take place at the **MGM Grand Garden Arena**; phone (702) 891-7777 for event information. The **Las Vegas Convention Center** and **Caesars Palace** also host fights.

Football

UNLV also supplies the city's big-time gridiron action, with the football Rebels scrapping in the

Mountain West Conference against the likes of Air Force, BYU and Wyoming. The Rebels' home games are August through November at **Sam Boyd Stadium** east of campus; phone (702) 739-3267.

Rodeo

Every visitor to America's West should attend at least one quality rodeo to complete the regional experience. Winter visitors to Las Vegas can see one of the very best every December when the National Finals Rodeo takes place over 2 weeks at the Thomas & Mack Center on the UNLV campus; phone (702) 739-3267 for ticket information.

Recreation

Las Vegas and its environs offer a royal flush of recreational pursuits that include golf, tennis, racquetball and swimming. The desert climate, despite scalding summer days, invites outdoor recreation all year.

Golf

Golf enthusiasts enjoy the excellent playing conditions of Las Vegas' desert climate. Numerous championship and less demanding golf courses are open to the public.

All of the following golf courses offer 18 holes: Angel Park Golf Club, (702) 254-4653 (two 18-hole courses), 10 miles west via Summerlin Parkway to 100 S. Rampart Blvd.; Craig Ranch, (702) 642-9700, 2.5 miles west off I-15 at 628 W. Craig Rd. (North Las Vegas); Desert Pines, (702) 388-4400, 2 miles east of I-15 off Eastern Avenue at 3415 E. Bonanza Rd.; Desert Rose Golf Course, (702) 431-4653, 6 miles east of I-15 off Sahara Avenue at 5483 Clubhouse Dr.; Summerlin Golf Club, (702) 254-7010, at 10201 Sun City Blvd.; and Las Vegas Golf Club, (702) 646-3003, at 4300 Washington Ave.

Others include Snow Mountain (Nu-Wav Kaiv) and Sun Mountain (Tav-Ai Kaiv), the two 18-hole courses at Las Vegas Paiute Golf Resort, (702) 658-1400, 23 miles northwest via US 95 at 10325 Nu-Wav Kaiv Blvd.; the Legacy Golf Club, (702) 897-2187, 130 Par Excellence Dr. in Henderson; and Los Prados Golf Course, (702) 645-5696, 2.5 miles west of US 95 via Lone Mountain Road and Los Prados Boulevard at 5150 Los Prados Cir.

All courses include a clubhouse, golf shop, equipment rental and some food service. None are lighted for night play. Early starts are recommended during the summer months.

Horseback Riding

Nobody but Dan Tanna would ride a palomino into the lounge at Caesars, but you can sit tall in the saddle if you giddyup to the outskirts of town. **Bonnie Springs Old Nevada** offers an Old West experience that includes rides through the beautiful Red Rock Canyon area west of Las Vegas; phone (702) 875-4191.

Jogging and Walking

Drive out of the city to public land trails, drive a few blocks to a city park or to the university track, or just step outside your hotel door and pound the Strip. Serious runners will find the nearby mountain trails a tempting respite from summer's oven heat. Realize, however, that elevations above 3,000 feet hold different challenges.

Try these urban areas: **Bob Baskin Park**, 2801 W. Oakey, is nestled in a quiet residential area, and the park's walking path is cushioned; **Pueblo Park**, at Buffalo Drive and Lake Mead Boulevard west of the Strip, has a delightfully undeveloped feeling; conversely, **Sunset Park**, 2601 E. Sunset Rd., is bustling and urban.

About 20 miles west of the city, the **Red Rock Canyon National Conservation Area** *(see attraction listing p. 238)* has several trails of varying lengths from which to choose—not to mention spectacular scenery. A trail map is free at the visitor center.

Tennis

Tennis players seldom have difficulty finding an empty court, since there are many public courts scattered throughout the city. Those that follow have at least two lighted courts: **Paradise Park Recreation Center,** 4770 S. Harrison Dr.; **Sunrise Recreation Center,** 2240 Linn Ln.; **Sunset Park,** 2601 E. Sunset Rd.; **Whitney Community Center,** Missouri Avenue and Boulder Highway; **Winchester Recreation Center,** 3130 S. McLeod; and **Winterwood Park,** Sahara Avenue and Winterwood Boulevard. Phone Clark County Recreation at (702) 455-8200 for more information about municipal facilities.

Many resort hotels and private clubs have tennis courts that visitors are allowed to use, but it is always a good idea to confirm the hotel's current visitor policy by phone. Hotels with tennis facilities include **Bally's Las Vegas** and **Paris Las Vegas,** (702) 739-4111; and the **Flamingo Las Vegas,** (702) 733-3111.

The **Frank and Vicki Fertitta Tennis Complex** on the UNLV campus requires reservations and charges a fee, but it is considered the city's finest tennis facility; phone (702) 895-4489.

Water Sports

Many swimming pools are open daily Memorial Day through Labor Day. Contact the Las Vegas Parks and Recreation Department for information about pools and their schedules; phone (702) 229-6309.

The 1.5 million acres of the **Lake Mead National Recreation Area** *(see place listing p. 252)*, which is twice the size of Rhode Island, hold nearly limitless outdoor recreation opportunities—all just 35 miles east of the neon Strip. **Lake Mead** and **Lake Mohave** *(see attraction listings p. 252 and p. 252)* serve up great sport fishing for rainbow trout, striped bass, channel catfish, crappie and blue gill. Steady breezes and large expanses of open water lure board and boat sailors as well as powered watercraft. Annual passes are available by mail; write Lake Mead NRA Fee Office, 601 Nevada Hwy., Boulder City, NV 89005; phone (702) 293-8491.

Winter Sports

Less than an hour's drive northwest of Las Vegas is **Humboldt-Toiyabe National Forest** *(see place listing p. 226)*. Within the forest is **Mount Charleston**, which includes the **Las Vegas Ski and Snowboard Resort**. The resort, which has a day lodge and three double chairlifts, is open Thanksgiving to Easter. Phone (702) 593-9500 for snow conditions, (702) 385-2754 for general information or (702) 645-2754 to make ski reservations.

Other Diversions

Flyaway Indoor Skydiving, 200 Convention Center Dr., offers a 15-minute simulated sky-diving experience in a 21-foot vertical wind tunnel; phone (702) 731-4768 or (877) 545-8093.

Shopping

If you have any money left over after a date with the gaming tables or a rendezvous with a slot machine, Las Vegas has any number of shopping opportunities. Souvenirs head the list, of course, and there are more than enough T-shirts, fuzzy dice and gambling mementoes to satisfy the most ardent hunter. Most of the major hotels have their own shopping arcades containing clothing, gift and specialty boutiques, often on the expensive side. In between are the area malls and shopping centers.

Fashion Show Mall / © Richard Cummins / Photophile

Malls

The **Fashion Show Mall,** at the heart of the Strip, 3200 Las Vegas Blvd. S., is Las Vegas' flagship mall. An impressive set of anchors—Dillard's, Macy's, Neiman Marcus and Robinsons-May, Saks Fifth Avenue—is accompanied by smaller stores and a fine selection of restaurants. In addition to the regular mall shops, Fashion Show has such upscale retailers as Louis Vuitton, Ann Taylor and Williams-Sonoma.

Boulevard Mall, the city's oldest, is at 3528 S. Maryland Pkwy., a few blocks east of the Strip. Anchored by Dillard's, Macy's, JCPenney and Sears, the Boulevard has more than 140 shops ranging from Victoria's Secret to The Gap. **Meadows Mall**, 4300 Meadows Ln., is a little farther off the beaten path. Dillard's, Macy's, JCPenney, Sears and more than 140 specialty shops provide ample opportunity to spend any money earned (or spared) at the casinos.

Rampart Commons, an open-air retail center at Charleston and Rampart boulevards in northwest Las Vegas, features Ann Taylor, Banana Republic, The Gap, Pottery Barn, Talbots and Williams-Sonoma.

In nearby Henderson is **Galleria at Sunset**, 1300 W. Sunset Rd., which is anchored by Dillard's, JCPenney, Mervyn's California and Robinsons-May, and has a skylit food court as well as more than 130 boutiques, including the Disney Store and Eddie Bauer.

Outlets

Outlet shopping is another option in Las Vegas. **Belz Factory Outlet World**, 7400 Las Vegas Blvd. S., has an Off 5th-Saks Fifth Avenue Outlet as its anchor store, plus more than 150 other outlets, including Lenox and Nike.

The Spanish-flavored **Vegas Pointe Plaza**, 9155 Las Vegas Blvd. S. (about 5 miles south of Tropicana Avenue), contains about 50 stores, including Izod, London Fog, Mikasa and Van Heusen.

Specialty Districts

The **Forum Shops at Caesars Palace**, 3500 Las Vegas Blvd. S., is an upscale complex with 108 specialty shops and restaurants—including **Planet Hollywood**—in a setting designed to recall a winding street in Italy. Take the moving sidewalk from the Strip into this shopper's wonderland, which creates a self-contained ambience right from the start: A cloud-flecked, domed ceiling gradually changes from cerulean blue to deep twilight and back again, giving this upscale collection of specialty stores and eateries its own version of night and day.

The mall's design resembles a fantasy re-creation of an ancient Roman streetscape, with storefronts clustered under portals and arches. A central piazza is dominated by the dramatic Fountain of the Gods, which has statues of Neptune, winged stallions and two spear-bearing warriors. Anchoring the mall's east wing is the Festival Fountain, where an animatronic statue of Bacchus (looking a bit inebriated) holds court with Apollo, Venus and other deities.

Among the tony names at the Forum are Bernini, Christian Dior, Escada, Gianni Versace, Gucci and Louis Vuitton. There also are clothing, jewelry and specialty gift shops, art galleries and stores catering to kids. Atlantis, an enormous fountain, also features lifelike animatronic figures. It stands in the Roman Great Hall, an open space 85 feet high and 160 feet in diameter that also contains a 50,000-gallon aquarium filled with tropical fish. Retail outlets here include Emporio Armani, FAO Schwarz, Fendi and a Virgin Megastore. Also within Caesars Palace is Appian Way, a much smaller but no less exclusive arcade of shops and galleries that includes a branch of Cartier.

On April 27, 1998, the 32-year-old Aladdin Hotel-Casino came crashing down—the result of a carefully controlled implosion—to make way for an expanded hotel and casino. The new resort includes **Desert Passage**, an extensive shopping facility made up of 130 stores divided into four themed areas: Morocco Gate, The Lost City, India Gate and Merchant's Harbor. Ornate iron grills, glazed mosaic tiles, Moorish gateways and interior building facades with domes and minarets give shoppers the impression that they are strolling through a North African bazaar.

To reach the 31 stores at **The Tower Shops**, at the Stratosphere Casino Hotel & Tower, 2000 Las Vegas Blvd. S., guests pass through themed street scenes of Hong Kong, Paris and New York. Other extensive retail areas can be found at Bally's Las Vegas, Excalibur, the Flamingo Las Vegas, the Luxor, MGM Grand and Treasure Island.

More than 70 specialty stores and restaurants line a replica of an Italian canal in the **Grand Canal Shoppes** of The Venetian, 3355 Las Vegas Blvd. S. The **Rue de la Paix** shopping district of Paris Las Vegas, 3655 Las Vegas Blvd. S., offers upscale French boutiques as well as pastry and wine and cheese shops.

Performing Arts

Popular images of Las Vegas lean more toward the spangled theatrics of razzle-dazzle showmanship than they do the rarified heights of serious theater. That does not mean, however, that the fine arts receive short shrift. Plays, concerts and dance performances are presented at several area locations. *Neon* magazine, the entertainment guide included with the Friday edition of the *Las Vegas Review-Journal,* carries listings of cultural events.

Dance

The **Nevada Ballet Theatre** presents ballets at **Artemus W. Ham Concert Hall** on the UNLV campus; phone (702) 243-2623. Ballroom dancing takes place at two Las Vegas locations. On Friday evenings the music starts at 8 p.m. at **Dance Charisma,** 3650 S. Jones Blvd., Suite 16. Admission is $10; phone (702) 364-8700. **Step by Step Dance Studios,** 1801 E. Tropicana Ave., Suite 22, offers ballroom and Latin dancing in the evenings. Admission is $5; phone (702) 795-0041.

Film

Repertory film series, musical performances and art exhibits are presented at the **Winchester Community Center** at 3130 S. McLeod Dr.; for schedule information phone (702) 455-7340.

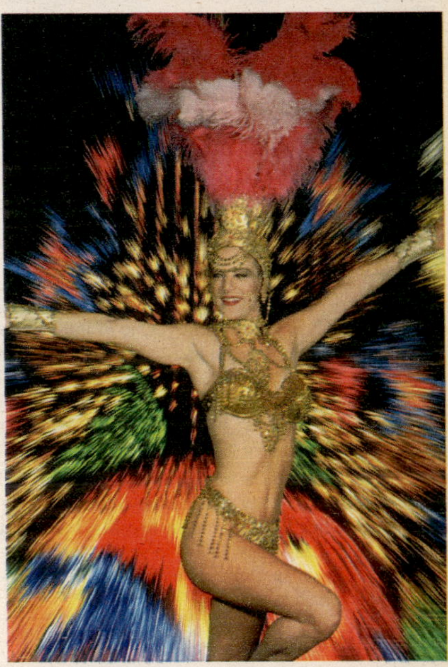

Las Vegas showgirl / © Jim Zuckerman / Corbis

Music

Concerts are presented periodically at **Reed Whipple Cultural Center** on Las Vegas Boulevard and at **Charleston Heights Arts Center**, on Brush Street west of Decatur Boulevard north of Charleston Boulevard.

Symphony, jazz and chamber music performances, including concerts by internationally recognized musicians, are presented at **Artemus W. Ham Concert Hall** just a few miles from the Strip. Phone (702) 895-2787 for schedule information.

The **Nevada Symphony Orchestra** participates in a Moonlight Concert Series held in the **Clark County Government Center Amphitheater**, 500 S. Grand Central Pkwy. (just west of downtown); phone (702) 455-8200.

Theater

The award-winning **Theatre Department of the University of Nevada, Las Vegas** stages both contemporary plays and the classics throughout the year in the 600-seat **Judy Bayley Theatre** on Maryland Parkway.

The city's **Rainbow Company** stages productions at the Reed Whipple Cultural Center and the Charleston Heights Arts Center; phone (702) 229-6553.

Special Events

Events in Las Vegas are as varied as entertainment on the Strip. The desert floor rumbles in early February when thousands of runners from around the globe compete in the annual Las Vegas International Marathon. The Invitational Native American

Arts Festival is held in late March. Prize livestock are proudly exhibited during the 4-day Clark County Fair, which is held in late March or early April.

The Old West is relived in May during Helldorado Days, which features Western costumes, parades and a championship rodeo. Also in May is the World Series of Poker. The city's Spanish heritage is celebrated in mid-September during a day of music and culture at the Las Vegas International Mariachi Festival.

Computer enthusiasts should be sure to include COMDEX/Fall in their itinerary. One of the world's largest computer conventions, the event is held in November at the Las Vegas Convention Center and other locations. COMDEX/Fall is massive and preregistration is required; phone (650) 372-7050 for more information.

Las Vegas' sports events are of the indoor and outdoor varieties. They include the Showboat Invitational Bowling Tournament in late May; the Best in the Desert Las Vegas "200" in spring; the Invensys Golf Classic in October; and the National Rodeo Finals which takes place in December.

Nightlife

Las Vegas is as much a mecca for entertainment as it is for gambling. On any given night visitors have their pick of some of the biggest marquee names in the business—Copperfield, Dion, Humperdinck, Iglesias, Minelli, Newton, Rickles, Rivers, Seinfeld—illusionists Penn & Teller and musical acts from oldies to pop and country superstars to the latest hip alternatives, electrifying production spectaculars, and a whole galaxy of lesser lights who may be tomorrow's stars.

Comedy Clubs

Stand-up comics have the most demanding job on the nightclub circuit, and Las Vegas has been their proving ground since 1948, when the upstart team of Dean Martin and Jerry Lewis made their bow at the Flamingo. Today the top comics perform in comedy clubs rather than the casino lounges. The **Riviera Comedy Club,** on the second floor of Mardi Gras Pavilion at the Riviera, has two shows nightly; phone (702) 794-9433.

Comedy Stop, at the Tropicana, has two shows nightly—the early show is nonsmoking; phone (702) 739-2714. **An Evening at the Improv,** on the second floor of Harrah's Las Vegas, presents two shows per night Tues.-Sun.; phone (702) 369-5000. **The Cabaret Theatre,** at New York-New York, offers nightly comedy; phone (702) 740-6815.

Dance Clubs

Club Rio, in the Rio Suite Hotel, attracts a young, chic crowd that takes over the Copacabana Showroom. The setting is plush, the dance floor large and the DJ-spun tunes loud, with state-of-the-art sound and lighting. The club also features occasional live bands. Doors open Thurs.-Sat. around 11:30 p.m. A strict dress code is enforced, and there also is a cover charge; phone (702) 252-7777.

Pulsing techno music, Caribbean-style food and a variety of rum drinks distinguish upscale **rumjungle** in Mandalay Bay, 3950 Las Vegas Blvd. S. Doors open at 11 p.m.; phone (702) 632-7777. Almost hidden away at the Hard Rock Hotel & Casino, 4455 Paradise Rd., **Baby's** cultivates an underground nightclub ambience with its simplistic but stylish decor and off-the-beaten-path location. Cozy booths distributed among several levels let patrons opt out of the crowd for private conversations when they choose. The club opens Thurs.-Sat. at midnight; phone (702) 693-5555.

The Beach, 365 Convention Center Dr. (at Paradise Road), is a big, casual club frequented by locals as well as tourists. There's a sports bar, slot and video poker machines, and a dance floor. Depending on the night, The Beach has DJ music, local bands or concerts by well-known rock bands. It is open daily 24 hours; phone (702) 731-1925.

Jazz

Located on the 51st floor of the Rio Suite Hotel & Casino, the **VooDoo Lounge** showcases blues, contemporary and jazz ensembles seven nights a week in addition to offering breathtaking views of the city; phone (702) 252-7777.

Production Shows

Following is a representative sampling of current production shows that are scheduled to run for the foreseeable future. For showtimes, ticket prices, reservations, showroom policies and other information, contact the hotel box office.

"Blue Man Group: Live at Luxor" (Luxor Theater, Luxor Las Vegas) is a wild and weird combination of performance art, highbrow humor and percussive music centered around three bald men in blue greasepaint. The trio silently creates a theater experience that is, despite the lack of dialogue, quite loud, thanks to their homemade instruments and a 16-piece band. The "Live at Luxor" production is the largest for this unusual New York-based theater troupe. Phone (702) 262-4400.

"Bottoms Up" (Flamingo Showroom, Flamingo Las Vegas) features the comedy ensemble of Breck Wall, Sue Motsinger and David Harris, who perform rapid pace skits reminiscent of "Rowan and Martin's Laugh-In." Backing up the trio is a troupe of topless dancers, making this an adults-only show. Phone (702) 733-3333.

"Céline Dion" (The Colosseum, Caesars Palace) headlines the show, accompanied by some 70 dancers, acrobats and musicians. Directed by Cirque du Soleil creator Franco Dragone, the show features stunning visual effects, including a piano that soars into the audience. The 4,000-seat theater, modeled after the ancient Roman amphitheater, was specially built to accommodate the production. All seats are within 120 feet of the stage. (702) 866-1400.

"Clint Holmes" (Clint Holmes Theater, Harrah's Las Vegas) stars multitalented entertainer Clint

Holmes in a classic Vegas-style variety show featuring singing, dancing and improvisation. Backed by a 12-piece band with a five-piece horn section, Holmes performs popular tunes from yesterday and today. Phone (702) 369-5111.

"Danny Gans" (Danny Gans Theatre, The Mirage) is a fast-paced act focusing on impressions. The multitalented Gans, whose long run of sold-out shows makes him one of the city's top entertainers, impersonates a mind-boggling variety of celebrity notables, from singers to presidents to cartoon characters. His Elvis impression stands out in a town full of them. Phone (702) 792-7777.

"An Evening at La Cage" (Mardi Gras Showrooms, Riviera) is one of several female impersonator revues playing in Las Vegas. This one, although it contains some bawdy humor, is pitched at mainstream audiences. Frank Marino emcees in the guise of Joan Rivers, sashaying out in a different gown to introduce each "lady." The performers lip-synch to recorded music. The impersonations of Patti LaBelle, Cher, Céline Dion, Judy Garland, Bette Midler, and Michael Jackson (the only male portrayed) are amazingly persuasive, and there is a wickedly funny take on Madonna by a rotund cast member. Phone (702) 794-9433.

"Folies Bergere" (Tiffany Theater, Tropicana), still going strong after nearly 40 years, is one of the few old-fashioned shows left in town. This exuberant musical variety production celebrates turn-of-the-20th-century Paris and features lavishly costumed (and topless) showgirls, chorus lines, comedy routines and a salute to American music that includes gospel, swing and big-band numbers. Phone (702) 739-2411.

"Jubilee!" (Jubilee Theater, Bally's Las Vegas) is a typical Vegas spectacle—outsize props, stunning costumes (including enormous feathered headdresses worn by topless showgirls) and lavish set pieces loosely built around a tribute to Tinseltown (the show opened in 1981 at the old, Hollywood-themed MGM Grand Hotel). Highlights include a re-creation of the sinking of the Titanic and the fiery destruction of a temple that climaxes a sultry interlude between Samson and Delilah. Phone (800) 237-7469.

"Lance Burton: Master Magician" (Lance Burton Theatre, Monte Carlo) performs in a specifically designed theater that echoes the turn-of-the-20th-century opulence of the Monte Carlo itself. He specializes in the classic tricks of the magician's trade—sleight of hand, levitation, escapes—and is backed up by dancers and beauteous showgirls. Phone (702) 730-7000.

"Legends in Concert" (Imperial Theatre, Imperial Palace) has been wowing audiences since 1983. Instead of female impersonators, a talented group of celebrity impersonators offer remarkable imitations of such entertainers as the Blues Brothers, Buddy Holly, Liberace, Madonna, Marilyn Monroe, Roy Orbison and a host of others. The roster varies from show to show (although Elvis always makes an appearance), and the performers sing (not lip-synch) and play their own instruments. Phone (702) 731-3311.

"Mystère" (Cirque du Soleil Showroom, Treasure Island) just might be the most distinctive show in town. Although it takes place within a single ring, "Mystère" in no way resembles a traditional three-ring circus. For one thing, the audience becomes intimately involved with this show. The music and lighting effects are ethereally beautiful, and the international cast of acrobats, clowns, jugglers, trapeze artists, dancers and musicians are uniformly superb. Suitable for all ages, this is a must-see. Phone (702) 796-9999 or (800) 392-1999.

"O" (Bellagio Theatre, Bellagio) is Cirque du Soleil's first venture into aquatic theater. In what may be the troupe's most innovative show yet, an international cast of 81 performs in, on and above a 1.5-million-gallon tank of water. By combining circus art, drama, choreography, aerial acrobatics and synchronized swimming, the show pays tribute to the age-old magic of theater. International music performed by a 10-piece orchestra accompanies the 90-minute show. Phone (702) 796-9999 or (888) 488-7111.

"The Scintas" (Copacabana Showroom, Rio All-Suite Casino Resort) are a family of four entertainers whose act features musical numbers, comedy and celebrity impersonations. Intermixed with Motown and popular music hits are impressions of Billy Joel, Johnny Mathis, Frank Sinatra and others. Phone (702) 252-7776 or (800) 752-9746.

Siegfried and Roy / © Neil Preston / Corbis

"Second City" (Bugsy's Celebrity Theatre, Flamingo Las Vegas) features the Chicago-based comedy company whose name is synonymous with innovative humor. Working with minimal props, staging and costumes, the unadorned comedy shines through in a series of fast-paced skits and improvisational acts. Some of Las Vegas' most flamboyant real-life and fictional characters are lampooned. Phone (702) 733-3333.

"Tournament of Kings" (King Arthur's Arena, Excalibur) is a family-oriented dinner show continuing the hotel's medieval theme. There are jousting matches, sword fights, costumed knights and ladies, equestrian stunt riding and fireworks. Dinner is eaten with the fingers. This show is similar to other medieval-themed dinner attractions that have opened in various U.S. cities over the last decade. Phone (702) 597-7600.

"Wayne Newton" (Wayne Newton Theatre, Stardust), "Mr. Las Vegas" himself, performs the hits that made him famous with the help of special effects, backup singers and a 20-piece orchestra. The charismatic Vegas veteran and consummate entertainer takes his audiences back in time as he sings his signature tunes from years past. Phone (702) 732-6325.

"Zumanity" (Zumanity Theatre, New York-New York). Known as "The Human Zoo," is Cirque du Soleil's creative approach to desire, love, passion and a celebration of the human body. Eclectic performers from around the world wrap delight, excitement and surprise into 90 minutes of acrobatics, dance and uninhibited costumes. Due to the mature nature of the show, under age 18 are not permitted. (702) 740-6815.

Other Shows: The hotel showrooms that don't feature ongoing productions continue the Las Vegas tradition of presenting celebrity headliners, along with rock concerts and occasional sporting events. Major venues include the **Jubilee Room** at Bally's Las Vegas, the **Hollywood Theatre** at the MGM Grand and the **Congo Room** at the Sahara.

A different kind of nightly show can be found at the **Fremont Street Experience**, which boasts a canopy of more than 2 million lights arching across a four-block expanse of downtown Las Vegas. This pedestrian gambling mall features animated sound and light shows—for 6-minute periods each hour the glittering casino lights are turned off and visitors are treated to themed productions of computer-generated graphics and music. Also lighting up Fremont Street are classic neon signs from the 1940s, '50s and '60s which have been restored and installed at various locations through the efforts of the **Neon Museum**, which is dedicated to preserving Las Vegas' high-wattage history. Placards provide a brief description of each sign.

Rock

The Joint, a live concert venue in the Hard Rock Hotel & Casino, 4455 Paradise Rd., showcases a variety of mainstream rock, pop and blues performers. Ticket prices range from $12 to upwards of $100, depending upon the performer. For recorded concert information phone (702) 226-4650.

The Las Vegas Vicinity

BLUE DIAMOND (E-5) pop. 282, elev. 3,400′

Established in the 1940s as a company town for employees of a gypsum producer, Blue Diamond is at the southern entrance to Red Rock Canyon National Conservation Area. Gypsum still is mined in the area.

GEM **SPRING MOUNTAIN RANCH STATE PARK,** 6 mi. n. on Blue Diamond Rd., is in a scenic location at the base of Wilson Cliffs. German actress Vera Krupp was the most notorious resident; although she sold the ranch to Howard Hughes in 1967, it is not known whether Hughes himself ever visited. Visitors can explore the main ranch house and the grounds. A guided tour includes the bunkhouse and other outbuildings as well as the Wilson cemetery and an interpretive trail with native plants. Picnicking is permitted. Allow 1 hour, 30 minutes minimum. Daily 8-5. Guided tours are offered daily at noon, 1, and 2 (also Sat.-Sun. at 3). Admission $5 per private vehicle. Phone (702) 875-4141.

BOULDER CITY (F-6) pop. 14,966, elev. 2,501′

Industrial necessity and civic idealism marked Boulder City's birth in 1931. With construction of the massive Hoover Dam project underway the federal government needed a site to house thousands of workers in the remote desert. Since the completed dam also would require a permanent workforce to operate it, temporary housing was impractical. Seizing upon the spirit of New Deal optimism, the Bureau of Reclamation commissioned noted city planner S.R. DeBoer to design an ideal town that exemplified hope for a brighter future. Indeed, thanks to rapid growth and plentiful jobs, Boulder City's early citizens were largely sheltered from the harsh reality of the Great Depression.

With dam construction complete, the town's population stabilized in the 1940s and it flourished as a civic-minded community. The federal government controlled all aspects of growth until deeding the city over to its citizens in the early 1960s. In tribute to its past, present-day Boulder City stands alone as being the only Nevada city to prohibit gambling. Nearby Lake Mead National Recreation Area *(see place listing p. 252)*, provides year-round outdoor activities.

Boulder City Chamber of Commerce: 1305 Arizona St., Boulder City, NV 89005; phone (702) 293-2034.

Self-guiding tours: A map and brochure featuring a walking tour of the historic district is available at the chamber of commerce.

BOULDER CITY HOOVER DAM MUSEUM, 1305 Arizona St., chronicles the story behind the dam's construction during the Great Depression. Desperate families from around the country moved to the city, hoping to find employment with what was then the U.S. government's largest public works project. Exhibits depict dangers encountered by the workers as well as challenges families faced as they started new lives in a desert company town.

Food is available. Allow 1 hour minimum. Mon.-Sat. 10-5, Sun. noon-5; closed Jan. 1, Easter, Mother's Day, Thanksgiving and Dec. 25. Admission $2; over 54 and under 18, $1. Phone (702) 294-1988.

HENDERSON (F-5) pop. 175,381, elev. 1,881′

Henderson was settled during World War II as a housing area for employees of a magnesium plant. The town since has expanded into Nevada's main industrial center, with many plants concerned principally with chemical and metal production. Henderson is the southwest terminus of scenic SR 147, which follows the spectacular Lake Mead shoreline from Hoover Dam to Overton Beach.

Henderson Convention Center and Visitors Bureau: 200 S. Water St., Henderson, NV 89015; phone (702) 565-2171 or (877) 775-5252.

SAVE **CLARK COUNTY MUSEUM,** 1830 S. Boulder Hwy., offers three exhibit areas: a chronological history of southern Nevada, from dinosaurs to the first white settlements; a group of historic residential and commercial structures called Heritage Street; and a re-created ghost town with a number of original structures and old railroad cars. Allow 1 hour minimum. Daily 9-4:30; closed Jan. 1 and Dec. 25. Admission $1.50; over 55 and ages 3-15, $1. Phone (702) 455-7955.

DID YOU KNOW

There are no clocks in Las Vegas casinos.

ETHEL M. CHOCOLATE FACTORY AND CACTUS GARDEN is in the Green Valley Business Park at 2 Cactus Garden Dr. The factory makes gourmet chocolates. Adjacent is the Cactus Garden, a 2.5-acre collection of more than 350 species of desert plants from the Southwest and other arid areas. Self-guiding tours of the chocolate factory and Cactus Garden are available daily 8:30-7; closed Dec. 25. Free. Phone (702) 433-2500 or (702) 458-8864.

GEM LAKE MEAD NATIONAL RECREATION AREA (E-5)

Extending about 140 miles along the Colorado River from Grand Canyon National Park, Ariz., to Bullhead City, Ariz., Lake Mead National Recreation Area embraces 1.5 million acres in western Arizona and southern Nevada. Included are Lake Mohave and Lake Mead as well as an isolated pocket of land north of the lower portion of Grand Canyon National Park.

Three of America's four desert ecosystems—the Mojave, the Great Basin and the Sonoran deserts—meet in Lake Mead National Recreation Area. Therefore the area is home to numerous plants and animals, including bighorn sheep, mule deer, coyotes, foxes and bobcats as well as lizards and snakes. Such threatened and endangered species as the desert tortoise and peregrine falcon also live here.

Fishing is popular in both lakes all year; licenses are required. Largemouth bass, striped bass and catfish are the chief catches in Lake Mead, while rainbow trout and bass are plentiful in Lake Mohave. The recreation area can be enjoyed year-round and is a prime destination for swimming, boating, skiing and fishing.

Area open daily 24 hours. Admission $5 per private vehicle, $3 per person arriving by other means. Passes are valid for up to 5 days. For further information contact the Superintendent, Lake Mead National Recreation Area, 601 Nevada Hwy., Boulder City, NV 89005; phone (702) 293-8907. *See Recreation Chart and the AAA California & Nevada CampBook.*

GEM **HOOVER DAM,** on SR 93, stands 726 feet high and is one of the highest concrete dams ever constructed. Completed in 1935 for flood control and water storage, it impounds Lake Mead, one of the largest man-made lakes in the United States.

The self-guiding Discovery Tour of the Hoover Dam Visitor Center includes a 25-minute film about construction of the dam and a theater presentation depicting how irrigation from the Colorado River turned desert into farmland. The power plant's eight generators may be explored via an elevator that descends 500 feet into Black Canyon. An exhibit gallery highlights the region's natural history and an overlook atop the visitor center provides scenic views. Talks are presented every 15 minutes at the overlook and at other locations.

Visitor center daily 9-4:45; closed Thanksgiving and Dec. 25. Last admission is 30 minutes before closing. Overlook closes at 5:30. Admission $10; over 61 and military with ID, $8; ages 7-16, $4. Parking $5. AX, MC, VI. Phone (702) 597-5970 or (866) 291-8687.

LAKE MEAD, 110 miles long and averaging 200 feet deep, has a 550-mile shoreline. There are six major recreational centers with marinas and launch facilities.

Films and exhibits about natural and cultural history are offered at the Alan Bible Visitor Center, 4 miles east of Boulder City at US 93 and Lakeshore Road, overlooking Lake Mead. A botanical garden surrounds the visitor center. Visitor center daily 8:30-4:30; closed Jan. 1, Thanksgiving and Dec. 25. Free. Phone (702) 293-8990. *See Recreation Chart and the AAA California & Nevada CampBook.*

SAVE **Lake Mead Cruises** depart from the Lake Mead Cruises Landing on Lakeshore Rd. (SR 166). Excursion cruises on a paddlewheeler include a narration about area history and the construction of Hoover Dam. Eco-tours and breakfast, dinner and dance cruises also are available. Ninety-minute round-trip excursion cruises depart daily at noon, 2 and 4. Fare $19; ages 2-11, $9. Reservations are recommended. AX, DS, MC, VI. Phone (702) 293-6180.

LAKE MOHAVE extends 67 mi. s. from Hoover Dam to Davis Dam. Launching ramps, trailer sites, refreshment concessions, boat rentals and overnight accommodations are available at Katherine Landing, about 35 miles west of Kingman, Ariz., and at Cottonwood Cove, 14 miles east of Searchlight. Willow Beach, 28 miles east of Boulder City on US 93, offers a launch ramp and concession facilities. Information regarding recreational facilities is available at all three sites.

LAUGHLIN (F-6) pop. 7,076

Laughlin, near the California border and across the Colorado River from Arizona, was little more than a nameless bait shack on the Colorado River in 1970. It is now a gambling mecca in the middle of the desert, a destination that attracts several million visitors per year. Buses and ferries provide transportation between the glittery casinos in Laughlin and parking areas in nearby Bullhead, Ariz.

Laughlin Chamber of Commerce: 1585 Casino Dr., P.O. Box 77777, Laughlin, NV 89028; phone (702) 298-2214 or (800) 227-5245.

OVERTON (E-6) elev. 1,250′

Founded by Mormon pioneers, Overton lies just north of the site of a prehistoric Anasazi Indian Pueblo, Pueblo Grande de Nevada, known as the Lost City, which extended 30 miles on both sides of the Muddy River. The Puebloans of Lost City were farmers who built above-ground dwellings with several rooms that were used to store crops.

Overton also lies at the northern end of a scenic route that follows the northwestern shore of Lake Mead. The route is made up of SR 169 to Overton Beach and SR 147 from Overton Beach to US 95/93 and Hoover Dam.

Moapa Valley Chamber of Commerce: P.O. Box 361, Overton, NV 89040; phone (702) 397-2160.

LOST CITY MUSEUM OF ARCHEOLOGY, 721 S. Moapa Valley Blvd., preserves and interprets the prehistory of the Moapa Valley, focusing on the Anasazi settlement. The museum contains artifacts of the Anasazi Indians, who settled the Moapa Valley during the first century.

An actual archeological site is interpreted within the museum. In addition, changing art and traveling exhibits are featured. Several Pueblo-type houses of wattle and daub are reconstructed on their original foundations. Allow 30 minutes minimum. Daily 8:30-4:30; closed Jan. 1, Thanksgiving and Dec. 25. Admission $2, under 18 free. Phone (702) 397-2193.

VALLEY OF FIRE STATE PARK, 14 mi. s.w. on SR 169, occupies a basin about 6 miles long and 3 to 4 miles wide. The rough floor and jagged walls contain formations of eroded red sandstone, said to date back 150 million years, that often appear to be on fire when reflecting the sun's rays.Exhibits about the park's history, geology and ecology are housed in the visitor center on SR 169, about 7 miles east of the park boundary.

Park daily dawn-dusk. Visitor center daily 8:30-4:30. Closed Dec. 25. Admission $5 per private vehicle. Phone (702) 397-2088. *See Recreation Chart and the AAA California & Nevada CampBook.*

Neon Museum at Fremont Street Experience / © Richard Cummins / Photophile

This ends listings for the Las Vegas Vicinity. The following page resumes the alphabetical listings of cities in Nevada.

LAUGHLIN—*see Las Vegas p. 252.*

LOVELOCK (B-3) pop. 2,003, elev. 3,900′

Lovelock is an agricultural town founded by immigrant pioneers as a stopping point before beginning a 40-mile desert crossing. It is said to have the only round courthouse in use in the country and offers such recreational diversions as gaming casinos, stock car races and rodeos. Hunting and fishing are profitable in the surrounding area. Small Tufa Park, 5 miles west of town, features geological deposits created by ancient Lake Lahontan, which covered the area thousands of years ago.

About 22 miles northeast is the 20,241-acre Rye Patch State Recreation Area, with facilities for camping, fishing, swimming, boating and picnicking. *See Recreation Chart and the AAA California & Nevada CampBook.*

Lovelock/Pershing County Chamber of Commerce: 1440 Cornell Ave., P.O. Box 821, Lovelock, NV 89419; phone (775) 273-7213.

MARZEN HOUSE, at the s.w. end of Cornell Ave., houses the Pershing County Museum. Displays of antiques, mineral ores, pioneer memorabilia and Paiute Indian artifacts are exhibited in the 1874 two-story frame house. A cave exhibit, an old fire engine and an ambulance also are featured. Mon.-Fri. 10:30-4, Sat.-Sun. 1:30-4, May-Oct.; otherwise varies. Closed Jan. 1, Thanksgiving and Dec. 25. Donations. Phone (775) 273-2115.

OVERTON—*see Las Vegas p. 252.*

PIOCHE (D-6) pop. 800, elev. 6,018′

Pioche was one of the roughest mining camps in the West during the 1870s. The town's Boot Hill boasted 75 graves before its first interment due to natural causes. Residents balanced their lack of creativity in solving disagreements with such epitaphs as "Fanny Peterson, July 12, 1872. They loved til death did them part. He killed her."

Pioche is known for its Million Dollar Courthouse, a $30,000 building that cost the county almost $1 million by the time it was completed in the late 1800s. Condemned in 1933, the building and the four lots on which it stands were sold 25 years later for $150. The courthouse has been restored and is open for guided tours.

Pioche Chamber of Commerce: P.O. Box 127, Pioche, NV 89043; phone (775) 962-5544 or (775) 962-5245.

LINCOLN COUNTY HISTORICAL MUSEUM, on Main St. next to the library, houses local historical items that include mining tools, furniture, musical instruments, photographs, documents and early 20th-century clothing. Daily 10-1 and 2-4; closed Thanksgiving and Dec. 25. Donations. Phone (775) 962-5207.

RENO (C-2) pop. 180,480, elev. 4,490′

Full of stage shows and gambling establishments that operate 24 hours a day, Reno is a city of diverse extremes, calling itself "The Biggest Little City in the World." Its neon lights supply the same excitement as Las Vegas, but Reno also is an important distribution and merchandising center, has extensive residential areas and is the home of the University of Nevada, Reno.

Reno's sunny, dry climate attracts summer and winter sports enthusiasts. Skiers flock to the Sierra Nevada in California for downhill and cross-country skiing. Facilities for boating, biking, snowmobiling, hiking and white-water rafting are available in the Reno area.

A more sedate side of Reno can be found along the banks of the Truckee River. The brass and marble Truckee River Walk features several fountains and is the location for various family events throughout the year.

The Silver Legacy Resort Casino, 407 N. Virginia St., features a 120-foot-tall mining rig that mints coins before your eyes, while free circus acts are offered at Circus Circus Hotel/Casino, 500 N. Sierra St.

Reno is at the southwestern end of a scenic route consisting of SRs 445, 446 and 447. These highways run through Pyramid Lake Indian Reservation and follow the southern shoreline of Pyramid Lake *(see attraction listing p. 256).*

Reno/Sparks Convention and Visitor Authority: 4590 S. Virginia St., P.O. Box 837, Reno, NV 89504; phone (775) 827-7600 or (800) 367-7366.

ANIMAL ARK NATURE CENTER AND WILDLIFE SANCTUARY is off US 395 exit 78, 11.5 mi. e. on Red Rock Rd., then 1 mi. s. on Deerlodge Rd. This refuge in the rural hills north of Reno features North American predators and exotic animals that are unable to live in their natural habitats. Educational programs and demonstrations focus on animal behavior and the role of predators in the wild. Wolves, birds of prey, foxes, a black bear, an Asian tiger, a snow leopard and other large cats are on display. Picnicking is permitted. Allow 1 hour minimum. Tues.-Sun. 10-4:30, Apr.-Oct. (weather permitting). Admission $6; over 65, $5; ages 3-12, $4. Phone (775) 970-3111.

CHURCH FINE ARTS BUILDING, at the University of Nevada, Reno, presents changing exhibits, principally of contemporary art, in Sheppard Fine Arts Gallery. Theatrical productions are staged by the university in the Church Fine Arts Theatre, and concerts are held in Nightingale Music Hall. Allow 30 minutes minimum. Building open Mon.-Fri. 8-5; closed major holidays and during school breaks. Building free. Phone (775) 784-6682, (775) 784-6839 or (775) 784-6145 for the music hall.

GEM SAVE **FLEISCHMANN PLANETARIUM,** at the n. edge of the University of Nevada, Reno campus on N. Virginia St., presents programs about the night sky. Periodically changing Star Shows depict astronomical events of the past, present and future. Films shown on the Skydome screen surround the audience with realistic images. Each performance includes planetarium and Skydome shows. Astronomy and earth science exhibits also are featured. Hours and programs vary.

Allow 1 hour, 30 minutes minimum. Mon.-Fri. 8-8, Sat.-Sun. 11-8; closed Jan. 1, Thanksgiving and Dec. 24-25 and 31. Star Show schedule varies; phone ahead. Planetarium free. Star Show and Skydome movie $7; over 59 and under 13, $5. Under 6 are admitted to daytime shows only. DS, MC, VI. Phone (775) 784-4811 for recorded show information, or (775) 784-4812 for reservations, or (775) 784-1759 for recorded Skyline information.

GEM SAVE **NATIONAL AUTOMOBILE MUSEUM,** 10 Lake St. S., displays more than 200 antique, vintage, classic and special-interest automobiles. Four street scenes with period automobiles and artifacts depict different eras of the 20th century. The facility also offers interactive exhibits, a multimedia theater presentation, antique clothing and an automotive research library.

Food is available in the summer. Allow 1 hour, 30 minutes minimum. Mon.-Sat. 9:30-5:30, Sun. 10-4; closed Thanksgiving and Dec. 25. Admission $8; over 62, $7; ages 6-18, $3. AX, DS, MC, VI. Phone (775) 333-9300. *See ad.*

NEVADA HISTORICAL SOCIETY MUSEUM is at 1650 N. Virginia St. Founded in 1904, the state's oldest museum chronicles Nevada history. Displays contain American Indian basketry, pottery and relics, pioneer and mining artifacts, and Las Vegas memorabilia, including neon signs and casino souvenirs. A research library contains records dating from 1859. Museum Mon.-Sat. 10-5. Library Tues.-Sat. noon-4. Closed major holidays. Admission $2, under 18 free. Phone (775) 688-1190.

NEVADA MUSEUM OF ART, 2 blks. w. of Virginia St. at 160 W. Liberty St., houses fine art exhibits relating to the state's history, culture, environment and political issues. Allow 1 hour minimum. Tues.-Sun. 11-6 (also Thurs. 6-8); closed Jan. 1, Easter and Dec. 25. Admission $5; over 60, $3; ages 6-12, $1. Phone (775) 329-3333.

PYRAMID LAKE—*see Sutcliffe p. 256.*

WILBUR D. MAY CENTER is in Rancho San Rafael Park at 1502 Washington St. The center includes the Wilbur D. May Museum, Arboretum and Botanical Garden and Great Basin Adventure. Containing objects collected by adventurer Wilbur D. May during his world travels, the museum is a replica of his Double Diamond Ranch. Highlights of the collection include souvenirs from African safaris, rare Tang Dynasty horse sculptures and 18th-century sterling silver.

Picnicking is permitted. Allow 1 hour minimum. Museum Mon.-Sat. 10-5, Sun. noon-5. Hours may vary; phone ahead. Arboretum daily 8-dusk. Great Basin Adventure Tues.-Sat. 10-5, Sun. noon-5, Memorial Day weekend-Labor Day. Museum $4.50; over 54, $3.50; ages 3-12, $2.50. Arboretum free. Great Basin Adventure $5; ages 3-12, $3.50. Pony and flume rides $1 each. Phone (775) 785-5961 for the museum, or (775) 785-4153 for the arboretum, (775) 785-4844 for Great Basin Adventure.

RHYOLITE (E-5)

On a dirt road 2.5 miles west of Beatty, Rhyolite was a city of 12,000 inhabitants in 1907. Mine failure caused its desertion, and only stone foundations and brick fronts remain. The town once boasted telephone service, water companies, saloons, hundreds of houses, an opera house, electric street lights and a red-light district.

An elaborate railroad depot and a house constructed almost entirely of bottles are two of the few surviving structures in Rhyolite; neither is open to the public. Visitors are cautioned to be careful if climbing the old remains; trembling caused by mining in nearby areas could make it dangerous.

Beatty Chamber of Commerce: P.O. Box 956, Beatty, NV 89003; phone (775) 553-2424.

SILVER SPRINGS (C-3)

pop. 4,708, elev. 4,209′

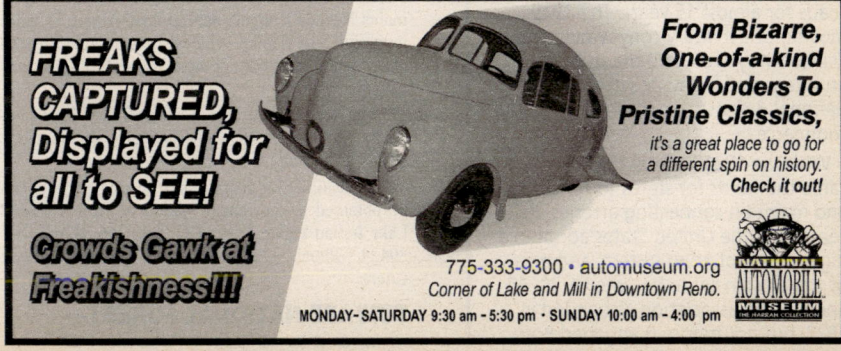

FORT CHURCHILL STATE HISTORIC PARK is 7 mi. s. on US 95A, then 1 mi. w. on Old Fort Churchill Rd. Built in 1860 as protection against American Indian attacks, this U.S. Army outpost also guarded the Pony Express and other mail routes. Although the fort is now in ruins, the site is

The Lincoln Highway

The horseless carriage rolled onto the American landscape in the 1890s. By 1910 there were more than 450,000 registered automobiles, yet the country still lacked a public road system.

Organized movements for better roads brought issues to the attention of the federal government, which had not participated in major road construction since it funded the National Road project in 1806.

But one particular initiative captured the public's support with a unique idea. In 1913 Carl Fisher—the man who built the Indianapolis Motor Speedway in 1909—and automobile industry leaders chartered the Lincoln Highway Association for the purpose of defining a direct coast-to-coast automobile route.

The LHA's first official act was to delineate a 3,389-mile, 12-state continuous route from New York to California—one that would be passable before the opening of the 1915 Panama-Pacific International Exposition in San Francisco. Although not perfect, the throughway was ready as promised, and a motion picture of America's transcontinental highway was shown at the exposition. Over time, the association improved surfaces by using better materials, shortened the driving distance with realignments and published guidebooks about the Lincoln Highway. Automobile touring had never been so good.

Through example, the LHA educated the public as well as state and federal governments about the value of good roads for almost 15 years. The 1919 moving of a military convoy over the "Lincolnway" foretold the utility of an integrated highway system for national defense and interstate commerce.

With the 1921 Federal Highway Act came the funds for states to construct and maintain connecting arteries. Four years later the United States adopted a highway numbering system, and most of the Lincoln route became US 30, 40 and 50. The association disbanded in 1928, but not before it engaged Boy

a 4,461-acre park with an interpretive trail. A visitor center reconstructs the fort's colorful history with exhibits.

Park daily 24 hours. Visitor center daily 8-4, Memorial Day-Labor Day; otherwise varies. Admission Memorial Day-Labor Day $3 per private vehicle. Admission rest of year $1. Camping $8. Phone (775) 577-2345. *See Recreation Chart.*

SPARKS (C-3) pop. 66,346, elev. 4,407′

Sparks was established in 1904 when railroad buildings were moved by the Southern Pacific Railroad to Reno's eastern border. It was named after the state's governor, John Sparks.

An outdoor railroad exhibit, the chamber of commerce and a number of casinos are on Victorian Avenue. Victorian Square Plaza, a pedestrian mall off I-80 via Rock Boulevard or Pyramid Way, holds events year-round. During summer an interactive sidewalk fountain presents water shows choreographed to music.

Sparks Chamber of Commerce: 831 Victorian Ave., P.O. Box 1776, Sparks, NV 89432-1776; phone (775) 358-1976.

SPARKS HERITAGE MUSEUM, 820 Victorian Ave., features memorabilia and displays depicting the history of Sparks and the surrounding Sierra Nevada region. Particular emphasis is placed on railroad history since the city owes its existence to the Central Pacific Railroad, whose booming industry fueled the town's economy until the mid-20th century. Allow 30 minutes minimum. Tues.-Fri. 11-4, Sat. 1-4. Donations. Phone (775) 355-1144.

SAVE **WILD ISLAND,** I-80E and Sparks Blvd. at 250 Wild Island Ct., has 10 outdoor water rides, a wave pool, a volleyball court, a children's play area, a game arcade, miniature golf and miniature race tracks. Picnicking is permitted. Food is available. Daily 11-7, mid-June through Labor Day. Admission $18.95; under 48 inches tall $14.95; over 59, $4.95. Golf $4.95. Indy racers $4.95. Sprint racers $2.75. DS, MC, VI. Phone (775) 359-2927.

SUTCLIFFE (B-2) pop. 281, elev. 3,900′

PYRAMID LAKE is off SR 445. Pyramid Lake remains Nevada's largest natural lake. About 30 miles long and 7 to 9 miles wide, it is surrounded by red and brown sandstone mountains and porous rock islands.

Long before it became a 475,000-acre Paiute Indian reservation in 1874, the lake area served as the tribe's homeland.

Applications for fishing and boating permits can be obtained at the ranger station or from Pyramid Lake Indian Paiute Tribe, P.O. Box 256, Nixon, NV 89424. Phone (775) 574-1000. *See Recreation Chart.*

TOIYABE NATIONAL FOREST—

see Humboldt-Toiyabe National Forest p. 226.

TONOPAH (D-4) pop. 2,627, elev. 6,030′

Tonopah had its beginning in 1900 when prospector Jim Butler idly chipped away at a ledge that sheltered him during a thunderstorm and noticed that the rock looked like silver ore. By the time the boom he started reached its peak 13 years later, production in the area had netted $9.5 million. The town shared the area's mineral wealth with nearby Goldfield.

Tonopah Chamber of Commerce: 301 Brougher Ave., P.O. Box 869, Tonopah, NV 89049; phone (775) 482-3859.

CENTRAL NEVADA MUSEUM, 1900 Logan Field Rd. s. of Nye Regional Medical Center, depicts the history of the area through displays about American Indians, settlements, boomtowns, railroads and mining. A research library also is available. The grounds contain heavy industrial and mining equipment. Allow 30 minutes minimum. Daily 9-5, Apr.-Sept.; Mon.-Sat. 11-5, rest of year. Closed Jan. 1, Thanksgiving and Dec. 25. Donations. Phone (775) 482-9676.

VIRGINIA CITY (C-2) elev. 6,220′

With nearly 30,000 residents, more than 100 saloons, a multitude of banks, churches and theaters, and the only elevator between Chicago and San Francisco, the Virginia City of the 1870s was the West's mining metropolis. The Comstock Lode had given the town unequaled prosperity. The ore extracted from the Consolidated Virginia Mine has been estimated to have a gross value of at least $234 million, some of which was used to build San Francisco and finance the Union Army during the Civil War.

Notable residents included Mark Twain and Bret Harte, who worked as reporters on the *Territorial Enterprise,* Nevada's first newspaper and one known for occasionally making up the news. The International Championship Camel Races, held on the first weekend in September, began as a fictitious story in 1959 and has since become one of the state's major events.

Much has been done to restore Virginia City to its 1870 boomtown appearance. Many small museums along C Street preserve the town's illustrious past. They include the Nevada Gambling Museum, The Way It Was Museum and Ponderosa Mine, which offers underground mine tours every 20 minutes.

Mark Twain Bookstore, on C and Taylor streets, contains a collection of historic memorabilia and rare books; phone (775) 847-0454.

Saint Mary's in the Mountains is a brick church built on the site of a church destroyed by fire in 1875. The building has been restored and can be visited daily in summer and on weekends all year.

Virginia City lies along a scenic route consisting of SR 341 northwest to the junction of US 395. From that point the route follows SR 431 through

The Lincoln Highway (continued)

Scout troops across the country to place some 3,000 concrete Lincoln Highway markers along the route in all 12 states: New York, New Jersey, Pennsylvania, Ohio, Indiana, Illinois, Iowa, Nebraska, Wyoming, Utah, Nevada and California. Many of these markers still exist.

The original 440-mile Nevada section of the Lincoln Highway entered the state from Ibapah, Utah and traversed several ranches on a southward path to **Ely.** In the early days some ranches offered meals, lodging and camping as well as radiator water. From Ely the route continued westward, passing through **Eureka, Austin** and **Fallon** on a sparsely populated corridor that eventually became US 50—sometimes referred to as "The Loneliest Road in America." The summit near Austin was one of the highest points on the Nevada Lincolnway.

The final leg to California ran through **Sparks,** then **Reno;** or, if the longer alternate route was chosen, through **Carson City** and around Lake Tahoe. **Look for these Nevada Lincoln Highway landmark towns in this TourBook guide.**

For more information about the old Lincoln Highway contact the new Lincoln Highway Association, P.O. Box 308, Franklin Grove, IL 61031; phone (815) 456-3030.

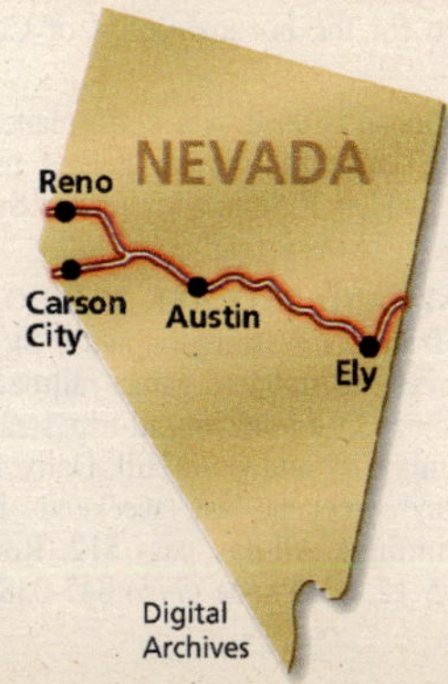

Digital Archives

Humboldt-Toiyabe National Forest to the northern shore of Lake Tahoe.

Virginia City Chamber of Commerce: 86 S. C St., P.O. Box 464, Virginia City, NV 89440; phone (775) 847-0311.

THE CASTLE, 190 S. B St., is an 1868 structure that reflects the prosperity of mining towns through original antique furnishings, 200-year-old Czechoslovakian crystal chandeliers, Italian marble fireplaces and silver doorknobs. Allow 30 minutes minimum. Guided tours are given daily 11-5, Memorial Day weekend-last Sun. in Oct. Fee $4.50; ages 13-17, $2; ages 6-12, 50c. Phone (775) 847-0275.

CHOLLAR MINE, on S. F St., is an 1861 Comstock gold and silver mine with original square-set timbering. Allow 30 minutes minimum. Sat.-Thurs. noon-5, June-Sept.; Sat.-Thurs. 1-4 in May and Oct. (weather permitting). Admission $5; ages 4-14, $2. Phone (775) 847-0155.

COMSTOCK FIREMEN'S MUSEUM, 125 S. C St., displays antique fire wagons dating from 1859 as well as firefighters' uniforms, leather helmets, photographs and firefighting accessories. The collection spans the volunteer fire department period in the Virginia City-Gold Hill area 1861-77 and includes relics from later periods. Daily 10-5, May-Oct. Donations. Phone (775) 847-0717.

MACKAY MANSION, 129 S. D St., is a 10-room, 1860 building that served as the original headquarters of the Gould and Curry Mine Co. Later it was the residence of silver king John Mackay, owner of the Consolidated Virginia Mine and an early leader of Virginia City who donated millions to Nevada education.

Daily 11-6 (weather permitting). Admission $4, under 14 free. Phone (775) 826-3934.

PIPER'S OPERA HOUSE, B and Union sts., witnessed the coming of age of many traveling players following its construction in the 1880s. Such greats as Maude Adams, Wilson Barrett, David Belasco, Edwin Booth, Lotta Crabtree and Adah Isaacs Menken performed for the bonanza kings of Comstock silver wealth.

The opera house is used as a performance venue throughout the year. Ten-minute guided tours are available. Daily 11-4:30, mid-May to late Sept. Donations. Phone (775) 847-0433.

SAVE **VIRGINIA AND TRUCKEE RAILROAD,** departing from the Washington and F St. station, is a partially restored standard gauge railroad. It operates a narrated 35-minute round-trip steam train between Virginia City and Gold Hill. Daily 10:30-5, Memorial Day weekend-last weekend in Oct. (weather permitting). All-day pass $12. Round-trip fare $6; ages 5-12, $3. Phone (775) 847-0380.

WELLS (A-5) pop. 1,346, elev. 5,625'

Wells took its name from a number of calm springs. This area, where I-80 and US 93 intersect, was an important stop for late 19th-century pioneers following the Humboldt Trail. The ruts left by the iron-rimmed wheels of their wagons still can be seen in nearby rocks.

For a panorama of the area, summer visitors can hike on trails leading from nearby Angel Lake *(see Recreation Chart and the AAA California & Nevada CampBook)* to the 11,000-foot "Hole-in-the-Mountain Peak." Angel Lake is accessible from Wells mid-June through September via SR 582, a precipitous two-lane road.

Wells Chamber of Commerce: 395 6th St., P.O. Box 615, Wells, NV 89835; phone (775) 752-3540.

WINNEMUCCA (B-3) pop. 7,174, elev. 4,324'

Thousands of pioneers passed through Winnemucca on their way to California and Oregon. In 1845 children in a wagon train bound for California played a game of tossing pebbles into blue buckets hanging from the wagons. The "pebbles" were later identified as gold nuggets, and although many have searched, the "Blue Bucket Mine" never has been found.

The infamous Butch Cassidy and the Sundance Kid were said to have left their mark on Winnemucca. In 1900 they purportedly celebrated their robbery of the First National Bank by sending the bank president a studio portrait of themselves.

The town also is home to one of the largest Basque populations in North America. The early Basque immigrants found the open range of the Great Basin suitable for raising sheep. Today their customs, food and language flourish in Winnemucca. The Basque Festival, held in June, celebrates this heritage

Humboldt Museum, at Maple Avenue and Jungo Road, chronicles the region's history with antiques and memorabilia, including a collection of vintage cars and American Indian artifacts. The excavation of a 13,000-year-old mammoth from nearby Black Rock Desert is chronicled in the ice age exhibit and video presentation; phone (775) 623-2912. Minerals found in the area include gold, silver, tungsten, barite and mercury, in addition to opals and turquoise.

Winnemucca Convention and Visitor Authority: 50 W. Winnemucca Blvd., Winnemucca, NV 89445; phone (775) 623-5071 or (800) 962-2638.

Self-guiding tours: Walking tour maps highlighting mining, Western and Basque history are available at the visitor authority.

ZEPHYR COVE—

see Lake Tahoe Area in California p. 89.

San Francisco's Golden Gate Bridge / © Bob and Suzanne Clemenz

Northern California Orientation Map to Destinations

Wine Country (see p. 762)

Major destinations are color-coded to index boxes, which display vicinity communities you will find listed within that destination's section of the book.
Cities outside major destination vicinities are listed in alphabetical order throughout the book.
Use the *Comprehensive City Index* at the back of this book to find every city's listing locations.

AHWAHNEE —*See also YOSEMITE NATIONAL PARK.*

WHERE TO STAY

THE HOMESTEAD **Phone:** (559)683-0495

Cottage

All Year [CP] 1P: $129-$189 2P: $134-$199 XP: $50

Location: 4.5 mi n of jct SR 41 and 49, 2.5 mi sw of SR 49 on CR 600. Located in a secluded area. 41110 Rd 600 93601. Fax: 559/683-8165. **Facility:** Oak-studded acreage surrounds these individual adobe, stone and cedar cottages, which include one studio unit; horse stalls are also available. Smoke free premises. 5 cottages. 1 story, exterior corridors. *Bath:* combo or shower only. **Parking:** on-site. **Terms:** 2 night minimum stay - weekends, 7 day cancellation notice. **Amenities:** irons, hair dryers. **Leisure Activities:** bicycles, hiking trails. **Cards:** AX, DS, MC, VI.

SOME UNITS

ALAMEDA pop. 72,259 (See map and index starting on p. 516)

WHERE TO STAY

CORAL REEF MOTEL & SUITES *Book at aaa.com* **Phone:** 510/521-2330 63

Motel

All Year 1P: $84 2P: $84

Location: I-880, exit 23rd Ave, 1 mi se. 400 Park St 94501. Fax: 510/521-4707. **Facility:** 93 units. 38 one-bedroom standard units with kitchens. 55 one-bedroom suites ($99) with kitchens. 2 stories (no elevator), exterior corridors. **Parking:** on-site. **Terms:** age restrictions may apply, weekly rates available, [CP] meal plan available. **Amenities:** voice mail, irons, hair dryers. **Pool(s):** heated outdoor. **Guest Services:** coin laundry. **Business Services:** conference facilities. **Cards:** AX, CB, DC, DS, MC, VI. *(See color ad below)*

SOME UNITS

HAWTHORN SUITES LTD-OAKLAND/ALAMEDA *Book at aaa.com* **Phone:** (510)522-1000 61

Small-scale Hotel

All Year [BP] 1P: $99-$169 2P: $99-$169 XP: $10 F16

Location: I-880, exit Broadway to Webster Tube. 1628 Webster St 94501. Fax: 510/522-1011. **Facility:** 50 one-bedroom suites. 3 stories, interior corridors. *Bath:* some combo or shower only. **Parking:** on-site. **Amenities:** high-speed Internet, dual phone lines, voice mail, irons, hair dryers. *Some:* DVD players. **Leisure Activities:** whirlpool. **Guest Services:** complimentary evening beverages: Wed, coin laundry. **Business Services:** meeting rooms, business center. **Cards:** AX, CB, DC, DS, JC, MC, VI. **Special Amenities: free full breakfast and preferred room (subject to availability with advanced reservations).** *(See color ad p 520)*

SOME UNITS

MARINA VILLAGE INN *Book at aaa.com* **Phone:** (510)523-9450 62

Small-scale Hotel

All Year [CP] 1P: $106-$159 2P: $106-$159 XP: $10 F16

Location: I-880, exit Broadway to Webster Tube. 1151 Pacific Marina 94501. Fax: 510/523-6315. **Facility:** 51 units. 49 one-bedroom standard units. 2 one-bedroom suites ($159). 2 stories (no elevator), exterior corridors. *Bath:* combo or shower only. **Parking:** on-site. **Amenities:** high-speed Internet, voice mail, safes, irons, hair dryers. **Pool(s):** heated outdoor. **Business Services:** meeting rooms. **Cards:** AX, DC, DS, MC, VI. **Special Amenities: free continental breakfast and free local telephone calls.** *(See color ad p 524)*

WHERE TO DINE

PASTA PELICAN **Lunch:** $7-$15 **Dinner:** $9-$18 **Phone:** 510/864-7427 37

Italian

Location: I-880 N, exit Broadway, just left thru tunnel. 2455 Mariner Square Dr 94501. **Hours:** 11 am-2 & 5-9 pm. Closed: 11/25, 12/24, 12/25. **Reservations:** suggested. **Features:** A home away from home for scores of residents, the restaurant specializes in Northern Italian cuisine. Dishes are built around fresh seafood from local markets, steaks and pasta. Casual dress; cocktails. **Parking:** on-site. **Cards:** AX, DC, MC, VI.

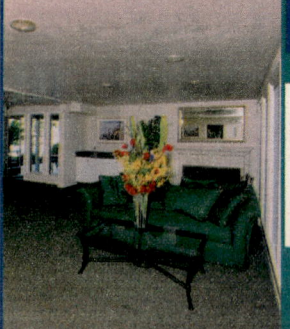

ALBION —See Wine Country p. 764.

ALTURAS pop. 2,892—See also CEDARVILLE.

WHERE TO STAY

BEST WESTERN TRAILSIDE INN Book at aaa.com **Phone:** 530/233-4111

Motel

5/1-10/31 [CP]	1P: $70-$75	2P: $75-$80	XP: $5	F12
2/1-4/30 & 11/1-1/31 [CP]	1P: $70	2P: $75	XP: $5	F12

Location: On US 395. 343 N Main St 96101. Fax: 530/233-3180. **Facility:** 38 one-bedroom standard units. 2 stories (no elevator), exterior corridors. **Parking:** on-site. **Terms:** age restrictions may apply, 7 day cancellation notice-fee imposed, pets ($5 extra charge). **Amenities:** irons, hair dryers. **Pool(s):** outdoor. **Cards:** AX, CB, DC, DS, MC, VI. **Special Amenities: free continental breakfast and free newspaper.**

SOME UNITS

FEE

SUPER 8 MOTEL **Phone:** (530)233-3545

Motel

6/1-1/31	1P: $66-$71	2P: $66-$71	XP: $5	F12
2/1-5/31	1P: $64-$69	2P: $64-$69	XP: $5	F12

Location: On US 395. 511 N Main St 96101. Fax: 530/233-3305. **Facility:** 48 one-bedroom standard units. 2 stories (no elevator), exterior corridors. **Parking:** on-site. **Terms:** age restrictions may apply. **Amenities:** *Some:* irons. **Cards:** AX, CB, DC, DS, JC, MC, VI. **Special Amenities: free local telephone calls and free room upgrade (subject to availability with advanced reservations).**

SOME UNITS

WHERE TO DINE

ANTONIO'S **Lunch:** $6-$9 **Dinner:** $10-$14 **Phone:** 530/233-5600

Traditional Italian

Location: On US 395; center of town. 220 S Main St 96101. **Hours:** 11 am-10 pm. Closed: 11/25, 12/25. **Features:** The small family restaurant offers pizza, pasta, sandwiches and beer, and is located in the center of downtown within walking distance of hotels. Casual dress; beer & wine only. **Parking:** on-site. **Cards:** VI.

AMADOR CITY pop. 196

WHERE TO DINE

IMPERIAL HOTEL RESTAURANT **Dinner:** $12-$25 **Phone:** 209/267-9172

Continental

Location: Center. 14202 Hwy 49 95601. **Hours:** 5 pm-9 pm. Closed: 12/24, 12/25; also Mon & Tues. **Reservations:** suggested. **Features:** The restaurant is rustic early California in design, and serves steaks, fish and chicken that is Continental in style of preparation and service. Casual dress; cocktails. **Parking:** on-site. **Cards:** AX, DS, MC, VI.

ANDERSON pop. 9,022

WHERE TO STAY

AMERIHOST INN-ANDERSON Book at aaa.com **Phone:** (530)365-6100

Motel

All Year [ECP]	1P: $62-$69	2P: $72-$79	XP: $10	F16

Location: I-5, exit Factory Outlet Dr, just w. 2040 Factory Outlet Dr 96007. Fax: 530/365-3231. **Facility:** 61 one-bedroom standard units, some with whirlpools. 2 stories (no elevator), interior corridors. *Bath:* combo or shower only. **Parking:** on-site. **Terms:** age restrictions may apply, weekly rates available, small pets only ($10 fee). **Amenities:** high-speed Internet, dual phone lines, safes, irons, hair dryers. **Pool(s):** heated indoor. **Leisure Activities:** sauna, whirlpool, exercise room. **Business Services:** meeting rooms. **Cards:** AX, CB, DC, DS, JC, MC, VI.

SOME UNITS

FEE

BEST WESTERN KNIGHTS INN Book at aaa.com **Phone:** (530)365-2753

Motel

All Year	1P: $55-$70	2P: $60-$80	XP: $8	F12

Location: I-5, exit Central Anderson eastbound; exit Lassen Park westbound, just e. 2688 Gateway Dr 96007. Fax: 530/365-6083. **Facility:** 40 one-bedroom standard units. 2 stories (no elevator), exterior corridors. **Parking:** on-site. **Terms:** age restrictions may apply, small pets only. **Amenities:** irons, hair dryers. **Pool(s):** outdoor. **Cards:** AX, CB, DC, DS, MC, VI. **Special Amenities: free local telephone calls and early check-in/late check-out.**

SOME UNITS

WHERE TO DINE

AMIGO'S ON THE RIVER — **Lunch:** $7-$12 — **Dinner:** $9-$14 — **Phone:** 530/365-6142

Mexican

Location: I-5, exit Riverside, just e; 1 mi to Sacramento River. 1542 Claude Ln 96007. **Hours:** 11 am-9 pm, Fri & Sat-10 pm. Closed: 4/11, 11/25, 12/25. **Features:** On the Sacramento River, the small, hacienda-like restaurant presents a menu of Mexican fare. Casual dress; cocktails. **Parking:** on-site. **Cards:** AX, DS, MC, VI.

ANGELS CAMP pop. 2,400

WHERE TO STAY

ANGELS HACIENDA — *Book at aaa.com* — **Phone:** (209)785-8533

Bed & Breakfast

All Year [BP]	2P: $129-$179	XP: $20	D10

Location: 7 mi on SR 4, then 5 mi. (4871 Hunt Rd, FARMINGTON, 95230). Fax: 209/785-8536. **Facility:** The hacienda has all the flourish and decor of old Hollywood; the scenic setting with acres and acres of ranch land is a perfect setting for romance. 8 one-bedroom standard units, some with whirlpools. 2 stories (no elevator), interior corridors. *Bath:* combo or shower only. **Parking:** on-site. **Terms:** office hours 8 am-8 pm, 2 night minimum stay - weekends, 14 day cancellation notice-fee imposed, package plans, pets ($10 extra charge, outside kennel). **Amenities:** video library, CD players, irons, hair dryers. **Pool(s):** heated outdoor. **Leisure Activities:** spa. **Guest Services:** gift shop, complimentary evening beverages. **Business Services:** meeting rooms. **Cards:** DS, MC, VI.

SOME UNITS — FEE

ANGELS INN MOTEL — **Phone:** (209)736-4242

SAVE — Motel

5/1-9/30	1P: $85-$105	2P: $85-$105	XP: $10	F12
2/1-4/30 & 10/1-1/31	1P: $75-$105	2P: $75-$105	XP: $10	F12

Location: SR 49, north end of town. 600 N Main St 95221 (PO Box 1121). Fax: 209/736-6758. **Facility:** 58 one-bedroom standard units. 2 stories (no elevator), exterior corridors. **Parking:** on-site. **Terms:** cancellation fee imposed, pets ($50 deposit, $10 extra charge). **Amenities:** high-speed Internet, irons, hair dryers. *Fee:* video library, video games. **Pool(s):** outdoor. **Guest Services:** coin laundry. **Business Services:** meeting rooms. **Cards:** AX, DS, MC, VI. *(See color ad below)*

FEE — SOME UNITS

BEST WESTERN CEDAR INN & SUITES — *Book at aaa.com* — **Phone:** (209)736-4000

SAVE — Motel

3/1-9/30 [ECP]	1P: $99-$169	2P: $99-$169	XP: $10	F12
2/1-2/29 & 10/1-1/31 [ECP]	1P: $89-$149	2P: $89-$149	XP: $10	F12

Location: On SR 49; center of town. 444 S Main St 95222 (PO Box 50). Fax: 209/736-4142. **Facility:** Smoke free premises. 38 units. 31 one-bedroom standard units, some with whirlpools. 7 one-bedroom suites ($129-$189), some with whirlpools. 2 stories (no elevator), interior/exterior corridors. *Bath:* combo or shower only. **Parking:** on-site. **Terms:** pets ($10 extra charge). **Amenities:** dual phone lines, voice mail, irons, hair dryers. **Pool(s):** outdoor. **Leisure Activities:** whirlpool, boat parking, exercise room. **Guest Services:** coin laundry. **Cards:** AX, CB, DC, DS, JC, MC, VI. **Special Amenities: free expanded continental breakfast and free local telephone calls.**

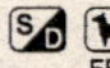

FEE

GOLD COUNTRY INN Phone: (209)736-4611

Motel

All Year 1P: $60-$85 2P: $70-$180 XP: $5 F12

Location: 1 mi s of jct SR 49 and 4. 720 S Main St 95222 (PO Box 188). Fax: 209/736-4832. **Facility:** 40 one-bedroom standard units. 2 stories (no elevator), exterior corridors. **Parking:** on-site. **Terms:** cancellation fee imposed, pets ($50 deposit, $15 extra charge). **Cards:** AX, DS, MC, VI. **Special Amenities: preferred room (subject to availability with advanced reservations).**

SOME UNITS

FEE

GREENHORN CREEK RESORT *Book at aaa.com* Phone: (209)736-8120

Vacation Home

All Year 1P: $165-$395 2P: $165-$395 XP: $25 F13

Location: Just s of SR 49. 711 McCauley Ranch Rd 95222. Fax: 209/736-6210. **Facility:** The scenic Sierra Nevada foothills form a backdrop to these individual homes, which are located along an 18-hole golf course. 59 one-bedroom standard units with kitchens. 1 story, exterior corridors. **Parking:** on-site. **Terms:** office hours 8:30 am-10 pm, age restrictions may apply, 7 day cancellation notice. **Amenities:** dual phone lines, voice mail, irons, hair dryers. **Pool(s):** 2 heated outdoor. **Leisure Activities:** golf-18 holes, 2 tennis courts, exercise room. *Fee:* massage. **Guest Services:** gift shop. **Business Services:** meeting rooms, business center. **Cards:** AX, MC, VI.

ASK VCR DATA PORT

JUMPING FROG MOTEL Phone: (209)736-2191

Motel

All Year 1P: $41-$108 XP: $5 F12

Location: SR 49, n of Angels Camp Center, just left. 330 Murphys Grade Rd 95221 (PO Box 27). Fax: 209/736-4832. **Facility:** 15 units. 13 one- and 2 two-bedroom standard units. 1 story, exterior corridors. *Bath:* combo or shower only. **Parking:** on-site. **Terms:** office hours 7 am-10 pm, cancellation fee imposed, pets ($15). **Amenities:** voice mail. *Some:* irons, hair dryers. **Cards:** AX, DS, MC, VI. **Special Amenities: free local telephone calls.**

SOME UNITS

FEE

ANTIOCH pop. 90,532

WHERE TO STAY

BEST WESTERN HERITAGE INN *Book at aaa.com* Phone: (925)778-2000

Motel

All Year [CP] 1P: $67-$76 2P: $67-$76 XP: $10 F12

Location: SR 4, exit Somersville Rd. 3210 Delta Fair Blvd 94509. Fax: 925/778-6015. **Facility:** 73 one-bedroom standard units, some with whirlpools. 3 stories, exterior corridors. **Parking:** on-site. **Amenities:** irons, hair dryers. **Pool(s):** outdoor. **Leisure Activities:** whirlpool. **Business Services:** meeting rooms. **Cards:** AX, CB, DC, DS, MC, VI. **Special Amenities: free continental breakfast and free local telephone calls.**

(See color ad p 283)

SOME UNITS

DATA PORT

COMFORT SUITES ANTIOCH-OAKLEY *Book at aaa.com* Phone: (925)755-1222

Small-scale Hotel

2/1-11/30 [ECP] 1P: $99-$119 2P: $99-$119

12/1-1/31 [ECP] 1P: $89-$109 2P: $89-$109

Location: In Oakley; just e of SR 160 and 4, just n of Main St. 5549 Bridgehead Rd 94561. Fax: 925/755-1221. **Facility:** Smoke free premises. 80 one-bedroom standard units, some with whirlpools. 3 stories, interior corridors. *Bath:* combo or shower only. **Parking:** on-site. **Amenities:** video games (fee), high-speed Internet, dual phone lines, voice mail, safes, irons, hair dryers. **Pool(s):** outdoor. **Leisure Activities:** whirlpool, exercise room. **Business Services:** meeting rooms, business center. **Cards:** AX, CB, DC, DS, MC, VI. **Special Amenities: free expanded continental breakfast and free local telephone calls.** *(See color ad below)*

DATA PORT

APTOS pop. 9,396—*See also CAPITOLA, FELTON, SANTA CRUZ & SCOTTS VALLEY.*

WHERE TO STAY

BAYVIEW HOTEL *Book at aaa.com* **Phone:** (831)688-8654

Country Inn

All Year 1P: $149-$269 2P: $149-$269

Location: SR 1, exit Seacliff, 1 mi ne; in Aptos Village. 8041 Soquel Dr 95003. Fax: 831/688-5128. **Facility:** Smoke free premises. 12 one-bedroom standard units. 3 stories (no elevator), interior corridors. *Bath:* combo or shower only. **Parking:** on-site. **Terms:** 10 day cancellation notice-fee imposed. **Amenities:** video library. *Some:* CD players. **Cards:** AX, MC, VI.

SOME UNITS

BEST WESTERN SEACLIFF INN *Book at aaa.com* **Phone:** (831)688-7300

Motel

5/28-9/6 [BP] 1P: $139-$169 2P: $139-$169 XP: $10 F17
2/1-5/27 & 9/7-1/31 [BP] 1P: $119-$139 2P: $119-$139 XP: $10 F17

Location: SR 1, exit State Park Dr, just n. 7500 Old Dominion Ct 95003. Fax: 831/685-3603. **Facility:** 149 one-bedroom standard units, some with whirlpools. 2 stories (no elevator), interior/exterior corridors. *Bath:* combo or shower only. **Parking:** on-site. **Amenities:** video games (fee), voice mail, irons, hair dryers. *Some:* dual phone lines. **Dining:** 6:30 am-9 pm, cocktails, entertainment. **Pool(s):** outdoor. **Leisure Activities:** whirlpool, exercise room. **Guest Services:** valet and coin laundry. **Business Services:** meeting rooms. **Cards:** AX, CB, DC, DS, MC, VI. **Special Amenities: free full breakfast and free local telephone calls.** *(See color ad p 710)*

SOME UNITS

FEE FEE

RIO SANDS MOTEL **Phone:** (831)688-3207

Motel

5/28-8/31 [ECP] 2P: $140-$170 XP: $10 F6
2/1-5/27 & 9/1-10/31 [ECP] 2P: $79-$140 XP: $10 F6
11/1-1/31 [ECP] 2P: $69-$110 XP: $10 F6

Location: SR 1, exit Rio Del Mar Blvd, 1.5 mi w. 116 Aptos Beach Dr 95003. Fax: 831/688-6107. **Facility:** 50 one-bedroom standard units, some with kitchens. 2 stories (no elevator), interior/exterior corridors. *Bath:* combo or shower only. **Parking:** on-site. **Terms:** 2 night minimum stay - weekends, weekly rates available. **Amenities:** voice mail. **Pool(s):** heated outdoor. **Leisure Activities:** whirlpool. **Cards:** AX, DS, MC, VI. **Special Amenities: free continental breakfast.** *(See color ad p 715)*

SOME UNITS

SEASCAPE RESORT **Phone:** (831)688-6800

Resort Large-scale Hotel

5/28-9/5 1P: $265-$540 2P: $265-$540
2/1-5/27 & 9/6-1/31 1P: $245-$495 2P: $245-$495

Location: 1 mi w of SR 1, exit San Andreas Rd, n on Seascape Blvd. One Seascape Resort Dr 95003. Fax: 831/685-0615. **Facility:** This resort property, on a hillside overlooking the Pacific Ocean, offers condos with gas fireplaces and private patios. Smoke free premises. 285 units. 84 one- and 201 two-bedroom suites ($265-$540), some with efficiencies or kitchens. 3 stories, exterior corridors. *Bath:* combo or shower only. **Parking:** on-site (fee). **Terms:** check-in 4 pm, 2-3 night minimum stay - in season, 3 day cancellation notice. **Amenities:** voice mail, irons, hair dryers. *Fee:* video games, high-speed Internet. *Some:* CD players, dual phone lines. **Dining:** 7 am-10 pm, cocktails. **Pool(s):** 3 heated outdoor. **Leisure Activities:** whirlpools, recreation programs, badminton, volleyball. *Fee:* golf course privileges, kids camp in summer, massage. **Guest Services:** complimentary laundry, area transportation-within 5 mi. **Business Services:** conference facilities, business center. **Cards:** AX, CB, DC, DS, MC, VI. *(See color ad below)*

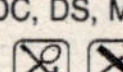
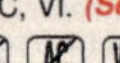
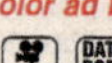

FEE

WHERE TO DINE

CAFE RIO **Dinner:** $18 **Phone:** 831/688-8917

Steak & Seafood

Location: SR 1, exit Rio Del Mar Blvd, 1.2 mi w. 131 Esplanade 95003. **Hours:** 5 pm-9:30 pm, Sun from 4 pm. Closed: 11/25, 12/25. **Reservations:** suggested. **Features:** The dining room's casual feel is befitting of its beach location. Fresh, local ingredients go into menu preparations. Dressy casual; cocktails. **Parking:** on-site. **Cards:** AX, MC, VI.

PALAPAS RESTAURANT AND CANTINA **Lunch:** $8-$14 **Dinner:** $10-$23 **Phone:** 831/662-9000

Mexican

Location: SR 1, exit San Andreas Rd, 1 mi w, then n on Seascape Blvd. 21 Seascape Village 95003. **Hours:** 11:30 am-2:30 & 5-10 pm. Closed: 11/25, 12/24, 12/25. **Reservations:** suggested. **Features:** Selections, many of which center on seafood, are made from fresh ingredients, including made-on-the-premises sauces. Casual dress; cocktails. **Parking:** on-site. **Cards:** AX, DC, DS, MC, VI.

ARCATA pop. 16,651

WHERE TO STAY

ARCATA SUPER 8 *Book at aaa.com* **Phone:** 707/822-8888

Small-scale Hotel

6/2-9/5 [CP]	1P: $50-$90	2P: $50-$90	XP: $6	F17
2/1-6/1 & 9/6-1/31 [CP]	1P: $45-$68	2P: $45-$68	XP: $6	F17

Location: US 101, exit Guintoli Ln, 2 mi n. 4887 Valley West Blvd 95521. Fax: 707/822-2513. **Facility:** 60 one-bedroom standard units. 2 stories (no elevator), interior corridors. **Parking:** on-site. **Terms:** age restrictions may apply, small pets only ($50 deposit). **Amenities:** *Some:* irons. **Cards:** AX, DS, MC, VI. **Special Amenities: free local telephone calls and free room upgrade (subject to availability with advanced reservations).**

SOME UNITS FEE

BEST WESTERN ARCATA INN *Book at aaa.com* **Phone:** (707)826-0313

Motel

All Year [ECP]	1P: $62-$103	2P: $62-$103	XP: $5	F12

Location: US 101, exit Guintoli Ln, 2 mi n. 4827 Valley West Blvd 95521. Fax: 707/826-0365. **Facility:** 62 one-bedroom standard units, some with whirlpools. 2 stories (no elevator), exterior corridors. *Bath:* combo or shower only. **Parking:** on-site. **Terms:** age restrictions may apply, [CP] meal plan available, pets ($10 extra charge). **Amenities:** irons, hair dryers. **Pool(s):** heated indoor/outdoor. **Leisure Activities:** whirlpool. **Guest Services:** coin laundry. **Cards:** AX, DC, DS, MC, VI. **Special Amenities: free expanded continental breakfast and early check-in/late check-out.**

SOME UNITS FEE

COMFORT INN *Book at aaa.com* **Phone:** (707)826-2827

Motel

5/14-9/15	1P: $65-$99	2P: $70-$99		
9/16-1/31	1P: $55-$99	2P: $60-$99		
2/1-5/13	1P: $55-$99	2P: $60-$99	XP: $6	F18

Location: US 101, exit Guintoli Ln, 2 mi n. 4701 Valley West Blvd 95521. Fax: 707/826-9344. **Facility:** 55 units. 54 one- and 1 two-bedroom standard units, some with whirlpools. 2 stories (no elevator), exterior corridors. *Bath:* combo or shower only. **Parking:** on-site. **Terms:** age restrictions may apply, [ECP] meal plan available, pets ($5 fee, limit 1 dog). **Amenities:** irons, hair dryers. **Pool(s):** heated indoor. **Leisure Activities:** whirlpool. **Cards:** AX, CB, DC, DS, JC, MC, VI. **Special Amenities: free expanded continental breakfast and early check-in/late check-out.**

(See color ad below)

SOME UNITS FEE

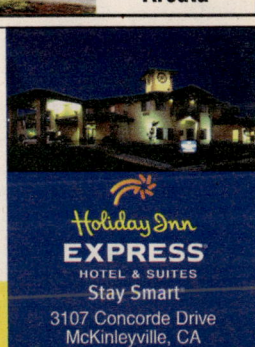

HOTEL ARCATA — Phone: (707)826-0217

Historic Small-scale Hotel

All Year 2P: $80-$130

Location: At Central Plaza. 708 9th St 95521. Fax: 707/826-1737. **Facility:** Refurbished 1915 hotel. 32 units. 26 one- and 2 two-bedroom standard units. 4 one-bedroom suites ($140-$200). 3 stories, interior corridors. **Parking:** street. **Terms:** age restrictions may apply, cancellation fee imposed, [CP] meal plan available, pets ($50 deposit). **Amenities:** *Some:* irons, hair dryers. **Dining:** 11 am-2:30 & 5-9 pm; Fri & Sat-11 pm in summer. **Guest Services:** gift shop. **Business Services:** meeting rooms. **Cards:** AX, CB, DC, DS, JC, MC, VI. **Special Amenities: free continental breakfast and early check-in/late check-out.**

SOME UNITS

FEE

HOWARD JOHNSON EXPRESS INN *Book at aaa.com* — Phone: (707)826-9660

Small-scale Hotel

7/1-9/15 [CP]	1P: $66-$120	2P: $75-$150	XP: $8	F17
5/1-6/30 [CP]	1P: $60-$120	2P: $70-$150	XP: $8	F17
9/16-1/31 [CP]	1P: $55-$90	2P: $60-$110	XP: $8	F17
2/1-4/30 [CP]	1P: $51-$80	2P: $56-$90	XP: $8	F17

Location: US 101, exit Guintoli Ln, 2 mi n. 4700 Valley West Blvd 95521. Fax: 707/826-9319. **Facility:** 48 units. 45 one- and 3 two-bedroom standard units, some with whirlpools. 2 stories (no elevator), interior corridors. **Parking:** on-site. **Terms:** age restrictions may apply, 3 day cancellation notice. **Amenities:** irons, hair dryers. **Pool(s):** heated indoor. **Leisure Activities:** whirlpool, exercise room. **Guest Services:** coin laundry. **Business Services:** meeting rooms. **Cards:** AX, CB, DC, DS, MC, VI. **Special Amenities: free continental breakfast and free local telephone calls.**

SOME UNITS

NORTH COAST INN — Phone: 707/822-4861

Small-scale Hotel

4/1-8/31 [CP]	2P: $85-$120
2/1-3/31 & 9/1-1/31 [CP]	2P: $65-$110

Location: US 101, exit Guintoli Ln, 2 mi n. 4975 Valley West Blvd 95521. Fax: 707/822-2036. **Facility:** 74 one-bedroom standard units. 2 stories (no elevator), interior corridors. **Parking:** on-site. **Terms:** age restrictions may apply. **Amenities:** voice mail. *Some:* irons, hair dryers. **Pool(s):** heated indoor. **Leisure Activities:** whirlpool. **Guest Services:** coin laundry. **Business Services:** conference facilities. **Cards:** AX, DS, MC, VI.

SOME UNITS

QUALITY INN-ARCATA *Book at aaa.com* — Phone: (707)822-0409

Small-scale Hotel

5/14-9/6 [ECP]	1P: $69-$139	2P: $69-$139	XP: $10	F16
2/1-5/13 & 9/7-1/31 [ECP]	1P: $59-$79	2P: $59-$79	XP: $10	F16

Location: US 101, exit Guintoli Ln/Janes Rd, 2 mi n. 3535 Janes Rd 95521. Fax: 707/822-1074. **Facility:** 64 one-bedroom standard units, some with whirlpools. 2 stories (no elevator), interior corridors. **Parking:** on-site. **Terms:** age restrictions may apply, cancellation fee imposed, pets ($50 deposit, $10 extra charge). **Amenities:** irons, hair dryers. **Pool(s):** heated outdoor. **Leisure Activities:** whirlpool, tennis court, playground, exercise room, sports court. *Fee:* game room. **Guest Services:** coin laundry. **Business Services:** meeting rooms. **Cards:** AX, DC, DS, MC, VI. **Special Amenities: free expanded continental breakfast and free local telephone calls.** *(See ad p 325)*

SOME UNITS

FEE FEE FEE

WHERE TO DINE

ABRUZZI — Dinner: $10-$25 — Phone: 707/826-2345

Italian

Location: On ground level of Jacoby's Storehouse; at Central Plaza. 791 8th St 95521. **Hours:** 5:30 pm-9 pm. Closed: 11/25, 12/25. **Reservations:** suggested. **Features:** In the Old Town section, the Italian restaurant matches its delicious pasta and fish dishes to selections from its excellent wine list. Casual dress; cocktails. **Parking:** on-site. **Cards:** AX, DC, DS, MC, VI.

PLAZA GRILL — Dinner: $8-$19 — Phone: 707/826-0860

California

Location: 3rd floor of Jacoby's Storehouse; at Central Plaza. 791 8th St 95521. **Hours:** 5 pm-9:30 pm, Fri-11 pm, Sat-10:30 pm. Closed: 12/25. **Reservations:** suggested. **Features:** On the town square, the restaurant serves California cuisine, including preparations of fresh fish and steaks. Produce comes from the farmers market. Casual dress; cocktails. **Parking:** on-site. **Cards:** AX, DS, MC, VI.

ARNOLD pop. 4,218

WHERE TO STAY

ARNOLD BLACK BEAR INN — Phone: 209/795-8999

Bed & Breakfast

All Year [BP] 1P: $185-$225 XP: $5

Location: SR 4, just w. 1343 Oak Cir 95223 (PO Box 109). Fax: 209/795-5723. **Facility:** Near the National Forest, this 4000-square-foot timber-framed lodge, with its ceiling-to-floor windows, is a great place to see nature at its best. Smoke free premises. 5 one-bedroom standard units, some with whirlpools. 1 story, interior corridors. *Bath:* combo or shower only. **Parking:** on-site. **Terms:** office hours 8 am-9 pm, 2 night minimum stay - weekends, 14 day cancellation notice-fee imposed. **Amenities:** hair dryers. *Some:* irons. **Leisure Activities:** whirlpool. *Fee:* massage. **Guest Services:** gift shop, complimentary evening beverages. **Cards:** AX, MC, VI.

TIMBERLINE LODGE — Phone: 209/795-1053

Motel

All Year 1P: $69-$159 2P: $69-$159

Location: East end of town. 890 Hwy 4 95223 (PO Box 6180). Fax: 209/795-3299. **Facility:** Smoke free premises. 20 one-bedroom standard units. 1 story, exterior corridors. *Bath:* combo or shower only. **Parking:** on-site. **Terms:** office hours 9 am-9 pm, 2-3 night minimum stay - weekends, 5 day cancellation notice-fee imposed. **Amenities:** video library (fee). **Cards:** AX, CB, DC, DS, MC, VI. **Special Amenities: free local telephone calls.**

SOME UNITS

FEE FEE FEE

YELLOW DOG INN — **Phone:** (209)795-1980

Bed & Breakfast

All Year	1P: $115-$150	2P: $120-$155	XP: $20	D16

Location: SR 4, e on Pine Dr, then 1 mi n. 1320 Pine Dr 95223 (PO Box 629). Fax: 209/795-8050. **Facility:** 4 one-bedroom standard units. 2 stories (no elevator), interior/exterior corridors. *Bath:* combo or shower only. **Parking:** on-site. **Terms:** office hours 9 am-9 pm, 2-3 night minimum stay - seasonal & weekends, 7 day cancellation notice-fee imposed, package plans. **Amenities:** hair dryers. *Some:* irons. **Guest Services:** gift shop. **Cards:** DS, MC, VI. **Special Amenities: free local telephone calls and early check-in/late check-out.**

ARROYO GRANDE pop. 15,851

WHERE TO STAY

BEST WESTERN CASA GRANDE INN — Book at aaa.com — **Phone:** (805)481-7398

Motel

5/23-1/31	1P: $69-$198	2P: $69-$198	XP: $15	F17
2/1-5/22	1P: $69-$148	2P: $69-$148	XP: $15	F17

Location: US 101, exit Oak Park Rd, just e. Located adjacent to several shopping malls. 850 Oak Park Rd 93420. Fax: 805/481-4859. **Facility:** 114 units. 92 one- and 12 two-bedroom standard units, some with efficiencies. 9 one- and 1 two-bedroom suites. 3 stories, interior/exterior corridors. *Bath:* combo or shower only. **Parking:** on-site. **Terms:** pets ($10 extra charge). **Amenities:** irons, hair dryers. **Pool(s):** heated outdoor. **Leisure Activities:** saunas, whirlpool, exercise room. **Guest Services:** valet and coin laundry. **Business Services:** meeting rooms. **Cards:** AX, CB, DC, DS, JC, MC, VI. **Special Amenities: free continental breakfast and free local telephone calls.**

SOME UNITS

FEE

ECONO LODGE — Book at aaa.com — **Phone:** (805)489-9300

Motel

All Year	1P: $55-$140	2P: $55-$140	XP: $10	F18

Location: US 101, exit Brisco northbound; exit Halcyon Rd southbound. Located in a residential area. 611 El Camino Real 93420. Fax: 805/473-8318. **Facility:** 40 one-bedroom standard units. 2 stories (no elevator), exterior corridors. *Bath:* combo or shower only. **Parking:** on-site. **Terms:** [CP] meal plan available. **Pool(s):** small heated outdoor. **Cards:** AX, CB, DC, DS, JC, MC, VI. **Special Amenities: free continental breakfast and free local telephone calls.**

SOME UNITS

GRAND AVE MOTEL — **Phone:** (805)489-5633

Motel

All Year	1P: $40-$80	2P: $50-$110	XP: $10	F18

Location: US 101, exit Grand Ave, 0.5 mi w. 617 Grand Ave 93420. Fax: 805/489-3471. **Facility:** Smoke free premises. 15 one-bedroom standard units. 2 stories (no elevator), exterior corridors. **Parking:** on-site. **Terms:** office hours 8 am-10 pm, 2 night minimum stay - weekends, 7 day cancellation notice-fee imposed, package plans. **Cards:** AX, DS, MC, VI. **Special Amenities: free local telephone calls and preferred room (subject to availability with advanced reservations).**

SOME UNITS

PREMIER INNS — **Phone:** (805)481-4774

Motel

All Year	1P: $35-$105	2P: $40-$110	XP: $5	F17

Location: US 101, exit Oak Park Rd, just e. 555 Camino Mercado 93420. Fax: 805/481-9023. **Facility:** 100 one-bedroom standard units. 2 stories (no elevator), exterior corridors. *Bath:* combo or shower only. **Parking:** on-site. **Terms:** weekly rates available, [CP] meal plan available. **Amenities:** voice mail. **Pool(s):** heated outdoor. **Leisure Activities:** whirlpool. *Fee:* game room. **Guest Services:** coin laundry. **Cards:** AX, MC, VI. **Special Amenities: free continental breakfast and free local telephone calls.**

SOME UNITS

ATASCADERO pop. 26,411

WHERE TO STAY

BEST WESTERN COLONY INN — Book at aaa.com — **Phone:** (805)466-4449

Motel

3/26-10/17 [ECP]	1P: $79-$169	2P: $79-$179	XP: $10	F17
2/1-3/25 [ECP]	1P: $69-$129	2P: $79-$139	XP: $10	F17
10/18-1/31 [ECP]	1P: $75-$129	2P: $75-$139	XP: $10	F17

Location: US 101, exit San Anselmo Rd, just e, then 0.5 mi n. 3600 El Camino Real 93422. Fax: 805/466-2119. **Facility:** 75 one-bedroom standard units, some with whirlpools. 2-3 stories, interior corridors. **Parking:** on-site. **Terms:** 2-3 night minimum stay - weekends. **Amenities:** dual phone lines, voice mail, irons, hair dryers. **Pool(s):** outdoor. **Leisure Activities:** saunas, whirlpool. **Guest Services:** valet laundry. **Business Services:** meeting rooms. **Cards:** AX, CB, DC, DS, MC, VI. **Special Amenities: free expanded continental breakfast and free local telephone calls.**

SOME UNITS

SUPER 8 MOTEL — **Phone:** (805)466-0794

Motel

All Year	1P: $49-$149	2P: $59-$159	XP: $10	F10

Location: US 101, exit SR 41 (Morro Rd), just w. 6505 Morro Rd 93422. Fax: 805/461-9500. **Facility:** 30 one-bedroom standard units. 2 stories, exterior corridors. **Parking:** on-site. **Terms:** 3 day cancellation notice, [CP] meal plan available. **Amenities:** hair dryers. *Some:* irons. **Cards:** AX, DC, DS, MC, VI. **Special Amenities: free continental breakfast and free local telephone calls.**

SOME UNITS

The following lodging was either not evaluated or did not meet AAA rating requirements but is listed for your information only.

THE CARLTON HOTEL **Phone:** 805/461-5100

fyi

	7/1-9/14	2P: $180-$380	XP: $25	F10
	6/1-6/30	2P: $170-$340	XP: $25	F10
Small-scale Hotel	9/15-1/31	2P: $160-$300	XP: $25	F10

Too new to rate, opening scheduled for November 2003. **Location:** US 101, exit Traffic Way, just e. 6005 El Camino Real 93422. Fax: 805/461-5116. **Amenities:** 52 units, restaurant, coffeemakers, refrigerators. **Terms:** open 6/1-1/31, 3 day cancellation notice. **Cards:** AX, DS, MC, VI.

WHERE TO DINE

GENIE'S STEAK HOUSE **Lunch:** $6-$13 **Dinner:** $9-$33 **Phone:** 805/466-6515

Steak House

Location: US 101, exit SR 41 (Morro Rd), just e. 7030 El Camino Real 93422. **Hours:** 11 am-9 pm, Fri-9:30 pm, Sat 10 am-9:30 pm, Sun 10 am-9 pm. Closed: 11/25, 12/25. **Reservations:** suggested. **Features:** Aged choice beef, pasta and seafood choices line the restaurant's menu. Live piano music adds to the ambience Thursday through Saturday evenings. Casual dress; cocktails; entertainment. **Parking:** on-site. **Cards:** AX, DS, MC, VI.

SALSITAS **Lunch:** $4-$10 **Dinner:** $6-$12 **Phone:** 805/461-5500

Mexican

Location: US 101, exit Santa Rosa Rd, just e, then just n; in Atascadero Oaks Shopping Center. 8783 El Camino Real 93422. **Hours:** 11 am-8 pm, Fri-8:30 pm, Sat noon-8:30 pm, Sun noon-8 pm. **Features:** Guests can sit indoors or on the patio at the informal restaurant. Among offerings are tacos, tostadas, burritos and an imaginative selection of beef, chicken and seafood specialties. Casual dress; beer & wine only. **Parking:** on-site. **Cards:** AX, DS, MC, VI.

VILLAGE CAFFE' **Lunch:** $6-$9 **Dinner:** $15-$23 **Phone:** 805/462-1900

Italian

Location: US 101, exit Curbaril Ave, just e, then just n; in Adobe Plaza Shopping Center. 7377 El Camino Real 93422. **Hours:** 11:30 am-9 pm, Sat-Mon from 5:30 pm. Closed major holidays. **Reservations:** suggested; weekends. **Features:** The diverse menu blends well-prepared pasta, chicken, veal and seafood dishes. Casual dress; beer & wine only. **Parking:** on-site. **Cards:** AX, MC, VI.

AUBURN pop. 12,462

WHERE TO STAY

BEST WESTERN GOLDEN KEY *Book at aaa.com* **Phone:** (530)885-8611

AAA SAVE — Motel

All Year	1P: $79-$115	2P: $79-$115	XP: $4	F18

Location: I-80, exit Foresthill Rd. 13450 Lincoln Way 95603. Fax: 530/888-0319. **Facility:** 68 one-bedroom standard units. 2 stories, exterior corridors. *Bath:* combo or shower only. **Parking:** on-site. **Terms:** [CP] meal plan available, pets ($15 extra charge). **Amenities:** irons, hair dryers. **Pool(s):** heated indoor. **Leisure Activities:** whirlpool. **Guest Services:** coin laundry. **Cards:** AX, DC, DS, MC, VI. **Special Amenities: free expanded continental breakfast and free local telephone calls.**

FEE SOME UNITS

COMFORT INN *Book at aaa.com* **Phone:** (530)885-1800

AAA SAVE — Motel

All Year [CP]	1P: $79-$99	2P: $79-$114	XP: $10	F18

Location: I-80 N, exit Foresthill and Auburn Ravine rds. 1875 Auburn Ravine Rd 95603. Fax: 530/888-6424. **Facility:** 79 one-bedroom standard units. 2 stories, interior corridors. *Bath:* combo or shower only. **Parking:** on-site. **Amenities:** irons, hair dryers. **Pool(s):** outdoor. **Leisure Activities:** whirlpool, exercise room. **Guest Services:** coin laundry. **Cards:** AX, CB, DC, DS, JC, MC, VI. **Special Amenities: free continental breakfast and free local telephone calls.**

SOME UNITS

FOOTHILLS MOTEL **Phone:** 530/885-8444

Motel

All Year 1P: $50-$90 2P: $55-$95 XP: $5 D12

Location: I-80, exit Foresthill Rd. 13431 Bowman Rd 95603. Fax: 530/823-8507. **Facility:** 62 one-bedroom standard units, some with kitchens. 1 story, exterior corridors. *Bath:* shower only. **Parking:** on-site. **Terms:** weekly rates available, small pets only ($10 fee). **Pool(s):** outdoor. **Leisure Activities:** whirlpool. **Cards:** AX, DS, MC, VI.

SOME UNITS

FEE

HOLIDAY INN-AUBURN **Book at aaa.com** **Phone:** (530)887-8787

Motel

All Year 1P: $119-$159 2P: $119-$159

Location: Jct I-80 and SR 49. 120 Grass Valley Hwy 95603. Fax: 530/887-9824. **Facility:** 96 units. 94 one-bedroom standard units. 2 one-bedroom suites ($159-$169). 2-3 stories, interior corridors. **Parking:** on-site. **Terms:** pets ($20 fee, dogs only). **Amenities:** video games, voice mail, irons, hair dryers. **Pool(s):** heated outdoor. **Leisure Activities:** whirlpool, exercise room. **Guest Services:** valet laundry. **Business Services:** meeting rooms. **Cards:** AX, CB, DC, DS, JC, MC, VI. ***(See color ad p 272)***

SOME UNITS

ASK FEE DATA PORT

MOTEL 6 **Book at aaa.com** **Phone:** 530/888-7829

Motel

All Year 1P: $56-$62 2P: $62-$68 XP: $6 F17

Location: I-80, exit Foresthill and Auburn Ravine rds. 1819 Auburn Ravine Rd 95603. Fax: 530/888-6200. **Facility:** 57 one-bedroom standard units. 3 stories (no elevator), interior corridors. *Bath:* shower only. **Parking:** on-site. **Pool(s):** outdoor. **Leisure Activities:** whirlpool. **Cards:** AX, DC, DS, MC, VI. **Special Amenities: free local telephone calls.**

SOME UNITS

DATA PORT

SUPER 8 MOTEL **Book at aaa.com** **Phone:** 530/888-8808

Motel

All Year [CP] 1P: $66-$100 2P: $66-$100 XP: $5 F16

Location: I-80 N, exit Foresthill and Auburn Ravine rds. 140 E Hillcrest Dr 95603. Fax: 530/885-3588. **Facility:** 52 one-bedroom standard units, some with whirlpools. 2 stories, exterior corridors. **Parking:** on-site. **Terms:** cancellation fee imposed. **Pool(s):** outdoor. **Leisure Activities:** whirlpool. **Cards:** AX, CB, DC, DS, MC, VI.

SOME UNITS

ASK

TRAVELODGE **Book at aaa.com** **Phone:** (530)885-7025

Motel

2/1-11/30 [CP] 1P: $60-$85 2P: $60-$85 XP: $5 F14
12/1-1/31 [CP] 1P: $60-$75 2P: $60-$75 XP: $5 F14

Location: I-80, exit Foresthill Rd. 13490 Lincoln Way 95603. Fax: 530/885-9503. **Facility:** 77 one-bedroom standard units. 2 stories, interior/exterior corridors. *Bath:* combo or shower only. **Parking:** on-site. **Terms:** weekly rates available, small pets only ($10 fee). **Pool(s):** outdoor. **Leisure Activities:** whirlpool. **Cards:** AX, CB, DC, DS, JC, MC, VI. **Special Amenities: free continental breakfast and free local telephone calls.**

SOME UNITS

FEE DATA PORT

WHERE TO DINE

THE HEADQUARTER HOUSE AT RASPBERRY HILL **Lunch:** $7-$16 **Dinner:** $16-$39 **Phone:** 530/878-1906

American

Location: 1.5 mi e; s off I-80 via Bell Rd. 14500 Musso Rd 95603. **Hours:** 11:30 am-9 pm, Sat-10 pm, Sun 10 am-9:30 pm. Closed: 12/25. **Reservations:** suggested. **Features:** On the Dunipace Angus Ranch, the restaurant is nestled amid tall pines. Beef, seafood and chicken dishes make up most of the menu. Casual dress; cocktails; entertainment. **Parking:** on-site. **Cards:** AX, CB, DC, DS, MC, VI.

LATITUDES **Lunch:** $8-$12 **Dinner:** $10-$19 **Phone:** 530/885-9535

Ethnic

Location: I-80, exit SR 49 (Placerville), 0.3 mi s to Lincoln Way, 0.3 mi w to Maple St; opposite the County Court House. 130 Maple St #200 95603. **Hours:** 11:30 am-3 & 5-9 pm, Sat & Sun-10 pm, Sunday brunch 10 am-3 pm. Closed: 12/25; also Mon & for dinner Tues. **Reservations:** suggested. **Features:** Dishes from several cultural regions are prepared with natural ingredients. Casual dress; cocktails. **Parking:** on-site. **Cards:** AX, MC, VI.

BADGER

—See KINGS CANYON NATIONAL PARK, SEQUOIA NATIONAL PARK & VISALIA.

BAKER

WHERE TO DINE

BUN BOY RESTAURANT **Lunch:** $6-$15 **Dinner:** $6-$15 **Phone:** 760/733-4660

American

Location: I-15, exit SR 127 (Baker Blvd); in Bun Boy Motel. 72155 Baker Blvd 92309. **Hours:** 6 am-midnight. **Features:** The restaurant is a refreshing respite for travelers on their way to or from Las Vegas. Service is folksy and friendly, and the menu's variety is sure to please almost any taste. Honey-dipped chicken and the pastrami burger are reliable choices. Desert pie—a large cookie topped with ice cream, hot fudge and whipped cream—is a favorite dessert. Casual dress; beer & wine only. **Parking:** on-site. **Cards:** AX, DS, MC, VI.

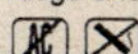

BAKERSFIELD pop. 247,057

WHERE TO STAY

BAKERSFIELD RED LION HOTEL Book at aaa.com **Phone:** (661)327-0681

Small-scale Hotel

All Year [BP] 1P: $71-$152 2P: $71-$152 XP: $10 F18

Location: SR 99, exit SR 58 (Rosedale Hwy), just s. 2400 Camino Del Rio Ct 93308. Fax: 661/637-1822. **Facility:** 165 units. 143 one-bedroom standard units. 22 one-bedroom suites ($91-$152), some with whirlpools. 2 stories, interior/exterior corridors. **Parking:** on-site. **Terms:** small pets only ($25 fee). **Amenities:** voice mail, irons, hair dryers. **Pool(s):** outdoor. **Leisure Activities:** whirlpool, exercise room. **Guest Services:** coin laundry, area transportation. **Business Services:** meeting rooms, business center. **Cards:** AX, CB, DC, DS, JC, MC, VI. ***(See color ad below)***

ASK · FEE · DATA PORT / VCR · SOME UNITS · FEE /

BEST INN Book at aaa.com **Phone:** (661)764-5221

AAA SAVE

Motel

All Year [ECP] 1P: $49-$59 2P: $49-$59 XP: $5 F16

Location: I-5, exit Stockdale Hwy, 15 mi w. 200 Trask St 93314. Fax: 661/764-5505. **Facility:** 53 one-bedroom standard units. 2 stories, exterior corridors. **Parking:** on-site. **Terms:** pets ($5 extra charge). **Amenities:** *Some:* irons, hair dryers. **Pool(s):** outdoor. **Business Services:** fax (fee). **Cards:** AX, DC, DS, MC, VI. **Special Amenities: free expanded continental breakfast and free local telephone calls.**

FEE · DATA PORT / SOME UNITS /

BEST WESTERN CRYSTAL PALACE INN & SUITES Book at aaa.com **Phone:** (661)327-9651

AAA SAVE

Small-scale Hotel

All Year [BP] 1P: $59-$99 2P: $59-$99 XP: $10 F12

Location: SR 99, exit Buck Owens Blvd northbound; exit Rosedale Hwy southbound. 2620 Buck Owens Blvd 93308. Fax: 661/334-1820. **Facility:** 195 one-bedroom standard units. 2 stories, interior corridors. **Parking:** on-site. **Terms:** pets ($10 extra charge). **Amenities:** voice mail, irons, hair dryers. **Dining:** 6 am-10 pm, cocktails. **Pool(s):** outdoor. **Leisure Activities:** whirlpool, exercise room. **Guest Services:** valet and coin laundry. **Business Services:** meeting rooms, fax (fee). **Cards:** AX, CB, DC, DS, JC, MC, VI. **Special Amenities: free full breakfast and free local telephone calls.** *(See color ad p 275)*

FEE · DATA PORT / SOME UNITS · FEE /

BEST WESTERN HERITAGE INN Book at aaa.com **Phone:** (661)764-6268

AAA SAVE

Motel

All Year 1P: $70-$89 2P: $79-$109 XP: $5 F17

Location: I-5, exit Stockdale Hwy, 15 mi w. 253 Trask St 93312. Fax: 661/764-5181. **Facility:** 47 one-bedroom standard units, some with whirlpools. 2 stories, exterior corridors. **Parking:** on-site. **Terms:** [ECP] meal plan available, small pets only ($10 extra charge). **Amenities:** irons, hair dryers. **Pool(s):** outdoor. **Business Services:** fax (fee). **Cards:** AX, CB, DC, DS, JC, MC, VI. **Special Amenities: free expanded continental breakfast and free local telephone calls.**

FEE · DATA PORT / SOME UNITS /

BEST WESTERN HILL HOUSE Book at aaa.com **Phone:** (661)327-4064

AAA SAVE

Small-scale Hotel

All Year [ECP] 1P: $59-$89 2P: $59-$99 XP: $10 F18

Location: SR 99, exit California Ave, just e, just n on Oak St, then 1.5 mi e. 700 Truxtun Ave St 93301. Fax: 661/327-1247. **Facility:** 97 one-bedroom standard units. 2 stories, interior corridors. **Parking:** on-site. **Terms:** [AP] meal plan available, pets ($10 extra charge). **Amenities:** voice mail, irons, hair dryers. **Dining:** 7 am-9 pm, Sun 7 am-2 pm, cocktails. **Pool(s):** outdoor. **Leisure Activities:** exercise room. **Business Services:** meeting rooms, fax (fee). **Cards:** AX, DS, JC, MC, VI. **Special Amenities: free expanded continental breakfast and early check-in/late check-out.**

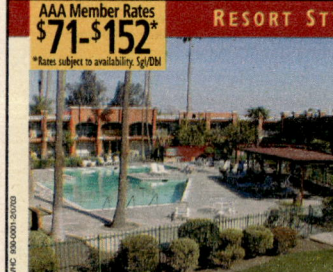

CALIFORNIA INN — **Phone:** (661)328-1100

AAA SAVE — Motel

All Year [CP] 1P: $45-$49 2P: $49-$59 XP: $4 F18

Location: SR 99, exit California Ave, just w, then s. 3400 Chester Ln 93309. Fax: 661/328-0433. **Facility:** 74 one-bedroom standard units, some with whirlpools. 3 stories, interior corridors. **Parking:** on-site. **Terms:** 7 day cancellation notice. **Amenities:** *Some:* irons, hair dryers. **Pool(s):** outdoor. **Leisure Activities:** sauna, whirlpool. **Guest Services:** coin laundry. **Business Services:** fax (fee). **Cards:** AX, DC, MC, VI.

SOME UNITS

CLARION HOTEL — *Book at aaa.com* — **Phone:** (661)326-1111

AAA SAVE — Small-scale Hotel

All Year [ECP] 1P: $85-$95 2P: $95-$110 XP: $10 F

Location: SR 99, just w on SR 58 (Rosedale Hwy). 3540 Rosedale Hwy 93308. Fax: 661/326-1513. **Facility:** 122 one-bedroom standard units. 5 stories, interior corridors. **Parking:** on-site. **Terms:** [AP] meal plan available. **Amenities:** voice mail, irons, hair dryers. **Dining:** 6 am-10 pm. **Pool(s):** outdoor. **Leisure Activities:** whirlpool. **Guest Services:** valet laundry. **Business Services:** meeting rooms, business center. **Cards:** AX, CB, DC, DS, JC, MC, VI. **Special Amenities: free expanded continental breakfast and free local telephone calls.**

SOME UNITS

COMFORT INN — *Book at aaa.com* — **Phone:** (661)833-1000

AAA SAVE — Motel

11/1-1/31 [ECP]	1P: $64-$69	2P: $130-$140	XP: $5	F18
5/1-10/31 [ECP]	1P: $67-$72	2P: $125-$135	XP: $5	F18
2/1-4/30 [ECP]	1P: $62-$67	2P: $125-$135	XP: $5	F18

Location: SR 99, exit White Ln, just n. 3620 Wible Rd 93309. Fax: 661/832-3212. **Facility:** 60 one-bedroom standard units, some with whirlpools. 2 stories, exterior corridors. **Parking:** on-site. **Amenities:** hair dryers. *Some:* irons. **Pool(s):** outdoor. **Leisure Activities:** whirlpool. **Guest Services:** valet and coin laundry. **Business Services:** fax (fee). **Cards:** AX, CB, DC, DS, JC, MC, VI.

SOME UNITS

COMFORT SUITES — *Book at aaa.com* — **Phone:** (661)325-8000

Small-scale Hotel

All Year 1P: $89-$149 2P: $109-$169 XP: $10 F12

Location: SR 99, exit Buck Owens Blvd, just w. 3115 Camino Del Rio Ct 93308. Fax: 661/325-8001. **Facility:** Designated smoking area. 57 one-bedroom standard units, some with whirlpools. 3 stories, interior corridors. **Parking:** on-site. **Terms:** cancellation fee imposed, [CP] meal plan available. **Amenities:** high-speed Internet, dual phone lines, voice mail, irons, hair dryers. *Some:* DVD players, video games. **Pool(s):** heated outdoor. **Leisure Activities:** whirlpool. **Guest Services:** sundries, coin laundry. **Business Services:** meeting rooms, business center. **Cards:** AX, CB, DC, DS, JC, MC, VI.

SOME UNITS

COURTYARD BY MARRIOTT *Book at aaa.com* **Phone:** (661)324-6660

Small-scale Hotel

All Year 1P: $109 2P: $109

Location: SR 99, exit SR 58 (Rosedale Hwy), then s on Camino Del Rio Ct. 3601 Marriott Dr 93308. Fax: 661/324-1185. **Facility:** 146 units. 134 one-bedroom standard units. 12 one-bedroom suites ($134). 3 stories, interior corridors. **Parking:** on-site. **Terms:** [BP] meal plan available. **Amenities:** voice mail, irons, hair dryers. **Pool(s):** outdoor. **Leisure Activities:** whirlpool, exercise room. **Guest Services:** coin laundry. **Business Services:** meeting rooms, fax (fee). **Cards:** AX, DC, DS, MC, VI.

SOME UNITS

DAYS INN *Book at aaa.com* **Phone:** (661)324-5555

Motel

All Year 1P: $69-$89 2P: $79-$109 XP: $10 F18

Location: SR 99, exit SR 58 (Rosedale Hwy) southbound, just e to Pierce Rd, then 0.7 mi n; exit Airport Dr northbound to Buck Owens Blvd, then just s. 4500 Buck Owens Blvd 93308. Fax: 661/325-0106. **Facility:** 203 one-bedroom standard units, some with efficiencies. 3 stories, exterior corridors. **Parking:** on-site. **Terms:** [CP] meal plan available, pets ($20 extra charge). **Amenities:** voice mail, hair dryers. *Some:* irons. **Pool(s):** outdoor. **Leisure Activities:** whirlpool. **Guest Services:** coin laundry. **Business Services:** meeting rooms, fax (fee). **Cards:** AX, CB, DC, DS, MC, VI.
(See color ad below)

SOME UNITS

FEE

DOUBLETREE HOTEL *Book at aaa.com* **Phone:** (661)323-7111

Large-scale Hotel

All Year 1P: $89-$165 2P: $89-$165 XP: $10 F18

Location: SR 99, exit SR 58 (Rosedale Hwy), just w. 3100 Camino Del Rio Ct 93308. Fax: 661/323-0331. **Facility:** 262 units. 255 one-bedroom standard units. 7 one-bedroom suites ($800-$1000), some with whirlpools. 3 stories, interior corridors. **Parking:** on-site. **Terms:** cancellation fee imposed, pets ($15 extra charge). **Amenities:** dual phone lines, voice mail, irons, hair dryers. *Some:* high-speed Internet. **Dining:** California Grill, see separate listing. **Pool(s):** outdoor. **Leisure Activities:** whirlpool, exercise room. **Guest Services:** gift shop, valet laundry, area transportation. **Business Services:** conference facilities, business center. **Cards:** AX, CB, DC, DS, MC, VI.

SOME UNITS

FEE FEE FEE FEE

FOUR POINTS BY SHERATON BAKERSFIELD *Book at aaa.com* **Phone:** 661/325-9700

AAA SAVE

Small-scale Hotel

All Year 1P: $89 2P: $99 XP: $10 F18

Location: SR 99, exit California Ave, 1.3 mi w. Located in a business park area. 5101 California Ave 93309. Fax: 661/323-3508. **Facility:** 198 one-bedroom standard units. 2 stories, interior corridors. **Parking:** on-site. **Amenities:** video games, high-speed Internet, dual phone lines, voice mail, irons, hair dryers. **Dining:** The Bistro, see separate listing. **Pool(s):** heated outdoor. **Leisure Activities:** whirlpool, exercise room. **Guest Services:** valet laundry, area transportation-within 5 mi. **Business Services:** conference facilities, fax (fee). **Cards:** AX, CB, DC, DS, JC, MC, VI. **Special Amenities: free newspaper and free room upgrade (subject to availability with advanced reservations).**

SOME UNITS

HAMPTON INN *Book at aaa.com* **Phone:** (661)633-0333

Small-scale Hotel

All Year [ECP] 1P: $80-$85 2P: $90-$95

Location: SR 99, exit California Ave. 1017 Oak St 93304. Fax: 661/633-0669. **Facility:** 95 one-bedroom standard units, some with whirlpools. 4 stories, interior corridors. **Parking:** on-site. **Amenities:** voice mail, irons, hair dryers. **Pool(s):** heated outdoor. **Leisure Activities:** exercise room. **Guest Services:** valet laundry. **Business Services:** meeting rooms, fax (fee). **Cards:** AX, CB, DC, DS, MC, VI.

SOME UNITS

HOLIDAY INN EXPRESS **Phone:** (661)833-3000

AAA SAVE

Small-scale Hotel

All Year [CP] 1P: $76 2P: $76 XP: $10 F18

Location: SR 99, exit White Ln, 0.3 mi e, just s. 4400 Hughes Ln 93304. Fax: 661/833-3736. **Facility:** 108 one-bedroom standard units, some with whirlpools. 4 stories, interior corridors. **Parking:** on-site. **Terms:** cancellation fee imposed. **Amenities:** voice mail, irons, hair dryers. **Pool(s):** outdoor. **Leisure Activities:** whirlpool. **Guest Services:** coin laundry. **Business Services:** meeting rooms, business center. **Cards:** AX, DC, DS, MC, VI. **Special Amenities: free continental breakfast and free local telephone calls.**
(See color ad p 277)

SOME UNITS

HOLIDAY INN SELECT CONVENTION CENTER *Book at aaa.com* **Phone:** (661)323-1900

Large-scale Hotel

All Year 1P: $85-$119 2P: $85-$119

Location: SR 99, exit California Ave, 1.2 mi e, then 0.4 mi n on Chester Ave; downtown. Located adjacent to Convention Center. 801 Truxtun Ave 93301. Fax: 661/324-7794. **Facility:** 258 units. 252 one-bedroom standard units. 6 one-bedroom suites, some with whirlpools. 9 stories, interior corridors. **Parking:** on-site. **Terms:** pets ($50 fee). **Amenities:** high-speed Internet, voice mail, irons, hair dryers. **Dining:** 6 am-10 pm, cocktails. **Pool(s):** outdoor. **Leisure Activities:** sauna, whirlpool, exercise room. **Guest Services:** gift shop, valet laundry. **Business Services:** conference facilities, business center. **Cards:** AX, CB, DC, DS, MC, VI. **Special Amenities: free newspaper.** *(See color ad below)*

SOME UNITS FEE FEE FEE

HOWARD JOHNSON EXPRESS INN *Book at aaa.com* **Phone:** (661)396-1425

Motel

All Year 1P: $60 2P: $65 XP: $5 F15

Location: SR 99, exit White Ln, then just e. 2700 White Ln 93304. Fax: 661/396-9258. **Facility:** 149 one-bedroom standard units. 2 stories, interior corridors. **Parking:** on-site. **Terms:** 15 day cancellation notice, [CP] meal plan available. **Amenities:** voice mail, irons, hair dryers. **Pool(s):** outdoor. **Leisure Activities:** whirlpool. **Guest Services:** coin laundry. **Business Services:** fax. **Cards:** AX, DC, MC, VI.

ASK SOME UNITS

LA QUINTA INN *Book at aaa.com* **Phone:** 661/325-7400

Motel

All Year 1P: $75-$85 2P: $81-$91 XP: $6 F18

Location: SR 99, exit SR 58 (Rosedale Hwy) southbound; exit Buck Owens Blvd northbound, just n of Rosedale Hwy. 3232 Riverside Dr 93308. Fax: 661/324-6032. **Facility:** 129 units. 126 one-bedroom standard units. 3 one-bedroom suites. 3 stories, exterior corridors. **Parking:** on-site. **Terms:** [ECP] meal plan available, small pets only. **Amenities:** video games, high-speed Internet, voice mail, irons, hair dryers. **Pool(s):** heated outdoor. **Guest Services:** coin laundry. **Business Services:** fax (fee). **Cards:** AX, CB, DC, DS, JC, MC, VI.

SOME UNITS

LIBERTY INN MOTEL **Phone:** 661/366-1630

Motel

All Year 1P: $46-$52 2P: $52-$55 XP: $4 F14

Location: SR 99, 7 mi e on SR 58, exit SR 284 (Weed Patch Hwy), just n, then just e. 8230 E Brundage Ln 93307. Fax: 661/363-5505. **Facility:** 40 one-bedroom standard units. 2 stories, interior corridors. **Parking:** on-site. **Terms:** office hours 7 am-11 pm, pets ($5 extra charge). **Amenities:** *Some:* irons. **Pool(s):** heated indoor. **Leisure Activities:** sauna, whirlpool. **Guest Services:** coin laundry. **Business Services:** fax (fee). **Cards:** AX, DC, MC, VI. **Special Amenities: free local telephone calls and preferred room (subject to availability with advanced reservations).**

SOME UNITS FEE

QUALITY INN *Book at aaa.com* **Phone:** (661)833-8000

Motel

All Year 1P: $64-$99 2P: $64-$99

Location: SR 99, exit White Ln, just e. 2514 White Ln 93304. Fax: 661/833-3861. **Facility:** 66 one-bedroom standard units, some with efficiencies and/or whirlpools. 2 stories, exterior corridors. **Parking:** on-site. **Terms:** cancellation fee imposed, [ECP] meal plan available. **Amenities:** irons, hair dryers. **Pool(s):** outdoor. **Leisure Activities:** whirlpool. **Business Services:** fax (fee). **Cards:** AX, CB, DC, DS, JC, MC, VI. **Special Amenities: free local telephone calls and free newspaper.**

SOME UNITS

QUALITY INN *Book at aaa.com* **Phone:** (661)325-0772

Motel

All Year [BP] 1P: $61-$125 2P: $66-$130 XP: $10 F17

Location: SR 99, exit California Ave, just e, then just s. 1011 Oak St 93304. Fax: 661/325-4646. **Facility:** 89 one-bedroom standard units. 2 stories, interior/exterior corridors. **Parking:** on-site. **Terms:** pets ($10 extra charge). **Amenities:** voice mail, irons, hair dryers. **Pool(s):** heated outdoor. **Leisure Activities:** whirlpool, exercise room. **Guest Services:** coin laundry. **Business Services:** fax (fee). **Cards:** AX, CB, DC, DS, JC, MC, VI. **Special Amenities: free full breakfast and free local telephone calls.**

SOME UNITS

FEE

RAMADA LIMITED SUITES *Book at aaa.com* **Phone:** (661)322-9988

Small-scale Hotel

All Year 1P: $95-$115 2P: $95-$115

Location: SR 99, exit California Ave, just s. 828 Real Rd 93309. Fax: 661/322-3668. **Facility:** 80 units. 79 one-bedroom standard units, some with whirlpools. 1 one-bedroom suite ($95-$115). 4 stories, interior corridors. **Parking:** on-site. **Terms:** cancellation fee imposed, [CP] meal plan available. **Amenities:** voice mail, irons, hair dryers. **Pool(s):** outdoor. **Leisure Activities:** whirlpool, exercise room. **Guest Services:** valet and coin laundry. **Business Services:** business center. **Cards:** AX, CB, DC, DS, JC, MC, VI. **Special Amenities: free continental breakfast and free local telephone calls.**

SOME UNITS

RESIDENCE INN BY MARRIOTT *Book at aaa.com* **Phone:** (661)321-9800

Small-scale Hotel

All Year 1P: $124-$146

Location: SR 99, exit California Ave, just w, then just n. 4241 Chester Ln 93309. Fax: 661/321-0721. **Facility:** 114 units. 80 one-bedroom standard units with kitchens. 6 one- and 28 two-bedroom suites with kitchens. 2 stories, exterior corridors. **Parking:** on-site. **Terms:** [ECP] meal plan available, pets ($40-$60 fee, $6 extra charge). **Amenities:** voice mail, irons, hair dryers. **Pool(s):** heated outdoor. **Leisure Activities:** whirlpool, putting green, exercise room, sports court. **Guest Services:** complimentary evening beverages: Mon-Thurs, coin laundry, area transportation. **Business Services:** meeting rooms, fax (fee). **Cards:** AX, DC, DS, MC, VI.

SOME UNITS

ASK FEE FEE

RIO BRAVO RESORT **Phone:** (661)872-5000

Resort
Large-scale Hotel

All Year 1P: $85-$119 2P: $85-$119

Location: SR 99, exit SR 178, 12 mi e, then 2.5 mi n on Alfred Harrell Hwy. 11200 Lake Ming Rd 93306. Fax: 661/871-8998. **Facility:** The resort is popular for family and corporate outings; rooms have views of the southern Sierras and Kern River. 106 units. 101 one-bedroom standard units. 5 one-bedroom suites, some with kitchens. 2 stories, interior corridors. **Parking:** on-site. **Terms:** cancellation fee imposed, pets ($10 fee). **Amenities:** voice mail, safes, irons, hair dryers. **Pool(s):** 2 outdoor. **Leisure Activities:** saunas, whirlpools, 14 lighted tennis courts, hiking trails, basketball, game room. *Fee:* massage. **Guest Services:** sundries, coin laundry. **Business Services:** conference facilities, fax (fee). **Cards:** AX, CB, DC, DS, MC, VI.

SOME UNITS

ASK FEE FEE FEE

ROYAL OAK INN **Phone:** 661/324-9686

Motel

All Year 1P: $38-$48 2P: $42-$68 XP: $10 F12

Location: SR 99, exit California Ave, then just se. 889 Oak St 93304. Fax: 661/325-4437. **Facility:** 41 one-bedroom standard units. 2 stories, exterior corridors. *Bath:* some combo or shower only. **Parking:** on-site. **Terms:** [CP] meal plan available, small pets only ($5 extra charge). **Amenities:** *Some:* irons, hair dryers. **Pool(s):** outdoor. **Guest Services:** coin laundry. **Business Services:** fax (fee). **Cards:** AX, CB, DC, DS, JC, MC, VI.

SOME UNITS

FEE FEE

SUPER 8 MOTEL BAKERSFIELD **Phone:** (661)322-1012

Motel

All Year [CP] 1P: $49-$65 2P: $60-$70 XP: $5 F12

Location: SR 99, exit California Ave, just w, then just s. 901 Real Rd 93309. Fax: 661/322-7636. **Facility:** 87 one-bedroom standard units. 3 stories, exterior corridors. **Parking:** on-site. **Terms:** pets ($10 extra charge). **Amenities:** *Some:* irons. **Pool(s):** outdoor. **Leisure Activities:** whirlpool. **Business Services:** fax (fee). **Cards:** AX, DC, DS, MC, VI.

SOME UNITS

ASK FEE

TRAVELRITE MOTEL *Book at aaa.com* **Phone:** (661)324-6666

Motel

All Year 1P: $49-$79 2P: $49-$79 XP: $10 F18

Location: SR 99, exit California Ave, just sw. 818 Real Rd 93309. Fax: 661/637-1822. **Facility:** 174 one-bedroom standard units. 2 stories, interior/exterior corridors. **Parking:** on-site. **Amenities:** *Some:* irons, hair dryers. **Pool(s):** outdoor. **Leisure Activities:** waterslide, exercise room. **Guest Services:** coin laundry, area transportation. **Business Services:** meeting rooms, fax (fee). **Cards:** AX, CB, DC, DS, JC, MC, VI.

SOME UNITS

ASK FEE FEE

VAGABOND INN NORTH Book at aaa.com **Phone:** (661)392-1800

Motel

All Year 1P: $36 2P: $42 XP: $5 F18

Location: SR 99, exit Olive Dr, west side. 6100 Knudsen Dr 93308. Fax: 661/392-1612. **Facility:** 154 one-bedroom standard units. 2 stories, exterior corridors. **Parking:** on-site. **Terms:** [CP] meal plan available, pets ($5 extra charge, in designated units). **Amenities:** hair dryers. *Some:* irons. **Pool(s):** outdoor. **Business Services:** fax (fee). **Cards:** AX, DC, MC, VI. **Special Amenities: free continental breakfast.**

SOME UNITS

FEE

VAGABOND INN SOUTH Book at aaa.com **Phone:** (661)831-9200

Motel

All Year 1P: $36 2P: $42 XP: $5 F18

Location: SR 99, exit Panama Ln, just e, then just s. 6501 Colony St 93307. Fax: 661/831-0214. **Facility:** 134 one-bedroom standard units, some with efficiencies (no utensils). 2 stories, exterior corridors. **Parking:** on-site. **Terms:** [CP] meal plan available, pets ($5 extra charge). **Amenities:** voice mail, hair dryers. *Some:* irons. **Pool(s):** outdoor. **Guest Services:** coin laundry, area transportation-within 5 mi. **Business Services:** fax (fee). **Cards:** AX, DC, MC, VI. **Special Amenities: free continental breakfast and free local telephone calls.**

SOME UNITS

FEE

WHERE TO DINE

BENJIS FRENCH BASQUE RESTAURANT **Lunch:** $7-$13 **Dinner:** $14-$19 **Phone:** 661/328-0400

Basque

Location: SR 99, exit SR 58 (Rosedale Hwy), 0.5 mi w. 4001 Rosedale Hwy 93308. **Hours:** 11:30 am-2 & 5:30-9:30 pm. Closed major holidays; also Tues. **Features:** Among menu items served in the traditional Basque style are soups and salads that complement any entree. Oxtail stew, when available, is especially good, as are the kebabs and the frog legs appetizer. When it is busy, which is often, the service can be a little hurried, but the staff is friendly and knowledgeable. Casual dress; cocktails. **Parking:** on-site. **Cards:** AX, DS, MC, VI.

THE BISTRO **Lunch:** $8-$18 **Dinner:** $15-$25 **Phone:** 661/323-3905

Continental

Location: SR 99, exit California Ave, 1.3 mi w; in Four Points by Sheraton Bakersfield. 5101 California Ave 93309. **Hours:** 6:30-10 am, 11-2 & 6-10 pm, Sat & Sun from 7:30 am. **Reservations:** suggested. **Features:** Contributing to the restaurant's upscale feel are rich wood accents, upholstered booths and chairs, subdued lighting and illuminated framed prints. The service staff is friendly, professional and well-versed in the preparation and fresh ingredients used in creating menu selections. The wide-reaching choices range from appetizers and entree salads to succulent steaks and fresh fish. Homemade desserts are worth the indulgence. Dressy casual; cocktails. **Parking:** on-site. **Cards:** AX, DC, DS, MC, VI.

BUCK OWENS' CRYSTAL PALACE **Dinner:** $7-$30 **Phone:** 661/328-7560

American

Location: SR 99, exit Buck Owens Blvd northbound; exit SR 58 (Rosedale Hwy) southbound, just e, then 0.8 mi n on Pierce Rd. 2800 Buck Owens Blvd 93308. **Hours:** 5 pm-10 pm; Sunday brunch 9:30 am-2 pm. Closed: 11/25, 12/25. **Reservations:** suggested. **Features:** The isn't the place for a quiet, romantic evening out. Bring dancing boots, cowboy hats and a hearty appetite for great steak and barbecue. Country music memorabilia, much of which is Buck Owens' own, adorns the dining room. Phone ahead, as food service hours and reservation policy may vary due to the many concerts scheduled here. Casual dress; cocktails; entertainment. **Parking:** on-site. **Cards:** AX, CB, DC, DS, MC, VI.

CALIFORNIA GRILL **Lunch:** $7-$15 **Phone:** 661/323-7111

American

Location: SR 99, exit SR 58 (Rosedale Hwy), just w; in DoubleTree Hotel. 3100 Camino Del Rio Ct 93308. **Hours:** 11:30 am-1:30 pm, Sun 9 am-2 pm. **Reservations:** suggested. **Features:** The menu blends a nice selection of steaks, seafood, sandwiches and all-you-can-eat pasta dishes. The lunch buffet changes daily. Save room for one of the sumptuous desserts. Casual dress; cocktails. **Parking:** on-site. **Cards:** AX, CB, DC, DS, JC, MC, VI.

CHALET BASQUE **Lunch:** $7-$12 **Dinner:** $14-$20 **Phone:** 661/327-2915

Basque

Location: SR 99, exit Stockdale Hwy/Brundage Ln, just e, then just n. 200 Oak St 93304. **Hours:** 11:30 am-2 & 5:30-9:30 pm, Fri & Sat 11:30 am-2 & 5-9:30 pm. Closed major holidays; also Sun & Mon. **Reservations:** accepted. **Features:** Complete meals—which include soup, salad, condiments and entrees—center on the specialty lamb or chicken, beef or fish. Service adheres to the friendly Basque tradition. Brick walls contribute to a homey, comfortable environment. Casual dress; cocktails. **Parking:** on-site. **Cards:** AX, MC, VI.

URICCHIO'S TRATTORIA **Lunch:** $7-$16 **Dinner:** $10-$26 **Phone:** 661/326-8870

Italian

Location: SR 99, exit California Ave, 1.2 mi e, then just n on Chester Ave. 1400 17th St 93301. **Hours:** 11 am-2 & 5-9 pm, Fri-10 pm, Sat 5 pm-10 pm. Closed major holidays; also Sun. **Reservations:** suggested. **Features:** Casual, contemporary dining is the mode in the restored downtown building. It can be crowded, but the wait is worthwhile. Upscale decor punctuates the cozy bar area and patio. The wait staff is friendly and eager to please. On the menu are traditional Italian entrees and appetizers, dinner steaks and noteworthy signature desserts. Casual dress; cocktails. **Parking:** street. **Cards:** AX, CB, DC, DS, MC, VI.

BARSTOW pop. 21,119

WHERE TO STAY

BARSTOW-SUPER 8 MOTEL *Book at aaa.com* **Phone:** 760/256-8443

Motel

All Year 1P: $58 2P: $58-$72 XP: $8 F12

Location: I-15/40, exit E Main St, 0.3 mi w, then just s. 170 Coolwater Ln 92311. Fax: 760/256-0997. **Facility:** 52 one-bedroom standard units. 2 stories, exterior corridors. **Parking:** on-site. **Terms:** pets ($5 extra charge). **Amenities:** irons, hair dryers. **Pool(s):** outdoor. **Business Services:** fax (fee). **Cards:** AX, DC, DS, MC, VI. **Special Amenities: free local telephone calls.**

SOME UNITS FEE

BEST MOTEL **Phone:** 760/256-6836

Motel

All Year [CP] 1P: $30-$33 2P: $33-$36 XP: $3

Location: I-15/40, exit E Main St, 0.5 mi w. 1281 E Main St 92311. Fax: 760/255-1029. **Facility:** 29 one-bedroom standard units. 2 stories, exterior corridors. **Parking:** on-site. **Terms:** weekly rates available, small pets only. **Amenities:** *Some:* irons, hair dryers. **Pool(s):** outdoor. **Business Services:** fax (fee). **Cards:** AX, DS, MC, VI.

SOME UNITS

BEST WESTERN DESERT VILLA INN *Book at aaa.com* **Phone:** (760)256-1781

Motel

All Year [ECP] 1P: $59-$139 2P: $59-$139 XP: $10 F17

Location: I-15/40, exit Main St westbound; exit Montara eastbound, 0.5 mi e of I-15. 1984 E Main St 92311. Fax: 760/256-9265. **Facility:** 95 one-bedroom standard units, some with efficiencies (no utensils) and/or whirlpools. 2 stories, exterior corridors. **Parking:** on-site. **Terms:** cancellation fee imposed, pets ($10 fee). **Amenities:** irons, hair dryers. **Dining:** 4 pm-8 pm, cocktails. **Pool(s):** outdoor. **Leisure Activities:** whirlpool. **Guest Services:** sundries, coin laundry. **Business Services:** fax (fee). **Cards:** AX, DS, JC, MC, VI. **Special Amenities: free expanded continental breakfast and free local telephone calls.**

SOME UNITS FEE

DAYS INN *Book at aaa.com* **Phone:** (760)256-1737

Motel

All Year [CP] 1P: $40-$59 2P: $49-$59 XP: $10 F12

Location: I-15/40, exit E Main St, just w, then just s on Roberta St. 1590 Coolwater Ln 92311. Fax: 760/256-7771. **Facility:** 113 one-bedroom standard units. 2 stories, exterior corridors. **Parking:** on-site. **Terms:** pets (in designated units). **Amenities:** hair dryers. *Some:* irons. **Pool(s):** outdoor. **Guest Services:** coin laundry. **Business Services:** fax. **Cards:** AX, DC, DS, MC, VI. **Special Amenities: free continental breakfast and early check-in/late check-out.**

SOME UNITS

ECONO LODGE *Book at aaa.com* **Phone:** (760)256-2133

Motel

All Year 1P: $39-$59 2P: $44-$64 XP: $5 F12

Location: I-15/40, exit E Main St, 0.8 mi w. 1230 E Main St 92311. Fax: 760/256-7999. **Facility:** 50 units. 49 one-bedroom standard units, some with efficiencies. 1 one-bedroom suite with efficiency. 2 stories, exterior corridors. *Bath:* combo or shower only. **Parking:** on-site. **Terms:** office hours 6 am-11 pm, weekly rates available, [CP] meal plan available, pets ($5 extra charge). **Amenities:** *Some:* irons, hair dryers. **Pool(s):** outdoor. **Business Services:** fax (fee). **Cards:** AX, CB, DC, DS, MC, VI.

SOME UNITS FEE

EXECUTIVE INN **Phone:** (760)256-7581

Motel

All Year 1P: $30-$50 2P: $35-$60 XP: $5 F

Location: I-15/40, exit E Main St, 0.8 mi w. 1261 E Main St 92311. Fax: 760/256-0155. **Facility:** 33 one-bedroom standard units, some with kitchens (no utensils). 2 stories, exterior corridors. **Parking:** on-site. **Terms:** cancellation fee imposed, weekly rates available, small pets only. **Amenities:** *Some:* irons, hair dryers. **Pool(s):** outdoor. **Business Services:** fax (fee). **Cards:** AX, DC, MC, VI. **Special Amenities: free continental breakfast and free local telephone calls.**

SOME UNITS

GATEWAY MOTEL **Phone:** (760)256-8931

Motel

All Year 1P: $31-$55 2P: $31-$85 XP: $10 F

Location: I-15/40, exit E Main St, just e. 1630 E Main St 92311. **Facility:** 33 one-bedroom standard units. 2 stories, exterior corridors. **Parking:** on-site. **Terms:** office hours 9 am-10 pm, small pets only ($10 extra charge, in designated units). **Pool(s):** outdoor. **Cards:** AX, CB, DC, DS, MC, VI. **Special Amenities: free local telephone calls and early check-in/late check-out.**

SOME UNITS FEE

HOLIDAY INN EXPRESS, BARSTOW-HISTORIC ROUTE 66 *Book at aaa.com* **Phone:** (760)256-1300

Small-scale Hotel

All Year 1P: $89-$109 2P: $89-$109 XP: $6 F17

Location: I-15/40, exit W Main St, 0.8 mi ne. 1861 W Main St 92311. Fax: 760/256-6807. **Facility:** 65 one-bedroom standard units. 3 stories, interior corridors. *Bath:* combo or shower only. **Parking:** on-site. **Terms:** [ECP] meal plan available, pets ($20 deposit). **Amenities:** high-speed Internet, voice mail, irons, hair dryers. **Pool(s):** outdoor. **Leisure Activities:** limited exercise equipment. **Guest Services:** coin laundry. **Business Services:** fax. **Cards:** AX, CB, DC, DS, JC, MC, VI.

SOME UNITS

FEE

HOLIDAY INN EXPRESS HOTEL & SUITES Book at aaa.com Phone: (760)253-9200

Small-scale Hotel

All Year [ECP] 1P: $89-$159 2P: $89-$159 XP: $10 F18

Location: I-15/40, exit Lenwood Rd, just e, then 0.5 mi s. 2700 Lenwood Rd 92311. Fax: 760/253-9201. **Facility:** 110 units. 106 one-bedroom standard units, some with whirlpools. 4 one-bedroom suites, some with whirlpools. 3 stories. **Parking:** on-site. **Terms:** package plans, pets ($25 deposit). **Amenities:** high-speed Internet. **Pool(s):** heated outdoor. **Leisure Activities:** whirlpool, exercise room. **Guest Services:** sundries, coin laundry. **Business Services:** meeting rooms, business center. **Cards:** AX, CB, DC, DS, JC, MC, VI.

SOME UNITS

ASK FEE DATA PORT

MOTEL 6 BARSTOW Book at aaa.com Phone: 760/256-1752

Motel

Property failed to provide current rates

Location: I-15/40, exit E Main St, 0.5 mi w, then just s. 150 N Yucca Ave 92311. Fax: 760/256-9110. **Facility:** 121 one-bedroom standard units. 2 stories, exterior corridors. *Bath:* combo or shower only. **Parking:** on-site. **Pool(s):** outdoor. **Business Services:** fax (fee).

SOME UNITS

DATA PORT

OAK TREE INN Book at aaa.com Phone: 760/254-1148

SAVE

Small-scale Hotel

All Year 1P: $60-$65 2P: $65-$70 XP: $5 F12

Location: I-15/40, exit Ghost Town Rd, just e, then just s. 35450 Yermo Rd 92398 (PO Box 456, YERMO). Fax: 760/254-1153. **Facility:** Designated smoking area. 65 one-bedroom standard units. 3 stories, interior corridors. **Parking:** on-site. **Terms:** office hours 7 am-11 pm, pets ($10 fee). **Amenities:** *Some:* irons, hair dryers. **Pool(s):** heated outdoor. **Leisure Activities:** exercise room. **Guest Services:** coin laundry. **Business Services:** fax (fee). **Cards:** AX, DC, DS, MC, VI. **Special Amenities: free continental breakfast and free local telephone calls.**

SOME UNITS

FEE DATA PORT

QUALITY INN Book at aaa.com Phone: (760)256-6891

SAVE

Motel

All Year 1P: $35-$65 2P: $35-$75 XP: $6 F16

Location: I-15/40, exit E Main St, 0.3 mi w. 1520 E Main St 92311. Fax: 760/256-3850. **Facility:** 100 one-bedroom standard units. 2 stories, exterior corridors. **Parking:** on-site. **Terms:** pets ($10 extra charge, in smoking units). **Amenities:** *Some:* irons, hair dryers. **Dining:** 6 am-10 & 4-9 pm, cocktails. **Pool(s):** outdoor. **Guest Services:** coin laundry. **Business Services:** meeting rooms, fax (fee). **Cards:** AX, CB, DC, DS, MC, VI. **Special Amenities: free local telephone calls and free newspaper.**

SOME UNITS

FEE DATA PORT

RAMADA INN Phone: (760)256-5673

Small-scale Hotel

All Year 1P: $89-$99 2P: $89-$99 XP: $10 F18

Location: I-15/40, exit E Main St, 0.3 mi w. 1511 E Main St 92311. Fax: 760/256-5917. **Facility:** 148 one-bedroom standard units. 3 stories, interior corridors. **Parking:** on-site. **Terms:** office hours 6 am-10 pm, pets ($20 fee). **Amenities:** voice mail, irons, hair dryers. **Pool(s):** outdoor. **Leisure Activities:** whirlpool. **Guest Services:** valet laundry. **Business Services:** meeting rooms, fax (fee). **Cards:** AX, DC, DS, MC, VI.

SOME UNITS

ASK FEE DATA PORT

RED ROOF INN Book at aaa.com Phone: (760)253-2121

Motel

All Year 1P: $35-$59 2P: $35-$59 XP: $6 F16

Location: I-15/40, exit Lenwood Rd, just w; 8 mi s of town. 2551 Commerce Pkwy 92311. Fax: 760/253-2086. **Facility:** 110 one-bedroom standard units. 3 stories, exterior corridors. **Parking:** on-site. **Amenities:** *Some:* irons, hair dryers. **Pool(s):** outdoor. **Leisure Activities:** whirlpool. **Guest Services:** coin laundry. **Business Services:** fax (fee). **Cards:** AX, DC, DS, MC, VI.

SOME UNITS

ASK DATA PORT

STARDUST INN Phone: (760)256-7116

SAVE

Motel

All Year 1P: $30-$35 2P: $35-$50 XP: $5 F9

Location: I-15/40, exit Barstow Rd, 0.8 mi n, then 0.4 mi e. 901 E Main St 92311. Fax: 760/256-1408. **Facility:** 24 one-bedroom standard units, some with kitchens (no utensils). 2 stories, exterior corridors. **Parking:** on-site. **Terms:** cancellation fee imposed, small pets only (with prior approval). **Pool(s):** outdoor. **Business Services:** fax (fee). **Cards:** AX, CB, DC, MC, VI. **Special Amenities: early check-in/late check-out and preferred room (subject to availability with advanced reservations).**

SOME UNITS

DATA PORT

WHERE TO DINE

DI NAPOLI'S FIREHOUSE **Lunch:** $5-$15 **Dinner:** $5-$20 **Phone:** 760/256-1094

Italian

Location: I-15/40, exit E Main St, 0.4 mi w. 1358 E Main St 92311. **Hours:** 11 am-9 pm. Closed major holidays; also Sun. **Features:** This well-established family restaurant is festively decorated in firehouse memorabilia and offers an excellent selection of Italian specialties, hand-tossed pizzas and delicious homemade Italian desserts. Friendly servers will assist you in making your selections. Casual dress; beer & wine only. **Parking:** on-site. **Cards:** AX, DS, MC, VI.

IDLE SPURS STEAK HOUSE **Lunch:** $7-$11 **Dinner:** $12-$19 **Phone:** 760/256-8888

Steak House

Location: I-15/40, exit Barstow Rd, 1 mi n to Main St, just w, 1 mi n on First Ave, then w on Old SR 58. 690 Old Hwy 58 92311. **Hours:** 11 am-9 pm, Sat & Sun from 4 pm. Closed major holidays; also 12/24, 12/31. **Features:** Just north of town, the steakhouse has been a local staple since the 1950s. Rustic country decor and old-fashioned friendly service makes patrons feel comfortable and welcomed. Homemade clam chowder is superb, and portions of steak and other entrees are generous. The signature homemade cherry cobbler is sublime. Casual dress; cocktails. **Parking:** on-site. **Cards:** AX, DS, MC, VI.

PEGGY SUE'S DINER — **Lunch:** $5-$10 **Dinner:** $5-$10 **Phone:** 760/254-3370

American

Location: I-15/40, exit Ghost Town Rd, just s; 7 mi ne of town of Yermo. 35654 Yermo Rd 92398. **Hours:** 6 am-9 pm, Fri-Sun to 10 pm. Closed: 12/25. **Features:** Restored in 1987, the 1954 roadside diner—decorated with the requisite movie, TV and rock 'n' roll memorabilia—was made for tourists. Seating is offered in three dining rooms or outdoors amid the man-made lagoons of Paradise Park. Pizza, old-fashioned burgers, sandwiches and such ice cream parlor treats as malts and sodas are representative of the fare. Sassy servers in '50s garb ensure guests are well taken care of. Casual dress; beer & wine only. **Parking:** on-site. **Cards:** AX, MC, VI.

ROSITA'S MEXICAN & AMERICAN RESTAURANT — **Lunch:** $6-$15 **Dinner:** $6-$20 **Phone:** 760/256-1058

Mexican

Location: I-15/40, exit W Main St, just w. 540 W Main St 92311. **Hours:** 11 am-9 pm, Sun-8 pm. Closed major holidays; also Mon. **Features:** This family-owned Mexican restaurant has been serving the area for nearly 50 years. There is a wide selection of Mexican and American entrees as well as a buffet available on Wednesdays. Try the Mexican-style hamburger steak or the New Mexico cheese and onion enchiladas with eggs. Be sure to save room for an apple burrito or fried ice cream for dessert. Casual dress; cocktails. **Parking:** on-site. **Cards:** AX, DS, MC, VI.

BASS LAKE —*See also YOSEMITE NATIONAL PARK.*

WHERE TO STAY

THE PINES RESORT — Book at aaa.com — **Phone:** (559)642-3121

Cottage

6/11-9/6	1P: $159-$219	2P: $159-$219	XP: $10	F16
9/7-1/31	1P: $129-$209	2P: $129-$209	XP: $10	F16
4/1-6/10	1P: $129-$189	2P: $129-$189	XP: $10	F16
2/1-3/31	1P: $89-$139	2P: $89-$139	XP: $10	F16

Location: 6 mi e of SR 41, exit CR 222, e on CR 274, then s on CR 434. Located in Pine Village. 54432 Road 432 93604 (PO Box 109). Fax: 559/642-3902. **Facility:** 84 cottages. 2 stories (no elevator), exterior corridors. **Parking:** on-site. **Terms:** check-in 4 pm, 3 night minimum stay - seasonal, 7 day cancellation notice. **Amenities:** voice mail, irons, hair dryers. **Pool(s):** outdoor. **Leisure Activities:** whirlpool, fishing, 2 tennis courts, playground. *Fee:* boats, marina, waterskiing, massage. **Guest Services:** gift shop, coin laundry. **Business Services:** meeting rooms. **Cards:** AX, DC, DS, MC, VI.

SOME UNITS

THE PINES RESORT — Phone: (559)642-3121

Small-scale Hotel

6/11-9/6 [CP]	1P: $219-$369	2P: $219-$369	XP: $10	F16
4/1-6/10 & 9/7-1/31 [CP]	1P: $189-$309	2P: $189-$309	XP: $10	F16
2/1-3/31 [CP]	1P: $169-$299	2P: $169-$299	XP: $10	F16

Location: 6 mi e of SR 41, exit CR 222, e on CR 274, then s on CR 434. Located in Pine Village. 54432 Road 432 93604 (PO Box 109). Fax: 559/642-3902. **Facility:** 20 units. 18 one-bedroom standard units, some with whirlpools. 2 one-bedroom suites with whirlpools. 2 stories, interior corridors. **Parking:** on-site. **Terms:** 3 night minimum stay - seasonal, 7 day cancellation notice. **Amenities:** dual phone lines, voice mail, irons, hair dryers. **Pool(s):** outdoor. **Leisure Activities:** whirlpool, fishing, 2 tennis courts, playground. *Fee:* boats, marina, waterskiing, massage. **Guest Services:** gift shop, valet and coin laundry. **Business Services:** meeting rooms, fax (fee). **Cards:** AX, DC, DS, MC, VI.

SOME UNITS

BEAR VALLEY pop. 133

WHERE TO STAY

THE BEAR VALLEY LODGE — Phone: 209/753-2327

Small-scale Hotel

2/1-4/17 & 11/24-1/31	1P: $110-$195	2P: $110-$195	XP: $25
4/18-11/23	1P: $85-$135	2P: $85-$135	XP: $25

Location: SR 4 (Bear Valley Rd), just n. 3 Bear Valley Rd 95223 (PO Box 5440). Fax: 209/753-6218. **Facility:** 51 units. 48 one-bedroom standard units. 1 one- and 2 two-bedroom suites. 3 stories, interior corridors. *Bath:* combo or shower only. **Parking:** on-site. **Terms:** 2 night minimum stay - weekends in winter, 7 day cancellation notice, in winter-fee imposed. **Amenities:** *Some:* irons, hair dryers. **Pool(s):** outdoor. **Leisure Activities:** downhill skiing, ice skating, bicycles, hiking trails, jogging. **Guest Services:** gift shop, area transportation. **Business Services:** meeting rooms. **Cards:** AX, MC, VI.

SOME UNITS

BELMONT —See San Francisco p. 660.

BENICIA pop. 26,865

WHERE TO STAY

BEST WESTERN HERITAGE INN — *Book at aaa.com* — Phone: (707)746-0401

Small-scale Hotel

(See color ad below)

All Year	1P: $80-$120	2P: $80-$120	XP: $10	F17

Location: I-780, exit Central Benicia/E 2nd St, just e. 1955 E 2nd St 94510. Fax: 707/745-0842. **Facility:** 100 one-bedroom standard units, some with whirlpools. 3 stories, interior corridors. **Parking:** on-site. **Terms:** [CP] meal plan available, small pets only ($25 fee). **Amenities:** irons, hair dryers. **Pool(s):** outdoor. **Leisure Activities:** whirlpool. **Guest Services:** valet and coin laundry. **Business Services:** meeting rooms. **Cards:** AX, DC, DS, MC, VI. **Special Amenities: free continental breakfast and free newspaper.**

SOME UNITS

FEE

BEN LOMOND pop. 2,364

WHERE TO STAY

ECONO LODGE — *Book at aaa.com* — Phone: (831)336-2292

Motel

5/1-9/30	1P: $89-$169	2P: $89-$169	XP: $12	F16
2/1-4/30 & 10/1-1/31	1P: $69-$109	2P: $69-$109	XP: $12	F16

Location: SR 9, 0.3 mi n; on San Lorenzo River. 9733 Hwy 9 95005. Fax: 831/336-0554. **Facility:** 21 one-bedroom standard units. 2 stories (no elevator), exterior corridors. *Bath:* combo or shower only. **Parking:** on-site. **Terms:** 2-10 night minimum stay - weekends & seasonal, 3 day cancellation notice-fee imposed, [CP] meal plan available. **Amenities:** irons. **Pool(s):** outdoor. **Leisure Activities:** fishing. **Cards:** AX, DS, MC, VI.

SOME UNITS

JAYE'S TIMBERLANE RESOURT — **Phone:** (831)336-5479

Cottage

All Year 1P: $95-$115 2P: $95-$140 XP: $15 F7

Location: SR 9, 0.5 mi s. 8705 Hwy 9 95005. **Facility:** 10 cottages. 1 story, exterior corridors. *Bath:* shower only. **Parking:** on-site. **Terms:** 2-3 night minimum stay - weekends, 7 day cancellation notice-fee imposed, weekly rates available. **Pool(s):** outdoor. **Cards:** MC, VI.

SOME UNITS

BERKELEY pop. 102,743 (See map and index starting on p. 516)

WHERE TO STAY

THE CLAREMONT RESORT AND SPA Book at aaa.com — **Phone:** (510)843-3000 28

Historic Large-scale Hotel

5/1-11/20 1P: $219-$349 2P: $219-$349 XP: $30 F17
2/1-4/30 & 11/21-1/31 1P: $199-$329 2P: $199-$329 XP: $30 F17

Location: SR 13 and 24, 1 mi n, exit SR 24 (Claremont Ave); in Berkeley Hills. 41 Tunnel Rd 94705. Fax: 510/848-6208. **Facility:** San Francisco Bay serves as a scenic backdrop for many of this 1915 Victorian landmark's guest rooms; manicured grounds complete the picture. 279 units. 273 one-bedroom standard units, some with whirlpools. 6 one-bedroom suites ($450-$950), some with whirlpools. 7 stories, interior corridors. *Bath:* some combo or shower only. **Parking:** on-site (fee) and valet. **Terms:** check-in 4 pm, age restrictions may apply, cancellation fee imposed, [AP] & [BP] meal plans available, package plans, $12 service charge. **Amenities:** video games, CD players, dual phone lines, voice mail, safes, honor bars, irons, hair dryers. **Dining:** Jordan's At The Claremont, see separate listing. **Pool(s):** 2 heated outdoor. **Leisure Activities:** saunas, whirlpools, 10 tennis courts (6 lighted), jogging, spa. **Guest Services:** gift shop, valet laundry, area transportation. **Business Services:** meeting rooms, business center. **Cards:** AX, CB, DC, DS, JC, MC, VI.

SOME UNITS

FEE

DOUBLETREE HOTEL AND EXECUTIVE MEETING CENTER BERKELEY MARINA — **Phone:** (510)548-7920 30

Small-scale Hotel

All Year 1P: $139-$228 XP: $10 F

Location: I-80, exit University Ave, 0.5 mi w. Located on Berkeley Marina. 200 Marina Blvd 94710. Fax: 510/548-7944. **Facility:** 369 one-bedroom standard units, some with whirlpools. 1-4 stories, interior corridors. *Bath:* combo or shower only. **Parking:** on-site. **Terms:** age restrictions may apply, weekly rates available. **Amenities:** high-speed Internet, dual phone lines, voice mail, irons, hair dryers. **Pool(s):** 2 heated indoor. **Leisure Activities:** sauna, whirlpools, boat dock, jogging, exercise room. **Guest Services:** gift shop, coin laundry, area transportation. **Business Services:** conference facilities, business center. **Cards:** AX, CB, DC, DS, JC, MC, VI.

SOME UNITS

FEE

HOLIDAY INN EXPRESS HOTEL & SUITES Book at aaa.com — **Phone:** (510)548-1700 31

Motel

All Year [CP] 1P: $111-$139 2P: $111-$139 XP: $10 F17

Location: I-80, exit University Ave E. 1175 University Ave 94702. Fax: 510/548-1705. **Facility:** 69 units. 67 one- and 1 two-bedroom standard units, some with kitchens. 1 one-bedroom suite ($169-$229) with whirlpool. 3 stories, interior corridors. *Bath:* combo or shower only. **Parking:** on-site. **Terms:** age restrictions may apply, cancellation fee imposed. **Amenities:** video library, high-speed Internet, dual phone lines, voice mail, irons, hair dryers. **Leisure Activities:** exercise room. **Guest Services:** coin laundry. **Business Services:** meeting rooms, fax. **Cards:** AX, DC, DS, JC, MC, VI. ***(See color ad p 260)***

SOME UNITS

(See map and index starting on p. 516)

HOTEL DURANT Book at aaa.com **Phone:** (510)845-8981 29

SAVE

Small-scale Hotel

All Year 1P: $140-$170 2P: $150-$180 XP: $10 F16

Location: E off I-80 on Ashby to Telegraph, n to Durant; westbound from SR 13 and 24, exit Berkeley, w on Ashby to Telegraph, then n to Durant at Bowditch. 2600 Durant Ave 94704. Fax: 510/486-8336. **Facility:** 144 units. 138 one-bedroom standard units. 6 one-bedroom suites ($290-$450). 6 stories, interior corridors. *Bath:* combo or shower only. **Parking:** on-site (fee). **Terms:** age restrictions may apply, cancellation fee imposed. **Amenities:** voice mail, irons, hair dryers. **Dining:** 7 am-10 & 11-10 pm, cocktails. **Guest Services:** valet laundry. **Business Services:** meeting rooms. **Cards:** AX, DC, DS, JC, MC, VI. **Special Amenities: free newspaper and early check-in/late check-out.**

SOME UNITS

FEE FEE

WHERE TO DINE

CAFE ROUGE **Lunch:** $6-$14 **Dinner:** $12-$28 **Phone:** 510/525-1440 18

Continental

Location: I-80, exit University Ave, just s; between Hearst and Delaware. 1782 4th St 94710. **Hours:** 11:30 am-10 pm, Fri & Sat-10:30 pm, Sun 5 pm-9:30 pm. Closed major holidays. **Reservations:** suggested. **Features:** A grocery story is attached to the cozy, casual cafe. Southern, French and Italian items are prepared with flair. Casual dress; cocktails. **Parking:** on-site. **Cards:** AX, MC, VI.

CHEZ PANISSE **Lunch:** $10-$25 **Dinner:** $12-$28 **Phone:** 510/548-5525 16

Regional American

Location: At Cedar St. 1517 Shattuck Ave 94709. **Hours:** 6 pm & 9 pm seatings; Cafe Panisse 11:30 am-3 & 5-10:30 pm, Fri & Sat-11:30 pm. Closed major holidays; also Sun. **Reservations:** required; 1 month advance. **Features:** California, French and strong Mediterranean influences mingle in the restaurant's intriguing dishes. At the same location, the more casual Cafe Panisse serves a full menu for lunch and has a less-restrictive reservation policy. Dressy casual; beer & wine only. **Parking:** street. **Cards:** AX, CB, DC, DS, MC, VI.

JORDAN'S AT THE CLAREMONT **Lunch:** $12-$18 **Dinner:** $23-$34 **Phone:** 510/843-3000 15

Regional American

Location: SR 13 and 24, 1 mi n, exit SR 24 (Claremont Ave); in Berkeley Hills; in The Claremont Resort and Spa. 41 Tunnel Rd 94705. **Hours:** 6:30-11 am, 11:30-2:30 & 6-10 pm, Fri & Sat-11 pm, Sun 6:30-9:30 am, 10-2 & 6-10 pm; Sunday brunch. **Reservations:** suggested. **Features:** From the warm, luxurious dining room, diners are privileged to extraordinary views of the sunset over San Francisco Bay. Innovative, nutritionally balanced items are prepared from seasonal, local ingredients. Herbs are grown in the Claremont's own garden. Casual dress; cocktails. **Parking:** on-site and valet. **Cards:** AX, CB, DC, DS, JC, MC, VI.

SKATES ON THE BAY **Lunch:** $9-$15 **Dinner:** $15-$30 **Phone:** 510/549-1900 17

American

Location: I-80, exit University Ave, 0.3 mi w; on Berkeley Marina. 100 Seawall Dr 94710. **Hours:** 11:30 am-10 pm, Fri & Sat-10:30 pm, Sun 10:30 am-2:30 & 4-10 pm. Closed: 11/25, 12/25. **Reservations:** suggested. **Features:** Dining on the bay is pleasant due to the beautiful setting. The extensive menu comprises flavorful, interestingly prepared dishes. Casual dress; cocktails. **Parking:** on-site. **Cards:** AX, MC, VI.

BERRY CREEK

WHERE TO STAY

LAKE OROVILLE BED & BREAKFAST **Phone:** (530)589-0700

Bed & Breakfast

All Year 1P: $125-$165 2P: $125-$165 XP: $10 D18

Location: SR 162, exit SR 70, 15 mi e on SR 162 to Bell Ranch Rd, 0.5 mi w. 240 Sunday Dr 95916. Fax: 530/589-3800. **Facility:** Picturesque setting overlooking Lake Oroville. 6 one-bedroom standard units, some with whirlpools. 1 story, interior corridors. **Parking:** on-site. **Terms:** office hours 7 am-10 pm, age restrictions may apply, 5 day cancellation notice, [BP] meal plan available, package plans - midweek, small pets only ($10 fee). **Amenities:** video library, CD players. *Some:* irons, hair dryers. **Leisure Activities:** horseshoes. **Cards:** AX, DS, MC, VI.

SOME UNITS

ASK FEE

BIG PINE pop. 1,350

WHERE TO STAY

BIG PINE MOTEL **Phone:** 760/938-2282

SAVE

Motel

All Year 1P: $36-$56 2P: $42-$62 XP: $4

Location: On US 395. 370 S Main 93513 (PO Box 759). **Facility:** 14 one-bedroom standard units, some with efficiencies. 1 story, exterior corridors. *Bath:* combo or shower only. **Parking:** on-site. **Terms:** pets ($4 extra charge). **Amenities:** *Some:* irons, hair dryers. **Cards:** AX, CB, DC, DS, JC, MC, VI. **Special Amenities: free local telephone calls and preferred room (subject to availability with advanced reservations).**

SOME UNITS

FEE

BRISTLECONE MOTEL **Phone:** 760/938-2067

SAVE

Motel

All Year 1P: $36-$68 2P: $40-$68 XP: $4

Location: On US 395. 101 N Main St 93513 (PO Box 849). Fax: 760/938-3107. **Facility:** 17 one-bedroom standard units, some with kitchens. 1 story, exterior corridors. *Bath:* combo or shower only. **Parking:** on-site. **Terms:** weekly rates available. **Amenities:** voice mail. *Some:* irons, hair dryers. **Guest Services:** coin laundry. **Cards:** AX, DC, DS, MC, VI. **Special Amenities: free local telephone calls and early check-in/late check-out.**

SOME UNITS

STARLIGHT MOTEL **Phone:** 760/938-2011

Motel

All Year 1P: $38-$50 2P: $45-$65 XP: $5 F12

Location: On US 395. 511 S Main St 93513 (PO Box 575). Fax: 760/938-2525. **Facility:** Designated smoking area. 8 one-bedroom standard units. 1 story, exterior corridors. *Bath:* shower only. **Parking:** on-site. **Amenities:** *Some:* irons, hair dryers. **Leisure Activities:** fish cleaning & freezing facilities. **Business Services:** fax. **Cards:** AX, DS, MC, VI. **Special Amenities: free local telephone calls and preferred room (subject to availability with advanced reservations).**

WHERE TO DINE

ROSSI'S STEAK & SPAGHETTI **Dinner:** $11-$19 **Phone:** 760/938-2254

American

Location: On US 395. 100 N Main St 93513. **Hours:** 5:30 pm-10 pm; from 4:30 pm in winter. Closed major holidays; also Mon. **Reservations:** suggested; weekends. **Features:** Warm and comfortable describes the surroundings, decor and staff. Farmhouse memorabilia, old-time framed photographs and leaded-glass chandeliers give diners the feeling they're sitting down to a meal at Aunt Bessie's farm. Food served family style is wonderful. Entrees come with warm bread, salad, spaghetti, coffee and dessert. Casual dress; cocktails. **Parking:** on-site. **Cards:** AX, CB, DC, DS, MC, VI.

BIG SUR

WHERE TO STAY

BIG SUR LODGE *Book at aaa.com* **Phone:** (831)667-3100

Motel

4/1-9/30	1P: $149-$229	2P: $149-$229
2/1-3/31 & 10/1-11/30	1P: $119-$199	2P: $119-$199
12/1-1/31	1P: $99-$179	2P: $99-$179

Location: 26 mi s of Carmel. Located in Pfeiffer Big Sur State Park. 47225 Hwy 1 93920. Fax: 831/667-3110. **Facility:** 61 units. 21 one- and 40 two-bedroom standard units, some with kitchens. 1 story, exterior corridors. *Bath:* combo or shower only. **Parking:** on-site. **Terms:** check-in 4 pm, 3-4 night minimum stay - weekends, 3 day cancellation notice. **Dining:** The Restaurant at Big Sur Lodge, see separate listing. **Pool(s):** outdoor. **Leisure Activities:** hiking trails, jogging. **Guest Services:** gift shop. **Business Services:** meeting rooms. **Cards:** AX, MC, VI. ***(See color ad below)***

VENTANA INN & SPA *Book at aaa.com* **Phone:** (831)667-2331

Small-scale Hotel

All Year [ECP] 1P: $399-$1000 2P: $399-$1000 XP: $50

Location: Off SR 1, 0.3 mi e. SR 1 93920. Fax: 831/667-2419. **Facility:** 60 units. 57 one-bedroom standard units, some with whirlpools. 3 one-bedroom suites ($975) with whirlpools. 2 stories, exterior corridors. *Bath:* combo or shower only. **Parking:** on-site. **Terms:** check-in 4 pm, 2-3 night minimum stay - weekends, age restrictions may apply, 14 day cancellation notice-fee imposed, [MAP] meal plan available, package plans - seasonal. **Amenities:** video library. **Dining:** Cielo Restaurant, see separate listing. **Pool(s):** 2 heated outdoor. **Leisure Activities:** sauna, whirlpools, hiking trails, jogging, exercise room, spa. **Guest Services:** gift shop, complimentary evening beverages. **Business Services:** meeting rooms. **Cards:** AX, DC, DS, MC, VI.

SOME UNITS

WHERE TO DINE

CIELO RESTAURANT **Lunch:** $12-$18 **Dinner:** $24-$32 **Phone:** 831/667-4242

American

Location: Off SR 1, 0.3 mi e; in Ventana Inn & Spa. Hwy 1 93920. **Hours:** noon-3 & 5:30-9 pm, Sat-9:30 pm. **Reservations:** suggested. **Features:** California Mediterranean cuisine is prepared on an oak-wood broiler. Several prix fixe meal options are offered. On a wooded hilltop, the dining room is casually comfortable. Casual dress; cocktails. **Parking:** on-site. **Cards:** AX, DC, DS, MC, VI.

THE RESTAURANT AT BIG SUR LODGE **Lunch:** $7-$13 **Dinner:** $10-$21 **Phone:** 831/667-3111

American

Location: 26 mi s of Carmel; in Big Sur Lodge. 47225 Hwy 1 93920. **Hours:** 7:30 am-9 pm. **Features:** Fresh seafood is prepared California style using local produce. The casual, creekside setting lets patrons unwind. Casual dress; beer & wine only. **Parking:** on-site. **Cards:** AX, MC, VI.

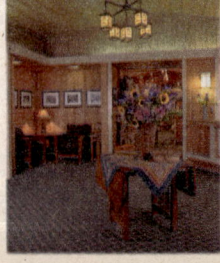

BISHOP pop. 3,575

WHERE TO STAY

BEST WESTERN BISHOP HOLIDAY SPA LODGE *Book at aaa.com* **Phone:** (760)873-3543

AAA SAVE

Motel

All Year [ECP]	1P: $69-$79	2P: $79-$119	XP: $5	F12

Location: On US 395. 1025 N Main St 93514. Fax: 760/872-4777. **Facility:** 89 units. 88 one-bedroom standard units. 1 one-bedroom suite. 2 stories, exterior corridors. **Parking:** on-site. **Terms:** cancellation fee imposed, small pets only. **Amenities:** voice mail, irons, hair dryers. **Pool(s):** outdoor. **Leisure Activities:** whirlpool, fish cleaning & freezing facilities, barbecue. **Guest Services:** coin laundry. **Cards:** AX, DC, DS, MC, VI. **Special Amenities: free expanded continental breakfast and free local telephone calls.**

SOME UNITS

BEST WESTERN CREEKSIDE INN *Book at aaa.com* **Phone:** 760/872-3044

AAA SAVE

Small-scale Hotel

6/1-9/30	1P: $119-$149	2P: $149-$189	XP: $15	F12
2/1-5/31 & 10/1-1/31	1P: $109-$129	2P: $109-$129	XP: $15	F12

Location: On US 395. 725 N Main St 93514. Fax: 760/872-1300. **Facility:** Designated smoking area. 89 units. 88 one-bedroom standard units, some with kitchens. 1 one-bedroom suite. 2 stories, interior corridors. **Parking:** on-site. **Terms:** check-in 4 pm, cancellation fee imposed, [ECP] meal plan available, pets ($10 fee). **Amenities:** voice mail, irons, hair dryers. **Pool(s):** outdoor. **Leisure Activities:** whirlpool, fish cleaning & freezing facilities. **Guest Services:** valet and coin laundry. **Business Services:** fax (fee). **Cards:** AX, CB, DC, DS, MC, VI. **Special Amenities: free continental breakfast and free newspaper.** *(See color ad below)*

SOME UNITS

FEE

BISHOP DAYS INN *Book at aaa.com* **Phone:** (760)872-1095

AAA SAVE

Motel

4/1-10/31	1P: $59-$79	2P: $69-$99	XP: $10	F10
2/1-3/31 & 11/1-1/31	1P: $59-$69	2P: $69-$89	XP: $10	F10

Location: US 395, 0.4 mi w on SR 168. 724 W Line St 93514. Fax: 760/872-1097. **Facility:** 33 one-bedroom standard units, some with whirlpools. 2 stories, exterior corridors. **Parking:** on-site. **Terms:** office hours 6 am-11 pm, 3 day cancellation notice, [CP] meal plan available. **Amenities:** irons, hair dryers. **Pool(s):** outdoor. **Leisure Activities:** whirlpool, fish cleaning facilities. **Guest Services:** coin laundry. **Business Services:** fax (fee). **Cards:** AX, DC, DS, MC, VI. **Special Amenities: free continental breakfast and free local telephone calls.**

SOME UNITS

CHALFANT HOUSE BED & BREAKFAST **Phone:** 760/872-1790

Bed & Breakfast

All Year [BP] 1P: $80-$105 2P: $80-$105 XP: $10 D

Location: On US 395, just w. 213 Academy St 93514. Fax: 760/872-1790. **Facility:** Charming Victorian decor in a restored 1898 house. Smoke free premises. 7 units. 5 one-bedroom standard units. 2 one-bedroom suites ($105). 2 stories, interior/exterior corridors. *Bath:* combo or shower only. **Parking:** on-site. **Terms:** office hours 7 am-9 pm, cancellation fee imposed. **Amenities:** video library. *Some:* irons, hair dryers. **Business Services:** fax (fee). **Cards:** DC, MC, VI.

SOME UNITS

COMFORT INN Book at aaa.com **Phone:** (760)873-4284

SAVE

Motel

All Year [ECP] 1P: $59-$79 2P: $79-$109 XP: $5

Location: On US 395. 805 N Main St 93514. Fax: 760/873-8563. **Facility:** 54 one-bedroom standard units, some with whirlpools. 2 stories, exterior corridors. **Parking:** on-site. **Amenities:** voice mail, irons, hair dryers. **Pool(s):** outdoor. **Leisure Activities:** whirlpool, fish cleaning & freezing facilities. **Guest Services:** coin laundry. **Cards:** AX, CB, DC, DS, MC, VI.

SOME UNITS

DATA PORT

EL RANCHO MOTEL **Phone:** (760)872-9251

SAVE

Motel

4/15-10/31 1P: $42-$55 2P: $48-$67 XP: $5 D10

2/1-4/14 & 11/1-1/31 1P: $38-$50 2P: $42-$62 XP: $5 D10

Location: US 395, just w. 274 Lagoon St 93514. **Facility:** 16 one-bedroom standard units, some with kitchens. 1 story, exterior corridors. *Bath:* combo or shower only. **Parking:** on-site. **Terms:** office hours 7 am-midnight, 3 day cancellation notice. **Amenities:** *Some:* irons. **Leisure Activities:** fish freezing & cleaning facilities. **Cards:** DS, MC, VI. **Special Amenities: preferred room (subject to availability with advanced reservations).**

SOME UNITS

HOLIDAY INN EXPRESS HOTEL & SUITES Book at aaa.com **Phone:** (760)872-2423

SAVE

Small-scale Hotel

5/1-10/31 [ECP] 1P: $109-$179 2P: $119-$189 XP: $10 F19

2/1-4/30 & 11/1-1/31 [ECP] 1P: $99-$149 2P: $99-$159 XP: $10 F19

Location: On US 395. Located adjacent to city park. 636 N Main St 93514. Fax: 760/872-2239. **Facility:** Smoke free premises. 66 one-bedroom standard units, some with whirlpools. 2 stories (no elevator), interior corridors. *Bath:* combo or shower only. **Parking:** on-site. **Amenities:** voice mail, irons, hair dryers. **Pool(s):** heated indoor. **Leisure Activities:** sauna, whirlpool, fish cleaning & freezing facilities, exercise room. **Guest Services:** coin laundry. **Business Services:** fax (fee). **Cards:** AX, CB, DC, DS, JC, MC, VI. **Special Amenities: free expanded continental breakfast and free local telephone calls.**

SOME UNITS

DATA PORT VCR

JOSEPH HOUSE INN **Phone:** (760)872-3389

Bed & Breakfast

All Year [BP] 2P: $145-$165

Location: 0.3 mi w of US 395. 376 W Yaney St 93514. Fax: 760/872-4410. **Facility:** This beautifully resorted home boasts individually appointed rooms and baths, lush rose gardens and a huge yard complete with creek, pond and fountains. Smoke free premises. 5 one-bedroom standard units. 1 story, interior corridors. *Bath:* combo or shower only. **Parking:** on-site. **Terms:** 2-3 night minimum stay - weekends, 14 day cancellation notice, package plans - seasonal & midweek, no pets allowed (owner's pet on premises). **Amenities:** video library, hair dryers. *Some:* irons. **Leisure Activities:** Fee: massage. **Guest Services:** complimentary evening beverages. **Business Services:** fax (fee). **Cards:** AX, DS, MC, VI.

ASK VCR

MOTEL 6 - 4094 Book at aaa.com **Phone:** 760/873-8426

Motel

All Year 1P: $39-$79 2P: $49-$89 XP: $10 F17

Location: On US 395. 1005 N Main St 93514. Fax: 760/873-8060. **Facility:** 51 one-bedroom standard units. 2 stories, exterior corridors. **Parking:** on-site. **Terms:** small pets only. **Amenities:** voice mail. *Some:* irons, hair dryers. **Pool(s):** outdoor. **Leisure Activities:** whirlpool. **Guest Services:** coin laundry. **Cards:** AX, CB, DC, DS, MC, VI.

SOME UNITS

DATA PORT

MOUNTAIN VIEW MOTEL **Phone:** (760)873-4242

SAVE

Motel

All Year [ECP] 1P: $55-$77 2P: $67-$99 XP: $10 F12

Location: On US 395, 0.4 mi w on SR 168. 730 W Line St 93514. Fax: 760/873-3409. **Facility:** 35 units. 33 one-bedroom standard units, some with kitchens. 2 one-bedroom suites ($125-$165) with kitchens. 2 stories, exterior corridors. *Bath:* combo or shower only. **Parking:** on-site. **Terms:** office hours 6 am-11 pm. **Amenities:** *Some:* irons, hair dryers. **Pool(s):** outdoor. **Leisure Activities:** fish cleaning & freezing facilities, gas barbecue & picnic area. **Business Services:** fax. **Cards:** AX, DS, MC, VI. **Special Amenities: free expanded continental breakfast and free local telephone calls.**

SOME UNITS

VCR FEE

RAMADA LIMITED Book at aaa.com **Phone:** (760)872-1771

Motel

All Year [ECP] 1P: $59-$69 2P: $69-$89 XP: $10 F

Location: On US 395, just e. 155 E Elm St 93514. Fax: 760/872-3090. **Facility:** 52 one-bedroom standard units, some with efficiencies. 2 stories, exterior corridors. **Parking:** on-site. **Terms:** pets ($15 extra charge). **Amenities:** voice mail, irons, hair dryers. **Pool(s):** outdoor. **Leisure Activities:** whirlpool. **Business Services:** fax (fee). **Cards:** AX, DC, DS, MC, VI.

SOME UNITS

ASK FEE DATA PORT

SUPER 8 MOTEL *Book at aaa.com* **Phone:** (760)872-1386

Motel

4/1-9/30 1P: $58-$65 2P: $65-$75 XP: $5 F12
2/1-3/31 & 10/1-1/31 1P: $48-$55 2P: $55-$65 XP: $5 F12

Location: On US 395. 535 S Main St 93514. Fax: 760/872-3262. **Facility:** 43 one-bedroom standard units. 2 stories, exterior corridors. **Parking:** on-site. **Terms:** office hours 7 am-11 pm, cancellation fee imposed. **Amenities:** *Some:* irons, hair dryers. **Pool(s):** outdoor. **Guest Services:** coin laundry. **Business Services:** fax (fee). **Cards:** AX, DC, DS, JC, MC, VI.

SOME UNITS

THUNDERBIRD MOTEL **Phone:** 760/873-4215

Motel

2/1-10/15 1P: $55-$150 2P: $65-$150 XP: $5 F12
10/16-1/31 1P: $50-$150 2P: $55-$150 XP: $5 F12

Location: On US 395, just w. 190 W Pine St 93514. Fax: 760/873-6870. **Facility:** 22 one-bedroom standard units. 2 stories, exterior corridors. **Parking:** on-site. **Terms:** small pets only ($4 extra charge). **Amenities:** hair dryers. *Some:* irons. **Business Services:** fax (fee). **Cards:** AX, CB, DC, DS, MC, VI.

SOME UNITS

FEE

VAGABOND INN *Book at aaa.com* **Phone:** (760)873-6351

AAA SAVE

Motel

All Year [ECP] 1P: $81 2P: $90 XP: $10 F18

Location: On US 395. 1030 N Main St 93514. Fax: 760/873-3067. **Facility:** 80 one-bedroom standard units. 2 stories, exterior corridors. **Parking:** on-site. **Terms:** pets ($5 extra charge). **Amenities:** hair dryers. *Some:* irons. **Pool(s):** outdoor. **Leisure Activities:** sauna, whirlpool, fish cleaning & freezing facilities, barbecue area with picnic table, horseshoes. **Guest Services:** coin laundry. **Business Services:** fax (fee). **Cards:** AX, DC, DS, MC, VI. **Special Amenities: free expanded continental breakfast.**

SOME UNITS

FEE

WHERE TO DINE

BAR-B-Q BILL'S **Lunch:** $6-$10 **Dinner:** $10-$18 **Phone:** 760/872-5535

Barbecue

Location: On US 395. 187 S Main St 93514. **Hours:** 11 am-8:30 pm, Fri & Sat-9 pm; to 9 pm, Fri & Sat-9:30 pm in summer. Closed: 11/25, 12/25. **Features:** This family restaurant was established in 1966 and has remained in the family since that time. All of the meat is freshly carved. There is also an all-you-can-eat soup and salad bar. Western decor and memorabilia creates a friendly atmosphere. Casual dress; beer & wine only. **Parking:** on-site. **Cards:** AX, CB, DC, DS, JC, MC, VI.

FIREHOUSE GRILL **Lunch:** $4-$8 **Dinner:** $15-$24 **Phone:** 760/873-4888

American

Location: On US 395. 635 N Main St 93514. **Hours:** 11 am-3 & 4-10 pm. **Features:** In the center of town, the easy-to-find restaurant has a big fire bell out front. Inside is firehouse decor, including scores of fire dog memorabilia. Soups, salads and sandwiches are among lunch offerings, while dinners center on such dishes as prime rib, steak Diane, teriyaki chicken and boar chops. Nice complements include quality California wines and homemade desserts. Casual dress; cocktails. **Parking:** on-site. **Cards:** AX, DS, MC, VI.

IMPERIAL GOURMET **Lunch:** $8-$30 **Dinner:** $8-$30 **Phone:** 760/872-1144

Chinese

Location: On US 395; on the 2nd floor of Cottonwood Shopping Plaza. 758 N Main St 93514. **Hours:** 11 am-9:30 pm, Fri & Sat-10 pm. Closed: 11/25. **Features:** Accessible by stairs or elevator, the established, second-floor restaurant treats patrons to an excellent array of traditional appetizers and entrees. A large aquarium contributes to the nice decor. Service is gracious and attentive. Casual dress; cocktails. **Parking:** on-site. **Cards:** AX, CB, DC, MC, VI.

UPPER CRUST PIZZA COMPANY **Lunch:** $6-$11 **Dinner:** $9-$13 **Phone:** 760/872-8153

Italian

Location: On US 395. 1180 N Main St 93514. **Hours:** 11 am-8 pm; to 9:30 pm in summer. Closed: 7/4, 11/25, 12/25. **Features:** Fresh pasta dishes and wood-fired gourmet pizzas made over a wood fire are favorites at the casual restaurant. Views of the mountains are particularly beautiful from the outdoor seats. Casual dress; beer & wine only. **Parking:** on-site. **Cards:** AX, MC, VI.

WHISKEY CREEK AT BISHOP **Lunch:** $6-$19 **Dinner:** $10-$22 **Phone:** 760/873-7174

American

Location: On US 395. 524 N Main St 93514. **Hours:** 11 am-9 pm, Sat 8 am-10 pm, Sun 8 am-9 pm. Closed: 12/25. **Reservations:** suggested. **Features:** A convenient stop when passing through town, the family restaurant treats diners to friendly service and delicious homemade desserts from the on-site bakery. Patio seating is popular, weather permitting. Casual dress; cocktails. **Parking:** on-site. **Cards:** AX, CB, DC, DS, MC, VI.

BLAIRSDEN pop. 50

WHERE TO DINE

GRIZZLY GRILL **Dinner:** $12-$22 **Phone:** 530/836-1300

American

Location: Center. 250 Bonta St 96103. **Hours:** Open 2/1-1/1; 5:30 pm-9 pm. Closed: 11/25, 12/25. **Reservations:** suggested. **Features:** Early bird specials. Casual dress; cocktails. **Parking:** street. **Cards:** MC, VI.

BODEGA BAY —*See Wine Country p. 764.*

BOULDER CREEK pop. 4,081

WHERE TO STAY

MERRYBROOK LODGE **Phone:** 831/338-6813

Cottage

All Year 1P: $80-$130 2P: $90-$150 XP: $15

Location: Just n on SR 236. 13420 Big Basin Way 95006 (PO Box 845). **Facility:** Smoke free premises. 9 cottages. 1 story, exterior corridors. *Bath:* shower only. **Parking:** on-site. **Terms:** 2-3 night minimum stay - weekends, 15 day cancellation notice. **Cards:** MC, VI.

BRENTWOOD pop. 23,302

WHERE TO STAY

HOLIDAY INN EXPRESS Book at aaa.com **Phone:** (925)634-6400

Small-scale Hotel

All Year 1P: $109-$129 2P: $109-$129 XP: $10 F19

Location: Just s of Balfour Rd. 8820 Brentwood Blvd 94513. Fax: 925/634-5700. **Facility:** 50 one-bedroom standard units, some with whirlpools. 2 stories (no elevator), interior corridors. **Parking:** on-site. **Terms:** cancellation fee imposed, [ECP] meal plan available. **Amenities:** video games (fee), dual phone lines, voice mail, irons, hair dryers. **Pool(s):** small outdoor. **Leisure Activities:** exercise room. **Business Services:** meeting rooms. **Cards:** AX, CB, DC, DS, JC, MC, VI. **Special Amenities: free continental breakfast and free local telephone calls.** *(See color ad p 260)*

SOME UNITS

BRIDGEPORT

WHERE TO STAY

BEST WESTERN RUBY INN Book at aaa.com **Phone:** (760)932-7241

Motel

4/23-10/31 [CP]	1P: $95-$150	2P: $105-$150	XP: $10	F12
11/1-1/31 [CP]	1P: $95-$125	2P: $105-$125	XP: $10	F12
2/1-4/22 [CP]	1P: $80-$125	2P: $90-$125	XP: $10	F12

Location: On US 395; center. 333 Main St 93517 (PO Box 475). Fax: 760/932-7531. **Facility:** Designated smoking area. 30 units. 29 one-bedroom standard units. 1 one-bedroom suite. 1-2 stories, exterior corridors. **Parking:** on-site. **Terms:** office hours 7:30 am-10:30 pm, small pets only. **Amenities:** irons, hair dryers. **Leisure Activities:** whirlpool, fishing cleaning & freezing facilities. **Guest Services:** sundries. **Business Services:** fax (fee). **Cards:** AX, CB, DC, DS, MC, VI. **Special Amenities: free continental breakfast and early check-in/late check-out.**

THE CAIN HOUSE **Phone:** (760)932-7040

Bed & Breakfast

4/25-10/30 1P: $100-$145 2P: $100-$145

Location: On US 395; center. 340 Main St 93517 (PO Box 428). Fax: 760/932-7811. **Facility:** This vintage home designed in the Western style has been decorated with an informal elegance. Smoke free premises. 7 one-bedroom standard units. 2 stories (no elevator), interior corridors. **Parking:** on-site. **Terms:** open 4/25-10/30, 3 day cancellation notice, [BP] meal plan available. **Amenities:** hair dryers. *Some:* irons. **Guest Services:** complimentary evening beverages. **Business Services:** fax (fee). **Cards:** AX, DS, MC, VI. **Special Amenities: free full breakfast and preferred room (subject to availability with advanced reservations).**

SOME UNITS

REDWOOD MOTEL **Phone:** (760)932-7060

Motel

6/18-9/7	1P: $67-$106	2P: $73-$149	XP: $10	D10
9/8-10/31	1P: $59-$94	2P: $66-$139	XP: $5	D10
4/1-6/17 & 11/1-1/3	1P: $50-$79	2P: $56-$99	XP: $5	D10

Location: On US 395; at the north side of town. 425 Main St 93517 (PO Box 674). **Facility:** 19 one-bedroom standard units. 1 story, exterior corridors. *Bath:* combo or shower only. **Parking:** on-site. **Terms:** open 4/1-1/3, office hours 8:30 am-midnight, pets ($5 fee, with prior approval). **Amenities:** *Some:* irons, hair dryers. **Leisure Activities:** fish cleaning & freezing facilities. **Business Services:** fax (fee). **Cards:** AX, DC, DS, MC, VI. **Special Amenities: free local telephone calls and early check-in/late check-out.**

SOME UNITS

FEE

SILVER MAPLE INN **Phone:** 760/932-7383

Motel

4/25-11/15 1P: $70-$85 2P: $75-$95 XP: $10

Location: On US 395; center. 310 Main St 93517 (PO Box 327). Fax: 760/932-7811. **Facility:** 20 one-bedroom standard units. 1 story, exterior corridors. *Bath:* combo or shower only. **Parking:** on-site. **Terms:** open 4/25-11/15, office hours 10 am-10 pm, 3 day cancellation notice-fee imposed. **Amenities:** irons. *Some:* hair dryers. **Leisure Activities:** fish cleaning & freezing facilities. **Cards:** AX, DS, MC, VI. **Special Amenities: free local telephone calls and preferred room (subject to availability with advanced reservations).**

SOME UNITS

WALKER RIVER LODGE **Phone:** 760/932-7021

Motel

4/1-11/15 [CP]	1P: $75-$135	2P: $85-$145	XP: $10
2/1-3/31 & 11/16-1/31 [CP]	1P: $50-$110	2P: $55-$125	XP: $10

Location: US 395; at south end of town. 100 Main St 93517 (PO Box 717). Fax: 760/932-7914. **Facility:** 36 units. 30 one-bedroom standard units. 3 one- and 3 two-bedroom suites ($120-$350), some with kitchens. 1-2 stories, exterior corridors. **Parking:** on-site. **Terms:** office hours 8 am-10 pm, cancellation fee imposed. **Amenities:** video library. *Some:* irons, hair dryers. **Pool(s):** outdoor. **Leisure Activities:** whirlpool, fishing, fish cleaning & freezing facilities, barbecue pits, picnic tables. **Guest Services:** gift shop. **Business Services:** fax (fee). **Cards:** AX, CB, DC, DS, MC, VI. **Special Amenities: free continental breakfast and free local telephone calls.**

SOME UNITS

FEE

WHERE TO DINE

RESTAURANT 1881 Historic **Dinner:** $15-$40 **Phone:** 760/932-1918

Continental

Location: On US 395; at the center of town. 362 Main St 93517. **Hours:** Open 4/15-1/1; 5:30 pm-9 pm, Fri & Sat-10 pm. **Features:** Built in 1881, the beautifully restored home provides an uncommon dining experience. Antique furnishings and chandeliers lend to an elegant atmosphere. The chef goes to great lengths to satisfy a wide range of tastes. Smoked sirloin with asparagus roulade is a great appetizer, and leek and asparagus soup is excellent. Osso buco, prepared from braised buffalo short ribs and homemade meatloaf, is a local favorite. Hummingbird cake is a treat. Casual dress; beer & wine only. **Parking:** street. **Cards:** AX, DS, MC, VI.

BRISBANE *—See San Francisco p. 660.*

BURLINGAME *—See San Francisco p. 661.*

BURNEY pop. 3,217

WHERE TO STAY

BURNEY MOTEL **Phone:** 530/335-4500

Motel

All Year 1P: $39-$69 2P: $45-$79 XP: $10

Location: 0.8 mi e on SR 299. 37448 Main St 96013. **Facility:** 10 units. 5 one- and 5 two-bedroom standard units, some with kitchens. 1 story, exterior corridors. *Bath:* combo or shower only. **Parking:** on-site. **Terms:** age restrictions may apply, 3 day cancellation notice-fee imposed, pets ($7 extra charge). **Amenities:** *Some:* irons, hair dryers. **Leisure Activities:** putting green, picnic area, horseshoes. **Cards:** AX, DS, MC, VI. **Special Amenities: free local telephone calls.**

SOME UNITS

FEE

CHARM MOTEL **Phone:** (530)335-2254

Motel

4/30-11/15 [CP]	1P: $59-$75	2P: $66-$82	XP: $7	D12
2/1-4/29 & 11/16-1/31 [CP]	1P: $39-$53	2P: $46-$58	XP: $5	D12

Location: 0.8 mi e on SR 299. 37363 Main St 96013. Fax: 530/335-4147. **Facility:** 42 units. 41 one- and 1 two-bedroom standard units, some with kitchens. 2 stories (no elevator), exterior corridors. *Bath:* combo or shower only. **Parking:** on-site. **Terms:** office hours 7 am-10 pm, age restrictions may apply, 3 day cancellation notice, weekly rates available, package plans, pets ($10 extra charge, with prior approval). **Amenities:** *Some:* irons, hair dryers. **Leisure Activities:** pool privileges, fish cleaning facility, barbecue, picnic area. **Business Services:** fax. **Cards:** AX, CB, DC, DS, JC, MC, VI. **Special Amenities: free continental breakfast and free local telephone calls.**

SOME UNITS

FEE

GREEN GABLES MOTEL **Phone:** (530)335-2264

Motel

4/30-11/15 [CP]	1P: $59-$75	2P: $66-$82	XP: $7	D12
2/1-4/29 & 11/16-1/31 [CP]	1P: $39-$53	2P: $46-$58	XP: $5	D12

Location: 0.8 mi e on SR 299. 37385 Main St 96013. Fax: 530/335-5037. **Facility:** Smoke free premises. 26 units. 24 one-bedroom standard units, some with kitchens. 2 two-bedroom suites with kitchens. 1 story, exterior corridors. *Bath:* combo or shower only. **Parking:** on-site. **Terms:** age restrictions may apply, 3 day cancellation notice, weekly rates available, package plans, small pets only ($5 extra charge, with prior approval). **Amenities:** *Some:* irons, hair dryers. **Pool(s):** heated outdoor. **Leisure Activities:** fish cleaning facility, barbecue, picnic area. **Business Services:** fax. **Cards:** AX, CB, DC, DS, JC, MC, VI. **Special Amenities: free continental breakfast and free local telephone calls.** *(See color ad below)*

SOME UNITS

FEE

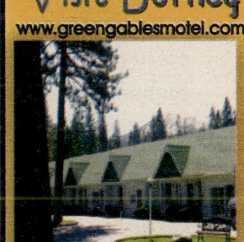

SHASTA PINES MOTEL **Phone:** 530/335-2201

AAA SAVE

Motel

All Year 1P: $42-$85 2P: $46-$95 XP: $7

Location: 0.8 mi e on SR 299. 37386 Main St 96013. Fax: 530/335-2202. **Facility:** 30 one-bedroom standard units, some with efficiencies. 1-2 stories (no elevator), exterior corridors. *Bath:* combo or shower only. **Parking:** on-site. **Terms:** age restrictions may apply, 5 day cancellation notice-fee imposed, pets ($7 extra charge, in limited units). **Amenities:** *Some:* irons, hair dryers. **Pool(s):** heated outdoor. **Leisure Activities:** sauna, whirlpool, barbecue, picnic area. **Cards:** AX, DC, DS, MC, VI. **Special Amenities: free local telephone calls.**

SOME UNITS

FEE

WHERE TO DINE

HUNGRY MOOSE **Lunch:** $6-$8 **Dinner:** $8-$11 **Phone:** 530/335-5152

Traditional American

Location: I-5, exit SR 299 E, Center. 37453 Hwy 299 E 96013. **Hours:** 5 am-11 pm. **Features:** The diner-type restaurant, owned by same family for years, features a seniors' menu, a children's menu and a little something for everyone. Casual dress. **Parking:** on-site. **Cards:** DS, MC, VI.

BUTTONWILLOW pop. 1,266

WHERE TO STAY

SUPER 8 MOTEL **Phone:** 661/764-5117

Motel

All Year 1P: $37-$39 2P: $42-$49 XP: $5 F12

Location: I-5, exit SR 58. 20681 Tracy Ave 93206 (PO Box 921). Fax: 661/764-6676. **Facility:** 86 one-bedroom standard units. 2 stories, exterior corridors. *Bath:* combo or shower only. **Parking:** on-site. **Terms:** [CP] meal plan available. **Amenities:** *Some:* irons, hair dryers. **Pool(s):** outdoor. **Leisure Activities:** whirlpool. **Guest Services:** coin laundry. **Business Services:** fax (fee). **Cards:** AX, DC, DS, MC, VI.

SOME UNITS

ASK

FEE

CALISTOGA —See Wine Country p. 766.

CAMBRIA pop. 6,232

WHERE TO STAY

BEST WESTERN FIRESIDE INN BY THE SEA *Book at aaa.com* **Phone:** (805)927-8661

AAA SAVE

Motel

6/18-9/4 [ECP]	1P: $169-$269	2P: $169-$269	XP: $10	F12
5/2-6/17 [ECP]	1P: $119-$249	2P: $119-$249	XP: $10	F12
2/1-5/1 & 9/5-1/31 [ECP]	1P: $99-$249	2P: $99-$249	XP: $10	F12

Location: SR 1, exit Moonstone Beach Dr, just w, then 0.5 mi s. 6700 Moonstone Beach Dr 93428. Fax: 805/927-8584. **Facility:** Smoke free premises. 46 one-bedroom standard units, some with whirlpools. 1 story, interior/exterior corridors. **Parking:** on-site. **Terms:** office hours 7 am-11 pm, 2 night minimum stay - weekends. **Amenities:** safes (fee), irons, hair dryers. **Pool(s):** heated outdoor. **Leisure Activities:** whirlpool. **Cards:** AX, CB, DC, MC, VI. *(See color ad below)*

BLUEBIRD MOTEL **Phone:** 805/927-4634

AAA SAVE

Motel

4/15-9/30	1P: $70-$180	2P: $70-$180	XP: $6	F
2/1-4/14 & 10/1-1/31	1P: $48-$180	2P: $48-$180	XP: $6	F

Location: SR 1, exit Main St northbound, 1.9 mi ne; exit Cambria Dr southbound, 0.5 mi se. Located in the East Village area. 1880 Main St 93428. Fax: 805/927-5215. **Facility:** 37 units. 35 one-bedroom standard units. 2 one-bedroom suites. 1-2 stories (no elevator), exterior corridors. *Bath:* combo or shower only. **Parking:** on-site. **Terms:** office hours 7:30 am-10 pm, weekly rates available, [CP] meal plan available, no pets allowed (owner's pet on premises). **Amenities:** irons, hair dryers. **Cards:** AX, CB, DC, DS, JC, MC, VI. **Special Amenities: free continental breakfast and free local telephone calls.**

SOME UNITS

VCR

BLUE WHALE INN BED & BREAKFAST — **Phone:** 805/927-4647

AAA SAVE — Bed & Breakfast

	1P	2P	XP	
All Year	1P: $190-$310	2P: $190-$310	XP: $40	

Location: SR 1, exit Moonstone Beach Dr, just w, then 0.5 mi s. 6736 Moonstone Beach Dr 93428. Fax: 805/927-3852. **Facility:** From the sitting room, guests can watch sunsets over the ocean and glimpse the occasional dolphin or whale; cozy guest rooms include gas fireplaces. Smoke free premises. 6 one-bedroom standard units with whirlpools. 1 story, exterior corridors. **Parking:** on-site. **Terms:** 10 day cancellation notice-fee imposed, [BP] meal plan available. **Amenities:** DVD players, irons, hair dryers. *Some:* CD players. **Cards:** MC, VI.

BURTON INN — **Phone:** 805/927-5125

AAA SAVE — Small-scale Hotel

	1P	2P	XP	
6/1-9/30 [CP]	1P: $129-$289	2P: $139-$299	XP: $10	F12
10/1-1/31 [CP]	1P: $109-$239	2P: $119-$249	XP: $10	F12
2/1-5/31 [CP]	1P: $89-$119	2P: $99-$229	XP: $10	F12

Location: SR 1, exit Burton Dr, 1 mi ne. Located in the East Village area. 4022 Burton Dr 93428. Fax: 805/927-9637. **Facility:** Smoke free premises. 11 units. 6 one-bedroom standard units. 4 one- and 1 two-bedroom suites ($200-$399), some with kitchens. 2 stories (no elevator), interior/exterior corridors. **Parking:** on-site. **Terms:** office hours 8 am-10 pm, 2 night minimum stay - weekends, 7 day cancellation notice, no pets allowed (owner's pet on premises). **Amenities:** video library, voice mail, hair dryers. **Cards:** AX, DS, MC, VI. **Special Amenities: free continental breakfast and free local telephone calls.**

CAMBRIA LANDING ON MOONSTONE BEACH — **Phone:** (805)927-1619

AAA SAVE — Motel

	1P	2P	XP	
All Year [CP]	1P: $95-$350	2P: $95-$350	XP: $20	

Location: SR 1, exit Moonstone Beach Dr, just w, then 0.6 mi s. 6530 Moonstone Beach Dr 93428. Fax: 805/927-9850. **Facility:** 26 one-bedroom standard units, some with whirlpools. 1-2 stories (no elevator), interior/exterior corridors. **Parking:** on-site. **Terms:** office hours 9 am-10 pm, 7 day cancellation notice. **Amenities:** video library, hair dryers. *Some:* irons. **Leisure Activities:** whirlpools. **Cards:** MC, VI. **Special Amenities: free continental breakfast and free newspaper.**

SOME UNITS

CAMBRIA SHORES INN — **Phone:** 805/927-8644

Motel

	1P	2P	XP	
6/20-9/1 [CP]	1P: $150-$180	2P: $150-$180	XP: $10	F12
9/2-11/1 [CP]	1P: $125-$180	2P: $125-$180	XP: $10	F12
2/1-6/19 & 11/2-1/31 [CP]	1P: $105-$180	2P: $105-$180	XP: $10	F12

Location: SR 1, exit Moonstone Beach Dr, just w, then 0.8 mi s. 6276 Moonstone Beach Dr 93428. Fax: 805/927-4070. **Facility:** Smoke free premises. 24 one-bedroom standard units. 1 story, exterior corridors. *Bath:* combo or shower only. **Parking:** on-site. **Terms:** office hours 7:30 am-9 pm, 2 night minimum stay - weekends, 7 day cancellation notice-fee imposed, pets ($10 extra charge). **Amenities:** video library, irons, hair dryers. **Guest Services:** complimentary evening beverages. **Cards:** AX, DS, MC, VI. ***(See color ad below)***

FEE

CAPTAIN'S COVE INN — **Phone:** 805/927-8581

AAA SAVE — Motel

	1P	2P	XP	
6/15-9/15 [CP]	1P: $155-$250	2P: $155-$250	XP: $10	F
2/1-6/14 & 9/16-1/31 [CP]	1P: $95-$225	2P: $95-$225	XP: $10	F

Location: SR 1, exit Moonstone Beach Dr, just w, then 0.7 mi s. 6454 Moonstone Beach Dr 93428. Fax: 805/927-8581. **Facility:** Smoke free premises. 5 one-bedroom standard units, some with whirlpools. 1 story, exterior corridors. **Parking:** on-site. **Terms:** office hours 9 am-9 pm, 2 night minimum stay - seasonal & weekends, 3 day cancellation notice-fee imposed. **Amenities:** video library (fee), irons, hair dryers. **Cards:** MC, VI. **Special Amenities: free local telephone calls.**

CASTLE INN BY THE SEA — **Phone:** 805/927-8605

AAA SAVE — Motel

	1P	2P	XP	
All Year		2P: $100-$160	XP: $10	F8

Location: SR 1, exit Moonstone Beach Dr, just w, then 0.5 mi s. 6620 Moonstone Beach Dr 93428. Fax: 805/927-3179. **Facility:** Smoke free premises. 31 one-bedroom standard units. 2 stories (no elevator), exterior corridors. *Bath:* combo or shower only. **Parking:** on-site. **Terms:** office hours 8 am-10 pm, 2-3 night minimum stay - some weekends, 7 day cancellation notice-fee imposed, [CP] meal plan available. **Pool(s):** heated outdoor. **Leisure Activities:** whirlpool. **Cards:** AX, DS, MC, VI. **Special Amenities: free continental breakfast.**

(See color ad p 294)

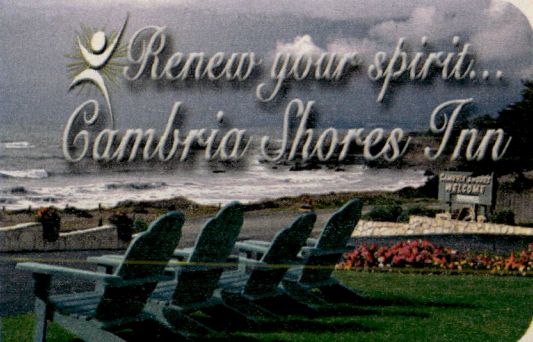

FOG CATCHER INN *Book at aaa.com* **Phone:** (805)927-1400

Motel

3/1-8/31 [ECP]	1P: $199-$309	2P: $199-$309	XP: $10	F5
9/1-10/31 [ECP]	1P: $169-$289	2P: $169-$289	XP: $10	F5
2/1-2/29 & 11/1-1/31 [ECP]	1P: $119-$159	2P: $119-$159	XP: $10	F5

Location: SR 1, exit Moonstone Beach Dr, just w, then 0.7 mi s. 6400 Moonstone Beach Dr 93428. Fax: 805/927-0204. **Facility:** Smoke free premises. 60 units. 57 one-bedroom standard units. 2 one- and 1 two-bedroom suites. 1-2 stories (no elevator), exterior corridors. **Parking:** on-site. **Terms:** 3 night minimum stay - with Saturday stayover, 3 day cancellation notice-fee imposed, package plans - excluding weekends, pets ($25 fee, in designated units). **Amenities:** voice mail, honor bars, irons, hair dryers. **Pool(s):** heated outdoor. **Leisure Activities:** whirlpool. **Cards:** AX, CB, DC, DS, JC, MC, VI. ***(See color ad p 295)***

ASK DATA PORT FEE

THE J PATRICK HOUSE BED AND BREAKFAST INN **Phone:** (805)927-3812

AAA SAVE

Bed & Breakfast

All Year [BP]	1P: $155-$205	2P: $155-$205

Location: SR 1, exit Burton Dr, 0.5 mi ne. 2990 Burton Dr 93428. Fax: 805/927-6759. **Facility:** On grounds dotted with tall pines and colorful flower beds, this B&B offers guest rooms with fireplaces in a main log home and a rear carriage house. Smoke free premises. 8 one-bedroom standard units. 2 stories (no elevator), interior corridors. *Bath:* combo or shower only. **Parking:** on-site. **Terms:** 2-3 night minimum stay - weekends, 10 day cancellation notice-fee imposed. **Amenities:** hair dryers. *Some:* CD players, irons. **Guest Services:** gift shop, complimentary evening beverages. **Cards:** DS, MC, VI. **Special Amenities: free local telephone calls.**

LITTLE SUR INN **Phone:** (805)927-1329

Motel

All Year	1P: $130-$250	2P: $130-$250	XP: $10	F6

Location: SR 1, exit Moonstone Beach Dr, just w, then 1 mi s. 6190 Moonstone Beach Dr 93428. Fax: 805/927-1581. **Facility:** Smoke free premises. 17 one-bedroom standard units, some with whirlpools. 1-2 stories (no elevator), exterior corridors. **Parking:** on-site. **Terms:** office hours 8 am-10 pm, 3 day cancellation notice, [ECP] meal plan available. **Amenities:** video library (fee), hair dryers. **Guest Services:** complimentary evening beverages. **Cards:** AX, DS, MC, VI.

ASK VCR DATA PORT

MARINERS INN BY THE SEA **Phone:** (805)927-4624

AAA SAVE

Motel

All Year [CP]	1P: $79-$239	2P: $79-$239	XP: $15	F9

Location: SR 1, exit Moonstone Beach Dr, just w, then 1 mi s. 6180 Moonstone Beach Dr 93428. Fax: 805/927-3425. **Facility:** Smoke free premises. 26 one-bedroom standard units, some with whirlpools. 1 story, exterior corridors. **Parking:** on-site. **Terms:** office hours 8 am-10 pm, 5 day cancellation notice-fee imposed, pets ($15 fee, in designated units). **Amenities:** *Some:* hair dryers. **Leisure Activities:** whirlpool, sun deck. **Cards:** AX, DC, MC, VI. **Special Amenities: free continental breakfast.**

SOME UNITS

FEE

MOONSTONE INN **Phone:** (805)927-4815

Motel

6/2-10/31 [CP]	1P: $129-$169	2P: $129-$169	XP: $20 F
2/1-6/1 & 11/1-1/31 [CP]	1P: $119-$159	2P: $119-$159	XP: $10 F

Location: SR 1, exit Moonstone Beach Dr, just w, then 1.2 mi s. 5860 Moonstone Beach Dr 93428. Fax: 805/927-5790. **Facility:** Smoke free premises. 10 one-bedroom standard units. 1-2 stories (no elevator), exterior corridors. *Bath:* combo or shower only. **Parking:** on-site. **Terms:** 2 night minimum stay - weekends, [ECP] meal plan available. **Amenities:** video library, hair dryers. **Leisure Activities:** whirlpool. **Cards:** AX, DC, MC, VI.

(See color ad p 294)

MOONSTONE LANDING **Phone:** (805)927-0012

Motel

All Year		2P: $100-$250	XP: $10 F

Location: SR 1, exit Moonstone Beach Dr, just w, then 0.8 mi s. 6240 Moonstone Beach Dr 93428. Fax: 805/927-0014. **Facility:** Smoke free premises. 29 one-bedroom standard units, some with whirlpools. 2 stories (no elevator), interior corridors. **Parking:** on-site. **Terms:** office hours 8 am-10 pm, 3 day cancellation notice, [ECP] meal plan available. **Amenities:** video library, DVD players, hair dryers. **Leisure Activities:** whirlpool. **Guest Services:** complimentary evening beverages. **Cards:** AX, DC, DS, MC, VI.

OLALLIEBERRY INN **Phone:** (805)927-3222

Historic Bed & Breakfast

5/28-9/6	1P: $135-$240	2P: $130-$240	XP: $25
9/7-1/31	1P: $120-$240	2P: $120-$240	XP: $25
2/1-5/27	1P: $120-$230	2P: $120-$230	XP: $25

Location: SR 1, exit Main St northbound, 1.4 mi nw; exit Cambria Dr southbound, 1 mi se. Located in the East Village area. 2476 Main St 93428. Fax: 805/927-0202. **Facility:** Built as a home in 1873, the inn is one of the oldest buildings in Cambria; guest rooms, in the main house and an outbuilding, have individual decor. Smoke free premises. 9 one-bedroom standard units. 2 stories (no elevator), interior/exterior corridors. *Bath:* combo, shower or tub only. **Parking:** on-site. **Terms:** 2 night minimum stay - weekends, 11 day cancellation notice-fee imposed, [BP] meal plan available, package plans - seasonal. **Amenities:** hair dryers. **Leisure Activities:** Fee: massage. **Guest Services:** complimentary evening beverages. **Cards:** AX, MC, VI.

PELICAN SUITES ***Book at aaa.com*** **Phone:** (805)927-1500

Small-scale Hotel

All Year	1P: $179-$329	2P: $179-$329	XP: $10

Location: SR 1, exit Moonstone Beach Dr, just w, then 0.8 mi s. 6316 Moonstone Beach Dr 93428. Fax: 805/927-0218. **Facility:** Reminiscent of a European inn, the property offers guest rooms with decorator fabrics, period furniture, down comforters and upscale accessories. Smoke free premises. 26 units. 25 one-bedroom standard units, some with whirlpools. 1 two-bedroom suite ($389-$479) with kitchen and whirlpool. 2 stories (no elevator), interior corridors. **Parking:** on-site. **Terms:** 2-3 night minimum stay - weekends & seasonal, 3 day cancellation notice-fee imposed, [BP] meal plan available. **Amenities:** video library, irons, hair dryers. **Pool(s):** heated outdoor. **Guest Services:** complimentary evening beverages. **Cards:** AX, DC, DS, MC, VI. *(See color ad below)*

SAN SIMEON PINES SEASIDE RESORT **Phone:** 805/927-4648

Motel

All Year	1P: $96	2P: $150

Location: SR 1, exit Moonstone Beach Dr, just w, then just s. 7200 Moonstone Beach Dr 93428. **Facility:** Smoke free premises. 58 one-bedroom standard units. 1-2 stories, exterior corridors. *Bath:* combo or shower only. **Parking:** on-site. **Terms:** office hours 7:30 am-10 pm, 3 day cancellation notice, [CP] meal plan available. **Amenities:** safes. **Pool(s):** heated outdoor. **Leisure Activities:** golf-9 holes, playground, shuffleboard. **Business Services:** meeting rooms. **Cards:** AX, MC, VI. *(See color ad p 703)*

SEA OTTER INN *Book at aaa.com* **Phone:** (805)927-5888

Motel

7/1-8/31	1P: $169-$259	2P: $169-$259	XP: $10	F5
4/1-6/30 & 9/1-1/31	1P: $119-$229	2P: $119-$229	XP: $10	F5
2/1-3/31	1P: $99-$229	2P: $99-$229	XP: $10	F5

Location: SR 1, exit Moonstone Beach Dr, just w, then 0.5 mi s. 6656 Moonstone Beach Dr 93428. Fax: 805/927-0204. **Facility:** Smoke free premises. 25 units. 23 one-bedroom standard units, some with whirlpools. 2 one-bedroom suites with whirlpools. 1 story, exterior corridors. **Parking:** on-site. **Terms:** office hours 7:30 am-8 pm, 2 night minimum stay - with Saturday stayover, 3 day cancellation notice-fee imposed, pets ($25 extra charge, in designated units). **Amenities:** video library (fee), hair dryers. **Pool(s):** heated outdoor. **Leisure Activities:** whirlpool. **Cards:** AX, DC, DS, MC, VI. ***(See color ad p 295)***

FEE

THE SQUIBB HOUSE BED & BREAKFAST **Phone:** (805)927-9600

Historic Bed & Breakfast

All Year [CP] 1P: $105-$175 2P: $105-$175

Location: SR 1, exit Burton Dr, 1 mi ne. Located in the East Village area. 4063 Burton Dr 93428. Fax: 805/927-9606. **Facility:** Built as a residence in 1877, the Squibb House is in town among shops and restaurants; rooms vary from small to average-size, with simple decor. Smoke free premises. 5 one-bedroom standard units. 2 stories (no elevator), interior corridors. *Bath:* combo or shower only. **Parking:** on-site. **Terms:** 2 night minimum stay - weekends, 7 day cancellation notice-fee imposed. **Cards:** AX, MC, VI.

WHITE WATER INN **Phone:** 805/927-1066

Motel

All Year 1P: $90-$180 2P: $90-$180 XP: $10

Location: SR 1, exit Moonstone Beach Dr, just w, then 0.4 mi s. 6790 Moonstone Beach Dr 93428. Fax: 805/927-0921. **Facility:** Smoke free premises. 17 one-bedroom standard units, some with whirlpools. 1 story, exterior corridors. **Parking:** on-site. **Terms:** 2 night minimum stay - weekends, 7 day cancellation notice-fee imposed, [CP] meal plan available, package plans - seasonal. **Amenities:** video library, irons, hair dryers. *Some:* DVD players. **Cards:** DS, MC, VI. **Special Amenities: free continental breakfast and free local telephone calls.**

WHERE TO DINE

BISTRO SOLE **Lunch:** $8-$10 **Dinner:** $9-$22 **Phone:** 805/927-0887

California

Location: SR 1, exit Main St northbound, 1.9 mi ne; exit Cambria Dr southbound, 0.5 mi se. 1980 Main St 93428. **Hours:** 11 am-2:30 & 5-9 pm; to 10 pm in season. Closed: 11/25, 12/25. **Reservations:** required. **Features:** Contemporary dining is the mode in the charming cottage or on the large garden patio. The menu features a nice variety of seafood, pasta, steak, roasted duck and rack of lamb. Casual dress; beer & wine only. **Parking:** on-site. **Cards:** MC, VI.

THE BRAMBLES DINNER HOUSE **Lunch:** $11-$25 **Dinner:** $11-$25 **Phone:** 805/927-4716

American

Location: SR 1, exit Burton Dr, 1 mi ne. 4005 Burton Dr 93428. **Hours:** 4 pm-9:30 pm, Sat-10 pm, Sun 9:30 am-2 & 4-9:30 pm. **Reservations:** suggested. **Features:** This restaurant has long been popular for its prime rib, but there is a large selection of well-prepared meat, fish and poultry dishes to choose from as well. Centrally located in the East Village area, it was originally built as a mill 100 years ago with later additions and renovations when it was opened as a restaurant. Casual dress; cocktails. **Parking:** on-site. **Cards:** AX, CB, DC, DS, MC, VI.

HARMONY PASTA FACTORY **Lunch:** $5-$11 **Dinner:** $11-$20 **Phone:** 805/927-5882

Italian

Location: Between East and West Villages; just off Main St; in Cambria Village Square. 1316 Tamson Dr 93428. **Hours:** 11:30 am-9 pm. Closed: 11/25, 12/25. **Reservations:** accepted. **Features:** On a hill with a nice view of the pines, the restaurant offers patrons a good selection of pasta entrees and friendly service. Casual dress; cocktails. **Parking:** on-site. **Cards:** AX, MC, VI.

LINN'S **Lunch:** $8-$12 **Dinner:** $9-$14 **Phone:** 805/927-0371

American

Location: SR 1, exit Main St northbound, 1.5 mi nw; exit Cambria Dr southound, 0.7 mi se. 2277 Main St 93428. **Hours:** 8 am-10 pm; 7:30 am-10 pm in summer; 8 am-9:30 pm weekends in winter. Closed: 12/25. **Features:** The restaurant is located in an old brick building in the East Village section of Cambria. The menu includes a good selection of "comfort food" including chicken and beef, pot pies, meat loaf and home made pastries, jams and jellies. You may want to visit the bakery and gift shop. Casual dress; beer & wine only. **Parking:** on-site. **Cards:** AX, DS, MC, VI.

MOONSTONE BEACH BAR & GRILL **Lunch:** $8-$13 **Dinner:** $15-$32 **Phone:** 805/927-3859

American

Location: SR 1, exit Moonstone Beach Dr, just w, then 0.6 mi s. 6550 Moonstone Beach Dr 93428. **Hours:** 8 am-9 pm, Sun from 10 am. Closed: 12/25. **Reservations:** suggested. **Features:** Ocean views are lovely from the attractive dining room and the cozy patio, where smoking is permitted. Casual dress; cocktails. **Parking:** on-site. **Cards:** MC, VI.

MUSTACHE PETE'S ITALIAN EATERY **Lunch:** $6-$8 **Dinner:** $11-$21 **Phone:** 805/927-8589

Italian

Location: SR 1, exit Burton Dr, 1 mi ne. 4090 Burton Dr 93428. **Hours:** 11 am-10 pm. Closed: 12/25. **Features:** This is a casual and friendly Italian restaurant located in the East Village area. The varieties of pizza available are limited only by your imagination. You may want to dine outside on the patio if you enjoy people watching. Casual dress; cocktails. **Parking:** on-site. **Cards:** AX, CB, DC, DS, MC, VI.

ROBIN'S — **Lunch:** $7-$11 — **Dinner:** $10-$20 — **Phone:** 805/927-5007

International

Location: SR 1, exit Burton Dr, 1 mi ne. 4095 Burton Dr 93428. **Hours:** 11 am-9 pm. Closed: 11/25, 12/25. **Reservations:** suggested. **Features:** Diners unwind in the charming dining room or on the semi-enclosed patio. Among the ethnic cuisines represented on the diverse menu are Mexican, Italian, Indian, Thai and Chinese. Casual dress; beer & wine only. **Parking:** on-site. **Cards:** MC, VI.

SEA CHEST RESTAURANT & OYSTER BAR — **Dinner:** $14-$20 — **Phone:** 805/927-4514

Seafood

Location: SR 1, exit Moonstone Beach Dr, just w, then 0.8 mi s. 6216 Moonstone Beach Dr 93428. **Hours:** Open 2/1-11/30 & 12/27-1/31; 5:30 pm-9 pm, Fri & Sat-9:30 pm. Closed: Tues. **Features:** A California coast atmosphere punctuates the seafood restaurant. Reservations and credit cards are not accepted. Casual dress; beer & wine only. **Parking:** on-site.

THE SOW'S EAR CAFE — **Dinner:** $17-$25 — **Phone:** 805/927-4865

California

Location: SR 1, exit Main St northbound, 1.5 mi nw; exit Cambria Dr southbound, 0.7 mi se. 2248 Main St 93428. **Hours:** 5 pm-9 pm, Fri & Sat-9:30 pm. Closed: 12/24, 12/25. **Reservations:** suggested. **Features:** The cozy, comfortable restaurant's menu lists a nice selection of fresh seafood, baby back ribs and chicken. Bread and desserts are made on the premises. Casual dress; beer & wine only. **Parking:** street. **Cards:** DS, MC, VI.

CAMERON PARK pop. 14,549

WHERE TO STAY

BEST WESTERN CAMERON PARK INN — Book at aaa.com — **Phone:** (530)677-2203

Motel

All Year [ECP] — 1P: $69-$149 — 2P: $79-$149 — XP: $10 — F16

Location: 12 mi w of Placerville on US 50, exit Cameron Park Dr. 3361 Coach Ln 95682. Fax: 530/676-1422. **Facility:** 63 one-bedroom standard units, some with kitchens. 2 stories, exterior corridors. **Parking:** on-site. **Terms:** small pets only. **Amenities:** irons, hair dryers. **Pool(s):** outdoor. **Leisure Activities:** whirlpool, exercise room. **Guest Services:** coin laundry. **Business Services:** meeting rooms. **Cards:** AX, DC, DS, JC, MC, VI.

SOME UNITS

SUPER 8 MOTEL — Book at aaa.com — **Phone:** 530/677-7177

Motel

Property failed to provide current rates

Location: 12 mi w of Placerville on US 50, exit Cameron Park Dr. 3444 Coach Ln 95682. Fax: 530/672-1980. **Facility:** 60 one-bedroom standard units. 2 stories, interior corridors. **Parking:** on-site. **Pool(s):** small outdoor. **Leisure Activities:** whirlpool. **Guest Services:** coin laundry. **Business Services:** meeting rooms.

SOME UNITS

FEE

CAMINO

WHERE TO STAY

CAMINO HOTEL-SEVEN MILE HOUSE — **Phone:** (530)644-7740

Bed & Breakfast

All Year [BP] — 1P: $68-$98 — 2P: $68-$98 — XP: $10

Location: US 50, exit at Camino, just n. 4103 Carson Rd 95709 (PO Box 1197). Fax: 530/647-1416. **Facility:** 9 one-bedroom standard units. 2 stories, interior corridors. *Bath:* some shared or private, combo or shower only. **Parking:** on-site. **Terms:** 2 night minimum stay - weekends 9/1-1/31, 7 day cancellation notice, 9/1-1/31, package plans, small pets only. **Leisure Activities:** Fee: massage. **Guest Services:** TV in common area. **Cards:** AX, CB, DC, DS, MC, VI.

CAMPBELL pop. 38,138

WHERE TO STAY

BEST WESTERN BRISTOL HOTEL — Book at aaa.com — **Phone:** (408)559-3330

Small-scale Hotel

All Year — 1P: $119-$179 — 2P: $119-$179 — XP: $20 — F12

Location: SR 85, 0.5 mi n. 3341 South Bascom 95008. Fax: 408/559-3363. **Facility:** Smoke free premises. 47 one-bedroom standard units. 2 stories, interior corridors. **Parking:** on-site. **Terms:** [MAP] meal plan available. **Amenities:** high-speed Internet, dual phone lines, voice mail, irons, hair dryers. **Guest Services:** complimentary evening beverages: Mon-Fri, coin laundry. **Business Services:** business center. **Cards:** AX, DC, DS, MC, VI. **Special Amenities: free full breakfast and early check-in/late check-out.**

SOME UNITS

FEE

BEST WESTERN CARLYLE HOTEL — Book at aaa.com — **Phone:** (408)559-3600

Small-scale Hotel

All Year — 1P: $99-$129 — 2P: $99-$129 — XP: $15 — F12

Location: SR 17, exit Camden Ave E. 1300 Camden Ave 95008. Fax: 408/371-5721. **Facility:** Smoke free premises. 38 one-bedroom standard units, some with whirlpools. 3 stories, interior corridors. *Bath:* combo or shower only. **Parking:** on-site. **Terms:** [BP] meal plan available, package plans. **Amenities:** irons, hair dryers. **Guest Services:** complimentary laundry. **Cards:** AX, DC, DS, MC, VI. **Special Amenities: free full breakfast and early check-in/late check-out.**

CAMPBELL INN *Book at aaa.com* **Phone:** (408)374-4300

AAA SAVE — Motel

All Year 1P: $89-$229 2P: $89-$229 XP: $15 F12

Location: SR 17, exit Hamilton Ave E, 0.3 mi to Bascom Ave, 0.3 mi s, then 0.3 mi w. 675 E Campbell Ave 95008. Fax: 408/379-0695. **Facility:** 95 one-bedroom standard units, some with whirlpools. 2 stories, exterior corridors. **Parking:** on-site. **Terms:** [BP] meal plan available. **Amenities:** video library, dual phone lines, irons, hair dryers. **Pool(s):** heated outdoor. **Leisure Activities:** whirlpool, lighted tennis court, bicycles, jogging. **Guest Services:** complimentary evening beverages: Mon-Thurs, valet laundry. **Business Services:** meeting rooms. **Cards:** AX, DC, DS, MC, VI. **Special Amenities: free full breakfast and early check-in/late check-out.**

SOME UNITS

LARKSPUR LANDING *Book at aaa.com* **Phone:** (408)364-1514

AAA SAVE — Small-scale Hotel

All Year 1P: $129-$149 2P: $129-$149

Location: SR 17, exit Hamilton Ave, 1 mi w. 550 W Hamilton Ave 95008. Fax: 408/364-1600. **Facility:** 116 units. 81 one-bedroom standard units with kitchens. 35 one-bedroom suites with kitchens. 4 stories, interior corridors. *Bath:* combo or shower only. **Parking:** on-site. **Terms:** cancellation fee imposed, [CP] meal plan available. **Amenities:** video library, CD players, high-speed Internet, dual phone lines, voice mail, irons, hair dryers. **Leisure Activities:** whirlpool, exercise room. **Guest Services:** complimentary laundry. **Business Services:** business center. **Cards:** AX, DC, DS, JC, MC, VI. **Special Amenities: free local telephone calls and free newspaper.**

(See color ad below)

SOME UNITS

THE PRUNEYARD INN Book at aaa.com Phone: (408)559-4300

Small-scale Hotel

All Year [ECP] 1P: $155-$179 2P: $155-$179 XP: $10 F18

Location: SR 17, exit Hamilton Ave, 0.3 mi e, then s. Located adjacent to Pruneyard Shopping Center. 1995 S Bascom Ave 95008. Fax: 408/559-9919. **Facility:** 171 one-bedroom standard units, some with efficiencies and/or whirlpools. 3 stories, interior corridors. *Bath:* combo or shower only. **Parking:** on-site. **Amenities:** video library, DVD players, high-speed Internet (fee), dual phone lines, voice mail, irons, hair dryers. **Pool(s):** heated outdoor. **Leisure Activities:** whirlpool, bicycles, exercise room. **Guest Services:** valet laundry, airport transportation-San Jose International Airport. **Business Services:** meeting rooms, business center. **Cards:** AX, CB, DC, DS, JC, MC, VI. **Special Amenities: free local telephone calls and free newspaper.** *(See color ad p 299)*

SOME UNITS

RESIDENCE INN BY MARRIOTT-SAN JOSE Book at aaa.com Phone: (408)559-1551

Motel

All Year 1P: $149-$179

Location: SR 17, exit Camden Ave E, just n. 2761 S Bascom Ave 95008. Fax: 408/371-9808. **Facility:** 80 units. 60 one-bedroom standard units with kitchens. 20 two-bedroom suites with kitchens. 2 stories (no elevator), exterior corridors. **Parking:** on-site. **Terms:** [ECP] meal plan available, pets ($75 fee, $10 extra charge). **Amenities:** voice mail, irons, hair dryers. **Pool(s):** heated outdoor. **Leisure Activities:** whirlpool. **Guest Services:** coin laundry. **Cards:** AX, CB, DC, DS, JC, MC, VI.

SOME UNITS

FEE

CAPAY pop. 200

WHERE TO STAY

CAPAY VALLEY BED & BREAKFAST Phone: (530)796-3738

Bed & Breakfast

All Year [BP] 1P: $79-$155 2P: $79-$155 XP: $25 F14

Location: I-505, exit SR 16, 10 mi w. 15875 State Hwy 16 95607. **Facility:** With over 70 animals and 142 acres, guests can take part in farm activities or just relax by the pool. 4 one-bedroom standard units, some with whirlpools. 1 story, interior corridors. *Bath:* some shared or private. **Parking:** on-site. **Terms:** 3 day cancellation notice-fee imposed. **Amenities:** irons, hair dryers. **Pool(s):** heated outdoor. **Leisure Activities:** hiking trails, horseshoes. **Cards:** MC, VI. **Special Amenities: free full breakfast and free local telephone calls.**

CAPITOLA pop. 10,033—*See also APTOS, FELTON, SANTA CRUZ & SCOTTS VALLEY.*

WHERE TO STAY

BEST WESTERN CAPITOLA BY-THE-SEA INN & SUITES Book at aaa.com Phone: (831)477-0607

Small-scale Hotel

5/16-9/15 [ECP]	1P: $99-$199	2P: $99-$199	XP: $10	F12
2/1-5/15 & 9/16-1/31 [ECP]	1P: $79-$179	2P: $79-$179	XP: $10	F12

Location: SR 1, exit 41st Ave, 4 blks w. 1435 41st Ave 95010. Fax: 831/477-7008. **Facility:** Smoke free premises. 54 units. 50 one-bedroom standard units, some with whirlpools. 4 one-bedroom suites ($99-$219), some with whirlpools. 3 stories, interior corridors. *Bath:* combo or shower only. **Parking:** on-site. **Terms:** pets ($50 deposit, $10 extra charge). **Amenities:** high-speed Internet, dual phone lines, voice mail, irons, hair dryers. **Pool(s):** heated outdoor. **Leisure Activities:** whirlpool, exercise room. **Guest Services:** coin laundry. **Business Services:** meeting rooms. **Cards:** AX, CB, DC, DS, JC, MC, VI. **Special Amenities: free expanded continental breakfast and free newspaper.**

FEE

CAPITOLA INN Phone: (831)462-3004

Motel

5/24-9/3 [CP]	1P: $105-$125	2P: $115-$135	XP: $10	F12
2/1-5/23 [CP]	1P: $85-$105	2P: $95-$115	XP: $10	F12
9/4-10/31 [CP]	1P: $75-$95	2P: $85-$105	XP: $10	F12
11/1-1/31 [CP]	1P: $70-$90	2P: $80-$100	XP: $10	F12

Location: SR 1, exit Bay Ave, just w. 822 Bay Ave 95010. Fax: 831/462-0835. **Facility:** 56 one-bedroom standard units. 2 stories (no elevator), interior/exterior corridors. **Parking:** on-site. **Terms:** cancellation fee imposed, small pets only ($20 extra charge, with prior approval). **Pool(s):** outdoor. **Business Services:** meeting rooms. **Cards:** AX, DC, DS, MC, VI.

SOME UNITS

FEE FEE FEE

THE INN AT DEPOT HILL Phone: (831)462-3376

Bed & Breakfast

7/2-9/6 [BP]	1P: $229-$399	2P: $229-$399	XP: $15
2/1-7/1 & 9/7-1/31 [BP]	1P: $225-$375	2P: $225-$375	XP: $15

Location: SR 1, exit Park Ave, 1 mi w. 250 Monterey Ave 95010. Fax: 831/462-3697. **Facility:** Occupying a converted former railroad station and annex, the inn has several fireplaces and offers individually decorated accommodations. Smoke free premises. 12 one-bedroom standard units, some with whirlpools. 2 stories, interior corridors. *Bath:* combo or shower only. **Parking:** on-site. **Terms:** 2 night minimum stay - weekends, 7 day cancellation notice-fee imposed. **Amenities:** video library, dual phone lines, hair dryers. *Some:* CD players, irons. **Leisure Activities:** whirlpool. **Business Services:** meeting rooms. **Cards:** AX, DS, MC, VI. **Special Amenities: free continental breakfast and free local telephone calls.** *(See color ad p 469)*

SOME UNITS

WHERE TO DINE

OSTRICH GRILL **Dinner:** $10-$27 **Phone:** 831/477-9181

American

Location: At Crossroads Center, on 2nd floor. 820 Bay Ave 95010. **Hours:** 5:30 pm-9 pm, Sat-9:30 pm. Closed: 11/25, 12/25. **Reservations:** accepted. **Features:** Wood-grilled meats, including ostrich, make up the core of the dinner menu. The shopping-center eatery nurtures a laid-back atmosphere. Casual dress; cocktails. **Parking:** on-site. **Cards:** AX, MC, VI.

SHADOWBROOK Lunch: $9-$15 Dinner: $13-$28 Phone: 831/475-1511

Regional American

Location: 0.5 mi s of SR 1, exit 41st Ave, then 0.5 mi e on Capitola Rd. 1750 Wharf Rd 95010. **Hours:** 11:30 am-9:30 pm, Sat 4 pm-10 pm, Sun 10 am-2:30 & 4-9 pm. **Reservations:** suggested. **Features:** The rustic setting overlooks a creek and lush, surrounding landscaping. A funicular railway leads down to the dining rooms. Prime rib and fresh, ocean-caught fish stand out on a menu of seasonal California specialties. Entertainment is lined up on weekends. Dressy casual; cocktails. **Parking:** on-site. **Cards:** AX, CB, DC, DS, MC, VI.

CARMEL-BY-THE-SEA —*See Monterey Peninsula p. 466.*

CARMEL VALLEY —*See Monterey Peninsula p. 483.*

CARNELIAN BAY —*See Lake Tahoe Area p. 371.*

CASTRO VALLEY pop. 57,292 (See map and index starting on p. 516)

WHERE TO STAY

CASTRO VALLEY COMFORT SUITES *Book at aaa.com* Phone: (510)889-9300 **5**

Small-scale Hotel

All Year [ECP] 1P: $79-$109 2P: $79-$109 XP: $10 F17

Location: I-580, exit Castro Valley Blvd, just n. 2419 Castro Valley Blvd 94546. Fax: 510/889-1010. **Facility:** 54 one-bedroom standard units, some with whirlpools. 3 stories, interior corridors. *Bath:* combo or shower only. **Parking:** on-site. **Terms:** cancellation fee imposed. **Amenities:** high-speed Internet, dual phone lines, voice mail, safes, irons, hair dryers. **Leisure Activities:** sauna, whirlpool, exercise room. **Guest Services:** coin laundry. **Cards:** AX, CB, DC, DS, JC, MC, VI.

SOME UNITS

ECONO LODGE *Book at aaa.com* Phone: (510)537-8833 **6**

SAVE

Motel

All Year 1P: $66-$77 2P: $66-$77 XP: $10 F12

Location: I-580, exit Crow Canyon Rd eastbound; exit Castro Valley Blvd westbound, 0.3 mi e. 3928 E Castro Valley Blvd 94552. Fax: 510/538-9584. **Facility:** 33 one-bedroom standard units. 2 stories (no elevator), exterior corridors. **Parking:** on-site. **Terms:** cancellation fee imposed, [CP] meal plan available. **Amenities:** hair dryers. **Pool(s):** small outdoor. **Leisure Activities:** whirlpool. **Cards:** AX, CB, DC, DS, JC, MC, VI. **Special Amenities: free continental breakfast.**

SOME UNITS

HOLIDAY INN EXPRESS *Book at aaa.com* Phone: (510)538-9501 **7**

Small-scale Hotel

5/1-9/30 [ECP] 1P: $89-$179 2P: $89-$179 XP: $10 F18
2/1-4/30 & 10/1-1/31 [ECP] 1P: $79-$179 2P: $79-$179 XP: $10 F18

Location: I-580, exit Castro Valley Blvd, 0.3 mi n. 2532 Castro Valley Blvd 94546. Fax: 510/538-9487. **Facility:** 62 one-bedroom units, some with whirlpools. 3 stories, interior corridors. **Parking:** on-site. **Amenities:** high-speed Internet, voice mail, irons, hair dryers. **Pool(s):** small heated outdoor. **Business Services:** meeting rooms. **Cards:** AX, CB, DC, DS, JC, MC, VI. ***(See color ad p 260)***

SOME UNITS

FEE

The following lodging was either not evaluated or did not meet AAA rating requirements but is listed for your information only.

CASTRO VALLEY INN Phone: 510/538-5757

fyi

Motel

All Year 1P: $66-$77 2P: $66-$77 XP: $10 F12

Too new to rate, opening scheduled for November 2003. **Location:** I-580, exit Crow Canyon Rd eastbound; exit Castro Valley westbound, 0.3 mi e. 3954 E Castro Valley Blvd 94552. **Amenities:** 49 units, coffeemakers, microwaves, refrigerators. **Terms:** cancellation fee imposed. **Cards:** AX, CB, DC, DS, JC, MC, VI.

CAYUCOS pop. 2,943

WHERE TO STAY

BEACHWALKER INN Phone: 805/995-2133

SAVE

Motel

5/15-9/15 [CP] 1P: $95-$180 2P: $95-$180 XP: $15 F12
2/1-5/14 & 9/16-1/31 [CP] 1P: $85-$160 2P: $85-$160 XP: $15 F12

Location: On SR 1 business route. 501 S Ocean Ave 93430. Fax: 805/995-3139. **Facility:** Smoke free premises. 24 units. 12 one-bedroom standard units. 12 one-bedroom suites ($95-$285) with kitchens. 2 stories (no elevator), exterior corridors. **Parking:** on-site. **Terms:** office hours 7:30 am-10 pm, 3 day cancellation notice-fee imposed. **Amenities:** hair dryers. **Business Services:** meeting rooms. **Cards:** AX, CB, DC, DS, JC, MC, VI. **Special Amenities: free continental breakfast and free newspaper.**

SOME UNITS

CAYUCOS BEACH INN Phone: 805/995-2828

Motel

All Year 1P: $75-$175 2P: $75-$175 XP: $10 F3

Location: On SR 1 business route. 333 S Ocean Ave 93430 (PO Box 227). Fax: 805/995-0131. **Facility:** Smoke free premises. 37 units. 30 one-bedroom standard units. 7 one-bedroom suites. 2 stories (no elevator), exterior corridors. *Bath:* combo or shower only. **Parking:** on-site. **Terms:** office hours 7 am-10 pm, cancellation fee imposed, weekly rates available, [ECP] meal plan available, pets ($10 extra charge). **Amenities:** video library, hair dryers. **Guest Services:** coin laundry. **Cards:** DS, MC, VI.

FEE

CAYUCOS PIERPOINTE INN **Phone:** 805/995-3200

Small-scale Hotel

4/1-9/30 [ECP] 1P: $200-$295 2P: $200-$295 XP: $20
2/1-3/31 & 10/1-1/31 [ECP] 1P: $135-$225 2P: $135-$225 XP: $20

Location: On SR 1 business route. 181 N Ocean Ave 93430. Fax: 805/995-9350. **Facility:** Smoke free premises. 14 one-bedroom standard units with whirlpools. 2 stories, interior corridors. **Parking:** on-site. **Terms:** office hours 8 am-10 pm, 2 night minimum stay - weekends 6/1-9/30, 3 day cancellation notice, package plans - mid-week & seasonal. **Amenities:** video library (fee), DVD players, irons, hair dryers. **Leisure Activities:** whirlpool. *Fee:* massage. **Guest Services:** complimentary evening beverages. **Cards:** AX, DS, MC, VI.

CAYUCOS SUNSET INN **Phone:** 805/995-2500

Bed & Breakfast

All Year 1P: $150-$250 2P: $150-$325 XP: $35

Location: On SR 1 business route. 95 S Ocean Ave 93430 (PO Box 151). Fax: 805/995-2999. **Facility:** A well-appointed B&B; all of the large one-room lodgings or two-room suites have spa tubs, fireplaces and a private deck or patio. Smoke free premises. 9 units. 4 one-bedroom standard units with whirlpools. 5 one-bedroom suites with whirlpools. 2 stories (no elevator), interior/exterior corridors. **Parking:** on-site. **Terms:** office hours 7 am-9 pm, 10 day cancellation notice-fee imposed, [BP] & [MAP] meal plans available. **Amenities:** DVD players, high-speed Internet, voice mail, irons, hair dryers. **Guest Services:** sundries. **Business Services:** meeting rooms. **Cards:** MC, VI. **Special Amenities: free full breakfast and free newspaper.**

CYPRESS TREE MOTEL **Phone:** (805)995-3917

Motel

6/1-9/30 1P: $57-$97 2P: $57-$97 XP: $10 F16
2/1-5/31 & 10/1-1/31 1P: $39-$79 2P: $39-$79 XP: $10 F16

Location: On SR 1 business route. 125 S Ocean Ave 93430. Fax: 805/995-3981. **Facility:** 12 units. 9 one- and 3 two-bedroom standard units, some with kitchens. 1-2 stories (no elevator), exterior corridors. *Bath:* combo or shower only. **Parking:** on-site. **Terms:** pets ($10 extra charge). **Cards:** AX, CB, DC, DS, MC, VI. **Special Amenities: free local telephone calls and preferred room (subject to availability with advanced reservations).**

SOME UNITS

FEE

DOLPHIN INN **Phone:** (805)995-3810

Motel

4/1-9/30 1P: $69-$129 2P: $79-$159
2/1-3/31 1P: $59-$119 2P: $69-$139
10/1-1/31 1P: $49-$109 2P: $59-$129

Location: On SR 1 business route. 399 S Ocean Ave 93430. Fax: 805/995-0618. **Facility:** Smoke free premises. 19 units. 12 one-bedroom standard units. 7 cottages, some with whirlpools. 1 story, exterior corridors. *Bath:* combo or shower only. **Parking:** on-site. **Terms:** office hours 8 am-9 pm, 3 day cancellation notice, [CP] meal plan available, pets ($10 extra charge). **Cards:** AX, DS, MC, VI. **Special Amenities: free local telephone calls.**

FEE

ESTERO BAY MOTEL **Phone:** (805)995-3614

Motel

6/1-9/30 1P: $59-$135 2P: $69-$145 XP: $10 F
2/1-5/31 & 10/1-1/31 1P: $49-$109 2P: $49-$109 XP: $10 F

Location: On SR 1 business route. 25 S Ocean Ave 93430. Fax: 805/995-5088. **Facility:** Smoke free premises. 12 one-bedroom standard units, some with kitchens. 1 story, exterior corridors. *Bath:* combo or shower only. **Parking:** on-site. **Terms:** office hours 7 am-midnight, 3 day cancellation notice, weekly rates available, [CP] meal plan available, pets ($15 extra charge, dogs only). **Amenities:** irons, hair dryers. **Cards:** AX, DC, MC, VI. **Special Amenities: free local telephone calls and preferred room (subject to availability with advanced reservations).**

FEE

SHORELINE INN **Phone:** 805/995-3681

Motel

6/2-8/31 [ECP] 1P: $105-$160 2P: $105-$160
2/1-6/1 & 9/1-1/31 [ECP] 1P: $80-$125 2P: $80-$125

Location: On SR 1 business route. 1 N Ocean Ave 93430 (PO Box 376). Fax: 805/995-2627. **Facility:** 29 one-bedroom standard units. 2 stories (no elevator), exterior corridors. **Parking:** on-site. **Terms:** office hours 6 am-10 pm, pets ($10 extra charge). **Amenities:** voice mail, hair dryers. **Business Services:** meeting rooms. **Cards:** AX, DS, MC, VI. **Special Amenities: free expanded continental breakfast and preferred room (subject to availability with advanced reservations).**

SOME UNITS

FEE

TIDE WATER INN **Phone:** (805)995-3670

Motel

All Year [CP] 1P: $55-$110 2P: $55-$110 XP: $12 F12

Location: On SR 1 business route. 20 S Ocean Ave 93430. **Facility:** Smoke free premises. 6 one-bedroom standard units. 1 story, exterior corridors. *Bath:* shower only. **Parking:** on-site. **Terms:** office hours 7 am-10 pm, 3 day cancellation notice-fee imposed. **Cards:** AX, DS, MC, VI. **Special Amenities: free continental breakfast and free local telephone calls.**

CEDARVILLE —*See also ALTURAS.*

WHERE TO STAY

SUNRISE MOTEL **Phone:** 530/279-2161

Motel

All Year 1P: $46-$50 2P: $55-$60 XP: $10 D9

Location: 0.5 mi w on SR 299. Located in a quiet area. 54889 Hwy 299 96104 (PO Box 345). Fax: 530/279-6261. **Facility:** 15 units. 14 one-bedroom standard units. 1 vacation home ($150-$400). 1 story, exterior corridors. *Bath:* combo or shower only. **Parking:** on-site. **Terms:** office hours 7 am-10:30 pm, age restrictions may apply, cancellation fee imposed, small pets only. **Amenities:** *Some:* irons, hair dryers. **Leisure Activities:** horseshoes. **Cards:** AX, CB, DC, DS, MC, VI. **Special Amenities: free local telephone calls and free newspaper.**

SOME UNITS

CHESTER pop. 2,316

WHERE TO STAY

THE BIDWELL HOUSE Phone: 530/258-3338

SAVE — Bed & Breakfast

All Year [BP] 2P: $80-$170 XP: $35 F

Location: On SR 36. 1 Main St 96020 (PO Box 1790). Fax: 530/258-3338. **Facility:** This renovated 1901 farmhouse at the east edge of town near Lake Almanor offers wood-burning fireplaces in three guest rooms. 14 units. 13 one-bedroom standard units, some with efficiencies and/or whirlpools. 1 cottage. 2 stories (no elevator), interior corridors. *Bath:* some shared or private, combo or shower only. **Parking:** on-site. **Terms:** 3 day cancellation notice, weekly rates available. **Cards:** MC, VI. **Special Amenities: free local telephone calls and free newspaper.**

SOME UNITS

CHESTER MANOR MOTEL Phone: 530/258-2441

SAVE — Motel

All Year 1P: $57-$79 2P: $69-$94 XP: $10 F4

Location: On SR 36. 306 Main St 96020 (PO Box 1688). Fax: 530/258-3523. **Facility:** 18 units. 8 one- and 6 two-bedroom standard units. 4 one-bedroom suites. 1 story, exterior corridors. *Bath:* shower only. **Parking:** on-site. **Terms:** age restrictions may apply, weekly rates available. **Amenities:** hair dryers. *Some:* irons. **Guest Services:** airport transportation-Chester Airport, area transportation. **Business Services:** administrative services (fee), fax. **Cards:** AX, DS, MC, VI. **Special Amenities: free local telephone calls and preferred room (subject to availability with advanced reservations).**

CHICO pop. 59,954

WHERE TO STAY

BEST WESTERN HERITAGE INN - CHICO *Book at aaa.com* Phone: (530)894-8600

SAVE — Small-scale Hotel

All Year 1P: $77-$102 2P: $83-$112 XP: $7 F12

Location: Just e of SR 99, via Cohasset Rd. 25 Heritage Ln 95926. Fax: 530/894-8600. **Facility:** 101 one-bedroom standard units, some with whirlpools. 3 stories, interior corridors. **Parking:** on-site. **Terms:** age restrictions may apply, [ECP] meal plan available. **Amenities:** irons, hair dryers. **Pool(s):** outdoor. **Leisure Activities:** whirlpool. **Business Services:** meeting rooms. **Cards:** AX, CB, DC, DS, MC, VI. **Special Amenities: free expanded continental breakfast and free local telephone calls.** *(See color ad below)*

SOME UNITS

DAYS INN *Book at aaa.com* Phone: (530)343-3286

SAVE — Motel

7/1-10/31 [CP]	1P: $69-$89	2P: $79-$99	XP: $10	F12
4/1-6/30 [CP]	1P: $59-$79	2P: $69-$89	XP: $10	F12
2/1-3/31 & 11/1-1/31 [CP]	1P: $49-$69	2P: $59-$79	XP: $10	F12

Location: SR 99, exit SR 32, west corner of Broadway and SR 32. 740 Broadway 95928. Fax: 530/894-7864. **Facility:** 39 one-bedroom standard units, some with whirlpools. 2 stories (no elevator), exterior corridors. *Bath:* combo or shower only. **Parking:** on-site. **Terms:** age restrictions may apply. **Amenities:** voice mail, irons, hair dryers. **Pool(s):** heated outdoor. **Business Services:** meeting rooms. **Cards:** AX, DC, DS, MC, VI. **Special Amenities: free continental breakfast and free newspaper.**

SOME UNITS

DELUXE INN Phone: (530)342-8386

SAVE — Motel

All Year [CP] 1P: $39-$59 2P: $39-$69 XP: $5 F10

Location: 2 mi n on SR 99 business route. 2507 Esplanade 95926. Fax: 530/342-8383. **Facility:** 36 one-bedroom standard units. 1 story, exterior corridors. *Bath:* combo or shower only. **Parking:** on-site. **Terms:** age restrictions may apply, 7 day cancellation notice, weekly rates available, small pets only ($4 extra charge). **Amenities:** *Some:* irons, hair dryers. **Pool(s):** outdoor. **Guest Services:** coin laundry. **Cards:** AX, CB, DC, DS, MC, VI. **Special Amenities: free continental breakfast.**

SOME UNITS

FEE

THE ESPLANADE BED & BREAKFAST — Phone: (530)345-8084

Bed & Breakfast

All Year [BP] 1P: $75-$95 2P: $75-$95 XP: $10 D

Location: 0.3 mi n; downtown. 620 The Esplanade 95926. **Facility:** This in-town inn, built in the California Bungalow style, features eclectic decor and comfortable accommodations. Smoke free premises. 5 one-bedroom standard units, some with whirlpools. 2 stories (no elevator), interior corridors. **Parking:** on-site. **Terms:** age restrictions may apply. **Amenities:** hair dryers. **Cards:** DC, MC, VI.

HERITAGE INN EXPRESS *Book at aaa.com* — **Phone:** (530)343-4527

SAVE — Motel

All Year 1P: $64-$91 2P: $72-$100 XP: $10 F12

Location: SR 32, exit SR 99, 1 mi w. 725 Broadway 95928. Fax: 530/343-4940. **Facility:** 39 units. 33 one-bedroom standard units. 6 one-bedroom suites ($91-$105) with whirlpools. 2 stories (no elevator), exterior corridors. **Parking:** on-site. **Terms:** age restrictions may apply, [BP] meal plan available. **Amenities:** irons, hair dryers. **Pool(s):** outdoor. **Guest Services:** coin laundry. **Cards:** AX, CB, DC, DS, MC, VI. **Special Amenities: free expanded continental breakfast and free local telephone calls.**

SOME UNITS

HOLIDAY INN OF CHICO *Book at aaa.com* — **Phone:** (530)345-2491

SAVE — Motel

All Year [BP] 1P: $125-$175 2P: $125-$175 XP: $10 F18

Location: Just w of SR 99, via Cohasset Rd. 685 Manzanita Ct 95926. Fax: 530/893-3040. **Facility:** Smoke free premises. 172 units. 165 one-bedroom standard units. 7 one-bedroom suites. 5 stories, interior corridors. **Parking:** on-site. **Terms:** check-in 4 pm, age restrictions may apply, cancellation fee imposed, [AP] meal plan available. **Amenities:** video games, high-speed Internet, dual phone lines, voice mail, irons, hair dryers. **Dining:** 6:30 am-1 & 4:30-9:30 pm, cocktails. **Pool(s):** outdoor. **Leisure Activities:** whirlpool. **Guest Services:** coin laundry. **Business Services:** conference facilities. **Cards:** AX, CB, DC, DS, JC, MC. **Special Amenities: free full breakfast and free local telephone calls.**

SOME UNITS

JOHNSON'S COUNTRY INN — **Phone:** (530)345-7829

Bed & Breakfast

All Year [BP] 1P: $85 2P: $125 XP: $10 F5

Location: 2 mi w on W 5th St. 3935 Morehead Ave 95928. Fax: 530/891-4589. **Facility:** Almond-tree orchards and flowering gardens surround the inn with greenery. Designated smoking area. 4 one-bedroom standard units, some with whirlpools. 2 stories, interior corridors. *Bath:* combo or shower only. **Parking:** on-site. **Terms:** office hours 9 am-8 pm, age restrictions may apply, cancellation fee imposed. **Cards:** AX, MC, VI.

SOME UNITS

MUSIC EXPRESS INN — **Phone:** (530)345-8376

Bed & Breakfast

All Year [BP] 1P: $76-$125 2P: $86-$125 XP: $20 F4

Location: SR 99, exit SR 32, 1 mi e to El Monte Ave, just n. 1091 El Monte Ave 95928. Fax: 530/893-8521. **Facility:** A family-oriented B&B featuring a swimming pool and spacious lodgings, the inn is walking distance from Bidwell Park. 9 one-bedroom standard units, some with whirlpools. 2 stories (no elevator), interior/exterior corridors. **Parking:** on-site. **Terms:** age restrictions may apply. **Amenities:** video library, irons. *Some:* hair dryers. **Cards:** AX, DS, MC, VI.

OXFORD SUITES *Book at aaa.com* — **Phone:** (530)899-9090

Small-scale Hotel

All Year [BP] 1P: $79-$159 2P: $79-$159 XP: $10 F10

Location: SR 99, exit 20th St E. 2035 Business Ln 95928. Fax: 530/899-9476. **Facility:** 183 one-bedroom standard units, some with whirlpools. 4 stories, interior corridors. **Parking:** on-site. **Terms:** age restrictions may apply, small pets only ($25 extra charge). **Amenities:** video library, voice mail, irons, hair dryers. **Pool(s):** outdoor, heated outdoor. **Leisure Activities:** whirlpool. **Guest Services:** gift shop, complimentary evening beverages, coin laundry. **Business Services:** meeting rooms, business center. **Cards:** AX, DC, DS, MC, VI.

SOME UNITS

FEE

SAFARI GARDEN MOTEL *Book at aaa.com* — **Phone:** (530)343-3201

SAVE — Motel

All Year 1P: $43 2P: $48 XP: $10 F12

Location: 2 mi n on SR 99 business route. 2352 Esplanade 95926. Fax: 530/343-2364. **Facility:** 50 one-bedroom standard units, some with kitchens. 1-2 stories (no elevator), exterior corridors. *Bath:* combo or shower only. **Parking:** on-site. **Terms:** age restrictions may apply, weekly rates available, small pets only ($25 deposit). **Amenities:** irons. **Pool(s):** outdoor. **Cards:** AX, CB, DC, DS, JC, MC, VI. **Special Amenities: free continental breakfast and free local telephone calls.**

SOME UNITS

FEE

SUPER 8 MOTEL *Book at aaa.com* — **Phone:** (530)345-2533

SAVE — Motel

All Year 1P: $50-$130 2P: $70-$150 XP: $5 F12

Location: Just w of SR 99, via Cohasset Rd. 655 Manzanita Ct 95926. Fax: 530/345-6762. **Facility:** 52 one-bedroom standard units. 3 stories (no elevator), interior corridors. *Bath:* combo or shower only. **Parking:** on-site. **Terms:** age restrictions may apply, [CP] meal plan available, small pets only ($4 fee). **Amenities:** *Some:* irons, hair dryers. **Pool(s):** outdoor. **Guest Services:** coin laundry. **Cards:** AX, CB, DC, DS, MC, VI. **Special Amenities: free continental breakfast and free local telephone calls.**

SOME UNITS

FEE

TOWN HOUSE MOTEL *Book at aaa.com* — **Phone:** 530/343-1621

SAVE — Motel

All Year 1P: $40-$59 2P: $49-$69 XP: $10 F5

Location: 1.8 mi n on SR 99 business route. 2231 Esplanade 95926. Fax: 530/894-6159. **Facility:** 29 one-bedroom standard units, some with whirlpools. 1 story, exterior corridors. **Parking:** on-site. **Terms:** age restrictions may apply, weekly rates available, [CP] meal plan available. **Pool(s):** outdoor. **Cards:** AX, DS, MC, VI. **Special Amenities: free continental breakfast and free local telephone calls.**

SOME UNITS

WHERE TO DINE

ALBATROSS RESTAURANT — **Dinner:** $15-$33 — **Phone:** 530/345-6037

American

Location: SR 99, exit Orland/Chico Rd "32", w to Main, then n. 3312 Esplanade 95973. **Hours:** 5:30 pm-10 pm. Closed major holidays. **Reservations:** suggested. **Features:** Enveloped by stately trees and green lawns, the converted 1940s California bungalow exudes the charming ambience of past years. Small dining areas are intimate. Casual dress; cocktails. **Parking:** on-site. **Cards:** AX, MC, VI.

BLACK CROW GRILL & TAPROOM — **Lunch:** $6-$13 — **Dinner:** $12-$23 — **Phone:** 530/892-1391

Traditional Continental

Location: Downtown. 209 Salem St 95928. **Hours:** 11:30 am-3:30 & 5-9:30 pm, Sun from 5 pm. Closed major holidays. **Features:** Located within the college area, the eatery serves inexpensive, quality dinners; the menu features Mexican, fresh fish and steak. Casual dress; cocktails. **Parking:** street. **Cards:** AX, MC, VI.

THE RAWBAR RESTAURANT & SUSHI — **Lunch:** $7-$11 — **Dinner:** $9-$16 — **Phone:** 530/897-0626

Asian

Location: SR 99, exit Orland/Chico Rd, w to Main St, n to 3rd St, then s. 346 Broadway 95928. **Hours:** 11:30 am-2:30 & 5-9 pm, Fri & Sat 5 pm-10 pm. Closed major holidays; also Sun. **Reservations:** suggested. **Features:** Across the street from the downtown green, the restaurant occupies a rustic former store. Asian decor lends visual appeal. Casual dress; beer & wine only. **Parking:** on-site. **Cards:** AX, MC, VI.

RED TAVERN — **Dinner:** $15-$20 — **Phone:** 530/894-3463

Mediterranean

Location: SR 99, exit Orland/Chico Rd, just w to Main St (changes to Esplanade), then n. 1250 Esplanade 95926. **Hours:** 5:30 pm-9 pm, Fri & Sat-10 pm. Closed major holidays; also Sun. **Reservations:** suggested. **Features:** In an old section of town with wide streets and majestic trees, the restaurant is housed in a cream-colored building with an all-glass front. Casual dress; cocktails. **Parking:** on-site. **Cards:** AX, MC, VI.

CHOWCHILLA pop. 11,127

WHERE TO STAY

CHOWCHILLA TRAVELODGE — *Book at aaa.com* — **Phone:** (559)665-8700

Motel

All Year — 1P: $79-$89 — 2P: $89-$99 — XP: $10 — F16

Location: SR 99, exit Robertson Blvd E. 205 Carlyle Way 93610. Fax: 559/665-8705. **Facility:** 49 one-bedroom standard units, some with kitchens and/or whirlpools. 2 stories (no elevator), exterior corridors. *Bath:* combo or shower only. **Parking:** on-site. **Terms:** [CP] meal plan available. **Amenities:** irons, hair dryers. **Pool(s):** outdoor. **Guest Services:** coin laundry. **Cards:** AX, CB, DC, MC, VI.

ASK / SOME UNITS

DAYS INN — *Book at aaa.com* — **Phone:** (559)665-4821

AAA SAVE — Motel

All Year — 1P: $48-$58 — 2P: $58-$68 — XP: $10 — F12

Location: SR 99, exit Robertson Blvd W. 220 E Robertson Blvd 93610. Fax: 559/665-4821. **Facility:** 30 one-bedroom standard units. 2 stories (no elevator), exterior corridors. **Parking:** on-site. **Terms:** cancellation fee imposed, small pets only ($5 extra charge). **Amenities:** irons, hair dryers. **Pool(s):** outdoor. **Guest Services:** coin laundry. **Cards:** AX, CB, DC, DS, JC, MC, VI. **Special Amenities: free continental breakfast and early check-in/late check-out.**

FEE / SOME UNITS

CITRUS HEIGHTS pop. 85,071 (See map and index starting on p. 565)

WHERE TO STAY

OLIVE GROVE INN & SUITES — **Phone:** (916)725-0100 — 70

AAA SAVE — Motel

All Year — 1P: $99-$150 — 2P: $99-$150 — XP: $7 — F18

Location: I-80, exit Greenback Ln, 1 mi s. 6143 Auburn Blvd 95621-4701. Fax: 916/726-5091. **Facility:** 80 one-bedroom suites with kitchens. 2 stories, exterior corridors. **Parking:** on-site. **Terms:** small pets only ($250 deposit, $10 fee). **Amenities:** dual phone lines, irons, hair dryers. **Guest Services:** coin laundry. **Cards:** AX, DC, MC, VI. **Special Amenities: early check-in/late check-out and preferred room (subject to availability with advanced reservations).**

FEE / SOME UNITS

CLEARLAKE —*See Wine Country p. 768.*

CLEARLAKE OAKS —*See Wine Country p. 768.*

CLIO pop. 90

WHERE TO STAY

MOLLY'S BED & BREAKFAST — **Phone:** (530)836-4436

Bed & Breakfast

All Year — 2P: $90-$110 — XP: $30 — D12

Location: Just e of SR 89. 276 Lower Main St 96106 (PO Box 269). Fax: 530/836-4432. **Facility:** 4 one-bedroom standard units. 2 stories (no elevator), interior corridors. *Bath:* combo or shower only. **Parking:** on-site. **Terms:** office hours 9 am-9 pm, 2-3 night minimum stay - weekends, 7 day cancellation notice-fee imposed, weekly rates available, [BP] meal plan available, package plans - seasonal, small pets only ($10 fee, in designated units). **Amenities:** hair dryers. *Some:* irons. **Guest Services:** gift shop. **Cards:** AX, MC, VI.

ASK / FEE

CLOVERDALE —See Wine Country p. 769.

CLOVIS pop. 68,468

WHERE TO STAY

BEST WESTERN CLOVIS COLE *Book at aaa.com* **Phone:** 559/299-1547

SAVE Motel

All Year [ECP] 1P: $84-$125 2P: $89-$135 XP: $8 F12

Location: SR 168 at 4th St; center. 415 Clovis Ave 93612. Fax: 559/325-9128. **Facility:** 58 units. 50 one-bedroom standard units. 8 one-bedroom suites ($120-$140). 3 stories, interior corridors. *Bath:* combo or shower only. **Parking:** on-site. **Terms:** 3 day cancellation notice. **Amenities:** irons, hair dryers. **Pool(s):** outdoor. **Leisure Activities:** sauna, whirlpool, exercise room. **Guest Services:** coin laundry. **Business Services:** fax. **Cards:** AX, CB, DC, DS, JC, MC, VI. **Special Amenities: free expanded continental breakfast and free newspaper.**

SOME UNITS

COALINGA pop. 11,668

WHERE TO STAY

BEST WESTERN BIG COUNTRY INN *Book at aaa.com* **Phone:** (559)935-0866

SAVE Motel

6/1-10/31 [CP] 1P: $79-$109 2P: $89-$129 XP: $7 F12
2/1-5/31 & 11/1-1/31 [CP] 1P: $69-$99 2P: $79-$109 XP: $7 F12

Location: I-5, exit SR 198/Hanford-Lemoore, just w. 25020 W Dorris Ave 93210. Fax: 559/935-0644. **Facility:** 48 one-bedroom standard units. 1 story, exterior corridors. **Parking:** on-site. **Terms:** cancellation fee imposed, small pets only ($10 extra charge). **Amenities:** video library (fee), irons, hair dryers. **Pool(s):** outdoor. **Guest Services:** coin laundry. **Cards:** AX, CB, DC, DS, MC, VI. **Special Amenities: free continental breakfast and early check-in/late check-out.** *(See color ad below)*

FEE SOME UNITS FEE

THE INN AT HARRIS RANCH **Phone:** (559)935-0717

SAVE Small-scale Hotel

All Year 1P: $110-$250 2P: $116-$250 XP: $8 F12

Location: I-5, exit SR 198, just e; at Hanford-Lemoore off-ramp. 24505 W Dorris Ave 93210 (Rt 1, Box 777). Fax: 559/935-5061. **Facility:** 153 units. 108 one-bedroom standard units. 45 one-bedroom suites ($128-$250), some with whirlpools. 2-3 stories, interior/exterior corridors. *Bath:* combo or shower only. **Parking:** on-site. **Terms:** package plans, pets ($10 extra charge). **Amenities:** dual phone lines, voice mail, honor bars, hair dryers. *Some:* irons. **Dining:** 6 am-11 pm, also, Harris Ranch Steak House, see separate listing. **Pool(s):** heated outdoor. **Leisure Activities:** whirlpools, exercise room, private airstrip. **Guest Services:** coin laundry. **Cards:** AX, DC, DS, MC, VI. **Special Amenities: free local telephone calls.**

FEE SOME UNITS

WHERE TO DINE

HARRIS RANCH STEAK HOUSE **Dinner:** $16-$32 **Phone:** 559/935-0717

Steak House

Location: I-5, exit SR 198, just e; at Hanford-Lemoore off-ramp; in The Inn at Harris Ranch. 24505 W Dorris Ave 93210. **Hours:** 5:30 pm-9:30 pm, Fri & Sat-10 pm. **Reservations:** suggested. **Features:** The combination coffee shop and dining room specializes in Harris-raised beef and Harris-grown produce. The dining room evokes an early California elegance. Casual dress; cocktails. **Parking:** on-site. **Cards:** AX, CB, DC, MC, VI.

COLUMBIA pop. 2,405

WHERE TO STAY

COLUMBIA CITY HOTEL *Book at aaa.com* **Phone:** (209)532-1479

Historic Bed & Breakfast

All Year 1P: $80-$120 2P: $85-$125 XP: $10 F4

Location: Center; in Columbia State Historic Park. Main St 95310 (PO Box 1870). Fax: 209/532-7027. **Facility:** Restoration has preserved many authentic touches at this 1856 Gold Rush-era hotel; phone for seasonal closures. Smoke free premises. 10 one-bedroom standard units. 2 stories (no elevator), interior corridors. *Bath:* combo or shower only. **Parking:** on-site. **Terms:** office hours 7:30 am-9 pm, 3 day cancellation notice, [ECP] meal plan available, package plans. **Dining:** restaurant, see separate listing. **Cards:** AX, DS, MC, VI.

SOME UNITS

ASK / /

COLUMBIA GEM MOTEL **Phone:** 209/532-4508

Cabin

All Year 1P: $79-$139 2P: $79-$139

Location: 3 mi n of Sonora; 1 mi from Columbia State Historic Park. 22131 Parrotts Ferry Rd 95370 (PO Box 874, 95310). Fax: 209/536-0515. **Facility:** 10 units. 3 one-bedroom standard units. 1 one-bedroom suite ($139). 6 cabins. 1 story, exterior corridors. *Bath:* combo or shower only. **Parking:** on-site. **Terms:** 7 day cancellation notice, pets (with prior approval). **Cards:** AX, DC, DS, JC, MC, VI.

SOME UNITS

/ /

FALLON HOTEL *Book at aaa.com* **Phone:** (209)532-1470

Historic Bed & Breakfast

All Year 1P: $60-$65 2P: $65-$135 XP: $10 F4

Location: Entrance to Columbia State Historic Park. Located adjacent to Fallon Theatre. 11175 Washington St 95310 (PO Box 1870). Fax: 209/532-7027. **Facility:** Built in 1857, this Victorian hotel has been authentically restored; phone for seasonal closures. Smoke free premises. 14 one-bedroom standard units. 2 stories (no elevator), interior corridors. *Bath:* some shower only. **Parking:** on-site. **Terms:** age restrictions may apply, 3 day cancellation notice, [ECP] meal plan available, package plans. **Cards:** DS, MC, VI.

ASK

HARLAN HOUSE **Phone:** 209/533-4862

Bed & Breakfast

All Year 2P: $95-$150 XP: $20 F4

Location: SR 49, exit Parrots Ferry Rd, n to Pacific, then 0.5 mi e. 22890 School House St 95310. **Facility:** 4 one-bedroom standard units, some with whirlpools. 2 stories (no elevator), interior corridors. **Parking:** on-site. **Terms:** office hours 7 am-9 pm, 5 day cancellation notice-fee imposed, [BP] meal plan available. **Amenities:** video library. **Pool(s):** small heated outdoor. **Cards:** AX, DC, MC, VI.

SOME UNITS

VCR / /

WHERE TO DINE

COLUMBIA CITY HOTEL RESTAURANT Historic **Dinner:** $17-$25 **Phone:** 209/532-1479

French

Location: Center; in Columbia State Historic Park; in Columbia City Hotel. 22768 Main St 95310. **Hours:** 5 pm-9 pm, Sat-9:30 pm; Sunday brunch 11 am-2 pm. Closed: 12/24, 12/25; also Mon & first two weeks of Jan. **Reservations:** suggested. **Features:** Housed in a restored 1870s landmark, the dining room is furnished to elicit the feel of a saloon in the gold rush days. The wine selection favors California vintages. Casual dress; cocktails. **Parking:** on-site. **Cards:** AX, DS, MC, VI.

CONCORD pop. 121,780

WHERE TO STAY

BEST WESTERN HERITAGE INN *Book at aaa.com* **Phone:** (925)686-4466

AAA SAVE

Motel

All Year 1P: $75-$115 2P: $75-$115 XP: $5 F12

Location: 3 mi e at Wharton Way. 4600 Clayton Rd 94521. Fax: 925/825-0581. **Facility:** 125 one-bedroom standard units. 2 stories, exterior corridors. **Parking:** on-site. **Terms:** [ECP] meal plan available. **Amenities:** irons, hair dryers. **Pool(s):** outdoor. **Leisure Activities:** whirlpool. **Guest Services:** coin laundry. **Business Services:** meeting rooms. **Cards:** AX, DC, DS, MC, VI. **Special Amenities: free continental breakfast and free local telephone calls.** *(See color ad p 283)*

SOME UNITS

DATA PORT / /

FEE

COMFORT INN *Book at aaa.com* **Phone:** (925)827-8998

AAA SAVE

Small-scale Hotel

5/1-9/30	1P: $94-$114	2P: $94-$114	XP: $5	F18
2/1-4/30 & 10/1-1/31	1P: $84-$104	2P: $84-$104	XP: $5	F18

Location: I-680, exit Monument Blvd northbound; exit Gregory Ln southbound, 0.5 mi e. 1370 Monument Blvd 94520. Fax: 925/798-3374. **Facility:** 41 one-bedroom standard units. 3 stories, interior corridors. *Bath:* combo or shower only. **Parking:** on-site. **Terms:** [ECP] meal plan available. **Amenities:** video library (fee), dual phone lines, voice mail, irons, hair dryers. **Pool(s):** outdoor. **Leisure Activities:** exercise room. **Guest Services:** coin laundry. **Business Services:** meeting rooms. **Cards:** AX, DC, DS, MC, VI. **Special Amenities: free continental breakfast and free local telephone calls.**

SOME UNITS

DATA PORT / VCR /

CONCORD HILTON *Book at aaa.com* **Phone:** (925)827-2000

AAA SAVE

Large-scale Hotel

All Year 1P: $89-$259 XP: $10 F17

Location: I-680, exit Willow Pass Rd, just e. 1970 Diamond Blvd 94520. Fax: 925/671-0984. **Facility:** 329 units. 323 one-bedroom standard units. 6 one-bedroom suites, some with whirlpools. 11 stories, interior corridors. **Parking:** on-site. **Amenities:** high-speed Internet (fee), dual phone lines, voice mail, irons, hair dryers. **Dining:** 6:30 am-10 pm, Sat & Sun 7 am-11 & 5-10 pm, cocktails. **Pool(s):** heated outdoor. **Leisure Activities:** whirlpool, exercise room. **Guest Services:** gift shop, valet laundry, area transportation-mall & Bart. **Business Services:** meeting rooms. **Cards:** AX, CB, DC, DS, MC, VI. **Special Amenities: free newspaper.**

SOME UNITS

DATA PORT / /

FEE FEE

ECONOMY INN — **Phone:** (925)682-7850

Motel

All Year 1P: $64-$84 2P: $79-$89

Location: 1 mi e at Babel Rd. 3606 Clayton Rd 94521. Fax: 925/676-7547. **Facility:** 63 one-bedroom standard units. 2 stories (no elevator), exterior corridors. **Parking:** on-site. **Terms:** cancellation fee imposed, [CP] meal plan available. **Pool(s):** outdoor. **Cards:** AX, DS, MC, VI.

SOME UNITS

EL MONTE MOTOR INN — **Phone:** (925)682-1601

Motel

All Year [CP] 1P: $69-$89 2P: $69-$89 XP: $10 F6

Location: Jct I-680 and SR 24, exit SR 242 at Clayton Rd, 2 mi e. 3555 Clayton Rd 94519. Fax: 925/827-4756. **Facility:** 43 one-bedroom standard units, some with kitchens. 2 stories (no elevator), interior/exterior corridors. *Bath:* combo or shower only. **Parking:** on-site. **Terms:** weekly rates available. **Amenities:** *Some:* hair dryers. **Pool(s):** small outdoor. **Leisure Activities:** whirlpool. **Guest Services:** coin laundry. **Cards:** AX, CB, DC, MC, VI.

SOME UNITS

HOLIDAY INN CONCORD *Book at aaa.com* — **Phone:** (925)687-5500

Small-scale Hotel

All Year 1P: $89-$129 2P: $89-$129

Location: I-680, exit E Concord Ave, Diamond Ave S, Burnett Ave W. 1050 Burnett Ave 94520. Fax: 925/363-5443. **Facility:** 198 one-bedroom standard units. 6 stories, interior/exterior corridors. **Parking:** on-site. **Terms:** [MAP] meal plan available, small pets only ($5 extra charge). **Amenities:** dual phone lines, voice mail, irons, hair dryers. **Dining:** 6:30 am-10 & 5-10 pm, cocktails. **Pool(s):** outdoor. **Leisure Activities:** exercise room. **Guest Services:** valet laundry, area transportation-within 5 mi. **Business Services:** meeting rooms, business center. **Cards:** AX, DC, DS, JC, MC, VI. **Special Amenities: free continental breakfast and free local telephone calls.** *(See color ad below)*

SOME UNITS

FEE FEE FEE

HOLIDAY INN EXPRESS *Book at aaa.com* — **Phone:** (925)674-9400

Motel

All Year 1P: $99-$169 2P: $99-$169 XP: $10 F

Location: 6.5 mi e of jct I-680 and SR 24; exit SR 242 (Clayton Rd), 5.5 mi e. 5370 Clayton Rd 94521. Fax: 925/674-9595. **Facility:** 33 one-bedroom standard units. 2 stories (no elevator), exterior corridors. **Parking:** on-site. **Terms:** [ECP] meal plan available. **Amenities:** video library (fee), dual phone lines, voice mail, irons, hair dryers. **Leisure Activities:** whirlpool. **Guest Services:** valet laundry. **Cards:** AX, CB, DC, DS, JC, MC, VI. **Special Amenities: free continental breakfast and free local telephone calls.**

SOME UNITS

PREMIER INNS — **Phone:** (925)674-0888

Motel

All Year 1P: $52-$75 2P: $57-$80 XP: $5 F17

Location: SR 242, exit Clayton Rd northbound; exit Concord Ave southbound, just e. 1581 Concord Ave 94520. Fax: 925/798-8277. **Facility:** 136 one-bedroom standard units. 2 stories, exterior corridors. *Bath:* combo or shower only. **Parking:** on-site. **Terms:** weekly rates available, [CP] meal plan available, small pets only. **Amenities:** voice mail. **Pool(s):** outdoor. **Leisure Activities:** whirlpool. **Cards:** AX, MC, VI. **Special Amenities: free continental breakfast and free local telephone calls.**

SOME UNITS

SHERATON CONCORD HOTEL *Book at aaa.com* — **Phone:** (925)825-7700

Small-scale Hotel

All Year 1P: $79-$199 2P: $89-$209 XP: $15 F12

Location: I-680, exit Concord Ave, just e. 45 John Glenn Dr 94520. Fax: 925/674-9567. **Facility:** 324 one-bedroom standard units. 3 stories, interior corridors. *Bath:* combo or shower only. **Parking:** on-site. **Terms:** [AP] meal plan available. **Amenities:** dual phone lines, voice mail, irons, hair dryers. *Some:* fax. **Pool(s):** heated indoor. **Leisure Activities:** whirlpool, putting green, exercise room. **Guest Services:** gift shop, valet laundry. **Business Services:** meeting rooms, business center. **Cards:** AX, CB, DC, MC, VI.

SOME UNITS

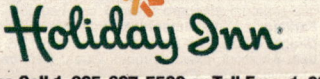

FEE FEE

COPPEROPOLIS pop. 2,363

WHERE TO STAY

LAKE TULLOCH RESORT Book at aaa.com Phone: (209)785-8200

Motel

4/1-10/31	1P: $120-$150	2P: $120-$150	XP: $20
2/1-3/31 & 11/1-1/31	1P: $99-$120	2P: $99-$120	XP: $20

Location: 5 mi n off SR 108/120; 7 mi s off SR 4. 7260 O'Byrnes Ferry Rd 95228. Fax: 209/785-8202. **Facility:** 46 one-bedroom standard units. 2 stories, exterior corridors. *Bath:* combo or shower only. **Parking:** on-site. **Terms:** check-in 4 pm, 2 night minimum stay - weekends 5/1-10/1, 3 day cancellation notice, [AP] meal plan available. **Pool(s):** heated outdoor. **Leisure Activities:** boating, sailboats, marina, waterskiing, fishing. **Business Services:** meeting rooms. **Cards:** AX, DS, MC, VI.

SOME UNITS

CORCORAN pop. 14,458

WHERE TO STAY

BUDGET INN Phone: (559)992-3171

Motel

All Year	1P: $43-$68	2P: $43-$100	XP: $8	F12

Location: SR 43, exit Whitley Ave, 1 mi w. 1224 Whitley Ave 93212. Fax: 559/992-5681. **Facility:** 45 one-bedroom standard units. 3 stories (no elevator), exterior corridors. **Parking:** on-site. **Terms:** [CP] meal plan available. **Amenities:** hair dryers. **Cards:** AX, DS, MC, VI. **Special Amenities: free continental breakfast and free local telephone calls.**

SOME UNITS

CORCORAN COUNTRY INN Phone: 559/992-5724

Motel

All Year [CP]	1P: $45-$60	2P: $55-$70	XP: $6	F12

Location: SR 43, exit Whitley Ave, 1.5 mi w. 2111 W Whitley Ave 93212. Fax: 559/992-8149. **Facility:** 19 one-bedroom standard units. 2 stories, exterior corridors. *Bath:* shower or tub only. **Parking:** on-site. **Amenities:** hair dryers. *Some:* irons. **Pool(s):** small outdoor. **Cards:** AX, DC, MC, VI. **Special Amenities: free continental breakfast and free local telephone calls.**

SOME UNITS

CORNING pop. 6,741

WHERE TO STAY

AMERIHOST INN-CORNING Book at aaa.com Phone: (530)824-5200

Motel

All Year [ECP]	1P: $62-$99	2P: $69-$99	XP: $10	F17

Location: I-5, exit 631 (Solano St), just e. 910 Hwy 99 W 96021. Fax: 530/824-5400. **Facility:** 60 one-bedroom standard units, some with whirlpools. 2 stories (no elevator), interior corridors. *Bath:* combo or shower only. **Parking:** on-site. **Terms:** age restrictions may apply, pets ($10 extra charge). **Amenities:** voice mail, safes, irons, hair dryers. **Pool(s):** heated indoor. **Leisure Activities:** whirlpool, exercise room. **Cards:** AX, DC, DS, MC, VI. **Special Amenities: free expanded continental breakfast and free local telephone calls.**

SOME UNITS

DATA PORT FEE

BEST WESTERN INN CORNING Book at aaa.com Phone: (530)824-2468

Motel

All Year	1P: $59-$89	2P: $65-$99	XP: $10	F8

Location: I-5 E, exit Corning, 1 blk e. 2165 Solano St 96021. Fax: 530/824-1688. **Facility:** 41 one-bedroom standard units. 2 stories (no elevator), exterior corridors. **Parking:** on-site. **Terms:** age restrictions may apply, [ECP] meal plan available. **Amenities:** irons, hair dryers. **Pool(s):** outdoor. **Cards:** AX, CB, DC, DS, JC, MC, VI. **Special Amenities: free continental breakfast and early check-in/late check-out.**

SOME UNITS

BUDGET INN Phone: 530/824-5103

Motel

All Year	1P: $39-$79	2P: $45-$99	XP: $10	F12

Location: I-5, exit Solano St, 0.3 mi e. 2104 Solano St 96021. Fax: 530/824-2928. **Facility:** 14 one-bedroom standard units. 1 story, exterior corridors. *Bath:* combo or shower only. **Parking:** on-site. **Terms:** age restrictions may apply, [CP] meal plan available. **Amenities:** irons. **Cards:** AX, DS, MC, VI. **Special Amenities: free local telephone calls and early check-in/late check-out.**

SOME UNITS

DAYS INN Book at aaa.com Phone: (530)824-2000

Motel

All Year	1P: $50-$100	2P: $50-$130	XP: $5	F13

Location: I-5, exit South Ave, 0.3 mi s. 3475 Hwy 99 W 96021. Fax: 530/824-2736. **Facility:** 62 one-bedroom standard units. 2 stories (no elevator), interior corridors. *Bath:* combo or shower only. **Parking:** on-site. **Terms:** [ECP] meal plan available, small pets only ($5 extra charge). **Amenities:** hair dryers. *Some:* irons. **Pool(s):** small outdoor. **Guest Services:** coin laundry. **Cards:** AX, CB, DC, DS, JC, MC, VI. **Special Amenities: free expanded continental breakfast and free local telephone calls.**

SOME UNITS

FEE

— WHERE TO DINE —

D2 (SQUARED) **Lunch:** $7-$12 **Dinner:** $10-$20 **Phone:** 530/824-417

Continental

Location: I-5, exit 631 (Central Corning), 1 mi. 410 Solano St 96021. **Hours:** 11:30 am-2 & 5-9 pm, Sat from pm. Closed: 1/1, 11/25, 12/25; also Sun (except Mothers Day) & Mon. **Reservations:** suggeste **Features:** The restaurant sustains a comfortable atmosphere. Creative dishes show an emphasis on fres ingredients. Casual dress; beer & wine only. **Parking:** on-site. **Cards:** DS, MC, VI.

HERITAGE DINNERHOUSE **Dinner:** $11-$19 **Phone:** 530/824-855

Traditional American

Location: I-5, exit 631 (Solano St). 965 Hwy 99 W 96021. **Hours:** 5 pm-9:30 pm. Closed: Sun. **Features:** Th restaurant is an old-fashioned dinner house, surrounded by open country fields and pastures. The menu' variety of American cuisine offers a little something for everyone. Casual dress; cocktails. **Parking:** on-site **Cards:** DC, MC, VI.

CORTE MADERA —*See San Francisco p. 664.*

COULTERVILLE —*See YOSEMITE NATIONAL PARK.*

CRESCENT CITY pop. 4,006

— WHERE TO STAY —

ANCHOR BEACH INN **Phone:** (707)464-260

AAA SAVE

Motel

7/1-9/30 [CP]	1P: $60-$110	2P: $70-$140	XP: $10	F1
5/24-6/30 [CP]	1P: $55-$95	2P: $66-$120	XP: $10	F1
2/1-5/23 & 10/1-1/31 [CP]	1P: $50-$75	2P: $59-$95	XP: $10	F1

Location: US 101 at Anchor Way. 880 Hwy US 101 S 95531. Fax: 707/464-1874. **Facility:** 52 one-bedroom stan dard units, some with whirlpools. 2 stories (no elevator), exterior corridors. *Bath:* combo or shower only **Parking:** on-site. **Terms:** age restrictions may apply. **Amenities:** high-speed Internet, dual phone lines, irons hair dryers. *Some:* fax, safes. **Leisure Activities:** whirlpool. **Guest Services:** coin laundry. **Cards:** AX, DC, DS, JC, MC, VI **Special Amenities: free continental breakfast and early check-in/late check-out.** *(See ad below)*

SOME UNITS

BAY VIEW INN **Phone:** 707/465-205

Motel

6/1-1/31	1P: $59-$95	2P: $59-$95
2/1-5/31	1P: $55-$95	2P: $55-$95

Location: W of US 101 S. 310 Hwy 101 S 95531. Fax: 707/465-3690. **Facility:** 65 one-bedroom standard units some with whirlpools. 3 stories (no elevator), interior/exterior corridors. *Bath:* combo or shower only. **Parking:** on-site. **Terms:** age restrictions may apply. **Amenities:** irons. *Some:* hair dryers. **Guest Services:** coin laundry. **Business Services:** meeting rooms. **Cards:** AX, DC, DS, MC, VI.

SOME UNITS

BEST VALUE INN *Book at aaa.com* **Phone:** (707)464-414

Motel

5/21-9/30	1P: $54-$69	2P: $59-$84	XP: $5	F1
2/1-5/20 & 10/1-1/31	1P: $45-$55	2P: $55-$65	XP: $5	F1

Location: On US 101. 440 Hwy 101 N 95531 (PO Box 595). Fax: 707/465-3274. **Facility:** 61 units. 58 one- and 3 two-bedroom standard units. 2 stories (no elevator), exterior corridors. *Bath:* some combo or shower only. **Parking:** on-site. **Terms:** age restrictions may apply, [CP] meal plan available, small pets only ($5 extra charge, dogs only). **Amenities:** video library. *Some:* irons, hair dryers. **Leisure Activities:** sauna, whirlpool. **Cards:** AX, MC, VI.

SOME UNITS

FEE

BEST WESTERN NORTHWOODS INN Book at aaa.com Phone: (707)464-9771

Motel

6/19-9/5 [BP]	1P: $89-$135	2P: $99-$150	XP: $10	F12
5/29-6/18 & 9/6-1/31 [BP]	1P: $79-$119	2P: $89-$119	XP: $10	F12
2/1-5/28 [BP]	1P: $69-$109	2P: $79-$109	XP: $10	F12

Location: E of US 101 S. 655 US 101 S 95531. Fax: 707/464-9461. **Facility:** 89 units. 87 one-bedroom standard units. 2 one-bedroom suites ($125-$175), some with whirlpools. 2 stories (no elevator), interior/exterior corridors. **Parking:** on-site. **Terms:** age restrictions may apply. **Amenities:** high-speed Internet, voice mail, irons, hair dryers. **Dining:** Northwood's Restaurant, see separate listing. **Pool(s):** heated indoor. **Leisure Activities:** whirlpools, barbecue, picnic area, exercise room. **Guest Services:** coin laundry. **Business Services:** meeting rooms. **Cards:** AX, DC, DS, MC, VI. **Special Amenities: free full breakfast and free local telephone calls.** *(See color ad below)*

SOME UNITS

COMFORT INN & SUITES Book at aaa.com Phone: (707)464-3885

Motel

5/16-9/15 [ECP]	1P: $82-$107	2P: $88-$108	XP: $10	F12
9/16-1/31 [ECP]	1P: $68-$101	2P: $78-$107	XP: $10	F12
2/1-5/15 [ECP]	1P: $70-$99	2P: $78-$105	XP: $10	F12

Location: W of Citizen Dock and US 101 S. 100 Walton St 95531. Fax: 707/464-5311. **Facility:** 46 one-bedroom standard units, some with kitchens and/or whirlpools. 2 stories (no elevator), exterior corridors. *Bath:* combo or shower only. **Parking:** on-site. **Terms:** age restrictions may apply, 3 day cancellation notice. **Amenities:** irons, hair dryers. **Guest Services:** coin laundry. **Business Services:** meeting rooms. **Cards:** AX, CB, DC, DS, JC, MC, VI.

SOME UNITS

CRESCENT CITY TRAVELODGE Book at aaa.com Phone: (707)464-6124

Motel

6/26-8/31 [CP]	1P: $65-$75	2P: $70-$80	XP: $5	F17
5/28-6/25 & 9/1-1/31 [CP]	1P: $49-$59	2P: $55-$65	XP: $5	F17
2/1-5/27 [CP]	1P: $45-$55	2P: $49-$59	XP: $5	F17

Location: Between US 101 northbound and southbound at 4th St. 353 L St 95531. Fax: 707/464-4781. **Facility:** 27 one-bedroom standard units. 2 stories (no elevator), exterior corridors. *Bath:* combo or shower only. **Parking:** on-site. **Terms:** age restrictions may apply. **Amenities:** *Some:* irons, hair dryers. **Leisure Activities:** sauna. **Cards:** AX, DS, MC, VI. **Special Amenities: free continental breakfast and free local telephone calls.**

SOME UNITS

CURLY REDWOOD LODGE — Phone: 707/464-2137

Motel

7/1-9/30	1P: $55-$76	2P: $55-$76	XP: $5
6/1-6/30	1P: $55-$69	2P: $55-$69	XP: $5
2/1-5/31 & 10/1-1/31	1P: $43-$55	2P: $43-$55	XP: $5

Location: S on US 101. 701 Redwood Hwy 101 S 95531. Fax: 707/464-1655. **Facility:** 36 units. 33 one- and 3 two-bedroom standard units. 1-2 stories (no elevator), interior/exterior corridors. *Bath:* combo or shower only. **Parking:** on-site. **Terms:** age restrictions may apply. **Cards:** AX, CB, DC, MC, VI. **Special Amenities: free local telephone calls and early check-in/late check-out.** *(See ad below)*

SOME UNITS

ECONO LODGE — Book at aaa.com — Phone: 707/464-6106

Motel

7/1-9/30 [CP]	1P: $69-$99	2P: $79-$109	XP: $10	F18
3/1-6/30 [CP]	1P: $49-$79	2P: $54-$89	XP: $5	F18
10/1-1/31 [CP]	1P: $55-$79	2P: $59-$85	XP: $5	F18
2/1-2/29 [CP]	1P: $49-$69	2P: $54-$75	XP: $5	F18

Location: On US 101 N. 725 Hwy 101 N 95531. Fax: 707/464-2781. **Facility:** 52 one-bedroom standard units. 1 story, exterior corridors. **Parking:** on-site. **Terms:** age restrictions may apply, cancellation fee imposed. **Amenities:** *Some:* irons, hair dryers. **Leisure Activities:** sauna, whirlpool. **Guest Services:** coin laundry. **Cards:** AX, DS, MC, VI. **Special Amenities: free continental breakfast and free local telephone calls.**

SOME UNITS

HIOUCHI MOTEL — Phone: 707/458-3041

Motel

All Year	1P: $35-$65	2P: $55-$65	XP: $5	F12

Location: US 101, exit US 199, 5 mi e. 2097 Hwy 199 95531. Fax: 707/458-4312. **Facility:** 17 one-bedroom standard units. 2 stories (no elevator), exterior corridors. *Bath:* combo or shower only. **Parking:** on-site. **Terms:** office hours 9 am-9 pm, age restrictions may apply, pets (with prior approval). **Cards:** MC, VI.

SOME UNITS

LIGHT HOUSE INN — Phone: 707/464-3993

Small-scale Hotel

6/1-1/31 [ECP]	1P: $79-$140	2P: $84-$140	XP: $5	F6
2/1-5/31 [ECP]	1P: $64-$125	2P: $69-$125	XP: $5	F6

Location: Center. 681 Hwy 101 S 95531. Fax: 707/464-9035. **Facility:** 65 units. 63 one- and 2 two-bedroom standard units, some with whirlpools. 3 stories, interior corridors. **Parking:** on-site. **Terms:** age restrictions may apply. **Amenities:** irons, hair dryers. **Guest Services:** coin laundry. **Business Services:** meeting rooms, business center. **Cards:** AX, DS, MC, VI.

SOME UNITS

PACIFIC INN — Phone: (707)464-9553

Motel

5/2-9/15	1P: $55-$65	2P: $65-$75	XP: $5	F15
9/16-10/31	1P: $50-$55	2P: $55-$65	XP: $5	F15
2/1-5/1 & 11/1-1/31	1P: $45-$50	2P: $50-$55	XP: $5	F15

Location: On US 101 N. 220 M St 95531. **Facility:** 25 one-bedroom standard units. 1 story, exterior corridors. **Parking:** on-site. **Terms:** age restrictions may apply, cancellation fee imposed. **Amenities:** hair dryers. *Some:* irons. **Cards:** AX, CB, DC, DS, MC, VI. **Special Amenities: free continental breakfast and free local telephone calls.**

SOME UNITS

SUPER 8 — Book at aaa.com — Phone: (707)464-4111

Motel

5/26-9/30	1P: $60-$80	2P: $65-$85	XP: $8	F12
2/1-5/25 & 10/1-1/31	1P: $40-$60	2P: $45-$65	XP: $5	F12

Location: E of US 101 S. Located opposite harbor. 685 Hwy 101 S 95531. Fax: 707/465-8916. **Facility:** 49 one-bedroom standard units. 2 stories (no elevator), exterior corridors. *Bath:* combo or shower only. **Parking:** on-site. **Terms:** age restrictions may apply, [CP] meal plan available, pets ($10 extra charge, small dogs only, with prior approval, in smoking units). **Amenities:** *Some:* irons, hair dryers. **Guest Services:** coin laundry. **Cards:** AX, DC, DS, MC, VI. **Special Amenities: free continental breakfast and free local telephone calls.**

SOME UNITS

FEE

The following lodging was either not evaluated or did not meet AAA rating requirements but is listed for your information only.

HAMPTON INN & SUITES-CRESCENT CITY **Phone:** 707/465-5400

fyi

Small-scale Hotel					
	5/16-10/31 [BP]	1P: $129-$159	2P: $139-$159	XP: $10	F18
	11/1-1/31 [BP]	1P: $99-$129	2P: $109-$139	XP: $10	F18
	2/1-5/15 [BP]	1P: $89-$119	2P: $99-$129	XP: $10	F18

Too new to rate, opening scheduled for November 2003. **Location:** US 101, exit Front St, just w. 100 A St 95531. Fax: 707/465-0962. **Amenities:** 53 units, pets, coffeemakers, microwaves, refrigerators. **Terms:** cancellation fee imposed. **Cards:** AX, CB, DC, DS, JC, MC, VI.

WHERE TO DINE

HARBOR VIEW GROTTO **Lunch:** $4-$11 **Dinner:** $4-$23 **Phone:** 707/464-3815

Steak & Seafood

Location: US 101, exit Anchor Way, just n. 150 Starfish Way 95531. **Hours:** 11:30 am-10 pm; to 9 pm in winter. Closed: 1/1, 11/25, 12/24, 12/25. **Reservations:** suggested. **Features:** Surrounding 180-degree windows offer lovely views of the ocean. The catch of the day rarely disappoints. Casual dress; cocktails. **Parking:** on-site. **Cards:** DS, MC, VI.

NORTHWOOD'S RESTAURANT **Lunch:** $6-$11 **Dinner:** $6-$20 **Phone:** 707/465-5656

American

Location: E of US 101 S; in Best Western Northwoods Inn. 675 Hwy 101 S 95531. **Hours:** 6 am-9 pm; to 10 pm in summer. Closed: 12/25. **Features:** Steaks, pasta, seafood and sandwiches are among the varied dishes. Casual dress; cocktails. **Parking:** on-site. **Cards:** AX, DC, DS, MC, VI.

CROMBERG pop. 290

WHERE TO STAY

LONG VALLEY RESORT **Phone:** (530)836-0754

Cottage

All Year 1P: $55-$75 2P: $55-$75 XP: $7 F12

Location: SR 70. 59532 Hwy 70 96103 (PO Box 30121). Fax: 530/836-0435. **Facility:** 13 units. 4 one-bedroom standard units. 9 cottages ($89-$150). 1 story, exterior corridors. *Bath:* combo or shower only. **Parking:** on-site. **Terms:** office hours 8 am-9 pm, 2 night minimum stay - in cottages, 14 day cancellation notice-fee imposed, pets (with prior approval). **Amenities:** video library. *Some:* irons, hair dryers. **Leisure Activities:** horseshoes, volleyball. **Guest Services:** gift shop. **Cards:** AX, DS, MC, VI.

SOME UNITS

/ VCR /

CUPERTINO pop. 50,546

WHERE TO STAY

COURTYARD BY MARRIOTT *Book at aaa.com* **Phone:** (408)252-9100

Small-scale Hotel

All Year [BP] 2P: $74-$159

Location: I-280, exit Wolfe Rd N, w on Pruneridge Rd. 10605 N Wolfe Rd 95014. Fax: 408/252-0632. **Facility:** 149 one-bedroom standard units. 3 stories, interior corridors. **Parking:** on-site. **Amenities:** high-speed Internet (fee), dual phone lines, voice mail, irons, hair dryers. **Pool(s):** heated outdoor. **Leisure Activities:** whirlpool, exercise room. **Guest Services:** valet and coin laundry. **Business Services:** meeting rooms. **Cards:** AX, DC, DS, MC, VI.

SOME UNITS

ASK DATA PORT / /

CUPERTINO INN *Book at aaa.com* **Phone:** (408)996-7700

Motel

All Year 1P: $99-$199 2P: $114-$214 XP: $15 F14

Location: I-280, exit Sunnyvale-Saratoga Rd, just n. 10889 N De Anza Blvd 95014. Fax: 408/257-0578. **Facility:** 125 one-bedroom standard units, some with whirlpools. 4 stories, interior corridors. **Parking:** on-site. **Terms:** check-in 4 pm, [BP] meal plan available. **Amenities:** video library, voice mail, honor bars, irons, hair dryers. *Some:* dual phone lines. **Pool(s):** heated outdoor. **Leisure Activities:** whirlpool. **Guest Services:** complimentary evening beverages, valet laundry. **Business Services:** meeting rooms. **Cards:** AX, CB, DC, DS, JC, MC, VI.

SOME UNITS

VCR DATA PORT / /

HILTON GARDEN INN *Book at aaa.com* **Phone:** 408/777-8787

Small-scale Hotel

All Year [BP] 1P: $79-$319 2P: $79-$319 XP: $10 F18

Location: I-280, exit Wolfe Rd N, w on Pruneridge Rd. 10741 N Wolfe Rd 95014. Fax: 408/777-8040. **Facility:** 165 one-bedroom standard units. 5 stories, interior corridors. *Bath:* combo or shower only. **Parking:** on-site. **Terms:** cancellation fee imposed. **Amenities:** video games (fee), CD players, high-speed Internet, dual phone lines, voice mail, irons, hair dryers. **Pool(s):** heated outdoor. **Leisure Activities:** whirlpool, exercise room. **Guest Services:** valet and coin laundry, area transportation. **Business Services:** meeting rooms, business center. **Cards:** AX, DC, DS, JC, MC, VI.

SOME UNITS

DATA PORT / VCR /

FEE

WHERE TO DINE

FONTANA'S ITALIAN RESTAURANT **Lunch:** $8-$21 **Dinner:** $12-$23 **Phone:** 408/725-0188

Italian

Location: I-280, exit Sunnyvale-Saratoga Rd, 0.3 mi w. 20840 Stevens Creek Blvd 95014. **Hours:** 11 am-10 pm, Sat from 5 pm, Sun 4:30 pm-9:30 pm. Closed: 11/25, 12/25. **Reservations:** suggested. **Features:** Diners can sit near the cozy fireplace and watch the activity in the display kitchen. The menu lists varied fresh fish dishes, as well as homemade pasta entrees and sinful desserts. Casual dress; beer & wine only. **Parking:** on-site. **Cards:** AX, DC, MC, VI.

DALY CITY —*See San Francisco p. 665.*

DANVILLE pop. 41,715 (See map and index starting on p. 516)

WHERE TO STAY

BEST WESTERN DANVILLE SYCAMORE INN Phone: (925)855-8888 51

Motel

All Year 1P: $79-$159 2P: $79-$169 XP: $10 F12

Location: I-680, exit Sycamore Valley Rd, just e. 803 Camino Ramon 94526. Fax: 925/255-8889. **Facility:** 62 one-bedroom standard units. 2 stories (no elevator), interior/exterior corridors. **Parking:** on-site. **Terms:** [CP] meal plan available. **Amenities:** irons, hair dryers. **Pool(s):** small heated outdoor. **Cards:** AX, CB, DC, DS, JC, MC, VI. ***(See color ad p 521 & below)***

SOME UNITS

ASK / /

WHERE TO DINE

BLACKHAWK GRILLE **Lunch:** $9-$15 **Dinner:** $16-$27 **Phone:** 925/736-4295 35

Regional American

Location: Intersection of Sycamore Valley, Crow Canyon Rd and Camino Tassajara; in Blackhawk Plaza. 3540 Blackhawk Plaza Cir 94506. **Hours:** 11:30 am-2:30 & 5:30-10 pm, Sat-10:30 pm, Sun 11 am-3 & 5-9 pm. Closed: 12/25. **Reservations:** suggested. **Features:** In an upscale shopping center, the cozy restaurant and its seasonal patio overlook a pond. An emphasis on fresh and local ingredients is evident in menu selections. Dressy casual; cocktails; entertainment. **Parking:** on-site. **Cards:** AX, CB, DC, DS, MC, VI.

DAVIS pop. 60,308

WHERE TO STAY

AGGIE INN **Phone:** (530)756-0352

AAA SAVE

Motel

All Year 1P: $85-$154 2P: $85-$154

Location: I-80, exit Davis, 0.5 mi n, w of First St, then 2 blks. 245 First St 95616. Fax: 530/753-5738. **Facility:** 34 units. 29 one-bedroom standard units, some with whirlpools. 5 one-bedroom suites, some with whirlpools. 2 stories, interior/exterior corridors. **Parking:** on-site. **Terms:** [CP] meal plan available. **Amenities:** voice mail, irons, hair dryers. **Leisure Activities:** sauna, whirlpool. **Cards:** AX, MC, VI. **Special Amenities: free continental breakfast and preferred room (subject to availability with advanced reservations).**

BEST WESTERN PALM COURT HOTEL *Book at aaa.com* **Phone:** (530)753-7100

AAA SAVE

Small-scale Hotel

All Year 1P: $144-$219 XP: $10 F12

Location: I-80, exit Central/Davis; downtown. 234 D St 95616. Fax: 530/753-8761. **Facility:** Centrally located in the downtown area, this elegantly furnished property offers spacious rooms and is walking distance from the University of California Davis campus. Smoke free premises. 27 one-bedroom suites, some with whirlpools. 3 stories, interior corridors. **Parking:** on-site. **Terms:** [ECP] meal plan available. **Amenities:** voice mail, irons, hair dryers. **Leisure Activities:** sauna, whirlpool, exercise room. **Guest Services:** complimentary laundry. **Business Services:** conference facilities. **Cards:** AX, DC, MC, VI. **Special Amenities: free continental breakfast and free newspaper.**

SOME UNITS

/ VCR /

BEST WESTERN UNIVERSITY LODGE *Book at aaa.com* **Phone:** (530)756-7890

AAA SAVE

Motel

All Year [ECP] 1P: $75-$95 2P: $75-$95 XP: $5 F

Location: Just e of University of California Campus. 123 B St 95616. Fax: 530/756-0245. **Facility:** 53 units. 51 one-bedroom standard units. 2 one-bedroom suites with kitchens. 2 stories, exterior corridors. *Bath:* combo or shower only. **Parking:** on-site. **Terms:** weekly rates available, small pets only ($5 extra charge). **Amenities:** voice mail, irons, hair dryers. **Leisure Activities:** whirlpool, bicycles, exercise room. **Cards:** AX, CB, DC, DS, JC, MC, VI. **Special Amenities: free continental breakfast and early check-in/late check-out.**

SOME UNITS

FEE / /

COMFORT SUITES *Book at aaa.com* **Phone:** (530)297-1500

Motel

4/1-9/30 [ECP]	1P: $99-$199	2P: $99-$199	XP: $10	F17
2/1-3/31 & 10/1-1/31 [ECP]	1P: $89-$139	2P: $89-$149	XP: $10	F17

Location: I-80, exit Richards Blvd, just s. 1640 Research Park Dr 95616. Fax: 530/297-1600. **Facility:** 71 units. 69 one-bedroom standard units. 2 one-bedroom suites ($139-$209) with whirlpools. 3 stories, interior corridors. **Parking:** on-site. **Amenities:** dual phone lines, voice mail, irons, hair dryers. **Pool(s):** heated outdoor. **Leisure Activities:** whirlpool. **Guest Services:** coin laundry. **Business Services:** meeting rooms. **Cards:** AX, DC, DS, MC, VI.

SOME UNITS

HALLMARK INN *Book at aaa.com* **Phone:** (530)753-3600

Motel

All Year [ECP]	1P: $95	2P: $95

Location: I-80, exit Davis westbound; exit Central Davis eastbound. Located within easy access to University of California campus. 110 F St 95616. Fax: 530/758-8623. **Facility:** 135 units. 129 one-bedroom standard units. 6 one-bedroom suites ($120-$150). 2-3 stories, interior corridors. **Parking:** on-site. **Amenities:** voice mail, irons, hair dryers. **Pool(s):** heated outdoor. **Guest Services:** gift shop, complimentary evening beverages. **Business Services:** meeting rooms. **Cards:** AX, DC, DS, MC, VI.

SOME UNITS

HOLIDAY INN EXPRESS HOTEL & SUITES *Book at aaa.com* **Phone:** (530)758-2600

SAVE

Motel

All Year	1P: $85-$199	2P: $85-$199	XP: $10	F18

Location: I-80, exit Richards Blvd, 2 blks e. 1771 Research Park Dr 95616. Fax: 530/758-1771. **Facility:** 50 one-bedroom standard units, some with whirlpools. 3 stories, interior corridors. **Parking:** on-site. **Terms:** [CP] & [ECP] meal plans available. **Amenities:** dual phone lines, voice mail, irons, hair dryers. **Pool(s):** heated outdoor. **Leisure Activities:** whirlpool. **Guest Services:** coin laundry. **Business Services:** meeting rooms. **Cards:** AX, CB, DC, DS, JC, MC, VI. **Special Amenities: free expanded continental breakfast and free newspaper.** *(See color ad below & p 260)*

SOME UNITS

HOWARD JOHNSON HOTEL *Book at aaa.com* **Phone:** (530)792-0800

SAVE

Motel

5/1-9/30 [BP]	1P: $89-$109	2P: $89-$109	XP: $10	F
2/1-4/30 & 10/1-1/31 [BP]	1P: $79-$99	2P: $79-$99	XP: $10	F

Location: I-80, exit Mace Blvd, just s, then 0.3 mi w. 4100 Chiles Rd 95616. Fax: 530/753-0225. **Facility:** 80 one-bedroom standard units. 2 stories, interior corridors. *Bath:* combo or shower only. **Parking:** on-site. **Terms:** small pets only ($10 fee). **Amenities:** voice mail, irons, hair dryers. **Dining:** cocktails. **Pool(s):** outdoor. **Leisure Activities:** volleyball. **Guest Services:** coin laundry. **Business Services:** meeting rooms, business center. **Cards:** AX, DC, DS, MC, VI. **Special Amenities: free full breakfast and free local telephone calls.**

SOME UNITS

FEE

UNIVERSITY PARK INN & SUITES *Book at aaa.com* **Phone:** (530)756-0910

Motel

All Year	1P: $75-$129	2P: $75-$129	XP: $10	F12

Location: I-80, exit Richards Blvd, just n. 1111 Richards Blvd 95616. Fax: 530/758-0978. **Facility:** 45 units. 25 one-bedroom standard units. 20 one-bedroom suites ($94-$129), some with whirlpools. 2 stories, exterior corridors. **Parking:** on-site. **Amenities:** voice mail, irons, hair dryers. *Some:* dual phone lines. **Pool(s):** outdoor. **Leisure Activities:** exercise room. **Business Services:** meeting rooms. **Cards:** AX, DC, MC, VI.

SOME UNITS

DEATH VALLEY NATIONAL PARK

WHERE TO STAY

FURNACE CREEK INN — Phone: (303)297-2757

Historic Small-scale Hotel

2/1-5/9 & 10/15-1/31	1P: $270-$320	2P: $270-$320	XP: $20	F18
5/10-10/14	1P: $180-$200	2P: $180-$200	XP: $20	F18

Location: On SR 190; 1 mi s of visitor center. SR 190 92328 (PO Box 1). Fax: 760/786-2514. **Facility:** Baths formed by natural springs are featured on the grounds of the inn, an imposing Mission-style structure of stone and adobe. Designated smoking area. 66 units. 64 one-bedroom standard units, some with whirlpools. 2 one-bedroom suites ($350-$370). 3-4 stories, interior/exterior corridors. *Bath:* combo or shower only. **Parking:** on-site. **Terms:** check-in 4 pm, 2-3 night minimum stay - some weekends. **Amenities:** video games, voice mail, irons, hair dryers. **Dining:** The Inn Dining Room, see separate listing. **Pool(s):** heated outdoor. **Leisure Activities:** saunas, 4 lighted tennis courts, exercise room. *Fee:* golf-18 holes, horseback riding, massage. **Guest Services:** gift shop. **Business Services:** meeting rooms, business center. **Cards:** AX, DC, DS, JC, MC, VI.

ASK DATA PORT

FURNACE CREEK RANCH — Phone: (303)297-2757

Motel

2/1-5/9 & 10/15-1/31	1P: $138-$164	2P: $138-$164	XP: $20	F18
5/10-10/14	1P: $118-$149	2P: $118-$149	XP: $20	F18

Location: On SR 190. Located adjacent to visitor center. (PO Box 1). Fax: 760/786-2514. **Facility:** Designated smoking area. 224 one-bedroom standard units. 2 stories, interior/exterior corridors. *Bath:* combo or shower only. **Parking:** on-site. **Terms:** check-in 4 pm, 2-3 night minimum stay - some weekends. **Amenities:** video games. *Some:* irons, hair dryers. **Pool(s):** heated outdoor. **Leisure Activities:** 2 lighted tennis courts, playground. *Fee:* golf-18 holes, horseback riding, massage. **Guest Services:** coin laundry. **Business Services:** fax (fee). **Cards:** AX, DC, DS, JC, MC, VI.

SOME UNITS

ASK

The following lodging was either not evaluated or did not meet AAA rating requirements but is listed for your information only.

STOVEPIPE WELLS VILLAGE — Phone: 760/786-2387

fyi

Motel

Did not meet all AAA rating requirements for some guest rooms at time of last evaluation on 01/28/2003. **Location:** On SR 190; 24 mi nw of visitor center. SR 190 92328. Facilities, services, and decor characterize a mid-range property.

WHERE TO DINE

THE INN DINING ROOM — **Lunch:** $10-$16 — **Dinner:** $21-$28 — **Phone:** 760/786-2345

American

Location: On SR 190; 1 mi s of visitor center; in Furnace Creek Inn. **Hours:** 7 am-10:30, noon-2:30 & 5:30-9:30 pm; dinner 7 pm-9 pm in summer. **Reservations:** suggested. **Features:** The "desert oasis" treats guests to a delightful fine-dining experience. The luxuriously appointed dining room affords beautiful mountain and desert sunset views. An extensive wine list incorporates appropriate selections for such choices as the rattlesnake taco appetizer, chicken liver tortilla soup, whole-leaf Caesar salad and delicious steaks and seafood dishes. Professional, knowledgeable servers eagerly assist with selections. Attention to detail is exceptional. Semi-formal attire; cocktails. **Parking:** on-site. **Cards:** AX, DC, DS, MC, VI.

DELANO pop. 38,824

WHERE TO STAY

BEST WESTERN LIBERTY INN — *Book at aaa.com* — Phone: (661)725-0976

AAA SAVE

Motel

All Year [ECP]	1P: $59-$79	2P: $65-$85	XP: $6	F12

Location: SR 99, exit County Line Rd. 14394 County Line Rd 93215. Fax: 661/725-6743. **Facility:** 51 one-bedroom standard units. 2 stories, interior corridors. **Parking:** on-site. **Amenities:** irons, hair dryers. **Pool(s):** heated indoor. **Leisure Activities:** sauna, whirlpool. **Business Services:** fax (fee). **Cards:** AX, CB, DC, DS, MC, VI. **Special Amenities: free expanded continental breakfast and free newspaper.** *(See ad below)*

SOME UNITS

DATA PORT VCR

COMFORT INN *Book at aaa.com* **Phone:** (661)725-1022

Motel

All Year [CP] 1P: $50-$60 2P: $60-$70 XP: $5 F14

Location: SR 99, exit County Line Rd, just e. 2211 Girard St 93215. Fax: 661/725-1104. **Facility:** 45 one-bedroom standard units, some with whirlpools. 2 stories, exterior corridors. **Parking:** on-site. **Terms:** small pets only ($10 extra charge). **Amenities:** irons, hair dryers. **Pool(s):** outdoor. **Business Services:** fax (fee). **Cards:** AX, DC, DS, MC, VI. **Special Amenities: free continental breakfast and free local telephone calls.**

SOME UNITS

FEE

DINUBA pop. 16,844

WHERE TO STAY

BEST WESTERN AMERICANA *Book at aaa.com* **Phone:** 559/595-8401

Motel

All Year 1P: $72-$85 2P: $80-$95 XP: $10 F12

Location: 0.6 mi sw of downtown. 1450 S Alta Ave 93618. Fax: 559/595-9450. **Facility:** 39 units. 35 one-bedroom standard units. 4 one-bedroom suites ($115-$145). 2 stories, interior corridors. *Bath:* combo or shower only. **Parking:** on-site. **Terms:** office hours 6 am-10 pm, 2 night minimum stay - weekends, cancellation fee imposed, [CP] & [ECP] meal plans available, package plans. **Amenities:** voice mail, irons, hair dryers. **Pool(s):** outdoor. **Leisure Activities:** whirlpool. **Guest Services:** coin laundry. **Business Services:** fax (fee). **Cards:** AX, DC, JC, MC, VI. **Special Amenities: free continental breakfast and early check-in/late check-out.**

SOME UNITS

REEDLEY COUNTRY INN **Phone:** 559/393-1810

Historic Bed & Breakfast

Property failed to provide current rates

Location: SR 99, exit Manning Ave, 8 mi e, 1 mi s on Rd 52 (Reed Ave). (43137 Rd 52, REEDLEY, 93654). Fax: 559/638-8099. **Facility:** A rose garden surrounds these two restored country farmhouses; an on-site gift shop specializes in lace. Smoke free premises. 5 units. 4 one-bedroom standard units, some with whirlpools. 1 one-bedroom suite. 1-2 stories, interior/exterior corridors. *Bath:* combo or shower only. **Parking:** on-site. **Amenities:** video library (fee). *Some:* irons, hair dryers. **Leisure Activities:** whirlpool. **Business Services:** meeting rooms, fax (fee).

DIXON pop. 16,103

WHERE TO STAY

BEST WESTERN INN DIXON *Book at aaa.com* **Phone:** (707)678-1400

Motel

4/1-9/30 [ECP] 1P: $100-$125 2P: $110-$135 XP: $10 F12

2/1-3/31 & 10/1-1/31 [ECP] 1P: $85-$105 2P: $95-$115 XP: $10 F12

Location: I-80, exit Pitt School Rd, 8 mi w of University of California Davis Campus. 1345 Commercial Way 95620. Fax: 707/678-0754. **Facility:** 105 units. 97 one-bedroom standard units, some with whirlpools. 8 one-bedroom suites ($145-$180) with whirlpools. 2 stories, interior/exterior corridors. **Parking:** on-site. **Terms:** small pets only ($10 fee). **Amenities:** dual phone lines, voice mail, irons, hair dryers. **Pool(s):** outdoor. **Leisure Activities:** sauna, whirlpool. **Guest Services:** coin laundry. **Business Services:** meeting rooms. **Cards:** AX, CB, DC, DS, MC, VI. **Special Amenities: free expanded continental breakfast and free local telephone calls.**

(See color ad below)

SOME UNITS

    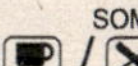

FEE FEE

MICROTEL INN & SUITES *Book at aaa.com* **Phone:** (707)693-0606

Motel

All Year 1P: $69-$89 2P: $69-$89 XP: $10 F16

Location: I-80, exit Pitt School Rd, just s. 1480 Ary Ln 95620. Fax: 707/693-0694. **Facility:** 60 one-bedroom standard units. 3 stories, interior corridors. **Parking:** on-site. **Terms:** cancellation fee imposed, weekly rates available, package plans. **Pool(s):** outdoor. **Leisure Activities:** whirlpool. **Guest Services:** coin laundry. **Cards:** AX, DC, DS, JC, MC, VI. **Special Amenities: free continental breakfast and free local telephone calls.**

SOME UNITS

DUBLIN pop. 29,973

WHERE TO STAY

AMERISUITES (SAN FRANCISCO/DUBLIN) *Book at aaa.com* **Phone:** (925)828-9006

Small-scale Hotel

All Year 1P: $162 2P: $162

Location: I-580, exit Hacienda Dr, then n. 4950 Hacienda Dr 94568. Fax: 925/828-9030. **Facility:** 128 one-bedroom suites. 6 stories, interior corridors. *Bath:* combo or shower only. **Parking:** on-site. **Terms:** [ECP] meal plan available, small pets only. **Amenities:** high-speed Internet, voice mail, irons, hair dryers. *Fee:* video library, video games. *Some:* dual phone lines. **Pool(s):** heated outdoor. **Leisure Activities:** exercise room. **Guest Services:** coin laundry. **Business Services:** meeting rooms. **Cards:** AX, DC, DS, JC, MC, VI. **Special Amenities: free expanded continental breakfast and free newspaper.** *(See color ad below)*

SOME UNITS

HOLIDAY INN EXPRESS HOTEL & SUITES *Book at aaa.com* **Phone:** (925)828-9393

Small-scale Hotel

All Year [CP] 1P: $69-$99 XP: $10 F18

Location: I-580, exit Hopyard/Dougherty Rd, just n. 6275 Dublin Blvd 94568. Fax: 925/828-9002. **Facility:** 91 one-bedroom standard units, some with whirlpools. 3 stories, interior corridors. *Bath:* combo or shower only. **Parking:** on-site. **Amenities:** video games (fee), high-speed Internet, dual phone lines, voice mail, irons, hair dryers. **Pool(s):** heated outdoor. **Leisure Activities:** whirlpool, exercise room. **Guest Services:** coin laundry. **Business Services:** meeting rooms. **Cards:** AX, CB, DC, DS, JC, MC, VI. ***(See color ad p 260)***

SOME UNITS

RADISSON DUBLIN *Book at aaa.com* **Phone:** (925)828-7750

Small-scale Hotel

All Year 1P: $109-$149 2P: $109-$149 XP: $10 F18

Location: At northwest quadrant of I-580 and 680. 6680 Regional St 94568. Fax: 925/828-3650. **Facility:** 234 one-bedroom standard units. 3 stories, interior corridors. **Parking:** on-site. **Terms:** pets ($35 fee). **Amenities:** dual phone lines, voice mail, irons, hair dryers. *Fee:* video games, high-speed Internet. **Dining:** 6 am-10 & 5-9 pm; closed Sun. **Pool(s):** heated indoor. **Leisure Activities:** sauna, whirlpool, exercise room. *Fee:* massage. **Guest Services:** valet and coin laundry. **Business Services:** conference facilities, business center. **Cards:** AX, DC, MC, VI. **Special Amenities: free continental breakfast and early check-in/late check-out.** *(See color ad p 629)*

SOME UNITS

FEE

DUNNIGAN

WHERE TO STAY

BEST VALUE INN *Book at aaa.com* **Phone:** (530)724-3333

Motel

5/1-10/31 [CP]	1P: $60-$90	2P: $65-$100	XP: $5	F12
2/1-4/30 & 11/1-1/31 [CP]	1P: $53-$75	2P: $63-$85	XP: $5	F12

Location: I-5, exit Dunnigan. 3930 Road 89 95937 (PO Box 740). Fax: 530/724-4233. **Facility:** 40 one-bedroom standard units. 2 stories, interior corridors. **Parking:** on-site. **Terms:** small pets only. **Pool(s):** outdoor. **Guest Services:** coin laundry. **Cards:** AX, DS, MC, VI.

SOME UNITS

BEST WESTERN COUNTRY *Book at aaa.com* **Phone:** (530)724-3471

Motel

5/2-10/31 [ECP] 1P: $65-$120 2P: $75-$125 XP: $5 F15
2/1-5/1 & 11/1-1/31 [ECP] 1P: $59-$100 2P: $69-$105 XP: $5 F15

Location: I-5, exit Dunnigan. 3930 Road 89 95937 (PO Box 740). Fax: 530/724-4233. **Facility:** 55 units. 51 one-bedroom standard units. 4 one-bedroom suites ($75-$125) with kitchens. 1 story, exterior corridors. **Parking:** on-site. **Terms:** small pets only. **Amenities:** irons, hair dryers. **Pool(s):** outdoor. **Leisure Activities:** whirlpool. **Guest Services:** coin laundry. **Business Services:** meeting rooms. **Cards:** AX, CB, DC, DS, MC, VI. **Special Amenities: free expanded continental breakfast and preferred room (subject to availability with advanced reservations).**

SOME UNITS

BUDGET 8 MOTEL **Phone:** (530)724-3411

Motel

All Year 1P: $45-$55 2P: $45-$55 XP: $5 F12

Location: I-5, exit CR 8, just e. 4930 CR 99 W 95937 (PO Box 95). Fax: 530/724-4205. **Facility:** 24 one-bedroom standard units. 1 story, exterior corridors. *Bath:* shower only. **Parking:** on-site. **Terms:** weekly rates available, small pets only ($5 extra charge). **Cards:** AX, DC, DS, MC, VI.

SOME UNITS

FEE

DUNSMUIR pop. 1,923

WHERE TO STAY

CABOOSE MOTEL-RAILROAD PARK RESORT **Phone:** (530)235-4440

Motel

4/16-10/15 1P: $80-$95 2P: $85-$100 XP: $8 D
2/1-4/15 & 10/16-1/31 1P: $70-$90 2P: $75-$95 XP: $8 D

Location: I-5, exit 778 (Railroad Park Rd), 1 mi s. 100 Railroad Park Rd 96025. Fax: 530/235-4470. **Facility:** 27 one-bedroom standard units. *Bath:* combo or shower only. **Parking:** on-site. **Terms:** office hours 8 am-9:30 pm, age restrictions may apply, small pets only ($10 extra charge, with prior approval). **Amenities:** *Some:* irons, hair dryers. **Dining:** Railroad Park Dinner House & Lounge, see separate listing. **Pool(s):** outdoor. **Leisure Activities:** whirlpool. **Guest Services:** gift shop. **Cards:** MC, VI.

SOME UNITS

FEE

CEDAR LODGE MOTEL **Phone:** (530)235-4331

Motel

5/2-9/1 1P: $48-$64 2P: $55-$75 XP: $5 F5
2/1-5/1 & 9/2-1/31 1P: $46-$62 2P: $52-$70 XP: $5 F5

Location: I-5, exit 730 (Dunsmuir/Siskiyou), 0.5 mi w. 4201 Dunsmuir Ave 96025. Fax: 530/235-4000. **Facility:** 15 units. 12 one- and 3 two-bedroom standard units, some with kitchens. 1 story, exterior corridors. *Bath:* combo or shower only. **Parking:** on-site. **Terms:** age restrictions may apply, 4 day cancellation notice, weekly rates available, small pets only ($5 extra charge, no cats). **Amenities:** hair dryers. *Some:* irons. **Leisure Activities:** whirlpool. **Cards:** AX, DS, MC, VI. **Special Amenities: free local telephone calls.**

SOME UNITS

FEE

DUNSMUIR TRAVELODGE *Book at aaa.com* **Phone:** (530)235-4395

Motel

All Year 1P: $55-$125 2P: $55-$125

Location: I-5, exit 730 (Central Dunsmuir). 5400 Dunsmuir Ave 96025. Fax: 530/235-0229. **Facility:** 18 one-bedroom standard units. 2 stories, exterior corridors. **Parking:** on-site. **Terms:** age restrictions may apply, [CP] meal plan available. **Amenities:** hair dryers. *Some:* irons. **Cards:** AX, DC, DS, MC, VI. **Special Amenities: free continental breakfast and free local telephone calls.** *(See color ad p 507)*

SOME UNITS

WHERE TO DINE

RAILROAD PARK DINNER HOUSE & LOUNGE **Dinner:** $12-$28 **Phone:** 530/235-4611

American

Location: I-5, exit 778 (Railroad Park Rd), 1 mi s; in Caboose Motel-Railroad Park Resort. 100 Railroad Park Rd 96025. **Hours:** Open 4/2-12/31; 5 pm-9 pm; to 10 pm in summer; hours vary in winter. Closed: 1/1, 11/25, 12/25; also Mon & Tues. **Reservations:** suggested. **Features:** Diners can sit in restored railroads cars more than 100 years old while tasting good steaks and fish. Call in advance because the restaurant is open only at selected times of the year. Casual dress; cocktails. **Parking:** on-site. **Cards:** AX, DS, MC, VI.

EL CERRITO pop. 22,900

WHERE TO STAY

BEST INN-EL CERRITO *Book at aaa.com* **Phone:** (510)232-0900

Small-scale Hotel

5/1-9/30 [ECP] 1P: $80-$110 2P: $85-$120 XP: $10 F12
2/1-4/30 & 10/1-1/31 [ECP] 1P: $70-$110 2P: $75-$120 XP: $10 F12

Location: I-80, exit Potrero Ave eastbound; exit Cutting Blvd westbound; S Cutting; W San Pablo; S Potrero Ave. 6009 Potrero Ave 94530. Fax: 510/231-0209. **Facility:** 48 one-bedroom standard units, some with whirlpools. 3 stories, interior corridors. *Bath:* combo or shower only. **Parking:** on-site. **Terms:** age restrictions may apply. **Amenities:** hair dryers. *Some:* high-speed Internet, irons. **Cards:** AX, CB, DC, DS, MC, VI. **Special Amenities: free expanded continental breakfast and free local telephone calls.** *(See color ad p 284)*

SOME UNITS

ELK —*See Wine Country p. 769.*

ELK GROVE pop. 59,984

WHERE TO STAY

HOLIDAY INN EXPRESS HOTEL & SUITES *Book at aaa.com* **Phone:** (916)478-9000

Motel

All Year [ECP] 1P: $110-$130 2P: $110-$130 XP: $10 F18

Location: SR 99, exit Laguna Blvd. 9175 W Stockton Blvd 95758. Fax: 916/478-9049. **Facility:** 116 units. 106 one-bedroom standard units. 10 one-bedroom suites ($140-$165). 3 stories, interior corridors. **Parking:** on-site. **Terms:** cancellation fee imposed. **Amenities:** dual phone lines, voice mail, irons, hair dryers. **Pool(s):** heated outdoor. **Leisure Activities:** whirlpool, exercise room. **Guest Services:** coin laundry. **Business Services:** meeting rooms, business center. **Cards:** AX, CB, DC, DS, JC, MC, VI. **Special Amenities: free continental breakfast and free local telephone calls.** *(See color ad p 260)*

SOME UNITS

The following lodging was either not evaluated or did not meet AAA rating requirements but is listed for your information only.

COMFORT SUITES **Phone:** 916/478-5200

fyi

Small-scale Hotel

All Year [ECP] 1P: $99-$139 2P: $109-$149 XP: $10 F12

Too new to rate, opening scheduled for September 2003. **Location:** I-5, exit Elk Grove Blvd, just e. 2460 Maritime Dr 95758. **Amenities:** 65 units, coffeemakers, microwaves, refrigerators, pool. **Terms:** 14 day cancellation notice. **Cards:** AX, CB, DC, DS, JC, MC, VI.

EL PORTAL —*See also YOSEMITE NATIONAL PARK.*

WHERE TO STAY

CEDAR LODGE **Phone:** (209)379-2612

Motel

4/1-10/31 1P: $96-$149 2P: $96-$149 XP: $10

2/1-3/31 & 11/1-1/31 1P: $59-$109 2P: $59-$109 XP: $10

Location: 6 mi w of Yosemite National Park West Gate. 9966 Hwy 140 95318 (PO Box C). Fax: 209/379-2712. **Facility:** 209 units. 192 one-bedroom standard units, some with efficiencies and/or whirlpools. 14 one- and 3 three-bedroom suites, some with kitchens and/or whirlpools. 2 stories (no elevator), exterior corridors. *Bath:* combo or shower only. **Parking:** on-site. **Terms:** 7 day cancellation notice-fee imposed. **Dining:** 7 am-10 pm in season, cocktails. **Pool(s):** heated outdoor, heated indoor. **Leisure Activities:** whirlpool. **Guest Services:** gift shop. **Business Services:** conference facilities. **Cards:** AX, MC, VI. *(See color ad p 819)*

SOME UNITS

FEE

YOSEMITE VIEW LODGE **Phone:** (209)379-2681

Motel

4/1-10/25 1P: $129-$249 2P: $129-$249

2/1-3/31 & 10/26-1/31 1P: $85-$135 2P: $85-$135

Location: Just w of Yosemite National Park West Gate. 11136 Hwy 140 95318 (PO Box D). Fax: 209/379-2704. **Facility:** 345 units. 339 one-bedroom standard units, some with efficiencies and/or whirlpools. 6 one-bedroom suites with efficiencies and whirlpools. 1-3 stories, exterior corridors. *Bath:* combo or shower only. **Parking:** on-site. **Terms:** 7 day cancellation notice-fee imposed, pets ($10 extra charge). **Amenities:** *Some:* irons, hair dryers. **Pool(s):** 2 heated outdoor, heated indoor. **Leisure Activities:** whirlpools, fishing, hiking trails. **Guest Services:** gift shop, coin laundry. **Business Services:** meeting rooms. **Cards:** AX, MC, VI. *(See color ad p 819)*

SOME UNITS

FEE

EMERYVILLE pop. 6,882 (See map and index starting on p. 516)

WHERE TO STAY

COURTYARD BY MARRIOTT EMERYVILLE Book at aaa.com Phone: (510)652-8777 32

Large-scale Hotel All Year 1P: $89-$179 2P: $89-$179

Location: I-80, exit Powell St westbound, just e. 5555 Shellmound St 94608. Fax: 510/601-4195. **Facility:** 295 one-bedroom standard units, some with whirlpools. 11 stories. *Bath:* combo or shower only. **Parking:** on-site. **Terms:** off-site registration, cancellation fee imposed, [MAP] meal plan available, package plans - weekends & seasonal. **Amenities:** video games, dual phone lines, voice mail, irons, hair dryers. **Pool(s):** heated indoor. **Leisure Activities:** whirlpool, exercise room. **Guest Services:** gift shop. **Business Services:** meeting rooms, business center. **Cards:** AX, CB, DC, DS, JC, MC, VI.

SOME UNITS DATA PORT

FOUR POINTS BY SHERATON-SAN FRANCISCO BAY BRIDGE Book at aaa.com Phone: (510)547-7888 35

Large-scale Hotel All Year 1P: $129-$149 2P: $129-$149 XP: $10 F18

Location: I-80, exit Powell St westbound; exit Shellmound St eastbound, 1 mi s. 1603 Powell St 94608. Fax: 510/652-4426. **Facility:** 153 one-bedroom standard units. 7 stories, interior corridors. **Parking:** on-site. **Terms:** [MAP] meal plan available. **Amenities:** video games, dual phone lines, voice mail, irons, hair dryers. **Pool(s):** outdoor. **Leisure Activities:** whirlpool, exercise room. **Guest Services:** coin laundry. **Business Services:** meeting rooms, business center. **Cards:** AX, CB, DC, DS, JC, MC, VI.

ASK DATA PORT SOME UNITS

HOLIDAY INN-BAY BRIDGE Book at aaa.com Phone: (510)658-9300 34

Large-scale Hotel All Year 1P: $159-$219 2P: $169-$229 XP: $10 F19

Location: I-80, exit Powell St westbound; exit Shellmound St eastbound, w to Christie, then n. 1800 Powell St 94608. Fax: 510/547-8166. **Facility:** 279 units. 278 one-bedroom standard units. 1 one-bedroom suite. 12 stories, interior corridors. *Bath:* combo or shower only. **Parking:** on-site. **Amenities:** video games, high-speed Internet, dual phone lines, voice mail, irons, hair dryers. **Dining:** 6 am-2 & 5-10 pm, cocktails. **Leisure Activities:** whirlpool, exercise room. **Guest Services:** valet laundry. **Business Services:** meeting rooms, business center. **Cards:** AX, DC, DS, JC, MC, VI. **Special Amenities: free newspaper.** *(See color ad below)*

SOME UNITS DATA PORT FEE FEE

WOODFIN SUITE HOTEL SAN FRANCISCO BAY BRIDGE Book at aaa.com Phone: (510)601-5880 33

Large-scale Hotel All Year 1P: $144 2P: $144

Location: I-80, exit Powell St. 5800 Shellmound St 94608. Fax: 510/601-5833. **Facility:** 234 units. 32 one-bedroom standard units. 202 one-bedroom suites ($144) with kitchens. 12 stories, interior corridors. *Bath:* combo or shower only. **Parking:** on-site. **Terms:** [BP] meal plan available. **Amenities:** video library, high-speed Internet, dual phone lines, voice mail, irons, hair dryers. *Some:* safes. **Pool(s):** heated outdoor. **Leisure Activities:** whirlpool, exercise room. *Fee:* massage. **Guest Services:** gift shop. **Business Services:** meeting rooms, business center. **Cards:** AX, DC, DS, JC, MC, VI.

ASK VCR DATA PORT SOME UNITS

ETNA pop. 781

WHERE TO STAY

MOTEL ETNA Phone: 530/467-5330

Motel All Year 1P: $37 2P: $42 XP: $5 F

Location: Just w of SR 3. 317 Collier Way 96027 (PO Box 754). **Facility:** 10 one-bedroom standard units. 1 story, exterior corridors. *Bath:* combo or shower only. **Parking:** on-site. **Terms:** office hours 7 am-10 pm, cancellation fee imposed. **Amenities:** *Some:* irons, hair dryers. **Cards:** AX, DS, MC, VI.

EUREKA pop. 26,128

WHERE TO STAY

ABIGAIL'S ELEGANT VICTORIAN MANSION BED & BREAKFAST INN — **Phone:** 707/444-3144

Bed & Breakfast

5/1-10/31 [ECP]	1P: $84-$185	2P: $135-$255	XP: $75
2/1-4/30 & 11/1-1/31 [ECP]	1P: $84-$165	2P: $125-$195	XP: $70

Location: US 101, exit C St, 0.5 mi e. Located in a quiet, residential area. 1406 C St 95501. Fax: 707/442-3295. **Facility:** An 1878 National Landmark, this symbol of opulence, grace and grandeur is breathtakingly authentic, with all the nostalgic trimmings of a century ago. Smoke free premises. 4 one-bedroom standard units. 2 stories (no elevator), interior corridors. *Bath:* shared or private, combo or shower only. **Parking:** on-site. **Terms:** office hours 10 am-4 pm, age restrictions may apply, 14 day cancellation notice-fee imposed, [BP] meal plan available. **Amenities:** video library. *Some:* irons, hair dryers. **Leisure Activities:** sauna, bicycles. **Guest Services:** complimentary laundry. **Business Services:** meeting rooms. **Cards:** MC, VI.

SOME UNITS

BAYVIEW MOTEL — **Phone:** 707/442-1673

Motel

5/1-9/30	1P: $85-$150	2P: $85-$150	XP: $10	F18
2/1-4/30 & 10/1-1/31	1P: $75-$130	2P: $75-$130	XP: $10	F18

Location: E of US 101, exit Henderson, at top of hill, just n. 2844 Fairfield St 95501. Fax: 707/268-8681. **Facility:** 17 units. 14 one- and 3 two-bedroom standard units, some with whirlpools. 2 stories (no elevator), exterior corridors. *Bath:* combo or shower only. **Parking:** on-site. **Terms:** office hours 7 am-10 pm, age restrictions may apply, pets ($5 extra charge). **Amenities:** irons, hair dryers. **Business Services:** meeting rooms. **Cards:** AX, DS, MC, VI.

FEE

BEST WESTERN BAYSHORE INN *Book at aaa.com* — **Phone:** (707)268-8005

SAVE — Motel

5/16-9/15 [BP]	1P: $109-$134	2P: $121-$149	XP: $5	F12
2/1-5/15 & 9/16-1/31 [BP]	1P: $84-$120	2P: $88-$135	XP: $5	F12

Location: US 101, s of Bayshore Mall. 3500 Broadway 95503. Fax: 707/268-8002. **Facility:** 81 units. 70 one- and 7 two-bedroom standard units, some with whirlpools. 4 one-bedroom suites ($108-$146) with whirlpools. 3 stories, exterior corridors. *Bath:* combo or shower only. **Parking:** on-site. **Terms:** [AP] meal plan available, package plans, pets ($20 extra charge). **Amenities:** video games, voice mail, irons, hair dryers. *Some:* high-speed Internet, dual phone lines. **Dining:** 7:30 am-10 pm, Fri & Sat-11 pm, cocktails. **Pool(s):** heated indoor/outdoor. **Leisure Activities:** sauna, whirlpool, exercise room. **Guest Services:** coin laundry. **Business Services:** conference facilities, business center. **Cards:** AX, CB, DC, DS, MC, VI. **Special Amenities: free full breakfast and free local telephone calls.**

SOME UNITS

FEE

BEST WESTERN HUMBOLDT BAY INN *Book at aaa.com* — **Phone:** (707)443-2234

SAVE — Motel

7/1-9/30 [ECP]	1P: $79-$139	2P: $79-$139	XP: $5	F12
2/1-6/30 & 10/1-1/31 [ECP]	1P: $69-$129	2P: $69-$129	XP: $5	F12

Location: US 101 at Broadway. 232 W 5th St 95501. Fax: 707/443-3489. **Facility:** 112 units. 110 one- and 1 two-bedroom standard units, some with whirlpools. 1 one-bedroom suite ($99-$199). 2 stories (no elevator), exterior corridors. *Bath:* combo or shower only. **Parking:** on-site. **Amenities:** video library, video games, irons, hair dryers. *Some:* DVD players, high-speed Internet. **Dining:** 6 am-10 pm, wine/beer only. **Pool(s):** heated outdoor. **Leisure Activities:** whirlpool, Pool table. **Guest Services:** coin laundry. **Business Services:** meeting rooms. **Cards:** AX, CB, DC, DS, JC, MC, VI. **Special Amenities: free expanded continental breakfast and free local telephone calls.** *(See color ad below & p 521)*

SOME UNITS

FEE

CARTER HOUSE INNS Book at aaa.com **Phone:** (707)444-8062

Classic Small-scale Hotel

All Year [BP] 1P: $105-$497 2P: $126-$497 XP: $25 F12

Location: Just w of US 101 S. 301 L St 95501. Fax: 707/444-8067. **Facility:** Accommodations are offered in the main inn as well as in a separate five-unit house and three-unit cottage; a one-unit cottage is across the street. Smoke free premises. 32 units. 20 one-bedroom standard units. 2 one-bedroom suites ($250-$426). 1 vacation home ($750-$1476) and 9 cottages ($497). 3 stories, interior corridors. *Bath:* combo or shower only. **Parking:** on-site. **Terms:** cancellation fee imposed, 18% service charge. **Amenities:** video library, CD players, voice mail, honor bars, irons, hair dryers. **Dining:** 301 At Carter House Inns, see separate listing. **Leisure Activities:** Fee: massage. **Guest Services:** complimentary evening beverages. **Cards:** AX, CB, DC, DS, MC, VI. **Special Amenities: free full breakfast and free local telephone calls.**

SOME UNITS

COMFORT INN Book at aaa.com **Phone:** (707)444-0401

Motel

5/14-9/15 1P: $70-$150 2P: $75-$150 XP: $6 F18

2/1-5/13 & 9/16-1/31 1P: $55-$99 2P: $65-$99 XP: $6 F18

Location: US 101 southbound, corner of 4th and V sts. 2014 4th St 95501. Fax: 707/442-8145. **Facility:** 30 one-bedroom standard units, some with whirlpools. 2 stories (no elevator), exterior corridors. *Bath:* combo or shower only. **Parking:** on-site. **Terms:** [ECP] meal plan available. **Amenities:** irons, hair dryers. **Cards:** AX, CB, DC, DS, JC, MC, VI. **Special Amenities: free continental breakfast and free local telephone calls.**

SOME UNITS

CORNELIUS DALY INN-BED & BREAKFAST Book at aaa.com **Phone:** 707/445-3638

Historic Bed & Breakfast

All Year [BP] 1P: $90-$180 2P: $90-$180 XP: $20 F4

Location: E of US 101. Located in a residential area. 1125 H St 95501. Fax: 707/444-3636. **Facility:** This exquisite Colonial Revival mansion was built in 1905 and features lovely Victorian gardens and a unique, third-floor Christmas ballroom. Smoke free premises. 5 one-bedroom standard units. 2 stories (no elevator), interior corridors. **Parking:** on-site. **Terms:** office hours 4 pm-10 pm, check-in 4 pm, age restrictions may apply, 7 day cancellation notice-fee imposed. **Amenities:** video library, hair dryers. *Some:* irons. **Guest Services:** complimentary evening beverages. **Cards:** AX, DS, MC, VI.

SOME UNITS

DAYS INN EUREKA Book at aaa.com **Phone:** (707)444-2019

Motel

6/1-9/15 [CP] 1P: $79-$99 2P: $79-$110 XP: $10 F12

2/1-5/31 & 9/16-1/31 [CP] 1P: $65-$75 2P: $69-$85 XP: $10 F12

Location: On US 101, south end of town. 4260 Broadway 95503. Fax: 707/445-9166. **Facility:** 48 one-bedroom standard units. 2 stories (no elevator), interior corridors. *Bath:* combo or shower only. **Parking:** on-site. **Amenities:** hair dryers. *Some:* irons. **Pool(s):** heated indoor. **Leisure Activities:** whirlpool. **Business Services:** fax. **Cards:** AX, DS, MC, VI. **Special Amenities: free continental breakfast and free newspaper.**

(See color ad below)

SOME UNITS

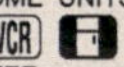

EUREKA RAMADA LIMITED Book at aaa.com **Phone:** (707)443-2206

Motel

5/16-9/15 [ECP] 1P: $69-$74 2P: $74-$81 XP: $8 F16

2/1-5/15 & 9/16-1/31 [ECP] 1P: $64-$72 2P: $69-$72 XP: $8 F16

Location: On US 101 northbound. 270 5th St 95501. Fax: 707/443-2029. **Facility:** 40 units. 39 one-bedroom standard units. 1 one-bedroom suite ($75-$120). 3 stories, interior corridors. **Parking:** on-site. **Terms:** small pets only ($8 extra charge). **Amenities:** voice mail, irons, hair dryers. **Leisure Activities:** sauna, whirlpool. **Business Services:** meeting rooms. **Cards:** AX, CB, DC, DS, MC, VI. **Special Amenities: free expanded continental breakfast and free local telephone calls.** *(See color ad p 324)*

SOME UNITS

FEE FEE

EUREKA SUPER 8 MOTEL — **Phone:** (707)443-3193

SAVE — Motel

6/1-9/15 [CP]	1P: $70-$90	2P: $75-$99	XP: $10	F12
2/1-5/31 & 9/16-1/31 [CP]	1P: $59-$69	2P: $65-$75	XP: $10	F12

Location: US 101 S at N St; downtown. 1304 4th St 95501. Fax: 707/444-2739. **Facility:** 50 one-bedroom standard units. 2 stories (no elevator), interior/exterior corridors. *Bath:* combo or shower only. **Parking:** on-site. **Amenities:** *Some:* irons. **Pool(s):** heated indoor. **Leisure Activities:** sauna, whirlpool. **Cards:** AX, DS, MC, VI. **Special Amenities: free continental breakfast and free newspaper.** *(See color ad below)*

SOME UNITS

EUREKA TOWN HOUSE MOTEL — **Phone:** 707/443-4536

SAVE — Motel

7/1-9/11	1P: $48-$75	2P: $50-$85	XP: $6	D12
5/14-6/30	1P: $45-$75	2P: $48-$85	XP: $6	D12
2/1-5/13 & 9/12-1/31	1P: $42-$75	2P: $45-$75	XP: $6	D12

Location: US 101 southbound, corner of 4th and K sts. 933 4th St 95501. Fax: 707/444-2099. **Facility:** 20 units. 16 one- and 4 two-bedroom standard units, some with whirlpools. 2 stories (no elevator), exterior corridors. *Bath:* combo or shower only. **Parking:** on-site. **Terms:** small pets only ($5 extra charge). **Amenities:** high-speed Internet. *Some:* irons, hair dryers. **Cards:** AX, CB, DC, DS, MC, VI. **Special Amenities: early check-in/late check-out.**

SOME UNITS

FEE FEE FEE

EUREKA TRAVELODGE — *Book at aaa.com* — **Phone:** 707/443-6345

Motel

6/16-9/30	1P: $59-$150	2P: $65-$150	XP: $10	F12
5/1-6/15	1P: $55-$150	2P: $60-$150	XP: $5	F12
2/1-4/30	1P: $49-$55	2P: $54-$59	XP: $5	F12
10/1-1/31	1P: $49-$54	2P: $54-$59	XP: $5	F12

Location: On US 101; corner of 4th and B sts. 4 4th St 95501. Fax: 707/443-1486. **Facility:** 46 one-bedroom standard units. 2 stories (no elevator), exterior corridors. *Bath:* combo or shower only. **Parking:** on-site. **Terms:** 10 day cancellation notice, package plans. **Amenities:** *Some:* irons, hair dryers. **Pool(s):** small heated outdoor. **Cards:** AX, DS, MC, VI.

SOME UNITS

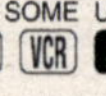

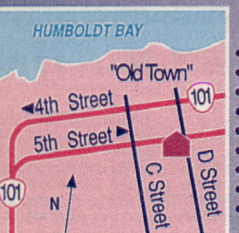

HOLIDAY INN EXPRESS *Book at aaa.com* **Phone:** (707)442-3261

AAA SAVE — Motel

6/2-10/1 [ECP]	1P: $85-$140	2P: $85-$140	XP: $5	F19
2/1-6/1 & 10/2-1/31 [ECP]	1P: $80-$100	2P: $80-$100	XP: $5	F19

Location: Exit US 101 northbound, w on V St, n on 3rd; exit US 101 southbound at X St. 2223 4th St 95501. Fax: 707/442-2317. **Facility:** 68 one-bedroom standard units, some with whirlpools. 2 stories, interior/exterior corridors. *Bath:* combo or shower only. **Parking:** on-site. **Amenities:** voice mail, irons, hair dryers. **Pool(s):** heated indoor. **Leisure Activities:** boating, sailboats, scuba diving, fishing, bicycles, hiking trails, exercise room. **Guest Services:** coin laundry. **Cards:** AX, CB, DC, DS, JC, MC, VI. **Special Amenities: free continental breakfast and free local telephone calls.**

SOME UNITS

QUALITY INN EUREKA *Book at aaa.com* **Phone:** (707)443-1601

AAA SAVE — Motel

5/30-9/30 [CP]	1P: $89-$200	2P: $89-$200	XP: $10	F12
2/1-5/29 & 10/1-1/31 [CP]	1P: $75-$120	2P: $75-$120	XP: $10	F12

Location: US 101 southbound, between M and N sts. 1209 4th St 95501. Fax: 707/444-8365. **Facility:** 60 units. 56 one- and 4 two-bedroom standard units. 2 stories (no elevator), exterior corridors. **Parking:** on-site. **Terms:** cancellation fee imposed. **Amenities:** irons, hair dryers. **Pool(s):** heated outdoor, wading. **Leisure Activities:** sauna, whirlpool. **Cards:** AX, CB, DC, DS, JC, MC, VI. **Special Amenities: free continental breakfast and free local telephone calls.** *(See ad below)*

SOME UNITS

RED LION HOTEL *Book at aaa.com* **Phone:** (707)445-0844

Motel

All Year 1P: $169-$179 2P: $169-$179 XP: $10 F

Location: US 101 southbound; between T and V sts. 1929 4th St 95501. Fax: 707/445-2752. **Facility:** 175 units. 165 one- and 9 two-bedroom standard units. 1 one-bedroom suite ($179-$189). 3 stories, interior corridors. *Bath:* combo or shower only. **Parking:** on-site. **Terms:** cancellation fee imposed, package plans, pets ($15 extra charge). **Amenities:** voice mail, irons, hair dryers. **Dining:** 6 am-10 pm, cocktails. **Pool(s):** heated outdoor. **Leisure Activities:** whirlpool, exercise room. **Guest Services:** valet laundry. **Business Services:** meeting rooms, business center. **Cards:** AX, CB, DC, DS, JC, MC, VI. **Special Amenities: free local telephone calls and early check-in/late check-out.** *(See color ad below)*

SOME UNITS

FEE FEE FEE

SUNRISE INN & SUITES **Phone:** (707)443-9751

Motel

5/15-9/30 1P: $45-$55 2P: $52-$69 XP: $6 F10

2/1-5/14 & 10/1-1/31 1P: $39-$49 2P: $45-$55 XP: $6 F10

Location: US 101, exit C St southbound; exit C St W northbound; downtown. 129 4th St 95501. Fax: 707/443-9751. **Facility:** 25 units. 20 one- and 5 two-bedroom standard units, some with whirlpools. 2 stories (no elevator), exterior corridors. *Bath:* combo or shower only. **Parking:** on-site. **Terms:** cancellation fee imposed, [CP] meal plan available, small pets only ($6 extra charge). **Amenities:** hair dryers. *Some:* irons. **Business Services:** PC, fax. **Cards:** AX, DS, MC, VI. **Special Amenities: free continental breakfast and free local telephone calls.**

SOME UNITS

FEE FEE FEE

WHERE TO DINE

301 AT CARTER HOUSE INNS **Dinner:** $20-$38 **Phone:** 707/444-8062

American

Location: Just w of US 101 S; in Carter House Inns. 301 L St 95501. **Hours:** 7:30 am-10 & 6-10 pm. **Reservations:** suggested. **Features:** Weekly seasonal specials, prepared from fresh ingredients, show noteworthy creativity. A concert on Thursday. Casual dress; cocktails. **Parking:** street. **Cards:** AX, CB, DC, DS, MC, VI.

CAFE MARINA **Lunch:** $7-$14 **Dinner:** $13-$20 **Phone:** 707/443-2233

Seafood

Location: On Woodley Island; US 101, exit SR 255, w to marina. 601 Startare Dr 95501. **Hours:** 7 am-9 pm; to 10 pm in summer. Closed: 11/25, 12/25; also Closed at 2 pm 12/24. **Features:** The menu is built around fresh local seafood. The casual dining room, as well as the seasonal patio, overlooks the marina. Casual dress; cocktails. **Parking:** on-site. **Cards:** AX, DS, MC, VI.

HURRICANE KATE'S **Lunch:** $7-$12 **Dinner:** $8-$25 **Phone:** 707/444-1405

New World

Location: US 101, w on F St to Second St; between F and G sts. 511 Second St 95501. **Hours:** 11:30 am-3 & 5-9 pm, Fri & Sat-10 pm. Closed: 1/1, 11/25, 12/25; also Sun & Mon. **Reservations:** suggested. **Features:** Located in old town Eureka, this restaurant has a French bistro, art-deco look, and is surrounded by boutique shops. The cuisine has a varied theme, from country to international, and adds a fresh seafood side as well. The easy dining style fits well with the contemporary music, with a weekend set aside after dining hours for jazz/blues concerts. Casual dress; cocktails. **Parking:** street. **Cards:** MC, VI.

THE RIB ROOM **Dinner:** $16-$24 **Phone:** 707/442-6441

Continental

Location: E of US 101 N; in Eureka Inn. 518 Seventh St 95501. **Hours:** 5:30 pm-10 pm. **Reservations:** suggested. **Features:** English Tudor decor, which is particularly attractive when it's dressed up for the holidays, adorns one of the city's oldest hotels. The menu features international cuisine. Service is excellent. Dressy casual; cocktails; entertainment. **Parking:** on-site. **Cards:** AX, CB, DC, DS, MC, VI.

SAMOA COOKHOUSE Historic **Lunch:** $9 **Dinner:** $13 **Phone:** 707/442-1659

American

Location: US 101, exit SR 255, w via Samoa Bridge on Samoa Peninsula. Samoa Rd 95501. **Hours:** 7 am-3:30 & 5-9 pm, Sun 7 am-9 pm; to 10 pm in summer; noon-8 pm 11/28. Closed: 12/25. **Features:** Built in 1885, the eatery is a holdout among the West's lumber-camp cookhouses. Families are welcomed to browse the relics of bygone days and sample hearty food. Casual dress. **Parking:** on-site. **Cards:** AX, DS, MC, VI.

THE SEA GRILL **Lunch:** $7-$12 **Dinner:** $15-$23 **Phone:** 707/443-7187

Seafood

Location: W off US 101. 316 E St 95501. **Hours:** 11 am-2 & 5-9 pm, Sat & Mon from 5 pm. Closed major holidays; also 12/24, Sun & 11/1-11/12. **Reservations:** suggested. **Features:** In the main downtown area, the established favorite specializes in seafood, steaks and pastas. Casual dress; cocktails. **Parking:** on-site. **Cards:** DC, DS, MC, VI.

EXETER pop. 9,168

WHERE TO STAY

BEST WESTERN EXETER INN & SUITES *Book at aaa.com* **Phone:** (559)592-8118

Motel

5/1-8/31 [ECP]	1P: $72-$79	2P: $72-$79	XP: $5	F12
9/1-1/31 [ECP]	1P: $69-$79	2P: $69-$79	XP: $5	F12
2/1-4/30 [ECP]	1P: $69-$75	2P: $69-$75	XP: $5	F12

Location: On SR 65, 0.5 mi s of town center. Located in a rural area. 805 S Kaweah Ave 93221. Fax: 559/592-5226. **Facility:** 32 one-bedroom standard units, some with whirlpools. 2 stories, exterior corridors. **Parking:** on-site. **Amenities:** voice mail, irons, hair dryers. **Pool(s):** outdoor. **Leisure Activities:** whirlpool, exercise room. **Guest Services:** coin laundry. **Business Services:** fax (fee). **Cards:** AX, CB, DC, DS, MC, VI. **Special Amenities: free expanded continental breakfast and free local telephone calls.**

SOME UNITS

KAWEAH MOTEL **Phone:** (559)592-2961

Motel

4/1-9/30	1P: $48-$60	2P: $48-$60	XP: $5	D14
2/1-3/31 & 10/1-1/31	1P: $48-$55	2P: $48-$55	XP: $5	D14

Location: On SR 65, just se of downtown. 319 S Kaweah Ave 93221. Fax: 559/592-4393. **Facility:** 19 one-bedroom standard units. 1 story, exterior corridors. *Bath:* shower only. **Parking:** on-site. **Amenities:** hair dryers. *Some:* irons. **Pool(s):** outdoor. **Cards:** AX, DS, MC, VI. **Special Amenities: free local telephone calls and preferred room (subject to availability with advanced reservations).**

SOME UNITS

FAIRFIELD pop. 96,178

WHERE TO STAY

BEST WESTERN CORDELIA INN *Book at aaa.com* **Phone:** (707)864-2029

AAA SAVE — Motel

All Year 1P: $68-$94 2P: $74-$106 XP: $10 F12

Location: I-80, exit Suisun Valley Rd, just e. Located in a quiet area. 4373 Central Pl 94585. Fax: 707/864-5834. **Facility:** 60 one-bedroom standard units. 2 stories, exterior corridors. **Parking:** on-site. **Terms:** 14 day cancellation notice, [ECP] meal plan available. **Amenities:** dual phone lines, voice mail, irons, hair dryers. **Pool(s):** heated outdoor. **Leisure Activities:** whirlpool. **Guest Services:** coin laundry. **Cards:** AX, CB, DC, DS, JC, MC, VI. **Special Amenities: free continental breakfast and free room upgrade (subject to availability with advanced reservations).** *(See color ad below)*

SOME UNITS

HAMPTON INN *Book at aaa.com* **Phone:** (707)864-1446

AAA SAVE — Motel

All Year [ECP] 1P: $99-$129 2P: $99-$129

Location: I-80, exit Suisun Valley Rd. 4441 Central Pl 94534. Fax: 707/864-4288. **Facility:** 57 units. 54 one-bedroom standard units. 3 one-bedroom suites ($155-$200) with whirlpools. 3 stories, interior/exterior corridors. **Parking:** on-site. **Terms:** check-in 4 pm, 3 day cancellation notice. **Amenities:** video games, high-speed Internet, voice mail, irons, hair dryers. **Pool(s):** heated outdoor. **Leisure Activities:** exercise room. **Guest Services:** coin laundry. **Business Services:** meeting rooms. **Cards:** AX, CB, DC, DS, MC, VI. **Special Amenities: free expanded continental breakfast and free local telephone calls.** *(See color ad below)*

SOME UNITS

FEE FEE

HOLIDAY INN EXPRESS HOTEL & SUITES *Book at aaa.com* **Phone:** (707)864-3797

Small-scale Hotel

4/1-11/14 [ECP]	1P: $89-$229	2P: $89-$229	XP: $10	F18
2/1-3/31 & 11/15-1/31 [ECP]	1P: $89-$179	2P: $89-$179	XP: $10	F18

Location: I-80, exit Suisun Valley Rd, just e. 316 Pittman Rd 94585. Fax: 707/864-3897. **Facility:** 60 one-bedroom standard units, some with whirlpools. 3 stories, interior corridors. *Bath:* combo or shower only. **Parking:** on-site. **Terms:** cancellation fee imposed. **Amenities:** dual phone lines, voice mail, irons, hair dryers. **Pool(s):** small heated outdoor. **Leisure Activities:** whirlpool, exercise room. **Business Services:** meeting rooms, business center. **Cards:** AX, CB, DC, DS, JC, MC, VI. *(See color ad p 792)*

SOME UNITS

HOLIDAY INN SELECT Book at aaa.com Phone: (707)422-4111

Small-scale Hotel

All Year	1P: $116-$269	2P: $116-$269

Location: I-80, exit Travis Blvd W, 0.3 mi s. 1350 Holiday Ln 94533. Fax: 707/428-3452. **Facility:** 142 units. 141 one-bedroom standard units. 1 one-bedroom suite ($269). 4 stories, interior corridors. **Parking:** on-site. **Amenities:** video games, high-speed Internet, voice mail, irons, hair dryers. **Pool(s):** heated outdoor. **Leisure Activities:** exercise room. **Guest Services:** coin laundry. **Business Services:** conference facilities, business center. **Cards:** AX, CB, DC, DS, JC, MC, VI.

SOME UNITS

FEE FEE

FALL RIVER MILLS pop. 648

WHERE TO STAY

HI-MONT MOTEL **Phone:** (530)336-5541

Motel

4/30-11/15 [CP]	1P: $59-$79	2P: $67-$87	XP: $8	D12
2/1-4/29 & 11/16-1/31 [CP]	1P: $39-$59	2P: $45-$65	XP: $6	D12

Location: 1 mi w on SR 299. 43021 Bridge St 96028 (PO Box 353). Fax: 530/336-7051. **Facility:** Smoke free premises. 31 one-bedroom standard units, some with kitchens. 2 stories, exterior corridors. *Bath:* combo or shower only. **Parking:** on-site. **Terms:** age restrictions may apply, 3 day cancellation notice, weekly rates available, package plans, pets ($10 extra charge). **Amenities:** *Some:* irons, hair dryers. **Leisure Activities:** barbecue, picnic area. **Business Services:** fax. **Cards:** AX, CB, DC, DS, JC, MC, VI. **Special Amenities: free continental breakfast and free local telephone calls.**

SOME UNITS

FEE

PIT RIVER LODGE **Phone:** (530)336-5005

Country Inn

4/23-12/31	1P: $115-$150	2P: $115-$150

Location: I-299 E, exit Pit One PowerHouse Rd. 24500 Pit One PowerHouse Rd 96028. Fax: 530/336-5013. **Facility:** 9 units. 5 one-bedroom standard units. 4 cottages ($230-$330). 1-2 stories, interior corridors. **Parking:** on-site. **Terms:** open 4/23-12/31, office hours 7:30 am-11 pm, 14 day cancellation notice, [ECP] & [MAP] meal plans available, package plans, pets ($250 deposit, in cottages with prior approval). **Amenities:** hair dryers. **Leisure Activities:** fishing. **Guest Services:** sundries. **Business Services:** meeting rooms. **Cards:** AX, DC, JC, MC.

SOME UNITS

FEE

FELTON pop. 1,051—*See also APTOS, CAPITOLA, SANTA CRUZ & SCOTTS VALLEY.*

WHERE TO STAY

FERN RIVER RESORT **Phone:** 831/335-4412

Cottage

5/15-9/26	1P: $80-$135	2P: $80-$135	XP: $10	F3
9/27-1/31	1P: $60-$135	2P: $60-$135	XP: $10	F3
4/1-5/14	1P: $60-$119	2P: $60-$119	XP: $10	F3
2/1-3/31	1P: $60-$105	2P: $60-$105	XP: $10	F3

Location: 1 mi s on SR 9; across river from Henry Cowell State Park. 5250 Hwy 9 95018. **Facility:** Designated smoking area. 15 cottages. 1 story, exterior corridors. *Bath:* combo or shower only. **Parking:** on-site. **Terms:** 30 day cancellation notice-fee imposed, weekly rates available. **Leisure Activities:** whirlpool, fishing, putting green, ping pong, hiking trails, playground, horseshoes, volleyball. **Cards:** AX, MC, VI.

FERNDALE pop. 1,382

WHERE TO STAY

COLLINGWOOD INN BED & BREAKFAST **Phone:** (707)786-9219

Bed & Breakfast

4/1-10/31 [BP]	1P: $110-$203	2P: $110-$203	XP: $55	F12
2/1-3/31 & 11/1-1/31 [BP]	1P: $99-$165	2P: $99-$165	XP: $55	F12

Location: US 101, exit Ferndale, 5 mi w. 831 Main St 95536. Fax: 707/786-9219. **Facility:** The romantic bed and breakfast is a historic original dating back to 1885; a charming inn in a charming town. 4 one-bedroom standard units. 2 stories (no elevator), interior corridors. **Parking:** on-site. **Terms:** office hours 6:30 am-11 pm, 2 night minimum stay - weekends, age restrictions may apply, 14 day cancellation notice-fee imposed, pets ($25 fee). **Amenities:** *Some:* voice mail, irons, hair dryers. **Guest Services:** gift shop, complimentary evening beverages. **Cards:** AX, MC, VI.

SOME UNITS

FEE

GINGERBREAD MANSION **Phone:** (707)786-4000

Historic Bed & Breakfast

All Year [BP]	1P: $150-$400	2P: $150-$400	XP: $40

Location: Just e of Main St. 400 Berding St 95536 (PO Box 40). Fax: 707/786-4381. **Facility:** This 1899 Victorian mansion in Queen Anne and Eastlake style features formal English gardens with sitting areas; some guest baths include fireplaces. Smoke free premises. 11 one-bedroom standard units. 3 stories (no elevator), interior corridors. *Bath:* combo or shower only. **Parking:** on-site. **Terms:** age restrictions may apply, 14 day cancellation notice-fee imposed. **Amenities:** CD players, hair dryers. **Guest Services:** gift shop. **Cards:** AX, MC, VI. **Special Amenities: free full breakfast.**

SOME UNITS

SHAW HOUSE BED & BREAKFAST INN — **Phone:** (707)786-9958

Bed & Breakfast

4/1-1/5 [BP]	1P: $85-$185	2P: $85-$185	XP: $15	F12
2/1-3/31 & 1/6-1/31 [BP]	1P: $75-$165	2P: $75-$165	XP: $15	F12

Location: US 101, exit Main St W. 703 Main St 95536 (PO Box 1369). Fax: 707/786-9758. **Facility:** Said to have once been the residence of the city's founder, this 1854 Carpenter Gothic house is on an acre of landscaped grounds. Smoke free premises. 8 one-bedroom standard units. 2 stories (no elevator), interior corridors. *Bath:* combo, shower or tub only. **Parking:** on-site. **Terms:** office hours 10 am-9 pm, check-in 4 pm, age restrictions may apply, 7 day cancellation notice-fee imposed. **Amenities:** *Some:* irons, hair dryers. **Guest Services:** gift shop, complimentary evening beverages. **Cards:** DS, MC, VI. **Special Amenities: free local telephone calls.**

SOME UNITS

VICTORIAN INN — *Book at aaa.com* — **Phone:** (707)786-4949

Bed & Breakfast

All Year [BP]	1P: $85-$225	2P: $85-$225	XP: $25

Location: Center. 400 Ocean Ave 95536 (PO Box 96). Fax: 707/786-4558. **Facility:** The late-1890 mansion of exquisite craftmanship embodies the romance and elegance of the Timber Boom era. 12 one-bedroom standard units. 2 stories (no elevator), interior corridors. *Bath:* combo or shower only. **Parking:** street. **Terms:** 2 night minimum stay - weekends in summer, age restrictions may apply, 7 day cancellation notice. **Amenities:** CD players. **Dining:** Curley's Grill, see separate listing. **Cards:** AX, DS, MC, VI.

SOME UNITS

WHERE TO DINE

CURLEY'S GRILL — **Lunch:** $6-$13 — **Dinner:** $13-$25 — **Phone:** 707/786-9696

Armenian

Location: Center; in Victorian Inn. 400 Ocean Ave 95536. **Hours:** 11:30 am-9 pm, Sat 8 am-11 & 11:30-9 pm, Sun 8 am-3 & 11:30-9 pm. Closed: 12/25. **Reservations:** suggested. **Features:** Located in the Victorian Inn, this bistro-style restaurant offers creative dishes from a simple fare. Casual dress; cocktails. **Parking:** street. **Cards:** DS, MC, VI.

FIREBAUGH pop. 5,743

WHERE TO STAY

The following lodging was either not evaluated or did not meet AAA rating requirements but is listed for your information only.

FIREBAUGH RIVERFRONT INN — **Phone:** 559/659-8324

fyi

Not evaluated. **Location:** 28 mi w of Fresno. 875 Q St 93622. Facilities, services, and decor characterize a basic property.

FISH CAMP —*See also YOSEMITE NATIONAL PARK.*

WHERE TO STAY

APPLE TREE INN — *Book at aaa.com* — **Phone:** (559)683-5111

Cottage

5/28-9/6 [ECP]	1P: $159-$209	2P: $159-$209	XP: $10	F3
9/7-1/31 [ECP]	1P: $129-$209	2P: $129-$209	XP: $10	F3
4/1-5/27 [ECP]	1P: $129-$149	2P: $129-$149	XP: $10	F3
2/1-3/31 [ECP]	1P: $99-$119	2P: $99-$119	XP: $10	F3

Location: 2 mi from South Gate to Yosemite National Park. 1110 Hwy 41 93623 (PO Box 41). Fax: 559/642-6280. **Facility:** Forested grounds surround these 17 duplex and triplex lodging buildings; most rooms have a fireplace, deck or porch. 53 units. 36 one-bedroom standard units. 17 one-bedroom suites ($119-$209). 2 stories, exterior corridors. **Parking:** on-site. **Terms:** cancellation fee imposed, pets ($50 fee). **Amenities:** video library (fee), irons, hair dryers. **Pool(s):** heated indoor. **Leisure Activities:** whirlpool, cross country skiing, hiking trails. *Fee:* racquetball court, horseback riding. **Guest Services:** gift shop, coin laundry. **Business Services:** meeting rooms. **Cards:** AX, CB, DC, DS, MC, VI. ***(See color ad p 818)***

FEE

THE NARROW GAUGE INN — **Phone:** (559)683-7720

Motel

4/1-10/31 [CP]	1P: $129-$195	2P: $129-$195	XP: $10	F6
2/1-3/31 & 11/1-1/31 [CP]	1P: $79-$129	2P: $79-$129	XP: $10	F6

Location: 4 mi from South Gate to Yosemite National Park. 48571 Hwy 41 93623. Fax: 559/683-2139. **Facility:** 26 one-bedroom standard units. 2 stories (no elevator), exterior corridors. *Bath:* combo or shower only. **Parking:** on-site. **Terms:** 4 day cancellation notice, pets ($25 fee, in limited units). **Dining:** restaurant, see separate listing. **Pool(s):** heated outdoor. **Leisure Activities:** whirlpool, hiking trails. **Guest Services:** gift shop. **Business Services:** fax. **Cards:** DC, DS, MC, VI. ***(See ad p 204 & p 821)***

SOME UNITS

FEE

OWL'S NEST LODGING — **Phone:** 559/683-3484

Cottage

All Year	1P: $90-$150	2P: $90-$150	XP: $20

Location: 2 mi from South Gate to Yosemite National Park. 1237 Hwy 41 93623 (PO Box 33). Fax: 559/683-3486. **Facility:** 4 one-bedroom standard units, some with kitchens. 2 stories (no elevator), exterior corridors. *Bath:* combo or shower only. **Parking:** on-site. **Terms:** 2-3 night minimum stay - seasonal & weekends, 15 day cancellation notice-fee imposed. **Cards:** MC, VI.

SOME UNITS

TENAYA LODGE AT YOSEMITE Book at aaa.com Phone: (559)683-6555

Large-scale Hotel

All Year 1P: $149-$319 XP: $15 F18

Location: 2 mi from South Gate to Yosemite National Park. 1122 Hwy 41 93623 (PO Box 159). Fax: 559/683-8684. **Facility:** On landscaped grounds surrounded by a national forest, the lodge is convenient to many seasonal activity areas. Smoke free premises. 244 units. 238 one-bedroom standard units, some with whirlpools. 6 one-bedroom suites ($209-$669), some with whirlpools. 3-4 stories, interior corridors. *Bath:* combo or shower only. **Parking:** on-site and valet. **Terms:** 10 day cancellation notice. **Amenities:** video games (fee), dual phone lines, voice mail, safes, irons, hair dryers. *Some:* honor bars. **Dining:** 3 restaurants, 7 am-11 pm, cocktails, also, Sierra Restaurant, see separate listing. **Pool(s):** heated outdoor, heated indoor. **Leisure Activities:** saunas, whirlpools, steamrooms, cross country skiing, recreation programs, hiking trails, horseshoes. *Fee:* downhill skiing, bicycles, horseback riding, massage. **Guest Services:** gift shop, valet and coin laundry. **Business Services:** conference facilities, business center. **Cards:** AX, DC, DS, MC, VI. **Special Amenities: free continental breakfast and free newspaper.** *(See color ad p 820)*

SOME UNITS

FEE FEE

WHERE TO DINE

THE NARROW GAUGE INN **Dinner:** $13-$36 **Phone:** 559/683-6446

American

Location: 4 mi from South Gate to Yosemite National Park; in The Narrow Gauge Inn. 48571 Hwy 41 93623. **Hours:** Open 2/1-4/15 & 11/1-1/31; 5:30 pm-9 pm. **Reservations:** suggested. **Features:** Friendly service makes the restaurant a favorite of both locals and tourists. Dressy casual; cocktails. **Parking:** on-site. **Cards:** DC, DS, MC, VI. ***(See ad p 204)***

SIERRA RESTAURANT **Dinner:** $17-$31 **Phone:** 559/683-6555

American

Location: 2 mi from South Gate to Yosemite National Park; in Tenaya Lodge at Yosemite. 1122 Highway 41 93623. **Hours:** 6:30 am-11 & 5-10 pm. **Reservations:** suggested. **Features:** Comfortable setting overlooking the pool area. Casual dress; cocktails. **Parking:** on-site and valet. **Cards:** AX, DC, DS, JC, MC, VI. ***(See color ad p 820)***

FOLSOM pop. 51,884 (See map and index starting on p. 565)

WHERE TO STAY

HILTON GARDEN INN Book at aaa.com **Phone:** (916)353-1717 150

Small-scale Hotel

All Year 1P: $62-$152 XP: $10 F18

Location: US 50, exit Folsom Blvd, 0.5 mi n to Iron Point Rd, then 0.3 mi e. 221 Iron Point Rd 95630. Fax: 916/353-1021. **Facility:** 100 one-bedroom standard units, some with whirlpools. 4 stories, interior corridors. **Parking:** on-site. **Terms:** cancellation fee imposed. **Amenities:** video games, high-speed Internet (fee), dual phone lines, voice mail, irons, hair dryers. **Pool(s):** heated outdoor. **Leisure Activities:** whirlpool, exercise room. **Guest Services:** coin laundry. **Business Services:** business center. **Cards:** AX, DC, DS, JC, MC, VI. **Special Amenities: free local telephone calls and free newspaper.**

SOME UNITS

LAKE NATOMA INN Book at aaa.com **Phone:** (916)351-1500 148

Small-scale Hotel

All Year 1P: $89-$129 2P: $89-$129 XP: $10 F16

Location: US 50, exit Folsom Blvd, 3 mi n; behind The Lakes Specialty Shopping Center. Located in a rural setting. 702 Gold Lake Dr 95630. Fax: 916/351-1511. **Facility:** 132 units. 120 one-bedroom standard units. 12 one-bedroom suites ($219) with whirlpools. 4 stories, interior corridors. **Parking:** on-site. **Terms:** cancellation fee imposed. **Amenities:** voice mail, irons, hair dryers. **Pool(s):** heated outdoor. **Leisure Activities:** saunas, whirlpool, putting green, basketball, volleyball. *Fee:* bicycles, massage. **Guest Services:** gift shop. **Business Services:** meeting rooms, business center. **Cards:** AX, CB, DC, DS, JC, MC, VI. ***(See color ad below)***

SOME UNITS

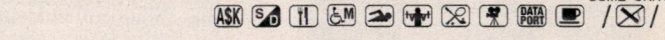

(See map and index starting on p. 565)

LARKSPUR LANDING HOME SUITE HOTEL Book at aaa.com Phone: (916)355-1616 149

Small-scale Hotel

All Year 1P: $79-$179 2P: $89-$189 XP: $10 F18

Location: US 50, exit Folsom Blvd, 0.5 mi n to Iron Point Rd, then 0.3 mi e. 121 Iron Point Rd 95630. Fax: 916/355-1766. **Facility:** 84 units. 58 one-bedroom standard units with kitchens. 26 one-bedroom suites with kitchens. 4 stories, interior corridors. **Parking:** on-site. **Amenities:** video games, CD players, high-speed Internet (fee), dual phone lines, voice mail, irons, hair dryers. **Leisure Activities:** whirlpool, exercise room. **Guest Services:** complimentary laundry. **Business Services:** meeting rooms, business center. **Cards:** AX, DC, DS, MC, VI. **Special Amenities: free local telephone calls and free newspaper.** *(See color ad below)*

SOME UNITS

RESIDENCE INN BY MARRIOTT Book at aaa.com Phone: (916)983-7289 152

Small-scale Hotel

All Year 1P: $79-$169

Location: US 50, exit Bidwell St, just n. 2555 Iron Point Rd 95630. Fax: 916/983-8637. **Facility:** 107 units. 43 one-bedroom standard units with kitchens. 43 one- and 21 two-bedroom suites with kitchens. 3 stories, interior corridors. **Parking:** on-site. **Terms:** [BP] meal plan available. **Amenities:** dual phone lines, voice mail, irons, hair dryers. **Pool(s):** heated indoor. **Leisure Activities:** whirlpool, exercise room, sports court. **Guest Services:** complimentary evening beverages: Mon-Thurs, coin laundry. **Business Services:** meeting rooms. **Cards:** AX, DC, DS, JC, MC, VI.

SOME UNITS

LOOK FOR THE RED

Next time you pore over a AAA TourBook® guide in search of a lodging establishment, take note of the vibrant red AAA logo, SAVE icon, and Diamond rating just under a select group of property names! These Official Appointment properties place a high value on the business they receive from dedicated AAA travelers and offer members great room rates*.

** See TourBook Navigator section, page 14, for complete details.*

FORESTVILLE —*See Wine Country p. 769.*

FORT BRAGG —*See Wine Country p. 769.*

FORTUNA pop. 10,497

WHERE TO STAY

BEST WESTERN COUNTRY INN Book at aaa.com **Phone:** (707)725-6822

SAVE Motel

5/1-9/30 [BP]	1P: $79-$110	2P: $79-$110	XP: $5	F12
2/1-4/30 & 10/1-1/31 [BP]	1P: $64-$89	2P: $64-$89	XP: $5	F12

Location: US 101, exit Kenmar Rd/Riverwalk Dr, just w. 2025 Riverwalk Dr 95540. Fax: 707/725-5270. **Facility:** 66 units. 64 one- and 2 two-bedroom standard units, some with whirlpools. 2 stories (no elevator), exterior corridors. *Bath:* combo or shower only. **Parking:** on-site. **Terms:** age restrictions may apply, small pets only. **Amenities:** voice mail, irons, hair dryers. **Pool(s):** small heated indoor/outdoor. **Leisure Activities:** whirlpool. **Guest Services:** coin laundry. **Business Services:** business center. **Cards:** AX, DC, DS, MC, VI. **Special Amenities: free full breakfast and free local telephone calls.**

SOME UNITS

COMFORT INN AND SUITES Book at aaa.com **Phone:** (707)725-7025

SAVE Motel

7/1-9/15 [ECP]	1P: $79-$149	2P: $79-$149	XP: $7	F17
5/1-6/30 [ECP]	1P: $69-$139	2P: $69-$139	XP: $7	F17
2/1-4/30 & 9/16-1/31 [ECP]	1P: $59-$129	2P: $64-$129	XP: $7	F17

Location: US 101, exit Kenmar Rd/Riverwalk Dr, just w. 1583 Riverwalk Dr 95540. Fax: 707/725-7088. **Facility:** 51 units. 45 one- and 6 two-bedroom standard units, some with whirlpools. 3 stories, interior corridors. *Bath:* combo or shower only. **Parking:** on-site. **Terms:** age restrictions may apply. **Amenities:** voice mail, irons, hair dryers. *Some:* dual phone lines. **Pool(s):** heated indoor. **Leisure Activities:** whirlpool, exercise room. **Guest Services:** coin laundry. **Business Services:** meeting rooms, fax. **Cards:** AX, CB, DC, DS, JC, MC, VI.

SOME UNITS

FORTUNA SUPER 8 Book at aaa.com **Phone:** (707)725-2888

SAVE Motel

5/1-9/30 [CP]	1P: $55-$85	2P: $65-$95	XP: $6	F12
2/1-4/30 & 10/1-1/31 [CP]	1P: $50-$80	2P: $55-$85	XP: $6	F12

Location: US 101, exit Kenmar Rd/Riverwalk Dr, just w. 1805 Alamar Way 95540. Fax: 707/725-1895. **Facility:** 47 one-bedroom standard units. 2 stories (no elevator), exterior corridors. *Bath:* combo or shower only. **Parking:** on-site. **Terms:** age restrictions may apply, pets ($10 extra charge). **Amenities:** irons, hair dryers. **Guest Services:** coin laundry. **Cards:** AX, CB, DC, DS, MC, VI.

SOME UNITS

FEE

HOLIDAY INN EXPRESS Book at aaa.com **Phone:** (707)725-5500

SAVE Motel

5/1-9/30	1P: $79-$179	2P: $79-$179	XP: $10	F19
10/1-1/31	1P: $79-$149	2P: $79-$149	XP: $10	F19
2/1-4/30	1P: $74-$139	2P: $74-$139	XP: $10	F19

Location: US 101, exit Kenmar Rd/Riverwalk Dr, just w. 1859 Alamar Way 95540. Fax: 707/725-2379. **Facility:** 46 one-bedroom standard units, some with whirlpools. 2 stories, exterior corridors. **Parking:** on-site. **Terms:** age restrictions may apply, [ECP] meal plan available, pets ($10 deposit). **Amenities:** voice mail, irons, hair dryers. *Some:* high-speed Internet. **Pool(s):** heated indoor/outdoor. **Leisure Activities:** whirlpool, ping pong, barbecue, bicycles. **Guest Services:** coin laundry. **Business Services:** meeting rooms, business center. **Cards:** AX, CB, DC, DS, JC, MC, VI.

(See color ad p 325)

SOME UNITS

FEE FEE

FOSTER CITY —*See San Francisco p. 665.*

FREMONT pop. 203,413

WHERE TO STAY

AMERISUITES (SILICON VALLEY/FREMONT) Book at aaa.com **Phone:** (510)623-6000

SAVE Small-scale Hotel

All Year	1P: $69-$109	2P: $69-$109	XP: $10	F17

Location: I-880, exit Warren Ave/Mission Blvd, just w. 3101 W Warren Ave 94538. Fax: 510/623-6001. **Facility:** 151 one-bedroom suites. 7 stories, interior corridors. *Bath:* combo or shower only. **Parking:** on-site. **Terms:** [ECP] meal plan available. **Amenities:** voice mail, irons, hair dryers. *Fee:* video games, high-speed Internet. *Some:* dual phone lines. **Pool(s):** heated outdoor. **Leisure Activities:** exercise room. **Guest Services:** valet and coin laundry, area transportation-within 5 mi. **Business Services:** meeting rooms. **Cards:** AX, DC, DS, JC, MC, VI. **Special Amenities: free expanded continental breakfast and free newspaper.** *(See color ad p 334)*

SOME UNITS

BEST WESTERN GARDEN COURT INN Book at aaa.com **Phone:** (510)792-4300

SAVE Small-scale Hotel

All Year	1P: $79-$159	2P: $79-$159	XP: $10	F

Location: I-880, exit Mowry Ave, just e. 5400 Mowry Ave 94538. Fax: 510/792-2643. **Facility:** 125 one-bedroom standard units. 3 stories, interior corridors. **Parking:** on-site. **Terms:** [ECP] meal plan available, pets ($10 extra charge). **Amenities:** high-speed Internet, voice mail, irons, hair dryers. **Pool(s):** outdoor. **Leisure Activities:** whirlpool. **Guest Services:** valet laundry. **Business Services:** meeting rooms. **Cards:** AX, DC, DS, MC, VI. **Special Amenities: free expanded continental breakfast and free local telephone calls.**

(See color ad p 334 & p 521)

SOME UNITS

FEE FEE FEE

COURTYARD BY MARRIOTT *Book at aaa.com* **Phone:** (510)656-1800

Small-scale Hotel All Year 1P: $54-$124

Location: I-880, exit Gateway Blvd northbound; exit Warren Ave southbound, just w. 47000 Lakeview Blvd 94538. Fax: 510/656-2441. **Facility:** 146 units. 134 one-bedroom standard units. 12 one-bedroom suites. 3 stories, interior corridors. *Bath:* combo or shower only. **Parking:** on-site. **Terms:** [BP] meal plan available. **Amenities:** high-speed Internet (fee), dual phone lines, voice mail, irons, hair dryers. **Pool(s):** heated outdoor. **Leisure Activities:** whirlpool, exercise room. **Guest Services:** coin laundry. **Business Services:** meeting rooms. **Cards:** AX, CB, DC, DS, JC, MC, VI.

SOME UNITS

ASK / /

CRAWFORD SUITES *Book at aaa.com* **Phone:** (510)651-7373

Small-scale Hotel All Year [CP] 1P: $129-$189 2P: $129-$189 XP: $10 F12

Location: I-880, exit Automall Pkwy, just w, n on Christy, then e. 42200 Albrae St 94538. Fax: 510/651-7362. **Facility:** 127 one-bedroom standard units, some with efficiencies. 4 stories, interior corridors. *Bath:* combo or shower only. **Parking:** on-site. **Terms:** pets ($75 fee, $50 deposit). **Amenities:** video games (fee), high-speed Internet, dual phone lines, voice mail, irons, hair dryers. **Pool(s):** heated outdoor. **Leisure Activities:** whirlpool, exercise room. **Guest Services:** valet and coin laundry. **Business Services:** meeting rooms, business center. **Cards:** AX, CB, DC, DS, JC, MC, VI.

SOME UNITS

ASK FEE / /

FREMONT ECONO LODGE *Book at aaa.com* **Phone:** (510)656-2800

Small-scale Hotel All Year 1P: $55-$59 2P: $55-$59 XP: $10 F18

Location: I-880, exit Warren Ave, just e to Mission Blvd, then 0.5 mi n. 46101 Warm Springs Blvd 94539. Fax: 510/659-0352. **Facility:** 49 one-bedroom standard units. 3 stories, interior corridors. *Bath:* combo or shower only. **Parking:** on-site. **Terms:** weekly rates available, [CP] meal plan available. **Amenities:** high-speed Internet (fee), voice mail, irons, hair dryers. **Cards:** AX, CB, DC, DS, JC, MC, VI.

SOME UNITS

ASK / /

FREMONT MARRIOTT *Book at aaa.com* **Phone:** 510/413-3700

AAA SAVE

Large-scale Hotel All Year 1P: $69-$139 2P: $69-$139 XP: $10 F

Location: I-880, exit Fremont Blvd/Cushing Pkwy, then w. 46100 Landing Pkwy 94538. Fax: 510/413-3710. **Facility:** 357 units. 355 one-bedroom standard units. 2 one-bedroom suites. 10 stories, interior corridors. *Bath:* combo or shower only. **Parking:** on-site. **Terms:** cancellation fee imposed, small pets only. **Amenities:** dual phone lines, voice mail, irons, hair dryers. *Fee:* video games, high-speed Internet. **Dining:** 6 am-10 pm, Sat & Sun from 7 am, cocktails. **Pool(s):** heated outdoor. **Leisure Activities:** whirlpool, exercise room. **Guest Services:** gift shop, coin laundry. **Business Services:** meeting rooms. **Cards:** AX, CB, DC, DS, JC, MC.

SOME UNITS

/ /

GOOD NITE INN **Book at aaa.com** **Phone:** (510)656-9307

Motel

All Year 1P: $39-$49 2P: $39-$49
Location: I-880, exit Fremont Blvd/Cushing Pkwy, just w. 4135 Cushing Pkwy 94538. Fax: 510/656-9110. **Facility:** 120 one-bedroom standard units. 3 stories, exterior corridors. **Parking:** on-site. **Amenities:** voice mail. **Pool(s):** outdoor. **Leisure Activities:** whirlpool. **Guest Services:** coin laundry. **Cards:** AX, DC, DS, MC, VI.

SOME UNITS

HAMPTON INN **Book at aaa.com** **Phone:** (510)498-1900

Motel

All Year 1P: $109-$149 2P: $119-$169 XP: $10 F16
Location: I-880, exit W Gateway northbound, 0.5 mi n on Bayside. 46500 Landing Pkwy 94538. Fax: 510/498-1992. **Facility:** 100 one-bedroom standard units. 3 stories, interior corridors. *Bath:* combo or shower only. **Parking:** on-site. **Terms:** [ECP] meal plan available. **Amenities:** video games (fee), dual phone lines, voice mail, irons, hair dryers. **Pool(s):** outdoor. **Leisure Activities:** exercise room. **Guest Services:** coin laundry. **Cards:** AX, CB, DC, DS, MC, VI.

SOME UNITS

HOLIDAY INN EXPRESS FREMONT-MILPITAS **Book at aaa.com** **Phone:** (510)490-2900

Small-scale Hotel

All Year [ECP] 1P: $49-$129 2P: $49-$129 XP: $10 F14
Location: I-880, exit Warren, just e. 47031 Kato Rd 94538. Fax: 510/659-8353. **Facility:** 114 one-bedroom standard units, some with whirlpools. 3 stories, interior corridors. **Parking:** on-site. **Terms:** cancellation fee imposed. **Amenities:** high-speed Internet, dual phone lines, voice mail, irons, hair dryers. **Pool(s):** heated outdoor. **Leisure Activities:** whirlpool, exercise room. **Cards:** AX, CB, DC, DS, MC, VI. ***(see color ad p 260)***

SOME UNITS

HOMESTEAD STUDIO SUITES HOTEL-FREMONT **Book at aaa.com** **Phone:** (510)353-1664

Small-scale Hotel

All Year 1P: $72-$92 2P: $77-$97 XP: $5 F17
Location: I-880, exit Fremont Blvd/Cushing Pkwy, just w. 46080 Fremont Blvd 94538. Fax: 510/353-9144. **Facility:** 128 one-bedroom standard units with efficiencies. 3 stories, interior corridors. *Bath:* combo or shower only. **Parking:** on-site. **Terms:** weekly rates available, small pets only ($75 extra charge). **Amenities:** high-speed Internet (fee), dual phone lines, voice mail, irons, hair dryers. **Guest Services:** coin laundry. **Cards:** AX, CB, DC, DS, JC, MC, VI.

SOME UNITS

FEE FEE

LA QUINTA INN & SUITES **Book at aaa.com** **Phone:** 510/445-0808

Small-scale Hotel

All Year 1P: $80-$109 2P: $90-$119 XP: $10 F18
Location: I-880, exit Fremont Blvd/Cushing Pkwy, just w. 46200 Landing Pkwy 94538. Fax: 510/445-1818. **Facility:** 148 units. 143 one-bedroom standard units. 5 one-bedroom suites ($115-$175). 5 stories, interior corridors. *Bath:* combo or shower only. **Parking:** on-site. **Terms:** [ECP] meal plan available. **Amenities:** video games (fee), dual phone lines, voice mail, irons, hair dryers. *Some:* high-speed Internet. **Pool(s):** outdoor. **Leisure Activities:** whirlpool, exercise room. **Guest Services:** coin laundry, area transportation. **Business Services:** meeting rooms. **Cards:** AX, CB, DC, DS, JC, MC, VI. ***(See color ad p 660)***

SOME UNITS

LORD BRADLEY'S INN **Phone:** (510)490-0520

Bed & Breakfast

All Year 1P: $99-$165 2P: $99-$165
Location: I-680, exit Mission Blvd (SR 237), 0.5 mi e. Adjacent to San Jose Mission. 43344 Mission Blvd 94539. Fax: 510/490-3015. **Facility:** Located adjacent the mission, this inn offers guests beautifully landscaped gardens and well-appointed guest units. Smoke free premises. 8 one-bedroom standard units, some with whirlpools. 2 stories, interior corridors. *Bath:* shower only. **Parking:** on-site. **Terms:** cancellation fee imposed, [ECP] meal plan available. **Amenities:** video library, hair dryers. **Cards:** AX, DS, MC, VI.

SOME UNITS

RESIDENCE INN BY MARRIOTT **Book at aaa.com** **Phone:** (510)794-5900

Motel

All Year [MAP] 1P: $129 2P: $129
Location: I-880, exit Mowry Ave, just e. 5400 Farwell Pl 94536. Fax: 510/793-6587. **Facility:** 80 units. 60 one-bedroom standard units with kitchens. 20 two-bedroom suites with kitchens. 2 stories, exterior corridors. **Parking:** on-site. **Terms:** pets ($75 fee, $10 extra charge). **Amenities:** dual phone lines, voice mail, irons, hair dryers. **Pool(s):** heated outdoor. **Leisure Activities:** whirlpool, exercise room, sports court. **Guest Services:** complimentary evening beverages: Mon-Thurs, coin laundry, area transportation. **Cards:** AX, CB, DC, DS, JC, MC, VI.

SOME UNITS

FEE

WHERE TO DINE

FREMONT MARKET BROILER **Lunch:** $5-$12 **Dinner:** $8-$25 **Phone:** 510/791-8675

Steak & Seafood

Location: I-880, exit Mowry, just e, 0.3 mi s; in Mowry East Shopping Center. 39195 Farwell Dr 94538. **Hours:** 11 am-10 pm, Fri & Sat-11 pm. Closed: 11/25, 12/25. **Features:** Mesquite-grilled seafood, fresh pasta and steak are at the heart of the casual, friendly restaurant's menu. A fish market is on the premises. Casual dress; cocktails. **Parking:** on-site. **Cards:** AX, DS, MC, VI.

PEARL'S CAFE **Lunch:** $9-$16 **Dinner:** $18-$27 **Phone:** 510/490-2190

American

Location: I-680, exit Washington, 1 mi w, just s. 4096 Bay St 94560. **Hours:** 11 am-3 & 5-9 pm, Sat 5 pm-9:30 pm. Closed major holidays; also Sun, Mon & for lunch Sat. **Reservations:** suggested. **Features:** Creative and unique preparations have made this restaurant a favorite with the local crowd. Casual dress; beer & wine only. **Parking:** street. **Cards:** AX, DS, MC, VI.

FRESNO pop. 427,652

WHERE TO STAY

BEST VALUE WATER TREE INN Book at aaa.com **Phone:** (559)222-4445

SAVE — Motel

All Year [ECP] 1P: $69-$89 2P: $69-$89 XP: $4 F12

Location: SR 41, exit Ashlan Ave, 0.3 mi w. 4141 N Blackstone Ave 93726. Fax: 559/226-4589. **Facility:** 134 one-bedroom standard units. 2 stories (no elevator), interior corridors. **Parking:** on-site. **Pool(s):** outdoor. **Business Services:** meeting rooms. **Cards:** AX, CB, DC, DS, MC, VI. **Special Amenities: free expanded continental breakfast and free newspaper.** *(See color ad below)*

SOME UNITS

FEE

BEST WESTERN VILLAGE INN Book at aaa.com **Phone:** (559)226-2110

SAVE — Motel

All Year [ECP] 1P: $59-$79 2P: $69-$89 XP: $4 F12

Location: SR 41, exit Shields Ave, 0.3 mi w. 3110 N Blackstone Ave 93703. Fax: 559/226-0539. **Facility:** 153 one-bedroom standard units. 2 stories (no elevator), interior corridors. **Parking:** on-site. **Amenities:** irons, hair dryers. **Pool(s):** outdoor. **Leisure Activities:** whirlpool. **Cards:** AX, CB, DC, DS, MC, VI. **Special Amenities: free expanded continental breakfast and free local telephone calls.**

SOME UNITS

CHATEAU INN BY PICCADILLY INN HOTELS Book at aaa.com **Phone:** (559)456-1418

SAVE — Motel

All Year 1P: $65-$106 2P: $71-$106 XP: $6 F17

Location: SR 41, exit McKinley Ave, 4 mi e. 5113 E McKinley Ave 93727. Fax: 559/456-4643. **Facility:** 78 one-bedroom standard units. 2 stories (no elevator), interior corridors. *Bath:* combo or shower only. **Parking:** on-site. **Terms:** 3 day cancellation notice. **Amenities:** irons, hair dryers. **Pool(s):** outdoor. **Cards:** AX, CB, DC, DS, JC, MC, VI. **Special Amenities: free local telephone calls and early check-in/late check-out.**

SOME UNITS

COMFORT INN **Phone:** (559)275-2374

SAVE — Motel

All Year 1P: $77-$125 2P: $79-$127 XP: $5 F12

Location: SR 99, exit Shaw Ave. 5455 W Shaw Ave 93711. Fax: 559/275-7674. **Facility:** 69 one-bedroom standard units, some with whirlpools. 2 stories, interior corridors. *Bath:* combo or shower only. **Parking:** on-site. **Terms:** [ECP] meal plan available, package plans - seasonal. **Amenities:** safes (fee), irons, hair dryers. **Pool(s):** outdoor. **Leisure Activities:** whirlpool, exercise room. **Business Services:** meeting rooms, fax. **Cards:** AX, CB, DC, DS, JC, MC, VI. **Special Amenities: free expanded continental breakfast and free local telephone calls.**

SOME UNITS

COMFORT SUITES Book at aaa.com **Phone:** (559)435-5650

SAVE — Motel

All Year 1P: $110-$139 2P: $118-$139 XP: $8 F18

Location: SR 41, exit Herndon Ave, just w. 102 E Herndon Ave 93720. Fax: 559/435-0175. **Facility:** 70 one-bedroom standard units. 3 stories, interior corridors. *Bath:* combo or shower only. **Parking:** on-site. **Terms:** 3 day cancellation notice. **Amenities:** dual phone lines, voice mail, irons, hair dryers. **Pool(s):** heated indoor/outdoor. **Leisure Activities:** whirlpool. **Guest Services:** coin laundry. **Business Services:** meeting rooms, fax (fee). **Cards:** AX, CB, DC, DS, JC, MC, VI. **Special Amenities: free continental breakfast and free local telephone calls.** *(See color ad p 337)*

SOME UNITS

COUNTRY INN & SUITES — Phone: (559)435-5838

Motel

All Year — 1P: $80-$95 — 2P: $80-$95

Location: SR 41, exit Bullard Ave, just e. 6065 N Thesta Ave 93710. Fax: 559/435-6439. **Facility:** 62 one-bedroom standard units. 3 stories, interior corridors. *Bath:* combo or shower only. **Parking:** on-site. **Terms:** cancellation fee imposed. **Amenities:** irons, hair dryers. **Pool(s):** heated indoor. **Leisure Activities:** whirlpool. **Cards:** AX, DC, DS, MC, VI.

ASK / DATA PORT / SOME UNITS

COURTYARD BY MARRIOTT-AIRPORT — *Book at aaa.com* — Phone: (559)251-5200

Small-scale Hotel

All Year — 1P: $89-$93 — 2P: $89-$93 — XP: $10 — F18

Location: SR 41, exit McKinley Ave, 4 mi e. 1551 N Peach Ave 93727. Fax: 559/454-0552. **Facility:** 116 one-bedroom standard units. 4 stories, interior corridors. **Parking:** on-site. **Terms:** cancellation fee imposed, [BP] meal plan available. **Amenities:** video games (fee), voice mail, irons, hair dryers. **Pool(s):** outdoor. **Leisure Activities:** whirlpool, exercise room. **Guest Services:** coin laundry. **Business Services:** meeting rooms, business center. **Cards:** AX, CB, DC, DS, JC, MC, VI.

ASK / DATA PORT / SOME UNITS

COURTYARD BY MARRIOTT-SHAW AVE — *Book at aaa.com* — Phone: (559)221-6000

Small-scale Hotel

All Year — 1P: $79-$129

Location: SR 41, exit Shaw Ave, just w. 140 E Shaw Ave 93710. Fax: 559/221-0368. **Facility:** 146 one-bedroom standard units. 3 stories, interior corridors. *Bath:* combo or shower only. **Parking:** on-site. **Terms:** cancellation fee imposed, package plans. **Amenities:** voice mail, irons, hair dryers. **Pool(s):** outdoor. **Leisure Activities:** whirlpool, exercise room. **Guest Services:** valet and coin laundry. **Business Services:** meeting rooms, fax. **Cards:** AX, CB, DC, DS, JC, MC, VI.

DATA PORT / SOME UNITS

DAYS INN — *Book at aaa.com* — Phone: (559)237-6644

AAA SAVE

Motel

6/1-9/30 [CP] — 1P: $69-$89 — 2P: $99-$109 — XP: $10 — F12
2/1-5/31 & 10/1-1/31 [CP] — 1P: $59-$79 — 2P: $89-$99 — XP: $10 — F12

Location: SR 99, exit Jensen Ave, just e. 2640 S Second St 93706. Fax: 559/237-0705. **Facility:** 148 one-bedroom standard units. 2 stories (no elevator), exterior corridors. **Parking:** on-site. **Terms:** weekly rates available. **Amenities:** voice mail, safes (fee), hair dryers. *Some:* irons. **Pool(s):** outdoor. **Leisure Activities:** whirlpool, exercise room. **Guest Services:** coin laundry. **Business Services:** meeting rooms. **Cards:** AX, DC, DS, MC, VI. **Special Amenities: free continental breakfast and free local telephone calls.**

DATA PORT / SOME UNITS

DAYS INN-PARKWAY — *Book at aaa.com* — Phone: (559)268-6211

AAA SAVE

Motel

All Year — 1P: $43-$89 — 2P: $49-$99 — XP: $6 — F17

Location: SR 99, exit Olive St, just w. 1101 N Parkway Dr 93728. Fax: 559/268-6211. **Facility:** 98 one-bedroom standard units. 2 stories (no elevator), exterior corridors. **Parking:** on-site. **Terms:** [CP] meal plan available, pets ($5 extra charge). **Amenities:** hair dryers. **Pool(s):** outdoor. **Cards:** AX, CB, DC, DS, MC, VI. **Special Amenities: free continental breakfast and free local telephone calls.**

SOME UNITS / FEE / FEE FEE

FOUR POINTS BY SHERATON FRESNO — *Book at aaa.com* — Phone: (559)226-2200

AAA SAVE

Small-scale Hotel

All Year — 1P: $89-$120 — 2P: $89-$125 — XP: $5 — F17

Location: SR 41, exit Shields Ave, 0.3 mi w. 3737 N Blackstone Ave 93726. Fax: 559/222-7147. **Facility:** 204 one-bedroom standard units. 2 stories (no elevator), interior corridors. *Bath:* combo or shower only. **Parking:** on-site. **Amenities:** video games (fee), dual phone lines, voice mail, irons, hair dryers. **Dining:** 6:30-10:30 am, 11-3 & 5-10 pm, Sun-9 pm, cocktails, also, Smuggler's Restaurant, see separate listing. **Pool(s):** outdoor. **Leisure Activities:** whirlpool, exercise room. **Guest Services:** valet and coin laundry. **Business Services:** meeting rooms, business center. **Cards:** AX, CB, DC, DS, JC, MC, VI. **Special Amenities: free local telephone calls and free newspaper.** *(See color ad p 338)*

DATA PORT / SOME UNITS

GARDEN INN AND SUITES **Phone:** (559)277-3888

AAA SAVE

Motel

All Year [ECP] 1P: $89-$129 2P: $89-$129 XP: $10 F12

Location: SR 99, exit Shaw Ave, just s. 4949 N Forestiere Ave 93722. Fax: 559/277-3888. **Facility:** 40 one-bedroom standard units. 2 stories (no elevator), exterior corridors. **Parking:** on-site. **Amenities:** high-speed Internet, voice mail, irons, hair dryers. *Some:* safes. **Pool(s):** outdoor. **Leisure Activities:** whirlpool. **Guest Services:** coin laundry. **Business Services:** meeting rooms. **Cards:** AX, DS, MC, VI. **Special Amenities: free expanded continental breakfast.**

SOME UNITS

FEE

HOLIDAY INN-AIRPORT *Book at aaa.com* **Phone:** (559)252-3611

Small-scale Hotel

All Year 1P: $121-$126 2P: $121-$126

Location: SR 41, exit McKinley Ave, 4 mi e. 5090 E Clinton Ave 93727. Fax: 559/456-8243. **Facility:** 210 one-bedroom standard units. 2 stories (no elevator), interior corridors. *Bath:* combo or shower only. **Parking:** on-site. **Amenities:** voice mail, irons, hair dryers. **Dining:** Skyline Cafe, see separate listing. **Pool(s):** outdoor, heated indoor. **Leisure Activities:** whirlpool, exercise room. **Guest Services:** valet and coin laundry, area transportation. **Business Services:** meeting rooms, fax. **Cards:** AX, DC, DS, MC, VI. ***(See color ad below)***

SOME UNITS

FEE FEE

HOLIDAY INN EXPRESS-BARCUS *Book at aaa.com* **Phone:** (559)277-5700

AAA SAVE

Motel

All Year 1P: $99-$119 2P: $99-$119

Location: SR 99, exit Shaw Ave, just e. 5046 N Barcus 93722. Fax: 559/277-2244. **Facility:** 50 one-bedroom standard units, some with kitchens. 3 stories, interior corridors. **Parking:** on-site. **Terms:** [ECP] meal plan available, pets ($20 fee). **Amenities:** dual phone lines, voice mail, irons, hair dryers. **Pool(s):** indoor/outdoor. **Guest Services:** coin laundry. **Cards:** AX, CB, DC, DS, JC, MC, VI. **Special Amenities: free local telephone calls and free newspaper.** *(See color ad p 260)*

SOME UNITS

FEE

HOLIDAY INN EXPRESS-THESTA *Book at aaa.com* **Phone:** (559)435-6593

Motel

All Year 1P: $75-$79 2P: $75-$79 XP: $10 F18

Location: SR 41, exit Bullard Ave, just e. 6051 N Thesta Ave 93710. Fax: 559/435-8694. **Facility:** 56 one-bedroom standard units. 2 stories (no elevator), exterior corridors. *Bath:* combo or shower only. **Parking:** on-site. **Terms:** [CP] meal plan available. **Amenities:** irons, hair dryers. **Pool(s):** outdoor. **Business Services:** meeting rooms. **Cards:** AX, CB, DC, MC, VI.

SOME UNITS

KNIGHTS INN Book at aaa.com Phone: (559)275-7766

SAVE

Motel

All Year [CP] 1P: $45-$59 2P: $49-$69 XP: $5 F12

Location: SR 99, exit Shields Ave eastbound; exit Clinton northbound, just w. 3093 N Parkway 93722. Fax: 559/271-7966. **Facility:** 85 one-bedroom standard units. 2 stories, exterior corridors. *Bath:* combo or shower only. **Parking:** on-site. **Terms:** cancellation fee imposed, pets ($5 extra charge). **Pool(s):** outdoor. **Guest Services:** coin laundry. **Business Services:** meeting rooms. **Cards:** AX, DS, MC, VI. **Special Amenities: free continental breakfast and early check-in/late check-out.**

SOME UNITS

FEE / VCR FEE FEE FEE /

KNIGHTS INN-BLACKSTONE Phone: (559)439-6500

Motel

All Year 1P: $55-$95 2P: $69-$110 XP: $6 F12

Location: SR 41, exit Bullard Ave, just n. 6090 N Blackstone Ave 93710. Fax: 559/432-8635. **Facility:** 55 units. 52 one- and 3 two-bedroom standard units. 2 stories (no elevator), exterior corridors. *Bath:* shower only. **Parking:** on-site. **Terms:** [CP] meal plan available. **Pool(s):** outdoor. **Cards:** AX, DS, MC, VI.

SOME UNITS

ASK / /

LA QUINTA INN Book at aaa.com Phone: 559/442-1110

SAVE

Motel

All Year 1P: $66-$80 2P: $72-$86 XP: $6 F18

Location: SR 99, exit Fresno St, 2 mi e. 2926 Tulare St 93721. Fax: 559/237-0415. **Facility:** 130 one-bedroom standard units. 3 stories, exterior corridors. **Parking:** on-site. **Terms:** [ECP] meal plan available. **Amenities:** voice mail, irons, hair dryers. *Fee:* video games, high-speed Internet. **Pool(s):** heated outdoor. **Business Services:** meeting rooms, fax. **Cards:** AX, CB, DC, DS, JC, MC, VI.

SOME UNITS

DATA PORT / /

PICCADILLY INN-AIRPORT Book at aaa.com Phone: (559)251-6000

SAVE

Small-scale Hotel

All Year 1P: $85-$150 2P: $85-$150 XP: $10 F17

Location: SR 41, exit McKinley Ave, 4 mi e. 5115 E McKinley Ave 93727. Fax: 559/251-6956. **Facility:** 185 one-bedroom standard units. 2 stories (no elevator), interior corridors. **Parking:** on-site. **Terms:** 3 day cancellation notice. **Amenities:** voice mail, irons, hair dryers. **Dining:** 2 restaurants, 6 am-10 pm, cocktails. **Pool(s):** outdoor. **Leisure Activities:** whirlpool, exercise room. **Guest Services:** valet and coin laundry, area transportation. **Business Services:** conference facilities, business center. **Cards:** AX, CB, DC, DS, JC, MC, VI. **Special Amenities: free local telephone calls and early check-in/late check-out.**

SOME UNITS

24 DATA PORT / /

PICCADILLY INN-SHAW Book at aaa.com Phone: (559)226-3850

SAVE

Motel

All Year [ECP] 1P: $85-$150 2P: $85-$150 XP: $10 F17

Location: SR 99, exit Shaw Ave, 3 mi e. Located in a quiet area. 2305 W Shaw Ave 93711. Fax: 559/226-2448. **Facility:** 194 one-bedroom standard units. 2 stories (no elevator), interior/exterior corridors. **Parking:** on-site. **Terms:** 3 day cancellation notice. **Amenities:** voice mail, irons, hair dryers. **Dining:** 4 pm-9 pm, cocktails. **Pool(s):** outdoor. **Leisure Activities:** whirlpool, exercise room. **Guest Services:** valet and coin laundry. **Business Services:** meeting rooms, fax. **Cards:** AX, DC, DS, MC, VI. **Special Amenities: free expanded continental breakfast and free local telephone calls.**

SOME UNITS

24 DATA PORT / /

PICCADILLY INN-UNIVERSITY Book at aaa.com Phone: (559)224-4200

SAVE

Motel

All Year [ECP] 1P: $85-$150 2P: $85-$150 XP: $10 F17

Location: E of SR 41, exit Shaw Ave, 1.5 mi e. 4961 N Cedar Ave 93726. Fax: 559/227-2382. **Facility:** 190 one-bedroom standard units, some with whirlpools. 3 stories, interior corridors. *Bath:* combo or shower only. **Parking:** on-site. **Terms:** 3 day cancellation notice. **Amenities:** voice mail, irons, hair dryers. **Pool(s):** outdoor. **Leisure Activities:** whirlpool, exercise room. **Guest Services:** valet and coin laundry. **Business Services:** meeting rooms, fax. **Cards:** AX, CB, DC, DS, JC, MC, VI. **Special Amenities: free expanded continental breakfast and free local telephone calls.**

SOME UNITS

DATA PORT / /

QUALITY INN Book at aaa.com Phone: (559)275-2727

Motel

2/1-10/31 1P: $99-$119 2P: $109-$129 XP: $10 F18

11/1-1/31 1P: $89-$109 2P: $99-$119 XP: $10 F18

Location: SR 99, exit Ashlan Ave, just w. 4278 W Ashlan Ave 93722. Fax: 559/275-9103. **Facility:** 123 one-bedroom standard units. 2 stories (no elevator), exterior corridors. **Parking:** on-site. **Terms:** [BP] meal plan available, package plans - seasonal, pets ($20 extra charge, dogs only). **Amenities:** voice mail, irons, hair dryers. **Pool(s):** outdoor. **Guest Services:** coin laundry. **Business Services:** meeting rooms. **Cards:** AX, DC, DS, MC, VI.

SOME UNITS

ASK FEE DATA PORT / /

QUALITY INN & SUITES Book at aaa.com Phone: (559)229-5811

Motel

All Year 1P: $98-$109 2P: $98-$109 XP: $10 F18

Location: SR 41, exit Shaw Ave, just e. 480 E Shaw Ave 93710. Fax: 559/229-5911. **Facility:** Smoke free premises. 55 units. 2 one-bedroom standard units. 53 one-bedroom suites. 3 stories, interior corridors. *Bath:* combo or shower only. **Parking:** on-site. **Terms:** weekly rates available, [CP] meal plan available. **Amenities:** voice mail, irons, hair dryers. **Pool(s):** heated outdoor. **Leisure Activities:** whirlpool. **Guest Services:** coin laundry. **Business Services:** meeting rooms, fax. **Cards:** AX, CB, DC, DS, JC, MC, VI.

ASK FEE DATA PORT

RADISSON HOTEL *Book at aaa.com* **Phone:** (559)268-1000

Large-scale Hotel

All Year 1P: $99-$149 2P: $104-$154 XP: $5 F12

Location: SR 99, exit Ventura St, just e. Adjacent to the convention center. 2233 Ventura St 93721. Fax: 559/441-2954. **Facility:** 321 units. 292 one-bedroom standard units. 29 one-bedroom suites. 8 stories, interior corridors. *Bath:* combo or shower only. **Parking:** on-site. **Terms:** check-in 3:30 pm, pets ($50 deposit, in limited units). **Amenities:** voice mail, irons, hair dryers. *Fee:* video games, high-speed Internet. **Pool(s):** indoor/outdoor. **Leisure Activities:** saunas, whirlpool, exercise room. *Fee:* game room. **Guest Services:** gift shop. **Business Services:** conference facilities, fax. **Cards:** AX, CB, DC, DS, JC, MC, VI. ***(See color ad p 629)***

SOME UNITS

FEE / FEE FEE /

RAMADA INN-UNIVERSITY *Book at aaa.com* **Phone:** (559)224-4040

SAVE

Small-scale Hotel

All Year 1P: $95-$115 2P: $105-$125 XP: $10 F18

Location: SR 41, exit Shaw Ave, just e. 324 E Shaw Ave 93710. Fax: 559/222-4017. **Facility:** 168 one-bedroom standard units. 2 stories (no elevator), interior/exterior corridors. **Parking:** on-site. **Terms:** 3 day cancellation notice. **Amenities:** video games (fee), voice mail, irons, hair dryers. **Dining:** 2 restaurants, 6:30 am-10 pm, Sat & Sun 7 am-9 pm, cocktails. **Pool(s):** outdoor. **Leisure Activities:** whirlpool. **Guest Services:** valet laundry. **Business Services:** meeting rooms, fax. **Cards:** AX, CB, DC, DS, JC, MC, VI. **Special Amenities: free local telephone calls and free newspaper.** *(See color ad below)*

SOME UNITS

RED ROOF INN *Book at aaa.com* **Phone:** (559)276-1910

SAVE

Motel

6/1-10/31 1P: $49 2P: $59 XP: $6 F

2/1-5/31 & 11/1-1/31 1P: $45 2P: $56 XP: $6 F

Location: SR 99, exit Shaw Ave. 5021 N Barcus Ave 93722. Fax: 559/276-2974. **Facility:** 86 one-bedroom standard units. 2 stories (no elevator), exterior corridors. **Parking:** on-site. **Terms:** pets ($10 fee). **Amenities:** voice mail. **Pool(s):** outdoor. **Cards:** AX, CB, DC, DS, MC, VI. **Special Amenities: free local telephone calls and free newspaper.**

SOME UNITS

FEE / FEE FEE /

RED ROOF INN *Book at aaa.com* **Phone:** (559)431-3557

SAVE

Motel

All Year [CP] 1P: $45-$75 2P: $50-$80 XP: $5 F18

Location: SR 41, exit Herndon Ave, then w. 6730 N Blackstone Ave 93710. Fax: 559/439-7824. **Facility:** 138 one-bedroom standard units. 3 stories, exterior corridors. **Parking:** on-site. **Terms:** pets ($25 deposit). **Amenities:** video games (fee). **Pool(s):** outdoor. **Leisure Activities:** whirlpool. **Guest Services:** coin laundry. **Business Services:** meeting rooms. **Cards:** AX, CB, DC, DS, MC, VI. **Special Amenities: free local telephone calls and free newspaper.**

SOME UNITS

FEE / FEE FEE /

RESIDENCE INN BY MARRIOTT *Book at aaa.com* **Phone:** 559/222-8900

Motel

All Year [ECP] 1P: $119-$124

Location: SR 41, exit Shaw Ave, 0.3 mi w, n on Blackstone Ave, then e on Barstow Ave. 5322 N Diana Ave 93710. Fax: 559/222-9089. **Facility:** 120 units. 102 one- and 18 two-bedroom standard units with kitchens. 3 stories, interior corridors. *Bath:* combo or shower only. **Parking:** on-site. **Terms:** pets ($50 fee, $5 extra charge). **Amenities:** voice mail, irons, hair dryers. **Pool(s):** outdoor. **Leisure Activities:** whirlpool, exercise room, sports court, basketball. **Guest Services:** complimentary evening beverages: Mon-Thurs, coin laundry. **Business Services:** meeting rooms, fax. **Cards:** AX, CB, DC, DS, MC, VI.

SOME UNITS

FEE / /

THE SAN JOAQUIN **Phone:** (559)225-1309

Motel

All Year [ECP] 1P: $109-$219 2P: $109-$219

Location: SR 99, exit Shaw Ave, 3.5 mi e. 1309 W Shaw Ave 93711. Fax: 559/225-6021. **Facility:** 68 units. 60 one- and 8 two-bedroom standard units. 3 stories, exterior corridors. *Bath:* combo or shower only. **Parking:** on-site. **Terms:** 3 day cancellation notice-fee imposed. **Amenities:** irons, hair dryers. **Pool(s):** outdoor. **Leisure Activities:** whirlpool. **Guest Services:** valet and coin laundry. **Business Services:** meeting rooms, fax. **Cards:** AX, DC, DS, MC, VI.

SOME UNITS

SUPER 8-DOWNTOWN Book at aaa.com **Phone:** (559)268-0621

AAA SAVE — Motel

All Year 1P: $50-$70 2P: $60-$80 XP: $5 F12

Location: SR 99, exit Ventura St, 0.5 mi e. 2127 Inyo St 93721. Fax: 559/233-9300. **Facility:** 50 one-bedroom standard units. 2 stories (no elevator), exterior corridors. **Parking:** on-site. **Terms:** 2-3 night minimum stay - seasonal, 3 day cancellation notice-fee imposed, [CP] meal plan available, pets ($10 extra charge). **Amenities:** irons, hair dryers. **Pool(s):** outdoor. **Cards:** AX, DC, MC, VI. **Special Amenities: free continental breakfast and free local telephone calls.**

FEE SOME UNITS FEE FEE

SUPER 8-PARKWAY **Phone:** (559)268-0741

AAA SAVE — Motel

All Year 1P: $49-$79 2P: $55-$85 XP: $5 F12

Location: SR 99, exit Olive Ave, just w. 1087 N Parkway Dr 93728. Fax: 559/237-2293. **Facility:** 48 one-bedroom standard units. 2 stories (no elevator), exterior corridors. **Parking:** on-site. **Terms:** cancellation fee imposed, [CP] meal plan available, pets ($10 extra charge). **Pool(s):** outdoor. **Cards:** AX, DS, MC, VI. **Special Amenities: free continental breakfast and free local telephone calls.**

SOME UNITS FEE

TOWNEPLACE SUITES BY MARRIOTT Book at aaa.com **Phone:** (559)435-4600

AAA SAVE — Motel

All Year 1P: $69-$129 2P: $69-$129

Location: SR 41, exit Herndon Ave E. 7127 N Fresno St 93720. Fax: 559/435-4613. **Facility:** 92 units. 72 one- and 20 two-bedroom standard units with kitchens. 3 stories, interior corridors. *Bath:* combo or shower only. **Parking:** on-site. **Terms:** pets ($50 fee, $10 extra charge). **Amenities:** high-speed Internet, voice mail, irons, hair dryers. **Pool(s):** outdoor. **Leisure Activities:** whirlpool, exercise room. **Guest Services:** valet and coin laundry. **Business Services:** meeting rooms, PC, fax. **Cards:** AX, CB, DC, DS, MC, VI. **Special Amenities: free local telephone calls and early check-in/late check-out.**

SOME UNITS FEE

TRAVELODGE Book at aaa.com **Phone:** 559/276-7745

AAA SAVE — Motel

All Year [CP] 1P: $59-$119 2P: $64-$129 XP: $5 F12

Location: SR 99, exit Sheilds Ave southbound; exit Clinton northbound, just w. 3093 N Parkway 93722. Fax: 559/271-7966. **Facility:** 115 one-bedroom standard units, some with whirlpools. 2 stories (no elevator), exterior corridors. *Bath:* combo or shower only. **Parking:** on-site. **Terms:** cancellation fee imposed, pets ($5 extra charge). **Pool(s):** outdoor. **Guest Services:** coin laundry. **Cards:** AX, DS, MC, VI. **Special Amenities: free continental breakfast and free local telephone calls.**

SOME UNITS FEE FEE FEE FEE

UNIVERSITY INN **Phone:** (559)294-0224

AAA SAVE — Motel

All Year [CP] 1P: $43-$76 2P: $52-$85 XP: $4 F18

Location: SR 41, exit Shaw Ave, 1.5 mi e. 2655 E Shaw Ave 93710. Fax: 559/292-0851. **Facility:** 110 one-bedroom standard units. 2 stories (no elevator), exterior corridors. **Parking:** on-site. **Terms:** pets ($20 fee). **Amenities:** voice mail. **Pool(s):** heated outdoor. **Leisure Activities:** whirlpool. **Guest Services:** coin laundry. **Cards:** AX, CB, DC, DS, MC, VI. **Special Amenities: free local telephone calls and early check-in/late check-out.**

SOME UNITS FEE FEE FEE

VILLAGER LODGE **Phone:** 559/233-3913

AAA SAVE — Motel

All Year 1P: $32-$40 2P: $35-$45 XP: $5 F12

Location: SR 99, exit Olive Ave, then w. 933 N Parkway Dr 93728. Fax: 559/498-8526. **Facility:** 107 one-bedroom standard units. 3 stories, exterior corridors. *Bath:* shower only. **Parking:** on-site. **Terms:** weekly rates available, pets ($6 extra charge, in limited units). **Guest Services:** coin laundry. **Cards:** AX, CB, DC, DS, MC, VI. **Special Amenities: free continental breakfast and early check-in/late check-out.**

SOME UNITS FEE

WHERE TO DINE

GIULIA'S ITALIAN RESTAURANT **Lunch:** $8-$18 **Dinner:** $12-$50 **Phone:** 559/276-3573

AAA — Italian

Location: In Target Shopping Center. 3050 W Shaw Ave #116 93711. **Hours:** 11 am-2 & 5-9 pm, Sat from 5 pm. Closed major holidays; also Sun. **Reservations:** suggested. **Features:** Tucked amid shops, the conveniently located restaurant comes through with good food and service. Dressy casual; cocktails. **Parking:** on-site. **Cards:** AX, MC, VI.

MANHATTAN STEAKHOUSE AND BAR **Dinner:** $13-$25 **Phone:** 559/449-1731

American

Location: SR 99, exit Bullard Ave, 5 mi e. 1731 W Bullard Ave 93711. **Hours:** 4 pm-midnight. Closed major holidays. **Reservations:** suggested. **Features:** The restaurant offers a nice combination of fine dining and friendly, professional service. The relaxed atmosphere shows a backdrop of the famous New York skyline. Dressy casual; cocktails. **Parking:** on-site. **Cards:** AX, DC, MC, VI.

SKYLINE CAFE **Lunch:** $7-$19 **Dinner:** $7-$19 **Phone:** 559/252-3611

American

Location: SR 41, exit McKinley Ave, 4 mi e; in Holiday Inn-Airport. 5090 E Clinton Ave 93727. **Hours:** 6 am-2 & 5-10 pm. **Reservations:** accepted. **Features:** Near the airport, the cafe is a nice place for a quick but relaxing meal. The salad bar is among popular choices at this breakfast, lunch and dinner spot. Casual dress; cocktails. **Parking:** on-site. **Cards:** AX, CB, DC, DS, JC, MC, VI.

SMUGGLER'S RESTAURANT **Lunch:** $6-$14 **Dinner:** $9-$21 **Phone:** 559/226-2200

California

Location: SR 41, exit Shields Ave, 0.3 mi w; in Four Points by Sheraton Fresno. 3787 N Blackstone Ave 93726. **Hours:** 6 am-2:30 & 5-10 pm, Sun 4 pm-9 pm. **Reservations:** suggested. **Features:** A city landmark for more than 30 years, the restaurant employs a friendly staff. The adjacent lounge is popular with tourists, businesspeople and locals alike. Dressy casual; cocktails. **Parking:** on-site. **Cards:** AX, CB, DC, DS, MC, VI.

GALT pop. 19,472

WHERE TO STAY

HOLIDAY INN EXPRESS-GALT *Book at aaa.com* **Phone:** (209)745-9500

Motel

All Year	1P: $83-$105	2P: $83-$105	XP: $10	F12

Location: SR 99, exit Simmerhorn Rd northbound; exit Pringle Ave southbound. 620 N Lincoln Way 95632. Fax: 209/745-9300. **Facility:** 44 one-bedroom standard units, some with whirlpools. 2 stories, interior corridors. **Parking:** on-site. **Terms:** [CP] meal plan available. **Amenities:** irons, hair dryers. **Pool(s):** outdoor. **Leisure Activities:** whirlpool. **Business Services:** meeting rooms. **Cards:** AX, CB, DC, DS, MC.

SOME UNITS

ASK DATA PORT

ROYAL DELTA INN **Phone:** (209)745-9181

AAA SAVE

Motel

All Year	1P: $45	2P: $51	XP: $6

Location: SR 99, exit Pringle Ave. 1040 N Lincoln Way 95632. Fax: 209/745-1112. **Facility:** 104 one-bedroom standard units. 2 stories, exterior corridors. **Parking:** on-site. **Terms:** weekly rates available, pets (dogs only). **Pool(s):** outdoor. **Guest Services:** coin laundry. **Cards:** AX, CB, DC, DS, MC, VI. **Special Amenities: free full breakfast.**

SOME UNITS

GARBERVILLE

WHERE TO STAY

BENBOW INN **Phone:** (707)923-2124

AAA SAVE

Historic Country Inn

7/2-10/2 & 12/23-1/2	1P: $125-$205	2P: $125-$205	XP: $20	F12
4/2-7/1 & 10/3-12/22	1P: $99-$205	2P: $99-$205	XP: $20	F12

Location: US 101, exit Benbow, 2 mi s. 445 Lake Benbow Dr 95542. Fax: 707/923-2897. **Facility:** A spot of tea with scones is an afternoon tradition at this English Tudor-style inn; guest rooms are provided with complimentary sherry. Smoke free premises. 55 one-bedroom standard units, some with whirlpools. 3 stories (no elevator), interior corridors. *Bath:* combo or shower only. **Parking:** on-site. **Terms:** open 4/2-1/2, 5 day cancellation notice, package plans. **Amenities:** video library, irons, hair dryers. **Dining:** Benbow Inn Restaurant, see separate listing. **Leisure Activities:** pool privileges, bicycles. **Guest Services:** gift shop. **Business Services:** meeting rooms. **Cards:** AX, DS, MC, VI. **Special Amenities: free room upgrade (subject to availability with advanced reservations).**

SOME UNITS

VCR

BEST WESTERN HUMBOLDT HOUSE INN *Book at aaa.com* **Phone:** (707)923-2771

AAA SAVE

Motel

6/1-10/31	1P: $99-$125	2P: $99-$125	XP: $5	F12
11/1-1/31	1P: $79-$98	2P: $88-$98	XP: $5	F12
2/1-5/31	1P: $75-$92	2P: $85-$95	XP: $5	F12

Location: US 101, 1st exit. 701 Redwood Dr 95542. Fax: 707/923-4259. **Facility:** 76 units. 70 one- and 5 two-bedroom standard units, some with kitchens. 1 one-bedroom suite with kitchen. 3 stories (no elevator), exterior corridors. *Bath:* combo or shower only. **Parking:** on-site. **Terms:** cancellation fee imposed, [ECP] meal plan available, small pets only. **Pool(s):** outdoor. **Leisure Activities:** whirlpool. **Guest Services:** complimentary evening beverages, coin laundry. **Business Services:** meeting rooms. **Cards:** AX, CB, DC, DS, MC, VI. **Special Amenities: free expanded continental breakfast and free newspaper.** *(See color ad p 342)*

SOME UNITS

HUMBOLDT REDWOODS INN **Phone:** 707/923-2451

AAA SAVE

Motel

5/22-9/30	1P: $55-$95	2P: $55-$95	XP: $5	D12
2/1-5/21 & 10/1-1/31	1P: $49-$59	2P: $55-$69	XP: $5	D12

Location: On US 101 business route. 987 Redwood Dr 95542 (PO Box 98). Fax: 707/923-2451. **Facility:** 22 units. 21 one- and 1 two-bedroom standard units. 1 story, exterior corridors. *Bath:* combo or shower only. **Parking:** on-site. **Terms:** office hours 3:30 am-10 pm. **Amenities:** *Some:* irons. **Pool(s):** small outdoor. **Cards:** AX, CB, DC, DS, JC, MC, VI. **Special Amenities: free local telephone calls and preferred room (subject to availability with advanced reservations).**

SOME UNITS

MOTEL GARBERVILLE **Phone:** (707)923-2422

AAA SAVE

Motel

5/1-9/30	1P: $49-$69	2P: $59-$79	XP: $5	F12
2/1-4/30 & 10/1-1/31	1P: $39-$49	2P: $49-$69	XP: $5	F12

Location: On US 101 business route. 948 Redwood Dr 95542. Fax: 707/923-2427. **Facility:** 30 one-bedroom standard units. 1 story, exterior corridors. *Bath:* combo or shower only. **Parking:** on-site. **Terms:** pets (in limited units). **Amenities:** *Some:* irons, hair dryers. **Cards:** AX, CB, DC, DS, MC, VI. **Special Amenities: free local telephone calls and free room upgrade (subject to availability with advanced reservations).**

SOME UNITS

SHERWOOD FOREST MOTEL **Phone:** (707)923-2721

AAA SAVE

Motel

6/1-10/31	1P: $74-$84	2P: $86-$96	XP: $5	F6
2/1-5/31 & 11/1-1/31	1P: $64-$74	2P: $76-$86	XP: $5	F6

Location: On US 101 business route. 814 Redwood Dr 95542. Fax: 707/923-3677. **Facility:** 32 units. 31 one- and 1 two-bedroom standard units. 1 story, exterior corridors. *Bath:* combo or shower only. **Parking:** on-site. **Terms:** office hours 8 am-10 pm, small pets only (in limited units). **Amenities:** hair dryers. **Pool(s):** heated outdoor. **Leisure Activities:** whirlpool. **Guest Services:** coin laundry. **Cards:** AX, DS, MC, VI. **Special Amenities: free local telephone calls.**

SOME UNITS

WHERE TO DINE

BENBOW INN RESTAURANT Historic **Lunch:** $8-$16 **Dinner:** $18-$30 **Phone:** 707/923-2124

Regional California

Location: US 101, exit Benbow, 2 mi s; in Benbow Inn. 445 Lake Benbow Dr 95542. **Hours:** Open 3/20-1/2; 8 am-11, noon-2 & 6-9 pm, Sun 8 am-1:30 & 6-9 pm; holiday hours vary. Closed: for lunch 9/15-5/31. **Reservations:** suggested. **Features:** Listed as a national historic landmark, the restaurant is an oasis for pleasant dining and good food made from fresh ingredients. The patio is a great spot for relaxing. Wine selections are plentiful. Casual dress; cocktails. **Parking:** on-site. **Cards:** AX, DS, MC, VI.

GEYSERVILLE —*See Wine Country p. 777.*

GILROY pop. 41,464

WHERE TO STAY

COMFORT INN *Book at aaa.com* **Phone:** (408)848-3500

AAA SAVE

Motel

All Year	1P: $59-$159	2P: $59-$159	XP: $5	F18

Location: US 101, exit Leavesley Rd, just w. 8292 Murray Ave 95020. Fax: 408/848-1569. **Facility:** 65 one-bedroom standard units. 2 stories (no elevator), exterior corridors. **Parking:** on-site. **Terms:** cancellation fee imposed, [ECP] meal plan available, small pets only ($100 deposit). **Amenities:** irons, hair dryers. **Pool(s):** outdoor. **Leisure Activities:** whirlpool. **Guest Services:** coin laundry. **Business Services:** meeting rooms. **Cards:** AX, DC, DS, MC, VI. **Special Amenities: free expanded continental breakfast and free newspaper.**

SOME UNITS

FEE

FOREST PARK INN **Phone:** (408)848-5144

AAA SAVE

Small-scale Hotel

All Year	1P: $60-$70	2P: $70-$82	XP: $10

Location: US 101, exit Leavesley Rd, just w. 375 Leavesley Rd 95020. Fax: 408/848-1138. **Facility:** 123 one-bedroom standard units. 3 stories, interior corridors. **Parking:** on-site. **Terms:** 4 day cancellation notice. **Amenities:** video games (fee), voice mail, hair dryers. **Pool(s):** outdoor. **Leisure Activities:** sauna, whirlpool, tennis court. **Guest Services:** coin laundry. **Business Services:** meeting rooms. **Cards:** AX, CB, DC, DS, MC, VI.

SOME UNITS

HILTON GARDEN INN GILROY *Book at aaa.com* **Phone:** (408)840-7000

SAVE

5/28-9/6	1P: $119-$179	2P: $129-$189	XP: $10	F18
9/7-11/18	1P: $109-$139	2P: $119-$149	XP: $10	F18
2/1-5/27	1P: $99-$129	2P: $109-$139	XP: $10	F18
11/19-1/31	1P: $89-$119	2P: $99-$129	XP: $10	F18

Small-scale Hotel **Location:** US 101, exit Monterey St, just w. 6070 Monterey St 95020-9502. Fax: 408/840-7022. **Facility:** 137 units. 135 one-bedroom standard units. 2 one-bedroom suites with whirlpools. 4 stories, interior corridors. *Bath:* combo or shower only. **Parking:** on-site. **Terms:** cancellation fee imposed. **Amenities:** dual phone lines, voice mail, irons, hair dryers. *Fee:* video games, high-speed Internet. **Dining:** 6-10 am, 11-1 & 5-9 pm, wine/beer only. **Leisure Activities:** whirlpool, exercise room. **Guest Services:** coin laundry. **Business Services:** meeting rooms, business center. **Cards:** AX, CB, DC, DS, MC, VI. *(See color ad below)*

SOME UNITS

LEAVESLEY INN **Phone:** (408)847-5500

SAVE

All Year	1P: $55-$75	2P: $68-$75	XP: $10	F12

Motel **Location:** US 101, exit Leavesley Rd, just w. 8430 Murray Ave 95020. Fax: 408/847-2241. **Facility:** 47 one-bedroom standard units. 2 stories (no elevator), exterior corridors. **Parking:** on-site. **Terms:** pets ($20 extra charge). **Amenities:** video library (fee). **Pool(s):** outdoor. **Leisure Activities:** whirlpool. **Guest Services:** coin laundry. **Business Services:** meeting rooms. **Cards:** AX, CB, DC, MC, VI. **Special Amenities: free continental breakfast.**

SOME UNITS

FEE

RAMADA LIMITED *Book at aaa.com* **Phone:** (408)848-1467

All Year	1P: $59-$159	2P: $59-$159	XP: $5	F18

Motel **Location:** US 101, exit Leavesley Rd, just w. 360 Leavesley Rd 95020. Fax: 408/848-1424. **Facility:** 41 units. 40 one- and 1 two-bedroom standard units. 2 stories (no elevator), exterior corridors. **Parking:** on-site. **Terms:** [ECP] meal plan available. **Amenities:** voice mail, irons, hair dryers. **Pool(s):** outdoor. **Leisure Activities:** whirlpool. **Guest Services:** coin laundry. **Cards:** AX, DC, DS, MC, VI. **Special Amenities: free expanded continental breakfast and free local telephone calls.**

SOME UNITS

RODEWAY INN *Book at aaa.com* **Phone:** (408)847-0688

SAVE

6/1-9/30 [CP]	1P: $59-$69	2P: $69-$79	XP: $10	F16
2/1-5/31 & 10/1-1/31 [CP]	1P: $49-$59	2P: $55-$65	XP: $10	F16

Motel **Location:** US 101, exit Leavesley Rd, just e. 611 Leavesley Rd 95020. Fax: 408/847-4400. **Facility:** 44 one-bedroom standard units. 2 stories (no elevator), exterior corridors. *Bath:* combo or shower only. **Parking:** on-site. **Terms:** 3 day cancellation notice. **Pool(s):** small outdoor. **Cards:** AX, DC, DS, MC, VI. **Special Amenities: free continental breakfast and free local telephone calls.**

SOME UNITS

SUPER 8 MOTEL **Phone:** (408)848-4108

SAVE

4/2-8/1	1P: $59-$73	2P: $63-$73
2/1-4/1 & 8/2-1/31	1P: $55-$69	2P: $59-$73

Motel **Location:** US 101, exit Leavesley Rd, just e. 8435 San Ysidro 95020. Fax: 408/848-2651. **Facility:** 52 one-bedroom standard units. 3 stories, interior corridors. **Parking:** on-site. **Terms:** weekly rates available. **Amenities:** *Some:* hair dryers. **Pool(s):** outdoor. **Guest Services:** coin laundry. **Cards:** AX, DC, MC, VI. **Special Amenities: free continental breakfast and free local telephone calls.**

SOME UNITS

GLEN ELLEN —See Wine Country p. 777.

GLENNVILLE

WHERE TO STAY

THE BUNKHOUSE MOTEL — **Phone:** (661)536-9100

Motel

All Year 1P: $65-$75 2P: $65-$75

Location: On SR 155 at Granite Rd. 12044 Hwy 15 S 93226 (PO Box 711). Fax: 661/536-8483. **Facility:** 8 one-bedroom standard units. 1 story, exterior corridors. **Parking:** on-site. **Terms:** [CP] meal plan available, small pets only ($10 deposit). **Amenities:** hair dryers. *Some:* irons. **Cards:** AX, DS, MC, VI.

SOME UNITS

FEE

GRAEAGLE pop. 831—*See also PORTOLA & QUINCY.*

WHERE TO STAY

GRAEAGLE MEADOWS — **Phone:** 530/836-1100

Ranch

All Year 2P: $320-$350 XP: $25 F12

Location: 0.3 mi s on SR 89, 1.5 mi s of jct SR 70 (Feather River Hwy). (PO Box 766). Fax: 530/836-1629. **Facility:** These two- and three-bedroom, two-bath, duplex homes feature fireplaces, patios and laundry facilities. 52 one-bedroom standard units. 1 story, exterior corridors. **Parking:** on-site. **Terms:** office hours 9 am-6 pm, 2 night minimum stay, 30 day cancellation notice-fee imposed, package plans - seasonal. **Leisure Activities:** fishing, golf-18 holes, bicycles, hiking trails. *Fee:* 4 tennis courts, horseback riding.

SOME UNITS

GRASS VALLEY pop. 10,922

WHERE TO STAY

ALTA SIERRA VILLAGE INN — **Phone:** (530)273-9102

SAVE

Motel

All Year 1P: $64-$185 2P: $64-$185 XP: $10 F18

Location: 6 mi s, 1.1 mi e on Alta Sierra Dr, 0.8 mi w on Norlene, 0.5 mi e on Tammy, follow signs to Alta Sierra Country Club. 11858 Tammy Way 95949. Fax: 530/273-8031. **Facility:** 16 units. 14 one-bedroom standard units. 1 one- and 1 two-bedroom suites ($125-$185), some with kitchens. 1 story, exterior corridors. *Bath:* combo or shower only. **Parking:** on-site. **Terms:** 2-3 night minimum stay - weekends, 10 day cancellation notice-fee imposed, pets ($10 extra charge). **Cards:** AX, DC, MC, VI. **Special Amenities: free local telephone calls and preferred room (subject to availability with advanced reservations).**

SOME UNITS

FEE

ANNIE HORAN'S BED & BREAKFAST — **Phone:** 530/272-1516

Historic Bed & Breakfast

All Year [BP] 1P: $69-$109 2P: $69-$109 XP: $10 F12

Location: SR 49, exit Central Grass Valley. 415 W Main St 95945. **Facility:** The 140-year-old Victorian home features generous porches for sun bathing or just relaxing and great views of the pine-covered hillsides. 4 one-bedroom standard units. 2 stories (no elevator), interior corridors. *Bath:* combo or shower only. **Parking:** on-site. **Terms:** 2 night minimum stay - weekends, 10 day cancellation notice-fee imposed. **Amenities:** hair dryers. **Guest Services:** complimentary evening beverages. **Cards:** AX, MC, VI.

SOME UNITS

BEST WESTERN GOLD COUNTRY INN *Book at aaa.com* — **Phone:** (530)273-1393

SAVE

Motel

4/1-11/1 [ECP]	1P: $99-$119	2P: $99-$119	XP: $10	F12
2/1-3/31 & 11/2-1/31 [ECP]	1P: $98-$109	2P: $98-$109	XP: $10	F12

Location: SR 20 and 49, exit Brunswick Rd, just e; midway between Grass Valley and Nevada City. 11972 Sutton Way 95945. Fax: 530/273-4229. **Facility:** 84 units. 81 one-bedroom standard units. 3 one-bedroom suites. 1-2 stories, exterior corridors. **Parking:** on-site. **Terms:** 2 night minimum stay - summer weekends, pets ($10 extra charge). **Amenities:** irons, hair dryers. **Pool(s):** outdoor. **Leisure Activities:** whirlpool. **Guest Services:** coin laundry. **Cards:** AX, CB, DC, DS, JC, MC, VI. **Special Amenities: free expanded continental breakfast and free local telephone calls.** *(See color ad below)*

SOME UNITS

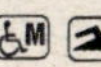

FEE

COACH N' FOUR MOTEL — **Phone:** (530)273-8009

AAA SAVE · Motel

4/17-1/31	1P: \$56-\$92	2P: \$62-\$122	XP: \$6
2/1-4/16	1P: \$56-\$89	2P: \$60-\$120	XP: \$6

Location: SR 49, exit E Empire St, 0.3 mi e, then just s. 628 S Auburn St 95945. Fax: 530/273-0827. **Facility:** 17 one-bedroom standard units. 2 stories, exterior corridors. *Bath:* combo or shower only. **Parking:** on-site. **Terms:** 2 night minimum stay - weekends 5/15-10/1, 3 day cancellation notice, [CP] meal plan available, pets (\$10 fee, \$50 deposit). **Amenities:** *Some:* irons, hair dryers. **Cards:** AX, DS, MC, VI.

SOME UNITS

FEE

ELAM BIGGS BED AND BREAKFAST — **Phone:** (530)477-0906

Bed & Breakfast

All Year [BP]	1P: \$80-\$115	2P: \$85-\$120	XP: \$20	F3

Location: Just e of jct of SR 49 and 174 (Colfax Hwy). 220 Colfax Ave 95945. **Facility:** Well-maintained gardens and a residential setting enhance this restored 1892 Queen Anne Victorian B&B. 4 one-bedroom standard units. 2 stories, interior corridors. **Parking:** on-site. **Terms:** 2 night minimum stay - weekends 4/1-12/31, 7 day cancellation notice. **Cards:** AX, MC, VI.

ASK

GOLDEN CHAIN RESORT MOTEL *Book at aaa.com* — **Phone:** (530)273-7279

AAA SAVE · Motel

5/1-10/15	1P: \$62-\$92	2P: \$72-\$102	XP: \$15	F13
10/16-1/31	1P: \$55-\$92	2P: \$65-\$102	XP: \$10	F13
2/1-4/30	1P: \$52-\$72	2P: \$62-\$82	XP: \$10	F13

Location: 2.5 mi s on SR 49. 13413 SR 49 95949. Fax: 530/273-7766. **Facility:** 21 one-bedroom standard units. 1 story, exterior corridors. *Bath:* combo or shower only. **Parking:** on-site. **Terms:** 1-2 night minimum stay - weekends, [CP] meal plan available, pets (\$10 extra charge, in limited units). **Amenities:** irons, hair dryers. **Pool(s):** heated outdoor. **Leisure Activities:** putting green. **Cards:** AX, DS, MC, VI. **Special Amenities: free continental breakfast and free local telephone calls.** *(See color ad p 345)*

DATA PORT

FEE

GRASS VALLEY COURTYARD SUITES — **Phone:** (530)272-7696

Motel

All Year	1P: \$115-\$260	2P: \$115-\$260	XP: \$15	F12

Location: SR 49, exit Central Grass Valley. 210 N Auburn St 95945. Fax: 530/272-1203. **Facility:** 32 one-bedroom standard units, some with kitchens. 2 stories, exterior corridors. **Parking:** on-site. **Terms:** 2 night minimum stay - weekends, 3 day cancellation notice-fee imposed, package plans, small pets only (\$25 fee, dogs only). **Amenities:** voice mail, irons, hair dryers. **Pool(s):** heated outdoor. **Leisure Activities:** sauna, whirlpool, exercise room. **Guest Services:** coin laundry. **Business Services:** meeting rooms. **Cards:** AX, DS, MC, VI. *(See color ad below)*

SOME UNITS

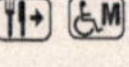

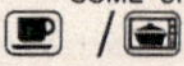

FEE

HOLBROOKE HOTEL **Phone:** (530)273-1353

Historic Small-scale Hotel

4/1-1/31 [CP]	1P: $85-$250	2P: $85-$250	XP: $15	F6
2/1-3/31 [CP]	1P: $75-$200	2P: $75-$200	XP: $15	F6

Location: SR 49, exit Central Grass Valley. 212 W Main St 95945. Fax: 530/273-0434. **Facility:** Even the addition maintains historic character at this property, an 1851 hotel with a Victorian-style annex that was built in 1870. 28 units. 27 one-bedroom standard units. 1 one-bedroom suite ($130-$250). 2 stories, interior corridors. *Bath:* combo or shower only. **Parking:** on-site. **Terms:** 2 night minimum stay - seasonal weekends. **Amenities:** irons, hair dryers. **Dining:** 11:30 am-2 & 5:30-9 pm; Sunday brunch 10 am-1 pm, cocktails. **Business Services:** meeting rooms. **Cards:** AX, DC, DS, MC, VI. **Special Amenities: free continental breakfast.**

DATA PORT

STAGECOACH MOTEL *Book at aaa.com* **Phone:** 530/272-3701

Motel

5/1-9/30 [CP]	1P: $75-$95	2P: $80-$95	XP: $5	F12
10/1-12/31 [CP]	1P: $70-$95	2P: $75-$90	XP: $5	F12
2/1-4/30 & 1/1-1/31 [CP]	1P: $60-$80	2P: $65-$90	XP: $5	F12

Location: SR 49, exit Colfax Ave, 0.4 mi s. 405 S Auburn St 95945. Fax: 530/272-9297. **Facility:** 16 one-bedroom standard units. 2 stories, exterior corridors. **Parking:** on-site. **Terms:** weekly rates available. **Cards:** AX, MC, VI. **Special Amenities: free continental breakfast and free local telephone calls.**

(See color ad p 345)

SOME UNITS

WHERE TO DINE

PAULETTE'S COUNTRY KITCHEN **Lunch:** $4-$9 **Phone:** 530/273-4008

American

Location: Jct SR 49 and 20, exit Brunswick Rd, just n. 11875 Sutton Way 95945. **Hours:** 6 am-3 pm, Sat & Sun from 7 am. Closed: 1/1, 11/25, 12/25. **Reservations:** suggested. **Features:** Family restaurant located in shopping center. Casual dress; beer & wine only. **Parking:** on-site. **Cards:** AX, DS, MC, VI.

SCHEIDEL'S RESTAURANT **Dinner:** $10-$32 **Phone:** 530/273-5553

German

Location: 6 mi s on SR 49; at entrance to Alta Sierra Dr. 10100 Alta Sierra Dr 95949. **Hours:** Open 2/4-12/31; 5:30 pm-10 pm, Sun 4 pm-9:30 pm. Closed major holidays. **Reservations:** suggested. **Features:** A charming Bavarian atmosphere is befitting the menu, which lists European and Continental specialties. The comfortable setting is nice for families. Casual dress; cocktails. **Parking:** on-site. **Cards:** MC, VI.

GREENVILLE pop. 1,160

WHERE TO STAY

YORKSHIRE HOUSE B&B **Phone:** 530/284-1794

Bed & Breakfast

All Year [BP]	1P: $85-$100	2P: $85-$100	XP: $15	F4

Location: N on SR 89, then 1 mi. 421 Main St 95947. Fax: 530/284-1821. **Facility:** The small, cozy B&B is quiet and serene and located in a small Northern California town, where neighbors know each other. 4 one-bedroom standard units, some with whirlpools. 2 stories (no elevator), interior corridors. **Parking:** on-site and street. **Terms:** office hours 8 am-9 pm, age restrictions may apply, 7 day cancellation notice, package plans. **Amenities:** video library, hair dryers. *Some:* irons. **Leisure Activities:** bicycles, hiking trails, jogging. *Fee:* massage. **Guest Services:** gift shop. **Cards:** AX, DC, MC, VI.

SOME UNITS

VCR

GRIDLEY pop. 5,382

WHERE TO STAY

GRIDLEY INN **Phone:** (530)846-4520

Motel

All Year	1P: $69-$89	2P: $69-$89	XP: $5	F12

Location: 1 mi s on SR 99. 1490 Hwy 99, Suite A 95948. Fax: 530/846-4569. **Facility:** 25 one-bedroom standard units. 2 stories (no elevator), exterior corridors. **Parking:** on-site. **Terms:** office hours 7 am-10 pm, small pets only ($50 deposit). **Amenities:** *Some:* irons, hair dryers. **Pool(s):** outdoor. **Leisure Activities:** whirlpool. **Guest Services:** coin laundry. **Cards:** AX, CB, DC, DS, JC, MC, VI. **Special Amenities: free local telephone calls.**

SOME UNITS

FEE

PACIFIC MOTEL **Phone:** 530/846-4580

Motel

All Year	1P: $48-$58	2P: $50-$60	XP: $5	F8

Location: 1 mi s on SR 99. 1308 Hwy 99 95948. **Facility:** 15 one-bedroom standard units. 1 story, exterior corridors. *Bath:* combo or shower only. **Parking:** on-site. **Terms:** office hours 7 am-10 pm, age restrictions may apply, weekly rates available, [CP] meal plan available, pets ($3 extra charge). **Amenities:** *Some:* irons, hair dryers. **Pool(s):** outdoor. **Cards:** AX, CB, MC, VI. **Special Amenities: free continental breakfast and free local telephone calls.**

SOME UNITS

FEE

GROVELAND —See also YOSEMITE NATIONAL PARK.

WHERE TO STAY

BEST VALUE YOSEMITE WESTGATE BUCKMEADOWS LODGE Book at aaa.com **Phone:** 209/962-5281

SAVE

Motel

5/1-10/31	1P: $99-$169	2P: $99-$179	XP: $10	F12
2/1-4/30	1P: $79-$149	2P: $79-$169	XP: $10	F12
11/1-1/31	1P: $69-$149	2P: $69-$169	XP: $10	F12

Location: On SR 120, 12 mi e. 7633/7647 Hwy 120 95321. Fax: 209/962-5285. **Facility:** 55 one-bedroom standard units. 1-2 stories (no elevator), exterior corridors. *Bath:* combo or shower only. **Parking:** on-site. **Terms:** 3 day cancellation notice-fee imposed, pets ($10 extra charge). **Amenities:** hair dryers. **Pool(s):** heated outdoor. **Leisure Activities:** whirlpool. **Guest Services:** coin laundry. **Cards:** AX, CB, DC, DS, MC, VI. **Special Amenities: free local telephone calls and preferred room (subject to availability with advanced reservations).** *(See color ad p 818)*

FEE / SOME UNITS

GROVELAND HOTEL AT YOSEMITE NATIONAL PARK **Phone:** 209/962-4000

SAVE

Historic Country Inn

All Year [ECP]	1P: $145	2P: $165	XP: $25	D12

Location: Center. 18767 Main St 95321 (PO Box 481). Fax: 209/962-6674. **Facility:** This eclectic property includes an 1849 adobe and a 1914 Queen Anne hotel said to be modeled after the first American mansion. 17 units. 14 one-bedroom standard units. 3 one-bedroom suites ($225-$265) with whirlpools. 2 stories (no elevator), interior corridors. *Bath:* combo or shower only. **Parking:** on-site. **Terms:** cancellation fee imposed, package plans - mid-week & seasonal, $3 service charge, pets ($25 deposit). **Amenities:** voice mail, hair dryers. *Some:* CD players, irons. **Dining:** Victorian Room at The Groveland Hotel, see separate listing. **Leisure Activities:** Pine Mountain Lake Golf privileges. **Guest Services:** gift shop. **Business Services:** meeting rooms. **Cards:** AX, CB, DC, DS, JC, MC, VI. **Special Amenities: free local telephone calls and preferred room (subject to availability with advanced reservations).**

DATA PORT / VCR / FEE / SOME UNITS

YOSEMITE ROSE BED & BREAKFAST **Phone:** 209/962-6548

Bed & Breakfast

All Year	1P: $145-$190	2P: $145-$190

Location: On SR 120, 7.5 mi e, 2.7 mi n. 22830 Ferretti Rd 95321. Fax: 209/962-7750. **Facility:** The inn is a great place to stay at night while you explore nature's majesty in Yosemite National Park during the day. 5 one-bedroom standard units. 2 stories (no elevator), interior/exterior corridors. *Bath:* combo or shower only. **Parking:** on-site. **Terms:** 2 night minimum stay - weekends, 14 day cancellation notice-fee imposed, [BP] meal plan available. **Guest Services:** complimentary laundry. **Cards:** AX, DS, MC, VI.

SOME UNITS / VCR

WHERE TO DINE

VICTORIAN ROOM AT THE GROVELAND HOTEL **Lunch:** $8-$15 **Dinner:** $14-$28 **Phone:** 209/962-4000

California

Location: Center; in Groveland Hotel at Yosemite National Park. 18767 Main St 95321. **Hours:** 11 am-2 & 6-10 pm. **Reservations:** suggested; req for lunch. **Features:** In the historic Groveland Hotel, the casually elegant restaurant presents a menu of well-prepared beef, pork, chicken and seafood dishes. The staff is friendly and attentive. Casual dress; cocktails. **Parking:** on-site. **Cards:** AX, CB, DC, DS, MC, VI.

GROVER BEACH pop. 13,067

WHERE TO STAY

HOLIDAY INN EXPRESS-PISMO BEACH/GROVER BEACH Book at aaa.com **Phone:** (805)481-4448

Motel

5/24-9/15	1P: $85-$120	2P: $85-$120	XP: $10	F17
2/1-5/23 & 9/16-1/31	1P: $65-$95	2P: $65-$95	XP: $10	F17

Location: US 101, exit Oak Park Blvd, just w. 775 Oak Park Blvd 93433. Fax: 805/473-3609. **Facility:** 78 one-bedroom standard units, some with whirlpools. 3 stories, interior corridors. **Parking:** on-site. **Terms:** [ECP] meal plan available. **Amenities:** irons, hair dryers. **Pool(s):** heated outdoor. **Leisure Activities:** whirlpool. **Guest Services:** valet laundry. **Business Services:** meeting rooms. **Cards:** AX, DC, DS, MC, VI. *(See color ad p 535)*

ASK / DATA PORT / SOME UNITS

GUALALA —See Point Arena & Wine Country p. 777.

GUERNEVILLE —See Monte Rio & Wine Country p. 779.

HALF MOON BAY —See San Francisco p. 666.

HANFORD pop. 41,686

WHERE TO STAY

BEST WESTERN HANFORD INN Book at aaa.com **Phone:** (559)583-7300

SAVE — Motel

All Year [CP] 1P: $58-$78 2P: $60-$80 XP: $6 F12

Location: SR 198, exit 11th Ave eastbound; exit Redington St westbound, just s. 755 Cadillac Ln 93230. Fax: 559/582-8455. **Facility:** 40 one-bedroom standard units. 2 stories, exterior corridors. **Parking:** on-site. **Amenities:** irons, hair dryers. **Pool(s):** outdoor. **Guest Services:** coin laundry. **Cards:** AX, CB, DC, DS, MC, VI. **Special Amenities: free continental breakfast.**

SOME UNITS

COMFORT INN Book at aaa.com **Phone:** (559)584-9300

SAVE — Small-scale Hotel

4/1-9/30 1P: $79-$99 2P: $79-$99 XP: $5 F12
2/1-3/31 & 10/1-1/31 1P: $69-$89 2P: $69-$89 XP: $5 F12

Location: SR 198, exit Redington St westbound; exit Douty Rd eastbound. 10 N Irwin St 93230. Fax: 559/584-0300. **Facility:** 65 units. 58 one-bedroom standard units, some with whirlpools. 7 one-bedroom suites, some with whirlpools. 3 stories, interior corridors. **Parking:** on-site. **Terms:** [ECP] meal plan available. **Amenities:** high-speed Internet, dual phone lines, voice mail, safes (fee), irons, hair dryers. **Pool(s):** outdoor. **Leisure Activities:** whirlpool, exercise room. **Guest Services:** valet and coin laundry. **Business Services:** meeting rooms, fax (fee). **Cards:** AX, CB, DC, DS, JC, MC, VI. **Special Amenities: free expanded continental breakfast and free newspaper.**

SOME UNITS — FEE FEE

IRWIN STREET INN Book at aaa.com **Phone:** (559)583-8000

Bed & Breakfast

All Year 1P: $79-$150 2P: $79-$150 XP: $5 F10

Location: Downtown Hanford Historic District. 522 N Irwin St 93230. Fax: 559/583-8793. **Facility:** Designated smoking area. 27 units. 24 one-bedroom standard units. 3 one-bedroom suites ($113-$150). 2 stories (no elevator), exterior corridors. *Bath:* combo or shower only. **Parking:** on-site. **Terms:** cancellation fee imposed, [ECP] meal plan available. **Amenities:** voice mail, irons. **Pool(s):** small outdoor. **Cards:** AX, DC, DS, MC, VI.

(See color ad below)

SEQUOIA INN **Phone:** (559)582-0338

SAVE — Small-scale Hotel

All Year [ECP] 1P: $65-$105 2P: $65-$105 XP: $6 F18

Location: SR 198, exit 12th Ave, then n. 1655 Mall Dr 93230. Fax: 559/582-1392. **Facility:** 58 one-bedroom standard units. 3 stories, interior corridors. *Bath:* combo or shower only. **Parking:** on-site. **Terms:** small pets only ($100 deposit). **Amenities:** voice mail, irons, hair dryers. **Pool(s):** outdoor. **Leisure Activities:** whirlpool, exercise room. **Guest Services:** coin laundry. **Cards:** AX, CB, DC, DS, JC, MC, VI. **Special Amenities: free expanded continental breakfast and free local telephone calls.**

SOME UNITS — FEE FEE FEE

HAYWARD pop. 140,030

WHERE TO STAY

BEST WESTERN INN OF HAYWARD Book at aaa.com **Phone:** (510)785-8700

SAVE Motel

All Year 1P: $79-$89 2P: $99-$109 XP: $8 D12

Location: I-880, exit A St, just e. 360 West A St 94541. Fax: 510/782-0850. **Facility:** 91 one-bedroom standard units, some with kitchens and/or whirlpools. 3 stories, interior/exterior corridors. *Bath:* combo or shower only. **Parking:** on-site. **Terms:** [ECP] meal plan available. **Amenities:** voice mail, irons, hair dryers. **Pool(s):** outdoor. **Leisure Activities:** sauna, whirlpool. **Guest Services:** valet laundry. **Business Services:** meeting rooms. **Cards:** AX, CB, DC, DS, MC, VI. **Special Amenities: free newspaper and free room upgrade (subject to availability with advanced reservations).**

SOME UNITS

COMFORT INN Book at aaa.com **Phone:** (510)538-4466

SAVE Motel

All Year [ECP] 1P: $79-$150 2P: $79-$150 XP: $10 F17

Location: 1.8 mi e of I-880, exit Jackson Blvd/SR 92, 0.5 mi s on SR 238 (Mission Blvd). 24997 Mission Blvd 94544. Fax: 510/581-8029. **Facility:** 62 one-bedroom standard units, some with whirlpools. 2 stories, exterior corridors. **Parking:** on-site. **Terms:** cancellation fee imposed. **Amenities:** high-speed Internet, voice mail, irons, hair dryers. **Leisure Activities:** sauna. **Guest Services:** coin laundry. **Business Services:** meeting rooms. **Cards:** AX, CB, DC, DS, MC, VI. **Special Amenities: free expanded continental breakfast and free newspaper.** *(See color ad p 617)*

SOME UNITS

DAYS INN AIRPORT Book at aaa.com **Phone:** (510)670-0555

SAVE Motel

All Year [CP] 1P: $69-$95 2P: $74-$99 XP: $5 F17

Location: I-880, exit A St, just w. 450 West A St 94541. Fax: 510/670-0440. **Facility:** 32 one-bedroom standard units, some with whirlpools. 3 stories, exterior corridors. **Parking:** on-site. **Terms:** cancellation fee imposed, $5 service charge. **Amenities:** dual phone lines, irons, hair dryers. **Cards:** AX, CB, DC, DS, JC, MC, VI. **Special Amenities: free continental breakfast and free newspaper.**

SOME UNITS

DISCOVERY INN **Phone:** (510)886-7111

SAVE Motel

All Year 1P: $69-$89 2P: $69-$99 XP: $10

Location: I-880, exit SR 92 (Jackson St), 1 mi e. 333 Jackson Blvd 94544. Fax: 510/727-1412. **Facility:** 21 one-bedroom standard units, some with whirlpools. 2 stories, exterior corridors. **Parking:** on-site. **Terms:** 3 day cancellation notice-fee imposed, [CP] meal plan available. **Amenities:** hair dryers. **Cards:** AX, CB, DC, DS, MC, VI. **Special Amenities: early check-in/late check-out and preferred room (subject to availability with advanced reservations).**

SOME UNITS

HAMPTON INN-HAYWARD Book at aaa.com **Phone:** 510/247-1555

SAVE Small-scale Hotel

1/1-1/31 [ECP] 1P: $95 2P: $95 XP: $10 F18
2/1-12/31 [ECP] 1P: $91 2P: $91 XP: $10 F18

Location: 1.8 mi e of I-880; exit Jackson Blvd/SR 92, just s on SR 238 (Mission Blvd). 24137 Mission Blvd 94544. Fax: 510/247-1313. **Facility:** 70 one-bedroom standard units, some with whirlpools. 3 stories, interior corridors. *Bath:* combo or shower only. **Parking:** on-site. **Amenities:** dual phone lines, voice mail, irons, hair dryers. **Pool(s):** heated outdoor. **Leisure Activities:** exercise room. **Guest Services:** coin laundry, airport transportation-Oakland & Hayward airports, area transportation-within 3 mi. **Business Services:** meeting rooms. **Cards:** AX, DC. **Special Amenities: free expanded continental breakfast and free local telephone calls.**

SOME UNITS

LA QUINTA INN & SUITES Book at aaa.com **Phone:** (510)732-6300

SAVE Small-scale Hotel

All Year [CP] 1P: $79-$109 2P: $79-$109 XP: $10 F17

Location: I-880, exit A St, 0.5 mi w. 20777 Hesperian Blvd 94541. Fax: 510/783-2265. **Facility:** 146 one-bedroom standard units. 3 stories, interior corridors. *Bath:* combo or shower only. **Parking:** on-site. **Terms:** pets ($25 deposit). **Amenities:** video games (fee), dual phone lines, voice mail, irons, hair dryers. *Some:* high-speed Internet. **Pool(s):** heated outdoor. **Leisure Activities:** whirlpool, exercise room. **Guest Services:** coin laundry. **Business Services:** conference facilities. **Cards:** AX, CB, DC, DS, MC, VI. **Special Amenities: free expanded continental breakfast and free local telephone calls.**

SOME UNITS

FEE

MAINSTAY SUITES Book at aaa.com **Phone:** (510)731-3571

SAVE Small-scale Hotel

5/1-8/31 [ECP] 1P: $89-$109 2P: $89-$129 XP: $10 F16
9/1-1/31 [ECP] 1P: $69-$99 2P: $69-$99 XP: $10 F16
2/1-4/30 [ECP] 1P: $69-$89 2P: $69-$89 XP: $10 F16

Location: I-880, exit A St, just w. 835 West A St 94541. Fax: 510/731-3572. **Facility:** 47 one-bedroom standard units with efficiencies. 3 stories, interior corridors. *Bath:* combo or shower only. **Parking:** on-site. **Terms:** cancellation fee imposed, weekly rates available, pets ($15 fee). **Amenities:** dual phone lines, voice mail, irons, hair dryers. *Some:* high-speed Internet. **Pool(s):** small outdoor. **Leisure Activities:** exercise room. **Guest Services:** coin laundry. **Cards:** AX, DC, DS, MC, VI. **Special Amenities: free expanded continental breakfast and early check-in/late check-out.** *(See ad p 351)*

SOME UNITS

FEE

PHOENIX LODGE **Phone:** (510)786-2844

Small-scale Hotel

All Year 1P: $50-$70 2P: $59-$80 XP: $6 F12

Location: I-880, exit Whipple/Industrial northbound, just w. Truck parking located on site. 2286 Industrial Pkwy W 94545. Fax: 510/786-0255. **Facility:** 70 one-bedroom standard units. 3 stories (no elevator), interior corridors. *Bath:* combo or shower only. **Parking:** on-site. **Terms:** 3 day cancellation notice. **Dining:** 5:30 am-9:30 pm. **Guest Services:** coin laundry. **Cards:** AX, MC, VI.

SOME UNITS

QUALITY INN & SUITES Book at aaa.com **Phone:** (510)782-5000

Small-scale Hotel

4/1-9/1	1P: $119-$129	2P: $129-$139	XP: $10	F18
2/1-3/31	1P: $109-$119	2P: $119-$129		
9/2-1/31	1P: $109-$119	2P: $119-$129	XP: $10	F18

Location: SR 92, exit Industrial Blvd, just n. 25921 Industrial Blvd 94545. Fax: 510/782-5222. **Facility:** 84 units. 65 one-bedroom standard units, some with kitchens. 19 one-bedroom suites ($149-$199). 3 stories, interior corridors. *Bath:* combo or shower only. **Parking:** on-site. **Terms:** cancellation fee imposed, [ECP] meal plan available. **Amenities:** high-speed Internet, dual phone lines, voice mail, irons, hair dryers. **Leisure Activities:** sauna, whirlpool, exercise room. **Business Services:** meeting rooms, business center. **Cards:** AX, CB, DC, DS, JC, MC, VI. **Special Amenities: free expanded continental breakfast and free local telephone calls.** *(See color ad below)*

SOME UNITS

RAMADA LIMITED Book at aaa.com **Phone:** (510)538-4380

Motel

All Year 1P: $69-$99 2P: $69-$99 XP: $10 F12

Location: Se of I-580 and 238 interchange. 21598 Foothill Blvd 94541. Fax: 510/889-0728. **Facility:** 70 one-bedroom standard units. 2 stories, exterior corridors. *Bath:* combo or shower only. **Parking:** on-site. **Terms:** [CP] meal plan available. **Amenities:** high-speed Internet, voice mail, irons, hair dryers. **Pool(s):** outdoor. **Guest Services:** coin laundry. **Cards:** AX, CB, DC, DS, JC, MC, VI. **Special Amenities: free expanded continental breakfast and free local telephone calls.**

SOME UNITS

WHERE TO DINE

RUE DE MAIN RESTAURANT FRANCAIS **Lunch:** $9-$17 **Dinner:** $14-$34 **Phone:** 510/537-0812

French

Location: I-880, exit A St, 1.5 mi e; s on Main St; between B and C sts. 22622 Main St 94541. **Hours:** 11:30 am-2:30 & 5:30-9 pm, Fri & Sat from 5:30 pm. Closed: Sun & Mon. **Reservations:** suggested. **Features:** Creative preparation and presentation marks well-thought-out dishes. Paris street-cafe decor lends to the pleasant, quiet atmosphere. Casual dress; beer & wine only. **Parking:** on-site. **Cards:** AX, CB, DC, MC, VI.

HEALDSBURG —See Wine Country p. 780.

HOLLISTER pop. 34,413

WHERE TO STAY

BEST WESTERN SAN BENITO INN Book at aaa.com **Phone:** (831)637-9248

SAVE Motel

6/1-7/31	1P: $180	2P: $200	XP: $10	F16
4/1-5/31	1P: $109	2P: $119	XP: $10	F16
8/1-1/31	1P: $109	2P: $109	XP: $10	F16
2/1-3/31	1P: $99	2P: $109	XP: $10	F16

Location: 1.5 mi n on SR 25 and 156. 660 San Felipe Rd 95023. Fax: 831/637-4584. **Facility:** 42 one-bedroom standard units. 2 stories (no elevator), exterior corridors. **Parking:** on-site. **Terms:** cancellation fee imposed, [CP] meal plan available. **Amenities:** high-speed Internet, voice mail, irons, hair dryers. **Pool(s):** outdoor. **Cards:** AX, CB, DC, DS, MC, VI. **Special Amenities: free continental breakfast.**

SOME UNITS

CASA DE FRUTA GARDEN MOTEL **Phone:** 408/842-9316

Motel

All Year	1P: $79-$149	2P: $79-$149	XP: $5	F10

Location: Just s of SR 152. 10031 Pacheco Pass Hwy 95023. Fax: 408/848-3793. **Facility:** Smoke free premises. 14 one-bedroom standard units. 1 story, exterior corridors. **Parking:** on-site. **Terms:** [CP] meal plan available. **Amenities:** voice mail, hair dryers. **Pool(s):** outdoor. **Leisure Activities:** playground. **Guest Services:** gift shop, coin laundry. **Business Services:** meeting rooms. **Cards:** DS, MC, VI.

ASK

HOLLISTER INN **Phone:** 831/637-1641

SAVE Motel

All Year	1P: $59-$190	2P: $69-$190	XP: $10

Location: Just n on SR 25 and 156. Located across from shopping mall. 152 San Felipe Rd 95023. Fax: 831/637-8423. **Facility:** 31 one-bedroom standard units. 2 stories (no elevator), exterior corridors. **Parking:** on-site. **Terms:** 3 day cancellation notice-fee imposed, [CP] meal plan available. **Amenities:** hair dryers. *Some:* DVD players. **Cards:** AX, CB, DC, DS, MC, VI. **Special Amenities: early check-in/late check-out and preferred room (subject to availability with advanced reservations).**

SOME UNITS

VCR

RIDGEMARK GUEST COTTAGES **Phone:** (831)637-8151

SAVE Cottage

All Year	1P: $99-$110	2P: $104-$120	XP: $10	F

Location: 2.5 mi se on SR 25; at Ridgemark Golf and Country Club. 3800 Airline Hwy 95023. Fax: 831/636-3168. **Facility:** Located just outside of town, the property and the guest room cottages offer views of the the golf course and surrounding rolling hills. 32 cottages, some with whirlpools. 1 story, exterior corridors. **Parking:** on-site. **Terms:** 2 night minimum stay - weekends 5/1-10/31, cancellation fee imposed, package plans. **Amenities:** voice mail, hair dryers. *Some:* irons. **Dining:** 2 restaurants, 7 am-9 pm. **Leisure Activities:** 6 lighted tennis courts. *Fee:* golf-36 holes. **Cards:** AX, CB, DC, DS, MC, VI.

SOME UNITS

HOOPA

WHERE TO STAY

TSEWENALDIN INN **Phone:** (530)625-4294

SAVE Motel

5/1-9/30	1P: $62-$100	2P: $66-$110	XP: $5	F
2/1-4/30 & 10/1-1/31	1P: $58-$75	2P: $62-$85	XP: $5	F

Location: On Hoopa Indian Reservation. Located at Hoopa Shopping Center. Hwy 96 95546 (PO Box 219). Fax: 530/625-4351. **Facility:** 21 one-bedroom standard units. 2 stories (no elevator), exterior corridors. **Parking:** on-site. **Terms:** age restrictions may apply, cancellation fee imposed. **Amenities:** hair dryers. *Some:* irons. **Pool(s):** small outdoor. **Leisure Activities:** whirlpool. **Business Services:** conference facilities. **Cards:** AX, CB, DC, DS, JC, MC, VI. **Special Amenities: free local telephone calls and early check-in/late check-out.**

SOME UNITS

HOPLAND —See Wine Country p. 781.

INDEPENDENCE pop. 574

WHERE TO STAY

RAY'S DEN MOTEL **Phone:** (760)878-2122

SAVE Motel

5/1-10/31	1P: $57-$72	2P: $57-$72
11/1-1/31	1P: $54-$69	2P: $54-$69
2/1-4/30	1P: $49-$63	2P: $49-$63

Location: On US 395. 405 N Edwards 93526 (PO Box 68). **Facility:** 8 one-bedroom standard units. 1 story, exterior corridors. *Bath:* shower only. **Parking:** on-site. **Terms:** office hours 7 am-11 pm, pets ($6 extra charge). **Amenities:** *Some:* irons. **Cards:** AX, DS, MC, VI. **Special Amenities: free local telephone calls and preferred room (subject to availability with advanced reservations).**

SOME UNITS

FEE

INVERNESS pop. 1,421

WHERE TO STAY

MOTEL INVERNESS — Phone: 415/669-1081

Motel — All Year 1P: $89-$350 2P: $89-$350

Location: 4 mi w of SR 1. 12718 Sir Francis Drake Blvd 94937 (PO Box 958). Fax: 415/669-1906. **Facility:** 8 units. 7 one-bedroom standard units, some with kitchens. 1 two-bedroom suite ($150-$350) with kitchen and whirlpool. 1 story, exterior corridors. *Bath:* combo or shower only. **Parking:** on-site. **Terms:** 7 day cancellation notice-fee imposed. **Amenities:** hair dryers. **Cards:** MC, VI.

ASK

JACKSON pop. 3,989

WHERE TO STAY

AMADOR MOTEL — Phone: 209/223-0970

AAA SAVE — Motel — All Year 1P: $49-$60 2P: $54-$66 XP: $10

Location: 1.5 mi n at jct SR 49 and 88 on Frontage Rd. 12408 Kennedy Flat Rd 95642. **Facility:** 10 one-bedroom standard units. Exterior corridors. *Bath:* shower only. **Parking:** on-site. **Terms:** office hours 8 am-11 pm, 5 day cancellation notice-fee imposed. **Pool(s):** small outdoor. **Leisure Activities:** outdoor barbecue & picnic facilities. **Cards:** AX, DS, MC, VI. **Special Amenities: free local telephone calls.**

BEST WESTERN AMADOR INN *Book at aaa.com* — Phone: (209)223-0211

AAA SAVE — Small-scale Hotel — All Year 1P: $75-$109 2P: $85-$119 XP: $10 F17

Location: On SR 49. 200 S Hwy 49 95642. Fax: 209/223-4836. **Facility:** 117 one-bedroom standard units, some with kitchens. 2 stories (no elevator), interior corridors. **Parking:** on-site. **Terms:** pets (in limited units). **Amenities:** voice mail, irons, hair dryers. **Pool(s):** outdoor. **Leisure Activities:** exercise room. **Guest Services:** valet laundry. **Business Services:** meeting rooms. **Cards:** AX, DC, MC, VI. **Special Amenities: free newspaper.** *(See color ad below)*

DATA PORT / VCR / SOME UNITS

EL CAMPO CASA RESORT MOTEL — Phone: 209/223-0100

AAA SAVE — Motel — 2/1-12/31 1P: $52-$102 2P: $52-$102 XP: $10

Location: 1.5 mi w in Martell, at jct SR 49 and 88 on Frontage Rd; approach off SR 88. 12548 Kennedy Flat Rd 95642. **Facility:** 14 units. 13 one-bedroom standard units. 1 one-bedroom suite. 2 stories (no elevator), exterior corridors. *Bath:* shower only. **Parking:** on-site. **Terms:** open 2/1-12/31, office hours 8 am-10 pm, cancellation fee imposed, pets ($10 extra charge, in designated unit). **Pool(s):** outdoor. **Leisure Activities:** barbecue & picnic facilities, playground. **Cards:** AX, DS, MC, VI.

FEE

GATE HOUSE INN — Phone: 209/223-3500

Historic Bed & Breakfast — All Year [BP] 2P: $135-$180 XP: $25

Location: 2 mi n on SR 49, then 1.5 mi e. 1330 Jackson Gate Rd 95642. Fax: 209/223-1299. **Facility:** A turn-of-the-century rural Victorian. 6 units. 3 one-bedroom standard units. 1 one-bedroom suite ($155-$205). 2 cottages ($205-$265) with whirlpools. 2 stories (no elevator), interior corridors. *Bath:* combo or shower only. **Parking:** on-site. **Terms:** office hours 10 am-6 pm, 2 night minimum stay - weekends, age restrictions may apply, 10 day cancellation notice-fee imposed. **Pool(s):** outdoor. **Cards:** DS, MC, VI.

ASK / SOME UNITS

THE WEDGEWOOD INN — Phone: (209)296-4300

AAA SAVE — Bed & Breakfast — All Year [BP] 1P: $145-$165 2P: $155-$175

Location: 6.5 mi e of jct SR 49 and 88, exit SR 88 Irishtown-Clinton rds, right on Clinton Rd, 0.6 mi s to Narcissus Rd, 0.4 mi e to Wedgewood Dr (don't exit W Clinton). 11941 Narcissus Rd 95642. Fax: 209/296-4301. **Facility:** English country-style grounds surround this replica Queen Anne Victorian furnished with European and American antiques and memorabilia. Smoke free premises. 5 units. 3 one-bedroom standard units. 2 one-bedroom suites ($185-$205) with whirlpools. 3 stories (no elevator), interior corridors. **Parking:** on-site. **Terms:** office hours 7 am-9 pm, age restrictions may apply, 7 day cancellation notice-fee imposed. **Amenities:** video library, hair dryers. *Some:* irons. **Leisure Activities:** croquet, parlor games, horseshoes. **Guest Services:** gift shop, complimentary evening beverages. **Cards:** AX, DS, MC, VI.

VCR / SOME UNITS

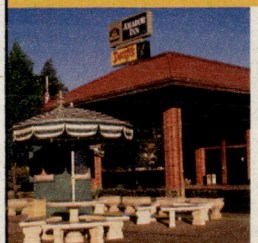

WINDROSE INN

Phone: (209)223-3650

Historic Bed & Breakfast

All Year [BP] 1P: $89-$185 2P: $99-$185

Location: 2 mi n on SR 49, then 1.5 mi e. 1407 Jackson Gate Rd 95642. Fax: 209/223-3793. **Facility:** Near town on one-acre grounds featuring gardens and a creek, this Victorian farmhouse dates to the late 1890s. Smoke free premises. 4 one-bedroom standard units, some with whirlpools. 2 stories (no elevator), interior corridors. **Parking:** on-site. **Terms:** office hours 8 am-6 pm, 2 night minimum stay - weekends, 7 day cancellation notice. **Amenities:** *Some:* irons, hair dryers. **Guest Services:** complimentary evening beverages. **Cards:** AX, MC, VI.

SOME UNITS

WHERE TO DINE

UPSTAIRS RESTAURANT & STREETSIDE BISTRO **Lunch:** $5-$10 **Dinner:** $14-$30 **Phone:** 209/223-3342

West American

Location: Center. 164 Main St 95642. **Hours:** 11:30 am-2:30 & 5:30-9 pm, Sat & Sun 11:30 am-3:30 & 5:30-9 pm. Closed: 12/25; also Mon, Tues & 1/1-1/15. **Reservations:** suggested. **Features:** In the center of downtown, the casual restaurant serves American fare. The decor is in keeping with the gold-mining era. Casual dress; beer & wine only. **Parking:** street. **Cards:** AX, DS, MC, VI.

JAMESTOWN pop. 3,017

WHERE TO STAY

1859 HISTORIC NATIONAL HOTEL, A COUNTRY INN

Phone: 209/984-3446

SAVE

Country Inn

All Year 1P: $90-$140 2P: $90-$140 XP: $15 F

Location: Downtown. 18183 Main St 95327 (PO Box 502). Fax: 209/984-5620. **Facility:** You will find outstanding accomodations and lovely service in this prize historical hotel, built in 1859. 9 one-bedroom standard units. 2 stories (no elevator), interior corridors. *Bath:* shower only. **Parking:** street. **Terms:** office hours 8 am-9 pm, 3 day cancellation notice-fee imposed, package plans, pets ($10 extra charge). **Amenities:** hair dryers. **Dining:** National Hotel Restaurant, see separate listing. **Cards:** AX, CB, DC, DS, JC, MC, VI. **Special Amenities: free continental breakfast and early check-in/late check-out.**

SOME UNITS

FEE

COUNTRY INN SONORA *Book at aaa.com*

Phone: (209)984-0315

Motel

5/1-10/1 1P: $59-$139 2P: $79-$159 XP: $10 F16

2/1-4/30 & 10/2-1/31 1P: $54-$139 2P: $64-$159 XP: $10 F16

Location: On SR 108 and 49, 1 mi e of town. 18730 Hwy 108 95327 (18730 Hwy 108, SONORA). Fax: 209/984-4849. **Facility:** 61 one-bedroom standard units. 3 stories (no elevator), exterior corridors. **Parking:** on-site. **Terms:** check-in 4 pm, cancellation fee imposed, [CP] meal plan available, small pets only ($10 extra charge). **Amenities:** high-speed Internet, voice mail, irons, hair dryers. **Pool(s):** outdoor. **Guest Services:** valet laundry. **Cards:** AX, CB, DC, DS, JC, MC, VI. ***(See color ad p 729)***

SOME UNITS

FEE

JAMESTOWN HOTEL

Phone: (209)984-3902

SAVE

Bed & Breakfast

All Year [BP] 1P: $85-$200 2P: $85-$200 XP: $25

Location: Downtown. 18153 Main St 95327. Fax: 209/984-4149. **Facility:** The hotel's original building, from the gold era of the 1850s, offers guest rooms equipped with modern conveniences but otherwise authentic in style. Smoke free premises. 11 units. 10 one-bedroom standard units, some with whirlpools. 1 two-bedroom suite. 2 stories (no elevator), interior corridors. *Bath:* combo or shower only. **Parking:** street. **Terms:** office hours 8 am-9 pm, 7 day cancellation notice-fee imposed, package plans. **Amenities:** video library, hair dryers. **Dining:** 11 am-9 pm, Sun 10 am-2 & 5-9 pm; closed Tues & Wed. **Business Services:** PC. **Cards:** AX, DC, DS, MC, VI. **Special Amenities: free continental breakfast and free local telephone calls.**

SOME UNITS

JAMESTOWN RAILTOWN MOTEL

Phone: (209)984-3332

SAVE

Motel

5/1-9/30 1P: $60-$65 2P: $75-$85 XP: $3 F3

2/1-4/30 & 10/1-1/31 1P: $49-$59 2P: $69-$79 XP: $5 F3

Location: Just s of Main St. 10301 Willow St 95327 (PO Box 1039). Fax: 209/532-6401. **Facility:** 20 one-bedroom standard units, some with whirlpools. 2 stories (no elevator), exterior corridors. **Parking:** on-site. **Terms:** 3 day cancellation notice, small pets only ($5 fee). **Amenities:** *Some:* irons, hair dryers. **Pool(s):** outdoor. **Leisure Activities:** whirlpool. **Cards:** AX, CB, DC, DS, JC, MC, VI. **Special Amenities: free local telephone calls.**

SOME UNITS

FEE

PALM HOTEL BED & BREAKFAST

Phone: (209)984-3429

Historic Bed & Breakfast

All Year 1P: $95-$175 2P: $95-$175 XP: $15

Location: Center. 10382 Willow St 95327. Fax: 209/984-4929. **Facility:** Themes such as stained glass and Victorian decor dress the guest rooms at this quaint, two-story B&B. Smoke free premises. 8 one-bedroom standard units. 2 stories (no elevator), interior corridors. *Bath:* shower or tub only. **Parking:** on-site. **Terms:** office hours 9 am-9 pm, 2 night minimum stay - weekends, 5 day cancellation notice-fee imposed. **Cards:** AX, MC, VI.

SOME UNITS

ROYAL CARRIAGE INN

Phone: 209/984-5271

Small-scale Hotel

All Year 1P: $70-$125 2P: $70-$135

Location: SR 108 and 49, exit Central Business District. 18239 Main St 95327. Fax: 209/984-1675. **Facility:** 25 units. 15 one-bedroom standard units. 10 cottages. 2 stories (no elevator), interior corridors. *Bath:* shower only. **Parking:** on-site. **Terms:** office hours 8 am-9 pm, 2 night minimum stay - weekends, 7 day cancellation notice, [CP] meal plan available. **Business Services:** meeting rooms. **Cards:** DS, MC, VI.

SOME UNITS

WHERE TO DINE

NATIONAL HOTEL RESTAURANT — Lunch: $7-$13 — Dinner: $7-$24 — Phone: 209/984-3446

Continental

Location: Downtown; in 1859 Historic National Hotel, A Country Inn. 18183 Main St 95327. **Hours:** 11:30 am-4:30 & 5-10 pm, Sun 10 am-3 & 4:30-10 pm. Closed: 12/25. **Reservations:** suggested. **Features:** Casual elegance marks the restaurant, occupying a restored landmark established in 1859. Casual dress; cocktails. **Parking:** street. **Cards:** AX, CB, DC, DS, MC, VI.

JENNER *—See Wine Country p. 781.*

JOHNSVILLE pop. 21

WHERE TO DINE

THE IRON DOOR — Dinner: $13-$24 — Phone: 530/836-2376

Continental

Location: 5 mi w of Graegle on SR A14. 5417 Main St 96103. **Hours:** Open 4/8-11/6; 5 pm-9 pm. Closed: Tues. **Reservations:** suggested. **Features:** Located 10 minutes from Graeagle, this restaurant serves American style cuisine including steak, seafood and pasta. Dressy casual; cocktails. **Parking:** on-site. **Cards:** MC, VI.

JUNE LAKE

WHERE TO STAY

BOULDER LODGE — **Phone:** (760)648-7533

Motel

2/1-10/31 & 12/17-1/31	1P: $68-$350	2P: $68-$350	XP: $10
11/1-12/16	1P: $48-$240	2P: $48-$240	XP: $10

Location: On SR 158; just e of the village. 2282 Hwy 158 93529 (PO Box 68). Fax: 760/648-7330. **Facility:** 57 units. 27 one-bedroom standard units, some with kitchens. 19 one- and 3 two-bedroom suites with kitchens. 8 cabins. 1-2 stories, exterior corridors. *Bath:* combo or shower only. **Parking:** on-site. **Terms:** office hours 9 am-9 pm, check-in 4 pm, 30 day cancellation notice-fee imposed, weekly rates available, package plans - seasonal, no pets allowed (owner's pet on premises). **Amenities:** *Some:* irons, hair dryers. **Pool(s):** indoor. **Leisure Activities:** sauna, whirlpool, fishing, fish cleaning & freezing facilities, tennis court, playground. **Business Services:** fax (fee). **Cards:** AX, DS, MC, VI. **Special Amenities: early check-in/late check-out and preferred room (subject to availability with advanced reservations).**

SOME UNITS

DOUBLE EAGLE RESORT/SPA, INC — **Phone:** (760)648-7004

Cabin

All Year	1P: $287-$319	2P: $287-$319

Location: On SR 158, 3 mi w of the village. 5587 Hwy 158 93529 (PO Box 736). Fax: 760/648-7017. **Facility:** On 13 acres of open and wooded grounds at the foot of Carson Peak, the resort offers two-bedroom cabins with kitchens and fireplaces. Designated smoking area. 14 units. 1 vacation home and 13 cabins. 1 story, exterior corridors. *Bath:* combo or shower only. **Parking:** on-site. **Terms:** office hours 7:30 am-7 pm, check-in 4 pm, 30 day cancellation notice-fee imposed, package plans - seasonal, pets (in designated cabins). **Amenities:** voice mail, irons, hair dryers. **Dining:** Eagle's Landing Restaurant, see separate listing. **Pool(s):** heated indoor. **Leisure Activities:** whirlpools, fishing, cross country skiing, snowmobiling, ice skating, hiking trails, spa, volleyball. *Fee:* bicycles, horseback riding. **Business Services:** meeting rooms, fax (fee). **Cards:** AX, DC, MC, VI. **Special Amenities: early check-in/late check-out.**

GULL LAKE LODGE — **Phone:** 760/648-7516

Motel

4/26-11/15	1P: $87-$149	2P: $87-$149
2/1-4/25 & 11/16-1/31	1P: $65-$149	2P: $65-$149

Location: Just n of SR 158; via Knoll and Bruce sts. Located in the village. 132 Leonard Ave 93529 (PO Box 25). Fax: 760/648-7266. **Facility:** Designated smoking area. 14 units. 13 one-bedroom suites with kitchens. 1 cabin ($115-$170). 2 stories, exterior corridors. *Bath:* combo or shower only. **Parking:** on-site. **Terms:** office hours 8 am-8 pm, 14 day cancellation notice, pets ($6 extra charge). **Amenities:** *Some:* irons, hair dryers. **Guest Services:** coin laundry. **Business Services:** fax. **Cards:** AX, DS, MC, VI.

FEE

JUNE LAKE MOTEL & CABINS — **Phone:** 760/648-7547

Motel

4/16-11/15	2P: $60-$90	XP: $10	D18
11/16-1/31	2P: $75-$88	XP: $10	D18
2/1-4/15	2P: $79-$84	XP: $10	D18

Location: On SR 158; in center of village. 2716 Boulder Dr 93529 (PO Box 98). Fax: 760/648-7147. **Facility:** 31 units. 19 one-bedroom standard units, some with kitchens. 2 two-bedroom suites ($102-$122) with kitchens. 10 cabins ($100-$195). 1-2 stories, exterior corridors. *Bath:* combo or shower only. **Parking:** on-site. **Terms:** office hours 8 am-9 pm, check-in 4 pm, 2 night minimum stay - weekends, 14 day cancellation notice-fee imposed, no pets allowed (owner's pet on premises). **Amenities:** voice mail. *Some:* irons, hair dryers. **Leisure Activities:** sauna, whirlpool, fish cleaning & freezing facilities. **Business Services:** fax (fee). **Cards:** DC, MC, VI. **Special Amenities: early check-in/late check-out and preferred room (subject to availability with advanced reservations).**

SOME UNITS

JUNE LAKE VILLAGER — **Phone:** 760/648-7712

Motel

2/1-4/30 & 11/1-1/31	2P: $35-$250	XP: $10
5/1-10/31	2P: $45-$125	XP: $10

Location: On SR 158; in center of village. 85 Boulder Dr 93529 (PO Box 127). Fax: 760/648-7003. **Facility:** Smoke free premises. 24 units. 15 one-bedroom standard units, some with efficiencies. 6 one- and 2 two-bedroom suites with kitchens. 1 cabin. 2 stories, exterior corridors. *Bath:* combo or shower only. **Parking:** on-site. **Terms:** office hours 9 am-9 pm, check-in 4 pm, 2 night minimum stay - weekends, 14 day cancellation notice-fee imposed, package plans, no pets allowed (owner's pet on premises). **Amenities:** *Some:* irons, hair dryers. **Leisure Activities:** whirlpool, fishing cleaning & freezing facilities. **Guest Services:** coin laundry. **Cards:** AX, DC, MC, VI. **Special Amenities: free local telephone calls and preferred room (subject to availability with advanced reservations).**

SOME UNITS

WHISPERING PINES CHALETS & MOTEL **Phone:** (760)648-7762

AAA SAVE

Motel

8/1-8/31 [CP]	1P: $79-$199	2P: $89-$199	XP: $10	F5
4/26-7/31 & 9/1-1/31 [CP]	1P: $49-$199	2P: $59-$199	XP: $10	F5
2/1-4/25 [CP]	1P: $39-$199	2P: $49-$199	XP: $10	F5

Location: On SR 158, 3 mi w of the village. (Rt 3, Box 14B). Fax: 760/648-7589. **Facility:** Smoke free premises. 24 units. 14 one-bedroom standard units with kitchens. 4 one-bedroom suites, some with kitchens. 6 cabins. 1-2 stories, exterior corridors. *Bath:* combo or shower only. **Parking:** on-site. **Terms:** office hours 7:30 am-10 pm, check-in 4 pm, 14 day cancellation notice. **Amenities:** video library (fee), voice mail. *Some:* irons. **Leisure Activities:** sauna, whirlpool, fish cleaning & freezing facilities. **Business Services:** meeting rooms, fax (fee). **Cards:** AX, DS, MC, VI. **Special Amenities: free room upgrade and preferred room (each subject to availability with advanced reservations).**

S/D VCR DATA PORT

WHERE TO DINE

CARSON PEAK INN **Dinner:** $11-$20 **Phone:** 760/648-7575

American

Location: On SR 158; 2 mi w of the village. **Hours:** 5 pm-10 pm. **Reservations:** suggested. **Features:** The restaurant occupies a beautiful country setting at the foot of Carson Peak. The menu lists steaks, seafood, barbecue ribs, combination plates and excellent homemade soups. Service is friendly and casual. Casual dress; beer & wine only. **Parking:** on-site. **Cards:** AX, DS, MC, VI.

EAGLE'S LANDING RESTAURANT **Lunch:** $7-$10 **Dinner:** $13-$25 **Phone:** 760/648-7897

American

Location: On SR 158, 3 mi w of the village; in Double Eagle Resort/Spa Inc. 5587 Hwy 158 93529. **Hours:** 7 am-9 pm. **Reservations:** suggested. **Features:** Views of the mountains are spectacular, particularly from the patio. The lounge is especially inviting, the food is good, and the staff is friendly and accommodating. Casual dress; cocktails. **Parking:** on-site. **Cards:** AX, DS, MC, VI.

SIERRA INN **Lunch:** $7-$9 **Dinner:** $12-$24 **Phone:** 760/648-7774

American

Location: On SR 158; in the village. 2588 Hwy 158 93529. **Hours:** 7 am-9:30 pm, Fri & Sat-10 pm. **Features:** Overlooking June Lake, the restaurant serves a selection of seafood, chicken, steaks, pasta and pizza; on Saturdays the buffet dinner draws a hungry crowd. Casual dress; cocktails. **Parking:** street. **Cards:** AX, DS, MC, VI.

TIGER BAR & CAFE **Lunch:** $6-$9 **Dinner:** $6-$16 **Phone:** 760/648-7551

American

Location: On SR 158; in the village. 2620 Hwy 158 93529. **Hours:** 8 am-10 pm. **Features:** This rustic restaurant and bar was established in 1932 and, with its full bar and friendly service, is a great place to grab a quick bite or just hang out. Try the country fried chicken or the homemade meat loaf. All sandwiches come with "tiger chips," which are deep-fried homemade potato chips. There is also a selection of Mexican specialties. Casual dress; cocktails. **Parking:** on-site. **Cards:** DS, MC, VI.

KELSEYVILLE *—See Wine Country p. 781.*

KERNVILLE pop. 1,736

WHERE TO STAY

BAREWOOD MOTEL **Phone:** 760/376-1910

Motel

4/2-10/15	1P: $70-$95	2P: $85-$125	XP: $10
2/1-4/1 & 10/16-1/31	1P: $60-$90	2P: $80-$100	XP: $10

Location: In Wofford Heights. 7013 Wofford Blvd 93285 (PO Box 3791, WOFFORD HEIGHTS). Fax: 760/376-1931. **Facility:** Smoke free premises. 10 one-bedroom standard units, some with whirlpools. 1 story, exterior corridors. *Bath:* combo or shower only. **Parking:** on-site. **Terms:** office hours 9 am-5 pm, 3 day cancellation notice-fee imposed, weekly rates available. **Amenities:** *Some:* irons, hair dryers. **Leisure Activities:** playground. **Business Services:** fax. **Cards:** AX, MC, VI.

SOME UNITS

ASK S/D / /

THE KERN LODGE **Phone:** 760/376-2223

Motel

All Year	2P: $80-$140	XP: $10	F18

Location: At Sierra Way, just n of Kernville Rd. 67 Valley View Dr 93238. Fax: 760/376-1879. **Facility:** Designated smoking area. 15 units. 13 one-bedroom standard units, some with kitchens and/or whirlpools. 2 one-bedroom suites ($110-$140). 1 story, exterior corridors. *Bath:* combo or shower only. **Parking:** on-site. **Terms:** 3 day cancellation notice, no pets allowed (owner's pet on premises). **Amenities:** *Some:* irons, hair dryers. **Pool(s):** outdoor. **Business Services:** fax (fee). **Cards:** DS, MC, VI.

SOME UNITS

ASK S/D / VCR DATA PORT /

KERN RIVER INN BED & BREAKFAST **Phone:** (760)376-6750

AAA SAVE

Bed & Breakfast

All Year [BP]	1P: $115-$145	2P: $115-$145	XP: $20

Location: Just s of Kernville Rd. 119 Kern River Dr 93238 (PO Box 1725). Fax: 760/376-6643. **Facility:** Gourmet breakfasts are available at this service-oriented inn across from the scenic Kern River and adjacent to downtown shopping. Smoke free premises. 5 one-bedroom standard units, some with whirlpools. 2 stories (no elevator), interior corridors. **Parking:** on-site. **Terms:** 2 night minimum stay - weekends, 7 day cancellation notice. **Amenities:** *Some:* irons, hair dryers. **Guest Services:** complimentary evening beverages. **Cards:** AX, MC, VI. **Special Amenities: free local telephone calls.**

KERNVILLE INN **Phone:** (760)376-2206

Motel

All Year 1P: $59-$159 2P: $59-$159 XP: $20

Location: Center. Located across from Circle Park. 11042 Kernville Rd 93238 (PO Box 2026). Fax: 760/376-3735. **Facility:** Smoke free premises. 26 one-bedroom standard units, some with kitchens. 1 story, exterior corridors. *Bath:* combo or shower only. **Parking:** on-site. **Terms:** 2-3 night minimum stay - some weekends, 3 day cancellation notice. **Amenities:** *Some:* irons, hair dryers. **Pool(s):** outdoor. **Guest Services:** sundries, coin laundry. **Business Services:** fax (fee). **Cards:** AX, CB, DC, DS, JC, MC, VI.

SOME UNITS

RIVER VIEW LODGE **Phone:** 760/376-6019

Motel

4/1-10/1 1P: $79-$109 2P: $89-$129 XP: $15
2/1-3/31 & 10/2-1/31 1P: $69-$99 2P: $79-$119 XP: $15

Location: On Kernville Rd, at the bridge; center. 2 Sirretta St 93238 (PO Box 887). Fax: 760/376-3157. **Facility:** Designated smoking area. 10 one-bedroom standard units, some with whirlpools. 1 story, exterior corridors. *Bath:* combo or shower only. **Parking:** on-site. **Terms:** office hours 9 am-11 pm, 2 night minimum stay - weekends, 14 day cancellation notice-fee imposed, weekly rates available, small pets only ($10 extra charge, in designated units). **Amenities:** hair dryers. *Some:* irons. **Leisure Activities:** fishing, hiking trails. **Business Services:** fax (fee). **Cards:** AX, DC, MC, VI. **Special Amenities: free expanded continental breakfast and free local telephone calls.**

FEE

SEQUOIA LODGE **Phone:** 760/376-2535

Motel

All Year 1P: $79-$109 2P: $79-$129 XP: $10 F6

Location: 2.5 mi n. Located on the river. 16123 Sierra Way 93238. Fax: 760/376-4771. **Facility:** Smoke free premises. 14 one-bedroom standard units. 1 story, exterior corridors. *Bath:* shower only. **Parking:** on-site. **Terms:** office hours 8 am-10 pm, 2 night minimum stay - weekends, 3 day cancellation notice. **Amenities:** voice mail. *Some:* irons, hair dryers. **Leisure Activities:** fishing, fish cleaning facilities. **Business Services:** fax. **Cards:** AX, DS, MC, VI. **Special Amenities: free local telephone calls.**

WHISPERING PINES LODGE BED & BREAKFAST **Phone:** (760)376-3733

Bed & Breakfast

All Year [BP] 1P: $109-$259 2P: $109-$259 XP: $20

Location: 0.3 mi n of town. 13745 Sierra Way 93238 (Rt 1, Box 41). Fax: 760/376-6513. **Facility:** Marigolds and other flowers color the gardens on this lodge's grounds, which offer vantage points onto the Kern River and surrounding mountains. Smoke free premises. 17 units. 14 one-bedroom standard units, some with kitchens and/or whirlpools. 3 one-bedroom suites, some with kitchens and/or whirlpools. 1-2 stories (no elevator), exterior corridors. *Bath:* combo, shower or tub only. **Parking:** on-site. **Terms:** 2-3 night minimum stay - weekends, 3 day cancellation notice. **Amenities:** CD players. *Some:* irons, hair dryers. **Pool(s):** outdoor. **Business Services:** fax. **Cards:** AX, CB, DC, DS, JC, MC, VI. **Special Amenities: free full breakfast.**

SOME UNITS

WHERE TO DINE

JOHNNY MCNALLY'S FAIRVIEW LODGE **Dinner:** $10-$35 **Phone:** 760/376-2430

Steak House

Location: 15 mi ne of town center; on Sierra Way. **Hours:** 5 pm-9 pm, Sun 3:30 pm-8 pm; 5 pm-10 pm, Sun 3:30 pm-9 pm in summer. Closed: 12/1-2/15, open weekends only 2/16-3/31 & 11/1-11/30. **Reservations:** suggested. **Features:** The extra drive is worth the inconvenience for prompt service and mouthwatering steaks. The in-house butcher ensures the cut you order—including the "logger," a massive, 40-ounce porterhouse—is just how you like it. Among other choices are chicken and seafood dishes, including deep-fried white catfish. Casual dress; cocktails. **Parking:** on-site. **Cards:** MC, VI.

PEACOCK INN **Lunch:** $5-$7 **Dinner:** $9-$13 **Phone:** 760/376-3937

Chinese

Location: Just e of bridge and n of Kernville Rd. 21 Sierra Dr 93238. **Hours:** 11 am-9 pm. Closed: 11/25, 12/25; also Tues. **Reservations:** suggested. **Features:** Near the bridge on the northeast end of town, the restaurant offers diners an excellent selection of Szechwan and Mandarin entrees. Garlic chicken is a favorite. Servers are casual and friendly, and special requests are handled graciously. Oriental artwork, hanging lanterns and abundant plants lend to the comfortable dining environment. Beer & wine only. **Parking:** on-site. **Cards:** AX, MC, VI.

THAT'S ITALIAN RESTAURANT **Lunch:** $6-$8 **Dinner:** $9-$17 **Phone:** 760/376-6020

Italian

Location: Center of town at Circle Park. 9 Big Blue Rd 93238. **Hours:** 4 pm-9 pm, Fri & Sat also 11 am-3 pm; 4 pm-8 pm in winter. Closed: 1/1. **Features:** A nice variety of pasta, chicken and seafood entrees awaits diners hungry after a full day of hiking, swimming or rafting. Servers are friendly, and the atmosphere is fun. Casual dress; beer & wine only. **Parking:** on-site. **Cards:** AX, CB, DC, DS, MC, VI.

KETTLEMAN CITY pop. 1,499

WHERE TO STAY

BEST WESTERN KETTLEMAN INN AND SUITES *Book at aaa.com* **Phone:** 559/386-0804

Motel

4/1-9/30 [ECP]	1P: $72-$159	2P: $72-$159	XP: $5	F12
2/1-3/31 & 10/1-1/31 [ECP]	1P: $72-$119	2P: $72-$119	XP: $5	F12

Location: E of and adjacent to I-5, exit SR 41 N, 0.3 mi to Bernard, then 0.3 mi n. 33410 Powers Dr 93239 (PO Box 539). Fax: 559/386-4526. **Facility:** 73 units. 56 one-bedroom standard units, some with whirlpools. 17 one-bedroom suites ($119-$159), some with whirlpools. 2 stories (no elevator), exterior corridors. **Parking:** on-site. **Terms:** small pets only ($6 extra charge). **Amenities:** irons, hair dryers. *Some:* dual phone lines. **Pool(s):** small outdoor. **Leisure Activities:** whirlpool. **Guest Services:** coin laundry. **Cards:** AX, CB, DC, DS, MC, VI. **Special Amenities: free expanded continental breakfast and free local telephone calls.** *(See color ad below)*

SOME UNITS — FEE — FEE

SUPER 8 **Phone:** 559/386-9530

Motel

All Year	1P: $50-$62	2P: $55-$65	XP: $5	F12

Location: E of and adjacent to I-5, exit SR 41 N, 0.3 mi to Bernard, then 0.3 mi n. 33415 Powers Dr 93239. Fax: 559/386-9530. **Facility:** 60 one-bedroom standard units. 2 stories, exterior corridors. *Bath:* combo or shower only. **Parking:** on-site. **Terms:** pets ($10 fee, $40 deposit). **Pool(s):** small outdoor. **Cards:** AX, CB, DC, MC, VI.

SOME UNITS — FEE

KING CITY pop. 11,094

WHERE TO STAY

BEST WESTERN KING CITY INN *Book at aaa.com* **Phone:** (831)385-6733

Motel

3/14-9/18 [ECP]	1P: $89-$99	2P: $99-$109	XP: $8	F17
2/1-3/13 & 9/19-1/31 [ECP]	1P: $69-$89	2P: $79-$99	XP: $8	F17

Location: US 101, exit Broadway, just e. 1190 Broadway 93930. Fax: 831/385-0714. **Facility:** 47 one-bedroom standard units. 2 stories (no elevator), exterior corridors. **Parking:** on-site. **Amenities:** voice mail, irons, hair dryers. **Pool(s):** small outdoor. **Leisure Activities:** whirlpool. **Cards:** AX, DC, JC, MC, VI. **Special Amenities: free continental breakfast and early check-in/late check-out.**

SOME UNITS — FEE

COURTESY INN **Phone:** (831)385-4646

Motel

5/16-9/30	1P: $59-$119	2P: $59-$119	XP: $6	F13
2/1-5/15 & 10/1-1/31	1P: $39-$89	2P: $39-$89	XP: $6	F13

Location: US 101, exit Broadway, just w. 4 Broadway Cir 93930. Fax: 831/385-6024. **Facility:** 63 one-bedroom standard units, some with whirlpools. 2 stories (no elevator), exterior corridors. **Parking:** on-site. **Terms:** cancellation fee imposed, [CP] meal plan available, pets ($10 extra charge). **Amenities:** video library (fee), hair dryers. **Pool(s):** small outdoor. **Leisure Activities:** whirlpool. **Guest Services:** coin laundry. **Business Services:** meeting rooms. **Cards:** AX, CB, DS, MC, VI. **Special Amenities: free continental breakfast.** *(See color ad below)*

SOME UNITS

FEE

DAYS INN *Book at aaa.com* **Phone:** (831)385-5921

Motel

All Year	1P: $40-$89	2P: $45-$109	XP: $6	F12

Location: US 101, exit Broadway, then e. 1130 Broadway St 93930. Fax: 831/385-6508. **Facility:** 30 one-bedroom standard units. 2 stories (no elevator), exterior corridors. **Parking:** on-site. **Terms:** [CP] meal plan available. **Amenities:** hair dryers. **Guest Services:** coin laundry. **Cards:** AX, DC, DS, MC, VI. **Special Amenities: free continental breakfast and free local telephone calls.**

SOME UNITS

KEEFER'S INN **Phone:** 831/385-4843

Motel

All Year	1P: $49-$79	2P: $55-$89	XP: $8	F12

Location: US 101, exit Canal St, just w. 615 Canal St 93930. Fax: 831/385-1254. **Facility:** 47 one-bedroom standard units. 2 stories (no elevator), interior/exterior corridors. **Parking:** on-site. **Terms:** [CP] meal plan available. **Pool(s):** small outdoor. **Leisure Activities:** whirlpool. **Guest Services:** coin laundry. **Cards:** AX, DC, DS, MC, VI. **Special Amenities: free continental breakfast and early check-in/late check-out.** *(See color ad below)*

SOME UNITS

WHERE TO DINE

KEEFER'S RESTAURANT **Lunch:** $7-$15 **Dinner:** $12-$23 **Phone:** 831/385-3543

American

Location: US 101, exit Canal St, just w. 611 Canal St 93930. **Hours:** 7 am-9 pm, Sat-9:30 pm. Closed: 12/25. **Reservations:** suggested. **Features:** The casual, comfortable restaurant presents a menu of selections that appeal to all members of the family. Casual dress; cocktails. **Parking:** on-site. **Cards:** AX, MC, VI. *(See color ad below)*

KINGS BEACH —See Lake Tahoe Area p. 371.

KINGSBURG pop. 9,199

WHERE TO STAY

SWEDISH INN **Phone:** (559)897-1022

Motel

All Year 1P: $58 2P: $68-$129 XP: $5 F18

Location: SR 99, exit Conejo St, just w. 401 Conejo St 93631. Fax: 559/897-0134. **Facility:** 47 one-bedroom standard units. 2 stories (no elevator), exterior corridors. **Parking:** on-site. **Pool(s):** outdoor. **Leisure Activities:** whirlpool. **Cards:** AX, DC, DS, MC, VI. **Special Amenities: free local telephone calls.**

SOME UNITS

KINGS CANYON NATIONAL PARK —See also SEQUOIA NATIONAL PARK

WHERE TO STAY

CEDAR GROVE LODGE **Phone:** (559)452-1081

Small-scale Hotel

5/6-10/10 1P: $99-$110 2P: $99-$110 XP: $12 F12

Location: On SR 180, 31 mi ne of Grant Grove, via winding mountain road. Kings Canyon National Park 93633 (5755 E Kings Canyon Rd, Suite 101, FRESNO, 93727). Fax: 559/452-1353. **Facility:** Smoke free premises. 21 one-bedroom standard units. 2 stories, interior corridors. *Bath:* shower only. **Parking:** on-site. **Terms:** open 5/6-10/10, check-in 4 pm, 14 day cancellation notice-fee imposed. **Amenities:** high-speed Internet. **Leisure Activities:** fishing, hiking trails. **Guest Services:** gift shop, coin laundry. **Cards:** AX, DS, MC, VI.

JOHN MUIR LODGE AT GRANT GROVE VILLAGE **Phone:** (559)452-1081

Small-scale Hotel

All Year 1P: $140-$150 2P: $140-$150 XP: $12 F12

Location: On SR 180; in Grant Grove Village. Kings Canyon National Park 93633 (5755 E Kings Canyon Rd, Suite 101, FRESNO, 93727). Fax: 559/452-1353. **Facility:** Smoke free premises. 30 one-bedroom standard units. 2 stories, interior corridors. **Parking:** on-site. **Terms:** check-in 4 pm. **Amenities:** voice mail. *Some:* hair dryers. **Dining:** 7 am-9 pm; to 8 pm off-season. **Leisure Activities:** visitor center, hiking trails. **Guest Services:** gift shop. **Cards:** AX, DS, MC, VI. *(See color ad p 724)*

The following lodging was either not evaluated or did not meet AAA rating requirements but is listed for your information only.

MONTECITO-SEQUOIA LODGE **Phone:** 559/565-3388

fyi

Small-scale Hotel

Did not meet all AAA rating requirements for some guest rooms at time of last evaluation on 06/02/2003. **Location:** 8 mi s of SR 180 off General's Hwy; between King's Canyon and Sequoia National Parks. 8000 General's Hwy 93633 (PO Box 858, Grant Grove). Facilities, services, and decor characterize a basic property. *(See ad p 725)*

KIT CARSON

WHERE TO STAY

KIT CARSON LODGE **Phone:** (209)258-8500

Cabin

6/11-10/10 2P: $95-$240

Location: 0.3 mi off SR 88, on Silver Lake. 32000 Kit Carson Rd 95644. Fax: 209/258-8315. **Facility:** Smoke free premises. 27 cabins. 1 story, exterior corridors. *Bath:* shower only. **Parking:** on-site. **Terms:** open 6/11-10/10, check-in 4 pm, 7 day cancellation notice-fee imposed. **Dining:** Kit Carson Restaurant, see separate listing. **Leisure Activities:** boating, rental canoes, boat dock, fishing. **Guest Services:** gift shop, coin laundry. **Cards:** MC, VI.

SOME UNITS

WHERE TO DINE

The following restaurant has not been evaluated by AAA but is listed for your information only.

KIT CARSON RESTAURANT **Phone:** 209/258-8500

fyi

Not evaluated. **Location:** 0.3 mi off SR 88, on Silver Lake; in Kit Carson Lodge. 32000 Kit Carson Rd 95644. **Features:** Open most days for breakfast and dinner, this quaint eatery sits near Silver Lake and has a wonderfully relaxing atmosphere.

KLAMATH pop. 651

WHERE TO STAY

MOTEL TREES **Phone:** (707)482-3152

Motel

3/14-11/29	1P: $59-$65	2P: $65-$86	XP: $5	F3
2/1-3/13 & 11/30-1/31 [CP]	1P: $45-$48	2P: $48-$63	XP: $5	F3

Location: 4 mi n on US 101. Located opposite Trees of Mystery. 15495 Hwy 101 N 95548 (PO Box 309). Fax: 707/482-2005. **Facility:** 23 units. 19 one- and 4 two-bedroom standard units. 1 story, exterior corridors. *Bath:* combo or shower only. **Parking:** on-site. **Terms:** cancellation fee imposed, package plans, small pets only ($10 fee). **Amenities:** *Some:* irons, hair dryers. **Leisure Activities:** tennis court. **Guest Services:** gift shop. **Cards:** AX, DC, DS, MC, VI. **Special Amenities: early check-in/late check-out and preferred room (subject to availability with advanced reservations).**

SOME UNITS

FEE

RAVENWOOD A MOTEL — Phone: 707/482-5911

Motel

All Year 1P: $58 2P: $58 XP: $10 F5

Location: US 101, exit Klamath Blvd, just e. 151 Klamath Blvd 95548 (PO Box 1004). Fax: 707/482-1330. **Facility:** Designated smoking area. 16 one-bedroom standard units, some with kitchens. Exterior corridors. **Parking:** on-site. **Terms:** 3 day cancellation notice-fee imposed, [CP] meal plan available. **Amenities:** voice mail, hair dryers. *Some:* irons. **Leisure Activities:** fishing, bicycles, hiking trails. **Cards:** AX, DS, MC, VI. **Special Amenities: free local telephone calls and early check-in/late check-out.**

SOME UNITS

KYBURZ

WHERE TO STAY

KYBURZ RESORT MOTEL — Phone: 530/293-3382

Motel

All Year 1P: $50-$75 2P: $60-$90

Location: On US 50, halfway between Placerville and South Lake Tahoe. 13660 Hwy 50 95720 (PO Box 27). **Facility:** 19 one-bedroom standard units. 2 stories, exterior corridors. *Bath:* shower only. **Parking:** on-site. **Terms:** package plans - seasonal & weekends, small pets only ($10 fee). **Cards:** AX, DS, MC, VI. **Special Amenities: free continental breakfast and free local telephone calls.**

FEE

LAFAYETTE pop. 23,908 (See map and index starting on p. 516)

WHERE TO STAY

LAFAYETTE PARK HOTEL & SPA — *Book at aaa.com* — Phone: (925)283-3700 — 36

Small-scale Hotel

All Year 1P: $225-$475 2P: $225-$475 XP: $10 F18

Location: SR 24, exit Pleasant Hill Rd, just s. 3287 Mt Diablo Blvd 94549. Fax: 925/284-1621. **Facility:** Featuring flower gardens and a courtyard with a fountain, the property offers elegant surroundings and spacious, well-appointed guest rooms. Smoke free premises. 139 units. 133 one-bedroom standard units. 6 one-bedroom suites ($475-$1275). 3 stories, interior corridors. **Parking:** on-site (fee). **Terms:** cancellation fee imposed. **Amenities:** CD players, high-speed Internet (fee), voice mail, honor bars, irons, hair dryers. **Dining:** 6:30 am-11 pm, cocktails, also, The Duck Club Restaurant, see separate listing. **Pool(s):** outdoor. **Leisure Activities:** sauna, whirlpool, exercise room, spa. **Guest Services:** complimentary evening beverages, valet laundry. **Business Services:** meeting rooms. **Cards:** AX, DC, DS, MC, VI. **Special Amenities: free newspaper.** *(See color ad inside back cover)*

SOME UNITS

WHERE TO DINE

THE DUCK CLUB RESTAURANT — **Lunch:** $7-$15 — **Dinner:** $18-$30 — **Phone:** 925/283-7108 — 25

American

Location: SR 24, exit Pleasant Hill Rd, just s; in Lafayette Park Hotel & Spa. 3287 Mt Diablo Blvd 94549. **Hours:** 6:30-11 am, 11:30-2 & 6-9 pm, Sunday champagne brunch 10:30 am-2:30 pm. Closed: for lunch Sat. **Reservations:** suggested. **Features:** Artistic, light fare exhibits a Continental influence. The surroundings are comfortable and attractive. Casual dress; cocktails. **Parking:** valet. **Cards:** AX, CB, DC, DS, MC, VI. ***(See color ad inside back cover & p 764)***

LAKE ISABELLA pop. 3,315—*See KERNVILLE.*

LAKEPORT —*See Wine Country p. 782.*

Destination Lake Tahoe Area

Lake Tahoe has a season and an activity for nearly everyone and every vacation budget.

Summer months offer water skiing, sailing, swimming and fishing, while snow skiing is the favorite winter activity. Accommodations range from campsites in the national forests to suites in gambling mecca Stateline.

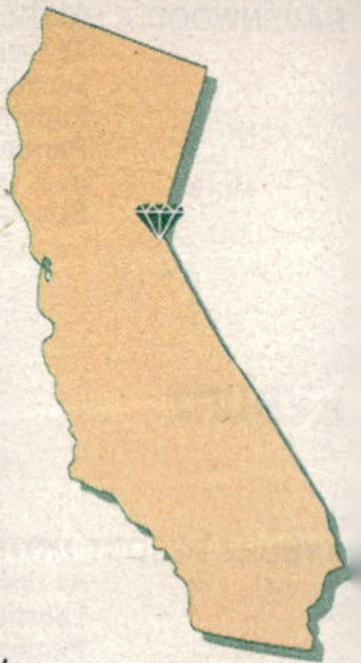

© Mark Gibson Index Stock

Restaurants and shops, Tahoe City. After experiencing all that the outdoors has to offer, there's always time for dining and shopping.

Sailboats on Lake Tahoe. The clear, deep blue water of Lake Tahoe is a favorite with sailboaters.

© Gibson Stock Photography

Horseback riding in the Lake Tahoe Area. The scenic beauty of the Lake Tahoe area also can be seen by horseback.

© Gibson Stock Photography

Lake Tahoe Area

Truckee, Olympic Valley, Tahoe Vista, Incline Village, Carnelian Bay, Kings Beach, Tahoe City, Zephyr Cove, Stateline, South Lake Tahoe, CALIFORNIA, NEVADA, 80, 89, 267, 28, 50

See Vicinity map page 363

The beach at Zephyr Cove, Nev. Enjoy the lake from the shore and also on a sightseeing cruise aboard the MS *Dixie II*. (See listing page 89)

© Gibson Stock Photography

Places included in this AAA Destination Area:

LAKE TAHOE AREA
ACCOMMODATIONS
Scale in Miles
Scale in Kilometers
To Graeagle
To Reno
Truckee Tahoe Airport
Martis Creek Lake
Donner Lake
Donner Memorial State Park
Truckee
To Nevada City
Tahoe
Nat'l.
Forest
Olympic Valley
Burton Creek State Park
Tahoe State Recreation Area
Tahoe City
Tahoe Vista
Kings Beach
Carnelian Bay
Crystal Bay
Incline Village
Humboldt-
Toiyabe
Nat'l.
Forest
Sand Harbor Beach State Recreation Area
Lake Tahoe State Park
Marlette Lake
Spooner Lake
To Carson City
CAVE ROCK TUNNEL
Lake
Tahoe
Tahoma
Sugar Pine Point State Park
Visitor Center
Miller Lake
D.L. Bliss State Park
Emerald Bay State Park
Nevada Beach
SEE INSET MAP FOR DETAIL
Kingsbury Grade
Pope Beach
Cascade Lake
Fallen Leaf Lake
Lake Tahoe Airport
South Lake Tahoe
Eldorado National Forest
To Pollock Pines
Stateline
© AAA
1833-L

Lake Tahoe Area

This index helps you "spot" where approved accommodations and restaurants are located on the corresponding detailed maps. Lodging rate ranges are for comparison only and show the property's high season; rates are per night, unless only weekly (W) rates are available. Restaurant rate range is for dinner, unless only lunch (L) is served. Turn to the listing page for more detailed rate information and consult display ads for special promotions.

Spotter/Map Page Number	OA	TRUCKEE - Lodgings	Diamond Rating	Rate Range High Season	Listing Page
3 / p. 363	AAA	**Donner Lake Village Resort** - see color ad p 400	3 diamonds	$130-$275 SAVE	399
5 / p. 363	AAA	**Holiday Inn Express** - see color ad p 400	3 diamonds	$114-$189 SAVE	399
6 / p. 363		The Inn at Truckee - see color ad p 401	2 diamonds	$90-$135	401
7 / p. 363		Alpine Country Lodge	1 diamond	$75-$160	399
8 / p. 363		Richardson House	3 diamonds	$100-$175	401
9 / p. 363	AAA	**Best Western Truckee Tahoe Inn** - see color ad p 399	3 diamonds	$106-$179 SAVE	399
10 / p. 363	AAA	**Northstar at Tahoe**	3 diamonds	$155-$900 SAVE	401
		TAHOE VISTA - Lodgings			
25 / p. 363	AAA	**Tahoe Vistana Inn** - see color ad p 398	2 diamonds	$46-$116 SAVE	398
27 / p. 363	AAA	**Cedar Glen Lodge-Best Value Inn & Suites** - see color ad p 396	2 diamonds	$75-$160 SAVE	396
28 / p. 363	AAA	**Mourelatos Lakeshore Resort** - see color ad p 397	3 diamonds	$99-$355 SAVE	397
31 / p. 363	AAA	**Franciscan Lakeside Lodge** - see color ad p 369	2 diamonds	$70-$325 SAVE	396
32 / p. 363	AAA	**Firelite Lodge** - see color ad p 368	2 diamonds	$58-$102 SAVE	396
33 / p. 363	AAA	**Shore House at Lake Tahoe, The**	3 diamonds	$220-$310 SAVE	397
34 / p. 363		Holiday House	1 diamond	$115-$215	397
35 / p. 363		Red Wolf Lakeside Lodge	3 diamonds	$150-$275	397
36 / p. 363		Tahoe Edgelake Beach Club	3 diamonds	$175-$225	397
		TAHOE VISTA - Restaurant			
1 / p. 363		Le Petit Pier	3 diamonds	$19-$40	399
		CARNELIAN BAY - Lodgings			
42 / p. 363		Shooting Star Bed & Breakfast	3 diamonds	$165-$275	371
		CARNELIAN BAY - Restaurant			
8 / p. 363	AAA	**Gar Woods Grill & Pier**	3 diamonds	$13-$26	371
		KINGS BEACH - Lodgings			
49 / p. 363	AAA	**Goldcrest Resort Motel**	1 diamond	$90-$295 SAVE	371
50 / p. 363	AAA	**Crown Motel**	2 diamonds	$70-$175 SAVE	371
53 / p. 363	AAA	**Sun N' Sand Lodge**	1 diamond	$79-$140 SAVE	371
54 / p. 363	AAA	**Stevenson's Holliday Inn**	1 diamond	$39-$129 SAVE	371
		INCLINE VILLAGE, NV - Lodgings			
63 / p. 363		Club Tahoe	3 diamonds	$190-$250	402
64 / p. 363	AAA	**The Inn at Incline**	2 diamonds	$99-$179 SAVE	402

Spotter/Map Page Number	OA	INCLINE VILLAGE, NV - Lodgings (continued)	Diamond Rating	Rate Range High Season	Listing Page
66 / p. 363	AAA	**Hyatt Regency Lake Tahoe Resort & Casino** - see color ad p 402	4 diamonds	$195-$345 SAVE	402
		INCLINE VILLAGE, NV - Restaurants			
15 / p. 363		Azzara's Italian Restaurant	2 diamonds	$10-$17	402
16 / p. 363		Cafe 333	2 diamonds	$14-$26	403
		OLYMPIC VALLEY - Lodgings			
80 / p. 363		Red Wolf Lodge at Squaw Valley	3 diamonds	$200-$400	372
81 / p. 363	AAA	**Resort at Squaw Creek**	4 diamonds	$379-$469 SAVE	372
82 / p. 363		The Village at Squaw Valley USA - see color ad p 372	3 diamonds	$279-$699	372
83 / p. 363	AAA	**Squaw Valley Lodge** - see color ad p 369	4 diamonds	$375-$1025 SAVE	372
		OLYMPIC VALLEY - Restaurant			
30 / p. 363		Glissandi	4 diamonds	$27-$39	373
		TAHOE CITY - Lodgings			
95 / p. 363		River Ranch Lodge	2 diamonds	$85-$175	395
97 / p. 363	AAA	**Lake of the Sky Motor Inn** - see color ad p 395	2 diamonds	$79-$139 SAVE	394
98 / p. 363		Pepper Tree Inn	2 diamonds	$89-$159	395
99 / p. 363	AAA	**Tahoe City Travelodge** - see color ad p 369	2 diamonds	$98-$153 SAVE	395
100 / p. 363	AAA	**Granlibakken Resort & Conference Center**	3 diamonds	$110-$216 SAVE	394
101 / p. 363		Cottage Inn at Lake Tahoe	3 diamonds	$150-$280	394
102 / p. 363		Sunnyside Resort	3 diamonds	$100-$300	395
103 / p. 363		Chaney House	3 diamonds	$165-$220	394
		TAHOE CITY - Restaurants			
45 / p. 363		Christy Hill Restaurant	3 diamonds	$20-$38	396
46 / p. 363		Tahoe House	1 diamond	$6-$10	396
		STATELINE, NV - Lodgings			
140 / p. 363		Horizon Casino Resort	3 diamonds	$119-$199	403
141 / p. 363		Lake Village Resort	3 diamonds	$145-$425	404
142 / p. 363	AAA	**Caesars Tahoe**	3 diamonds	$79-$300 SAVE	403
143 / p. 363	AAA	**Harveys Casino & Resort**	4 diamonds	$165-$230 SAVE	403
144 / p. 363	AAA	**Harrah's Hotel & Casino**	4 diamonds	$176-$253 SAVE	403
145 / p. 363		Tahoe Summit Village	3 diamonds	$90-$445	404
146 / p. 363	AAA	**Lakeside Inn and Casino** - see color ad p 387	3 diamonds	$89-$149 SAVE	403
147 / p. 363	AAA	**The Ridge Tahoe** - see color ad p 388	3 diamonds	$160-$280 SAVE	404
		STATELINE, NV - Restaurants			
60 / p. 363		Taberna	2 diamonds	$5-$15	405
61 / p. 363		El Vaquero	2 diamonds	$12-$25	404
62 / p. 363		The Broiler Room	3 diamonds	$18-$60	404
63 / p. 363	AAA	**Llewellyn's**	4 diamonds	$17-$27	405

Spotter/Map Page Number	OA	**STATELINE, NV** - Restaurants (continued)	Diamond Rating	Rate Range High Season	Listing Page
64 / p. 363		Sage Room Steak House	◆◆◆	$23-$56	405
65 / p. 363	AAA	**The Summit Room**	◆◆◆◆	$26-$75	405
66 / p. 363		Josh's	◆◆◆	$13-$30	404
68 / p. 363		Friday's Station	◆◆◆	$25-$45	404
69 / p. 363		Timber House Restaurant	◆◆	$7-$23	405
		SOUTH LAKE TAHOE - Lodgings			
162 / p. 363	AAA	**Royal Valhalla Motor Lodge**	◆◆◆	$109 SAVE	388
163 / p. 363	AAA	**Cedar Inn & Suites**	◆	$99-$139 SAVE	380
164 / p. 363	AAA	**Capri Motel**	◆	$60-$100 SAVE	378
165 / p. 363	AAA	**Cal Va Rado Motel**	◆	$49-$79 SAVE	378
166 / p. 363	AAA	**7 Seas Inn at Tahoe** - see color ad p 373	◆	$49-$109 SAVE	373
167 / p. 363		Lampliter Inn	◆◆	$79-$199	386
169 / p. 363	AAA	**Blue Jay Lodge** - see color ad p 378	◆◆	$59-$109 SAVE	377
170 / p. 363	AAA	**Best Tahoe West Inn** - see color ad p 368	◆◆	$55-$104 SAVE	375
171 / p. 363		Green Lantern Motel	◆	$49-$99	383
172 / p. 363	AAA	**Stardust Lodge** - see color ad p 389	◆◆◆	$95-$145 SAVE	389
173 / p. 363	AAA	**El Dorado Motel**	◆	$79-$109 SAVE	382
174 / p. 363		Beachside Inn, Suites, Spas & Cappuccino Bar	◆◆	Failed to provide	375
175 / p. 363		Embassy Suites-Lake Tahoe Resort - see color ad p 382	◆◆◆◆	$229-$499	382
179 / p. 363	AAA	**Holiday Lodge** - see color ad p 385	◆◆	$74-$94 SAVE	384
180 / p. 363	AAA	**Ambassador Motor Lodge**	◆◆	$60-$110 SAVE	374
181 / p. 363	AAA	**Viking Motor Lodge**	◆◆	$75-$95 SAVE	393
182 / p. 363		Tahoe Lakeside Lodge	◆	$49-$125	392
183 / p. 363	AAA	**Best Western Station House Inn** - see color ad p 376	◆◆◆	$98-$138 SAVE	375
184 / p. 363	AAA	**Alpenrose Inn** - see color ad p 374	◆◆	$49-$130 SAVE	374
186 / p. 363	AAA	**Cedar Lodge**	◆◆	$55-$100 SAVE	380
187 / p. 363		Alpine Inn & Spa	◆	$30-$185	374
188 / p. 363	AAA	**3 Peaks Resort & Beach Club**	◆◆	$69-$199 SAVE	373
191 / p. 363	AAA	**Mark Twain Motel**	◆	$32-$250 SAVE	387
192 / p. 363	AAA	**Paradice Motel**	◆	$28-$250 SAVE	387
194 / p. 363	AAA	**Days Inn-Casino Area/South Lake Tahoe** - see color ad p 380	◆◆	$41-$199 SAVE	380
197 / p. 363	AAA	**Tahoe Colony Inn**	◆	$60-$80 SAVE	390
198 / p. 363	AAA	**Stateline Travelodge** - see color ad p 379	◆◆	$74-$139 SAVE	389

Spotter/Map Page Number	OA	**SOUTH LAKE TAHOE - Lodgings (continued)**	Diamond Rating	Rate Range High Season	Listing Page
199 / p. 363	AAA	**Forest Suites Resorts** - see color ad p 383	◆◆◆	$69-$189 SAVE	383
200 / p. 363	AAA	**Casino Area Travelodge** - see color ad p 379	◆◆	$74-$139 SAVE	379
201 / p. 363	AAA	**Holiday Inn Express** - see color ad p 384	◆◆◆	$109-$169 SAVE	384
202 / p. 363		Thunderchief Motel	◆	$30-$200	393
203 / p. 363	AAA	**Elizabeth Lodge**	◆	$25-$199 SAVE	382
204 / p. 363	AAA	**South Shore Inn**	◆◆	$48-$189 SAVE	389
205 / p. 363	AAA	**The Lodge at Lake Tahoe**	◆◆	$104-$130 SAVE	387
206 / p. 363	AAA	**Tahoe Chalet Inn**	◆◆	$40-$220 SAVE	390
207 / p. 363		National 9 Inn	◆	Failed to provide	387
208 / p. 363		Tahoe Hacienda Motel	◆◆	$48-$250	391
209 / p. 363	AAA	**Quality Inn & Suites** - see color ad p 381	◆◆	$59-$400 SAVE	388
210 / p. 363	AAA	**Tahoe Keys Resort** - see color ad p 391	◆◆◆	$100-$1300 SAVE	391
211 / p. 363	AAA	**Inn By The Lake** - see color ad p 386	◆◆◆	$108-$228 SAVE	384
212 / p. 363	AAA	**Royal Inn**	◆	$29-$250 SAVE	388
214 / p. 363	AAA	**South Tahoe Travelodge**	◆◆	$59-$124 SAVE	389
215 / p. 363		Tahoe Lakeshore Lodge and Spa - see color ad p 392	◆◆◆	$179-$249	392
216 / p. 363	AAA	**Lakeland Village Beach & Mountain Resort** - see color ad p 385	◆◆◆	$189-$319 SAVE	385
217 / p. 363	AAA	**Days Inn Lake Tahoe** - see color ad p 381	◆◆	$39-$250 SAVE	380
219 / p. 363	AAA	**Tahoe Beach & Ski Club**	◆◆◆	$120-$295 SAVE	390
220 / p. 363	AAA	**Best Western Timber Cove Lodge** - see color ad p 377	◆◆◆	$119-$215 SAVE	375
221 / p. 363	AAA	**Super 8** - see color ad p 390	◆◆	$40-$205 SAVE	389
222 / p. 363		Embassy Vacation Resort	◆◆◆	$79-$169	382
223 / p. 363	AAA	**Bavarian Village**	◆◆	$129-$381 SAVE	375
224 / p. 363	AAA	**The Tahoe Seasons Resort**	◆◆◆	$122-$196 SAVE	393
225 / p. 363	AAA	**Alder Inn**	◆◆	$48-$140 SAVE	373
226 / p. 363	AAA	**Econo Lodge** - see color ad p 381	◆	$32-$220 SAVE	381
228 / p. 363		Dream Inn	◆	$35-$150	380
229 / p. 363	AAA	**Tahoe Valley Lodge** - see ad p 392	◆◆	$75-$295 SAVE	393
230 / p. 363	AAA	**Apex Inn**	◆	$30-$150 SAVE	374
232 / p. 363	AAA	**Tahoe Sundowner Motel**	◆	$30-$250 SAVE	393
233 / p. 363	AAA	**High Country Lodge**	◆◆	$30-$150 SAVE	383
236 / p. 363	AAA	**Ridgewood Inn**	◆	$59-$135 SAVE	388
238 / p. 363	AAA	**Budget Inn**	◆	$39-$150 SAVE	378

Spotter/Map Page Number	OA	SOUTH LAKE TAHOE - Lodgings (continued)	Diamond Rating	Rate Range High Season	Listing Page
239 / p. 363	AAA	**Americana Village** - see color ad p 375	◆◆	$85-$450 SAVE	374
321 / p. 363		Fireside Lodge B & B	◆◆	$69-$155	383
		SOUTH LAKE TAHOE - Restaurants			
86 / p. 363	AAA	**LewMarNel's** - see color ad p 376	◆◆◆	$14-$30	394
89 / p. 363		Heidi's Pancake House	◆◆	$6-$12(L)	394
90 / p. 363	AAA	**Tep's Villa Roma**	◆◆	$9-$19	394
92 / p. 363	AAA	**The Swiss Chalet**	◆◆	$13-$22	394
93 / p. 363		Evans American Gourmet Cafe	◆◆◆	$18-$26	393
95 / p. 363	AAA	**Chef Lee China Bistro**	◆◆	$6-$16	393

Get the Complete Picture.

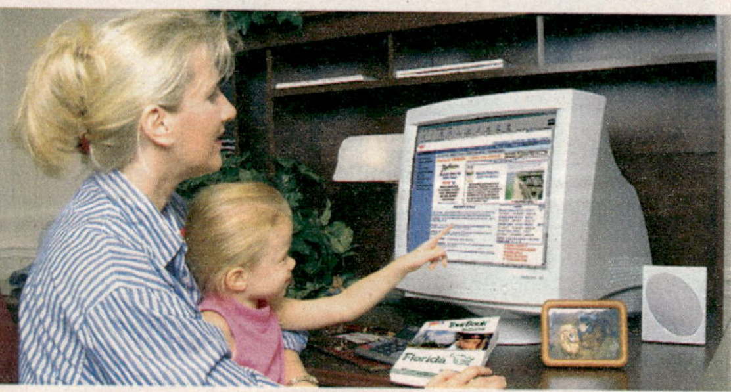

When making travel plans online at **aaa.com**, look for lodgings and attractions with an online photo gallery or online TourBook® ad. The photographs and descriptive text allow you to "virtually" experience the property or attraction prior to making your reservations or buying your tickets. Properties with a photo gallery or an ad are easily located in the online TourBook or Internet TripTik®/Traveler of aaa.com. Simply begin your search by entering your trip criteria such as destination, and then look for the listings featuring the camera icon.

So, the next time you're making travel plans look to aaa.com for <u>complete</u> travel information.

CARNELIAN BAY (See map and index starting on p. 363)

WHERE TO STAY

SHOOTING STAR BED & BREAKFAST — Phone: (530)546-8903 — 42

Bed & Breakfast

All Year [BP] 1P: $165-$275 2P: $165-$275 XP: $50

Location: SR 28, just n on Carnelian Bay Ave. 315 Olive St 96140 (PO Box 1573). Fax: 530/546-2742. **Facility:** Located on Lake Tahoe's north shore, the inn invites guests to stroll to the beach or take part in the numerous other activities available. 4 one-bedroom standard units, some with whirlpools. 2 stories, interior corridors. *Bath:* combo or shower only. **Parking:** on-site. **Terms:** cancellation fee imposed. **Amenities:** irons, hair dryers. **Guest Services:** complimentary evening beverages. **Cards:** AX, CB, DC, DS, MC, VI.

WHERE TO DINE

GAR WOODS GRILL & PIER — Lunch: $8-$13 — Dinner: $13-$26 — Phone: 530/546-3366 — 8

Traditional Continental

Location: SR 28, 6 mi e of SR 89. 5000 N Lake Blvd 96140. **Hours:** 5:30 pm-9:30 pm, Fri & Sat 11:30 am-10 pm, Sun 10 am-9:30 pm. **Reservations:** suggested. **Features:** Lakefront view on Tahoe's north shore. Dressy casual. **Parking:** on-site. **Cards:** AX, MC, VI.

KINGS BEACH pop. 4,037 (See map and index starting on p. 363)

WHERE TO STAY

CROWN MOTEL — Phone: (530)546-3388 — 50

Motel — SAVE

	1P	2P	XP	
12/19-1/31	$70-$175	$75-$175	$5	F16
6/18-9/11	$65-$160	$70-$175		
2/1-6/17 & 9/12-12/18	$45-$150	$50-$160		

Location: SR 28, 0.3 mi e of SR 267. 8200 N Lake Blvd 96143 (PO Box 845). Fax: 530/546-3851. **Facility:** 45 units. 37 one- and 8 two-bedroom standard units, some with efficiencies. 2 stories, exterior corridors. *Bath:* combo or shower only. **Parking:** on-site. **Terms:** 1-4 night minimum stay - weekends & seasonal, 7 day cancellation notice-fee imposed, package plans. **Pool(s):** outdoor. **Leisure Activities:** whirlpool. **Cards:** AX, DC, MC, VI. **Special Amenities: free local telephone calls and preferred room (subject to availability with advanced reservations).**

SOME UNITS

GOLDCREST RESORT MOTEL — Phone: (530)546-3301 — 49

Motel — SAVE

	1P	2P
12/17-1/31 [CP]	$90-$215	$125-$295
6/16-9/16 [CP]	$65-$225	$99-$295
2/1-6/15 & 9/17-12/16 [CP]	$45-$180	$45-$275

Location: SR 28, 0.3 mi e of SR 267. 8194 N Lake Blvd 96143 (PO Box 579). Fax: 530/546-4395. **Facility:** 25 units. 21 one-bedroom standard units. 4 one-bedroom suites with kitchens. 1-2 stories, exterior corridors. *Bath:* combo or shower only. **Parking:** on-site. **Terms:** 2-4 night minimum stay - seasonal & weekends, 10 day cancellation notice-fee imposed. **Pool(s):** heated outdoor. **Leisure Activities:** whirlpool. **Cards:** AX, CB, DC, DS, MC, VI. **Special Amenities: free continental breakfast and free local telephone calls.**

SOME UNITS

STEVENSON'S HOLLIDAY INN — Phone: (530)546-2269 — 54

Motel — SAVE

	1P	2P	XP
9/16-1/31	$39-$99	$79-$129	$5
6/15-9/15	$59-$99	$69-$129	$5
2/1-6/14	$39-$99	$69-$99	$5

Location: SR 28, 1 mi e of SR 267. 8742 N Lake Blvd 96143 (PO Box 235). Fax: 530/546-2896. **Facility:** 22 units. 18 one-bedroom standard units. 4 one-bedroom suites ($99-$139), some with kitchens. 1 story, exterior corridors. *Bath:* combo or shower only. **Parking:** on-site. **Terms:** 2-3 night minimum stay - weekends, 7 day cancellation notice-fee imposed, small pets only ($5 fee). **Pool(s):** heated outdoor. **Leisure Activities:** whirlpool. **Cards:** AX, DC, MC, VI. **Special Amenities: free continental breakfast and free local telephone calls.**

SOME UNITS

FEE

SUN N' SAND LODGE — Phone: 530/546-2515 — 53

Motel — SAVE

	1P	2P	XP
6/16-9/15	$79-$140	$79-$140	$10
2/1-6/15 & 9/16-1/31	$79-$110	$79-$110	$10

Location: SR 28, 0.3 mi e of SR 267. 8308 N Lake Blvd 96143 (PO Box 5). Fax: 530/546-0112. **Facility:** 26 one-bedroom standard units. 2 stories, exterior corridors. *Bath:* shower only. **Parking:** on-site. **Terms:** 2-3 night minimum stay - weekends, 7 day cancellation notice-fee imposed. **Leisure Activities:** whirlpool. **Cards:** AX, DC, MC, VI. **Special Amenities: free continental breakfast.**

SOME UNITS

OLYMPIC VALLEY (See map and index starting on p. 363)

WHERE TO STAY

RED WOLF LODGE AT SQUAW VALLEY Phone: (530)583-7226 80

Motel

2/1-4/21 & 12/12-1/31 1P: $200-$400
4/22-12/11 1P: $160-$330

Location: Located at Squaw Valley Ski Area. 2000 Squaw Loop Rd 96146 (PO Box 2612). Fax: 530/583-8808. **Facility:** 31 units. 16 one-bedroom standard units with kitchens. 12 one- and 3 two-bedroom suites with kitchens and whirlpools. 3 stories, interior corridors. *Bath:* combo or shower only. **Parking:** on-site. **Terms:** 2 night minimum stay - weekends, cancellation fee imposed. **Leisure Activities:** saunas, whirlpools, game room. **Cards:** AX, CB, DC, MC, VI.

ASK SOME UNITS

RESORT AT SQUAW CREEK *Book at aaa.com* Phone: (530)583-6300 81

AAA SAVE

Resort Large-scale Hotel

12/17-1/8 1P: $379-$469 2P: $379-$469 XP: $20 F1
2/1-12/16 & 1/9-1/31 1P: $179-$469 2P: $179-$469 XP: $20 F1

Location: 0.3 mi from entrance to Squaw Valley. 400 Squaw Creek Rd 96146 (PO Box 3333). Fax: 530/581-5407. **Facility:** Among this all-season resort's notable recreational facilities is an 18-hole golf course; rooms have mountain or valley views. 405 units. 387 one-bedroom standard units. 18 two-bedroom suites ($229-$3500) with kitchens. 9 stories, interior corridors. **Parking:** valet. **Terms:** check-in 4 pm, 7 day cancellation notice-fee imposed, package plans, $14 service charge. **Amenities:** voice mail, honor bars, irons, hair dryers. **Dining:** 3 restaurants, 6:30 am-10 pm, cocktails, also, Glissandi, see separate listing. **Pool(s):** 3 heated outdoor, wading. **Leisure Activities:** saunas, whirlpools, ice skating, recreation programs, rental bicycles, spa. *Fee:* golf-18 holes, 2 tennis courts, downhill skiing, horseback riding. **Business Services:** conference facilities. **Cards:** AX, DC, DS, MC, VI.

FEE DATA PORT SOME UNITS

SQUAW VALLEY LODGE Phone: (530)583-5500 83

AAA SAVE

Resort Condominium

12/17-1/1 1P: $375-$1025 2P: $375-$1025
2/1-4/10 & 1/2-1/31 1P: $190-$875 2P: $190-$875
4/11-12/16 1P: $170-$420 2P: $170-$420

Location: Located at Squaw Valley Ski Area. 201 Squaw Peak Rd 96146 (PO Box 2364). Fax: 530/583-0326. **Facility:** At the foot of the ski slopes, 150 feet from the cable car, the lodge features views of the mountain or valley from most rooms. Smoke free premises. 125 units. 85 one-bedroom standard units with kitchens. 25 one- and 15 two-bedroom suites with kitchens. 3 stories, interior corridors. **Parking:** on-site and valet. **Terms:** check-in 4 pm, 2-4 night minimum stay - weekends, 30 day cancellation notice-fee imposed. **Amenities:** voice mail, irons, hair dryers. **Pool(s):** heated outdoor. **Leisure Activities:** sauna, whirlpools, 2 tennis courts, recreation programs, exercise room. *Fee:* downhill skiing. **Guest Services:** coin laundry. **Cards:** AX, DC, MC, VI. **Special Amenities: free newspaper.**
(See color ad p 369)

VCR DATA PORT

THE VILLAGE AT SQUAW VALLEY USA *Book at aaa.com* Phone: (530)584-1000 82

Resort Condominium

11/24-1/31 1P: $279-$699
2/1-4/13 1P: $259-$499
4/14-11/23 1P: $199-$399

Location: Located at Squaw Valley Ski Area. 1735 Squaw Valley Rd 96146 (PO Box 2025). Fax: 530/584-6290. **Facility:** 286 units. 133 one-, 127 two- and 26 three-bedroom suites. 4 stories, interior corridors. **Parking:** on-site. **Terms:** check-in 4 pm, 14 day cancellation notice-fee imposed. **Amenities:** DVD players, CD players, high-speed Internet, dual phone lines, voice mail, irons, hair dryers. **Leisure Activities:** saunas, whirlpools, hiking trails, jogging, exercise room, game room. *Fee:* golf-18 holes, downhill & cross country skiing, snowmobiling, ice skating, horseback riding, massage. **Guest Services:** gift shop, coin laundry. **Business Services:** meeting rooms. **Cards:** AX, DC, DS, MC, VI.
(See color ad below)

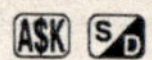

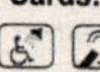
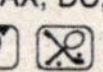

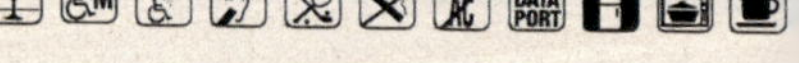

(See map and index starting on p. 363)

WHERE TO DINE

GLISSANDI · Dinner: $27-$39 Phone: 530/581-6621 (30)

French

Location: 0.3 mi from entrance to Squaw Valley; in Resort At Squaw Creek. 400 Squaw Creek Rd 96146. **Hours:** 6 pm-10 pm. Closed: Sun & Mon. **Reservations:** required. **Features:** Menu features contemporary gourmet cuisine made from the freshest seasonal ingredients. Dressy casual; cocktails. **Parking:** valet. **Cards:** AX, CB, DC, DS, MC, VI.

The following restaurant has not been evaluated by AAA but is listed for your information only.

MOTHER BARCLAY'S CAFE **Phone:** 530/581-3251

fyi

Not evaluated. **Location:** SR 89, 8 mi s, then 2 mi w. 1990 Squaw Valley Rd 96146. **Features:** Located in the heart of the Squaw Valley ski area, the eatery has a 7-day-a-week schedule during the winter season.

SOUTH LAKE TAHOE pop. 23,609 (See map and index starting on p. 363)—*See also STATELINE*

WHERE TO STAY

3 PEAKS RESORT & BEACH CLUB *Book at aaa.com* **Phone:** (530)544-4131 (188)

AAA SAVE

Motel

All Year	1P: $69-$199	2P: $69-$199	XP: $15	F12

Location: 6 blks w of casino center; 2 blks n off US 50 toward lake at Park and Manzanita aves. 931 Park Ave 96150. **Fax:** 530/543-1480. **Facility:** 57 units. 45 one- and 12 two-bedroom standard units, some with kitchens and/or whirlpools. 2 stories (no elevator), exterior corridors. **Parking:** on-site. **Terms:** 2 night minimum stay - seasonal, 10 day cancellation notice-fee imposed, pets ($15 extra charge). **Amenities:** *Some:* irons, hair dryers. **Pool(s):** heated outdoor. **Leisure Activities:** whirlpool. **Cards:** AX, DC, DS, MC, VI.

SOME UNITS

FEE

7 SEAS INN AT TAHOE **Phone:** (530)544-7031 (166)

AAA SAVE

Motel

6/11-9/30 [CP]	1P: $49-$89	2P: $55-$109	XP: $10	D12
12/17-1/31 [CP]	1P: $39-$69	2P: $49-$89	XP: $10	D12
2/1-6/10 [CP]	1P: $39-$69	2P: $45-$79	XP: $10	D12
10/1-12/16 [CP]	1P: $35-$59	2P: $42-$65	XP: $10	D12

Location: 2 blks from casino center; 2 blks n off US 50 towards lake. 4145 Manzanita Ave 96150. **Fax:** 530/544-1208. **Facility:** 17 one-bedroom standard units. 2 stories (no elevator), exterior corridors. *Bath:* combo or shower only. **Parking:** on-site. **Terms:** 2-4 night minimum stay - weekends, 5 day cancellation notice-fee imposed, package plans. **Leisure Activities:** whirlpool. **Cards:** AX, CB, DS, MC, VI. **Special Amenities: free local telephone calls and free room upgrade (subject to availability with advanced reservations).** *(See color ad below)*

SOME UNITS

ALDER INN **Phone:** (530)544-4485 (225)

AAA SAVE

Motel

5/1-10/31 [CP]	1P: $48-$125	2P: $80-$140	XP: $10	F18
1/1-1/31 [CP]	1P: $65-$90	2P: $70-$95	XP: $10	F18
2/1-4/30 & 11/1-12/31 [CP]	1P: $48-$85	2P: $65-$95	XP: $10	F18

Location: 2.5 blks s off US 50 on Ski Run Blvd; 0.8 mi below Heavenly Valley ski lift terminal. Located in a quiet area. 1072 Ski Run Blvd 96150. **Fax:** 530/541-4816. **Facility:** 24 one-bedroom standard units. 2 stories (no elevator), exterior corridors. **Parking:** on-site. **Terms:** 15 day cancellation notice-fee imposed, pets ($12 extra charge). **Pool(s):** heated outdoor. **Leisure Activities:** whirlpool. **Cards:** AX, DS, MC, VI. **Special Amenities: free continental breakfast and early check-in/late check-out.**

SOME UNITS

FEE

(See map and index starting on p. 363)

ALPENROSE INN Phone: (530)544-2985 184

Motel

6/13-9/11 [CP]	1P: $49-$120	2P: $59-$130	XP: $10	F12
9/12-1/31 [CP]	1P: $40-$120	2P: $59-$130	XP: $10	F12
2/1-4/17 [CP]	1P: $49-$99	2P: $59-$120	XP: $10	F12
4/18-6/12 [CP]	1P: $40-$85	2P: $50-$99	XP: $10	F12

Location: 0.3 mi n of US 50 via Park Ave. 4074 Pine Blvd 96150. Fax: 530/543-0299. **Facility:** 19 one-bedroom standard units. 2 stories (no elevator), exterior corridors. *Bath:* combo or shower only. **Parking:** on-site. **Terms:** 2-3 night minimum stay - weekends, 7 day cancellation notice, small pets only ($50 deposit, $10 extra charge, in limited units). **Amenities:** video library. **Leisure Activities:** whirlpool. **Cards:** AX, CB, DC, DS, MC, VI. **Special Amenities: free continental breakfast and free local telephone calls.** *(See color ad below)*

SOME UNITS
FEE FEE

ALPINE INN & SPA Phone: 530/544-3340 187

Motel

All Year	1P: $30-$185	2P: $30-$185	XP: $10	F

Location: Just s of casino center. 920 Stateline Ave 96150. Fax: 530/544-2850. **Facility:** 38 one-bedroom standard units, some with whirlpools. 2 stories (no elevator), exterior corridors. *Bath:* combo or shower only. **Parking:** on-site. **Terms:** 10 day cancellation notice-fee imposed. **Pool(s):** outdoor. **Leisure Activities:** whirlpool. **Cards:** AX, CB, DC, DS, JC, MC, VI.

SOME UNITS

AMBASSADOR MOTOR LODGE Phone: 530/544-6461 180

Motel

5/1-9/30 [CP]	1P: $60-$100	2P: $60-$110	XP: $10	F
2/1-4/30 & 10/1-1/31 [CP]	1P: $45-$55	2P: $45-$75	XP: $10	F

Location: Just s of US 50 on Stateline Ave. 4130 Manzanita Ave 96150. Fax: 530/544-8061. **Facility:** 57 one-bedroom standard units, some with kitchens. 2 stories (no elevator), exterior corridors. **Parking:** on-site. **Terms:** small pets only ($10 extra charge, in limited units). **Pool(s):** heated outdoor. **Cards:** AX, DS, MC, VI. **Special Amenities: free continental breakfast and free local telephone calls.**

SOME UNITS
FEE

AMERICANA VILLAGE Phone: 530/541-8022 239

Motel

6/15-10/15	2P: $85-$450
2/1-6/14 & 10/16-1/31	2P: $75-$300

Location: 0.7 mi w of casino center. 3845 Pioneer Tr 96150. Fax: 530/541-1474. **Facility:** 74 units. 64 one-bedroom standard units. 8 one- and 2 two-bedroom suites, some with whirlpools. 2 stories (no elevator), exterior corridors. *Bath:* combo or shower only. **Parking:** on-site. **Terms:** check-in 4 pm, 3 day cancellation notice, weekly rates available, [CP] meal plan available. **Amenities:** *Some:* CD players. **Pool(s):** heated outdoor. **Leisure Activities:** sauna, whirlpool, playground, exercise room, basketball, horseshoes, volleyball. **Guest Services:** complimentary laundry, area transportation. **Business Services:** meeting rooms, business center. **Cards:** AX, DS, MC, VI. **Special Amenities: free continental breakfast and free local telephone calls.** *(See color ad p 375)*

SOME UNITS

APEX INN Phone: (530)541-2940 230

Motel

All Year	1P: $30-$150	2P: $35-$150	XP: $5	F

Location: US 50, 0.5 mi n of airport. 1171 Emerald Bay Rd 96150. Fax: 530/544-1750. **Facility:** 15 one-bedroom standard units. 2 stories (no elevator), exterior corridors. *Bath:* shower only. **Parking:** on-site. **Terms:** 7 day cancellation notice-fee imposed. **Leisure Activities:** whirlpool. **Cards:** AX, DS, MC, VI. **Special Amenities: free local telephone calls and free room upgrade (subject to availability with advanced reservations).**

SOME UNITS

(See map and index starting on p. 363)

BAVARIAN VILLAGE Phone: (530)541-8191 223

AAA SAVE — Condominium

12/20-1/31	1P: $129-$381	2P: $129-$381
6/13-9/14	1P: $129-$199	2P: $129-$199
2/1-6/12	1P: $99-$199	2P: $129-$199
9/15-12/19	1P: $99-$199	2P: $99-$199

Location: Just w of Ski Run Blvd, 0.3 mi s of US 50. 1140-B Herbert Ave 96150 (PO Box 709, 96156). Fax: 530/544-3082. **Facility:** 55 three-bedroom suites with kitchens. 2 stories (no elevator), exterior corridors. **Parking:** on-site. **Terms:** 14 day cancellation notice-fee imposed. **Amenities:** video library (fee). **Pool(s):** heated outdoor. **Leisure Activities:** whirlpool, playground.

VCR

BEACHSIDE INN, SUITES, SPAS & CAPPUCCINO BAR Phone: 530/544-2400 174

Motel

Property failed to provide current rates

Location: 3 blks from casino center. 930 Park Ave 96150. Fax: 530/544-0600. **Facility:** 15 one-bedroom standard units, some with whirlpools. 2 stories (no elevator), exterior corridors. *Bath:* combo or shower only. **Parking:** on-site. **Leisure Activities:** sauna, whirlpool.

SOME UNITS

BEST TAHOE WEST INN Phone: (530)544-6455 170

AAA SAVE — Motel

6/25-9/11 [CP]	1P: $55-$99	2P: $55-$104
9/12-10/30 [CP]	1P: $40-$80	2P: $47-$99
2/1-6/24 & 10/31-1/31 [CP]	1P: $35-$79	2P: $35-$99

Location: N off US 50 via Park Ave; between Stateline and Park aves. 4107 Pine Blvd 96150. Fax: 530/544-0508. **Facility:** 61 one-bedroom standard units, some with efficiencies and/or whirlpools. 2-3 stories (no elevator), exterior corridors. **Parking:** on-site. **Terms:** 2-3 night minimum stay - weekends, 3 day cancellation notice-fee imposed. **Pool(s):** heated outdoor. **Leisure Activities:** sauna, whirlpool. **Guest Services:** coin laundry. **Cards:** AX, CB, DC, DS, JC, MC, VI. **Special Amenities: free newspaper and early check-in/late check-out.** *(See color ad p 368)*

SOME UNITS

DATA PORT / FEE

BEST WESTERN STATION HOUSE INN Book at aaa.com Phone: (530)542-1101 183

AAA SAVE — Motel

2/1-3/31 & 6/16-10/15 [BP]	1P: $98-$138	2P: $98-$138
10/16-1/31 [BP]	1P: $78-$138	2P: $78-$138
4/1-6/15 [BP]	1P: $78-$128	2P: $78-$128

Location: 3.5 blks from casino center; just n off US 50 via Lake Park Ave. 901 Park Ave 96150. Fax: 530/542-1714. **Facility:** 101 units. 100 one- and 1 two-bedroom standard units, some with kitchens and/or whirlpools. 2 stories (no elevator), exterior corridors. *Bath:* combo or shower only. **Parking:** on-site. **Terms:** 2 night minimum stay - with Saturday stayover, cancellation fee imposed. **Amenities:** voice mail, irons, hair dryers. **Dining:** 5:30 pm-10 pm, also, LewMarNel's, see separate listing. **Pool(s):** heated outdoor. **Leisure Activities:** whirlpool. **Business Services:** meeting rooms. **Cards:** AX, CB, DC, DS, MC, VI. **Special Amenities: free full breakfast and free local telephone calls.**
(See color ad p 376)

SOME UNITS

DATA PORT

BEST WESTERN TIMBER COVE LODGE Book at aaa.com Phone: (530)541-6722 220

AAA SAVE — Motel

6/18-9/30 [BP]	1P: $119-$205	2P: $129-$215	XP: $20	F12
12/27-1/31 [BP]	1P: $69-$199	2P: $79-$209	XP: $20	F12
2/1-6/17 & 10/1-12/26 [BP]	1P: $69-$139	2P: $79-$149	XP: $20	F12

Location: 1.5 mi w of casino center, 0.5 mi w of Ski Run Blvd. Located on lake. 3411 Lake Tahoe Blvd 96150. Fax: 530/541-7959. **Facility:** 262 one-bedroom standard units. 3 stories, exterior corridors. *Bath:* combo or shower only. **Parking:** on-site. **Terms:** 2 night minimum stay - with Saturday stayover 6/18-9/30, cancellation fee imposed, $1 service charge, pets ($20 extra charge, in limited units). **Amenities:** video games (fee), voice mail, irons, hair dryers. **Dining:** 7 am-10 pm; to 9 pm in winter, cocktails. **Pool(s):** heated outdoor. **Leisure Activities:** whirlpool, rental boats, marina, waterskiing, fishing, exercise room. *Fee:* massage. **Guest Services:** coin laundry. **Business Services:** meeting rooms. **Cards:** AX, CB, DC, DS, MC, VI. **Special Amenities: free full breakfast and free local telephone calls.**
(See color ad p 377)

SOME UNITS

FEE

(See map and index starting on p. 363)

BLUE JAY LODGE Phone: (530)544-5232 

7/2-8/31	1P: $59-$99	2P: $69-$109	XP: $10	F17
2/1-7/1 & 9/1-1/31	1P: $49-$89	2P: $59-$99	XP: $10	F17

Motel

Location: 2 blks from casino center. 4133 Cedar Ave 96150. Fax: 530/544-0453. **Facility:** 65 one-bedroom standard units, some with efficiencies. 2 stories (no elevator), exterior corridors. *Bath:* combo or shower only. **Parking:** on-site. **Terms:** [CP] meal plan available, pets ($10 extra charge). **Amenities:** voice mail, hair dryers. *Some:* dual phone lines, safes. **Pool(s):** heated outdoor. **Leisure Activities:** whirlpool. **Guest Services:** coin laundry. **Cards:** AX, CB, DC, DS, MC, VI. **Special Amenities: early check-in/late check-out and free room upgrade (subject to availability with advanced reservations).** *(See color ad p 378)*

FEE SOME UNITS FEE

(See map and index starting on p. 363)

BUDGET INN Phone: 530/544-2834 238

AAA SAVE

Motel

6/16-9/30	1P: $39-$150	2P: $39-$150	XP: $5	F
2/1-3/15 & 10/1-1/31	1P: $32-$150	2P: $39-$150	XP: $5	F
3/16-6/15	1P: $35-$150	2P: $35-$150	XP: $5	F

Location: On US 50, 1.5 mi w of casino center. 3496 Lake Tahoe Blvd 96150. Fax: 530/544-7987. **Facility:** 28 units. 22 one- and 6 two-bedroom standard units. 1 story, exterior corridors. *Bath:* shower only. **Parking:** on-site. **Terms:** 3 day cancellation notice-fee imposed, pets ($5 extra charge). **Amenities:** hair dryers. **Pool(s):** heated outdoor. **Cards:** AX, JC, MC. **Special Amenities: free continental breakfast and free local telephone calls.**

SOME UNITS

FEE

CAL VA RADO MOTEL Phone: 530/541-3900 165

AAA SAVE

Motel

6/1-9/30	1P: $49-$79	2P: $49-$79	XP: $5	F
2/1-5/31 & 10/1-1/31	1P: $39-$69	2P: $39-$69	XP: $5	F

Location: Just n of US 50; near casino center. 988 Stateline Ave 96150. Fax: 530/542-2067. **Facility:** 20 units. 19 one-bedroom standard units. 1 one-bedroom suite ($75-$119). 1-2 stories, exterior corridors. *Bath:* combo or shower only. **Parking:** on-site. **Terms:** package plans, small pets only. **Cards:** AX, DS, MC, VI.

SOME UNITS

CAPRI MOTEL Phone: 530/544-3665 164

AAA SAVE

Motel

5/1-9/30 [CP]	1P: $60-$100	2P: $60-$100	XP: $10	F
2/1-4/30 & 10/1-1/31 [CP]	1P: $45-$55	2P: $45-$75	XP: $10	F

Location: Just s of US 50. 932 Stateline Ave 96150. Fax: 530/544-1576. **Facility:** 25 units. 23 one-bedroom standard units. 2 one-bedroom suites ($95-$120). 2 stories (no elevator), exterior corridors. *Bath:* combo or shower only. **Parking:** on-site. **Terms:** small pets only ($10 extra charge, in limited units). **Pool(s):** heated outdoor. **Cards:** AX, DS, MC, VI. **Special Amenities: free continental breakfast and free local telephone calls.**

FEE

(See map and index starting on p. 363)

CASINO AREA TRAVELODGE — **Phone:** (530)541-5000 — 200

AAA SAVE — Motel

5/1-10/31 [CP]	1P: $74-$129	2P: $79-$139	XP: $10	F18
1/1-1/31 [CP]	1P: $65-$90	2P: $70-$100	XP: $10	F18
2/1-4/30 & 11/1-12/31 [CP]	1P: $62-$87	2P: $67-$97	XP: $10	F18

Location: US 50, just w of casino center. 4003 Lake Tahoe Blvd 96150. Fax: 530/544-6910. **Facility:** 66 one-bedroom standard units. 2 stories (no elevator), exterior corridors. *Bath:* shower only. **Parking:** on-site. **Amenities:** voice mail, hair dryers. **Dining:** 11 am-11 pm. **Pool(s):** heated outdoor. **Leisure Activities:** whirlpool. **Cards:** AX, CB, DC, DS, JC, MC, VI. **Special Amenities: free continental breakfast and free local telephone calls.** *(See color ad below)*

SOME UNITS

(See map and index starting on p. 363)

CEDAR INN & SUITES Phone: (530)543-0159 163

Motel

12/24-1/31	1P: $99-$129	2P: $109-$139
6/16-9/30	1P: $49-$69	2P: $59-$79
10/1-12/23	1P: $39-$59	2P: $59-$79
2/1-6/15	1P: $39-$59	2P: $49-$69

Location: US 50, 2 blks n, at Stateline and Manzanita aves. 890 Stateline Ave 96150. Fax: 530/543-0304. **Facility:** 39 one-bedroom standard units, some with efficiencies. 2 stories, exterior corridors. *Bath:* combo or shower only. **Parking:** on-site. **Terms:** weekly rates available, package plans - seasonal, pets ($10 extra charge, in limited units). **Pool(s):** heated outdoor. **Leisure Activities:** whirlpool. **Cards:** AX, DS, MC, VI. **Special Amenities: free continental breakfast and free local telephone calls.**

SOME UNITS FEE

CEDAR LODGE Phone: (530)544-6453 186

Motel

6/21-9/13 [CP]	1P: $55-$95	2P: $55-$100
2/1-3/31 [CP]	1P: $45-$80	2P: $45-$85
4/1-6/20 & 9/14-1/31 [CP]	1P: $40-$65	2P: $40-$70

Location: N off US 50, toward the lake; at Cedar and Friday aves; 3 blks from the casino center. 4069 Cedar Ave 96150. Fax: 530/542-1290. **Facility:** 56 units. 54 one- and 2 two-bedroom standard units. 2 stories (no elevator), exterior corridors. *Bath:* combo or shower only. **Parking:** on-site. **Terms:** 2-3 night minimum stay - seasonal, small pets only ($10 fee, $50 deposit, dogs only, in limited units). **Pool(s):** heated outdoor. **Leisure Activities:** whirlpools. **Cards:** AX, MC, VI. **Special Amenities: free continental breakfast and early check-in/late check-out.**

SOME UNITS FEE

DAYS INN-CASINO AREA/SOUTH LAKE TAHOE Phone: (530)541-4800 194

Motel

9/22-1/31 [CP]	1P: $41-$189	2P: $41-$199	XP: $8	F12
6/16-9/21 [CP]	1P: $49-$135	2P: $49-$145	XP: $8	F12
2/1-4/14 [CP]	1P: $44-$118	2P: $44-$129	XP: $8	F12
4/15-6/15 [CP]	1P: $41-$105	2P: $41-$115	XP: $8	F12

Location: 3 blks w of casino center, 1 blk n off US 50 toward lake at Park and Cedar aves. 968 Park Ave 96150 (PO Box 562581, 96156). Fax: 530/544-4643. **Facility:** 59 one-bedroom standard units. 3 stories, interior corridors. **Parking:** on-site. **Terms:** 3 day cancellation notice-fee imposed, pets ($10 extra charge, in limited units). **Amenities:** hair dryers. **Pool(s):** small outdoor. **Leisure Activities:** sauna, whirlpool. **Cards:** AX, CB, DC, DS, MC, VI. **Special Amenities: free continental breakfast and free newspaper.** *(See color ad below)*

SOME UNITS FEE

DAYS INN LAKE TAHOE Book at aaa.com Phone: (530)544-3445 217

Motel

All Year	1P: $39-$250	2P: $39-$250	XP: $10	F16

Location: US 50, 1.5 mi w of casino center. 3530 Lake Tahoe Blvd 96150. Fax: 530/544-3466. **Facility:** 42 one-bedroom standard units. 1 story, exterior corridors. *Bath:* combo or shower only. **Parking:** on-site. **Terms:** [CP] meal plan available. **Amenities:** hair dryers. **Pool(s):** heated outdoor. **Leisure Activities:** whirlpool. **Cards:** AX, CB, DC, DS, MC, VI. **Special Amenities: free continental breakfast and free newspaper.** *(See color ad p 381)*

SOME UNITS

DREAM INN Phone: 530/544-6228 228

Motel

6/16-9/30	1P: $35-$150	2P: $35-$150	XP: $10	D12
2/1-3/31 & 10/1-1/31	1P: $35-$125	2P: $35-$140	XP: $10	D12
4/1-6/15	1P: $28-$99	2P: $28-$99	XP: $5	D12

Location: 0.5 mi s of US 50. 1200 Ski Run Blvd 96150. Fax: 530/544-2560. **Facility:** 23 one-bedroom standard units, some with whirlpools. 2 stories (no elevator), exterior corridors. *Bath:* combo or shower only. **Parking:** on-site. **Terms:** 7 day cancellation notice-fee imposed. **Amenities:** video library. **Cards:** AX, DS, MC, VI.

SOME UNITS FEE

(See map and index starting on p. 363)

ECONO LODGE *Book at aaa.com* **Phone:** (530)544-2036 226

Motel

All Year 1P: $32-$220 2P: $32-$220 XP: $10 F16

Location: On US 50, 1.5 mi w of casino center. 3536 Lake Tahoe Blvd 96150. Fax: 530/544-3466. **Facility:** 36 one-bedroom standard units. 1-2 stories (no elevator), exterior corridors. *Bath:* combo or shower only. **Parking:** on-site. **Terms:** check-in 3:30 pm. **Amenities:** hair dryers. **Pool(s):** heated outdoor. **Leisure Activities:** whirlpool. **Cards:** AX, CB, DC, DS, JC, MC, VI. **Special Amenities: free local telephone calls.** *(See color ad below)*

SOME UNITS

(See map and index starting on p. 363)

EL DORADO MOTEL Book at aaa.com — Phone: (530)544-5757 — 173

SAVE — Motel

6/1-9/30	1P: $79-$109	2P: $79-$109
2/1-3/31 & 10/1-1/31	1P: $69-$99	2P: $69-$99
4/1-5/31	1P: $59-$79	2P: $59-$79

Location: Near casino center. 4139 Lake Tahoe Blvd 96150. Fax: 530/544-4829. **Facility:** 26 one-bedroom standard units. 2 stories (no elevator), exterior corridors. *Bath:* combo or shower only. **Parking:** on-site. **Terms:** cancellation fee imposed, [CP] meal plan available. **Amenities:** *Some:* irons, hair dryers. **Cards:** MC, VI.

SOME UNITS

ELIZABETH LODGE — Phone: (530)544-2417 — 203

SAVE — Motel

All Year	1P: $25-$129	2P: $35-$199	XP: $5	F9

Location: 4 blks w of casino center. 3918 Pioneer Tr 96150. Fax: 530/543-1746. **Facility:** 20 one-bedroom standard units. 1 story, exterior corridors. *Bath:* combo or shower only. **Parking:** on-site. **Terms:** cancellation fee imposed. **Cards:** AX, MC, VI. **Special Amenities: free local telephone calls and early check-in/late check-out.**

SOME UNITS FEE

EMBASSY SUITES-LAKE TAHOE RESORT Book at aaa.com — Phone: (530)544-5400 — 175

Large-scale Hotel

12/19-1/4 [BP]	1P: $229-$499	2P: $229-$499	XP: $30	F12
2/1-9/30 [BP]	1P: $169-$349	2P: $169-$349	XP: $30	F12
1/5-1/31 [BP]	1P: $159-$299	2P: $159-$299	XP: $30	F12
10/1-12/18 [BP]	1P: $149-$269	2P: $149-$269	XP: $30	F12

Location: At casino center. 4130 Lake Tahoe Blvd 96150. Fax: 530/544-7643. **Facility:** Nicely appointed rooms with ample amenities add to the appeal of this property conveniently located near Lake Tahoe. 400 one-bedroom suites. 9 stories, interior corridors. *Bath:* combo or shower only. **Parking:** on-site (fee). **Terms:** check-in 4:30 pm, 2-3 night minimum stay - seasonal weekends, 3 day cancellation notice-fee imposed, package plans - seasonal. **Amenities:** dual phone lines, voice mail, safes, honor bars, irons, hair dryers. *Fee:* video games, high-speed Internet. **Pool(s):** heated indoor. **Leisure Activities:** sauna, whirlpool, exercise room. **Guest Services:** gift shop, complimentary evening beverages, valet and coin laundry. **Business Services:** meeting rooms, business center. **Cards:** AX, CB, DC, DS, JC, MC, VI. ***(See color ad below)***

ASK FEE DATA PORT SOME UNITS

EMBASSY VACATION RESORT Book at aaa.com — Phone: (530)541-6122 — 222

Small-scale Hotel

	1P
All Year	1P: $79-$169

Location: Jct US 50 and Ski Run Blvd, 1 mi w of casino center. Located adjacent to Ski Run Marina. 901 Ski Run Blvd 96150. Fax: 530/541-2028. **Facility:** 276 units. 138 one-bedroom standard units. 138 one-bedroom suites with kitchens and whirlpools. 6 stories, interior corridors. **Parking:** on-site. **Terms:** check-in 4 pm. **Amenities:** voice mail, safes, irons, hair dryers. *Some:* CD players. **Pool(s):** heated indoor/outdoor. **Leisure Activities:** whirlpools, exercise room. *Fee:* game room. **Guest Services:** gift shop, coin laundry. **Cards:** AX, DC, DS, JC, MC, VI.

ASK DATA PORT SOME UNITS

(See map and index starting on p. 363)

FIRESIDE LODGE B & B Phone: (530)542-1717 321

Bed & Breakfast

All Year [ECP] 1P: $69-$155 2P: $69-$155

Location: SR 89, 1 mi n of US 50. 515 Emerald Bay Rd 96150. Fax: 530/543-0416. **Facility:** Designated smoking area. 9 one-bedroom standard units. 1 story, exterior corridors. *Bath:* shower only. **Parking:** on-site. **Terms:** 2-7 night minimum stay - seasonal weekends, 30 day cancellation notice-fee imposed, package plans, pets ($100 deposit, $20 extra charge). **Amenities:** video library. **Leisure Activities:** bicycles. *Fee:* sailboats, downhill skiing. **Guest Services:** complimentary evening beverages. **Business Services:** meeting rooms, fax. **Cards:** AX, DS, MC, VI.

FEE

FOREST SUITES RESORTS *Book at aaa.com* Phone: (530)541-6655 199

Motel

All Year [ECP] 1P: $69-$189 2P: $69-$189

Location: Just se off US 50. Located adjacent to the casinos. 1 Lake Pkwy 96150. Fax: 530/544-3135. **Facility:** 119 units. 70 one- and 49 two-bedroom standard units, some with kitchens and/or whirlpools. 3 stories, interior/exterior corridors. *Bath:* combo or shower only. **Parking:** on-site. **Terms:** check-in 4 pm, 1-5 night minimum stay - seasonal & weekends, 7 day cancellation notice-fee imposed. **Amenities:** safes (fee), irons, hair dryers. **Pool(s):** 2 heated outdoor. **Leisure Activities:** sauna, whirlpools, steamroom, exercise room. *Fee:* downhill skiing, bicycles, massage. **Guest Services:** coin laundry. **Business Services:** meeting rooms. **Cards:** AX, DC, DS, MC, VI. **Special Amenities: free continental breakfast.** *(See color ad below)*

DATA PORT / SOME UNITS

GREEN LANTERN MOTEL Phone: (530)544-6336 171

Motel

6/15-10/14 [CP]	1P: $49-$89	2P: $54-$99	XP: $5	F13
10/15-1/31 [CP]	1P: $39-$79	2P: $44-$89	XP: $5	F13
2/1-6/14 [CP]	1P: $39-$69	2P: $44-$79	XP: $5	F13

Location: 3 blks toward the lake from casino area, at Poplar St. 4097 Manzanita Ave 96150. Fax: 530/544-0276. **Facility:** 36 one-bedroom standard units. 2 stories (no elevator), exterior corridors. *Bath:* shower only. **Parking:** on-site. **Terms:** 2 night minimum stay, 5 day cancellation notice. **Pool(s):** outdoor. **Leisure Activities:** whirlpool. **Cards:** AX, CB, DC, DS, JC, MC, VI. **Special Amenities: free continental breakfast and free local telephone calls.**

HIGH COUNTRY LODGE Phone: (530)541-0508 233

Motel

All Year 1P: $30-$150 2P: $35-$150 XP: $5 D10

Location: US 50, 0.5 mi n of airport. 1227 Emerald Bay Rd 96150. Fax: 530/544-7518. **Facility:** 15 one-bedroom standard units. 1 story, exterior corridors. *Bath:* shower only. **Parking:** on-site. **Terms:** 3 day cancellation notice-fee imposed, pets ($50 deposit, $5 extra charge). **Leisure Activities:** whirlpool. **Cards:** AX, DC, MC, VI. **Special Amenities: free local telephone calls and preferred room (subject to availability with advanced reservations).**

FEE / SOME UNITS FEE FEE

(See map and index starting on p. 363)

HOLIDAY INN EXPRESS Book at aaa.com

Phone: (530)544-5900 201

AAA SAVE — Motel

6/25-8/28 [ECP]	1P: $109-$169	2P: $109-$169
2/1-4/3 [ECP]	1P: $89-$149	2P: $89-$149
4/4-6/24 & 8/29-1/31 [ECP]	1P: $69-$119	2P: $69-$119

Location: 0.3 mi w of casino center on US 50; at Pioneer Tr. 3961 Lake Tahoe Blvd 96150. Fax: 530/544-5333. **Facility:** 89 one-bedroom standard units, some with kitchens. 3 stories (no elevator), exterior corridors. **Parking:** on-site. **Terms:** 2 night minimum stay - seasonal, with Saturday stayover, cancellation fee imposed. **Amenities:** dual phone lines, voice mail, irons, hair dryers. **Pool(s):** heated outdoor. **Leisure Activities:** sauna, whirlpools. **Guest Services:** valet and coin laundry. **Cards:** AX, CB, DC, DS, MC, VI. **Special Amenities: free expanded continental breakfast and free local telephone calls.** *(See color ad below)*

HOLIDAY LODGE Book at aaa.com

Phone: (530)544-4101 179

AAA SAVE — Motel

2/1-3/31 & 6/18-9/19 [CP]	1P: $74-$94	2P: $74-$94	XP: $5 F12
4/1-6/17 & 9/20-1/31 [CP]	1P: $59-$79	2P: $59-$79	XP: $5 F12

Location: Just w of casinos and US 50. 4095 Laurel Ave 96157. Fax: 530/542-4932. **Facility:** 165 units. 149 one-bedroom standard units, some with kitchens (no utensils) and/or whirlpools. 16 one-bedroom suites ($79-$114). 1-2 stories (no elevator), exterior corridors. *Bath:* combo or shower only. **Parking:** on-site. **Terms:** 2 night minimum stay - seasonal & weekends, 3 day cancellation notice. **Pool(s):** heated outdoor, heated indoor. **Leisure Activities:** sauna, whirlpool. **Guest Services:** coin laundry. **Cards:** AX, MC, VI. **Special Amenities: free continental breakfast and free local telephone calls.** *(See color ad p 385)*

SOME UNITS

INN BY THE LAKE Book at aaa.com

Phone: (530)542-0330 211

AAA SAVE — Motel

6/25-9/4	1P: $108-$228	2P: $108-$228
2/1-6/24 & 9/5-1/31	1P: $98-$188	2P: $98-$188

Location: US 50, 2 mi s of casino center. 3300 Lake Tahoe Blvd 96150. Fax: 530/541-6596. **Facility:** 99 units. 97 one- and 2 two-bedroom standard units, some with kitchens and/or whirlpools. 3 stories, interior corridors. *Bath:* combo or shower only. **Parking:** on-site. **Terms:** 2-5 night minimum stay - weekends, [ECP] meal plan available, package plans - seasonal, pets ($20 extra charge, in limited units). **Amenities:** video games (fee), voice mail, irons, hair dryers. **Pool(s):** heated outdoor. **Leisure Activities:** sauna, whirlpool, bicycles. **Guest Services:** coin laundry. **Business Services:** meeting rooms, business center. **Cards:** AX, CB, DC, DS, MC, VI. **Special Amenities: free continental breakfast.** *(See color ad p 386)*

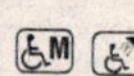

SOME UNITS

FEE FEE FEE

(See map and index starting on p. 363)

LAKELAND VILLAGE BEACH & MOUNTAIN RESORT Book at aaa.com Phone: (530)544-1685 216

AAA SAVE

Condominium

12/21-1/31	1P: $189-$239	2P: $189-$319
6/19-9/5	1P: $135-$279	2P: $135-$279
2/1-6/18	1P: $89-$239	2P: $89-$259
9/6-12/20	1P: $89-$159	2P: $89-$179

Location: US 50, 1.3 mi w of casino center. 3535 Lake Tahoe Blvd 96150. Fax: 530/541-6278. **Facility:** Spacious grounds. Some units on lakefront. 210 units. 110 one- and 100 two-bedroom standard units, some with kitchens. 1-3 stories, interior/exterior corridors. **Parking:** on-site. **Terms:** check-in 4 pm, 1-6 night minimum stay - seasonal, 30 day cancellation notice. **Amenities:** video library (fee), voice mail, irons, hair dryers. **Pool(s):** 2 heated outdoor, wading. **Leisure Activities:** sauna, whirlpools, boat dock, exercise room. *Fee:* 2 tennis courts, downhill skiing. **Guest Services:** gift shop, coin laundry, area transportation-within 5 mi. **Business Services:** meeting rooms. **Cards:** AX, DS, MC, VI. **Special Amenities: preferred room (subject to availability with advanced reservations).** *(See color ad below)*

SOME UNITS

VCR DATA PORT

(See map and index starting on p. 363)

LAMPLITER INN Book at aaa.com Phone: (530)544-2936 167

Motel

10/1-1/31	1P: $79-$199	2P: $79-$199	XP: $10	F12
6/1-9/30	1P: $69-$199	2P: $69-$199	XP: $10	F12
2/1-5/31	1P: $49-$119	2P: $49-$119	XP: $10	F12

Location: 2 blks n of US 50. 4143 Cedar Ave 96150. Fax: 530/544-5249. **Facility:** 28 one-bedroom standard units, some with whirlpools. 2 stories (no elevator), exterior corridors. *Bath:* combo or shower only. **Parking:** on-site. **Terms:** 2-3 night minimum stay - weekends, cancellation fee imposed, package plans, pets ($100 deposit, $10 extra charge, in limited units). **Leisure Activities:** whirlpool. **Cards:** AX, DC, DS, MC, VI.

SOME UNITS

ASK FEE

(See map and index starting on p. 363)

THE LODGE AT LAKE TAHOE Book at aaa.com — Phone: (530)541-6226 — 205

AAA SAVE — Motel

2/1-3/31 & 5/22-10/15	1P: $104-$115	2P: $117-$130
4/1-5/21 & 10/16-1/31	1P: $81-$90	2P: $95-$105

Location: 0.7 mi w of casino center. 3840 Pioneer Tr 96150. Fax: 530/541-1389. **Facility:** 45 units. 37 one-bedroom standard units, some with kitchens. 8 two-bedroom suites with kitchens. 2 stories (no elevator), exterior corridors. *Bath:* combo or shower only. **Parking:** on-site. **Terms:** check-in 4 pm, 3 day cancellation notice-fee imposed. **Amenities:** irons, hair dryers. **Pool(s):** heated outdoor. **Leisure Activities:** whirlpool, playground, horseshoes, volleyball. **Guest Services:** coin laundry, area transportation-casinos. **Cards:** AX, DS, MC, VI.

FEE

MARK TWAIN MOTEL — Phone: (530)544-5733 — 191

AAA SAVE — Motel

6/16-1/31	1P: $32-$250	2P: $32-$250	XP: $10	F10
2/1-6/15	1P: $32-$120	2P: $32-$120	XP: $10	F10

Location: 1 blk n of US 50, toward the lake. 947 Park Ave 96150. Fax: 530/544-2482. **Facility:** 21 one-bedroom standard units. 2 stories (no elevator), exterior corridors. *Bath:* shower only. **Parking:** on-site. **Pool(s):** outdoor. **Leisure Activities:** whirlpool. **Cards:** AX, DC, DS, MC, VI.

SOME UNITS

NATIONAL 9 INN — Phone: 530/541-2119 — 207

Motel

Property failed to provide current rates

Location: 0.4 mi w of casino center on US 50. 3901 Pioneer Tr 96150. Fax: 530/542-2015. **Facility:** 32 units. 31 one- and 1 two-bedroom standard units. 2 stories (no elevator), exterior corridors. **Parking:** on-site. **Amenities:** hair dryers. **Pool(s):** outdoor. **Leisure Activities:** whirlpool.

SOME UNITS

PARADICE MOTEL — Phone: (530)544-6800 — 192

AAA SAVE — Motel

All Year	1P: $28-$250	2P: $28-$250	XP: $10	F10

Location: Just n of US 50, toward the lake. 953 Park Ave 96150. Fax: 530/544-9145. **Facility:** 14 one-bedroom standard units. 2 stories (no elevator), exterior corridors. *Bath:* combo or shower only. **Parking:** on-site. **Cards:** AX, DC, DS, MC, VI.

SOME UNITS

(See map and index starting on p. 363)

QUALITY INN & SUITES Book at aaa.com

Phone: (530)541-5400 209

SAVE — Motel

12/19-1/31	1P: $59-$300	2P: $69-$400	XP: $10	F15
6/11-9/30	1P: $59-$250	2P: $69-$300	XP: $10	F15
2/1-6/10 & 10/1-12/18	1P: $49-$200	2P: $59-$250	XP: $10	F15

Location: US 50, 0.7 mi w of casino center. 3838 Lake Tahoe Blvd 96150. Fax: 530/541-7170. **Facility:** 120 one-bedroom standard units, some with kitchens. 2 stories (no elevator), exterior corridors. *Bath:* combo or shower only. **Parking:** on-site. **Terms:** check-in 4 pm, 3 day cancellation notice-fee imposed. **Amenities:** irons, hair dryers. **Pool(s):** outdoor. **Leisure Activities:** whirlpool. **Business Services:** meeting rooms. **Cards:** AX, CB, DC, DS, JC, MC, VI. *(See color ad p 381)*

SOME UNITS

RIDGEWOOD INN

Phone: 530/541-8589 236

SAVE — Motel

6/18-9/25	1P: $59-$135	2P: $59-$135	XP: $10	F13
2/1-4/24	1P: $55-$135	2P: $55-$135	XP: $10	F13
4/25-6/17 & 9/26-1/31	1P: $49-$135	2P: $49-$135	XP: $10	F13

Location: US 50, 0.5 mi n of airport. 1341 Emerald Bay Rd 96150. Fax: 530/542-4638. **Facility:** 12 units. 11 one-bedroom standard units, some with efficiencies. 1 one-bedroom suite ($99-$149) with kitchen. 1 story, exterior corridors. *Bath:* combo or shower only. **Parking:** on-site. **Terms:** 2 night minimum stay - weekends, 3 day cancellation notice, pets ($10 extra charge). **Cards:** AX, DS, MC, VI. **Special Amenities: free local telephone calls.**

SOME UNITS

FEE

ROYAL INN

Phone: (530)544-1177 212

SAVE — Motel

All Year	1P: $29-$199	2P: $39-$250	XP: $7	F12

Location: US 50, 1.5 mi w of casino center. 3520 Lake Tahoe Blvd 96150. Fax: 530/542-3638. **Facility:** 33 units. 32 one- and 1 two-bedroom standard units. 2 stories (no elevator), exterior corridors. *Bath:* shower only. **Parking:** on-site. **Terms:** 2-5 night minimum stay, 3 day cancellation notice-fee imposed. **Pool(s):** outdoor. **Guest Services:** coin laundry. **Cards:** AX, CB, DC, MC, VI. **Special Amenities: free local telephone calls and free room upgrade (subject to availability with advanced reservations).**

SOME UNITS

ROYAL VALHALLA MOTOR LODGE

Phone: (530)544-2233 162

SAVE — Motel

2/1-9/30 & 12/12-1/4	1P: $109	2P: $109	XP: $10	F
10/1-12/11 & 1/5-1/31	1P: $71-$101	2P: $71-$101	XP: $10	F

Location: N off US 50; at Lakeshore Blvd and Stateline Ave. 4104 Lakeshore Blvd 96150. Fax: 530/544-1436. **Facility:** 92 one-bedroom standard units, some with efficiencies or kitchens. 3 stories, interior/exterior corridors. *Bath:* combo or shower only. **Parking:** on-site. **Terms:** [ECP] meal plan available. **Amenities:** irons. **Pool(s):** heated outdoor. **Leisure Activities:** whirlpool. **Guest Services:** coin laundry. **Cards:** AX, CB, DC, MC, VI. **Special Amenities: free continental breakfast and free local telephone calls.**

SOME UNITS

(See map and index starting on p. 363)

SOUTH SHORE INN Phone: (530)544-1000 204

Motel

2/1-3/31 & 6/16-9/15	1P: $48-$168	2P: $55-$189	XP: $10	F10
4/1-6/15 & 9/16-1/31	1P: $38-$125	2P: $43-$135	XP: $10	F10

Location: 4 blks w of casino area. Located in a quiet area. 3900 Pioneer Tr 96150. Fax: 530/544-2019. **Facility:** 22 units. 20 one-bedroom standard units. 1 one- and 1 two-bedroom suites ($109-$325). 2 stories (no elevator), exterior corridors. **Parking:** on-site. **Terms:** cancellation fee imposed, no pets allowed (owner's pet on premises). **Cards:** MC, VI. **Special Amenities: free local telephone calls and early check-in/late check-out.**

SOME UNITS

SOUTH TAHOE TRAVELODGE Phone: (530)541-4000 214

Motel

5/1-10/31 [CP]	1P: $59-$114	2P: $64-$124	XP: $10	F18
1/1-1/31 [CP]	1P: $50-$75	2P: $55-$85	XP: $10	F18
2/1-4/30 & 11/1-12/31 [CP]	1P: $47-$72	2P: $52-$82	XP: $10	F18

Location: 1.5 mi w of casino center. 3489 Lake Tahoe Blvd 96150. Fax: 530/544-6985. **Facility:** 59 one-bedroom standard units. 2 stories (no elevator), exterior corridors. *Bath:* combo or shower only. **Parking:** on-site. **Amenities:** voice mail, hair dryers. **Dining:** Heidi's Pancake House, see separate listing. **Pool(s):** outdoor. **Leisure Activities:** whirlpool. **Cards:** AX, CB, DC, DS, JC, MC, VI. **Special Amenities: free continental breakfast and free local telephone calls.**

SOME UNITS

DATA PORT

STARDUST LODGE Book at aaa.com Phone: (530)544-5211 172

Motel

~~6/15-10/15~~	~~1P: $95-$145~~	~~2P: $95-$145~~	~~XP: $10~~	F12
2/1-6/14 & 10/16-1/31	1P: $75-$110	2P: $75-$110	XP: $10	F12

Location: US 50, just w of casino center. 4061 Lake Tahoe Blvd 96150. Fax: 530/544-3617. **Facility:** 86 units. 42 one-bedroom standard units. 40 one- and 4 two-bedroom suites, some with kitchens. 2 stories (no elevator), exterior corridors. *Bath:* combo or shower only. **Parking:** on-site. **Terms:** check-in 4 pm, [CP] meal plan available. **Amenities:** video library, CD players, hair dryers. **Pool(s):** 2 heated outdoor. **Leisure Activities:** whirlpools, exercise room. **Guest Services:** complimentary laundry. **Cards:** AX, DS, MC, VI. **Special Amenities: free continental breakfast and free local telephone calls.** *(See color ad below)*

SOME UNITS

VCR

STATELINE TRAVELODGE Book at aaa.com Phone: (530)544-6000 198

Motel

5/1-10/31 [CP]	1P: $74-$129	2P: $79-$139	XP: $10	F18
1/1-1/31 [CP]	1P: $65-$90	2P: $70-$100	XP: $10	F18
2/1-4/30 & 11/1-12/31 [CP]	1P: $62-$87	2P: $67-$97	XP: $10	F18

Location: US 50, just w of casino center. 4011 Lake Tahoe Blvd 96150. Fax: 530/544-6869. **Facility:** 50 units. 48 one- and 2 two-bedroom standard units. 2 stories, exterior corridors. *Bath:* combo or shower only. **Parking:** on-site. **Amenities:** voice mail, hair dryers. **Pool(s):** heated outdoor. **Leisure Activities:** whirlpool. **Cards:** AX, CB, DC, DS, JC, MC, VI. **Special Amenities: free continental breakfast and free local telephone calls.** *(See color ad p 379)*

SOME UNITS

DATA PORT

SUPER 8 Book at aaa.com Phone: (530)544-3476 221

Motel

12/24-1/31	1P: $40-$205	2P: $40-$205
6/25-9/30	1P: $50-$175	2P: $50-$175
2/1-6/24	1P: $40-$155	2P: $40-$155
10/1-12/23	1P: $40-$65	2P: $40-$65

Location: US 50, just w of Ski Run Blvd. 3600 Lake Tahoe Blvd 96150. Fax: 530/542-4011. **Facility:** 108 units. 103 one-bedroom standard units. 5 one-bedroom suites. 2 stories (no elevator), exterior corridors. *Bath:* combo or shower only. **Parking:** on-site. **Terms:** [CP] meal plan available. **Amenities:** voice mail, hair dryers. **Dining:** 4 pm-10 pm, Sat & Sun from 11 am. **Pool(s):** heated outdoor. **Leisure Activities:** whirlpool, playground, shuffleboard. **Business Services:** meeting rooms. **Cards:** AX, DC, DS, MC, VI. **Special Amenities: free continental breakfast and free local telephone calls.** *(See color ad p 390)*

SOME UNITS

DATA PORT

(See map and index starting on p. 363)

TAHOE BEACH & SKI CLUB Book at aaa.com **Phone:** 530/541-6220 219

AAA SAVE

Condominium

6/24-9/30	1P: $120-$295	2P: $120-$295
10/1-1/31	1P: $85-$295	2P: $85-$295
2/1-4/6	1P: $110-$250	2P: $110-$250
4/7-6/23	1P: $85-$210	2P: $85-$210

Location: US 50, 1.5 mi w of casino center. 3601 Lake Tahoe Blvd 96150. Fax: 530/541-6187. **Facility:** Buffered by extensive grounds, the club offers some units with lake views and many with whirlpool baths. 140 units. 94 one-bedroom standard units, some with whirlpools. 41 one- and 4 two-bedroom suites, some with kitchens and/or whirlpools. 1 cabin ($250-$295). 2-3 stories, interior corridors. *Bath:* combo or shower only. **Parking:** on-site. **Terms:** check-in 4 pm, 3 day cancellation notice. **Amenities:** video library (fee), voice mail, hair dryers. **Pool(s):** heated outdoor. **Leisure Activities:** saunas, whirlpools, tennis court, playground, exercise room, horseshoes, volleyball. **Guest Services:** gift shop, coin laundry, area transportation-casinos. **Cards:** AX, DS, MC, VI.

SOME UNITS

TAHOE CHALET INN **Phone:** (530)544-3311 206

AAA SAVE

Motel

All Year	1P: $40-$220	2P: $40-$220

Location: 0.5 mi s of casino center. 3860 Lake Tahoe Blvd 96150. Fax: 530/544-4069. **Facility:** 66 units. 58 one-bedroom standard units, some with whirlpools. 8 one-bedroom suites ($125-$225) with kitchens (no utensils). 1-2 stories (no elevator), exterior corridors. *Bath:* combo or shower only. **Parking:** on-site. **Terms:** 2 night minimum stay - some weekends, 3 day cancellation notice-fee imposed, [CP] meal plan available. **Amenities:** *Some:* hair dryers. **Pool(s):** outdoor. **Leisure Activities:** whirlpool. **Guest Services:** coin laundry. **Cards:** AX, CB, DC, MC, VI. **Special Amenities: free continental breakfast.**

SOME UNITS

TAHOE COLONY INN Book at aaa.com **Phone:** (530)544-6481 197

AAA SAVE

Motel

6/15-9/30 [CP]	1P: $60-$70	2P: $70-$80	XP: $10
2/1-6/14 & 10/1-1/31 [CP]	1P: $50-$60	2P: $60-$70	XP: $10

Location: Just s of US 50. 3794 Montreal Rd 96150. Fax: 530/544-2775. **Facility:** 91 one-bedroom standard units. 2 stories (no elevator), interior corridors. **Parking:** on-site. **Terms:** cancellation fee imposed, weekly rates available, pets ($40 deposit, in limited units). **Pool(s):** heated outdoor. **Leisure Activities:** whirlpool. **Guest Services:** complimentary laundry. **Cards:** AX, DS, MC, VI. **Special Amenities: free continental breakfast and free local telephone calls.**

SOME UNITS

FEE

(See map and index starting on p. 363)

TAHOE HACIENDA MOTEL Book at aaa.com Phone: (530)541-3805 208

Motel

6/16-9/30 & 12/1-1/31	1P: $48-$250	2P: $48-$250
2/1-6/15 & 10/1-11/30	1P: $38-$150	2P: $38-$150

Location: US 50, 0.7 mi w of casino center. 3820 Lake Tahoe Blvd 96150. Fax: 530/541-5567. **Facility:** 33 one-bedroom standard units, some with whirlpools. 1-2 stories (no elevator), exterior corridors. *Bath:* combo or shower only. **Parking:** on-site. **Terms:** 2-3 night minimum stay - weekends & seasonal, 3 day cancellation notice. **Pool(s):** heated outdoor. **Leisure Activities:** whirlpool. **Cards:** AX, DS, MC, VI.

SOME UNITS

ASK

TAHOE KEYS RESORT Book at aaa.com Phone: (530)544-5397 210

AAA SAVE

Condominium

All Year	1P: $100-$1300	2P: $100-$1300

Location: US 50, exit Tahoe Keys Blvd, 1 mi w. 599 Tahoe Keys Blvd 96150. Fax: 530/544-2741. **Facility:** Waterfront condos, homes and villas. 137 units. 21 one-bedroom standard units with kitchens. 22 two- and 94 three-bedroom suites with kitchens. 2 stories (no elevator), exterior corridors. **Parking:** on-site. **Terms:** 2-7 night minimum stay - seasonal, cancellation fee imposed, pets ($100 deposit, $25 extra charge, in limited units). **Amenities:** *Some:* irons. **Pool(s):** heated indoor. **Leisure Activities:** whirlpool, boating, marina, fishing, bicycles. *Fee:* 6 lighted tennis courts. **Guest Services:** complimentary laundry. **Business Services:** meeting rooms, fax (fee). **Cards:** AX, DS, MC, VI. **Special Amenities:** free local telephone calls. *(See color ad below)*

SOME UNITS

FEE VCR

(See map and index starting on p. 363)

TAHOE LAKESHORE LODGE AND SPA *Book at aaa.com* **Phone:** (530)541-2180 **215**

Motel

6/25-9/5 [CP]	1P: $179-$249	2P: $179-$249
9/6-1/31 [CP]	1P: $129-$199	2P: $129-$199
2/1-6/24 [CP]	1P: $129-$159	2P: $129-$159

Location: 1.5 mi w of casino center; off US 50. Located on lake. 930 Bal BiJou Rd 96150. Fax: 530/544-7759. **Facility:** 71 units. 45 one-bedroom standard units, some with kitchens and/or whirlpools. 11 one-, 6 two- and 9 three-bedroom suites with kitchens. 3-4 stories, interior/exterior corridors. *Bath:* combo or shower only. **Parking:** on-site. **Terms:** check-in 4 pm, 2-5 night minimum stay - seasonal, 14 day cancellation notice-fee imposed, package plans - seasonal. **Amenities:** irons, hair dryers. **Pool(s):** heated outdoor. **Leisure Activities:** sauna, whirlpool. *Fee:* massage. **Cards:** MC, VI. ***(See color ad below)***

TAHOE LAKESIDE LODGE **Phone:** (530)544-9655 **182**

Motel

All Year	1P: $49-$115	2P: $69-$125	XP: $25 F12

Location: 0.3 mi n of US 50. 942 Poplar St 96150. Fax: 530/544-9657. **Facility:** 12 one-bedroom standard units. 1 story, exterior corridors. *Bath:* combo or shower only. **Parking:** on-site. **Pool(s):** outdoor. **Cards:** AX, DS, MC, VI.

ASK

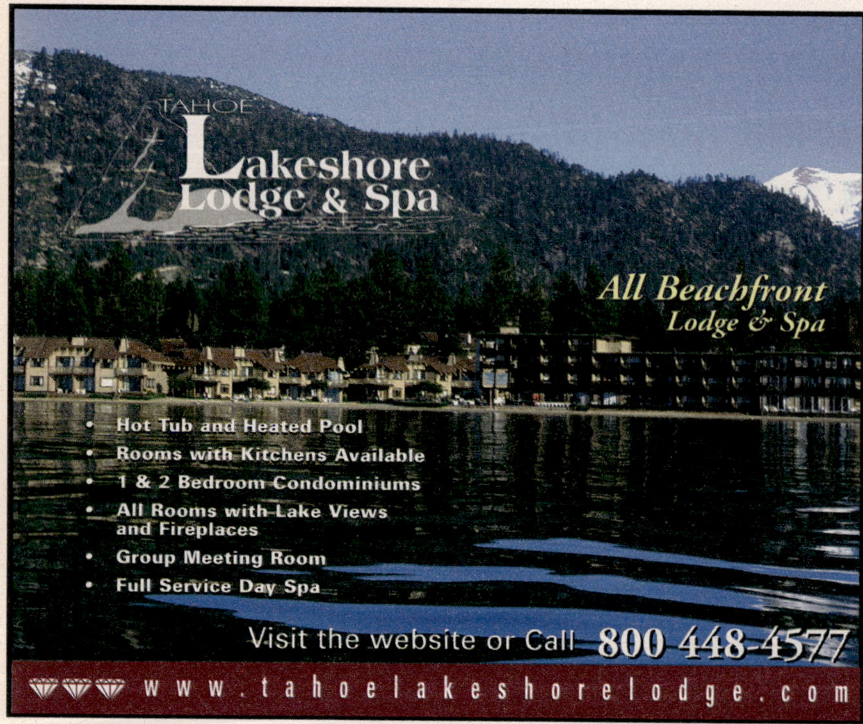

(See map and index starting on p. 363)

THE TAHOE SEASONS RESORT **Phone:** (530)541-6700 224

AAA SAVE

Small-scale Hotel

2/1-4/3 & 6/18-9/25	1P: $122-$196	2P: $122-$196
4/4-6/17 & 9/26-1/31	1P: $86-$196	2P: $86-$196

Location: 1.3 mi se off US 50; 0.5 mi ne on Saddle Rd. Located across from Heavenly Valley ski area. Saddle Rd at Keller Rd 96157 (PO Box 5656). Fax: 530/541-3143. **Facility:** 183 units. 171 one- and 12 two-bedroom standard units, some with whirlpools. 8 stories, interior corridors. *Bath:* combo or shower only. **Parking:** valet and street. **Terms:** check-in 4 pm. **Amenities:** voice mail, irons. **Dining:** 7 am-noon & 5-9 pm; closed Mon & Tues, cocktails. **Pool(s):** heated outdoor. **Leisure Activities:** whirlpool, 2 tennis courts, recreation programs, volleyball. *Fee:* downhill skiing, snowmobiling, tobogganing. **Guest Services:** gift shop, valet laundry, area transportation-casinos. **Business Services:** meeting rooms, fax. **Cards:** AX, DC, MC, VI.

TAHOE SUNDOWNER MOTEL **Phone:** 530/541-2282 232

AAA SAVE

Motel

All Year	1P: $30-$195	2P: $35-$250	XP: $10	F5

Location: US 50, 0.5 mi n of airport. 1211 Emerald Bay Rd 96150. Fax: 530/541-6388. **Facility:** 16 units. 15 one- and 1 two-bedroom standard units. 1 story, exterior corridors. *Bath:* shower only. **Parking:** on-site. **Terms:** 5 day cancellation notice-fee imposed, pets ($50 deposit, $5 extra charge, in limited units). **Leisure Activities:** whirlpool. **Cards:** AX, DS, MC, VI. **Special Amenities: free local telephone calls and preferred room (subject to availability with advanced reservations).**

SOME UNITS

FEE

TAHOE VALLEY LODGE *Book at aaa.com* **Phone:** (530)541-0353 229

AAA SAVE

Motel

All Year	1P: $75-$195	2P: $95-$295	XP: $30

Location: 0.5 mi e of jct US 50 and SR 89, at Tahoe Keys Blvd. 2241 Lake Tahoe Blvd 96150. Fax: 530/541-6289. **Facility:** 19 units. 17 one-bedroom standard units. 2 one-bedroom suites ($145-$395). 2 stories, exterior corridors. *Bath:* combo or shower only. **Parking:** on-site. **Terms:** 7 day cancellation notice-fee imposed, pets ($10 extra charge, small dogs only, in limited units). **Pool(s):** outdoor. **Leisure Activities:** whirlpool. **Cards:** AX, CB, DC, DS, MC, VI. *(See ad p 392)*

SOME UNITS

FEE

THUNDERCHIEF MOTEL **Phone:** (530)541-6231 202

Motel

All Year	1P: $30-$175	2P: $35-$200	XP: $5	F10

Location: Corner of Echo Rd and Pioneer Tr. 1008 Echo Rd 96150. Fax: 530/544-3820. **Facility:** 15 one-bedroom standard units. 2 stories, exterior corridors. *Bath:* shower only. **Parking:** on-site. **Terms:** 3 day cancellation notice-fee imposed. **Cards:** AX, DC, MC, VI.

SOME UNITS

ASK

VIKING MOTOR LODGE **Phone:** (530)541-5155 181

AAA SAVE

Motel

6/11-9/11 [CP]	1P: $75-$85	2P: $75-$95	XP: $5	F12
2/1-6/10 & 9/12-1/31 [CP]	1P: $55-$60	2P: $55-$70	XP: $5	F12

Location: US 50, exit Friday Ave, toward lake on Cedar Ave; near casino center. 4083 Cedar Ave 96150. Fax: 530/541-5643. **Facility:** 74 units. 73 one- and 1 two-bedroom standard units, some with efficiencies. 2 stories (no elevator), exterior corridors. *Bath:* combo or shower only. **Parking:** on-site. **Terms:** 2 night minimum stay - weekends 6/12-9/11, package plans. **Pool(s):** heated outdoor. **Leisure Activities:** whirlpool. **Cards:** AX, CB, DC, DS, MC, VI. **Special Amenities: free continental breakfast and free local telephone calls.**

SOME UNITS

The following lodgings were either not evaluated or did not meet AAA rating requirements but are listed for your information only.

LAKE TAHOE ACCOMMODATIONS **Phone:** 530/544-3234

fyi

Not evaluated. **Location:** 2048 Dunlap Dr, Suite 4 96150. Facilities, services, and decor characterize a mid-range property. ***(See color ad p 370)***

STATE LINE LODGE **Phone:** 530/544-3075

fyi

Motel

Did not meet all AAA rating requirements for some property operations at time of last evaluation on 12/07/2002. **Location:** 0.3 mi w of casino center. 913 Friday Ave 96150. Facilities, services, and decor characterize a basic property.

WHERE TO DINE

CHEF LEE CHINA BISTRO **Lunch:** $6-$9 **Dinner:** $6-$16 **Phone:** 530/542-4568 95

AAA

Chinese

Location: SR 89; 0.5 mi n of US 50. 871 Emerald Bay Rd 96150. **Hours:** 11:30 am-9:30 pm. **Reservations:** accepted. **Features:** Lunch and dinner guests appreciate the authentic look and taste of dishes on the extensive Mandarin menu. Meals are served family style. Casual dress; beer & wine only. **Parking:** on-site. **Cards:** AX, MC, VI.

EVANS AMERICAN GOURMET CAFE **Dinner:** $18-$26 **Phone:** 530/542-1990 93

American

Location: On SR 89, 1 mi n of US 50. 536 Emerald Bay Rd 96150. **Hours:** 5:30 pm-9:30 pm, Sat-10 pm. Closed major holidays. **Reservations:** suggested. **Features:** The atmosphere in the dining room is quiet and cozy. Creative California cuisine emphasizes fresh ingredients. Dressy casual; cocktails. **Parking:** on-site. **Cards:** DC, DS, MC, VI.

(See map and index starting on p. 363)

HEIDI'S PANCAKE HOUSE **Lunch:** $6-$12 **Phone:** 530/544-8113 (89)

American

Location: 1.5 mi w of casino center; in South Tahoe Travelodge. 3485 Lake Tahoe Blvd 96150. **Hours:** 7 am-2 pm. **Features:** An area tradition for more than 40 years, the Bavarian eatery appeals to tourists and locals alike. Tried-and-true breakfast favorites include huge, four-egg omelets, waffles and crepes. The lunch menu has a good selection. Casual dress. **Parking:** on-site. **Cards:** MC, VI.

LEWMARNEL'S **Lunch:** $5-$10 **Dinner:** $14-$30 **Phone:** 530/542-1072 (86)

Continental

Location: 3.5 blks from casino center; just n off US 50 via Lake Park Ave; in Best Western Station House Inn. 901 Park Ave 96157. **Hours:** 7:30-10 am, 11-4 & 5:30-10 pm, Sat & Sun 7 am-4 & 5:30-10:30 pm. Closed: Wed & 12/1-12/17. **Reservations:** suggested. **Features:** A rustic, western atmosphere invites diners to relax. On the varied menu are plenty of steak and seafood choices. Dressy casual; cocktails. **Parking:** on-site. **Cards:** AX, CB, DC, MC, VI. *(See color ad p 376)*

THE SWISS CHALET **Dinner:** $13-$22 **Phone:** 530/544-3304 (92)

Continental

Location: 4 mi w of Stateline; on US 50 at Sierra Blvd. 2544 Lake Tahoe Blvd Blvd 96158. **Hours:** 5 pm-10 pm. Closed: 4/11, 12/25; also Mon & 11/15-12/3. **Reservations:** suggested. **Features:** Chalet decor lends a warm, cozy feel to the casual restaurant. European, German and Swiss selections line a menu that also includes steak and seafood. Casual dress; cocktails. **Parking:** on-site. **Cards:** AX, MC, VI.

TEP'S VILLA ROMA **Dinner:** $9-$19 **Phone:** 530/541-8227 (90)

Italian

Location: 1.5 mi w of Stateline. 3450 Lake Tahoe Blvd 96150. **Hours:** 5 pm-10 pm, Sat-10:30 pm. Closed: 11/25. **Features:** Patrons of the laid-back restaurant can order from an array of fresh seafood specialties. The salad bar lines up a nice variety. Casual dress; cocktails. **Parking:** on-site. **Cards:** AX, MC, VI.

TAHOE CITY (See map and index starting on p. 363)

WHERE TO STAY

CHANEY HOUSE **Phone:** (530)525-7333 (103)

Bed & Breakfast

5/21-10/31 [BP]	1P: $165-$220	2P: $165-$220	XP: $25	D
2/1-5/20 & 11/1-1/31 [BP]	1P: $140-$195	2P: $140-$195	XP: $25	D

Location: SR 89, 0.5 mi s. 4725 W Lake Blvd 96145 (PO Box 7852). Fax: 530/525-4413. **Facility:** This house across from Lake Tahoe offers picturesque views of the surrounding mountains. 4 one-bedroom standard units. 2 stories, interior corridors. *Bath:* combo or shower only. **Parking:** on-site. **Terms:** 2 night minimum stay - weekends & 6/1-9/30, 14 day cancellation notice-fee imposed. **Amenities:** hair dryers. **Cards:** DC, MC, VI.

SOME UNITS

COTTAGE INN AT LAKE TAHOE **Phone:** (530)581-4073 (101)

Bed & Breakfast

All Year	1P: $150-$280	2P: $150-$280	XP: $20

Location: SR 89, 2 mi s. 1690 W Lake Blvd 96145 (PO Box 66). Fax: 530/581-0226. **Facility:** In a wooded area of mature trees, the inn offers attractively appointed guest units within walking distance of Lake Tahoe. 20 one-bedroom standard units, some with kitchens and/or whirlpools. 1 story, exterior corridors. *Bath:* combo or shower only. **Parking:** on-site. **Terms:** 2 night minimum stay - weekends, 14 day cancellation notice-fee imposed, [BP] meal plan available. **Leisure Activities:** sauna. **Cards:** MC, VI.

GRANLIBAKKEN RESORT & CONFERENCE CENTER **Phone:** (530)583-4242 (100)

SAVE

Resort Motel

All Year [BP]	1P: $110-$216	2P: $110-$216	XP: $25

Location: 0.8 mi s of jct SR 89 and 28, 0.6 mi w. 725 Granlibakken Rd 96145 (PO Box 6329). Fax: 530/583-7641. **Facility:** The resort, on 74 scenic wooded acres, is walking distance from Lake Tahoe; the main building includes a few smaller rooms. 110 units. 80 one-bedroom standard units. 20 two- and 10 three-bedroom suites ($242-$309) with kitchens. 3 stories, interior/exterior corridors. **Parking:** on-site. **Terms:** 2-5 night minimum stay - weekends, 30 day cancellation notice-fee imposed. **Amenities:** voice mail, hair dryers. **Pool(s):** heated outdoor. **Leisure Activities:** whirlpool, 5 tennis courts, tobogganing, hiking trails, jogging. *Fee:* downhill skiing. **Guest Services:** coin laundry. **Business Services:** conference facilities, PC. **Cards:** AX, DC, DS, MC, VI.

SOME UNITS

LAKE OF THE SKY MOTOR INN **Phone:** (530)583-3305 (97)

SAVE

Motel

7/1-8/21 [ECP]	1P: $79-$139	2P: $79-$139	XP: $5	F12
2/1-3/27 & 8/22-1/31 [ECP]	1P: $69-$119	2P: $69-$119	XP: $5	F12
3/28-6/30 [ECP]	1P: $59-$109	2P: $59-$109	XP: $5	F12

Location: 1 mi e of jct SR 89. 955 N Lake Blvd 96145 (PO Box 227). Fax: 530/583-7621. **Facility:** 23 one-bedroom standard units. 1 story, exterior corridors. *Bath:* shower only. **Parking:** on-site. **Terms:** 2 night minimum stay - seasonal & weekends, 3 day cancellation notice-fee imposed, package plans - seasonal & midweek. **Pool(s):** heated outdoor. **Business Services:** meeting rooms. **Cards:** AX, CB, DC, DS, MC, VI. **Special Amenities: free continental breakfast and free local telephone calls.** *(See color ad p 395)*

SOME UNITS

(See map and index starting on p. 363)

PEPPER TREE INN Book at aaa.com Phone: (530)583-3711 98

Motel

9/16-1/31 2P: $89-$159
2/1-9/15 2P: $54-$149

Location: SR 28, 0.5 mi e of SR 89. 645 N Lake Blvd 96145 (PO Box 29). Fax: 530/583-6938. **Facility:** 51 one-bedroom standard units. 7 stories, exterior corridors. *Bath:* combo or shower only. **Parking:** on-site. **Amenities:** irons, hair dryers. **Pool(s):** heated outdoor. **Leisure Activities:** whirlpool. **Guest Services:** coin laundry. **Cards:** AX, DC, MC, VI.

SOME UNITS

RIVER RANCH LODGE Phone: 530/583-4264 95

Motel

9/26-1/31 [ECP] 1P: $85-$175 2P: $85-$175 XP: $15 F7
2/1-4/17 & 6/11-9/25 [ECP] 1P: $115-$170 2P: $115-$170 XP: $15 F7
4/18-6/10 [ECP] 1P: $85-$130 2P: $85-$130 XP: $15 F7

Location: I-80, exit SR 89, 11 mi s. Adjacent to Alpine Meadows Ski Resort. SR 89 & Alpine Meadows Rd 96145 (PO Box 197). Fax: 530/583-7237. **Facility:** 19 one-bedroom standard units. 2 stories, interior/exterior corridors. *Bath:* combo or shower only. **Parking:** on-site. **Terms:** 2-3 night minimum stay - weekends, 3 day cancellation notice. **Amenities:** voice mail. **Leisure Activities:** hiking trails, jogging. **Cards:** AX, MC, VI.

SUNNYSIDE RESORT Phone: (530)583-7200 102

Country Inn

All Year [ECP] 1P: $100-$300 2P: $100-$300 XP: $10 F4

Location: SR 89, 2 mi s. 1850 W Lake Blvd 96145 (PO Box 5969). Fax: 530/583-2551. **Facility:** This refurbished 1908 residence offers comfortably furnished lodgings, most facing the lake, some with a fireplace. 23 one-bedroom standard units. 2 stories, interior/exterior corridors. **Parking:** on-site. **Terms:** 2-5 night minimum stay - weekends, 3 day cancellation notice-fee imposed. **Amenities:** irons, hair dryers. **Leisure Activities:** rental boats, rental canoes, fishing. *Fee:* sailboats, boat dock, waterskiing. **Business Services:** conference facilities. **Cards:** AX, DS, MC, VI.

SOME UNITS

TAHOE CITY TRAVELODGE Book at aaa.com Phone: (530)583-3766 99

SAVE

Motel

6/24-9/5 [CP] 1P: $98-$153 2P: $103-$153 XP: $10 F17
12/17-1/31 [CP] 1P: $93-$135 2P: $100-$135 XP: $10 F17
2/1-6/23 [CP] 1P: $74-$130 2P: $79-$130 XP: $10 F17
9/6-12/16 [CP] 1P: $63-$123 2P: $66-$128 XP: $10 F17

Location: SR 28, 0.3 mi e of jct SR 89. 455 N Lake Blvd 96145 (PO Box 84). Fax: 530/583-8045. **Facility:** 47 one-bedroom standard units. 2 stories, interior/exterior corridors. *Bath:* combo or shower only. **Parking:** on-site. **Terms:** 2 night minimum stay - seasonal weekends, 3 day cancellation notice, package plans - seasonal. **Amenities:** voice mail, irons, hair dryers. **Pool(s):** heated outdoor. **Leisure Activities:** sauna, whirlpool. **Cards:** AX, CB, DC, DS, MC, VI. **Special Amenities: free continental breakfast and free newspaper.** *(See color ad p 369)*

SOME UNITS

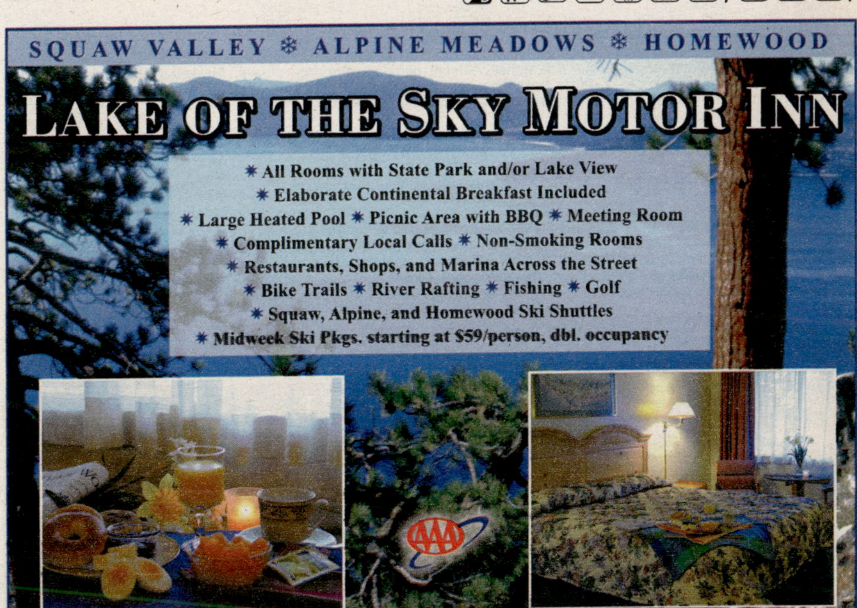

(See map and index starting on p. 363)

The following lodging was either not evaluated or did not meet AAA rating requirements but is listed for your information only.

LAKE TAHOE ACCOMMODATIONS **Phone:** 530/544-3234

Not evaluated. **Location:** SR 89 S. 905 N Lake Blvd 96145. Facilities, services, and decor characterize a mid-range property.

WHERE TO DINE

CHRISTY HILL RESTAURANT **Dinner:** $20-$38 **Phone:** 530/583-8551 (45)

American

Location: E off SR 28 toward lake. 115 Grove St, Tahoe City 96145. **Hours:** 5:30 pm-9:30 pm. Closed: 11/25, 12/25; also Mon & first 2 weeks in December. **Reservations:** suggested. **Features:** Menu offerings—made from such local ingredients as Pacific seafood—show an emphasis on California and French cooking. Furnished in attractive decor, the dining room affords views of the lake. Dressy casual; beer & wine only. **Parking:** on-site. **Cards:** AX, MC, VI.

TAHOE HOUSE **Lunch:** $6-$10 **Dinner:** $6-$10 **Phone:** 530/583-1377 (46)

Deli/Subs Sandwiches

Location: 0.8 mi s of Tahoe City on SR 89. 625 W Lake Blvd 96145. **Hours:** 6 am-6 pm. **Reservations:** suggested. **Features:** The European-style restaurant's menu lists choices of Swiss and California cuisine. Freshly baked breads and homemade desserts are delicious. Beer & wine only. **Parking:** on-site. **Cards:** AX, CB, DC, MC, VI.

TAHOE VISTA pop. 1,668 (See map and index starting on p. 363)

WHERE TO STAY

CEDAR GLEN LODGE-BEST VALUE INN & SUITES **Phone:** (530)546-4281 (27)

Motel

All Year	1P: $75-$120	2P: $75-$160

Location: SR 28, 1.5 mi w of SR 267; 3 mi w of casino center. 6589 N Lake Blvd 96148 (PO Box 188). Fax: 530/546-2250. **Facility:** 31 units. 7 one-bedroom standard units. 7 one-bedroom suites, some with efficiencies or kitchens. 17 cottages. 1-2 stories, exterior corridors. *Bath:* combo or shower only. **Parking:** on-site. **Terms:** 2-3 night minimum stay - weekends, 14 day cancellation notice-fee imposed, package plans. **Pool(s):** outdoor. **Leisure Activities:** sauna, whirlpool, playground. **Guest Services:** coin laundry. **Cards:** AX, DS, MC, VI. **Special Amenities: free newspaper.** *(See color ad below)*

SOME UNITS

FIRELITE LODGE **Phone:** (530)546-7222 (32)

Motel

2/1-3/31 [CP]	1P: $58-$98	2P: $62-$102
6/16-1/31 [CP]	1P: $59-$86	2P: $59-$94
4/1-6/15 [CP]	1P: $48-$62	2P: $48-$69

Location: SR 28, 1 mi w of SR 267. 7035 N Lake Blvd 96148 (PO Box 135). Fax: 530/546-7770. **Facility:** 27 one-bedroom standard units. 2 stories, exterior corridors. **Parking:** on-site. **Amenities:** hair dryers. **Pool(s):** heated outdoor. **Leisure Activities:** whirlpool. **Guest Services:** coin laundry. **Cards:** AX, DC, MC, VI. **Special Amenities: free continental breakfast and free local telephone calls.** *(See color ad p 368)*

SOME UNITS

FRANCISCAN LAKESIDE LODGE **Phone:** 530/546-6300 (31)

Motel

2/1-4/15 & 6/16-10/1	1P: $70	2P: $325	XP: $10	F12
4/16-6/15 & 10/2-1/31	1P: $52	2P: $245	XP: $10	F12

Location: SR 28, 1 mi w of SR 267. 6944 N Lake Blvd 96148 (PO Box 280). Fax: 530/546-0348. **Facility:** 63 units. 37 one-bedroom standard units with kitchens. 12 one-, 6 two- and 1 three-bedroom suites with kitchens. 7 cottages ($185-$250). 1-2 stories, exterior corridors. *Bath:* combo or shower only. **Parking:** on-site. **Terms:** 2-3 night minimum stay - seasonal, 14 day cancellation notice-fee imposed, package plans. **Pool(s):** heated outdoor. **Leisure Activities:** fishing, playground. **Cards:** AX, MC, VI. **Special Amenities: free local telephone calls.** *(See color ad p 369)*

SOME UNITS

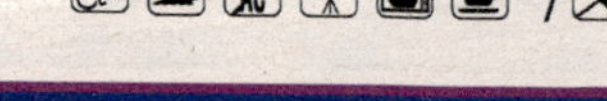

(See map and index starting on p. 363)

HOLIDAY HOUSE — Phone: (530)546-2369 (34)

Motel

All Year 1P: $115-$215 2P: $115-$215 XP: $15

Location: SR 28, 1 mi w of SR 267. 7276 N Lake Blvd 96148 (PO Box 229). Fax: 530/546-1438. **Facility:** 7 units. 6 one-bedroom standard units with kitchens. 1 one-bedroom suite ($115-$215) with kitchen. 2 stories, exterior corridors. **Parking:** on-site. **Terms:** 14 day cancellation notice, small pets only ($30 fee, $100 deposit). **Amenities:** hair dryers. **Leisure Activities:** whirlpool. **Guest Services:** coin laundry. **Cards:** DC, DS, MC, VI.

FEE

MOURELATOS LAKESHORE RESORT — Phone: 530/546-9500 (28)

SAVE

Motel

All Year 1P: $99-$355 2P: $99-$355 XP: $15

Location: SR 28, 1.2 mi w of SR 267. Located in a secluded area. 6834 N Lake Blvd 96148 (PO Box 77). Fax: 530/546-2744. **Facility:** 32 one-bedroom standard units, some with kitchens and/or whirlpools. 2 stories, exterior corridors. **Parking:** on-site. **Terms:** cancellation fee imposed. **Amenities:** hair dryers. **Leisure Activities:** whirlpools. **Business Services:** meeting rooms. **Cards:** AX, DC, DS, MC, VI. **Special Amenities: free local telephone calls and early check-in/late check-out.** *(See color ad below)*

DATA PORT

RED WOLF LAKESIDE LODGE — Phone: (530)546-6262 (35)

Motel

2/1-4/15 & 5/15-9/30 1P: $150-$275
10/1-1/31 1P: $125-$275
4/16-5/14 1P: $125-$175

Location: SR 28, just w of SR 267. 7630 N Lake Blvd 96148. Fax: 530/546-1572. **Facility:** 27 units. 5 one-bedroom standard units with kitchens and whirlpools. 16 one- and 6 two-bedroom suites with kitchens and whirlpools. 2 stories, exterior corridors. **Parking:** on-site. **Terms:** 4 day cancellation notice. **Amenities:** irons, hair dryers. **Pool(s):** heated outdoor. **Leisure Activities:** whirlpool. **Guest Services:** coin laundry. **Cards:** AX, DS, MC, VI.

ASK DATA PORT SOME UNITS

SHORE HOUSE AT LAKE TAHOE, THE — Phone: (530)546-7270 (33)

SAVE

Bed & Breakfast

5/28-10/2 [BP] 1P: $220-$310 2P: $220-$310
10/3-1/31 [BP] 1P: $210-$285 2P: $210-$285
2/1-5/27 [BP] 1P: $190-$255 2P: $190-$255

Location: SR 28, 1 mi w of jct SR 28 and 267. 7170 N Lake Blvd 96148 (PO Box 499). Fax: 530/546-7130. **Facility:** The property is on the northern shore of Lake Tahoe and offers lake access and a private dock; all guests units have gas fireplaces. 9 one-bedroom standard units, some with whirlpools. 2 stories, exterior corridors. *Bath:* combo or shower only. **Parking:** on-site. **Terms:** 2-3 night minimum stay - weekends, 14 day cancellation notice-fee imposed. **Amenities:** CD players. **Leisure Activities:** whirlpool. *Fee:* massage. **Guest Services:** complimentary evening beverages. **Cards:** DS, MC, VI.

TAHOE EDGELAKE BEACH CLUB — Phone: 530/546-5974 (36)

Condominium

All Year 1P: $175-$225 2P: $175-$225

Location: SR 28, just w of SR 267. 7680 N Lake Blvd 96148 (PO Box 318). Fax: 530/546-5112. **Facility:** The resort, located on 240 feet of sandy beach and the clear blue water of Lake Tahoe, invites guests to lounge by the outdoor pool and spa. 32 units. 11 one-, 20 two- and 1 three-bedroom suites with kitchens. 2 stories, exterior corridors. **Parking:** on-site. **Terms:** 30 day cancellation notice-fee imposed, [ECP] meal plan available. **Amenities:** DVD players, CD players, voice mail, irons, hair dryers. **Pool(s):** heated outdoor. **Leisure Activities:** whirlpool, playground, exercise room. **Cards:** AX, DC, DS, MC, VI.

ASK DATA PORT

(See map and index starting on p. 363)

TAHOE VISTANA INN

Motel

Phone: (530)546-2529 25

All Year 1P: $46-$106 2P: $46-$116 XP: $6

Location: SR 28, 1.5 mi w of SR 267. Located opposite the beach. 6549 N Lake Blvd 96148 (PO Box 316). Fax: 530/546-0308. **Facility:** 29 units. 27 one-bedroom standard units, some with efficiencies. 2 one-bedroom suites with kitchens, some with whirlpools. 1 story, exterior corridors. *Bath:* combo or shower only. **Parking:** on-site. **Terms:** 2-3 night minimum stay - seasonal, 3 day cancellation notice-fee imposed. **Pool(s):** heated outdoor. **Leisure Activities:** whirlpool. **Cards:** AX, DC, MC, VI. **Special Amenities: free local telephone calls.** *(See color ad below)*

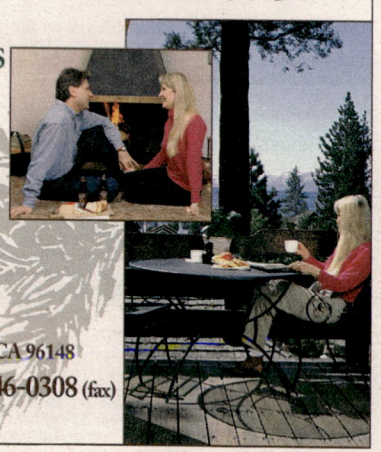

AAA TourBookMark

Lodging Listing Symbols

Member Values

(see pg. 14)

- Official Appointment
- Offers minimum 10% discount
- SYC&S chain partners
- May offer discount
- Offers senior discount
- Informational listing only

Member Services

- Airport transportation
- Pets allowed
- Restaurant on premises
- Restaurant off premises (walking distance)
- 24-hour room service
- Cocktail lounge
- Child care

Accessibility Features

(see pg. 18)

- Accessibility features
- Roll-in showers
- Hearing impaired

Leisure Activities

- Full Service Casino
- Pool
- Health Club on premises
- Health Club off premises
- Recreational activities

In-Room Amenities

- Non-smoking rooms
- No air conditioning
- No TV
- No Cable TV
- VCR
- Movies
- Data port/modem line
- No telephones
- Refrigerator
- Microwave
- Coffee maker

Call property for detailed information about fees & restrictions relating to the lodging listing symbols.

CHOICE HOTELS INTERNATIONAL®

(See map and index starting on p. 363)

WHERE TO DINE

LE PETIT PIER — Dinner: $19-$40 — Phone: 530/546-4464 (1)

French

Location: SR 28, 0.5 mi w of SR 267. 7238 N Lake Blvd 96148. **Hours:** 5:30 pm-10 pm. Closed: Tues. **Reservations:** suggested. **Features:** View of lake and mountains; quiet atmosphere. Dressy casual; cocktails. **Parking:** on-site. **Cards:** AX, DC, MC, VI.

TRUCKEE pop. 13,864 (See map and index starting on p. 363)

WHERE TO STAY

ALPINE COUNTRY LODGE — Phone: 530/587-3801 (7)

Motel

12/16-1/31	1P: $75-$160	2P: $75-$160
2/1-12/15	1P: $60-$150	2P: $60-$150

Location: I-80, exit Donner Pass Rd, just s. 12260 Deerfield Dr 96161. Fax: 530/587-3692. **Facility:** 28 units. 15 one-bedroom standard units. 13 one-bedroom suites ($98-$160), some with kitchens. 2 stories, exterior corridors. **Parking:** on-site. **Terms:** 2 night minimum stay - weekends, cancellation fee imposed, small pets only ($10 fee). **Cards:** AX, DS, MC, VI.

SOME UNITS

FEE

BEST WESTERN TRUCKEE TAHOE INN — *Book at aaa.com* — Phone: (530)587-4525 (9)

SAVE

Motel

2/1-4/10 & 6/11-9/30 [ECP]	1P: $106-$179	2P: $113-$179	XP: $7	F13
10/1-1/31 [ECP]	1P: $88-$179	2P: $95-$179	XP: $7	F13
4/11-6/10 [ECP]	1P: $88-$106	2P: $95-$115	XP: $7	F13

Location: I-80, exit 267, 1.5 mi se. 11331 Brockway Rd 96161. Fax: 530/587-8173. **Facility:** Smoke free premises. 100 one-bedroom standard units. 2 stories, interior corridors. **Parking:** on-site. **Terms:** package plans - seasonal. **Amenities:** video library, irons, hair dryers. **Dining:** 11 am-10 pm, Sat & Sun from 4 pm. **Pool(s):** heated outdoor. **Leisure Activities:** sauna, whirlpool, exercise room. **Guest Services:** coin laundry. **Business Services:** meeting rooms. **Cards:** AX, CB, DC, DS, MC, VI. **Special Amenities: free expanded continental breakfast and free local telephone calls.** *(See color ad below)*

DONNER LAKE VILLAGE RESORT — Phone: (530)587-6081 (3)

SAVE

Motel

5/28-10/4 & 12/17-1/31	1P: $130-$275	2P: $130-$275	XP: $10	F12
2/1-5/27	1P: $90-$225	2P: $90-$225	XP: $10	F12
10/5-12/16	1P: $80-$185	2P: $80-$185	XP: $10	F12

Location: I-80, exit Donner Lake, 4 mi w, on Old Hwy 40 at west end of lake. 15695 Donner Pass Rd 96161. Fax: 530/587-8782. **Facility:** 64 units. 58 one-bedroom standard units, some with kitchens. 6 one-bedroom suites with kitchens. 2 stories, interior/exterior corridors. **Parking:** on-site. **Terms:** 2-5 night minimum stay - weekends, 5 day cancellation notice. **Leisure Activities:** saunas, rental boats, rental canoes, rental paddleboats, marina, waterskiing, fishing, hiking trails. *Fee:* jet ski. **Guest Services:** coin laundry. **Cards:** AX, DS, MC, VI. **Special Amenities: early check-in/late check-out and free room upgrade (subject to availability with advanced reservations).** *(See color ad p 400)*

SOME UNITS

FEE

HOLIDAY INN EXPRESS — *Book at aaa.com* — Phone: (530)582-9999 (5)

SAVE

Motel

2/1-4/3 & 7/3-1/31 [ECP]	1P: $114-$189	2P: $114-$189
4/4-7/2 [ECP]	1P: $89-$139	2P: $89-$139

Location: I-80, exit Donner Pass Rd. Located adjacent to Donner Memorial State Park. 10527 Cold Stream Rd 96161. Fax: 530/582-9996. **Facility:** 65 one-bedroom standard units. 3 stories, interior corridors. **Parking:** on-site. **Terms:** cancellation fee imposed. **Amenities:** dual phone lines, voice mail, irons, hair dryers. **Pool(s):** heated outdoor. **Leisure Activities:** whirlpool. **Guest Services:** coin laundry. **Cards:** AX, CB, DC, DS, JC, MC, VI. **Special Amenities: free local telephone calls and free newspaper.** *(See color ad p 400)*

(See map and index starting on p. 363)

THE INN AT TRUCKEE *Book at aaa.com* **Phone:** (530)587-8888 6

Motel

6/18-9/11 & 12/10-1/31	1P: $90-$125	2P: $100-$135
2/1-6/17	1P: $69-$110	2P: $79-$135
9/12-12/9	1P: $69-$110	2P: $79-$120

Location: I-80, exit SR 89, just s. 11506 Deerfield Dr 96161. Fax: 530/587-1568. **Facility:** 43 one-bedroom standard units. 3 stories (no elevator), interior corridors. **Parking:** on-site. **Terms:** 3 day cancellation notice, [CP] meal plan available, small pets only ($11 fee). **Leisure Activities:** sauna, whirlpool. **Guest Services:** coin laundry. **Cards:** AX, DS, MC, VI. ***(See color ad below)***

SOME UNITS

FEE

NORTHSTAR AT TAHOE **Phone:** (530)562-1010 10

SAVE

Resort Condominium

All Year	1P: $155-$900	2P: $155-$900

Location: I-80, exit SR 267, 7 mi se; exit SR 28 at Kings Beach SR 267, 6 mi n. SR 267 & Northstar Dr 96160 (PO Box 129). Fax: 530/562-2215. **Facility:** On spacious grounds in a mountain setting, the property offers one- to four-bedroom housekeeping units, most with fireplaces. 254 units. 164 one-bedroom standard units, some with kitchens. 69 two-bedroom suites ($150-$300) with kitchens. 21 vacation homes ($400-$900). 2-3 stories (no elevator), interior/exterior corridors. **Parking:** on-site. **Terms:** check-in 4 pm, 2 night minimum stay, 14 day cancellation notice-fee imposed, package plans. **Dining:** 2 restaurants, 8 am-9 pm, cocktails. **Pool(s):** heated outdoor. **Leisure Activities:** saunas, whirlpools, 10 tennis courts, recreation programs, rental bicycles. *Fee:* golf-18 holes, downhill & cross country skiing, ski equipment, horseback riding. **Guest Services:** coin laundry. **Cards:** AX, DS, MC, VI. **Special Amenities: free local telephone calls.**

SOME UNITS

RICHARDSON HOUSE **Phone:** 530/587-5388 8

Historic Bed & Breakfast

All Year [BP]	1P: $100-$175	2P: $100-$175	XP: $25

Location: Just up the hill overlooking historic downtown. 10154 High St 96161 (PO Box 2011). Fax: 530/587-0927. **Facility:** Richardson House is within walking distance of several restaurants. Smoke free premises. 8 one-bedroom standard units. 2 stories (no elevator), interior corridors. *Bath:* some shared or private, combo or shower only. **Parking:** on-site. **Terms:** 2-4 night minimum stay - seasonal & weekends, age restrictions may apply, 8 day cancellation notice-fee imposed, package plans. **Cards:** AX, DC, DS, MC, VI.

SOME UNITS

Nearby Nevada

INCLINE VILLAGE pop. 9,952 (See map and index starting on p. 363)

WHERE TO STAY

CLUB TAHOE Phone: (775)831-5750 63

Condominium

6/11-9/9	1P: $190-$250	2P: $190-$250
2/1-4/15	1P: $165-$250	2P: $165-$250
4/16-6/10 & 9/10-1/31	1P: $145-$250	2P: $145-$250

Location: SR 28 at N Village Blvd, 0.3 mi e. Located in North Lake Tahoe area. 914 Northwood Blvd 89451 (PO Box 7440, 89452). Fax: 775/832-9400. **Facility:** Featuring fireplaces, decks, lofts and laundry facilities, these two-bedroom units are on pine-shaded, manicured grounds alongside a creek. 92 two-bedroom suites with kitchens. 2 stories, exterior corridors. **Parking:** on-site. **Terms:** check-in 4 pm, 2-7 night minimum stay - seasonal, 14 day cancellation notice, weekly rates available. **Amenities:** voice mail, irons. **Pool(s):** heated outdoor. **Leisure Activities:** sauna, whirlpools, 2 lighted tennis courts, racquetball courts, recreation programs. **Business Services:** meeting rooms. **Cards:** DS, MC, VI.

HYATT REGENCY LAKE TAHOE RESORT & CASINO *Book at aaa.com* Phone: (775)832-1234 66

AAA SAVE

Large-scale Hotel

5/23-9/6 & 12/19-1/31	1P: $195-$345	2P: $195-$345	XP: $25	F18
2/1-5/22 & 9/7-12/18	1P: $130-$250	2P: $130-$250	XP: $25	F18

Location: 0.5 mi w of SR 28, toward lake via Country Club Dr; 2 mi s of Mt Rose Hwy. Lakeshore at Country Club Dr 89450 (PO Box 3239). Fax: 775/831-7508. **Facility:** Nestled in the pines, the resort offers extensive recreational facilities and manicured grounds; some rooms front on a private Lake Tahoe beach. 424 units. 397 one-bedroom standard units. 27 one-bedroom suites. 12 stories, interior corridors. **Parking:** valet. **Terms:** 14 day cancellation notice-fee imposed, $10 service charge. **Amenities:** voice mail, irons, hair dryers. **Dining:** 3 restaurants, 24 hours, cocktails. **Pool(s):** heated outdoor, heated indoor/outdoor, wading. **Leisure Activities:** saunas, whirlpools, 2 tennis courts, recreation programs, rental bicycles, spa. *Fee:* sailboats, jet ski, kayak. **Guest Services:** valet laundry. **Business Services:** conference facilities. **Cards:** AX, CB, DC, DS, JC, MC, VI. *(See color ad below)*

SOME UNITS

THE INN AT INCLINE *Book at aaa.com* Phone: 775/831-1052 64

AAA SAVE

Motel

6/1-9/30 [CP]	1P: $99-$179	2P: $99-$179	XP: $15	F12
2/1-5/31 & 10/1-1/31	1P: $69-$149	2P: $69-$149	XP: $15	F12

Location: On SR 28, e of Country Club Dr. Located in North Lake Tahoe area. 1003 Tahoe Blvd 89451. Fax: 775/831-3016. **Facility:** 38 one-bedroom standard units. 2 stories, interior/exterior corridors. **Parking:** on-site. **Terms:** 2 night minimum stay - weekends & seasonal 6/1-9/30, 7 day cancellation notice. **Pool(s):** heated indoor. **Leisure Activities:** sauna, whirlpool. **Cards:** AX, DS, MC, VI. **Special Amenities: free continental breakfast and free local telephone calls.**

The following lodging was either not evaluated or did not meet AAA rating requirements but is listed for your information only

LAKE TAHOE ACCOMMODATIONS Phone: 775/832-4475

fyi

Not evaluated. **Location:** SR 267 S to SR 28 N. 800 Southwood Blvd, Suite 112 89451. Facilities, services, and decor characterize a mid-range property.

WHERE TO DINE

AZZARA'S ITALIAN RESTAURANT **Dinner:** $10-$17 Phone: 775/831-0346 15

Italian

Location: On SR 28 (Tahoe Blvd). 930 Tahoe Blvd 89450. **Hours:** 5 pm-9:30 pm. Closed: 4/11, 11/25, 12/24, 12/25; also Mon. **Features:** European decor gives the dining room a charming feel. Seafood is prominent on the varied menu. Casual dress; cocktails. **Parking:** on-site. **Cards:** AX, MC, VI.

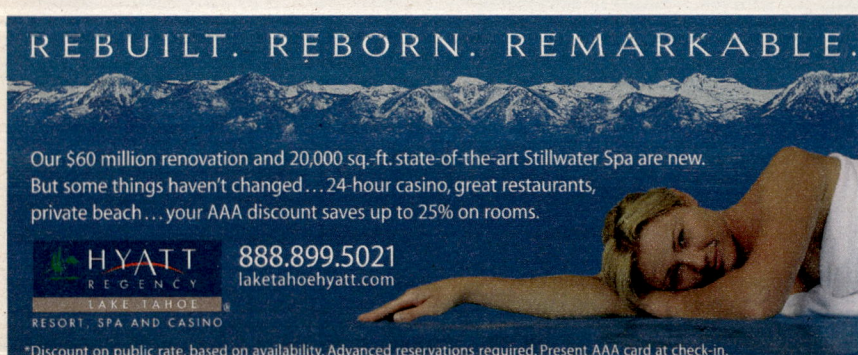

(See map and index starting on p. 363)

CAFE 333 Lunch: $7-$12 Dinner: $14-$26 Phone: 775/832-7333 (16)

Traditional American

Location: 0.3 mi n of SR 28. 333 Village Blvd 89451. **Hours:** 7 am-3 & 5:30-9 pm. Closed: 12/25. **Reservations:** suggested. **Features:** The dining room is adorned in pretty French country decor, while the beautiful garden area overlooks a waterfall. Casual dress; cocktails. **Parking:** on-site. **Cards:** MC, VI.

STATELINE pop. 1,215 (See map and index starting on p. 363)

WHERE TO STAY

CAESARS TAHOE Book at aaa.com Phone: (775)588-3515 142

12/21-1/31	1P: $79-$300	2P: $79-$300	XP: $20	F16
6/1-8/31	1P: $130-$250	2P: $130-$250	XP: $20	F16
2/1-5/31	1P: $90-$180	2P: $90-$180	XP: $20	F16
9/1-12/20	1P: $70-$165	2P: $70-$165	XP: $20	F16

Large-scale Hotel **Location:** At casino center. 55 Hwy 50 89449 (PO Box 5800). Fax: 775/586-2068. **Facility:** 440 units. 401 one-bedroom standard units, some with whirlpools. 30 one- and 9 two-bedroom suites with whirlpools. 14 stories, interior corridors. *Bath:* combo or shower only. **Parking:** on-site and valet. **Terms:** 4 day cancellation notice-fee imposed. **Amenities:** high-speed Internet (fee), voice mail, safes, irons, hair dryers. **Dining:** 3 restaurants, 24 hours; buffet $8-$21, cocktails, also, The Broiler Room, see separate listing, nightclub, name entertainment. **Pool(s):** heated indoor. **Leisure Activities:** saunas, whirlpool. *Fee:* 4 lighted tennis courts, massage. **Guest Services:** gift shop, valet laundry, area transportation. **Business Services:** meeting rooms, business center. **Cards:** AX, DC, DS, JC, MC, VI.

SOME UNITS

FEE

HARRAH'S HOTEL & CASINO Book at aaa.com Phone: (775)588-6611 144

6/13-9/20	1P: $176-$253	2P: $176-$253	XP: $20
2/1-6/12 & 9/21-1/31	1P: $132-$231	2P: $132-$231	XP: $20

Large-scale Hotel **Location:** In casino area. Hwy 50 89449 (PO Box 8). Fax: 775/586-6607. **Facility:** The property, which offers many rooms with views of a lake and mountains, has well-maintained public areas featuring shops and restaurants. 531 units. 517 one-bedroom standard units. 14 one-bedroom suites with whirlpools. 18 stories, interior corridors. *Bath:* combo or shower only. **Parking:** on-site and valet. **Terms:** check-in 4 pm, 3 day cancellation notice-fee imposed, pets ($15 extra charge, in kennel). **Amenities:** video games (fee), voice mail, honor bars, irons, hair dryers. *Some:* dual phone lines, safes. **Dining:** 6 restaurants, 24 hours; buffet $12-$26, cocktails, also, The Summit Room, Friday's Station, see separate listings, entertainment. **Pool(s):** heated indoor. **Leisure Activities:** whirlpools. *Fee:* massage, game room. **Guest Services:** gift shop, valet laundry, area transportation. **Business Services:** conference facilities. **Cards:** AX, DC, DS, MC, VI.

SOME UNITS

FEE FEE FEE

HARVEYS CASINO & RESORT Book at aaa.com Phone: (775)588-2411 143

6/13-9/20	1P: $165-$230	2P: $165-$230	XP: $20
2/1-6/12 & 9/21-1/31	1P: $121-$187	2P: $121-$187	XP: $20

Large-scale Hotel **Location:** US 50, in casino center. (PO Box 128). Fax: 775/588-6643. **Facility:** Near recreation areas, this property offers on-site shops and restaurants as well as many rooms with a view. 740 units. 714 one-bedroom standard units. 26 one-bedroom suites with whirlpools. 19 stories, interior corridors. *Bath:* combo or shower only. **Parking:** on-site and valet. **Terms:** check-in 4 pm, 3 day cancellation notice-fee imposed, pets ($15 extra charge, in kennel). **Amenities:** video games (fee), voice mail, irons, hair dryers. *Some:* safes, honor bars. **Dining:** 6 restaurants, 24 hours; buffet $12-$26, cocktails, also, Sage Room Steak House, Llewellyn's, Josh's, El Vaquero, see separate listings, entertainment. **Pool(s):** heated outdoor. **Leisure Activities:** whirlpool. *Fee:* massage, game room. **Guest Services:** gift shop, valet laundry, area transportation. **Business Services:** conference facilities, business center. **Cards:** AX, DC, DS, MC, VI.

SOME UNITS

FEE FEE FEE

HORIZON CASINO RESORT Book at aaa.com Phone: (775)588-6211 140

All Year	1P: $119-$199	2P: $119-$199	XP: $10	F12

Large-scale Hotel **Location:** Located in the casino area. 50 Hwy 50 89449 (PO Box C). Fax: 775/588-1344. **Facility:** 539 units. 535 one-bedroom standard units, some with whirlpools. 4 one-bedroom suites ($300-$500) with whirlpools. 9-15 stories, interior corridors. **Parking:** on-site and valet. **Terms:** check-in 4 pm, cancellation fee imposed, package plans - seasonal. **Amenities:** voice mail, irons, hair dryers. **Dining:** Josh's, see separate listing. **Pool(s):** heated outdoor, wading. **Leisure Activities:** whirlpools, exercise room. *Fee:* game room. **Guest Services:** gift shop, valet laundry. **Business Services:** meeting rooms, business center. **Cards:** AX, DC, DS, MC, VI.

SOME UNITS

LAKESIDE INN AND CASINO Book at aaa.com Phone: (775)588-7777 146

6/1-8/31	2P: $89-$149	XP: $10	F16
2/1-5/31 & 9/1-1/31	2P: $49-$109	XP: $10	F16

Motel **Location:** On US 50; 1 mi e of state line at Kingsbury Grade. 168 Hwy 50 89449 (PO Box 5640). Fax: 775/588-4092. **Facility:** 124 units. 122 one-bedroom standard units. 2 one-bedroom suites ($150-$250) with whirlpools. 2 stories, interior/exterior corridors. *Bath:* combo or shower only. **Parking:** on-site. **Terms:** check-in 3:30 pm, 1-2 night minimum stay - seasonal & weekends, cancellation fee imposed, [AP] meal plan available, package plans - seasonal & weekends. **Amenities:** voice mail, irons, hair dryers. **Dining:** 2 restaurants, 24 hours, cocktails, also, Taberna, Timber House Restaurant, see separate listings. **Pool(s):** heated outdoor. **Leisure Activities:** whirlpool. **Cards:** AX, DC, MC, VI. *(See color ad p 387)*

SOME UNITS

(See map and index starting on p. 363)

LAKE VILLAGE RESORT Phone: (775)589-6065 141

Condominium

All Year 1P: $145-$425 2P: $145-$425

Location: Near casino center. 301 Hwy 50 89449 (PO box 4827). Fax: 775/589-6056. **Facility:** Enjoy all the comforts of home while taking in all the casinos as well as the snow skiing and Lake Tahoe water sports. 30 units. 12 two- and 18 three-bedroom suites, some with whirlpools. Exterior corridors. **Parking:** on-site. **Terms:** 2-7 night minimum stay - seasonal weekends, 30 day cancellation notice-fee imposed, weekly rates available, package plans, pets ($100 deposit, $20 extra charge, in limited units). **Amenities:** irons. *Some:* hair dryers. **Pool(s):** heated outdoor. **Leisure Activities:** saunas, whirlpool, 4 tennis courts, playground. *Fee:* sailboats, downhill skiing, massage. **Guest Services:** complimentary laundry. **Business Services:** meeting rooms, fax. **Cards:** AX, DS, MC, VI.

SOME UNITS

FEE

THE RIDGE TAHOE Book at aaa.com Phone: (775)588-3553 147

SAVE

Condominium

2/1-3/25 & 6/18-9/5 1P: $160-$175 2P: $265-$280

3/26-6/17 & 9/6-1/31 1P: $115-$175 2P: $190-$280

Location: 3 mi e of US 50 via Kingsbury Grade, 0.8 mi s via Tramway Dr, then 1.3 mi e on Quaking Aspen Ln. 400 Ridge Club Dr 89449 (PO Box 5790). Fax: 775/588-7099. **Facility:** Perched at 7,600 feet, the property has a gondola to the ski lift and offers a range of accommodations, including some with kitchens and fireplaces. 539 units. 237 one-bedroom standard units. 242 one- and 60 two-bedroom suites ($190-$495), some with kitchens and/or whirlpools. 4-11 stories, interior/exterior corridors. **Parking:** on-site. **Terms:** check-in 4 pm, 3 day cancellation notice-fee imposed. **Amenities:** voice mail, safes, irons, hair dryers. *Some:* CD players. **Dining:** 11 am-2:30 & 5-8 pm; Sunday brunch 10 am-1:30 pm, cocktails. **Pool(s):** 2 heated outdoor, heated indoor/outdoor. **Leisure Activities:** saunas, whirlpool, putting green, 4 tennis courts (1 indoor, 2 lighted), racquetball courts, recreation programs, children's sled area, playground. *Fee:* downhill skiing, game room. **Guest Services:** complimentary laundry, area transportation-casinos. **Business Services:** meeting rooms, fax. **Cards:** AX, DS, MC, VI. *(See color ad p 388)*

SOME UNITS

TAHOE SUMMIT VILLAGE Book at aaa.com Phone: (775)588-8571 145

Condominium

All Year 1P: $90-$445

Location: 3 mi e of US 50 via Kingsbury Grade, 0.7 mi s via Tramway Dr. 750 Wells Fargo Ln 89449 (PO Box 4917). Fax: 775/588-5521. **Facility:** While the property is situated in the middle of great snow skiing, you'll also appreciate the convenience to Lake Tahoe and the casinos. 29 units. 19 two- and 10 three-bedroom suites with kitchens and whirlpools. 3-4 stories (no elevator), exterior corridors. **Parking:** on-site. **Terms:** check-in 4 pm. **Amenities:** video library (fee), voice mail, irons, hair dryers. **Leisure Activities:** sauna, whirlpool, playground, exercise room. **Guest Services:** area transportation. **Business Services:** fax (fee). **Cards:** AX, MC, VI.

The following lodging was either not evaluated or did not meet AAA rating requirements but is listed for your information only.

LAKE TAHOE ACCOMMODATIONS Phone: 775/588-5684

fyi

Not evaluated. **Location:** 275 Kingsbury Grade 89449. Facilities, services, and decor characterize a mid-range property.

WHERE TO DINE

THE BROILER ROOM **Dinner:** $18-$60 **Phone:** 775/588-3515 62

Steak & Seafood

Location: At casino center; in Caesars Tahoe. 55 Hwy 50 89449. **Hours:** 6 pm-10:30 pm. **Reservations:** suggested. **Features:** High-grade steaks and seafood are prepared in an elegant yet comfortable setting. Rich wood accents add to the appeal of the dining room. Desserts are delicious. Dressy casual; cocktails. **Parking:** on-site and valet. **Cards:** AX, CB, DC, DS, JC, MC, VI.

EL VAQUERO **Dinner:** $12-$25 **Phone:** 775/588-2411 61

Mexican

Location: US 50, in casino center; in Harveys Casino & Resort. Hwy 50 89449. **Hours:** 5 pm-10 pm. Closed: Mon & Tues. **Reservations:** suggested. **Features:** After a day at the lake or mountains, guests can savor dinner in the comfortable dining room or in the lounge, where they can watch the big-screen TV. Good-size portions and friendly service await. Casual dress; cocktails. **Parking:** on-site and valet. **Cards:** MC, VI.

FRIDAY'S STATION **Dinner:** $25-$45 **Phone:** 775/588-6611 68

Steak House

Location: In casino area; in Harrah's Hotel & Casino. Hwy 50 89449. **Hours:** 5:30 pm-9 pm. **Reservations:** suggested. **Features:** Named after a famous Pony Express stop, the steakhouse sits high and offers wonderful views of the Lake Tahoe area. Good food and service complement the beautiful scenery. Dressy casual; cocktails. **Parking:** on-site and valet. **Cards:** AX, CB, DC, DS, JC, MC, VI.

JOSH'S **Dinner:** $13-$30 **Phone:** 775/588-6211 66

American

Location: US 50, in casino center; in Horizon Casino Resort. 50 Hwy 50 89449. **Hours:** 5:30 pm-10 pm. **Reservations:** suggested. **Features:** Tucked away from the main casino floor, the elegant dining room features a wide selection of steak, seafood and chicken preparations. Guests find this place a great way to relax after a busy day at the lake or mountains. Dressy casual; cocktails. **Parking:** on-site and valet. **Cards:** AX, CB, DC, DS, MC, VI.

(See map and index starting on p. 363)

LLEWELLYN'S **Lunch:** $6-$17 **Dinner:** $17-$27 **Phone:** 775/588-2411 (63)

Continental

Location: US 50, in casino center; in Harveys Casino & Resort. **Hours:** 11:30 am-2:30 & 6-9:30 pm, Sat-10 pm, Sun 10 am-2 pm & 6-9:30 pm. Closed: for lunch Mon & Tues. **Reservations:** suggested; in season. **Features:** Elegant surroundings befit the refined restaurant, where diners take in spectacular views of Lake Tahoe and the mountains. Innovative preparation marks each dish. Semi-formal attire; cocktails; entertainment. **Parking:** on-site. **Cards:** AX, CB, DC, MC, VI.

SAGE ROOM STEAK HOUSE **Dinner:** $23-$56 **Phone:** 775/588-2411 (64)

Steak House

Location: US 50, in casino center; in Harveys Casino & Resort. **Hours:** 6 pm-10 pm, Sat & Sun from 5:30 pm. **Reservations:** suggested. **Features:** An extensive selection of beef dishes is prepared in a quiet, rustic atmosphere. Dressy casual; cocktails. **Parking:** on-site and valet. **Cards:** AX, CB, DS, MC, VI.

THE SUMMIT ROOM **Dinner:** $26-$75 **Phone:** 775/588-6611 (65)

Continental

Location: In casino area; in Harrah's Hotel & Casino. US 50 89449. **Hours:** 5:30 pm-9 pm, Sat-10 pm. Closed: Mon & Tues. **Reservations:** suggested. **Features:** On the 16th floor, the premier restaurant at Harrah's Lake Tahoe looks out over the Sierra Nevada. Excellently prepared dishes are served in a sophisticated, intimate environment. Semi-formal attire; cocktails; entertainment. **Parking:** on-site and valet. **Cards:** AX, CB, DC, MC, VI.

TABERNA **Lunch:** $5-$15 **Dinner:** $5-$15 **Phone:** 775/588-7777 (60)

Mexican

Location: On US 50; 1 mi e of state line at Kingsbury Grade; in Lakeside Inn and Casino. 168 Hwy 50 89449. **Hours:** 8 am-10 pm. **Features:** For casual Mexican fare served by a friendly staff, give this popular room a try. Right off the casino's sports book and lounge, this place enables patrons to keep track of their favorite game. Casual dress; cocktails. **Parking:** on-site. **Cards:** AX, MC, VI.

TIMBER HOUSE RESTAURANT **Lunch:** $5-$15 **Dinner:** $7-$23 **Phone:** 775/588-7777 (69)

American

Location: On US 50; 1 mi e of state line at Kingsbury Grade; in Lakeside Inn and Casino. 168 Hwy 50 89449. **Hours:** 24 hours. **Features:** A comfortable, rustic look fits perfectly with the atmosphere of the area. The 24-hour room is great for breakfast, lunch or dinner. Prime rib is the dinner specialty. Casual dress; cocktails. **Parking:** on-site. **Cards:** AX, MC, VI.

ZEPHYR COVE pop. 1,649

WHERE TO DINE

ZEPHYR COVE LODGE RESTAURANT **Lunch:** $6-$9 **Dinner:** $11-$21 **Phone:** 775/589-4968

American

Location: 4 mi n of state line. 760 Hwy 50 89448. **Hours:** 7 am-9 pm. Closed: 11/25. **Reservations:** No reservation accepted. **Features:** Friendly staff serves up three squares a day with a good selection of American food. Located at Lake Tahoe. Casual dress; cocktails. **Parking:** on-site. **Cards:** AX, DS, MC, VI.

This ends listings for the Lake Tahoe Area.
The following page resumes the alphabetical listings of cities in Northern California.

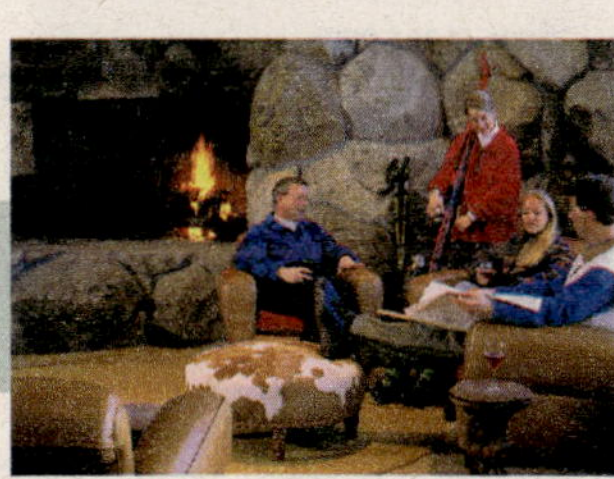

LARKSPUR —*See San Francisco p. 669.*

LASSEN VOLCANIC NATIONAL PARK —*See also RED BLUFF & REDDING.*

WHERE TO STAY

The following lodging was either not evaluated or did not meet AAA rating requirements but is listed for your information only.

DRAKESBAD GUEST RANCH **Phone:** 530/529-1512

fyi

Not evaluated. **Location:** I-5, exit Red Bluff, then e on SR 36 to enter from the south, then n on SR 89; exit Redding, then e on SR 44 to enter from the north. CR Chester-Warner Valley 96020. Facilities, services, and decor characterize a basic property.

LATHROP pop. 10,445

WHERE TO STAY

COMFORT INN *Book at aaa.com* **Phone:** 209/983-1177

Motel

All Year 1P: $66-$70 2P: $76-$80

Location: I-5, exit Lathrop Rd. 14730 S Harlan Rd 95330. Fax: 209/983-1171. **Facility:** 41 units. 37 one-bedroom standard units. 4 one-bedroom suites. 3 stories, interior corridors. **Parking:** on-site. **Amenities:** high-speed Internet, irons, hair dryers. **Pool(s):** heated indoor. **Leisure Activities:** sauna, whirlpool, exercise room. **Guest Services:** coin laundry. **Business Services:** meeting rooms. **Cards:** AX, DC, DS, MC, VI.

SOME UNITS

ASK VCR DATA PORT

DAYS INN *Book at aaa.com* **Phone:** 209/982-1959

Motel

All Year 1P: $65-$70 2P: $75-$82

Location: I-5, exit Lathrop Rd. 14750 S Harlan Rd 95330. Fax: 209/982-4978. **Facility:** 40 units. 38 one-bedroom standard units. 2 one-bedroom suites with whirlpools. 2 stories, interior corridors. **Parking:** on-site. **Terms:** pets ($10 extra charge). **Amenities:** hair dryers. **Pool(s):** outdoor. **Leisure Activities:** sauna. **Guest Services:** coin laundry. **Cards:** AX, DS, MC, VI.

SOME UNITS

ASK FEE DATA PORT

HOLIDAY INN EXPRESS *Book at aaa.com* **Phone:** (209)858-1234

AAA SAVE

Motel

All Year [ECP] 1P: $89-$119 2P: $99-$149 XP: $10 F18

Location: I-5, exit Louise Rd. 16855 S Harlan Rd 95330. Fax: 209/858-1800. **Facility:** 65 units. 58 one-bedroom standard units. 7 one-bedroom suites with whirlpools. 2 stories, exterior corridors. **Parking:** on-site. **Amenities:** dual phone lines, voice mail, irons, hair dryers. **Pool(s):** outdoor. **Leisure Activities:** sauna, whirlpool, exercise room. **Guest Services:** coin laundry. **Business Services:** meeting rooms. **Cards:** AX, CB, DC, DS, MC, VI. **Special Amenities: free expanded continental breakfast and free newspaper.**

(See color ad p 260 & p 732)

SOME UNITS

DATA

LEE VINING

WHERE TO STAY

BEST WESTERN LAKE VIEW LODGE *Book at aaa.com* **Phone:** (760)647-6543

AAA SAVE

Motel

4/21-10/31	1P: $59-$149	2P: $59-$149	XP: $4	F12
11/1-1/31	1P: $59-$99	2P: $59-$99	XP: $4	F12
2/1-4/20	1P: $59-$89	2P: $59-$89	XP: $4	F12

Location: On US 395; in town. 30 Main St 93541 (PO Box 345). Fax: 760/647-6325. **Facility:** Designated smoking area. 46 units. 44 one-bedroom standard units, some with kitchens. 2 one-bedroom suites. 2 stories, exterior corridors. **Parking:** on-site. **Terms:** check-in 4 pm. **Amenities:** irons, hair dryers. **Business Services:** fax (fee). **Cards:** AX, CB, DC, DS, JC, MC, VI. **Special Amenities: free local telephone calls and early check-in/late check-out.**

SOME UNITS

DATA PORT

MURPHEY'S MOTEL **Phone:** 760/647-6316

AAA SAVE

Motel

All Year 1P: $48-$88 2P: $53-$108 XP: $5

Location: On US 395; in town. 51493 Hwy 395 93541 (PO Box 57). Fax: 760/647-6044. **Facility:** 43 one-bedroom standard units, some with kitchens. 2 stories, exterior corridors. *Bath:* combo or shower only. **Parking:** on-site. **Terms:** small pets only ($5 extra charge). **Amenities:** *Some:* irons, hair dryers. **Business Services:** meeting rooms, fax (fee). **Cards:** AX, DS, MC, VI.

SOME UNITS

FEE

WHERE TO DINE

THE MONO INN RESTAURANT & ANSEL ADAMS GALLERY **Dinner:** $15-$25 **Phone:** 760/647-6581

American

Location: On US 395; 4 mi n of town. 55620 Hwy 395 93541. **Hours:** 5 pm-10 pm; to 9 pm 12/1-3/30. Closed: Tues in summer; Mon-Wed in winter. **Reservations:** suggested. **Features:** A spectacular view of Mono Lake enhance patrons' meals at the fine-dining restaurant. During warmer months, terrace seating is available. Food is carefully prepared to diners' tastes, and service is gracious. Casual dress; cocktails. **Parking:** on-site. **Cards:** AX, DS, MC, VI.

NICELY'S RESTAURANT **Lunch:** $5-$8 **Dinner:** $6-$15 **Phone:** 760/647-6477

American

Location: On US 395. US Hwy 395 At 4th St 93541. **Hours:** 6 am-9 pm; to 8 pm in winter. Closed: 1/1, 11/25, 12/25; also Wed in winter. **Features:** This restaurant is a favorite stop for a delicious breakfast including homemade pork sausage, or for a variety of good lunch or dinner selections including oyster stew, Chinese chicken salad or grilled ham steak. There is something sure to please any taste, and you'll find the atmosphere comfortable and the staff friendly. Casual dress; cocktails. **Parking:** street. **Cards:** MC, VI.

LEGGETT —*See Wine Country p. 783.*

LEMON COVE pop. 298

WHERE TO STAY

PLANTATION BED & BREAKFAST **Phone:** (559)597-2555

Bed & Breakfast

All Year [BP] 1P: $129-$219 2P: $129-$219

Location: On SR 198, 18 mi w of entrance to Sequoia National Park. 33038 Sierra Hwy 198 93244. Fax: 559/597-2551. **Facility:** The B&B, in a small citrus community close to downtown Visalia and Sequoia National Park, has a "Gone With the Wind" setting and themed guest rooms. Designated smoking area. 7 one-bedroom standard units, some with whirlpools. 2 stories, interior/exterior corridors. *Bath:* combo or shower only. **Parking:** on-site. **Terms:** office hours 6 am-9 pm, check-in 4 pm, 7 day cancellation notice. **Amenities:** video library. *Some:* irons, hair dryers. **Pool(s):** heated outdoor. **Leisure Activities:** whirlpool. **Guest Services:** complimentary evening beverages. **Cards:** AX, DC, DS, MC, VI.

SOME UNITS

LEMOORE pop. 19,712

WHERE TO STAY

BEST WESTERN VINEYARD INN Book at aaa.com **Phone:** (559)924-1261

AAA SAVE

Motel

All Year 1P: $80-$90 2P: $85-$95

Location: SR 198, exit Houston St, 0.8 ni nw. 877 East D St 93245. Fax: 559/924-4270. **Facility:** 66 one-bedroom standard units. 2 stories, exterior corridors. **Parking:** on-site. **Terms:** [CP] & [ECP] meal plans available, pets ($50 deposit, in limited units). **Amenities:** high-speed Internet (fee), irons, hair dryers. **Pool(s):** small outdoor. **Leisure Activities:** barbecue & picnic facilities, horseshoes. **Guest Services:** coin laundry. **Business Services:** fax (fee). **Cards:** AX, CB, DC, DS, MC, VI. **Special Amenities: free expanded continental breakfast and free newspaper.**

SOME UNITS

FEE

HOLIDAY INN EXPRESS Book at aaa.com **Phone:** (559)924-3200

Motel

All Year [ECP] 1P: $81-$103 2P: $81-$103 XP: $7 F18

Location: SR 198, exit Houston St, 0.8 mi nw. 820 E Bush St 93245. Fax: 559/924-0198. **Facility:** 60 one-bedroom standard units, some with whirlpools. 2 stories, exterior corridors. **Parking:** on-site. **Amenities:** dual phone lines, voice mail, irons, hair dryers. **Pool(s):** small outdoor. **Leisure Activities:** whirlpool. **Guest Services:** coin laundry. **Cards:** AX, DC, DS, JC, MC, VI.

ASK

LINDSAY pop. 10,297

WHERE TO STAY

SUPER 8 MOTEL Book at aaa.com **Phone:** (559)562-5188

AAA SAVE

Motel

All Year 1P: $55-$85 2P: $65-$95 XP: $5 F12

Location: On SR 65. 390 N Hwy 65 93247. Fax: 559/562-2113. **Facility:** 51 one-bedroom standard units. 2 stories, exterior corridors. **Parking:** on-site. **Terms:** [ECP] meal plan available, pets ($10 extra charge). **Amenities:** *Some:* irons, hair dryers. **Pool(s):** outdoor. **Leisure Activities:** whirlpool. **Guest Services:** coin laundry. **Business Services:** fax (fee). **Cards:** AX, CB, DC, DS, JC, MC, VI. **Special Amenities: free expanded continental breakfast and free local telephone calls.**

SOME UNITS

FEE

LITTLE RIVER —*See Wine Country p. 783.*

LIVE OAK pop. 6,229

WHERE TO DINE

PASQUINI'S **Dinner:** $14-$22 **Phone:** 530/695-3384

Italian

Location: SR 99, end of town, south side. 6241 Live Oak Hwy 95953. **Hours:** 4:30 pm-9 pm, Sat 4:30 pm-10 pm. Closed: 12/25; also Sun. **Features:** The comfortable restaurant is housed in an adobe-style, cream-colored building. Casual dress; cocktails. **Parking:** on-site. **Cards:** AX, DS, MC, VI.

LIVERMORE pop. 73,345

WHERE TO STAY

COMFORT INN *Book at aaa.com* **Phone:** (925)606-6200

Motel

All Year 1P: $99-$139 2P: $109-$149 XP: $10 F16

Location: I-580, exit Airway/Collier Canyon Rd N. 2625 Constitution Dr 94551. Fax: 925/606-6014. **Facility:** 60 one-bedroom standard units, some with whirlpools. 2 stories, exterior corridors. **Parking:** on-site. **Terms:** [CP] meal plan available. **Amenities:** voice mail, irons, hair dryers. **Pool(s):** outdoor. **Leisure Activities:** whirlpool, exercise room. **Guest Services:** valet laundry. **Business Services:** meeting rooms. **Cards:** AX, CB, DC, DS, MC, VI. **Special Amenities: free continental breakfast and free local telephone calls.**

SOME UNITS

COURTYARD BY MARRIOTT - LIVERMORE *Book at aaa.com* **Phone:** (925)243-1000

Small-scale Hotel

All Year 1P: $119-$129 2P: $119-$129

Location: I-580, exit Airway Blvd, just n. 2929 Constitution Dr 94550. Fax: 925/243-1010. **Facility:** 121 one-bedroom standard units, some with whirlpools. 3 stories, interior corridors. *Bath:* combo or shower only. **Parking:** on-site. **Terms:** cancellation fee imposed. **Amenities:** high-speed Internet, dual phone lines, voice mail, irons, hair dryers. **Dining:** 6:30-10 am, Sat & Sun 7-11 am. **Pool(s):** heated indoor. **Leisure Activities:** whirlpool, exercise room. **Guest Services:** coin laundry. **Business Services:** meeting rooms. **Cards:** AX, CB, DC, DS, JC, MC, VI. **Special Amenities: free newspaper and preferred room (subject to availability with advanced reservations).**

SOME UNITS

DOUBLETREE CLUB HOTEL LIVERMORE *Book at aaa.com* **Phone:** (925)443-4950

Large-scale Hotel

All Year 1P: $65-$159 2P: $65-$159 XP: $10 F16

Location: I-580, exit Springtown Blvd, just n. 720 Las Flores Rd 94551. Fax: 925/449-9059. **Facility:** 125 one-bedroom standard units. 4 stories, interior corridors. **Parking:** on-site. **Terms:** [AP] meal plan available. **Amenities:** dual phone lines, voice mail, irons, hair dryers. **Pool(s):** outdoor. **Leisure Activities:** exercise room. **Guest Services:** coin laundry. **Business Services:** conference facilities, business center. **Cards:** AX, CB, DC, DS, JC, MC, VI.

SOME UNITS

HAMPTON INN *Book at aaa.com* **Phone:** (925)606-6400

Small-scale Hotel

All Year 1P: $129 2P: $139

Location: I-580, exit Airway/Collier Canyon Rd N. 2850 Constitution Dr 94551. Fax: 925/606-6410. **Facility:** 80 one-bedroom standard units. 2 stories, interior corridors. *Bath:* combo or shower only. **Parking:** on-site. **Terms:** [ECP] meal plan available. **Amenities:** video games (fee), high-speed Internet, dual phone lines, voice mail, irons, hair dryers. **Pool(s):** outdoor. **Leisure Activities:** exercise room. **Guest Services:** valet laundry, area transportation. **Business Services:** meeting rooms, business center. **Cards:** AX, CB, DC, DS, JC, MC, VI.

SOME UNITS

HAWTHORN SUITES *Book at aaa.com* **Phone:** (925)606-6060

Small-scale Hotel

All Year [BP] 1P: $79-$119 2P: $79-$119

Location: I-580, exit N Livermore Ave, just s. 1700 N Livermore Ave 94551. Fax: 925/606-8050. **Facility:** 62 one-bedroom standard units, some with efficiencies. 3 stories, interior corridors. *Bath:* combo or shower only. **Parking:** on-site. **Amenities:** high-speed Internet, dual phone lines, voice mail, irons, hair dryers. **Pool(s):** small heated outdoor. **Leisure Activities:** whirlpool, exercise room. **Guest Services:** valet and coin laundry. **Business Services:** meeting rooms. **Cards:** AX, CB, DC, DS, JC, MC, VI. **Special Amenities: free full breakfast and free local telephone calls.**

SOME UNITS

HILTON GARDEN INN LIVERMORE *Book at aaa.com* **Phone:** (925)292-2000

Small-scale Hotel

All Year 1P: $129-$159 XP: $10 F17

Location: I-580, exit Airway Blvd, Just n. 2801 Constitution Dr 94551. Fax: 925/292-2100. **Facility:** 97 units. 79 one-bedroom standard units, some with whirlpools. 18 one-bedroom suites ($159-$209) with whirlpools. 2 stories, interior corridors. *Bath:* combo or shower only. **Parking:** on-site. **Terms:** cancellation fee imposed. **Amenities:** video games (fee), high-speed Internet, dual phone lines, voice mail, irons, hair dryers. **Pool(s):** heated indoor. **Leisure Activities:** sauna, whirlpool, exercise room. **Guest Services:** valet and coin laundry. **Business Services:** meeting rooms, business center. **Cards:** AX, CB, DC, DS, JC, MC.

SOME UNITS

RAMADA LIMITED *Book at aaa.com* **Phone:** (925)456-5422

Small-scale Hotel

All Year [ECP] 1P: $89-$129 2P: $99-$139 XP: $10 F18

Location: I-580, exit N Greenville Rd, just s. 7600 Southfront Rd 94550. Fax: 925/456-3055. **Facility:** 66 one-bedroom standard units, some with whirlpools. 3 stories, interior corridors. **Parking:** on-site. **Terms:** weekly rates available, package plans - weekends & seasonal. **Amenities:** high-speed Internet, dual phone lines, voice mail, irons, hair dryers. **Pool(s):** heated outdoor. **Leisure Activities:** exercise room. **Guest Services:** coin laundry. **Cards:** AX, DC, DS, MC, VI.

SOME UNITS

RESIDENCE INN BY MARRIOTT *Book at aaa.com* **Phone:** (925)373-1800

Motel

All Year [BP] 1P: $119-$174 2P: $119-$174

Location: I-580, exit Airway/Collier Canyon Rd, just n. 1000 Airway Blvd 94551. Fax: 925/373-7252. **Facility:** 96 units. 80 one-bedroom standard units with kitchens. 16 two-bedroom suites with kitchens. 2 stories (no elevator), exterior corridors. *Bath:* combo or shower only. **Parking:** on-site. **Terms:** cancellation fee imposed, 8% service charge, pets ($75 extra charge). **Amenities:** voice mail, irons, hair dryers. **Pool(s):** outdoor. **Leisure Activities:** sauna, whirlpool, exercise room, sports court. **Guest Services:** coin laundry. **Business Services:** meeting rooms. **Cards:** AX, DC, DS, MC, VI.

SOME UNITS

FEE

WHERE TO DINE

WENTE VINEYARDS RESTAURANT **Lunch:** $10-$20 **Dinner:** $18-$40 **Phone:** 925/456-2460

American

Location: I-580, exit N Livermore Ave, 1.2 mi s to 1st St, 0.8 mi w to S L St, 4.5 mi s via L St and Arroyo Rd. 5050 Arroyo Rd 94550. **Hours:** 11:30 am-2:30 & 5-9:30 pm, Sun from 10:30 am. Closed major holidays; also 12/24. **Reservations:** suggested. **Features:** In the middle of Wente Vineyards, the relaxed restaurant looks out over the surrounding valley. Fresh herb gardens produce outstanding seasonings for the delicious food. Dressy casual; wine only. **Parking:** on-site. **Cards:** AX, MC, VI.

LOCKEFORD pop. 3,179

WHERE TO STAY

THE INN AT LOCKE HOUSE **Phone:** 209/727-5715

Historic Bed & Breakfast

All Year 1P: $115-$120 2P: $120-$125

Location: SR 99, exit SR 12 E, 9 mi e to Elliott Rd, just n. 19960 Elliott Rd 95237 (PO Box 1510). Fax: 209/727-0873. **Facility:** The inn is named for the doctor said to have built it between 1865 and 1882. Smoke free premises. 5 units. 4 one-bedroom standard units. 1 one-bedroom suite ($185-$195). 2 stories, interior corridors. *Bath:* combo or shower only. **Parking:** on-site. **Terms:** 14 day cancellation notice-fee imposed, [BP] & [MAP] meal plans available, package plans. **Amenities:** CD players, hair dryers. **Cards:** AX, CB, DC, DS, MC, VI.

DATA PORT

LODI pop. 56,999

WHERE TO STAY

BEST WESTERN ROYAL HOST INN *Book at aaa.com* **Phone:** (209)369-8484

AAA SAVE — Motel

All Year [ECP] 1P: $70-$85 2P: $85-$100 XP: $8 F12

Location: 0.8 mi s on SR 99 business route. 710 S Cherokee Ln 95240. Fax: 209/369-0654. **Facility:** 48 units. 46 one-bedroom standard units. 2 one-bedroom suites. 2 stories, exterior corridors. *Bath:* combo or shower only. **Parking:** on-site. **Amenities:** voice mail, irons, hair dryers. **Pool(s):** outdoor. **Business Services:** meeting rooms. **Cards:** AX, CB, DC, DS, MC, VI. **Special Amenities: free continental breakfast and free local telephone calls.**

SOME UNITS

DATA PORT

COMFORT INN *Book at aaa.com* **Phone:** (209)367-4848

AAA SAVE — Motel

All Year 1P: $65 2P: $84 XP: $5 F12

Location: 0.3 mi on SR 99 business route. 118 N Cherokee Ln 95240. Fax: 209/367-4898. **Facility:** 53 one-bedroom standard units. 2 stories, exterior corridors. **Parking:** on-site. **Terms:** [ECP] meal plan available. **Amenities:** irons, hair dryers. **Pool(s):** outdoor. **Leisure Activities:** whirlpool, exercise room. **Cards:** AX, CB, DC, DS, JC, MC, VI. **Special Amenities: free continental breakfast and free local telephone calls.**

(See color ad below)

SOME UNITS

DATA PORT VCR FEE

EL RANCHO MOTEL *Book at aaa.com* **Phone:** (209)368-0651

AAA SAVE — Motel

All Year 1P: $45-$55 2P: $55 XP: $5 F12

Location: SR 99, exit Turner Rd, just s. 603 N Cherokee Ln 95240. Fax: 209/368-0697. **Facility:** 33 one-bedroom standard units. 2 stories, exterior corridors. *Bath:* combo or shower only. **Parking:** on-site. **Terms:** cancellation fee imposed, weekly rates available, pets ($10 fee). **Pool(s):** outdoor. **Cards:** AX, DC, DS, MC, VI. **Special Amenities: free continental breakfast and free local telephone calls.**

SOME UNITS

FEE

HOLIDAY INN EXPRESS-LODI Book at aaa.com **Phone:** (209)334-6422

AAA SAVE
Motel

All Year [ECP]	1P: $80-$105	2P: $80-$105	XP: $10	F18

Location: SR 99, exit SR 12 W, just w. 1140 S Cherokee Ln 95240. Fax: 209/368-7967. **Facility:** 95 one-bedroom standard units. 2 stories, exterior corridors. **Parking:** on-site. **Terms:** cancellation fee imposed. **Amenities:** voice mail, irons, hair dryers. **Pool(s):** outdoor. **Leisure Activities:** sauna, whirlpool, exercise room. **Guest Services:** coin laundry. **Business Services:** meeting rooms. **Cards:** AX, CB, DC, DS, JC, MC, VI. **Special Amenities: free continental breakfast and free local telephone calls.**

(See color ad p 260)

SOME UNITS

MICROTEL INN & SUITES Book at aaa.com **Phone:** (209)367-9700

Motel

All Year	1P: $69-$139	2P: $69-$139	XP: $5	F17

Location: I-5, exit SR 12, southeast corner. 6428 W Banner St 95242. Fax: 209/367-0907. **Facility:** 51 one-bedroom standard units. 3 stories, interior corridors. **Parking:** on-site. **Terms:** cancellation fee imposed. **Pool(s):** heated outdoor. **Guest Services:** coin laundry. **Business Services:** meeting rooms. **Cards:** AX, DC, DS, MC, VI.

SOME UNITS

WINE & ROSES HOTEL AND RESTAURANT **Phone:** (209)334-6988

AAA SAVE
Country Inn

All Year [CP]	1P: $155-$215	2P: $155-$215	XP: $20	F12

Location: I-5, exit Turner Rd, 5 mi e; SR 99, exit Turner Rd, 2 mi w. 2505 W Turner Rd 95242. Fax: 209/371-6049. **Facility:** Five manicured acres surround this 1902 estate. 36 units. 32 one-bedroom standard units. 4 one-bedroom suites ($275-$395) with whirlpools. 2 stories, interior corridors. *Bath:* combo or shower only. **Parking:** on-site. **Terms:** 7 day cancellation notice-fee imposed, weekly rates available. **Amenities:** voice mail, irons, hair dryers. **Dining:** 11:30 am-1:30 & 6-9 pm, Tues-1:30 pm, Sat 6 pm-9 pm, Sunday brunch 10:30 am-2 pm, cocktails. **Business Services:** meeting rooms. **Cards:** AX, DC, DS, MC, VI.

SOME UNITS

LONE PINE pop. 1,655

WHERE TO STAY

BEST WESTERN FRONTIER MOTEL Book at aaa.com **Phone:** (760)876-5571

AAA SAVE
Motel

3/25-10/15	1P: $54-$98	2P: $59-$103	XP: $5	F12
2/1-3/24 & 10/16-1/31	1P: $44-$76	2P: $49-$81	XP: $5	F12

Location: On US 395, at south end of town. 1008 S Main St 93545. Fax: 760/876-5357. **Facility:** 73 one-bedroom standard units, some with whirlpools. 1 story, exterior corridors. *Bath:* combo or shower only. **Parking:** on-site. **Terms:** check-in 4 pm, [ECP] meal plan available. **Amenities:** voice mail, irons, hair dryers. **Pool(s):** heated outdoor. **Guest Services:** coin laundry. **Business Services:** meeting rooms, fax (fee). **Cards:** AX, CB, DC, DS, MC, VI.

SOME UNITS

COMFORT INN **Phone:** (760)876-8700

AAA SAVE
Small-scale Hotel

5/1-8/31	1P: $79-$129	2P: $79-$129	XP: $10	F12
9/1-10/31	1P: $69-$109	2P: $69-$109	XP: $10	F12
11/1-1/31	1P: $59-$89	2P: $59-$89	XP: $10	F12
2/1-4/30	1P: $59-$79	2P: $59-$79	XP: $10	F12

Location: US 395, 1.5 mi s of town. 1920 S Main St 93545 (PO Box C). Fax: 760/876-8704. **Facility:** 58 one-bedroom standard units, some with efficiencies. 2 stories, interior corridors. **Parking:** on-site. **Terms:** [ECP] meal plan available, pets ($10 extra charge). **Amenities:** hair dryers. *Some:* irons. **Pool(s):** outdoor. **Guest Services:** coin laundry. **Business Services:** fax (fee). **Cards:** AX, DC, MC, VI.

SOME UNITS

FEE

DOW VILLA MOTEL **Phone:** (760)876-5521

AAA SAVE
Motel

4/1-10/31	1P: $82-$92	2P: $82-$92
2/1-3/31 & 11/1-1/31	1P: $60-$64	2P: $60-$64

Location: On US 395. 310 S Main St 93545 (PO Box 205). Fax: 760/876-5643. **Facility:** 42 one-bedroom standard units, some with whirlpools. 1-2 stories, exterior corridors. **Parking:** on-site. **Terms:** check-in 4 pm, pets (in smoking units). **Amenities:** video library, irons, hair dryers. **Pool(s):** heated outdoor. **Leisure Activities:** whirlpool. **Business Services:** meeting rooms, fax (fee). **Cards:** AX, CB, DC, DS, MC, VI. **Special Amenities: free local telephone calls and preferred room (subject to availability with advanced reservations).**

SOME UNITS

LONE PINE BUDGET INN MOTEL **Phone:** 760/876-5655

AAA SAVE
Motel

3/1-10/31	1P: $49-$89	2P: $54-$99	XP: $5	D10
2/1-2/29 & 11/1-1/31	1P: $39-$59	2P: $45-$69	XP: $5	D10

Location: US 395, just w. 138 W Willow St 93545 (PO Box 216). Fax: 760/876-5655. **Facility:** 16 one-bedroom standard units, some with whirlpools. 1 story, exterior corridors. **Parking:** on-site. **Terms:** 3 day cancellation notice-fee imposed, small pets only ($10 extra charge, with prior approval). **Amenities:** hair dryers. *Some:* irons. **Business Services:** fax. **Cards:** AX, DC, DS, MC, VI. **Special Amenities: free continental breakfast and free local telephone calls.**

SOME UNITS

FEE

MT. WHITNEY MOTEL **Phone:** 760/876-4207

Motel

3/1-10/31	1P: $49-$89	2P: $79-$95	XP: $5	D10
2/1-2/29 & 11/1-1/31	1P: $36-$49	2P: $45-$69	XP: $5	D10

Location: On US 395. 305 N Main St 93545 (PO Box 722). Fax: 760/876-8818. **Facility:** 29 one-bedroom standard units, some with whirlpools. 2 stories, exterior corridors. *Bath:* combo or shower only. **Parking:** on-site. **Terms:** office hours 7 am-midnight, 3 day cancellation notice-fee imposed. **Amenities:** hair dryers. *Some:* irons. **Pool(s):** small outdoor. **Business Services:** fax (fee). **Cards:** AX, DC, DS, MC, VI. **Special Amenities: free local telephone calls and preferred room (subject to availability with advanced reservations).**

SOME UNITS

NATIONAL 9 TRAILS MOTEL **Phone:** (760)876-5555

Motel

3/1-10/31 [CP]	1P: $49-$89	2P: $54-$99	XP: $5	F10
2/1-2/29 & 11/1-1/31 [CP]	1P: $39-$59	2P: $45-$69	XP: $5	F10

Location: On US 395. 633 S Main St 93545 (PO Box 65). Fax: 760/876-4650. **Facility:** 17 one-bedroom standard units. 1 story, exterior corridors. *Bath:* combo or shower only. **Parking:** on-site. **Terms:** 3 day cancellation notice-fee imposed, pets ($5 extra charge, in smoking units). **Amenities:** hair dryers. **Pool(s):** outdoor. **Leisure Activities:** fish freezing facilities. **Cards:** AX, DC, DS, MC, VI. **Special Amenities: free continental breakfast and free local telephone calls.**

FEE SOME UNITS

THE PORTAL MOTEL **Phone:** 760/876-5930

Motel

3/1-10/31	1P: $49-$89	2P: $79-$95	XP: $5	D10
2/1-2/29 & 11/1-1/31	1P: $36-$49	2P: $45-$69	XP: $5	D10

Location: On US 395. 425 S Main St 93545 (PO Box 97). Fax: 760/876-5930. **Facility:** 17 one-bedroom standard units. 1 story, exterior corridors. *Bath:* combo or shower only. **Parking:** on-site. **Terms:** 3 day cancellation notice-fee imposed. **Amenities:** hair dryers. *Some:* irons. **Business Services:** fax (fee). **Cards:** AX, DS, MC, VI. **Special Amenities: free local telephone calls and preferred room (subject to availability with advanced reservations).**

SOME UNITS

WHERE TO DINE

MERRY GO ROUND DINNER HOUSE **Dinner:** $10-$22 **Phone:** 760/876-4115

American

Location: On US 395; center. 212 S Main St 93545. **Hours:** 5 pm-8:30 pm; to 10 pm 5/15-10/15. Closed: 11/25, 12/25. **Reservations:** suggested. **Features:** The small, cozy restaurant prepares charbroiled steaks, lamb chops, chicken and seafood. Seating in the round gives diners the feeling they are on a merry-go-round. Lace curtains, mirrored walls and a decorative ceiling add visual appeal. The staff is friendly and accommodating. Casual dress; beer & wine only. **Parking:** street. **Cards:** CB, DC, DS, MC, VI.

SEASONS RESTAURANT **Dinner:** $15-$22 **Phone:** 760/876-8927

Continental

Location: On US 395. 206 S Main St 93545. **Hours:** 5 pm-9 pm. Closed: 1/1-1/31. **Reservations:** suggested. **Features:** On the popular restaurant's menu are chicken, seafood, lamb, veal, steak and pasta preparations. Servers are especially gracious, and the surroundings are comfortable and relaxing. Casual dress; cocktails. **Parking:** on-site. **Cards:** AX, DS, MC, VI.

LOS ALTOS pop. 27,693

WHERE TO STAY

COURTYARD BY MARRIOTT-PALO ALTO/LOS ALTOS *Book at aaa.com* **Phone:** 650/941-9900

Motel

All Year 1P: $89-$259

Location: US 101, exit San Antonio Rd, 2 mi w to SR 82, then just n. 4320 El Camino Real 94022. Fax: 650/941-2866. **Facility:** 190 units. 185 one-bedroom standard units. 5 one-bedroom suites ($209-$259). 3 stories, interior corridors. **Parking:** on-site. **Terms:** cancellation fee imposed, [BP] meal plan available. **Amenities:** high-speed Internet, dual phone lines, voice mail, irons, hair dryers. **Pool(s):** heated outdoor. **Leisure Activities:** whirlpools, exercise room. **Guest Services:** valet and coin laundry. **Business Services:** conference facilities, business center. **Cards:** AX, CB, DC, DS, JC, MC, VI.

MARRIOTT RESIDENCE INN-PALO ALTO/LOS ALTOS *Book at aaa.com* **Phone:** (650)559-7890

Motel

All Year [ECP] 1P: $94-$184 2P: $94-$184

Location: US 101, exit San Antonio Rd, just n. 4460 El Camino Real 94022. Fax: 650/559-7891. **Facility:** 156 units. 118 one-bedroom standard units with kitchens. 27 one- and 11 two-bedroom suites with kitchens. 3 stories, interior corridors. **Parking:** on-site. **Terms:** weekly rates available. **Amenities:** video games (fee), high-speed Internet, dual phone lines, voice mail, irons, hair dryers. **Pool(s):** heated outdoor. **Leisure Activities:** whirlpool, exercise room, sports court. **Guest Services:** complimentary evening beverages, valet and coin laundry. **Business Services:** meeting rooms, business center. **Cards:** AX, CB, DC, DS, JC, MC, VI. ***(See color ad p 528)***

SOME UNITS FEE

LOS BANOS pop. 25,869

WHERE TO STAY

BEST WESTERN EXECUTIVE INN *Book at aaa.com* **Phone:** (209)827-0954

Small-scale Hotel

All Year [ECP] 1P: $65-$75 2P: $65-$75 XP: $6 F12

Location: On SR 152. 301 W Pacheco Blvd 93635. Fax: 209/827-8891. **Facility:** 57 one-bedroom standard units. 3 stories, interior corridors. **Parking:** on-site. **Terms:** small pets only ($10 fee). **Amenities:** irons, hair dryers. **Pool(s):** outdoor. **Leisure Activities:** sauna, whirlpool, exercise room. **Guest Services:** coin laundry. **Cards:** AX, DC, DS, MC, VI. **Special Amenities: free expanded continental breakfast and free local telephone calls.**

FEE / SOME UNITS / FEE FEE

REGENCY INN **Phone:** (209)826-3871

Motel

All Year 1P: $39-$48 2P: $49-$55 XP: $5 F12

Location: On SR 152; center of town. 349 W Pacheco Blvd 93635. Fax: 209/826-2063. **Facility:** 37 one-bedroom standard units, some with whirlpools. 2 stories (no elevator), exterior corridors. *Bath:* combo or shower only. **Parking:** on-site. **Terms:** small pets only ($20 deposit, $5 extra charge). **Amenities:** *Some:* irons, hair dryers. **Pool(s):** small outdoor. **Cards:** AX, CB, DC, DS, MC, VI. **Special Amenities: preferred room (subject to availability with advanced reservations).**

FEE / SOME UNITS

LOS GATOS pop. 28,592

WHERE TO STAY

LA HACIENDA INN **Phone:** (408)354-9230

Motel

All Year [ECP] 1P: $110-$145 2P: $110-$145

Location: SR 9, 1 mi w. 18840 Saratoga-Los Gatos Rd 95030. Fax: 408/354-7590. **Facility:** 20 units. 18 one-bedroom standard units, some with kitchens. 2 one-bedroom suites ($110-$160) with kitchens. 1 story, exterior corridors. *Bath:* combo or shower only. **Parking:** on-site. **Terms:** weekly rates available. **Amenities:** video library, irons, hair dryers. **Dining:** La Hacienda Restaurant, see separate listing. **Pool(s):** outdoor. **Leisure Activities:** exercise room. **Guest Services:** valet and coin laundry. **Business Services:** meeting rooms. **Cards:** AX, CB, DC, DS, JC, MC, VI.

LODGE AT VILLA FELICE **Phone:** (408)395-6710

Small-scale Hotel

All Year [CP] 1P: $99-$170 2P: $99-$170 XP: $10 F

Location: SR 17, exit Lark Ave or Los Gatos, just w. 15350 S Winchester Blvd 95030. Fax: 408/354-1826. **Facility:** 33 one-bedroom standard units, some with whirlpools. 2 stories, interior corridors. *Bath:* combo or shower only. **Parking:** on-site. **Pool(s):** outdoor. **Leisure Activities:** whirlpool. **Guest Services:** valet laundry. **Business Services:** meeting rooms. **Cards:** AX, DC, MC, VI. **Special Amenities: free continental breakfast and free newspaper.**

SOME UNITS

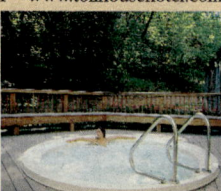

LOS GATOS LODGE *Book at aaa.com* **Phone:** (408)354-3300

SAVE

Motel

All Year 1P: $99-$149 2P: $109-$159

Location: SR 17, exit E Los Gatos, just e. 50 Los Gatos-Saratoga Rd 95032. Fax: 408/354-5451. **Facility:** 128 units. 115 one-bedroom standard units, some with efficiencies. 13 one-bedroom suites ($129-$189). 2 stories, interior/exterior corridors. *Bath:* combo or shower only. **Parking:** on-site. **Terms:** small pets only. **Amenities:** voice mail, irons, hair dryers. *Some:* DVD players. **Dining:** 7 am-8:30 pm, Fri & Sat-9:30 pm, Sun 8 am-2 pm, cocktails. **Pool(s):** outdoor. **Leisure Activities:** whirlpool, putting green, exercise room. **Guest Services:** coin laundry. **Business Services:** meeting rooms. **Cards:** AX, DC, DS, MC, VI.

SOME UNITS

DATA PORT / VCR /

LOS GATOS MOTOR INN **Phone:** (408)356-9191

Motel

All Year [CP] 1P: $89 2P: $110 XP: $5 F12

Location: SR 17, exit E Los Gatos, just e. Located in a quiet area. 55 Los Gatos-Saratoga Rd 95032. Fax: 408/356-7502. **Facility:** 60 one-bedroom standard units. 2 stories, exterior corridors. *Bath:* combo or shower only. **Parking:** on-site. **Pool(s):** outdoor. **Cards:** AX, CB, DC, DS, MC, VI.

SOME UNITS

ASK DATA PORT / /

LOS GATOS VILLAGE INN **Phone:** (408)354-8120

SAVE

Motel

All Year 1P: $95-$145 2P: $100-$150 XP: $5 F7

Location: SR 17 W, exit Saratoga-Los Gatos Rd. 235 W Main St 95030. Fax: 408/354-8121. **Facility:** 23 one-bedroom standard units. 2 stories, exterior corridors. *Bath:* combo or shower only. **Parking:** on-site. **Terms:** cancellation fee imposed, package plans. **Amenities:** high-speed Internet (fee), voice mail, irons, hair dryers. *Some:* DVD players. **Pool(s):** outdoor. **Guest Services:** valet laundry. **Cards:** AX, CB, DC, DS, JC, MC, VI.

SOME UNITS

DATA PORT / VCR /

TOLL HOUSE HOTEL *Book at aaa.com* **Phone:** (408)395-7070

Small-scale Hotel

All Year [ECP] 1P: $119-$205 2P: $129-$215 XP: $12 F18

Location: I-880/SR 17, exit SR 9, 0.3 mi w. 140 S Santa Cruz Ave 95030. Fax: 408/395-3730. **Facility:** Smoke free premises. 114 units. 106 one-bedroom standard units, some with whirlpools. 8 one-bedroom suites ($350-$475) with whirlpools. 3 stories, interior corridors. **Parking:** on-site. **Terms:** package plans. **Amenities:** dual phone lines, voice mail, irons, hair dryers. *Fee:* video games, high-speed Internet. *Some:* DVD players, CD players, safes, honor bars. **Leisure Activities:** whirlpool, exercise room. **Guest Services:** coin laundry. **Business Services:** meeting rooms, business center. **Cards:** AX, CB, DC, DS, MC, VI. ***(See color ad p 412)***

SOME UNITS

ASK DATA PORT / VCR /

WHERE TO DINE

LA HACIENDA RESTAURANT **Lunch:** $12-$16 **Dinner:** $18-$27 **Phone:** 408/354-6669

Continental

Location: SR 9, 1 mi w; in La Hacienda Inn. 18840 Saratoga-Los Gatos Rd 95030. **Hours:** 11 am-2 & 5-10 pm, Sat-11 pm, Sun 10 am-2 & 5-9 pm. Closed: 7/4, 12/25. **Reservations:** suggested. **Features:** This casual yet intimate restaurant offers its diners a variety of choices including Italian specialties and pasta. Dressy casual; cocktails; entertainment. **Parking:** on-site. **Cards:** AX, CB, DC, DS, MC, VI.

LOS OSOS

WHERE TO STAY

BACK BAY INN **Phone:** 805/528-1233

Motel

5/14-10/31 1P: $115-$240 2P: $115-$240 XP: $40

2/1-5/13 & 11/1-1/31 1P: $100-$200 2P: $100-$200 XP: $40

Location: SR 1, exit Los Osos/Baywood Park, 2.5 mi s on S Bay Blvd, 1 mi w on Santa Ysabel, 0.3 mi s. Located in Baywood Park. 1391 2nd St 93402. Fax: 805/528-7481. **Facility:** Smoke free premises. 13 one-bedroom standard units. 2 stories (no elevator), exterior corridors. **Parking:** on-site. **Terms:** office hours 8 am-8 pm, 2 night minimum stay - weekends, 3 day cancellation notice. **Guest Services:** complimentary evening beverages. **Cards:** AX, MC, VI.

DATA PORT

SEA PINES GOLF RESORT **Phone:** (805)528-5252

SAVE

Motel

6/1-9/30 1P: $99-$189

2/1-5/31 & 10/1-1/31 1P: $89-$169

Location: SR 1, exit Los Osos/Baywood Park, 4 mi s on S Bay Blvd, 1.6 mi w on Los Osos Valley Rd, 0.3 mi n on Pecho Rd, then just w on Skyline Dr. 1945 Solano St 93402. Fax: 805/528-8231. **Facility:** 44 units. 39 one-bedroom standard units. 5 one-bedroom suites ($119-$199). 2 stories (no elevator), exterior corridors. **Parking:** on-site. **Terms:** package plans. **Amenities:** irons, hair dryers. *Some:* dual phone lines. **Dining:** 7:30 am-9 pm. **Leisure Activities:** whirlpool, putting green, exercise room, horseshoes. *Fee:* golf-9 holes, driving range. **Business Services:** meeting rooms. **Cards:** AX, DS, MC, VI. **Special Amenities: free newspaper and early check-in/late check-out.**

SOME UNITS

DATA PORT / VCR /

LOST HILLS pop. 1,938

WHERE TO STAY

DAYS INN OF LOST HILLS *Book at aaa.com* **Phone:** (661)797-2371

Motel

All Year 1P: $35-$70 2P: $44-$98 XP: $5 F16

Location: I-5, exit SR 46, just w. 14684 Aloma St 93249 (PO Box 295). Fax: 661/797-2021. **Facility:** 76 one-bedroom standard units. 2 stories, exterior corridors. **Parking:** on-site. **Terms:** weekly rates available, pets ($6 fee). **Amenities:** hair dryers. *Some:* irons. **Pool(s):** outdoor. **Guest Services:** coin laundry. **Business Services:** fax (fee). **Cards:** AX, CB, DC, DS, JC, MC, VI.

SOME UNITS

ASK FEE DATA PORT / VCR /

MADERA pop. 43,207

WHERE TO STAY

BEST WESTERN MADERA VALLEY INN Book at aaa.com **Phone:** (559)664-0100

AAA SAVE — Motel

All Year [ECP] 1P: $75-$105 2P: $79-$109 XP: $10 F13

Location: SR 99, exit Central Madera, just e. 317 North G St 93637. Fax: 559/664-0200. **Facility:** 93 one-bedroom standard units. 5 stories, interior corridors. **Parking:** on-site. **Terms:** pets ($15 fee). **Amenities:** irons, hair dryers. **Dining:** 6 am-9 pm, cocktails. **Pool(s):** outdoor. **Leisure Activities:** exercise room. **Business Services:** meeting rooms, PC. **Cards:** AX, CB, DC, DS, JC, MC, VI. **Special Amenities: free expanded continental breakfast and free local telephone calls.**

SOME UNITS

FEE

HOLIDAY INN EXPRESS Book at aaa.com **Phone:** (559)661-7400

AAA SAVE — Motel

All Year [CP] 1P: $99-$109 2P: $99-$109 XP: $10 F

Location: SR 99, exit Ave 16 Gateway, just w. 2290 Market Place Dr 93637. Fax: 559/673-4800. **Facility:** 62 one-bedroom standard units, some with whirlpools. 3 stories, interior corridors. *Bath:* combo or shower only. **Parking:** on-site. **Terms:** cancellation fee imposed. **Amenities:** high-speed Internet, dual phone lines, voice mail, irons, hair dryers. **Pool(s):** heated outdoor. **Leisure Activities:** whirlpool, exercise room. **Guest Services:** valet and coin laundry. **Business Services:** meeting rooms, fax. **Cards:** AX, CB, DC, DS, JC, MC, VI.

SOME UNITS

LIBERTY INN **Phone:** (559)675-8697

AAA SAVE — Motel

All Year 1P: $49-$65 2P: $53-$85 XP: $9

Location: SR 99, exit Ave 18 1/2, just w. Located adjacent to truck stop. 22683 Ave 18 1/2 93637. Fax: 559/662-8938. **Facility:** 40 one-bedroom standard units. 2 stories (no elevator), interior corridors. *Bath:* combo or shower only. **Parking:** on-site. **Terms:** 3 day cancellation notice-fee imposed, small pets only ($25 deposit, $5 extra charge). **Amenities:** video library (fee), irons, hair dryers. **Pool(s):** heated indoor. **Leisure Activities:** sauna, whirlpool, pool table. **Guest Services:** coin laundry. **Business Services:** fax (fee). **Cards:** AX, DC, MC. **Special Amenities: free continental breakfast and free local telephone calls.**

SOME UNITS

ASK FEE

SUPER 8 Book at aaa.com **Phone:** (559)661-1131

Motel

All Year 1P: $55 2P: $65

Location: SR 99, exit Cleveland Ave, just w. 1855 W Cleveland Ave 93637. Fax: 559/661-0224. **Facility:** 80 one-bedroom standard units. 2 stories (no elevator), exterior corridors. **Parking:** on-site. **Terms:** [CP] meal plan available, pets ($5 extra charge, with prior approval). **Amenities:** hair dryers. **Pool(s):** heated outdoor. **Guest Services:** coin laundry. **Cards:** AX, CB, DC, DS, MC, VI.

SOME UNITS

ASK FEE FEE FEE

MAMMOTH LAKES pop. 7,093

WHERE TO STAY

THE 1849 CONDOMINIUMS **Phone:** 760/934-7525

AAA SAVE — Condominium

All Year 1P: $245-$300 2P: $265-$500

Location: From Old Mammoth Rd, take SR 203 (Main St) and Lake Mary Rd, 1.3 mi w, then 0.4 mi nw. 826 Lakeview Blvd 93546 (PO Box 835). Fax: 760/934-6501. **Facility:** The property is within walking distance of ski lifts and offers a wide variety of individually furnished units. 64 units. 38 two- and 26 three-bedroom suites with kitchens. 3 stories, interior/exterior corridors. **Parking:** on-site. **Terms:** office hours 8 am-10 pm, 3-4 night minimum stay - seasonal. **Amenities:** video library (fee). *Some:* DVD players, CD players, irons, hair dryers. **Pool(s):** outdoor. **Leisure Activities:** sauna, whirlpools. **Guest Services:** coin laundry, area transportation. **Cards:** AX, DS, MC, VI. **Special Amenities: free newspaper.**

SOME UNITS

VCR

ALPENHOF LODGE **Phone:** 760/934-6330

AAA SAVE — Motel

2/1-4/30 & 11/15-1/31 1P: $95-$130 2P: $115-$150 XP: $10 F12
5/1-11/14 1P: $75-$100 2P: $80-$115 XP: $10 F12

Location: SR 203, 1.1 mi w of Old Mammoth Rd. 6080 Minaret Rd 93546 (PO Box 1157). Fax: 760/934-7614. **Facility:** Smoke free premises. 60 units. 57 one-bedroom standard units, some with kitchens. 3 cottages. 2-3 stories (no elevator), interior/exterior corridors. *Bath:* combo or shower only. **Parking:** on-site. **Terms:** 2-3 night minimum stay - seasonal, 7 day cancellation notice-fee imposed. **Amenities:** hair dryers. *Some:* DVD players, irons. **Pool(s):** outdoor. **Leisure Activities:** sauna, whirlpool. **Guest Services:** coin laundry. **Business Services:** fax (fee). **Cards:** AX, DS, MC, VI. **Special Amenities: preferred room (subject to availability with advanced reservations).**

SOME UNITS

VCR

AUSTRIA HOF LODGE Book at aaa.com **Phone:** (760)934-2764

AAA SAVE — Small-scale Hotel

2/1-4/30 & 10/16-1/31 1P: $110-$195 2P: $110-$195 XP: $15
6/1-10/15 1P: $69-$99 2P: $69-$99 XP: $15

Location: Old Mammoth Rd, take SR 203 (Main St), 1 mi w, just w on Lake Mary Rd, then 1 mi nw. 924 Canyon Blvd 93546 (Box 607). Fax: 760/934-1880. **Facility:** Smoke free premises. 23 one-bedroom standard units, some with kitchens. Interior corridors. *Bath:* combo or shower only. **Parking:** on-site. **Terms:** open 2/1-4/30 & 6/1-1/31, office hours 8 am-10 pm, 14 day cancellation notice-fee imposed, [CP] meal plan available. **Amenities:** irons, hair dryers. **Dining:** Austria Hof Restaurant, see separate listing. **Leisure Activities:** whirlpool, downhill & cross country skiing, snowmobiling. **Guest Services:** sundries. **Business Services:** fax (fee). **Cards:** AX, DC, DS, MC, VI.

SOME UNITS

CINNAMON BEAR INN BED & BREAKFAST Book at aaa.com **Phone:** (760)934-2873

Bed & Breakfast

All Year [BP] 1P: $104-$135 2P: $115-$155 XP: $10

Location: Just s of SR 203 and w of Old Mammoth Rd. 113 Center St 93546 (PO Box 3338). Fax: 760/934-2873. **Facility:** This B&B offers a variety of rooms and suites, some with four-poster canopy beds and some with fireplaces. Smoke free premises. 22 units. 16 one-bedroom standard units. 6 one-bedroom suites ($129-$169), some with efficiencies or kitchens. 2 stories, exterior corridors. *Bath:* combo or shower only. **Parking:** on-site. **Terms:** 21 day cancellation notice-fee imposed, package plans. **Amenities:** *Some:* irons, hair dryers. **Leisure Activities:** whirlpool. **Guest Services:** complimentary evening beverages. **Business Services:** fax (fee). **Cards:** AX, DS, MC, VI. **Special Amenities: free full breakfast and free local telephone calls.**

SOME UNITS

DISCOVERY 4 CONDOMINIUMS **Phone:** (760)934-6410

Condominium

2/1-4/30 & 11/1-1/31	1P: $152-$280
5/1-10/31	1P: $115-$170

Location: Old Mammoth Rd, take SR 203 (Main St) and Lake Mary Rd, 1.5 mi w, just nw on Davidson Rd, then just s. 25 Lee Rd 93546 (PO Box 789). Fax: 760/934-2558. **Facility:** A variety of nicely decorated apartments. Smoke free premises. 51 units. 25 one-, 20 two- and 6 three-bedroom suites with kitchens. 2 stories, exterior corridors. **Parking:** on-site. **Terms:** office hours 10 am-10 pm, check-in 5 pm, 30 day cancellation notice-fee imposed, weekly rates available, pets ($10 extra charge, in limited units). **Amenities:** video library (fee). *Some:* DVD players, CD players, irons, hair dryers. **Pool(s):** outdoor. **Leisure Activities:** sauna, whirlpool, barbecue areas, game room. **Guest Services:** coin laundry. **Cards:** MC, VI. **Special Amenities: free newspaper and early check-in/late check-out.**

FEE

ECONO LODGE WILDWOOD INN Book at aaa.com **Phone:** (760)934-6855

Motel

10/1-1/31 [CP]	1P: $69-$79	2P: $79-$149	XP: $10	F18
2/1-4/30 [CP]	1P: $69-$89	2P: $69-$149	XP: $10	F18
5/1-9/30 [CP]	1P: $59-$69	2P: $69-$129	XP: $10	F18

Location: SR 203 (Main St), 0.7 mi w of Old Mammoth Rd. 3626 Main St 93546 (PO Box 568). Fax: 760/934-8208. **Facility:** 32 one-bedroom standard units. 2 stories, exterior corridors. **Parking:** on-site. **Terms:** office hours 7 am-11 pm, 3-6 night minimum stay - seasonal, 7 day cancellation notice-fee imposed, package plans - seasonal, pets ($10 fee, in designated units). **Amenities:** hair dryers. *Some:* irons. **Pool(s):** outdoor. **Leisure Activities:** whirlpool, fish cleaning & freezing facilities. **Business Services:** fax (fee). **Cards:** AX, DC, DS, MC, VI. **Special Amenities: free continental breakfast and free local telephone calls.**

SOME UNITS

FEE

HOLIDAY HAUS **Phone:** 760/934-2414

Motel

2/1-5/1 & 10/16-1/31	1P: $50-$90	2P: $60-$135	XP: $20	F16
5/2-10/15	1P: $45-$75	2P: $55-$85	XP: $10	F16

Location: SR 203, 0.7 mi w. 3905 Main St 93546 (PO Box 107). **Facility:** Smoke free premises. 19 units. 12 one-bedroom standard units. 1 cabin and 6 cottages. 2 stories, exterior corridors. *Bath:* combo or shower only. **Parking:** on-site. **Terms:** 14 day cancellation notice. **Amenities:** *Some:* irons, hair dryers. **Leisure Activities:** whirlpool. **Cards:** AX, MC, VI.

SOME UNITS

HOLIDAY INN HOTEL & SUITES Book at aaa.com **Phone:** (760)924-1234

Small-scale Hotel

12/17-1/31	1P: $170	2P: $170	XP: $10	F12
2/1-5/8 & 6/20-12/16	1P: $129	2P: $129	XP: $10	F12
5/9-6/19	1P: $111	2P: $111	XP: $10	F12

Location: SR 203 (Main St), just w of jct Old Mammoth Rd. 3236 Main St 93546 (PO Box 390). Fax: 760/934-3626. **Facility:** Smoke free premises. 71 one-bedroom standard units, some with efficiencies and/or whirlpools. 3 stories, interior corridors. **Parking:** on-site. **Amenities:** dual phone lines, voice mail, irons, hair dryers. *Fee:* video library, high-speed Internet. **Pool(s):** heated indoor. **Leisure Activities:** whirlpool, exercise room. **Guest Services:** gift shop, coin laundry. **Business Services:** meeting rooms. *Fee:* PC, fax. **Cards:** AX, CB, DC, DS, MC, VI.

SOME UNITS

ASK

FEE

JUNIPER SPRINGS LODGE **Phone:** (760)924-1102

Condominium

12/17-1/31	1P: $385-$395	2P: $595-$650
2/1-4/19 & 11/26-12/16	1P: $210-$310	2P: $440-$480
4/20-11/25	1P: $155-$175	2P: $245-$338

Location: SR 203, 0.4 mi s on Old Mammoth Rd, then 1 mi w. Located at chair lifts 15 and 24. 4000 Meridian Blvd 93546 (PO Box 2129). Fax: 760/924-8152. **Facility:** The lodge offers studio, one-, two- and three-bedroom condominiums with fireplaces. Smoke free premises. 208 units. 12 one-bedroom standard units with kitchens. 95 one-, 94 two- and 7 three-bedroom suites with kitchens. 5 stories, interior corridors. **Parking:** on-site. **Terms:** check-in 4 pm, 14 day cancellation notice-fee imposed, [CP] meal plan available. **Amenities:** video library (fee), voice mail, irons, hair dryers. *Some:* CD players. **Pool(s):** 2 heated outdoor. **Leisure Activities:** whirlpools, limited exercise equipment. **Guest Services:** gift shop, coin laundry, area transportation. **Business Services:** meeting rooms, business center. **Cards:** AX, MC, VI.

ASK

MAMMOTH MOUNTAIN INN **Phone:** (760)934-2581

Large-scale Hotel

11/5-1/31	1P: $165-$289	2P: $165-$289
2/1-4/24	1P: $155-$275	2P: $155-$275
4/25-11/4	1P: $115-$175	2P: $115-$175

Location: 5 mi w of town on SR 203; at Mammoth Mountain ski area. 1 Minaret Rd 93546 (PO Box 353). Fax: 760/934-0701. **Facility:** 213 units. 170 one-bedroom standard units. 24 one- and 19 two-bedroom suites ($315-$600) with kitchens, some with whirlpools. 3 stories, interior corridors. **Parking:** on-site. **Terms:** check-in 4 pm, 3 night minimum stay - weekends, 14 day cancellation notice-fee imposed, package plans - midweek. **Amenities:** voice mail, irons, hair dryers. **Pool(s):** heated outdoor. **Leisure Activities:** whirlpools, downhill & cross country skiing, snowmobiling, recreation programs, hiking trails, jogging. *Fee:* bicycles, game room. **Guest Services:** gift shop, coin laundry, area transportation. **Business Services:** conference facilities, fax (fee). **Cards:** AX, MC, VI.

SOME UNITS

ASK

MAMMOTH SKI & RACQUET CLUB — **Phone:** (760)934-7368

Condominium

2/1-4/30 & 11/1-1/31	1P: $130-$285	2P: $150-$322
5/1-10/31	1P: $105-$110	2P: $105-$125

Location: From Old Mammoth Rd, take SR 203, 1 mi w; SR 203, just n, Canyon Blvd, 0.8 mi w, then just s. 248 Mammoth Slopes Dr 93546 (PO Box 3846). Fax: 760/934-7080. **Facility:** 68 units. 54 one- and 14 two-bedroom suites with kitchens. 2-3 stories, interior corridors. **Parking:** on-site. **Terms:** check-in 5 pm, 28 day cancellation notice-fee imposed, weekly rates available, package plans, pets ($20 extra charge, in limited units). **Amenities:** video library (fee). *Some:* DVD players, CD players, irons, hair dryers. **Pool(s):** outdoor. **Leisure Activities:** sauna, whirlpools, 3 lighted tennis courts. *Fee:* game room. **Guest Services:** coin laundry. **Business Services:** fax (fee). **Cards:** AX, MC, VI.

ASK FEE VCR

MOUNTAINBACK CONDOMINIUMS — **Phone:** 760/934-5000

AAA SAVE

Condominium

All Year	2P: $135-$551

Location: From Old Mammoth Rd, take SR 203 and Lake Mary Rd, 1.3 mi w, then just nw. 435 Lakeview Blvd 93546 (PO Box 1838). Fax: 760/934-5254. **Facility:** Lofts are featured in some of these individually decorated two-bedroom condominiums. Smoke free premises. 60 units. 23 two- and 37 three-bedroom suites with kitchens. 2-3 stories, interior corridors. **Parking:** on-site. **Terms:** office hours 9 am-6 pm, check-in 5 pm, 2 night minimum stay, 30 day cancellation notice-fee imposed, package plans. **Amenities:** video library (fee). *Some:* CD players, irons, hair dryers. **Pool(s):** outdoor. **Leisure Activities:** sauna, whirlpools. **Guest Services:** complimentary laundry. **Cards:** MC, VI.

VCR DATA PORT

QUALITY INN *Book at aaa.com* — **Phone:** (760)934-5114

AAA SAVE

Small-scale Hotel

2/1-4/30 & 11/15-1/31 [CP]	1P: $105-$199	2P: $105-$199	XP: $10	F18
5/1-11/14 [CP]	1P: $89-$139	2P: $89-$139	XP: $10	F18

Location: SR 203, 0.5 mi w of Old Mammoth Rd. 3537 Main St 93546 (PO Box 3507). Fax: 760/934-5165. **Facility:** 61 one-bedroom standard units, some with kitchens and/or whirlpools. 2 stories, interior corridors. **Parking:** on-site. **Terms:** 3 day cancellation notice-fee imposed. **Amenities:** irons, hair dryers. **Leisure Activities:** whirlpool. **Business Services:** fax (fee). **Cards:** AX, CB, DC, DS, JC, MC, VI. **Special Amenities:** **free continental breakfast and free local telephone calls.**

DATA PORT SOME UNITS

ROYAL PINES RESORT **Phone:** 760/934-2306

Motel

All Year	1P: $79-$139	2P: $79-$139	XP: $10	F7

Location: Adjacent to SR 203, 0.8 mi w of Old Mammoth Rd. 3814 View Point Rd 93546 (PO Box 348). Fax: 760/934-2306. **Facility:** 28 units. 21 one-bedroom standard units, some with efficiencies. 7 one-bedroom suites with kitchens. 1-2 stories, interior/exterior corridors. *Bath:* combo or shower only. **Parking:** on-site. **Terms:** office hours 8 am-10 pm, 7 day cancellation notice-fee imposed, pets ($5 fee, in designated units). **Amenities:** *Some:* irons, hair dryers. **Leisure Activities:** whirlpool. **Business Services:** fax. **Cards:** DS, MC, VI. **Special Amenities: free local telephone calls and preferred room (subject to availability with advanced reservations).**

SOME UNITS

FEE

SIERRA LODGE *Book at aaa.com* **Phone:** (760)934-8881

Small-scale Hotel

2/1-5/1 & 11/1-1/31	1P: $79-$179	2P: $79-$179	XP: $10	F12
5/2-10/31	1P: $69-$169	2P: $69-$169	XP: $10	F12

Location: SR 203, 0.6 mi w of Old Mammoth Rd. 3540 Main St 93546 (PO Box 9228). Fax: 760/934-7231. **Facility:** Smoke free premises. 36 one-bedroom standard units. 2 stories (no elevator), interior corridors. **Parking:** on-site. **Terms:** office hours 7 am-11 pm, cancellation fee imposed, [CP] meal plan available, package plans - seasonal, pets ($10 extra charge, in designated units). **Amenities:** voice mail, hair dryers. *Some:* irons. **Leisure Activities:** whirlpool. **Business Services:** *Fee:* PC, fax. **Cards:** AX, DS, MC, VI. **Special Amenities: free continental breakfast and free local telephone calls.** *(See ad below)*

SOME UNITS

FEE FEE

SIERRA NEVADA RODEWAY INN *Book at aaa.com* **Phone:** (760)934-2515

Small-scale Hotel

12/19-1/31	1P: $169-$239	2P: $179-$249	XP: $10	F
11/16-12/18	1P: $89-$159	2P: $99-$169	XP: $10	F
2/1-5/31	1P: $79-$149	2P: $89-$169	XP: $10	F
6/1-11/15	1P: $69-$149	2P: $89-$169	XP: $10	F

Location: Just s of SR 203. 164 Old Mammoth Rd 93546 (PO Box 918). Fax: 760/934-7319. **Facility:** 156 units. 148 one-bedroom standard units, some with kitchens. 8 one-bedroom suites ($139-$349) with kitchens. 2 stories, interior/exterior corridors. *Bath:* combo or shower only. **Parking:** on-site. **Terms:** cancellation fee imposed, [CP] meal plan available, pets (in designated units). **Amenities:** *Some:* irons, hair dryers. **Pool(s):** outdoor. **Leisure Activities:** sauna, whirlpool, fish cleaning & freezing facilities. **Guest Services:** sundries, coin laundry. **Business Services:** meeting rooms, fax (fee). **Cards:** AX, CB, DC, MC, VI. **Special Amenities: free continental breakfast.** *(See color ad below)*

SOME UNITS

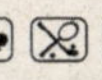

SUMMIT CONDOMINIUMS Book at aaa.com Phone: (760)934-5771

Condominium

All Year 1P: $89-$168 2P: $89-$168

Location: 1 mi w of Old Mammoth Rd. 3253 Meridian Blvd 93546 (PO Box 2187). Fax: 760/934-4251. **Facility:** Smoke free premises. 100 units. 91 one-, 5 two- and 4 three-bedroom suites with kitchens. 2 stories, interior corridors. **Parking:** on-site. **Terms:** office hours 9 am-6 pm, check-in 5 pm. **Amenities:** *Some:* irons. **Pool(s):** 2 outdoor. **Leisure Activities:** whirlpools, 3 tennis courts, exercise room. **Guest Services:** coin laundry. **Business Services:** fax (fee). **Cards:** AX, DC, DS, MC, VI.

SWISS CHALET MOTEL Phone: 760/934-2403

Motel

All Year [CP] 1P: $65-$120 2P: $65-$120 XP: $15 F14

Location: Adjacent to SR 203, 0.7 mi w of Old Mammoth Rd. 3776 Viewpoint Rd 93546 (PO Box 16). Fax: 760/934-2403. **Facility:** Designated smoking area. 20 one-bedroom standard units, some with efficiencies. 2 stories, exterior corridors. *Bath:* shower only. **Parking:** on-site. **Terms:** office hours 7 am-9 pm, 7 day cancellation notice-fee imposed, package plans, pets ($5 fee). **Amenities:** hair dryers. *Some:* irons. **Leisure Activities:** sauna, whirlpool. **Guest Services:** sundries. **Business Services:** fax (fee). **Cards:** AX, DS, MC, VI.

SOME UNITS

FEE

TRAVELODGE Book at aaa.com Phone: (760)934-8892

Small-scale Hotel

2/1-4/30 & 10/1-1/31 [CP] 1P: $69-$79 2P: $89-$149 XP: $10 F18

5/1-9/30 [CP] 1P: $59-$69 2P: $79-$129 XP: $10 F18

Location: Just n of SR 203, 0.6 mi w of Old Mammoth Rd. 54 Sierra Blvd 93546 (PO Box 568). Fax: 760/934-3496. **Facility:** Smoke free premises. 40 one-bedroom standard units. 2 stories, interior corridors. *Bath:* combo or shower only. **Parking:** on-site. **Terms:** office hours 7 am-11 pm, 3-6 night minimum stay - seasonal, 5 day cancellation notice-fee imposed, package plans - seasonal, small pets only ($10 extra charge). **Amenities:** hair dryers. *Some:* irons. **Leisure Activities:** sauna, whirlpool. **Guest Services:** coin laundry. **Business Services:** fax (fee). **Cards:** AX, DC, DS, MC, VI.

SOME UNITS

ASK DATA PORT

FEE

WHERE TO DINE

ALPENROSE RESTAURANT Lunch: $6-$10 Dinner: $13-$25 Phone: 760/934-3077

Continental

Location: Just s of SR 203. 343 Old Mammoth Rd 93546. **Hours:** 11:30 am-2 & 5-9 pm; Sunday brunch 9 am-3 pm. **Reservations:** suggested. **Features:** The charming, cozy restaurant builds its menu on European cuisine. Attractive, hand-painted walls contribute to a Bavarian theme. The summer patio is a nice place to relax. This place is closed for two weeks in the spring and fall. Casual dress; beer & wine only. **Parking:** on-site. **Cards:** AX, MC, VI.

ANGEL'S RESTAURANT Lunch: $6-$10 Dinner: $8-$16 Phone: 760/934-7427

American

Location: On SR 203, 0.5 mi w of Old Mammoth Rd. 3516 Main St 93546. **Hours:** 11:30 am-10 pm. **Features:** The casually informal restaurant serves salads, sandwiches, Mexican cuisine and barbecue specialties. Among good choices are the excellent homemade soups and the ultimate pork sandwich, made with marinated pork shoulder smothered with barbecue sauce, grilled onions and jack cheese. Cocktails. **Parking:** on-site. **Cards:** AX, CB, DC, DS, MC, VI.

AUSTRIA HOF RESTAURANT Dinner: $17-$28 Phone: 760/934-2764

German

Location: Old Mammoth Rd, take SR 203 (Main St), 1 mi w, just w on Lake Mary Rd, then 1 mi nw; in Austria Hof Lodge. 924 Canyon Blvd 93546. **Hours:** 5 pm-9 pm. Closed: 5/1-5/31 & 10/16-11/15. **Reservations:** suggested; weekends. **Features:** The cozy, well-appointed restaurant has high-back booths, stained-glass windows, lantern-style sconces and plants. Professional, friendly servers guide diners through a selection of German entrees or such dishes as venison medallions, steak, lamb or rainbow trout. Delicious desserts, including strudel, are homemade. Casual dress; cocktails. **Parking:** on-site. **Cards:** AX, CB, DC, DS, MC, VI.

CAFE VERMEER Lunch: $7-$10 Phone: 760/934-4203

Deli/Subs Sandwiches

Location: On SR 203, 0.3 mi w of Old Mammoth Rd; in Schats' Bakery building. 3305 Main St 93546. **Hours:** 7 am-11:30 & noon-2 pm. Closed major holidays. **Features:** This small deli-style restaurant is a great place for breakfast or for a quick bite before or after hitting the slopes. Try the Wisconsin smoked ham sandwich or the blackened salmon salad. Service is friendly and the atmosphere relaxed. Casual dress. **Parking:** on-site. **Cards:** MC, VI.

CERVINO'S Dinner: $16-$25 Phone: 760/934-4734

Northern Italian

Location: Adjacent to SR 203; 0.7 mi w of Old Mammoth Rd. 3752 Viewpoint Rd 93546. **Hours:** 5 pm-10 pm. Closed: 11/25. **Reservations:** suggested. **Features:** The hillside location affords lovely mountain views. On the menu is a selection of imaginative pasta, seafood, lamb and veal preparations. Old World decor and semi-private booths lend to the sophisticated feel of the dining room. Servers are well versed in ingredients and preparation styles and willingly accommodate special requests. Casual dress; beer & wine only. **Parking:** on-site. **Cards:** AX, CB, DC, DS, MC, VI.

THE LAKEFRONT RESTAURANT **Dinner:** $20-$25 **Phone:** 760/934-3534

French

Location: 3 mi sw via SR 203 and Lake Mary Rd; in Tamarack Lodge. **Hours:** 5:30 pm-9:30 pm; from 5 pm in winter; open for lunch in season. Closed: Tues & Wed in Spring and Fall. **Reservations:** accepted. **Features:** The charming, cozy dining room overlooks Twin Lakes. On the menu is excellently prepared French-California cuisine. Beer & wine only. **Parking:** on-site. **Cards:** AX, MC, VI.

THE MOGUL RESTAURANT **Dinner:** $13-$26 **Phone:** 760/934-3039

American

Location: Just s of SR 203, then just w of Old Mammoth Rd. 1528 Tavern Rd 93546. **Hours:** 5:30 pm-9:30 pm; 5 pm-10 pm in winter. **Features:** Country decor adorns the dining room, where patrons sit down for a meal of steak, prime rib, chicken or seafood. Casual dress; cocktails. **Parking:** on-site. **Cards:** AX, DS, MC, VI.

NEVADOS **Dinner:** $16-$24 **Phone:** 760/934-4466

American

Location: SR 203, 1 mi w of Old Mammoth Rd. Minaret Rd at Main St 93546. **Hours:** 5:30 pm-10 pm. **Reservations:** suggested. **Features:** The restaurant—with its upscale decor and pretty mountain views—provides a relaxing atmosphere in which patrons can enjoy a three-course prix fixe menu or such entrees as the favorite roast duck. Servers are friendly, casual and eager to please. Casual dress; cocktails. **Parking:** on-site. **Cards:** AX, DC, DS, MC, VI.

OCEAN HARVEST RESTAURANT **Dinner:** $14-$20 **Phone:** 760/934-8539

Seafood

Location: Just s of SR 203. 242 Old Mammoth Rd 93546. **Hours:** 5:30 pm-10 pm; to 9:30 pm in summer. Closed: 6/1-6/15 & 10/15-11/15. **Reservations:** suggested. **Features:** Mesquite-broiled seafood is at the heart of a menu that also lists steak and chicken entrees. The decor is nautical in theme, with plenty of rich woods, and fish mounted on the walls. Service is cordial and efficient. Casual dress; cocktails. **Parking:** on-site. **Cards:** AX, CB, DC, DS, MC, VI.

PERRY'S ITALIAN CAFE **Lunch:** $8-$12 **Dinner:** $9-$20 **Phone:** 760/934-6521

Italian

Location: On SR 203, 0.3 mi w of Old Mammoth Rd; in Factory Outlet Mall. 3399 Main St 93546. **Hours:** 6:30 am-10 pm. **Features:** The long-established cafe presents a menu of Italian and American favorites, including pizza. Patio dining is available, weather permitting. Casual dress; cocktails. **Parking:** on-site. **Cards:** AX, CB, DC, DS, MC, VI.

THE RESTAURANT AT CONVICT LAKE **Lunch:** $8-$22 **Dinner:** $16-$45 **Phone:** 760/934-3803

Continental

Location: 9 mi se of town; 2 mi w of US 395 from Convict Lake turnoff. **Hours:** 5:30 pm-9 pm, Fri & Sat-9:30 pm; also 11 am-2 pm in summer. **Reservations:** suggested. **Features:** A short drive south, the restaurant welcomes diners to a rustic but elegant setting. While taking in gorgeous mountain views, patrons can sample carefully prepared and beautifully presented menu items from salads to steaks. The light raspberry sorbet rounds out a good meal. Servers are helpful in making recommendations. Casual dress; cocktails. **Parking:** on-site. **Cards:** AX, DS, MC, VI.

SLOCUMS GRILL **Dinner:** $10-$30 **Phone:** 760/934-7647

Steak House

Location: On SR 203, just w of Old Mammoth Rd. 3221 Main St 93546. **Hours:** 5:30 pm-9:30 pm, Fri & Sat-10 pm. **Reservations:** suggested. **Features:** A favorite of tourists and locals for more than 18 years, the restaurant is an old-fashioned haven, decorated with polished brass and wood paneling. Steaks, ribs, seafood and pasta are delicious, as are the mouthwatering burgers. Hickory-smoked prime rib is a big draw on Friday and Saturday. Casual dress; cocktails. **Parking:** on-site. **Cards:** AX, DS, MC, VI.

WHISKEY CREEK RESTAURANT & MAMMOTH BREWING CO **Dinner:** $14-$24 **Phone:** 760/934-2555

American

Location: SR 203, 1 mi w of Old Mammoth Rd. 24 Lake Mary Rd 93546. **Hours:** 5:30 pm-10 pm; from 5 pm in winter. **Reservations:** suggested. **Features:** The restaurant—with its pretty mountain views, rich use of wood paneling, rock fireplace, upstairs lounge with dance floor and on-premises microbrewery—nurtures a friendly, lively atmosphere. Specialty beers mix well with such entrees as South Carolina cola pork chops and bacon-wrapped meatloaf. Service is upbeat and casual. Casual dress; cocktails. **Parking:** on-site. **Cards:** AX, CB, DC, DS, MC, VI.

MANTECA pop. 49,258

— WHERE TO STAY —

BEST WESTERN EXECUTIVE INN & SUITES *Book at aaa.com* **Phone:** (209)825-1415

Motel

All Year	1P: $65-$73	2P: $73-$89	XP: $8	F14

Location: Jct SR 99 and 120, exit Yosemite Ave. 1415 E Yosemite Ave 95336. Fax: 209/825-4251. **Facility:** 101 one-bedroom standard units, some with whirlpools. 3 stories, exterior corridors. **Parking:** on-site. **Terms:** [ECP] meal plan available, small pets only ($20 extra charge). **Amenities:** irons, hair dryers. **Pool(s):** outdoor. **Leisure Activities:** whirlpool. **Guest Services:** coin laundry. **Business Services:** meeting rooms. **Cards:** AX, CB, DC, DS, MC, VI. **Special Amenities: free continental breakfast and free local telephone calls.**

SOME UNITS

FEE

COMFORT INN *Book at aaa.com* **Phone:** (209)239-6115

Motel

All Year [ECP]	1P: $69-$100	2P: $75-$100	XP: $10	F18

Location: SR 99, exit SR 120, 0.5 mi e. 1920 E Yosemite Ave 95336. Fax: 209/239-9011. **Facility:** 58 one-bedroom standard units, some with whirlpools. 2 stories, exterior corridors. **Parking:** on-site. **Amenities:** irons, hair dryers. **Pool(s):** small outdoor. **Leisure Activities:** sauna, whirlpool, exercise room. **Guest Services:** coin laundry. **Business Services:** meeting rooms. **Cards:** AX, CB, DC, DS, JC, MC, VI. **Special Amenities: free expanded continental breakfast and free local telephone calls.** *(See color ad below)*

SOME UNITS

The following lodging was either not evaluated or did not meet AAA rating requirements but is listed for your information only.

HOLIDAY INN EXPRESS HOTEL & SUITES **Phone:** 916/952-6552

fyi

6/1-8/31	1P: $69-$89	2P: $84-$104	XP: $5	F18
2/1-5/31 & 9/1-10/31	1P: $49-$69	2P: $54-$74	XP: $5	F18
11/1-1/31	1P: $39-$59	2P: $44-$64	XP: $5	F18

Too new to rate, opening scheduled for September 2003. **Location:** 179 Commerce Ave 95336 (8803 Liscarney Way, SACRAMENTO, 95828). **Amenities:** 72 units, coffeemakers, microwaves, refrigerators, pool. **Cards:** AX, CB, DC, DS, JC, MC, VI. *(See ad below)*

MARICOPA pop. 1,111

WHERE TO STAY

MOTEL 8 Phone: 661/769-8291

Motel

All Year	1P: $30-$48	2P: $48-$58	XP: $10	F12

Location: Jct SR 166 and 33. 600 Poso St 93252 (PO Box 608). Fax: 661/769-8852. **Facility:** 40 one-bedroom standard units. 2 stories (no elevator), exterior corridors. **Parking:** on-site. **Amenities:** *Some:* irons, hair dryers. **Pool(s):** outdoor. **Business Services:** fax (fee). **Cards:** AX, DS, MC, VI. **Special Amenities: free continental breakfast and free local telephone calls.**

SOME UNITS

MARINA —*See Monterey Peninsula p. 483.*

MARIPOSA pop. 1,373—*See also YOSEMITE NATIONAL PARK.*

WHERE TO STAY

BEST VALUE MARIPOSA LODGE Book at aaa.com Phone: (209)966-3607

Motel

5/15-10/31	1P: $69-$129	2P: $69-$129	XP: $10	F10
4/1-5/14	1P: $59-$79	2P: $59-$79	XP: $10	F10
2/1-3/31 & 11/1-1/31	1P: $49-$69	2P: $49-$69	XP: $10	F10

Location: Center. 5052 Hwy 140 95338 (PO Box 733). Fax: 209/742-7038. **Facility:** 44 one-bedroom standard units. 2 stories (no elevator), exterior corridors. *Bath:* combo or shower only. **Parking:** on-site. **Terms:** pets ($10 extra charge). **Amenities:** irons, hair dryers. **Pool(s):** small outdoor. **Leisure Activities:** whirlpool. **Cards:** AX, CB, DC, DS, MC, VI. **Special Amenities: free local telephone calls and preferred room (subject to availability with advanced reservations).** *(See color ad below & p 817)*

SOME UNITS

FEE

BEST WESTERN YOSEMITE WAY STATION MOTEL Book at aaa.com Phone: (209)966-7545

Motel

4/1-9/8 [CP]	1P: $74-$96	2P: $74-$96	XP: $10	F12
9/9-11/30 [CP]	1P: $74-$86	2P: $74-$86	XP: $10	F12
2/1-3/31 & 12/1-1/31 [CP]	1P: $44-$69	2P: $44-$69	XP: $10	F12

Location: SR 140 at SR 49 S. 4999 Hwy 140 95338 (PO Box 1989). Fax: 209/966-6353. **Facility:** 78 one-bedroom standard units. 2-3 stories (no elevator), exterior corridors. *Bath:* combo or shower only. **Parking:** on-site. **Terms:** small pets only ($5 extra charge). **Amenities:** irons, hair dryers. **Pool(s):** outdoor. **Leisure Activities:** whirlpool. **Business Services:** meeting rooms. **Cards:** AX, CB, DC, DS, JC, MC, VI. **Special Amenities: free continental breakfast and free local telephone calls.** *(See color ad p 819)*

SOME UNITS

FEE

COMFORT INN-MARIPOSA Book at aaa.com Phone: (209)966-4344

Motel

4/1-10/31 [CP]	1P: $79-$99	2P: $79-$99	XP: $10	F18
2/1-3/31 & 11/1-1/31 [CP]	1P: $49-$79	2P: $49-$79	XP: $10	F18

Location: Just e of jct SR 140 and 49 S. 4994 Bullion St 95338 (PO Box 1989). Fax: 209/966-4655. **Facility:** 61 one-bedroom standard units. 2-3 stories (no elevator), exterior corridors. *Bath:* combo or shower only. **Parking:** on-site. **Terms:** check-in 4 pm. **Amenities:** irons, hair dryers. **Pool(s):** outdoor. **Leisure Activities:** whirlpool. **Guest Services:** gift shop. **Business Services:** meeting rooms. **Cards:** AX, CB, DC, DS, JC, MC, VI. **Special Amenities: free continental breakfast and free newspaper.** *(See color ad p 819)*

SOME UNITS

E.C. LODGE YOSEMITE — **Phone:** (209)742-6800

Motel

4/1-9/30 [ECP]	2P: $58-$121	XP: $10	F6
2/1-3/31 & 10/1-1/31 [ECP]	2P: $39-$89	XP: $10	F6

Location: Jct SR 49 and 140 N. 5180 Jones St 95338 (PO Box 339). Fax: 209/742-6719. **Facility:** 27 one-bedroom standard units. 2 stories (no elevator), exterior corridors. *Bath:* combo or shower only. **Parking:** on-site. **Terms:** weekly rates available. **Amenities:** high-speed Internet, irons, hair dryers. **Pool(s):** small outdoor. **Leisure Activities:** whirlpool. **Business Services:** meeting rooms, PC, fax. **Cards:** AX, DC, DS, MC, VI. **Special Amenities: free expanded continental breakfast and free local telephone calls.** *(See color ad p 818)*

SOME UNITS

LITTLE VALLEY INN AT THE CREEK — Book at aaa.com — **Phone:** 209/742-6204

Bed & Breakfast

All Year	1P: $104	2P: $104	XP: $20

Location: SR 49, 7 mi s. 3483 Brooks Rd 95338. Fax: 209/742-5099. **Facility:** 6 one-bedroom standard units, some with kitchens. 1 story, exterior corridors. **Parking:** on-site. **Terms:** check-in 4 pm, 3 day cancellation notice. **Leisure Activities:** bicycles, hiking trails. **Cards:** JC, MC, VI.

SOME UNITS

MINERS INN — Book at aaa.com — **Phone:** (209)742-7777

Motel

4/1-9/30	1P: $59	2P: $69	XP: $6	F6
2/1-3/31	1P: $49	2P: $59	XP: $6	F6
10/1-1/31	1P: $45	2P: $55	XP: $6	F6

Location: On SR 49, n at SR 140. 5181 Hwy 49 N 95338 (PO Box 2248). Fax: 209/966-2343. **Facility:** 78 units. 76 one-bedroom standard units, some with efficiencies and/or whirlpools. 2 one-bedroom suites ($110-$149) with efficiencies and whirlpools. 2 stories (no elevator), interior/exterior corridors. *Bath:* combo or shower only. **Parking:** on-site. **Terms:** cancellation fee imposed, pets ($5 extra charge). **Dining:** Miners Inn Restaurant, see separate listing. **Pool(s):** outdoor. **Leisure Activities:** whirlpool. **Guest Services:** gift shop. **Business Services:** meeting rooms, fax (fee). **Cards:** AX, DS, MC, VI. *(See color ad p 823)*

FEE SOME UNITS

SUPER 8 MOTEL — Book at aaa.com — **Phone:** (209)966-4288

Motel

All Year [CP]	1P: $69-$109	2P: $89-$119	XP: $10	F4

Location: Center. 5059 Hwy 140 95338 (PO Box 2193). Fax: 209/966-4788. **Facility:** 46 one-bedroom standard units. 4 stories, interior corridors. **Parking:** on-site. **Amenities:** irons, hair dryers. **Pool(s):** small outdoor. **Cards:** AX, CB, DC, MC, VI.

SOME UNITS

WHERE TO DINE

MINERS INN RESTAURANT — **Lunch:** $6-$10 — **Dinner:** $7-$17 — **Phone:** 209/966-2444

American

Location: On SR 49, n at SR 140; in Miners Inn. 5159 Hwy 140 95338. **Hours:** 7 am-9 pm, Sat-10 pm. **Features:** On the way to or from Yosemite National Park, the popular eatery is a great stop for breakfast, lunch or dinner. Casual dress; cocktails. **Parking:** on-site. **Cards:** AX, DC, MC, VI.

SAVOURY'S — **Dinner:** $11-$19 — **Phone:** 209/966-7677

American

Location: Center. 5027 Hwy 140 95338. **Hours:** 5 pm-9 pm. Closed: 4/11; also Wed & Sun. **Reservations:** suggested. **Features:** Guests can take a seat by the window and watch small-town-style hustle and bustle. On the way to scenic Yosemite National Park, the dinner-only dining room has lots of charm and good food. Casual dress; beer & wine only. **Parking:** on-site and street. **Cards:** MC, VI.

MARKLEEVILLE pop. 197

WHERE TO STAY

THE WOODFORDS INN — **Phone:** (530)694-2410

Motel

All Year	1P: $88-$110	2P: $88-$110	XP: $10	F12

Location: On SR 89, 0.3 mi s of jct SR 89/88. 20960 Hwy 89 96120 (1925 S Winchester Blvd, Suite 203, CAMPBELL, 95008). Fax: 530/694-9696. **Facility:** 20 one-bedroom standard units. 2 stories (no elevator), exterior corridors. *Bath:* shower only. **Parking:** on-site. **Amenities:** hair dryers. **Leisure Activities:** whirlpool. **Cards:** MC, VI. **Special Amenities: early check-in/late check-out.**

MARTINEZ pop. 35,866

WHERE TO STAY

BEST WESTERN JOHN MUIR INN — Book at aaa.com — **Phone:** (925)229-1010

Small-scale Hotel

All Year [ECP]	1P: $104-$119	2P: $109-$124	XP: $10	F16

Location: Jct I-680 and SR 4, 2.3 mi w, exit SR 4 at Pine/Center. 445 Muir Station Rd 94553. Fax: 925/228-4810. **Facility:** 116 one-bedroom standard units, some with efficiencies or kitchens. 3 stories, interior corridors. **Parking:** on-site. **Amenities:** video games (fee), voice mail, irons, hair dryers. *Some:* dual phone lines. **Pool(s):** small heated outdoor. **Leisure Activities:** whirlpool. **Guest Services:** complimentary evening beverages: Mon-Thurs, valet laundry. **Business Services:** meeting rooms, business center. **Cards:** AX, CB, DC, DS, JC, MC, VI. **Special Amenities: free expanded continental breakfast and early check-in/late check-out.** *(See color ad p 612)*

SOME UNITS

MARYSVILLE pop. 12,268

WHERE TO STAY

AMERIHOST INN-MARYSVILLE Book at aaa.com **Phone:** (530)742-2700

Motel

5/1-9/30 [ECP]	1P: $89-$99	2P: $95-$99	XP: $5	F17
2/1-4/30 [ECP]	1P: $79-$89	2P: $85-$99	XP: $5	F17
10/1-1/31 [ECP]	1P: $79-$89	2P: $79-$89	XP: $5	F17

Location: 0.5 mi s on SR 70, exit N Beale Rd (Yuba College). 1111 N Beale Rd 95901. Fax: 530/742-2733. **Facility:** 62 units. 60 one-bedroom standard units, some with whirlpools. 2 one-bedroom suites ($129-$169) with whirlpools. 2 stories, interior corridors. *Bath:* combo or shower only. **Parking:** on-site. **Amenities:** voice mail, irons, hair dryers. **Pool(s):** heated indoor. **Leisure Activities:** whirlpool, exercise room. **Guest Services:** coin laundry. **Business Services:** meeting rooms. **Cards:** AX, CB, DC, DS, JC, MC, VI. **Special Amenities: free expanded continental breakfast and free local telephone calls.**

SOME UNITS

BEST VALUE INN Book at aaa.com **Phone:** (530)743-1531

Motel

All Year 1P: $45-$75 2P: $50-$80 XP: $5 F12

Location: Jct SR 70 and 20. 904 E St 95901. Fax: 530/741-3119. **Facility:** 40 one-bedroom standard units. 2 stories, exterior corridors. *Bath:* combo or shower only. **Parking:** on-site. **Terms:** cancellation fee imposed, pets ($5 fee). **Cards:** AX, DS, MC, VI. **Special Amenities: early check-in/late check-out and free room upgrade (subject to availability with advanced reservations).**

SOME UNITS

FEE

SUPER 8 MOTEL Book at aaa.com **Phone:** (530)742-8238

Motel

All Year 1P: $40-$80 2P: $50-$80 XP: $3 F11

Location: 0.5 mi s on SR 70, exit N Beale Rd (Yuba College) southbound; exit Feather River Blvd northbound. 1078 N Beale Rd 95901. Fax: 530/742-7989. **Facility:** 40 one-bedroom standard units. 2 stories, exterior corridors. **Parking:** on-site. **Amenities:** hair dryers. **Pool(s):** outdoor. **Cards:** AX, DC, DS, MC, VI. **Special Amenities: free continental breakfast and free local telephone calls.**

SOME UNITS

TRAVELODGE Book at aaa.com **Phone:** (530)742-8586

Motel

All Year 1P: $45-$75 2P: $50-$85 XP: $5 F12

Location: SR 20, 0.5 mi w of SR 70. 721 10th St 95901. Fax: 530/742-0132. **Facility:** 43 one-bedroom standard units. 2 stories, exterior corridors. **Parking:** on-site. **Terms:** cancellation fee imposed, [CP] meal plan available. **Amenities:** voice mail, hair dryers. **Pool(s):** outdoor. **Cards:** AX, DS, MC, VI. **Special Amenities: free continental breakfast and free local telephone calls.**

SOME UNITS

MCCLOUD pop. 1,343

WHERE TO STAY

MCCLOUD HOTEL BED & BREAKFAST **Phone:** (530)964-2822

Bed & Breakfast

4/1-10/31 [BP]	1P: $119-$154	2P: $119-$154	XP: $25
2/1-3/31 & 11/1-1/31 [BP]	1P: $99-$154	2P: $99-$154	XP: $25

Location: I-5. 408 Main St 96057 (PO Box 730). Fax: 530/964-2844. **Facility:** Large communal parlors and a fieldstone fireplace add character to this 1916 hotel; across the street is the Shasta Sunset Dinner Train. 16 one-bedroom standard units, some with whirlpools. 2 stories, interior corridors. **Parking:** on-site. **Terms:** office hours 7 am-11 pm, age restrictions may apply, 10 day cancellation notice-fee imposed. **Amenities:** video library, hair dryers. *Some:* DVD players, irons. **Dining:** 7 am-9 pm. **Guest Services:** gift shop. **Business Services:** meeting rooms. **Cards:** AX, DS, MC, VI. **Special Amenities: free local telephone calls and early check-in/late check-out.**

(See ad p 507)

SOME UNITS

VCR

MCCLOUD RIVER INN BED & BREAKFAST **Phone:** (530)964-2130

Historic Bed & Breakfast

6/1-10/31 [BP]	1P: $96-$115	2P: $96-$115	XP: $15
2/1-5/31 & 11/1-1/31 [BP]	1P: $82-$115	2P: $82-$115	XP: $15

Location: I-5. 325 Lawndale Ct 96057 (PO Box 1560). Fax: 530/964-2730. **Facility:** A two-story home built in the 1900s, this B&B just off the town's main thoroughfare is painted yellow and white and is surrounded by wooden decks. Smoke free premises. 5 one-bedroom standard units, some with whirlpools. 2 stories, interior corridors. *Bath:* combo or shower only. **Parking:** on-site. **Terms:** office hours 9 am-5 pm, 2 night minimum stay - seasonal weekends, age restrictions may apply, 7 day cancellation notice, package plans - mid-week in winter. **Amenities:** irons, hair dryers. **Leisure Activities:** Fee: massage. **Guest Services:** gift shop. **Business Services:** meeting rooms. **Cards:** AX, DS, MC, VI. **Special Amenities: free local telephone calls.**

SOME UNITS

MCCLOUD RIVER SKI LODGE **Phone:** 530/964-2700

Motel

All Year [CP] 1P: $65-$80 XP: $10 F

Location: W on SR 89. 140 Squaw Valley Rd 96057 (PO Box 656). **Facility:** 5 one-bedroom standard units with whirlpools. 1 story, exterior corridors. **Parking:** on-site. **Terms:** age restrictions may apply, 3 day cancellation notice. **Amenities:** *Some:* irons, hair dryers. **Cards:** AX, DS, MC, VI.

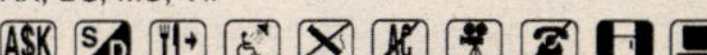

WHERE TO DINE

BRIARPATCH RESTAURANT Dinner: $5-$15 Phone: 530/964-2700

American

Location: W on SR 89; in the McCloud River Ski Lodge. 140 Squaw Valley Rd 96057. **Hours:** 5 pm-9 pm. **Features:** Interesting aspects of the Mexican restaurant are the wood stove and pool table in the dining area. Guests can sit outdoors in good weather. Casual dress; cocktails; entertainment. **Parking:** on-site. **Cards:** AX, DS, MC, VI.

MCKINLEYVILLE pop. 13,599

WHERE TO STAY

HOLIDAY INN EXPRESS & SUITES Book at aaa.com Phone: (707)840-9305

Small-scale Hotel

6/1-9/30	1P: $89-$149	2P: $89-$149	XP: $5	F19
10/1-1/31	1P: $79-$149	2P: $79-$149	XP: $5	F19
2/1-5/31	1P: $79-$139	2P: $79-$139	XP: $5	F19

Location: US 101, exit Arcata Airport Rd, just s of Boeing. 3107 Concord Dr 95519. Fax: 707/840-9417. **Facility:** 70 one-bedroom standard units, some with whirlpools. 2 stories, interior corridors. *Bath:* combo or shower only. **Parking:** on-site. **Terms:** age restrictions may apply, [ECP] meal plan available. **Amenities:** high-speed Internet, voice mail, irons, hair dryers. **Pool(s):** heated indoor. **Leisure Activities:** whirlpool. **Guest Services:** coin laundry. **Business Services:** business center. **Cards:** AX, DC, DS, MC, VI. **Special Amenities: free expanded continental breakfast and free local telephone calls.** *(See color ad p 269)*

SOME UNITS

MENDOCINO —See Wine Country p. 784.

MENLO PARK pop. 30,785 (See map and index starting on p. 599)

WHERE TO STAY

BEST WESTERN RIVIERA Book at aaa.com Phone: (650)321-8772 483

Motel

All Year [ECP] 1P: $109-$159 2P: $119-$169 XP: $15 F12

Location: On SR 82. Located adjacent to Stanford University campus. 15 El Camino Real 94025. Fax: 650/321-2137. **Facility:** 36 one-bedroom standard units. 3 stories, exterior corridors. **Parking:** on-site. **Terms:** 7 day cancellation notice. **Amenities:** high-speed Internet, voice mail, irons, hair dryers. **Pool(s):** small outdoor. **Leisure Activities:** sauna, whirlpool, exercise room. **Guest Services:** coin laundry. **Cards:** AX, CB, DC, DS, JC, MC, VI. **Special Amenities: free expanded continental breakfast and free local telephone calls.**

SOME UNITS

MENLO PARK INN Book at aaa.com Phone: (650)326-7530 482

Motel

All Year [ECP] 1P: $99-$149 2P: $109-$159 XP: $10 F17

Location: On SR 82 at Valparaiso. Located in a commercial area. 1315 El Camino Real 94025. Fax: 650/328-7539. **Facility:** 30 one-bedroom standard units, some with whirlpools. 2 stories, exterior corridors. **Parking:** on-site. **Amenities:** voice mail, irons, hair dryers. **Guest Services:** valet laundry. **Cards:** AX, CB, DC, DS, JC, MC, VI. **Special Amenities: free expanded continental breakfast and free newspaper.** *(See color ad below)*

SOME UNITS

RED COTTAGE INN Book at aaa.com Phone: (650)326-9010 481

Motel

All Year 1P: $74-$119 2P: $74-$119

Location: On SR 82. 1704 El Camino Real 94025. Fax: 650/326-4002. **Facility:** 28 units. 27 one-bedroom standard units. 1 two-bedroom suite ($109-$159) with kitchen and whirlpool. 2 stories, exterior corridors. *Bath:* combo or shower only. **Parking:** on-site. **Terms:** [ECP] meal plan available. **Amenities:** irons, hair dryers. **Pool(s):** heated outdoor. **Cards:** AX, CB, DC, DS, JC, MC, VI. **Special Amenities: free continental breakfast and free room upgrade (subject to availability with advanced reservations).**

(See map and index starting on p. 599)

STANFORD PARK HOTEL *Book at aaa.com* **Phone:** (650)322-1234 480

SAVE

Large-scale Hotel

All Year 1P: $159-$725 2P: $159-$725 XP: $15 F12

Location: On SR 82, 0.5 mi ne of Stanford University. 100 El Camino Real 94025. Fax: 650/322-0975. **Facility:** Fireplaces are featured in some guest rooms at this elegantly appointed hotel surrounded by manicured grounds. Smoke free premises. 163 units. 155 one-bedroom standard units. 8 one-bedroom suites ($230-$725), some with whirlpools. 4 stories, interior corridors. **Parking:** valet. **Terms:** cancellation fee imposed. **Amenities:** video games, CD players, high-speed Internet, dual phone lines, voice mail, honor bars, irons, hair dryers. **Dining:** 6:30 am-2 & 5:30-10 pm, cocktails. **Pool(s):** heated outdoor. **Leisure Activities:** sauna, whirlpool, exercise room. **Guest Services:** gift shop, complimentary evening beverages, valet laundry. **Business Services:** conference facilities, business center. **Cards:** AX, CB, DC, DS, JC, MC, VI. **Special Amenities: free newspaper.**

(See color ad inside back cover)

SOME UNITS

24 DATA PORT / VCR /

WHERE TO DINE

GAYLORD INDIA RESTAURANT **Lunch:** $12-$17 **Dinner:** $13-$24 **Phone:** 650/326-8761 225

Indian

Location: On SR 82 at Encinal Ave. 1706 El Camino Real 94027. **Hours:** 11:45 am-2:30 & 5-10 pm. Closed: 11/25, 12/25. **Reservations:** suggested. **Features:** The varied menu includes many vegetarian and seafood specialties. At lunch, the buffet lines up an appealing choice of dishes. The surroundings are attractive and cozy. Casual dress; cocktails. **Parking:** on-site. **Cards:** AX, CB, DC, DS, MC, VI.

MERCED pop. 63,893

WHERE TO STAY

BEST WESTERN INN *Book at aaa.com* **Phone:** (209)723-2163

SAVE

Motel

All Year [ECP] 1P: $69-$89 2P: $69-$89

Location: SR 99, exit Childs Ave or SR 140, just e. 1033 Motel Dr 95340. Fax: 209/384-7272. **Facility:** 42 one-bedroom standard units, some with whirlpools. 2 stories (no elevator), exterior corridors. **Parking:** on-site. **Amenities:** voice mail, irons, hair dryers. **Pool(s):** outdoor. **Leisure Activities:** exercise room. **Guest Services:** coin laundry. **Cards:** AX, CB, DC, DS, MC, VI. **Special Amenities: free expanded continental breakfast and free newspaper.**

SOME UNITS

DATA PORT / VCR /

DAYS INN *Book at aaa.com* **Phone:** (209)722-2726

SAVE

Motel

All Year 1P: $59-$79 2P: $59-$108 XP: $10 F18

Location: SR 99, exit Childs Ave or SR 140, just e. 1199 Motel Dr 95340. Fax: 209/722-7083. **Facility:** 24 one-bedroom standard units. 1 story, exterior corridors. *Bath:* combo or shower only. **Parking:** on-site. **Terms:** [CP] meal plan available. **Amenities:** dual phone lines, voice mail, safes, irons, hair dryers. **Pool(s):** outdoor. **Leisure Activities:** exercise room. **Guest Services:** coin laundry. **Cards:** AX, CB, DC, DS, MC, VI. **Special Amenities: free continental breakfast and free local telephone calls.**

SOME UNITS

VCR DATA PORT / /

MERCED-YOSEMITE TRAVELODGE *Book at aaa.com* **Phone:** (209)722-6224

SAVE

Motel

5/1-9/30 [CP] 1P: $55-$75 2P: $55-$75 XP: $5 F17

2/1-4/30 & 10/1-1/31 [CP] 1P: $45-$65 2P: $45-$65 XP: $5 F17

Location: SR 99, exit SR 140, just e. 1260 Yosemite Pkwy 95340. Fax: 209/726-3224. **Facility:** 46 one-bedroom standard units, some with whirlpools. 2 stories (no elevator), exterior corridors. *Bath:* combo or shower only. **Parking:** on-site. **Terms:** cancellation fee imposed, pets ($25 deposit, $10 extra charge). **Amenities:** voice mail, hair dryers. **Pool(s):** outdoor. **Cards:** AX, CB, DC, DS, JC, MC, VI. **Special Amenities: free continental breakfast and free local telephone calls.** *(See color ad below)*

SOME UNITS

FEE DATA PORT / /

RAMADA INN Book at aaa.com **Phone:** (209)723-3121

Motel

All Year 1P: $79-$129 2P: $79-$129 XP: $15 F17

Location: SR 99, exit Childs Ave, just e. 2000 E Childs Ave 95340. Fax: 209/723-0127. **Facility:** 110 one-bedroom standard units, some with whirlpools. 2 stories (no elevator), interior/exterior corridors. **Parking:** on-site. **Terms:** cancellation fee imposed. **Amenities:** voice mail, irons, hair dryers. *Some:* high-speed Internet. **Dining:** Eagles Nest, see separate listing. **Pool(s):** outdoor. **Business Services:** meeting rooms. **Cards:** AX, CB, DC, DS, JC, MC, VI. **Special Amenities: early check-in/late check-out and free room upgrade (subject to availability with advanced reservations).** *(See color ad p 821 & below)*

SOME UNITS

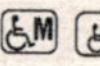   

SUPER 8 Book at aaa.com **Phone:** (209)384-1303

Motel

All Year [ECP] 1P: $60-$65 2P: $65-$70 XP: $10 F

Location: SR 99, exit Childs Ave, just e. 1983 E Childs Ave 95340. Fax: 209/384-1304. **Facility:** 80 one-bedroom standard units. 2 stories, interior corridors. *Bath:* combo or shower only. **Parking:** on-site. **Amenities:** voice mail. **Pool(s):** outdoor. **Cards:** AX, DS, MC, VI.

SOME UNITS

WHERE TO DINE

THE BRANDING IRON Lunch: $5-$12 Dinner: $10-$30 Phone: 209/722-1822

American

Location: 0.5 mi e of SR 99. 640 W 16th St 95340. **Hours:** 11:30 am-2 & 5:30-9:30 pm, Sat from 5:30 pm, Sun 5 pm-9 pm. Closed major holidays. **Reservations:** suggested. **Features:** Casual, Western decor gives the dining room a homey feel. Quality food is served in ample portions. Service is prompt and friendly. Patio seating is a seasonal option. Dressy casual; cocktails. **Parking:** on-site. **Cards:** AX, MC, VI.

EAGLES NEST Lunch: $5-$14 Dinner: $10-$25 Phone: 209/723-1041

American

Location: SR 99, exit Childs Ave, just e; in Ramada Inn. 2000 E Childs Ave 95340. **Hours:** 6 am-10 pm. Closed: 12/25. **Reservations:** suggested. **Features:** Just off the highway, the upscale family restaurant serves California cuisine prepared with fresh ingredients. Casual dress; cocktails. **Parking:** on-site. **Cards:** AX, CB, DC, DS, MC, VI. *(See color ad p 821 & p 426)*

SIR JAMES Dinner: $15-$38 Phone: 209/723-5552

American

Location: SR 99, exit Childs Ave or SR 140, just e. 1111 Motel Dr 95340. **Hours:** 5 pm-9:30 pm. Closed major holidays; also Sun. **Reservations:** suggested. **Features:** Well-prepared steak, seafood and poultry dishes line the menu at the comfortable restaurant. The staff is friendly. Casual dress; cocktails; entertainment. **Parking:** on-site. **Cards:** AX, CB, DC, DS, MC, VI.

MIDDLETOWN —*See Wine Country p. 788.*

MILLBRAE —*See San Francisco p. 669.*

MILL VALLEY —*See San Francisco p. 672.*

MILPITAS pop. 62,698

WHERE TO STAY

BEST VALUE INN & SUITES Book at aaa.com **Phone:** (408)946-8383

SAVE

Motel

All Year 1P: $69-$99 2P: $69-$99 XP: $5 F12

Location: I-880, exit Calaveras Blvd (SR 237), 0.5 mi e, then just s. 485 S Main St 95035. Fax: 408/262-6128. **Facility:** 82 one-bedroom standard units, some with whirlpools. 2-3 stories (no elevator), exterior corridors. **Parking:** on-site. **Terms:** weekly rates available, [CP] meal plan available. **Amenities:** voice mail. **Guest Services:** coin laundry. **Cards:** AX, DC, DS, JC, MC, VI. **Special Amenities: free continental breakfast and early check-in/late check-out.**

SOME UNITS

DATA PORT

BEST WESTERN BROOKSIDE INN Book at aaa.com **Phone:** (408)263-5566

SAVE

Motel

All Year [ECP] 1P: $89-$119 2P: $89-$119 XP: $10 F16

Location: I-880, exit Calaveras Blvd (SR 237/N Abbott Ave), just e. 400 Valley Way 95035. Fax: 408/262-6866. **Facility:** 78 one-bedroom standard units. 2 stories (no elevator), interior/exterior corridors. *Bath:* combo or shower only. **Parking:** on-site. **Terms:** pets ($15 extra charge). **Amenities:** voice mail, irons, hair dryers. **Pool(s):** heated outdoor. **Leisure Activities:** whirlpool, steamroom, exercise room. **Guest Services:** coin laundry. **Business Services:** meeting rooms. **Cards:** AX, CB, DC, DS, JC, MC, VI. **Special Amenities: free expanded continental breakfast and early check-in/late check-out.**

SOME UNITS

FEE DATA PORT VCR

BEVERLY HERITAGE HOTEL Book at aaa.com **Phone:** 408/943-9080

SAVE

Large-scale Hotel

All Year 1P: $229 2P: $229

Location: Northwest quadrant of I-880 and Montague Expwy. 1820 Barber Ln 95035. Fax: 408/432-8617. **Facility:** 237 units. 172 one-bedroom standard units. 65 one-bedroom suites ($239), some with whirlpools. 3 stories, interior corridors. *Bath:* combo or shower only. **Parking:** on-site. **Terms:** 19% service charge. **Amenities:** dual phone lines, voice mail, irons, hair dryers. *Fee:* video games, high-speed Internet. **Dining:** Brandon's, see separate listing. **Pool(s):** outdoor. **Leisure Activities:** whirlpool, bicycles, jogging, exercise room. **Guest Services:** valet laundry, airport transportation-San Jose Airport, area transportation-within 3 mi. **Business Services:** conference facilities, business center. **Cards:** AX, DS, MC, VI. **Special Amenities: free newspaper and free room upgrade (subject to availability with advanced reservations).** *(See color ad p 426)*

SOME UNITS

DATA PORT

CANDLEWOOD SUITES-MILIPITAS/SILICON VALLEY Book at aaa.com **Phone:** (408)719-1212

SAVE

Small-scale Hotel

All Year 1P: $59-$129 2P: $69-$139 XP: $10 F18

Location: SR 237, exit McCarthy, just n. 40 Ranch Dr 95035. Fax: 408/719-9080. **Facility:** 126 one-bedroom standard units with efficiencies. 4 stories, interior corridors. *Bath:* combo or shower only. **Parking:** on-site. **Terms:** cancellation fee imposed, pets ($75 fee, $10 extra charge). **Amenities:** video library, video games (fee), CD players, high-speed Internet, dual phone lines, voice mail, irons, hair dryers. **Leisure Activities:** whirlpool, exercise room. **Guest Services:** complimentary laundry, area transportation-within 5 mi. **Cards:** AX, CB, DC, DS, JC, MC, VI. **Special Amenities: free local telephone calls and free newspaper.** *(See color ad p 428)*

SOME UNITS

FEE VCR DATA PORT

COMFORT INN Book at aaa.com Phone: (408)262-7666

Motel

All Year [ECP] 1P: $79-$125 2P: $79-$125 XP: $5 F16

Location: I-880, exit Calaveras Blvd (SR 237), 0.5 mi e, just s. 66 S Main St 95035. Fax: 408/262-2026. **Facility:** 53 one-bedroom standard units, some with whirlpools. 3 stories, exterior corridors. **Parking:** on-site. **Amenities:** high-speed Internet, voice mail, irons, hair dryers. **Pool(s):** small outdoor. **Leisure Activities:** whirlpool. **Guest Services:** coin laundry. **Cards:** AX, CB, DC, DS, MC, VI. **Special Amenities: free expanded continental breakfast and free local telephone calls.**

SOME UNITS

CROWNE PLAZA HOTEL AND RESORT SAN JOSE/SILICON VALLEY Book at aaa.com Phone: (408)321-9500

Large-scale Hotel

All Year 1P: $79-$179 2P: $79-$179 XP: $10 F18

Location: Southwest quadrant of I-880 and SR 237, Ranch Dr/McCarthy Ranch Rd, then just s. 777 Bellew Dr 95035. Fax: 408/321-9599. **Facility:** 305 units. 285 one-bedroom standard units. 20 one-bedroom suites ($109-$209). 12 stories, interior corridors. *Bath:* combo or shower only. **Parking:** on-site. **Amenities:** video games (fee), CD players, dual phone lines, voice mail, irons, hair dryers. *Some:* high-speed Internet (fee). **Pool(s):** heated outdoor. **Leisure Activities:** sauna, whirlpool, exercise room. **Guest Services:** gift shop, valet and coin laundry, area transportation. **Business Services:** conference facilities, business center. **Cards:** AX, CB, DC, DS, JC, MC, VI.

SOME UNITS

EMBASSY SUITES MILPITAS/SILICON VALLEY Book at aaa.com Phone: (408)942-0400

Large-scale Hotel

All Year [BP] 1P: $109-$209 2P: $129-$229 XP: $10 F17

Location: I-680, exit Calaveras Blvd W (SR 237). 901 E Calaveras Blvd 95035. Fax: 408/262-8604. **Facility:** 266 one-bedroom suites. 8 stories, interior corridors. **Parking:** on-site. **Amenities:** video games (fee), dual phone lines, voice mail, irons, hair dryers. *Some:* high-speed Internet (fee). **Pool(s):** heated indoor. **Leisure Activities:** sauna, whirlpool, steamroom. **Guest Services:** gift shop, complimentary evening beverages, coin laundry, area transportation. **Business Services:** conference facilities. **Cards:** AX, CB, DC, DS, JC, MC, VI. ***(See color ad p 621)***

SOME UNITS

FEE FEE

HAMPTON INN Book at aaa.com Phone: (408)428-9090

Small-scale Hotel

All Year 1P: $79-$159 2P: $89-$169

Location: SR 237, exit McCarthy, just s. 215 Barber Ct 95035. Fax: 408/428-9012. **Facility:** 93 one-bedroom standard units. 4 stories, interior corridors. *Bath:* combo or shower only. **Parking:** on-site. **Terms:** [ECP] meal plan available. **Amenities:** video games (fee), dual phone lines, voice mail, irons, hair dryers. **Pool(s):** heated outdoor. **Leisure Activities:** exercise room. **Guest Services:** valet and coin laundry. **Cards:** AX, CB, DC, DS, JC, MC, VI. **Special Amenities: free expanded continental breakfast and free local telephone calls.**

SOME UNITS

HILTON GARDEN INN-SAN JOSE/MILPITAS Book at aaa.com Phone: (408)719-1313

Small-scale Hotel

All Year 1P: $59-$179 2P: $69-$189 XP: $10 F18

Location: SR 237, exit McCarthy, just n. 30 Ranch Dr 95035. Fax: 408/719-0191. **Facility:** 161 one-bedroom standard units, some with whirlpools. 4 stories, interior corridors. *Bath:* combo or shower only. **Parking:** on-site. **Terms:** cancellation fee imposed, [BP] & [CP] meal plans available. **Amenities:** video games (fee), high-speed Internet, dual phone lines, voice mail, irons, hair dryers. **Dining:** 6-10 am, Sat & Sun 7 am-noon, cocktails. **Pool(s):** outdoor. **Leisure Activities:** whirlpool, exercise room. **Guest Services:** coin laundry, area transportation-within 5 mi. **Business Services:** meeting rooms, business center. **Cards:** AX, CB, DC, DS, JC, MC, VI. **Special Amenities: free local telephone calls and free newspaper.**

SOME UNITS

HOMESTEAD STUDIO SUITES HOTEL-MILPITAS/SILICON VALLEY Book at aaa.com Phone: (408)433-9700

Motel

All Year 1P: $81-$101 2P: $86-$106 XP: $5 F17

Location: SR 237, exit McCarthy S. 330 Cypress Dr 95035. Fax: 408/433-9790. **Facility:** 161 one-bedroom standard units with efficiencies. 2 stories (no elevator), interior/exterior corridors. *Bath:* combo or shower only. **Parking:** on-site. **Terms:** weekly rates available, pets ($75 fee). **Amenities:** high-speed Internet (fee), dual phone lines, voice mail, irons, hair dryers. **Leisure Activities:** exercise room. **Guest Services:** valet and coin laundry. **Business Services:** meeting rooms, business center. **Cards:** AX, CB, DC, DS, JC, MC, VI.

SOME UNITS

FEE

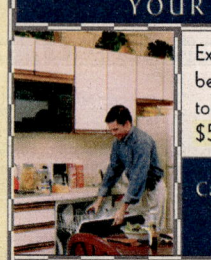

INNS OF AMERICA *Book at aaa.com* **Phone:** (408)946-8889

AAA SAVE

Motel

All Year 1P: $69-$109 2P: $69-$109

Location: I-880, exit Calaveras Blvd (SR 237), just e. Located adjacent to Serra Shopping Center. 270 S Abbott Ave 95035. Fax: 408/946-0748. **Facility:** 123 one-bedroom standard units. 3 stories, exterior corridors. **Parking:** on-site. **Terms:** [ECP] meal plan available, small pets only ($10 fee). **Amenities:** video games (fee), dual phone lines, voice mail, irons, hair dryers. *Some:* high-speed Internet. **Pool(s):** heated outdoor. **Guest Services:** coin laundry. **Business Services:** meeting rooms. **Cards:** AX, DC, MC, VI. **Special Amenities: free continental breakfast.**

SOME UNITS

FEE

MILPITAS COURTYARD BY MARRIOTT *Book at aaa.com* **Phone:** (408)719-1966

Small-scale Hotel

All Year 1P: $69-$179

Location: I-680, exit Montague Expwy W, just w, then just n. 1480 Falcon Dr 95035. Fax: 408/719-1962. **Facility:** 155 units. 149 one-bedroom standard units, some with whirlpools. 6 one-bedroom suites ($89-$199). 3 stories, interior corridors. *Bath:* combo or shower only. **Parking:** on-site. **Terms:** [BP] meal plan available. **Amenities:** high-speed Internet (fee), dual phone lines, voice mail, irons, hair dryers. **Pool(s):** heated outdoor. **Leisure Activities:** whirlpool, exercise room. **Guest Services:** coin laundry. **Business Services:** meeting rooms. **Cards:** AX, DC, DS, JC, MC, VI.

SOME UNITS

MILPITAS TRAVELODGE *Book at aaa.com* **Phone:** (408)263-0500

AAA SAVE

Motel

All Year 1P: $65-$99 2P: $75-$99

Location: I-880, exit Calaveras Blvd E (SR 237), 4 mi n of San Jose Airport. 378 W Calaveras Blvd 95035. Fax: 408/263-0416. **Facility:** 39 one-bedroom standard units. 2 stories (no elevator), exterior corridors. *Bath:* combo or shower only. **Parking:** on-site. **Terms:** cancellation fee imposed. **Amenities:** voice mail, safes (fee), hair dryers. **Pool(s):** outdoor. **Cards:** AX, CB, DC, DS, MC, VI. **Special Amenities: free newspaper and preferred room (subject to availability with advanced reservations).**

SOME UNITS

RESIDENCE INN BY MARRIOTT *Book at aaa.com* **Phone:** (408)941-9222

Small-scale Hotel

All Year 1P: $99-$139 2P: $99-$139

Location: I-880, exit Dixon Landing Rd E, just s. 1501 California Cir 95035. Fax: 408/941-0800. **Facility:** 120 units. 96 one-bedroom standard units with kitchens. 24 two-bedroom suites with kitchens. 3 stories, interior corridors. *Bath:* combo or shower only. **Parking:** on-site. **Terms:** [BP] meal plan available, pets ($10 fee, $75 extra charge). **Amenities:** dual phone lines, voice mail, irons, hair dryers. *Fee:* video games, high-speed Internet. **Pool(s):** heated outdoor. **Leisure Activities:** whirlpool, exercise room, sports court. **Guest Services:** complimentary evening beverages: Mon-Thurs, coin laundry. **Business Services:** meeting rooms. **Cards:** AX, DC, DS, MC, VI.

SOME UNITS

FEE

SHERATON SAN JOSE AT SILICON VALLEY *Book at aaa.com* **Phone:** (408)943-0600

AAA SAVE

Large-scale Hotel

All Year 1P: $89-$199 2P: $89-$209 XP: $10 F17

Location: 4 mi n of San Jose Airport; 0.3 mi nw of I-880 and Montague Expwy. 1801 Barber Ln 95035. Fax: 408/943-0484. **Facility:** Accenting the hotel's exterior are attractively landscaped gardens and a pool courtyard; guest rooms and common areas are spacious. 229 one-bedroom standard units. 2-9 stories, interior/exterior corridors. **Parking:** on-site. **Amenities:** dual phone lines, voice mail, irons, hair dryers. *Fee:* video games, high-speed Internet. *Some:* fax. **Dining:** 6:30 am-10 pm, cocktails. **Pool(s):** heated outdoor. **Leisure Activities:** whirlpool, jogging, exercise room. **Guest Services:** gift shop, valet laundry, area transportation-Great Mall. **Business Services:** conference facilities, business center. **Cards:** AX, CB, DC, DS, JC, MC, VI. **Special Amenities: free newspaper and free room upgrade (subject to availability with advanced reservations).** *(See color ad below)*

SOME UNITS

TOWNEPLACE SUITES BY MARRIOTT *Book at aaa.com* **Phone:** 408/719-1959

Small-scale Hotel

All Year 1P: $59-$119

Location: I-880, exit Montague Expwy, e to Great Mall Pkwy, turn left; turn right on Mustang Dr, right on Great Mall Dr, then just right. 1428 Falcon Dr 95035. Fax: 408/719-1952. **Facility:** 143 units. 83 one-bedroom standard units with kitchens. 60 two-bedroom suites ($89-$139) with kitchens. 4 stories, interior corridors. *Bath:* combo or shower only. **Parking:** on-site. **Terms:** pets ($75 fee, $12 extra charge). **Amenities:** dual phone lines, voice mail, irons, hair dryers. *Fee:* video games, high-speed Internet. **Pool(s):** heated outdoor. **Leisure Activities:** exercise room. **Cards:** AX, CB, DC, DS, JC, MC, VI.

SOME UNITS

FEE

WHERE TO DINE

BRANDON'S Lunch: $11-$18 Dinner: $15-$35 Phone: 408/570-5470

American

Location: Northwest quadrant of I-880 and Montague Expwy; in Beverly Heritage Hotel. 1800 Barber Ln 95035. **Hours:** 6:30-11 am, 11:30-2 & 5:30-9 pm, Sat & Sun 7 am-11:30 & 5-11 pm. Closed: 11/25, 12/25. **Reservations:** suggested; lunch & brunch. **Features:** Fresh seafood is at the heart of a menu of California cuisine. The busy but relaxed dining room is attractive. Dressy casual; cocktails. **Parking:** on-site. **Cards:** AX, CB, DC, DS, MC, VI.

MIRANDA

WHERE TO STAY

MIRANDA GARDENS RESORT Phone: 707/943-3011

Condominium

5/1-11/1 [ECP] 2P: $65-$225
4/1-4/30 & 11/2-1/2 [ECP] 2P: $55-$185

Location: US 101, exit Avenue of the Giants E. Located in quiet village area. 6766 Avenue of the Giants 95553 (PO Box 186). Fax: 707/943-3584. **Facility:** On large, shaded grounds, this resort in the redwoods offers cozy single or duplex cottages, some with a fireplace and a whirlpool. Designated smoking area. 16 units. 6 one-bedroom standard units, some with whirlpools. 10 cottages. 1 story. *Bath:* combo or shower only. **Parking:** on-site. **Terms:** open 4/1-1/2, office hours 7 am-11 pm, 2 night minimum stay - weekends, 7 day cancellation notice-fee imposed, pets ($100 deposit, $10 extra charge). **Amenities:** *Some:* irons, hair dryers. **Pool(s):** small outdoor. **Leisure Activities:** recreation programs. **Cards:** AX, DS, MC, VI.

FEE

MI-WUK VILLAGE pop. 1,485

WHERE TO STAY

CHRISTMAS TREE INN Phone: (209)586-1005

Motel

All Year 1P: $59-$79 2P: $69-$89 XP: $10 D16

Location: 15 mi e of Sonora. 24685 Hwy 108 95346 (PO Box 700). Fax: 209/586-2247. **Facility:** 16 one-bedroom standard units. 2 stories (no elevator), exterior corridors. **Parking:** on-site. **Terms:** 2-3 night minimum stay - seasonal, 7 day cancellation notice-fee imposed, weekly rates available, package plans - weekends. **Pool(s):** heated outdoor. **Leisure Activities:** whirlpool. **Cards:** AX, DS, MC, VI. **Special Amenities: free local telephone calls and preferred room (subject to availability with advanced reservations).**

MI-WUK VILLAGE INN & RESORT Phone: (209)586-3031

Motel

All Year 1P: $89-$160 2P: $98-$160 XP: $10

Location: 15 mi e of Sonora. 24680 SR 108 95346 (PO Box 70). Fax: 209/586-1737. **Facility:** 25 one-bedroom standard units, some with efficiencies, kitchens and/or whirlpools. 1-2 stories (no elevator), exterior corridors. *Bath:* combo or shower only. **Parking:** on-site. **Terms:** office hours 8 am-8 pm, 2-3 night minimum stay - weekends, 7 day cancellation notice, 21 days in season-fee imposed, [ECP] meal plan available, pets ($10 extra charge, with prior approval). **Amenities:** video library. *Some:* irons, hair dryers. **Pool(s):** small heated outdoor. **Leisure Activities:** whirlpool. *Fee:* massage. **Guest Services:** coin laundry. **Business Services:** meeting rooms. **Cards:** AX, MC, VI.

SOME UNITS

FEE

MODESTO pop. 188,856

WHERE TO STAY

BEST WESTERN TOWN HOUSE LODGE *Book at aaa.com* Phone: (209)524-7261

Motel

All Year [ECP] 1P: $70-$78 2P: $78-$85 XP: $8 F12

Location: SR 99, exit Central Modesto at I St, 1 mi e. 909 16th St 95354. Fax: 209/579-9546. **Facility:** 56 one-bedroom standard units. 2 stories, exterior corridors. *Bath:* combo or shower only. **Parking:** on-site. **Terms:** small pets only ($20 deposit). **Amenities:** voice mail, irons, hair dryers. **Pool(s):** outdoor. **Leisure Activities:** whirlpool. **Guest Services:** valet laundry. **Cards:** AX, CB, DC, DS, MC, VI. **Special Amenities: free expanded continental breakfast and free local telephone calls.**

SOME UNITS

FEE

CHALET MOTEL Phone: (209)529-4370

Motel

All Year [ECP] 1P: $55 2P: $60 XP: $10 F18

Location: Downtown. 115 Downey Ave 95354. Fax: 209/579-9545. **Facility:** 40 one-bedroom standard units, some with whirlpools. 2 stories, exterior corridors. *Bath:* combo or shower only. **Parking:** on-site. **Terms:** small pets only ($20 deposit). **Pool(s):** outdoor. **Cards:** AX, DC, DS, MC, VI.

SOME UNITS

FEE

COURTYARD BY MARRIOTT *Book at aaa.com* Phone: (209)577-3825

Motel

All Year 1P: $114 2P: $114

Location: SR 99, exit Briggsmore Ave, 0.3 mi n. 1720 Sisk Rd 95350. Fax: 209/577-1717. **Facility:** 126 one-bedroom standard units, some with whirlpools. 2 stories, interior corridors. *Bath:* combo or shower only. **Parking:** on-site. **Terms:** [BP] meal plan available. **Amenities:** high-speed Internet (fee), voice mail, irons, hair dryers. **Dining:** 6:30 am-10 & 5:30-10 pm, Sat & Sun 7 am-11 & 5:30-10 pm. **Pool(s):** outdoor. **Leisure Activities:** whirlpool, exercise room. **Guest Services:** valet and coin laundry. **Business Services:** meeting rooms, fax. **Cards:** AX, CB, DC, DS, JC, MC, VI. **Special Amenities: free newspaper and preferred room (subject to availability with advanced reservations).**

SOME UNITS

DAYS INN *Book at aaa.com* Phone: 209/527-1010

Motel

All Year [CP] 1P: $69-$89 2P: $75-$95 XP: $6 F17

Location: SR 108, exit Briggsmore Ave, 1.8 mi n; SR 99, 2.3 mi e, then 0.5 mi s. 1312 McHenry Ave 95350. Fax: 209/527-2033. **Facility:** 101 one-bedroom standard units. 2 stories, interior/exterior corridors. *Bath:* combo or shower only. **Parking:** on-site. **Terms:** package plans. **Amenities:** hair dryers. **Pool(s):** heated outdoor. **Leisure Activities:** whirlpool. **Guest Services:** coin laundry. **Business Services:** meeting rooms. **Cards:** AX, DS, MC, VI. **Special Amenities: free continental breakfast and free local telephone calls.**

(See color ad p 431)

SOME UNITS

DOUBLETREE *Book at aaa.com* **Phone:** (209)526-6000

Large-scale Hotel

All Year 1P: $69-$169 2P: $69-$169 XP: $20 F18

Location: SR 99 exit Central Modesto northbound; exit Maze Blvd southbound. Located at Convention Center Plaza. 1150 9th St 95354. Fax: 209/526-6096. **Facility:** 258 units. 252 one-bedroom standard units. 6 one-bedroom suites with whirlpools. 15 stories, interior corridors. **Parking:** on-site. **Terms:** cancellation fee imposed, weekly rates available, pets ($100 deposit). **Amenities:** video games, voice mail, irons, hair dryers. **Pool(s):** heated outdoor. **Leisure Activities:** whirlpool. **Guest Services:** gift shop, valet laundry. **Business Services:** conference facilities, business center. **Cards:** AX, DC, DS, JC, MC, VI. ***(See color ad below)***

SOME UNITS

FEE

ECONO LODGE *Book at aaa.com* **Phone:** (209)578-5400

AAA SAVE

Motel

All Year [CP] 1P: $49-$69 2P: $49-$89 XP: $5 F14

Location: SR 99, exit Kansas Ave. 500 Kansas Ave 95351. Fax: 209/578-5415. **Facility:** 69 one-bedroom standard units. 3 stories (no elevator), interior corridors. *Bath:* combo or shower only. **Parking:** on-site. **Amenities:** hair dryers. **Dining:** 6 am-8 pm, Sat-2 pm; closed Sun, wine/beer only. **Pool(s):** heated outdoor. **Guest Services:** coin laundry. **Cards:** AX, DC, DS, MC, VI. **Special Amenities: free continental breakfast and free local telephone calls.**

SOME UNITS

HOLIDAY INN EXPRESS *Book at aaa.com* **Phone:** (209)543-9000

AAA SAVE

Motel

All Year [ECP] 1P: $89-$129 2P: $99-$149 XP: $10 F18

Location: SR 99, exit Pelandale Ave, just w. 4100 Salida Blvd 95358. Fax: 209/543-9500. **Facility:** 66 one-bedroom standard units, some with whirlpools. 2 stories, exterior corridors. *Bath:* combo or shower only. **Parking:** on-site. **Amenities:** high-speed Internet, dual phone lines, voice mail, irons, hair dryers. **Pool(s):** heated outdoor. **Leisure Activities:** sauna, whirlpool, exercise room. **Guest Services:** coin laundry. **Business Services:** meeting rooms. **Cards:** AX, CB, DC, DS, MC, VI. **Special Amenities: free expanded continental breakfast and free newspaper.** *(See color ad p 432)*

SOME UNITS

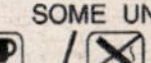

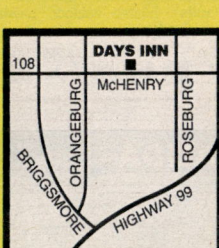

HOWARD JOHNSON EXPRESS INN *Book at aaa.com* **Phone:** (209)537-4821

Motel

All Year [ECP] 1P: $60-$65 2P: $65-$90 XP: $10 F17

Location: SR 99, exit Hatch Rd, then s. 1672 Herndon Rd 95307. Fax: 209/537-1040. **Facility:** 50 one-bedroom standard units. 1-2 stories, exterior corridors. *Bath:* combo or shower only. **Parking:** on-site. **Terms:** pets ($15 deposit). **Amenities:** irons, hair dryers. **Pool(s):** outdoor. **Guest Services:** valet laundry. **Business Services:** meeting rooms. **Cards:** AX, CB, DC, DS, MC, VI. **Special Amenities: free expanded continental breakfast and free local telephone calls.**

FEE SOME UNITS FEE

MICROTEL INN & SUITES *Book at aaa.com* **Phone:** (209)538-6466

Motel

All Year [CP] 1P: $64-$79 2P: $79-$99 XP: $10 F17

Location: SR 99, exit Hatch Rd E, then just s. 1760 Herndon Rd 95307. Fax: 209/538-6366. **Facility:** 59 one-bedroom standard units. 3 stories, interior corridors. **Parking:** on-site. **Terms:** small pets only ($25 fee). **Amenities:** voice mail, safes, irons, hair dryers. **Pool(s):** outdoor. **Leisure Activities:** whirlpool, exercise room. **Guest Services:** coin laundry. **Business Services:** meeting rooms. **Cards:** AX, CB, DC, DS, MC, VI.

FEE SOME UNITS

QUALITY INN *Book at aaa.com* **Phone:** (209)544-2000

Motel

All Year [ECP] 1P: $54-$79 2P: $54-$99 XP: $5 F14

Location: SR 99, exit Briggsmore Ave. 2025 W Orangeburg Ave 95350. Fax: 209/575-4118. **Facility:** 77 one-bedroom standard units, some with whirlpools. 3 stories, interior corridors. **Parking:** on-site. **Amenities:** voice mail, irons, hair dryers. **Pool(s):** outdoor. **Business Services:** meeting rooms, business center. **Cards:** AX, DC, DS, MC, VI. **Special Amenities: free expanded continental breakfast and free local telephone calls.**

SOME UNITS

RAMADA INN *Book at aaa.com* **Phone:** (209)521-9000

Motel

All Year [ECP] 1P: $79-$92 2P: $89-$102 XP: $10 F18

Location: SR 99, exit Briggsmore Ave, just s. 2001 W Orangeburg Ave 95350. Fax: 209/521-6034. **Facility:** 114 one-bedroom standard units, some with whirlpools. 2 stories, exterior corridors. **Parking:** on-site. **Terms:** cancellation fee imposed. **Amenities:** safes (fee), irons, hair dryers. **Pool(s):** heated outdoor. **Leisure Activities:** whirlpool. **Guest Services:** coin laundry. **Business Services:** meeting rooms. **Cards:** AX, CB, DC, DS, JC, MC, VI.

SOME UNITS

RED LION *Book at aaa.com* **Phone:** (209)521-1612

Small-scale Hotel

All Year 1P: $89-$129 2P: $89-$129

Location: SR 99, exit Briggsmore Ave. 1612 Sisk Rd 95350. Fax: 209/527-5074. **Facility:** 185 units. 182 one-bedroom standard units. 3 one-bedroom suites ($255-$325). 2 stories, interior corridors. **Parking:** on-site. **Terms:** cancellation fee imposed. **Amenities:** voice mail, irons, hair dryers. **Pool(s):** outdoor, heated indoor, wading. **Leisure Activities:** sauna, whirlpool, playground. **Guest Services:** valet and coin laundry. **Business Services:** meeting rooms, business center. **Cards:** AX, CB, DC, DS, MC, VI. ***(See color ad p 326)***

SOME UNITS

ASK / FEE

TRAVELODGE *Book at aaa.com* **Phone:** 209/524-3251

SAVE

Motel

5/16-10/15	1P: $50-$70	2P: $60-$75	XP: $10	D
2/1-5/15 & 10/16-1/31	1P: $45-$65	2P: $50-$70	XP: $10	D

Location: SR 99, exit Kansas Ave, then w. 722 Kansas Ave 95351. Fax: 209/578-1250. **Facility:** 99 one-bedroom standard units. 2 stories, exterior corridors. *Bath:* shower only. **Parking:** on-site. **Terms:** cancellation fee imposed, [CP] meal plan available, small pets only ($10 fee, $25 deposit). **Amenities:** hair dryers. **Pool(s):** outdoor. **Cards:** AX, DC, DS, MC, VI. **Special Amenities: free continental breakfast and free local telephone calls.**

SOME UNITS

FEE

MOJAVE pop. 3,836

WHERE TO STAY

BEST VALUE INN *Book at aaa.com* **Phone:** (661)824-9317

SAVE

Motel

All Year [CP] 1P: $40-$55 2P: $55-$65 XP: $5 F8

Location: On SR 14 and 58. 16352 Sierra Hwy 93501. Fax: 661/824-9393. **Facility:** 25 one-bedroom standard units. 2 stories, exterior corridors. **Parking:** on-site. **Terms:** pets ($5-$10 extra charge). **Amenities:** hair dryers. *Some:* irons. **Pool(s):** outdoor. **Leisure Activities:** whirlpool. **Business Services:** fax (fee). **Cards:** AX, DC, DS, JC, MC, VI. **Special Amenities: free continental breakfast and free local telephone calls.**

SOME UNITS

FEE

BEST WESTERN DESERT WINDS *Book at aaa.com* **Phone:** (661)824-3601

SAVE

Motel

All Year [CP] 1P: $65-$70 2P: $70-$75 XP: $10 F13

Location: On SR 14 and 58. 16200 Sierra Hwy 93501. Fax: 661/824-3605. **Facility:** 51 one-bedroom standard units. 2 stories, exterior corridors. **Parking:** on-site. **Terms:** cancellation fee imposed, pets ($10 extra charge). **Amenities:** high-speed Internet, irons, hair dryers. **Pool(s):** outdoor. **Leisure Activities:** whirlpool. **Guest Services:** coin laundry. **Business Services:** fax. **Cards:** AX, DC, DS, MC, VI. **Special Amenities: free continental breakfast and free local telephone calls.**

SOME UNITS

FEE / VCR

DESERT INN **Phone:** (661)824-2518

SAVE

Motel

All Year [CP] 1P: $42-$54 2P: $46-$54 XP: $5 F11

Location: Just e of SR 14. 1954 Hwy 58 93501. Fax: 661/824-5392. **Facility:** 18 one-bedroom standard units. 1 story, exterior corridors. *Bath:* combo or shower only. **Parking:** on-site. **Amenities:** hair dryers. *Some:* irons. **Business Services:** fax. **Cards:** AX, DC, DS, MC, VI. **Special Amenities: free continental breakfast and free local telephone calls.**

SOME UNITS

ECONO LODGE *Book at aaa.com* **Phone:** (661)824-2463

SAVE

Motel

All Year [CP] 1P: $34-$49 2P: $39-$69 XP: $5 F12

Location: Just e of SR 14. 2145 Hwy 58 93501. Fax: 661/824-9508. **Facility:** 33 one-bedroom standard units. 2 stories, exterior corridors. **Parking:** on-site. **Terms:** weekly rates available, pets ($5 extra charge). **Amenities:** *Some:* irons, hair dryers. **Pool(s):** outdoor. **Guest Services:** coin laundry. **Business Services:** fax (fee). **Cards:** AX, CB, DC, DS, MC, VI. **Special Amenities: free continental breakfast and early check-in/late check-out.**

SOME UNITS

FEE

MARIAH COUNTRY INN & SUITES **Phone:** 661/824-4980

SAVE

Small-scale Hotel

All Year 1P: $90 2P: $95 XP: $5 F

Location: 1.5 mi e of SR 14. 1385 Hwy 58 93501. Fax: 661/824-4906. **Facility:** 50 one-bedroom standard units, some with whirlpools. 2 stories, interior corridors. *Bath:* combo or shower only. **Parking:** on-site. **Terms:** small pets only ($10 extra charge). **Amenities:** irons, hair dryers. **Dining:** 6:30 am-2 & 4:30-9:30 pm. **Pool(s):** outdoor. **Leisure Activities:** whirlpool. **Guest Services:** coin laundry. **Business Services:** meeting rooms, fax (fee). **Cards:** AX, DC, DS, MC, VI. **Special Amenities: free continental breakfast and early check-in/late check-out.**

SOME UNITS

FEE

Destination Monterey Peninsula

The Monterey Peninsula is the place to build memories that will last a lifetime.

The coastal and inland scenery is a feast for the eyes and the camera lens. For the more active there are such watersports as scuba diving, kayaking and fishing, and such land sports as golfing, hiking and cycling. And don't forget the palate-pleasing seafood.

© Craig Lovell / Corbis

Golfing in Monterey.
You can experience Monterey's hilly terrain up close and personal on one of its many fine golf courses.

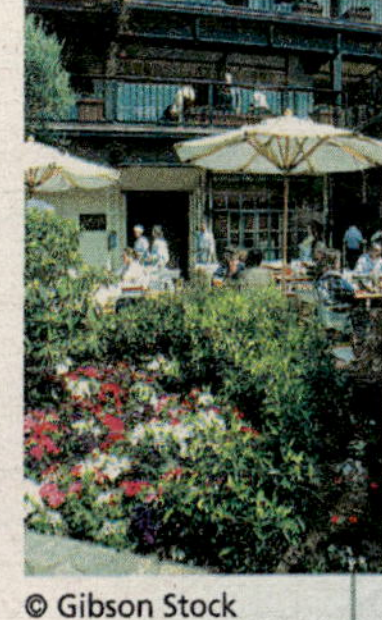

© Gibson Stock Photography

Outdoor dining, Carmel.
Charming outdoor cafes and distinctive shops tempt those out for a stroll.

© Morton Beebe / Corbis

Mexican dancers.
California's multicultural heritage is celebrated at festivals throughout the year.

Seventeen-Mile Drive.
The peninsula's spectacular coastline is best seen along this scenic stretch. (See listing page 104)

Places included in this AAA Destination Area:

© Jaye Phillips Index Stock

1891-L
MONTEREY PENINSULA
ACCOMMODATIONS
Scale in Miles 0 0.5
Scale in Kilometers 0 0.7
PACIFIC
OCEAN
Monterey
Carmel
Bay
Pacific Grove
Pacific Grove Municipal G.C.
Point Pinos Lighthouse Reservation
Asilomar State Beach
Monterey Bay Aquarium
Municipal Wharf #2
Fisherman's Wharf
Presidio of Monterey U.S. Military Reservation
Monterey
Spanish Bay G.C.
LIGHTHOUSE GATE (TOLL)
Monterey Peninsula Country Club Dunes Course
Monterey Peninsula Country Club Shore Course
S.B.F. Morse Bot. Res.
Spyglass Hill Golf Course
Poppy Hills G.C.
Cypress Point Golf Course
Pebble Beach
Pebble Beach Golf Links
HI-WAY ONE GATE (TOLL)
CARMEL GATE (TOLL)
Carmel-by-the-Sea
SEE DOWNTOWN CARMEL-BY-THE-SEA INSET
Carmel Beach City Park
Mission San Carlos Borromeo Del Rio Carmelo
Carmel River State Beach
To San Simeon, Big Sur, 110, 112 & 50, 54
28 THRU 42
SEVENTEEN MILE DR.
SPANISH BAY DR.
SLOAT RD.
LOPEZ RD.
SUNRIDGE RD.
COSTANILLA WAY
SCENIC DR.
CARMEL HWY.
PACIFIC GROVE
FOREST AVE.
SUNSET DR.
ASILOMAR BLVD.
MILE DR.
LIGHTHOUSE AVE.
SINEX AVE.
OCEAN VIEW BLVD.
Marine Gardens Park
CENTRAL AVE.
WAVE ST.
FOAM ST.
CANNERY ROW
LIGHTHOUSE
PACIFIC ST.
MUNRAS AVE.
SOLEDAD DR.
AGUAJITO
DOLORES ST.
SIERRA AVE.
DRIVE
PALMERO WAY
SAN ANTONIO AVE.
JUNIPERO AVE.
SANTA LUCIA AVE.
RIO RD.

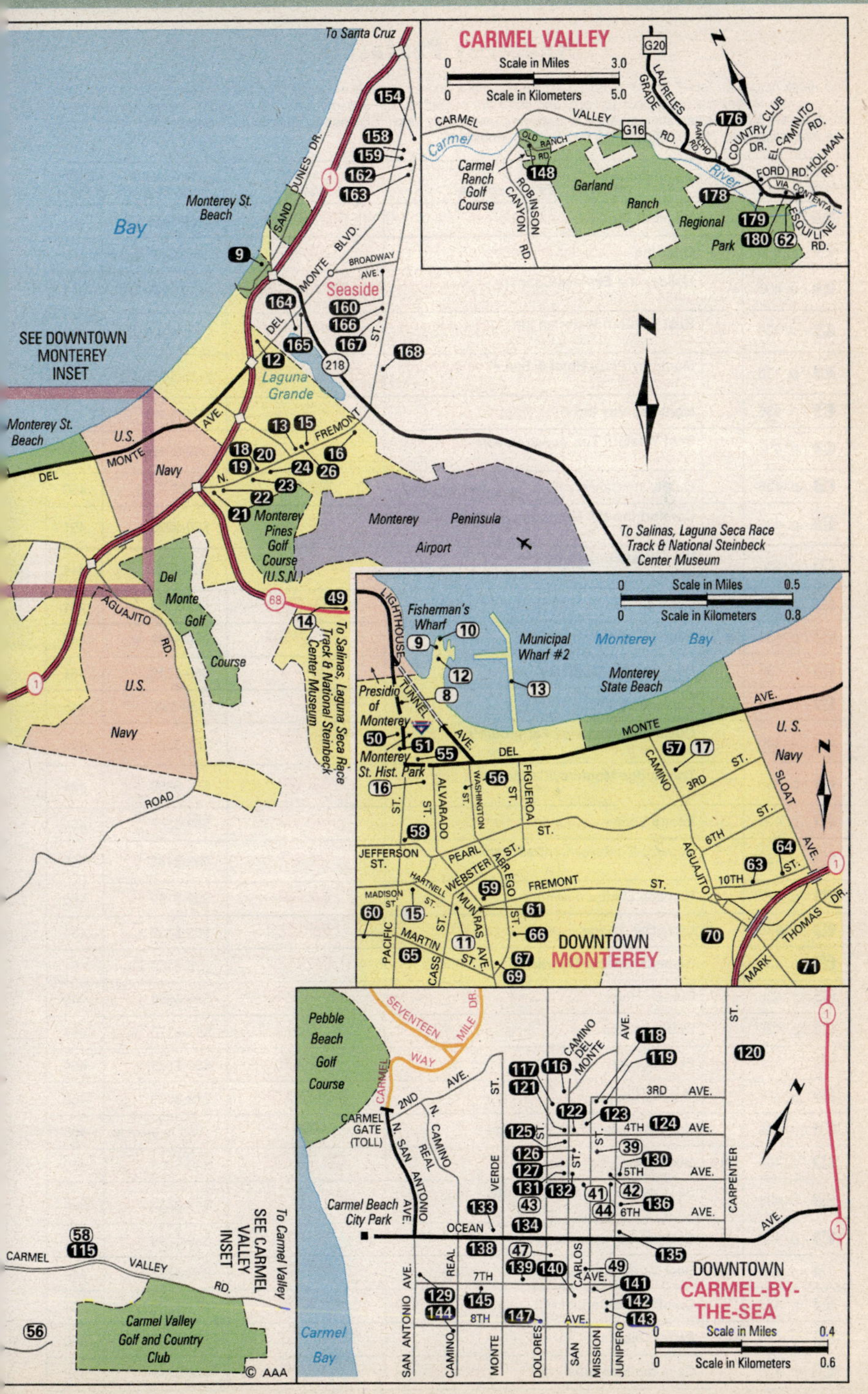

CARMEL VALLEY
Scale in Miles
Scale in Kilometers
Carmel Ranch Golf Course
Garland Ranch Regional Park
Monterey Bay
Seaside
Laguna Grande
SEE DOWNTOWN MONTEREY INSET
Monterey Peninsula Airport
Monterey Pines Golf Course (U.S.N.)
Del Monte Golf Course
U.S. Navy
To Santa Cruz
To Salinas, Laguna Seca Race Track & National Steinbeck Center Museum
Fisherman's Wharf
Municipal Wharf #2
Monterey State Beach
Presidio of Monterey
Monterey St. Hist. Park
DOWNTOWN MONTEREY
Pebble Beach Golf Course
CARMEL GATE (TOLL)
Carmel Beach City Park
Carmel Bay
DOWNTOWN CARMEL-BY-THE-SEA
Carmel Valley Golf and Country Club
SEE CARMEL VALLEY INSET
To Carmel Valley
© AAA

Monterey Peninsula

This index helps you "spot" where approved accommodations and restaurants are located on the corresponding detailed maps. Lodging rate ranges are for comparison only and show the property's high season; rates are per night, unless only weekly (W) rates are available. Restaurant rate range is for dinner, unless only lunch (L) is served. Turn to the listing page for more detailed rate information and consult display ads for special promotions.

Spotter/Map Page Number	OA	**MONTEREY** - Lodgings	Diamond Rating	Rate Range High Season	Listing Page
2 / p. 436	AAA	**Spindrift Inn** - see color ad p 447	◆◆◆	$169-$479 SAVE	461
3 / p. 436	AAA	**Otter Inn** - see color ad p 460	◆◆	$89-$399 SAVE	459
4 / p. 436	AAA	**Holiday Inn Express-Cannery** - see color ad p 455	◆◆◆	$159-$399 SAVE	454
5 / p. 436	AAA	**Best Western Victorian Inn** - see color ad p 447	◆◆◆	$125-$369 SAVE	447
7 / p. 436	AAA	**Monterey Plaza Hotel & Spa** - see color ad inside back cover	◆◆◆◆	$185-$445 SAVE	459
8 / p. 436	AAA	**Monterey Bay Inn** - see color ad p 447	◆◆◆	$179-$349 SAVE	456
9 / p. 436	AAA	**Best Western The Beach Resort** - see color ad p 446	◆◆◆	$99-$389 SAVE	447
11 / p. 436		Quality Inn Cannery Row - see color ad p 460	◇◇	$89-$399	460
12 / p. 436	AAA	**Comfort Inn-Del Monte Beach** - see color ad p 460	◆◆	$69-$299 SAVE	451
13 / p. 436	AAA	**Best Western De Anza Inn** - see color ad p 445	◆◆◆	$129-$249 SAVE	444
15 / p. 436	AAA	**Cypress Tree Inn** - see color ad p 452	◆◆	$64-$159 SAVE	451
16 / p. 436	AAA	**Best Western Ramona Inn**	◆◆◆	$89-$199 SAVE	446
18 / p. 436	AAA	**Rodeway Inn Monterey** - see color ad p 453	◆◆	$69-$249 SAVE	461
19 / p. 436	AAA	**Casa Verde inn**	◆	$59-$98 SAVE	448
20 / p. 436	AAA	**Quality Inn Monterey Fairgrounds** - see color ad p 461	◆◆	$69-$329 SAVE	460
21 / p. 436	AAA	**Travelodge-Monterey/Carmel** - see color ad p 463	◆◆	$79-$239 SAVE	464
22 / p. 436	AAA	**Econo Lodge** - see color ad p 453	◆◆	$59-$259 SAVE	454
23 / p. 436	AAA	**Super 8-Monterey/Central/Carmel** - see color ad p 462	◆◆	$59-$169 SAVE	462
24 / p. 436	AAA	**Ramada Limited-Fremont**	◆◆	$89-$189 SAVE	460
26 / p. 436	AAA	**Lone Oak Lodge** - see color ad p 443	◆◆	$68-$138 SAVE	456
28 / p. 436	AAA	**Ramada Limited-Munras**	◆◆	$99-$189 SAVE	461
29 / p. 436	AAA	**Clarion Hotel** - see color ad p 449	◆◆◆	$99-$399 SAVE	449
30 / p. 436	AAA	**El Dorado Inn**	◆	$59-$175 SAVE	454
31 / p. 436	AAA	**El Adobe Inn**	◆◆	$59-$175 SAVE	454
32 / p. 436	AAA	**Munras Lodge** - see color ad p 459	◆◆◆	$89-$299 SAVE	459
33 / p. 436		Howard Johnson Montero Lodge	◇	Failed to provide	455
34 / p. 436	AAA	**Quality Inn** - see color ad p 449	◆◆◆	$99-$299 SAVE	460
35 / p. 436	AAA	**Best Western Park Crest Motel** - see color ad p 446	◆◆◆	$79-$219 SAVE	446
36 / p. 436	AAA	**Cypress Gardens Resort Inn**	◆◆	$59-$299 SAVE	451
37 / p. 436	AAA	**Best Value Surf Inn**	◆◆	$79-$298 SAVE	444
38 / p. 436	AAA	**Comfort Inn-Carmel Hill** - see color ad p 450	◆◆◆	$74-$199 SAVE	451
39 / p. 436	AAA	**Padre Oaks**	◆◆	$64-$199 SAVE	460
40 / p. 436	AAA	**Days Inn-Monterey** - see color ad p 453	◆◆	$79-$249 SAVE	452

Spotter/Map Page Number	OA	**MONTEREY** - Lodgings (continued)	Diamond Rating	Rate Range High Season	Listing Page
42 / p. 436	AAA	**Comfort Inn-Munras** - see color ad p 450	◆◆◆	$79-$199 SAVE	451
43 / p. 436		Del Monte Pines Motel	◆	$69-$229	453
44 / p. 436	AAA	**Steinbeck Lodge**	◆◆	$59-$209 SAVE	462
45 / p. 436	AAA	**Carmel Hill Lodge**	◆◆	$59-$199 SAVE	448
46 / p. 436	AAA	**Mariposa Inn** - see color ad p 456	◆◆◆	$129-$169 SAVE	456
47 / p. 436	AAA	**Bay Park Hotel** - see color ad p 444	◆◆◆	$119-$249 SAVE	443
49 / p. 436	AAA	**Way Station Inn** - see color ad p 463	◆◆	$89-$199 SAVE	464
50 / p. 436	AAA	**Hotel Pacific** - see color ad p 447	◆◆◆◆	$179-$399 SAVE	455
51 / p. 436		Merritt House	◆◆◆	$161-$235	456
55 / p. 436		Doubletree Hotel	◆◆◆	$189-$209	453
56 / p. 436		The Monterey Hotel - see color ad p 458	◆◆◆	$99-$199	458
57 / p. 436	AAA	**Monterey Bay Lodge** - see color ad p 457	◆◆	$109-$319 SAVE	457
58 / p. 436		Monterey Marriott	◆◆◆	$169-$229	459
59 / p. 436	AAA	**Monterey Downtown Travelodge** - see color ad p 458	◆◆	$89-$199 SAVE	458
60 / p. 436	AAA	**Old Monterey Inn**	◆◆◆◆	$240-$350 SAVE	459
61 / p. 436	AAA	**Casa Munras Garden Hotel** - see color ad p 448	◆◆◆	$149-$219 SAVE	448
63 / p. 436	AAA	**Best Value Stage Coach Lodge** - see color ad p 443	◆◆	$69-$199 SAVE	444
64 / p. 436	AAA	**Monterey Fireside Lodge**	◆◆	$59-$309 SAVE	458
65 / p. 436	AAA	**Colton Inn** - see color ad p 449	◆◆◆	$109-$199 SAVE	449
66 / p. 436	AAA	**Sand Dollar Inn** - see color ad p 462	◆◆◆	$109-$209 SAVE	461
67 / p. 436	AAA	**Best Western Monterey Inn** - see color ad p 445	◆◆◆	$109-$199 SAVE	445
69 / p. 436	AAA	**Days Inn-Downtown Monterey/San Carlos Inn** - see color ad p 452	◆◆	$79-$299 SAVE	452
70 / p. 436	AAA	**Hilton-Monterey** - see color ad p 454	◆◆◆	$134-$184 SAVE	454
71 / p. 436	AAA	**Hyatt Regency-Monterey Resort & Conference Center** - see color ad p 623	◆◆◆	$109-$295 SAVE	455
		MONTEREY - Restaurants			
1 / p. 436		The Fish Hopper	◆◆	$10-$24	465
4 / p. 436	AAA	**Whaling Station Prime Steaks & Seafood**	◆◆◆	$17-$30	466
5 / p. 436	AAA	**Blue Moon**	◆◆◆	$13-$50	465
6 / p. 436	AAA	**Sardine Factory**	◆◆◆◆	$22-$50	465
7 / p. 436		The Duck Club - see color ad inside back cover	◆◆◆◆	$15-$26	465
8 / p. 436		Fresh Cream	◆◆◆◆	$25-$45	465
9 / p. 436	AAA	**Cafe Fina**	◆◆	$15-$27	465
10 / p. 436	AAA	**Abalonetti Seafood Trattoria**	◆◆	$11-$26	464
11 / p. 436		The Whaler Steak House	◆◆	$12-$32	466
12 / p. 436	AAA	**Domenico's on The Wharf**	◆◆◆	$15-$36	465
13 / p. 436		Sandbar & Grill	◆◆	$11-$21	465
14 / p. 436		Tarpy's Roadhouse	◆◆◆	$6-$35	465
15 / p. 436		Stokes Adobe Restaurant	◆◆◆	$13-$18	465

Spotter/Map Page Number	OA	**MONTEREY** - Restaurants (continued)	Diamond Rating	Rate Range High Season	Listing Page
16 / p. 436		Montrio Bistro	◆◆◆	$16-$22	465
17 / p. 436		Ann Kelly's By The Lake	◆	$8-$22	464
		PACIFIC GROVE - Lodgings			
74 / p. 436		Sea Breeze Inn and Cottages - see color ad p 488	◆◆	$79-$189	490
75 / p. 436		Green Gables Inn	◆◆◆	$130-$195	488
76 / p. 436	AAA	**Olympia Motor Lodge**	◆◆	$88-$160 SAVE	489
77 / p. 436	AAA	**Bide-A-Wee Inn & Cottages**	◆◆	$99-$149 SAVE	487
78 / p. 436	AAA	**Borg's Ocean Front Motel**	◆	$72-$135 SAVE	487
79 / p. 436	AAA	**Best Western Monarch Resort** - see color ad p 486	◆◆◆	$100-$240 SAVE	486
80 / p. 436	AAA	**The Wilkies Inn** - see color ad p 490	◆◆	$89-$299 SAVE	491
81 / p. 436	AAA	**Lovers Point Inn**	◆	$59-$289 SAVE	488
82 / p. 436	AAA	**The Centrella Inn** - see color ad p 469	◆◆◆	$159-$259 SAVE	487
83 / p. 436		Old St. Angela Inn	◆◆◆	$110-$210	489
84 / p. 436	AAA	**The Gatehouse Inn**	◆◆◆	$125-$195 SAVE	488
85 / p. 436	AAA	**The Inn at 213 Seventeen Mile Drive**	◆◆◆	$145-$240 SAVE	488
86 / p. 436		Pacific Grove Motel - see color ad p 488	◆	$89-$169	490
87 / p. 436	AAA	**Butterfly Grove Inn** - see color ad p 487	◆◆	$79-$299 SAVE	487
88 / p. 436	AAA	**Pacific Gardens Inn**	◆◆◆	$130-$250 SAVE	489
89 / p. 436	AAA	**Howard Johnson Express Inn** - see color ad p 455	◆◆◆	$129-$229 SAVE	488
90 / p. 436		Asilomar - see color ad p 485	◆◆	$99-$122	485
91 / p. 436	AAA	**Rosedale Inn** - see color ad p 490	◆◆◆	$145-$180 SAVE	490
92 / p. 436		Deer Haven Inn & Suites - see color ad p 488	◆◆	$89-$299	487
93 / p. 436	AAA	**Pacific Grove Inn** - see color ad p 489	◆◆◆	$129-$229 SAVE	489
94 / p. 436		Anton Inn	◆◆	$89-$300	485
		PACIFIC GROVE - Restaurants			
25 / p. 436		Old Bath House	◆◆◆	$20-$35	491
27 / p. 436	AAA	**Fandango**	◆◆	$11-$25	491
28 / p. 436		Passionfish	◆◆	$13-$22	491
		PEBBLE BEACH - Lodgings			
99 / p. 436		Casa Palmero	◆◆◆◆	$655-$725	491
100 / p. 436		The Inn at Spanish Bay	◆◆◆◆	$450-$600	491
101 / p. 436		The Lodge at Pebble Beach	◆◆◆◆	$425-$1650	491
		PEBBLE BEACH - Restaurants			
32 / p. 436		Roy's	◆◆◆	$17-$35	492
35 / p. 436		Stillwater Bar and Grill	◆◆◆	$22-$65	492
36 / p. 436		Club XIX	◆◆◆◆	$20-$30	492
		CARMEL-BY-THE-SEA - Lodgings			
106 / p. 436	AAA	**Sandpiper Inn by the Sea**	◆◆◆	$135-$220 SAVE	480
109 / p. 436	AAA	**Colonial Terrace Inn** - see color ad p 476	◆◆◆	$129-$249 SAVE	475
110 / p. 436	AAA	**Highlands Inn-A Park Hyatt Hotel**	◆◆◆◆	$215-$445 SAVE	476

Spotter/Map Page Number	OA	CARMEL-BY-THE-SEA - Lodgings (continued)	Diamond Rating	Rate Range High Season	Listing Page
112 / p. 436	AAA	**Tickle Pink Inn** - see color ad p 481	4 diamonds	$269-$529 SAVE	480
113 / p. 436	AAA	**Carmel River Inn** - see color ad p 472	2 diamonds	$125-$250 SAVE	470
114 / p. 436	AAA	**Best Western Carmel Mission Inn** - see color ad p 447	3 diamonds	$79-$329 SAVE	467
115 / p. 436	AAA	**Quail Lodge** - see color ad p 480	4 diamonds	$225-$425 SAVE	478
116 / p. 436	AAA	**Hofsas House** - see color ad p 477	2 diamonds	$100-$250 SAVE	477
117 / p. 436		Carmel Country Inn	3 diamonds	$150-$325	469
118 / p. 436		Carmel Tradewinds Inn	3 diamonds	$250-$475	473
119 / p. 436	AAA	**Horizon Inn Ocean View Lodge & Annex** - see color ad p 478	3 diamonds	$135-$275 SAVE	477
120 / p. 436	AAA	**Best Value Carmel Resort Inn** - see color ad p 466	2 diamonds	$125-$300 SAVE	466
121 / p. 436	AAA	**Svendsgaard's** - see color ad p 469	3 diamonds	$150-$289 SAVE	480
122 / p. 436	AAA	**Dolphin Inn** - see color ad p 469	3 diamonds	$150-$225 SAVE	476
123 / p. 436		Carmel Wayfarer Inn	2 diamonds	$129-$229	474
124 / p. 436	AAA	**Carmel Garden Court** - see color ad p 471	3 diamonds	$150-$245 SAVE	470
125 / p. 436	AAA	**Carmel Fireplace Inn** - see color ad p 470	3 diamonds	$125-$285 SAVE	470
126 / p. 436	AAA	**Briarwood Inn** - see color ad p 468	3 diamonds	$120-$235 SAVE	468
127 / p. 436	AAA	**Candle Light Inn** - see color ad p 469	3 diamonds	$189-$299 SAVE	468
129 / p. 436		San Antonio House Inn - see color ad p 471	2 diamonds	$160-$225	479
130 / p. 436	AAA	**Chateau de Carmel** - see color ad p 475	3 diamonds	$79-$225 SAVE	474
131 / p. 436	AAA	**Best Western Carmel's Town House Lodge**	3 diamonds	$109-$249 SAVE	468
132 / p. 436	AAA	**Carmel Sands Lodge** - see color ad p 473	3 diamonds	$85-$199 SAVE	471
133 / p. 436		Lobos Lodge	3 diamonds	$99-$150	477
134 / p. 436		Pine Inn - see color ad p 479	3 diamonds	$135-$260	478
135 / p. 436		Carmel Village Inn & Annex - see color ad p 474	3 diamonds	$149-$189	473
136 / p. 436	AAA	**Best Western Carmel Bay View Inn** - see color ad p 467	3 diamonds	$149-$299 SAVE	466
138 / p. 436	AAA	**Normandy Inn** - see color ad p 479	3 diamonds	$98-$250 SAVE	478
139 / p. 436		Cypress Inn	3 diamonds	$125-$395	475
140 / p. 436	AAA	**Coachman's Inn** - see color ad p 475	3 diamonds	$135-$425 SAVE	474
141 / p. 436	AAA	**Wayside Inn** - see color ad p 469	3 diamonds	$150-$299 SAVE	480
142 / p. 436	AAA	**Carriage House Inn** - see color ad p 469	4 diamonds	$299-$350 SAVE	474
143 / p. 436		Cobblestone Inn	3 diamonds	$130-$185	475
144 / p. 436		La Playa Hotel	3 diamonds	$165-$325	477
145 / p. 436		Green Lantern Inn Bed & Breakfast	2 diamonds	$129-$249	476
147 / p. 436	AAA	**Adobe Inn-Carmel**	4 diamonds	$199-$495 SAVE	466
148 / p. 436	AAA	**Carmel Valley Ranch-A Wyndham Luxury Resort**	4 diamonds	$299-$399 SAVE	473
		CARMEL-BY-THE-SEA - Restaurants			
39 / p. 436		Le Coq D'Or	3 diamonds	$19-$25	482
41 / p. 436		Casanova	3 diamonds	$25-$47	482
42 / p. 436	AAA	**The French Poodle Restaurant**	4 diamonds	$16-$60	482

Spotter/Map Page Number	OA	CARMEL-BY-THE-SEA - Restaurants (continued)	Diamond Rating	Rate Range High Season	Listing Page
43 / p. 436		Sans Souci	◆◆◆	$31-$58	482
44 / p. 436		The Forge In The Forest	◆◆	$12-$29	482
47 / p. 436	AAA	**Tutto Mondo Trattoria**	◆◆◆	$10-$23	483
49 / p. 436	AAA	**Anton & Michel**	◆◆◆	$18-$29	482
50 / p. 436		California Market	◆◆◆	$18-$25	482
53 / p. 436		From Scratch Restaurant	◆	$7-$8(L)	482
54 / p. 436		Pacific's Edge	◆◆◆◆	$40-$75	482
56 / p. 436		Rio Grill	◆◆◆	$7-$29	482
58 / p. 436		The Covey - see color ad p 480	◆◆◆	$26-$40	482
		SEASIDE - Lodgings			
154 / p. 436	AAA	**Thunderbird Motel**	◆	$46-$145 SAVE	494
158 / p. 436	AAA	**Sandcastle Inn**	◆◆	$55-$145 SAVE	494
159 / p. 436	AAA	**Seaside Inn**	◆◆	$45-$135 SAVE	494
160 / p. 436	AAA	**Econo Lodge Bay Breeze - see color ad p 461**	◆◆	$69-$249 SAVE	493
162 / p. 436	AAA	**Howard Johnson Express Inn**	◆◆	$49-$179 SAVE	493
163 / p. 436	AAA	**Best Western Magic Carpet Lodge - see color ad p 486**	◆◆	$59-$269 SAVE	492
164 / p. 436		Holiday Inn Express	◆◆◆	$99-$249	493
165 / p. 436	AAA	**Embassy Suites Hotel & Conference Center - see color ad p 493**	◆◆◆	$169-$299 SAVE	493
166 / p. 436	AAA	**Pacific Best Inn**	◆◆	$69-$199 SAVE	494
167 / p. 436	AAA	**Economy Inn**	◆	$49-$174 SAVE	493
168 / p. 436	AAA	**Discovery Inn**	◆	$65-$179 SAVE	493
		CARMEL VALLEY - Lodgings			
176 / p. 436	AAA	**Los Laureles Lodge**	◆◆◆	$130-$155 SAVE	483
178 / p. 436	AAA	**Carmel Valley Lodge**	◆◆◆	$179-$219 SAVE	483
179 / p. 436	AAA	**Hidden Valley Inn-Country Garden Inns - see color ad p 469**	◆◆◆	$85-$269 SAVE	483
180 / p. 436	AAA	**Acacia Lodge-Country Garden Inns - see color ad p 469**	◆◆◆	$85-$269 SAVE	483
		CARMEL VALLEY - Restaurant			
62 / p. 436		Will's Fargo Restaurant	◆◆	$14-$27	483

MONTEREY pop. 29,674 (See map and index starting on p. 436)

WHERE TO STAY

BAY PARK HOTEL Book at aaa.com Phone: (831)649-1020 47

SAVE

Small-scale Hotel

7/1-10/31	1P: $119-$249	2P: $119-$249	XP: $10	F18
4/1-6/30	1P: $99-$199	2P: $99-$199	XP: $10	F18
2/1-3/31 & 11/1-1/31	1P: $89-$169	2P: $89-$169	XP: $10	F18

Location: SR 1, exit Munras Ave, just w. Located across from Del Monte Shopping Center. 1425 Munras Ave 93940. Fax: 831/373-4258. **Facility:** 80 one-bedroom standard units. 3 stories, interior corridors. *Bath:* combo or shower only. **Parking:** on-site. **Terms:** small pets only ($20 extra charge). **Amenities:** voice mail, irons, hair dryers. **Dining:** 6:30 am-11 & 11:30-9 pm, cocktails. **Pool(s):** outdoor. **Leisure Activities:** whirlpool, exercise room. **Guest Services:** valet laundry. **Business Services:** meeting rooms. **Cards:** AX, CB, DC, DS, MC, VI. **Special Amenities: early check-in/late check-out and free room upgrade (subject to availability with advanced reservations).** *(See color ad p 444)*

FEE SOME UNITS

(See map and index starting on p. 436)

BEST VALUE STAGE COACH LODGE *Book at aaa.com* **Phone:** (831)373-3632 **63**

AAA SAVE ◆◆ Motel

5/1-10/31 [CP]	1P: $69-$199	2P: $69-$199	XP: $15	F12
2/1-4/30 & 11/1-1/31 [CP]	1P: $49-$119	2P: $49-$119	XP: $15	F12

Location: SR 1, exit Aguajito Rd or Monterey, just w. 1111 Tenth St 93940. Fax: 831/648-1734. **Facility:** 25 one-bedroom standard units. 2 stories (no elevator), exterior corridors. **Parking:** on-site. **Terms:** 2-3 night minimum stay - weekends, 3 day cancellation notice-fee imposed. **Pool(s):** small outdoor. **Leisure Activities:** sauna, exercise room. **Guest Services:** coin laundry. **Cards:** AX, CB, DC, DS, MC, VI. **Special Amenities: free continental breakfast and early check-in/late check-out.** *(See color ad p 443)*

SOME UNITS

BEST VALUE SURF INN *Book at aaa.com* **Phone:** (831)372-5821 **37**

AAA SAVE ◆◆ Motel

6/1-9/30 [ECP]	1P: $79-$298	2P: $89-$298	XP: $10	F12
10/1-11/30 [ECP]	1P: $52-$199	2P: $56-$199	XP: $10	F12
2/1-5/31 [ECP]	1P: $35-$199	2P: $40-$199	XP: $10	F12
12/1-1/31 [ECP]	1P: $39-$179	2P: $45-$189	XP: $10	F12

Location: SR 1, exit Soledad Dr/Munras Ave, 0.5 mi w. 1200 Munras Ave 93940. Fax: 831/372-4866. **Facility:** 27 one-bedroom standard units. 1 story, exterior corridors. *Bath:* combo or shower only. **Parking:** on-site. **Terms:** 3 day cancellation notice, package plans. **Amenities:** hair dryers. **Pool(s):** small outdoor. **Cards:** AX, CB, DC, DS, JC, MC, VI. **Special Amenities: free expanded continental breakfast and free room upgrade (subject to availability with advanced reservations).**

SOME UNITS

BEST WESTERN DE ANZA INN *Book at aaa.com* **Phone:** (831)646-8300 **13**

AAA SAVE ◆◆◆ Small-scale Hotel

8/1-8/31 [CP]	1P: $129-$239	2P: $139-$249	XP: $10	F17
7/1-7/31 [CP]	1P: $99-$179	2P: $109-$189	XP: $10	F17
2/1-6/30 & 9/1-1/31 [CP]	1P: $59-$159	2P: $69-$169	XP: $8	F17

Location: SR 1, exit Casa Verde Way or Fremont St, 0.4 mi e. 2141 Fremont St 93940. Fax: 831/646-8130. **Facility:** Smoke free premises. 43 one-bedroom standard units. 3 stories, interior corridors. **Parking:** on-site. **Terms:** 2 night minimum stay - weekends, 7 day cancellation notice. **Amenities:** irons, hair dryers. **Pool(s):** small outdoor. **Leisure Activities:** whirlpool. **Guest Services:** valet laundry. **Business Services:** meeting rooms. **Cards:** AX, CB, DC, DS, JC, MC, VI. **Special Amenities: free continental breakfast and free newspaper.** *(See color ad p 445)*

SOME UNITS

(See map and index starting on p. 436)

BEST WESTERN MONTEREY INN *Book at aaa.com* **Phone:** (831)373-5345 67

6/1-10/31 [ECP]	1P: $109-$189	2P: $109-$199	XP: $10	F12
2/1-5/31 & 11/1-1/31 [ECP]	1P: $69-$119	2P: $69-$129	XP: $10	F12

SAVE

Small-scale Hotel

Location: SR 1, exit Munras Ave, 0.7 mi w. 825 Abrego St 93940. Fax: 831/373-3246. **Facility:** 80 one-bedroom standard units. 3 stories, interior corridors. *Bath:* combo or shower only. **Parking:** on-site. **Terms:** 2-3 night minimum stay - seasonal weekends. **Amenities:** voice mail, irons, hair dryers. **Pool(s):** small outdoor. **Leisure Activities:** whirlpool. **Cards:** AX, CB, DC, DS, MC, VI. **Special Amenities: free expanded continental breakfast and early check-in/late check-out.** *(See color ad below)*

SOME UNITS

DATA PORT / VCR /

(See map and index starting on p. 436)

BEST WESTERN PARK CREST MOTEL Book at aaa.com Phone: (831)372-4576 35

AAA SAVE

Motel

6/1-10/31 [CP]	1P: $79-$209	2P: $89-$219	XP: $10	F13
2/1-5/31 [CP]	1P: $69-$199	2P: $79-$219	XP: $10	F13
11/1-1/31 [CP]	1P: $59-$169	2P: $69-$179	XP: $10	F13

Location: SR 1, exit Soledad Dr/Munras Ave, 0.5 mi w. 1100 Munras Ave 93940. Fax: 831/372-2317. **Facility:** 53 one-bedroom standard units. 2 stories (no elevator), exterior corridors. *Bath:* combo or shower only. **Parking:** on-site. **Terms:** cancellation fee imposed. **Amenities:** irons, hair dryers. **Pool(s):** heated outdoor. **Cards:** AX, CB, DC, DS, JC, MC, VI. **Special Amenities: free continental breakfast and free room upgrade (subject to availability with advanced reservations).** *(See color ad below)*

SOME UNITS

BEST WESTERN RAMONA INN Book at aaa.com Phone: (831)373-2445 16

AAA SAVE

Motel

6/1-10/31 [ECP]	1P: $89-$199	2P: $99-$199	XP: $10	F17
2/1-5/31 [ECP]	1P: $69-$159	2P: $79-$159	XP: $10	F17
11/1-1/31 [ECP]	1P: $59-$149	2P: $69-$159	XP: $10	F17

Location: SR 1, exit Del Rey Oaks or Fremont St, 0.7 mi e. 2332 Fremont St 93940. Fax: 831/373-6358. **Facility:** 34 one-bedroom standard units. 2 stories (no elevator), exterior corridors. **Parking:** on-site. **Terms:** 3 day cancellation notice-fee imposed. **Amenities:** irons, hair dryers. **Pool(s):** small heated outdoor. **Leisure Activities:** whirlpool. **Cards:** AX, CB, DC, DS, JC, MC, VI. **Special Amenities: free expanded continental breakfast and free local telephone calls.**

SOME UNITS

(See map and index starting on p. 436)

BEST WESTERN THE BEACH RESORT *Book at aaa.com* **Phone:** (831)394-3321 9

AAA SAVE

Small-scale Hotel

4/1-10/31	1P: $99-$389	2P: $99-$389	XP: $15	F12
2/1-3/31 & 11/1-1/31	1P: $99-$259	2P: $99-$259	XP: $15	F12

Location: SR 1, exit Del Rey Oaks, just w. 2600 Sand Dunes Dr 93940. Fax: 831/393-1912. **Facility:** 196 one-bedroom standard units. 4 stories, exterior corridors. **Parking:** on-site. **Terms:** check-in 4 pm, cancellation fee imposed, [BP] & [CP] meal plans available, $4 service charge, small pets only ($25 extra charge). **Amenities:** dual phone lines, voice mail, irons, hair dryers. **Dining:** 7 am-1:30 & 5:30-10 pm, entertainment. **Pool(s):** outdoor. **Leisure Activities:** whirlpool, exercise room. **Guest Services:** valet laundry. **Business Services:** conference facilities, fax. **Cards:** AX, CB, DC, DS, MC. **Special Amenities: free local telephone calls.** *(See color ad p 446)*

FEE

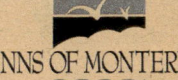

BEST WESTERN VICTORIAN INN *Book at aaa.com* **Phone:** (831)373-8000 5

AAA SAVE

Motel

All Year [CP]	1P: $125-$369	2P: $125-$369	XP: $10

Location: SR 1, exit Monterey, 3.4 mi w. 487 Foam St 93940. Fax: 831/373-4815. **Facility:** 68 one-bedroom standard units, some with whirlpools. 3 stories, interior/exterior corridors. *Bath:* combo or shower only. **Parking:** on-site (fee). **Terms:** check-in 4 pm, 2 night minimum stay - some weekends, cancellation fee imposed, package plans - seasonal, pets ($35 fee, $75 deposit). **Amenities:** video library (fee), dual phone lines, voice mail, irons, hair dryers. *Some:* CD players. **Leisure Activities:** whirlpool. **Guest Services:** valet laundry. **Business Services:** meeting rooms, PC (fee). **Cards:** AX, DC, DS, JC, MC, VI. **Special Amenities: free continental breakfast.** *(See color ad below)*

SOME UNITS

FEE

(See map and index starting on p. 436)

CARMEL HILL LODGE Phone: (831)373-3252 45

5/1-9/30	1P: $59-$179	2P: $69-$199	XP: $10	F5
2/1-4/30	1P: $49-$139	2P: $59-$179	XP: $10	F5
10/1-11/30	1P: $49-$109	2P: $59-$149	XP: $10	F5
12/1-1/31	1P: $39-$119	2P: $49-$149	XP: $10	F5

Motel

Location: SR 1, exit Munras Ave, just w. 1374 Munras Ave 93940. Fax: 831/655-2420. **Facility:** 38 one-bedroom standard units. 2 stories (no elevator), exterior corridors. *Bath:* combo or shower only. **Parking:** on-site. **Terms:** 3 day cancellation notice-fee imposed, [CP] meal plan available. **Amenities:** hair dryers. **Pool(s):** outdoor. **Cards:** AX, DC, MC, VI. **Special Amenities: free continental breakfast and free local telephone calls.**

SOME UNITS

CASA MUNRAS GARDEN HOTEL Book at aaa.com Phone: (831)375-2411 61

7/1-10/31	1P: $149-$209	2P: $159-$219	XP: $15	F12
4/1-6/30	1P: $129-$189	2P: $139-$199	XP: $15	F12
2/1-3/31 & 11/1-1/31	1P: $119-$169	2P: $119-$169	XP: $15	F12

Motel

Location: SR 1, exit Munras Ave, 0.8 mi w. 700 Munras Ave 93940 (PO Box 1351). Fax: 831/375-1365. **Facility:** 166 one-bedroom standard units. 1-2 stories (no elevator), interior/exterior corridors. *Bath:* combo or shower only. **Parking:** on-site. **Amenities:** voice mail, irons, hair dryers. **Dining:** 7 am-2 & 5-9 pm, Sat & Sun 7 am-1 & 5-9 pm, cocktails. **Pool(s):** heated outdoor. **Guest Services:** valet laundry. **Business Services:** conference facilities. **Cards:** AX, CB, DC, MC, VI. *(See color ad below)*

SOME UNITS

CASA VERDE INN Phone: 831/375-5407 19

5/1-10/31	1P: $59-$89	2P: $69-$98	XP: $8	F16
2/1-4/30	1P: $39-$42	2P: $45-$54	XP: $8	F16
11/1-1/31	1P: $35-$39	2P: $40-$49	XP: $8	F16

Motel

Location: SR 1, exit Casa Verde Way or Fremont St, just s. 2113 N Fremont St 93940. Fax: 831/373-7261. **Facility:** 18 one-bedroom standard units. 1 story, exterior corridors. *Bath:* combo or shower only. **Parking:** on-site. **Terms:** cancellation fee imposed. **Cards:** AX, DS, MC, VI. **Special Amenities: free room upgrade and preferred room (each subject to availability with advanced reservations).**

SOME UNITS

FEE FEE

(See map and index starting on p. 436)

CLARION HOTEL *Book at aaa.com* **Phone:** (831)373-1337 29

AAA SAVE — Motel

5/15-10/31	1P: $99-$399	2P: $99-$399	XP: $10	F17
2/1-5/14 & 11/1-1/31	1P: $79-$299	2P: $79-$299	XP: $10	F17

Location: SR 1, exit Munras Ave, 0.5 mi w. 1046 Munras Ave 93940. Fax: 831/372-2451. **Facility:** Smoke free premises. 52 units. 42 one- and 10 two-bedroom standard units, some with kitchens and/or whirlpools. 2 stories (no elevator), exterior corridors. **Parking:** on-site. **Terms:** 3 day cancellation notice-fee imposed, [ECP] meal plan available. **Amenities:** voice mail, irons, hair dryers. **Pool(s):** heated indoor. **Leisure Activities:** sauna, whirlpool. **Cards:** AX, DC, DS, JC, MC, VI. **Special Amenities: free continental breakfast and free local telephone calls.** *(See color ad below)*

COLTON INN **Phone:** (831)649-6500 65

AAA SAVE — Motel

6/1-10/31	1P: $109-$199	2P: $109-$199	XP: $10	F17
2/1-5/31	1P: $99-$199	2P: $99-$199	XP: $10	F17
11/1-1/31	1P: $79-$199	2P: $79-$199	XP: $10	F17

Location: In Old Monterey. 707 Pacific St 93940. Fax: 831/373-6987. **Facility:** Designated smoking area. 50 one-bedroom standard units, some with whirlpools. 3 stories, exterior corridors. **Parking:** on-site. **Terms:** 3 day cancellation notice, [ECP] meal plan available. **Amenities:** video library, irons, hair dryers. **Leisure Activities:** sauna, sun deck. **Business Services:** meeting rooms. **Cards:** AX, DC, DS, MC, VI. **Special Amenities: free continental breakfast.** *(See color ad below)*

SOME UNITS

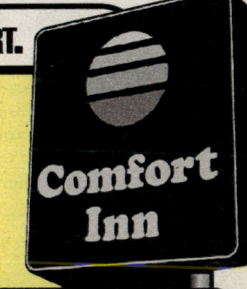

(See map and index starting on p. 436)

COMFORT INN-CARMEL HILL Book at aaa.com — **Phone:** (831)372-2908 — 38

SAVE — Motel

7/1-10/15 [ECP]	1P: $74-$169	2P: $84-$199	XP: $10	F16
5/1-6/30 [ECP]	1P: $64-$149	2P: $64-$169	XP: $10	F16
10/16-1/31 [ECP]	1P: $54-$119	2P: $54-$149	XP: $10	F16
2/1-4/30 [ECP]	1P: $54-$119	2P: $54-$119	XP: $10	F16

Location: SR 1, exit Munras Ave, just s. 1252 Munras Ave 93940. Fax: 831/372-7608. **Facility:** 31 one-bedroom standard units. 2 stories, exterior corridors. *Bath:* combo or shower only. **Parking:** on-site. **Terms:** cancellation fee imposed. **Amenities:** dual phone lines, voice mail, irons, hair dryers. **Pool(s):** small heated outdoor. **Cards:** AX, CB, DC, DS, JC, MC, VI. **Special Amenities: free expanded continental breakfast and free local telephone calls.** *(See color ad p 450)*

SOME UNITS

COMFORT INN-DEL MONTE BEACH Book at aaa.com — **Phone:** (831)373-7100 — 12

SAVE — Motel

All Year	1P: $69-$299	2P: $69-$299	XP: $10	F

Location: SR 1, exit Seaside/Del Rey Oaks, just e. 2401 Del Monte Ave 93940. Fax: 831/373-4813. **Facility:** Smoke free premises. 47 one-bedroom standard units. 3 stories, interior corridors. **Parking:** on-site. **Terms:** 3 day cancellation notice, package plans - seasonal. **Amenities:** irons, hair dryers. **Cards:** AX, DC, DS, MC, VI. **Special Amenities: free continental breakfast and free local telephone calls.** *(See color ad p 460)*

SOME UNITS

COMFORT INN-MUNRAS Book at aaa.com — **Phone:** (831)372-8088 — 42

SAVE — Motel

7/1-10/15 [ECP]	1P: $79-$169	2P: $89-$199	XP: $10	F16
5/1-6/30 [ECP]	1P: $69-$149	2P: $69-$169	XP: $10	F16
2/1-4/30 & 10/16-1/31 [ECP]	1P: $59-$119	2P: $59-$149	XP: $10	F16

Location: SR 1, exit Munras Ave, just w. 1262 Munras Ave 93940. Fax: 831/373-5829. **Facility:** 36 one-bedroom standard units, some with whirlpools. 2 stories, exterior corridors. *Bath:* combo or shower only. **Parking:** on-site. **Terms:** cancellation fee imposed. **Amenities:** dual phone lines, voice mail, irons, hair dryers. **Cards:** AX, CB, DC, DS, JC, MC, VI. **Special Amenities: free expanded continental breakfast and free local telephone calls.** *(See color ad p 450)*

SOME UNITS

CYPRESS GARDENS RESORT INN Book at aaa.com — **Phone:** 831/373-2761 — 36

SAVE — Motel

All Year	1P: $59-$299	2P: $59-$299	XP: $10	F18

Location: SR 1, exit Munras Ave, 0.5 mi w. 1150 Munras Ave 93940. Fax: 831/649-1329. **Facility:** Smoke free premises. 46 one-bedroom standard units. 2 stories, exterior corridors. **Parking:** on-site. **Terms:** 3 day cancellation notice, [ECP] meal plan available. **Amenities:** irons, hair dryers. **Pool(s):** heated outdoor. **Leisure Activities:** whirlpool, exercise room. **Cards:** AX, DS, MC, VI. **Special Amenities: free continental breakfast and free local telephone calls.**

CYPRESS TREE INN — **Phone:** 831/372-7586 — 15

SAVE — Motel

6/1-9/30	1P: $64-$159	2P: $64-$159	XP: $5	F10
2/1-5/31	1P: $64-$119	2P: $64-$119	XP: $8	F10
10/1-1/31	1P: $54-$94	2P: $54-$94	XP: $8	F10

Location: SR 1, exit Del Rey Oaks or Fremont St, 0.6 mi e. 2227 N Fremont St 93940. Fax: 831/372-2940. **Facility:** 55 one-bedroom standard units, some with efficiencies. 2 stories (no elevator), interior/exterior corridors. *Bath:* combo or shower only. **Parking:** on-site. **Terms:** cancellation fee imposed. **Amenities:** voice mail, irons, hair dryers. **Leisure Activities:** sauna, whirlpool. **Guest Services:** coin laundry. **Cards:** AX, CB, DC, DS, MC, VI. **Special Amenities: free continental breakfast and free local telephone calls.** *(See color ad p 452)*

SOME UNITS

(See map and index starting on p. 436)

DAYS INN-DOWNTOWN MONTEREY/SAN CARLOS INN *Book at aaa.com* **Phone:** (831)649-6332 **69**

SAVE	5/1-10/31 [CP]	1P: $79-$199	2P: $89-$299	XP: $10	F12
	2/1-4/30 [CP]	1P: $59-$189	2P: $69-$199	XP: $10	F12
Motel	11/1-1/31 [CP]	1P: $49-$99	2P: $49-$99	XP: $10	F12

Location: SR 1, exit Fremont St or Munras Ave, 0.8 mi w. 850 Abrego St 93940. Fax: 831/649-6353. **Facility:** 55 one-bedroom standard units. 2-4 stories, exterior corridors. *Bath:* combo or shower only. **Parking:** on-site. **Terms:** 3 day cancellation notice, package plans - seasonal. **Amenities:** irons, hair dryers. **Leisure Activities:** whirlpool. **Cards:** AX, CB, DC, DS, JC, MC, VI. **Special Amenities: free continental breakfast and free local telephone calls.** *(See color ad below)*

SOME UNITS

DAYS INN-MONTEREY *Book at aaa.com* **Phone:** (831)375-2168 **40**

SAVE	6/16-8/31	1P: $79-$239	2P: $79-$249	XP: $10	F12
	9/1-1/31	1P: $39-$239	2P: $39-$239	XP: $10	F12
Motel	2/1-6/15	1P: $39-$139	2P: $39-$149	XP: $10	F12

Location: SR 1, exit Munras Ave, just w. 1288 Munras Ave 93940. Fax: 831/375-0368. **Facility:** 35 one-bedroom standard units, some with whirlpools. 1-2 stories (no elevator), exterior corridors. *Bath:* combo or shower only. **Parking:** on-site. **Terms:** cancellation fee imposed, [CP] meal plan available. **Amenities:** video library (fee), hair dryers. **Cards:** AX, CB, DC, DS, MC, VI. **Special Amenities: free continental breakfast and free newspaper.** *(See color ad p 453)*

SOME UNITS

(See map and index starting on p. 436)

DEL MONTE PINES MOTEL Book at aaa.com Phone: (831)375-2323 43

Motel

6/16-9/30 [CP]	1P: $69-$229	2P: $79-$229	XP: $10	F12
10/1-1/31 [CP]	1P: $35-$189	2P: $39-$199	XP: $10	F12
5/1-6/15 [CP]	1P: $39-$189	2P: $49-$189	XP: $10	F12
2/1-4/30 [CP]	1P: $35-$189	2P: $38-$189	XP: $10	F12

Location: SR 1, exit Munras Ave, just w. Located across from Del Monte Shopping Center. 1298 Munras Ave 93940. Fax: 831/655-2539. **Facility:** 19 one-bedroom standard units, some with whirlpools. 2 stories (no elevator); exterior corridors. *Bath:* combo or shower only. **Parking:** on-site. **Terms:** 2-4 night minimum stay - weekends, 3 day cancellation notice-fee imposed. **Pool(s):** small outdoor. **Cards:** AX, CB, DC, DS, JC, MC, VI.

SOME UNITS

DOUBLETREE HOTEL Book at aaa.com Phone: (831)649-4511 55

Large-scale Hotel

6/1-11/15	1P: $189-$209	2P: $189-$209	XP: $20	F
3/1-5/31	1P: $169-$189	2P: $169-$189	XP: $20	F
2/1-2/29 & 11/16-1/31	1P: $159-$179	2P: $159-$179	XP: $20	F

Location: 2 mi w of SR 1, exit Del Monte or Munras aves; near Fisherman's Wharf; downtown. 2 Portola Plaza 93940. Fax: 831/372-0620. **Facility:** Smoke free premises. 380 one-bedroom standard units, some with whirlpools. 1-7 stories, interior corridors. *Bath:* combo or shower only. **Parking:** on-site. **Terms:** [BP], [CP] & [ECP] meal plans available. **Amenities:** voice mail, irons, hair dryers. *Fee:* video games, high-speed Internet. **Pool(s):** outdoor. **Leisure Activities:** whirlpool. *Fee:* massage. **Guest Services:** gift shop, valet laundry. **Business Services:** conference facilities, business center. **Cards:** AX, DC, DS, JC, MC, VI.

SOME UNITS

FEE FEE FEE

(See map and index starting on p. 436)

ECONO LODGE Book at aaa.com **Phone:** (831)372-5851 22

Motel

6/1-9/30 [CP]	1P: $59-$169	2P: $69-$259	XP: $10	F12
2/1-5/31 & 10/1-1/31 [CP]	1P: $45-$109	2P: $49-$159	XP: $10	F12

Location: SR 1, exit Fremont St or Casa Verde Way, just e. 2042 Fremont St 93940. Fax: 831/372-4228. **Facility:** 47 one-bedroom standard units, some with efficiencies (no utensils). 1-2 stories (no elevator), exterior corridors. *Bath:* combo or shower only. **Parking:** on-site. **Terms:** 2-5 night minimum stay - weekends & seasonal, cancellation fee imposed. **Pool(s):** small outdoor. **Leisure Activities:** whirlpool. **Cards:** AX, DC, DS, MC, VI. **Special Amenities: free continental breakfast and free local telephone calls.** *(See color ad p 453)*

SOME UNITS

EL ADOBE INN Book at aaa.com **Phone:** 831/372-5409 31

Motel

4/15-10/31 [CP]	1P: $59-$175	2P: $59-$175	XP: $10	F12
2/1-4/14 & 11/1-1/31 [CP]	1P: $45-$119	2P: $45-$119	XP: $10	F12

Location: SR 1, exit Munras Ave, 0.6 mi w. 936 Munras Ave 93940. Fax: 831/375-7236. **Facility:** Smoke free premises. 26 one-bedroom standard units. 2 stories (no elevator), exterior corridors. *Bath:* combo or shower only. **Parking:** on-site. **Terms:** 3 day cancellation notice, pets ($10 extra charge). **Amenities:** irons. **Leisure Activities:** whirlpool. **Cards:** AX, CB, DC, DS, JC, MC, VI. **Special Amenities: free continental breakfast and free local telephone calls.**

SOME UNITS

FEE

EL DORADO INN **Phone:** 831/373-2921 30

Motel

4/15-10/31 [CP]	1P: $59-$175	2P: $59-$175	XP: $10	F12
2/1-4/14 & 11/1-1/31 [CP]	1P: $45-$115	2P: $45-$115	XP: $10	F12

Location: SR 1, exit Munras Ave, 0.6 mi w. 900 Munras Ave 93940. Fax: 831/373-5838. **Facility:** 15 one-bedroom standard units. 2 stories (no elevator), exterior corridors. *Bath:* shower only. **Parking:** on-site. **Terms:** 3 day cancellation notice. **Amenities:** hair dryers. **Cards:** AX, CB, DC, DS, JC, MC, VI. **Special Amenities: free continental breakfast and free local telephone calls.**

SOME UNITS

HILTON-MONTEREY Book at aaa.com **Phone:** 831/373-6141 70

Small-scale Hotel

7/1-10/31	1P: $134-$184	2P: $134-$184	XP: $10	F18
6/1-6/30	1P: $104-$184	2P: $104-$184	XP: $10	F18
2/1-5/31 & 11/1-1/31	1P: $74-$154	2P: $74-$154	XP: $10	F18

Location: SR 1, exit Aguajito Rd or Fisherman's Wharf, just w. 1000 Aguajito Rd 93940. Fax: 831/655-8608. **Facility:** 204 one-bedroom standard units. 3 stories, interior corridors. **Parking:** on-site (fee). **Terms:** check-in 4 pm, cancellation fee imposed. **Amenities:** dual phone lines, voice mail, irons, hair dryers. *Fee:* video games, high-speed Internet. **Dining:** 6:30 am-2 & 5-10 pm, cocktails. **Pool(s):** outdoor. **Leisure Activities:** whirlpool, putting green, 2 tennis courts, exercise room. **Guest Services:** valet and coin laundry. **Business Services:** conference facilities, business center. **Cards:** AX, DC, DS, JC, MC, VI. **Special Amenities: free newspaper.** *(See color ad below)*

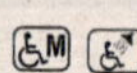

SOME UNITS

FEE FEE

HOLIDAY INN EXPRESS-CANNERY Book at aaa.com **Phone:** (831)372-1800 4

Motel

6/1-10/31 [ECP]	1P: $159-$399	2P: $159-$399	XP: $10	F19
2/1-5/31 & 11/1-1/31 [ECP]	1P: $99-$399	2P: $99-$399	XP: $10	F19

Location: SR 1, exit Monterey, 3 mi w. 443 Wave St 93940. Fax: 831/372-1969. **Facility:** 43 one-bedroom standard units. 3 stories, exterior corridors. **Parking:** on-site. **Amenities:** high-speed Internet, dual phone lines, voice mail, irons, hair dryers. **Leisure Activities:** whirlpool. **Guest Services:** complimentary evening beverages, valet laundry. **Business Services:** meeting rooms. **Cards:** AX, CB, DC, DS, JC, MC, VI. **Special Amenities: free expanded continental breakfast and free local telephone calls.** *(See color ad p 455)*

SOME UNITS

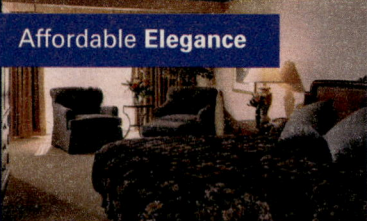

(See map and index starting on p. 436)

HOTEL PACIFIC Book at aaa.com **Phone:** (831)373-5700 50

AAA SAVE

Motel

All Year [ECP] 1P: $179-$399 2P: $179-$399 XP: $10

Location: SR 1, exit Del Monte Ave, 2.2. mi w; near conference center. 300 Pacific St 93940. Fax: 831/373-6921. **Facility:** Adobe-style architecture and attractive gardens give the hotel distinction; all units have decks and gas fireplaces. Smoke free premises. 105 units. 104 one- and 1 two-bedroom suites. 4 stories, interior/exterior corridors. *Bath:* combo or shower only. **Parking:** on-site (fee). **Terms:** check-in 4 pm, 2 night minimum stay - some weekends, cancellation fee imposed, package plans - seasonal. **Amenities:** video library (fee), CD players, voice mail, honor bars, irons, hair dryers. **Leisure Activities:** whirlpools. **Guest Services:** valet laundry. **Business Services:** meeting rooms, PC, fax. **Cards:** AX, DC, DS, JC, MC, VI. **Special Amenities: free expanded continental breakfast.** *(See color ad p 447)*

HOWARD JOHNSON MONTERO LODGE Book at aaa.com **Phone:** 831/375-6002 33

Motel

Property failed to provide current rates

Location: SR 1, exit Soledad Dr/Munras Ave, 0.5 mi w. 1240 Munras Ave 93940. Fax: 831/333-1603. **Facility:** Smoke free premises. 20 one-bedroom standard units. 2 stories (no elevator), exterior corridors. *Bath:* combo or shower only. **Parking:** on-site. **Amenities:** high-speed Internet, voice mail, irons, hair dryers. *Some:* DVD players (fee).

SOME UNITS

FEE

HYATT REGENCY-MONTEREY RESORT & CONFERENCE CENTER Book at aaa.com **Phone:** (831)372-1234 71

AAA SAVE

Large-scale Hotel

All Year 1P: $109-$295 2P: $109-$295 XP: $15 F18

Location: SR 1, exit Aguajito Rd northbound; exit Monterey southbound, just e. 1 Old Golf Course Rd 93940. Fax: 831/375-3960. **Facility:** 575 units. 516 one-bedroom standard units. 59 one-bedroom suites. 2-4 stories, interior corridors. *Bath:* combo or shower only. **Parking:** on-site. **Terms:** cancellation fee imposed, pets ($50 fee, in limited units). **Amenities:** voice mail, irons, hair dryers. *Some:* dual phone lines. *Fee:* high-speed Internet. **Dining:** 6:30 am-11 pm, cocktails. **Pool(s):** 2 outdoor. **Leisure Activities:** whirlpools, recreation programs, croquet, ping pong, rental bicycles, jogging, basketball, volleyball, game room. *Fee:* golf-18 holes, 6 tennis courts (2 lighted), massage. **Guest Services:** gift shop, valet and coin laundry. **Business Services:** conference facilities, business center. **Cards:** AX, CB, DC, DS, JC, MC, VI. *(See color ad p 623)*

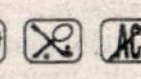

FEE SOME UNITS FEE FEE

(See map and index starting on p. 436)

LONE OAK LODGE Book at aaa.com — Phone: (831)372-4924 — 26

AAA SAVE — Motel

	1P	2P	XP	
7/1-9/30	1P: $68-$138	2P: $68-$138	XP: $6	F12
5/1-6/30	1P: $60-$116	2P: $60-$116	XP: $6	F12
2/1-4/30	1P: $54-$108	2P: $54-$108	XP: $6	F12
10/1-1/31	1P: $54-$94	2P: $54-$94	XP: $6	F12

Location: SR 1, exit Del Rey Oaks or Fremont St, 0.6 mi e. 2221 N Fremont St 93940. Fax: 831/372-4985. **Facility:** 46 units. 36 one- and 10 two-bedroom standard units, some with kitchens and/or whirlpools. 1 story, exterior corridors. *Bath:* combo or shower only. **Parking:** on-site. **Amenities:** CD players, high-speed Internet, dual phone lines, voice mail, hair dryers. **Leisure Activities:** sauna, whirlpool, exercise room. **Business Services:** meeting rooms. **Cards:** AX, CB, DC, DS, JC, MC, VI. **Special Amenities: free local telephone calls.** *(See color ad p 443)*

SOME UNITS

MARIPOSA INN Book at aaa.com — Phone: (831)649-1414 — 46

AAA SAVE — Motel

	1P	2P	XP	
5/2-10/16 [ECP]	1P: $129-$169	2P: $129-$169	XP: $10	F17
2/1-5/1 & 10/17-1/31 [ECP]	1P: $79-$139	2P: $79-$139	XP: $10	F17

Location: SR 1, exit Soledad Dr/Munras Ave, just w. 1386 Munras Ave 93940. Fax: 831/649-5308. **Facility:** 50 one-bedroom standard units, some with whirlpools. 3-4 stories, interior/exterior corridors. *Bath:* combo or shower only. **Parking:** on-site. **Terms:** 2 night minimum stay - seasonal & weekends, 3 day cancellation notice-fee imposed. **Amenities:** high-speed Internet, irons, hair dryers. **Pool(s):** heated outdoor. **Leisure Activities:** whirlpool. **Guest Services:** valet laundry. **Cards:** AX, CB, DC, DS, MC, VI. **Special Amenities: free continental breakfast and free local telephone calls.** *(See color ad below)*

SOME UNITS

MERRITT HOUSE — Phone: 831/646-9686 — 51

Motel

	1P	2P	XP	
All Year	1P: $161-$235	2P: $161-$235	XP: $15	F12

Location: SR 1, exit Munras Ave, 2 mi w. 386 Pacific St 93940. Fax: 831/646-5392. **Facility:** 25 one-bedroom standard units. 2 stories (no elevator), exterior corridors. **Parking:** on-site. **Terms:** cancellation fee imposed, [ECP] meal plan available, package plans. **Amenities:** high-speed Internet (fee), irons, hair dryers. **Guest Services:** valet laundry. **Cards:** AX, DC, DS, MC, VI.

ASK

MONTEREY BAY INN Book at aaa.com — Phone: (831)373-6242 — 8

AAA SAVE — Motel

	1P	2P	XP
All Year [CP]	1P: $179-$349	2P: $179-$349	XP: $10

Location: SR 1, exit Monterey, 3.5 mi w. 242 Cannery Row 93940. Fax: 831/373-7603. **Facility:** 47 one-bedroom standard units. 4 stories, interior corridors. **Parking:** on-site (fee). **Terms:** check-in 4 pm, 2 night minimum stay - some weekends, cancellation fee imposed, package plans - seasonal. **Amenities:** video library (fee), CD players, dual phone lines, voice mail, honor bars, irons, hair dryers. **Leisure Activities:** sauna, whirlpools, lockers for scuba gear. *Fee:* massage. **Business Services:** meeting rooms. **Cards:** AX, DC, DS, JC, MC, VI. **Special Amenities: free continental breakfast and free newspaper.** *(See color ad p 447)*

(See map and index starting on p. 436)

MONTEREY BAY LODGE Phone: (831)372-8057 57

7/1-10/31	1P: $109-$269	2P: $159-$319	XP: $15	F12
4/30-6/30	1P: $99-$199	2P: $119-$209	XP: $15	F12
11/1-1/31	1P: $79-$169	2P: $89-$179	XP: $15	F12
2/1-4/29	1P: $89-$159	2P: $99-$169	XP: $15	F12

SAVE · Motel

Location: SR 1, exit Aguajito Rd, just w. Located across from El Estero Lagoon and Park. 55 Camino Aguajito 93940. Fax: 831/655-2933. **Facility:** Designated smoking area. 45 units. 43 one- and 2 two-bedroom standard units. 2 stories (no elevator), exterior corridors. *Bath:* combo or shower only. **Parking:** on-site. **Terms:** 2-3 night minimum stay - some weekends, package plans. **Amenities:** high-speed Internet, dual phone lines, voice mail, safes, irons, hair dryers. **Dining:** 6:30 am-2 & 4:30-9 pm. **Pool(s):** heated outdoor. **Leisure Activities:** whirlpool. **Cards:** AX, DC, DS, MC, VI. **Special Amenities: free local telephone calls.** *(See color ad below)*

SOME UNITS

FEE

(See map and index starting on p. 436)

MONTEREY DOWNTOWN TRAVELODGE Book at aaa.com **Phone:** (831)373-1876 59

Motel

All Year 1P: $89-$199 2P: $89-$199 XP: $12 F17

Location: SR 1, exit Fremont St or Munras Ave, 0.7 mi w. 675 Munras Ave 93940. Fax: 831/373-8693. **Facility:** 51 one-bedroom standard units. 3 stories, exterior corridors. *Bath:* combo or shower only. **Parking:** on-site. **Amenities:** irons, hair dryers. **Pool(s):** outdoor. **Cards:** AX, CB, DC, DS, JC, MC, VI. **Special Amenities: free local telephone calls and free newspaper.** *(See color ad below)*

SOME UNITS

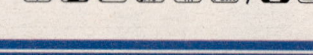

MONTEREY FIRESIDE LODGE **Phone:** (831)373-4172 64

Motel

All Year 1P: $59-$299 2P: $69-$309 XP: $10 F9

Location: SR 1, exit Aguajito Rd or Monterey, just w. 1131 10th St 93940. Fax: 831/655-5640. **Facility:** 24 one-bedroom standard units. 2 stories (no elevator), exterior corridors. **Parking:** on-site. **Terms:** 3 day cancellation notice-fee imposed, [CP] meal plan available, pets ($20 extra charge). **Leisure Activities:** whirlpool. **Cards:** AX, DC, DS, MC, VI. **Special Amenities: free continental breakfast and preferred room (subject to availability with advanced reservations).**

SOME UNITS

FEE

THE MONTEREY HOTEL Book at aaa.com **Phone:** (831)375-3184 56

Historic Small-scale Hotel

All Year 1P: $99-$199 2P: $99-$199

Location: Downtown. 406 Alvarado St 93940. Fax: 831/373-2899. **Facility:** This Victorian hotel built in 1904 has some small guest rooms and a few featuring gas fireplaces and wet bars. Smoke free premises. 45 units. 41 one-bedroom standard units. 4 one-bedroom suites ($149-$309). 4 stories, interior corridors. **Parking:** valet. **Terms:** 3 day cancellation notice, [CP] meal plan available, package plans - seasonal. **Amenities:** dual phone lines, voice mail, hair dryers. **Leisure Activities:** spa. **Guest Services:** complimentary evening beverages, valet laundry. **Business Services:** meeting rooms. **Cards:** AX, CB, DC, DS, JC, MC, VI. *(See color ad below)*

SOME UNITS

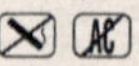

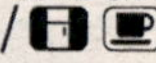

(See map and index starting on p. 436)

MONTEREY MARRIOTT *Book at aaa.com* **Phone:** (831)649-4234 58

Large-scale Hotel

7/1-10/31 1P: $169-$229
5/1-6/30 1P: $129-$209
2/1-4/30 & 11/1-1/31 1P: $119-$209

Location: SR 1, exit Del Monte or Munras aves, 2 mi w. Located opposite conference center. 350 Calle Principal 93940. Fax: 831/372-2968. **Facility:** Smoke free premises. 341 units. 320 one-bedroom standard units. 21 one-bedroom suites. 10 stories, interior corridors. *Bath:* combo or shower only. **Parking:** valet. **Terms:** cancellation fee imposed, [AP] & [BP] meal plans available. **Amenities:** dual phone lines, voice mail, irons, hair dryers. *Fee:* video games, high-speed Internet. **Pool(s):** outdoor. **Leisure Activities:** whirlpool, exercise room, spa. **Guest Services:** gift shop, valet and coin laundry. **Business Services:** conference facilities, business center. **Cards:** AX, DC, DS, MC, VI.

SOME UNITS / VCR FEE /

MONTEREY PLAZA HOTEL & SPA *Book at aaa.com* **Phone:** (831)646-1700 7

SAVE Large-scale Hotel

All Year 1P: $185-$445 2P: $185-$445 XP: $20 F17

Location: SR 1, exit Del Monte or Munras aves, 3 mi w. 400 Cannery Row 93940. Fax: 831/646-5937. **Facility:** On historic Cannery Row overlooking Monterey Bay and the Pacific Ocean, this property offers many units with balconies and bay views. 290 units. 279 one-bedroom standard units. 11 one-bedroom suites ($740-$2500), some with whirlpools. 3-5 stories, interior corridors. *Bath:* combo or shower only. **Parking:** valet. **Terms:** check-in 4 pm, 2 night minimum stay - most weekends, cancellation fee imposed. **Amenities:** CD players, voice mail, honor bars, irons, hair dryers. **Dining:** 11:30 am-11 pm, also, The Duck Club, see separate listing. **Leisure Activities:** Fee: kayaking, bicycles, exercise room, massage. **Guest Services:** gift shop, valet laundry. **Business Services:** conference facilities, business center. **Cards:** AX, CB, DC, DS, MC, VI. **Special Amenities: free newspaper.**
(See color ad inside back cover)

SOME UNITS / AC VCR /

MUNRAS LODGE *Book at aaa.com* **Phone:** (831)646-9696 32

SAVE Motel

All Year 1P: $89-$299 2P: $89-$299 XP: $10 F17

Location: SR 1, exit Soledad Dr/Munras Ave, 0.7 mi w. 1010 Munras Ave 93940. Fax: 831/647-8248. **Facility:** 29 one-bedroom standard units, some with whirlpools. 2 stories (no elevator), interior corridors. **Parking:** on-site. **Terms:** 3 day cancellation notice-fee imposed. **Amenities:** irons. **Leisure Activities:** sauna, whirlpool. **Cards:** AX, DS, MC, VI. **Special Amenities: free continental breakfast.** *(See color ad below)*

OLD MONTEREY INN **Phone:** (831)375-8284 60

SAVE Bed & Breakfast

All Year [BP] 1P: $240-$350 2P: $240-$350 XP: $50

Location: SR 1, exit Soledad Dr/Munras Ave, 1 mi w; 1 mi s from Fishermans Wharf on Pacific St to Martin St, 2 blks w. 500 Martin St 93940. Fax: 831/375-6730. **Facility:** This 1929 Tudor-style garden home is on a wooded hillside and features individually decorated rooms, most with feather beds and some with fireplaces. Smoke free premises. 10 units. 7 one-bedroom standard units. 3 one-bedroom suites ($390), some with whirlpools. 1-3 stories (no elevator), interior/exterior corridors. *Bath:* combo or shower only. **Parking:** on-site. **Terms:** 10 day cancellation notice. **Amenities:** video library, CD players, irons, hair dryers. **Cards:** MC, VI. **Special Amenities: free local telephone calls and free newspaper.**

AC VCR DATA PORT

OTTER INN *Book at aaa.com* **Phone:** (831)375-2299 3

SAVE Motel

All Year 1P: $89-$399 2P: $89-$399 XP: $10 F

Location: SR 1, exit Monterey, 3.5 mi w. Located in Cannery Row area. 571 Wave St 93940. Fax: 831/375-2352. **Facility:** 33 one-bedroom standard units, some with whirlpools. 4 stories, exterior corridors. **Parking:** on-site. **Terms:** 3 day cancellation notice, package plans - seasonal. **Amenities:** irons, hair dryers. **Leisure Activities:** whirlpool. **Cards:** AX, DC, DS, MC, VI. **Special Amenities: free continental breakfast and free local telephone calls.** *(See color ad p 460)*

(See map and index starting on p. 436)

PADRE OAKS — Phone: (831)373-3741 — 39

AAA SAVE — Two Diamonds — Motel

7/1-8/31 [CP]	1P: $64-$189	2P: $69-$199	XP: $10
9/1-10/31 [CP]	1P: $39-$169	2P: $49-$179	XP: $10
2/1-6/30 [CP]	1P: $39-$149	2P: $39-$159	XP: $10
11/1-1/31 [CP]	1P: $39-$139	2P: $39-$149	XP: $10

Location: SR 1, exit Soledad Dr/Munras Ave, 0.3 mi w. 1278 Munras Ave 93940. Fax: 831/333-0413. **Facility:** 20 one-bedroom standard units. 1 story, exterior corridors. *Bath:* shower only. **Parking:** on-site. **Terms:** 3 day cancellation notice-fee imposed. **Pool(s):** small outdoor. **Cards:** AX, DS, MC, VI. **Special Amenities: free continental breakfast and early check-in/late check-out.**

SOME UNITS — FEE FEE

QUALITY INN — *Book at aaa.com* — Phone: (831)372-3381 — 34

AAA SAVE — Three Diamonds — Motel

5/15-10/31	1P: $99-$299	2P: $99-$299	XP: $10	F17
2/1-5/14 & 11/1-1/31	1P: $69-$299	2P: $69-$299	XP: $10	F17

Location: SR 1, exit Munras Ave, 0.5 mi w. 1058 Munras Ave 93940. Fax: 831/372-4687. **Facility:** 56 one-bedroom standard units. 2 stories (no elevator), exterior corridors. **Parking:** on-site. **Terms:** 2-3 night minimum stay - weekends, 3 day cancellation notice-fee imposed, [ECP] meal plan available. **Amenities:** voice mail, irons, hair dryers. **Cards:** AX, DC, DS, JC, MC, VI. **Special Amenities: free continental breakfast and free local telephone calls.** *(See color ad p 449)*

SOME UNITS

QUALITY INN CANNERY ROW — *Book at aaa.com* — Phone: (831)649-8580 — 11

Two Diamonds — Motel

All Year	1P: $89-$399	2P: $89-$399	XP: $10	F

Location: SR 1, exit Monterey, 3 mi w. Located in Cannery Row area. 200 Foam St 93940. Fax: 831/649-2566. **Facility:** 32 units. 31 one- and 1 two-bedroom standard units. 3 stories, interior corridors. **Parking:** on-site. **Terms:** 3 day cancellation notice, package plans - seasonal. **Amenities:** irons, hair dryers. **Cards:** AX, DC, DS, MC, VI. ***(See color ad below)***

QUALITY INN MONTEREY FAIRGROUNDS — *Book at aaa.com* — Phone: (831)373-5551 — 20

AAA SAVE — Two Diamonds — Motel

5/1-10/31 [ECP]	1P: $69-$329	2P: $69-$329	XP: $10	F10
2/1-4/30 & 11/1-1/31 [ECP]	1P: $59-$299	2P: $59-$299	XP: $10	F10

Location: SR 1, exit Fremont St or Casa Verde Way, just e. 2075 Fremont St 93940. Fax: 831/373-4250. **Facility:** 42 units. 31 one- and 11 two-bedroom standard units. 2 stories (no elevator), exterior corridors. *Bath:* combo or shower only. **Parking:** on-site. **Amenities:** irons, hair dryers. **Pool(s):** small outdoor. **Guest Services:** coin laundry. **Cards:** AX, DC, DS, MC, VI. **Special Amenities: free continental breakfast and early check-in/late check-out.** *(See color ad p 461)*

SOME UNITS

RAMADA LIMITED-FREMONT — *Book at aaa.com* — Phone: (831)375-9511 — 24

AAA SAVE — Two Diamonds — Motel

6/2-10/31 [CP]	1P: $89-$149	2P: $89-$189	XP: $10	F16
4/16-6/1 [CP]	1P: $69-$109	2P: $79-$129	XP: $10	F16
11/1-1/31 [CP]	1P: $69-$89	2P: $69-$109	XP: $10	F16
2/1-4/15 [CP]	1P: $69-$89	2P: $69-$99	XP: $10	F16

Location: SR 1, exit Fremont St or Casa Verde Way, 0.3 mi e. 2058 N Fremont St 93940. Fax: 831/375-9701. **Facility:** 47 one-bedroom standard units. 1-2 stories, exterior corridors. *Bath:* combo or shower only. **Parking:** on-site. **Terms:** 2-3 night minimum stay - seasonal, 3 day cancellation notice-fee imposed, package plans - seasonal. **Amenities:** voice mail, irons, hair dryers. **Pool(s):** small heated outdoor. **Leisure Activities:** sauna, whirlpool. **Cards:** AX, DC, DS, MC, VI.

SOME UNITS

(See map and index starting on p. 436)

RAMADA LIMITED-MUNRAS *Book at aaa.com* Phone: (831)375-2679 28

Motel

6/2-10/31 [CP]	1P: $99-$149	2P: $99-$189	XP: $10	F16
4/16-6/1 [CP]	1P: $79-$129	2P: $89-$139	XP: $10	F16
2/1-4/15 & 11/1-1/31 [CP]	1P: $69-$99	2P: $79-$109	XP: $10	F16

Location: SR 1, exit Munras Ave, 0.5 mi w. 1182 Cass St 93940. Fax: 831/643-2837. **Facility:** Smoke free premises. 19 units. 18 one- and 1 two-bedroom standard units. 2 stories (no elevator), exterior corridors. **Parking:** on-site. **Terms:** 2-3 night minimum stay - seasonal, 3 day cancellation notice-fee imposed. **Amenities:** voice mail, hair dryers. *Some:* irons. **Pool(s):** small outdoor. **Cards:** AX, DC, DS, MC, VI. **Special Amenities: free continental breakfast and free local telephone calls.**

SOME UNITS

RODEWAY INN MONTEREY *Book at aaa.com* Phone: (831)373-2911 18

Motel

5/1-9/30 [CP]	1P: $69-$199	2P: $79-$249	XP: $10	F17
10/1-1/31 [CP]	1P: $49-$99	2P: $59-$139	XP: $10	F17
2/1-4/30 [CP]	1P: $59-$99	2P: $69-$119	XP: $10	F17

Location: SR 1, exit Fremont St or Casa Verde Way, 0.3 mi e. 2041 Fremont St 93940. Fax: 831/655-3450. **Facility:** 22 one-bedroom standard units. 2 stories (no elevator), exterior corridors. **Parking:** on-site. **Terms:** 3 day cancellation notice-fee imposed. **Cards:** AX, CB, DC, DS, JC, MC, VI. **Special Amenities: free continental breakfast and free local telephone calls.** *(See color ad p 453)*

SOME UNITS

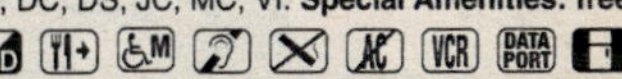

SAND DOLLAR INN Phone: (831)372-7551 66

Motel

6/1-9/30 [ECP]	1P: $109-$209	2P: $109-$209	XP: $10	F12
2/1-5/31 & 10/1-1/31 [ECP]	1P: $89-$189	2P: $89-$189	XP: $10	F12

Location: SR 1, exit Fremont St, 0.8 mi w. 755 Abrego St 93940. Fax: 831/372-0916. **Facility:** Smoke free premises. 63 one-bedroom standard units. 3 stories, interior/exterior corridors. **Parking:** on-site. **Terms:** cancellation fee imposed. **Amenities:** video library (fee), irons, hair dryers. *Some:* DVD players. **Pool(s):** heated outdoor. **Leisure Activities:** whirlpool. **Cards:** AX, MC, VI. **Special Amenities: free continental breakfast and early check-in/late check-out.** *(See color ad p 462)*

SPINDRIFT INN *Book at aaa.com* Phone: (831)646-8900 2

Motel

All Year [CP]	1P: $169-$479	2P: $169-$479	XP: $10

Location: SR 1, exit Monterey, 3.7 mi w. 652 Cannery Row 93940. Fax: 831/646-5342. **Facility:** Smoke free premises. 42 one-bedroom standard units. 4 stories, interior corridors. **Parking:** on-site (fee). **Terms:** check-in 4 pm, 2 night minimum stay - some weekends, cancellation fee imposed, package plans - seasonal. **Amenities:** video library (fee), CD players, dual phone lines, voice mail, honor bars, hair dryers. **Guest Services:** valet laundry. **Business Services:** fax (fee). **Cards:** AX, DC, DS, JC, MC, VI. **Special Amenities: free continental breakfast and free newspaper.** *(See color ad p 447)*

(See map and index starting on p. 436)

STEINBECK LODGE — **Phone:** (831)373-3203 — 44

AAA SAVE — Motel

5/1-9/30	1P: $59-$199	2P: $69-$209	XP: $10	F5
2/1-4/30 & 10/1-11/30	1P: $49-$179	2P: $59-$199	XP: $10	F5
12/1-1/31	1P: $39-$179	2P: $49-$199	XP: $10	F5

Location: SR 1, exit Munras Ave, just w. 1300 Munras Ave 93940. Fax: 831/372-3505. **Facility:** 34 one-bedroom standard units. 2 stories (no elevator), exterior corridors. **Parking:** on-site. **Terms:** 3 day cancellation notice-fee imposed, [CP] meal plan available. **Amenities:** high-speed Internet, irons, hair dryers. **Pool(s):** outdoor. **Cards:** AX, DC, MC, VI. **Special Amenities: free continental breakfast and free local telephone calls.**

SOME UNITS

SUPER 8-MONTEREY/CENTRAL/CARMEL — *Book at aaa.com* — **Phone:** (831)373-3081 — 23

AAA SAVE — Motel

6/16-9/15 [ECP]	1P: $59-$159	2P: $69-$169	XP: $10	F16
9/16-1/31 [ECP]	1P: $49-$159	2P: $59-$169	XP: $10	F16
2/1-6/15 [ECP]	1P: $49-$159	2P: $49-$169	XP: $10	F16

Location: SR 1, exit Fremont St or Casa Verde Way, 0.3 mi e. Located across from fairgrounds. 2050 N Fremont St 93940. Fax: 831/372-6730. **Facility:** 48 one-bedroom standard units. 2 stories (no elevator), exterior corridors. *Bath:* combo or shower only. **Parking:** on-site. **Terms:** cancellation fee imposed. **Amenities:** dual phone lines, voice mail. **Leisure Activities:** sauna, whirlpools. **Cards:** AX, CB, DC, DS, MC, VI. **Special Amenities: free expanded continental breakfast and free local telephone calls.** *(See color ad below)*

SOME UNITS

FEE FEE

(See map and index starting on p. 436)

TRAVELODGE-MONTEREY/CARMEL *Book at aaa.com* **Phone:** (831)373-3381 **21**

SAVE — Motel

7/1-9/30	1P: $79-$239	2P: $89-$239	XP: $10	F16
6/1-6/30	1P: $69-$239	2P: $79-$239	XP: $10	F16
2/1-5/31 & 10/1-1/31	1P: $59-$169	2P: $69-$169	XP: $10	F16

Location: Jct SR 1 and Fremont St at SR 68. 2030 N Fremont St 93940. Fax: 831/649-8741. **Facility:** 104 one-bedroom standard units. 2 stories (no elevator), interior/exterior corridors. *Bath:* combo or shower only. **Parking:** on-site. **Terms:** package plans. **Amenities:** safes, irons, hair dryers. **Dining:** 7:30 am-9:30 pm. **Pool(s):** heated outdoor. **Guest Services:** valet and coin laundry. **Business Services:** meeting rooms. **Cards:** AX, CB, DC, DS, MC, VI. **Special Amenities: early check-in/late check-out and free room upgrade (subject to availability with advanced reservations).** *(See color ad p 463)*

SOME UNITS

WAY STATION INN *Book at aaa.com* **Phone:** (831)372-2945 **49**

SAVE — Motel

7/1-9/30	1P: $89-$189	2P: $99-$199	XP: $15
4/1-6/30	1P: $79-$179	2P: $89-$179	XP: $15
2/1-3/31 & 10/1-1/31	1P: $69-$169	2P: $79-$179	XP: $15

Location: SR 1, exit Airport-Salinas, 1.5 mi e on SR 68. Located across from airport. 1200 Olmstead Rd 93940. Fax: 831/375-6267. **Facility:** 46 one-bedroom standard units. 2 stories (no elevator), exterior corridors. **Parking:** on-site. **Terms:** 7 day cancellation notice-fee imposed, [CP] meal plan available. **Cards:** AX, CB, DC, DS, JC, MC, VI. **Special Amenities: free continental breakfast and early check-in/late check-out.** *(See color ad p 463)*

SOME UNITS

WHERE TO DINE

ABALONETTI SEAFOOD TRATTORIA **Lunch:** $11-$21 **Dinner:** $11-$26 **Phone:** 831/373-1851 **10**

Steak & Seafood

Location: On Fisherman's Wharf. 57 Fisherman's Wharf 93940. **Hours:** 11 am-10 pm. Closed: 12/25. **Reservations:** accepted. **Features:** Calamari is a specialty among the many listed appetizers. Fresh seafood comes in from the restaurant's own boat. Casual dress; cocktails. **Parking:** on-site (fee). **Cards:** AX, CB, DC, DS, JC, MC, VI.

ANN KELLY'S BY THE LAKE **Lunch:** $5-$10 **Dinner:** $8-$22 **Phone:** 831/646-2002 **17**

American

Location: SR 1, exit Aguajito Rd, then w. 55 Camino Aguajito 93940. **Hours:** 6:30 am-2 & 4:30-9 pm. Closed: 11/25, 12/25; also Sun. **Reservations:** suggested. **Features:** A local favorite, the casual restaurant overlooks a small lake surrounded by marine wildlife and birds. Dishes are prepared from fresh, local ingredients. Casual dress; beer & wine only. **Parking:** street. **Cards:** AX, CB, DC, DS, JC, MC, VI.

(See map and index starting on p. 436)

BLUE MOON Lunch: $9-$16 Dinner: $13-$50 Phone: 831/375-4155 (5)

Seafood

Location: Adjacent to Spindrift Inn. 654 Cannery Row 93940. **Hours:** 11 am-10 pm. Closed: 12/25. **Reservations:** suggested. **Features:** Overlooking Monterey Bay from its location on Cannery Row, the restaurant prepares California and Mediterranean dishes. The dining room has a comfortable, laid-back feel. Casual dress; cocktails. **Parking:** street. **Cards:** AX, CB, DC, MC, VI.

CAFE FINA Lunch: $10-$19 Dinner: $15-$27 Phone: 831/372-5200 (9)

Seafood

Location: At Old Fisherman's Wharf. 47 Fisherman's Wharf 93940. **Hours:** 11:30 am-2:30 & 5-10 pm, Sat & Sun 11:30 am-3 & 5-10 pm. Closed: 11/25, 12/25. **Reservations:** suggested. **Features:** Mesquite-broiled seafood, pizzas baked in a brick oven and homemade pasta dishes are foremost on the menu. The neat, small dining area includes a few tables on the second level. Dressy casual; cocktails. **Parking:** on-site (fee). **Cards:** AX, CB, DC, DS, JC, MC, VI.

DOMENICO'S ON THE WHARF Lunch: $7-$19 Dinner: $15-$36 Phone: 831/372-3655 (12)

Seafood

Location: On Fisherman's Wharf. 50 Fisherman's Wharf 93940. **Hours:** 11:30 am-2:30 & 4-9:30 pm, Fri & Sat-10 pm. Closed: 11/25, 12/25. **Reservations:** suggested. **Features:** This restaurant overlooks the marina and Monterey Bay. Mesquite-grilled seafood and pasta dishes emphasize fresh, local ingredients. Casual dress; cocktails. **Parking:** on-site (fee). **Cards:** AX, CB, DC, DS, MC, VI.

THE DUCK CLUB Dinner: $15-$26 Phone: 831/646-1700 (7)

American

Location: SR 1, exit Del Monte or Munras aves, 3 mi w; in Monterey Plaza Hotel & Spa. 400 Cannery Row 93940. **Hours:** 6:30 am-11 & 5:30-9:30 pm, Sat & Sun 6:30 am-noon & 5:30-9:30 pm. Closed: Mon. **Reservations:** suggested. **Features:** Seats in the sophisticated dining room afford beautiful views of Monterey Bay. Imaginative California specialties center on fresh fish and grilled steak. Casual dress; cocktails; entertainment. **Parking:** valet. **Cards:** AX, CB, DC, DS, JC, MC, VI. ***(See color ad inside back cover)***

THE FISH HOPPER Lunch: $8-$17 Dinner: $10-$24 Phone: 831/372-8543 (1)

Seafood

Location: On Cannery Row. 700 Cannery Row 93940. **Hours:** 11 am-10 pm. Closed: 12/24, 12/25. **Reservations:** suggested. **Features:** Over the water on Monterey Bay and Cannery Row, the restaurant houses an oyster bar and a cozy dining deck. Casual dress; cocktails. **Parking:** street. **Cards:** AX, DS, MC, VI.

FRESH CREAM Dinner: $25-$45 Phone: 831/375-9798 (8)

Regional French

Location: At Heritage Harbor/Fisherman's Wharf. 99 Pacific St #100 C 93940. **Hours:** 5:30 pm-10 pm. Closed: 4/11; also 12/24. **Reservations:** suggested. **Features:** California accents distinguish classic French dishes. Seats afford stunning views of Fisherman's Wharf and Monterey Bay. Dressy casual; cocktails. **Parking:** on-site (fee). **Cards:** AX, CB, DC, DS, MC, VI.

MONTRIO BISTRO Dinner: $16-$22 Phone: 831/648-8880 (16)

Regional California

Location: Downtown. 414 Calle Principal 93940. **Hours:** 5 pm-10 pm, Sat-11 pm. Closed: 7/4, 11/25, 12/25. **Reservations:** suggested. **Features:** The charming bistro channels influences from Italy, France and America. The open kitchen features a wood-burning rotisserie. Casual dress; cocktails. **Parking:** street. **Cards:** AX, DS, MC, VI.

SANDBAR & GRILL Lunch: $6-$11 Dinner: $11-$21 Phone: 831/373-2818 (13)

Seafood

Location: Just n of Fisherman's Wharf. **Hours:** 11:30 am-11 pm, Sat & Sun 10:30 am-midnight. Closed: 11/25. **Features:** Overlooking the marina and Monterey Bay, the cozy restaurant presents a menu of pasta, steak and rib choices. Casual dress; cocktails; entertainment. **Parking:** on-site (fee). **Cards:** AX, DC, DS, MC, VI.

SARDINE FACTORY Dinner: $22-$50 Phone: 831/373-3775 (6)

Regional Continental

Location: In Cannery Row area. 701 Wave St 93940. **Hours:** 5 pm-10:30 pm, Fri-Sun to 11 pm. Closed: 12/20-12/25. **Reservations:** suggested. **Features:** The menu comprises preparations of fresh seafood, steak and pasta. Diners can sit in one of four individually decorated dining rooms, from the casual, glass-domed "Conservatory" to the refined "Cannery Row Room.". Dressy casual; cocktails. **Parking:** valet. **Cards:** AX, CB, DC, DS, MC, VI.

STOKES ADOBE RESTAURANT Lunch: $7-$9 Dinner: $13-$18 Phone: 831/373-1110 (15)

Regional California

Location: Downtown. 500 Hartnell St 93940. **Hours:** 11:30 am-10 pm, Sun from 4 pm. Closed: 12/25. **Reservations:** suggested. **Features:** In a restored, two-story adobe downtown, the restaurant presents a menu of regional cuisine made from local ingredients, including fresh fish. Casual dress; cocktails. **Parking:** on-site. **Cards:** AX, DC, MC, VI.

TARPY'S ROADHOUSE Lunch: $6-$35 Dinner: $6-$35 Phone: 831/647-1444 (14)

Regional American

Location: On SR 68, 2.5 mi e of jct SR 1. 2999 Monterey-Salinas Hwy 93940. **Hours:** 11:30 am-10 pm. Closed major holidays. **Reservations:** suggested. **Features:** Distinctive dining rooms and intimate garden patios contribute to the attractive, relaxed setting. Dressy casual; entertainment. **Parking:** on-site. **Cards:** AX, DC, DS, MC, VI.

(See map and index starting on p. 436)

THE WHALER STEAK HOUSE **Dinner:** $12-$32 **Phone:** 831/373-1933 (11)

Steak & Seafood

Location: Downtown. 635 Cass St 93940. **Hours:** 4:30 pm-9 pm, Sat-9:30 pm. Closed: Mon. **Reservations:** accepted. **Features:** Local ingredients add to the authentic taste of California regional dishes. The atmosphere is relaxed. Casual dress; cocktails. **Parking:** on-site. **Cards:** AX, MC, VI.

WHALING STATION PRIME STEAKS & SEAFOOD **Dinner:** $17-$30 **Phone:** 831/373-3778 (4)

Steak & Seafood

Location: In Cannery Row area. 763 Wave St 93940. **Hours:** 5 pm-10 pm. Closed: 12/25. **Reservations:** suggested. **Features:** Tuscan decor gives the dining room an upscale feel. Prime beef and fresh seafood are prepared over a mesquite-wood broiler. Dressy casual; cocktails. **Parking:** on-site. **Cards:** AX, CB, DC, DS, JC, MC, VI.

CARMEL-BY-THE-SEA pop. 4,081 (See map and index starting on p. 436)

WHERE TO STAY

ADOBE INN-CARMEL **Phone:** (831)624-3933 (147)

Motel

6/1-10/31 [ECP]	1P: $199-$495	2P: $199-$495	XP: $20	F17
3/1-5/31 [ECP]	1P: $170-$495	2P: $170-$495	XP: $20	F17
2/1-2/29 & 11/1-1/31 [ECP]	1P: $155-$495	2P: $155-$495	XP: $20	F17

Location: Just s off Ocean Ave, at Dolores St and 8th Ave. (PO Box 4115, CARMEL, 93921). Fax: 831/624-8636. **Facility:** Many of the inn's spacious and attractively decorated guests units feature balcony and wet bar, and some include gas fireplaces. 20 one-bedroom standard units. 2 stories, exterior corridors. **Parking:** on-site. **Terms:** 2-3 night minimum stay - weekends, 5 day cancellation notice. **Amenities:** irons, hair dryers. **Pool(s):** small outdoor. **Leisure Activities:** sauna. **Cards:** AX, CB, DC, DS, JC, MC, VI. **Special Amenities: free expanded continental breakfast and free newspaper.**

SOME UNITS

BEST VALUE CARMEL RESORT INN **Phone:** (831)624-3113 (120)

Cottage

All Year	1P: $125-$180	2P: $159-$300	XP: $10

Location: SR 1, exit Carpenter St, 0.5 mi w. (PO Box 2266, 93921). Fax: 831/624-5456. **Facility:** Smoke free premises. 31 units. 28 one- and 3 two-bedroom standard units, some with efficiencies. 1 story, exterior corridors. **Parking:** on-site. **Terms:** 3 day cancellation notice-fee imposed. **Amenities:** irons, hair dryers. **Cards:** AX, CB, DC, DS, MC, VI. **Special Amenities: free continental breakfast and free local telephone calls.** *(See color ad below)*

BEST WESTERN CARMEL BAY VIEW INN **Phone:** (831)624-1831 (136)

Motel

6/1-8/31 [CP]	1P: $149-$299	2P: $149-$299	XP: $10	F12
9/1-10/31 [CP]	1P: $129-$299	2P: $129-$299	XP: $10	F12
2/1-5/31 [CP]	1P: $109-$259	2P: $109-$259	XP: $10	F12
11/1-1/31 [CP]	1P: $109	2P: $109	XP: $10	F12

Location: Just n off Ocean Ave on Junipero St. Junipero St between 5th & 6th aves 93923 (PO Box 3715, 93921). Fax: 831/625-2336. **Facility:** Smoke free premises. 58 units. 50 one-bedroom standard units. 6 one- and 2 two-bedroom suites. 1-5 stories, exterior corridors. *Bath:* combo or shower only. **Parking:** on-site. **Terms:** 3 day cancellation notice. **Amenities:** irons, hair dryers. **Pool(s):** outdoor. **Cards:** AX, DC, MC, VI. **Special Amenities: free continental breakfast.** *(See color ad p 467)*

SOME UNITS

(See map and index starting on p. 436)

BEST WESTERN CARMEL MISSION INN Book at aaa.com **Phone:** (831)624-1841 114

AAA SAVE — Small-scale Hotel

All Year 1P: $79-$329 2P: $79-$329 XP: $15 F16

Location: 1 mi s on SR 1. 3665 Rio Rd 93923. Fax: 831/624-8684. **Facility:** 165 units. 163 one-bedroom standard units. 2 one-bedroom suites. 4 stories, interior/exterior corridors. **Parking:** on-site. **Terms:** check-in 4 pm, cancellation fee imposed, pets ($35 fee). **Amenities:** voice mail, irons, hair dryers. **Dining:** 7 am-10 & 5-10 pm, Sat & Sun 7 am-11 & 5-10 pm, cocktails. **Pool(s):** outdoor. **Leisure Activities:** whirlpools. **Guest Services:** valet laundry. **Business Services:** conference facilities, business center. **Cards:** AX, CB, DC, DS, JC, MC, VI. **Special Amenities: free room upgrade (subject to availability with advanced reservations).**

(See color ad p 447)

SOME UNITS

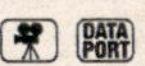

FEE

(See map and index starting on p. 436)

BEST WESTERN CARMEL'S TOWN HOUSE LODGE — Phone: (831)624-1261 — 131

AAA SAVE — Motel

7/1-10/31 [CP]	1P: $109-$249	2P: $109-$249	XP: $10	F10
4/1-6/30 [CP]	1P: $89-$229	2P: $89-$229	XP: $10	F10
2/1-3/31 & 11/1-1/31 [CP]	1P: $79-$199	2P: $79-$199	XP: $10	F10

Location: 2 blks n off Ocean Ave at 5th Ave and San Carlos St. Corner of San Carlos St & 5th Ave 93923 (PO Box 3574, 93921). Fax: 831/625-6783. **Facility:** Smoke free premises. 28 units. 25 one- and 3 two-bedroom standard units. 2 stories, exterior corridors. *Bath:* combo or shower only. **Parking:** on-site. **Terms:** 2 night minimum stay - weekends, 7 day cancellation notice. **Amenities:** voice mail, irons, hair dryers. **Pool(s):** small heated outdoor. **Leisure Activities:** sun deck with fireplace. **Cards:** AX, CB, DC, DS, MC, VI. **Special Amenities: free continental breakfast and free newspaper.**

BRIARWOOD INN — Phone: (831)626-9056 — 126

AAA SAVE — Bed & Breakfast

6/1-10/31 [CP]	1P: $120-$235	2P: $120-$235	XP: $20	F5
2/1-5/31 & 11/1-1/31 [CP]	1P: $110-$235	2P: $110-$235	XP: $20	F5

Location: 3 blks n off Ocean Ave at San Carlos St and 4th Ave. (PO Box 5245, 93921). Fax: 831/626-8900. **Facility:** Most rooms have a fireplace and some have a wet bar; a garden beautifies the well-maintained grounds. Smoke free premises. 12 units. 11 one- and 1 two-bedroom standard units, some with kitchens and/or whirlpools. 1-2 stories, exterior corridors. *Bath:* combo or shower only. **Parking:** on-site. **Terms:** 1-3 night minimum stay - weekends, 7 day cancellation notice-fee imposed. **Amenities:** video library, irons, hair dryers. **Guest Services:** complimentary evening beverages. **Cards:** AX, MC, VI. **Special Amenities: free continental breakfast and free local telephone calls.** *(See color ad below)*

SOME UNITS

CANDLE LIGHT INN — Phone: (831)624-6451 — 127

AAA SAVE — Motel

7/2-9/6 [CP]	1P: $189-$299	2P: $189-$299	XP: $15	F13
2/1-7/1 & 9/7-1/31 [CP]	1P: $99-$259	2P: $99-$259	XP: $15	F13

Location: 2 blks n off ocean on San Carlos St, between 4th and 5th aves. (PO Box 1900, 93921). Fax: 831/624-6732. **Facility:** Smoke free premises. 20 units. 19 one- and 1 two-bedroom standard units, some with kitchens and/or whirlpools. 2 stories, exterior corridors. *Bath:* combo or shower only. **Parking:** on-site. **Terms:** 2 night minimum stay - weekends, 7 day cancellation notice-fee imposed. **Amenities:** irons, hair dryers. **Leisure Activities:** whirlpool. **Guest Services:** valet laundry. **Business Services:** fax. **Cards:** AX, DS, MC, VI. **Special Amenities: free continental breakfast and free local telephone calls.** *(See color ad p 469)*

SOME UNITS

(See map and index starting on p. 436)

CARMEL COUNTRY INN — Phone: 831/625-3263 — 117

Bed & Breakfast — All Year — 1P: $150-$325 — 2P: $150-$325 — XP: $20

Location: 4 blks n of Ocean Ave at Dolores St and 3rd Ave. (PO Box 3756, 93921). Fax: 831/625-2945. **Facility:** Well-maintained grounds surround these spacious, attractively appointed guest rooms; all have wet bars and most have gas fireplaces. Smoke free premises. 12 units. 2 one-bedroom standard units. 5 one- and 5 two-bedroom suites, some with whirlpools. 2 stories, exterior corridors. *Bath:* combo or shower only. **Parking:** on-site. **Terms:** 2 night minimum stay - weekends, 7 day cancellation notice-fee imposed, pets ($20 extra charge, in limited units). **Amenities:** irons, hair dryers. **Cards:** AX, MC, VI.

ASK FEE DATA PORT

(See map and index starting on p. 436)

CARMEL FIREPLACE INN — Phone: (831)624-4862 — 125

Motel

6/1-10/31 [CP]	1P: $125-$285	2P: $125-$285	XP: $15	F5
2/1-5/31 & 11/1-1/31 [CP]	1P: $99-$265	2P: $99-$265	XP: $15	F5

Location: 3 blks n off Ocean Ave at San Carlos St and 4th Ave. (PO Box 4082, 93921). Fax: 831/626-1981. **Facility:** Smoke free premises. 18 units. 17 one- and 1 two-bedroom standard units. 2 stories, exterior corridors. *Bath:* combo or shower only. **Parking:** on-site. **Terms:** 1-3 night minimum stay - weekends, 7 day cancellation notice-fee imposed. **Amenities:** video library, irons, hair dryers. **Guest Services:** complimentary evening beverages. **Cards:** AX, MC, VI. **Special Amenities: free continental breakfast and free local telephone calls.** *(See color ad below)*

CARMEL GARDEN COURT — Phone: (831)624-6926 — 124

Bed & Breakfast

All Year	1P: $150-$245	XP: $20	D12

Location: 3 blks n off Ocean Ave, at 4th Ave and Torres St. (PO Box 6226, 93921). Fax: 831/624-4935. **Facility:** Fountains accent the award-winning garden at this property, which offers a wood-burning fireplace and some flower-filled private patios. Smoke free premises. 10 one-bedroom standard units. 1 story, exterior corridors. *Bath:* combo or shower only. **Parking:** on-site. **Terms:** check-in 4 pm, 2 night minimum stay - weekends, 7 day cancellation notice-fee imposed, [ECP] meal plan available, small pets only ($50 fee). **Amenities:** video library, hair dryers. **Cards:** AX, MC, VI. *(See color ad p 471)*

SOME UNITS

FEE

CARMEL RIVER INN *Book at aaa.com* — Phone: (831)624-1575 — 113

Motel

All Year	1P: $125-$250	2P: $125-$250	XP: $20

Location: 1 mi s on SR 1, n of Carmel River Bridge at Oliver Rd. (PO Box 221609). Fax: 831/624-0290. **Facility:** 43 one-bedroom standard units. 2 stories, exterior corridors. *Bath:* combo or shower only. **Parking:** on-site. **Terms:** 2 night minimum stay - weekends, 3 day cancellation notice, pets ($25 extra charge). **Amenities:** voice mail, irons, hair dryers. *Some:* DVD players. **Pool(s):** heated outdoor. **Cards:** AX, CB, DC, DS, JC, MC, VI. **Special Amenities: free room upgrade and preferred room (each subject to availability with advanced reservations).** *(See color ad p 472)*

SOME UNITS

FEE

(See map and index starting on p. 436)

CARMEL SANDS LODGE — **Phone:** 831/624-1255 (132)

AAA SAVE — Motel

6/20-10/31	1P: $85-$199	2P: $85-$199	XP: $20
2/1-6/19 & 11/1-1/31	1P: $68-$159	2P: $68-$159	XP: $20

Location: 2 blks n off Ocean Ave; on San Carlos St and 5th Ave. (PO Box 951, 93921). Fax: 831/624-2576. **Facility:** 37 one-bedroom standard units. 2 stories, interior/exterior corridors. *Bath:* combo or shower only. **Parking:** on-site. **Terms:** 5 day cancellation notice. **Amenities:** voice mail. *Some:* hair dryers. **Pool(s):** outdoor. **Cards:** AX, CB, DC, DS, MC, VI. *(See color ad p 473)*

SOME UNITS

(See map and index starting on p. 436)

CARMEL TRADEWINDS INN — **Phone:** (831)624-2776 — 118

Motel

6/15-10/31	1P: $250-$475	2P: $250-$475	XP: $20
2/1-6/14	1P: $225-$475	2P: $225-$475	XP: $20
11/1-1/31	1P: $150-$375	2P: $150-$375	XP: $20

Location: 4 blks n off Ocean Ave; at Mission St and 3rd Ave. (PO Box 3403, 93921). Fax: 831/624-0634. **Facility:** Smoke free premises. 28 units. 26 one-bedroom standard units, some with whirlpools. 2 one-bedroom suites ($350-$550) with whirlpools. 1-3 stories (no elevator), exterior corridors. *Bath:* combo or shower only. **Parking:** on-site. **Terms:** [ECP] meal plan available, pets ($25 extra charge, in designated units). **Amenities:** voice mail, irons, hair dryers. **Business Services:** meeting rooms. **Cards:** AX, MC, VI.

FEE

CARMEL VALLEY RANCH-A WYNDHAM LUXURY RESORT — *Book at aaa.com* — **Phone:** (831)625-9500 — 148

AAA SAVE

Resort
Large-scale Hotel

5/21-11/13	1P: $299-$399	2P: $299-$399	XP: $20	F18
3/26-5/20	1P: $249-$299	2P: $249-$299	XP: $20	F18
2/1-3/25 & 11/14-1/31	1P: $199-$249	2P: $199-$249	XP: $20	F18

Location: 6.3 mi e of SR 1 via Carmel Valley Rd, exit Robinson Canyon Rd, follow signs. One Old Ranch Rd 93923. Fax: 831/624-2858. **Facility:** Hillside, overlooking the Carmel Valley and a golf course, the resort offers spacious units with wood-burning fireplaces. 144 units. 10 one-bedroom standard units. 132 one- and 2 two-bedroom suites ($249-$899), some with whirlpools. 1 story, exterior corridors. **Parking:** on-site. **Terms:** check-in 4 pm, 14 day cancellation notice-fee imposed. **Amenities:** CD players, dual phone lines, voice mail, safes, honor bars, irons, hair dryers. *Fee:* video games, high-speed Internet. *Some:* fax. **Dining:** 3 restaurants, 7 am-2 & 6-10 pm, cocktails. **Pool(s):** 2 heated outdoor. **Leisure Activities:** saunas, whirlpools, 2 clay tennis courts, exercise room. *Fee:* golf-18 holes, 12 tennis courts, horseback riding, massage. **Guest Services:** valet laundry. **Business Services:** meeting rooms, fax (fee). **Cards:** AX, DC, DS, MC, VI.

SOME UNITS
VCR
FEE FEE

CARMEL VILLAGE INN & ANNEX — **Phone:** (831)624-3864 — 135

Motel

7/1-8/31 [ECP]	1P: $149-$189	2P: $149-$189	XP: $20	F3
9/1-10/31 [ECP]	1P: $129-$169	2P: $129-$169	XP: $20	F3
2/1-6/30 & 11/1-1/31 [ECP]	1P: $99-$139	2P: $99-$139	XP: $20	F3

Location: At Ocean Ave and Junipero St. (PO Box 5275, 93921). Fax: 831/626-6763. **Facility:** 53 units. 48 one-bedroom standard units, some with kitchens. 5 one-bedroom suites ($129-$379). 2 stories, exterior corridors. **Parking:** on-site. **Terms:** 2-4 night minimum stay - weekends, 3 day cancellation notice. **Cards:** AX, MC, VI. ***(See color ad p 474)***

SOME UNITS
ASK

(See map and index starting on p. 436)

CARMEL WAYFARER INN — **Phone:** (831)624-2711 — 123

Bed & Breakfast

6/16-9/30 [ECP]	1P: $129-$229	2P: $129-$229	XP: $20	F10
2/1-6/15 & 10/1-1/31 [ECP]	1P: $89-$159	2P: $89-$159	XP: $20	F10

Location: 3 blks n off Ocean at 4th Ave and Mission St. Mission St & 4th Ave 93921 (PO Box 1896). Fax: 831/625-1210. **Facility:** Smoke free premises. 16 one-bedroom standard units, some with efficiencies. 2 stories, exterior corridors. **Parking:** on-site. **Terms:** 2-3 night minimum stay - weekends, 3 day cancellation notice. **Amenities:** video library. **Cards:** AX, DC, DS, MC, VI.

CARRIAGE HOUSE INN — **Phone:** (831)625-2585 — 142

AAA SAVE — **Bed & Breakfast**

7/2-9/6 [ECP]	1P: $299-$350	2P: $299-$350	XP: $15	F13
2/1-7/1 & 9/7-1/31 [ECP]	1P: $229-$325	2P: $229-$325	XP: $15	F13

Location: 2 blks s off Ocean Ave, on Junipero St between 7th and 8th aves. (PO Box 1900, 93921). Fax: 831/626-6974. **Facility:** Guest rooms are spacious and attractively appointed and all have fireplaces, giving the inn a warm ambience. 13 units. 12 one-bedroom standard units, some with whirlpools. 1 one-bedroom suite ($279-$399) with whirlpool. 2 stories, exterior corridors. **Parking:** on-site. **Terms:** 2 night minimum stay - weekends, 7 day cancellation notice-fee imposed. **Amenities:** video library, CD players, safes, honor bars, irons, hair dryers. **Guest Services:** complimentary evening beverages, valet laundry. **Business Services:** fax. **Cards:** AX, DS, MC, VI. **Special Amenities: free continental breakfast and free local telephone calls.** *(See color ad p 469)*

CHATEAU DE CARMEL — **Phone:** (831)624-1900 — 130

AAA SAVE — **Motel**

All Year [CP]	1P: $79-$225	2P: $79-$225	XP: $10

Location: 2 blks n of Ocean Ave at Junipero St and 5th Ave. (PO Box 1295, 93921). Fax: 831/624-1571. **Facility:** Smoke free premises. 20 units. 15 one-bedroom standard units. 5 one-bedroom suites. 2 stories, exterior corridors. **Parking:** on-site. **Terms:** 2-3 night minimum stay - seasonal, 7 day cancellation notice-fee imposed. **Amenities:** hair dryers. *Some:* irons. **Pool(s):** small heated outdoor. **Cards:** AX, CB, DC, DS, MC, VI. **Special Amenities: free continental breakfast and free newspaper.** *(See color ad p 475)*

SOME UNITS

COACHMAN'S INN — **Phone:** (831)624-6421 — 140

AAA SAVE — **Motel**

All Year	1P: $135-$425	2P: $135-$425	XP: $15	F16

Location: Just s of Ocean Ave, San Carlos St between 7th and 8th aves. (PO Box C-1, 93921). Fax: 831/624-3311. **Facility:** Smoke free premises. 30 one-bedroom standard units, some with efficiencies and/or whirlpools. 3 stories (no elevator), exterior corridors. **Parking:** on-site. **Terms:** 3 day cancellation notice, [CP] meal plan available, pets ($20 extra charge, small dogs only). **Amenities:** video library, voice mail, irons, hair dryers. **Leisure Activities:** whirlpool. **Cards:** AX, DS, MC, VI. **Special Amenities: free continental breakfast.**

(See color ad p 475)

FEE

(See map and index starting on p. 436)

COBBLESTONE INN — **Phone:** (831)625-5222 — 143

Bed & Breakfast

All Year — 2P: $130-$185 — XP: $20

Location: S off Ocean Ave on Junipero St between 7th and 8th aves. (PO Box 3185, 93921). Fax: 831/625-0478. **Facility:** The inn offers a garden and attractive common areas; gas fireplaces are featured in all accommodations. Smoke free premises. 24 units. 22 one-bedroom standard units, some with whirlpools. 2 one-bedroom suites ($200-$275), some with whirlpools. 2 stories (no elevator), interior/exterior corridors. *Bath:* combo or shower only. **Parking:** street. **Terms:** cancellation fee imposed, package plans - seasonal. **Amenities:** voice mail, hair dryers. *Some:* irons. **Guest Services:** complimentary evening beverages. **Cards:** AX, DC, MC, VI.

COLONIAL TERRACE INN — **Phone:** (831)624-2741 — 109

AAA SAVE

Bed & Breakfast

All Year [ECP] — 1P: $129-$249 — 2P: $129-$249 — XP: $20 — F6

Location: On San Antonio, between 12th and 13th aves. (PO Box 1375, 93921). Fax: 831/626-2715. **Facility:** The inn, offering attractive gardens and some ocean views, features gas fireplaces in all guest rooms. Smoke free premises. 25 units. 24 one-bedroom standard units, some with whirlpools. 1 one-bedroom suite ($249-$359) with whirlpool. 2 stories (no elevator), exterior corridors. *Bath:* combo or shower only. **Parking:** on-site. **Terms:** 2-3 night minimum stay - weekends, 7 day cancellation notice. **Cards:** AX, MC, VI. **Special Amenities: free expanded continental breakfast and free newspaper.** *(See color ad p 476)*

SOME UNITS

CYPRESS INN — **Phone:** (831)624-3871 — 139

Classic Small-scale Hotel

All Year — 2P: $125-$395 — XP: $25

Location: Just s off Ocean Ave at Lincoln St and 7th Ave. (PO Box Y, 93921). Fax: 831/624-8216. **Facility:** Built in 1929 in the Spanish Mediterranean style, this inn centers on a garden courtyard. Smoke free premises. 34 one-bedroom standard units, some with whirlpools. 2 stories, interior/exterior corridors. *Bath:* combo or shower only. **Parking:** street. **Terms:** check-in 4 pm, 3 night minimum stay - weekends, 3 day cancellation notice-fee imposed, [ECP] meal plan available, pets ($20 extra charge). **Amenities:** CD players, high-speed Internet (fee), voice mail, irons, hair dryers. **Guest Services:** valet laundry. **Cards:** AX, MC, VI.

FEE

(See map and index starting on p. 436)

DOLPHIN INN — **Phone:** (831)624-5356 — 122

Motel

7/2-9/6 [CP]	1P: $150-$225	2P: $150-$225	XP: $15	F13
2/1-7/1 & 9/7-1/31 [CP]	1P: $89-$205	2P: $89-$205	XP: $15	F13

Location: 3 blks n off Ocean Ave at San Carlos St and 4th Ave. (PO Box 1900, 93921). Fax: 831/624-4891. **Facility:** Smoke free premises. 26 units. 23 one-bedroom standard units. 3 one-bedroom suites ($189-$299), some with efficiencies and/or whirlpools. 2 stories, exterior corridors. **Parking:** on-site. **Terms:** 2 night minimum stay - weekends, 7 day cancellation notice-fee imposed. **Amenities:** irons, hair dryers. **Pool(s):** small heated outdoor. **Business Services:** fax. **Cards:** AX, DS, MC, VI. **Special Amenities: free continental breakfast and free local telephone calls.** *(See color ad p 469)*

GREEN LANTERN INN BED & BREAKFAST — **Phone:** (831)624-4392 — 145

Bed & Breakfast

6/16-9/30 [ECP]	1P: $129-$249	2P: $129-$249	XP: $20	F10
2/1-6/15 [ECP]	1P: $89-$199	2P: $89-$199	XP: $20	F10
10/1-1/31 [ECP]	1P: $89-$129	2P: $89-$129	XP: $20	F10

Location: Just s of Ocean Ave, at 7th Ave and Casanova St. (PO Box 1114, CARMEL, 93921). Fax: 831/624-9591. **Facility:** Smoke free premises. 18 one-bedroom standard units. 2 stories (no elevator), exterior corridors. *Bath:* combo or shower only. **Parking:** on-site. **Terms:** 2 night minimum stay - weekends, 3 day cancellation notice. **Amenities:** video library, hair dryers. **Cards:** AX, DC, DS, MC, VI.

HIGHLANDS INN-A PARK HYATT HOTEL — Book at aaa.com — **Phone:** (831)620-1234 — 110

Small-scale Hotel

All Year	1P: $215-$445	2P: $215-$445	XP: $25	F18

Location: 4 mi s on SR 1. Located in Carmel Highlands. 120 Highlands Dr 93923. Fax: 831/626-8105. **Facility:** Outstanding ocean view. Units with woodburning fireplace. Some small units. Designated smoking area. 142 units. 39 one-bedroom standard units. 98 one- and 5 two-bedroom suites with whirlpools. 2-3 stories (no elevator), exterior corridors. *Bath:* combo or shower only. **Parking:** on-site. **Terms:** check-in 4 pm, 3 day cancellation notice-fee imposed. **Amenities:** CD players, voice mail, irons, hair dryers. *Some:* DVD players. **Dining:** 7 am-10 pm, also, Pacific's Edge, California Market, see separate listings, entertainment. **Pool(s):** outdoor. **Leisure Activities:** whirlpools, bicycles, exercise room. **Guest Services:** gift shop, valet laundry. **Business Services:** conference facilities, business center. **Cards:** AX, CB, DC, DS, JC, MC, VI.

SOME UNITS

(See map and index starting on p. 436)

HOFSAS HOUSE **Phone:** (831)624-2745 **116**

Motel

7/1-1/31 [CP]	1P: $100-$250	2P: $110-$250	XP: $15	F
5/1-6/30 [CP]	1P: $90-$230	2P: $100-$230	XP: $15	F
2/1-4/30 [CP]	1P: $75-$200	2P: $85-$200	XP: $15	F

Location: 3 blks n off Ocean Ave, between 3rd and 4th aves on San Carlos St. (PO Box 1195, 93921). Fax: 831/624-0159. **Facility:** 38 units. 33 one- and 5 two-bedroom standard units, some with efficiencies. 4 stories (no elevator), exterior corridors. *Bath:* combo or shower only. **Parking:** on-site. **Terms:** 2 night minimum stay - weekends 3/1-10/31, 3 day cancellation notice. **Amenities:** voice mail. *Some:* irons, hair dryers. **Pool(s):** heated outdoor. **Leisure Activities:** sauna. **Business Services:** meeting rooms. **Cards:** AX, DS, MC, VI. *(See color ad below)*

SOME UNITS

HORIZON INN OCEAN VIEW LODGE & ANNEX **Phone:** 831/624-5327 **119**

Motel

7/1-10/31 [CP]	1P: $135-$275	2P: $135-$275	XP: $15	F12
2/1-6/30 & 11/1-1/31 [CP]	1P: $81-$259	2P: $81-$259	XP: $15	F12

Location: 4 blks n off Ocean Ave. 3rd & Junipero SWC 93921 (PO Box 1693). Fax: 831/626-8253. **Facility:** Smoke free premises. 29 units. 23 one-bedroom standard units, some with efficiencies, kitchens and/or whirlpools. 6 one-bedroom suites with whirlpools. 2 stories, exterior corridors. **Parking:** on-site. **Terms:** 2-3 night minimum stay - weekends, 3 day cancellation notice. **Amenities:** voice mail, irons, hair dryers. **Leisure Activities:** whirlpool. **Cards:** AX, DC, DS, MC, VI. **Special Amenities: free continental breakfast and free newspaper.**

(See color ad p 478)

SOME UNITS

LA PLAYA HOTEL *Book at aaa.com* **Phone:** (831)624-6476 **144**

Historic Small-scale Hotel

All Year	1P: $165-$325	2P: $165-$325	XP: $15	F17

Location: Just s of Ocean Ave Camino Real at 8th Ave 93921 (PO Box 900). Fax: 831/624-7966. **Facility:** A tile staircase and stained-glass window accent the lobby of this Mediterranean-style 1904 mansion; guest rooms range in size. Smoke free premises. 80 units. 75 one-bedroom standard units. 5 cottages ($325-$650). 4 stories (no elevator), interior/exterior corridors. *Bath:* combo or shower only. **Parking:** on-site. **Terms:** 2 night minimum stay - weekends. **Amenities:** irons, hair dryers. **Pool(s):** heated outdoor. **Guest Services:** valet laundry. **Business Services:** conference facilities, business center. **Cards:** AX, DC, MC, VI.

LOBOS LODGE **Phone:** (831)624-3874 **133**

Motel

All Year	1P: $99-$150	2P: $99-$150	XP: $25	F4

Location: At Ocean Ave and Monte Verde St. (PO Box L-1, 93921). Fax: 831/624-0135. **Facility:** 30 one-bedroom standard units, some with kitchens. 2 stories, exterior corridors. **Parking:** on-site. **Terms:** 2 night minimum stay - weekends, 3 day cancellation notice, [CP] meal plan available. **Amenities:** hair dryers. **Cards:** AX, MC, VI.

SOME UNITS

(See map and index starting on p. 436)

NORMANDY INN Phone: 831/624-3825 **138**

Motel

All Year 1P: $98-$250 2P: $98-$250 XP: $10 F5

Location: On Ocean Ave, between Monte Verde St and Casanova. (PO Box 1706, 93921). Fax: 831/624-4614. **Facility:** Smoke free premises. 48 units. 43 one-bedroom standard units, some with efficiencies. 2 one-bedroom suites ($150-$350). 3 vacation homes. 2 stories, exterior corridors. *Bath:* combo or shower only. **Parking:** on-site. **Terms:** 2-3 night minimum stay - weekends, 3 day cancellation notice, [CP] meal plan available. **Amenities:** irons, hair dryers. **Pool(s):** small heated outdoor. **Cards:** AX, DC, MC, VI.

(See color ad p 479)

SOME UNITS / FEE

PINE INN Phone: (831)624-3851 **134**

Historic Small-scale Hotel

All Year 1P: $135-$260 2P: $135-$260

Location: Between Lincoln and Monte Verde St. Ocean Ave & Monte Verde St 93923 (PO Box 250, 93921). Fax: 831/624-3030. **Facility:** The beautifully restored 1889 turn-of-the-century hotel features elegant furnishings and fabrics decorating the guest rooms. Smoke free premises. 49 one-bedroom standard units. 3 stories (no elevator), interior/exterior corridors. **Parking:** on-site. **Terms:** check-in 4 pm, 2 night minimum stay - weekends. **Amenities:** voice mail, irons, hair dryers. **Guest Services:** valet laundry. **Business Services:** meeting rooms. **Cards:** AX, CB, DC, DS, JC, MC, VI. ***(See color ad p 479)***

SOME UNITS

QUAIL LODGE *Book at aaa.com* Phone: (831)624-2888 **115**

Resort Small-scale Hotel

All Year 1P: $225-$425 2P: $225-$425 XP: $35 F12

Location: 3.5 mi e of SR 1, via Carmel Valley Rd. 8205 Valley Greens Dr 93923. Fax: 831/624-3726. **Facility:** Well-kept country club grounds and an 18-hole golf course surround the lodgings; some units have fireplaces and patios or balconies. Smoke free premises. 97 units. 79 one-bedroom standard units. 18 one-bedroom suites ($430-$795), some with whirlpools. 2 stories, exterior corridors. **Parking:** on-site. **Terms:** check-in 4 pm, 3 day cancellation notice-fee imposed, package plans, $15 service charge. **Amenities:** video library, high-speed Internet (fee), dual phone lines, voice mail, safes, honor bars, irons, hair dryers. *Some:* CD players. **Dining:** 7 am-3 pm, also, The Covey, see separate listing. **Pool(s):** 2 heated outdoor. **Leisure Activities:** whirlpool, recreation programs, fitness walk, hiking trails, jogging, exercise room, spa. *Fee:* golf-18 holes, 4 tennis courts. **Guest Services:** gift shop, valet laundry. **Business Services:** meeting rooms. **Cards:** AX, CB, DC, DS, JC, MC, VI. **Special Amenities: free continental breakfast and free newspaper.** Affiliated with A Preferred Hotel. *(See color ad p 480)*

SOME UNITS / FEE

(See map and index starting on p. 436)

SAN ANTONIO HOUSE INN — Phone: (831)624-4334 — 129

Bed & Breakfast — All Year — 1P: $160-$225 — XP: $20 — D12

Location: Just s of Ocean Ave on San Antonio; between Ocean and 7th aves. (PO Box 6226, CARMEL, 93921). Fax: 831/624-4935. **Facility:** Smoke free premises. 5 units. 4 one- and 1 two-bedroom standard units, some with kitchens. 2 stories (no elevator), exterior corridors. *Bath:* combo or shower only. **Parking:** street. **Terms:** check-in 4 pm, 2 night minimum stay - weekends, 7 day cancellation notice-fee imposed, [ECP] meal plan available. **Amenities:** video library, hair dryers. **Cards:** AX, MC, VI. *(See color ad p 471)*

SOME UNITS

(See map and index starting on p. 436)

SANDPIPER INN BY THE SEA Phone: (831)624-6433 106

Bed & Breakfast

	1P	2P	XP	
5/1-10/31 [ECP]	1P: $135-$220	2P: $135-$220	XP: $20	F12
2/1-4/30 & 11/1-1/31 [ECP]	1P: $115-$180	2P: $115-$180	XP: $20	F12

Location: Just s of Ocean Ave on Scenic Dr, 0.6 mi e on Santa Lucia, then s. 2408 Bay View Ave 93923. Fax: 831/624-5964. **Facility:** This early California 1929 inn is located in a quiet residential area; some units have views of the Pacific Ocean. Smoke free premises. 17 one-bedroom standard units. 2 stories (no elevator), interior/exterior corridors. *Bath:* combo or shower only. **Parking:** street. **Terms:** 2 night minimum stay - weekends, 7 day cancellation notice-fee imposed. **Cards:** AX, DS, MC, VI. **Special Amenities: free continental breakfast and preferred room (subject to availability with advanced reservations).**

SOME UNITS

SVENDSGAARD'S Phone: (831)624-1511 121

Motel

	1P	2P	XP	
7/2-9/6 [CP]	1P: $150-$289	2P: $150-$289	XP: $15	F13
2/1-7/1 & 9/7-1/31 [CP]	1P: $89-$259	2P: $89-$259	XP: $15	F13

Location: 3 blks n off Ocean Ave, at San Carlos St and 4th Ave. (PO Box 1900, 93921). Fax: 831/624-5661. **Facility:** Smoke free premises. 34 units. 31 one- and 1 two-bedroom standard units, some with efficiencies and/or whirlpools. 2 one-bedroom suites ($179-$325) with whirlpools. 2 stories, exterior corridors. *Bath:* combo or shower only. **Parking:** on-site. **Terms:** 2 night minimum stay - weekends, 7 day cancellation notice-fee imposed. **Amenities:** irons, hair dryers. **Pool(s):** heated outdoor. **Guest Services:** valet laundry. **Business Services:** fax. **Cards:** AX, DS, MC, VI. **Special Amenities: free continental breakfast and free local telephone calls.** *(See color ad p 469)*

SOME UNITS

TICKLE PINK INN Phone: (831)624-1244 112

Motel

	1P	2P	XP
All Year [ECP]	1P: $269-$529	2P: $269-$529	XP: $50

Location: 4 mi s on SR 1. Located in Carmel Highlands. 155 Highland Dr 93923. Fax: 831/626-9516. **Facility:** Sweeping views are a highlight of this hillside inn, which offers spacious accommodations, most with balconies and some with fireplaces. 35 units. 30 one-bedroom standard units, some with whirlpools. 4 one-bedroom suites. 1 cottage. 2-3 stories (no elevator), exterior corridors. *Bath:* combo or shower only. **Parking:** on-site. **Terms:** 1-3 night minimum stay - weekends, 7 day cancellation notice. **Amenities:** video library, CD players, irons, hair dryers. **Leisure Activities:** whirlpool. **Guest Services:** complimentary evening beverages. **Business Services:** meeting rooms. **Cards:** AX, DC, MC, VI. **Special Amenities: free expanded continental breakfast and free newspaper.** *(See color ad p 481)*

SOME UNITS

WAYSIDE INN Phone: (831)624-5336 141

Motel

	1P	2P	XP	
7/2-9/6 [CP]	1P: $150-$299	2P: $150-$299	XP: $15	F13
2/1-7/1 & 9/7-1/31 [CP]	1P: $99-$299	2P: $99-$299	XP: $15	F13

Location: 1 blk s off Ocean Ave, at Mission St and 7th Ave. (PO Box 1900, 93921). Fax: 831/626-6974. **Facility:** Smoke free premises. 22 units. 20 one- and 1 two-bedroom standard units, some with kitchens and/or whirlpools. 1 one-bedroom suite ($229-$399) with kitchen. 2 stories, exterior corridors. *Bath:* combo or shower only. **Parking:** on-site. **Terms:** 2 night minimum stay - weekends, 7 day cancellation notice-fee imposed, small pets only. **Amenities:** video library, irons, hair dryers. **Guest Services:** valet laundry. **Business Services:** fax. **Cards:** AX, DS, MC, VI. **Special Amenities: free continental breakfast and free local telephone calls.** *(See color ad p 469)*

SOME UNITS

(See map and index starting on p. 436)

WHERE TO DINE

ANTON & MICHEL **Lunch:** $10-$18 **Dinner:** $18-$29 **Phone:** 831/624-2406 (49)

Continental

Location: Just s off Ocean Ave, on Mission St at 7th Ave. **Hours:** 11:30 am-3 & 5:30-9:30 pm, Sat-10 pm. **Reservations:** suggested. **Features:** Guests who unwind in the romantic solarium setting are treated to attractive courtyard views. Lamb and seafood are specialties on the ambitious menu. Tableside service is traditional. Dressy casual; cocktails. **Parking:** street. **Cards:** AX, CB, DC, DS, MC, VI.

CALIFORNIA MARKET **Lunch:** $13-$22 **Dinner:** $18-$25 **Phone:** 831/620-1234 (50)

California

Location: 4 mi s on SR 1; in Highlands Inn-A Park Hyatt Hotel. 120 Highlands Dr 93923. **Hours:** 7 am-10 pm. **Features:** Located on a bluff overlooking the Pacific Ocean, the eatery offers guests spectacular views. Patio dining is available, weather permitting. Casual dress; cocktails. **Parking:** on-site. **Cards:** AX, CB, DC, DS, JC, MC, VI.

CASANOVA **Lunch:** $9-$16 **Dinner:** $25-$47 **Phone:** 831/625-0501 (41)

French

Location: Just n off Ocean Ave on 5th Ave; between Mission and San Carlos sts. **Hours:** 11:30 am-3 & 5-10 pm, Fri & Sat-10:30 pm, Sun from 10 am. Closed: 12/25. **Reservations:** suggested. **Features:** A cozy, country atmosphere invites patrons to relax. On the menu are Northern Italian and Mediterranean specialties. Casual dress; cocktails. **Parking:** street. **Cards:** DS, MC, VI.

THE COVEY **Dinner:** $26-$40 **Phone:** 831/620-8860 (58)

Continental

Location: 3.5 mi e of SR 1, via Carmel Valley Rd; in Quail Lodge. 8205 Valley Greens Dr 93923. **Hours:** 7 am-10 & 5:30-9:30 pm, Sat-10 pm. Closed: Sun. **Reservations:** suggested. **Features:** Overlooking the golf course and a duck pond, the restaurant prepares California specialties from fresh local produce. Dressy casual; cocktails; entertainment. **Parking:** on-site. **Cards:** AX, CB, DC, DS, MC, VI. ***(See color ad p 480)***

THE FORGE IN THE FOREST **Lunch:** $10-$17 **Dinner:** $12-$29 **Phone:** 831/624-2233 (44)

Regional American

Location: Southwest corner of 5th Ave and Junipero St. **Hours:** 11:30 am-9 pm, Fri & Sat-11 pm, Sun 11 am-9 pm. **Reservations:** suggested. **Features:** Located in the heart of downtown Carmel, this restaurant is owned and operated by its employees. Unique and creative specialities make it a favorite among locals and visitors alike. Outside dining is available. Casual dress; cocktails. **Parking:** street. **Cards:** AX, DS, MC, VI.

THE FRENCH POODLE RESTAURANT **Dinner:** $16-$60 **Phone:** 831/624-8643 (42)

French

Location: Just n off Ocean Ave; at Junipero St and 5th Ave. **Hours:** 5:30 pm-9:30 pm. Closed: 12/25; also Sun. **Reservations:** suggested. **Features:** Decorated with lovely paintings, the elegant dining room sustains a warm, charming atmosphere. Dishes are prepared in the classic French tradition. Dressy casual; beer & wine only. **Parking:** street. **Cards:** AX, DC, MC, VI.

FROM SCRATCH RESTAURANT **Lunch:** $7-$8 **Phone:** 831/625-2448 (53)

American

Location: SR 1, exit Carmel Valley Rd, 1 mi s; in Barnyard Shopping Center. 3626 The Barnyard 93923. **Hours:** 8 am-3 pm. Closed: 11/25, 12/25. **Reservations:** suggested. **Features:** In an upscale shopping center, the restaurant does as its name suggests—prepares homemade food from scratch. The atmosphere is friendly and comfortable. Casual dress; beer & wine only. **Parking:** on-site. **Cards:** AX, CB, DC, MC, VI.

LE COQ D'OR **Dinner:** $19-$25 **Phone:** 831/626-9319 (39)

Continental

Location: 3 blks n off Ocean Ave on Mission St; between 4th and 5th sts. **Hours:** 5 pm-9 pm. **Reservations:** suggested. **Features:** The diverse menu dabbles in lavishly flavored European, German and French dishes. The homey, country-style environment is cozy, as is the small, heated patio. Casual dress; beer & wine only. **Parking:** street. **Cards:** AX, MC, VI.

PACIFIC'S EDGE **Dinner:** $40-$75 **Phone:** 831/622-5445 (54)

Regional American

Location: 4 mi s on SR 1; in Carmel Highlands; in Highlands Inn-A Park Hyatt Hotel. 120 Highlands Dr 93923. **Hours:** 5:30 pm-10 pm. **Reservations:** suggested. **Features:** Views of the Pacific Ocean are spectacular from the casually elegant dining room. Light, robustly flavored dishes are made from fresh, local ingredients. Semi-formal attire; cocktails. **Parking:** on-site. **Cards:** AX, CB, DC, DS, MC, VI.

RIO GRILL **Lunch:** $5-$18 **Dinner:** $7-$29 **Phone:** 831/625-5436 (56)

California

Location: Just e of SR 1; in Crossroads Shopping Center. 101 Crossroads Blvd 93923. **Hours:** 11:30 am-10 pm, Fri & Sat-11 pm. Closed: 7/4, 11/25, 12/25. **Reservations:** suggested. **Features:** The Southwestern atmosphere is upbeat and welcoming. California cuisine is creatively prepared with a Western flair. Fresh ingredients are emphasized. Casual dress; cocktails. **Parking:** on-site. **Cards:** AX, DC, MC, VI.

SANS SOUCI **Dinner:** $31-$58 **Phone:** 831/624-6220 (43)

French

Location: Just n of Ocean Ave on Lincoln St; between 5th and 6th aves. **Hours:** 5:30 pm-9:30 pm. Closed: 12/25; also Wed & 11/29-12/3. **Reservations:** suggested. **Features:** Fresh seafood dishes are made from local ingredients. The cozy dining room is warm and quiet. Dressy casual; cocktails. **Parking:** street. **Cards:** AX, MC, VI.

(See map and index starting on p. 436)

TUTTO MONDO TRATTORIA **Lunch:** $6-$14 **Dinner:** $10-$23 **Phone:** 831/624-8977 (47)

Italian

Location: Just s off Ocean Ave on Dolores St; between Ocean and 7th aves. **Hours:** 11:30 am-3 & 5:30-10:30 pm. Closed major holidays. **Reservations:** suggested. **Features:** The varied menu lists traditional dishes of both Northern and Southern Italy. Sinful desserts are homemade. Casual dress; beer & wine only. **Parking:** street. **Cards:** AX, MC, VI.

CARMEL VALLEY pop. 4,700 (See map and index starting on p. 436)

WHERE TO STAY

ACACIA LODGE-COUNTRY GARDEN INNS **Phone:** (831)659-2297 (180)

7/1-9/30	1P: $85-$269	2P: $85-$269	XP: $20	F3
2/1-6/30 & 10/1-1/31	1P: $85-$195	2P: $85-$195	XP: $20	F3

Motel

Location: 12.8 mi e of SR 1. Located in a quiet, secluded area in Carmel Valley Village. 20 Via Contenta 93924 (PO Box 87). Fax: 831/659-2392. **Facility:** Smoke free premises. 19 one-bedroom standard units, some with kitchens. 1 story, exterior corridors. *Bath:* combo or shower only. **Parking:** on-site. **Terms:** 2-4 night minimum stay - seasonal weekends, 3 day cancellation notice, [ECP] meal plan available. **Amenities:** irons, hair dryers. **Pool(s):** outdoor. **Leisure Activities:** whirlpool. **Business Services:** meeting rooms. **Cards:** AX, DS, MC, VI.
(See color ad p 469)

DATA PORT

CARMEL VALLEY LODGE **Phone:** (831)659-2261 (178)

4/26-10/24 [ECP]	1P: $179-$219	2P: $179-$219	XP: $15	F12
10/25-1/31 [ECP]	1P: $159-$199	2P: $159-$199	XP: $15	F12
2/1-4/25 [ECP]	1P: $149-$189	2P: $149-$189	XP: $15	F12

Motel

Location: 11.5 mi e of SR 1; at Carmel Valley and Ford rds. Located in a quiet area. 8 Ford Rd 93924 (PO Box 93). Fax: 831/659-4558. **Facility:** 31 units. 23 one- and 4 two-bedroom standard units, some with kitchens. 4 one-bedroom suites ($249-$269) with efficiencies. 2 stories, exterior corridors. **Parking:** on-site. **Terms:** 2 night minimum stay - weekends, 7 day cancellation notice, pets ($10 extra charge, dogs only). **Amenities:** video library, irons, hair dryers. **Pool(s):** heated outdoor. **Leisure Activities:** sauna, whirlpool, exercise room. **Business Services:** meeting rooms. **Cards:** AX, MC, VI.

SOME UNITS

FEE VCR DATA PORT

HIDDEN VALLEY INN-COUNTRY GARDEN INNS *Book at aaa.com* **Phone:** (831)659-5361 (179)

7/1-9/30	1P: $85-$269	2P: $85-$269	XP: $20	F3
2/1-6/30 & 10/1-1/31	1P: $85-$195	2P: $85-$195	XP: $20	F3

Motel

Location: 11 mi e of SR 1. Located in a quiet area. 102 W Carmel Valley Rd 93924 (PO Box 504). Fax: 831/659-2392. **Facility:** Smoke free premises. 26 one-bedroom standard units, some with efficiencies. 2 stories, exterior corridors. *Bath:* combo or shower only. **Parking:** on-site. **Terms:** 2-4 night minimum stay - seasonal & weekends, 3 day cancellation notice, [ECP] meal plan available. **Amenities:** irons, hair dryers. **Pool(s):** outdoor. **Business Services:** meeting rooms. **Cards:** AX, DS, MC, VI. *(See color ad p 469)*

SOME UNITS

DATA PORT

LOS LAURELES LODGE *Book at aaa.com* **Phone:** (831)659-2233 (176)

5/1-10/31 [ECP]	1P: $130-$155	2P: $130-$155	XP: $20	F12
2/1-4/30 & 11/1-1/31 [ECP]	1P: $105-$135	2P: $105-$135	XP: $20	F12

Motel

Location: 10.5 mi e of SR 1. 313 W Carmel Valley Rd 93924 (PO Box 2310). Fax: 831/659-0481. **Facility:** 31 one-bedroom standard units, some with kitchens and/or whirlpools. 1 story, exterior corridors. *Bath:* combo or shower only. **Parking:** on-site. **Terms:** 2-3 night minimum stay - weekends & seasonal, 3 day cancellation notice, small pets only ($20 extra charge). **Amenities:** irons. **Dining:** 11 am-9:30 pm, cocktails. **Pool(s):** outdoor. **Leisure Activities:** Fee: horseback riding. **Guest Services:** gift shop. **Business Services:** meeting rooms. **Cards:** AX, MC, VI. **Special Amenities: free continental breakfast and free local telephone calls.**

SOME UNITS

FEE

WHERE TO DINE

WILL'S FARGO RESTAURANT **Dinner:** $14-$27 **Phone:** 831/659-2774 (62)

Steak House

Location: In the village. **Hours:** 5 pm-10 pm. Closed: 1/1, 12/25. **Reservations:** suggested. **Features:** The attractive garden setting displays 1880s decor. Cut-to-order steaks are among selections on the diverse menu. Dressy casual; cocktails. **Parking:** street. **Cards:** AX, CB, DC, MC, VI.

MARINA pop. 25,101

WHERE TO STAY

BEST WESTERN BEACH DUNES INN *Book at aaa.com* **Phone:** (831)883-0300

7/1-9/30 [CP]	1P: $69-$209	2P: $79-$229	XP: $10	F14
2/1-6/30 [CP]	1P: $59-$149	2P: $69-$159	XP: $10	F14
10/1-1/31 [CP]	1P: $59-$99	2P: $69-$109	XP: $10	F14

Motel

Location: SR 1, exit Reservation Rd, just w. 3290 Dunes Dr 93933. Fax: 831/384-8137. **Facility:** 84 one-bedroom standard units. 2 stories (no elevator), exterior corridors. **Parking:** on-site. **Terms:** 3 day cancellation notice. **Amenities:** hair dryers. **Leisure Activities:** whirlpool, playground. **Guest Services:** coin laundry. **Cards:** AX, CB, DC, DS, JC, MC, VI. **Special Amenities: free continental breakfast and free local telephone calls.**
(See color ad p 521)

SOME UNITS

COMFORT INN *Book at aaa.com*

Phone: (831)883-4000

AAA SAVE

Motel

6/1-9/30	1P: $79-$229	2P: $89-$239	XP: $10	F16
2/1-5/31 & 10/1-1/31	1P: $69-$179	2P: $79-$189	XP: $10	F16

Location: SR 1, exit Reservation Rd, just e. 140 Reservation Rd 93933. Fax: 831/883-4001. **Facility:** 62 one-bedroom standard units. 3 stories, interior corridors. *Bath:* combo or shower only. **Parking:** on-site. **Terms:** [CP] meal plan available. **Amenities:** irons. *Some:* hair dryers. **Leisure Activities:** sauna, exercise room. **Guest Services:** coin laundry. **Business Services:** meeting rooms. **Cards:** AX, DC, DS, JC, MC, VI.

SOME UNITS

HOLIDAY INN EXPRESS MONTEREY-MARINA *Book at aaa.com*

Phone: (831)884-2500

AAA SAVE

Small-scale Hotel

5/1-8/31	1P: $149-$169	2P: $149-$169	XP: $10	F17
9/1-10/31	1P: $119-$139	2P: $119-$139	XP: $10	F17
2/1-4/30 & 11/1-1/31	1P: $109-$129	2P: $109-$129	XP: $10	F17

Location: SR 1, exit Reservation Rd, 0.5 mi e, then just s. 189 Seaside Cir 93933. Fax: 831/884-2510. **Facility:** 80 units. 78 one-bedroom standard units. 2 one-bedroom suites ($129-$259). 3 stories, interior corridors. *Bath:* combo or shower only. **Parking:** on-site. **Terms:** [ECP] meal plan available, package plans. **Amenities:** video games (fee), high-speed Internet, dual phone lines, voice mail, irons, hair dryers. **Leisure Activities:** sauna, whirlpool, exercise room. **Guest Services:** valet and coin laundry. **Business Services:** meeting rooms. **Cards:** AX, DC, DS, MC, VI. **Special Amenities: free expanded continental breakfast and free local telephone calls.** *(See color ad below)*

SOME UNITS

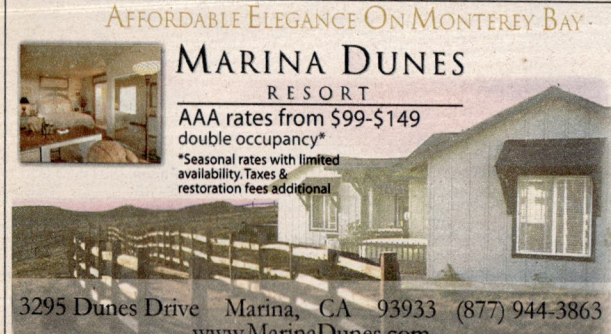

MARINA DUNES RESORT Book at aaa.com Phone: (831)883-9478

Motel

7/1-10/20	1P: $199-$399	2P: $199-$399
4/1-6/30	1P: $129-$349	2P: $129-$349
10/21-1/31	1P: $119-$319	2P: $119-$319
2/1-3/31	1P: $109-$299	2P: $109-$299

Location: SR 1, exit Reservation Rd, just w. 3295 Dunes Dr 93933. Fax: 831/883-9477. **Facility:** 60 units. 30 one-bedroom standard units. 30 one-bedroom suites. 2 stories (no elevator), exterior corridors. **Parking:** on-site. **Terms:** check-in 4 pm, 2-3 night minimum stay - some weekends, 3 day cancellation notice, package plans - seasonal, $15 service charge. **Amenities:** CD players, voice mail, irons, hair dryers. **Pool(s):** heated outdoor. **Leisure Activities:** whirlpool, spa. **Guest Services:** valet laundry. **Business Services:** meeting rooms. **Cards:** AX, CB, DC, DS, MC, VI. ***(See color ad p 484)***

SOME UNITS

ASK / DATA PORT /

SUPER 8 Book at aaa.com Phone: (831)384-1800

AAA SAVE

Motel

7/1-9/30 [CP]	1P: $59-$129	2P: $64-$195	XP: $5	F14
2/1-6/30 & 10/1-1/31 [CP]	1P: $49-$99	2P: $59-$109	XP: $5	F14

Location: SR 1, exit Reservation Rd, just w. 3280 Dunes Dr 93933. Fax: 831/384-5279. **Facility:** 114 one-bedroom standard units. 3 stories (no elevator), exterior corridors. **Parking:** on-site. **Leisure Activities:** whirlpool. **Business Services:** meeting rooms. **Cards:** AX, CB, DC, DS, JC, MC, VI. **Special Amenities: free continental breakfast.** ***(See color ad p 521)***

SOME UNITS

DATA PORT / /

PACIFIC GROVE pop. 15,522 (See map and index starting on p. 436)

WHERE TO STAY

ANTON INN Phone: 831/373-4429 94

Motel

All Year 1P: $89-$300 2P: $89-$300

Location: Just w of Seventeen Mile Dr. 1095 Lighthouse Ave 93950. Fax: 831/647-1566. **Facility:** Smoke free premises. 12 one-bedroom standard units, some with whirlpools. 1 story, exterior corridors. **Parking:** on-site. **Terms:** cancellation fee imposed, [CP] meal plan available. **Amenities:** irons, hair dryers. **Cards:** MC, VI.

ASK DATA PORT

ASILOMAR Book at aaa.com Phone: (831)372-8016 90

Historic Motel

All Year [BP]	1P: $99-$115	2P: $106-$122	XP: $13	D12

Location: Just n of SR 68. Located at Asilomar State Beach and Conference grounds. 800 Asilomar Blvd 93950. Fax: 831/372-7227. **Facility:** Located in a beautifully mature wood area, the spacious exterior grounds offer guests forest or ocean views. Smoke free premises. 312 one-bedroom standard units. 1-2 stories, interior/exterior corridors. *Bath:* combo or shower only. **Parking:** on-site. **Amenities:** *Some:* hair dryers. **Pool(s):** outdoor. **Leisure Activities:** rental bicycles, hiking trails, volleyball. **Guest Services:** gift shop. **Business Services:** conference facilities. **Cards:** AX, MC, VI. ***(See color ad below)***

SOME UNITS

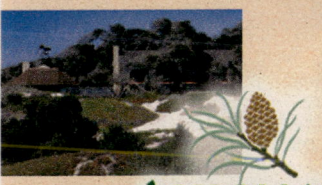

(See map and index starting on p. 436)

BEST WESTERN MONARCH RESORT *Book at aaa.com* **Phone:** (831)646-8885 **79**

AAA SAVE

Motel

5/23-10/31 [ECP]	1P: $100-$230	2P: $110-$240	XP: $20	F12
3/16-5/22 [ECP]	1P: $90-$200	2P: $100-$220	XP: $20	F12
11/1-1/31 [ECP]	1P: $80-$200	2P: $90-$220	XP: $20	F12
2/1-3/15 [ECP]	1P: $80-$180	2P: $90-$200	XP: $20	F12

Location: Just w of Seventeen Mile Dr. 1111 Lighthouse Ave 93950. Fax: 831/375-5567. **Facility:** 49 units. 44 one-bedroom standard units. 5 one-bedroom suites ($150-$700) with efficiencies. 2 stories, interior corridors. **Parking:** on-site. **Terms:** check-in 4 pm, 2-4 night minimum stay - seasonal weekends, 3 day cancellation notice-fee imposed. **Amenities:** irons, hair dryers. **Pool(s):** outdoor. **Leisure Activities:** sauna, whirlpool. **Guest Services:** complimentary evening beverages. **Business Services:** meeting rooms. **Cards:** AX, CB, DC, DS, JC, MC, VI. **Special Amenities: free expanded continental breakfast.** *(See color ad below)*

SOME UNITS

(See map and index starting on p. 436)

BIDE-A-WEE INN & COTTAGES — Phone: (831)372-2330 — 77

AAA SAVE — Motel

7/1-10/31 [CP]	1P: $99-$129	2P: $109-$149	XP: $10	F13
3/16-6/30 [CP]	1P: $69-$129	2P: $79-$139	XP: $10	F13
2/1-3/15 & 11/1-1/31 [CP]	1P: $59-$109	2P: $69-$119	XP: $10	F13

Location: 1 mi n of SR 68. 221 Asilomar Ave 93950. Fax: 831/372-3947. **Facility:** Smoke free premises. 19 units. 17 one- and 2 two-bedroom standard units, some with efficiencies. 1-2 stories, exterior corridors. *Bath:* combo or shower only. **Parking:** on-site. **Terms:** 3 day cancellation notice, pets ($10 extra charge). **Amenities:** voice mail, irons, hair dryers. **Cards:** AX, DC, DS, MC, VI. **Special Amenities: early check-in/late check-out and preferred room (subject to availability with advanced reservations).**

DATA PORT FEE

BORG'S OCEAN FRONT MOTEL — Phone: 831/375-2406 — 78

AAA SAVE — Motel

6/11-10/30	1P: $72-$135	2P: $72-$135
2/1-6/10 & 10/31-1/31	1P: $59-$115	2P: $59-$115

Location: 0.5 mi n on Monterey Bay; at Lovers Point. 635 Ocean View Blvd 93950. Fax: 831/375-7173. **Facility:** Smoke free premises. 60 units. 54 one- and 6 two-bedroom standard units. 2 stories, exterior corridors. *Bath:* combo or shower only. **Parking:** on-site. **Terms:** 3 day cancellation notice-fee imposed. **Cards:** AX, MC, VI. **Special Amenities: free local telephone calls.**

DATA PORT

BUTTERFLY GROVE INN — Phone: (831)373-4921 — 87

AAA SAVE — Motel

6/1-9/30 [CP]	1P: $79-$269	2P: $89-$299	XP: $10	F12
2/1-5/31 [CP]	1P: $69-$199	2P: $79-$209	XP: $10	F12
10/1-1/31 [CP]	1P: $59-$199	2P: $69-$209	XP: $10	F12

Location: Just w of Seventeen Mile Dr. 1073 Lighthouse Ave 93950. Fax: 831/373-7596. **Facility:** Smoke free premises. 30 one-bedroom standard units, some with whirlpools. 2 stories, exterior corridors. *Bath:* combo or shower only. **Parking:** on-site. **Terms:** 2-3 night minimum stay - weekends, 3 day cancellation notice-fee imposed. **Amenities:** video library (fee), irons, hair dryers. **Pool(s):** heated outdoor. **Leisure Activities:** whirlpool. **Cards:** AX, CB, DC, DS, JC, MC, VI. **Special Amenities: free continental breakfast and free room upgrade (subject to availability with advanced reservations).** *(See color ad below)*

VCR DATA PORT

THE CENTRELLA INN Book at aaa.com — Phone: (831)372-3372 — 82

AAA SAVE — Bed & Breakfast

7/2-9/6 [BP]	1P: $159-$259	2P: $159-$259	XP: $15	F13
2/1-7/1 & 9/7-1/31 [BP]	1P: $119-$229	2P: $119-$229	XP: $15	F13

Location: At 17th St; center. 612 Central Ave 93950. Fax: 831/372-2036. **Facility:** Accommodations are offered in a restored 1890s Victorian and five cottages; some have gas fireplaces. Smoke free premises. 26 one-bedroom standard units, some with whirlpools. 3 stories (no elevator), interior/exterior corridors. *Bath:* combo or shower only. **Parking:** street. **Terms:** 2 night minimum stay - weekends, 7 day cancellation notice-fee imposed. **Amenities:** irons, hair dryers. **Cards:** AX, DS, MC, VI. **Special Amenities: free continental breakfast and free local telephone calls.** *(See color ad p 469)*

SOME UNITS / VCR /

DEER HAVEN INN & SUITES Book at aaa.com — Phone: (831)373-7784 — 92

Motel

6/16-10/15 [CP]	1P: $89-$299	2P: $89-$299	XP: $10	F12
2/1-6/15 [CP]	1P: $79-$219	2P: $79-$219	XP: $10	F12
10/16-1/31 [CP]	1P: $69-$199	2P: $69-$199	XP: $10	F12

Location: Just e of SR 68 via Sinex Ave. 740 Crocker Ave 93950 (1100 Lighthouse Ave). Fax: 831/655-5048. **Facility:** 48 units. 41 one- and 7 two-bedroom standard units, some with kitchens. 2 stories, exterior corridors. **Parking:** on-site. **Terms:** 2 night minimum stay - with Saturday stayover. **Amenities:** irons, hair dryers. **Guest Services:** coin laundry. **Cards:** AX, DS, MC, VI. *(See color ad p 488)*

ASK

(See map and index starting on p. 436)

THE GATEHOUSE INN — Phone: (831)649-8436 — 84

AAA SAVE — Bed & Breakfast

All Year 1P: $125-$195 2P: $125-$195 XP: $20 D12

Location: Center. 225 Central Ave 93950. Fax: 831/648-8044. **Facility:** Offering impressive views of Monterey Bay, this Italianate Victorian has been restored and accented with well-tended gardens. Smoke free premises. 9 one-bedroom standard units. 2 stories (no elevator), interior/exterior corridors. *Bath:* combo or shower only. **Parking:** on-site. **Terms:** 2-3 night minimum stay - weekends, age restrictions may apply, 3 day cancellation notice. **Amenities:** voice mail, hair dryers. **Guest Services:** complimentary evening beverages. **Cards:** AX, DS, MC, VI. **Special Amenities: free expanded continental breakfast and free local telephone calls.**

GREEN GABLES INN — Phone: (831)375-2095 — 75

Bed & Breakfast

All Year 2P: $130-$195 XP: $20 F5

Location: At 5th St. 301 Ocean View Blvd 93950. Fax: 831/375-5437. **Facility:** The inn, across from the bay, offers spacious, elegantly appointed public areas and some units with ocean views. Smoke free premises. 11 one-bedroom standard units, some with whirlpools. 2-3 stories (no elevator). *Bath:* some shared or private, combo, shower or tub only. **Parking:** on-site. **Terms:** 7 day cancellation notice-fee imposed, package plans - seasonal. **Amenities:** video library, irons. *Some:* hair dryers. **Guest Services:** complimentary evening beverages. **Cards:** AX, DC, MC, VI.

SOME UNITS

HOWARD JOHNSON EXPRESS INN — *Book at aaa.com* — Phone: (831)373-8777 — 89

AAA SAVE — Motel

5/16-10/31	1P: $129-$229	2P: $129-$229	XP: $10	F12
2/1-5/15	1P: $89-$159	2P: $89-$159	XP: $10	F12
11/1-1/31	1P: $79-$129	2P: $79-$129	XP: $10	F12

Location: Just e of SR 68 via Sinex Ave. Located in a quiet area. 660 Dennett Ave 93950. Fax: 831/373-2698. **Facility:** 30 units. 20 one- and 10 two-bedroom standard units, some with kitchens. 2 stories, exterior corridors. **Parking:** on-site. **Terms:** 3 day cancellation notice-fee imposed, [ECP] meal plan available. **Amenities:** irons, hair dryers. **Business Services:** meeting rooms. **Cards:** AX, DC, DS, MC, VI. **Special Amenities: free expanded continental breakfast and free newspaper.** *(See color ad p 455)*

SOME UNITS

THE INN AT 213 SEVENTEEN MILE DRIVE — *Book at aaa.com* — Phone: (831)642-9514 — 85

AAA SAVE — Historic Bed & Breakfast

All Year 1P: $145-$240 2P: $145-$240 XP: $20 F5

Location: At Lighthouse Ave. 213 Seventeen Mile Dr 93950. Fax: 831/642-9546. **Facility:** Craftsman in style, this attractively appointed inn offers some units with ocean views; gardens enhance the grounds. Smoke free premises. 14 one-bedroom standard units. 2 stories (no elevator), interior/exterior corridors. *Bath:* combo or shower only. **Parking:** on-site. **Terms:** 2 night minimum stay - weekends, 3 day cancellation notice-fee imposed. **Amenities:** irons, hair dryers. **Leisure Activities:** whirlpool. **Guest Services:** complimentary evening beverages. **Cards:** AX, MC, VI. **Special Amenities: free local telephone calls and preferred room (subject to availability with advanced reservations).**

LOVERS POINT INN — Phone: (831)373-4771 — 81

AAA SAVE — Motel

All Year [CP] 1P: $59-$289 2P: $59-$289 XP: $10 F8

Location: 0.5 mi n. 625 Ocean View Blvd 93950. Fax: 831/373-4215. **Facility:** 51 one-bedroom standard units. 3 stories, exterior corridors. **Parking:** on-site. **Terms:** 4 day cancellation notice-fee imposed. **Cards:** AX, CB, DC, DS, JC, MC, VI. **Special Amenities: free continental breakfast.**

SOME UNITS

(See map and index starting on p. 436)

OLD ST. ANGELA INN — Phone: (831)372-3246 — 83

Bed & Breakfast

All Year 1P: $110-$210 2P: $110-$210 XP: $20 D12

Location: At Forest Ave; center. 321 Central Ave 93950. Fax: 831/372-8560. **Facility:** Country elegance characterizes the rooms of this handsomely restored 1910 Cape Cod on well-landscaped grounds. Smoke free premises. 9 one-bedroom standard units, some with whirlpools. 2 stories (no elevator), interior/exterior corridors. *Bath:* combo or shower only. **Parking:** on-site. **Terms:** 2-3 night minimum stay - weekends, 3 day cancellation notice. **Amenities:** voice mail, hair dryers. **Guest Services:** complimentary evening beverages. **Cards:** DS, MC, VI.

ASK

OLYMPIA MOTOR LODGE — Phone: 831/373-2777 — 76

SAVE

Motel

All Year 1P: $88-$160 2P: $88-$160 XP: $10 F

Location: 1 mi w. 1140 Lighthouse Ave 93950. Fax: 831/375-8741. **Facility:** 38 one-bedroom standard units. 2 stories (no elevator), exterior corridors. **Parking:** on-site. **Terms:** 3 day cancellation notice-fee imposed, [CP] meal plan available, pets ($20 fee). **Pool(s):** heated outdoor. **Guest Services:** coin laundry. **Cards:** AX, DC, MC, VI. **Special Amenities: free continental breakfast and early check-in/late check-out.**

SOME UNITS

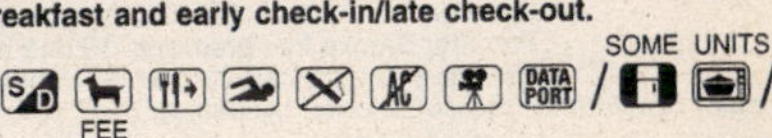

FEE

PACIFIC GARDENS INN — Phone: (831)646-9414 — 88

Motel

All Year [CP] 1P: $130-$250 2P: $130-$250 XP: $10 F12

Location: Just n of SR 68; across conference grounds. 701 Asilomar Blvd 93950. Fax: 831/647-0555. **Facility:** 28 units. 26 one- and 2 two-bedroom standard units, some with kitchens. 2 stories, exterior corridors. **Parking:** on-site. **Terms:** cancellation fee imposed. **Leisure Activities:** whirlpools. **Guest Services:** complimentary evening beverages, coin laundry. **Business Services:** meeting rooms. **Cards:** AX, MC, VI.

SOME UNITS

PACIFIC GROVE INN — Phone: (831)375-2825 — 93

SAVE

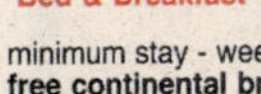

Bed & Breakfast

6/16-9/30 [ECP] 1P: $129-$229 2P: $129-$229 XP: $20 F10

2/1-6/15 & 10/1-1/31 [ECP] 1P: $99-$189 2P: $99-$189 XP: $20 F10

Location: 3.5 mi w of SR 1 via SR 68 and Forest Ave. 581 Pine Ave 93950. Fax: 831/375-0752. **Facility:** Housed in a charming 1904 Queen Anne Victorian and annex, the inn is walking distance from downtown and offers some rooms with ocean views. Smoke free premises. 16 units. 13 one- and 3 two-bedroom standard units. 2-3 stories (no elevator), interior corridors. *Bath:* combo or shower only. **Parking:** on-site. **Terms:** 2-3 night minimum stay - weekends, 3 day cancellation notice. **Amenities:** video library. **Cards:** AX, DC, DS, MC, VI. **Special Amenities: free continental breakfast and free local telephone calls.** *(See color ad below)*

VCR

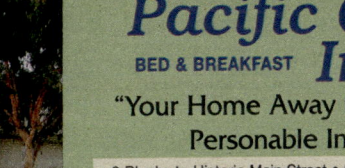

(See map and index starting on p. 436)

PACIFIC GROVE MOTEL — Phone: (831)372-3431 — 86

Motel

7/1-10/18 [CP]	1P: $89-$169	2P: $89-$169	XP: $10	F12
4/1-6/30 [CP]	1P: $59-$119	2P: $69-$129	XP: $10	F12
10/19-1/31 [CP]	1P: $59-$129	2P: $59-$129	XP: $10	F12
2/1-3/31 [CP]	1P: $59-$119	2P: $59-$119	XP: $10	F12

Location: Just w of Seventeen Mile Dr. 1101 Lighthouse Ave 93950 (1100 Lighthouse Ave). Fax: 831/643-0235. **Facility:** Smoke free premises. 29 one-bedroom standard units. 1 story, exterior corridors. *Bath:* combo or shower only. **Parking:** on-site. **Terms:** 2 night minimum stay - with Saturday stayover, pets ($20-$50 extra charge). **Amenities:** irons, hair dryers. **Pool(s):** small outdoor. **Leisure Activities:** whirlpool. **Cards:** AX, DS, MC, VI. ***(See color ad p 488)***

FEE

ROSEDALE INN — Phone: (831)655-1000 — 91

SAVE

Motel

6/1-10/1 [ECP]	1P: $145-$180	2P: $145-$180	XP: $10	F18
10/2-1/31 [ECP]	1P: $135-$170	2P: $135-$170	XP: $10	F18
2/1-5/31 [ECP]	1P: $125-$160	2P: $125-$160	XP: $10	F18

Location: Just n of SR 68; across conference grounds. 775 Asilomar Blvd 93950. Fax: 831/655-0691. **Facility:** Smoke free premises. 19 one-bedroom standard units. 1 story, exterior corridors. **Parking:** on-site. **Terms:** 3 day cancellation notice. **Amenities:** video library (fee), hair dryers. **Cards:** AX, DC, DS, MC, VI. **Special Amenities: free continental breakfast.** ***(See color ad below)***

SEA BREEZE INN AND COTTAGES — ***Book at aaa.com*** — Phone: (831)372-7771 — 74

Motel

6/16-10/15 [CP]	1P: $79-$189	2P: $79-$189	XP: $10	F12
10/16-1/31 [CP]	1P: $69-$179	2P: $69-$179	XP: $10	F12
2/1-6/15 [CP]	1P: $69-$129	2P: $69-$129	XP: $10	F12

Location: Just w of Seventeen Mile Dr; Lighthouse and Grove Acre. 1100 Lighthouse Ave 93950. Fax: 831/643-0235. **Facility:** Smoke free premises. 30 one-bedroom standard units, some with efficiencies or kitchens. 2 stories (no elevator), interior/exterior corridors. *Bath:* combo or shower only. **Parking:** on-site. **Terms:** 2 night minimum stay - with Saturday stayover, pets ($20-$50 extra charge). **Amenities:** voice mail, irons, hair dryers. **Cards:** AX, DS, MC, VI. ***(See color ad p 488)***

SOME UNITS

FEE

(See map and index starting on p. 436)

THE WILKIES INN — **Phone:** (831)372-5960 (80)

Motel

7/1-10/31	1P: $89-$289	2P: $89-$299	XP: $15	F12
5/1-6/30	1P: $69-$189	2P: $69-$199	XP: $15	F12
2/1-4/30 & 11/1-1/31	1P: $59-$169	2P: $59-$179	XP: $15	F12

Location: Just w of Seventeen Mile Dr. 1038 Lighthouse Ave 93950. Fax: 831/655-1681. **Facility:** Smoke free premises. 24 one-bedroom standard units, some with whirlpools. 2 stories, exterior corridors. *Bath:* combo or shower only. **Parking:** on-site. **Terms:** 2-3 night minimum stay - seasonal & weekends, 3 day cancellation notice-fee imposed, [ECP] meal plan available. **Amenities:** hair dryers. **Cards:** AX, DS, MC, VI. **Special Amenities: early check-in/late check-out and free room upgrade (subject to availability with advanced reservations).**

(See color ad p 490)

SOME UNITS

WHERE TO DINE

FANDANGO — **Lunch:** $8-$18 **Dinner:** $11-$25 **Phone:** 831/372-3456 (27)

Steak & Seafood

Location: Center. 223 17th St 93950. **Hours:** 11:30 am-2:30 & 5-9 pm, Sun 10 am-2:30 & 5-9 pm. **Reservations:** accepted. **Features:** Mesquite-grilled seafood and meats are at the heart of a menu of European specialties. The informal dining room evokes a Mediterranean feel. Casual dress; cocktails. **Parking:** on-site. **Cards:** AX, CB, DC, DS, MC, VI.

OLD BATH HOUSE — **Dinner:** $20-$35 **Phone:** 831/375-5195 (25)

Continental

Location: 0.5 mi n at Lovers Point. 620 Ocean View Blvd 93950. **Hours:** 5 pm-10 pm, Sat & Sun from 4 pm. **Reservations:** suggested. **Features:** The location treats diners to spectacular views of Monterey Bay. Fresh local seafood, including many mesquite-grilled preparations, is at the heart of a menu of California fare. Dressy casual; cocktails. **Parking:** street. **Cards:** AX, CB, DC, DS, MC, VI.

PASSIONFISH — **Dinner:** $13-$22 **Phone:** 831/655-3311 (28)

Seafood

Location: Center. 701 Lighthouse Ave 93950. **Hours:** 5 pm-10 pm. Closed: 11/25, 12/25; also Tues. **Reservations:** suggested. **Features:** In the heart of downtown, the restaurant uses fresh local fish in its menu preparations. The mood is relaxed. Casual dress; beer & wine only. **Parking:** street. **Cards:** AX, DC, DS, MC, VI.

PEBBLE BEACH (See map and index starting on p. 436)

WHERE TO STAY

CASA PALMERO — **Phone:** (831)622-6650 (99)

Small-scale Hotel

All Year [CP]	1P: $655-$725	2P: $655-$725	XP: $50	F17

Location: Off SR 1, on Seventeen Mile Dr. 1518 Cypress Dr 93953 (PO Box 1128). Fax: 831/622-6655. **Facility:** Elegantly appointed guest rooms and public areas and extensive spa facilities are features of this property adjacent to Pebble Beach Resort. Smoke free premises. 24 units. 21 one-bedroom standard units, some with whirlpools. 3 one-bedroom suites ($995-$2050) with whirlpools. 2 stories, exterior corridors. **Parking:** on-site. **Terms:** 10 day cancellation notice-fee imposed, $20 service charge. **Amenities:** CD players, dual phone lines, voice mail, safes, honor bars, irons, hair dryers. *Fee:* video games, high-speed Internet. **Pool(s):** heated outdoor. **Leisure Activities:** spa. **Guest Services:** gift shop, complimentary evening beverages, valet laundry. **Business Services:** business center. **Cards:** AX, DC, DS, JC, MC, VI.

THE INN AT SPANISH BAY — **Phone:** 831/647-7500 (100)

Resort Large-scale Hotel

All Year	2P: $450-$600

Location: 3.5 mi w of SR 1, exit SR 68. 2700 Seventeen Mile Dr 93953. Fax: 831/644-7955. **Facility:** Rooms at this inn bordered by a golf course all have bay or forest views and feature a gas-burning fireplace; many rooms have a balcony or patio. 269 units. 252 one-bedroom standard units. 17 one-bedroom suites ($825-$1900) with whirlpools. 3-5 stories, interior corridors. *Bath:* combo or shower only. **Parking:** valet. **Terms:** check-in 4 pm, 2 night minimum stay - weekends, 10 day cancellation notice-fee imposed. **Amenities:** dual phone lines, voice mail, safes, honor bars, irons, hair dryers. *Fee:* video games, high-speed Internet. *Some:* CD players. **Dining:** Roy's, see separate listing. **Pool(s):** heated outdoor. **Leisure Activities:** saunas, whirlpool, scuba diving, recreation programs, rental bicycles, hiking trails, jogging. *Fee:* golf-18 holes, 8 tennis courts (2 lighted), horseback riding, massage. **Guest Services:** gift shop, valet laundry, area transportation (fee). **Business Services:** conference facilities, business center. **Cards:** AX, DC, DS, JC, MC, VI.

SOME UNITS

FEE

THE LODGE AT PEBBLE BEACH — **Phone:** (831)624-3811 (101)

Resort Large-scale Hotel

All Year	1P: $425-$1650	2P: $425-$1650	XP: $50	F18

Location: Off SR 1. Seventeen Mile Dr 93953 (PO Box 1128). Fax: 831/625-8598. **Facility:** Notable for its sweeping views of Monterey Bay, the lodge features spacious guest units, many with wood-burning fireplaces. 161 units. 150 one-bedroom standard units, some with whirlpools. 11 one-bedroom suites ($895-$1650), some with whirlpools. 2-3 stories, interior/exterior corridors. **Parking:** on-site. **Terms:** check-in 4 pm, 2 night minimum stay - weekends, 3 day cancellation notice-fee imposed, package plans, $15 service charge, small pets only. **Amenities:** CD players, dual phone lines, voice mail, safes, honor bars, irons, hair dryers. *Fee:* video games, high-speed Internet. **Dining:** Club XIX, Stillwater Bar and Grill, see separate listings. **Pool(s):** 2 heated outdoor, wading. **Leisure Activities:** sauna, whirlpool, rental bicycles, jogging, spa. *Fee:* golf-18 holes, 12 tennis courts, horseback riding. **Guest Services:** gift shop, valet laundry, area transportation (fee). **Business Services:** conference facilities, business center. **Cards:** AX, CB, DC, DS, JC, MC, VI.

(See map and index starting on p. 436)

WHERE TO DINE

CLUB XIX — French

Lunch: $8-$20 **Dinner:** $20-$30 **Phone:** 831/625-8519 (36)

Location: Off SR 1; in The Lodge at Pebble Beach. Seventeen Mile Dr 93953. **Hours:** 11:30 am-4 & 6:30-10 pm. **Reservations:** suggested. **Features:** French and California cuisine is served in a casually elegant dining room that overlooks the greens. Dressy casual; cocktails. **Parking:** on-site. **Cards:** AX, DC, DS, JC, MC, VI.

ROY'S — Asian

Lunch: $13-$28 **Dinner:** $17-$35 **Phone:** 831/647-7423 (32)

Location: 3.5 mi w of SR 1, exit SR 68; in The Inn at Spanish Bay. 2700 Seventeen Mile Dr 93953. **Hours:** 6:30-11 am, 11:30-3 & 5:30-10 pm. **Reservations:** suggested. **Features:** Delicious Euro-Asian cooking and a friendly, relaxed atmosphere draw diners to the restaurant. The dining room looks out over Monterey Bay and Spanish Links Golf Course. Dressy casual; cocktails. **Parking:** on-site. **Cards:** AX, CB, DC, DS, MC, VI.

STILLWATER BAR AND GRILL — Regional American

Lunch: $13-$65 **Dinner:** $22-$65 **Phone:** 831/625-8524 (35)

Location: Off SR 1; in The Lodge at Pebble Beach. Seventeen Mile Dr 93953. **Hours:** 7 am-10 pm. **Reservations:** suggested. **Features:** This casual yet upscale restaurant offers diners views of the golf course and Monterey Bay. Dressy casual; cocktails. **Parking:** on-site. **Cards:** AX, CB, DC, DS, JC, MC, VI.

SEASIDE pop. 31,696 (See map and index starting on p. 436)

WHERE TO STAY

BEST WESTERN MAGIC CARPET LODGE — *Book at aaa.com* — SAVE — Motel

Phone: (831)899-4221 (163)

All Year 1P: $59-$249 2P: $69-$269 XP: $15

Location: SR 1, exit Seaside, 1.5 mi e. 1875 Fremont Blvd 93955. Fax: 831/899-3377. **Facility:** 43 one-bedroom standard units. 3 stories, interior/exterior corridors. **Parking:** on-site. **Terms:** cancellation fee imposed, [CP] meal plan available. **Amenities:** irons, hair dryers. **Pool(s):** heated outdoor. **Cards:** AX, CB, DC, DS, JC, MC, VI. **Special Amenities: free continental breakfast and free local telephone calls.**

(See color ad p 486)

SOME UNITS — FEE FEE

(See map and index starting on p. 436)

DISCOVERY INN — Phone: (831)394-3113 — 168

Motel

8/1-9/30	1P: $65-$149	2P: $79-$179	XP: $10	F
5/1-7/31	1P: $45-$139	2P: $65-$159	XP: $10	F
2/1-4/30	1P: $39-$79	2P: $45-$89	XP: $10	F
10/1-1/31	1P: $39-$65	2P: $45-$79	XP: $10	F

Location: SR 1, exit Seaside/Del Rey Oaks, 2 mi e. 1106 Fremont Blvd 93955. **Facility:** 20 one-bedroom standard units. 1 story, exterior corridors. **Parking:** on-site. **Terms:** 2-3 night minimum stay - seasonal, cancellation fee imposed. **Cards:** AX, DS, MC, VI.

SOME UNITS

ECONO LODGE BAY BREEZE — Phone: (831)899-7111 — 160

Motel

5/1-10/31 [ECP]	1P: $69-$249	2P: $69-$249	XP: $10	F
2/1-4/30 & 11/1-1/31 [ECP]	1P: $49-$199	2P: $49-$199	XP: $10	F

Location: SR 1, exit Sand City/Seaside, just e. 2049 Fremont Blvd 93955. Fax: 831/899-7211. **Facility:** 50 one-bedroom standard units. 2 stories, interior/exterior corridors. **Parking:** on-site. **Terms:** pets (small dogs only). **Cards:** AX, DC, DS, MC, VI. **Special Amenities: free expanded continental breakfast and early check-in/late check-out.** *(See color ad p 461)*

SOME UNITS

ECONOMY INN — *Book at aaa.com* — Phone: 831/899-2700 — 167

Motel

5/1-9/30	1P: $49-$159	2P: $59-$174	XP: $10	F13
2/1-4/30 & 10/1-1/31	1P: $32-$99	2P: $42-$109	XP: $10	F13

Location: SR 1, exit Seaside, 2 mi e. 1131 Fremont Blvd 93955. Fax: 831/899-0469. **Facility:** 17 one-bedroom standard units. 2 stories (no elevator), exterior corridors. **Parking:** on-site. **Terms:** cancellation fee imposed, [CP] meal plan available. **Cards:** AX, DC, DS, MC, VI. **Special Amenities: free local telephone calls.**

SOME UNITS

EMBASSY SUITES HOTEL & CONFERENCE CENTER — *Book at aaa.com* — Phone: (831)393-1115 — 165

Large-scale Hotel

6/1-1/31 [BP]	1P: $169-$299	2P: $169-$299	XP: $20	F17
2/1-5/31 [BP]	1P: $154-$249	2P: $154-$249	XP: $20	F17

Location: SR 1, exit Seaside/Del Rey Oaks, just e. 1441 Canyon Del Rey 93955. Fax: 831/393-1113. **Facility:** 225 one-bedroom suites. 12 stories, interior corridors. *Bath:* combo or shower only. **Parking:** on-site. **Terms:** check-in 4 pm, 3 day cancellation notice-fee imposed. **Amenities:** video games (fee), dual phone lines, voice mail, irons, hair dryers. **Dining:** 11 am-11 pm. **Pool(s):** heated indoor. **Leisure Activities:** sauna, whirlpool, exercise room. *Fee:* massage. **Guest Services:** gift shop, complimentary evening beverages, valet and coin laundry, airport transportation-Monterey Airport. **Business Services:** conference facilities, business center. **Cards:** AX, CB, DC, DS, JC, MC. **Special Amenities: free full breakfast and free newspaper.** *(See color ad below)*

SOME UNITS

HOLIDAY INN EXPRESS — *Book at aaa.com* — Phone: (831)394-5335 — 164

Motel

6/1-10/31	1P: $99-$249	2P: $99-$249
4/1-5/31	1P: $99-$199	2P: $99-$199
2/1-3/31 & 11/1-1/31	1P: $89-$159	2P: $89-$159

Location: SR 1, exit Seaside/Del Rey Oaks, just e. 1400 Del Monte Blvd 93955. Fax: 831/394-7125. **Facility:** 143 one-bedroom standard units. 5 stories, exterior corridors. *Bath:* combo or shower only. **Parking:** on-site. **Terms:** [ECP] meal plan available. **Amenities:** video games (fee), dual phone lines, voice mail, irons, hair dryers. **Pool(s):** heated outdoor. **Leisure Activities:** whirlpool, exercise room. **Guest Services:** valet laundry. **Cards:** AX, CB, DC, DS, JC, MC, VI.

SOME UNITS

HOWARD JOHNSON EXPRESS INN — *Book at aaa.com* — Phone: (831)394-8566 — 162

Motel

6/1-9/30 [ECP]	1P: $49-$179	2P: $49-$179	XP: $10	F15
2/1-5/31 & 10/1-1/31 [ECP]	1P: $49-$139	2P: $49-$139	XP: $10	F15

Location: SR 1, exit Seaside, 1.2 mi e. 1893 Fremont Blvd 93955. Fax: 831/394-8568. **Facility:** 38 one-bedroom standard units. 2 stories (no elevator), exterior corridors. **Parking:** on-site. **Terms:** cancellation fee imposed. **Amenities:** high-speed Internet, voice mail, irons, hair dryers. **Leisure Activities:** whirlpool. **Guest Services:** coin laundry. **Cards:** AX, DC, MC, VI.

SOME UNITS

(See map and index starting on p. 436)

PACIFIC BEST INN **Phone:** (831)899-1881 166

Motel

All Year 1P: $69-$189 2P: $79-$199 XP: $20 F7

Location: SR 1, exit Fremont Blvd, then e. 1141 Fremont Blvd 93955. Fax: 831/392-1300. **Facility:** 23 one-bedroom standard units. 2 stories (no elevator), exterior corridors. **Parking:** on-site. **Terms:** cancellation fee imposed, [CP] meal plan available. **Business Services:** meeting rooms. **Cards:** AX, DC, MC, VI.

SOME UNITS / VCR FEE FEE FEE /

SANDCASTLE INN **Phone:** (831)394-6556 158

Motel

6/1-9/30 [CP] 1P: $55-$125 2P: $65-$145 XP: $10 F17

2/1-5/31 & 10/1-1/31 [CP] 1P: $45-$89 2P: $55-$109 XP: $10 F17

Location: SR 1, exit Sand City/Seaside, just e. 1011 Auto Center Pkwy 93955. Fax: 831/394-1578. **Facility:** 34 one-bedroom standard units. 2 stories (no elevator), exterior corridors. **Parking:** on-site. **Amenities:** high-speed Internet. **Guest Services:** coin laundry. **Cards:** AX, DC, DS, MC, VI. **Special Amenities: free continental breakfast and early check-in/late check-out.**

SOME UNITS DATA PORT / FEE FEE /

SEASIDE INN **Phone:** (831)394-4041 159

Motel

All Year 1P: $45-$125 2P: $55-$135 XP: $10 F3

Location: SR 1, exit Sand City/Seaside, just e. 1986 Del Monte Blvd 93955. Fax: 831/394-2806. **Facility:** 17 one-bedroom standard units. 1-2 stories (no elevator), exterior corridors. **Parking:** on-site. **Terms:** 3 day cancellation notice-fee imposed, weekly rates available. **Cards:** AX, DC, MC, VI. **Special Amenities: free continental breakfast and free local telephone calls.**

SOME UNITS DATA PORT / /

THUNDERBIRD MOTEL **Phone:** (831)394-6797 154

Motel

4/1-9/30 1P: $46-$125 2P: $65-$145 XP: $10 F6

2/1-3/31 & 10/1-1/31 1P: $41-$120 2P: $55-$135 XP: $10 F6

Location: SR 1 business route, 0.3 mi n. 1933 Fremont Blvd 93955. Fax: 831/394-5568. **Facility:** 33 one-bedroom standard units. 2 stories (no elevator), exterior corridors. *Bath:* combo or shower only. **Parking:** on-site. **Pool(s):** small outdoor. **Cards:** AX, CB, DC, DS, MC, VI. **Special Amenities: free continental breakfast.**

SOME UNITS DATA PORT / /

This ends listings for the Monterey Peninsula.
The following page resumes the alphabetical listings of cities in Northern California.

MONTE RIO
—See Guerneville & Wine Country p. 789.

MORGAN HILL pop. 33,556

WHERE TO STAY

BEST WESTERN COUNTRY INN Book at aaa.com **Phone:** (408)779-0447

Motel

All Year 1P: $59-$109 2P: $59-$109 XP: $6 F16

Location: US 101, exit Tennant Ave or E Dunne Ave, just e. 16525 Condit Rd 95037. Fax: 408/778-7170. **Facility:** 83 one-bedroom standard units. 2 stories (no elevator), interior corridors. **Parking:** on-site. **Terms:** [ECP] meal plan available, small pets only ($10 fee). **Amenities:** dual phone lines, voice mail, irons, hair dryers. **Pool(s):** outdoor. **Leisure Activities:** whirlpool. **Guest Services:** coin laundry. **Business Services:** meeting rooms. **Cards:** AX, CB, DC, DS, JC, MC, VI. **Special Amenities: free continental breakfast and free newspaper.** *(See color ad below & p 521)*

SOME UNITS

FEE

COMFORT INN & SUITES Book at aaa.com **Phone:** (408)778-3400

Motel

All Year 1P: $89-$149 2P: $99-$159 XP: $10 F15

Location: US 101, exit Tennant Ave, just e. 16225 Condit Rd 95037. Fax: 408/782-2300. **Facility:** 53 one-bedroom standard units, some with whirlpools. 3 stories, interior corridors. **Parking:** on-site. **Terms:** cancellation fee imposed, [CP] meal plan available. **Amenities:** dual phone lines, voice mail, irons, hair dryers. *Some:* DVD players. **Pool(s):** small outdoor. **Leisure Activities:** sauna, whirlpool, exercise room. **Guest Services:** coin laundry. **Business Services:** meeting rooms, administrative services, fax. **Cards:** AX, DC, DS, JC, MC, VI. **Special Amenities: free continental breakfast and free local telephone calls.**

SOME UNITS

COURTYARD BY MARRIOTT Book at aaa.com **Phone:** (408)782-6034

Small-scale Hotel

All Year 1P: $129

Location: US 101, exit Cochrane W, then n. 18610 Madrone Pkwy 95037. Fax: 408/782-1064. **Facility:** 90 units. 87 one-bedroom standard units. 3 one-bedroom suites. 3 stories, interior corridors. **Parking:** on-site. **Terms:** [BP] meal plan available. **Amenities:** dual phone lines, voice mail, irons, hair dryers. **Pool(s):** indoor. **Leisure Activities:** whirlpool, exercise room. **Guest Services:** valet and coin laundry. **Business Services:** meeting rooms. **Cards:** AX, DC, DS, MC, VI.

SOME UNITS

EXECUTIVE INN Book at aaa.com **Phone:** (408)778-0404

Motel

All Year 1P: $79-$129 2P: $79-$129

Location: US 101, exit Dunne Ave, just e. 16505 Condit Rd 95037. Fax: 408/778-2090. **Facility:** 30 units. 3 one-bedroom standard units. 27 one-bedroom suites, some with whirlpools. 2 stories (no elevator), exterior corridors. **Parking:** on-site. **Terms:** [CP] meal plan available. **Amenities:** video library, irons, hair dryers. **Pool(s):** outdoor. **Guest Services:** complimentary laundry. **Cards:** AX, CB, DC, DS, MC, VI. **Special Amenities: free expanded continental breakfast and early check-in/late check-out.**

SOME UNITS

HOLIDAY INN EXPRESS HOTEL & SUITES Book at aaa.com **Phone:** (408)776-7676

Small-scale Hotel

All Year 1P: $109-$149 2P: $109-$149

Location: US 101, exit Dunne Ave, then e. 17035 Condit Rd 95037. Fax: 408/776-1577. **Facility:** 84 units. 62 one-bedroom standard units, some with whirlpools. 22 one-bedroom suites ($159-$229), some with whirlpools. 3 stories, interior corridors. *Bath:* combo or shower only. **Parking:** on-site. **Terms:** [ECP] meal plan available. **Amenities:** video library, video games (fee), high-speed Internet, dual phone lines, voice mail, irons, hair dryers. *Some:* DVD players. **Pool(s):** heated indoor. **Leisure Activities:** sauna, whirlpool, exercise room. **Guest Services:** complimentary evening beverages, complimentary laundry. **Business Services:** meeting rooms, business center. **Cards:** AX, CB, DC, DS, JC, MC, VI. ***(See color ad p 260)***

SOME UNITS

INN AT MORGAN HILL **Book at aaa.com** **Phone:** (408)779-7666

Small-scale Hotel

All Year [BP] 1P: $139-$319 2P: $154-$319 XP: $15 F11

Location: US 101, exit Tennant Ave, just e. 16115 Condit Rd 95037. Fax: 408/779-8757. **Facility:** 100 units. 95 one-bedroom standard units, some with whirlpools. 5 one-bedroom suites with whirlpools, some with efficiencies. 3 stories, interior corridors. *Bath:* combo or shower only. **Parking:** on-site. **Terms:** check-in 4 pm. **Amenities:** video library, video games (fee), high-speed Internet, dual phone lines, voice mail, honor bars, irons, hair dryers. **Pool(s):** outdoor. **Leisure Activities:** whirlpool, exercise room. **Guest Services:** complimentary evening beverages, coin laundry. **Business Services:** meeting rooms, fax. **Cards:** AX, DC, DS, MC, VI.

SOME UNITS

ASK VCR DATA PORT

RESIDENCE INN BY MARRIOTT **Book at aaa.com** **Phone:** (408)782-8311

Small-scale Hotel

5/21-9/6	1P: $112-$138	2P: $112-$138
2/1-5/20 & 9/7-1/31	1P: $108-$135	2P: $108-$135

Location: US 101, exit Cochrane W, just n. 18620 Madrone Pkwy 95037. Fax: 408/782-8322. **Facility:** 90 units. 73 one-bedroom standard units with kitchens. 17 two-bedroom suites with kitchens. 3 stories, interior corridors. **Parking:** on-site. **Terms:** [BP] meal plan available, pets ($200 fee, $15 extra charge). **Amenities:** dual phone lines, voice mail, irons, hair dryers. *Some:* high-speed Internet (fee). **Pool(s):** heated indoor. **Leisure Activities:** whirlpool, exercise room. **Guest Services:** valet and coin laundry. **Business Services:** meeting rooms. **Cards:** AX, DC, DS, MC, VI.

SOME UNITS

ASK FEE DATA PORT

WHERE TO DINE

GOLDEN OAK **Lunch:** $6-$20 **Dinner:** $15-$30 **Phone:** 408/779-8085

Continental

Location: US 101, exit Tennant Ave or E Dunne Ave, just e. 16695 Condit Rd 95037. **Hours:** 11 am-3 & 5-10 pm, Sat from 5 pm, Sun from 4 pm. Closed major holidays. **Reservations:** accepted. **Features:** Converted from an old winery, the restaurant is spacious and attractive in design. The menu comprises fresh pasta and California dishes. Casual dress; cocktails. **Parking:** on-site. **Cards:** AX, DC, MC, VI.

MORRO BAY pop. 10,350

WHERE TO STAY

ASCOT INN *Book at aaa.com* **Phone:** (805)772-4437

AAA SAVE — Motel

6/1-9/30 [CP]	1P: $79-$199	2P: $79-$199	XP: $10	F12
4/1-5/31 [CP]	1P: $59-$149	2P: $59-$149	XP: $10	F12
2/1-3/31 & 10/1-1/31 [CP]	1P: $49-$129	2P: $49-$129	XP: $10	F12

Location: SR 1, exit Morro Bay Blvd, 0.7 mi w. 845 Morro Ave 93442. Fax: 805/772-8860. **Facility:** Smoke free premises. 25 units. 24 one- and 1 two-bedroom standard units. 2 stories (no elevator), exterior corridors. *Bath:* combo or shower only. **Parking:** on-site. **Terms:** 3 day cancellation notice, [ECP] meal plan available, package plans - seasonal. **Amenities:** voice mail. **Cards:** AX, CB, DC, DS, MC, VI. **Special Amenities: free continental breakfast and free local telephone calls.** *(See color ad below)*

SOME UNITS

ASCOT SUITES Book at aaa.com **Phone:** (805)772-4437

AAA SAVE — Small-scale Hotel

7/1-9/30 [ECP]	1P: $169-$349	2P: $169-$349	XP: $10	F12
4/1-6/30 [ECP]	1P: $139-$259	2P: $139-$259	XP: $10	F12
2/1-3/31 & 10/1-1/31 [ECP]	1P: $129-$199	2P: $129-$199	XP: $10	F12

Location: SR 1, exit Morro Bay Blvd, 0.7 mi w. 260 Morro Bay Blvd 93442. Fax: 805/772-8860. **Facility:** Well-tended flower beds and an arched green-canvas awning mark the entry to this three-story motel with Tudor-style architecture. Smoke free premises. 32 units. 29 one-bedroom standard units, some with whirlpools. 3 one-bedroom suites ($199-$369) with whirlpools. 3 stories, interior corridors. **Parking:** on-site. **Terms:** 3 day cancellation notice, weekly rates available, package plans - seasonal. **Amenities:** voice mail, safes, honor bars, irons, hair dryers. *Some:* dual phone lines. **Leisure Activities:** sun deck. *Fee:* massage. **Guest Services:** complimentary evening beverages, valet laundry. **Business Services:** meeting rooms. **Cards:** AX, CB, DC, DS, MC, VI. **Special Amenities: free expanded continental breakfast and free local telephone calls.** *(See color ad p 497)*

S/D · VCR · DATA PORT

BAY VIEW INN **Phone:** (805)772-2771

AAA SAVE — Motel

All Year	1P: $69-$229	2P: $69-$229	XP: $10	F12

Location: SR 1, exit Morro Bay Blvd, 0.8 mi w to Market Ave, just n. 225 Harbor St 93442. Fax: 805/772-0411. **Facility:** Smoke free premises. 22 one-bedroom standard units. 2 stories (no elevator), exterior corridors. *Bath:* combo or shower only. **Parking:** on-site. **Terms:** office hours 8 am-10 pm, cancellation fee imposed, [CP] meal plan available. **Amenities:** video library, irons. **Leisure Activities:** whirlpool. **Cards:** AX, DS, MC, VI.

S/D · AC · VCR

BEST WESTERN EL RANCHO Book at aaa.com **Phone:** (805)772-2212

AAA SAVE — Motel

6/1-9/15	1P: $69-$149	2P: $69-$149	XP: $10	F12
2/1-5/31 & 9/16-1/31	1P: $59-$139	2P: $59-$139	XP: $10	F12

Location: SR 1, exit SR 41, 0.5 mi n. 2460 Main St 93442. Fax: 805/772-2212. **Facility:** 27 one-bedroom standard units. 1 story, exterior corridors. *Bath:* combo or shower only. **Parking:** on-site. **Terms:** office hours 8 am-10 pm, pets ($10 extra charge). **Amenities:** video library, irons, hair dryers. **Dining:** 7 am-10 pm, wine/beer only. **Pool(s):** heated outdoor. **Guest Services:** coin laundry. **Cards:** AX, CB, DC, DS, MC, VI. **Special Amenities: free local telephone calls and early check-in/late check-out.** *(See ad below)*

S/D · FEE · AC · VCR · DATA PORT / SOME UNITS /

BEST WESTERN SAN MARCOS INN Book at aaa.com **Phone:** (805)772-2248

AAA SAVE — Motel

6/11-8/28	2P: $99-$179	XP: $10
2/1-6/10 & 8/29-10/30	2P: $69-$169	XP: $10
10/31-1/31	2P: $59-$169	XP: $10

Location: SR 1, exit Morro Bay Blvd, 0.8 mi w, just s on Morro Ave. 250 Pacific St 93442. Fax: 805/772-6844. **Facility:** Smoke free premises. 32 one-bedroom standard units. 3 stories, interior corridors. *Bath:* shower only. **Parking:** on-site. **Terms:** office hours 7:30 am-10 pm, 3 day cancellation notice, [ECP] meal plan available. **Amenities:** voice mail, irons, hair dryers. **Leisure Activities:** large indoor hydra-therapy spa. **Guest Services:** complimentary evening beverages. **Cards:** AX, CB, DC, DS, JC, MC, VI. **Special Amenities: free expanded continental breakfast and free local telephone calls.** *(See color ad p 501)*

S/D · AC · DATA PORT / SOME UNITS / VCR /

BEST WESTERN TRADEWINDS MOTEL Book at aaa.com **Phone:** (805)772-7376

AAA SAVE — Motel

All Year [CP]	1P: $59-$199	2P: $59-$199	XP: $10	F12

Location: SR 1, exit Morro Bay Blvd, 0.8 mi w to Market Ave, then 0.3 mi n. 225 Beach St 93442. Fax: 805/772-2090. **Facility:** Smoke free premises. 24 one-bedroom standard units. 2 stories (no elevator), exterior corridors. **Parking:** on-site. **Terms:** office hours 7 am-10 pm, 2-3 night minimum stay - seasonal weekends, 3 day cancellation notice, weekly rates available. **Amenities:** irons, hair dryers. **Leisure Activities:** whirlpool. **Cards:** AX, CB, DC, DS, JC, MC, VI. **Special Amenities: free continental breakfast and free local telephone calls.**

S/D · DATA PORT / SOME UNITS /

BLUE SAIL INN — **Phone:** 805/772-2766

SAVE — Motel

2/1-10/31	1P: $80-$150	2P: $80-$150
11/1-1/31	1P: $65-$145	2P: $65-$145

Location: SR 1, exit Morro Bay Blvd, 0.8 mi w. 851 Market Ave 93442. Fax: 805/772-8406. **Facility:** 48 one-bedroom standard units. 3 stories, interior/exterior corridors. **Parking:** on-site. **Terms:** office hours 8 am-10 pm. **Amenities:** hair dryers. *Some:* irons. **Leisure Activities:** whirlpool. **Cards:** AX, DS, MC, VI. **Special Amenities: free local telephone calls and free newspaper.**

SOME UNITS

BREAKERS MOTEL — **Phone:** 805/772-7317

SAVE — Motel

All Year	2P: $95-$135	XP: $10	F12

Location: SR 1, exit Morro Bay Blvd, 0.8 mi w. 780 Market Ave 93442. Fax: 805/772-4771. **Facility:** 25 one-bedroom standard units. 3 stories (no elevator), exterior corridors. *Bath:* combo or shower only. **Parking:** on-site. **Terms:** office hours 8 am-10 pm, 2 night minimum stay - weekends, 3 day cancellation notice, [CP] meal plan available. **Amenities:** irons, hair dryers. **Pool(s):** heated outdoor. **Leisure Activities:** whirlpool. **Cards:** AX, DS, MC, VI. **Special Amenities: free continental breakfast and free newspaper.**

SOME UNITS

ECONO LODGE *Book at aaa.com* — **Phone:** (805)772-5609

SAVE — Motel

5/1-9/30	1P: $69-$189	2P: $79-$198	XP: $8	F12
2/1-4/30	1P: $54-$169	2P: $64-$189	XP: $8	F12
10/1-1/31	1P: $54-$149	2P: $64-$169	XP: $8	F12

Location: SR 1, exit Morro Bay Blvd, 0.7 mi w, then just n. 1100 Main St 93442. Fax: 805/772-1051. **Facility:** 18 units. 17 one- and 1 two-bedroom standard units. 2 stories (no elevator), exterior corridors. **Parking:** on-site. **Terms:** office hours 7:30 am-10 pm. **Cards:** AX, CB, DC, DS, MC, VI.

SOME UNITS

EL MORRO MASTERPIECE MOTEL — **Phone:** (805)772-5633

SAVE — Small-scale Hotel

6/11-8/28	2P: $89-$179	XP: $10
2/1-6/10 & 8/29-10/30	2P: $69-$169	XP: $10
10/31-1/31	2P: $59-$169	XP: $10

Location: SR 1 southbound, 0.3 mi s; exit Morro Bay Blvd northbound, 0.7 mi w, then 0.4 mi n. 1206 Main St 93442. Fax: 805/772-1404. **Facility:** Smoke free premises. 27 one-bedroom standard units, some with whirlpools. 2 stories, interior corridors. **Parking:** on-site. **Terms:** office hours 7:30 am-10 pm, 3 day cancellation notice, [ECP] meal plan available. **Amenities:** hair dryers. *Some:* irons. **Leisure Activities:** whirlpool, exercise room. **Guest Services:** complimentary evening beverages, coin laundry. **Cards:** AX, CB, DC, DS, JC, MC, VI. **Special Amenities: free expanded continental breakfast and free local telephone calls.** *(See color ad p 501)*

SOME UNITS

EMBARCADERO INN *Book at aaa.com* — **Phone:** 805/772-2700

SAVE — Motel

(See color ad below)

All Year [CP]	1P: $95-$155	2P: $95-$155	XP: $10	F12

Location: SR 1, exit Morro Bay Blvd, 0.7 mi w to Main St, 0.3 mi s to Marina St, just w, then just s. 456 Embarcadero 93442 (1148 Market St). Fax: 805/772-1060. **Facility:** 32 units. 30 one-bedroom standard units. 2 one-bedroom suites ($225). 3 stories, exterior corridors. **Parking:** on-site. **Terms:** office hours 7 am-11 pm, 3 day cancellation notice. **Amenities:** video library, irons, hair dryers. **Leisure Activities:** whirlpools. **Cards:** AX, CB, DC, DS, JC, MC, VI. **Special Amenities: free continental breakfast and free local telephone calls.**

SOME UNITS

FIRESIDE INN MOTEL

Motel

Phone: 805/772-2244

All Year 1P: $49-$129 2P: $52-$149 XP: $10

Location: SR 1, exit Morro Bay Blvd, 0.7 mi w, just s. 730 Morro Ave 93442. Fax: 805/772-0308. **Facility:** 24 one-bedroom standard units. 2 stories (no elevator), exterior corridors. *Bath:* combo or shower only. **Parking:** on-site. **Terms:** office hours 7 am-11 pm, 3 day cancellation notice-fee imposed, [CP] meal plan available. **Cards:** AX, DC, MC, VI. **Special Amenities: free continental breakfast and free local telephone calls.**

SOME UNITS

HOLLAND INN

Motel

Phone: (805)772-2650

4/26-8/31 [CP] 1P: $38-$245 2P: $38-$245 XP: $8 D5

2/1-4/25 & 9/1-1/31 [CP] 1P: $30-$85 2P: $30-$85 XP: $5 D5

Location: SR 1, exit SR 41, 1 mi n. 2630 Main St 93442. Fax: 805/772-7796. **Facility:** Smoke free premises. 23 units. 19 one- and 4 two-bedroom standard units, some with whirlpools. 1 story, exterior corridors. *Bath:* combo or shower only. **Parking:** on-site. **Terms:** office hours 6 am-11:30 pm, 3 day cancellation notice. **Amenities:** hair dryers. **Cards:** AX, DC, DS, MC, VI. **Special Amenities: free continental breakfast and early check-in/late check-out.**

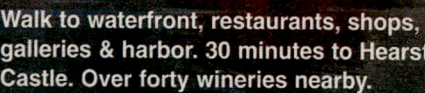

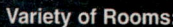

SOME UNITS

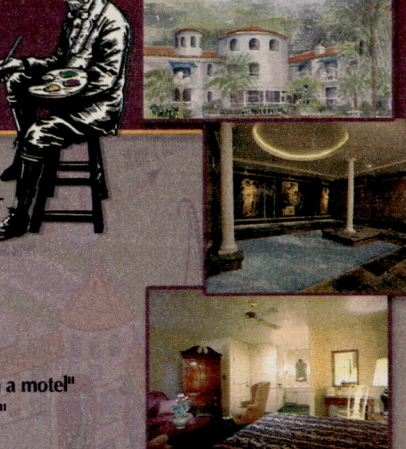

THE INN AT MORRO BAY Book at aaa.com **Phone:** (805)772-5651

Small-scale Hotel

6/1-9/30	2P: $129-$350	XP: $25	F12
2/1-5/31 & 10/1-1/31	2P: $99-$299	XP: $25	F12

Location: SR 1, exit Morro Bay Blvd, 0.7 mi w, 1 mi s on Main St. Located at the entrance to Morro Bay State Park. 60 State Park Rd 93442. Fax: 805/772-4779. **Facility:** Smoke free premises. 98 one-bedroom standard units, some with whirlpools. 2 stories (no elevator), exterior corridors. *Bath:* combo or shower only. **Parking:** on-site. **Terms:** check-in 4 pm, 2 night minimum stay - weekends 7/1-8/31, cancellation fee imposed. **Amenities:** CD players, voice mail, irons, hair dryers. **Dining:** 7 am-10 pm, also, The Dining Room at Inn of Morro Bay, see separate listing. **Pool(s):** heated outdoor. **Leisure Activities:** bicycles. *Fee:* massage. **Guest Services:** valet laundry. **Business Services:** meeting rooms. **Cards:** AX, DC, DS, MC, VI. *(See color ad below)*

LA SERENA INN **Phone:** (805)772-5665

Small-scale Hotel

6/11-8/28	2P: $89-$179	XP: $10
2/1-6/10 & 8/29-10/30	2P: $69-$169	XP: $10
10/31-1/31	2P: $59-$169	XP: $10

Location: SR 1, exit Morro Bay Blvd, 0.7 mi w, then just n. 990 Morro Ave 93442. Fax: 805/772-1044. **Facility:** 38 one-bedroom standard units. 3 stories, interior corridors. **Parking:** on-site. **Terms:** office hours 7:30 am-10 pm, 3 day cancellation notice, [ECP] meal plan available. **Amenities:** hair dryers. **Leisure Activities:** sauna. **Guest Services:** complimentary evening beverages: Fri & Sat. **Cards:** AX, CB, DC, DS, JC, MC, VI. **Special Amenities: free expanded continental breakfast and free local telephone calls.** *(See color ad p 500)*

SOME UNITS

MARINA STREET INN **Phone:** (805)772-4016

Bed & Breakfast

5/2-9/15 [BP]	1P: $119-$160	2P: $129-$170	XP: $15
2/1-5/1 & 9/16-1/31 [BP]	1P: $109-$150	2P: $119-$160	XP: $15

Location: SR 1, exit Morro Bay Blvd, 0.8 mi w, then just s on Morro Ave. 305 Marina St 93442. Fax: 805/772-0667. **Facility:** Set among wildflowers, this modern, yellow inn has views of Morro Bay; guest rooms are cozy and individually themed. Smoke free premises. 4 one-bedroom standard units. 2 stories (no elevator), interior corridors. *Bath:* shower only. **Parking:** on-site. **Terms:** 2-3 night minimum stay - weekends, 4 day cancellation notice. **Guest Services:** complimentary evening beverages. **Cards:** MC, VI.

MORRO BAY SANDPIPER/KEYSTONE INN **Phone:** (805)772-7503

Motel

All Year	1P: $49-$169	2P: $49-$169	XP: $10

Location: SR 1, exit Morro Bay Blvd, 0.7 mi w, then 0.4 mi s. 540 Main St 93442. **Facility:** 21 one-bedroom standard units. 2 stories (no elevator), exterior corridors. **Parking:** on-site. **Terms:** office hours 9 am-9 pm, 3 day cancellation notice-fee imposed, weekly rates available, pets (in designated units). **Amenities:** hair dryers. **Cards:** AX, DS, MC, VI. **Special Amenities: free room upgrade and preferred room (each subject to availability with advanced reservations).**

SOME UNITS

MORRO CREST INN Book at aaa.com **Phone:** 805/772-7740

Motel

5/15-9/30	1P: $32-$195	2P: $38-$215	XP: $5	F12
2/1-5/14	1P: $32-$135	2P: $35-$145	XP: $5	F12
10/1-1/31	1P: $30-$125	2P: $32-$130	XP: $5	F12

Location: SR 1, exit Morro Bay Blvd, 0.7 mi w, just s. 670 Main St 93442. Fax: 805/772-7796. **Facility:** 17 one-bedroom standard units. 2 stories (no elevator), exterior corridors. *Bath:* shower only. **Parking:** on-site. **Terms:** office hours 7 am-11:30 pm, cancellation fee imposed, [CP] meal plan available. **Amenities:** *Some:* irons, hair dryers. **Cards:** AX, MC, VI. **Special Amenities: free local telephone calls and preferred room (subject to availability with advanced reservations).**

SOME UNITS

SUNDOWN MOTEL **Phone:** (805)772-7381

Motel

6/11-9/30	1P: $45-$135	2P: $45-$135	XP: $6	F10
2/1-6/10 & 10/1-1/31	1P: $36-$95	2P: $38-$95	XP: $6	F10

Location: SR 1, exit Morro Bay Blvd, 0.7 mi w, then just s. 640 Main St 93442. Fax: 805/772-7381. **Facility:** 17 one-bedroom standard units. 1 story, exterior corridors. *Bath:* shower only. **Parking:** on-site. **Terms:** office hours 7:30 am-11 pm, weekly rates available, small pets only ($8 extra charge 10/1-4/30, in designated units). **Amenities:** *Some:* irons, hair dryers. **Cards:** AX, DS, MC, VI. **Special Amenities: free local telephone calls and preferred room (subject to availability with advanced reservations).**

SOME UNITS

FEE

SUNSET TRAVELODGE Book at aaa.com **Phone:** (805)772-1259

Motel

All Year 1P: $59-$199 2P: $59-$199 XP: $10 F16

Location: SR 1, exit Morro Bay Blvd, 0.8 mi w, just n. 1080 Market Ave 93442. Fax: 805/772-8967. **Facility:** Smoke free premises. 31 units. 29 one- and 2 two-bedroom standard units, some with whirlpools. 1-2 stories (no elevator), exterior corridors. *Bath:* combo or shower only. **Parking:** on-site. **Terms:** office hours 7:30 am-midnight, 2-3 night minimum stay - seasonal & weekends, 3 day cancellation notice-fee imposed, [CP] meal plan available. **Amenities:** irons, hair dryers. **Pool(s):** heated outdoor. **Cards:** AX, DC, DS, MC, VI. **Special Amenities: free continental breakfast and free local telephone calls.**

TWIN DOLPHIN INN Book at aaa.com **Phone:** (805)772-4483

Motel

All Year 1P: $79-$249 2P: $79-$249 XP: $10 F12

Location: SR 1, exit Morro Bay Blvd, 0.7 mi w, just s. 590 Morro Ave 93442. **Facility:** 31 one-bedroom standard units. 3 stories, interior corridors. *Bath:* shower only. **Parking:** on-site. **Terms:** office hours 7:30 am-10 pm, cancellation fee imposed, [CP] meal plan available. **Amenities:** *Some:* irons, hair dryers. **Leisure Activities:** whirlpool. **Cards:** AX, DS, MC, VI. **Special Amenities: free continental breakfast and free local telephone calls.**

SOME UNITS

VILLAGER MOTEL **Phone:** 805/772-1235

Motel

5/1-10/31	1P: $49-$189	2P: $59-$199	XP: $10	F10
2/1-4/30	1P: $45-$149	2P: $55-$159	XP: $10	F10
11/1-1/31	1P: $40-$105	2P: $50-$115	XP: $10	F10

Location: SR 1, exit Morro Bay Blvd, 0.7 mi w, then just n. 1098 Main St 93442. Fax: 805/772-3317. **Facility:** 22 one-bedroom standard units. 2 stories (no elevator), exterior corridors. *Bath:* shower only. **Parking:** on-site. **Terms:** office hours 7 am-11:30 pm, 3 day cancellation notice-fee imposed, [CP] meal plan available, small pets only ($20 extra charge). **Amenities:** irons, hair dryers. **Leisure Activities:** whirlpool. **Cards:** AX, DC, MC, VI. **Special Amenities: free continental breakfast and free local telephone calls.**

SOME UNITS

FEE

WHERE TO DINE

THE DINING ROOM AT INN OF MORRO BAY **Dinner:** $15-$30 **Phone:** 805/772-5651

American

Location: SR 1, exit Morro Bay Blvd, 0.7 mi w, 1 mi s on Main St; at entrance to Morro Bay State Park; in The Inn at Morro Bay. 60 State Park Rd 93442. **Hours:** 5 pm-9 pm. **Reservations:** suggested. **Features:** The upscale restaurant affords nice views of the bay, both from the dining room and the relaxed patio. Dressy casual; cocktails. **Parking:** on-site. **Cards:** AX, CB, DC, DS, MC, VI. ***(See color ad p 502)***

DORN'S BREAKERS CAFE **Lunch:** $8-$11 **Dinner:** $9-$23 **Phone:** 805/772-4415

American

Location: Corner of Morro Bay Blvd. 801 Market Ave 93442. **Hours:** 7 am-9 pm; to 10 pm in season. Closed: 12/25. **Reservations:** suggested. **Features:** This family restaurant, which sits on a bluff overlooking the bay and embarcadero areas with a good view of Morro Rock, has been a part of the local scene for years. The menu offers a large selection of fish as well as chicken and meat entrees. The clam chowder is always well-seasoned and full of chewy clams. Also a great place for breakfast. Casual dress; cocktails. **Parking:** on-site. **Cards:** DS, MC, VI.

GALLEY RESTAURANT **Lunch:** $6-$22 **Dinner:** $14-$22 **Phone:** 805/772-2806

Seafood

Location: Main St, just w on Harbor Dr. 899 Embarcadero 93442. **Hours:** Open 2/1-11/30 & 12/26-1/31; 11 am-8:30 pm; Sat & Sun-9:30 pm 6/1-9/15. **Reservations:** suggested. **Features:** On the waterfront overlooking the bay, the long-established, family-operated restaurant serves a variety of seafood, beef and chicken dishes. It may close earlier in the off-season. Casual dress; beer & wine only. **Parking:** on-site. **Cards:** AX, DS, MC, VI.

GREAT AMERICAN FISH COMPANY **Lunch:** $6-$12 **Dinner:** $15-$23 **Phone:** 805/772-4407

Seafood

Location: Main St, just w on Harbor Dr. 1185 Embarcadero 93442. **Hours:** 11 am-10 pm; to 9 pm 11/1-4/1. Closed: 11/25. **Features:** The restaurant is located on the waterfront, with a view of Morro Rock from any seat in the house. As you dine, you may be able to enjoy the antics of local sea otters. Although the restaurant specializes in mesquite-grilled seafood, there is also a good selection of beef and poultry on the menu. Casual dress; cocktails. **Parking:** on-site. **Cards:** AX, DS, MC, VI.

HARADA JAPANESE RESTAURANT & SUSHI BAR **Lunch:** $10-$15 **Dinner:** $19-$30 **Phone:** 805/772-1410

Japanese

Location: Main St, just w on Harbor Dr. 630 Embarcadero 93442. **Hours:** 11:30 am-2 & 5-10 pm. **Reservations:** suggested. **Features:** Attractive Japanese decor adds character to the cozy restaurant, which occupies the upper level and overlooks the bay. Casual dress; beer & wine only. **Parking:** on-site. **Cards:** AX, MC, VI.

HARBOR HUT RESTAURANT **Lunch:** $8-$16 **Dinner:** $10-$24 **Phone:** 805/772-2255

Seafood

Location: Main St, just w on Harbor Dr. 1205 Embarcadero 93442. **Hours:** 11 am-10 pm; to 9 pm 11/1-4/1. **Reservations:** suggested. **Features:** The restarant is a triangular-shaped, weathered wood building facing the bay with Polynesian decor including bamboo and tiki wood furnishings. The menu includes fresh seafood, salads and very good clam chowder. Casual dress; cocktails. **Parking:** on-site. **Cards:** AX, DS, MC, VI.

WINDOWS ON THE WATER — Dinner: $14-$21 — Phone: 805/772-0677

Continental

Location: SR 1, exit Main St southbound, 0.5 mi s to Harbor Blvd, 0.3 mi w, then just s; exit Morro Bay Blvd northbound, just w, 0.7 mi w on Harbor Blvd, then just s. 699 Embarcadero 93442. **Hours:** 5 pm-9 pm, Sat-10 pm. Closed: 1/1, 12/25. **Reservations:** suggested. **Features:** On the second floor of Marina Square, the restaurant features picture windows that afford views of the bay and Morro Rock. The menu lists seafood, pasta, pheasant, steak and lamb choices. Casual dress; cocktails. **Parking:** street. **Cards:** AX, DC, DS, MC, VI.

MOUNTAIN VIEW pop. 70,708

WHERE TO STAY

BEST WESTERN MOUNTAIN VIEW INN — *Book at aaa.com* — **Phone:** (650)962-9912

Motel

All Year [ECP] — 1P: $89-$129 — 2P: $99-$139 — XP: $10 — F12

Location: US 101, exit Rengstorff Rd, 1.3 mi s. 2300 El Camino Real W 94040. Fax: 650/962-9011. **Facility:** 71 one-bedroom standard units. 2-3 stories (no elevator), exterior corridors. *Bath:* combo or shower only. **Parking:** on-site. **Amenities:** voice mail, irons, hair dryers. **Pool(s):** outdoor. **Leisure Activities:** whirlpool, exercise room. **Guest Services:** valet and coin laundry. **Business Services:** meeting rooms, business center. **Cards:** AX, CB, DC, DS, JC, MC, VI. **Special Amenities: free expanded continental breakfast and free local telephone calls.**

SOME UNITS

COMFORT INN-MOUNTAIN VIEW — *Book at aaa.com* — **Phone:** (650)967-7888

Motel

All Year [CP] — 1P: $99-$119 — 2P: $99-$129 — XP: $10 — F12

Location: US 101, exit Shoreline Blvd, 2 mi to SR 82, just n. 1561 W El Camino Real 94040. Fax: 650/967-3579. **Facility:** 44 one-bedroom standard units, some with whirlpools. 3 stories, interior corridors. **Parking:** on-site. **Terms:** cancellation fee imposed. **Amenities:** voice mail, irons, hair dryers. **Pool(s):** small outdoor. **Leisure Activities:** whirlpool. **Guest Services:** coin laundry. **Cards:** AX, CB, DC, DS, JC, MC, VI. **Special Amenities: free continental breakfast and free newspaper.**

SOME UNITS

COUNTY INN — *Book at aaa.com* — **Phone:** (650)961-1131

Motel

All Year — 1P: $79-$129 — 2P: $89-$139 — XP: $10 — F10

Location: US 101, exit Moffett Blvd, just s. Located in a quiet, residential area. 850 Leong Dr 94043. Fax: 650/965-9099. **Facility:** 53 units. 52 one-bedroom standard units, some with whirlpools. 1 two-bedroom suite ($119-$149) with kitchen and whirlpool. 2 stories, exterior corridors. **Parking:** on-site. **Terms:** [BP] meal plan available, package plans. **Amenities:** video library, dual phone lines, voice mail, irons, hair dryers. *Some:* safes, honor bars. **Pool(s):** heated outdoor. **Leisure Activities:** exercise room. **Cards:** AX, DC, DS, MC, VI.

SOME UNITS

CRESTVIEW HOTEL — *Book at aaa.com* — **Phone:** (650)966-8848

Motel

All Year [BP] — 2P: $139-$149 — XP: $10 — F18

Location: SR 82, 0.5 mi e of SR 85. 901 E El Camino Real 94040. Fax: 650/966-8884. **Facility:** 66 units. 58 one-bedroom standard units with efficiencies, some with whirlpools. 8 one-bedroom suites with efficiencies and whirlpools. 3 stories, interior corridors. **Parking:** on-site. **Terms:** cancellation fee imposed, weekly rates available. **Amenities:** video games, CD players, voice mail, irons, hair dryers. **Guest Services:** valet and coin laundry. **Cards:** AX, CB, DC, DS, JC, MC, VI. **Special Amenities: free continental breakfast and free newspaper.**

SOME UNITS

HILTON GARDEN INN — *Book at aaa.com* — **Phone:** (650)964-1700

Small-scale Hotel

All Year — 1P: $89-$199 — 2P: $89-$199 — XP: $10 — F

Location: US 101, exit SR 85 W, s on SR 82, U-turn. 840 E El Camino Real 94040. Fax: 650/964-7900. **Facility:** 160 one-bedroom standard units. 4 stories, interior corridors. *Bath:* combo or shower only. **Parking:** on-site. **Terms:** cancellation fee imposed, [AP] meal plan available. **Amenities:** video games, high-speed Internet, dual phone lines, voice mail, irons, hair dryers. **Pool(s):** heated outdoor. **Leisure Activities:** whirlpool, exercise room. **Guest Services:** gift shop, coin laundry. **Business Services:** meeting rooms, business center. **Cards:** AX, CB, DC, DS, JC, MC, VI.

SOME UNITS

HOLIDAY INN EXPRESS HOTEL & SUITES *Book at aaa.com* **Phone:** (650)967-6957

AAA SAVE

Motel

All Year [ECP]	1P: $109-$189	2P: $109-$189	XP: $10	F16

Location: US 101, exit SR 237 northbound, 3 mi w, just n on SR 82; exit SR 85 southbound, 0.5 mi s, exit Grant Rd, just n on SR 82. 93 El Camino Real W 94040. Fax: 650/967-4834. **Facility:** 58 units. 53 one-bedroom standard units, some with efficiencies or kitchens. 5 one-bedroom suites ($135-$199). 2 stories, exterior corridors. **Parking:** on-site. **Terms:** package plans, 10% service charge. **Amenities:** DVD players, CD players, high-speed Internet, dual phone lines, voice mail, irons, hair dryers. *Some:* safes. **Pool(s):** small heated outdoor. **Leisure Activities:** whirlpool, exercise room. **Guest Services:** valet and coin laundry. **Cards:** AX, CB, DC, DS, JC, MC, VI. **Special Amenities: free local telephone calls and free newspaper.** *(See color ad p 260 & p 504)*

SOME UNITS

HOLIDAY INN EXPRESS HOTEL & SUITES *Book at aaa.com* **Phone:** (650)559-9115

AAA SAVE

Motel

2/1-10/31 [ECP]	1P: $159	2P: $159	XP: $10	F
11/1-1/31 [ECP]	1P: $139	2P: $139	XP: $10	F

Location: US 101, exit San Antonio W, 0.5 mi n on SR 82. 2700 W El Camino Real 94040. Fax: 650/559-9045. **Facility:** 98 units. 82 one-bedroom standard units, some with whirlpools. 16 one-bedroom suites ($179-$199). 2-3 stories, interior corridors. *Bath:* combo or shower only. **Parking:** on-site. **Terms:** [CP] meal plan available. **Amenities:** high-speed Internet, dual phone lines, voice mail, irons, hair dryers. **Pool(s):** heated outdoor. **Leisure Activities:** whirlpool, exercise room. **Guest Services:** valet and coin laundry. **Cards:** AX, CB, DC, DS, JC, MC, VI. **Special Amenities: free continental breakfast and free local telephone calls.**

SOME UNITS

HOMESTEAD STUDIO SUITES HOTEL-MOUNTAIN VIEW/SILICON VALLEY *Book at aaa.com* **Phone:** (650)962-1500

Motel

All Year	1P: $95-$115	2P: $100-$120	XP: $5	F17

Location: On SR 82, just w of SR 85. 190 E El Camino Real 94040. Fax: 650/962-1977. **Facility:** 132 one-bedroom standard units with efficiencies. 2 stories, exterior corridors. *Bath:* combo or shower only. **Parking:** on-site. **Terms:** weekly rates available, pets ($150 extra charge). **Amenities:** dual phone lines, voice mail, irons, hair dryers. **Guest Services:** coin laundry. **Cards:** AX, CB, DC, DS, JC, MC, VI.

SOME UNITS

FEE FEE FEE

HOTEL AVANTE *Book at aaa.com* **Phone:** (650)940-1000

Small-scale Hotel

1/1-1/31 [ECP]	1P: $230	2P: $230	XP: $20
2/1-12/31 [ECP]	1P: $225	2P: $225	XP: $20

Location: US 101, exit at SR 85 S, exit at El Camino Real, then just e. 860 E El Camino Real 94040. Fax: 650/968-7870. **Facility:** 91 one-bedroom standard units. 4 stories, interior corridors. **Parking:** on-site. **Terms:** package plans. **Amenities:** CD players, high-speed Internet, dual phone lines, voice mail, honor bars, irons, hair dryers. **Pool(s):** outdoor. **Leisure Activities:** whirlpool, exercise room. **Guest Services:** complimentary evening beverages. **Business Services:** meeting rooms, business center. **Cards:** AX, DC, DS, MC, VI.

QUALITY INN & SUITES *Book at aaa.com* **Phone:** (650)934-0155

AAA SAVE

Small-scale Hotel

All Year 1P: $79-$129 2P: $79-$129 XP: $10 F17

Location: US 101, exit Moffett Blvd. 5 Fairchild Dr 94043. Fax: 650/968-9562. **Facility:** 70 units. 43 one-bedroom standard units. 27 one-bedroom suites. 3 stories, interior corridors. **Parking:** on-site. **Terms:** [BP] meal plan available. **Amenities:** high-speed Internet, dual phone lines, voice mail, irons, hair dryers. **Leisure Activities:** exercise room. **Guest Services:** coin laundry. **Business Services:** meeting rooms, business center. **Cards:** AX, CB, DC, DS, JC, MC, VI. **Special Amenities: free continental breakfast and free local telephone calls.** *(See color ad p 505)*

SOME UNITS

DATA PORT / /

RAMADA LIMITED *Book at aaa.com* **Phone:** (650)967-6856

AAA SAVE

Motel

All Year [ECP] 1P: $80-$110 2P: $80-$110 XP: $5 F17

Location: US 101, exit Ellis St, 0.5 mi n. 55 Fairchild Dr 94043. Fax: 650/964-4542. **Facility:** 50 one-bedroom standard units, some with whirlpools. 2 stories, exterior corridors. **Parking:** on-site. **Terms:** 3 day cancellation notice. **Amenities:** high-speed Internet, voice mail, irons, hair dryers. **Pool(s):** heated outdoor. **Leisure Activities:** whirlpool, exercise room. **Guest Services:** coin laundry. **Business Services:** meeting rooms. **Cards:** AX, CB, DC, DS, MC, VI. **Special Amenities: free expanded continental breakfast and free local telephone calls.**

SOME UNITS

DATA PORT / VCR /

SAN ANTONIO INN **Phone:** 650/948-1036

AAA SAVE

Motel

All Year 1P: $49-$129 2P: $59-$139

Location: US 101, exit San Antonio Rd, just n. 2650 El Camino Real 94040. Fax: 650/948-7214. **Facility:** 58 one-bedroom standard units. 2 stories, exterior corridors. *Bath:* combo or shower only. **Parking:** on-site. **Terms:** [CP] meal plan available. **Amenities:** voice mail, hair dryers. **Pool(s):** outdoor. **Guest Services:** coin laundry. **Business Services:** meeting rooms. **Cards:** AX, CB, DC, JC, MC, VI. **Special Amenities: free continental breakfast and free local telephone calls.**

SOME UNITS

VCR DATA PORT / /

SUPER 8 MOTEL *Book at aaa.com* **Phone:** (650)969-9641

AAA SAVE

Motel

6/11-8/31 [CP]	1P: $80-$90	2P: $80-$90	XP: $10	F12
2/1-6/10 [CP]	1P: $75-$85	2P: $75-$85	XP: $10	F12
9/1-1/31 [CP]	1P: $70-$80	2P: $70-$80	XP: $10	F12

Location: US 101, exit Shoreline Blvd, 2 mi to SR 82, just n. 1665 El Camino Real 94040. Fax: 650/938-3791. **Facility:** 31 one-bedroom standard units. 2 stories, exterior corridors. **Parking:** on-site. **Terms:** cancellation fee imposed. **Amenities:** voice mail, irons, hair dryers. **Leisure Activities:** whirlpool. **Cards:** AX, DC, DS, MC, VI. **Special Amenities: free continental breakfast.**

SOME UNITS

DATA PORT / /

TROPICANA LODGE **Phone:** (650)961-0220

AAA SAVE

Motel

All Year 1P: $70-$100 2P: $75-$105 XP: $5 F12

Location: US 101, exit Shoreline Blvd, 2 mi to SR 82, just n. 1720 El Camino Real W 94040. Fax: 650/961-1471. **Facility:** 59 one-bedroom standard units. 2 stories, interior/exterior corridors. *Bath:* combo or shower only. **Parking:** on-site. **Terms:** [CP] meal plan available, pets (with prior approval). **Amenities:** hair dryers. *Some:* irons. **Pool(s):** outdoor. **Leisure Activities:** sauna. **Cards:** AX, CB, DC, DS, JC, MC, VI. **Special Amenities: free continental breakfast and free local telephone calls.** *(See color ad p 505)*

SOME UNITS

DATA PORT / /

WHERE TO DINE

ZUCCA RISTORANTE **Lunch:** $8-$16 **Dinner:** $11-$21 **Phone:** 650/864-9940

Mediterranean

Location: US 101, exit Moffett Blvd, 1 mi w. 186 Castro St 94041. **Hours:** 11:30 am-2:30 & 5-11 pm. Closed major holidays. **Reservations:** suggested. **Features:** Many foods and flavors infuse the chef's flair-filled preparations, making the restaurant popular with the locals. The martinis are worth noting. Dressy casual; cocktails. **Parking:** on-site. **Cards:** AX, MC, VI.

MOUNT SHASTA pop. 3,621

WHERE TO STAY

A-1 CHOICE INN **Phone:** 530/926-4811

AAA SAVE

Motel

All Year 1P: $49-$79 2P: $59-$89 XP: $10

Location: I-5, exit McCloud/SR 89, just n at first left, then 1 mi. 1340 S Mt Shasta Blvd 96067. Fax: 530/926-4811. **Facility:** 29 one-bedroom standard units. 2 stories (no elevator), exterior corridors. *Bath:* combo or shower only. **Parking:** on-site. **Terms:** 2-4 night minimum stay - seasonal weekends, age restrictions may apply, 3 day cancellation notice-fee imposed, pets ($10 fee, in designated units). **Amenities:** hair dryers. **Pool(s):** small heated outdoor. **Leisure Activities:** whirlpool. **Cards:** AX, CB, DC, DS, JC, MC, VI.

SOME UNITS

FEE CTV / VCR FEE /

BEST WESTERN TREE HOUSE MOTOR INN Book at aaa.com **Phone:** 530/926-3101

Motel

All Year [BP] 1P: $91-$159 2P: $91-$159 XP: $6 F12

Location: I-5, exit Central Mt Shasta (2nd exit), just e. 111 Morgan Way 96067. Fax: 530/926-3542. **Facility:** 98 units. 92 one- and 4 two-bedroom standard units. 2 one-bedroom suites. 2-3 stories, interior/exterior corridors. *Bath:* combo or shower only. **Parking:** on-site. **Terms:** age restrictions may apply, pets ($10 extra charge, in limited units). **Amenities:** irons, hair dryers. **Dining:** Tree House Restaurant, see separate listing. **Pool(s):** indoor, heated indoor. **Leisure Activities:** whirlpool. **Business Services:** meeting rooms. **Cards:** AX, CB, DC, DS, MC, VI. **Special Amenities: free full breakfast and free local telephone calls.** *(See ad below)*

SOME UNITS

FEE

ECONO LODGE *Book at aaa.com* **Phone:** (530)926-3145

SAVE

Motel

4/1-9/1	1P: $55-$75	2P: $65-$85
2/1-3/31 & 9/2-1/31	1P: $45-$75	2P: $55-$85

Location: I-5, exit Central, 0.5 mi e, then 0.5 mi s. 908 S Mt Shasta Blvd 96067. Fax: 530/926-5897. **Facility:** 20 units. 15 one- and 5 two-bedroom standard units, some with kitchens. 2 stories (no elevator), exterior corridors. *Bath:* combo or shower only. **Parking:** on-site. **Terms:** age restrictions may apply, cancellation fee imposed, pets ($20 deposit). **Amenities:** hair dryers. *Some:* irons. **Pool(s):** heated outdoor. **Leisure Activities:** whirlpool. **Cards:** AX, DS, MC, VI. **Special Amenities: free local telephone calls and early check-in/late check-out.**

SOME UNITS

FEE

EVERGREEN LODGE **Phone:** 530/926-2143

SAVE

Motel

All Year	1P: $49-$59	2P: $59-$79	XP: $10	D6

Location: I-5, exit McCloud/SR 89, just n at first left, then 1 mi. 1312 S Mt Shasta Blvd 96067. Fax: 530/926-2143. **Facility:** 20 units. 14 one- and 4 two-bedroom standard units, some with kitchens (no utensils). 2 one-bedroom suites ($89-$125). 1 story, exterior corridors. **Parking:** on-site. **Terms:** age restrictions may apply, 3 day cancellation notice-fee imposed, pets ($10 extra charge). **Pool(s):** small heated outdoor. **Leisure Activities:** whirlpool. **Cards:** AX, CB, DC, DS, JC, MC, VI. **Special Amenities: free room upgrade and preferred room (each subject to availability with advanced reservations).**

SOME UNITS

FEE

MOUNT SHASTA RESORT **Phone:** (530)926-3030

Resort
Small-scale Hotel

5/16-10/31	1P: $112-$127	2P: $112-$127		
11/1-1/31	1P: $109-$127	2P: $109-$127		
2/1-5/15	1P: $99-$112	2P: $99-$112	XP: $5	F12

Location: I-5, exit Central Mt Shasta, just w, s on Old Stage Rd to W A Barr Rd, then just n. 1000 Siskiyou Lake Blvd 96067. Fax: 530/926-0333. **Facility:** The resort is not conducive to boredom, as activities are plentiful, including restaurants, golf, swimming and tennis. 65 units. 15 one-bedroom standard units. 50 cottages ($144-$289). Exterior corridors. *Bath:* combo or shower only. **Parking:** on-site. **Terms:** office hours 6 am-2 am, check-in 4 pm, 2-3 night minimum stay - seasonal weekends, age restrictions may apply, 3 day cancellation notice-fee imposed, weekly rates available, package plans - seasonal. **Amenities:** *Some:* irons, hair dryers. **Leisure Activities:** whirlpool, boating, fishing, golf-18 holes, 4 tennis courts, cross country skiing, bicycles, hiking trails. **Guest Services:** gift shop. **Business Services:** meeting rooms, fax. **Cards:** AX, CB, DC, DS, MC, VI.

SOME UNITS

SWISS HOLIDAY LODGE **Phone:** (530)926-3446

SAVE

Motel

All Year	1P: $35-$65	2P: $48-$75	XP: $5	F5

Location: I-5, exit McCloud/SR 89, just n at first left. 2400 S Mt Shasta Blvd 96067 (PO Box 335). Fax: 530/926-3091. **Facility:** 21 units. 20 one-bedroom standard units. 1 one-bedroom suite with kitchen. 2 stories (no elevator), exterior corridors. *Bath:* shower only. **Parking:** on-site. **Terms:** age restrictions may apply, cancellation fee imposed, weekly rates available, [CP] meal plan available, small pets only ($5 extra charge). **Amenities:** *Some:* irons, hair dryers. **Pool(s):** heated outdoor. **Leisure Activities:** whirlpool. **Cards:** AX, DC, DS, MC, VI. **Special Amenities: free continental breakfast and free local telephone calls.**

SOME UNITS

FEE FEE FEE

WHERE TO DINE

LILY'S **Lunch:** $8-$11 **Dinner:** $10-$25 **Phone:** 530/926-3372

California

Location: I-5, exit Central, 0.5 mi e, then 0.3 mi s. 1013 S Mt Shasta Blvd 96067. **Hours:** 8 am-9 pm; 7 am-10 pm in summer. Closed: 12/25. **Reservations:** suggested. **Features:** Pleasant surroundings and a good selection of seafood, pasta, Mexican and vegetarian specialties make the restaurant a popular stop. Casual dress; cocktails. **Parking:** on-site. **Cards:** AX, DS, MC, VI.

MICHAEL'S RESTAURANT **Lunch:** $6-$12 **Dinner:** $12-$25 **Phone:** 530/926-5288

Regional California

Location: I-5, exit Central, 0.3 mi e. 313 N Mt Shasta Blvd 96067. **Hours:** 11 am-2:30 & 5-9 pm, Sat noon-9 pm. Closed major holidays; also Sun & Mon. **Reservations:** suggested. **Features:** The varied menu comprises homemade soups, steaks, salads. The restaurant is on the town's main street. Casual dress; beer & wine only. **Parking:** street. **Cards:** AX, DS, MC, VI.

SERGE'S RESTAURANT **Dinner:** $13-$19 **Phone:** 530/926-1276

French

Location: I-5, exit Central E, 0.5 mi to Chestnut, then just n. 531 Chestnut St 96067. **Hours:** 5 pm-9 pm, Fri & Sat-9:30 pm. Closed: Mon & Tues. **Reservations:** suggested. **Features:** Quality ingredients go into classical French dishes, including some low-fat selections. From the sun deck, guests are treated to a lovely view of Mount Shasta. Casual dress; beer & wine only. **Parking:** street. **Cards:** AX, MC, VI.

TREE HOUSE RESTAURANT **Dinner:** $10-$25 **Phone:** 530/926-3101

American

Location: I-5, exit Central Mt Shasta (2nd exit), just e; in Best Western Tree House Motor Inn. 111 Morgan Way 96067. **Hours:** 6:30 am-10:30 & 4:30-9:30 pm. **Reservations:** suggested. **Features:** Adding to the charmingly rustic decor is a huge fireplace, open to both the restaurant and lobby. All seats afford a view of spectacular Mount Shasta. Diners can savor pasta, steak or prime rib by candlelight. Casual dress; cocktails. **Parking:** on-site. **Cards:** AX, DS, MC, VI.

MURPHYS pop. 2,061

WHERE TO STAY

DUNBAR HOUSE 1880

Phone: (209)728-2897

Bed & Breakfast

All Year [BP] 2P: $190-$245

Location: 9 mi n of jct SR 49 and 4; exit Main St Murphys. 271 Jones St 95247. Fax: 209/728-1451. **Facility:** A large porch overlooks the attractive gardens at this Italianate-style home built in 1880. Smoke free premises. 5 one-bedroom standard units. 2 stories (no elevator), interior corridors. **Parking:** on-site. **Terms:** office hours 7 am-9 pm, 2 night minimum stay - weekends, 10 day cancellation notice-fee imposed, package plans. **Amenities:** video library, CD players, irons, hair dryers. **Guest Services:** complimentary evening beverages. **Cards:** AX, MC, VI. **Special Amenities: free local telephone calls and preferred room (subject to availability with advanced reservations).**

MURPHYS HISTORIC HOTEL & LODGE

Phone: 209/728-3444

Motel

All Year 2P: $75-$100 XP: $10 F18

Location: Center. 457 Main St 95247. Fax: 209/728-1590. **Facility:** 29 one-bedroom standard units. 1-2 stories, interior/exterior corridors. *Bath:* some shower only. **Parking:** on-site. **Terms:** cancellation fee imposed. **Amenities:** *Some:* irons, hair dryers. **Business Services:** meeting rooms. **Cards:** AX, DC, MC, VI.

SOME UNITS

MURPHYS INN MOTEL

Phone: (209)728-1818

Motel

5/1-9/30	1P: $85-$105	2P: $85-$105	XP: $10	F12
2/1-4/30 & 10/1-1/31	1P: $75-$105	2P: $75-$105	XP: $10	F12

Location: Jct SR 4 and Main St. 76 Main St 95247 (PO Box 882). Fax: 209/728-2944. **Facility:** Smoke free premises. 37 units. 36 one-bedroom standard units. 1 one-bedroom suite ($115-$220). 2 stories (no elevator), interior corridors. **Parking:** on-site. **Terms:** cancellation fee imposed. **Amenities:** video library (fee), irons, hair dryers. **Pool(s):** outdoor. **Leisure Activities:** exercise room. **Guest Services:** coin laundry. **Business Services:** PC. **Cards:** AX, DS, MC, VI. *(See color ad p 266)*

SOME UNITS

MURPHYS SUITES

Phone: (209)728-2121

Small-scale Hotel

5/1-9/30	1P: $119-$159	2P: $119-$159	XP: $10	F12
2/1-4/30 & 10/1-1/31	1P: $109-$159	2P: $109-$159	XP: $10	F12

Location: SR 4. 134 Hwy 4 95247 (PO Box 882). Fax: 209/736-0269. **Facility:** 70 units. 16 one-bedroom standard units. 54 one-bedroom suites ($169-$220). 2 stories, interior corridors. **Parking:** on-site. **Terms:** cancellation fee imposed. **Amenities:** video library, irons, hair dryers. **Pool(s):** outdoor. **Leisure Activities:** sauna, whirlpool, exercise room. **Guest Services:** coin laundry. **Business Services:** conference facilities, business center. **Cards:** AX, DS, MC, VI. **Special Amenities: free continental breakfast.** *(See color ad p 266)*

VICTORIA INN

Phone: 209/728-8933

Bed & Breakfast

All Year 1P: $50 2P: $60 XP: $10 F4

Location: SR 49 "to Angels Camp," e to SR 4. 402 Main St 95247. Fax: 209/728-8914. **Facility:** Smoke free premises. 14 units. 12 one-bedroom standard units, some with whirlpools. 2 cottages, some with whirlpools. 2 stories (no elevator), interior corridors. *Bath:* combo or shower only. **Parking:** on-site. **Terms:** office hours 8:30 am-8:30 pm, 3 day cancellation notice. **Amenities:** CD players, hair dryers. *Some:* irons. **Guest Services:** gift shop, complimentary evening beverages. **Cards:** AX, MC, VI. **Special Amenities: free expanded continental breakfast and free local telephone calls.**

SOME UNITS

WHERE TO DINE

AUBERGE 1899 RESTAURANT

Dinner: $14-$32 **Phone:** 209/728-1899

French

Location: SR 4, just e. 498 Main St 95247. **Hours:** 5 pm-close. Closed: 1/1, 12/25; also Mon & Tues. **Reservations:** suggested. **Features:** Wonderful French dining with fine wines. Enjoy dry-aged meats, the freshest seafood, the finest hand-crafted sauces, Raclette and fondue (in the winter months). Everything is made from scratch and all natural. Casual dress; beer & wine only. **Parking:** street. **Cards:** DS, MC, VI.

MYERS FLAT

WHERE TO STAY

MYERS INN

Phone: (707)943-3259

Bed & Breakfast

All Year [ECP] 1P: $125-$195 2P: $125-$195

Location: W of and adjacent to US 101. 12913 Avenue of the Giants 95554 (PO Box 173). Fax: 707/943-1800. **Facility:** Smoke free premises. 11 units. 10 one-bedroom standard units. 1 cottage. 2 stories (no elevator), interior corridors. **Parking:** on-site. **Terms:** office hours 9 am-9 pm, check-in 4 pm, 7 day cancellation notice. **Amenities:** *Some:* irons. **Cards:** AX, MC, VI. **Special Amenities: free continental breakfast and free room upgrade (subject to availability with advanced reservations).**

NAPA *—See Wine Country p. 789.*

NEVADA CITY pop. 3,001

WHERE TO STAY

DEER CREEK INN — Historic Bed & Breakfast — **Phone:** (530)265-0363

All Year 2P: $115-$190 XP: $20

Location: In the historic district. 116 Nevada St 95959. Fax: 530/265-0980. **Facility:** A creek runs along the manicured grounds of this restored 1860s Queen Anne Victorian. 5 one-bedroom standard units. 3 stories (no elevator), interior corridors. *Bath:* combo or shower only. **Parking:** on-site. **Terms:** 2 night minimum stay - weekends, 10 day cancellation notice-fee imposed, [BP] meal plan available. **Cards:** AX, MC, VI.

SOME UNITS

EMMA NEVADA HOUSE Book at aaa.com — SAVE — Historic Bed & Breakfast — **Phone:** 530/265-4415

All Year [BP] 1P: $130-$200 2P: $130-$200 XP: $40

Location: In the historic district. Located in a quiet, residential area. 528 E Broad St 95959. Fax: 530/265-4416. **Facility:** A fireplace warms the living room of this restored 1856 house; two guest rooms include a fireplace and a whirlpool. 6 one-bedroom standard units, some with whirlpools. 2 stories, interior corridors. *Bath:* combo or shower only. **Parking:** on-site. **Terms:** 2 night minimum stay - weekends, 7 day cancellation notice. **Cards:** AX, DS, MC, VI. **Special Amenities: free local telephone calls.**

SOME UNITS

GRANDMERE'S INN — Historic Bed & Breakfast — **Phone:** (530)265-4660

All Year 1P: $156-$220 2P: $156-$220 XP: $20

Location: In the historic district. 449 Broad St 95959. Fax: 530/265-4561. **Facility:** Built in 1856, the inn is Colonial Revival in style and offers two rooms with private entrances; the historic downtown is within walking distance. 6 one-bedroom standard units. 2 stories, interior corridors. *Bath:* combo or shower only. **Parking:** on-site. **Terms:** 2 night minimum stay - weekends 5/1-12/31, 7 day cancellation notice-fee imposed, package plans - seasonal & weekends. **Cards:** AX, DS, MC, VI.

SOME UNITS

NEVADA CITY INN Book at aaa.com — SAVE — Motel — **Phone:** (530)265-2253

All Year [ECP] 1P: $59-$139 2P: $59-$139 XP: $20 F18

Location: SR 20 and 49, exit Gold Flat/Ridge Rd, 0.3 mi w, then 0.3 mi n. 760 Zion St 95959. Fax: 530/265-3310. **Facility:** 27 units. 20 one-bedroom standard units. 7 cottages ($109-$239). 2 stories, exterior corridors. *Bath:* combo or shower only. **Parking:** on-site. **Terms:** 5 day cancellation notice, small pets only ($10 fee). **Cards:** AX, CB, DC, DS, JC, MC, VI. **Special Amenities: free continental breakfast and free local telephone calls.** *(See color ad p 346)*

SOME UNITS

FEE

NORTHERN QUEEN INN — Motel — **Phone:** 530/265-5824

All Year 1P: $80-$125 2P: $80-$125 XP: $5 F5

Location: SR 20 and 49, exit Sacramento St, 0.5 mi w. 400 Railroad Ave 95959. Fax: 530/265-3720. **Facility:** 86 units. 70 one-bedroom standard units. 8 cabins ($125) and 8 cottages ($110). 2 stories, exterior corridors. *Bath:* combo or shower only. **Parking:** on-site. **Terms:** cancellation fee imposed. **Amenities:** voice mail. **Pool(s):** heated outdoor. **Leisure Activities:** whirlpool. **Business Services:** meeting rooms. **Cards:** AX, DC, DS, MC, VI.

SOME UNITS

PIETY HILL COTTAGES — Bed & Breakfast — **Phone:** (530)265-2245

All Year [BP] 1P: $90-$145 2P: $95-$165 XP: $20 F3

Location: SR 20 and 49, exit Sacramento St. 523 Sacramento St 95959. Fax: 530/265-6528. **Facility:** 9 cottages. 1 story, exterior corridors. *Bath:* combo or shower only. **Parking:** on-site. **Terms:** 2 night minimum stay - weekends, 7 day cancellation notice, weekly rates available, [CP] & [ECP] meal plans available. **Leisure Activities:** whirlpool. **Cards:** AX, MC, VI.

SOME UNITS

NEWARK pop. 42,471

WHERE TO STAY

COURTYARD BY MARRIOTT NEWARK/SILICON VALLEY Book at aaa.com — Small-scale Hotel — **Phone:** (510)792-5200

All Year 1P: $69-$119 2P: $69-$119

Location: SR 84, exit Newark Blvd, just s. 34905 Newark Blvd 94560. Fax: 510/792-5255. **Facility:** 181 units. 176 one-bedroom standard units, some with whirlpools. 5 one-bedroom suites ($129-$149). 6 stories, interior corridors. *Bath:* combo or shower only. **Parking:** on-site. **Terms:** cancellation fee imposed, package plans - weekends. **Amenities:** high-speed Internet (fee), dual phone lines, voice mail, irons, hair dryers. **Pool(s):** heated outdoor. **Leisure Activities:** whirlpool, exercise room. **Guest Services:** valet and coin laundry, area transportation. **Business Services:** meeting rooms. **Cards:** AX, CB, DC, DS, MC, VI.

SOME UNITS

HILTON HOTEL Book at aaa.com — SAVE — Large-scale Hotel — **Phone:** (510)490-8390

All Year 1P: $69-$169 2P: $69-$169 XP: $20 F

Location: I-880, exit Stevenson Blvd, just w. 39900 Balentine Dr 94560. Fax: 510/651-7828. **Facility:** 313 one-bedroom standard units. 2-7 stories, interior corridors. **Parking:** on-site. **Terms:** cancellation fee imposed, [BP] meal plan available, package plans - seasonal & weekends. **Amenities:** high-speed Internet (fee), voice mail, irons, hair dryers. **Dining:** 6 am-10 pm, cocktails. **Pool(s):** outdoor. **Leisure Activities:** sauna, whirlpool, exercise room. **Guest Services:** gift shop, valet laundry. **Business Services:** conference facilities. **Cards:** AX, DC, DS, MC, VI. **Special Amenities: free newspaper and early check-in/late check-out.** *(See color ad p 690)*

SOME UNITS

FEE FEE

HOLIDAY INN EXPRESS HOTEL & SUITES *Book at aaa.com* **Phone:** (510)795-7995

Small-scale Hotel

All Year [ECP] 1P: $79-$109 2P: $79-$109 XP: $10 F18

Location: I-880, exit Mowry Ave, 0.5 mi w. 5977 Mowry Ave 94560. Fax: 510/795-0295. **Facility:** 101 units. 69 one-bedroom standard units. 32 one-bedroom suites ($109-$124). 4 stories, interior corridors. **Parking:** on-site. **Amenities:** video games (fee), high-speed Internet, dual phone lines, voice mail, irons, hair dryers. **Pool(s):** outdoor. **Business Services:** meeting rooms. **Cards:** AX, CB, DC, DS, JC, MC, VI. **Special Amenities: free expanded continental breakfast and free newspaper.** *(See ad below & color ad p 260)*

SOME UNITS

HOMEWOOD SUITES BY HILTON *Book at aaa.com* **Phone:** (510)791-7700

Small-scale Hotel

All Year 1P: $129 2P: $129

Location: I-880, exit Mowry Ave, w to Cedar Blvd, then 0.3 mi s. 39270 Cedar Blvd 94560. Fax: 510/791-8200. **Facility:** 192 units. 161 one- and 31 two-bedroom standard units, some with kitchens. 4 stories, interior corridors. *Bath:* combo or shower only. **Parking:** on-site. **Terms:** cancellation fee imposed, [BP] meal plan available, pets ($150 extra charge). **Amenities:** video games (fee), dual phone lines, voice mail, irons, hair dryers. **Pool(s):** heated outdoor. **Leisure Activities:** whirlpool, exercise room, sports court. **Guest Services:** complimentary evening beverages: Mon-Thurs, valet and coin laundry. **Business Services:** meeting rooms, business center. **Cards:** AX, CB, DC, DS, MC.

SOME UNITS

FEE

RESIDENCE INN BY MARRIOTT NEWARK/SILICON VALLEY *Book at aaa.com* **Phone:** (510)739-6000

Small-scale Hotel

All Year [BP] 1P: $64-$129 2P: $89-$159

Location: SR 84, exit Newark Blvd, just s. 34566 Dumbarton Ct 94560. Fax: 510/739-6606. **Facility:** 168 units. 70 one-bedroom standard units with kitchens. 71 one- and 27 two-bedroom suites with kitchens. 6 stories, interior corridors. *Bath:* combo or shower only. **Parking:** on-site. **Terms:** weekly rates available, pets ($75 fee, $10 extra charge). **Amenities:** video games (fee), high-speed Internet, voice mail, irons, hair dryers. *Some:* dual phone lines. **Pool(s):** heated outdoor. **Leisure Activities:** whirlpool, exercise room. **Guest Services:** complimentary evening beverages, valet and coin laundry, area transportation. **Business Services:** meeting rooms. **Cards:** AX, DC, DS, MC, VI.

SOME UNITS

FEE

TOWNEPLACE SUITES NEWARK *Book at aaa.com* **Phone:** 510/657-4600

Small-scale Hotel

All Year 1P: $89-$119

Location: I-880, exit Mowry Ave, just w to Cedar, then s. 39802 Cedar Blvd 94560. Fax: 510/657-4646. **Facility:** 127 units. 59 one-bedroom standard units with kitchens. 38 one- and 30 two-bedroom suites with kitchens. 4 stories, interior corridors. *Bath:* combo or shower only. **Parking:** on-site. **Terms:** cancellation fee imposed, pets ($75 deposit, $10 extra charge). **Amenities:** dual phone lines, voice mail, irons, hair dryers. **Pool(s):** heated outdoor. **Leisure Activities:** exercise room. **Guest Services:** coin laundry. **Business Services:** business center. **Cards:** AX, DC, DS, MC, VI.

SOME UNITS

FEE

WOODFIN SUITES *Book at aaa.com* **Phone:** (510)795-1200

Motel

All Year [BP] 1P: $89-$129 2P: $89-$129 XP: $10 F

Location: I-880, exit Mowry Ave, just w, 0.3 mi s. 39150 Cedar Blvd 94560. Fax: 510/795-8874. **Facility:** Smoke free premises. 148 units. 132 one- and 16 two-bedroom suites with kitchens. 2 stories, exterior corridors. *Bath:* combo or shower only. **Parking:** on-site. **Terms:** weekly rates available, [CP] & [ECP] meal plans available, pets ($50 fee, $200 deposit). **Amenities:** video library, dual phone lines, voice mail, irons, hair dryers. *Some:* CD players. **Pool(s):** heated outdoor. **Leisure Activities:** whirlpool. **Guest Services:** complimentary evening beverages: Mon-Thurs, coin laundry, area transportation. **Business Services:** meeting rooms, business center. **Cards:** AX, DC, DS, MC, VI.

FEE

NICE
—See Wine Country p. 795.

NIPOMO pop. 12,626

WHERE TO STAY

KALEIDOSCOPE INN & GARDENS B&B

Phone: 805/929-5444

Historic Bed & Breakfast

All Year [BP] 1P: $125 2P: $125 XP: $20 F12

Location: US 101, exit Tefft St, 0.7 mi e, just s on Thompson Rd, then just e. 130 E Dana St 93444. Fax: 805/929-5440. **Facility:** Attractive lawn and garden area. Historical Victorian house built in 1887. Smoke free premises. 4 one-bedroom standard units, some with whirlpools. 2 stories (no elevator), interior/exterior corridors. *Bath:* combo or shower only. **Parking:** on-site. **Terms:** 7 day cancellation notice, pets (in cottage only). **Amenities:** video library, CD players, hair dryers. **Guest Services:** TV in common area. **Cards:** MC, VI.

NOVATO pop. 47,630

WHERE TO STAY

BEST WESTERN NOVATO OAKS INN *Book at aaa.com*

Phone: (415)883-4400

SAVE

Small-scale Hotel

All Year [ECP] 1P: $99-$149 2P: $99-$149 XP: $5 F18

Location: US 101, exit W Alameda del Prado. 215 Alameda del Prado 94949. Fax: 415/883-4128. **Facility:** 105 one-bedroom standard units, some with kitchens and/or whirlpools. 3 stories, interior corridors. **Parking:** on-site. **Amenities:** voice mail, irons, hair dryers. *Some:* high-speed Internet. **Pool(s):** heated outdoor. **Leisure Activities:** whirlpool, exercise room. **Guest Services:** valet laundry, area transportation-restaurants. **Business Services:** meeting rooms, business center. **Cards:** AX, CB, DC, DS, JC, MC, VI. **Special Amenities: free expanded continental breakfast and free newspaper.** *(See color ad p 807)*

SOME UNITS

FEE

COURTYARD BY MARRIOTT *Book at aaa.com*

Phone: (415)883-8950

Small-scale Hotel

5/1-10/31 1P: $119-$139 2P: $119-$139

2/1-4/30 & 11/1-1/31 1P: $89-$119 2P: $89-$119

Location: US 101, exit Hamilton Field, just e. 1400 N Hamilton Pkwy 94949. Fax: 415/883-8960. **Facility:** 136 units. 130 one-bedroom standard units. 6 one-bedroom suites ($119-$189) with whirlpools. 4 stories, interior corridors. **Parking:** on-site. **Terms:** [BP] meal plan available. **Amenities:** dual phone lines, voice mail, irons, hair dryers. **Pool(s):** heated outdoor. **Leisure Activities:** whirlpool, exercise room. **Guest Services:** coin laundry. **Business Services:** meeting rooms. **Cards:** AX, DC, DS, MC, VI.

SOME UNITS

INN MARIN *Book at aaa.com*

Phone: (415)883-5952

SAVE

Motel

All Year 1P: $89-$139 2P: $89-$139 XP: $10 F18

Location: US 101, exit Ignacio Blvd, just w, then just n on Enfrente Rd. 250 Entrada Dr 94949. Fax: 415/883-5058. **Facility:** 70 units. 66 one-bedroom standard units. 4 one-bedroom suites ($119-$179), some with whirlpools. 1 story, exterior corridors. *Bath:* combo or shower only. **Parking:** on-site. **Terms:** [ECP] meal plan available, small pets only ($20 fee). **Amenities:** high-speed Internet (fee), dual phone lines, voice mail, irons, hair dryers. *Some:* DVD players. **Pool(s):** heated outdoor. **Leisure Activities:** whirlpool, exercise room. **Guest Services:** valet and coin laundry. **Business Services:** meeting rooms. **Cards:** AX, DC, DS, MC, VI. **Special Amenities: free continental breakfast and early check-in/late check-out.**

SOME UNITS

FEE FEE FEE

NOVATO DAYS INN *Book at aaa.com*

Phone: (415)897-7111

SAVE

Motel

5/1-10/31 1P: $79-$109 2P: $79-$109 XP: $5 F18

2/1-4/30 & 11/1-1/31 1P: $69-$99 2P: $69-$99 XP: $5 F18

Location: US 101, exit San Marin Dr, 1 mi n. 8141 Redwood Blvd 94945. Fax: 415/897-8367. **Facility:** 57 units. 55 one-bedroom standard units. 2 one-bedroom suites ($125-$175). 2 stories, exterior corridors. **Parking:** on-site. **Terms:** [CP] meal plan available. **Amenities:** safes, irons, hair dryers. **Dining:** 11:30 am-2 & 4:30-9:30 pm, Sun from 4:30 pm, wine/beer only. **Pool(s):** outdoor. **Leisure Activities:** whirlpool, exercise room. **Guest Services:** coin laundry. **Business Services:** meeting rooms. **Cards:** AX, CB, DC, DS, JC, MC, VI. **Special Amenities: free continental breakfast and free newspaper.**

SOME UNITS

NOVATO TRAVELODGE *Book at aaa.com*

Phone: (415)892-7500

SAVE

Motel

All Year [ECP] 1P: $59-$79 2P: $69-$89 XP: $5 F12

Location: US 101, exit San Marin Dr, just w. 7600 Redwood Blvd 94945. Fax: 415/898-0828. **Facility:** 55 units. 53 one-bedroom standard units. 2 one-bedroom suites ($99-$129) with whirlpools. 3 stories, exterior corridors. **Parking:** on-site. **Terms:** small pets only ($10 fee). **Amenities:** irons, hair dryers. **Pool(s):** outdoor. **Leisure Activities:** whirlpool. **Guest Services:** coin laundry. **Cards:** AX, DC, DS, MC, VI. **Special Amenities: free expanded continental breakfast and free local telephone calls.**

SOME UNITS

FEE

OAKDALE pop. 15,503

WHERE TO STAY

BEST WESTERN RAMA INN *Book at aaa.com* **Phone:** (209)845-2500

SAVE Motel

4/1-9/30 [ECP]	1P: $69-$89		XP: $10	F12
2/1-3/31 & 10/1-1/31 [ECP]	1P: $59-$79		XP: $10	F12

Location: 1 mi e jct SR 108 and 120. 1450 East F St 95361. Fax: 209/845-2523. **Facility:** 47 one-bedroom standard units, some with whirlpools. 3 stories, interior corridors. *Bath:* combo or shower only. **Parking:** on-site. **Terms:** cancellation fee imposed, weekly rates available, package plans - seasonal. **Amenities:** voice mail, irons, hair dryers. **Pool(s):** heated indoor. **Leisure Activities:** sauna, whirlpool, exercise room. **Guest Services:** valet laundry. **Business Services:** meeting rooms. **Cards:** AX, DC, DS, JC, MC, VI. **Special Amenities: free expanded continental breakfast.** *(See color ad below)*

SOME UNITS

HOLIDAY INN EXPRESS *Book at aaa.com* **Phone:** (209)847-9121

SAVE Motel

5/1-9/30 [ECP]	1P: $75-$99	2P: $75-$99	XP: $5	F17
2/1-4/30 & 10/1-1/31 [ECP]	1P: $65-$85	2P: $65-$85	XP: $5	F17

Location: 0.8 mi e on SR 108 and 120. 828 East F St 95361. Fax: 209/848-0367. **Facility:** 50 one-bedroom standard units, some with whirlpools. 2 stories (no elevator), interior/exterior corridors. **Parking:** on-site. **Terms:** 3 day cancellation notice. **Amenities:** high-speed Internet, dual phone lines, voice mail, irons, hair dryers. **Pool(s):** outdoor. **Guest Services:** coin laundry. **Business Services:** meeting rooms. **Cards:** AX, CB, DC, DS, MC, VI. **Special Amenities: free expanded continental breakfast and free local telephone calls.** *(See color ad p 260 & p 822)*

SOME UNITS

HOLIDAY MOTEL **Phone:** (209)847-7023

SAVE Motel

4/1-10/31	1P: $50-$55	2P: $65-$80	XP: $8	F10
1/1-1/31	1P: $40-$45	2P: $50-$60	XP: $8	F10
2/1-3/31 & 11/1-12/31	1P: $45-$49	2P: $51-$56	XP: $8	F10

Location: 1 mi e on SR 108 and 120. 950 East F St 95361. Fax: 209/847-3165. **Facility:** 32 units. 31 one-bedroom standard units. 1 one-bedroom suite ($98-$150). 1 story, exterior corridors. *Bath:* combo or shower only. **Parking:** on-site. **Terms:** cancellation fee imposed. **Pool(s):** outdoor. **Cards:** AX, DC, DS, MC, VI. **Special Amenities: free continental breakfast and preferred room (subject to availability with advanced reservations).**

SOME UNITS

RAMADA INN *Book at aaa.com* **Phone:** (209)847-8181

SAVE Motel

4/9-9/30 [CP]	1P: $79-$97	2P: $85-$103	XP: $6	F18
2/1-4/8 & 10/1-1/31 [CP]	1P: $73-$91	2P: $79-$97	XP: $6	F18

Location: 0.8 mi e on SR 108 and 120. 825 East F St 95361. Fax: 209/847-9546. **Facility:** 70 one-bedroom standard units. 2 stories (no elevator), exterior corridors. *Bath:* combo or shower only. **Parking:** on-site. **Terms:** 14 day cancellation notice-fee imposed, [AP] & [BP] meal plans available. **Amenities:** voice mail, irons, hair dryers. **Pool(s):** heated outdoor. **Leisure Activities:** whirlpool. **Guest Services:** valet laundry. **Business Services:** meeting rooms. **Cards:** AX, CB, DC, DS, MC, VI. **Special Amenities: free continental breakfast and free newspaper.**

SOME UNITS

FEE FEE

OAKHURST pop. 2,868—*See also YOSEMITE NATIONAL PARK.*

WHERE TO STAY

BEST WESTERN YOSEMITE GATEWAY INN Book at aaa.com **Phone:** (559)683-2378

AAA SAVE — Motel

5/23-10/11	1P: $82-$102	2P: $89-$102	XP: $10	F12
10/12-11/29	1P: $56-$69	2P: $62-$73	XP: $10	F12
2/1-5/22	1P: $54-$69	2P: $59-$72	XP: $10	F12
11/30-1/31	1P: $46-$49	2P: $49-$58	XP: $10	F12

Location: SR 49, 0.8 mi n. 40530 Hwy 41 93644. Fax: 559/683-3813. **Facility:** 122 units. 104 one- and 18 two-bedroom standard units, some with kitchens. 2 stories (no elevator), exterior corridors. *Bath:* combo or shower only. **Parking:** on-site. **Terms:** [BP] & [MAP] meal plans available, small pets only (dogs only). **Amenities:** irons, hair dryers. **Pool(s):** heated outdoor, heated indoor. **Leisure Activities:** whirlpools, playground, exercise room. **Guest Services:** gift shop, coin laundry. **Business Services:** meeting rooms, fax (fee). **Cards:** AX, CB, DC, DS, MC. **Special Amenities: free local telephone calls and preferred room (subject to availability with advanced reservations).** *(See color ad p 817 & p 521)*

SOME UNITS

CHATEAU DU SUREAU **Phone:** (559)683-6860

AAA — Country Inn

2/1-1/3 & 1/27-1/31	1P: $350-$2500	2P: $350-$2500	XP: $75	F3

Location: Just w of jct SR 41 and 49. 48688 Victoria Ln 93644 (PO Box 577). Fax: 559/683-0800. **Facility:** Seven acres of terraced gardens give this property an atmosphere of Provence; rooms are individually appointed with antiques, oils and objects d'art. 12 units. 10 one-bedroom standard units, some with whirlpools. 2 one-bedroom suites ($1000-$1800) with whirlpools. 1-2 stories (no elevator), interior corridors. *Bath:* combo or shower only. **Parking:** valet. **Terms:** open 2/1-1/3 & 1/27-1/31, 2-3 night minimum stay - weekends, 14 day cancellation notice-fee imposed, [BP] meal plan available. **Amenities:** video library, CD players, hair dryers. **Dining:** Erna's Elderberry House Restaurant, see separate listing. **Pool(s):** small outdoor. **Leisure Activities:** library in all units, bocci, outdoor granite chess court, secluded picnic area with pond & gazebo, hiking trails. *Fee:* massage. **Guest Services:** gift shop, complimentary evening beverages. **Business Services:** meeting rooms. **Cards:** AX, MC, VI.

SOME UNITS

COMFORT INN-OAKHURST Book at aaa.com **Phone:** (559)683-8282

AAA SAVE — Motel

4/1-10/31 [CP]	1P: $79-$109	2P: $79-$109	XP: $10	F18
11/1-1/31 [CP]	1P: $49-$99	2P: $49-$99	XP: $10	F18
2/1-3/31 [CP]	1P: $49-$89	2P: $49-$89	XP: $10	F18

Location: SR 49, 0.5 mi n. 40489 Hwy 41 93644. Fax: 559/658-7030. **Facility:** 114 units. 111 one- and 3 two-bedroom standard units. 2 stories (no elevator), exterior corridors. **Parking:** on-site. **Terms:** small pets only ($5 extra charge, in limited units). **Amenities:** video library (fee). **Pool(s):** outdoor. **Leisure Activities:** whirlpool. **Guest Services:** gift shop. **Business Services:** fax (fee). **Cards:** AX, CB, DC, DS, MC, VI. **Special Amenities: free continental breakfast and free newspaper.** *(See color ad p 819)*

FEE SOME UNITS FEE

DAYS INN Book at aaa.com **Phone:** 559/642-2525

AAA SAVE — Motel

5/1-8/31 [CP]	1P: $67-$99	2P: $76-$99	XP: $10	F12
9/1-10/11 [CP]	1P: $52-$69	2P: $59-$69	XP: $10	F12
10/12-1/31 [CP]	1P: $44-$59	2P: $50-$59	XP: $10	F12
2/1-4/30 [CP]	1P: $37-$49	2P: $42-$49	XP: $10	F12

Location: SR 49, 0.8 mi n. 40662 Hwy 41 93644. Fax: 559/658-8481. **Facility:** 42 one-bedroom standard units, some with whirlpools. 4 stories (no elevator), exterior corridors. **Parking:** on-site. **Amenities:** safes (fee), irons, hair dryers. **Pool(s):** outdoor. **Cards:** AX, MC, VI.

SOME UNITS

HOUNDS TOOTH INN **Phone:** (559)642-6600

Bed & Breakfast

All Year [ECP]	1P: $89-$169	2P: $95-$175	XP: $20	F10

Location: North end of town. 42071 Hwy 41 93644. Fax: 559/658-2946. **Facility:** Fireplaces are featured in some accommodations at the inn, which is convenient to the national park; smoking is permitted on patios only. Smoke free premises. 13 one-bedroom standard units, some with whirlpools. 2 stories (no elevator), interior/exterior corridors. *Bath:* combo or shower only. **Parking:** on-site. **Terms:** 3 day cancellation notice, no pets allowed (owner's pet on premises). **Amenities:** hair dryers. **Guest Services:** complimentary evening beverages. **Cards:** AX, DC, DS, MC, VI.

SOME UNITS

OAKHURST LODGE Book at aaa.com **Phone:** (559)683-4417

AAA SAVE — Motel

5/16-10/15	1P: $65-$75	2P: $75-$85	XP: $5	F12
2/1-5/15	1P: $45-$65	2P: $55-$70	XP: $5	F12
10/16-1/31	1P: $40-$50	2P: $55-$65	XP: $5	F12

Location: SR 49 at CR 426, just n. 40302 Hwy 41 93644. Fax: 559/683-4417. **Facility:** 60 one-bedroom standard units. 1-2 stories (no elevator), exterior corridors. *Bath:* combo or shower only. **Parking:** on-site. **Terms:** cancellation fee imposed, package plans. **Pool(s):** outdoor. **Guest Services:** coin laundry. **Business Services:** fax (fee). **Cards:** AX, DS, MC, VI. **Special Amenities: free local telephone calls and preferred room (subject to availability with advanced reservations).** *(See color ad p 822)*

SOME UNITS

RAMADA LIMITED YOSEMITE *Book at aaa.com* **Phone:** 559/658-5500

Motel

4/1-12/31 1P: $89-$139
2/1-3/31 & 1/1-1/31 1P: $69-$99

Location: SR 41, just s of SR 49. 48800 Royal Oaks Dr 93644. Fax: 559/658-5505. **Facility:** 69 one-bedroom standard units, some with whirlpools. 2 stories (no elevator), interior corridors. *Bath:* combo or shower only. **Parking:** on-site. **Amenities:** voice mail, irons, hair dryers. **Pool(s):** outdoor. **Leisure Activities:** whirlpool. **Guest Services:** coin laundry. **Business Services:** meeting rooms. **Cards:** AX, CB, DS, MC, VI. **Special Amenities: free expanded continental breakfast and free local telephone calls.**

SOME UNITS

FEE

WHERE TO DINE

ERNA'S ELDERBERRY HOUSE RESTAURANT **Dinner:** $82 **Phone:** 559/683-6800

French

Location: Just w of jct SR 41 and 49; in Chateau du Sureau. 48688 Victoria Ln 93644. **Hours:** 5:30 pm-8:30 pm. Closed: first 3 weeks in Jan. **Reservations:** suggested. **Features:** Elegant decor and the finest table settings are among special touches that enable the dining room to exude warm country French ambience. European influences punctuate inventive preparations of California cuisine. Kitchen-garden items crown a fresh seasonal menu. Cigars are welcomed in the sophisticated smoking garden. Service is impeccable. Semi-formal attire; cocktails. **Parking:** on-site. **Cards:** AX, MC, VI.

OAKLAND/BERKELEY
ACCOMMODATIONS
RAPID TRANSIT
STATION
Scale in Miles
Scale in Kilometers
0
1.8
0
2.8
1620-L
To Richmond
Berkeley
University of California
Emeryville
Oakland
Alameda
San Leandro
Redwood Regional Park
Oakland Army Base
Naval Supply Center
Alameda Point
Oakland Mus. of California
Lake Merritt
Robert W. Crown Mem. State Beach
Oakland Alameda Co. Coliseum Complex
Oakland International Airport
San Francisco Bay
San Leandro Bay
Inner Harbor
CALDECOTT TUNNEL
SAN FRANCISCO-OAKLAND BAY BRIDGE
(TOLL WEST BOUND)
To San Francisco
WEBSTER ST. TUBE
POSEY TUBE

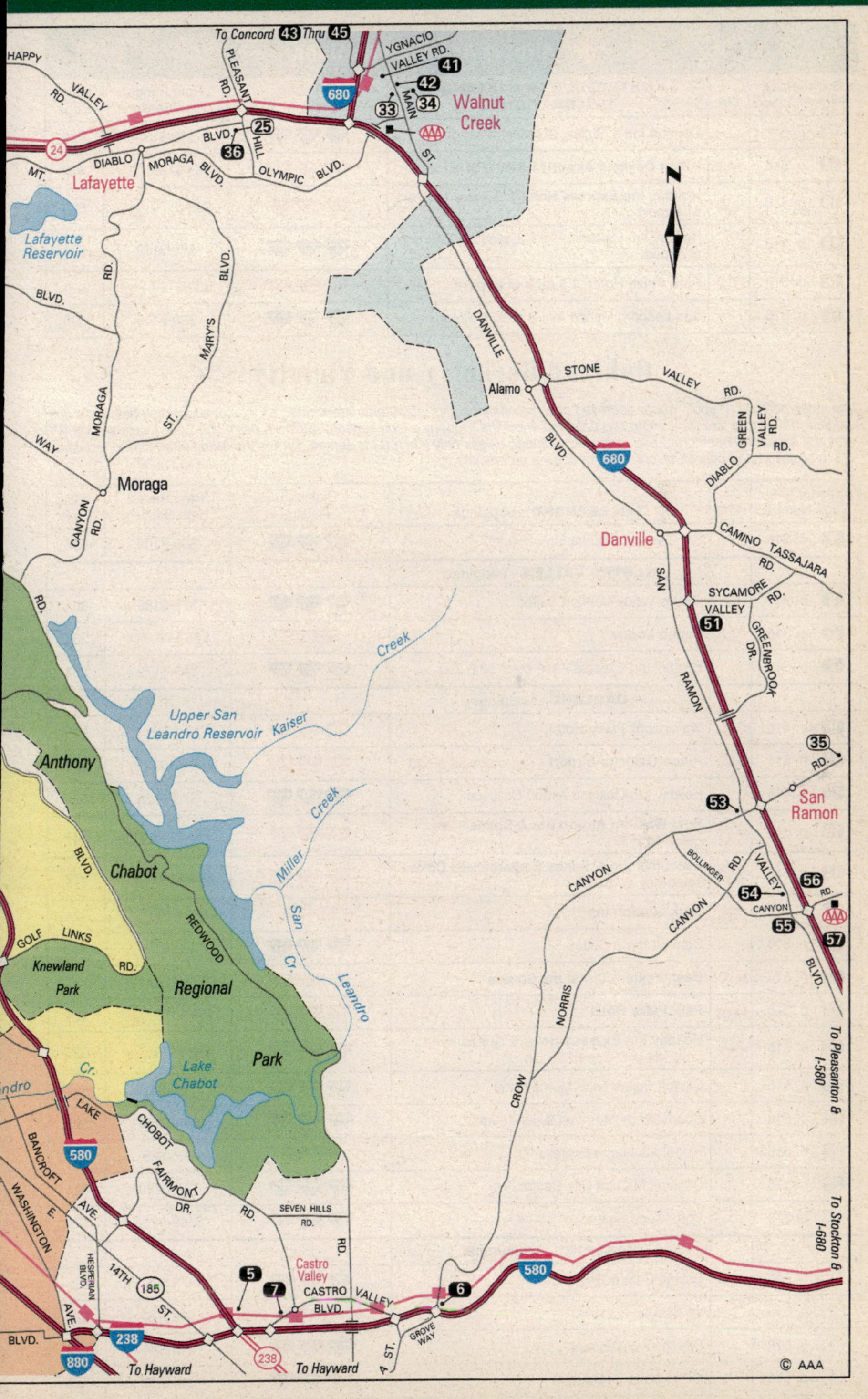
To Concord 43 Thru 45
Walnut Creek
Lafayette
Lafayette Reservoir
Moraga
Alamo
Danville
San Ramon
Upper San Leandro Reservoir
Anthony Chabot Regional Park
Knewland Park
Lake Chabot
Castro Valley
To Hayward
To Pleasanton & I-580
To Stockton & I-680
© AAA

Airport Accommodations

Spotter/Map Page Number	OA	METROPOLITAN OAKLAND INTERNATIONAL	Diamond Rating	Rate Range High Season	Listing Page
16 / p. 516		Comfort Inn & Suites, 2.3 mi e of airport	◆◆◆	$99-$139	522
11 / p. 516	AAA	**Hilton Oakland Airport, 1.3 mi e of airport**	◆◆◆	$89-$189 SAVE	523
19 / p. 516	AAA	**Holiday Inn Express Hotel & Suites, 1 mi e of airport**	◆◆◆	$99-$179 SAVE	523
12 / p. 516		Holiday Inn-Oakland Airport/Coliseum, 2.3 mi e of airport	◆◆◆	$79-$129	524
18 / p. 516	AAA	**Park Plaza Hotel, 1.5 mi e of airport**	◆◆◆	$99-$139 SAVE	524
1 / p. 516		San Leandro Marina Inn, 3 mi s of airport	◆◆◆	$99-$109	696

Oakland/Berkeley and Vicinity

This index helps you "spot" where approved accommodations and restaurants are located on the corresponding detailed maps. Lodging rate ranges are for comparison only and show the property's high season; rates are per night, unless only weekly (W) rates are available. Restaurant rate range is for dinner, unless only lunch (L) is served. Turn to the listing page for more detailed rate information and consult display ads for special promotions.

Spotter/Map Page Number	OA	SAN LEANDRO - Lodgings	Diamond Rating	Rate Range High Season	Listing Page
1 / p. 516		San Leandro Marina Inn	◆◆◆	$99-$109	696
		CASTRO VALLEY - Lodgings			
5 / p. 516		Castro Valley Comfort Suites	◆◆◆	$79-$109	301
6 / p. 516	AAA	**Econo Lodge**	◆◆	$66-$77 SAVE	301
7 / p. 516		Holiday Inn Express - see color ad p 260	◆◆◆	$89-$179	301
		OAKLAND - Lodgings			
10 / p. 516	AAA	**Waterfront Plaza Hotel**	◆◆◆	$179-$225 SAVE	525
11 / p. 516	AAA	**Hilton Oakland Airport - see color ad p 523**	◆◆◆	$89-$189 SAVE	523
12 / p. 516		Holiday Inn-Oakland Airport/Coliseum	◆◆◆	$79-$129	524
13 / p. 516	AAA	**Best Western Airport Inn & Suites - see color ad p 521**	◆◆◆	$89-$149 SAVE	521
14 / p. 516	AAA	**Executive Inn & Suites Embarcadero Cove - see color ad p 522**	◆◆◆	$99-$149 SAVE	522
15 / p. 516	AAA	**Jack London Inn**	◆◆	$109-$199 SAVE	524
16 / p. 516		Comfort Inn & Suites	◆◆◆	$99-$139	522
17 / p. 516	AAA	**Best Western Inn at the Square**	◆◆◆	$109-$169 SAVE	521
18 / p. 516	AAA	**Park Plaza Hotel**	◆◆◆	$99-$139 SAVE	524
19 / p. 516	AAA	**Holiday Inn Express Hotel & Suites - see color ad p 260, p 523**	◆◆◆	$99-$179 SAVE	523
20 / p. 516		Clarion Suites Lake Merritt Hotel	◆◆◆	$199-$319	522
21 / p. 516		Courtyard by Marriott-Oakland Airport	◆◆◆	$99-$159	522
22 / p. 516		Howard Johnson Express Inn	◆◆	$65-$85	524
23 / p. 516		Oakland Marriott City Center	◆◆◆	$89-$229	524
24 / p. 516		Homewood Suites	◆◆◆	$169-$299	524
		OAKLAND - Restaurants			
1 / p. 516		Oliveto Cafe & Restaurant	◆◆◆	$12-$32	525
2 / p. 516		Le Cheval	◆◆	$10-$20	525
3 / p. 516		Bay Wolf Restaurant	◆◆◆	$16-$24	525
4 / p. 516		Il Pescatore Restaurant	◆◆◆	$14-$28	525

Spotter/Map Page Number	OA	OAKLAND - Restaurants (continued)	Diamond Rating	Rate Range High Season	Listing Page
5 / p. 516		Madison's	◆◆◆	$13-$22	525
6 / p. 516	AAA	**Quinn's Lighthouse Restaurant & Pub**	◆◆	$8-$22	525
8 / p. 516		Garibaldi's on College	◆◆◆	$15-$30	525
		BERKELEY - Lodgings			
28 / p. 516		The Claremont Resort and Spa	◆◆◆◆	$219-$349	284
29 / p. 516	AAA	**Hotel Durant**	◆◆	$140-$180 SAVE	285
30 / p. 516		Doubletree Hotel and Executive Meeting Center Berkeley Marina	◆◆◆	$139-$228	284
31 / p. 516		Holiday Inn Express Hotel & Suites - see color ad p 260	◆◆◆	$111-$139	284
		BERKELEY - Restaurants			
15 / p. 516		Jordan's At The Claremont	◆◆◆◆	$23-$34	285
16 / p. 516		Chez Panisse	◆◆◆	$12-$28	285
17 / p. 516		Skates on the Bay	◆◆◆	$15-$30	285
18 / p. 516		Cafe Rouge	◆◆	$12-$28	285
		EMERYVILLE - Lodgings			
32 / p. 516		Courtyard by Marriott Emeryville	◆◆◆	$89-$179	321
33 / p. 516		Woodfin Suite Hotel San Francisco Bay Bridge	◆◆◆	$144	321
34 / p. 516	AAA	**Holiday Inn-Bay Bridge - see color ad p 321**	◆◆◆	$159-$229 SAVE	321
35 / p. 516		Four Points by Sheraton-San Francisco Bay Bridge	◆◆◆	$129-$149	321
		LAFAYETTE - Lodgings			
36 / p. 516	AAA	**Lafayette Park Hotel & Spa - see color ad inside back cover**	◆◆◆◆	$225-$475 SAVE	361
		LAFAYETTE - Restaurant			
25 / p. 516		The Duck Club Restaurant - see color ad inside back cover, p 764	◆◆◆◆	$18-$30	361
		WALNUT CREEK - Lodgings			
41 / p. 516		Marriott Hotel	◆◆◆	$85-$209	755
42 / p. 516	AAA	**Walnut Creek Motor Lodge**	◆◆	$75-$90 SAVE	756
43 / p. 516	AAA	**Holiday Inn Walnut Creek - see color ad p 755**	◆◆◆	$79-$199 SAVE	755
44 / p. 516	AAA	**Embassy Suites Hotel - see color ad p 755**	◆◆◆	$116-$189 SAVE	754
45 / p. 516	AAA	**Renaissance Club Sport**	◆◆◆◆	$119-$219 SAVE	755
		WALNUT CREEK - Restaurants			
33 / p. 516		California Cafe Bar & Grill	◆◆◆	$10-$20	756
34 / p. 516		Massimo Ristorante	◆◆◆	$11-$27	756
		DANVILLE - Lodgings			
51 / p. 516		Best Western Danville Sycamore Inn - see color ad p 521, p 314	◆◆	$79-$169	314
		DANVILLE - Restaurant			
35 / p. 516		Blackhawk Grille	◆◆◆	$16-$27	314
		SAN RAMON - Lodgings			
53 / p. 516		Sierra Suites Hotel San Ramon	◆◆◆	$79-$200	702
54 / p. 516		Homestead Studio Suites Hotel-San Ramon	◆◆	$90-$115	701
55 / p. 516		Courtyard by Marriott	◆◆◆	$64-$144	701
56 / p. 516		San Ramon Marriott at Bishop Ranch	◆◆◆	$79-$199	702

Spotter/Map Page Number	OA	**SAN RAMON** - Lodgings (continued)	Diamond Rating	Rate Range High Season	Listing Page
57 / p. 516		Residence Inn by Marriott	◆◆◆	$199-$249	702
		ALAMEDA - Lodgings			
61 / p. 516	AAA	**Hawthorn Suites Ltd-Oakland/Alameda** - see color ad below	◆◆◆	$99-$169 SAVE	264
62 / p. 516	AAA	**Marina Village Inn** - see color ad p 524	◆◆◆	$106-$159 SAVE	264
63 / p. 516	AAA	**Coral Reef Motel & Suites** - see color ad p 264	◆◆◆	$84 SAVE	264
		ALAMEDA - Restaurant			
37 / p. 516		Pasta Pelican	◆◆	$9-$18	264

OAKLAND pop. 399,484 (See map and index starting on p. 516)

WHERE TO STAY

BEST WESTERN AIRPORT INN & SUITES Book at aaa.com Phone: (510)633-0500 13

Small-scale Hotel

All Year	1P: $89-$139	2P: $99-$149	XP: $10	F13

Location: I-880, exit Hengenber Airport, just left; n on I-880, cross over, then just left. 170 Hengenberger Loop 94621. Fax: 510/633-1040. **Facility:** 76 one-bedroom standard units, some with whirlpools. 3 stories, interior corridors. *Bath:* combo or shower only. **Parking:** on-site. **Terms:** cancellation fee imposed, [BP] meal plan available. **Amenities:** high-speed Internet, dual phone lines, voice mail, safes, irons, hair dryers. **Pool(s):** heated indoor. **Leisure Activities:** whirlpool, exercise room. **Guest Services:** coin laundry, airport transportation-Oakland Airport. **Business Services:** meeting rooms, business center. **Cards:** AX, CB, DC, DS, JC, MC, VI. **Special Amenities: free expanded continental breakfast and free local telephone calls.** *(See color ad below)*

DATA PORT

BEST WESTERN INN AT THE SQUARE Book at aaa.com Phone: (510)452-4565 17

Small-scale Hotel

5/1-10/31	1P: $109-$169	2P: $109-$169	XP: $10	F17
2/1-4/30 & 11/1-1/31	1P: $99-$139	2P: $99-$139	XP: $10	F17

Location: I-880, exit Broadway northbound, 0.3 mi w; exit 12th westbound, w to 7th St, s to Broadway. Located at entrance to Jack London Square. 233 Broadway 94607. Fax: 510/452-4634. **Facility:** 100 units. 99 one-bedroom standard units. 1 one-bedroom suite. 3 stories, interior corridors. *Bath:* combo or shower only. **Parking:** on-site. **Amenities:** voice mail, irons, hair dryers. **Pool(s):** heated outdoor. **Leisure Activities:** exercise room. **Guest Services:** coin laundry. **Cards:** AX, DC, DS, MC, VI. **Special Amenities: free newspaper and free room upgrade (subject to availability with advanced reservations).**

DATA PORT / SOME UNITS FEE FEE /

(See map and index starting on p. 516)

CLARION SUITES LAKE MERRITT HOTEL Book at aaa.com Phone: (510)832-2300 20

Historic Small-scale Hotel

All Year 1P: $199-$319 2P: $199-$319 XP: $20 F18

Location: I-880, exit Broadway, 0.8 mi e to 17th St, then just s. 1800 Madison St 94612. Fax: 510/832-7150. **Facility:** Most units in this refurbished 1927 art deco-style hotel overlook Lake Merritt. 51 units. 9 one-bedroom standard units. 42 one-bedroom suites with efficiencies, some with whirlpools. 6 stories, interior corridors. *Bath:* combo or shower only. **Parking:** valet. **Terms:** pets ($150 deposit). **Amenities:** voice mail, irons, hair dryers. **Dining:** Madison's, see separate listing. **Leisure Activities:** exercise room. **Guest Services:** valet laundry, area transportation. **Business Services:** meeting rooms. **Cards:** AX, CB, DC, DS, JC, MC, VI.

SOME UNITS

ASK / FEE / DATA PORT / VCR /

COMFORT INN & SUITES Book at aaa.com Phone: (510)568-1500 16

Large-scale Hotel

6/1-8/31 1P: $99-$139 2P: $99-$139 XP: $10 F17

2/1-5/31 & 9/1-1/31 1P: $89-$129 2P: $89-$129 XP: $10 F17

Location: I-880, exit Hegenberger Rd, 2.3 mi e of Oakland Airport. 8452 Edes Ave 94621. Fax: 510/430-8360. **Facility:** 104 one-bedroom standard units, some with kitchens. 3 stories, interior corridors. *Bath:* combo or shower only. **Parking:** on-site. **Terms:** [CP] meal plan available, package plans. **Amenities:** high-speed Internet, dual phone lines, voice mail, irons, hair dryers. *Some:* safes. **Leisure Activities:** sauna, whirlpool, steamroom, exercise room. **Guest Services:** coin laundry, area transportation. **Business Services:** meeting rooms, business center. **Cards:** AX, CB, DC, DS, JC, MC, VI.

SOME UNITS

ASK / DATA PORT / /

COURTYARD BY MARRIOTT-OAKLAND AIRPORT Book at aaa.com Phone: (510)568-7600 21

Large-scale Hotel

All Year 1P: $99-$159 2P: $99-$159

Location: I-880, exit Hegenberger Rd W, 0.5 mi e of Oakland Airport. 350 Hegenberger Rd 94621. Fax: 510/568-7695. **Facility:** 156 units. 152 one-bedroom standard units, some with whirlpools. 4 one-bedroom suites ($159-$199). 3 stories, interior corridors. *Bath:* combo or shower only. **Parking:** on-site. **Terms:** [BP], [CP] & [MAP] meal plans available. **Amenities:** video games, dual phone lines, voice mail, irons, hair dryers. **Pool(s):** heated outdoor. **Leisure Activities:** whirlpool, exercise room. **Guest Services:** complimentary evening beverages, valet and coin laundry, area transportation. **Business Services:** meeting rooms, business center. **Cards:** AX, CB, DC, DS, JC, MC, VI.

SOME UNITS

ASK / DATA PORT / /

EXECUTIVE INN & SUITES EMBARCADERO COVE Book at aaa.com Phone: (510)536-6633 14

AAA SAVE

Small-scale Hotel

All Year [ECP] 1P: $99-$149 2P: $99-$149 XP: $15 F17

Location: I-880, exit 16th/Embarcadero southbound, just w; exit 5th Ave/Embarcadero northbound. 1755 Embarcadero 94606. Fax: 510/536-6006. **Facility:** 228 one-bedroom standard units. 3 stories, interior corridors. *Bath:* combo or shower only. **Parking:** on-site. **Amenities:** video games, voice mail, irons, hair dryers. *Some:* high-speed Internet, dual phone lines, safes. **Pool(s):** heated outdoor. **Leisure Activities:** whirlpool, fishing, limited exercise equipment. **Guest Services:** coin laundry. **Business Services:** meeting rooms, business center. **Cards:** AX, DC, DS, MC, VI. **Special Amenities: free continental breakfast and free newspaper.**
(See color ad below)

SOME UNITS

DATA PORT / /

(See map and index starting on p. 516)

HILTON OAKLAND AIRPORT Book at aaa.com **Phone:** 510/635-5000 11

AAA SAVE All Year 1P: $89-$189 2P: $89-$189 XP: $20 F18

Large-scale Hotel

Location: I-880, exit Hegenberger Rd, 1 mi w, 1.3 mi e of Oakland Airport. 1 Hegenberger Rd 94621. Fax: 510/383-4090. **Facility:** 363 units. 356 one-bedroom standard units. 7 one-bedroom suites. 3 stories, interior corridors. *Bath:* combo or shower only. **Parking:** on-site. **Terms:** [AP], [BP] & [CP] meal plans available, small pets only ($200 deposit). **Amenities:** video games, high-speed Internet, dual phone lines, voice mail, irons, hair dryers. *Some:* honor bars. **Dining:** 2 restaurants, 6:30 am-midnight, cocktails. **Pool(s):** heated outdoor. **Leisure Activities:** exercise room. **Guest Services:** gift shop, valet laundry, area transportation-BART & Jack London Square. **Business Services:** meeting rooms, business center. **Cards:** AX, CB, DC, DS, MC, VI. **Special Amenities:** **free newspaper.** *(See color ad below)*

SOME UNITS

FEE

HOLIDAY INN EXPRESS HOTEL & SUITES Book at aaa.com **Phone:** (510)569-4400 19

AAA SAVE All Year 1P: $99-$179 2P: $99-$179 XP: $10 F

Small-scale Hotel

Location: I-880, exit Hegenberger Rd W, jct Doolittle and airport access road. 66 Airport Access Rd 94603. Fax: 510/569-4441. **Facility:** 69 units. 65 one-bedroom standard units. 4 one-bedroom suites, some with kitchens and/or whirlpools. 3 stories, interior corridors. *Bath:* combo or shower only. **Parking:** on-site. **Terms:** [ECP] meal plan available. **Amenities:** dual phone lines, voice mail, irons, hair dryers. **Leisure Activities:** whirlpool, exercise room. **Guest Services:** coin laundry. **Business Services:** meeting rooms, business center. **Cards:** AX, CB, DC, DS, JC, MC, VI. **Special Amenities:** **free local telephone calls and free newspaper.** *(See color ad below & p 260)*

SOME UNITS

(See map and index starting on p. 516)

HOLIDAY INN-OAKLAND AIRPORT/COLISEUM *Book at aaa.com* **Phone:** (510)562-5311 **12**

Large-scale Hotel

All Year 1P: $79-$129 2P: $79-$129 XP: $10 F18

Location: I-880, exit Hegenberger Rd, 2.3 mi e of Oakland Airport. 500 Hegenberger Rd 94621. Fax: 510/632-7019. **Facility:** 293 units. 291 one-bedroom standard units. 2 one-bedroom suites with efficiencies. 2-6 stories, interior/exterior corridors. *Bath:* combo or shower only. **Parking:** on-site. **Terms:** cancellation fee imposed. **Amenities:** video games, voice mail, irons, hair dryers. **Pool(s):** outdoor. **Leisure Activities:** exercise room. **Guest Services:** coin laundry, area transportation. **Business Services:** meeting rooms. **Cards:** AX, CB, DC, DS, MC, VI.

SOME UNITS

HOMEWOOD SUITES *Book at aaa.com* **Phone:** (510)663-2700 **24**

Small-scale Hotel

All Year [ECP] 1P: $169-$299 2P: $169-$299 XP: $10 F12

Location: I-880, exit 5th/Embarcadero southbound; exit 16th/Embarcadero northbound. 1103 Embarcadero 94606. Fax: 510/663-2701. **Facility:** 132 units. 116 one-bedroom standard units, some with efficiencies or kitchens. 8 one- and 8 two-bedroom suites with kitchens. 3 stories, interior corridors. *Bath:* combo or shower only. **Parking:** on-site. **Terms:** pets ($300 deposit). **Amenities:** video games, high-speed Internet, dual phone lines, voice mail, irons, hair dryers. **Pool(s):** heated outdoor. **Leisure Activities:** whirlpool, limited exercise equipment. **Guest Services:** gift shop, coin laundry. **Business Services:** meeting rooms, business center. **Cards:** AX, CB, DC, DS, MC, VI.

SOME UNITS

FEE

HOWARD JOHNSON EXPRESS INN *Book at aaa.com* **Phone:** (510)451-6316 **22**

Motel

All Year 1P: $65-$85 2P: $65-$85 XP: $10 F12

Location: I-880, exit Broadway, right to 7th St; I-880 S, exit Broadway/Alameda, then right. 423 7th St 94607. Fax: 510/663-3700. **Facility:** 115 one-bedroom standard units. 3-4 stories, interior corridors. **Parking:** on-site. **Terms:** weekly rates available, [ECP] meal plan available. **Amenities:** *Some:* irons, hair dryers. **Leisure Activities:** exercise room. **Business Services:** meeting rooms, fax. **Cards:** AX, DS, MC, VI.

SOME UNITS

JACK LONDON INN *Book at aaa.com* **Phone:** (510)444-2032 **15**

SAVE

Small-scale Hotel

5/15-10/1 [CP]	1P: $109-$199	2P: $109-$199	XP: $10	F12
2/1-5/14 & 10/2-1/31 [CP]	1P: $99-$179	2P: $99-$179	XP: $10	F12

Location: End of Broadway. Located in the heart of historic Jack London Square. 444 Embarcadero W 94607. Fax: 510/834-3074. **Facility:** 110 one-bedroom standard units, some with efficiencies. 4 stories, interior corridors. *Bath:* combo or shower only. **Parking:** on-site. **Amenities:** voice mail, irons, hair dryers. **Dining:** 24 hours, cocktails. **Pool(s):** small outdoor. **Leisure Activities:** exercise room. **Guest Services:** valet laundry. **Business Services:** meeting rooms. **Cards:** AX, CB, DC, DS, MC, VI. **Special Amenities: free continental breakfast and free newspaper.**

SOME UNITS

FEE

OAKLAND MARRIOTT CITY CENTER *Book at aaa.com* **Phone:** (510)451-4000 **23**

Large-scale Hotel

All Year 1P: $89-$229

Location: I-880, exit Broadway northbound. 1001 Broadway 94607. Fax: 510/835-3466. **Facility:** 487 units. 479 one-bedroom standard units. 8 two-bedroom suites. 21 stories, interior corridors. *Bath:* some combo or shower only. **Parking:** valet. **Amenities:** video games, high-speed Internet, voice mail, irons, hair dryers. **Pool(s):** heated outdoor. **Leisure Activities:** whirlpool, exercise room. **Guest Services:** gift shop, valet and coin laundry. **Business Services:** meeting rooms, business center. **Cards:** AX, DC, DS, MC, VI.

SOME UNITS

FEE

PARK PLAZA HOTEL *Book at aaa.com* **Phone:** (510)635-5300 **18**

SAVE

Large-scale Hotel

All Year 1P: $99 2P: $139

Location: I-880, exit Hegenberger Rd, 0.8 mi w, 1.5 mi e of Oakland Airport W. 150 Hegenberger Rd 94621. Fax: 510/635-9661. **Facility:** 189 one-bedroom standard units. 6 stories, interior corridors. *Bath:* combo or shower only. **Parking:** on-site. **Terms:** cancellation fee imposed, package plans. **Amenities:** video games, voice mail, irons, hair dryers. **Dining:** 6 am-10 pm, Sat & Sun from 7 am, cocktails. **Pool(s):** outdoor. **Leisure Activities:** saunas, whirlpool, exercise room. **Guest Services:** coin laundry, area transportation-BART & Jack London Square. **Business Services:** meeting rooms. **Cards:** AX, CB, DC, DS, MC, VI. **Special Amenities: free newspaper and early check-in/late check-out.**

SOME UNITS

FEE FEE

(See map and index starting on p. 516)

WATERFRONT PLAZA HOTEL Book at aaa.com **Phone:** (510)836-3800 10

AAA SAVE All Year 1P: $179-$225 2P: $179-$225

Large-scale Hotel **Location:** I-880, exit Broadway, 0.5 mi w. Located in Jack London Square. Ten Washington St 94607. Fax: 510/832-5695. **Facility:** 145 one-bedroom standard units. 5 stories, interior corridors. *Bath:* combo or shower only. **Parking:** valet. **Amenities:** video games, voice mail, safes, honor bars, irons, hair dryers. **Dining:** 6:30 am-midnight, cocktails. **Pool(s):** heated outdoor. **Leisure Activities:** sauna, exercise room. *Fee:* boat dock. **Guest Services:** gift shop, valet laundry, area transportation-within 3 mi. **Business Services:** meeting rooms, business center. **Cards:** AX, CB, DC, DS, MC, VI. **Special Amenities: free newspaper and early check-in/late check-out.**

SOME UNITS

FEE

WHERE TO DINE

BAY WOLF RESTAURANT **Lunch:** $9-$17 **Dinner:** $16-$24 **Phone:** 510/655-6004 3

California **Location:** I-580, exit Oakland Ave, 2 blks e on Piedmont Ave, 0.3 mi n on Mac Arthur Blvd. 3853 Piedmont Ave 94611. **Hours:** 11:30 am-2 & 6-9:30 pm, Sat & Sun from 5:30 pm. Closed major holidays. **Reservations:** suggested. **Features:** The pretty converted house invites diners to sample California cuisine made with a strong Mediterranean influence. Semi-formal attire; beer & wine only. **Parking:** street. **Cards:** AX, MC, VI.

GARIBALDI'S ON COLLEGE **Lunch:** $8-$16 **Dinner:** $15-$30 **Phone:** 510/595-4000 8

California **Location:** SR 24, exit Claremont Ave. 5356 College Ave 94618. **Hours:** 11:30 am-2:30 & 5:30-10 pm, Fri & Sat-10:30 pm, Sunday brunch 10 am-2 pm. Closed: 7/4, 12/24, 12/25; also 5/29 for lunch. **Reservations:** suggested. **Features:** A Southern Mediterranean influence, although light on the herbs, is evident in the style and preparation of menu offerings. Casual dress; cocktails. **Parking:** street. **Cards:** AX, MC, VI.

IL PESCATORE RESTAURANT **Lunch:** $12-$16 **Dinner:** $14-$28 **Phone:** 510/465-2188 4

Italian **Location:** At Jack London Square. 57 Jack London Sq 94607. **Hours:** 11:30 am-10 pm, Sat from 11 am, Sun 10:30 am-9 pm. **Reservations:** suggested. **Features:** Fresh seafood and homemade pasta are prepared in the Tuscan style. Overlooking the marina, the dining room plays host to opera singers on the last Thursday of the month during dinner. Casual dress; cocktails. **Parking:** valet. **Cards:** AX, CB, DC, MC, VI.

LE CHEVAL **Lunch:** $6-$8 **Dinner:** $10-$20 **Phone:** 510/763-8495 2

Vietnamese **Location:** At 11th St. 1007 Clay St 94607. **Hours:** 11 am-9:30 pm, Sun from 5 pm. Closed: 11/25, 12/24, 12/25. **Reservations:** suggested. **Features:** The cuisine is a mixture of French and South Vietnamese, including delicacies to appeal to discriminating guests. Casual dress; cocktails. **Parking:** on-site. **Cards:** AX, DC, DS, MC, VI.

MADISON'S **Lunch:** $10-$14 **Dinner:** $13-$22 **Phone:** 510/832-2300 5

California **Location:** I-880, exit Broadway, 0.8 mi e to 17th St, then just s; in Clarion Suites Lake Merritt Hotel. 1800 Madison St 94612. **Hours:** 11:30 am-2 & 5-9:30 pm. Closed major holidays. **Reservations:** suggested. **Features:** Overlooking Lake Meritt, the classy restaurant sports a 1930s Art Deco design. California cuisine is made with a Pacific Rim flair. Casual dress; cocktails; entertainment. **Parking:** valet. **Cards:** AX, DC, DS, JC, MC, VI.

OLIVETO CAFE & RESTAURANT **Lunch:** $12-$15 **Dinner:** $12-$32 **Phone:** 510/547-5356 1

Italian **Location:** Opposite Rockridge Bart station; in Market Hall Building. 5655 College Ave 94618. **Hours:** 7 am-2:30 & 5:30-9:30 pm, Sat 11:30 am-2 & 5:30-10 pm, Sun 5 pm-9 pm. Closed major holidays. **Reservations:** suggested. **Features:** Fresh seasonal ingredients are prepared in the Italian tradition. Casual dress; cocktails. **Parking:** on-site. **Cards:** AX, DC, MC, VI.

QUINN'S LIGHTHOUSE RESTAURANT & PUB **Lunch:** $7-$12 **Dinner:** $8-$22 **Phone:** 510/536-2050 6

AAA American **Location:** I-880, exit 16th Ave southbound; exit 5th Ave northbound, just w, then 0.3 mi s. 51 Embarcadero Cove 94606. **Hours:** 11:30 am-9 pm, Fri & Sat-10 pm, Sun from 11 am. Closed: 1/1, 12/25; also 11/23-11/27. **Reservations:** suggested. **Features:** In a historic 1890 lighthouse, the restaurant presents a menu of contemporary fare, including preparations of seafood, pasta and chicken. The upstairs deck is a beautiful lookout. Casual dress; cocktails. **Parking:** street. **Cards:** AX, MC, VI.

OCCIDENTAL —See Wine Country p. 796.

OLEMA

WHERE TO STAY

POINT REYES SEASHORE LODGE **Phone:** 415/663-9000

3/1-11/30	1P: $135-$295	2P: $135-$295	XP: $25	F6
2/1-2/29 & 12/1-1/31	1P: $105-$250	2P: $105-$250	XP: $25	F6

Motel **Location:** Center. Located adjacent to Golden Gate National Recreation Area. 10021 State Rt #1 94950 (PO Box 39). Fax: 415/663-9030. **Facility:** 23 units. 19 one-bedroom standard units, some with whirlpools. 3 one-bedroom suites ($175-$230) with whirlpools, some with kitchens. 1 cottage ($250-$295). 2 stories, exterior corridors. *Bath:* combo or shower only. **Parking:** on-site. **Terms:** 2 night minimum stay - weekends, 7 day cancellation notice, weekly rates available. **Business Services:** meeting rooms. **Cards:** AX, DS, MC, VI. ***(See color ad p 159)***

SOME UNITS

OLYMPIC VALLEY —See Lake Tahoe Area p. 372.

ORLAND pop. 6,281

WHERE TO STAY

AMBER LIGHT INN MOTEL

AAA SAVE — Motel

Phone: 530/865-7655

All Year 1P: $45-$48 2P: $49-$54 XP: $5 F12

Location: I-5, exit Chico (SR 32), 0.3 mi e. 828 Newville Rd 95963. Fax: 530/865-4627. **Facility:** 39 one-bedroom standard units, some with whirlpools. 2 stories, exterior corridors. *Bath:* combo or shower only. **Parking:** on-site. **Terms:** office hours 7 am-11 pm, cancellation fee imposed, weekly rates available, small pets only. **Amenities:** *Some:* irons, hair dryers. **Pool(s):** outdoor. **Leisure Activities:** whirlpool. **Cards:** AX, DC, DS, MC, VI. **Special Amenities: free local telephone calls and early check-in/late check-out.**

SOME UNITS

ORLAND INN

AAA SAVE — Motel

Phone: (530)865-7632

All Year 1P: $49-$55 2P: $53-$59 XP: $5 F17

Location: I-5, exit South St, 0.5 mi s; northbound exit I-5 E via Orland-Fairgrounds; southbound exit I-5 E via CR 16. Located in Stony Creek Shopping Center. 1052 South St 95963. Fax: 530/865-8731. **Facility:** 40 one-bedroom standard units. 2 stories, exterior corridors. **Parking:** on-site. **Terms:** office hours 7 am-11 pm, weekly rates available, pets ($5 extra charge). **Amenities:** *Some:* irons, hair dryers. **Pool(s):** outdoor. **Cards:** AX, CB, DC, DS, JC, MC, VI. **Special Amenities: free local telephone calls and early check-in/late check-out.**

FEE SOME UNITS

OROVILLE pop. 13,004

WHERE TO STAY

BEST VALUE INN *Book at aaa.com*

AAA SAVE — Motel

Phone: (530)533-7070

All Year 1P: $55-$110 2P: $65-$110 XP: $5 F12

Location: SR 70, exit Oroville Dam Blvd, 0.3 mi e. 580 Oro Dam Blvd 95965. Fax: 530/532-0402. **Facility:** 71 units. 70 one-bedroom standard units, some with whirlpools. 1 one-bedroom suite ($140-$155) with whirlpool. 1 story, exterior corridors. *Bath:* combo or shower only. **Parking:** on-site. **Terms:** cancellation fee imposed, pets ($20 deposit). **Amenities:** hair dryers. *Some:* irons. **Guest Services:** coin laundry. **Cards:** AX, CB, DC, DS, MC, VI. **Special Amenities: free continental breakfast and free local telephone calls.**

FEE SOME UNITS

COMFORT INN *Book at aaa.com*

AAA SAVE — Motel

Phone: (530)533-9673

All Year [CP] 1P: $74-$89 2P: $74-$89 XP: $10 F18

Location: SR 70, exit E Montgomery St. 1470 Feather River Blvd 95965. Fax: 530/533-5862. **Facility:** 54 units. 51 one-bedroom standard units. 3 one-bedroom suites ($99-$135). 3 stories, interior corridors. *Bath:* combo or shower only. **Parking:** on-site. **Terms:** pets ($100, with prior approval deposit). **Amenities:** irons, hair dryers. **Pool(s):** outdoor. **Leisure Activities:** sauna, whirlpool, exercise room. **Guest Services:** coin laundry. **Cards:** AX, CB, DC, DS, JC, MC, VI. **Special Amenities: free continental breakfast and free room upgrade (subject to availability with advanced reservations).**

DATA PORT FEE SOME UNITS

DAYS INN-OROVILLE *Book at aaa.com*

AAA SAVE — Motel

Phone: (530)533-3297

5/1-10/31 1P: $55-$70 2P: $60-$75 XP: $5 F14

2/1-4/30 & 11/1-1/31 1P: $50-$65 2P: $55-$70 XP: $5 F14

Location: SR 70, exit E Montgomery St, just e to Feather River Blvd, then 0.5 mi s. 1745 Feather River Blvd 95965. Fax: 530/533-4809. **Facility:** 38 one-bedroom standard units. 2 stories (no elevator), exterior corridors. *Bath:* combo or shower only. **Parking:** on-site. **Terms:** cancellation fee imposed, [CP] meal plan available, small pets only ($10 extra charge). **Amenities:** hair dryers. *Some:* irons. **Pool(s):** outdoor. **Cards:** AX, DC, MC, VI. **Special Amenities: free continental breakfast and free local telephone calls.**

FEE SOME UNITS

RIVERSIDE BED & BREAKFAST

Bed & Breakfast

Phone: 530/533-1413

All Year 1P: $100-$160 2P: $100-$160 XP: $20

Location: SR 70, exit Oroville Dam Blvd, 0.3 mi w to Middlehoff Ln, then 0.3 mi n. 1142 Middlehoff Ln 95965 (PO Box 2334). **Facility:** 8 one-bedroom standard units, some with whirlpools. 1 story, interior corridors. *Bath:* combo or shower only. **Parking:** on-site. **Terms:** age restrictions may apply, 7 day cancellation notice-fee imposed, weekly rates available, [BP] meal plan available, package plans. **Leisure Activities:** fishing. **Cards:** MC, VI.

SOME UNITS

SUNSET INN *Book at aaa.com*

AAA SAVE

Motel

Phone: (530)533-8201

All Year 1P: $45-$150 XP: $10 F12

Location: SR 70, exit E Montgomery St, 0.5 mi s. 1835 Feather River Blvd 95965. Fax: 530/533-7515. **Facility:** 42 one-bedroom standard units. 2 stories (no elevator), exterior corridors. *Bath:* combo or shower only. **Parking:** on-site. **Terms:** age restrictions may apply, cancellation fee imposed, [CP] meal plan available, small pets only. **Amenities:** *Some:* irons, hair dryers. **Pool(s):** outdoor. **Cards:** AX, DS, MC, VI. **Special Amenities: free continental breakfast and free local telephone calls.**

SOME UNITS

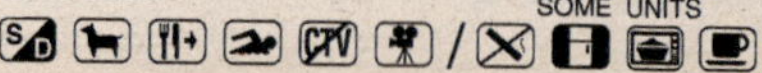

VILLA COURT INN Phone: (530)533-3930

Motel

All Year 1P: $46-$75 2P: $55-$90 XP: $10 F16
Location: SR 70, exit E Montgomery St, 0.3 mi e; SR 162 (Oroville Dam Blvd), 0.5 mi n. 1527 Feather River Blvd 95965. Fax: 530/533-1002. **Facility:** 20 one-bedroom standard units. 1 story, exterior corridors. *Bath:* shower only. **Parking:** on-site. **Terms:** age restrictions may apply, cancellation fee imposed, weekly rates available. **Amenities:** *Some:* irons, hair dryers. **Pool(s):** outdoor. **Business Services:** PC. **Cards:** AX, MC, VI. **Special Amenities: free expanded continental breakfast and free local telephone calls.**

SOME UNITS

WHERE TO DINE

THE DEPOT **Lunch:** $6-$11 **Dinner:** $9-$22 **Phone:** 530/534-9101

Steak & Seafood

Location: I-70, exit Montgomery St, corner of Oliver and High St. 2191 High St 95965. **Hours:** 11 am-9 pm, Fri-10 pm, Sat 4 pm-10 pm, Sun 3:30 pm-9 pm. Closed: 12/25. **Features:** Varied menu. Casual dress; cocktails. **Parking:** on-site. **Cards:** AX, DS, MC, VI.

PACIFICA —*See San Francisco p. 673.*

PACIFIC GROVE —*See Monterey Peninsula p. 485.*

PALO ALTO pop. 58,598

WHERE TO STAY

COUNTRY INN MOTEL **Phone:** 650/948-9154

Motel

All Year [CP] 1P: $64-$98 2P: $64-$98 XP: $10 F12
Location: US 101, exit San Antonio, just n on SR 82. 4345 El Camino Real 94306. Fax: 650/949-4190. **Facility:** 27 one-bedroom standard units, some with kitchens. 1-2 stories, exterior corridors. *Bath:* combo or shower only. **Parking:** on-site. **Terms:** cancellation fee imposed, weekly rates available. **Amenities:** irons. **Pool(s):** heated outdoor. **Cards:** AX, CB, DC, DS, JC, MC, VI.

SOME UNITS

CREEKSIDE INN *Book at aaa.com* **Phone:** (650)493-2411

Motel

All Year 1P: $139-$249 2P: $149-$259
Location: SR 82, 0.3 mi s of Oregon Expwy/Page Mill Rd. 3400 El Camino Real 94306. Fax: 650/493-6787. **Facility:** 136 units. 130 one-bedroom standard units, some with kitchens. 6 one-bedroom suites with kitchens. 4 stories, interior/exterior corridors. *Bath:* combo or shower only. **Parking:** on-site. **Terms:** cancellation fee imposed. **Amenities:** high-speed Internet, voice mail, irons, hair dryers. **Pool(s):** heated outdoor. **Leisure Activities:** exercise room. **Guest Services:** coin laundry, area transportation-within 5 mi. **Business Services:** meeting rooms. **Cards:** AX, CB, DC, DS, JC, MC, VI. *(See color ad below)*

SOME UNITS FEE

CROWNE PLAZA HOTEL AND RESORT CABANA HOTEL *Book at aaa.com*

Small-scale Hotel

Phone: (650)857-0787

All Year 1P: $99-$279 2P: $99-$279 XP: $15 F18

Location: US 101, exit San Antonio Rd, 0.4 mi n. 4290 El Camino Real 94306. Fax: 650/496-1939. **Facility:** 194 units. 182 one-bedroom standard units. 12 one-bedroom suites ($399-$599) with whirlpools. 2-8 stories, interior/exterior corridors. *Bath:* combo or shower only. **Parking:** on-site. **Terms:** cancellation fee imposed, pets ($100 deposit). **Amenities:** high-speed Internet, dual phone lines, voice mail, irons, hair dryers. **Pool(s):** outdoor. **Leisure Activities:** whirlpool. **Guest Services:** gift shop, valet laundry. **Business Services:** conference facilities, business center. **Cards:** AX, CB, DC, DS, MC, VI.

ASK FEE SOME UNITS

DAYS INN *Book at aaa.com*

AAA SAVE

Motel

Phone: (650)493-4222

All Year 1P: $69-$129 2P: $79-$159 XP: $10 F12

Location: US 101, exit San Antonio Rd, 2 mi w to SR 82, then 1 mi n on SR 82. 4238 El Camino Real 94306. Fax: 650/494-6112. **Facility:** 23 one-bedroom standard units. 2 stories, exterior corridors. **Parking:** on-site. **Terms:** [CP] meal plan available. **Amenities:** high-speed Internet, dual phone lines, voice mail, irons, hair dryers. **Cards:** AX, CB, DC, DS, JC, MC, VI. **Special Amenities: free continental breakfast and free local telephone calls.**

DATA PORT SOME UNITS

DINAH'S GARDEN HOTEL *Book at aaa.com*

AAA SAVE

Motel

Phone: (650)493-2844

All Year 1P: $109-$189 2P: $109-$189

Location: US 101, exit San Antonio Rd, just n on SR 82. 4261 El Camino Real 94306-4405. Fax: 650/856-4713. **Facility:** 146 units. 48 one-bedroom standard units, some with efficiencies. 97 one- and 1 two-bedroom suites ($189-$249), some with efficiencies, kitchens and/or whirlpools. 1-3 stories, interior/exterior corridors. *Bath:* combo or shower only. **Parking:** on-site. **Terms:** cancellation fee imposed. **Amenities:** high-speed Internet, dual phone lines, voice mail, safes, honor bars, irons, hair dryers. **Dining:** 2 restaurants, 6:30 am-9:30 pm, cocktails. **Pool(s):** 2 heated outdoor. **Leisure Activities:** sauna, exercise room. **Guest Services:** coin laundry. **Business Services:** conference facilities. **Cards:** AX, DC, DS, JC, MC, VI.

DATA PORT SOME UNITS VCR FEE

HOWARD JOHNSON EXPRESS INN *Book at aaa.com*

AAA SAVE

Motel

Phone: (650)493-2760

All Year 1P: $89-$159 2P: $99-$169 XP: $10 F12

Location: US 101, exit Oregon Expwy/Page Mill Rd, 2 mi w to SR 82, then se on SR 82 to Ventura. 3901 El Camino Real 94306. Fax: 650/494-7833. **Facility:** 53 one-bedroom standard units. 1-2 stories, exterior corridors. *Bath:* combo or shower only. **Parking:** on-site. **Terms:** [ECP] meal plan available, package plans - weekends. **Amenities:** voice mail, irons, hair dryers. *Some:* high-speed Internet. **Cards:** AX, DC, DS, MC, VI. **Special Amenities: early check-in/late check-out and preferred room (subject to availability with advanced reservations).**

DATA PORT SOME UNITS

HYATT RICKEYS *Book at aaa.com*

AAA SAVE

Motel

Phone: (650)493-8000

All Year 1P: $99-$209 2P: $99-$209 XP: $25 F18

Location: US 101, exit San Antonio Rd, 1 mi n on SR 82. 4219 El Camino Real 94306. Fax: 650/424-0836. **Facility:** 350 units. 342 one-bedroom standard units. 8 one-bedroom suites. 1-6 stories, interior/exterior corridors. *Bath:* combo or shower only. **Parking:** on-site. **Terms:** cancellation fee imposed. **Amenities:** voice mail, irons, hair dryers. **Dining:** 6:30 am-4 & 5-10:30 pm, cocktails. **Pool(s):** outdoor. **Leisure Activities:** exercise room. **Guest Services:** valet laundry, area transportation-within 5 mi. **Business Services:** conference facilities, business center. **Cards:** AX, CB, DC, DS, JC, MC, VI. *(See color ad p 623)*

FEE DATA PORT SOME UNITS VCR FEE

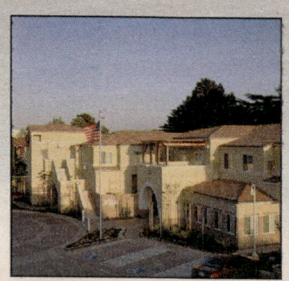

QUALITY INN-PALO ALTO *Book at aaa.com* **Phone:** (650)493-3141

Motel

All Year [ECP] 1P: $69-$159 2P: $69-$169 XP: $10 F17
Location: US 101, exit Oregon Expwy/Page Mill Rd, then 1 mi s. 3945 El Camino Real 94306. Fax: 650/493-6313. **Facility:** 70 one-bedroom standard units. 2 stories, exterior corridors. *Bath:* combo or shower only. **Parking:** on-site. **Amenities:** high-speed Internet, voice mail, irons, hair dryers. **Cards:** AX, CB, DC, DS, JC, MC, VI. **Special Amenities: free expanded continental breakfast and free newspaper.**

SHERATON PALO ALTO HOTEL *Book at aaa.com* **Phone:** 650/328-2800

Small-scale Hotel

All Year 1P: $299 2P: $299
Location: US 101, exit Embarcadero W to SR 82, then 0.5 mi n. Located opposite Stanford University. 625 El Camino Real 94301. Fax: 650/327-7362. **Facility:** 346 one-bedroom standard units, some with whirlpools. 4 stories, interior corridors. **Parking:** on-site. **Terms:** cancellation fee imposed, small pets only. **Amenities:** video games, dual phone lines, voice mail, irons, hair dryers. *Some:* high-speed Internet, fax. **Pool(s):** heated outdoor. **Leisure Activities:** exercise room. **Guest Services:** gift shop, coin laundry, area transportation. **Business Services:** conference facilities, business center. **Cards:** AX, CB, DC, DS, JC, MC, VI.

ASK FEE SOME UNITS FEE

SKY RANCH INN **Phone:** (650)493-7221

Motel

All Year [CP] 1P: $65-$100 2P: $70-$105 XP: $10 D
Location: 2.5 mi s of Stanford University campus. 4234 El Camino Real 94306. Fax: 650/493-0858. **Facility:** 27 one-bedroom standard units. 1-2 stories, exterior corridors. *Bath:* combo or shower only. **Parking:** on-site. **Terms:** 3 day cancellation notice-fee imposed. **Amenities:** voice mail, irons. *Some:* hair dryers. **Guest Services:** coin laundry. **Cards:** AX, CB, DC, DS, JC, MC, VI. **Special Amenities: free continental breakfast and preferred room (subject to availability with advanced reservations).** *(See color ad below)*

SOME UNITS

STANFORD TERRACE INN *Book at aaa.com* **Phone:** (650)857-0333

Motel

All Year [ECP] 1P: $179-$209 2P: $189-$219 XP: $10 F12
Location: W off SR 82. Adjacent to Stanford University campus. 531 Stanford Ave 94306. Fax: 650/857-0343. **Facility:** 80 units. 78 one-bedroom standard units, some with kitchens. 2 one-bedroom suites ($230-$270) with kitchens. 2-3 stories, exterior corridors. *Bath:* combo or shower only. **Parking:** on-site. **Terms:** cancellation fee imposed. **Amenities:** voice mail, honor bars, irons, hair dryers. **Pool(s):** heated outdoor. **Leisure Activities:** exercise room. **Guest Services:** coin laundry, area transportation-within 5 mi. **Business Services:** meeting rooms. **Cards:** AX, DC, DS, MC, VI. **Special Amenities: free continental breakfast and free newspaper.**

SOME UNITS

SUPER 8 *Book at aaa.com* **Phone:** (650)493-9085

AAA SAVE — Motel

6/11-8/31 [CP]	1P: $85-$95	2P: $85-$95	XP: $10	F12
2/1-6/10 [CP]	1P: $80-$90	2P: $80-$90	XP: $10	F12
9/1-1/31 [CP]	1P: $75-$85	2P: $75-$85	XP: $10	F12

Location: 0.3 mi s of Oregon Expwy. Located in a commercial area. 3200 El Camino Real 94306. Fax: 650/493-8405. **Facility:** 36 units. 32 one- and 4 two-bedroom standard units. 2 stories, exterior corridors. **Parking:** on-site. **Terms:** cancellation fee imposed. **Amenities:** voice mail, irons, hair dryers. **Pool(s):** outdoor. **Cards:** AX, DC, DS, MC, VI. **Special Amenities: free continental breakfast and free local telephone calls.**

SOME UNITS

TOWNHOUSE INN *Book at aaa.com* **Phone:** (650)493-4492

AAA SAVE — Motel

All Year [CP] 1P: $84-$114 2P: $92-$121 XP: $8 F12

Location: US 101, exit Oregon Expwy, 3 mi w to SR 82 SE. 4164 El Camino Real 94306. Fax: 650/493-3418. **Facility:** 37 units. 34 one-bedroom standard units. 2 one- and 1 two-bedroom suites ($150-$210), some with efficiencies, kitchens and/or whirlpools. 1-2 stories, exterior corridors. **Parking:** on-site. **Amenities:** voice mail, irons, hair dryers. **Leisure Activities:** whirlpool, exercise room. **Guest Services:** coin laundry. **Business Services:** meeting rooms. **Cards:** AX, DC, DS, MC, VI. *(See color ad p 529)*

SOME UNITS

TRAVELODGE PALO ALTO *Book at aaa.com* **Phone:** (650)493-6340

Motel

All Year 1P: $79 2P: $89

Location: US 101, exit Oregon Expwy, 2 mi w to SR 82. 3255 El Camino Real 94306. Fax: 650/424-9535. **Facility:** 29 one-bedroom standard units. 2 stories, exterior corridors. *Bath:* combo or shower only. **Parking:** on-site. **Terms:** [CP] meal plan available, pets ($50 extra charge). **Amenities:** safes, irons, hair dryers. **Pool(s):** heated outdoor. **Cards:** AX, DC, DS, JC, MC, VI.

SOME UNITS

FEE

THE WESTIN PALO ALTO *Book at aaa.com* **Phone:** (650)321-4422

Large-scale Hotel

All Year 1P: $139-$279 2P: $139-$279 XP: $15 F16

Location: US 101, exit to Embarcadero, right on El Camino Real, just n. 675 El Camino Real 94301. Fax: 650/321-5522. **Facility:** 184 units. 180 one-bedroom standard units, some with whirlpools. 4 one-bedroom suites ($179-$379). 5 stories, interior corridors. **Parking:** valet. **Amenities:** video games, CD players, dual phone lines, voice mail, safes, honor bars, irons, hair dryers. **Pool(s):** heated outdoor. **Leisure Activities:** whirlpool, exercise room. **Guest Services:** gift shop, valet laundry, area transportation. **Business Services:** meeting rooms, business center. **Cards:** AX, CB, DC, DS, JC, MC, VI.

SOME UNITS

WHERE TO DINE

CALIFORNIA CAFE BAR & GRILL **Lunch:** $7-$14 **Dinner:** $13-$27 **Phone:** 650/325-2233

Regional American

Location: SR 82, exit Palm Dr, s to Arboreteum, w to Quarry; at Stanford Barn. 700 Welch Rd 94304. **Hours:** 11:30 am-10 pm, Sun 11 am-8 pm. Closed: 1/1, 12/25, 12/26; also Super Bowl Sun. **Reservations:** suggested. **Features:** Contemporary California cuisine is prepared with a decidedly Continental flair. Dressy casual; cocktails. **Parking:** on-site. **Cards:** AX, DC, MC, VI.

MANDARIN GOURMET **Lunch:** $8-$28 **Dinner:** $8-$28 **Phone:** 650/328-8898

Chinese

Location: Between University and Lytton. 420 Ramona St 94301. **Hours:** 11:30 am-2:30 & 5-10 pm, Sun 5 pm-9 pm. Closed: 11/25. **Reservations:** suggested. **Features:** Modern and attractive, the restaurant tempts diners with well-prepared traditional dishes. Casual dress; cocktails. **Parking:** street. **Cards:** AX, MC, VI.

MING'S RESTAURANT **Lunch:** $9-$19 **Dinner:** $11-$29 **Phone:** 650/856-7700

Regional Chinese

Location: US 101, just e. 1700 Embarcadero Rd 94303. **Hours:** 11 am-9:30 pm, Sat-10 pm. **Reservations:** suggested. **Features:** Among choices are dim sum on carts, fresh seafood, Chinese barbecue and Cantonese favorites. Seating is comfortable. Casual dress; cocktails. **Parking:** on-site. **Cards:** AX, DC, DS, MC, VI.

SCOTT'S SEAFOOD GRILL & BAR **Lunch:** $9-$30 **Dinner:** $15-$40 **Phone:** 650/856-1046

Steak & Seafood

Location: US 101, exit Embarcadero Rd E. 2300 E Bayshore Rd 94303. **Hours:** 7 am-10:30 & 11-9:30 pm. Closed major holidays. **Reservations:** suggested. **Features:** The dining room nurtures a casual, New England atmosphere. On the menu are pasta, chicken and prime steak dishes. Casual dress; cocktails. **Parking:** on-site. **Cards:** AX, CB, DC, DS, MC, VI.

SUNDANCE MINE COMPANY **Lunch:** $10-$24 **Dinner:** $15-$37 **Phone:** 650/321-6798

AAA — American

Location: On SR 82, between Oregon Expwy and Embarcadero Rd. 1921 El Camino Real 94306. **Hours:** 11:30 am-2 & 5-10 pm, Sat 5 pm-10:30 pm, Sun 5 pm-9 pm. Closed major holidays. **Reservations:** suggested. **Features:** Steak, prime rib and seafood specials line the comfortable and modern restaurant's menu. Soft lighting, mahogany paneling and light jazz music mingle to create an intimate dining experience. The wine list is lengthy. Dressy casual; cocktails. **Parking:** on-site. **Cards:** AX, DC, DS, MC, VI.

PARADISE pop. 26,408

WHERE TO STAY

COMFORT INN

Motel

Book at aaa.com — **Phone:** (530)876-0191

All Year [CP] 1P: $69-$94 2P: $69-$94 XP: $10 F18

Location: SR 191, 0.5 mi s of Pearson Rd. 5475 Clark Rd 95969. Fax: 530/876-9936. **Facility:** 62 units. 60 one-bedroom standard units. 2 one-bedroom suites. 3 stories, interior corridors. *Bath:* combo or shower only. **Parking:** on-site. **Terms:** pets ($100 deposit, $6 extra charge). **Amenities:** voice mail, irons, hair dryers. **Pool(s):** heated outdoor. **Leisure Activities:** whirlpool, exercise room. **Guest Services:** coin laundry. **Business Services:** fax. **Cards:** AX, CB, DC, DS, JC, MC, VI. **Special Amenities: free continental breakfast and free local telephone calls.**

FEE SOME UNITS

LANTERN INN

Motel

Phone: 530/877-5553

All Year [CP] 1P: $49-$69 2P: $59-$89 XP: $5 F12

Location: 1 blk w off Skyway. Located in a quiet area. 5799 Wildwood Ln 95969. Fax: 530/877-3944. **Facility:** 16 one-bedroom standard units. 1 story, exterior corridors. *Bath:* shower only. **Parking:** on-site. **Terms:** office hours 7 am-11 pm, weekly rates available. **Amenities:** voice mail. *Some:* irons, hair dryers. **Pool(s):** small outdoor. **Cards:** AX, DC, DS, MC, VI. **Special Amenities: free local telephone calls.**

SOME UNITS

PARADISE INN

Motel

Phone: (530)877-2127

All Year 1P: $49-$79 2P: $59-$99 XP: $5 F12

Location: 1.5 mi w. 5423 Skyway 95969. Fax: 530/877-2756. **Facility:** 17 units. 14 one- and 3 two-bedroom standard units. 1-2 stories (no elevator), exterior corridors. *Bath:* combo or shower only. **Parking:** on-site. **Terms:** office hours 8 am-10 pm. **Amenities:** irons, hair dryers. **Pool(s):** small heated outdoor. **Cards:** AX, DC, DS, MC, VI. **Special Amenities: free local telephone calls.**

PONDEROSA GARDENS MOTEL
Motel

Phone: (530)872-9094

All Year [ECP] 1P: $72-$95 2P: $78-$105 XP: $6 F5

Location: 2 blks e; center. Located in a secluded area. 7010 Skyway 95969. Fax: 530/872-2993. **Facility:** 48 units. 47 one-bedroom standard units, some with kitchens and/or whirlpools. 1 one-bedroom suite ($120) with kitchen. 1 story, exterior corridors. **Parking:** on-site. **Terms:** office hours 7 am-10:30 pm, pets ($6 extra charge). **Amenities:** hair dryers. *Some:* irons. **Pool(s):** outdoor. **Leisure Activities:** whirlpool. **Guest Services:** gift shop, coin laundry. **Business Services:** meeting rooms. **Cards:** AX, CB, DC, MC, VI.

FEE SOME UNITS

WHERE TO DINE

SMOKIE MOUNTAIN DINNERHOUSE & LOUNGE
American

Dinner: $12-$22 **Phone:** 530/872-3323

Location: SR 99, exit Skyway S. 7059 Skyway 95969. **Hours:** 5 pm-9 pm, Fri & Sat-10 pm. Closed: Sun & Mon. **Features:** Small elegant restaurant, fine dining, fine service and a variety of fare- leaning towards American/Cajun. Beautifully crafted wood paneling & local artis wall covering. **Parking:** on-site. **Cards:** AX, MC, VI.

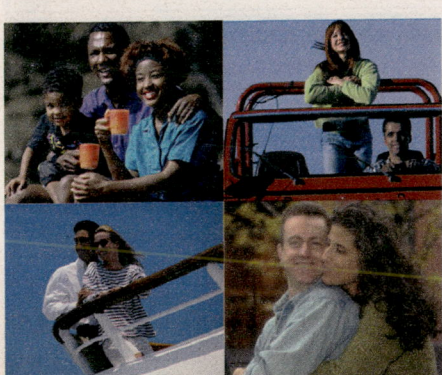

PASO ROBLES pop. 24,297

WHERE TO STAY

ADELAIDE INN — **Phone:** (805)238-2770

Motel

4/30-10/17 [CP]	1P: $55-$99	2P: $60-$99	XP: $6
2/1-4/29 & 10/18-1/31 [CP]	1P: $50-$85	2P: $55-$85	XP: $6

Location: US 101, exit SR 46 (Fresno/Bakersfield), just w. 1215 Ysabel Ave 93446. Fax: 805/238-3497. **Facility:** 67 one-bedroom standard units. 1-2 stories (no elevator), exterior corridors. *Bath:* combo or shower only. **Parking:** on-site. **Terms:** 3 day cancellation notice. **Amenities:** irons, hair dryers. *Some: Fee:* high-speed Internet. **Pool(s):** heated outdoor. **Leisure Activities:** sauna, whirlpool, 3-hole micro golf putting green. **Guest Services:** coin laundry. **Cards:** AX, CB, DC, DS, MC, VI. **Special Amenities: free local telephone calls and free newspaper.** *(See color ad below)*

SOME UNITS DATA PORT / FEE FEE /

BEST WESTERN BLACK OAK MOTOR LODGE Book at aaa.com — **Phone:** (805)238-4740

Motel

All Year	1P: $75-$130	2P: $75-$130	XP: $10 F12

Location: US 101, exit SR 46 (Fresno/Bakersfield), just w. 1135 24th St 93446. Fax: 805/238-0726. **Facility:** 110 one-bedroom standard units, some with whirlpools. 2 stories (no elevator), exterior corridors. *Bath:* combo or shower only. **Parking:** on-site. **Amenities:** video library (fee), voice mail, irons, hair dryers. *Some:* safes. **Dining:** 6 am-9 pm, wine/beer only. **Pool(s):** heated outdoor, wading. **Leisure Activities:** sauna, whirlpool, picnic tables & barbecue grills, playground. **Guest Services:** valet and coin laundry. **Cards:** AX, CB, DC, DS, JC, MC, VI. **Special Amenities: free local telephone calls and free newspaper.**

SOME UNITS DATA PORT / VCR /

HAMPTON INN & SUITES Book at aaa.com — **Phone:** (805)226-9988

Small-scale Hotel

5/11-9/27 [ECP]	1P: $109-$149	2P: $115-$154
9/28-1/31 [ECP]	1P: $89-$139	2P: $95-$145
3/9-5/10 [ECP]	1P: $89-$135	2P: $95-$145
2/1-3/8 [ECP]	1P: $79-$125	2P: $85-$131

Location: US 101, exit SR 46 W, just sw. 212 Alexa Ct 93446. Fax: 805/226-9073. **Facility:** 81 one-bedroom standard units. 3 stories, interior corridors. **Parking:** on-site. **Terms:** cancellation fee imposed, pets ($50 deposit). **Amenities:** video games (fee), dual phone lines, voice mail, irons, hair dryers. **Pool(s):** heated outdoor. **Leisure Activities:** whirlpool, exercise room. **Guest Services:** gift shop, complimentary evening beverages: Mon-Thurs. **Business Services:** meeting rooms. **Cards:** AX, DC, DS, MC, VI.

SOME UNITS ASK FEE DATA PORT / /

HOLIDAY INN EXPRESS HOTEL & SUITES Book at aaa.com Phone: (805)238-6500

Small-scale Hotel

3/16-9/30 [ECP]	1P: $99-$179	2P: $99-$179
2/1-3/15 & 10/1-1/31 [ECP]	1P: $89-$179	2P: $89-$179

Location: US 101, exit SR 46 E (Fresno/Bakersfield), just w, then just n. Located across from Mid-State Fairgrounds. 2455 Riverside Ave 93446. Fax: 805/238-0500. **Facility:** Smoke free premises. 62 one-bedroom standard units, some with whirlpools. 3 stories, interior corridors. **Parking:** on-site. **Terms:** 3 day cancellation notice-fee imposed, package plans. **Amenities:** dual phone lines, voice mail, irons, hair dryers. **Pool(s):** heated indoor. **Leisure Activities:** whirlpool, exercise room. **Guest Services:** valet and coin laundry. **Cards:** AX, DC, DS, MC, VI.

ASK

MELODY RANCH MOTEL Phone: 805/238-3911

SAVE

Motel

4/1-10/31	1P: $50-$64	2P: $56-$69	XP: $3
2/1-3/31 & 11/1-1/31	1P: $48-$58	2P: $56-$64	XP: $3

Location: US 101, exit Spring St northbound, 0.6 mi n; exit 16th St southbound, just w, then 0.6 mi s. 939 Spring St 93446. **Facility:** 19 one-bedroom standard units. 1 story, exterior corridors. *Bath:* shower only. **Parking:** on-site. **Terms:** office hours 7:30 am-11 pm. **Amenities:** *Some:* irons, hair dryers. **Pool(s):** heated outdoor. **Cards:** AX, CB, DC, DS, MC, VI. **Special Amenities: free newspaper and preferred room (subject to availability with advanced reservations).**

SOME UNITS

PASO ROBLES INN Book at aaa.com Phone: (805)238-2660

SAVE

Historic Small-scale Hotel

4/1-10/31	1P: $115-$255	2P: $115-$255	XP: $10	F17
2/1-3/31 & 11/1-1/31	1P: $105-$195	2P: $105-$195	XP: $10	F17

Location: US 101, exit Spring St northbound, 0.8 mi n; exit 16th St southbound, just w, then just s. 1103 Spring St 93446. Fax: 805/238-4707. **Facility:** Trees shade the manicured grounds of this inn, which has an early-California atmosphere and includes 10 units in the original 1890 building. 100 one-bedroom standard units, some with whirlpools. 2 stories (no elevator), interior/exterior corridors. *Bath:* combo or shower only. **Parking:** on-site. **Terms:** 3 day cancellation notice. **Amenities:** voice mail, hair dryers. *Some:* irons. **Dining:** 2 restaurants, 6 am-9 pm, Fri & Sat-10 pm, cocktails. **Pool(s):** heated outdoor. **Leisure Activities:** whirlpool, exercise room. **Guest Services:** valet laundry. **Business Services:** meeting rooms. **Cards:** AX, CB, DC, DS, JC, MC, VI. *(See color ad p 532)*

SOME UNITS

SUMMERWOOD INN — Phone: 805/227-1111

Bed & Breakfast — All Year [BP] 1P: $195-$295 2P: $225-$360 XP: $65

Location: US 101, exit SR 46 W, 1 mi w. Located at Summerwood Winery. 2130 Arbor Rd 93446. Fax: 805/227-1112. **Facility:** Set amid vineyards and a large manicured lawn, this modern Victorian offers tastefully decorated rooms, all with a fireplace and balcony. Smoke free premises. 9 one-bedroom standard units, some with whirlpools. 2 stories (no elevator), interior/exterior corridors. **Parking:** on-site. **Terms:** 2 night minimum stay - with Saturday stay-over. **Amenities:** CD players, voice mail, irons, hair dryers. **Guest Services:** gift shop, complimentary evening beverages. **Business Services:** meeting rooms. **Cards:** AX, MC, VI.

WHERE TO DINE

BISTRO LAURENT — **Lunch:** $5-$13 **Dinner:** $15-$24 **Phone:** 805/226-8191

French

Location: US 101, exit SR 46 (Fresno/Bakersfield), 0.5 mi w on 24th St, 1 mi s on Spring St, then just e on 12th St. 1202 Pine St 93446. **Hours:** 11:30 am-2:30 & 5:30-10 pm. Closed: 1/1, 11/25, 12/25; also Sun. **Features:** The small, casual restaurant serves excellent fish, beef and poultry entrees. From 11:30 am to 2:30 pm, the patio opens for lunch as "Le Petite Morsel". Casual dress; beer & wine only. **Parking:** street. **Cards:** MC, VI.

BUSI'S ON THE PARK — **Lunch:** $5-$7 **Dinner:** $8-$15 **Phone:** 805/238-1390

American

Location: US 101, exit SR 46 (Fresno/Bakersfield), 0.5 mi w on 24th St, 1 mi s on Spring St, then just e on 11th St. 1122 Pine St 93446. **Hours:** 11 am-4 & 5-9 pm. Closed: 7/4, 12/25. **Reservations:** suggested. **Features:** In the center of town, the small, casual restaurant makes decadent pastries and desserts on the premises. Casual dress; cocktails. **Parking:** street. **Cards:** AX, MC, VI.

LOLO'S — **Lunch:** $6-$9 **Dinner:** $6-$10 **Phone:** 805/239-5777

Mexican

Location: US 101, exit SR 46 (Fresno/Bakersfield), 0.5 mi w on 24th St, then 1.6 mi s. 305 Spring St 93446. **Hours:** 11 am-8 pm; to 9 pm in summer. Closed: 11/25, 12/24, 12/25; also 3/29-3/31. **Features:** In a restored home with a breezy, comfortable patio, the restaurant offers patrons a casual dining experience. Casual dress; beer & wine only. **Parking:** on-site. **Cards:** AX, MC, VI.

VILLA CREEK RESTAURANT — **Dinner:** $14-$27 **Phone:** 805/238-3000

Southwestern

Location: Downtown; across from city park. 1144 Pine St 93446. **Hours:** 5 pm-10 pm. Closed major holidays. **Reservations:** suggested. **Features:** Early California decor distinguishes the casual dining room. An impressive choice of wines matches well with early California and Mexican dishes. Casual dress; cocktails. **Parking:** street. **Cards:** AX, DS, MC, VI.

PATTERSON pop. 11,606

WHERE TO STAY

BEST WESTERN VILLA DEL LAGO INN — *Book at aaa.com* — **Phone:** (209)892-5300

SAVE

Small-scale Hotel — All Year 1P: $68-$78 2P: $68-$78 XP: $10 F17

Location: I-5, exit Patterson, just e. 2959 Speno Dr 95363. Fax: 209/892-5303. **Facility:** 82 units. 80 one-bedroom standard units, some with whirlpools. 2 one-bedroom suites ($155-$165) with whirlpools. 3 stories, interior corridors. **Parking:** on-site. **Terms:** 3 day cancellation notice, [MAP] meal plan available. **Amenities:** video games (fee), dual phone lines, voice mail, irons, hair dryers. **Dining:** 11 am-10 pm. **Pool(s):** outdoor. **Leisure Activities:** sauna, whirlpool, exercise room. **Guest Services:** coin laundry. **Business Services:** meeting rooms, business center. **Cards:** AX, DC, DS, MC, VI. **Special Amenities: free continental breakfast and early check-in/late check-out.** *(See color ad below)*

SOME UNITS FEE FEE

PEBBLE BEACH —*See Monterey Peninsula p. 491.*

PETALUMA —*See Wine Country p. 796.*

PINECREST

WHERE TO STAY

PINECREST LAKE RESORT — **Phone:** 209/965-3411

Motel — All Year 1P: $80-$250 2P: $80-$250

Location: Center. 421 Pinecrest Lake Rd 95364. Fax: 209/965-4032. **Facility:** 27 units. 6 one-bedroom standard units. 7 cabins and 14 cottages. 1 story, exterior corridors. *Bath:* combo or shower only. **Parking:** on-site. **Terms:** office hours 9 am-6 pm, 2 night minimum stay - weekends, 30 day cancellation notice-fee imposed. **Leisure Activities:** boating, canoeing, paddleboats, sailboats, windsurfing, boat dock, 2 tennis courts, downhill & cross country skiing, bicycles, hiking trails. **Cards:** MC, VI.

PINOLE pop. 19,039

WHERE TO STAY

DAYS INN-SF/PINOLE Book at aaa.com — **Phone:** (510)222-9400

Motel — All Year 1P: $59-$89 2P: $69-$99

Location: I-80, exit Appian Way, 0.3 mi s. 2600 Appian Way 94564. Fax: 510/669-1614. **Facility:** 50 one-bedroom standard units. 2 stories (no elevator), exterior corridors. **Parking:** on-site. **Terms:** age restrictions may apply. **Amenities:** hair dryers. *Some:* irons. **Leisure Activities:** sauna, whirlpool, exercise room. **Guest Services:** coin laundry. **Cards:** AX, CB, DC, MC, VI.

SOME UNITS

PIONEER

WHERE TO STAY

PIONEER RESORTS LODGE — **Phone:** 209/295-3490

Motel — All Year 1P: $66-$100 2P: $66-$100 XP: $5 F

Location: East end of town. 24144 Hwy 88 95689 (P O Box 677, 95666). Fax: 209/295-3481. **Facility:** 25 one-bedroom standard units, some with kitchens. 2 stories (no elevator), exterior corridors. **Parking:** on-site. **Terms:** [CP] meal plan available. **Pool(s):** outdoor. **Leisure Activities:** whirlpool. **Cards:** AX, DS, MC, VI.

SOME UNITS

PISMO BEACH pop. 8,551

WHERE TO STAY

BEACHCOMBER INN — **Phone:** (805)773-5505

AAA SAVE — Motel — All Year [CP] 1P: $79-$179 2P: $99-$179

Location: US 101, exit Price St northbound, 0.5 mi n to Hines Ave, just w; exit Hines Ave southbound, just w. 541 Cypress St 93449. Fax: 805/773-0880. **Facility:** Smoke free premises. 7 one-bedroom standard units. 2 stories (no elevator), exterior corridors. **Parking:** on-site. **Terms:** office hours 8 am-8 pm. **Amenities:** voice mail, hair dryers. **Cards:** AX, DS, MC, VI. **Special Amenities: free continental breakfast and free local telephone calls.**

BEST WESTERN SHELTER COVE LODGE *Book at aaa.com* **Phone:** (805)773-3511

AAA SAVE — Motel

5/1-9/30 [ECP]	1P: $158-$310	2P: $158-$310	XP: $10	F18
12/24-1/31 [ECP]	1P: $148-$268	2P: $148-$268	XP: $10	F18
2/1-4/30 [ECP]	1P: $98-$268	2P: $98-$268	XP: $10	F18
10/1-12/23 [ECP]	1P: $88-$218	2P: $88-$218	XP: $10	F18

Location: US 101, exit Shell Beach Rd northbound, just w, 0.3 mi n; exit Price St southbound, just w, 0.4 mi n. 2651 Price St 93449. Fax: 805/773-0368. **Facility:** Smoke free premises. 53 one-bedroom standard units. 2 stories, exterior corridors. **Parking:** on-site. **Terms:** 3 day cancellation notice-fee imposed. **Amenities:** voice mail, irons, hair dryers. **Pool(s):** heated outdoor. **Leisure Activities:** whirlpool. **Business Services:** meeting rooms. **Cards:** AX, DC, DS, MC, VI. **Special Amenities: free expanded continental breakfast and free newspaper.** *(See color ad below)*

BEST WESTERN SHORE CLIFF LODGE *Book at aaa.com* **Phone:** (805)773-4671

AAA SAVE — Small-scale Hotel

4/1-10/31 [CP]	1P: $129-$289	2P: $129-$289	XP: $10	F17
2/1-3/31 [CP]	1P: $99-$269	2P: $99-$269	XP: $10	F17
11/1-1/31 [CP]	1P: $89-$269	2P: $89-$269	XP: $10	F17

Location: US 101, exit Shell Beach Rd northbound; exit Price St southbound, just w. 2555 Price St 93449. Fax: 805/773-2341. **Facility:** Smoke free premises. 99 units. 93 one-bedroom standard units. 6 one-bedroom suites ($199-$339). 2-3 stories, interior/exterior corridors. **Parking:** on-site. **Terms:** 3 day cancellation notice. **Amenities:** video games (fee), voice mail, irons, hair dryers. **Dining:** Shore Cliff Restaurant, see separate listing. **Pool(s):** heated outdoor. **Leisure Activities:** sauna, whirlpool, 2 lighted tennis courts. **Guest Services:** valet laundry. **Business Services:** meeting rooms. **Cards:** AX, CB, DC, DS, JC, MC, VI. **Special Amenities: free continental breakfast and free room upgrade (subject to availability with advanced reservations).** *(See color ad p 537)*

CLIFFS RESORT *Book at aaa.com* **Phone:** (805)773-5000

Small-scale Hotel

5/28-9/18	1P: $169-$319	2P: $169-$319	XP: $10	F12
9/19-11/13	1P: $159-$279	2P: $159-$279	XP: $10	F12
11/14-1/31	1P: $149-$269	2P: $149-$269	XP: $10	F12
2/1-5/27	1P: $139-$269	2P: $139-$269	XP: $10	F12

Location: US 101, exit Spyglass Dr northbound; exit Shell Beach Rd southbound, just w, then just n. 2757 Shell Beach Rd 93449. Fax: 805/773-0764. **Facility:** Smoke free premises. 165 units. 155 one-bedroom standard units, some with whirlpools. 10 one-bedroom suites ($199-$429) with whirlpools. 5 stories, interior corridors. *Bath:* combo or shower only. **Parking:** on-site and valet. **Terms:** 2 night minimum stay - some weekends, 3 day cancellation notice-fee imposed, weekly rates available, package plans - midweek. **Amenities:** video games (fee), voice mail, irons, hair dryers. **Dining:** Sea Cliffs Restaurant, see separate listing. **Pool(s):** heated outdoor. **Leisure Activities:** sauna, whirlpools, bicycles, exercise room, volleyball. *Fee:* massage. **Guest Services:** gift shop, valet and coin laundry, area transportation. **Business Services:** conference facilities, business center. **Cards:** AX, CB, DC, DS, JC, MC, VI. ***(See color ad p 538)***

SOME UNITS

COTTAGE INN BY THE SEA *Book at aaa.com* **Phone:** (805)773-4617

Motel

6/11-10/31 [ECP] 1P: $119-$249 2P: $119-$249
2/1-6/10 & 11/1-1/31 [ECP] 1P: $89-$229 2P: $89-$229

Location: US 101, exit Shell Beach Rd northbound, just w, 0.5 mi s; exit Price St southbound, just w, then just s. 2351 Price St 93449. Fax: 805/773-8336. **Facility:** Smoke free premises. 79 one-bedroom standard units. 1-2 stories (no elevator), exterior corridors. **Parking:** on-site. **Terms:** pets ($10 fee, in designated units). **Amenities:** voice mail, irons, hair dryers. *Fee:* video games, safes. **Pool(s):** heated outdoor. **Leisure Activities:** whirlpool. **Guest Services:** valet laundry. **Business Services:** fax. **Cards:** AX, DC, DS, JC, MC, VI. **Special Amenities: free expanded continental breakfast.** *(See color ad p 539)*

FEE

EDGEWATER INN & SUITES *Book at aaa.com* **Phone:** (805)773-4811

Motel

All Year [CP] 1P: $99-$190 2P: $99-$190 XP: $10 F18

Location: US 101, exit Wadsworth Ave northbound, just w; exit Price St southbound, just w, then 0.4 mi s on Doliver St. 280 Wadsworth Ave 93449. Fax: 805/773-5121. **Facility:** 101 units. 81 one-bedroom standard units, some with whirlpools. 19 one- and 1 two-bedroom suites ($109-$230) with kitchens, some with whirlpools. 2-3 stories, exterior corridors. *Bath:* combo or shower only. **Parking:** on-site. **Terms:** 2 night minimum stay - weekends. **Amenities:** *Some:* irons. **Pool(s):** heated outdoor. **Leisure Activities:** whirlpool. **Guest Services:** coin laundry. **Business Services:** meeting rooms. **Cards:** AX, CB, DC, DS, JC, MC, VI. **Special Amenities: free continental breakfast and free local telephone calls.** *(See color ad p 538)*

SOME UNITS

KON TIKI INN **Phone:** (805)773-4833

Motel

4/2-9/6 [CP] 1P: $126-$146 2P: $126-$146 XP: $16
9/7-1/31 [CP] 1P: $96-$124 2P: $96-$124 XP: $16
2/1-4/1 [CP] 1P: $94-$124 2P: $94-$124 XP: $16

Location: US 101, exit Shell Beach Rd northbound, just w, then 0.6 mi s; exit SR 1 southbound, just w. 1621 Price St 93449. Fax: 805/773-6541. **Facility:** Smoke free premises. 86 one-bedroom standard units. 3-4 stories, exterior corridors. **Parking:** on-site. **Terms:** office hours 7 am-midnight, 2 night minimum stay - weekends, 3 day cancellation notice. **Amenities:** dual phone lines, voice mail. **Pool(s):** heated outdoor. **Leisure Activities:** sauna, whirlpools, steamroom, lighted tennis court, racquetball courts. *Fee:* massage. **Guest Services:** coin laundry. **Business Services:** meeting rooms. **Cards:** AX, DS, MC, VI.

OCEAN PALMS MOTEL **Phone:** (805)773-4669

Motel

All Year 1P: $45-$160 2P: $55-$170 XP: $10 F12

Location: US 101, exit Price St northbound; exit Hinds St southbound, just s. 390 Ocean View Ave 93449. Fax: 805/556-0878. **Facility:** 22 one-bedroom standard units. 2 stories (no elevator), exterior corridors. *Bath:* combo or shower only. **Parking:** on-site. **Terms:** office hours 8 am-10 pm, 3 day cancellation notice. **Amenities:** hair dryers. **Pool(s):** heated outdoor. **Leisure Activities:** whirlpool. **Cards:** AX, DC, DS, MC, VI. **Special Amenities: free continental breakfast and free local telephone calls.**

SOME UNITS

OXFORD SUITES RESORT *Book at aaa.com* **Phone:** (805)773-3773

AAA SAVE

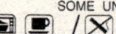

Small-scale Hotel

5/28-10/30 [BP]	1P: $99-$149	2P: $109-$179	XP: $15	F9
10/31-1/31 [BP]	1P: $89-$139	2P: $99-$159	XP: $15	F9
2/1-5/27 [BP]	1P: $89-$129	2P: $99-$139	XP: $15	F9

Location: US 101, exit 4th St, just w, then just n. 651 Five Cities Dr 93449. Fax: 805/773-5177. **Facility:** 133 one-bedroom suites. 2 stories (no elevator), exterior corridors. **Parking:** on-site. **Terms:** weekly rates available, package plans, pets ($10 extra charge). **Amenities:** video library (fee), irons, hair dryers. **Pool(s):** heated outdoor, wading. **Leisure Activities:** whirlpool. **Guest Services:** gift shop, complimentary evening beverages, valet and coin laundry. **Business Services:** meeting rooms. **Cards:** AX, CB, DC, DS, MC, VI. **Special Amenities: free full breakfast and free local telephone calls.**

FEE SOME UNITS

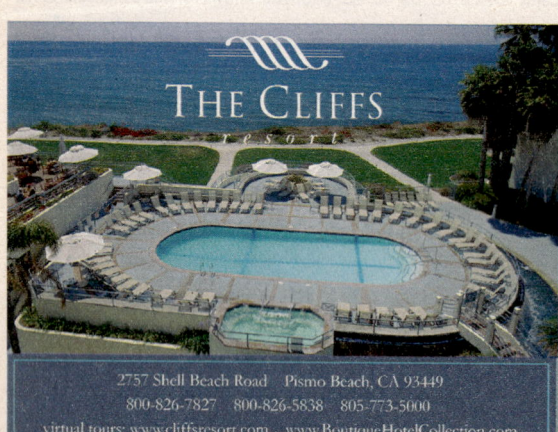

PISMO BEACH INN — Phone: 805/773-1234

Motel

All Year	1P: $79-$179		XP: $10	F5

Location: US 101, exit Shell Beach Rd northbound, just w, then just s; exit SR 1 S southbound, just w, then 0.5 mi s. 371 Pismo St 93449. Fax: 805/773-2727. **Facility:** Smoke free premises. 13 one-bedroom standard units, some with kitchens. 1-2 stories (no elevator), exterior corridors. *Bath:* combo or shower only. **Parking:** on-site. **Terms:** office hours 8 am-8 pm, 2-3 night minimum stay - weekends, 10 day cancellation notice-fee imposed, [CP] meal plan available, package plans - seasonal. **Amenities:** voice mail, irons, hair dryers. **Leisure Activities:** barbecue grill, bicycles. **Guest Services:** coin laundry. **Business Services:** fax (fee). **Cards:** AX, DS, MC, VI. **Special Amenities: free continental breakfast and free local telephone calls.**

PISMO LIGHTHOUSE SUITES *Book at aaa.com* — Phone: (805)773-2411

Motel

6/1-9/30 [ECP]	1P: $199-$375	2P: $199-$375	XP: $10	F17
10/1-1/31 [ECP]	1P: $179-$355	2P: $179-$355	XP: $10	F17
3/1-5/31 [ECP]	1P: $169-$355	2P: $169-$355	XP: $10	F17
2/1-2/29 [ECP]	1P: $149-$305	2P: $149-$305	XP: $10	F17

Location: US 101, exit Shell Beach Rd northbound, just w, 0.5 mi s; exit Price St southbound, just w, then just s. 2411 Price St 93449. Fax: 805/773-1508. **Facility:** Smoke free premises. 70 units. 40 two-bedroom standard units. 30 one-bedroom suites ($149-$375), some with whirlpools. 2-3 stories, exterior corridors. **Parking:** on-site. **Terms:** 3 day cancellation notice. **Amenities:** video games (fee), dual phone lines, voice mail, irons, hair dryers. **Pool(s):** heated outdoor. **Leisure Activities:** whirlpool, putting green, ping pong, bicycles, exercise room. **Guest Services:** coin laundry. **Cards:** AX, CB, DC, DS, JC, MC, VI. **Special Amenities: free expanded continental breakfast.** *(See color ad below)*

SANDCASTLE INN *Book at aaa.com* — Phone: (805)773-2422

Motel

5/16-9/15 [ECP]	1P: $129-$329	2P: $129-$329
9/16-1/31 [ECP]	1P: $109-$329	2P: $109-$329
2/1-5/15 [ECP]	1P: $99-$279	2P: $99-$279

Location: US 101, exit Price St northbound, 0.3 mi s, just w; exit Hinds Ave southbound, just w, then just s. 100 Stimson Ave 93449. Fax: 805/773-0771. **Facility:** Smoke free premises. 75 units. 73 one-bedroom standard units. 2 one-bedroom suites. 3 stories, interior/exterior corridors. **Parking:** on-site. **Terms:** 2 night minimum stay - weekends 6/1-10/31, pets ($100 deposit, $10 extra charge, in limited units). **Amenities:** video games (fee), voice mail, irons, hair dryers. **Leisure Activities:** whirlpool. **Guest Services:** valet laundry. **Business Services:** fax (fee). **Cards:** AX, DC, DS, MC, VI. **Special Amenities: free expanded continental breakfast.** *(See color ad p 539)*

SOME UNITS

FEE

SEA CREST RESORT MOTEL — **Phone:** 805/773-4608

AAA SAVE — Motel

5/29-9/1	1P: $100-$125	2P: $100-$125	XP: $10	F12
4/11-5/28 & 9/2-1/31	1P: $90-$115	2P: $90-$115	XP: $10	F12
2/1-4/10	1P: $85-$105	2P: $85-$105	XP: $10	F12

Location: US 101, exit Shell Beach Rd northbound, just w, then 0.5 mi s; exit Price St southbound, just w, then just s. 2241 Price St 93449. Fax: 805/773-4525. **Facility:** 160 units. 155 one-bedroom standard units, some with whirlpools. 5 two-bedroom suites ($150-$175). 2-4 stories, interior/exterior corridors. *Bath:* combo or shower only. **Parking:** on-site. **Terms:** office hours 7 am-11 pm, check-in 4 pm, 2 night minimum stay - weekends. **Amenities:** voice mail. *Some:* irons, hair dryers. **Pool(s):** heated outdoor. **Leisure Activities:** whirlpools, picnic area with barbecues. **Guest Services:** coin laundry. **Business Services:** meeting rooms. **Cards:** AX, DC, DS, MC, VI.

SOME UNITS

SEA GYPSY MOTEL — **Phone:** 805/773-1801

Condominium

6/1-9/15	1P: $70-$165	2P: $80-$165	XP: $10	F3
9/16-1/31	1P: $55-$140	2P: $60-$140	XP: $10	F3
2/1-5/31	1P: $45-$135	2P: $50-$135	XP: $10	F3

Location: US 101, exit Price St northbound, 0.5 mi n to Pismo Ave, then just w; exit Hines Ave southbound, 0.3 mi w, then just n. 1020 Cypress St 93449. Fax: 805/773-9286. **Facility:** 77 one-bedroom standard units, some with kitchens. 3 stories (no elevator), interior/exterior corridors. *Bath:* combo or shower only. **Parking:** on-site. **Terms:** office hours 7 am-11 pm, check-in 3:30 pm, 2 night minimum stay - weekends, weekly rates available, pets ($15 extra charge). **Amenities:** *Some:* irons. **Pool(s):** heated outdoor. **Leisure Activities:** whirlpool. **Guest Services:** coin laundry. **Cards:** AX, DS, MC, VI.

SOME UNITS

FEE

All rooms and suites with a private balcony mineral spa.

Therapeutic massage and facial services

Outdoor redwood mineral spas

Gourmet dining at the **Gardens of Avila Restaurant**

SEAVENTURE RESORT Book at aaa.com **Phone:** (805)773-4994

AAA SAVE — Small-scale Hotel

5/26-9/7 [ECP]	1P: $139-$349	2P: $139-$349
2/1-5/25 & 9/8-1/31 [ECP]	1P: $119-$299	2P: $119-$299

Location: US 101, exit Price St northbound, just n; exit Hinds St southbound, just w, just s on Price St, then just w. 100 Ocean View Ave 93449. Fax: 805/773-0924. **Facility:** Designated smoking area. 50 one-bedroom standard units, some with whirlpools. 2-3 stories, interior corridors. *Bath:* combo or shower only. **Parking:** on-site. **Terms:** check-in 4 pm, 2 night minimum stay - weekends, cancellation fee imposed. **Amenities:** video library (fee), CD players, irons, hair dryers. **Dining:** 4 pm-9 pm, Fri-10 pm, Sat noon-3 & 4-10 pm, Sun 10 am-2 & 5-9 pm; Sunday brunch, cocktails. **Leisure Activities:** whirlpool, barbecue, bicycles. *Fee:* pedal surreys, massage. **Guest Services:** gift shop, valet laundry. **Business Services:** meeting rooms. **Cards:** AX, DC, DS, MC, VI. **Special Amenities: free expanded continental breakfast and free newspaper.** *(See color ad p 541)*

VCR DATA PORT

SHELL BEACH MOTEL **Phone:** (805)773-4373

AAA SAVE — Motel

6/11-9/6	1P: $109-$169	2P: $109-$169	XP: $10	F17
2/1-6/10 & 9/7-1/31	1P: $71-$132	2P: $71-$132	XP: $10	F17

Location: US 101, exit Shell Beach Rd northbound, just w, then 1.2 mi s; exit Price St southbound, just w, then 1 mi n. Located in Shell Beach area. 653 Shell Beach Rd 93449. Fax: 805/773-6208. **Facility:** Smoke free premises. 9 one-bedroom standard units. 1 story, exterior corridors. *Bath:* combo or shower only. **Parking:** on-site. **Terms:** 1-3 night minimum stay - weekends, pets ($15 extra charge). **Amenities:** irons, hair dryers. **Pool(s):** heated outdoor. **Cards:** AX, DC, DS, MC, VI.

FEE DATA PORT

SPYGLASS INN Book at aaa.com **Phone:** (805)773-4855

AAA SAVE — Small-scale Hotel

6/1-8/31	1P: $119-$239	2P: $119-$239
9/1-1/31	1P: $89-$239	2P: $89-$239
4/1-5/31	1P: $99-$179	2P: $99-$179
2/1-3/31	1P: $79-$159	2P: $79-$159

Location: US 101, exit Spyglass Dr northbound; exit Shell Beach Rd southbound, just w, then just n. 2705 Spyglass Dr 93449. Fax: 805/773-5298. **Facility:** Smoke free premises. 82 units. 80 one-bedroom standard units. 2 one-bedroom suites with kitchens. 2-3 stories (no elevator), exterior corridors. *Bath:* combo or shower only. **Parking:** on-site. **Terms:** 2-3 night minimum stay - weekends. **Amenities:** video games (fee), voice mail, irons, hair dryers. **Dining:** 7 am-9 pm, Fri & Sat-10 pm, cocktails. **Pool(s):** heated outdoor. **Leisure Activities:** whirlpool. **Business Services:** meeting rooms. **Cards:** AX, DC, DS, MC, VI. *(See color ad p 539)*

SOME UNITS

DATA PORT

WHERE TO DINE

F MCLINTOCK'S SALOON & DINING HOUSE **Dinner:** $16-$29 **Phone:** 805/773-1892

American

Location: US 101, exit Spyglass Dr northbound, just e, then 1 mi s; exit Shell Beach Rd southbound, just e, then 1 mi s. 750 Mattie Rd 93449. **Hours:** 4:30 pm-9:30 pm, Sat 3 pm-10:30 pm, Sun 9 am-9:30 pm. Closed: 1/1, 11/25, 12/24, 12/25. **Reservations:** suggested; Sun-Thurs. **Features:** This popular, long established restaurant is known for its great steaks but also offers a variety of seafood, chicken and rib plates. The atmosphere is family-friendly with a touch of the Old West. Before or after dinner, you may want to stop at the butcher shop or the gift shop. Casual dress; cocktails; entertainment. **Parking:** on-site. **Cards:** AX, DS, MC, VI.

GIUSEPPE'S CUCINA ITALIANA **Lunch:** $6-$9 **Dinner:** $10-$22 **Phone:** 805/773-2870

Italian

Location: US 101, exit Price St northbound; exit Hinds Ave southbound, just w. 891 Price St 93449. **Hours:** 11:30 am-3 & 4:30-10 pm, Fri-Sun 4:30 pm-11 pm. Closed major holidays; also 1st week in Jan. **Features:** A favorite of families, the downtown neighborhood restaurant combines fresh produce, seafood and organically grown herbs in its well-prepared dishes. Service is friendly and knowledgeable. Casual dress; cocktails. **Parking:** on-site. **Cards:** AX, MC, VI.

OLD VIENNA RESTAURANT **Dinner:** $12-$24 **Phone:** 805/773-4521

German

Location: US 101, exit Shell Beach Rd northbound, 0.4 mi s; exit Price St southbound, 1.3 mi nw. 1527 Shell Beach Rd 93449. **Hours:** 5 pm-9 pm. Closed: 1/1, 12/25; also Mon. **Reservations:** suggested. **Features:** The delightful, family-owned and operated restaurant serves traditional German cuisine. Casual dress; beer & wine only. **Parking:** on-site. **Cards:** AX, DS, MC, VI.

ROSA'S RISTORANTE ITALIANO **Lunch:** $6-$10 **Dinner:** $9-$20 **Phone:** 805/773-0551

AAA — Italian

Location: US 101, exit Price St northbound; exit Hinds St southbound, just w. 491 Price St 93449. **Hours:** 11:30 am-2 & 4-9:30 pm, Fri-10 pm, Sat 4 pm-10 pm, Sun 4 pm-9:30 pm. Closed: 11/25, 12/25. **Features:** On the charming, family-owned restaurant's menu are pizza and preparations of pasta, seafood, chicken and veal. The patio is a relaxed seating option. Casual dress; cocktails. **Parking:** on-site. **Cards:** AX, DC, DS, MC, VI.

SEA CLIFFS RESTAURANT **Lunch:** $6-$17 **Dinner:** $11-$24 **Phone:** 805/773-5000

California

Location: US 101, exit Spyglass Dr northbound; exit Shell Beach Rd southbound, just w, then just n; in Cliffs Resort. 2757 Shell Beach Rd 93449. **Hours:** 6:30 am-9:30 pm, Fri & Sat-10 pm. **Reservations:** suggested. **Features:** The menu blends preparations of pasta, seafood, chicken, steak and lamb. The mood is relaxed on the large patio, which affords nice views of the ocean. Casual dress; cocktails. **Parking:** on-site and valet. **Cards:** AX, DC, DS, MC, VI.

SHORE CLIFF RESTAURANT **Lunch:** $6-$12 **Dinner:** $11-$28 **Phone:** 805/773-4671

American

Location: US 101, exit Shell Beach Rd northbound; exit Price St southbound, just w; in Best Western Shore Cliff Lodge. 2555 Price St 93449. **Hours:** 11 am-2:30 & 5-10 pm. **Reservations:** suggested. **Features:** Guests can see the Pacific Ocean from most seats in the restaurant. Soft lights and good food are the ingredients for a relaxing evening. Casual dress; cocktails; entertainment. **Parking:** on-site. **Cards:** AX, DC, DS, MC, VI. *(See color ad p 537)*

STEAMERS OF PISMO Lunch: $8-$12 Dinner: $12-$27 Phone: 805/773-4711

Steak & Seafood

Location: US 101, exit Shell Beach Rd northbound, 0.6 mi s, just w; exit SR 1 southbound, then just w. 1601 Price St 93448. **Hours:** 11:30 am-3 & 4:30-9 pm, Fri & Sat-10 pm, Sun 4 pm-9 pm. **Features:** This popular restaurant features ocean view dining, a cozy fireplace and background music from the big band era, The menu includes a large selection of fresh fish prepared "as you like it". Casual dress; cocktails. **Parking:** on-site. **Cards:** AX, DS, MC, VI.

PLACERVILLE pop. 9,610

WHERE TO STAY

BEST WESTERN PLACERVILLE INN Book at aaa.com Phone: (530)622-9100

Motel

All Year [ECP]	1P: $69-$99	2P: $79-$109	XP: $10	F15

Location: US 50, exit Missouri Flat Rd S, 2 mi w. 6850 Green Leaf Dr 95667. Fax: 530/622-9376. **Facility:** 105 one-bedroom standard units. 3 stories, interior corridors. **Parking:** on-site. **Terms:** [BP] meal plan available. **Amenities:** voice mail, irons, hair dryers. **Pool(s):** heated outdoor. **Leisure Activities:** whirlpool, exercise room. **Guest Services:** coin laundry. **Business Services:** meeting rooms. **Cards:** AX, CB, DC, DS, JC, MC, VI. **Special Amenities: free full breakfast and free local telephone calls.** *(See color ad below)*

SOME UNITS

DATA PORT

THE CHICHESTER-MCKEE HOUSE Phone: (530)626-1882

Historic Bed & Breakfast

All Year [BP]	1P: $90-$125	2P: $105-$140	XP: $20	D18

Location: US 50, exit Spring St (SR 49), just n. 800 Spring St 95667. Fax: 530/626-7801. **Facility:** A hill overlooking the historic downtown is the setting for this restored 1892 Victorian. 4 one-bedroom standard units. 2 stories, interior corridors. *Bath:* combo or shower only. **Parking:** on-site. **Terms:** 5 day cancellation notice-fee imposed. **Cards:** AX, DS, MC, VI.

SOME UNITS

GOLD COUNTRY INN Phone: (530)622-3124

Motel

7/1-10/31 [CP]	1P: $62-$87	2P: $62-$87	XP: $5	F12
4/1-6/30 [CP]	1P: $57-$82	2P: $57-$82	XP: $5	F12
2/1-3/31 & 11/1-1/31 [CP]	1P: $51-$64	2P: $51-$64	XP: $5	F12

Location: US 50, exit S Schnell School Rd; downtown. 1332 Broadway 95667. Fax: 530/622-2080. **Facility:** 45 one-bedroom standard units. 2 stories, exterior corridors. *Bath:* combo or shower only. **Parking:** on-site. **Terms:** 3 day cancellation notice-fee imposed. **Cards:** AX, DS, MC, VI. **Special Amenities: free continental breakfast and free local telephone calls.**

SOME UNITS

DATA PORT

HISTORIC CARY HOUSE HOTEL Book at aaa.com Phone: (530)622-4271

Historic Small-scale Hotel

All Year [CP]	1P: $110-$135	2P: $115-$140	XP: $10	F10

Location: Just s of US 50; downtown. Located in historic district. 300 Main St 95667. Fax: 530/622-0696. **Facility:** Built in 1857, centrally located. 38 one-bedroom standard units, some with kitchens. 4 stories, interior corridors. *Bath:* combo or shower only. **Parking:** on-site. **Amenities:** irons. **Business Services:** meeting rooms. **Cards:** AX, DS, MC, VI. **Special Amenities: free continental breakfast and free room upgrade (subject to availability with advanced reservations).**

SOME UNITS

MOTHER LODE MOTEL Phone: 530/622-0895

Motel

5/15-10/31	1P: $52-$56	2P: $54-$62	XP: $10	F6
2/1-5/14 & 11/1-1/31	1P: $42-$52	2P: $44-$52	XP: $5	F6

Location: 2 mi e, adjacent to US 50, exit Point View Dr. 1940 Broadway 95667. Fax: 530/344-0159. **Facility:** 21 one-bedroom standard units, some with whirlpools. 1 story, exterior corridors. *Bath:* combo or shower only. **Parking:** on-site. **Terms:** 3 day cancellation notice-fee imposed, small pets only ($5 extra charge). **Pool(s):** outdoor. **Cards:** AX, DS, MC, VI. **Special Amenities: free local telephone calls and early check-in/late check-out.**

SOME UNITS

FEE

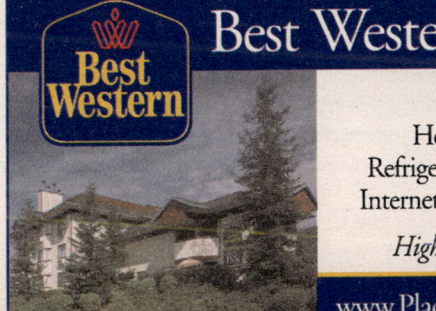

NATIONAL 9 INN **Phone:** 530/622-3884

Motel

All Year 1P: $45-$50 2P: $55-$65 XP: $10

Location: US 50, exit Schnell School Rd. 1500 Broadway 95667. **Facility:** 24 one-bedroom standard units. 2 stories, exterior corridors. *Bath:* combo or shower only. **Parking:** on-site. **Terms:** 3 day cancellation notice-fee imposed, [ECP] meal plan available. **Cards:** AX, MC, VI. **Special Amenities: free continental breakfast and free local telephone calls.**

SOME UNITS

SHADOWRIDGE RANCH & LODGE *Book at aaa.com* **Phone:** (530)295-1000

Bed & Breakfast

All Year [BP] 1P: $145-$275 2P: $145-$275 XP: $15 D12

Location: US 50, exit Point View Dr/New Towne Rd, 3 mi se on New Towne Rd, then 2 mi s. 3700 Fort Jim Rd 95667. Fax: 530/626-5613. **Facility:** The lodge is on a large rural parcel with picturesque views of surrounding foothills; a fireplace warms the breakfast area. 4 one-bedroom standard units. 1 story, exterior corridors. **Parking:** on-site. **Terms:** 2 night minimum stay - weekends, 5 day cancellation notice. **Guest Services:** complimentary evening beverages. **Cards:** AX, MC, VI.

PLEASANT HILL pop. 32,837

WHERE TO STAY

COURTYARD BY MARRIOTT-PLEASANT HILL *Book at aaa.com* **Phone:** 925/691-1444

Small-scale Hotel

All Year 1P: $69-$139 2P: $69-$139

Location: I-680, exit Gregory Ln southbound, just w; exit Monument Blvd northbound. 2250 Contra Costa Blvd 94523. Fax: 925/691-0616. **Facility:** 135 one-bedroom standard units, some with whirlpools. 4 stories, interior corridors. *Bath:* combo or shower only. **Parking:** on-site. **Terms:** cancellation fee imposed, [BP] meal plan available. **Amenities:** high-speed Internet (fee), dual phone lines, voice mail, irons, hair dryers. **Pool(s):** heated indoor. **Leisure Activities:** whirlpool, exercise room. **Guest Services:** coin laundry. **Business Services:** meeting rooms. **Cards:** AX, DC, DS, JC, MC, VI.

SOME UNITS

RESIDENCE INN BY MARRIOTT-PLEASANT HILL *Book at aaa.com* **Phone:** (925)689-1010

Motel

All Year [ECP] 1P: $89-$179 2P: $89-$179

Location: I-680, exit Willow Pass Rd to Taylor W; S Contra Costa Blvd, e on Ellinwood Dr, then n. 700 Ellinwood Way 94523. Fax: 925/689-1098. **Facility:** 126 units. 98 one- and 28 two-bedroom standard units with kitchens. 2 stories (no elevator), interior/exterior corridors. **Parking:** on-site. **Terms:** cancellation fee imposed, small pets only ($75 fee, $6 extra charge). **Amenities:** voice mail, irons, hair dryers. **Pool(s):** outdoor. **Leisure Activities:** whirlpool, exercise room, sports court. **Guest Services:** complimentary evening beverages: Mon-Thurs, valet and coin laundry, area transportation. **Business Services:** meeting rooms. **Cards:** AX, DC, DS, MC, VI.

SOME UNITS

FEE

SUMMERFIELD SUITES BY WYNDHAM-PLEASANT HILL *Book at aaa.com* **Phone:** (925)934-3343

Small-scale Hotel

All Year 1P: $104-$169 2P: $104-$169

Location: I-680, exit Contra Costa Blvd, then w. 2611 Contra Costa Blvd 94523. Fax: 925/934-5973. **Facility:** 142 units. 56 one-bedroom standard units with efficiencies. 58 one- and 28 two-bedroom suites ($104-$209) with efficiencies. 4 stories, interior corridors. *Bath:* combo or shower only. **Parking:** on-site. **Terms:** cancellation fee imposed, [MAP] meal plan available, pets ($75 deposit). **Amenities:** video library (fee), CD players, high-speed Internet, dual phone lines, voice mail, irons, hair dryers. **Pool(s):** heated outdoor. **Leisure Activities:** whirlpool, exercise room, sports court. **Guest Services:** complimentary evening beverages: Mon-Thurs, valet and coin laundry. **Business Services:** meeting rooms, business center. **Cards:** AX, CB, DC, DS, JC, MC, VI.

SOME UNITS

FEE

PLEASANTON pop. 63,634

WHERE TO STAY

CANDLEWOOD SUITES Book at aaa.com **Phone:** (925)463-1212

Small-scale Hotel

All Year 1P: $129 2P: $129 XP: $10 F16

Location: I-580, exit Hopyard Rd S, w on Owen. 5535 Johnson Dr 94588. Fax: 925/463-6080. **Facility:** 126 one-bedroom standard units with efficiencies. 4 stories, interior corridors. **Parking:** on-site. **Terms:** cancellation fee imposed, package plans - weekends, pets ($75-$150 fee extra charge). **Amenities:** video library, CD players, dual phone lines, voice mail, irons, hair dryers. *Fee:* video games, high-speed Internet. **Leisure Activities:** whirlpool, exercise room. **Guest Services:** complimentary laundry. **Cards:** AX, DC, DS, JC, MC, VI. **Special Amenities: free local telephone calls and free newspaper.** *(See color ad below)*

SOME UNITS

FEE

COURTYARD BY MARRIOTT Book at aaa.com **Phone:** (925)463-1414

Small-scale Hotel

All Year 1P: $79-$159

Location: I-580, exit Hopyard Rd, 0.5 mi s. 5059 Hopyard Rd 94588. Fax: 925/463-0113. **Facility:** 145 one-bedroom standard units. 2-3 stories, interior corridors. *Bath:* combo or shower only. **Parking:** on-site. **Terms:** cancellation fee imposed, [AP], [BP] & [CP] meal plans available. **Amenities:** high-speed Internet (fee), dual phone lines, voice mail, irons, hair dryers. **Pool(s):** outdoor. **Leisure Activities:** whirlpool, exercise room. **Guest Services:** coin laundry. **Business Services:** meeting rooms. **Cards:** AX, CB, DC, DS, JC, MC, VI.

SOME UNITS

ASK

CROWNE PLAZA HOTEL AND RESORT PLEASANTON Book at aaa.com **Phone:** (925)847-6000

Small-scale Hotel

All Year 1P: $69-$161 2P: $69-$161

Location: I-580, exit Foothill Rd, 0.3 mi s. 11950 Dublin Canyon Rd 94588. Fax: 925/463-2585. **Facility:** 244 one-bedroom standard units. 6 stories, interior corridors. *Bath:* combo or shower only. **Parking:** on-site. **Terms:** [AP], [BP] & [CP] meal plans available. **Amenities:** voice mail, irons, hair dryers. *Some:* dual phone lines. *Fee:* high-speed Internet. **Pool(s):** outdoor. **Leisure Activities:** whirlpool, exercise room. **Guest Services:** coin laundry, area transportation. **Business Services:** conference facilities, business center. **Cards:** AX, CB, DC, DS, MC, VI.

SOME UNITS

ASK

FEE

EVERGREEN BED & BREAKFAST **Phone:** 925/426-0901

Bed & Breakfast

All Year 1P: $135-$250 2P: $135-$250

Location: I-680, exit Bernal Ave W, 0.3 mi s on Foothill Rd. Located adjacent to Augustin Bernal Park and the Pleasanton Ridge. 9104 Longview Dr 94588. Fax: 925/426-9568. **Facility:** The B&B, on a hillside overlooking Pleasanton Valley, features mature landscaping and attractively appointed gardens highlighted by a cascading pond. 5 one-bedroom standard units, some with whirlpools. 3 stories (no elevator), interior corridors. *Bath:* combo or shower only. **Parking:** on-site. **Terms:** [BP] meal plan available. **Amenities:** hair dryers. *Some:* CD players. **Leisure Activities:** whirlpool, hiking trails, exercise room. **Cards:** AX, MC, VI.

SOME UNITS

FOUR POINTS HOTEL BY SHERATON Book at aaa.com **Phone:** (925)460-8800

Small-scale Hotel

All Year 1P: $79-$139 2P: $79-$139 XP: $10 F16

Location: 0.5 mi e of jct I-680 and 580, exit I-580 at Hopyard Rd, then 0.5 mi s. 5115 Hopyard Rd 94588. Fax: 925/847-9455. **Facility:** 214 one-bedroom standard units. 2 stories, interior corridors. **Parking:** on-site. **Terms:** cancellation fee imposed. **Amenities:** video games (fee), high-speed Internet, dual phone lines, voice mail, irons, hair dryers. **Dining:** 6:30 am-10 pm. **Pool(s):** heated outdoor. **Leisure Activities:** whirlpool, exercise room. **Guest Services:** valet laundry, area transportation-within 7 mi. **Business Services:** conference facilities, fax. **Cards:** AX, CB, DC, DS, JC, MC, VI. **Special Amenities: free newspaper and free room upgrade (subject to availability with advanced reservations).** *(See color ad p 546)*

SOME UNITS

HILTON PLEASANTON AT THE CLUB Book at aaa.com Phone: (925)463-8000

Large-scale Hotel

All Year 1P: $79-$199 2P: $79-$199 XP: $10 F18

Location: In southeast quadrant at jct I-580 and 680. 7050 Johnson Dr 94588. Fax: 925/463-3801. **Facility:** 294 one-bedroom standard units. 5 stories, interior corridors. **Parking:** on-site. **Terms:** [BP] & [CP] meal plans available, package plans. **Amenities:** video games (fee), dual phone lines, voice mail, irons, hair dryers. **Pool(s):** 4 heated outdoor. **Leisure Activities:** whirlpools. *Fee:* 18 tennis courts (14 indoor, 4 lighted), racquetball courts. **Guest Services:** gift shop, valet laundry, area transportation. **Business Services:** conference facilities, fax. **Cards:** AX, DC, DS, JC, MC, VI.

SOME UNITS FEE

RAMADA INN Phone: (925)463-1300

Motel

All Year 1P: $59-$109 2P: $59-$109

Location: I-580, exit Hopyard Rd, just s. 5375 Owens Ct 94588. Fax: 925/734-8843. **Facility:** Smoke free premises. 102 one-bedroom standard units. 3 stories, exterior corridors. **Parking:** on-site. **Terms:** small pets only ($10 extra charge). **Amenities:** voice mail, irons, hair dryers. **Pool(s):** outdoor. **Leisure Activities:** whirlpool. **Cards:** AX, CB, DC, DS, JC, MC, VI.

FEE SOME UNITS FEE FEE

RESIDENCE INN BY MARRIOTT Book at aaa.com Phone: (925)227-0500

AAA SAVE

Small-scale Hotel

All Year 1P: $69-$139 2P: $69-$139

Location: I-580, exit Foothill Blvd S, then w. 11920 Dublin Canyon Rd 94588. Fax: 925/828-1199. **Facility:** 135 units. 123 one- and 12 two-bedroom standard units with kitchens. 3 stories, interior corridors. *Bath:* combo or shower only. **Parking:** on-site. **Terms:** weekly rates available, [MAP] meal plan available, 8% service charge, pets ($100 deposit, $10 extra charge). **Amenities:** voice mail, irons, hair dryers. *Fee:* video games, high-speed Internet. **Pool(s):** heated outdoor. **Leisure Activities:** whirlpool, exercise room, sports court. **Guest Services:** complimentary evening beverages, complimentary laundry. **Business Services:** meeting rooms, business center. **Cards:** AX, DC, DS, MC, VI. **Special Amenities: free continental breakfast and free newspaper.**

FEE SOME UNITS FEE

THE ROSE HOTEL Book at aaa.com Phone: (925)846-8802

AAA SAVE

Bed & Breakfast

All Year 1P: $229 2P: $229

Location: I-580, exit Santa Rita, 3 mi s. 807 Main St 94566. Fax: 925/846-2272. **Facility:** Located in historic downtown within walking distance to many shops and restaurants. Guest units are spacious and elegantly appointed. Smoke free premises. 38 units. 35 one-bedroom standard units with whirlpools. 3 one-bedroom suites ($429-$695), some with whirlpools. 3 stories, interior corridors. **Parking:** on-site. **Terms:** cancellation fee imposed, [ECP] meal plan available. **Amenities:** video library, DVD players, CD players, high-speed Internet, dual phone lines, voice mail, safes, honor bars, irons, hair dryers. **Leisure Activities:** exercise room. **Guest Services:** valet laundry. **Business Services:** meeting rooms, administrative services, fax. **Cards:** AX, DC, DS, MC, VI. **Special Amenities: free continental breakfast and free room upgrade (subject to availability with advanced reservations).**

SIERRA SUITES HOTEL Book at aaa.com Phone: (925)730-0000

Small-scale Hotel

All Year [ECP] 1P: $69-$159 2P: $69-$159

Location: I-580, exit Hopyard Rd, 1 mi s, e on Stoneridge Dr, then s. Located in a business park. 4555 Chabot Dr 94588. Fax: 925/730-0050. **Facility:** 112 one-bedroom standard units with efficiencies. 3 stories, interior corridors. *Bath:* combo or shower only. **Parking:** on-site. **Terms:** pets ($100 fee, $5 extra charge). **Amenities:** high-speed Internet (fee), dual phone lines, voice mail, irons, hair dryers. **Pool(s):** heated outdoor. **Leisure Activities:** exercise room. **Guest Services:** valet and coin laundry. **Cards:** AX, CB, DC, DS, JC, MC, VI.

SOME UNITS FEE

SUMMERFIELD SUITES BY WYNDHAM-PLEASANTON Book at aaa.com **Phone:** (925)730-0070

Motel

All Year 1P: $99-$199 2P: $99-$199

Location: I-580, exit Hopyard Rd, 1 mi s, e on Stoneridge Dr, then s. Located in a business park. 4545 Chabot Dr 94588. Fax: 925/730-0075. **Facility:** 128 units. 74 one-bedroom standard units with kitchens. 54 two-bedroom suites ($99-$249) with kitchens. 3 stories (no elevator), exterior corridors. *Bath:* combo or shower only. **Parking:** on-site. **Terms:** cancellation fee imposed, [MAP] meal plan available, pets ($150 fee, $10 extra charge). **Amenities:** dual phone lines, voice mail, irons, hair dryers. *Fee:* video library, high-speed Internet. **Pool(s):** heated outdoor. **Leisure Activities:** whirlpool, exercise room, sports court. **Guest Services:** complimentary evening beverages, valet and coin laundry. **Business Services:** meeting rooms. **Cards:** AX, DC, DS, MC, VI.

SOME UNITS

FEE

WYNDHAM GARDEN HOTEL-PLEASANTON Book at aaa.com **Phone:** (925)463-3330

Small-scale Hotel

All Year 1P: $59-$109 2P: $59-$119 XP: $10 F17

Location: Jct I-580 and 680, 0.5 mi sw; I-580, exit Foothill Rd, 0.3 mi s, then 0.3 mi e on Canyon Way. Located opposite Stoneridge Mall. 5990 Stoneridge Mall Rd 94588. Fax: 925/463-3315. **Facility:** 171 one-bedroom standard units. 6 stories, interior corridors. *Bath:* combo or shower only. **Parking:** on-site. **Terms:** cancellation fee imposed. **Amenities:** voice mail, irons, hair dryers. *Fee:* video games, high-speed Internet. **Dining:** 6:30 am-2 & 5-10 pm, Sat & Sun 7 am-noon & 5-10 pm. **Pool(s):** outdoor. **Leisure Activities:** sauna, whirlpool, exercise room. **Guest Services:** valet laundry. **Business Services:** meeting rooms. **Cards:** AX, CB, DC, DS, MC, VI.

SOME UNITS

FEE FEE

WHERE TO DINE

MAESTRO'S CAFFE ITALIANO **Lunch:** $7-$20 **Dinner:** $8-$20 **Phone:** 925/463-8773

Italian

Location: I-580, exit Hopyard Rd, 0.3 mi s. 5100 Hopyard Rd 94566. **Hours:** 11:30 am-2:30 & 4:30-9:30 pm, Sat & Sun from 4 pm. Closed major holidays. **Reservations:** suggested. **Features:** Attractive surroundings lend to the comfortable, casual atmosphere. The menu centers on seafood dishes. Casual dress; cocktails. **Parking:** on-site. **Cards:** AX, DC, DS, MC, VI.

PLEASANTON HOTEL RESTAURANT Historic **Lunch:** $6-$15 **Dinner:** $12-$26 **Phone:** 925/846-8106

American

Location: I-680, exit Bernal Ave, 2 mi e; historic downtown. 855 Main St 94566. **Hours:** 11:30 am-2:30 & 5-9 pm, Sun 10 am-2 & 4:30-8:30 pm. Closed major holidays. **Reservations:** suggested. **Features:** In an 1851 downtown building, the restaurant presents a varied menu. The feel of the dining room is cozy and cordial. Casual dress; cocktails; entertainment. **Parking:** on-site. **Cards:** AX, CB, DC, DS, MC, VI.

PLYMOUTH pop. 980

WHERE TO STAY

SHENANDOAH INN **Phone:** 209/245-4491

Motel

6/1-9/15 [ECP]	1P: $85-$99	2P: $98-$112	XP: $10	F12
3/1-5/31 & 9/16-1/31 [ECP]	1P: $79-$94	2P: $93-$108	XP: $10	F12
2/1-2/29 [ECP]	1P: $72-$89	2P: $86-$103	XP: $10	F12

Location: 1 mi s on SR 49. 17674 Village Dr 95669 (PO Box 758, JACKSON, 95642). Fax: 209/245-4498. **Facility:** 47 units. 46 one-bedroom standard units. 1 one-bedroom suite ($121-$140). 2 stories (no elevator), exterior corridors. **Parking:** on-site. **Terms:** cancellation fee imposed. **Amenities:** voice mail. *Some:* irons, hair dryers. **Pool(s):** outdoor. **Leisure Activities:** whirlpool. **Business Services:** meeting rooms. **Cards:** AX, DS, MC, VI. **Special Amenities: free continental breakfast and preferred room (subject to availability with advanced reservations).**

SOME UNITS

POINT ARENA —*See Gualala & Wine Country p. 797.*

POLLOCK PINES pop. 4,728

WHERE TO STAY

BEST WESTERN STAGECOACH INN **Phone:** (530)644-2029

Motel

All Year [ECP] 1P: $89-$119 2P: $99-$129 XP: $10 F12

Location: US 50, exit Pollock Pines eastbound, 1 mi e; exit Sly Park westbound; 12 mi e of Placerville. 5940 Pony Express Tr 95726 (PO Box 657). Fax: 530/644-6937. **Facility:** 26 units. 24 one-bedroom standard units, some with efficiencies. 2 one-bedroom suites ($219-$249) with kitchens. 2 stories. **Parking:** on-site. **Terms:** 8% service charge, small pets only ($5 extra charge). **Amenities:** irons, hair dryers. **Pool(s):** outdoor. **Cards:** AX, CB, DC, DS, MC, VI. **Special Amenities: free expanded continental breakfast and preferred room (subject to availability with advanced reservations).**

FEE

WESTHAVEN INN Book at aaa.com **Phone:** 530/644-7800

Motel

Property failed to provide current rates

Location: US 50, exit Pollock Pines, just n. 5658 Pony Express Tr 95726 (PO Box 1616). Fax: 530/644-1673. **Facility:** 21 one-bedroom standard units. 2 stories, exterior corridors. **Parking:** on-site. **Terms:** small pets only ($25 deposit).

SOME UNITS

FEE

WHERE TO DINE

HAVEN RESTAURANT | **Lunch:** $5-$12 | **Dinner:** $11-$23 | **Phone:** 530/644-3448

American

Location: Off US 50 at Sly Park, 0.5 mi w. 6396 Pony Express Tr 95726. **Hours:** 11 am-4:30 & 5-9 pm. Closed major holidays; also 12/10-12/25. **Features:** A variety of sandwiches, omelets and a few hot entrees line the restaurant's tried-and-true menu. Casual dress; beer & wine only. **Parking:** on-site. **Cards:** MC, VI.

PORTERVILLE pop. 39,615

WHERE TO STAY

BEST WESTERN PORTERVILLE INN *Book at aaa.com* **Phone:** 559/781-7411

SAVE

Small-scale Hotel

All Year [BP] 1P: $79-$84 2P: $89-$94 XP: $8 F12

Location: SR 65, 0.8 mi e, just s on Jaya St, then just e; adjacent to SR 190. 350 W Montgomery Ave 93257. Fax: 559/781-8910. **Facility:** 113 units. 112 one-bedroom standard units. 1 one-bedroom suite ($99-$109). 2 stories, interior corridors. **Parking:** on-site. **Amenities:** video games, irons, hair dryers. **Dining:** 6 am-11 pm, cocktails. **Pool(s):** heated outdoor. **Leisure Activities:** whirlpool. *Fee:* massage. **Guest Services:** coin laundry. **Business Services:** meeting rooms, business center. **Cards:** AX, CB, DC, DS, JC, MC, VI. **Special Amenities: free full breakfast and free newspaper.**

SOME UNITS

DATA PORT

WHERE TO DINE

APPLE ANNIE'S | **Lunch:** $5-$10 | **Dinner:** $5-$12 | **Phone:** 559/781-4088

American

Location: SR 65, exit Henderson Ave, 0.3 mi w. 1213 W Henderson Ave 93257. **Hours:** 6 am-10 pm. Closed: 1/1, 11/25, 12/25. **Features:** The polular country-style restaurant presents a menu of sandwiches and salads, as well as all-day breakfast dishes, including omelets. Dinner entrees are available after 4 pm. For dessert, guests can choose from several tasty apple recipes. Eager-to-please servers are "down-home" friendly. Casual dress; beer & wine only. **Parking:** on-site. **Cards:** AX, DS, MC, VI.

OAK PIT STEAK HOUSE | **Lunch:** $7-$9 | **Dinner:** $11-$21 | **Phone:** 559/781-7427

Steak & Seafood

Location: SR 65, exit Henderson Ave, 1 mi e, then just s. 615 N Main St 93257. **Hours:** 11 am-9 pm, Sat from 5 pm. Closed major holidays; also Sun. **Features:** Western decor—including mounted game on the walls and an old-fashioned saloon—lends to the homey feel of the casual steakhouse, where steak and barbecue specialties dominate a menu that also lists some chicken and seafood entrees. As an appetizer, try jalapeno peppers or waffle fries. Country-style ribs and barbecue beef skewers are favorites. Casual dress; cocktails. **Parking:** on-site. **Cards:** AX, CB, DC, DS, MC, VI.

PORTOLA pop. 2,227—*See also GRAEAGLE & QUINCY.*

WHERE TO STAY

PULLMAN INN **Phone:** (530)832-0107

Bed & Breakfast

5/1-10/31 1P: $65-$85 2P: $75-$95 XP: $20 D16
2/1-4/30 & 11/1-1/31 1P: $55-$80 2P: $65-$90 XP: $20 D16

Location: Just s of SR 70 via Gulling St. 256 Commercial St 96122. Fax: 530/832-6323. **Facility:** Smoke free premises. 6 one-bedroom standard units. 2 stories (no elevator), interior corridors. *Bath:* combo or shower only. **Parking:** on-site. **Terms:** office hours 8 am-9 pm, 7 day cancellation notice-fee imposed, [CP] meal plan available. **Amenities:** video library, irons, hair dryers. **Cards:** AX, MC, VI.

SOME UNITS

ASK VCR

SLEEPY PINES MOTEL **Phone:** 530/832-4291

Motel

All Year 1P: $56-$120 2P: $61-$120

Location: On SR 70. 74631 Hwy 70 96122. Fax: 530/832-5101. **Facility:** 17 units. 15 one-bedroom standard units, some with efficiencies. 2 cabins. 1 story, exterior corridors. *Bath:* combo or shower only. **Parking:** on-site. **Terms:** pets (in selected units). **Amenities:** *Some:* irons, hair dryers. **Guest Services:** gift shop. **Cards:** AX, DC, DS, MC, VI.

SOME UNITS

QUINCY pop. 1,879—*See also GRAEAGLE & PORTOLA.*

WHERE TO STAY

THE FEATHERBED **Phone:** 530/283-0102

Bed & Breakfast

All Year 1P: $85-$140 2P: $95-$150 XP: $12 F8

Location: Just s of SR 70 at Court St; downtown. 542 Jackson St 95971 (PO Box 3200). Fax: 530/283-0167. **Facility:** On the square in Quincy, the property features a large, old-fashioned front porch perfect for people watching; a cottage is also on the grounds. 7 units. 5 one-bedroom standard units. 2 cottages ($140-$150). 2 stories (no elevator), exterior corridors. *Bath:* combo or shower only. **Parking:** on-site. **Terms:** age restrictions may apply, 7 day cancellation notice-fee imposed, [BP] meal plan available. **Leisure Activities:** bicycles. **Cards:** AX, DC, DS, MC, VI.

SOME UNITS

HASKINS VALLEY INN Phone: 530/283-9667

Bed & Breakfast

All Year [BP] 1P: $110-$135 2P: $110-$135

Location: 17 mi w. 16860 Bucks Lake Rd 95971 (PO Box 4217). Fax: 530/283-9668. **Facility:** Built specifically as a B&B, this inn in the snow country offers gourmet meals and proximity to a snowmobile pass. 6 one-bedroom standard units, some with whirlpools. 2 stories (no elevator), interior corridors. *Bath:* combo or shower only. **Parking:** on-site. **Terms:** office hours 8 am-7 pm, age restrictions may apply, 14 day cancellation notice-fee imposed. **Amenities:** *Some:* irons, hair dryers. **Guest Services:** TV in common area. **Cards:** MC, VI.

LARIAT LODGE Phone: 530/283-1000

Motel

All Year [CP] 1P: $55-$80 2P: $62-$90 XP: $10 F5

Location: On SR 70 and 89, south side. 2370 E Main St 95971. Fax: 530/283-2064. **Facility:** 19 units. 18 one- and 1 two-bedroom standard units. 1 story, exterior corridors. *Bath:* combo or shower only. **Parking:** on-site. **Terms:** age restrictions may apply, 3 day cancellation notice, $2 service charge. **Amenities:** *Some:* irons, hair dryers. **Pool(s):** outdoor. **Cards:** AX, DS, MC, VI.

SOME UNITS

PINE HILL MOTEL Phone: 530/283-1670

Motel

All Year 1P: $55-$70 2P: $65-$75 XP: $5

Location: 1 mi s. 42075 Hwy 70 95971 (PO Box 3289). Fax: 530/283-1950. **Facility:** 12 units. 1 vacation home and 11 cabins ($125-$175). 1 story, exterior corridors. **Parking:** on-site. **Terms:** office hours 8 am-10 pm, age restrictions may apply, cancellation fee imposed, pets ($5 fee, with prior approval). **Amenities:** voice mail. *Some:* irons, hair dryers. **Leisure Activities:** bicycles, hiking trails, basketball. **Cards:** AX, CB, DC, DS, MC, VI. **Special Amenities: free local telephone calls.**

SOME UNITS

FEE

RANCHO CORDOVA pop. 55,060 (See map and index starting on p. 565)

WHERE TO STAY

AMERISUITES (SACRAMENTO/RANCHO CORDOVA) Book at aaa.com Phone: (916)635-4799 86

Small-scale Hotel

All Year 1P: $69 2P: $129 XP: $10 F17

Location: US 50, exit Zinfandel Dr, just s. 10744 Gold Center Dr 95670. Fax: 916/635-3799. **Facility:** 128 one-bedroom standard units. 6 stories, interior corridors. **Parking:** on-site. **Terms:** [ECP] meal plan available, small pets only. **Amenities:** video games, high-speed Internet (fee), voice mail, irons, hair dryers. **Pool(s):** heated outdoor. **Leisure Activities:** exercise room. **Guest Services:** coin laundry. **Business Services:** meeting rooms, business center. **Cards:** AX, DC, DS, JC, MC, VI. **Special Amenities: free expanded continental breakfast and free newspaper.** *(See color ad p 569)*

SOME UNITS

BEST CHOICE INN Phone: (916)638-2500 89

Motel

All Year [CP] 1P: $49-$59 2P: $59-$69 XP: $5 F12

Location: US 50, exit Zinfandel Dr, just n. 10800 Olson Dr 95670. Fax: 916/638-2672. **Facility:** 136 one-bedroom standard units. 3 stories, exterior corridors. **Parking:** on-site. **Terms:** weekly rates available. **Amenities:** hair dryers. **Pool(s):** outdoor. **Leisure Activities:** whirlpool. **Cards:** AX, CB, DC, MC, VI.

SOME UNITS

ASK

BEST WESTERN HERITAGE INN Book at aaa.com Phone: (916)635-4040 83

Motel

All Year 1P: $99 2P: $99

Location: US 50, exit Sunrise Blvd S; 12 mi e of Sacramento. 11269 Point East Dr 95742. Fax: 916/635-7198. **Facility:** 122 one-bedroom standard units, some with whirlpools. 3 stories, interior corridors. **Parking:** on-site. **Terms:** cancellation fee imposed, [BP] meal plan available, package plans - seasonal, small pets only ($15 fee). **Amenities:** irons, hair dryers. **Dining:** 6-9 am. **Pool(s):** outdoor. **Leisure Activities:** whirlpool. **Guest Services:** valet laundry. **Business Services:** meeting rooms. **Cards:** AX, DC, MC, VI. **Special Amenities: free expanded continental breakfast and free local telephone calls.** *(See color ad p 570)*

SOME UNITS

FEE

COURTYARD BY MARRIOTT Book at aaa.com Phone: (916)638-3800 87

Motel

All Year 1P: $69-$124 2P: $69-$124

Location: S of and adjacent to US 50, exit Zinfandel Dr; 11 mi e of Sacramento. 10683 White Rock Rd 95670. Fax: 916/638-6776. **Facility:** 145 units. 133 one-bedroom standard units. 12 one-bedroom suites ($104-$154). 3 stories, interior corridors. **Parking:** on-site. **Terms:** [BP] meal plan available, 12% service charge. **Amenities:** dual phone lines, voice mail, irons, hair dryers. **Pool(s):** heated outdoor. **Leisure Activities:** whirlpool, exercise room. **Guest Services:** coin laundry. **Business Services:** meeting rooms. **Cards:** AX, DC, DS, MC, VI.

SOME UNITS

FAIRFIELD INN BY MARRIOTT Book at aaa.com Phone: (916)631-7500 84

Motel

All Year 1P: $59-$99 2P: $69-$109

Location: S of and adjacent to US 50, exit Zinfandel Dr; 11 mi e of Sacramento. 10713 White Rock Rd 95670. Fax: 916/635-0301. **Facility:** 116 one-bedroom standard units. 3 stories, interior/exterior corridors. **Parking:** on-site. **Terms:** [ECP] meal plan available. **Amenities:** voice mail, irons, hair dryers. **Pool(s):** heated outdoor. **Cards:** AX, CB, DC, DS, JC, MC, VI.

SOME UNITS

ASK

(See map and index starting on p. 565)

HALLMARK SUITES *Book at aaa.com* **Phone:** (916)638-4141 82

Motel

All Year [BP] 1P: $127-$147 2P: $127-$147

Location: US 50, exit Sunrise Blvd S; 12 mi e of Sacramento. 11260 Point East Dr 95742. Fax: 916/638-4287. **Facility:** 159 units. 127 one-bedroom standard units. 32 one-bedroom suites with kitchens. 3 stories, interior corridors. **Parking:** on-site. **Terms:** 12% service charge. **Amenities:** voice mail, irons, hair dryers. **Pool(s):** heated outdoor. **Leisure Activities:** whirlpool, exercise room. **Guest Services:** complimentary evening beverages, coin laundry. **Business Services:** meeting rooms. **Cards:** AX, DC, MC, VI.

SOME UNITS

ASK S/D VCR DATA PORT

HAMPTON INN *Book at aaa.com* **Phone:** (916)638-4800 85

Motel

2/1-11/1 [ECP] 1P: $64-$99 2P: $74-$109
11/2-1/31 [ECP] 1P: $59-$79 2P: $69-$89

Location: US 50, exit Zinfandel Dr. 10755 Gold Center Dr 95670. Fax: 916/638-3594. **Facility:** 87 one-bedroom standard units. 3 stories, interior corridors. **Parking:** on-site. **Terms:** 7 day cancellation notice-fee imposed. **Amenities:** dual phone lines, voice mail, irons, hair dryers. **Pool(s):** indoor. **Leisure Activities:** whirlpool. **Guest Services:** valet and coin laundry. **Business Services:** meeting rooms. **Cards:** AX, CB, DC, DS, MC, VI.

SOME UNITS

ASK S/D DATA PORT

HAWTHORN SUITES *Book at aaa.com* **Phone:** (916)351-9192 88

Motel

All Year [BP] 1P: $109 2P: $109

Location: US 50, exit Hazel Ave, just n. 12180 Tributary Point Dr 95670. Fax: 916/355-1752. **Facility:** 61 one-bedroom standard units, some with kitchens. 3 stories, interior corridors. **Parking:** on-site. **Terms:** cancellation fee imposed. **Amenities:** dual phone lines, voice mail, irons, hair dryers. **Pool(s):** heated outdoor. **Leisure Activities:** whirlpool, exercise room. **Guest Services:** valet and coin laundry. **Business Services:** meeting rooms. **Cards:** AX, DC, DS, MC, VI.

SOME UNITS

ASK S/D DATA PORT

HOLIDAY INN *Book at aaa.com* **Phone:** (916)638-1111 79

AAA SAVE

Motel

All Year 1P: $119-$129 2P: $139-$149

Location: US 50, exit Sunrise Blvd S; 12 mi e of Sacramento. 11131 Folsom Blvd 95670. Fax: 916/635-3297. **Facility:** 130 one-bedroom standard units. 5 stories, interior corridors. **Parking:** on-site. **Terms:** [ECP] meal plan available. **Amenities:** high-speed Internet (fee), voice mail, irons, hair dryers. **Pool(s):** heated outdoor. **Leisure Activities:** whirlpool, exercise room. **Guest Services:** valet and coin laundry. **Business Services:** meeting rooms. **Cards:** AX, CB, DC, DS, MC, VI. **Special Amenities: free continental breakfast and free newspaper.** *(See color ad p 578)*

SOME UNITS

S/D DATA PORT

INNS OF AMERICA *Book at aaa.com* **Phone:** (916)351-1213 78

AAA SAVE

Motel

All Year 1P: $69-$77 2P: $69-$77

Location: US 50, exit Hazel Ave, then just s. 12249 Folsom Blvd 95670. Fax: 916/351-1817. **Facility:** 123 one-bedroom standard units. 3 stories, exterior corridors. **Parking:** on-site. **Terms:** [CP] meal plan available, small pets only ($5 fee). **Pool(s):** heated outdoor. **Guest Services:** coin laundry. **Business Services:** meeting rooms. **Cards:** AX, MC, VI. **Special Amenities: free continental breakfast.**

SOME UNITS

S/D FEE DATA PORT

(See map and index starting on p. 565)

QUALITY INN & SUITES Book at aaa.com Phone: (916)363-3344 90

Motel

All Year [BP] 1P: $69-$139 2P: $69-$139

Location: US 50, exit Mather Field Rd; 9 mi e of Sacramento. 3240 Mather Field Rd 95670. Fax: 916/363-1988. **Facility:** 110 units. 104 one-bedroom standard units. 6 one-bedroom suites ($99-$139). 4 stories, exterior corridors. **Parking:** on-site. **Amenities:** irons, hair dryers. **Pool(s):** outdoor. **Leisure Activities:** whirlpool. **Guest Services:** coin laundry. **Business Services:** meeting rooms. **Cards:** AX, DS, MC, VI. **Special Amenities: free full breakfast and early check-in/late check-out.** *(See color ad p 550)*

SOME UNITS

FEE

RESIDENCE INN Book at aaa.com Phone: (916)851-1550 80

Motel

All Year 1P: $130-$170 2P: $130-$170

Location: US 50, exit Zinfandel Dr. 2779 Prospect Park Dr 95670. Fax: 916/851-1550. **Facility:** 90 units. 42 one-bedroom standard units with kitchens. 33 one- and 15 two-bedroom suites with kitchens. 3 stories, interior corridors. **Parking:** on-site. **Terms:** [BP] meal plan available. **Amenities:** dual phone lines, voice mail, irons, hair dryers. **Pool(s):** indoor. **Leisure Activities:** whirlpool, exercise room, sports court. **Guest Services:** valet and coin laundry. **Business Services:** meeting rooms. **Cards:** AX, DC, DS, MC, VI.

SOME UNITS

ASK

SACRAMENTO MARRIOTT RANCHO CORDOVA Book at aaa.com Phone: (916)638-1100 81

Large-scale Hotel

All Year 1P: $179-$199 2P: $189-$209

Location: US 50, exit Sunrise Blvd, just s; 9 mi e of Sacramento. 11211 Point East Dr 95742. Fax: 916/635-8356. **Facility:** This renovated property offers attractively appointed and spacious guest units; the pool is surrounded by well-tended gardens. 265 units. 254 one-bedroom standard units. 11 one-bedroom suites ($250-$379). 11 stories, interior corridors. **Parking:** on-site. **Terms:** cancellation fee imposed. **Amenities:** video games, high-speed Internet, dual phone lines, voice mail, irons, hair dryers. **Dining:** 6 am-10:30 pm, cocktails. **Pool(s):** heated outdoor. **Leisure Activities:** whirlpool. **Guest Services:** gift shop, complimentary laundry. **Business Services:** conference facilities, business center. **Cards:** AX, CB, DC, DS, JC, MC, VI.

SOME UNITS

RED BLUFF pop. 13,147—*See also LASSEN VOLCANIC NATIONAL PARK.*

WHERE TO STAY

BEST VALUE INN & SUITES Book at aaa.com Phone: (530)529-2028

Motel

All Year 1P: $50-$55 2P: $55-$75 XP: $6 F13

Location: I-5, exit SR 36 W (Central District), just s. 30 Gilmore Rd 96080. Fax: 530/527-1702. **Facility:** 60 one-bedroom standard units. 2 stories (no elevator), exterior corridors. **Parking:** on-site. **Terms:** age restrictions may apply, 3 day cancellation notice, [CP] meal plan available, small pets only ($5 extra charge). **Amenities:** hair dryers. *Some:* irons. **Pool(s):** small outdoor. **Guest Services:** coin laundry. **Cards:** AX, DC, DS, MC, VI. **Special Amenities: free continental breakfast and free room upgrade (subject to availability with advanced reservations).** *(See color ad below)*

SOME UNITS

FEE

CINDERELLA RIVERVIEW MOTEL **Phone:** 530/527-5490

Motel

All Year 1P: $37-$55 2P: $45-$65 XP: $6 F5

Location: I-5, exit SR 36 W (Central District), 0.4 mi w on Antelope Blvd. 600 Rio St 96080. Fax: 530/527-7051. **Facility:** 39 one-bedroom standard units. 2 stories (no elevator), exterior corridors. *Bath:* combo or shower only. **Parking:** on-site. **Terms:** age restrictions may apply, 3 day cancellation notice, weekly rates available, [CP] meal plan available, pets ($5 extra charge). **Amenities:** *Some:* irons, hair dryers. **Pool(s):** outdoor. **Leisure Activities:** fishing. **Guest Services:** coin laundry. **Cards:** AX, DC, MC, VI. **Special Amenities: free continental breakfast and free local telephone calls.**

SOME UNITS

FEE

COMFORT INN *Book at aaa.com* **Phone:** (530)529-7060

Motel

All Year [CP] 1P: $79-$109 2P: $79-$109 XP: $10 F18

Location: I-5, exit Susanville/Lassen Park, 0.3 mi e. 90 Sale Ln 96080. Fax: 530/529-7077. **Facility:** 67 units. 65 one-bedroom standard units. 2 one-bedroom suites ($104-$159). 3 stories, interior corridors. **Parking:** on-site. **Terms:** age restrictions may apply. **Amenities:** irons, hair dryers. **Pool(s):** outdoor. **Leisure Activities:** whirlpool, exercise room. **Guest Services:** coin laundry. **Cards:** AX, CB, DC, DS, JC, MC, VI. **Special Amenities: free continental breakfast and free local telephone calls.**

SOME UNITS

DAYS INN & SUITES *Book at aaa.com* **Phone:** 530/527-6130

Motel

All Year 1P: $50-$95 2P: $50-$95 XP: $5 F11

Location: I-5, exit S Main St southbound, just right; exit S Main St northbound, cross over bridge, just right. 5 John Sutter St 96080. Fax: 530/527-1251. **Facility:** 47 one-bedroom standard units. 2 stories (no elevator), exterior corridors. **Parking:** on-site. **Terms:** age restrictions may apply, small pets only ($5 fee). **Amenities:** hair dryers. *Some:* irons. **Pool(s):** outdoor. **Cards:** AX, DC, DS, MC, VI. **Special Amenities: free continental breakfast and free newspaper.**

SOME UNITS

FEE

LAMPLIGHTER LODGE **Phone:** (530)527-1150

Motel

All Year [CP] 1P: $50-$55 2P: $55-$65 XP: $10 F12

Location: I-5, exit via business loop. 210 S Main St 96080. Fax: 530/527-5878. **Facility:** 50 one-bedroom standard units. 2 stories (no elevator), exterior corridors. *Bath:* combo or shower only. **Parking:** on-site. **Terms:** age restrictions may apply. **Amenities:** *Some:* irons, hair dryers. **Pool(s):** outdoor. **Cards:** AX, CB, DC, DS, JC, MC, VI. **Special Amenities: free continental breakfast and free local telephone calls.**

SOME UNITS

RIVER INN *Book at aaa.com* **Phone:** (530)528-8890

Motel

All Year 1P: $39-$85 2P: $45-$90 XP: $5 F12

Location: I-5, exit 351 northbound, just s; exit Antelope Blvd southbound, 0.5 mi w, then just n. 1142 N Main St 96080. **Facility:** 29 units. 27 one- and 2 two-bedroom standard units. 2 stories (no elevator), exterior corridors. *Bath:* combo or shower only. **Parking:** on-site. **Terms:** age restrictions may apply, weekly rates available, [CP] meal plan available, pets ($5 extra charge). **Amenities:** hair dryers. *Some:* irons. **Pool(s):** small outdoor. **Cards:** AX, DC, DS, MC, VI.

SOME UNITS

FEE

SPORTSMAN LODGE — **Phone:** (530)527-2888

AAA SAVE — Motel

All Year 1P: $40-$80 2P: $50-$100 XP: $6 F6

Location: I-5, exit Susanville/Lassen Park, 1.5 mi e. 768 Antelope Blvd 96080. Fax: 530/527-2889. **Facility:** 19 one-bedroom standard units. 1 story, exterior corridors. *Bath:* shower only. **Parking:** on-site. **Terms:** age restrictions may apply, 3 day cancellation notice-fee imposed, pets ($7 extra charge). **Amenities:** *Some:* irons, hair dryers. **Pool(s):** outdoor. **Cards:** AX, DS, MC, VI.

FEE — SOME UNITS

SUPER 8 MOTEL *Book at aaa.com* — **Phone:** (530)527-8882

AAA SAVE — Motel

All Year [ECP] 1P: $55-$85 2P: $60-$90 XP: $5 F17

Location: I-5, exit Susanville/Lassen Park. 203 Antelope Blvd 96080. Fax: 530/527-5078. **Facility:** 68 one-bedroom standard units. 2 stories (no elevator), interior corridors. **Parking:** on-site. **Terms:** age restrictions may apply, pets ($5 deposit). **Amenities:** hair dryers. *Some:* irons. **Pool(s):** outdoor. **Cards:** AX, DC, DS, MC, VI. **Special Amenities: free expanded continental breakfast and free local telephone calls.**

FEE — SOME UNITS

TRAVELODGE RED BLUFF *Book at aaa.com* — **Phone:** (530)527-6020

AAA SAVE — Motel

5/1-10/31 1P: $55-$60 2P: $60-$75 XP: $6 F16
2/1-4/30 & 11/1-1/31 1P: $50-$55 2P: $55-$75 XP: $6 F16

Location: I-5, exit 36 W (Central District), just w. 38 Antelope Blvd 96080. Fax: 530/527-4653. **Facility:** 41 one-bedroom standard units. 2 stories (no elevator), exterior corridors. *Bath:* combo or shower only. **Parking:** on-site. **Terms:** [CP] meal plan available, pets ($5 fee). **Amenities:** hair dryers. *Some:* irons. **Pool(s):** outdoor. **Cards:** AX, DC, DS, MC, VI. **Special Amenities: free continental breakfast and free local telephone calls.** *(See color ad p 552)*

FEE — SOME UNITS

VILLAGER LODGE — **Phone:** (530)527-3545

AAA SAVE — Motel

All Year 1P: $40-$75 2P: $50-$100 XP: $5 F12

Location: I-5, exit SR 36 W (Central District), 0.5 mi w on Antelope Blvd, then 0.7 mi s. 250 S Main St 96080. Fax: 530/527-3035. **Facility:** 34 one-bedroom standard units. 1 story, exterior corridors. *Bath:* combo or shower only. **Parking:** on-site. **Terms:** age restrictions may apply, weekly rates available, [CP] meal plan available, pets ($5 extra charge). **Amenities:** *Some:* irons, hair dryers. **Pool(s):** small outdoor. **Cards:** AX, DC, DS, MC, VI. **Special Amenities: free continental breakfast and free local telephone calls.**

FEE — SOME UNITS

WHERE TO DINE

GREEN BARN RESTAURANT — **Lunch:** $7-$14 **Dinner:** $22 **Phone:** 530/527-3161

Steak House

Location: I-5, exit SR 36 (Susanville/Lassen Park), 1 mi e. 5 Chestnut Ave 96080. **Hours:** 11 am-9 pm, Sat-10 pm, Sun 4 pm-9 pm. Closed major holidays. **Features:** Long established, family atmosphere, varied menu. Casual dress; cocktails. **Parking:** on-site. **Cards:** AX, DC, MC, VI.

REDCREST

WHERE TO STAY

REDCREST RESORT — **Phone:** (707)722-4208

AAA SAVE — Cabin

5/1-10/31 1P: $60-$115 2P: $60-$115 XP: $8
2/1-4/30 & 11/1-1/31 1P: $55-$95 2P: $55-$95 XP: $8

Location: US 101, exit Redcrest, just n. 26459 Avenue of the Giants 95569 (PO Box 235). Fax: 707/722-4403. **Facility:** Designated smoking area. 10 cabins. 1 story, exterior corridors. *Bath:* shower only. **Parking:** on-site. **Terms:** 14 day cancellation notice-fee imposed, weekly rates available, pets ($5 extra charge). **Amenities:** *Some:* irons, hair dryers. **Leisure Activities:** whirlpool, barbecue, bicycles, hiking trails, playground, horseshoes, volleyball. **Cards:** MC, VI.

FEE — SOME UNITS

REDDING pop. 80,865—*See also LASSEN VOLCANIC NATIONAL PARK & SHASTA LAKE.*

WHERE TO STAY

BEST WESTERN HILLTOP INN *Book at aaa.com* — **Phone:** (530)221-6100

AAA SAVE — Motel

4/12-1/31 [BP] 1P: $129 2P: $149 XP: $15 F16
2/1-4/11 [BP] 1P: $119 2P: $139 XP: $15 F16

Location: I-5, exit Cypress Ave E, 0.3 mi n. 2300 Hilltop Dr 96002. Fax: 530/221-2867. **Facility:** 114 one-bedroom standard units. 2 stories, exterior corridors. *Bath:* combo or shower only. **Parking:** on-site. **Terms:** age restrictions may apply. **Amenities:** dual phone lines, irons, hair dryers. **Dining:** C.R. Gibbs American Grill, see separate listing. **Pool(s):** heated outdoor. **Leisure Activities:** whirlpool. **Guest Services:** valet and coin laundry. **Business Services:** meeting rooms, business center. **Cards:** AX, CB, DC, DS, MC, VI. **Special Amenities: free full breakfast and free local telephone calls.** *(See color ad p 554 & p 521)*

SOME UNITS

BEST WESTERN HOSPITALITY HOUSE *Book at aaa.com* **Phone:** 530/241-6464

Motel

4/15-10/15 [ECP]	1P: $70-$89	2P: $76-$95	XP: $6	F10
2/1-4/14 & 10/16-1/31 [ECP]	1P: $60-$79	2P: $66-$85	XP: $6	F10

Location: I-5, exit Lake Blvd northbound, just w, 0.5 mi to Market St, then 0.5 mi s; exit Market St southbound, then 2 mi s. 532 N Market St 96003. Fax: 530/244-1998. **Facility:** 62 units. 61 one-bedroom standard units. 1 two-bedroom suite. 2 stories, exterior corridors. *Bath:* some combo or shower only. **Parking:** on-site. **Terms:** age restrictions may apply, small pets only ($30 deposit, $10 extra charge). **Amenities:** voice mail, irons, hair dryers. **Dining:** 7 am-8:30 pm. **Pool(s):** outdoor. **Leisure Activities:** whirlpool. **Guest Services:** coin laundry. **Cards:** AX, DC, DS, MC, VI. **Special Amenities: free expanded continental breakfast and free local telephone calls.**

FEE SOME UNITS

BEST WESTERN PONDEROSA INN *Book at aaa.com* **Phone:** (530)241-6300

Motel

All Year [CP]	1P: $59-$64	2P: $59-$70	XP: $10	F12

Location: I-5, exit Cypress Ave, 1.5 mi w. Located in a commercial area. 2220 Pine St 96001. Fax: 530/241-4959. **Facility:** 69 units. 68 one- and 1 two-bedroom standard units. 2 stories (no elevator), exterior corridors. **Parking:** on-site. **Terms:** age restrictions may apply, pets ($100 deposit). **Amenities:** irons, hair dryers. **Pool(s):** outdoor, wading. **Business Services:** meeting rooms. **Cards:** AX, DC, DS, MC, VI. **Special Amenities: free continental breakfast.**

FEE SOME UNITS

COMFORT INN *Book at aaa.com* **Phone:** (530)221-6530

Motel

All Year [ECP]	1P: $79-$109	2P: $79-$109	XP: $6	F12

Location: I-5, exit Cypress Ave E, 0.3 mi n. 2059 Hilltop Dr 96002. Fax: 530/221-3687. **Facility:** 88 one-bedroom standard units. 2-3 stories (no elevator), exterior corridors. **Parking:** on-site. **Terms:** pets ($15 extra charge). **Amenities:** video games, irons, hair dryers. **Pool(s):** outdoor. **Cards:** AX, DC, DS, MC, VI. **Special Amenities: free expanded continental breakfast and free local telephone calls.**

FEE SOME UNITS FEE

GRAND MANOR INN *Book at aaa.com* **Phone:** (530)221-4472

Motel

All Year [CP]	1P: $74-$129	2P: $79-$129	XP: $10	F18

Location: I-5, exit Cypress Ave E, 0.8 mi n on Hilltop Dr. 850 Mistletoe Ln 96002. Fax: 530/222-8106. **Facility:** 71 one-bedroom standard units. 3 stories, interior corridors. *Bath:* combo or shower only. **Parking:** on-site. **Terms:** age restrictions may apply. **Amenities:** irons, hair dryers. **Pool(s):** outdoor. **Leisure Activities:** whirlpool, exercise room. **Cards:** AX, CB, DC, DS, JC, MC, VI. **Special Amenities: free continental breakfast and free local telephone calls.**

SOME UNITS

HOLIDAY INN *Book at aaa.com* **Phone:** (530)221-7500

Motel

All Year 1P: $99-$159 2P: $119-$179 XP: $10 F18

Location: I-5, exit Hilltop Dr, just s. 1900 Hilltop Dr 96002. Fax: 530/223-9644. **Facility:** 126 one-bedroom standard units. 2 stories, interior corridors. *Bath:* combo or shower only. **Parking:** on-site. **Terms:** age restrictions may apply. **Amenities:** high-speed Internet, dual phone lines, voice mail, irons, hair dryers. **Dining:** 2 restaurants, 6 am-9 pm, cocktails. **Pool(s):** outdoor. **Leisure Activities:** whirlpool, exercise room. **Guest Services:** valet and coin laundry. **Business Services:** conference facilities, fax. **Cards:** AX, CB, DC, DS, JC, MC, VI. **Special Amenities: free local telephone calls and early check-in/late check-out.**

SOME UNITS

HOLIDAY INN EXPRESS *Book at aaa.com* **Phone:** (530)241-5500

Motel

4/17-5/20	1P: $110-$140	2P: $110-$140	XP: $10	F19
5/21-9/2	1P: $99-$140	2P: $99-$140	XP: $10	F19
2/1-4/16 & 9/3-1/31	1P: $94-$120	2P: $94-$120	XP: $10	F19

Location: I-5, exit Twin View Blvd, just w. 1080 Twin View Blvd 96003. Fax: 530/241-5674. **Facility:** 50 one-bedroom standard units, some with whirlpools. 2 stories, interior corridors. **Parking:** on-site. **Terms:** age restrictions may apply, [ECP] meal plan available, pets ($30 extra charge). **Amenities:** irons, hair dryers. **Pool(s):** outdoor. **Leisure Activities:** exercise room. **Cards:** AX, CB, DC, DS, MC, VI. **Special Amenities: free local telephone calls and free newspaper.** *(See ad below)*

FEE SOME UNITS FEE

HOWARD JOHNSON EXPRESS *Book at aaa.com* **Phone:** (530)223-1935

Motel

All Year 1P: $69 2P: $79 XP: $10 F12

Location: I-5, exit Cypress Ave W, 0.5 mi s. 2731 Bechelli Ln 96002. Fax: 530/223-1176. **Facility:** 75 one-bedroom standard units, some with efficiencies. 2 stories, exterior corridors. **Parking:** on-site. **Amenities:** *Some:* irons, hair dryers. **Pool(s):** small outdoor. **Cards:** AX, DC, DS, MC, VI.

SOME UNITS

LA QUINTA INN *Book at aaa.com* **Phone:** 530/221-8200

Motel

All Year 1P: $75-$115 2P: $75-$115

Location: I-5, exit Cypress Ave E, 0.5 mi n. 2180 Hilltop Dr 96002. Fax: 530/223-4727. **Facility:** 141 units. 140 one-bedroom standard units. 1 one-bedroom suite. 3 stories, interior corridors. *Bath:* combo or shower only. **Parking:** on-site. **Terms:** [ECP] meal plan available, small pets only. **Amenities:** video games (fee), irons, hair dryers. **Pool(s):** heated outdoor. **Leisure Activities:** whirlpool, exercise room. **Guest Services:** valet and coin laundry. **Business Services:** meeting rooms. **Cards:** AX, CB, DC, DS, JC, MC, VI.

SOME UNITS FEE FEE

OXFORD SUITES *Book at aaa.com* **Phone:** (530)221-0100

Motel

All Year [BP] 1P: $88-$135 2P: $88-$135 XP: $10 F

Location: I-5, exit Cypress Ave E, 0.5 mi n. 1967 Hilltop Dr 96002. Fax: 530/221-8265. **Facility:** 139 units. 137 one- and 2 two-bedroom suites. 3-4 stories, interior/exterior corridors. **Parking:** on-site. **Terms:** small pets only ($25 extra charge). **Amenities:** video library (fee), voice mail, irons, hair dryers. **Pool(s):** heated outdoor. **Leisure Activities:** whirlpool. **Guest Services:** gift shop, complimentary evening beverages, valet and coin laundry. **Business Services:** meeting rooms, fax. **Cards:** AX, CB, DC, DS, MC, VI.

SOME UNITS FEE

RAMADA LIMITED *Book at aaa.com* **Phone:** (530)246-2222

Motel

6/1-9/30 [ECP]	1P: $91-$101	2P: $101-$111
4/1-5/31 & 10/1-1/31 [ECP]	1P: $81-$91	2P: $91-$101
2/1-3/31 [ECP]	1P: $71-$81	2P: $81-$91

Location: I-5, exit Twin View Blvd E, just n. 1286 Twin View Blvd 96003. Fax: 530/246-3151. **Facility:** 63 one-bedroom standard units, some with whirlpools. 3 stories, interior corridors. *Bath:* combo or shower only. **Parking:** on-site. **Terms:** pets ($15 extra charge). **Amenities:** voice mail, irons, hair dryers. **Pool(s):** heated indoor. **Leisure Activities:** whirlpool, exercise room. **Guest Services:** coin laundry. **Business Services:** meeting rooms. **Cards:** AX, CB, DC, DS, JC, MC, VI. **Special Amenities: free expanded continental breakfast and free newspaper.**

SOME UNITS FEE

REDDING TRAVELODGE **Phone:** (530)243-5291

SAVE Motel

5/16-10/15	1P: $69-$99	2P: $75-$105	XP: $6	F17
10/16-1/31	1P: $59-$84	2P: $65-$89	XP: $6	F17
2/1-5/15	1P: $59-$79	2P: $65-$85	XP: $6	F17

Location: I-5, exit Lake Blvd southbound, 1 mi to Market St, then make left; exit SR 273 northbound, SR 90 S 2 mi. 540 N Market St 96003. Fax: 530/243-8328. **Facility:** 42 units. 41 one- and 1 two-bedroom standard units, some with kitchens. 2 stories (no elevator), exterior corridors. **Parking:** on-site. **Terms:** cancellation fee imposed, [ECP] meal plan available, pets (with prior approval). **Amenities:** irons, hair dryers. **Pool(s):** heated outdoor. **Leisure Activities:** whirlpool. **Guest Services:** coin laundry. **Business Services:** meeting rooms. **Cards:** AX, DC, DS, MC, VI. **Special Amenities: free expanded continental breakfast and free local telephone calls.** *(See color ad below)*

SOME UNITS

RED LION HOTEL *Book at aaa.com* **Phone:** (530)221-8700

Motel

7/1-8/31	1P: $104	2P: $124
4/1-6/30	1P: $94	2P: $114
2/1-3/31 & 9/1-1/31	1P: $89	2P: $109

Location: I-5, exit SR 44 and 299 (Hilltop Dr). 1830 Hilltop Dr 96002. Fax: 530/221-0324. **Facility:** 192 units. 190 one-bedroom standard units. 2 one-bedroom suites. 2 stories (no elevator), interior corridors. *Bath:* combo or shower only. **Parking:** on-site. **Terms:** pets ($50 extra charge). **Amenities:** voice mail, irons, hair dryers. *Some:* dual phone lines. **Pool(s):** outdoor, wading. **Leisure Activities:** whirlpool, exercise room. **Guest Services:** valet laundry, area transportation. **Business Services:** conference facilities, business center. **Cards:** AX, DC, DS, MC, VI. *(See ad below)*

SOME UNITS FEE FEE

RIVER INN *Book at aaa.com* **Phone:** (530)241-9500

SAVE Motel

5/2-9/30	1P: $75-$85	2P: $75-$85	XP: $10
2/1-5/1 & 10/1-1/31	1P: $65-$75	2P: $65-$75	XP: $10

Location: I-5, exit SR 299 W; 1 mi w, exit Park Marina Dr. 1835 Park Marina Dr 96001. Fax: 530/241-5345. **Facility:** 79 one-bedroom standard units. 2 stories (no elevator), exterior corridors. **Parking:** on-site. **Terms:** age restrictions may apply, 7 day cancellation notice, pets ($6 extra charge). **Amenities:** *Some:* irons, hair dryers. **Pool(s):** outdoor. **Leisure Activities:** sauna, whirlpool. **Guest Services:** coin laundry. **Cards:** AX, CB, DC, DS, MC, VI.

SOME UNITS FEE

SUPER 8 MOTEL — Phone: 530/221-8881

Motel

	1P	2P	XP	
5/28-9/4	1P: $59-$65	2P: $68-$75	XP: $5	F12
1/1-1/31	1P: $57-$69	2P: $65-$75	XP: $5	F12
2/1-5/27 & 9/5-12/31	1P: $55-$65	2P: $60-$69	XP: $5	F12

Location: I-5, exit Churn Creek Rd E. 5175 Churn Creek Rd 96002. Fax: 530/221-8881. **Facility:** 80 one-bedroom standard units. 2 stories, interior corridors. **Parking:** on-site. **Amenities:** *Some:* irons, hair dryers. **Pool(s):** outdoor. **Leisure Activities:** sauna, whirlpool. **Cards:** AX, CB, DC, MC, VI.

SOME UNITS

DATA PORT / /

TIFFANY HOUSE BED & BREAKFAST INN — Phone: (530)244-3225

Bed & Breakfast

	1P	2P	XP	
All Year	1P: $100-$150	2P: $100-$150	XP: $30	F6

Location: I-5, exit Lake Blvd, 0.8 mi w to Market, 0.8 mi s to Benton W, then just n. Located in residential neighborhood. 1510 Barbara Rd 96003. **Facility:** A canopy of aged oaks adds a tranquil ambience to this 1930s home offering a pool, a spa and views of Lassen Peak. Smoke free premises. 4 units. 3 one-bedroom standard units. 1 cottage. 2 stories (no elevator), interior/exterior corridors. *Bath:* combo or shower only. **Parking:** on-site. **Terms:** office hours 8 am-9 pm, check-in 4 pm, age restrictions may apply, 7 day cancellation notice-fee imposed, [BP] meal plan available. **Amenities:** hair dryers. **Pool(s):** outdoor. **Cards:** AX, DS, MC, VI.

SOME UNITS

DATA PORT / /

The following lodging was either not evaluated or did not meet AAA rating requirements but is listed for your information only.

AMERIHOST INN & SUITES-REDDING — Phone: 530/722-9100

fyi

Small-scale Hotel

Property failed to provide current rates

Too new to rate, opening scheduled for October 2003. **Location:** I-5, exit Larkspur Ln, just e, then left. 2600 Larkspur Ln 96002. Fax: 530/722-9969. **Amenities:** 84 units, coffeemakers, microwaves, refrigerators, pool. ***(See color ad p 554)***

WHERE TO DINE

C.R. GIBBS AMERICAN GRILL — **Lunch:** $7-$14 — **Dinner:** $9-$20 — **Phone:** 530/221-2335

American

Location: I-5, exit Cypress Ave E, 0.3 mi n; in Best Western Hilltop Inn. 2300 Hilltop Dr 96002. **Hours:** 10 am-11 pm. Closed: 12/25. **Reservations:** suggested. **Features:** Guests can watch meals being prepared in the open kitchen or shift their gaze to the breathtaking view of Mt Lassen. Casual dress; cocktails. **Parking:** on-site. **Cards:** AX, CB, DC, DS, MC, VI. ***(See color ad p 554)***

DE MECURIO'S RESTAURANT — **Dinner:** $18-$30 — **Phone:** 530/222-1307

Continental

Location: I-5, exit Cypress Ave, 1 mi e, just e to Churn Creek, 0.4 mi s to Hartnell Ave, then 0.5 mi e. 1647 Hartnell Ave #21 96002. **Hours:** 5 pm-9 pm. Closed: 1/1, 12/24-12/26; also Sun & Mon. **Reservations:** suggested. **Features:** Specializing in French, Italian and American dishes, the restaurant sustains a quiet, comfortable atmosphere. Casual dress; cocktails. **Parking:** on-site. **Cards:** AX, DC, DS, MC, VI.

HATCHCOVER RESTAURANT — **Lunch:** $4-$10 — **Dinner:** $8-$29 — **Phone:** 530/223-5606

Steak & Seafood

Location: I-5, exit Cypress Ave W, 0.5 mi n. 202 Hemsted Dr 96002. **Hours:** 11:30 am-2 & 5:30-9 pm, Fri-10 pm, Sat 5:30 pm-10 pm, Sun 5 pm-9 pm. Closed: 1/1, 11/25, 12/25. **Features:** The menu lists a good variety of fresh fish and seafood, as well as prime rib, chicken, pasta and beef dishes. Casual dress; cocktails. **Parking:** on-site. **Cards:** AX, DC, DS, MC, VI.

REDWAY pop. 1,188

WHERE TO STAY

DEAN CREEK RESORT — **Phone:** (707)923-2555

AAA SAVE

Motel

	1P	2P
5/1-10/31	1P: $75-$130	2P: $75-$130
11/1-1/31	1P: $60-$100	2P: $60-$100
2/1-4/30	1P: $55-$90	2P: $55-$90

Location: US 101, exit Redwood Dr northbound; exit Redway/Shelter Cove southbound, just w. Located next to the Avenue of the Giants. 4112 Redwood Dr 95560 (PO Box 157). Fax: 707/923-2547. **Facility:** 11 one-bedroom standard units, some with efficiencies or kitchens. 1 story, exterior corridors. *Bath:* combo or shower only. **Parking:** on-site. **Terms:** office hours 8 am-9 pm, 3 day cancellation notice-fee imposed, pets (with prior approval). **Amenities:** *Some:* irons, hair dryers. **Pool(s):** small heated outdoor. **Leisure Activities:** sauna, whirlpool. **Guest Services:** coin laundry. **Cards:** DC, MC, VI. **Special Amenities: free local telephone calls and preferred room (subject to availability with advanced reservations).**

SOME UNITS

DATA PORT / /

REDWOOD CITY pop. 75,402 (See map and index starting on p. 599)

WHERE TO STAY

BEST INN *Book at aaa.com* — **Phone:** (650)369-1731 468

Motel

	1P	2P	XP	
All Year	1P: $69-$89	2P: $69-$89	XP: $5	F12

Location: Just w to SR 82, then just n. 1090 El Camino Real 94063. Fax: 650/299-9428. **Facility:** 39 one-bedroom standard units, some with whirlpools. 2 stories, exterior corridors. **Parking:** on-site. **Amenities:** high-speed Internet, voice mail, irons, hair dryers. **Pool(s):** outdoor. **Business Services:** fax. **Cards:** AX, DC, DS, MC, VI.

SOME UNITS

ASK DATA PORT / VCR /

(See map and index starting on p. 599)

BEST WESTERN EXECUTIVE SUITES *Book at aaa.com* **Phone:** (650)366-5794 **469**

SAVE — Motel

All Year [CP] 1P: $119-$129 2P: $119-$129 XP: $10 F12

Location: US 101, exit SR 84, 1 mi w, 1.5 mi s on SR 82, then just e. 25 5th Ave 94063. Fax: 650/365-1429. **Facility:** 29 one-bedroom standard units, some with whirlpools. 2 stories, exterior corridors. **Parking:** on-site. **Amenities:** voice mail, irons, hair dryers. **Leisure Activities:** sauna, whirlpool, steamroom, exercise room. **Guest Services:** coin laundry. **Cards:** AX, CB, DC, DS, MC, VI. **Special Amenities: free continental breakfast and free local telephone calls.**

SOME UNITS

BEST WESTERN INN *Book at aaa.com* **Phone:** (650)366-3808 **466**

SAVE — Motel

All Year [ECP] 1P: $69-$119 2P: $79-$129 XP: $10 F17

Location: US 101, exit Whipple Ave, 0.5 mi w to SR 82, 0.3 mi n. 316 El Camino Real 94062. Fax: 650/364-9380. **Facility:** 31 one-bedroom standard units. 2 stories, exterior corridors. **Parking:** on-site. **Amenities:** voice mail, irons, hair dryers. **Pool(s):** outdoor. **Cards:** AX, CB, DC, DS, MC, VI. **Special Amenities: free expanded continental breakfast and free local telephone calls.** *(See color ad below)*

SOME UNITS

COMFORT INN *Book at aaa.com* **Phone:** (650)599-9636 **467**

SAVE — Motel

All Year 1P: $49-$89 2P: $59-$99 XP: $5 F18

Location: US 101, exit Whipple Ave, 0.5 mi w to SR 82, then 1 mi s. 1818 El Camino Real 94063. Fax: 650/369-6481. **Facility:** 52 one-bedroom standard units, some with efficiencies and/or whirlpools. 2 stories, interior corridors. **Parking:** on-site. **Terms:** [ECP] meal plan available. **Amenities:** irons, hair dryers. **Pool(s):** heated outdoor. **Leisure Activities:** sauna. **Business Services:** meeting rooms. **Cards:** AX, DS, MC, VI. **Special Amenities: free expanded continental breakfast and free newspaper.**

SOME UNITS

DAYS INN *Book at aaa.com* **Phone:** (650)369-9200 **470**

SAVE — Motel

6/1-10/31 [CP] 1P: $75-$80 2P: $75-$85 XP: $5 F12
2/1-5/31 & 11/1-1/31 [CP] 1P: $70 2P: $70-$80 XP: $5 F12

Location: 1 mi s on SR 82; 0.3 mi s of jct SR 84. 2650 El Camino Real 94061. Fax: 650/363-8167. **Facility:** 68 units. 64 one-bedroom standard units. 4 one-bedroom suites ($110-$140) with kitchens. 2 stories, exterior corridors. *Bath:* combo or shower only. **Parking:** on-site. **Terms:** cancellation fee imposed, weekly rates available. **Amenities:** hair dryers. **Pool(s):** heated outdoor. **Leisure Activities:** sauna, whirlpool, exercise room. **Guest Services:** coin laundry. **Business Services:** meeting rooms. **Cards:** AX, CB, DC, DS, JC, MC, VI. **Special Amenities: free continental breakfast and free newspaper.**

SOME UNITS

HOLIDAY INN EXPRESS *Book at aaa.com* **Phone:** (650)366-2000 **471**

Motel

5/16-10/31 [ECP] 1P: $99-$139 2P: $109-$149 XP: $10 F18
2/1-5/15 & 11/1-1/31 [ECP] 1P: $89-$129 2P: $99-$139 XP: $10 F18

Location: 0.5 mi s of jct SR 84 and US 101, exit US 101 at Woodside Rd (SR 84), 0.5 mi w, then 1.3 mi s. 2834 El Camino Real 94061. Fax: 650/365-4434. **Facility:** 38 one-bedroom standard units. 2 stories, exterior corridors. **Parking:** on-site. **Terms:** cancellation fee imposed. **Amenities:** dual phone lines, voice mail, irons, hair dryers. **Leisure Activities:** sauna, whirlpool, steamroom, exercise room. **Cards:** AX, CB, DC, DS, JC, MC, VI. ***(See color ad p 260)***

SOME UNITS

HOTEL SOFITEL SAN FRANCISCO BAY AT REDWOOD SHORES *Book at aaa.com* **Phone:** (650)598-9000 **465**

Large-scale Hotel

All Year 1P: $99-$349 2P: $99-$349 XP: $20 F11

Location: US 101, exit Marine World Pkwy E, 0.5 mi s. 223 Twin Dolphin Dr 94065. Fax: 650/598-0459. **Facility:** The hotel's handsome lobby includes a restaurant and lounge; some units overlook a lagoon and the bay. 421 units. 400 one-bedroom standard units. 21 one-bedroom suites. 8 stories, interior corridors. **Parking:** valet. **Terms:** cancellation fee imposed, [BP] meal plan available, pets ($25 extra charge). **Amenities:** high-speed Internet, dual phone lines, voice mail, honor bars, irons, hair dryers. *Some:* CD players. **Pool(s):** heated outdoor. **Leisure Activities:** exercise room. **Guest Services:** gift shop, valet laundry. **Business Services:** conference facilities, business center. **Cards:** AX, DC, MC, VI.

FEE SOME UNITS FEE

(See map and index starting on p. 599)

TOWNEPLACE SUITES BY MARRIOTT Book at aaa.com **Phone:** (650)593-4100 464

Motel

All Year [CP] 1P: $69-$179 2P: $69-$179

Location: US 101, exit Redwood Shores Pkwy, 0.3 mi e, then just s. 1000 Twin Dolphin Dr 94065. Fax: 650/593-8600. **Facility:** 95 units. 77 one-bedroom standard units with kitchens. 15 one- and 3 two-bedroom suites with kitchens. 4 stories, interior corridors. **Parking:** on-site. **Terms:** cancellation fee imposed, small pets only ($75 fee). **Amenities:** high-speed Internet, dual phone lines, voice mail, irons, hair dryers. **Leisure Activities:** whirlpool, exercise room. **Guest Services:** valet and coin laundry. **Business Services:** meeting rooms, business center. **Cards:** AX, CB, DC, DS, MC, VI.

SOME UNITS

FEE

WHERE TO DINE

The following restaurants have not been evaluated by AAA but are listed for your information only.

D'ASARO **Phone:** 650/995-9800

fyi

Not evaluated. **Location:** 1041 Middlefield Rd 94061. **Features:** Classic Italian cuisine is served in a casual but stylish rustic trattoria setting.

MILAGROS **Phone:** 650/369-4730

fyi

Not evaluated. **Location:** 1099 Middlefield Rd 94061. **Features:** The menu specializes in entrees from the Oaxaca region of Mexico. Guests can dine indoors amid thousands of imported Mexican art pieces or out on the patio.

REEDLEY pop. 20,756

WHERE TO STAY

EDGEWATER INN **Phone:** (559)637-7777

SAVE

Motel

All Year [CP] 1P: $64-$77 2P: $74-$84 XP: $10 F8

Location: 12 mi e of SR 99 via Manning Ave. 1977 W Manning Ave 93654. Fax: 559/637-2228. **Facility:** 48 units. 46 one-bedroom standard units. 1 one- and 1 two-bedroom suites ($110-$155). 2 stories, exterior corridors. **Parking:** on-site. **Terms:** small pets only ($7 extra charge). **Amenities:** video library. **Pool(s):** outdoor. **Leisure Activities:** whirlpool. **Cards:** AX, CB, DC, DS, MC, VI. **Special Amenities: free continental breakfast and free local telephone calls.**

SOME UNITS

FEE

WHERE TO DINE

THE GOURMET GARDEN **Lunch:** $6-$10 **Dinner:** $12-$18 **Phone:** 559/638-4489

Regional American

Location: Downtown. 1043 G St 93654. **Hours:** 10 am-2 & 5:30-9 pm. Closed major holidays; also Sun, Mon & 12-24-12/30. **Reservations:** suggested. **Features:** The downtown restaurant sustains a comfortable, laid-back atmosphere. Fresh local ingredients mingle in the tasty food. Casual dress. **Parking:** street. **Cards:** AX, CB, DC, DS, MC, VI.

JON'S BEAR CLUB **Lunch:** $9-$17 **Dinner:** $17-$30 **Phone:** 559/638-2396

Regional California

Location: Center. 1695 E Manning Ave 93654. **Hours:** 11:30 am-2 & 5:30-8:30 pm, Sat 5:30 pm-9:30 pm. Closed: Sun. **Reservations:** suggested. **Features:** A good selection of steak, seafood and chicken dishes and a friendly, relaxed setting add up to a nice overall dining experience. Casual dress; cocktails. **Parking:** on-site. **Cards:** DC, MC, VI.

RICHMOND pop. 99,216

WHERE TO STAY

COURTYARD BY MARRIOTT Book at aaa.com **Phone:** (510)262-0700

Small-scale Hotel

All Year 1P: $79-$155 2P: $84-$155 XP: $10 F12

Location: I-80, exit Hilltop Dr N. 3150 Garrity Way 94806. Fax: 510/262-0927. **Facility:** 149 units. 141 one-bedroom standard units. 8 one-bedroom suites ($165-$195). 5 stories, interior corridors. **Parking:** on-site. **Terms:** [BP] & [CP] meal plans available. **Amenities:** video games, voice mail, irons, hair dryers. **Pool(s):** outdoor. **Leisure Activities:** whirlpool, exercise room. **Business Services:** meeting rooms. **Cards:** AX, DC, DS, MC, VI.

SOME UNITS

QUALITY INN & SUITES Book at aaa.com **Phone:** (510)237-3000

SAVE

Motel

All Year [CP] 1P: $75-$159 2P: $75-$159 XP: $10 F12

Location: I-580, exit Canal Blvd, just s. 915 Cutting Blvd 94804. Fax: 510/237-1175. **Facility:** 106 one-bedroom standard units, some with whirlpools. 2 stories (no elevator), exterior corridors. *Bath:* combo or shower only. **Parking:** on-site. **Terms:** cancellation fee imposed. **Amenities:** voice mail, irons, hair dryers. **Pool(s):** outdoor. **Leisure Activities:** exercise room. **Guest Services:** coin laundry. **Business Services:** conference facilities, business center. **Cards:** AX, CB, DC, DS, JC, MC, VI. **Special Amenities: free continental breakfast and free newspaper.**

SOME UNITS

WHERE TO DINE

HOTEL MAC RESTAURANT Lunch: $5-$22 Dinner: $14-$25 Phone: 510/233-0576

Continental

Location: I-580, exit Pt Richmond/Richmond Pkwy, 1 mi e. 50 Washington Ave 94801. **Hours:** 11:30 am-2:30 & 5:30-10 pm, Sat from 5:30 pm, Sun 4:30 pm-9 pm. Closed: 1/1, 7/4, 12/25. **Reservations:** suggested. **Features:** In a nicely restored building downtown, the sophisticated restaurant presents a diverse menu. Casual dress; cocktails. **Parking:** on-site. **Cards:** DS, MC, VI.

SALUTE RISTORANTE AT MARINA BAY Lunch: $10-$17 Dinner: $12-$17 Phone: 510/215-0803

Italian

Location: I-580, exit Marina Bay Pkwy, 0.3 mi s to Regatta, just w to Melville, then just s. 1900 Esplanade Dr 94804. **Hours:** 11 am-10 pm, Fri & Sat-11 pm. Closed: 1/1, 12/25. **Reservations:** suggested. **Features:** Seats in the charming house's attractive dining rooms look out over the marina. The menu blends traditional and modern dishes, each creatively prepared with fresh ingredients. Casual dress; cocktails. **Parking:** on-site. **Cards:** AX, DC, MC, VI.

RIDGECREST pop. 24,927

WHERE TO STAY

BEST WESTERN CHINA LAKE INN Book at aaa.com Phone: (760)371-2300

Motel

All Year 1P: $72 2P: $77 XP: $5 F13

Location: On US 395 business route. 400 S China Lake Blvd 93555. Fax: 760/375-8785. **Facility:** 46 one-bedroom standard units. 2 stories, exterior corridors. **Parking:** on-site. **Terms:** cancellation fee imposed, [ECP] meal plan available, pets ($10 extra charge). **Amenities:** irons, hair dryers. **Pool(s):** outdoor. **Leisure Activities:** whirlpool. **Guest Services:** coin laundry. **Business Services:** fax (fee). **Cards:** AX, CB, DC, DS, JC, MC, VI. **Special Amenities: free continental breakfast and free local telephone calls.**

SOME UNITS

FEE

CARRIAGE INN Book at aaa.com Phone: (760)446-7910

Motel

All Year [BP] 1P: $110-$170 2P: $120-$180 XP: $10 F16

Location: On SR 178 and US 395 business route. 901 N China Lake Blvd 93555. Fax: 760/446-6408. **Facility:** 162 units. 154 one-bedroom standard units. 8 one-bedroom suites ($120-$190). 2 stories, exterior corridors. **Parking:** on-site. **Terms:** cancellation fee imposed, pets ($25 extra charge, in designated units). **Amenities:** video games, high-speed Internet, voice mail, irons, hair dryers. *Some:* CD players. **Dining:** 2 restaurants, 6 am-10 pm, cocktails. **Pool(s):** heated outdoor. **Leisure Activities:** sauna, whirlpool, exercise room. **Guest Services:** valet laundry. **Business Services:** conference facilities, fax (fee). **Cards:** AX, DC, DS, MC, VI.

SOME UNITS

FEE

ECONO LODGE Book at aaa.com Phone: (760)446-2551

Motel

All Year [CP] 1P: $55-$65 2P: $55-$70

Location: On SR 178 and US 395 business route, just w of China Lake Blvd. 201 Inyokern Rd 93555. Fax: 760/446-5740. **Facility:** 85 one-bedroom standard units. 2 stories, exterior corridors. **Parking:** on-site. **Terms:** office hours 6 am-11 pm, pets (small dogs only). **Amenities:** voice mail, hair dryers. *Some:* irons. **Pool(s):** outdoor. **Business Services:** fax (fee). **Cards:** AX, CB, DC, DS, MC, VI. **Special Amenities: free continental breakfast and free local telephone calls.**

SOME UNITS

HERITAGE INN & SUITES Phone: (760)446-7951

Small-scale Hotel

All Year [BP] 1P: $75-$88 2P: $75-$88 XP: $7 F16

Location: On US 395 business route, just w. 1050 N Norma 93555. Fax: 760/446-2884. **Facility:** 169 units. 123 one-bedroom standard units, some with efficiencies and/or whirlpools. 46 one-bedroom suites with kitchens. 2 stories, interior corridors. **Parking:** on-site. **Terms:** [AP] meal plan available, pets ($100 deposit). **Amenities:** voice mail, irons, hair dryers. **Dining:** 5:30 am-11 & 5-10 pm, Sat & Sun from 6:30 am, cocktails. **Pool(s):** 2 heated outdoor. **Leisure Activities:** whirlpools, limited exercise equipment. **Guest Services:** coin laundry. **Business Services:** conference facilities, fax (fee). **Cards:** AX, CB, DC, DS, JC, MC, VI. **Special Amenities: free full breakfast and free local telephone calls.**

SOME UNITS

FEE

QUALITY INN Book at aaa.com Phone: (760)375-9731

Motel

All Year 1P: $79-$89 2P: $79-$89 XP: $10 F12

Location: On US 395 business route. 507 S China Lake Blvd 93555. Fax: 760/375-4684. **Facility:** 57 units. 53 one-bedroom standard units. 4 one-bedroom suites. 2 stories, exterior corridors. **Parking:** on-site. **Terms:** pets (in smoking units). **Amenities:** high-speed Internet, voice mail, irons, hair dryers. **Pool(s):** outdoor. **Business Services:** fax (fee). **Cards:** AX, CB, DC, DS, MC, VI. **Special Amenities: free local telephone calls and free newspaper.**

SOME UNITS

VAGABOND INN Book at aaa.com Phone: (760)375-2220

Motel

All Year 1P: $65-$70 2P: $70-$75 XP: $5 F18

Location: On US 395 business route. 426 China Lake Blvd 93555. Fax: 760/384-1909. **Facility:** 33 one-bedroom standard units. 2 stories, exterior corridors. **Parking:** on-site. **Terms:** [CP] meal plan available, pets ($10 extra charge). **Amenities:** *Some:* irons, hair dryers. **Business Services:** fax (fee). **Cards:** AX, CB, DC, DS, JC, MC, VI. **Special Amenities: free continental breakfast and free local telephone calls.**

SOME UNITS

FEE

WHERE TO DINE

TEXAS CATTLE CO — **Lunch:** $8-$10 **Dinner:** $8-$20 **Phone:** 760/446-6602

Steak House

Location: On US 395 business route, just s of SR 178. 1429 N China Lake Blvd 93555. **Hours:** 11 am-9 pm, Fri-Sun from 8 am. Closed major holidays. **Features:** True to its name, the restaurant serves up Texas steakhouse food and down-home service from staffers who treat everyone like a local. Diners won't find any petite servings; even the many varied burgers are a minimum half-pound. A special treat is the rustler combo: baby back ribs and charbroiled chicken. The decor is country all the way, including wood-plank floors and Mexican tile tabletops. Casual dress; beer & wine only. **Parking:** on-site. **Cards:** AX, CB, DC, DS, MC, VI.

RIO DELL pop. 3,174

WHERE TO STAY

HUMBOLDT GABLES MOTEL — **Phone:** (707)764-5609

Motel

All Year 1P: $44-$50 2P: $50-$58 XP: $8 F12

Location: US 101, exit Rio Dell/Davis St W. 40 W Davis St 95562. **Facility:** 18 one-bedroom standard units. 1 story, exterior corridors. *Bath:* combo or shower only. **Parking:** on-site. **Terms:** pets (with prior approval). **Amenities:** hair dryers. *Some:* irons. **Special Amenities: free local telephone calls.**

SOME UNITS

RIO VISTA pop. 4,571

WHERE TO DINE

THE POINT WATERFRONT RESTAURANT — **Lunch:** $8-$13 **Dinner:** $12-$21 **Phone:** 707/374-5400

Seafood

Location: 0.5 mi s of SR 12; adjacent to the Sacramento River. 120 Marina Dr 94571. **Hours:** 11 am-3 & 4:30-9 pm, Fri & Sat-10 pm. Closed: Mon & 12/24-12/30. **Reservations:** accepted. **Features:** On the river, the restaurant offers docking facilities for guests who arrive by boat. The glassed-in garden room on the deck is ideal for brunch or lunch. Menu choices are varied. Casual dress; cocktails. **Parking:** on-site. **Cards:** AX, DS, MC, VI.

ROCKLIN pop. 36,330 (See map and index starting on p. 565)

WHERE TO STAY

BEST WESTERN ROCKLIN PARK HOTEL *Book at aaa.com* **Phone:** (916)630-9400 **114**

AAA SAVE

Small-scale Hotel

All Year 1P: $139-$169 2P: $149-$179 XP: $10 F17

Location: I-80, exit Rocklin Rd, just e, s on Aguilar Rd, then e. 5450 China Garden Rd 95677. Fax: 916/630-9448. **Facility:** A beamed ceiling adds character to the hotel's common area; the grounds are beautified by a terraced rose garden. 67 units. 66 one-bedroom standard units, some with whirlpools. 1 one-bedroom suite. 2 stories, interior corridors. **Parking:** on-site. **Terms:** weekly rates available, [AP], [BP] & [CP] meal plans available, 8% service charge. **Amenities:** dual phone lines, voice mail, safes, irons, hair dryers. **Dining:** 11:30 am-2:30 & 5:30-9 pm, Fri & Sat-10 pm, cocktails. **Pool(s):** outdoor. **Leisure Activities:** sauna, whirlpool, bicycles, hiking trails, exercise room. **Guest Services:** gift shop, valet laundry. **Business Services:** meeting rooms, business center. **Cards:** AX, CB, DC, DS, JC, MC, VI. **Special Amenities: free local telephone calls and free newspaper.**

SOME UNITS

COMFORT SUITES *Book at aaa.com* **Phone:** (916)315-1300 **109**

Motel

All Year [ECP] 1P: $89-$169 2P: $99-$179 F

Location: I-80, exit Stanford Ranch Rd. 6830 Five Star Blvd 95677. Fax: 916/315-3366. **Facility:** 72 units. 70 one-bedroom standard units, some with whirlpools. 2 one-bedroom suites ($129-$189) with whirlpools. 3 stories, interior corridors. **Parking:** on-site. **Terms:** cancellation fee imposed. **Amenities:** dual phone lines, voice mail, irons, hair dryers. **Pool(s):** outdoor. **Leisure Activities:** whirlpool. **Guest Services:** coin laundry. **Business Services:** meeting rooms, fax. **Cards:** AX, CB, DC, DS, JC, MC, VI.

SOME UNITS

DAYS INN-SACRAMENTO/ROCKLIN *Book at aaa.com* **Phone:** (916)632-0101 **110**

Motel

All Year 1P: $59-$79 2P: $69-$89 XP: $10 F12

Location: I-80, exit Rocklin Rd, 0.3 mi to Granite Dr, then 0.5 mi e. 4515 Granite Dr 95677. Fax: 916/632-0335. **Facility:** 65 one-bedroom standard units, some with kitchens and/or whirlpools. 2 stories, exterior corridors. **Parking:** on-site. **Terms:** cancellation fee imposed. **Amenities:** hair dryers. *Some:* irons. **Pool(s):** outdoor. **Leisure Activities:** sauna, whirlpool, exercise room. **Guest Services:** coin laundry. **Business Services:** meeting rooms. **Cards:** AX, DC, DS, MC, VI.

SOME UNITS

(See map and index starting on p. 565)

HOWARD JOHNSON HOTEL Book at aaa.com Phone: (916)624-4500 112

AAA SAVE Motel

5/1-9/30 [BP] 1P: $89-$114 2P: $89-$114 XP: $7 F12
2/1-4/30 & 10/1-1/31 [BP] 1P: $84-$109 2P: $84-$109 XP: $7 F12

Location: I-80 E, exit Rocklin Rd. 4420 Rocklin Rd 95677. Fax: 916/624-5982. **Facility:** 124 units. 112 one-bedroom standard units. 12 one-bedroom suites ($139-$189), some with whirlpools. 3 stories, interior corridors. *Bath:* combo or shower only. **Parking:** on-site. **Terms:** pets ($20 extra charge). **Amenities:** dual phone lines, voice mail, safes, irons, hair dryers. **Pool(s):** heated outdoor. **Leisure Activities:** whirlpool, exercise room. **Guest Services:** complimentary evening beverages: Mon-Fri, coin laundry. **Business Services:** meeting rooms, business center. **Cards:** AX, CB, DC, DS, JC, MC, VI. **Special Amenities: free full breakfast and free newspaper.**
(See color ad p 562)

FEE SOME UNITS

RAMADA LIMITED Book at aaa.com Phone: (916)632-3366 113

Motel

All Year [ECP] 1P: $53-$93 2P: $53-$93 XP: $5 F18

Location: I-80, exit Rocklin Rd. 4480 Rocklin Rd 95677. Fax: 916/632-3895. **Facility:** 102 one-bedroom standard units. 3 stories, interior corridors. **Parking:** on-site. **Terms:** weekly rates available, small pets only ($25 fee). **Amenities:** irons, hair dryers. **Pool(s):** outdoor. **Leisure Activities:** whirlpool. **Business Services:** meeting rooms. **Cards:** AX, CB, DC, DS, JC, MC, VI.

ASK FEE SOME UNITS

ROHNERT PARK —*See Wine Country p. 798.*

ROSEVILLE pop. 79,921 (See map and index starting on p. 565)

WHERE TO STAY

BEST WESTERN ROSEVILLE INN Book at aaa.com Phone: 916/782-4434 134

AAA SAVE Motel

All Year 1P: $75-$80 2P: $80-$90 XP: $5 F12

Location: I-80, exit Douglas Blvd, just w, then just n. 220 Harding Blvd 95678. Fax: 916/782-8335. **Facility:** 126 one-bedroom standard units, some with kitchens and/or whirlpools. 2 stories, exterior corridors. *Bath:* combo or shower only. **Parking:** on-site. **Terms:** 5 day cancellation notice, [ECP] meal plan available, pets ($10 extra charge). **Amenities:** irons, hair dryers. **Pool(s):** outdoor. **Business Services:** meeting rooms. **Cards:** AX, CB, DC, DS, MC, VI. **Special Amenities: free expanded continental breakfast and free local telephone calls.** *(See color ad p 570)*

FEE SOME UNITS

COURTYARD BY MARRIOTT Book at aaa.com Phone: (916)772-5555 129

Small-scale Hotel

All Year 1P: $99 2P: $99

Location: I-80, exit Eureka-Taylor Rd, just s. 1920 Taylor Rd 95661. Fax: 916/772-5555. **Facility:** 90 units. 87 one-bedroom standard units. 3 one-bedroom suites. 3 stories, interior corridors. *Bath:* combo or shower only. **Parking:** on-site. **Terms:** [BP] meal plan available. **Amenities:** dual phone lines, voice mail, irons, hair dryers. **Pool(s):** heated indoor. **Leisure Activities:** whirlpool, exercise room. **Guest Services:** valet and coin laundry. **Business Services:** conference facilities. **Cards:** AX, DC, DS, MC, VI.

ASK SOME UNITS

FAIRFIELD INN BY MARRIOTT Book at aaa.com Phone: 916/772-3500 133

Motel

All Year [ECP] 1P: $89

Location: I-80, exit Eureka-Taylor Rd, just s. 1910 Taylor Rd 95661. Fax: 916/772-3500. **Facility:** 82 one-bedroom standard units. 3 stories, interior corridors. **Parking:** on-site. **Amenities:** voice mail, irons, hair dryers. **Pool(s):** indoor. **Leisure Activities:** whirlpool. **Business Services:** meeting rooms. **Cards:** AX, DC, DS, MC, VI.

ASK SOME UNITS

(See map and index starting on p. 565)

HERITAGE INN Book at aaa.com **Phone:** (916)782-4466 127

Motel

All Year 1P: $65-$95 2P: $65-$95 XP: $10 F18

Location: I-80, exit Douglas Blvd, just w, then just n. 204 Harding Blvd 95678. Fax: 916/782-4461. **Facility:** 95 one-bedroom standard units, some with whirlpools. 2 stories, exterior corridors. **Parking:** on-site. **Terms:** weekly rates available. **Amenities:** irons, hair dryers. **Pool(s):** outdoor. **Leisure Activities:** whirlpool. **Business Services:** meeting rooms. **Cards:** AX, CB, DC, DS, MC, VI. **Special Amenities: free continental breakfast and free local telephone calls.** *(See color ad p 570)*

SOME UNITS

HILTON GARDEN INN Book at aaa.com **Phone:** (916)773-7171 125

Small-scale Hotel

All Year 1P: $99-$154 2P: $99-$154

Location: I-80, exit Eureka-Taylor Rd, 0.3 mi ne. 1951 Taylor Rd 95661. Fax: 916/773-7138. **Facility:** 131 one-bedroom standard units, some with whirlpools. 3 stories, interior corridors. **Parking:** on-site. **Amenities:** video games, high-speed Internet, dual phone lines, voice mail, irons, hair dryers. **Pool(s):** heated outdoor. **Leisure Activities:** whirlpool, exercise room. **Guest Services:** coin laundry. **Business Services:** meeting rooms, business center. **Cards:** AX, CB, DC, DS, MC, VI. **Special Amenities: free local telephone calls and free newspaper.**

SOME UNITS

LARKSPUR LANDING Book at aaa.com **Phone:** (916)773-1717 128

Small-scale Hotel

All Year 1P: $129-$159

Location: I-80, exit Eureka-Taylor Rd, 0.3 mi ne. 1931 Taylor Rd 95661. Fax: 916/773-1765. **Facility:** 90 units. 62 one-bedroom standard units with kitchens. 28 one-bedroom suites with kitchens. 3 stories, interior corridors. *Bath:* combo or shower only. **Parking:** on-site. **Terms:** cancellation fee imposed. **Amenities:** video games, high-speed Internet, dual phone lines, voice mail, irons, hair dryers. **Leisure Activities:** whirlpool, exercise room. **Guest Services:** complimentary laundry. **Business Services:** meeting rooms, business center. **Cards:** AX, DC, DS, JC, MC, VI. **Special Amenities: free local telephone calls and free newspaper.** *(See color ad p 563)*

SOME UNITS

OXFORD SUITES Book at aaa.com **Phone:** (916)784-2222 135

Motel

All Year [BP] 1P: $89-$149 2P: $89-$149 XP: $10 F10

Location: I-80, exit Douglas Blvd, just e, then 0.3 mi n. 130 N Sunrise Ave 95661. Fax: 916/782-9034. **Facility:** 184 units. 180 one-bedroom standard units. 4 one-bedroom suites with whirlpools. 3 stories, interior/exterior corridors. **Parking:** on-site. **Terms:** small pets only ($15 fee). **Amenities:** voice mail, irons, hair dryers. **Pool(s):** heated outdoor. **Leisure Activities:** whirlpool, exercise room. **Guest Services:** gift shop, complimentary evening beverages, coin laundry. **Business Services:** meeting rooms. **Cards:** AX, DC, DS, MC, VI.

SOME UNITS

FEE

RESIDENCE INN Book at aaa.com **Phone:** (916)772-5500 126

Small-scale Hotel

All Year 1P: $134-$179 2P: $134-$179

Location: I-80, exit Eureka-Taylor Rd, just s. 1930 Taylor Rd 95661. Fax: 916/772-9441. **Facility:** 90 units. 42 one-bedroom standard units with kitchens. 33 one- and 15 two-bedroom suites with kitchens. 3 stories, interior corridors. **Parking:** on-site. **Terms:** [BP] meal plan available, small pets only ($100 fee, $10 extra charge). **Amenities:** dual phone lines, voice mail, irons, hair dryers. **Pool(s):** heated indoor. **Leisure Activities:** whirlpool, exercise room, sports court. **Guest Services:** complimentary evening beverages, valet and coin laundry. **Business Services:** meeting rooms. **Cards:** AX, DC, DS, MC, VI.

SOME UNITS

FEE

RUTHERFORD —*See Wine Country p. 798.*

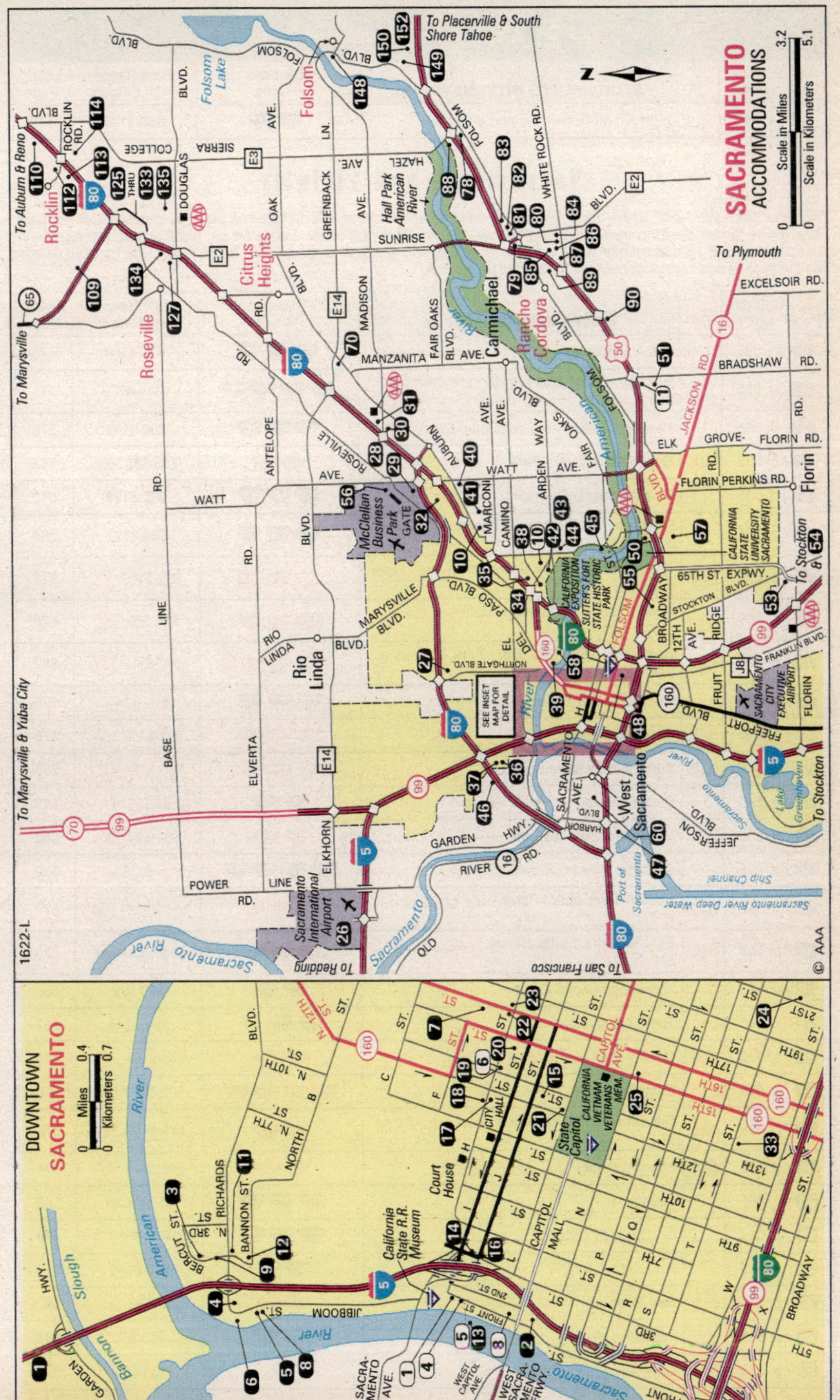
SACRAMENTO
ACCOMMODATIONS
Scale in Miles
Scale in Kilometers
0
3.2
5.1
1622-L
SEE INSET MAP FOR DETAIL
To Auburn & Reno
To Marysville
To Marysville & Yuba City
To Redding
To San Francisco
To Stockton
To Placerville & South Shore Tahoe
To Plymouth
Rocklin
Roseville
Citrus Heights
Folsom
Folsom Lake
Carmichael
Rancho Cordova
Rio Linda
West Sacramento
Florin
Hall Park American River
McClellan Business Park
Sacramento International Airport
Sacramento City Executive Airport
California State University Sacramento
California Exposition
Sutter's Fort State Historic Park
Port of Sacramento
Sacramento River Deep Water Ship Channel
Sacramento River
American River
Lake Greenhaven
DOWNTOWN
SACRAMENTO
Miles
Kilometers
0
0.4
0.7
California State R.R. Museum
Court House
City Hall
State Capitol
California Vietnam Veterans Mem.
Bannon Slough
American River
Sacramento River
© AAA

Airport Accommodations

Spotter/Map Page Number	OA	SACRAMENTO INTERNATIONAL	Diamond Rating	Rate Range High Season	Listing Page
26 / p. 565		Host Airport Hotel, at airport entrance	◆◆	$80-$140	579

Sacramento and Vicinity

This index helps you "spot" where approved accommodations and restaurants are located on the corresponding detailed maps. Lodging rate ranges are for comparison only and show the property's high season; rates are per night, unless only weekly (W) rates are available. Restaurant rate range is for dinner, unless only lunch (L) is served. Turn to the listing page for more detailed rate information and consult display ads for special promotions.

Spotter/Map Page Number	OA	SACRAMENTO - Lodgings	Diamond Rating	Rate Range High Season	Listing Page
1 / p. 565		Hilton Garden Inn	◆◆◆	$79-$169	576
2 / p. 565		Embassy Suites Sacramento - see color ad p 575	◆◆◆◆	$119-$279	575
3 / p. 565		Hawthorn Suites - see color ad p 576	◆◆◆	$89-$149	575
4 / p. 565	AAA	**Super 8-Discovery Park**	◆◆	$55-$90 SAVE	583
5 / p. 565		Comfort Suites- Downtown	◆◆◆	$89-$199	572
6 / p. 565		La Quinta Inn-Sacramento Downtown - see color ad p 580	◆◆◆	$86-$121	580
7 / p. 565	AAA	**Holiday Inn Express Sacramento - see color ad p 573**	◆◆◆	$89-$119 SAVE	577
8 / p. 565	AAA	**Best Western Sandman Motel - see color ad p 571**	◆◆◆	$70-$89 SAVE	570
9 / p. 565	AAA	**Ramada Limited-Discovery Park - see ad p 581**	◆◆◆	$79-$110 SAVE	582
10 / p. 565		Hampton Inn & Suites	◆◆◆	$99-$144	575
11 / p. 565	AAA	**Governors Inn - see color ad p 576**	◆◆◆	$82-$102 SAVE	575
12 / p. 565	AAA	**Super 8 Executive Suites**	◆◆◆	$55-$125 SAVE	583
13 / p. 565		Delta King Hotel	◆◆	$139-$184	573
14 / p. 565	AAA	**Vagabond Executive Inn**	◆◆	$84-$90 SAVE	583
15 / p. 565		Sheraton Grand Sacramento Hotel	◆◆◆◆	$335	582
16 / p. 565	AAA	**Holiday Inn Capitol Plaza - see color ad p 577**	◆◆◆	$154-$184 SAVE	577
17 / p. 565	AAA	**Best Western Sutter House - see color ad p 571, p 521**	◆◆◆	$89-$190 SAVE	570
18 / p. 565		Travelodge Capitol Center	◆◆	$59-$99	583
19 / p. 565		The Sterling Hotel	◆◆◆	$99-$249	582
20 / p. 565	AAA	**Quality Inn - see ad p 581**	◆◆	$84-$104 SAVE	581
21 / p. 565	AAA	**Hyatt Regency - see color ad p 579**	◆◆◆◆	$99-$269 SAVE	579
22 / p. 565	AAA	**Clarion Hotel Mansion Inn - see color ad p 573**	◆◆	$79-$109 SAVE	572
23 / p. 565	AAA	**Econo Lodge - see color ad p 574**	◆◆	$65-$119 SAVE	574
24 / p. 565		Vizcaya	◆◆◆	$159-$249	583
25 / p. 565		Inn Off Capitol Park	◆◆◆	$79-$169	579
26 / p. 565		Host Airport Hotel	◆◆	$80-$140	579
27 / p. 565	AAA	**Red Roof Inn**	◆◆	$50-$90 SAVE	582
28 / p. 565		Vagabond Inn	◆◆	$43-$64	583
29 / p. 565		Days Inn	◆	$59-$89	573

Spotter/Map Page Number	OA	**SACRAMENTO** - Lodgings (continued)	Diamond Rating	Rate Range High Season	Listing Page
30 / p. 565		La Quinta Inn-North - see color ad p 580	◆◆◆	$80-$101	579
31 / p. 565	AAA	**Holiday Inn Sacramento Northeast** - see color ad p 578	◆◆◆	$139 SAVE	578
32 / p. 565		Travelodge	◆	$50-$96	583
33 / p. 565		Capitol Park Bed & Breakfast Inn	◆◆◆	$129-$189	572
34 / p. 565	AAA	**Hilton Sacramento Arden West** - see color ad p 577	◆◆◆	$99-$249 SAVE	577
35 / p. 565	AAA	**Red Lion Hotel Sacramento** - see ad p 582	◆◆◆	$129-$159 SAVE	582
36 / p. 565		Residence Inn by Marriott	◆◆◆	$154-$184	582
37 / p. 565		Homestead Studio Suites Hotel-Sacramento	◆◆	$72-$97	579
38 / p. 565		Doubletree Hotel - see color ad p 574	◆◆◆	$89-$225	574
39 / p. 565	AAA	**Radisson Hotel** - see color ad p 629	◆◆◆	$105-$185 SAVE	581
40 / p. 565	AAA	**Econo Lodge**	◆◆	$59-$99 SAVE	574
41 / p. 565		Quality Inn Hotel & Conference Center - see color ad p 572	◆◆	$69	581
42 / p. 565	AAA	**Vagabond Executive Inn**	◆◆◆	$69-$79 SAVE	583
43 / p. 565		Marriott Residence Inn	◆◆◆	$159	580
44 / p. 565	AAA	**Best Western Expo Inn** - see ad p 569	◆◆	$85-$150 SAVE	569
45 / p. 565	AAA	**Candlewood Suites** - see color ad p 571	◆◆◆	$124-$149 SAVE	571
46 / p. 565	AAA	**Microtel Inn & Suites** - see color ad p 580	◆◆	$60-$75 SAVE	580
47 / p. 565	AAA	**Best Western Harbor Inn & Suites** - see ad p 570	◆◆◆	$69-$159 SAVE	569
48 / p. 565	AAA	**Amber House Bed & Breakfast Inn**	◆◆◆◆	$149-$289 SAVE	569
50 / p. 565	AAA	**Good Nite Inn**	◆◆	$53 SAVE	575
51 / p. 565		Relax Inn & Suites	fyi	$44-$79	584
53 / p. 565	AAA	**Gold Star National 9 Inn**	◆	$59-$70 SAVE	575
54 / p. 565	AAA	**Best Western John Jay Inn**	◆◆◆	$78-$118 SAVE	570
55 / p. 565	AAA	**Courtyard by Marriott**	◆◆◆	$79-$139 SAVE	572
56 / p. 565		Lions Gate Hotel	◆◆◆	$99-$119	580
57 / p. 565	AAA	**Comfort Inn & Suites**	◆◆◆	$84-$129 SAVE	572
58 / p. 565		Canterbury Inn	◆◆	$49-$89	572
60 / p. 565		Holiday Inn Express - see color ad p 578	◆◆◆	$99-$199	577
		SACRAMENTO - Restaurants			
1 / p. 565		California Fat's Asia Grill & Dim Sum Bar	◆◆	$10-$20	584
4 / p. 565		Fat City Bar & Cafe'	◆◆	$9-$20	584
5 / p. 565		Pilothouse Restaurant	◆◆◆	$13-$25	584
6 / p. 565		Chanterelle	◆◆◆	$16-$24	584
8 / p. 565		The Firehouse	◆◆◆	$17-$49	584
10 / p. 565		California Cafe Bar & Grill	◆◆	$12-$24	584
11 / p. 565		Bradshaws Restaurant	◆◆	$7-$15	584
		CITRUS HEIGHTS - Lodgings			
70 / p. 565	AAA	**Olive Grove Inn & Suites**	◆◆◆	$99-$150 SAVE	305

Spotter/Map Page Number	OA	RANCHO CORDOVA - Lodgings	Diamond Rating	Rate Range High Season	Listing Page
78 / p. 565	AAA	**Inns of America**	◆◆	$69-$77 SAVE	550
79 / p. 565	AAA	**Holiday Inn** - see color ad p 578	◆◆◆	$119-$149 SAVE	550
80 / p. 565		Residence Inn	◆◆◆	$130-$170	551
81 / p. 565	AAA	**Sacramento Marriott Rancho Cordova**	◆◆◆◆	$179-$209 SAVE	551
82 / p. 565		Hallmark Suites	◆◆◆	$127-$147	550
83 / p. 565	AAA	**Best Western Heritage Inn** - see color ad p 570	◆◆◆	$99 SAVE	549
84 / p. 565		Fairfield Inn by Marriott	◆◆	$59-$109	549
85 / p. 565		Hampton Inn	◆◆◆	$64-$109	550
86 / p. 565	AAA	**AmeriSuites (Sacramento/Rancho Cordova)** - see color ad p 569	◆◆◆	$69-$129 SAVE	549
87 / p. 565		Courtyard by Marriott	◆◆◆	$69-$124	549
88 / p. 565		Hawthorn Suites	◆◆◆	$109	550
89 / p. 565		Best Choice Inn	◆	$49-$69	549
90 / p. 565	AAA	**Quality Inn & Suites** - see color ad p 550	◆◆	$69-$139 SAVE	551
		ROCKLIN - Lodgings			
109 / p. 565		Comfort Suites	◆◆◆	$89-$179	562
110 / p. 565		Days Inn-Sacramento/Rocklin	◆◆	$59-$89	562
112 / p. 565	AAA	**Howard Johnson Hotel** - see color ad p 562	◆◆◆	$89-$114 SAVE	563
113 / p. 565		Ramada Limited	◆◆	$53-$93	563
114 / p. 565	AAA	**Best Western Rocklin Park Hotel**	◆◆◆◆	$139-$179 SAVE	562
		ROSEVILLE - Lodgings			
125 / p. 565	AAA	**Hilton Garden Inn**	◆◆◆	$99-$154 SAVE	564
126 / p. 565		Residence Inn	◆◆◆	$134-$179	564
127 / p. 565	AAA	**Heritage Inn** - see color ad p 570	◆◆	$65-$95 SAVE	564
128 / p. 565	AAA	**Larkspur Landing** - see color ad p 563	◆◆◆	$129-$159 SAVE	564
129 / p. 565		Courtyard By Marriott	◆◆◆	$99	563
133 / p. 565		Fairfield Inn By Marriott	◆◆	$89	563
134 / p. 565	AAA	**Best Western Roseville Inn** - see color ad p 570	◆◆	$75-$90 SAVE	563
135 / p. 565		Oxford Suites	◆◆◆	$89-$149	564
		FOLSOM - Lodgings			
148 / p. 565		Lake Natoma Inn - see color ad p 331	◆◆◆	$89-$129	331
149 / p. 565	AAA	**Larkspur Landing Home Suite Hotel** - see color ad p 332	◆◆◆	$79-$189 SAVE	332
150 / p. 565	AAA	**Hilton Garden Inn**	◆◆◆	$62-$152 SAVE	331
152 / p. 565		Residence Inn by Marriott	◆◆◆	$79-$169	332

SACRAMENTO pop. 407,018 (See map and index starting on p. 565)

WHERE TO STAY

AMBER HOUSE BED & BREAKFAST INN — **Phone:** (916)444-8085 — 48

AAA SAVE — Historic Bed & Breakfast

All Year [BP] 1P: $149-$269 2P: $169-$289

Location: Business Rt 80, exit SR 160 (16th St), 0.8 mi n to N St, then 0.5 mi e. 1315 22nd St 95816. Fax: 916/552-6529. **Facility:** Four historic Craftsman-style mansions, all restored, make up this residential-area property. 18 one-bedroom standard units, some with whirlpools. 2 stories, interior corridors. **Parking:** on-site. **Terms:** check-in 4 pm, 7 day cancellation notice. **Amenities:** CD players, high-speed Internet, voice mail, irons, hair dryers. **Cards:** AX, CB, DC, DS, MC, VI. **Special Amenities: free local telephone calls and free newspaper.**

BEST WESTERN EXPO INN *Book at aaa.com* — **Phone:** (916)922-9833 — 44

AAA SAVE — Motel

All Year [ECP] 1P: $85-$150 2P: $85-$150

Location: Jct SR 16 and US 50, exit Howe Ave, 2.5 mi n. 1413 Howe Ave 95825. Fax: 916/922-3384. **Facility:** 125 units. 75 one-bedroom standard units. 50 one-bedroom suites with efficiencies. 2 stories, interior corridors. **Parking:** on-site. **Terms:** pets ($100 deposit). **Amenities:** dual phone lines, irons, hair dryers. **Pool(s):** outdoor. **Leisure Activities:** whirlpool, exercise room. **Guest Services:** coin laundry, area transportation. **Business Services:** meeting rooms. **Cards:** AX, CB, DC, DS, JC, MC, VI. **Special Amenities: free local telephone calls and early check-in/late check-out.** *(See ad below)*

SOME UNITS

FEE

BEST WESTERN HARBOR INN & SUITES *Book at aaa.com* — **Phone:** (916)371-2100 — 47

AAA SAVE — Motel

All Year 1P: $69-$149 2P: $79-$159 XP: $10 F17

Location: 4 mi w; exit Business Rt 80 via Harbor Blvd. 1250 Halyard Dr 95691. Fax: 916/373-1507. **Facility:** 138 units. 123 one-bedroom standard units. 15 one-bedroom suites with whirlpools. 2-4 stories, interior/exterior corridors. **Parking:** on-site. **Terms:** package plans, pets ($100 deposit, $10 extra charge). **Amenities:** high-speed Internet (fee), voice mail, safes, irons, hair dryers. **Pool(s):** outdoor. **Leisure Activities:** whirlpools, exercise room. **Guest Services:** valet and coin laundry. **Business Services:** meeting rooms. **Cards:** AX, CB, DC, DS, JC, MC, VI. **Special Amenities: free continental breakfast and early check-in/late check-out.** *(See ad p 570)*

SOME UNITS

FEE

(See map and index starting on p. 565)

BEST WESTERN JOHN JAY INN *Book at aaa.com* **Phone:** (916)689-4425 54

SAVE

Motel

All Year [ECP] 1P: $78-$110 2P: $88-$118 XP: $8 F12

Location: SR 99, exit Stockton Blvd northbound, 0.8 mi n; exit Mack Rd southbound, 0.8 mi ne. 15 Massie Ct 95823. Fax: 916/689-8045. **Facility:** 58 units. 55 one-bedroom standard units. 3 one-bedroom suites ($120-$145). 3 stories, interior corridors. **Parking:** on-site. **Terms:** 3 day cancellation notice. **Amenities:** irons, hair dryers. **Pool(s):** outdoor. **Leisure Activities:** sauna, whirlpool, exercise room. **Guest Services:** coin laundry. **Cards:** AX, CB, DC, DS, JC, MC, VI. **Special Amenities: free expanded continental breakfast and free newspaper.**

SOME UNITS

BEST WESTERN SANDMAN MOTEL *Book at aaa.com* **Phone:** (916)443-6515 8

SAVE

Motel

5/1-9/30 [ECP] 1P: $70-$85 2P: $74-$89 XP: $6 F12
2/1-4/30 & 10/1-1/31 [ECP] 1P: $68-$83 2P: $72-$87 XP: $6 F12

Location: I-5, exit Richards Blvd, 2.3 mi nw of Business Rt 80. 236 Jibboom St 95814. Fax: 916/443-8346. **Facility:** 116 one-bedroom standard units. 2 stories, exterior corridors. **Parking:** on-site. **Terms:** 3 day cancellation notice. **Amenities:** irons, hair dryers. **Pool(s):** heated outdoor. **Leisure Activities:** whirlpool. **Guest Services:** coin laundry. **Cards:** AX, CB, DC, DS, MC, VI. **Special Amenities: free expanded continental breakfast and free room upgrade (subject to availability with advanced reservations).** *(See color ad p 571)*

SOME UNITS

BEST WESTERN SUTTER HOUSE *Book at aaa.com* **Phone:** (916)441-1314 17

SAVE

Motel

All Year [CP] 1P: $89-$185 2P: $99-$190 XP: $10 F12

Location: 3 blks from state capitol, between 11th and 12th sts; downtown. 1100 H St 95814. Fax: 916/441-5961. **Facility:** 98 one-bedroom standard units. 3 stories, interior/exterior corridors. **Parking:** on-site. **Terms:** 3 day cancellation notice-fee imposed. **Amenities:** voice mail, fax, irons, hair dryers. **Pool(s):** outdoor. **Guest Services:** valet laundry. **Business Services:** meeting rooms. **Cards:** AX, CB, DC, DS, MC, VI. **Special Amenities: free continental breakfast and free newspaper.** *(See color ad p 571 & p 521)*

SOME UNITS

(See map and index starting on p. 565)

CANDLEWOOD SUITES *Book at aaa.com* **Phone:** (916)646-1212 **45**

AAA SAVE

Small-scale Hotel

All Year 1P: $124-$149

Location: US 50, exit Howe Ave, 1.5 mi n. 555 Howe Ave 95825. Fax: 916/646-1216. **Facility:** 126 units. 86 one-bedroom standard units with kitchens. 40 one-bedroom suites with kitchens. 4 stories, interior corridors. **Parking:** on-site. **Terms:** cancellation fee imposed, small pets only ($75 fee). **Amenities:** video games, CD players, high-speed Internet (fee), dual phone lines, voice mail, irons, hair dryers. **Leisure Activities:** whirlpool, exercise room. **Guest Services:** complimentary laundry. **Cards:** AX, DC, DS, MC, VI. **Special Amenities: free local telephone calls and free newspaper.**

(See color ad below)

FEE SOME UNITS

Best Western Sutter House

Located in the heart of Sacramento's attractions, the State Capitol and Convention Center are just three blocks away • Complimentary deluxe continental breakfast • Solar heated outdoor pool with private courtyard • On premises restaurant, bar • 100% Non-Smoking

800/830-1314
916/441-1314

1100 H Street
Sacramento, CA 95814

A PACIFIC PLAZA HOTEL • www.PacificPlazaHotels.com

GATEWAY TO THE GOLD COUNTRY

A SUITE IN SACRAMENTO.
THE BEST EXECUTIVE DECISION YOU'VE MADE IN A WHILE.

Experience a space made with you in mind. Our spacious studios, and one bedroom suites offer families and business travelers everything from full kitchens to an executive desk complete with free in-room internet. Call for our amazing $89, dbl. occ., weekend Medallion Rate, or the best available mid-week rate.

Call 1.888.CANDLEWOOD Visit larkspurhotels.com
555 Howe Avenue Sacramento, CA 95825

CANDLEWOOD SUITES

(See map and index starting on p. 565)

CANTERBURY INN — Phone: (916)927-0927 — 58

Motel — All Year — 1P: $49-$79 — 2P: $59-$89 — XP: $5 — D12

Location: Business Rt 80, exit Exposition Blvd, 0.4 mi w to Leisure Ln, then just n of SR 160. 1900 Canterbury Rd 95815. Fax: 916/641-8594. **Facility:** 150 one-bedroom standard units. 2 stories, exterior corridors. **Parking:** on-site. **Terms:** small pets only ($10 fee). **Amenities:** irons, hair dryers. **Pool(s):** outdoor. **Guest Services:** coin laundry. **Cards:** AX, DC, MC, VI.

SOME UNITS

FEE

CAPITOL PARK BED & BREAKFAST INN — Phone: 916/414-1300 — 33

Historic Bed & Breakfast — All Year — 1P: $129-$159 — 2P: $149-$189

Location: 0.5 mi s of state capitol. 1300 T St 95814. Fax: 916/414-1304. **Facility:** This stately, Federalist-style B&B, built in 1910, is in the city center a short walk from the state capitol. 4 one-bedroom standard units, some with whirlpools. 2 stories, interior corridors. *Bath:* combo or shower only. **Parking:** on-site. **Terms:** age restrictions may apply, cancellation fee imposed, [BP] meal plan available. **Amenities:** irons, hair dryers. **Guest Services:** complimentary evening beverages. **Cards:** AX, DC, MC, VI.

CLARION HOTEL MANSION INN — Book at aaa.com — Phone: (916)444-8000 — 22

SAVE — Small-scale Hotel — All Year — 1P: $79-$109 — XP: $10 — F17

Location: On SR 160, 1.3 mi n of Business Rt 80, exit 16th St. Located opposite the Governor's Mansion State Historic Park. 700 16th St 95814. Fax: 916/444-9412. **Facility:** Designated smoking area. 106 units. 105 one-bedroom standard units. 1 one-bedroom suite. 2-3 stories, interior corridors. *Bath:* shower only. **Parking:** on-site. **Terms:** 3 day cancellation notice. **Amenities:** irons, hair dryers. **Dining:** 6:30 am-2:30 & 6-10 pm, cocktails. **Pool(s):** outdoor. **Guest Services:** valet laundry. **Business Services:** conference facilities, business center. **Cards:** AX, CB, DC, DS, JC, MC, VI. **Special Amenities: free newspaper and free room upgrade (subject to availability with advanced reservations).** *(See color ad p 573)*

COMFORT INN & SUITES — Book at aaa.com — Phone: (916)379-0400 — 57

SAVE — Motel — All Year [BP] — 1P: $84-$129 — 2P: $84-$129 — XP: $10 — F12

Location: US 50, exit Howe Ave, just s. 21 Howe Ave 95826. Fax: 916/379-0700. **Facility:** 68 units. 65 one-bedroom standard units. 3 one-bedroom suites ($99-$189). 3 stories, interior corridors. **Parking:** on-site. **Terms:** cancellation fee imposed. **Amenities:** high-speed Internet (fee), dual phone lines, voice mail, irons, hair dryers. **Pool(s):** indoor. **Leisure Activities:** whirlpool, exercise room. **Guest Services:** valet and coin laundry. **Business Services:** conference facilities, business center. **Cards:** AX, CB, DC, DS, JC, MC, VI. **Special Amenities: free full breakfast and free local telephone calls.**

SOME UNITS

COMFORT SUITES- DOWNTOWN — Book at aaa.com — Phone: (916)446-9400 — 5

Motel — All Year [ECP] — 1P: $89-$189 — 2P: $99-$199 — XP: $10 — F

Location: I-5, exit Richards Blvd, just w. 226 Jibboom St 95814. Fax: 916/442-1100. **Facility:** 53 units. 50 one-bedroom standard units, some with whirlpools. 3 one-bedroom suites ($149-$199). 3 stories, interior corridors. **Parking:** on-site. **Terms:** cancellation fee imposed. **Amenities:** dual phone lines, voice mail, irons, hair dryers. **Pool(s):** outdoor. **Leisure Activities:** whirlpool. **Guest Services:** coin laundry. **Business Services:** meeting rooms. **Cards:** AX, CB, DC, DS, JC, MC, VI.

SOME UNITS

COURTYARD BY MARRIOTT — Book at aaa.com — Phone: 916/455-6800 — 55

SAVE — Small-scale Hotel — All Year — 1P: $79-$139

Location: Adjacent to the University of California Medical Center. 4422 Y St 95817. Fax: 916/669-1031. **Facility:** 139 units. 136 one-bedroom standard units, some with kitchens. 3 one-bedroom suites ($144-$164) with kitchens. 4 stories, interior corridors. **Parking:** on-site. **Terms:** [AP], [BP], [CP] & [ECP] meal plans available, package plans. **Amenities:** high-speed Internet, dual phone lines, voice mail, irons, hair dryers. **Dining:** 6-10 am, 11:30-2 & 5-10 pm, cocktails. **Pool(s):** outdoor. **Leisure Activities:** whirlpool, exercise room. **Guest Services:** coin laundry. **Business Services:** conference facilities, business center. **Cards:** AX, CB, DC, DS, MC, VI. **Special Amenities: free newspaper and preferred room (subject to availability with advanced reservations).**

SOME UNITS

(See map and index starting on p. 565)

DAYS INN Book at aaa.com — Phone: (916)488-4100 29

Motel

5/1-8/1 [ECP]	1P: $59-$89	2P: $59-$89	XP: $10	F17
8/2-12/31 [ECP]	1P: $52-$89	2P: $52-$89	XP: $10	F17
1/1-1/31 [ECP]	1P: $49-$89	2P: $49-$89	XP: $10	F17
2/1-4/30 [ECP]	1P: $47-$67	2P: $47-$67	XP: $10	F17

Location: I-80, exit Watt Ave, just n. 3425 Orange Grove Ave 95660. Fax: 916/489-0286. **Facility:** 141 one-bedroom standard units. 2 stories, exterior corridors. **Parking:** on-site. **Amenities:** hair dryers. **Pool(s):** outdoor. **Business Services:** meeting rooms. **Cards:** DS, MC, VI.

SOME UNITS

DELTA KING HOTEL Book at aaa.com — Phone: (916)444-5464 13

Small-scale Hotel

All Year	1P: $139-$184	2P: $139-$184

Location: I-5, exit J St (Old Sacramento). 1000 Front St 95814. Fax: 916/444-5314. **Facility:** 44 one-bedroom standard units. 5 stories, interior/exterior corridors. *Bath:* combo or shower only. **Parking:** valet. **Terms:** check-in 4 pm, [ECP] meal plan available, package plans - weekends. **Amenities:** hair dryers. **Dining:** Pilothouse Restaurant, see separate listing. **Guest Services:** gift shop, valet laundry. **Business Services:** meeting rooms. **Cards:** AX, DC, DS, MC, VI.

(See map and index starting on p. 565)

DOUBLETREE HOTEL *Book at aaa.com* **Phone:** (916)929-8855 38

Large-scale Hotel

1/1-1/31	1P: $89-$225	2P: $89-$225	XP: $15	F18
2/1-12/31	1P: $89-$215	2P: $89-$215	XP: $15	F18

Location: 1 blk off Business Rt 80, exit via Arden Way, 3 mi e. 2001 Point West Way 95815. Fax: 916/924-4913. **Facility:** 448 units. 433 one-bedroom standard units. 15 one-bedroom suites ($249-$515), some with whirlpools. 3-4 stories, interior corridors. **Parking:** on-site. **Terms:** cancellation fee imposed, [AP] meal plan available, small pets only ($25 fee). **Amenities:** voice mail, irons, hair dryers. **Pool(s):** outdoor. **Leisure Activities:** whirlpool, exercise room. **Guest Services:** gift shop, valet laundry. **Business Services:** conference facilities, business center. **Cards:** AX, DC, DS, MC, VI. *(See color ad below)*

SOME UNITS FEE

ECONO LODGE *Book at aaa.com* **Phone:** 916/482-2300 40

Motel

All Year [CP]	1P: $59-$99	2P: $95-$99	XP: $6	F12

Location: I-80, exit Watt Ave. 2912 Auburn Blvd 95821. Fax: 916/486-4294. **Facility:** 47 units. 42 one-bedroom standard units. 5 one-bedroom suites ($99-$115). 2 stories, exterior corridors. **Parking:** on-site. **Pool(s):** outdoor. **Leisure Activities:** whirlpool, exercise room. **Cards:** AX, DC, DS, MC, VI. **Special Amenities: free continental breakfast and early check-in/late check-out.**

SOME UNITS

ECONO LODGE *Book at aaa.com* **Phone:** (916)443-6631 23

Motel

5/15-9/15	1P: $65-$109	2P: $69-$119	XP: $4	F18
9/16-1/31	1P: $59-$109	2P: $65-$119	XP: $4	F18
2/1-5/14	1P: $55-$99	2P: $60-$109	XP: $4	F18

Location: Business Rt 80, exit 15th St eastbound; exit 16th St westbound; I-5, exit J St. 711 16th St 95814. Fax: 916/442-7251. **Facility:** 41 units. 39 one-bedroom standard units. 2 one-bedroom suites. 3 stories, exterior corridors. *Bath:* combo or shower only. **Parking:** on-site. **Terms:** [CP] meal plan available, pets ($6 extra charge). **Amenities:** hair dryers. **Cards:** AX, CB, DC, DS, MC, VI. **Special Amenities: free continental breakfast and free room upgrade (subject to availability with advanced reservations).** *(See color ad below)*

SOME UNITS FEE FEE

(See map and index starting on p. 565)

EMBASSY SUITES SACRAMENTO *Book at aaa.com* **Phone:** 916/326-5000 **2**

Large-scale Hotel

All Year [BP] 1P: $119-$279 2P: $119-$279 XP: $15 F

Location: I-5, exit J St, just s on 3rd St, then w on Capitol Mall. Located on the Sacramento River, adjacent to Old Sacramento. 100 Capitol Mall 95814. Fax: 916/326-5001. **Facility:** Offers high end furnishings and a rich collection of works by local artists depicting historic Old Sacramento, the Capitol and life on the river. 242 one-bedroom suites. 8 stories, interior corridors. **Parking:** on-site (fee) and valet. **Amenities:** video games, dual phone lines, voice mail, safes, irons, hair dryers. **Pool(s):** heated indoor. **Leisure Activities:** whirlpool, exercise room. **Guest Services:** gift shop, complimentary evening beverages, valet and coin laundry. **Business Services:** conference facilities, business center. **Cards:** AX, DC, DS, MC, VI. ***(See color ad below)***

SOME UNITS

GOLD STAR NATIONAL 9 INN **Phone:** (916)399-8077 **53**

Motel

All Year 1P: $59-$64 2P: $65-$70 XP: $10 F5

Location: SR 99, exit 47th Ave, 1 mi e to Stockton Blvd, 0.5 mi s. 6610 Stockton Blvd 95823. Fax: 916/422-9317. **Facility:** 31 one-bedroom standard units, some with kitchens. 2 stories, exterior corridors. *Bath:* combo or shower only. **Parking:** on-site. **Cards:** AX, CB, DC, MC, VI.

SOME UNITS

GOOD NITE INN *Book at aaa.com* **Phone:** (916)386-8408 **50**

Motel

All Year 1P: $53 2P: $53

Location: Southwest corner of jct SR 50 and Howe Ave. 25 Howe Ave 95826. Fax: 916/386-1608. **Facility:** 102 one-bedroom standard units. 3 stories, exterior corridors. **Parking:** on-site. **Terms:** [CP] meal plan available. **Pool(s):** outdoor. **Guest Services:** coin laundry. **Cards:** AX, CB, DC, DS, MC, VI. **Special Amenities: free continental breakfast.**

SOME UNITS

GOVERNORS INN *Book at aaa.com* **Phone:** (916)448-7224 **11**

Motel

All Year [ECP] 1P: $82-$92 2P: $92-$102 XP: $10 F12

Location: I-5, exit E Richards Blvd, 2.3 mi nw of Business Loop 80. 210 Richards Blvd 95814. Fax: 916/448-7382. **Facility:** 134 units. 122 one-bedroom standard units. 12 one-bedroom suites. 3 stories, interior corridors. *Bath:* combo or shower only. **Parking:** on-site. **Terms:** 3 day cancellation notice, [CP] meal plan available. **Amenities:** irons, hair dryers. **Pool(s):** outdoor. **Leisure Activities:** whirlpool, exercise room. **Guest Services:** complimentary evening beverages: Mon-Thurs, valet laundry. **Business Services:** meeting rooms. **Cards:** AX, DC, DS, MC, VI. *(See color ad p 576)*

SOME UNITS

HAMPTON INN & SUITES *Book at aaa.com* **Phone:** (916)927-2222 **10**

Small-scale Hotel

All Year [ECP] 1P: $99-$134 2P: $105-$144 XP: $10 F12

Location: Business Rt 80, exit Howe Ave. 2230 Auburn Blvd 95821. Fax: 916/927-2014. **Facility:** 67 units. 60 one-bedroom standard units. 7 one-bedroom suites with whirlpools. 3 stories, interior corridors. **Parking:** on-site. **Amenities:** voice mail, irons, hair dryers. **Pool(s):** outdoor. **Leisure Activities:** exercise room. **Guest Services:** valet and coin laundry. **Business Services:** meeting rooms. **Cards:** AX, CB, DC, DS, JC, MC, VI.

SOME UNITS

HAWTHORN SUITES *Book at aaa.com* **Phone:** (916)441-1200 **3**

Small-scale Hotel

All Year 1P: $89-$139 2P: $99-$149 XP: $15 F

Location: I-5, exit Richards Blvd, 2.3 mi nw of Business Rt 80. 321 Bercut Dr 95814. Fax: 916/441-6530. **Facility:** 272 units. 240 one-bedroom standard units, some with kitchens. 32 two-bedroom suites with kitchens. 3 stories, interior corridors. **Parking:** on-site. **Terms:** cancellation fee imposed. **Amenities:** dual phone lines, voice mail, irons, hair dryers. **Pool(s):** heated outdoor. **Leisure Activities:** whirlpool, exercise room, sports court. **Guest Services:** gift shop, complimentary evening beverages: Mon-Thurs, coin laundry, area transportation. **Business Services:** conference facilities. **Cards:** AX, DC, DS, MC, VI. ***(See color ad p 576)***

SOME UNITS

(See map and index starting on p. 565)

HILTON GARDEN INN *Book at aaa.com* **Phone:** (916)568-5400

Small-scale Hotel All Year 1P: $79-$169 2P: $79-$169

Location: I-5, exit Garden Hwy, 0.3 mi w to Gateway Oaks Dr, then 0.3 mi n. 2540 Venture Oaks Way 95833. Fax: 916/568-5072. **Facility:** 154 one-bedroom standard units. 3 stories, interior corridors. **Parking:** on-site. **Terms:** $1 service charge. **Amenities:** high-speed Internet (fee), dual phone lines, voice mail, irons, hair dryers. **Pool(s):** heated outdoor. **Leisure Activities:** whirlpool, exercise room. **Guest Services:** coin laundry. **Business Services:** meeting rooms, business center. **Cards:** AX, DC, DS, MC, VI.

SOME UNITS

ASK DATA PORT

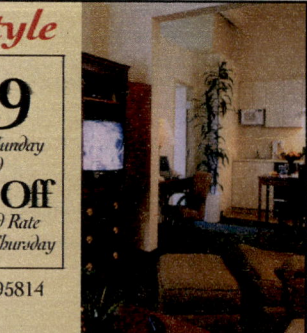

(See map and index starting on p. 565)

HILTON SACRAMENTO ARDEN WEST Book at aaa.com Phone: (916)922-4700 34

AAA SAVE

Large-scale Hotel

All Year 1P: $99-$239 2P: $109-$249 XP: $10 F18

Location: At jct Business Rt 80 and Arden Way, exit W Arden Way. 2200 Harvard St 95815. Fax: 916/922-8418. **Facility:** 331 units. 323 one-bedroom standard units. 8 one-bedroom suites with whirlpools. 12 stories, interior corridors. **Parking:** on-site. **Terms:** cancellation fee imposed, $1 service charge. **Amenities:** high-speed Internet (fee), dual phone lines, voice mail, irons, hair dryers. **Dining:** 6 am-2 & 5-10 pm, cocktails. **Pool(s):** heated outdoor. **Leisure Activities:** sauna, whirlpool, exercise room. **Guest Services:** gift shop, valet laundry, area transportation-within 5 mi. **Business Services:** conference facilities, business center. **Cards:** AX, CB, DC, MC, VI. **Special Amenities: early check-in/late check-out and preferred room (subject to availability with advanced reservations).** *(See color ad below)*

SOME UNITS

HOLIDAY INN CAPITOL PLAZA Book at aaa.com Phone: (916)446-0100 16

AAA SAVE

Large-scale Hotel

All Year 1P: $154-$184 XP: $10 F18

Location: I-5, exit J St (Old Sacramento). Adjacent to downtown plaza shopping mall. 300 J St 95814. Fax: 916/446-0117. **Facility:** 364 one-bedroom standard units. 16 stories, interior corridors. **Parking:** on-site. **Terms:** [AP] meal plan available, package plans - seasonal. **Amenities:** dual phone lines, voice mail, irons, hair dryers. **Dining:** 6 am-2 & 5-10 pm, cocktails. **Pool(s):** heated outdoor. **Leisure Activities:** exercise room. **Guest Services:** gift shop, valet laundry. **Business Services:** meeting rooms, business center. **Cards:** AX, DC, DS, MC, VI. **Special Amenities: free newspaper.** *(See color ad below)*

SOME UNITS

HOLIDAY INN EXPRESS Book at aaa.com Phone: 916/372-6900 60

Motel

All Year 1P: $99-$199 2P: $99-$199 XP: $10 F12

Location: I-80, exit Harbor Blvd, just n. 2761 Evergreen Ave 95691. Fax: 916/372-6306. **Facility:** 55 one-bedroom standard units, some with whirlpools. 4 stories, interior corridors. **Parking:** on-site. **Terms:** cancellation fee imposed, [ECP] meal plan available. **Amenities:** high-speed Internet, dual phone lines, voice mail, irons, hair dryers. **Leisure Activities:** whirlpool, exercise room. **Business Services:** business center. **Cards:** AX, CB, DC, DS, JC, MC, VI. *(See color ad p 578)*

SOME UNITS

HOLIDAY INN EXPRESS SACRAMENTO Book at aaa.com Phone: (916)444-4436 7

AAA SAVE

Small-scale Hotel

All Year [ECP] 1P: $89-$119 2P: $89-$119 XP: $10 F17

Location: ON SR 160. 728 16th St 95814. Fax: 916/444-0066. **Facility:** 132 one-bedroom standard units. 4 stories, interior corridors. **Parking:** on-site. **Terms:** 3 day cancellation notice. **Amenities:** dual phone lines, voice mail, irons, hair dryers. **Pool(s):** outdoor. **Leisure Activities:** exercise room. **Guest Services:** valet laundry. **Business Services:** meeting rooms. **Cards:** AX, CB, DC, DS, JC, MC, VI. **Special Amenities: free expanded continental breakfast and free newspaper.** *(See color ad p 573)*

(See map and index starting on p. 565)

HOLIDAY INN SACRAMENTO NORTHEAST *Book at aaa.com* **Phone:** (916)338-5800 **31**

AAA SAVE

Small-scale Hotel

All Year 1P: $139 2P: $139

Location: I-80, exit Madison Ave, 9 mi e. 5321 Date Ave 95841. Fax: 916/334-2868. **Facility:** 230 units. 218 one-bedroom standard units. 12 one-bedroom suites ($169). 6 stories, interior corridors. **Parking:** on-site. **Terms:** cancellation fee imposed, [BP] & [CP] meal plans available. **Amenities:** video games, voice mail, irons, hair dryers. **Dining:** 6 am-10 pm, cocktails. **Pool(s):** heated outdoor. **Leisure Activities:** whirlpool, exercise room. **Guest Services:** gift shop, coin laundry. **Business Services:** conference facilities, business center. **Cards:** AX, DC, DS, MC, VI. *(See color ad below)*

SOME UNITS

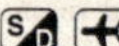

(See map and index starting on p. 565)

HOMESTEAD STUDIO SUITES HOTEL-SACRAMENTO *Book at aaa.com* **Phone:** (916)564-7500 37

Motel

All Year 1P: $72-$92 2P: $77-$97 XP: $5 F17

Location: I-5, exit W El Camino Ave, just w, then 0.4 mi n. 2810 Gateway Oaks Dr 95833. Fax: 916/564-7515. **Facility:** 143 one-bedroom standard units with efficiencies. 2 stories, exterior corridors. **Parking:** on-site. **Terms:** weekly rates available, small pets only ($75 fee). **Amenities:** voice mail, irons, hair dryers. **Guest Services:** coin laundry. **Cards:** AX, CB, DC, DS, JC, MC, VI.

ASK FEE SOME UNITS

HOST AIRPORT HOTEL *Book at aaa.com* **Phone:** (916)922-8071 26

Motel

All Year [CP] 1P: $80-$140 2P: $80-$140 XP: $10 F12

Location: 11 mi nw of state capitol; 6 mi nw of I-80, off I-5. Located at the Sacramento Metropolitan Airport. 6945 Airport Blvd 95837. Fax: 916/929-8636. **Facility:** 84 one-bedroom standard units. 2 stories, exterior corridors. **Parking:** on-site. **Terms:** cancellation fee imposed, pets ($50 extra charge). **Amenities:** voice mail, irons, hair dryers. **Leisure Activities:** whirlpool, exercise room. **Business Services:** conference facilities. **Cards:** AX, DC, DS, MC, VI.

FEE SOME UNITS VCR FEE

HYATT REGENCY *Book at aaa.com* **Phone:** (916)443-1234 21

AAA SAVE

Large-scale Hotel

All Year 1P: $99-$269 2P: $99-$269 XP: $25 F18

Location: 1/2 blk from capitol at 12th and L sts. Located accross from the state capitol and convention center. 1209 L St 95814. Fax: 916/321-6699. **Facility:** Lavish appointments adorn the lobby and common areas of this centrally located hotel. 502 units. 490 one-bedroom standard units. 12 one-bedroom suites with whirlpools. 15 stories, interior corridors. **Parking:** on-site (fee) and valet. **Terms:** cancellation fee imposed. **Amenities:** dual phone lines, voice mail, honor bars, irons, hair dryers. **Dining:** 2 restaurants, 6 am-11 pm, cocktails, nightclub, entertainment. **Pool(s):** heated outdoor. **Leisure Activities:** whirlpool, exercise room. **Guest Services:** gift shop, valet laundry. **Business Services:** conference facilities, business center. **Cards:** AX, CB, DC, DS, JC, MC, VI.

(See color ad below)

FEE SOME UNITS VCR FEE FEE FEE

INN OFF CAPITOL PARK *Book at aaa.com* **Phone:** (916)447-8100 25

Motel

2/1-6/30 [CP]	1P: $79-$169	2P: $84-$169	XP: $10	F17
9/1-11/15 [CP]	1P: $79-$129	2P: $84-$129	XP: $10	F17
11/16-1/31 [CP]	1P: $79-$119	2P: $84-$119	XP: $10	F17
7/1-8/31 [CP]	1P: $79-$99	2P: $79-$119	XP: $10	F17

Location: 0.3 mi e of capitol; downtown. 1530 N St 95814. Fax: 916/341-0798. **Facility:** 38 units. 22 one-bedroom standard units. 16 one-bedroom suites. 3 stories, interior corridors. **Parking:** on-site. **Amenities:** dual phone lines, voice mail, irons, hair dryers. **Cards:** AX, DC, DS, MC, VI.

ASK

LA QUINTA INN-NORTH *Book at aaa.com* **Phone:** 916/348-0900 30

Motel

All Year 1P: $80-$95 2P: $86-$101 XP: $6 F18

Location: I-80, exit Madison Ave, 9 mi e. 4604 Madison Ave 95841. Fax: 916/331-7160. **Facility:** 127 one-bedroom standard units. 3 stories, exterior corridors. **Parking:** on-site. **Terms:** [ECP] meal plan available, small pets only. **Amenities:** video games, voice mail, irons, hair dryers. **Pool(s):** heated outdoor. **Leisure Activities:** whirlpool. **Guest Services:** coin laundry. **Business Services:** meeting rooms. **Cards:** AX, CB, DC, DS, JC, MC, VI.

(See color ad p 580)

SOME UNITS

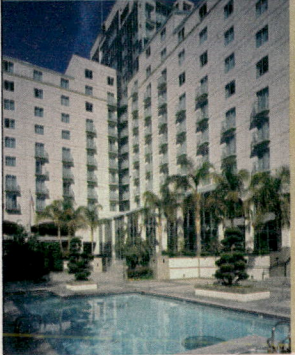

(See map and index starting on p. 565)

LA QUINTA INN-SACRAMENTO DOWNTOWN *Book at aaa.com* **Phone:** 916/448-8100 **6**

Motel

All Year 1P: $86-$115 2P: $92-$121 XP: $6 F18

Location: I-5, exit Richards Blvd W, 2.3 mi nw of Business Loop 80. 200 Jibboom St 95814. Fax: 916/447-3621. **Facility:** 168 units. 165 one-bedroom standard units. 3 one-bedroom suites. 3 stories, exterior corridors. **Parking:** on-site. **Terms:** [ECP] meal plan available, small pets only. **Amenities:** video games, voice mail, irons, hair dryers. **Pool(s):** heated outdoor. **Leisure Activities:** whirlpool, exercise room. **Guest Services:** coin laundry. **Business Services:** meeting rooms. **Cards:** AX, CB, DC, DS, JC, MC, VI. ***(See color ad below)***

SOME UNITS

LIONS GATE HOTEL *Book at aaa.com* **Phone:** 916/643-6222 **56**

Motel

All Year 1P: $99-$119 2P: $99-$119 XP: $10 F16

Location: I-80, exit Watt Ave, 1.5 mi n to Palm St. 3410 Westover St 95652. Fax: 916/643-9511. **Facility:** 110 units. 80 one-bedroom standard units. 20 one- and 10 two-bedroom suites ($129-$179). 2 stories, interior/exterior corridors. **Parking:** on-site. **Terms:** [AP] meal plan available. **Amenities:** irons, hair dryers. **Pool(s):** heated outdoor. **Leisure Activities:** whirlpool. **Guest Services:** coin laundry. **Business Services:** conference facilities, business center. **Cards:** AX, CB, DC, DS, MC, VI.

MARRIOTT RESIDENCE INN *Book at aaa.com* **Phone:** (916)920-9111 **43**

Motel

All Year [BP] 1P: $159 2P: $159

Location: 2.5 mi n of jct SR 16 and US 50, exit Howe Ave. 1530 Howe Ave 95825. Fax: 916/921-5664. **Facility:** 176 units. 143 one-bedroom standard units with kitchens. 22 one- and 11 two-bedroom suites with kitchens. 2 stories, exterior corridors. **Parking:** on-site. **Terms:** cancellation fee imposed, pets ($100 fee). **Amenities:** voice mail, irons, hair dryers. **Pool(s):** heated outdoor. **Leisure Activities:** whirlpools, exercise room. **Guest Services:** coin laundry. **Business Services:** meeting rooms. **Cards:** AX, CB, DC, DS, MC, VI.

SOME UNITS

FEE

MICROTEL INN & SUITES *Book at aaa.com* **Phone:** (916)920-4451 **46**

SAVE

Motel

4/1-9/30 [CP] 1P: $60-$75 2P: $60-$75 XP: $5 F12
2/1-3/31 & 10/1-1/31 [CP] 1P: $50-$65 2P: $50-$65 XP: $5 F12

Location: I-80, exit W El Camino Ave. 2654 El Centro Rd 95833. Fax: 916/561-0665. **Facility:** 56 one-bedroom standard units. 3 stories, interior corridors. **Parking:** on-site. **Terms:** [ECP] meal plan available. **Cards:** AX, CB, DC, DS, JC, MC, VI. **Special Amenities: free continental breakfast and free local telephone calls.** *(See color ad below)*

SOME UNITS

(See map and index starting on p. 565)

QUALITY INN Book at aaa.com **Phone:** (916)444-3980 20

Motel

	1P	2P	XP	
All Year	1P: $84-$104	2P: $84-$104	XP: $5	F12

Location: I-5, exit J St, 0.8 mi e to 14th St, n on 14th St, e on H St, then s; from Business Rt 80/SR 99 exit SR 160 (16th St), 1 mi n, then just w on I St. 818 15th St 95814. Fax: 916/444-2991. **Facility:** 41 units. 37 one-bedroom standard units. 4 one-bedroom suites ($104-$115). 3 stories, exterior corridors. *Bath:* combo or shower only. **Parking:** on-site. **Amenities:** irons, hair dryers. **Pool(s):** outdoor. **Cards:** AX, CB, DC, DS, JC, MC, VI. **Special Amenities: free continental breakfast and free local telephone calls.** *(See ad below)*

SOME UNITS

QUALITY INN HOTEL & CONFERENCE CENTER **Phone:** (916)487-7600 41

Motel

	1P	2P	XP
6/15-9/5	1P: $69	2P: $69	XP: $10
2/1-6/14 & 9/6-1/31	1P: $64	2P: $64	XP: $10

Location: Business Rt 80, exit Fulton Ave. 2600 Auburn Blvd 95821. Fax: 916/481-7112. **Facility:** 180 one-bedroom standard units. 4 stories, interior corridors. **Parking:** on-site. **Terms:** [BP] meal plan available, package plans, pets ($100 deposit). **Amenities:** safes, hair dryers. **Pool(s):** outdoor. **Leisure Activities:** exercise room. **Guest Services:** coin laundry. **Business Services:** meeting rooms. **Cards:** AX, CB, DC, DS, MC, VI. ***(See color ad p 572)***

SOME UNITS

FEE

RADISSON HOTEL Book at aaa.com **Phone:** (916)922-2020 39

Small-scale Hotel

	1P	2P	XP	
All Year	1P: $105-$185	2P: $105-$185	XP: $10	F16

Location: Business Rt 80, exit Exposition Blvd, 0.4 mi w. 500 Leisure Ln 95815. Fax: 916/649-9463. **Facility:** 309 units. 297 one-bedroom standard units. 12 one-bedroom suites. 1-2 stories, exterior corridors. **Parking:** on-site. **Terms:** check-in 4 pm, pets ($100 deposit). **Amenities:** dual phone lines, voice mail, irons, hair dryers. **Dining:** 6 am-10 pm, cocktails. **Pool(s):** heated outdoor. **Leisure Activities:** whirlpool, rental paddleboats, rental bicycles, exercise room. **Guest Services:** gift shop, valet laundry. **Business Services:** conference facilities, business center. **Cards:** AX, DC, DS, MC, VI. **Special Amenities: free newspaper and free room upgrade (subject to availability with advanced reservations).** *(See color ad p 629)*

SOME UNITS

FEE

(See map and index starting on p. 565)

RAMADA LIMITED-DISCOVERY PARK *Book at aaa.com* **Phone:** 916/442-6971 **9**

Motel

All Year 1P: $79-$110 2P: $79-$110
Location: I-5, exit E Richards Blvd, 2.3 mi nw of Business Loop 80. 350 Bercut Dr 95814. Fax: 916/444-2809. **Facility:** 100 one-bedroom standard units. 2 stories, exterior corridors. **Parking:** on-site. **Terms:** [ECP] meal plan available. **Amenities:** hair dryers. **Pool(s):** outdoor. **Leisure Activities:** whirlpool. **Guest Services:** valet laundry. **Business Services:** meeting rooms. **Cards:** AX, CB, DC, DS, JC, MC, VI. **Special Amenities: free continental breakfast and free room upgrade (subject to availability with advanced reservations).** *(See ad p 581)*

SOME UNITS

RED LION HOTEL SACRAMENTO *Book at aaa.com* **Phone:** (916)922-8041 **35**

Motel

All Year 1P: $129-$159 2P: $129-$159 XP: $10 F
Location: Exit Business Rt 80 via Arden Way. Located in Arden Fair Shopping Plaza. 1401 Arden Way 95815. Fax: 916/922-0386. **Facility:** 376 units. 370 one-bedroom standard units. 6 one-bedroom suites. 2 stories, interior/exterior corridors. *Bath:* combo or shower only. **Parking:** on-site. **Terms:** cancellation fee imposed, [AP], [BP], [CP] & [ECP] meal plans available, small pets only ($25 deposit). **Amenities:** voice mail, irons, hair dryers. **Dining:** 6 am-10 pm, Fri & Sat-11 pm, cocktails. **Pool(s):** 2 outdoor, heated outdoor, wading. **Leisure Activities:** whirlpool, putting green, exercise room. **Guest Services:** gift shop, valet laundry. **Business Services:** conference facilities. **Cards:** AX, CB, DC, DS, JC, MC, VI. **Special Amenities: free room upgrade and preferred room (each subject to availability with advanced reservations).** *(See ad below)*

SOME UNITS
FEE

RED ROOF INN *Book at aaa.com* **Phone:** (916)927-7117 **27**

Motel

All Year 1P: $50-$90 XP: $6 F18
Location: I-80, exit Northgate Blvd, just s. 3796 Northgate Blvd 95834. Fax: 916/646-1433. **Facility:** 132 one-bedroom standard units. 3 stories, exterior corridors. **Parking:** on-site. **Pool(s):** outdoor. **Leisure Activities:** whirlpool. **Business Services:** meeting rooms. **Cards:** AX, DC, DS, MC, VI. **Special Amenities: free local telephone calls and free newspaper.**

SOME UNITS

RESIDENCE INN BY MARRIOTT *Book at aaa.com* **Phone:** (916)649-1300 **36**

Motel

All Year [BP] 1P: $154-$184 2P: $154-$184
Location: I-5, exit W El Camino Ave. 2410 W El Camino Ave 95833. Fax: 916/649-1395. **Facility:** 126 units. 94 one-bedroom standard units with kitchens. 32 two-bedroom suites with kitchens. 2 stories, exterior corridors. **Parking:** on-site. **Terms:** cancellation fee imposed, small pets only ($6 fee, $50 deposit). **Amenities:** voice mail, irons, hair dryers. **Pool(s):** heated outdoor. **Leisure Activities:** whirlpool, sports court. **Guest Services:** coin laundry. **Business Services:** meeting rooms. **Cards:** AX, CB, DC, DS, JC, MC, VI.

SOME UNITS
FEE

SHERATON GRAND SACRAMENTO HOTEL *Book at aaa.com* **Phone:** (916)447-1700 **15**

Large-scale Hotel

All Year 1P: $335 2P: $335 XP: $25 F17
Location: I-5, exit J St, 1 mi e. Adjacent to the Sacramento Convention Center. 1230 J St 95814. Fax: 916/447-1701. **Facility:** Located in the beautifully restored historic Public Market Building, the hotel is steps away from the convention center and the State Capitol. 503 units. 476 one-bedroom standard units. 27 one-bedroom suites ($435). 27 stories, interior corridors. **Parking:** on-site (fee) and valet. **Terms:** cancellation fee imposed, [ECP] meal plan available. **Amenities:** video games, dual phone lines, voice mail, irons, hair dryers. **Pool(s):** heated outdoor. **Leisure Activities:** exercise room. **Guest Services:** gift shop, valet laundry. **Business Services:** conference facilities, business center. **Cards:** AX, CB, DC, DS, JC, MC, VI.

SOME UNITS

THE STERLING HOTEL *Book at aaa.com* **Phone:** (916)448-1300 **19**

Small-scale Hotel

All Year [ECP] 1P: $99-$249
Location: 3 blks n of state capitol; downtown. 1300 H St 95814. Fax: 916/448-8066. **Facility:** Designated smoking area. 17 one-bedroom standard units with whirlpools. 3 stories, interior corridors. **Parking:** on-site (fee). **Amenities:** CD players, voice mail, irons, hair dryers. **Dining:** Chanterelle, see separate listing. **Business Services:** conference facilities. **Cards:** AX, DC, DS, MC, VI.

SOME UNITS
FEE

(See map and index starting on p. 565)

SUPER 8-DISCOVERY PARK Book at aaa.com **Phone:** (916)442-7777 4

AAA SAVE Motel

All Year 1P: $55-$75 2P: $65-$90 XP: $7 F12

Location: I-5, exit Richards Blvd, 2.3 mi nw of Business Loop 80. 221 Jibboom St 95814. Fax: 916/442-0479. **Facility:** 28 one-bedroom standard units, some with whirlpools. 2 stories, exterior corridors. **Parking:** on-site. **Amenities:** hair dryers. **Cards:** AX, DC, DS, MC, VI. **Special Amenities: free continental breakfast and free local telephone calls.**

SOME UNITS

SUPER 8 EXECUTIVE SUITES Book at aaa.com **Phone:** (916)447-5400 12

AAA SAVE Motel

All Year 1P: $55-$99 2P: $60-$125 XP: $7 F12

Location: I-5, exit E Richards Blvd, 2.3 mi nw of Business Rt 80. 216 Bannon St 95814. Fax: 916/447-5153. **Facility:** 40 one-bedroom standard units, some with whirlpools. 3 stories, exterior corridors. **Parking:** on-site. **Terms:** [ECP] meal plan available. **Amenities:** high-speed Internet, irons, hair dryers. **Leisure Activities:** sauna, whirlpool. **Guest Services:** coin laundry. **Business Services:** meeting rooms. **Cards:** AX, CB, DC, DS, JC, MC, VI. **Special Amenities: free expanded continental breakfast and free local telephone calls.**

SOME UNITS

TRAVELODGE Book at aaa.com **Phone:** 916/971-9440 32

Motel

3/1-1/31 1P: $50-$61 2P: $56-$96 XP: $6 F10

2/1-2/29 1P: $46-$56 2P: $50-$86 XP: $6 F10

Location: I-80, exit Watt Ave, just s. 4325 N Watt Ave 95660. Fax: 916/483-3836. **Facility:** 89 one-bedroom standard units. 3 stories (no elevator), exterior corridors. **Parking:** on-site. **Guest Services:** coin laundry. **Cards:** AX, DC, MC, VI.

SOME UNITS

TRAVELODGE CAPITOL CENTER Book at aaa.com **Phone:** (916)444-8880 18

Motel

All Year [CP] 1P: $59-$89 2P: $69-$99 XP: $10 F12

Location: Between 11th and 12th sts; downtown. 1111 H St 95814. Fax: 916/447-7540. **Facility:** 71 one-bedroom standard units. 3-4 stories, exterior corridors. *Bath:* combo or shower only. **Parking:** on-site. **Terms:** 14 day cancellation notice. **Amenities:** safes, irons, hair dryers. **Business Services:** meeting rooms. **Cards:** AX, CB, DC, DS, JC, MC, VI.

SOME UNITS

VAGABOND EXECUTIVE INN Book at aaa.com **Phone:** (916)929-5600 42

AAA SAVE Motel

All Year [ECP] 1P: $69-$79 2P: $69-$79 XP: $5 F18

Location: Business Rt 80, exit Arden Way, 1 mi e. 2030 Arden Way 95825. Fax: 916/929-2419. **Facility:** 190 units. 184 one-bedroom standard units, some with efficiencies. 6 one-bedroom suites ($85-$150), some with efficiencies or kitchens. 2 stories, exterior corridors. **Parking:** on-site. **Amenities:** voice mail, irons, hair dryers. **Pool(s):** outdoor. **Leisure Activities:** whirlpool. **Guest Services:** coin laundry. **Business Services:** meeting rooms. **Cards:** AX, CB, DC, DS, MC, VI. **Special Amenities: free continental breakfast and free local telephone calls.**

SOME UNITS

VAGABOND EXECUTIVE INN Book at aaa.com **Phone:** (916)446-1481 14

AAA SAVE Motel

All Year [ECP] 1P: $84-$90 2P: $88-$90 XP: $10 F18

Location: I-5, exit J St (Old Sacramento), 8 blks w of capitol. Adjacent to Chinese Cultural Ctr and Old Sacramento Historic Qtr. 909 3rd St 95814. Fax: 916/448-0364. **Facility:** 107 one-bedroom standard units. 3 stories, exterior corridors. **Parking:** on-site. **Terms:** pets ($5 fee). **Amenities:** dual phone lines, irons, hair dryers. **Pool(s):** heated outdoor. **Leisure Activities:** whirlpool, exercise room. **Guest Services:** valet laundry. **Business Services:** meeting rooms, business center. **Cards:** AX, CB, DC, DS, MC, VI. **Special Amenities: free continental breakfast and free local telephone calls.**

SOME UNITS

FEE

VAGABOND INN Book at aaa.com **Phone:** (916)334-7430 28

Motel

All Year 1P: $43-$59 2P: $48-$64 XP: $5 F18

Location: I-80, exit Madison Ave, just n. 4317 Madison Ave 95842. Fax: 916/331-8916. **Facility:** 128 one-bedroom standard units. 2-3 stories, interior corridors. **Parking:** on-site. **Terms:** [CP] meal plan available. **Pool(s):** outdoor. **Cards:** AX, DS, MC, VI.

SOME UNITS

VIZCAYA Book at aaa.com **Phone:** (916)455-5243 24

Bed & Breakfast

All Year 1P: $159-$249 2P: $159-$249

Location: Between T and U sts; downtown. 2019 21st St 95818. Fax: 916/455-6102. **Facility:** A renovated turn-of-the-20th-century Victorian mansion, Vizcaya features extensive convention and banquet facilities. 9 units. 8 one-bedroom standard units, some with whirlpools. 1 one-bedroom suite with whirlpool. 2 stories, interior/exterior corridors. *Bath:* combo or shower only. **Parking:** on-site. **Terms:** [BP] meal plan available. **Amenities:** irons, hair dryers. **Business Services:** meeting rooms. **Cards:** AX, DC, MC, VI.

(See map and index starting on p. 565)

The following lodging was either not evaluated or did not meet AAA rating requirements but is listed for your information only.

RELAX INN & SUITES — **Phone:** (916)361-3131 (51)

fyi — Motel

All Year 1P: $44-$74 2P: $48-$79 XP: $8 F12

Under major renovation, scheduled to be completed April 2003. **Last rated:** (1 diamond) **Location:** Exit US 50 at Bradshaw Rd, just s. 9646 Micron Way 95827. Fax: 916/361-9674. **Facility:** 93 one-bedroom standard units. 3 stories, exterior corridors. **Parking:** on-site. **Terms:** 3 day cancellation notice-fee imposed. **Pool(s):** outdoor. **Cards:** AX, DS, MC, VI.

SOME UNITS

WHERE TO DINE

BRADSHAWS RESTAURANT — **Lunch:** $6-$10 **Dinner:** $7-$15 **Phone:** 916/362-3274 (11)

American

Location: On south side of US 50 at Bradshaw Rd. 9647 Micron Ave 95827. **Hours:** 6:30 am-10 pm, Fri & Sat-11 pm. Closed: 12/25. **Reservations:** required. **Features:** Country charm pervades the cozy restaurant, an area favorite for its homemade soups, desserts and entrees, as well as the varied salad bar. Casual dress; beer & wine only. **Parking:** on-site. **Cards:** AX, DS, MC, VI.

CALIFORNIA CAFE BAR & GRILL — **Lunch:** $8-$15 **Dinner:** $12-$24 **Phone:** 916/925-2233 (10)

American

Location: Business Rt 80, exit E Arden Way; in Arden Fair Shopping Plaza. 1689 Arden Way 95815. **Hours:** 11 am-9:30 pm, Fri & Sat-10 pm, Sun-8:30 pm. Closed: 11/25, 12/25. **Reservations:** suggested. **Features:** Contemporary California cuisine is prepared in a casual and inviting atmosphere. Casual dress; cocktails. **Parking:** on-site. **Cards:** AX, CB, DC, DS, MC, VI.

CALIFORNIA FAT'S ASIA GRILL & DIM SUM BAR — **Lunch:** $8-$14 **Dinner:** $10-$20 **Phone:** 916/441-7966 (1)

Asian

Location: In Old Sacramento historic area. 1015 Front St 95814. **Hours:** 11:30 am-3 & 5-10 pm, Sun 4 pm-9 pm. Closed: 11/25, 12/25; also Mon & Tues for lunch. **Reservations:** suggested. **Features:** Eastern seasonings flavor California-Pacific wok and grill cuisine. Bold, rustic-modern design characterizes the three dining levels. Casual dress; cocktails. **Parking:** on-site (fee). **Cards:** AX, MC, VI.

CHANTERELLE — **Lunch:** $8-$15 **Dinner:** $16-$24 **Phone:** 916/442-0451 (6)

Continental

Location: 3 blks n of state capitol; downtown; in The Sterling Hotel. 1300 H St 95814. **Hours:** 11:30 am-2 & 5:30-9 pm, Sat from 5:30 pm, Sun 9 am-2 & 5:30-9 pm. Closed major holidays. **Reservations:** suggested. **Features:** Varied menu with California French cuisine. Dressy casual; cocktails. **Parking:** on-site. **Cards:** AX, MC, VI.

FAT CITY BAR & CAFE' — **Lunch:** $8-$14 **Dinner:** $9-$20 **Phone:** 916/446-6768 (4)

American

Location: In Old Sacramento historic area. 1001 Front St 95814. **Hours:** 11:30 am-2:30 & 4-10 pm, Fri-11 pm, Sat 10:30 am-2:30 & 5-11 pm, Sun 10:30 am-2:30 & 5-10 pm. Closed: 11/25, 12/25. **Features:** Turn-of-the-century cafe. Casual dress; cocktails. **Parking:** on-site (fee). **Cards:** AX, MC, VI.

THE FIREHOUSE — **Lunch:** $9-$16 **Dinner:** $17-$49 **Phone:** 916/442-4772 (8)

Continental

Location: In Old Sacramento historic area. 1112 2nd St 95814. **Hours:** 11:30 am-2:15 & 5:30-10 pm, Sat from 5:30 pm. Closed major holidays; also Sun. **Reservations:** suggested. **Features:** In the former quarters of Sacramento Fire Company, the restaurant displays period decor. Dressy casual; cocktails. **Parking:** on-site (fee). **Cards:** AX, MC, VI.

PILOTHOUSE RESTAURANT — **Lunch:** $8-$14 **Dinner:** $13-$25 **Phone:** 916/441-4440 (5)

Continental

Location: I-5, exit J St (Old Sacramento); in Delta King Hotel. 1000 Front St 95814. **Hours:** 11:30 am-2 & 5-10 pm, Sun from 10 am. **Reservations:** suggested. **Features:** Turn-of-the-century decor. Casual dress; cocktails. **Parking:** on-site. **Cards:** AX, DC, DS, MC, VI.

The following restaurants have not been evaluated by AAA but are listed for your information only.

ENOTRIA CAFE & WINE BAR — **Phone:** 916/922-6792

fyi

Not evaluated. **Location:** At Arden Way. 1431 Del Paso Blvd 95815. **Features:** Near the Iceland Skating Rink, this cafe offers many wine dinners and a great place to relax.

LA TRATTORIA BOHEMIA — **Phone:** 916/455-7803

fyi

Not evaluated. **Location:** 3649 J St 95816. **Features:** A little slice of Europe in East Sacramento. Feast on Czechoslovakian specialties and Italian delights. A plus is that the entire menu can be ordered "to go".

ST. HELENA

—See Wine Country p. 799.

SALIDA

WHERE TO STAY

FAIRFIELD INN & SUITES BY MARRIOTT *Book at aaa.com* **Phone:** (209)543-7800

Motel

6/1-9/30 [ECP]	1P: $89-$109	2P: $89-$109	XP: $10	F17
2/1-5/31 & 10/1-1/31 [ECP]	1P: $79-$99	2P: $79-$99	XP: $10	F17

Location: SR 99, exit Pelandale, just w, then just n. 4342 Salida Blvd 95368. Fax: 209/543-1250. **Facility:** 68 units. 67 one-bedroom standard units, some with whirlpools. 1 one-bedroom suite with whirlpool. 2 stories, interior corridors. *Bath:* combo or shower only. **Parking:** on-site. **Terms:** cancellation fee imposed. **Amenities:** high-speed Internet, dual phone lines, voice mail, irons, hair dryers. **Pool(s):** outdoor. **Leisure Activities:** sauna, whirlpool, exercise room. **Guest Services:** coin laundry. **Business Services:** meeting rooms. **Cards:** AX, CB, DC, DS, JC, MC, VI. ***(See color ad p 432)***

SOME UNITS

HAMPTON INN & SUITES *Book at aaa.com* **Phone:** (209)543-3650

AAA SAVE

Motel

All Year [ECP]	1P: $85-$120	2P: $90-$125	XP: $5	F

Location: SR 99, exit SR 219, just e. 4921 Sisk Rd 95368. Fax: 209/543-3655. **Facility:** 70 one-bedroom standard units, some with whirlpools. 3 stories, interior corridors. **Parking:** on-site. **Terms:** package plans - weekends. **Amenities:** high-speed Internet, dual phone lines, voice mail, irons, hair dryers. **Pool(s):** heated outdoor. **Leisure Activities:** exercise room. **Guest Services:** valet and coin laundry. **Business Services:** meeting rooms, business center. **Cards:** AX, CB, DC, DS, JC, MC, VI. **Special Amenities: free expanded continental breakfast and free local telephone calls.**

SOME UNITS

SALINAS pop. 151,060

WHERE TO STAY

BEST WESTERN JOHN JAY INN *Book at aaa.com* **Phone:** (831)784-0176

AAA SAVE

Small-scale Hotel

5/1-10/31 [ECP]	1P: $76-$130	2P: $82-$155	XP: $8	F12
2/1-4/30 & 11/1-1/31 [ECP]	1P: $72-$120	2P: $79-$145	XP: $8	F12

Location: US 101, exit Market St, just n. 175 Kern St 93905. Fax: 831/772-0292. **Facility:** 58 one-bedroom standard units. 3 stories, interior/exterior corridors. *Bath:* combo or shower only. **Parking:** on-site. **Terms:** 7 day cancellation notice. **Amenities:** irons, hair dryers. **Pool(s):** outdoor. **Leisure Activities:** sauna, whirlpool, exercise room. **Cards:** AX, CB, DC, DS, JC, MC, VI. **Special Amenities: free expanded continental breakfast and free newspaper.**

SOME UNITS

BEST WESTERN SALINAS VALLEY INN & SUITES *Book at aaa.com* **Phone:** (831)751-6411

AAA SAVE

Small-scale Hotel

5/1-10/31 [ECP]	1P: $89-$165	2P: $99-$189	XP: $8	F12
2/1-4/30 & 11/1-1/31 [ECP]	1P: $79-$150	2P: $89-$179	XP: $8	F12

Location: US 101, exit Market St, just e. 187 Kern St 93905. Fax: 831/751-6890. **Facility:** Smoke free premises. 62 units. 45 one-bedroom standard units. 17 one-bedroom suites ($105-$230), some with whirlpools. 3 stories, interior corridors. *Bath:* combo or shower only. **Parking:** on-site. **Terms:** 7 day cancellation notice. **Amenities:** dual phone lines, voice mail, irons, hair dryers. **Pool(s):** heated outdoor. **Leisure Activities:** sauna, whirlpool, exercise room. **Cards:** AX, CB, DC, DS, JC, MC, VI. **Special Amenities: free expanded continental breakfast and free newspaper.**

SOME UNITS

COMFORT INN *Book at aaa.com* **Phone:** (831)758-8850

AAA SAVE

Motel

All Year [CP]	1P: $79-$199	2P: $89-$199	XP: $8	F18

Location: US 101, exit Market St, just e. 144 Kern St 93905. Fax: 831/758-3611. **Facility:** 32 one-bedroom standard units. 3 stories, exterior corridors. **Parking:** on-site. **Terms:** 2-3 night minimum stay - weekends. **Amenities:** voice mail, hair dryers. *Some:* irons. **Cards:** AX, CB, DC, DS, JC, MC, VI. **Special Amenities: free continental breakfast and free local telephone calls.** *(See color ad p 451)*

SOME UNITS

DAYS INN *Book at aaa.com* **Phone:** 831/759-9900

AAA SAVE

Motel

All Year	1P: $68-$175	2P: $68-$175	XP: $12	F12

Location: US 101, exit Airport Blvd, just e. 1226 de la Torre St 93905. Fax: 831/759-2133. **Facility:** Smoke free premises. 32 one-bedroom standard units. 2 stories (no elevator), exterior corridors. **Parking:** on-site. **Terms:** cancellation fee imposed, [CP] meal plan available. **Amenities:** irons, hair dryers. **Cards:** AX, CB, DC, DS, JC, MC, VI. **Special Amenities: free continental breakfast.**

ECONO LODGE *Book at aaa.com* **Phone:** (831)422-5111

AAA SAVE

Motel

All Year	1P: $69-$120	2P: $79-$140	XP: $10	F18

Location: US 101, exit Sanborn Rd or Fairview Ave, just e. 180 S Sanborn Rd 93905. Fax: 831/783-0307. **Facility:** 59 one-bedroom standard units. 3 stories (no elevator), exterior corridors. *Bath:* combo or shower only. **Parking:** on-site. **Terms:** 3 day cancellation notice-fee imposed, [CP] meal plan available. **Amenities:** safes (fee). *Some:* irons, hair dryers. **Cards:** AX, DS, MC, VI. **Special Amenities: free continental breakfast and free local telephone calls.**

SOME UNITS

VCR FEE FEE

LAUREL INN

Phone: (831)449-2474

Motel

All Year 1P: $62-$140 2P: $69-$140

Location: US 101, exit Laurel Dr, just e. 801 W Laurel Dr 93906. Fax: 831/449-2476. **Facility:** 146 one-bedroom standard units. 2 stories (no elevator), exterior corridors. *Bath:* combo or shower only. **Parking:** on-site. **Terms:** 3 day cancellation notice. **Amenities:** hair dryers. **Pool(s):** outdoor. **Leisure Activities:** sauna, whirlpool. **Business Services:** meeting rooms. **Cards:** AX, CB, DC, DS, MC, VI.

SOME UNITS

QUALITY INN OF SALINAS Book at aaa.com

Phone: 831/770-1400

Small-scale Hotel

3/12-9/16 [ECP] 1P: $89-$109 2P: $109-$129

2/1-3/11 & 9/17-1/31 [ECP] 1P: $69-$89 2P: $89-$109

Location: US 101, exit Market St, just e. 181 Kern St 93905. Fax: 831/770-1600. **Facility:** 61 one-bedroom standard units. 3 stories, interior corridors. **Parking:** on-site. **Terms:** 3 day cancellation notice. **Amenities:** dual phone lines, voice mail, irons, hair dryers. **Pool(s):** heated indoor. **Leisure Activities:** exercise room. **Cards:** AX, DC, DS, JC, MC, VI.

ASK SOME UNITS

RAMADA LIMITED Book at aaa.com

Phone: (831)424-4801

SAVE

Motel

5/1-10/31 [ECP] 1P: $79-$149 2P: $89-$159 XP: $10 F16

2/1-4/30 & 11/1-1/31 [ECP] 1P: $59-$99 2P: $69-$109 XP: $10 F16

Location: US 101, exit John St, 0.7 mi w. 109 John St 93901. Fax: 831/758-1300. **Facility:** 39 one-bedroom standard units. 2 stories (no elevator), exterior corridors. *Bath:* combo or shower only. **Parking:** on-site. **Terms:** cancellation fee imposed, small pets only ($25 deposit). **Amenities:** high-speed Internet, voice mail, irons, hair dryers. **Leisure Activities:** exercise room. **Business Services:** meeting rooms. **Cards:** AX, CB, DC, DS, JC, MC, VI. **Special Amenities: free expanded continental breakfast and free local telephone calls.**

SOME UNITS

FEE

SUPER 8 MOTEL

Phone: (831)422-6486

SAVE

Motel

All Year [CP] 1P: $69-$129 2P: $79-$139 XP: $10 F18

Location: US 101, exit Sanborn Rd or Fairview Ave, just e. 1030 Fairview Ave 93905. Fax: 831/422-8712. **Facility:** 44 one-bedroom standard units. 2 stories (no elevator), exterior corridors. **Parking:** on-site. **Terms:** 3 day cancellation notice-fee imposed. **Amenities:** safes (fee). **Cards:** AX, CB, DC, DS, MC, VI. **Special Amenities: free continental breakfast and free local telephone calls.**

SOME UNITS

VAGABOND INN Book at aaa.com

Phone: (831)758-4693

SAVE

Motel

All Year 1P: $60-$160 2P: $70-$170 XP: $5 F17

Location: US 101, exit Market St, just e. 131 Kern St 93905. Fax: 831/758-9835. **Facility:** 70 one-bedroom standard units. 2 stories (no elevator), exterior corridors. **Parking:** on-site. **Terms:** pets ($10 extra charge). **Amenities:** *Some:* hair dryers. **Pool(s):** outdoor. **Cards:** AX, CB, DC, DS, MC, VI. **Special Amenities: free continental breakfast and free local telephone calls.**

SOME UNITS

FEE FEE FEE

SAN ANDREAS pop. 2,615

WHERE TO STAY

THE ROBINS NEST Book at aaa.com

Phone: (209)754-1076

Historic Bed & Breakfast

All Year [BP] 1P: $85-$125 2P: $90-$150 XP: $15 D12

Location: SR 49; north end of town. 247 W St. Charles St 95249 (PO Box 1090). Fax: 209/754-3975. **Facility:** This 1895 Queen Anne Victorian features attractively landscaped gardens. 9 one-bedroom standard units. 2 stories (no elevator), interior corridors. *Bath:* combo or shower only. **Parking:** on-site. **Terms:** 7 day cancellation notice, weekly rates available, pets (with prior approval). **Amenities:** hair dryers. *Some:* DVD players. **Leisure Activities:** whirlpool, limited exercise equipment. **Guest Services:** complimentary evening beverages, complimentary laundry. **Cards:** AX, DS, MC, VI.

ASK SOME UNITS

SAN BRUNO —See San Francisco p. 674.

SAN CARLOS —See San Francisco p. 675.

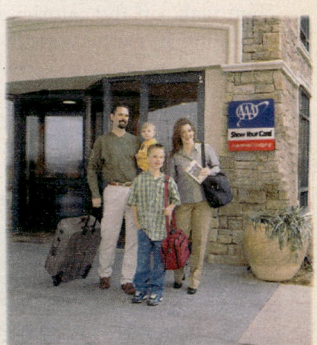

Destination San Francisco

pop. 776,733

Spectacular views are commonplace in San Francisco, as are marvelous accommodations and superb restaurants.

Hop on a cable car and have lunch or an early dinner in one of the multitude of eateries in Chinatown. Then walk off the calories while indulging in exotic window-shopping. *This* is a San Francisco treat.

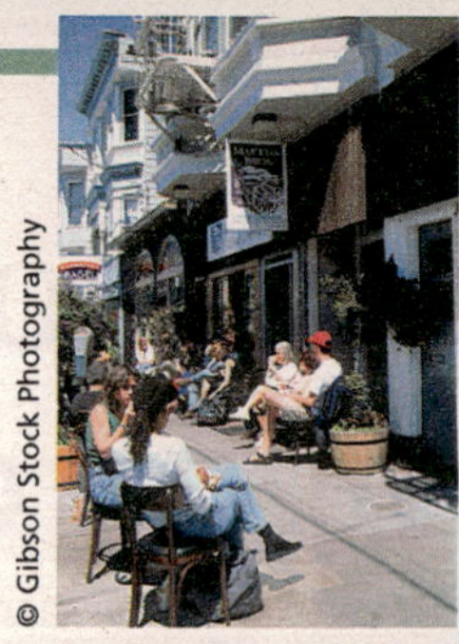

© Gibson Stock Photography

San Francisco neighborhoods.
The city's many distinctive neighborhoods retain their own personality and architecture.

© Gibson Stock Photography

Volleyball game, San Francisco.
The expansive grounds of Golden Gate Park provide the setting for many recreational pursuits. (See listing page 141)

© Gibson Stock Photography

Farmers market, San Francisco.
Stalls with the best fresh produce the Bay area has to offer tempt shoppers at the Ferry Plaza Farmers Market each Saturday morning.

Places included in this AAA Destination City:

Boating in San Francisco Bay. Both fishing and whale-watching excursions are popular pastimes in San Francisco Bay.

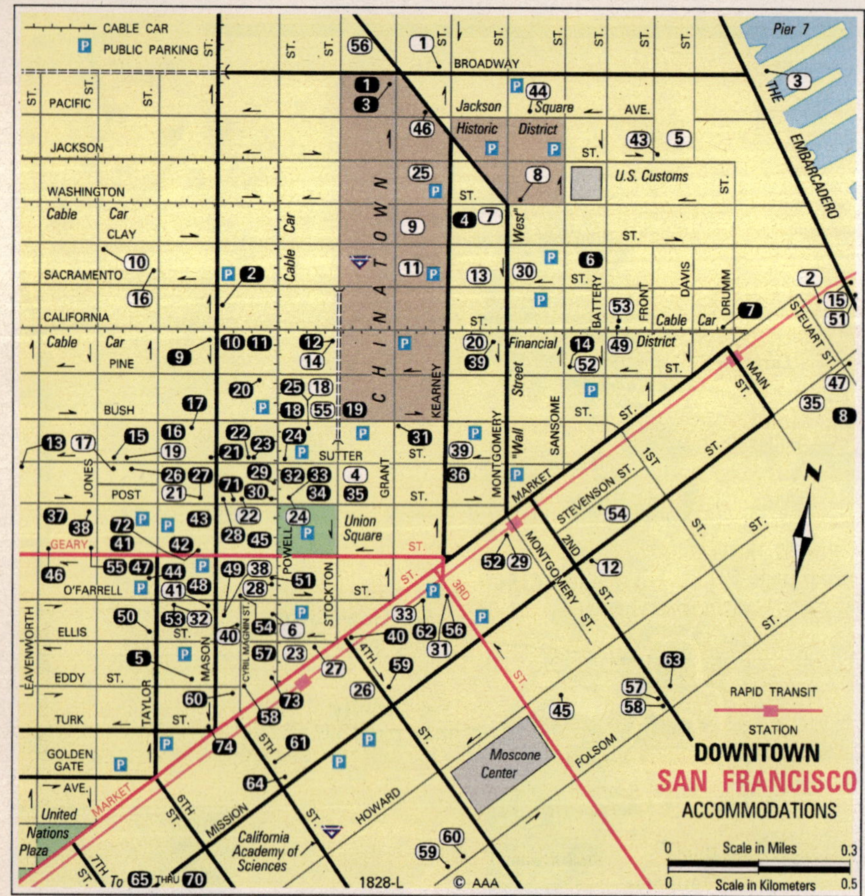

Downtown San Francisco

This index helps you "spot" where approved accommodations and restaurants are located on the corresponding detailed maps. Lodging rate ranges are for comparison only and show the property's high season; rates are per night, unless only weekly (W) rates are available. Restaurant rate range is for dinner, unless only lunch (L) is served. Turn to the listing page for more detailed rate information and consult display ads for special promotions.

Spotter/Map Page Number	OA	**SAN FRANCISCO** - Lodgings	Diamond Rating	Rate Range High Season	Listing Page
1 / above	AAA	**Royal Pacific Motor Inn** - see color ad p 642		$106 SAVE	643
2 / above		The Fairmont San Francisco		$189-$289	621
3 / above	AAA	**SW Hotel**		$119-$149 SAVE	645
4 / above	AAA	**Holiday Inn Select & Spa Downtown** - see color ad p 619		$119-$279 SAVE	625
5 / above		Hotel Bijou - see color ad p 617		$125-$145	626
6 / above	AAA	**Park Hyatt Hotel** - see color ad p 635		$155-$295 SAVE	636
7 / above	AAA	**Hyatt Regency-San Francisco** - see color ad p 623		$89-$240 SAVE	629
8 / above	AAA	**Harbor Court Hotel**		$120-$235 SAVE	624
9 / below		Huntington Hotel		$295-$1130	628

Spotter/Map Page Number	OA	SAN FRANCISCO - Lodgings (continued)	Diamond Rating	Rate Range High Season	Listing Page
10 / p. 590	AAA	**Mark Hopkins Inter-Continental**	◆◆◆◆	$395-$525 SAVE	631
11 / p. 590	AAA	**Renaissance Stanford Court Hotel**	◆◆◆◆	$199-$459 SAVE	642
12 / p. 590	AAA	**The Ritz-Carlton, San Francisco**	◆◆◆◆◆	$319	642
13 / p. 590		York Hotel	◆◆◆	Failed to provide	648
14 / p. 590		Mandarin Oriental, San Francisco	◆◆◆◆	$490-$745	630
15 / p. 590	AAA	**Best Western Canterbury Hotel** - see color ad p 610	◆◆◆	$99-$295 SAVE	610
16 / p. 590		Petite Auberge	◆◆◆	$135-$245	636
17 / p. 590		White Swan Inn	◆◆◆	$180-$285	648
18 / p. 590	AAA	**Executive Hotel Vintage Court**	◆◆◆	$109-$179 SAVE	620
19 / p. 590	AAA	**Hotel Juliana**	◆◆◆	$189-$219 SAVE	627
20 / p. 590		Nob Hill Lambourne	◆◆◆	$189-$249	633
21 / p. 590	AAA	**Hotel Beresford** - see color ad p 626	◆◆	$92-$119 SAVE	626
22 / p. 590		Hotel Rex	◆◆◆	$205-$245	628
23 / p. 590		Cartwright Hotel	◆◆	$99-$139	613
24 / p. 590	AAA	**Crowne Plaza Union Square** - see color ad p 619	◆◆◆	$139-$309 SAVE	618
25 / p. 590	AAA	**The Orchard Hotel**	◆◆◆	$159-$269 SAVE	634
26 / p. 590	AAA	**The Commodore Hotel** - see color ad p 617	◆◆	$89-$275 SAVE	617
27 / p. 590		The Pan Pacific Hotel	◆◆◆◆	$265-$365	635
28 / p. 590	AAA	**Maxwell Hotel**	◆◆◆	$145-$175 SAVE	632
29 / p. 590	AAA	**Chancellor Hotel on Union Square** - see color ad p 614	◆◆◆	$148-$175 SAVE	615
30 / p. 590	AAA	**Inn @ Union Square**	◆◆◆	$143-$199 SAVE	630
31 / p. 590	AAA	**Hotel Triton** - see color ad p 628	◆◆◆	$139-$199 SAVE	628
32 / p. 590	AAA	**Sir Francis Drake Hotel** - see color ad p 645	◆◆◆	$169-$239 SAVE	644
33 / p. 590	AAA	**The Prescott Hotel** - see color ad p 636	◆◆◆◆	$275-$1200 SAVE	637
34 / p. 590	AAA	**Grand Hyatt San Francisco** - see color ad p 623	◆◆◆◆	$159-$319 SAVE	622
35 / p. 590		Campton Place Hotel	◆◆◆◆	$335-$470	613
36 / p. 590	AAA	**Galleria Park Hotel**	◆◆◆	$119-$235 SAVE	622
37 / p. 590	AAA	**Clarion Hotel Cosmo**	◆◆	$89-$159 SAVE	615
38 / p. 590	AAA	**Beresford Arms** - see color ad p 608	◆◆◆	$109-$129 SAVE	608
39 / p. 590		Omni San Francisco Hotel	◆◆◆◆	$159-$299	633
40 / p. 590	AAA	**Hotel Palomar**	◆◆◆◆	$169-$349 SAVE	627
41 / p. 590	AAA	**Hotel Adagio**	◆◆◆	$189-$695 SAVE	626
42 / p. 590	AAA	**Warwick Regis Hotel** - see color ad p 607	◆◆◆	$169-$249 SAVE	646
43 / p. 590		The Donatello	◆◆◆	$199-$295	620
44 / p. 590	AAA	**Serrano Hotel**	◆◆◆	$139-$219 SAVE	643
45 / p. 590	AAA	**The Westin St. Francis**	◆◆◆◆	$129-$569 SAVE	647
46 / p. 590		Savoy Hotel - see color ad p 617	◆◆◆	$89-$159	643
47 / p. 590	AAA	**Hotel Monaco**	◆◆◆◆	$170-$359 SAVE	627
48 / p. 590	AAA	**King George Hotel** - see color ad p 631	◆◆◆	$109-$195 SAVE	630

Spotter/Map Page Number	OA	**SAN FRANCISCO** - Lodgings (continued)	Diamond Rating	Rate Range High Season	Listing Page
49 / p. 590	AAA	**Hotel Nikko**	◆◆◆◆	$175 SAVE	627
50 / p. 590	AAA	**Ramada Mark Twain-Union Square**	◆◆◆	$140-$180 SAVE	639
51 / p. 590	AAA	**Villa Florence Hotel**	◆◆◆	$139-$209 SAVE	646
52 / p. 590		Palace Hotel	◆◆◆◆	$550-$650	635
53 / p. 590		Hilton San Francisco	◆◆◆◆	$139-$269	624
54 / p. 590	AAA	**The Handlery Union Square Hotel** - **see color ad p 624**	◆◆◆	$189-$299 SAVE	624
55 / p. 590	AAA	**Quality Inn Union Square** - **see color ad p 637**	◆◆	$79-$169 SAVE	637
56 / p. 590	AAA	**The Argent Hotel** - **see color ad p 607**	◆◆◆◆	$349 SAVE	605
57 / p. 590	AAA	**Monticello Inn**	◆◆◆	$129-$199 SAVE	632
58 / p. 590		The Powell Hotel	◆◆	$94-$164	636
59 / p. 590		San Francisco Marriott	◆◆◆◆	Failed to provide	643
60 / p. 590		Renaissance Parc 55 Hotel - see color ad p 641	◆◆◆◆	$159-$269	640
61 / p. 590	AAA	**Hotel Milano**	◆◆◆	$139-$219 SAVE	627
62 / p. 590		Four Seasons San Francisco	◆◆◆◆	$469-$600	622
63 / p. 590		San Francisco Downtown Courtyard	◆◆◆	$199-$259	643
64 / p. 590		The Pickwick Hotel	◆◆	$59-$99	636
65 / p. 590	AAA	**Best Western Americania** - **see color ad p 609**	◆◆◆	$139-$189 SAVE	608
67 / p. 590	AAA	**Best Western Carriage Inn** - **see color ad p 609**	◆◆◆	$149-$199 SAVE	610
68 / p. 590	AAA	**Best Western Flamingo Inn** - **see color ad p 609**	◆◆	$99-$129 SAVE	611
70 / p. 590	AAA	**Britton Hotel** - **see color ad p 609**	◆◆	$119-$159 SAVE	612
71 / p. 590		Kensington Park Hotel	◆◆	$125-$159	630
72 / p. 590		Diva Hotel	◆◆◆	$145-$205	620
73 / p. 590		Hotel Union Square	◆◆◆	$95-$165	628
74 / p. 590		Hotel Metropolis	◆◆	Failed to provide	627
		SAN FRANCISCO - Restaurants			
1 / p. 590		Enrico's	◆◆	$12-$26	652
2 / p. 590		One Market Restaurant	◆◆◆	$21-$30	655
3 / p. 590		The Waterfront Restaurant	◆◆◆	$14-$39	658
4 / p. 590		Campton Place Restaurant	◆◆◆◆	$29-$39	650
5 / p. 590	AAA	**L'Olivier Restaurant**	◆◆◆	$15-$22	654
6 / p. 590		Millennium Restaurant	◆◆◆	$12-$20	655
7 / p. 590		Tommy Toy's Haute Cusine	◆◆◆	$15-$35	658
8 / p. 590		Elisabeth Daniel	◆◆◆◆	$25-$38	651
9 / p. 590		Empress of China	◆◆	$31-$50	651
10 / p. 590		Charles Nob Hill	◆◆◆◆	$27-$45	650
11 / p. 590		Kan's	◆◆	$15-$30	654
12 / p. 590		Roy's	◆◆◆◆	$28-$39	657
13 / p. 590		Palio D'Asti	◆◆◆	$16-$25	656
14 / p. 590	AAA	**The Dining Room**	◆◆◆◆◆	$67-$82	651

Spotter/Map Page Number	OA	SAN FRANCISCO - Restaurants (continued)	Diamond Rating	Rate Range High Season	Listing Page
15 / p. 590		Sinbad's Pier II	◆◆	$18-$29	658
16 / p. 590		Nob Hill Cafe	◆◆	$8-$15	655
17 / p. 590		Fleur de Lys	◆◆◆◆	$65-$85	652
18 / p. 590		Solea Restaurant	◆◆◆	$16-$26	658
19 / p. 590		Lehr's Greenhouse	◆◆	$12-$28	654
20 / p. 590		Carnelian Room	◆◆◆	$28-$65	650
21 / p. 590		Pacific	◆◆◆◆	$25-$38	656
22 / p. 590		Farallon	◆◆◆	$25-$33	652
23 / p. 590	AAA	**John's Grill**	◆◆	$17-$27	653
24 / p. 590		Postrio	◆◆◆	$26-$36	657
25 / p. 590		Pearl City	◆◆	$8-$20	656
26 / p. 590		Fifth Floor	◆◆◆◆	$18-$43	652
27 / p. 590	AAA	**Puccini & Pinetti**	◆◆	$12-$25(L)	657
28 / p. 590	AAA	**Kuleto's**	◆◆◆	$7-$23	654
29 / p. 590		The Garden Court	◆◆◆	$14-$20(L)	652
30 / p. 590		Rubicon	◆◆◆	$17-$30	657
31 / p. 590		Jester's Restaurant	◆◆◆	$14-$20	653
32 / p. 590		Cityscape Bar & Restaurant	◆◆◆	$18-$36	651
33 / p. 590		Seasons Restaurant	◆◆◆◆	$15-$40	657
35 / p. 590		The Cosmopolitan Cafe	◆◆◆	$17-$28	651
38 / p. 590		Anzu Restaurant	◆◆◆	$25-$45	649
39 / p. 590		Cafe Metropol	◆◆	$10-$17	650
40 / p. 590		First Crush Restaurant Wine Bar & Lounge	◆◆	$13-$19	652
41 / p. 590		Lori's Diner	◆	$10-$13	654
43 / p. 590		MacArthur Park	◆◆	$9-$28	654
44 / p. 590		mc2	◆◆◆	$10-$21	655
45 / p. 590		Hawthorne Lane	◆◆◆◆	$21-$29	653
46 / p. 590		Brandy Ho's Hunan Food	◆◆	$8-$12	650
47 / p. 590		Boulevard	◆◆◆	$26-$33	650
49 / p. 590		Aqua Restaurant	◆◆◆	$41-$80	649
51 / p. 590		Shanghai 1930	◆◆◆	$13-$18	657
52 / p. 590		Silks	◆◆◆◆	$26-$36	658
53 / p. 590		Tadich Grill	◆◆	$12-$19	658
54 / p. 590		Yank Sing	◆◆	$4-$12(L)	658
55 / p. 590		Masa's	◆◆◆◆	$65-$109	654
56 / p. 590		The Stinking Rose	◆◆	$12-$25	658
57 / p. 590		Maya Restaurant	◆◆◆	$19-$26	655
58 / p. 590		Fly Trap	◆◆◆	$16-$26	652
59 / p. 590		Azie	◆◆◆	$15-$25	649
60 / p. 590		Restaurant Lulu	◆◆	$12-$27	657

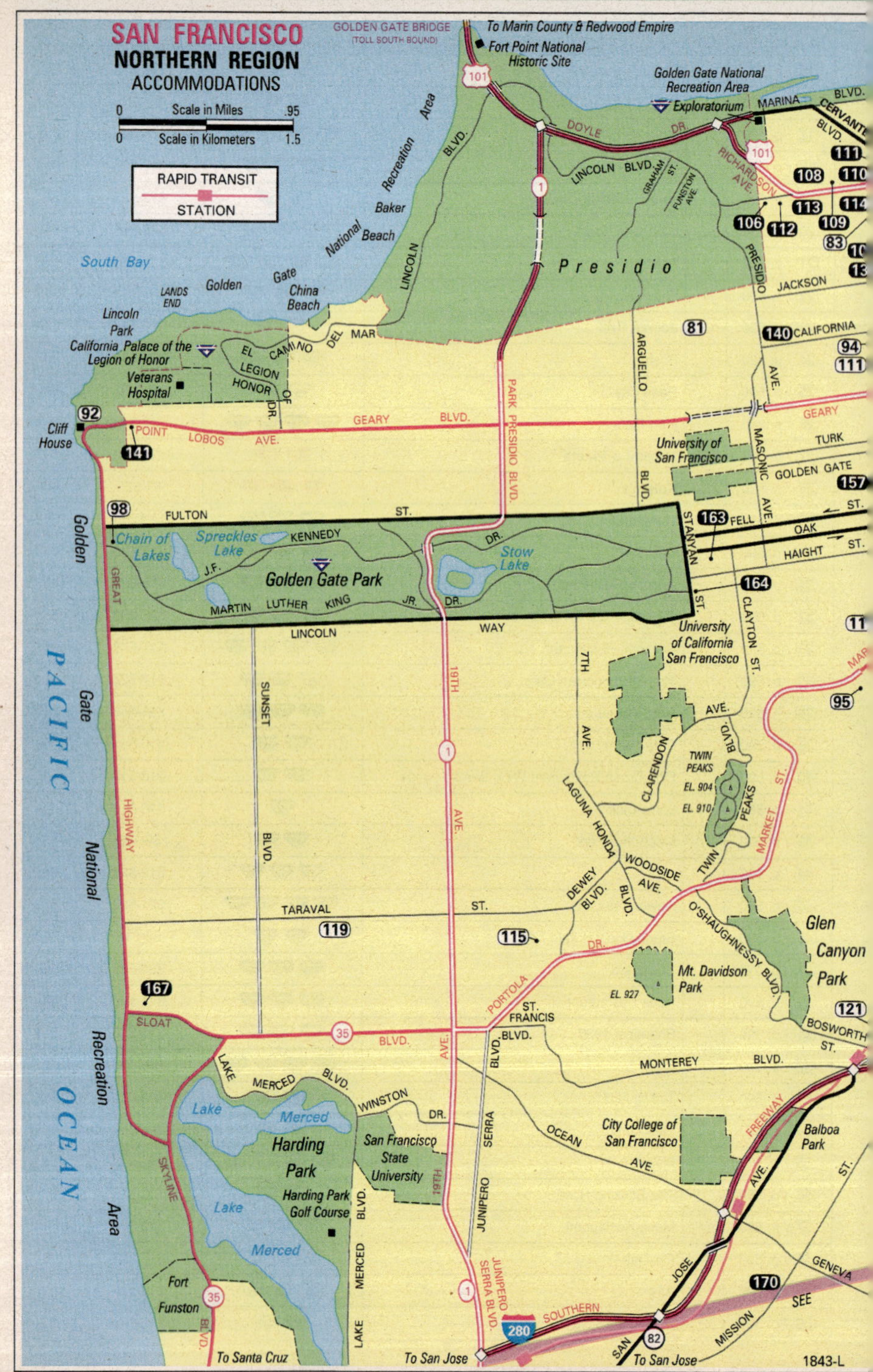
SAN FRANCISCO
NORTHERN REGION
ACCOMMODATIONS
Scale in Miles
Scale in Kilometers
RAPID TRANSIT
STATION
GOLDEN GATE BRIDGE (TOLL SOUTH BOUND)
To Marin County & Redwood Empire
Fort Point National Historic Site
Golden Gate National Recreation Area
Exploratorium
Presidio
South Bay
Lands End
Golden Gate National Recreation Area
Baker Beach
China Beach
Lincoln Park
California Palace of the Legion of Honor
Veterans Hospital
Cliff House
University of San Francisco
Golden Gate Park
Chain of Lakes
Spreckles Lake
Stow Lake
University of California San Francisco
Twin Peaks
Glen Canyon Park
Mt. Davidson Park
Lake Merced
Harding Park
Harding Park Golf Course
San Francisco State University
City College of San Francisco
Balboa Park
Fort Funston
PACIFIC OCEAN
To Santa Cruz
To San Jose
To San Jose
1843-L

To Treasure Island
To Oakland & East Bay Cities
YERBA BUENA ISLAND
U.S. Coast Guard Reservation
SEE DOWNTOWN ACCOMMODATIONS MAP
SAN FRANCISCO- OAKLAND BAY BRIDGE (TOLL WEST BOUND)
San Francisco Bay
Pacific Bell Park
China Basin
Central Basin
Indian Basin
South Basin
San Francisco Bay Naval Shipyard
SOUTHERN REGION ACCOMMODATIONS MAP
SAN FRANCISCO
Mc Laren Park
San Francisco Stadium at Candlestick Point
Bay View Park
To San Francisco International Airport & San Jose
Mission San Francisco de Asis
San Francisco General Hospital
Civic Center
© AAA

San Francisco Northern Region

This index helps you "spot" where approved accommodations and restaurants are located on the corresponding detailed maps. Lodging rate ranges are for comparison only and show the property's high season; rates are per night, unless only weekly (W) rates are available. Restaurant rate range is for dinner, unless only lunch (L) is served. Turn to the listing page for more detailed rate information and consult display ads for special promotions.

Spotter/Map Page Number	OA	**SAN FRANCISCO** - Lodgings	Diamond Rating	Rate Range High Season	Listing Page
100 / p. 594		Courtyard By Marriott at Fisherman's Wharf	◆◆◆	$129-$199	618
101 / p. 594	AAA	**Radisson Hotel Fisherman's Wharf** - see color ad p 638, p 629	◆◆◆	$149-$189 SAVE	638
104 / p. 594	AAA	**Greenwich Inn**	◆◆	$80-$135 SAVE	623
105 / p. 594	AAA	**The Wharf Inn** - see color ad p 647, p 521	◆◆	$139-$185 SAVE	648
106 / p. 594	AAA	**Best Inn**	◆◆	$85-$95 SAVE	608
107 / p. 594		Lombard Plaza Motel	◆	Failed to provide	630
108 / p. 594	AAA	**Super 8 Motel**	◆◆	$59-$170 SAVE	645
109 / p. 594		Days Inn Lombard	◆◆	$85-$175	620
110 / p. 594	AAA	**Cow Hollow Motor Inn & Suites** - see color ad p 616, p 618	◆◆◆	$86-$125 SAVE	618
111 / p. 594	AAA	**Ramada Limited-Golden Gate**	◆◆	$99-$145 SAVE	639
112 / p. 594	AAA	**Presidio Inn & Suites** - see color ad p 637	◆◆	$89-$159 SAVE	637
113 / p. 594	AAA	**Pacific Motor Inn**	◆◆	$72-$172 SAVE	635
114 / p. 594	AAA	**Chelsea Motor Inn** - see color ad p 616	◆◆◆	$86-$125 SAVE	615
115 / p. 594	AAA	**Coventry Motor Inn** - see color ad p 616	◆◆◆	$86-$125 SAVE	618
116 / p. 594	AAA	**Star Motel** - see color ad p 606	◆◆	$99-$129 SAVE	645
117 / p. 594	AAA	**Buena Vista Motor Inn** - see color ad p 606	◆◆◆	$79-$139 SAVE	612
118 / p. 594	AAA	**Redwood Inn** - see color ad p 641	◆◆	$90-$150 SAVE	640
119 / p. 594		Marina Inn	◆◆	$85-$135	630
120 / p. 594	AAA	**Francisco Bay Inn** - see color ad p 622	◆◆	$85-$145 SAVE	622
121 / p. 594	AAA	**Lombard Motor Inn** - see color ad p 616	◆◆◆	$86-$125 SAVE	630
122 / p. 594	AAA	**Comfort Inn by the Bay** - see color ad p 605	◆◆	$115-$195 SAVE	617
123 / p. 594	AAA	**Travelodge By The Bay** - see color ad p 645	◆◆	$99-$119 SAVE	646
124 / p. 594	AAA	**Holiday Inn Express & Suites at Fishermans Wharf** - see color ad p 260, p 619	◆◆◆	$124-$299 SAVE	625
125 / p. 594	AAA	**Holiday Inn Fisherman's Wharf** - see color ad p 619	◆◆◆	$129-$299 SAVE	625
126 / p. 594	AAA	**Hyatt Fisherman's Wharf** - see color ad p 623	◆◆◆	$109-$269 SAVE	628
127 / p. 594	AAA	**Sheraton at Fisherman's Wharf** - see color ad p 644	◆◆◆◆	$159-$229 SAVE	644
128 / p. 594	AAA	**Best Western Tuscan Inn at Fisherman's Wharf** - see ad p 611	◆◆◆	$189-$269 SAVE	611
129 / p. 594	AAA	**Hilton San Francisco Fisherman's Wharf**	◆◆◆	$179-$289 SAVE	624
130 / p. 594		The Sherman House	◆◆◆	$300-$600	644
131 / p. 594		Hotel Del Sol - see color ad p 617	◆◆	$135-$185	627
132 / p. 594	AAA	**Capri Motel**	◆	$70-$80 SAVE	613
133 / p. 594	AAA	**Pacific Heights Inn** - see color ad p 634	◆◆	$95-$150 SAVE	635
135 / p. 594		San Francisco Marriott Fisherman's Wharf	◆◆◆	$169-$239	643
136 / p. 594	AAA	**Columbus Motor Inn** - see color ad p 615	◆◆◆	$90-$135 SAVE	615
137 / p. 594	AAA	**Broadway Manor Inn** - see color ad p 612	◆	$59-$99 SAVE	612

Spotter/Map Page Number	OA	**SAN FRANCISCO** - Lodgings (continued)	Diamond Rating	Rate Range High Season	Listing Page
138 / p. 594	AAA	**Castle Inn** - see color ad p 613	◆◆	$85-$165 SAVE	614
139 / p. 594	AAA	**Nob Hill Motor Inn** - see color ad p 633	◆◆◆	$85-$145 SAVE	633
140 / p. 594	AAA	**The Laurel Inn**	◆◆◆	$150-$185 SAVE	630
141 / p. 594	AAA	**Seal Rock Inn**	◆◆	$115-$153 SAVE	643
142 / p. 594	AAA	**Best Western Miyako Inn** - see ad p 611	◆◆	$89-$119 SAVE	611
143 / p. 594	AAA	**Best Inn Fishermans Wharf**	◆◆	$89-$149 SAVE	608
144 / p. 594	AAA	**Radisson Miyako Hotel** - see color ad p 639, p 629	◆◆◆	$159-$219 SAVE	638
145 / p. 594		Richelieu Hotel	◆◆◆	$139-$179	642
146 / p. 594		Cathedral Hill Hotel - see color ad p 614	◆◆◆	$169	614
147 / p. 594	AAA	**Holiday Inn Golden Gateway Nob Hill (Area)** - see color ad p 625	◆◆◆	$129-$179 SAVE	625
148 / p. 594	AAA	**Carlton Hotel** - see color ad p 617	◆◆	$79-$260 SAVE	613
149 / p. 594		Nob Hill Hotel	◆◆◆	$79-$185	633
150 / p. 594	AAA	**The Monarch Hotel**	◆◆	$74-$139 SAVE	632
151 / p. 594		Queen Anne Hotel	◆◆◆	$139-$199	637
152 / p. 594	AAA	**Days Inn-Geary** - see color ad p 620	◆◆	$80-$120 SAVE	620
154 / p. 594		Oasis Inn - see color ad p 634	◆◆	$89-$99	633
155 / p. 594		The Phoenix Hotel - see color ad p 617	◆◆	$120-$180	636
156 / p. 594		Inn at the Opera	◆◆◆	$165	629
157 / p. 594		The Archbishop's Mansion	◆◆◆	$195-$425	605
158 / p. 594	AAA	**Days Inn-Civic Center** - see color ad p 619	◆◆	$95-$149 SAVE	619
160 / p. 594	AAA	**Ramada Plaza Hotel Downtown** - see color ad p 640	◆◆	$89-$179 SAVE	640
161 / p. 594	AAA	**Holiday Inn Civic Center** - see color ad p 619	◆◆◆	$94-$229 SAVE	625
162 / p. 594	AAA	**Ramada Limited Downtown** - see color ad p 639	◆◆	$89-$179 SAVE	638
163 / p. 594		Inn 1890	◆◆◆	$79-$129	629
164 / p. 594	AAA	**Stanyan Park Hotel**	◆◆◆	$135-$190 SAVE	645
165 / p. 594	AAA	**Best Western Civic Center Motor Inn** - see color ad p 610	◆◆	$109-$149 SAVE	610
166 / p. 594	AAA	**Beck's Motor Lodge** - see color ad p 607	◆◆	$109-$159 SAVE	605
167 / p. 594	AAA	**Days Inn at The Beach**	◆◆	$90-$125 SAVE	618
170 / p. 594	AAA	**Mission Inn** - see color ad p 632	◆◆	$75-$110 SAVE	632
		SAN FRANCISCO - Restaurants			
61 / p. 594	AAA	**Pompei's Grotto**	◆◆	$9-$24	656
63 / p. 594		McCormick & Kuleto's Seafood Restaurant	◆◆◆	$25-$50	655
65 / p. 594	AAA	**Scoma's Restaurant**	◆◆◆	$12-$55	657
66 / p. 594	AAA	**Alioto's**	◆◆	$12-$47	649
67 / p. 594		Dante's	◆◆	$17-$24	651
68 / p. 594		Lolli's Castagnola	◆◆	$12-$40	654
69 / p. 594		Chic's Seafood	◆◆	$9-$34	651
71 / p. 594		Pier Market Seafood Restaurant	◆◆	$8-$23	656
72 / p. 594		Ana Mandara	◆◆◆	$15-$28	649
73 / p. 594	AAA	**Julius' Castle**	◆◆◆	$18-$36	653

Spotter/Map Page Number	OA	SAN FRANCISCO - Restaurants (continued)	Diamond Rating	Rate Range High Season	Listing Page
74 / p. 594		Gary Danko		$55-$74	652
75 / p. 594		Pasta Pomodoro		$6-$11	656
77 / p. 594		Moose's		$11-$32	655
78 / p. 594		Rose Pistola		$13-$29	657
79 / p. 594		L'Osteria del Forno		$8-$12	654
80 / p. 594		Pasta Pomodoro-Cow Hollow		$6-$10	656
81 / p. 594		Pasta Pomodoro-Laurel Village		$6-$10	656
82 / p. 594		Golden Turtle		$12-$25	652
83 / p. 594		Night Monkey		$10-$24	655
84 / p. 594		Harris'		$17-$38	652
85 / p. 594		Figaro		$9-$17	652
86 / p. 594		Betelnut		$6-$20	650
87 / p. 594		La Folie		$25-$50	654
89 / p. 594		Hyde Street Seafood House and Raw Bar		$10-$20	653
90 / p. 594		Acquerello		$29-$32	649
91 / p. 594		House of Prime Rib		$22-$29	653
92 / p. 594		**The Cliff House**		$16-$25	651
93 / p. 594		Venture Frogs		$7-$18	658
94 / p. 594		Julia		$17-$26	653
95 / p. 594		Pasta Pomodoro-Noe Valley		$6-$10	656
96 / p. 594		Maharani		$8-$25	654
97 / p. 594		Suppenkuche		$15	658
98 / p. 594		Beach Chalet Brewery and Restaurant		$12-$18	650
99 / p. 594		The Slanted Door		$9-$27	658
100 / p. 594		Jardiniere		$24-$35	653
103 / p. 594		Hayes Street Grill		$17-$28	653
104 / p. 594		Bacar Restaurant		$41-$75	649
106 / p. 594		MoMo's		$10-$28	655
107 / p. 594		Acme Chophouse		$17-$45	649
108 / p. 594		Zuni Cafe		$10-$30	659
110 / p. 594		Pasta Pomodoro-Castro		$6-$10	656
111 / p. 594		Pasta Pomodoro-Kabuki		$6-$10	656
112 / p. 594		Home		$7-$13	653
113 / p. 594		Mecca		$16-$29	655
115 / p. 594		Pasta Pomodoro-Sunset		$6-$10	656
116 / p. 594		Chez Spencer		$19-$29	651
117 / p. 594		Delfina		$13-$19	651
118 / p. 594		Chez Papa Bistro		$16-$24	650
119 / p. 594		**Rick's Restaurant & Bar**		$13-$20	657
121 / p. 594		Chenery Park		$9-$20	650

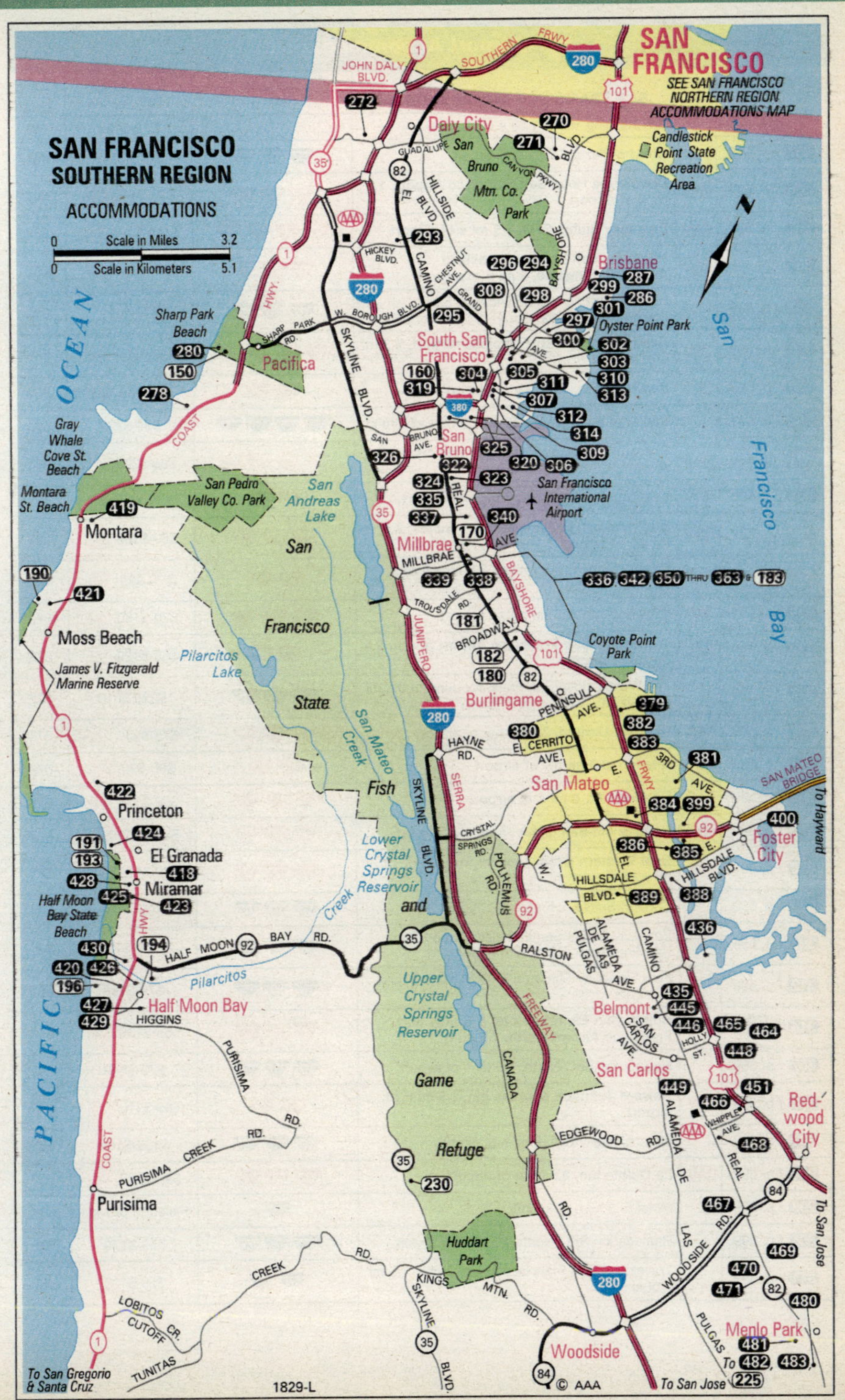
SAN FRANCISCO
SOUTHERN REGION
ACCOMMODATIONS
Scale in Miles
Scale in Kilometers
SAN FRANCISCO
SEE SAN FRANCISCO NORTHERN REGION ACCOMMODATIONS MAP
Candlestick Point State Recreation Area
Daly City
San Bruno Mtn. Co. Park
Brisbane
Oyster Point Park
South San Francisco
Pacifica
Sharp Park Beach
Gray Whale Cove St. Beach
Montara St. Beach
Montara
San Pedro Valley Co. Park
San Andreas Lake
San Bruno
San Francisco International Airport
Millbrae
Moss Beach
James V. Fitzgerald Marine Reserve
Pilarcitos Lake
San Francisco State Fish and Game Refuge
Coyote Point Park
Burlingame
San Mateo
SAN MATEO BRIDGE
To Hayward
Foster City
Lower Crystal Springs Reservoir
Upper Crystal Springs Reservoir
Princeton
El Granada
Miramar
Half Moon Bay State Beach
Half Moon Bay
Belmont
San Carlos
Redwood City
Huddart Park
Purisima
Woodside
Menlo Park
To San Jose
To San Gregorio & Santa Cruz
PACIFIC OCEAN
San Francisco Bay
1829-L
© AAA

Airport Accommodations

Spotter/Map Page Number	OA	SAN FRANCISCO INTERNATIONAL	Diamond Rating	Rate Range High Season	Listing Page
N/A		Bay Landing Hotel, 1 mi s of terminal		$79-$129	663
357 / p. 599		Crowne Plaza, 2.5 mi s of airport	♦♦♦	$249-$349	661
356 / p. 599	AAA	**Doubletree Hotel-San Francisco Airport, 1.3 mi s of airport**	♦♦♦	$79-$149 SAVE	661
355 / p. 599	AAA	**Embassy Suites-SFO, 1.5 mi s of airport**	♦♦♦♦	$119-$199 SAVE	662
351 / p. 599	AAA	**Hilton Garden Inn San Francisco Airport/Burlingame, 2 mi s of airport**	♦♦♦	$78-$268 SAVE	662
353 / p. 599		Holiday Inn Express Burlingame, San Francisco Intl Airport South, 2.5 mi s of airport	♦♦♦	$72-$119	662
350 / p. 599	AAA	**Hyatt Regency-San Francisco Airport, 2.5 mi s of airport**	♦♦♦♦	$99-$209 SAVE	663
360 / p. 599	AAA	**Red Roof Inn, 1.5 mi s of airport**	♦♦	$59-$89 SAVE	663
362 / p. 599		San Francisco Airport Marriott, 2 mi s of airport	♦♦♦♦	$99-$229	663
361 / p. 599	AAA	**Sheraton Gateway Hotel San Francisco Airport, 1.5 mi s of airport**	♦♦♦♦	$99-$209 SAVE	663
363 / p. 599	AAA	**Vagabond Inn-Airport, 1 mi s of airport**	♦♦	$55-$80 SAVE	663
340 / p. 599	AAA	**Best Western El Rancho Inn & Suites, 2.5 mi sw of airport**	♦♦♦	$89-$169 SAVE	669
337 / p. 599	AAA	**Comfort Inn-Airport West, 2.5 mi sw of airport**	♦♦	$79-$99 SAVE	669
335 / p. 599	AAA	**Millwood Inn, 2.5 mi sw of airport**	♦♦♦	$79-$150 SAVE	672
339 / p. 599	AAA	**Travelodge San Francisco Airport South, 2.5 mi sw of airport**	♦♦	$69-$129 SAVE	672
342 / p. 599		The Westin Hotel-San Francisco Airport, 0.5 mi s of airport	♦♦♦	$299-$319	672
322 / p. 599	AAA	**Ramada Limited, 2.5 mi nw of airport**	♦♦♦	$75-$100 SAVE	675
324 / p. 599	AAA	**Ritz Inn, 2.5 mi nw of airport**	♦♦	$60-$90 SAVE	675
383 / p. 599	AAA	**Comfort Inn, 5 mi s of airport**	♦♦♦	$59-$129 SAVE	676
382 / p. 599	AAA	**Holiday Inn-San Mateo, 5 mi s of airport**	♦♦♦	$89-$159 SAVE	677
306 / p. 599	AAA	**Best Western Grosvenor Airport Hotel, 1.5 mi n of airport**	♦♦♦	$79-$129 SAVE	681
300 / p. 599		Comfort Suites, 2.5 mi n of airport	♦♦♦	$99-$129	681
303 / p. 599		Embassy Suites San Francisco Airport-South San Francisco, 2.5 mi n of airport	♦♦♦	$109-$199	681
312 / p. 599		Four Points by Sheraton SFO North, 1.5 mi n of airport	♦♦♦	$79-$199	681
314 / p. 599	AAA	**Holiday Inn Express Hotel & Suites San Francisco Airport North, 1.5 mi n**	♦♦♦	$65-$139 SAVE	682
307 / p. 599		Holiday Inn SFO-North, 1.5 mi n of airport	♦♦♦	$79-$249	682
308 / p. 599	AAA	**Howard Johnson Express Inn, 1.5 mi n of airport**	♦♦	$59-$119 SAVE	682
301 / p. 599		Inn at Oyster Point, 2 mi n of airport	♦♦♦	$139-$189	682
304 / p. 599	AAA	**La Quinta Inn, 2.5 mi n of airport**	♦♦♦	$90-$169 SAVE	683
298 / p. 599		Motel 6, 2 mi n of airport	♦	Failed to provide	684
305 / p. 599		Ramada Inn SFO North, 1.5 mi n of airport	♦♦♦	$69-$179	685
311 / p. 599		Travelodge San Francisco Airport North, 1.5 mi n of airport	♦♦	$59-$119	685

San Francisco Southern Region

This index helps you "spot" where approved accommodations and restaurants are located on the corresponding detailed maps. Lodging rate ranges are for comparison only and show the property's high season; rates are per night, unless only weekly (W) rates are available. Restaurant rate range is for dinner, unless only lunch (L) is served. Turn to the listing page for more detailed rate information and consult display ads for special promotions.

Spotter/Map Page Number	OA	DALY CITY - Lodgings	Diamond Rating	Rate Range High Season	Listing Page
270 / p. 599	AAA	**Royal Palace Inn**	◆	$75-$85 SAVE	665
271 / p. 599	AAA	**Days Inn** - see color ad p 665	◆◆	$75-$150 SAVE	665
272 / p. 599		Hampton Inn	◆◆◆	$99-$139	665
		PACIFICA - Lodgings			
278 / p. 599	AAA	**Holiday Inn Express & Suites** - see color ad p 260, p 673	◆◆◆	$139-$229 SAVE	673
280 / p. 599	AAA	**Best Western Lighthouse Hotel** - see color ad p 673	◆◆◆	$99-$280 SAVE	673
		PACIFICA - Restaurant			
150 / p. 599		Moonraker Restaurant	◆◆◆	$20-$40	674
		BRISBANE - Lodgings			
286 / p. 599		Homewood Suites	◆◆◆	$129-$189	660
287 / p. 599		Radisson Hotel San Francisco Airport at Sierra Point - see color ad p 629	◆◆◆	$99-$219	660
		SOUTH SAN FRANCISCO - Lodgings			
293 / p. 599	AAA	**Travelers Inn** - see color ad p 684	◆◆	$69-$102 SAVE	685
294 / p. 599		Ramada Limited All Suites	◆◆	$89-$119	685
295 / p. 599	AAA	**Americana Inn**	◆◆	$49-$99 SAVE	680
296 / p. 599	AAA	**Economy Inn**	◆	$69-$79 SAVE	681
297 / p. 599		Courtyard by Marriott	◆◆◆	$69-$179	681
298 / p. 599		Motel 6	◆	Failed to provide	684
299 / p. 599		Days Inn-SFO North	◆◆	$79-$109	681
300 / p. 599		Comfort Suites	◆◆◆	$99-$129	681
301 / p. 599		Inn at Oyster Point	◆◆◆	$139-$189	682
302 / p. 599		Hampton Inn	◆◆◆	$89-$159	681
303 / p. 599		Embassy Suites San Francisco Airport-South San Francisco - see color ad p 621	◆◆◆	$109-$199	681
304 / p. 599	AAA	**La Quinta Inn** - see color ad p 660	◆◆◆	$90-$169 SAVE	683
305 / p. 599		Ramada Inn SFO North - see ad p 683	◆◆◆	$69-$179	685
306 / p. 599	AAA	**Best Western Grosvenor Airport Hotel**	◆◆◆	$79-$129 SAVE	681
307 / p. 599		Holiday Inn SFO-North - see ad p 683	◆◆◆	$79-$249	682
308 / p. 599	AAA	**Howard Johnson Express Inn**	◆◆	$59-$119 SAVE	682
309 / p. 599	AAA	**Quality Inn & Suites** - see color ad p 684	◆◆◆	$79-$89 SAVE	684
310 / p. 599	AAA	**Larkspur Landing** - see color ad p 683	◆◆◆	$79-$139 SAVE	684
311 / p. 599		Travelodge San Francisco Airport North	◆◆	$59-$119	685
312 / p. 599		Four Points by Sheraton SFO North	◆◆◆	$79-$199	681
313 / p. 599	AAA	**Hilton Garden Inn**	◆◆◆	$99-$139 SAVE	682
314 / p. 599	AAA	**Holiday Inn Express Hotel & Suites San Francisco Airport North** - see color ad p 682	◆◆◆	$65-$139 SAVE	682

Spotter/Map Page Number	OA	SOUTH SAN FRANCISCO - Restaurant	Diamond Rating	Rate Range High Season	Listing Page
160 / p. 599		South City Steakhouse	◆◆	$10-$25	686
		SAN BRUNO - Lodgings			
319 / p. 599	AAA	**Summerfield Suites by Wyndham-San Francisco**	◆◆◆	$89-$139 SAVE	675
320 / p. 599	AAA	**Best Inn & Suites**	◆◆◆	$49-$99 SAVE	674
322 / p. 599	AAA	**Ramada Limited** - see color ad p 674	◆◆◆	$75-$100 SAVE	675
323 / p. 599		Days Inn-SFO Int'l-West	◆◆◆	Failed to provide	674
324 / p. 599	AAA	**Ritz Inn**	◆◆	$60-$90 SAVE	675
325 / p. 599	AAA	**Regency Inn**	◆◆	$75 SAVE	675
326 / p. 599		Cal West Inn	◆◆	$65-$75	674
		MILLBRAE - Lodgings			
335 / p. 599	AAA	**Millwood Inn** - see color ad p 671	◆◆◆	$79-$150 SAVE	672
336 / p. 599		Clarion Hotel-San Francisco Airport	◆◆◆	$99-$129	669
337 / p. 599	AAA	**Comfort Inn-Airport West**	◆◆	$79-$99 SAVE	669
338 / p. 599	AAA	**Quality Suites** - see color ad p 671, p 521	◆◆◆	$89-$129 SAVE	672
339 / p. 599	AAA	**Travelodge San Francisco Airport South** - see color ad p 671	◆◆	$69-$129 SAVE	672
340 / p. 599	AAA	**Best Western El Rancho Inn & Suites** - see color ad p 670	◆◆◆	$89-$169 SAVE	669
342 / p. 599		The Westin Hotel-San Francisco Airport	◆◆◆	$299-$319	672
		MILLBRAE - Restaurant			
170 / p. 599		Terrace Cafe - see color ad p 670	◆◆◆	$9-$20	672
		BURLINGAME - Lodgings			
350 / p. 599	AAA	**Hyatt Regency-San Francisco Airport** - see color ad p 623	◆◆◆◆	$99-$209 SAVE	663
351 / p. 599	AAA	**Hilton Garden Inn San Francisco Airport/Burlingame** - see color ad p 662	◆◆◆	$78-$268 SAVE	662
353 / p. 599		Holiday Inn Express Burlingame, San Francisco Intl Airport South	◆◆◆	$72-$119	662
355 / p. 599	AAA	**Embassy Suites-SFO** - see color ad p 621	◆◆◆◆	$119-$199 SAVE	662
356 / p. 599	AAA	**Doubletree Hotel-San Francisco Airport** - see color ad p 661	◆◆◆	$79-$149 SAVE	661
357 / p. 599		Crowne Plaza	◆◆◆	$249-$349	661
360 / p. 599	AAA	**Red Roof Inn**	◆◆	$59-$89 SAVE	663
361 / p. 599	AAA	**Sheraton Gateway Hotel San Francisco Airport**	◆◆◆◆	$99-$209 SAVE	663
362 / p. 599		San Francisco Airport Marriott	◆◆◆◆	$99-$229	663
363 / p. 599	AAA	**Vagabond Inn-Airport**	◆◆	$55-$80 SAVE	663
		BURLINGAME - Restaurants			
180 / p. 599		Cafe' La Scala	◆◆◆	$17	663
181 / p. 599		Kuleto's Trattoria	◆◆◆	$8-$19	664
182 / p. 599		Pisces	◆◆◆	$24-$38	664
183 / p. 599		Gulliver's	◆◆	$18-$29	664
		SAN MATEO - Lodgings			
379 / p. 599	AAA	**Super 8 Motel**	◆◆	$69-$110 SAVE	678
380 / p. 599		Coxhead House Bed & Breakfast	◆◆◆	$120-$250	676

Spotter/Map Page Number	OA	SAN MATEO - Lodgings (continued)	Diamond Rating	Rate Range High Season	Listing Page
381 / p. 599		Hilton Garden Inn San Mateo	◆◆◆	$79-$189	677
382 / p. 599	AAA	**Holiday Inn-San Mateo**	◆◆◆	$89-$159 SAVE	677
383 / p. 599	AAA	**Comfort Inn**	◆◆◆	$59-$129 SAVE	676
384 / p. 599	AAA	**Marriott San Mateo/San Francisco Airport** - see color ad p 677	◆◆◆◆	$99-$349 SAVE	678
385 / p. 599		Residence Inn by Marriott	◆◆◆	$104-$151	678
386 / p. 599		Homestead Studio Suites Hotel-San Mateo/SFO	◆◆	$86-$111	677
388 / p. 599	AAA	**Best Western San Mateo/Los Prados Inn**	◆◆	$89-$189 SAVE	676
389 / p. 599		Radisson Villa Hotel - see color ad p 677, p 629	◆◆◆	$185	678
		FOSTER CITY - Lodgings			
399 / p. 599		Crowne Plaza Hotel and Resort Foster City	◆◆◆	$99-$129	666
400 / p. 599		Courtyard by Marriott	◆◆◆	$79-$149	665
		HALF MOON BAY - Lodgings			
418 / p. 599		Landis Shores Oceanfront Inn	◆◆◆	$275-$345	667
419 / p. 599		Goose & Turrets Bed & Breakfast Inn	◆◆	$160-$215	666
420 / p. 599	AAA	**The Ritz-Carlton, Half Moon Bay**	◆◆◆◆◆	$275-$625	668
421 / p. 599	AAA	**Seal Cove Inn**	◆◆◆◆	$200-$300 SAVE	668
422 / p. 599	AAA	**Harbor View Inn**	◆◆	$76-$176 SAVE	667
423 / p. 599	AAA	**Miramar Lodge & Conference Center**	◆◆◆	$99-$189 SAVE	668
424 / p. 599	AAA	**Cypress Inn on Miramar Beach** - see color ad p 469	◆◆◆	$225-$385 SAVE	666
425 / p. 599		Ramada Limited	◆◆	$90-$325	668
426 / p. 599	AAA	**Mill Rose Inn, Spa & Garden Suites**	◆◆◆◆	$190-$360 SAVE	667
427 / p. 599		Old Thyme Inn	◆◆◆	$130-$300	668
428 / p. 599		Beach House Inn & Conference Center - see color ad p 666	◆◆◆	$185-$425	666
429 / p. 599	AAA	**Half Moon Bay Lodge** - see color ad p 667	◆◆◆	$195-$220 SAVE	667
430 / p. 599	AAA	**Holiday Inn Express**	◆◆◆	$99-$139 SAVE	667
		HALF MOON BAY - Restaurants			
190 / p. 599	AAA	**Moss Beach Distillery**	◆◆	$25-$45	669
191 / p. 599	AAA	**Half Moon Bay Brewing Company**	◆◆	$7-$14	668
193 / p. 599		Miramar Beach Restaurant	◆◆	$17-$25	668
194 / p. 599		Pasta Moon Ristorante	◆◆	$15-$32	669
196 / p. 599		Navio	◆◆◆◆	$10-$36	669
		BELMONT - Lodgings			
435 / p. 599	AAA	**Holiday Inn Express Hotel & Suites** - see color ad p 260	◆◆◆	$149 SAVE	660
436 / p. 599		Summerfield Suites by Wyndham-Belmont/Redwood Shores	◆◆◆	$79-$139	660
		SAN CARLOS - Lodgings			
445 / p. 599	AAA	**Days Inn-San Carlos**	◆◆	$69-$99 SAVE	676
446 / p. 599	AAA	**Comfort Inn & Suites** - see color ad p 675	◆◆◆	$89-$139 SAVE	675
448 / p. 599	AAA	**Inns of America**	◆◆◆	$69-$109 SAVE	676
449 / p. 599	AAA	**San Carlos Travelodge** - see color ad p 674	◆◆	$70-$100 SAVE	676

Spotter/Map Page Number	OA	**SAN CARLOS** - Lodgings (continued)	Diamond Rating	Rate Range High Season	Listing Page
451 / p. 599		Homestead Studio Suites Hotel-San Carlos/Redwood Shores	◆◆	$95-$120	676
		REDWOOD CITY - Lodgings			
464 / p. 599		TownePlace Suites by Marriott	◆◆◆	$69-$179	559
465 / p. 599		Hotel Sofitel San Francisco Bay at Redwood Shores	◆◆◆◆	$99-$349	558
466 / p. 599	AAA	**Best Western Inn** - see color ad p 558	◆◆◆	$69-$129 SAVE	558
467 / p. 599	AAA	**Comfort Inn**	◆◆	$49-$99 SAVE	558
468 / p. 599		Best Inn	◆◆	$69-$89	557
469 / p. 599	AAA	**Best Western Executive Suites**	◆◆◆	$119-$129 SAVE	558
470 / p. 599	AAA	**Days Inn**	◆◆	$75-$85 SAVE	558
471 / p. 599		Holiday Inn Express - see color ad p 260	◆◆◆	$99-$149	558
		MENLO PARK - Lodgings			
480 / p. 599	AAA	**Stanford Park Hotel** - see color ad inside back cover	◆◆◆◆	$159-$725 SAVE	425
481 / p. 599	AAA	**Red Cottage Inn**	◆◆	$74-$119 SAVE	424
482 / p. 599	AAA	**Menlo Park Inn** - see color ad p 424	◆◆◆	$99-$159 SAVE	424
483 / p. 599	AAA	**Best Western Riviera**	◆◆◆	$109-$169 SAVE	424
		MENLO PARK - Restaurant			
225 / p. 599		Gaylord India Restaurant	◆◆◆	$13-$24	425
		WOODSIDE - Restaurant			
230 / p. 599		Bella Vista Restaurant	◆◆	$25-$55	816

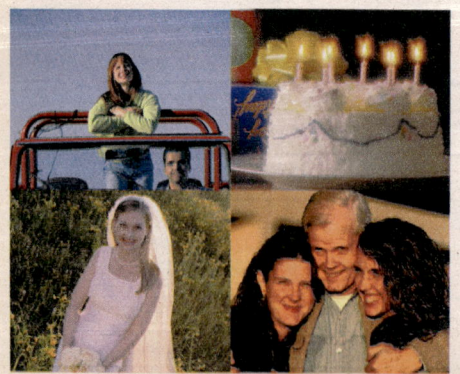

SAN FRANCISCO pop. 776,733 (See map and index starting on p. 590)

WHERE TO STAY

THE ARCHBISHOP'S MANSION Book at aaa.com Phone: (415)563-7872 157

Historic Bed & Breakfast

7/15-10/31	1P: $195-$425	2P: $195-$425	XP: $20	F12
5/1-7/14 & 11/1-1/31	1P: $165-$355	2P: $165-$355	XP: $20	F12
2/1-4/30	1P: $135-$325	2P: $135-$325	XP: $20	F12

Location: US 101 (Van Ness Ave), 1.1 mi w. Located at Alamo Square. 1000 Fulton St 94117. Fax: 415/885-3193. **Facility:** European antiques bring an elegant ambience to this restored 1904 French chateau; many units have fireplaces. 15 units. 14 one-bedroom standard units, some with whirlpools. 1 one-bedroom suite. 3 stories, interior corridors. *Bath:* combo or shower only. **Parking:** on-site. **Terms:** 2 night minimum stay - weekends, 7 day cancellation notice-fee imposed, weekly rates available. **Amenities:** video library, CD players, irons, hair dryers. **Guest Services:** complimentary evening beverages, valet laundry. **Business Services:** meeting rooms. **Cards:** AX, CB, DC, DS, MC, VI.

SOME UNITS

FEE

THE ARGENT HOTEL Book at aaa.com Phone: (415)974-6400 56

Large-scale Hotel

All Year	1P: $349	2P: $349	XP: $25	F16

Location: 1 1/2 blks n of Moscone Convention Center. 50 3rd St 94103. Fax: 415/543-8268. **Facility:** With each of its guest rooms featuring a dramatic floor-to-ceiling window, the hotel offers sweeping views of scenic San Francisco. 667 units. 647 one-bedroom standard units. 20 one-bedroom suites ($599). 36 stories, interior corridors. *Bath:* combo or shower only. **Parking:** valet. **Terms:** age restrictions may apply, cancellation fee imposed. **Amenities:** high-speed Internet, dual phone lines, voice mail, safes, honor bars, irons, hair dryers. **Dining:** Jester's Restaurant, see separate listing. **Leisure Activities:** saunas, exercise room. *Fee:* massage. **Guest Services:** gift shop, valet laundry. **Business Services:** conference facilities, business center. **Cards:** AX, CB, DC, DS, JC, MC, VI. **Special Amenities: free newspaper.** *(See color ad p 607)*

SOME UNITS

FEE

BECK'S MOTOR LODGE Phone: (415)621-8212 166

Motel

5/1-10/31	1P: $109-$159	2P: $109-$159	XP: $10	F18
2/1-4/30 & 11/1-1/31	1P: $99-$139	2P: $99-$139	XP: $10	F18

Location: 0.6 mi w of US 101 (Van Ness Ave); near Castro St. 2222 Market St 94114. Fax: 415/241-0435. **Facility:** 58 one-bedroom standard units. 3 stories, interior/exterior corridors. *Bath:* combo or shower only. **Parking:** on-site. **Amenities:** voice mail, irons. *Some:* hair dryers. **Guest Services:** coin laundry. **Cards:** AX, CB, DC, DS, JC, MC, VI. **Special Amenities: early check-in/late check-out and free room upgrade (subject to availability with advanced reservations).** *(See color ad p 607)*

SOME UNITS

(See map and index starting on p. 590)

BERESFORD ARMS Book at aaa.com — Phone: (415)673-2600 — 38

Small-scale Hotel

	1P	2P	XP	
4/1-10/31 [CP]		2P: $109-$129	XP: $10	F12
2/1-3/31 & 11/1-1/31 [CP]	1P: $99-$119	2P: $99-$119	XP: $10	F12

Location: 3 blks w of Union Square. 701 Post St 94109. Fax: 415/929-1535. **Facility:** 96 units. 84 one-bedroom standard units, some with efficiencies and/or whirlpools. 12 one-bedroom suites ($139-$179) with kitchens and whirlpools. 7 stories, interior corridors. *Bath:* combo or shower only. **Parking:** on-site (fee) and valet. **Terms:** pets (on 3rd floor, in smoking units). **Amenities:** video library, honor bars, irons. **Guest Services:** complimentary evening beverages, valet laundry. **Business Services:** meeting rooms. **Cards:** AX, CB, DC, DS, JC, MC, VI. **Special Amenities: free continental breakfast.** *(See color ad below)*

SOME UNITS FEE

BEST INN Book at aaa.com — Phone: (415)567-2425 — 106

Motel

	1P	2P	XP	
5/1-9/30 [CP]	1P: $85	2P: $85-$95	XP: $10	F10
10/1-12/31 [CP]	1P: $58	2P: $65-$75	XP: $10	F10
2/1-4/30 & 1/1-1/31 [CP]	1P: $58-$65	2P: $58-$75	XP: $10	F10

Location: Just w of Divisadero St. 2707 Lombard St 94123. Fax: 415/567-8222. **Facility:** 23 one-bedroom standard units. 2 stories (no elevator), exterior corridors. **Parking:** on-site. **Amenities:** voice mail, irons, hair dryers. **Cards:** AX, CB, DC, DS, JC, MC, VI.

SOME UNITS FEE

BEST INN FISHERMANS WHARF — Phone: (415)776-3220 — 143

Motel

	1P	2P	XP	
5/1-10/31	1P: $89-$149	2P: $89-$149		
11/1-1/31	1P: $69-$89	2P: $69-$89		
2/1-4/30	1P: $69-$89	2P: $69-$89	XP: $10	F12

Location: On US 101 at Chestnut. 2850 Van Ness Ave 94109. Fax: 415/921-7451. **Facility:** 42 one-bedroom standard units. 3 stories, exterior corridors. **Parking:** on-site. **Terms:** cancellation fee imposed, [CP] meal plan available. **Business Services:** fax. **Cards:** AX, DC, DS, MC, VI. **Special Amenities: free continental breakfast and preferred room (subject to availability with advanced reservations).**

BEST WESTERN AMERICANIA Book at aaa.com — Phone: (415)626-0200 — 65

Motel

	1P	2P	XP	
4/1-10/31	1P: $139-$189	2P: $139-$189	XP: $10	F17
2/1-3/31 & 11/1-1/31	1P: $129-$169	2P: $129-$169	XP: $15	F17

Location: Just s of Market St. 121 7th St 94103. Fax: 415/863-2529. **Facility:** 143 units. 126 one- and 11 two-bedroom standard units. 6 one-bedroom suites. 4 stories, exterior corridors. *Bath:* combo or shower only. **Parking:** on-site. **Amenities:** video games (fee), voice mail, irons, hair dryers. **Dining:** 2 restaurants, 6:30 am-10 pm, cocktails. **Pool(s):** heated outdoor. **Leisure Activities:** saunas, exercise room. **Guest Services:** valet and coin laundry, area transportation-Union Square. **Business Services:** meeting rooms, fax. **Cards:** AX, CB, DC, DS, JC, MC, VI. **Special Amenities: free local telephone calls.** *(See color ad p 609)*

SOME UNITS FEE

(See map and index starting on p. 590)

BEST WESTERN CANTERBURY HOTEL *Book at aaa.com* **Phone:** (415)474-6464 **15**

AAA SAVE ◆◆◆ Small-scale Hotel

4/1-10/31	1P: $99-$295	2P: $99-$295	XP: $15	F17
2/1-3/31 & 11/1-1/31	1P: $79-$195	2P: $79-$195	XP: $15	F17

Location: Between Taylor and Jones sts. 750 Sutter St 94109. Fax: 415/474-5856. **Facility:** 254 units. 248 one-bedroom standard units, some with whirlpools. 6 one-bedroom suites. 10 stories, interior corridors. *Bath:* combo or shower only. **Parking:** on-site (fee) and valet. **Terms:** cancellation fee imposed. **Amenities:** video games, dual phone lines, voice mail, irons, hair dryers. **Dining:** 6:30 am-9 pm, cocktails, also, Lehr's Greenhouse, see separate listing. **Guest Services:** gift shop, valet laundry. **Business Services:** conference facilities, business center. **Cards:** AX, DC, DS, JC, MC, VI. **Special Amenities: free local telephone calls and early check-in/late check-out.** *(See color ad below)*

FEE / SOME UNITS

BEST WESTERN CARRIAGE INN *Book at aaa.com* **Phone:** (415)552-8600 **67**

AAA SAVE ◆◆◆ Small-scale Hotel

4/1-10/31	1P: $149-$199	2P: $149-$199	XP: $15	F17
2/1-3/31 & 11/1-1/31	1P: $139-$169	2P: $139-$169	XP: $15	F17

Location: 1 1/2 blks s of Market St. 140 7th St 94103. Fax: 415/626-3973. **Facility:** 48 one-bedroom standard units. 4 stories, interior corridors. **Parking:** on-site (fee). **Terms:** [ECP] meal plan available. **Amenities:** video games (fee), voice mail, irons, hair dryers. *Some:* dual phone lines. **Leisure Activities:** whirlpool. **Guest Services:** complimentary evening beverages, valet laundry, area transportation-Union Square. **Business Services:** fax. **Cards:** AX, CB, DC, DS, JC, MC, VI. **Special Amenities: free continental breakfast and free newspaper.** *(See color ad p 609)*

FEE / SOME UNITS

BEST WESTERN CIVIC CENTER MOTOR INN *Book at aaa.com* **Phone:** (415)621-2826 **165**

AAA SAVE ◆◆ Motel

5/28-10/31 [CP]	1P: $109-$149	2P: $109-$149	XP: $10	F18
4/1-5/27 [CP]	1P: $99-$139	2P: $99-$139	XP: $10	F18
2/1-3/31 & 11/1-1/31 [CP]	1P: $89-$129	2P: $89-$129	XP: $10	F18

Location: Just n off freeway; exit civic center, at Harrison St. 364 9th St 94103. Fax: 415/621-0833. **Facility:** 57 one-bedroom standard units. 2 stories, exterior corridors. *Bath:* combo or shower only. **Parking:** on-site. **Amenities:** voice mail, irons, hair dryers. **Dining:** 7 am-2 pm, Sat & Sun-11 am. **Pool(s):** small heated outdoor. **Guest Services:** coin laundry. **Cards:** AX, CB, DC, DS, JC, MC, VI. **Special Amenities: free continental breakfast and free local telephone calls.** *(See color ad below)*

FEE / SOME UNITS

(See map and index starting on p. 590)

BEST WESTERN FLAMINGO INN Book at aaa.com **Phone:** (415)621-0701 68

Motel

4/1-10/31	1P: $99-$129	2P: $99-$129	XP: $10	F17
2/1-3/31 & 11/1-1/31	1P: $89-$109	2P: $89-$109	XP: $10	F17

Location: Just s of Market St; 3 blks from civic center. 114 7th St 94103. Fax: 415/621-4069. **Facility:** Smoke free premises. 38 one-bedroom standard units. 2 stories, exterior corridors. *Bath:* shower only. **Parking:** on-site. **Amenities:** video games (fee), voice mail, irons, hair dryers. **Guest Services:** valet laundry, area transportation-Union Square. **Cards:** AX, CB, DC, DS, JC, MC, VI. **Special Amenities: free continental breakfast and free local telephone calls.** *(See color ad p 609)*

SOME UNITS

FEE

BEST WESTERN MIYAKO INN Book at aaa.com **Phone:** (415)921-4000 142

Small-scale Hotel

4/1-10/31	1P: $89-$109	2P: $99-$119	XP: $10	F18
2/1-3/31 & 11/1-1/31	1P: $79-$99	2P: $89-$109	XP: $10	F18

Location: 1 mi w of Union Square; 5 blks w of US 101 (Van Ness Ave) at Sutter and Buchanan sts; 1 blk from the Japan Center. 1800 Sutter St 94115. Fax: 415/923-1064. **Facility:** 125 one-bedroom standard units. 8 stories, interior corridors. **Parking:** on-site (fee). **Terms:** cancellation fee imposed. **Amenities:** video games (fee), voice mail, irons, hair dryers. **Dining:** 7 am-11:30 pm, cocktails. **Guest Services:** gift shop, valet laundry. **Business Services:** meeting rooms, fax. **Cards:** AX, CB, DC, DS, JC, MC, VI. *(See ad below)*

SOME UNITS

BEST WESTERN TUSCAN INN AT FISHERMAN'S WHARF Book at aaa.com **Phone:** (415)561-1100 128

Small-scale Hotel

5/1-10/31	1P: $189-$269	2P: $189-$269	XP: $20	F17
2/1-4/30 & 11/1-1/31	1P: $169-$219	2P: $169-$219	XP: $20	F17

Location: Just s of Fisherman's Wharf at Mason St. 425 Northpoint St 94133. Fax: 415/561-1199. **Facility:** 221 units. 209 one-bedroom standard units. 12 one-bedroom suites ($239-$349). 4 stories, interior corridors. **Parking:** on-site (fee). **Terms:** 2 night minimum stay - weekends, cancellation fee imposed, package plans, small pets only ($50 fee). **Amenities:** video games (fee), voice mail, honor bars, irons, hair dryers. *Some:* CD players. **Dining:** 7 am-10 pm, Fri & Sat-11 pm, cocktails. **Guest Services:** complimentary evening beverages, valet laundry. **Business Services:** meeting rooms, fax. **Cards:** AX, CB, DC, DS, JC, MC, VI. **Special Amenities: free local telephone calls and free room upgrade (subject to availability with advanced reservations).** *(See ad below)*

SOME UNITS

FEE FEE

(See map and index starting on p. 590)

BRITTON HOTEL *Book at aaa.com* **Phone:** (415)621-7001 **70**

SAVE — Small-scale Hotel

	1P	2P	XP	
4/1-10/31	1P: $119-$159	2P: $119-$159	XP: $10	F17
2/1-3/31 & 11/1-1/31	1P: $99-$129	2P: $99-$129	XP: $10	F17

Location: Just s of Market St; 3 blks s of civic center. 112 7th St 94103. Fax: 415/621-4069. **Facility:** 79 units. 74 one- and 5 two-bedroom standard units. 5 stories, interior corridors. *Bath:* combo or shower only. **Parking:** on-site (fee). **Amenities:** video games (fee), voice mail. *Some:* irons, hair dryers. **Dining:** 11 am-11 pm. **Guest Services:** complimentary evening beverages, valet laundry, area transportation-Union Square. **Cards:** AX, CB, DC, DS, JC, MC, VI. *(See color ad p 609)*

SOME UNITS

FEE

BROADWAY MANOR INN *Book at aaa.com* **Phone:** (415)776-7900 **137**

SAVE — Motel

	1P	2P	XP	
All Year	1P: $59-$99	2P: $59-$99	XP: $10	F11

Location: On US 101 (Van Ness Ave) at Broadway. 2201 Van Ness Ave 94109. Fax: 415/928-0460. **Facility:** 56 one-bedroom standard units. 4 stories, exterior corridors. **Parking:** on-site. **Terms:** 3 day cancellation notice, [BP] meal plan available, package plans - in winter. **Amenities:** *Some:* high-speed Internet. **Cards:** AX, CB, DC, DS, JC, MC, VI. **Special Amenities: early check-in/late check-out and preferred room (subject to availability with advanced reservations).** *(See color ad below)*

SOME UNITS

BUENA VISTA MOTOR INN **Phone:** (415)923-9600 **117**

SAVE — Motel

2/1-6/15 & 11/1-1/31	1P: $79-$129	2P: $89-$139
6/16-10/31	1P: $129	2P: $139

Location: At Gough St. 1599 Lombard St 94123. Fax: 415/441-4775. **Facility:** 50 one-bedroom standard units. 3 stories, interior corridors. *Bath:* combo or shower only. **Parking:** on-site. **Terms:** cancellation fee imposed. **Amenities:** irons, hair dryers. **Cards:** AX, CB, DC, DS, MC, VI. *(See color ad p 606)*

SOME UNITS

FEE

(See map and index starting on p. 590)

CAMPTON PLACE HOTEL Book at aaa.com

Phone: (415)781-5555 **35**

Small-scale Hotel

All Year 1P: $335-$470 2P: $335-$470

Location: Just n of Union Square. 340 Stockton St 94108. Fax: 415/955-5536. **Facility:** A service-oriented staff and a Union Square location enhance this elegant small hotel decorated in the French style. 110 units. 101 one-bedroom standard units. 9 one-bedroom suites. 17 stories, interior corridors. *Bath:* combo or shower only. **Parking:** valet. **Terms:** cancellation fee imposed, pets ($35 extra charge). **Amenities:** video games, CD players, high-speed Internet, dual phone lines, voice mail, safes, honor bars, irons, hair dryers. **Dining:** Campton Place Restaurant, see separate listing. **Leisure Activities:** exercise room. **Guest Services:** valet laundry. **Business Services:** meeting rooms, fax. **Cards:** AX, CB, DC, JC, MC, VI.

SOME UNITS

FEE FEE

CAPRI MOTEL

Phone: 415/346-4667 **132**

Motel

All Year 1P: $70-$80

Location: Just s of US 101 (Van Ness Ave) at Buchanan St. 2015 Greenwich St 94123. Fax: 415/346-3256. **Facility:** 46 units. 44 one-bedroom standard units. 2 one-bedroom suites with efficiencies. 3 stories, exterior corridors. *Bath:* combo or shower only. **Parking:** on-site. **Terms:** cancellation fee imposed. **Amenities:** voice mail. **Cards:** AX, CB, DC, DS, MC, VI.

SOME UNITS

CARLTON HOTEL Book at aaa.com

Phone: (415)673-0242 **148**

Large-scale Hotel

All Year 1P: $79-$260 2P: $79-$260 XP: $20 F12

Location: 5 blks w of Union Square. 1075 Sutter St 94109. Fax: 415/673-4904. **Facility:** 165 units. 164 one-bedroom standard units. 1 one-bedroom suite. 9 stories, interior corridors. **Parking:** valet. **Terms:** [BP], [CP] & [MAP] meal plans available. **Amenities:** voice mail, honor bars, irons, hair dryers. **Dining:** 7 am-11 & 5-9 pm. **Guest Services:** complimentary evening beverages, valet laundry. **Business Services:** meeting rooms. **Cards:** AX, CB, DC, DS, JC, MC, VI. **Special Amenities: early check-in/late check-out and free room upgrade (subject to availability with advanced reservations).** *(See color ad p 617)*

SOME UNITS

FEE FEE

CARTWRIGHT HOTEL Book at aaa.com

Phone: (415)421-2865 **23**

Small-scale Hotel

All Year [CP] 1P: $99-$139 2P: $99-$139 XP: $20 F17

Location: Union Square at Powell St. 524 Sutter St 94102. Fax: 415/983-6244. **Facility:** 114 units. 109 one-bedroom standard units. 5 one-bedroom suites. 8 stories, interior corridors. **Parking:** on-site (fee) and valet. **Terms:** cancellation fee imposed. **Amenities:** video games (fee), voice mail, honor bars, hair dryers. *Some:* irons. **Guest Services:** valet laundry. **Business Services:** meeting rooms. **Cards:** AX, CB, DC, DS, MC, VI.

SOME UNITS

FEE FEE

(See map and index starting on p. 590)

CASTLE INN *Book at aaa.com* **Phone:** (415)441-1155 **138**

AAA SAVE

Motel

5/1-10/31 [CP]	1P: $85-$125	2P: $85-$165	XP: $10	F17
2/1-4/30 & 11/1-1/31 [CP]	1P: $85-$105	2P: $85-$145	XP: $10	F17

Location: Just e of US 101 (Van Ness Ave). 1565 Broadway 94109. Fax: 415/775-2237. **Facility:** 26 one-bedroom standard units. 5 stories, exterior corridors. **Parking:** on-site. **Terms:** 3 day cancellation notice. **Amenities:** voice mail, irons, hair dryers. **Cards:** AX, CB, DC, DS, JC, MC, VI. **Special Amenities: free continental breakfast and preferred room (subject to availability with advanced reservations).**

(See color ad p 613)

FEE SOME UNITS

CATHEDRAL HILL HOTEL *Book at aaa.com* **Phone:** (415)776-8200 **146**

Large-scale Hotel

All Year	1P: $169	2P: $169	XP: $20	F17

Location: On US 101 (Van Ness Ave); between Geary and Post sts. 1101 Van Ness Ave 94109. Fax: 415/441-2841. **Facility:** 400 one-bedroom standard units. 8 stories, interior corridors. **Parking:** on-site (fee). **Terms:** cancellation fee imposed. **Amenities:** video games (fee), voice mail, irons, hair dryers. **Pool(s):** heated outdoor. **Leisure Activities:** exercise room. **Guest Services:** gift shop, valet laundry. **Business Services:** conference facilities, fax. **Cards:** AX, DC, DS, MC, VI. *(See color ad below)*

FEE SOME UNITS FEE

(See map and index starting on p. 590)

CHANCELLOR HOTEL ON UNION SQUARE Book at aaa.com **Phone:** (415)362-2004 29

AAA SAVE
Small-scale Hotel

All Year 1P: $148-$160 2P: $163-$175 XP: $15

Location: Just n of Union Square. 433 Powell St 94102. Fax: 415/362-1403. **Facility:** Smoke free premises. 137 units. 135 one-bedroom standard units. 2 one-bedroom suites ($250-$300). 15 stories, interior corridors. **Parking:** on-site (fee) and valet. **Terms:** package plans - seasonal. **Amenities:** video games, high-speed Internet, dual phone lines, voice mail, safes, irons, hair dryers. *Some:* CD players. **Dining:** 7 am-2 & 5-9:30 pm, Sun-3 pm, cocktails. **Guest Services:** gift shop, valet laundry. **Business Services:** meeting rooms. **Cards:** AX, CB, DC, DS, JC, MC, VI. **Special Amenities: free local telephone calls and preferred room (subject to availability with advanced reservations).** *(See color ad p 614)*

SOME UNITS
FEE

CHELSEA MOTOR INN **Phone:** 415/563-5600 114

AAA SAVE
Motel

All Year 1P: $86-$125 2P: $86-$125 XP: $10 F5

Location: US 101 (Van Ness Ave) at Fillmore St. 2095 Lombard St 94123 (3210 Fillmore St, #3, SAN FRANCISCO). Fax: 415/567-6475. **Facility:** Smoke free premises. 60 one-bedroom standard units. 4 stories, interior corridors. *Bath:* combo or shower only. **Parking:** on-site. **Amenities:** hair dryers. **Cards:** AX, CB, DC, MC, VI. **Special Amenities: free local telephone calls.** *(See color ad p 616)*

SOME UNITS
FEE

CLARION HOTEL COSMO Book at aaa.com **Phone:** (415)673-6040 37

AAA SAVE
Small-scale Hotel

All Year 1P: $89-$159 2P: $89-$159 XP: $10 F17

Location: 3 1/2 blks w of Union Square. 761 Post St 94109. Fax: 415/563-6739. **Facility:** 144 units. 137 one-bedroom standard units. 7 one-bedroom suites ($129-$299). 17 stories, interior corridors. **Parking:** on-site (fee) and valet. **Terms:** [BP], [CP] & [ECP] meal plans available, small pets only. **Amenities:** video games, voice mail, honor bars, irons, hair dryers. **Dining:** 6:30 am-11 & 5-11 pm, cocktails. **Guest Services:** complimentary evening beverages, valet laundry. **Business Services:** meeting rooms. **Cards:** AX, CB, DC, DS, JC, MC, VI. **Special Amenities: free newspaper and preferred room (subject to availability with advanced reservations).**

SOME UNITS
FEE

COLUMBUS MOTOR INN **Phone:** 415/885-1492 136

AAA SAVE
Small-scale Hotel

All Year 1P: $90-$135 2P: $90-$135 XP: $10 F5

Location: Just s of Fisherman's Wharf; between Francisco and Chestnut sts. 1075 Columbus Ave 94133 (3210 Fillmore St, #3, SAN FRANCISCO, 94123). Fax: 415/928-2174. **Facility:** Smoke free premises. 45 units. 39 one- and 6 two-bedroom standard units. 5 stories, interior corridors. **Parking:** on-site. **Business Services:** fax. **Cards:** AX, CB, DC, MC, VI. **Special Amenities: free local telephone calls.** *(See color ad below)*

(See map and index starting on p. 590)

COMFORT INN BY THE BAY *Book at aaa.com* **Phone:** (415)928-5000 **122**

AAA SAVE ◆◆ Small-scale Hotel

5/14-10/31 [ECP]	1P: $115-$195	2P: $115-$195	XP: $10	F18
4/1-5/13 [ECP]	1P: $100-$160	2P: $100-$160	XP: $10	F18
11/1-1/31 [ECP]	1P: $90-$155	2P: $90-$155	XP: $10	F18
2/1-3/31 [ECP]	1P: $90-$150	2P: $90-$150	XP: $10	F18

Location: On US 101 (Van Ness Ave) at Lombard St. 2775 Van Ness Ave 94109. Fax: 415/441-3990. **Facility:** 138 one-bedroom standard units. 11 stories, interior corridors. *Bath:* combo or shower only. **Parking:** on-site (fee). **Terms:** check-in 4 pm. **Amenities:** irons, hair dryers. *Fee:* video games, safes. **Business Services:** fax. **Cards:** AX, DC, DS, JC, MC, VI. **Special Amenities: free expanded continental breakfast.** *(See color ad p 605)*

SOME UNITS

THE COMMODORE HOTEL *Book at aaa.com* **Phone:** (415)923-6800 **26**

AAA SAVE ◆◆ Small-scale Hotel

All Year	1P: $89-$275	2P: $89-$275	XP: $15	F12

Location: 2 1/2 blks nw of Union Square. 825 Sutter St 94109. Fax: 415/923-6804. **Facility:** 110 one-bedroom standard units. 6 stories, interior corridors. **Parking:** on-site (fee) and valet. **Amenities:** voice mail, irons, hair dryers. **Dining:** 7 am-2 & 5-2 am. **Guest Services:** valet laundry. **Business Services:** meeting rooms. **Cards:** AX, CB, DC, DS, JC, MC, VI. **Special Amenities: early check-in/late check-out.** *(See color ad below)*

SOME UNITS

FEE

(See map and index starting on p. 590)

COURTYARD BY MARRIOTT AT FISHERMAN'S WHARF Book at aaa.com Phone: (415)775-3800 100

Small-scale Hotel 4/1-10/31 1P: $129 2P: $199
2/1-3/31 & 11/1-1/31 1P: $99 2P: $159

Location: Between Jones and Leavenworth sts. Located adjacent to the Cannery. 580 Beach St 94133. Fax: 415/441-7307. **Facility:** 127 one-bedroom standard units. 4 stories, interior corridors. *Bath:* combo or shower only. **Parking:** on-site (fee). **Terms:** [BP] meal plan available. **Amenities:** voice mail, irons, hair dryers. **Leisure Activities:** exercise room. **Guest Services:** coin laundry. **Cards:** AX, CB, DC, DS, JC, MC, VI.

SOME UNITS

COVENTRY MOTOR INN Phone: 415/567-1200 115

Motel All Year 1P: $86-$125 2P: $86-$125 XP: $10 F5

Location: US 101 (Van Ness Ave) at Buchanan St. 1901 Lombard St 94123 (3210 Fillmore St #3, SAN FRANCISCO). Fax: 415/921-8745. **Facility:** Smoke free premises. 69 one-bedroom standard units. 4 stories, interior corridors. *Bath:* combo or shower only. **Parking:** on-site. **Amenities:** hair dryers. **Cards:** AX, CB, DC, MC, VI. **Special Amenities: free local telephone calls.** *(See color ad p 616)*

COW HOLLOW MOTOR INN & SUITES Phone: 415/921-5800 110

Motel All Year 1P: $86-$125 2P: $86-$125 XP: $10 F5

Location: US 101 (Van Ness Ave) at Steiner St. 2190 Lombard St 94123 (3210 Fillmore St, #3, SAN FRANCISCO). Fax: 415/922-8515. **Facility:** Smoke free premises. 129 one-bedroom standard units. 4 stories, interior corridors. *Bath:* combo or shower only. **Parking:** on-site. **Amenities:** hair dryers. **Cards:** AX, CB, DC, MC, VI. **Special Amenities: free local telephone calls.** *(See color ad p 616 & below)*

SOME UNITS

CROWNE PLAZA UNION SQUARE Book at aaa.com Phone: (415)398-8900 24

Large-scale Hotel All Year 1P: $139-$309 2P: $139-$309 XP: $20 F19

Location: Just n off Union Square; corner of Powell St. 480 Sutter St 94108. Fax: 415/989-8823. **Facility:** 403 units. 396 one-bedroom standard units. 7 one-bedroom suites. 30 stories, interior corridors. *Bath:* combo or shower only. **Parking:** on-site (fee) and valet. **Terms:** pets ($100 deposit). **Amenities:** CD players, high-speed Internet, voice mail, irons, hair dryers. *Some:* dual phone lines. **Dining:** 2 restaurants, 6 am-11 pm, cocktails. **Leisure Activities:** exercise room. **Guest Services:** gift shop, valet laundry. **Business Services:** conference facilities, business center. **Cards:** AX, CB, DC, DS, JC, MC, VI. *(See color ad p 619)*

SOME UNITS

FEE FEE FEE

DAYS INN AT THE BEACH Book at aaa.com Phone: 415/665-9000 167

Small-scale Hotel 3/1-9/30 [CP] 1P: $90-$125 2P: $90-$125 XP: $10 F17
2/1-2/29 & 10/1-1/31 [CP] 1P: $70-$105 2P: $70-$105 XP: $10 F17

Location: Just e of the beach. Across the street from San Francisco Zoo. 2600 Sloat Blvd 94116. Fax: 415/665-5440. **Facility:** 33 one-bedroom standard units, some with efficiencies. 2 stories (no elevator), interior/exterior corridors. *Bath:* combo or shower only. **Parking:** on-site. **Amenities:** irons, hair dryers. **Cards:** AX, DC, DS, MC, VI. **Special Amenities: free continental breakfast and free newspaper.**

SOME UNITS

(See map and index starting on p. 590)

DAYS INN-CIVIC CENTER *Book at aaa.com* **Phone:** (415)864-4040 158

AAA SAVE

Motel

6/1-10/31 [CP]	1P: $95-$149	2P: $105-$149	XP: $10	F12
2/1-5/31 [CP]	1P: $75-$135	2P: $80-$135	XP: $10	F12
11/1-1/31 [CP]	1P: $69-$135	2P: $79-$135	XP: $10	F12

Location: 2 1/2 blks w of US 101 (Van Ness Ave). 465 Grove St 94102. Fax: 415/552-4914. **Facility:** 40 one-bedroom standard units, some with whirlpools. 4 stories, exterior corridors. **Parking:** on-site. **Terms:** cancellation fee imposed. **Amenities:** voice mail, irons, hair dryers. **Cards:** AX, CB, DC, DS, JC, MC, VI. **Special Amenities: free continental breakfast and free newspaper.** *(See color ad below)*

SOME UNITS

(See map and index starting on p. 590)

DAYS INN-GEARY *Book at aaa.com* **Phone:** (415)441-8220 **152**

SAVE · Motel

All Year [ECP] 1P: $80-$120 2P: $80-$120

Location: Just e of US 101 (Van Ness Ave), exit Larkin St. 895 Geary St 94109. Fax: 415/771-5667. **Facility:** 73 one-bedroom standard units. 4 stories, interior corridors. **Parking:** on-site. **Amenities:** voice mail, irons, hair dryers. **Cards:** AX, CB, DC, DS, MC, VI. **Special Amenities: free expanded continental breakfast and free newspaper.** *(See color ad below)*

SOME UNITS

DAYS INN LOMBARD *Book at aaa.com* **Phone:** (415)922-2010 **109**

Motel

4/1-10/31	1P: $85-$150	2P: $85-$175	XP: $10	F12
11/1-1/31	1P: $65-$95	2P: $65-$95		
2/1-3/31	1P: $65-$95	2P: $65-$95	XP: $10	F12

Location: 0.5 mi w of US 101 (Van Ness Ave). 2358 Lombard St 94123. Fax: 415/931-0603. **Facility:** 22 one-bedroom standard units. 2 stories (no elevator), exterior corridors. **Parking:** on-site. **Terms:** cancellation fee imposed, weekly rates available, [CP] meal plan available, pets ($10 extra charge). **Amenities:** hair dryers. **Cards:** AX, CB, DC, DS, JC, MC, VI.

SOME UNITS

FEE

DIVA HOTEL *Book at aaa.com* **Phone:** (415)885-0200 **72**

Small-scale Hotel

5/1-10/31	1P: $145-$205	XP: $10	F12
2/1-4/30	1P: $135-$195	XP: $10	F12
11/1-1/31	1P: $115-$175	XP: $10	F12

Location: Just w of Union Square. 440 Geary St 94102. Fax: 415/346-6613. **Facility:** 115 units. 104 one-bedroom standard units. 11 one-bedroom suites ($275-$395). 7 stories, interior corridors. **Parking:** on-site. **Amenities:** video games, CD players, high-speed Internet, dual phone lines, voice mail, safes, irons, hair dryers. **Leisure Activities:** exercise room. *Fee:* massage. **Guest Services:** complimentary evening beverages, valet laundry. **Business Services:** meeting rooms, business center. **Cards:** AX, CB, DC, DS, JC, MC, VI.

SOME UNITS

FEE

THE DONATELLO *Book at aaa.com* **Phone:** (415)441-7100 **43**

Large-scale Hotel

All Year 1P: $199-$295 2P: $199-$295

Location: Just w of Union Square at Mason St. 501 Post St 94102. Fax: 415/885-8825. **Facility:** 94 one-bedroom standard units with efficiencies. 15 stories, interior corridors. **Parking:** valet. **Terms:** age restrictions may apply, cancellation fee imposed. **Amenities:** video games, CD players, high-speed Internet, voice mail, irons, hair dryers. **Leisure Activities:** saunas, whirlpool, exercise room. *Fee:* massage. **Guest Services:** valet laundry. **Business Services:** meeting rooms, fax. **Cards:** AX, DC, DS, MC, VI.

SOME UNITS

FEE

EXECUTIVE HOTEL VINTAGE COURT *Book at aaa.com* **Phone:** (415)392-4666 **18**

SAVE · Small-scale Hotel

All Year [CP] 1P: $109-$179 2P: $109-$179 XP: $20 F

Location: 2 blks n of Union Square. 650 Bush St 94108. Fax: 415/433-4065. **Facility:** Smoke free premises. 107 units. 106 one-bedroom standard units. 1 one-bedroom suite ($200-$375) with whirlpool. 8 stories, interior corridors. *Bath:* combo or shower only. **Parking:** on-site (fee) and valet. **Terms:** pets ($50 deposit). **Amenities:** video games, voice mail, honor bars, irons, hair dryers. **Guest Services:** complimentary evening beverages, valet laundry. **Business Services:** meeting rooms. **Cards:** AX, CB, DC, DS, JC, MC, VI. **Special Amenities: free continental breakfast and free newspaper.**

SOME UNITS

FEE FEE

(See map and index starting on p. 590)

THE FAIRMONT SAN FRANCISCO Book at aaa.com Phone: (415)772-5000 2

Large-scale Hotel

All Year 1P: $189-$289 2P: $189-$289 XP: $30 F17

Location: Atop Nob Hill at California St. 950 Mason St 94108. Fax: 415/772-5013. **Facility:** Newly renovated, this historic hotel features a prime location, an impressive lobby and a selection of fine shops and restaurants. 591 units. 526 one-bedroom standard units. 55 one- and 10 two-bedroom suites ($429-$729), some with whirlpools. 7-22 stories, interior corridors. **Parking:** on-site (fee) and valet. **Terms:** cancellation fee imposed, small pets only. **Amenities:** dual phone lines, voice mail, fax, safes, honor bars, irons, hair dryers. *Fee:* video games, high-speed Internet. *Some:* CD players. **Leisure Activities:** Fee: massage. **Guest Services:** gift shop, valet laundry. **Business Services:** conference facilities, business center. **Cards:** AX, CB, DC, DS, JC, MC, VI.

SOME UNITS

ASK FEE FEE DATA PORT

(See map and index starting on p. 590)

FOUR SEASONS SAN FRANCISCO *Book at aaa.com* **Phone:** (415)633-3000 **62**

Large-scale Hotel

All Year 1P: $469-$600 2P: $469-$600

Location: Between 3rd and 4th sts. 757 Market St 94103. Fax: 415/633-3009. **Facility:** Well-tended common areas and elegant, spacious rooms distinguish this downtown hotel, which is convenient to public transportation. 277 units. 241 one-bedroom standard units. 31 one-, 3 two- and 2 three-bedroom suites ($800-$3900). 17 stories, interior corridors. **Parking:** on-site (fee) and valet. **Terms:** cancellation fee imposed, [BP] meal plan available, package plans, small pets only. **Amenities:** DVD players, CD players, dual phone lines, voice mail, safes, honor bars, irons, hair dryers. *Fee:* video games, high-speed Internet. *Some:* fax. **Dining:** Seasons Restaurant, see separate listing. **Pool(s):** heated indoor. **Leisure Activities:** saunas, spa. **Guest Services:** gift shop, valet laundry, area transportation. **Business Services:** conference facilities, business center. **Cards:** AX, DC, DS, JC, MC, VI.

ASK FEE DATA PORT / SOME UNITS VCR /

FRANCISCO BAY INN *Book at aaa.com* **Phone:** (415)474-3030 **120**

AAA SAVE Motel

All Year [CP] 1P: $85-$145 2P: $85-$145 XP: $10 F11

Location: US 101 (Van Ness Ave) at Franklin. 1501 Lombard St 94123. Fax: 415/567-7082. **Facility:** 39 one-bedroom standard units. 4 stories, exterior corridors. **Parking:** on-site. **Terms:** 3 day cancellation notice, package plans - seasonal. **Amenities:** high-speed Internet, voice mail, hair dryers. *Some:* DVD players. **Cards:** AX, CB, DC, DS, JC, MC, VI. **Special Amenities: free continental breakfast and preferred room (subject to availability with advanced reservations).** *(See color ad below)*

DATA PORT / SOME UNITS VCR /

GALLERIA PARK HOTEL *Book at aaa.com* **Phone:** (415)781-3060 **36**

AAA SAVE Small-scale Hotel

All Year [CP] 1P: $119-$235 2P: $119-$235 XP: $20 F16

Location: 2 blks ne of Union Square. 191 Sutter St 94104. Fax: 415/433-4409. **Facility:** 177 units. 169 one-bedroom standard units. 8 one-bedroom suites, some with whirlpools. 9 stories, interior corridors. *Bath:* combo or shower only. **Parking:** on-site (fee) and valet. **Terms:** package plans. **Amenities:** video games, dual phone lines, voice mail, fax, honor bars, irons, hair dryers. *Some:* CD players. **Dining:** 7 am-10 pm. **Leisure Activities:** exercise room. **Guest Services:** complimentary evening beverages, valet laundry. **Business Services:** meeting rooms, business center. **Cards:** AX, DC, DS, MC, VI. **Special Amenities: early check-in/late check-out.**

FEE DATA PORT / SOME UNITS /

GRAND HYATT SAN FRANCISCO *Book at aaa.com* **Phone:** (415)398-1234 **34**

AAA SAVE Large-scale Hotel

All Year 1P: $159-$319 2P: $159-$319 XP: $25 F18

Location: On Union Square at Post St. 345 Stockton St 94108. Fax: 415/391-1780. **Facility:** Centrally located, the hotel is walking distance from the Financial District and convention center. 685 units. 625 one-bedroom standard units. 25 one- and 35 two-bedroom suites, some with whirlpools. 36 stories, interior corridors. **Parking:** valet. **Terms:** age restrictions may apply, cancellation fee imposed. **Amenities:** voice mail, honor bars, irons, hair dryers. **Dining:** 6:30 am-11 pm, cocktails. **Guest Services:** gift shop, valet laundry, area transportation-within 5 mi. **Business Services:** conference facilities, business center. **Cards:** AX, CB, DC, DS, JC, MC, VI. *(See color ad p 623)*

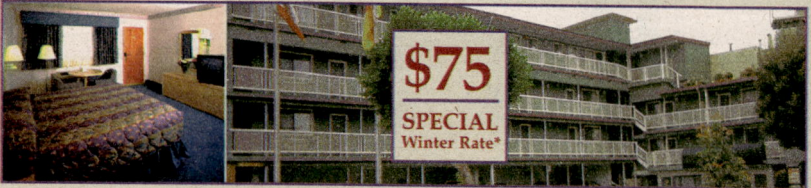

FEE  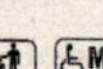   / SOME UNITS VCR / FEE

(See map and index starting on p. 590)

GREENWICH INN Book at aaa.com **Phone:** (415)921-5162 104

AAA SAVE

Motel

7/1-10/31	1P: $80-$115	2P: $90-$135	XP: $10	F15
5/1-6/30	1P: $75-$108	2P: $80-$125	XP: $10	F15
2/1-4/30 & 11/1-1/31	1P: $55-$80	2P: $65-$90	XP: $10	F15

Location: Just s of Lombard St. 3201 Steiner St 94123. Fax: 415/921-3602. **Facility:** 32 one-bedroom standard units. 2 stories (no elevator), exterior corridors. *Bath:* shower only. **Parking:** on-site. **Terms:** package plans - weekends. **Amenities:** *Some:* dual phone lines. **Cards:** AX, CB, DC, DS, MC, VI. **Special Amenities: free newspaper.**

SOME UNITS

(See map and index starting on p. 590)

THE HANDLERY UNION SQUARE HOTEL Book at aaa.com Phone: (415)781-7800 54

SAVE

Large-scale Hotel

(See color ad below)

All Year 1P: $189-$299 2P: $189-$299 XP: $10 F15

Location: Just sw of Union Square. 351 Geary St 94102. Fax: 415/781-0269. **Facility:** 377 units. 349 one-bedroom standard units. 28 one-bedroom suites ($249-$750). 8 stories, interior corridors. *Bath:* combo or shower only. **Parking:** valet. **Amenities:** video games, high-speed Internet, voice mail, safes, irons, hair dryers. **Dining:** 7 am-11 pm. **Pool(s):** heated outdoor. **Leisure Activities:** sauna. **Guest Services:** gift shop, valet laundry. **Business Services:** meeting rooms. **Cards:** AX, CB, DC, DS, JC, MC, VI.

FEE SOME UNITS

HARBOR COURT HOTEL Book at aaa.com Phone: (415)882-1300 8

SAVE

Small-scale Hotel

All Year 1P: $120-$235 2P: $120-$235

Location: On Embarcadero; between Howard and Mission sts. 165 Steuart St 94105. Fax: 415/882-1313. **Facility:** 131 one-bedroom standard units. 8 stories, interior corridors. *Bath:* combo or shower only. **Parking:** on-site (fee) and valet. **Terms:** cancellation fee imposed, [CP] meal plan available, 14% service charge. **Amenities:** video games (fee), dual phone lines, voice mail, fax, honor bars, irons, hair dryers. *Some:* high-speed Internet. **Dining:** 11:30 am-2 & 5:30-10 pm, Sat & Sun from 5:30 pm, cocktails. **Pool(s):** heated indoor. **Guest Services:** complimentary evening beverages, valet laundry. **Cards:** AX, DC, DS, JC, MC, VI. **Special Amenities: early check-in/late check-out.**

SOME UNITS

HILTON SAN FRANCISCO Book at aaa.com Phone: 415/771-1400 53

Large-scale Hotel

All Year 1P: $139-$269 XP: $20 F18

Location: Just w of Union Square at Mason St. 333 O'Farrell St 94102. Fax: 415/771-6807. **Facility:** In a convenient location with several fine restaurants and shops, the hotel offers some units with city views. 1907 units. 1850 one-bedroom standard units. 57 one-bedroom suites ($450-$2250). 19-46 stories, interior corridors. *Bath:* combo or shower only. **Parking:** on-site (fee) and valet. **Terms:** cancellation fee imposed. **Amenities:** video games (fee), dual phone lines, voice mail, irons, hair dryers. *Some:* CD players, high-speed Internet (fee), honor bars. **Dining:** Cityscape Bar & Restaurant, see separate listing. **Pool(s):** heated outdoor. **Leisure Activities:** whirlpool, steamrooms. *Fee:* massage. **Guest Services:** gift shop, valet laundry. **Business Services:** conference facilities, business center. **Cards:** AX, CB, DC, DS, JC, MC.

FEE SOME UNITS

HILTON SAN FRANCISCO FISHERMAN'S WHARF Book at aaa.com Phone: (415)885-4700 129

SAVE

Large-scale Hotel

7/1-10/31	1P: $179-$289	2P: $179-$289	XP: $20	F18
5/1-6/30 & 11/1-1/31	1P: $159-$279	2P: $159-$279	XP: $20	F18
2/1-4/30	1P: $139-$269	2P: $139-$269	XP: $20	F18

Location: Just sw of Fisherman's Wharf; at Columbus Ave and Jones St. 2620 Jones St 94133. Fax: 415/771-8945. **Facility:** 234 units. 225 one-bedroom standard units. 9 one-bedroom suites. 4 stories, interior corridors. *Bath:* combo or shower only. **Parking:** on-site (fee). **Terms:** [AP] meal plan available, package plans. **Amenities:** dual phone lines, voice mail, safes, hair dryers. *Some:* irons. **Dining:** 6:30 am-10 pm, cocktails. **Leisure Activities:** exercise room. **Guest Services:** valet laundry. **Business Services:** conference facilities, business center. **Cards:** AX, CB, DC, DS, JC, MC, VI. **Special Amenities: free newspaper.**

SOME UNITS

(See map and index starting on p. 590)

HOLIDAY INN CIVIC CENTER Book at aaa.com **Phone:** (415)626-6103 161

SAVE Large-scale Hotel

All Year 1P: $94-$229 2P: $94-$229 XP: $15 F19

Location: 2 blks from civic auditorium; just s of Market St and BART Station. 50 8th St 94103. Fax: 415/552-0184. **Facility:** 394 one-bedroom standard units. 14 stories, interior corridors. *Bath:* combo or shower only. **Parking:** on-site (fee). **Terms:** small pets only ($75 fee). **Amenities:** voice mail, irons, hair dryers. *Fee:* video games, safes. **Dining:** 6 am-11 & 5:30-11 pm, cocktails. **Pool(s):** heated outdoor. **Leisure Activities:** exercise room. **Guest Services:** gift shop, coin laundry. **Business Services:** meeting rooms, business center. **Cards:** AX, CB, DC, DS, JC, MC, VI. *(See color ad p 619)*

FEE FEE SOME UNITS FEE

HOLIDAY INN EXPRESS & SUITES AT FISHERMANS WHARF Book at aaa.com **Phone:** (415)409-4600 124

SAVE Small-scale Hotel

All Year [ECP] 1P: $124-$299 2P: $124-$299 XP: $20 F19

Location: Just s of Fisherman's Wharf. 550 North Point 94133. Fax: 415/409-5111. **Facility:** 252 one-bedroom standard units. 4 stories, interior corridors. *Bath:* combo or shower only. **Parking:** on-site (fee) and valet. **Amenities:** dual phone lines, voice mail, safes, irons, hair dryers. *Fee:* video games, high-speed Internet. **Leisure Activities:** exercise room. **Business Services:** meeting rooms, business center. **Cards:** AX, CB, DC, DS, JC, MC, VI. **Special Amenities: free expanded continental breakfast and free local telephone calls.** *(See color ad p 260 & p 619)*

FEE SOME UNITS FEE FEE

HOLIDAY INN FISHERMAN'S WHARF Book at aaa.com **Phone:** (415)771-9000 125

SAVE Large-scale Hotel

All Year 1P: $129-$299 2P: $129-$299 XP: $20 F19

Location: Across from bay. 1300 Columbus Ave 94133. Fax: 415/771-7006. **Facility:** 585 one-bedroom standard units. 5 stories, interior corridors. *Bath:* combo or shower only. **Parking:** on-site (fee). **Amenities:** voice mail, safes, irons, hair dryers. *Some:* dual phone lines. **Dining:** 2 restaurants, 24 hours, cocktails. **Pool(s):** heated outdoor. **Leisure Activities:** exercise room. **Guest Services:** gift shop, valet and coin laundry, airport transportation (fee)-San Francisco International Airport. **Business Services:** meeting rooms, business center. **Cards:** AX, CB, DC, DS, JC, MC, VI. *(See color ad p 619)*

FEE SOME UNITS FEE

HOLIDAY INN GOLDEN GATEWAY NOB HILL (AREA) Book at aaa.com **Phone:** (415)441-4000 147

SAVE Large-scale Hotel

All Year 1P: $129-$179 2P: $129-$179

Location: US 101 (Van Ness Ave) at Pine St. 1500 Van Ness Ave 94109. Fax: 415/776-7155. **Facility:** 499 one-bedroom standard units. 26 stories, interior corridors. *Bath:* combo or shower only. **Parking:** on-site (fee). **Terms:** check-in 4 pm, cancellation fee imposed. **Amenities:** voice mail, irons, hair dryers. *Fee:* video games, high-speed Internet. **Dining:** 6:30-10:30 am, 11:30-2 & 4:30-10 pm, cocktails. **Pool(s):** heated outdoor. **Leisure Activities:** exercise room. **Guest Services:** gift shop, valet laundry. **Business Services:** conference facilities, business center. **Cards:** AX, CB, DC, DS, JC, MC, VI. *(See color ad below)*

FEE SOME UNITS FEE FEE

HOLIDAY INN SELECT & SPA DOWNTOWN Book at aaa.com **Phone:** (415)433-6600 4

SAVE Large-scale Hotel

All Year 1P: $119-$279 2P: $119-$279 XP: $20 F19

Location: Adjacent to North Beach. 750 Kearny St 94108. Fax: 415/765-7891. **Facility:** 565 units. 562 one-bedroom standard units. 3 one-bedroom suites. 27 stories, interior corridors. **Parking:** on-site (fee). **Terms:** small pets only ($100 fee). **Amenities:** voice mail, irons, hair dryers. **Dining:** 6:30 am-10:30 & 5:30-10 pm, cocktails. **Pool(s):** heated outdoor. **Leisure Activities:** exercise room, spa. **Guest Services:** gift shop, coin laundry. **Business Services:** conference facilities, business center. **Cards:** AX, CB, DC, DS, JC, MC, VI. *(See color ad p 619)*

FEE FEE SOME UNITS FEE

(See map and index starting on p. 590)

HOTEL ADAGIO *Book at aaa.com* **Phone:** (415)775-5000 **41**

AAA SAVE

Large-scale Hotel

All Year 1P: $189-$695 2P: $189-$695 XP: $20 F12

Location: 3 blks w of Union Square; between Jones and Taylor sts. 550 Geary St 94102. Fax: 415/775-9388. **Facility:** 171 units. 169 one-bedroom standard units. 2 one-bedroom suites ($269-$695). 15 stories, interior corridors. *Bath:* combo or shower only. **Parking:** on-site (fee) and valet. **Terms:** cancellation fee imposed, [BP], [CP], [ECP] & [MAP] meal plans available. **Amenities:** video games, CD players, high-speed Internet, dual phone lines, voice mail, safes, honor bars, irons, hair dryers. **Dining:** 6:30 am-11 & 5-10 pm, cocktails. **Guest Services:** sundries, valet laundry. **Business Services:** meeting rooms, business center. **Cards:** AX, CB, DC, DS, JC, MC, VI. **Special Amenities: free newspaper and early check-in/late check-out.**

SOME UNITS

FEE

HOTEL BERESFORD *Book at aaa.com* **Phone:** (415)673-9900 **21**

AAA SAVE

Small-scale Hotel

4/1-10/31 [CP] 1P: $92-$119 2P: $92-$119 XP: $10 F12

2/1-3/31 & 11/1-1/31 [CP] 1P: $87-$105 2P: $87-$105 XP: $10 F12

Location: 1 blk nw of Union Square at Mason St. 635 Sutter St 94102. Fax: 415/474-0449. **Facility:** 114 one-bedroom standard units, some with whirlpools. 7 stories, interior corridors. *Bath:* combo or shower only. **Parking:** valet. **Terms:** small pets only (in smoking units). **Amenities:** honor bars, irons. **Dining:** 7 am-2 & 5:30-10 pm; closed for dinner Sun & Mon. **Guest Services:** valet laundry. **Cards:** AX, CB, DC, DS, JC, MC, VI. **Special Amenities: free continental breakfast.** *(See color ad below)*

SOME UNITS

HOTEL BIJOU *Book at aaa.com* **Phone:** (415)771-1200 **5**

Small-scale Hotel

All Year [CP] 1P: $125-$145 2P: $125-$145 XP: $10 F12

Location: US 101. 111 Mason St 94102. Fax: 415/346-3196. **Facility:** 65 one-bedroom standard units. 3 stories, interior corridors. *Bath:* combo or shower only. **Parking:** valet. **Terms:** age restrictions may apply, package plans. **Amenities:** dual phone lines, voice mail, irons, hair dryers. **Guest Services:** valet laundry. **Business Services:** meeting rooms, PC. **Cards:** AX, DC, DS, MC, VI. *(See color ad p 617)*

SOME UNITS

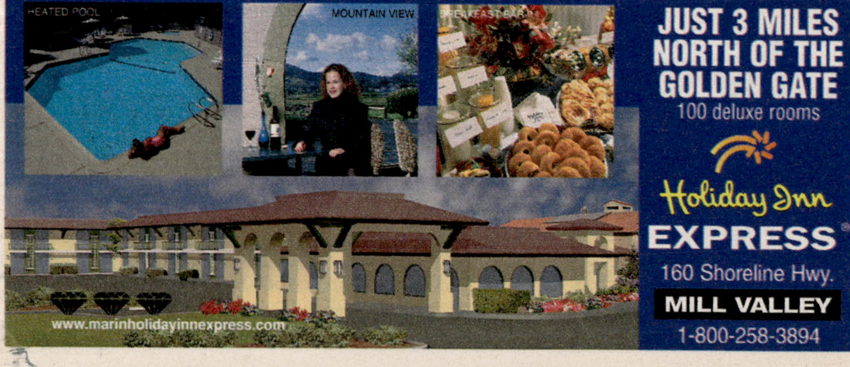

(See map and index starting on p. 590)

HOTEL DEL SOL **Book at aaa.com** **Phone:** (415)921-5520 131

Motel

All Year [CP] 1P: $135-$185 2P: $135-$185 XP: $20 F17

Location: Just w of US 101 (Van Ness Ave) at Greenwich St. 3100 Webster St 94123. Fax: 415/931-4137. **Facility:** 57 units. 47 one-bedroom standard units. 10 one-bedroom suites ($205-$235). 3 stories, exterior corridors. *Bath:* combo or shower only. **Parking:** on-site. **Terms:** cancellation fee imposed. **Amenities:** CD players, high-speed Internet (fee), dual phone lines, voice mail, safes, irons, hair dryers. **Pool(s):** outdoor. **Leisure Activities:** sauna. **Guest Services:** valet laundry. **Business Services:** fax. **Cards:** AX, DC, DS, MC, VI. ***(See color ad p 617)***

SOME UNITS

FEE FEE FEE

HOTEL JULIANA **Book at aaa.com** **Phone:** (415)392-2540 19

AAA SAVE

Small-scale Hotel

4/1-11/15 1P: $189-$219 2P: $189-$219 XP: $20 F17

2/1-3/31 & 11/16-1/31 1P: $169-$199 2P: $169-$199 XP: $20 F17

Location: Downtown. 590 Bush St 94108. Fax: 415/986-2880. **Facility:** 107 units. 82 one-bedroom standard units. 25 one-bedroom suites ($189-$249). 8 stories, interior corridors. *Bath:* combo or shower only. **Parking:** on-site (fee) and valet. **Amenities:** video games, voice mail, honor bars, irons, hair dryers. **Leisure Activities:** exercise room. **Guest Services:** complimentary evening beverages, valet laundry. **Cards:** AX, DC, DS, JC, MC, VI. **Special Amenities: early check-in/late check-out.**

SOME UNITS

FEE

HOTEL METROPOLIS **Book at aaa.com** **Phone:** 415/775-4600 74

Small-scale Hotel

Property failed to provide current rates

Location: US 101, exit Market St, just w. 25 Mason St 94102. Fax: 415/775-4606. **Facility:** 105 units. 100 one-bedroom standard units. 4 one- and 1 two-bedroom suites. 11 stories, interior corridors. *Bath:* combo or shower only. **Parking:** on-site (fee) and valet. **Terms:** pets ($50 fee, with prior approval). **Amenities:** video games, dual phone lines, voice mail, irons, hair dryers. *Some:* CD players, high-speed Internet. **Leisure Activities:** limited exercise equipment. **Guest Services:** complimentary evening beverages, valet laundry. **Business Services:** meeting rooms, business center.

SOME UNITS

FEE FEE

HOTEL MILANO **Book at aaa.com** **Phone:** (415)543-8555 61

AAA SAVE

Small-scale Hotel

All Year 1P: $139-$219 2P: $139-$219 XP: $20 F12

Location: Just s of Market St; between Mission and Market sts. 55 5th St 94103. Fax: 415/543-5885. **Facility:** 108 one-bedroom standard units, some with whirlpools. 7 stories, interior corridors. **Parking:** on-site (fee) and valet. **Terms:** cancellation fee imposed. **Amenities:** video games, voice mail, safes, honor bars, irons, hair dryers. **Dining:** 7 am-10 pm, cocktails. **Leisure Activities:** sauna, whirlpool, steamroom, exercise room. **Guest Services:** valet laundry. **Business Services:** meeting rooms. **Cards:** AX, DC, DS, MC, VI.

SOME UNITS

HOTEL MONACO **Book at aaa.com** **Phone:** (415)292-0100 47

AAA SAVE

Large-scale Hotel

All Year 1P: $170-$359 2P: $170-$359 XP: $15 F17

Location: Just w of Union Square at Taylor St. 501 Geary St 94102. Fax: 415/292-8129. **Facility:** Distinctive architecture, eclectic decor and attention to service characterize this restored 1910 American Beaux Arts hotel. 201 units. 177 one-bedroom standard units. 24 one-bedroom suites, some with whirlpools. 7 stories, interior corridors. *Bath:* combo or shower only. **Parking:** on-site (fee) and valet. **Terms:** cancellation fee imposed. **Amenities:** video games, CD players, high-speed Internet, dual phone lines, voice mail, fax, safes, honor bars, irons, hair dryers. **Dining:** 2 restaurants, 7 am-10 pm, Fri & Sat-11 pm, cocktails. **Leisure Activities:** sauna, whirlpool, exercise room. **Guest Services:** complimentary evening beverages, valet laundry, area transportation. **Business Services:** meeting rooms, business center. **Cards:** AX, CB, DC, DS, JC, MC. **Special Amenities: early check-in/late check-out.**

SOME UNITS

FEE

HOTEL NIKKO **Book at aaa.com** **Phone:** (415)394-1111 49

AAA SAVE

Large-scale Hotel

All Year 1P: $175 2P: $175 XP: $30 F18

Location: 3 blks w of Union Square. 222 Mason St 94102. Fax: 415/394-1106. **Facility:** Contemporary Japanese styling. 532 units. 516 one-bedroom standard units. 16 one-bedroom suites ($285-$2500), some with whirlpools. 25 stories, interior corridors. **Parking:** valet. **Terms:** cancellation fee imposed, [AP], [BP] & [CP] meal plans available, small pets only. **Amenities:** CD players, high-speed Internet, dual phone lines, voice mail, fax, honor bars, irons, hair dryers. *Some:* safes. **Dining:** 6:30 am-10 pm, cocktails, also, Anzu Restaurant, see separate listing. **Pool(s):** heated indoor. **Leisure Activities:** sauna, whirlpool. *Fee:* massage. **Guest Services:** gift shop, valet laundry. **Business Services:** conference facilities, business center. **Special Amenities: preferred room (subject to availability with advanced reservations).**

SOME UNITS

FEE FEE

HOTEL PALOMAR **Phone:** (415)348-1111 40

AAA SAVE

Small-scale Hotel

All Year 1P: $169-$349 2P: $169-$349 XP: $15 F16

Location: At Market St; downtown. Located in Union Square. 12 Fourth St 94103. Fax: 415/348-0302. **Facility:** Distinguished by its sleekly designed, finely tailored interior and emphasis on service, this refurbished landmark hotel was built in 1908. 198 units. 182 one-bedroom standard units. 16 one-bedroom suites with whirlpools. 9 stories, interior corridors. *Bath:* combo or shower only. **Parking:** valet. **Terms:** age restrictions may apply, pets (dogs only, in designated units). **Amenities:** video games, CD players, high-speed Internet, dual phone lines, voice mail, fax, safes, honor bars, irons, hair dryers. **Dining:** 7 am-10 & 4-10:30 pm, Sat & Sun 8 am-11 & 4-11:30 pm, also, Fifth Floor, see separate listing. **Leisure Activities:** exercise room. *Fee:* massage. **Guest Services:** valet laundry. **Business Services:** meeting rooms. **Cards:** AX, DC, DS, JC, MC, VI. **Special Amenities: early check-in/late check-out.**

SOME UNITS

FEE

(See map and index starting on p. 590)

HOTEL REX *Book at aaa.com* **Phone:** (415)433-4434 22

Small-scale Hotel

All Year [CP] 1P: $205-$245 2P: $205-$245 XP: $20 F12

Location: Just nw of Union Square. 562 Sutter St 94102. Fax: 415/433-3695. **Facility:** 94 units. 92 one-bedroom standard units. 2 one-bedroom suites. 7 stories, interior corridors. **Parking:** valet. **Terms:** cancellation fee imposed, [AP], [BP] & [ECP] meal plans available. **Amenities:** CD players, dual phone lines, voice mail, honor bars, irons, hair dryers. *Some:* high-speed Internet. **Guest Services:** valet laundry. **Business Services:** meeting rooms, business center. **Cards:** AX, DC, DS, MC, VI.

SOME UNITS

FEE FEE

HOTEL TRITON *Book at aaa.com* **Phone:** (415)394-0500 31

SAVE

Small-scale Hotel

All Year 1P: $139-$199 2P: $139-$199 XP: $15 F17

Location: Near Union Square at Bush St. 342 Grant Ave 94108. Fax: 415/394-0555. **Facility:** 140 one-bedroom standard units, some with whirlpools. 7 stories, interior corridors. *Bath:* combo or shower only. **Parking:** on-site (fee) and valet. **Terms:** cancellation fee imposed, [AP], [BP] & [CP] meal plans available, package plans. **Amenities:** video games (fee), CD players, high-speed Internet, dual phone lines, voice mail, fax, honor bars, irons, hair dryers. *Some:* DVD players. **Leisure Activities:** exercise room. **Guest Services:** complimentary evening beverages, valet laundry. **Business Services:** meeting rooms, business center. **Cards:** AX, CB, DC, DS, JC, MC, VI. **Special Amenities: early check-in/late check-out.** *(See color ad below)*

SOME UNITS

HOTEL UNION SQUARE *Book at aaa.com* **Phone:** (415)397-3000 73

Small-scale Hotel

5/2-10/31	1P: $95-$165	2P: $95-$165	XP: $10	F12
11/1-1/31	1P: $79-$129	2P: $79-$129	XP: $10	F12
2/1-5/1	1P: $85-$125	2P: $85-$125	XP: $10	F12

Location: US 101, exit Market E to Powell St, just n of cable car turnaround. 114 Powell St 94102. Fax: 415/399-1874. **Facility:** 131 units. 130 one-bedroom standard units. 1 one-bedroom suite ($175-$350). 5 stories, interior corridors. *Bath:* combo or shower only. **Parking:** on-site (fee). **Terms:** pets ($50 fee). **Amenities:** video games, voice mail, hair dryers. *Some:* safes, irons. **Guest Services:** valet laundry. **Business Services:** business center. **Cards:** AX, CB, DC, DS, JC, MC, VI.

SOME UNITS

FEE FEE

HUNTINGTON HOTEL *Book at aaa.com* **Phone:** (415)474-5400 9

Large-scale Hotel

All Year 1P: $295-$1130 2P: $320-$1130 XP: $30 F5

Location: Atop Nob Hill. 1075 California St 94108. Fax: 415/474-6227. **Facility:** 135 units. 95 one-bedroom standard units. 40 one-bedroom suites ($465-$1130), some with efficiencies. 12 stories, interior corridors. **Parking:** valet. **Terms:** cancellation fee imposed. **Amenities:** high-speed Internet, dual phone lines, voice mail, fax, hair dryers. *Some:* DVD players (fee). **Pool(s):** heated indoor. **Leisure Activities:** spa. **Guest Services:** gift shop, valet laundry. **Cards:** AX, CB, DC, DS, JC, MC, VI.

SOME UNITS

FEE

HYATT FISHERMAN'S WHARF *Book at aaa.com* **Phone:** (415)563-1234 126

SAVE

Large-scale Hotel

All Year 1P: $109-$269 2P: $109-$269 XP: $25 F18

Location: Just s of Fisherman's Wharf at Taylor St. 555 N Point St 94133. Fax: 415/749-6122. **Facility:** 313 units. 307 one-bedroom standard units. 6 one-bedroom suites, some with whirlpools. 5 stories, interior corridors. *Bath:* combo or shower only. **Parking:** on-site (fee). **Terms:** cancellation fee imposed. **Amenities:** dual phone lines, voice mail, irons, hair dryers. *Some:* high-speed Internet (fee). **Dining:** 6:30 am-11 pm. **Pool(s):** heated outdoor. **Leisure Activities:** sauna, whirlpool, exercise room. **Guest Services:** coin laundry, area transportation-within 2 mi. **Business Services:** conference facilities, business center. **Cards:** AX, CB, DC, DS, JC, MC, VI. *(See color ad p 623)*

SOME UNITS

FEE

(See map and index starting on p. 590)

HYATT REGENCY-SAN FRANCISCO Book at aaa.com Phone: (415)788-1234 7

Large-scale Hotel

All Year 1P: $89-$240 2P: $89-$240 XP: $25 F18

Location: Foot of California and Market sts. Located in the financial district. 5 Embarcadero Center 94111. Fax: 415/398-2567. **Facility:** The rooftop restaurant at this high-rise offers great views of the city; tourist draws Union Square and Fisherman's Wharf are conveniently close. 805 units. 775 one-bedroom standard units. 30 one-bedroom suites. 17 stories, interior corridors. *Bath:* combo or shower only. **Parking:** valet. **Terms:** cancellation fee imposed. **Amenities:** high-speed Internet, dual phone lines, voice mail, safes, honor bars, irons, hair dryers. **Dining:** 3 restaurants, 6 am-midnight, cocktails, entertainment. **Leisure Activities:** exercise room. *Fee:* massage. **Guest Services:** gift shop, valet laundry. **Business Services:** conference facilities, business center. **Cards:** AX, CB, DC, DS, JC, MC, VI. *(See color ad p 623)*

FEE SOME UNITS

INN AT THE OPERA Book at aaa.com Phone: (415)863-8400 156

Small-scale Hotel

All Year [ECP] 1P: $165 2P: $165

Location: Just w of US 101 (Van Ness Ave); between Franklin and Gough sts. 333 Fulton St 94102. Fax: 415/861-0821. **Facility:** Smoke free premises. 48 units. 30 one-bedroom standard units. 6 one- and 12 two-bedroom suites ($195-$235). 7 stories, interior corridors. **Parking:** valet. **Amenities:** voice mail, hair dryers. *Some:* CD players, irons. **Guest Services:** valet laundry. **Cards:** AX, CB, DC, DS, JC, MC, VI.

ASK VCR DATA PORT

INN 1890 Book at aaa.com Phone: (415)386-0486 163

Historic Bed & Breakfast

All Year [ECP] 1P: $79-$129 2P: $79-$129 XP: $10 F3

Location: 1 blk e of Golden Gate Park. 1890 Page St 94117. Fax: 415/386-3626. **Facility:** The inn offers comfortable accommodations in a residential area that's walking distance from Golden Gate Park. Smoke free premises. 16 units. 12 one-bedroom standard units, some with kitchens. 3 one-bedroom suites ($129-$159), some with kitchens. 1 cottage ($119-$129). 3 stories (no elevator), interior corridors. *Bath:* shared or private, combo or shower only. **Parking:** on-site (fee). **Terms:** age restrictions may apply, weekly rates available. **Amenities:** voice mail. *Some:* irons, hair dryers. **Guest Services:** coin laundry. **Business Services:** PC. **Cards:** MC, VI.

ASK DATA PORT SOME UNITS

(See map and index starting on p. 590)

INN @ UNION SQUARE *Book at aaa.com* **Phone:** (415)397-3510 **30**

SAVE — Historic Small-scale Hotel

6/1-1/31	1P: $143-$199	2P: $143-$199
2/1-5/31	1P: $125-$189	2P: $125-$189

Location: 1 blk w of Union Square. 440 Post St 94102. Fax: 415/989-0529. **Facility:** One of several small boutique hotels in the San Francisco area, the inn is close to the newly renovated Union Square. Smoke free premises. 30 units. 23 one-bedroom standard units. 7 one-bedroom suites, some with whirlpools. 6 stories, interior corridors. *Bath:* combo or shower only. **Parking:** no self-parking. **Terms:** age restrictions may apply, cancellation fee imposed, [ECP] meal plan available. **Amenities:** high-speed Internet, dual phone lines, voice mail, irons, hair dryers. **Guest Services:** valet laundry. **Business Services:** meeting rooms. **Cards:** AX, DC, DS, MC, VI. **Special Amenities: free continental breakfast and free room upgrade (subject to availability with advanced reservations).**

KENSINGTON PARK HOTEL *Book at aaa.com* **Phone:** (415)788-6400 **71**

Small-scale Hotel

All Year	1P: $125-$159	2P: $125-$159	XP: $20 F12

Location: US 101, exit 5th St, r to Ellis St, r on Taylor St. 450 Post St 94102. Fax: 415/399-9484. **Facility:** 90 units. 89 one-bedroom standard units, some with whirlpools. 1 one-bedroom suite with whirlpool. 12 stories, interior corridors. *Bath:* combo or shower only. **Parking:** valet. **Terms:** pets ($50 fee). **Amenities:** video games, dual phone lines, voice mail, irons, hair dryers. **Dining:** Farallon, see separate listing. **Leisure Activities:** limited exercise equipment. **Guest Services:** valet laundry. **Business Services:** business center. **Cards:** AX, CB, DC, DS, JC, MC, VI.

SOME UNITS

ASK / FEE

KING GEORGE HOTEL *Book at aaa.com* **Phone:** (415)781-5050 **48**

SAVE — Small-scale Hotel

6/1-11/15	1P: $109-$175	2P: $109-$195
11/16-1/31	1P: $99-$165	2P: $99-$195
2/1-5/31	1P: $99-$165	2P: $99-$185

Location: Just w of Union Square. 334 Mason St 94102. Fax: 415/391-6976. **Facility:** 154 units. 153 one-bedroom standard units. 1 one-bedroom suite ($165-$255). 9 stories, interior corridors. *Bath:* combo or shower only. **Parking:** valet. **Terms:** age restrictions may apply, cancellation fee imposed, [ECP] meal plan available, package plans. **Amenities:** *Some:* video games, high-speed Internet (fee), voice mail, safes, irons, hair dryers. **Guest Services:** valet laundry. **Business Services:** meeting rooms, business center. **Cards:** AX, CB, DC, DS, JC, MC, VI.

(See color ad p 631)

SOME UNITS

FEE / 24

THE LAUREL INN *Book at aaa.com* **Phone:** (415)567-8467 **140**

SAVE — Motel

All Year	1P: $150-$185	2P: $150-$185	XP: $10 F12

Location: 1 mi w of US 101 (Van Ness Ave), 1 mi e of Park Presidio Blvd (SR 1) at California St. 444 Presidio Ave 94115. Fax: 415/928-1866. **Facility:** 49 one-bedroom standard units, some with efficiencies. 4 stories, interior corridors. *Bath:* combo or shower only. **Parking:** on-site. **Terms:** 1-2 night minimum stay - weekends, cancellation fee imposed. **Amenities:** CD players, dual phone lines, voice mail, irons, hair dryers. **Guest Services:** valet laundry. **Business Services:** PC. **Cards:** AX, DC, DS, JC, MC, VI. **Special Amenities: free continental breakfast and free newspaper.**

SOME UNITS

FEE / VCR

LOMBARD MOTOR INN **Phone:** 415/441-6000 **121**

SAVE — Motel

All Year	1P: $86-$125	2P: $86-$125	XP: $10 F5

Location: US 101 (Van Ness Ave) at Franklin St. 1475 Lombard St 94123 (3210 Fillmore St #3, SAN FRANCISCO). Fax: 415/441-4291. **Facility:** 48 one-bedroom standard units. 4 stories, interior corridors. *Bath:* combo or shower only. **Parking:** on-site. **Amenities:** hair dryers. **Cards:** AX, CB, DC, MC, VI. **Special Amenities: free local telephone calls.** *(See color ad p 616)*

LOMBARD PLAZA MOTEL **Phone:** 415/921-2444 **107**

Motel

Property failed to provide current rates

Location: On US 101 (Van Ness Ave). 2026 Lombard St 94123. Fax: 415/921-5275. **Facility:** 29 one-bedroom standard units. 2-3 stories (no elevator), exterior corridors. *Bath:* combo or shower only. **Parking:** on-site.

SOME UNITS

MANDARIN ORIENTAL, SAN FRANCISCO *Book at aaa.com* **Phone:** (415)276-9888 **14**

Large-scale Hotel

9/6-1/31	1P: $490-$720	2P: $515-$745	XP: $45	F12
2/1-9/5	1P: $470-$700	2P: $495-$725	XP: $45	F12

Location: US 101, s on Lombard St, e on Bush, then s. 222 Sansome St 94104. Fax: 415/433-0289. **Facility:** Top 11 floors of 48 story First Interstate Center Bldg. View of bay. 158 units. 154 one-bedroom standard units. 3 one- and 1 two-bedroom suites ($1400-$3000), some with whirlpools. 47 stories, interior corridors. *Bath:* combo or shower only. **Parking:** valet. **Terms:** cancellation fee imposed, pets (with prior approval). **Amenities:** video library, video games, CD players, high-speed Internet, dual phone lines, voice mail, safes, honor bars, irons, hair dryers. *Some:* DVD players, fax. **Dining:** Silks, see separate listing. **Leisure Activities:** exercise room, spa. **Guest Services:** gift shop, valet laundry. **Business Services:** meeting rooms, business center. **Cards:** AX, CB, DC, DS, JC, MC, VI.

SOME UNITS

ASK / VCR

MARINA INN *Book at aaa.com* **Phone:** (415)928-1000 **119**

Motel

	2P		
6/1-10/31	2P: $85-$135	XP: $10	F5
3/1-5/31	2P: $75-$125	XP: $10	F5
2/1-2/29 & 11/1-1/31	2P: $65-$115	XP: $10	F5

Location: At Lombard St. 3110 Octavia St 94123. Fax: 415/928-5909. **Facility:** Smoke free premises. 40 one-bedroom standard units. 4 stories, interior corridors. **Parking:** street. **Terms:** cancellation fee imposed, package plans - seasonal. **Amenities:** *Some:* irons, hair dryers. **Guest Services:** complimentary evening beverages. **Cards:** AX, DC, MC, VI.

ASK

(See map and index starting on p. 590)

MARK HOPKINS INTER-CONTINENTAL *Book at aaa.com* **Phone:** (415)392-3434 **10**

AAA SAVE

Historic Large-scale Hotel

All Year 1P: $395-$495 2P: $425-$525 XP: $30 F17

Location: Corner of California and Mason sts. 1 Nob Hill 94108. Fax: 415/421-3302. **Facility:** Centered in the city, this refined hotel is notable for its panoramic views. 383 units. 336 one-bedroom standard units, some with whirlpools. 47 one-bedroom suites ($650-$7750), some with whirlpools. 17 stories, interior corridors. **Parking:** on-site (fee). **Terms:** cancellation fee imposed. **Amenities:** video games (fee), dual phone lines, voice mail, safes, honor bars, irons, hair dryers. **Dining:** 6:30 am-10:30 pm, cocktails, entertainment. **Leisure Activities:** exercise room. *Fee:* massage. **Guest Services:** gift shop, valet laundry, area transportation. **Business Services:** conference facilities, business center. **Cards:** AX, CB, DC, DS, JC, MC, VI.

FEE SOME UNITS FEE

(See map and index starting on p. 590)

MAXWELL HOTEL Book at aaa.com **Phone:** (415)986-2000 **28**

Large-scale Hotel

All Year	1P: $145-$175	2P: $145-$175	XP: $15	F18

Location: Just w of Union Square. 386 Geary St 94102. Fax: 415/397-2447. **Facility:** 153 units. 150 one-bedroom standard units. 3 one-bedroom suites ($175-$205). 12 stories, interior corridors. *Bath:* combo or shower only. **Parking:** no self-parking. **Terms:** age restrictions may apply, package plans. **Amenities:** video games, voice mail, safes, irons, hair dryers. *Some:* high-speed Internet. **Dining:** 7 am-11 pm, Fri & Sat from 8 am, cocktails. **Guest Services:** valet laundry. **Business Services:** meeting rooms, business center. **Cards:** AX, CB, DC, DS, JC, MC, VI. **Special Amenities: early check-in/late check-out and free room upgrade (subject to availability with advanced reservations).**

SOME UNITS / FEE / VCR /

MISSION INN Book at aaa.com **Phone:** (415)584-5020 **170**

Motel

5/28-9/30	1P: $75-$95	2P: $75-$110	XP: $10	F12
2/1-5/27 & 10/1-1/31	1P: $70-$95	2P: $75-$100	XP: $7	F12

Location: 1 mi e of I-280, exit Geneva Ave, just s. 5630 Mission St 94112. Fax: 415/584-1752. **Facility:** 52 units. 41 one- and 11 two-bedroom standard units, some with efficiencies. 2-4 stories, exterior corridors. *Bath:* combo or shower only. **Parking:** on-site. **Terms:** package plans. **Guest Services:** coin laundry. **Cards:** AX, CB, DC, DS, MC, VI. *(See color ad below)*

SOME UNITS / FEE FEE /

THE MONARCH HOTEL Book at aaa.com **Phone:** (415)673-5232 **150**

Small-scale Hotel

4/1-10/31	1P: $74-$129	2P: $84-$139	XP: $10	F12
2/1-3/31 & 11/1-1/31	1P: $55-$109	2P: $55-$109	XP: $10	F12

Location: Just e of US 101 (Van Ness Ave). 1015 Geary Blvd 94109. Fax: 415/885-2802. **Facility:** 101 one-bedroom standard units. 6 stories, interior corridors. **Parking:** on-site (fee). **Amenities:** safes (fee). *Some:* irons, hair dryers. **Dining:** 7 am-2:30 pm. **Business Services:** meeting rooms. **Cards:** AX, CB, DC, DS, JC, MC, VI. **Special Amenities: free local telephone calls and early check-in/late check-out.**

SOME UNITS / /

MONTICELLO INN Book at aaa.com **Phone:** (415)392-8800 **57**

Small-scale Hotel

All Year	1P: $129-$199	2P: $129-$199	XP: $20	F17

Location: Just w of Union Square. 127 Ellis St 94102. Fax: 415/398-2650. **Facility:** 91 units. 70 one-bedroom standard units. 21 one-bedroom suites ($199-$299), some with whirlpools. 5 stories, interior corridors. *Bath:* combo or shower only. **Parking:** valet. **Terms:** cancellation fee imposed, [BP] & [CP] meal plans available, pets (with prior approval). **Amenities:** video games, dual phone lines, voice mail, honor bars, irons, hair dryers. **Dining:** 11 am-10 pm, Sun 5 pm-11 pm. **Leisure Activities:** book readings. **Guest Services:** complimentary evening beverages, valet laundry. **Business Services:** meeting rooms, business center. **Cards:** AX, DC, DS, JC, MC, VI. **Special Amenities: early check-in/late check-out.**

SOME UNITS FEE / /

(See map and index starting on p. 590)

NOB HILL HOTEL Book at aaa.com Phone: (415)885-2987 149

Small-scale Hotel
5/1-11/30 [CP] 1P: $79-$185 2P: $79-$185
3/1-4/30 [CP] 1P: $59-$119 2P: $59-$119
2/1-2/29 & 12/1-1/31 [CP] 1P: $55-$119 2P: $55-$119

Location: 5 blks nw of Union Square. 835 Hyde St 94109. Fax: 415/345-3646. **Facility:** Smoke free premises. 50 units. 47 one-bedroom standard units. 3 one-bedroom suites with whirlpools. 5 stories, interior corridors. *Bath:* combo or shower only. **Parking:** on-site (fee). **Terms:** weekly rates available. **Amenities:** CD players, voice mail, irons, hair dryers. *Some:* high-speed Internet, fax. **Guest Services:** complimentary evening beverages, coin laundry. **Business Services:** business center. **Cards:** AX, DC, DS, MC, VI.

SOME UNITS

NOB HILL LAMBOURNE Book at aaa.com Phone: (415)433-2287 20

Small-scale Hotel
All Year [ECP] 1P: $189-$249 2P: $189-$249 XP: $20 F12

Location: Just n of Union Square. 725 Pine St 94108. Fax: 415/433-0975. **Facility:** 20 units. 15 one-bedroom standard units with efficiencies. 5 one-bedroom suites ($229-$299) with efficiencies. 3 stories, interior corridors. **Parking:** on-site (fee) and valet. **Terms:** cancellation fee imposed. **Amenities:** CD players, dual phone lines, voice mail, fax, honor bars, irons, hair dryers. **Leisure Activities:** Fee: massage. **Guest Services:** complimentary evening beverages, valet laundry. **Business Services:** meeting rooms. **Cards:** AX, DC, DS, MC, VI.

NOB HILL MOTOR INN Book at aaa.com Phone: (415)775-8160 139

AAA SAVE
Motel
All Year [CP] 1P: $85-$145 2P: $85-$145 XP: $10 F11

Location: Just e of US 101 (Van Ness Ave). 1630 Pacific Ave 94109. Fax: 415/673-8842. **Facility:** Smoke free premises. 29 units. 25 one- and 2 two-bedroom standard units. 2 one-bedroom suites ($145-$175). 3 stories, exterior corridors. *Bath:* combo or shower only. **Parking:** on-site. **Terms:** 3 day cancellation notice, package plans - seasonal. **Amenities:** DVD players, high-speed Internet, voice mail, irons, hair dryers. **Cards:** AX, CB, DC, DS, JC, MC, VI. **Special Amenities: free continental breakfast and preferred room (subject to availability with advanced reservations).** *(See color ad below)*

SOME UNITS

OASIS INN Book at aaa.com Phone: (415)885-6865 154

Motel
All Year 1P: $89 2P: $89-$99 XP: $10 F12

Location: Just w of US 101 (Van Ness Ave) at Eddy St. 900 Franklin St 94109. Fax: 415/474-1652. **Facility:** 59 one-bedroom standard units. 4 stories, exterior corridors. **Parking:** on-site. **Amenities:** irons, hair dryers. **Leisure Activities:** whirlpool, exercise room. **Guest Services:** valet laundry. **Business Services:** meeting rooms. **Cards:** AX, MC, VI. ***(See color ad p 634)***

SOME UNITS

FEE

OMNI SAN FRANCISCO HOTEL Book at aaa.com Phone: (415)677-9494 39

Large-scale Hotel
9/2-10/31 1P: $159-$299 2P: $159-$299 XP: $20 F17
2/1-9/1 & 11/1-1/31 1P: $159-$269 2P: $159-$269 XP: $20 F17

Location: Downtown financial district; at Montgomery St. 500 California St 94104. Fax: 415/273-3038. **Facility:** Located downtown in the heart of San Francisco's Financial District, the hotel offers spacious and elegantly appointed guest rooms and public areas. 362 units. 348 one-bedroom standard units. 14 one-bedroom suites, some with whirlpools. 17 stories, interior corridors. **Parking:** on-site (fee). **Terms:** pets ($50 fee). **Amenities:** CD players, dual phone lines, voice mail, safes, honor bars, irons, hair dryers. *Fee:* video games, high-speed Internet. *Some:* DVD players, fax. **Leisure Activities:** exercise room. **Guest Services:** valet laundry. **Business Services:** conference facilities, business center. **Cards:** AX, CB, DC, DS, JC, MC, VI.

SOME UNITS

FEE FEE

(See map and index starting on p. 590)

THE ORCHARD HOTEL *Book at aaa.com* **Phone:** (415)362-8878 25

Small-scale Hotel

All Year 1P: $159-$269 2P: $159-$269 XP: $25 F12

Location: Just s of Stockton St. 665 Bush St 94108. Fax: 415/362-8088. **Facility:** 105 units. 96 one-bedroom standard units. 9 one-bedroom suites ($249-$359). 10 stories, interior corridors. *Bath:* combo or shower only. **Parking:** on-site (fee). **Terms:** [ECP] meal plan available. **Amenities:** video library, DVD players, CD players, high-speed Internet (fee), dual phone lines, voice mail, safes, honor bars, irons, hair dryers. **Dining:** 11 am-3 & 5:30-10 pm, cocktails, also, Solea Restaurant, see separate listing. **Leisure Activities:** exercise room. **Guest Services:** valet laundry, area transportation-Financial District. **Business Services:** meeting rooms, fax. **Cards:** AX, DC, DS, JC, MC, VI. **Special Amenities: free newspaper and early check-in/late check-out.**

FEE

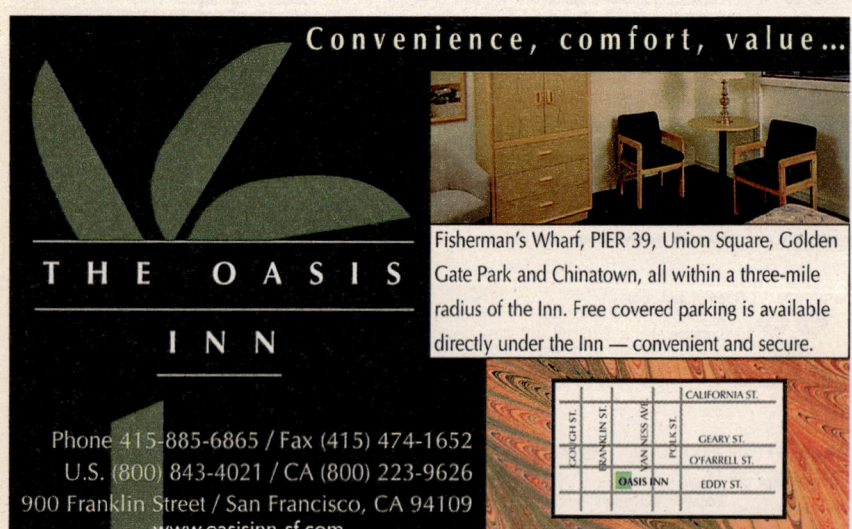

(See map and index starting on p. 590)

PACIFIC HEIGHTS INN — Phone: (415)776-3310 — 133

Motel

5/1-10/31 — 1P: $95-$150 — 2P: $95-$150
2/1-4/30 & 11/1-1/31 — 1P: $85-$125 — 2P: $85-$125

Location: Just w of US 101 (Van Ness Ave). 1555 Union St 94123. Fax: 415/776-8176. **Facility:** 40 units. 35 one- and 5 two-bedroom standard units, some with efficiencies. 2 stories, exterior corridors. *Bath:* combo or shower only. **Parking:** on-site. **Terms:** [CP] meal plan available, small pets only (with prior approval). **Cards:** AX, CB, DC, DS, MC, VI. *(See color ad p 634)*

SOME UNITS

PACIFIC MOTOR INN — *Book at aaa.com* — Phone: (415)346-4664 — 113

Motel

All Year [CP] — 1P: $72-$172 — 2P: $72-$172 — XP: $10 — F6

Location: US 101 at Broderick. 2599 Lombard St 94123. Fax: 415/346-4665. **Facility:** 42 one-bedroom standard units. 3 stories, exterior corridors. *Bath:* combo or shower only. **Parking:** on-site. **Cards:** AX, MC, VI.

SOME UNITS

PALACE HOTEL — *Book at aaa.com* — Phone: (415)512-1111 — 52

Historic Large-scale Hotel

All Year — 1P: $550-$610 — 2P: $590-$650 — XP: $40 — F17

Location: Just e of Union Square at Market St. 2 New Montgomery St 94105. Fax: 415/543-0671. **Facility:** A 1909 San Francisco landmark, the hotel has been restored and offers attractively furnished guest rooms and common areas. 553 units. 519 one-bedroom standard units. 34 one-bedroom suites ($775-$4400). 8 stories, interior corridors. *Bath:* combo or shower only. **Parking:** on-site (fee) and valet. **Terms:** cancellation fee imposed. **Amenities:** video games, dual phone lines, voice mail, safes, irons, hair dryers. *Some:* honor bars. **Dining:** The Garden Court, see separate listing. **Pool(s):** heated indoor. **Leisure Activities:** sauna, whirlpool. *Fee:* massage. **Guest Services:** gift shop, valet laundry. **Business Services:** conference facilities, business center. **Cards:** AX, CB, DC, DS, JC, MC, VI.

SOME UNITS

FEE

THE PAN PACIFIC HOTEL — *Book at aaa.com* — Phone: (415)771-8600 — 27

Large-scale Hotel

All Year — 1P: $265-$365 — 2P: $265-$365 — XP: $25 — F12

Location: Just w of Union Square at Mason St. 500 Post St 94102. Fax: 415/398-0267. **Facility:** An area landmark designed by John Portman, this service-oriented hotel strives for the highest levels of luxury. 329 units. 311 one-bedroom standard units. 14 one-, 3 two- and 1 three-bedroom suites ($445-$2800), some with whirlpools. 21 stories, interior corridors. *Bath:* combo or shower only. **Parking:** valet. **Terms:** cancellation fee imposed, package plans - seasonal & weekends, small pets only ($75 deposit). **Amenities:** video games, high-speed Internet, dual phone lines, voice mail, safes, honor bars, irons, hair dryers. **Dining:** Pacific, see separate listing. **Guest Services:** valet laundry. **Business Services:** conference facilities, business center. **Cards:** AX, CB, DC, DS, JC, MC, VI.

SOME UNITS

FEE FEE FEE FEE

(See map and index starting on p. 590)

PARK HYATT HOTEL *Book at aaa.com* **Phone:** (415)392-1234 **6**

Large-scale Hotel

All Year 1P: $155-$295 2P: $155-$295 XP: $25 F18

Location: At Clay St. Located in the financial district. 333 Battery St 94111. Fax: 415/421-2433. **Facility:** The hotel, downtown in the financial district, offers a few units with views of San Francisco Bay; some rooms have balconies. 360 units. 320 one-bedroom standard units. 40 one-bedroom suites, some with whirlpools. 24 stories, interior corridors. *Bath:* combo or shower only. **Parking:** valet. **Terms:** cancellation fee imposed. **Amenities:** CD players, high-speed Internet (fee), dual phone lines, voice mail, safes, honor bars, irons, hair dryers. **Dining:** 6 am-10 pm, cocktails, entertainment. **Leisure Activities:** exercise room. **Guest Services:** valet laundry, area transportation-downtown. **Business Services:** conference facilities, business center. **Cards:** AX, CB, DC, DS, JC, MC, VI. *(See color ad p 635)*

FEE / SOME UNITS /

PETITE AUBERGE *Book at aaa.com* **Phone:** (415)673-7214 **16**

Small-scale Hotel

All Year [BP] 1P: $135-$245 2P: $135-$245 XP: $20 F5

Location: US 101 (Van Ness Ave), exit Bush St, 6 1/2 blks e. 863 Bush St 94108. Fax: 415/775-5717. **Facility:** 26 one-bedroom standard units. 5 stories, interior corridors. *Bath:* combo or shower only. **Parking:** on-site (fee) and valet. **Terms:** age restrictions may apply, cancellation fee imposed. **Amenities:** voice mail, hair dryers. *Some:* irons. **Guest Services:** complimentary evening beverages, valet laundry. **Cards:** AX, DC, DS, MC, VI.

SOME UNITS

THE PHOENIX HOTEL *Book at aaa.com* **Phone:** (415)776-1380 **155**

Motel

All Year [CP] 1P: $120-$180 2P: $120-$180 XP: $20 F17

Location: Just e of US 101 (Van Ness Ave) at Larkin. 601 Eddy St 94109. Fax: 415/885-3109. **Facility:** 44 units. 42 one-bedroom standard units. 2 one-bedroom suites ($225). 2 stories, exterior corridors. **Parking:** on-site. **Terms:** cancellation fee imposed. **Amenities:** voice mail. **Pool(s):** heated outdoor. **Guest Services:** valet laundry. **Business Services:** fax. **Cards:** AX, DC, DS, MC, VI. ***(See color ad p 617)***

FEE / SOME UNITS /

THE PICKWICK HOTEL *Book at aaa.com* **Phone:** (415)421-7500 **64**

Small-scale Hotel

All Year 1P: $59-$99 2P: $59-$99 XP: $20 F17

Location: 1 blk s of Market St at Mission St. 85 5th St 94103. Fax: 415/243-8066. **Facility:** 188 units. 186 one-bedroom standard units. 2 one-bedroom suites ($139-$179). 8 stories, interior corridors. **Parking:** on-site (fee). **Terms:** cancellation fee imposed. **Amenities:** video games, dual phone lines, voice mail, irons, hair dryers. **Guest Services:** valet laundry. **Business Services:** meeting rooms. **Cards:** AX, CB, DC, DS, JC, MC, VI.

FEE / SOME UNITS /

THE POWELL HOTEL *Book at aaa.com* **Phone:** (415)398-3200 **58**

Small-scale Hotel

5/1-10/31 1P: $94-$154 2P: $104-$164 XP: $15 F12

2/1-4/30 & 11/1-1/31 1P: $75-$134 2P: $80-$144 XP: $15 F12

Location: At Powell St cable car turnaround; downtown. 28 Cyrill Magnin St 94102. Fax: 415/398-3654. **Facility:** 126 units. 118 one-bedroom standard units. 8 one-bedroom suites. 6 stories, interior corridors. *Bath:* combo or shower only. **Parking:** valet. **Terms:** age restrictions may apply, [ECP] meal plan available, 14% service charge. **Amenities:** dual phone lines, voice mail, irons, hair dryers. **Guest Services:** valet laundry. **Business Services:** fax. **Cards:** AX, CB, DC, DS, JC, MC, VI.

FEE / SOME UNITS /

(See map and index starting on p. 590)

THE PRESCOTT HOTEL *Book at aaa.com* **Phone:** (415)563-0303 33

SAVE

Large-scale Hotel

All Year 1P: $275-$1200 2P: $275-$1200

Location: Just w of Union Square. 545 Post St 94102. Fax: 415/563-6831. **Facility:** Elegant decor and a high standard of service give The Prescott a retreat-like ambience. 164 units. 103 one-bedroom standard units. 61 one-bedroom suites, some with whirlpools. 7 stories, interior corridors. **Parking:** valet. **Terms:** age restrictions may apply, cancellation fee imposed, small pets only. **Amenities:** video games, CD players, dual phone lines, voice mail, fax, honor bars, irons, hair dryers. *Some:* high-speed Internet. **Dining:** Postrio, see separate listing. **Leisure Activities:** exercise room. *Fee:* massage. **Guest Services:** complimentary evening beverages, valet laundry. **Business Services:** meeting rooms, business center. **Cards:** AX, CB, DC, DS, JC, MC, VI. **Special Amenities: early check-in/late check-out.** *(See color ad p 636)*

SOME UNITS

FEE

PRESIDIO INN & SUITES *Book at aaa.com* **Phone:** (415)931-7810 112

SAVE

Motel

All Year 1P: $89-$149 2P: $99-$159 XP: $10 F17

Location: US 101 (Lombard St); between Scott and Pierce sts. 2361 Lombard St 94123. Fax: 415/931-5318. **Facility:** 24 one-bedroom standard units. 4 stories, exterior corridors. *Bath:* combo or shower only. **Parking:** on-site. **Amenities:** voice mail, hair dryers. **Cards:** AX, CB, DC, DS, JC, MC, VI. *(See color ad below)*

SOME UNITS

QUALITY INN UNION SQUARE *Book at aaa.com* **Phone:** (415)673-9221 55

SAVE

Small-scale Hotel

All Year [CP] 1P: $79-$159 2P: $89-$169 XP: $10 F12

Location: US 101 (Van Ness Ave), 5 blks from jct Jones and Geary sts. 610 Geary St 94102. Fax: 415/928-2434. **Facility:** 90 one-bedroom standard units, some with whirlpools. 7 stories, interior corridors. *Bath:* combo or shower only. **Parking:** valet. **Terms:** age restrictions may apply, cancellation fee imposed. **Amenities:** voice mail, safes, irons, hair dryers. **Dining:** 7 am-9 pm. **Cards:** AX, CB, DC, DS, JC, MC, VI. **Special Amenities: free continental breakfast and free local telephone calls.** *(See color ad below)*

SOME UNITS

QUEEN ANNE HOTEL *Book at aaa.com* **Phone:** (415)441-2828 151

Small-scale Hotel

All Year [ECP] 1P: $139-$199 2P: $139-$199 XP: $10 F12

Location: Just w of US 101 (Van Ness Ave) at Octavia St. 1590 Sutter St 94109. Fax: 415/775-5212. **Facility:** 48 one-bedroom standard units, some with whirlpools. 4 stories, interior corridors. *Bath:* combo or shower only. **Parking:** on-site (fee). **Terms:** weekly rates available, package plans. **Amenities:** voice mail, irons, hair dryers. **Guest Services:** complimentary evening beverages, valet laundry. **Business Services:** meeting rooms, fax (fee). **Cards:** AX, CB, DC, DS, JC, MC, VI.

SOME UNITS

ASK

FEE FEE FEE

(See map and index starting on p. 590)

RADISSON HOTEL FISHERMAN'S WHARF Book at aaa.com Phone: (415)392-6700 **101**

6/1-10/31	1P: $149-$189	2P: $149-$189	XP: $10	F
4/1-5/31	1P: $139-$179	2P: $139-$179	XP: $10	F
2/1-3/31	1P: $129-$169	2P: $129-$169	XP: $10	F
11/1-1/31	1P: $119-$159	2P: $119-$159	XP: $10	F

Large-scale Hotel **Location:** At Powell St. 250 Beach St 94133. Fax: 415/986-7853. **Facility:** 355 one-bedroom standard units. 4 stories, interior corridors. *Bath:* combo or shower only. **Parking:** on-site. **Amenities:** video games (fee), voice mail, irons, hair dryers. **Pool(s):** heated outdoor. **Leisure Activities:** exercise room. **Business Services:** meeting rooms, business center. **Cards:** AX, DC, DS, MC, VI. *(See color ad below & p 629)*

SOME UNITS

RADISSON MIYAKO HOTEL Book at aaa.com Phone: (415)922-3200 **144**

5/1-10/31	1P: $159-$219	2P: $159-$219	XP: $20	F18
2/1-4/30 & 11/1-1/31	1P: $149-$209	2P: $149-$209	XP: $20	F18

Large-scale Hotel **Location:** 1 mi w of Union Square at Laguna St. Located in Japan Center. 1625 Post St 94115. Fax: 415/921-0417. **Facility:** 218 units. 209 one-bedroom standard units, some with whirlpools. 9 one-bedroom suites ($219-$299), some with whirlpools. 16 stories, interior corridors. *Bath:* combo or shower only. **Parking:** valet. **Terms:** cancellation fee imposed. **Amenities:** dual phone lines, voice mail, irons, hair dryers. *Some:* fax. **Dining:** 6:30 am-10:30 & 5:30-10 pm, cocktails. **Leisure Activities:** exercise room. **Guest Services:** valet laundry. **Business Services:** conference facilities, business center. **Cards:** AX, CB, DC, DS, JC, MC, VI. **Special Amenities: free local telephone calls and free newspaper.** *(See color ad p 639 & p 629)*

SOME UNITS

RAMADA LIMITED DOWNTOWN Book at aaa.com Phone: (415)861-6469 **162**

5/28-10/31	1P: $89-$179	2P: $89-$179	XP: $10	F16
2/1-5/27 & 11/1-1/31	1P: $79-$159	2P: $79-$159	XP: $10	F16

Motel **Location:** Just s of Market St; between Folsom and Howard sts. 240 7th St 94103 (PO Box 1968, BURLINGAME, 94011-1966). Fax: 415/626-4041. **Facility:** 68 units. 64 one-bedroom standard units. 4 two-bedroom suites ($129-$179). 3 stories, interior/exterior corridors. *Bath:* combo or shower only. **Parking:** on-site. **Terms:** cancellation fee imposed, [ECP] meal plan available. **Amenities:** voice mail, irons, hair dryers. **Guest Services:** coin laundry. **Business Services:** meeting rooms. **Cards:** AX, DC, DS, JC, MC, VI. **Special Amenities: free continental breakfast and free newspaper.** *(See color ad p 639)*

SOME UNITS

FEE

(See map and index starting on p. 590)

RAMADA LIMITED-GOLDEN GATE *Book at aaa.com* **Phone:** (415)775-8116 **111**

SAVE — Motel

7/1-9/4 [CP]	1P: $99-$135	2P: $110-$145	XP: $10	F18
5/2-6/30 [CP]	1P: $75-$125	2P: $85-$135	XP: $10	F18
9/5-1/31 [CP]	1P: $65-$110	2P: $75-$125	XP: $10	F18
2/1-5/1 [CP]	1P: $65-$99	2P: $75-$110	XP: $10	F18

Location: 0.3 mi w of US 101 (Van Ness Ave). 1940 Lombard St 94123. Fax: 415/775-9937. **Facility:** 37 one-bedroom standard units, some with whirlpools. 3 stories (no elevator), interior/exterior corridors. **Parking:** on-site. **Terms:** cancellation fee imposed. **Amenities:** voice mail, irons, hair dryers. **Business Services:** fax. **Cards:** AX, CB, DC, DS, JC, MC, VI. **Special Amenities: free newspaper and early check-in/late check-out.**

SOME UNITS   
FEE FEE

RAMADA MARK TWAIN-UNION SQUARE *Book at aaa.com* **Phone:** (415)673-2332 **50**

SAVE — Small-scale Hotel

All Year 1P: $140-$180 2P: $140-$180 XP: $20 F18

Location: Just w of Union Square; downtown. 345 Taylor St 94102. Fax: 415/673-0529. **Facility:** 118 units. 116 one-bedroom standard units. 2 one-bedroom suites ($260-$300). 8 stories, interior corridors. **Parking:** valet. **Terms:** age restrictions may apply. **Amenities:** video games, voice mail, safes, irons. *Some:* hair dryers. **Dining:** 7 am-2:30 & 5-10 pm. **Leisure Activities:** exercise room. **Guest Services:** valet laundry. **Business Services:** meeting rooms. **Cards:** AX, CB, DC, DS, JC, MC, VI.

SOME UNITS

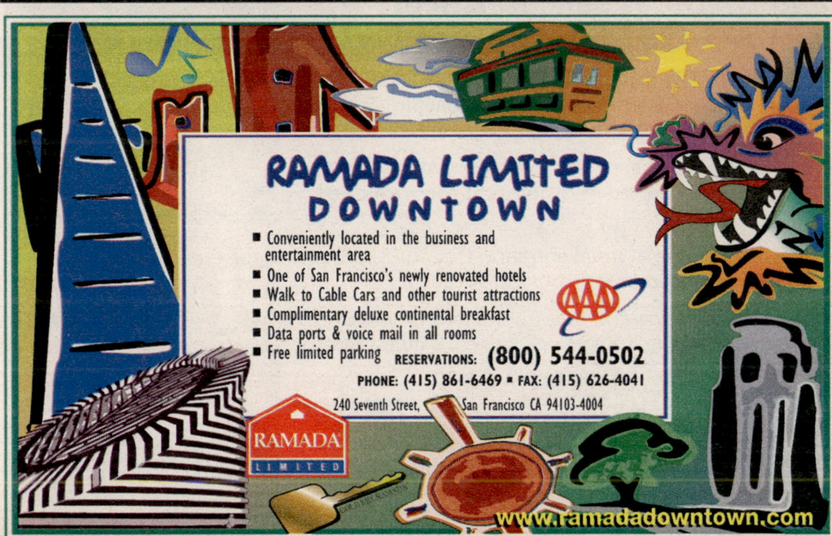

(See map and index starting on p. 590)

RAMADA PLAZA HOTEL DOWNTOWN *Book at aaa.com* **Phone:** (415)626-8000 160

Large-scale Hotel

All Year 1P: $89-$169 2P: $99-$179 XP: $20 F18

Location: 1 blk from civic auditorium. 1231 Market St 94103. Fax: 415/861-1460. **Facility:** 458 units. 445 one-bedroom standard units. 13 one-bedroom suites ($269-$369). 8 stories, interior corridors. *Bath:* combo or shower only. **Parking:** on-site (fee). **Terms:** 3 day cancellation notice. **Amenities:** voice mail, irons, hair dryers. **Dining:** 6:30 am-2 & 5-10 pm, cocktails. **Leisure Activities:** exercise room. **Guest Services:** gift shop, valet laundry. **Business Services:** meeting rooms, business center. **Cards:** AX, DC, DS, MC, VI. **Special Amenities: free room upgrade and preferred room (each subject to availability with advanced reservations).** *(See color ad below)*

SOME UNITS FEE FEE

REDWOOD INN **Phone:** 415/776-3800 118

Motel

5/1-10/31	1P: $90-$120	2P: $110-$150	XP: $10	F5
2/1-4/30 & 11/1-1/31	1P: $75-$100	2P: $90-$130	XP: $10	F5

Location: On US 101 (Van Ness Ave). 1530 Lombard St 94123. Fax: 415/928-1934. **Facility:** 33 one-bedroom standard units. 2-4 stories, exterior corridors. **Parking:** on-site. **Guest Services:** coin laundry. **Cards:** AX, DC, DS, MC, VI. *(See color ad p 641)*

SOME UNITS

RENAISSANCE PARC 55 HOTEL *Book at aaa.com* **Phone:** (415)392-8000 60

Large-scale Hotel

All Year 1P: $159-$269 2P: $159-$269 XP: $20 F18

Location: 3 blks w of Union Square. 55 Cyril Magnin St 94102. Fax: 415/403-6602. **Facility:** Tiered exterior affording maximum views. 1010 units. 995 one-bedroom standard units. 15 one-bedroom suites, some with whirlpools. 32 stories, interior corridors. *Bath:* combo or shower only. **Parking:** valet. **Terms:** [AP] meal plan available. **Amenities:** video games, high-speed Internet, voice mail, irons, hair dryers. *Some:* CD players, dual phone lines, safes. **Leisure Activities:** sauna. *Fee:* massage. **Guest Services:** gift shop, valet laundry. **Business Services:** conference facilities, business center. **Cards:** AX, CB, DC, DS, JC, MC, VI. ***(See color ad p 641)***

SOME UNITS FEE

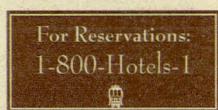

(See map and index starting on p. 590)

RENAISSANCE STANFORD COURT HOTEL Book at aaa.com Phone: (415)989-3500 11

SAVE

Large-scale Hotel

All Year 1P: $199-$459 XP: $20 F17

Location: Atop Nob Hill at Powell St. 905 California St 94108. Fax: 415/391-0513. **Facility:** A long heritage distinguishes this service-oriented luxury hotel offering sweeping views of the city's famous skyline. 393 units. 387 one-bedroom standard units. 6 one-bedroom suites, some with whirlpools. 8 stories, interior corridors. *Bath:* combo or shower only. **Parking:** valet. **Amenities:** dual phone lines, voice mail, irons, hair dryers. *Fee:* video games, high-speed Internet. *Some:* CD players. **Dining:** 6:30 am-2:30 & 5:30-10 pm, Fri & Sat-11 pm, cocktails. **Leisure Activities:** exercise room. **Guest Services:** gift shop, valet laundry. **Business Services:** conference facilities, business center. **Cards:** AX, DC, DS, MC, VI.

SOME UNITS

DATA PORT / VCR /

FEE

RICHELIEU HOTEL Book at aaa.com Phone: (415)673-4711 145

Small-scale Hotel

6/1-9/30	1P: $139-$179	2P: $139-$179	XP: $10	F16
2/1-5/31 & 10/1-1/31	1P: $109-$169	2P: $109-$169	XP: $10	F16

Location: On US 101 (Van Ness Ave). 1050 Van Ness Ave 94109. Fax: 415/673-9362. **Facility:** 168 one-bedroom standard units. 5 stories, interior corridors. *Bath:* combo or shower only. **Parking:** on-site. **Amenities:** voice mail, irons, hair dryers. **Leisure Activities:** exercise room. **Guest Services:** valet and coin laundry. **Cards:** AX, DS, MC, VI.

SOME UNITS

ASK DATA PORT / /

THE RITZ-CARLTON, SAN FRANCISCO Book at aaa.com Phone: (415)296-7465 12

Large-scale Hotel

9/3-11/13	1P: $319	2P: $319
2/1-9/2 & 11/14-1/31	1P: $265	2P: $265

Location: Just n of Union Square at California St. 600 Stockton St 94108. Fax: 415/364-3455. **Facility:** The new-classical architecture of this Nob Hill landmark blends well with its sophisticated surroundings. 336 units. 294 one-bedroom standard units. 42 one-bedroom suites. 9 stories, interior corridors. **Parking:** on-site (fee) and valet. **Terms:** cancellation fee imposed. **Amenities:** CD players, dual phone lines, voice mail, safes, honor bars, irons, hair dryers. *Fee:* video games, high-speed Internet. **Dining:** 2 restaurants, 6:30 am-10:30 pm, also, The Dining Room, see separate listing, entertainment. **Pool(s):** heated indoor. **Leisure Activities:** saunas, whirlpool, steamrooms. *Fee:* massage. **Guest Services:** gift shop, valet laundry, area transportation-financial district. **Business Services:** conference facilities, business center. **Cards:** AX, CB, DC, DS, JC, MC, VI. **Special Amenities: free newspaper and preferred room (subject to availability with advanced reservations).**

SOME UNITS

ASK 24 DATA PORT / /

FEE

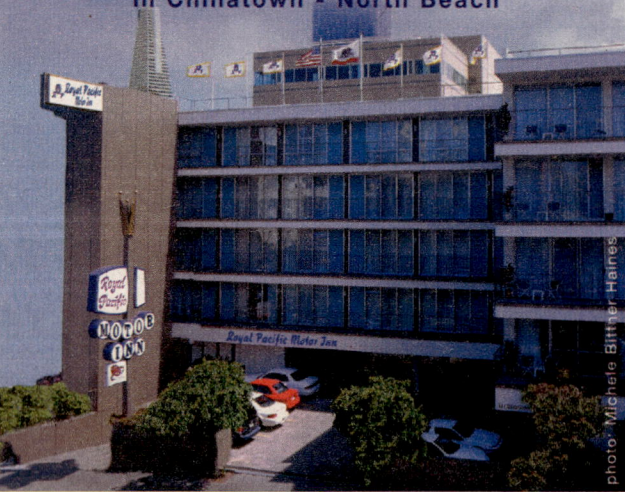

(See map and index starting on p. 590)

ROYAL PACIFIC MOTOR INN Phone: (415)781-6661 1

Motel

All Year 1P: $106 2P: $106 XP: $6 F12

Location: Between Grant Ave and Stockton St. Located in Chinatown area. 661 Broadway 94133. Fax: 415/781-6688. **Facility:** 74 one-bedroom standard units. 5 stories, exterior corridors. *Bath:* combo or shower only. **Parking:** on-site. **Amenities:** hair dryers. **Leisure Activities:** sauna, exercise room. **Guest Services:** coin laundry. **Cards:** AX, CB, DC, MC, VI. *(See color ad p 642)*

SOME UNITS FEE

SAN FRANCISCO DOWNTOWN COURTYARD *Book at aaa.com* **Phone:** (415)947-0700 63

Large-scale Hotel

All Year 1P: $199-$259 2P: $199-$259 XP: $20 F18

Location: US 101 N to I-280, n to King St, then 2 mi w to 2nd St; corner of 2nd and Folsom sts. 299 2nd St 94105. Fax: 415/947-0800. **Facility:** 405 units. 376 one-bedroom standard units. 29 one-bedroom suites. 16 stories, interior corridors. *Bath:* combo or shower only. **Parking:** valet. **Amenities:** video games, high-speed Internet, dual phone lines, voice mail, irons, hair dryers. **Pool(s):** heated indoor. **Leisure Activities:** whirlpool, exercise room. **Guest Services:** gift shop, valet and coin laundry. **Business Services:** meeting rooms, PC. **Cards:** AX, DC, DS, JC, MC, VI.

SOME UNITS

SAN FRANCISCO MARRIOTT *Book at aaa.com* **Phone:** 415/896-1600 59

Large-scale Hotel

Property failed to provide current rates

Location: Just s of Union Square; just n of Moscone Center. 55 Fourth St 94103. Fax: 415/777-2799. **Facility:** This service-oriented property has a distinctly upscale ambience. 1498 units. 1364 one-bedroom standard units. 134 one-bedroom suites, some with whirlpools. 39 stories, interior corridors. **Parking:** on-site (fee) and valet. **Amenities:** high-speed Internet, voice mail, honor bars, irons, hair dryers. **Pool(s):** heated indoor. **Leisure Activities:** sauna, whirlpool, steamroom, exercise room. *Fee:* massage. **Guest Services:** gift shop, valet laundry. **Business Services:** conference facilities, business center.

SOME UNITS FEE

SAN FRANCISCO MARRIOTT FISHERMAN'S WHARF *Book at aaa.com* **Phone:** 415/775-7555 135

Large-scale Hotel

All Year 1P: $169-$239 2P: $169-$239 XP: $15 F17

Location: Just s of Fisherman's Wharf at Bay St. 1250 Columbus Ave 94133. Fax: 415/474-2099. **Facility:** 285 one-bedroom standard units. 5 stories, interior corridors. *Bath:* combo or shower only. **Parking:** on-site (fee). **Terms:** check-in 4 pm, cancellation fee imposed, small pets only ($100 fee, $5 extra charge). **Amenities:** dual phone lines, voice mail, honor bars, irons, hair dryers. **Leisure Activities:** sauna, exercise room. **Guest Services:** gift shop, valet laundry. **Business Services:** meeting rooms, business center. **Cards:** AX, CB, DC, DS, JC, MC, VI.

SOME UNITS FEE FEE FEE

SAVOY HOTEL *Book at aaa.com* **Phone:** (415)441-2700 46

Small-scale Hotel

All Year 1P: $89-$159 2P: $89-$159 XP: $10 F12

Location: 3 blks w of Union Square. 580 Geary St 94102. Fax: 415/441-0124. **Facility:** 83 units. 70 one-bedroom standard units. 13 one-bedroom suites. 7 stories, interior corridors. **Parking:** valet. **Terms:** [CP] meal plan available. **Amenities:** video games, voice mail, safes, honor bars, irons, hair dryers. *Some:* CD players, high-speed Internet. **Dining:** Millennium Restaurant, see separate listing. **Guest Services:** valet laundry. **Business Services:** meeting rooms, business center. **Cards:** AX, CB, DC, DS, MC, VI. *(See color ad p 617)*

SOME UNITS

SEAL ROCK INN **Phone:** (415)752-8000 141

Motel

5/16-9/15 1P: $115-$143 2P: $125-$153 XP: $10 D16

2/1-5/15 & 9/16-1/31 1P: $95-$127 2P: $105-$137 XP: $10 D16

Location: From beach, 5 mi w of civic center. 545 Point Lobos Ave 94121. Fax: 415/752-6034. **Facility:** 27 one-bedroom standard units, some with efficiencies (utensils extra charge). 4 stories, exterior corridors. *Bath:* combo or shower only. **Parking:** on-site. **Terms:** 2 night minimum stay - weekends, 3 day cancellation notice-fee imposed. **Amenities:** voice mail, irons, hair dryers. **Dining:** 6 am-4 pm, Sat & Sun-6 pm. **Pool(s):** outdoor. **Cards:** AX, CB, DC, MC, VI.

SERRANO HOTEL *Book at aaa.com* **Phone:** (415)885-2500 44

Small-scale Hotel

All Year 1P: $139-$179 2P: $179-$219 XP: $15 F18

Location: Just w of Union Square. 405 Taylor St 94102. Fax: 415/474-4879. **Facility:** 236 units. 217 one-bedroom standard units. 19 one-bedroom suites, some with whirlpools. 17 stories, interior corridors. *Bath:* some combo or shower only. **Parking:** valet. **Terms:** cancellation fee imposed, 14% service charge. **Amenities:** video games, high-speed Internet, dual phone lines, voice mail, fax, safes, honor bars, irons, hair dryers. *Some:* CD players. **Dining:** 7 am-10 & 4:30-midnight, cocktails. **Leisure Activities:** sauna, exercise room. *Fee:* massage. **Guest Services:** complimentary evening beverages, valet laundry. **Business Services:** meeting rooms, business center. **Cards:** AX, DC, DS, JC, MC, VI. **Special Amenities: early check-in/late check-out.**

SOME UNITS FEE

(See map and index starting on p. 590)

SHERATON AT FISHERMAN'S WHARF *Book at aaa.com* **Phone:** (415)362-5500 **127**

AAA SAVE

Large-scale Hotel

6/15-11/14	1P: $159-$229	2P: $159-$229	XP: $20	F18
4/1-6/14	1P: $139-$229	2P: $139-$229	XP: $20	F18
2/1-3/31 & 11/15-1/31	1P: $129-$229	2P: $129-$229	XP: $20	F18

Location: Just se of Fisherman's Wharf at Beach St. 2500 Mason St 94133. Fax: 415/956-5275. **Facility:** Centrally located, the hotel is within walking distance of Pier 39, shops, restaurants and attractions. 529 units. 521 one-bedroom standard units. 8 one-bedroom suites, some with whirlpools. 4 stories, interior corridors. *Bath:* combo or shower only. **Parking:** on-site (fee). **Terms:** cancellation fee imposed. **Amenities:** voice mail, irons, hair dryers. *Fee:* video games, high-speed Internet. *Some:* dual phone lines, safes. **Dining:** 2 restaurants, 6:30 am-10:30 pm, cocktails. **Pool(s):** heated outdoor. **Leisure Activities:** exercise room. **Guest Services:** gift shop, area transportation-financial district & civic center. **Business Services:** conference facilities, business center. **Cards:** AX, CB, DC, DS, JC, MC, VI. *(See color ad below)*

FEE / SOME UNITS / FEE

THE SHERMAN HOUSE *Book at aaa.com* **Phone:** (415)563-3600 **130**

Historic Small-scale Hotel

All Year	1P: $300-$600	2P: $300-$600

Location: US 101 (Lombard St), exit Fillmore St, 4 blks s. 2160 Green St 94123. Fax: 415/563-1882. **Facility:** Built in 1876, The Sherman House is in the French-Italianate Victorian style and features wood-burning fireplaces. Smoke free premises. 14 units. 13 one-bedroom standard units, some with whirlpools. 1 one-bedroom suite with whirlpool. 3-4 stories (no elevator), interior corridors. **Parking:** street. **Terms:** check-in 4 pm, 7 day cancellation notice, [BP] meal plan available. **Amenities:** CD players, hair dryers. *Some:* safes. **Guest Services:** complimentary evening beverages, valet laundry. **Business Services:** meeting rooms. **Cards:** AX, CB, DC, DS, MC, VI.

ASK / SOME UNITS

SIR FRANCIS DRAKE HOTEL *Book at aaa.com* **Phone:** (415)392-7755 **32**

AAA SAVE

Historic Large-scale Hotel

5/1-11/15	1P: $169-$239	2P: $169-$239	XP: $20	F12
11/16-1/31	1P: $159-$179	2P: $159-$179	XP: $20	F12
2/1-4/30	1P: $149-$169	2P: $149-$169	XP: $20	F12

Location: Just off Union Square at Sutter St. 450 Powell St 94102. Fax: 415/391-8719. **Facility:** Charm of a bygone era. 417 units. 412 one-bedroom standard units. 3 one- and 2 two-bedroom suites ($499-$699), some with whirlpools. 24 stories, interior corridors. *Bath:* combo or shower only. **Parking:** valet. **Terms:** cancellation fee imposed, [BP] & [CP] meal plans available. **Amenities:** video games, voice mail, honor bars, irons, hair dryers. *Some:* CD players. **Dining:** 2 restaurants, 6:30 am-11 pm, cocktails, nightclub, entertainment. **Leisure Activities:** exercise room. **Guest Services:** valet laundry. **Business Services:** meeting rooms, PC, fax. **Cards:** AX, CB, DC, DS, MC, VI. **Special Amenities: early check-in/late check-out.** *(See color ad p 645)*

FEE / SOME UNITS

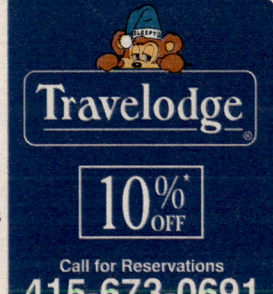

(See map and index starting on p. 590)

STANYAN PARK HOTEL Book at aaa.com **Phone:** (415)751-1000 **164**

Historic Bed & Breakfast

5/1-1/31 [ECP] 1P: $135-$190 2P: $135-$190
2/1-4/30 [ECP] 1P: $130-$185 2P: $130-$185

Location: 2.5 mi w. 750 Stanyan St 94117. Fax: 415/668-5454. **Facility:** Some rooms of this restored Victorian hotel overlook Golden Gate Park. Smoke free premises. 36 units. 30 one-bedroom standard units. 4 one- and 2 two-bedroom suites ($265-$315) with kitchens. 3 stories, interior corridors. **Parking:** on-site (fee). **Amenities:** voice mail, hair dryers. *Some:* irons. **Cards:** AX, DC, DS, MC, VI. **Special Amenities: free continental breakfast.**

FEE

STAR MOTEL **Phone:** (415)346-8250 **116**

Motel

6/16-10/31 1P: $99-$109 2P: $119-$129 XP: $5 F14
11/1-1/31 1P: $69-$99 2P: $89-$129 XP: $5 F14
2/1-6/15 1P: $66-$99 2P: $89-$129 XP: $5 F14

Location: On US 101 (Van Ness Ave). 1727 Lombard St 94123. Fax: 415/441-4469. **Facility:** 52 one-bedroom standard units. 2 stories (no elevator), exterior corridors. *Bath:* combo or shower only. **Parking:** on-site. **Amenities:** hair dryers. **Cards:** AX, CB, DC, DS, MC, VI. *(See color ad p 606)*

SOME UNITS

FEE

SUPER 8 MOTEL Book at aaa.com **Phone:** (415)922-0244 **108**

Motel

All Year 1P: $59-$160 2P: $69-$170 XP: $10 F12

Location: On US 101 (Van Ness Ave); between Scott and Divisadero sts. 2440 Lombard St 94123. Fax: 415/922-8887. **Facility:** 32 one-bedroom standard units, some with whirlpools. 3 stories (no elevator), exterior corridors. **Parking:** on-site. **Terms:** cancellation fee imposed. **Amenities:** irons, hair dryers. **Leisure Activities:** sauna, sun deck. **Cards:** AX, CB, DC, DS, JC, MC, VI. **Special Amenities: free continental breakfast.**

SOME UNITS

SW HOTEL Book at aaa.com **Phone:** 415/362-2999 **3**

Small-scale Hotel

All Year 1P: $119-$139 2P: $119-$149

Location: Between Stockton St and Grant Ave. Located in Chinatown area. 615 Broadway St 94133. Fax: 415/362-1808. **Facility:** 81 units. 79 one-bedroom standard units. 2 one-bedroom suites ($245-$345). 4 stories, interior corridors. *Bath:* combo or shower only. **Parking:** on-site (fee). **Terms:** cancellation fee imposed, [CP] meal plan available. **Amenities:** voice mail, irons, hair dryers. **Business Services:** meeting rooms, PC. **Cards:** AX, DC, MC, VI. **Special Amenities: free continental breakfast.**

SOME UNITS

(See map and index starting on p. 590)

TRAVELODGE BY THE BAY Book at aaa.com Phone: (415)673-0691 123

Motel

5/16-10/31	1P: $99-$109	2P: $109-$119	XP: $10	F12
2/1-5/15 & 11/1-1/31	1P: $69-$79	2P: $79-$89	XP: $10	F12

Location: On US 101 (Van Ness Ave). 1450 Lombard St 94123. Fax: 415/673-3232. **Facility:** 72 one-bedroom standard units. 2-3 stories, exterior corridors. *Bath:* combo or shower only. **Parking:** on-site (fee). **Terms:** cancellation fee imposed, [AP] & [BP] meal plans available, small pets only ($20 extra charge). **Amenities:** hair dryers. **Business Services:** fax. **Cards:** AX, CB, DC, DS, JC, MC, VI. **Special Amenities:** free newspaper. *(See color ad p 645)*

SOME UNITS

FEE

VILLA FLORENCE HOTEL Book at aaa.com Phone: (415)397-7700 51

Small-scale Hotel

All Year	1P: $139-$209	2P: $139-$209	XP: $20	F17

Location: Just s of Union Square. 225 Powell St 94107. Fax: 415/397-1006. **Facility:** 183 one-bedroom standard units. 7 stories, interior corridors. *Bath:* combo or shower only. **Parking:** valet. **Terms:** cancellation fee imposed, [CP] meal plan available. **Amenities:** video games, CD players, voice mail, honor bars, irons, hair dryers. **Dining:** Kuleto's, see separate listing. **Guest Services:** complimentary evening beverages, valet laundry. **Business Services:** meeting rooms. **Cards:** AX, DC, DS, JC, MC, VI. **Special Amenities:** early check-in/late check-out.

SOME UNITS

FEE

WARWICK REGIS HOTEL Book at aaa.com Phone: (415)928-7900 42

Small-scale Hotel

3/1-10/31	1P: $169-$249	2P: $169-$249	XP: $20	F12
12/31-1/31	1P: $169-$239	2P: $169-$239	XP: $20	F12
2/1-2/29 & 11/1-12/30	1P: $159-$239	2P: $159-$239	XP: $20	F12

Location: 2 blks w of Union Square. 490 Geary St 94102. Fax: 415/441-8788. **Facility:** 74 units. 58 one-bedroom standard units. 16 one-bedroom suites. 8 stories, interior corridors. *Bath:* combo or shower only. **Parking:** valet. **Terms:** cancellation fee imposed. **Amenities:** video games, high-speed Internet, voice mail, safes, honor bars, irons, hair dryers. *Some:* CD players. **Dining:** 7 am-10:30 & 5-11 pm, Fri & Sat-midnight. **Guest Services:** valet laundry. **Business Services:** meeting rooms, business center. **Cards:** AX, CB, DC, DS, JC, MC, VI. *(See color ad p 607)*

SOME UNITS

FEE

(See map and index starting on p. 590)

THE WESTIN ST. FRANCIS *Book at aaa.com* **Phone:** (415)397-7000 45

AAA SAVE All Year 1P: $129-$569 2P: $129-$569 XP: $30 F

Large-scale Hotel

Location: On Union Square. 335 Powell St 94102. Fax: 415/774-0124. **Facility:** Nationally famous hotel. Outstanding facilities. 1189 units. 1153 one-bedroom standard units. 36 one-bedroom suites ($250-$3300), some with whirlpools. 32 stories. *Bath:* combo or shower only. **Parking:** on-site (fee). **Terms:** cancellation fee imposed, small pets only ($25 fee). **Amenities:** dual phone lines, voice mail, safes, honor bars, irons, hair dryers. *Some:* high-speed Internet. **Dining:** 3 restaurants, 6 am-11:30 pm, cocktails, entertainment. **Leisure Activities:** steamroom, spa. **Guest Services:** gift shop, valet laundry. **Business Services:** conference facilities, business center. **Cards:** AX, CB, DC, DS, JC, MC, VI. **Special Amenities: free room upgrade and preferred room (each subject to availability with advanced reservations).**

SOME UNITS

FEE

(See map and index starting on p. 590)

THE WHARF INN *Book at aaa.com* **Phone:** (415)673-7411 105

Motel

6/1-8/31	1P: $139-$185	2P: $139-$185
3/1-5/31	1P: $119-$145	2P: $119-$145
9/1-1/31	1P: $95-$145	2P: $95-$145
2/1-2/29	1P: $95-$119	2P: $95-$119

Location: Adjacent to Fisherman's Wharf and Bay; at Beach St. 2601 Mason St 94133. Fax: 415/776-2181. **Facility:** 51 units. 50 one-bedroom standard units. 1 two-bedroom suite ($299-$425) with kitchen. 3 stories, exterior corridors. *Bath:* combo or shower only. **Parking:** on-site. **Cards:** AX, CB, DC, DS, JC, MC, VI.
(See color ad p 647 & p 521)

FEE SOME UNITS

WHITE SWAN INN *Book at aaa.com* **Phone:** (415)775-1755 17

Small-scale Hotel

All Year [BP] 1P: $180-$285 2P: $180-$285 XP: $20 F5

Location: US 101 (Van Ness Ave), exit Bush St. 845 Bush St 94108. Fax: 415/775-5717. **Facility:** Smoke free premises. 26 one-bedroom standard units. 4 stories, interior corridors. *Bath:* combo or shower only. **Parking:** on-site (fee) and valet. **Terms:** age restrictions may apply, cancellation fee imposed. **Amenities:** voice mail, irons, hair dryers. **Leisure Activities:** exercise room. **Guest Services:** complimentary evening beverages, valet laundry. **Business Services:** meeting rooms. **Cards:** AX, DC, DS, MC, VI.

SOME UNITS

YORK HOTEL *Book at aaa.com* **Phone:** 415/885-6800 13

Small-scale Hotel

Property failed to provide current rates

Location: Just w of Union Square. 940 Sutter St 94109. Fax: 415/885-2115. **Facility:** Smoke free premises. 96 units. 90 one-bedroom standard units. 6 one-bedroom suites. 8 stories, interior corridors. *Bath:* combo or shower only. **Parking:** valet. **Terms:** age restrictions may apply. **Amenities:** video games, high-speed Internet, voice mail, safes, honor bars, hair dryers. *Some:* irons. **Leisure Activities:** exercise room. **Guest Services:** valet and coin laundry. **Business Services:** meeting rooms.

SOME UNITS

Savings at Your Fingertips

When you have a AAA TourBook® guide in your hand, you have a world of savings right at your fingertips. AAA Official Appointment lodgings that display the bright-red AAA logo, SAVE icon and Diamond rating in their listing want business from AAA Members, and many offer discounts and special amenities to them*.

So, when planning your next vacation, be sure to consult your AAA TourBook for the familiar red SAVE icon.

**See TourBook Navigator, page 14, for details.*

SAVE

(See map and index starting on p. 590)

The following lodging was either not evaluated or did not meet AAA rating requirements but is listed for your information only.

ARGONAUT HOTEL — **Phone:** 415/563-0800

fyi

5/1-11/20	2P: $259-$289	XP: $20	F18
2/1-4/30 & 11/21-1/31	2P: $179-$209	XP: $20	F18

Large-scale Hotel Too new to rate. **Location:** Fisherman's Wharf; adjacent The Cannery. 495 Jefferson St 94109. Fax: 415/563-2800. **Amenities:** 252 units, pets, restaurant, coffeemakers. **Cards:** AX, CB, DC, DS, JC, MC, VI.

(See color ad p 648)

WHERE TO DINE

ACME CHOPHOUSE — **Lunch:** $10-$20 — **Dinner:** $17-$45 — **Phone:** 415/644-0240 — (107)

American

Location: At Third St; at Pacific Bell Ball Park. 24 Willie Mays Plaza 94107. **Hours:** 5:30 pm-10 pm; open for lunch 10 am-3 pm during baseball season day games. Closed: Mon 10/1-3/31. **Reservations:** suggested. **Features:** In Pacific Bell Park, the upscale steakhouse also serves good seafood dishes. This spot is reminiscent of one of the old San Francisco grills. Try the rib-eye or double-cut pork chops. Casual dress; cocktails. **Parking:** valet and street. **Cards:** AX, MC, VI.

ACQUERELLO — **Dinner:** $29-$32 — **Phone:** 415/567-5432 — (90)

Italian

Location: US 101. 1722 Sacramento St 94109. **Hours:** 5:30 pm-10:30 pm. Closed major holidays; also Sun & Mon. **Reservations:** suggested. **Features:** The intimate, cozy restaurant serves elegant Northern Italian cuisine. On the seasonally changing menu are some constant favorites, including spinach salad, salmon with fresh anchovy and pork loin encrusted with parsley and peppercorn. Those who can't make up their mind might choose the prix fixe dinner. Semi-formal attire; cocktails. **Parking:** street. **Cards:** AX, DS, MC, VI.

ALIOTO'S — **Lunch:** $12-$47 — **Dinner:** $12-$47 — **Phone:** 415/673-0183 — (66)

AAA

Seafood

Location: 8 Fisherman's Wharf 94133. **Hours:** 11 am-11 pm. Closed: 12/25. **Reservations:** suggested. **Features:** Established in 1928, the third-floor restaurant overlooks the fishing fleet. Seafood specialties are at the heart of the menu. Parking is validated for the lot across the street. Casual dress; cocktails. **Parking:** no self-parking. **Cards:** AX, CB, DC, MC, VI.

ANA MANDARA — **Lunch:** $9-$20 — **Dinner:** $15-$28 — **Phone:** 415/771-6800 — (72)

Vietnamese

Location: Just w of Larkin St; at Ghiradelli Square. 891 Beach St 94109. **Hours:** 11:30 am-2 & 5:30-10 pm, Fri-11 pm, Sat 5:30 pm-11 pm, Sun 5:30 pm-10 pm. Closed major holidays. **Reservations:** required. **Features:** Just west of the wharf, the restaurant nurtures a calm atmosphere and soothing, quiet elegance. Dishes reflect intriguing flavors, textures and ingredients. Mekong basa, a mild white fish, comes with snow pea sprouts and a blend of sauces that contain red pepper heat and sweet orange flavors. Homemade sorbets and ice creams are refreshing and tangy. Dressy casual; cocktails. **Parking:** valet and street. **Cards:** AX, CB, DC, DS, JC, MC, VI.

ANZU RESTAURANT — **Lunch:** $20-$35 — **Dinner:** $25-$45 — **Phone:** 415/394-1100 — (38)

California

Location: 3 blks w of Union Square; in Hotel Nikko. 222 Mason St 94102. **Hours:** 6:30-11 am, 11:30-2:30 & 5:30-10 pm. **Reservations:** required. **Features:** Featuring fine aged beef and masterfully prepared sushi from chef Kazuhito Takahashi, the restaurant stands out among hotel eateries. An elegant dining room sets the scene for equally refined service. Dressy casual; cocktails. **Parking:** valet. **Cards:** AX, DS, JC, MC, VI.

AQUA RESTAURANT — **Lunch:** $20-$30 — **Dinner:** $41-$80 — **Phone:** 415/956-9662 — (49)

Seafood

Location: Between Front and Battery sts; in the financial district. 252 California St 94110. **Hours:** 11:30 am-2:30 & 5:30-10:30 pm, Fri & Sat 5:30 pm-11 pm, Sun 5:30 pm-9:30 pm. **Reservations:** required. **Features:** Representative of innovative seafood served in the sophisticated setting are Russian caviar and Hawaiian swordfish. A few non-seafood entrees, including dishes on the five-course vegetarian tasting menu, are always available. The sleek dining room displays extravagant flower arrangements and large mirrors. Dressy casual; cocktails. **Parking:** valet and street. **Cards:** AX, CB, DC, DS, MC, VI.

AZIE — **Dinner:** $15-$25 — **Phone:** 415/538-0918 — (59)

Asian

Location: Between 4th and 5th sts, just sw of Moscone Convention Center. 826 Folsom St 94105. **Hours:** 5:30 pm-10 pm, Fri & Sat 5 pm-11 pm, Sun 5 pm-10 pm. Closed major holidays. **Reservations:** suggested. **Features:** The most recent addition to a small chain in San Francisco, the restaurant serves Asian-inspired French cuisine. This place has received many accolades. An excellent wine list that also includes several sake selections matches with a wide selection of lamb, duck, chicken, fish, beef and vegetarian entrees. Dressy casual; cocktails. **Parking:** valet and street. **Cards:** AX, DC, DS, MC, VI.

BACAR RESTAURANT — **Dinner:** $41-$75 — **Phone:** 415/904-4100 — (104)

Mediterranean

Location: Located south of Market St between 3rd and 4th sts. 448 Brannan St 94107. **Hours:** 5:30 pm-midnight, Fri & Sat-1 am, Sun-11 pm. **Reservations:** suggested. **Features:** South of Market, the dramatic and lively modern brasserie's offerings range from pan-roasted quail to New Zealand venison and also include more traditional steak, lamb and seafood dishes. All are prepared with a Mediterranean flair. Mahogany, glass and steel accents characterize the dining room. Live jazz adds to the atmosphere. Dressy casual; cocktails. **Parking:** valet and street. **Cards:** AX, CB, DC, JC, MC, VI.

(See map and index starting on p. 590)

BEACH CHALET BREWERY AND RESTAURANT **Lunch:** $9-$16 **Dinner:** $12-$18 **Phone:** 415/386-8439 (98)

American

Location: Northwest corner of Golden Gate Park, below the Dutch Windmill facing the Pacific Ocean; near JFK Dr. 1000 Great Hwy 94121-3268. **Hours:** 9 am-11 pm, Fri & Sat-midnight. Closed: 12/25. **Reservations:** suggested. **Features:** The eatery is popular with tourists, as it affords a great view of the ocean and easy access to Golden Gate Park. The menu lists American bistro fare, such as salads, sandwiches, burgers, ribs, fish and chips and several handcrafted ales. Casual dress; cocktails; entertainment. **Parking:** on-site. **Cards:** MC, VI.

BETELNUT **Lunch:** $6-$20 **Dinner:** $6-$20 **Phone:** 415/929-8855 (86)

Asian

Location: Between Buchanan and Webster sts; in the Cow Hollow District. 2030 Union St 94123. **Hours:** 11:30 am-11 pm, Fri & Sat-midnight. Closed: 11/25, 12/25. **Reservations:** suggested. **Features:** The Asian beer house serves a tasty selection of Korean, Thai and Chinese dishes that reflect the compelling flavors of exotic Far Eastern street foods. Sidewalk seating is an option. Casual dress; cocktails. **Parking:** street. **Cards:** CB, DS, MC, VI.

BOULEVARD **Lunch:** $17-$28 **Dinner:** $26-$33 **Phone:** 415/543-6084 (47)

American

Location: Jct of Steuart St; at the Embarcadero. 1 Mission St 94105. **Hours:** 11:30 am-2 & 5:30-10 pm, Sat & Sun from 5:30 pm. Closed major holidays. **Reservations:** suggested. **Features:** With exceptional food and spectacular views of the San Francisco Bay, the restaurant offers an elegant dining experience perfect for special occasions. Dressy casual; cocktails. **Parking:** valet and street. **Cards:** AX, CB, DC, DS, MC, VI.

BRANDY HO'S HUNAN FOOD **Lunch:** $8-$12 **Dinner:** $8-$12 **Phone:** 415/788-7527 (46)

Chinese

Location: Jct Pacific Ave, just nw. 219 Columbus Ave 94133. **Hours:** 11:30 am-11 pm. Closed: 11/25, 12/25. **Reservations:** No reservation accepted. **Features:** Long popular with the folks who live and work in the area, the busy eatery serves spicy Hunan chicken, beef, pork and seafood. Guests may choose the level of piquancy: mild, medium or hot. Casual dress; cocktails. **Parking:** street. **Cards:** AX, DS, MC, VI.

CAFE METROPOL **Lunch:** $10-$17 **Dinner:** $10-$17 **Phone:** 415/732-7777 (39)

Continental

Location: Between Kearney and Montgomery sts. 168 Sutter St 94104. **Hours:** 9 am-9 pm, Sat noon-4 pm. Closed major holidays; also Sun. **Reservations:** accepted. **Features:** Dishes are prepared in the local custom of several European countries at the downtown eatery. Pizza, pasta and cafe specialties of beef, pork and chicken, as well as lighter fare, are available. Casual dress; cocktails. **Parking:** street. **Cards:** AX, DC, DS, MC, VI.

CAMPTON PLACE RESTAURANT **Lunch:** $17-$30 **Dinner:** $29-$39 **Phone:** 415/955-5555 (4)

French

Location: Just n of Union Square; in Campton Place Hotel. 340 Stockton St 94108. **Hours:** 7-10:30 am, 11:30-2 & 5:30-10 pm, Sat 8 am-11, noon-2 & 5:30-10:30 pm, Sun 8 am-2 & 5:30-9:30 pm. **Reservations:** suggested. **Features:** Inventive, eclectic American dishes show a French influence. Artful presentation distinguishes each selection. The atmosphere is intimate and elegant. Semi-formal attire; cocktails. **Parking:** valet. **Cards:** AX, CB, DC, JC, MC, VI.

CARNELIAN ROOM **Dinner:** $28-$65 **Phone:** 415/433-7500 (20)

Continental

Location: Atop Bank of America Center on 52nd floor. 555 California St 94104. **Hours:** 6 pm-11 pm, Sat from 5 pm, Sun 10 am-2 & 6-11 pm. Closed: 1/1. **Reservations:** suggested. **Features:** Spectacular panoramic views spread out from the sophisticated dining room. Seasonal California cuisine is well-prepared. Semi-formal attire; cocktails. **Parking:** on-site (fee). **Cards:** AX, CB, DC, DS, MC, VI.

CHARLES NOB HILL **Dinner:** $27-$45 **Phone:** 415/771-5400 (10)

French

Location: At Clay St. 1250 Jones St 94109. **Hours:** 5:30 pm-10 pm, Sun-9:30 pm. Closed: 1/1, 4/11, 12/25; also Mon & Tues. **Reservations:** required. **Features:** Knowledgeable diners favor the distinguished restaurant for its California-French food, elegant surroundings and thoughtful service. Semi-formal attire; cocktails. **Parking:** on-site (fee). **Cards:** AX, DS, MC, VI.

CHENERY PARK **Dinner:** $9-$20 **Phone:** 415/337-8537 (121)

American

Location: Just ne of jct of Diamond St; in Glen Park area. 683 Chenery St 94131. **Hours:** 5:30 pm-9:30 pm, Fri & Sat-10 pm. **Reservations:** suggested. **Features:** The comfortable and quiet restaurant offers Southern-style food with a Californian twist. Dressy casual; cocktails. **Parking:** street. **Cards:** AX, MC, VI.

CHEZ PAPA BISTRO **Lunch:** $9-$16 **Dinner:** $16-$24 **Phone:** 415/824-8210 (118)

French

Location: Corner of Missouri St; Potrero Hill. 1401 18th St 94110. **Hours:** 11:30 am-3 & 5:30-11 pm, Sun from 5:30 pm. Closed major holidays. **Features:** The Southern French menu takes its influences from Provence and features items such as grilled salmon, roast half chicken and the signature lamb daube. A short but smart wine list accompanies. Rest assured, this is not a stuffy restaurant, but rather a trendy bistro with cool metallic tables, rich, red walls and abundant black accents. The small size of the dining room ensures a wait for dinner and an energetic atmosphere. Casual dress; cocktails. **Parking:** street. **Cards:** AX, MC, VI.

(See map and index starting on p. 590)

CHEZ SPENCER **Dinner:** $19-$29 **Phone:** 415/864-2191 (116)

French

Location: Just e of Folsom St; in Mission District. 82 14th St 94103. **Hours:** 5:30 pm-10:30 pm. Closed major holidays; also 12/24, Sun & Mon. **Reservations:** suggested. **Features:** Ignore the street, and head inside to sample French-influenced culinary delights prepared by chef Yasu Ueno. Experienced service and tasteful offerings from foie gras to poached asparagus to olive-crusted ling cod with sauteed eggplant make for a delightful dining experience. Save room for a cheese course or mouthwatering creme brulee. Casual dress; cocktails. **Parking:** street. **Cards:** AX, CB, DC, DS, JC, MC, VI.

CHIC'S SEAFOOD **Lunch:** $9-$34 **Dinner:** $9-$34 **Phone:** 415/421-2442 (69)

Steak & Seafood

Location: On Pier 39 at Fisherman's Wharf. Pier 39 #213 94133. **Hours:** 9 am-11 pm. **Features:** Early San Francisco decor lends character to the dining room, where guests can look out over the marina and bay. Dinners and lighter fare are served all day. Casual dress; cocktails. **Parking:** on-site (fee). **Cards:** AX, CB, DC, DS, MC, VI.

CITYSCAPE BAR & RESTAURANT **Dinner:** $18-$36 **Phone:** 415/923-5002 (32)

American

Location: Just w of Union Square at Mason St; in Hilton San Francisco. 333 O'Farrell St 94102. **Hours:** 5:30 pm-10 pm, Fri & Sat-11 pm, Sun 10 am-2 & 5:30-10 pm. **Reservations:** suggested. **Features:** Panoramic views of the city draw diners to the appropriately named restaurant. Dance music plays from 9 pm until midnight. Dressy casual; cocktails; entertainment. **Parking:** on-site (fee). **Cards:** AX, CB, DC, DS, JC, MC, VI.

THE CLIFF HOUSE **Lunch:** $8-$23 **Dinner:** $16-$25 **Phone:** 415/386-3330 (92)

AAA

American

Location: At Ocean Beach; 6 mi w of downtown. 1090 Point Lobos Ave (#993) 94121. **Hours:** 9 am-3:30 & 4:30-10 pm; Sat & Sun 8:30 am-3:30 & 4:30-10:30 pm. **Reservations:** suggested. **Features:** Upstairs from the Seafood and Beverage Co., the landmark restaurant overlooks Seal Rocks and the ocean. Specialty omelets and the Sunday brunch and buffet appeal to guests. Casual dress; cocktails. **Parking:** street. **Cards:** AX, MC, VI.

THE COSMOPOLITAN CAFE **Lunch:** $14-$18 **Dinner:** $17-$28 **Phone:** 415/543-4001 (35)

American

Location: Just s of Mission St; in Financial District. 121 Spear St, Unit B-8 94105. **Hours:** 11:15 am-2 & 5:30-9:30 pm, Thurs & Fri-10 pm, Sat 5:30 pm-10:30 pm. Closed major holidays; also Sun. **Reservations:** required. **Features:** In the "meeting and greeting" place, the high energy of San Francisco meets culinary delights such as peppercorn-seared yellowfin tuna and grilled Niman Ranch pork chops. The expert wait staff guides guests through selections and becomes friends along the way. Dressy casual; cocktails. **Parking:** on-site (fee) and street. **Cards:** AX, DC, MC, VI.

DANTE'S **Lunch:** $9-$17 **Dinner:** $17-$24 **Phone:** 415/421-5778 (67)

Seafood

Location: On Pier 39. **Hours:** 11 am-9 pm, Fri & Sat-10 pm. Closed: 12/25. **Reservations:** suggested. **Features:** Attractive decor punctuates the dining room, from which diners can look out over the harbor. California cuisine reflects a Mediterranean twist. Casual dress; cocktails. **Parking:** on-site (fee). **Cards:** AX, CB, DC, DS, JC, MC, VI.

DELFINA **Dinner:** $13-$19 **Phone:** 415/552-4055 (117)

American

Location: Between Guerrero and Dolores sts. 3621 18th St 94110. **Hours:** 5:30 pm-10 pm, Fri & Sat-11 pm. Closed: 1/1, 11/25, 12/25. **Reservations:** accepted. **Features:** Pasta, chicken, seafood and beef dishes, as well as frequently changing specialty items and a wide variety of wines, await customers of the restaurant with a bistro atmosphere. Casual dress; beer & wine only. **Parking:** street. **Cards:** MC, VI.

THE DINING ROOM **Dinner:** $67-$82 **Phone:** 415/773-6168 (14)

AAA

Nouvelle French

Location: Just n of Union Square at California St; in The Ritz-Carlton, San Francisco. 600 Stockton St 94108. **Hours:** 6 pm-9:30 pm. Closed: 4/11, 11/25; also Sun & Mon. **Reservations:** accepted. **Features:** Exceptional, quality ingredients mingle in original, imaginative cuisine. Three- to five-course dinners present an exceptional sampling. Expect impeccable service in an elegant atmosphere. Semi-formal attire; cocktails; entertainment. **Parking:** on-site (fee) and valet. **Cards:** AX, CB, DC, DS, MC, VI.

ELISABETH DANIEL **Dinner:** $25-$38 **Phone:** 415/397-6129 (8)

French

Location: Just n of Transamerica Pyramid; between Montgomery and Sansome sts. 550 Washington St 94111. **Hours:** 6 pm-10 pm, Sat from 5:30 pm. Closed major holidays. **Features:** A blend of elegance and charm, the classic French nouveau restaurant presents an award-winning wine list beside an ever-changing menu of French/California fusion cuisine. Garden-fresh ingredients mingle to create scintillating flavors. Semi-formal attire; beer & wine only. **Parking:** on-site (fee). **Cards:** AX, DC, MC, VI.

EMPRESS OF CHINA **Lunch:** $10-$20 **Dinner:** $31-$50 **Phone:** 415/434-1345 (9)

Chinese

Location: In Chinatown; on top floor of China Trade Center Building. 838 Grant Ave 94108. **Hours:** 11 am-10:30 pm, Sun from noon. **Reservations:** suggested. **Features:** Oriental decor; Regional specialties. Dressy casual; cocktails. **Parking:** on-site. **Cards:** AX, CB, DC, MC, VI.

(See map and index starting on p. 590)

ENRICO'S — Italian — **Lunch:** $7-$12 **Dinner:** $12-$26 **Phone:** 415/982-6223 (1)

Location: Between Columbus Ave and Montgomery St; near Chinatown. 504 Broadway 94133. **Hours:** 11:30 am-1 am. Closed: 11/25, 12/25. **Reservations:** suggested. **Features:** Cuisine is referred to as California Mediterranean with a strong Italian influence. Dish selections emphasize seafood, beef and pasta. The restaurant is one of the city's first to offer patio seating. Jazz combinations are offered nightly. Casual dress; cocktails. **Parking:** valet and street. **Cards:** AX, MC, VI.

FARALLON — Seafood — **Lunch:** $18-$20 **Dinner:** $25-$33 **Phone:** 415/956-6969 (22)

Location: US 101, exit 5th St, r to Ellis St, r on Taylor St; in Kensington Park Hotel. 450 Post St 94102. **Hours:** 11:30 am-2 & 5:30-10 pm, Fri & Sat-10:30 pm, Sun 5 pm-10 pm. Closed major holidays. **Reservations:** suggested. **Features:** The sophisticated, softly illuminated seafood restaurant is near Union Square. Professional servers deliver dishes that show a flair for presentation. Casual dress; cocktails. **Parking:** valet. **Cards:** AX, MC, VI.

FIFTH FLOOR — French — **Dinner:** $18-$43 **Phone:** 415/348-1555 (26)

Location: At Market St; downtown; in Hotel Palomar. 12 Fourth St 94103. **Hours:** 5:30 pm-9:30 pm, Fri & Sat-10:30 pm. Closed major holidays; also Sun. **Reservations:** suggested. **Features:** This high scale restaurant is close to the famous trolley stop on Powell. The comfortable interior is adorned with beautifully sculpted mahogany woodwork, sculptured chairs, fine fabric, crystal chandeliers and impeccable linen. Cuisine leans toward the game side, but with a staple of at least one steak and one chicken dish prepared with a French accent. Dressy casual; cocktails. **Parking:** on-site (fee). **Cards:** AX, DC, DS, MC, VI.

FIGARO — Italian — **Lunch:** $7-$17 **Dinner:** $9-$17 **Phone:** 415/398-1300 (85)

Location: Between Vallejo and Green sts; North Beach. 414 Columbus Ave 94133. **Hours:** 10 am-11 pm; Fri-Sun to midnight. **Reservations:** accepted. **Features:** The North Beach restaurant may be known as the house of gnocchi, but its menu lists many other Italian favorites, including pizza, calzones, pasta and risottos. Lending to the warm European feel is sidewalk seating. Casual dress; cocktails. **Parking:** street. **Cards:** AX, CB, DC, DS, MC, VI.

FIRST CRUSH RESTAURANT WINE BAR & LOUNGE — American — **Lunch:** $7-$14 **Dinner:** $13-$19 **Phone:** 415/982-7874 (40)

Location: Corner of Cyril Magnin and Ellis sts. 101 Cyril Magnin St 94102. **Hours:** 11 am-3 & 5-midnight, Thurs-Sat to 1 am, Sun 5 pm-midnight. Closed: 11/25, 12/25. **Reservations:** accepted. **Features:** Diners can enjoy entrees of beef, lamb, chicken or seafood, as well as salads, in the downtown location near Union Square. Casual dress; beer & wine only. **Parking:** street. **Cards:** AX, CB, DC, MC, VI.

FLEUR DE LYS — French — **Dinner:** $65-$85 **Phone:** 415/673-7779 (17)

Location: Between Taylor and Jones sts. 777 Sutter St 94109. **Hours:** 6 pm-9 pm, Fri & Sat 5:30 pm-10 pm. Closed major holidays; also Sun. **Reservations:** required. **Features:** A Mediterranean touch influences contemporary French cuisine served in the elegant dining area. The restaurant presents two prix fixe menus, one of which is designed for vegetarians. Formal attire; cocktails. **Parking:** valet and street. **Cards:** AX, DC, MC, VI.

FLY TRAP — American — **Lunch:** $11-$15 **Dinner:** $16-$26 **Phone:** 415/243-0580 (58)

Location: Folsom and 2nd sts. 606 Folsom St 94107. **Hours:** 11:30 am-9:30 pm, Sat from 5 pm. Closed major holidays; also Sun. **Reservations:** accepted. **Features:** San Francisco favorites such as Dungeness crab cake appetizers accompany thick grilled meats, fresh seafood, pasta and daily specials in the upscale restaurant. Brass accents natural wood in the warm atmosphere. Casual dress; cocktails. **Parking:** street. **Cards:** AX, DC, MC, VI.

THE GARDEN COURT — American — **Lunch:** $14-$20 **Phone:** 415/512-1111 (29)

Location: Just e of Union Square at Market St; in Palace Hotel. 2 New Montgomery St 94105. **Hours:** 6:30 am-10:30 & 11:30-1:30 pm, Sun 6:30 am-1:30 pm. Closed: 7/1-7/7. **Reservations:** suggested. **Features:** An Old World atmosphere punctuates the elegantly restored 1909 landmark. Contributing to the style are a glass-domed atrium, lavish crystal chandeliers and marble and gold-leaf accents. Classically inspired cuisine is exceptional. Dressy casual; cocktails; entertainment. **Parking:** valet. **Cards:** AX, MC, VI.

GARY DANKO — Continental — **Dinner:** $55-$74 **Phone:** 415/749-2060 (74)

Location: Just e of Ghiradelli Square at Hyde St. 800 North Point 94109. **Hours:** 5:30 pm-9:30 pm, Thurs-Sat to 10 pm. Closed: 7/4, 11/25, 12/25; also 12/31. **Reservations:** required. **Features:** An elegant and intimate space without being stiff, the restaurant provides both luxury and comfort, and serves lively, seasonal dishes prepared with a careful eye toward classical techniques; try the roast lobster! Formal attire; cocktails. **Parking:** valet and street. **Cards:** AX, CB, DC, DS, JC, MC, VI.

GOLDEN TURTLE — Ethnic — **Dinner:** $12-$25 **Phone:** 415/441-4419 (82)

Location: On US 101 (Van Ness Ave). 2211 Van Ness Ave 94109. **Hours:** 5 pm-11 pm. Closed: Mon & 12/24-12/30. **Reservations:** suggested. **Features:** Custom ethnic appointments decorate the cozy dining room, a favorite haunt for Vietnamese cuisine. Dressy casual; beer & wine only. **Parking:** on-site (fee). **Cards:** AX, MC, VI.

HARRIS' — Steak House — **Dinner:** $17-$38 **Phone:** 415/673-1888 (84)

Location: On US 101 (Van Ness Ave) at Pacific Ave. 2100 Van Ness Ave 94109. **Hours:** 5:30 pm-9:30 pm, Sat & Sun from 5 pm. Closed: 1/1, 7/4, 12/25. **Reservations:** suggested. **Features:** An old San Francisco atmosphere pervades the modestly sophisticated restaurant, where patrons linger over dry-aged, Midwestern beef and fresh seafood. Smoking is permitted only in the lounge. Dressy casual; cocktails. **Parking:** on-site (fee). **Cards:** AX, CB, DC, DS, MC, VI.

(See map and index starting on p. 590)

HAWTHORNE LANE **Lunch:** $12-$15 **Dinner:** $21-$29 **Phone:** 415/777-9779 (45)

California

Location: Adjacent to the San Francisco Museum of Modern Art. 22 Hawthorne St 94105. **Hours:** 11:30 am-1:30 & 5:30-9 pm, Fri & Sat-10:30 pm, Sun from 5:30 pm. Closed major holidays. **Reservations:** suggested. **Features:** While San Francisco boasts many great places to dine, this may one of the few that satisfies all of the senses. From its understated but impressive interior to the pleasing sounds and smells coming from the open kitchen to the inviting fusion of flavors it leaves on the palate, the restaurant will leave a lasting impression. The seasonal menu has a prominent Asian influence and is so perfectly designed it makes a choice difficult. Casual dress; cocktails. **Parking:** on-site (fee). **Cards:** CB, DC, DS, JC, MC, VI.

HAYES STREET GRILL **Lunch:** $9-$19 **Dinner:** $17-$28 **Phone:** 415/863-5545 (103)

Seafood

Location: 320 Hayes St 94102. **Hours:** 11:30 am-2 & 5-9:30 pm, Fri & Sat 5:30 pm-10:30 pm, Sun 5 pm-8:30 pm. Closed major holidays. **Reservations:** suggested. **Features:** Mesquite-grilled seafood is prepared in the California style with an array of fresh ingredients. Casual dress; cocktails. **Parking:** no self-parking. **Cards:** AX, CB, DC, DS, MC, VI.

HOME **Lunch:** $7-$10 **Dinner:** $7-$13 **Phone:** 415/503-0333 (112)

American

Location: Jct of Church and 14th sts; Castro. 2100 Market St 94114. **Hours:** 11:30 am-2:30 & 5-10:30 pm, Fri 11:30 am-2:30 & 5:30-11 pm, Sat 5:30 pm-11 pm, Sun 11 am-3 & 5:30-11 pm. Closed: 7/4, 11/25, 12/25. **Reservations:** suggested. **Features:** Representative of comfort food done with flair are braised pot roast, split pea soup and macaroni and cheese. While ceviche, pate and crispy polenta may not bring thoughts of dishes from Mom's kitchen, they are an example of the menu's diversity. Because of the restaurant's location, the scene is young but mixed. Seating may require patience, a sense of humor or a total lack of want for privacy. Loyalists like the $5 cocktail list and early bird specials. Casual dress; cocktails. **Parking:** valet. **Cards:** AX, MC, VI.

HOUSE OF PRIME RIB **Dinner:** $22-$29 **Phone:** 415/885-4605 (91)

American

Location: US 101 (Van Ness Ave). 1906 Van Ness Ave 94109. **Hours:** 5:30 pm-10 pm, Sat from 4:30 pm, Sun from 4 pm. Closed: 12/25. **Reservations:** accepted. **Features:** A cart is brought to the table to enable guests to select individual cuts. Also on the menu are fresh fish and specialty items. Dressy casual; cocktails. **Parking:** on-site (fee). **Cards:** AX, MC, VI.

HYDE STREET SEAFOOD HOUSE AND RAW BAR 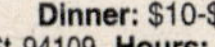 **Dinner:** $10-$20 **Phone:** 415/931-3474 (89)

Seafood

Location: Jct Jackson St, just n. 1509 Hyde St 94109. **Hours:** 5 pm-10 pm, Fri & Sat-10:30 pm. Closed: 1/1, 11/25, 12/25. **Reservations:** suggested. **Features:** Nautical decor and friendly service, as well as fine seafood prepared in a variety of styles, are what patrons find at the neighborhood restaurant. Dungeness crab Mornay teases palates with its delicate taste. Casual dress; beer & wine only. **Parking:** street. **Cards:** AX, MC, VI.

JARDINIERE **Dinner:** $24-$35 **Phone:** 415/861-5555 (100)

French

Location: US 101 (Van Ness Ave), just w at Franklin St. 300 Grove St 94102. **Hours:** 5:30 pm-10:30 pm, Fri & Sat-11:30 pm. Closed major holidays. **Reservations:** required; 1 week prior. **Features:** Contributing to the sophisticated surroundings are an oval atrium and glowing, gold dome. Pewter-colored railings swoop gracefully between softly lit lampposts that, filled with ice, double as champagne buckets. Instrumental musicians perform nightly. Menu offerings change daily. A temperature-controlled "cave" keeps a good selection of cheese fresh. Semi-formal attire; cocktails; entertainment. **Parking:** on-site (fee) and valet. **Cards:** AX, CB, DS, MC, VI.

JESTER'S RESTAURANT **Lunch:** $7-$15 **Dinner:** $14-$20 **Phone:** 415/974-7046 (31)

American

Location: 1 1/2 blks n of Moscone Convention Center; in The Argent Hotel. 50 Third St 94103. **Hours:** 6:30 am-10:30 pm. **Reservations:** suggested. **Features:** The eclectic restaurant provides fare for even the fussiest diners. Continental dishes reflect an Asian accent. The gardens, lounge and dining area carefully entwine. Casual dress; cocktails; entertainment. **Parking:** valet. **Cards:** AX, CB, DC, DS, MC, VI.

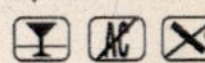

JOHN'S GRILL **Lunch:** $6-$22 **Dinner:** $17-$27 **Phone:** 415/986-0069 (23)

Continental

Location: 2.5 blks s of Union Square. 63 Ellis St 94102. **Hours:** Open 2/1-11/27 & 12/26-1/31; 11 am-10 pm, Sun from 5 pm. Closed: 11/25, 12/25. **Reservations:** suggested. **Features:** Established in 1908, the relaxed restaurant is furnished in turn-of-the-20th-century decor. This place was a setting in "The Maltese Falcon" by author Dashiell Hammett. Casual dress; cocktails; entertainment. **Parking:** no self-parking. **Cards:** AX, DC, MC, VI.

JULIA **Dinner:** $17-$26 **Phone:** 415/441-2101 (94)

American

Location: Southwest corner of Sutter and Steiner sts; near the Kabuki Theater. 2101 Sutter St 94115. **Hours:** 5:30 pm-10 pm, Mon-9 pm. Closed major holidays. **Reservations:** suggested. **Features:** The decor is somewhat distinctive, with eccentric, oversized mirrors, iron light fixtures, a bold awning and stuffed animals in the men's restroom. The diversified menu lists seafood, beef and chicken dishes that are sure to please the palate. The house specialty is skewered chicken livers with bacon and vinegary greens and pot roast with mashed potatoes and root vegetables. Casual dress; cocktails. **Parking:** valet and street. **Cards:** AX, MC, VI.

JULIUS' CASTLE Historic **Dinner:** $18-$36 **Phone:** 415/392-2222 (73)

Italian

Location: Just e of Coit Tower. 1541 Montgomery St 94133. **Hours:** 5 pm-9:30 pm. **Reservations:** suggested. **Features:** Excellent views and a cozy setting make the restaurant, near Coit Tower, ideal for a romantic evening. Sophisticated Italian dishes make up the bulk of the menu. Dressy casual; cocktails. **Parking:** on-site (fee). **Cards:** AX, CB, DC, DS, MC, VI.

(See map and index starting on p. 590)

KAN'S — Chinese — **Lunch:** $15-$25 **Dinner:** $15-$30 **Phone:** 415/362-5267 (11)

Location: In Chinatown. Upstairs at 708 Grant Ave 94108. **Hours:** 11:30 am-10 pm, Sun from 4 pm. **Reservations:** suggested. **Features:** Cantonese dishes make up most of the menu at the long-established Chinese restaurant. Casual dress; cocktails. **Parking:** street. **Cards:** AX, DC, MC, VI.

KULETO'S — AAA — Italian — **Lunch:** $7-$23 **Dinner:** $7-$23 **Phone:** 415/397-7720 (28)

Location: Just s of Union Square; in Villa Florence Hotel. 221 Powell St 94102. **Hours:** 7 am-10:30 & 11:30-11 pm, Sat & Sun from 8 am. Closed major holidays. **Reservations:** suggested. **Features:** In-house cured prosciutto and other flavorful foods are served in an upscale, lively atmosphere. Casual dress; cocktails. **Parking:** on-site (fee). **Cards:** AX, CB, DC, DS, MC, VI.

LA FOLIE — French — **Dinner:** $25-$50 **Phone:** 415/776-5577 (87)

Location: In Russian Hill district. 2316 Polk St 94109. **Hours:** 5:30 pm-10 pm. Closed major holidays; also Sun. **Reservations:** suggested. **Features:** Whimsical, intimate and dreamlike decor contrasts with classic French specialties, such as foie gras with fresh figs in wine reduction. Service is attentive yet unobtrusive. Dressy casual; cocktails. **Parking:** valet and street. **Cards:** AX, MC, VI.

LEHR'S GREENHOUSE — California — **Lunch:** $8-$18 **Dinner:** $12-$28 **Phone:** 415/474-6478 (19)

Location: Between Taylor and Jones sts; in Best Western Canterbury Hotel. 740 Sutter St 94109. **Hours:** 6:30 am-10 pm. Closed: 1/1. **Reservations:** suggested. **Features:** Indoor garden dining. California cuisine. Dressy casual; cocktails. **Parking:** valet. **Cards:** AX, CB, DC, DS, JC, MC, VI.

L'OLIVIER RESTAURANT — AAA — Regional French — **Lunch:** $14-$18 **Dinner:** $15-$22 **Phone:** 415/981-7824 (5)

Location: Off Jackson St; in Golden Gateway Center. 465 Davis Ct 94111. **Hours:** 11:30 am-2:30 & 5:30-10 pm. Closed major holidays; also Sun. **Reservations:** suggested. **Features:** Award-winning bouillabaisse and other French delights are served in a quiet, relaxing atmosphere. Dressy casual; cocktails. **Parking:** valet. **Cards:** AX, CB, DC, DS, MC, VI.

LOLLI'S CASTAGNOLA — Seafood — **Lunch:** $7-$20 **Dinner:** $12-$40 **Phone:** 415/776-5015 (68)

Location: 1 blk w of Fisherman's Wharf at Jones St. 286 Jefferson St 94133. **Hours:** 11 am-10 pm, Sat-11 pm. Closed: 12/25. **Reservations:** suggested. **Features:** Since 1952, the established eatery has prepared Italian specialties, along with many seafood selections. The view overlooks the boat marina. Casual dress; cocktails. **Parking:** on-site (fee). **Cards:** AX, CB, DC, MC.

LORI'S DINER — American — **Lunch:** $10-$13 **Dinner:** $10-$13 **Phone:** 415/677-9999 (41)

Location: Between O'Farrell and Ellis sts; near Union Square. 149 Powell St 94102. **Hours:** 7 am-10 pm, Fri & Sat-11 pm. **Features:** The 1950s diner prepares great burgers, shakes, fries and appetizers. Mexican dishes, as well as steamed vegetables and Chinese chicken salads, are also available. Lending to the decor are neon, red vinyl, chrome and buxom waitress pinup pictures. Casual dress. **Parking:** street. **Cards:** AX, DS, MC, VI.

L'OSTERIA DEL FORNO — Italian — **Lunch:** $8-$12 **Dinner:** $8-$12 **Phone:** 415/982-1124 (79)

Location: S of Fisherman's Wharf at Green St. 519 Columbus Ave 94133. **Hours:** 11:30 am-10 pm, Fri & Sat-10:30 pm. Closed: 1/1, 12/25; also Tues. **Features:** The dining room is small, so patrons might experience a wait for a table. However, it will be worth it. The restaurant is known for its thin-crust pizzas and focaccia sandwiches. Try pumpkin ravioli or milk-braised roast pork. Casual dress; cocktails. **Parking:** street.

MACARTHUR PARK — American — **Lunch:** $9-$15 **Dinner:** $9-$28 **Phone:** 415/398-5700 (43)

Location: Corner of Front and Jackson sts; across from Jackson Square. 607 Front St 94111. **Hours:** 11:30 am-10 pm, Fri-11 pm, Sat 5 pm-11 pm, Sun 4:30 pm-10 pm. Closed: 12/25. **Reservations:** accepted. **Features:** The restaurant's early 1900s renovated warehouse building overlooks Walton Park. Barbecue is the forte, with steak and seafood dishes also available. On the lunch menu is a good variety of salads, soups and sandwiches. Casual dress; cocktails. **Parking:** street. **Cards:** AX, DC, MC, VI.

MAHARANI — Ethnic — **Lunch:** $8-$25 **Dinner:** $8-$25 **Phone:** 415/775-1988 (96)

Location: US 101 (Van Ness Ave), just e. 1122 Post St 94109. **Hours:** 11:30 am-2:30 & 5-10 pm, Sun from 5 pm. Closed: Sun for lunch. **Reservations:** required; for dinner. **Features:** The menu focuses on the cuisine of India. Lunch is served in the main dining room, while guests can opt to have dinner instead in the traditional, cushioned and curtained fantasy room. Casual dress; cocktails. **Parking:** on-site (fee). **Cards:** AX, DC, MC, VI.

MASA'S — French — **Dinner:** $65-$109 **Phone:** 415/989-7154 (55)

Location: Just s of Stockton St. 648 Bush St 94108. **Hours:** 5:30 pm-9:30 pm. Closed major holidays; also Sun, first 2 weeks in Jan & 1st week in July. **Reservations:** required. **Features:** The elegant, sophisticated restaurant offers diners a choice of two fixed menus. In the dining room, the atmosphere is quiet and cozy. Semi-formal attire; cocktails. **Parking:** on-site (fee). **Cards:** AX, CB, DC, DS, MC, VI.

(See map and index starting on p. 590)

MAYA RESTAURANT **Lunch:** $11-$17 **Dinner:** $19-$26 **Phone:** 415/543-2928 (57)

Mexican

Location: Just e of Folsom and 2nd sts; in the South of Market area; downtown. 303 2nd St 94107. **Hours:** 11:30 am-2 & 5:30-10 pm, Sat from 5:30 pm, Sun 5:30 pm-9 pm. Closed major holidays. **Reservations:** suggested. **Features:** The beautifully decorated dining room is appointed with original art and prehistoric masks. Upscale Mexican dishes use fresh, interesting ingredients. Capable servers offer items such as tamal al chipotle, mole poblano and chayote relleno. Dressy casual; cocktails. **Parking:** on-site (fee). **Cards:** AX, DS, MC, VI.

MCCORMICK & KULETO'S SEAFOOD RESTAURANT **Lunch:** $10-$25 **Dinner:** $25-$50 **Phone:** 415/929-1730 (63)

Seafood

Location: Ghiradelli Square. 900 N Point St 94109. **Hours:** 11:30 am-11 pm, Sun from 10:30 am. **Reservations:** suggested. **Features:** The restaurant affords spectacular views of San Francisco Bay and its bridges. Dressy casual; cocktails. **Parking:** on-site (fee). **Cards:** AX, CB, DC, DS, MC, VI.

MC2 Historic **Lunch:** $7-$14 **Dinner:** $10-$21 **Phone:** 415/956-0666 (44)

California

Location: Just s of North Beach, e of jct Pacific Ave and Montgomery St. 470 Pacific Ave 94133. **Hours:** 11:30 am-2:30 & 5:30-10 pm, Fri & Sat-11 pm. Closed major holidays; also Sun. **Reservations:** suggested. **Features:** Chef Todd Davies offers refined and flavorful cooking with seasonally influenced items, tasting courses and wine pairings. Mesquite-grilled Colorado rack of lamb with eggplant caviar, smoked Columbia River sturgeon and grilled Cervena venison chop are just a few of the entrees capably served in a 120-year-old building just south of North Beach. The wine list is extensive, and by-the-glass selections are offered. Casual dress; cocktails. **Parking:** valet and street. **Cards:** AX, CB, DC, DS, MC, VI.

MECCA **Dinner:** $16-$29 **Phone:** 415/621-7000 (113)

Asian

Location: 14th and Market sts, just ne. 2029 Market St 94114. **Hours:** 6 pm-11 pm, Thurs-Sat 5:30 pm-midnight, Sun 5 pm-10 pm. Closed: 1/1, 11/25, 12/25. **Reservations:** suggested. **Features:** The stylish, svelte restaurant is one of those places people go to see and be seen. The lounge is a lively spot. The specialty is in the delicate tastes of New Asian cuisine, as found in such dishes as Maine lobster risotto. Dressy casual; cocktails. **Parking:** street. **Cards:** AX, DC, MC, VI.

MILLENNIUM RESTAURANT **Dinner:** $12-$20 **Phone:** 415/345-3900 (6)

Vegetarian

Location: 3 blks w of Union Square; in Savoy Hotel. 580 Geary St 94102. **Hours:** 5 pm-10 pm, Sun also 10:30 am-1 pm. Closed: 12/25. **Reservations:** suggested. **Features:** Healthy, environmentally friendly foods with fresh produce (organic when available) are used to create a gourmet dining experience. Dressy casual; cocktails. **Parking:** valet and street. **Cards:** AX, CB, DC, DS, MC, VI.

MOMO'S **Lunch:** $8-$17 **Dinner:** $10-$28 **Phone:** 415/227-8660 (106)

American

Location: At King; across from Pacific Bell Park. 760 Second St 94107. **Hours:** 11:30 am-9:30 pm, Sat-10 pm. **Reservations:** suggested. **Features:** Across from the ballpark, the restaurant can be extremely busy on game day. American-style cuisine includes such favorites as crispy onion strings, wood-grilled pork chops with garlic mashed potatoes, baby back ribs in bourbon sauce and crisp, thin-crust pizzas. Finish the meal with a tangy blackberry crisp. Dressy casual; cocktails. **Parking:** on-site (fee) and valet. **Cards:** AX, CB, DC, DS, JC, MC, VI.

MOOSE'S **Lunch:** $8-$15 **Dinner:** $11-$32 **Phone:** 415/989-7800 (77)

American

Location: Just n of Union St; in North Beach. 1652 Stockton St 94133. **Hours:** 5:30 pm-10:30 pm, Thurs also 11:30 am-2:30 pm, Fri & Sat 11:30 am-2:30 & 5:30-11 pm, Sun 10 am-2:30 & 5-10 pm. Closed: 1/1, 12/25. **Reservations:** suggested. **Features:** The upbeat atmosphere and live entertainment set the tone as patrons enjoy the competent staff and friendly service in the North Beach eatery. Featuring local organic produce, free-range fowl and beef, the eclectic menu beckons to discriminating diners with palate-pleasing options. Casual dress; cocktails. **Parking:** on-site (fee) and valet. **Cards:** AX, CB, DC, DS, JC, MC, VI.

NIGHT MONKEY **Dinner:** $10-$24 **Phone:** 415/775-1130 (83)

American

Location: Jct of Fillmore St; in Cow Hollow Area. 2223 Union St 94123. **Hours:** 6 pm-midnight. Closed major holidays; also Sun. **Reservations:** accepted. **Features:** The restaurant offers late-night dining on cooked-to-order food. All meats are free-range and hormone-free, while the fruits and vegetables are organic. Casual dress; beer & wine only. **Parking:** street. **Cards:** AX, DC, DS, MC, VI.

NOB HILL CAFE **Lunch:** $8-$15 **Dinner:** $8-$15 **Phone:** 415/776-6500 (16)

Italian

Location: Between Sacramento and Clay sts; atop Nob Hill. 1152 Taylor St 94108. **Hours:** 11 am-3 & 5-10 pm. Closed major holidays. **Features:** A regular meeting place for locals, the quaint bistro is perched out of the mainstream. The menu centers on homemade pasta, pizza and light antipasto and is perfect for a quick lunch or casual dinner. No reservations are accepted, and there is often a wait. Casual dress; beer & wine only. **Parking:** street. **Cards:** DC, MC, VI.

ONE MARKET RESTAURANT **Lunch:** $15-$18 **Dinner:** $21-$30 **Phone:** 415/777-5577 (2)

American

Location: Southeast corner of Market and Steuart sts; near Embarcadero Station. 1 Market St 94105. **Hours:** 11:30 am-2 & 5:30-9 pm, Sat from 5:30 pm. Closed major holidays; also Sun. **Reservations:** suggested. **Features:** At the end of Market Street within view of the Bay Bridge, the popular restaurant has received accolades from San Francisco Focus magazine, Wine Spectator and Where Magazine. A prime seating spot is the chef's table in the open exhibition kitchen. Although the main feature is seafood, the menu also lists selections in beef, lamb and chicken. Casual dress; cocktails. **Parking:** valet and street. **Cards:** AX, DC, DS, MC, VI.

(See map and index starting on p. 590)

PACIFIC — Regional California — Lunch: $15-$20 Dinner: $25-$38 Phone: 415/929-2087 (21)
Location: Just w of Union Square at Mason St; in The Pan Pacific Hotel. 500 Post St 94102. **Hours:** 7-11 am, 11:30-2:30 & 5:30-9:30 pm, Sun & Mon-2:30 pm. **Reservations:** suggested. **Features:** French influences are evident in selections of California cuisine. The elegant dining room is open and airy. Dressy casual; cocktails. **Parking:** valet. **Cards:** AX, CB, DC, DS, MC, VI.

PALIO D'ASTI — Italian — **Lunch:** $13-$25 **Dinner:** $16-$25 **Phone:** 415/395-9800 (13)
Location: In Financial District. 640 Sacramento St 94111. **Hours:** 11:30 am-2:30 & 5:30-9 pm. Closed major holidays; also Sat & Sun. **Reservations:** suggested. **Features:** The menu comprises traditional favorites as well as regional specialties. The high-tech atmosphere is relaxed. Casual dress; cocktails. **Parking:** no self-parking. **Cards:** AX, CB, DC, DS, MC, VI.

PASTA POMODORO — Italian — **Lunch:** $6-$9 **Dinner:** $6-$11 **Phone:** 415/399-0300 (75)
Location: 1 mi e of Van Ness Ave (US 101) at Columbus. 655 Union St 94133. **Hours:** 11 am-10:30 pm. **Features:** The restaurant is well known for its large, reasonably priced portions. Heart-healthy items are available. Casual dress; beer & wine only. **Parking:** street. **Cards:** MC, VI.

PASTA POMODORO-CASTRO — Italian — **Lunch:** $6-$10 **Dinner:** $6-$10 **Phone:** 415/558-8123 (110)
Location: At 16th St. 2304 Market St 94114. **Hours:** 11 am-10:30 pm. **Features:** In a vibrant neighborhood and offering both inside and outside seating, the location is popular with locals and tourists alike. Fresh food and upbeat servers abound. Casual dress; beer & wine only. **Parking:** street. **Cards:** MC, VI.

PASTA POMODORO-COW HOLLOW — Italian — **Lunch:** $6-$10 **Dinner:** $6-$10 **Phone:** 415/771-7900 (80)
Location: At Laguna. 1875 Union St 94123. **Hours:** 11 am-10:30 pm. **Features:** Great for people-watching, the restaurant lets guests grab a seat near the window to enjoy the hustle and bustle of Union Street. Delicious food is prepared before diners' eyes in the centrally located bar area. Casual dress; beer & wine only. **Parking:** street. **Cards:** MC, VI.

PASTA POMODORO-KABUKI — Italian — **Lunch:** $6-$10 **Dinner:** $6-$10 **Phone:** 415/674-1826 (111)
Location: At Fillmore. 1865 Post St 94115. **Hours:** 11 am-10:30 pm. **Features:** People patronize the restaurant for quick or relaxed dining before or after enjoying a flick at the nearby cinema complex. Both downstairs and upstairs seating is available. Casual dress; beer & wine only. **Parking:** street. **Cards:** MC, VI.

PASTA POMODORO-LAUREL VILLAGE — Italian — **Lunch:** $6-$10 **Dinner:** $6-$10 **Phone:** 415/831-0900 (81)
Location: At Spruce. 3611 California St 94118. **Hours:** 11 am-10:30 pm. **Features:** Those who stop in will find a dining room that's popular with local business owners, medical staff and visitors to nearby hospitals. Guests can enjoy a quick meal or sit back and relax while the friendly staff serves. Casual dress; beer & wine only. **Parking:** street. **Cards:** MC, VI.

PASTA POMODORO-NOE VALLEY — Italian — **Lunch:** $6-$10 **Dinner:** $6-$10 **Phone:** 415/920-9904 (95)
Location: At Noe. 4000 24th St 94114. **Hours:** 11 am-10:30 pm. **Features:** An integral part of the neighborhood, the cozy spot offers expanded sidewalk seating. Diners from all parts of the city enjoy the service and tasty preparations. Casual dress; beer & wine only. **Parking:** street. **Cards:** MC, VI.

PASTA POMODORO-SUNSET — Italian — **Lunch:** $6-$10 **Dinner:** $6-$10 **Phone:** 415/566-0900 (115)
Location: At 9th Ave. 816 Irving St 94122. **Hours:** 11 am-10:30 pm. **Features:** At the entrance to Golden Gate Park and the inner Sunset District, the location lures a loyal local clientele. Fresh food, friendly service and both inside and patio seating are available. Casual dress; beer & wine only. **Parking:** street. **Cards:** MC, VI.

PEARL CITY — Chinese — **Lunch:** $8-$20 **Dinner:** $8-$20 **Phone:** 415/398-8383 (25)
Location: At Kearney; in Chinatown. 641 Jackson St 94133. **Hours:** 8 am-10 pm. **Reservations:** accepted. **Features:** The restaurant is the place for dim sum, and the prices are reasonable. Expect a wait on the weekends, as this spot is popular with the locals. Casual dress; beer & wine only. **Parking:** street. **Cards:** MC, VI.

PIER MARKET SEAFOOD RESTAURANT — Seafood — **Lunch:** $8-$23 **Dinner:** $8-$23 **Phone:** 415/989-7437 (71)
Location: At Fisherman's Wharf. Pier 39, Space 213 94133. **Hours:** 11 am-11 pm. **Features:** The seaside restaurant beckons to tourists and locals. Seafood and friendly service await. Casual dress; cocktails. **Parking:** on-site (fee). **Cards:** AX, DS, JC, MC, VI.

POMPEI'S GROTTO — AAA — Seafood — **Lunch:** $7-$13 **Dinner:** $9-$24 **Phone:** 415/776-9265 (61)
Location: At Fisherman's Wharf. 340 Jefferson St 94133. **Hours:** 10 am-11 pm. Closed: 12/24, 12/25. **Reservations:** suggested. **Features:** Homemade pasta and Northern Italian dishes are what diners can expect at the cozy restaurant, which is in a popular tourist area. Casual dress; cocktails. **Parking:** on-site (fee). **Cards:** AX, MC, VI.

(See map and index starting on p. 590)

POSTRIO Lunch: $13-$18 Dinner: $26-$36 Phone: 415/776-7825 (24)

American

Location: Just w of Union Square; in The Prescott Hotel. 545 Post St 94102. **Hours:** 7-10 am, 11:30-2 & 5:30-10 pm, Sat-10:30 pm, Sun 10 am-2 & 5:30-10 pm. Closed: 7/4, 11/25, 12/25. **Reservations:** required. **Features:** The lively restaurant's California cuisine reflects Asian and Mediterranean influences. Casual dress; cocktails. **Parking:** valet. **Cards:** AX, CB, DC, MC, VI. ***(See color ad p 636)***

PUCCINI & PINETTI **Lunch:** $12 **Dinner:** $25 **Phone:** 415/392-5500 (27)

Italian

Location: 1 blk n on Market St; downtown. 129 Ellis St 94102. **Hours:** 11:30 am-3:30 & 4-10 pm, Fri & Sat-11 pm, Sun 4 pm-10 pm. Closed: 11/25, 12/25. **Reservations:** suggested. **Features:** Patrons feast on creative works of art, such as polenta cakes drizzled with balsamic reduction and adorned with chantrels and roasted garlic. Dressy casual; cocktails. **Parking:** no self-parking. **Cards:** AX, CB, DC, DS, JC, MC, VI.

RESTAURANT LULU **Lunch:** $8-$22 **Dinner:** $12-$27 **Phone:** 415/495-5775 (60)

French

Location: Intersection 5th and Folsom sts, just ne. 816 Folsom St 94107. **Hours:** 11:30 am-3 & 5:30-10:30 pm, Fri 11:30 am-3 & 5-11:30 pm, Sat 5 pm-11:30 pm, Sun 11:30-3 & 5-10:30 pm. Closed: 1/1, 11/25, 12/25. **Reservations:** suggested. **Features:** The restaurant's specialty is California French cuisine, with crusty bread, fine olive oil, eclectic soups, salads and entrees. In combination with a light, bright, cheery look, patrons have everything necessary for a pleasant dining experience. Good choices are the leg of lamb sandwich and portobello mushroom soup. Dressy casual; cocktails. **Parking:** street. **Cards:** AX, DC, DS, MC, VI.

RICK'S RESTAURANT & BAR **Dinner:** $13-$20 **Phone:** 415/731-8900 (119)

American

Location: Between 29th and 30th aves. 1940 Taraval St 94116. **Hours:** 4:30 pm-10 pm, Sat 5 pm-10:30 pm, Sun 4 pm-10 pm. Closed: 1/1, 12/25. **Reservations:** suggested. **Features:** Local ingredients factor heavily in well-prepared dishes of San Francisco cuisine. The upscale dining room sustains a lively atmosphere. Dressy casual; cocktails; entertainment. **Parking:** on-site (fee). **Cards:** AX, DS, MC, VI.

ROSE PISTOLA **Lunch:** $13-$27 **Dinner:** $13-$29 **Phone:** 415/399-0499 (78)

Italian

Location: Just s of Union St. 532 Columbus Ave 94133. **Hours:** 11:30 am-4 & 5:30-11 pm, Fri & Sat 5:30 pm-midnight. Closed major holidays. **Reservations:** required. **Features:** A delightful decor, friendly, casual service and an excellent selection of freshly prepared dishes are found at the popular, busy restaurant. An excellent selection of wines complements the pasta, pizza and seasonal antipasto choices. Casual dress; cocktails. **Parking:** valet and street. **Cards:** AX, DS, MC, VI.

ROY'S **Lunch:** $15-$30 **Dinner:** $28-$39 **Phone:** 415/777-0277 (12)

Nouvelle Hawaiian

Location: Just off Market St; downtown. 101 2nd St 94105. **Hours:** 11:30 am-4 & 5-10 pm, Fri & Sat-10:30 pm, Sun 5 pm-10 pm. Closed: 1/1, 11/25. **Reservations:** suggested. **Features:** A fusion of freshness and creativity from Hawaii and California is proffered in an artsy, upbeat, dressy-casual atmosphere. Dressy casual; cocktails. **Parking:** no self-parking. **Cards:** AX, CB, DC, DS, JC, MC, VI.

RUBICON **Lunch:** $12-$18 **Dinner:** $17-$30 **Phone:** 415/434-4100 (30)

French

Location: Jct Montgomery St, just e. 558 Sacramento St 94111. **Hours:** 11:30 am-2:30 & 5:30-10:30 pm, Thurs from 5:30 pm, Fri & Sat 5:30 pm-11:30 pm. Closed major holidays; also Sun. **Reservations:** suggested. **Features:** In the financial district, the upscale restaurant sustains a refined setting, with crisp, white linens and excellent American fine-dining cuisine. Service is competent and unobtrusive. Dressy casual; beer & wine only. **Parking:** on-site (fee) and valet. **Cards:** AX, DC, DS, MC, VI.

SCOMA'S RESTAURANT **Lunch:** $12-$55 **Dinner:** $12-$55 **Phone:** 415/771-4383 (65)

Seafood

Location: On Fisherman's Wharf. Fisherman's Wharf Pier 47 94133. **Hours:** 11:30 am-10:30 pm, Sat-11 pm. Closed: 11/25, 12/24, 12/25. **Features:** A casual mood pervades the landmark restaurant. Picturesque views of the harbor invite wistful daydreaming. Casual dress; cocktails. **Parking:** on-site (fee). **Cards:** AX, CB, DC, DS, JC, MC, VI.

SEASONS RESTAURANT **Lunch:** $10-$20 **Dinner:** $15-$40 **Phone:** 415/633-3000 (33)

California

Location: Between 3rd and 4th sts; in Four Seasons San Francisco. 757 Market St 94103. **Hours:** 6:30-10:30 am, 11:30-2:30 & 6-10 pm, Fri & Sat from 5:30 pm. **Reservations:** suggested. **Features:** Patrons unwind in the elegant yet informal room over California-style cuisine prepared with a French influence. Cityscape views are captivating from any seat. The decor incorporates rich wood paneling and granite floors. Dressy casual; cocktails. **Parking:** on-site (fee). **Cards:** AX, CB, DC, DS, JC, MC, VI.

SHANGHAI 1930 **Lunch:** $13-$18 **Dinner:** $13-$18 **Phone:** 415/896-5600 (51)

Asian

Location: Between Mission and Howard sts. 133 Steuart St 94105. **Hours:** 11 am-2 & 5-10 pm, Fri & Sat-11 pm, Sun 5 pm-9 pm. Closed major holidays. **Reservations:** accepted. **Features:** On offer at the themed restaurant is a full range of dishes prepared in the Southeast Asian tradition. Patrons can savor appetizers and entrees that include prawns, chicken, duck, beef or lamb. Casual dress; cocktails. **Parking:** street. **Cards:** AX, DC, DS, JC, MC, VI.

(See map and index starting on p. 590)

SILKS **Lunch:** $18-$26 **Dinner:** $26-$36 **Phone:** 415/986-2020 (52)

Northern California

Location: US 101, s on Lombard St, e on Bush, then s; in Mandarin Oriental, San Francisco. 222 Sansome St 94104. **Hours:** 6:30-10:30 am, 11:30-2 & 6-9:30 pm, Sat & Sun 7 am-11 & 6-9:30 pm. **Reservations:** suggested. **Features:** Reminiscent of Southern Europe and Asia, the exceptional cuisine is primarily contemporary California cuisine with a touch of Asian influences. Cocktails. **Parking:** valet. **Cards:** AX, CB, DC, DS, JC, MC, VI.

SINBAD'S PIER II **Lunch:** $7-$21 **Dinner:** $18-$29 **Phone:** 415/781-2555 (15)

Seafood

Location: Located at Pier 2 on San Francisco's Bay/Embarcadero. Pier 2 94111. **Hours:** 11 am-10:30 pm. Closed major holidays. **Reservations:** accepted. **Features:** Right on the water, the restaurant affords incredible views of the bay and serves only the freshest seafood, steak and pasta. This place is a must-see for San Francisco visitors. Casual dress; cocktails. **Parking:** on-site and valet. **Cards:** AX, CB, DC, DS, MC, VI.

THE SLANTED DOOR **Lunch:** $8-$17 **Dinner:** $9-$27 **Phone:** 415/861-8032 (99)

Vietnamese

Location: I-280 N, to King St and then Embarcadero, then w. 100 Brannan St 94107. **Hours:** 11:30 am-3 & 5:30-10 pm. Closed major holidays; also first 2 weeks of Jan & Vietnamese New Year. **Reservations:** suggested. **Features:** The restaurant serves creative Vietnamese cuisine in an above-average atmosphere. Guests are treated to a fantastic view of the Bay Bridge. Dressy casual. **Parking:** street. **Cards:** AX, MC, VI.

SOLEA RESTAURANT **Lunch:** $9-$18 **Dinner:** $16-$26 **Phone:** 415/837-1680 (18)

California

Location: Just s of Stockton St; in The Orchard Hotel. 665 Bush St 94108. **Hours:** 6-11 am, 11:30-3 & 5:30-10 pm, Sat-10:30 pm. **Reservations:** suggested. **Features:** An upscale decor welcomes guests, and leisurely service follows. Dishes of fresh California cuisine delight the eye and taste buds. Top off the meal with one of the master pastry chef's desserts, such as dome chocolate cake. Dressy casual; cocktails. **Parking:** valet. **Cards:** AX, MC, VI.

THE STINKING ROSE **Lunch:** $12-$25 **Dinner:** $12-$25 **Phone:** 415/781-7673 (56)

Italian

Location: Between Vallejo and Broadway sts; in the North Beach area. 325 Columbus Ave 94133. **Hours:** 11 am-11:30 pm, Fri & Sat-midnight. **Reservations:** suggested. **Features:** In the city's "little Italy," the restaurant is known for its abundant use of garlic, which it publicizes via its motto: "We season our garlic with food." The menu features grilled, baked and roasted dishes all cooked with plenty of garlic. Those who prefer can get some selections without the pungent herb. A huge garlic braid winds through the establishment. Casual dress; cocktails. **Parking:** street. **Cards:** AX, DS, MC, VI.

SUPPENKUCHE **Dinner:** $15 **Phone:** 415/252-9289 (97)

Traditional German

Location: Jct Hayes St. 525 Laguna St 94102. **Hours:** 5 pm-10 pm, Sun 10 am-2:30 pm. Closed major holidays. **Reservations:** suggested. **Features:** Rustic decor sets the mood for the German kitchen. Intriguing selections include venison medallions, pork loin and some vegetarian dishes. Casual dress; beer & wine only. **Parking:** valet and street. **Cards:** AX, MC, VI.

TADICH GRILL Classic Historic **Lunch:** $12-$19 **Dinner:** $12-$19 **Phone:** 415/391-1849 (53)

Seafood

Location: Between Battery and Front sts; near Embarcadero Station. 240 California St 94111. **Hours:** 11 am-9:30 pm, Sat from 11:30 am. Closed major holidays; also Sun. **Features:** Established in 1849, the original restaurant began during the California Gold Rush and is listed with the California Historical Society. This popular spot usually bustles, so be prepared to wait for a table. Varied beef, chicken and pasta dishes are available, but the fish plates star. Waiters are somewhat "rough around the edges," but this adds to the ambience. Casual dress; cocktails. **Parking:** street. **Cards:** MC, VI.

TOMMY TOY'S HAUTE CUISINE **Lunch:** $12-$25 **Dinner:** $15-$35 **Phone:** 415/397-4888 (7)

Nouvelle Chinese

Location: Downtown; in Financial District. 655 Montgomery St 94111. **Hours:** 11:30 am-2:30 & 6-9:30 pm, Sat & Sun from 6 pm. Closed: 1/1, 12/25. **Reservations:** suggested. **Features:** Reminiscent of an Imperial Palace, the fantastic dining room is the setting for classic French service and artistic presentations. Dressy casual; cocktails. **Parking:** no self-parking. **Cards:** AX, CB, DC, DS, JC, MC, VI.

VENTURE FROGS **Lunch:** $6-$8 **Dinner:** $7-$18 **Phone:** 415/409-2550 (93)

Chinese

Location: On US 101 (Van Ness Ave); in AMC Movie Theater building. 1000 Van Ness Ave 94109. **Hours:** noon-11 pm. **Reservations:** suggested. **Features:** The eatery offers friendly service in a casual atmosphere, and the menu features a variety of Chinese specialties. Casual dress; cocktails. **Parking:** on-site (fee). **Cards:** AX, DC, MC, VI.

THE WATERFRONT RESTAURANT **Lunch:** $9-$26 **Dinner:** $14-$39 **Phone:** 415/391-2696 (3)

Seafood

Location: Just n of the Ferry Building; on the Embarcadero. Pier 7 94111. **Hours:** 11:30 am-4 & 5-10:30 pm, Sun from 10 am. Closed: 12/26 & 12/27. **Reservations:** suggested. **Features:** Innovative cuisine is on the menu at the ground-floor cafe terrace on the bay. The second-story restaurant, which overlooks Bay Bridge, tempts diners with Asian specialties. Dressy casual; cocktails. **Parking:** valet. **Cards:** AX, DC, MC, VI.

YANK SING **Lunch:** $4-$12 **Phone:** 415/541-4949 (54)

Chinese

Location: Between 1st and 2nd sts; near Union Square. 49 Stevenson St 94105. **Hours:** 11 am-3 pm. **Features:** No menus are needed here, as diners just point as dishes are rolled by. Among choices are more than 60 varieties of fresh dim sum, including such specialties as pot stickers, steamed dumplings and spring rolls. Casual dress; beer & wine only. **Parking:** street. **Cards:** AX, DC, MC, VI.

(See map and index starting on p. 590)

ZUNI CAFE **Lunch:** $9-$12 **Dinner:** $10-$30 **Phone:** 415/552-2522 (108)

California

Location: At Gough. 1658 Market St 94102. **Hours:** 11:30 am-midnight. Closed: Mon. **Reservations:** suggested. **Features:** Popular with the local crowd since it opened more than 20 years ago, the restaurant is where to head for Mediterranean cuisine in a casual atmosphere. Patrons can sample fresh shucked oysters at the copper-topped bar downstairs or dine in one of the many dining rooms on the first or second floor. Dressy casual; cocktails. **Parking:** street. **Cards:** AX, MC, VI.

The following restaurants have not been evaluated by AAA but are listed for your information only.

42 DEGREES **Phone:** 415/777-5558

fyi Not evaluated. **Location:** 235 16th St 94107. **Features:** The restaurant is named for the latitude line that passes through most of the Mediterranean, from which this place's food is derived. Among specialties are Iberian sausage, lamb shank with eggplant and spaghetti carbonara. Those with daring palates might opt for the roasted veal bone marrow and toast points starter.

CAFE JACQUELINE **Phone:** 415/981-5565

fyi Not evaluated. **Location:** 1454 Grant Ave 94133. **Features:** While guests can start with a soup or salad, everything else is souffles, and the kitchen staff is talented at making them. For an entree, patrons can choose from a number of items, including corn, lobster, black truffles, gruyere, prosciutto and others. Don't forget a dessert souffle.

FRINGALE **Phone:** 415/543-0573

fyi Not evaluated. **Location:** 570 4th St 94107. **Features:** In the SOMA district, the restaurant provides quality, reasonably priced French cuisine that is served in a casual, cozy, hometown atmosphere. Favorite entrees include roasted quail stuffed with apple risotto in foie gras jus; crab salad with mango and red pepper salsa; and pork tenderloin confit with cabbage, onion and apple marmalade. Among can't-miss desserts are coffee and almanac parfait and the flattened goat cheese souffle with creme fraiche and berries.

PANCHO VILLA TAQUERIA **Phone:** 415/864-8840

fyi Not evaluated. **Location:** 3071 16th St 94103. **Features:** In the Mission District, the restaurant is extremely popular with locals desiring good Mexican cuisine. The dining room is basic but comfortable. Lines move quickly, so this place shouldn't be passed up by those who are in the neighborhood.

ZARZUELA **Phone:** 415/346-0800

fyi Not evaluated. **Location:** 2000 Hyde St 94109. **Features:** The restaurant serves fine tapas selections in an authentic Madrid setting complete with Spanish music. The seafood stew is where the restaurant name originates. Other popular entrees include poached octopus, spicy shrimp with aioli, paella and escalivada. A good selection of Spanish wines is available.

The San Francisco Vicinity

BELMONT pop. 25,123 (See map and index starting on p. 599)

WHERE TO STAY

HOLIDAY INN EXPRESS HOTEL & SUITES Book at aaa.com **Phone:** (650)654-4000 435

AAA SAVE

Motel

All Year [ECP] 1P: $149 2P: $149

Location: US 101, exit Ralston Ave, w to SR 82, just s. 1650 El Camino Real 94002. Fax: 650/654-4001. **Facility:** 82 units. 77 one-bedroom standard units. 5 one-bedroom suites with whirlpools. 3 stories, interior corridors. *Bath:* combo or shower only. **Parking:** on-site. **Terms:** cancellation fee imposed. **Amenities:** video games, high-speed Internet, dual phone lines, voice mail, irons, hair dryers. **Leisure Activities:** exercise room. **Guest Services:** valet laundry. **Business Services:** meeting rooms. **Cards:** AX, CB, DC, DS, MC, VI. **Special Amenities: free expanded continental breakfast and free local telephone calls.** *(See color ad p 260)*

SOME UNITS

SUMMERFIELD SUITES BY WYNDHAM-BELMONT/REDWOOD SHORES Book at aaa.com **Phone:** (650)591-8600 436

Motel

All Year 1P: $79-$139 2P: $79-$139 XP: $10 F17

Location: US 101, exit Marine World Pkwy, just e, then just n on Oracle Pkwy. 400 Concourse Dr 94002. Fax: 650/592-8900. **Facility:** 132 units. 67 one- and 65 two-bedroom suites ($109-$169) with kitchens. 3 stories, exterior corridors. **Parking:** on-site. **Terms:** cancellation fee imposed, [MAP] meal plan available, pets ($150 fee). **Amenities:** high-speed Internet (fee), voice mail, irons, hair dryers. **Pool(s):** heated outdoor. **Leisure Activities:** whirlpool, exercise room. **Guest Services:** coin laundry. **Business Services:** meeting rooms. **Cards:** AX, CB, DC, DS, JC, MC, VI.

FEE SOME UNITS

BRISBANE pop. 3,597 (See map and index starting on p. 599)

WHERE TO STAY

HOMEWOOD SUITES Book at aaa.com **Phone:** (650)589-1600 286

Small-scale Hotel

All Year [ECP] 1P: $129-$189 2P: $129-$189

Location: US 101, exit Sierra Point Pkwy, just e. 2000 Shoreline Ct 94005. Fax: 650/589-2622. **Facility:** 177 units. 116 one-bedroom standard units with kitchens. 56 one- and 5 two-bedroom suites ($129-$189) with kitchens. 4 stories, interior corridors. *Bath:* combo or shower only. **Parking:** on-site. **Amenities:** dual phone lines, voice mail, irons, hair dryers. *Fee:* video games, high-speed Internet. **Pool(s):** lap. **Leisure Activities:** exercise room. **Guest Services:** sundries, complimentary evening beverages: Mon-Thurs, coin laundry. **Business Services:** meeting rooms, business center. **Cards:** AX, CB, DC, DS, MC, VI.

SOME UNITS

RADISSON HOTEL SAN FRANCISCO AIRPORT AT SIERRA POINT Book at aaa.com **Phone:** (415)467-4400 287

Large-scale Hotel

All Year 1P: $99-$219 2P: $99-$219 XP: $20 F16

Location: US 101, exit Sierra Point Pkwy, just e. 5000 Sierra Point Pkwy 94005. Fax: 415/467-4440. **Facility:** 210 units. 203 one-bedroom standard units. 7 one-bedroom suites ($149-$299). 8 stories, interior corridors. *Bath:* combo or shower only. **Parking:** on-site. **Terms:** cancellation fee imposed. **Amenities:** video games, high-speed Internet (fee), dual phone lines, voice mail, safes, irons, hair dryers. *Some:* CD players. **Pool(s):** heated indoor. **Leisure Activities:** whirlpool, exercise room. **Guest Services:** gift shop. **Business Services:** conference facilities, business center. **Cards:** AX, CB, DC, DS, MC, VI. ***(See color ad p 629)***

SOME UNITS

BURLINGAME pop. 28,158 (See map and index starting on p. 599)

WHERE TO STAY

CROWNE PLAZA *Book at aaa.com* **Phone:** (650)342-9200 357

Large-scale Hotel

All Year 1P: $249-$349 2P: $249-$349 XP: $10 F18

Location: US 101, exit Broadway-Burlingame or Old Bayshore, just e. 1177 Airport Blvd 94010. Fax: 650/342-1655. **Facility:** 309 units. 299 one-bedroom standard units. 10 one-bedroom suites, some with whirlpools. 10 stories, interior corridors. **Parking:** on-site (fee). **Terms:** cancellation fee imposed, [BP] meal plan available, pets ($100 deposit). **Amenities:** video games, CD players, high-speed Internet (fee), dual phone lines, voice mail, irons, hair dryers. **Pool(s):** heated indoor. **Leisure Activities:** whirlpool, exercise room. **Guest Services:** gift shop, valet laundry. **Business Services:** meeting rooms, business center. **Cards:** AX.

SOME UNITS

FEE FEE

DOUBLETREE HOTEL-SAN FRANCISCO AIRPORT *Book at aaa.com* **Phone:** (650)344-5500 356

AAA SAVE

Large-scale Hotel

All Year 1P: $79-$149 2P: $79-$149 XP: $10 F18

Location: US 101, exit Broadway-Burlingame or Anza Blvd, just e. 835 Airport Blvd 94010. Fax: 650/340-8851. **Facility:** 390 units. 383 one-bedroom standard units. 7 one-bedroom suites ($389-$589). 8 stories, interior corridors. *Bath:* combo or shower only. **Parking:** on-site. **Terms:** package plans, pets ($20 extra charge). **Amenities:** video games, high-speed Internet, dual phone lines, voice mail, irons, hair dryers. *Some:* fax. **Dining:** 6:30 am-10 pm, cocktails. **Leisure Activities:** exercise room. **Guest Services:** gift shop, valet laundry, airport transportation-San Francisco International Airport, area transportation-within 5 mi. **Business Services:** meeting rooms, business center. **Cards:** AX, CB, DC, DS, JC, MC, VI. **Special Amenities: free newspaper.** *(See color ad below)*

SOME UNITS

(See map and index starting on p. 599)

EMBASSY SUITES-SFO Book at aaa.com Phone: (650)342-4600 355

AAA SAVE All Year 1P: $119-$199 XP: $15 F17

Large-scale Hotel

Location: US 101, exit Broadway-Burlingame or Anza Blvd, just e. 150 Anza Blvd 94010. Fax: 650/343-8137. **Facility:** Lavish arrangements of fresh flowers and greenery are displayed in the hotel's common areas; in the lobby is a garden atrium and koi pond. 340 one-bedroom suites. 9 stories, interior corridors. *Bath:* combo or shower only. **Parking:** on-site. **Terms:** [BP] meal plan available, pets ($50 extra charge). **Amenities:** video games, high-speed Internet, dual phone lines, voice mail, irons, hair dryers. **Dining:** 11:30 am-2:30 & 5-10 pm, Fri & Sat-11 pm, cocktails, entertainment. **Pool(s):** heated indoor. **Leisure Activities:** sauna, whirlpools, exercise room. *Fee:* massage. **Guest Services:** gift shop, complimentary evening beverages, valet and coin laundry, airport transportation-San Francisco International Airport. **Business Services:** meeting rooms, administrative services. **Cards:** AX, CB, DC, DS, JC, MC, VI. **Special Amenities: free full breakfast and free newspaper.** *(See color ad p 621)*

SOME UNITS
FEE FEE

HILTON GARDEN INN SAN FRANCISCO AIRPORT/BURLINGAME Book at aaa.com Phone: (650)347-7800 351

AAA SAVE All Year 1P: $78-$268 2P: $78-$268 XP: $10 F18

Small-scale Hotel

Location: US 101, exit Broadway-Burlingame or Anza Blvd, just e. 765 Airport Blvd 94010. Fax: 650/347-4898. **Facility:** 132 one-bedroom standard units, some with whirlpools. 6 stories, interior corridors. **Parking:** on-site. **Terms:** [BP] meal plan available. **Amenities:** video games, high-speed Internet, dual phone lines, voice mail, irons, hair dryers. **Pool(s):** heated indoor. **Leisure Activities:** whirlpool, exercise room. **Guest Services:** valet and coin laundry, airport transportation-San Francisco International Airport. **Business Services:** meeting rooms, business center. **Cards:** AX, CB, DC, DS, JC, MC, VI. **Special Amenities: free newspaper and early check-in/late check-out.** *(See color ad below)*

SOME UNITS

HOLIDAY INN EXPRESS BURLINGAME, SAN FRANCISCO INTL AIRPORT SOUTH Book at aaa.com Phone: (650)347-2381 353

All Year [ECP] 1P: $72-$119 2P: $72-$119

Small-scale Hotel

Location: US 101, exit Broadway-Burlingame or Old Bayshore Hwy, just e. 1250 Old Bayshore Hwy 94010. Fax: 650/348-8838. **Facility:** 147 units. 140 one-bedroom standard units. 7 one-bedroom suites ($135-$155). 3 stories, interior corridors. **Parking:** on-site. **Terms:** cancellation fee imposed, 10% service charge. **Amenities:** video games, high-speed Internet, dual phone lines, voice mail, irons, hair dryers. **Pool(s):** outdoor. **Leisure Activities:** exercise room. **Guest Services:** valet laundry. **Business Services:** meeting rooms, business center. **Cards:** AX, CB, DC, DS, MC, VI.

ASK SOME UNITS

(See map and index starting on p. 599)

HYATT REGENCY-SAN FRANCISCO AIRPORT Book at aaa.com **Phone:** (650)347-1234 350

AAA SAVE — Large-scale Hotel

All Year 1P: $99-$209 2P: $99-$209 XP: $25 F18

Location: US 101, exit Broadway-Burlingame or Old Bayshore Hwy, just e. 1333 Old Bayshore Hwy 94010. Fax: 650/696-2669. **Facility:** The hotel centers on an eight-story atrium with a translucent fabric roof; some units have views of San Francisco Bay or the surrounding hills. 793 units. 767 one-bedroom standard units. 26 one-bedroom suites. 9 stories, interior corridors. *Bath:* combo or shower only. **Parking:** valet. **Terms:** cancellation fee imposed. **Amenities:** high-speed Internet, dual phone lines, voice mail, irons, hair dryers. *Some:* DVD players, CD players, fax. **Dining:** 3 restaurants, 6:30 am-11 pm, cocktails, nightclub. **Pool(s):** heated outdoor. **Leisure Activities:** sauna, whirlpool. *Fee:* massage. **Guest Services:** gift shop, valet laundry. **Business Services:** conference facilities, business center. **Cards:** AX, CB, DC, DS, JC, MC, VI. *(See color ad p 623)*

SOME UNITS

RED ROOF INN Book at aaa.com **Phone:** 650/342-7772 360

AAA SAVE — Motel

All Year 1P: $59-$89 2P: $59-$89

Location: US 101, exit Broadway-Burlingame or E Anza Blvd; just s of airport. 777 Airport Blvd 94010. Fax: 650/342-2635. **Facility:** 213 one-bedroom standard units. 5 stories, exterior corridors. *Bath:* combo or shower only. **Parking:** on-site. **Amenities:** video games, high-speed Internet, voice mail, irons, hair dryers. *Some:* safes. **Pool(s):** heated outdoor. **Guest Services:** airport transportation-San Francisco International Airport. **Cards:** AX, CB, DC, DS, MC, VI. **Special Amenities: free local telephone calls and free newspaper.**

SOME UNITS

SAN FRANCISCO AIRPORT MARRIOTT Book at aaa.com **Phone:** (650)692-9100 362

Large-scale Hotel

All Year 1P: $99-$229 2P: $99-$229 XP: $10 F18

Location: US 101, exit Millbrae Ave, just e. 1800 Old Bayshore Hwy 94010. Fax: 650/692-8016. **Facility:** Views of San Francisco Bay are featured from many of the hotel's rooms; the attractively appointed lobby includes a restaurant and lounge. 684 units. 668 one-bedroom standard units. 16 one-bedroom suites. 11 stories, interior corridors. **Parking:** valet. **Terms:** small pets only. **Amenities:** video games, high-speed Internet, voice mail, irons, hair dryers. *Some:* CD players, dual phone lines. **Pool(s):** heated indoor. **Leisure Activities:** saunas, whirlpool, exercise room. **Guest Services:** gift shop, valet and coin laundry. **Business Services:** conference facilities, business center. **Cards:** AX, CB, DC, DS, JC, MC, VI.

SOME UNITS

SHERATON GATEWAY HOTEL SAN FRANCISCO AIRPORT Book at aaa.com **Phone:** (650)340-8500 361

AAA SAVE — Large-scale Hotel

All Year 1P: $99-$199 2P: $109-$209 XP: $15 F18

Location: US 101, exit Broadway-Burlingame or Anza Blvd, 0.3 mi e. 600 Airport Blvd 94010. Fax: 650/340-0599. **Facility:** Many of the hotel's guest rooms overlook San Francisco Bay; a restaurant and lounge are featured in the spacious lobby. 404 units. 400 one-bedroom standard units. 4 one-bedroom suites. 15 stories, interior corridors. **Parking:** on-site. **Amenities:** high-speed Internet (fee), dual phone lines, voice mail, irons, hair dryers. *Some:* fax. **Dining:** 6 am-11 pm, cocktails. **Pool(s):** heated indoor. **Leisure Activities:** sauna, whirlpool, exercise room. **Guest Services:** gift shop, valet laundry, airport transportation-San Francisco International Airport, area transportation. **Business Services:** meeting rooms, business center. **Cards:** AX, CB, DC, DS, JC, MC, VI. **Special Amenities: free newspaper and free room upgrade (subject to availability with advanced reservations).**

SOME UNITS

FEE

VAGABOND INN-AIRPORT Book at aaa.com **Phone:** (650)692-4040 363

AAA SAVE — Motel

All Year [CP] 1P: $55-$75 2P: $60-$80 XP: $5 F18

Location: US 101, exit Millbrae Ave, just e. 1640 Bayshore Hwy 94010. Fax: 650/692-5314. **Facility:** 93 one-bedroom standard units. 3 stories, exterior corridors. **Parking:** on-site. **Terms:** pets ($10 extra charge). **Amenities:** voice mail, irons, hair dryers. **Guest Services:** coin laundry. **Cards:** AX, CB, DC, DS, MC, VI. **Special Amenities: free continental breakfast and free local telephone calls.**

SOME UNITS

FEE

The following lodgings were either not evaluated or did not meet AAA rating requirements but are listed for your information only.

BAY LANDING HOTEL **Phone:** 650/259-9000

fyi — Small-scale Hotel

All Year [ECP] 1P: $79-$129 XP: $10 F5

Too new to rate, opening scheduled for October 2003. **Location:** US 101, exit Broadway/Burlingame, e to Bayshore Hwy, then n. 1550 Bayshore Hwy 94010. Fax: 650/259-9099. **Amenities:** 130 units, coffeemakers, microwaves, refrigerators. **Cards:** AX, CB, DC, MC, VI. *(See color ad p 661)*

HAMPTON INN & SUITES **Phone:** 650/697-5736

fyi — Motel

Property failed to provide current rates

Too new to rate, opening scheduled for September 2003. **Location:** 1755 Bayshore Hwy 94010. Fax: 650/697-5736. **Amenities:** 77 units, coffeemakers, microwaves, refrigerators.

WHERE TO DINE

CAFE' LA SCALA **Lunch:** $11 **Dinner:** $17 **Phone:** 650/347-3035 180

Italian

Location: US 101, exit Broadway, 1.1 mi s, then just w. 1219 Burlingame Ave 94010. **Hours:** 11 am-10 pm, Fri & Sat-11 pm, Sun noon-10 pm. Closed: 12/25. **Reservations:** accepted. **Features:** Families and groups enjoy the cozy, bustling trattoria. Start with the arugula salad, follow with house lasagna and finish with one of the homemade ice creams. Casual dress. **Parking:** street. **Cards:** AX, CB, DC, DS, JC, MC, VI.

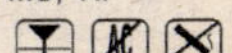

(See map and index starting on p. 599)

GULLIVER'S   **Lunch:** $10-$18   **Dinner:** $18-$29   **Phone:** 650/692-6060   (183)

American

Location: US 101, exit Millbrae Ave, just e. 1699 Old Bayshore Hwy 94010. **Hours:** 11:30 am-2:30 & 5:30-9:30 pm, Fri & Sat 5 pm-10 pm. **Reservations:** suggested. **Features:** English pub atmosphere. Prime rib and seafood. Casual dress; cocktails. **Parking:** on-site. **Cards:** AX, MC, VI.

KULETO'S TRATTORIA   **Lunch:** $8-$19   **Dinner:** $8-$19   **Phone:** 650/342-4922   (181)

Italian

Location: US 101, exit Burlingame Ave, just w. 1095 Rollins Rd 94010. **Hours:** 11:30 am-10 pm, Sat 5 pm-11 pm, Sun 4 pm-10 pm. Closed major holidays. **Reservations:** accepted. **Features:** An oak-wood grill is the centerpiece of the exhibition kitchen. The dining room's atmosphere is upscale. Dressy casual; cocktails. **Parking:** on-site. **Cards:** AX, CB, DC, DS, MC, VI.

PISCES   **Dinner:** $24-$38   **Phone:** 650/401-7500   (182)

West Seafood

Location: US 101, exit Broadway W, then s. 1190 California Dr 94010. **Hours:** 5:30 pm-10 pm, Fri & Sat-11 pm. Closed major holidays; also Sun. **Reservations:** suggested. **Features:** In the city's historic train station, the restaurant nurtures a casually elegant atmosphere. The menu focus is on seafood entrees. Try the Pisces five-course tasting menu, phyllo-crusted sand dabs or the favorite miso-glazed Chilean sea bass. Dressy casual; cocktails. **Parking:** on-site. **Cards:** AX, DC, DS, MC, VI.

CORTE MADERA pop. 9,100

WHERE TO STAY

BEST WESTERN CORTE MADERA INN   *Book at aaa.com*   **Phone:** (415)924-1502

AAA SAVE

Motel

All Year	1P: $119-$169	2P: $119-$169	XP: $10	F17

Location: US 101, exit Madera Blvd southbound; exit Tamalpias Rd/Paradise Dr northbound, 1 blk w, then 3 blks n. 56 Madera Blvd 94925. Fax: 415/924-5419. **Facility:** 110 units. 104 one-bedroom standard units. 6 one-bedroom suites ($179-$249), some with kitchens and/or whirlpools. 2 stories, exterior corridors. *Bath:* combo or shower only. **Parking:** on-site. **Amenities:** high-speed Internet, voice mail, irons, hair dryers. **Pool(s):** heated outdoor. **Leisure Activities:** whirlpools, playground, exercise room. **Guest Services:** coin laundry. **Business Services:** meeting rooms, business center. **Cards:** AX, CB, DC, DS, MC, VI. **Special Amenities: free continental breakfast and free local telephone calls.** *(See color ad below)*

SOME UNITS

MARIN SUITES HOTEL Book at aaa.com Phone: (415)924-3608

Motel

All Year 1P: $154-$220 2P: $154-$220

Location: US 101, exit Tamalpais Rd/Paradise Dr. 45 Tamal Vista Blvd 94925. Fax: 415/924-0761. **Facility:** 100 units. 16 one-bedroom standard units with efficiencies. 58 one- and 26 two-bedroom suites with kitchens. 3 stories, exterior corridors. **Parking:** on-site. **Terms:** small pets only ($10 fee). **Amenities:** voice mail, irons, hair dryers. **Pool(s):** heated outdoor. **Leisure Activities:** sauna, exercise room. **Guest Services:** coin laundry. **Business Services:** meeting rooms. **Cards:** AX, CB, DC, DS, JC, MC, VI. **Special Amenities: free continental breakfast and free local telephone calls.** *(See color ad p 664)*

SOME UNITS

FEE

DALY CITY pop. 103,621 (See map and index starting on p. 599)

WHERE TO STAY

DAYS INN Book at aaa.com Phone: (415)467-5600 271

Motel

All Year 1P: $75-$150 2P: $85-$150 XP: $10 F12

Location: US 101, exit Cow Palace/Brisbane, 0.5 mi w. Located across from P G and E sub-station. 3255 Geneva Ave 94014. Fax: 415/467-0491. **Facility:** 35 one-bedroom standard units, some with whirlpools. 2 stories, exterior corridors. **Parking:** on-site. **Terms:** cancellation fee imposed, [CP] meal plan available. **Amenities:** irons, hair dryers. **Cards:** AX, DC, DS, MC, VI. **Special Amenities: free continental breakfast and free local telephone calls.** *(See color ad below)*

SOME UNITS

HAMPTON INN Book at aaa.com Phone: (650)755-7500 272

Motel

All Year [ECP] 1P: $99-$129 2P: $99-$139

Location: I-280, exit Mission St northbound; exit Junipero Serra Blvd southbound. 2700 Junipero Serra Blvd 94015. Fax: 650/755-9400. **Facility:** 86 one-bedroom standard units. 3 stories, interior corridors. *Bath:* combo or shower only. **Parking:** on-site. **Amenities:** video games, high-speed Internet, dual phone lines, voice mail, irons, hair dryers. **Pool(s):** heated indoor. **Leisure Activities:** exercise room. **Guest Services:** coin laundry. **Business Services:** meeting rooms, business center. **Cards:** AX, DC, DS, MC, VI.

SOME UNITS

ROYAL PALACE INN Phone: (415)468-4550 270

Motel

All Year 1P: $75-$85 2P: $75-$85 XP: $10 F13

Location: US 101, exit Cow Palace/Brisbane, 0.6 mi w. Located across from P G and E sub-station. 2929 Geneva Ave 94014. **Facility:** 20 one-bedroom standard units, some with whirlpools. 2 stories, exterior corridors. **Parking:** on-site. **Terms:** 4 day cancellation notice. **Amenities:** hair dryers. **Cards:** AX, CB, DC, DS, MC, VI.

SOME UNITS

FOSTER CITY pop. 28,803 (See map and index starting on p. 599)

WHERE TO STAY

COURTYARD BY MARRIOTT Book at aaa.com Phone: (650)377-0600 400

Motel

All Year 1P: $79-$149

Location: SR 92, exit Foster City Blvd S; se of jct US 101 and SR 92. 550 Shell Blvd 94404. Fax: 650/377-1983. **Facility:** 147 units. 134 one-bedroom standard units. 13 one-bedroom suites ($159-$199). 3 stories, interior corridors. *Bath:* combo or shower only. **Parking:** on-site. **Amenities:** high-speed Internet, dual phone lines, voice mail, irons, hair dryers. **Pool(s):** heated indoor. **Leisure Activities:** whirlpool, exercise room. **Guest Services:** valet and coin laundry. **Business Services:** meeting rooms. **Cards:** AX, JC, MC, VI.

SOME UNITS

FEE

(See map and index starting on p. 599)

CROWNE PLAZA HOTEL AND RESORT FOSTER CITY *Book at aaa.com* **Phone:** (650)570-5700 399

Large-scale Hotel

All Year 1P: $99-$129 2P: $99-$129 XP: $10 F18

Location: Jct US 101 and SR 92; 1 mi e, exit SR 92 at Foster City Blvd, 0.3 mi n. 1221 Chess Dr 94404. Fax: 650/570-0540. **Facility:** 350 units. 340 one-bedroom standard units. 10 one-bedroom suites, some with whirlpools. 6 stories, interior corridors. *Bath:* combo or shower only. **Parking:** valet. **Terms:** cancellation fee imposed, $2 service charge. **Amenities:** video games, CD players, dual phone lines, voice mail, irons, hair dryers. *Some:* safes. **Pool(s):** heated indoor/outdoor. **Leisure Activities:** sauna, whirlpool, exercise room. **Guest Services:** gift shop, valet laundry, area transportation. **Business Services:** conference facilities, business center. **Cards:** AX, CB, DC, DS, JC, MC, VI.

ASK / SOME UNITS / FEE

HALF MOON BAY pop. 11,842 (See map and index starting on p. 599)

WHERE TO STAY

BEACH HOUSE INN & CONFERENCE CENTER *Book at aaa.com* **Phone:** (650)712-0220 428

Small-scale Hotel

5/1-11/30 1P: $185-$425 2P: $185-$425 XP: $25 F17
2/1-4/30 & 12/1-1/31 1P: $175-$395 2P: $175-$395 XP: $25 F17

Location: 3 mi n of jct SR 92 and 1. 4100 Hwy 1 N 94019 (PO Box 129). Fax: 650/712-0693. **Facility:** Smoke free premises. 54 one-bedroom standard units. 3 stories, interior corridors. *Bath:* combo or shower only. **Parking:** on-site. **Terms:** check-in 4 pm, 3 day cancellation notice-fee imposed. **Amenities:** CD players, high-speed Internet, voice mail, irons, hair dryers. **Pool(s):** small heated outdoor. **Leisure Activities:** whirlpool, exercise room. *Fee:* massage. **Business Services:** meeting rooms. **Cards:** AX, CB, DC, DS, MC, VI. ***(See color ad below)***

CYPRESS INN ON MIRAMAR BEACH **Phone:** (650)726-6002 424

AAA SAVE

Bed & Breakfast

7/2-9/6 [BP] 1P: $225-$385 2P: $225-$385 XP: $15
2/1-7/1 & 9/7-1/31 [BP] 1P: $215-$365 2P: $215-$365 XP: $15

Location: 3 mi n of jct SR 92 and 1, w of SR 1 at Medio Ave. 407 Mirada Rd 94019. Fax: 650/712-0380. **Facility:** This hotel opposite the beach has an upscale, contemporary, Spanish-influenced decor; features include gas fireplaces and some ocean-view balconies. Smoke free premises. 18 one-bedroom standard units, some with whirlpools. 3 stories, interior/exterior corridors. *Bath:* combo or shower only. **Parking:** on-site. **Terms:** 2 night minimum stay - weekends, 7 day cancellation notice-fee imposed. **Amenities:** video library, irons, hair dryers. *Some:* CD players. **Leisure Activities:** Fee: massage. **Guest Services:** complimentary evening beverages. **Business Services:** meeting rooms. **Cards:** AX, DS, MC, VI. **Special Amenities: free continental breakfast and free local telephone calls.** ***(See color ad p 469)***

DATA PORT / VCR / SOME UNITS

GOOSE & TURRETS BED & BREAKFAST INN **Phone:** (650)728-5451 419

Bed & Breakfast

All Year [BP] 1P: $160-$215 2P: $160-$215 XP: $30 D12

Location: 7.5 mi n of jct SR 92 and 1; e of SR 1, exit 2nd St, s on Main St, then 0.5 mi e on 3rd. Located in a quiet, residential area. 835 George St 94037 (PO Box 370937, MONTARA, 94037-0937). Fax: 650/728-0141. **Facility:** Smoke free premises. 5 one-bedroom standard units. 1 story, interior corridors. *Bath:* combo or shower only. **Parking:** on-site. **Terms:** check-in 4 pm, cancellation fee imposed. **Cards:** AX, DC, DS, MC, VI.

ASK

(See map and index starting on p. 599)

HALF MOON BAY LODGE *Book at aaa.com* **Phone:** (650)726-9000 429

Motel

All Year 1P: $195-$220 2P: $195-$220 XP: $10 F17

Location: 2.5 mi s of jct SR 92 and 1, just w. 2400 S Cabrillo Hwy 94019. Fax: 650/726-7951. **Facility:** 80 one-bedroom standard units, some with whirlpools. 2 stories, exterior corridors. **Parking:** on-site. **Terms:** check-in 3:30 pm. **Amenities:** dual phone lines, voice mail, honor bars, irons, hair dryers. **Pool(s):** heated outdoor. **Leisure Activities:** sauna, whirlpool, exercise room. **Guest Services:** valet laundry. **Business Services:** conference facilities, fax. **Cards:** AX, DC, DS, JC, MC, VI. **Special Amenities: free continental breakfast and free newspaper.** *(See color ad below)*

SOME UNITS / VCR /

HARBOR VIEW INN *Book at aaa.com* **Phone:** (650)726-2329 422

Motel

All Year [CP] 1P: $76-$176 2P: $86-$176

Location: 4 mi n of jct SR 92 and 1; e of SR 1. Located in El Granada. 51 Ave Alhambra 94018 (PO Box 127, EL GRANADA). Fax: 650/726-2573. **Facility:** Smoke free premises. 17 one-bedroom standard units. 2 stories, exterior corridors. *Bath:* shower only. **Parking:** on-site. **Terms:** pets ($10 fee, with prior approval). **Amenities:** dual phone lines, irons, hair dryers. **Cards:** AX, DS, MC, VI. **Special Amenities: free continental breakfast and preferred room (subject to availability with advanced reservations).**

SOME UNITS
FEE

HOLIDAY INN EXPRESS *Book at aaa.com* **Phone:** 650/726-3400 430

Motel

4/1-10/31 2P: $99-$139 XP: $10 F18
2/1-3/31 & 11/1-1/31 2P: $99-$109 XP: $10 F18

Location: On SR 1, just s of SR 92. 230 S Cabrillo Hwy 94019. Fax: 650/726-1256. **Facility:** Smoke free premises. 52 one-bedroom standard units. 2 stories (no elevator), exterior corridors. **Parking:** on-site. **Terms:** [CP] meal plan available, pets ($10 extra charge). **Amenities:** voice mail, irons, hair dryers. **Cards:** AX, DC, DS, JC, MC, VI. **Special Amenities: free expanded continental breakfast and free local telephone calls.**

SOME UNITS
FEE

LANDIS SHORES OCEANFRONT INN **Phone:** (650)726-6642 418

Bed & Breakfast

All Year [BP] 1P: $275-$345 2P: $275-$345 XP: $30

Location: 3 mi n of jct SR 92 and 1, exit SR 1 W (Medio Rd), just n. 211 Mirada Rd 94019. Fax: 650/726-6644. **Facility:** Heated stone floors are among the special touches at this contemporary property across from the beach; all rooms have a balcony and gas fireplace. Smoke free premises. 8 one-bedroom standard units, some with whirlpools. 3 stories, interior corridors. *Bath:* combo or shower only. **Parking:** on-site. **Terms:** 7 day cancellation notice-fee imposed. **Amenities:** video library, CD players, high-speed Internet, voice mail, irons, hair dryers. **Leisure Activities:** exercise room. **Guest Services:** complimentary evening beverages. **Business Services:** meeting rooms. **Cards:** AX, DC, DS, MC, VI.

SOME UNITS VCR

MILL ROSE INN, SPA & GARDEN SUITES **Phone:** (650)726-8750 426

Bed & Breakfast

All Year 1P: $190-$360 2P: $190-$360 XP: $50

Location: Just w of historic Main St. 615 Mill St 94019. Fax: 650/726-3031. **Facility:** Fireplaces and claw-foot tubs add a romantic ambience to the country-style inn; attractively landscaped gardens, including a Gazebo, surround the inn. 6 units. 4 one-bedroom standard units. 2 one-bedroom suites ($310-$360), some with whirlpools. 2 stories, exterior corridors. *Bath:* combo or shower only. **Parking:** on-site. **Terms:** 2 night minimum stay - weekends, 14 day cancellation notice-fee imposed, [BP] meal plan available. **Amenities:** video library, CD players, irons, hair dryers. **Leisure Activities:** whirlpool. **Guest Services:** complimentary evening beverages, valet laundry. **Business Services:** meeting rooms. **Cards:** AX, DC, MC, VI. **Special Amenities: free local telephone calls and free newspaper.**

VCR

(See map and index starting on p. 599)

MIRAMAR LODGE & CONFERENCE CENTER Book at aaa.com **Phone:** (650)712-1999 423

SAVE

Motel

8/1-10/31 [CP]	1P: $99-$189	2P: $99-$189	XP: $10	F
6/1-7/31 [CP]	1P: $119-$159	2P: $119-$159	XP: $10	F
2/1-5/31 [CP]	1P: $89-$139	2P: $89-$139	XP: $10	F
11/1-1/31 [CP]	1P: $89-$109	2P: $89-$109	XP: $10	F

Location: On SR 1. 2930 N Cabrillo Hwy 94019. Fax: 650/712-4412. **Facility:** Smoke free premises. 53 one-bedroom standard units, some with whirlpools. 2 stories, exterior corridors. *Bath:* combo or shower only. **Parking:** on-site. **Terms:** package plans, pets ($20 extra charge). **Amenities:** voice mail, irons, hair dryers. **Leisure Activities:** exercise room. **Business Services:** meeting rooms, fax. **Cards:** AX, DC, DS, MC, VI. **Special Amenities: free continental breakfast and free newspaper.**

FEE

OLD THYME INN Book at aaa.com **Phone:** (650)726-1616 427

Bed & Breakfast

All Year [BP]	1P: $130-$300	2P: $130-$300	XP: $25

Location: Just e of SR 1 and s of SR 92; center of town. 779 Main St 94019. Fax: 650/726-6394. **Facility:** Feather beds and two-person whirlpools are among the guest-room amenities enhancing this 1899 Queen Anne Victorian. Designated smoking area. 7 one-bedroom standard units, some with whirlpools. 2 stories, interior corridors. **Parking:** on-site. **Terms:** 2 night minimum stay - weekends, 14 day cancellation notice-fee imposed. **Amenities:** video library, hair dryers. *Some:* CD players, irons. **Guest Services:** complimentary evening beverages. **Business Services:** meeting rooms. **Cards:** AX, DS, MC, VI.

SOME UNITS

ASK VCR

RAMADA LIMITED Book at aaa.com **Phone:** (650)726-9700 425

Motel

4/1-10/31 [ECP]	1P: $90-$325	2P: $90-$325	XP: $10	F17
2/1-3/31 & 11/1-1/31 [ECP]	1P: $70-$275	2P: $70-$275	XP: $10	F17

Location: 2 mi n of jct SR 92 and 1, w of SR 1. 3020 N Cabrillo Hwy 94019. Fax: 650/726-5269. **Facility:** 27 one-bedroom standard units, some with whirlpools. 2 stories, exterior corridors. **Parking:** on-site. **Terms:** cancellation fee imposed, pets ($20 extra charge). **Amenities:** voice mail, irons, hair dryers. **Cards:** AX, DC, DS, MC, VI.

SOME UNITS

ASK FEE DATA PORT VCR FEE

THE RITZ-CARLTON, HALF MOON BAY Book at aaa.com **Phone:** (650)712-7000 420

Large-scale Hotel

3/15-11/14	1P: $275-$625	2P: $275-$625	XP: $30	F12
2/1-3/14 & 11/15-1/31	1P: $250-$595	2P: $250-$595	XP: $30	F12

Location: 3 mi s of jct SR 92 and 1, w of SR 1 at Miramontes Point Rd. 1 Miramontes Point Rd 94019. Fax: 650/712-7070. **Facility:** This beautifully appointed resort-style hotels offers guests many amenities and luxuries, and spectacular views of the ocean and the golf course. 261 units. 239 one-bedroom standard units. 22 one-bedroom suites ($625-$2500). 6 stories, interior/exterior corridors. *Bath:* combo or shower only. **Parking:** on-site (fee) and valet. **Terms:** 7 day cancellation notice-fee imposed, package plans - seasonal & weekends. **Amenities:** video games (fee), CD players, high-speed Internet, dual phone lines, voice mail, safes, honor bars, irons, hair dryers. *Some:* DVD players. **Dining:** 6:30 am-11 pm, cocktails, also, Navio, see separate listing. **Pool(s):** heated indoor, heated indoor/outdoor. **Leisure Activities:** sauna, whirlpools, 6 lighted tennis courts, bicycles, jogging, spa. *Fee:* golf-18 holes. **Guest Services:** gift shop, valet laundry, area transportation-within 5 mi. **Business Services:** conference facilities, business center. **Cards:** AX, CB, DC, DS, MC, VI.

SOME UNITS

ASK FEE 24 DATA PORT

SEAL COVE INN **Phone:** (650)728-4114 421

SAVE

Bed & Breakfast

All Year [BP]	1P: $200-$300	2P: $200-$300	XP: $30	F3

Location: 6 mi n of jct SR 92 and 1, w of SR 1. Located in Moss Beach; adjacent to Fitzgerald Marine Reserve. (221 Cypress Ave, MOSS BEACH, 94038). Fax: 650/728-4116. **Facility:** Guest rooms are spacious and attractively furnished; the property also offers access to a tide pool and beach area. Smoke free premises. 10 one-bedroom standard units, some with whirlpools. 2 stories, interior corridors. **Parking:** on-site. **Terms:** 2 night minimum stay - with Saturday stayover, 7 day cancellation notice-fee imposed. **Amenities:** video library, honor bars, irons, hair dryers. **Leisure Activities:** hiking trails. **Guest Services:** complimentary evening beverages. **Business Services:** meeting rooms. **Cards:** AX, DS, MC, VI. **Special Amenities: free local telephone calls and free newspaper.**

VCR DATA PORT

WHERE TO DINE

HALF MOON BAY BREWING COMPANY **Lunch:** $7-$14 **Dinner:** $7-$14 **Phone:** 650/728-2739 191

Seafood

Location: SR 1, just w. 390 Capistrano Rd 94037. **Hours:** 11:30 am-10 pm. Closed: 11/25, 12/24, 12/25. **Reservations:** suggested. **Features:** Coastsiders and visitors alike patronize the friendly restaurant/brew pub. Microbrews complement menu offerings of seafood right off the dock, as well as pasta, steak and salad. Seating is offered indoors in front of the fireplace or outside on the patio, weather permitting. Casual dress; cocktails. **Parking:** on-site. **Cards:** AX, DS, MC, VI.

MIRAMAR BEACH RESTAURANT **Lunch:** $9-$21 **Dinner:** $17-$25 **Phone:** 650/726-9053 193

Steak & Seafood

Location: 2.7 mi n of jct SR 92 and 1, then w. 131 Mirada Rd 94019. **Hours:** noon-3:30 & 5-9 pm, Sat 11:30 am-3:30 & 5-9:30 pm, Sun 11 am-3 & 4:30-9 pm. Closed: 11/25, 12/24, 12/25. **Reservations:** suggested. **Features:** Inside, guests' attention is drawn to the spectacular view of the ocean and many surrounding photos of the 1920s era. Among the chef's distinctive seafood dishes is prawns etouffee, a preparation of Texas prawns simmered in Creole sauce with cold bay shrimp and basmati rice. Casual dress; cocktails. **Parking:** on-site. **Cards:** AX, DS, MC, VI.

(See map and index starting on p. 599)

MOSS BEACH DISTILLERY **Lunch:** $10-$20 **Dinner:** $25-$45 **Phone:** 650/728-5595 (190)

Seafood

Location: SR 1, exit Cypress St, 6 mi n of jct SR 92. 140 Beach Way 94038. **Hours:** noon-3 & 4:30-8:30 pm, Sat-9 pm, Sun 10 am-2:30 & 4:30-8:30 pm. Closed: 12/1-12/7. **Reservations:** suggested. **Features:** The resident ghost, Blue Lady, occupies the restaurant on a bluff overlooking the Pacific. Sunset views are spectacular. Casual dress; cocktails. **Parking:** on-site. **Cards:** AX, DC, DS, MC, VI.

NAVIO **Lunch:** $9-$31 **Dinner:** $10-$36 **Phone:** 650/712-7040 (196)

American

Location: 3 mi s of jct SR 92 and 1, w of SR 1 at Miramontes Point Rd; in The Ritz-Carlton, Half Moon Bay. 1 Miramontes Point Rd 94019. **Hours:** 6:30 am-10:30, noon-3 & 6-10 pm; Sunday brunch 11:30 am-2 pm. **Reservations:** suggested. **Features:** Though casual, this upscale restaurant has become a favorite with the San Francisco Bay area. The open grill kitchen and views of the Pacific Ocean and golf course add to the overall dining experience. Dressy casual; cocktails. **Parking:** valet. **Cards:** AX, CB, DC, DS, JC, MC, VI.

PASTA MOON RISTORANTE **Lunch:** $13-$24 **Dinner:** $15-$32 **Phone:** 650/726-5125 (194)

Italian

Location: Just s of SR 92, e of SR 1. 315 Main St 94019. **Hours:** 11:30 am-2:30 & 5:30-9:30 pm, Sat noon-3 & 5:30-10 pm, Sun 11 am-3 & 5:30-9:30 pm. Closed: 12/25. **Reservations:** suggested. **Features:** Daily specials and homemade soups are among selections that emphasize fresh ingredients and unusual preparation. A large orchid plant serves as both decor and a serving table. Dressy casual; cocktails. **Parking:** street. **Cards:** AX, DC, MC, VI.

LARKSPUR pop. 11,100

WHERE TO STAY

COURTYARD BY MARRIOTT *Book at aaa.com* **Phone:** (415)925-1800

Small-scale Hotel

All Year 1P: $109-$159 2P: $109-$159

Location: US 101, exit E Sir Francis Drake Blvd, 0.3 mi e. 2500 Larkspur Landing Cir 94939. Fax: 415/925-1107. **Facility:** 146 units. 134 one-bedroom standard units. 12 one-bedroom suites ($159-$199). 3 stories, interior corridors. **Parking:** on-site. **Terms:** check-in 4 pm, cancellation fee imposed. **Amenities:** dual phone lines, voice mail, irons, hair dryers. **Pool(s):** heated outdoor. **Leisure Activities:** whirlpool, exercise room. **Guest Services:** coin laundry. **Business Services:** meeting rooms. **Cards:** AX, DC, DS, JC, MC, VI.

SOME UNITS

DATA PORT

WHERE TO DINE

LARK CREEK INN Historic **Lunch:** $12-$17 **Dinner:** $18-$32 **Phone:** 415/924-7766

Regional American

Location: US 101, exit Tamalpais Dr, 1.3 mi w. 234 Magnolia Ave 94939. **Hours:** 11:30 am-2 & 5:30-10 pm, Sat from 5 pm, Sun 10 am-2 & 5-9 pm. Closed major holidays. **Reservations:** suggested. **Features:** Built in 1888, the restored Victorian home occupies a pleasant garden setting. Smoking is not permitted. Dressy casual; cocktails. **Parking:** on-site. **Cards:** AX, MC, VI.

MILLBRAE pop. 20,718 (See map and index starting on p. 599)

WHERE TO STAY

BEST WESTERN EL RANCHO INN & SUITES *Book at aaa.com* **Phone:** (650)588-8500 (340)

SAVE

Motel

All Year 1P: $89-$169 2P: $89-$169 XP: $10 F

Location: US 101, exit Millbrae Ave, 0.3 mi sw, then 0.8 mi n on SR 82. 1100 El Camino Real 94030. Fax: 650/871-7150. **Facility:** 306 units. 220 one-bedroom standard units. 8 one- and 78 two-bedroom suites ($125-$180) with kitchens. 2 stories, exterior corridors. *Bath:* some combo or shower only. **Parking:** on-site. **Terms:** cancellation fee imposed, weekly rates available, [CP] meal plan available, package plans. **Amenities:** voice mail, irons, hair dryers. **Dining:** Terrace Cafe, see separate listing. **Pool(s):** 2 heated outdoor. **Leisure Activities:** whirlpools, exercise room. **Guest Services:** coin laundry. **Business Services:** meeting rooms. **Cards:** AX, CB, DC, DS, JC, MC, VI. **Special Amenities: free continental breakfast and free room upgrade (subject to availability with advanced reservations).** *(See color ad p 670)*

SOME UNITS

DATA PORT VCR

CLARION HOTEL-SAN FRANCISCO AIRPORT *Book at aaa.com* **Phone:** (650)692-6363 (336)

Large-scale Hotel

All Year 1P: $99-$129 2P: $99-$129 XP: $10 F12

Location: US 101, exit Millbrae Ave, just e. 401 E Millbrae Ave 94030. Fax: 650/697-8735. **Facility:** 440 units. 434 one-bedroom standard units, some with whirlpools. 6 one-bedroom suites ($159-$259) with whirlpools. 6 stories, interior corridors. **Parking:** on-site. **Terms:** cancellation fee imposed, pets ($30 extra charge). **Amenities:** dual phone lines, voice mail, irons, hair dryers. *Some:* high-speed Internet. **Pool(s):** heated outdoor. **Leisure Activities:** whirlpool, exercise room. **Guest Services:** gift shop, valet laundry. **Business Services:** conference facilities, business center. **Cards:** AX, DC, DS, JC, MC, VI.

SOME UNITS

ASK DATA PORT FEE

COMFORT INN-AIRPORT WEST *Book at aaa.com* **Phone:** (650)952-3200 (337)

SAVE

Motel

All Year [ECP] 1P: $79-$89 2P: $89-$99 XP: $5 F18

Location: 0.3 mi sw of US 101, exit Millbrae Ave; 1 mi n on SR 82. 1390 El Camino Real 94030. Fax: 650/952-0474. **Facility:** 100 units. 98 one-bedroom standard units, some with kitchens and/or whirlpools. 2 one-bedroom suites. 3 stories, exterior corridors. **Parking:** on-site. **Amenities:** voice mail, irons, hair dryers. **Pool(s):** heated outdoor. **Leisure Activities:** sauna, whirlpool. **Guest Services:** coin laundry. **Business Services:** meeting rooms. **Cards:** AX, CB, DC, DS, JC, MC, VI. **Special Amenities: free expanded continental breakfast and free local telephone calls.**

SOME UNITS

DATA PORT

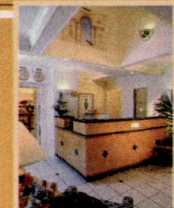

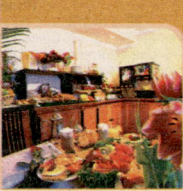

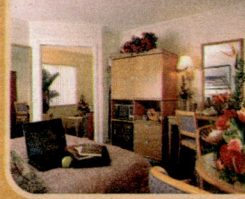

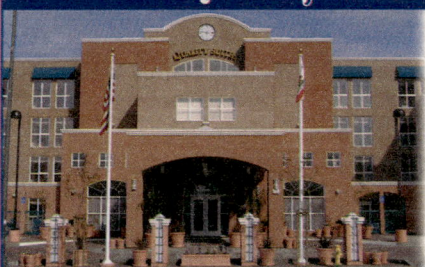

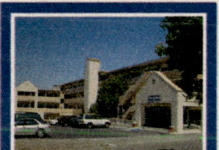

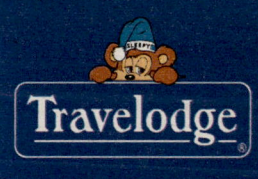

(See map and index starting on p. 599)

MILLWOOD INN Book at aaa.com Phone: (650)583-3935 335

Motel

All Year [ECP] 1P: $79-$150 2P: $79-$150 XP: $5 F15

Location: 0.3 mi sw of US 101, exit Millbrae Ave, 1 mi n on SR 82. 1375 El Camino Real 94030. Fax: 650/875-4354. **Facility:** 34 units. 29 one-bedroom standard units. 5 one-bedroom suites ($99-$150). 1-2 stories, exterior corridors. *Bath:* combo or shower only. **Parking:** on-site. **Terms:** package plans. **Amenities:** high-speed Internet, dual phone lines, voice mail, irons, hair dryers. **Leisure Activities:** exercise room. **Guest Services:** coin laundry. **Cards:** AX, CB, DC, DS, JC, MC, VI. **Special Amenities: free continental breakfast and free local telephone calls.** *(See color ad p 671)*

SOME UNITS

QUALITY SUITES Book at aaa.com Phone: (650)259-0400 338

Motel

6/1-9/30 [BP] 1P: $89-$129 2P: $89-$129
2/1-5/31 & 10/1-1/31 [BP] 1P: $79-$129 2P: $79-$129

Location: US 101, exit Millbrae Ave, 0.3 mi w, then 0.3 mi n. 250 El Camino Real 94030. Fax: 650/692-5511. **Facility:** 86 units. 78 one-bedroom standard units. 8 one-bedroom suites, some with whirlpools. 4 stories, interior corridors. **Parking:** on-site. **Amenities:** voice mail, irons, hair dryers. **Leisure Activities:** whirlpool, exercise room. **Guest Services:** gift shop, complimentary evening beverages, valet laundry. **Business Services:** meeting rooms, business center. **Cards:** AX, CB, DC, DS, JC, MC, VI. **Special Amenities: free full breakfast and free local telephone calls.** *(See color ad p 671 & p 521)*

SOME UNITS

TRAVELODGE SAN FRANCISCO AIRPORT SOUTH Book at aaa.com Phone: (650)697-7373 339

Motel

All Year 1P: $69-$129 2P: $79-$129 XP: $6 F18

Location: 1.5 mi sw of US 101, exit Millbrae Ave, just s on SR 82. 110 S El Camino Real 94030. Fax: 650/697-7387. **Facility:** 58 one-bedroom standard units. 3 stories, interior/exterior corridors. *Bath:* combo or shower only. **Parking:** on-site. **Terms:** [CP] meal plan available. **Amenities:** voice mail, safes, irons, hair dryers. **Cards:** AX, CB, DC, DS, JC, MC, VI. **Special Amenities: free continental breakfast and free local telephone calls.** *(See color ad p 671)*

SOME UNITS

THE WESTIN HOTEL-SAN FRANCISCO AIRPORT Book at aaa.com Phone: (650)692-3500 342

Large-scale Hotel

All Year 1P: $299-$319 2P: $299-$319 XP: $20 F17

Location: Just e of US 101, exit Millbrae Ave. 1 Old Bayshore Hwy 94030. Fax: 650/872-8111. **Facility:** 393 units. 390 one-bedroom standard units, some with whirlpools. 3 two-bedroom suites ($350-$750). 7 stories, interior corridors. **Parking:** on-site and valet. **Terms:** cancellation fee imposed, small pets only. **Amenities:** high-speed Internet, voice mail, safes, honor bars, irons, hair dryers. **Pool(s):** heated indoor. **Leisure Activities:** whirlpool, hiking trails, exercise room. *Fee:* massage. **Guest Services:** gift shop, valet laundry. **Business Services:** conference facilities, business center. **Cards:** AX, DC, DS, MC, VI.

SOME UNITS

WHERE TO DINE

TERRACE CAFE **Lunch:** $5-$11 **Dinner:** $9-$20 **Phone:** 650/742-5588 170

American

Location: US 101, exit Millbrae Ave, 0.3 mi sw, then 0.8 mi n on SR 82; in Best Western El Rancho Inn & Suites. 1100 El Camino Real 94030. **Hours:** 7:30-11 am, 11:30-2 & 5-10 pm. Closed: 11/25, 12/25. **Reservations:** suggested. **Features:** Contemporary preparation marks thoughtfully planned seafood dishes made from fresh ingredients and American cuisine. Casual dress; cocktails. **Parking:** on-site. **Cards:** AX, CB, DC, DS, MC, VI. ***(See color ad p 670)***

MILL VALLEY pop. 13,600

WHERE TO STAY

ACQUA HOTEL Book at aaa.com **Phone:** (415)380-0400

Small-scale Hotel

All Year [ECP] 1P: $150-$220 2P: $150-$220 XP: $20 F16

Location: US 101, exit Seminary Dr. 555 Redwood Hwy 94941. Fax: 415/380-9696. **Facility:** 50 one-bedroom standard units. 3 stories, interior/exterior corridors. **Parking:** on-site. **Terms:** cancellation fee imposed. **Amenities:** CD players, dual phone lines, voice mail, irons, hair dryers. **Leisure Activities:** exercise room. **Business Services:** meeting rooms. **Cards:** AX, DC, DS, JC, MC, VI. **Special Amenities: free expanded continental breakfast and free room upgrade (subject to availability with advanced reservations).**

HOLIDAY INN EXPRESS Book at aaa.com **Phone:** 415/332-5700

Small-scale Hotel

Property failed to provide current rates

Location: 4 mi n of Golden Gate Bridge; w off US 101 at the Richardson Bay Bridge on the Stinson Beach turn-off. 160 Shoreline Hwy 94941. Fax: 415/331-1859. **Facility:** 100 one-bedroom standard units. 2 stories, interior corridors. **Parking:** on-site. **Amenities:** dual phone lines, voice mail, irons, hair dryers. **Pool(s):** heated outdoor. **Leisure Activities:** exercise room. **Guest Services:** valet laundry. **Business Services:** meeting rooms, business center. ***(See color ad p 260 & p 626)***

SOME UNITS

MILL VALLEY INN Book at aaa.com **Phone:** (415)389-6608

Small-scale Hotel

All Year [ECP] 1P: $160-$399 XP: $15

Location: Center. 165 Throckmorton Ave 94941. Fax: 415/389-5051. **Facility:** 25 one-bedroom standard units. 3 stories, interior corridors. **Parking:** on-site. **Terms:** check-in 4 pm, 2-3 night minimum stay - seasonal & weekends, 7 day cancellation notice-fee imposed, package plans - seasonal. **Amenities:** CD players, voice mail, irons, hair dryers. **Business Services:** meeting rooms. **Cards:** AX, DC, DS, MC, VI. **Special Amenities: free expanded continental breakfast and early check-in/late check-out.**

SOME UNITS

MILL VALLEY/SAUSALITO TRAVELODGE *Book at aaa.com* **Phone:** (415)383-0340

AAA SAVE — Motel

5/1-6/12 & 10/1-1/31	1P: $79-$89
6/13-9/30	1P: $89
2/1-4/30	1P: $69-$79

Location: US 101, exit Seminary Dr. 707 Redwood Hwy 94941. Fax: 415/383-0312. **Facility:** 50 units. 48 one-bedroom standard units, some with whirlpools. 2 one-bedroom suites ($109-$129) with whirlpools. 2 stories, exterior corridors. *Bath:* combo or shower only. **Parking:** on-site. **Amenities:** hair dryers. **Cards:** AX, MC, VI. **Special Amenities: free continental breakfast and free newspaper.**

SOME UNITS

PACIFICA pop. 38,390 (See map and index starting on p. 599)

WHERE TO STAY

BEST WESTERN LIGHTHOUSE HOTEL *Book at aaa.com* **Phone:** (650)355-6300 280

AAA SAVE — Small-scale Hotel

All Year	1P: $99-$280	2P: $99-$280	XP: $10	F12

Location: Just w off SR 1. 105 Rockaway Beach Ave 94044 (1933 Cliff Dr, Suite 1, SANTA BARBARA, 93109). Fax: 650/359-4036. **Facility:** Smoke free premises. 97 units. 96 one-bedroom standard units. 1 one-bedroom suite ($159-$350) with whirlpool. 4 stories, interior corridors. **Parking:** on-site. **Terms:** check-in 4 pm, 10% service charge. **Amenities:** video games (fee), dual phone lines, voice mail, irons, hair dryers. **Dining:** Moonraker Restaurant, see separate listing. **Pool(s):** heated outdoor. **Leisure Activities:** sauna, whirlpool, exercise room. **Guest Services:** gift shop. **Business Services:** meeting rooms. **Cards:** AX, DC, DS, MC, VI.

(See color ad below)

SOME UNITS

HOLIDAY INN EXPRESS & SUITES *Book at aaa.com* **Phone:** 650/355-5000 278

AAA SAVE — Small-scale Hotel

5/2-10/30 [ECP]	1P: $139-$219	2P: $149-$229	XP: $10	F12
2/1-5/1 [ECP]	1P: $129-$209	2P: $139-$219	XP: $10	F12
10/31-1/31 [ECP]	1P: $119-$199	2P: $129-$209	XP: $10	F12

Location: W of SR 1, exit Rockaway Beach. 519 Nick Gust Way 94044. Fax: 650/355-5959. **Facility:** 38 units. 36 one-bedroom standard units, some with whirlpools. 2 one-bedroom suites ($179-$239) with whirlpools. 2 stories, interior corridors. **Parking:** on-site. **Terms:** cancellation fee imposed. **Amenities:** high-speed Internet, voice mail, irons, hair dryers. *Some:* safes. **Guest Services:** coin laundry. **Business Services:** meeting rooms. **Cards:** AX, CB, DC, DS, JC, MC, VI. **Special Amenities: free expanded continental breakfast and free local telephone calls.**

(See color ad below & p 260)

SOME UNITS

(See map and index starting on p. 599)

WHERE TO DINE

MOONRAKER RESTAURANT Dinner: $20-$40 Phone: 650/359-0303 (150)

Seafood

Location: Just w off SR 1; in Best Western Lighthouse Hotel. 105 Rockaway Beach Ave 94044. **Hours:** 5 pm-10 pm; Sunday brunch 10 am-2 pm. Closed: Mon. **Reservations:** suggested. **Features:** Diners are treated to excellent ocean views from most tables. Seafood specialties are made from fresh ingredients. Dressy casual; cocktails. **Parking:** on-site. **Cards:** AX, DC, MC, VI.

SAN BRUNO pop. 40,165 (See map and index starting on p. 599)

WHERE TO STAY

BEST INN & SUITES Book at aaa.com Phone: (650)589-5089 (320)

AAA SAVE

Motel

All Year	1P: $49-$89	2P: $59-$99	XP: $5	F18

Location: US 101, exit San Bruno Ave, 0.4 mi w. 611 San Bruno Ave 94066. Fax: 650/837-9701. **Facility:** 29 one-bedroom standard units, some with whirlpools. 2 stories, interior corridors. **Parking:** on-site. **Terms:** [ECP] meal plan available. **Amenities:** high-speed Internet, voice mail, irons, hair dryers. **Business Services:** meeting rooms. **Cards:** AX, DS, JC, MC, VI. **Special Amenities: free continental breakfast and early check-in/late check-out.**

SOME UNITS

CAL WEST INN Book at aaa.com Phone: (650)624-0999 (326)

Motel

4/1-6/30	1P: $65	2P: $75	XP: $10	D17
7/1-9/30	1P: $60	2P: $65	XP: $10	D17
2/1-3/31 & 10/1-1/31	1P: $55	2P: $60	XP: $10	D17

Location: US 101 to I-380, exit El Camino Real S. 421 El Camino Real 94066. Fax: 650/225-0448. **Facility:** 54 one-bedroom standard units, some with whirlpools. 3 stories, interior corridors. **Parking:** on-site. **Terms:** cancellation fee imposed, [CP] & [ECP] meal plans available. **Amenities:** irons, hair dryers. **Leisure Activities:** exercise room. **Cards:** AX, DC, DS, JC, MC, VI.

SOME UNITS

DAYS INN-SFO INT'L-WEST Book at aaa.com Phone: 650/616-9600 (323)

Motel

Property failed to provide current rates

Location: US 101 to I-380, exit El Camino Real S. 1550 El Camino Real 94066. Fax: 650/616-9575. **Facility:** 48 one-bedroom standard units, some with whirlpools. 3 stories, interior corridors. **Parking:** on-site. **Amenities:** voice mail, irons, hair dryers.

SOME UNITS

(See map and index starting on p. 599)

RAMADA LIMITED Book at aaa.com **Phone:** (650)871-4000 322

Motel

All Year [ECP] 1P: $75-$100 2P: $75-$100 XP: $5 F12
Location: US 101 to I-380, exit El Camino Real S; 2.8 mi nw of airport. 500 El Camino Real 94066. Fax: 650/871-5754. **Facility:** 61 one-bedroom standard units, some with efficiencies, kitchens and/or whirlpools. 3 stories, interior corridors. **Parking:** on-site. **Amenities:** voice mail, irons, hair dryers. **Leisure Activities:** sauna, whirlpool, exercise room. **Guest Services:** coin laundry. **Cards:** AX, CB, DC, DS, MC, VI. **Special Amenities: free expanded continental breakfast and free newspaper.** *(See color ad p 674)*

SOME UNITS

REGENCY INN Book at aaa.com **Phone:** (650)589-7535 325

Motel

All Year 1P: $75 2P: $75 XP: $10 F17
Location: US 101, exit San Bruno Ave, 0.4 mi w. 411 E San Bruno Ave 94066. Fax: 650/244-9782. **Facility:** 31 one-bedroom standard units. 2 stories, exterior corridors. **Parking:** on-site. **Terms:** [CP] meal plan available, small pets only ($50 deposit). **Amenities:** voice mail, irons, hair dryers. **Guest Services:** coin laundry. **Cards:** AX, DC, DS, JC, MC, VI. **Special Amenities: free continental breakfast and free newspaper.**

SOME UNITS

FEE

RITZ INN **Phone:** 650/589-3553 324

Motel

All Year 1P: $60-$75 2P: $75-$90 XP: $5 F6
Location: US 101 to I-380, exit El Camino Real S; 2.5 mi nw of airport. 151 El Camino Real 94066. Fax: 650/873-2476. **Facility:** 23 one-bedroom standard units. 2 stories, exterior corridors. *Bath:* combo or shower only. **Parking:** on-site. **Terms:** [CP] meal plan available. **Amenities:** irons, hair dryers. **Cards:** AX, DS, MC, VI. **Special Amenities: free continental breakfast.**

SOME UNITS

SUMMERFIELD SUITES BY WYNDHAM-SAN FRANCISCO Book at aaa.com **Phone:** (650)588-0770 319

Motel

All Year 1P: $89-$139 2P: $89-$139 XP: $20 F17
Location: I-380, exit El Camino Real N, e on Sneath Ln. 1350 Huntington Ave 94066. Fax: 650/588-0892. **Facility:** 92 units. 41 one- and 51 two-bedroom suites with kitchens. 3 stories (no elevator), exterior corridors. **Parking:** on-site. **Terms:** cancellation fee imposed, [MAP] meal plan available, pets ($150-$200 fee, $10 extra charge). **Amenities:** CD players, voice mail, irons, hair dryers. *Fee:* video library, high-speed Internet. **Pool(s):** heated outdoor. **Leisure Activities:** whirlpool, exercise room, sports court. **Guest Services:** gift shop, coin laundry. **Business Services:** meeting rooms, fax. **Cards:** AX, DC, DS, JC, MC, VI.

SOME UNITS

FEE

SAN CARLOS pop. 27,718 (See map and index starting on p. 599)

WHERE TO STAY

COMFORT INN & SUITES Book at aaa.com **Phone:** (650)508-1800 446

Motel

5/1-9/30 [ECP] 1P: $89 2P: $139 XP: $10 F
2/1-4/30 & 10/1-1/31 [ECP] 1P: $79 2P: $109 XP: $10 F
Location: N of US 101, exit Holly St, 0.3 mi n on SR 82. 251 El Camino Real 94070. Fax: 650/593-6100. **Facility:** 50 one-bedroom standard units, some with whirlpools. 3 stories, interior corridors. **Parking:** on-site. **Amenities:** high-speed Internet, dual phone lines, voice mail, irons, hair dryers. **Pool(s):** heated outdoor. **Leisure Activities:** exercise room. **Guest Services:** valet laundry. **Business Services:** meeting rooms. **Cards:** AX, CB, DC, DS, JC, MC, VI. **Special Amenities: free expanded continental breakfast and free local telephone calls.** *(See color ad below)*

SOME UNITS

(See map and index starting on p. 599)

DAYS INN-SAN CARLOS *Book at aaa.com* **Phone:** (650)591-5771 445

AAA SAVE

Motel

All Year [CP] 1P: $69 2P: $99 XP: $10 F17

Location: US 101, exit Holly St northbound, w to El Camino Real, then 0.3 mi n; exit Ralston southbound, w to El Camino Real, 0.5 mi s. 26 El Camino Real 94070. Fax: 650/508-1476. **Facility:** 29 one-bedroom standard units, some with whirlpools. 2 stories, exterior corridors. **Parking:** on-site. **Amenities:** voice mail, irons, hair dryers. **Pool(s):** outdoor. **Cards:** AX, CB, DC, DS, JC, MC, VI.

SOME UNITS

HOMESTEAD STUDIO SUITES HOTEL-SAN CARLOS/REDWOOD SHORES *Book at aaa.com* **Phone:** (650)368-2600 451

Motel

All Year 1P: $95-$115 2P: $100-$120 XP: $5 F17

Location: US 101, exit Whipple Ave, w to Industrial, then just n. Located in an industrial park. 3 Circle Star Way 94070. Fax: 650/368-5815. **Facility:** 116 one-bedroom standard units with efficiencies. 3 stories, interior corridors. *Bath:* combo or shower only. **Parking:** on-site. **Terms:** weekly rates available, small pets only ($75 extra charge). **Amenities:** high-speed Internet (fee), dual phone lines, voice mail, irons, hair dryers. **Guest Services:** coin laundry. **Business Services:** meeting rooms. **Cards:** AX, CB, DC, DS, JC, MC, VI.

SOME UNITS

FEE FEE FEE

INNS OF AMERICA *Book at aaa.com* **Phone:** (650)631-0777 448

AAA SAVE

Motel

All Year [ECP] 1P: $69-$109 2P: $69-$109

Location: US 101, exit Holly St/Redwood Shores, e to Airport Blvd, then just s. 555 Skyway Rd 94070. Fax: 650/631-9610. **Facility:** 122 one-bedroom standard units. 3 stories, interior corridors. *Bath:* combo or shower only. **Parking:** on-site. **Terms:** weekly rates available, small pets only ($10 fee). **Amenities:** video games, voice mail, irons, hair dryers. *Some:* dual phone lines. **Pool(s):** heated outdoor. **Leisure Activities:** exercise room. **Guest Services:** coin laundry, area transportation-within 5 mi. **Business Services:** meeting rooms. **Cards:** AX, DC, MC, VI.

SOME UNITS

FEE

SAN CARLOS TRAVELODGE *Book at aaa.com* **Phone:** (650)591-6655 449

AAA SAVE

Motel

All Year [CP] 1P: $70-$100 2P: $70-$100 XP: $5 F12

Location: W of US 101, exit Holly St, 1 mi s on SR 82. 1562 El Camino Real 94070. Fax: 650/802-9139. **Facility:** 32 one-bedroom standard units, some with efficiencies (no utensils) and/or whirlpools. 2 stories, exterior corridors. **Parking:** on-site. **Amenities:** irons, hair dryers. **Leisure Activities:** sauna, whirlpool. **Cards:** AX, CB, DC, DS, MC, VI. **Special Amenities: free continental breakfast and early check-in/late check-out.** *(See color ad p 674)*

SOME UNITS

WHERE TO DINE

The following restaurant has not been evaluated by AAA but is listed for your information only.

A TAVOLA **Phone:** 650/595-5914

fyi

Not evaluated. **Location:** 716 Laurel Ave 94074. **Features:** The California-influenced Italian menu changes often but is always enjoyable. The intimate dining room is elegant but casual. A good selection of wines is available.

SAN MATEO pop. 92,482 (See map and index starting on p. 599)

WHERE TO STAY

BEST WESTERN SAN MATEO/LOS PRADOS INN *Book at aaa.com* **Phone:** (650)341-3300 388

AAA SAVE

Motel

All Year 1P: $89-$159 2P: $89-$189 XP: $10 F17

Location: Just e of and adjacent to US 101, exit E Hillsdale Ave. 2940 S Norfolk St 94403. Fax: 650/341-9999. **Facility:** 116 one-bedroom standard units. 2-3 stories, interior/exterior corridors. *Bath:* combo or shower only. **Parking:** on-site. **Terms:** [CP] meal plan available. **Amenities:** voice mail, irons, hair dryers. **Leisure Activities:** whirlpool, exercise room. **Guest Services:** valet laundry, airport transportation-San Francisco International Airport. **Business Services:** meeting rooms. **Cards:** AX, CB, DC, DS, JC, MC, VI. **Special Amenities: free continental breakfast.**

SOME UNITS

COMFORT INN *Book at aaa.com* **Phone:** (650)344-6376 383

AAA SAVE

Motel

All Year [CP] 1P: $59-$129 2P: $59-$129 XP: $10 F18

Location: US 101, Dore Ave northbound; exit 3rd Ave E southbound, re-enter US 101 N, then exit Dore Ave. 350 N Bayshore Blvd 94401. Fax: 650/343-7108. **Facility:** 111 units. 108 one-bedroom standard units. 3 one-bedroom suites ($89-$139). 4 stories, interior/exterior corridors. *Bath:* combo or shower only. **Parking:** on-site. **Amenities:** dual phone lines, voice mail, irons, hair dryers. **Guest Services:** coin laundry. **Business Services:** meeting rooms. **Cards:** AX, CB, DC, DS, JC, MC, VI. **Special Amenities: free continental breakfast and free local telephone calls.**

SOME UNITS

COXHEAD HOUSE BED & BREAKFAST *Book at aaa.com* **Phone:** (650)685-1600 380

Historic Bed & Breakfast

All Year [BP] 1P: $120-$250 2P: $120-$250 XP: $30

Location: US 101, exit 3rd Ave, w to SR 82 (El Camino Real), 0.6 mi n, then just e. 37 E Santa Inez Ave 94401. Fax: 650/685-1684. **Facility:** A quiet neighborhood is the setting for this Tudor Revival-style inn built in 1891. 5 one-bedroom standard units, some with whirlpools. 2 stories, interior corridors. *Bath:* shared or private, combo or shower only. **Parking:** on-site. **Terms:** check-in 4 pm, 7 day cancellation notice. **Amenities:** *Some:* irons, hair dryers. **Business Services:** business center. **Cards:** AX, DC, DS, MC, VI.

SOME UNITS

(See map and index starting on p. 599)

HILTON GARDEN INN SAN MATEO *Book at aaa.com* **Phone:** (650)522-9000 381

Small-scale Hotel

All Year 1P: $79-$189 2P: $79-$189 XP: $10 F18

Location: N of SR 92, exit Mariners Island eastbound, n to Fashion Island, then e. Located in the Bridgepointe Shopping/Office complex. 2000 Bridgepoint Cir 94404. Fax: 650/522-9099. **Facility:** 156 one-bedroom standard units. 6 stories, interior corridors. *Bath:* combo or shower only. **Parking:** on-site. **Terms:** weekly rates available, [AP], [BP] & [CP] meal plans available. **Amenities:** video games, high-speed Internet, dual phone lines, voice mail, irons, hair dryers. **Pool(s):** small heated outdoor. **Leisure Activities:** whirlpool, exercise room. **Guest Services:** gift shop, valet and coin laundry, area transportation. **Business Services:** meeting rooms, business center. **Cards:** AX, CB, DC, DS, JC, MC, VI.

SOME UNITS

HOLIDAY INN-SAN MATEO *Book at aaa.com* **Phone:** (650)344-3219 382

SAVE

Small-scale Hotel

All Year 1P: $89-$159 2P: $89-$159 XP: $10 F12

Location: US 101, exit Dore Ave E northbound; exit 3rd Ave E southbound, re-enter US 101, then exit Dore Ave. 330 N Bayshore Blvd 94401. Fax: 650/344-9012. **Facility:** 109 units. 98 one-bedroom standard units. 11 one-bedroom suites ($179-$269). 4 stories, interior corridors. *Bath:* some combo or shower only. **Parking:** on-site. **Amenities:** dual phone lines, voice mail, irons, hair dryers. **Dining:** 6:30 am-2 & 5:30-10 pm, Sat from 7 am, Sun 8 am-1 pm. **Leisure Activities:** sauna, whirlpool, exercise room. **Guest Services:** valet and coin laundry. **Business Services:** conference facilities. **Cards:** AX, CB, DC, DS, JC, MC, VI. **Special Amenities: free newspaper and free room upgrade (subject to availability with advanced reservations).**

SOME UNITS

HOMESTEAD STUDIO SUITES HOTEL-SAN MATEO/SFO *Book at aaa.com* **Phone:** (650)574-1744 386

Motel

All Year 1P: $86-$106 2P: $91-$111 XP: $5 F17

Location: SR 92, exit Edgewater Blvd, se of jct US 101 and SR 92. 1830 Gateway Dr 94404. Fax: 650/574-1757. **Facility:** 137 one-bedroom standard units, some with efficiencies. 2 stories, exterior corridors. *Bath:* combo or shower only. **Parking:** on-site. **Terms:** weekly rates available, small pets only ($75 fee). **Amenities:** dual phone lines, voice mail, irons, hair dryers. *Some:* high-speed Internet. **Guest Services:** coin laundry. **Cards:** AX, CB, DC, DS, JC, MC, VI.

SOME UNITS

FEE

(See map and index starting on p. 599)

MARRIOTT SAN MATEO/SAN FRANCISCO AIRPORT *Book at aaa.com* **Phone:** (650)653-6000 384

SAVE

Large-scale Hotel

All Year 1P: $99-$349 2P: $99-$349 XP: $10 F12

Location: Nw of jct US 101 and SR 92; SR 92, exit Delaware St, e on Concar Dr. 1770 S Amphlett Blvd 94402. Fax: 650/653-6084. **Facility:** Designed in a classic American style, this service-oriented hotel has a relaxed yet sophisticated ambience. 476 units. 396 one-bedroom standard units. 80 one-bedroom suites ($110-$369). 6 stories, interior corridors. **Parking:** valet. **Terms:** 3 day cancellation notice. **Amenities:** video games, high-speed Internet, dual phone lines, voice mail, irons, hair dryers. *Some:* CD players. **Dining:** 6 am-10 pm, cocktails. **Pool(s):** heated outdoor. **Leisure Activities:** whirlpool, exercise room. **Guest Services:** gift shop, valet laundry. **Business Services:** conference facilities, business center. **Cards:** AX, CB, DC, DS, JC, MC, VI. **Special Amenities: free newspaper and early check-in/late check-out.** *(See color ad p 677)*

SOME UNITS

RADISSON VILLA HOTEL *Book at aaa.com* **Phone:** (650)341-0966 389

Small-scale Hotel

All Year 1P: $185 2P: $185 XP: $10 F18

Location: 8 mi s of San Francisco International Airport; US 101, exit W Hillsdale Blvd, 0.5 mi s on SR 82. 4000 S El Camino Real 94403. Fax: 650/573-0164. **Facility:** 286 units. 272 one-bedroom standard units. 14 one-bedroom suites ($285-$425). 2-4 stories, interior/exterior corridors. *Bath:* combo or shower only. **Parking:** on-site. **Terms:** [AP] meal plan available, $2 service charge, pets ($100 deposit). **Amenities:** high-speed Internet, dual phone lines, voice mail, irons, hair dryers. *Some:* DVD players. **Pool(s):** heated outdoor. **Leisure Activities:** exercise room. **Guest Services:** gift shop, valet laundry, area transportation. **Business Services:** conference facilities, business center. **Cards:** AX, CB, DC, DS, JC, MC, VI. ***(See color ad p 677 & p 629)***

SOME UNITS

ASK FEE

RESIDENCE INN BY MARRIOTT *Book at aaa.com* **Phone:** (650)574-4700 385

Motel

All Year [ECP] 1P: $104-$151

Location: 0.8 mi se from jct US 101 and SR 92; exit SR 92 via Edgewater Blvd. 2000 Winward Way 94404. Fax: 650/572-9084. **Facility:** 159 units. 120 one-bedroom standard units with kitchens. 39 two-bedroom suites with kitchens. 2 stories, exterior corridors. *Bath:* combo or shower only. **Parking:** on-site. **Terms:** check-in 4 pm, pets ($75 fee, $6 extra charge). **Amenities:** video games, dual phone lines, voice mail, irons, hair dryers. **Pool(s):** heated outdoor. **Leisure Activities:** whirlpools, sports court. **Guest Services:** complimentary evening beverages: Mon-Thurs, coin laundry, area transportation. **Business Services:** meeting rooms, PC, fax. **Cards:** AX, CB, DC, DS, JC, MC, VI.

SOME UNITS

ASK FEE

SUPER 8 MOTEL *Book at aaa.com* **Phone:** (650)342-3273 379

SAVE

Motel

6/16-10/31 [CP] 1P: $69-$99 2P: $79-$110 XP: $10 F12
2/1-6/15 & 11/1-1/31 [CP] 1P: $59-$89 2P: $69-$99 XP: $10 F12

Location: US 101, exit Dore Ave, just right. 140 N Bayshore Blvd 94401. Fax: 650/342-4619. **Facility:** 53 one-bedroom standard units, some with whirlpools. 2 stories, exterior corridors. **Parking:** on-site. **Amenities:** irons, hair dryers. **Cards:** AX, CB, DC, DS, JC, MC, VI. **Special Amenities: free continental breakfast.**

SOME UNITS

WHERE TO DINE

The following restaurants have not been evaluated by AAA but are listed for your information only.

CENTRAL PARK BISTRO **Phone:** 650/558-8401

fyi

Not evaluated. **Location:** Downtown. 181 E 4th Ave 94401. **Features:** The restaurant offers a comfortable stainless steel bar and cherry wood tables with a view of the open kitchen.

THE DINING ROOM **Phone:** 650/349-5552

fyi

Not evaluated. **Location:** 1602 S El Camino Real 94402. **Features:** In a cottage, the upscale French restaurant changes its menu seasonally to promote available ingredients. Jackets are required.

KINGFISH **Phone:** 650/343-1226

fyi

Not evaluated. **Location:** 201 S "B" St 94401. **Features:** From the decor to the food, guests might feel as though they're in a New Orleans eatery. The casually elegant restaurant also presents an extensive wine list.

VIOGNIER **Phone:** 650/685-3727

fyi

Not evaluated. **Location:** 222 E 4th Ave 94401. **Features:** Menu items are a creation of classic French technique combined with California cuisine. For a start-to-finish example of this cooking style, order the grand tasting menu, then sit back and enjoy each course.

SAN RAFAEL pop. 56,063

WHERE TO STAY

EMBASSY SUITES HOTEL *Book at aaa.com* **Phone:** (415)499-9222

Large-scale Hotel

All Year [BP] 1P: $129-$349 2P: $129-$359 XP: $15 F

Location: US 101, exit E San Pedro Dr northbound; exit Freitas Pkwy southbound. Adjacent to Marin County Civic Center. 101 McInnis Pkwy 94903. Fax: 415/499-9268. **Facility:** A garden atrium, a koi pond and fresh flowers and greenery bring a touch of the outdoors to the hotel's common areas. 235 one-bedroom suites. 5 stories, interior corridors. **Parking:** on-site. **Amenities:** video library, dual phone lines, voice mail, irons, hair dryers. **Pool(s):** heated indoor. **Leisure Activities:** whirlpool, exercise room. **Guest Services:** gift shop, complimentary evening beverages, coin laundry. **Business Services:** conference facilities. **Cards:** AX, CB, DC, DS, JC, MC, VI. ***(See color ad p 621)***

SOME UNITS

FOUR POINTS BY SHERATON SAN RAFAEL *Book at aaa.com* **Phone:** 415/479-8800

Small-scale Hotel

All Year 1P: $89-$189 2P: $89-$189 XP: $10 F18

Location: US 101, exit Terra Linda, 3 mi n. Located in Terra Linda. 1010 Northgate Dr 94903. Fax: 415/479-2342. **Facility:** 235 units. 231 one-bedroom standard units. 4 one-bedroom suites. 4-5 stories, interior corridors. **Parking:** on-site. **Terms:** cancellation fee imposed, [AP] & [BP] meal plans available. **Amenities:** dual phone lines, voice mail, irons, hair dryers. **Pool(s):** heated outdoor. **Leisure Activities:** whirlpool, exercise room. **Guest Services:** gift shop, valet laundry. **Business Services:** meeting rooms. **Cards:** AX, CB, DC, DS, JC, MC, VI.

SOME UNITS

GERSTLE PARK INN **Phone:** (415)721-7611

Historic Bed & Breakfast

All Year [BP] 1P: $179-$275 2P: $179-$275 XP: $25

Location: US 101, exit Central San Rafael, 0.5 mi w on 4th St, 0.5 mi s on D St, then just w on San Rafael Ave. 34 Grove St 94901. Fax: 415/721-7600. **Facility:** Settled amongst the foothills, the one-and-a-half acre grounds overlook San Rafael and contain oak, cedar, redwood and fruit trees. 12 units. 8 one-bedroom standard units, some with whirlpools. 4 one-bedroom suites with kitchens, some with whirlpools. 2 stories, interior/exterior corridors. **Parking:** on-site. **Amenities:** CD players, voice mail, irons, hair dryers. **Guest Services:** complimentary evening beverages. **Business Services:** meeting rooms.

SAN RAFAEL INN **Phone:** 415/454-9470

AAA SAVE

Motel

6/15-10/15 1P: $75-$85 2P: $85-$105 XP: $10

2/1-6/14 & 10/16-1/31 1P: $60-$75 2P: $75-$85 XP: $10

Location: US 101, exit E Francisco Blvd, just n. 865 Francisco Blvd E 94901. Fax: 415/457-2512. **Facility:** 32 units. 30 one-bedroom standard units. 2 one-bedroom suites with whirlpools. 2 stories, exterior corridors. *Bath:* combo or shower only. **Parking:** on-site. **Terms:** 3 day cancellation notice-fee imposed. **Pool(s):** heated outdoor. **Leisure Activities:** whirlpool. **Cards:** AX, CB, DC, DS, MC, VI. **Special Amenities: free continental breakfast.** *(See color ad below)*

SOME UNITS

VILLA INN **Phone:** 415/456-4975

Motel

All Year 1P: $60-$85 2P: $65-$90 XP: $10 F12

Location: Off US 101 at Lincoln Ave off-ramp; exit Central San Rafael northbound, 0.3 mi w on Fourth St, 0.5 mi n. Located in a residential setting. 1600 Lincoln Ave 94901. Fax: 415/456-1520. **Facility:** 60 units. 57 one-bedroom standard units, some with kitchens. 3 one-bedroom suites with kitchens. 2 stories, exterior corridors. *Bath:* combo or shower only. **Parking:** on-site. **Terms:** cancellation fee imposed, [CP] meal plan available, small pets only ($20 deposit, no cats). **Amenities:** hair dryers. **Pool(s):** heated outdoor. **Leisure Activities:** whirlpool. **Guest Services:** coin laundry. **Business Services:** meeting rooms. **Cards:** AX, DC, MC, VI. *(See color ad below)*

SOME UNITS

FEE

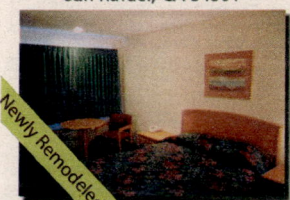

WHERE TO DINE

CHALET BASQUE RESTAURANT — **Lunch:** $6-$12 **Dinner:** $14-$22 **Phone:** 415/479-1070

Basque

Location: 1 mi e of Marin Civic Center. 405 N San Pedro Rd 94903. **Hours:** 11:30 am-2 & 5-9 pm, Sat from 4 pm, Sun 10:30 am-2 & 4-9 pm. Closed: 12/25; also Mon. **Reservations:** suggested. **Features:** Family dinners. Patio dining, weather permitting. Dressy casual; cocktails. **Parking:** on-site. **Cards:** AX, DS, MC, VI.

SALUTE RISTORANTE — **Lunch:** $15-$25 **Dinner:** $25-$35 **Phone:** 415/453-7596

Italian

Location: US 101, exit W Central San Rafael, on 3rd St to Tamalpias. 706 3rd St 94901. **Hours:** 11 am-10 pm. Closed major holidays. **Reservations:** suggested. **Features:** Turn-of-the-20th-century decor punctuates the dining room, where diners try traditional and modern dishes. Dressy casual; cocktails. **Parking:** on-site. **Cards:** AX, CB, DC, DS, JC, MC, VI.

SAUSALITO pop. 7,330

WHERE TO STAY

CASA MADRONA HOTEL *Book at aaa.com* — **Phone:** (415)332-0502

AAA SAVE — Small-scale Hotel

All Year [CP] 1P: $180-$360 2P: $180-$360 XP: $25 F12

Location: US 101, exit Alexander Ave, 1.5 mi to Bridgeway. 801 Bridgeway 94965. Fax: 415/332-2537. **Facility:** Smoke free premises. 65 units. 57 one-bedroom standard units. 8 one-bedroom suites ($360), some with kitchens. 3 stories, interior/exterior corridors. *Bath:* combo or shower only. **Parking:** on-site (fee). **Terms:** 3 day cancellation notice-fee imposed. **Amenities:** video library, CD players, dual phone lines, voice mail, honor bars, irons, hair dryers. **Dining:** 6 pm-10 pm; Sunday brunch 10 am-2:30 pm, cocktails. **Leisure Activities:** whirlpool, spa. **Guest Services:** complimentary evening beverages, valet laundry. **Business Services:** meeting rooms. **Cards:** AX, DC, MC, VI. **Special Amenities: free continental breakfast and free newspaper.**

SOME UNITS

THE GABLES INN-SAUSALITO — **Phone:** (415)289-1100

Bed & Breakfast

4/1-10/31 2P: $155-$325 XP: $15 F5
2/1-3/31 & 11/1-1/31 2P: $135-$305 XP: $15 F5

Location: US 101, exit Alexander Ave, 1.5 mi to Bridgeway. 62 Princess St 94965. Fax: 415/339-0536. **Facility:** Picturesque views of San Francisco Bay are featured from this inn set on a hillside just above the historic downtown area. Designated smoking area. 9 one-bedroom standard units, some with whirlpools. 2 stories, interior corridors. *Bath:* combo or shower only. **Parking:** on-site. **Terms:** 7 day cancellation notice, [CP] meal plan available. **Amenities:** video library, voice mail, irons, hair dryers. **Cards:** AX, CB, DC, DS, MC, VI.

ASK

THE INN ABOVE TIDE *Book at aaa.com* — **Phone:** (415)332-9535

Motel

All Year [ECP] 1P: $250-$450 2P: $250-$450 XP: $15 F5

Location: US 101, exit Alexander Ave, 1.5 mi to Bridgeway. 30 El Portal 94965. Fax: 415/332-6714. **Facility:** 30 units. 28 one-bedroom standard units, some with whirlpools. 2 one-bedroom suites ($495-$780), some with whirlpools. 3 stories, interior/exterior corridors. **Parking:** on-site (fee). **Terms:** 2 night minimum stay - weekends, cancellation fee imposed. **Amenities:** CD players, high-speed Internet, dual phone lines, voice mail, honor bars, hair dryers. **Guest Services:** complimentary evening beverages. **Business Services:** meeting rooms. **Cards:** AX, DC, MC, VI.

WHERE TO DINE

HOTEL ALTA MIRA DINING ROOM — **Lunch:** $10-$22 **Dinner:** $18-$29 **Phone:** 415/332-1350

American

Location: W on Princess St from Bridgeway, then n; center. 125 Bulkley Ave 94966. **Hours:** Open 2/1-1/1; 7:30 am-11 pm. **Reservations:** suggested. **Features:** The hillside location, including the nice terrace, affords an excellent view of the San Francisco Bay area. This place is busy during lunch and Sunday brunch. Dressy casual; beer & wine only. **Parking:** on-site. **Cards:** AX, CB, MC, VI.

THE SPINNAKER — **Lunch:** $10-$19 **Dinner:** $13-$27 **Phone:** 415/332-1500

Seafood

Location: Town center; adjacent to yacht harbor. 100 Spinnaker Dr 94965. **Hours:** 11 am-11 pm. Closed: 11/25, 12/24, 12/25. **Reservations:** suggested. **Features:** Dining room over water. Varied menu. Dressy casual; cocktails. **Parking:** on-site. **Cards:** AX, DC, DS, MC, VI.

SOUTH SAN FRANCISCO pop. 60,552 (See map and index starting on p. 599)

WHERE TO STAY

AMERICANA INN — **Phone:** (650)589-0404 295

AAA SAVE — Motel

All Year 1P: $49-$89 2P: $59-$99 XP: $5 F18

Location: 3 mi nw of airport on SR 82; US 101 to I-380, exit El Camino Real. 760 El Camino Real 94080. Fax: 650/873-2516. **Facility:** 17 one-bedroom standard units. 2 stories, exterior corridors. **Parking:** on-site. **Leisure Activities:** sauna. **Cards:** AX, DS, MC, VI. **Special Amenities: free local telephone calls and early check-in/late check-out.**

SOME UNITS

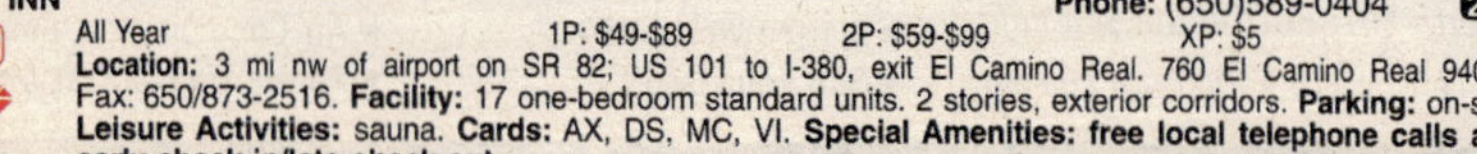

(See map and index starting on p. 599)

BEST WESTERN GROSVENOR AIRPORT HOTEL Book at aaa.com **Phone:** (650)873-3200 306

Small-scale Hotel

All Year 1P: $79-$129 2P: $79-$129 XP: $10 F12

Location: US 101, exit S Airport Blvd, just e. 380 S Airport Blvd 94080. Fax: 650/589-3495. **Facility:** 207 units. 198 one-bedroom standard units. 9 one-bedroom suites. 8 stories, interior corridors. **Parking:** on-site. **Terms:** $4 service charge. **Amenities:** voice mail, irons, hair dryers. **Dining:** 6 am-2 & 5-10 pm; closed for lunch Sat & Sun, cocktails. **Pool(s):** small outdoor. **Leisure Activities:** exercise room. **Guest Services:** valet laundry. **Business Services:** meeting rooms. **Cards:** AX, CB, DC, DS, JC, MC, VI. **Special Amenities: free continental breakfast and free local telephone calls.**

SOME UNITS

COMFORT SUITES Book at aaa.com **Phone:** (650)589-7100 300

Motel

4/1-10/31 [CP] 1P: $99-$129 2P: $99-$129 XP: $10 F17
2/1-3/31 & 11/1-1/31 [CP] 1P: $69-$89 2P: $69-$89 XP: $10 F17

Location: US 101, exit Grand Ave, just e. Located adjacent to railroad tracks. 121 E Grand Ave 94080. Fax: 650/589-7796. **Facility:** 169 one-bedroom standard units. 3 stories, exterior corridors. *Bath:* combo or shower only. **Parking:** on-site. **Terms:** cancellation fee imposed. **Amenities:** video games, voice mail, irons, hair dryers. **Leisure Activities:** whirlpool. **Guest Services:** coin laundry. **Cards:** AX, CB, DC, DS, JC, MC, VI.

SOME UNITS

FEE

COURTYARD BY MARRIOTT Book at aaa.com **Phone:** (650)871-4100 297

Small-scale Hotel

All Year 1P: $69-$179 2P: $69-$179

Location: US 101, exit Oyster Point, just e. 1300 Veterans Blvd 94080. Fax: 650/871-4700. **Facility:** 198 units. 186 one-bedroom standard units, some with whirlpools. 12 one-bedroom suites ($159-$199). 4 stories, interior corridors. *Bath:* combo or shower only. **Parking:** on-site. **Terms:** cancellation fee imposed, [BP] meal plan available. **Amenities:** dual phone lines, voice mail, irons, hair dryers. **Pool(s):** heated indoor. **Leisure Activities:** whirlpool, exercise room. **Guest Services:** gift shop, coin laundry. **Business Services:** meeting rooms, business center. **Cards:** AX, CB, DC, DS, JC, MC, VI.

SOME UNITS

DAYS INN-SFO NORTH Book at aaa.com **Phone:** (650)873-9300 299

Motel

All Year [CP] 1P: $79-$99 2P: $89-$109 XP: $10 F12

Location: US 101, exit Oyster Point, just w. 1113 Airport Blvd 94080. Fax: 650/873-6200. **Facility:** 25 one-bedroom standard units. 3 stories, exterior corridors. **Parking:** on-site. **Amenities:** irons, hair dryers. **Cards:** AX, CB, DC, DS, JC, MC, VI.

SOME UNITS

ECONOMY INN **Phone:** 650/952-2505 296

Motel

All Year 1P: $69-$79 2P: $69-$79 XP: $5

Location: US 101, exit Grand Ave or S San Francisco, just w. 701 Airport Blvd 94080. Fax: 650/952-8311. **Facility:** 23 one-bedroom standard units. 2 stories, exterior corridors. **Parking:** on-site. **Cards:** AX, DC, DS, MC, VI. **Special Amenities: free continental breakfast and preferred room (subject to availability with advanced reservations).**

SOME UNITS

EMBASSY SUITES SAN FRANCISCO AIRPORT-SOUTH SAN FRANCISCO Book at aaa.com **Phone:** (650)589-3400 303

Large-scale Hotel

All Year [BP] 1P: $109-$199 2P: $109-$199 XP: $10 F18

Location: US 101, exit Grand Ave, just e. 250 Gateway Blvd 94080. Fax: 650/876-0305. **Facility:** 312 one-bedroom suites. 10 stories, interior corridors. **Parking:** on-site. **Terms:** check-in 4 pm, cancellation fee imposed. **Amenities:** high-speed Internet, dual phone lines, voice mail, irons, hair dryers. **Pool(s):** heated indoor. **Leisure Activities:** sauna, whirlpool. **Guest Services:** gift shop, complimentary evening beverages. **Business Services:** conference facilities, fax. **Cards:** AX, CB, DC, DS, JC, MC, VI. ***(See color ad p 621)***

SOME UNITS

FOUR POINTS BY SHERATON SFO NORTH Book at aaa.com **Phone:** (650)588-4683 312

Small-scale Hotel

All Year 1P: $79-$199 2P: $79-$199 XP: $10 F16

Location: US 101, exit S Airport Blvd, just e. 264 S Airport Blvd 94080. Fax: 650/553-9466. **Facility:** 100 units. 84 one-bedroom standard units. 16 one-bedroom suites. 4 stories, interior corridors. **Parking:** on-site. **Terms:** cancellation fee imposed. **Amenities:** high-speed Internet, dual phone lines, voice mail, safes, irons, hair dryers. **Leisure Activities:** exercise room. **Guest Services:** gift shop, valet and coin laundry. **Business Services:** meeting rooms, business center. **Cards:** AX, CB, DC, DS, MC, VI.

SOME UNITS

HAMPTON INN Book at aaa.com **Phone:** (650)876-0200 302

Motel

5/16-10/15 [ECP] 1P: $89-$149 2P: $99-$159 XP: $10 F18
2/1-5/15 & 10/16-1/31 [ECP] 1P: $69-$129 2P: $79-$139 XP: $10 F18

Location: US 101, exit Grand Ave, just e. 300 Gateway Blvd 94080. Fax: 650/876-0600. **Facility:** 100 units. 97 one-bedroom standard units, some with whirlpools. 3 one-bedroom suites ($129-$169). 4 stories, interior corridors. **Parking:** on-site. **Terms:** cancellation fee imposed. **Amenities:** video games, high-speed Internet (fee), dual phone lines, voice mail, safes, irons, hair dryers. **Pool(s):** heated indoor. **Leisure Activities:** exercise room. **Guest Services:** gift shop, coin laundry. **Business Services:** business center. **Cards:** AX, DC, DS, MC, VI.

SOME UNITS

(See map and index starting on p. 599)

HILTON GARDEN INN Book at aaa.com **Phone:** 650/872-1515 313

AAA SAVE — Small-scale Hotel

All Year 1P: $99-$139 2P: $99-$139 XP: $10 F18

Location: US 101, exit Grand Ave, just e. 670 Gateway Blvd 94080. Fax: 650/872-1064. **Facility:** 169 one-bedroom standard units. 7 stories, interior corridors. **Parking:** on-site. **Terms:** check-in 4 pm, cancellation fee imposed, [MAP] meal plan available. **Amenities:** video games, high-speed Internet (fee), dual phone lines, voice mail, irons, hair dryers. **Dining:** 6 am-10 & 5-10 pm, cocktails. **Pool(s):** small heated indoor/outdoor. **Leisure Activities:** whirlpool, exercise room. **Guest Services:** complimentary laundry. **Business Services:** meeting rooms, business center. **Cards:** AX, CB, DC, DS, JC, MC, VI. **Special Amenities: free local telephone calls and free newspaper.**

SOME UNITS

HOLIDAY INN EXPRESS HOTEL & SUITES SAN FRANCISCO AIRPORT NORTH Book at aaa.com **Phone:** (650)589-0600 314

AAA SAVE — Small-scale Hotel

5/1-9/30 [ECP] 1P: $65-$139 2P: $65-$139 XP: $5
2/1-4/30 [ECP] 1P: $69-$129 2P: $69-$129 XP: $5
10/1-1/31 [ECP] 1P: $59-$129 2P: $59-$129 XP: $5

Location: US 101, exit S Airport Blvd, just e. 373 S Airport Blvd 94080. Fax: 650/589-0682. **Facility:** 89 units. 86 one-bedroom standard units. 3 one-bedroom suites ($135-$159) with whirlpools. 4 stories, interior corridors. **Parking:** on-site. **Terms:** package plans. **Amenities:** video games (fee), high-speed Internet, dual phone lines, voice mail, safes, irons, hair dryers. **Leisure Activities:** whirlpool, exercise room. **Guest Services:** valet and coin laundry. **Business Services:** meeting rooms, business center. **Cards:** AX, CB, DC, DS, JC, MC, VI. **Special Amenities: free local telephone calls and free newspaper.** *(See color ad below)*

SOME UNITS

HOLIDAY INN SFO-NORTH Book at aaa.com **Phone:** (650)873-3550 307

Small-scale Hotel

All Year 1P: $79-$249 2P: $79-$249 XP: $10 F18

Location: US 101, exit S Airport Blvd, just e. Located adjacent to the convention center. 275 S Airport Blvd 94080. Fax: 650/873-4524. **Facility:** 224 units. 223 one-bedroom standard units. 1 one-bedroom suite. 5 stories, interior corridors. **Parking:** on-site. **Terms:** cancellation fee imposed, [AP], [BP], [CP] & [ECP] meal plans available. **Amenities:** video games, high-speed Internet (fee), voice mail, irons, hair dryers. **Leisure Activities:** exercise room. **Guest Services:** gift shop. **Business Services:** meeting rooms, business center. **Cards:** AX, CB, DC, DS, JC, MC, VI. *(See ad p 683)*

SOME UNITS FEE FEE

HOWARD JOHNSON EXPRESS INN Book at aaa.com **Phone:** (650)589-9055 308

AAA SAVE — Motel

6/1-9/6 1P: $59-$119 2P: $59-$119 XP: $10 F12
2/1-5/31 & 9/7-1/31 1P: $49-$99 2P: $49-$99 XP: $10 F12

Location: US 101, exit S Airport Blvd, just e. 222 S Airport Blvd 94080 (1655 Pacific Hwy, SAN DIEGO, 92101). Fax: 650/871-1290. **Facility:** 51 one-bedroom standard units. 2 stories, exterior corridors. **Parking:** on-site. **Terms:** pets ($10 extra charge, in limited units). **Amenities:** safes. **Business Services:** fax. **Cards:** AX, CB, DC, DS, JC, MC, VI. **Special Amenities: free continental breakfast and early check-in/late check-out.**

FEE SOME UNITS

INN AT OYSTER POINT Book at aaa.com **Phone:** (650)737-7633 301

Motel

All Year [ECP] 1P: $139-$179 2P: $149-$189 XP: $10 F12

Location: 0.7 mi e of US 101, exit Oyster Point Blvd or S San Francisco. 425 Marina Blvd 94080. Fax: 650/737-0795. **Facility:** 30 one-bedroom standard units. 3 stories, interior corridors. **Parking:** on-site. **Amenities:** honor bars, irons, hair dryers. **Leisure Activities:** jogging. **Business Services:** meeting rooms. **Cards:** AX, CB, DC, DS, JC, MC, VI.

SOME UNITS FEE

(See map and index starting on p. 599)

LA QUINTA INN Book at aaa.com Phone: 650/583-2223 304

AAA SAVE

Motel

All Year 1P: $90-$159 2P: $100-$169 XP: $10 F18

Location: US 101, exit S Airport Blvd, just w. Located adjacent to industrial property and railroad tracks. 20 S Airport Blvd 94080. Fax: 650/589-6770. **Facility:** 171 units. 167 one-bedroom standard units. 4 one-bedroom suites. 4 stories, interior corridors. **Parking:** on-site. **Terms:** [ECP] meal plan available, small pets only. **Amenities:** video games, high-speed Internet, voice mail, irons, hair dryers. **Pool(s):** small heated outdoor. **Leisure Activities:** whirlpool, exercise room. **Guest Services:** coin laundry. **Business Services:** meeting rooms. **Cards:** AX, CB, DC, DS, JC, MC, VI. *(See color ad p 660)*

SOME UNITS

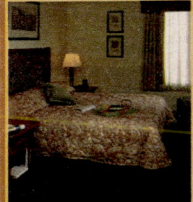

(See map and index starting on p. 599)

LARKSPUR LANDING *Book at aaa.com* **Phone:** 650/827-1515 310

Small-scale Hotel

All Year 1P: $79-$139 2P: $79-$139

Location: US 101, exit Grand Ave, just e. 690 Gateway Blvd 94080. Fax: 650/827-1058. **Facility:** 111 units. 75 one-bedroom standard units with kitchens. 36 one-bedroom suites with kitchens. 4 stories, interior corridors. *Bath:* combo or shower only. **Parking:** on-site. **Terms:** check-in 4 pm, cancellation fee imposed, [MAP] meal plan available. **Amenities:** video games, high-speed Internet (fee), dual phone lines, voice mail, irons, hair dryers. **Leisure Activities:** whirlpool, exercise room. **Guest Services:** complimentary laundry. **Business Services:** meeting rooms, business center. **Cards:** AX, CB, DC, DS, JC, MC, VI. **Special Amenities: free local telephone calls and free newspaper.** *(See color ad p 683)*

SOME UNITS

MOTEL 6 **Phone:** 650/877-0770 298

Motel

Property failed to provide current rates

Location: US 101, exit S Airport Blvd, just e. 111 Mitchell Ave 94080. Fax: 650/871-8377. **Facility:** 117 one-bedroom standard units. 3 stories, interior corridors. **Parking:** on-site. **Amenities:** *Some:* safes.

SOME UNITS

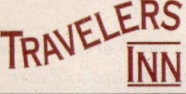

QUALITY INN & SUITES *Book at aaa.com* **Phone:** (650)875-7878 309

Motel

6/1-10/31 [BP]	1P: $79-$89	2P: $79-$89	XP: $10	F12
2/1-5/31 [BP]	1P: $69-$89	2P: $69-$89	XP: $10	F12
11/1-1/31 [BP]	1P: $59-$69	2P: $59-$69	XP: $10	F12

Location: US 101, exit S Airport Blvd, just e. 410 S Airport Blvd 94080. Fax: 650/875-0961. **Facility:** 45 one-bedroom standard units. 3 stories, interior corridors. **Parking:** on-site. **Terms:** package plans. **Amenities:** high-speed Internet, voice mail, irons, hair dryers. **Leisure Activities:** exercise room. **Guest Services:** valet laundry, airport transportation-San Francisco International Airport. **Business Services:** meeting rooms. **Cards:** AX, DC, DS, MC, VI. **Special Amenities: free full breakfast and free room upgrade (subject to availability with advanced reservations).** *(See color ad below)*

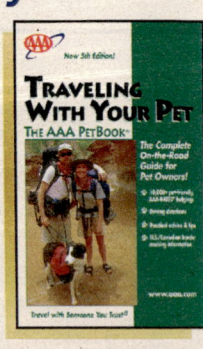

(See map and index starting on p. 599)

RAMADA INN SFO NORTH **Book at aaa.com** **Phone:** (650)589-7200 305

Motel

All Year [CP] 1P: $69-$179 2P: $69-$179 XP: $10 F18

Location: US 101, exit S Airport Blvd, just e. Located adjacent to the convention center. 245 S Airport Blvd 94080. Fax: 650/588-5007. **Facility:** 323 units. 320 one-bedroom standard units. 3 one-bedroom suites. 2 stories, exterior corridors. **Parking:** on-site. **Terms:** cancellation fee imposed. **Amenities:** video games, high-speed Internet (fee), voice mail, irons, hair dryers. **Pool(s):** heated outdoor. **Leisure Activities:** whirlpool. **Guest Services:** gift shop, coin laundry. **Business Services:** meeting rooms. **Cards:** AX, CB, DC, DS, JC, MC, VI.

SOME UNITS

FEE FEE

RAMADA LIMITED ALL SUITES **Book at aaa.com** **Phone:** (650)583-7300 294

Motel

All Year [ECP] 1P: $89-$109 2P: $99-$119 XP: $10 F12

Location: US 101, exit Grand Ave, just w. 721 Airport Blvd 94080. Fax: 650/583-7400. **Facility:** 45 one-bedroom standard units, some with whirlpools. 3 stories, interior corridors. *Bath:* combo or shower only. **Parking:** on-site. **Amenities:** high-speed Internet, dual phone lines, voice mail, irons, hair dryers. **Cards:** AX, CB, DC, DS, JC, MC, VI.

SOME UNITS

FEE

TRAVELERS INN **Phone:** 650/755-9556 293

AAA SAVE

Motel

All Year 1P: $69-$102 2P: $69-$102 XP: $10 F

Location: I-280, exit Hickey Blvd E, just e. 100 Hickey Blvd 94080. Fax: 650/755-2558. **Facility:** 20 one-bedroom standard units. 1 story, exterior corridors. *Bath:* shower only. **Parking:** on-site. **Amenities:** hair dryers. **Cards:** AX, MC, VI. **Special Amenities: early check-in/late check-out and free room upgrade (subject to availability with advanced reservations).** *(See color ad p 684)*

SOME UNITS

TRAVELODGE SAN FRANCISCO AIRPORT NORTH **Book at aaa.com** **Phone:** (650)583-9600 311

Motel

All Year 1P: $59-$119 2P: $59-$119 XP: $10 F17

Location: US 101, exit S Airport Blvd, then e. 326 S Airport Blvd 94080. Fax: 650/873-9392. **Facility:** 197 one-bedroom standard units. 2 stories, exterior corridors. *Bath:* combo or shower only. **Parking:** on-site. **Amenities:** video games, voice mail, safes, hair dryers. **Pool(s):** heated outdoor. **Cards:** AX, CB, DC, DS, MC, VI.

SOME UNITS

(See map and index starting on p. 599)

WHERE TO DINE

SOUTH CITY STEAKHOUSE — Dinner: $10-$25 — Phone: 650/737-7900 (160)

Steak House

Location: Just w of El Camino Real. 101 Brentwood Dr 94080. **Hours:** 4:30 pm-9 pm, Fri & Sat-10 pm. Closed: 12/25. **Reservations:** accepted. **Features:** Family restaurant. Casual dress; cocktails. **Parking:** on-site. **Cards:** MC, VI.

TIBURON pop. 8,666

WHERE TO STAY

TIBURON LODGE — Book at aaa.com — **Phone:** 415/435-3133

Motel

5/1-10/31	1P: $179-$339	2P: $194-$339	XP: $15	F12
2/1-4/30 & 11/1-1/31	1P: $159-$319	2P: $174-$319	XP: $15	F12

Location: US 101, exit Tiburon-Belvedere, 4 mi e; in village; 1 blk from bay. 1651 Tiburon Blvd 94920. Fax: 415/435-2451. **Facility:** 107 units. 101 one-bedroom standard units, some with whirlpools. 6 one-bedroom suites ($295-$315) with whirlpools, some with efficiencies or kitchens. 2-3 stories, exterior corridors. *Bath:* combo or shower only. **Parking:** on-site. **Terms:** 3 day cancellation notice-fee imposed. **Amenities:** voice mail, irons, hair dryers. **Pool(s):** heated outdoor. **Business Services:** meeting rooms, business center. **Cards:** AX, DS, MC, VI. ***(See color ad p 646)***

SOME UNITS

THE WATERS EDGE HOTEL — Book at aaa.com — **Phone:** (415)789-5999

Small-scale Hotel

All Year [ECP]	1P: $225-$325	2P: $225-$325	XP: $20	F17

Location: US 101, exit Tiburon-Belvedere, 4 mi e. 25 Main St 94920. Fax: 415/789-5888. **Facility:** 23 units. 21 one-bedroom standard units. 2 one-bedroom suites ($425). 2 stories, interior corridors. **Parking:** on-site. **Terms:** 2 night minimum stay - weekends in summer, 7 day cancellation notice-fee imposed. **Amenities:** CD players, dual phone lines, voice mail, irons, hair dryers. **Guest Services:** complimentary evening beverages. **Business Services:** meeting rooms. **Cards:** AX, DC, DS, MC, VI.

Maritime Museum / © Richard Cummins / Photophile

This ends listings for the San Francisco Vicinity. The following page resumes the alphabetical listings of cities in Northern California.

SANGER pop. 18,931

WHERE TO STAY

TOWN HOUSE MOTEL — **Phone:** (559)875-5531

AAA SAVE — Motel

All Year 1P: $45-$49 2P: $45-$49 XP: $5

Location: 1.3 mi s of SR 180 at Academy Ave, then 0.7 mi n. 1308 Church Ave 93657. Fax: 559/875-5201. **Facility:** 19 one-bedroom standard units. 2 stories (no elevator), exterior corridors. *Bath:* combo or shower only. **Parking:** on-site. **Pool(s):** outdoor. **Cards:** AX, DS, MC, VI.

SOME UNITS

WONDER VALLEY RANCH RESORT — **Phone:** (559)787-2551

Country Inn

4/1-11/1 [ECP] 1P: $142-$203 2P: $142-$203 XP: $20 F4
2/1-3/31 & 11/2-1/31 [ECP] 1P: $113-$162 2P: $113-$162 XP: $20 F4

Location: 35 mi e of SR 99; 5 mi between Piedra Rd and SR 180. 6450 Elwood Rd 93657. Fax: 559/787-2556. **Facility:** 53 one-bedroom standard units. 1 story, exterior corridors. *Bath:* combo or shower only. **Parking:** on-site. **Terms:** [AP] meal plan available, package plans. **Amenities:** voice mail. **Pool(s):** 2 outdoor. **Leisure Activities:** whirlpool, canoeing, sailboats, putting green, 2 tennis courts, jogging, horseback riding, playground, sports court, horseshoes, volleyball. **Guest Services:** gift shop, coin laundry. **Business Services:** meeting rooms, fax. **Cards:** MC, VI.

ASK — SOME UNITS

SAN JOSE pop. 894,943

WHERE TO STAY

ADLON HOTEL — Book at aaa.com — **Phone:** 408/282-1000

AAA SAVE — Small-scale Hotel

All Year [MAP] 1P: $109-$169 2P: $109-$169 XP: $10

Location: US 101, exit N 1st St, 0.5 mi s to Rosemary St E. 1275 N 4th St 95112. Fax: 408/282-1002. **Facility:** 57 one-bedroom standard units. 4 stories, interior corridors. **Parking:** on-site. **Terms:** cancellation fee imposed. **Amenities:** high-speed Internet, dual phone lines, voice mail, irons, hair dryers. **Guest Services:** complimentary laundry. **Cards:** AX, DC, DS, MC, VI. **Special Amenities: free full breakfast and early check-in/late check-out.**

SOME UNITS

ARENA HOTEL — Book at aaa.com — **Phone:** (408)294-6500

AAA SAVE — Small-scale Hotel

All Year [BP] 1P: $89 2P: $99 XP: $10 F12

Location: Downtown. Located adjacent to the arena. 817 The Alameda 95126. Fax: 408/294-6585. **Facility:** 89 one-bedroom standard units, some with efficiencies and/or whirlpools. 3 stories, interior corridors. **Parking:** on-site. **Terms:** cancellation fee imposed, [MAP] meal plan available. **Amenities:** CD players, voice mail, irons, hair dryers. *Fee:* video games, high-speed Internet. **Guest Services:** coin laundry. **Business Services:** meeting rooms. **Cards:** AX, DC, DS, MC, VI. **Special Amenities: free continental breakfast and free room upgrade (subject to availability with advanced reservations).**

SOME UNITS

BEST WESTERN AIRPORT PLAZA — Book at aaa.com — **Phone:** 408/243-2400

Small-scale Hotel

All Year [ECP] 2P: $99-$129 XP: $10

Location: I-880, exit The Alameda, just w. 2118 The Alameda 95126. Fax: 408/243-5478. **Facility:** 40 one-bedroom standard units, some with whirlpools. 3 stories, interior corridors. **Parking:** on-site. **Amenities:** video library, high-speed Internet, dual phone lines, voice mail, safes, irons, hair dryers. **Pool(s):** heated outdoor. **Leisure Activities:** whirlpool. **Guest Services:** valet laundry. **Cards:** AX, CB, DC, DS, MC, VI.

ASK — SOME UNITS

BEST WESTERN GATEWAY INN Book at aaa.com

Phone: (408)435-8800

AAA SAVE

Motel

All Year [ECP] 1P: $99-$109 2P: $99-$109 XP: $10 F18

Location: US 101, exit Trimble Rd E; 1 mi ne of San Jose International Airport. 2585 Seaboard Ave 95131. Fax: 408/435-8879. **Facility:** 150 one-bedroom standard units. 2 stories, interior corridors. **Parking:** on-site. **Terms:** cancellation fee imposed. **Amenities:** dual phone lines, voice mail, irons, hair dryers. **Pool(s):** heated outdoor. **Leisure Activities:** whirlpool. **Guest Services:** coin laundry, area transportation-within 8 mi. **Business Services:** meeting rooms. **Cards:** AX, DC, DS, JC, MC, VI. **Special Amenities: free expanded continental breakfast and free local telephone calls.** *(See color ad p 687)*

SOME UNITS

BEST WESTERN LANAI GARDEN INN & SUITES Book at aaa.com

Phone: (408)929-8100

AAA SAVE

Motel

All Year [ECP] 1P: $79-$129 2P: $89-$139 XP: $10 F12

Location: US 101, exit Tully Rd, just e. 1575 Tully Rd 95122. Fax: 408/929-8140. **Facility:** 52 units. 37 one-bedroom standard units, some with whirlpools. 15 one-bedroom suites. 2 stories, interior corridors. *Bath:* combo or shower only. **Parking:** on-site. **Amenities:** high-speed Internet, dual phone lines, voice mail, irons, hair dryers. **Pool(s):** heated outdoor. **Guest Services:** complimentary laundry. **Business Services:** meeting rooms. **Cards:** AX, CB, DC, DS, JC, MC, VI. **Special Amenities: free expanded continental breakfast and free newspaper.**

SOME UNITS

BEST WESTERN SAN JOSE LODGE Book at aaa.com

Phone: (408)453-7750

AAA SAVE

Motel

All Year 1P: $79-$99 2P: $79-$99 XP: $5 F16

Location: 1 mi e of San Jose International Airport; s off US 101. 1440 N 1st St 95112. Fax: 408/437-9519. **Facility:** 75 one-bedroom standard units. 2 stories (no elevator), exterior corridors. *Bath:* combo or shower only. **Parking:** on-site. **Terms:** [CP] meal plan available. **Amenities:** irons, hair dryers. **Pool(s):** outdoor. **Guest Services:** valet laundry. **Business Services:** fax (fee). **Cards:** AX, CB, DC, DS, MC, VI. **Special Amenities: free continental breakfast and free local telephone calls.**

SOME UNITS

THE CLARION PRESIDENT INN Book at aaa.com

Phone: (408)972-2200

AAA SAVE

Motel

All Year 1P: $79-$299 2P: $79-$299 XP: $10 F18

Location: US 101, exit Tully, just s. 3200 Monterey Rd 95111. Fax: 408/972-2632. **Facility:** 47 units. 44 one-bedroom standard units, some with whirlpools. 3 one-bedroom suites with whirlpools. 2-3 stories, interior corridors. **Parking:** on-site. **Terms:** [ECP] meal plan available. **Amenities:** high-speed Internet, dual phone lines, voice mail, irons, hair dryers. **Pool(s):** heated outdoor. **Leisure Activities:** whirlpool, exercise room. **Guest Services:** valet and coin laundry. **Cards:** AX, DC, DS, JC, MC, VI. **Special Amenities: free expanded continental breakfast and free newspaper.**

SOME UNITS

COMFORT INN Book at aaa.com

Phone: (408)287-9380

Small-scale Hotel

All Year [ECP] 1P: $89-$129 2P: $94-$134 XP: $5 F16

Location: US 101, exit 13th St/Old Oakland Rd, just w. Located in a industrial area. 875 N 13th St 95112. Fax: 408/287-9950. **Facility:** 45 units. 43 one-bedroom standard units. 2 one-bedroom suites ($119-$159). 3 stories, interior corridors. **Parking:** on-site. **Terms:** cancellation fee imposed. **Amenities:** high-speed Internet, dual phone lines, voice mail, irons, hair dryers. **Business Services:** meeting rooms. **Cards:** AX, CB, DC, DS, JC, MC, VI.

SOME UNITS

COMFORT SUITES AIRPORT Book at aaa.com

Phone: (408)392-9009

Small-scale Hotel

All Year [BP] 1P: $89-$139 2P: $89-$139

Location: US 101, exit 1st St, just s. 1510 N 1st St 95112. Fax: 408/392-9020. **Facility:** 51 one-bedroom standard units. 3 stories, interior corridors. *Bath:* combo or shower only. **Parking:** on-site. **Amenities:** video library, high-speed Internet, dual phone lines, voice mail, irons, hair dryers. **Leisure Activities:** exercise room. **Guest Services:** valet and coin laundry. **Business Services:** meeting rooms. **Cards:** AX, CB, DC, DS, JC, MC, VI.

SOME UNITS

CROWNE PLAZA HOTEL AND RESORT SAN JOSE Book at aaa.com

Phone: (408)998-0400

AAA SAVE

Large-scale Hotel

All Year 1P: $129-$189 2P: $129-$189

Location: 6 blks n off I-280, exit Almaden-Vine. Located opposite convention center. 282 Almaden Blvd 95113. Fax: 408/289-9081. **Facility:** 239 one-bedroom standard units. 9 stories, interior corridors. **Parking:** on-site (fee). **Terms:** cancellation fee imposed. **Amenities:** dual phone lines, voice mail, irons, hair dryers. *Fee:* video games, high-speed Internet. **Dining:** 6 am-10 pm, cocktails. **Leisure Activities:** exercise room. **Guest Services:** gift shop, valet laundry. **Business Services:** meeting rooms, business center. **Cards:** AX, CB, DC, DS, MC, VI. *(See color ad p 694)*

SOME UNITS

DOUBLETREE HOTEL Book at aaa.com

Phone: (408)453-4000

AAA SAVE

Large-scale Hotel

All Year 1P: $79-$259 2P: $79-$259 XP: $10 F18

Location: 0.3 mi e of San Jose International Airport via Airport Blvd; w of US 101, exit N 1st St; US 101 northbound, exit Brokaw Rd. 2050 Gateway Pl 95110. Fax: 408/437-2898. **Facility:** Extensive conference facilities are featured at this hotel, which has spacious, well-appointed guest rooms and public areas. 505 units. 495 one-bedroom standard units. 10 one-bedroom suites ($695-$895) with whirlpools. 10 stories, interior corridors. **Parking:** on-site. **Terms:** cancellation fee imposed, pets ($100 deposit). **Amenities:** dual phone lines, voice mail, irons, hair dryers. *Fee:* video games, high-speed Internet. *Some:* CD players. **Dining:** 2 restaurants, 6 am-10 pm, also, Madrone, see separate listing. **Pool(s):** heated outdoor. **Leisure Activities:** whirlpool, exercise room. **Guest Services:** gift shop, valet laundry. **Business Services:** conference facilities, business center. **Cards:** AX, CB, DC, DS, JC, MC, VI. **Special Amenities: free newspaper.** *(See color ad p 689)*

SOME UNITS

FEE FEE

EXECUTIVE INN-AIRPORT *Book at aaa.com* **Phone:** (408)453-1100

Motel

All Year 1P: $79-$109 2P: $79-$109 XP: $10 F12

Location: 1 mi e of San Jose Airport at E Rosemary St. 1310 N 1st St 95112. Fax: 408/453-1890. **Facility:** Smoke free premises. 56 one-bedroom standard units. 2 stories, exterior corridors. **Parking:** on-site. **Terms:** [CP] meal plan available. **Amenities:** irons, hair dryers. **Pool(s):** small heated outdoor. **Leisure Activities:** whirlpool. **Guest Services:** coin laundry. **Cards:** AX, DC, DS, MC, VI. **Special Amenities: free expanded continental breakfast and early check-in/late check-out.**

EXECUTIVE INN SUITES *Book at aaa.com* **Phone:** (408)281-8700

Motel

All Year 1P: $79-$109 2P: $79-$109

Location: On SR 82, just n of jct CR 6-21. 3930 Monterey Rd 95111. Fax: 408/578-6799. **Facility:** 25 one-bedroom standard units. 2 stories (no elevator), exterior corridors. **Parking:** on-site. **Terms:** [CP] meal plan available. **Amenities:** dual phone lines, voice mail, irons, hair dryers. **Cards:** AX, DC, DS, MC, VI. **Special Amenities: free expanded continental breakfast and early check-in/late check-out.**

SOME UNITS

FAIRFIELD INN AND SUITES *Book at aaa.com* **Phone:** (408)453-3133

Small-scale Hotel

All Year [ECP] 1P: $79-$159 2P: $79-$159 XP: $10 F18

Location: US 101, exit N 1st St, just w. 1755 N 1st St 95112. Fax: 408/452-1849. **Facility:** 186 one-bedroom standard units. 3 stories, interior corridors. *Bath:* combo or shower only. **Parking:** on-site. **Amenities:** video games (fee), high-speed Internet, dual phone lines, voice mail, safes, irons, hair dryers. **Pool(s):** heated outdoor. **Leisure Activities:** whirlpool, exercise room. **Guest Services:** valet and coin laundry, area transportation-within 3 mi. **Business Services:** conference facilities, business center. **Cards:** AX, CB, DC, DS, JC, MC, VI. **Special Amenities: free expanded continental breakfast and free local telephone calls.**

SOME UNITS

FEE

THE FAIRMONT SAN JOSE *Book at aaa.com* **Phone:** 408/998-1900

Large-scale Hotel

Property failed to provide current rates

Location: At Fairmont Plaza. 170 S Market St 95113. Fax: 408/287-1648. **Facility:** The hotel, walking distance from the convention center, has an elegant ambience; poolside lanais adjoin some rooms. 805 units. 731 one-bedroom standard units. 74 one-bedroom suites. 20 stories, interior corridors. **Parking:** on-site (fee). **Terms:** small pets only ($50 fee). **Amenities:** video games (fee), dual phone lines, voice mail, honor bars, irons, hair dryers. *Some:* CD players, safes. *Fee:* DVD players, high-speed Internet. **Pool(s):** heated outdoor. **Leisure Activities:** saunas. *Fee:* massage. **Guest Services:** gift shop, valet laundry. **Business Services:** conference facilities, business center.

SOME UNITS

FEE FEE

HAMPTON INN AND SUITES *Book at aaa.com* **Phone:** (408)298-7373

Motel

All Year [ECP] 1P: $69-$299 2P: $79-$309

Location: US 101, exit Tully Rd, 1 mi w, then just s on Seventh St/Old Tully Rd. 55 Old Tully Rd 95111. Fax: 408/291-0303. **Facility:** 80 units. 59 one-bedroom standard units. 21 one-bedroom suites ($109-$399). 3 stories, interior corridors. *Bath:* combo or shower only. **Parking:** on-site. **Terms:** cancellation fee imposed, package plans - weekends. **Amenities:** video games (fee), high-speed Internet, dual phone lines, voice mail, irons, hair dryers. **Pool(s):** heated outdoor. **Leisure Activities:** exercise room. **Guest Services:** complimentary laundry. **Business Services:** meeting rooms. **Cards:** AX, CB, DC, DS, JC, MC. **Special Amenities: free expanded continental breakfast and free local telephone calls.**

SOME UNITS

HAYES MANSION CONFERENCE CENTER *Book at aaa.com* **Phone:** 408/226-3200

Large-scale Hotel

All Year 1P: $135-$295 2P: $135-$295 XP: $15 F12

Location: US 101, exit Blossom Hill Rd W, 1 mi n on Lean Ave. 200 Edenvale Ave 95136. Fax: 408/362-2377. **Facility:** 214 units. 192 one-bedroom standard units. 22 one-bedroom suites ($195-$895). 2-3 stories, interior corridors. **Parking:** on-site. **Terms:** cancellation fee imposed, package plans - weekends. **Amenities:** video games (fee), dual phone lines, voice mail, safes, irons, hair dryers. *Some:* CD players, high-speed Internet. **Pool(s):** heated outdoor. **Leisure Activities:** whirlpool, exercise room, spa. **Guest Services:** area transportation. **Business Services:** conference facilities, business center. **Cards:** AX, DC, DS, MC, VI.

SOME UNITS

FEE

HILTON SAN JOSE & TOWERS Book at aaa.com **Phone:** (408)287-2100

Large-scale Hotel

All Year 1P: $89-$249 2P: $89-$249 XP: $20 F18

Location: Downtown. Located adjacent to the convention center. 300 Almaden Blvd 95110. Fax: 408/947-4489. **Facility:** 355 units. 340 one-bedroom standard units. 15 one-bedroom suites ($119-$279), some with whirlpools. 18 stories, interior corridors. **Parking:** on-site (fee). **Terms:** check-in 4 pm, cancellation fee imposed, small pets only (credit card deposit). **Amenities:** dual phone lines, voice mail, irons, hair dryers. *Fee:* video games, high-speed Internet. *Some:* fax, honor bars. **Dining:** 6 am-midnight, cocktails. **Pool(s):** heated outdoor. **Leisure Activities:** whirlpool, exercise room. **Guest Services:** gift shop, valet and coin laundry. **Business Services:** conference facilities, business center. **Cards:** AX, CB, DC, DS, JC, MC, VI. *(See ad below)*

SOME UNITS

HOLIDAY INN EXPRESS CENTRAL CITY Book at aaa.com **Phone:** (408)279-6600

Motel

All Year [CP] 2P: $79-$109

Location: US 101, exit Tully W, just s. 2660 Monterey Rd 95111. Fax: 408/279-1064. **Facility:** 57 one-bedroom standard units, some with whirlpools. 2 stories (no elevator), exterior corridors. *Bath:* combo or shower only. **Parking:** on-site. **Terms:** cancellation fee imposed, package plans - weekends. **Amenities:** high-speed Internet, dual phone lines, voice mail, irons, hair dryers. **Pool(s):** outdoor. **Leisure Activities:** sauna, whirlpool, exercise room. **Guest Services:** valet and coin laundry. **Business Services:** meeting rooms. **Cards:** AX, CB, DC, DS, JC, MC. **Special Amenities: free newspaper and early check-in/late check-out.** *(See color ad p 260)*

SOME UNITS

FEE

HOLIDAY INN EXPRESS-SAN JOSE INTERNATIONAL AIRPORT *Book at aaa.com* **Phone:** (408)467-1789

Motel

All Year [ECP] 1P: $129-$165 2P: $129-$165

Location: US 101, exit N 1st St, 0.5 mi s to Rosemary St E. 1350 N 4th St 95112. Fax: 408/467-1788. **Facility:** 126 units. 85 one-bedroom standard units. 41 one-bedroom suites ($135-$165) with efficiencies. 3 stories, interior corridors. **Parking:** on-site. **Amenities:** video games (fee), dual phone lines, voice mail, irons, hair dryers. **Pool(s):** outdoor. **Leisure Activities:** whirlpool, exercise room. **Guest Services:** coin laundry. **Business Services:** meeting rooms. **Cards:** AX, CB, DC, DS, JC, MC, VI. **Special Amenities: free expanded continental breakfast and free local telephone calls.** *(See color ad p 260)*

SOME UNITS

HOLIDAY INN SOUTH SAN JOSE *Book at aaa.com* **Phone:** (408)972-7800

Small-scale Hotel

All Year 1P: $79-$109

Location: US 101, exit Bernal Rd E. 399 Silicon Valley Blvd 95138. Fax: 408/972-0157. **Facility:** 208 units. 184 one-bedroom standard units. 24 one-bedroom suites ($109-$139). 3 stories, interior corridors. **Parking:** on-site. **Terms:** cancellation fee imposed, [AP] meal plan available, package plans, 15% service charge. **Amenities:** dual phone lines, voice mail, irons, hair dryers. **Pool(s):** heated outdoor. **Leisure Activities:** whirlpool, exercise room. **Guest Services:** valet laundry. **Business Services:** meeting rooms. **Cards:** AX, CB, DC, DS, JC, MC, VI. ***(See color ad below)***

SOME UNITS

FEE FEE

HOMESTEAD STUDIO SUITES HOTEL-SAN JOSE *Book at aaa.com* **Phone:** (408)573-0648

Small-scale Hotel

All Year 1P: $90-$110 2P: $95-$115 XP: $5 F17

Location: 1 mi e of San Jose International Airport; US 101, exit N 1st St, then s. 1560 N 1st St 95112. Fax: 408/573-0647. **Facility:** 153 one-bedroom standard units with efficiencies. 3 stories, interior corridors. *Bath:* combo or shower only. **Parking:** on-site. **Terms:** weekly rates available, small pets only ($75 fee). **Amenities:** high-speed Internet (fee), dual phone lines, voice mail, irons, hair dryers. **Guest Services:** coin laundry. **Cards:** AX, CB, DC, DS, JC, MC, VI.

SOME UNITS

FEE FEE

HOMEWOOD SUITES BY HILTON *Book at aaa.com* **Phone:** (408)428-9900

Motel

All Year 1P: $159-$199

Location: 2 mi ne of San Jose International Airport; US 101, exit Trimble Rd, 1.3 mi e. 10 W Trimble Rd 95131. Fax: 408/428-0222. **Facility:** 140 units. 127 one- and 13 two-bedroom suites with efficiencies. 2-3 stories, interior/exterior corridors. **Parking:** on-site. **Terms:** [BP] meal plan available, pets ($75 fee). **Amenities:** video games (fee), dual phone lines, voice mail, irons, hair dryers. **Pool(s):** heated outdoor. **Leisure Activities:** whirlpool, exercise room, sports court. **Guest Services:** gift shop, complimentary evening beverages: Mon-Thurs, valet and coin laundry, area transportation. **Business Services:** conference facilities, business center. **Cards:** AX, CB, DC, DS, JC, MC, VI.

SOME UNITS

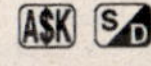

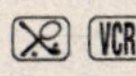
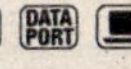

FEE

HOTEL DE ANZA Book at aaa.com

Large-scale Hotel

All Year 1P: $109-$399 2P: $109-$399 XP: $15 F12 Phone: (408)286-1000

Location: Downtown. 233 W Santa Clara St 95113. Fax: 408/286-0500. **Facility:** This attractively restored 1931 hotel has reintroduced elegance to the downtown San Jose area; its guest units and public areas are well appointed. 101 units. 95 one-bedroom standard units. 6 one-bedroom suites ($350-$1500) with whirlpools. 10 stories, interior corridors. **Parking:** valet. **Terms:** cancellation fee imposed. **Amenities:** video library, CD players, high-speed Internet (fee), dual phone lines, voice mail, honor bars, irons, hair dryers. **Dining:** 11 am-10 pm, cocktails, entertainment. **Leisure Activities:** exercise room. **Guest Services:** valet laundry, airport transportation (fee)-San Jose & San Francisco International airports. **Business Services:** meeting rooms, business center. **Cards:** AX, DC, DS, JC, MC, VI. **Special Amenities: free newspaper.**

SOME UNITS FEE

HOWARD JOHNSON Book at aaa.com

Motel

All Year 1P: $89-$149 2P: $99-$149 XP: $5 D16 Phone: (408)280-5300

Location: Jct I-280 and SR 82, 0.8 mi s. 1215 S 1st St 95110. Fax: 408/280-0569. **Facility:** 57 one-bedroom standard units, some with whirlpools. 2 stories, exterior corridors. **Parking:** on-site. **Terms:** [ECP] meal plan available. **Amenities:** irons, hair dryers. **Guest Services:** valet laundry. **Cards:** AX, CB, DC, DS, MC, VI. **Special Amenities: free continental breakfast and free newspaper.**

SOME UNITS

HYATT SAINTE CLAIRE-DOWNTOWN SAN JOSE Book at aaa.com

Historic Large-scale Hotel

All Year 1P: $99-$249 2P: $99-$249 XP: $20 F18 Phone: (408)885-1234

Location: Opposite convention center. 302 S Market St 95113-2889. Fax: 408/977-0403. **Facility:** This beautifully restored 1926 Hotel is located downtown, and features spacious and attractively appointed public areas. 171 one-bedroom standard units. 6 stories, interior corridors. **Parking:** valet. **Terms:** cancellation fee imposed. **Amenities:** high-speed Internet (fee), dual phone lines, voice mail, safes, honor bars, irons, hair dryers. **Dining:** 7 am-11 pm, Fri-midnight, Sat 8 am-midnight, Sun 8 am-11 pm, cocktails. **Leisure Activities:** exercise room. **Guest Services:** valet laundry. **Business Services:** conference facilities. **Cards:** AX, CB, DC, DS, JC, MC, VI.

SOME UNITS FEE

HYATT SAN JOSE Book at aaa.com

Large-scale Hotel

All Year 1P: $79-$229 2P: $79-$229 XP: $20 F18 Phone: (408)993-1234

Location: 0.5 mi e of San Jose International Airport via Airport Pkwy; w of US 101, exit N 1st St. 1740 N 1st St 95112. Fax: 408/453-0259. **Facility:** 512 units. 500 one-bedroom standard units. 12 one-bedroom suites, some with whirlpools. 2-3 stories, interior corridors. *Bath:* combo or shower only. **Parking:** on-site. **Terms:** cancellation fee imposed. **Amenities:** high-speed Internet, dual phone lines, voice mail, irons, hair dryers. **Dining:** 2 restaurants, 11 am-2 & 5-10 pm, cocktails. **Pool(s):** heated outdoor. **Leisure Activities:** whirlpool, jogging, exercise room. **Guest Services:** gift shop, valet laundry. **Business Services:** conference facilities. **Cards:** AX, CB, DC, DS, JC, MC, VI.

SOME UNITS

THE MOORPARK HOTEL Book at aaa.com

Small-scale Hotel

All Year 1P: $189-$209 2P: $189-$209 XP: $10 F12 Phone: (408)864-0300

Location: I-280, exit Saratoga, just w. 4241 Moorpark Ave 95129. Fax: 408/864-0350. **Facility:** Smoke free premises. 79 one-bedroom standard units. 3 stories, interior corridors. *Bath:* combo or shower only. **Parking:** on-site. **Terms:** cancellation fee imposed, [BP] & [CP] meal plans available. **Amenities:** video library, DVD players, CD players, high-speed Internet, dual phone lines, voice mail, honor bars, irons, hair dryers. **Pool(s):** heated outdoor. **Leisure Activities:** whirlpool, exercise room. **Guest Services:** complimentary evening beverages. **Business Services:** meeting rooms, business center. **Cards:** AX, CB, DC, DS, MC, VI.

PARK PLAZA Book at aaa.com

Motel

All Year 1P: $69-$149 XP: $10 F12 Phone: (408)453-5340

Location: 0.5 mi e of San Jose International Airport; US 101, exit N 1st St, 0.5 mi s to Rosemary St E. Located in a quiet area. 1355 N Fourth St 95112. Fax: 408/453-5208. **Facility:** 194 one-bedroom standard units. 2 stories, exterior corridors. **Parking:** on-site. **Terms:** package plans. **Amenities:** voice mail, irons, hair dryers. *Fee:* video games, high-speed Internet. **Pool(s):** heated outdoor. **Leisure Activities:** whirlpool, putting green, exercise room. **Guest Services:** valet and coin laundry, area transportation. **Business Services:** meeting rooms. **Cards:** AX, CB, DC, DS, JC, MC, VI. ***(See color ad p 693)***

SOME UNITS FEE FEE

RADISSON PLAZA HOTEL, SAN JOSE AIRPORT Book at aaa.com

Large-scale Hotel

All Year 1P: $79-$209 2P: $79-$209 XP: $10 F18 Phone: (408)452-0200

Location: 0.5 mi n of San Jose International Airport; US 101, exit N 1st St. 1471 N 4th St 95112. Fax: 408/437-8819. **Facility:** 196 units. 187 one-bedroom standard units. 9 one-bedroom suites. 5 stories, interior corridors. **Parking:** on-site. **Terms:** cancellation fee imposed. **Amenities:** dual phone lines, voice mail, irons, hair dryers. *Fee:* video games, high-speed Internet. **Pool(s):** heated outdoor. **Leisure Activities:** exercise room. **Business Services:** meeting rooms. **Cards:** AX, CB, DC, DS, JC, MC, VI. ***(See color ad p 629)***

SOME UNITS FEE

RESIDENCE INN BY MARRIOTT Book at aaa.com

Small-scale Hotel

Property failed to provide current rates Phone: 408/226-7676

Location: US 101, exit Bernal Rd, then e. 6111 San Ignacio Ave 95119. Fax: 408/226-9916. **Facility:** 150 units. 64 one-bedroom standard units with kitchens. 62 one- and 24 two-bedroom suites with kitchens. 3 stories, interior corridors. *Bath:* combo or shower only. **Parking:** on-site. **Terms:** pets ($75 fee, $10 extra charge). **Amenities:** video games (fee), dual phone lines, voice mail, irons, hair dryers. **Pool(s):** outdoor. **Leisure Activities:** whirlpool, exercise room, sports court. **Guest Services:** valet and coin laundry. **Business Services:** meeting rooms.

SAN JOSE AIRPORT COURTYARD *Book at aaa.com* **Phone:** 408/441-6111

Small-scale Hotel

All Year 1P: $149-$169

Location: 0.5 mi e of San Jose International Airport via Airport Pkwy; US 101, exit N 1st St, 0.3 mi w to Skyport Dr. 1727 Technology Dr 95110. Fax: 408/441-8039. **Facility:** 151 units. 143 one-bedroom standard units. 8 one-bedroom suites. 4 stories, interior corridors. **Parking:** on-site. **Terms:** cancellation fee imposed. **Amenities:** high-speed Internet (fee), dual phone lines, voice mail, irons, hair dryers. **Pool(s):** heated outdoor. **Leisure Activities:** whirlpool, exercise room. **Guest Services:** coin laundry. **Business Services:** meeting rooms. **Cards:** AX, CB, DC, DS, JC, MC.

SOME UNITS

SAN JOSE RAMADA LIMITED *Book at aaa.com* **Phone:** (408)298-3500

AAA SAVE

Motel

All Year [ECP] 1P: $95-$149 2P: $105-$169 XP: $5 F17

Location: SR 82, just e. 455 S 2nd St 95113. Fax: 408/298-2477. **Facility:** 72 one-bedroom standard units. 3 stories, exterior corridors. *Bath:* combo or shower only. **Parking:** on-site. **Amenities:** voice mail, irons, hair dryers. **Pool(s):** outdoor. **Leisure Activities:** exercise room. **Business Services:** meeting rooms. **Cards:** AX, CB, DC, DS, JC, MC, VI. **Special Amenities: free expanded continental breakfast and free newspaper.**

SOME UNITS

SIERRA SUITES *Book at aaa.com* **Phone:** (408)453-3000

Small-scale Hotel

All Year [ECP] 1P: $79-$179 2P: $79-$179

Location: US 101, exit First St/Brokaw Rd, just e. 55 E Brokaw Rd 95112. Fax: 408/453-3066. **Facility:** 138 one-bedroom standard units with efficiencies. 4 stories, interior corridors. *Bath:* combo or shower only. **Parking:** on-site. **Amenities:** high-speed Internet, dual phone lines, voice mail, irons, hair dryers. **Pool(s):** heated outdoor. **Leisure Activities:** whirlpool, exercise room. **Guest Services:** coin laundry. **Cards:** AX, CB, DC, DS, JC, MC, VI.

SOME UNITS

SUMMERFIELD SUITES BY WYNDHAM-SAN JOSE/SILICON VALLEY *Book at aaa.com* **Phone:** (408)436-1600

AAA SAVE

Motel

All Year 1P: $89-$159 2P: $89-$159 XP: $20 F18

Location: US 101, exit Brokaw Rd E, 0.4 mi to Bering S, then 0.5 mi. 1602 Crane Ct 95112. Fax: 408/436-1075. **Facility:** 114 units. 58 one- and 56 two-bedroom suites ($89-$209) with kitchens. 3 stories, exterior corridors. **Parking:** on-site. **Terms:** cancellation fee imposed, [MAP] meal plan available, pets ($100-$200 fee, $10 extra charge). **Amenities:** CD players, dual phone lines, voice mail, irons, hair dryers. *Fee:* video library, high-speed Internet. **Pool(s):** heated outdoor. **Leisure Activities:** whirlpool, exercise room. **Guest Services:** gift shop, valet laundry, area transportation-within 3 mi. **Business Services:** meeting rooms, fax. **Cards:** AX, CB, DC, DS, JC, MC, VI.

SOME UNITS

FEE

SUPER 8-SAN JOSE *Book at aaa.com* **Phone:** (408)293-9361

AAA SAVE — Motel

All Year 1P: $75-$95 2P: $85-$110 XP: $7 F12

Location: I-880, exit The Alameda, just e. 1860 The Alameda 95126. Fax: 408/293-5170. **Facility:** 55 one-bedroom standard units, some with whirlpools. 2 stories, exterior corridors. *Bath:* combo or shower only. **Parking:** on-site. **Amenities:** voice mail, irons, hair dryers. **Pool(s):** outdoor. **Cards:** AX, CB, DC, DS, JC, MC, VI. **Special Amenities: early check-in/late check-out and preferred room (subject to availability with advanced reservations).**

SOME UNITS

FEE

TRAVELODGE-SAN JOSE CONVENTION CENTER *Book at aaa.com* **Phone:** (408)993-1711

AAA SAVE — Motel

All Year 1P: $69-$129 2P: $69-$129 XP: $5 F17

Location: 1 mi s of I-280 and SR 82 via S 1st St. 1415 Monterey Rd 95110. Fax: 408/993-8744. **Facility:** 26 one-bedroom standard units. 2 stories, exterior corridors. **Parking:** on-site. **Terms:** cancellation fee imposed, [CP] meal plan available. **Amenities:** voice mail, hair dryers. **Cards:** AX, CB, DC, DS, MC, VI. **Special Amenities: free continental breakfast and free newspaper.**

SOME UNITS

VAGABOND *Book at aaa.com* **Phone:** (408)453-8822

AAA SAVE — Motel

All Year [CP] 1P: $59-$89 2P: $59-$89 XP: $5 F18

Location: I-880, exit N 1st St, then w. 1488 N 1st St 95112. Fax: 408/453-0559. **Facility:** 76 one-bedroom standard units. 2 stories (no elevator), exterior corridors. **Parking:** on-site. **Terms:** small pets only ($25 deposit). **Amenities:** voice mail. *Some:* irons, hair dryers. **Pool(s):** heated outdoor. **Leisure Activities:** whirlpool. **Guest Services:** coin laundry. **Cards:** AX, CB, DC, DS, MC, VI. **Special Amenities: free continental breakfast and free local telephone calls.**

SOME UNITS

FEE

VALLEY INN *Book at aaa.com* **Phone:** (408)241-8500

AAA SAVE — Motel

All Year [CP] 1P: $69-$79 2P: $79-$89 XP: $10 F5

Location: I-880, exit The Alameda, just w. 2155 The Alameda 95126. Fax: 408/241-8573. **Facility:** 26 one-bedroom standard units. 2 stories (no elevator), exterior corridors. *Bath:* combo or shower only. **Parking:** on-site. **Terms:** cancellation fee imposed. **Cards:** AX, CB, DC, DS, MC, VI. **Special Amenities: free continental breakfast and free local telephone calls.**

SOME UNITS

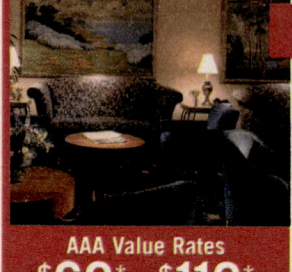

VALLEY PARK HOTEL Book at aaa.com **Phone:** (408)293-5000

AAA SAVE

Small-scale Hotel

All Year 1P: $99 2P: $129 XP: $10 F15

Location: I-880, exit W San Carlos, 0.3 mi e. 2404 Stevens Creek Blvd 95128. Fax: 408/293-5287. **Facility:** 55 one-bedroom standard units with efficiencies (no utensils) and whirlpools. 3 stories, interior corridors. **Parking:** on-site. **Terms:** cancellation fee imposed, [BP] meal plan available. **Amenities:** video games (fee), dual phone lines, voice mail, irons, hair dryers. **Guest Services:** coin laundry. **Business Services:** meeting rooms. **Cards:** AX, CB, DC, DS, JC, MC, VI. **Special Amenities: free continental breakfast and free newspaper.**

SOME UNITS

WYNDHAM SAN JOSE Book at aaa.com **Phone:** (408)453-6200

AAA SAVE

Large-scale Hotel

All Year 1P: $69-$129 2P: $69-$139 XP: $10 F18

Location: US 101, exit N 1st St, 0.3 mi s; 1 mi e of San Jose International Airport via Airport Pkwy, just s. 1350 N 1st St 95112. Fax: 408/437-9693. **Facility:** 355 one-bedroom standard units. 9 stories, interior corridors. *Bath:* combo or shower only. **Parking:** on-site. **Terms:** cancellation fee imposed. **Amenities:** voice mail, irons, hair dryers. *Fee:* video games, high-speed Internet. **Dining:** 2 restaurants, 6 am-2 & 5-10 pm, cocktails. **Pool(s):** heated outdoor. **Leisure Activities:** exercise room. **Guest Services:** gift shop, valet laundry. **Business Services:** conference facilities, PC, fax. **Cards:** AX, CB, DC, DS, JC, MC, VI. *(See color ad p 694)*

SOME UNITS

FEE

The following lodgings were either not evaluated or did not meet AAA rating requirements but are listed for your information only.

HOTEL VALENCIA SANTANA ROW **Phone:** 408/551-0010

fyi

Small-scale Hotel

All Year 1P: $295-$355 2P: $295-$355 XP: $25 F18

Too new to rate, opening scheduled for September 2003. **Location:** I-880, Stevens Creek Blvd, just w. Located in the Santana Row Shopping area. 355 Santana Row 95128. Fax: 408/551-0550. **Amenities:** 213 units, restaurant, microwaves, refrigerators, pool. **Terms:** cancellation fee imposed. **Cards:** AX, CB, DC, DS, JC, MC, VI.

SLEEP INN SILICON VALLEY **Phone:** 408/434-9330

fyi

Motel

5/1-9/30 [ECP] 1P: $79-$109 2P: $89-$119 XP: $10 F18

2/1-4/30 & 10/1-1/31 [ECP] 1P: $69-$89 2P: $79-$99 XP: $10 F18

Too new to rate, opening scheduled for September 2003. **Location:** I-880, exit Montague Expwy, then e. 2390 Harris Way 95131. Fax: 408/434-9915. **Amenities:** 49 units, coffeemakers, microwaves, refrigerators. **Cards:** AX, DC, DS, MC, VI.

WHERE TO DINE

EIGHT FORTY NORTH FIRST **Lunch:** $11-$20 **Dinner:** $13-$27 **Phone:** 408/282-0840

Continental

Location: 3 blks w of I-880. 840 N 1st St 95112. **Hours:** 11:30 am-9 pm, Sat from 5 pm. Closed major holidays; also Sun. **Reservations:** suggested. **Features:** An extensive wine lists complements diverse preparations of fresh fish and pasta. The comfortable dining room has a casual feel. Dressy casual; cocktails. **Parking:** on-site. **Cards:** AX, DC, DS, MC, VI.

EMILES RESTAURANT **Dinner:** $24-$35 **Phone:** 408/289-1960

French

Location: Center. 545 S 2nd St 95112. **Hours:** 6 pm-10 pm. Closed: 1/1, 12/25; also Sun, Mon & first week of Jan. **Reservations:** suggested. **Features:** Classic French specialties reflect an emphasis on healthy preparation. The atmosphere is warm and inviting. Dressy casual; cocktails. **Parking:** valet. **Cards:** AX, CB, DC, DS, MC, VI.

EULIPIA RESTAURANT & BAR **Dinner:** $15-$30 **Phone:** 408/280-6161

American

Location: 374 S 1st St 95113. **Hours:** 5:30 pm-10 pm, Sun 4:30 pm-9 pm. Closed: 1/1, 7/4, 11/25; also Mon. **Reservations:** suggested. **Features:** Creative and contemporary cuisine lines the restaurant's menu. Attractive decor contributes to the comfortable atmosphere. Casual dress; cocktails. **Parking:** on-site (fee). **Cards:** AX, CB, DC, DS, MC, VI.

GARDEN CITY CASINO & RESTAURANT **Lunch:** $5-$13 **Dinner:** $9-$55 **Phone:** 408/244-4443

American

Location: I-280, exit Saratoga Ave, just n. 360 S Saratoga Ave 95129. **Hours:** 7:30 am-3 am. **Reservations:** suggested. **Features:** A comfortable and attractive interior, marked by a pretty piano, invites guests to unwind. Daily specials rarely disappoint. A casino is adjacent. Casual dress; cocktails; entertainment. **Parking:** on-site. **Cards:** AX, MC, VI.

LOU'S VILLAGE **Lunch:** $11-$27 **Dinner:** $18-$47 **Phone:** 408/293-4570

AAA

Seafood

Location: 3.5 mi s on SR 17 from jct US 101, 1.3 mi e. 1465 W San Carlos St 95126. **Hours:** 11:30 am-10 pm, Sat 4:30 pm-10:30 pm, Sun 4:30 pm-9 pm. Closed: 1/1, 12/25. **Reservations:** suggested. **Features:** Cheerful surroundings and a casual atmosphere make the family-owned restaurant, an area institution since 1946, a good place for the family. On the varied menu are pasta, beef and poultry dishes. Dressy casual; cocktails. **Parking:** on-site. **Cards:** AX, MC, VI.

MADRONE **Lunch:** $9-$18 **Dinner:** $13-$28 **Phone:** 408/453-4000

California

Location: 0.3 mi e of San Jose International Airport via Airport Pkwy; w of US 101, exit N 1st St; US 101 northbound, exit Brokaw Rd; in Doubletree Hotel. 2050 Gateway Pl 95110. **Hours:** 11:30 am-2 & 5-10 pm, Sat & Sun from 5 pm. **Reservations:** suggested. **Features:** Representative of Northern California cuisine are preparations of seafood, chicken, lamb, veal and beef. Dressy casual; cocktails. **Parking:** on-site. **Cards:** AX, CB, DS, MC, VI. ***(See color ad p 689)***

PAOLO'S RESTAURANT **Lunch:** $9-$18 **Dinner:** $15-$34 **Phone:** 408/294-2558

Italian

Location: Just e of SR 87. 333 W San Carlos, Suite 150 95110. **Hours:** 11 am-2:30 & 5:30-10 pm, Sat from 5:30 pm. Closed major holidays; also Sun. **Reservations:** suggested. **Features:** The contemporary Italian menu lists pasta, veal and salmon preparations. Guests can unwind in the attractive dining room. Dressy casual; cocktails. **Parking:** on-site. **Cards:** AX, CB, DC, DS, MC, VI.

SAN JUAN BAUTISTA pop. 1,549

WHERE TO STAY

SAN JUAN INN

Motel

Phone: (831)623-4380

All Year 1P: $69-$89 2P: $79-$99 XP: $10 F

Location: Jct SR 156. Located in a quiet area. 410 The Alameda 95045. Fax: 831/623-0689. **Facility:** 42 one-bedroom standard units. 2 stories (no elevator), exterior corridors. **Parking:** on-site. **Terms:** 2-3 night minimum stay - some weekends, weekly rates available, pets ($15 extra charge). **Pool(s):** outdoor. **Leisure Activities:** whirlpool. **Cards:** AX, DC, MC, VI. **Special Amenities: early check-in/late check-out and free room upgrade (subject to availability with advanced reservations).**

SOME UNITS

FEE

SAN LEANDRO pop. 79,452 (See map and index starting on p. 516)

WHERE TO STAY

SAN LEANDRO MARINA INN *Book at aaa.com*

Phone: (510)895-1311 1

Small-scale Hotel

All Year [ECP] 1P: $99-$109 2P: $99-$109

Location: I-880, exit Marina Blvd, 1.3 mi w. 68 San Leandro Marina 94577. Fax: 510/483-4078. **Facility:** 131 one-bedroom standard units. 3 stories, interior corridors. *Bath:* combo or shower only. **Parking:** on-site. **Amenities:** video games (fee), voice mail, safes, irons, hair dryers. **Pool(s):** outdoor. **Leisure Activities:** whirlpool, bicycles. **Guest Services:** valet laundry, area transportation. **Business Services:** meeting rooms. **Cards:** AX, DC, MC, VI.

SOME UNITS

ASK DATA PORT

SAN LUIS OBISPO pop. 44,174

WHERE TO STAY

APPLE FARM INN

Small-scale Hotel

Phone: (805)544-2040

7/1-8/31	1P: $219-$399	2P: $219-$399	XP: $20	F
2/1-6/30 & 9/1-1/31	1P: $199-$299	2P: $199-$299	XP: $20	F

Location: US 101, exit Monterey St, just s. 2015 Monterey St 93401. Fax: 805/546-9495. **Facility:** This Victorian-style inn painted crisp white with a green roof is surrounded by large trees, colorful flower beds and overflowing hanging baskets. Smoke free premises. 69 one-bedroom standard units, some with whirlpools. 3 stories, interior corridors. **Parking:** on-site. **Terms:** check-in 4 pm, 2 night minimum stay - weekends, package plans. **Amenities:** CD players, voice mail, irons, hair dryers. **Dining:** Apple Farm Restaurant, see separate listing. **Pool(s):** heated outdoor. **Leisure Activities:** whirlpool. *Fee:* massage. **Guest Services:** gift shop, complimentary evening beverages, valet laundry, area transportation-Amtrak station. **Business Services:** meeting rooms, fax (fee). **Cards:** AX, DS, MC, VI. **Special Amenities: free local telephone calls and free newspaper.** *(See color ad below)*

DATA PORT

APPLE FARM TRELLIS COURT

Motel

Phone: (805)544-2040

7/1-8/31	1P: $129-$239	2P: $129-$239	XP: $20	F
2/1-6/30 & 9/1-1/31	1P: $99-$239	2P: $99-$239	XP: $20	F

Location: US 101, exit Monterey St, just s. 2015 Monterey St 93401. Fax: 805/546-9495. **Facility:** Smoke free premises. 35 units. 33 one- and 2 two-bedroom standard units, some with whirlpools. 1-2 stories (no elevator), exterior corridors. *Bath:* combo or shower only. **Parking:** on-site. **Terms:** office hours 9 am-6 pm, check-in 4 pm, 2 night minimum stay - weekends, package plans. **Amenities:** CD players, voice mail, hair dryers. **Pool(s):** heated outdoor. **Leisure Activities:** whirlpool. *Fee:* massage. **Guest Services:** gift shop, complimentary evening beverages, valet laundry, area transportation-Amtrak station. **Business Services:** meeting rooms. **Cards:** AX, DS, MC, VI. **Special Amenities: free local telephone calls and free newspaper.**

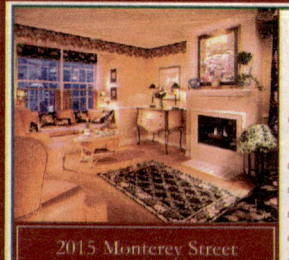

BEST WESTERN ROYAL OAK HOTEL Book at aaa.com Phone: 805/544-4410

Motel

All Year 1P: $79-$150 2P: $79-$150 XP: $10 F12

Location: US 101, exit Madonna Rd, just s. 214 Madonna Rd 93405. Fax: 805/544-3026. **Facility:** 99 one-bedroom standard units. 2 stories (no elevator), interior/exterior corridors. **Parking:** on-site. **Terms:** [ECP] meal plan available, small pets only ($10 extra charge). **Amenities:** voice mail, irons, hair dryers. **Pool(s):** heated outdoor. **Leisure Activities:** whirlpool. **Guest Services:** coin laundry. **Business Services:** meeting rooms. **Cards:** AX, DC, DS, MC, VI. **Special Amenities: free continental breakfast.** *(See color ad p 521)*

SOME UNITS

FEE

DAYS INN Book at aaa.com Phone: (805)549-9911

Motel

All Year 1P: $59-$189 2P: $69-$189 XP: $5 F

Location: US 101, exit Monterey St, just sw. 2050 Garfield St 93401. Fax: 805/546-0734. **Facility:** 75 units. 66 one- and 5 two-bedroom standard units, some with whirlpools. 4 one-bedroom suites. 3 stories, exterior corridors. *Bath:* combo or shower only. **Parking:** on-site. **Terms:** cancellation fee imposed, pets ($10 fee, $50 deposit, dogs only, with prior approval). **Amenities:** high-speed Internet, voice mail, irons, hair dryers. *Some:* dual phone lines. **Pool(s):** heated outdoor. **Leisure Activities:** whirlpool, exercise room. **Guest Services:** valet and coin laundry. **Cards:** AX, CB, DC, DS, JC, MC, VI.

SOME UNITS

FEE

EMBASSY SUITES HOTEL Book at aaa.com Phone: (805)549-0800

Small-scale Hotel

6/1-8/31 [BP]	1P: $129-$269	2P: $139-$279	XP: $10	F18
2/1-5/31 [BP]	1P: $109-$199	2P: $119-$209	XP: $10	F18
9/1-1/31 [BP]	1P: $119-$129	2P: $129-$139	XP: $10	F18

Location: US 101, 0.5 mi sw. Located at east end of SLO Promenade. 333 Madonna Rd 93405. Fax: 805/543-5273. **Facility:** 196 one-bedroom standard units, some with whirlpools. 4 stories, interior corridors. **Parking:** on-site. **Amenities:** voice mail, irons, hair dryers. *Fee:* video games, high-speed Internet. **Dining:** 11:30 am-2 & 5-10 pm. **Pool(s):** heated indoor. **Leisure Activities:** whirlpools, exercise room. **Guest Services:** complimentary evening beverages, valet and coin laundry, area transportation-Amtrak station. **Business Services:** conference facilities. **Cards:** AX, CB, DC, DS, JC, MC, VI. **Special Amenities: free full breakfast and free newspaper.**

SOME UNITS

GARDEN STREET INN BED & BREAKFAST Book at aaa.com Phone: (805)545-9802

Historic Bed & Breakfast

All Year 1P: $140-$200 2P: $140-$200

Location: US 101, exit Marsh St, 0.5 mi e; downtown. 1212 Garden St 93401. Fax: 805/545-9403. **Facility:** Sunlight streaming through stained-glass windows brightens the breakfast room of this 1887 Victorian home; an adjoining library has a fireplace. Smoke free premises. 13 units. 11 one-bedroom standard units, some with whirlpools. 2 one-bedroom suites ($180-$200). 2 stories (no elevator), interior corridors. **Parking:** on-site. **Terms:** 2-3 night minimum stay - weekends, 7 day cancellation notice, [BP] meal plan available, package plans. **Amenities:** hair dryers. *Some:* CD players. **Guest Services:** complimentary evening beverages. **Cards:** AX, MC, VI.

SOME UNITS

HERITAGE INN BED & BREAKFAST Phone: 805/544-7440

Historic Bed & Breakfast

All Year 1P: $85-$185 2P: $85-$185 XP: $10 F18

Location: US 101, exit SR 1/Morro Bay northbound, just w on Santa Rosa St, then just s; exit Santa Rosa St southbound, just ne. 978 Olive St 93405. Fax: 805/544-2819. **Facility:** A turn-of-the-20th-century home with a nicely landscaped sitting area overlooking a creek, the B&B features four rooms with gas fireplaces. Smoke free premises. 7 one-bedroom standard units. 2 stories (no elevator), interior corridors. *Bath:* some shared or private, shower or tub only. **Parking:** on-site. **Terms:** 2 night minimum stay - weekends, 7 day cancellation notice-fee imposed, [BP] meal plan available, small pets only ($25 deposit, $25 extra charge). **Amenities:** hair dryers. **Cards:** AX, CB, DS, MC, VI.

FEE

HOLIDAY INN EXPRESS *Book at aaa.com* **Phone:** (805)544-8600

SAVE

Small-scale Hotel

All Year [CP] 1P: $99-$219 2P: $99-$219 XP: $10 F17

Location: US 101, exit Monterey St, just w. 1800 Monterey St 93401. Fax: 805/541-4698. **Facility:** Smoke free premises. 100 units. 99 one-bedroom standard units. 1 one-bedroom suite. 3 stories, interior corridors. **Parking:** on-site. **Terms:** 2 night minimum stay - seasonal, pets ($25 fee). **Amenities:** video games (fee), dual phone lines, voice mail, irons, hair dryers. **Dining:** 11:30 am-9:30 pm, Fri-Sun to midnight, cocktails. **Pool(s):** heated outdoor. **Leisure Activities:** whirlpool. **Guest Services:** valet laundry. **Business Services:** meeting rooms. **Cards:** AX, DC, DS, MC, VI. **Special Amenities: free continental breakfast and free local telephone calls.**

DATA PORT

FEE

LA CUESTA INN *Book at aaa.com* **Phone:** (805)543-2777

SAVE

Small-scale Hotel

All Year [ECP] 1P: $89-$179 2P: $89-$179 XP: $10 F12

Location: US 101, exit Monterey St, just s. 2074 Monterey St 93401. Fax: 805/544-0696. **Facility:** Smoke free premises. 72 one-bedroom standard units. 4 stories, interior corridors. **Parking:** on-site. **Terms:** cancellation fee imposed. **Amenities:** video library (fee), dual phone lines, voice mail, irons, hair dryers. **Pool(s):** heated outdoor. **Leisure Activities:** whirlpool. **Guest Services:** valet laundry. **Business Services:** meeting rooms. **Cards:** AX, CB, DC, DS, JC, MC, VI. **Special Amenities: free expanded continental breakfast and free local telephone calls.** *(See color ad p 697)*

SOME UNITS

DATA PORT / VCR /

FEE

MORGAN'S MANSIONS LODGING **Phone:** (805)541-1122

SAVE

Small-scale Hotel

All Year [ECP] 1P: $79-$250 2P: $79-$250 XP: $15 F12

Location: US 101, exit Monterey St, just e. 1941 Monterey St 93401. Fax: 805/541-2475. **Facility:** Smoke free premises. 25 one-bedroom standard units, some with whirlpools. 2 stories (no elevator), interior/exterior corridors. *Bath:* combo or shower only. **Parking:** on-site. **Terms:** office hours 7 am-11 pm, check-in 4 pm, weekly rates available. **Amenities:** DVD players, CD players, dual phone lines, voice mail, irons, hair dryers. **Guest Services:** valet laundry. **Cards:** AX, DC, DS, MC, VI. **Special Amenities: free expanded continental breakfast and free local telephone calls.**

PEACH TREE INN — **Phone:** 805/543-3170

Motel

All Year 1P: $59-$150 2P: $69-$175 XP: $10 F5

Location: US 101, exit Monterey St, just s. 2001 Monterey St 93401. Fax: 805/543-7673. **Facility:** Smoke free premises. 37 one-bedroom standard units. 1 story, exterior corridors. *Bath:* combo or shower only. **Parking:** on-site. **Terms:** office hours 7 am-10 pm, cancellation fee imposed, [CP] meal plan available. **Cards:** AX, DS, MC, VI.

ASK

PETIT SOLEIL BED & BREAKFAST — **Phone:** 805/549-0321

Bed & Breakfast

All Year 1P: $125-$225 2P: $125-$225 XP: $10 F13

Location: US 101, exit Monterey St, 0.3 mi sw. 1473 Monterey St 93401. Fax: 805/549-0383. **Facility:** An intimate country inn with a feel of Provence, featuring a cobblestone courtyard leading to guestrooms that are named to match their decor. Smoke free premises. 15 one-bedroom standard units. 2 stories (no elevator), exterior corridors. *Bath:* combo or shower only. **Parking:** on-site. **Terms:** office hours 7 am-10 pm. **Amenities:** CD players, high-speed Internet, voice mail, irons, hair dryers. **Guest Services:** complimentary laundry. **Business Services:** meeting rooms. **Cards:** AX, DS, MC, VI.

QUALITY SUITES *Book at aaa.com* — **Phone:** (805)541-5001

AAA SAVE

Motel

5/21-9/25	1P: $129-$249	2P: $139-$259	XP: $10	F18
9/26-1/31	1P: $119-$199	2P: $129-$209	XP: $10	F18
2/1-5/20	1P: $109-$189	2P: $119-$199	XP: $10	F18

Location: US 101, exit Monterey St, 0.3 mi sw. 1631 Monterey St 93401. Fax: 805/546-9475. **Facility:** 138 one-bedroom suites. 2-3 stories, exterior corridors. **Parking:** on-site. **Amenities:** video library (fee), voice mail, irons, hair dryers. *Some:* dual phone lines. **Pool(s):** heated outdoor, wading. **Leisure Activities:** whirlpool. **Guest Services:** sundries, complimentary evening beverages, valet and coin laundry, area transportation-Amtrak station. **Business Services:** meeting rooms, business center. **Cards:** AX, DC, DS, MC, VI. **Special Amenities: free full breakfast and free newspaper.** *(See color ad below)*

SOME UNITS

RAMADA INN OLIVE TREE *Book at aaa.com* — **Phone:** (805)544-2800

AAA SAVE

Motel

6/1-9/30 [CP]	1P: $69-$179	2P: $79-$199	XP: $10	F12
2/1-5/31 & 10/1-1/31 [CP]	1P: $59-$169	2P: $69-$189	XP: $5	F12

Location: US 101, exit Morro Bay northbound, just w on Santa Rosa St, then just s; exit Santa Rosa St southbound, just ne. 1000 Olive St 93405. Fax: 805/787-0814. **Facility:** Smoke free premises. 48 units. 40 one-bedroom standard units, some with efficiencies. 4 one- and 4 two-bedroom suites ($99-$289) with kitchens. 2 stories (no elevator), exterior corridors. **Parking:** on-site. **Terms:** office hours 7 am-11 pm, 3 day cancellation notice-fee imposed, weekly rates available, small pets only ($25 deposit, $10 extra charge). **Amenities:** voice mail, safes (fee), irons, hair dryers. **Pool(s):** heated outdoor. **Leisure Activities:** sauna. **Guest Services:** coin laundry. **Cards:** AX, CB, DC, DS, JC, MC, VI. **Special Amenities: free continental breakfast and free newspaper.**

FEE

SANDS SUITES & MOTEL **Phone:** (805)544-0500

Motel

5/31-9/15 [ECP]	1P: $69-$219	2P: $69-$219	XP: $10	F12
9/16-12/31 [ECP]	1P: $69-$179	2P: $69-$179	XP: $10	F12
2/1-5/30 & 1/1-1/31 [ECP]	1P: $59-$179	2P: $59-$179	XP: $10	F12

Location: US 101, exit Monterey St, just sw. 1930 Monterey St 93401. Fax: 805/544-3529. **Facility:** 70 units. 56 one-bedroom standard units, some with whirlpools. 14 one-bedroom suites ($89-$289). 2 stories (no elevator), exterior corridors. *Bath:* combo or shower only. **Parking:** on-site. **Terms:** pets ($10 extra charge). **Amenities:** video library, voice mail, irons. *Some:* hair dryers. **Pool(s):** heated outdoor. **Leisure Activities:** whirlpool. **Guest Services:** valet and coin laundry. **Business Services:** meeting rooms. **Cards:** AX, CB, DC, DS, MC, VI. **Special Amenities: free expanded continental breakfast and free local telephone calls.** *(See color ad p 698)*

FEE FEE SOME UNITS

SAN LUIS OBISPO TRAVELODGE Book at aaa.com **Phone:** 805/543-5110

Motel

6/11-9/30	1P: $79-$179	2P: $89-$189	XP: $10
3/17-6/10	1P: $69-$119	2P: $79-$139	XP: $8
2/1-3/16 & 10/1-1/31	1P: $65-$119	2P: $75-$139	XP: $8

Location: US 101, exit Grand Ave northbound, just s, then just e; exit Monterey St southbound. 1825 Monterey St 93401. Fax: 805/543-3406. **Facility:** 39 one-bedroom standard units. 2 stories, exterior corridors. *Bath:* combo or shower only. **Parking:** on-site. **Terms:** office hours 7 am-11 pm, [CP] meal plan available. **Amenities:** hair dryers. **Pool(s):** heated outdoor. **Cards:** AX, CB, DC, DS, MC, VI. **Special Amenities: free continental breakfast and free local telephone calls.**

SOME UNITS

SUPER 8 MOTEL **Phone:** (805)544-6888

Motel

All Year	1P: $49-$119	2P: $59-$129	XP: $5	F17

Location: US 101, exit Monterey St, just e. 1951 Monterey St 93401. Fax: 805/783-0988. **Facility:** 49 one-bedroom standard units. 2 stories (no elevator), exterior corridors. **Parking:** on-site. **Terms:** 1-2 night minimum stay - seasonal & weekends, cancellation fee imposed, small pets only ($50 deposit, $10 extra charge, in designated units). **Amenities:** irons. **Pool(s):** small heated outdoor. **Cards:** AX, CB, DC, DS, JC, MC, VI.

FEE SOME UNITS

SYCAMORE MINERAL SPRINGS Book at aaa.com **Phone:** (805)595-7302

Small-scale Hotel

All Year 2P: $145-$195

Location: US 101, exit Avila Beach Dr, 1 mi w. 1215 Avila Beach Dr 93405. Fax: 805/595-4007. **Facility:** Smoke free premises. 74 units. 26 one-bedroom standard units with whirlpools. 45 one- and 2 two-bedroom suites ($260-$290) with whirlpools. 1 vacation home ($410-$695) with whirlpool. 1-2 stories, exterior corridors. **Parking:** on-site. **Terms:** check-in 4 pm, 3 day cancellation notice. **Amenities:** voice mail, irons, hair dryers. *Some:* dual phone lines. **Pool(s):** heated outdoor. **Leisure Activities:** hiking trails, spa. **Guest Services:** gift shop, valet laundry. **Business Services:** meeting rooms, fax (fee). **Cards:** AX, DS, MC, VI. *(See color ad p 541)*

SOME UNITS

TRAVELODGE DOWNTOWN Book at aaa.com **Phone:** (805)543-6443

Motel

5/27-9/6 [CP]	1P: $80-$100	2P: $90-$110	XP: $10	F18
2/1-5/26 & 9/7-1/31 [CP]	1P: $60-$80	2P: $80-$100	XP: $10	F18

Location: US 101, exit Marsh St, just e. 345 Marsh St 93401. Fax: 805/545-0951. **Facility:** 51 units. 49 one- and 2 two-bedroom standard units. 2 stories (no elevator), exterior corridors. *Bath:* combo or shower only. **Parking:** on-site. **Terms:** office hours 7 am-11 pm, cancellation fee imposed. **Amenities:** hair dryers. **Cards:** AX, CB, DC, DS, MC, VI. **Special Amenities: early check-in/late check-out and free room upgrade (subject to availability with advanced reservations).**

SOME UNITS

The following lodging was either not evaluated or did not meet AAA rating requirements but is listed for your information only.

MADONNA INN **Phone:** 805/543-3000

fyi

Not evaluated. **Location:** US 101, exit Madonna Rd, just w. 100 Madonna Rd 93405. Facilities, services, and decor characterize a basic property.

WHERE TO DINE

ALEX MADONNA'S GOLD RUSH STEAK HOUSE **Dinner:** $20-$26 **Phone:** 805/543-3000

Steak House

Location: US 101, exit Madonna Rd, just w; in Madonna Inn. 100 Madonna Rd 93405. **Hours:** 5:30 pm-10 pm. **Reservations:** suggested. **Features:** Great for special occasions and casual dining, the ornate, distinctively decorated restaurant is splashed definitively in pink. The menu comprises steakhouse fare. Casual dress; cocktails; entertainment. **Parking:** on-site. **Cards:** AX, JC, MC, VI.

APPLE FARM RESTAURANT **Lunch:** $7-$9 **Dinner:** $11-$18 **Phone:** 805/544-6100

American

Location: US 101, exit Monterey St, just s; in Apple Farm Inn. 2015 Monterey St 93401. **Hours:** 7 am-9 pm, Fri & Sat-10 pm; to 10 pm in summer. **Reservations:** suggested. **Features:** Country charm lends to the down-home feel of the busy restaurant. Home-style soups, entrees and desserts are filling and reliably good. Homemade ice cream is a treat. Casual dress; cocktails. **Parking:** on-site. **Cards:** AX, DS, MC, VI.

BENVENUTI RISTORANTE **Lunch:** $7-$11 **Dinner:** $10-$22 **Phone:** 805/541-5393

Italian

Location: US 101, exit Marsh St, 0.3 mi n. 450 Marsh St 93401. **Hours:** 11:30 am-2 & 5-10 pm, Sat & Sun from 5 pm. Closed major holidays. **Reservations:** suggested. **Features:** In a restored home, the charming restaurant offers some seating on the smoker-friendly patio. Tableside food preparation adds a touch of elegance. Casual dress; cocktails. **Parking:** on-site. **Cards:** AX, DC, DS, MC, VI.

BUONA TAVOLA **Lunch:** $7-$14 **Dinner:** $10-$25 **Phone:** 805/545-8000

Italian

Location: US 101, exit Santa Rosa St, 0.4 mi se; next to Fremont Theater. 1037 Monterey St 93401. **Hours:** 11:30 am-2:30 & 5:30-9:30 pm, Fri-10 pm, Sat 5:30 pm-10 pm, Sun 5:30 pm-9:30 pm. Closed major holidays. **Reservations:** suggested. **Features:** Patrons can dine inside the small restaurant or on the patio. The varied menu lists many pasta and antipasto dishes. Casual dress; beer & wine only. **Parking:** street. **Cards:** AX, DS, MC, VI.

CAFE ROMA **Lunch:** $8-$12 **Dinner:** $10-$25 **Phone:** 805/541-6800

Italian

Location: US 101, exit Marsh St northbound, 0.9 mi n to Santa Rosa St, then 0.4 mi e; exit Santa Rosa St southbound, 1 mi e. 1020 Railroad Ave 93401. **Hours:** 11:30 am-2:30 & 5:30-10:30 pm, Sat from 5:30 pm. Closed major holidays; also Sun. **Reservations:** suggested. **Features:** The large, locally popular restaurant serves a nice selection of pasta, veal, chicken, scampi and pizza. Smoking is permitted on the pleasant patio. Casual dress; cocktails. **Parking:** on-site. **Cards:** AX, CB, DC, DS, MC, VI.

LINN'S RESTAURANT **Lunch:** $4-$12 **Dinner:** $9-$18 **Phone:** 805/546-8444

American

Location: US 101, exit Marsh St, 0.6 mi n. 1141 Chorro St 93401. **Hours:** 8 am-10 pm, Fri & Sat-11 pm, Sun-9 pm. Closed: 12/25. **Features:** Although the Reuben sandwich is a staple, this place offers much more, including homemade chicken and beef pot pies, creamy pastries and lip-smacking jams and jellies. Casual dress; beer & wine only. **Parking:** street. **Cards:** AX, DS, MC, VI.

SAN MATEO —See San Francisco p. 676.

SAN MIGUEL pop. 1,427

WHERE TO STAY

WESTERN STATES INN **Phone:** 805/467-3674

SAVE

Motel

All Year 1P: $49-$89 2P: $59-$109 XP: $10 F4

Location: US 101, exit 10th St, just e, then just n. 1099 K St 93451 (PO Box 58). Fax: 805/467-3935. **Facility:** 17 one-bedroom standard units. 2 stories (no elevator), exterior corridors. **Parking:** on-site. **Terms:** 7 day cancellation notice-fee imposed. **Amenities:** *Some:* irons. **Cards:** AX, MC, VI. **Special Amenities: free local telephone calls and preferred room (subject to availability with advanced reservations).**

SOME UNITS

SAN PABLO pop. 30,215

WHERE TO STAY

HOLIDAY INN EXPRESS HOTEL & SUITES *Book at aaa.com* **Phone:** (510)965-1900

Small-scale Hotel

All Year [ECP] 1P: $99-$129 2P: $99-$139 XP: $10 F12

Location: I-80, exit San Pablo Dam Rd N. 2525 San Pablo Dam Rd 94806. Fax: 510/965-1300. **Facility:** 77 units. 73 one-bedroom standard units, some with whirlpools. 4 one-bedroom suites ($159-$229). 3 stories, interior corridors. *Bath:* combo or shower only. **Parking:** on-site. **Terms:** age restrictions may apply, cancellation fee imposed, weekly rates available. **Amenities:** video games, high-speed Internet, dual phone lines, voice mail, irons, hair dryers. **Leisure Activities:** whirlpool, limited exercise equipment. **Guest Services:** coin laundry. **Business Services:** meeting rooms. **Cards:** AX, DC, DS, MC, VI.

SOME UNITS

ASK / DATA PORT

SAN RAFAEL —See San Francisco p. 678.

SAN RAMON pop. 44,722 (See map and index starting on p. 516)

WHERE TO STAY

COURTYARD BY MARRIOTT *Book at aaa.com* **Phone:** (925)866-2900 55

Small-scale Hotel

All Year 1P: $64-$144 2P: $64-$144

Location: I-680, exit Bollinger Canyon Rd W, then s. 18090 San Ramon Valley Blvd 94583. Fax: 925/866-8983. **Facility:** 136 units. 130 one-bedroom standard units. 6 one-bedroom suites with whirlpools. 4 stories, interior corridors. **Parking:** on-site. **Terms:** cancellation fee imposed, package plans. **Amenities:** dual phone lines, voice mail, irons, hair dryers. **Pool(s):** heated outdoor. **Leisure Activities:** whirlpool, exercise room. **Guest Services:** valet and coin laundry. **Business Services:** meeting rooms. **Cards:** AX, DC, DS, JC, MC, VI.

SOME UNITS

ASK / DATA PORT

HOMESTEAD STUDIO SUITES HOTEL-SAN RAMON *Book at aaa.com* **Phone:** (925)277-0833 54

Motel

All Year 1P: $90-$110 2P: $95-$115 XP: $5 F17

Location: I-680, exit Bollinger Canyon Rd E, just n. 18000 San Ramon Valley Blvd 94583. Fax: 925/277-0881. **Facility:** 148 one-bedroom standard units with efficiencies. 3 stories, exterior corridors. *Bath:* combo or shower only. **Parking:** on-site. **Terms:** weekly rates available, pets ($75 extra charge). **Amenities:** dual phone lines, voice mail, irons, hair dryers. **Guest Services:** valet and coin laundry. **Cards:** AX, CB, DC, DS, JC, MC, VI.

SOME UNITS

ASK / FEE / DATA PORT / VCR / FEE

(See map and index starting on p. 516)

RESIDENCE INN BY MARRIOTT *Book at aaa.com* **Phone:** (925)277-9292 57

Small-scale Hotel

All Year [ECP]	1P: $199-$249	2P: $199-$249

Location: I-680, exit Bollinger Canyon Rd E, 0.5 mi e. 1071 Market Pl 94583. Fax: 925/277-0687. **Facility:** 106 units. 82 one- and 24 two-bedroom standard units with kitchens. 2 stories, exterior corridors. *Bath:* combo or shower only. **Parking:** on-site. **Terms:** pets ($125 fee, $5 extra charge). **Amenities:** voice mail, irons, hair dryers. **Pool(s):** heated outdoor. **Leisure Activities:** whirlpool, exercise room, sports court. **Guest Services:** complimentary evening beverages: Mon-Thurs, coin laundry. **Business Services:** meeting rooms. **Cards:** AX, CB, DC, DS, JC, MC, VI.

SOME UNITS

ASK FEE DATA PORT

SAN RAMON MARRIOTT AT BISHOP RANCH *Book at aaa.com* **Phone:** (925)867-9200 56

Large-scale Hotel

All Year	1P: $79-$199

Location: I-680, exit Bollinger Canyon E, n on Sunset, then just w. 2600 Bishop Dr 94583. Fax: 925/830-9326. **Facility:** 368 one-bedroom standard units. 6 stories, interior corridors. **Parking:** on-site. **Terms:** cancellation fee imposed, [BP], [CP] & [ECP] meal plans available, pets ($75 deposit). **Amenities:** video games (fee), voice mail, irons, hair dryers. **Pool(s):** heated outdoor. **Leisure Activities:** saunas, whirlpool, exercise room. **Guest Services:** gift shop, valet and coin laundry. **Business Services:** conference facilities, business center. **Cards:** AX, CB, DC, DS, JC, MC, VI.

SOME UNITS

FEE DATA PORT

SIERRA SUITES HOTEL SAN RAMON *Book at aaa.com* **Phone:** (925)743-1882 53

Small-scale Hotel

All Year [ECP]	1P: $79-$200

Location: I-680, exit Crow Canyon W, just n. 2323 San Ramon Valley Blvd 94583. Fax: 925/743-1784. **Facility:** 142 units. 99 one-bedroom standard units with efficiencies. 43 one-bedroom suites with efficiencies. 4 stories, interior corridors. *Bath:* combo or shower only. **Parking:** on-site. **Terms:** pets ($100-$150 extra charge). **Amenities:** video library (fee), high-speed Internet, voice mail, irons, hair dryers. **Pool(s):** heated outdoor. **Leisure Activities:** whirlpool, exercise room. **Guest Services:** valet and coin laundry. **Business Services:** meeting rooms, business center. **Cards:** AX, DC, DS, MC, VI.

SOME UNITS

ASK FEE VCR DATA PORT

SAN SIMEON

WHERE TO STAY

INNS OF CALIFORNIA-SAN SIMEON **Phone:** (805)927-8659

Motel

7/1-9/15	1P: $64-$149	2P: $79-$229	XP: $5	F14
4/1-6/30	1P: $59-$104	2P: $62-$189	XP: $5	F14
2/1-3/31	1P: $39-$149	2P: $42-$189	XP: $5	F14
9/16-1/31	1P: $39-$79	2P: $49-$129	XP: $5	F14

Location: Just e of SR 1. 9280 Castillo Dr 93452. Fax: 805/927-4800. **Facility:** 48 one-bedroom standard units. 2 stories (no elevator), interior corridors. **Parking:** on-site. **Terms:** office hours 8 am-10 pm. **Amenities:** hair dryers. **Leisure Activities:** whirlpool. *Fee:* game room. **Cards:** AX, DC, DS, MC, VI.

SOME UNITS

ASK VCR DATA PORT

MOTEL 6 PREMIERE - 1212 *Book at aaa.com* **Phone:** 805/927-8691

Small-scale Hotel

6/10-10/2	1P: $67-$89	2P: $73-$95	XP: $3	F17
4/8-6/9	1P: $41-$61	2P: $47-$67	XP: $3	F17
10/3-1/31	1P: $41-$51	2P: $47-$57	XP: $3	F17
2/1-4/7	1P: $39-$49	2P: $45-$55	XP: $3	F17

Location: Just e of SR 1. 9070 Castillo Dr 93452. Fax: 805/927-5341. **Facility:** 100 one-bedroom standard units. 2 stories (no elevator), interior corridors. **Parking:** on-site. **Terms:** pets (limit 1). **Pool(s):** heated outdoor. **Guest Services:** coin laundry. **Cards:** AX, CB, DC, DS, MC, VI.

SOME UNITS

DATA PORT

SANDS BY THE SEA **Phone:** 805/927-3243

Motel

6/1-8/31 [CP]	1P: $85-$125	2P: $85-$150	XP: $5	F
9/1-1/31 [CP]	1P: $50-$100	2P: $50-$130	XP: $5	F
2/1-5/31 [CP]	1P: $45-$95	2P: $45-$110	XP: $5	F

Location: Just w of SR 1. 9355 Hearst Dr 93452. **Facility:** 33 one-bedroom standard units. 2 stories (no elevator), exterior corridors. *Bath:* combo or shower only. **Parking:** on-site. **Terms:** office hours 7:30 am-10 pm. **Amenities:** video library (fee). **Pool(s):** heated indoor. **Cards:** AX, DC, MC, VI.

SOME UNITS

DATA PORT VCR

SAN SIMEON LODGE *Book at aaa.com* **Phone:** (805)927-4601

Small-scale Hotel

7/1-9/6	1P: $75-$135	2P: $75-$135
2/1-6/30 & 9/7-10/31	1P: $65-$85	2P: $65-$85
11/1-1/31	1P: $45-$65	2P: $45-$65

Location: On SR 1. 9520 Castillo Dr 93452. Fax: 805/927-2374. **Facility:** 62 one-bedroom standard units. 2 stories (no elevator), exterior corridors. *Bath:* combo or shower only. **Parking:** on-site. **Terms:** office hours 7 am-10 pm. **Pool(s):** heated outdoor. **Cards:** AX, DS, MC, VI. ***(See color ad p 703)***

SOME UNITS

ASK DATA PORT

SILVER SURF MOTEL Book at aaa.com **Phone:** (805)927-4661

7/1-9/15	1P: $69-$176	2P: $69-$176	XP: $5
4/1-6/30 & 9/16-1/31	1P: $49-$156	2P: $49-$156	XP: $5
2/1-3/31	1P: $39-$142	2P: $39-$142	XP: $5

SAVE Motel

Location: Just e of SR 1. 9390 Castillo Dr 93452. Fax: 805/927-3225. **Facility:** 72 one-bedroom standard units. 2 stories (no elevator), exterior corridors. *Bath:* combo or shower only. **Parking:** on-site. **Terms:** office hours 7 am-10 pm, pets ($10 extra charge). **Pool(s):** small heated indoor/outdoor. **Leisure Activities:** whirlpool. **Guest Services:** coin laundry. **Business Services:** meeting rooms. **Cards:** AX, DC, DS, MC, VI. **Special Amenities: free local telephone calls.**

FEE SOME UNITS

WHERE TO DINE

MANTA REY RESTAURANT **Dinner:** $10-$21 **Phone:** 805/924-1032

American

Location: East side of SR 1. 9240 Castillo Dr 93452. **Hours:** 5 pm-9 pm. Closed: 12/1-12/25. **Reservations:** accepted. **Features:** The small, family-owned and operated eatery focuses its menu on fresh seafood and pasta. Casual dress; beer & wine only. **Parking:** on-site. **Cards:** AX, DS, MC, VI.

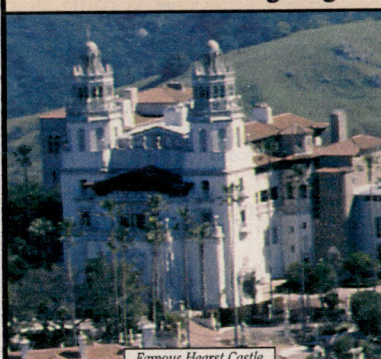

SANTA CLARA pop. 102,361

WHERE TO STAY

BEST WESTERN INN SANTA CLARA *Book at aaa.com* **Phone:** (408)244-3366

SAVE — Motel

All Year 1P: $69-$129 2P: $69-$129 XP: $5 F17

Location: SR 82, 2 blks w of Lawrence Expwy. 4341 El Camino Real 95051. Fax: 408/246-1387. **Facility:** 52 one-bedroom standard units. 2 stories (no elevator), exterior corridors. **Parking:** on-site. **Terms:** cancellation fee imposed, [CP] meal plan available. **Amenities:** video library, dual phone lines, voice mail, irons, hair dryers. **Pool(s):** outdoor. **Guest Services:** coin laundry. **Cards:** AX, CB, DC, DS, MC, VI. **Special Amenities: free continental breakfast and free newspaper.**

SOME UNITS

BILTMORE HOTEL & SUITES/SILICON VALLEY *Book at aaa.com* **Phone:** (408)988-8411

SAVE — Small-scale Hotel

All Year 1P: $59-$129 2P: $59-$129 XP: $10 F17

Location: US 101, exit Montague Expwy, just e; 1 mi s of Great America Pkwy. 2151 Laurelwood Rd 95054. Fax: 408/988-0225. **Facility:** 262 units. 128 one-bedroom standard units. 134 one-bedroom suites. 2-9 stories, interior/exterior corridors. **Parking:** on-site. **Terms:** 3 day cancellation notice, [AP], [BP] & [MAP] meal plans available. **Amenities:** video games (fee), dual phone lines, voice mail, irons, hair dryers. *Some:* honor bars. **Dining:** 6 am-10 pm, cocktails, also, Montague's Cafe, see separate listing. **Pool(s):** heated outdoor. **Leisure Activities:** whirlpool, exercise room. **Guest Services:** valet laundry, area transportation-within 5 mi. **Business Services:** conference facilities, business center. **Cards:** AX, CB, DC, MC, VI.

SOME UNITS

FEE FEE

EMBASSY SUITES HOTEL *Book at aaa.com* **Phone:** (408)496-6400

Large-scale Hotel

All Year 1P: $95-$210 2P: $95-$210 XP: $15 F18

Location: US 101, exit Great America Pkwy, then w. 2885 Lakeside Dr 95054. Fax: 408/988-7529. **Facility:** 257 one-bedroom suites. 10 stories, interior corridors. *Bath:* combo or shower only. **Parking:** on-site. **Terms:** cancellation fee imposed, [BP] meal plan available. **Amenities:** video games (fee), dual phone lines, voice mail, irons, hair dryers. **Pool(s):** heated indoor. **Leisure Activities:** sauna, whirlpool, exercise room. **Guest Services:** gift shop, complimentary evening beverages, valet and coin laundry. **Business Services:** conference facilities. **Cards:** AX, CB, DC, DS, JC, MC, VI. ***(See color ad p 621)***

ASK — SOME UNITS

GRANADA INN-SILICON VALLEY **Phone:** 408/241-2841

Motel

Property failed to provide current rates

Location: US 101, exit San Tomas Expwy, 3 mi s, then just w. 2515 El Camino Real 95051. Fax: 408/241-8559. **Facility:** 67 one-bedroom standard units with efficiencies. 2 stories, interior corridors. *Bath:* combo or shower only. **Parking:** on-site. **Amenities:** video library, dual phone lines, irons, hair dryers. **Guest Services:** complimentary laundry, area transportation. **Business Services:** meeting rooms.

SOME UNITS

GUESTHOUSE INTERNATIONAL INN & SUITES-SILICON VALLEY USA *Book at aaa.com* **Phone:** (408)241-3010

SAVE — Motel

All Year 1P: $79-$129 2P: $89-$145

Location: SR 82, 0.5 mi w of San Tomas Expwy; US 101, exit S Bowers Ave. 2930 El Camino Real 95051 (PO Box 2841). Fax: 408/247-0623. **Facility:** 70 units. 52 one- and 18 two-bedroom standard units, some with kitchens. 2 stories (no elevator), exterior corridors. **Parking:** on-site. **Terms:** 3 day cancellation notice, [ECP] meal plan available, package plans, pets ($10 extra charge). **Amenities:** video library (fee), voice mail, irons, hair dryers. **Pool(s):** small heated outdoor. **Guest Services:** valet laundry. **Business Services:** meeting rooms. **Cards:** AX, CB, DC, DS, JC, MC, VI. **Special Amenities: free continental breakfast and free local telephone calls.** *(See color ad p 705)*

SOME UNITS

FEE

HAWTHORN SUITES *Book at aaa.com* **Phone:** (408)241-6444

Small-scale Hotel — All Year [BP] 1P: $99-$239 2P: $99-$239

Location: Just w of San Tomas Expwy. 2455 El Camino Real 95051. Fax: 408/241-6446. **Facility:** 97 one-bedroom standard units, some with whirlpools. 3 stories, interior corridors. **Parking:** on-site. **Amenities:** video library, high-speed Internet, dual phone lines, voice mail, safes, irons, hair dryers. **Pool(s):** heated outdoor. **Leisure Activities:** whirlpool, exercise room. **Guest Services:** complimentary laundry, area transportation. **Cards:** AX, DC, DS, MC, VI. ***(See color ad below)***

SOME UNITS

HILTON SANTA CLARA HOTEL *Book at aaa.com* **Phone:** 408/330-0001

AAA SAVE

Large-scale Hotel — All Year 1P: $109-$319 2P: $109-$319 XP: $20 F18

Location: US 101, exit Great America Pkwy, 0.5 mi n. 4949 Great America Pkwy 95054. Fax: 408/330-0011. **Facility:** Silicon Valley is the setting for this centrally located hotel offering manicured grounds and attractively appointed accommodations. 280 units. 272 one-bedroom standard units. 8 one-bedroom suites. 8 stories, interior corridors. **Parking:** on-site. **Terms:** [AP] meal plan available, package plans - weekends. **Amenities:** dual phone lines, voice mail, irons, hair dryers. *Fee:* video games, high-speed Internet. *Some:* CD players. **Dining:** 6 am-10 pm, cocktails. **Pool(s):** heated outdoor. **Leisure Activities:** whirlpool, exercise room. **Guest Services:** gift shop, valet laundry. **Business Services:** meeting rooms, business center. **Cards:** AX, DC, DS, MC, VI. **Special Amenities: free newspaper and free room upgrade (subject to availability with advanced reservations).**

(See color ad p 706)

SOME UNITS

FEE

HOLIDAY INN EXPRESS & SUITES *Book at aaa.com* **Phone:** 408/554-9200

Small-scale Hotel — All Year 1P: $110-$150 XP: $10 F12

Location: E of San Tomas Expwy. 1700 El Camino Real 95050. Fax: 408/554-8917. **Facility:** 47 one-bedroom standard units. 2 stories, interior corridors. *Bath:* combo or shower only. **Parking:** on-site. **Amenities:** high-speed Internet, dual phone lines, voice mail, irons, hair dryers. **Business Services:** business center. **Cards:** AX, CB, DC, DS, JC, MC, VI.

SOME UNITS

HOLIDAY INN-GREAT AMERICA/SILICON VALLEY **Book at aaa.com** **Phone:** (408)235-8900

Motel

All Year 1P: $79-$179 2P: $79-$179

Location: 0.5 mi e off US 101, exit Great America Pkwy; 0.8 mi s of Great America Theme Park. 4200 Great America Pkwy 95054. Fax: 408/988-2888. **Facility:** 168 one-bedroom standard units. 4 stories, exterior corridors. **Parking:** on-site. **Amenities:** dual phone lines, voice mail, irons, hair dryers. *Fee:* video games, high-speed Internet. **Pool(s):** heated outdoor. **Leisure Activities:** whirlpool, exercise room. **Guest Services:** valet and coin laundry, area transportation. **Business Services:** meeting rooms. **Cards:** AX, CB, DC, DS, JC, MC, VI.

SOME UNITS

MARIANI'S INN **Book at aaa.com** **Phone:** (408)243-1431

Motel

All Year [BP] 1P: $69-$129 2P: $76-$136 XP: $10 F15

Location: US 101, exit San Tomas Expwy, 3 mi s, then just w. 2500 El Camino Real 95051. Fax: 408/243-5745. **Facility:** 143 units. 139 one- and 4 two-bedroom standard units, some with kitchens. 2 stories, exterior corridors. *Bath:* combo or shower only. **Parking:** on-site. **Terms:** [MAP] meal plan available. **Amenities:** voice mail. *Some:* irons, hair dryers. **Dining:** Mariani's, see separate listing. **Pool(s):** heated outdoor. **Leisure Activities:** whirlpool. **Guest Services:** coin laundry. **Business Services:** meeting rooms. **Cards:** AX, DC, DS, MC, VI. **Special Amenities: free continental breakfast and free local telephone calls.**

SOME UNITS

THE PLAZA SUITES **Book at aaa.com** **Phone:** (408)748-9800

Small-scale Hotel

All Year 1P: $149-$169 2P: $159-$179 XP: $10 F7

Location: W of US 101, exit Lawrence Expwy, s on Oakmead at Peterson Way. 3100 Lakeside Dr 95054. Fax: 408/748-1476. **Facility:** 220 one-bedroom suites. 7 stories, interior corridors. **Parking:** on-site. **Terms:** package plans - weekends. **Amenities:** high-speed Internet, voice mail, honor bars, irons, hair dryers. *Fee:* video library, video games. *Some:* safes. **Pool(s):** heated outdoor. **Leisure Activities:** whirlpool, exercise room. **Guest Services:** gift shop, complimentary evening beverages, valet and coin laundry. **Business Services:** conference facilities, fax. **Cards:** AX, CB, DC, DS, JC, MC, VI. **Special Amenities: free continental breakfast.**

SOME UNITS

RAMADA LIMITED **Book at aaa.com** **Phone:** (408)244-8313

Motel

All Year [ECP] 1P: $65-$85 2P: $70-$90 XP: $15 F18

Location: I-880, exit The Alameda, 2 mi w. 1655 El Camino Real 95050. Fax: 408/554-9167. **Facility:** 68 one-bedroom standard units. 2 stories, exterior corridors. *Bath:* combo or shower only. **Parking:** on-site. **Amenities:** high-speed Internet, dual phone lines, voice mail, irons, hair dryers. **Pool(s):** outdoor. **Business Services:** meeting rooms. **Cards:** AX, MC, VI.

SOME UNITS

SANTA CLARA DAYS INN **Book at aaa.com** **Phone:** (408)244-2840

Motel

All Year [ECP] 1P: $65-$85 2P: $70-$90 XP: $10 F12

Location: SR 82 at Lafayette. 859 El Camino Real 95050. Fax: 408/984-5720. **Facility:** 44 one-bedroom standard units, some with whirlpools. 2 stories (no elevator), exterior corridors. **Parking:** on-site. **Terms:** package plans. **Amenities:** high-speed Internet, dual phone lines, voice mail, irons, hair dryers. **Cards:** AX, CB, DC, MC, VI.

SOME UNITS

SANTA CLARA MARRIOTT HOTEL *Book at aaa.com* **Phone:** (408)988-1500

SAVE

Large-scale Hotel

All Year 1P: $80-$229 2P: $80-$229 XP: $20 F18

Location: 0.5 mi e off US 101, exit Great America Pkwy; 0.8 mi s of Great America Theme Park. 2700 Mission College 95054. Fax: 408/352-4353. **Facility:** 759 one-bedroom standard units. 2-15 stories, interior corridors. **Parking:** on-site (fee). **Terms:** cancellation fee imposed, pets ($100 deposit, on 1st floor). **Amenities:** dual phone lines, voice mail, irons, hair dryers. *Fee:* video games, high-speed Internet. *Some:* safes. **Dining:** 2 restaurants, 6 am-midnight, cocktails. **Pool(s):** heated outdoor. **Leisure Activities:** whirlpool, 4 lighted tennis courts, exercise room, sports court. **Guest Services:** gift shop, valet laundry. **Business Services:** conference facilities, business center. **Cards:** AX, CB, DC, DS, JC, MC, VI. **Special Amenities: free newspaper and preferred room (subject to availability with advanced reservations).**

FEE SOME UNITS FEE

TRAVELODGE *Book at aaa.com* **Phone:** (408)984-3364

SAVE

Motel

All Year 1P: $69-$149 2P: $69-$149 XP: $10 F17

Location: 3477 El Camino Real 95051. Fax: 408/244-5561. **Facility:** 43 one-bedroom standard units. 2 stories, exterior corridors. **Parking:** on-site. **Terms:** 3 day cancellation notice-fee imposed. **Amenities:** video library, high-speed Internet, voice mail, hair dryers. **Cards:** AX, DS, MC, VI. **Special Amenities: free continental breakfast and free local telephone calls.**

SOME UNITS

THE VAGABOND INN *Book at aaa.com* **Phone:** (408)241-0771

SAVE

Motel

All Year 1P: $44-$99 2P: $44-$109 XP: $10 F18

Location: On SR 82, southeast corner of Lawrence Expwy cloverleaf. 3580 El Camino Real 95051. Fax: 408/247-3386. **Facility:** 70 one-bedroom standard units. 2 stories (no elevator), exterior corridors. **Parking:** on-site. **Terms:** [CP] meal plan available, small pets only ($10 extra charge). **Amenities:** dual phone lines, voice mail. *Some:* hair dryers. **Pool(s):** heated outdoor. **Guest Services:** coin laundry. **Cards:** AX, CB, DC, DS, MC, VI. **Special Amenities: free continental breakfast and free room upgrade (subject to availability with advanced reservations).**

FEE SOME UNITS

WELLESLEY INN (SANTA CLARA) *Book at aaa.com* **Phone:** (408)257-8600

SAVE

Small-scale Hotel

All Year 1P: $79-$89 2P: $79-$89

Location: I-280 and Lawrence Expwy, exit Stevens Creek Blvd, just w. 5405 Stevens Creek Blvd 95051. Fax: 408/446-2936. **Facility:** 96 one-bedroom standard units. 2 stories, interior corridors. **Parking:** on-site. **Terms:** [ECP] meal plan available, small pets only. **Amenities:** high-speed Internet (fee), dual phone lines, voice mail, irons, hair dryers. **Pool(s):** outdoor. **Guest Services:** valet and coin laundry. **Business Services:** meeting rooms. **Cards:** AX, DC, DS, JC, MC, VI. **Special Amenities: free expanded continental breakfast and free newspaper.** *(See color ad p 704)*

SOME UNITS

THE WESTIN HOTEL-SANTA CLARA *Book at aaa.com* **Phone:** (408)986-0700

Large-scale Hotel

All Year 1P: $99-$239 2P: $99-$239 XP: $20 F18

Location: 0.8 mi e off US 101, exit Great America Pkwy. Located at Santa Clara Convention Center. 5101 Great America Pkwy 95054. Fax: 408/980-3990. **Facility:** Manicured lawns and gardens with fountains surround this high-rise hotel. 505 units. 497 one-bedroom standard units. 8 one-bedroom suites ($500-$750), some with whirlpools. 14 stories, interior corridors. **Parking:** on-site. **Terms:** cancellation fee imposed, package plans - seasonal & weekends, pets ($35 fee). **Amenities:** dual phone lines, voice mail, safes, honor bars, irons, hair dryers. *Fee:* video games, high-speed Internet. **Pool(s):** heated outdoor. **Leisure Activities:** sauna, whirlpool, exercise room. *Fee:* golf-18 holes, 4 lighted tennis courts. **Guest Services:** gift shop, valet laundry. **Business Services:** conference facilities, business center. **Cards:** AX, CB, DC, DS, JC, MC, VI.

ASK FEE SOME UNITS

WOODCREST HOTEL *Book at aaa.com* **Phone:** (408)446-9636

Small-scale Hotel

All Year 1P: $79-$225 2P: $79-$225 XP: $25 F12

Location: I-280 and Lawrence Expwy, exit Stevens Creek Blvd, just w. 5415 Stevens Creek Blvd 95051. Fax: 408/446-9739. **Facility:** 60 units. 54 one-bedroom standard units, some with whirlpools. 6 one-bedroom suites ($109-$225). 4 stories, interior corridors. *Bath:* combo or shower only. **Parking:** on-site. **Terms:** [BP] & [MAP] meal plans available, package plans. **Amenities:** video library, high-speed Internet, dual phone lines, voice mail, irons, hair dryers. **Business Services:** meeting rooms. **Cards:** AX, DC, MC, VI.

ASK SOME UNITS

WHERE TO DINE

ARTHUR'S RESTAURANT **Lunch:** $9-$19 **Dinner:** $19-$39 **Phone:** 408/980-1666

American

Location: US 101, exit Great America Pkwy W. 2875 Lakeside Dr 95054. **Hours:** 11 am-2:30 & 5-10 pm, Sat from 5 pm. Closed major holidays; also Sun. **Reservations:** suggested. **Features:** A loyal local clientele patronizes the elegantly decorated restaurant. Continental influences are evident in many dishes on the varied menu. Semi-formal attire; cocktails; entertainment. **Parking:** on-site. **Cards:** AX, CB, DC, DS, MC, VI.

CALIFORNIA CAFE BAR & GRILL **Lunch:** $7-$14 **Dinner:** $9-$24 **Phone:** 408/296-2233

Regional American

Location: In Valley Fair Shopping Center. 2855 Stevens Creek Blvd 95050. **Hours:** 11 am-10 pm, Sun-8 pm. Closed: 11/25, 12/25. **Reservations:** suggested. **Features:** In a shopping mall, the family-friendly restaurant prepares California cuisine from fresh ingredients. Casual dress; cocktails. **Parking:** on-site. **Cards:** AX, CB, DC, DS, MC, VI.

MARIANI'S **Lunch:** $8-$16 **Dinner:** $13-$20 **Phone:** 408/243-1431

Continental

Location: US 101, exit San Tomas Expwy, 3 mi s, then just w; in Mariani's Inn. 2500 El Camino Real 95051. **Hours:** 6:30 am-10:30 pm, Sun-10 pm. Closed major holidays. **Reservations:** suggested. **Features:** Guests can relax amid modern, comfortable decor to sample foods from a menu featuring pasta, seafood, chops and poultry. Casual dress; cocktails; entertainment. **Parking:** on-site. **Cards:** AX, CB, DC, DS, MC, VI.

MONTAGUE'S CAFE **Lunch:** $5-$11 **Dinner:** $5-$21 **Phone:** 408/988-8411

American

Location: US 101, exit Montague Expwy, just e; 1 mi s of Great America Pkwy; in Biltmore Hotel & Suites/Silicon Valley. 2151 Laurelwood Rd 95054. **Hours:** 6 am-3 & 5-10 pm, Sat & Sun 6 am-11 & 5-10 pm. **Features:** Freshly prepared homestyle cooking has made this restaurant a favorite with the local clientele. Casual dress; cocktails. **Parking:** on-site. **Cards:** AX, CB, DC, DS, JC, MC, VI.

PASAND INDIA CUISINE **Lunch:** $6-$8 **Dinner:** $6-$15 **Phone:** 408/241-5150

Ethnic

Location: W of Lawrence Expwy. 3701 El Camino Real 95051. **Hours:** 11:30 am-10 pm. Closed: 12/25; also Mon. **Features:** Specializing in food from Southern India, the comfortably relaxed restaurant has a loyal clientele. Casual dress; beer & wine only. **Parking:** on-site. **Cards:** AX, CB, DC, DS, MC, VI.

SANTA CRUZ pop. 54,593—*See also APTOS, CAPITOLA, FELTON & SCOTTS VALLEY.*

WHERE TO STAY

BABBLING BROOK BED & BREAKFAST INN **Phone:** (831)427-2437

AAA SAVE

Bed & Breakfast

7/2-9/6 [ECP]	1P: $189-$275	2P: $189-$275	XP: $15
2/1-7/1 & 9/7-1/31 [ECP]	1P: $129-$249	2P: $129-$249	XP: $15

Location: Just s of US 1. 1025 Laurel St 95060. Fax: 831/427-2457. **Facility:** In a shaded setting along a brook with a water wheel, this B&B features extensively landscaped grounds and many units with fireplaces. Smoke free premises. 13 one-bedroom standard units, some with whirlpools. 2 stories (no elevator), interior corridors. *Bath:* combo or shower only. **Parking:** on-site. **Terms:** 2 night minimum stay - weekends, cancellation fee imposed. **Amenities:** video library, hair dryers. *Some:* CD players. **Cards:** AX, DS, MC, VI. **Special Amenities: free continental breakfast and free local telephone calls.** *(See color ad p 469)*

BAY FRONT INN *Book at aaa.com* **Phone:** 831/423-8564

AAA SAVE

Motel

All Year	1P: $48-$175	2P: $48-$185

Location: 6 blks se of SR 1. 325 Pacific Ave 95060. Fax: 831/469-0218. **Facility:** 38 one-bedroom standard units. 1-2 stories, exterior corridors. *Bath:* combo or shower only. **Parking:** on-site. **Terms:** small pets only ($10 fee). **Amenities:** voice mail, irons, hair dryers. **Pool(s):** outdoor. **Cards:** AX, DC, DS, MC, VI. **Special Amenities: free continental breakfast and free local telephone calls.** *(See color ad below)*

SOME UNITS

FEE

BEACH VIEW INN *Book at aaa.com* **Phone:** (831)426-3575

AAA SAVE

Motel

5/1-9/30 [CP]	1P: $90-$200	2P: $90-$200	XP: $10	F5
2/1-4/30 [CP]	1P: $70-$150	2P: $70-$150	XP: $10	F5
10/1-1/31 [CP]	1P: $60-$150	2P: $60-$150	XP: $10	F5

Location: 1 blk from beach. 50 Front St 95060. Fax: 831/421-9218. **Facility:** 22 one-bedroom standard units, some with whirlpools. 2 stories (no elevator), exterior corridors. **Parking:** on-site. **Terms:** check-in 4 pm. **Amenities:** hair dryers. **Cards:** AX, CB, DC, DS, MC, VI. **Special Amenities: free continental breakfast.**

SOME UNITS

BEST INN AND SUITES *Book at aaa.com* **Phone:** (831)458-9660

Motel

6/1-9/30 [ECP]	1P: $122-$131	2P: $122-$131	XP: $5	F18
2/1-5/31 & 10/1-1/31 [ECP]	1P: $78-$86	2P: $78-$86	XP: $5	F18

Location: 4 blks from beach. 600 Riverside Ave 95060. Fax: 831/426-8775. **Facility:** 79 one-bedroom standard units, some with whirlpools. 3 stories, exterior corridors. **Parking:** on-site. **Terms:** cancellation fee imposed. **Amenities:** irons, hair dryers. **Pool(s):** outdoor. **Leisure Activities:** whirlpools. **Guest Services:** valet laundry. **Cards:** AX, DC, DS, MC, VI. **Special Amenities: free expanded continental breakfast and free local telephone calls.** *(See color ad below)*

SOME UNITS

BEST VALUE INN *Book at aaa.com* **Phone:** (831)426-7766

Motel

8/1-10/31	1P: $89-$159	2P: $109-$189	XP: $10	F12
5/1-7/31	1P: $69-$149	2P: $109-$189	XP: $10	F12
2/1-4/30	1P: $69-$110	2P: $79-$149	XP: $10	F12
11/1-1/31	1P: $69-$89	2P: $89-$109	XP: $10	F12

Location: Jct SR 1 and 17, exit Ocean St, just w. 522 Ocean St 95060. Fax: 831/457-9201. **Facility:** 22 units. 18 one- and 4 two-bedroom standard units. 2 stories (no elevator), exterior corridors. **Parking:** on-site. **Terms:** cancellation fee imposed. **Cards:** AX, DS, MC, VI. **Special Amenities: free continental breakfast and early check-in/late check-out.**

SOME UNITS

BEST WESTERN ALL SUITES INN *Book at aaa.com* **Phone:** (831)458-9898

Small-scale Hotel

5/1-9/30	1P: $99-$199	2P: $109-$209	XP: $10
2/1-4/30 & 10/1-1/31	1P: $89-$189	2P: $99-$199	XP: $10

Location: Jct SR 1 and 17, exit Central District. 500 Ocean St 95060. Fax: 831/429-1903. **Facility:** 40 one-bedroom standard units with whirlpools. 3 stories, interior corridors. **Parking:** on-site. **Terms:** 3 day cancellation notice-fee imposed, [ECP] meal plan available. **Amenities:** irons, hair dryers. **Pool(s):** lap. **Leisure Activities:** sauna. **Guest Services:** coin laundry. **Cards:** AX, CB, DC, DS, JC, MC, VI. **Special Amenities: free continental breakfast and free newspaper.**

SOME UNITS

BEST WESTERN INN *Book at aaa.com* **Phone:** (831)425-4717

Motel

6/1-8/1 [ECP]	1P: $99-$160	2P: $99-$160
3/1-5/31 & 8/2-1/31 [ECP]	1P: $79-$119	2P: $79-$119
2/1-2/29 [ECP]	1P: $65-$99	2P: $65-$99

Location: Jct SR 1 and 17; east side of Ocean St. 126 Plymouth St 95060. Fax: 831/425-0643. **Facility:** 28 one-bedroom standard units, some with whirlpools. 2 stories, exterior corridors. **Parking:** on-site. **Amenities:** irons, hair dryers. **Leisure Activities:** sauna, whirlpool. **Cards:** AX, CB, DC, DS, JC, MC, VI. **Special Amenities: free expanded continental breakfast and free newspaper.**

SOME UNITS

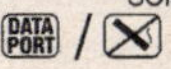

BEST WESTERN TORCH-LITE INN *Book at aaa.com* **Phone:** (831)426-7575

	Dates	1P	2P	XP	
SAVE	6/2-10/31	1P: $199-$225	2P: $225-$259	XP: $10	F10
	4/1-6/1	1P: $169-$189	2P: $189-$225	XP: $10	F10
	11/1-1/31	1P: $89-$109	2P: $109-$129	XP: $10	F10
Motel	2/1-3/31	1P: $89-$109	2P: $109	XP: $10	F10

Location: 3 blks from beach. 500 Riverside Ave 95060. Fax: 831/460-1470. **Facility:** Smoke free premises. 38 one-bedroom standard units, some with kitchens and/or whirlpools. 2 stories (no elevator), interior/exterior corridors. *Bath:* combo or shower only. **Parking:** on-site. **Terms:** 2 night minimum stay - seasonal, cancellation fee imposed, [CP] meal plan available. **Amenities:** voice mail, irons, hair dryers. **Pool(s):** heated outdoor. **Guest Services:** valet and coin laundry. **Cards:** AX, CB, DC, DS, JC, MC, VI. **Special Amenities: free continental breakfast and free local telephone calls.**

SOME UNITS

DATA PORT / VCR /

FEE

CAROUSEL MOTEL **Phone:** (831)425-7090

Motel

5/28-9/5 [CP]	1P: $109-$179	2P: $109-$179	XP: $10	F15
9/6-10/31 [CP]	1P: $69-$159	2P: $69-$159	XP: $10	F15
2/1-5/27 [CP]	1P: $59-$159	2P: $59-$159	XP: $10	F15
11/1-1/31 [CP]	1P: $59-$109	2P: $59-$109	XP: $10	F15

Location: Near the boardwalk and beach. 110 Riverside Ave 95060. Fax: 831/423-4801. **Facility:** 34 one-bedroom standard units, some with whirlpools. 3 stories, interior corridors. *Bath:* combo or shower only. **Parking:** on-site. **Terms:** 2-3 night minimum stay - with Saturday stayover, package plans. **Amenities:** voice mail. **Cards:** AX, DC, DS, MC, VI. **Special Amenities: free continental breakfast.** *(See color ad p 710)*

SOME UNITS

CHAMINADE AT SANTA CRUZ *Book at aaa.com* **Phone:** (831)475-5600

Large-scale Hotel

All Year	1P: $149-$219	2P: $149-$219	XP: $35	F15

Location: 1.5 mi e of SR 1 and 17; exit SR 1, exit Soquel Ave, just w to Paul Sweet Rd, then 0.5 mi n. Located in a quiet area. 1 Chaminade Ln 95065 (PO Box 2788, 95063). Fax: 831/476-4942. **Facility:** A hillside setting gives this property good views of Santa Cruz and the ocean; grounds are well tended and recreational facilities are extensive. Smoke free premises. 153 one-bedroom standard units. 2 stories (no elevator), interior corridors. **Parking:** on-site. **Terms:** check-in 4 pm, 2 night minimum stay - weekends in summer, 3 day cancellation notice. **Amenities:** dual phone lines, voice mail, safes, irons, hair dryers. *Fee:* video games, high-speed Internet. *Some:* CD players. **Dining:** 3 restaurants, 7 am-11 pm, cocktails. **Pool(s):** heated outdoor. **Leisure Activities:** saunas, whirlpools, men's & women's therapy pools, 4 lighted tennis courts, hiking trails, exercise room, spa. **Guest Services:** gift shop, valet laundry. **Business Services:** conference facilities, business center. **Cards:** AX, DC, DS, MC, VI.

SOME UNITS

FEE

COAST SANTA CRUZ HOTEL *Book at aaa.com* **Phone:** 831/426-4330

Small-scale Hotel

6/29-8/24	1P: $250-$289	2P: $250-$289
5/30-6/28	1P: $209-$289	2P: $209-$289
8/25-1/31	1P: $167-$197	2P: $167-$197
2/1-5/29	1P: $129-$195	2P: $129-$195

Location: At the Wharf. 175 W Cliff Dr 95060. Fax: 831/427-2025. **Facility:** 163 units. 151 one-bedroom standard units. 12 one-bedroom suites ($200-$500). 3-10 stories, interior corridors. **Parking:** on-site. **Terms:** check-in 4 pm, cancellation fee imposed, [AP] meal plan available, pets ($10 extra charge). **Amenities:** video games (fee), voice mail, safes, irons, hair dryers. **Dining:** 2 restaurants, 6:30 am-10 pm, Sat & Sun from 7 am, cocktails. **Pool(s):** heated outdoor. **Leisure Activities:** whirlpool. **Guest Services:** valet laundry. **Business Services:** business center. **Cards:** AX, DC, DS, MC, VI. **Special Amenities: free newspaper.**

SOME UNITS

FEE

COMFORT INN BEACH BOARDWALK *Book at aaa.com* **Phone:** (831)471-9999

Motel

6/1-8/31 [ECP]	1P: $79-$259	2P: $79-$279	XP: $10	F18
4/1-5/31 [ECP]	1P: $69-$199	2P: $69-$249	XP: $10	F18
9/1-1/31 [ECP]	1P: $59-$199	2P: $59-$199	XP: $10	F18
2/1-3/31 [ECP]	1P: $59-$169	2P: $59-$169	XP: $10	F18

Location: 1 blk from boardwalk. 314 Riverside Ave 95060. Fax: 831/429-5000. **Facility:** 28 one-bedroom standard units, some with whirlpools. Exterior corridors. **Parking:** on-site. **Terms:** cancellation fee imposed. **Amenities:** high-speed Internet, voice mail, irons, hair dryers. **Pool(s):** small heated outdoor. **Cards:** AX, DC, DS, MC, VI.

SOME UNITS

COMFORT INN-SANTA CRUZ *Book at aaa.com* **Phone:** (831)426-2664

AAA SAVE — Motel

5/1-9/30 [ECP]	1P: $89-$169	2P: $99-$269	XP: $10	F18
10/1-1/31 [ECP]	1P: $69-$129	2P: $79-$169	XP: $10	F18
2/1-4/30 [ECP]	1P: $59-$119	2P: $69-$129	XP: $10	F18

Location: Jct SR 1 and 17; south side of Ocean St. 110 Plymouth St 95060. Fax: 831/426-0923. **Facility:** 61 one-bedroom standard units, some with whirlpools. 2 stories (no elevator), exterior corridors. **Parking:** on-site. **Amenities:** irons, hair dryers. **Pool(s):** heated outdoor. **Leisure Activities:** sauna, whirlpool. **Cards:** AX, DC, DS, MC, VI. **Special Amenities: free expanded continental breakfast and free local telephone calls.** *(See color ad p 711)*

SOME UNITS

COMPASSION FLOWER INN **Phone:** (831)466-0420

Historic Bed & Breakfast

All Year [BP]	1P: $115-$175	2P: $115-$175

Location: Jct SR 1 and 17 W via Ocean St, 1 mi w to Broadway Ave, then turn right; Broadway Ave becomes Laurel St. 216 Laurel St 95060. Fax: 831/466-0431. **Facility:** The attractively restored 1860's gothic revival Victorian is withinwalking distance of downtown shops, the beach and wharf. Smoke free premises. 4 one-bedroom standard units. 2 stories, interior corridors. *Bath:* shared or private, combo or shower only. **Parking:** on-site. **Terms:** check-in 4 pm, 2 night minimum stay - weekends, 10 day cancellation notice-fee imposed. **Cards:** AX, DS, MC, VI.

CONTINENTAL INN **Phone:** (831)429-1221

AAA SAVE — Motel

All Year [CP]	1P: $75-$260	2P: $75-$260	XP: $10

Location: 5 blks from beach; between Broadway and Soquel aves. 414 Ocean St 95060. Fax: 831/426-8561. **Facility:** 47 one-bedroom standard units, some with whirlpools. 2 stories, exterior corridors. *Bath:* combo or shower only. **Parking:** on-site. **Terms:** 7 day cancellation notice, small pets only. **Amenities:** voice mail, irons, hair dryers. **Pool(s):** heated outdoor. **Leisure Activities:** whirlpool. **Cards:** AX, CB, DC, DS, JC, MC, VI. **Special Amenities: free continental breakfast and free newspaper.**

SOME UNITS

ECONO LODGE *Book at aaa.com* **Phone:** (831)426-3626

AAA SAVE — Motel

4/16-9/30	1P: $75-$175	2P: $75-$199	XP: $10	F17
2/1-4/15 & 10/1-1/31	1P: $55-$110	2P: $55-$125	XP: $10	F17

Location: 3 blks from beach. 550 Second St 95060. Fax: 831/458-3603. **Facility:** 20 one-bedroom standard units, some with kitchens (utensil deposit required). 2 stories (no elevator), exterior corridors. **Parking:** on-site. **Terms:** [CP] meal plan available. **Pool(s):** outdoor. **Cards:** AX, CB, DC, DS, JC, MC, VI. **Special Amenities: free continental breakfast and free local telephone calls.**

SOME UNITS

GUESTHOUSE INTERNATIONAL PACIFIC INN *Book at aaa.com* **Phone:** (831)425-3722

AAA SAVE — Motel

6/16-8/31 [CP]	1P: $99-$199	2P: $118-$199	XP: $10	D18
9/1-1/31 [CP]	1P: $59-$129	2P: $79-$169	XP: $10	D18
4/1-6/15 [CP]	1P: $79-$129	2P: $89-$149	XP: $10	D18
2/1-3/31 [CP]	1P: $59-$99	2P: $69-$119	XP: $10	D18

Location: 1 mi from jct SR 1 and 17. 330 Ocean St 95060. Fax: 831/425-4983. **Facility:** 36 one-bedroom standard units, some with whirlpools. 2 stories, interior corridors. **Parking:** on-site. **Terms:** 2 night minimum stay - seasonal & weekends, cancellation fee imposed, pets ($10 extra charge). **Amenities:** video library (fee), high-speed Internet, voice mail, irons, hair dryers. **Pool(s):** heated indoor. **Leisure Activities:** whirlpool. **Cards:** AX, DC, DS, MC, VI. **Special Amenities: free local telephone calls and early check-in/late check-out.**

SOME UNITS

FEE

HAMPTON INN *Book at aaa.com* **Phone:** (831)457-8000

SAVE Motel

5/28-9/1 [ECP]	1P: $109-$189	2P: $119-$199	XP: $10	F16
9/2-10/31 [ECP]	1P: $99-$159	2P: $109-$169	XP: $10	F16
2/1-5/27 & 11/1-1/31 [ECP]	1P: $89-$159	2P: $99-$169	XP: $10	F16

Location: Jct SR 1 and 17. 1505 Ocean St 95060. Fax: 831/457-8900. **Facility:** Smoke free premises. 46 one-bedroom standard units. 3 stories, interior corridors. **Parking:** on-site. **Amenities:** dual phone lines, voice mail, irons, hair dryers. *Fee:* video library, high-speed Internet. **Pool(s):** small heated indoor. **Cards:** AX, CB, DC, DS, JC, MC, VI. **Special Amenities: free expanded continental breakfast and free local telephone calls.**

(See color ad p 712)

SOME UNITS FEE FEE

THE INN AT PASATIEMPO *Book at aaa.com* **Phone:** (831)423-5000

SAVE Motel

All Year [CP]	1P: $150-$200	2P: $150-$200	XP: $10	F18

Location: 0.8 mi n of jct SR 1 and 17; exit SR 17, exit Pasatiempo Dr. 555 Hwy 17 95060. Fax: 831/426-1737. **Facility:** 54 one-bedroom standard units. 1 story, exterior corridors. *Bath:* combo or shower only. **Parking:** on-site. **Terms:** 2-7 night minimum stay - in season weekends, package plans. **Amenities:** irons, hair dryers. *Some:* CD players, dual phone lines. **Dining:** 11:30 am-10 pm, cocktails. **Pool(s):** outdoor. **Cards:** AX, CB, DC, DS, MC, VI. *(See color ad below)*

SOME UNITS

MISSION INN **Phone:** (831)425-5455

SAVE Motel

6/1-9/30 [ECP]	1P: $110-$180	2P: $110-$180	XP: $10	F12
2/1-5/31 & 10/1-1/31 [ECP]	1P: $85-$180	2P: $85-$180	XP: $10	F12

Location: Jct SR 1 and SR 17; 2.5 mi sw on SR 1 northbound. 2250 Mission St 95060. Fax: 831/469-4870. **Facility:** 53 one-bedroom standard units. 2 stories (no elevator), exterior corridors. **Parking:** on-site. **Terms:** check-in 4 pm. **Amenities:** voice mail, hair dryers. **Leisure Activities:** sauna, whirlpool. **Cards:** AX, DS, MC, VI. **Special Amenities: free continental breakfast and free local telephone calls.**

(See color ad p 714)

SOME UNITS FEE

NATIONAL 9 MOTEL **Phone:** (831)426-4515

SAVE Motel

5/16-9/30	1P: $65-$129	2P: $79-$149	XP: $10	F10
10/1-1/31	1P: $39-$89	2P: $49-$119	XP: $10	F10
4/1-5/15	1P: $49-$99	2P: $59-$99	XP: $10	F10
2/1-3/31	1P: $39-$79	2P: $49-$89	XP: $10	F10

Location: Jct SR 1 and 17; east side of Ocean St. 130 Plymouth St 95060. Fax: 831/429-2046. **Facility:** 21 one-bedroom standard units. 2 stories (no elevator), exterior corridors. **Parking:** on-site. **Terms:** 3 day cancellation notice-fee imposed. **Pool(s):** outdoor. **Cards:** AX, CB, DC, DS, MC, VI. **Special Amenities: free local telephone calls and preferred room (subject to availability with advanced reservations).**

SOME UNITS

OCEAN PACIFIC LODGE Phone: (831)457-1234

Motel

5/28-9/6	1P: $105-$140	2P: $105-$140	XP: $10	F12
9/7-1/31	1P: $75-$110	2P: $75-$110	XP: $10	F12
3/1-5/27	1P: $70-$105	2P: $70-$105	XP: $10	F12
2/1-2/29	1P: $60-$90	2P: $60-$90	XP: $10	F12

Location: SR 1 and 17, exit w via Ocean St, 1 mi w to Broadway, turn right, left on Front St to Pacific Ave, then just right. 120 Washington 95060. Fax: 831/457-0861. **Facility:** 57 units. 44 one-bedroom standard units, some with whirlpools. 13 one-bedroom suites ($104-$205), some with whirlpools. 3 stories, exterior corridors. **Parking:** on-site. **Terms:** cancellation fee imposed, [ECP] meal plan available, small pets only ($20 extra charge). **Amenities:** video library (fee), voice mail. **Pool(s):** outdoor. **Leisure Activities:** whirlpools. **Guest Services:** coin laundry. **Business Services:** meeting rooms. **Cards:** AX, CB, DC, DS, MC, VI. **Special Amenities: free continental breakfast.**

SOME UNITS

FEE

PLEASURE POINT INN BED AND BREAKFAST Phone: (831)475-4657

Bed & Breakfast

All Year 1P: $220-$265

Location: SR 1, exit 41st Ave, 1.3 mi w, turn right on Portola Dr, left on 36th Ave, then left. Located across the street from Pacific Ocean. 2-3665 E Cliff Dr 95062. Fax: 831/479-0459. **Facility:** Located directly across from the Pacific Ocean, this inn combines a beachside setting with the warmth and comfort of a bed and breakfast. Smoke free premises. 4 one-bedroom standard units, some with whirlpools. 2 stories (no elevator), interior corridors. *Bath:* combo or shower only. **Parking:** on-site. **Terms:** 14 day cancellation notice-fee imposed, [ECP] meal plan available, package plans. **Amenities:** safes, irons, hair dryers. **Leisure Activities:** whirlpool. **Cards:** MC, VI.

SOME UNITS

QUALITY INN *Book at aaa.com* Phone: 831/427-1616

Motel

6/1-9/30	1P: $79-$299	2P: $79-$299	XP: $12	F12
2/1-5/31	1P: $69-$299	2P: $69-$299	XP: $12	F12
10/1-1/31	1P: $59-$299	2P: $69-$299	XP: $12	F12

Location: 3 blks w off SR 1 and 17, exit Central District. 1101 Ocean St 95060. Fax: 831/427-9053. **Facility:** 42 one-bedroom standard units. 2-3 stories (no elevator), exterior corridors. **Parking:** on-site. **Amenities:** dual phone lines, voice mail, irons, hair dryers. **Pool(s):** outdoor. **Cards:** AX, CB, DC, DS, JC, MC, VI. **Special Amenities: free local telephone calls and free newspaper.**

SOME UNITS

RAMADA LIMITED *Book at aaa.com* Phone: (831)426-6111

Motel

6/1-8/31 [CP]	1P: $89-$169	2P: $99-$199	XP: $10	F16
9/1-10/31 [CP]	1P: $79-$159	2P: $89-$179	XP: $10	F16
2/1-5/31 [CP]	1P: $79-$149	2P: $89-$169	XP: $10	F16
11/1-1/31 [CP]	1P: $69-$89	2P: $89-$109	XP: $10	F16

Location: 0.4 mi w of jct SR 1 and 17, just s. 516 Water St 95060. Fax: 831/426-2242. **Facility:** 50 one-bedroom standard units. 1-2 stories (no elevator), exterior corridors. **Parking:** on-site. **Terms:** 3 day cancellation notice-fee imposed. **Amenities:** voice mail, irons. **Pool(s):** outdoor. **Cards:** AX, CB, DC, DS, JC, MC, VI. **Special Amenities: free continental breakfast and free local telephone calls.**

SOME UNITS

RAMADA LIMITED *Book at aaa.com* Phone: (831)423-7737

Motel

5/1-9/30 [CP]	1P: $79-$185	2P: $89-$185	XP: $10	F18
2/1-4/30 & 10/1-12/31 [CP]	1P: $69-$120	2P: $79-$125	XP: $10	F18
1/1-1/31 [CP]	1P: $62-$102	2P: $62-$102	XP: $10	F18

Location: 2 blks from beach. 130 W Cliff Dr 95060. Fax: 831/429-6200. **Facility:** 30 one-bedroom standard units, some with efficiencies (no utensils). 2 stories (no elevator), exterior corridors. **Parking:** on-site. **Amenities:** high-speed Internet, voice mail, irons, hair dryers. **Leisure Activities:** whirlpool. **Guest Services:** coin laundry. **Cards:** AX, CB, DC, DS, JC, MC, VI. **Special Amenities: free continental breakfast and free local telephone calls.** *(See color ad p 716)*

SOME UNITS

SEA & SAND INN — **Phone:** (831)427-3400

Motel

5/28-9/5 [CP]	1P: $159-$359	2P: $159-$359	XP: $10	F11
9/6-10/31 [CP]	1P: $129-$349	2P: $129-$349	XP: $10	F11
2/1-5/27 [CP]	1P: $99-$349	2P: $99-$349	XP: $10	F11
11/1-1/31 [CP]	1P: $99-$269	2P: $99-$269	XP: $10	F11

Location: Overlooking the wharf. 201 W Cliff Dr 95060. Fax: 831/466-9882. **Facility:** 20 one-bedroom standard units, some with whirlpools. 2 stories (no elevator), exterior corridors. *Bath:* shower only. **Parking:** on-site. **Terms:** 2-3 night minimum stay - weekends. **Amenities:** video library (fee), irons. *Some:* high-speed Internet. **Cards:** AX, DC, DS, MC, VI. ***(See color ad p 710)***

SOME UNITS

SUNSET INN — **Phone:** 831/423-7500

SAVE — Motel

5/1-9/30	1P: $75-$185	2P: $85-$195	XP: $10	F12
2/1-4/30	1P: $55-$165	2P: $65-$175	XP: $10	F12
10/1-1/31	1P: $55-$165	2P: $55-$175	XP: $10	F12

Location: SR 1, exit Mission St, 2.5 mi w. 2424 Mission St 95060. Fax: 831/423-7595. **Facility:** 32 units. 31 one- and 1 two-bedroom standard units, some with whirlpools. 2 stories (no elevator), exterior corridors. **Parking:** on-site. **Terms:** cancellation fee imposed, [CP] meal plan available. **Amenities:** voice mail. *Some:* hair dryers. **Leisure Activities:** sauna, whirlpool. **Cards:** AX, DS, JC, MC, VI. **Special Amenities: free continental breakfast and free local telephone calls.**

SOME UNITS

SUPER 8-BOARDWALK Book at aaa.com — **Phone:** (831)423-9449

SAVE — Motel

All Year	1P: $49-$199	2P: $59-$299

Location: 2 blks from beach and boardwalk. 321 Riverside Ave 95060. Fax: 831/425-5100. **Facility:** 23 one-bedroom standard units, some with whirlpools. 2 stories, exterior corridors. **Parking:** on-site. **Terms:** [CP] meal plan available. **Amenities:** dual phone lines, voice mail, hair dryers. **Pool(s):** small outdoor. **Leisure Activities:** whirlpool. **Cards:** AX, DC, DS, MC, VI. **Special Amenities: free continental breakfast and free local telephone calls.**

SOME UNITS

SUPER 8 MOTEL-BEACH BOARDWALK Book at aaa.com — **Phone:** (831)426-3707

SAVE — Motel

All Year	1P: $49-$199	2P: $59-$299

Location: 2 blks from beach and boardwalk. 338 Riverside Ave 95060. Fax: 831/426-0547. **Facility:** 24 one-bedroom standard units, some with whirlpools. 2 stories, exterior corridors. **Parking:** on-site. **Terms:** [CP] meal plan available. **Amenities:** high-speed Internet, dual phone lines, hair dryers. **Pool(s):** small heated outdoor. **Cards:** AX, DC, DS, MC, VI. **Special Amenities: free continental breakfast and free local telephone calls.**

SOME UNITS

TRAVELODGE BEACH BOARDWALK Book at aaa.com — **Phone:** (831)423-9515

SAVE — Motel

5/21-9/10	1P: $69-$199	2P: $89-$199	XP: $10	F12
2/1-5/20	1P: $45-$149	2P: $59-$149	XP: $10	F12
9/11-1/31	1P: $45-$139	2P: $49-$139	XP: $10	F12

Location: 3 blks from beach. 619 Riverside Ave 95060. Fax: 831/423-1159. **Facility:** 63 units. 32 one- and 31 two-bedroom standard units, some with kitchens (no utensils). 2 stories (no elevator), exterior corridors. **Parking:** on-site. **Pool(s):** heated indoor. **Leisure Activities:** whirlpool. **Cards:** AX, DC, DS, MC, VI. **Special Amenities: free newspaper and free room upgrade (subject to availability with advanced reservations).**

SOME UNITS

TRAVELODGE SANTA CRUZ Book at aaa.com — **Phone:** (831)426-2300

SAVE — Motel

6/1-9/30	1P: $79-$129	2P: $89-$189	XP: $10	F12
10/1-1/31	1P: $59-$109	2P: $79-$129	XP: $10	F12
2/1-5/31	1P: $59-$89	2P: $79-$99	XP: $10	F12

Location: Jct SR 1 and 17, exit Ocean St Beach. 525 Ocean St 95060. Fax: 831/426-1126. **Facility:** 55 one-bedroom standard units. 2 stories (no elevator), interior/exterior corridors. *Bath:* combo or shower only. **Parking:** on-site. **Terms:** 3 day cancellation notice-fee imposed. **Amenities:** dual phone lines, voice mail, hair dryers. **Pool(s):** heated outdoor. **Cards:** AX, DC, DS, JC, MC, VI. **Special Amenities: free newspaper and preferred room (subject to availability with advanced reservations).**

SOME UNITS

VILLAGER LODGE *Book at aaa.com* **Phone:** (831)423-6020

Motel

5/23-9/1 [CP]	1P: $59-$225	2P: $79-$250	XP: $10	F12
2/1-5/22 & 9/2-1/31 [CP]	1P: $39-$155	2P: $49-$165	XP: $10	F12

Location: 3 blks from beach and boardwalk. 510 Leibrandt Ave 95060. Fax: 831/426-7574. **Facility:** 26 one-bedroom standard units. 2 stories (no elevator), exterior corridors. *Bath:* combo or shower only. **Parking:** on-site. **Terms:** 7 day cancellation notice-fee imposed. **Pool(s):** small outdoor. **Guest Services:** coin laundry. **Cards:** AX, CB, DC, DS, JC, MC, VI. **Special Amenities: free continental breakfast.**

SOME UNITS

WHERE TO DINE

CROW'S NEST **Lunch:** $8-$14 **Dinner:** $14-$22 **Phone:** 831/476-4560

Seafood

Location: 1.3 mi e; at South Shore Santa Cruz Small Crafts Harbor via Murray St Bridge. 2218 E Cliff Dr 95062. **Hours:** 11:30 am-2:30 & 5:30-10 pm, Sat 11:30 am-3 & 4:30-10:30 pm, Sun 11:30 am-3 & 4:30-9:30 pm. Closed: 12/25. **Reservations:** suggested. **Features:** Diners are treated to picturesque views of the bay and Pacific Ocean, as well as well-prepared selections of fresh local seafood. The lively atmosphere makes this place popular with locals. Casual dress; cocktails; entertainment. **Parking:** on-site (fee). **Cards:** AX, CB, DC, MC, VI.

HOLLINS HOUSE RESTAURANT **Dinner:** $13-$26 **Phone:** 831/459-9177

Continental

Location: 0.5 mi n of jct SR 1 and 17; w of SR 17, exit Pasatiempo Dr; at golf course. 20 Club House Rd 95060. **Hours:** 5:30 pm-9:30 pm, Sun 10 am-1:30 pm. Closed major holidays; also Mon, Tues & 1/1-1/15. **Reservations:** suggested. **Features:** From its perch atop a hill, the restaurant overlooks the city, bay and Pacific Ocean. The feel is casual yet elegant. Dressy casual; cocktails. **Parking:** on-site. **Cards:** AX, MC, VI.

SANTA MARIA pop. 77,423

WHERE TO STAY

BEST WESTERN BIG AMERICA *Book at aaa.com* **Phone:** (805)922-5200

Motel

All Year [ECP]	1P: $89-$149	2P: $89-$149	XP: $10	F18

Location: US 101, exit Broadway, 0.5 mi w. 1725 N Broadway 93454. Fax: 805/922-9865. **Facility:** 106 units. 90 one-bedroom standard units. 16 one-bedroom suites ($99-$169). 2 stories, exterior corridors. **Parking:** on-site. **Amenities:** video library (fee), high-speed Internet, voice mail, irons, hair dryers. **Pool(s):** heated outdoor. **Leisure Activities:** whirlpool. **Guest Services:** airport transportation-Santa Maria Municipal Airport. **Business Services:** meeting rooms. **Cards:** AX, CB, DC, DS, JC, MC, VI. **Special Amenities: free expanded continental breakfast and free newspaper.** *(See color ad below)*

SOME UNITS

FEE FEE

COMFORT INN Book at aaa.com **Phone:** (805)922-5891

Motel

5/16-9/30 [CP]	1P: $79-$179	2P: $79-$179	XP: $10	F18
2/1-5/15 & 10/1-1/31 [CP]	1P: $69-$109	2P: $69-$109	XP: $10	F18

Location: US 101, exit Main St, just e, then just s. 210 S Nicholson Ave 93454. Fax: 805/928-9222. **Facility:** 64 one-bedroom standard units. 2 stories, interior corridors. **Parking:** on-site. **Terms:** small pets only ($10 extra charge). **Amenities:** high-speed Internet, irons, hair dryers. **Pool(s):** heated outdoor, wading. **Leisure Activities:** whirlpool, playground. **Guest Services:** coin laundry. **Business Services:** fax. **Cards:** AX, DC, DS, MC, VI. **Special Amenities: free continental breakfast and free local telephone calls.**

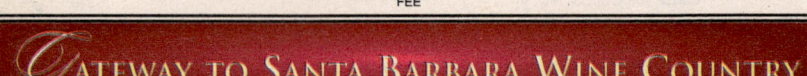

SOME UNITS

FEE

HISTORIC SANTA MARIA INN Book at aaa.com **Phone:** (805)928-7777

Historic Large-scale Hotel

All Year	1P: $119-$149	2P: $119-$149	XP: $10	F18

Location: US 101, exit Main St, 1 mi w, then 0.5 mi s. 801 S Broadway 93454. Fax: 805/928-5690. **Facility:** An Old English country motif unifies the hotel's original restored building and newer tower section; rooms vary in size. 164 units. 149 one-bedroom standard units. 15 one-bedroom suites ($129-$300), some with kitchens. 2-6 stories, interior corridors. **Parking:** on-site. **Terms:** 7 day cancellation notice, pets ($50 fee). **Amenities:** video games (fee), dual phone lines, voice mail, irons, hair dryers. **Dining:** Garden Room at Historic Santa Maria Inn, see separate listing. **Pool(s):** heated outdoor. **Leisure Activities:** sauna, whirlpool, exercise room. *Fee:* massage. **Guest Services:** gift shop, valet and coin laundry. **Business Services:** meeting rooms, fax. **Cards:** AX, CB, DC, DS, MC, VI.
(See color ad below)

SOME UNITS

FEE

HOLIDAY INN HOTEL & SUITES *Book at aaa.com* **Phone:** (805)928-6000

6/1-9/30	1P: $140	2P: $140	XP: $10	F19
2/1-5/31 & 10/1-1/31	1P: $120	2P: $120	XP: $10	F19

Large-scale Hotel

Location: US 101, exit Broadway, just w. 2100 N Broadway 93454. Fax: 805/928-0356. **Facility:** 207 units. 195 one-bedroom standard units with efficiencies. 12 two-bedroom suites ($139-$199) with efficiencies. 4 stories, interior corridors. **Parking:** on-site. **Terms:** check-in 4 pm. **Amenities:** voice mail, irons, hair dryers. *Fee:* video games, high-speed Internet. *Some:* dual phone lines. **Dining:** Mesquite Bar & Grill, see separate listing. **Pool(s):** heated outdoor. **Leisure Activities:** whirlpool, exercise room. **Guest Services:** valet and coin laundry. **Business Services:** meeting rooms, fax (fee). **Cards:** AX, CB, DC, DS, JC, MC, VI. **Special Amenities: free room upgrade (subject to availability with advanced reservations).** *(See color ad p 168 & p 718)*

SOME UNITS

RADISSON HOTEL SANTA MARIA *Book at aaa.com* **Phone:** (805)928-8000

All Year	1P: $129-$149	2P: $129-$149	XP: $10	F18

Large-scale Hotel

Location: US 101, exit Betteravia Rd, 2.3 mi w, then 1.8 mi s on Skyway Dr. Located next to the Santa Maria Airport. 3455 Skyway Dr 93455. Fax: 805/928-5251. **Facility:** 183 one-bedroom standard units. 4 stories, interior/exterior corridors. **Parking:** on-site. **Terms:** cancellation fee imposed, [AP] meal plan available. **Amenities:** video games, dual phone lines, voice mail, irons, hair dryers. **Pool(s):** heated outdoor. **Leisure Activities:** sauna, whirlpool, exercise room. **Guest Services:** valet laundry. **Business Services:** meeting rooms. **Cards:** AX, DS, MC, VI.

SOME UNITS

WHERE TO DINE

CENTRAL CITY BROILER **Lunch:** $6-$11 **Dinner:** $10-$23 **Phone:** 805/922-3700

American

Location: US 101, exit Donovan Rd, 0.7 mi w, then just s. 1520 N Broadway 93454. **Hours:** 11:30 am-2 & 5-9 pm, Fri-10 pm, Sat 5 pm-10 pm, Sun 5 pm-9 pm. Closed: 11/25, 12/25. **Features:** Early American decor adorns the dining room, where patrons relax to sample large portions of steak, chicken and seafood or the succulent prime rib. Meat is cooked over an open oak-pit barbecue. On Tuesday nights, the all-you-can-eat crab is a big draw. Casual dress; cocktails. **Parking:** on-site. **Cards:** AX, DC, DS, MC, VI.

FAR WESTERN TAVERN **Lunch:** $7-$11 **Dinner:** $7-$39 **Phone:** 805/343-2211

Steak House

Location: US 101, exit Main St, 9 mi w; in Guadalupe. 899 Guadalupe St 93434. **Hours:** 11 am-9 pm, Fri & Sat-10 pm, Sun 9 am-9 pm. Closed: 11/25, 12/25. **Reservations:** suggested. **Features:** The established, family-operated steakhouse serves quality meats in ample portions. Casual dress; cocktails. **Parking:** on-site. **Cards:** AX, DS, MC, VI.

GARDEN ROOM AT HISTORIC SANTA MARIA INN **Lunch:** $8-$13 **Dinner:** $13-$24 **Phone:** 805/928-7777

American

Location: US 101, exit Main St, 1 mi w, then 0.5 mi s; in Historic Santa Maria Inn. 801 S Broadway 93454. **Hours:** 6 am-2 & 5-9 pm, Fri & Sat-10 pm. **Reservations:** suggested. **Features:** In the original section built in 1917, the dining room is a charming spot, as is the cozy patio. On the menu is a selection of prime rib, steak, seafood and chicken dishes. Guests can request cellar wines, primarily the California regional variety, from 4:30 to 9:30 pm Monday through Saturday. Cocktails. **Parking:** on-site. **Cards:** AX, DC, DS, JC, MC, VI. ***(See color ad p 718)***

MESQUITE BAR & GRILL **Lunch:** $8-$10 **Dinner:** $11-$22 **Phone:** 805/928-6000

American

Location: I-101, exit Broadway, just w; in Holiday Inn Hotel & Suites. 2100 N Broadway 93454. **Hours:** 6 am-10 & 5-9 pm, Sat & Sun 6 am-11 & 5-9 pm. **Features:** Featuring an upscale but relaxed ambiance, the restaurant offers a dinner menu that features regional specialties such as beef and seafood complemented by fine regional wines. The Mesquite coffee is a perfect way to end your dinner: a blend of fresh Folger's coffee with brandy, Kahlua and Bailey's Irish creme. Enjoy Holiday Inn's Best 4 Breakfast, plus American and Continental breakfast buffets. Casual dress; cocktails. **Parking:** on-site. **Cards:** AX, MC, VI.

SANTA NELLA

WHERE TO STAY

BEST WESTERN ANDERSEN'S INN *Book at aaa.com* **Phone:** (209)826-5534

6/1-9/30	1P: $70-$95	2P: $70-$95	XP: $8	F12
2/1-5/31 & 10/1-1/31	1P: $68-$95	2P: $68-$95	XP: $8	F12

Motel

Location: I-5, exit SR 33, just e. 12367 Hwy 33 S 95322. Fax: 209/827-1448. **Facility:** 94 one-bedroom standard units. 2 stories (no elevator), exterior corridors. **Parking:** on-site. **Terms:** cancellation fee imposed, [ECP] meal plan available, small pets only ($10 extra charge). **Amenities:** irons, hair dryers. **Pool(s):** heated outdoor. **Guest Services:** coin laundry. **Cards:** AX, CB, DC, DS, MC, VI. **Special Amenities: free expanded continental breakfast and free local telephone calls.** *(See color ad below & p 721)*

SOME UNITS FEE

COMFORT INN *Book at aaa.com* **Phone:** (209)827-8700

6/1-8/31 [BP]	1P: $65-$80	2P: $65-$80	XP: $5	F13
2/1-5/31 & 9/1-1/31 [BP]	1P: $59-$65	2P: $59-$65	XP: $5	F13

Motel

Location: 3 mi w of I-5; SR 152, exit Gonzaga Rd, just s. 28821 W Gonzaga Rd 95322. Fax: 209/827-1497. **Facility:** 64 one-bedroom standard units. 2 stories (no elevator), exterior corridors. *Bath:* combo or shower only. **Parking:** on-site. **Terms:** 14 day cancellation notice, [ECP] meal plan available, pets ($10 fee extra charge). **Amenities:** irons, hair dryers. **Pool(s):** heated outdoor. **Leisure Activities:** whirlpool. **Cards:** AX, DC, DS, MC, VI. **Special Amenities: free full breakfast and free room upgrade (subject to availability with advanced reservations).** *(See color ad p 721)*

SOME UNITS FEE

HOLIDAY INN EXPRESS *Book at aaa.com* **Phone:** (209)826-8282

6/1-9/30	1P: $70-$85	2P: $70-$85	XP: $8	F20
2/1-5/31 & 10/1-1/31	1P: $65-$80	2P: $65-$80	XP: $8	F20

Motel

Location: I-5, exit SR 33, just e. 28976 W Plaza Dr 95322. Fax: 209/826-9039. **Facility:** 100 one-bedroom standard units. 2 stories, exterior corridors. **Parking:** on-site. **Terms:** [ECP] meal plan available. **Amenities:** voice mail, irons, hair dryers. **Pool(s):** heated outdoor. **Leisure Activities:** whirlpool, exercise room. **Guest Services:** coin laundry. **Cards:** AX, CB, DC, DS, MC, VI. **Special Amenities: free expanded continental breakfast and free local telephone calls.** *(See color ad p 721)*

SOME UNITS

RAMADA INN MISSION DE ORO *Book at aaa.com* **Phone:** (209)826-4444

Small-scale Hotel

6/2-1/31	1P: $71-$91	2P: $71-$91	XP: $10	F18
2/1-6/1	1P: $67-$87	2P: $67-$87	XP: $10	F18

Location: I-5, exit SR 33, just w. 13070 Hwy 33 S 95322. Fax: 209/826-8071. **Facility:** 161 one-bedroom standard units. 2 stories, interior/exterior corridors. **Parking:** on-site. **Terms:** cancellation fee imposed, pets ($10 extra charge). **Amenities:** voice mail, irons, hair dryers. **Pool(s):** outdoor. **Leisure Activities:** whirlpool. **Guest Services:** coin laundry. **Business Services:** conference facilities. **Cards:** AX, CB, DC, DS, MC, VI. ***(See color ad below)***

ASK S/D FEE DATA PORT SOME UNITS

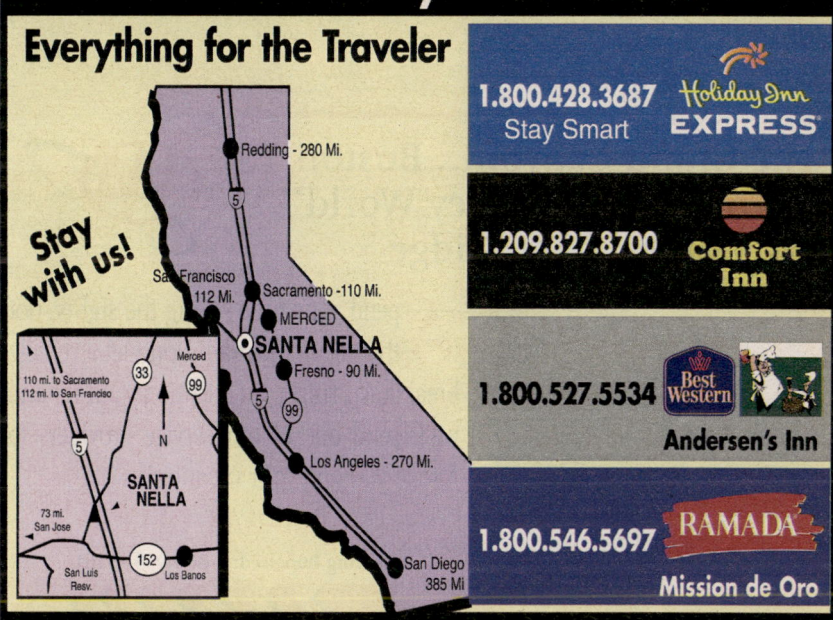

SANTA ROSA —See Wine Country p. 800.

SARATOGA pop. 29,843

WHERE TO STAY

THE INN AT SARATOGA *Book at aaa.com* **Phone:** (408)867-5020

Small-scale Hotel

All Year [ECP] 1P: $179 2P: $179 XP: $20 F18

Location: Just n of SR 9; center. 20645 Fourth St 95070. Fax: 408/741-0981. **Facility:** Smoke free premises. 45 units. 41 one-bedroom standard units, some with whirlpools. 4 one-bedroom suites ($375-$575) with whirlpools. 5 stories, interior corridors. **Parking:** on-site. **Amenities:** video library, high-speed Internet, dual phone lines, voice mail, honor bars, irons, hair dryers. **Leisure Activities:** exercise room. **Guest Services:** complimentary evening beverages. **Business Services:** meeting rooms. **Cards:** AX, CB, DC, MC, VI.

SARATOGA OAKS LODGE *Book at aaa.com* **Phone:** 408/867-3307

AAA SAVE

Motel

All Year 1P: $125-$250 2P: $125-$250 XP: $10 D18

Location: SR 85, exit Saratoga Ave, 2 mi w. 14626 Big Basin Way 95070. Fax: 408/867-6765. **Facility:** Smoke free premises. 26 units. 20 one-bedroom standard units. 6 one-bedroom suites ($225-$450). 2 stories, exterior corridors. *Bath:* combo or shower only. **Parking:** on-site. **Terms:** 3 day cancellation notice, [CP] meal plan available. **Amenities:** high-speed Internet, voice mail, hair dryers. *Some:* irons. **Guest Services:** valet laundry. **Business Services:** meeting rooms. **Cards:** AX, DS, MC, VI. **Special Amenities: free continental breakfast and early check-in/late check-out.**

WHERE TO DINE

LA MERE MICHELLE **Lunch:** $10-$20 **Dinner:** $20-$45 **Phone:** 408/867-5272

French

Location: 0.3 mi sw on SR 9. 14467 Big Basin Way 95070. **Hours:** 11:30 am-2 & 6-9 pm, Sat-10 pm. Closed major holidays; also Mon. **Reservations:** suggested. **Features:** Quiet and refined, the dining room is appointed in casually elegant decor. Smoking is permitted only on the terrace. Dressy casual; cocktails. **Parking:** on-site. **Cards:** AX, CB, DC, MC, VI.

THE PLUMED HORSE **Dinner:** $20-$36 **Phone:** 408/867-4711

French

Location: 0.3 mi sw on SR 9. 14555 Big Basin Way 95070. **Hours:** 5:30 pm-10 pm. Closed major holidays; also Sun. **Reservations:** suggested. **Features:** Old World charm permeates the relaxing dining room. The often-changing menu occasionally includes a prix fixe dinner, and dishes are prepared from fresh seasonal products. The wine cellar is outstanding. Dressy casual; cocktails; entertainment. **Parking:** valet. **Cards:** AX, DC, DS, MC, VI.

SAUSALITO —See San Francisco p. 680.

SCOTTS VALLEY pop. 11,385—*See also APTOS, CAPITOLA, FELTON & SANTA CRUZ.*

—— WHERE TO STAY ——

BEST WESTERN INN SCOTTS VALLEY *Book at aaa.com* **Phone:** (831)438-6666

AAA SAVE — Motel

6/1-9/6 [ECP]	1P: $89-$225	2P: $89-$225	XP: $6	F12
4/1-5/31 & 9/7-1/31 [ECP]	1P: $89-$99	2P: $89-$99	XP: $6	F12
2/1-3/31 [ECP]	1P: $79-$89	2P: $79-$89	XP: $6	F12

Location: SR 17, exit Granite Creek, just w. 6020 Scotts Valley Dr 95066. Fax: 831/439-8752. **Facility:** 58 units. 55 one-bedroom standard units. 3 one-bedroom suites ($120-$225) with whirlpools. 2 stories, exterior corridors. **Parking:** on-site. **Amenities:** irons, hair dryers. **Pool(s):** small outdoor. **Leisure Activities:** whirlpool. **Guest Services:** coin laundry. **Business Services:** meeting rooms. **Cards:** AX, CB, DC, DS, MC, VI. **Special Amenities: free expanded continental breakfast and free local telephone calls.**

SOME UNITS

HILTON SAN JOSE SOUTH/SCOTTS VALLEY *Book at aaa.com* **Phone:** (831)440-1000

AAA SAVE — Small-scale Hotel

5/21-10/24	1P: $149-$349	2P: $149-$349
2/1-5/20 & 10/25-1/31	1P: $119-$249	2P: $119-$249

Location: SR 17, exit Mt Hermon Rd. 6001 La Madrona Dr 95066. Fax: 831/440-1111. **Facility:** Smoke free premises. 177 units. 159 one-bedroom standard units. 18 one-bedroom suites ($249-$379) with whirlpools. 4 stories, interior corridors. **Parking:** on-site. **Terms:** check-in 4 pm, cancellation fee imposed, pets ($25 extra charge). **Amenities:** video library, video games (fee), high-speed Internet, dual phone lines, voice mail, honor bars, irons, hair dryers. **Dining:** 6:30 am-10 pm, Fri & Sat-11 pm, cocktails. **Pool(s):** heated outdoor. **Leisure Activities:** whirlpool, exercise room. **Guest Services:** gift shop, coin laundry. **Business Services:** conference facilities, business center. **Cards:** AX, DC, DS, MC, VI. **Special Amenities: free newspaper.** *(See color ad below)*

FEE

SEA RANCH —*See Wine Country p. 806.*

SEASIDE —*See Monterey Peninsula p. 492.*

SEBASTOPOL —*See Wine Country p. 806.*

SELMA pop. 19,444

WHERE TO STAY

BEST WESTERN COLONIAL INN *Book at aaa.com* **Phone:** 559/891-0300

Small-scale Hotel

All Year 1P: $69-$130 2P: $79-$150 XP: $10 F12

Location: SR 99, exit Floral Ave, just e. 2799 Floral Ave 93662. Fax: 559/891-1538. **Facility:** 57 one-bedroom standard units. 3 stories, interior corridors. **Parking:** on-site. **Terms:** cancellation fee imposed, [CP] meal plan available. **Amenities:** irons, hair dryers. **Pool(s):** outdoor. **Leisure Activities:** sauna, whirlpool, exercise room. **Guest Services:** coin laundry. **Cards:** AX, DC, DS, MC, VI. **Special Amenities: free continental breakfast.**

SOME UNITS / FEE FEE

HOLIDAY INN-SWAN COURT *Book at aaa.com* **Phone:** (559)891-8000

Small-scale Hotel

All Year 1P: $83-$129 2P: $83-$129

Location: SR 99, exit Floral Ave, just w. 2950 Pea Soup Andersen Blvd 93662. Fax: 559/891-9575. **Facility:** 66 units. 60 one-bedroom standard units. 6 one-bedroom suites ($165), some with whirlpools. 3 stories, interior corridors. **Parking:** on-site. **Terms:** cancellation fee imposed, [AP] meal plan available. **Amenities:** voice mail, irons, hair dryers. **Pool(s):** outdoor. **Leisure Activities:** whirlpool, exercise room. **Guest Services:** valet and coin laundry. **Business Services:** conference facilities. **Cards:** AX, DC, DS, JC, MC, VI.

SOME UNITS / ASK

SUPER 8 MOTEL *Book at aaa.com* **Phone:** 559/896-2800

Small-scale Hotel

All Year 1P: $52-$64 2P: $58-$70 XP: $6 F10

Location: SR 99, exit Floral Ave. 3142 S Highland Ave 93662. Fax: 559/896-7244. **Facility:** 39 one-bedroom standard units. 2 stories (no elevator), interior corridors. **Parking:** on-site. **Terms:** [ECP] meal plan available, pets ($5 fee, $20 deposit). **Pool(s):** outdoor. **Cards:** AX, CB, DC, DS, MC, VI. **Special Amenities: free continental breakfast and free local telephone calls.**

SOME UNITS / FEE

SEQUOIA NATIONAL PARK —*See also KINGS CANYON NATIONAL PARK*

WHERE TO STAY

STONY CREEK LODGE **Phone:** (559)452-1081

Small-scale Hotel

5/13-9/19 1P: $125 2P: $125 XP: $12 F12

Location: On General's Hwy, between Grant Grove and Giant Forest, 13 mi s of jct SR 180. General's Hwy 93633 (5755 E Kings Canyon Rd, Suite 101, FRESNO, 93727). Fax: 559/452-1353. **Facility:** Smoke free premises. 11 one-bedroom standard units. 2 stories, interior corridors. *Bath:* combo or shower only. **Parking:** on-site. **Terms:** open 5/13-9/19, check-in 4 pm, 14 day cancellation notice-fee imposed. **Amenities:** voice mail. *Some:* irons, hair dryers. **Dining:** 11:30 am-2 & 5-8 pm. **Leisure Activities:** fishing, hiking trails. **Guest Services:** gift shop, coin laundry. **Cards:** AX, DS, MC, VI. *(See color ad below)*

WUKSACHI VILLAGE & LODGE Book at aaa.com Phone: (559)565-4070

Small-scale Hotel

4/30-10/30	1P: $165-$229	2P: $165-$229	XP: $10	F12
10/31-1/31	1P: $96-$143	2P: $96-$143	XP: $10	F12
2/1-4/29	1P: $96-$133	2P: $96-$133	XP: $10	F12

Location: 6 mi n of Giant Forest on Generals Hwy. 64740 Wuksachi Way 93262 (PO Box 89). Fax: 559/565-4098. **Facility:** 102 units. 84 one-bedroom standard units. 18 one-bedroom suites. 3 stories, interior corridors. **Parking:** on-site. **Terms:** check-in 4 pm. **Amenities:** irons, hair dryers. **Dining:** dining room, see separate listing. **Leisure Activities:** cross country skiing, hiking trails. **Guest Services:** gift shop. **Business Services:** meeting rooms, fax (fee). **Cards:** AX, DC, DS, MC, VI. ***(See color ad below)***

SOME UNITS

WHERE TO DINE

WUKSACHI VILLAGE & LODGE DINING ROOM **Lunch:** $6-$9 **Dinner:** $8-$22 **Phone:** 559/565-4070

American

Location: 6 mi n of Giant Forest on Generals Hwy; at Wuksachi Village & Lodge. 64740 Wuksachi Way 93262. **Hours:** 7-10 am, 11:30-2 & 5-10 pm; hours vary in winter. **Reservations:** accepted. **Features:** Picture windows in the large dining room look toward the forest and mountains. Luncheon features include sandwiches, soups and salads, while the dinner menu lists a limited selection of beef, seafood, chicken and pasta dishes. Patrons can order boxed lunches to go. Casual dress; cocktails. **Parking:** on-site. **Cards:** AX, CB, DC, DS, MC, VI.

SHASTA LAKE pop. 9,008—*See also REDDING.*

WHERE TO STAY

BRIDGE BAY RESORT **Phone:** (530)275-3021

AAA SAVE

Motel

5/1-9/30	1P: $103-$175	2P: $103-$175	XP: $10	F5
2/1-4/30 & 10/1-1/31	1P: $78-$138	2P: $78-$138	XP: $10	F5

Location: I-5, exit 690, e of I-5, exit Bridge Bay Rd; 12 mi n of Redding. Located on Lake Shasta. (10300 Bridge Bay Rd, REDDING, 96003). Fax: 530/275-8365. **Facility:** 40 units. 32 one-bedroom standard units. 8 one-bedroom suites ($135-$175) with kitchens. 2 stories, exterior corridors. *Bath:* shower or tub only. **Parking:** on-site. **Terms:** 2 night minimum stay - in suites, age restrictions may apply, 3 day cancellation notice, pets ($25 deposit, $5 extra charge). **Amenities:** *Some:* irons, hair dryers. **Dining:** 8 am-2 & 5-9 pm, Sat & Sun-10 pm. **Pool(s):** outdoor. **Leisure Activities:** rental boats, boat ramp, waterskiing, fishing. *Fee:* houseboats, patioboats, sea-doos. **Business Services:** meeting rooms. **Cards:** DS, MC, VI.

SOME UNITS

FEE

FAWNDALE LODGE & RV RESORT **Phone:** (530)275-8000

AAA SAVE

Motel

4/1-9/30 [CP]	1P: $69-$79	2P: $77-$87	XP: $8	D12
10/1-1/31	1P: $69-$79	2P: $69-$79	XP: $8	D12
2/1-3/31	1P: $59-$67	2P: $59-$67	XP: $8	D12

Location: I-5, exit 689, 1 mi s of Shasta Lake; e of I-5, exit Fawndale Rd; 10 mi n of Redding. (15215 Fawndale Rd, REDDING, 96003). Fax: 530/275-1863. **Facility:** 7 units. 2 one- and 3 two-bedroom standard units, some with kitchens. 2 one-bedroom suites ($110-$118) with kitchens. 1 story, exterior corridors. *Bath:* shower only. **Parking:** on-site. **Terms:** office hours 7 am-10 pm, age restrictions may apply, 4 day cancellation notice-fee imposed, weekly rates available, pets ($6 fee, $50 deposit). **Amenities:** *Some:* irons, hair dryers. **Pool(s):** outdoor. **Leisure Activities:** badminton, barbecue pavilion, croquet, horseshoes, volleyball. **Guest Services:** coin laundry. **Cards:** AX, DS, MC, VI. **Special Amenities: free continental breakfast and free local telephone calls.**

SOME UNITS

VCR

FEE

O'BRIEN MOUNTAIN INN BED & BREAKFAST **Phone:** (530)238-8026

Bed & Breakfast

All Year [BP]	1P: $125-$265	2P: $135-$275	XP: $25	F12

Location: 4 mi n of Lake Shasta/Pit River Bridge; I-5, exit O'Brien/Shasta Caverns, 0.3 mi w. 18026 O'Brien Inlet Rd (PO Box 27, O'BRIEN, 96070-0027). Fax: 530/238-2027. **Facility:** Nestled in the mountainside, the inn overlooks Lassen Peak, Castle Crags Wilderness and the permanently snow-capped Mt Shasta. Smoke free premises. 7 units. 4 one-bedroom standard units, some with whirlpools. 3 one-bedroom suites ($225-$275) with efficiencies, some with whirlpools. 2 stories (no elevator), interior corridors. *Bath:* combo or shower only. **Parking:** on-site. **Terms:** office hours 9 am-9 pm, check-in 4 pm, 7 day cancellation notice-fee imposed. **Amenities:** video library, CD players. *Some:* DVD players, irons, hair dryers. **Leisure Activities:** game room. **Guest Services:** complimentary evening beverages. **Cards:** AX, DS, MC, VI.

(See color ad below)

SOME UNITS

VCR DATA PORT

SHASTA DAM MOTEL **Phone:** (530)275-1065

AAA SAVE

Motel

All Year [CP]	1P: $49-$59	2P: $56-$66	XP: $7	D12

Location: I-5, exit 685 (Shasta Dam Blvd), just w, then just n on Union School Rd; 6 mi s of Lake Shasta. 1529 Cascade Blvd 96079 (PO Box 71033, PROJECT CITY). Fax: 530/549-5722. **Facility:** 14 one-bedroom standard units. 1 story, exterior corridors. *Bath:* shower only. **Parking:** on-site. **Terms:** office hours 7 am-9 pm, age restrictions may apply, 3 day cancellation notice, weekly rates available, package plans. **Pool(s):** outdoor. **Leisure Activities:** barbecue, picnic area. **Business Services:** fax. **Cards:** AX, CB, DC, DS, JC, MC, VI. **Special Amenities: free continental breakfast and free local telephone calls.**

SOME UNITS

DATA PORT

SHAVER LAKE pop. 705

WHERE TO STAY

DINKEY CREEK INN & CHALETS — Phone: 559/841-3435

Cottage

All Year — 2P: $85-$100

Location: SR 168, 13.5 mi e. 53861 Dinkey Creek Rd 93664. Fax: 559/841-3435. **Facility:** 4 cottages. 1 story, exterior corridors. *Bath:* shower only. **Parking:** on-site. **Terms:** weekly rates available, pets ($25 fee). **Leisure Activities:** cross country skiing, snowmobiling, bicycles, hiking trails, horseshoes, volleyball. **Cards:** DC, MC, VI.

FEE

ELLIOTT HOUSE BED & BREAKFAST — Phone: (559)841-8601

Bed & Breakfast

All Year [BP] — 1P: $109-$149 — 2P: $109-$149 — XP: $15 — F10

Location: Center. 42062 Tollhouse Rd 93664 (PO Box 297). Fax: 559/841-8602. **Facility:** 4 one-bedroom standard units. 2 stories (no elevator), interior corridors. *Bath:* combo or shower only. **Parking:** on-site. **Terms:** 2 night minimum stay - weekends, 14 day cancellation notice. **Amenities:** hair dryers. **Guest Services:** complimentary evening beverages. **Cards:** AX, DS, MC, VI.

ASK

SHELTER COVE

WHERE TO STAY

SHELTER COVE MOTOR INN — **Phone:** 707/986-7521

AAA SAVE — Motel

5/1-9/30 — 2P: $88-$120 — XP: $10 — F12

2/1-4/30 & 10/1-1/31 — 2P: $75-$105 — XP: $10 — F12

Location: 23 mi w of US 101 via Shelter Cove Rd, 1 mi n on Upper Pacific Rd, w on Lower Pacific Rd. 205 Wave Dr 95589. Fax: 707/986-7521. **Facility:** Smoke free premises. 16 one-bedroom standard units with efficiencies. 3 stories (no elevator), exterior corridors. **Parking:** on-site. **Terms:** office hours 8 am-10 pm. **Amenities:** hair dryers. *Some:* irons. **Guest Services:** coin laundry. **Cards:** MC, VI.

VCR

SIERRA CITY

WHERE TO STAY

HERRINGTON'S SIERRA PINES — **Phone:** 530/862-1151

AAA SAVE — Motel

5/1-10/31 — 1P: $65-$89 — 2P: $65-$89 — XP: $5

Location: 0.5 mi w on SR 49. 104 Main St 96125 (PO Box 235). **Facility:** 19 one-bedroom standard units, some with kitchens. 1 story, exterior corridors. *Bath:* shower only. **Parking:** on-site. **Terms:** open 5/1-10/31, 2 night minimum stay - with Saturday stayover, 7 day cancellation notice. **Amenities:** *Some:* irons, hair dryers. **Dining:** 8 am-11 & 5-9 pm, cocktails. **Leisure Activities:** picnic tables by the river. *Fee:* fishing. **Guest Services:** gift shop. **Cards:** DS, MC, VI.

HOLLY HOUSE — **Phone:** 530/862-1123

AAA SAVE — Historic Bed & Breakfast

5/28-9/7 — 1P: $90-$140 — 2P: $90-$140 — XP: $15 — D23

Location: SR 4. 119 Main St 96125 (PO Box 350). Fax: 530/862-1040. **Facility:** Historic 1886 Italiante Victorian. 6 one-bedroom standard units, some with whirlpools. 2 stories (no elevator), interior corridors. *Bath:* some combo or shower only. **Parking:** on-site. **Terms:** open 5/28-9/7, office hours 7 am-8 pm, check-in 4 pm, 2 night minimum stay - weekends, age restrictions may apply, 7 day cancellation notice-fee imposed, [BP] meal plan available. **Amenities:** video library, hair dryers. *Some:* irons. **Cards:** AX, DS, MC, VI.

SOME UNITS

VCR

RIVERSIDE INN — **Phone:** (530)289-1000

Motel

All Year [CP] — 1P: $63-$70 — 2P: $63-$70 — XP: $10 — F16

Location: Downieville Hwy 49; center of town. 206 Commercial St 95936 (PO Box 176, DOWNIEVILLE). Fax: 530/289-1025. **Facility:** 11 one-bedroom standard units, some with kitchens. 2 stories (no elevator), exterior corridors. **Parking:** on-site. **Terms:** 3 day cancellation notice, pets ($10 fee). **Leisure Activities:** fishing, bicycles, hiking trails. **Cards:** AX, DS, MC, VI.

SOME UNITS

FEE

SMITH RIVER

WHERE TO STAY

SHIP ASHORE MOTEL — **Phone:** (707)487-3141

Motel

6/16-10/31 & 12/31-1/31 — 1P: $63-$90 — 2P: $69-$90 — XP: $6 — F12

2/1-6/15 & 11/1-12/30 — 1P: $54-$83 — 2P: $60-$86 — XP: $6 — F12

Location: 2.8 mi n on US 101; 3 mi s of OR-CA state line. 12370 Hwy 101 95567. Fax: 707/487-7070. **Facility:** 50 units. 48 one- and 2 two-bedroom standard units, some with kitchens and/or whirlpools. 2 stories (no elevator), exterior corridors. **Parking:** on-site. **Terms:** age restrictions may apply, small pets only (with prior approval). **Amenities:** irons, hair dryers. **Leisure Activities:** boat ramp, fishing. **Guest Services:** gift shop, coin laundry. **Business Services:** conference facilities. **Cards:** AX, DS, MC, VI.

SOME UNITS

WHITE ROSE MANSION INN Phone: 707/487-9260

Historic Bed & Breakfast

All Year [BP] 2P: $118-$275 XP: $45

Location: US 101, exit Fred Haight Dr, then w. 149 S Fred Haight Dr 95567 (PO Box 428). Fax: 707/487-0303. **Facility:** Built in 1869, the mansion is on grounds which feature a gazebo, a bubbling fountain and a lush forest of rhododendrons and cedars. 7 units. 6 one-bedroom standard units, some with whirlpools. 1 cottage. 2 stories (no elevator), interior/exterior corridors. *Bath:* combo, shower or tub only. **Parking:** on-site. **Terms:** age restrictions may apply, 10 day cancellation notice-fee imposed. **Amenities:** CD players, hair dryers. *Some:* irons. **Business Services:** meeting rooms. **Cards:** DS, MC, VI. **Special Amenities: free local telephone calls.**

SOME UNITS

SODA SPRINGS pop. 450

WHERE TO STAY

ICE LAKES LODGE Phone: (530)426-7660

Motel

2/1-4/25	1P: $110-$170	2P: $110-$170
9/20-1/31	1P: $90-$170	2P: $90-$170
6/5-9/19	1P: $105-$150	2P: $105-$150
4/26-6/4	1P: $90-$125	2P: $90-$125

Location: I-80, exit Soda Springs, 3 mi s. 1111 Soda Springs Rd 95128 (PO Box 850, 95728). Fax: 530/426-7667. **Facility:** 26 one-bedroom standard units. 2 stories, interior corridors. **Parking:** on-site. **Terms:** 14 day cancellation notice - fee imposed. **Amenities:** hair dryers. **Cards:** AX, DS, MC, VI.

SOLEDAD pop. 11,263

WHERE TO STAY

BEST WESTERN VALLEY HARVEST INN *Book at aaa.com* Phone: (831)678-3833

Motel

4/1-10/31 [CP]	1P: $89-$170	2P: $89-$170	XP: $10	F12
2/1-3/31 & 11/1-1/31 [CP]	1P: $79-$150	2P: $79-$150	XP: $10	F12

Location: US 101, exit Soledad, just e. 1155 Front St 93960. Fax: 831/678-3011. **Facility:** 59 one-bedroom standard units. 2 stories, interior/exterior corridors. **Parking:** on-site. **Terms:** small pets only ($10 fee). **Amenities:** irons, hair dryers. **Dining:** 2 restaurants, 5:30 am-10:30 pm. **Pool(s):** outdoor. **Leisure Activities:** whirlpool. **Business Services:** meeting rooms. **Cards:** AX, CB, DC, DS, MC, VI. **Special Amenities: free continental breakfast and free local telephone calls.**

SOME UNITS

FEE FEE FEE

SOLEDAD MOTEL 8 Phone: 831/678-3814

Motel

All Year 1P: $55-$88

Location: US 101, exit 2nd Soledad southbound; exit 1st Soledad northbound. 1013 S Front St 93960. Fax: 831/678-3141. **Facility:** 60 one-bedroom standard units. 2 stories, exterior corridors. *Bath:* combo or shower only. **Parking:** on-site. **Amenities:** *Some:* irons. **Cards:** AX, DS, MC, VI.

SOME UNITS

SONOMA

—See Wine Country p. 807.

SONORA pop. 4,423

WHERE TO STAY

ALADDIN MOTOR INN Phone: (209)533-4971

Motel

All Year [ECP] 1P: $68-$102 2P: $76-$102 XP: $8 F6

Location: On SR 108, 3.5 mi e. 14260 Mono Way (Hwy 108) 95370 (PO Box 356, STANDARD, 95373). Fax: 209/532-1522. **Facility:** 61 one-bedroom standard units. 2 stories (no elevator), interior/exterior corridors. **Parking:** on-site. **Terms:** pets ($5 extra charge, in limited units). **Amenities:** video library. **Pool(s):** heated outdoor. **Leisure Activities:** whirlpool. **Guest Services:** coin laundry. **Cards:** AX, DC, DS, MC, VI.

SOME UNITS

FEE FEE

BARRETTA GARDENS INN Phone: (209)532-6039

Bed & Breakfast

All Year [BP] 2P: $100-$260 XP: $15 F9

Location: Downtown. 700 S Barretta St 95370. Fax: 209/532-8257. **Facility:** Within the historic district, this turn-of-the-20th-century Victorian home offers shady porches, fragrant gardens and a cozy living room fireplace. Smoke free premises. 5 units. 4 one-bedroom standard units, some with whirlpools. 1 one-bedroom suite. 2 stories (no elevator), interior corridors. *Bath:* combo or shower only. **Parking:** on-site. **Terms:** 2 night minimum stay - with Saturday stayover, 7 day cancellation notice. **Amenities:** video library. **Guest Services:** gift shop. **Cards:** AX, DS, MC, VI. **Special Amenities: free local telephone calls.**

BEST WESTERN SONORA OAKS *Book at aaa.com* Phone: (209)533-4400

Motel

5/1-10/15	1P: $85-$95	2P: $85-$95
2/1-4/30 & 10/16-1/31	1P: $79-$95	2P: $79-$95

Location: 3.5 mi e on SR 108. 19551 Hess Ave 95370. Fax: 209/532-1964. **Facility:** 101 units. 97 one- and 1 two-bedroom standard units, some with whirlpools. 3 one-bedroom suites ($139-$179). 2 stories (no elevator), interior/exterior corridors. *Bath:* combo or shower only. **Parking:** on-site. **Terms:** package plans - seasonal, small pets only ($20 extra charge, in limited units). **Amenities:** irons, hair dryers. *Fee:* video library, video games. **Pool(s):** heated outdoor. **Leisure Activities:** whirlpool. **Guest Services:** valet laundry. **Business Services:** meeting rooms. **Cards:** AX, CB, DC, DS, JC, MC, VI. **Special Amenities: free continental breakfast and free newspaper.**

SOME UNITS

FEE

BRADFORD PLACE INN AND GARDENS Phone: (209)536-6075

AAA SAVE — Bed & Breakfast

All Year [BP] 1P: $120-$180 2P: $135-$195

Location: Just w of SR 49; downtown. 56 W Bradford St 95370. Fax: 209/532-6303. **Facility:** Known as the Keil-Birgson House, this 1889 Victorian home offers guests a peaceful setting reminiscent of a bygone era. 4 one-bedroom standard units, some with whirlpools. 2 stories (no elevator), interior corridors. **Parking:** on-site. **Terms:** office hours 7 am-9 pm. **Amenities:** video library, CD players, irons, hair dryers. **Guest Services:** complimentary laundry. **Business Services:** fax. **Cards:** AX, MC, VI. **Special Amenities: free local telephone calls.** *(See color ad below)*

SOME UNITS

INNS OF CALIFORNIA Phone: (209)532-3633

AAA SAVE — Motel

5/1-10/31	1P: $70-$155	2P: $70-$155	XP: $5	F12
2/1-4/30 & 11/1-1/31	1P: $60-$125	2P: $60-$125	XP: $5	F12

Location: 3 blks e on SR 108 business route. 350 S Washington St 95370. Fax: 209/532-9000. **Facility:** 112 one-bedroom standard units, some with whirlpools. 3 stories (no elevator), exterior corridors. *Bath:* combo or shower only. **Parking:** on-site. **Terms:** cancellation fee imposed. **Pool(s):** outdoor. **Leisure Activities:** whirlpool, game room. **Guest Services:** complimentary laundry. **Cards:** AX, CB, DC, DS, JC, MC, VI. **Special Amenities: free local telephone calls and early check-in/late check-out.**

SOME UNITS

LAVENDER HILL B & B INN Phone: (209)532-9024

AAA SAVE — Bed & Breakfast

All Year [BP] 1P: $85-$140 2P: $95-$150 XP: $25

Location: SR 108 E to downtown. 683 S Barretta St 95370. **Facility:** The 1900's Victorian overlooking the historic goldrush town features a wrap-around porch with a year round garden, making for a memorable experience. 4 one-bedroom standard units. 2 stories (no elevator), interior corridors. *Bath:* combo or shower only. **Parking:** on-site. **Terms:** office hours 8 am-9 pm, 2 night minimum stay - weekends 4/1-10/31, cancellation fee imposed, weekly rates available. **Amenities:** video library, CD players. *Some:* irons, hair dryers. **Leisure Activities:** Fee: massage. **Guest Services:** gift shop, complimentary evening beverages. **Cards:** AX, DC, DS, MC, VI. **Special Amenities: free full breakfast and free local telephone calls.**

SOME UNITS

MINERS MOTEL Phone: (209)532-7850

AAA SAVE — Motel

5/1-9/30	1P: $50-$60	2P: $65-$75	XP: $5	F3
2/1-4/30 & 10/1-1/31	1P: $39-$49	2P: $59-$69	XP: $5	F3

Location: On SR 108 and 49, 1 mi e of Jamestown. 18740 SR 108 95327. Fax: 209/532-6401. **Facility:** 18 one-bedroom standard units. 1-2 stories (no elevator), exterior corridors. *Bath:* combo or shower only. **Parking:** on-site. **Terms:** 3 day cancellation notice, [CP] meal plan available, small pets only ($5 extra charge). **Pool(s):** small outdoor. **Cards:** AX, CB, DC, DS, JC, MC, VI. **Special Amenities: free continental breakfast and free local telephone calls.**

SOME UNITS

FEE

SONORA DAYS INN *Book at aaa.com* **Phone:** (209)532-2400

Motel

4/2-9/1	1P: $79-$89	2P: $83-$93	XP: $10	F12
2/1-4/1 & 9/2-1/31	1P: $71-$87	2P: $73-$89	XP: $6	F12

Location: Downtown. 160 S Washington St 95370. Fax: 209/532-4542. **Facility:** 64 one-bedroom standard units. 3 stories, interior/exterior corridors. *Bath:* combo or shower only. **Parking:** on-site. **Terms:** cancellation fee imposed, [CP] meal plan available, pets ($10 extra charge). **Amenities:** *Some:* irons, hair dryers. **Dining:** 5 pm-10 pm. **Pool(s):** small outdoor. **Business Services:** meeting rooms. **Cards:** AX, DC, DS, MC, VI. **Special Amenities: free continental breakfast and free newspaper.** *(See color ad below)*

FEE SOME UNITS

SONORA GOLD LODGE **Phone:** (209)532-3952

Motel

4/1-10/31 [ECP]	1P: $49-$99	2P: $69-$109	XP: $9
2/1-3/31 & 11/1-1/31 [ECP]	1P: $39-$89	2P: $49-$99	XP: $5

Location: 0.5 mi sw on SR 108 business route and 49. 480 Stockton St 95370. Fax: 209/532-2759. **Facility:** 42 one-bedroom standard units. 1 story, exterior corridors. *Bath:* combo or shower only. **Parking:** on-site. **Terms:** office hours 7 am-11 pm, weekly rates available, package plans, $3 service charge, pets ($10 extra charge). **Pool(s):** small outdoor. **Leisure Activities:** sauna, whirlpool, exercise room. **Cards:** AX, DS, MC, VI. **Special Amenities: free continental breakfast and early check-in/late check-out.**

FEE SOME UNITS

STERLING GARDENS **Phone:** 209/533-9300

Bed & Breakfast

All Year [BP]	1P: $100-$110	2P: $100-$110	XP: $25

Location: 1.5 mi s of SR 108. 18047 Lime Kiln Rd 95370. Fax: 209/532-0498. **Facility:** This English-style country home on land once owned by a mining company, features a flower garden that compliments a vista of a pond and wooded hills. Smoke free premises. 4 one-bedroom standard units. 2 stories (no elevator), interior corridors. *Bath:* combo or tub only. **Parking:** on-site. **Terms:** office hours 7 am-9 pm, 5 day cancellation notice-fee imposed. **Amenities:** video library, hair dryers. **Cards:** AX, CB, DC, DS, MC, VI.

SOUTH LAKE TAHOE —See Lake Tahoe Area p. 373.

SOUTH SAN FRANCISCO —See San Francisco p. 680.

SPRINGVILLE pop. 1,109

WHERE TO STAY

ANNIE'S BED & BREAKFAST — **Phone:** (559)539-3827

Bed & Breakfast

All Year [ECP] 1P: $85 2P: $95 XP: $25

Location: 3.2 mi sw on SR 190, then 0.3 mi s. 33024 Globe Dr 93265. Fax: 559/539-2179. **Facility:** Smoke free premises. 3 one-bedroom standard units. 1 story, interior/exterior corridors. *Bath:* combo or shower only. **Parking:** on-site. **Terms:** 14 day cancellation notice, weekly rates available. **Pool(s):** outdoor. **Leisure Activities:** whirlpool. **Guest Services:** complimentary evening beverages. **Cards:** AX, CB, DC, MC, VI.

SOME UNITS

STOCKTON pop. 243,771

WHERE TO STAY

COMFORT INN — *Book at aaa.com* — **Phone:** 209/931-9341

Motel

Property failed to provide current rates

Location: E of SR 99 at jct SR 88. 3951 E Budweiser Ct 95215. Fax: 209/931-6243. **Facility:** 67 one-bedroom standard units. 3 stories (no elevator), interior corridors. *Bath:* combo or shower only. **Parking:** on-site. **Amenities:** irons, hair dryers. **Pool(s):** outdoor. **Guest Services:** coin laundry.

SOME UNITS

COMFORT INN & SUITES — *Book at aaa.com* — **Phone:** (209)478-4300

AAA SAVE — Motel

All Year [ECP] 1P: $59-$130 2P: $64-$135 XP: $5 F18

Location: I-5, exit March Ln, just e. 2654 W March Ln 95207. Fax: 209/478-1872. **Facility:** 123 units. 104 one-bedroom standard units. 19 one-bedroom suites ($90-$150). 3 stories, exterior corridors. **Parking:** on-site. **Amenities:** video games. *Some:* irons, hair dryers. **Pool(s):** outdoor. **Leisure Activities:** whirlpool. **Business Services:** meeting rooms. **Cards:** AX, CB, DC, DS, MC, VI. **Special Amenities: free expanded continental breakfast and free local telephone calls.**

SOME UNITS

COURTYARD BY MARRIOTT — *Book at aaa.com* — **Phone:** (209)472-9700

AAA SAVE — Small-scale Hotel

All Year 1P: $124-$199 2P: $124-$199

Location: I-5, exit March Ln, 0.5 mi w. 3252 W March Ln 95219. Fax: 209/472-9722. **Facility:** 89 units. 85 one-bedroom standard units. 4 one-bedroom suites ($154-$199) with whirlpools. 3 stories, interior corridors. **Parking:** on-site. **Terms:** [BP] meal plan available. **Amenities:** video games, voice mail, irons, hair dryers. **Pool(s):** heated outdoor. **Leisure Activities:** whirlpool, exercise room. **Guest Services:** coin laundry. **Business Services:** meeting rooms. **Cards:** AX, DC, DS, MC, VI. **Special Amenities: free newspaper and preferred room (subject to availability with advanced reservations).**

SOME UNITS

DATA PORT

ECONO LODGE OF STOCKTON — *Book at aaa.com* — **Phone:** (209)466-5741

AAA SAVE — Motel

5/1-8/31 1P: $54-$59 2P: $58-$62
9/1-1/31 1P: $48-$54 2P: $56-$60
2/1-4/30 1P: $49-$55 2P: $55-$60 XP: $6 F12

Location: I-5, exit 8th St, 0.3 mi s of jct SR 4. 2210 S Manthey Rd 95206. Fax: 209/463-1255. **Facility:** 69 units. 67 one-bedroom standard units. 2 one-bedroom suites. 3 stories (no elevator), interior corridors. *Bath:* combo or shower only. **Parking:** on-site. **Terms:** cancellation fee imposed, small pets only ($25 deposit). **Pool(s):** outdoor. **Guest Services:** coin laundry. **Cards:** AX, DC, DS, MC, VI. **Special Amenities: free local telephone calls.**

SOME UNITS

FEE

GUEST INN

Motel

Phone: (209)931-6675

All Year 1P: $55-$65 2P: $60-$70 XP: $8 F12

Location: E of SR 99 at jct SR 88. 2533 N Piccoli Rd 95215. Fax: 209/931-8351. **Facility:** 27 one-bedroom standard units, some with whirlpools. 2 stories, exterior corridors. **Parking:** on-site. **Terms:** cancellation fee imposed. **Amenities:** hair dryers. **Guest Services:** coin laundry. **Cards:** AX, DC, DS, MC, VI. **Special Amenities: free local telephone calls and free room upgrade (subject to availability with advanced reservations).**

SOME UNITS

HAMPTON INN & SUITES *Book at aaa.com*

Motel

Phone: (209)946-1234

All Year [ECP] 1P: $89-$119 2P: $99-$139 XP: $10 F18

Location: SR 99, exit Arch Rd, just e. 5045 S State Rt 99-E Frontage Rd 95215. Fax: 209/466-6500. **Facility:** 73 units. 70 one-bedroom standard units, some with whirlpools. 3 one-bedroom suites ($99-$149) with whirlpools. 3 stories, interior corridors. **Parking:** on-site. **Amenities:** high-speed Internet, dual phone lines, voice mail, irons, hair dryers. **Pool(s):** heated indoor. **Leisure Activities:** whirlpool, exercise room. **Guest Services:** coin laundry. **Business Services:** meeting rooms, business center. **Cards:** AX, CB, DC, DS, MC, VI. **Special Amenities: free local telephone calls and free newspaper.** *(See color ad p 731)*

SOME UNITS

HOLIDAY INN *Book at aaa.com*

Small-scale Hotel

Phone: (209)474-3301

All Year 1P: $89-$159 2P: $89-$159 XP: $10 F18

Location: I-5, exit March Ln, 2 mi e; corner of El Dorado St. 111 E March Ln 95207. Fax: 209/474-1701. **Facility:** 202 units. 196 one-bedroom standard units. 6 one-bedroom suites ($169-$299) with whirlpools. 3 stories, interior corridors. **Parking:** on-site. **Terms:** 2-3 night minimum stay - seasonal, cancellation fee imposed, [BP] meal plan available. **Amenities:** voice mail, irons, hair dryers. **Dining:** 6:30 am-11 & 6-9 pm, cocktails. **Pool(s):** outdoor. **Leisure Activities:** whirlpool, exercise room. **Guest Services:** valet and coin laundry. **Business Services:** meeting rooms, business center. **Cards:** AX, DS, MC, VI.

SOME UNITS

HOWARD JOHNSON EXPRESS INN-MARINA *Book at aaa.com*

Motel

Phone: (209)948-6151

1/1-1/31 1P: $65-$70 2P: $70-$75 XP: $7 F12

2/1-12/31 1P: $59-$69 2P: $65-$70 XP: $7 F12

Location: 1 blk n; w off El Dorado St via Weber; SR 99 southbound, exit Wilson Way; SR 99 northbound, w via Mariposa Rd to Charter Way; I-5, exit downtown. 33 N Center St 95202. Fax: 209/948-1220. **Facility:** 96 one-bedroom standard units. 3 stories, exterior corridors. **Parking:** on-site. **Terms:** cancellation fee imposed, [CP] meal plan available, small pets only ($20 deposit, $5 extra charge). **Amenities:** hair dryers. *Some:* irons. **Pool(s):** outdoor. **Business Services:** meeting rooms. **Cards:** AX, DC, DS, MC, VI.

SOME UNITS

FEE

INN CAL

Motel

Phone: (209)473-2000

All Year 1P: $49-$89 2P: $54-$89 XP: $5 F17

Location: I-5, exit W Hammer Ln, just w. 3473 W Hammer Ln 95219 (1919 Grand Canal Blvd, Suite B-5, 95207). Fax: 209/478-0876. **Facility:** 122 one-bedroom standard units. 3 stories, exterior corridors. **Parking:** on-site. **Terms:** 3 day cancellation notice. **Pool(s):** outdoor. **Guest Services:** coin laundry. **Cards:** AX, CB, DC, DS, MC, VI.

SOME UNITS

LA QUINTA INN *Book at aaa.com*

Motel

Phone: 209/952-7800

All Year 1P: $80-$95 2P: $86-$101 XP: $6 F18

Location: I-5, exit March Ln, just w. 2710 W March Ln 95219-6571. Fax: 209/472-0732. **Facility:** 153 one-bedroom standard units. 3 stories, exterior corridors. **Parking:** on-site. **Terms:** [ECP] meal plan available, small pets only. **Amenities:** voice mail, irons, hair dryers. **Pool(s):** outdoor. **Guest Services:** valet laundry. **Business Services:** meeting rooms. **Cards:** AX, CB, DC, DS, JC, MC, VI.

SOME UNITS

RADISSON HOTEL STOCKTON *Book at aaa.com* **Phone:** (209)957-9090

Small-scale Hotel

All Year 1P: $89-$119 2P: $89-$119 XP: $10 F17

Location: I-5, exit March Ln, 0.4 mi e. 2323 Grand Canal Blvd 95207. Fax: 209/473-0739. **Facility:** 198 units. 190 one-bedroom standard units. 8 one-bedroom suites ($160-$350). 5 stories, interior corridors. **Parking:** on-site. **Amenities:** voice mail, irons, hair dryers. **Pool(s):** outdoor. **Leisure Activities:** whirlpool, exercise room. **Guest Services:** valet and coin laundry. **Business Services:** conference facilities, business center. **Cards:** AX, DC, DS, MC, VI. *(See color ad below & p 629)*

SOME UNITS

RESIDENCE INN BY MARRIOTT *Book at aaa.com* **Phone:** (209)472-9800

Small-scale Hotel

All Year 1P: $139-$279 2P: $139-$279

Location: I-5, exit March Ln, 0.5 mi w. 3240 W March Ln 95219. Fax: 209/472-9888. **Facility:** 104 units. 51 one-bedroom standard units with kitchens. 29 one- and 24 two-bedroom suites with kitchens. 3 stories, interior corridors. **Parking:** on-site. **Terms:** cancellation fee imposed, pets ($60 deposit, $6 extra charge). **Amenities:** video games, high-speed Internet (fee), voice mail, irons, hair dryers. **Pool(s):** heated outdoor. **Leisure Activities:** whirlpool, exercise room, sports court. **Guest Services:** coin laundry. **Business Services:** meeting rooms. **Cards:** AX, DC, DS, MC, VI. **Special Amenities: free full breakfast and free newspaper.**

SOME UNITS

FEE

SUPER 8 MOTEL *Book at aaa.com* **Phone:** (209)477-5576

Motel

All Year [CP] 1P: $54-$94 2P: $59-$94 XP: $5 F17

Location: I-5, exit March Ln, just w. 2717 W March Ln 95219 (1919 Grand Canal Blvd, Suite B, 95207). Fax: 209/477-5968. **Facility:** 167 one-bedroom standard units. 2 stories, exterior corridors. **Parking:** on-site. **Terms:** 3 day cancellation notice. **Pool(s):** outdoor. **Guest Services:** coin laundry. **Cards:** AX, CB, DC, DS, MC, VI. **Special Amenities: free continental breakfast.**

SOME UNITS

WHERE TO DINE

LE BISTRO

Continental

Lunch: $10-$20 **Dinner:** $23-$52 **Phone:** 209/951-0885
Location: I-5, exit Benjamin Holt Dr; in Village Square Center, behind Lyons. 3121 W Benjamin Holt Dr 95219. **Hours:** 11:30 am-3 & 5-9 pm, Sat & Sun 5 pm-10 pm. Closed: 1/1, 12/25. **Reservations:** suggested. **Features:** Menu offers a French Continental cuisine including a variety of fish, meat and poultry entrees. Semi-formal attire; cocktails. **Parking:** on-site. **Cards:** AX, DC, DS, MC, VI.

ON LOCK SAM

Chinese

Lunch: $5-$9 **Dinner:** $12-$19 **Phone:** 209/466-4561
Location: I-5, exit downtown, 3 blks s. 333 S Sutter St 95203. **Hours:** 11 am-9 pm, Fri & Sat-10 pm. Closed: 11/25, 12/25. **Reservations:** suggested. **Features:** Menu offers a traditional Cantonese cuisine since 1898. Casual dress; cocktails. **Parking:** on-site. **Cards:** AX, MC, VI.

YE OLDE HOOSIER INN

American

Lunch: $4-$8 **Dinner:** $6-$13 **Phone:** 209/463-0271
Location: 1 mi ne on SR 99 business route. 1537 N Wilson Way 95205. **Hours:** 7 am-9 pm, Sat-9:30 pm, Sun-8:30 pm. Closed: 1/1, 7/4, 12/25. **Features:** Family restaurant. Furnished in antiques. Casual dress. **Parking:** on-site. **Cards:** MC, VI.

SUGAR PINE

WHERE TO STAY

ALL SEASONS SUGAR PINE RESORT **Phone:** (209)586-2007

Country Inn

2/1-4/1 & 11/2-1/31	1P: $125-$325	2P: $125-$325
4/2-11/1	1P: $85-$225	2P: $85-$225

Location: 2 mi e on SR 108, just n. 19958 Middle Camp 95383 (PO Box 244, 95321). Fax: 209/586-2002. **Facility:** The unique B&B features fantastic views of the valley and theme rooms that everyone will be pleased to have as something out of the ordinary. Smoke free premises. 5 units. 2 one-bedroom standard units. 3 one-bedroom suites. 3 stories (no elevator), interior corridors. *Bath:* combo or shower only. **Parking:** on-site. **Terms:** check-in 4 pm, age restrictions may apply, 3 day cancellation notice-fee imposed. **Amenities:** video library, DVD players, CD players, irons, hair dryers. **Leisure Activities:** whirlpool. **Cards:** MC, VI.

SUNNYVALE pop. 131,760

WHERE TO STAY

BEST WESTERN INN & SUITES *Book at aaa.com* **Phone:** (408)245-2520

Motel

All Year [BP]	1P: $59-$109	2P: $59-$109	XP: $5	F7

Location: On SR 82, just w of Wolfe Rd. 820 E El Camino Real 94087. Fax: 408/736-9851. **Facility:** 79 one-bedroom standard units, some with whirlpools. 2 stories, exterior corridors. **Parking:** on-site. **Terms:** package plans - seasonal. **Amenities:** video library, high-speed Internet, dual phone lines, voice mail, safes, irons, hair dryers. **Pool(s):** heated outdoor. **Leisure Activities:** whirlpool, putting green, exercise room. **Guest Services:** complimentary laundry. **Business Services:** meeting rooms. **Cards:** AX, DC, DS, MC, VI. **Special Amenities: free full breakfast and early check-in/late check-out.**

SOME UNITS

BEST WESTERN SILICON VALLEY INN *Book at aaa.com* **Phone:** (408)735-7800

Small-scale Hotel

All Year [BP]	1P: $59-$139	2P: $79-$159	XP: $10	F13

Location: US 101, exit Mathilda Ave, just s. 600 N Mathilda Ave 94085. Fax: 408/739-5439. **Facility:** 101 one-bedroom standard units, some with efficiencies and/or whirlpools. 2 stories (no elevator), interior corridors. **Parking:** on-site. **Terms:** cancellation fee imposed. **Amenities:** high-speed Internet, dual phone lines, voice mail, safes, irons, hair dryers. **Leisure Activities:** exercise room. **Guest Services:** valet and coin laundry. **Business Services:** business center. **Cards:** AX, CB, DC, DS, JC, MC, VI. **Special Amenities: free full breakfast and free local telephone calls.**

SOME UNITS

BEST WESTERN SUNNYVALE INN *Book at aaa.com* **Phone:** (408)734-3742

Small-scale Hotel

All Year [ECP]	1P: $59-$139	2P: $79-$159	XP: $10	F13

Location: N off and adjacent to US 101, exit Mathilda Ave, just e on Ross Dr. 940 Weddell Dr 94089. Fax: 408/734-9519. **Facility:** 90 one-bedroom standard units, some with whirlpools. 3 stories, interior corridors. *Bath:* combo or shower only. **Parking:** on-site. **Terms:** cancellation fee imposed. **Amenities:** video library, dual phone lines, voice mail, safes, irons, hair dryers. **Pool(s):** heated outdoor. **Leisure Activities:** exercise room. **Guest Services:** complimentary laundry. **Cards:** AX, CB, DC, DS, MC, VI. **Special Amenities: free newspaper.**

SOME UNITS

COMFORT INN *Book at aaa.com* **Phone:** (408)749-8000

Small-scale Hotel

All Year [ECP]	1P: $69-$149	2P: $79-$169	XP: $10	F17

Location: US 101, exit Mathilda Ave. 595 N Mathilda Ave 94085. Fax: 408/749-0367. **Facility:** 52 one-bedroom standard units, some with whirlpools. 2 stories (no elevator), interior corridors. **Parking:** on-site. **Amenities:** video library, high-speed Internet, dual phone lines, voice mail, safes, irons, hair dryers. **Leisure Activities:** sauna, whirlpool. **Guest Services:** complimentary laundry. **Cards:** AX, CB, DC, DS, JC, MC, VI. **Special Amenities: free expanded continental breakfast and free local telephone calls.**

SOME UNITS

COMFORT INN SUNNYVALE *Book at aaa.com* **Phone:** (408)244-9000

SAVE

Small-scale Hotel

All Year [ECP] 1P: $59-$159 2P: $69-$169 XP: $10 F16

Location: SR 82, 0.3 mi w of Lawrence Expwy. 1071 E El Camino Real 94087. Fax: 408/244-7354. **Facility:** Smoke free premises. 63 one-bedroom standard units. 3 stories, interior corridors. **Parking:** on-site. **Terms:** package plans. **Amenities:** voice mail, irons, hair dryers. **Pool(s):** small outdoor. **Leisure Activities:** whirlpool. **Cards:** AX, DC, DS, JC, MC, VI. **Special Amenities: free expanded continental breakfast and early check-in/late check-out.** *(See color ad below)*

CORPORATE INN/SUNNYVALE *Book at aaa.com* **Phone:** (408)220-1000

Small-scale Hotel

All Year [ECP] 1P: $130-$165 2P: $130-$165 XP: $10 F12

Location: On SR 82, just w of Wolfe Rd. 805 E El Camino Real 94087. Fax: 408/220-1001. **Facility:** Smoke free premises. 73 one-bedroom standard units with efficiencies. 3 stories, interior corridors. *Bath:* combo or shower only. **Parking:** on-site. **Terms:** cancellation fee imposed, weekly rates available, package plans - weekends. **Amenities:** high-speed Internet, dual phone lines, voice mail, safes, irons, hair dryers. **Pool(s):** small heated outdoor. **Leisure Activities:** whirlpool, steamroom, exercise room. **Guest Services:** valet and coin laundry. **Business Services:** meeting rooms. **Cards:** AX, CB, DC, DS, JC, MC, VI.

ASK VCR DATA PORT

DAYS INN *Book at aaa.com* **Phone:** (408)737-1177

SAVE

Small-scale Hotel

All Year [ECP] 1P: $62-$79 2P: $62-$79 XP: $5 F

Location: US 101, exit Mathilda Ave, 0.3 mi s. 590 N Mathilda Ave 94086. Fax: 408/738-6666. **Facility:** 35 one-bedroom standard units, some with whirlpools. 2 stories, interior corridors. **Parking:** on-site. **Terms:** weekly rates available, [CP] meal plan available. **Amenities:** dual phone lines, irons, hair dryers. *Some:* high-speed Internet. **Guest Services:** coin laundry. **Cards:** AX, DC, DS, JC, MC, VI. **Special Amenities: free expanded continental breakfast and early check-in/late check-out.**

DATA PORT / VCR / SOME UNITS

FOUR POINTS BY SHERATON SUNNYVALE *Book at aaa.com* **Phone:** (408)738-4888

SAVE

Small-scale Hotel

All Year 1P: $109 2P: $109

Location: US 101, exit Lawrence Expwy S, e on Oakmead. 1250 Lakeside Dr 94085-4010. Fax: 408/737-7147. **Facility:** 378 one-bedroom standard units. 3 stories, interior corridors. **Parking:** on-site. **Terms:** weekly rates available, package plans - weekends. **Amenities:** video games (fee), dual phone lines, voice mail, irons, hair dryers. **Dining:** 2 restaurants, 6:30 am-10 pm, cocktails. **Pool(s):** heated outdoor. **Leisure Activities:** whirlpool, exercise room. **Guest Services:** gift shop, valet laundry, area transportation-within 5 mi. **Business Services:** conference facilities, business center. **Cards:** AX, CB, DC, DS, JC, MC, VI. **Special Amenities: free newspaper and early check-in/late check-out.**

DATA PORT / / SOME UNITS

GRAND HOTEL *Book at aaa.com* **Phone:** (408)720-8500

Small-scale Hotel

All Year 1P: $119-$249 2P: $134-$264 XP: $15 F14

Location: W of Mathilda Ave. 865 W El Camino Real 94086. Fax: 408/720-1997. **Facility:** Smoke free premises. 104 units. 100 one-bedroom standard units, some with kitchens and/or whirlpools. 4 one-bedroom suites with whirlpools. 4 stories, interior/exterior corridors. **Parking:** on-site. **Terms:** check-in 4 pm, [BP] meal plan available. **Amenities:** dual phone lines, voice mail, honor bars, irons, hair dryers. *Some:* high-speed Internet. **Pool(s):** heated outdoor. **Leisure Activities:** whirlpool. **Guest Services:** complimentary evening beverages, area transportation. **Business Services:** meeting rooms. **Cards:** AX, CB, DC, DS, JC, MC, VI.

DATA PORT / / SOME UNITS

HOMESTEAD STUDIO SUITES HOTEL-SUNNYVALE/SANTA CLARA *Book at aaa.com* **Phone:** (408)734-3431

Motel

All Year 1P: $86-$106 2P: $91-$111 XP: $5 F

Location: N of SR 237, exit Mathilda Ave, then e on Moffett Park Dr. 1255 Orleans Dr 94089. Fax: 408/744-1146. **Facility:** 145 one-bedroom standard units with kitchens. 2 stories, exterior corridors. *Bath:* combo or shower only. **Parking:** on-site. **Terms:** weekly rates available, pets ($10 fee, $150 deposit). **Amenities:** dual phone lines, voice mail, irons, hair dryers. *Fee:* video games, high-speed Internet. **Guest Services:** valet and coin laundry. **Cards:** AX, CB, DC, DS, JC, MC, VI.

ASK FEE DATA PORT / VCR FEE / SOME UNITS

LARKSPUR LANDING Book at aaa.com **Phone:** (408)733-1212

SAVE

Small-scale Hotel

All Year 1P: $129-$159 2P: $129-$159 XP: $10 F

Location: US 101, exit Mathilda Ave, then just s. 748 N Mathilda Ave 94086. Fax: 408/733-3343. **Facility:** 126 units. 88 one-bedroom standard units with efficiencies. 38 one-bedroom suites ($149-$179) with efficiencies. 4 stories, interior corridors. *Bath:* combo or shower only. **Parking:** on-site. **Terms:** [CP] meal plan available. **Amenities:** video library, CD players, high-speed Internet, dual phone lines, voice mail, irons, hair dryers. **Leisure Activities:** whirlpool, exercise room. **Guest Services:** valet laundry. **Business Services:** meeting rooms, business center. **Cards:** AX, CB, DC, DS, JC, MC, VI. **Special Amenities: free local telephone calls and free newspaper.** *(See color ad below)*

SOME UNITS

MAPLE TREE INN Book at aaa.com **Phone:** (408)720-9700

SAVE

Small-scale Hotel

All Year 1P: $185-$195 2P: $195-$205 XP: $10 F12

Location: SR 82; between Fair Oaks and Wolfe Rd; 2.5 mi w of US 101. 711 E El Camino Real 94087. Fax: 408/738-5665. **Facility:** 181 one-bedroom standard units. 3 stories, interior corridors. **Parking:** on-site. **Terms:** [ECP] meal plan available. **Amenities:** video games (fee), voice mail, irons, hair dryers. *Some:* dual phone lines. **Pool(s):** heated outdoor. **Guest Services:** valet and coin laundry. **Business Services:** meeting rooms. **Cards:** AX, CB, DC, DS, JC, MC, VI. **Special Amenities: free continental breakfast and free newspaper.** *(See color ad below)*

SOME UNITS

FEE

QUALITY INN-SUNNYVALE Book at aaa.com **Phone:** (408)744-1100

SAVE

Small-scale Hotel

All Year [ECP] 1P: $59-$159 2P: $65-$165 XP: $10 F16

Location: US 101, exit Lawrence Expwy N, 1 mi n to Persian Dr, then 0.3 mi w. 1280 Persian Dr 94089. Fax: 408/744-1688. **Facility:** 72 one-bedroom standard units. 2 stories, interior corridors. **Parking:** on-site. **Terms:** package plans, small pets only ($50 deposit, $10 extra charge). **Amenities:** video library, high-speed Internet, voice mail, irons, hair dryers. *Some:* DVD players. **Pool(s):** heated outdoor. **Leisure Activities:** exercise room. **Guest Services:** valet laundry. **Cards:** AX, DC, DS, JC, MC, VI. **Special Amenities: free expanded continental breakfast and early check-in/late check-out.** *(See color ad p 737)*

SOME UNITS

FEE

QUALITY INN SUNNYVALE CIVIC CENTER Book at aaa.com **Phone:** (408)773-1234

SAVE

Small-scale Hotel

All Year 1P: $79-$149 2P: $89-$169 XP: $10 F16

Location: W of Mathilda Ave. 852 W El Camino Real 94087. Fax: 408/773-0420. **Facility:** 59 one-bedroom standard units. 3 stories, interior corridors. **Parking:** on-site. **Terms:** [BP] meal plan available. **Amenities:** voice mail, irons, hair dryers. **Guest Services:** valet laundry. **Cards:** AX, CB, DC, DS, JC, MC, VI. **Special Amenities: free continental breakfast and free newspaper.**

SOME UNITS

RADISSON INN-SUNNYVALE *Book at aaa.com* **Phone:** (408)247-0800

Small-scale Hotel

All Year [BP] 1P: $79-$149 2P: $79-$149 XP: $10 F12

Location: SR 82; 0.3 mi w of Lawrence Expwy. 1085 E El Camino Real 94087. Fax: 408/984-7120. **Facility:** 136 one-bedroom standard units, some with whirlpools. 3 stories, interior corridors. **Parking:** on-site. **Terms:** cancellation fee imposed, small pets only ($10 extra charge). **Amenities:** video games (fee), dual phone lines, voice mail, honor bars, irons, hair dryers. **Pool(s):** heated outdoor. **Leisure Activities:** whirlpool, exercise room. **Guest Services:** valet laundry. **Business Services:** conference facilities. **Cards:** AX, CB, DC, DS, JC, MC, VI. ***(See color ad p 629)***

SOME UNITS

ASK FEE DATA PORT

RAMADA INN-SILICON VALLEY *Book at aaa.com* **Phone:** (408)245-5330

AAA SAVE

Motel

All Year 1P: $59-$99 2P: $59-$99 XP: $15 F

Location: US 101, exit Lawrence Expwy N, just n. 1217 Wildwood Ave 94089. Fax: 408/732-2628. **Facility:** 176 one-bedroom standard units. 2 stories, exterior corridors. **Parking:** on-site. **Amenities:** dual phone lines, voice mail, safes (fee), irons, hair dryers. **Dining:** 2 restaurants, 6 am-2 & 5-10 pm, cocktails. **Pool(s):** heated outdoor. **Leisure Activities:** whirlpool. **Guest Services:** valet and coin laundry, area transportation-within 5 mi. **Business Services:** meeting rooms. **Cards:** AX, CB, DC, DS, JC, MC, VI. **Special Amenities: free local telephone calls and free newspaper.**

SOME UNITS

DATA PORT

RESIDENCE INN BY MARRIOTT *Book at aaa.com* **Phone:** 408/720-1000

Motel

All Year [BP] 1P: $159 2P: $159

Location: US 101, exit Lawrence Expwy S, then e on Oakmead. 750 Lakeway Dr 94086. Fax: 408/737-9722. **Facility:** 231 units. 173 one-bedroom standard units with kitchens. 58 two-bedroom suites with kitchens. 2 stories, exterior corridors. **Parking:** on-site. **Terms:** cancellation fee imposed, pets ($75 fee, $10 extra charge). **Amenities:** video games (fee), dual phone lines, voice mail, irons, hair dryers. **Pool(s):** heated outdoor. **Leisure Activities:** whirlpools, exercise room, sports court. **Guest Services:** complimentary evening beverages, valet and coin laundry, area transportation. **Business Services:** business center. **Cards:** AX, CB, DC, DS, JC, MC, VI.

SOME UNITS

ASK FEE DATA PORT VCR

RESIDENCE INN BY MARRIOTT *Book at aaa.com* **Phone:** 408/720-8893

Motel

All Year [BP] 1P: $79-$169 2P: $79-$169

Location: US 101, exit Lawrence Expwy S, Duane Ave W. 1080 Stewart Dr 94086. Fax: 408/720-8749. **Facility:** 247 units. 185 one-bedroom standard units with kitchens. 62 two-bedroom suites ($79-$169) with kitchens. 2 stories, exterior corridors. **Parking:** on-site. **Terms:** small pets only ($75 deposit, $10 extra charge). **Amenities:** video games (fee), voice mail, irons, hair dryers. **Pool(s):** heated outdoor. **Leisure Activities:** whirlpools, exercise room, sports court. **Guest Services:** coin laundry, area transportation. **Business Services:** meeting rooms. **Cards:** AX, CB, DC, DS, JC, MC, VI.

SOME UNITS

ASK FEE DATA PORT

SHERATON SUNNYVALE *Book at aaa.com* **Phone:** (408)745-6000

AAA SAVE

Small-scale Hotel

All Year 1P: $65-$185 2P: $65-$185 XP: $10 F17

Location: US 101, exit Mathilda Ave. 1100 N Mathilda Ave 94089. Fax: 408/734-8276. **Facility:** 173 one-bedroom standard units. 2 stories, interior corridors. **Parking:** on-site. **Terms:** cancellation fee imposed, [AP] meal plan available. **Amenities:** dual phone lines, voice mail, irons, hair dryers. *Fee:* video games, high-speed Internet. **Dining:** 6:30 am-10:30 pm. **Pool(s):** heated outdoor. **Leisure Activities:** whirlpool, exercise room. **Guest Services:** valet laundry, area transportation-within 5 mi. **Business Services:** conference facilities, business center. **Cards:** AX, CB, DC, DS, JC, MC, VI. **Special Amenities: free newspaper and free room upgrade (subject to availability with advanced reservations).** *(See color ad p 691)*

SOME UNITS

DATA PORT FEE

SILICON WAY INN *Book at aaa.com* **Phone:** (408)734-0555

AAA SAVE — Small-scale Hotel

All Year 1P: $59-$129 2P: $69-$139

Location: N off and adjacent to US 101, exit Mathilda Ave, just e on Ross Dr. 331 E Weddell 94089. Fax: 408/752-2739. **Facility:** Smoke free premises. 14 one-bedroom standard units, some with whirlpools. 2 stories, interior corridors. **Parking:** on-site. **Terms:** cancellation fee imposed, [CP] meal plan available. **Amenities:** dual phone lines, voice mail, irons, hair dryers. **Cards:** AX, DS, JC, MC, VI. **Special Amenities: free continental breakfast and free local telephone calls.**

SUMMERFIELD SUITES BY WYNDHAM-SUNNYVALE/SILICON VALLEY *Book at aaa.com* **Phone:** (408)745-1515

AAA SAVE — Motel

All Year 1P: $89-$129 2P: $89-$129 XP: $20 F18

Location: SR 237, exit Mathilda Ave S, w on Ross. 900 Hamlin Ct 94089. Fax: 408/745-0540. **Facility:** 138 units. 86 one- and 52 two-bedroom suites ($89-$159) with kitchens. 3 stories, exterior corridors. **Parking:** on-site. **Terms:** cancellation fee imposed, [MAP] meal plan available, pets ($150-$200 fee). **Amenities:** voice mail, irons, hair dryers. *Fee:* video library, high-speed Internet. *Some:* dual phone lines. **Pool(s):** heated outdoor. **Leisure Activities:** whirlpool, putting green, exercise room, sports court. **Guest Services:** gift shop, complimentary evening beverages: Mon-Thurs, valet and coin laundry. **Business Services:** meeting rooms. **Cards:** AX, CB, DC, DS, JC, MC, VI.

SOME UNITS

FEE

SUNDOWNER INN *Book at aaa.com* **Phone:** (408)734-9900

Motel

All Year 1P: $79-$129 2P: $89-$139 XP: $10 F10

Location: SW corner of SR 237 and Mathilda Ave; e off US 101. 504 Ross Dr 94089. Fax: 408/747-0580. **Facility:** 105 one-bedroom standard units, some with whirlpools. 2 stories, interior/exterior corridors. **Parking:** on-site. **Terms:** [BP] meal plan available, package plans. **Amenities:** video games (fee), high-speed Internet, dual phone lines, voice mail, irons, hair dryers. *Some:* safes, honor bars. **Pool(s):** heated outdoor. **Leisure Activities:** sauna, exercise room. **Guest Services:** complimentary laundry. **Business Services:** meeting rooms. **Cards:** AX, DC, DS, MC, VI. ***(See color ad below)***

SOME UNITS

VAGABOND INN *Book at aaa.com* **Phone:** (408)734-4607

AAA SAVE — Motel

All Year 1P: $49-$199 2P: $54-$209 XP: $10 F18

Location: US 101, exit Mathilda Ave S, then s. 816 Ahwanee Ave 94086. Fax: 408/734-1675. **Facility:** 60 one-bedroom standard units. 2 stories, exterior corridors. **Parking:** on-site. **Terms:** cancellation fee imposed, weekly rates available, [CP] meal plan available, pets ($10 extra charge). **Amenities:** safes (fee), irons. *Some:* dual phone lines, hair dryers. **Pool(s):** heated outdoor. **Cards:** AX, DC, DS, MC, VI. **Special Amenities: free continental breakfast and free local telephone calls.**

SOME UNITS

FEE

WILD PALMS HOTEL *Book at aaa.com* **Phone:** (408)738-0500

Motel

All Year [ECP] 1P: $89-$169 2P: $89-$169 XP: $20 F12

Location: I-280, exit Wolfe Rd, just e. 910 E Fremont Ave 94087. Fax: 408/245-4167. **Facility:** 208 units. 204 one-bedroom standard units. 4 one-bedroom suites. 2 stories (no elevator), exterior corridors. **Parking:** on-site. **Terms:** cancellation fee imposed. **Amenities:** video games (fee), dual phone lines, voice mail, safes, irons, hair dryers. *Some:* CD players, high-speed Internet. **Pool(s):** heated outdoor. **Leisure Activities:** whirlpool, exercise room. **Guest Services:** valet laundry. **Business Services:** meeting rooms, business center. **Cards:** AX, CB, DC, DS, MC, VI.

SOME UNITS

WOODFIN SUITES Book at aaa.com Phone: (408)738-1700

Motel

All Year [BP] 1P: $99-$189 2P: $99-$189

Location: US 101, exit Fair Oaks, 2.5 mi w to SR 82 E. 635 E El Camino Real 94087. Fax: 408/738-0840. **Facility:** 88 units. 81 one- and 7 two-bedroom standard units with kitchens. 2 stories, exterior corridors. **Parking:** on-site. **Terms:** cancellation fee imposed, small pets only ($150 deposit, $5 extra charge). **Amenities:** video library, CD players, high-speed Internet, voice mail, irons, hair dryers. **Pool(s):** small outdoor. **Leisure Activities:** whirlpool. **Guest Services:** complimentary evening beverages, coin laundry. **Business Services:** business center. **Cards:** AX, CB, DC, DS, JC, MC, VI.

ASK FEE DATA PORT

WYNDHAM SUNNYVALE Book at aaa.com Phone: (408)747-0999

Large-scale Hotel

All Year 1P: $79-$155 2P: $79-$155 XP: $20 F17

Location: US 101, exit Lawrence Expwy N; at northwest quadrant of SR 237 and Lawrence Expwy. 1300 Chesapeake Terr 94089. Fax: 408/745-0759. **Facility:** 180 one-bedroom standard units. 5 stories, interior corridors. **Parking:** on-site. **Terms:** cancellation fee imposed. **Amenities:** voice mail, irons, hair dryers. *Fee:* video games, high-speed Internet. *Some:* CD players. **Pool(s):** heated outdoor. **Leisure Activities:** whirlpool, exercise room, sports court. **Guest Services:** valet laundry. **Business Services:** conference facilities, business center. **Cards:** AX, CB, DC, DS, JC, MC, VI.

SOME UNITS

ASK DATA PORT / /

WHERE TO DINE

PEZZELLA'S Lunch: $8-$19 Dinner: $8-$30 Phone: 408/738-2400

AAA

Italian

Location: W of Mary Ave. 1025 W El Camino Real 94087. **Hours:** Open 2/1-8/13 & 9/4-1/31; 11:30 am-2:30 & 5-10:30 pm, Sat from 5 pm. Closed major holidays; also Sun & Mon. **Reservations:** suggested. **Features:** Patrons can sample seafood, steak, veal and pasta dishes in a comfortable, attractive dining room. The restaurant has been family owned for three generations. Dressy casual; cocktails. **Parking:** on-site. **Cards:** AX, CB, DC, DS, MC, VI.

SUSANVILLE pop. 13,541

WHERE TO STAY

AMERICA'S BEST INNS Phone: (530)257-4522

Motel

7/2-9/1 [CP]	1P: $50-$54	2P: $54-$60	XP: $5	F12
4/2-7/1 [CP]	1P: $48-$52	2P: $52-$60	XP: $5	F12
2/1-4/1 & 9/2-1/31 [CP]	1P: $42-$46	2P: $46-$50	XP: $5	F12

Location: 1.5 mi e on SR 36. 2705 Main St 96130. Fax: 530/257-2881. **Facility:** 25 units. 23 one-bedroom standard units, some with kitchens. 2 one-bedroom suites ($75-$105). 1 story, exterior corridors. *Bath:* combo or shower only. **Parking:** on-site. **Terms:** cancellation fee imposed, small pets only ($10 fee). **Cards:** AX, CB, DC, DS, JC, MC, VI.

SOME UNITS

ASK FEE DATA PORT / /

APPLE INN MOTEL Phone: 530/257-4726

Motel

All Year 1P: $35-$45 2P: $46-$57 XP: $3

Location: 1.5 mi e on SR 36. 2720 Main St 96130. **Facility:** 10 units. 9 one- and 1 two-bedroom standard units. 1 story, exterior corridors. *Bath:* combo or shower only. **Parking:** on-site. **Terms:** cancellation fee imposed. **Guest Services:** gift shop. **Cards:** AX, DS, MC, VI.

SOME UNITS

/ /

BEST WESTERN TRAILSIDE Book at aaa.com Phone: (530)257-4123

AAA SAVE

Motel

6/1-1/31	1P: $70-$105	2P: $70-$105	XP: $5	F12
2/1-5/31	1P: $68-$100	2P: $68-$100	XP: $5	F12

Location: 1.5 mi e on SR 36. 2785 Main St 96130 (PO Box 759). Fax: 530/257-2665. **Facility:** 85 units. 83 one-bedroom standard units, some with whirlpools. 2 one-bedroom suites. 2 stories, exterior corridors. **Parking:** on-site. **Terms:** [ECP] meal plan available. **Amenities:** irons, hair dryers. **Pool(s):** heated outdoor. **Business Services:** meeting rooms, administrative services (fee), fax. **Cards:** AX, CB, DC, DS, JC, MC, VI. **Special Amenities: free continental breakfast and free local telephone calls.**

SOME UNITS

DATA PORT / VCR /

HIGH COUNTRY INN Phone: (530)257-3450

AAA SAVE

Motel

5/1-10/31 [ECP]	1P: $71-$87	2P: $75-$87	XP: $5
2/1-4/30 & 11/1-1/31 [ECP]	1P: $62-$82	2P: $66-$86	XP: $5

Location: SR 36, 1.9 mi e. 3015 E Riverside Dr 96130. Fax: 530/257-2460. **Facility:** 66 units. 63 one-bedroom standard units. 3 one-bedroom suites ($100-$120). 2 stories (no elevator), interior corridors. *Bath:* combo or shower only. **Parking:** on-site. **Amenities:** irons, hair dryers. **Pool(s):** heated outdoor. **Leisure Activities:** whirlpool, exercise room. **Cards:** AX, CB, DC, DS, MC, VI. **Special Amenities: free continental breakfast and free local telephone calls.**

SOME UNITS

DATA PORT / /

RIVER INN Phone: (530)257-6051

AAA SAVE

Motel

5/1-10/31	1P: $48-$52	2P: $56-$58	XP: $5
2/1-4/30 & 11/1-1/31	1P: $42-$44	2P: $46-$48	XP: $5

Location: 0.8 mi e on SR 36. 1710 Main St 96130. Fax: 530/257-6093. **Facility:** 49 one-bedroom standard units. 2 stories, exterior corridors. **Parking:** on-site. **Terms:** office hours 7 am-11 pm, cancellation fee imposed, pets ($10 extra charge, in limited units with prior approval). **Amenities:** *Some:* irons. **Pool(s):** outdoor. **Cards:** AX, DS, MC, VI. **Special Amenities: free continental breakfast and free local telephone calls.**

SOME UNITS

FEE

SUPER 8 MOTEL *Book at aaa.com* **Phone:** (530)257-2782

Motel

4/2-10/1	1P: $54-$60	2P: $62-$64	XP: $5	F12
2/1-4/1 & 10/2-1/31	1P: $48-$52	2P: $54-$56	XP: $5	F12

Location: SR 36, 1.8 mi e. 2975 Johnstonville Rd 96130. Fax: 530/257-4956. **Facility:** 69 one-bedroom standard units. 2 stories (no elevator), exterior corridors. **Parking:** on-site. **Terms:** [CP] meal plan available, pets ($5 extra charge in limited units). **Amenities:** *Some:* irons. **Pool(s):** small outdoor. **Business Services:** meeting rooms. **Cards:** AX, DC, DS, MC, VI. **Special Amenities: free continental breakfast and free local telephone calls.**

SOME UNITS
FEE FEE FEE

SUTTER CREEK pop. 2,303

WHERE TO STAY

THE FOXES INN OF SUTTER CREEK BED & BREAKFAST **Phone:** 209/267-5882

Bed & Breakfast

All Year 2P: $155-$210

Location: Center. 77 Main St 95685 (PO Box 159). Fax: 209/267-0712. **Facility:** A gazebo and gardens enhance the grounds of this attractively appointed inn. 7 units. 6 one-bedroom standard units. 1 one-bedroom suite. 2 stories (no elevator), interior/exterior corridors. *Bath:* combo or shower only. **Parking:** on-site. **Terms:** office hours 10 am-8 pm, 2 night minimum stay - with Saturday stayover, age restrictions may apply, 10 day cancellation notice-fee imposed, [BP] meal plan available, package plans. **Amenities:** video library, hair dryers. *Some:* CD players, irons. **Cards:** AX, DS, MC, VI. **Special Amenities: free full breakfast and free newspaper.**

SOME UNITS

GREY GABLES BED & BREAKFAST INN **Phone:** (209)267-1039

Bed & Breakfast

All Year 1P: $110-$280 2P: $110-$280 XP: $30

Location: 0.3 mi n on SR 49. 161 Hanford St 95685 (PO Box 1687). Fax: 209/267-0998. **Facility:** Views of the garden enhance some guest rooms at this English country-style manor. 8 one-bedroom standard units. 3 stories (no elevator), interior corridors. *Bath:* combo or shower only. **Parking:** on-site. **Terms:** office hours 8 am-9:30 pm, 2 night minimum stay - weekends, age restrictions may apply, 10 day cancellation notice-fee imposed, [BP] meal plan available. **Amenities:** hair dryers. **Guest Services:** complimentary evening beverages. **Cards:** AX, CB, DC, DS, MC, VI. **Special Amenities: free local telephone calls.**

SOME UNITS

HANFORD HOUSE BED AND BREAKFAST INN *Book at aaa.com* **Phone:** (209)267-0747

Bed & Breakfast

All Year [BP] 1P: $115-$249 2P: $115-$249 XP: $30 F10

Location: Downtown. 61 Hanford St (SR 49) 95685 (PO Box 1450). Fax: 209/267-1825. **Facility:** Vine-covered red bricks form the facade of this B&B set within wine country and the Sierra Foothills; shops and restaurants are nearby. Smoke free premises. 10 units. 7 one-bedroom standard units, some with whirlpools. 3 one-bedroom suites ($169-$249). 2 stories (no elevator), interior corridors. **Parking:** on-site. **Terms:** office hours 6:30 am-10 pm, 2 night minimum stay - weekends, age restrictions may apply, 10 day cancellation notice-fee imposed, package plans. **Amenities:** video library, CD players, irons, hair dryers. **Guest Services:** complimentary evening beverages. **Cards:** AX, DS, MC, VI. **Special Amenities: free local telephone calls and free newspaper.**

SUTTER CREEK INN **Phone:** 209/267-5606

Bed & Breakfast

All Year [BP] 1P: $80-$185 2P: $80-$185 XP: $25

Location: Center. 75 Main St 95685 (PO Box 385). Fax: 209/267-9287. **Facility:** 17 one-bedroom standard units. 1-2 stories, interior/exterior corridors. *Bath:* combo, shower or tub only. **Parking:** on-site. **Terms:** 4 day cancellation notice-fee imposed. **Amenities:** *Some:* irons, hair dryers. **Guest Services:** complimentary evening beverages. **Cards:** MC, VI.

SOME UNITS

TAFT pop. 6,400

WHERE TO STAY

HOLLAND INN & SUITES **Phone:** 661/763-5211

Small-scale Hotel

All Year 1P: $74-$94 XP: $5 F12

Location: SR 33, 0.3 mi n on 6th St. 531 Warren St 93268. Fax: 661/763-1536. **Facility:** 22 one-bedroom standard units. 2 stories, interior corridors. *Bath:* combo or shower only. **Parking:** on-site. **Terms:** office hours 7 am-10 pm, cancellation fee imposed, [CP] meal plan available. **Amenities:** *Some:* irons, hair dryers. **Leisure Activities:** whirlpool. **Business Services:** fax. **Cards:** AX, DC, DS, MC, VI. **Special Amenities: free local telephone calls and free newspaper.**

SOME UNITS

TAHOE CITY —*See Lake Tahoe Area p. 394.*

TAHOE VISTA —*See Lake Tahoe Area p. 396.*

TEHACHAPI pop. 10,957

WHERE TO STAY

BEST WESTERN MOUNTAIN INN *Book at aaa.com* **Phone:** (661)822-5591

Motel

All Year 1P: $69-$79 2P: $79-$89

Location: SR 58, exit SR 202, then 1 mi e. 418 W Tehachapi Blvd 93561. Fax: 661/822-6197. **Facility:** 73 one-bedroom standard units. 2 stories, exterior corridors. **Parking:** on-site. **Terms:** weekly rates available. **Amenities:** voice mail, irons, hair dryers. **Pool(s):** heated outdoor. **Leisure Activities:** whirlpool. **Guest Services:** coin laundry. **Business Services:** fax (fee). **Cards:** AX, CB, DC, DS, JC, MC, VI. *(See ad below)*

SOME UNITS

TEHACHAPI SUMMIT TRAVELODGE *Book at aaa.com* **Phone:** (661)823-8000

Motel

All Year 1P: $72 2P: $78 XP: $7 F18

Location: SR 58, exit Monolith eastbound; exit Tehachapi Blvd westbound. 500 Steuber Rd 93581 (PO Box 670). Fax: 661/823-8006. **Facility:** 76 units. 74 one-bedroom standard units. 2 one-bedroom suites ($83-$120), some with kitchens and/or whirlpools. 2 stories, interior corridors. **Parking:** on-site. **Terms:** [AP] meal plan available, pets ($7 extra charge, in designated units). **Amenities:** voice mail. *Some:* irons, hair dryers. **Pool(s):** outdoor. **Leisure Activities:** whirlpool, spa. **Guest Services:** gift shop. **Business Services:** meeting rooms, fax (fee). **Cards:** AX, CB, DC, DS, JC, MC, VI. **Special Amenities: free local telephone calls and free newspaper.** *(See color ad below)*

FEE SOME UNITS

TEMPLETON pop. 4,687

WHERE TO DINE

A J SPURS

American

Dinner: $17-$30 **Phone:** 805/434-2700

Location: US 101, exit Main St, 1 mi to town center. 508 Main St 93465. **Hours:** 5 pm-9 pm, Sat & Sun from 4 pm. Closed major holidays. **Reservations:** suggested; except Sat. **Features:** A casual western atmosphere prevails at the family-friendly steakhouse. Steaks, barbecued foods, seafood and pasta are served in large portions. Casual dress; cocktails. **Parking:** on-site. **Cards:** AX, DC, DS, MC, VI.

MCPHEE'S GRILL

American

Lunch: $8-$12 **Dinner:** $10-$25 **Phone:** 805/434-3204

Location: US 101, exit Main St, 1 mi to town center. 416 Main St 93465. **Hours:** 11:30 am-2 & 5-9 pm, Sun-8:30 pm; Sunday brunch 10 am-2 pm. Closed: 7/4, 12/25. **Reservations:** suggested. **Features:** In a restored store in downtown Templeton, the restaurant mingles fresh regional products in its classic California/Mediterranean food. Lending warmth to the dining rooms are old depressed wood paneling and tables covered with oil cloth. Casual dress; beer & wine only. **Parking:** on-site. **Cards:** MC, VI.

THREE RIVERS pop. 2,248—

See also KINGS CANYON NATIONAL PARK, SEQUOIA NATIONAL PARK & VISALIA.

WHERE TO STAY

BEST WESTERN HOLIDAY LODGE *Book at aaa.com* **Phone:** (559)561-4119

Motel

5/1-10/31 [ECP]	1P: $79-$119	2P: $89-$129	XP: $5	F12
2/1-4/30 & 11/1-1/31 [ECP]	1P: $59-$99	2P: $69-$109	XP: $5	F12

Location: SR 198, 2 mi sw of town center. 40105 Sierra Dr 93271. Fax: 559/561-3427. **Facility:** Smoke free premises. 54 units. 53 one-bedroom standard units. 1 one-bedroom suite. 1-2 stories, exterior corridors. *Bath:* combo or shower only. **Parking:** on-site. **Terms:** cancellation fee imposed, pets ($5 extra charge). **Amenities:** irons, hair dryers. **Pool(s):** outdoor. **Leisure Activities:** whirlpool, fishing, hiking trails, playground. **Guest Services:** coin laundry. **Business Services:** fax (fee). **Cards:** AX, DC, DS, MC, VI. **Special Amenities: free expanded continental breakfast and early check-in/late check-out.**

SOME UNITS

FEE

BUCKEYE TREE LODGE **Phone:** (559)561-5900

Motel

4/1-10/31 [CP]	1P: $82-$99	2P: $94-$118	XP: $5
2/1-3/31 & 11/1-1/31 [CP]	1P: $59-$89	2P: $69-$99	XP: $4

Location: SR 198, 6 mi ne of town center; 0.5 mi sw of entrance to Sequoia National Park. 46000 Sierra Dr 93271. Fax: 559/561-4611. **Facility:** 12 units. 11 one-bedroom standard units, some with efficiencies. 1 cottage ($120-$200). 1-2 stories, exterior corridors. *Bath:* combo or shower only. **Parking:** on-site. **Terms:** office hours 8 am-9 pm, 2-3 night minimum stay - seasonal weekends, 3 day cancellation notice, pets ($5 extra charge). **Amenities:** video library (fee), hair dryers. *Some:* irons. **Pool(s):** outdoor. **Leisure Activities:** fishing, barbecue & picnic area. **Business Services:** fax (fee). **Cards:** AX, CB, DC, DS, MC, VI. **Special Amenities: free continental breakfast and free local telephone calls.**

SOME UNITS

FEE

GATEWAY LODGE **Phone:** (559)561-4133

Motel

All Year	1P: $69-$119

Location: SR 198, 6 mi ne of town center; 0.5 mi sw of entrance to Sequoia National Park. 45978 Sierra Dr 93271. Fax: 559/561-3656. **Facility:** Smoke free premises. 7 units. 5 one-bedroom standard units. 2 cottages. 1 story, exterior corridors. *Bath:* combo or shower only. **Parking:** on-site. **Terms:** office hours 10 am-10 pm, 3 day cancellation notice, pets ($10 extra charge). **Amenities:** CD players, hair dryers. *Some:* irons. **Dining:** Gateway Restaurant, see separate listing. **Guest Services:** coin laundry. **Business Services:** fax. **Cards:** AX, DC, DS, MC, VI.

SOME UNITS

FEE

HOLIDAY INN EXPRESS *Book at aaa.com* **Phone:** (559)561-9000

Motel

5/1-9/30 [ECP]	1P: $109-$139	2P: $109-$139	XP: $10	F19
2/1-4/30 [ECP]	1P: $89-$109	2P: $89-$109	XP: $10	F19
10/1-1/31 [ECP]	1P: $79-$99	2P: $79-$99	XP: $10	F19

Location: SR 198, 1.5 mi sw of town center. 40820 Sierra Dr 93271 (PO Box 1149). Fax: 559/561-9010. **Facility:** Designated smoking area. 103 one-bedroom standard units, some with whirlpools. 2 stories, exterior corridors. **Parking:** on-site. **Terms:** check-in 4 pm, 3 day cancellation notice. **Amenities:** dual phone lines, irons, hair dryers. **Pool(s):** outdoor. **Leisure Activities:** sauna, whirlpool, limited exercise equipment. **Guest Services:** coin laundry. **Business Services:** fax. **Cards:** AX, CB, DC, DS, JC, MC, VI. **Special Amenities: early check-in/late check-out.**

SOME UNITS

LAZY J RANCH MOTEL *Book at aaa.com* **Phone:** (559)561-4449

Motel

5/1-10/31 [CP]	1P: $85-$95	2P: $95-$105	XP: $5
2/1-4/30 & 11/1-1/31 [CP]	1P: $70-$80	2P: $85-$95	XP: $5

Location: SR 198, 2.5 mi sw of town center. 39625 Sierra Dr 93271. Fax: 559/561-4889. **Facility:** 18 units. 10 one-bedroom standard units. 1 one- and 2 two-bedroom suites ($200-$222), some with kitchens. 5 cottages ($130-$140). 1 story, exterior corridors. *Bath:* combo or shower only. **Parking:** on-site. **Terms:** office hours 8 am-10 pm, 3 day cancellation notice, pets ($5 extra charge). **Amenities:** video library (fee), hair dryers. *Some:* irons. **Pool(s):** outdoor. **Leisure Activities:** fishing, barbecues, picnic areas, hiking trails, playground, volleyball. **Guest Services:** coin laundry. **Business Services:** fax (fee). **Cards:** AX, DC, DS, MC, VI. **Special Amenities: free continental breakfast and free local telephone calls.** Affiliated with Best Value Inn Brand Membership.

SOME UNITS

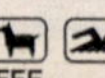
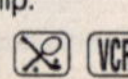

FEE

THE RIVER INN **Phone:** (559)561-4367

Motel

4/1-10/31 [CP]	1P: $89-$119	2P: $89-$119	XP: $10	F17
2/1-3/31 & 11/1-1/31 [CP]	1P: $64-$94	2P: $64-$94	XP: $10	F17

Location: SR 198, 5 mi ne of town center; 1.5 mi sw of entrance to Sequoia National Park. 45176 Sierra Dr 93271 (PO Box 1064). Fax: 559/561-4931. **Facility:** Smoke free premises. 10 one-bedroom standard units. 2 stories, exterior corridors. *Bath:* combo or shower only. **Parking:** on-site. **Terms:** 3 day cancellation notice. **Amenities:** hair dryers. **Leisure Activities:** barbecue & picnic areas. **Cards:** AX, CB, DC, DS, JC, MC, VI. **Special Amenities: free continental breakfast and free local telephone calls.**

SEQUOIA VILLAGE INN **Phone:** (559)561-3652

Cottage

5/1-10/31	1P: $87-$127	2P: $87-$249	XP: $8	F5
2/1-4/30 & 11/1-1/31	1P: $60-$85	2P: $69-$198	XP: $8	F5

Location: SR 198, 6 mi ne of town center; 0.5 mi sw of entrance to Sequoia National Park. 45971 Sierra Dr 93271 (Box 1014). Fax: 559/561-3628. **Facility:** Designated smoking area. 8 units. 3 one-bedroom standard units, some with kitchens. 5 cottages ($69-$127). 2 stories, exterior corridors. *Bath:* combo or shower only. **Parking:** on-site. **Terms:** office hours 8 am-9 pm, 14 day cancellation notice, pets ($5 extra charge). **Amenities:** video library (fee). *Some:* irons, hair dryers. **Pool(s):** outdoor. **Leisure Activities:** whirlpool. **Guest Services:** complimentary laundry. **Business Services:** fax. **Cards:** AX, MC, VI. **Special Amenities: free local telephone calls and free room upgrade (subject to availability with advanced reservations).**

FEE

SIERRA LODGE **Phone:** (559)561-3681

Motel

All Year	1P: $36-$86	2P: $46-$96	XP: $10	D10

Location: SR 198, 1 mi se of town center; 3 mi sw of entrance to Sequoia National Park. 43175 Sierra Dr 93271. Fax: 559/561-3264. **Facility:** 22 units. 17 one-bedroom standard units. 2 one- and 3 two-bedroom suites ($95-$210), some with efficiencies or kitchens. 1-2 stories, exterior corridors. *Bath:* combo or shower only. **Parking:** on-site. **Terms:** 14 day cancellation notice-fee imposed, [CP] meal plan available, pets ($20 deposit, $5 extra charge, in designated units). **Amenities:** *Some:* irons, hair dryers. **Pool(s):** outdoor. **Leisure Activities:** barbecue & picnic areas. **Business Services:** meeting rooms, fax. **Cards:** AX, DC, DS, MC, VI. **Special Amenities: free local telephone calls and free room upgrade (subject to availability with advanced reservations).**

SOME UNITS

FEE FEE

WHERE TO DINE

GATEWAY RESTAURANT **Lunch:** $6-$10 **Dinner:** $13-$25 **Phone:** 559/561-4133

American

Location: SR 198, 6 mi ne of town center; 0.5 mi sw of entrance to Sequoia National Park; in Gateway Lodge. 45978 Sierra Dr 93271. **Hours:** 11 am-9 pm, Sat from 9 am, Sun from 8 am. **Features:** The lovely mountain setting overlooks the river, and guests who sit on the deck have a particularly good vantage point. The menu brings together fish, poultry, meat and pasta dishes. Casual dress; cocktails. **Parking:** on-site. **Cards:** AX, DC, DS, MC, VI.

TIBURON —*See San Francisco p. 686.*

TOMALES pop. 210

WHERE TO STAY

THE CONTINENTAL INN **Phone:** 707/878-2396

Small-scale Hotel

5/1-11/30	1P: $110-$169	2P: $110-$169	XP: $20	F12
2/1-4/30 & 12/1-1/31	1P: $100-$149	2P: $100-$149	XP: $20	F12

Location: On SR 1 at Dillon Beach Rd. 26985 Highway One 94971. Fax: 707/878-2119. **Facility:** 8 one-bedroom standard units. 2 stories, interior corridors. **Parking:** on-site. **Terms:** 7 day cancellation notice-fee imposed. **Cards:** AX, MC, VI. **Special Amenities: free continental breakfast and preferred room (subject to availability with advanced reservations).**

TRACY pop. 56,929

WHERE TO STAY

BEST WESTERN LUXURY INN *Book at aaa.com* **Phone:** (209)832-0271

Motel

All Year	1P: $79-$99	2P: $79-$99	XP: $5	F17

Location: I-205, exit Central Tracy. 811 W Clover Rd 95376. Fax: 209/832-0388. **Facility:** 59 units. 53 one-bedroom standard units. 6 one-bedroom suites ($99-$150). 3 stories, interior corridors. *Bath:* combo or shower only. **Parking:** on-site. **Terms:** 3 day cancellation notice, [ECP] meal plan available, pets ($50 deposit). **Amenities:** voice mail, irons, hair dryers. **Pool(s):** outdoor. **Leisure Activities:** sauna, whirlpool, exercise room. **Guest Services:** coin laundry. **Cards:** AX, DC, DS, MC, VI. **Special Amenities: free expanded continental breakfast and free local telephone calls.**

SOME UNITS

FEE

FAIRFIELD INN BY MARRIOTT *Book at aaa.com* **Phone:** (209)833-0135

Motel

All Year [ECP]	1P: $69-$84	2P: $69-$84

Location: I-205, exit Grantline/Naglee Rd, just n. 2410 Naglee Rd 95304. Fax: 209/833-0135. **Facility:** 64 one-bedroom standard units. 3 stories, interior corridors. *Bath:* combo or shower only. **Parking:** on-site. **Amenities:** irons, hair dryers. **Pool(s):** heated indoor. **Leisure Activities:** whirlpool. **Guest Services:** valet laundry. **Business Services:** meeting rooms. **Cards:** AX, DC, DS, MC, VI.

SOME UNITS

HAMPTON INN-TRACY *Book at aaa.com* **Phone:** (209)833-0483

Motel

All Year [ECP] 1P: $74-$84 2P: $74-$84

Location: I-205, exit Grantline/Naglee Rd, just n. 2400 Naglee Rd 95376. Fax: 209/833-1128. **Facility:** 63 one-bedroom standard units. 3 stories, interior corridors. *Bath:* combo or shower only. **Parking:** on-site. **Amenities:** dual phone lines, voice mail, irons. *Some:* hair dryers. **Pool(s):** heated indoor. **Leisure Activities:** whirlpool. **Guest Services:** valet laundry. **Cards:** AX, DC, DS, MC, VI.

SOME UNITS FEE FEE

HOLIDAY INN EXPRESS HOTEL & SUITES *Book at aaa.com* **Phone:** (209)830-8500

SAVE

Small-scale Hotel

All Year [CP] 1P: $89-$110 2P: $89-$110 XP: $10 F18

Location: I-205, exit Central Tracy. 3751 Tracy Blvd 95304. Fax: 209/836-3424. **Facility:** 103 units. 86 one-bedroom standard units. 17 one-bedroom suites ($99-$159), some with whirlpools. 3 stories, interior corridors. *Bath:* combo or shower only. **Parking:** on-site. **Terms:** cancellation fee imposed. **Amenities:** dual phone lines, voice mail, irons, hair dryers. **Pool(s):** outdoor. **Leisure Activities:** sauna, whirlpool, exercise room. **Guest Services:** coin laundry. **Business Services:** meeting rooms. **Cards:** AX, CB, DC, DS, JC, MC, VI. **Special Amenities: free continental breakfast and free local telephone calls.** *(See color ad p 260)*

SOME UNITS

PHOENIX LODGE **Phone:** (209)835-1335

SAVE

Motel

5/1-10/31 1P: $55-$75 2P: $61-$81 XP: $6 F12

2/1-4/30 & 11/1-1/31 1P: $50-$70 2P: $56-$76 XP: $6 F12

Location: I-205, exit Central Tracy. 3511 N Tracy Blvd 95376. Fax: 209/835-8041. **Facility:** 59 one-bedroom standard units. 3 stories (no elevator), interior corridors. *Bath:* combo or shower only. **Parking:** on-site. **Terms:** 3 day cancellation notice, pets ($20 deposit). **Pool(s):** small outdoor. **Guest Services:** coin laundry. **Cards:** AX, MC, VI.

SOME UNITS FEE

TRINIDAD pop. 311

WHERE TO STAY

BISHOP PINE LODGE **Phone:** 707/677-3314

SAVE

Cabin

2/1-12/31 1P: $80 2P: $80 XP: $10

Location: Just w on US 101, exit Trinidad northbound, then 2 mi n; exit Seawood southbound, then 1 mi s. 1481 Patricks Point Dr 95570. Fax: 707/677-3444. **Facility:** Smoke free premises. 12 cabins. 1 story, exterior corridors. *Bath:* combo or shower only. **Parking:** on-site. **Terms:** open 2/1-12/31, office hours 8:30 am-7 pm, 2 night minimum stay - weekends, age restrictions may apply, pets ($10 extra charge). **Amenities:** safes, hair dryers. *Some:* irons. **Leisure Activities:** barbecue area with individual barbecues, exercise room. **Cards:** AX, MC, VI. **Special Amenities: free local telephone calls.**

SOME UNITS FEE

LOST WHALE BED & BREAKFAST INN **Phone:** (707)677-3425

SAVE

Bed & Breakfast

5/1-10/31 [BP] 1P: $160-$190 2P: $170-$200 XP: $25 F3

2/1-4/30 & 11/1-1/31 [BP] 1P: $130-$160 2P: $140-$170 XP: $25 F3

Location: US 101, exit Seawood, then w. 3452 Patrick's Point Dr 95570. Fax: 707/677-0284. **Facility:** 6 one-bedroom standard units. 2 stories (no elevator), interior corridors. *Bath:* combo or shower only. **Parking:** on-site. **Terms:** office hours 8 am-5 pm, 2 night minimum stay - 6/1-9/30, age restrictions may apply, 7 day cancellation notice-fee imposed, [MAP] meal plan available. **Amenities:** hair dryers. *Some:* irons. **Leisure Activities:** whirlpool. **Cards:** AX, DS, MC, VI. **Special Amenities: free full breakfast and preferred room (subject to availability with advanced reservations).**

SOME UNITS

TRINIDAD BAY BED & BREAKFAST **Phone:** 707/677-0840

Bed & Breakfast

5/1-10/31 [BP] 2P: $150-$190 XP: $20 F12

2/1-4/30 & 11/1-11/30 [BP] 2P: $135-$190 XP: $20 F12

Location: US 101. 560 Edwards St 95570 (PO Box 849). Fax: 707/677-9245. **Facility:** Sweeping Pacific views are a key feature of this traditional B&B just opposite the Trinidad lighthouse. Smoke free premises. 4 one-bedroom standard units. 2 stories (no elevator), interior/exterior corridors. *Bath:* combo or shower only. **Parking:** on-site. **Terms:** open 2/1-11/30, office hours 9:30 am-7 pm, 2 night minimum stay - weekends, age restrictions may apply, 5 day cancellation notice-fee imposed. **Amenities:** *Some:* irons, hair dryers. **Cards:** MC, VI.

SOME UNITS

TRINIDAD INN **Phone:** (707)677-3349

SAVE

Motel

All Year 1P: $75-$90 2P: $75-$90 XP: $10

Location: US 101, exit Trinidad northbound, 1.5 mi w; exit Seawood southbound, 1.5 mi s. 1170 Patricks Point Dr 95570. **Facility:** Smoke free premises. 10 units. 7 one-bedroom standard units with kitchens. 1 one-bedroom suite ($130-$145) with kitchen. 2 cabins. 1 story, exterior corridors. *Bath:* combo or shower only. **Parking:** on-site. **Terms:** office hours 9 am-9 pm, age restrictions may apply, 5 day cancellation notice, pets ($20 deposit, $10 extra charge). **Amenities:** *Some:* irons, hair dryers. **Cards:** AX, CB, DC, DS, MC, VI.

SOME UNITS FEE

TURTLE ROCKS OCEANFRONT INN — **Phone:** 707/677-3707

Bed & Breakfast

5/1-10/31 [BP] 1P: $135-$230 2P: $135-$230 XP: $30
2/1-4/30 & 11/1-1/31 [BP] 1P: $130-$190 2P: $130-$190 XP: $30

Location: 5 mi n, w of US 101, exit Patrick's Point Dr, then 1.5 mi s. 3392 Patrick's Point Dr 95570. **Facility:** Nature takes center stage at this gabled house overlooking a bluff; minimalist decor helps keep the focus simple. Designated smoking area. 6 one-bedroom standard units. 2 stories (no elevator), interior corridors. *Bath:* combo or shower only. **Parking:** on-site. **Terms:** office hours 6 am-10 pm, 2 night minimum stay - weekends & 7/1-8/31, age restrictions may apply, 7 day cancellation notice-fee imposed. **Amenities:** *Some:* irons, hair dryers. **Cards:** AX, DS, MC, VI.

DATA PORT

VIEW CREST LODGE — **Phone:** (707)677-3393

SAVE

Cottage

All Year 1P: $85-$135 2P: $85-$135 XP: $10

Location: 5 mi n; w of US 101, exit Patrick's Point Dr, then 1.5 mi s. 3415 Patrick's Point Dr 95570. Fax: 707/677-9363. **Facility:** The lodge features well-groomed gardens and modern, individual cottages whose private decks offer vistas of the Pacific. Smoke free premises. 11 cottages ($110-$145), some with whirlpools. 1 story, exterior corridors. *Bath:* combo or shower only. **Parking:** on-site. **Terms:** age restrictions may apply, 14 day cancellation notice. **Amenities:** irons, hair dryers. **Guest Services:** coin laundry. **Cards:** DS, MC, VI. **Special Amenities: free local telephone calls.**

SOME UNITS

/ VCR /

WHERE TO DINE

SEASCAPE RESTAURANT — **Lunch:** $5-$13 **Dinner:** $8-$23 **Phone:** 707/677-3762

Seafood

Location: 0.3 mi w of US 101; at the pier. **Hours:** 7 am-10 pm; to 8:30 pm in winter. Closed: 11/25, 12/25. **Reservations:** suggested. **Features:** On the beach at Trinidad Harbor, the rustic restaurant affords views of the pier and bay. Fresh seafood specials—as well as omelets and beef, chicken and pasta selections—make up the menu. Casual dress; beer & wine only. **Parking:** on-site. **Cards:** DS, MC, VI.

TRINIDAD BAY EATERY — **Lunch:** $5-$10 **Dinner:** $9-$17 **Phone:** 707/677-3777

American

Location: US 101, exit Trinidad, 0.5 mi w. 607 Parker St 95570. **Hours:** 8 am-3 pm, Fri & Sat-8 pm; to 8 pm in summer. Closed: 11/25, 12/25; also Tues. **Reservations:** suggested. **Features:** The small, family-owned restaurant specializes in preparing a fresh fish of the day and homemade desserts. Casual dress; beer & wine only. **Parking:** street. **Cards:** AX, DS, MC, VI.

TRINITY CENTER

WHERE TO STAY

CARRVILLE INN B&B — **Phone:** (530)266-3511

Bed & Breakfast

4/15-11/3 [BP] 1P: $125-$160 2P: $125-$160 XP: $20

Location: 6 mi n of Trinity Center on SR 3, exit Carrville Loop Rd, 0.5 mi. 3536 Carrville Loop Rd 96091. Fax: 530/266-3778. **Facility:** Surrounded by the picturesque Trinity Alps, the inn offers comfortable accommodations in a quaint setting. 5 one-bedroom standard units. 2 stories, interior corridors. *Bath:* some shower or tub only. **Parking:** on-site. **Terms:** open 4/15-11/3, office hours 10 am-8 pm, 2 night minimum stay - weekends, 10 day cancellation notice-fee imposed. **Amenities:** video library. *Some:* DVD players, irons, hair dryers. **Pool(s):** small outdoor. **Leisure Activities:** boating, canoeing, hiking trails, jogging, horseback riding. **Guest Services:** complimentary evening beverages.

SOME UNITS

ASK / /

COFFEE CREEK RANCH — **Phone:** (530)266-3343

SAVE

Ranch

4/1-12/1 Wkly [AP] 1P: $300-$1128 2P: $300-$1128

Location: 8 mi n of Trinity Center on SR 3, then 5 mi w. Located in a quiet location. 4940 Coffee Creek Rd 96091 (HC 2, Box 4940). Fax: 530/266-3597. **Facility:** Surrounded by the Trinity Alps Wilderness area, the ranch offers comfortable cabins scattered on a forested hillside above a creek. Designated smoking area. 16 one-bedroom standard units. 1 story, exterior corridors. *Bath:* combo or shower only. **Parking:** on-site. **Terms:** open 4/1-12/1, office hours 8 am-5 pm, 2-6 night minimum stay - in summer, cancellation fee imposed, daily rates available, package plans - weekends, 15% service charge. **Dining:** 7:30-9:30 am, 12:30-1:30 & 5:30-7 pm, wine/beer only, entertainment. **Pool(s):** outdoor. **Leisure Activities:** whirlpool, paddleboats, fishing, recreation programs, trap shooting, gold panning, hiking trails, playground, exercise room, sports court. *Fee:* horseback riding, massage. **Guest Services:** gift shop, coin laundry. **Business Services:** conference facilities, fax. **Cards:** AX, CB, DS, MC, VI. **Special Amenities: early check-in/late check-out.**

TRUCKEE —*See Lake Tahoe Area p. 399.*

TULARE pop. 43,994

WHERE TO STAY

BEST WESTERN TOWN & COUNTRY LODGE — Book at aaa.com — **Phone:** (559)688-7537

SAVE

Motel

All Year [BP] 1P: $64-$125 2P: $70-$150 XP: $6 F12

Location: SR 99, exit Prosperity Ave, just w. 1051 N Blackstone St 93274. Fax: 559/688-2163. **Facility:** 93 units. 91 one-bedroom standard units. 2 one-bedroom suites. 2 stories, interior corridors. *Bath:* combo or shower only. **Parking:** on-site. **Terms:** cancellation fee imposed, small pets only ($10 extra charge, for dog shows). **Amenities:** voice mail, irons, hair dryers. **Pool(s):** outdoor. **Leisure Activities:** whirlpool, limited exercise equipment. **Guest Services:** coin laundry. **Business Services:** meeting rooms, fax (fee). **Cards:** AX, CB, DC, DS, MC, VI. **Special Amenities: free full breakfast and free local telephone calls.** *(See ad p 746)*

SOME UNITS

CHARTER INN *Book at aaa.com* **Phone:** (559)685-9500

Small-scale Hotel

All Year [BP] 1P: $69-$109 2P: $69-$109 XP: $5 F12

Location: SR 99, just e. 1016 E Prosperity Ave 93274. Fax: 559/685-9559. **Facility:** 70 one-bedroom standard units. 3 stories, interior corridors. *Bath:* combo or shower only. **Parking:** on-site. **Terms:** pets ($100 deposit). **Amenities:** voice mail, irons, hair dryers. **Pool(s):** outdoor. **Leisure Activities:** whirlpool, exercise room. **Guest Services:** coin laundry. **Business Services:** meeting rooms, business center. **Cards:** AX, DC, DS, MC, VI. **Special Amenities: free full breakfast and free local telephone calls.** *(See color ad below)*

SOME UNITS

FEE

COMFORT SUITES *Book at aaa.com* **Phone:** (559)687-1246

Motel

All Year 1P: $68-$88 2P: $72-$88 XP: $10 F18

Location: SR 99, exit Prosperity Ave, just s. 1021 N Blackstone St 93274. Fax: 559/687-1524. **Facility:** 50 one-bedroom standard units, some with whirlpools. 2 stories, interior corridors. **Parking:** on-site. **Terms:** [BP] meal plan available. **Amenities:** voice mail, irons, hair dryers. **Pool(s):** outdoor. **Leisure Activities:** whirlpool, putting green, exercise room. **Guest Services:** valet laundry. **Business Services:** fax (fee). **Cards:** AX, CB, DC, DS, MC, VI. **Special Amenities: free full breakfast and free local telephone calls.**

SOME UNITS

DAYS INN *Book at aaa.com* **Phone:** 559/686-0985

Motel

All Year 1P: $55 2P: $60 XP: $5 F10

Location: SR 99, exit Prosperity Ave, just w. 1183 N Blackstone St 93274. Fax: 559/688-6814. **Facility:** 89 one-bedroom standard units. 3 stories, exterior corridors. **Parking:** on-site. **Terms:** pets ($5 extra charge). **Amenities:** hair dryers. *Some:* irons. **Pool(s):** outdoor. **Guest Services:** coin laundry. **Business Services:** fax (fee). **Cards:** AX, DC, DS, MC, VI. **Special Amenities: free continental breakfast and free local telephone calls.** *(See color ad p 747)*

SOME UNITS

FEE

QUALITY INN *Book at aaa.com* **Phone:** (559)686-3432

Motel

All Year 1P: $63-$75 2P: $69-$75 XP: $10 F18

Location: SR 99, exit Prosperity Ave, just e. Located next to factory outlet shopping mall. 1010 E Prosperity Ave 93274. Fax: 559/686-3378. **Facility:** 58 units. 50 one-bedroom standard units. 8 one-bedroom suites ($79-$109). 3 stories, interior corridors. *Bath:* combo or shower only. **Parking:** on-site. **Terms:** cancellation fee imposed, [BP] meal plan available, pets (small dogs only). **Amenities:** hair dryers. *Some:* irons. **Pool(s):** outdoor. **Leisure Activities:** sauna, whirlpool, exercise room. **Guest Services:** coin laundry. **Business Services:** meeting rooms, PC (fee). **Cards:** AX, CB, DC, DS, JC, MC, VI. **Special Amenities: free full breakfast and free local telephone calls.** *(See color ad p 747)*

SOME UNITS

WHERE TO DINE

APPLE ANNIE'S RESTAURANT **Lunch:** $7-$8 **Dinner:** $7-$12 **Phone:** 559/686-3411

American

Location: SR 99, exit Prosperity Ave, just e. 1165 N Blackstone St 93274. **Hours:** 6 am-9 pm, Sun-3 pm. Closed: 1/1, 11/25, 12/25. **Features:** The popular country-style restaurant presents a menu of sandwiches and salads, as well as all-day breakfast dishes, including omelets. Dinner entrees are available after 4 pm. For dessert, guests can choose from several tasty apple recipes. Eager-to-please servers are "down-home" friendly. Casual dress; beer & wine only. **Parking:** on-site. **Cards:** AX, MC, VI.

EMERTON CLUB **Lunch:** $8-$13 **Dinner:** $16-$27 **Phone:** 559/684-1264

Continental

Location: SR 99, exit SR 137 (Central Tulare Ave), 1 mi w. 210 E Tulare Ave 93274. **Hours:** 11:30 am-2 & 5-9 pm, Sat from 5 pm. Closed major holidays; also Sun. **Reservations:** suggested. **Features:** The modestly elegant dining room features a rich use a woods and nicely appointed booths and tables. A large skylight accentuates the relaxing fountain below in the center of the room. The menu blends steak and seafood entrees, as well as lamb and pasta. Prime rib is a highlight on Friday and Saturday nights. Cocktails. **Parking:** on-site. **Cards:** AX, CB, DC, DS, MC, VI.

TURLOCK pop. 55,810

WHERE TO STAY

BEST WESTERN ORCHARD INN *Book at aaa.com* **Phone:** (209)667-2827

Motel

All Year [ECP] 1P: $74-$78 2P: $80-$86 XP: $8 F12

Location: SR 99, exit Taylor Rd, 5 mi n. 5025 N Golden State Blvd 95380. Fax: 209/634-6588. **Facility:** 72 one-bedroom standard units, some with efficiencies and/or whirlpools. 2 stories, exterior corridors. *Bath:* combo or shower only. **Parking:** on-site. **Amenities:** voice mail, irons, hair dryers. **Pool(s):** outdoor. **Leisure Activities:** whirlpool. **Guest Services:** valet laundry. **Business Services:** meeting rooms. **Cards:** AX, CB, DC, DS, MC, VI. **Special Amenities: free expanded continental breakfast and free local telephone calls.**

SOME UNITS

THE TREE INN *Book at aaa.com* **Phone:** (209)668-3400

Motel

All Year 1P: $60-$75 2P: $64-$75 XP: $8 F12

Location: SR 99, exit Lander. Located in a rural setting. 201 W Glenwood Ave 95380. Fax: 209/668-0144. **Facility:** 92 one-bedroom standard units. 2 stories, exterior corridors. *Bath:* combo or shower only. **Parking:** on-site. **Terms:** [CP] meal plan available, small pets only. **Pool(s):** outdoor. **Leisure Activities:** whirlpool. **Business Services:** meeting rooms. **Cards:** AX, CB, DC, DS, JC, MC, VI. **Special Amenities: free continental breakfast and preferred room (subject to availability with advanced reservations).**

SOME UNITS

TWAIN HARTE pop. 2,586

WHERE TO STAY

MCCAFFREY HOUSE B & B INN **Phone:** 209/586-0757

Bed & Breakfast

All Year [BP] 1P: $110-$135 2P: $125-$185 XP: $15

Location: 0.5 mi on SR 108; just beyond 4000' elevation marker. Located in a quiet area. 23251 Hwy 108 95383 (PO Box 67). Fax: 209/586-3689. **Facility:** Country inn nestled in a forest setting. Smoke free premises. 8 units. 7 one- and 1 two-bedroom standard units. 3 stories (no elevator), interior corridors. **Parking:** on-site. **Terms:** 2 night minimum stay - weekends, age restrictions may apply, 8 day cancellation notice-fee imposed, weekly rates available. **Amenities:** video library, CD players, irons, hair dryers. **Guest Services:** complimentary evening beverages. **Cards:** AX, MC, VI. **Special Amenities: free local telephone calls.**

SOME UNITS

VCR DATA PORT

WILDWOOD INN **Phone:** (209)586-2900

Motel

5/1-10/1 [CP] 1P: $64-$79 2P: $64-$79 XP: $5 F

2/1-4/30 & 10/2-1/31 [CP] 1P: $60-$71 2P: $60-$71 XP: $5 F

Location: Center. 22960 Meadow Dr 95383 (PO Box 222). Fax: 209/586-1408. **Facility:** 21 one-bedroom standard units. 2 stories (no elevator), exterior corridors. *Bath:* shower only. **Parking:** on-site. **Terms:** office hours 8 am-10 pm, 3 day cancellation notice, weekly rates available, package plans. **Amenities:** *Some:* irons, hair dryers. **Pool(s):** outdoor. **Leisure Activities:** whirlpool. **Cards:** MC, VI. **Special Amenities: free continental breakfast and free local telephone calls.**

SOME UNITS

UKIAH —*See Wine Country p. 809.*

UNION CITY pop. 66,869

WHERE TO STAY

CROWNE PLAZA OAKLAND SOUTH/UNION CITY — **Phone:** (510)489-2200

Large-scale Hotel

All Year — 1P: $99-$129 — 2P: $99-$129 — XP: $15 — F17

Location: I-880, exit Alvarado-Niles Rd, just e. 32083 Alvarado-Niles Rd 94587. Fax: 510/489-7642. **Facility:** 271 units. 270 one-bedroom standard units. 1 one-bedroom suite. 6 stories, interior corridors. *Bath:* combo or shower only. **Parking:** on-site. **Terms:** cancellation fee imposed. **Amenities:** video games (fee), dual phone lines, voice mail, irons, hair dryers. **Pool(s):** outdoor. **Leisure Activities:** whirlpool, racquetball court, exercise room. **Guest Services:** gift shop, coin laundry. **Business Services:** meeting rooms. **Cards:** AX, CB, DC, DS, JC, MC, VI.
(See color ad below & p 629)

ASK / SOME UNITS / FEE FEE

HOLIDAY INN EXPRESS UNION CITY — Book at aaa.com — **Phone:** (510)475-0600

Small-scale Hotel

All Year [ECP] — 1P: $99-$129 — 2P: $99-$139 — XP: $10 — F15

Location: I-880, exit Alvarado-Niles Rd, just w. 31140 Alvarado-Niles Rd 94587. Fax: 510/475-0910. **Facility:** 77 one-bedroom standard units. 4 stories, interior corridors. *Bath:* combo or shower only. **Parking:** on-site. **Amenities:** video games (fee), high-speed Internet, dual phone lines, voice mail, irons, hair dryers. **Pool(s):** heated outdoor. **Leisure Activities:** whirlpool, exercise room. **Guest Services:** valet and coin laundry. **Business Services:** meeting rooms. **Cards:** AX, CB, DC, DS, MC, VI.

ASK / SOME UNITS

UPPER LAKE —*See Wine Country p. 812.*

VACAVILLE pop. 88,625

WHERE TO STAY

BEST VALUE VACA VALLEY INN — Book at aaa.com — **Phone:** (707)446-8888

AAA SAVE — Motel

All Year [CP] — 1P: $66-$76 — 2P: $71-$81 — XP: $5 — F17

Location: I-80, exit Leisure Town Rd, just s; just e of I-505 interchange. 950 Leisure Town Rd 95687. Fax: 707/449-0109. **Facility:** 119 one-bedroom standard units. 2 stories, exterior corridors. *Bath:* combo or shower only. **Parking:** on-site. **Pool(s):** outdoor. **Leisure Activities:** whirlpool. **Guest Services:** coin laundry. **Business Services:** meeting rooms. **Cards:** AX, CB, DC, DS, MC, VI. **Special Amenities: free continental breakfast and free local telephone calls.** *(See color ad below)*

SOME UNITS

BEST WESTERN HERITAGE INN *Book at aaa.com* **Phone:** 707/448-8453

AAA SAVE

Motel

All Year 1P: $78-$100 2P: $78-$100 XP: $5 F12

Location: I-80, exit Monte Vista Ave, just n. 1420 E Monte Vista Ave 95688. Fax: 707/447-8649. **Facility:** 41 one-bedroom standard units. 2 stories, exterior corridors. **Parking:** on-site. **Terms:** [ECP] meal plan available, pets ($35 deposit). **Amenities:** irons, hair dryers. **Pool(s):** outdoor. **Cards:** AX, CB, DC, DS, JC, MC, VI. **Special Amenities: free expanded continental breakfast and free local telephone calls.**

SOME UNITS

FEE

COURTYARD BY MARRIOTT *Book at aaa.com* **Phone:** (707)451-9000

AAA SAVE

Small-scale Hotel

All Year 1P: $129-$149 2P: $129-$149 XP: $10 F18

Location: I-80, exit Orange Dr eastbound, just w; exit Monte Vista westbound, freeway overpass to E Nut Tree Pkwy, just w. 120 Nut Tree Pkwy 95687. Fax: 707/449-3952. **Facility:** 127 units. 123 one-bedroom standard units. 4 one-bedroom suites. 2 stories, interior corridors. *Bath:* combo or shower only. **Parking:** on-site. **Terms:** [BP] & [ECP] meal plans available. **Amenities:** video library, video games, dual phone lines, voice mail, irons, hair dryers. **Dining:** 6:30-10 am, Sat & Sun 7-11 am. **Pool(s):** heated outdoor. **Leisure Activities:** whirlpool, exercise room. **Guest Services:** coin laundry. **Business Services:** meeting rooms. **Cards:** AX, CB, DC, DS, JC, MC, VI. **Special Amenities: free newspaper and preferred room (subject to availability with advanced reservations).**

SOME UNITS

FAIRFIELD INN BY MARRIOTT-VACAVILLE *Book at aaa.com* **Phone:** (707)469-0800

Small-scale Hotel

5/1-9/30 [ECP] 1P: $89-$109
2/1-4/30 & 10/1-1/31 [ECP] 1P: $79-$89

Location: I-80, exit Orange Dr eastbound, 0.5 mi s; exit Monte Vista westbound, freeway overpass to E Nut Tree Pkwy. 370 Orange Dr 95687. Fax: 707/469-0800. **Facility:** 81 one-bedroom standard units. 3 stories (no elevator), interior corridors. *Bath:* combo or shower only. **Parking:** on-site. **Amenities:** voice mail, irons, hair dryers. **Pool(s):** heated indoor. **Leisure Activities:** whirlpool. **Cards:** AX, CB, DC, DS, MC, VI.

SOME UNITS

HAMPTON INN & SUITES VACAVILLE/NAPA VALLEY *Book at aaa.com* **Phone:** (707)469-6200

AAA SAVE

Small-scale Hotel

All Year [ECP] 1P: $99-$129

Location: I-80, exit Davis St eastbound; exit Mason St westbound. 800 Mason St 95688. Fax: 707/469-6300. **Facility:** 83 one-bedroom standard units, some with whirlpools. 3 stories, interior corridors. **Parking:** on-site. **Terms:** cancellation fee imposed. **Amenities:** high-speed Internet, dual phone lines, voice mail, irons, hair dryers. **Pool(s):** heated outdoor. **Leisure Activities:** whirlpool, exercise room. **Guest Services:** coin laundry. **Business Services:** meeting rooms, business center. **Cards:** AX, CB, DC, DS, JC, MC, VI. **Special Amenities: free expanded continental breakfast and free local telephone calls.** *(See color ad below)*

SOME UNITS

HOLIDAY INN EXPRESS *Book at aaa.com* **Phone:** 707/451-3500

Small-scale Hotel

Property failed to provide current rates

Location: I-80, exit Orange Dr eastbound; exit Monte Vista westbound. 151 Lawrence Dr 95687. Fax: 707/451-2613. **Facility:** 91 one-bedroom standard units, some with whirlpools. 3 stories, interior corridors. **Parking:** on-site. **Amenities:** dual phone lines, voice mail, irons, hair dryers. **Pool(s):** heated indoor. **Leisure Activities:** whirlpool, exercise room. **Guest Services:** coin laundry. **Business Services:** meeting rooms, business center.

SOME UNITS

RESIDENCE INN BY MARRIOTT *Book at aaa.com* **Phone:** (707)469-0300

Small-scale Hotel

5/21-9/6 1P: $124-$152 2P: $124-$152
2/1-5/20 & 9/7-1/31 1P: $122-$144 2P: $122-$144

Location: I-80, exit Orange Dr eastbound, 0.5 mi; exit Monte Vista westbound, freeway overpass to E Nut Tree Pkwy. 360 Orange Dr 95687. Fax: 707/469-0300. **Facility:** 78 units. 33 one-bedroom standard units. 33 one- and 12 two-bedroom suites, some with efficiencies or kitchens. 3 stories, interior corridors. **Parking:** on-site. **Terms:** [BP] meal plan available, pets ($100 deposit, $10 extra charge). **Amenities:** voice mail, irons, hair dryers. **Pool(s):** heated indoor. **Leisure Activities:** whirlpool, exercise room, sports court. **Guest Services:** coin laundry. **Business Services:** conference facilities. **Cards:** AX, DC, DS, MC, VI.

SOME UNITS

FEE FEE

ROYAL MOTEL — Phone: (707)448-6482

Motel

5/16-10/15	1P: $95	2P: $110
4/1-5/15	1P: $75	2P: $75
10/16-1/31	1P: $70	2P: $75
2/1-3/31	1P: $70	2P: $70

Location: I-80, exit E Monte Vista. 1571 E Monte Vista Ave 95688. Fax: 707/448-8731. **Facility:** 86 one-bedroom standard units. 1-2 stories, exterior corridors. *Bath:* combo or shower only. **Parking:** on-site. **Terms:** [CP] meal plan available. **Amenities:** hair dryers. **Pool(s):** outdoor. **Leisure Activities:** whirlpool. **Guest Services:** coin laundry. **Business Services:** meeting rooms. **Cards:** AX, CB, DC, DS, MC, VI.

SOME UNITS

ASK

VACAVILLE SUPER 8 — *Book at aaa.com* — Phone: (707)449-8884

Motel

All Year [CP]	1P: $59-$79	2P: $64-$84	XP: $5	F12

Location: I-80, exit Monte Vista Ave, just n. Located in a quiet area. 101 Allison Ct 95688. Fax: 707/449-9132. **Facility:** 53 one-bedroom standard units. 3 stories, interior corridors. **Parking:** on-site. **Terms:** pets ($10 extra charge, dogs only). **Amenities:** video games, safes. **Pool(s):** outdoor. **Guest Services:** coin laundry. **Cards:** AX, CB, DC, DS, MC, VI.

SOME UNITS

ASK FEE DATA PORT

WHERE TO DINE

BLACK OAK RESTAURANT — **Lunch:** $5-$13 **Dinner:** $6-$19 **Phone:** 707/448-1311

American

Location: South side of I-80 at jct I-505. 320 Orange Dr 95687. **Hours:** 7 am-9 pm, Fri & Sat 6 pm-10 pm. **Features:** Booth seating lends to the roadside restaurant's casual appeal. The menu lists extensive selections. Casual dress; beer & wine only. **Parking:** on-site. **Cards:** AX, MC, VI.

VACA JOE'S RESTAURANT — **Lunch:** $6-$15 **Dinner:** $8-$15 **Phone:** 707/447-4633

Italian

Location: I-80, exit Leisure Town Rd. 980 Leisure Town Rd 95687. **Hours:** 7 am-9 pm, Fri & Sat-10 pm. Closed: Mon. **Reservations:** suggested. **Features:** Varied menu, seafood, beef with a Italian flavor. Casual dress; cocktails. **Parking:** on-site. **Cards:** AX, DC, DS, MC, VI.

VALLEJO pop. 116,760

WHERE TO STAY

BEST WESTERN INN AT MARINE WORLD — *Book at aaa.com* — Phone: (707)554-9655

Motel

5/1-8/31	1P: $89-$109	2P: $89-$109	XP: $10	F13
9/1-10/31	1P: $79-$89	2P: $79-$89	XP: $5	F13
2/1-4/30 & 11/1-1/31	1P: $49-$59	2P: $49-$59	XP: $5	F13

Location: I-80, exit SR 37 N, 0.3 mi w. 1596 Fairgrounds Dr 94589. Fax: 707/554-3951. **Facility:** 117 one-bedroom standard units. 3 stories, interior corridors. *Bath:* combo or shower only. **Parking:** on-site. **Terms:** cancellation fee imposed, package plans - seasonal. **Amenities:** video games, voice mail, irons, hair dryers. **Pool(s):** heated outdoor. **Leisure Activities:** whirlpool. **Guest Services:** coin laundry, area transportation. **Business Services:** meeting rooms. **Cards:** AX, DC, DS, MC, VI.

SOME UNITS

ASK DATA PORT

COMFORT INN — *Book at aaa.com* — Phone: (707)648-1400

AAA SAVE

Motel

6/1-9/15 [ECP]	1P: $74-$109	2P: $84-$114	XP: $10	F16
9/16-1/31 [ECP]	1P: $69-$84	2P: $79-$89	XP: $10	F16
4/1-5/31 [ECP]	1P: $59-$79	2P: $64-$89	XP: $10	F16
2/1-3/31 [ECP]	1P: $49-$69	2P: $54-$74	XP: $10	F16

Location: I-80, exit Columbus Pkwy, 0.5 mi e, then 0.3 mi s. 1185 Admiral Callaghan Ln 94591. Fax: 707/552-8623. **Facility:** 80 one-bedroom standard units, some with whirlpools. 2 stories, interior corridors. **Parking:** on-site. **Terms:** 3 day cancellation notice. **Amenities:** irons, hair dryers. **Pool(s):** outdoor. **Leisure Activities:** whirlpool. **Guest Services:** coin laundry. **Business Services:** meeting rooms. **Cards:** AX, DC, DS, MC, VI. **Special Amenities: free expanded continental breakfast and free local telephone calls.**

SOME UNITS

DATA PORT

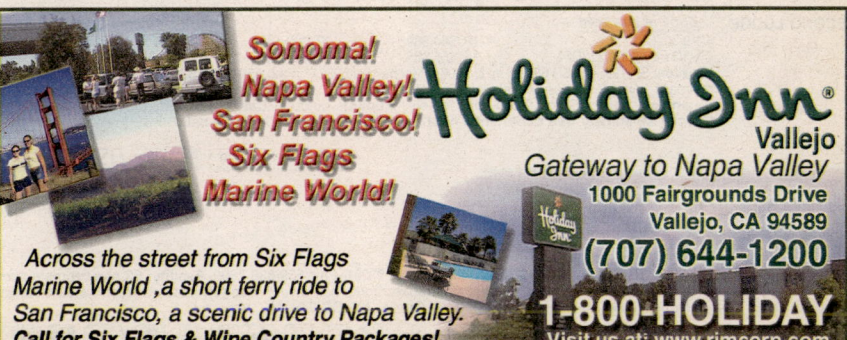

HOLIDAY INN AT NAPA GATEWAY Book at aaa.com **Phone:** (707)644-1200

AAA SAVE

Small-scale Hotel

5/1-9/30	1P: $129-$149	2P: $129-$149
2/1-4/30 & 10/1-1/31	1P: $109-$129	2P: $109-$129

Location: I-80, exit Marine World Pkwy (SR 37), 0.3 mi n. Located opposite Marine World Theme Park. 1000 Fairgrounds Dr 94589. Fax: 707/643-7011. **Facility:** 170 one-bedroom standard units, some with whirlpools. 5 stories, interior corridors. **Parking:** on-site. **Terms:** 11% service charge, pets ($25 extra charge). **Amenities:** video games, dual phone lines, voice mail, irons, hair dryers. **Dining:** 6 am-10 & 5-9 pm, weekends 7 am-11 am, cocktails. **Pool(s):** heated outdoor. **Leisure Activities:** whirlpool, exercise room. **Guest Services:** coin laundry. **Business Services:** meeting rooms. **Cards:** AX, CB, DC, DS, JC, MC, VI. **Special Amenities: free local telephone calls and free newspaper.** *(See color ad p 751)*

SOME UNITS

FEE

RAMADA INN Book at aaa.com **Phone:** (707)643-2700

Motel

All Year	1P: $89-$109	2P: $99-$109

Location: I-80 S, exit Columbus Pkwy, 0.5 mi w. 1000 Admiral Callaghan Ln 94591. Fax: 707/642-1148. **Facility:** 129 one-bedroom standard units. 3 stories, exterior corridors. **Parking:** on-site. **Terms:** cancellation fee imposed, [ECP] meal plan available, pets ($25 deposit). **Amenities:** high-speed Internet, voice mail, safes, irons, hair dryers. **Pool(s):** outdoor. **Leisure Activities:** whirlpool. **Guest Services:** coin laundry, area transportation. **Business Services:** meeting rooms. **Cards:** AX, CB, DC, DS, JC, MC, VI.

ASK SOME UNITS

FEE

VISALIA pop. 91,565—

See also KINGS CANYON NATIONAL PARK, SEQUOIA NATIONAL PARK & THREE RIVERS.

WHERE TO STAY

BEN MADDOX HOUSE Book at aaa.com **Phone:** 559/739-0721

Historic Bed & Breakfast

All Year [BP]	1P: $75-$110	2P: $100-$130	XP: $17

Location: SR 198, exit Central Visalia, just n; at corner of Encina St and Race; downtown. Located in the historic district. 601 N Encina St 93291. Fax: 559/625-0420. **Facility:** This property built in 1886, is surrounded by some of the oldest homes in the Central Valley; shading the grounds are 100-year-old trees. Smoke free premises. 5 one-bedroom standard units, some with whirlpools. 1 story, interior/exterior corridors. *Bath:* combo or shower only. **Parking:** on-site. **Terms:** office hours 10 am-8 pm, check-in 4 pm, 7 day cancellation notice-fee imposed. **Amenities:** video library, irons, hair dryers. **Pool(s):** outdoor. **Business Services:** fax (fee). **Cards:** AX, DC, MC, VI.

ASK SOME UNITS VCR

BEST WESTERN VISALIA INN Book at aaa.com **Phone:** (559)732-4561

AAA SAVE

Motel

All Year	1P: $79-$85	2P: $79-$85	XP: $5	F12

Location: SR 198, exit Mooney Blvd, just n, then just 0.9 mi e. 623 W Main St 93291. Fax: 559/738-0562. **Facility:** 41 one-bedroom standard units. 2 stories, exterior corridors. **Parking:** on-site. **Terms:** pets ($10 extra charge, small dogs only, limit 1). **Amenities:** voice mail, irons, hair dryers. *Some:* high-speed Internet. **Pool(s):** outdoor. **Business Services:** meeting rooms, fax (fee). **Cards:** AX, CB, DC, DS, JC, MC, VI. **Special Amenities: free full breakfast and free newspaper.**

SOME UNITS

FEE

COMFORT SUITES Book at aaa.com **Phone:** (559)738-1700

AAA SAVE

Small-scale Hotel

5/1-10/31 [ECP]	1P: $89-$119	2P: $89-$119	XP: $5	F12
2/1-4/30 & 11/1-1/31 [ECP]	1P: $79-$109	2P: $79-$109	XP: $5	F12

Location: SR 198, exit Central Visalia, just n on Mineral King, just w on Court St, then just n. 210 E Acequia Ave 93291. Fax: 559/738-8300. **Facility:** 72 one-bedroom standard units, some with whirlpools. 4 stories, interior corridors. **Parking:** on-site. **Amenities:** high-speed Internet, voice mail, safes, irons, hair dryers. **Leisure Activities:** whirlpool, limited exercise equipment. **Guest Services:** valet and coin laundry. **Business Services:** meeting rooms, fax (fee). **Cards:** AX, CB, DC, DS, JC, MC, VI. **Special Amenities: free expanded continental breakfast and free newspaper.**

SOME UNITS

ECONO LODGE Book at aaa.com **Phone:** (559)732-6641

AAA SAVE

Motel

4/1-9/30 [CP]	1P: $64-$89	2P: $69-$89	XP: $5	F12
2/1-3/31 & 10/1-1/31 [CP]	1P: $55-$85	2P: $59-$89	XP: $5	F12

Location: SR 198, exit SR 63, 0.5 mi s. 1400 S Mooney Blvd 93277. Fax: 559/739-7520. **Facility:** 50 one-bedroom standard units. 2 stories (no elevator), exterior corridors. *Bath:* combo or shower only. **Parking:** on-site. **Amenities:** safes. *Some:* irons, hair dryers. **Pool(s):** outdoor. **Cards:** AX, CB, DC, DS, JC, MC, VI. **Special Amenities: free continental breakfast and free local telephone calls.**

SOME UNITS

FAIRFIELD INN Book at aaa.com **Phone:** (559)636-7600

Small-scale Hotel

2/1-2/29 [ECP]	1P: $79-$149
5/1-9/30 [ECP]	1P: $89-$94
3/1-4/30 & 10/1-1/31 [ECP]	1P: $79-$84

Location: SR 198, exit Akers St, just n. 140 S Akers 93291. Fax: 559/636-7600. **Facility:** 63 one-bedroom standard units. 3 stories, interior corridors. **Parking:** on-site. **Amenities:** irons, hair dryers. **Pool(s):** heated indoor. **Leisure Activities:** whirlpool. **Business Services:** meeting rooms, fax (fee). **Cards:** AX, DC, DS, MC, VI.

SOME UNITS

JOHN JAY INN & SUITES — **Phone:** (559)651-3700

Small-scale Hotel

All Year [ECP] 1P: $70-$83 2P: $76-$89 XP: $7 F12

Location: SR 99, exit SR 198, just e to Plaza Dr, then just s. Located next to Visalia Airport. 9300 W Airport Dr 93277. Fax: 559/651-4884. **Facility:** 64 units. 47 one-bedroom standard units. 17 one-bedroom suites ($85-$156), some with whirlpools. 3 stories, interior corridors. **Parking:** on-site. **Terms:** 7 day cancellation notice. **Amenities:** irons, hair dryers. **Pool(s):** outdoor. **Leisure Activities:** sauna, whirlpool, exercise room. **Guest Services:** coin laundry. **Cards:** AX, CB, DC, DS, JC, MC, VI.

SOME UNITS

LAMP LITER INN — **Phone:** (559)732-4511

Motel

All Year [CP] 1P: $69-$109 2P: $69-$109 XP: $10 F15

Location: 0.5 mi w of jct SR 63 (Mooney Blvd); adjacent to SR 198. 3300 W Mineral King Ave 93291 (3130 W Main St, Suite A). Fax: 559/732-1840. **Facility:** 100 units. 96 one-bedroom standard units. 4 cottages ($159-$199). 2 stories, exterior corridors. *Bath:* combo or shower only. **Parking:** on-site. **Terms:** cancellation fee imposed. **Amenities:** voice mail. *Some:* irons, hair dryers. **Dining:** 5:30 am-10 pm, Sun-2 pm, cocktails. **Pool(s):** outdoor. **Leisure Activities:** exercise room. **Business Services:** meeting rooms, fax (fee). **Cards:** AX, CB, DC, DS, JC, MC, VI. **Special Amenities: free continental breakfast and free local telephone calls.**

SOME UNITS

RADISSON HOTEL-VISALIA **Book at aaa.com** — **Phone:** (559)636-1111

Small-scale Hotel

All Year 1P: $168 2P: $168

Location: SR 198, exit Central Visalia/SR 63, just n. Located adjacent to convention center. 300 S Court St 93291. Fax: 559/636-8224. **Facility:** 201 units. 195 one-bedroom standard units. 6 one-bedroom suites, some with kitchens and/or whirlpools. 8 stories, interior corridors. **Parking:** on-site. **Terms:** cancellation fee imposed, package plans. **Amenities:** video games, voice mail, irons, hair dryers. *Some:* high-speed Internet, dual phone lines, honor bars. **Pool(s):** outdoor. **Leisure Activities:** whirlpool, exercise room. **Guest Services:** valet laundry, area transportation. **Business Services:** conference facilities. *Fee:* PC, fax. **Cards:** AX, DC, DS, MC. ***(See color ad p 629)***

SOME UNITS

FEE

THE SPALDING HOUSE BED & BREAKFAST INN — **Phone:** (559)739-7877

Bed & Breakfast

All Year [BP] 1P: $85-$95 2P: $95-$105 XP: $10 F12

Location: SR 198, exit Central Visalia/Court St, 0.4 mi n to Murray St, then just w; downtown. 631 N Encina St 93291. Fax: 559/625-0902. **Facility:** Built in 1907 by lumberman W.R. Spalding, this B&B boasts picturesque, manicured grounds and Colonial Revival architecture. Designated smoking area. 3 one-bedroom standard units. 2 stories (no elevator), interior corridors. *Bath:* shower only. **Parking:** street. **Terms:** 3 day cancellation notice, no pets allowed (owner's pet on premises). **Amenities:** hair dryers. *Some:* irons. **Cards:** AX, MC, VI.

SUPER 8 — **Phone:** 559/627-2885

Motel

All Year [CP] 1P: $55-$105 2P: $60-$105 XP: $5 F18

Location: SR 198, exit Akers St, just s, then 0.5 mi e on frontage road. 4801 W Noble Ave 93277. Fax: 559/732-7114. **Facility:** 39 one-bedroom standard units. 2 stories (no elevator), exterior corridors. **Parking:** on-site. **Amenities:** *Some:* irons, hair dryers. **Pool(s):** outdoor. **Guest Services:** coin laundry. **Cards:** AX, CB, DC, DS, MC, VI. **Special Amenities: free continental breakfast and free local telephone calls.**

SOME UNITS

VISALIA HOLIDAY INN HOTEL & CONFERENCE CENTER *Book at aaa.com* **Phone:** (559)651-5000

AAA SAVE

Large-scale Hotel

All Year 1P: $109-$159

Location: SR 99, exit SR 198, just e to Plaza Dr. Located next to Visalia Airport. 9000 W Airport Dr 93277. Fax: 559/651-5014. **Facility:** 256 units. 242 one-bedroom standard units. 14 one-bedroom suites ($169-$199). 3-5 stories, interior corridors. **Parking:** on-site. **Terms:** pets ($25 fee). **Amenities:** video games, high-speed Internet, voice mail, irons, hair dryers. **Dining:** 6 am-2 & 5-10 pm, cocktails. **Pool(s):** heated outdoor, heated indoor. **Leisure Activities:** whirlpool, exercise room. **Guest Services:** gift shop, coin laundry. **Business Services:** conference facilities, business center. **Cards:** AX, CB, DC, DS, JC, MC, VI. **Special Amenities: free local telephone calls and free room upgrade (subject to availability with advanced reservations).** *(See color ad p 753)*

SOME UNITS

FEE FEE

WHERE TO DINE

CAFE 225 **Lunch:** $6-$10 **Dinner:** $10-$18 **Phone:** 559/733-2967

American

Location: SR 198, exit Court St, just n; downtown. 225 W Main St 92391. **Hours:** 7 am-10 pm. Closed: 1/1, 11/25, 12/25. **Features:** Diners can expect contemporary-style dining. On the menu is a selection of pasta dishes, pizzas, rotisserie chicken preparations and house specialties. Street parking is at a premium and may require a short walk. Uniformed servers are gracious and attentive. Casual dress; beer & wine only. **Parking:** street. **Cards:** AX, CB, DC, DS, MC, VI.

THE DEPOT RESTAURANT **Lunch:** $6-$9 **Dinner:** $13-$22 **Phone:** 559/732-8611

Continental

Location: SR 198, exit Court St, 0.5 mi n, then just e. 207 E Oak St 93291. **Hours:** 11 am-2:30 & 5-10 pm. Closed major holidays; also Sun. **Reservations:** suggested; weekends. **Features:** A fine-dining experience awaits diners in the historic restaurant, originally an 1897 railroad depot. Elegant Spanish-style decor and excellent food and service make the well-established spot a favorite. Casual dress; cocktails. **Parking:** on-site. **Cards:** AX, DS, MC, VI.

DOUBLE LL STEAKHOUSE **Dinner:** $15-$40 **Phone:** 559/627-1126

Steak House

Location: SR 198, exit Court St, just n, then just e; downtown. 401 E Center St 93291. **Hours:** 4:30 pm-10 pm, Sat-10:30 pm, Sun-9:30 pm. Closed: 11/25, 12/25. **Reservations:** suggested. **Features:** Attractive western decor contributes to the steakhouse atmosphere. An extensive wine list complements large portions of steak, prime rib, barbecue, ribs and seafood. A menu of lighter fare also is offered. Casual dress; cocktails. **Parking:** street. **Cards:** AX, DS, MC, VI.

SOMETHING FRESH AMERICAN BAR & GRILL **Lunch:** $7-$10 **Dinner:** $8-$15 **Phone:** 559/732-6572

American

Location: SR 198, exit Akers St eastbound, 0.5 mi e on Noble Ave; exit Demaree St westbound, 0.5 mi w on Mineral King Ave to Noble Ave, then just s. 505 S Chinowth Rd 93291. **Hours:** 10:30 am-10 pm. Closed major holidays. **Features:** In a restored farmhouse, the casual restaurant tempts patrons with friendly, attentive service; tasty salads, sandwiches and entrees; and scrumptious homemade desserts, including bananas Foster creme brulee. Pretty landscaping distinguishes the beautiful exterior. Inside are hardwood floors and antique hanging lamps. Cocktails. **Parking:** on-site. **Cards:** AX, CB, DC, DS, MC, VI.

THE VINTAGE PRESS **Lunch:** $6-$14 **Dinner:** $13-$35 **Phone:** 559/733-3033

California

Location: SR 198, exit Court St, just n to Center St, then just w; downtown. 216 N Willis St 93291. **Hours:** 11:30 am-2 & 5:30-10 pm, Sun 10 am-2 & 5-9 pm. Closed: 12/25. **Reservations:** suggested. **Features:** The large restaurant has a garden patio and several attractive dining areas beautifully decorated with rich woods and stained glass. An extensive wine list complements such favorites as the portobello mushroom sandwich. Among great desserts is blackberry crisp with honey ice cream. Casual dress; cocktails. **Parking:** on-site. **Cards:** AX, CB, DC, MC, VI.

WAGON WHEEL STEAK HOUSE **Lunch:** $6-$11 **Dinner:** $11-$20 **Phone:** 559/734-7427

Steak House

Location: Just n of Main St; downtown. 400 N Willis Ave 93291. **Hours:** 11 am-10 pm, Sat & Sun from 4 pm. Closed major holidays. **Features:** Although the emphasis is on steak at the Western-themed restaurant, diners will find an ample selection of seafood, chicken and Mexican dishes. Casual dress; cocktails. **Parking:** on-site. **Cards:** AX, DC, DS, MC, VI.

WALNUT CREEK pop. 64,296 (See map and index starting on p. 516)

WHERE TO STAY

EMBASSY SUITES HOTEL *Book at aaa.com* **Phone:** (925)934-2500 44

AAA SAVE

Large-scale Hotel

All Year 1P: $116-$189 2P: $116-$186

Location: I-680, exit Treat Blvd northbound; exit Oak Park Blvd southbound, then e; at Pleasant Hill Bart Station. 1345 Treat Blvd 94597. Fax: 925/256-7233. **Facility:** 249 one-bedroom suites. 8 stories, interior corridors. *Bath:* combo or shower only. **Parking:** on-site (fee). **Terms:** cancellation fee imposed, [AP] meal plan available. **Amenities:** dual phone lines, voice mail, irons, hair dryers. *Fee:* video games, high-speed Internet. **Dining:** 11 am-10 pm, Fri & Sat-11 pm. **Pool(s):** heated indoor. **Leisure Activities:** sauna, whirlpool, library, exercise room. **Guest Services:** gift shop, complimentary evening beverages, coin laundry. **Business Services:** meeting rooms, fax. **Cards:** AX, DC, DS, MC, VI. **Special Amenities: free full breakfast and free local telephone calls.** *(See color ad p 755)*

SOME UNITS

FEE

(See map and index starting on p. 516)

HOLIDAY INN WALNUT CREEK *Book at aaa.com* **Phone:** (925)932-3332 43

AAA SAVE — Small-scale Hotel

All Year 1P: $79-$199 2P: $79-$199 XP: $10 F18

Location: I-680, exit N Main St, just n. 2730 N Main St 94596. Fax: 925/256-7672. **Facility:** 156 one-bedroom standard units. 2 stories, interior corridors. **Parking:** on-site. **Terms:** cancellation fee imposed, [BP] meal plan available, pets ($25 fee). **Amenities:** dual phone lines, voice mail, irons, hair dryers. **Dining:** 6 am-11 & 5-9 pm, cocktails. **Pool(s):** heated outdoor. **Leisure Activities:** whirlpool, exercise room. **Guest Services:** valet laundry. **Business Services:** meeting rooms, fax. **Cards:** AX, DC, DS, JC, MC, VI. **Special Amenities:** free newspaper. *(See color ad below)*

SOME UNITS — FEE — FEE FEE

MARRIOTT HOTEL *Book at aaa.com* **Phone:** (925)934-2000 41

Small-scale Hotel

All Year 1P: $85-$209

Location: I-680, exit N Main St, 0.3 mi e, s at Parkside Dr. 2355 N Main 94596. Fax: 925/934-6374. **Facility:** 338 one-bedroom standard units. 6 stories, interior corridors. **Parking:** on-site (fee). **Amenities:** dual phone lines, voice mail, irons, hair dryers. *Fee:* video games, high-speed Internet. **Pool(s):** heated outdoor. **Leisure Activities:** whirlpool, exercise room. *Fee:* game room. **Guest Services:** gift shop, valet laundry, area transportation. **Business Services:** meeting rooms, business center. **Cards:** AX, DC, DS, JC, MC, VI.

SOME UNITS

RENAISSANCE CLUB SPORT *Book at aaa.com* **Phone:** 925/938-8700 45

AAA SAVE — Large-scale Hotel

All Year 1P: $119 2P: $219

Location: I-680, exit Geary Rd/Treat Blvd, just e. 2805 Jones Rd 94597. Fax: 925/938-8707. **Facility:** This attractively appointed hotel doubles as a fitness resort offering guests access to various sport activities including a full service spa. Smoke free premises. 175 units. 170 one-bedroom standard units. 5 one-bedroom suites. 6 stories, interior corridors. **Parking:** on-site (fee) and valet. **Terms:** [AP] meal plan available. **Amenities:** video games (fee), CD players, high-speed Internet, dual phone lines, voice mail, irons, hair dryers. **Dining:** 6 am-10:30 pm. **Pool(s):** 2 heated outdoor, lap. **Leisure Activities:** saunas, whirlpools, spa, sports court, basketball, volleyball. **Guest Services:** gift shop, valet laundry. **Business Services:** conference facilities, business center. **Cards:** AX, CB, DC, DS, MC, VI. **Special Amenities: free newspaper.**

SOME UNITS

(See map and index starting on p. 516)

WALNUT CREEK MOTOR LODGE — **Phone:** 925/932-2811 — 42

Motel

All Year — 1P: $75-$80 — 2P: $85-$90 — XP: $5 — F17

Location: Just e off I-680 and SR 24; exit e via Ygnacio Valley Rd northbound; exit e via N Main St southbound. 1960 N Main St 94596. Fax: 925/932-5989. **Facility:** 71 one-bedroom standard units. 2 stories, exterior corridors. **Parking:** on-site. **Amenities:** hair dryers. **Pool(s):** outdoor. **Leisure Activities:** whirlpool. **Cards:** AX, DC, MC, VI. **Special Amenities: free local telephone calls and preferred room (subject to availability with advanced reservations).**

SOME UNITS

WHERE TO DINE

CALIFORNIA CAFE BAR & GRILL — **Lunch:** $8-$13 — **Dinner:** $10-$20 — **Phone:** 925/938-9977 — 33

Regional American

Location: I-680, exit Ygnacio Valley Rd, 0.3 mi e, then 0.8 mi s. 1540 N California Blvd 94596. **Hours:** 11:30 am-2:30 & 5:30-9:30 pm, Sat 5 pm-10 pm, Sun 10:30 am-2:30 & 5-9 pm. **Reservations:** suggested. **Features:** The casual, downtown restaurant's innovative menu preparations show a focus on fresh ingredients. Dressy casual; cocktails. **Parking:** valet. **Cards:** AX, DC, MC, VI.

MASSIMO RISTORANTE — **Lunch:** $8-$17 — **Dinner:** $11-$27 — **Phone:** 925/932-1474 — 34

Northern Italian

Location: I-680 and SR 24, exit Ygnacio Valley Rd, s on California Blvd, then e on La Cassie. 1604 Locust St 94596. **Hours:** 11:30 am-3 & 5-9 pm, Sat-11 pm. Closed major holidays; also for lunch Sat & Sun. **Reservations:** suggested. **Features:** Attractive, contemporary decor punctuates the downtown restaurant. Diners can relax in the casual and friendly atmosphere. Dressy casual; cocktails. **Parking:** on-site. **Cards:** AX, DC, MC, VI.

WATSONVILLE pop. 44,265

WHERE TO STAY

BEST WESTERN ROSE GARDEN INN — Book at aaa.com — **Phone:** (831)724-3367

Motel

5/16-9/15 [ECP]	1P: $79-$129	2P: $79-$129	XP: $10	F12
9/16-1/31 [ECP]	1P: $69-$129	2P: $69-$129	XP: $10	F12
2/1-5/15 [ECP]	1P: $69-$99	2P: $69-$99	XP: $10	F12

Location: On SR 152. 740 Freedom Blvd 95076. Fax: 831/761-1785. **Facility:** 43 one-bedroom standard units, some with efficiencies (no utensils). 2 stories (no elevator), exterior corridors. *Bath:* combo or shower only. **Parking:** on-site. **Terms:** small pets only ($5 extra charge). **Amenities:** voice mail, irons, hair dryers. *Some:* dual phone lines. **Pool(s):** small heated outdoor. **Leisure Activities:** whirlpool. **Guest Services:** coin laundry. **Cards:** AX, CB, DC, DS, JC, MC, VI. **Special Amenities: free expanded continental breakfast and free newspaper.**

SOME UNITS

FEE FEE

ECONOMY INN — **Phone:** (831)724-4755

Motel

5/1-10/15	1P: $69-$109	2P: $79-$129	XP: $10	F12
2/1-4/30	1P: $45-$55	2P: $50-$59	XP: $10	F12
10/16-1/31	1P: $49-$55	2P: $49-$59	XP: $10	F12

Location: SR 1, exit SR 152, 1 mi e. 584 Auto Center Dr 95076. Fax: 831/761-1120. **Facility:** 30 one-bedroom standard units. 1 story, exterior corridors. *Bath:* combo or shower only. **Parking:** on-site. **Terms:** 7 day cancellation notice, weekly rates available, [CP] meal plan available. **Cards:** AX, CB, DS, MC, VI.

SOME UNITS

HOLIDAY INN EXPRESS HOTEL & SUITES — Book at aaa.com — **Phone:** (831)728-3600

Small-scale Hotel

5/1-9/30	1P: $119-$169	2P: $119-$169	XP: $10	F18
10/1-1/31	1P: $99-$129	2P: $99-$129		
2/1-4/30	1P: $99-$129	2P: $99-$129	XP: $10	F18

Location: SR 1, exit SR 152/Main St southbound; exit S Green Valley Rd northbound. 1855 Main St 95077. Fax: 831/728-9600. **Facility:** Smoke free premises. 64 one-bedroom standard units, some with whirlpools. 3 stories, interior corridors. *Bath:* combo or shower only. **Parking:** on-site. **Terms:** [ECP] meal plan available. **Amenities:** dual phone lines, voice mail, irons, hair dryers. **Pool(s):** heated indoor. **Leisure Activities:** whirlpool, exercise room. **Guest Services:** coin laundry. **Cards:** AX, CB, DC, DS, MC, VI.

RED ROOF INN — Book at aaa.com — **Phone:** (831)740-4520

Small-scale Hotel

6/1-8/26	1P: $85	2P: $90
5/1-5/31	1P: $75	2P: $80
2/1-4/30 & 8/27-1/31	1P: $70	2P: $75

Location: SR 1, exit Riverside Dr (SR 129), just w. 1620 W Beach St 95076. Fax: 831/740-4401. **Facility:** 95 one-bedroom standard units. 3 stories, interior corridors. *Bath:* combo or shower only. **Parking:** on-site. **Terms:** weekly rates available, [ECP] meal plan available, package plans, small pets only. **Amenities:** video games (fee), hair dryers. *Some:* high-speed Internet. **Pool(s):** heated outdoor. **Cards:** AX, CB, DC, DS, JC, MC, VI.

SOME UNITS

FEE FEE

The following lodging was either not evaluated or did not meet AAA rating requirements but is listed for your information only.

COMFORT INN WATSONVILLE — **Phone:** 831/728-2300

fyi

Motel

6/1-9/30 [ECP]	1P: $89-$250	2P: $89-$250	XP: $10
4/1-5/31 [ECP]	1P: $79-$180	2P: $79-$180	XP: $10
2/1-3/31 & 10/1-1/31 [ECP]	1P: $59-$109	2P: $59-$109	XP: $10

Too new to rate, opening scheduled for October 2003. **Location:** US 1, 1 mi e. 112 Airport Blvd 95019. Fax: 831/728-3700. **Amenities:** 41 units, pets, coffeemakers, microwaves, refrigerators. **Cards:** AX, CB, DC, DS, JC, MC, VI.

WHERE TO DINE

MT MADONNA INN RESTAURANT — **Lunch:** $5-$13 **Dinner:** $12-$24 **Phone:** 831/724-2275

Continental

Location: 7 mi e on SR 152 at summit. 1285 Hecker Pass Rd 95076. **Hours:** noon-10 pm, Sun from 10 am. Closed: 12/25; also Mon-Wed. **Reservations:** accepted. **Features:** Panoramic views of the valleys and cities below are impressive from the dining room. The menu comprises diverse fresh seafood dishes. Dressy casual; cocktails; entertainment. **Parking:** on-site. **Cards:** AX, CB, DC, MC, VI.

WEAVERVILLE pop. 3,554

WHERE TO STAY

49ER MOTEL — **Phone:** 530/623-4937

Motel

5/1-10/31	1P: $40-$55	2P: $50-$60	XP: $5	F5
2/1-4/30 & 11/1-1/31	1P: $38-$50	2P: $48-$55	XP: $5	F5

Location: On SR 299. 718 Main St 96093 (PO Box 1608). Fax: 530/623-4937. **Facility:** 24 one-bedroom standard units, some with whirlpools. 1 story, exterior corridors. *Bath:* combo or shower only. **Parking:** on-site. **Terms:** 3 day cancellation notice. **Amenities:** *Some:* irons, hair dryers. **Pool(s):** outdoor. **Cards:** AX, DS, MC, VI. **Special Amenities: free continental breakfast and free local telephone calls.**

SOME UNITS

BEST WESTERN WEAVERVILLE VICTORIAN INN — *Book at aaa.com* — **Phone:** 530/623-4432

Motel

5/16-10/15	1P: $88-$198	2P: $98-$198	XP: $10	F12
2/1-5/15 & 10/16-1/31	1P: $55-$198	2P: $65-$198	XP: $10	F12

Location: On SR 299. 1709 Main St 96093 (PO Box 2400). Fax: 530/623-4264. **Facility:** 65 one-bedroom standard units, some with whirlpools. 2 stories (no elevator), exterior corridors. **Parking:** on-site. **Terms:** age restrictions may apply, cancellation fee imposed, small pets only ($10 deposit). **Amenities:** irons, hair dryers. **Dining:** 7 am-9 pm; hours vary in summer; closed Wed & Thurs, cocktails. **Pool(s):** small outdoor. **Business Services:** meeting rooms. **Cards:** AX, CB, DC, DS, JC, MC, VI. **Special Amenities: free continental breakfast.**

SOME UNITS

FEE FEE

MOTEL TRINITY — **Phone:** (530)623-2129

Motel

5/1-10/31	1P: $40-$80	2P: $50-$90	XP: $5	F9
2/1-4/30 & 11/1-1/31	1P: $35-$70	2P: $40-$80	XP: $5	F9

Location: 1112 Main St 96093 (PO Box 1179). Fax: 530/623-6007. **Facility:** 25 one-bedroom standard units, some with kitchens and/or whirlpools. 1 story, exterior corridors. *Bath:* combo or shower only. **Parking:** on-site. **Terms:** age restrictions may apply, 3 day cancellation notice-fee imposed. **Amenities:** *Some:* irons, hair dryers. **Pool(s):** outdoor. **Cards:** AX, DS, MC, VI. **Special Amenities: free local telephone calls and preferred room (subject to availability with advanced reservations).**

SOME UNITS

RED HILL MOTEL — **Phone:** 530/623-4331

Cottage

All Year	1P: $30-$75	2P: $35-$75	XP: $5	F12

Location: SR 299, just w of SR 3. Red Hill Rd 96093 (PO Box 234). Fax: 530/623-4341. **Facility:** 14 units. 7 one- and 1 two-bedroom standard units. 6 cabins. 1 story, exterior corridors. *Bath:* combo or shower only. **Parking:** on-site. **Terms:** office hours 8 am-11 pm, age restrictions may apply. **Amenities:** *Some:* irons, hair dryers. **Cards:** AX, DS, MC, VI.

SOME UNITS

WHERE TO DINE

LA GRANGE CAFE — **Lunch:** $7-$9 **Dinner:** $9-$24 **Phone:** 530/623-5325

Nouvelle California

Location: On US 299. 216 Main St 96093. **Hours:** 11 am-2 & 4-10 pm. Closed: 12/25. **Features:** The elegant restaurant occupies a former drugstore in the town's historic section. Soft lights, brick walls and hardwood floors add to the refined setting, while old standards playing in the background set the mood. Casual dress; cocktails. **Parking:** on-site. **Cards:** AX, DS, MC, VI.

VICTORIAN RESTAURANT — **Dinner:** $10-$24 **Phone:** 530/623-9411

American

Location: SR 299. 1701 Main St 96093. **Hours:** 4 pm-8:30 pm. Closed: 11/25, 12/25; also Mon-Thurs & Sun. **Features:** Traditional American dishes, as well as daily specials, are dished in generous portions. Vintage memorabilia is spread throughout the restaurant. Casual dress; cocktails. **Parking:** on-site. **Cards:** AX, MC, VI.

WEED pop. 2,978

WHERE TO STAY

COMFORT INN — *Book at aaa.com* — **Phone:** 530/938-1982

Motel

All Year [CP]	1P: $69-$99	2P: $69-$99	XP: $10	F18

Location: I-5, exit S Weed, just e. 1844 Shastina Dr 96094. Fax: 530/938-1983. **Facility:** 56 units. 54 one-bedroom standard units. 2 one-bedroom suites ($81-$119). 3 stories, interior corridors. *Bath:* some combo or shower only. **Parking:** on-site. **Terms:** age restrictions may apply, pets ($100 deposit, $10 extra charge). **Amenities:** irons, hair dryers. **Pool(s):** outdoor. **Leisure Activities:** whirlpool, exercise room. **Guest Services:** coin laundry. **Business Services:** meeting rooms. **Cards:** AX, CB, DC, DS, JC, MC, VI. **Special Amenities: free continental breakfast and free local telephone calls.**

SOME UNITS

FEE

HOLIDAY INN EXPRESS *Book at aaa.com* **Phone:** (530)938-1308

AAA SAVE — Motel

All Year [ECP] 1P: $71-$79 2P: $80-$89 XP: $6 F19

Location: Just e of I-5, in town. 1830 Black Butte Dr 96094. Fax: 530/938-1349. **Facility:** 50 one-bedroom standard units, some with whirlpools. 2 stories (no elevator), interior corridors. **Parking:** on-site. **Terms:** age restrictions may apply, pets ($10 extra charge). **Amenities:** irons, hair dryers. **Leisure Activities:** whirlpool. **Cards:** AX, DC, DS, MC, VI.

SOME UNITS — FEE

SIS-Q-INN MOTEL **Phone:** (530)938-4194

AAA SAVE — Motel

All Year 1P: $40 2P: $100

Location: I-5, exit S Weed. 1825 Shastina Dr 96094. Fax: 530/938-4195. **Facility:** 22 one-bedroom standard units. 2 stories, interior corridors. **Parking:** on-site. **Terms:** age restrictions may apply, cancellation fee imposed, [CP] meal plan available, pets ($5 extra charge). **Leisure Activities:** whirlpool. **Cards:** AX, DS, MC, VI. **Special Amenities: free continental breakfast and free local telephone calls.**

SOME UNITS — FEE FEE FEE

WESTLEY pop. 747

— WHERE TO STAY —

ECONO LODGE *Book at aaa.com* **Phone:** (209)894-3900

AAA SAVE — Motel

5/1-10/31 1P: $55-$65 2P: $70-$90 XP: $10 F12

2/1-4/30 & 11/1-1/31 1P: $50-$60 2P: $65-$85 XP: $10 F12

Location: I-5, exit Westley E. 7100 McCracken Rd 95387 (PO Box 990). Fax: 209/894-3905. **Facility:** 37 one-bedroom standard units. 2 stories (no elevator), exterior corridors. **Parking:** on-site. **Terms:** 3 day cancellation notice, [CP] meal plan available, small pets only ($5 extra charge). **Amenities:** hair dryers. **Pool(s):** heated outdoor. **Leisure Activities:** whirlpool. **Guest Services:** coin laundry. **Cards:** AX, DC, DS, MC, VI. **Special Amenities: free continental breakfast and free local telephone calls.**

SOME UNITS — FEE

HOLIDAY INN EXPRESS *Book at aaa.com* **Phone:** (209)894-8940

AAA SAVE — Small-scale Hotel

All Year [ECP] 1P: $59-$89 2P: $89-$99 XP: $10 F18

Location: I-5, exit Westley. 4525 Howard Rd 95387 (PO Box 307). Fax: 209/894-3800. **Facility:** 65 one-bedroom standard units, some with whirlpools. 3 stories, interior corridors. *Bath:* combo or shower only. **Parking:** on-site. **Amenities:** voice mail, irons, hair dryers. **Pool(s):** outdoor. **Leisure Activities:** whirlpool, exercise room. **Guest Services:** coin laundry. **Cards:** AX, CB, DC, DS, MC, VI. **Special Amenities: free expanded continental breakfast and free newspaper.** *(See color ad p 733)*

SOME UNITS

WESTPORT —*See Wine Country p. 812.*

WILLIAMS pop. 3,670

— WHERE TO STAY —

COMFORT INN *Book at aaa.com* **Phone:** (530)473-2381

Motel

All Year [CP] 1P: $59-$75 2P: $70-$85 XP: $6 F12

Location: I-5, exit Williams, just w on E St, then just n on 4th St. 400 C St 95987 (PO Box 1149). Fax: 530/473-2418. **Facility:** 60 one-bedroom standard units. 2 stories (no elevator), exterior corridors. **Parking:** on-site. **Terms:** age restrictions may apply, small pets only ($5 extra charge). **Amenities:** hair dryers. **Pool(s):** small outdoor. **Leisure Activities:** whirlpool. **Cards:** AX, DC, DS, MC, VI. **Special Amenities: free continental breakfast and free local telephone calls.**

FEE / SOME UNITS /

GRANZELLA'S INN **Phone:** (530)473-3310

Motel

All Year 1P: $75-$100 2P: $75-$100 XP: $5 F18

Location: I-5, exit Williams, 0.5 mi w. 391 6th St 95987. Fax: 530/473-3486. **Facility:** 43 one-bedroom standard units. 2 stories (no elevator), interior corridors. *Bath:* combo or shower only. **Parking:** on-site. **Terms:** age restrictions may apply, [CP] meal plan available, small pets only ($10 extra charge). **Amenities:** hair dryers. *Some:* irons. **Dining:** 6:30 am-10 pm. **Pool(s):** outdoor. **Leisure Activities:** whirlpool. **Guest Services:** coin laundry. **Business Services:** meeting rooms. **Cards:** AX, CB, DC, DS, MC, VI. *(See color ad below)*

FEE / SOME UNITS /

HOLIDAY INN EXPRESS HOTEL & SUITES *Book at aaa.com* **Phone:** (530)473-5120

Motel

All Year [ECP] 1P: $79-$99 2P: $79-$99 XP: $5 F19

Location: I-5, exit Williams, just e. 374 Ruggieri Way 95987. Fax: 530/473-5113. **Facility:** 51 one-bedroom standard units, some with whirlpools. 2 stories, interior corridors. *Bath:* combo or shower only. **Parking:** on-site. **Terms:** cancellation fee imposed. **Amenities:** dual phone lines, voice mail, irons, hair dryers. **Leisure Activities:** exercise room. **Guest Services:** coin laundry. **Cards:** AX, DC, DS, MC, VI. **Special Amenities: early check-in/late check-out.**

SOME UNITS /

STAGE STOP INN **Phone:** 530/473-2281

Motel

All Year 1P: $36-$42 2P: $43-$50 XP: $6 F14

Location: I-5, exit SR 20 business route, 3 blks w. 300 N 7th St 95987 (PO Box 1226). Fax: 530/473-2166. **Facility:** 23 one-bedroom standard units. 1 story, exterior corridors. *Bath:* combo or shower only. **Parking:** on-site. **Terms:** age restrictions may apply, pets ($5 extra charge). **Pool(s):** outdoor. **Cards:** AX, DC, DS, MC, VI.

FEE / SOME UNITS /

— WHERE TO DINE —

GRANZELLA'S RESTAURANT & DELI **Lunch:** $6-$12 **Dinner:** $9-$18 **Phone:** 530/473-5496

American

Location: I-5, exit Williams, 0.5 mi w. 451 6th St 95987. **Hours:** 6 am-10 pm. Closed: 12/25. **Reservations:** accepted. **Features:** In a large barn-like facility, the rustic restaurant serves simple, basic food. There is also a deli/gourmet shop. Casual dress; cocktails. **Parking:** on-site. **Cards:** AX, DC, DS, MC, VI. ***(See color ad below)***

WILLITS —*See Wine Country p. 812.*

WILLOW CREEK pop. 1,743

WHERE TO STAY

BIGFOOT MOTEL **Phone:** 530/629-2142

Motel

All Year 1P: $50-$85 2P: $55-$95

Location: SR 299; center of town. 39039 Hwy 299 95573 (PO Box 957). **Facility:** 24 units. 22 one- and 2 two-bedroom standard units, some with kitchens. 2 stories (no elevator), exterior corridors. *Bath:* combo or shower only. **Parking:** on-site. **Terms:** age restrictions may apply, pets ($5 extra charge). **Amenities:** *Some:* irons, hair dryers. **Pool(s):** small outdoor. **Cards:** AX, DC, DS, MC, VI. **Special Amenities: free local telephone calls.**

SOME UNITS

FEE

WILLOWS pop. 6,220

WHERE TO STAY

AMERIHOST INN & SUITES-WILLOWS *Book at aaa.com* **Phone:** (530)934-9700

Small-scale Hotel

All Year [ECP] 1P: $62-$159 2P: $72-$169 XP: $10 F16

Location: I-5, exit Willows, then right. 199 N Humboldt Ave 95988. Fax: 530/934-3431. **Facility:** 71 one-bedroom standard units, some with whirlpools. 2 stories (no elevator), interior corridors. *Bath:* combo or shower only. **Parking:** on-site. **Amenities:** voice mail, irons, hair dryers. **Pool(s):** heated indoor. **Leisure Activities:** whirlpool, limited exercise equipment. **Business Services:** meeting rooms. **Cards:** AX, CB, DC, DS, JC, MC, VI.

SOME UNITS

BEST VALUE INN *Book at aaa.com* **Phone:** (530)934-7026

Motel

All Year [CP] 1P: $39-$89 2P: $44-$119 XP: $6 F6

Location: I-5, exit Willow-Elk Creek-Glenn Rd, just e. 452 N Humboldt Ave 95988. Fax: 530/934-4121. **Facility:** 41 one-bedroom standard units. 2 stories, exterior corridors. **Parking:** on-site. **Terms:** cancellation fee imposed. **Amenities:** hair dryers. *Some:* irons. **Pool(s):** outdoor. **Cards:** AX, CB, DC, DS, JC, MC, VI. **Special Amenities: free continental breakfast and free local telephone calls.**

SOME UNITS

BEST WESTERN GOLDEN PHEASANT INN *Book at aaa.com* **Phone:** (530)934-4603

Motel

All Year [ECP] 1P: $69-$100 2P: $79-$150 XP: $10

Location: I-5, exit Willow-Elk Creek-Glenn Rd, just e. 249 N Humboldt Ave 95988 (PO Box 758, JACKSON, 95642). Fax: 530/934-4275. **Facility:** 104 one-bedroom standard units, some with whirlpools. 1 story, exterior corridors. *Bath:* combo or shower only. **Parking:** on-site. **Terms:** pets ($10 fee). **Amenities:** video library, voice mail, irons, hair dryers. **Dining:** Casa Ramos, see separate listing. **Pool(s):** 2 outdoor. **Business Services:** meeting rooms. **Cards:** AX, DC, DS, MC, VI. **Special Amenities: free expanded continental breakfast and free local telephone calls.**

SOME UNITS

FEE

DAYS INN *Book at aaa.com* **Phone:** (530)934-4444

Motel

All Year 1P: $50-$55 2P: $50-$60 XP: $10 F12

Location: I-5, exit Willow-Elk Creek-Glenn Rd, just e. 475 N Humboldt Ave 95988. Fax: 530/934-0222. **Facility:** 50 one-bedroom standard units, some with whirlpools. 2 stories, exterior corridors. *Bath:* combo or shower only. **Parking:** on-site. **Terms:** cancellation fee imposed, [CP] meal plan available. **Amenities:** hair dryers. *Some:* irons. **Pool(s):** outdoor. **Leisure Activities:** whirlpool. **Cards:** AX, MC, VI. **Special Amenities: free continental breakfast and free local telephone calls.**

SOME UNITS

ECONOMY INN **Phone:** 530/934-4224

Motel

All Year 1P: $35-$55 2P: $50-$70 XP: $5 F3

Location: I-5. 435 N Tehama St 95988. Fax: 530/934-4947. **Facility:** 20 one-bedroom standard units, some with kitchens (no utensils). 1 story, exterior corridors. *Bath:* shower only. **Parking:** on-site. **Terms:** age restrictions may apply, cancellation fee imposed, weekly rates available. **Cards:** AX, DS, MC, VI. **Special Amenities: free local telephone calls and early check-in/late check-out.**

SOME UNITS

SUPER 8 MOTEL OF WILLOWS *Book at aaa.com* **Phone:** (530)934-2871

Motel

7/1-10/31 1P: $49-$52 2P: $54-$57 XP: $5 F12
2/1-6/30 & 11/1-1/31 1P: $44-$48 2P: $49-$51 XP: $5 F12

Location: I-5, exit Willow-Elk Creek-Glenn Rd. 457 Humboldt Ave 95988. Fax: 530/934-5512. **Facility:** 41 one-bedroom standard units. 2 stories, interior corridors. **Parking:** on-site. **Terms:** 5-10 night minimum stay - midweek, age restrictions may apply, weekly rates available, package plans - midweek, pets ($20 deposit). **Amenities:** *Some:* irons, hair dryers. **Pool(s):** outdoor. **Cards:** AX, DC, MC, VI.

SOME UNITS

FEE

WHERE TO DINE

CASA RAMOS

Mexican

Lunch: $6-$8 **Dinner:** $6-$15 **Phone:** 530/934-2878

Location: I-5, exit Willow-Elk Creek-Glenn Rd, just e; in Best Western Golden Pheasant Inn. 247 N Humboldt 95988. **Hours:** 6-9 am, 11-2:30 & 5-9 pm, Sun 10 am-2:30 & 5-9 pm. **Reservations:** accepted. **Features:** The tastefully decorated Mexican restaurant offers large amounts of food and easy access from the Interstate. Casual dress; cocktails. **Parking:** on-site. **Cards:** AX, CB, DC, DS, MC, VI.

FRANCO'S

Italian

Lunch: $5-$11 **Dinner:** $9-$20 **Phone:** 530/934-4273

Location: 0.5 mi s on Old Hwy 99. 610 S Tehama St 95988. **Hours:** 11 am-2 & 4:30-10 pm, Sat from 5 pm, Sun 4 pm-9 pm. Closed major holidays. **Reservations:** suggested. **Features:** Family-style, Italian American cuisine. Casual dress; cocktails. **Parking:** on-site. **Cards:** AX, DS, MC, VI.

Destination Wine Country

Wining and dining are two popular activities in Wine Country.

And what goes better with wine than scrumptious California cuisine? Nearly every restaurant has an extensive wine list, and menus offer creative entree combinations and decadent desserts. To work off the calories, go bicycling, canoeing or kayaking amid dramatic scenery. Then soothe your sore muscles with a massage or mineral bath.

© Craig Tuttle / Corbis

Vineyards.
The fruits of the vine are what Wine Country is all about.

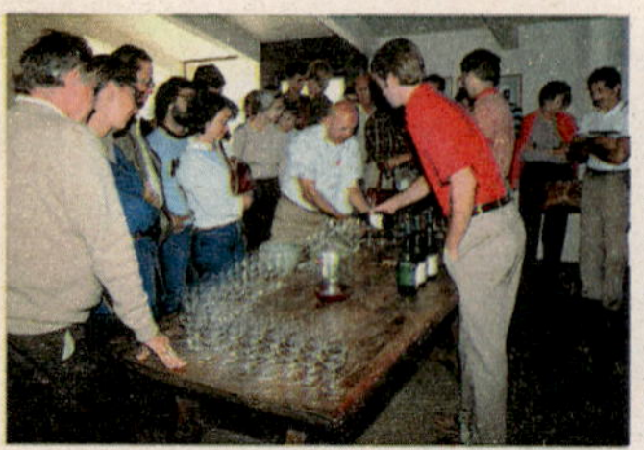

© Gibson Stock Photography

Wine tasting.
Start with a white wine and move to heavier reds; maybe try a reserve wine—often the winemaker's finest—if it's offered.

Dining in Wine Country.
Restaurants utilize fresh, seasonal ingredients to create dishes that complement locally produced wines.

© Gibson Stock Photography

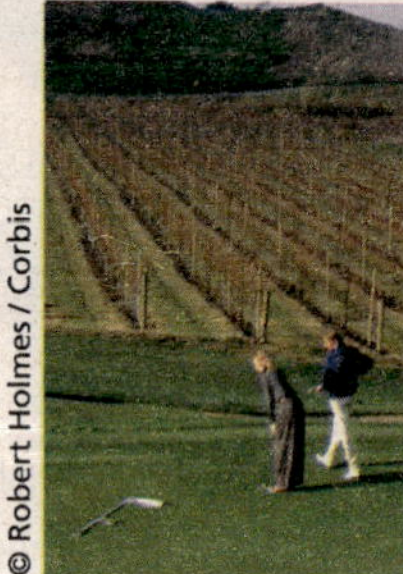

© Robert Holmes / Corbis

Putting on the green.
Perhaps these golfers will celebrate a well-played round with a glass of wine from a neighboring vineyard.

Places included in this AAA Destination Area:

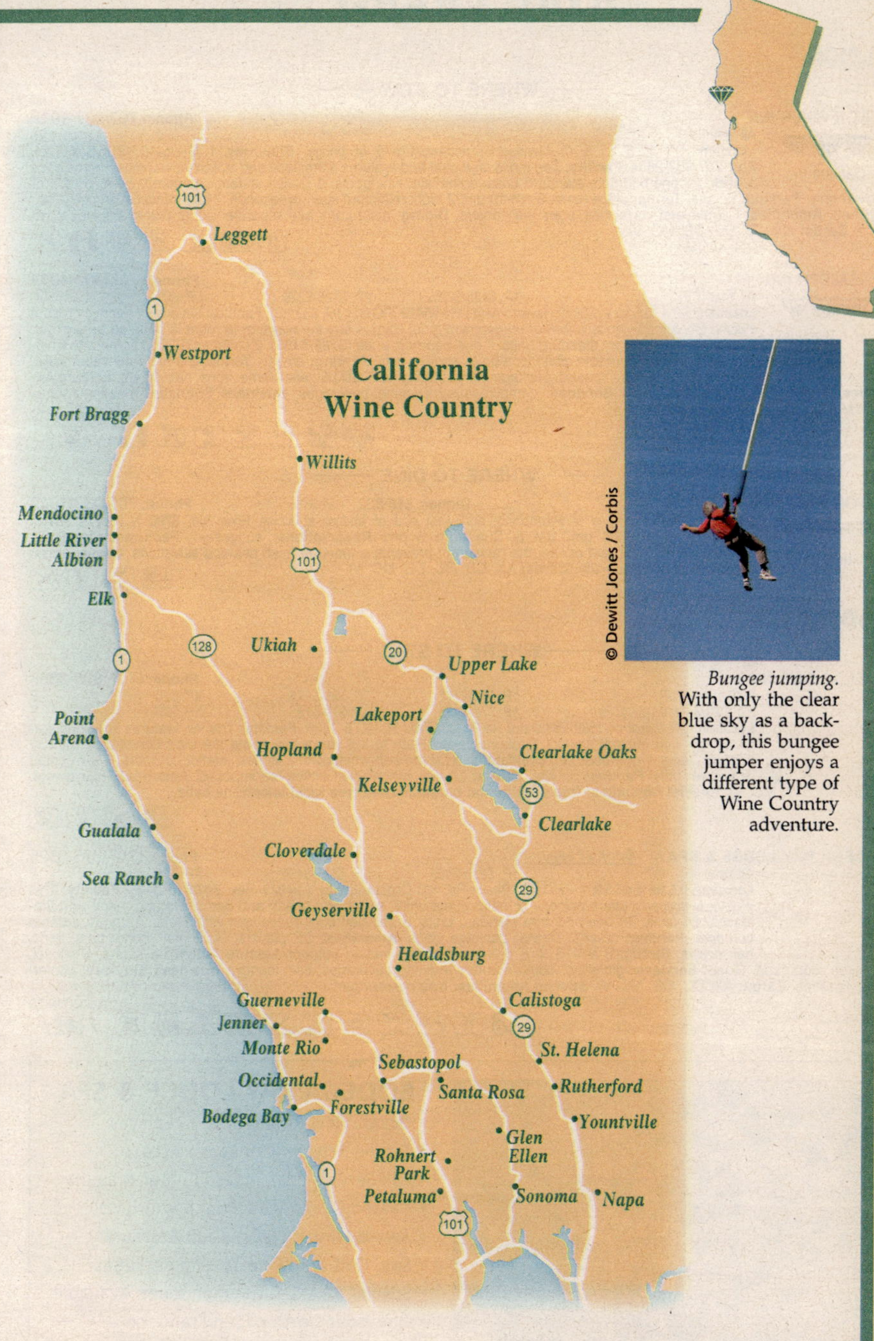

Bungee jumping. With only the clear blue sky as a backdrop, this bungee jumper enjoys a different type of Wine Country adventure.

Wine Country

ALBION

WHERE TO STAY

ALBION RIVER INN — **Phone:** 707/937-1919

Country Inn

All Year [BP] 2P: $160-$310 XP: $20 F6

Location: SR 1, 6 mi s of Mendocino; northwest end of bridge. 3790 Hwy 1 N 95410 (PO Box 100). Fax: 707/937-2604. **Facility:** The inn is on a bluff and features a fireplace and ocean views; most rooms have a deck. 20 one-bedroom standard units, some with whirlpools. 2 stories, exterior corridors. *Bath:* combo or shower only. **Parking:** on-site. **Terms:** office hours 8 am-10 pm, 2 night minimum stay - weekends, 7 day cancellation notice-fee imposed. **Amenities:** CD players, voice mail, irons, hair dryers. **Dining:** restaurant, see separate listing. **Guest Services:** gift shop. **Cards:** AX, CB, DC, DS, MC, VI.

DATA PORT

FENSALDEN INN — **Phone:** (707)937-4042

Bed & Breakfast

All Year [BP] 1P: $125-$225 2P: $125-$225 XP: $20

Location: SR 1, 0.5 mi e. 33810 Navarro Ridge Rd 95410 (PO Box 99, 952110). **Facility:** On a bluff overlooking the Pacific Ocean, the inn is a former stagecoach stop; rumors say the Hawthorne room is haunted by a ghost. 8 units. 5 one-bedroom standard units. 1 one-bedroom suite ($180-$185). 2 cottages ($225), some with whirlpools. 2 stories (no elevator), interior corridors. *Bath:* combo or shower only. **Parking:** on-site. **Terms:** 2-3 night minimum stay - weekends, 7 day cancellation notice-fee imposed, package plans. **Amenities:** CD players. *Some:* irons, hair dryers. **Leisure Activities:** horseshoes, volleyball. **Guest Services:** complimentary evening beverages. **Business Services:** meeting rooms. **Cards:** AX, MC, VI.

SOME UNITS

ASK

WHERE TO DINE

ALBION RIVER INN RESTAURANT — **Dinner:** $18-$32 — **Phone:** 707/937-1919

American

Location: SR 1, 6 mi s of Mendocino; northwest end of bridge; at Albion River Inn. 3790 N Hwy 1 95410. **Hours:** 5:30 pm-9:30 pm, Sat & Sun from 5 pm. **Reservations:** suggested. **Features:** On a cliff overlooking the river and ocean, the restaurant presents a menu of fresh seafood selections. Casual dress; cocktails. **Parking:** on-site. **Cards:** AX, CB, DC, DS, MC, VI.

BODEGA BAY pop. 1,423

WHERE TO STAY

BODEGA BAY INN — **Phone:** (707)875-3388

AAA SAVE

Bed & Breakfast

5/30-10/31 [CP]	1P: $99-$175	2P: $99-$175	XP: $20	F
2/1-5/29 & 11/1-1/31 [CP]	1P: $79-$135	2P: $79-$135	XP: $20	F

Location: SR 1, just w. 1588 Eastshore Rd 94923. Fax: 707/875-2905. **Facility:** The inn features spacious surroundings with original artwork throughout; ask Ruth to tell you a tale about the inn's connection with Sir Francis Drake. 7 one-bedroom standard units, some with whirlpools. 2 stories, interior corridors. *Bath:* combo or shower only. **Parking:** on-site. **Terms:** 10 day cancellation notice-fee imposed. **Amenities:** hair dryers. **Cards:** AX, DS, MC, VI. **Special Amenities: free continental breakfast and free local telephone calls.**

BODEGA BAY LODGE & SPA — *Book at aaa.com* — **Phone:** (707)875-3525

AAA SAVE

Motel

All Year 1P: $225-$465 2P: $225-$465 XP: $25 F

Location: 0.5 mi s off SR 1 via Doran Beach Rd. 103 Coast Highway 1 94923. Fax: 707/875-2428. **Facility:** This bay-view property offers balcony or patio guest units, some with ocean and bay views and many with fireplaces. 84 units. 78 one-bedroom standard units. 6 one-bedroom suites with whirlpools. 2 stories, exterior corridors. **Parking:** on-site. **Terms:** package plans. **Amenities:** CD players, voice mail, honor bars, irons, hair dryers. **Dining:** 8 am-10:30 & 6-9 pm. **Pool(s):** heated outdoor. **Leisure Activities:** sauna, whirlpool, exercise room, spa. **Guest Services:** gift shop, complimentary evening beverages, coin laundry. **Business Services:** conference facilities. **Cards:** AX, DC, DS, MC, VI. **Special Amenities: free newspaper.** *(See color ad inside back cover & below)*

SOME UNITS

DATA PORT

BODEGA COAST INN — Phone: 707/875-2217

6/1-1/31	1P: $189-$279	2P: $189-$279	XP: $20	F18
2/1-5/31	1P: $159-$239	2P: $159-$239	XP: $20	F18

AAA SAVE — Motel

Location: 2 blks s. 521 SR 1 N 94923 (PO Box 55). Fax: 707/875-2964. **Facility:** 45 one-bedroom standard units, some with whirlpools. 3 stories, exterior corridors. **Parking:** on-site. **Terms:** cancellation fee imposed, [CP] meal plan available, pets (in designated units). **Amenities:** CD players, dual phone lines, voice mail, irons, hair dryers. **Leisure Activities:** whirlpool. **Business Services:** meeting rooms. **Cards:** AX, DC, DS, MC, VI. *(See color ad below)*

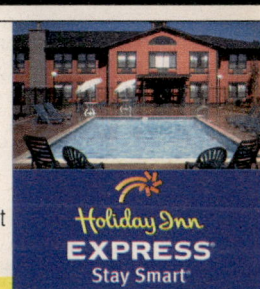

INN AT THE TIDES *Book at aaa.com* **Phone:** (707)875-2751

SAVE Motel

6/16-11/15	1P: $209-$269	2P: $209-$269	XP: $20	F12
11/16-1/31	1P: $199-$269	2P: $199-$269	XP: $20	F12
2/1-6/15	1P: $189-$259	2P: $189-$259	XP: $20	F12

Location: Center. 800 SR 1 94923 (PO Box 640). Fax: 707/875-2669. **Facility:** 86 one-bedroom standard units. 2 stories, exterior corridors. **Parking:** on-site. **Amenities:** irons, hair dryers. **Dining:** 5 pm-10 pm; closed Mon & Tues, cocktails. **Pool(s):** heated outdoor. **Leisure Activities:** sauna, whirlpool. **Guest Services:** coin laundry. **Business Services:** meeting rooms. **Cards:** AX, DC, DS, MC, VI. *(See color ad p 765)*

SOME UNITS / VCR / FEE

WHERE TO DINE

LUCAS WHARF RESTAURANT **Lunch:** $8-$23 **Dinner:** $8-$23 **Phone:** 707/875-3522

Seafood

Location: Center. 595 SR 1 94923. **Hours:** 11 am-9:30 pm, Fri & Sat-10 pm. Closed: 11/25, 12/25. **Features:** Also, steak and pasta. On the bay. Casual dress; cocktails. **Parking:** on-site. **Cards:** DS, MC, VI.

CALISTOGA pop. 5,190

WHERE TO STAY

AURORA PARK COTTAGES **Phone:** (707)942-6733

Bed & Breakfast

4/1-10/31	2P: $225-$265	XP: $50
2/1-3/31 & 11/1-1/31	2P: $185-$225	XP: $50

Location: On SR 128, 0.5 mi n of jct SR 29. 1807 Foothill Blvd 94515. **Facility:** 6 cottages. 1 story, exterior corridors. *Bath:* shower only. **Parking:** on-site. **Terms:** 2-3 night minimum stay - weekends, cancellation fee imposed, [ECP] meal plan available, package plans. **Amenities:** hair dryers. **Cards:** AX, MC, VI.

BEST WESTERN STEVENSON MANOR INN *Book at aaa.com* **Phone:** (707)942-1112

SAVE Motel

3/1-11/30 & 12/22-1/31 [ECP]	1P: $109-$199	2P: $119-$299	XP: $10	F18
2/1-2/29 & 12/1-12/21 [ECP]	1P: $84-$179	2P: $89-$199	XP: $10	F18

Location: 0.5 mi n on SR 29. 1830 Lincoln Ave 94515. Fax: 707/942-0318. **Facility:** 34 one-bedroom standard units. 2 stories, exterior corridors. *Bath:* combo or shower only. **Parking:** on-site. **Amenities:** voice mail, irons, hair dryers. **Pool(s):** heated outdoor. **Leisure Activities:** sauna, whirlpool, steamroom. *Fee:* massage. **Cards:** AX, CB, DC, DS, JC, MC, VI. **Special Amenities: free expanded continental breakfast and free local telephone calls.**

CARLIN COUNTRY COTTAGES **Phone:** 707/942-9102

Cottage

4/1-10/31	1P: $94-$205	2P: $94-$205	XP: $15	F12
2/1-3/31 & 11/1-1/31	1P: $89-$195	2P: $89-$195	XP: $15	F12

Location: W of SR 29 via Lincoln Ave (SR 29). 1623 Lake St 94515. Fax: 707/942-2295. **Facility:** 15 units. 8 one-bedroom standard units with kitchens, some with whirlpools. 3 one-bedroom suites. 4 cottages. 1 story, exterior corridors. *Bath:* combo or shower only. **Parking:** on-site. **Terms:** 2 night minimum stay - weekends, 7 day cancellation notice-fee imposed. **Amenities:** irons. *Some:* hair dryers. **Pool(s):** heated outdoor. **Leisure Activities:** whirlpool. **Cards:** AX, DC, MC, VI.

SOME UNITS

ASK / /

CHRISTOPHER'S INN **Phone:** (707)942-5755

SAVE Bed & Breakfast

All Year [ECP]	1P: $175-$425	2P: $175-$425	XP: $25

Location: On SR 29, just s of intersection of Lincoln Ave. 1010 Foothill Blvd 94515. Fax: 707/942-6895. **Facility:** Smoke free premises. 19 one-bedroom standard units, some with whirlpools. 2 stories (no elevator), interior corridors. *Bath:* combo or shower only. **Parking:** on-site. **Terms:** 7 day cancellation notice-fee imposed, package plans. **Amenities:** irons, hair dryers. **Special Amenities: free continental breakfast and free local telephone calls.**

SOME UNITS / VCR /

COMFORT INN NAPA VALLEY NORTH *Book at aaa.com* **Phone:** (707)942-9400

SAVE Motel

3/1-11/30 & 12/23-1/31 [ECP]	1P: $94-$174	2P: $99-$179	XP: $10	F18
2/1-2/29 & 12/1-12/22 [ECP]	1P: $70-$120	2P: $75-$140	XP: $10	F18

Location: 0.5 mi n on SR 29. 1865 Lincoln Ave 94515. Fax: 707/942-5262. **Facility:** 55 units. 54 one-bedroom standard units. 1 one-bedroom suite. 2 stories, exterior corridors. **Parking:** on-site. **Amenities:** voice mail, irons, hair dryers. **Pool(s):** small heated outdoor. **Leisure Activities:** sauna, whirlpool, small geothermal pool. **Cards:** AX, CB, DC, DS, JC, MC, VI.

SOME UNITS / /

COTTAGE GROVE INN **Phone:** 707/942-8400

Cottage

All Year	1P: $250-$325	2P: $250-$325	XP: $50

Location: On SR 29, at Wapoo St. 1711 Lincoln Ave 94515. Fax: 707/942-2653. **Facility:** These cozy, individually decorated cottages each include a fireplace, wet bar and stereo system. Smoke free premises. 16 cottages with whirlpools. 1 story, exterior corridors. **Parking:** on-site. **Terms:** 2 night minimum stay - weekends, 7 day cancellation notice-fee imposed. **Amenities:** video library, CD players, voice mail, safes, irons, hair dryers. **Leisure Activities:** bicycles, hiking trails. **Guest Services:** complimentary evening beverages. **Cards:** AX, DC, DS, MC, VI.

DR. WILKINSON'S HOT SPRINGS RESORT *Book at aaa.com* **Phone:** (707)942-4102

Resort Motel

All Year 1P: $109-$209 XP: $12 D

Location: Center. 1507 Lincoln Ave 94515. Fax: 707/942-4412. **Facility:** Family owned for 50 years, the resort offers motel rooms, bungalows and a refurbished 1880s Victorian house with sunny patios. 42 units. 38 one-bedroom standard units, some with kitchens. 4 cottages. 2 stories, interior/exterior corridors. *Bath:* combo or shower only. **Parking:** on-site. **Amenities:** voice mail, hair dryers. *Some:* irons. **Pool(s):** 2 heated outdoor, heated indoor. **Leisure Activities:** whirlpool, spa. **Guest Services:** gift shop. **Cards:** AX, MC, VI. **Special Amenities: free local telephone calls and preferred room (subject to availability with advanced reservations).**

FOOTHILL HOUSE BED & BREAKFAST **Phone:** 707/942-6933

Bed & Breakfast

All Year 1P: $165-$375 2P: $175-$375 XP: $50 F6

Location: SR 128, 1.5 mi n of jct SR 29. 3037 Foothill Blvd 94515. Fax: 707/942-5692. **Facility:** A shaded patio, formal flower garden and gas fireplaces are featured at this restored 1892 farmhouse. 4 one-bedroom standard units, some with kitchens and/or whirlpools. 1 story, exterior corridors. **Parking:** on-site. **Terms:** 2 night minimum stay - weekends, 14 day cancellation notice-fee imposed, [BP] meal plan available. **Amenities:** video library, video games, CD players, irons, hair dryers. **Leisure Activities:** whirlpool. **Guest Services:** complimentary evening beverages, complimentary laundry. **Cards:** AX, DC, MC, VI. **Special Amenities: free local telephone calls and free newspaper.**

SOME UNITS

GARNETT CREEK INN **Phone:** (707)942-9797

Bed & Breakfast

All Year 1P: $155-$295 2P: $155-$295

Location: On SR 29. 1139 Lincoln Ave 94515. Fax: 707/942-8021. **Facility:** Combining old world elegance with modern luxury, the inn also features a fabulous location on a tree-lined corner of the historic main street. 5 one-bedroom standard units. 2 stories, interior corridors. **Parking:** on-site. **Terms:** 2 night minimum stay - weekends in season, 7 day cancellation notice. **Amenities:** irons, hair dryers. **Cards:** MC, VI.

HIDEAWAY COTTAGES **Phone:** (707)942-4108

Cottage

All Year 1P: $139-$550 2P: $139-$550

Location: 1412 Fairway 94515. Fax: 707/942-4412. **Facility:** 15 units. 6 one-bedroom standard units with efficiencies. 9 cottages. 1 story, exterior corridors. *Bath:* combo or shower only. **Parking:** on-site. **Terms:** 3 day cancellation notice, package plans. **Amenities:** video library, irons, hair dryers. *Some:* CD players. **Pool(s):** heated outdoor. **Leisure Activities:** whirlpool, hiking trails, jogging. *Fee:* massage. **Cards:** AX, MC, VI.

SOME UNITS

MOUNT VIEW HOTEL & SPA **Phone:** (707)942-6877

Historic Small-scale Hotel

7/1-11/15 [CP]	1P: $180-$310	2P: $180-$310
3/1-6/30 [CP]	1P: $165-$300	2P: $165-$300
11/16-1/31 [CP]	1P: $160-$290	2P: $160-$290
2/1-2/29 [CP]	1P: $140-$260	2P: $140-$260

Location: On SR 29; center. 1457 Lincoln Ave 94515. Fax: 707/942-6904. **Facility:** A private courtyard, hot mineral whirlpool and large outdoor pool all invite you to relax at this 1917 historic hotel. 32 units. 27 one-bedroom standard units. 2 one-bedroom suites ($195-$305). 3 cottages ($250-$350) with whirlpools. 2 stories, interior corridors. *Bath:* combo or shower only. **Parking:** on-site. **Terms:** 2-3 night minimum stay - with Saturday stay-over, 14 day cancellation notice-fee imposed, package plans - seasonal & midweek. **Amenities:** voice mail, irons, hair dryers. **Dining:** 11:30 am-9:30 pm, cocktails. **Pool(s):** heated outdoor. **Leisure Activities:** sauna, whirlpool, spa. **Cards:** AX, DC, DS, MC, VI. **Special Amenities: free continental breakfast and free newspaper.**

SOME UNITS

ROMAN SPA HOT SPRINGS RESORT Phone: 707/942-4441

Resort Motel

6/11-9/5 2P: $134-$325 XP: $16
9/6-11/13 2P: $100-$325 XP: $16
2/1-6/10 & 11/14-1/31 2P: $92-$325 XP: $16

Location: Just n of Lincoln Ave (SR 29). 1300 Washington St 94515. **Facility:** Lodging buildings with well-landscaped patios are clustered on grounds featuring ponds, arbors, sunning areas and a barbecue patio. 60 units. 58 one- and 2 two-bedroom standard units, some with kitchens and/or whirlpools. 2 stories, exterior corridors. *Bath:* combo or shower only. **Parking:** on-site. **Terms:** 2 night minimum stay - weekends, 3 day cancellation notice-fee imposed. **Amenities:** hair dryers. *Some:* irons. **Leisure Activities:** saunas, 3 geothermal mineral pools, 2 with jets, 1 indoor, spa. **Guest Services:** coin laundry. **Cards:** AX, DS, MC, VI. **Special Amenities:** **free local telephone calls.** *(See color ad p 767)*

SOME UNITS

WASHINGTON STREET LODGING Phone: 707/942-6968

Cottage

All Year [CP] 1P: $95-$140 2P: $95-$140 XP: $10 F

Location: On SR 29. 1605 Washington St 94515. Fax: 707/942-0775. **Facility:** 5 cottages. 1 story, exterior corridors. *Bath:* shower only. **Parking:** on-site. **Terms:** 2 night minimum stay - weekends, 3 day cancellation notice-fee imposed, pets ($15 fee). **Amenities:** irons, hair dryers.

FEE

WHERE TO DINE

BRANNAN'S GRILL Lunch: $10-$16 Dinner: $13-$28 Phone: 707/942-2233

American

Location: On SR 29; center of town. 1374 Lincoln Ave 94515. **Hours:** 11:30 am-3 & 4:30-9 pm. Closed: 12/25. **Reservations:** suggested. **Features:** The beautiful club-like restaurant has high-beamed ceilings, dyed cement floors and contemporary artwork. Dressy casual; cocktails. **Parking:** on-site. **Cards:** AX, MC, VI.

CLEARLAKE pop. 13,142

WHERE TO STAY

BEST WESTERN EL GRANDE INN *Book at aaa.com* Phone: (707)994-2000

Motel

4/1-10/31 1P: $89-$139 2P: $89-$139
2/1-3/31 & 11/1-1/31 1P: $79-$95 2P: $89-$139

Location: SR 53, exit Lakeshore Dr, just w. 15135 Lakeshore Dr 95422 (PO Box 4598). Fax: 707/994-2042. **Facility:** 68 units. 44 one-bedroom standard units. 24 one-bedroom suites. 4 stories, interior corridors. *Bath:* combo or shower only. **Parking:** on-site. **Terms:** age restrictions may apply, [AP] meal plan available. **Amenities:** irons, hair dryers. **Dining:** 7 am-1:30 & 4-9:30 pm, cocktails. **Pool(s):** small heated indoor. **Leisure Activities:** whirlpool. **Business Services:** conference facilities. **Cards:** AX, DC, DS, MC, VI.

SOME UNITS

HIGHLANDS INN Phone: 707/994-8982

Motel

5/1-9/30 1P: $85-$95 2P: $95-$115 XP: $15 F6
10/1-1/31 1P: $55-$65 2P: $75-$85 XP: $10 F6
2/1-4/30 1P: $55-$75 2P: $65-$85 XP: $10 F6

Location: SR 53, exit Lakeshore Dr, 3 mi w. 13865 Lakeshore Dr 95422 (PO Box 5983, 95422-5983). Fax: 707/994-0613. **Facility:** 20 units. 18 one-bedroom standard units. 2 one-bedroom suites ($145). 2 stories (no elevator), exterior corridors. **Parking:** on-site. **Terms:** 2 night minimum stay - weekends, age restrictions may apply, 3 day cancellation notice-fee imposed, package plans - seasonal & weekends. **Amenities:** *Some:* irons, hair dryers. **Pool(s):** outdoor. **Leisure Activities:** boat dock, waterskiing, fishing. **Guest Services:** coin laundry. **Cards:** AX, DS, MC, VI. **Special Amenities: early check-in/late check-out and free room upgrade (subject to availability with advanced reservations).**

SOME UNITS

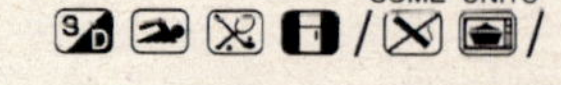

TRAVELODGE *Book at aaa.com* Phone: 707/994-1499

Motel

5/1-9/30 1P: $73-$110 2P: $73-$120 XP: $10 F17
2/1-4/30 & 10/1-1/31 1P: $73-$85 2P: $73-$85 XP: $10 F17

Location: SR 53, exit Clearlake on Lakeshore Dr. 4775 Old Hwy 53 95422. Fax: 707/994-5941. **Facility:** 31 one-bedroom standard units. 2 stories (no elevator), exterior corridors. **Parking:** on-site. **Terms:** office hours 8 am-11 pm, age restrictions may apply, 3 day cancellation notice. **Amenities:** irons, hair dryers. **Pool(s):** outdoor. **Leisure Activities:** whirlpool. **Guest Services:** complimentary laundry. **Cards:** AX, CB, DC, DS, MC, VI. **Special Amenities: free continental breakfast and free local telephone calls.**

SOME UNITS

CLEARLAKE OAKS

WHERE TO STAY

LAKE POINT LODGE Phone: 707/998-4350

Motel

5/1-10/31 1P: $60-$98 2P: $72-$98 XP: $10
2/1-4/30 & 11/1-1/31 1P: $54-$92 2P: $68-$92 XP: $10

Location: SR 53, 3 mi nw. 13470 E Hwy 20 95423 (PO Box 708). Fax: 707/998-2144. **Facility:** 40 one-bedroom standard units. 2 stories (no elevator), exterior corridors. **Parking:** on-site. **Terms:** age restrictions may apply, 4 day cancellation notice, [CP] meal plan available. **Amenities:** *Some:* irons, hair dryers. **Pool(s):** outdoor. **Leisure Activities:** whirlpool. **Guest Services:** coin laundry. **Cards:** AX, DC, MC, VI. **Special Amenities: free continental breakfast and free local telephone calls.**

SOME UNITS

CLOVERDALE pop. 6,831

WHERE TO STAY

THE SHELFORD HOUSE BED & BREAKFAST **Phone:** (707)894-5956

Bed & Breakfast

All Year 2P: $115-$250 XP: $35

Location: US 101, exit Citrus Fair Dr, 0.5 mi n on Asti Rd, then 1 mi e on Crocker Rd. 29955 River Rd 95425. Fax: 707/894-8621. **Facility:** The original 1885 Queen Anne-style Victorian invites guests to sit out on the wrap-around porch and savor the picturesque views of the vineyards. 7 units. 6 one-bedroom standard units. 1 one-bedroom suite with whirlpool. 2 stories (no elevator), interior corridors. *Bath:* combo or shower only. **Parking:** on-site. **Terms:** 1-2 night minimum stay - weekends, 7 day cancellation notice-fee imposed, [BP] meal plan available. **Leisure Activities:** whirlpool. **Cards:** AX, DS, MC, VI.

SOME UNITS

VINEYARD VALLEY INN **Phone:** (707)894-0707

Motel

All Year [CP] 1P: $45-$119 2P: $55-$129 XP: $10 F14

Location: US 101, exit 128 W (Fort Bragg/Mendocino). 721 N Cloverdale Blvd 95425. Fax: 707/894-0606. **Facility:** 15 one-bedroom standard units. 1 story, exterior corridors. *Bath:* combo or shower only. **Parking:** on-site. **Terms:** 2-3 night minimum stay - some weekends, 3 day cancellation notice-fee imposed. **Cards:** AX, CB, DC, DS, MC, VI. **Special Amenities: free continental breakfast and free newspaper.**

The following lodging was either not evaluated or did not meet AAA rating requirements but is listed for your information only.

BEST WESTERN CLOVERDALE INN

fyi Motel

Property failed to provide current rates **Phone:** 707/894-7500

Too new to rate. **Location:** US 101, exit Citrus Fair Dr, 0.4 mi w to S Cloverdale Blvd, then just s. 324 S Cloverdale Blvd 95425. **Amenities:** 62 units, coffeemakers, pool.

ELK

WHERE TO STAY

ELK COVE INN **Phone:** (707)877-3321

Bed & Breakfast

6/1-10/31 [BP] 1P: $130-$350 2P: $130-$350 XP: $30 D12
2/1-5/31 & 11/1-1/31 [BP] 1P: $100-$325 2P: $100-$325 XP: $30 D12

Location: W off SR 1, 6.3 mi s of jct SR 128. 6300 S Hwy 1 95432 (PO Box 367). Fax: 707/877-1808. **Facility:** Built in the late 1800's, this property, a former lumber baron's estate, is nestled in peaceful seclusion atop a bluff on the Mendocino Coast. 15 one-bedroom standard units, some with whirlpools. 2 stories (no elevator), interior/exterior corridors. *Bath:* combo or shower only. **Parking:** on-site. **Terms:** office hours 8 am-10 pm, 2 night minimum stay - with Saturday stayover, age restrictions may apply, 14 day cancellation notice-fee imposed, package plans - seasonal. **Amenities:** hair dryers. *Some:* CD players, irons. **Leisure Activities:** whirlpool, spa. **Business Services:** meeting rooms. **Cards:** AX, DC, DS, MC, VI.

SOME UNITS

FORESTVILLE pop. 2,370

WHERE TO STAY

FARMHOUSE INN & RESTAURANT **Phone:** 707/887-3300

Historic Country Inn

All Year [BP] 2P: $175-$275 XP: $25

Location: US 101, exit River Rd, 7 mi w. 7871 River Rd 95436. Fax: 707/887-3311. **Facility:** Enjoy the attractively landscaped grounds with an on-site demonstration vineyard and rose garden, or relax in the private sauna found in each room. 8 one-bedroom standard units with whirlpools. 1 story, exterior corridors. **Parking:** on-site. **Terms:** 2 night minimum stay - weekends, 10 day cancellation notice-fee imposed. **Amenities:** irons, hair dryers. **Cards:** AX, DS, MC, VI.

VCR DATA PORT

FORT BRAGG pop. 7,026

WHERE TO STAY

ANCHOR LODGE **Phone:** 707/964-4283

Motel

4/1-10/31 1P: $55-$175 2P: $55-$175 XP: $15 F11
2/1-3/31, 11/1-12/31 & 1/11-1/31 1P: $45-$135 2P: $45-$135 XP: $15 F11

Location: SR 1, exit N Harbor Dr, 1.5 mi e. 32260 N Harbor Dr 95437 (PO Box 1429). Fax: 707/964-0254. **Facility:** 17 units. 16 one-bedroom standard units. 1 one-bedroom suite with kitchen. 2 stories (no elevator), interior/exterior corridors. *Bath:* shower only. **Parking:** on-site. **Terms:** open 2/1-12/31 & 1/11-1/31, office hours 7 am-11 pm, age restrictions may apply, cancellation fee imposed. **Amenities:** *Some:* voice mail, irons. **Leisure Activities:** boating, fishing, bicycles, hiking trails. **Business Services:** meeting rooms. **Cards:** DS, MC, VI.

SOME UNITS

ASK / DATA PORT /

ANNIE'S JUGHANDLE BEACH BED & BREAKFAST INN **Phone:** 707/964-1415

Bed & Breakfast

Property failed to provide current rates

Location: Just e of SR 1; between Mendocino and Fort Bragg. Gibney Ln & Hwy 1 95437 (PO Box 228, MENDOCINO, 95460). Fax: 707/961-1473. **Facility:** Opposite the Jughead Natural Reserve, this charming B&B reflects charm and elegance of a bygone era. 7 one-bedroom standard units, some with whirlpools. 2 stories (no elevator), interior/exterior corridors. *Bath:* combo or shower only. **Parking:** on-site. **Terms:** office hours 8 am-9 pm, age restrictions may apply. **Amenities:** CD players. *Some:* irons, hair dryers.

SOME UNITS

AVALON HOUSE — Phone: (707)964-5555

Bed & Breakfast

All Year [BP] 1P: $85-$155 2P: $85-$155 XP: $10 F5

Location: Just w of SR 1 via Pine St, then just n. 561 Stewart St 95437. Fax: 707/964-5555. **Facility:** 6 one-bedroom standard units, some with whirlpools. 3 stories (no elevator), interior corridors. *Bath:* combo or shower only. **Parking:** on-site. **Terms:** office hours 9 am-9 pm, 2-3 night minimum stay - weekends, age restrictions may apply, 3 day cancellation notice. **Amenities:** *Some:* irons, hair dryers. **Guest Services:** complimentary evening beverages. **Cards:** AX, DS, MC, VI.

SOME UNITS

BEACHCOMBER MOTEL — Phone: (707)964-2402

AAA SAVE — Motel

(See color ad below)

6/1-10/31 [CP]	1P: $69-$250	2P: $69-$250	XP: $10	F
2/1-5/31 & 11/1-1/31 [CP]	1P: $59-$175	2P: $59-$175	XP: $10	F

Location: 1111 N Main St 95437. Fax: 707/964-8925. **Facility:** 72 one-bedroom standard units, some with efficiencies and/or whirlpools. 2 stories (no elevator), exterior corridors. *Bath:* combo or shower only. **Parking:** on-site. **Terms:** age restrictions may apply, pets ($10 extra charge, in limited units). **Amenities:** video library. *Some:* irons, hair dryers. **Leisure Activities:** exercise room. **Cards:** AX, CB, DC, DS, MC, VI.

FEE SOME UNITS

BEACH HOUSE INN — Phone: 707/961-1700

AAA SAVE — Motel

All Year 1P: $79-$175 2P: $79-$175 XP: $10 F12

Location: 0.7 mi n on SR 1. 100 Pudding Creek Rd 95437. Fax: 707/961-1627. **Facility:** 30 one-bedroom standard units, some with whirlpools. 2 stories (no elevator), interior corridors. **Parking:** on-site. **Terms:** age restrictions may apply, small pets only ($10 fee). **Amenities:** irons, hair dryers. **Leisure Activities:** boating. **Cards:** AX, DC, MC, VI. **Special Amenities: free local telephone calls.** *(See color ad p 771)*

FEE SOME UNITS

BEST WESTERN VISTA MANOR LODGE — Book at aaa.com — Phone: (707)964-4776

AAA SAVE — Motel

6/15-9/4 [CP]	1P: $109-$119	2P: $109-$119	XP: $10	F12
9/5-10/27 [CP]	1P: $79-$109	2P: $79-$109		
2/1-6/14 & 10/28-1/31 [CP]	1P: $69-$99	2P: $69-$99		

Location: 1 mi n on SR 1. 1100 N Main St 95437. Fax: 707/964-4779. **Facility:** 55 units. 53 one-bedroom standard units. 2 cottages ($129-$299). 2 stories (no elevator), exterior corridors. *Bath:* combo or shower only. **Parking:** on-site. **Terms:** age restrictions may apply, cancellation fee imposed. **Amenities:** irons, hair dryers. **Pool(s):** heated indoor. **Leisure Activities:** horseshoes, volleyball. **Business Services:** fax. **Cards:** AX, DC, DS, MC, VI. **Special Amenities: free continental breakfast and free local telephone calls.**

SOME UNITS

CLEONE GARDENS INN **Phone:** (707)964-2788

Motel

All Year 1P: $86-$140 2P: $86-$140 XP: $12

Location: 3 mi n on SR 1. Located in Cleone. 24600 N Hwy 1 95437. **Facility:** 10 units. 6 one- and 2 two-bedroom standard units, some with kitchens. 1 vacation home and 1 cottage. 1 story, exterior corridors. *Bath:* combo or shower only. **Parking:** on-site. **Terms:** office hours 8 am-8 pm, age restrictions may apply, 3 day cancellation notice-fee imposed, [BP] meal plan available, pets ($6 extra charge, dogs only, in designated units). **Amenities:** *Some:* irons, hair dryers. **Leisure Activities:** whirlpool. **Cards:** AX, DC, MC, VI.

FEE FEE / SOME UNITS /

COUNTRY INN BED & BREAKFAST **Phone:** (707)964-3737

SAVE

Bed & Breakfast

All Year [BP] 1P: $90-$145 2P: $90-$145 XP: $25 F

Location: 0.5 mi n on SR 1. 632 N Main St 95437. Fax: 707/964-0289. **Facility:** This 1890s residence has been renovated into a comfortably appointed B&B. 8 one-bedroom standard units, some with whirlpools. 2 stories (no elevator), interior corridors. *Bath:* combo, shower or tub only. **Parking:** on-site. **Terms:** office hours 7 am-10 pm, age restrictions may apply, 7 day cancellation notice-fee imposed. **Amenities:** *Some:* irons, hair dryers. **Leisure Activities:** whirlpool. **Cards:** AX, DS, MC, VI. **Special Amenities: free local telephone calls and free newspaper.**

EBB TIDE LODGE — **Phone:** (707)964-5321

Motel

7/1-9/30	1P: $59-$149	2P: $65-$159	XP: $10	F12
5/1-6/30	1P: $55-$79	2P: $65-$89	XP: $10	F12
2/1-4/30 & 10/1-1/31	1P: $45-$69	2P: $55-$79	XP: $10	F12

Location: Just s on SR 1. 250 S Main St 95437. Fax: 707/964-6730. **Facility:** 31 one-bedroom standard units. 2 stories (no elevator), exterior corridors. *Bath:* combo or shower only. **Parking:** on-site. **Terms:** age restrictions may apply, cancellation fee imposed. **Amenities:** hair dryers. *Some:* irons. **Leisure Activities:** whirlpool. **Cards:** AX, DC, DS, MC, VI. **Special Amenities: free local telephone calls and free room upgrade (subject to availability with advanced reservations).** *(See color ad p 771)*

SOME UNITS

THE EMERALD DOLPHIN INN — **Phone:** (707)964-6699

Motel

6/1-10/31 [CP]	1P: $80-$160	2P: $80-$160	XP: $10	F11
2/1-5/31 & 11/1-1/31 [CP]	1P: $50-$110	2P: $60-$120	XP: $10	F11

Location: On SR 1. 1211 S Main St 95437. Fax: 707/962-0338. **Facility:** 43 one-bedroom standard units, some with whirlpools. 2 stories (no elevator), exterior corridors. **Parking:** on-site. **Terms:** age restrictions may apply, package plans. **Amenities:** safes. *Some:* irons, hair dryers. **Leisure Activities:** fishing, hiking trails. **Guest Services:** area transportation. **Business Services:** fax. **Cards:** AX, DC, MC, VI.

ASK SOME UNITS

THE GREY WHALE INN — **Phone:** (707)964-0640

Bed & Breakfast

All Year [BP]	1P: $100-$200	2P: $110-$210	XP: $25

Location: 0.5 mi n on SR 1. 615 N Main St 95437. Fax: 707/964-4408. **Facility:** Common areas include a tea parlor, a lounge with a fireplace and a VCR-equipped TV room; some rooms have private decks, fireplaces and ocean views. Smoke free premises. 14 one-bedroom standard units, some with efficiencies and/or whirlpools. 4 stories (no elevator), interior corridors. *Bath:* combo or shower only. **Parking:** on-site. **Terms:** office hours 8 am-8 pm, 2 night minimum stay - seasonal weekends, age restrictions may apply, 7 day cancellation notice-fee imposed. **Amenities:** video library, hair dryers. *Some:* DVD players, high-speed Internet, irons. **Leisure Activities:** foos ball, pool table. **Business Services:** PC. **Cards:** AX, MC, VI. **Special Amenities: free local telephone calls.**

SOME UNITS

HARBOR LITE LODGE — **Phone:** 707/964-0221

Motel

6/12-9/11	1P: $79-$104	2P: $79-$104	XP: $7	F3
2/1-6/11 & 9/12-1/31	1P: $76-$95	2P: $76-$95	XP: $7	F3

Location: SR 1, 0.5 mi s at north end of Noyo River Bridge. 120 N Harbor Dr 95437. Fax: 707/964-8748. **Facility:** 79 one-bedroom standard units. 2 stories, exterior corridors. *Bath:* combo or shower only. **Parking:** on-site. **Terms:** 2 night minimum stay - weekends, age restrictions may apply, cancellation fee imposed, [CP] meal plan available. **Amenities:** voice mail. *Some:* irons, hair dryers. **Leisure Activities:** sauna. **Cards:** AX, CB, DC, DS, MC, VI. **Special Amenities: free continental breakfast and free local telephone calls.** *(See color ad below)*

SOME UNITS

HISTORIC OLD COAST HOTEL — **Phone:** 707/961-4488

Small-scale Hotel

All Year [ECP]	1P: $95-$175	2P: $95-$175	XP: $25	D12

Location: Just e of SR 1 on Oak St. 101 N Franklin St 95437. Fax: 707/961-4480. **Facility:** 15 one-bedroom standard units. 2 stories (no elevator), interior/exterior corridors. *Bath:* combo or shower only. **Parking:** on-site. **Terms:** office hours 8 am-9 pm, age restrictions may apply, cancellation fee imposed. **Dining:** 4 pm-9 pm, Fri & Sat noon-10 pm, dining room, see separate listing. **Cards:** MC, VI.

HOLIDAY INN EXPRESS *Book at aaa.com* **Phone:** (707)964-1100

Small-scale Hotel

6/1-10/31 [ECP]	1P: $69-$159	2P: $69-$159	XP: $10	F
2/1-5/31 & 11/1-1/31 [ECP]	1P: $65-$139	2P: $65-$139	XP: $10	F

Location: On SR 20. 250 Hwy 20 95437. Fax: 707/964-1177. **Facility:** 54 one-bedroom standard units. 3 stories, interior corridors. *Bath:* combo or shower only. **Parking:** on-site. **Terms:** age restrictions may apply. **Amenities:** dual phone lines, voice mail, irons, hair dryers. **Pool(s):** heated indoor. **Leisure Activities:** whirlpool, exercise room. **Cards:** AX, CB, DC, DS, JC, MC, VI.

SOME UNITS

THE LODGE AT NOYO RIVER **Phone:** (707)964-8045

AAA SAVE

Bed & Breakfast

5/1-10/1 [ECP]	1P: $95-$175	2P: $95-$175	XP: $15	F5
2/1-4/30 & 10/2-1/31 [ECP]	1P: $75-$175	2P: $75-$175	XP: $15	F5

Location: 3 blks e of SR 1 via Harbor Dr. 500 Casa del Noyo Dr 95437. Fax: 707/964-9366. **Facility:** Guest-room features range from views of the river and its fishing fleet to fireplaces, balconies and soaking tubs. 17 units. 15 one-bedroom standard units. 2 one-bedroom suites. 2 stories (no elevator), interior corridors. *Bath:* combo or shower only. **Parking:** on-site. **Terms:** office hours 7 am-9 pm, 5-9 night minimum stay - weekends, age restrictions may apply, 3 day cancellation notice. **Amenities:** *Some:* irons, hair dryers. **Cards:** AX, MC, VI.

SOME UNITS

NORTH CLIFF HOTEL **Phone:** 707/962-2500

Motel

5/28-10/31	1P: $169-$225	2P: $169-$225	XP: $20	D12
2/1-5/27	1P: $125-$175	2P: $125-$175	XP: $20	D12
11/1-1/31	1P: $99-$149	2P: $99-$149	XP: $20	D12

Location: North end of Noyo River Bridge. 1005 S Main St 95437. Fax: 707/962-2572. **Facility:** 39 one-bedroom standard units, some with whirlpools. 3 stories (no elevator), exterior corridors. *Bath:* shower only. **Parking:** on-site. **Terms:** office hours 7 am-10 pm, check-in 4 pm, age restrictions may apply. **Amenities:** voice mail, irons, hair dryers. **Business Services:** fax. **Cards:** AX, DC, DS, MC, VI.

OCEAN VIEW LODGE **Phone:** 707/964-1951

AAA SAVE

Motel

5/1-9/30	1P: $125-$245	2P: $125-$255	XP: $15	F
10/1-1/31	1P: $125-$225	2P: $125-$235	XP: $15	F
2/1-4/30	1P: $125-$185	2P: $125-$185	XP: $15	F

Location: 1 mi n on SR 1. 1141 N Main St 95437. Fax: 707/964-7592. **Facility:** 30 units. 25 one- and 5 two-bedroom standard units, some with whirlpools. 2 stories (no elevator), exterior corridors. *Bath:* combo or shower only. **Parking:** on-site. **Terms:** age restrictions may apply, cancellation fee imposed. **Amenities:** safes (fee), hair dryers. *Some:* irons. **Business Services:** fax. **Cards:** AX, DC, DS, MC, VI. **Special Amenities: free local telephone calls and preferred room (subject to availability with advanced reservations).** *(See color ad below)*

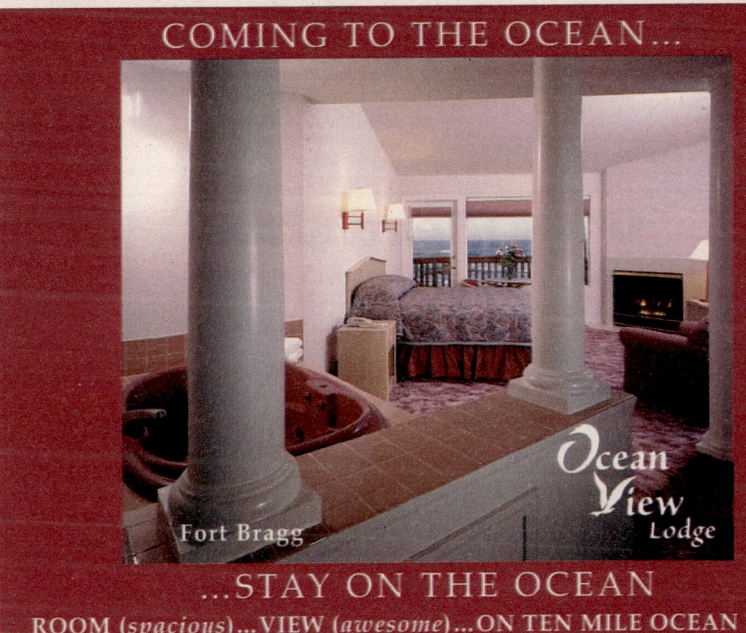

OLD STEWART HOUSE INN — Phone: 707/961-0775

AAA SAVE — Bed & Breakfast

6/1-10/31 [BP]	2P: $115-$145	XP: $15	F5
2/1-5/31 & 11/1-1/31 [BP]	2P: $100-$130	XP: $15	F5

Location: Just w of SR 1 via Pine St. Located in the Old Historic District. 511 Stewart St 95437. Fax: 707/962-0559. **Facility:** 5 units. 3 one-bedroom standard units, some with whirlpools. 2 cabins. 2 stories (no elevator), interior/exterior corridors. *Bath:* combo or shower only. **Parking:** on-site. **Terms:** office hours 7 am-11 pm, 2 night minimum stay - weekends, age restrictions may apply, 7 day cancellation notice-fee imposed, pets (in limited units). **Amenities:** hair dryers. *Some:* irons. **Cards:** AX, MC, VI. **Special Amenities: free local telephone calls and early check-in/late check-out.** *(See color ad p 785)*

SOME UNITS

PINE BEACH INN & SUITES — Phone: (707)964-5603

AAA SAVE — Motel

5/1-9/30	1P: $89-$149	2P: $89-$149	XP: $10	F10
2/1-4/30 & 10/1-1/31	1P: $69-$109	2P: $69-$109	XP: $10	F10

Location: 4 mi s on SR 1. 16801 N Hwy 1 95437 (PO Box 1173). Fax: 707/964-8381. **Facility:** 50 units. 41 one- and 7 two-bedroom standard units. 2 one-bedroom suites ($99-$179) with whirlpools. 1-2 stories (no elevator), exterior corridors. *Bath:* combo or shower only. **Parking:** on-site. **Terms:** office hours 7:30 am-10:30 pm, 2 night minimum stay - weekends in summer, age restrictions may apply, 3 day cancellation notice-fee imposed, weekly rates available, package plans. **Amenities:** *Some:* irons, hair dryers. **Dining:** 7-10:30 am & 5:30-9 pm; Sunday brunch 7 am-2 pm 4/1-10/31, cocktails. **Leisure Activities:** fishing, 2 tennis courts, barbecue, playground. **Cards:** AX, MC, VI. *(See color ad below)*

SOME UNITS
FEE FEE

SEABIRD LODGE Book at aaa.com — Phone: (707)964-4731

AAA SAVE — Motel

5/28-10/31	1P: $75-$100	2P: $85-$110
2/1-5/27 & 11/1-1/31	1P: $60-$85	2P: $70-$95

Location: 0.8 mi n of Noyo River Bridge; 1 blk e off SR 1. 191 South St 95437. Fax: 707/961-1779. **Facility:** 65 one-bedroom standard units. 2 stories (no elevator), exterior corridors. **Parking:** on-site. **Terms:** age restrictions may apply, small pets only ($8 extra charge, 1st floor only). **Amenities:** *Some:* irons, hair dryers. **Pool(s):** heated indoor. **Leisure Activities:** whirlpool. **Guest Services:** coin laundry. **Cards:** AX, MC, VI. **Special Amenities: free local telephone calls and preferred room (subject to availability with advanced reservations).** Affiliated with Best Value Inn Brand Membership. *(See color ad p 775)*

SOME UNITS
FEE

SURF MOTEL — Phone: (707)964-5361

AAA SAVE — Motel

5/16-10/25 [CP]	1P: $73-$110	2P: $73-$110	XP: $6	F15
4/4-5/15 [CP]	1P: $63-$90	2P: $63-$90	XP: $6	F15
2/1-4/3 & 10/26-1/31 [CP]	1P: $51-$80	2P: $51-$80	XP: $9	F15

Location: 1 mi s on SR 1; s of Noyo River Bridge; 0.3 mi n of jct SR 20. 1220 S Main St 95437 (PO Box 488). Fax: 707/964-3187. **Facility:** 54 units. 52 one-bedroom standard units. 2 one-bedroom suites ($125-$190) with kitchens. 1 story, exterior corridors. *Bath:* combo or shower only. **Parking:** on-site. **Terms:** age restrictions may apply. **Amenities:** voice mail, hair dryers. *Some:* irons. **Leisure Activities:** fish cleaning facilities, barbecue & picnic area. **Business Services:** fax. **Cards:** AX, DS, MC, VI.

SOME UNITS
FEE FEE

SURF 'N SAND LODGE

Motel

5/1-9/30	1P: $89-$175	2P: $89-$175	XP: $10	F10
10/1-12/31	1P: $79-$165	2P: $79-$165	XP: $10	F10
2/1-4/30 & 1/1-1/31	1P: $69-$150	2P: $69-$150	XP: $10	F10

Phone: (707)964-9383

Location: 1 mi n on SR 1. 1131 N Main St 95437. Fax: 707/964-0314. **Facility:** 30 one-bedroom standard units, some with whirlpools. 2 stories (no elevator), interior corridors. **Parking:** on-site. **Terms:** office hours 7 am-11 pm, 2 night minimum stay - weekends, age restrictions may apply, 3 day cancellation notice. **Amenities:** video library, irons, hair dryers. **Business Services:** fax. **Cards:** AX, DS, MC, VI. **Special Amenities: free local telephone calls and early check-in/late check-out.** *(See color ad p 775)*

TRADEWINDS LODGE

Motel

5/28-10/31	1P: $69-$150	2P: $69-$150	XP: $10	F12
2/1-5/27	1P: $59-$125	2P: $59-$125	XP: $10	F12
11/1-1/31	1P: $49-$115	2P: $49-$115	XP: $10	F12

Phone: 707/964-4761

Location: 6 blks s on SR 1. 400 S Main St 95437. Fax: 707/964-0372. **Facility:** 92 units. 80 one- and 10 two-bedroom standard units. 2 one-bedroom suites with kitchens. 2 stories (no elevator), exterior corridors. *Bath:* combo or shower only. **Parking:** on-site. **Terms:** package plans, pets ($10 extra charge). **Amenities:** voice mail, irons, hair dryers. **Dining:** 4 am-midnight, cocktails. **Pool(s):** heated indoor. **Leisure Activities:** whirlpool, exercise room, spa. **Guest Services:** gift shop, coin laundry. **Business Services:** meeting rooms. **Cards:** AX, DC, DS, MC, VI. *(See color ad below)*

FEE SOME UNITS

THE WELLER HOUSE INN

Historic Bed & Breakfast

All Year	1P: $95-$170	2P: $95-$170	XP: $25	F

Phone: (707)964-4415

Location: Just w of SR 1 via Pine St, then just n. 524 Stewart St 95437. Fax: 707/964-4198. **Facility:** This historic inn was built in 1886. Smoke free premises. 10 one-bedroom standard units, some with whirlpools. 3 stories (no elevator), interior corridors. *Bath:* combo or shower only. **Parking:** on-site. **Terms:** office hours 7 am-9 pm, 2 night minimum stay - weekends in summer, age restrictions may apply, 10 day cancellation notice-fee imposed, [BP] meal plan available. **Amenities:** video library, hair dryers. *Some:* irons. **Guest Services:** complimentary evening beverages. **Cards:** AX, CB, DC, DS, MC, VI.

SOME UNITS

WHERE TO DINE

CLIFF HOUSE

American

Dinner: $10-$24 **Phone:** 707/961-0255

Location: SR 1, at south end of Noyo River Bridge. 1011 S Main St 95437. **Hours:** 4 pm-9 pm, Sat-10 pm. Closed: 12/24, 12/25. **Reservations:** suggested. **Features:** Overlooking the ocean and Noyo River, the four dining levels have a graceful appeal. Italian preparations of steak, chicken and seafood are thoughtfully done. Casual dress; cocktails. **Parking:** on-site. **Cards:** AX, DS, MC, VI.

OLD COAST HOTEL

American

Lunch: $5-$11 **Dinner:** $9-$23 **Phone:** 707/961-4488

Location: Just e of SR 1 on Oak St; in Historic Old Coast Hotel. 101 N Franklin 95437. **Hours:** 4 pm-9 pm, Fri-Sun noon-10 pm. Closed: 12/25; also Wed. **Reservations:** suggested. **Features:** The well-established restaurant and lodge blend a sports-bar atmosphere with fine-dining embellishments. Casual dress; cocktails. **Parking:** on-site. **Cards:** AX, MC, VI.

THE RESTAURANT — American — Dinner: $19-$26 — **Phone:** 707/964-9800

Location: Just n on SR 1. 418 N Main St 95437. **Hours:** 5 pm-9 pm; Sunday brunch 10 am-1 pm. Closed: 12/25; also Tues & Wed. **Reservations:** suggested. **Features:** The longtime family-owned restaurant is known for its wild-game preparations and natural foods. Casual dress; beer & wine only. **Parking:** on-site. **Cards:** AX, DC, MC, VI.

THE WHARF RESTAURANT — Seafood — **Lunch:** $6-$12 — **Dinner:** $15-$25 — **Phone:** 707/964-4283

Location: SR 1, exit N Harbor Dr, 1.5 mi e. 32260 N Harbor Dr 95437. **Hours:** 11 am-10 pm. Closed: 1/2-1/15. **Reservations:** suggested. **Features:** Situated right on the wharf of the Noyo River, this family-style restaurant offers a surprising ninety degree view of the inlet, including boaters, fisherman and a pair of sea lions, all for the entertainment of the diner. Casual dress; cocktails. **Parking:** on-site. **Cards:** DC, MC, VI.

GEYSERVILLE

WHERE TO STAY

GEYSERVILLE INN — SAVE — Motel — **Phone:** (707)857-4343

4/1-11/15	1P: $105-$185	2P: $105-$185	XP: $10	F18
2/1-3/31 & 11/16-1/31	1P: $89-$150	2P: $89-$150	XP: $10	F18

Location: US 101, exit E Canyon Rd, just s. 21714 Geyersville Ave 95441. Fax: 707/857-4411. **Facility:** Smoke free premises. 38 one-bedroom standard units. 2 stories, interior corridors. *Bath:* combo or shower only. **Parking:** on-site. **Terms:** 2 night minimum stay - weekends, 7 day cancellation notice-fee imposed. **Amenities:** voice mail, irons, hair dryers. **Pool(s):** outdoor. **Leisure Activities:** whirlpool. **Business Services:** meeting rooms. **Cards:** AX, DC, MC, VI. *(See color ad p 803)*

HOPE-MERRILL HOUSE — SAVE — Historic Bed & Breakfast — **Phone:** (707)857-3356

All Year [BP]	1P: $104-$186	2P: $122-$218	XP: $30

Location: US 101, exit Geyserville Ave/SR 128 E, 0.5 mi e. 21253 Geyserville Ave 95441. Fax: 707/857-4673. **Facility:** The Hope-Merrill House is a late-1800s Victorian; four units are also available at the Hope-Bosworth House across the street. Smoke free premises. 12 one-bedroom standard units, some with whirlpools. 2 stories, interior corridors. *Bath:* combo or shower only. **Parking:** on-site. **Terms:** check-in 3:30 pm, 2 night minimum stay - weekends, 7 day cancellation notice-fee imposed. **Amenities:** hair dryers. *Some:* irons. **Pool(s):** heated outdoor. **Guest Services:** gift shop. **Business Services:** PC. **Cards:** AX, DS, MC, VI.

SOME UNITS

GLEN ELLEN pop. 992

WHERE TO STAY

GAIGE HOUSE INN — Bed & Breakfast — **Phone:** (707)935-0237

	2P	XP
All Year [BP]	2P: $275-$550	XP: $50

Location: SR 12, exit Arnold Dr, 0.5 mi w. 13540 Arnold Dr 95442. Fax: 707/935-6411. **Facility:** Set within the Sonoma Valley, this centrally located property is beside a creek and features a large pool and patio area. 15 one-bedroom standard units, some with whirlpools. 2 stories, interior/exterior corridors. *Bath:* combo or shower only. **Parking:** on-site. **Terms:** 2 night minimum stay - weekends, 7 day cancellation notice. **Amenities:** CD players, voice mail, irons, hair dryers. **Pool(s):** heated outdoor. **Leisure Activities:** whirlpool. **Guest Services:** complimentary evening beverages. **Cards:** AX, DC, MC, VI.

SOME UNITS

GUALALA

WHERE TO STAY

BREAKERS INN — Motel — **Phone:** (707)884-3200

All Year	1P: $95-$255	2P: $95-$255	XP: $15	F5

Location: Center. 39300 S Hwy 1 95445 (PO Box 389, 95445-0389). Fax: 707/884-3400. **Facility:** 28 units. 27 one-bedroom standard units, some with whirlpools. 1 vacation home. 3 stories (no elevator), exterior corridors. **Parking:** on-site. **Terms:** 5 day cancellation notice-fee imposed, [ECP] meal plan available, package plans - seasonal, midweek & weekends 11/1-4/30. **Amenities:** video library, hair dryers. *Some:* irons. **Cards:** AX, DS, MC, VI. ***(See color ad p 778)***

SOME UNITS

ASK / VCR FEE

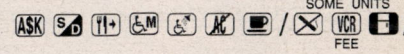

GUALALA COUNTRY INN — Motel — **Phone:** (707)884-4343

	1P	2P
All Year	1P: $110-$165	2P: $110-$165

Location: East side of SR 1. 47955 Center St 95445 (PO Box 697). Fax: 707/884-1018. **Facility:** 20 one-bedroom standard units. 2 stories (no elevator), interior/exterior corridors. **Parking:** on-site. **Terms:** office hours 8 am-10 pm, age restrictions may apply, 3 day cancellation notice, [CP] meal plan available, pets ($10 extra charge). **Amenities:** *Some:* irons, hair dryers. **Cards:** AX, CB, DC, DS, MC, VI. ***(See color ad p 778)***

SOME UNITS

NORTH COAST COUNTRY INN

Phone: (707)884-4537

Bed & Breakfast

All Year [BP] 1P: $175-$215 2P: $175-$215 XP: $25 F5

Location: 4 mi n. 34591 S Hwy 1 95445. Fax: 707/884-1833. **Facility:** The inn's six cottages, nestled on a hillside overlooking the Pacific Ocean, feature antique furnishings and handmade quilts. 6 one-bedroom standard units, some with kitchens and/or whirlpools. 2 stories, exterior corridors. *Bath:* combo or shower only. **Parking:** on-site. **Terms:** office hours 8 am-9 pm, 2 night minimum stay - weekends, age restrictions may apply, 5 day cancellation notice. **Amenities:** irons, hair dryers. **Leisure Activities:** whirlpool. **Cards:** AX, MC, VI.

SOME UNITS

ASK

SURF MOTEL

Phone: (707)884-3571

Motel

All Year 1P: $95-$179 2P: $95-$179

Location: West side of SR 1. 39170 S Hwy 1 95445 (PO Box 695). Fax: 707/884-3009. **Facility:** 20 one-bedroom standard units, some with kitchens. 1 story, exterior corridors. *Bath:* combo or shower only. **Parking:** on-site. **Terms:** age restrictions may apply, pets ($10 extra charge). **Amenities:** *Some:* irons, hair dryers. **Cards:** AX, CB, DC, DS, MC, VI. ***(See color ad below)***

SOME UNITS

VCR DATA PORT

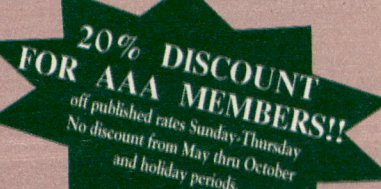

FEE

WHERE TO DINE

ST ORRES — Dinner: $40 — **Phone:** 707/884-3335

California

Location: 2 mi n. 36601 S Hwy 1 95445. **Hours:** Open 2/1-1/1; 6 pm-9 pm, Sat 5 pm-10 pm. Closed: Tues & Wed in winter. **Reservations:** suggested. **Features:** Representative of the distinctive Russian architecture is the three-story domed dining room. Three-course dinners include a choice of several entrees. Daily specials often center on wild game. Fresh appetizers and desserts are delicious. Casual dress; beer & wine only. **Parking:** on-site. **Cards:** MC, VI.

GUERNEVILLE pop. 2,441

WHERE TO STAY

BROOKSIDE LODGE — **Phone:** (707)869-2874

Motel

5/1-10/1	1P: $125-$275	2P: $125-$275	XP: $12
2/1-4/30 & 10/2-1/31	1P: $92-$184	2P: $92-$184	XP: $12

Location: Just n of SR 116. 14100 Brookside Ln 95446 (PO Box 382). Fax: 707/869-0714. **Facility:** 35 units. 30 one- and 2 two-bedroom standard units, some with whirlpools. 3 cottages. 1-2 stories, exterior corridors. **Parking:** on-site. **Terms:** 2 night minimum stay - 5/1-10/31, 14 day cancellation notice-fee imposed. **Amenities:** *Some:* hair dryers. **Pool(s):** heated outdoor. **Leisure Activities:** sauna, whirlpool. **Cards:** AX, DS, MC, VI. *(See color ad below)*

SOME UNITS

FERNGROVE COTTAGES — **Phone:** 707/869-8105

Cottage

All Year [ECP]	1P: $79-$219	2P: $79-$219	XP: $25	D12

Location: On SR 116. 16650 Hwy 116 95446. Fax: 707/869-1615. **Facility:** Smoke free premises. 21 units. 10 one-bedroom standard units, some with kitchens and/or whirlpools. 11 cottages. 1 story, exterior corridors. *Bath:* combo or shower only. **Parking:** on-site. **Terms:** 2 night minimum stay - in season & weekends, 3 day cancellation notice-fee imposed, small pets only ($15 fee). **Pool(s):** outdoor. **Leisure Activities:** bicycles, hiking trails, jogging. **Cards:** AX, DS, MC, VI.

SOME UNITS

FEE

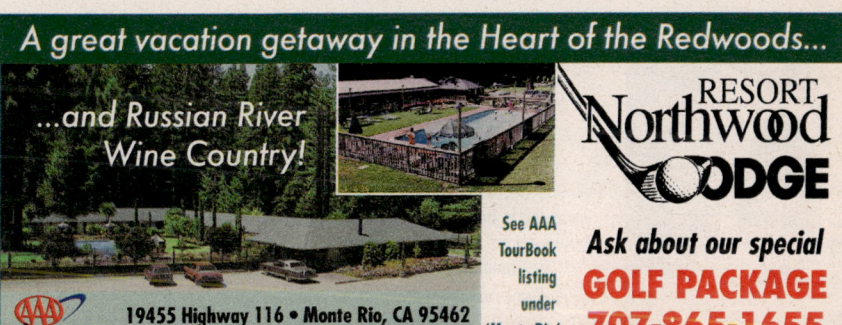

HEALDSBURG pop. 10,722

WHERE TO STAY

BEST WESTERN DRY CREEK INN *Book at aaa.com* **Phone:** (707)433-0300

AAA SAVE — Motel

4/11-11/30 [CP]	1P: $89-$199	2P: $89-$199	XP: $10	F16
2/1-4/10 & 12/1-1/31 [CP]	1P: $84-$175	2P: $84-$175	XP: $10	F16

Location: US 101, exit Dry Creek Rd, just e. 198 Dry Creek Rd 95448. Fax: 707/433-1129. **Facility:** 103 one-bedroom standard units. 3 stories, exterior corridors. **Parking:** on-site. **Terms:** 2 night minimum stay - weekends & 4/1-10/31, small pets only ($20 fee). **Amenities:** voice mail, irons, hair dryers. **Pool(s):** outdoor. **Leisure Activities:** whirlpool, exercise room. **Guest Services:** coin laundry. **Cards:** AX, CB, DC, DS, MC, VI. **Special Amenities: free continental breakfast and free local telephone calls.** *(See color ad below)*

SOME UNITS
FEE

DUCHAMP **Phone:** 707/431-1300

Cottage

All Year [ECP]	2P: $225-$375	XP: $75

Location: US 101, exit Central Healdsburg. 421 Foss St 95448. Fax: 707/431-1333. **Facility:** The property offers modern amenities and unparalleled contemporary design; unwind in the heated pool or relax on your private patio. Smoke free premises. 10 units. 6 one-bedroom standard units. 4 cottages. 1 story, exterior corridors. *Bath:* shower only. **Parking:** on-site. **Terms:** 2 night minimum stay - weekends, age restrictions may apply, 14 day cancellation notice-fee imposed, package plans - seasonal & weekends, pets ($50 fee, $500 deposit, in selected units). **Amenities:** video library, CD players, safes, irons, hair dryers. **Pool(s):** heated outdoor. **Leisure Activities:** whirlpool. **Cards:** AX, MC, VI.

FEE

FAIRVIEW MOTEL **Phone:** 707/433-5548

AAA SAVE — Motel

4/1-10/31	1P: $69-$139	2P: $69-$139	XP: $10	F10
2/1-3/31 & 11/1-1/31	1P: $59-$139	2P: $59-$139	XP: $10	F10

Location: US 101, exit Central Healdsburg, just e; exit N Guernville/Westside Rd. 74 Healdsburg Ave 95448. Fax: 707/433-4512. **Facility:** 18 one-bedroom standard units. 1 story, exterior corridors. *Bath:* combo or shower only. **Parking:** on-site. **Terms:** [CP] meal plan available, small pets only ($10 fee). **Amenities:** irons, hair dryers. **Pool(s):** outdoor. **Leisure Activities:** whirlpool, playground. **Cards:** AX, MC, VI. **Special Amenities: free continental breakfast and free local telephone calls.**

SOME UNITS
FEE

THE GRAPE LEAF INN **Phone:** (707)433-8140

AAA SAVE — Historic Bed & Breakfast

All Year [BP]	1P: $165-$325	2P: $165-$325	XP: $35

Location: US 101, exit Central Healdsburg, just e. 539 Johnson St 95448. Fax: 707/433-3140. **Facility:** Queen Anne and Victorian styling is evident in this meticulously restored 1900 home. 12 units. 11 one-bedroom standard units, some with whirlpools. 1 one-bedroom suite with whirlpool. 3 stories, interior corridors. *Bath:* combo or shower only. **Parking:** on-site. **Terms:** check-in 4 pm, 2 night minimum stay - weekends, 7 day cancellation notice-fee imposed. **Amenities:** hair dryers. *Some:* irons. **Guest Services:** gift shop, complimentary evening beverages. **Cards:** MC, VI. **Special Amenities: free local telephone calls and preferred room (subject to availability with advanced reservations).**

SOME UNITS

THE HONOR MANSION **Phone:** (707)433-4277

AAA SAVE — Historic Bed & Breakfast

12/26-1/31	1P: $190-$550	2P: $190-$550
2/1-12/21	1P: $190	2P: $190

Location: Just e of US 101, exit Dry Creek Rd, just s. 14891 Grove St 95448. Fax: 707/431-7173. **Facility:** Decks and a koi pond provide outside interest at this 1883 Italianate Victorian mansion; also featured are a studio cottage, a water tower and suites. 13 units. 6 one-bedroom standard units. 7 one-bedroom suites with whirlpools. 2 stories (no elevator), interior/exterior corridors. *Bath:* combo or shower only. **Parking:** on-site. **Terms:** open 2/1-12/21 & 12/26-1/31, check-in 4 pm, 2-4 night minimum stay - weekends, age restrictions may apply, 15 day cancellation notice-fee imposed. **Amenities:** video library, CD players, voice mail, irons, hair dryers. **Pool(s):** heated outdoor. **Leisure Activities:** tennis court, exercise room. *Fee:* massage. **Guest Services:** gift shop, complimentary evening beverages. **Cards:** AX, MC, VI.

HOTEL HEALDSBURG **Book at aaa.com** **Phone:** (707)431-2800

Small-scale Hotel

5/2-11/30	1P: $295-$740	2P: $295-$740	XP: $25	F16
2/1-5/1 & 12/1-1/31	1P: $185-$625	2P: $185-$625	XP: $25	F16

Location: On the plaza. 25 Matheson St 95448. Fax: 707/431-0414. **Facility:** Smoke free premises. 55 units. 49 one-bedroom standard units. 6 one-bedroom suites. 3 stories, interior corridors. *Bath:* combo or shower only. **Parking:** on-site. **Terms:** 2 night minimum stay - weekends, 7 day cancellation notice, [ECP] meal plan available. **Amenities:** CD players, high-speed Internet, dual phone lines, voice mail, honor bars, irons, hair dryers. **Pool(s):** heated outdoor. **Leisure Activities:** whirlpool, exercise room, spa. **Guest Services:** gift shop, valet laundry. **Business Services:** meeting rooms, business center. **Cards:** AX, DC, MC, VI.

ASK VCR DATA PORT

VILLA MESSINA **Phone:** 707/433-6655

Bed & Breakfast

All Year [BP]	1P: $200-$350	2P: $200-$350

Location: US 101, exit Dry Creek Rd, just e to Grove St, 0.5 mi n to Chiquita Rd, then 0.5 mi w. 316 Burgundy Rd 95448. Fax: 707/433-4515. **Facility:** The elegant Italian villa features a 360-degree panoramic view overlooking the Alexander, Dry Creek and Russian River Valleys. 5 one-bedroom standard units, some with whirlpools. 2 stories, interior corridors. **Parking:** on-site. **Terms:** 2 night minimum stay - weekends. **Amenities:** CD players, irons, hair dryers. **Pool(s):** heated outdoor. **Guest Services:** complimentary evening beverages. **Cards:** CB, DC, DS, MC, VI.

VCR DATA PORT

WINE COUNTRY TRAVELODGE **Book at aaa.com** **Phone:** (707)433-0101

AAA SAVE

Motel

4/16-11/30 [CP]	1P: $69-$169	2P: $69-$169	XP: $10	F14
2/1-4/15 & 12/1-1/31 [CP]	1P: $59-$139	2P: $59-$139	XP: $10	F14

Location: US 101, exit Dry Creek Rd, just e. 178 Dry Creek Rd 95448. Fax: 707/433-1466. **Facility:** 23 one-bedroom standard units. 3 stories (no elevator), interior corridors. **Parking:** on-site. **Terms:** 2-3 night minimum stay - some weekends, 3 day cancellation notice-fee imposed. **Amenities:** *Some:* irons, hair dryers. **Leisure Activities:** sauna, whirlpool. **Cards:** AX, CB, DC, DS, JC, MC, VI. **Special Amenities: free continental breakfast and free newspaper.**

SOME UNITS

DATA PORT

HOPLAND

WHERE TO STAY

THE HOPLAND INN **Phone:** 707/744-1890

AAA SAVE

Historic Country Inn

6/21-9/30 [CP]	1P: $115	XP: $10	D12
2/1-6/20 & 10/1-1/31 [CP]	1P: $105	XP: $10	D12

Location: Center. 13401 S Hwy 101 95449 (PO Box 660). Fax: 707/744-1219. **Facility:** With its hardwood paneling and floors, and spacious guest rooms, this restored 1890s Victorian recalls the fashion of a long-ago era. Smoke free premises. 21 one-bedroom standard units. 3 stories (no elevator), interior corridors. *Bath:* combo, shower or tub only. **Parking:** on-site. **Terms:** office hours 6:30 am-11 pm, cancellation fee imposed. **Amenities:** irons, hair dryers. **Dining:** 5:30 pm-9:30 pm, Fri & Sat-10 pm; closed Wed, cocktails. **Pool(s):** small outdoor. **Business Services:** meeting rooms. **Cards:** AX, MC, VI. **Special Amenities: free continental breakfast.**

SOME UNITS

DATA PORT

JENNER

WHERE TO STAY

JENNER INN **Phone:** (707)865-2377

Country Inn

All Year [BP]	1P: $98-$268	2P: $98-$268	XP: $20	F6

Location: On SR 1 at jct SR 116. 10400 Hwy 1 95450 (PO Box 69). Fax: 707/865-0829. **Facility:** The inn includes several cottages, some on a bluff overlooking the river; rooms with fireplaces are available. 20 units. 13 one-bedroom standard units. 3 one-bedroom suites ($218-$268) with kitchens, some with whirlpools. 4 cottages ($158-$278). 2 stories, exterior corridors. *Bath:* combo or shower only. **Parking:** on-site. **Terms:** 2 night minimum stay - weekends, 10 day cancellation notice-fee imposed, small pets only ($35 extra charge, in limited units). **Amenities:** *Some:* CD players, hair dryers. **Leisure Activities:** sauna, whirlpool. **Cards:** AX, MC, VI.

SOME UNITS

FEE

KELSEYVILLE pop. 2,928

WHERE TO STAY

BELL HAVEN RESORT **Phone:** (707)279-4329

Cabin

All Year	1P: $95-$125	2P: $95-$125

Location: SR 29, exit SR 281, 6 mi e. Located at Soda Bay. 3415 White Oak Way 95451. Fax: 707/279-8993. **Facility:** 10 units. 8 cabins and 2 cottages ($125-$145). 1 story, exterior corridors. *Bath:* combo or shower only. **Parking:** on-site. **Terms:** office hours 9 am-9 pm, 2 night minimum stay - weekends, age restrictions may apply, 15 day cancellation notice, weekly rates available, pets ($5 deposit, with prior approval). **Amenities:** video library. *Some:* irons, hair dryers. **Leisure Activities:** boating, sailboats, boat dock, fishing. **Guest Services:** coin laundry. **Cards:** DC, MC, VI.

VCR

FEE

KONOCTI HARBOR RESORT & SPA

Phone: (707)279-4281

Large-scale Hotel	5/2-11/1	1P: $109-$129	2P: $109-$129
	2/1-5/1 & 11/2-1/31	1P: $99-$129	2P: $99-$129

Location: 5 mi ne of SR 29 via SR 281. 8727 Soda Bay Rd 95451. Fax: 707/279-9205. **Facility:** 252 units. 162 one-bedroom standard units. 90 one-bedroom suites ($169-$259) with kitchens, some with whirlpools. 2 stories (no elevator), exterior corridors. *Bath:* combo or shower only. **Parking:** on-site. **Terms:** check-in 4 pm, cancellation fee imposed, weekly rates available, package plans - midweek in season. **Amenities:** video games, voice mail, irons, hair dryers. **Pool(s):** 2 heated outdoor, heated indoor, 2 wading. **Leisure Activities:** saunas, whirlpools, steamrooms, rental boats, rental canoes, rental paddleboats, waterskiing, fishing, 8 lighted tennis courts, recreation programs, hiking trails, playground, spa. *Fee:* marina, charter fishing, miniature golf. **Guest Services:** gift shop, coin laundry. **Business Services:** conference facilities. **Cards:** AX, DS, MC, VI.

SOME UNITS

LAKEPORT pop. 4,820

WHERE TO STAY

ANCHORAGE INN

Phone: (707)263-5417

Motel

All Year	1P: $65-$75	2P: $69-$85	XP: $10	F5

Location: SR 29, exit 11th St, 1 mi e. 950 N Main St 95453. Fax: 707/263-5453. **Facility:** 34 units. 14 one-bedroom standard units. 12 one- and 8 two-bedroom suites ($89-$110) with kitchens (no utensils). 2 stories (no elevator), exterior corridors. *Bath:* combo or shower only. **Parking:** on-site. **Terms:** 2 night minimum stay - weekends in summer, age restrictions may apply, 5 day cancellation notice. **Amenities:** *Some:* irons, hair dryers. **Pool(s):** small outdoor. **Leisure Activities:** sauna, whirlpool, waterskiing, fishing. *Fee:* boat dock. **Guest Services:** coin laundry. **Cards:** AX, DS, MC, VI. **Special Amenities: free local telephone calls and early check-in/late check-out.**

SOME UNITS

ARBOR HOUSE INN

Phone: 707/263-6444

Bed & Breakfast

All Year	1P: $79-$139	2P: $89-$139	XP: $15	D17

Location: SR 29 (W Scotts Valley) to Main St, left 1 blk, then left. 150 Clearlake Ave 95453. **Facility:** This 1890s Victorian home has been renovated to incorporate modern conveniences while preserving its period appeal. Smoke free premises. 5 one-bedroom standard units with whirlpools. 1 story. **Parking:** on-site. **Terms:** office hours 7 am-9 pm, age restrictions may apply, 7 day cancellation notice. **Amenities:** video library. *Some:* irons, hair dryers. **Leisure Activities:** sauna, whirlpool. **Guest Services:** complimentary evening beverages. **Cards:** AX, DC, DS, MC, VI.

SOME UNITS

FORBESTOWN INN

Phone: 707/263-7858

Bed & Breakfast

5/1-10/31 [BP]	1P: $84-$115	2P: $95-$125	XP: $20	D12
11/1-1/31 [BP]	1P: $84	2P: $99	XP: $20	D12
2/1-4/30 [BP]	1P: $84	2P: $95	XP: $20	D12

Location: SR 29, exit 11th St, 1 mi e. 825 Forbes St 95453. Fax: 707/263-7878. **Facility:** 1863 Victorian farmhouse, attractive corner lot. 4 one-bedroom standard units. 2 stories (no elevator), interior corridors. *Bath:* combo or shower only. **Parking:** on-site. **Terms:** office hours 8 am-9 pm, 7 day cancellation notice-fee imposed, package plans - seasonal. **Amenities:** video library. *Some:* irons, hair dryers. **Pool(s):** outdoor. **Guest Services:** complimentary evening beverages. **Cards:** AX, DC, DS, MC, VI.

SOME UNITS

LAKEPORT ENGLISH INN

Phone: (707)263-4317

Bed & Breakfast

All Year [BP]	1P: $135-$195	2P: $135-$195	XP: $25	F10

Location: SR 29, exit 11th St, then right. 675 N Main St 95453. Fax: 707/263-4317. **Facility:** Two historical Victorian homes surrounding an English village garden, the inn's charming small-town setting is enhanced by the state's largest lake. 5 one-bedroom standard units, some with whirlpools. 2 stories (no elevator), interior corridors. *Bath:* combo or shower only. **Parking:** street. **Terms:** office hours 8 am-8 pm, 8 day cancellation notice-fee imposed. **Amenities:** video library, CD players, high-speed Internet, voice mail, hair dryers. *Some:* irons. **Guest Services:** gift shop, complimentary evening beverages. **Business Services:** meeting rooms. **Cards:** AX, MC, VI.

SOME UNITS

SKYLARK SHORES MOTEL RESORT

Phone: (707)263-6151

Motel

5/28-9/27	1P: $91-$141	2P: $91-$141	XP: $8
9/28-11/2	1P: $75-$116	2P: $75-$116	XP: $8
2/1-5/27	1P: $67-$116	2P: $67-$116	XP: $8
11/3-1/31	1P: $67-$102	2P: $67-$102	XP: $8

Location: SR 29, exit 11th St, 1 mi e. 1120 N Main St 95453. Fax: 707/263-7733. **Facility:** 45 units. 37 one-bedroom standard units, some with kitchens. 3 two-bedroom suites with kitchens. 5 cabins. 1-2 stories (no elevator), exterior corridors. *Bath:* combo or shower only. **Parking:** on-site. **Terms:** office hours 7 am-10 pm, age restrictions may apply, 3 day cancellation notice. **Amenities:** hair dryers. *Some:* irons. **Pool(s):** outdoor. **Leisure Activities:** boating, boat dock, waterskiing, fishing, playground. **Cards:** AX, CB, DC, DS, JC, MC, VI.

SOME UNITS

WHERE TO DINE

ANTHONY'S

Italian

Dinner: $10-$20

Phone: 707/263-4905

Location: 0.8 mi n on SR 29 business route. 2509 Lakeshore Blvd 95453. **Hours:** 5 pm-10 pm. Closed: 4/11, 11/25, 12/25; also Sun-Wed. **Reservations:** suggested. **Features:** Across the highway from Clear Lake, the old-time steak/chop restaurant devised its menu before calories counted. Large baked potatoes are among the good old favorites. Casual dress; cocktails. **Parking:** on-site. **Cards:** AX, DS, MC, VI.

LEGGETT

WHERE TO STAY

REDWOODS RIVER RESORT — **Phone:** 707/925-6249

Cabin

Dates	1P	2P	XP	
5/1-10/31		2P: $71-$120	XP: $6	F3
11/1-1/31		2P: $49-$109		
2/1-4/30		2P: $49-$109	XP: $6	F3

Location: US 101. 75000 Hwy 101 95585. Fax: 707/925-6413. **Facility:** Smoke free premises. 15 units. 6 one- and 2 two-bedroom standard units with kitchens. 7 cabins ($78-$110). 2 stories (no elevator), exterior corridors. *Bath:* combo or shower only. **Parking:** on-site. **Terms:** office hours 8 am-10 pm, 2 night minimum stay - seasonal weekends, 7 day cancellation notice-fee imposed. **Amenities:** *Some:* irons, hair dryers. **Leisure Activities:** fishing. **Guest Services:** coin laundry. **Cards:** DS, MC, VI.

STONEGATE VILLA'S — **Phone:** 707/925-6226

Motel

Dates	1P	2P
2/1-10/15	1P: $39	2P: $49
10/16-1/31	1P: $35	2P: $45

Location: US 101, exit Drive Thru Tree Rd, 0.7 mi e. Located in a quiet area. 65260 Drive Thru Tree Rd 95585 (PO Box 239). Fax: 707/925-6226. **Facility:** Designated smoking area. 7 units. 5 one- and 2 two-bedroom standard units, some with kitchens. 1 story, exterior corridors. *Bath:* shower only. **Parking:** on-site. **Terms:** age restrictions may apply, 3 day cancellation notice. **Amenities:** *Some:* irons. **Cards:** AX, MC, VI.

LITTLE RIVER

WHERE TO STAY

AUBERGE MENDOCINO — **Phone:** (707)937-0088

Bed & Breakfast

Dates	2P	XP	
All Year	2P: $135-$325	XP: $20	D12

Location: 2 mi s of Mendocino, w of SR 1. 8200 N Hwy 1 95456 (PO Box 134, MENDOCINO, 95460). Fax: 707/937-3620. **Facility:** Occupying an 1860s farmhouse and converted barn, the inn features many units with fireplaces and balconies, and one with a piano and an ocean view. 10 units. 6 one-bedroom standard units. 3 one-bedroom suites ($215-$250), some with whirlpools. 1 cottage ($275-$325). 2 stories (no elevator), interior corridors. *Bath:* combo, shower or tub only. **Parking:** on-site. **Terms:** office hours 6 am-10 pm, 2-4 night minimum stay - seasonal & weekends, 14 day cancellation notice-fee imposed, weekly rates available, [BP] meal plan available, package plans. **Amenities:** *Some:* irons, hair dryers. **Leisure Activities:** bicycles, hiking trails. **Cards:** AX, DS, MC, VI.

SOME UNITS

DENNEN'S VICTORIAN FARMHOUSE — **Phone:** 707/937-0697

Bed & Breakfast

Dates	2P	XP
All Year [BP]	2P: $105-$225	XP: $25

Location: 3 mi s of Mendocino; e of Coast Hwy. 7001 N Hwy 1 95456 (PO Box 661, MENDOCINO, 95460). Fax: 707/937-5238. **Facility:** On grounds graced by gardens and a creek, this 1877 farmhouse built as a family home is said to have been used as a model by artist Thomas Kinkade. 10 units. 8 one-bedroom standard units. 1 one-bedroom suite ($195). 1 cottage ($225). 2 stories (no elevator), exterior corridors. *Bath:* combo or shower only. **Parking:** on-site. **Terms:** office hours 9:30 am-9:30 pm, 2 night minimum stay - weekends, cancellation fee imposed, weekly rates available. **Amenities:** CD players. *Some:* irons, hair dryers. **Cards:** AX, MC, VI. **Special Amenities: free local telephone calls and early check-in/late check-out.** *(See color ad below)*

SOME UNITS

GLENDEVEN INN — **Phone:** 707/937-0083

Bed & Breakfast

Dates	1P	2P
5/29-10/26	1P: $135-$235	2P: $135-$235
2/1-5/28 & 10/27-1/31	1P: $120-$215	2P: $120-$215

Location: 2 mi s of Mendocino, e of SR 1. 8205 N Hwy 1 95456 (PO Box 914, MENDOCINO, 95460). Fax: 707/937-6108. **Facility:** A New England Federalist-style farmhouse built in 1867 serves as the core of this appealing country inn. Smoke free premises. 11 units. 8 one-bedroom standard units. 2 one-bedroom suites. 1 vacation home with whirlpool. 2-3 stories (no elevator), interior/exterior corridors. *Bath:* shower only. **Parking:** on-site. **Terms:** office hours 9 am-7 pm, 7 day cancellation notice-fee imposed. **Amenities:** CD players, irons, hair dryers. **Cards:** AX, DS, MC, VI.

SOME UNITS

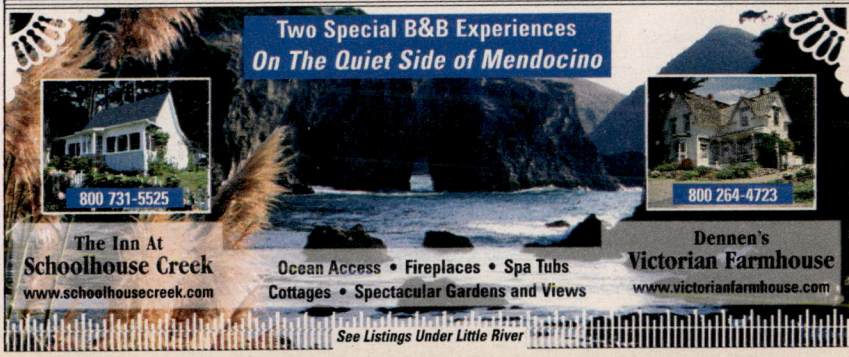

HERITAGE HOUSE Book at aaa.com **Phone:** (707)937-5885

AAA SAVE — Country Inn

5/1-10/31 1P: $150-$500 2P: $150-$500 XP: $20 F12
2/1-4/30 & 11/1-1/31 1P: $135-$425 2P: $135-$425 XP: $20 F12

Location: 3 mi n of jct SR 128 and 1; w of SR 1; 5 mi s of Mendocino. 5200 N Hwy 1 95456. Fax: 707/937-0318. **Facility:** Thirty-seven acres of forested grounds surround this 1877 farmhouse and cottages on a hillside above the Pacific Ocean. 66 units. 64 one-bedroom standard units, some with whirlpools. 2 two-bedroom suites, some with whirlpools. 2 stories (no elevator), exterior corridors. *Bath:* combo or shower only. **Parking:** on-site. **Terms:** age restrictions may apply, 5 day cancellation notice. **Amenities:** hair dryers. *Some:* CD players, irons. **Dining:** 8 am-11 & 6-9 pm, Sat-1 pm, cocktails. **Leisure Activities:** Fee: massage. **Guest Services:** gift shop. **Cards:** AX, MC, VI. **Special Amenities: free newspaper.**

SOME UNITS

THE INN AT SCHOOLHOUSE CREEK **Phone:** (707)937-5525

AAA SAVE — Bed & Breakfast

All Year [BP] 2P: $130-$175 XP: $15 F12

Location: 3 mi s of Mendocino; e of Coast Hwy. 7051 N Hwy 1 (PO Box 1637, MENDOCINO, 95460). Fax: 707/937-2012. **Facility:** The main building in this complex is a farmhouse dating from 1862; sharing the grounds are cottages and cabins, all in rustic decor. 15 units. 4 one-bedroom standard units. 3 one-bedroom suites ($235), some with efficiencies and/or whirlpools. 8 cottages ($185-$195), some with whirlpools. 1 story, exterior corridors. *Bath:* combo or shower only. **Parking:** on-site. **Terms:** office hours 6:30 am-9:30 pm, 2 night minimum stay - weekends, 14 day cancellation notice-fee imposed, pets (in limited units). **Amenities:** video library, CD players, hair dryers. *Some:* irons. **Leisure Activities:** whirlpool, picnic area. **Guest Services:** complimentary evening beverages. **Cards:** AX, DC, DS, MC, VI. **Special Amenities: free full breakfast and free local telephone calls.** *(See color ad p 783)*

SOME UNITS

STEVENSWOOD LODGE **Phone:** (707)937-2810

Country Inn

All Year [BP] 1P: $125-$150 2P: $125-$250 XP: $25 D12

Location: 2 mi s of Mendocino; e of SR 1. Located in a quiet area. 8211 N Hwy 1 95456 (PO Box 170, MENDOCINO, 95460). Fax: 707/937-1237. **Facility:** An award-winning restaurant and abundance of hot tubs are featured at this lodge characterized by a woodland setting and simple decor. Smoke free premises. 10 one-bedroom standard units. 2 stories (no elevator), interior corridors. *Bath:* combo or shower only. **Parking:** on-site. **Terms:** office hours 8 am-8 pm, 2 night minimum stay - weekends, 7 day cancellation notice-fee imposed. **Amenities:** honor bars, hair dryers. *Some:* irons. **Dining:** dining room, see separate listing. **Leisure Activities:** whirlpools, hiking trails. **Business Services:** meeting rooms. **Cards:** AX, DC, DS, MC, VI.

WHERE TO DINE

LITTLE RIVER INN RESTAURANT Country Inn **Dinner:** $19-$28 **Phone:** 707/937-5942

California

Location: East side of SR 1; on a knoll. 7901 N Hwy 1 95456. **Hours:** 7:30 am-10:30 & 6-9 pm, Sat & Sun 7:30 am-noon & 6-9:30 pm. **Reservations:** suggested. **Features:** Succulent prime rib is the special every Saturday at the restaurant, which occupies a charming, 1853 Victorian inn. Garden views are beautiful. Casual dress; cocktails. **Parking:** on-site. **Cards:** AX, MC, VI.

STEVENSWOOD **Dinner:** $26-$38 **Phone:** 707/937-2810

West California

Location: 2 mi s of Mendocino; e of SR 1; in Stevenswood Lodge. 8211 N Hwy 1 95460. **Hours:** Open 2/1-1/1; 8 am-10 & 5:30-9 pm. Closed: Wed, Thurs 11/1-5/31. **Reservations:** suggested. **Features:** Upon entering the tasteful, sophisticated dining room, diners catch sight of large French doors, flanked by big bay windows, that lead to the beautiful gardens. Adding to the visual appeal are a rustic fireplace, candles in artfully designed holders, soft lighting and linen-draped tables. An extensive wine list complements Mediterranean-influenced dishes thoughtfully created by chef Marc Dyn. Semi-formal attire; beer & wine only. **Parking:** on-site. **Cards:** AX, DC, DS, MC, VI.

MENDOCINO pop. 824

WHERE TO STAY

AGATE COVE INN **Phone:** 707/937-0551

AAA SAVE — Cottage

All Year 1P: $129-$299 2P: $129-$299 XP: $30

Location: SR 1, exit Little Lake Rd; exit Lansing St, 0.5 mi nw. 11201 N Lansing St 95460 (PO Box 1150). Fax: 707/937-0550. **Facility:** Consisting of a simply styled 1860s farmhouse and a cluster of cottages, the inn is on a bluff overlooking the Pacific Ocean. 10 cottages, some with whirlpools. 1 story, exterior corridors. *Bath:* combo or shower only. **Parking:** on-site. **Terms:** office hours 7:30 am-8 pm, 2-3 night minimum stay - weekends, age restrictions may apply, 7 day cancellation notice-fee imposed, [BP] meal plan available, package plans - midweek 11/1-3/31. **Amenities:** video library, CD players, irons, hair dryers. **Cards:** MC, VI. **Special Amenities: free local telephone calls and free newspaper.**

BLACKBERRY INN **Phone:** 707/937-5281

AAA SAVE — Motel

6/11-11/28 1P: $115-$180 2P: $115-$180 XP: $10 D18
2/1-6/10 & 11/29-1/31 1P: $90-$180 2P: $90-$180 XP: $10 D18

Location: SR 1, exit Larkin Rd, just e. 44951 Larkin Rd 95460. **Facility:** 17 units. 16 one-bedroom standard units, some with efficiencies and/or whirlpools. 1 cottage ($175-$215) with whirlpool. 1 story, exterior corridors. **Parking:** on-site. **Terms:** office hours 8 am-10 pm, 2-3 night minimum stay - weekends, age restrictions may apply, 4 day cancellation notice-fee imposed, [CP] meal plan available, pets ($10 extra charge, in limited units). **Amenities:** irons. *Some:* hair dryers. **Cards:** MC, VI. *(See color ad p 786)*

SOME UNITS

FEE

BREWERY GULCH INN — **Phone:** (707)937-4752

AAA SAVE — Bed & Breakfast

5/1-11/1 [BP]		2P: $195-$295	XP: $25	D12
2/1-4/30 & 11/2-1/31 [BP]		2P: $150-$250	XP: $25	D12

Location: SR 1, 1 mi s to Mendocino Village, just e. 9401 Coast Hwy One N 95460. Fax: 707/937-1279. **Facility:** Vintage redwood was salvaged for use in the construction of this inn overlooking Smuggler's Cove; lush gardens give it a retreatlike ambience. Smoke free premises. 10 one-bedroom standard units, some with whirlpools. 2 stories (no elevator), interior corridors. *Bath:* combo or shower only. **Parking:** on-site. **Terms:** office hours 7 am-7 pm, 2-3 night minimum stay - weekends, age restrictions may apply, 7 day cancellation notice-fee imposed. **Amenities:** video library, CD players, voice mail, hair dryers. *Some:* irons. **Leisure Activities:** canoeing, fishing, bicycles, hiking trails. **Guest Services:** gift shop, complimentary evening beverages. **Cards:** AX, MC, VI. **Special Amenities: free full breakfast and free local telephone calls.**

SOME UNITS

VCR DATA PORT / /

C.O. PACKARD HOUSE — **Phone:** (707)937-2677

Bed & Breakfast

6/1-10/31 [BP]	1P: $145-$245	2P: $155-$255	XP: $25
2/1-5/31 & 11/1-1/31 [BP]	1P: $125-$245	2P: $135-$255	XP: $25

Location: SR 1, exit Main St, right on Kasten. 45170 Little Lake St 95460 (PO Box 1065). Fax: 707/937-1323. **Facility:** One of four landmark homes on executive row, this Gothic Victorian built in the late 1870s displays a museum-quality art collection. Smoke free premises. 5 units. 4 one-bedroom standard units with whirlpools. 1 cottage with whirlpool. 2 stories (no elevator), interior corridors. **Parking:** street. **Terms:** office hours 8 am-8 pm, 2 night minimum stay - weekends, age restrictions may apply, 14 day cancellation notice-fee imposed. **Amenities:** video library, CD players. **Leisure Activities:** bicycles, hiking trails. **Guest Services:** gift shop, complimentary evening beverages. **Cards:** MC, VI.

VCR

THE HEADLANDS INN *Book at aaa.com* — **Phone:** 707/937-4431

Historic Bed & Breakfast

7/1-10/31 [BP]	1P: $105-$205	2P: $105-$205
11/1-1/31 [BP]	1P: $91-$179	2P: $105-$205
2/1-6/30 [BP]	1P: $91-$179	2P: $91-$179

Location: SR 1, exit Little Lake Rd, just w. Albion & Howard sts 95460 (PO Box 132). Fax: 707/937-0421. **Facility:** Remodeled 1868 Victorian; fireplaces. Smoke free premises. 7 units. 6 one-bedroom standard units. 1 cottage. 3 stories (no elevator), interior corridors. *Bath:* combo or shower only. **Parking:** on-site. **Terms:** office hours 8 am-9 pm, 2-3 night minimum stay - weekends 7/1-10/31, age restrictions may apply, 14 day cancellation notice-fee imposed. **Amenities:** hair dryers. *Some:* irons. **Cards:** AX, DS, MC, VI.

SOME UNITS

ASK / VCR /

HILL HOUSE INN — **Phone:** (707)937-0554

Country Inn

5/16-10/15	1P: $167-$250	2P: $167-$250	XP: $15	F13
2/1-5/15 & 10/16-1/31	1P: $117-$185	2P: $117-$185	XP: $15	F13

Location: SR 1, exit Little Lake St, just w to stop sign, right to entrance. 10701 Pallette Dr 95460 (PO Box 625). Fax: 707/937-1123. **Facility:** Fans of the series "Murder, She Wrote" may recognize this hillside, New England-style country home from the show's opening credits. 44 one-bedroom standard units, some with whirlpools. 2 stories (no elevator), interior/exterior corridors. **Parking:** on-site. **Terms:** age restrictions may apply, 5 day cancellation notice-fee imposed, pets ($25 extra charge). **Amenities:** video library, voice mail, irons, hair dryers. **Leisure Activities:** Fee: massage. **Business Services:** meeting rooms. **Cards:** AX, DS, MC, VI.

SOME UNITS

ASK FEE / VCR /

JOHN DOUGHERTY HOUSE — **Phone:** (707)937-5266

Historic Bed & Breakfast

7/1-10/31	1P: $135-$240	XP: $20
2/1-6/30 & 11/1-1/31	1P: $110-$205	XP: $20

Location: Center. 571 Ukiah St 95460 (PO Box 817). Fax: 707/937-4139. **Facility:** Styled like a New England saltbox, John Dougherty House was built in 1867; also on the grounds are cottages, a water tower and English gardens. 8 one-bedroom standard units. 2 stories (no elevator), interior/exterior corridors. *Bath:* combo or shower only. **Parking:** on-site. **Terms:** office hours 7 am-8 pm, age restrictions may apply, 7 day cancellation notice-fee imposed, [BP] meal plan available. **Amenities:** *Some:* high-speed Internet, irons, hair dryers. **Cards:** DS, MC, VI.

SOME UNITS

/ VCR /

JOSHUA GRINDLE INN Phone: (707)937-4143

AAA SAVE

Historic Bed & Breakfast

2/1-12/24 & 12/26-1/31 [BP] 1P: $140-$260 2P: $140-$260 XP: $30

Location: Just w of SR 1. 44800 Little Lake Rd 95460 (PO Box 647). **Facility:** Early American antiques decorate this 1879 Victorian farmhouse, cottage and water tower surrounded by well-groomed gardens. 10 units. 8 one-bedroom standard units, some with whirlpools. 2 cottages with whirlpools. 2 stories, interior/exterior corridors. *Bath:* combo or shower only. **Parking:** on-site. **Terms:** open 2/1-12/24 & 12/26-1/31, office hours 8 am-8 pm, 2-4 night minimum stay - weekends, age restrictions may apply, 14 day cancellation notice-fee imposed. **Amenities:** hair dryers. *Some:* DVD players, CD players, irons. **Cards:** MC, VI.

SOME UNITS

MACCALLUM HOUSE INN Phone: (707)937-0289

Bed & Breakfast

All Year [BP] 1P: $120-$295 2P: $120-$295 XP: $25 F6

Location: Center. 45020 Albion St 95460 (PO Box 206). **Facility:** This 1882 Victorian features beautiful gardens with a sitting area. Smoke free premises. 20 units. 10 one- and 2 two-bedroom standard units, some with kitchens and/or whirlpools. 8 cottages, some with whirlpools. 3 stories (no elevator), interior/exterior corridors. *Bath:* combo or shower only. **Parking:** street. **Terms:** office hours 8 am-10 pm, check-in 4 pm, 2 night minimum stay - weekends, age restrictions may apply, 7 day cancellation notice-fee imposed, package plans, pets ($25 extra charge). **Amenities:** video library, DVD players. *Some:* irons, hair dryers. **Dining:** MacCallum House Restaurant, see separate listing. **Leisure Activities:** whirlpool. *Fee:* bicycles. **Business Services:** meeting rooms, PC. **Cards:** AX, DS, MC, VI.

ASK FEE SOME UNITS

MCELROY'S INN Phone: 707/937-1734

Bed & Breakfast

All Year 1P: $85-$125 2P: $85-$125 XP: $20 F4

Location: SR 1, exit Main St, just w. 998 Main St 95460 (PO Box 1881). Fax: 707/937-2569. **Facility:** 4 units. 2 one-bedroom standard units. 2 one-bedroom suites. 2 stories (no elevator), interior corridors. *Bath:* shower only. **Parking:** on-site. **Terms:** office hours 8:30 am-6 pm, 2 night minimum stay - weekends 4/1-12/31, age restrictions may apply, 7 day cancellation notice-fee imposed, [CP] meal plan available. **Amenities:** *Some:* irons, hair dryers. **Cards:** MC, VI.

SOME UNITS

MENDOCINO HOTEL & GARDEN SUITES *Book at aaa.com* Phone: (707)937-0511

Historic Small-scale Hotel

All Year 1P: $95-$295 2P: $95-$295 XP: $20 F12

Location: SR 1, exit Main St, just w. 45080 Main St 95460 (PO Box 587). Fax: 707/937-0513. **Facility:** Built in 1878, this restored Victorian hotel has a few small rooms and also some large, modern, garden units. 51 units. 46 one-bedroom standard units. 5 one-bedroom suites. 2-3 stories (no elevator), interior/exterior corridors. *Bath:* some shared or private, combo or shower only. **Parking:** on-site. **Terms:** check-in 4 pm, 2 night minimum stay - weekends, age restrictions may apply, 3 day cancellation notice, package plans. **Amenities:** hair dryers. *Some:* safes, irons. **Dining:** restaurant, see separate listing. **Business Services:** meeting rooms. **Cards:** AX, MC, VI.

ASK SOME UNITS

MENDOCINO SEASIDE COTTAGES Phone: (707)485-0239

AAA SAVE

Bed & Breakfast

All Year 1P: $187-$391 2P: $187-$391

Location: SR 1, exit Little Lake Rd; exit Lansing St, 0.6 mi nw. 10940 Lansing St 95460 (1050 Wallace Dr, REDWOOD VALLEY, 95470). Fax: 707/485-9746. **Facility:** Built in 1997 as a replica of Victorian seaside cottages, these accommodations orient toward the headlands, providing an unobstructed view. 4 one-bedroom standard units. 2 stories, interior/exterior corridors. *Bath:* combo or shower only. **Parking:** on-site. **Terms:** office hours 8 am-10 pm, age restrictions may apply, 14 day cancellation notice-fee imposed, weekly rates available, [CP] meal plan available, package plans, pets ($80 deposit). **Amenities:** CD players, irons, hair dryers. **Leisure Activities:** hiking trails. **Special Amenities: free continental breakfast and free local telephone calls.**

FEE DATA PORT SOME UNITS

NICHOLSON HOUSE INN **Phone:** (707)937-0934

Bed & Breakfast

6/1-10/31	2P: $99-$189
3/1-5/31	2P: $95-$169
2/1-2/29 & 11/1-1/31	2P: $90-$149

Location: Center. 951 Ukiah St 95460 (PO Box 707). Fax: 707/937-2349. **Facility:** 7 units. 5 one-bedroom standard units. 2 one-bedroom suites with kitchens. 2 stories (no elevator), interior corridors. *Bath:* combo or shower only. **Parking:** street. **Terms:** office hours 8 am-8 pm, 2 night minimum stay - weekends, 7 day cancellation notice-fee imposed, weekly rates available. **Amenities:** *Some:* irons, hair dryers. **Cards:** AX, MC, VI.

SOME UNITS

REED MANOR **Phone:** 707/937-5446

Bed & Breakfast

All Year [CP]	1P: $175-$550	2P: $175-$550	XP: $50

Location: SR 1, exit Little Lake Rd, just w, right on Lansing, then right on Palette. (PO Box 127). **Facility:** Car buffs will appreciate the large collection of miniature autos displayed in the contemporary common areas of this large, French Manor-style home. Designated smoking area. 5 one-bedroom standard units with whirlpools. 2 stories, interior corridors. **Parking:** on-site. **Terms:** office hours 8 am-8 pm, 2-3 night minimum stay - weekends, age restrictions may apply, 14 day cancellation notice-fee imposed. **Amenities:** irons, hair dryers. **Cards:** AX, MC, VI.

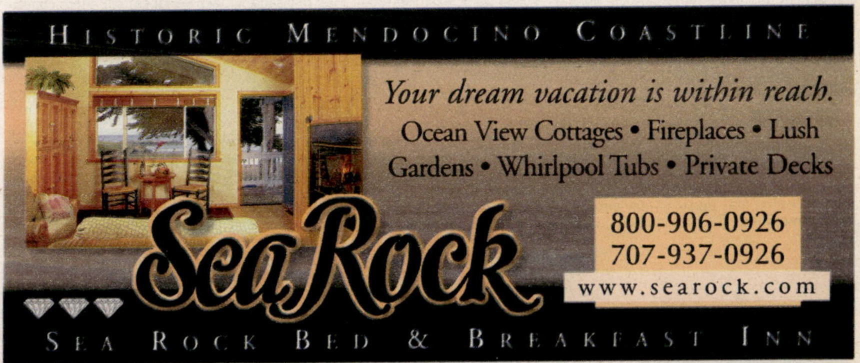

SEA ROCK BED & BREAKFAST INN — **Phone:** 707/937-0926

Bed & Breakfast

All Year [ECP] 1P: $150-$300 2P: $150-$300 XP: $20

Location: SR 1, exit Little Lake Rd; exit Lansing St, 0.5 mi nw. 11101 Lansing St 95460 (PO Box 906). **Facility:** The B&B offers a range of accommodations including individual cottages; most have a fireplace, a deck and ocean or garden views. 14 units. 4 one-bedroom standard units. 4 one-bedroom suites ($279), some with kitchens and/or whirlpools. 6 cottages ($150-$250). 1-2 stories (no elevator), exterior corridors. *Bath:* combo or shower only. **Parking:** on-site. **Terms:** 2 night minimum stay - weekends, 14 day cancellation notice-fee imposed, package plans - midweek 11/4-1/5. **Amenities:** video library, irons, hair dryers. **Cards:** AX, CB, DC, DS, MC, VI. **Special Amenities: free expanded continental breakfast and free local telephone calls.** *(See color ad p 787)*

SOME UNITS

STANFORD INN BY THE SEA-BIG RIVER LODGE — **Phone:** (707)937-5615

Country Inn

All Year 1P: $195-$395 2P: $225-$465 XP: $45 D18

Location: SR 1, exit Comptche-Ukiah Rd, 0.5 mi e. PO Box 487 95460. Fax: 707/937-0305. **Facility:** Spacious grounds, a rustic setting and many rooms with ocean views add to the lodge's appeal; llamas and an organic farm share the grounds. 41 units. 32 one-bedroom standard units. 6 one-bedroom suites. 3 cottages. 2-3 stories (no elevator), exterior corridors. *Bath:* combo or shower only. **Parking:** on-site. **Terms:** office hours 7:30 am-11:30 pm, check-in 4 pm, age restrictions may apply, 7 day cancellation notice-fee imposed, [BP] meal plan available, package plans, pets ($25 extra charge). **Amenities:** video library, DVD players, CD players, dual phone lines, voice mail, irons, hair dryers. **Dining:** 8 am-10:30 & 6-9 pm, wine/beer only. **Pool(s):** heated indoor. **Leisure Activities:** sauna, whirlpool, rental canoes, bicycles, hiking trails, exercise room. *Fee:* massage. **Guest Services:** gift shop, complimentary evening beverages. **Business Services:** conference facilities, business center. **Cards:** AX, CB, DC, DS, MC, VI.
(See color ad p 787)

 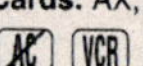  

FEE

WHITEGATE INN — **Phone:** (707)937-4892

Historic Bed & Breakfast

6/30-10/31 1P: $179-$289 2P: $179-$289 XP: $30 D18
2/1-6/29 & 11/1-1/31 1P: $159-$289 2P: $159-$289 XP: $30 D18

Location: SR 1, exit Little Lake Rd, just w. 499 Howard St 95460 (PO Box 150). Fax: 707/937-1131. **Facility:** Sweeping views of the ocean are a main draw at the inn, which was built as a family home in 1883. Smoke free premises. 6 one-bedroom standard units, some with whirlpools. 2 stories (no elevator), exterior corridors. *Bath:* combo or shower only. **Parking:** on-site. **Terms:** office hours 7:30 am-7 pm, 2 night minimum stay - weekends, age restrictions may apply, 14 day cancellation notice-fee imposed, weekly rates available, [BP] meal plan available, package plans. **Amenities:** CD players, irons, hair dryers. **Guest Services:** gift shop, complimentary evening beverages. **Cards:** AX, MC, VI.

SOME UNITS

WHERE TO DINE

CAFE BEAJOULIS — **Dinner:** $21-$32 — **Phone:** 707/937-5614

California

Location: SR 1, exit Little Lake W to Lansing, then w. 961 Ukiak St 95460. **Hours:** Open 2/1-11/30 & 1/1-1/31; 5:45 pm-9 pm. **Reservations:** suggested. **Features:** The bungalow cottage restaurant features wood floors and whitewashed walls. Cuisine is fresh organic with a hint of French; service is impeccable. Casual dress; beer & wine only. **Parking:** street. **Cards:** AX, DS, MC, VI.

MACCALLUM HOUSE RESTAURANT — **Dinner:** $21-$32 — **Phone:** 707/937-5763

American

Location: Center; in MacCallum House Inn. 45020 Albion St 95460. **Hours:** Open 2/1-1/1; 5:30 pm-9 pm. **Reservations:** suggested. **Features:** The elegant restaurant occupies the main floor of the historic bed and breakfast. Casual dress; cocktails. **Parking:** street. **Cards:** MC, VI.

MENDOCINO HOTEL VICTORIAN RESTAURANT — **Dinner:** $19-$30 — **Phone:** 707/937-0511

Continental

Location: SR 1, exit Main St, just w; in Mendocino Hotel & Garden Suites. 45080 Main St 95460. **Hours:** 6 pm-9:30 pm, Fri & Sat-10 pm. **Reservations:** required. **Features:** Victorian decor adorns the dining room and the glass-enclosed courtyard, a popular lunching spot. The menu centers on California cuisine. Casual dress; cocktails. **Parking:** street. **Cards:** AX, MC, VI.

THE RAVENS — **Dinner:** $15-$20 — **Phone:** 707/937-5615

Vegetarian

Location: SR 1, exit Comptche-Ukiak Rd, just e. 44850 Comptche-Ukiah Rd 95460. **Hours:** 5:30 pm-8:30 pm. **Reservations:** required. **Features:** Known for its delectable hearty cuisine and monthly changing vegetarian menu, the restaurant gets most produce from its own private gardens. Beer & wine only. **Parking:** on-site. **Cards:** AX, CB, DC, DS, MC, VI.

MIDDLETOWN pop. 1,020

WHERE TO STAY

WILLOW OAK PLANTATION — **Phone:** (707)987-9000

Bed & Breakfast

All Year [BP] 2P: $200-$350 XP: $50

Location: On SR 29. 20650 Hwy 29 95461 (PO Box 951). Fax: 707/987-4781. **Facility:** The two-story red brick Southern mansion, located in the heart of Napa Valley, features lush foliage and a swimming pool and spa. 4 one-bedroom standard units, some with whirlpools. 2 stories (no elevator), interior corridors. *Bath:* combo or shower only. **Parking:** on-site. **Terms:** 10 day cancellation notice-fee imposed, weekly rates available, package plans. **Amenities:** hair dryers. *Some:* irons. **Pool(s):** heated outdoor. **Leisure Activities:** whirlpool, badminton. **Guest Services:** area transportation-local restaurants. **Cards:** AX, DS, MC, VI. **Special Amenities: free full breakfast.**

SOME UNITS

MONTE RIO pop. 1,104

WHERE TO STAY

NORTHWOOD LODGE & RESORT — **Phone:** (707)865-1655

SAVE — Motel

5/1-10/31	1P: $79-$159	2P: $110-$179	XP: $10	F12
2/1-4/30 & 11/1-1/31	1P: $79-$109	2P: $99-$139	XP: $10	F12

Location: On SR 116. 19455 Hwy 116 95462. Fax: 707/865-1657. **Facility:** 26 units. 20 one-bedroom standard units. 6 cottages ($189-$289). 1 story, exterior corridors. **Parking:** on-site. **Terms:** 2-3 night minimum stay - seasonal weekends, 14 day cancellation notice-fee imposed, package plans. **Amenities:** *Some:* irons, hair dryers. **Pool(s):** heated outdoor. **Guest Services:** coin laundry. **Cards:** AX, DS, MC, VI.

(See color ad p 779)

RIO VILLA BEACH RESORT — **Phone:** 707/865-1143

Motel

All Year	1P: $89-$199	2P: $89-$199	XP: $10

Location: Center. 20292 Hwy 116 95462. Fax: 707/865-0115. **Facility:** 13 units. 9 one- and 2 two-bedroom standard units, some with kitchens and/or whirlpools. 2 cottages. 1 story, exterior corridors. *Bath:* combo or shower only. **Parking:** on-site. **Terms:** 2 night minimum stay - weekends, 7 day cancellation notice-fee imposed. **Amenities:** video library. *Some:* CD players, irons, hair dryers. **Guest Services:** gift shop. **Cards:** AX, DS, MC, VI.

SOME UNITS

NAPA pop. 72,585

WHERE TO STAY

THE 1801 INN — **Phone:** 707/224-3739

Historic Bed & Breakfast

All Year	1P: $250-$395	2P: $250-$395	XP: $50

Location: SR 29, exit 1st St (downtown), 0.5 mi e to Jefferson St, just n. 1801 1st St 94559. Fax: 707/224-3932. **Facility:** Occupying a restored 1903 Queen Anne Victorian, the inn also includes cottages with private patios and colorful flower gardens. 8 one-bedroom standard units, some with whirlpools. 2 stories (no elevator), interior/exterior corridors. **Parking:** on-site. **Terms:** 2 night minimum stay - weekends, cancellation fee imposed, [BP] meal plan available. **Amenities:** irons, hair dryers. **Guest Services:** complimentary evening beverages. **Cards:** AX, DC, DS, MC, VI.

SOME UNITS

BEL ABRI — **Phone:** 707/226-5825

Bed & Breakfast

6/1-11/15	1P: $149-$299	2P: $149-$299	XP: $15	F3
5/1-5/31	1P: $149-$269	2P: $149-$269	XP: $15	F3
11/16-1/31	1P: $125-$245	2P: $125-$245	XP: $15	F3
2/1-4/30	1P: $119-$239	2P: $119-$239	XP: $15	F3

Location: SR 29, exit 1st St, just e. 837 California Blvd 94559. Fax: 707/226-5321. **Facility:** Centered in the Napa Valley, this new-construction B&B offers spacious and attractively appointed guest units. 15 one-bedroom standard units, some with whirlpools. 3 stories, interior corridors. **Parking:** on-site. **Terms:** 2 night minimum stay - weekends, 7 day cancellation notice, [ECP] meal plan available, 12% service charge. **Amenities:** CD players, voice mail, irons, hair dryers. **Guest Services:** complimentary evening beverages. **Cards:** AX, CB, DC, DS, MC, VI.

BEST WESTERN ELM HOUSE INN *Book at aaa.com* **Phone:** (707)255-1831

AAA SAVE — Small-scale Hotel

6/17-11/14 [ECP]	1P: $149-$299	2P: $149-$299	XP: $10	F12
5/1-6/16 [ECP]	1P: $129-$199	2P: $129-$199	XP: $10	F12
2/1-4/30 & 11/15-1/31 [ECP]	1P: $109-$199	2P: $109-$199	XP: $10	F12

Location: SR 29, exit 1st St, 1.5 blks s. Located in a residential area. 800 California Blvd 94559 (1275 4th St #119, SANTA ROSA, 95404). Fax: 707/255-8609. **Facility:** 22 one-bedroom standard units, some with whirlpools. 3 stories, interior corridors. *Bath:* combo or shower only. **Parking:** on-site. **Terms:** 2-3 night minimum stay - weekends. **Amenities:** CD players, dual phone lines, voice mail, honor bars, irons, hair dryers. **Leisure Activities:** whirlpool. **Guest Services:** coin laundry. **Business Services:** meeting rooms. **Cards:** AX, CB, DC, DS, JC, MC, VI. **Special Amenities: free expanded continental breakfast and free local telephone calls.** *(See color ad p 789)*

BEST WESTERN INN AT THE VINES *Book at aaa.com* **Phone:** (707)257-1930

AAA SAVE — Motel

5/1-1/31 [BP]	1P: $129-$275	2P: $139-$275	XP: $10	F
4/1-4/30 [BP]	1P: $115-$265	2P: $125-$265	XP: $10	F
3/1-3/31 [BP]	1P: $100-$260	2P: $110-$260	XP: $10	F
2/1-2/29 [BP]	1P: $95-$150	2P: $100-$150	XP: $10	F

Location: Jct SR 121 and Soscol Ave. 100 Soscol Ave 94559. Fax: 707/255-0709. **Facility:** 68 one-bedroom standard units. 2-3 stories, interior/exterior corridors. **Parking:** on-site. **Terms:** 5-9 night minimum stay - seasonal & weekends. **Amenities:** voice mail, irons, hair dryers. **Pool(s):** heated outdoor. **Leisure Activities:** whirlpool. **Business Services:** meeting rooms. **Cards:** AX, DC, DS, MC, VI. **Special Amenities: free full breakfast and free local telephone calls.**

BLACKBIRD INN **Phone:** (707)226-2450

Bed & Breakfast

4/1-10/31	2P: $165-$295	XP: $20	F5
2/1-3/31 & 11/1-1/31	2P: $145-$245	XP: $20	F5

Location: SR 29, exit 1st St (downtown), 0.5 mi e to Jefferson St, just n. 1755 1st St 94559. Fax: 707/258-6391. **Facility:** A spacious front porch, huge stone fireplace and liberal use of fine woods help the inn stand out as an example of early-20th-century craftsmanship. 8 one-bedroom standard units, some with whirlpools. 2 stories, interior corridors. *Bath:* combo or shower only. **Parking:** on-site. **Terms:** 7 day cancellation notice-fee imposed, package plans - seasonal. **Amenities:** irons, hair dryers. **Guest Services:** complimentary evening beverages. **Cards:** AX, DC, MC, VI.

CEDAR GABLES INN **Phone:** (707)224-7969

AAA SAVE — Historic Bed & Breakfast

All Year	1P: $229-$369	2P: $229-$369	XP: $50

Location: Just s of downtown. 486 Coombs St 94559. Fax: 707/224-4838. **Facility:** The inn occupies a historic building designed by English architect Ernest Coxhead and constructed in 1892; phone for seasonal closures. 9 units. 7 one-bedroom standard units, some with whirlpools. 2 one-bedroom suites. 2 stories, interior corridors. **Parking:** on-site. **Terms:** 2 night minimum stay - seasonal, 7 day cancellation notice, weekly rates available, package plans - seasonal & mid-week. **Amenities:** irons, hair dryers. **Guest Services:** TV in common area, complimentary evening beverages. **Cards:** AX, DS, MC, VI. **Special Amenities: free room upgrade (subject to availability with advanced reservations).**

THE CHATEAU *Book at aaa.com* **Phone:** (707)253-9300

Motel

6/1-11/13 [CP]	1P: $119-$169	2P: $119-$169	XP: $10	F12
4/1-5/31 [CP]	1P: $99-$129	2P: $99-$129	XP: $10	F12
2/1-3/31 & 11/14-1/31 [CP]	1P: $99	2P: $99	XP: $10	F12

Location: West of and adjacent to SR 29 at Wine Country Ave. 4195 Solano Ave 94558. Fax: 707/253-0906. **Facility:** 115 units. 109 one-bedroom standard units. 6 one-bedroom suites ($149-$239). 2 stories, interior corridors. **Parking:** on-site. **Terms:** cancellation fee imposed. **Amenities:** hair dryers. **Pool(s):** heated outdoor. **Leisure Activities:** whirlpool. **Business Services:** meeting rooms. **Cards:** AX, DC, DS, MC, VI. *(See color ad below)*

SOME UNITS

EMBASSY SUITES NAPA VALLEY **Book at aaa.com** **Phone:** (707)253-9540

Small-scale Hotel

All Year 1P: $154-$284 2P: $164-$294 XP: $15 F18

Location: SR 29, exit 1st St E. 1075 California Blvd 94559. Fax: 707/253-9202. **Facility:** 205 one-bedroom suites. 3 stories, interior/exterior corridors. **Parking:** on-site. **Terms:** cancellation fee imposed, 8% service charge. **Amenities:** dual phone lines, voice mail, irons, hair dryers. **Pool(s):** heated outdoor, heated indoor. **Leisure Activities:** sauna, whirlpool, rental bicycles. **Guest Services:** complimentary evening beverages, valet laundry. **Business Services:** conference facilities. **Cards:** AX, CB, DC, MC, VI. ***(See color ad below)***

SOME UNITS

ASK

HAWTHORN INN & SUITES **Book at aaa.com** **Phone:** (707)226-1878

Motel

5/1-10/31 [BP] 1P: $129-$199 2P: $129-$199
2/1-4/30 & 11/1-1/31 [BP] 1P: $109-$169 2P: $109-$169

Location: SR 29, exit downtown Napa. 314 Soscol Ave 94559. Fax: 707/226-1448. **Facility:** 60 units. 54 one-bedroom standard units. 6 one-bedroom suites ($139-$239) with whirlpools. 3 stories, exterior corridors. **Parking:** on-site. **Terms:** cancellation fee imposed. **Amenities:** high-speed Internet, dual phone lines, voice mail, irons, hair dryers. **Pool(s):** heated indoor. **Leisure Activities:** whirlpool, exercise room. **Business Services:** meeting rooms. **Cards:** AX, CB, DC, DS, JC, MC, VI. ***(See color ad below)***

SOME UNITS

ASK

HILTON GARDEN INN-NAPA *Book at aaa.com* **Phone:** 707/252-0444

Motel

5/16-11/15	1P: $200-$389	2P: $200-$389	XP: $10	F18
2/1-5/15	1P: $120-$200	2P: $120-$200	XP: $10	F18
11/16-1/31	1P: $99-$200	2P: $99-$200	XP: $10	F18

Location: SR 29, exit Redwood Rd, just n. 3585 Solano Ave 94558. Fax: 707/252-0244. **Facility:** 80 units. 62 one-bedroom standard units. 18 one-bedroom suites with whirlpools. 3 stories, interior corridors. **Parking:** on-site. **Terms:** [MAP] meal plan available, package plans. **Amenities:** high-speed Internet, dual phone lines, voice mail, irons, hair dryers. **Pool(s):** heated outdoor. **Leisure Activities:** whirlpool, exercise room. **Guest Services:** coin laundry. **Business Services:** meeting rooms, business center. **Cards:** AX, DC, DS, MC, VI.

SOME UNITS

JOHN MUIR INN **Phone:** (707)257-7220

AAA SAVE

Small-scale Hotel

5/1-10/31	1P: $140-$230	2P: $140-$230	XP: $10	F14
11/1-1/31	1P: $115-$195	2P: $115-$195	XP: $10	F14
2/1-4/30	1P: $115-$185	2P: $115-$185	XP: $10	F14

Location: SR 29, exit E Trower Ave. 1998 Trower Ave 94558. Fax: 707/258-0943. **Facility:** Smoke free premises. 59 one-bedroom standard units, some with efficiencies and/or whirlpools. 3 stories, interior corridors. **Parking:** on-site. **Terms:** 2 night minimum stay - weekends 5/1-11/30. **Amenities:** irons, hair dryers. **Pool(s):** heated outdoor. **Leisure Activities:** whirlpool. **Guest Services:** valet laundry. **Business Services:** meeting rooms. **Cards:** AX, DC, DS, MC, VI. **Special Amenities: free continental breakfast and free local telephone calls.**

SOME UNITS

THE NAPA INN *Book at aaa.com* **Phone:** 707/257-1444

AAA SAVE

Historic Bed & Breakfast

5/1-10/31	1P: $140-$295	2P: $140-$295	XP: $30	D3
11/1-1/31	1P: $125-$260	2P: $125-$260	XP: $30	D3
2/1-4/30	1P: $120-$250	2P: $120-$250	XP: $30	D3

Location: SR 29, exit 1st St, 0.5 mi e, 0.3 mi n. 1137 Warren St 94559. Fax: 707/257-0251. **Facility:** The inn retains the romantic aura of this turn-of-the-century Queen Anne Victorian; relax in the quiet gardens or in front of the fireplace. 14 one-bedroom standard units, some with whirlpools. 2 stories, interior corridors. *Bath:* combo or shower only. **Parking:** on-site. **Terms:** 2-3 night minimum stay - weekends, cancellation fee imposed, [BP] meal plan available, small pets only ($20 fee). **Amenities:** voice mail, irons, hair dryers. **Guest Services:** complimentary evening beverages. **Cards:** AX, DC, DS, MC, VI. **Special Amenities: free full breakfast and free local telephone calls.**

SOME UNITS

FEE

NAPA RIVER INN *Book at aaa.com* **Phone:** (707)251-8500

Motel

4/1-11/15 [BP]	1P: $179-$399	2P: $179-$399	XP: $25
2/1-3/31 & 11/16-1/31 [BP]	1P: $159-$349	2P: $159-$349	XP: $25

Location: Downtown. 500 Main St 94559. Fax: 707/251-8504. **Facility:** 66 one-bedroom standard units. 3 stories, interior corridors. **Parking:** on-site. **Terms:** small pets only ($25 fee). **Amenities:** CD players, dual phone lines, voice mail, irons, hair dryers. **Leisure Activities:** exercise room. **Guest Services:** complimentary evening beverages, valet laundry. **Business Services:** meeting rooms. **Cards:** AX, CB, DC, DS, JC, MC, VI.

ASK

FEE

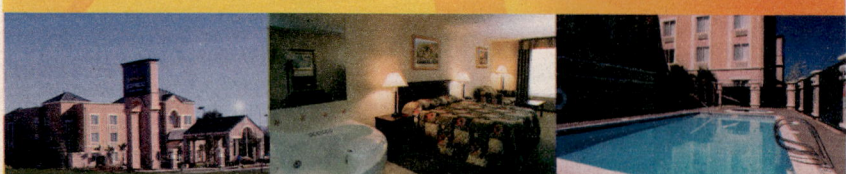

NAPA VALLEY MARRIOTT **Book at aaa.com** **Phone:** (707)253-7433

Small-scale Hotel

5/2-11/13	1P: $189-$249	
2/1-5/1 & 11/14-1/31	1P: $159-$189	

Location: 1 blk w off SR 29 via Redwood Rd, 0.5 blk n. 3425 Solano Ave 94558. Fax: 707/258-1320. **Facility:** 274 units. 272 one-bedroom standard units. 2 one-bedroom suites ($350-$500). 2 stories, interior corridors. **Parking:** on-site. **Terms:** package plans. **Amenities:** high-speed Internet (fee), voice mail, irons, hair dryers. *Some:* safes. **Pool(s):** heated outdoor. **Leisure Activities:** whirlpool, exercise room, spa. **Guest Services:** gift shop, complimentary evening beverages, valet and coin laundry. **Business Services:** conference facilities, business center. **Cards:** AX, DC, DS, JC, MC, VI. *(See color ad p 794)*

SOME UNITS

NAPA VALLEY REDWOOD INN **Phone:** 707/257-6111

AAA SAVE

Motel

5/1-10/31 [CP]	1P: $83-$150	2P: $83-$150	XP: $10	F16
2/1-4/30 & 11/1-1/31 [CP]	1P: $67-$99	2P: $67-$99	XP: $10	F16

Location: Just w off SR 29 via Redwood Rd, then just s. 3380 Solano Ave 94558. Fax: 707/252-2702. **Facility:** 58 one-bedroom standard units. 2 stories, exterior corridors. *Bath:* shower only. **Parking:** on-site. **Terms:** pets ($10 extra charge). **Amenities:** high-speed Internet. **Pool(s):** outdoor. **Cards:** AX, CB, DC, DS, MC, VI. *(See color ad below)*

FEE

NAPA VALLEY TRAVELODGE HOTEL & SUITES **Book at aaa.com** **Phone:** (707)226-1871

Motel

5/1-11/30	1P: $149-$299	2P: $149-$299	XP: $20	F12
2/1-4/30	1P: $129-$249	2P: $129-$249	XP: $20	F12
12/1-1/31	1P: $109-$199	2P: $109-$199	XP: $20	F12

Location: At 2nd and Coombs sts. Located across from the courthouse. 853 Coombs St 94559. Fax: 707/226-1707. **Facility:** 44 one-bedroom standard units. 3 stories, exterior corridors. **Parking:** on-site. **Terms:** 7 day cancellation notice-fee imposed. **Amenities:** irons, hair dryers. **Pool(s):** small outdoor. **Cards:** AX, CB, DC, DS, MC, VI.

SOME UNITS

THE OLD WORLD INN — **Phone:** (707)257-0112

Historic Bed & Breakfast

4/1-11/30	1P: $145-$275	2P: $155-$275	XP: $40
2/1-3/31 & 12/1-1/31	1P: $100-$225	2P: $125-$225	XP: $40

Location: SR 29, exit Lincoln Ave E, 0.5 mi e to Jefferson St, then 0.5 mi s. 1301 Jefferson St 94559. Fax: 707/257-0118. **Facility:** This 1906 home is an ecletic combination of architectural styles detailed with wood shingles, wide shady porches and leaded and beveled glass. 10 one-bedroom standard units, some with whirlpools. 2 stories, interior corridors. **Parking:** on-site. **Terms:** 2 night minimum stay - weekends, 7 day cancellation notice-fee imposed, [BP] meal plan available. **Amenities:** irons, hair dryers. **Leisure Activities:** whirlpool. **Guest Services:** complimentary evening beverages. **Cards:** AX, DC, MC, VI.

SOME UNITS

SILVERADO RESORT Book at aaa.com Phone: (707)257-0200

Resort Large-scale Hotel

3/1-11/26	1P: $290	2P: $290		
11/27-1/31	1P: $185	2P: $185		
2/1-2/29	1P: $170	2P: $170		

Location: 5.8 mi e of Napa via SR 121. 1600 Atlas Peak Rd 94558. Fax: 707/257-5400. **Facility:** Notable for its recreational facilities, the resort offers cottages and one- to three-bedroom, kitchen or efficiency apartments, many with fireplaces. 280 units. 80 one-, 180 two- and 20 three-bedroom suites, some with efficiencies or kitchens. 2 stories, exterior corridors. **Parking:** valet. **Terms:** check-in 5 pm, 2 night minimum stay - weekends 5/1-10/31. **Amenities:** CD players, voice mail, honor bars, irons, hair dryers. **Pool(s):** 7 outdoor, heated outdoor. **Leisure Activities:** rental bicycles, spa. *Fee:* golf-36 holes, 14 tennis courts (3 lighted). **Guest Services:** gift shop, valet laundry. **Business Services:** conference facilities, business center. **Cards:** AX, CB, DC, DS, JC, MC, VI.

SOME UNITS

ASK FEE DATA PORT

STAHLECKER HOUSE Phone: 707/257-1588

AAA SAVE

Bed & Breakfast

4/1-10/31 [BP]	1P: $160-$248	2P: $160-$248	XP: $75	D18
2/1-3/31 & 11/1-1/31 [BP]	1P: $144-$223	2P: $144-$223	XP: $50	D18

Location: SR 29, exit 1st St, 0.5 mi w. 1042 Easum Dr 94558. Fax: 707/224-7429. **Facility:** This property is beside a creek and has attractively landscaped grounds; some units have fireplaces. 4 one-bedroom standard units, some with whirlpools. 1 story, interior corridors. *Bath:* combo or shower only. **Parking:** on-site. **Terms:** 2 night minimum stay - weekends, 7 day cancellation notice-fee imposed. **Amenities:** irons, hair dryers. **Cards:** AX, DS, MC, VI.

WINE VALLEY LODGE Book at aaa.com Phone: (707)224-7911

AAA SAVE

Motel

5/1-11/30 [CP]	1P: $119-$165	2P: $119-$165	XP: $20	F18
3/1-4/30 [CP]	1P: $89-$165	2P: $89-$165	XP: $20	F18
2/1-2/29 & 12/1-1/31 [CP]	1P: $69-$165	2P: $69-$165	XP: $20	F18

Location: SR 29, exit Imola Ave (SR 121), 0.5 mi e to S Coombs St, then just n. 200 S Coombs St 94559. Fax: 707/224-9152. **Facility:** 54 one-bedroom standard units. 1 story, exterior corridors. *Bath:* combo or shower only. **Parking:** on-site. **Terms:** cancellation fee imposed. **Pool(s):** heated outdoor. **Cards:** AX, CB, DC, DS, MC, VI. **Special Amenities: free continental breakfast and free room upgrade (subject to availability with advanced reservations).**

SOME UNITS

WHERE TO DINE

CHANTERELLE RESTAURANT **Lunch:** $8-$15 **Dinner:** $12-$22 **Phone:** 707/253-7300

Continental

Location: Downtown. 804 1st St 94559. **Hours:** 11 am-4 & 5-9:30 pm, Sun 10:30 am-2:30 & 5-9 pm. Closed major holidays. **Reservations:** suggested. **Features:** Conveniently located in downtown area. Dressy casual; cocktails. **Parking:** on-site. **Cards:** MC, VI.

JONESY'S FAMOUS STEAK HOUSE **Lunch:** $6-$25 **Dinner:** $10-$26 **Phone:** 707/255-2003

Steak House

Location: At Napa County Airport. 2044 Airport Rd 94558. **Hours:** 10 am-8 pm, Fri-Sun to 9 pm. Closed: 1/1, 11/25; also Mon & 12/21-12/26. **Reservations:** suggested. **Features:** Also, chicken and fresh fish. Casual dress; cocktails. **Parking:** on-site. **Cards:** AX, DC, DS, MC, VI.

NAPA VALLEY WINE TRAIN **Lunch:** $35-$88 **Dinner:** $70-$125 **Phone:** 707/253-2111

AAA

Continental

Location: SR 29, exit 1st St, 0.8 mi e on 1st St, then 4 blks n on Soscal Ave. 1275 McKinstry St 94559. **Hours:** Seatings at 11:30 am & 6:30 pm, Sat & Sun seatings at 12:20 pm & 6 pm. Closed: 1/1, 12/25. **Reservations:** required. **Features:** Diners can sit back in restored turn-of-the-20th-century Pullman cars for a three-hour, 36-mile excursion through scenic wine country. Prix fixe menus list three entree choices. Dressy casual; cocktails. **Parking:** on-site. **Cards:** AX, CB, DC, MC, VI. *(See color ad p 196)*

RUFFINO'S **Lunch:** $7-$16 **Dinner:** $10-$19 **Phone:** 707/255-4455

Northern Italian

Location: 645 1st St 94559. **Hours:** 5 pm-9:30 pm, Tues-Fri also 11:30 am-2 pm. Closed major holidays; also Mon. **Reservations:** suggested. **Features:** Specializing in Northern Italian cuisine. Also offering steak and seafood entrees. Centrally located between downtown Napa and the Silverado Trail. Casual dress; cocktails. **Parking:** on-site. **Cards:** AX, DC, MC, VI.

NICE pop. 2,509

WHERE TO STAY

FEATHERBED RAILROAD CO. Phone: (707)274-4434

AAA SAVE

Bed & Breakfast

5/1-9/30 [ECP]	1P: $123-$182	2P: $123-$182	XP: $10	D12
2/1-4/30 & 10/1-1/31 [ECP]	1P: $117-$167	2P: $117-$167	XP: $10	D12

Location: 0.5 mi s of SR 20. 2870 Lakesshore Blvd 95464 (PO Box 4016). Fax: 707/274-1415. **Facility:** These authentically restored caboose cars, each in a different decor theme, share a tree-shaded, parklike setting. 9 one-bedroom standard units, some with whirlpools. 1 story. **Parking:** on-site. **Terms:** office hours 10 am-8 pm, 3 day cancellation notice-fee imposed, package plans. **Amenities:** video library. *Some:* irons, hair dryers. **Pool(s):** outdoor. **Leisure Activities:** whirlpool, boat dock, fishing, croquet, ping pong, bicycles. **Cards:** AX, DS, MC, VI. **Special Amenities: free newspaper and free room upgrade (subject to availability with advanced reservations).**

VCR

GINGERBREAD COTTAGES Phone: (707)274-0200

AAA SAVE

Bed & Breakfast

All Year [CP]	1P: $140-$185	2P: $140-$185	XP: $35	

Location: On SR 20. 4057 E Hwy 20 95464 (PO Box 4004). **Facility:** All cottages face lake. 6 cottages. *Bath:* combo or shower only. **Parking:** on-site. **Terms:** office hours 7 am-9 pm, 2 night minimum stay - weekends, age restrictions may apply, 7 day cancellation notice-fee imposed, package plans. **Amenities:** video library, CD players, irons, hair dryers. **Pool(s):** small outdoor. **Leisure Activities:** whirlpool, boating, boat dock, waterskiing, fishing, bicycles, hiking trails, jogging. **Guest Services:** gift shop. **Business Services:** fax. **Cards:** AX, DS, MC, VI. **Special Amenities: free continental breakfast and free local telephone calls.**

VCR DATA PORT

OCCIDENTAL pop. 1,272

WHERE TO STAY

THE INN AT OCCIDENTAL Book at aaa.com **Phone:** (707)874-1047

Bed & Breakfast

4/1-11/30 [BP]	1P: $195-$350	2P: $195-$350	XP: $75
2/1-3/31 & 12/1-1/31 [BP]	1P: $195-$320	2P: $195-$320	XP: $75

Location: Town center. 3657 Church St 95465 (PO Box 857). Fax: 707/874-1078. **Facility:** Covered porches with wicker furnishings enhance the exterior of this elegantly restored 1860 Victorian; most rooms have a fireplace. 16 one-bedroom standard units, some with whirlpools. 3 stories, interior corridors. *Bath:* combo or shower only. **Parking:** on-site. **Terms:** 2 night minimum stay - weekends, 10 day cancellation notice-fee imposed. **Amenities:** hair dryers. **Guest Services:** complimentary evening beverages. **Business Services:** meeting rooms, business center. **Cards:** AX, DS, MC, VI. **Special Amenities: free full breakfast and free local telephone calls.**

OCCIDENTAL LODGE **Phone:** (707)874-3623

Motel

All Year	1P: $48-$109	2P: $58-$119	XP: $10	F11

Location: In the village. 3610 Bohemian Hwy 95465 (PO Box 84). Fax: 707/525-1276. **Facility:** 26 units. 24 one-bedroom standard units. 2 one-bedroom suites ($89-$139) with kitchens. 2 stories, exterior corridors. **Parking:** on-site. **Terms:** small pets only ($8 extra charge). **Pool(s):** outdoor. **Cards:** AX, DC, DS, MC, VI. **Special Amenities: free local telephone calls.**

FEE

PETALUMA pop. 54,548

WHERE TO STAY

BEST WESTERN PETALUMA INN Book at aaa.com **Phone:** (707)763-0994

Motel

All Year	1P: $69-$139	2P: $79-$139	XP: $10	F12

Location: US 101, exit Washington St, 1 blk e. 200 S McDowell Blvd 94954. Fax: 707/778-3111. **Facility:** 73 units. 72 one-bedroom standard units. 1 one-bedroom suite. 2 stories, exterior corridors. *Bath:* combo or shower only. **Parking:** on-site. **Amenities:** dual phone lines, voice mail, irons, hair dryers. **Pool(s):** heated outdoor. **Guest Services:** coin laundry. **Business Services:** meeting rooms. **Cards:** AX, CB, DC, DS, MC, VI. **Special Amenities: free continental breakfast and free newspaper.** *(See color ad below)*

SOME UNITS

THE OLD PALMS — Phone: (707)658-2554

Historic Bed & Breakfast

All Year [BP] 1P: $145-$220

Location: US 101, exit Washington St, 1 mi w. 2 Liberty St 94952. Fax: 707/658-2539. **Facility:** The Carlsbad Spas of Bohemia are credited with inspiring the European ambience which characterizes this downtown property. 5 one-bedroom standard units. 2 stories (no elevator), interior corridors. **Parking:** on-site. **Terms:** 30 day cancellation notice-fee imposed, package plans - weekends, 10% service charge. **Amenities:** irons, hair dryers. **Guest Services:** TV in common area. **Cards:** MC, VI.

SOME UNITS

QUALITY INN-PETALUMA *Book at aaa.com* — Phone: (707)664-1155

SAVE

Motel

5/1-10/30 [ECP]	1P: $95-$180	2P: $95-$180	XP: $10	F18
2/1-4/30 & 10/31-1/31 [ECP]	1P: $90-$170	2P: $90-$170	XP: $10	F18

Location: US 101, exit Old Redwood Hwy-Penngrove northbound; exit Petaluma Blvd N-Penngrove southbound (east side). 5100 Montero Way 94954. Fax: 707/664-8566. **Facility:** 110 units. 106 one-bedroom standard units, some with whirlpools. 4 one-bedroom suites, some with whirlpools. 2 stories, interior/exterior corridors. *Bath:* combo or shower only. **Parking:** on-site. **Terms:** cancellation fee imposed, small pets only ($15 fee). **Amenities:** irons, hair dryers. *Some:* dual phone lines. **Pool(s):** heated outdoor. **Leisure Activities:** sauna, whirlpool, exercise room. **Guest Services:** valet and coin laundry. **Cards:** AX, CB, DC, DS, JC, MC, VI. **Special Amenities: free expanded continental breakfast and free room upgrade (subject to availability with advanced reservations).**

SOME UNITS

FEE

SHERATON SONOMA COUNTY-PETALUMA *Book at aaa.com* — Phone: (707)283-2888

SAVE

Small-scale Hotel

5/1-10/31	1P: $230-$310	2P: $230-$310	XP: $25	F17
1/1-1/31	1P: $225-$300	2P: $225-$300	XP: $25	F17
2/1-4/30 & 11/1-12/31	1P: $215-$290	2P: $215-$290	XP: $25	F17

Location: US 101, exit SR 116 (Lakeville Hwy), just e. 745 Baywood Dr 94954. Fax: 707/283-2828. **Facility:** 183 units. 180 one-bedroom standard units. 3 one-bedroom suites ($320-$650). 4 stories, interior corridors. **Parking:** on-site. **Amenities:** voice mail, irons, hair dryers. **Dining:** 6:30 am-9:30 pm, cocktails, also, Jellyfish, see separate listing. **Pool(s):** outdoor. **Leisure Activities:** whirlpool, exercise room. **Guest Services:** valet and coin laundry. **Business Services:** conference facilities, business center. **Cards:** AX, CB, DC, DS, MC, VI. **Special Amenities: free newspaper and preferred room (subject to availability with advanced reservations).**

SOME UNITS

WHERE TO DINE

JELLYFISH — **Lunch:** $18-$24 **Dinner:** $18-$24 — **Phone:** 707/283-2900

California

Location: US 101, exit SR 116 (Lakeville Hwy), just e; in Sheraton Sonoma County-Petaluma. 745 Baywood Dr 94954. **Hours:** 6:30-11 am, 11-2:30 & 5:30-9 pm, Fri & Sat-10 pm. **Reservations:** accepted. **Features:** Casual dining with views of the hotel's pool and local marina. Experience an explosive fusion of flavors complimented by global wine list. Casual dress; cocktails. **Parking:** on-site. **Cards:** AX, CB, DC, DS, JC, MC, VI.

POINT ARENA pop. 474

WHERE TO STAY

BEST WESTERN INN *Book at aaa.com* — Phone: (707)882-3171

Motel

All Year	1P: $75-$200	2P: $75-$200	XP: $20	F

Location: 1 mi w of SR 1; at wharf via Iversen Ave or Port Rd. Located in a quiet, secluded area. 785 Port Rd 95468 (PO Box 674). Fax: 707/882-4114. **Facility:** 25 one-bedroom standard units, some with whirlpools. 2 stories (no elevator), exterior corridors. *Bath:* combo or tub only. **Parking:** on-site. **Terms:** 5 day cancellation notice-fee imposed, [ECP] meal plan available. **Amenities:** video library, irons, hair dryers. **Leisure Activities:** scuba diving, snorkeling, fishing, hiking trails. **Business Services:** meeting rooms. **Cards:** AX, CB, DS, MC, VI.

SOME UNITS

ROHNERT PARK pop. 42,236

WHERE TO STAY

BEST WESTERN INN *Book at aaa.com* **Phone:** (707)584-7435

Motel

5/1-9/30 [ECP]	1P: $70-$80	2P: $76-$89	XP: $6	F12
2/1-4/30 & 10/1-1/31 [ECP]	1P: $68-$78	2P: $73-$85	XP: $6	F12

Location: US 101, exit Rohnert Park Expwy, just w. 6500 Redwood Dr 94928. Fax: 707/584-3848. **Facility:** 145 one-bedroom standard units. 2 stories, exterior corridors. **Parking:** on-site. **Terms:** 3 day cancellation notice, small pets only. **Amenities:** irons, hair dryers. **Pool(s):** heated outdoor. **Leisure Activities:** whirlpool. **Guest Services:** coin laundry. **Business Services:** meeting rooms. **Cards:** AX, CB, DC, DS, MC, VI. **Special Amenities: free expanded continental breakfast and free room upgrade (subject to availability with advanced reservations).** *(See color ad below)*

SOME UNITS

DOUBLETREE HOTEL SONOMA WINE COUNTRY *Book at aaa.com* **Phone:** (707)584-5466

Large-scale Hotel

All Year 1P: $89-$239

Location: US 101, exit Golf Course Dr; 3 mi s of Santa Rosa. One Doubletree Dr 94928. Fax: 707/586-9726. **Facility:** Featuring California Spanish architecture, this recently renovated property has attractively appointed and spacious guest units. 245 units. 239 one-bedroom standard units. 6 one-bedroom suites ($400-$800) with whirlpools. 3 stories, interior corridors. **Parking:** on-site. **Terms:** cancellation fee imposed, package plans - seasonal. **Amenities:** voice mail, irons, hair dryers. **Dining:** 6:30 am-11 pm. **Pool(s):** heated outdoor. **Leisure Activities:** whirlpool, 2 tennis courts, exercise room. **Guest Services:** gift shop, valet laundry. **Business Services:** conference facilities, business center. **Cards:** AX, CB, DC, DS, JC, MC, VI. **Special Amenities: free newspaper and early check-in/late check-out.**

SOME UNITS

RAMADA LIMITED *Book at aaa.com* **Phone:** 707/584-1600

Motel

Property failed to provide current rates

Location: US 101, exit W Rohnert Park Expwy. 6288 Redwood Dr 94928. Fax: 707/584-1305. **Facility:** 138 one-bedroom standard units. 2 stories, exterior corridors. **Parking:** on-site. **Amenities:** irons, hair dryers. **Pool(s):** outdoor. **Business Services:** meeting rooms.

SOME UNITS

The following lodging was either not evaluated or did not meet AAA rating requirements but is listed for your information only.

GOOD NITE INN **Phone:** 707/584-8180

fyi Motel

Did not meet all AAA rating requirements for some property operations at time of last evaluation on 06/09/2003. **Location:** US 101, exit Golf Course Dr, just w. 5040 Redwood Dr 94928. Facilities, services, and decor characterize a basic property.

RUTHERFORD

WHERE TO STAY

RANCHO CAYMUS **Phone:** 707/963-1777

Motel

4/1-11/30 [CP]	1P: $225-$365	2P: $225-$365	XP: $25	F5
12/1-1/31 [CP]	1P: $195-$355	2P: $195-$355	XP: $25	F5
2/1-3/31 [CP]	1P: $195-$345	2P: $195-$345	XP: $25	F5

Location: 4 mi s of St Helena; just e of SR 29 and 128. 1140 Rutherford Rd 94573 (PO Box 78). Fax: 707/963-5387. **Facility:** 26 units. 24 one-bedroom standard units, some with kitchens and/or whirlpools. 2 one-bedroom suites with kitchens and whirlpools. 2 stories, exterior corridors. **Parking:** on-site. **Terms:** 2-3 night minimum stay - weekends, 3 day cancellation notice-fee imposed. **Amenities:** voice mail, irons, hair dryers. **Business Services:** meeting rooms. **Cards:** AX, MC, VI. ***(See color ad p 794)***

ST. HELENA pop. 5,950

WHERE TO STAY

ADAGIO INN — Bed & Breakfast — **Phone:** (707)963-2238

All Year [BP] 1P: $200-$275 2P: $200-$275 XP: $50 F5

Location: SR 29, just w on Adams. Located in a quiet residential area. 1417 Kearney St 94574. Fax: 707/963-5598. **Facility:** Just west of downtown, this inn is nicely appointed and offers a warm atmosphere. Designated smoking area. 4 one-bedroom standard units, some with whirlpools. 2 stories, interior corridors. **Parking:** street. **Terms:** 2-3 night minimum stay - weekends, 21 day cancellation notice, package plans. **Amenities:** hair dryers. **Cards:** MC, VI.

EL BONITA MOTEL — Motel — **Phone:** 707/963-3216

Dates	2P
5/28-11/29	$140-$289
3/12-5/27	$120-$269
11/30-1/31	$90-$209
2/1-3/11	$89-$199

Location: 0.8 mi s on SR 29. 195 Main St 94574. Fax: 707/963-8838. **Facility:** 42 units. 38 one- and 2 two-bedroom standard units, some with efficiencies and/or whirlpools. 1 one- and 1 two-bedroom suites with efficiencies and whirlpools. 2 stories, exterior corridors. *Bath:* combo or shower only. **Parking:** on-site. **Terms:** 2 night minimum stay - weekends, 3 day cancellation notice-fee imposed, small pets only. **Amenities:** irons, hair dryers. **Pool(s):** heated outdoor. **Leisure Activities:** sauna, whirlpool. **Cards:** AX, CB, DC, DS, JC, MC, VI.

HARVEST INN — *Book at aaa.com* — AAA SAVE — Small-scale Hotel — **Phone:** (707)963-9463

Dates	1P	2P	XP	
4/1-11/30	$315-$675	$315-$675	$25	F16
2/1-3/31 & 12/1-1/31	$249-$675	$249-$675	$25	F16

Location: 1.5 mi s on SR 29. One Main St 94574. Fax: 707/963-4402. **Facility:** English Tudor in design, the inn is surrounded by vineyards and offers spacious units, many with fireplaces and antique furnishings. 54 units. 51 one-bedroom standard units. 3 one-bedroom suites with whirlpools. 2 stories, exterior corridors. **Parking:** on-site. **Terms:** check-in 4 pm, 2 night minimum stay - weekends, 7 day cancellation notice-fee imposed, [ECP] meal plan available, small pets only ($75 fee). **Amenities:** CD players, voice mail, honor bars, irons, hair dryers. **Pool(s):** 2 heated outdoor. **Leisure Activities:** whirlpools, rental bicycles. **Business Services:** meeting rooms. **Cards:** AX, CB, DC, DS, JC, MC, VI. *(See color ad below)*

FEE

HOTEL ST. HELENA — Historic Small-scale Hotel — **Phone:** (707)963-4388

All Year 1P: $185-$275 2P: $185-$275

Location: On SR 29; center. 1309 Main St 94574. Fax: 707/963-5402. **Facility:** 1888 Victorian Hotel. 18 units. 17 one-bedroom standard units. 1 one-bedroom suite ($325). 2 stories, interior corridors. *Bath:* some shared or private, combo or shower only. **Parking:** on-site. **Terms:** 3 day cancellation notice-fee imposed, [CP] meal plan available. **Amenities:** hair dryers. **Guest Services:** complimentary evening beverages. **Cards:** AX, DC, DS, JC, MC, VI.

SOME UNITS

THE INK HOUSE BED & BREAKFAST — Historic Bed & Breakfast — **Phone:** (707)963-3890

All Year [BP] 1P: $120-$230 2P: $120-$230 XP: $25 F6

Location: On SR 29, 1.5 mi s. 1575 St Helena Hwy 94574. Fax: 707/968-0739. **Facility:** Casual Victorian elegance characterizes this landmark home built in 1884. 7 one-bedroom standard units. 2 stories (no elevator), interior corridors. *Bath:* some shared or private, combo or shower only. **Parking:** on-site. **Terms:** 7 day cancellation notice-fee imposed, package plans. **Amenities:** irons, hair dryers. **Leisure Activities:** bicycles, game room. **Guest Services:** TV in common area, complimentary evening beverages. **Cards:** MC, VI.

MEADOWOOD NAPA VALLEY Book at aaa.com **Phone:** (707)963-3646

Resort Small-scale Hotel

4/1-11/30	1P: $575-$1250	2P: $575-$1250	XP: $25	F12
12/1-1/31	1P: $525-$1000	2P: $525-$1000	XP: $25	F12
2/1-3/31	1P: $470-$975	2P: $470-$975	XP: $25	F12

Location: Jct SR 29 and 12, exit Pope St, 0.8 mi e to Silverado Tr, just n, then 1 blk e on Howell Mountain Rd. 900 Meadowood Ln 94574. Fax: 707/963-3532. **Facility:** A 250-acre, private, wooded reserve wraps around these country-style lodges; many accommodations have wood-burning fireplaces. 85 units. 40 one-bedroom standard units. 20 one-, 15 two- and 10 three-bedroom suites. 2 stories, exterior corridors. *Bath:* combo or shower only. **Parking:** on-site. **Terms:** check-in 4 pm, 2 night minimum stay - weekends, 14 day cancellation notice-fee imposed. **Amenities:** dual phone lines, voice mail, safes, honor bars, irons, hair dryers. **Dining:** The Restaurant At Meadowood, see separate listing. **Pool(s):** 2 heated outdoor. **Leisure Activities:** whirlpool, recreation programs, exercise room. *Fee:* golf-9 holes, 7 tennis courts. **Guest Services:** gift shop, valet laundry. **Business Services:** conference facilities, business center. **Cards:** AX, CB, DC, DS, JC, MC, VI. Affiliated with A Preferred Hotel.

SOME UNITS DATA PORT / VCR /

VINEYARD COUNTRY INN **Phone:** (707)963-1000

AAA SAVE

Bed & Breakfast

All Year [ECP]	1P: $170-$295	2P: $170-$295	XP: $15	F5

Location: 0.8 mi s on SR 29. 201 Main St 94574. Fax: 707/963-1794. **Facility:** Wood-burning fireplaces are featured in all of the inn's rooms, while some have patios, decks or views of the vineyard. 21 one-bedroom suites. 2 stories, exterior corridors. **Parking:** on-site. **Terms:** check-in 4 pm, 2-3 night minimum stay - weekends, 3 day cancellation notice. **Amenities:** hair dryers. **Pool(s):** heated outdoor. **Leisure Activities:** whirlpool. **Cards:** AX, CB, DC, MC, VI. **Special Amenities: free continental breakfast and free local telephone calls.** *(See color ad p 794)*

DATA PORT

WHERE TO DINE

THE RESTAURANT AT MEADOWOOD **Dinner:** $65-$125 **Phone:** 707/963-3646

AAA

South French

Location: Jct SR 29 and 12, exit Pope St, 0.8 mi e to Silverado Tr, just n, then 1 blk e on Howell Mountain Rd; in Meadowood Napa Valley. 900 Meadowood Ln 94574. **Hours:** 6 pm-9:30 pm, Fri & Sat-10 pm. Closed: 1st week of June. **Reservations:** suggested. **Features:** View of the wooded hillsides are particularly scenic from the relaxed, seasonal deck. Dressy casual; cocktails. **Parking:** on-site. **Cards:** AX, CB, DC, DS, MC, VI.

TRA VIGNE **Lunch:** $9-$24 **Dinner:** $14-$24 **Phone:** 707/963-4444

Italian

Location: 0.5 mi s on SR 29. 1050 Charter Oak Ave 94574. **Hours:** 11:30 am-10 pm. Closed major holidays. **Reservations:** suggested. **Features:** The restaurant is set in an attractive location in the heart of Napa Valley. Dressy casual; cocktails. **Parking:** on-site. **Cards:** DC, MC, VI.

WINE SPECTATOR GREYSTONE RESTAURANT **Lunch:** $15-$27 **Dinner:** $15-$27 **Phone:** 707/967-1010

California

Location: 1.5 mi n on SR 29. 2555 Main St 94574. **Hours:** 11:15 am-9 pm, Fri & Sat-10 pm. Closed major holidays; also 1/1-1/21. **Reservations:** suggested. **Features:** Located on the grounds of the old Christian Brothers winery, the restaurant features students from the Culinary Institute of America, and local, seasonal ingredients are the inspiration for the cuisine. Dressy casual; cocktails. **Parking:** on-site. **Cards:** AX, DC, DS, MC, VI.

SANTA ROSA pop. 147,595

WHERE TO STAY

BEST WESTERN GARDEN INN Book at aaa.com **Phone:** (707)546-4031

AAA SAVE

Motel

6/1-9/30	1P: $89-$129	2P: $89-$129	XP: $10	F12
10/1-1/31	1P: $84-$124	2P: $84-$124	XP: $10	F12
2/1-5/31	1P: $79-$119	2P: $79-$119	XP: $10	F12

Location: US 101, exit Baker Ave northbound; exit Corby Ave southbound. 1500 Santa Rosa Ave 95404. Fax: 707/526-4903. **Facility:** 78 units. 72 one-bedroom standard units. 6 one-bedroom suites. 2 stories, exterior corridors. *Bath:* combo or shower only. **Parking:** on-site. **Terms:** small pets only ($15 extra charge). **Amenities:** irons, hair dryers. **Dining:** 6:30-11 am. **Pool(s):** 2 outdoor. **Guest Services:** coin laundry. **Business Services:** meeting rooms. **Cards:** AX, CB, DC, DS, JC, MC, VI. **Special Amenities: early check-in/late check-out and free room upgrade (subject to availability with advanced reservations).** *(See color ad below & p 521)*

SOME UNITS FEE DATA PORT / /

COMFORT INN *Book at aaa.com* **Phone:** (707)542-5544

Motel

5/28-9/30	1P: $79-$119	2P: $79-$119	XP: $6	F
2/1-5/27 & 10/1-1/31	1P: $59-$89	2P: $59-$89	XP: $6	F

Location: US 101, exit Steele Ln, 1 mi n. 2632 Cleveland Ave 95403. Fax: 707/542-9738. **Facility:** 100 one-bedroom standard units. 3 stories, interior corridors. **Parking:** on-site. **Pool(s):** outdoor. **Cards:** AX, DC, MC, VI. **Special Amenities: free continental breakfast and free newspaper.** *(See color ad below)*

SOME UNITS

COURTYARD BY MARRIOTT *Book at aaa.com* **Phone:** 707/573-9000

Small-scale Hotel

4/30-10/30	1P: $129-$209	2P: $129-$209
10/31-1/31	1P: $109-$169	2P: $109-$169
2/1-4/29	1P: $99-$169	2P: $99-$169

Location: US 101, exit downtown west; jct 3rd and Railroad sts. Adjacent to Railroad Square, Old Town. 175 Railroad St 95401. Fax: 707/573-0272. **Facility:** 138 units. 133 one-bedroom standard units. 5 one-bedroom suites ($129-$239). 5 stories, interior corridors. **Parking:** on-site. **Terms:** 2-4 night minimum stay - some weekends in summer. **Amenities:** dual phone lines, voice mail, irons, hair dryers. **Dining:** 6:30-10 am, Sat & Sun 7-11 am. **Pool(s):** outdoor. **Leisure Activities:** whirlpool, exercise room. **Guest Services:** coin laundry. **Business Services:** meeting rooms. **Cards:** AX, CB, DC, DS, MC, VI. **Special Amenities: free newspaper and preferred room (subject to availability with advanced reservations).** *(See color ad below)*

SOME UNITS

DAYS INN *Book at aaa.com* **Phone:** (707)568-1011

Motel

6/1-9/30 [CP]	1P: $79-$89	2P: $89-$99	XP: $10	F7
2/1-5/31 & 10/1-1/31 [CP]	1P: $69-$75	2P: $79-$85	XP: $10	F7

Location: US 101, exit Todd Rd, 0.5 mi n. 3345 Santa Rosa Ave 95407. Fax: 707/568-1022. **Facility:** 104 one-bedroom standard units. 2 stories, exterior corridors. **Parking:** on-site. **Terms:** 2 night minimum stay - in season, cancellation fee imposed. **Amenities:** hair dryers. **Pool(s):** outdoor. **Leisure Activities:** whirlpool. **Guest Services:** coin laundry. **Business Services:** meeting rooms. **Cards:** AX, CB, DC, DS, MC, VI. **Special Amenities: free expanded continental breakfast.**

SOME UNITS

FEE

FLAMINGO RESORT HOTEL *Book at aaa.com* **Phone:** (707)545-8530

Small-scale Hotel

All Year	1P: $99-$179	XP: $10	F12

Location: Off SR 12; at Farmers Ln. 2777 Fourth St 95405. Fax: 707/528-1404. **Facility:** 170 units. 156 one-bedroom standard units. 14 one-bedroom suites ($199-$249), some with whirlpools. 2 stories, interior corridors. **Parking:** on-site. **Terms:** 2 night minimum stay - seasonal weekends, cancellation fee imposed. **Amenities:** voice mail, irons, hair dryers. *Some:* high-speed Internet. **Dining:** 6:30 am-9 pm, Fri & Sat-10 pm, cocktails. **Pool(s):** heated outdoor. **Leisure Activities:** whirlpool, 5 tennis courts, spa. **Guest Services:** valet and coin laundry. **Business Services:** conference facilities, business center. **Cards:** AX, CB, MC, VI. *(See color ad p 802)*

FEE FEE

FOUNTAINGROVE INN, HOTEL & CONFERENCE CENTER *Book at aaa.com* **Phone:** (707)578-6101

SAVE

Small-scale Hotel

6/1-10/31 [ECP]	1P: $139-$159	2P: $139-$159	XP: $15	F13
2/1-5/31 [ECP]	1P: $129-$139	2P: $129-$139	XP: $15	F13
11/1-1/31 [ECP]	1P: $119-$129	2P: $119-$129	XP: $15	F13

Location: 2 mi n off US 101, exit Mendocino Ave/Old Redwood Hwy, 0.3 mi s. 101 Fountain Grove Pkwy 95403. Fax: 707/544-3126. **Facility:** Accents of natural wood and stone impart elegance to this hotel's lobby, but its most striking feature is a stone wall with cascading sheets of water. 124 units. 122 one-bedroom standard units. 2 one-bedroom suites with whirlpools. 2 stories, interior corridors. **Parking:** on-site. **Terms:** check-in 4 pm. **Amenities:** dual phone lines, voice mail, irons, hair dryers. **Dining:** Equus Restaurant, see separate listing. **Pool(s):** heated outdoor. **Leisure Activities:** whirlpool. **Guest Services:** gift shop, valet laundry. **Business Services:** conference facilities, fax. **Cards:** AX, DC, DS, JC, MC, VI. **Special Amenities: free continental breakfast and free newspaper.** *(See color ad below)*

SOME UNITS

DATA PORT

THE GABLES INN **Phone:** (707)585-7777

SAVE

Historic Bed & Breakfast

All Year [BP]	1P: $175-$300	2P: $175-$300	XP: $50

Location: 4 mi s of downtown. 4257 Petaluma Hill Rd 95404. Fax: 707/584-5634. **Facility:** This 1877 Victorian mansion is in a tranquil country setting. 8 one-bedroom standard units, some with kitchens and/or whirlpools. 2 stories, interior corridors. **Parking:** on-site. **Terms:** 2 night minimum stay - weekends, 14 day cancellation notice-fee imposed. **Amenities:** irons, hair dryers. **Cards:** AX, DC, DS, MC, VI. **Special Amenities: free full breakfast and free local telephone calls.**

HILLSIDE INN MOTEL **Phone:** (707)546-9353

SAVE

Motel

All Year	1P: $78-$98	2P: $82-$98	XP: $4	F11

Location: US 101, 2.5 mi e on SR 12; at Farmers Ln and 4th St. 2901 4th St 95409. Fax: 707/526-1470. **Facility:** 36 units. 29 one-bedroom standard units, some with efficiencies or kitchens. 7 one-bedroom suites with kitchens. 2 stories, exterior corridors. **Parking:** on-site. **Terms:** 3 day cancellation notice, pets (with prior approval). **Dining:** 6:30 am-2:30 pm, wine/beer only. **Pool(s):** outdoor. **Guest Services:** coin laundry. **Cards:** AX, CB, DC, DS, MC, VI. *(See color ad p 803)*

SOME UNITS

DATA PORT

HILTON SONOMA COUNTY/SANTA ROSA *Book at aaa.com* **Phone:** (707)523-7555

Small-scale Hotel — All Year 1P: $109-$199 2P: $119-$209 XP: $10 F18

Location: US 101, exit e via Mendocino-Old Redwood Hwy; 3 blks n top of the hill. 3555 Round Barn Blvd 95403. Fax: 707/569-5555. **Facility:** 247 one-bedroom standard units. 3 stories, interior corridors. **Parking:** on-site. **Amenities:** dual phone lines, voice mail, irons, hair dryers. **Pool(s):** outdoor. **Leisure Activities:** whirlpool, exercise room. **Guest Services:** valet laundry. **Business Services:** conference facilities, business center. **Cards:** AX. *(See ad below)*

SOME UNITS

HOLIDAY INN EXPRESS Book at aaa.com

Motel

Phone: (707)545-9000

5/1-8/31 [ECP]	1P: $109-$199	2P: $109-$199	XP: $10	F19
2/1-4/30 & 9/1-1/31 [ECP]	1P: $99-$169	2P: $99-$169	XP: $10	F19

Location: US 101, exit Mendocino/Hopper Ave, just w. 870 Hopper Ave 95403. Fax: 707/571-0145. **Facility:** 96 units. 91 one-bedroom standard units. 5 one-bedroom suites with whirlpools. 2 stories, exterior corridors. **Parking:** on-site. **Amenities:** irons, hair dryers. **Pool(s):** outdoor. **Leisure Activities:** exercise room. **Business Services:** conference facilities. **Cards:** AX, CB, DC, DS, JC, MC, VI. **Special Amenities: free expanded continental breakfast and free local telephone calls.** *(See color ad below & p 260)*

SOME UNITS

HOTEL LA ROSE Book at aaa.com

Historic Small-scale Hotel

Phone: (707)579-3200

5/1-10/31 [BP]	1P: $129-$249	2P: $144-$264	XP: $15
2/1-4/30 & 11/1-1/31 [BP]	1P: $109-$249	2P: $124-$264	XP: $15

Location: 2 blks w off US 101, exit downtown Santa Rosa. Located on Railroad Square. 308 Wilson St 95401. Fax: 707/579-3247. **Facility:** Cobblestones were used in the construction of this historic hotel, which was built in 1907. 49 units. 39 one-bedroom standard units. 10 one-bedroom suites, some with whirlpools. 2-4 stories, interior/exterior corridors. *Bath:* combo or shower only. **Parking:** on-site. **Amenities:** high-speed Internet, dual phone lines, irons, hair dryers. **Dining:** 11:30 am-2 & 5:30-9:30 pm, Sat 5:30 pm-9 pm; closed Sun & Mon, cocktails. **Leisure Activities:** whirlpool. **Guest Services:** valet laundry. **Business Services:** meeting rooms, business center. **Cards:** AX, CB, DC, DS, MC, VI. **Special Amenities: free continental breakfast and free local telephone calls.**

SOME UNITS

FEE

MICROTEL INN & SUITES Book at aaa.com

Motel

Phone: (707)544-6464

5/1-12/31	1P: $59-$69	2P: $69-$89	XP: $10	F16
2/1-4/30 & 1/1-1/31	1P: $49-$59	2P: $59-$69	XP: $10	F16

Location: US 101, exit Todd Rd, 1.3 mi n. 3000 Santa Rosa Ave 95407. Fax: 707/568-3274. **Facility:** 64 one-bedroom standard units. 2 stories, interior corridors. **Parking:** on-site. **Terms:** cancellation fee imposed, weekly rates available. **Business Services:** meeting rooms. **Cards:** AX, DC, DS, JC, MC, VI.

SOME UNITS

RAMADA LIMITED Book at aaa.com

Motel

Phone: (707)575-4600

5/1-10/31	1P: $89-$129	2P: $89-$149	XP: $10	F17
2/1-4/30 & 11/1-1/31	1P: $59-$99	2P: $59-$99	XP: $10	F17

Location: US 101, exit Mendocino/Hopper Ave. 866 Hopper Ave 95403. Fax: 707/575-0945. **Facility:** 34 one-bedroom standard units, some with whirlpools. 2 stories, exterior corridors. **Parking:** on-site. **Terms:** [ECP] meal plan available. **Amenities:** irons, hair dryers. **Pool(s):** heated outdoor. **Cards:** AX, CB, DC, DS, MC, VI.

SOME UNITS

SANDMAN MOTEL Book at aaa.com

Motel

Phone: (707)544-8570

All Year [ECP]	1P: $71-$82	2P: $77-$88	XP: $6	F12

Location: US 101, exit W Mendocino Ave. 3421 Cleveland Ave 95403. Fax: 707/544-8710. **Facility:** 136 one-bedroom standard units. 2 stories, exterior corridors. **Parking:** on-site. **Terms:** check-in 4 pm, 3 day cancellation notice. **Amenities:** voice mail, irons, hair dryers. **Pool(s):** heated outdoor. **Leisure Activities:** whirlpool, exercise room. **Guest Services:** valet and coin laundry. **Business Services:** meeting rooms. **Cards:** AX, CB, DC, DS, MC, VI. *(See color ad p 805)*

SOME UNITS

SANTA ROSA DOWNTOWN TRAVELODGE Book at aaa.com

Motel

Phone: (707)544-4141

6/1-9/30	1P: $60-$120	2P: $60-$120	XP: $5	F12
2/1-5/31 & 10/1-1/31	1P: $50-$95	2P: $50-$95	XP: $5	F12

Location: 3 blks off US 101 via College Ave, at Mendocino Ave. 635 Healdsburg Ave 95401. Fax: 707/542-4403. **Facility:** 44 one-bedroom standard units. 3 stories, exterior corridors. *Bath:* combo or shower only. **Parking:** on-site. **Terms:** cancellation fee imposed, [CP] meal plan available. **Amenities:** hair dryers. **Pool(s):** outdoor. **Cards:** AX, DS, MC, VI.

SOME UNITS

SANTA ROSA MOTOR INN *Book at aaa.com* **Phone:** (707)523-3480

AAA SAVE

Motel

All Year [CP] 1P: $60-$80 2P: $65-$89 XP: $5 D12

Location: US 101, northbound exit Baker Ave; southbound exit Corby Ave. 1800 Santa Rosa Ave 95407. Fax: 707/542-9243. **Facility:** 43 one-bedroom standard units. 2 stories, exterior corridors. **Parking:** on-site. **Terms:** cancellation fee imposed, small pets only ($10 fee). **Cards:** AX, DS, MC, VI. **Special Amenities: free continental breakfast and early check-in/late check-out.**

SOME UNITS

FEE

VINEYARD CREEK HOTEL, SPA & CONFERENCE CENTER *Book at aaa.com* **Phone:** (707)636-7100

AAA SAVE

Small-scale Hotel

All Year 1P: $159-$249 2P: $159-$249 XP: $15 F12

Location: US 101, exit downtown, just w. 170 Railroad St 95401. Fax: 707/636-7130. **Facility:** Located at Historic Railroad Square, the hotel offers richly detailed Mediterranean architecture which conveys a sense of privacy, romance and charm. 155 one-bedroom standard units, some with whirlpools. 3 stories, interior corridors. **Parking:** on-site. **Terms:** cancellation fee imposed, [AP] & [CP] meal plans available. **Amenities:** video games, CD players, high-speed Internet, voice mail, safes, honor bars, irons, hair dryers. **Pool(s):** heated outdoor. **Leisure Activities:** sauna, whirlpool, exercise room, spa. **Guest Services:** valet laundry. **Business Services:** conference facilities, business center. **Cards:** AX, CB, DC, DS, MC, VI. **Special Amenities: free newspaper and preferred room (subject to availability with advanced reservations).**

SOME UNITS

DATA PORT

VINEYARD LODGE *Book at aaa.com* **Phone:** 707/542-3472

AAA SAVE

Motel

6/1-1/31	1P: $69-$89	2P: $79-$99	XP: $5	D12
2/1-5/31	1P: $59-$69	2P: $69-$79	XP: $5	D12

Location: 1.5 mi s on US 101 business route; exit US 101 via Baker Ave northbound; exit Santa Rosa Ave-Corby southbound. 1815 Santa Rosa Ave 95407. Fax: 707/542-5038. **Facility:** 31 units. 27 one-bedroom standard units. 4 one-bedroom suites. 1 story, exterior corridors. *Bath:* combo or shower only. **Parking:** on-site. **Terms:** [CP] meal plan available, pets ($20 deposit). **Pool(s):** outdoor. **Guest Services:** valet laundry. **Cards:** AX, DC, DS, MC, VI. **Special Amenities: free continental breakfast.**

SOME UNITS

FEE

VINTNERS INN *Book at aaa.com* **Phone:** (707)575-7350

AAA SAVE

Small-scale Hotel

8/28-10/30 [BP]	1P: $220-$395	2P: $220-$395	XP: $30	F10
4/18-8/27 [BP]	1P: $210-$375	2P: $210-$375	XP: $30	F10
10/31-1/31 [BP]	1P: $178-$323	2P: $178-$323	XP: $30	F10
2/1-4/17 [BP]	1P: $173-$318	2P: $173-$318	XP: $30	F10

Location: 2 mi n on US 101, exit w off US 101 via River Rd-Mark West Springs Rd. 4350 Barnes Rd 95403. Fax: 707/575-1426. **Facility:** Among the property's attributes are the scenic vineyards which surround it; some rooms feature fireplaces. 44 one-bedroom standard units. 2 stories, interior corridors. **Parking:** on-site. **Terms:** 2 night minimum stay - weekends, 7 day cancellation notice, [AP] meal plan available. **Amenities:** CD players, dual phone lines, voice mail, safes, honor bars, irons, hair dryers. **Dining:** John Ash & Co, see separate listing. **Leisure Activities:** whirlpool, exercise room. **Guest Services:** valet laundry. **Business Services:** meeting rooms, fax. **Cards:** AX, DC, MC, VI. **Special Amenities: free continental breakfast and free newspaper.**

DATA PORT

WHERE TO DINE

EQUUS RESTAURANT Lunch: $7-$14 Dinner: $17-$25 Phone: 707/578-0149

Continental

Location: 2 mi n off US 101, exit Mendocino Ave/Old Redwood Hwy, 0.3 mi s; in Fountaingrove Inn, Hotel & Conference Center. 101 FountainGrove Pkwy 95403. **Hours:** 11:30 am-2:30 & 5:30-9:30 pm, Sat from 5:30 pm, Sun 10 am-2 & 5-9 pm. **Reservations:** suggested. **Features:** The Gallery of Sonoma County Wines displays approximately 300 premium wines chosen by each local winery's winemaker. Dressy casual; cocktails. **Parking:** on-site. **Cards:** AX, DC, DS, MC, VI. ***(See color ad p 802)***

JOHN ASH & CO Lunch: $10-$22 Dinner: $18-$29 Phone: 707/527-7687

American

Location: 2 mi n on US 101, exit w off US 101 via River Rd-Mark West Springs Rd; in Vintners Inn. 4330 Barnes Rd 95403. **Hours:** 11:30 am-2:30 & 5:30-9 pm, Sat 5:30 pm-10 pm, Sun from 11 am. Closed: 1/1, 7/4, 12/25. **Reservations:** suggested. **Features:** Emphasis on local foods. Dressy casual; cocktails. **Parking:** on-site. **Cards:** AX, DS, MC, VI.

LA GARE FRENCH RESTAURANT Dinner: $15-$22 Phone: 707/528-4355

French

Location: US 101, exit downtown, just w; just s of Railroad Square. 208 Wilson St 95401. **Hours:** 5:30 pm-10 pm, Sun 5 pm-9 pm. Closed: 1/1, 11/25, 12/25; also Mon, Tues & 7/1-7/14. **Reservations:** suggested. **Features:** This restaurant is appropriately located near Santa Rosa's historic Railroad Square. The menu offers a variety of traditional country-style French cuisine. Dressy casual; beer & wine only. **Parking:** on-site. **Cards:** AX, CB, DC, DS, MC, VI.

LISA HEMENWAY'S Lunch: $8-$17 Dinner: $15-$29 Phone: 707/526-5111

American

Location: US 101, exit College Ave, 1 mi e to McDonald Ave, then 0.5 mi n. 1612 Terrace Way 95405. **Hours:** 11:30 am-3 & 5-9:30 pm. Closed: 1/1, 7/4, 12/25; also Sun & Mon. **Reservations:** suggested. **Features:** Fresh Sonoma County products are key ingredients in the restaurant's California cuisine. Dressy casual; beer & wine only. **Parking:** on-site. **Cards:** DC, MC, VI.

SEA RANCH

WHERE TO STAY

SEA RANCH LODGE *Book at aaa.com* Phone: (707)785-2371

Small-scale Hotel

All Year 1P: $205 2P: $395 XP: $30

Location: Just w of SR 1. 60 Sea Walk Dr 95497 (PO Box 44). Fax: 707/785-2917. **Facility:** 20 units. 18 one- and 2 two-bedroom standard units, some with whirlpools. 2 stories, exterior corridors. **Parking:** on-site. **Terms:** office hours 8 am-10 pm, 2 night minimum stay - seasonal & weekends 7/1-10/31, cancellation fee imposed, [BP] meal plan available. **Amenities:** voice mail, irons, hair dryers. **Dining:** restaurant, see separate listing. **Leisure Activities:** bicycles, hiking trails, jogging. **Guest Services:** gift shop. **Business Services:** meeting rooms. **Cards:** AX, MC, VI. **Special Amenities: free newspaper and free room upgrade (subject to availability with advanced reservations).**

SOME UNITS

WHERE TO DINE

SEA RANCH LODGE RESTAURANT Lunch: $9-$21 Dinner: $18-$29 Phone: 707/785-2371

Regional California

Location: Just w of SR 1; in Sea Ranch Lodge. 60 Sea Walk Dr 95497. **Hours:** 8-10:30 am, 11:30-2 & 5:30-8:30 pm, Sun 8-10 am, 11-2 & 5:30-8:30 pm. **Reservations:** suggested. **Features:** The oceanview restaurant entices diners with a menu of California cuisine prepared with local produce. Casual dress; cocktails. **Parking:** on-site. **Cards:** AX, MC, VI.

SEBASTOPOL pop. 7,774

WHERE TO STAY

FOUNTAIN BLEU ESTATE Phone: (707)823-7755

Bed & Breakfast

All Year 1P: $150-$200 2P: $150-$200 XP: $20 D12

Location: 2 mi n on SR 116, 1.5 mi w on Occidental Rd, 0.5 mi s on Mill Station Rd, then 0.5 mi w. 10017 Cherry Ridge Rd 95472. Fax: 707/823-8855. **Facility:** This B&B offers a quiet country setting with picturesque views of the surrounding foothills. 6 units. 5 one-bedroom standard units. 1 one-bedroom suite with whirlpool. 2 stories, interior corridors. **Parking:** on-site. **Terms:** 10 day cancellation notice-fee imposed, [CP] meal plan available. **Amenities:** irons, hair dryers. **Leisure Activities:** sauna, bicycles, game room. **Business Services:** meeting rooms. **Cards:** AX, MC, VI.

HOLIDAY INN EXPRESS HOTEL & SUITES *Book at aaa.com* Phone: (707)829-6677

Motel

All Year 1P: $89-$179 2P: $89-$179 XP: $5 F18

Location: US 101, exit SR 116 W northbound, 8 mi w; exit SR 12 southbound, 7 mi w to Main St. 1101 Gravenstein Hwy S 95472. Fax: 707/829-2618. **Facility:** 82 units. 81 one-bedroom standard units. 1 one-bedroom suite. 3 stories, interior corridors. **Parking:** on-site. **Terms:** 2 night minimum stay - with Saturday stayover 5/1-10/31, [ECP] meal plan available. **Amenities:** dual phone lines, voice mail, irons, hair dryers. **Pool(s):** heated outdoor. **Leisure Activities:** whirlpool, exercise room. **Guest Services:** coin laundry. **Business Services:** meeting rooms. **Cards:** AX, CB, DC, DS, JC, MC, VI. **Special Amenities: free expanded continental breakfast and free local telephone calls.** *(See color ad p 260 & p 765)*

SOME UNITS

SEBASTOPOL INN *Book at aaa.com* **Phone:** (707)829-2500

Motel

5/1-10/31	1P: $148-$218	2P: $148-$218	XP: $20	F13
11/1-1/31	1P: $138-$208	2P: $138-$208	XP: $20	F13
2/1-4/30	1P: $128-$198	2P: $128-$198	XP: $20	F13

Location: US 101, exit SR 12, 7 mi w. 6751 Sebastopol Ave 95472. Fax: 707/823-1535. **Facility:** Smoke free premises. 31 units. 29 one-bedroom standard units. 2 one-bedroom suites with whirlpools. 2 stories, exterior corridors. **Parking:** on-site. **Terms:** 1-2 night minimum stay - weekends, 3 day cancellation notice-fee imposed. **Amenities:** voice mail, irons, hair dryers. **Pool(s):** heated outdoor. **Leisure Activities:** whirlpool. **Cards:** AX, DC, DS, MC, VI. **Special Amenities: free newspaper and free room upgrade (subject to availability with advanced reservations).**

SOME UNITS

SONOMA pop. 9,128

WHERE TO STAY

BEST WESTERN SONOMA VALLEY INN *Book at aaa.com* **Phone:** 707/938-9200

Motel

5/1-10/31	1P: $139-$314	2P: $139-$314	XP: $10	F
2/1-4/30 & 11/1-1/31	1P: $114-$249	2P: $114-$249	XP: $10	F

Location: 1 blk w of Town Plaza. 550 2nd St W 95476. Fax: 707/938-0935. **Facility:** 70 units. 73 one-bedroom standard units. 7 one-bedroom suites with whirlpools. 2 stories, exterior corridors. **Parking:** on-site. **Terms:** 3 day cancellation notice-fee imposed, [CP] meal plan available, small pets only ($15 extra charge). **Amenities:** CD players, voice mail, irons, hair dryers. **Pool(s):** heated outdoor. **Leisure Activities:** whirlpool, exercise room. **Guest Services:** valet laundry. **Business Services:** conference facilities. **Cards:** AX, CB, DC, DS, JC, MC, VI. **Special Amenities: free continental breakfast and free newspaper.** *(See color ad below)*

SOME UNITS

FEE

THE BRICK HOUSE BUNGALOWS **Phone:** 707/996-8091

Bed & Breakfast

4/1-11/30 [BP]	2P: $230-$280	XP: $25	F10
2/1-3/31 [BP]	2P: $135-$260	XP: $25	F10
12/1-1/31 [BP]	2P: $130-$260	XP: $25	F10

Location: Just n of Sonoma Plaza. 313 First St E 95476. Fax: 707/996-7301. **Facility:** Built in classic California Bungalow style, these accommodations offer private patios as well as a large central courtyard with a fountain. 5 units. 1 one-bedroom suite ($130-$230) with kitchen. 4 cottages. 1 story, exterior corridors. *Bath:* combo or shower only. **Parking:** on-site. **Terms:** 2 night minimum stay, 7 day cancellation notice-fee imposed, package plans - seasonal & midwek. **Amenities:** irons, hair dryers. **Cards:** MC, VI.

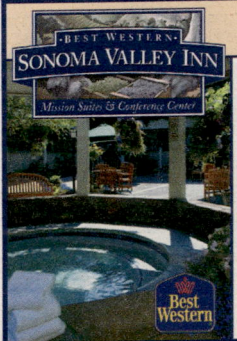

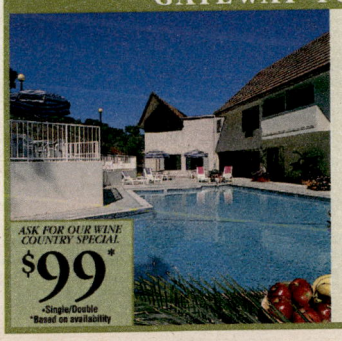

EL PUEBLO INN

Motel

Phone: 707/996-3651

5/1-12/31 [ECP]	1P: $120-$260	2P: $120-$260	XP: $20	F18
3/1-4/30 [ECP]	1P: $110-$230	2P: $110-$230	XP: $20	F18
2/1-2/29 & 1/1-1/31 [ECP]	1P: $90-$160	2P: $90-$160	XP: $20	F18

Location: SR 12, 1 mi w of town plaza. 896 W Napa St 95476. Fax: 707/935-5988. **Facility:** 52 units. 51 one-bedroom standard units. 1 one-bedroom suite. 2 stories, exterior corridors. **Parking:** on-site. **Amenities:** DVD players, voice mail, irons, hair dryers. **Pool(s):** heated outdoor. **Leisure Activities:** whirlpool, exercise room. **Business Services:** meeting rooms. **Cards:** AX, DC, DS, MC, VI.

THE FAIRMONT SONOMA MISSION INN & SPA *Book at aaa.com*

Resort Large-scale Hotel

Phone: (707)938-9000

5/1-10/31	1P: $345-$425	2P: $345-$425	XP: $50	F18
11/1-1/31	1P: $325-$405	2P: $325-$405	XP: $50	F18
2/1-4/30	1P: $310-$390	2P: $310-$390	XP: $50	F18

Location: 2.5 mi n on SR 12. 18140 Sonoma Hwy 95476 (PO Box 1447). Fax: 707/938-4250. **Facility:** A mixture of Mediterranean and Spanish-Californian architecture distinguishes this inn set on spacious, landscaped grounds; a spa is featured. 228 units. 218 one-bedroom standard units. 10 one-bedroom suites ($455-$1200) with whirlpools. 3 stories, interior/exterior corridors. *Bath:* combo or shower only. **Parking:** valet. **Terms:** check-in 4 pm, 14 day cancellation notice, 9% service charge. **Amenities:** high-speed Internet (fee), dual phone lines, voice mail, safes, honor bars, irons, hair dryers. *Some:* CD players. **Dining:** 2 restaurants, 7 am-10 pm, cocktails. **Pool(s):** heated outdoor. **Leisure Activities:** sauna, whirlpools, bicycles, hiking trails, spa. *Fee:* golf-18 holes. **Guest Services:** gift shop, complimentary evening beverages, valet laundry. **Business Services:** conference facilities, business center. **Cards:** AX, MC, VI.

SOME UNITS

FEE

INN AT SONOMA

Bed & Breakfast

Phone: (707)939-1340

6/16-10/31	2P: $155-$250	XP: $20	F5
2/1-6/15 & 11/1-1/31	2P: $135-$195	XP: $20	F5

Location: On SR 12, 0.3 mi s of Sonoma Plaza. 630 Broadway 95476. Fax: 707/939-8834. **Facility:** The inn invites guests to relax on their own private balcony and enjoy the quiet pace and beautiful vistas of the wine country. 19 one-bedroom standard units. 2 stories, interior corridors. **Parking:** on-site. **Terms:** 7 day cancellation notice-fee imposed, package plans - seasonal. **Amenities:** DVD players, voice mail, irons, hair dryers. **Leisure Activities:** whirlpool. **Guest Services:** complimentary evening beverages, valet laundry. **Cards:** AX, DC, MC, VI.

SOME UNITS

THE LODGE AT SONOMA *Book at aaa.com*

Small-scale Hotel

Phone: (707)935-6600

4/1-10/31	1P: $189-$389	2P: $189-$389	XP: $20	F17
11/1-1/31	1P: $189-$339	2P: $189-$339	XP: $20	F17
2/1-3/31	1P: $169-$319	2P: $169-$319	XP: $20	F17

Location: SR 12, 1 mi s of Sonoma Plaza. 1325 Broadway 95476. Fax: 707/935-6829. **Facility:** 182 units. 178 one-bedroom standard units. 4 one-bedroom suites ($450-$650). 2 stories, interior/exterior corridors. **Parking:** on-site. **Terms:** 2 night minimum stay - seasonal & with Saturday stayover, 7 day cancellation notice-fee imposed, package plans. **Amenities:** dual phone lines, voice mail, irons, hair dryers. **Pool(s):** heated outdoor. **Leisure Activities:** sauna, whirlpool, spa. **Guest Services:** gift shop. **Business Services:** conference facilities, business center. **Cards:** AX, CB, DC, DS, JC, MC, VI. Affiliated with Renaissance Hotels & Resorts.

FEE

MACARTHUR PLACE

Country Inn

Phone: (707)938-2929

4/1-11/30 [ECP]	1P: $249-$729	2P: $249-$729	XP: $25	F11
2/1-3/31 & 12/1-1/31 [ECP]	1P: $199-$650	2P: $199-$650	XP: $25	F11

Location: Just e of SR 12 (Broadway). 29 E MacArthur St 95476. Fax: 707/933-9833. **Facility:** The property includes a Victorian manor house built in the 1860s as well as several new-construction cottages designed to replicate its vintage style. 64 units. 60 one-bedroom standard units, some with whirlpools. 4 one-bedroom suites with whirlpools. 2 stories (no elevator), interior/exterior corridors. *Bath:* combo or shower only. **Parking:** on-site. **Terms:** 2 night minimum stay - weekends, 7 day cancellation notice-fee imposed. **Amenities:** DVD players, CD players, dual phone lines, voice mail, irons, hair dryers. **Pool(s):** heated outdoor. **Leisure Activities:** whirlpool, spa. **Guest Services:** complimentary evening beverages. **Business Services:** meeting rooms. **Cards:** AX, DS, MC, VI.

FEE

MAGLIULO'S ROSE GARDEN INN

Historic Bed & Breakfast

Phone: 707/996-1031

Property failed to provide current rates

Location: SR 12, 0.3 mi s of Sonoma Plaza. 681 Broadway 95476. **Facility:** The very romantic Victorian is located two blocks south of the historic Sonoma Plaza and near world famous wineries. 4 one-bedroom standard units. 1 story, interior corridors. *Bath:* some shared or private, combo or shower only. **Parking:** on-site.

SONOMA CREEK INN

Motel

Phone: (707)939-9463

6/16-10/31	2P: $99-$169	XP: $25	F5
2/1-6/15 & 11/1-1/31	2P: $79-$159	XP: $25	F5

Location: SR 12, 0.5 mi w. 239 Boyes Blvd 95476. Fax: 707/938-3042. **Facility:** 16 one-bedroom standard units. 2 stories, exterior corridors. **Parking:** on-site. **Terms:** 7 day cancellation notice-fee imposed, package plans - seasonal. **Amenities:** dual phone lines, irons, hair dryers. **Cards:** AX, DC, MC, VI.

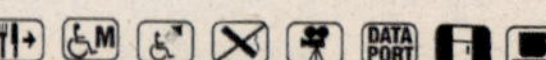

SONOMA HOTEL — **Phone:** 707/996-2996

Historic Small-scale Hotel

5/1-10/31 [CP]	1P: $145-$245	2P: $145-$245	XP: $20	F6
2/1-4/30 & 11/1-1/31 [CP]	1P: $110-$195	2P: $110-$195	XP: $20	F6

Location: Located in the historic Sonoma Plaza. 110 W Spain St 95476. Fax: 707/996-7014. **Facility:** Originally a dry goods store, this hotel built in 1880 includes a second floor that once served as the community social hall. Designated smoking area. 16 one-bedroom standard units. 3 stories (no elevator), interior corridors. *Bath:* combo or shower only. **Parking:** street. **Terms:** 2 night minimum stay - weekends 5/1-10/31, 3 day cancellation notice-fee imposed. **Guest Services:** complimentary evening beverages. **Cards:** AX, DC, DS, MC, VI.

ASK DATA PORT

TROJAN HORSE INN — **Phone:** (707)996-2430

Bed & Breakfast

4/1-11/30 [BP]	1P: $160-$185	2P: $160-$185	XP: $30	F12
2/1-3/31 & 12/1-1/31 [BP]	1P: $135-$155	2P: $135-$155	XP: $30	F12

Location: 1 mi w of Sonoma Plaza. 19455 Sonoma Hwy 95476. Fax: 707/996-9185. **Facility:** The inn offers well-appointed guest units and attractively landscaped grounds. 6 one-bedroom standard units, some with whirlpools. 2 stories, interior corridors. *Bath:* combo or shower only. **Parking:** on-site. **Terms:** 2 night minimum stay - weekends, 7 day cancellation notice-fee imposed. **Leisure Activities:** whirlpool. **Cards:** AX, DS, MC, VI.

ASK

WHERE TO DINE

THE GENERAL'S DAUGHTER — **Lunch:** $9-$17 — **Dinner:** $16-$30 — **Phone:** 707/938-4004

AAA — Continental

Location: 4 blks w of Sonoma Plaza. 400 W Spain St 95476. **Hours:** 11:30 am-2:30 & 5:30-9:30 pm, Sun-8:30 pm. Closed: 1/1, 12/25; also Mon. **Reservations:** suggested. **Features:** The renovated Victorian home was built in 1864 for Natalia, the third daughter of pioneer California statesman Gen. M.G. Vallejo. Dressy casual; cocktails. **Parking:** on-site. **Cards:** AX, DS, MC, VI.

LA CASA RESTAURANT & BAR — **Lunch:** $8-$16 — **Dinner:** $8-$17 — **Phone:** 707/996-3406

Mexican

Location: Opposite San Francisco Solano Mission. 121 E Spain St 95476. **Hours:** 11:30 am-10 pm, Sat-noon. Closed: 11/25, 12/25. **Reservations:** suggested. **Features:** Traditional specialties. Casual dress; cocktails. **Parking:** street. **Cards:** AX, CB, DC, MC, VI.

UKIAH pop. 15,497

WHERE TO STAY

BEST WESTERN ORCHARD INN — *Book at aaa.com* — **Phone:** (707)462-1514

AAA SAVE — Small-scale Hotel

5/1-9/30	1P: $79-$99	2P: $79-$99	XP: $5	F12
2/1-4/30 & 10/1-1/31	1P: $69-$89	2P: $69-$89	XP: $5	F12

Location: US 101, exit Gobbi St, 0.5 mi w. 555 S Orchard Ave 95482. Fax: 707/462-1237. **Facility:** 54 one-bedroom standard units. 2 stories (no elevator), interior corridors. *Bath:* combo or shower only. **Parking:** on-site. **Terms:** age restrictions may apply, cancellation fee imposed, [ECP] meal plan available. **Amenities:** dual phone lines, voice mail, irons, hair dryers. **Pool(s):** small outdoor. **Leisure Activities:** whirlpool, limited exercise equipment. **Guest Services:** coin laundry. **Business Services:** meeting rooms. **Cards:** AX, DC, DS, MC, VI. **Special Amenities: free expanded continental breakfast and preferred room (subject to availability with advanced reservations).**

SOME UNITS

DATA PORT

DAYS INN — *Book at aaa.com* — **Phone:** (707)462-7584

AAA SAVE — Motel

5/1-9/30	1P: $69-$110	2P: $79-$129	XP: $10	F12
10/1-1/31	1P: $59-$99	2P: $69-$110	XP: $10	F12
2/1-4/30	1P: $50-$70	2P: $60-$80	XP: $10	F12

Location: US 101, exit N State St, 0.5 mi s. Located in Old Town. 950 N State St 95482. Fax: 707/463-1218. **Facility:** 54 units. 53 one-bedroom standard units. 1 two-bedroom suite ($110-$169). 2 stories, exterior corridors. **Parking:** on-site. **Terms:** age restrictions may apply, 7 day cancellation notice-fee imposed, [CP] meal plan available, small pets only ($10 extra charge). **Amenities:** hair dryers. *Some:* irons. **Pool(s):** outdoor. **Cards:** AX, DS, MC, VI. **Special Amenities: free continental breakfast and free local telephone calls.**

SOME UNITS

FEE DATA PORT

DISCOVERY INN — *Book at aaa.com* — **Phone:** (707)462-8873

AAA SAVE — Motel

5/1-9/30 [ECP]	1P: $69-$87	2P: $74-$92	XP: $6	F12
2/1-4/30 & 10/1-1/31 [ECP]	1P: $65-$82	2P: $69-$87	XP: $6	F12

Location: 1.5 mi n on US 101 business route; US 101, exit N State St. 1340 N State St 95482. Fax: 707/462-1249. **Facility:** 175 one-bedroom standard units, some with kitchens. 2 stories, exterior corridors. *Bath:* combo or shower only. **Parking:** on-site. **Terms:** age restrictions may apply, 3 day cancellation notice. **Amenities:** voice mail, irons, hair dryers. **Pool(s):** heated outdoor. **Leisure Activities:** whirlpools, exercise room. **Guest Services:** coin laundry. **Cards:** AX, CB, DC, DS, MC, VI. *(See color ad p 810)*

SOME UNITS

DATA PORT

ECONOMY INN — **Phone:** (707)462-8611

AAA SAVE — Motel

5/1-9/30	1P: $49-$59	2P: $59-$69	XP: $5	F12
2/1-4/30 & 10/1-1/31	1P: $39-$49	2P: $49-$59	XP: $5	F12

Location: Just 2 blks s on US 101 business route; US 101 W, exit Perkins off-ramp northbound; exit Central off-ramp southbound. 406 S State St 95482. Fax: 707/468-9476. **Facility:** 40 one-bedroom standard units. 2 stories, exterior corridors. *Bath:* combo or shower only. **Parking:** on-site. **Terms:** age restrictions may apply. **Amenities:** *Some:* irons, hair dryers. **Pool(s):** outdoor. **Cards:** AX, CB, DC, DS, MC, VI. **Special Amenities: free local telephone calls and free room upgrade (subject to availability with advanced reservations).**

SOME UNITS

HAMPTON INN UKIAH *Book at aaa.com*

Small-scale Hotel

Phone: (707)462-6555

6/1-9/15	1P: $99-$179	2P: $109-$199		
9/16-11/20	1P: $89-$159	2P: $99-$199		
2/1-5/31	1P: $89-$159	2P: $99-$199	XP: $10	F16
11/21-1/31	1P: $89-$119	2P: $89-$119		

Location: US 101, exit Talmage Rd W. 1160 Airport Park Blvd 95482. Fax: 707/463-2382. **Facility:** Smoke free premises. 76 one-bedroom standard units, some with whirlpools. 3 stories, interior corridors. *Bath:* combo or shower only. **Parking:** on-site. **Terms:** age restrictions may apply, [ECP] meal plan available, pets ($250 deposit). **Amenities:** video games, high-speed Internet, dual phone lines, voice mail, irons, hair dryers. *Some:* DVD players (fee), safes. **Pool(s):** heated outdoor. **Leisure Activities:** whirlpool, limited exercise equipment. *Fee:* massage. **Guest Services:** complimentary evening beverages, coin laundry. **Business Services:** meeting rooms, business center. **Cards:** AX, CB, DC, DS, MC, VI.

FEE SOME UNITS FEE

HOLIDAY INN EXPRESS *Book at aaa.com*

Motel

Phone: (707)462-5745

All Year [ECP]	1P: $59-$149	2P: $59-$149	XP: $10	F18

Location: US 101, exit N State St. 1720 N State St 95482. Fax: 707/462-8804. **Facility:** 55 one-bedroom standard units, some with efficiencies (no utensils) and/or whirlpools. 2 stories, exterior corridors. *Bath:* combo or shower only. **Parking:** on-site. **Terms:** age restrictions may apply, cancellation fee imposed. **Amenities:** high-speed Internet, dual phone lines, voice mail, irons, hair dryers. *Some:* safes. **Pool(s):** outdoor. **Leisure Activities:** whirlpool. **Guest Services:** coin laundry. **Business Services:** meeting rooms, business center. **Cards:** AX, CB, DC, DS, JC, MC, VI. **Special Amenities: free continental breakfast and free local telephone calls.**

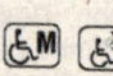

SOME UNITS

RAMADA LIMITED *Book at aaa.com*

Motel

Phone: (707)462-8868

5/1-9/30 [ECP]	1P: $59-$79	2P: $69-$89	XP: $5	F12
2/1-4/30 & 10/1-1/31 [ECP]	1P: $49-$69	2P: $59-$79	XP: $5	F12

Location: E off US 101 Bypass, exit Talmage Rd off-ramp. 601 Talmage Rd 95482. Fax: 707/468-9043. **Facility:** 39 one-bedroom standard units. 2 stories, exterior corridors. **Parking:** on-site. **Terms:** age restrictions may apply. **Amenities:** dual phone lines, voice mail, irons, hair dryers. **Pool(s):** outdoor. **Leisure Activities:** whirlpool. **Cards:** AX, CB, DC, DS, MC, VI. **Special Amenities: free expanded continental breakfast and free local telephone calls.**

SOME UNITS

RODEWAY INN *Book at aaa.com*

Motel

Phone: (707)462-2906

6/1-9/30 [ECP]	1P: $60-$75	2P: $69-$89	XP: $7	F17
2/1-5/31 [ECP]	1P: $55-$70	2P: $59-$79	XP: $7	F17
10/1-1/31 [ECP]	1P: $55-$70	2P: $59-$70	XP: $7	F17

Location: US 101, exit Talmage Rd off-ramp, 0.5 mi w. 1050 S State St 95482. Fax: 707/462-3040. **Facility:** 43 units. 41 one- and 2 two-bedroom standard units, some with whirlpools. 2 stories (no elevator), exterior corridors. *Bath:* combo or shower only. **Parking:** on-site. **Terms:** age restrictions may apply, package plans. **Amenities:** hair dryers. *Some:* irons. **Pool(s):** outdoor. **Cards:** AX, DC, DS, MC, VI. **Special Amenities: free local telephone calls and early check-in/late check-out.**

SOME UNITS

SUNRISE INN — Book at aaa.com — **Phone:** (707)462-6601

AAA SAVE — Motel

5/1-9/30	1P: $48-$65	2P: $55-$85	XP: $5	F12
2/1-4/30 & 10/1-1/31	1P: $42-$52	2P: $45-$65	XP: $5	F12

Location: US 101, exit Gobbi St, 0.5 mi w to S State St, just n. 650 S State St 95482. Fax: 707/462-6009. **Facility:** 24 one-bedroom standard units. 1 story, exterior corridors. *Bath:* combo or shower only. **Parking:** on-site. **Terms:** age restrictions may apply. **Amenities:** *Some:* irons, hair dryers. **Cards:** AX, DC, DS, MC, VI.

SOME UNITS

SUPER 8 MOTEL — Book at aaa.com — **Phone:** (707)462-6657

AAA SAVE — Motel

6/1-9/30 [CP]	1P: $69-$89	2P: $89-$125	XP: $6	F12
10/1-1/31 [CP]	1P: $49-$69	2P: $69-$89	XP: $6	F12
3/1-5/31 [CP]	1P: $49-$59	2P: $69-$89	XP: $6	F12
2/1-2/29 [CP]	1P: $39-$59	2P: $59-$69	XP: $6	F12

Location: US 101, exit Talmage Rd, 1 mi w. 1070 S State St 95482. Fax: 707/468-8665. **Facility:** 30 one-bedroom standard units. 2 stories (no elevator), exterior corridors. **Parking:** on-site. **Terms:** age restrictions may apply, pets ($10 deposit, $5 extra charge). **Amenities:** *Some:* irons, hair dryers. **Pool(s):** outdoor. **Cards:** AX, DC, MC, VI. **Special Amenities: free continental breakfast and free local telephone calls.**

SOME UNITS

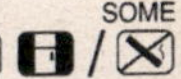

FEE

VICHY HOT SPRINGS RESORT AND INN — **Phone:** (707)462-9515

Historic Bed & Breakfast

All Year [ECP]	1P: $115-$265	2P: $150-$265	XP: $40

Location: US 101, exit E Perkins St/Vichy Springs Rd, 3 mi e. 2605 Vichy Springs Rd 95482. Fax: 707/462-9516. **Facility:** The oldest building on this resort's grounds dates from 1854 and houses a few of the smaller guest rooms. 26 units. 18 one-bedroom standard units. 8 cottages ($265). 1 story, exterior corridors. *Bath:* combo or shower only. **Parking:** on-site. **Terms:** office hours 8:30 am-8 pm, 2 night minimum stay - weekends in summer, age restrictions may apply, 7 day cancellation notice-fee imposed. **Pool(s):** outdoor. **Leisure Activities:** whirlpool, hiking trails. *Fee:* massage. **Cards:** AX, CB, DC, DS, JC, MC, VI.

WESTERN TRAVELER MOTEL — **Phone:** (707)468-9167

AAA SAVE — Motel

5/16-10/31 [ECP]	1P: $59-$79	2P: $59-$79	XP: $10	F12
2/1-5/15 & 11/1-1/31 [ECP]	1P: $49-$69	2P: $49-$69	XP: $10	F12

Location: US 101, exit Gobbi St W. Located in a commercial area. 693 S Orchard Ave 95482. Fax: 707/468-8268. **Facility:** 56 units. 54 one- and 2 two-bedroom standard units. 2 stories, exterior corridors. **Parking:** on-site. **Terms:** age restrictions may apply, small pets only ($5 extra charge). **Amenities:** video library. *Some:* irons, hair dryers. **Pool(s):** outdoor. **Leisure Activities:** whirlpool. **Cards:** AX, DC, DS, MC, VI. **Special Amenities: free continental breakfast and free local telephone calls.** *(See color ad below)*

SOME UNITS

DATA PORT — VCR

FEE

WHERE TO DINE

ANGELO'S — **Lunch:** $6-$11 — **Dinner:** $10-$20 — **Phone:** 707/462-0448

Italian

Location: I-101, exit N Ukiah, s to N State St; corner of N State and Lowgap sts. 920 N State St 95482. **Hours:** 11 am-2 & 5-9:30 pm, Sat from 5 pm, Sun 5 pm-9 pm. Closed: 4/11, 11/25, 12/25. **Reservations:** suggested. **Features:** The family-style restaurant, with a patio for outdoor dining weather permitting, serves cusine that is Northern Italy, with a touch of California. Casual dress; cocktails. **Parking:** on-site. **Cards:** AX, CB, DC, DS, JC, MC, VI.

UPPER LAKE pop. 989

— WHERE TO STAY —

SUPER 8 MOTEL — AAA SAVE — Motel — **Phone:** 707/275-0888

4/1-9/30 [CP]	1P: $60-$80	2P: $70-$90	XP: $10	F12
2/1-3/31 & 10/1-1/31 [CP]	1P: $55-$75	2P: $65-$85	XP: $10	F12

Location: SR 29, 0.5 mi e. 450 E Hwy 20 95485 (PO Box 67). Fax: 707/275-2566. **Facility:** 34 one-bedroom standard units, some with efficiencies (no utensils) and/or whirlpools. 2 stories (no elevator), exterior corridors. **Parking:** on-site. **Terms:** age restrictions may apply. **Amenities:** hair dryers. *Some:* irons. **Pool(s):** small outdoor. **Leisure Activities:** whirlpool. **Guest Services:** coin laundry. **Cards:** AX, DC, DS, MC, VI. **Special Amenities: free continental breakfast and free local telephone calls.**

SOME UNITS

WESTPORT

— WHERE TO STAY —

DE HAVEN VALLEY FARM — AAA SAVE — Bed & Breakfast — **Phone:** 707/961-1660

All Year [MAP]	2P: $89-$144	XP: $25	F6

Location: SR 1, 18 mi n of jct SR 20, just n of Branscomb Rd. 39247 N Hwy 1 95488. Fax: 707/961-1677. **Facility:** A stream, meadow and woods beautify the 20 acres of rolling hills surrounding this 1875 Victorian farmhouse. 9 units. 6 one-bedroom standard units. 3 cottages ($134-$144). 2 stories (no elevator), interior/exterior corridors. *Bath:* shared or private, combo or shower only. **Parking:** on-site. **Terms:** 2 night minimum stay - seasonal & weekends, age restrictions may apply, cancellation fee imposed, pets (in selected units). **Leisure Activities:** whirlpool. **Guest Services:** complimentary evening beverages. **Cards:** AX, DS, MC, VI. **Special Amenities: free full breakfast and free local telephone calls.**

SOME UNITS

WILLITS pop. 5,000

— WHERE TO STAY —

BAECHTEL CREEK INN & SPA — *Book at aaa.com* — Motel — **Phone:** (707)459-9063

5/1-9/30 [ECP]	1P: $69-$150	2P: $69-$150	XP: $5	F12
2/1-4/30 [ECP]	1P: $59-$140	2P: $69-$150	XP: $5	F12
10/1-1/31 [ECP]	1P: $59-$140	2P: $69-$140	XP: $5	F12

Location: US 101, just w. 101 Gregory Ln 95490. Fax: 707/459-0226. **Facility:** 43 one-bedroom standard units. 2 stories (no elevator), exterior corridors. **Parking:** on-site. **Terms:** age restrictions may apply, cancellation fee imposed, package plans, small pets only ($10 extra charge, in limited units). **Amenities:** voice mail, hair dryers. *Some:* irons. **Pool(s):** heated outdoor. **Leisure Activities:** whirlpool, spa. **Business Services:** meeting rooms. **Cards:** AX, DC, DS, MC, VI.
(See color ad below)

FEE
SOME UNITS

BEST WESTERN WILLITS INN Book at aaa.com **Phone:** 707/459-5800

AAA SAVE — Motel

5/1-9/30 [ECP]	1P: $69-$79	2P: $69-$89	XP: $5	F
2/1-4/30 & 10/1-1/31 [ECP]	1P: $59-$69	2P: $69-$79	XP: $5	F

Location: US 101, 1.3 mi s of jct SR 20. 1777 S Main St 95490. Fax: 707/459-9367. **Facility:** 44 one-bedroom standard units. 2 stories (no elevator), exterior corridors. **Parking:** on-site. **Terms:** age restrictions may apply. **Amenities:** irons, hair dryers. **Pool(s):** heated outdoor. **Leisure Activities:** whirlpool. **Guest Services:** coin laundry. **Cards:** AX, CB, DC, DS, MC, VI. **Special Amenities: free expanded continental breakfast and free room upgrade (subject to availability with advanced reservations).**

SOME UNITS

CREEKSIDE INN SUPER 8 Book at aaa.com **Phone:** 707/459-3388

AAA SAVE — Motel

5/1-9/30 [ECP]	1P: $59-$79	2P: $69-$99	XP: $6	F5
10/1-12/31 [ECP]	1P: $55-$75	2P: $65-$81	XP: $6	F5
2/1-4/30 & 1/1-1/31 [ECP]	1P: $49-$59	2P: $59-$69	XP: $6	F5

Location: SR 20, just n. 1119 S Main St 95490. Fax: 707/459-1478. **Facility:** 44 one-bedroom standard units, some with kitchens and/or whirlpools. 2 stories (no elevator), exterior corridors. **Parking:** on-site. **Terms:** age restrictions may apply. **Amenities:** voice mail. *Some:* irons, hair dryers. **Pool(s):** outdoor. **Leisure Activities:** whirlpool, spa. **Guest Services:** coin laundry. **Business Services:** meeting rooms. **Cards:** AX, CB, DC, DS, JC, MC, VI. **Special Amenities: free expanded continental breakfast and free local telephone calls.**

SOME UNITS

HOLIDAY LODGE MOTEL **Phone:** (707)459-5361

AAA SAVE — Motel

5/15-10/15	1P: $49-$99	2P: $59-$140	XP: $6	F6
2/1-5/14 & 10/16-1/31	1P: $39-$59	2P: $59-$89	XP: $6	F6

Location: US 101, 1 mi s of jct SR 20. 1540 S Main St 95490. Fax: 707/459-2334. **Facility:** 16 one-bedroom standard units. 1 story, exterior corridors. *Bath:* combo or shower only. **Parking:** on-site. **Terms:** age restrictions may apply, cancellation fee imposed. **Amenities:** *Some:* irons, hair dryers. **Pool(s):** outdoor. **Cards:** AX, DS, MC, VI. **Special Amenities: free continental breakfast and free local telephone calls.**

SOME UNITS

OLD WEST INN **Phone:** (707)459-4201

AAA SAVE — Motel

All Year [CP]	1P: $45-$150	2P: $45-$150	XP: $10	D12

Location: US 101, 0.5 mi s of jct SR 20. 1221 S Main St 95490. Fax: 707/459-3009. **Facility:** 18 one-bedroom standard units. 2 stories (no elevator), exterior corridors. **Parking:** on-site. **Terms:** age restrictions may apply, 3 day cancellation notice. **Amenities:** *Some:* irons, hair dryers. **Pool(s):** outdoor. **Business Services:** fax. **Cards:** AX, DC, DS, MC, VI. **Special Amenities: free continental breakfast and free local telephone calls.**

SOME UNITS

YOUNTVILLE pop. 2,916

WHERE TO STAY

LAVENDER **Phone:** (707)944-1388

Bed & Breakfast

4/1-10/31	2P: $200-$250	XP: $20	F5
2/1-3/31 & 11/1-1/31	2P: $150-$200	XP: $20	F5

Location: SR 29, exit Yountville. 2020 Webber Ave 94599. Fax: 707/944-1579. **Facility:** In a quiet residential area, this property is walking distance from downtown; most rooms have private patios or balconies. 8 units. 7 one-bedroom standard units. 1 one-bedroom suite. 1 story, exterior corridors. **Parking:** on-site. **Terms:** 7 day cancellation notice-fee imposed, package plans - seasonal. **Amenities:** irons, hair dryers. **Guest Services:** complimentary evening beverages. **Cards:** AX, DC, MC, VI.

MAISON FLEURIE **Phone:** (707)944-2056

Bed & Breakfast

4/1-11/30	2P: $135-$235	XP: $20	F5
2/1-3/31 & 12/1-1/31	2P: $125-$200	XP: $20	F5

Location: SR 29, exit Yountville; center. 6529 Yount St 94599. Fax: 707/944-9342. **Facility:** 13 one-bedroom standard units, some with whirlpools. 2 stories (no elevator), interior/exterior corridors. *Bath:* combo or shower only. **Parking:** on-site. **Terms:** 7 day cancellation notice-fee imposed, package plans - seasonal. **Amenities:** irons, hair dryers. **Pool(s):** heated outdoor. **Leisure Activities:** whirlpool. **Guest Services:** complimentary evening beverages. **Cards:** AX, DC, MC, VI.

SOME UNITS

NAPA VALLEY LODGE Book at aaa.com **Phone:** (707)944-2468

AAA SAVE — Small-scale Hotel

6/1-11/30 [ECP]	1P: $302-$382	2P: $302-$382	XP: $25	F3
3/1-5/31 [ECP]	1P: $272-$352	2P: $272-$352	XP: $25	F3
2/1-2/29 & 12/1-1/31 [ECP]	1P: $212-$292	2P: $212-$292	XP: $25	F3

Location: SR 29, exit Madison St, 0.5 mi n. 2230 Madison St 94599. Fax: 707/944-9362. **Facility:** Fireplaces are featured in many of the lodge's guest rooms, some of which overlook vineyards and surrounding hills. 55 units. 54 one-bedroom standard units, some with whirlpools. 1 one-bedroom suite ($395-$495) with whirlpool. 2 stories, exterior corridors. **Parking:** on-site. **Terms:** 2 night minimum stay - weekends, 7 day cancellation notice-fee imposed. **Amenities:** CD players, honor bars, irons, hair dryers. **Pool(s):** heated outdoor. **Leisure Activities:** sauna, whirlpool, exercise room. **Guest Services:** complimentary evening beverages, valet laundry. **Business Services:** meeting rooms. **Cards:** AX, DC, DS, MC, VI. **Special Amenities: free newspaper.** *(See color ad inside back cover & p 793)*

VILLAGIO INN & SPA

Phone: (707)944-8877

8/1-11/28 [BP]	1P: $310-$430	2P: $310-$430	XP: $25	F12
4/1-7/31 [BP]	1P: $250-$390	2P: $250-$390	XP: $25	F12
2/1-3/31 & 11/29-1/31 [BP]	1P: $215-$330	2P: $215-$330	XP: $25	F12

Small-scale Hotel

Location: SR 29, exit Yountville. 6481 Washington St 94599. Fax: 707/944-8855. **Facility:** Extensive spa facilities and a spacious pool area are featured; many guest rooms have fireplaces and private balconies or patios. 112 units. 88 one-bedroom standard units. 24 one-bedroom suites ($325-$545) with whirlpools. 2 stories, exterior corridors. **Parking:** on-site. **Terms:** check-in 4 pm, 2 night minimum stay - weekends, 7 day cancellation notice. **Amenities:** dual phone lines, voice mail, irons, hair dryers. **Pool(s):** heated outdoor. **Leisure Activities:** sauna, whirlpool, 2 tennis courts, spa. **Guest Services:** gift shop, valet laundry. **Business Services:** conference facilities, business center. **Cards:** AX, DC, DS, MC, VI. **Special Amenities: free continental breakfast and free newspaper.**

FEE

VINTAGE INN *Book at aaa.com*

Phone: (707)944-1112

8/1-11/28 [ECP]	1P: $310-$430	2P: $310-$430	XP: $25	F12
4/1-7/31 [ECP]	1P: $250-$350	2P: $250-$350	XP: $25	F12
2/1-3/31 & 11/29-1/31 [ECP]	1P: $215-$330	2P: $215-$330	XP: $25	F12

Small-scale Hotel

Location: SR 29, exit Yountville; center. 6541 Washington St 94599. Fax: 707/944-1617. **Facility:** Picturesque vineyard, mountain and town views can be seen from the inn's many balconies and patios; all rooms have fireplaces and whirlpool tubs. 80 one-bedroom standard units with whirlpools. 2 stories, exterior corridors. **Parking:** on-site. **Terms:** check-in 4 pm, 2 night minimum stay - weekends, 7 day cancellation notice-fee imposed, small pets only ($35 fee). **Amenities:** voice mail, irons, hair dryers. **Pool(s):** heated outdoor. **Leisure Activities:** whirlpool, 2 tennis courts, rental bicycles. **Guest Services:** valet laundry. **Business Services:** meeting rooms. **Cards:** AX, CB, DC, DS, MC, VI. **Special Amenities: free continental breakfast and free newspaper.**

FEE

WHERE TO DINE

DOMAINE CHANDON — **Lunch:** $40-$55 — **Dinner:** $65-$80 — **Phone:** 707/944-2892

French

Location: W off SR 29; adjacent to Veteran's Home. 1 California Dr 94599. **Hours:** 11:30 am-2:30 & 6-9:30 pm. Closed: 1/1, 12/25; also for dinner Mon & Tues; first 3 weeks in Jan. **Reservations:** required; 14-day advance. **Features:** The upscale restaurant's lunch menu focuses on California cuisine, while dinner offerings are more French in scope. Semi-formal attire; wine only. **Parking:** on-site. **Cards:** AX, DC, MC, VI.

NAPA VALLEY GRILLE — **Lunch:** $8-$18 — **Dinner:** $12-$24 — **Phone:** 707/944-8686

American

Location: SR 29, exit Madison St; in Washington Square. 6795 Washington St 94599. **Hours:** 11:30 am-9:30 pm, Sat-10 pm, Sun 11 am-9:30 pm. Closed: 12/25. **Reservations:** suggested. **Features:** Fresh grilled meats and fish are prepared in the contemporary California style. Dressy casual; cocktails. **Parking:** on-site. **Cards:** AX, DC, DS, MC, VI.

PIATTI RISTORANTE — **Lunch:** $8-$15 — **Dinner:** $13-$22 — **Phone:** 707/944-2070

Italian

Location: SR 29, exit E Yountville-Veterans Home, 1 blk n. 6480 Washington St 94599. **Hours:** 11:30 am-9 pm. Closed: 11/25, 12/25. **Reservations:** suggested. **Features:** Few tables with view of vineyard. Dressy casual; cocktails. **Parking:** on-site. **Cards:** AX, MC, VI.

The following restaurant has not been evaluated by AAA but is listed for your information only.

THE FRENCH LAUNDRY — **Phone:** 707/944-2380

fyi

Not evaluated. **Location:** SR 29, exit Madison St, then right. 6640 Washington St 94599. **Features:** Built in the 1890s as a French steam laundry, the rustic two-story stone house is surrounded by lush country gardens. Reservations only taken 60 days in advance.

This ends listings for the Wine Country.
The following page resumes the alphabetical listings of cities in Northern California.

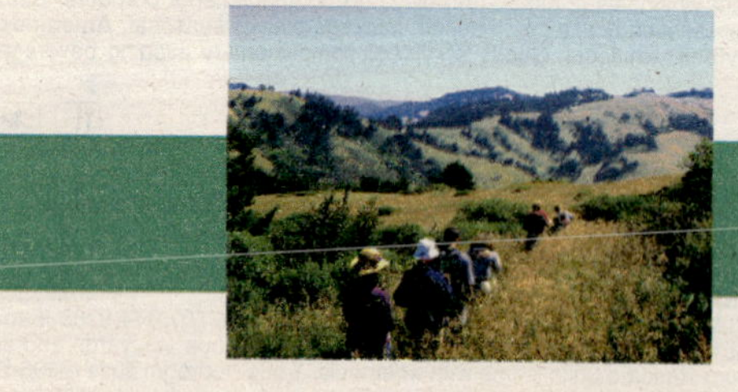

WOODLAND pop. 49,151

WHERE TO STAY

BEST WESTERN SHADOW INN *Book at aaa.com* **Phone:** (530)666-1251

Motel

All Year [CP] 1P: $84-$98 2P: $84-$98 XP: $4 F12

Location: I-5, exit Yuba City/Davis (SR 113 N), 0.3 mi w. 584 N East St 95776. Fax: 530/662-2804. **Facility:** 118 one-bedroom standard units. 2 stories, exterior corridors. **Parking:** on-site. **Terms:** cancellation fee imposed. **Amenities:** voice mail, irons, hair dryers. **Pool(s):** heated outdoor. **Leisure Activities:** whirlpools. **Guest Services:** valet and coin laundry. **Business Services:** meeting rooms. **Cards:** AX, DC, DS, MC, VI.

SOME UNITS

CINDERELLA MOTEL **Phone:** (530)662-1091

SAVE Motel

All Year 1P: $48-$58 2P: $68 XP: $10

Location: 0.8 mi w on I-5 business loop; I-5, exit Main St northbound, 2 mi w; exit West St southbound, 1.5 mi s to Main St, just w. 99 W Main St 95695. Fax: 530/668-0332. **Facility:** 30 one-bedroom standard units, some with whirlpools. 2 stories, exterior corridors. *Bath:* combo or shower only. **Parking:** on-site. **Terms:** cancellation fee imposed. **Amenities:** hair dryers. **Pool(s):** outdoor. **Leisure Activities:** whirlpool. **Cards:** AX, CB, DC, DS, JC, MC, VI. **Special Amenities: free continental breakfast.**

SOME UNITS

COMFORT INN *Book at aaa.com* **Phone:** 530/666-3050

SAVE Motel

All Year 1P: $64-$94 2P: $69-$99 XP: $6 F17

Location: I-5, exit Main St (Woodland) northbound; exit SR 113 (Davis) southbound. 1562 E Main St 95776. Fax: 530/666-1119. **Facility:** 51 units. 48 one-bedroom standard units. 3 one-bedroom suites ($99-$160) with whirlpools. 2 stories, exterior corridors. **Parking:** on-site. **Terms:** [ECP] meal plan available. **Amenities:** voice mail, irons, hair dryers. **Pool(s):** outdoor. **Leisure Activities:** whirlpool. **Guest Services:** coin laundry. **Cards:** AX, DC, DS, MC, VI. **Special Amenities: free continental breakfast and free local telephone calls.** *(See color ad below)*

SOME UNITS

DAYS INN *Book at aaa.com*

Motel

Phone: 530/666-3800

All Year 1P: $59-$89 2P: $65-$95 XP: $6 F17

Location: I-5, exit Main St (Woodland) northbound; exit SR 113 (Davis) southbound. 1524 E Main St 95776. Fax: 530/666-2281. **Facility:** 51 one-bedroom standard units. 3 stories (no elevator), interior corridors. *Bath:* combo or shower only. **Parking:** on-site. **Terms:** [CP] meal plan available, small pets only ($10 fee). **Amenities:** voice mail, irons, hair dryers. **Pool(s):** outdoor. **Guest Services:** coin laundry. **Business Services:** meeting rooms. **Cards:** AX, DC, DS, MC, VI. **Special Amenities: free continental breakfast and free local telephone calls.**

SOME UNITS

FEE

VALLEY OAKS INN

Motel

Phone: (530)666-5511

All Year [ECP] 1P: $45-$55 2P: $45-$60

Location: I-5, exit Yuba City. 600 N East St 95776. Fax: 530/666-5511. **Facility:** 62 one-bedroom standard units. 2 stories, exterior corridors. **Parking:** on-site. **Pool(s):** outdoor. **Leisure Activities:** whirlpool. **Guest Services:** coin laundry. **Cards:** AX, MC, VI.

SOME UNITS

The following lodging was either not evaluated or did not meet AAA rating requirements but is listed for your information only.

HOLIDAY INN EXPRESS HOTEL & SUITES

fyi

Phone: 530/662-7750

Property failed to provide current rates

Too new to rate. **Location:** I-5, exit CR 102. 2070 Freeway Dr 95726. Fax: 530/666-9970. **Amenities:** 69 units, coffeemakers, microwaves, refrigerators, pool. ***(See color ad p 815)***

WOODSIDE pop. 5,352 (See map and index starting on p. 599)

WHERE TO DINE

BELLA VISTA RESTAURANT

Continental

Dinner: $25-$55 **Phone:** 650/851-1229 230

Location: On SR 35, between SR 92 and 84; n of SR 84. 13451 Skyline Blvd 94062. **Hours:** 5 pm-10 pm. Closed: 1/1, 12/24, 12/25; also Sun. **Reservations:** suggested. **Features:** In the redwoods. Some tables with a view. Dressy casual; cocktails. **Parking:** on-site. **Cards:** AX, DC, DS, MC, VI.

YOSEMITE NATIONAL PARK—*See also AHWAHNEE, BASS LAKE, EL PORTAL, FISH CAMP, GROVELAND, MARIPOSA & OAKHURST.*

Reservations should be made well in advance for all types of accommodations: write Yosemite Concession Services, Inc., Yosemite National Park, CA 95389, or phone (559)252-4848; also The Redwoods, PO Box 2085, Wawona, CA 95389 or phone (209)375-6666. Rates may be revised or adjusted in fall & spring with NPS approval.

WHERE TO STAY

THE AHWAHNEE *Book at aaa.com* **Phone:** (209)372-1407

AAA SAVE

Historic Large-scale Hotel

4/5-1/31	1P: $371-$1189	2P: $371-$1189	XP: $21	F11
2/1-4/4	1P: $357-$1141	2P: $357-$1141	XP: $21	F11

Location: 0.8 mi e; beyond park headquarters. In Yosemite Valley 95389. Fax: 559/456-0542. **Facility:** Spacious, shaded grounds offer scenic views of the park; though some guest rooms are compact, the property features impressive common areas. For reservations call 559-252-4848. 123 units. 119 one-bedroom standard units, some with whirlpools. 4 one-bedroom suites ($784-$1141). 1-7 stories, interior/exterior corridors. *Bath:* combo or shower only. **Parking:** on-site and valet. **Terms:** check-in 5 pm, 3 day cancellation notice, [AP] meal plan available, package plans - seasonal. **Amenities:** voice mail, irons, hair dryers. *Some:* CD players. **Dining:** 7 am-9 pm, cocktails, dining room, see separate listing. **Pool(s):** heated outdoor. **Leisure Activities:** fishing, 2 tennis courts, hiking trails. *Fee:* downhill & cross country skiing, ice skating, bicycles, horseback riding. **Guest Services:** gift shop, coin laundry, area transportation. **Business Services:** meeting rooms, fax. **Cards:** AX, DC, DS, JC, MC, VI.

SOME UNITS

AAA members receive up to 25% off published room rates*
Tenaya Lodge
AT YOSEMITE
Escape to Tenaya Lodge and discover a mountain of High Sierra adventure. Experience mountain hospitality in a comfortable, Four-Diamond rated family resort nestled adjacent to Yosemite National Park. The lodge features 244 Guestrooms, 3 Restaurants, Spa Facilities, Indoor and Outdoor Pools, Children's Programs and activities for the entire family!
Tenaya Lodge enhances the experience with discounts for AAA members and two full buffet breakfasts.
AAA Four Diamond Award
Delaware North Companies
PARKS & RESORTS
TENAYA LODGE
AT YOSEMITE
800-332-3135
tenayalodge.com
*Rates are subject to availability. Blackout dates may apply.
All rights reserved. ©2004 Tenaya Lodge at Yosemite, Inc.
See our listing under Fish Camp

THE REDWOODS IN YOSEMITE Book at aaa.com Phone: (209)375-6666

Vacation Home

All Year 1P: $135-$672 2P: $135-$672 XP: $25 F4

Location: 6 mi inside the southern entrance via SR 41 and Chilnualna Falls Rd. Located in Wawona. 8038 Chilnualna Falls Rd 95389 (PO Box 2085). Fax: 209/375-6400. **Facility:** 129 vacation homes. 1-2 stories (no elevator), exterior corridors. *Bath:* combo or shower only. **Parking:** on-site. **Terms:** 2-3 night minimum stay - seasonal, 10 day cancellation notice-fee imposed, pets ($10 fee, in limited units). **Leisure Activities:** fishing, hiking trails. **Guest Services:** gift shop. **Business Services:** meeting rooms, business center. **Cards:** AX, DS, MC, VI. *(See color ad below)*

SOME UNITS

FEE

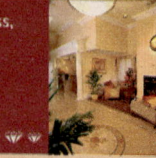

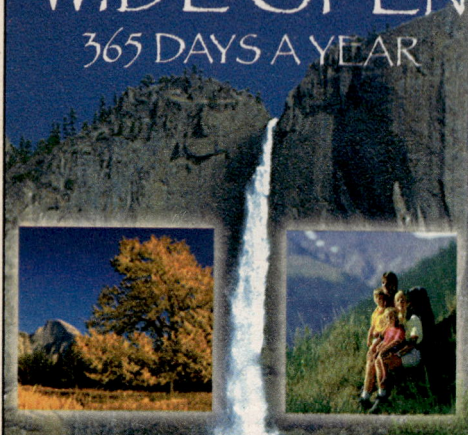

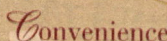

YOSEMITE LODGE — Phone: (209)372-1000

Motel

2/1-3/20 & 11/1-1/31	1P: $111-$144	2P: $111-$144
3/21-10/31	1P: $110-$146	

Location: In Yosemite Valley; 0.8 mi w of park headquarters. Located near Yosemite Falls. (PO Box 578, 95389). Fax: 559/456-0542. **Facility:** 245 one-bedroom standard units. 1-2 stories (no elevator), interior/exterior corridors. *Bath:* combo or shower only. **Parking:** on-site. **Terms:** check-in 5 pm, 3 day cancellation notice. **Amenities:** voice mail, irons, hair dryers. **Pool(s):** heated outdoor. **Leisure Activities:** fishing, recreation programs in summer, rental bicycles, hiking trails. *Fee:* downhill & cross country skiing, ice skating, horseback riding. **Guest Services:** gift shop, area transportation. **Business Services:** meeting rooms. **Cards:** AX, CB, DC, DS, JC, MC, VI.

SOME UNITS

WHERE TO DINE

THE AHWAHNEE DINING ROOM — **Lunch:** $11-$16 **Dinner:** $24-$36 **Phone:** 209/372-1489

Continental

Location: 0.8 mi e; in The Ahwahnee. In Yosemite Valley 95389. **Hours:** 7 am-10:30, 11:30-3 & 5:30-9 pm. **Reservations:** suggested. **Features:** Experienced staffers provide service in an elegant setting. Yosemite National Park serves as the backdrop. Be prepared to dress for the occasion, and call for a reservation. Semi-formal attire; cocktails. **Parking:** on-site and valet. **Cards:** AX, CB, DC, DS, JC, MC, VI.

YOUNTVILLE
—See Wine Country p. 813.

YREKA pop. 7,290

WHERE TO STAY

AMERIHOST INN-YREKA Book at aaa.com
Phone: (530)841-1300

AAA SAVE — Motel

6/1-11/1	1P: $79-$90	2P: $79-$90
2/1-5/31 & 11/2-1/31	1P: $69-$90	2P: $69-$90

Location: I-5, exit SR 3 (Fort Jones Rd). 148 Moonlit Oaks Ave 96097. Fax: 530/841-0399. **Facility:** 61 one-bedroom standard units, some with whirlpools. 2 stories, interior corridors. *Bath:* combo or shower only. **Parking:** on-site. **Terms:** age restrictions may apply, small pets only. **Amenities:** safes, irons, hair dryers. **Pool(s):** heated indoor. **Leisure Activities:** sauna, whirlpool, exercise room. **Business Services:** meeting rooms. **Cards:** AX, CB, DC, DS, MC, VI. **Special Amenities: free expanded continental breakfast and free local telephone calls.**

SOME UNITS

BEST WESTERN MINER'S INN Book at aaa.com
Phone: (530)842-4355

AAA SAVE — Motel

5/1-9/30 [CP]	1P: $68-$99	2P: $78-$99	XP: $5	F12
2/1-4/30 & 10/1-1/31 [CP]	1P: $65-$99	2P: $75-$99	XP: $5	F12

Location: I-5, exit Central Yreka, just w. 122 E Miner St 96097. Fax: 530/842-4480. **Facility:** 134 units. 119 one-bedroom standard units. 15 two-bedroom suites ($98-$119) with efficiencies. 2 stories (no elevator), exterior corridors. *Bath:* combo or shower only. **Parking:** on-site. **Terms:** age restrictions may apply, small pets only. **Amenities:** irons, hair dryers. **Pool(s):** 2 heated outdoor. **Leisure Activities:** picnic area, playground. **Business Services:** meeting rooms. **Cards:** AX, CB, DC, DS, JC, MC, VI. **Special Amenities: free continental breakfast and free local telephone calls.**

SOME UNITS

COMFORT INN
Phone: (530)842-1612

AAA SAVE — Motel

All Year [CP]	1P: $55-$85	2P: $69-$99	XP: $8	F12

Location: I-5, exit SR 3 (Fort Jones Rd). 1804-B Fort Jones Rd 96097. Fax: 530/842-0822. **Facility:** 50 one-bedroom standard units. 3 stories (no elevator), interior corridors. *Bath:* combo or shower only. **Parking:** on-site. **Terms:** age restrictions may apply, cancellation fee imposed, pets ($20 deposit, $5 extra charge). **Amenities:** irons, hair dryers. **Pool(s):** heated outdoor. **Cards:** AX, DC, DS, JC, MC, VI. **Special Amenities: free continental breakfast and free local telephone calls.**

SOME UNITS

FEE

ECONOMY INN
Phone: (530)842-4404

AAA SAVE — Motel

5/16-9/15	1P: $42-$80	2P: $49-$99	XP: $5	F5
2/1-5/15 [CP]	1P: $38-$60	2P: $44-$75	XP: $5	F5
9/16-1/31	1P: $38-$60	2P: $44-$75	XP: $5	F5

Location: I-5, exit Central Yreka, 0.3 mi s. 526 S Main St 96097. Fax: 530/841-0439. **Facility:** 44 one-bedroom standard units. 2 stories (no elevator), exterior corridors. *Bath:* shower only. **Parking:** on-site. **Terms:** age restrictions may apply, weekly rates available, pets ($5 extra charge, in designated units). **Amenities:** *Some:* irons, hair dryers. **Pool(s):** small outdoor. **Cards:** AX, DS, MC, VI. **Special Amenities: free continental breakfast and free local telephone calls.**

SOME UNITS

FEE

KLAMATH MOTOR LODGE
Phone: (530)842-2751

AAA SAVE — Motel

5/15-9/30	1P: $52-$300	2P: $59-$350	XP: $10	F12
2/1-5/14 & 10/1-1/31	1P: $49-$225	2P: $56-$275	XP: $8	F12

Location: I-5, exit SR 3 (Fort Jones Rd) northbound, 1.3 mi n; exit Central Yreka southbound, 0.8 mi s. 1111 S Main St 96097. Fax: 530/842-4703. **Facility:** 28 units. 26 one- and 2 two-bedroom standard units. 2 stories, exterior corridors. *Bath:* combo or shower only. **Parking:** on-site. **Terms:** age restrictions may apply, weekly rates available, package plans. **Amenities:** *Some:* irons, hair dryers. **Pool(s):** small heated outdoor. **Leisure Activities:** barbecue & picnic area. **Cards:** AX, DC, DS, MC, VI. **Special Amenities: free local telephone calls and free room upgrade (subject to availability with advanced reservations).**

SOME UNITS

SUPER 8-YREKA Book at aaa.com
Phone: 530/842-5781

AAA SAVE — Motel

5/16-9/30 [CP]	1P: $51-$56	2P: $56-$61	XP: $5	F12
2/1-5/15 & 10/1-1/31 [CP]	1P: $46-$51	2P: $51-$56	XP: $5	F12

Location: I-5, exit Montague Rd, just w. 136 Montague Rd 96097. Fax: 530/841-1821. **Facility:** 61 one-bedroom standard units, some with whirlpools. 2 stories (no elevator), exterior corridors. **Parking:** on-site. **Terms:** age restrictions may apply, cancellation fee imposed, pets ($5 extra charge). **Amenities:** hair dryers. **Pool(s):** outdoor. **Guest Services:** coin laundry. **Cards:** AX, DS, MC, VI. **Special Amenities: free continental breakfast and free local telephone calls.**

SOME UNITS

FEE

WAYSIDE INN
Phone: (530)842-4412

AAA SAVE — Motel

5/15-9/15	1P: $46-$68	2P: $50-$78	XP: $5	F12
2/1-5/14 & 9/16-1/31	1P: $40-$56	2P: $45-$72	XP: $5	F12

Location: I-5, SR 3 (Fort Jones Rd) northbound, 1 mi n; exit Central Yreka southbound, 1 mi s. 1235 S Main St 96097. Fax: 530/842-4412. **Facility:** 44 one-bedroom standard units, some with kitchens. 1 story, exterior corridors. *Bath:* combo or shower only. **Parking:** on-site. **Terms:** age restrictions may apply, weekly rates available, pets ($3 extra charge). **Amenities:** *Some:* irons. **Pool(s):** outdoor. **Leisure Activities:** whirlpool, picnic area. **Guest Services:** coin laundry. **Cards:** AX, CB, DC, DS, MC, VI. **Special Amenities: free continental breakfast.**

SOME UNITS

FEE

WHERE TO DINE

BOSTON SHAFT RESTAURANT **Lunch:** $6-$11 **Dinner:** $10-$18 **Phone:** 530/842-5768

Continental

Location: I-5, exit SR 3 (Fort Jones Rd). 1801 Fort Jones Rd 96097. **Hours:** 11 am-2:30 & 5-9:30 pm, Sat from 5 pm. Closed: 1/1, 12/24, 12/25; also Sun. **Reservations:** suggested. **Features:** The quaint, New England-style restaurant's varied American/European menu features beef, seafood and veal, as well as European desserts. Casual dress; cocktails. **Parking:** on-site. **Cards:** AX, CB, DC, DS, MC, VI.

YUBA CITY pop. 36,758

WHERE TO STAY

BEST WESTERN BONANZA INN *Book at aaa.com* **Phone:** (530)674-8824

Motel

All Year 1P: $79-$104 2P: $85-$104 XP: $10 F12

Location: 2 mi w of Marysville, 1 blk n off SR 20. 1001 Clark Ave 95991. Fax: 530/674-0563. **Facility:** 125 units. 119 one-bedroom standard units. 6 one-bedroom suites ($104-$157) with whirlpools. 2 stories, exterior corridors. **Parking:** on-site. **Terms:** cancellation fee imposed. **Amenities:** video games, voice mail, irons, hair dryers. *Some:* safes. **Dining:** 2 restaurants, 6 am-2 & 5-10 pm, cocktails. **Pool(s):** outdoor. **Leisure Activities:** whirlpool. **Guest Services:** valet laundry. **Business Services:** conference facilities. **Cards:** AX, CB, DC, DS, MC, VI. **Special Amenities: free local telephone calls.**

SOME UNITS

COMFORT INN *Book at aaa.com* **Phone:** (530)674-1592

Motel

4/1-10/31 [CP]	1P: $68-$99	2P: $73-$99	XP: $5	F12
11/1-1/31 [CP]	1P: $60-$85	2P: $65-$90	XP: $5	F12
2/1-3/31 [CP]	1P: $55-$85	2P: $65-$90	XP: $5	F12

Location: SR 99, exit Bridge St, 0.5 mi s of jct SR 20. 730 Palora Ave 95991. Fax: 530/674-3032. **Facility:** 53 one-bedroom standard units. 3 stories (no elevator), interior corridors. *Bath:* combo or shower only. **Parking:** on-site. **Terms:** cancellation fee imposed, weekly rates available, pets ($10 extra charge). **Amenities:** irons, hair dryers. **Pool(s):** small outdoor. **Guest Services:** coin laundry. **Cards:** AX, DC, DS, MC, VI.

SOME UNITS

FEE

DAYS INN & SUITES *Book at aaa.com* **Phone:** 530/674-0201

Motel

All Year 1P: $50-$68 2P: $55-$81 XP: $6 F12

Location: SR 99, 4.5 mi s of SR 20. 4228 S Hwy 99 95991. Fax: 530/671-5758. **Facility:** 61 units. 59 one-bedroom standard units, some with efficiencies. 2 one-bedroom suites ($150-$185) with efficiencies and whirlpools. 2 stories, exterior corridors. *Bath:* combo or shower only. **Parking:** on-site. **Terms:** weekly rates available, [CP] meal plan available. **Pool(s):** outdoor. **Leisure Activities:** whirlpool, exercise room. **Guest Services:** coin laundry. **Business Services:** meeting rooms. **Cards:** AX, DS, MC, VI.

SOME UNITS

DAYS INN-DOWNTOWN-YUBA CITY *Book at aaa.com* **Phone:** (530)674-1711

Motel

All Year 1P: $45-$70 2P: $45-$80 XP: $5 F12

Location: SR 99, exit Bridge St, 0.5 mi s of SR 20. 700 N Palora Ave 95991. Fax: 530/671-1937. **Facility:** 50 one-bedroom standard units. 2 stories, exterior corridors. *Bath:* combo or shower only. **Parking:** on-site. **Terms:** cancellation fee imposed, [CP] meal plan available, small pets only ($7 fee). **Amenities:** hair dryers. *Some:* irons. **Pool(s):** heated outdoor. **Cards:** AX, DC, DS, MC, VI. *(See ad below)*

SOME UNITS

FEE

THE HARKEY HOUSE **Phone:** (530)674-1942

Historic Bed & Breakfast

All Year 1P: $90-$185 2P: $100-$195 XP: $20 F

Location: Downtown. Located adjacent to Sutter County offices. 212 C St 95991. Fax: 530/674-1840. **Facility:** The property has attractively landscaped gardens and a pool area. 4 one-bedroom standard units. 2 stories, interior corridors. **Parking:** on-site. **Terms:** 7 day cancellation notice-fee imposed, weekly rates available, [BP] meal plan available. **Amenities:** CD players, hair dryers. **Pool(s):** outdoor. **Leisure Activities:** whirlpool. **Cards:** AX, CB, DC, DS, JC, MC, VI.

SOME UNITS

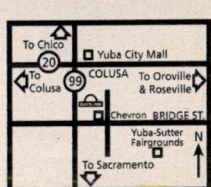

HOLIDAY INN EXPRESS-YUBA CITY Book at aaa.com **Phone:** (530)674-1650

Motel

All Year [ECP] 1P: $86-$125 2P: $86-$125 XP: $10 F18

Location: SR 99, 0.3 mi s of jct SR 20. 894 W Onstott Rd 95991. Fax: 530/674-1266. **Facility:** 91 one-bedroom standard units. 2 stories, exterior corridors. **Parking:** on-site. **Terms:** cancellation fee imposed. **Amenities:** video games, voice mail, irons, hair dryers. **Pool(s):** outdoor. **Leisure Activities:** sauna, whirlpool, exercise room. **Guest Services:** coin laundry. **Cards:** AX, CB, DC, DS, JC, MC, VI. **Special Amenities: free continental breakfast and free newspaper.** *(See color ad p 260)*

SOME UNITS

VILLAGER LODGE Book at aaa.com **Phone:** (530)671-1151

Motel

All Year 1P: $50-$55 2P: $55-$70 XP: $10 F

Location: SR 20, 0.5 mi e of SR 99. 545 Colusa Ave 95991. Fax: 530/673-8189. **Facility:** 40 units. 34 one-bedroom standard units. 6 one-bedroom suites with kitchens. 2 stories, exterior corridors. *Bath:* combo or shower only. **Parking:** on-site. **Terms:** cancellation fee imposed. **Cards:** AX, DS, MC, VI. **Special Amenities: free continental breakfast and free newspaper.**

SOME UNITS

WHERE TO DINE

THE REFUGE RESTAURANT & LOUNGE **Lunch:** $8-$12 **Dinner:** $16-$24 **Phone:** 530/673-7620

American

Location: SR 99, 1 blk w of SR 20, 3 blks n, then just w. 1501 Butte House Rd 95991. **Hours:** 11:30 am-2 & 5-9 pm, Sat 5 pm-10 pm, Sun 5 pm-9 pm. Closed: 7/4, 12/25. **Reservations:** suggested. **Features:** Prime rib, steak and fresh seafood. Dressy casual; cocktails. **Parking:** on-site. **Cards:** AX, DS, MC, VI.

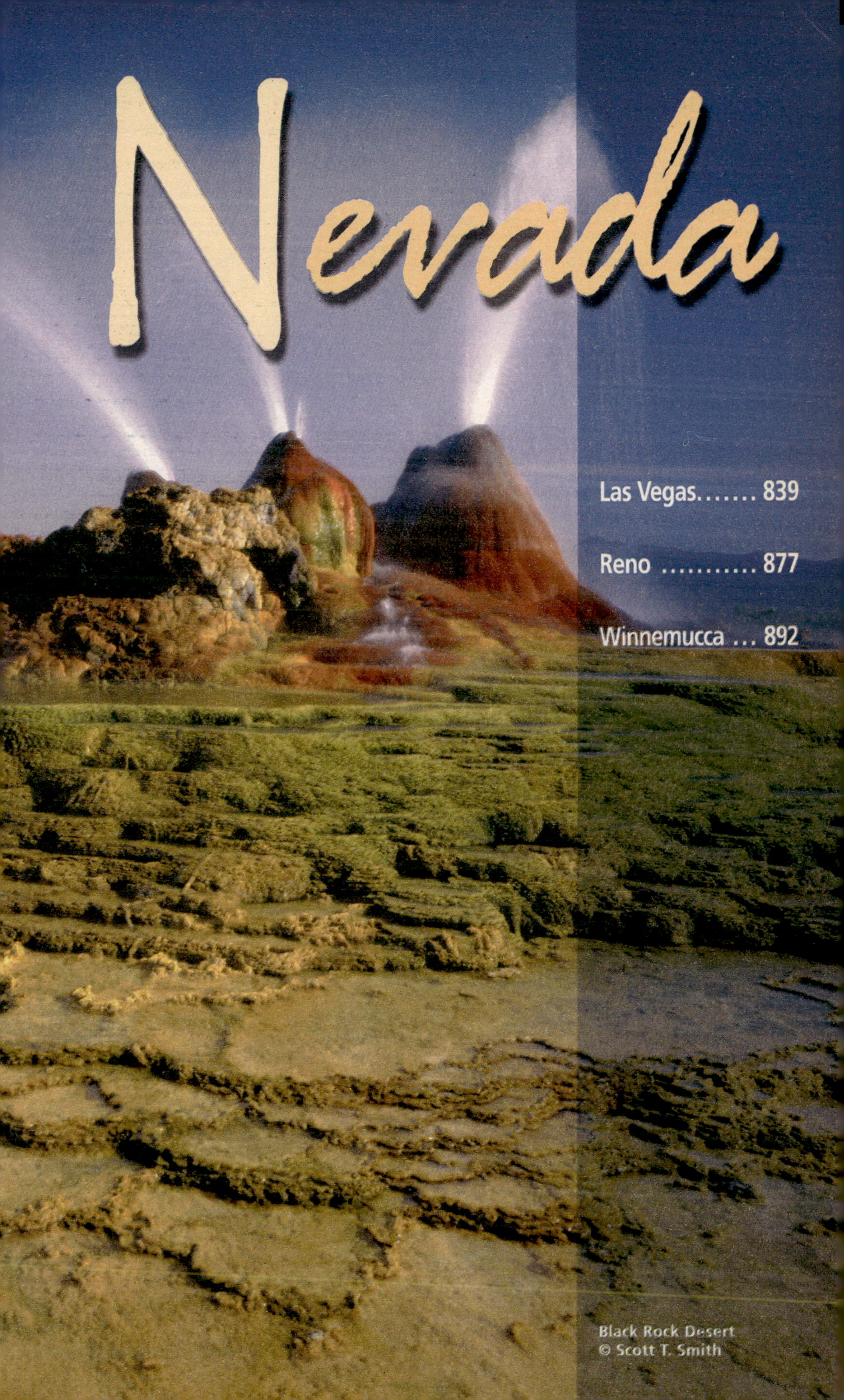

Nevada

Black Rock Desert
© Scott T. Smith

AMARGOSA VALLEY

WHERE TO STAY

LONGSTREET INN, CASINO & RV PARK **Phone:** 775/372-1777

Small-scale Hotel

All Year 1P: $60-$90 2P: $70-$100

Location: 7 mi n of jct SR 127 and 190 (Death Valley Jct) on SR 373; 15 mi s of jct SR 95 and 373 on SR 373. 373 Stateline 89020 (PO Box 559 HCR 70). Fax: 775/372-1280. **Facility:** The property features an attractively landscaped pool area with a gazebo and a pond. 60 one-bedroom standard units. 2 stories, interior corridors. *Bath:* shower only. **Parking:** on-site. **Terms:** 2 night minimum stay, weekly rates available, [AP], [BP], [CP], [ECP] & [MAP] meal plans available, package plans - seasonal & weekends, small pets only ($50 deposit). **Pool(s):** heated outdoor. **Leisure Activities:** whirlpool, horseshoes. **Guest Services:** sundries, coin laundry. **Cards:** AX, CB, DC, DS, MC, VI.

FEE

BATTLE MOUNTAIN pop. 2,871

WHERE TO STAY

BATTLE MOUNTAIN INN **Phone:** (775)635-5200

AAA SAVE

Motel

All Year 1P: $39-$49 2P: $49-$59

Location: I-80, exit 229 or 233, 0.5 mi e. 650 W Front St 89820. Fax: 775/635-5699. **Facility:** 70 one-bedroom standard units, some with whirlpools. 2 stories (no elevator), exterior corridors. **Parking:** on-site. **Terms:** cancellation fee imposed, [CP] meal plan available, pets ($10 fee). **Leisure Activities:** playground, exercise room. **Cards:** AX, DC, DS, MC, VI. **Special Amenities: free expanded continental breakfast and free local telephone calls.**

SOME UNITS

DATA PORT / FEE /

BIG CHIEF MOTEL **Phone:** 775/635-2416

AAA SAVE

Motel

All Year 1P: $35-$39 2P: $39-$49 XP: $5 F11

Location: I-80, exit 229 or 233, just n. 434 W Front St 89820. Fax: 775/635-2418. **Facility:** 56 one-bedroom standard units. 2 stories (no elevator), exterior corridors. *Bath:* combo or shower only. **Parking:** on-site. **Terms:** pets ($5 extra charge). **Pool(s):** heated outdoor. **Leisure Activities:** whirlpool. **Guest Services:** coin laundry. **Cards:** AX, DC, DS, MC, VI. **Special Amenities: free continental breakfast and free local telephone calls.**

SOME UNITS

FEE / /

COMFORT INN *Book at aaa.com* **Phone:** (775)635-5880

AAA SAVE

Motel

All Year [CP] 1P: $50-$89 2P: $56-$89 XP: $6 F18

Location: I-80, exit 229 or 233, just n. 521 E Front St 89820. Fax: 775/635-5788. **Facility:** 71 one-bedroom standard units. 3 stories, interior corridors. **Parking:** on-site. **Terms:** pets ($100 deposit). **Amenities:** irons, hair dryers. **Pool(s):** heated outdoor. **Leisure Activities:** whirlpool, exercise room. **Guest Services:** coin laundry. **Business Services:** meeting rooms. **Cards:** AX, CB, DC, DS, JC, MC, VI. **Special Amenities: free continental breakfast and free local telephone calls.**

SOME UNITS

DATA PORT / FEE / /

BEATTY pop. 1,154

WHERE TO STAY

BURRO INN **Phone:** (775)553-2225

Motel

All Year 1P: $35 2P: $40 XP: $5

Location: 4 blks s on SR 95. Third St & Hwy 95 89003 (PO Box 7). Fax: 775/553-2892. **Facility:** 62 one-bedroom standard units. 2 stories (no elevator), exterior corridors. **Parking:** on-site. **Terms:** pets ($25 deposit, $5 extra charge). **Guest Services:** gift shop, coin laundry. **Cards:** AX, MC, VI.

SOME UNITS

ASK FEE / /

EXCHANGE CLUB MOTEL & CASINO **Phone:** 775/553-2333

AAA SAVE

Motel

All Year 1P: $42-$63 2P: $48-$68 XP: $5 F12

Location: SR 95 at SR 374; downtown. 119 Main St 89003 (PO Box 444). Fax: 775/553-9348. **Facility:** 44 one-bedroom standard units. 2 stories (no elevator), exterior corridors. **Parking:** on-site. **Terms:** cancellation fee imposed. **Dining:** 2 restaurants, 24 hours, cocktails. **Guest Services:** coin laundry. **Cards:** AX, DC, MC, VI.

SOME UNITS

/ /

PHOENIX INN **Phone:** 775/553-2250

Motel

All Year 1P: $27-$43 2P: $31-$50 XP: $4 F7

Location: Just off SR 95. 350 First St 89003 (PO Box 503). Fax: 775/553-2260. **Facility:** 54 one-bedroom standard units. 1 story, exterior corridors. **Parking:** on-site. **Terms:** cancellation fee imposed, [CP] meal plan available, pets ($5 extra charge). **Guest Services:** coin laundry. **Business Services:** fax. **Cards:** AX, DC, DS, MC, VI.

SOME UNITS

STAGECOACH HOTEL CASINO & RV PARK Phone: 775/553-2419

AAA SAVE — Motel

All Year 1P: $35-$45 2P: $40-$48 XP: $5 F5

Location: North end of town, west side of US 95. Hwy 95 N 89003 (PO Box 836). Fax: 775/553-2548. **Facility:** 80 one-bedroom standard units. 2 stories (no elevator), interior/exterior corridors. *Bath:* combo or shower only. **Parking:** on-site. **Terms:** pets ($5 extra charge, in limited units). **Amenities:** voice mail. **Dining:** 24 hours, cocktails. **Pool(s):** outdoor. **Leisure Activities:** whirlpool. **Guest Services:** gift shop. **Business Services:** meeting rooms. **Cards:** AX, DC, MC, VI.

SOME UNITS

FEE

BOULDER CITY *—See Las Vegas p. 867.*

CARLIN pop. 2,161

WHERE TO STAY

COMFORT INN *Book at aaa.com* Phone: (775)754-6110

AAA SAVE — Motel

All Year [CP] 1P: $59-$89 2P: $59-$89 XP: $10 F18

Location: I-80, exit 280, just s. 1018 Fir St 89822 (PO Box 847). Fax: 775/754-6973. **Facility:** 61 units. 59 one-bedroom standard units. 2 one-bedroom suites ($75-$104). 3 stories, interior corridors. *Bath:* combo or shower only. **Parking:** on-site. **Terms:** pets ($100 deposit). **Amenities:** irons, hair dryers. **Leisure Activities:** exercise room. **Guest Services:** coin laundry. **Business Services:** fax. **Cards:** AX, CB, DC, DS, JC, MC, VI. **Special Amenities: free continental breakfast and free local telephone calls.**

SOME UNITS

FEE

CARSON CITY pop. 52,457

WHERE TO STAY

BEST VALUE INN *Book at aaa.com* Phone: (775)882-2007

AAA SAVE — Motel

5/1-10/31	1P: $33-$179	2P: $43-$199	XP: $5	F12
2/1-4/30	1P: $29-$109	2P: $33-$129	XP: $5	F12
11/1-1/31	1P: $29-$79	2P: $33-$99	XP: $5	F12

Location: 1.3 mi s on US 50 and 395. 2731 S Carson St 89701. Fax: 775/883-4182. **Facility:** 58 one-bedroom standard units. 2 stories (no elevator), exterior corridors. **Parking:** on-site. **Terms:** cancellation fee imposed, small pets only ($30 deposit). **Pool(s):** outdoor. **Leisure Activities:** whirlpool. **Guest Services:** coin laundry. **Cards:** AX, CB, DC, DS, JC, MC, VI. **Special Amenities: free local telephone calls and preferred room (subject to availability with advanced reservations).**

SOME UNITS

FEE FEE

BEST WESTERN CARSON STATION HOTEL/CASINO *Book at aaa.com* Phone: (775)883-0900

Small-scale Hotel

4/1-10/31	1P: $63-$120	2P: $63-$120	XP: $5	F13
2/1-3/31 & 11/1-1/31	1P: $58-$105	2P: $58-$105	XP: $5	F13

Location: South end of town. 900 S Carson 89701. Fax: 775/882-7569. **Facility:** 92 one-bedroom standard units. 5 stories, interior corridors. **Parking:** on-site. **Amenities:** voice mail, irons, hair dryers. **Guest Services:** gift shop, valet laundry. **Business Services:** meeting rooms. **Cards:** AX, DC, DS, MC, VI.

SOME UNITS

ASK

BEST WESTERN PINON PLAZA RESORT *Book at aaa.com* Phone: (775)885-9000

Small-scale Hotel

All Year 1P: $65-$145 2P: $65-$145 XP: $5 F13

Location: East end of town. 2171 Hwy 50 E 89701. Fax: 775/888-8003. **Facility:** 148 one-bedroom standard units, some with whirlpools. 3 stories, interior corridors. *Bath:* combo or shower only. **Parking:** on-site. **Terms:** package plans. **Amenities:** voice mail, irons, hair dryers. **Pool(s):** heated outdoor. **Leisure Activities:** sauna, whirlpool, exercise room. *Fee:* game room. **Guest Services:** gift shop, valet laundry. **Business Services:** conference facilities. **Cards:** AX, DC, DS, MC, VI.

SOME UNITS

ASK

BEST WESTERN TRAILSIDE INN *Book at aaa.com* Phone: (775)883-7300

AAA SAVE — Motel

5/1-9/30	1P: $59-$149	2P: $65-$179	XP: $6	F12
2/1-4/30 & 12/25-1/31	1P: $49-$109	2P: $55-$119	XP: $6	F12
10/1-12/24	1P: $49-$99	2P: $55-$109	XP: $6	F12

Location: 0.5 mi n on US 395. 1300 N Carson St 89701. Fax: 775/885-7506. **Facility:** 67 one-bedroom standard units. 2 stories (no elevator), exterior corridors. **Parking:** on-site. **Terms:** cancellation fee imposed, [CP] meal plan available, pets ($10 extra charge). **Amenities:** irons, hair dryers. **Pool(s):** heated outdoor. **Cards:** AX, CB, DC, MC, VI. **Special Amenities: free continental breakfast and early check-in/late check-out.**

SOME UNITS

FEE

BLISS MANSION Phone: (775)887-8988

Historic Bed & Breakfast

All Year 1P: $145-$215 2P: $145-$215

Location: W of US 395 and SR 50. Located across from Governor's Mansion. 710 W Robinson 89703. Fax: 775/887-0540. **Facility:** Antique furnishings and an upscale residential setting give this service-oriented property an elegant ambience. 5 one-bedroom standard units. 3 stories (no elevator), interior corridors. *Bath:* combo or shower only. **Parking:** on-site. **Terms:** 5 day cancellation notice. **Guest Services:** complimentary evening beverages. **Cards:** AX, CB, DC, DS, MC, VI.

CARSON CITY SUPER 8 *Book at aaa.com* **Phone:** (775)883-7800

AAA SAVE · Motel

7/1-9/30	1P: $35-$193	2P: $41-$199	XP: $6	F12
4/2-6/30	1P: $32-$145	2P: $38-$151	XP: $6	F12
10/1-1/31	1P: $28-$145	2P: $34-$151	XP: $6	F12
2/1-4/1	1P: $28-$125	2P: $34-$131	XP: $6	F12

Location: South end of town. 2829 S Carson 89701. Fax: 775/883-0376. **Facility:** 63 one-bedroom standard units. 2 stories (no elevator), interior corridors. **Parking:** on-site. **Terms:** cancellation fee imposed, pets ($25 deposit, $7 extra charge, in smoking units). **Cards:** AX, DC, MC, VI. **Special Amenities: early check-in/late check-out and preferred room (subject to availability with advanced reservations).**

SOME UNITS / FEE

DAYS INN **Phone:** (775)883-3343

AAA SAVE · Motel

All Year 1P: $45-$140 2P: $50-$140

Location: US 395 N, north end of city. 3103 N Carson St 89706. Fax: 775/887-0446. **Facility:** 61 one-bedroom standard units. 2 stories (no elevator), exterior corridors. **Parking:** on-site. **Terms:** [CP] meal plan available, 10% service charge, small pets only ($10 extra charge). **Amenities:** hair dryers. **Guest Services:** coin laundry. **Business Services:** PC. **Cards:** AX, DC, DS, MC, VI. **Special Amenities: free continental breakfast and free local telephone calls.**

SOME UNITS / FEE

PARK INN HARDMAN HOUSE *Book at aaa.com* **Phone:** (775)882-7744

AAA SAVE · Motel

All Year 1P: $80 2P: $80 XP: $10 F12

Location: US 395, just s of US 50; downtown. 917 N Carson St 89701. Fax: 775/887-0321. **Facility:** 62 one-bedroom standard units. 3 stories, interior corridors. **Parking:** on-site. **Terms:** [ECP] meal plan available. **Amenities:** irons, hair dryers. **Business Services:** meeting rooms. **Cards:** AX, CB, DC, JC, MC, VI. **Special Amenities: free continental breakfast and free newspaper.**

SOME UNITS / FEE / FEE

The following lodging was either not evaluated or did not meet AAA rating requirements but is listed for your information only.

HOLIDAY INN EXPRESS & SUITES **Phone:** 775/283-4055

fyi · Motel

All Year 1P: $69-$189 2P: $79-$199 XP: $10

Too new to rate, opening scheduled for November 2003. **Location:** US 395; north end of town. 4055 N Carson St 89701. **Amenities:** 85 units, coffeemakers, microwaves, refrigerators, pool.

WHERE TO DINE

ADELE'S RESTAURANT AND LOUNGE **Lunch:** $9-$18 **Dinner:** $17-$71 **Phone:** 775/882-3353

Continental

Location: Jct US 395 and 50. 1112 N Carson St 89701. **Hours:** 11 am-3 pm, Sat 11:30 am-2:30 & 5-10 pm. Closed major holidays; also Sun; first 3 weeks of Jan. **Reservations:** suggested. **Features:** Friendly service and good, creative food contribute to an enjoyable dining experience. The setting is distinctive. Dressy casual; cocktails. **Parking:** on-site. **Cards:** AX, MC, VI.

B'SGHETTI'S RESTAURANT **Lunch:** $6-$11 **Dinner:** $7-$15 **Phone:** 775/887-8879

Italian

Location: Center. 318 N Carson St 89701. **Hours:** 11 am-9 pm. Closed: 11/25, 12/25. **Features:** A breezy, relaxed and friendly setting awaits diners in the convenient, main-street setting. A loyal local clientele patronizes this place. Casual dress; cocktails. **Parking:** on-site. **Cards:** MC, VI.

HEIDI'S FAMILY RESTAURANT **Lunch:** $4-$8 **Phone:** 775/882-0486

American

Location: Jct US 395 and 50 E. 1020 N Carson St 89701. **Hours:** 6:30 am-2 pm. **Features:** Family restaurant noted for breakfast. Casual dress. **Parking:** on-site. **Cards:** MC, VI.

Q'S STEAKS, BAR-B-QUE & SALADS **Lunch:** $5-$9 **Dinner:** $5-$22 **Phone:** 775/841-7227

Barbecue

Location: US 395, exit Fairview Dr, just e. 230 Fairview Dr 89701. **Hours:** 11 am-9 pm, Sat-10 pm. Closed: 1/1, 12/25. **Reservations:** accepted. **Features:** Plentiful portions of Texas-style barbecue are served seven days a week. In a great location right off the main street, the friendly spot offers a wide selection from the Lone Star State. Casual dress; cocktails. **Parking:** on-site. **Cards:** AX, DS, MC, VI.

COTTONWOOD COVE *—See Las Vegas p. 868.*

ECHO BAY *—See Las Vegas p. 868.*

ELKO pop. 16,708

WHERE TO STAY

BEST WESTERN AMERITEL INN-ELKO *Book at aaa.com* **Phone:** (775)738-8787

Motel

All Year [ECP] 1P: $69-$99 2P: $69-$99 XP: $5 F17

Location: I-80, exit 303, 0.3 mi sw. 1930 Idaho St 89801. Fax: 775/753-7910. **Facility:** 109 units. 106 one-bedroom standard units, some with whirlpools. 3 one-bedroom suites with efficiencies. 2 stories (no elevator), interior corridors. **Parking:** on-site. **Amenities:** voice mail, irons, hair dryers. *Some:* high-speed Internet. **Pool(s):** heated indoor. **Leisure Activities:** whirlpool, exercise room. **Guest Services:** coin laundry. **Cards:** AX, CB, DC, DS, MC, VI.

ASK · SOME UNITS

BEST WESTERN GOLD COUNTRY MOTOR INN *Book at aaa.com* **Phone:** (775)738-8421

AAA SAVE — Motel

All Year 1P: $59-$99 2P: $69-$109 XP: $10 F16

Location: I-80, exit 303, just s. 2050 Idaho St 89801. Fax: 775/738-1798. **Facility:** Located in the famous "cowboy country," this friendly place has 24-hour dining and a casino that is always the place to be. 151 units. 146 one- and 5 two-bedroom standard units, some with kitchens. 2 stories (no elevator), exterior corridors. *Bath:* combo or shower only. **Parking:** on-site. **Terms:** check-in 4 pm, pets ($15 fee). **Amenities:** irons, hair dryers. **Dining:** 24 hours, cocktails, also, JR's Bar and Grill, see separate listing. **Pool(s):** heated outdoor. **Guest Services:** coin laundry, area transportation. **Cards:** AX, CB, DC, DS, JC, MC, VI. **Special Amenities: free local telephone calls and early check-in/late check-out.**

SOME UNITS

FEE

BUDGET INN **Phone:** (775)738-7000

AAA SAVE — Motel

2/1-9/15 1P: $34-$40 2P: $37-$46 XP: $4 F11
9/16-1/31 1P: $30-$39 2P: $34-$44 XP: $4 F11

Location: I-80, exit 301 or 303, 1 mi s. 1349 Idaho St 89801. Fax: 775/738-1216. **Facility:** 61 units. 57 one- and 4 two-bedroom standard units. 2 stories (no elevator), exterior corridors. **Parking:** on-site. **Terms:** weekly rates available, package plans. **Pool(s):** heated outdoor. **Cards:** AX, DS, MC, VI.

SOME UNITS

COMFORT INN *Book at aaa.com* **Phone:** 775/777-8762

AAA SAVE — Motel

6/2-9/15 1P: $79-$89 2P: $79-$89
2/1-6/1 & 9/16-1/31 1P: $59-$69 2P: $59-$69

Location: I-80, exit 303, just s, then just e. 2970 Idaho St 89801. Fax: 775/753-9439. **Facility:** 51 one-bedroom standard units, some with whirlpools. 2 stories (no elevator), interior corridors. *Bath:* combo or shower only. **Parking:** on-site. **Terms:** [ECP] meal plan available, pets ($10 extra charge, in limited units). **Amenities:** voice mail, irons, hair dryers. **Pool(s):** heated indoor. **Leisure Activities:** sauna, whirlpool, exercise room. **Guest Services:** coin laundry. **Business Services:** meeting rooms. **Cards:** AX, DC, DS, MC, VI. **Special Amenities: free expanded continental breakfast and free local telephone calls.**

SOME UNITS

FEE

DAYS INN *Book at aaa.com* **Phone:** 775/738-7245

AAA SAVE — Motel

6/1-9/15 1P: $45-$49 2P: $49-$59
9/16-1/31 1P: $35-$39 2P: $39-$45
2/1-5/31 1P: $35-$39 2P: $39-$45 XP: $4 F12

Location: I-80, exit 303, 1 mi s. 1500 Idaho St 89801. Fax: 775/738-7491. **Facility:** 33 one-bedroom standard units. 2 stories (no elevator), exterior corridors. **Parking:** on-site. **Terms:** weekly rates available, [ECP] meal plan available. **Amenities:** irons, hair dryers. **Guest Services:** coin laundry. **Cards:** AX, CB, DC, DS, MC, VI. **Special Amenities: free continental breakfast and free newspaper.**

SOME UNITS

ELKO INN EXPRESS **Phone:** 775/738-7261

Motel

All Year [CP] 1P: $59 2P: $64 XP: $10 F16

Location: I-80, exit 301 or 303, 1 mi s. 837 Idaho St 89801. Fax: 775/738-0118. **Facility:** 49 units. 46 one- and 3 two-bedroom standard units. 2 stories (no elevator), exterior corridors. **Parking:** on-site. **Terms:** cancellation fee imposed, pets ($10 extra charge). **Pool(s):** heated outdoor. **Cards:** AX, DC, MC, VI.

ASK — SOME UNITS

FEE

HIGH DESERT INN **Phone:** (775)738-8425

AAA SAVE — Small-scale Hotel

All Year 1P: $59 2P: $69 XP: $10 F18

Location: I-80, exit 303, just s. 3015 Idaho St 89801. Fax: 775/753-7906. **Facility:** 171 one-bedroom standard units. 4 stories, interior/exterior corridors. **Parking:** on-site. **Terms:** check-in 4 pm, small pets only ($15 fee). **Amenities:** irons, hair dryers. **Dining:** 6 am-2 & 5-10 pm, cocktails, also, High Desert Inn Cafe, see separate listing. **Pool(s):** heated indoor. **Leisure Activities:** whirlpool, exercise room. **Guest Services:** coin laundry, area transportation. **Business Services:** meeting rooms, fax. **Cards:** AX, DC, DS, MC, VI. **Special Amenities: free local telephone calls.**

SOME UNITS

FEE FEE FEE

HILTON GARDEN INN *Book at aaa.com* **Phone:** (775)777-1200

Small-scale Hotel

All Year 1P: $79-$119

Location: I-80, exit 303, just s. 3650 E Idaho St 89801. Fax: 775/777-1203. **Facility:** 84 units. 78 one-bedroom standard units. 6 one-bedroom suites ($99-$189) with efficiencies (no utensils) and whirlpools. 3 stories, interior corridors. *Bath:* combo or shower only. **Parking:** on-site. **Terms:** [AP] meal plan available, $2 service charge. **Amenities:** video games (fee), dual phone lines, voice mail, irons, hair dryers. **Pool(s):** heated indoor. **Leisure Activities:** whirlpool, exercise room. **Guest Services:** sundries, coin laundry. **Business Services:** meeting rooms, business center. **Cards:** AX, CB, DC, DS, JC, MC, VI. ***(See color ad p 832)***

ASK — SOME UNITS

HOLIDAY INN EXPRESS HOTEL & SUITES *Book at aaa.com* **Phone:** (775)777-0990

AAA SAVE — Motel

All Year [ECP] 1P: $89-$99 2P: $99-$109 XP: $10 F18

Location: I-80, exit 303, just s. 3019 Idaho St 89801. Fax: 775/777-0989. **Facility:** 77 units. 75 one-bedroom standard units. 2 one-bedroom suites ($109-$159) with kitchens. 3 stories, interior corridors. *Bath:* combo or shower only. **Parking:** on-site. **Terms:** check-in 4 pm, pets ($20 fee). **Amenities:** dual phone lines, voice mail, irons, hair dryers. **Leisure Activities:** pool & whirlpool privileges. **Guest Services:** area transportation. **Business Services:** meeting rooms, business center. **Cards:** AX, CB, DC, DS, JC, MC, VI. **Special Amenities: free local telephone calls and free newspaper.**

SOME UNITS

FEE

NATIONAL 9 EL NEVA MOTEL

SAVE

Motel

				Phone: (775)738-7152
5/16-9/6	1P: $36-$59	2P: $39-$59	XP: $5	F15
2/1-5/15 & 9/7-1/31	1P: $32-$59	2P: $35-$59	XP: $5	F15

Location: I-80, exit 301 or 303, 1 mi s. 736 Idaho St 89801. Fax: 775/738-3447. **Facility:** 27 one-bedroom standard units. 2 stories (no elevator), exterior corridors. **Parking:** on-site. **Amenities:** irons, hair dryers. **Cards:** AX, CB, DC, DS, MC, VI.

SOME UNITS

OAK TREE INN *Book at aaa.com*

SAVE

Motel

			Phone: (775)777-2222
All Year	1P: $49-$69	2P: $59-$79	

Location: I-80, exit 301, just n. 95 Spruce Rd 89802. Fax: 775/777-2236. **Facility:** 120 one-bedroom standard units. 4 stories, interior corridors. *Bath:* combo or shower only. **Parking:** on-site. **Terms:** weekly rates available, pets ($5 extra charge). **Amenities:** *Some:* irons, hair dryers. **Leisure Activities:** whirlpool, exercise room. **Guest Services:** coin laundry. **Business Services:** meeting rooms. **Cards:** AX, DC, DS, MC, VI. **Special Amenities: free continental breakfast and free local telephone calls.** *(See color ad below)*

FEE SOME UNITS

RED LION INN & CASINO *Book at aaa.com* **Phone:** (775)738-2111

Small-scale Hotel

All Year 1P: $79 2P: $89-$119 XP: $10 F18

Location: I-80, exit 303, just s. 2065 Idaho St 89801. Fax: 775/753-9859. **Facility:** 223 units. 216 one- and 5 two-bedroom standard units. 2 one-bedroom suites ($109-$259) with whirlpools. 3 stories, interior corridors. **Parking:** on-site. **Terms:** check-in 4 pm, pets ($15 fee). **Amenities:** voice mail, irons, hair dryers. **Dining:** 2 restaurants, 24 hours; buffet $7-$16, cocktails, also, Misty's Restaurant, see separate listing, entertainment. **Pool(s):** outdoor. **Leisure Activities:** Fee: game room. **Guest Services:** gift shop, area transportation. **Business Services:** meeting rooms. **Cards:** AX, CB, DC, DS, JC, MC, VI. **Special Amenities: free local telephone calls and free room upgrade (subject to availability with advanced reservations).** *(See color ad below)*

SOME UNITS

FEE

STOCKMEN'S HOTEL & CASINO **Phone:** 775/738-5141

Small-scale Hotel

All Year 1P: $32-$75 2P: $32-$75 XP: $10 F16

Location: Commercial and 4th sts; downtown. 340 Commercial St 89801. Fax: 775/777-0700. **Facility:** 141 one-bedroom standard units, some with whirlpools. 4 stories, interior/exterior corridors. **Parking:** on-site. **Pool(s):** outdoor. **Leisure Activities:** exercise room. *Fee:* game room. **Business Services:** meeting rooms. **Cards:** AX, CB, DC, DS, MC, VI.

SOME UNITS

THUNDERBIRD MOTEL **Phone:** 775/738-7115

Motel

All Year [BP] 1P: $49-$59 2P: $59-$69 XP: $10 F12

Location: I-80, exit 301 or 303, 1 mi s. 345 Idaho St 89801. Fax: 775/738-2694. **Facility:** 70 one-bedroom standard units. 2 stories (no elevator), exterior corridors. **Parking:** on-site. **Terms:** pets ($10 fee). **Pool(s):** heated outdoor. **Guest Services:** area transportation. **Business Services:** fax. **Cards:** AX, DC, DS, MC, VI. **Special Amenities: free local telephone calls.**

SOME UNITS

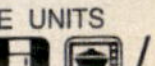

FEE

WHERE TO DINE

HIGH DESERT INN CAFE **Lunch:** $6-$9 **Dinner:** $6-$14 **Phone:** 775/738-8425

American

Location: I-80, exit 303, just s; in High Desert Inn. 3015 Idaho St 89801. **Hours:** 6 am-2 & 5-10 pm. **Reservations:** accepted. **Features:** Open for breakfast, lunch and dinner, the comfortable room is right off the motel lobby and lounge. Guests appreciate the good food and service. Casual dress; cocktails. **Parking:** on-site. **Cards:** AX, CB, DC, DS, MC, VI.

JR'S BAR AND GRILL — American — **Lunch:** $7-$13 **Dinner:** $8-$17 **Phone:** 775/778-0515

Location: I-80, exit 303, just s; in Best Western Gold Country Motor Inn. 2050 Idaho St 89801. **Hours:** 24 hours. **Features:** The bustling restaurant never closes. Patrons can watch the busy cooks as they scurry to fill orders from the wide-ranging menu. All food is also available for takeout. Casual dress; cocktails. **Parking:** on-site. **Cards:** AX, CB, DC, DS, JC, MC, VI.

MISTY'S RESTAURANT — Continental — **Dinner:** $12-$40 **Phone:** 775/738-2111

Location: I-80, exit 303, just s; in Red Lion Inn & Casino. 2065 Idaho St 89801. **Hours:** 5 pm-10 pm. **Reservations:** suggested. **Features:** Just off the casino floor, the warm, comfortable dining room is a spot for patrons to relax with an ample portion of good food. The staff is friendly and happy to serve. Dressy casual; cocktails. **Parking:** on-site. **Cards:** AX, DS, MC, VI.

NEVADA DINNER HOUSE — Basque — **Lunch:** $6-$11 **Dinner:** $15-$23 **Phone:** 775/738-8485

Location: I-80, 1.5 mi s, at 4th St. 351 Silver St 89801. **Hours:** 11:30 am-1:30 & 5-9:30 pm. Closed: 11/25, 12/25; also Mon. **Reservations:** accepted. **Features:** Diners can choose offerings of Basque cuisine, served family style, or American fare. Casual dress; cocktails. **Parking:** on-site. **Cards:** AX, MC, VI.

ELY pop. 4,041

WHERE TO STAY

BRISTLECONE MOTEL — Motel — **Phone:** 775/289-8838

All Year 1P: $44-$48 2P: $50-$56 XP: $2

Location: Just s of jct US 6, 50 and 93. 700 Ave I 89301. Fax: 775/289-6128. **Facility:** 31 one-bedroom standard units. 2 stories (no elevator), exterior corridors. **Parking:** on-site. **Amenities:** voice mail, hair dryers. **Cards:** AX, CB, DC, DS, MC, VI. **Special Amenities: free local telephone calls.**

SOME UNITS

FIRESIDE INN — Motel — **Phone:** (775)289-3765

All Year 1P: $42 2P: $46 XP: $4 D18

Location: 2 mi n on US 95. McGill Hwy 89301-9402 (HC 33, Box 33400, 89301). **Facility:** 14 one-bedroom standard units. 1 story, exterior corridors. **Parking:** on-site. **Terms:** weekly rates available, small pets only ($5 extra charge). **Amenities:** voice mail. **Cards:** AX, DS, MC, VI. **Special Amenities: free local telephone calls and early check-in/late check-out.**

SOME UNITS

FEE

HISTORIC HOTEL NEVADA & GAMBLING HALL — Historic Small-scale Hotel — **Phone:** (775)289-6665

5/1-10/31 1P: $38-$48 2P: $38-$48 XP: $5 F3
2/1-4/30 & 11/1-1/31 1P: $30-$40 2P: $30-$40 XP: $5 F3

Location: Downtown. 501 Aultman St 89301. Fax: 775/289-4715. **Facility:** When it was built in 1929, the hotel was the tallest building in Nevada. 63 units. 59 one- and 3 two-bedroom standard units. 1 two-bedroom suite ($85) with whirlpool. 6 stories, interior corridors. *Bath:* combo or shower only. **Parking:** on-site. **Terms:** pets (in limited units). **Amenities:** hair dryers. **Dining:** 24 hours, cocktails. **Business Services:** meeting rooms. **Cards:** AX, DC, DS, MC, VI.

SOME UNITS

HOLIDAY INN — *Book at aaa.com* — Motel — **Phone:** (775)289-8900

5/2-10/31 1P: $89 XP: $4 F12
2/1-5/1 & 11/1-1/31 1P: $75 XP: $4 F12

Location: 1.5 mi n on US 93. 1501 E Aultman St 89301. Fax: 775/289-4607. **Facility:** Newly renovated rooms make this a good choice for your stay in town; dining and a casino add to the appeal. 61 one-bedroom standard units. 2 stories (no elevator), interior corridors. *Bath:* combo or shower only. **Parking:** on-site. **Terms:** 10 day cancellation notice. **Amenities:** voice mail, irons, hair dryers. **Pool(s):** heated indoor. **Leisure Activities:** whirlpool, exercise room. **Guest Services:** coin laundry. **Business Services:** meeting rooms. **Cards:** AX, DC, DS, MC, VI.

ASK — SOME UNITS

RAMADA INN-COPPER QUEEN CASINO — *Book at aaa.com* — Motel — **Phone:** (775)289-4884

6/1-10/31 [ECP] 1P: $80-$105 2P: $85-$110 XP: $5 F18
5/1-5/31 [ECP] 1P: $69-$90 2P: $74-$95 XP: $5 F18
2/1-4/30 & 11/1-1/31 [ECP] 1P: $64-$85 2P: $69-$90 XP: $5 F18

Location: 0.3 mi s of jct US 6, 50 and 93. 805 Great Basin Blvd 89301. Fax: 775/289-1480. **Facility:** Hotel rooms and a slot casino are in a main building, with motel rooms available across the street. 65 one-bedroom standard units. 2 stories, interior/exterior corridors. **Parking:** on-site. **Amenities:** voice mail, irons, hair dryers. **Dining:** 7 am-9 pm, cocktails, also, Evah's, see separate listing. **Pool(s):** heated indoor. **Leisure Activities:** whirlpool. **Business Services:** meeting rooms. **Cards:** AX, CB, DC, DS, MC, VI.

SOME UNITS

WHERE TO DINE

EVAH'S — Italian — **Lunch:** $5-$12 **Dinner:** $5-$15 **Phone:** 775/289-4271

Location: 0.3 mi s of jct US 6, 50 and 93; in Ramada Inn-Copper Queen Casino. 805 Great Basin Blvd 89301. **Hours:** 11 am-9 pm. Closed: 11/25, 12/24, 12/25. **Features:** Sitting just above and overlooking the casino and indoor pool, the eatery serves good-tasting food from a varied menu. A couple TVs provide entertainment. Casual dress; cocktails. **Parking:** on-site. **Cards:** AX, CB, DC, DS, JC, MC, VI.

EUREKA

WHERE TO STAY

BEST WESTERN EUREKA INN *Book at aaa.com* **Phone:** (775)237-5247

Motel

All Year	1P: $79-$119	2P: $79-$119	XP: $5	F16

Location: On east side of Main St; center of town. 251 N Main St 89316 (PO Box 147). Fax: 775/237-5155. **Facility:** 42 units. 39 one-bedroom standard units. 3 one-bedroom suites. 2 stories (no elevator), interior corridors. *Bath:* combo or shower only. **Parking:** on-site. **Terms:** [ECP] meal plan available. **Amenities:** voice mail, irons, hair dryers. **Leisure Activities:** whirlpool, exercise room. **Business Services:** meeting rooms. **Cards:** AX, CB, DC, DS, MC, VI.

SOME UNITS

JACKSON HOUSE HOTEL, SALOON & RESTAURANT **Phone:** (775)237-5247

Historic Small-scale Hotel

All Year	1P: $79-$119	2P: $79-$119	XP: $5	F16

Location: On east side of Main St; downtown. 11 S Main St 89316 (PO Box 147). Fax: 775/237-5155. **Facility:** The charming property is situated right across the street from the Eureka County Courthouse in the center of town. Designated smoking area. 9 units. 7 one- and 2 two-bedroom standard units. 2 stories (no elevator), interior corridors. *Bath:* combo or shower only. **Parking:** on-site. **Terms:** [ECP] meal plan available. **Amenities:** hair dryers. **Cards:** AX, CB, DC, DS, MC, VI.

FALLON pop. 7,536

WHERE TO STAY

BEST WESTERN FALLON INN *Book at aaa.com* **Phone:** (775)423-6005

Motel

5/16-9/30 [ECP]	1P: $74-$84	2P: $80-$90	XP: $6	F12
2/1-5/15 & 10/1-1/31 [ECP]	1P: $70-$80	2P: $76-$86	XP: $6	F12

Location: 1035 W Williams Ave 89406. Fax: 775/423-7005. **Facility:** 54 units. 48 one-bedroom standard units, some with whirlpools. 6 one-bedroom suites ($100-$110). 2 stories (no elevator), exterior corridors. *Bath:* combo or shower only. **Parking:** on-site. **Amenities:** irons, hair dryers. **Pool(s):** heated outdoor. **Leisure Activities:** exercise room. **Guest Services:** coin laundry. **Business Services:** fax. **Cards:** AX, CB, DC, DS, JC, MC, VI. **Special Amenities: free expanded continental breakfast and free local telephone calls.**

SOME UNITS

COMFORT INN **Phone:** (775)423-5554

Motel

All Year	1P: $50-$150	2P: $60-$160	XP: $5	F18

Location: US 50, 1 mi w of US 95. 1830 W Williams Ave 89406. Fax: 775/423-0663. **Facility:** 82 one-bedroom standard units, some with whirlpools. 2 stories (no elevator), interior corridors. *Bath:* combo or shower only. **Parking:** on-site. **Terms:** [CP] meal plan available, small pets only (in limited units). **Amenities:** *Some:* hair dryers. **Pool(s):** heated indoor. **Leisure Activities:** whirlpool, exercise room. **Guest Services:** coin laundry. **Business Services:** meeting rooms. **Cards:** AX, CB, DC, DS, MC, VI. **Special Amenities: free continental breakfast and free local telephone calls.**

SOME UNITS

FEE FEE FEE

ECONO LODGE *Book at aaa.com* **Phone:** 775/423-2194

Motel

5/1-1/31	1P: $49-$75	2P: $65-$139	XP: $5	F18
2/1-4/30	1P: $36-$95	2P: $50-$109	XP: $5	F18

Location: US 50, e of US 95. 70 E Williams Ave 89406. Fax: 775/423-7187. **Facility:** 30 one-bedroom standard units. 2 stories, exterior corridors. *Bath:* combo or shower only. **Parking:** on-site. **Terms:** cancellation fee imposed, weekly rates available. **Amenities:** irons, hair dryers. **Pool(s):** heated outdoor. **Cards:** AX, CB, DC, DS, JC, MC, VI. **Special Amenities: free continental breakfast and free local telephone calls.**

SOME UNITS

FEE

HOLIDAY INN EXPRESS *Book at aaa.com* **Phone:** (775)428-2588

Small-scale Hotel

All Year [ECP]	1P: $79-$129	XP: $10	F19

Location: At Williams Ave, 0.8 mi w of US 95. 55 Commercial Way 89406. Fax: 775/428-2589. **Facility:** Set off the main road through town, this charming property offers an adjacent casino and two dining options. 98 units. 94 one-bedroom standard units, some with whirlpools. 4 one-bedroom suites ($89-$129) with whirlpools. 3 stories, interior corridors. **Parking:** on-site. **Amenities:** dual phone lines, voice mail, irons, hair dryers. **Dining:** Angelica's Steak House, see separate listing. **Pool(s):** outdoor, heated indoor. **Leisure Activities:** sauna, whirlpool, exercise room. **Guest Services:** valet and coin laundry. **Business Services:** meeting rooms, fax. **Cards:** AX, CB, DC, DS, JC, MC, VI.

SOME UNITS

LARIAT MOTEL **Phone:** (775)423-3181

Motel

All Year	1P: $34-$39	2P: $40-$44	XP: $8	

Location: US 50, 0.5 mi w of US 95. 850 W Williams Ave 89407 (PO Box 649). **Facility:** 18 one-bedroom standard units. 1 story, exterior corridors. *Bath:* shower only. **Parking:** on-site. **Pool(s):** heated outdoor. **Cards:** AX, MC, VI. **Special Amenities: free local telephone calls and preferred room (subject to availability with advanced reservations).**

SOME UNITS

MICROTEL INN & SUITES Book at aaa.com Phone: 775/428-0300

Motel

Property failed to provide current rates

Location: Just w of US 95. 1051 W Williams Ave 89406. Fax: 775/428-0301. **Facility:** 61 one-bedroom standard units. 2 stories (no elevator), interior corridors. *Bath:* combo or shower only. **Parking:** on-site. **Terms:** pets ($10 fee). **Amenities:** high-speed Internet, voice mail, hair dryers. **Guest Services:** coin laundry. **Business Services:** fax.

SOME UNITS FEE

MOTEL 6 Book at aaa.com Phone: 775/423-2277

SAVE Motel

3/1-10/31	1P: $43-$55	2P: $49-$63	XP: $6	F17
2/1-2/29 & 11/1-1/31	1P: $40-$50	2P: $46-$56	XP: $6	F17

Location: 0.5 mi s of US 50. 1705 S Taylor St 89406. Fax: 775/423-2271. **Facility:** 45 one-bedroom standard units. 1-2 stories (no elevator), exterior corridors. *Bath:* combo or shower only. **Parking:** on-site. **Terms:** 7 day cancellation notice-fee imposed, small pets only. **Pool(s):** small outdoor. **Guest Services:** coin laundry. **Cards:** AX, DC, DS, MC, VI.

SOME UNITS

WESTERN MOTEL Phone: (775)423-5118

SAVE Motel

All Year [CP]	1P: $37	2P: $41	XP: $8	F10

Location: US 95, just e. 125 S Carson St 89406. Fax: 775/423-4973. **Facility:** 22 one-bedroom standard units. 2 stories (no elevator), exterior corridors. *Bath:* combo or shower only. **Parking:** on-site. **Terms:** weekly rates available, small pets only ($5 extra charge, dogs only). **Amenities:** hair dryers. **Pool(s):** outdoor. **Cards:** AX, CB, DC, DS, MC, VI. **Special Amenities: free continental breakfast and free local telephone calls.**

SOME UNITS FEE

WHERE TO DINE

ANGELICA'S STEAK HOUSE **Dinner:** $12-$35 **Phone:** 775/423-2117

Steak House

Location: At Williams Ave, 0.8 mi w of US 95; in Stockman's Casino. 1560 W Williams Ave 89406. **Hours:** 5 pm-10 pm. Closed: Sun & Mon. **Reservations:** suggested. **Features:** Tucked in a busy casino, the quiet dining room lets guests savor a good selection of steaks, as well as seafood and fowl selections. The staff is friendly. Dressy casual; cocktails. **Parking:** on-site. **Cards:** AX, DC, DS, MC, VI.

FERNLEY pop. 8,543

WHERE TO STAY

BEST WESTERN FERNLEY INN Book at aaa.com Phone: (775)575-6776

SAVE Motel

5/16-9/30 [ECP]	1P: $73-$83	2P: $78-$88	XP: $5	F17
10/1-11/30 [ECP]	1P: $70-$80	2P: $75-$85	XP: $5	F17
2/1-5/15 [ECP]	1P: $66-$76	2P: $71-$81	XP: $5	F17
12/1-1/31 [ECP]	1P: $63-$73	2P: $68-$78	XP: $5	F17

Location: I-80, exit 48, just s. 1405 E Newlands Dr 89408. Fax: 775/575-6748. **Facility:** 66 one-bedroom standard units. 2 stories (no elevator), exterior corridors. **Parking:** on-site. **Terms:** pets ($7 extra charge, in limited units). **Amenities:** irons, hair dryers. **Pool(s):** heated indoor. **Leisure Activities:** whirlpool. **Guest Services:** coin laundry. **Cards:** AX, CB, DC, DS, MC, VI. **Special Amenities: free expanded continental breakfast and early check-in/late check-out.**

SOME UNITS FEE

SUPER 8 MOTEL Book at aaa.com Phone: 775/575-5555

Motel

All Year	1P: $55-$65	2P: $60-$70	XP: $6	F16

Location: I-80, exit 48, just s. 1350 Newlands Dr W 89408. Fax: 775/575-6546. **Facility:** 49 one-bedroom standard units. 2-3 stories, exterior corridors. **Parking:** on-site. **Terms:** [CP] meal plan available. **Amenities:** safes (fee). **Pool(s):** heated indoor. **Leisure Activities:** whirlpool. **Cards:** AX, CB, DC, DS, MC, VI.

ASK SOME UNITS

GARDNERVILLE pop. 3,357

WHERE TO STAY

HISTORIAN INN Phone: 775/783-1175

SAVE Motel

4/1-10/31 [CP]	1P: $69-$119	2P: $69-$119	XP: $6	F18
2/1-3/31 & 11/1-1/31 [CP]	1P: $59-$99	2P: $59-$99	XP: $6	F18

Location: Center. 1427 Hwy 395 N 89410 (PO Box 1848). Fax: 775/783-8620. **Facility:** 35 one-bedroom standard units. 2 stories (no elevator), exterior corridors. *Bath:* combo or shower only. **Parking:** on-site. **Amenities:** voice mail, irons, hair dryers. *Some:* dual phone lines. **Guest Services:** gift shop, valet laundry. **Business Services:** meeting rooms, fax. **Cards:** AX, MC, VI. **Special Amenities: free continental breakfast and early check-in/late check-out.**

SOME UNITS

TOPAZ LODGE Phone: 775/266-3338

SAVE Motel

All Year	1P: $55-$75	2P: $55-$75	XP: $10	F12

Location: US 395 S at Topaz Lake, 22 mi s. 1979 US 395 S 89410. Fax: 775/266-3046. **Facility:** All units with view of Topaz Lake. 102 one-bedroom standard units. 2-3 stories, exterior corridors. *Bath:* combo or shower only. **Parking:** on-site. **Terms:** pets ($8 extra charge, in limited units, no cats). **Dining:** 24 hours, cocktails. **Pool(s):** outdoor. **Leisure Activities:** playground. *Fee:* game room. **Guest Services:** gift shop. **Business Services:** meeting rooms. **Cards:** AX, DS, MC, VI. **Special Amenities: early check-in/late check-out and preferred room (subject to availability with advanced reservations).**

SOME UNITS

WESTERNER MOTEL Phone: 775/782-3602

AAA SAVE — Motel

4/30-10/26	1P: $40-$50	2P: $50-$65	XP: $5	F5
2/1-4/29	1P: $35-$45	2P: $45-$65	XP: $5	F5
10/27-1/31	1P: $32-$45	2P: $40-$55	XP: $5	F5

Location: US 395 S; end of town. 1353 US 395 N 89410 (PO Box 335). Fax: 775/782-8232. **Facility:** 25 one-bedroom standard units. 1 story, exterior corridors. **Parking:** on-site. **Terms:** pets ($50 deposit). **Pool(s):** heated outdoor. **Cards:** AX, DS, MC, VI. **Special Amenities: free local telephone calls and early check-in/late check-out.**

SOME UNITS

FEE

GENOA

WHERE TO STAY

THE LEGEND COUNTRY INN Phone: 775/783-0906

Bed & Breakfast

Property failed to provide current rates

Location: US 395, exit Genoa Ln, 3.5 mi w. 2292 Main St 89411. Fax: 775/783-1008. **Facility:** Set within a town known as Nevada's oldest permanent settlement, this charming inn promises an Old World atmosphere with a Western touch. 11 one-bedroom standard units. 2 stories (no elevator), exterior corridors. *Bath:* shower only. **Parking:** on-site. **Amenities:** voice mail, hair dryers.

DATA PORT

HAWTHORNE pop. 3,311

WHERE TO STAY

EL CAPITAN RESORT CASINO Phone: (775)945-3321

AAA SAVE — Motel

All Year 1P: $54-$60 2P: $54-$60

Location: Just n of US 95. 540 F St 89415 (PO Box 1000). Fax: 775/945-2193. **Facility:** Off the main roads. 103 units. 102 one-bedroom standard units. 1 one-bedroom suite. 1-2 stories (no elevator), exterior corridors. **Parking:** on-site. **Terms:** check-in 3:30 pm, small pets only ($10 fee). **Dining:** 6 am-2 am, cocktails. **Pool(s):** outdoor. **Leisure Activities:** Fee: golf-18 holes. **Guest Services:** gift shop. **Business Services:** meeting rooms. **Cards:** AX, CB, DC, DS, MC, VI. **Special Amenities: free local telephone calls and preferred room (subject to availability with advanced reservations).**

SOME UNITS

FEE

HENDERSON —*See Las Vegas p. 868.*

INCLINE VILLAGE —*See Lake Tahoe Area p. 402.*

INDIAN SPRINGS —*See Las Vegas p. 870.*

JACKPOT

WHERE TO STAY

CACTUS PETES RESORT CASINO Phone: (775)755-2321

AAA SAVE — Large-scale Hotel

5/1-10/31	1P: $59-$200	2P: $59-$200
2/1-4/30 & 11/1-1/31	1P: $49-$175	2P: $49-$175

Location: On SR 93. 1385 Hwy 93 89825 (PO Box 508). Fax: 775/755-2740. **Facility:** In addition to a casino, this service-oriented high-rise offers golf, tennis, entertainment and fine dining. 300 units. 296 one-bedroom standard units, some with whirlpools. 4 one-bedroom suites ($125-$200). 4-10 stories, interior corridors. *Bath:* combo or shower only. **Parking:** on-site. **Terms:** check-in 4 pm, package plans. **Amenities:** video games (fee), voice mail, irons, hair dryers. **Dining:** 2 restaurants, 24 hours; buffet $6-$11, cocktails, also, Plateau Room, see separate listing, entertainment. **Pool(s):** heated outdoor. **Leisure Activities:** whirlpool, 2 lighted tennis courts, recreation programs. *Fee:* golf-18 holes, game room. **Guest Services:** gift shop, area transportation. **Business Services:** conference facilities, fax. **Cards:** AX, DC, DS, MC, VI.

SOME UNITS

24

FOUR JACKS HOTEL & CASINO Phone: 775/755-2491

Motel

All Year 1P: $25-$45 2P: $25-$50 XP: $5 F

Location: On SR 93. 1702 Hwy 93 89825 (PO Box 468). Fax: 775/755-2934. **Facility:** 60 one-bedroom standard units, some with whirlpools. 2 stories (no elevator), interior corridors. **Parking:** on-site. **Amenities:** hair dryers. **Cards:** AX, DC, DS, MC, VI.

SOME UNITS

HORSESHU HOTEL & CASINO Phone: (775)755-7777

AAA SAVE — Small-scale Hotel

5/1-10/31	1P: $45-$85	2P: $45-$85
2/1-4/30	1P: $29-$77	2P: $29-$77
11/1-1/31	1P: $29-$69	2P: $29-$69

Location: On SR 93. 1385 Hwy 93 89825 (PO Box 508). Fax: 775/755-2769. **Facility:** Located right in the middle of town, this casino property offers a full service restaurant, casino and pool/spa. 120 one-bedroom standard units, some with whirlpools. 3 stories, interior corridors. **Parking:** on-site. **Terms:** check-in 4 pm, small pets only (in limited units). **Amenities:** voice mail, irons, hair dryers. **Dining:** 7 am-11 pm, Sat-midnight. **Pool(s):** heated outdoor. **Leisure Activities:** whirlpool, 2 lighted tennis courts. *Fee:* golf-18 holes. **Guest Services:** area transportation. **Cards:** AX, DC, DS, MC, VI.

SOME UNITS

WEST STAR RESORT

Motel

All Year [CP] 2P: $32-$75 **Phone:** (775)755-2600

Location: Just w of SR 93. Hwy 93 & Poker St 89825 (PO Box 775). Fax: 775/755-2980. **Facility:** Nice rooms, the distinction of being the first property on the north end of town and now a casino are among the reasons to check out this popular spot. 76 one-bedroom standard units. 3 stories, interior corridors. *Bath:* combo or shower only. **Parking:** on-site. **Terms:** cancellation fee imposed, pets ($5 extra charge, in limited units). **Amenities:** hair dryers. **Guest Services:** coin laundry, area transportation. **Business Services:** meeting rooms. **Cards:** AX, CB, DC, DS, MC.

ASK FEE DATA PORT SOME UNITS

WHERE TO DINE

PLATEAU ROOM

American

Dinner: $13-$44 **Phone:** 775/755-2321

Location: On SR 93; in Cactus Petes Resort Casino. 1385 Hwy 93 89825. **Hours:** 6 pm-10:30 pm. Closed: Mon & Tues. **Reservations:** suggested. **Features:** Fine dining in a quiet, elegant and intimate setting makes this a top choice. Choose from a varied menu and trust that you'll be served by a friendly and able staff. Dressy casual; cocktails. **Parking:** on-site. **Cards:** AX, CB, DC, DS, JC, MC, VI.

Destination Las Vegas

pop. 478,434

Las Vegas' bright lights beckon to the high roller in all of us. But like the flip side of a coin, this big city also offers a wealth of ways to venture beyond the neon.

Once you've had your fun on "the Strip," consider heading outdoors to complete your trip. Geological wonders and recreational fun are only minutes away. Taken together, Las Vegas' two faces make one winning combination.

© Richard Cummins Photophile

The Venetian. Many architectural glories of Venice, Italy, including Doge's Palace and St. Marks Square, are re-created in the desert. (See mention page 239)

© Richard Cummins Photophile

National Finals Rodeo. Bronco riding, calf roping and steer wrestling draw big crowds when the "super bowl of rodeos" comes to town in early December. (See mention page 240)

© Rick Doyle / Corbis

Lake Mead National Recreation Area, outside Boulder City. Catch the wind while boating or water skiing. It's the escape locals favor for beating the heat. (See mention page 241)

Mesquite
15
93
Indian Springs
95
See Vicinity map page 840
215
160
Overton
Echo Bay
Las Vegas
169
Pahrump
Henderson
NV
AZ
515
93
Boulder City
NEVADA
CALIFORNIA
95
15
Primm
Cottonwood Cove
68
163
Laughlin

Places included in this AAA Destination City:

© Richard Cummins / Photophile

Encore. In a town full of celebrity impersonators, the curtain never falls on the beloved entertainers who established Las Vegas as an entertainment mecca.

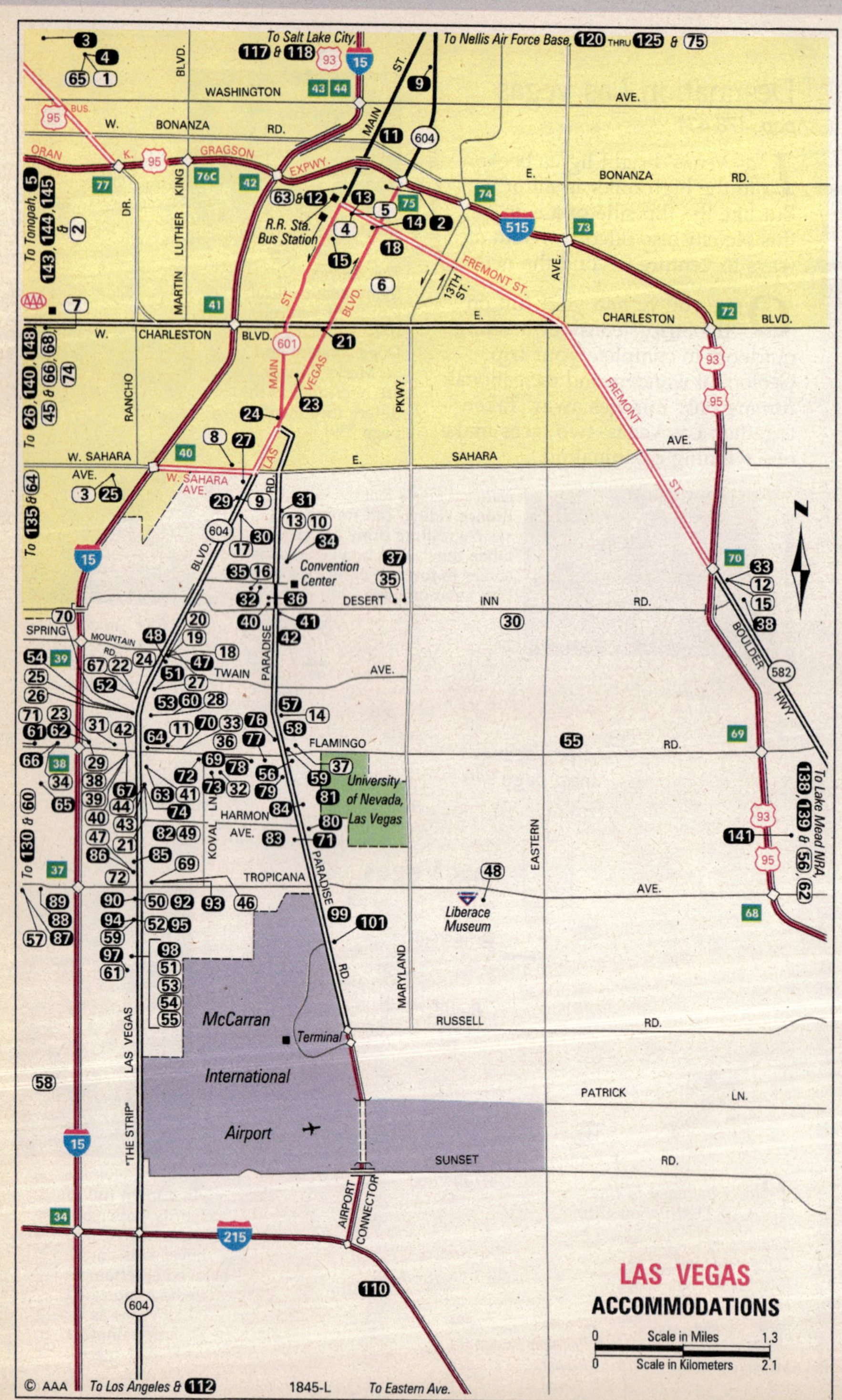

LAS VEGAS
ACCOMMODATIONS
Scale in Miles 0 1.3
Scale in Kilometers 0 2.1
To Salt Lake City, 117 & 118
To Nellis Air Force Base, 120 THRU 125 & 75
To Tonopah, 5, 143, 144, 145 & 2
To 26, 140, 148, 45 & 66, 68, 74
To 135 & 64
To 130 & 60
To Lake Mead NRA, 138, 139 & 56, 62
To Los Angeles & 112
To Eastern Ave.
WASHINGTON AVE.
W. BONANZA RD.
E. BONANZA RD.
ORAN K. GRAGSON EXPWY.
MARTIN LUTHER KING BLVD.
R.R. Sta.
Bus Station
FREMONT ST.
13TH ST.
W. CHARLESTON BLVD.
E. CHARLESTON BLVD.
RANCHO DR.
MAIN ST.
LAS VEGAS BLVD.
PKWY.
W. SAHARA AVE.
E. SAHARA AVE.
Convention Center
DESERT INN RD.
SPRING MOUNTAIN RD.
TWAIN AVE.
PARADISE RD.
FLAMINGO RD.
BOULDER HWY.
University of Nevada, Las Vegas
HARMON AVE.
KOVAL LN.
TROPICANA AVE.
EASTERN AVE.
Liberace Museum
MARYLAND PKWY.
RUSSELL RD.
McCarran International Airport
Terminal
PATRICK LN.
SUNSET RD.
"THE STRIP"
AIRPORT CONNECTOR
1845-L

Las Vegas

This index helps you "spot" where approved accommodations and restaurants are located on the corresponding detailed maps. Lodging rate ranges are for comparison only and show the property's high season; rates are per night, unless only weekly (W) rates are available. Restaurant rate range is for dinner, unless only lunch (L) is served. Turn to the listing page for more detailed rate information and consult display ads for special promotions.

Spotter/Map Page Number	OA	LAS VEGAS - Lodgings	Diamond Rating	Rate Range High Season	Listing Page
2 / p. 840		Park Plaza Las Vegas Lady Luck Casino Hotel	♦♦	$35-$125	857
3 / p. 840	AAA	**Fiesta Casino Hotel**	♦♦	$55-$110 SAVE	850
4 / p. 840	AAA	**Texas Station Gambling Hall & Hotel**	♦♦♦	$59-$149 SAVE	859
5 / p. 840	AAA	**Santa Fe Station Hotel Casino**	♦♦	$49-$129 SAVE	858
9 / p. 840	AAA	**Best Western Parkview Inn**	♦♦	$45-$149 SAVE	847
11 / p. 840	AAA	**Best Western Main Street Inn**	♦♦	$39-$149 SAVE	847
12 / p. 840		Main Street Station	♦♦♦	$60-$160	855
13 / p. 840	AAA	**Golden Nugget Hotel**	♦♦♦♦	$59-$129 SAVE	852
14 / p. 840	AAA	**Fitzgeralds Hotel & Casino**	♦♦♦	$39-$159 SAVE	852
15 / p. 840	AAA	**Budget Inn Hotel**	♦	$35-$69 SAVE	848
18 / p. 840	AAA	**Days Inn Downtown**	♦♦	$32-$129 SAVE	849
21 / p. 840	AAA	**Econo Lodge**	♦	$35-$209 SAVE	850
23 / p. 840	AAA	**Howard Johnson Las Vegas Strip**	♦♦	$39-$159 SAVE	854
24 / p. 840		Stratosphere	♦♦♦	$39-$199	859
25 / p. 840	AAA	**Palace Station Hotel & Casino**	♦♦♦	$50-$200 SAVE	857
26 / p. 840	AAA	**Suncoast Hotel & Casino**	♦♦♦	$59-$199 SAVE	859
27 / p. 840		Travelodge Las Vegas Strip	♦	$49-$79	860
29 / p. 840		Circus Circus Hotel, Casino & Themepark	♦♦♦	Failed to provide	849
30 / p. 840		Riviera Hotel and Casino	♦♦♦	$59-$149	858
31 / p. 840		Hilton Grand Vacations Club at the Las Vegas Hilton	♦♦♦	$129-$449	853
32 / p. 840		Marriott Suites Las Vegas	♦♦♦	$99-$329	856
33 / p. 840	AAA	**Boulder Station Hotel Casino**	♦♦♦	$49-$139 SAVE	848
34 / p. 840	AAA	**Las Vegas Hilton**	♦♦♦	$65-$365 SAVE	855
35 / p. 840	AAA	**Somerset House Motel**	♦♦	$35-$55 SAVE	859
36 / p. 840		Residence Inn Las Vegas Convention Center	♦♦♦	$119-$289	858
37 / p. 840		Homestead Studio Suites	♦♦	$60	854
38 / p. 840		Motel 6 Boulder Highway	♦	$30-$81	856
40 / p. 840	AAA	**Courtyard by Marriott-Convention Center**	♦♦♦	$99-$249 SAVE	849
41 / p. 840		Embassy Suites Convention Center	♦♦♦	$89-$239	850
42 / p. 840	AAA	**Best Western Mardi Gras Inn**	♦♦	$59-$119 SAVE	847
47 / p. 840		The Venetian Resort Hotel Casino	♦♦♦♦	$159-$899	860
48 / p. 840	AAA	**Casino Royale and Hotel**	♦♦	$49-$109 SAVE	848
51 / p. 840		Harrah's-Las Vegas	♦♦♦	$60-$250	853
52 / p. 840	AAA	**TI - Treasure Island**	♦♦♦♦	$69-$399 SAVE	860

Spotter/Map Page Number	OA	**LAS VEGAS - Lodgings (continued)**	Diamond Rating	Rate Range High Season	Listing Page
53 / p. 840		Hilton Grand Vacations Club	◆◆◆	$129-$449	853
54 / p. 840	AAA	**The Mirage**	◆◆◆◆	$89-$399 SAVE	856
55 / p. 840	AAA	**Wellesley Inn & Suites (Las Vegas/East Flamingo)**	◆◆◆	$59-$79 SAVE	860
56 / p. 840		Terrible's Hotel & Casino	◆◆	$29-$99	859
57 / p. 840		Fairfield Inn by Marriott	◆◆	$49-$189	850
58 / p. 840		La Quinta Inn Convention Center	◆◆◆	$70-$110	854
59 / p. 840		Candlewood Suites	◆◆◆	$89-$209	848
60 / p. 840	AAA	**Flamingo Las Vegas**	◆◆◆	$60-$260 SAVE	852
61 / p. 840	AAA	**Gold Coast Hotel**	◆◆◆	$49-$129 SAVE	852
62 / p. 840		Caesars Palace	◆◆◆◆	$129-$750	848
63 / p. 840		Bally's Las Vegas	◆◆◆	$69-$399	846
64 / p. 840		Leisure Resorts Las Vegas	◆◆◆	$85-$120	855
65 / p. 840		The Palms Casino Resort	◆◆◆	$109-$499	857
66 / p. 840		Rio All Suite Hotel & Casino	◆◆◆	$60-$250	858
67 / p. 840	AAA	**Bellagio**	◆◆◆◆◆	$159-$699 SAVE	847
69 / p. 840	AAA	**Best Western Tuscany Hotel & Casino**	◆◆◆	$89-$189 SAVE	847
70 / p. 840	AAA	**Barbary Coast Hotel**	◆◆◆	$49-$279 SAVE	846
71 / p. 840	AAA	**St. Tropez All Suite Hotel**	◆◆◆	$79-$259 SAVE	858
72 / p. 840		Econo Lodge By The Strip	◆◆	Failed to provide	850
73 / p. 840		Super 8 Motel Las Vegas Strip	◆◆	$61-$225	859
74 / p. 840		Paris Las Vegas	◆◆◆◆	$95-$350	857
76 / p. 840		Residence Inn-Hughes Center	◆◆◆	$99-$300	857
77 / p. 840		Key Largo Casino & Hotel at the Quality Inn	◆◆	$30-$150	854
78 / p. 840	AAA	**Clarion Hotel & Suites Emerald Springs**	◆◆◆	$89-$99 SAVE	849
79 / p. 840	AAA	**Crowne Plaza**	◆◆◆	$99-$259 SAVE	849
80 / p. 840	AAA	**AmeriSuites (Las Vegas/Paradise Road)**	◆◆◆	$79-$159 SAVE	846
81 / p. 840		Embassy Suites Hotel Las Vegas	◆◆◆	$89-$299	850
82 / p. 840	AAA	**Carriage House**	◆◆◆	$145-$300 SAVE	848
83 / p. 840		Alexis Park Resort Hotel	◆◆◆	$69-$169	846
84 / p. 840		Comfort Inn	◆◆	$59-$189	849
85 / p. 840	AAA	**Boardwalk Hotel & Casino**	◆◆◆	$49-$350 SAVE	848
86 / p. 840		Monte Carlo Resort & Casino	◆◆◆	$50-$450	856
87 / p. 840	AAA	**The Orleans**	◆◆◆	$45-$159 SAVE	857
88 / p. 840		Hampton Inn Tropicana	◆◆◆	$60-$210	853
89 / p. 840		Golden Palm Casino Hotel	◆◆	$29-$159	852
90 / p. 840		Excalibur Hotel & Casino - see color ad p 851	◆◆◆	$50-$300	850
92 / p. 840		Hawthorn Suites-Las Vegas	◆◆◆	$79-$309	853
93 / p. 840		MGM Grand Hotel & Casino	◆◆◆	$79-$499	856
94 / p. 840		Luxor Las Vegas	◆◆◆	$69-$399	855

Spotter/Map Page Number	OA	LAS VEGAS - Lodgings (continued)	Diamond Rating	Rate Range High Season	Listing Page
95 / p. 840	AAA	**Airport Inn Travelodge**	♦♦	$39-$179 SAVE	846
97 / p. 840	AAA	**Four Seasons Hotel Las Vegas**	♦♦♦♦♦	$300-$500	852
98 / p. 840	AAA	**Mandalay Bay Resort & Casino**	♦♦♦♦	$109-$2999 SAVE	856
99 / p. 840	AAA	**Best Western McCarran Inn**	♦♦	$59-$229 SAVE	847
101 / p. 840		Howard Johnson Airport Inn	♦	$49-$159	854
110 / p. 840	AAA	**DoubleTree Club Hotel Las Vegas Airport**	♦♦♦	$89-$149 SAVE	850
112 / p. 840		Silverton Hotel-Casino	♦♦	$35-$259	858
117 / p. 840		Ramada Inn-Speedway Casino	♦♦	$49-$169	857
118 / p. 840		Holiday Inn Express Hotel & Suites N Las Vegas	♦♦♦	$80	854
120 / p. 840	AAA	**Best Western Nellis Motor Inn**	♦♦	$54-$200 SAVE	847
121 / p. 840	AAA	**Barcelona Motel**	♦♦	$55-$95 SAVE	846
122 / p. 840		Hampton Inn Nellis	♦♦♦	$69-$99	853
123 / p. 840	AAA	**Comfort Inn**	♦♦♦	$59-$299 SAVE	849
124 / p. 840		Super 8 at Nellis	♦	$39-$89	859
125 / p. 840		La Quinta Inn-Nellis	♦♦♦	$79-$139	855
130 / p. 840	AAA	**La Quinta Inn**	♦♦♦	$69-$250 SAVE	854
135 / p. 840	AAA	**Holiday Inn Express**	♦♦♦	$79-$150 SAVE	853
138 / p. 840	AAA	**Sam's Town Hotel & Gambling Hall**	♦♦♦	$39-$160 SAVE	858
139 / p. 840		Nevada Palace	♦	$35-$100	856
140 / p. 840		Arizona Charlie's Decatur	♦♦	$35-$200	846
141 / p. 840	AAA	**Super 8 Motel-Boulder Hwy**	♦♦	$30-$88 SAVE	859
143 / p. 840	AAA	**Hampton Inn Las Vegas**	♦♦♦	$59-$99 SAVE	852
144 / p. 840		Courtyard by Marriott Las Vegas-Summerlin	♦♦♦	$89	849
145 / p. 840		La Quinta Las Vegas NW Tech Center	♦♦♦	$65-$96	855
148 / p. 840	AAA	**La Quinta Suites**	♦♦♦	$79-$199 SAVE	855
		LAS VEGAS - Restaurants			
1 / p. 840		Austins	♦♦♦	$25-$35	861
2 / p. 840		Taos Steakhouse	♦♦	$9-$35	866
3 / p. 840		The Broiler	♦♦	$14-$26	862
4 / p. 840		Lillie Langtry's	♦♦♦	$10-$29	864
5 / p. 840		Stefano's	♦♦♦	$14-$35	866
6 / p. 840		Andre's French Restaurant	♦♦♦	$22-$35	861
7 / p. 840		Country Inn	♦♦	$8-$15	862
8 / p. 840		Golden Steer	♦♦	$20-$60	863
9 / p. 840		Blue Iguana	♦♦	$8-$15	861
10 / p. 840		Andiamo	♦♦♦	$30-$70	861
11 / p. 840		Battista's Hole In The Wall	♦♦	$18-$35	861
12 / p. 840		Pasta Palace	♦♦	$9-$24	865
13 / p. 840		Hilton Steakhouse	♦♦♦	$20-$50	863

Spotter/Map Page Number	OA	**LAS VEGAS - Restaurants (continued)**	Diamond Rating	Rate Range High Season	Listing Page
14 / p. 840		Yolie's Brazilian Steak House	◆◆	$16-$27	867
15 / p. 840		Guadalajara Bar & Grille	◆◆	$5-$15	863
16 / p. 840		Piero's	◆◆◆	$20-$65	865
17 / p. 840		Ristorante Italiano	◆◆◆	$15-$30	866
18 / p. 840		Valentino Las Vegas	◆◆◆	$16-$40	867
19 / p. 840		Lutece	◆◆◆	$28-$45	864
20 / p. 840		Delmonico Steakhouse	◆◆◆	$27-$36	862
21 / p. 840		Mon Ami Gabi	◆◆◆	$20-$28	864
22 / p. 840		Francesco's	◆◆◆	$15-$40	863
23 / p. 840		Cafe Lago	◆◆	$9-$28	862
24 / p. 840		Buccaneer Bay	◆◆◆	$19-$36	862
25 / p. 840		Samba Brazillian Steakhouse	◆◆◆	$17-$30	866
26 / p. 840		Renoir	◆◆◆◆◆	$85	865
27 / p. 840		Range Steakhouse at Harrah's	◆◆◆	$20-$45	865
28 / p. 840		Conrad's	◆◆◆	$18-$33	862
29 / p. 840		Empress Court	◆◆◆	$15-$65	863
30 / p. 840		Tillerman	◆◆◆	$21-$54	866
31 / p. 840		Neros Steak and Seafood	◆◆◆	$26-$49	865
32 / p. 840		Palazzo Ristorante	◆◆◆	$15-$28	865
33 / p. 840		Michaels	◆◆◆◆	$35-$75	864
34 / p. 840		All American Bar & Grille	◆◆	$20-$60	861
35 / p. 840	AAA	**La Scala Restaurant**	◆◆◆	$12-$29	864
36 / p. 840		Lawry's The Prime Rib	◆◆◆	$24-$39	864
37 / p. 840	AAA	**Gandhi India's Cuisine**	◆◆	$13-$21	863
38 / p. 840		Le Cirque	◆◆◆◆◆	$80-$90	864
39 / p. 840		Prime Steakhouse	◆◆◆	$25-$74	865
40 / p. 840		Olives at Bellagio	◆◆◆	$12-$41	865
41 / p. 840		Al Dente	◆◆◆	$14-$35	860
42 / p. 840		Picasso	◆◆◆◆◆	$85-$95	865
43 / p. 840		Les Artistes Steakhouse	◆◆◆	$20-$35	864
44 / p. 840		Eiffel Tower Restaurant	◆◆◆◆	$26-$48	863
45 / p. 840		Primo's - A Place for Steaks	◆◆◆	$13-$37	865
46 / p. 840		Emeril's New Orleans Fish House	◆◆◆	$20-$35	863
47 / p. 840		Blackstone's	◆◆◆	$15-$40	861
48 / p. 840		Carluccio's Tivoli Gardens	◆◆	$9-$13	862
49 / p. 840		Joey Bistro & Bar	◆◆◆	$9-$16	863
50 / p. 840		The Steakhouse at Camelot	◆◆◆	$27-$39	866
51 / p. 840		3950 Restaurant	◆◆◆◆	$27-$58	860
52 / p. 840		Sacred Sea Room	◆◆◆	$22-$52	866
53 / p. 840		Border Grill	◆◆◆	$16-$30	861

Spotter/Map Page Number	OA	**LAS VEGAS - Restaurants (continued)**	Diamond Rating	Rate Range High Season	Listing Page
54 / p. 840		Aureole	♦♦♦♦	$60-$80	861
55 / p. 840		Shanghai Lilly	♦♦♦	$17-$65	866
56 / p. 840		Billy Bob's Steak House & Saloon	♦♦	$15-$41	861
57 / p. 840		Courtyard Cafe	♦♦	$5-$21	862
58 / p. 840		Blackjack Lodge	♦♦	$5-$17	861
59 / p. 840		Luxor Steakhouse	♦♦♦	$19-$52	864
60 / p. 840		Don Miguel's	♦♦	$8-$15	862
61 / p. 840		Charlie Palmer Steak	♦♦♦	$21-$38	862
62 / p. 840		Fresh Harvest Cafe	♦♦	$6-$13	863
63 / p. 840		Triple 7 Restaurant Brewery	♦♦	$5-$16	867
64 / p. 840		Rosemary's Restaurant	♦♦♦	$19-$36	866
65 / p. 840		San Lorenzo	♦♦♦	$10-$35	866
66 / p. 840		Fellini's Italian Dining	♦♦♦	$11-$27	863
67 / p. 840	AAA	**Kahunaville**	♦♦♦	$7-$19	864
68 / p. 840		Sourdough Cafe	♦	$8-$18	866
69 / p. 840		Craftsteak	♦♦♦	$24-$42	862
70 / p. 840		Kokomos	♦♦♦	$16-$50	864
71 / p. 840		Ping Pang Pong	♦♦	$8-$29	865
72 / p. 840		America	♦♦	$7-$16	861
74 / p. 840		Tre	♦♦♦	$12-$35	867
75 / p. 840		Waverly's Steak House	♦♦♦	$14-$26	867

LAS VEGAS pop. 478,434 (See map and index starting on p. 840)

Most establishments in Las Vegas do not confirm advance reservations at a definite rate. Advance reservations for Saturday only are extremely difficult.

WHERE TO STAY

AIRPORT INN TRAVELODGE Book at aaa.com Phone: (702)736-3600 95

SAVE Motel

All Year 1P: $39-$169 2P: $49-$179 XP: $10 F17

Location: I-15, exit Tropicana Ave, 0.5 mi e. 5075 S Koval Ln 89119. Fax: 702/736-0726. **Facility:** 106 one-bedroom standard units. 2 stories (no elevator), exterior corridors. **Parking:** on-site. **Terms:** cancellation fee imposed. **Amenities:** safes (fee), hair dryers. **Pool(s):** outdoor. **Leisure Activities:** exercise room. **Guest Services:** coin laundry, area transportation-convention center. **Cards:** AX, CB, DC, DS, JC, MC, VI. **Special Amenities: free local telephone calls and free newspaper.**

SOME UNITS

ALEXIS PARK RESORT HOTEL Book at aaa.com Phone: (702)796-3300 83

Small-scale Hotel

All Year 1P: $69-$169 2P: $69-$169 XP: $20 F12

Location: I-15, exit Tropicana Ave, just w to UNLV; 2 mi s of convention center. 375 E Harmon Ave 89109. Fax: 702/796-0766. **Facility:** 496 units. 484 one- and 12 two-bedroom standard units, some with whirlpools. 2 stories, exterior corridors. **Parking:** on-site. **Terms:** 3 day cancellation notice-fee imposed. **Amenities:** dual phone lines, voice mail, irons, hair dryers. **Pool(s):** 3 outdoor, heated outdoor. **Leisure Activities:** saunas, whirlpools. *Fee:* massage. **Guest Services:** gift shop, valet laundry. **Business Services:** conference facilities, business center. **Cards:** AX, CB, DC, DS, JC, MC, VI.

SOME UNITS

AMERISUITES (LAS VEGAS/PARADISE ROAD) Book at aaa.com Phone: (702)369-3366 80

SAVE Small-scale Hotel

9/16-11/30	1P: $79-$159	2P: $79-$159	XP: $10	F17
2/1-5/15 & 12/1-1/31	1P: $69-$149	2P: $69-$149	XP: $10	F17
5/16-9/15	1P: $59-$139	2P: $59-$139	XP: $10	F17

Location: Cross streets Harmon and Paradise, e of the Strip. 4520 Paradise Ave 89109. Fax: 702/369-0009. **Facility:** 202 one-bedroom standard units. 6 stories, interior corridors. *Bath:* combo or shower only. **Parking:** on-site. **Terms:** check-in 4 pm, [ECP] meal plan available, small pets only. **Amenities:** voice mail, irons, hair dryers. *Fee:* video games, high-speed Internet. *Some:* dual phone lines. **Pool(s):** heated outdoor. **Leisure Activities:** exercise room. **Guest Services:** coin laundry, area transportation-within 5 mi. **Business Services:** meeting rooms, business center. **Cards:** AX, DC, DS, JC, MC, VI. **Special Amenities: free expanded continental breakfast and free newspaper.**

SOME UNITS

ARIZONA CHARLIE'S DECATUR Phone: (702)258-5200 140

Small-scale Hotel

All Year 1P: $35-$200 2P: $35-$200 XP: $10 F12

Location: I-15, exit Charleston Blvd W, 7 mi nw. 740 S Decatur Blvd, Evergreen Ave 89107. Fax: 702/258-5192. **Facility:** Old West atmosphere. 257 units. 250 one-bedroom standard units. 5 one- and 2 two-bedroom suites with whirlpools. 3-7 stories, interior corridors. *Bath:* combo or shower only. **Parking:** on-site and valet. **Terms:** 3 day cancellation notice. **Dining:** Sourdough Cafe, see separate listing. **Pool(s):** outdoor. **Leisure Activities:** whirlpool. *Fee:* game room. **Guest Services:** gift shop, valet laundry, area transportation. **Business Services:** meeting rooms, fax. **Cards:** AX, DC, DS, MC, VI.

SOME UNITS

BALLY'S LAS VEGAS Book at aaa.com Phone: (702)739-4111 63

Large-scale Hotel

All Year 1P: $69-$399 2P: $69-$399 XP: $30 F18

Location: 4.5 mi s on the Strip. 3645 Las Vegas Blvd S 89109. Fax: 702/967-4405. **Facility:** A casino and common areas connect this property's two lodging towers. 2814 units. 2514 one-bedroom standard units. 300 one-bedroom suites. 26 stories, interior corridors. *Bath:* some combo or shower only. **Parking:** on-site and valet. **Terms:** 3 day cancellation notice. **Amenities:** voice mail, safes (fee), irons, hair dryers. *Some:* dual phone lines. **Dining:** Al Dente, see separate listing. **Pool(s):** outdoor. **Leisure Activities:** sauna, whirlpool, steamroom. *Fee:* 8 lighted tennis courts, massage, game room. **Guest Services:** gift shop, valet laundry. **Business Services:** conference facilities, business center. **Cards:** AX, DC, DS, JC, MC, VI.

SOME UNITS

FEE FEE

BARBARY COAST HOTEL Book at aaa.com Phone: (702)737-7111 70

SAVE Large-scale Hotel

All Year 1P: $49-$279 XP: $10 F12

Location: 1.8 mi s on the Strip. 3595 Las Vegas Blvd S 89109 (PO Box 19030, 89132). Fax: 702/737-6304. **Facility:** A large mural crafted in Tiffany-style stained glass adds distinction to this hotel. 200 units. 188 one-bedroom standard units. 12 one-bedroom suites, some with whirlpools. 5 stories, interior corridors. *Bath:* combo or shower only. **Parking:** on-site and valet. **Amenities:** voice mail, hair dryers. **Dining:** 3 restaurants, 24 hours, cocktails, also, Michaels, see separate listing. **Guest Services:** gift shop, valet laundry. **Business Services:** fax. **Cards:** AX, CB, DC, DS, JC, MC, VI. **Special Amenities: early check-in/late check-out.**

SOME UNITS

BARCELONA MOTEL Phone: (702)644-6300 121

SAVE Motel

All Year 1P: $55-$85 2P: $65-$95 XP: $10 F16

Location: I-15, exit 48 eastbound, 7 mi ne; 0.5 mi from Nellis AFB. 5011 E Craig Rd 89115. Fax: 702/644-6510. **Facility:** 172 one-bedroom standard units. 2 stories (no elevator), exterior corridors. *Bath:* combo or shower only. **Parking:** on-site. **Terms:** weekly rates available. **Amenities:** *Some:* safes (fee). **Dining:** 24 hours, cocktails, entertainment. **Pool(s):** outdoor. **Leisure Activities:** whirlpool, small casino. **Guest Services:** coin laundry. **Business Services:** meeting rooms, fax. **Cards:** AX, MC, VI.

SOME UNITS

(See map and index starting on p. 840)

BELLAGIO Book at aaa.com **Phone:** (702)693-7111 67

Large-scale Hotel

All Year 1P: $159-$699 2P: $159-$699 XP: $35

Location: I-15, exit E Flamingo Rd, on the Strip. 3600 Las Vegas Blvd S 89109 (PO Box 7700, 89177). Fax: 702/693-8546. **Facility:** Many of the spacious, nicely decorated guest rooms overlook the Strip; fountains and fine finishes distinguish the exterior. 3005 units. 2676 one-bedroom standard units, some with whirlpools. 250 one-, 68 two- and 11 three-bedroom suites ($350-$6000) with whirlpools. 36 stories, interior corridors. *Bath:* combo or shower only. **Parking:** on-site and valet. **Amenities:** CD players, high-speed Internet (fee), dual phone lines, voice mail, safes, honor bars, irons, hair dryers. **Dining:** 10 restaurants, 24 hours; buffet $13-$32, cocktails, also, Le Cirque, Olives at Bellagio, Prime Steakhouse, Picasso, see separate listings, entertainment. **Pool(s):** 6 heated outdoor. **Leisure Activities:** whirlpools, 39 pool cabanas, spa. *Fee:* game room. **Guest Services:** gift shop, valet laundry. **Business Services:** conference facilities, business center. **Cards:** AX, DC, DS, JC, MC, VI.

SOME UNITS / FEE / FEE FEE

BEST WESTERN MAIN STREET INN Book at aaa.com **Phone:** (702)382-3455 11

Motel

All Year 1P: $39-$149 2P: $39-$149 XP: $7 F12

Location: I-15, exit 43E northbound; exit 44E southbound. 1000 N Main St 89101. Fax: 702/382-1428. **Facility:** 91 one-bedroom standard units. 2-3 stories, exterior corridors. **Parking:** on-site. **Terms:** small pets only ($8 extra charge). **Amenities:** irons, hair dryers. **Dining:** 6 am-11 pm. **Pool(s):** outdoor. **Guest Services:** coin laundry. **Business Services:** meeting rooms, fax. **Cards:** AX, CB, DC, DS, JC, MC, VI. **Special Amenities: free local telephone calls and free room upgrade (subject to availability with advanced reservations).**

SOME UNITS / FEE FEE

BEST WESTERN MARDI GRAS INN Book at aaa.com **Phone:** (702)731-2020 42

Motel

All Year 1P: $59-$119 2P: $59-$119

Location: 0.5 mi s of convention center. 3500 Paradise Rd 89109. Fax: 702/731-4005. **Facility:** 314 one-bedroom standard units. 3 stories, exterior corridors. **Parking:** on-site. **Terms:** [CP] meal plan available, $3 service charge. **Amenities:** video library, video games, voice mail, safes (fee), irons, hair dryers. **Dining:** 6:30 am-10 pm, cocktails. **Pool(s):** outdoor. **Leisure Activities:** whirlpool, sun deck. **Guest Services:** gift shop, complimentary evening beverages, coin laundry, area transportation-the Strip. **Business Services:** conference facilities, fax. **Cards:** AX, CB, DC, DS, JC, MC, VI. **Special Amenities: free continental breakfast and free room upgrade (subject to availability with advanced reservations).**

SOME UNITS

BEST WESTERN MCCARRAN INN Book at aaa.com **Phone:** (702)798-5530 99

Motel

All Year [ECP] 1P: $59-$229 2P: $59-$229 XP: $10 F12

Location: I-15, exit Tropicana E, 5.5 blks. Located across from the airport. 4970 Paradise Rd 89119. Fax: 702/798-7627. **Facility:** 100 one-bedroom standard units. 3 stories, interior corridors. **Parking:** on-site. **Terms:** cancellation fee imposed. **Amenities:** irons, hair dryers. **Pool(s):** heated outdoor. **Leisure Activities:** exercise room. **Guest Services:** coin laundry, area transportation-within 2 mi. **Business Services:** business center. **Cards:** AX, CB, DC, DS, MC, VI. **Special Amenities: free expanded continental breakfast and free local telephone calls.**

SOME UNITS

BEST WESTERN NELLIS MOTOR INN Book at aaa.com **Phone:** (702)643-6111 120

Motel

All Year 1P: $54-$200 2P: $54-$200 XP: $5 F12

Location: I-15, exit 48 eastbound, 7 mi ne; 0.3 mi from Nellis AFB. 5330 E Craig Rd 89115. Fax: 702/643-8553. **Facility:** 52 one-bedroom standard units. 2 stories (no elevator), exterior corridors. **Parking:** on-site. **Terms:** check-in 4 pm, cancellation fee imposed, pets ($10 extra charge). **Amenities:** irons, hair dryers. **Pool(s):** outdoor. **Leisure Activities:** playground. **Guest Services:** coin laundry. **Cards:** AX, DC, DS, MC, VI. **Special Amenities: free full breakfast and free local telephone calls.**

SOME UNITS / FEE / FEE

BEST WESTERN PARKVIEW INN Book at aaa.com **Phone:** (702)385-1213 9

Motel

All Year [CP] 1P: $45-$149 2P: $49-$149 XP: $7 F12

Location: I-15, exit US 93-95, 0.3 mi n at Washington. 921 Las Vegas Blvd N 89101. Fax: 702/382-2380. **Facility:** 42 one-bedroom standard units. 2 stories (no elevator), exterior corridors. **Parking:** on-site. **Terms:** small pets only ($8 extra charge). **Amenities:** voice mail, irons, hair dryers. **Pool(s):** outdoor. **Guest Services:** coin laundry. **Business Services:** fax (fee). **Cards:** AX, CB, DC, DS, JC, MC, VI. **Special Amenities: free continental breakfast and early check-in/late check-out.**

SOME UNITS / FEE

BEST WESTERN TUSCANY HOTEL & CASINO Book at aaa.com **Phone:** (702)893-8933 69

Large-scale Hotel

12/1-1/31	1P: $89-$189	2P: $89-$189	XP: $10	F12
2/1-4/30 & 9/1-11/30	1P: $89-$159	2P: $89-$159	XP: $10	F12
5/1-8/31	1P: $79-$139	2P: $79-$139	XP: $10	F12

Location: I-15, exit E Flamingo Rd, 0.5 mi. 255 E Flamingo Rd 89109. Fax: 702/947-5994. **Facility:** 716 units. 712 one-bedroom standard units, some with efficiencies (no utensils). 4 two-bedroom suites with whirlpools. 3 stories, interior corridors. **Parking:** on-site and valet. **Amenities:** voice mail, safes, hair dryers. *Fee:* video games, high-speed Internet. **Dining:** 2 restaurants, 24 hours, cocktails, also, Palazzo Ristorante, see separate listing. **Pool(s):** heated outdoor, small heated indoor. **Leisure Activities:** whirlpool, exercise room. **Guest Services:** gift shop, valet laundry. **Business Services:** conference facilities, business center. **Cards:** AX, CB, DC, DS, JC, MC, VI. **Special Amenities: free local telephone calls and early check-in/late check-out.**

SOME UNITS

(See map and index starting on p. 840)

BOARDWALK HOTEL & CASINO Book at aaa.com **Phone:** (702)735-2400 85

Large-scale Hotel

All Year 1P: $49-$350 2P: $49-$350 XP: $15 F12

Location: I-15, exit Flamingo Rd, then s on the Strip. 3750 Las Vegas Blvd S 89109. Fax: 702/739-8152. **Facility:** 654 units. 651 one- and 3 two-bedroom standard units, some with whirlpools. 4-16 stories, interior/exterior corridors. *Bath:* combo or shower only. **Parking:** on-site. **Amenities:** voice mail, irons, hair dryers. **Dining:** 2 restaurants, 24 hours; buffet, cocktails. **Pool(s):** 2 outdoor. **Leisure Activities:** exercise room. **Guest Services:** gift shop, coin laundry. **Business Services:** meeting rooms, business center. **Cards:** AX, CB, DC, DS, JC, MC, VI.

SOME UNITS FEE

BOULDER STATION HOTEL CASINO Book at aaa.com **Phone:** (702)432-7777 83

Large-scale Hotel

All Year 1P: $49-$139 2P: $49-$139 XP: $12 F11

Location: Just s of Sahara Ave. 4111 Boulder Hwy 89121 (PO Box 12027, 89112-0027). Fax: 702/221-6510. **Facility:** Come out to Boulder Highway and enjoy the casino, movie theaters and wide selection of dining this longtime popular property has to offer. 300 units. 294 one-bedroom standard units. 6 one-bedroom suites, some with whirlpools. 13 stories, interior corridors. *Bath:* combo or shower only. **Parking:** on-site and valet. **Terms:** cancellation fee imposed. **Amenities:** high-speed Internet (fee), voice mail, irons, hair dryers. *Some:* safes. **Dining:** 5 restaurants, 24 hours; buffet $5-$12, cocktails, also, Pasta Palace, Guadalajara Bar & Grille, see separate listings, entertainment. **Pool(s):** outdoor. **Leisure Activities:** Fee: movie theater, game room. **Guest Services:** gift shop, valet laundry. **Business Services:** meeting rooms, fax. **Cards:** AX, CB, DC, DS, JC, MC, VI. **Special Amenities: free local telephone calls and early check-in/late check-out.**

SOME UNITS FEE

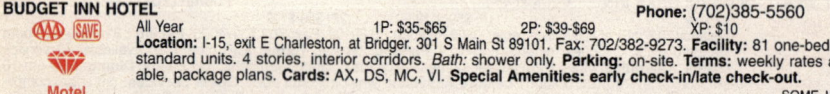

BUDGET INN HOTEL **Phone:** (702)385-5560 15

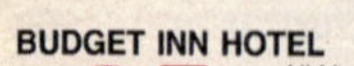

Motel

All Year 1P: $35-$65 2P: $39-$69 XP: $10 F3

Location: I-15, exit E Charleston, at Bridger. 301 S Main St 89101. Fax: 702/382-9273. **Facility:** 81 one-bedroom standard units. 4 stories, interior corridors. *Bath:* shower only. **Parking:** on-site. **Terms:** weekly rates available, package plans. **Cards:** AX, DS, MC, VI. **Special Amenities: early check-in/late check-out.**

SOME UNITS

CAESARS PALACE Book at aaa.com **Phone:** (702)731-7110 62

Large-scale Hotel

All Year 1P: $129-$750 2P: $129-$750 XP: $20 F18

Location: I-15, exit E Flamingo Rd, 0.5 mi e at the Strip. 3570 Las Vegas Blvd S 89109. Fax: 702/731-6636. **Facility:** The hotel's Forum Mall resembles a Roman streetscape with shops, art galleries and eateries; marble statues accent the manicured grounds. 2419 units. 2207 one-bedroom standard units, some with whirlpools. 212 one-bedroom suites ($350-$4000) with whirlpools. 14-29 stories, interior corridors. *Bath:* combo or shower only. **Parking:** on-site and valet. **Terms:** check-in 5 pm, 3 day cancellation notice-fee imposed. **Amenities:** voice mail, safes, irons, hair dryers. *Some:* dual phone lines. **Dining:** Empress Court, Neros Steak and Seafood, Cafe Lago, see separate listings. **Pool(s):** 3 heated outdoor. **Leisure Activities:** sauna, whirlpools. *Fee:* massage. **Guest Services:** gift shop, valet laundry. **Business Services:** conference facilities, business center. **Cards:** AX, DC, DS, MC, VI.

SOME UNITS FEE

CANDLEWOOD SUITES Book at aaa.com **Phone:** (702)836-3660 59

Small-scale Hotel

All Year 1P: $89-$209

Location: I-15, exit E Flamingo Rd to Paradise Rd, just ne. 4034 S Paradise Rd 89109. Fax: 702/836-3661. **Facility:** 276 units. 178 one-bedroom standard units with efficiencies. 98 one-bedroom suites with efficiencies. 4 stories, interior corridors. *Bath:* combo or shower only. **Parking:** on-site. **Terms:** cancellation fee imposed, weekly rates available, pets ($75 fee). **Amenities:** CD players, dual phone lines, voice mail, irons, hair dryers. **Pool(s):** heated outdoor. **Leisure Activities:** whirlpool, exercise room. **Guest Services:** sundries, complimentary laundry. **Business Services:** meeting rooms, fax. **Cards:** AX, DC, DS, MC, VI.

SOME UNITS FEE

CARRIAGE HOUSE Book at aaa.com **Phone:** (702)798-1020 82

Small-scale Hotel

All Year 1P: $145-$300 2P: $145-$300

Location: Just e off the Strip. 105 E Harmon Ave 89109. Fax: 702/798-1020. **Facility:** 155 units. 140 one- and 15 two-bedroom standard units, some with efficiencies or kitchens. 9 stories, interior corridors. *Bath:* combo or shower only. **Parking:** on-site. **Terms:** check-in 4 pm. **Amenities:** voice mail, safes, irons, hair dryers. *Fee:* video library, video games. **Dining:** Joey Bistro & Bar, see separate listing. **Pool(s):** outdoor. **Leisure Activities:** whirlpool, lighted tennis court. **Guest Services:** coin laundry, area transportation-the Strip. **Business Services:** fax. **Cards:** AX, DC, DS, MC, VI. **Special Amenities: free local telephone calls and free room upgrade (subject to availability with advanced reservations).**

SOME UNITS

CASINO ROYALE AND HOTEL **Phone:** (702)737-3500 48

Small-scale Hotel

All Year 1P: $49-$109 2P: $49-$109 XP: $10 F18

Location: Center of the Strip. 3411 Las Vegas Blvd S 89109. Fax: 702/650-4746. **Facility:** 151 units. 149 one-bedroom standard units. 2 one-bedroom suites ($150-$299) with whirlpools. 4 stories, interior corridors. **Parking:** on-site. **Terms:** check-in 4 pm. **Amenities:** voice mail, safes. *Some:* irons, hair dryers. **Dining:** 24 hours. **Pool(s):** heated outdoor. **Leisure Activities:** casino. **Guest Services:** valet laundry. **Cards:** AX, MC, VI. **Special Amenities: free local telephone calls.**

SOME UNITS

(See map and index starting on p. 840)

CIRCUS CIRCUS HOTEL, CASINO & THEMEPARK **Book at aaa.com** **Phone:** 702/734-0410 29

Property failed to provide current rates

Large-scale Hotel **Location:** 2.8 mi s on the Strip. 2880 Las Vegas Blvd S 89109 (PO Box 14967, 89114). Fax: 702/734-5897. **Facility:** The property includes guest rooms in its hotel towers and motel units in a three-story building. 3770 one-bedroom standard units, some with whirlpools. 2-35 stories, interior corridors. *Bath:* combo or shower only. **Parking:** on-site and valet. **Amenities:** dual phone lines, voice mail, safes, hair dryers. **Dining:** Blue Iguana, see separate listing. **Pool(s):** 3 heated outdoor. **Leisure Activities:** whirlpools. *Fee:* game room. **Guest Services:** gift shop, valet laundry. **Business Services:** conference facilities, business center.

SOME UNITS / FEE

CLARION HOTEL & SUITES EMERALD SPRINGS **Book at aaa.com** **Phone:** (702)732-9100 78

Small-scale Hotel All Year 1P: $89-$99 2P: $89-$99 XP: $20 F12

Location: I-15, exit E Flamingo Rd. 325 E Flamingo Rd 89109. Fax: 702/731-9784. **Facility:** 150 one-bedroom standard units, some with whirlpools. 3 stories, interior corridors. **Parking:** on-site. **Terms:** [AP], [BP], [ECP] & [MAP] meal plans available. **Amenities:** video games (fee), voice mail, irons, hair dryers. **Dining:** 6:30 am-9 pm, cocktails. **Pool(s):** outdoor. **Leisure Activities:** whirlpool, exercise room. **Guest Services:** valet laundry, airport transportation-by limo, area transportation-the Strip. **Business Services:** conference facilities, business center. **Cards:** AX, CB, DC, DS, JC, MC, VI. **Special Amenities: free newspaper and preferred room (subject to availability with advanced reservations).**

SOME UNITS / FEE

COMFORT INN **Book at aaa.com** **Phone:** (702)938-2000 84

Motel All Year [CP] 1P: $59-$189 2P: $59-$189 XP: $10 F18

Location: I-15, exit E Flamingo Rd. 4350 Paradise Rd 89109. Fax: 702/938-2001. **Facility:** 199 one-bedroom standard units with efficiencies. 2 stories (no elevator), exterior corridors. *Bath:* combo or shower only. **Parking:** on-site. **Amenities:** voice mail, irons, hair dryers. **Pool(s):** heated outdoor. **Guest Services:** coin laundry. **Business Services:** meeting rooms. **Cards:** AX, CB, DC, DS, JC, MC, VI.

SOME UNITS

COMFORT INN **Book at aaa.com** **Phone:** (702)399-1500 123

Motel All Year 1P: $59-$299 2P: $69-$299

Location: I-15, exit 46 (Cheyenne Ave W). 910 E Cheyenne Ave 89030. Fax: 702/399-2900. **Facility:** 59 one-bedroom standard units, some with whirlpools. 3 stories (no elevator), interior corridors. *Bath:* combo or shower only. **Parking:** on-site. **Terms:** cancellation fee imposed, [CP] & [ECP] meal plans available, pets ($5 extra charge). **Amenities:** irons, hair dryers. **Pool(s):** heated outdoor. **Leisure Activities:** whirlpool. **Guest Services:** gift shop, coin laundry. **Business Services:** meeting rooms. **Cards:** AX, CB, DC, DS, JC, MC, VI. **Special Amenities: free expanded continental breakfast and free local telephone calls.**

SOME UNITS / FEE

COURTYARD BY MARRIOTT-CONVENTION CENTER **Book at aaa.com** **Phone:** (702)791-3600 40

Small-scale Hotel All Year 1P: $99-$249 2P: $99-$249

Location: Just e of the Strip. Located near the convention center. 3275 Paradise Rd 89109. Fax: 702/796-7981. **Facility:** 149 one-bedroom standard units. 3 stories, interior corridors. *Bath:* combo or shower only. **Parking:** on-site. **Amenities:** high-speed Internet (fee), dual phone lines, voice mail, irons, hair dryers. **Dining:** 6:30-11 am, Sat & Sun 7 am-noon. **Pool(s):** heated outdoor. **Leisure Activities:** whirlpool, exercise room. **Guest Services:** coin laundry. **Business Services:** meeting rooms, fax. **Cards:** AX, CB, DC, DS, JC, MC, VI.

SOME UNITS

COURTYARD BY MARRIOTT LAS VEGAS-SUMMERLIN **Book at aaa.com** **Phone:** (702)646-4400 144

Small-scale Hotel

2/1-5/31 & 9/1-1/31 1P: $89 2P: $89

6/1-8/31 1P: $79 2P: $79

Location: US 95, exit Lake Mead Blvd, just e. 1901 N Rainbow Blvd 89108. Fax: 702/646-0337. **Facility:** 154 one-bedroom standard units, some with whirlpools. 3 stories, interior corridors. *Bath:* combo or shower only. **Parking:** on-site. **Terms:** [BP] meal plan available. **Amenities:** dual phone lines, voice mail, irons, hair dryers. **Pool(s):** heated outdoor. **Leisure Activities:** whirlpool, exercise room. **Guest Services:** valet and coin laundry. **Business Services:** meeting rooms, business center. **Cards:** AX, CB, DC, DS, JC, MC, VI.

SOME UNITS

CROWNE PLAZA **Book at aaa.com** **Phone:** (702)369-4400 79

Large-scale Hotel All Year 1P: $99-$259 2P: $99-$259 XP: $10 F12

Location: I-15, exit Flamingo Rd, 0.5 mi e to Paradise Rd, 0.3 mi s. 4255 S Paradise Rd 89109. Fax: 702/369-3770. **Facility:** 201 one-bedroom standard units. 6 stories, interior corridors. **Parking:** on-site. **Terms:** 3 day cancellation notice, pets ($200 deposit, on 1st floor). **Amenities:** video games (fee), dual phone lines, voice mail, irons, hair dryers. **Dining:** 6 am-10 pm, cocktails. **Pool(s):** heated outdoor. **Leisure Activities:** sauna, whirlpool, exercise room. **Guest Services:** gift shop, valet laundry, area transportation-the Strip. **Business Services:** meeting rooms, business center. **Cards:** AX, CB, DC, DS, JC, MC, VI. **Special Amenities: early check-in/late check-out and free room upgrade (subject to availability with advanced reservations).**

SOME UNITS / FEE

DAYS INN DOWNTOWN **Book at aaa.com** **Phone:** (702)388-1400 18

Motel All Year 1P: $32-$119 2P: $36-$129 XP: $5 F16

Location: On US 93 and 95 business route. 707 E Fremont St 89101. Fax: 702/388-9622. **Facility:** 147 one-bedroom standard units. 3 stories, exterior corridors. **Parking:** on-site. **Terms:** cancellation fee imposed, [AP] meal plan available. **Amenities:** hair dryers. **Dining:** 7 am-8 pm. **Pool(s):** outdoor. **Cards:** AX, CB, DC, DS, JC, MC, VI. **Special Amenities: free local telephone calls and free newspaper.**

SOME UNITS

(See map and index starting on p. 840)

DOUBLETREE CLUB HOTEL LAS VEGAS AIRPORT Book at aaa.com **Phone:** (702)948-4000 **110**

SAVE

Small-scale Hotel

2/1-5/30 & 8/2-1/31	1P: $89-$149	2P: $89-$149	XP: $15	F17
5/31-8/1	1P: $69-$119	2P: $69-$119	XP: $15	F17

Location: I-215, exit 7 (Warm Springs Rd). 7250 Pollock Dr 89119. Fax: 702/948-4100. **Facility:** 190 one-bedroom standard units. 6 stories, interior corridors. *Bath:* combo or shower only. **Parking:** on-site. **Amenities:** video games (fee), dual phone lines, voice mail, irons, hair dryers. **Dining:** 6 am-10 pm, cocktails. **Leisure Activities:** exercise room. **Guest Services:** valet laundry, area transportation-within 5 mi. **Business Services:** meeting rooms, business center. **Cards:** AX, CB, DC, DS, JC, MC, VI. **Special Amenities: free local telephone calls and free newspaper.**

SOME UNITS / FEE FEE

ECONO LODGE Book at aaa.com **Phone:** (702)382-6001 **21**

SAVE

Motel

All Year 1P: $35-$209

Location: I-15, exit 41 to Las Vegas Blvd, just s. 1150 Las Vegas Blvd S 89104. Fax: 702/382-9180. **Facility:** 121 one-bedroom standard units. 2 stories (no elevator), exterior corridors. **Parking:** on-site. **Pool(s):** outdoor. **Cards:** AX, DC, DS, JC, MC, VI. **Special Amenities: free local telephone calls.**

SOME UNITS

ECONO LODGE BY THE STRIP Book at aaa.com **Phone:** 702/733-7800 **72**

Motel

Property failed to provide current rates

Location: I-15, exit E Flamingo Rd at Koval Rd. 211 E Flamingo Rd 89109. Fax: 702/733-7353. **Facility:** 121 one-bedroom standard units. 2 stories (no elevator), exterior corridors. **Parking:** on-site. **Pool(s):** small outdoor.

SOME UNITS

EMBASSY SUITES CONVENTION CENTER Book at aaa.com **Phone:** (702)893-8000 **41**

Large-scale Hotel

All Year 1P: $89-$239 2P: $89-$239 XP: $10 F18

Location: I-15, exit Sahara Ave E, 0.5 mi s of convention center. 3600 Paradise Rd 89109. Fax: 702/893-0378. **Facility:** 286 one-bedroom suites. 11 stories, interior corridors. *Bath:* combo or shower only. **Parking:** on-site. **Terms:** [BP] meal plan available. **Amenities:** dual phone lines, voice mail, irons, hair dryers. *Fee:* video games, high-speed Internet. **Pool(s):** heated indoor. **Leisure Activities:** whirlpool, exercise room. **Guest Services:** gift shop, complimentary evening beverages, coin laundry, area transportation. **Business Services:** meeting rooms, fax. **Cards:** AX, CB, DC, DS, JC, MC, VI.

ASK SOME UNITS

EMBASSY SUITES HOTEL LAS VEGAS Book at aaa.com **Phone:** (702)795-2800 **81**

Large-scale Hotel

All Year 1P: $89-$299 2P: $89-$299 XP: $10 F18

Location: I-15, exit Tropicana Ave, just e, then just n. 4315 Swenson St 89119. Fax: 702/795-1520. **Facility:** 220 one-bedroom standard units. 6 stories, interior corridors. *Bath:* combo or shower only. **Parking:** on-site. **Terms:** [BP] meal plan available. **Amenities:** dual phone lines, voice mail, irons, hair dryers. **Pool(s):** heated outdoor. **Leisure Activities:** whirlpools, exercise room. **Guest Services:** gift shop, complimentary evening beverages, valet and coin laundry, area transportation. **Business Services:** meeting rooms. **Cards:** AX, CB, DC, DS, JC, MC, VI.

ASK SOME UNITS VCR FEE

EXCALIBUR HOTEL & CASINO Book at aaa.com **Phone:** (702)597-7777 **90**

Large-scale Hotel

All Year 1P: $50-$300 2P: $50-$300 XP: $15 F12

Location: I-15, exit E Tropicana Ave, on the Strip. 3850 Las Vegas Blvd S 89109 (PO Box 96778, 89193). Fax: 702/597-7163. **Facility:** Medieval castle theme. 3991 units. 3961 one-bedroom standard units, some with whirlpools. 30 one-bedroom suites. 28 stories, interior corridors. *Bath:* shower only. **Parking:** on-site and valet. **Amenities:** voice mail, irons, hair dryers. **Dining:** The Steakhouse at Camelot, see separate listing. **Pool(s):** heated outdoor. **Leisure Activities:** whirlpool. *Fee:* game room. **Guest Services:** gift shop, valet and coin laundry. **Business Services:** conference facilities, business center. **Cards:** AX, CB, DC, DS, JC, MC, VI. ***(See color ad p 851)***

ASK SOME UNITS FEE

FAIRFIELD INN BY MARRIOTT Book at aaa.com **Phone:** (702)791-0899 **57**

Motel

All Year 1P: $49-$189 2P: $49-$189

Location: I-15, exit E Flamingo Rd, 3 blks n of convention center. 3850 Paradise Rd 89109. Fax: 702/791-2705. **Facility:** 129 one-bedroom standard units. 4 stories, interior corridors. **Parking:** on-site. **Terms:** cancellation fee imposed, [ECP] meal plan available. **Amenities:** voice mail, irons. **Pool(s):** outdoor. **Leisure Activities:** whirlpool. **Business Services:** meeting rooms. **Cards:** AX, CB, DC, DS, JC, MC, VI.

ASK SOME UNITS

FIESTA CASINO HOTEL Book at aaa.com **Phone:** (702)631-7000 **3**

SAVE

Small-scale Hotel

All Year 1P: $55-$110 2P: $55-$110 XP: $15 F12

Location: 3 mi n; downtown. 2400 N Rancho Dr 89130. Fax: 702/638-3645. **Facility:** 100 one-bedroom standard units. 5 stories, interior corridors. *Bath:* combo or shower only. **Parking:** on-site and valet. **Terms:** cancellation fee imposed, $5 service charge. **Amenities:** voice mail, irons, hair dryers. **Dining:** 3 restaurants, 24 hours; buffet $5-$9. **Pool(s):** heated outdoor. **Guest Services:** gift shop. **Business Services:** meeting rooms. **Cards:** AX, DC, DS, MC, VI.

SOME UNITS

(See map and index starting on p. 840)

FITZGERALDS HOTEL & CASINO Book at aaa.com **Phone:** (702)388-2400 14

SAVE Large-scale Hotel

All Year 1P: $39-$159 2P: $49-$159 XP: $10 F17

Location: Downtown. Located in casino center. 301 Fremont St 89101. Fax: 702/388-2181. **Facility:** 640 units. 625 one-bedroom standard units, some with whirlpools. 15 one-bedroom suites with whirlpools. 34 stories, interior corridors. *Bath:* combo or shower only. **Parking:** on-site and valet. **Terms:** [AP] meal plan available. **Amenities:** safes, irons. *Some:* hair dryers. **Dining:** 3 restaurants, 24 hours; buffet, cocktails. **Guest Services:** gift shop. **Business Services:** meeting rooms. **Cards:** AX, CB, DC, DS, JC, MC, VI. **Special Amenities: early check-in/late check-out.**

SOME UNITS

FLAMINGO LAS VEGAS Book at aaa.com **Phone:** (702)733-3111 60

SAVE Large-scale Hotel

All Year 1P: $60-$260 2P: $60-$260 XP: $20 F17

Location: I-15, exit E Flamingo Rd, just n on the Strip. 3555 Las Vegas Blvd S 89109. Fax: 702/733-3528. **Facility:** 3565 units. 3511 one-bedroom standard units. 30 one- and 24 two-bedroom suites ($350-$700), some with whirlpools. 2-28 stories, interior corridors. *Bath:* combo or shower only. **Parking:** on-site and valet. **Terms:** 3 day cancellation notice-fee imposed. **Amenities:** voice mail, irons, hair dryers. *Fee:* high-speed Internet, safes. **Dining:** 8 restaurants, 24 hours; buffet $9-$14, cocktails, also, Conrad's, see separate listing, entertainment. **Pool(s):** 2 outdoor, heated outdoor, wading. **Leisure Activities:** whirlpools, waterslide. *Fee:* 4 lighted tennis courts, massage. **Guest Services:** gift shop, valet laundry. **Business Services:** conference facilities, business center. **Cards:** AX, CB, DC, DS, JC, MC, VI.

FEE SOME UNITS FEE

FOUR SEASONS HOTEL LAS VEGAS Book at aaa.com **Phone:** (702)632-5000 97

Large-scale Hotel

2/1-6/1 & 9/3-1/31 1P: $300-$500 2P: $300-$500 XP: $30 F18
6/2-9/2 1P: $250-$450 2P: $250-$450 XP: $30 F18

Location: I-15, exit E Tropicana Ave, just s on the Strip. 3960 Las Vegas Blvd S 89119. Fax: 702/632-5195. **Facility:** The hotel's spacious rooms, on floors 35 through 39 of a high-rise, overlook a mountain range; pampering appointments include extra-deep soaking tubs. 424 units. 338 one-bedroom standard units. 54 one- and 32 two-bedroom suites ($450-$4150), some with whirlpools. 5 stories, interior corridors. *Bath:* combo or shower only. **Parking:** on-site (fee). **Terms:** cancellation fee imposed, package plans, small pets only. **Amenities:** CD players, dual phone lines, voice mail, safes, honor bars, irons, hair dryers. *Fee:* video games, high-speed Internet. **Dining:** 2 restaurants, 6:30 am-10:30 pm, cocktails, also, Charlie Palmer Steak, see separate listing. **Pool(s):** small outdoor, heated outdoor. **Leisure Activities:** whirlpools, jogging, spa. **Guest Services:** gift shop, valet laundry. **Business Services:** conference facilities, business center. **Cards:** AX, DC, DS, JC, MC, VI.

FEE SOME UNITS

GOLD COAST HOTEL Book at aaa.com **Phone:** (702)367-7111 61

SAVE Large-scale Hotel

9/4-1/31 1P: $49-$129 2P: $49-$129
2/1-5/31 1P: $49-$129 2P: $49-$129 XP: $10 F15
6/1-9/3 1P: $39-$129 2P: $39-$129 XP: $10 F15

Location: I-15, exit W Flamingo Rd, just w. 4000 W Flamingo Rd 89103 (PO Box 80750, 89180). Fax: 702/367-8575. **Facility:** Colonial-Spanish architecture. 711 units. 700 one-bedroom standard units. 11 one-bedroom suites ($175-$350). 10 stories, interior corridors. *Bath:* combo or shower only. **Parking:** on-site and valet. **Terms:** cancellation fee imposed. **Amenities:** voice mail, irons, hair dryers. **Dining:** 5 restaurants, 24 hours; buffet $5-$12, cocktails, also, Ping Pang Pong, see separate listing, entertainment. **Pool(s):** outdoor. **Leisure Activities:** whirlpool, exercise room. *Fee:* bowling. **Guest Services:** gift shop, valet laundry, area transportation-the Strip. **Business Services:** conference facilities, fax. **Cards:** AX, DC, DS, MC, VI. **Special Amenities: early check-in/late check-out.**

SOME UNITS

GOLDEN NUGGET HOTEL Book at aaa.com **Phone:** (702)385-7111 13

SAVE Large-scale Hotel

All Year 2P: $59-$129 XP: $20

Location: Downtown. Located in casino center. 129 E Fremont St 89101 (PO Box 610, 89125). Fax: 702/386-8362. **Facility:** The property's two towers offer comfortable rooms and well-maintained common areas. 1907 units. 1805 one-bedroom standard units. 102 one-bedroom suites ($275-$375) with whirlpools. 10-22 stories, interior corridors. *Bath:* combo or shower only. **Parking:** on-site and valet. **Terms:** cancellation fee imposed, weekly rates available. **Amenities:** voice mail, safes, irons, hair dryers. *Some:* dual phone lines. **Dining:** 4 restaurants, 24 hours; buffet $7-$11, cocktails, also, Stefano's, Lillie Langtry's, see separate listings, entertainment. **Pool(s):** heated outdoor. **Leisure Activities:** whirlpool. *Fee:* massage. **Guest Services:** gift shop, valet laundry. **Business Services:** conference facilities, business center. **Cards:** AX, CB, DC, DS, JC, MC, VI.

FEE SOME UNITS FEE

GOLDEN PALM CASINO HOTEL Book at aaa.com **Phone:** (702)798-1111 89

Small-scale Hotel

All Year 1P: $29-$149 2P: $39-$159 XP: $10 F12

Location: I-15, exit W Tropicana Ave. 3111 W Tropicana Ave 89103. Fax: 702/798-7138. **Facility:** 150 one-bedroom standard units. 6 stories, interior corridors. **Parking:** on-site. **Terms:** cancellation fee imposed. **Amenities:** voice mail, hair dryers. *Some:* irons. **Pool(s):** outdoor. **Leisure Activities:** whirlpool. **Guest Services:** valet laundry. **Business Services:** meeting rooms. **Cards:** AX, DC, DS, MC, VI.

ASK SOME UNITS

HAMPTON INN LAS VEGAS Book at aaa.com **Phone:** (702)360-5700 143

SAVE Motel

All Year [ECP] 1P: $59-$99 2P: $59-$99

Location: I-95, exit W Cheyenne Ave, just s on Tenaya Way. 7100 Cascade Valley Ct 89128. Fax: 702/360-5757. **Facility:** 127 one-bedroom standard units. 3 stories, interior corridors. *Bath:* combo or shower only. **Parking:** on-site. **Terms:** 30 day cancellation notice-fee imposed, small pets only ($25 fee). **Amenities:** voice mail, irons, hair dryers. **Pool(s):** outdoor. **Leisure Activities:** whirlpool. **Business Services:** meeting rooms, business center. **Cards:** AX, CB, DC, DS, JC, MC, VI. **Special Amenities: free expanded continental breakfast and free newspaper.**

FEE SOME UNITS

(See map and index starting on p. 840)

HAMPTON INN NELLIS **Book at aaa.com** **Phone:** (702)644-5700 **122**

Motel

All Year 1P: $69-$89 2P: $79-$99 XP: $10 F18

Location: I-15, exit Craig Rd, 2.3 mi e, then just s. 4035 N Nellis Blvd 89115. Fax: 702/644-5701. **Facility:** 87 one-bedroom standard units. 3 stories, exterior corridors. *Bath:* combo or shower only. **Parking:** on-site. **Terms:** cancellation fee imposed. **Amenities:** video games (fee), voice mail, irons, hair dryers. **Pool(s):** heated outdoor. **Leisure Activities:** whirlpool, exercise room. **Guest Services:** coin laundry. **Business Services:** meeting rooms, business center. **Cards:** AX, CB, DC, DS, MC, VI.

SOME UNITS

HAMPTON INN TROPICANA **Book at aaa.com** **Phone:** (702)948-8100 **88**

Motel

All Year [ECP] 1P: $60-$200 2P: $70-$210

Location: I-15, exit W Tropicana Ave. 4975 S Industrial Rd 89118. Fax: 702/948-8101. **Facility:** 320 one-bedroom standard units. 6 stories, interior corridors. *Bath:* combo or shower only. **Parking:** on-site. **Terms:** 3 night minimum stay - weekends, cancellation fee imposed. **Amenities:** video library, video games, dual phone lines, voice mail, irons, hair dryers. **Pool(s):** heated outdoor. **Leisure Activities:** whirlpool, exercise room. **Guest Services:** sundries, coin laundry, area transportation. **Business Services:** conference facilities, business center. **Cards:** AX, DC, DS, JC, MC, VI.

SOME UNITS

HARRAH'S-LAS VEGAS **Book at aaa.com** **Phone:** (702)369-5000 **51**

Large-scale Hotel

All Year 1P: $60-$250 2P: $60-$250 XP: $20

Location: 4 mi s on the Strip. 3475 Las Vegas Blvd S 89109. Fax: 702/369-5008. **Facility:** Name entertainment, several restaurants and shops and a full casino are all here in the center of the strip. 2601 units. 2455 one-bedroom standard units. 146 one-bedroom suites with whirlpools. 15-35 stories, interior corridors. *Bath:* combo or shower only. **Parking:** on-site and valet. **Terms:** check-in 4 pm, 3 day cancellation notice. **Amenities:** video games (fee), voice mail, honor bars, irons, hair dryers. **Dining:** Range Steakhouse at Harrah's, see separate listing. **Pool(s):** heated outdoor. **Leisure Activities:** whirlpool. *Fee:* massage. **Guest Services:** gift shop, valet laundry, area transportation. **Business Services:** conference facilities, fax. **Cards:** AX, DC, DS, MC, VI.

SOME UNITS

FEE FEE

HAWTHORN SUITES-LAS VEGAS **Book at aaa.com** **Phone:** (702)739-7000 **92**

Motel

12/1-1/31 [ECP] 1P: $79-$309 2P: $79-$309
2/1-4/30 & 9/2-11/30 [ECP] 1P: $99-$209 2P: $99-$209
5/1-9/1 [ECP] 1P: $69-$159 2P: $69-$159

Location: I-15, exit E Tropicana Ave, 0.8 mi e to Duke Ellington Way, then just s. 5051 Duke Ellington Way 89119. Fax: 702/739-9350. **Facility:** 278 units. 217 one- and 61 two-bedroom suites. 3 stories, exterior corridors. *Bath:* combo or shower only. **Parking:** on-site. **Terms:** check-in 4 pm, cancellation fee imposed, small pets only ($25 fee). **Amenities:** video games (fee), voice mail, irons, hair dryers. **Pool(s):** outdoor. **Leisure Activities:** whirlpool, exercise room, sports court. **Guest Services:** sundries, complimentary evening beverages: Mon-Thurs, coin laundry. **Business Services:** meeting rooms. **Cards:** AX, CB, DC, DS, MC, VI.

SOME UNITS

FEE

HILTON GRAND VACATIONS CLUB **Book at aaa.com** **Phone:** (702)697-2900 **53**

Large-scale Hotel

All Year 1P: $129-$269 2P: $189-$449

Location: I-15, exit E Flamingo Rd, just n on the Strip. Located directly behind Flamingo Las Vegas. 3575 Las Vegas Blvd S 89109. Fax: 702/697-2910. **Facility:** 303 units. 191 one- and 112 two-bedroom standard units with whirlpools, some with efficiencies or kitchens. 17 stories, interior corridors. **Parking:** on-site and valet. **Terms:** check-in 4 pm, 3 day cancellation notice. **Amenities:** voice mail, safes, irons, hair dryers. **Pool(s):** heated outdoor, wading. **Leisure Activities:** sauna, whirlpools, exercise room. **Guest Services:** gift shop, valet laundry. **Business Services:** meeting rooms. **Cards:** AX, CB, DC, DS, MC, VI.

SOME UNITS

HILTON GRAND VACATIONS CLUB AT THE LAS VEGAS HILTON **Book at aaa.com** **Phone:** (702)946-9200 **31**

Large-scale Hotel

All Year 1P: $129-$269 2P: $189-$449

Location: At Paradise Rd. Located adjacent to Las Vegas Hilton. 455 Karen Ave 89109. Fax: 702/946-9212. **Facility:** 405 one-bedroom standard units, some with whirlpools. 16 stories, interior corridors. *Bath:* combo or shower only. **Parking:** on-site. **Terms:** check-in 4 pm, 3 day cancellation notice. **Amenities:** video library (fee), dual phone lines, voice mail, safes, irons, hair dryers. **Pool(s):** heated outdoor. **Leisure Activities:** whirlpools, jogging, exercise room. **Guest Services:** gift shop, complimentary laundry. **Business Services:** meeting rooms, fax. **Cards:** AX, CB, DC, DS, MC, VI.

SOME UNITS

HOLIDAY INN EXPRESS **Book at aaa.com** **Phone:** (702)256-3766 **135**

AAA SAVE

Motel

2/1-5/31 & 9/16-1/31 [ECP] 1P: $79-$150 2P: $79-$150 XP: $10 D16
6/1-9/15 [ECP] 1P: $69-$125 2P: $69-$125 XP: $10 D16

Location: I-15, exit Sahara Ave, 6.5 mi w at Durango. 8669 W Sahara Ave 89117. Fax: 702/256-3763. **Facility:** 59 one-bedroom standard units, some with whirlpools. 3 stories (no elevator), interior corridors. *Bath:* combo or shower only. **Parking:** on-site. **Terms:** 2-3 night minimum stay - weekends, cancellation fee imposed, pets ($20 fee, in smoking units). **Amenities:** irons, hair dryers. **Pool(s):** heated indoor. **Leisure Activities:** whirlpool. **Guest Services:** sundries, coin laundry. **Business Services:** meeting rooms, fax. **Cards:** AX, DC, DS, MC, VI. **Special Amenities: free expanded continental breakfast and free local telephone calls.**

SOME UNITS

FEE

(See map and index starting on p. 840)

HOLIDAY INN EXPRESS HOTEL & SUITES N LAS VEGAS Book at aaa.com Phone: (702)649-3000 118

Motel

5/1-8/31	1P: $80	2P: $80	XP: $10	F18
2/1-4/30	1P: $71	2P: $71	XP: $10	F18
9/1-1/31	1P: $62	2P: $62	XP: $10	F18

Location: I-15, exit W Craig Rd. 4540 Donovan Way 89031. Fax: 702/649-3997. **Facility:** 74 one-bedroom standard units, some with whirlpools. 3 stories, interior corridors. *Bath:* combo or shower only. **Parking:** on-site. **Terms:** [CP] meal plan available, pets ($25 fee). **Amenities:** dual phone lines, voice mail, irons, hair dryers. **Pool(s):** heated outdoor. **Leisure Activities:** whirlpool. **Guest Services:** sundries, valet and coin laundry. **Business Services:** meeting rooms, business center. **Cards:** AX, DC, DS, MC, VI.

ASK FEE DATA PORT / SOME UNITS /

HOMESTEAD STUDIO SUITES Book at aaa.com Phone: 702/369-1414 37

Motel

All Year	1P: $60	2P: $60	XP: $5	F18

Location: I-15, exit Sahara Ave E, just s. 3045 S Maryland Pkwy 89109. Fax: 702/369-2242. **Facility:** 123 one-bedroom standard units with efficiencies. 3 stories, interior corridors. *Bath:* combo or shower only. **Parking:** on-site. **Terms:** pets ($10 extra charge). **Amenities:** voice mail, irons. **Guest Services:** sundries, coin laundry. **Cards:** AX, DC, DS, JC, MC, VI.

FEE DATA PORT / SOME UNITS VCR FEE /

HOWARD JOHNSON AIRPORT INN Book at aaa.com Phone: (702)798-2777 101

Motel

All Year	1P: $49-$139	2P: $59-$159

Location: I-15, exit E Tropicana Ave, 1.8 mi to Paradise Rd, then 0.3 mi s. 5100 Paradise Rd 89119. Fax: 702/736-8295. **Facility:** 327 one-bedroom standard units. 2 stories (no elevator), exterior corridors. *Bath:* combo or shower only. **Parking:** on-site. **Terms:** 7 day cancellation notice, weekly rates available, [AP] meal plan available, pets ($50 fee, in limited units). **Amenities:** voice mail, irons, hair dryers. **Pool(s):** 2 outdoor. **Leisure Activities:** Fee: game room. **Guest Services:** coin laundry, area transportation. **Business Services:** meeting rooms. **Cards:** AX, CB, DC, DS, JC, MC, VI.

ASK FEE / SOME UNITS DATA PORT /

HOWARD JOHNSON LAS VEGAS STRIP Book at aaa.com Phone: (702)388-0301 23

AAA SAVE

Motel

5/1-1/31	1P: $39-$159	2P: $39-$159
2/1-4/30	1P: $49-$149	2P: $49-$149

Location: I-15, exit Las Vegas Blvd, just n. 1401 Las Vegas Blvd S 89104. Fax: 702/388-2506. **Facility:** 104 one-bedroom standard units, some with whirlpools. 3 stories, interior/exterior corridors. **Parking:** on-site. **Terms:** small pets only ($10 extra charge). **Amenities:** voice mail, safes (fee). **Dining:** 7 am-10 pm, wine/beer only. **Pool(s):** outdoor. **Leisure Activities:** Fee: game room. **Guest Services:** coin laundry. **Business Services:** meeting rooms. **Cards:** AX, CB, DC, DS, MC, VI. **Special Amenities: free local telephone calls and free newspaper.**

FEE DATA PORT / SOME UNITS /

KEY LARGO CASINO & HOTEL AT THE QUALITY INN Book at aaa.com Phone: (702)733-7777 77

Motel

All Year	1P: $30-$150	2P: $30-$150	XP: $10	F18

Location: I-15, exit E Flamingo Rd, 4 blks. 377 E Flamingo Rd 89109. Fax: 702/369-6911. **Facility:** Attractively landscaped grounds. 316 one-bedroom standard units. 3 stories, interior/exterior corridors. **Parking:** on-site. **Terms:** 2 night minimum stay - weekends, cancellation fee imposed. **Pool(s):** heated outdoor. **Leisure Activities:** whirlpool. **Guest Services:** gift shop, coin laundry, area transportation. **Business Services:** meeting rooms, fax. **Cards:** AX, CB, DC, DS, JC, MC, VI.

ASK DATA PORT / SOME UNITS /

LA QUINTA INN Book at aaa.com Phone: (702)798-7736 130

AAA SAVE

Motel

9/1-1/31 [ECP]	1P: $69-$250
3/2-5/31 [ECP]	1P: $69-$120
2/1-3/1 & 6/1-8/31 [ECP]	1P: $59-$89

Location: I-15, exit Tropicana Ave W. 4975 S Valley View Blvd 89118. Fax: 702/798-5951. **Facility:** 59 one-bedroom standard units, some with kitchens. 3 stories (no elevator), interior corridors. *Bath:* combo or shower only. **Parking:** on-site. **Amenities:** irons, hair dryers. **Pool(s):** heated indoor. **Leisure Activities:** whirlpool, exercise room. **Guest Services:** gift shop, valet and coin laundry. **Business Services:** meeting rooms. **Cards:** AX, CB, DC, DS, JC, MC, VI. **Special Amenities: free expanded continental breakfast and free local telephone calls.**

DATA PORT / SOME UNITS /

LA QUINTA INN CONVENTION CENTER Book at aaa.com Phone: 702/796-9000 58

Motel

All Year	1P: $70-$100	2P: $80-$110	XP: $10	F18

Location: I-15, exit E Flamingo Rd, 0.8 mi s of convention center; 0.5 mi e of the Strip. 3970 Paradise Rd 89109. Fax: 702/796-3537. **Facility:** 251 units. 221 one- and 30 two-bedroom standard units, some with whirlpools. 3 stories, interior corridors. *Bath:* combo or shower only. **Parking:** on-site. **Terms:** [ECP] meal plan available, small pets only. **Amenities:** video games (fee), voice mail, irons, hair dryers. **Pool(s):** 2 outdoor. **Leisure Activities:** whirlpool, exercise room. **Guest Services:** coin laundry, area transportation. **Business Services:** meeting rooms. **Cards:** AX, CB, DC, DS, JC, MC, VI.

DATA PORT / SOME UNITS /

(See map and index starting on p. 840)

LA QUINTA INN-NELLIS Book at aaa.com Phone: (702)632-0229 125

Motel

All Year 1P: $79-$139 2P: $79-$139 XP: $10 F18

Location: I-15, exit Craig St, e to N Las Vegas Blvd. 4288 N Nellis Blvd 89115. Fax: 702/643-2598. **Facility:** 59 one-bedroom standard units, some with whirlpools. 3 stories, interior corridors. *Bath:* combo or shower only. **Parking:** on-site. **Terms:** cancellation fee imposed, pets ($10 extra charge). **Amenities:** irons, hair dryers. **Pool(s):** heated indoor. **Leisure Activities:** whirlpool. **Guest Services:** coin laundry. **Business Services:** meeting rooms. **Cards:** AX, DC, DS, MC, VI.

SOME UNITS

FEE

LA QUINTA LAS VEGAS NW TECH CENTER Book at aaa.com Phone: 702/360-1200 145

Motel

All Year 1P: $65-$90 2P: $71-$96 XP: $6 F18

Location: US 95, exit W Cheyenne Ave. 7101 Cascade Valley Ct 89128-0455. Fax: 702/360-1222. **Facility:** 128 one-bedroom standard units. 5 stories, interior corridors. *Bath:* combo or shower only. **Parking:** on-site. **Terms:** [ECP] meal plan available. **Amenities:** video games (fee), voice mail, irons, hair dryers. **Pool(s):** heated outdoor. **Leisure Activities:** whirlpool, exercise room. **Guest Services:** coin laundry. **Business Services:** meeting rooms, fax. **Cards:** AX, CB, DC, DS, JC, MC, VI.

SOME UNITS

LA QUINTA SUITES Book at aaa.com Phone: (702)243-0356 148

AAA SAVE

Motel

All Year [ECP] 1P: $79-$199 2P: $79-$199 XP: $10 F18

Location: Just w of Fort Apache. 9570 W Sahara Ave 89117. Fax: 702/233-8023. **Facility:** 75 one-bedroom standard units, some with whirlpools. 3 stories, interior corridors. *Bath:* combo or shower only. **Parking:** on-site. **Terms:** 2 night minimum stay - weekends. **Amenities:** dual phone lines, voice mail, irons, hair dryers. **Pool(s):** heated outdoor. **Leisure Activities:** whirlpool, exercise room. **Guest Services:** valet and coin laundry. **Business Services:** meeting rooms, fax. **Cards:** AX, DC, DS, MC, VI. **Special Amenities: free expanded continental breakfast and free local telephone calls.**

SOME UNITS

LAS VEGAS HILTON Book at aaa.com Phone: (702)732-5111 34

AAA SAVE

Large-scale Hotel

All Year 1P: $65-$365 XP: $30 F18

Location: I-15, exit Sahara Ave, 2 mi e. Located adjacent to convention center. 3000 Paradise Rd 89109 (PO Box 93147, 89193). Fax: 702/732-5805. **Facility:** A range of restaurants, lounges and shops is featured at this hotel, which is next to the convention center and convenient to the Las Vegas Strip. 3174 units. 2949 one-bedroom standard units, some with whirlpools. 150 one- and 75 two-bedroom suites, some with whirlpools. 30 stories, interior corridors. *Bath:* combo or shower only. **Parking:** on-site and valet. **Terms:** 3 day cancellation notice, package plans - seasonal. **Amenities:** high-speed Internet (fee), voice mail, irons, hair dryers. *Some:* safes. **Dining:** 9 restaurants, 24 hours; buffet $9-$13, cocktails, also, Andiamo, Hilton Steakhouse, see separate listings, entertainment. **Pool(s):** heated outdoor. **Leisure Activities:** whirlpool, 6 lighted tennis courts. *Fee:* Star Trek experience, massage, game room. **Guest Services:** gift shop, valet laundry. **Business Services:** conference facilities, business center. **Cards:** AX, CB, DC, DS, JC, MC, VI.

SOME UNITS

FEE FEE FEE

LEISURE RESORTS LAS VEGAS Phone: 702/731-6100 64

Motel

All Year 1P: $85-$120 2P: $85-$120

Location: I-15, exit 38 to Audrie, just n. 100 Winnick Ave 89109. Fax: 702/731-6175. **Facility:** 489 units. 389 one- and 100 two-bedroom standard units, some with whirlpools. 3 stories, interior/exterior corridors. *Bath:* combo or shower only. **Parking:** on-site. **Terms:** check-in 4 pm, cancellation fee imposed. **Amenities:** voice mail, safes, irons, hair dryers. **Pool(s):** outdoor, 7 heated outdoor. **Leisure Activities:** saunas, whirlpools, exercise room. **Guest Services:** gift shop, coin laundry, area transportation. **Business Services:** fax. **Cards:** AX, DS, MC, VI.

SOME UNITS

LUXOR LAS VEGAS Book at aaa.com Phone: (702)262-4000 94

Large-scale Hotel

All Year 1P: $69-$399 2P: $69-$399 XP: $25 F11

Location: I-15, exit E Tropicana Ave, just s on the Strip; exit Russel Rd northbound, e to the Strip, then just n. 3900 Las Vegas Blvd S 89119-1000. Fax: 702/262-4454. **Facility:** A 350-foot, glass-faced pyramid crowned by a 40 billion candlepower vertical light beam is the central feature of this Egyptian-themed hotel. 4407 units. 4000 one-bedroom standard units, some with whirlpools. 372 one- and 35 two-bedroom suites ($169-$799), some with whirlpools. 30 stories, interior corridors. *Bath:* combo or shower only. **Parking:** on-site and valet. **Amenities:** voice mail, irons, hair dryers. **Dining:** Sacred Sea Room, Luxor Steakhouse, see separate listings. **Pool(s):** 2 heated outdoor, wading. **Leisure Activities:** saunas, whirlpools. *Fee:* massage, game room. **Guest Services:** gift shop, valet laundry. **Business Services:** conference facilities, business center. **Cards:** AX, CB, DC, DS, JC, MC, VI.

SOME UNITS

FEE FEE

MAIN STREET STATION Phone: (702)387-1896 12

Large-scale Hotel

All Year 1P: $60-$160 2P: $60-$160 XP: $10 F12

Location: Downtown. Located in casino center. 200 N Main St 89125 (PO Box 7625). Fax: 702/386-4406. **Facility:** 406 one-bedroom standard units. 17 stories, interior corridors. *Bath:* combo or shower only. **Parking:** on-site. **Terms:** check-in 4 pm. **Amenities:** video games (fee), voice mail, safes. **Dining:** Triple 7 Restaurant Brewery, see separate listing. **Guest Services:** gift shop. **Cards:** AX, CB, DC, DS, JC, MC, VI.

SOME UNITS

(See map and index starting on p. 840)

MANDALAY BAY RESORT & CASINO Book at aaa.com Phone: (702)632-7777 98

AAA SAVE — Large-scale Hotel

All Year 1P: $109-$2999 2P: $109-$2999 XP: $35

Location: I-15, exit E Tropicana Ave, just e. 3950 Las Vegas Blvd S 89119 (PO Box 98880). Fax: 702/632-7190. **Facility:** On the Strip, the property offers spacious rooms as well as a spa, pools, restaurants, a casino and shops. 3220 units. 3013 one-bedroom standard units, some with whirlpools. 114 one- and 93 two-bedroom suites ($159-$9999) with whirlpools. 42 stories, interior corridors. **Parking:** on-site and valet. **Terms:** cancellation fee imposed, package plans - seasonal. **Amenities:** dual phone lines, voice mail, safes, irons, hair dryers. **Dining:** 9 restaurants, 24 hours; buffet $10-$19, cocktails, also, Aureole, Shanghai Lilly, Border Grill, 3950 Restaurant, see separate listings, entertainment. **Pool(s):** 5 heated outdoor. **Leisure Activities:** whirlpools, poolside cabanas and bungalows, jogging. *Fee:* massage. **Guest Services:** gift shop, valet laundry, area transportation-to Excalibur, Luxor. **Business Services:** conference facilities, business center. **Cards:** AX, DC, DS, JC, MC, VI.

FEE / SOME UNITS /

MARRIOTT SUITES LAS VEGAS Book at aaa.com Phone: (702)650-2000 32

Large-scale Hotel

All Year 1P: $99-$329 2P: $99-$329

Location: At Paradise Rd. 325 Convention Center Dr 89109. Fax: 702/650-9466. **Facility:** 278 one-bedroom standard units. 17 stories, interior corridors. *Bath:* combo or shower only. **Parking:** on-site. **Terms:** [AP] meal plan available. **Amenities:** high-speed Internet (fee), voice mail, honor bars, irons, hair dryers. **Pool(s):** heated outdoor. **Leisure Activities:** whirlpool, exercise room. **Guest Services:** sundries, valet and coin laundry. **Business Services:** meeting rooms, business center. **Cards:** AX, CB, DC, DS, JC, MC, VI.

/ SOME UNITS VCR FEE /

MGM GRAND HOTEL & CASINO Book at aaa.com Phone: (702)891-1111 93

Large-scale Hotel

All Year 1P: $79-$499 2P: $79-$499 XP: $25 F12

Location: I-15, exit Tropicana Ave. 3799 Las Vegas Blvd S 89109. Fax: 702/891-1030. **Facility:** World's largest hotel. 5005 units. 4253 one-bedroom standard units. 679 one- and 73 two-bedroom suites ($119-$2000), some with whirlpools. 30 stories, interior corridors. *Bath:* combo or shower only. **Parking:** on-site and valet. **Terms:** package plans - seasonal. **Amenities:** voice mail, irons, hair dryers. *Some:* dual phone lines, safes. **Dining:** Emeril's New Orleans Fish House, Craftsteak, see separate listings. **Pool(s):** 4 heated outdoor. **Leisure Activities:** whirlpools. *Fee:* massage, game room. **Guest Services:** gift shop, valet laundry, area transportation (fee). **Business Services:** conference facilities, business center. **Cards:** AX, CB, DC, DS, JC, MC, VI.

FEE FEE / SOME UNITS /

THE MIRAGE Book at aaa.com Phone: (702)791-7111 54

AAA SAVE — Large-scale Hotel

All Year 1P: $89-$399 XP: $30

Location: I-15, exit Spring Mountain Rd, e to the Strip. 3400 Las Vegas Blvd S 89109. Fax: 702/791-7446. **Facility:** Home to a dolphin habitat and the famous performing white tigers, this property boasts lavish grounds and distinctive common areas. 3044 units. 2763 one-bedroom standard units, some with whirlpools. 187 one-, 92 two- and 2 three-bedroom suites ($275-$4000). 30 stories, interior corridors. *Bath:* combo or shower only. **Parking:** on-site and valet. **Terms:** cancellation fee imposed. **Amenities:** high-speed Internet (fee), dual phone lines, voice mail, safes, honor bars, irons, hair dryers. **Dining:** 8 restaurants, 24 hours; buffet $9-$20, cocktails, also, Samba Brazilian Steakhouse, Renoir, Kokomos, see separate listings, name entertainment. **Pool(s):** 2 heated outdoor. **Leisure Activities:** whirlpools, spa. *Fee:* game room. **Guest Services:** gift shop, valet laundry, area transportation-Treasure Island. **Business Services:** conference facilities, business center. **Cards:** AX, CB, DC, DS, MC, VI.

FEE / SOME UNITS VCR FEE FEE /

MONTE CARLO RESORT & CASINO Book at aaa.com Phone: (702)730-7777 86

Large-scale Hotel

All Year 1P: $50-$450 2P: $50-$450 XP: $25

Location: On the Strip between Flamingo Rd and Tropicana Ave. 3770 Las Vegas Blvd S 89109. Fax: 702/730-7250. **Facility:** The resort's great location makes it easy for guests to take advantage of everything it has to offer. 3002 units. 2974 one-bedroom standard units, some with whirlpools. 28 one-bedroom suites ($200-$5000), some with whirlpools. 32 stories, interior corridors. *Bath:* combo or shower only. **Parking:** on-site and valet. **Terms:** cancellation fee imposed. **Amenities:** voice mail, irons, hair dryers. **Dining:** Blackstone's, see separate listing. **Pool(s):** 3 heated outdoor, wading. **Leisure Activities:** sauna, whirlpool, steamroom. *Fee:* 3 lighted tennis courts, massage, game room. **Guest Services:** gift shop, valet laundry, area transportation. **Business Services:** conference facilities, business center. **Cards:** AX, DC, DS, JC, MC, VI.

FEE / SOME UNITS /

MOTEL 6 BOULDER HIGHWAY Book at aaa.com Phone: 702/457-8051 38

Motel

All Year 1P: $30-$75 2P: $36-$81 XP: $3 F18

Location: Just s of Sahara Ave. 4125 Boulder Hwy 89121. Fax: 702/457-0265. **Facility:** 161 one-bedroom standard units. 2 stories (no elevator), exterior corridors. *Bath:* combo or shower only. **Parking:** on-site. **Terms:** small pets only. **Pool(s):** outdoor. **Guest Services:** coin laundry. **Cards:** AX, DC, DS, MC, VI.

/ SOME UNITS /

NEVADA PALACE Book at aaa.com Phone: (702)458-8810 139

Motel

All Year 1P: $35-$100 2P: $35-$100 XP: $10 F12

Location: 0.5 mi n of Tropicana Ave. 5255 Boulder Hwy 89122. Fax: 702/458-3361. **Facility:** Located on the popular Boulder Highway, this property has dining, gambling and a friendly staff to serve you. 211 one-bedroom standard units. 3 stories, exterior corridors. **Parking:** on-site. **Pool(s):** outdoor. **Guest Services:** gift shop. **Business Services:** meeting rooms. **Cards:** AX, CB, DC, DS, MC, VI.

ASK / SOME UNITS /

(See map and index starting on p. 840)

THE ORLEANS Book at aaa.com **Phone:** (702)365-7111 87

AAA SAVE

Large-scale Hotel

All Year 1P: $45-$159 2P: $45-$159 XP: $10 F15

Location: I-15, exit Tropicana Ave, 1 mi w. 4500 W Tropicana Ave 89103. Fax: 702/365-7500. **Facility:** The property was recently expanded to include a new events center, more parking, restaurants, movie theaters, bowling and shops. 1426 units. 1368 one-bedroom standard units. 28 one- and 30 two-bedroom suites ($250-$325), some with whirlpools. 22 stories. *Bath:* combo or shower only. **Parking:** on-site and valet. **Terms:** 2-3 night minimum stay - weekends, package plans. **Amenities:** high-speed Internet (fee), voice mail, irons, hair dryers. **Dining:** 8 restaurants, 24 hours; buffet $6-$11, cocktails, also, Don Miguel's, Courtyard Cafe, see separate listings, entertainment. **Pool(s):** outdoor, wading. **Leisure Activities:** whirlpool, spa. *Fee:* bowling, movie theaters, game room. **Guest Services:** gift shop, valet laundry, area transportation-Barbary Coast, Gold Coast. **Business Services:** conference facilities, business center. **Cards:** AX, CB, DC, DS, JC, MC, VI. **Special Amenities: early check-in/late check-out.**

SOME UNITS

FEE FEE

PALACE STATION HOTEL & CASINO Book at aaa.com **Phone:** (702)367-2411 25

AAA SAVE

Large-scale Hotel

All Year 1P: $50-$200 XP: $10 F17

Location: I-15, exit W Sahara Ave, southwest corner of Sahara Ave and Rancho Dr. 2411 W Sahara Ave 89102. Fax: 702/367-2478. **Facility:** 1028 units. 1008 one-bedroom standard units, some with whirlpools. 20 one-bedroom suites with whirlpools. 2-21 stories, interior corridors. *Bath:* combo or shower only. **Parking:** on-site and valet. **Terms:** 2 night minimum stay - some weekends, $5 service charge. **Amenities:** voice mail. *Some:* safes (fee), irons, hair dryers. **Dining:** 10 restaurants, 24 hours; buffet $6-$16, cocktails, also, The Broiler, see separate listing. **Pool(s):** outdoor, heated outdoor. **Leisure Activities:** whirlpools, exercise room. *Fee:* game room. **Guest Services:** gift shop, valet laundry, area transportation-the Strip. **Business Services:** conference facilities, fax. **Cards:** AX, CB, DC, DS, JC, MC, VI. **Special Amenities: early check-in/late check-out and free room upgrade (subject to availability with advanced reservations).**

SOME UNITS

THE PALMS CASINO RESORT Book at aaa.com **Phone:** (702)942-7777 65

Large-scale Hotel

10/1-1/31	1P: $109-$499	2P: $109-$499	XP: $25
2/1-5/27	1P: $99-$499	2P: $99-$499	XP: $25
5/28-9/30	1P: $79-$499	2P: $79-$499	XP: $25

Location: I-15, exit W Flamingo Rd, 0.5 mi w. 4321 W Flamingo Rd 89103 (4205 S Valley View Dr). Fax: 702/942-6999. **Facility:** The property, located just off the famous Las Vegas strip, offers trendy restaurants, night clubs, movie theaters and gambling. 439 units. 394 one-bedroom standard units. 23 one- and 22 two-bedroom suites, some with whirlpools. 43 stories, interior corridors. *Bath:* combo or shower only. **Parking:** on-site and valet. **Terms:** 2 night minimum stay - weekends. **Amenities:** voice mail, safes, honor bars, irons, hair dryers. *Fee:* video games, high-speed Internet. *Some:* CD players, dual phone lines. **Pool(s):** heated outdoor. **Leisure Activities:** whirlpool. *Fee:* massage, game room. **Guest Services:** gift shop, area transportation. **Business Services:** conference facilities, business center. **Cards:** AX, CB, DC, DS, JC, MC, VI.

SOME UNITS

FEE FEE

PARIS LAS VEGAS Book at aaa.com **Phone:** (702)946-7000 74

Large-scale Hotel

All Year 1P: $95-$350 2P: $95-$350 XP: $30 F18

Location: I-15, exit E Flamingo Rd, just s on the Strip. 3655 Las Vegas Blvd S 89109. Fax: 702/946-4405. **Facility:** On the Strip but with a vibe that's pure Paris, the hotel is complete with a simulated Eiffel Tower offering sweeping views. 2916 units. 2621 one-bedroom standard units. 295 one-bedroom suites ($350-$2500) with whirlpools. 33 stories, interior corridors. *Bath:* combo or shower only. **Parking:** on-site and valet. **Terms:** 3 day cancellation notice, package plans. **Amenities:** high-speed Internet (fee), dual phone lines, voice mail, safes, irons, hair dryers. **Dining:** Les Artistes Steakhouse, Eiffel Tower Restaurant, Mon Ami Gabi, see separate listings. **Pool(s):** heated outdoor. **Leisure Activities:** whirlpools. *Fee:* 8 lighted tennis courts, massage. **Guest Services:** gift shop, valet laundry, area transportation (fee). **Business Services:** conference facilities, business center. **Cards:** AX, DC, DS, MC, VI.

SOME UNITS

FEE FEE

PARK PLAZA LAS VEGAS LADY LUCK CASINO HOTEL Book at aaa.com **Phone:** (702)477-3000 2

Large-scale Hotel

All Year 1P: $35-$125 2P: $35-$125 XP: $10

Location: Downtown. Located in casino center. 206 N Third St 89101. Fax: 702/383-0782. **Facility:** Few poolside units. 792 one-bedroom standard units, some with whirlpools. 17-25 stories, interior corridors. *Bath:* combo or shower only. **Parking:** on-site and valet. **Terms:** 10% service charge. **Amenities:** voice mail. **Pool(s):** heated outdoor. **Leisure Activities:** exercise room. **Guest Services:** gift shop. **Business Services:** meeting rooms. **Cards:** AX, MC, VI.

SOME UNITS

RAMADA INN-SPEEDWAY CASINO Book at aaa.com **Phone:** (702)399-3297 117

Motel

All Year 2P: $49-$169

Location: I-15, exit 46E (Cheyenne Ave). 3227 Civic Ctr Dr 89030. Fax: 702/399-4108. **Facility:** 95 one-bedroom standard units. 3 stories, interior corridors. *Bath:* combo or shower only. **Parking:** on-site. **Terms:** cancellation fee imposed, [AP] & [BP] meal plans available. **Amenities:** voice mail. **Pool(s):** heated outdoor. **Guest Services:** sundries, valet laundry. **Cards:** AX, CB, DC, DS, MC, VI.

SOME UNITS

RESIDENCE INN-HUGHES CENTER Book at aaa.com **Phone:** (702)650-0040 76

Motel

All Year 1P: $99-$300 2P: $99-$300

Location: I-15, exit Paradise Rd. 370 Hughes Center Dr 89109. Fax: 702/650-5510. **Facility:** 256 units. 144 one-bedroom standard units with kitchens. 71 one- and 41 two-bedroom suites with kitchens. 11 stories, interior corridors. *Bath:* combo or shower only. **Parking:** on-site. **Terms:** check-in 4 pm, [BP] meal plan available, pets ($50 fee, $10 extra charge). **Amenities:** voice mail, irons, hair dryers. **Pool(s):** heated outdoor. **Leisure Activities:** whirlpool, exercise room. **Guest Services:** complimentary evening beverages: Mon-Thurs, valet and coin laundry. **Cards:** AX, CB, DC, DS, JC, MC, VI.

SOME UNITS

FEE

(See map and index starting on p. 840)

RESIDENCE INN LAS VEGAS CONVENTION CENTER Book at aaa.com Phone: (702)796-9300 36

Motel

All Year [BP] 1P: $119-$289 2P: $119-$289

Location: Opposite the convention center. 3225 Paradise Rd 89109. Fax: 702/796-9562. **Facility:** 192 units. 144 one- and 48 two-bedroom standard units with kitchens. 2 stories (no elevator), exterior corridors. *Bath:* combo or shower only. **Parking:** on-site. **Terms:** check-in 4 pm, small pets only ($50 fee, $10 extra charge). **Amenities:** video games (fee), voice mail, irons, hair dryers. **Pool(s):** heated outdoor. **Leisure Activities:** whirlpools, sports court. **Guest Services:** sundries, complimentary evening beverages: Mon-Thurs, coin laundry. **Business Services:** meeting rooms, fax. **Cards:** AX, CB, DC, DS, JC, MC, VI.

FEE SOME UNITS

RIO ALL SUITE HOTEL & CASINO Book at aaa.com Phone: (702)777-7777 66

Large-scale Hotel

All Year 1P: $60-$250 2P: $60-$250 XP: $30

Location: I-15, exit Flamingo Rd, 0.3 mi w. 3700 W Flamingo Rd 89103. Fax: 702/777-2294. **Facility:** A white-sand beach borders the hotel's tropical swimming lagoon; carnival parades and shows are presented. 2548 units. 2454 one-bedroom standard units. 70 one- and 24 two-bedroom suites with whirlpools. 20-41 stories, interior corridors. *Bath:* combo or shower only. **Parking:** on-site and valet. **Terms:** check-in 4 pm, 3 day cancellation notice-fee imposed. **Amenities:** video games (fee), voice mail, safes, honor bars, irons, hair dryers. *Some:* high-speed Internet (fee), dual phone lines. **Dining:** All American Bar & Grille, see separate listing. **Pool(s):** 3 outdoor, heated outdoor. **Leisure Activities:** whirlpools. *Fee:* golf-18 holes, massage, game room. **Guest Services:** gift shop, valet laundry, area transportation. **Business Services:** conference facilities, business center. **Cards:** AX, CB, DC, DS, JC, MC, VI.

FEE SOME UNITS

RIVIERA HOTEL AND CASINO Book at aaa.com Phone: (702)734-5110 30

Large-scale Hotel

All Year 1P: $59-$149 2P: $59-$149 XP: $20

Location: I-15, exit E Sahara Ave; on the Strip. 2901 Las Vegas Blvd S 89109. Fax: 702/794-9451. **Facility:** Many large rooms. Wedding chapel. 2073 units. 1997 one-bedroom standard units. 76 one-bedroom suites ($125-$500), some with whirlpools. 24 stories, interior corridors. *Bath:* combo or shower only. **Parking:** on-site and valet. **Terms:** check-in 4 pm, cancellation fee imposed. **Amenities:** voice mail, safes (fee). *Some:* irons, hair dryers. **Dining:** Ristorante Italiano, see separate listing. **Pool(s):** heated outdoor. **Leisure Activities:** 2 lighted tennis courts. *Fee:* massage. **Guest Services:** gift shop, valet laundry. **Business Services:** conference facilities, business center. **Cards:** AX, CB, DC, DS, JC, MC, VI.

FEE SOME UNITS

ST. TROPEZ ALL SUITE HOTEL Book at aaa.com Phone: (702)369-5400 71

AAA SAVE

Motel

All Year [ECP] 1P: $79-$259 2P: $79-$259 XP: $10 F12

Location: 2 mi s of convention center at Paradise Rd. 455 E Harmon Ave 89109. Fax: 702/369-1150. **Facility:** 149 one-bedroom standard units, some with whirlpools. 2 stories, interior/exterior corridors. *Bath:* combo or shower only. **Parking:** on-site. **Terms:** 3 day cancellation notice. **Amenities:** voice mail, irons, hair dryers. *Some:* dual phone lines. **Pool(s):** heated outdoor. **Leisure Activities:** whirlpool, exercise room. **Guest Services:** valet laundry, area transportation-Bally's. **Business Services:** meeting rooms. **Cards:** AX, CB, DC, DS, JC, MC, VI. **Special Amenities: preferred room (subject to availability with advanced reservations).**

SOME UNITS

SAM'S TOWN HOTEL & GAMBLING HALL Book at aaa.com Phone: (702)456-7777 138

AAA SAVE

Large-scale Hotel

All Year 1P: $39-$160 2P: $39-$160 XP: $10 F12

Location: 1 mi e of I-515/SR 93 and 95, exit Flamingo Rd. 5111 Boulder Hwy 89122. Fax: 702/454-8014. **Facility:** This property centering on an indoor park with a waterfall presents nightly laser and water shows. 646 units. 613 one-bedroom standard units. 33 one-bedroom suites, some with whirlpools. 9 stories, interior corridors. *Bath:* combo or shower only. **Parking:** on-site and valet. **Terms:** $4 service charge. **Amenities:** voice mail, hair dryers. **Dining:** 6 restaurants, 24 hours; buffet $6-$12, cocktails, also, Billy Bob's Steak House & Saloon, Fresh Harvest Cafe, see separate listings, entertainment. **Pool(s):** heated outdoor. **Leisure Activities:** whirlpool. *Fee:* bowling, 18-screen movie complex, game room. **Guest Services:** gift shop, valet laundry, area transportation-the Strip & downtown. **Business Services:** conference facilities, fax. **Cards:** AX, CB, DC, DS, MC, VI. **Special Amenities: early check-in/late check-out.**

SOME UNITS FEE

SANTA FE STATION HOTEL CASINO Book at aaa.com Phone: (702)658-4900 5

AAA SAVE

Small-scale Hotel

All Year 1P: $49-$129 2P: $49-$129 XP: $15 F13

Location: US 95, exit Ann Rd, just e. 4949 N Rancho Rd 89130. Fax: 702/658-4919. **Facility:** A newly remodeled casino just adds to the appeal of this bustling property; choose from several restaurants or relax with a trip around the ice rink. 200 one-bedroom standard units. 5 stories, interior corridors. *Bath:* combo or shower only. **Parking:** on-site and valet. **Terms:** cancellation fee imposed, [CP] meal plan available, $5 service charge. **Amenities:** video games (fee), voice mail, irons, hair dryers. **Dining:** 3 restaurants, 24 hours, also, Taos Steakhouse, see separate listing. **Pool(s):** heated outdoor. **Leisure Activities:** whirlpool, ice skating, 60-lane bowling center. **Guest Services:** gift shop, valet laundry. **Business Services:** meeting rooms, fax. **Cards:** AX, CB, DC, DS, MC, VI. **Special Amenities: early check-in/late check-out.**

SOME UNITS

SILVERTON HOTEL-CASINO Book at aaa.com Phone: (702)263-7777 112

Small-scale Hotel

All Year 1P: $35-$259 2P: $35-$259 XP: $10 F12

Location: I-15, exit 33 (W Blue Diamond Rd). 3333 Blue Diamond Rd 89139. Fax: 702/896-5635. **Facility:** Replica of 1800s Old West frontier mining town. 304 units. 290 one-bedroom standard units. 14 one-bedroom suites with whirlpools. 4 stories, interior corridors. *Bath:* combo or shower only. **Parking:** on-site and valet. **Terms:** cancellation fee imposed. **Amenities:** voice mail. *Some:* hair dryers. **Pool(s):** heated outdoor, wading. **Leisure Activities:** whirlpool. **Guest Services:** gift shop, valet laundry, area transportation. **Business Services:** meeting rooms, fax. **Cards:** AX, CB, DC, DS, MC, VI.

SOME UNITS FEE FEE

(See map and index starting on p. 840)

SOMERSET HOUSE MOTEL Phone: 702/735-4411 35

AAA SAVE — Motel

All Year 1P: $35-$44 2P: $44-$55 XP: $5 F9

Location: Just e off the Strip; 1 blk w of convention center. 294 Convention Center Dr 89109. Fax: 702/369-2388. **Facility:** 104 one-bedroom standard units. 3 stories, exterior corridors. *Bath:* combo or shower only. **Parking:** on-site. **Terms:** 3 day cancellation notice-fee imposed. **Amenities:** hair dryers. **Pool(s):** heated outdoor. **Guest Services:** coin laundry. **Business Services:** meeting rooms. **Cards:** AX, CB, DC, MC, VI. **Special Amenities: early check-in/late check-out and free room upgrade (subject to availability with advanced reservations).**

SOME UNITS

STRATOSPHERE Book at aaa.com Phone: (702)380-7777 24

Large-scale Hotel

All Year 1P: $39-$199 2P: $39-$199 XP: $15 F12

Location: Just n of Sahara Ave. 2000 Las Vegas Blvd S 89104. Fax: 702/380-7701. **Facility:** Take a trip to the top and enjoy the panoramic views of the entire Las Vegas area; gambling and a good selection of dining are also available. 2444 units. 2411 one-bedroom standard units, some with whirlpools. 33 one-bedroom suites ($114-$1000), some with whirlpools. 9-24 stories, interior corridors. *Bath:* combo or shower only. **Parking:** on-site and valet. **Terms:** cancellation fee imposed, package plans, $3 service charge. **Amenities:** voice mail, irons, hair dryers. **Pool(s):** heated outdoor. **Leisure Activities:** whirlpool. *Fee:* massage. **Guest Services:** gift shop, valet and coin laundry, area transportation (fee). **Business Services:** meeting rooms, business center. **Cards:** AX, DC, DS, MC, VI.

SOME UNITS

FEE FEE FEE

SUNCOAST HOTEL & CASINO Phone: (702)636-7111 26

AAA SAVE — Large-scale Hotel

All Year 2P: $59-$199 XP: $10 F15

Location: US 95 to Rampart. 9090 Alta Dr. Fax: 702/636-7288. **Facility:** 427 units. 386 one-bedroom standard units. 30 one- and 11 two-bedroom suites ($199-$1000), some with whirlpools. 10 stories, interior corridors. *Bath:* combo or shower only. **Parking:** on-site and valet. **Terms:** 2-3 night minimum stay - seasonal & weekends. **Dining:** 4 restaurants, 24 hours; buffet $5-$11, cocktails, also, Primo's - A Place for Steaks, see separate listing. **Pool(s):** heated outdoor. **Leisure Activities:** whirlpool, bowling, movie theaters, exercise room. *Fee:* game room. **Guest Services:** gift shop, valet laundry, area transportation-Barbary Coast Hotel. **Business Services:** conference facilities, business center. **Cards:** AX, CB, DC, DS, JC, MC, VI.

SOME UNITS

SUPER 8 AT NELLIS Book at aaa.com Phone: (702)644-7878 124

Motel

All Year 1P: $39-$79 2P: $49-$89 XP: $7 F16

Location: I-15, exit Craig Rd E, 2.7 mi e to Las Vegas Blvd, then just n. 4435 Las Vegas Blvd N 89115. Fax: 702/644-1219. **Facility:** 105 one-bedroom standard units. 2 stories (no elevator), exterior corridors. **Parking:** on-site. **Terms:** cancellation fee imposed. **Pool(s):** heated outdoor. **Guest Services:** coin laundry. **Cards:** AX, DS, MC, VI.

SOME UNITS

SUPER 8 MOTEL-BOULDER HWY Book at aaa.com Phone: (702)435-8888 141

AAA SAVE — Motel

All Year 1P: $30-$88 2P: $30-$88 XP: $5 F12

Location: At Harmon. 5288 Boulder Hwy 89122. Fax: 702/435-6953. **Facility:** 150 one-bedroom standard units. 4 stories, interior corridors. **Parking:** on-site. **Terms:** cancellation fee imposed. **Dining:** 24 hours. **Pool(s):** outdoor. **Leisure Activities:** whirlpool, exercise room. **Guest Services:** gift shop, coin laundry. **Cards:** AX, CB, DC, DS, MC, VI. **Special Amenities: free local telephone calls and preferred room (subject to availability with advanced reservations).**

SOME UNITS

SUPER 8 MOTEL LAS VEGAS STRIP Book at aaa.com Phone: (702)794-0888 73

Motel

All Year 1P: $61-$225 2P: $61-$225

Location: I-15, exit S Koval Ln. 4250 S Koval Ln 89109. Fax: 702/794-3504. **Facility:** 288 one-bedroom standard units. 3 stories, interior corridors. **Parking:** on-site. **Terms:** cancellation fee imposed, small pets only ($15 extra charge, in smoking units). **Pool(s):** heated outdoor. **Leisure Activities:** whirlpool. **Guest Services:** coin laundry. **Business Services:** meeting rooms. **Cards:** AX, CB, DC, DS, JC, MC, VI.

SOME UNITS

FEE

TERRIBLE'S HOTEL & CASINO Book at aaa.com Phone: (702)733-7000 56

Small-scale Hotel

All Year 1P: $29-$99 2P: $29-$99 XP: $10 F12

Location: I-15, exit E Flamingo Rd, just e. 4100 S Paradise Rd 89109. Fax: 702/731-1997. **Facility:** Close to the famous Las Vegas Strip, this has quickly become a popular place for the locals to gamble and eat. 371 one-bedroom standard units. 3 stories, interior corridors. *Bath:* combo or shower only. **Parking:** on-site and valet. **Terms:** package plans. **Amenities:** video games (fee), voice mail, hair dryers. **Pool(s):** heated outdoor. **Leisure Activities:** whirlpool. **Guest Services:** gift shop, valet laundry. **Cards:** AX, DS, MC, VI.

SOME UNITS

TEXAS STATION GAMBLING HALL & HOTEL Book at aaa.com Phone: 702/631-1000 4

AAA SAVE — Small-scale Hotel

All Year 1P: $59-$149 2P: $59-$149 XP: $15 F

Location: Business US 95, 3 mi n of downtown. 2101 Texas Star Ln 89030. Fax: 702/631-8120. **Facility:** 200 one-bedroom standard units. 6 stories, interior corridors. *Bath:* combo or shower only. **Parking:** on-site and valet. **Amenities:** high-speed Internet (fee), voice mail, safes, irons, hair dryers. **Dining:** 4 restaurants, 24 hours; buffet $4-$11, also, Austins, San Lorenzo, see separate listings. **Pool(s):** heated outdoor. **Leisure Activities:** casino, 18-screen movie theater, 60-lane bowling. *Fee:* game room. **Guest Services:** gift shop, valet laundry. **Business Services:** conference facilities, business center. **Cards:** AX, DC, DS, MC, VI. **Special Amenities: free local telephone calls and preferred room (subject to availability with advanced reservations).**

SOME UNITS

(See map and index starting on p. 840)

TI - TREASURE ISLAND Book at aaa.com **Phone:** (702)894-7444 52

Large-scale Hotel

All Year 1P: $69-$399 2P: $69-$399 XP: $25

Location: 3.5 mi s on the Strip. 3300 Las Vegas Blvd S 89109 (PO Box 7711, 89177). Fax: 702/894-7446. **Facility:** The property offers comfortable rooms with views of the Vegas Strip and the mountains, and features several dining, retail and entertainment options. 2885 units. 2865 one-bedroom standard units, some with whirlpools. 20 one-bedroom suites ($150-$1200) with whirlpools. 36 stories, interior corridors. *Bath:* combo or shower only. **Parking:** on-site and valet. **Terms:** cancellation fee imposed. **Amenities:** voice mail, safes, irons, hair dryers. *Some: Fee:* high-speed Internet. **Dining:** 8 restaurants, 24 hours; buffet $8-$13, cocktails, also, Buccaneer Bay, Francesco's, Kahunaville, see separate listings, entertainment. **Pool(s):** heated outdoor, wading. **Leisure Activities:** whirlpool. *Fee:* massage, game room. **Guest Services:** gift shop, valet laundry, area transportation-The Mirage. **Business Services:** conference facilities, business center. **Cards:** AX, CB, DC, DS, JC, MC, VI.

FEE / SOME UNITS VCR FEE FEE /

TRAVELODGE LAS VEGAS STRIP Book at aaa.com **Phone:** (702)735-4222 27

Motel

All Year 1P: $49-$69 2P: $59-$79

Location: I-15, exit Sahara Ave E. 2830 Las Vegas Blvd S 89109. Fax: 702/733-7695. **Facility:** 100 one-bedroom standard units. 2 stories (no elevator), exterior corridors. *Bath:* combo or shower only. **Parking:** on-site. **Terms:** [CP] meal plan available. **Amenities:** safes (fee), hair dryers. **Pool(s):** heated outdoor. **Cards:** AX, CB, DC, DS, JC, MC, VI.

ASK / SOME UNITS FEE /

THE VENETIAN RESORT HOTEL CASINO Book at aaa.com **Phone:** (702)414-1000 47

Large-scale Hotel

All Year 1P: $159-$899 2P: $159-$899 XP: $35 F12

Location: On the Strip. 3355 Las Vegas Blvd S 89109. Fax: 702/414-4805. **Facility:** Centering on a lobby lush with artwork and marble, this attractive property offers restaurants, shops and large, comfortable lodgings. 4049 units. 3649 one-bedroom standard units. 382 one- and 18 two-bedroom suites with whirlpools. 23-36 stories, interior corridors. *Bath:* combo or shower only. **Parking:** on-site and valet. **Terms:** 3 day cancellation notice-fee imposed. **Amenities:** high-speed Internet (fee), dual phone lines, voice mail, fax, safes, honor bars, irons, hair dryers. *Some:* CD players. **Dining:** Delmonico Steakhouse, Lutece, Valentino Las Vegas, see separate listings. **Pool(s):** 5 heated outdoor. **Leisure Activities:** whirlpools. *Fee:* massage. **Guest Services:** gift shop, valet laundry. **Business Services:** conference facilities, business center. **Cards:** AX, CB, DC, DS, JC, MC, VI.

FEE FEE / SOME UNITS /

WELLESLEY INN & SUITES (LAS VEGAS/EAST FLAMINGO) Book at aaa.com **Phone:** (702)731-3111 55

Motel

2/1-5/1 & 8/1-11/30 1P: $59-$79 2P: $59-$79
5/2-7/31 & 12/1-1/31 1P: $49-$69 2P: $49-$69

Location: I-15, exit E Flamingo Rd, then 2 mi. 1550 E Flamingo Rd 89119. Fax: 702/731-3184. **Facility:** 125 one-bedroom standard units with efficiencies. 3 stories, interior corridors. *Bath:* combo or shower only. **Parking:** on-site. **Terms:** [ECP] meal plan available. **Amenities:** dual phone lines, voice mail, irons, hair dryers. *Fee:* video games, safes. **Pool(s):** heated outdoor. **Leisure Activities:** exercise room. **Guest Services:** coin laundry. **Business Services:** meeting rooms, fax. **Cards:** AX, CB, DC, DS, JC, MC, VI. **Special Amenities: free expanded continental breakfast and free newspaper.**

/ SOME UNITS /

The following lodgings were either not evaluated or did not meet AAA rating requirements but are listed for your information only.

NEW YORK NEW YORK HOTEL & CASINO **Phone:** 702/740-6969

fyi

Not evaluated. **Location:** I-15, exit E Tropicana Ave, just e. 3790 Las Vegas Blvd S 89109. Facilities, services, and decor characterize a mid-range property.

WESTGATE FLAMINGO BAY **Phone:** 702/251-3435

fyi

Not evaluated. **Location:** 5625 W Flamingo Rd 89103. Facilities, services, and decor characterize a mid-range property.

THE WESTIN CASUARINA LAS VEGAS **Phone:** 702/836-9775

fyi

Large-scale Hotel

All Year 1P: $99-$229 2P: $99-$229 XP: $20 F17

Too new to rate, opening scheduled for November 2003. **Location:** I-15, exit Flamingo E. 160 E Flamingo 89109. Fax: 702/836-9776. **Amenities:** 825 units, restaurant, coffeemakers, pool, exercise facilities. **Terms:** cancellation fee imposed. **Cards:** AX, CB, DC, DS, JC, MC, VI.

WHERE TO DINE

3950 RESTAURANT **Dinner:** $27-$58 **Phone:** 702/632-7414 51

Continental

Location: I-15, exit E Tropicana Ave, just e; in Mandalay Bay Resort & Casino. 3950 Las Vegas Blvd S 89119. **Hours:** 5:30 pm-11 pm. **Reservations:** suggested. **Features:** The upscale restaurant distinguishes itself through a menu of excellent Continental cuisine. Dressy casual; cocktails. **Parking:** on-site and valet. **Cards:** AX, CB, DS, MC, VI.

AL DENTE **Dinner:** $14-$35 **Phone:** 702/967-4656 41

Italian

Location: 4.5 mi s on the Strip; in Bally's Las Vegas. 3645 Las Vegas Blvd S 89109. **Hours:** 5:30 pm-11 pm. Closed: Wed & Thurs. **Reservations:** suggested. **Features:** The bustling dining room exudes an upbeat atmosphere. The menu centers on well-prepared Italian dishes. Service is attentive. Dressy casual; cocktails. **Parking:** on-site and valet. **Cards:** AX, CB, MC, VI.

(See map and index starting on p. 840)

ALL AMERICAN BAR & GRILLE — Lunch: $8-$19 Dinner: $20-$60 Phone: 702/252-7777 (34)

Steak House

Location: I-15, exit W Flamingo Rd, 0.3 mi w; in Rio All Suite Hotel & Casino. 3700 W Flamingo Rd 89103. **Hours:** 11 am-10 pm. **Reservations:** accepted. **Features:** Guests can dine either in the lounge area, while enjoying the game on TVs adjacent to the casino action, or in the more quiet dining room. A good meal of burgers, steaks or chops awaits. Casual dress; cocktails. **Parking:** on-site and valet. **Cards:** AX, DC, DS, MC, VI.

AMERICA — Lunch: $7-$16 Dinner: $7-$16 Phone: 702/740-6451 (72)

American

Location: I-15, exit E Tropicana, just e; in New York New York Hotel & Casino. 3790 Las Vegas Blvd S 89109. **Hours:** 24 hours. **Reservations:** accepted. **Features:** The casual restaurant builds its menu on home-style dishes. The decor centers on a huge curved map of the United States. Casual dress; cocktails. **Parking:** on-site and valet. **Cards:** AX, CB, DC, DS, JC, MC, VI.

ANDIAMO — Dinner: $30-$70 Phone: 702/732-5755 (10)

Regional Italian

Location: I-15, exit Sahara Ave, 2 mi e; in Las Vegas Hilton. 3000 Paradise Rd 89109. **Hours:** 5 pm-11 pm. **Reservations:** suggested. **Features:** Diners can choose from a good variety of dishes amid comfortable and elegant surroundings. Dressy casual; cocktails. **Parking:** on-site and valet. **Cards:** AX, CB, DC, DS, JC, MC, VI.

ANDRE'S FRENCH RESTAURANT — Dinner: $22-$35 Phone: 702/385-5016 (6)

French

Location: At Lewis St. 401 S 6th St 89101. **Hours:** Open 2/1-7/1 & 8/1-1/31; 6 pm-11 pm. Closed major holidays; also Sun. **Reservations:** suggested. **Features:** Charming country French decor adorns several dining rooms. A favorite with the locals for many years, the restaurant is convenient to downtown. Dressy casual; cocktails; entertainment. **Parking:** on-site. **Cards:** AX, CB, DC, MC, VI.

AUREOLE — Dinner: $60-$80 Phone: 702/632-7401 (54)

American

Location: I-15, exit E Tropicana Ave, just e; in Mandalay Bay Resort & Casino. 3950 Las Vegas Blvd 89119. **Hours:** 6 pm-11 pm. **Reservations:** suggested. **Features:** Chef Charlie Palmer presents a menu of classic dishes that appeal to the city's fine-dining aficionados. Dressy casual; cocktails. **Parking:** on-site and valet. **Cards:** AX, CB, DS, MC, VI.

AUSTINS — Dinner: $25-$35 Phone: 702/631-1033 (1)

Steak House

Location: Business US 95; 3 mi n of downtown; in Texas Station Gambling Hall & Hotel. 2101 Texas Star Ln 89032. **Hours:** 5 pm-10 pm, Fri & Sat-11 pm. **Reservations:** suggested. **Features:** Casino action going on outside the doors goes unnoticed as guests in the elegant dining room choose from a creative menu. The staff is proficient. Dressy casual; cocktails. **Parking:** on-site and valet. **Cards:** AX, DC, DS, MC, VI.

BATTISTA'S HOLE IN THE WALL — Dinner: $18-$35 Phone: 702/732-1424 (11)

Italian

Location: I-15, exit Flamingo Rd, 0.3 mi e; just e of the Strip. 4041 Audrie 89109. **Hours:** 5 pm-10:30 pm, Fri & Sat-11 pm. Closed: 11/25, 12/24, 12/25. **Reservations:** suggested. **Features:** A strolling accordion player adds a touch of charm to the rustic setting. The house wine and cappuccino accompany dinners. Casual dress; cocktails. **Parking:** on-site. **Cards:** AX, CB, DC, DS, MC, VI.

BILLY BOB'S STEAK HOUSE & SALOON — Dinner: $15-$41 Phone: 702/454-8031 (56)

Steak House

Location: 1 mi e of I-515/US 93 and 95, exit Flamingo Rd; in Sam's Town Hotel & Gambling Hall. 5111 Boulder Hwy 89122. **Hours:** 5 pm-11 pm. **Reservations:** suggested. **Features:** Friendly staff members serve large portions of steak, seafood and chicken. The dining room is just off an atrium. Casual dress; cocktails. **Parking:** on-site and valet. **Cards:** AX, DC, MC, VI.

BLACKJACK LODGE — Lunch: $5-$10 Dinner: $5-$17 Phone: 702/876-0551 (58)

American

Location: I-215, exit Rainbow N, just n. 6200 S Rainbow 89118. **Hours:** 24 hours. **Features:** Conveniently located in the southwest area of the city, the restaurant is an ideal spot for a casual meal with friends. Only Angus beef is served, and all sauces and dressings are made in house. Fish and chips seems to be one of the favorites. Casual dress; cocktails. **Parking:** on-site. **Cards:** AX, MC, VI.

BLACKSTONE'S — Dinner: $15-$40 Phone: 702/730-7777 (47)

Steak House

Location: I-15, On the Strip between Flamingo Rd and Tropicana Ave; in Monte Carlo Resort & Casino. 3770 Las Vegas Blvd S 89109. **Hours:** 5 pm-11 pm. **Reservations:** suggested. **Features:** Tucked away yet near busy casino action, the attractive dining room boasts stained-glass windows. Service is both attentive and friendly. Dressy casual; cocktails. **Parking:** on-site and valet. **Cards:** AX, CB, DC, DS, MC, VI.

BLUE IGUANA — Dinner: $8-$15 Phone: 702/734-0410 (9)

Mexican

Location: 2.8 mi s on the Strip; in Circus Circus Hotel, Casino & Themepark. 2880 Las Vegas Blvd S 89109. **Hours:** 5 pm-10:30 pm, Sat-11:30 pm. **Features:** Near an indoor theme park, the second floor dining room is splashed with colorful decor that complements the lively Mexican preparations. Servers are friendly. Casual dress; cocktails. **Parking:** on-site and valet. **Cards:** AX, CB, DC, DS, MC, VI.

BORDER GRILL — Lunch: $10-$18 Dinner: $16-$30 Phone: 702/632-7403 (53)

Mexican

Location: I-15, exit E Tropicana Ave, just e; in Mandalay Bay Resort & Casino. 3950 Las Vegas Blvd S 89119. **Hours:** 11:30 am-11 pm. Closed: 12/25. **Reservations:** suggested. **Features:** Diners can nosh on well-prepared Mexican food while sitting beachside, either indoors or on the patio. Pleasant servers are on hand. Casual dress; cocktails. **Parking:** on-site and valet. **Cards:** AX, CB, DC, DS, MC, VI.

(See map and index starting on p. 840)

THE BROILER — **Lunch:** $7-$16 **Dinner:** $14-$26 **Phone:** 702/367-2411 (3)

Steak & Seafood

Location: I-15, exit W Sahara Ave, southwest corner of Sahara Ave and Rancho Dr; in Palace Station Hotel & Casino. 2411 W Sahara Ave 89102. **Hours:** 11 am-11 pm. **Reservations:** accepted. **Features:** The 19th-century eatery includes brass fixtures and hardwood floors. Although lunch choices center primarily on seafood, juicy steaks have a prominent place on the dinner menu. Casual dress; cocktails. **Parking:** on-site and valet. **Cards:** AX, MC, VI.

BUCCANEER BAY — **Dinner:** $19-$36 **Phone:** 702/894-7350 (24)

Continental

Location: 3.5 mi s on the Strip; in TI - Treasure Island. 3300 Las Vegas Blvd S 89109. **Hours:** 5 pm-10:30 pm. **Reservations:** suggested. **Features:** The comfortably upscale, second-floor dining room overlooks staged pirate battles. On the menu are contemporary Continental dishes. The staff is inviting and friendly. Dressy casual; cocktails. **Parking:** on-site and valet. **Cards:** AX, CB, DC, DS, MC, VI.

CAFE LAGO — **Lunch:** $9-$28 **Dinner:** $9-$28 **Phone:** 702/731-7110 (23)

American

Location: I-15, exit E Flamingo Rd, 0.5 mi e at the Strip; in Caesars Palace. 3570 Las Vegas Blvd S 89109. **Hours:** 24 hours. **Features:** Patrons can choose from a wide-ranging menu or serve themselves at the popular buffet. Reservations are not needed, so diners can stop in anytime at the casual, 24-hour spot off the casino floor. Casual dress; cocktails. **Parking:** on-site and valet. **Cards:** AX, CB, DC, DS, JC, MC, VI.

CARLUCCIO'S TIVOLI GARDENS — **Dinner:** $9-$13 **Phone:** 702/795-3236 (48)

Italian

Location: 2.5 mi e of Las Vegas Blvd S; at Spencer in Liberace Plaza. 1775 E Tropicana 89119. **Hours:** 4:30 pm-10 pm. Closed major holidays; also Mon. **Features:** Established in 1984, the restaurant presents an extensive menu of traditional dishes. Cordial servers add to the inviting feel. Casual dress. **Parking:** on-site. **Cards:** AX, DS, MC, VI.

CHARLIE PALMER STEAK — **Dinner:** $21-$38 **Phone:** 702/632-5120 (61)

Steak House

Location: I-15, exit E Tropicana, just s on the Strip; in Four Seasons Hotel Las Vegas. 3960 Las Vegas Blvd S 89119. **Hours:** 5 pm-10 pm. Closed: 12/25. **Reservations:** suggested. **Features:** In addition to great steaks, patrons can sample fine appetizers, salads, desserts and a good selection of wine. Before or after dinner, the comfortable lounge is a nice spot for a drink. Dressy casual; cocktails. **Parking:** on-site and valet. **Cards:** AX, MC, VI.

CONRAD'S — **Dinner:** $18-$33 **Phone:** 702/733-3502 (28)

French

Location: I-15, exit E Flamingo Rd, just n on the Strip; in Flamingo Las Vegas. 3555 Las Vegas Blvd S 89109. **Hours:** 5:30 pm-10 pm. **Reservations:** suggested. **Features:** Fresh flowers and plush chairs arranged in the serene dining room set the stage for a fine-dining experience. In addition to delicious French entrees, the menu lists imaginative desserts. Dressy casual; cocktails. **Parking:** on-site and valet. **Cards:** AX, CB, DC, DS, MC, VI.

COUNTRY INN — **Lunch:** $7-$10 **Dinner:** $8-$15 **Phone:** 702/254-0521 (7)

American

Location: I-15, exit Charleston, 4 mi w or exit S Rainbow, then 0.3 mi. 1401 S Rainbow 89102. **Hours:** 7 am-9 pm. Closed: 12/25. **Features:** Attractive country decor lends to the restaurant's casual atmosphere. The food is good and the staff friendly. Casual dress; beer & wine only. **Parking:** on-site. **Cards:** AX, MC, VI.

COURTYARD CAFE — **Lunch:** $5-$21 **Dinner:** $5-$21 **Phone:** 702/365-7111 (57)

American

Location: I-15, exit Tropicana Ave, 1 mi w; in The Orleans. 4500 W Tropicana Ave 89103. **Hours:** 24 hours. **Features:** Open 24 hours a day, the restaurant lets diners select from a wide and varied menu, as well as a separate offering of Chinese food. Casual dress; cocktails. **Parking:** on-site and valet. **Cards:** AX, DC, DS, MC, VI.

CRAFTSTEAK — **Dinner:** $24-$42 **Phone:** 702/891-7318 (69)

Steak House

Location: I-15, exit Tropicana Ave E, at the Strip; in MGM Grand Hotel & Casino. 3799 Las Vegas Blvd S 89109. **Hours:** 5:30 pm-10:30 pm. **Reservations:** suggested. **Features:** Elegant simplicity is the culinary approach, and the results are good. Cooking emphasizing natural, pure ingredients translates into a satisfying experience. Signature dishes include porterhouse for two, beef short ribs and sea scallops. Dressy casual; cocktails. **Parking:** on-site and valet. **Cards:** AX, CB, DC, DS, JC, MC, VI.

DELMONICO STEAKHOUSE — **Lunch:** $12-$36 **Dinner:** $27-$36 **Phone:** 702/414-3737 (20)

Steak House

Location: On the Strip; in The Venetian Resort Hotel Casino. 3355 Las Vegas Blvd S 89109. **Hours:** 11:30 am-2 & 5:30-10:30 pm, Fri & Sat-11 pm. **Reservations:** suggested. **Features:** Famous for his New Orleans cooking, owner Emeril Lagasse adds his influence to the American steakhouse. The staff is friendly, and the modern decor is comfortable and inviting. Dressy casual; cocktails; entertainment. **Parking:** on-site and valet. **Cards:** AX, DC, DS, MC, VI.

DON MIGUEL'S — **Lunch:** $7-$9 **Dinner:** $8-$15 **Phone:** 702/365-7111 (60)

Mexican

Location: I-15, exit Tropicana Ave, 1 mi w; in The Orleans. 4500 W Tropicana Ave 89103. **Hours:** 11 am-11 pm. **Features:** Friendly server deliver traditional Mexican dishes to guests in the relaxed dining room. Casual dress; cocktails. **Parking:** on-site and valet. **Cards:** AX, DC, DS, MC, VI.

(See map and index starting on p. 840)

EIFFEL TOWER RESTAURANT Dinner: $26-$48 Phone: 702/948-6937 (44)

French

Location: I-15, exit E Flamingo Rd, just s on the Strip; in Paris Las Vegas. 3655 Las Vegas Blvd S 89109. **Hours:** 5:30 pm-10 pm, Fri & Sat-10:30 pm. **Reservations:** suggested. **Features:** Attractively presented gourmet French cuisine is served in a refined dining room that affords views of the lights of the Strip. Dressy casual; cocktails; entertainment. **Parking:** on-site and valet. **Cards:** AX, CB, DC, DS, MC, VI.

EMERIL'S NEW ORLEANS FISH HOUSE Lunch: $14-$25 Dinner: $20-$35 Phone: 702/891-7374 (46)

Creole

Location: I-15, exit Tropicana Ave, in MGM Grand Hotel Casino. 3799 Las Vegas Blvd S 89109. **Hours:** 11 am-2:30 & 5:30-10:30 pm. **Reservations:** suggested. **Features:** The flavors and culture of New Orleans are captured with a menu that features a wide selection of Creole and Cajun dishes. The well-stocked wine list adds to the sophistication factor. Dressy casual; cocktails. **Parking:** on-site and valet. **Cards:** AX, CB, DC, DS, MC, VI.

EMPRESS COURT Dinner: $15-$65 Phone: 702/731-7110 (29)

Chinese

Location: I-15, exit E Flamingo Rd, 0.5 mi e at the Strip; in Caesars Palace. 3570 Las Vegas Blvd S 89109. **Hours:** 6 pm-10:30 pm. Closed: Tues & Wed. **Reservations:** suggested. **Features:** In an elegant casino, the restaurant builds its menu on Chinese delicacies. Thoughtful service contributes to the fine-dining experience. Semi-formal attire; cocktails. **Parking:** on-site. **Cards:** AX, CB, DC, DS, MC, VI.

FELLINI'S ITALIAN DINING Dinner: $11-$27 Phone: 702/870-9999 (66)

Italian

Location: 4 mi w of the Strip. 5555 W Charleston Blvd 89146. **Hours:** 5 pm-10 pm, Sat-11 pm. Closed major holidays. **Reservations:** suggested. **Features:** Off the Strip, the restaurant is a haven for romantic dining. On the menu is a wide selection of Italian specialties and desserts. Soft piano music plays in the background. Dressy casual; cocktails; entertainment. **Parking:** on-site. **Cards:** AX, CB, DC, DS, MC, VI.

FRANCESCO'S Dinner: $15-$40 Phone: 702/894-7348 (22)

Italian

Location: 3.5 mi s on the Strip; in TI - Treasure Island. 3300 Las Vegas Blvd S 89109. **Hours:** 5:30 pm-11 pm. Closed: Mon & Tues. **Reservations:** suggested. **Features:** Diners can savor contemporary Italian cuisine while gazing at artwork from such celebrities as Tony Curtis. The exhibition kitchen adds to the enjoyable experience. Dressy casual; cocktails. **Parking:** on-site and valet. **Cards:** AX, CB, DC, DS, MC, VI.

FRESH HARVEST CAFE Lunch: $6-$13 Dinner: $6-$13 Phone: 702/456-7777 (62)

American

Location: 1 mi e of I-515/SR 93 and 95, exit Flamingo Rd; in Sam's Town Hotel & Gambling Hall. 5111 Boulder Hwy 89122. **Hours:** 24 hours. **Features:** For a break from the casino action, guests can stop in 24 hours a day for a nice, casual meal. Breakfast and lunch offerings include a buffet, in addition to an extensive menu. Casual dress; cocktails. **Parking:** on-site and valet. **Cards:** AX, DC, MC, VI.

GANDHI INDIA'S CUISINE Lunch: $8-$10 Dinner: $13-$21 Phone: 702/734-0094 (37)

Indian

Location: 0.5 mi e of the Strip at Flamingo Rd. 4080 Paradise Rd 89109. **Hours:** 11 am-2:30 & 5-10:30 pm. **Reservations:** suggested. **Features:** Dishes burst with the flavors of north and south India. An interesting sampling of food lines the daily lunch buffet. Casual dress; cocktails. **Parking:** on-site. **Cards:** AX, DC, DS, MC, VI.

GOLDEN STEER Dinner: $20-$60 Phone: 702/384-4470 (8)

Steak House

Location: I-15, exit Sahara Ave, 0.3 mi e, just w of the Strip. 308 W Sahara Ave 89102. **Hours:** 5 pm-11 pm, Sat-11:30 pm. Closed: 12/25. **Reservations:** suggested. **Features:** Italian specialties, as well as chicken, veal and seafood dishes, make up the restaurant's diverse menu. Dressy casual; cocktails. **Parking:** on-site. **Cards:** AX, CB, DC, MC, VI.

GUADALAJARA BAR & GRILLE Lunch: $5-$15 Dinner: $5-$15 Phone: 702/432-7777 (15)

Mexican

Location: Just s of Sahara Ave; in Boulder Station Hotel Casino. 4111 Boulder Hwy 89121. **Hours:** 11 am-10 pm, Fri & Sat-11 pm. **Reservations:** accepted. **Features:** Plenty of traditional flavors infuse dishes at the popular restaurant and watering hole. A salsa bar is an added benefit. The staff is friendly and attentive. Casual dress; cocktails. **Parking:** on-site and valet. **Cards:** AX, MC, VI.

HILTON STEAKHOUSE Dinner: $20-$50 Phone: 702/732-5645 (13)

Steak House

Location: I-15, exit Sahara Ave, 2 mi e; in Las Vegas Hilton. 3000 Paradise Rd 89109. **Hours:** 5 pm-11:30 pm. **Reservations:** suggested. **Features:** Mesquite-broiled steaks are the specialty in the comfortable dining room. Service is friendly and attentive. Dressy casual; cocktails. **Parking:** on-site and valet. **Cards:** AX, CB, DC, DS, MC, VI.

JOEY BISTRO & BAR Lunch: $5-$9 Dinner: $9-$16 Phone: 702/369-5639 (49)

Italian

Location: Just e off the Strip; in Carriage House. 105 E Harmon 89109. **Hours:** 7 am-11 pm. **Reservations:** suggested. **Features:** A great view awaits guests of the restaurant, which prepares a nice selection of Italian cuisine. Patrons are challenged to see how many of the pictured famous "Joes" they can name while eating. Dressy casual; cocktails. **Parking:** on-site. **Cards:** AX, MC, VI.

(See map and index starting on p. 840)

KAHUNAVILLE — **Lunch:** $7-$19 **Dinner:** $7-$19 **Phone:** 702/894-7390 (67)

American

Location: I-15, exit Spring Mountain Rd E, 3.5 mi s on the Strip; in TI - Treasure Island. 3300 Las Vegas Blvd S 89109. **Hours:** 8 am-11 pm, Sat-midnight. **Reservations:** accepted. **Features:** Guests might feel as though they've landed in a island paradise, and their taste buds will appreciate the trip. The extensive menu includes lots of seafood, beef and chicken. Seasonal poolside seating is an option. Casual dress; cocktails. **Parking:** on-site and valet. **Cards:** DC, MC, VI.

KOKOMOS — **Dinner:** $16-$50 **Phone:** 702/791-7111 (70)

Steak & Seafood

Location: I-15, exit Spring Mountain Rd E, e to the Strip; in The Mirage. 3400 Las Vegas Blvd S 89109. **Hours:** 5 pm-10 pm. **Reservations:** suggested. **Features:** For prime steaks, fresh seafood, lobster and chops, the exotic spot in a tropical rain forest setting is the place to be. The competent, friendly staff is ready to serve. Dressy casual; cocktails. **Parking:** on-site and valet. **Cards:** AX, CB, DC, DS, MC, VI.

LA SCALA RESTAURANT — **Lunch:** $10-$20 **Dinner:** $12-$29 **Phone:** 702/699-9980 (35)

Italian

Location: 2 mi e of the Strip; in Mark I Tower. 1020 E Desert Inn 89109. **Hours:** 11:30 am-2 & 5-10 pm, Sat & Sun from 5 pm. Closed major holidays. **Reservations:** suggested. **Features:** Popular with locals since its opening, the warm and inviting spot is convenient to the strip and convention center. Servers are friendly, and the food is well-prepared. Dressy casual; cocktails. **Parking:** on-site. **Cards:** AX, DC, DS, MC, VI.

LAWRY'S THE PRIME RIB — **Dinner:** $24-$39 **Phone:** 702/893-2223 (36)

American

Location: 1 mi e of the Strip, just off Flamingo Rd. 4043 Howard Hughes Pkwy 89109. **Hours:** 5 pm-10 pm, Sat-11 pm. Closed: 12/25. **Reservations:** suggested. **Features:** Roasted prime rib of beef is carved tableside from silver carts. The restaurant is convenient to the Strip and convention center. Dressy casual; cocktails. **Parking:** valet. **Cards:** AX, CB, DC, DS, MC, VI.

LE CIRQUE — **Dinner:** $80-$90 **Phone:** 702/693-8100 (38)

French

Location: I-15, exit E Flamingo Rd, on the Strip; in Bellagio. 3600 Las Vegas Blvd S 89109. **Hours:** 5:30 pm-10:30 pm. **Reservations:** required. **Features:** Located lakeside, this sophisticated, elegant yet relaxed dining room offers a classic French menu. The rich interior has a circus theme with plush mahogany furnishings. The staff is equally professional and friendly. Semi-formal attire; cocktails. **Parking:** on-site. **Cards:** AX, DC, DS, MC, VI.

LES ARTISTES STEAKHOUSE — **Dinner:** $20-$35 **Phone:** 702/967-7999 (43)

French

Location: I-15, exit E Flamingo Rd, just s on the Strip; in Paris Las Vegas. 3655 Las Vegas Blvd S 89109. **Hours:** 5:30 pm-11 pm. **Reservations:** suggested. **Features:** The two-story Art Deco dining room features an open kitchen, where slow-roasted fresh meats, poultry and fish are prepared. Servers are pleasant. Dressy casual; cocktails. **Parking:** on-site and valet. **Cards:** AX, CB, DC, DS, MC, VI.

LILLIE LANGTRY'S — **Dinner:** $10-$29 **Phone:** 702/385-7111 (4)

Chinese

Location: Downtown; in Golden Nugget Hotel. 129 E Fremont St 89101. **Hours:** 5 pm-11 pm. **Reservations:** suggested. **Features:** The menu comprises traditional Szechwan and Cantonese dishes, as well as mesquite-broiled prime steaks. The friendly staff serves in a comfortable, elegant dining room. Dressy casual; cocktails. **Parking:** on-site. **Cards:** AX, DC, DS, MC, VI.

LUTECE — **Dinner:** $28-$45 **Phone:** 702/414-2220 (19)

French

Location: On the Strip; in The Venetian Resort Hotel Casino. 3355 Las Vegas Blvd S 89109. **Hours:** 5:30 pm-10:30 pm. **Reservations:** suggested. **Features:** Modern French cuisine exhibits classic influences. The attractive and relaxing setting offers indoor and outdoor seating. Views of gondola canals and the Strip are picturesque. Dressy casual; cocktails. **Parking:** on-site and valet. **Cards:** AX, CB, DC, DS, MC, VI.

LUXOR STEAKHOUSE — **Dinner:** $19-$52 **Phone:** 702/262-4778 (59)

Steak House

Location: I-15, exit E Tropicana Ave, just s on the Strip; exit Russel Rd northbound, e to the Strip, then just n; in Luxor Las Vegas. 3900 Las Vegas Blvd S 89119. **Hours:** 5 pm-11 pm. **Reservations:** suggested. **Features:** The steakhouse is so quiet that patrons would never guess a busy casino is right outside the door. Good food includes steaks, seafood and chicken, all served by a friendly and efficient staff. Dressy casual; cocktails. **Parking:** on-site and valet. **Cards:** AX, CB, DC, DS, JC, MC, VI.

MICHAELS — **Dinner:** $35-$75 **Phone:** 702/737-7111 (33)

Continental

Location: 1.8 mi s on the Strip; in Barbary Coast Hotel. 3595 Las Vegas Blvd S 89109. **Hours:** 6 pm-10 pm. **Reservations:** suggested. **Features:** In the heart of the Strip, the cozy, romantic dining room is tended by a highly qualified staff. Semi-formal attire; cocktails. **Parking:** on-site and valet. **Cards:** AX, CB, DC, DS, JC, MC, VI.

MON AMI GABI — **Lunch:** $10-$28 **Dinner:** $20-$28 **Phone:** 702/944-4224 (21)

French

Location: I-15, exit E Flamingo Rd, just s on the Strip; in Paris Las Vegas. 3655 Las Vegas Blvd S 89109. **Hours:** 11:30 am-3:30 & 5-11 pm. **Reservations:** suggested. **Features:** Straight from the streets of Paris, the charming French bistro offers seating inside or at outdoor umbrella tables that afford views of the Las Vegas Strip scene. Casual dress; cocktails. **Parking:** on-site and valet. **Cards:** AX, CB, DC, DS, JC, MC, VI.

(See map and index starting on p. 840)

NEROS STEAK AND SEAFOOD **Dinner:** $26-$49 **Phone:** 702/731-7110 (31)

Steak & Seafood

Location: I-15, exit E Flamingo Rd, 0.5 mi e at the Strip; in Caesars Palace. 3570 Las Vegas Blvd S 89109. **Hours:** 5:30 pm-10:30 pm, Fri & Sat-11 pm. **Reservations:** suggested. **Features:** The bustling casino setting is great for people-watching. The appealing menu makes for a difficult choice between steak and seafood. Dressy casual; cocktails. **Parking:** on-site and valet. **Cards:** AX, CB, DC, DS, MC, VI.

OLIVES AT BELLAGIO **Lunch:** $8-$20 **Dinner:** $12-$41 **Phone:** 702/693-8181 (40)

Mediterranean

Location: I-15, exit E Flamingo Rd, on the Strip; in Bellagio. 3600 Las Vegas Blvd S 89109. **Hours:** 11 am-2:30 & 5-10:30 pm. **Reservations:** suggested. **Features:** The casual Mediterranean cafe nurtures a lively atmosphere and is a great meeting spot. The wine list comprises selections from around the world. Casual dress; cocktails. **Parking:** on-site and valet. **Cards:** AX, DC, DS, MC, VI.

PALAZZO RISTORANTE **Lunch:** $8-$15 **Dinner:** $15-$28 **Phone:** 702/947-5910 (32)

Italian

Location: I-15, exit Flamingo Rd E, 0.5 mi; in Best Western Tuscany Hotel & Casino. 255 E Flamingo Rd 89109. **Hours:** 11:30 am-3:30 & 5:30-11 pm. Closed: Sun. **Reservations:** suggested. **Features:** Patrons can choose from a wide selection of pasta, beef, chicken and fish dishes, as well as a nice special or two. Service is friendly in the comfortable and elegant dining room. Dressy casual; cocktails. **Parking:** on-site and valet. **Cards:** AX, DS, MC, VI.

PASTA PALACE **Dinner:** $9-$24 **Phone:** 702/432-7559 (12)

Italian

Location: Just s of Sahara Ave; in Boulder Station Hotel Casino. 4111 Boulder Hwy 89121. **Hours:** 5 pm-10 pm, Fri & Sat-11 pm, Sun 3 pm-9 pm. **Reservations:** suggested. **Features:** Diners can sample fresh pasta, pizza and other traditional favorites in an atmosphere that resembles Italy. Casual dress; cocktails. **Parking:** on-site and valet. **Cards:** AX, DC, DS, MC, VI.

PICASSO **Dinner:** $85-$95 **Phone:** 702/693-7111 (42)

French

Location: I-15, exit Flamingo Rd, on the Strip; in Bellagio. 3600 Las Vegas Blvd S 89109. **Hours:** 6 pm-10 pm. Closed: Tues. **Reservations:** suggested. **Features:** The Mediterranean restaurant displays Pablo Picasso's original paintings and ceramics in a flower-filled dining room that overlooks the Bellagio fountain. Award-winning chef Julian Serrano creates two prix fixe tasting menus. The accomplished staff provides impeccable service. Semi-formal attire; cocktails. **Parking:** on-site and valet. **Cards:** AX, CB, DC, DS, MC, VI.

PIERO'S **Dinner:** $20-$65 **Phone:** 702/369-2305 (16)

Italian

Location: I-15 E, at Sahara Ave 2 mi, 0.5 mi s on Paradise; opposite convention center. 355 Convention Center Dr 89109. **Hours:** 5:30 pm-10:30 pm. Closed: 12/25. **Reservations:** suggested. **Features:** Just off the Strip, the Italian restaurant is noted for its osso buco and fresh seafood dishes. Dressy casual; cocktails; entertainment. **Parking:** valet. **Cards:** AX, CB, DC, DS, MC, VI.

PING PANG PONG **Dinner:** $8-$29 **Phone:** 702/247-8136 (71)

Chinese

Location: I-15, exit W Flamingo Rd, just w; in Gold Coast Hotel. 4000 W Flamingo Rd 89103. **Hours:** 5 pm-3 am. **Features:** A multitude of specialty dishes from various regions of China adds to the restaurant's appeal. The dining room has a friendly and open look, and service won't disappoint. Casual dress; cocktails. **Parking:** on-site and valet. **Cards:** AX, CB, DC, DS, MC, VI.

PRIME STEAKHOUSE **Dinner:** $25-$74 **Phone:** 702/693-7111 (39)

Steak House

Location: I-15, exit E Flamingo Rd, on the Strip; in Bellagio. 3600 Las Vegas Blvd S 89109. **Hours:** 5:30 pm-10 pm. **Reservations:** suggested. **Features:** An extensive wine list complements delicious preparations of prime meat, chops and seafood. Exquisite decor furnishes the waterfront dining room. Dressy casual; cocktails. **Parking:** on-site and valet. **Cards:** AX, CB, DC, DS, MC, VI.

PRIMO'S - A PLACE FOR STEAKS **Dinner:** $13-$37 **Phone:** 702/636-7111 (45)

Steak House

Location: US 95 to Rampart; in Suncoast Hotel & Casino. 9090 Alta Dr 89145. **Hours:** 5 pm-10 pm. **Reservations:** suggested. **Features:** The menu blends a good selection of steak with seafood and chops preparations. Friendly servers circulate in the attractive restaurant, on the second floor of a hotel and casino. Dressy casual; cocktails. **Parking:** on-site and valet. **Cards:** AX, CB, DC, DS, MC, VI.

RANGE STEAKHOUSE AT HARRAH'S **Dinner:** $20-$45 **Phone:** 702/369-5084 (27)

Steak House

Location: I-15, 4 mi s on the Strip; in Harrah's-Las Vegas. 3475 Las Vegas Blvd S 89109. **Hours:** 5:30 pm-10:30 pm. **Reservations:** suggested. **Features:** The popular restaurant treats diners to a nice selection of steaks, chops, fish and fowl. Friendly service and a nice view of the Strip make for an enjoyable experience. Dressy casual; cocktails; entertainment. **Parking:** on-site and valet. **Cards:** AX, DC, DS, MC, VI.

RENOIR **Dinner:** $85 **Phone:** 702/791-7353 (26)

French

Location: I-15, exit Spring Mountain Rd, e to the Strip; in The Mirage. 3400 Las Vegas Blvd S 89109. **Hours:** 5:30 pm-9:30 pm. Closed: Sun & Mon. **Reservations:** suggested. **Features:** Innovative, Mediterranean-inspired French cuisine makes up both a la carte and prix fixe menus. Refined elegance characterizes the dining room. An impressive wine list centers on French vintages. Semi-formal attire; cocktails. **Parking:** on-site and valet. **Cards:** AX, CB, DC, DS, MC, VI.

(See map and index starting on p. 840)

RISTORANTE ITALIANO **Dinner:** $15-$30 **Phone:** 702/794-9363 (17)

Italian

Location: I-15, exit E Sahara Ave, exit E Sahara Ave; on the Strip; in Riviera Hotel and Casino. 2901 Las Vegas Blvd S 89109. **Hours:** 5:30 pm-11 pm. Closed: 11/25, 12/25; also Wed, Thurs & 11/21-12/27. **Reservations:** suggested. **Features:** The restaurant is tucked away from the bustle of the casino. Good food and thoughtful service appeal to both locals and tourists. Casual dress; cocktails. **Parking:** on-site and valet. **Cards:** AX, CB, DC, DS, MC, VI.

ROSEMARY'S RESTAURANT **Lunch:** $11-$15 **Dinner:** $19-$36 **Phone:** 702/869-2251 (64)

American

Location: I-15, exit W Sahara Ave, 6 mi w. 8125 W Sahara 89117. **Hours:** 11:30 am-2:30 & 5:30-10:30 pm, Sat & Sun from 5:30 pm. Closed: 1/1, 12/25. **Reservations:** suggested. **Features:** American fine dining with French influence best describes the cuisine. This "off strip" location is popular with tourists and locals alike. Enjoy friendly and attentive service while dining in the warm ambience of the dining room, which has a touch of New Orleans and the flare of a European bistro. Dressy casual; cocktails. **Parking:** on-site. **Cards:** AX, CB, DC, DS, MC, VI.

SACRED SEA ROOM **Dinner:** $22-$52 **Phone:** 702/262-4772 (52)

Seafood

Location: I-15, exit E Tropicana Ave, just s on the Strip; exit Russel Rd northbound, e to the Strip, then just n; in Luxor Las Vegas. 3900 Las Vegas Blvd S 89109. **Hours:** 5:30 pm-11 pm. Closed: Wed & Thurs. **Reservations:** suggested. **Features:** Freshwater and saltwater seafood is shipped in daily. The dining room is splashed in murals that reproduce fishing on the Nile. Dressy casual; cocktails. **Parking:** on-site and valet. **Cards:** AX, CB, DC, DS, MC, VI.

SAMBA BRAZILLIAN STEAKHOUSE **Dinner:** $17-$30 **Phone:** 702/791-7337 (25)

Brazilian

Location: I-15, exit Spring Mountain Rd, e to the Strip; in The Mirage. 3400 Las Vegas Blvd S 89109. **Hours:** 5:30 pm-10:30 pm. **Reservations:** suggested. **Features:** The Brazilian grill is a showcase for Brazilian "churrascaria de rodizio" cooking style. Meat, chicken and fish are skewered, carved tableside and served with traditional South American side dishes. Casual dress; cocktails. **Parking:** on-site and valet. **Cards:** AX, CB, DC, DS, MC, VI.

SAN LORENZO **Dinner:** $10-$35 **Phone:** 702/631-1023 (65)

Italian

Location: Business US 95, 3 mi n of downtown; in Texas Station Gambling Hall & Hotel. 2101 Texas Star Ln 89030. **Hours:** 5 pm-9:30 pm, Fri & Sat-10:30 pm. **Reservations:** suggested. **Features:** Patrons can sip a beverage in the "A" Lounge, which also is a great place to watch a game on TV or view the casino action. A nice array of delicious Italian fare is served in the comfortable dining room. Casual dress; cocktails. **Parking:** on-site and valet. **Cards:** AX, CB, DC, DS, MC, VI.

SHANGHAI LILLY **Dinner:** $17-$65 **Phone:** 702/632-7409 (55)

Chinese

Location: I-15, exit E Tropicana Ave, just e; in Mandalay Bay Resort & Casino. 3950 Las Vegas Blvd S 89119. **Hours:** 5:30 pm-11 pm. **Reservations:** suggested. **Features:** Imaginative Cantonese cuisine including selections of beef, seafood and pork. Attentive servers are available to help you with your selections while you enjoy the imaginative and elegant surroundings. Some private dining rooms are available. Dressy casual; cocktails. **Parking:** on-site and valet. **Cards:** AX, CB, DC, DS, JC, MC, VI.

SOURDOUGH CAFE **Lunch:** $5-$10 **Dinner:** $8-$18 **Phone:** 702/258-5200 (68)

American

Location: I-15, 7 mi nw; in Arizona Charlie's Decatur. 740 S Decatur Blvd 89107. **Hours:** 24 hours. **Features:** Big portions and friendly service draw locals and tourists alike to the 24-hour coffee shop. The menu is broad and the atmosphere relaxed. Casual dress; cocktails. **Parking:** on-site and valet. **Cards:** AX, DC, DS, MC, VI.

THE STEAKHOUSE AT CAMELOT **Dinner:** $27-$39 **Phone:** 702/597-7777 (50)

Steak House

Location: I-15, exit E Tropicana Ave, on the Strip; in Excalibur Hotel & Casino. 3850 Las Vegas Blvd S 89109. **Hours:** 5 pm-10 pm, Fri-Sun to 11 pm. **Reservations:** suggested. **Features:** Quality steaks, fine wines and delicious desserts are served in a comfortable setting. Dressy casual; cocktails. **Parking:** on-site and valet. **Cards:** AX, CB, DC, DS, MC, VI.

STEFANO'S **Dinner:** $14-$35 **Phone:** 702/385-7111 (5)

Italian

Location: Downtown; in Golden Nugget Hotel. 129 E Fremont St 89101. **Hours:** 6 pm-11 pm, Fri & Sat from 5:30 pm. **Reservations:** suggested. **Features:** The nicely appointed dining room setting is reminiscent of a romantic Italian countryside. Hand-blown glass chandeliers and fresh flowers abound. Talented "singing waiters" serve creative, flavorful dishes. Dressy casual; cocktails. **Parking:** on-site and valet. **Cards:** AX, CB, DC, DS, MC, VI.

TAOS STEAKHOUSE **Lunch:** $5-$13 **Dinner:** $9-$35 **Phone:** 702/515-4385 (2)

Steak House

Location: US 95, exit Ann Rd, just e; in Santa Fe Station Hotel Casino. 4949 N Rancho Rd 89130. **Hours:** 11 am-2 & 5-9 pm, Sat 5 pm-10 pm, Sun 5 pm-9 pm. **Reservations:** suggested. **Features:** A statue of a gigantic bear greets guests at the entrance to the steakhouse, right off the casino floor. The friendly staff serves a good selection of beef, chicken and fish dishes. Casual dress; cocktails. **Parking:** on-site and valet. **Cards:** AX, DS, MC, VI.

TILLERMAN **Dinner:** $21-$54 **Phone:** 702/731-4036 (30)

Steak & Seafood

Location: 3.5 mi e of Las Vegas Blvd S. 2245 E Flamingo Rd 89119. **Hours:** 5 pm-10 pm. Closed major holidays. **Reservations:** suggested. **Features:** Fresh seafood and steak are served in a distinctively and comfortably decorated dining room. Servers are cordial and prompt. Dressy casual; cocktails. **Parking:** on-site. **Cards:** DC, DS, MC, VI.

(See map and index starting on p. 840)

TRE — Dinner: $12-$35 — Phone: 702/946-6200 (74)

Mediterranean

Location: US 95 to Rampart, at W Charleston. 1050 S Rampart 89145. **Hours:** 5:30 pm-10:30 pm. Closed major holidays. **Reservations:** suggested. **Features:** The Mediterranean menu lists cuisine from Italy, Spain and France, including such popular dishes as braised beef short ribs with horseradish potato puree and Brunello sauce. The facility includes an upscale dining room and a bar/lounge. Dressy casual; cocktails. **Parking:** on-site. **Cards:** AX, MC, VI.

TRIPLE 7 RESTAURANT BREWERY — Lunch: $5-$16 — Dinner: $5-$16 — Phone: 702/387-1896 (63)

American

Location: Downtown; in Main Street Station. 200 N Main St 89125. **Hours:** 11 am-7 am. **Features:** Lots of beer choices complement plentiful food choices, including a good selection of sushi and oysters. A large-screen TV is nearby, so watching the big game is never a problem. Casual dress; cocktails. **Parking:** on-site and valet. **Cards:** AX, CB, DC, DS, MC, VI.

VALENTINO LAS VEGAS — Dinner: $16-$40 — Phone: 702/414-3000 (18)

Italian

Location: On the Strip; in The Venetian Resort Hotel Casino. 3355 Las Vegas Blvd S 89109. **Hours:** 5:30 pm-11 pm. **Reservations:** suggested. **Features:** Delicious Italian specialties line a seasonally changing menu. Many ingredients are imported directly from Italy and are used to create contemporary cuisine. Dressy casual; cocktails. **Parking:** on-site and valet. **Cards:** AX, DC, DS, MC, VI.

WAVERLY'S STEAK HOUSE — Dinner: $14-$26 — Phone: 702/507-5700 (75)

Steak House

Location: I-15, exit W Craig Rd, 1 mi w. 2121 E Craig Rd 89030. **Hours:** 5 pm-9:30 pm; Fri & Sat-10:30 pm. **Reservations:** suggested. **Features:** Big sellers are the fillets and prime rib, but it's hard to go wrong with any of the pasta, chicken or fish choices. A nice selection of breads starts off the meal, and several attractive and tasty desserts end it. Dressy casual; cocktails. **Parking:** on-site and valet. **Cards:** AX, MC, VI.

YOLIE'S BRAZILIAN STEAK HOUSE — Lunch: $8-$15 — Dinner: $16-$27 — Phone: 702/794-0700 (14)

Ethnic

Location: On upper level of Citybank Park Plaza. 3900 Paradise Rd 89109. **Hours:** 11 am-2 & 5-11 pm, Sat & Sun from 5 pm. Closed: 12/25. **Reservations:** suggested. **Features:** The informal restaurant's menu lists lamb, chicken and fish dishes, as well as a variety of meats served from a skewer. Dressy casual; cocktails. **Parking:** on-site. **Cards:** AX, CB, DC, DS, MC, VI.

The Las Vegas Vicinity

BOULDER CITY pop. 14,966

WHERE TO STAY

BEST WESTERN LIGHTHOUSE INN & RESORT — *Book at aaa.com* — **Phone:** (702)293-6444

AAA SAVE — Motel

3/2-7/15	1P: $69-$99	2P: $69-$99	XP: $5	F18
2/1-3/1 & 7/16-10/1	1P: $59-$69	2P: $59-$69	XP: $5	F18
10/2-1/31	1P: $49-$69	2P: $49-$69	XP: $5	F18

Location: 1 mi e on US 93. 110 Ville Dr 89005. Fax: 702/293-6547. **Facility:** 70 one-bedroom standard units, some with whirlpools. 3 stories (no elevator), exterior corridors. **Parking:** on-site. **Terms:** [CP] meal plan available, pets ($10 fee). **Amenities:** irons, hair dryers. **Pool(s):** outdoor. **Leisure Activities:** whirlpool. **Guest Services:** coin laundry. **Business Services:** conference facilities. **Cards:** AX, CB, DC, DS, JC, MC, VI. **Special Amenities: free continental breakfast and free room upgrade (subject to availability with advanced reservations).**

SOME UNITS — FEE — FEE

BOULDER DAM HOTEL — *Book at aaa.com* — **Phone:** (702)293-3510

Historic Small-scale Hotel

All Year [BP] — 1P: $89-$179 — 2P: $89-$179 — XP: $10

Location: Center. 1305 Arizona St 89005. Fax: 702/293-3093. **Facility:** This very charming historic hotel is right off the main street and has a museum that alone is worth the trip; dine in the lobby restaurant. 21 units. 18 one-bedroom standard units. 3 one-bedroom suites ($139-$179). 3 stories, interior corridors. *Bath:* combo or shower only. **Parking:** on-site. **Terms:** [AP] meal plan available. **Amenities:** voice mail, hair dryers. **Guest Services:** gift shop, complimentary evening beverages. **Cards:** AX, CB, DC, DS, MC, VI.

SOME UNITS — ASK — DATA PORT — VCR

EL RANCHO BOULDER MOTEL — **Phone:** 702/293-1085

AAA SAVE — Motel

All Year — 1P: $60 — 2P: $80

Location: On US 93. 725 Nevada Way 89005. Fax: 702/293-3021. **Facility:** 39 one-bedroom standard units. 2 stories (no elevator), exterior corridors. **Parking:** on-site. **Terms:** 7 night minimum stay, pets ($10 extra charge, dogs only). **Pool(s):** outdoor. **Cards:** AX, DS, MC, VI. **Special Amenities: free local telephone calls.**

SOME UNITS — FEE

SANDS MOTEL

Motel

All Year 1P: $46-$65 2P: $54-$74 XP: $15 F12

Phone: 702/293-2589

Location: On US 93. 809 Nevada Way 89005. Fax: 702/294-0160. **Facility:** 26 one-bedroom standard units. 1 story, exterior corridors. *Bath:* combo or shower only. **Parking:** on-site. **Terms:** 5 day cancellation notice, weekly rates available, [CP] & [ECP] meal plans available. **Cards:** AX, CB, DC, DS, JC, MC, VI. **Special Amenities: free expanded continental breakfast and free local telephone calls.**

SOME UNITS

SUPER 8 MOTEL *Book at aaa.com*

Motel

All Year [ECP] 1P: $50-$100 2P: $50-$100 XP: $7 F12

Phone: (702)294-8888

Location: On US 93. 704 Nevada Way 89005. Fax: 702/293-4344. **Facility:** 114 one-bedroom standard units, some with whirlpools. 3 stories, exterior corridors. *Bath:* combo or shower only. **Parking:** on-site. **Terms:** weekly rates available, small pets only ($10 fee). **Amenities:** voice mail. **Pool(s):** heated indoor. **Leisure Activities:** whirlpool. **Guest Services:** coin laundry. **Business Services:** meeting rooms. **Cards:** AX, CB, DC, MC, VI.

ASK FEE SOME UNITS

COTTONWOOD COVE

WHERE TO STAY

COTTONWOOD COVE MOTEL

Motel

5/22-11/1 1P: $108 2P: $108 XP: $10 F5
2/1-5/21 & 11/2-1/31 1P: $60 2P: $60 XP: $10 F5

Phone: (702)297-1464

Location: Between Las Vegas and Needles; off US 95. 14 mi e of Searchlight. 10000 Cottonwood Cove Rd 89046. Fax: 702/297-2036. **Facility:** 24 one-bedroom standard units. 1 story, exterior corridors. **Parking:** on-site. **Terms:** 14 day cancellation notice-fee imposed, [AP] meal plan available. **Dining:** 7 am-8 pm; to 6 pm 11/1-4/1. **Leisure Activities:** waterskiing, fishing, horseshoes, shuffleboard, volleyball. *Fee:* marina, houseboats, powerboats & equipment. **Guest Services:** gift shop, coin laundry. **Business Services:** meeting rooms. **Cards:** AX, DS, MC, VI.

SOME UNITS

ECHO BAY

WHERE TO STAY

ECHO BAY RESORT

Motel

All Year 1P: $85-$115 2P: $85-$115 XP: $6 F5

Phone: (702)394-4000

Location: 4 mi e of SR 167; on Lake Mead. (Lake Mead, OVERTON). Fax: 702/394-4180. **Facility:** 52 one-bedroom standard units. 2 stories (no elevator), interior corridors. *Bath:* combo or shower only. **Parking:** on-site. **Terms:** 3 day cancellation notice, pets ($50 deposit, $5 extra charge). **Amenities:** hair dryers. **Dining:** 7 am-9 pm; 10 am-4 pm 10/1-4/5, cocktails. **Leisure Activities:** rental boats, marina, waterskiing, fishing. *Fee:* houseboats. **Guest Services:** gift shop, coin laundry. **Business Services:** meeting rooms. **Cards:** DS, MC, VI.

FEE SOME UNITS

HENDERSON pop. 175,381

WHERE TO STAY

COURTYARD BY MARRIOTT *Book at aaa.com*

Small-scale Hotel

All Year 1P: $89-$99 2P: $89-$99

Phone: (702)434-4700

Location: I-215, exit Green Valley Pkwy, 2.5 mi n; near Sunset Rd. 2800 N Green Valley Pkwy 89014. Fax: 702/434-3888. **Facility:** 155 one-bedroom standard units, some with whirlpools. 3 stories, interior corridors. *Bath:* combo or shower only. **Parking:** on-site. **Terms:** [BP] meal plan available. **Amenities:** voice mail, irons, hair dryers. **Pool(s):** heated outdoor. **Leisure Activities:** whirlpool, exercise room. **Guest Services:** coin laundry, area transportation (fee). **Business Services:** meeting rooms, fax (fee). **Cards:** AX, CB, DC, DS, JC, MC, VI.

ASK DATA PORT SOME UNITS

FIESTA-HENDERSON *Book at aaa.com*

Small-scale Hotel

All Year 1P: $60-$120 2P: $60-$120 XP: $15 F12

Phone: (702)558-7000

Location: I-515, exit Lake Mead Dr. 777 W Lake Mead Dr 89015. Fax: 702/567-7373. **Facility:** 224 one-bedroom standard units, some with whirlpools. 9 stories, interior corridors. *Bath:* combo or shower only. **Parking:** on-site and valet. **Terms:** cancellation fee imposed, $5 service charge. **Amenities:** video games (fee), voice mail, hair dryers. **Dining:** 3 restaurants, 11 am-9 pm; buffet $7-$10, 24 hours, cocktails. **Pool(s):** heated outdoor. **Leisure Activities:** whirlpool. **Guest Services:** gift shop, valet laundry. **Business Services:** meeting rooms. **Cards:** AX, DC, DS, MC, VI. **Special Amenities: early check-in/late check-out.**

DATA PORT SOME UNITS FEE

GREEN VALLEY RANCH — Phone: (702)617-7777

AAA SAVE — Large-scale Hotel

All Year 1P: $159-$450 2P: $159-$450 XP: $12 F17

Location: I-215, exit Green Valley Pkwy, just s. 2300 S Paseo Verde Dr 89012. Fax: 702/617-7778. **Facility:** An adjacent casino offers gaming, dining and upscale lounges while the guest rooms are elegant and spacious. 201 units. 184 one-bedroom standard units. 8 one-, 8 two- and 1 three-bedroom suites ($300-$3500) with whirlpools. 5 stories. *Bath:* combo or shower only. **Parking:** on-site and valet. **Terms:** cancellation fee imposed. **Amenities:** CD players, high-speed Internet (fee), dual phone lines, voice mail, safes, honor bars, irons, hair dryers. **Dining:** 6 restaurants, 24 hours; buffet $6-$15, also, Bullshrimp, see separate listing, entertainment. **Pool(s):** heated outdoor, wading. **Leisure Activities:** whirlpool, 2 lighted tennis courts, bocci, movie theater, spa. *Fee:* game room. **Guest Services:** gift shop, complimentary evening beverages, valet laundry, area transportation-the Strip. **Business Services:** conference facilities, business center. **Cards:** AX, CB, DC, DS, JC, MC, VI.

SOME UNITS

HAMPTON INN HOTEL & SUITES — *Book at aaa.com* — Phone: (702)992-9292

Motel

All Year [ECP] 1P: $79-$125 2P: $79-$125 XP: $10 F18

Location: I-215, exit Stephanie St N, 1.8 mi; exit Warm Springs Rd, just e, then just s. 421 Astaire Dr 89014. Fax: 702/992-9293. **Facility:** 99 one-bedroom standard units. 3 stories, interior corridors. *Bath:* combo or shower only. **Parking:** on-site. **Terms:** cancellation fee imposed, weekly rates available. **Amenities:** video games (fee), high-speed Internet, dual phone lines, voice mail, irons, hair dryers. **Pool(s):** heated outdoor. **Leisure Activities:** whirlpool, exercise room. **Guest Services:** coin laundry. **Business Services:** meeting rooms, business center. **Cards:** AX, CB, DC, DS, MC, VI.

SOME UNITS

HAWTHORN INN & SUITES — *Book at aaa.com* — Phone: (702)568-7800

Motel

All Year [BP] 1P: $79-$139 2P: $79-$139 XP: $10 F18

Location: S of Lake Mead Blvd. 910 S Boulder Hwy 89015. Fax: 702/568-8430. **Facility:** 71 one-bedroom standard units, some with whirlpools. 3 stories, interior corridors. *Bath:* combo or shower only. **Parking:** on-site. **Terms:** cancellation fee imposed, pets ($15 fee). **Amenities:** voice mail, irons, hair dryers. **Pool(s):** heated indoor. **Leisure Activities:** whirlpool, exercise room. **Guest Services:** coin laundry. **Business Services:** meeting rooms. **Cards:** AX, DC, DS, MC, VI.

SOME UNITS

FEE

HOLIDAY INN EXPRESS & SUITES — *Book at aaa.com* — Phone: (702)990-2323

Motel

All Year 1P: $79-$199

Location: I-215, exit Stephanie St N, 1.8 mi; exit Warm Springs Rd, just e, then just s. 441 Astaire Dr 89014. Fax: 702/990-2324. **Facility:** 101 one-bedroom standard units. 3 stories, interior/exterior corridors. *Bath:* combo or shower only. **Parking:** on-site. **Terms:** [ECP] meal plan available. **Amenities:** high-speed Internet, dual phone lines, voice mail, irons, hair dryers. **Pool(s):** heated outdoor. **Leisure Activities:** whirlpool, exercise room. **Guest Services:** coin laundry. **Business Services:** meeting rooms, business center. **Cards:** AX, CB, DC, DS, JC, MC, VI.

SOME UNITS

HYATT REGENCY LAKE LAS VEGAS RESORT — *Book at aaa.com* — Phone: (702)567-1234

AAA SAVE — Large-scale Hotel

2/1-6/13 & 9/13-11/21	1P: $129-$374	2P: $129-$374	XP: $30	F18
6/14-9/12 & 11/22-1/31	1P: $99-$209	2P: $99-$209	XP: $30	F18

Location: I-215, e to end, then n on Lake Las Vegas Pkwy. 101 Montelago Blvd 89011. Fax: 702/567-6112. **Facility:** With its desert oasis setting imparting a Mediterranean feel, this multi-tiered resort offers many units with lake and golf course views. 493 units. 472 one-bedroom standard units. 21 one-bedroom suites, some with whirlpools. 9 stories, interior corridors. *Bath:* combo or shower only. **Parking:** on-site and valet. **Terms:** 3 day cancellation notice-fee imposed, $10 service charge. **Dining:** 2 restaurants, 24 hours, also, Japengo, see separate listing. **Pool(s):** 2 heated outdoor. **Leisure Activities:** whirlpool, rental canoes, rental paddleboats, putting green, rental bicycles. *Fee:* marina, massage. **Guest Services:** gift shop, valet laundry, area transportation-the Strip. **Business Services:** conference facilities, business center. **Cards:** AX, CB, DC, DS, JC, MC, VI.

SOME UNITS

LAKE MEAD MOTEL — *Book at aaa.com* — Phone: 702/564-1712

Motel

12/28-1/31 [CP]	1P: $99	2P: $99	XP: $5	F
5/16-9/15 [CP]	1P: $61-$66	2P: $66-$71	XP: $5	F
2/1-5/15 & 9/16-12/27 [CP]	1P: $56-$61	2P: $61-$66	XP: $5	F

Location: US 93/95, exit Lake Mead Dr, 1.5 mi e on SR 146. 85 W Lake Mead Dr 89015. Fax: 702/564-7642. **Facility:** 59 one-bedroom standard units. 2 stories, exterior corridors. *Bath:* combo or shower only. **Parking:** on-site. **Terms:** cancellation fee imposed. **Amenities:** irons, hair dryers. **Pool(s):** heated outdoor. **Guest Services:** coin laundry. **Cards:** AX, DC, DS, MC, VI.

SOME UNITS

RESIDENCE INN-GREEN VALLEY — *Book at aaa.com* — Phone: (702)434-2700

Motel

All Year [ECP] 1P: $114-$144 2P: $114-$144

Location: I-215, exit Green Valley Pkwy N. 2190 Olympic Ave 89014. Fax: 702/434-3999. **Facility:** 126 units. 63 one-bedroom standard units with kitchens. 36 one- and 27 two-bedroom suites with kitchens. 3 stories, interior corridors. *Bath:* combo or shower only. **Parking:** on-site. **Terms:** pets ($50 fee, $10 extra charge). **Amenities:** voice mail, irons, hair dryers. **Pool(s):** heated outdoor. **Leisure Activities:** whirlpool, exercise room, sports court. **Guest Services:** complimentary evening beverages: Mon-Thurs, valet and coin laundry. **Business Services:** meeting rooms, fax. **Cards:** AX, CB, DC, DS, JC, MC, VI.

SOME UNITS

FEE

THE RITZ-CARLTON, LAKE LAS VEGAS Book at aaa.com

Phone: (702)567-4700

Resort
Large-scale Hotel

4/1-5/30	1P: $269-$589	2P: $269-$589	XP: $30	F13
10/1-1/31	1P: $199-$589	2P: $199-$589	XP: $30	F13
2/1-3/31	1P: $269-$579	2P: $269-$579	XP: $30	F13
5/31-9/30	1P: $199-$489	2P: $199-$489	XP: $30	F13

Location: I-215, e to end, n on Lake Las Vegas Pkwy, then 0.5 mi on right. 1610 Lake Las Vegas Pkwy 89011. Fax: 702/567-4777. **Facility:** Accommodations are comfortable and luxurious at this Mediterranean-style resort, which offers golf, tennis, water sports and a relaxing pool. 349 units. 311 one-bedroom standard units. 38 one-bedroom suites ($415-$5000), some with whirlpools. 8 stories, interior corridors. *Bath:* combo or shower only. **Parking:** on-site (fee) and valet. **Terms:** cancellation fee imposed, pets ($250 deposit). **Amenities:** CD players, dual phone lines, voice mail, safes, honor bars, irons, hair dryers. *Fee:* video games, high-speed Internet. **Dining:** Medici Cafe and Terrace, see separate listing. **Pool(s):** heated outdoor. **Leisure Activities:** whirlpool, 4 lighted tennis courts, spa, volleyball. *Fee:* golf-54 holes. **Guest Services:** gift shop, valet laundry, area transportation. **Business Services:** conference facilities, business center. **Cards:** AX, DC, DS, JC, MC, VI.

ASK FEE FEE SOME UNITS / /

SUNSET STATION HOTEL & CASINO Book at aaa.com

Phone: (702)547-7777

SAVE
Large-scale Hotel

All Year 1P: $39-$169 XP: $15 F12

Location: I-15, exit I-215 to Warm Springs, 7 mi e to Stephanie St and Sunset Rd. 1301 W Sunset Rd 89014. Fax: 702/547-7744. **Facility:** Entertainment, multiple fine dining and fast food restaurants and a full casino are just some aspects that make this a great spot. 457 one-bedroom standard units, some with whirlpools. 21 stories, interior corridors. *Bath:* combo or shower only. **Parking:** on-site and valet. **Terms:** cancellation fee imposed, $4 service charge. **Amenities:** voice mail, irons, hair dryers. **Dining:** 8 restaurants, 24 hours; buffet $5-$17, cocktails, also, Sunset Cafe, see separate listing, nightclub, entertainment. **Pool(s):** outdoor. **Leisure Activities:** 13 movie screen complex, exercise room. *Fee:* game room. **Guest Services:** gift shop, valet laundry, area transportation. **Business Services:** conference facilities. **Cards:** AX, CB, DC, DS, JC, MC, VI.

WHERE TO DINE

BULLSHRIMP

Steak & Seafood

Lunch: $8-$18 Dinner: $19-$46 Phone: 702/942-4110

Location: I-215, exit Green Valley Pkwy, just s; in Green Valley Ranch. 2300 Paseo Verde Dr 89052. **Hours:** 11:30 am-2 & 5-10 pm, Fri & Sat 5 pm-11 pm, Sun 5 pm-10 pm. **Reservations:** suggested. **Features:** Friendly servers present a good selection of seafood and beef dishes in an eclectic setting. The dining room is tucked just off the casino floor. Dressy casual; cocktails. **Parking:** on-site and valet. **Cards:** AX, CB, DC, DS, JC, MC, VI.

JAPENGO

Pacific Rim

Dinner: $22-$45 Phone: 702/567-6125

Location: I-215, e to end, then n on Lake Las Vegas Pkwy; in Hyatt Regency Lake Las Vegas Resort. 101 Montelago Blvd 89011. **Hours:** 6 pm-10:30 pm. Closed: Mon. **Reservations:** suggested. **Features:** It's worth the drive to Lake Las Vegas to enjoy the dining experience. The menu has an Asian infusion not found at most restaurants. Throw in a friendly staff and a good view, and it's an all-around enjoyable experience. Dressy casual; cocktails. **Parking:** on-site and valet. **Cards:** AX, DC, DS, MC, VI.

MEDICI CAFE AND TERRACE

Mediterranean

Lunch: $10-$20 Dinner: $15-$50 Phone: 702/567-4700

Location: I-215, e to end, n on Lake Las Vegas Pkwy, then 0.5 mi on right; in The Ritz-Carlton, Lake Las Vegas. 1610 Lake Las Vegas Pkwy 89011. **Hours:** 7 am-11, noon-3 & 6-10 pm. **Reservations:** suggested. **Features:** The upscale restaurant's menu covers Spanish, French and Italian cuisine. All is prepared in the exhibition kitchen and can be enjoyed in the elegant dining room or outside on the patio. A good way to finish a meal is with the popular chef's dessert sampler. Dressy casual; cocktails. **Parking:** on-site and valet. **Cards:** AX, CB, DC, DS, JC, MC, VI.

SUNSET CAFE

American

Lunch: $5-$13 Dinner: $5-$13 Phone: 702/547-7777

Location: I-215, exit Stephanie St N, 7 mi e to Stephanie St and Sunset Rd; in Sunset Station Hotel & Casino. 1301 W Sunset Rd 89014. **Hours:** 24 hours. **Features:** Guests can break from the casino action and take advantage of the expanded 24-hour menu for a good meal. Breakfast is served anytime, and all the food is well-presented. Casual dress; cocktails. **Parking:** on-site and valet. **Cards:** AX, CB, DC, DS, JC, MC, VI.

INDIAN SPRINGS pop. 1,302

WHERE TO STAY

INDIAN SPRINGS MOTOR HOTEL

Motel

Phone: (702)879-3700

All Year 1P: $33-$42 2P: $39-$45

Location: On US 95, 45 mi n of Las Vegas. Adjacent to air base. 300 Tonopah Hwy 89018 (PO Box 630). Fax: 702/879-3221. **Facility:** 45 one-bedroom standard units. 2 stories (no elevator), interior corridors. **Parking:** on-site. **Terms:** weekly rates available, pets ($50 deposit, $5 extra charge). **Dining:** 24 hours. **Guest Services:** coin laundry. **Cards:** AX, CB, DC, DS, JC, MC, VI. **Special Amenities: free local telephone calls and early check-in/late check-out.**

LAUGHLIN pop. 7,076

WHERE TO STAY

AVI RESORT & CASINO — **Phone:** 702/535-5555

AAA SAVE — Small-scale Hotel

5/1-8/31	1P: $24-$109	2P: $24-$109	XP: $5	F21
2/1-4/30 & 9/1-1/31	1P: $19-$79	2P: $19-$79		

Location: 9 mi s on Needles Hwy via Casino Dr; I-40, exit W Broadway, 12 mi n. 10000 AHA Macav Pkwy 89028-7011 (PO Box 77011). Fax: 702/535-5514. **Facility:** On the Colorado River; spacious units. 456 one-bedroom standard units, some with whirlpools. 4 stories, interior corridors. *Bath:* combo or shower only. **Parking:** on-site and valet. **Dining:** 3 restaurants, 24 hours; buffet $6-$8, cocktails, entertainment. **Pool(s):** heated outdoor. **Leisure Activities:** whirlpool, rental boats, boat ramp, 8 screen movie theater, exercise room. *Fee:* sea doos, golf-18 holes, game room. **Guest Services:** gift shop, valet laundry. **Business Services:** conference facilities. **Cards:** AX, DC, DS, MC, VI.

COLORADO BELLE HOTEL & CASINO — **Phone:** (702)298-4000

Large-scale Hotel

All Year	1P: $25-$90	2P: $25-$90	XP: $4	F12

Location: 3 mi s of Davis Dam. 2100 S Casino Dr 89028 (PO Box 77000). Fax: 702/299-0669. **Facility:** On the Colorado River, riverboat design. 1177 one-bedroom standard units, some with whirlpools. 6 stories, interior/exterior corridors. *Bath:* shower only. **Parking:** on-site and valet. **Terms:** cancellation fee imposed. **Amenities:** safes. **Dining:** Mississippi Lounge and Seafood Bar, see separate listing. **Pool(s):** 2 heated outdoor. **Leisure Activities:** whirlpool, exercise room. *Fee:* game room. **Guest Services:** gift shop, valet laundry. **Business Services:** conference facilities. **Cards:** AX, CB, DC, DS, MC, VI.

SOME UNITS / FEE

DON LAUGHLIN'S RIVERSIDE RESORT HOTEL & CASINO — **Phone:** (702)298-2535

Large-scale Hotel

All Year	1P: $39-$199	2P: $39-$199

Location: 2 mi s of Davis Dam. 1650 S Casino Dr 89029 (PMB 500). Fax: 702/298-2614. **Facility:** On the Colorado River. 1404 units. 1395 one-bedroom standard units, some with whirlpools. 9 one-bedroom suites ($89-$399), some with whirlpools. 14-26 stories, interior corridors. *Bath:* combo or shower only. **Parking:** on-site and valet. **Terms:** 7 day cancellation notice-fee imposed, package plans - seasonal & weekends, small pets only ($100 deposit, $8 extra charge). **Dining:** The Gourmet Room, see separate listing. **Pool(s):** 2 outdoor. **Leisure Activities:** whirlpool. *Fee:* massage, game room. **Guest Services:** gift shop, valet laundry. **Business Services:** meeting rooms. **Cards:** AX, CB, DC, DS, MC, VI.

ASK — FEE — SOME UNITS / FEE

EDGEWATER HOTEL/CASINO Book at aaa.com

AAA SAVE

Large-scale Hotel

All Year 1P: $33-$80 2P: $33-$80 XP: $4 F12 **Phone:** (702)298-2453

Location: 2.3 mi s of Davis Dam. 2020 S Casino Dr 89028 (PO Box 30707). Fax: 702/298-8165. **Facility:** Southwestern decor. Native-American art. 1419 units. 1401 one-bedroom standard units. 18 one-bedroom suites, some with whirlpools. 3-26 stories, interior corridors. *Bath:* combo or shower only. **Parking:** on-site and valet. **Terms:** 3 day cancellation notice-fee imposed. **Amenities:** *Some:* safes, hair dryers. **Dining:** 5 restaurants, 24 hours; buffet $5-$8, cocktails, entertainment. **Pool(s):** heated outdoor. **Leisure Activities:** whirlpool. *Fee:* game room. **Guest Services:** gift shop, valet laundry. **Business Services:** meeting rooms. **Cards:** AX, DC, DS, MC, VI.

SOME UNITS

FLAMINGO LAUGHLIN Book at aaa.com

Large-scale Hotel

All Year 1P: $22-$399 2P: $22-$399 XP: $5 F4 **Phone:** (702)298-5111

Location: 2 mi s of Davis Dam. 1900 S Casino Dr 89029. Fax: 702/298-5129. **Facility:** Property located on the Colorado River. 1907 units. 1856 one-bedroom standard units. 34 one- and 17 two-bedroom suites. 18 stories, interior corridors. **Parking:** on-site and valet. **Terms:** 3 day cancellation notice. **Amenities:** video games (fee), high-speed Internet, voice mail. *Some:* irons, hair dryers. **Dining:** Beef Barron, see separate listing. **Pool(s):** heated outdoor. **Leisure Activities:** 3 lighted tennis courts, exercise room. *Fee:* massage, game room. **Guest Services:** gift shop, valet laundry. **Business Services:** conference facilities, business center. **Cards:** AX, CB, DC, DS, JC, MC, VI.

ASK DATA PORT SOME UNITS FEE

GOLDEN NUGGET LAUGHLIN

Small-scale Hotel

All Year 1P: $29-$149 2P: $29-$149 XP: $7 F14 **Phone:** 702/298-7111

Location: 3.5 mi s of Davis Dam. 2300 S Casino Dr 89028 (PO Box 77111). Fax: 702/298-7122. **Facility:** More than 500 tropical plants were imported to give the hotel's 30-foot, glass-topped atrium a rain forest feel. 300 units. 296 one-bedroom standard units. 4 one-bedroom suites ($99-$149). 4 stories, interior corridors. *Bath:* combo or shower only. **Parking:** on-site and valet. **Terms:** package plans - seasonal & weekends. **Amenities:** dual phone lines, voice mail, hair dryers. **Dining:** Jane's Grill, see separate listing. **Pool(s):** heated outdoor. **Leisure Activities:** whirlpool. *Fee:* game room. **Guest Services:** gift shop, valet laundry. **Cards:** AX, DS, MC, VI.

ASK DATA PORT SOME UNITS

HARRAH'S CASINO HOTEL Book at aaa.com

Large-scale Hotel

Phone: (702)298-4600

7/1-9/30	1P: $50-$89	2P: $50-$89	XP: $10
4/1-6/30	1P: $50-$85	2P: $50-$85	XP: $10
10/1-1/31	1P: $45-$80	2P: $45-$80	XP: $10
2/1-3/31	1P: $45-$75	2P: $45-$75	XP: $10

Location: 5 mi s of Davis Dam; on the river. 2900 S Casino Dr 89029. Fax: 702/298-6855. **Facility:** Southwest architecture. On the Colorado River. 1600 one-bedroom standard units. 15-20 stories, exterior corridors. *Bath:* combo or shower only. **Parking:** on-site and valet. **Terms:** 3 day cancellation notice-fee imposed. **Amenities:** voice mail, irons, hair dryers. **Dining:** Range Steakhouse, Baja Blue, see separate listings. **Pool(s):** outdoor, heated outdoor. **Leisure Activities:** whirlpools. *Fee:* massage, game room. **Guest Services:** gift shop, valet laundry. **Business Services:** conference facilities. **Cards:** AX, DC, DS, MC, VI.

FEE DATA PORT SOME UNITS

RAMADA EXPRESS HOTEL & CASINO Book at aaa.com

Large-scale Hotel

All Year 1P: $25-$200 2P: $25-$200 XP: $7 **Phone:** (702)298-4200

Location: 3 mi s of Davis Dam. 2121 S Casino Dr 89028 (PO Box 77771). Fax: 702/298-6403. **Facility:** A turn-of-the-20th-century railroad motif is the theme of this property, which includes one adults-only tower. 1501 units. 1492 one-bedroom standard units, some with whirlpools. 9 one-bedroom suites with whirlpools. 12-24 stories, interior corridors. *Bath:* combo or shower only. **Parking:** on-site and valet. **Terms:** 1-3 night minimum stay - seasonal, cancellation fee imposed. **Amenities:** *Some:* irons, hair dryers. **Pool(s):** heated outdoor. **Leisure Activities:** whirlpool. **Guest Services:** gift shop, valet laundry. **Business Services:** meeting rooms. **Cards:** AX, CB, DC, DS, MC, VI.

DATA PORT SOME UNITS FEE

WHERE TO DINE

BAJA BLUE

Mexican

Dinner: $9-$19 **Phone:** 702/298-4600

Location: 5 mi s of Davis Dam; on the river; in Harrah's Casino Hotel. 2900 S Casino Dr 89029. **Hours:** 5 pm-10 pm; Fri & Sat-11 pm. **Features:** Just off the lobby and casino is this popular Mexican eatery. Guests can listen for the good times being experienced by diners and the people enjoying games on the bar televisions. Casual dress; cocktails. **Parking:** on-site and valet. **Cards:** AX, DC, DS, MC, VI.

BEEF BARRON

Steak House

Dinner: $13-$28 **Phone:** 702/298-5111

Location: 2 mi s of Davis Dam; in Flamingo Laughlin Hotel. 1900 S Casino Dr 89029. **Hours:** 4 pm-10 pm. **Features:** Right off the casino floor, the established steakhouse serves good-size portions of beef and a few choices of fish and chicken. Casual dress; cocktails. **Parking:** on-site and valet. **Cards:** AX, CB, DC, DS, MC, VI.

THE GOURMET ROOM

Continental

Dinner: $19-$36 **Phone:** 702/298-2535

Location: 2 mi s of Davis Dam; in Don Laughlin's Riverside Resort Hotel & Casino. 1650 Casino Dr 89029. **Hours:** 5 pm-10 pm, Sat-11 pm. **Reservations:** suggested. **Features:** Guests can unwind in a relaxing, elegant dining room while taking in great views of the Colorado River. The staff is friendly and attentive. Casual dress; cocktails. **Parking:** on-site and valet. **Cards:** AX, CB, DC, DS, MC, VI.

JANE'S GRILL — American — **Lunch:** $6-$17 **Dinner:** $6-$17 **Phone:** 702/298-7111

Location: 3.5 mi s of Davis Dam; in Golden Nugget Laughlin. 2300 S Casino Dr 89028. **Hours:** 11 am-9 pm, Sat-10 pm, Sun 9 am-1:30 & 4-9 pm. **Features:** Long a staple for good food, the restaurant prepares enjoyable lunch and dinner selections. Guests can choose from pizzas, calzones, pastas, burgers and some nice salads. The staff is friendly. Casual dress; cocktails. **Parking:** on-site and valet. **Cards:** AX, DS, MC, VI.

MISSISSIPPI LOUNGE AND SEAFOOD BAR — Seafood — **Lunch:** $8-$40 **Dinner:** $8-$40 **Phone:** 702/298-4000

Location: 3 mi s of Davis Dam; in Colorado Belle Hotel & Casino. 2100 S Casino Dr 89029. **Hours:** noon-10 pm. **Features:** Upstairs in Colorado Belle Hotel and Casino, the casual and friendly restaurant overlooks the Colorado River. Seafood, including peel-and-eat shrimp, is at the heart of the menu. Casual dress; cocktails. **Parking:** on-site and valet. **Cards:** AX, CB, DC, DS, MC, VI.

RANGE STEAKHOUSE — American — **Dinner:** $20-$60 **Phone:** 702/298-4600

Location: 5 mi s of Davis Dam; on the river; in Harrah's Casino Hotel. 2900 S Casino Dr 89029. **Hours:** 5 pm-10 pm, Fri & Sat-11 pm. **Reservations:** suggested. **Features:** Overlooking the beautiful Colorado River, the steakhouse nurtures an intimate casino dining atmosphere. Patrons can select from a varied menu. Dressy casual; cocktails. **Parking:** on-site and valet. **Cards:** AX, DC, DS, MC, VI.

MESQUITE pop. 9,389

WHERE TO STAY

BUDGET INN & SUITES — Motel — **Phone:** (702)346-7444

All Year 1P: $44-$54 2P: $49-$69

Location: I-15, exit 122. 390 N Sandhill 89024. Fax: 702/346-7438. **Facility:** 66 one-bedroom standard units. 2 stories (no elevator), exterior corridors. *Bath:* combo or shower only. **Parking:** on-site. **Terms:** small pets only ($10 extra charge). **Pool(s):** heated outdoor. **Leisure Activities:** whirlpool. **Cards:** AX, DS, MC, VI.

ASK FEE DATA PORT SOME UNITS

CASA BLANCA RESORT & CASINO — Large-scale Hotel — **Phone:** 702/346-7529

All Year 1P: $39-$109 2P: $39-$109

Location: I-15, exit 120. 950 W Mesquite Blvd 89027 (PO Box 1620, 89024). Fax: 702/346-6888. **Facility:** Placed amid plush golf courses and manicured landscaping, this popular casino property also has a nice selection of dining. 488 one-bedroom standard units. 9 stories, interior corridors. *Bath:* combo or shower only. **Parking:** on-site and valet. **Terms:** cancellation fee imposed. **Amenities:** voice mail, irons, hair dryers. **Dining:** Katherine's at Casa Blanca, see separate listing. **Pool(s):** heated outdoor. **Leisure Activities:** whirlpool, golf-18 holes, 4 lighted tennis courts. *Fee:* massage, game room. **Guest Services:** gift shop, valet laundry, area transportation. **Business Services:** conference facilities, fax (fee). **Cards:** AX, MC, VI.

DATA PORT SOME UNITS

EUREKA HOTEL & CASINO — Small-scale Hotel — **Phone:** (702)346-4600

All Year 1P: $49-$99 2P: $49-$99

Location: I-15, exit 122 W, 0.5 mi nw. 275 Mesa Blvd 89027. Fax: 702/346-8526. **Facility:** The casino is very convenient to the rooms, offers a wide range of gambling options and has both casual and fine dining. 215 units. 207 one-bedroom standard units. 8 two-bedroom suites ($60-$129) with whirlpools. 4 stories, interior corridors. *Bath:* combo or shower only. **Parking:** on-site. **Terms:** cancellation fee imposed. **Amenities:** voice mail, irons, hair dryers. *Some:* dual phone lines. **Dining:** Tumbleweed Cafe, see separate listing. **Pool(s):** heated outdoor. **Leisure Activities:** whirlpool, exercise room. *Fee:* massage. **Guest Services:** coin laundry. **Business Services:** meeting rooms. **Cards:** AX, DC, DS, MC, VI.

ASK DATA PORT SOME UNITS FEE

OASIS RESORT CASINO GOLF AND SPA — Motel — **Phone:** 702/346-5232

All Year 1P: $29-$99

Location: I-15, exit 120. 897 W Mesquite Blvd 89024 (PO Box 360). Fax: 702/346-2746. **Facility:** Located only 80 miles from Las Vegas, this oasis in the desert has golf, a spa, gaming and a selection of restaurants. 952 units. 911 one-bedroom standard units. 41 one-bedroom suites ($69-$159). 3 stories, exterior corridors. *Bath:* combo or shower only. **Parking:** on-site and valet. **Pool(s):** outdoor, 4 heated outdoor. **Leisure Activities:** whirlpools, 2 lighted tennis courts. *Fee:* golf-36 holes, horseback riding, exercise room, massage, game room. **Guest Services:** gift shop, coin laundry. **Business Services:** conference facilities, fax (fee). **Cards:** AX, DC, DS, MC, VI.

SOME UNITS

VIRGIN RIVER HOTEL CASINO BINGO — Motel — **Phone:** (702)346-7777

All Year 1P: $19-$99 2P: $19-$99

Location: I-15, exit 122, just w. 100 Pioneer Blvd 89024 (PO Box 1620). Fax: 702/346-7771. **Facility:** Near Utah border. 716 units. 714 one-bedroom standard units. 2 one-bedroom suites ($250). 2-3 stories, exterior corridors. *Bath:* combo or shower only. **Parking:** on-site. **Terms:** pets ($25 deposit, in limited units). **Pool(s):** 2 heated outdoor. **Leisure Activities:** whirlpools. *Fee:* game room. **Guest Services:** gift shop, coin laundry. **Cards:** AX, DC, DS, MC, VI.

FEE SOME UNITS

WHERE TO DINE

KATHERINE'S AT CASA BLANCA — Steak & Seafood — **Dinner:** $18-$50 **Phone:** 702/346-7529

Location: I-15, exit 120; in Casa Blanca Resort & Casino. 950 W Mesquite Blvd 89027. **Hours:** 5 pm-10 pm. **Reservations:** suggested. **Features:** Steak, seafood or Italian, wonderful dishes are served by a friendly, well-trained staff. Guests can start a meal with one of the many cold and warm appetizers and finish it with a great dessert. Dressy casual; cocktails. **Parking:** on-site and valet. **Cards:** AX, DC, MC, VI.

TUMBLEWEED CAFE Lunch: $5-$10 Dinner: $5-$10 Phone: 702/346-4600

American

Location: I-15, exit 122 W, 0.5 mi nw; in Eureka Hotel & Casino. 275 Mesa Blvd 89027. **Hours:** 24 hours. **Features:** Just off the casino, the restaurant welcomes locals and tourists alike. The friendly staff serves breakfast, lunch and dinner at any hour of the day. Casual dress; cocktails. **Parking:** on-site. **Cards:** AX, DC, DS, MC, VI.

OVERTON

WHERE TO STAY

BEST WESTERN NORTH SHORE INN AT LAKE MEAD *Book at aaa.com* Phone: (702)397-6000

Motel

All Year [ECP] 1P: $55-$69 2P: $55-$69 XP: $5 F12

Location: I-15, exit 93, 10 mi ne on SR 169. 520 N Moapa Valley Blvd 89040 (PO Box 1650). Fax: 702/397-6008. **Facility:** 43 units. 42 one-bedroom standard units. 1 one-bedroom suite ($95-$120). 2 stories (no elevator), interior corridors. **Parking:** on-site. **Terms:** small pets only ($10 fee). **Amenities:** irons, hair dryers. **Pool(s):** heated outdoor. **Leisure Activities:** whirlpool. **Guest Services:** coin laundry. **Business Services:** meeting rooms. **Cards:** AX, CB, DS, MC, VI.

ASK FEE / SOME UNITS VCR FEE /

PAHRUMP pop. 24,631

WHERE TO STAY

BEST WESTERN PAHRUMP STATION *Book at aaa.com* Phone: 775/727-5100

AAA SAVE

Motel

All Year 1P: $51-$129 XP: $6 F17

Location: Downtown. 1101 S Hwy 160 89048 (PO Box 38, 89041). Fax: 775/751-1325. **Facility:** 90 units. 85 one-bedroom standard units, some with whirlpools. 5 one-bedroom suites, some with whirlpools. 1-2 stories (no elevator), exterior corridors. *Bath:* combo or shower only. **Parking:** on-site. **Terms:** [CP] meal plan available, pets ($6 extra charge, dogs only). **Amenities:** irons, hair dryers. **Pool(s):** heated outdoor. **Leisure Activities:** whirlpool, exercise room. **Cards:** AX, DC, DS, MC, VI. **Special Amenities: free continental breakfast and preferred room (subject to availability with advanced reservations).**

FEE / SOME UNITS FEE FEE /

PAHRUMP NUGGET HOTEL & GAMBLING HALL Phone: (775)751-6500

Small-scale Hotel

All Year 2P: $49-$65 XP: $5 F12

Location: Downtown. 681 S Hwy 160 89048. Fax: 775/751-6535. **Facility:** Plenty of options await visitors, including a bustling casino and both fine dining and fast food selections. 71 one-bedroom standard units. 3 stories, interior corridors. *Bath:* combo or shower only. **Parking:** on-site. **Terms:** check-in 4 pm, $3 service charge. **Dining:** The Nugget Steakhouse, see separate listing. **Leisure Activities:** Fee: game room. **Guest Services:** gift shop. **Business Services:** conference facilities, fax. **Cards:** AX, CB, DC, DS, MC, VI.

ASK / SOME UNITS /

SADDLE WEST HOTEL & CASINO Phone: (775)727-1111

AAA SAVE

Motel

All Year 1P: $46-$61 2P: $46-$61 XP: $5 F17

Location: Downtown. 1220 S Hwy 160 89048. Fax: 775/727-6749. **Facility:** 158 units. 154 one-bedroom standard units. 4 one-bedroom suites ($65-$107) with whirlpools. 2 stories (no elevator), exterior corridors. *Bath:* combo or shower only. **Parking:** on-site. **Terms:** package plans, small pets only ($100 deposit). **Amenities:** *Some:* hair dryers. **Dining:** 24 hours, cocktails. **Pool(s):** heated outdoor. **Leisure Activities:** whirlpool. *Fee:* game room. **Guest Services:** gift shop, coin laundry. **Business Services:** meeting rooms, fax. **Cards:** AX, CB, DC, DS, MC, VI. **Special Amenities: free continental breakfast and free room upgrade (subject to availability with advanced reservations).**

FEE / SOME UNITS FEE /

WHERE TO DINE

THE NUGGET STEAKHOUSE Dinner: $15-$40 Phone: 775/751-6500

Steak & Seafood

Location: Downtown; in Pahrump Nugget Hotel & Gambling Hall. 681 S Hwy 160 89048. **Hours:** 5 pm-10 pm. **Reservations:** suggested. **Features:** On the town's main street, the steakhouse is a quiet place to dine and relax in a comfortable setting just off the casino floor. Dressy casual; cocktails. **Parking:** on-site. **Cards:** AX, CB, DC, DS, JC, MC, VI.

PRIMM

WHERE TO STAY

BUFFALO BILL'S Phone: (702)382-1212

Large-scale Hotel

All Year 1P: $27-$60 2P: $27-$60 XP: $5 F16

Location: I-15, exit state line, just e; 45 mi s of Las Vegas. (PO Box 19129). Fax: 702/679-5424. **Facility:** The property offers lots to choose from, including all the gambling options, restaurants, shopping and even a popular roller coaster. 1240 units. 1220 one-bedroom standard units. 20 one-bedroom suites, some with whirlpools. 16 stories, interior corridors. *Bath:* shower only. **Parking:** on-site and valet. **Terms:** cancellation fee imposed. **Amenities:** voice mail. **Pool(s):** heated outdoor. **Leisure Activities:** whirlpool. *Fee:* golf-36 holes. **Guest Services:** gift shop, valet laundry, area transportation. **Business Services:** conference facilities, PC, fax. **Cards:** AX, DC, DS, MC, VI.

/ SOME UNITS FEE /

PRIMM VALLEY RESORT & CASINO Book at aaa.com **Phone:** (702)382-1212

Large-scale Hotel

All Year 1P: $35-$70 2P: $35-$70 XP: $5 F16

Location: I-15; 45 mi s of Las Vegas. 31900 S Las Vegas Blvd 89019 (PO Box 19119). Fax: 702/679-5424. **Facility:** 623 units. 588 one-bedroom standard units. 35 one-bedroom suites, some with whirlpools. 4 stories, interior corridors. *Bath:* combo or shower only. **Parking:** on-site and valet. **Terms:** cancellation fee imposed. **Amenities:** irons, hair dryers. **Dining:** GP's Restaurant, see separate listing. **Pool(s):** heated outdoor. **Leisure Activities:** whirlpool, playground. *Fee:* golf-36 holes, game room. **Guest Services:** gift shop, valet laundry, area transportation. **Business Services:** conference facilities. **Cards:** AX, DC, DS, MC, VI.

SOME UNITS

WHISKEY PETE'S HOTEL & CASINO **Phone:** (702)382-1212

Large-scale Hotel

All Year 1P: $35-$50 2P: $35-$50 XP: $5 F16

Location: I-15, exit state line, just w; 45 mi s of Las Vegas. (PO Box 19119, 89019-3718). Fax: 702/679-5424. **Facility:** The hotel offers plenty to see and do, including gambling and eating at one of the popular restaurants; it's convenient to shopping too. 777 units. 767 one-bedroom standard units. 10 one-bedroom suites, some with whirlpools. 2-19 stories, interior corridors. *Bath:* combo or shower only. **Parking:** on-site and valet. **Terms:** cancellation fee imposed. **Pool(s):** outdoor. **Leisure Activities:** whirlpool, waterslide. *Fee:* golf-36 holes, game room. **Guest Services:** gift shop, valet laundry, area transportation. **Business Services:** meeting rooms. **Cards:** AX, DC, DS, MC, VI.

SOME UNITS

WHERE TO DINE

GP'S RESTAURANT **Dinner:** $13-$20 **Phone:** 702/382-1212

American

Location: I-15, 45 mi s of Las Vegas; in Primm Valley Resort & Casino. 31900 S Las Vegas Blvd 89019. **Hours:** 5 pm-10 pm, Fri & Sat-11 pm. Closed: Mon & Tues. **Reservations:** suggested. **Features:** The restaurant presents a menu of American fare, including prime rib and seafood, especially lobster. Comfortable booths and tables are attractively arranged. Cocktails. **Parking:** on-site and valet. **Cards:** AX, CB, DC, MC, VI.

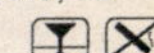

Neon Museum at Fremont Street Experience / © Richard Cummins / Photophile

This ends listings for the Las Vegas Vicinity. The following page resumes the alphabetical listings of cities in Nevada.

LAUGHLIN —*See Las Vegas p. 871.*

LOVELOCK pop. 2,003

WHERE TO STAY

RAMADA INN-STURGEON'S CASINO Book at aaa.com **Phone:** (775)273-2971

Motel

All Year 1P: $45-$52 2P: $53-$59 XP: $8 F17

Location: I-80, exit 105 or 107, just n. 1420 Cornell Ave 89419 (PO Box 56). Fax: 775/273-2278. **Facility:** Visitors can enjoy the casino scene or a nice meal that is also popular with locals at this hotel, located in a charming town right off the highway. 74 one-bedroom standard units, some with whirlpools. 2 stories (no elevator), exterior corridors. **Parking:** on-site. **Terms:** small pets only ($5 extra charge). **Amenities:** voice mail, hair dryers. **Pool(s):** heated indoor. **Leisure Activities:** Fee: game room. **Guest Services:** coin laundry. **Business Services:** meeting rooms. **Cards:** AX, DC, DS, MC, VI.

SOME UNITS

FEE

MESQUITE —*See Las Vegas p. 873.*

MINDEN pop. 2,836

WHERE TO STAY

BEST WESTERN MINDEN INN Book at aaa.com **Phone:** (775)782-7766

Motel

4/1-10/31	1P: $75-$129	2P: $75-$129	XP: $8	F16
2/1-3/31 & 11/1-1/31	1P: $59-$69	2P: $59-$69	XP: $8	F16

Location: US 395, exit Ironwood Dr W, 0.5 mi n of jct US 395 and SR 88. 1795 Ironwood Dr 89423. Fax: 775/782-7756. **Facility:** 83 one-bedroom standard units. 2 stories (no elevator), exterior corridors. *Bath:* combo or shower only. **Parking:** on-site. **Terms:** cancellation fee imposed, [CP] meal plan available, pets ($15 extra charge, in designated units, dogs only, with prior approval). **Amenities:** irons, hair dryers. **Pool(s):** heated outdoor. **Guest Services:** coin laundry. **Business Services:** fax. **Cards:** AX, DC, DS, MC, VI. **Special Amenities: free continental breakfast.**

SOME UNITS

FEE FEE FEE

CARSON VALLEY INN HOTEL & CASINO **Phone:** (775)782-9711

Small-scale Hotel

5/28-10/31	1P: $79-$109	2P: $79-$109	XP: $6	F12
4/2-5/27	1P: $69-$89	2P: $69-$89	XP: $6	F12
2/1-4/1 & 11/1-1/31	1P: $59-$79	2P: $59-$79	XP: $6	F12

Location: Center. 1627 US 395 N 89423. Fax: 775/782-7472. **Facility:** View of mountains or ranch land. 153 one-bedroom standard units. 4 stories, interior corridors. *Bath:* combo or shower only. **Parking:** on-site and valet. **Amenities:** voice mail, irons, hair dryers. **Dining:** 3 restaurants, 24 hours, cocktails, also, Michael's at the Inn, see separate listing, entertainment. **Pool(s):** heated indoor. **Leisure Activities:** whirlpools, exercise room. *Fee:* game room. **Guest Services:** gift shop, valet laundry. **Business Services:** meeting rooms. **Cards:** AX, CB, DC, DS, MC, VI.

SOME UNITS

FEE

CARSON VALLEY MOTOR LODGE **Phone:** (775)782-9711

Motel

5/28-10/31	1P: $59-$99	2P: $59-$99	XP: $6	F12
4/2-5/27	1P: $59-$69	2P: $59-$69	XP: $6	F12
2/1-4/1 & 11/1-1/31	1P: $49-$59	2P: $49-$59	XP: $6	F12

Location: Center. 1643 Hwy 395 N 89423. Fax: 775/782-7472. **Facility:** 76 one-bedroom standard units. 2 stories, exterior corridors. *Bath:* combo or shower only. **Parking:** on-site. **Amenities:** voice mail, hair dryers. **Pool(s):** heated indoor. **Leisure Activities:** whirlpools, exercise room. **Guest Services:** gift shop, valet laundry. **Business Services:** meeting rooms, fax. **Cards:** AX, CB, DC, DS, MC, VI.

SOME UNITS

HOLIDAY LODGE **Phone:** 775/782-2288

Motel

5/1-10/31	1P: $38-$46	2P: $41-$49	XP: $5
2/1-4/30 & 11/1-1/31	1P: $32-$38	2P: $38-$41	XP: $5

Location: Center. 1591 US 395 N 89423 (PO Box 848). Fax: 775/782-3765. **Facility:** 20 one-bedroom standard units. 1 story, exterior corridors. **Parking:** on-site. **Terms:** pets ($20 deposit, $5 extra charge, dogs only). **Pool(s):** heated outdoor. **Cards:** AX, DS, MC, VI.

SOME UNITS

FEE

WHERE TO DINE

FIONA'S BAR & GRILL **Dinner:** $16-$30 **Phone:** 775/782-9711

Steak & Seafood

Location: Center. 1627 US Hwy 395 N 89423. **Hours:** 4:30 pm-9:30 pm. Closed: Mon. **Reservations:** suggested. **Features:** On the main road through town, the restaurant is a relaxing place to enjoy dinner. Guests can choose among steaks, chops and seafood, and all entrees come with a trip to the soup and salad bar. Casual dress; cocktails. **Parking:** on-site. **Cards:** AX, CB, DC, DS, MC, VI.

MICHAEL'S AT THE INN **Dinner:** $19-$35 **Phone:** 775/782-9711

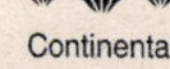

Continental

Location: Center; in Carson Valley Inn Hotel & Casino. 1627 US Hwy 359 N 89423. **Hours:** 5:30 pm-9 pm. Closed: Tues. **Reservations:** suggested. **Features:** Off the casino floor, the quiet spot offers casual, contemporary Continental cuisine. Servers are friendly and the menu varied. The nice dining experience draws a good base of locals. Dressy casual; cocktails. **Parking:** on-site and valet. **Cards:** AX, CB, MC, VI.

OVERTON —*See Las Vegas p. 874.*

PAHRUMP —*See Las Vegas p. 874.*

PRIMM —*See Las Vegas p. 874.*

RENO pop. 180,480

WHERE TO STAY

A&A'S RODEWAY INN & SPA *Book at aaa.com* **Phone:** (775)786-2500

AAA SAVE — Motel

All Year 1P: $30-$169 2P: $36-$169 XP: $10 F14

Location: I-395, exit W Mill St. 2050 Market St 89502. Fax: 775/786-3884. **Facility:** 91 one-bedroom standard units, some with kitchens (no utensils). 4 stories, interior corridors. **Parking:** on-site. **Terms:** pets ($10 extra charge). **Amenities:** voice mail. **Pool(s):** outdoor. **Leisure Activities:** sauna, whirlpool. **Guest Services:** coin laundry, area transportation-Harrah's & Hilton. **Cards:** AX, CB, DC, DS, JC, MC, VI. **Special Amenities: free continental breakfast and free local telephone calls.** *(See color ad below)*

SOME UNITS / DATA PORT / FEE

ATLANTIS CASINO RESORT - RENO *Book at aaa.com* **Phone:** (775)825-4700

AAA SAVE — Large-scale Hotel

All Year 1P: $39-$189 2P: $39-$189 XP: $10 F17

Location: 3 mi s on US 395. 3800 S Virginia St 89502. Fax: 775/826-7860. **Facility:** Some motel units. 980 units. 940 one-bedroom standard units, some with whirlpools. 40 one-bedroom suites ($109-$275), some with whirlpools. 2-27 stories, interior/exterior corridors. *Bath:* combo or shower only. **Parking:** on-site and valet. **Terms:** package plans - seasonal. **Amenities:** voice mail. *Some:* irons, hair dryers. **Dining:** 6 restaurants, 24 hours; buffet $7-$13, cocktails, also, Cafe Alfresco, Montevigna Italian Ristorante, see separate listings, entertainment. **Pool(s):** heated outdoor, heated indoor. **Leisure Activities:** sauna, whirlpools, concierge floors with restricted access, spa. *Fee:* game room. **Guest Services:** gift shop, valet laundry, area transportation-downtown. **Business Services:** conference facilities. **Cards:** AX, DC, DS, JC, MC, VI. *(See color ad p 878)*

SOME UNITS / FEE / DATA PORT

BEST WESTERN AIRPORT PLAZA HOTEL *Book at aaa.com* **Phone:** (775)348-6370

AAA SAVE — Small-scale Hotel

All Year 1P: $79-$249 2P: $79-$249 XP: $10 F

Location: US 395, exit E Plumb Villanova. 1981 Terminal Way 89502. Fax: 775/348-9722. **Facility:** 269 units. 265 one-bedroom standard units. 4 two-bedroom suites. 3 stories, interior corridors. *Bath:* combo or shower only. **Parking:** on-site. **Terms:** pets ($50 deposit, $10 extra charge, in limited units). **Amenities:** video games (fee), dual phone lines, voice mail, irons, hair dryers. **Dining:** 6 am-2 & 5-10 pm, cocktails. **Pool(s):** heated outdoor. **Leisure Activities:** sauna, whirlpool, putting green, exercise room. **Guest Services:** valet laundry, area transportation-Reno Hilton. **Business Services:** conference facilities, business center. **Special Amenities: free local telephone calls.**

SOME UNITS / FEE / DATA PORT / FEE

BOOMTOWN HOTEL CASINO **Phone:** (775)345-6000

Small-scale Hotel

3/1-10/31	1P: $79-$169	2P: $79-$169	XP: $10	F12
2/1-2/29 & 11/1-1/31	1P: $69-$159	2P: $69-$159	XP: $10	F12

Location: I-80, exit 4 (Boomtown/Garson Rd). Boomtown/Garson Rd 89439 (PO Box 399). Fax: 775/345-8693. **Facility:** Western-themed hotel and casino. 318 units. 292 one-bedroom standard units. 26 one-bedroom suites ($139-$299), some with whirlpools. 5 stories, interior corridors. *Bath:* combo or shower only. **Parking:** on-site and valet. **Terms:** check-in 4 pm. **Amenities:** video games (fee), high-speed Internet, voice mail, irons, hair dryers. **Dining:** 2 restaurants, 24 hours; buffet $8-$23, cocktails, also, Cassidy's, see separate listing, entertainment. **Pool(s):** heated indoor. **Leisure Activities:** Fee: game room. **Guest Services:** gift shop, valet laundry, area transportation. **Business Services:** conference facilities. **Cards:** AX, DS, MC, VI. **Special Amenities: early check-in/late check-out.** *(See color ad p 879)*

SOME UNITS

CIRCUS CIRCUS HOTEL & CASINO-RENO *Book at aaa.com* **Phone:** (775)329-0711

Large-scale Hotel

All Year	1P: $35-$189	2P: $35-$189	XP: $10	F12

Location: Corner of Sierra and 6th sts; just n off I-80 business route. 500 N Sierra St 89503 (PO Box 5880, 89513). Fax: 775/328-9585. **Facility:** Come on in for free circus acts, a choice of dining, a full-service casino and a friendly staff in the heart of Reno. 1572 units. 1542 one-bedroom standard units. 30 one-bedroom suites ($89-$300) with whirlpools. 23-28 stories, interior corridors. *Bath:* some combo or shower only. **Parking:** on-site and valet. **Terms:** package plans - seasonal. **Amenities:** voice mail, irons, hair dryers. *Fee:* video games, high-speed Internet. **Leisure Activities:** exercise room. *Fee:* massage, game room. **Guest Services:** gift shop, valet laundry. **Business Services:** meeting rooms. **Cards:** AX, CB, DC, DS, JC, MC, VI.

SOME UNITS FEE

COLONIAL MOTOR INN **Phone:** (775)786-5038

Motel

2/1-10/31	1P: $58-$111	2P: $58-$111	XP: $10	F12
11/1-1/31	1P: $30-$111	2P: $30-$111	XP: $10	F12

Location: 1 blk off I-80 business route; 1 blk from casinos. 232 West St 89501. Fax: 775/323-4588. **Facility:** 100 one-bedroom standard units. 5 stories, exterior corridors. **Parking:** on-site. **Terms:** cancellation fee imposed, weekly rates available. **Amenities:** hair dryers. **Pool(s):** heated outdoor. **Leisure Activities:** sauna. **Guest Services:** gift shop, valet laundry. **Cards:** AX, DS, MC, VI. *(See ad p 879)*

SOME UNITS

DANIEL'S MOTOR LODGE **Phone:** 775/329-1351

Motel

All Year	1P: $49-$125	2P: $49-$125	XP: $10	F16

Location: On US 395; jct I-80 business route. Located in casino area. 375 N Sierra St 89501. Fax: 775/329-2508. **Facility:** 82 one-bedroom standard units. 2-3 stories, exterior corridors. **Parking:** on-site. **Terms:** 14% service charge. **Cards:** AX, DC, DS, MC, VI.

SOME UNITS

DAYS INN *Book at aaa.com* **Phone:** (775)786-4070

AAA SAVE

Motel

8/5-9/25 [CP]	1P: $35-$175	2P: $35-$185	XP: $10	F12
9/26-1/31 [CP]	1P: $30-$115	2P: $30-$120	XP: $10	F12
5/30-8/4 [CP]	1P: $35-$99	2P: $35-$110	XP: $10	F12
2/1-5/29 [CP]	1P: $35-$99	2P: $35-$99	XP: $10	F12

Location: I-80, exit Wells Ave, just s. 701 E 7th St 89512. Fax: 775/329-4338. **Facility:** 138 one-bedroom standard units. 4 stories, exterior corridors. **Parking:** on-site. **Terms:** [CP] meal plan available, pets ($10 extra charge, in limited units). **Amenities:** safes (fee), hair dryers. **Pool(s):** heated outdoor. **Guest Services:** coin laundry. **Business Services:** meeting rooms, fax. **Cards:** AX, DC, DS, MC, VI. **Special Amenities: free continental breakfast and free newspaper.**

SOME UNITS

S/D FEE DATA PORT / FEE FEE /

EASY 8 MOTEL

AAA SAVE

Motel

Phone: (775)322-4588

All Year 1P: $29-$175 2P: $39-$200

Location: I-80, exit Keystone, 4 blks e. 255 W 5th St 89503. Fax: 408/926-0215. **Facility:** 21 one-bedroom standard units. 2 stories (no elevator), exterior corridors. **Parking:** on-site. **Terms:** small pets only ($25 deposit). **Cards:** DC, MC, VI. **Special Amenities: free local telephone calls and preferred room (subject to availability with advanced reservations).**

SOME UNITS

FEE

ECONO LODGE *Book at aaa.com*

AAA SAVE

Motel

Phone: (775)329-3125

All Year 1P: $29-$68 2P: $34-$79 XP: $5 F16

Location: I-80, exit Wells Ave, just s. 666 N Wells Ave 89512. Fax: 775/329-3755. **Facility:** 93 one-bedroom standard units. 2 stories (no elevator), exterior corridors. *Bath:* combo or shower only. **Parking:** on-site. **Terms:** [CP] meal plan available. **Cards:** AX, DC, MC, VI. **Special Amenities: free continental breakfast and free local telephone calls.** *(See color ad below)*

SOME UNITS

FEE FEE

ELDORADO HOTEL *Book at aaa.com*

Large-scale Hotel

Phone: (775)786-5700

All Year 1P: $49-$199 2P: $49-$199 XP: $10 F12

Location: 4th and Virginia sts. Located in casino area. 345 N Virginia St 89505 (PO Box 3399). Fax: 775/322-7124. **Facility:** Come in and enjoy the full casino experience at this longtime Reno favorite, located in the heart of the action. 816 units. 799 one-bedroom standard units, some with whirlpools. 17 one-bedroom suites ($99-$500), some with whirlpools. 11-26 stories, interior corridors. *Bath:* combo or shower only. **Parking:** on-site and valet. **Terms:** 2 night minimum stay - weekends, 14% service charge. **Amenities:** safes, honor bars, irons, hair dryers. *Fee:* video games, high-speed Internet. **Pool(s):** heated outdoor. **Leisure Activities:** whirlpool. **Guest Services:** gift shop, valet laundry. **Business Services:** meeting rooms, business center. **Cards:** AX, CB, DC, DS, JC, MC, VI.

SOME UNITS

FEE

FITZGERALDS CASINO/HOTEL — **Phone:** (775)786-3663

Large-scale Hotel

7/1-10/24	1P: $38-$120	2P: $38-$120	XP: $10	F13
3/1-6/30	1P: $34-$98	2P: $34-$98	XP: $10	F13
10/25-1/31	1P: $28-$98	2P: $28-$98	XP: $10	F13
2/1-2/29	1P: $24-$98	2P: $24-$98	XP: $10	F13

Location: I-80, exit Virginia St S. Located in casino area. 255 N Virginia St 89501. Fax: 775/785-3686. **Facility:** 351 units. 343 one-bedroom standard units. 8 one-bedroom suites ($98-$180). 16 stories, interior corridors. **Parking:** on-site and valet. **Terms:** 2 night minimum stay - with Saturday stayover. **Amenities:** video games (fee), voice mail. *Some:* irons, hair dryers. **Dining:** Limericks Pub & Grille, see separate listing. **Guest Services:** gift shop, valet laundry. **Business Services:** fax. **Cards:** AX, CB, DC, DS, MC, VI. ***(See color ad p 880)***

ASK FEE SOME UNITS

GATEKEEPER INN — **Phone:** (775)786-3500

AAA SAVE Motel

All Year	1P: $35-$300	2P: $45-$300	XP: $10	F3

Location: Corner of West and 5th sts. Adjacent to the casinos. 221 W 5th St 89503. Fax: 775/324-3318. **Facility:** 28 one-bedroom standard units. 3 stories, exterior corridors. **Parking:** on-site. **Cards:** AX, CB, DC, DS, MC, VI. **Special Amenities: free local telephone calls and preferred room (subject to availability with advanced reservations).**

SOME UNITS

GOLDEN PHOENIX HOTEL & CASINO — *Book at aaa.com* — **Phone:** (775)785-7100

Large-scale Hotel

6/1-9/30	1P: $39-$79
12/1-1/31	1P: $39-$59
2/1-5/31 & 10/1-11/30	1P: $29-$49

Location: I-80, exit S Virginia St. Located in casino area. 255 N Sierra St 89501. Fax: 775/785-7086. **Facility:** Located in the heart of the gambling action in "The Biggest Little City In The World," this property offers a wide range of activities to choose from. 604 units. 601 one-bedroom standard units, some with whirlpools. 3 one-bedroom suites ($129-$179) with whirlpools. 21 stories, interior corridors. *Bath:* combo or shower only. **Parking:** on-site and valet. **Terms:** pets ($150 deposit, $25 extra charge). **Amenities:** video games (fee), voice mail, hair dryers. *Some:* irons. **Leisure Activities:** exercise room. **Guest Services:** gift shop, valet laundry. **Business Services:** conference facilities, business center. **Cards:** AX, CB, DC, DS, JC, MC, VI. ***(See color ad below)***

ASK FEE SOME UNITS VCR FEE FEE

HARRAH'S — *Book at aaa.com* — **Phone:** (775)786-3232

Large-scale Hotel

7/1-10/31	1P: $69-$229	2P: $69-$229	XP: $10
3/1-6/30	1P: $49-$169	2P: $49-$169	XP: $10
2/1-2/29 & 11/1-1/31	1P: $39-$149	2P: $39-$149	XP: $10

Location: At Center and 2nd sts; downtown. 219 N Center St 89501 (PO Box 10, 89504). Fax: 775/788-2815. **Facility:** Visitors here have several choices to make for dining, entertainment and gambling, and all of the options are good ones. 946 units. 931 one-bedroom standard units. 12 one- and 3 two-bedroom suites, some with whirlpools. 24-26 stories, interior corridors. *Bath:* combo or shower only. **Parking:** on-site and valet. **Terms:** check-in 4 pm, 3 day cancellation notice-fee imposed, no pets allowed (kennel available). **Amenities:** video games (fee), voice mail, irons, hair dryers. **Dining:** Steak House, Cafe Napa, see separate listings. **Pool(s):** heated outdoor. **Leisure Activities:** saunas, whirlpools. *Fee:* massage, game room. **Guest Services:** gift shop, valet laundry. **Business Services:** conference facilities, business center. **Cards:** AX, DC, DS, MC, VI.

ASK FEE SOME UNITS

HOLIDAY INN-DOWNTOWN *Book at aaa.com* **Phone:** (775)786-5151

AAA SAVE

Small-scale Hotel

6/1-10/31 1P: $79-$299 2P: $79-$299 XP: $10 F17
2/1-5/31 & 11/1-1/31 1P: $69-$299 2P: $69-$299 XP: $10 F17

Location: I-80, exit Wells Ave, 12 blks e. 1000 E 6th St 89512. Fax: 775/786-2447. **Facility:** 283 units. 277 one-bedroom standard units. 6 one-bedroom suites. 13 stories, interior corridors. **Parking:** on-site. **Terms:** [BP] meal plan available, pets ($10 extra charge, in limited units). **Amenities:** video games (fee), voice mail, irons, hair dryers. **Dining:** 6:30 am-2 & 5-10 pm, cocktails. **Pool(s):** heated outdoor. **Leisure Activities:** exercise room. *Fee:* game room. **Guest Services:** gift shop, valet laundry, area transportation. **Business Services:** meeting rooms, business center. **Cards:** AX, DC, DS, MC, VI. **Special Amenities: free newspaper.**

SOME UNITS
FEE / FEE FEE

LA QUINTA INN *Book at aaa.com* **Phone:** 775/348-6100

Motel

All Year 1P: $65-$90 2P: $71-$96 XP: $6 F18

Location: US 395, exit airport northbound; exit Villanova Dr southbound. 4001 Market St 89502-3110. Fax: 775/348-8794. **Facility:** 130 one-bedroom standard units. 2 stories (no elevator), exterior corridors. **Parking:** on-site. **Terms:** [ECP] meal plan available, small pets only. **Amenities:** voice mail, irons, hair dryers. *Fee:* video games, high-speed Internet. **Pool(s):** outdoor. **Guest Services:** valet and coin laundry, area transportation. **Business Services:** fax. **Cards:** AX, CB, DC, DS, JC, MC, VI. ***(See color ad below)***

SOME UNITS
/ FEE FEE

QUALITY INN & SUITES *Book at aaa.com* **Phone:** (775)329-1001

AAA SAVE

Motel

All Year 1P: $60-$115 2P: $68-$125 XP: $10 F18

Location: US 395, exit Plumb Villanova, 1 mi w. 1885 S Virginia St 89502. Fax: 775/324-5402. **Facility:** 103 one-bedroom standard units. 2 stories, interior/exterior corridors. *Bath:* combo or shower only. **Parking:** on-site. **Amenities:** irons, hair dryers. **Dining:** 6 am-3 pm. **Pool(s):** heated outdoor. **Leisure Activities:** whirlpool. **Business Services:** fax. **Cards:** AX, CB, DC, DS, JC, MC, VI. **Special Amenities: free local telephone calls.**

SOME UNITS

RENO DOWNTOWN TRAVELODGE *Book at aaa.com* **Phone:** (775)329-3451

AAA SAVE

Motel

All Year [CP] 1P: $29-$199 2P: $29-$199 XP: $5 F17

Location: I-80, exit Keystone, just e. 655 W 4th St 89503. Fax: 775/329-3454. **Facility:** 98 units. 96 one-bedroom standard units. 2 one-bedroom suites with whirlpools. 2-3 stories (no elevator), exterior corridors. *Bath:* combo or shower only. **Parking:** on-site. **Terms:** cancellation fee imposed, small pets only ($8 extra charge, in limited units). **Amenities:** hair dryers. **Pool(s):** outdoor. **Cards:** AX, CB, DC, DS, JC, MC, VI. **Special Amenities: free newspaper and early check-in/late check-out.**

SOME UNITS
FEE

RENO HILTON *Book at aaa.com* **Phone:** (775)789-2000

Large-scale Hotel

All Year 1P: $69-$209 2P: $69-$209 XP: $10 F17

Location: 0.5 mi s of jct I-80 and US 395; US 395, exit Mill St. 2500 E 2nd St 89595. Fax: 775/789-2130. **Facility:** Located near two major highways, this full-service resort is popular for conventions and for all that enjoy tennis, entertainment, dining and gambling. 2003 units. 1603 one-bedroom standard units. 200 one-, 196 two- and 4 three-bedroom suites, some with whirlpools. 27 stories, interior corridors. *Bath:* combo or shower only. **Parking:** on-site and valet. **Amenities:** high-speed Internet (fee), voice mail, irons, hair dryers. **Pool(s):** outdoor. **Leisure Activities:** saunas, whirlpools. *Fee:* 5 lighted tennis courts, massage, game room. **Guest Services:** gift shop, valet laundry. **Business Services:** conference facilities, business center. **Cards:** AX, CB, DC, DS, JC, MC, VI. ***(See color ad p 883)***

SOME UNITS
FEE / FEE FEE

RESIDENCE INN BY MARRIOTT *Book at aaa.com* **Phone:** (775)853-8800

Motel

6/1-9/30 [ECP]	1P: $119-$209
2/1-5/31 & 10/1-1/31 [ECP]	1P: $109-$179

Location: US 395, exit S Meadows Pkwy, then e. 9845 Gateway Dr 89521. Fax: 775/853-8805. **Facility:** 120 units. 99 one- and 21 two-bedroom standard units with kitchens. 3 stories, interior corridors. *Bath:* combo or shower only. **Parking:** on-site. **Terms:** check-in 4 pm, cancellation fee imposed, pets ($90 fee, $6 extra charge). **Amenities:** video games (fee), voice mail, irons, hair dryers. **Pool(s):** heated outdoor. **Leisure Activities:** whirlpool, exercise room, sports court, basketball. **Guest Services:** complimentary evening beverages: Mon-Thurs, coin laundry. **Business Services:** meeting rooms, fax. **Cards:** AX, CB, DC, DS, JC, MC, VI.

SOME UNITS

FEE

SANDS REGENCY CASINO HOTEL *Book at aaa.com* **Phone:** (775)348-2200

Large-scale Hotel

All Year	1P: $29-$139	2P: $29-$139	XP: $10	F12

Location: Downtown. Located in casino area. 345 N Arlington Ave 89501. Fax: 775/348-2226. **Facility:** 836 one-bedroom standard units, some with whirlpools. 17 stories, interior corridors. **Parking:** on-site. **Amenities:** voice mail, hair dryers. **Pool(s):** heated outdoor. **Leisure Activities:** sauna, whirlpools. *Fee:* massage, game room. **Guest Services:** gift shop, valet laundry. **Business Services:** meeting rooms, fax. **Cards:** AX, CB, DC, DS, MC, VI. *(See color ad below)*

SOME UNITS

FEE

SEASONS INN **Phone:** 775/322-6000

Motel

All Year	1P: $35-$99	2P: $38-$129	XP: $6

Location: Corner of West and 5th sts; 1 blk w of casinos. 495 West St 89503. Fax: 775/324-6434. **Facility:** 56 one-bedroom standard units. 4 stories, exterior corridors. **Parking:** on-site. **Terms:** small pets only ($10 extra charge, dogs only). **Cards:** AX, CB, DC, DS, JC, MC. *(See color ad p 884)*

SOME UNITS

FEE

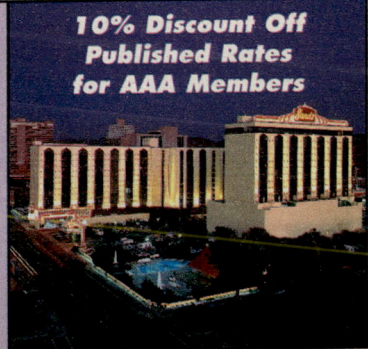

SIENA HOTEL SPA CASINO | **Phone:** (775)337-6260

Large-scale Hotel	6/1-10/31	1P: $89-$129	2P: $89-$129	XP: $20 F17
	2/1-5/31 & 11/1-1/31	1P: $69-$109	2P: $69-$109	XP: $20 F17

Location: I-80, exit Virginia St S. One S Lake St 89501. Fax: 775/337-6201. **Facility:** 214 units. 185 one-bedroom standard units. 29 one-bedroom suites, some with whirlpools. 9 stories, interior corridors. *Bath:* combo or shower only. **Parking:** on-site and valet. **Terms:** 2 night minimum stay - Sat arrival, cancellation fee imposed, [CP] meal plan available. **Amenities:** video games (fee), high-speed Internet, dual phone lines, voice mail, safes, irons, hair dryers. **Pool(s):** heated outdoor. **Leisure Activities:** whirlpool, exercise room. *Fee:* massage. **Guest Services:** gift shop, valet laundry. **Business Services:** conference facilities, business center. **Cards:** AX, DC, DS, MC, VI.

ASK SOME UNITS

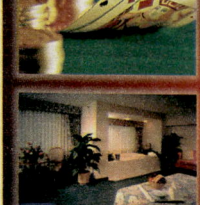

SILVER LEGACY *Book at aaa.com* **Phone:** (775)329-4777

Large-scale Hotel

All Year	1P: $65-$250	2P: $65-$250	XP: $10	F12

Location: I-80, exit S Virginia St; in casino center. 407 N Virginia St 89501. Fax: 775/325-7474. **Facility:** The place in Reno to be for name entertainment, the property offers several dining choices and a full menu of gambling options. 1720 one-bedroom standard units, some with whirlpools. 38 stories, interior corridors. *Bath:* combo or shower only. **Parking:** on-site and valet. **Terms:** 2-3 night minimum stay - weekends, cancellation fee imposed, $3 service charge. **Amenities:** voice mail, irons, hair dryers. **Dining:** 7 restaurants, 24 hours; buffet $9-$13, cocktails, also, Sterling's Seafood-Steakhouse, see separate listing, entertainment. **Pool(s):** heated outdoor. **Leisure Activities:** sauna, whirlpool. *Fee:* massage, game room. **Guest Services:** gift shop, valet laundry. **Business Services:** conference facilities, business center. **Cards:** AX, CB, DC, DS, JC, MC, VI. *(See color ad p 884)*

SOME UNITS

FEE

SPEAKEASY INN **Phone:** (775)329-7400

Small-scale Hotel

All Year	1P: $39-$179	2P: $39-$179	XP: $10	F16

Location: I-80, exit Wells Ave S, 3 blks w. 200 E 6th St 89501. Fax: 775/329-5934. **Facility:** 234 one-bedroom standard units. 11 stories, interior corridors. **Parking:** on-site. **Amenities:** voice mail. *Some:* irons, hair dryers. **Leisure Activities:** exercise room. **Guest Services:** valet laundry. **Business Services:** meeting rooms. **Cards:** AX, CB, DC, DS, MC.

SOME UNITS

SUPER 8 MOTEL AT MEADOW WOOD COURTYARD Book at aaa.com **Phone:** (775)829-4600

AAA SAVE — Motel

4/1-9/30 1P: $59-$139 2P: $59-$139
2/1-3/31 & 10/1-1/31 1P: $49-$59 2P: $49-$59

Location: US 395 at S McCarran Blvd. 5851 S Virginia St 89502. Fax: 775/826-3835. **Facility:** 155 one-bedroom standard units. 2 stories (no elevator), exterior corridors. **Parking:** on-site. **Terms:** 2 night minimum stay - seasonal weekends, [AP] meal plan available, pets ($10 extra charge, in limited units). **Amenities:** voice mail. **Dining:** 6 am-10 pm, cocktails. **Pool(s):** heated outdoor. **Leisure Activities:** whirlpool. **Guest Services:** valet and coin laundry. **Business Services:** meeting rooms. **Cards:** AX, DC, DS, MC, VI. **Special Amenities: free local telephone calls and early check-in/late check-out.** *(See color ad p 885)*

FEE — SOME UNITS

SUPER 8 MOTEL (MINERS INN) Book at aaa.com **Phone:** 775/329-3464

AAA SAVE — Motel

4/1-9/30 1P: $49-$140 2P: $49-$140
10/1-11/30 1P: $39-$140 2P: $49-$140
2/1-3/31 1P: $39-$140 2P: $39-$140
12/1-1/31 1P: $35-$140 2P: $39-$140

Location: Opposite University of Nevada. 1651 N Virginia St 89503. **Facility:** 70 one-bedroom standard units. 2 stories (no elevator), exterior corridors. **Parking:** on-site. **Terms:** [CP] meal plan available, pets ($40 deposit, $5 extra charge, in limited units). **Pool(s):** outdoor. **Cards:** AX, CB, DC, JC, MC, VI. **Special Amenities: free continental breakfast and early check-in/late check-out.**

FEE — SOME UNITS

TRAVELODGE AIRPORT Book at aaa.com **Phone:** (775)786-2506

Motel

All Year 1P: $35-$190 2P: $35-$190 XP: $10 F14

Location: I-395, exit W Mill St, just w. 2050-B Market St 89502. Fax: 775/786-3884. **Facility:** 118 one-bedroom standard units. 4 stories, interior corridors. **Parking:** on-site. **Terms:** pets ($10 extra charge). **Amenities:** voice mail. **Pool(s):** outdoor. **Leisure Activities:** sauna, whirlpool. **Guest Services:** area transportation. **Cards:** AX, CB, DC, DS, JC, MC, VI. ***(See color ad p 877)***

ASK — FEE — SOME UNITS — DATA PORT

TRUCKEE RIVER LODGE Book at aaa.com **Phone:** (775)786-8888

Motel

All Year 1P: $43 2P: $48 XP: $10 F5

Location: I-80, exit Virginia St, just w. 501 W 1st St 89503. Fax: 775/348-4769. **Facility:** 219 units. 201 one-bedroom standard units with kitchens (utensils extra charge). 16 one- and 2 two-bedroom suites ($89-$139) with kitchens (no utensils). 5 stories, interior/exterior corridors. *Bath:* combo or shower only. **Parking:** on-site. **Terms:** pets ($10 extra charge). **Amenities:** voice mail. **Leisure Activities:** exercise room. *Fee:* bicycles. **Guest Services:** gift shop, valet and coin laundry. **Business Services:** meeting rooms. **Cards:** AX, CB, DC, DS, MC, VI.

ASK — FEE

VAGABOND INN Book at aaa.com **Phone:** (775)825-7134

AAA SAVE — Motel

4/4-1/31 1P: $55-$79 2P: $60-$79
2/1-4/3 1P: $45-$79 2P: $50-$79

Location: 2.5 mi s on US 395. 3131 S Virginia St 89502. Fax: 775/825-3096. **Facility:** 129 units. 121 one- and 8 two-bedroom standard units. 2 stories (no elevator), exterior corridors. **Parking:** on-site. **Terms:** pets ($10 extra charge, in limited units). **Amenities:** *Some:* hair dryers. **Pool(s):** outdoor. **Guest Services:** area transportation-downtown. **Cards:** AX, DC, DS, MC, VI. **Special Amenities: free continental breakfast.**

FEE — SOME UNITS — DATA PORT

WONDER LODGE **Phone:** (775)786-6840

AAA SAVE — Motel

7/1-10/31 1P: $37-$44 2P: $37-$57
3/1-6/30 1P: $33-$42 2P: $33-$54
2/1-2/29 & 11/1-1/31 1P: $26-$32 2P: $26-$46

Location: 1 blk off I-80 business route; 2 blks from casinos. 430 Lake St 89501. Fax: 775/329-4257. **Facility:** 63 one-bedroom standard units. 4 stories, exterior corridors. **Parking:** on-site. **Terms:** weekly rates available, no pets allowed (owner's pet on premises). **Pool(s):** outdoor. **Cards:** AX, DS, MC, VI. **Special Amenities: free local telephone calls and preferred room (subject to availability with advanced reservations).**

SOME UNITS

WHERE TO DINE

CAFE ALFRESCO **Lunch:** $8-$10 **Dinner:** $8-$10 **Phone:** 775/825-4700

Italian

Location: 3 mi s on US 395; in Atlantis Casino Resort - Reno. 3800 S Virginia St 89502. **Hours:** 11:30 am-11 pm. **Features:** This fun place to dine lets patrons enjoy a meal while taking in the action from the casino. Among favorites are pasta dishes and pizzas cooked in a wood-fired brick oven. Casual dress; cocktails. **Parking:** on-site and valet. **Cards:** AX, CB, DC, DS, JC, MC, VI.

CAFE NAPA **Lunch:** $5-$17 **Dinner:** $7-$17 **Phone:** 775/786-3232

American

Location: At Center and 2nd sts; downtown; in Harrah's. 219 N Center 89501. **Hours:** 24 hours. **Reservations:** accepted. **Features:** Just upstairs from the bustling casino action, the 24-hour spot has not only a good selection of American food but Chinese fare as well. Casual dress; cocktails. **Parking:** on-site and valet. **Cards:** AX, DC, DS, MC, VI.

CASSIDY'S
Steak House

Dinner: $15-$29 **Phone:** 775/345-8500
Location: I-80, exit 4; in Boomtown Hotel. Boomtown/Garson Rd 89439. **Hours:** 5 pm-9 pm. **Reservations:** suggested. **Features:** Excellent prime rib—carved tableside from a large, rolling serving cart—is the house specialty, but seafood, chicken and pasta dishes are also good. Right off the casino floor, the dining room is a nice spot for a quiet meal. Service is friendly. Casual dress; cocktails. **Parking:** on-site and valet. **Cards:** AX, CB, DC, MC, VI.

FLOWING TIDE PUB
American

Lunch: $6-$9 **Dinner:** $7-$14 **Phone:** 775/747-7707
Location: I-80, exit W McCarran, 1 mi n. 10580 N McCarran 89523. **Hours:** 11 am-midnight, Sat from 9 am, Sun 9 am-11 pm. **Features:** Good food and friendly service can be expected at the neighborhood eatery, where patrons can enjoy a game on TV or shoot a game of pool. Casual dress; cocktails. **Parking:** on-site. **Cards:** AX, DC, MC, VI.

HEIDI'S FAMILY RESTAURANT
American

Lunch: $4-$11 **Phone:** 775/826-3336
Location: US 395, 2 mi s; adjacent to Park Lane Mall. 2450 S Virginia St 89502. **Hours:** 6:30 am-2 pm. **Features:** Family restaurant noted for breakfast. Casual dress. **Parking:** on-site. **Cards:** MC, VI.

LIMERICKS PUB & GRILLE
Steak House

Dinner: $8-$28 **Phone:** 775/785-3677
Location: I-80, exit Virginia St S; in casino area; in Fitzgeralds Casino/Hotel. 255 N Virginia St 89504. **Hours:** 5 pm-9 pm, Sat-10 pm. **Reservations:** suggested. **Features:** The steakhouse has a decidedly Irish-American flair. Friendly servers provide able assistance in the dining room, which is tucked away off the casino. After dinner, spring for an Irish coffee or another coffee drink. Dressy casual; cocktails. **Parking:** on-site. **Cards:** AX, DS, MC, VI.

MONTEVIGNA ITALIAN RISTORANTE
Italian

Dinner: $15-$50 **Phone:** 775/825-4700
Location: 3 mi s on US 395; in Atlantis Casino Resort - Reno. 3800 S Virginia St 89502. **Hours:** 5 pm-10 pm. **Features:** A feeling of the Tuscan countryside goes along with the menu, which lists delicious pastas, steaks and seafood. The piano lounge is a good place to start or finish the evening. Dressy casual; cocktails. **Parking:** on-site and valet. **Cards:** AX, CB, DC, DS, JC, MC, VI.

RAPSCALLION SEAFOOD HOUSE
Seafood

Lunch: $6-$15 **Dinner:** $13-$25 **Phone:** 775/323-1211
Location: 1555 S Wells 89502. **Hours:** 11:30 am-4 & 5-10 pm, Sat 5 pm-10:30 pm, Sun 10 am-2 & 5-10 pm. Closed: 7/4, 11/25, 12/25. **Reservations:** suggested. **Features:** Fresh seafood flown in daily. Dressy casual; cocktails. **Parking:** on-site. **Cards:** AX, MC, VI.

STEAK HOUSE
AAA
Continental

Lunch: $7-$11 **Dinner:** $17-$25 **Phone:** 775/788-2929
Location: At Center and 2nd sts; downtown; in Harrah's. 210 N Center St 89501. **Hours:** 11 am-2:30 & 5-10 pm, Sat-11 pm. Closed: for lunch Sat & Sun. **Reservations:** required. **Features:** Some of the flavorful dishes are prepared tableside. The staff is service-oriented. Dressy casual; cocktails. **Parking:** on-site and valet. **Cards:** AX, CB, DC, DS, JC, MC, VI.

STERLING'S SEAFOOD-STEAKHOUSE
Steak & Seafood

Dinner: $18-$72 **Phone:** 775/325-7573
Location: I-80, exit S Virginia St; in casino center; in Silver Legacy. 407 N Virginia St 89501. **Hours:** 5 pm-10 pm, Fri & Sat-11 pm. **Reservations:** suggested. **Features:** Specializing in steaks, the elegant dining room also offers good service by a friendly staff. Guests can treat themselves to a quiet meal despite the casino action going on nearby. Dressy casual; cocktails. **Parking:** on-site and valet. **Cards:** AX, CB, DC, DS, JC, MC, VI.

WHITE ORCHID
AAA
American

Dinner: $17-$65 **Phone:** 775/689-7300
Location: In Peppermill Hotel. 2707 S Virginia St 89502. **Hours:** 5:30 pm-9:30 pm, Fri & Sat-10 pm. Closed: Mon & Tues. **Reservations:** suggested. **Features:** Tucked away in a casino/hotel setting, the distinctive, elegant restaurant treats guests to a nice experience from start to finish. Service is attentive. Dressy casual; cocktails. **Parking:** on-site and valet. **Cards:** AX, CB, DC, DS, MC, VI.

SPARKS pop. 66,346

— WHERE TO STAY —

JOHN ASCUAGA'S NUGGET COURTYARD
Motel

Phone: (775)356-3300
All Year 1P: $79-$109 2P: $79-$109 XP: $10 F18
Location: I-80, exit Pyramid Way, on I-80 business loop. 1225 Victorian Ave 89431 (PO Box 797). Fax: 775/356-4198. **Facility:** 157 one-bedroom standard units. 5 stories, interior corridors. *Bath:* combo or shower only. **Parking:** on-site. **Amenities:** voice mail, irons. **Pool(s):** outdoor. **Guest Services:** sundries, valet laundry. **Cards:** AX, CB, DC, DS, MC, VI.

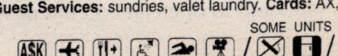

JOHN ASCUAGA'S NUGGET HOTEL TOWER Book at aaa.com

Large-scale Hotel

All Year 1P: $99-$169 2P: $99-$169 Phone: (775)356-3300 XP: $10 F18

Location: I-80, exit Nugget Ave eastbound; exit Pyramid Way westbound. 1100 Nugget Ave 89431. Fax: 775/356-4198. **Facility:** Guest rooms at the hotel are spacious and attractively appointed. 1407 units. 1395 one-bedroom standard units. 12 one-bedroom suites ($145-$295) with whirlpools. 29 stories, interior corridors. *Bath:* combo or shower only. **Parking:** on-site and valet. **Terms:** $3 service charge. **Amenities:** voice mail, irons, hair dryers. **Dining:** The Steakhouse Grill, see separate listing. **Pool(s):** heated indoor. **Leisure Activities:** whirlpool, exercise room. *Fee:* massage. **Guest Services:** gift shop, valet laundry. **Business Services:** conference facilities, business center. **Cards:** AX, CB, DC, DS, MC, VI.

SOME UNITS FEE FEE

QUALITY INN Book at aaa.com

Motel

All Year 1P: $69-$109 2P: $69-$109 Phone: 775/358-6900 XP: $10

Location: I-80, exit E McCarran Blvd, just s. 55 E Nugget Ave 89431. Fax: 775/359-6065. **Facility:** 220 one-bedroom standard units. 9 stories, interior corridors. *Bath:* combo or shower only. **Parking:** on-site. **Amenities:** voice mail, irons, hair dryers. **Pool(s):** heated outdoor. **Leisure Activities:** whirlpool. *Fee:* game room. **Guest Services:** area transportation. **Business Services:** meeting rooms, fax. **Cards:** AX, DC, MC, VI.

SOME UNITS

SILVER CLUB HOTEL & CASINO Book at aaa.com

AAA SAVE

Small-scale Hotel

Phone: (775)358-4771

12/25-1/31	1P: $29-$150	2P: $29-$150	XP: $10	F12
5/1-9/30	1P: $29-$135	2P: $29-$135	XP: $10	F12
2/1-4/30 & 10/1-12/24	1P: $29-$89	2P: $29-$89	XP: $10	F12

Location: I-80, exit Nugget Ave eastbound; exit Rock Blvd westbound. 1040 Victorian Ave 89431 (PO Box 3567, 89432). Fax: 775/356-1639. **Facility:** Placed right off the interstate and in the heart of town, the property invites visitors to join the casino action or enjoy a meal 24 hours a day. 204 units. 200 one-bedroom standard units. 4 one-bedroom suites ($75-$175). 6 stories, interior corridors. **Parking:** on-site. **Amenities:** video games (fee), voice mail. **Dining:** 2 restaurants, 24 hours; buffet $8, cocktails, entertainment. **Guest Services:** gift shop. **Business Services:** meeting rooms. **Cards:** AX, CB, DC, DS, MC, VI.

SOME UNITS

SUNRISE MOTEL

AAA SAVE

Motel

All Year 1P: $40-$125 2P: $40-$125 Phone: (775)358-7010 XP: $10 F14

Location: I-80, exit McCarren Blvd, 1 blk n to E Victorian Ave, then just w. 210 E Victorian Ave 89431. Fax: 775/358-7566. **Facility:** 20 one-bedroom standard units. 2 stories (no elevator), exterior corridors. **Parking:** on-site. **Terms:** 10 day cancellation notice, weekly rates available. **Amenities:** *Some:* hair dryers. **Cards:** AX, DC, MC, VI. **Special Amenities: free local telephone calls and preferred room (subject to availability with advanced reservations).**

SOME UNITS

WHERE TO DINE

THE STEAKHOUSE GRILL

Steak House

Lunch: $7-$17 Dinner: $17-$27 Phone: 775/356-3300

Location: I-80, exit Nugget Ave eastbound; exit Pyramid Way westbound; in John Ascuaga's Nugget Hotel Tower. 1100 Nugget Ave 89431. **Hours:** 11:30 am-2 & 5-10 pm, Sat & Sun from 5 pm. **Reservations:** suggested. **Features:** It's no wonder this dining room is popular with locals and tourists alike. It's a great place to go not only for steaks but also for seafood and chicken selections. Dressy casual; cocktails. **Parking:** on-site and valet. **Cards:** AX, CB, DC, DS, JC, MC, VI.

STATELINE

—See Lake Tahoe Area p. 403.

TONOPAH pop. 2,627

WHERE TO STAY

BEST WESTERN HI-DESERT INN *Book at aaa.com* **Phone:** (775)482-3511

AAA SAVE · Motel (3 diamonds)

All Year [CP] 1P: $59-$69 2P: $69-$89 XP: $6 F12

Location: On US 6 and 95. 320 Main St 89049 (PO Box 351). Fax: 775/482-3300. **Facility:** 62 one-bedroom standard units. 2 stories (no elevator), interior corridors. **Parking:** on-site. **Terms:** pets (no puppies or cats). **Amenities:** irons, hair dryers. **Pool(s):** heated outdoor. **Leisure Activities:** whirlpool. **Business Services:** business center. **Cards:** AX, CB, DC, DS, JC, MC, VI. **Special Amenities: free continental breakfast and free local telephone calls.** *(See color ad below)*

SOME UNITS

JIM BUTLER MOTEL **Phone:** 775/482-3577

AAA SAVE · Motel (2 diamonds)

All Year 1P: $44-$49 2P: $50-$56 XP: $8

Location: On US 6 and 95; downtown. Located across from casino. 100 S Main St 89049 (PO Box 1352). Fax: 775/482-5240. **Facility:** 25 one-bedroom standard units. 2 stories (no elevator), exterior corridors. **Parking:** on-site. **Terms:** small pets only (no puppies or cats). **Cards:** AX, CB, DC, DS, MC, VI. **Special Amenities: free local telephone calls and free newspaper.** *(See ad below)*

SOME UNITS

RAMADA INN-TONOPAH STATION Book at aaa.com

Motel

Phone: (775)482-9777

5/1-10/31	1P: $54	2P: $58	XP: $5	F18
2/1-4/30	1P: $50	2P: $54	XP: $5	F18
11/1-1/31	1P: $46	2P: $50	XP: $5	F18

Location: On US 6 and 95. 1100 Main St 89049. Fax: 775/482-9782. **Facility:** Newly re-opened and renovated, the property offers a casino and easy access to the bars and restaurants located on the main road through town. 75 one-bedroom standard units. 2 stories, interior corridors. *Bath:* combo or shower only. **Parking:** on-site. **Terms:** [AP] meal plan available, pets (in limited units). **Amenities:** voice mail, irons, hair dryers. **Leisure Activities:** exercise room. **Guest Services:** gift shop, coin laundry. **Business Services:** meeting rooms. **Cards:** AX, CB, DC, DS, JC, MC, VI.

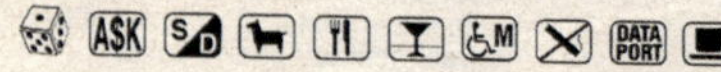

UNIONVILLE

WHERE TO STAY

OLD PIONEER GARDEN

Historic Bed & Breakfast

Phone: 775/538-7585

All Year	1P: $95	XP: $10

Location: I-80, exit 149, 16 mi s, then 2.5 mi w. 2805 Unionville Rd 89418. **Facility:** Stay in the real west when you spend the night at this historic B&B; take the time to browse in their antique shop. 9 one-bedroom standard units. 1-2 stories (no elevator), interior corridors. *Bath:* some shared or private, combo or shower only. **Parking:** on-site. **Terms:** [BP] meal plan available, pets (in designated units). **Leisure Activities:** game room. **Guest Services:** complimentary laundry.

VIRGINIA CITY

WHERE TO STAY

CHOLLAR MANSION B & B

Bed & Breakfast

Phone: 775/847-9777

All Year [BP]	1P: $75-$125	2P: $75-$125	XP: $40	D12

Location: South end of town. 565 S D St 89440 (PO Box 889). **Facility:** 4 one-bedroom standard units. 2 stories (no elevator), interior corridors. *Bath:* some shared or private. **Parking:** street. **Terms:** 14 day cancellation notice-fee imposed, $3 service charge, no pets allowed (owner's pet on premises).

SOME UNITS

GOLD HILL HOTEL

Historic Bed & Breakfast

Phone: (775)847-0111

All Year	1P: $50	2P: $50

Location: 1 mi s on SR 342. 1540 Main St 89440 (PO Box 710). Fax: 775/847-0604. **Facility:** It's been called Nevada's oldest hotel, and the Gold Hill retains the ambience of an earlier century; balconies adjoin some rooms. 18 units. 14 one-bedroom standard units. 4 cottages. 1-2 stories (no elevator), interior/exterior corridors. *Bath:* combo or shower only. **Parking:** on-site. **Terms:** [CP] meal plan available. **Amenities:** *Some:* hair dryers. **Guest Services:** gift shop. **Business Services:** fax. **Cards:** MC, VI.

SOME UNITS

WELLS pop. 1,346

WHERE TO STAY

BEST WESTERN SAGE INN Book at aaa.com

SAVE

Motel

Phone: (775)752-3353

5/1-9/30	1P: $49-$59	2P: $52-$65	XP: $5	F12
10/1-10/31	1P: $39-$54	2P: $49-$59	XP: $5	F12

Location: I-80, exit 352, 0.5 mi n. 576 6th St 89835 (PO Box 343). Fax: 775/752-3353. **Facility:** 24 units. 22 one- and 2 two-bedroom standard units. 1-2 stories (no elevator), exterior corridors. *Bath:* combo or shower only. **Parking:** on-site. **Terms:** open 5/1-10/31, [CP] meal plan available, small pets only ($5 extra charge, in limited units). **Amenities:** irons, hair dryers. **Pool(s):** heated outdoor. **Cards:** AX, DC, DS, MC, VI. **Special Amenities: early check-in/late check-out and free room upgrade (subject to availability with advanced reservations).**

SOME UNITS

FEE

SUPER 8 MOTEL

SAVE

Motel

Phone: (775)752-3384

5/16-9/15	1P: $54-$64	2P: $59-$69	XP: $5	F12
9/16-1/31	1P: $44-$54	2P: $55-$69	XP: $5	F12
2/1-5/15	1P: $44-$54	2P: $49-$64	XP: $3	F12

Location: I-80, 0.5 mi w of jct US 93. 930 6th St 89835 (PO Box 302). Fax: 775/752-3384. **Facility:** 57 one-bedroom standard units. 2 stories (no elevator), exterior corridors. *Bath:* combo or shower only. **Parking:** on-site. **Terms:** weekly rates available, small pets only ($5 extra charge, in limited units). **Pool(s):** heated outdoor. **Cards:** AX, CB, DC, DS, JC, MC, VI. **Special Amenities: free continental breakfast and free local telephone calls.**

SOME UNITS

FEE

WENDOVER pop. 1,537

WHERE TO STAY

BEST WESTERN SALT FLAT INN *Book at aaa.com* **Phone:** (435)665-7811

AAA SAVE

Motel

6/2-9/1	1P: $44-$64	2P: $54-$74	XP: $5	F12
4/1-6/1	1P: $34-$64	2P: $34-$74	XP: $5	F12
9/2-3/31	1P: $34-$64	2P: $34-$64	XP: $5	F12

Location: I-80, exit 2. 835 E Wendover Blvd 84083 (PO Box 400). Fax: 435/665-7811. **Facility:** 24 one-bedroom standard units. 2 stories (no elevator), exterior corridors. **Parking:** on-site. **Amenities:** irons, hair dryers. **Pool(s):** heated outdoor. **Leisure Activities:** sauna, whirlpool, steamroom. **Cards:** AX, CB, DC, DS, JC, MC, VI. **Special Amenities: early check-in/late check-out and free room upgrade (subject to availability with advanced reservations).**

SOME UNITS

DAYS INN OF WENDOVER *Book at aaa.com* **Phone:** 435/665-2215

Motel

Property failed to provide current rates

Location: I-80, exit 2. 685 E Wendover Blvd 84083 (PO Box 787). Fax: 435/665-7838. **Facility:** 80 units. 78 one-bedroom standard units. 2 one-bedroom suites with whirlpools. 3 stories, interior corridors. *Bath:* combo or shower only. **Parking:** on-site. **Terms:** small pets only ($5 fee, in limited units). **Amenities:** video library, irons, hair dryers. **Pool(s):** heated indoor. **Leisure Activities:** whirlpool. **Guest Services:** coin laundry. **Business Services:** meeting rooms.

SOME UNITS

FEE FEE

ECONO LODGE *Book at aaa.com* **Phone:** 435/665-2226

Motel

Property failed to provide current rates

Location: I-80, exit 2. 295 E Wendover Blvd 84083 (PO Box 787). Fax: 801/531-4080. **Facility:** 101 one-bedroom standard units. 2 stories (no elevator), interior/exterior corridors. **Parking:** on-site. **Terms:** small pets only ($5 fee). **Amenities:** video library (fee), voice mail. **Pool(s):** heated outdoor. **Leisure Activities:** whirlpool.

SOME UNITS

FEE

WESTERN RIDGE MOTEL **Phone:** (435)665-2211

Motel

All Year	1P: $20-$54	2P: $21-$64	XP: $5	F12

Location: I-80, exit 2. 895 E Wendover Blvd 84083 (PO Box 400). Fax: 435/665-7811. **Facility:** 55 units. 45 one- and 10 two-bedroom standard units. 2 stories (no elevator), exterior corridors. **Parking:** on-site. **Terms:** small pets only ($5 extra charge, in limited units). **Pool(s):** heated outdoor. **Guest Services:** coin laundry. **Cards:** AX, CB, DC, DS, JC, MC, VI.

SOME UNITS

ASK FEE

WEST WENDOVER pop. 4,721

WHERE TO STAY

PEPPERMILL HOTEL & CASINO **Phone:** 775/664-2255

Small-scale Hotel

Property failed to provide current rates

Location: I-80, exit 410 SW. 680 Wendover Blvd 89883 (PO Box 3700). Fax: 775/664-2837. **Facility:** Pamper yourself in unexpected comfort; watch the sun set over the high desert at this exciting hotel and casino. 302 one-bedroom standard units, some with whirlpools. 4 stories, interior corridors. *Bath:* some combo or shower only. **Parking:** on-site. **Amenities:** irons, hair dryers. **Guest Services:** gift shop. **Business Services:** conference facilities.

SOME UNITS

RED GARTER HOTEL & CASINO **Phone:** (775)664-2111

Small-scale Hotel

All Year	1P: $22-$85	2P: $22-$85	XP: $5	F8

Location: I-80, exit 410 SW, 0.5 mi w. 1225 W Wendover Blvd 89883 (PO Box 3999). Fax: 775/664-4700. **Facility:** Offering comfortably furnished rooms with a touch of elegance at a reasonable price, the hotel also has exciting casino and restaurants available. 106 one-bedroom standard units, some with whirlpools. 2 stories, interior corridors. **Parking:** on-site. **Terms:** check-in 4 pm, [AP] & [BP] meal plans available. **Amenities:** voice mail. *Some:* hair dryers. **Leisure Activities:** Fee: game room. **Guest Services:** gift shop. **Cards:** AX, DS, MC, VI.

SOME UNITS

WENDOVER SUPER 8 *Book at aaa.com* **Phone:** 775/664-2888

Motel

All Year	1P: $40-$100	2P: $40-$100

Location: I-80, exit 410, 0.5 mi w. 1325 Wendover Blvd 89883 (PO Box 2259). Fax: 775/664-2888. **Facility:** 74 one-bedroom standard units. 2 stories (no elevator), interior corridors. **Parking:** on-site. **Terms:** small pets only ($7.50 fee). **Guest Services:** coin laundry. **Cards:** AX, DC, DS, MC, VI.

SOME UNITS

ASK FEE

WINNEMUCCA pop. 7,174

WHERE TO STAY

BEST WESTERN GOLD COUNTRY INN *Book at aaa.com* **Phone:** (775)623-6999

SAVE

Motel

5/16-10/15	1P: $89-$109	2P: $99-$119	XP: $10	F18
2/1-5/15 & 10/16-1/31	1P: $79-$99	2P: $89-$109	XP: $10	F18

Location: I-80, exit 176 or 178, just s. 921 W Winnemucca Blvd 89445. Fax: 775/623-9190. **Facility:** 71 units. 70 one- and 1 two-bedroom standard units, some with kitchens. 2 stories (no elevator), interior corridors. **Parking:** on-site. **Terms:** check-in 4 pm, [CP] meal plan available, pets ($10 fee). **Amenities:** irons, hair dryers. **Pool(s):** heated outdoor. **Guest Services:** area transportation. **Business Services:** business center. **Cards:** AX, DC, DS, MC, VI. **Special Amenities: early check-in/late check-out and free room upgrade (subject to availability with advanced reservations).**

FEE SOME UNITS

BEST WESTERN HOLIDAY MOTEL *Book at aaa.com* **Phone:** (775)623-3684

SAVE

Motel

5/16-10/15	1P: $64-$84	2P: $74-$94	XP: $10	F18
2/1-5/15 & 10/16-1/31	1P: $49-$69	2P: $59-$89	XP: $10	F18

Location: I-80, exit 176 or 178, just s. 670 W Winnemucca Blvd 89445. Fax: 775/623-4221. **Facility:** 40 one-bedroom standard units. 2 stories (no elevator), exterior corridors. **Parking:** on-site. **Terms:** [CP] meal plan available. **Amenities:** irons, hair dryers. **Pool(s):** heated outdoor. **Cards:** AX, DC, DS, MC, VI. **Special Amenities: free continental breakfast and early check-in/late check-out.**

SOME UNITS

DAYS INN *Book at aaa.com* **Phone:** (775)623-3661

SAVE

Motel

5/16-10/15	1P: $59-$79	2P: $69-$99	XP: $10	F18
2/1-5/15 & 10/16-1/31	1P: $49-$69	2P: $59-$89	XP: $10	F18

Location: I-80, exit 176 or 178, just s. 511 W Winnemucca Blvd 89445. Fax: 775/623-4234. **Facility:** 50 one-bedroom standard units, some with efficiencies. 2 stories (no elevator), exterior corridors. **Parking:** on-site. **Terms:** [CP] meal plan available, small pets only ($10 fee). **Amenities:** irons, hair dryers. **Pool(s):** heated outdoor. **Cards:** AX, DC, DS, MC, VI. **Special Amenities: free continental breakfast and free local telephone calls.**

FEE SOME UNITS

HOLIDAY INN EXPRESS *Book at aaa.com* **Phone:** 775/625-3100

Motel

4/1-8/31	1P: $89-$99	XP: $5	F18
9/1-10/31	1P: $79-$89	XP: $5	F18
2/1-3/31 & 11/1-1/31	1P: $59-$79	XP: $5	F18

Location: I-80, exit 176, just s. 1987 W Winnemucca Blvd 89445. Fax: 775/625-3100. **Facility:** A convenient location just off the highway helps makes this a popular stopping point; plenty of dining choices are nearby. 72 units. 70 one-bedroom standard units, some with whirlpools. 2 one-bedroom suites ($99-$169). 3 stories, interior corridors. *Bath:* combo or shower only. **Parking:** on-site. **Terms:** 30 day cancellation notice-fee imposed, pets ($10 fee, $50 deposit). **Amenities:** irons, hair dryers. **Pool(s):** heated indoor. **Leisure Activities:** whirlpool. **Business Services:** meeting rooms. **Cards:** AX, DC, DS, MC, VI.

ASK FEE SOME UNITS

QUALITY INN & MODEL T CASINO *Book at aaa.com* **Phone:** (775)623-2588

Motel

5/1-9/30	1P: $45-$65	2P: $55-$70	XP: $5	F18
2/1-4/30 & 10/1-1/31	1P: $35-$55	2P: $40-$60	XP: $5	F18

Location: I-80, exit 176 or 178. 1130 W Winnemucca Blvd 89445 (P O Box 3500, 89446). Fax: 775/623-0771. **Facility:** Located in the center of town, the casino is popular with locals and tourists alike; for food, choose from a coffee shop or the nearby fast food row. 75 one-bedroom standard units. 3 stories, interior corridors. **Parking:** on-site. **Amenities:** irons, hair dryers. **Pool(s):** heated outdoor. **Leisure Activities:** Fee: game room. **Guest Services:** gift shop, coin laundry, area transportation. **Cards:** AX, DC, DS, MC, VI.

ASK SOME UNITS

RED LION HOTEL & CASINO *Book at aaa.com* **Phone:** (775)623-2565

SAVE

Small-scale Hotel

5/16-10/15	1P: $89-$109	2P: $99-$119	XP: $10	F18
2/1-5/15 & 10/16-1/31	1P: $79-$99	2P: $89-$109	XP: $10	F18

Location: I-80, exit 176 or 178, just s. 741 W Winnemucca Blvd 89445. Fax: 775/623-2527. **Facility:** A great location on the main road through town makes this property appealing; a 24-hour casino and dining make it a favorite. 105 units. 98 one- and 6 two-bedroom standard units. 1 one-bedroom suite with whirlpool. 2 stories (no elevator), interior corridors. **Parking:** on-site. **Terms:** [AP] meal plan available. **Amenities:** irons, hair dryers. **Dining:** 24 hours, cocktails, also, The Red Lion Coffee Garden, see separate listing. **Pool(s):** heated outdoor. **Leisure Activities:** Fee: game room. **Guest Services:** sundries, area transportation. **Business Services:** meeting rooms. **Cards:** AX, DC, DS, MC, VI. **Special Amenities: free local telephone calls and free room upgrade (subject to availability with advanced reservations).** *(See color ad p 893)*

SOME UNITS

SCOTT SHADY COURT MOTEL

Motel

Phone: 775/623-3646

All Year 1P: $38-$55 2P: $38-$55 XP: $5

Location: I-80, exit 176 or 178, 0.3 mi n on Pavilion. 400 First St 89445. Fax: 775/623-3410. **Facility:** 70 one-bedroom standard units. 1 story, exterior corridors. *Bath:* combo or shower only. **Parking:** on-site. **Pool(s):** heated indoor. **Leisure Activities:** playground. **Cards:** AX, DC, MC, VI. **Special Amenities: free local telephone calls.**

SUPER 8 MOTEL *Book at aaa.com*

Motel

Phone: (775)625-1818

6/1-8/31 [CP] 1P: $49-$57 2P: $55-$62 XP: $5 F12

2/1-5/31 & 9/1-1/31 [CP] 1P: $43-$49 2P: $48-$54 XP: $5 F12

Location: I-80, exit 176, 0.5 mi e. 1157 W Winnemucca Blvd 89446. Fax: 775/625-1818. **Facility:** 50 one-bedroom standard units, some with whirlpools. 2 stories (no elevator), interior corridors. **Parking:** on-site. **Terms:** pets ($10 extra charge). **Cards:** AX, DC, DS, MC, VI.

SOME UNITS

FEE

TOWN HOUSE MOTEL

Motel

			Phone: 775/623-3620
5/1-10/31	1P: $52	2P: $54-$58	XP: $5
2/1-4/30 & 11/1-1/31	1P: $38	2P: $40-$45	XP: $5

Location: I-80, exit 176 or 178, just s. 375 Monroe St 89445. **Facility:** 19 one-bedroom standard units. 1 story, exterior corridors. *Bath:* combo or shower only. **Parking:** on-site. **Terms:** small pets only. **Pool(s):** outdoor. **Cards:** AX, DC, DS, MC, VI. **Special Amenities: free local telephone calls.** *(See ad p 893)*

SOME UNITS

VAL-U MOTEL

Motel

Book at aaa.com

			Phone: (775)623-5248
All Year	1P: $40-$45	2P: $45-$49	XP: $5 F10

Location: I-80, exit 178, just s. 125 E Winnemucca Blvd 89445. Fax: 775/623-4722. **Facility:** 80 one-bedroom standard units. 3 stories (no elevator), interior corridors. **Parking:** on-site. **Terms:** small pets only. **Amenities:** hair dryers. **Pool(s):** heated outdoor. **Leisure Activities:** sauna. **Cards:** AX, DC, MC, VI.

SOME UNITS

WHERE TO DINE

ORMACHEA'S DINNER HOUSE — **Dinner:** $14-$30 — **Phone:** 775/623-3455

Ethnic

Location: On US 95 N at 2nd. 180 Melarkey St 89445. **Hours:** 4:30 pm-10 pm. Closed: 1/1, 11/25, 12/25; also Mon. **Features:** Basque and American entree dinners are served family style. Meals include a complimentary glass of wine and ice cream. Smoking is permitted only in the lounge. Casual dress; cocktails. **Parking:** on-site. **Cards:** AX, CB, DC, DS, MC, VI.

THE RED LION COFFEE GARDEN — **Lunch:** $5-$9 — **Dinner:** $10-$20 — **Phone:** 775/623-2565

American

Location: I-80, exit 176 or 178, just s; in Red Lion Hotel & Casino. 741 W Winnemucca Blvd 89445. **Hours:** 24 hours. **Features:** Located right off the casino floor, this restaurant has been popular for years with locals and tourists alike. Among extensive offerings are daily specials. Casual dress; cocktails. **Parking:** on-site. **Cards:** AX, DC, DS, MC, VI.

ZEPHYR COVE

—See Lake Tahoe Area p. 405.

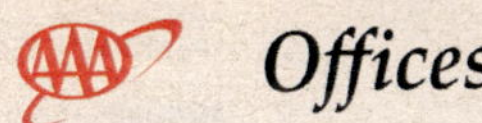

Offices

Cities with main offices are listed in **BOLD TYPE** and toll-free member service numbers in *ITALIC TYPE.* All are closed Saturdays, Sundays and holidays unless otherwise indicated.

The type of service provided is designated below the name of the city where the office is located:

- + Auto travel services, including books/maps, marked maps and on-demand Triptik maps
- ● Auto travel services, including books/maps, marked maps, but no on-demand Triptik maps
- ■ Provides books/maps only. No marked maps or on-demand Triptik maps available
- ▲ Travel agency services

NATIONAL OFFICE: 1000 AAA DRIVE, HEATHROW, FLORIDA 32746-5063, (407) 444-7000

NORTHERN CALIFORNIA

ANGELS CAMP—CALIFORNIA STATE AUTOMOBILE ASSN, 465 S MAIN HWY 49, 95222. MON-FRI 8:30-5:30. (209) 736-4517.+

ANTIOCH—CALIFORNIA STATE AUTOMOBILE ASSN, 1700 SOMERSVILLE RD, 94509. MON-FRI 8:30-5:30. (925) 754-2210.+▲

AUBURN—CALIFORNIA STATE AUTOMOBILE ASSN, 2495 BELL RD, 95603. MON-FRI 8:30-5:30. (530) 885-6561.+

BAKERSFIELD—AUTOMOBILE CLUB OF SO CALIFORNIA, 1500 COMMERCIAL WAY, 93309. MON-FRI 9-5. (661) 327-4661.+▲

BERKELEY—CALIFORNIA STATE AUTOMOBILE ASSN, 1775 UNIVERSITY AVE, 94703. MON-FRI 8:30-5:30. (510) 845-8890.+

BISHOP—AUTOMOBILE CLUB OF SO CALIFORNIA, 187 W PINE ST, 93514. MON-FRI 9-5. (760) 872-8241.+▲

CAPITOLA—CALIFORNIA STATE AUTOMOBILE ASSN, 4400 CAPITOLA RD #100, 95010. MON-FRI 8:30-5:30. (831) 479-9830.+▲

CHICO—CALIFORNIA STATE AUTOMOBILE ASSN, 2221 FOREST AVE, 95928. MON-FRI 8:30-5:30. (530) 891-8601.+▲

CLOVIS—CALIFORNIA STATE AUTOMOBILE ASSN, 1595 SHAW AVE, 93612. MON-FRI 8:30-5:30. (559) 298-9121.+▲

CONCORD—CALIFORNIA STATE AUTOMOBILE ASSN, 2055 MERIDIAN PARK BLVD, 94520. MON-FRI 8:30-5:30. (925) 671-2708.+▲

CRESCENT CITY—CALIFORNIA STATE AUTOMOBILE ASSN, 785 E WASHINGTON BLVD #1, 95531. MON-FRI 8:30-5:30. (707) 464-7428.+

CUPERTINO—CALIFORNIA STATE AUTOMOBILE ASSN, 1601 S DE ANZA BLVD #148, 95014. MON-FRI 8:30-5:30. (408) 996-3553.+▲

DALY CITY—CALIFORNIA STATE AUTOMOBILE ASSN, 455 HICKEY BLVD, 94015. MON-FRI 8:30-5:30. (650) 994-8400.+▲

DUBLIN—CALIFORNIA STATE AUTOMOBILE ASSN, 4460 TASSAJARA RD, 94568. MON-FRI 8:30-5:30. (925) 829-2021.+▲

EUREKA—CALIFORNIA STATE AUTOMOBILE ASSN, 707 L ST, 95501. MON-FRI 8:30-5:30. (707) 443-5087.+

FAIRFIELD—CALIFORNIA STATE AUTOMOBILE ASSN, 222 ACACIA ST, 94533. MON-FRI 8:30-5:30. (707) 422-1820.+

FRESNO—CALIFORNIA STATE AUTOMOBILE ASSN, 5040 N FORKNER AVE, 93711. MON-FRI 8:30-5:30. (559) 435-8450.+▲

GILROY—CALIFORNIA STATE AUTOMOBILE ASSN, 1395 FIRST ST, 95020. MON-FRI 8:30-5:30. (408) 847-2300.+

GRASS VALLEY—CALIFORNIA STATE AUTOMOBILE ASSN, 113 DORSEY DR, 95945. MON-FRI 8:30-5:30. (530) 272-9011.+

GREENBRAE—CALIFORNIA STATE AUTOMOBILE ASSN, 100 DRAKES LANDING RD, 94904. MON-FRI 8:30-5:30. (415) 925-1200.+▲

HANFORD—CALIFORNIA STATE AUTOMOBILE ASSN, 780 N IRWIN ST, 93230. MON-FRI 8:30-5:30. (559) 582-9071.+

HAYWARD—CALIFORNIA STATE AUTOMOBILE ASSN, 1580 CHABOT CT, 94545. MON-FRI 8:30-5:30. (510) 784-0900.+▲

HOLLISTER—CALIFORNIA STATE AUTOMOBILE ASSN, 351 TRES PINOS RD SUITE D, 95023. MON-FRI 8:30-5:30. (831) 637-7457.+

JACKSON—CALIFORNIA STATE AUTOMOBILE ASSN, 11974 STATE HWY 88 #2092, 95642. MON-FRI 8:30-5:30. (209) 223-2761.+

KINGS BEACH—CALIFORNIA STATE AUTOMOBILE ASSN, 7717 N LAKE BLVD, 96143. MON-FRI 8:30-5:30. (530) 546-4245.+

LAKEPORT—CALIFORNIA STATE AUTOMOBILE ASSN, 1464 PARALLEL DR, 95453. MON-FRI 8:30-5:30. (707) 263-4807.+

LODI—CALIFORNIA STATE AUTOMOBILE ASSN, 1335 S FAIRMONT AVE, 95240. MON-FRI 8:30-5:30. (209) 334-9671.+

LOS BANOS—CALIFORNIA STATE AUTOMOBILE ASSN, 919 W PACHECO BLVD, 93635. MON-FRI 8:30-5:30. (209) 826-1773.+

LOS GATOS—CALIFORNIA STATE AUTOMOBILE ASSN, 101 BLOSSOM HILL RD, 95032. MON-FRI 8:30-5:30. (408) 395-6411.+▲

MADERA—CALIFORNIA STATE AUTOMOBILE ASSN, 221 NORTH G ST, 93637. MON-FRI 8:30-5:30. (559) 673-3586.+

MANTECA—CALIFORNIA STATE AUTOMOBILE ASSN, 145 TREVINO AVE, 95337. MON-FRI 8:30-5:30. (209) 239-1252.+

MARYSVILLE—CALIFORNIA STATE AUTOMOBILE ASSN, 1205 D ST, 95901. MON-FRI 8:30-5:30. (530) 742-5531.+

MERCED—CALIFORNIA STATE AUTOMOBILE ASSN, 3065 M ST, 95348. MON-FRI 8:30-5:30. (209) 723-9143.+

MODESTO—CALIFORNIA STATE AUTOMOBILE ASSN, 3525 COFFEE RD, 95355. MON-FRI 8:30-5:30. (209) 523-9171.+▲

MONTEREY—CALIFORNIA STATE AUTOMOBILE ASSN, 53 SOLEDAD DR, 93940. MON-FRI 8:30-5:30. (831) 373-3021.+▲

MOUNTAIN VIEW—CALIFORNIA STATE AUTOMOBILE ASSN, 900 MIRAMONTE AVE, 94040. MON-FRI 8:30-5:30. (650) 965-7000.+▲

NAPA—CALIFORNIA STATE AUTOMOBILE ASSN, 800 TRANCAS ST, 94558. MON-FRI 8:30-5:30. (707) 226-9961.+▲

NEWARK—CALIFORNIA STATE AUTOMOBILE ASSN, 39600 BALENTINE DR, 94560. MON-FRI 8:30-5:30. (510) 770-9280.+▲

OAKLAND—CALIFORNIA STATE AUTOMOBILE ASSN, 380 W MACARTHUR BLVD, 94609. MON-FRI 8:30-5:30. (510) 652-1812.+▲

OROVILLE—CALIFORNIA STATE AUTOMOBILE ASSN, 1430 FEATHER RIVER BLVD, 95965. MON-FRI 8:30-5:30. (530) 533-3931.+

PALO ALTO—CALIFORNIA STATE AUTOMOBILE ASSN, 430 FOREST AVE, 94301. MON-FRI 8:30-5:30. (650) 321-0470.+▲

PARADISE—CALIFORNIA STATE AUTOMOBILE ASSN, 6332 CLARK RD, 95969. MON-FRI 8:30-5:30. (530) 872-2236.+

PETALUMA—CALIFORNIA STATE AUTOMOBILE ASSN, 111 LYNCH CREEK WAY, 94954. MON-FRI 8:30-5:30. (707) 763-0973.✚

PLACERVILLE—CALIFORNIA STATE AUTOMOBILE ASSN, 1323 BROADWAY, 95667. MON-FRI 8:30-5:30. (530) 622-4084.✚

PORTERVILLE—AUTOMOBILE CLUB OF SO CALIFORNIA, 24 W MORTON AVE, 93257. MON-FRI 9-5. (559) 784-6500.✚▲

QUINCY—CALIFORNIA STATE AUTOMOBILE ASSN, 20 CRESCENT ST, 95971. MON-FRI 8:30-5:30. (530) 283-1014.✚

RED BLUFF—CALIFORNIA STATE AUTOMOBILE ASSN, 151 SALE LN, 96080. MON-FRI 8:30-5:30. (530) 527-4304.✚

REDDING—CALIFORNIA STATE AUTOMOBILE ASSN, 943 MISSION DE ORO DR, 96003. MON-FRI 8:30-5:30. (530) 222-2722.✚▲

REDWOOD CITY—CALIFORNIA STATE AUTOMOBILE ASSN, 20 EL CAMINO REAL, 94062. MON-FRI 8:30-5:30. (650) 364-0620.✚

RICHMOND—CALIFORNIA STATE AUTOMOBILE ASSN, 3060 HILLTOP MALL RD, 94806. MON-FRI 8:30-5:30. (510) 223-8080.✚▲

ROSEVILLE—CALIFORNIA STATE AUTOMOBILE ASSN, 2100 PROFESSIONAL DR, 95661. MON-FRI 8:30-5:30. (916) 784-3232.✚▲

SACRAMENTO—CALIFORNIA STATE AUTOMOBILE ASSN, 15 BICENTENNIAL CIR, 95826. MON-FRI 8:30-5:30. (916) 381-3355.✚▲

SACRAMENTO—CALIFORNIA STATE AUTOMOBILE ASSN, 4333 FLORIN RD, 95823. MON-FRI 8:30-5:30. (916) 422-6511.✚▲

SACRAMENTO—CALIFORNIA STATE AUTOMOBILE ASSN, 4745 CHIPPENDALE DR, 95841. MON-FRI 8:30-5:30. (916) 331-7610.✚▲

SALINAS—CALIFORNIA STATE AUTOMOBILE ASSN, 1019 POST DR, 93907. MON-FRI 8:30-5:30. (831) 424-2521.✚

SAN FRANCISCO—CALIFORNIA STATE AUTOMOBILE ASSN,

150 VAN NESS AVE, 94102. MON-FRI 8:30-5:30. (415) 565-2012.✚▲

SAN JOSE—CALIFORNIA STATE AUTOMOBILE ASSN, 5340 THORNWOOD DR, 95123. MON-FRI 8:30-5:30. (408) 629-1911.✚▲

SAN LUIS OBISPO—AUTOMOBILE CLUB OF SO CALIFORNIA,

1445 CALLE JOAQUIN, 93405. MON-FRI 9-5. (805) 543-6454.✚▲

SAN MATEO—CALIFORNIA STATE AUTOMOBILE ASSN, 1650 S DELAWARE ST, 94402. MON-FRI 8:30-5:30. (650) 572-1160.✚▲

SAN RAFAEL—CALIFORNIA STATE AUTOMOBILE ASSN, 99 SMITH RANCH RD, 94903. MON-FRI 8:30-5:30. (415) 472-6700.✚▲

SAN RAMON—CALIFORNIA STATE AUTOMOBILE ASSN, 1081 MARKET PL, 94583. MON-FRI 8:30-5:30. (925) 830-9797.✚▲

SANTA CLARA—CALIFORNIA STATE AUTOMOBILE ASSN, 80 SARATOGA AVE, 95051. MON-FRI 8:30-5:30. (408) 985-9300.✚▲

SANTA MARIA—AUTOMOBILE CLUB OF SO CALIFORNIA, 2033 B SO BROADWAY, 93454. MON-FRI 9-5, SAT 10-2. (805) 922-5731.✚▲

SANTA ROSA—CALIFORNIA STATE AUTOMOBILE ASSN, 1500 FARMERS LN, 95405. MON-FRI 8:30-5:30. (707) 544-1010.✚▲

SONOMA—CALIFORNIA STATE AUTOMOBILE ASSN, 650 2ND ST W, 95476. MON-FRI 8:30-5:30. (707) 996-1083.✚

SONORA—CALIFORNIA STATE AUTOMOBILE ASSN, 1071 SANGUINETTI RD, 95370. MON-FRI 8:30-5:30. (209) 532-3134.✚

SOUTH LAKE TAHOE—CALIFORNIA STATE AUTOMOBILE

ASSN, 961 EMERALD BAY RD, 96150. MON-FRI 8:30-5:30. (530) 541-4434.✚

STOCKTON—CALIFORNIA STATE AUTOMOBILE ASSN, 3116 W MARCH LN SUITE 100, 95219. MON-FRI 8:30-5:30. (209) 952-4100.✚▲

SUSANVILLE—CALIFORNIA STATE AUTOMOBILE ASSN, 550 ASH ST, 96130. MON-FRI 8:30-5:30. (530) 257-6144.✚

TURLOCK—CALIFORNIA STATE AUTOMOBILE ASSN, 2160 GEER RD, 95382. MON-FRI 8:30-5:30. (209) 668-2722.✚

UKIAH—CALIFORNIA STATE AUTOMOBILE ASSN, 601 KINGS CT, 95482. MON-FRI 8:30-5:30. (707) 462-3861.✚

VACAVILLE—CALIFORNIA STATE AUTOMOBILE ASSN, 555 MASON ST SUITE 150, 95688. MON-FRI 8:30-5:30. (707) 453-0260.✚

VALLEJO—CALIFORNIA STATE AUTOMOBILE ASSN, 1183 ADMIRAL CALLAHAN LN, 94591. MON-FRI 8:30-5:30. (707) 552-0592.✚▲

VISALIA—AUTOMOBILE CLUB OF SO CALIFORNIA, 300 S MOONEY BLVD, 93291. MON-FRI 9-5. (559) 732-8045.✚▲

WALNUT CREEK—CALIFORNIA STATE AUTOMOBILE ASSN,

1276 CALIFORNIA BLVD, 94596. MON-FRI 8:30-5:30, SAT 10-5:30. (925) 988-1475.✚▲

WATSONVILLE—CALIFORNIA STATE AUTOMOBILE ASSN, 1195 S GREEN VALLEY RD, 95076. MON-FRI 8:30-5:30. (831) 722-8151.✚

WILLOWS—CALIFORNIA STATE AUTOMOBILE ASSN, 855 W WOOD ST, 95988. MON-FRI 8:30-5:30. (530) 934-4648.✚

WOODLAND—CALIFORNIA STATE AUTOMOBILE ASSN, 95 W LINCOLN AVE, 95695. MON-FRI 8:30-5:30. (530) 662-9344.✚

YREKA—CALIFORNIA STATE AUTOMOBILE ASSN, 1876 FORT JONES RD, 96097. MON-FRI 8:30-5:30. (530) 842-4416.✚

NEVADA

CARSON CITY—CALIFORNIA STATE AUTOMOBILE ASSN, 2901 S CARSON ST, 89701. MON-FRI 8:30-5:30. (775) 883-2470.✚

HENDERSON—CALIFORNIA STATE AUTOMOBILE ASSN, 601 WHITNEY RANCH DR #A, 89014. MON-FRI 8:30-5:30. (702) 458-2323.✚▲

LAS VEGAS—CALIFORNIA STATE AUTOMOBILE ASSN, 3312 W CHARLESTON BLVD, 89102. MON-FRI 8:30-5:30. (702) 870-9171.✚▲

LAS VEGAS—CALIFORNIA STATE AUTOMOBILE ASSN, 8440 W LAKE MEAD STE 203, 89128. MON-FRI 8:30-5:30. (702) 360-3151.✚▲

RENO—CALIFORNIA STATE AUTOMOBILE ASSN, 199 E MOANA LN, 89502. MON-FRI 8:30-5:30. (775) 826-8800.✚▲

GOLDEN PASSPORTS

Golden Passports, available in three types, offer benefits and significant savings to individuals who plan to visit federal recreation sites.

The Golden Eagle Passport, available for a **$65** annual fee, is valid for entrance only to all federal recreation areas that have an entrance fee. Sites include those operated by the National Forest Service, National Park Service, Bureau of Land Management and the U.S. Fish and Wildlife Service. The passport admits all occupants of a private vehicle at locations where entrance is on a per vehicle basis. At locations where a per person fee is charged, the pass covers the pass holder, spouse, parents and children.

Citizens or permanent residents of the United States who are 62 and older can obtain *Golden Age Passports* for a one-time **$10** fee. Proof of age is required.

Golden Access Passports are free to citizens or permanent residents of the United States (regardless of age) who are medically blind or permanently disabled.

Both *Golden Age* and *Golden Access passports* cover entrance fees for the holder and accompanying private party to all national parks and sites managed by the U.S. Fish and Wildlife Service, the U.S. Forest Service and the Bureau of Land Management, plus half off camping and other fees. When a per person fee is imposed, the pass covers the pass holder, spouse and children. Apply in person at a federally operated area where an entrance fee is charged.

NATIONAL PARKS PASS

The *National Parks Pass*, valid for 1 year from its first use in a park, allows unlimited admissions to all U.S. national parks. The **$50** pass covers all occupants of a private vehicle at parks where the entrance fee is per vehicle. At parks with individual entry fees, the pass covers the pass holder, spouse, parents and children.

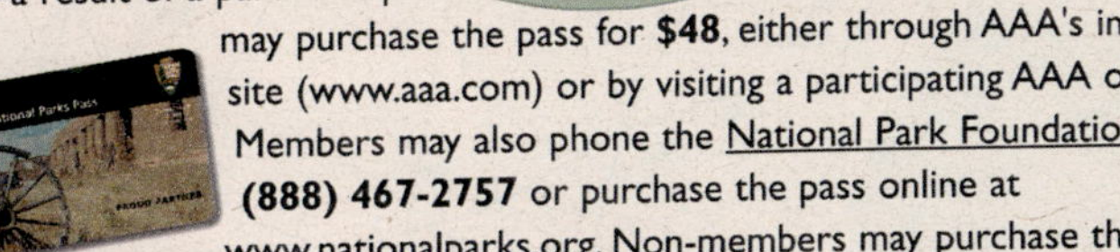

As a result of a partnership with the National Park Foundation, AAA members may purchase the pass for **$48**, either through AAA's internet site (www.aaa.com) or by visiting a participating AAA office. Members may also phone the National Park Foundation at **(888) 467-2757** or purchase the pass online at www.nationalparks.org. Non-members may purchase the pass through participating AAA offices for the full **$50** price or online at www.nationalparks.org.

For an upgrade fee of **$15**, a Golden Eagle hologram sticker can be added to a *National Parks Pass*. The hologram covers entrance fees not just at national parks, but at any federal recreation area that has an admission fee. Valid for the duration of the *National Parks Pass* to which it is affixed, the Golden Eagle hologram is available at National Park Service, Fish and Wildlife Service and Bureau of Land Management fee stations.

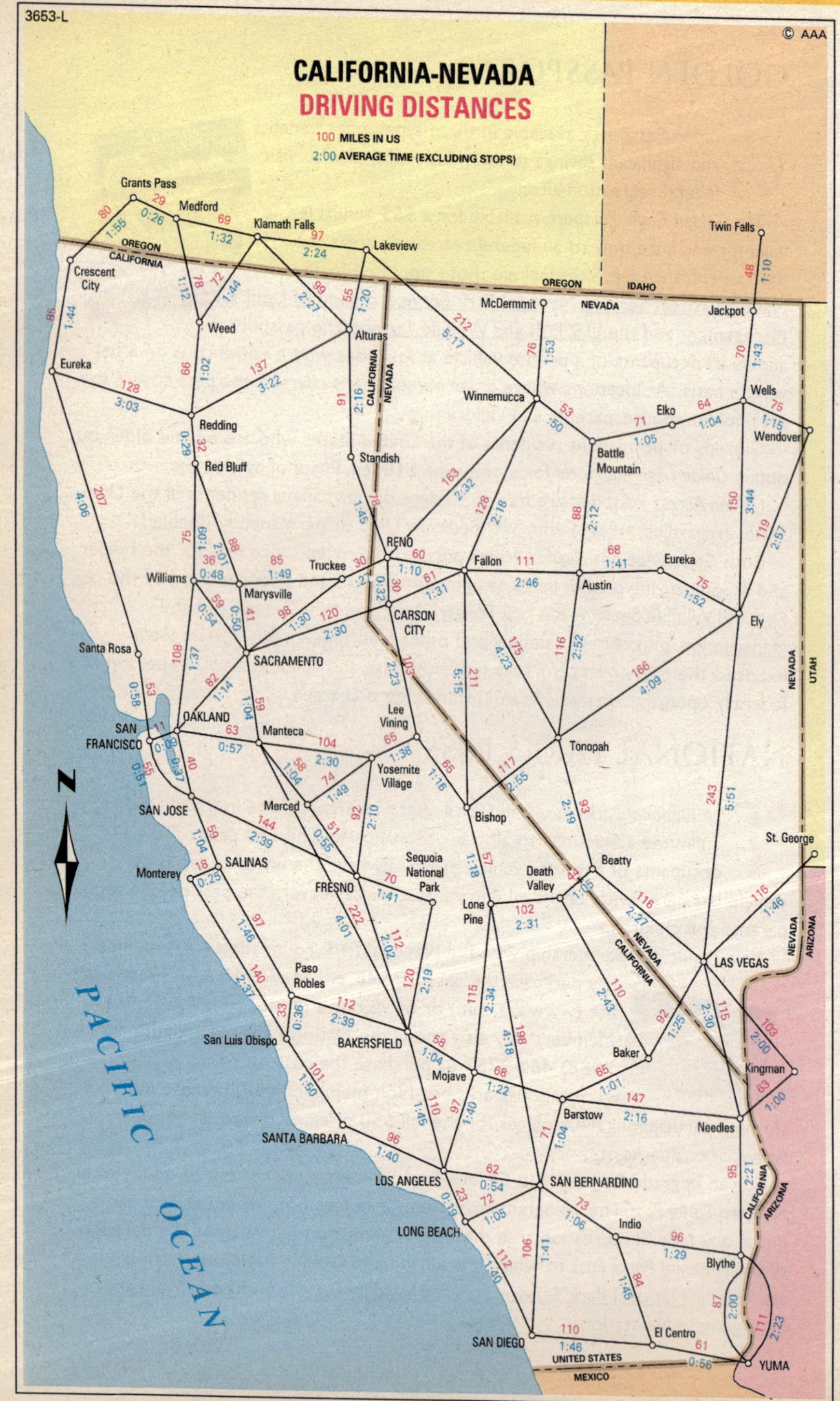
3653-L
© AAA
CALIFORNIA-NEVADA
DRIVING DISTANCES
100 MILES IN US
2:00 AVERAGE TIME (EXCLUDING STOPS)
Grants Pass
Medford
Klamath Falls
Lakeview
Twin Falls
Crescent City
OREGON
CALIFORNIA
NEVADA
IDAHO
UTAH
ARIZONA
McDermmit
Jackpot
Weed
Alturas
Eureka
Winnemucca
Wells
Elko
Wendover
Redding
Battle Mountain
Red Bluff
Standish
RENO
Fallon
Austin
Eureka
Truckee
Williams
Marysville
CARSON CITY
Ely
Santa Rosa
SACRAMENTO
Lee Vining
SAN FRANCISCO
OAKLAND
Manteca
Tonopah
Yosemite Village
SAN JOSE
Merced
Bishop
St. George
SALINAS
Monterey
Sequoia National Park
Beatty
FRESNO
Death Valley
Lone Pine
LAS VEGAS
Paso Robles
San Luis Obispo
BAKERSFIELD
Baker
Mojave
Kingman
Barstow
Needles
SANTA BARBARA
LOS ANGELES
SAN BERNARDINO
LONG BEACH
Indio
Blythe
El Centro
SAN DIEGO
YUMA
UNITED STATES
MEXICO
PACIFIC OCEAN
N

Points of Interest Index

Index Legend

NB....national battlefield
NBP....national battlefield park
NC....national cemetery
NF....national forest
NHM....national historic(al) monument
NHP....national historic(al) park
NHS....national historic(al) site
NL....national lakeshore
NME....national memorial
NMO....national monument
NMP....national military park
NP....national park
NRA....national recreation area
NR....national river
NS....national seashore
NWR....national wildlife refuge
PHP....provincial historic(al) park
PHS....provincial historic(al) site
PP....provincial park
SF....state forest
SHM....state historic(al) monument
SHP....state historic(al) park
SHS....state historic(al) site
SME....state memorial
SP....state park
SRA....state recreation area

GEM: Points of Interest Offering a *Great Experience for Members*®

CHURCHES-CHAPELS

CHURCHES-MISSIONS

CHURCHES-TEMPLES & SYNAGOGUES

COURTHOUSES

CULTURAL CENTERS & CIVIC CENTERS

DAMS

DUNES

EVENTS-GENERAL

EVENTS-FAIRS

EVENTS-FESTIVALS

EVENTS-FIESTAS

EVENTS-MUSIC

EVENTS-PAGEANTS, PARADES, DAYS

EVENTS-RODEOS

EVENTS-SHOWS

EVENTS-SPORTS

EXHIBITS & COLLECTIONS-GENERAL

EXHIBITS & COLLECTIONS-ANIMALS & BIRDS

EXHIBITS & COLLECTIONS-AVIATION

EXHIBITS & COLLECTIONS-CLOCKS

EXHIBITS & COLLECTIONS-DOLLS & TOYS

EXHIBITS & COLLECTIONS-HISTORICAL

EXHIBITS & COLLECTIONS-INDIAN

EXHIBITS & COLLECTIONS-MUSIC

EXHIBITS & COLLECTIONS-RELIGIOUS ITEMS

EXHIBITS & COLLECTIONS-SCIENCE

GEOLOGICAL FORMATIONS

GHOST TOWNS

GRAVES & TOMBS

HISTORIC BUILDINGS & HOUSES

HISTORIC DOCUMENTS, MANUSCRIPTS & RARE BOOKS

HISTORIC SITES

MONUMENTS, GENERAL

MONUMENTS, NATIONAL; STATE

MOUNTAINS

MURALS & MOSAICS

MUSEUMS

PARKS, NATIONAL

PIERS

PLANETARIUMS

RACETRACKS-AUTO

RACETRACKS-HORSE

RAILROADS

RAILROADS-LOCOMOTIVES & CARS

RAILROADS & SKI LIFTS, CABLE; COG; INCLINE; NARROW GAUGE

RANCHES

RECREATION-SUMMER ACTIVITIES

RECREATION-WINTER ACTIVITIES

RESEARCH ORGANIZATIONS

RESTORED VILLAGES & SETTLEMENTS

RIVERS

ROCKS

SCENIC DRIVES

SCHOOL BUILDINGS

SCHOOLS

SCHOOLS-ACADEMIES

SCHOOLS-COLLEGES & UNIVERSITIES

SCHOOLS-INSTITUTES

SELF-GUIDING TOURS

SHIPS & BOATS

SHOPS, FIRMS & STORES

SIGHTSEEING-AIRCRAFT RIDES & TOURS

SIGHTSEEING TOURS

SIGHTSEEING TOURS-BOATS

SIGHTSEEING TOURS-RAFTING & CANOEING

SOUND & LIGHT PRESENTATIONS

SPORTS ARENAS

SPRINGS

STATUES

STREETS, PLAZAS, SQUARES, CITY AREAS

THEATERS-BUILDINGS

THEATERS-PLAYS, DRAMAS & MUSICALS

TOWERS

TREES

VIEWS

VISITOR CENTERS

VISITOR INFORMATION

WALKING TOURS

WATERFALLS

WATER PARKS

WAX MUSEUMS

WILDERNESS AREAS

WILDLIFE SANCTUARIES

WINERIES

ZOOLOGICAL PARKS & EXHIBITS

ZOOLOGICAL PARKS & EXHIBITS-CHILDREN'S ZOOS

SAVE Attraction Admission Discount Index

Bed & Breakfast Lodgings Index

Some bed and breakfasts listed below might have historical significance. Those properties are also referenced in the Historical index. The indication that continental [CP] or full breakfast [BP] is included in the room rate reflects whether a property is a Bed-and-Breakfast facility.

NORTHERN CALIFORNIA

ACCOMMODATIONS

BED & BREAKFAST LODGINGS (CONT'D)

NEVADA

ACCOMMODATIONS

Country Inns Index

Some of the following country inns can also be considered as bed-and-breakfast operations. The indication that continental [CP] or full breakfast [BP] is included in the room rate reflects whether a property is a Bed-and-Breakfast facility.

NORTHERN CALIFORNIA

ACCOMMODATIONS

RESTAURANT

Historical Lodgings & Restaurants Index

Some of the following historical lodgings can also be considered as bed-and-breakfast operations. The indication that continental [CP] or full breakfast [BP] is included in the room rate reflects whether a property is a Bed-and-Breakfast facility.

NORTHERN CALIFORNIA

ACCOMMODATIONS

RESTAURANTS

NEVADA

ACCOMMODATIONS

Resorts Index

Many establishments are located in resort areas; however, the following places have extensive on-premises recreational facilities:

NORTHERN CALIFORNIA

ACCOMMODATIONS

NEVADA

ACCOMMODATION

Comprehensive City Index

Here is an alphabetical list of all cities appearing in this TourBook® guide. Cities are presented by state/province. Page numbers under the POI column indicate where points of interest text begins. Page numbers under the L&R column indicate where lodging and restaurant listings begin.

Comprehensive City Index (cont'd)

Comprehensive City Index (cont'd)

Which place is best for each vehicle to travel?

Help the car, the airplane and the cruise ship find a path to the right spot.

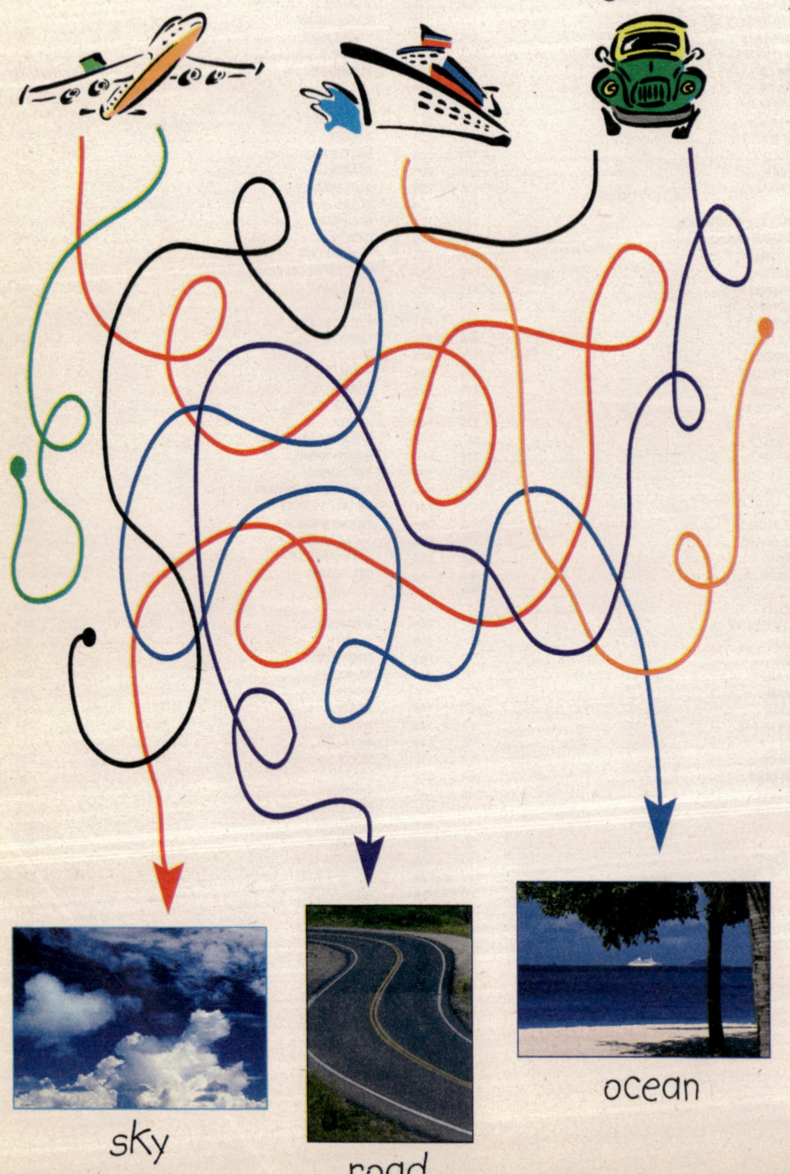

Word Search

A H T R E S T A U R A N T F D T A H M F C V N S Q H F H

G J H E R S P O O D A R D G V R J M A P N S T L C C V B

A S D S A P O E I H A K L D V A A K D F G H A A I W E U

T Y A E G H A H O T E L E Y P V O R T G T H E E J K W F

T H J R R B L N N W O G F P Y E F G H W A B U S S R E A

E I W V D T K E A O O E C V N L A P E D S E E N M S T I

K L E A H H S T P N P A D S A R S G M A D A N V D T Y R

C D A T E A B G U Y L O J D C A A W E Y T J S E I L N P

I E B I A L N G D Y A W H G I H F A P G J F U N V N M O

T E T O J I C X Z A N F T H I E E M A N E U I Z P W M R

F T M N M P Q A G J E R D S N Y T B R E W S T I J B S T

K F A M G H I U A A R E F P I B Y O K A B T C A R V J V

D L I F S A E G M T Y D I K A A C N O G D A A D Y T S A

R W C B B N F S A S O P L S R E F V B Z Q R S E E A N T

S A R H S B M E N O Z E M I T D R M C P F H E C I T Y S

Suitcase	Plane	Train	Swimming Pool
Travel	Time Zone	Reservation	Restaurant
Ticket	Hotel	Bus	City
Car	Beach	Theme Park	Highway
Map	Fun	Safety	Airport

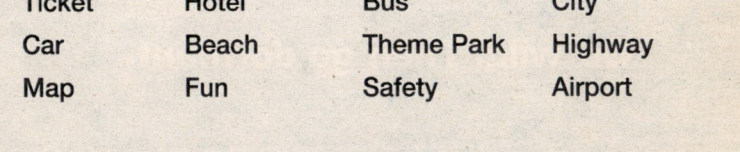

SLEEPY
Travelodge.